Congressional Roll Call 2009

A Chronology and Analysis of Votes in the House and Senate
111th Congress, First Session

CQ PRESS

A Division of SAGE
Washington, D.C.

CQ Press
2300 N Street, NW, Suite 800
Washington, DC 20037

Phone: 202-729-1900; toll-free, 1-866-4CQ-PRESS (1-866-427-7737)

Web: www.cqpress.com

14 13 12 11 10   1 2 3 4 5

ISBN 978-1-60871-027-0
ISSN 0191-1473

Table of Contents

Editor's Note: *Congressional Roll Call 2009* provides a member-by-member survey and analysis of votes in the House and Senate during the first session of the 111th Congress.

An introductory legislative summary is followed by three sections. The first contains Congressional Quarterly's special voting studies. These studies examine votes on which a majority of Democrats opposed a majority of Republicans, congressional support of the president's position on specific votes, and the percentage of all recorded votes on which members voted or took stands. Summaries and charts of the key votes are included in the second section.

The third section of the book contains a compilation of roll call votes in the House and Senate in 2009, followed by indexes of the roll call votes and bills on which roll call votes were taken.

INTRODUCTION

Rancorous Session, Landmark Year: Inauguration, Economy, Health Care

THE MOST SIGNIFICANT moment in the 2009 session came on the last day, when Senate Democrats succeeded in passing a historic overhaul of the nation's health care system. The Dec. 24 vote was the culmination of a yearlong drive by congressional Democrats to prevail on their new president's No. 1 priority. It also epitomized the dynamic that dominated the first session of the 111th Congress: Democrats eager to deliver on President Obama's hugely ambitious first-year agenda and Republicans intent on stopping them.

A handful of bills won near-unanimous support, and a few individuals struggled to find common ground on major issues such as health care and financial regulation. But neither party was willing to back off in the name of compromise, and both sides were willing to take the fight to such lengths that senators found themselves still at work in the Capitol on the morning of Christmas Eve.

The sharp divide meant that the Democratic majority had to maintain an exceptional level of party unity to get much done. As a result, the chief obstacles facing Senate Majority Leader Harry Reid, D-Nev., and House Speaker Nancy Pelosi, D-Calif., came not from Republicans but from members of their own party.

Just a handful of members regularly crossed their party's leaders, and just a few hot-button issues — gun rights, bank bailouts and war policy — unraveled the otherwise tight Democratic majorities. Democrats' ability to enact an economic stimulus package, move health care legislation through both chambers and push a climate change bill through the House depended almost entirely on resolving debates within the party and sometimes negotiating with a handful of Republicans — not on building a broad consensus on any of those issues.

MAKING HISTORY

For one day, however, the partisanship was nowhere in sight. On Jan. 20, the nation and many around the world watched the historic inauguration of Barack Obama as the 44th president of the United States and the first African-American ever to lead the country. Obama's journey to the White House was marked by a ceremony filled with grandeur and calls for personal sacrifice. The new president repeated the 35-word oath of office as his wife, Michelle, held the same gilt-edged Bible used for Abraham Lincoln's first inauguration. A record crowd, estimated at 1.8 million, filled the Mall and lined the nearby streets.

Even as he took office, Obama sought to dampen the high public expectations, which were reminiscent of those that accompanied

the inauguration of John F. Kennedy and Ronald Reagan, if not Franklin D. Roosevelt. His biggest immediate challenge — one that forced him to reorder his priorities — was responding to the most severe economic meltdown since the Great Depression. His economic team had worked closely for weeks with the outgoing administration, but there was no playbook for recovery.

He also inherited the wars in Iraq and Afghanistan, growing public anger over the massive use of federal funds to rescue Wall Street financial firms and a swollen federal deficit.

In his first week in office, Obama broke with his predecessor, President George W. Bush, on several high-profile issues. He ordered the detention center for terrorism suspects at Guantánamo Bay, Cuba, closed within a year, with the remaining prisoners released, transferred or sent to U.S. jails. He overturned the so-called Mexico City policy, which barred U.S. aid to international family groups that performed or "actively promoted" abortion with their own money. He subsequently reversed Bush's restrictions on federal funding for embryonic stem cell research.

Like the hopes for the Obama administration, expectations were high for Congress. With the return of one-party government, it was the Democrats who were expected to accomplish their goals, just as Republicans had been when they controlled Congress during most of the first six years of Bush's presidency. Liberals, in particular, saw Obama's election as a repudiation of GOP policies and a mandate for their own — and were often unprepared for the compromises that the Democratic leadership and the White House would make to get things done.

Although Republicans were coming off two devastating electoral losses — of Congress in 2006 and the White House in 2008 — their leaders clearly had no intention of retreating. They launched early rhetorical salvos at the Democrats and voted against bills such as the economic stimulus package. By late spring, they were taking the offensive, using parliamentary guerrilla tactics to frustrate Democratic initiatives and raise their own profile on issues such as taxes, spending, the deficit and, above all, the Democrats' marquee issue of health care.

The polarization was more evident in the Senate, where Republicans routinely threatened to filibuster legislation, forcing Democrats to round up the 60 votes needed to invoke cloture and limit floor debate. In some cases, the leaders simply agreed to require 60 votes without going through the lengthier process. As a consequence, 60 effectively replaced 51 as the number of floor votes required for actions as simple as proceeding to a bill.

Leaders: 111th Congress, 1st Session

SENATE

President of the Senate: Vice President Joseph R. Biden Jr.
President Pro Tempore: Robert C. Byrd, D-W.Va.

Democrats

Majority Leader	Harry Reid, Nev.	Steering and Outreach Committee Chairwoman	Debbie Stabenow, Mich.
Majority Whip	Richard J. Durbin, Ill.	Chief Deputy Whip	Barbara Boxer, Calif.
Caucus Vice Chairman	Charles E. Schumer, N.Y.	Democratic Senatorial Campaign Committee Chairman	Robert Menendez, N.J.
Policy Committee Chairman	Byron L. Dorgan, N.D.		
Conference Secretary	Patty Murray, Wash.		

Republicans

Minority Leader	Mitch McConnell, Ky.	Policy Committee Chairman	John Thune, S.D. *
Minority Whip	Jon Kyl, Ariz.	Chief Deputy Whip	Richard M. Burr, N.C.
Conference Chairman	Lamar Alexander, Tenn.	National Republican Senatorial Committee Chairman	John Cornyn, Texas
Conference Vice Chairwoman	Lisa Murkowski, Alaska*	Counsel & Adviser to the Leader	Robert F. Bennett, Utah

HOUSE

Speaker of the House: Nancy Pelosi, D-Calif.

Democrats

Majority Leader	Steny H. Hoyer, Md.	Democratic Congressional Campaign Committee Chairman	Chris Van Hollen, Md.
Majority Whip	James E. Clyburn, S.C.	Steering and Policy Committee Co-Chairwoman	Rosa DeLauro, Conn.
Caucus Chairman	John B. Larson, Conn.	Co-Chairman	George Miller, Calif.
Caucus Vice Chairman	Xavier Becerra, Calif.		
Assistant to the Speaker	Chris Van Hollen, Md.		
Senior Chief Deputy Whip	John Lewis, Ga.		

Republicans

Minority Leader	John A. Boehner, Ohio	Conference Secretary	John Carter, Texas
Minority Whip	Eric Cantor, Va.	Policy Committee Chairman	Thaddeus McCotter, Mich.
Conference Chairman	Mike Pence, Ind.	Chief Deputy Whip	Kevin McCarthy, Calif.
Conference Vice Chairwoman	Cathy McMorris Rogers, Wash.	National Republican Congressional Committee Chairman	Pete Sessions, Texas

*Lisa Murkowski became the conference vice chairwoman on June 25, replacing John Thune, who moved to become the chairman of the policy committee the same day. Thune replaced John Ensign, Nev., who resigned as policy committee chairman on June 17.

Reid began the year with 58 senators in his caucus, including two independents — a shortfall that required him to win the support of at least a few Republicans. In July, the Democratic caucus grew to 60 members, thanks to a party switch by former Republican Arlen Specter of Pennsylvania and the arrival of Minnesota Democrat Al Franken following an extended election dispute.

Senate Democrats had reached the magic number, but Reid's job was no easier. As the legislative stakes rose over the summer and fall, he had to work harder than ever to keep his party united.

The simultaneous rise in partisan conflict and party unity were reflected in Congressional Quarterly's annual vote studies, which showed that a record 72 percent of all Senate roll call votes pitted a majority of Democrats against a majority of Republicans. On average, Senate Democrats stuck with their party on 91 percent of those votes. Republicans averaged 85 percent, but two or three moderates who were sometimes open to voting with Democrats pulled down the score.

On the other side of the Capitol, the party divide was not as stark: A majority of House Democrats faced off against a majority of Republicans 57 percent of the time.

Pelosi was one of the most powerful Speakers in history and led the largest majority either party had had in 16 years, 256 members at the start of the year. She was unapologetic about her determination to prevail, which meant mustering 218 votes if every House member voted. But it often took all of her well-known skills at persuasion and dealmaking to build consensus in a caucus that included the Blue Dog Coalition of fiscal conservatives who fought to reduce the deficit, as well as members of the Congressional Progressive Caucus who were anxious to increase spending on social programs, and the Black Caucus, with its concerns about aiding minority and low-income communities.

The difficulty was reflected in the leadership's narrow victories on top-priority legislation. Pelosi mustered 219 votes for a global warming bill, 220 votes to pass the House health care overhaul, and 223 votes for a bill to create a new regulatory regime for the financial services industry. On average, Democrats voted with the leadership on 91 percent of the year's 502 party unity votes. Republicans were not too far behind, holding together 87 percent of the time.

JOB #1: THE ECONOMY

The shock from the collapse of the financial services sector and an economy in free fall was still fresh at the start of the year.

Unemployment had climbed to 7.4 percent in December 2009. Public anger was growing over government recovery efforts that seemed to favor Wall Street over Main Street, and there was fear that hundreds of billions more in taxpayer dollars might be required before the crisis was over. Although the meltdown and a $700 billion bailout of faltering financial firms had occurred under Bush, the Democrats were now in charge; it was their problem.

• **TARP funds.** The Senate handed Obama an important victory on Jan. 15, even before he was inaugurated, when it rejected a GOP joint resolution that would have prevented the president from using the second half of the $700 billion authorized in 2008 under the Troubled Asset Relief Program (TARP, PL 110-343). Obama's economic team had lobbied for weeks to ensure that the resolution of disapproval (S J Res 5) was defeated. In the House, 99 Democrats joined all but four Republicans to pass a companion measure (H J Res 3), but the action was symbolic: Both chambers had to endorse the disapproval resolution for it to take effect.

• **Stimulus bill.** Beyond preserving access to TARP funds, the first legislative priority for both congressional Democrats and the White House was enactment of an economic stimulus bill that had been in the works since soon after the 2008 election. The measure provided $575.3 billion in new spending over 11 years, primarily for programs intended to save or create jobs, assist unemployed workers and support education, to name a few. It also provided $211.8 billion in individual and business tax cuts.

The House passed an $819.5 billion version with relative ease Jan. 8, but the Senate was able to pass its bill only after a group of moderates negotiated a version that dropped some Democratic items, thereby winning the support of three Republicans and enabling Reid to clear the 60-vote hurdle. Liberal Democrats were not happy, but they had to accept some of the changes as the price of getting a final bill through the Senate. "How three senators could do this is beyond me," lamented Rep. Barbara Lee, D-Calif.

As Congress considered the legislation, Obama traveled to several hard-hit areas of the country and had the first news conference of his presidency in an effort to convince the nation that the bill was necessary to stimulate the sagging economy. The bill cleared on Feb. 13 and was signed four days later (PL 111-5).

Republicans made the huge package a centerpiece of their claim that Democrats' penchant for spending was out of control. They also argued, as they would throughout the session, that the majority was denying them any input in legislation.

CLEARING THE DECKS

Before Obama made his first address to Congress or submitted his budget, Democrats cleared away legislation that had been on their agenda for years but had been blocked under Bush.

• **Wage discrimination.** The first was a bill signed into law Jan. 29 (PL 111-2) that made it easier for employees to challenge wage discrimination.

The measure, which Democrats named the Lilly Ledbetter Fair Play Act, applied the statute of limitations in wage discrimination suits to each discriminatory paycheck, rather than to the first instance of discrimination, as required under previous law. The bill was named after a Goodyear Tire and Rubber Co. employee, who discovered after nearly 20 years that she had been paid less than men who were doing the same work. The Supreme Court ruled against her claim of gender discrimination in 2007 on the grounds that existing law required an employee to file a formal complaint within 180 days of the date the alleged discrimination first occurred.

The House had passed the same legislation in 2008, but Republicans blocked it in the Senate and the White House warned that Bush was likely to veto the bill if it reached his desk.

• **Children's health insurance.** On Feb. 4, Obama signed a bill expanding the Children's Health Insurance Program, which served children in low-income families that were not poor enough to qualify for Medicaid but could not afford private insurance. The measure (PL 111-3) added $32.8 billion in mandatory funds over five years to the amount already being spent on the joint state-federal program, enough to cover 4.1 million previously uninsured children. The extra cost was offset mainly through an increase in federal excise taxes on cigarettes and other tobacco products.

Bush had vetoed two versions of the bill in 2007, saying they cost too much and did not target the program to the truly poor.

• **Tobacco regulation.** Later in the year, Democrats crossed another to-do item off their list when Congress cleared legislation giving the Food and Drug Administration the power to regulate tobacco products. The bill authorized the FDA to regulate nicotine levels and required that tobacco packaging carry new, larger warning labels. It banned flavored cigarettes, which critics said were targeted at children, and barred the use of words such as "light" and "mild" in packaging and advertising. FDA enforcement of the new regulations was funded largely by user fees on tobacco products that were expected to bring in $5.4 billion over 10 years. The bill, which Obama signed June 22 (PL 111-31), did not permit the FDA to ban tobacco products, nor did it require companies to eliminate nicotine.

The House had passed similar legislation in 2008, but the bill died in the Senate. The Bush administration threatened to veto the measure, saying it would undermine the FDA and could lead the public to conclude that some tobacco products were safe. It also said the tax would fall disproportionately on low-income individuals.

SETTING NEW PRIORITIES

In an address to Congress on Feb. 24, Obama told lawmakers and the nation that while his top priority was the economy, he would not shy away from what he described as "bold action and big ideas." Two days later, he sent Congress a preliminary version of his $3.59 trillion fiscal 2010 budget, which reflected the same far-reaching strategy.

Obama called for overhauling the nation's health care system to reduce costs and put the United States on the path to universal coverage, and he included a $630 billion reserve fund in his budget to help finance the overhaul. He asked Congress to create a market-based cap-and-trade system to reduce carbon pollution that would also generate billions of dollars for investments in renewable energy. He called for wide-ranging improvements in education and a new system for regulating the banking and financial services industry that would prevent a repeat of the implosion of 2007-08.

On May 7, the White House released a detailed version of the budget that called on Congress to replace the tax and spending priorities of the previous decade. It included a $1.25 trillion cap on discretionary budget authority, with about $1.09 trillion available for the annual spending bills — 25 percent above the amount Bush requested in his fiscal 2009 budget. According to the Congressional

Highlights: 111th Congress, First Session

CONGRESS DID

- Inject $787 billion into the economy, principally for projects intended to save or create jobs, in a bid to stimulate an end to the deepest recession since the 1930s.
- Give the Food and Drug Administration broad authority to regulate the contents and marketing of tobacco products.
- Impose a range of new regulations and restrictions on the credit card industry, including limits on interest rate increases.
- Confirm Sonia Sotomayor as the first Hispanic justice ever on the Supreme Court.
- Appropriate $218.6 billion for the wars in Iraq and Afghanistan, pushing their combined cost to more than $1 trillion.
- Boost domestic discretionary spending about 10 percent, the biggest such increase this decade.
- Set conditions on the movement of wartime detainees and the closure of the prison at Guantánamo Bay, Cuba.
- Allocate $3 billion in cash incentives for consumers to trade in their cars and purchase more energy-efficient vehicles.
- Add new layers of oversight for Pentagon procurement practices.
- Broaden the federal hate crimes statute to include acts based on disdain for people who are gay, lesbian, bisexual or transgender.
- Expand federal national and community service programs.
- Increase funding and expand eligibility for the health insurance program for low-income children.

CONGRESS DID NOT

- Negotiate the final compromises on overhauling the nation's health care system, centered on an expansion of medical insurance coverage, which was President Obama's top first-year domestic priority.
- Complete legislation to combat global warming, mainly by creating a cap-and-trade system for carbon dioxide emissions.
- Finish an overhaul of the regulation of financial services, in part by creating a consumer-focused oversight agency.
- Grant unions easier federal regulations for organizing workplaces.
- Expand the authority of the Food and Drug Administration to regulate the safety of the food supply.
- Update the laws authorizing improvements to airports, highways and mass transit systems.
- Alter the tax treatment of estates before the onset of the one-year-only repeal of all estate taxes in 2010.
- Extend an assortment of tax breaks before their expiration at the end of the year.
- Revive the debate on overhauling federal immigration policy.
- Enact Obama's plan to make the federal government the sole originator of student loans.
- Grant the District of Columbia a full-fledged seat in the House.
- Increase the limit on the federal debt by a sufficient amount to permit new government borrowing after February 2010.

Budget Office (CBO), the total consisted of $687.2 billion for defense and $561.5 billion for non-defense programs.

To help pay for his priorities, Obama included tax increases on affluent Americans after years of reductions under Bush, and he took a large swing at a variety of special tax provisions for businesses. He also counted on raising $646 billion by selling carbon emissions credits to polluters as part of the cap-and-trade system. In keeping with a pledge made during his campaign, he proposed making the cuts in Bush's 2001 and 2003 tax laws (PL 107-16, PL 108-27) permanent for middle- and low-income households.

Congressional Democrats endorsed much of Obama's ambitious agenda in a $3.56 trillion fiscal 2010 budget resolution (S Con Res 13) that set the stage for the year's spending and tax debates. However, the lawmakers felt somewhat constrained by concern about the soaring deficit.

The resolution set a cap of $1.09 trillion for the 12 annual appropriations bills, about $10 billion less than Obama requested.

It also gave Democrats the option of pushing Obama's health care overhaul through Congress in the form of a reconciliation bill, which would not be subject to a filibuster in the Senate. As a result, Democrats would need only a simple majority to pass the bill, rather than the 60 votes required to invoke cloture. The budget resolution provided the same protection to legislation that would end the role of private lenders in providing government-subsidized student loans. (Democrats did not use the reconciliation instructions in the first session.)

A LONG APPROPRIATIONS SEASON

The 2009 appropriations season began before the session even started and lasted until virtually the last day. The path of the various spending bills closely tracked with the steady rise in partisan acrimony.

- **Stimulus.** The economic stimulus package was, in effect, the first appropriations bill. House Appropriations Committee Chairman David R. Obey, D-Wis., and other lead appropriators played a central role in assembling it, and the two Appropriations committees marked up the discretionary spending sections in January. The final bill included $311.2 billion in discretionary funds — about $50 billion less than in the House-passed version but $21 billion more than in the Senate bill. House Democrats were especially upset at the loss of funds they had set aside for construction at junior colleges, but it was part of the price for getting the bill through the Senate.

- **Fiscal 2009 omnibus.** The next task was to close the books on fiscal 2009. Democratic leaders deliberately left nine of the 12 annual spending bills unfinished at the end of the 110th Congress. They gambled that the November 2008 election would give them bigger majorities in both chambers and control of the White House, allowing increases in domestic spending that were not possible under Bush.

The gamble paid off. The $1.05 trillion omnibus appropriations package signed March 11 (PL 111-8) included $410 billion for discretionary programs — $19 billion above the amount Bush had said was acceptable — and allowed for many of the domestic

spending increases that Democrats had been unable to win in the last Congress.

- **Supplemental.** After about six weeks of work in May and early June, Congress sent Obama a $105.9 billion fiscal 2009 supplemental spending bill devoted mainly to operations in Iraq and Afghanistan and related costs such as aid to Afghanistan and Pakistan. Other items included $7.7 billion for pandemic flu preparation and $5 billion to support an additional U.S. contribution to the International Monetary Fund (IMF).

For many Democrats who had opposed war funding under Bush, it was a tough vote. Four months earlier, Obama had set a deadline of Aug. 31, 2010, for withdrawing combat troops from Iraq, but many Democrats were disappointed that he planned to leave as many as 50,000 soldiers there until the end of 2011 for training and other purposes. House leaders had to count on Republican support to pass the initial version of the bill.

The measure, which was signed June 24 (PL 111-32), was the second supplemental for the wars in fiscal 2009. A 2008 measure (PL 110-252) provided $65.9 billion in "bridge funding" for the first half of the fiscal year.

The final bill got fewer GOP votes than it otherwise would have, in part because of the IMF money. Republicans were also unhappy that the bill did not bar U.S. trials for Guantánamo detainees.

The detainee issue became a mainstay of GOP attacks on the Democratic majority and the Obama administration during the year. Democrats agreed to attach language to many of the regular appropriations bills barring Guantánamo prisoners from being released in the United States, but they held the line against a blanket ban on bringing any detainees into the country, even for trial.

- **Fiscal 2010 bills.** At about the time the fiscal 2010 appropriations process got under way in June, Republicans began to turn up the heat. They proposed more than 100 amendments to the Commerce-Justice-Science bill, the first spending measure to hit the House floor. Democrats reacted with a floor rule that allowed no more than 33 amendments. Republicans retaliated with a barrage of parliamentary delaying tactics that brought action to a crawl. On June 18, the House took 53 votes on the bill, a modern record for a single day.

From then on, House Democrats broke with tradition by using restrictive rules for every spending bill. Republicans still succeeded in slowing the pace, but Obey achieved his goal of passing all 12 of the bills before the end of July.

The process bogged down in the Senate, where individual senators have wide latitude and even non-controversial bills can consume days of floor time. The chamber passed just four spending bills before the August recess. That slow pace, and the amount of time consumed by the health care debate in the fall, left seven spending bills unfinished. Appropriators combined six of them into a single package that was cleared Dec. 13. The last appropriations bill, for Defense, was held back until the end as a vehicle for other unfinished legislation and was cleared Dec. 19.

The Defense appropriations and authorization bills had given rise to one of the few open disputes between Democrats and Obama. The issue arose over Pentagon plans to halt production of the F-22 fighter plane and end Congress' practice of requiring the Air Force to develop two competing engines for the F-35. Both programs had strong support from the defense committees. The Senate eventually backed down on the F-22 in the face of a direct

veto threat from Obama, and the House followed suit. Lawmakers modified the F-35 provisions but left them in both the authorization and appropriations bills, without provoking a veto.

A NEW SUPREME COURT JUSTICE

On Aug. 6, the Senate confirmed Sonia Sotomayor to become the Supreme Court's first Hispanic justice and the third woman ever to serve on the high court. She was sworn in two days later. Nine Republicans joined 57 Democrats and two independents in supporting the nomination. The remaining 31 Republicans voted "no."

Obama announced his selection of Sotomayor on May 26, following Justice David H. Souter's announcement earlier that month that he would retire.

Many Senate Republicans launched a concerted attack on Sotomayor, focusing in particular on a phrase she had used in several past speeches to the effect that "a wise Latina" judge would often reach a better conclusion than a white male. But GOP leaders chose not to mount a filibuster, which would have failed in any case, given the Democrats' new 60-vote majority.

Republicans also faced a delicate balancing act in trying to criticize Sotomayor without alienating Hispanic voters. She had strong legal credentials — the American Bar Association gave her its highest rating — and a compelling life story. She handled her nomination hearing well, and because she was not expected to change the ideological balance of the court, her nomination was not as fiercely disputed as it might have been.

A GLIMMER OF BIPARTISANSHIP

Although it was rarely easy, members of both parties were able to come together on some legislation, particularly bills aimed at aiding Americans who were hurt by the recession.

- **Credit card rules.** Legislation to curb what many saw as abusive practices by credit card companies sailed through Congress, reaching Obama's desk before Memorial Day, the date he had set as his target for the legislation. The measure (PL 111-24) imposed new disclosure requirements on credit card companies and new restrictions on when they could increase interest rates and fees. Many Republicans warned that credit card companies might revive annual fees, limit cash back and start assessing interest charges from the moment of purchase, instead of giving a grace period. Still, most Republicans in both chambers voted for the bill, underscoring its resonance with voters.

- **Aid to unemployed, homebuyers.** Another example came in November, when the Senate combined two popular proposals — more generous federal unemployment benefits and more help for homebuyers — into a single bill that won near-unanimous support in both chambers (PL 111-92). With the unemployment rate at 10 percent, there was wide support for a plan that added 14 weeks to the extra federal benefits already going to jobless workers who had exhausted their state benefits, with more for the hardest-hit states.

The homebuyer credit, first enacted in 2008, was aimed at propping up the housing sector, which was virtually paralyzed by the subprime mortgage crisis and the subsequent freezing-up of credit. Members of both parties agreed to extend the credit into 2010 and make it available to purchasers with higher incomes — up to $125,000 for individuals and $225,000 for couples — in an effort to help speed economic recovery.

111th Congress, First Session: By the Numbers

The first session of the 111th Congress began at 12 p.m. on Jan. 6, 2009. The House adjourned sine die at 10:31 a.m. on Dec. 24, 2009. The Senate adjourned sine die at 10:19 a.m. on Dec. 24, 2009. Following are some statistical comparisons of activities in the two chambers over the past decade:

		2009	2008	2007	2006	2005	2004	2003	2002	2001	2000	1999
Days in session	Senate	191	184	190	138	159	133	167	149	173	141	162
	House	159	118	164	101	140	110	133	123	142	135	137
Time in session (hours)	Senate	1,421	989	1,376	1,028	1,222	1,032	1,454	1,043	1,236	1,018	1,184
	House	1,247	890	1,478	850	1,067	879	1,015	772	922	1,054	1,125
Average length of daily session (hours)	Senate	7.4	5.4	7.2	7.4	7.7	7.8	8.7	7.0	7.1	7.2	7.3
	House	7.8	7.5	9.0	8.4	7.6	8.0	7.6	6.3	6.5	7.8	8.2
Public laws enacted [1]		125	285	175	321	161	300	198	269	108	410	170
Bills and resolutions introduced	Senate	3,380	1,590	3,033	2,302	2,618	1,318	2,398	1,558	2,212	1,546	2,352
	House	5,691	3,225	6,194	2,451	5,703	2,338	4,616	2,711	4,318	2,701	4,241
	Total	9,071	4,815	9,227	4,753	8,321	3,656	7,014	4,269	6,530	4,247	6,593
Roll calls	Senate	397	215	442	279	366	216	459	253	380	298	374
	House [2]	987	688	1,177	541	669	543	675	483	507	600	609
	House [3]	991	690	1,186	543	671	544	677	484	512	603	611
	Total [3]	1,388	905	1,628	822	1,037	760	1,136	737	892	901	985
Vetoes		1	4	7 [4]	1	0	0	0	0	0	7 [4]	5

SOURCE: Congressional Record   [1] Bills signed into law during congressional session   [2] Votes only; excludes quorum calls   [3] Includes quorum calls   [4] Includes pocket vetoes

UNFINISHED BUSINESS

In addition to the health care bill, a significant amount of other legislation was left unfinished at the end of the session, including two of Obama's main priorities for the year: climate change and financial regulation. The list also included bills to update the estate tax, reauthorize aviation and surface transportation laws and rewrite the rules for student loans.

• **Financial regulation.** The House passed a sweeping overhaul of the U.S. financial regulatory structure in December, taking aim at Wall Street in the first major regulatory response to the banking crisis of 2008. The bill, a priority for Financial Services Committee Chairman Barney Frank, D-Mass., included a process for managing — and, if necessary, dissolving — systemically risky financial institutions. It also proposed a new consumer protection agency to police consumer financial products such as credit cards and home mortgages, new restrictions on executive compensation and federal regulation of the multibillion-dollar over-the-counter market in financial derivatives.

In the Senate, the Banking, Housing and Urban Affairs Committee broke into bipartisan groups to work on various parts of a proposal by the chairman, Christopher J. Dodd, D-Conn., but the measure got no further.

• **Climate change.** A bill to combat global warming and move the nation toward cleaner energy squeaked through the House in June, marking the first time either chamber had passed a bill designed to curb greenhouse gas emissions. Winning over enough moderate Democrats to pass the bill required extensive concessions to members from coal-producing, manufacturing and farm states, plus furious White House lobbying. Even then, it took eight Republicans who broke with their party to provide a winning margin.

The House bill proposed a cap-and-trade system that would set specific limits on greenhouse gas emissions and require polluters to hold government-issued emissions certificates that could be traded in the marketplace. The bill also required that utilities supply a percentage of their electricity from renewable sources.

Similar legislation stalled in the Senate behind the effort to overhaul the health care system. Sharp differences over the cap-and-trade model, electricity requirements and other issues such as nuclear energy made it unlikely that the Senate would act on a global warming bill in the second session.

• **Estate tax.** Congress allowed the estate tax to expire Dec. 31 without a plan for the future. The 2001 tax law (PL 107-16) had put the estate tax on a downward trajectory until 2010, when it would vanish. But the 2001 law itself was due to expire at the end of 2010, which meant that without congressional action, the estate tax would bounce back up to the old level in 2011, with a smaller exclusion and higher rate than taxpayers had seen in years.

No one favored the yo-yo effect, but lawmakers disagreed over the best fix. Many Republicans wanted to repeal the tax for good, or at least keep it as low as possible. Most Democrats opposed a permanent repeal as too expensive, and the House passed a bill with a rate and exclusion that were higher than Republicans sought. The Senate's focus on the health care debate did not leave enough time to work out a compromise.

• **Student loans.** The House passed a bill proposing the most dramatic change to federal student loan programs in a decade; the Senate was expected to take up the legislation in 2010. Under the bill, the government would become the sole originator of federally backed student loans, cutting out the role of private companies as

middlemen in the loan-making process. CBO estimated the switch would save about $87 billion over 10 years, before administrative costs. Almost $40 billion of that was to go toward increasing the value and availability of Pell grants for low-income undergraduates. Most Republicans favored a role for private lenders; the bill received just six GOP votes in the House.

• **Highway, aviation programs.** Surface transportation and aviation programs were left limping along on short-term reauthorization bills in the absence of any consensus on the length of multi-year authorizations, the amount of money to approve or how to pay for the costs. Both short-term laws were good through March 2010.

The last surface transportation law expired Sept. 30. The Federal Aviation Administration had not had a full authorization law since Sept. 30, 2007.

• **Debt limit.** Lawmakers had no alternative but to increase the statutory limit on the federal debt once the Treasury Department warned that federal borrowing would hit the existing ceiling by the end of the year. The only question was the length of the extension. Democrats wanted a new ceiling to last until after the November 2010 elections so they would not have to vote for another increase before that. Republicans preferred to have another vote before the election, since it was the majority's job to ensure that the government did not default, while the minority would have an opportunity to remind the voters about the profligate ways of the other party.

Also, House and Senate Democrats wanted to attach budget enforcement language, but they disagreed over whether to add pay-as-you-go requirements for future legislation or create an independent budget commission to recommend ways to be more frugal. The upshot was a short-term increase (PL 111-123) to tide the government over until early 2010.

• **Job creation.** With unemployment hovering around 10 percent at the end of the year, Pelosi saw to it that her party went on record favoring a jobs bill. In its last vote of the session, the House narrowly passed the $154 billion "Jobs for Main Street Act." The proposed spending was broken into three broad categories: infrastructure investment, public service jobs and help for families and small businesses. The bulk of it was to be funded with leftover TARP money. Senators were too wrapped up in the health care debate to invest energy in jobs legislation, but the issue was ripe for consideration early in the next session.

WRANGLING OVER HEALTH CARE

The biggest unfinished business of all was the Democrats' health care bill.

In the summer and fall, Democrats turned to the monumental task of putting together legislation that would come as close as possible to achieving universal health care coverage, while slowing the growth in health care costs, making health insurance affordable to lower-income Americans and setting minimal coverage requirements for the health insurance industry.

The president and Democratic congressional leaders initially planned to finish the legislation by the end of the year, but they had seriously underestimated the difficulty of putting together a bill that could attract enough votes to pass in both chambers. When Congress left for the August recess neither the House nor the Senate had passed a health care bill.

Republicans used the August break to launch a nationwide campaign against what they called "Obamacare." Some GOP lawmakers took to the hustings, claiming that the government was trying to socialize health care and deprive individuals of making even the most private decisions about life and death. They charged that the Democrats were bent on a plan that would recklessly drive up health care costs, raise middle-class taxes, slash Medicare services and force employers to cut jobs in the middle of the recession.

Democrats regained at least some of the initiative when Congress returned in September and Obama went before a joint session of Congress in a nationally televised speech to explain and promote the legislation.

With Republicans solidly opposing her, Pelosi worked for weeks negotiating, cajoling and fine-tuning as she rounded up the necessary votes from within her own caucus. To nail down the last votes, she accepted anti-abortion language that she and most House Democrats opposed. The House passed the bill Nov. 7, with just two votes to spare.

In the Senate, Finance Committee Chairman Max Baucus, D-Mont., seemed at times close to producing a bipartisan bill, but he and a small group of senators from both parties were never able to nail down the final details. So, like Pelosi, Reid had to look to his own caucus. Unlike the Speaker, however, Reid had to deliver every one of his 58 Democrats and two independents. His goal, and that of Obama, was to pass the bill by the end of the session.

Minority Leader Mitch McConnell, R-Ky., vowed to use every parliamentary delaying tactic available to him to block a bill he said most Americans opposed. Reid's response was to keep the Senate in session seven days a week while he continued trying to lock down the 60 votes he needed to invoke cloture and overcome the stalling tactics. The marathon ultimately lasted for 25 days.

In pursuit of a 60-vote majority, Reid dropped a proposed public health insurance option, which was a core element of the House bill and a key part of the plan for liberals in both chambers. He agreed to pay part of the cost of the plan with an excise tax on high-cost insurance plans that unions and many House Democrats warned would hit not only the wealthy but members of the middle class. And he added anti-abortion language, although it was less restrictive than that in the House bill.

Finally, with 60 votes in hand, Reid filed the rewritten legislation on Saturday, Dec. 18. McConnell responded by forcing the Senate clerks to read the 383-page document aloud. On Dec. 21, Reid won a cloture vote, showing that he could overcome the Republican filibuster. But McConnell forced two more cloture votes before the Senate could pass the bill. Republicans also insisted on the full 30 hours of debate permitted after each successful cloture vote, although they relented and allowed a shorter debate before the final vote on Dec. 24 to allow members to get home by Christmas Day.

The two leaders' assessments were as opposite as their positions had been throughout the long debate.

"We are reshaping the nation. That's what we want to do. That's what we have to do," Reid said before the Dec. 21 cloture vote. "With this vote we're rejecting a system in which one class of people can afford to stay healthy while another cannot. For the first time in American history, good health will not depend on wealth."

McConnell's conclusion: "Mark my words, this legislation will reshape our nation, and Americans have already issued their verdict — they don't want it." ∎

VOTE STUDIES

Popular President Keeps His Caucus In Line, But the Stress Shows

A PUBLIC RECEPTIVE to Barack Obama's "Yes, we can" pledge to enact "change" in Washington not only swept him into the White House but granted his fellow Democrats expanded majorities in the House and the Senate. Expectations among his supporters were accordingly high, and they grew higher when Democrats secured a seemingly filibuster-proof Senate majority during the summer. And they also reached a high in December, when the Senate joined the House in passing bills to overhaul the nation's health care system, a goal that had eluded Congress since Harry S. Truman was president.

Along the way, Obama tested both flanks of his caucus, advancing a broad expansion of government that risked alienating deficit hawks over its spending and populists for its focus on rescuing big companies. Later, he endorsed a Senate health care bill far less sweeping than liberals wanted. All the while, his approach — allowing Congress to work out the details of major bills while he laid out just a few, shifting principles — was criticized for its malleability.

Still, if one accepts that legislating is a messy business and that the best measure of success is the final vote tally, Obama delivered. His success score — the share of votes on which Congress acceded to his clearly stated position — was a historic high, 96.7 percent. That toppled a 44-year-old record held by Lyndon B. Johnson by a margin of 3.6 percentage points and bested the tallies of every president since Congressional Quarterly began its voting studies in 1953.

So it seemed a bit surprising that the year closed with a foreboding sense of political danger for the new president and his party. Obama's public-approval rating sank in December to 49 percent, according to the Gallup polling firm. That rating tied Ronald Reagan for the lowest rating for any first-term, elected president since World War II, registered in December of Reagan's first year in office.

TOUGH VICTORIES

The contrast between Obama's legislative success and his approval rating could be explained by the fact that most of his victories came after lengthy and damaging battles that tested his party's unity in ways that belied the final tallies. As a result, much of his first-term agenda remained incomplete. And where Obama did win clear victories, some were unpopular with the public, particularly a historic increase in spending to counter the ailing economy and government intervention in the financial and automotive industries. To a skeptical public, Obama said these were steps he took only with reluctance. His hand was forced, he said, largely by circumstances left by his predecessor.

But on the signature issues where Obama pushed his own agenda — health care, regulation of financial services and climate change — the president won key votes, but no new laws. Only the final results of those debates could ultimately determine whether Obama would be viewed by historians as merely the beneficiary of an unlikely series of events, which handed Democrats their strongest overall congressional majorities since the late 1970s, or as a legislative mastermind every bit Johnson's equal. "If this Congress passes both health care reform and climate change legislation on top of the economic stuff, it will go down as a historic achievement," said Rich Fleisher, a political science

professor at Fordham University in New York City. "But unless they continue to manage the agenda in a way that is very, very careful, that could all fall apart."

To get his way, Obama relied heavily on his majorities in the House and the Senate, which held together with an unprecedented level of unity when voting on the president's agenda. Republicans provided only occasional support. *(Party unity, p. B-12)*

But as a perilous December health care vote demonstrated, Obama's success hinged, at key moments, on holding on to every single one of his party's votes in the Senate. And he would not have reached the 60-vote threshold without a series of fortuitous events, including

CQ Vote Study Guide

Congressional Quarterly has conducted studies analyzing the voting behavior of members of Congress since 1945. The three principal vote studies currently produced by CQ — presidential support, party unity and voting participation — have been conducted in a consistent manner since 1953. This is how the studies are carried out:

Selecting votes CQ bases its vote studies on all floor votes on which members were asked to vote "yea" or "nay." In 2009, there were 987 such roll call votes in the House and 397 in the Senate. The House total excludes quorum calls (there were four in 2009) because they require only that members vote "present."

The House total does include votes on procedural matters, including votes to approve the Journal (seven in 2009). The Senate total includes votes to instruct the sergeant at arms to request members' presence in the chamber (none in 2009).

The presidential support and party unity studies are based on votes selected from the total according to the criteria described on pp. B-7 and B-16.

Individual scores Members' scores in the accompanying charts are based only on the votes each member actually cast. This makes individual support and opposition scores add up to 100 percent. The same method is used to identify the leading scorers on pp. B-5 and B-14.

Overall scores For consistency with previous years, calculations of average scores by chamber, party and region are based on all eligible "yea" or "nay" votes, whether or not all members participated. As a result, the failure of one or more lawmakers to participate in a roll call vote reduces average support and opposition scores. Therefore, chamber and party averages are not strictly comparable with individual member scores.

Rounding Scores in the tables for the full House and Senate membership are rounded to the nearest percentage point, although rounding is not used to increase any score to 100 percent or to reduce any score to zero. Scores for party and chamber support and opposition leaders are reported to one decimal point to rank them more precisely.

How Often the President Wins

Barack Obama's success rate on roll call votes on which he took a clear position was the highest not only for the first year of any presidency, but for any year since Congressional Quarterly began this study 56 years ago. Typically, a president succeeds most often in the first or second year of his tenure. The data combines House and Senate figures.

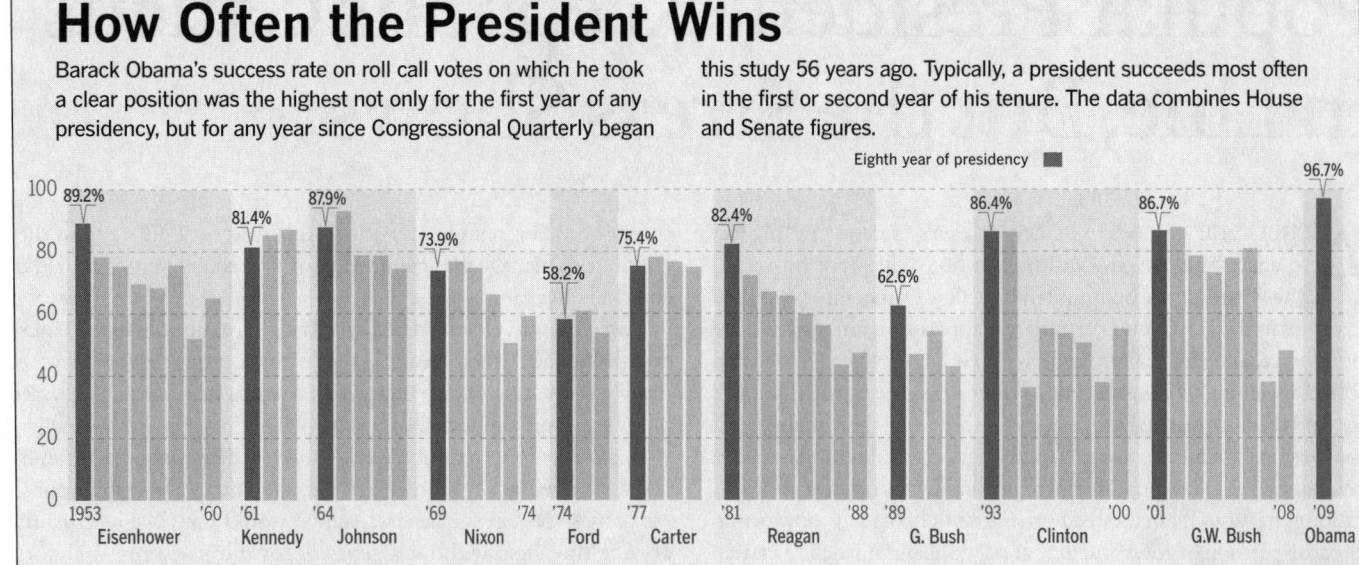

Eighth year of presidency ■

Al Franken's hard-fought recount victory over Minnesota Republican Norm Coleman and Pennsylvanian Arlen Specter's decision in April to switch parties and become a Democrat.

To push the Senate's health care bill over the finish line, and preserve his historic victory rating, Obama had to keep the entire Democratic caucus in line, including senators such as Ben Nelson of Nebraska, who were inclined from the start to oppose it.

"How you begin to understand his success is as a triumph of party government," said Steven Schier, a political scientist at Carleton College in Minnesota. "He's got the large and unified majorities, and those are the enabling conditions for his record high support score."

The situation in 1965 was far different. To pass the law creating Medicare, Johnson had to overcome a divided Democratic caucus, in which seven Southerners opposed him. The Medicare program to provide medical care to the elderly was created only with the help of 13 Republicans. And to win Senate passage, Johnson had to persuade seven Democrats — six from the South — to switch their positions on the issue, along with eight Republicans who'd previously opposed the program. The new votes were just enough to avoid a filibuster.

For Obama, by contrast, the task was less often about winning over Republicans than holding his own side together. Only a rule change in 1975 — setting 60 votes as the total needed for Senate cloture instead of two-thirds of those voting, as it was in Johnson's day — made such an approach possible.

It worked. Of the 79 Senate votes on which Obama expressed a clear position in 2009, he got his way 78 times — and in 70 of those cases, Democrats provided a strong enough margin that he did not need a single Republican vote. In the House, Obama needed Republicans on just 13 of the 68 votes he won, out of a total of 72 votes on which he'd expressed a position. The large number of votes both chambers took on spending bills, which Obama pushed because they helped him achieve his domestic policy goals, also help boost his score.

Instances where Republicans were able to hand Obama a defeat were exceedingly rare. Of the four House votes Obama lost, two were GOP victories: a vote to disapprove further spending under the Troubled Asset Relief Program to aid ailing banks that came two days after his inauguration and a July vote that fell short of the number

needed to pass a food safety overhaul bill. In the end, both votes proved meaningless. In the first case, the Senate already had voted not to halt the bank funding; in the latter, the House voted the next day under different procedures to pass the food safety measure.

The one Obama loss in the Senate came in May, when Republicans voted unanimously, along with a majority of Democrats, to adopt an amendment to the fiscal 2009 supplemental spending bill barring use of federal funds to transfer detainees at the Guantánamo Bay prison camp in Cuba to the United States. Notably, a month later the issue proved thorny in the House where, in a vote on a GOP amendment to the fiscal 2010 Commerce-Justice-Science appropriations bill, Democrats needed two Republicans to join them in defeating a similar effort to de-fund Guantánamo transfers. The Republicans' May Senate victory proved short-lived: The supplemental's final language grants permission to move detainees as long as certain conditions are met.

Instances in which Democrats parted with their president were just as rare, but they did demonstrate that the majority in Congress would protect its prerogatives when pushed. In the first such case, House Democrats passed a fiscal 2010 defense authorization bill that included $369 million to buy parts for a dozen F-22 Raptor fighter jets and $603 million to continue development of an alternative engine for the F-35 Joint Strike Fighter. Obama threatened to veto the bill if it included either provision, saying they were not needed. In the end, a compromise was reached. The final law ended production of the F-22 but proceeded with the alternative engine for the F-35.

The second split came in July, when House Democrats voted overwhelmingly for language overruling a signing statement Obama had issued the month before. The specific issue involved conditions Congress had placed on U.S. funding of the World Bank and International Monetary Fund, financial institutions that provide loans to poor and developing countries, in its fiscal 2009 supplemental spending law. Obama had pledged to ignore them. The back story here was important: George W. Bush had made regular use of such statements, in which a president expresses disagreement with some provisions of a bill while still signing it into law. The practice could leave the legality of

FOR MORE INFORMATION	
Top scorers	B-5
Background	B-7
Vote lists	B-8
Senators' scores	B-9
House members' scores	B-10

Leading Scorers: Presidential Support

Support indicates those who voted in 2009 most often for President Obama's position, when it was clearly known. **Opposition** shows those who voted most often against his position. Lawmakers who left office or who missed half or more of the votes are not listed. Scores are reported to one decimal point only here; those with identical scores are listed alphabetically. *(Complete scores, pp. B-9, B-10)*

SENATE

SUPPORT				OPPOSITION			
Democrats		**Republicans**		**Democrats**		**Republicans**	
Durbin, Ill.	100.0%	Collins, Maine	84.8%	Bayh, Ind.	23.1%	Coburn, Okla.	72.7%
Reed, R.I.	100.0	Snowe, Maine	81.0	McCaskill, Mo.	20.3	DeMint, S.C.	70.1
Rockefeller, W.Va.	100.0	Voinovich, Ohio	77.6	Feingold, Wis.	15.2	Bunning, Ky.	67.5
Whitehouse, R.I.	100.0	Bond, Mo.	69.0	Nelson, Neb.	10.1	Inhofe, Okla.	64.9
Cardin, Md.	98.7	Alexander, Tenn.	68.4	Begich, Alaska	6.8	Ensign, Nev.	61.6
Kaufman, Del.	98.7	Lugar, Ind.	68.4	Byrd, W.Va.	6.8	Burr, N.C.	60.5
Levin, Mich.	98.7	Gregg, N.H.	67.1	Webb, Va.	6.3	Sessions, Ala.	58.7
Menendez, N.J.	98.7	Murkowski, Alaska	65.8	Dorgan, N.D.	5.3	Thune, S.D.	58.2
Reid, Nev.	98.7	Cochran, Miss.	62.2	Murray, Wash.	5.3	Chambliss, Ga.	58.1
Schumer, N.Y.	98.7	Bennett, Utah	59.5	5 members	5.1	Vitter, La.	57.7
Mikulski, Md.	98.6	Brownback, Kan.	58.2			Enzi, Wyo.	57.1
5 members	97.5	Shelby, Ala.	58.2			McCain, Ariz.	56.6

HOUSE

SUPPORT				OPPOSITION			
Democrats		**Republicans**		**Democrats**		**Republicans**	
Becerra, Calif.	100.0%	Cao, La.	68.1%	Taylor, Miss.	50.0%	Flake, Ariz.	92.3%
Carnahan, Mo.	98.6	LoBiondo, N.J.	68.1	Bright, Ala.	45.8	Shadegg, Ariz.	91.4
Crowley, N.Y.	98.6	Murphy, Pa.	65.7	Kirkpatrick, Ariz.	33.3	Foxx, N.C.	90.3
Jackson, Ill.	98.6	Smith, N.J.	65.3	Mitchell, Ariz.	33.3	Franks, Ariz.	90.3
Moore, Wis.	98.6	LaTourette, Ohio	62.5	Kratovil, Md.	31.9	Broun, Ga.	90.1
Olver, Mass.	98.6	Turner, Ohio	61.1	Minnick, Idaho	31.9	Johnson, Texas	90.0
Reyes, Texas	98.6	Castle, Del.	55.6	Childers, Miss.	29.6	Lummis, Wyo.	90.0
Sarbanes, Md.	98.6	Miller, Mich.	55.6	Nye, Va.	29.2	Linder, Ga.	89.9
Waxman, Calif.	98.6	Reichert, Wash.	55.6	Adler, N.J.	26.1	Neugebauer, Texas	89.9
Brown, Fla.	98.5	Ehlers, Mich.	54.9	Marshall, Ga.	25.4	Barrett, S.C.	89.6
DeLauro, Conn.	98.5	King, N.Y.	53.5	Matheson, Utah	25.4	Bishop, Utah	88.9
Hastings, Fla.	98.5	Ros-Lehtinen, Fla.	52.8	Altmire, Pa.	25.0	Chaffetz, Utah	88.9
Larson, Conn.	98.5	Upton, Mich.	52.8	Boren, Okla.	25.0	Conaway, Texas	88.9
Fudge, Ohio	98.4	Gerlach, Pa.	50.7	Herseth Sandlin, S.D.	22.2	Miller, Fla.	88.9
Kennedy, R.I.	98.1	Kirk, Ill.	50.0	Teague, N.M.	22.2	Royce, Calif.	88.9
47 members	97.2	Platts, Pa.	47.9	Griffith, Ala.*	20.8	Blackburn, Tenn.	88.7
		Lance, N.J.	47.2	Shuler, N.C.	20.0	Hensarling, Texas	88.7
		Fortenberry, Neb.	46.5	3 members	18.1	McHenry, N.C.	88.7

Parker Griffith of Alabama switched his party affiliation to Republican after the session ended.

those provisions in dispute. Congress had denounced the practice, and House Democratic leaders wanted to make clear to the new president that they wouldn't tolerate it. "The notion that the administration can take the money and pick and choose what it wants to do with the conditions is unacceptable," said Barney Frank of Massachusetts, chairman of the House Financial Services Committee.

STICKING TOGETHER

Instances of division between the president and his party were otherwise few and far between. Almost as rare were votes on which Democrats were so divided in backing Obama's position that they needed Republicans to carry the day for the president. One of the few such instances came in December, when an amendment by North Dakota Democrat Byron L. Dorgan would have permitted the importation of pharmaceuticals from foreign countries as a way of reducing costs for consumers. Importing drugs had long been on liberal Democrats' health care wish list, but Obama opposed it for fear that it would blow up the delicately crafted health care overhaul. Senators agreed to require 60 votes for adoption, allowing 30 Democrats to join with 16 Republicans and one independent to kill it.

Share of Presidential Positions Declines

The House and Senate held 151 roll call votes in 2009 on which the editors of CQ Weekly determined that President Obama took a clear position. While the actual number of these presidential support votes rose, the figure as a share of all House and Senate votes fell to 10.9 percent. That was the fourth-lowest presidential support vote percentage since this study began in 1953.

Percentage of Presidential Support Votes *For Congress as a Whole*

1965: High: 59.7%
1976: Low: 7.7%
2009: 10.9%

But those were clear exceptions in a year when Democrats belied their reputation for fractiousness and walked in near lock step to support the president's agenda. Most members of the fiscally conservative Blue Dog Caucus of House Democrats, for instance, voted with Obama on at least 88 percent of votes, just 6 percentage points lower than most House Democrats and just 8 percentage points lower than members of the party's liberal wing, the Progressive Caucus. Of the 267 House Democrats who voted in 2009, 79 percent — 211 members — voted with Obama at least 90 percent of the time. By contrast, just 6 percent of them — 17 members — voted with him less than 80 percent of the time. Only two, Bobby Bright of Alabama and Gene Taylor of Mississippi, were on the president's side less than 60 percent of the time. As Speaker Nancy Pelosi, D-Calif., said: "To solve the pressing needs of our nation and put Americans back to work and strengthen our economy, Democrats in Congress had to be unified, organized, and disciplined."

In the Senate, the results were much the same. Just five members of the Democratic caucus parted with Obama on more than one vote out of 10. One of the senators who gave him the most trouble during the health care fight — independent (but Democrat-aligned) Joseph I. Lieberman of Connecticut — was not among them. Evan Bayh of Indiana was the Democrat most likely to disagree with the president, voting against him 23 percent of the time, followed by Claire McCaskill of Missouri (20 percent), Russ Feingold of Wisconsin (15 percent), independent Bernard Sanders of Vermont (14 percent) and Nelson (10 percent). Lieberman was actually more loyal than the Democratic average, voting for the president 96 percent of the time. The average

for the caucus was 92 percent.

Majority Leader Harry Reid, D-Nev., said the cohesion of his caucus was in large part a result of the mess he said President George W. Bush had left behind. "We have tackled an aggressive agenda, understanding that correcting eight years of poor decisions requires a unified effort," he said. And Pelosi said just prior to the end of the first session, "Next year will require the same focus."

REPUBLICANS TESTED

Although Republicans seemed as united in opposition as the Democrats were in support, in reality Obama tested GOP unity time and again. Nearly half of Senate Republicans sided with him on most votes on which he expressed a preference. Of those, Maine's Susan Collins (85 percent) and Olympia J. Snowe (81 percent) were regular converts and provided the crucial votes to approve the economic stimulus bill. The fact that about 40 percent of votes on which the president expressed a position were nominations also boosted his average support score with Senate Republicans.

In the House, more than one out of four Republicans gave Obama their votes in at least a third of the instances where he stated a position. GOP Leader John A. Boehner of Ohio pledged his willingness to work with Democrats if they reached across the aisle. "Republicans are ready to work with Democrats and President Obama to get things done for the American people," Boehner said. Still, he didn't hold out much hope of that in the second session: "Again and again over the past year, Democrats have chosen to go it alone, passing massive bills on a purely partisan basis," he said. ■

Presidential Support Background

Congressional Quarterly's editors select presidential support votes each year based on clear statements by the president or authorized spokesmen. **Support** scores show the percentage of roll call votes on which members of Congress voted in agreement with the president's position. **Success** shows the percentage of the selected votes on which the president prevailed.

Presidential Success by Issues

Economic affairs includes votes on taxes, trade, and omnibus and some supplemental spending bills, which may fund both domestic and defense/foreign policy programs. **Confirmation** votes in the Senate are included only in the chamber's overall scores.

	Defense/Foreign Policy		Domestic		Economic Affairs		Overall	
	2009	2008	2009	2008	2009	2008	2009	2008
House	85.7%	42.9%	97.6%	29.5%	93.8%	36.4%	94.4%	33.8%
Senate	93.8	71.4	100.0	59.3	100.0	69.2	98.7	68.5
Congress	90.0	52.4	98.4	40.8	96.2	48.6	96.7	47.8

House Average Presidential Support Scores

DEMOCRATS | REPUBLICANS

Eisenhower, R	DEM	REP
1954	44%	71%
1955	53	60
1956	52	72
1957	49	54
1958	44	67
1959	40	68
1960	44	59
Kennedy, D		
1961	73	37
1962	72	42
1963	72	32

Johnson, D	DEM	REP
1964	74%	38%
1965	74	41
1966	63	37
1967	69	46
1968	64	51
Nixon, R		
1969	48	57
1970	53	66
1971	47	72
1972	47	64
1973	35	62
1974	46	65

Ford, R	DEM	REP
1974	41%	51%
1975	38	63
1976	32	63
Carter, D		
1977	63	42
1978	60	36
1979	64	34
1980	63	40
Reagan, R		
1981	42	68
1982	39	64
1983	28	70
1984	34	60
1985	30	67

Year	DEM	REP
1986	25%	65%
1987	24	62
1988	25	57
G. Bush, R		
1989	36	69
1990	25	63
1991	34	72
1992	25	71
Clinton, D		
1993	77	39
1994	75	47
1995	75	22
1996	74	38
1997	71	30

Year	DEM	REP
1998	74%	26%
1999	73	23
2000	73	27
G.W. Bush, R		
2001	31	86
2002	32	82
2003	26	89
2004	30	80
2005	24	81
2006	31	85
2007	7	72
2008	16	64
Obama, D		
2009	90	26

Senate Average Presidential Support Scores

DEMOCRATS | REPUBLICANS

Eisenhower, R	DEM	REP
1954	38%	73%
1955	56	72
1956	39	72
1957	51	69
1958	44	67
1959	38	72
1960	43	66
Kennedy, D		
1961	65	36
1962	63	39
1963	63	44

Johnson, D	DEM	REP
1964	61%	45%
1965	64	48
1966	57	43
1967	61	53
1968	48	47
Nixon, R		
1969	47	66
1970	45	60
1971	40	64
1972	44	66
1973	37	61
1974	39	57

Ford, R	DEM	REP
1974	39%	55%
1975	47	68
1976	39	62
Carter, D		
1977	70	52
1978	66	41
1979	68	47
1980	62	45
Reagan, R		
1981	49	80
1982	43	74
1983	42	73
1984	41	76
1985	35	75

Year	DEM	REP
1986	37	78
1987	36%	64%
1988	47	68
G. Bush, R		
1989	55	82
1990	38	70
1991	41	83
1992	32	73
Clinton, D		
1993	87	29
1994	86	42
1995	81	29
1996	83	37
1997	85	60

Year	DEM	REP
1998	82	41
1999	84	34
2000	89%	46%
G.W. Bush, R		
2001	66	94
2002	71	89
2003	48	94
2004	60	91
2005	38	86
2006	51	85
2007	37	78
2008	34	70
Obama, D		
2009	92	50

2009 Presidential Position Votes

The following is a list of the 72 House and 79 Senate roll call votes in 2009 on which the president took a clear position, based on his statements or those of authorized spokesmen. A victory is a vote on which the president's position prevailed.

HOUSE

Defense and Foreign Policy

VOTE NUMBER	DESCRIPTION
12 Victories	
252	Weapons acquisitions
265	War spending
286	Weapons acquisitions
348	War spending
361	Detainee policy
517	State Department
520	Foreign aid spending
525	Foreign aid spending
529	Military construction
661	Weapons acquisitions
674	Defense spending
783	Detainee policy
2 Defeats	
460	Defense authorization
521	International banks

Domestic Policy

VOTE NUMBER	DESCRIPTION
41 Victories	
140	National service
169	National service
187	Tobacco regulation
314	Auto buyer subsidies
335	Tobacco regulation
359	Legal Services
367	Domestic spending
408	Domestic spending
420	Veterans' health care
443	Domestic spending
450	Domestic spending
468	Domestic spending
469	Climate change
475	Domestic spending
476	Climate change
477	Climate change
502	Domestic spending
510	Domestic spending
555	Executive powers
557	Domestic spending
558	Executive powers
571	Domestic spending
580	Domestic spending
592	Domestic spending
620	Housing spending
621	Transit spending
623	Domestic spending
637	Domestic spending
645	Domestic spending
646	Domestic spending
680	Food safety
682	Auto buyer subsidies
752	Domestic spending
761	Domestic spending
771	Veterans' health care
784	Domestic spending
793	HIV/AIDS
826	Domestic spending
885	Health care
887	Health care
909	Physicians' payments
1 Defeat	
657	Food safety

Economic Affairs and Trade

VOTE NUMBER	DESCRIPTION
15 Victories	
44	Economic stimulus
46	Economic stimulus
70	Economic stimulus
228	Credit card regulation
235	Financial fraud
268	Financial fraud
271	Mortgage modifications
276	Credit card regulation
612	Budget enforcement
712	Student loans
719	Student loans
943	Tax extensions
949	Omnibus spending
965	Financial regulation
968	Financial regulation
1 Defeat	
27	Financial bailout

House Success Score

Victories	68
Defeats	4
Total	72
Success rate	94.4%

SENATE

Defense and Foreign Policy

VOTE NUMBER	DESCRIPTION
15 Victories	
19	Global family planning
186	Weapons acquisitions
197	Weapons acquisitions
201	International banks
202	War spending
209	War spending
210	War spending
222	Defense spending
235	Weapons acquisitions
240	Weapons acquisitions
242	Defense programs
305	War policy
315	Defense spending
347	Detainee policy
348	Military construction
1 Defeat	
196	Detainee policy

Domestic Policy

VOTE NUMBER	DESCRIPTION
21 Victories	
115	National service
207	Tobacco regulation
229	Domestic spending
248	Domestic spending
259	Domestic spending
261	Domestic spending
270	Domestic spending
282	Domestic spending
287	Domestic spending
295	Executive powers
298	Domestic spending
318	Domestic spending
319	Domestic spending
322	Domestic spending
323	Domestic spending
331	Domestic spending
340	Domestic spending
358	Health care
377	Health care
385	Health care (cloture)
396	Health care

Economic Affairs and Trade

VOTE NUMBER	DESCRIPTION
10 Victories	
45	Economic stimulus
48	Economic stimulus
61	Economic stimulus
64	Economic stimulus
120	Budget limits
129	Budget limits
171	Financial fraud
185	Mortgage modifications
194	Credit card regulation
374	Omnibus spending

Nominations

VOTE NUMBER	DESCRIPTION
32 Victories	
6	Hillary Rodham Clinton
15	Timothy F. Geithner
17	Daniel K. Tarullo
32	Eric H. Holder Jr.
62	William Lynn
66	Hilda L. Solis
97	David W. Ogden
98	Thomas J. Perrelli
100	Ron Kirk
107	Elena Kagan
109	David S. Kris
155	Tony West
156	Lanny A. Breuer
157	Christine Anne Varney
159	Christopher Hill
172	Kathleen Sebelius
175	Thomas L. Strickland
187	R. Gil Kerlikowske
195	Gary Gensler
213	Harold Hongju Koh
262	Sonia Sotomayor
274	Cass R. Sunstein
288	Gerard E. Lynch
299	Jeffrey L. Viken
306	Thomas E. Perez
324	Roberto A. Lange
328	Irene Berger
341	Ignacia S. Moreno
342	Andre M. Davis
343	Charlene E. Honeywell
350	David F. Hamilton
354	Jacqueline H. Nguyen

Senate Success Score

Victories	78
Defeats	1
Total	79
Success rate	98.7%
Success rate, minus nominations	97.9%

SENATE

1. Presidential Support Score. Percentage of recorded votes cast in 2009 on which President Obama took a position and on which the senator voted "yea" or "nay" in agreement with the president's position. Failure to vote does not lower an individual's score.

2. Presidential Opposition Score. Percentage of recorded votes cast in 2009 on which President Obama took a position and on which the senator voted "yea" or "nay" in disagreement with the president's position. Failure to vote does not lower an individual's score.

3. Participation in Presidential Support Votes. Percentage of the recorded Senate votes in 2009 on which President Obama took a position and for which the senator was eligible and present and voted "yea" or "nay." There were a total of 79 such recorded votes.

[1] Sen. Michael Bennet, D-Colo., was sworn in Jan. 22, 2009, to fill the seat vacated by fellow Democrat Ken Salazar, who resigned Jan. 20 to become secretary of Interior. The first vote for which Bennet was eligible was vote 11; Salazar was not eligible for any presidential support votes in 2009.

[2] Sen. Ted Kaufman, D-Del., was sworn in Jan. 16, 2009, to fill the seat vacated by fellow Democrat Joseph R. Biden Jr., who resigned Jan. 15 to become vice president. The first vote for which Kaufman was eligible was vote 6; Biden was not eligible for any presidential support votes in 2009.

[3] Sen. George LeMieux, R-Fla., was sworn in Sept. 10 to fill the seat vacated by the Sept. 9 resignation of fellow Republican Mel Martinez. The first vote for which LeMieux was eligible was vote 274; the last vote for which Martinez was eligible was vote 272.

[4] Sen. Roland W. Burris, D-Ill., was sworn in Jan. 15, 2009, to fill the seat vacated by fellow Democrat Barack Obama, who resigned Nov. 16, 2008, to become president. The first vote for which Burris was eligible was vote 5.

[5] Sen. Paul G. Kirk Jr., D-Mass., was sworn in Sept. 25, 2009, to fill the seat vacated by fellow Democrat Edward M. Kennedy, who died Aug. 25. The first vote for which Kirk was eligible was vote 299; the last vote for which Kennedy was eligible was vote 270.

[6] Sen. Al Franken, D-Minn., was sworn in July 7, 2009, after he was certified the winner of that state's contested election. The first vote for which he was eligible was vote 218.

[7] Sen. Kirsten Gillibrand, D-N.Y., was sworn in Jan. 27, 2009, to fill the seat vacated by fellow Democrat Hillary Rodham Clinton, who resigned Jan. 21 to become secretary of State. The first vote for which Gillibrand was eligible was vote 16; Clinton did not participate in any presidential support votes in 2009.

[8] Pennsylvania Sen. Arlen Specter switched party affiliation from Republican to Democrat, effective April 30, 2009. The first vote he cast as a Democrat was vote 174. As a Republican, he was eligible for 25 presidential support votes in 2009; as a Democrat, he was eligible for 54 such votes. His scores in the table reflect his votes as a Democrat. As a Republican, Specter's presidential support score was 76 percent; opposition score, 24 percent; and participation rate, 100 percent.

	1	2	3		1	2	3
ALABAMA				**MONTANA**			
Shelby	58	42	100	Baucus	96	4	99
Sessions	41	59	95	Tester	97	3	100
ALASKA				**NEBRASKA**			
Murkowski	66	34	100	Nelson	90	10	100
Begich	93	7	92	**Johanns**	52	48	97
ARIZONA				**NEVADA**			
McCain	43	57	96	Reid	99	1	100
Kyl	45	55	96	**Ensign**	38	62	92
ARKANSAS				**NEW HAMPSHIRE**			
Lincoln	95	5	100	**Gregg**	67	33	92
Pryor	95	5	100	Shaheen	95	5	99
CALIFORNIA				**NEW JERSEY**			
Feinstein	96	4	99	Lautenberg	97	3	97
Boxer	96	4	97	Menendez	99	1	95
COLORADO				**NEW MEXICO**			
Salazar[1]	–	–	–	Bingaman	96	4	100
Udall	97	3	97	Udall	96	4	100
Bennet[1]	96	4	100	**NEW YORK**			
CONNECTICUT				Schumer	99	1	100
Dodd	97	3	95	Clinton[7]	–	–	0
Lieberman	96	4	94	Gillibrand[7]	97	3	100
DELAWARE				**NORTH CAROLINA**			
Biden[2]	–	–	–	**Burr**	39	61	96
Carper	97	3	97	Hagan	96	4	95
Kaufman[2]	99	1	100	**NORTH DAKOTA**			
FLORIDA				Conrad	95	5	100
Nelson	97	3	97	Dorgan	95	5	95
Martinez[3]	64	36	92	**OHIO**			
LeMieux[3]	50	50	100	**Voinovich**	78	22	96
GEORGIA				Brown	96	4	99
Chambliss	42	58	94	**OKLAHOMA**			
Isakson	45	55	94	**Inhofe**	35	65	97
HAWAII				**Coburn**	27	73	97
Inouye	96	4	100	**OREGON**			
Akaka	97	3	100	Wyden	97	3	95
IDAHO				Merkley	96	4	99
Crapo	48	52	100	**PENNSYLVANIA**			
Risch	47	53	97	Specter[8]	96	4	98
ILLINOIS				Casey	97	3	100
Durbin	100	0	97	**RHODE ISLAND**			
Burris[4]	97	3	99	Reed	100	0	99
INDIANA				Whitehouse	100	0	100
Lugar	68	32	100	**SOUTH CAROLINA**			
Bayh	77	23	99	**Graham**	49	51	97
IOWA				**DeMint**	30	70	97
Grassley	47	53	100	**SOUTH DAKOTA**			
Harkin	97	3	99	Johnson	96	4	96
KANSAS				**Thune**	42	58	100
Brownback	58	42	100	**TENNESSEE**			
Roberts	51	49	95	**Alexander**	68	32	100
KENTUCKY				**Corker**	54	46	100
McConnell	46	54	100	**TEXAS**			
Bunning	32	68	97	**Hutchison**	50	50	96
LOUISIANA				**Cornyn**	45	55	95
Landrieu	97	3	95	**UTAH**			
Vitter	42	58	99	**Hatch**	58	42	96
MAINE				**Bennett**	59	41	94
Snowe	81	19	100	**VERMONT**			
Collins	85	15	100	Leahy	96	4	97
MARYLAND				*Sanders*	86	14	99
Mikulski	99	1	91	**VIRGINIA**			
Cardin	99	1	100	Webb	94	6	100
MASSACHUSETTS				Warner	96	4	100
Kennedy[5]	100	0	4	**WASHINGTON**			
Kerry	97	3	92	Murray	95	5	95
Kirk[5]	100	0	100	Cantwell	95	5	100
MICHIGAN				**WEST VIRGINIA**			
Levin	99	1	100	Byrd	93	7	56
Stabenow	96	4	100	Rockefeller	100	0	76
MINNESOTA				**WISCONSIN**			
Klobuchar	97	3	99	Kohl	97	3	100
Franken[6]	97	3	100	Feingold	85	15	100
MISSISSIPPI				**WYOMING**			
Cochran	62	38	94	**Enzi**	43	57	97
Wicker	49	51	99	**Barrasso**	44	56	100
MISSOURI							
Bond	69	31	90				
McCaskill	80	20	100				

KEY **Republicans** Democrats *Independents*

HOUSE

1. **Presidential Support.** Percentage of recorded votes cast in 2009 on which President Obama took a position and on which the member voted "yea" or "nay" in agreement with the president's position. Failure to vote does not lower an individual's score.

2. **Presidential Opposition.** Percentage of recorded votes cast in 2009 on which President Obama took a position and on which the member voted "yea" or "nay" in disagreement with the president's position. Failure to vote does not lower an individual's score.

3. **Participation in Presidential Support Votes.** Percentage of the recorded House votes in 2009 on which President Obama took a position and for which the member was eligible and present and voted "yea" or "nay." There were a total of 72 such recorded votes.

		1	2	3
ALABAMA				
1	**Bonner**	22	78	100
2	**Bright**	54	46	100
3	**Rogers**	42	58	100
4	**Aderholt**	28	72	96
5	**Griffith**[1]	79	21	100
6	**Bachus**	29	71	100
7	Davis	86	14	97
ALASKA				
AL	**Young**	42	58	93
ARIZONA				
1	Kirkpatrick	67	33	100
2	**Franks**	10	90	100
3	**Shadegg**	9	91	97
4	Pastor	96	4	100
5	Mitchell	67	33	100
6	**Flake**	8	92	90
7	Grijalva	93	7	96
8	Giffords	90	10	100
ARKANSAS				
1	Berry	90	10	97
2	Snyder	97	3	100
3	**Boozman**	22	78	100
4	Ross	87	13	99
CALIFORNIA				
1	Thompson	96	4	100
2	**Herger**	16	84	96
3	**Lungren**	26	74	100
4	**McClintock**	13	87	100
5	Matsui	96	4	100
6	Woolsey	92	8	99
7	Miller, George	97	3	97
8	Pelosi[2]	100	0	21
9	Lee	93	7	100
10	Tauscher[3]	96	4	87
10	Garamendi[3]	100	0	100
11	McNerney	93	7	100
12	Speier	92	8	92
13	Stark	87	13	89
14	Eshoo	97	3	99
15	Honda	94	6	99
16	Lofgren	93	7	96
17	Farr	94	6	99
18	Cardoza	96	4	96
19	**Radanovich**	20	80	90
20	Costa	93	7	94
21	**Nunes**	18	82	94
22	**McCarthy**	24	76	99
23	Capps	97	3	100
24	**Gallegly**	25	75	99
25	**McKeon**	28	72	100
26	**Dreier**	28	72	100
27	Sherman	96	4	100
28	Berman	97	3	100
29	Schiff	97	3	100
30	Waxman	99	1	100
31	Becerra	100	0	96
32	Solis[4]	100	0	50
32	Chu[4]	100	0	100
33	Watson	94	6	99
34	Roybal-Allard	97	3	99
35	Waters	93	7	99
36	Harman	96	4	93
37	Richardson	94	6	99
38	Napolitano	93	7	99
39	Sánchez, Linda	95	5	86
40	**Royce**	11	89	100
41	**Lewis**	25	75	100
42	**Miller, Gary**	27	73	92
43	Baca	97	3	99
44	**Calvert**	24	76	100
45	**Bono Mack**	31	69	99
46	**Rohrabacher**	23	77	99
47	Sanchez, Loretta	94	6	93
48	**Campbell**	14	86	96
49	**Issa**	19	81	100
50	**Bilbray**	35	65	99
51	Filner	93	7	100
52	**Hunter**	21	79	100
53	Davis	97	3	100

		1	2	3
COLORADO				
1	DeGette	97	3	100
2	Polis	88	12	96
3	Salazar	93	7	94
4	Markey	84	16	97
5	**Lamborn**	13	87	100
6	**Coffman**	24	76	100
7	Perlmutter	97	3	97
CONNECTICUT				
1	Larson	98	2	92
2	Courtney	96	4	100
3	DeLauro	99	1	94
4	Himes	92	8	100
5	Murphy	97	3	96
DELAWARE				
AL	**Castle**	56	44	100
FLORIDA				
1	**Miller**	11	89	100
2	Boyd	86	14	97
3	Brown	99	1	93
4	**Crenshaw**	37	63	99
5	**Brown-Waite**	44	56	97
6	**Stearns**	26	74	100
7	**Mica**	19	81	97
8	Grayson	93	7	96
9	**Bilirakis**	31	69	99
10	**Young**	32	68	99
11	Castor	96	4	100
12	**Putnam**	37	63	97
13	**Buchanan**	41	59	94
14	**Mack**	13	87	99
15	**Posey**	22	78	100
16	**Rooney**	30	70	99
17	Meek	94	6	99
18	**Ros-Lehtinen**	53	47	100
19	Wexler	96	4	97
20	Wasserman Schultz	97	3	100
21	**Diaz-Balart, L.**	45	55	99
22	Klein	94	6	99
23	Hastings	98	2	90
24	Kosmas	85	15	99
25	**Diaz-Balart, M.**	44	56	99
GEORGIA				
1	**Kingston**	17	83	100
2	Bishop	94	6	99
3	**Westmoreland**	13	87	94
4	Johnson	96	4	99
5	Lewis	93	7	76
6	**Price**	11	89	97
7	**Linder**	10	90	96
8	Marshall	75	25	99
9	**Deal**	12	88	92
10	**Broun**	10	90	99
11	**Gingrey**	20	80	97
12	Barrow	85	15	100
13	Scott	93	7	100
HAWAII				
1	Abercrombie	97	3	96
2	Hirono	97	3	100
IDAHO				
1	Minnick	68	32	96
2	**Simpson**	32	68	100
ILLINOIS				
1	Rush	97	3	99
2	Jackson	99	1	100
3	Lipinski	90	10	99
4	Gutierrez	93	7	94
5	Quigley[5]	97	3	100
6	**Roskam**	26	74	100
7	Davis	97	3	97
8	Bean	83	17	99
9	Schakowsky	96	4	99
10	**Kirk**	50	50	100
11	Halvorson	92	8	100
12	Costello	87	13	97
13	**Biggert**	45	55	99
14	Foster	90	10	100
15	**Johnson**	27	73	97

KEY   **Republicans**   Democrats

[1] Alabama Rep. Parker Griffith switched party affiliation from Democrat to Republican, effective Dec. 23, 2009. All votes cast by Griffith in 2009 were as a Democrat.

[2] The Speaker votes only at her discretion.

[3] Rep. John Garamendi, D-Calif., was sworn in Nov. 5 to fill the seat vacated by fellow Democrat Ellen O. Tauscher, who resigned June 26 to become an undersecretary of State. The first vote for which Garamendi was eligible was vote 858; the last vote for which Tauscher was eligible was vote 477.

[4] Rep. Judy Chu, D-Calif., was sworn in July 16, 2009, to fill the seat vacated by fellow Democrat Hilda L. Solis, who resigned Feb. 24 to become secretary of Labor. The first vote for which Chu was eligible was vote 549; the last vote for which Solis was eligible was vote 79.

[5] Rep. Mike Quigley, D-Ill., was sworn in April 21, 2009, to fill the seat vacated by fellow Democrat Rahm Emanuel, who resigned Jan. 2 to become President Obama's chief of staff. The first vote for which Quigley was eligible was vote 194; Emanuel was not eligible for any votes in 2009.

[6] Rep. Scott Murphy, D-N.Y., was sworn in April 29, 2009, to fill the seat vacated by fellow Democrat Kirsten Gillibrand, who resigned Jan. 26 to become a senator. The first vote for which Murphy was eligible was vote 221; the last vote for which Gillibrand was eligible was vote 29.

[7] Rep. Bill Owens, D-N.Y., was sworn in Nov. 6 to fill the seat vacated by Republican John M. McHugh, who resigned Sept. 21 to become secretary of the Army. The first vote for which Owens was eligible was vote 867; the last vote for which McHugh was eligible was vote 719.

[8] Del. Gregorio Kilili Camacho Sablan of the Northern Mariana Islands, who was elected in 2008 as an independent, informed the Speaker on Feb. 23, 2009, that he wished to list his party affiliation as Democrat. The first vote in the Committee of the Whole for which he asked to be counted with the Democrats was vote 100.

Name	1	2	3
16 Manzullo	22	78	100
17 Hare	96	4	99
18 Schock	36	64	97
19 Shimkus	35	65	100
INDIANA			
1 Visclosky	93	7	100
2 Donnelly	85	15	100
3 Souder	34	66	99
4 Buyer	24	76	94
5 Burton	18	82	100
6 Pence	12	88	90
7 Carson	97	3	100
8 Ellsworth	89	11	100
9 Hill	83	17	99
IOWA			
1 Braley	97	3	96
2 Loebsack	97	3	99
3 Boswell	97	3	100
4 Latham	35	65	100
5 King	13	87	100
KANSAS			
1 Moran	21	79	100
2 Jenkins	22	78	100
3 Moore	94	6	100
4 Tiahrt	18	82	100
KENTUCKY			
1 Whitfield	30	70	97
2 Guthrie	32	68	100
3 Yarmuth	97	3	100
4 Davis	21	79	99
5 Rogers	35	65	100
6 Chandler	92	8	100
LOUISIANA			
1 Scalise	23	77	97
2 Cao	68	32	96
3 Melancon	85	15	94
4 Fleming	26	74	100
5 Alexander	27	73	99
6 Cassidy	37	63	100
7 Boustany	23	77	97
MAINE			
1 Pingree	90	10	100
2 Michaud	92	8	100
MARYLAND			
1 Kratovil	68	32	100
2 Ruppersberger	96	4	96
3 Sarbanes	99	1	99
4 Edwards	94	6	99
5 Hoyer	97	3	99
6 Bartlett	18	82	100
7 Cummings	97	3	97
8 Van Hollen	97	3	99
MASSACHUSETTS			
1 Olver	99	1	100
2 Neal	96	4	99
3 McGovern	94	6	100
4 Frank	97	3	97
5 Tsongas	94	6	97
6 Tierney	94	6	100
7 Markey	97	3	99
8 Capuano	96	4	93
9 Lynch	96	4	99
10 Delahunt	94	6	94
MICHIGAN			
1 Stupak	87	13	96
2 Hoekstra	20	80	99
3 Ehlers	55	45	99
4 Camp	36	64	100
5 Kildee	96	4	100
6 Upton	53	47	100
7 Schauer	96	4	100
8 Rogers	31	69	97
9 Peters	87	13	100
10 Miller	56	44	100
11 McCotter	37	63	100
12 Levin	96	4	99
13 Kilpatrick	96	4	96
14 Conyers	91	9	96
15 Dingell	96	4	99
MINNESOTA			
1 Walz	96	4	100
2 Kline	17	83	99
3 Paulsen	32	68	99
4 McCollum	96	4	96

Name	1	2	3
5 Ellison	95	5	92
6 Bachmann	14	86	90
7 Peterson	83	17	100
8 Oberstar	94	6	99
MISSISSIPPI			
1 Childers	70	30	99
2 Thompson	97	3	99
3 Harper	31	69	99
4 Taylor	50	50	97
MISSOURI			
1 Clay	96	4	100
2 Akin	17	83	97
3 Carnahan	99	1	99
4 Skelton	90	10	96
5 Cleaver	96	4	99
6 Graves	19	81	93
7 Blunt	24	76	92
8 Emerson	41	59	97
9 Luetkemeyer	27	73	99
MONTANA			
AL Rehberg	26	74	100
NEBRASKA			
1 Fortenberry	46	54	99
2 Terry	41	59	99
3 Smith	15	85	100
NEVADA			
1 Berkley	96	4	99
2 Heller	22	78	93
3 Titus	94	6	100
NEW HAMPSHIRE			
1 Shea-Porter	91	9	96
2 Hodes	93	7	100
NEW JERSEY			
1 Andrews	96	4	100
2 LoBiondo	68	32	100
3 Adler	74	26	96
4 Smith	65	35	100
5 Garrett	18	82	100
6 Pallone	97	3	99
7 Lance	47	53	100
8 Pascrell	97	3	94
9 Rothman	97	3	99
10 Payne	94	6	96
11 Frelinghuysen	42	58	100
12 Holt	97	3	99
13 Sires	97	3	100
NEW MEXICO			
1 Heinrich	87	13	100
2 Teague	78	22	100
3 Lujan	93	7	99
NEW YORK			
1 Bishop	97	3	100
2 Israel	97	3	97
3 King	54	46	99
4 McCarthy	97	3	83
5 Ackerman	97	3	94
6 Meeks	97	3	100
7 Crowley	99	1	99
8 Nadler	97	3	99
9 Weiner	94	6	100
10 Towns	96	4	94
11 Clarke	96	4	100
12 Velázquez	94	6	93
13 McMahon	87	13	100
14 Maloney	97	3	94
15 Rangel	96	4	97
16 Serrano	94	6	100
17 Engel	97	3	99
18 Lowey	97	3	100
19 Hall	96	4	97
20 Gillibrand [6]	0	100	100
20 Murphy [6]	88	12	92
21 Tonko	97	3	100
22 Hinchey	93	7	97
23 McHugh [7]	80	20	84
23 Owens [7]	86	14	100
24 Arcuri	83	17	100
25 Maffei	94	6	100
26 Lee	42	58	99
27 Higgins	97	3	99
28 Slaughter	95	5	92
29 Massa	82	18	100
NORTH CAROLINA			
1 Butterfield	97	3	100
2 Etheridge	97	3	99
3 Jones	36	64	97
4 Price	97	3	100

Name	1	2	3
5 Foxx	10	90	100
6 Coble	23	77	97
7 McIntyre	82	18	100
8 Kissell	89	11	99
9 Myrick	19	81	100
10 McHenry	11	89	99
11 Shuler	80	20	97
12 Watt	97	3	99
13 Miller	97	3	100
NORTH DAKOTA			
AL Pomeroy	96	4	99
OHIO			
1 Driehaus	85	15	99
2 Schmidt	22	78	94
3 Turner	61	39	100
4 Jordan	13	87	100
5 Latta	13	87	100
6 Wilson	94	6	97
7 Austria	35	65	100
8 Boehner	12	88	93
9 Kaptur	90	10	93
10 Kucinich	82	18	100
11 Fudge	98	2	89
12 Tiberi	41	59	99
13 Sutton	97	3	99
14 LaTourette	63	37	100
15 Kilroy	96	4	100
16 Boccieri	90	10	100
17 Ryan	97	3	96
18 Space	90	10	99
OKLAHOMA			
1 Sullivan	20	80	76
2 Boren	75	25	100
3 Lucas	17	83	92
4 Cole	22	78	100
5 Fallin	25	75	99
OREGON			
1 Wu	97	3	97
2 Walden	44	56	99
3 Blumenauer	93	7	100
4 DeFazio	90	10	99
5 Schrader	92	8	100
PENNSYLVANIA			
1 Brady	96	4	99
2 Fattah	97	3	99
3 Dahlkemper	90	10	97
4 Altmire	75	25	100
5 Thompson	27	73	99
6 Gerlach	51	49	99
7 Sestak	97	3	99
8 Murphy, P.	90	10	99
9 Shuster	27	73	97
10 Carney	88	12	90
11 Kanjorski	93	7	99
12 Murtha	97	3	93
13 Schwartz	96	4	99
14 Doyle	97	3	99
15 Dent	46	54	100
16 Pitts	22	78	100
17 Holden	89	11	99
18 Murphy, T.	66	34	97
19 Platts	48	52	99
RHODE ISLAND			
1 Kennedy	98	2	75
2 Langevin	97	3	100
SOUTH CAROLINA			
1 Brown	23	77	99
2 Wilson	18	82	100
3 Barrett	10	90	67
4 Inglis	22	78	100
5 Spratt	97	3	97
6 Clyburn	97	3	99
SOUTH DAKOTA			
AL Herseth Sandlin	78	22	100
TENNESSEE			
1 Roe	26	74	100
2 Duncan	17	83	100
3 Wamp	26	74	97
4 Davis	83	17	99
5 Cooper	85	15	99
6 Gordon	92	8	100
7 Blackburn	11	89	99
8 Tanner	86	14	92
9 Cohen	96	4	100

Name	1	2	3
TEXAS			
1 Gohmert	15	85	94
2 Poe	19	81	100
3 Johnson, S.	10	90	97
4 Hall	31	69	97
5 Hensarling	11	89	99
6 Barton	21	79	99
7 Culberson	14	86	100
8 Brady	11	89	97
9 Green, A.	97	3	100
10 McCaul	26	74	97
11 Conaway	11	89	100
12 Granger	21	79	87
13 Thornberry	14	86	100
14 Paul	14	86	87
15 Hinojosa	97	3	94
16 Reyes	99	1	99
17 Edwards	90	10	97
18 Jackson Lee	96	4	99
19 Neugebauer	10	90	96
20 Gonzalez	97	3	97
21 Smith	22	78	100
22 Olson	13	87	99
23 Rodriguez	93	7	100
24 Marchant	15	85	93
25 Doggett	89	11	100
26 Burgess	17	83	96
27 Ortiz	93	7	100
28 Cuellar	92	8	100
29 Green, G.	96	4	99
30 Johnson, E.	97	3	99
31 Carter	16	84	94
32 Sessions	12	88	94
UTAH			
1 Bishop	11	89	87
2 Matheson	75	25	99
3 Chaffetz	11	89	100
VERMONT			
AL Welch	92	8	99
VIRGINIA			
1 Wittman	31	69	100
2 Nye	71	29	100
3 Scott	96	4	94
4 Forbes	25	75	100
5 Perriello	83	17	99
6 Goodlatte	14	86	100
7 Cantor	21	79	100
8 Moran	97	3	99
9 Boucher	93	7	99
10 Wolf	43	57	100
11 Connolly	96	4	100
WASHINGTON			
1 Inslee	94	6	99
2 Larsen	97	3	99
3 Baird	87	13	100
4 Hastings	19	81	96
5 McMorris Rodgers	23	77	99
6 Dicks	97	3	99
7 McDermott	93	7	100
8 Reichert	56	44	100
9 Smith	94	6	99
WEST VIRGINIA			
1 Mollohan	94	6	94
2 Capito	44	56	97
3 Rahall	94	6	100
WISCONSIN			
1 Ryan	17	83	99
2 Baldwin	96	4	94
3 Kind	83	17	100
4 Moore	99	1	97
5 Sensenbrenner	15	85	100
6 Petri	26	74	100
7 Obey	97	3	100
8 Kagen	93	7	100
WYOMING			
AL Lummis	10	90	97
DELEGATES			
Faleomavaega (A.S.)	94	6	80
Norton (D.C.)	93	7	75
Bordallo (Guam)	93	7	75
Sablan (N. Marianas) [6]	95	5	100
Pierluisi (P.R.)	94	6	90
Christensen (V.I.)	94	6	85

An Ever Wider Line Between Parties

DEMOCRATS PROVED IN THE FIRST SESSION of the 111th Congress that they could move their agenda without Republican help. For their part, Republicans showed their determination to make the Democrats do just that. The voting patterns revealed in Congressional Quarterly's 57th annual study of partisanship in Congress depict a legislative body operating ever more purely as a partisan system.

Only a handful of members routinely broke with their party's leaders, and just a few hot-button issues — gun rights, bank bailouts and war policy — scrambled the otherwise tight Democratic majorities and presented the opportunity for a few Republican victories.

Democrats' ability to clear an economic stimulus package, move health care legislation through both chambers and push a climate change bill through the House depended almost entirely on resolving debates within the party and negotiating with a handful of Republicans — not on building a broad consensus on any of those issues.

The two chambers increasingly operated mechanically and predictably, as each party pursued its own distinct agenda as aggressively as its numbers in Congress and legislative procedures allow.

Consider the simplicity of the current system: Democrats campaign on one set of ideas and defeat Republicans, who campaign on an opposing ideological platform. Once in office, with few exceptions, Democrats try to implement those ideas, working within their own ranks to assemble the necessary votes rather than cooperating with the other team and adopting some of its principles. Republicans, in contrast, attempt to block nearly everything Democrats want to do in hopes that they will soon regain control and implement their own ideas.

Ideology and party have not always been so neatly aligned in Congress. A broad ideological range in each party was commonplace the last two times that Democrats controlled Congress by a big margin, during the presidencies of Lyndon B. Johnson and Jimmy Carter.

Those Congresses contained conservative Democrats and liberal Republicans whose voting records were virtually indistinguishable from their ideological fellow travelers in the opposite party.

Thanks to districts drawn to favor one party or the other, a perpetual campaign cycle, and an issue agenda chosen in part to avoid fractures, those crosscurrents barely exist any longer. Instead of working to persuade the other side, the two teams battle for numerical supremacy. As measured by roll call voting in 2009, that trend intensified.

"There are all those years that people claim there wasn't a dime's worth of difference between the two political parties," said Bruce Oppenheimer, a professor of public policy and education at Vanderbilt University. "At least on how they vote in Congress,

no one can claim that anymore."

The basic dynamics of moving legislation were similar in both chambers in 2009, because Democrats had enough votes to pass bills without any GOP help. But the customs and procedures in the Senate led to record-setting levels of partisanship in that chamber.

LESS SENATE DISSENT

Senate Republicans continued to make the threat of a filibuster routine for most legislation, forcing Democrats to file cloture and get 60 votes to cut off debate. Even when they did not formally go through the mechanics of filing cloture, Democratic and Republican leaders frequently agreed to set 60-vote thresholds for votes that would otherwise require simple majorities.

As a result, the Senate effectively functioned as if the Constitution required a three-fifths majority to pass a bill. Unlike the recent past, however, Democrats had those 60 votes: Their ranks had expanded from 51 to 58 members (including two independents) between 2008 and January 2009. In July, they reached 60 after the party switch of Arlen Specter of Pennsylvania and the seating of Minnesota's Al Franken following a contested election.

That numerical advantage — seemingly sizable, but in practice quite thin — meant Democrats often had to muster every single member of their caucus behind a vote. Leaders cajoled recalcitrant members and altered legislation to suit those senators most likely to defect, who were often (but not always) moderates. That pattern was most evident in December, when Majority Leader Harry Reid,

Democrats Dominate In Both Chambers

House Democrats won an all-time high of 94 percent of those roll call votes that divided the two parties in 2009, while their compatriots in the Senate were victorious on a record 92 percent of such party unity votes. Still, for a second straight year, Republicans across Capitol Hill voted unanimously far more often than did Democrats on party unity votes.

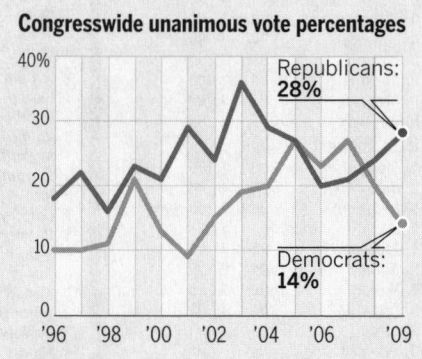

Congresswide unanimous vote percentages

Republicans: **28%**
Democrats: **14%**

'96 '98 '00 '02 '04 '06 '09

Majority party victory percentages

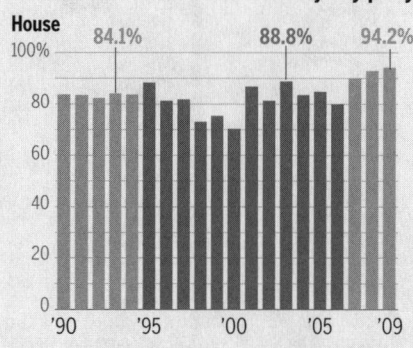

House
84.1% 88.8% 94.2%

'90 '95 '00 '05 '09

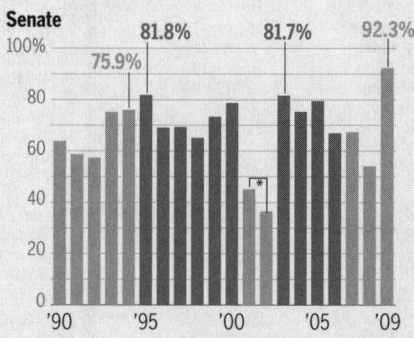

Senate
75.9% 81.8% 81.7% 92.3%

'90 '95 '00 '05 '09

*Sen. James M. Jeffords of Vermont changed parties, giving Democrats a majority.

Loyalty Rises in Senate, Steady in House

House Democrats on average voted with their party's majority 91 percent of the time in 2009 on roll call votes where the two parties divided, almost matching the 92 percent all-time high set during the previous two years. Senate Democrats also voted with their caucus colleagues 91 percent of the time on party unity votes in 2009, eclipsing their record of 89 percent set a decade earlier. House Republicans voted with their party's majority 87 percent of the time, equaling their performance of a year earlier. And Senate Republicans had an average 85 percent party unity score, higher than the 83 percent average posted in 2008.

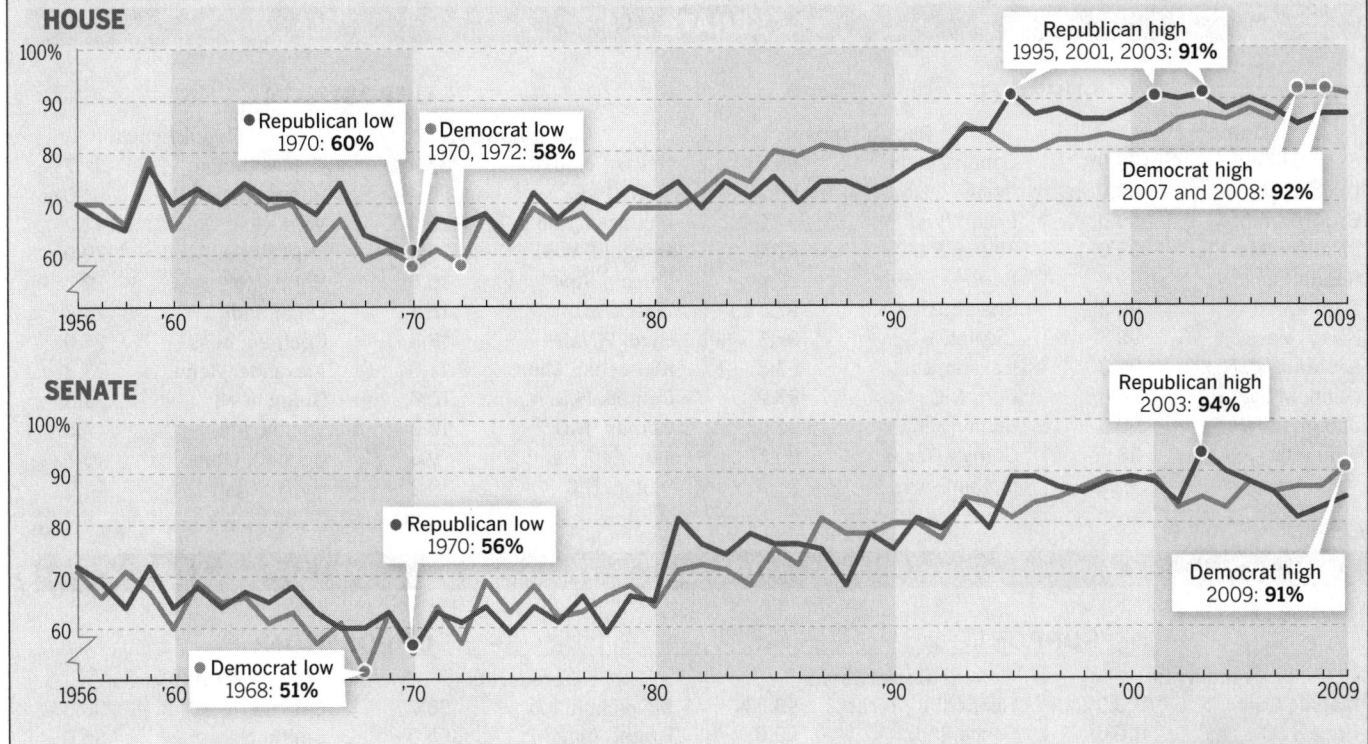

HOUSE

Republican high 1995, 2001, 2003: **91%**

Republican low 1970: **60%**

Democrat low 1970, 1972: **58%**

Democrat high 2007 and 2008: **92%**

SENATE

Republican high 2003: **94%**

Republican low 1970: **56%**

Democrat high 2009: **91%**

Democrat low 1968: **51%**

D-Nev., changed his health care bill in the final days of the session to suit Joseph I. Lieberman of Connecticut, an independent affiliated with the Democrats, and Democrat Ben Nelson of Nebraska.

The dynamic created the conditions for Senate Democrats to set records for party unity. In all, 72 percent of Senate votes in 2009 were what CQ labeled party unity votes, meaning they pitted a majority of one party against a majority of the other. That was the highest level in the study's history, topping the mark of 68.8 percent set in 1995, after Republicans regained the Senate majority following eight years in the minority. The 91 percent average party unity score for members of the caucus was the highest ever for Democrats, though still shy of the 94 percent mark set by Senate Republicans in 2003.

Because the Democrats' margin for success was so slim, they had only a handful of outliers, and one-time mavericks were pulled back into the party's orbit.

Louisiana's Mary L. Landrieu, for example, voted against her party 30.6 percent of the time in 2008, which was an election year for her. In 2009, that number dropped to 9.6 percent. "This Republican Party's not the one it used to be. There were moderates that would reach out with those of us that were moderate on the other side, but that's not the direction they're going in," she said. "I can only be a centrist if there's a center to hold on to."

The Republicans were not quite as cohesive, with an 85 percent party unity average. That mark was pulled downward by the handful of members who were often willing to vote with Democrats — Olympia J. Snowe and Susan Collins of Maine and George V. Voinovich of Ohio, as well as Specter before his switch.

The parties also set records on the outcome of party unity votes, with Democrats winning 92.3 percent — higher than the previous mark for a majority, set by Democrats in 1962 and 1963. Republicans managed to win 22 party unity votes.

HOUSE CHALLENGES

Reid often looked longingly across the Capitol at his House counterparts, who had almost the same share of seats under their control — 59 percent of the House total — but who benefited from rules that were much more favorable to the majority, allowing it to act quickly and decisively.

Speaker Nancy Pelosi of California — who finished the legislative session with 258 Democrats — enjoyed deep support in her caucus, which voted with the party's position 91 percent of the time. That was just shy of the 92 percent record that Pelosi and the Democrats set in 2007 and matched in 2008.

More than half of House Democrats voted with their party at least 98 percent

2009 DATA

AVERAGE PARTY UNITY SCORE

All Republicans: **87 percent**

All Democrats: **91 percent**

HOUSE

Republicans	Democrats
87%	91%

SENATE

Republicans	Democrats
85%	91%

VOTES

	SENATE	HOUSE
PARTISAN VOTES	286	502
TOTAL	397	987
	72%	51%

Leading Scorers: Party Unity

Support indicates those who voted most often with a majority of their party against a majority of the other party in 2009. **Opposition** shows those who voted most often against their party's majority. Lawmakers who left office or who missed half or more of the votes are not listed. Scores are reported to one decimal point only; those with identical scores are listed alphabetically. (Complete scores, pp. B-18, B-20)

SENATE

SUPPORT

Democrats		Republicans	
Burris, Ill.	100.0%	Coburn, Okla.	98.9%
Durbin, Ill.	100.0	Inhofe, Okla.	98.2
Brown, Ohio	99.6	Enzi, Wyo.	97.9
Mikulski, Md.	99.6	Thune, S.D.	97.9
Reed, R.I.	99.6	Barrasso, Wyo.	97.6
Cardin, Md.	99.3	Chambliss, Ga.	97.5
Kerry, Mass.	99.3	DeMint, S.C.	97.5
Lautenberg, N.J.	99.3	Isakson, Ga.	97.5
Levin, Mich.	99.0	Burr, N.C.	97.2
Schumer, N.Y.	99.0	Bunning, Ky.	96.6
4 members	98.9	Cornyn, Texas	96.5
		McCain, Ariz.	96.5

OPPOSITION

Democrats		Republicans	
Nelson, Neb.	37.1%	Collins, Maine	51.7%
Bayh, Ind.	36.4	Snowe, Maine	51.0
McCaskill, Mo.	28.1	Voinovich, Ohio	42.2
Feingold, Wis.	25.5	Murkowski, Alaska	29.9
Lincoln, Ark.	16.5	Bond, Mo.	28.7
Webb, Va.	16.1	Lugar, Ind.	26.7
Byrd, W.Va.	12.3	Cochran, Miss.	24.6
Klobuchar, Minn.	11.0	Alexander, Tenn.	23.3
Conrad, N.D.	10.6	Gregg, N.H.	21.8
Dorgan, N.D.	10.6	Shelby, Ala.	17.5
Landrieu, La.	9.6	Bennett, Utah	16.7
Hagan, N.C.	9.2	Hatch, Utah	14.9

HOUSE

SUPPORT

Democrats		Republicans	
Matsui, Calif.	100.0%	Hensarling, Texas	99.8%
Price, N.C.	100.0	Pence, Ind.	99.6
Capps, Calif.	99.8	Sessions, Texas	99.4
Carson, Ind.	99.8	Foxx, N.C.	99.2
Castor, Fla.	99.8	Franks, Ariz.	99.2
Clyburn, S.C.	99.8	King, Iowa	99.2
Davis, Ill.	99.8	Lamborn, Colo.	99.2
Green, Texas	99.8	Shadegg, Ariz.	99.2
Hirono, Hawaii	99.8	Jordan, Ohio	99.0
Larson, Conn.	99.8	McHenry, N.C.	99.0
McGovern, Mass.	99.8	Neugebauer, Texas	99.0
Miller, Calif.	99.8	Westmoreland, Ga.	98.9
Olver, Mass.	99.8	Blackburn, Tenn.	98.8
Roybal-Allard, Calif.	99.8	Barrett, S.C.	98.6
Schakowsky, Ill.	99.8	Conaway, Texas	98.5
Sutton, Ohio	99.8	Latta, Ohio	98.4
Watson, Calif.	99.8	Marchant, Texas	98.4
Waxman, Calif.	99.8	Thornberry, Texas	98.4

OPPOSITION

Democrats		Republicans	
Minnick, Idaho	58.7%	Cao, La.	36.6%
Bright, Ala.	55.0	Smith, N.J.	35.0
Taylor, Miss.	40.8	LoBiondo, N.J.	33.7
Childers, Miss.	37.4	Murphy, Pa.	32.2
Mitchell, Ariz.	37.3	Reichert, Wash.	32.1
Kratovil, Md.	32.3	Ros-Lehtinen, Fla.	30.3
Shuler, N.C.	32.0	LaTourette, Ohio	30.1
Nye, Va.	30.5	Turner, Ohio	29.4
Griffith, Ala.*	30.0	Jones, N.C.	29.3
Hill, Ind.	26.6	Young, Alaska	28.7
Kirkpatrick, Ariz.	25.8	Gerlach, Pa.	27.3
Murphy, N.Y.	24.0	Diaz-Balart, L., Fla.	26.8
Donnelly, Ind.	22.9	Dent, Pa.	26.7
Boren, Okla.	22.7	King, N.Y.	26.0
Ellsworth, Ind.	22.3	Diaz-Balart, M., Fla.	25.7
Altmire, Pa.	22.1	Platts, Pa.	25.5
Marshall, Ga.	20.7	Castle, Del.	24.1
Teague, N.M.	20.6	Ehlers, Mich.	23.9

*Parker Griffith of Alabama switched his party affiliation to Republican after the session ended.

of the time, meaning that Pelosi could count on 125 votes on almost every issue. There were only 22 votes on which fewer than 200 Democrats stuck with their leaders. The votes were mainly on gun rights, war funding and banking regulation.

The size of Pelosi's majority and the House's 50-percent-plus-one political structure meant that she could allow her most politically vulnerable members to vote against the party when it served their interests, often because they were seeking re-election in districts previously held by Republicans. And she could cut almost all of her deals inside the Democratic Party, because of the comfortable cushion afforded by the large majority.

However, major initiatives — such as the health care and climate change bills — barely passed the House and did so only because Pelosi and Democratic leaders shaped legislation that got just enough votes to survive.

The Democrats who did defect tended to be less senior and more conservative than the rest of the caucus, indicating that Pelosi was able to keep liberals on board. A majority of members of the Congressional Progressive Caucus had a party unity score of 99 percent or more, compared with 98 percent for all Democrats and 89 percent for the fiscally conservative Blue Dog Coalition. Freshman and sophomore Democrats voted less often with the party than more senior members, with half scoring below 95 percent.

One of those freshmen, Ann Kirkpatrick of Arizona, voted with the

Frequency of Party Unity Votes Increases

The number of roll call votes in 2009 in which a majority of Democrats opposed a majority of Republicans increased from 2008 in no small part because there were close to 50 percent more roll call votes taken last year. Congresswide, the percentage that were party unity votes rose a bit, and at almost 57 percent it was just above the 56 percent average for the past two decades.

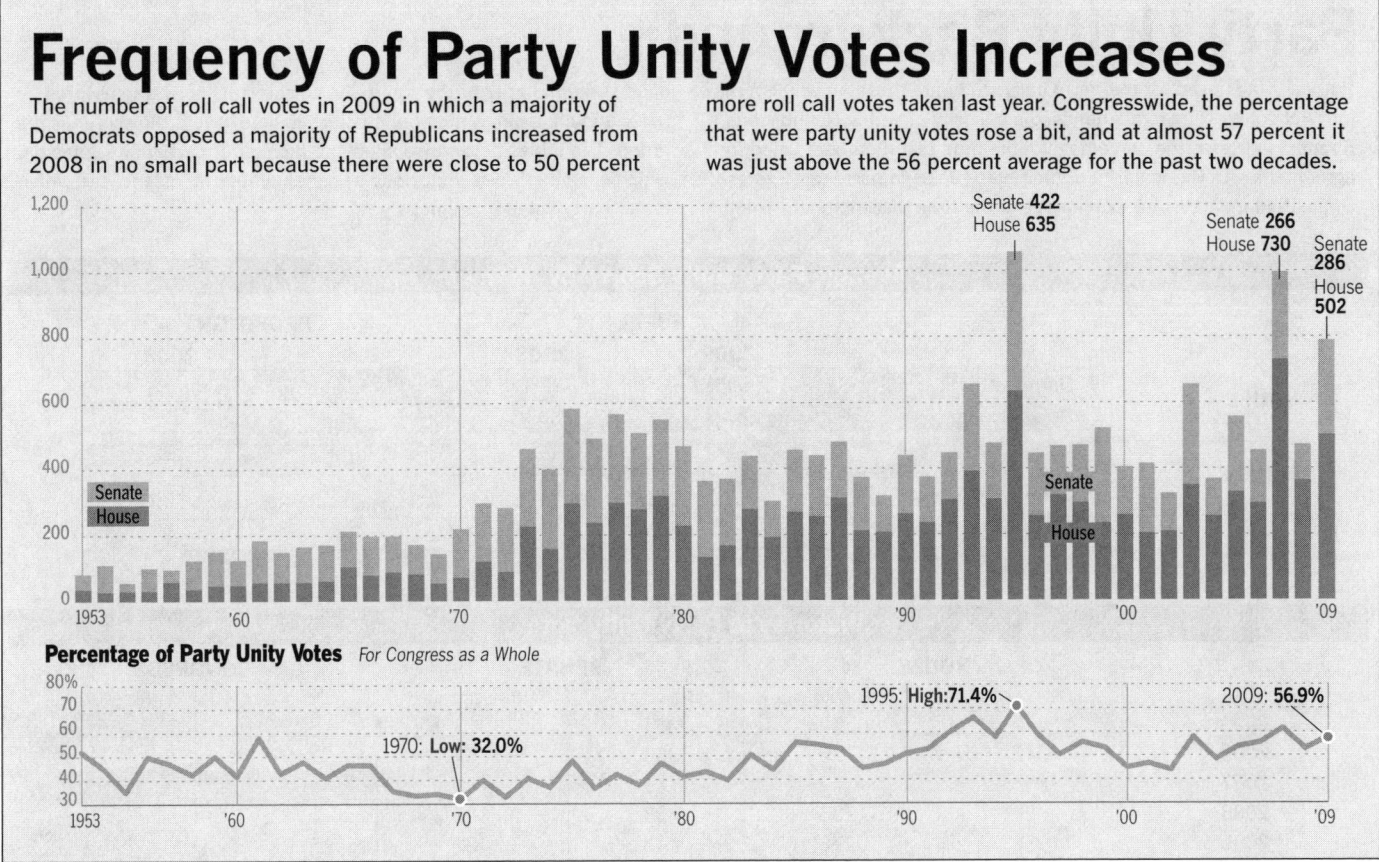

Percentage of Party Unity Votes *For Congress as a Whole*

Democrats just 74 percent of the time, bucking the majority on issues including climate change and gun rights. "I feel like I'm respected for my independent-mindedness," said Kirkpatrick, whose sprawling, largely rural district was previously held by a Republican.

As a result of such defections, House Democrats were rarely unanimous, hitting that mark on just 6 percent of party unity votes in 2009, compared with 29 percent for House Republicans, 28 percent for Senate Democrats and 26 percent for Senate Republicans.

That unanimity — particularly on major issues — was a point of pride for House Republicans, including Minority Whip Eric Cantor of Virginia, who cast that steady parade of "no" votes as a repudiation of Pelosi. "The partisan nature of her rule has necessarily translated into her having to insist upon her members being there, because there will be no sort of reciprocation, if you will, on our part, because we've not been allowed in the room," he said.

PARTISANS UNBOUND

Lawmakers and experts cited varied forces that continued to contribute to polarization in Congress, and few could see any near-term prospects that could reverse the trend.

One of the biggest factors was the perception that control in Congress was fleeting, giving the minority little incentive to negotiate and empowering the majority to push its own agenda as quickly as possible before the clock ran out. The 2010 election began hovering over congressional decision-making by the middle of 2009, particularly in the Senate, where Democrats' filibuster-resistant majority was fragile.

Before Republicans broke the Democrats' four-decade lock on the House in 1994, minority parties did not really regard party cohesion as a path toward regaining control because control seemed so unreachable, said David W. Rohde, a professor of political science

at Duke University. "Because of the aftermath of 1994 and majority control being in doubt, every choice these people make with regard to legislative activity is viewed in terms of what impact it might have on majority control, and majority control is everything in terms of policy," he said.

That pattern was exacerbated by the dynamics within each of the parties, where ideologically driven movements on the fringes played a powerful role in the selection of candidates. Threats from the wings and a constant focus on the next election dried up potential incentives for parties to cooperate. Republicans rarely saw fit to work in concert with the president, even during his post-inaugural honeymoon. *(Presidential support, p. B-3)*

On the other side, even the most conservative Democrats saw little electoral benefit in preventing their own party from compiling a record of success while it simultaneously held the House, Senate and White House in 2009 for the first time in 15 years.

Perhaps most importantly, no countertrend emerged to stem partisan polarization. The forces that once scrambled parties — primarily race and region — no longer served that function, and there was no issue on the horizon likely to cause Democrats to side frequently with Republicans, or vice versa.

Obama and congressional Democrats laid out an agenda for the year that put the role and scope of government at the center — a debate that neatly fit the clear divide between the two parties — and avoided social issues that tended to create different coalitions, such as immigration.

"We've had that kind of sorting process going on now for an awfully long time," said Steven S. Smith, professor of political science at Washington University in St. Louis, "without any major cross-cutting issues to upset the apple cart." ∎

Party Unity Background

Roll call votes used for the party unity study are those on which a majority of voting Democrats opposed a majority of voting Republicans. **Support** indicates the percentage of the time that members voted in agreement with the majority of their party on such party unity votes. **Opposition** indicates the percentage of the time that members voted against the majority of their party. In calculations of average scores by party and chamber, a member's failure to vote lowers the score for the group. The tables below also show the number of party unity votes on which each party was **victorious** and the number of instances in which either party voted **unanimously**.

Average Party Unity Scores by Chamber

		SUPPORT		OPPOSITION	
		2009	2008	2009	2008
HOUSE	Democrats	91%	92%	6%	3%
	Republicans	87	87	10	8
SENATE	Democrats	91	87	6	8
	Republicans	85	83	13	12
CONGRESS	Democrats	91	92	6	4
	Republicans	87	87	11	8

Victories in Party Unity Votes

	HOUSE		SENATE		CONGRESS	
YEAR	DEMOCRATS	REPUBLICANS	DEMOCRATS	REPUBLICANS	DEMOCRATS	REPUBLICANS
2009	473	29	264	22	737	51
2008	342	25	60	51	402	76
2007	658	72	179	87	837	159
2006	59	236	53	107	112	343
2005	50	278	47	182	97	460
2004	42	213	28	85	70	298
2003	39	310	56	250	95	560
2002	39	170	42	73	81	243
2001	27	177	95	115	122	292
2000	77	182	31	114	108	296
1999	58	177	77	211	135	388
1998	80	216	61	114	141	330
1997	58	261	46	104	104	365
1996	48	208	59	132	107	340
1995	74	561	77	345	151	906
1994	257	50	129	41	386	91
1993	329	62	199	66	528	128

Unanimous Voting by Parties

YEAR	DEMOCRATS	REPUBLICANS	DEMOCRATS	REPUBLICANS	DEMOCRATS	REPUBLICANS
2009	29	144	79	74	108	218
2008	66	96	30	19	96	115
2007	170	177	102	35	272	212
2006	70	62	34	30	104	92
2005	82	91	69	59	151	150
2004	70	77	3	31	73	108
2003	94	109	32	130	126	239
2002	37	54	12	23	49	77
2001	1	66	37	55	38	121
2000	1	67	52	19	53	86
1999	11	59	100	63	111	122
1998	8	42	46	33	54	75
1997	11	63	35	38	46	101
1996	10	32	35	47	45	79
1995	17	159	63	104	80	263
1994	7	38	37	19	44	57
1993	13	65	29	57	42	122

Party Unity History

The left section of the table below shows how frequently during roll call votes a majority of Democrats aligned against a majority of Republicans.

The center and right sections show the average party unity support score for each party in each chamber.

	Frequency of Unity Votes		House Average Scores		Senate Average Scores	
YEAR	HOUSE	SENATE	DEMOCRATS	REPUBLICANS	DEMOCRATS	REPUBLICANS
2009	50.9%	72.0%	91%	87%	91%	85%
2008	53.3	51.6	92	87	87	83
2007	62.0	60.2	92	85	87	81
2006	54.5	57.3	86	88	86	86
2005	49.0	62.6	88	90	88	88
2004	47.0	52.3	86	88	83	90
2003	51.7	66.7	87	91	85	94
2002	43.3	45.5	86	90	83	84
2001	40.2	55.3	83	91	89	88
2000	43.2	48.7	82	88	88	89
1999	47.3	62.8	83	86	89	88
1998	55.5	55.7	82	86	87	86
1997	50.4	50.3	82	88	85	87
1996	56.4	62.4	80	87	84	89
1995	73.2	68.8	80	91	81	89
1994	61.8	51.7	83	84	84	79
1993	65.5	67.1	85	84	85	84
1992	64.5	53.0	79	79	77	79
1991	55.1	49.3	81	77	80	81
1990	49.1	54.3	81	74	80	75
1989	56.3	35.3	81	72	78	78
1988	47.0	42.5	80	74	78	68
1987	63.7	40.7	81	74	81	75
1986	56.5	52.3	79	70	72	76
1985	61.0	49.6	80	75	75	76
1984	47.1	40.0	74	71	68	78
1983	55.6	43.7	76	74	71	74
1982	36.4	43.4	72	69	72	76
1981	37.4	47.8	69	74	71	81
1980	37.6	45.8	69	71	64	65
1979	47.3	46.7	69	73	68	66
1978	33.2	45.2	63	69	66	59
1977	42.2	42.4	68	71	63	66
1976	35.9	37.2	66	67	62	61
1975	48.4	47.8	69	72	68	64
1974	29.4	44.3	62	63	63	59
1973	41.8	39.9	68	68	69	64
1972	27.1	36.5	58	66	57	61
1971	37.8	41.6	61	67	64	63
1970	27.1	35.2	58	60	55	56
1969	31.1	36.3	61	62	63	63
1968	35.2	32.0	59	64	51	60
1967	36.3	34.6	67	74	61	60
1966	41.5	50.2	62	68	57	63
1965	52.2	41.9	70	71	63	68
1964	54.9	35.7	69	71	61	65
1963	48.7	47.2	73	74	66	67
1962	46.0	41.1	70	70	65	64
1961	50.0	62.3	72	73	69	68
1960	52.7	36.7	65	70	60	64
1959	55.2	47.9	79	77	67	72
1958	39.8	43.5	66	65	71	64
1957	59.0	35.5	70	67	66	69
1956	43.8	53.1	70	70	71	72
1955	40.8	29.9				
1954	38.2	48.0				
1953	52.1	51.7				

Tallying Party Unity Votes

In the House in 2009, the two parties aligned against each other on 502 of 987 roll call votes, or 50.9 percent of the time. In the Senate, the parties opposed each other on 286 of 397 roll calls, or 72.0 percent of the time. A list of roll call votes that pitted majorities of the two parties against each other is available upon request from Congressional Quarterly.

Calculations of average scores by chamber and party are based on all eligible "yea" or "nay" votes, whether or not all members participated. Under this methodology, average support and opposition scores are reduced when members choose not to vote. Because individual member scores are based on the number of votes cast, party and chamber averages are not strictly comparable to individual member scores. (Complete member scores, pp. B-18, B-20)

Also, in the member score tables, Sens. Joseph I. Lieberman, I-Conn., and Bernard Sanders, I-Vt., are treated as if they were Democrats when calculating their support and opposition scores. However, Lieberman's and Sanders' votes were not used to determine which roll calls were party unity votes, and they are not included in the Democratic Party averages for the Senate.

HOUSE

1. **Party Unity.** Percentage of recorded party unity votes in 2009 on which a member voted "yea" or "nay" in agreement with a majority of his or her party. (Party unity votes are those on which a majority of voting Democrats opposed a majority of voting Republicans.) Percentages are based on votes cast; thus, failure to vote does not lower a member's score.

2. **Party Opposition.** Percentage of recorded party unity votes in 2009 on which a member voted "yea" or "nay" in disagreement with a majority of his or her party. Percentages are based on votes cast; thus, failure to vote does not lower a member's score.

3. **Participation in Party Unity Votes.** Percentage of recorded party unity votes in 2009 for which a member was eligible and present and voted "yea" or "nay." There were 502 recorded party unity votes.

[1] Alabama Rep. Parker Griffith switched party affiliation from Democrat to Republican, effective Dec. 23, 2009. All votes cast by Griffith in 2009 were as a Democrat.

[2] The Speaker votes only at her discretion.

[3] Rep. John Garamendi, D-Calif., was sworn in Nov. 5, 2009, to fill the seat vacated by fellow Democrat Ellen O. Tauscher, who resigned June 26, 2009, to become an undersecretary of State. The first vote for which Garamendi was eligible was vote 858; the last vote for which Tauscher was eligible was vote 477.

[4] Rep. Judy Chu, D-Calif., was sworn in July 16, 2009, to fill the seat vacated by fellow Democrat Hilda L. Solis, who resigned Feb. 24, 2009, to become secretary of Labor. The first vote for which Chu was eligible was vote 549; the last vote for which Solis was eligible was vote 79.

[5] Rep. Mike Quigley, D-Ill., was sworn in April 21, 2009, to fill the seat vacated by fellow Democrat Rahm Emanuel, who resigned Jan. 2, 2009, to become President Obama's chief of staff. The first vote for which Quigley was eligible was vote 194; Emanuel was not eligible for any votes in 2009.

[6] Rep. Scott Murphy, D-N.Y., was sworn in April 29, 2009, to fill the seat vacated by fellow Democrat Kirsten Gillibrand, who resigned Jan. 26, 2009, to become a senator. The first vote for which Murphy was eligible was vote 221; the last vote for which Gillibrand was eligible was vote 29.

[7] Rep. Bill Owens, D-N.Y., was sworn in Nov. 6, 2009, to fill the seat vacated by Republican John M. McHugh, who resigned Sept. 21, 2009, to become secretary of the Army. The first vote for which Owens was eligible was vote 867; the last vote for which McHugh was eligible was vote 719.

[8] Del. Gregorio Kilili Camacho Sablan of the Northern Mariana Islands, who was elected in 2008 as an independent, informed the Speaker on Feb. 23, 2009, that he wished to list his party affiliation as Democrat. The first vote in the Committee of the Whole for which he asked to be counted with the Democrats was vote 100.

	1	2	3
ALABAMA			
1 **Bonner**	87	13	96
2 Bright	45	55	97
3 **Rogers**	80	20	99
4 **Aderholt**	84	16	96
5 Griffith [1]	70	30	98
6 **Bachus**	86	14	98
7 Davis	91	9	94
ALASKA			
AL **Young**	71	29	91
ARIZONA			
1 Kirkpatrick	74	26	99
2 **Franks**	99	1	99
3 **Shadegg**	99	1	98
4 Pastor	99	1	99
5 Mitchell	63	37	100
6 **Flake**	97	3	93
7 Grijalva	99	1	98
8 Giffords	82	18	99
ARKANSAS			
1 Berry	92	8	96
2 Snyder	94	6	97
3 **Boozman**	96	4	99
4 Ross	90	10	99
CALIFORNIA			
1 Thompson	98	2	99
2 **Herger**	98	2	99
3 **Lungren**	95	5	99
4 **McClintock**	97	3	99
5 Matsui	100	0	99
6 Woolsey	98	2	97
7 Miller, George	99	1	96
8 Pelosi [2]	100	0	7
9 Lee	99	1	99
10 Tauscher [3]	99	1	85
10 Garamendi [3]	100	0	98
11 McNerney	90	10	98
12 Speier	95	5	92
13 Stark	96	4	83
14 Eshoo	99	1	98
15 Honda	99	1	98
16 Lofgren	99	1	90
17 Farr	99	1	99
18 Cardoza	94	6	96
19 **Radanovich**	93	7	86
20 Costa	91	9	97
21 **Nunes**	97	3	94
22 **McCarthy**	96	4	99
23 Capps	99	1	98
24 **Gallegly**	90	10	98
25 **McKeon**	88	12	98
26 **Dreier**	86	14	99
27 Sherman	99	1	98
28 Berman	99	1	96
29 Schiff	99	1	99
30 Waxman	99	1	96
31 Becerra	99	1	96
32 Solis [4]	100	0	30
32 Chu [4]	100	0	99
33 Watson	99	1	98
34 Roybal-Allard	99	1	99
35 Waters	98	2	96
36 Harman	98	2	89
37 Richardson	98	2	96
38 Napolitano	99	1	98
39 Sánchez, Linda	99	1	82
40 **Royce**	98	2	99
41 **Lewis**	85	15	99
42 **Miller, Gary**	87	13	84
43 Baca	98	2	97
44 **Calvert**	86	14	99
45 **Bono Mack**	88	12	99
46 **Rohrabacher**	91	9	98
47 Sanchez, Loretta	97	3	92
48 **Campbell**	97	3	93
49 **Issa**	98	2	98
50 **Bilbray**	87	13	99
51 Filner	98	2	99
52 **Hunter**	95	5	99
53 Davis	99	1	99

	1	2	3
COLORADO			
1 DeGette	99	1	99
2 Polis	97	3	98
3 Salazar	95	5	97
4 Markey	89	11	98
5 **Lamborn**	99	1	99
6 **Coffman**	98	2	98
7 Perlmutter	97	3	98
CONNECTICUT			
1 Larson	99	1	92
2 Courtney	99	1	98
3 DeLauro	99	1	97
4 Himes	90	10	98
5 Murphy	97	3	98
DELAWARE			
AL **Castle**	76	24	100
FLORIDA			
1 **Miller**	98	2	99
2 Boyd	91	9	96
3 Brown	99	1	96
4 **Crenshaw**	84	16	98
5 **Brown-Waite**	82	18	96
6 **Stearns**	95	5	99
7 **Mica**	90	10	98
8 Grayson	98	2	99
9 **Bilirakis**	87	13	99
10 **Young**	77	23	94
11 Castor	99	1	96
12 **Putnam**	84	16	98
13 **Buchanan**	82	18	98
14 **Mack**	97	3	98
15 **Posey**	89	11	99
16 **Rooney**	90	10	99
17 Meek	97	3	98
18 **Ros-Lehtinen**	70	30	98
19 Wexler	99	1	95
20 Wasserman Schultz	99	1	98
21 **Diaz-Balart, L.**	73	27	95
22 Klein	96	4	98
23 Hastings	99	1	94
24 Kosmas	86	14	99
25 **Diaz-Balart, M.**	74	26	98
GEORGIA			
1 **Kingston**	95	5	98
2 Bishop	96	4	98
3 **Westmoreland**	99	1	91
4 Johnson	99	1	96
5 Lewis	99	1	77
6 **Price**	98	2	99
7 **Linder**	97	3	96
8 Marshall	79	21	99
9 **Deal**	97	3	86
10 **Broun**	98	2	97
11 **Gingrey**	95	5	98
12 Barrow	87	13	98
13 Scott	97	3	99
HAWAII			
1 Abercrombie	99	1	93
2 Hirono	99	1	98
IDAHO			
1 Minnick	41	59	98
2 **Simpson**	79	21	98
ILLINOIS			
1 Rush	97	3	96
2 Jackson	99	1	98
3 Lipinski	94	6	99
4 Gutierrez	98	2	94
5 Quigley [5]	96	4	99
6 **Roskam**	94	6	99
7 Davis	99	1	95
8 Bean	83	17	96
9 Schakowsky	99	1	99
10 **Kirk**	78	22	97
11 Halvorson	88	12	100
12 Costello	94	6	99
13 **Biggert**	76	24	99
14 Foster	85	15	99
15 **Johnson**	80	20	97

KEY   **Republicans**   Democrats

#	Member	1	2	3
16	Manzullo	94	6	99
17	Hare	99	1	99
18	Schock	84	16	97
19	Shimkus	92	8	99
INDIANA				
1	Visclosky	97	3	99
2	Donnelly	77	23	100
3	Souder	90	10	97
4	Buyer	89	11	95
5	Burton	98	2	99
6	Pence	99	1	95
7	Carson	99	1	100
8	Ellsworth	78	22	99
9	Hill	73	27	97
IOWA				
1	Braley	99	1	95
2	Loebsack	97	3	98
3	Boswell	96	4	97
4	Latham	81	19	97
5	King	99	1	98
KANSAS				
1	Moran	96	4	99
2	Jenkins	95	5	100
3	Moore	95	5	99
4	Tiahrt	92	8	99
KENTUCKY				
1	Whitfield	81	19	98
2	Guthrie	85	15	100
3	Yarmuth	99	1	98
4	Davis	90	10	99
5	Rogers	82	18	98
6	Chandler	93	7	94
LOUISIANA				
1	Scalise	98	2	97
2	Cao	63	37	93
3	Melancon	82	18	93
4	Fleming	97	3	99
5	Alexander	87	13	97
6	Cassidy	92	8	96
7	Boustany	97	3	97
MAINE				
1	Pingree	99	1	99
2	Michaud	92	8	99
MARYLAND				
1	Kratovil	68	32	99
2	Ruppersberger	97	3	94
3	Sarbanes	99	1	99
4	Edwards	99	1	99
5	Hoyer	99	1	99
6	Bartlett	90	10	99
7	Cummings	98	2	99
8	Van Hollen	99	1	98
MASSACHUSETTS				
1	Olver	99	1	97
2	Neal	99	1	98
3	McGovern	99	1	97
4	Frank	99	1	96
5	Tsongas	99	1	98
6	Tierney	98	2	98
7	Markey	99	1	98
8	Capuano	99	1	87
9	Lynch	98	2	98
10	Delahunt	99	1	93
MICHIGAN				
1	Stupak	93	7	94
2	Hoekstra	95	5	98
3	Ehlers	76	24	96
4	Camp	85	15	99
5	Kildee	98	2	99
6	Upton	80	20	99
7	Schauer	90	10	98
8	Rogers	90	10	95
9	Peters	91	9	100
10	Miller	77	23	100
11	McCotter	88	12	99
12	Levin	99	1	98
13	Kilpatrick	99	1	97
14	Conyers	98	2	91
15	Dingell	99	1	96
MINNESOTA				
1	Walz	94	6	99
2	Kline	98	2	97
3	Paulsen	89	11	99
4	McCollum	99	1	97

#	Member	1	2	3
5	Ellison	99	1	91
6	Bachmann	98	2	87
7	Peterson	87	13	99
8	Oberstar	97	3	98
MISSISSIPPI				
1	Childers	63	37	99
2	Thompson	99	1	96
3	Harper	93	7	98
4	Taylor	59	41	96
MISSOURI				
1	Clay	99	1	97
2	Akin	98	2	99
3	Carnahan	99	1	99
4	Skelton	92	8	97
5	Cleaver	99	1	99
6	Graves	98	2	95
7	Blunt	91	9	93
8	Emerson	77	23	97
9	Luetkemeyer	97	3	99
MONTANA				
AL	Rehberg	85	15	99
NEBRASKA				
1	Fortenberry	81	19	99
2	Terry	90	10	99
3	Smith	97	3	100
NEVADA				
1	Berkley	97	3	97
2	Heller	91	9	96
3	Titus	95	5	100
NEW HAMPSHIRE				
1	Shea-Porter	97	3	97
2	Hodes	93	7	99
NEW JERSEY				
1	Andrews	99	1	99
2	LoBiondo	66	34	100
3	Adler	84	16	98
4	Smith	65	35	98
5	Garrett	98	2	99
6	Pallone	99	1	98
7	Lance	78	22	99
8	Pascrell	98	2	95
9	Rothman	99	1	98
10	Payne	99	1	98
11	Frelinghuysen	77	23	99
12	Holt	99	1	98
13	Sires	98	2	98
NEW MEXICO				
1	Heinrich	94	6	99
2	Teague	79	21	99
3	Lujan	99	1	99
NEW YORK				
1	Bishop	96	4	99
2	Israel	99	1	97
3	King	74	26	99
4	McCarthy	97	3	88
5	Ackerman	99	1	96
6	Meeks	98	2	97
7	Crowley	99	1	97
8	Nadler	98	2	98
9	Weiner	99	1	97
10	Towns	99	1	97
11	Clarke	99	1	98
12	Velázquez	99	1	95
13	McMahon	87	13	99
14	Maloney	99	1	95
15	Rangel	99	1	93
16	Serrano	99	1	99
17	Engel	99	1	95
18	Lowey	99	1	99
19	Hall	97	3	98
20	Gillibrand[6]	94	6	100
20	Murphy[6]	76	24	94
21	Tonko	99	1	99
22	Hinchey	99	1	97
23	McHugh[7]	59	41	92
23	Owens[7]	87	13	100
24	Arcuri	83	17	99
25	Maffei	94	6	99
26	Lee	84	16	98
27	Higgins	98	2	98
28	Slaughter	99	1	94
29	Massa	90	10	99
NORTH CAROLINA				
1	Butterfield	99	1	94
2	Etheridge	95	5	99
3	Jones	71	29	99
4	Price	100	0	99

#	Member	1	2	3
5	Foxx	99	1	99
6	Coble	95	5	97
7	McIntyre	83	17	99
8	Kissell	93	7	99
9	Myrick	98	2	97
10	McHenry	99	1	98
11	Shuler	68	32	98
12	Watt	99	1	98
13	Miller	99	1	99
NORTH DAKOTA				
AL	Pomeroy	95	5	98
OHIO				
1	Driehaus	90	10	99
2	Schmidt	96	4	93
3	Turner	71	29	99
4	Jordan	99	1	99
5	Latta	98	2	100
6	Wilson	96	4	97
7	Austria	93	7	99
8	Boehner	98	2	92
9	Kaptur	94	6	95
10	Kucinich	90	10	99
11	Fudge	99	1	93
12	Tiberi	90	10	96
13	Sutton	99	1	97
14	LaTourette	70	30	98
15	Kilroy	98	2	99
16	Boccieri	88	12	99
17	Ryan	99	1	97
18	Space	88	12	98
OKLAHOMA				
1	Sullivan	97	3	74
2	Boren	77	23	100
3	Lucas	89	11	91
4	Cole	86	14	99
5	Fallin	97	3	99
OREGON				
1	Wu	98	2	98
2	Walden	83	17	96
3	Blumenauer	99	1	99
4	DeFazio	97	3	97
5	Schrader	95	5	98
PENNSYLVANIA				
1	Brady	99	1	99
2	Fattah	99	1	98
3	Dahlkemper	89	11	98
4	Altmire	78	22	100
5	Thompson	85	15	99
6	Gerlach	73	27	95
7	Sestak	96	4	91
8	Murphy, P.	95	5	95
9	Shuster	86	14	98
10	Carney	84	16	93
11	Kanjorski	96	4	99
12	Murtha	99	1	92
13	Schwartz	98	2	99
14	Doyle	99	1	96
15	Dent	73	27	97
16	Pitts	96	4	98
17	Holden	93	7	99
18	Murphy, T.	68	32	98
19	Platts	75	25	97
RHODE ISLAND				
1	Kennedy	99	1	76
2	Langevin	99	1	99
SOUTH CAROLINA				
1	Brown	86	14	97
2	Wilson	98	2	99
3	Barrett	99	1	69
4	Inglis	95	5	99
5	Spratt	97	3	99
6	Clyburn	99	1	97
SOUTH DAKOTA				
AL	Herseth Sandlin	88	12	98
TENNESSEE				
1	Roe	96	4	99
2	Duncan	92	8	99
3	Wamp	93	7	96
4	Davis	89	11	96
5	Cooper	83	17	99
6	Gordon	93	7	97
7	Blackburn	99	1	99
8	Tanner	89	11	93
9	Cohen	98	2	99

#	Member	1	2	3
TEXAS				
1	Gohmert	95	5	93
2	Poe	95	5	97
3	Johnson, S.	98	2	95
4	Hall	92	8	97
5	Hensarling	99	1	98
6	Barton	91	9	97
7	Culberson	89	11	96
8	Brady	97	3	98
9	Green, A.	99	1	99
10	McCaul	94	6	97
11	Conaway	99	1	95
12	Granger	88	12	88
13	Thornberry	98	2	100
14	Paul	89	11	91
15	Hinojosa	99	1	91
16	Reyes	99	1	96
17	Edwards	95	5	98
18	Jackson Lee	99	1	96
19	Neugebauer	99	1	96
20	Gonzalez	99	1	97
21	Smith	86	14	97
22	Olson	97	3	97
23	Rodriguez	96	4	99
24	Marchant	98	2	97
25	Doggett	95	5	99
26	Burgess	96	4	95
27	Ortiz	97	3	99
28	Cuellar	91	9	99
29	Green, G.	98	2	97
30	Johnson, E.	99	1	97
31	Carter	89	11	95
32	Sessions	99	1	96
UTAH				
1	Bishop	96	4	89
2	Matheson	84	16	99
3	Chaffetz	96	4	99
VERMONT				
AL	Welch	98	2	95
VIRGINIA				
1	Wittman	88	12	99
2	Nye	69	31	99
3	Scott	98	2	96
4	Forbes	90	10	99
5	Perriello	80	20	95
6	Goodlatte	96	4	99
7	Cantor	97	3	96
8	Moran	98	2	88
9	Boucher	95	5	94
10	Wolf	79	21	99
11	Connolly	97	3	99
WASHINGTON				
1	Inslee	98	2	99
2	Larsen	98	2	99
3	Baird	87	13	97
4	Hastings	89	11	96
5	McMorris Rodgers	95	5	99
6	Dicks	99	1	98
7	McDermott	99	1	98
8	Reichert	68	32	99
9	Smith	93	7	98
WEST VIRGINIA				
1	Mollohan	97	3	97
2	Capito	76	24	99
3	Rahall	97	3	99
WISCONSIN				
1	Ryan	97	3	99
2	Baldwin	99	1	95
3	Kind	86	14	98
4	Moore	99	1	97
5	Sensenbrenner	98	2	100
6	Petri	89	11	99
7	Obey	99	1	99
8	Kagen	98	2	97
WYOMING				
AL	Lummis	98	2	99
DELEGATES				
	Faleomavaega (A.S.)	98	2	79
	Norton (D.C.)	99	1	86
	Bordallo (Guam)	96	4	75
	Sablan (N. Marianas)[8]	99	1	94
	Pierluisi (P.R.)	99	1	86
	Christensen (V.I.)	100	0	89

SENATE

1. Party Unity. Percentage of recorded party unity votes in 2009 on which a senator voted "yea" or "nay" in agreement with a majority of his or her party. (Party unity votes are those on which a majority of voting Democrats opposed a majority of voting Republicans.) Percentages are based on votes cast; thus, failure to vote does not lower a senator's score.

2. Party Opposition. Percentage of recorded party unity votes in 2009 on which a senator voted "yea" or "nay" in disagreement with a majority of his or her party. Percentages are based on votes cast; thus, failure to vote does not lower a senator's score.

3. Participation in Party Unity Votes. Percentage of recorded party unity votes in 2009 for which a senator was eligible and present and voted "yea" or "nay." There were 286 recorded party unity votes.

[1] Sen. Michael Bennet, D-Colo., was sworn in Jan. 22, 2009, to fill the seat vacated by fellow Democrat Ken Salazar, who resigned Jan. 20, 2009, to become secretary of Interior. The first vote for which Bennet was eligible was vote 11; the last vote for which Salazar was eligible was vote 5.

[2] Sens. Joseph I. Lieberman, I-Conn., and Bernard Sanders, I-Vt., caucused with the Democrats, and their party unity scores are calculated as if they were Democrats.

[3] Sen. Ted Kaufman, D-Del., was sworn in Jan. 16, 2009, to fill the seat vacated by fellow Democrat Joseph R. Biden Jr., who resigned Jan. 15, 2009, to become vice president. The first vote for which Kaufman was eligible was vote 6; the last vote for which Biden was eligible was vote 5.

[4] Sen. George LeMieux, R-Fla., was sworn in Sept. 10, 2009, to fill the seat vacated by fellow Republican Mel Martinez, who resigned Sept. 9, 2009. The first vote for which LeMieux was eligible was vote 274; the last vote for which Martinez was eligible was vote 272.

[5] Sen. Roland W. Burris, D-Ill., was sworn in Jan. 15, 2009, to fill the seat vacated by fellow Democrat Barack Obama, who resigned Nov. 16, 2008, to become president. The first vote for which Burris was eligible was vote 5.

[6] Sen. Paul G. Kirk Jr., D-Mass., was sworn in Sept. 25, 2009, to fill the seat vacated by fellow Democrat Edward M. Kennedy, who died Aug. 25, 2009. The first vote for which Kirk was eligible was vote 299; the last vote for which Kennedy was eligible was vote 270.

[7] Sen. Al Franken, D-Minn., was sworn in July 7, 2009, after he was certified the winner of that state's contested election. The first vote for which he was eligible was vote 218.

[8] Sen. Kirsten Gillibrand, D-N.Y., was sworn in Jan. 27, 2009, to fill the seat vacated by fellow Democrat Hillary Rodham Clinton, who resigned Jan. 21, 2009, to become secretary of State. The first vote for which Gillibrand was eligible was vote 16; the last vote for which Clinton was eligible was vote 6.

[9] Sen. Arlen Specter of Pennsylvania switched party affiliation from Republican to Democrat, effective April 30, 2009. The first vote he cast as a Democrat was vote 174. As a Republican, he was eligible for 135 party unity votes in 2009; as a Democrat, he was eligible for 151 such votes. His scores in the table reflect his votes as a Democrat. As a Republican, Specter's party unity support score was 56 percent; opposition score, 44 percent; participation rate, 100 percent.

	1	2	3		1	2	3
ALABAMA				**MONTANA**			
Shelby	83	17	100	Baucus	92	8	99
Sessions	96	4	94	Tester	92	8	99
ALASKA				**NEBRASKA**			
Murkowski	70	30	98	Nelson	63	37	100
Begich	93	7	99	**Johanns**	94	6	91
ARIZONA				**NEVADA**			
McCain	96	4	99	Reid	96	4	100
Kyl	95	5	100	**Ensign**	95	5	99
ARKANSAS				**NEW HAMPSHIRE**			
Lincoln	83	17	99	**Gregg**	78	22	90
Pryor	91	9	100	Shaheen	95	5	99
CALIFORNIA				**NEW JERSEY**			
Feinstein	96	4	99	Lautenberg	99	1	99
Boxer	97	3	99	Menendez	98	2	100
COLORADO				**NEW MEXICO**			
Salazar [1]	100	0	100	Bingaman	95	5	100
Udall	93	7	99	Udall	96	4	99
Bennet [1]	92	8	100	**NEW YORK**			
CONNECTICUT				Schumer	99	1	100
Dodd	99	1	98	Clinton [8]	100	0	100
Lieberman [2]	90	10	98	Gillibrand [8]	99	1	99
DELAWARE				**NORTH CAROLINA**			
Biden [3]	100	0	50	**Burr**	97	3	99
Carper	93	7	100	Hagan	91	9	99
Kaufman [3]	98	2	99	**NORTH DAKOTA**			
FLORIDA				Conrad	89	11	95
Nelson	93	7	100	Dorgan	89	11	99
Martinez [4]	81	19	94	**OHIO**			
LeMieux [4]	93	7	100	**Voinovich**	58	42	97
GEORGIA				Brown	99	1	98
Chambliss	97	3	97	**OKLAHOMA**			
Isakson	97	3	98	**Inhofe**	98	2	96
HAWAII				**Coburn**	99	1	98
Inouye	99	1	99	**OREGON**			
Akaka	98	2	100	Wyden	98	2	99
IDAHO				Merkley	98	2	99
Crapo	94	6	99	**PENNSYLVANIA**			
Risch	95	5	100	Specter [9]	95	5	93
ILLINOIS				Casey	95	5	100
Durbin	100	0	99	**RHODE ISLAND**			
Burris [5]	100	0	98	Reed	99	1	99
INDIANA				Whitehouse	99	1	97
Lugar	73	27	99	**SOUTH CAROLINA**			
Bayh	64	36	99	**Graham**	94	6	98
IOWA				**DeMint**	98	2	99
Grassley	92	8	100	**SOUTH DAKOTA**			
Harkin	99	1	99	Johnson	95	5	98
KANSAS				**Thune**	98	2	100
Brownback	89	11	99	**TENNESSEE**			
Roberts	90	10	97	**Alexander**	77	23	99
KENTUCKY				**Corker**	87	13	99
McConnell	95	5	100	**TEXAS**			
Bunning	97	3	92	**Hutchison**	89	11	94
LOUISIANA				**Cornyn**	96	4	99
Landrieu	90	10	95	**UTAH**			
Vitter	96	4	99	**Hatch**	85	15	99
MAINE				**Bennett**	83	17	98
Snowe	49	51	100	**VERMONT**			
Collins	48	52	100	Leahy	98	2	98
MARYLAND				*Sanders* [2]	97	3	99
Mikulski	99	1	90	**VIRGINIA**			
Cardin	99	1	100	Webb	84	16	100
MASSACHUSETTS				Warner	92	8	99
Kennedy [6]	100	0	3	**WASHINGTON**			
Kerry	99	1	98	Murray	97	3	98
Kirk [6]	100	0	100	Cantwell	94	6	99
MICHIGAN				**WEST VIRGINIA**			
Levin	99	1	100	Byrd	88	12	63
Stabenow	97	3	99	Rockefeller	98	2	91
MINNESOTA				**WISCONSIN**			
Klobuchar	89	11	99	Kohl	95	5	100
Franken [7]	98	2	100	Feingold	74	26	100
MISSISSIPPI				**WYOMING**			
Cochran	75	25	99	**Enzi**	98	2	99
Wicker	88	12	99	**Barrasso**	98	2	100
MISSOURI							
Bond	71	29	96				
McCaskill	72	28	99				

KEY   **Republicans**   Democrats   *Independents*

Long Session Draws Record Votes

IN A DRAWN-OUT SESSION that saw the Senate voting on Christmas Eve for the first time since 1895, the House and Senate racked up a near-record number of votes. Only twice before had lawmakers been called upon to vote more often: in 1995, after Republicans took over both chambers for the first time since 1948, and in 2007, following the Democrats' return to power.

Undeterred by the frequency of roll call votes, members of both chambers responded and maintained relatively high participation rates, with participation defined as casting a "yea" or a "nay" vote and not merely answering "present."

The bells rang 991 times in the House during the session, summoning lawmakers for four quorum calls and 987 yea-or-nay votes. That was a 43 percent increase above the total for 2008 and was near the 2007 record of 1,177 votes. The House conducted a modern one-day record of 53 votes on June 18, after Republicans forced roll call after roll call to protest limits imposed by the majority party on the number of amendments to the first of 12 annual appropriations bills that came to the floor. Republicans had filed 103 amendments to the measure, and Democrats imposed a tighter limit to avoid having to debate them all. At that point, Republicans retaliated by forcing 14 procedural votes on top of votes on almost 40 amendments.

In the Senate, members were called to vote 397 times. That was almost twice as often as in 2008 and the fourth-highest total in two decades. Laboring under that workload, Senate leaders strained to pass a health care overhaul bill and forced the chamber into an unusual amount of weekend work. The intense drive to complete the landmark health care bill led senators to take 11 weekend votes, the most since a sweeping rewrite of the income tax code in 1986, when the chamber voted 15 times on a Saturday or Sunday. In 2009, the Senate spent 191 days in session, the most since 1997.

The average House member participated in 96 percent of roll calls during the session. That average was higher than in any of the previous seven years and roughly comparable to the chamber's average over the past two decades. Speaker Nancy Pelosi, D-Calif., who voted at her own discretion, participated in just 5 percent of the votes, the smallest percentage for a Speaker in at least a decade.

Senators voted on average 97 percent of the time, more than in the previous two years. More than half of all senators made at least 99 percent of the year's votes, though a few ailing lawmakers lowered the average. Edward M. Kennedy of Massachusetts, who died in August of complications from a brain tumor, participated in only 3 percent of the year's votes. Robert C. Byrd of West Virginia, at 92 the oldest member, was frequently hospitalized and made just three-fifths of the votes.

Perfect attendance was a bit higher in 2009. Six House members and 15 senators cast every possible vote, almost twice as many as in 2008. Republican Sen. Charles E. Grassley of Iowa— perfect since 1993 — had another spotless year. Four of the seven lawmakers who joined the Senate midyear also scored 100 percent, voting every time they could. ■

Participation in Floor Votes Rises Again

This past year marked a resurgence of lawmaker participation in roll call votes in both chambers. The average House member voted 96 percent of the time in 2009, the highest since 2001 and the fifth-highest on record. The average senator voted 97 percent of the time. While that's higher than in the previous two years (when participation was lowered by a large number of absences by senators running for president), the year's average attendance on roll call votes is only the 10th highest in the past two decades.

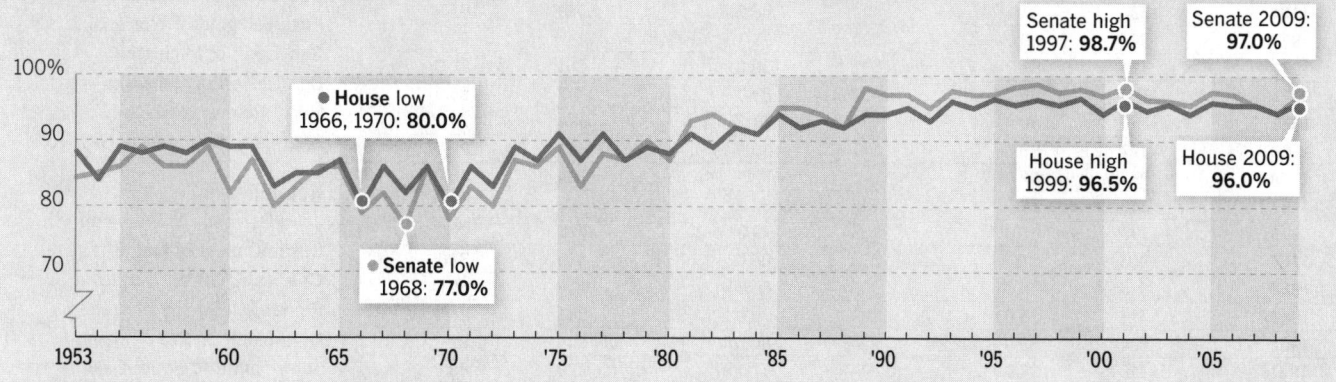

Voting Participation History

These tables show the number of roll call votes in each chamber and in Congress as a whole since 1953 and the frequency with which lawmakers on average cast "yea" or "nay" votes. Participation in floor votes had held close to 95 percent since the mid-1990s.

YEAR	House Roll Calls	Rate	Senate Roll Calls	Rate	Congress as a Whole Roll Calls	Rate
2009	987	96.0%	397	97.0%	1,384	96.1%
2008	688	94.3	215	94.3	903	94.3
2007	1,177	95.5	442	95.0	1,619	95.4
2006	541	95.5	279	97.1	820	95.7
2005	669	95.9	366	97.4	1,035	96.1
2004	543	94.1	216	95.5	759	94.2
2003	675	95.6	459	96.1	1,134	95.7
2002	483	94.6	253	96.3	736	94.8
2001	507	96.2	380	98.2	887	96.5
2000	600	94.1	298	96.9	898	94.4
1999	609	96.5	374	97.9	983	96.6
1998	533	95.5	314	97.4	847	95.7
1997	633	96.3	298	98.7	931	96.5
1996	454	95.5	306	98.2	760	95.8
1995	867	96.4	613	97.1	1,480	96.5
1994	497	95.0	329	97.0	826	95.0
1993	597	96.0	395	97.6	992	96.0
1992	473	93.0	270	95.0	743	93.4
1991	428	95.0	280	97.0	708	95.0
1990	536	94.0	326	97.0	862	95.0
1989	368	94.0	312	98.0	680	95.0
1988	451	92.0	379	92.0	830	92.0
1987	488	93.0	420	94.0	908	93.0
1986	451	92.0	354	95.0	805	93.0
1985	439	94.0	381	95.0	820	94.0
1984	408	91.0	275	91.0	683	91.0
1983	498	92.0	371	92.0	869	92.0
1982	459	89.0	465	94.0	924	90.0
1981	353	91.0	483	93.0	836	92.0
1980	604	88.0	531	87.0	1,135	87.0
1979	672	89.0	497	90.0	1,169	89.0
1978	834	87.0	516	87.0	1,350	87.0
1977	706	91.0	635	88.0	1,341	90.0
1976	661	87.0	688	83.0	1,349	86.0
1975	612	91.0	602	89.0	1,214	91.0
1974	537	87.0	544	86.0	1,081	87.0
1973	541	89.0	594	87.0	1,135	89.0
1972	329	83.0	532	80.0	861	82.0
1971	320	86.0	423	83.0	743	85.0
1970	266	80.0	418	78.0	684	79.0
1969	177	86.0	245	86.0	422	86.0
1968	233	82.0	281	77.0	514	80.0
1967	245	86.0	315	82.0	560	85.0
1966	193	80.0	235	79.0	428	79.0
1965	201	87.0	258	86.0	459	87.0
1964	113	85.0	305	86.0	418	85.0
1963	119	85.0	229	83.0	348	84.0
1962	124	83.0	224	80.0	348	82.0
1961	116	89.0	204	87.0	320	88.0
1960	93	89.0	207	82.0	300	87.0
1959	87	90.0	215	89.0	302	89.0
1958	93	88.0	200	86.0	293	87.0
1957	100	89.0	107	86.0	207	88.0
1956	73	88.0	130	89.0	203	88.0
1955	76	89.0	87	86.0	163	88.0
1954	76	84.0	171	85.0	247	84.0
1953	71	88.2	89	84.3	160	87.4

Perfect Records Of Attendance

Voting participation increased in the House and Senate in 2009, though it fell short of the records for either chamber. And the number of lawmakers with perfect attendance on roll call votes also rose. Six House members — one Democrat and five Republicans — participated in every vote. So did 15 senators: nine Democrats and six Republicans.

Perfect Attendance, House

Democrat
Jason Altmire of Pennsylvania

Republicans
Michael N. Castle of Delaware
Lynn Jenkins of Kansas
Bob Latta of Ohio
Frank A. LoBiondo of New Jersey
F. James Sensenbrenner Jr. of Wisconsin

Perfect Attendance, Senate

Democrats
Daniel K. Akaka of Hawaii
Jeff Bingaman of New Mexico
Benjamin L. Cardin of Maryland
Bob Casey of Pennsylvania
Russ Feingold of Wisconsin
Carl Levin of Michigan
Ben Nelson of Nebraska
Harry Reid of Nevada
Charles E. Schumer of New York

Republicans
John Barrasso of Wyoming
Susan Collins of Maine
Charles E. Grassley of Iowa
Richard C. Shelby of Alabama
Olympia J. Snowe of Maine
John Thune of South Dakota

(Democratic Sens. Michael Bennet of Colorado, Al Franken of Minnesota and Paul G. Kirk Jr. of Massachusetts and Republican George LeMieux of Florida had perfect attendance but weren't eligible for all votes in 2009.)

SENATE

1. Voting Participation. Percentage recorded votes in 2009 on which a senator was eligible and present, and voted "yea" or "nay." There were a total of 397 such recorded votes.

Voting participation excluding motions to instruct. Typically, Congressional Quarterly also calculates Senate voting percentages by excluding votes on motions to instruct the sergeant at arms to request the attendance of absent senators. In 2009, there were no such votes, so this study was eliminated for the past year only.

Absences because of illness. Congressional Quarterly no longer designates members who missed votes because of illness. In the past, notations to that effect were based on official statements published in the Congressional Record, but these were found to be inconsistently used.

Rounding. Scores are rounded to the nearest percentage point, except that no scores are rounded up to 100 percent. Senators with a 100 percent score participated in all recorded votes for which they were eligible.

State / Senator		State / Senator	
ALABAMA		**MONTANA**	
Shelby	100	Baucus	99
Sessions	95	Tester	99
ALASKA		**NEBRASKA**	
Murkowski	98	Nelson	100
Begich	97	**Johanns**	93
ARIZONA		**NEVADA**	
McCain	98	Reid	100
Kyl	99	**Ensign**	97
ARKANSAS		**NEW HAMPSHIRE**	
Lincoln	99	**Gregg**	89
Pryor	99	Shaheen	99
CALIFORNIA		**NEW JERSEY**	
Feinstein	99	Lautenberg	99
Boxer	99	Menendez	98
COLORADO		**NEW MEXICO**	
Salazar[1]	100	Bingaman	100
Udall	99	Udall	99
Bennet[1]	100		
CONNECTICUT		**NEW YORK**	
Dodd	97	Schumer	100
Lieberman	96	Clinton[7]	83
		Gillibrand[7]	99
DELAWARE		**NORTH CAROLINA**	
Biden[2]	40	**Burr**	98
Carper	99	Hagan	99
Kaufman[2]	99		
FLORIDA		**NORTH DAKOTA**	
Nelson	99	Conrad	97
Martinez[3]	93	Dorgan	98
LeMieux[3]	100		
GEORGIA		**OHIO**	
Chambliss	97	**Voinovich**	96
Isakson	97	Brown	98
HAWAII		**OKLAHOMA**	
Inouye	99	**Inhofe**	96
Akaka	100	**Coburn**	97
IDAHO		**OREGON**	
Crapo	99	Wyden	98
Risch	99	Merkley	99
ILLINOIS		**PENNSYLVANIA**	
Durbin	99	Specter[8]	96
Burris[4]	98	Casey	100
INDIANA		**RHODE ISLAND**	
Lugar	99	Reed	99
Bayh	99	Whitehouse	97
IOWA		**SOUTH CAROLINA**	
Grassley	100	**Graham**	97
Harkin	99	**DeMint**	99
KANSAS		**SOUTH DAKOTA**	
Brownback	99	Johnson	97
Roberts	95	**Thune**	100
KENTUCKY		**TENNESSEE**	
McConnell	99	**Alexander**	99
Bunning	92	**Corker**	99
LOUISIANA		**TEXAS**	
Landrieu	94	**Hutchison**	94
Vitter	98	**Cornyn**	97
MAINE		**UTAH**	
Snowe	100	**Hatch**	98
Collins	100	**Bennett**	96
MARYLAND		**VERMONT**	
Mikulski	89	Leahy	98
Cardin	100	*Sanders*	99
MASSACHUSETTS		**VIRGINIA**	
Kennedy[5]	3	Webb	99
Kerry	97	Warner	99
Kirk[5]	100		
MICHIGAN		**WASHINGTON**	
Levin	100	Murray	98
Stabenow	99	Cantwell	99
MINNESOTA		**WEST VIRGINIA**	
Klobuchar	99	Byrd	60
Franken[6]	100	Rockefeller	85
MISSISSIPPI		**WISCONSIN**	
Cochran	98	Kohl	99
Wicker	99	Feingold	100
MISSOURI		**WYOMING**	
Bond	95	**Enzi**	98
McCaskill	99	**Barrasso**	100

KEY   **Republicans**   Democrats   *Independents*

[1] Sen. Michael Bennet, D-Colo., was sworn in Jan. 22, 2009, to fill the seat vacated by fellow Democrat Ken Salazar, who resigned Jan. 20 to become secretary of Interior. The first vote for which Bennet was eligible was vote 11; the last vote for which Salazar was eligible was vote 5.

[2] Sen. Ted Kaufman, D-Del., was sworn in Jan. 16, 2009, to fill the seat vacated by fellow Democrat Joseph R. Biden Jr., who resigned Jan. 15 to become vice president. The first vote for which Kaufman was eligible was vote 6; the last vote for which Biden was eligible was vote 5.

[3] Sen. George LeMieux, R-Fla., was sworn in Sept. 10 to fill the seat vacated by the Sept. 9 resignation of fellow Republican Mel Martinez. The first vote for which LeMieux was eligible was vote 274; the last vote for which Martinez was eligible was vote 272.

[4] Sen. Roland W. Burris, D-Ill., was sworn in Jan. 15, 2009, to fill the seat vacated by fellow Democrat Barack Obama, who resigned Nov. 16, 2008, to become president. The first vote for which Burris was eligible was vote 5.

[5] Sen. Paul G. Kirk Jr., D-Mass., was sworn in Sept. 25, 2009, to fill the seat vacated by fellow Democrat Edward M. Kennedy, who died Aug. 25. The first vote for which Kirk was eligible was vote 299; the last vote for which Kennedy was eligible was vote 270.

[6] Sen. Al Franken, D-Minn., was sworn in July 7, 2009, after he was certified the winner of that state's contested election. The first vote for which he was eligible was vote 218.

[7] Sen. Kirsten Gillibrand, D-N.Y., was sworn in Jan. 27, 2009, to fill the seat vacated by fellow Democrat Hillary Rodham Clinton, who resigned Jan. 21 to become secretary of State. The first vote for which Gillibrand was eligible was vote 16; the last vote for which Clinton was eligible was vote 6.

[8] Pennsylvania Sen. Arlen Specter switched party affiliation from Republican to Democrat, effective April 30, 2009. The first vote he cast as a Democrat was vote 174.

HOUSE

1. Voting Participation. Percentage of recorded votes in 2009 on which a representative was eligible and present, and voted "yea" or "nay." There were a total of 987 such recorded votes. Quorum calls, although they are included in the House list of recorded roll calls, are not counted as votes because lawmakers are only asked to respond "present." There were four recorded quorum calls in 2009.

2. Voting Participation (without Journal votes). Percentage of recorded votes in 2009 on which a representative was eligible and present, and voted "yea" or "nay." There were a total of 980 such recorded votes. In this version of the study, seven votes on motions to approve the House Journal were excluded.

Absences because of illness. Congressional Quarterly no longer designates members who missed votes because of illness. In the past, notations to that effect were based on official statements published in the Congressional Record, but these were found to be inconsistently used.

Rounding. Scores are rounded to the nearest percentage point, except that no scores are rounded up to 100 percent. Members with a 100 percent score participated in all recorded votes for which they were eligible.

[1] Alabama Rep. Parker Griffith switched party affiliation from Democrat to Republican, effective Dec. 23, 2009. All votes cast by Griffith in 2009 were as a Democrat.

[2] The Speaker votes only at her discretion.

[3] Rep. John Garamendi, D-Calif., was sworn in Nov. 5 to fill the seat vacated by fellow Democrat Ellen O. Tauscher, who resigned June 26 to become an undersecretary of State. The first vote for which Garamendi was eligible was 858; the last vote for which Tauscher was eligible was vote 477.

[4] Rep. Judy Chu, D-Calif., was sworn in July 16, 2009, to fill the seat vacated by fellow Democrat Hilda L. Solis, who resigned Feb. 24 to become secretary of Labor. The first vote for which Chu was eligible was vote 549; the last vote for which Solis was eligible was 79.

[5] Rep. Mike Quigley, D-Ill., was sworn in April 21, 2009, to fill the seat vacated by fellow Democrat Rahm Emanuel, who resigned Jan. 2 to become President Obama's chief of staff. The first vote for which Quigley was eligible was vote 194; Emanuel was not eligible for any votes in 2009.

[6] Rep. Scott Murphy, D-N.Y., was sworn in April 29, 2009, to fill the seat vacated by fellow Democrat Kirsten Gillibrand, who resigned Jan. 26 to become a senator. The first vote for which Murphy was eligible was vote 221; the last vote for which Gillibrand was eligible was vote 29.

[7] Rep. Bill Owens, D-N.Y., was sworn in Nov. 6 to fill the seat vacated by Republican John M. McHugh, who resigned Sept. 21 to become secretary of the Army. The first vote for which Owens was eligible was 867; the last vote for which McHugh was eligible was 719.

[8] Del. Gregorio Kilili Camacho Sablan of the Northern Mariana Islands, who was elected in 2008 as an independent, informed the Speaker on Feb. 23, 2009, that he wished to list his party affiliation as Democrat. The first vote in the Committee of the Whole for which he asked to be counted with the Democrats was vote 100.

		1	2
ALABAMA			
1	**Bonner**	94	94
2	**Bright**	97	97
3	**Rogers**	99	99
4	**Aderholt**	95	95
5	**Griffith** [1]	98	98
6	**Bachus**	98	98
7	Davis	90	90
ALASKA			
AL	**Young**	90	90
ARIZONA			
1	Kirkpatrick	98	98
2	**Franks**	99	99
3	**Shadegg**	95	95
4	Pastor	99	99
5	Mitchell	99	99
6	**Flake**	95	94
7	Grijalva	89	89
8	Giffords	99	99
ARKANSAS			
1	Berry	97	97
2	Snyder	97	97
3	**Boozman**	99	99
4	Ross	99	99
CALIFORNIA			
1	Thompson	99	99
2	**Herger**	98	98
3	**Lungren**	99	99
4	**McClintock**	99	99
5	Matsui	99	99
6	Woolsey	96	96
7	Miller, George	96	96
8	Pelosi [2]	5	5
9	Lee	99	99
10	Tauscher [3]	89	89
10	Garamendi [3]	98	98
11	McNerney	99	99
12	Speier	89	89
13	Stark	78	78
14	Eshoo	98	98
15	Honda	97	97
16	Lofgren	91	91
17	Farr	97	97
18	Cardoza	95	95
19	**Radanovich**	83	83
20	Costa	96	96
21	**Nunes**	93	93
22	**McCarthy**	99	99
23	Capps	98	98
24	**Gallegly**	97	97
25	**McKeon**	98	98
26	**Dreier**	97	97
27	Sherman	99	99
28	Berman	95	95
29	Schiff	99	99
30	Waxman	96	96
31	Becerra	96	96
32	Solis [4]	24	25
32	Chu [4]	99	99
33	Watson	97	97
34	Roybal-Allard	99	99
35	Waters	94	93
36	Harman	89	89
37	Richardson	95	95
38	Napolitano	98	98
39	Sánchez, Linda	80	80
40	**Royce**	99	99
41	**Lewis**	99	99
42	**Miller, Gary**	83	83
43	Baca	98	98
44	**Calvert**	99	99
45	**Bono Mack**	98	98
46	**Rohrabacher**	92	92
47	Sanchez, Loretta	91	92
48	**Campbell**	90	91
49	**Issa**	98	98
50	**Bilbray**	98	98
51	Filner	99	99
52	**Hunter**	99	99
53	Davis	99	99

		1	2
COLORADO			
1	DeGette	98	98
2	Polis	98	98
3	Salazar	97	97
4	Markey	98	98
5	**Lamborn**	99	99
6	**Coffman**	98	98
7	Perlmutter	98	98
CONNECTICUT			
1	Larson	93	93
2	Courtney	98	98
3	DeLauro	98	98
4	Himes	98	98
5	Murphy	97	97
DELAWARE			
AL	**Castle**	100	100
FLORIDA			
1	**Miller**	99	99
2	Boyd	95	95
3	Brown	92	92
4	**Crenshaw**	96	96
5	**Brown-Waite**	96	96
6	**Stearns**	98	98
7	**Mica**	98	98
8	Grayson	98	98
9	**Bilirakis**	99	99
10	**Young**	90	91
11	Castor	96	96
12	**Putnam**	94	94
13	**Buchanan**	98	98
14	**Mack**	98	98
15	**Posey**	99	99
16	**Rooney**	99	99
17	Meek	98	98
18	**Ros-Lehtinen**	97	97
19	Wexler	91	91
20	Wasserman Schultz	96	96
21	**Diaz-Balart, L.**	96	96
22	Klein	97	97
23	Hastings	96	96
24	Kosmas	98	98
25	**Diaz-Balart, M.**	98	98
GEORGIA			
1	**Kingston**	97	97
2	Bishop	97	97
3	**Westmoreland**	91	91
4	Johnson	96	96
5	Lewis	80	80
6	**Price**	97	97
7	**Linder**	94	94
8	Marshall	98	98
9	**Deal**	81	82
10	**Broun**	95	95
11	**Gingrey**	97	97
12	Barrow	98	98
13	Scott	99	99
HAWAII			
1	Abercrombie	89	89
2	Hirono	98	98
IDAHO			
1	**Minnick**	99	99
2	**Simpson**	97	97
ILLINOIS			
1	Rush	91	92
2	Jackson	97	97
3	Lipinski	97	97
4	Gutierrez	89	89
5	Quigley [5]	99	99
6	**Roskam**	97	97
7	Davis	92	93
8	Bean	95	95
9	Schakowsky	98	98
10	**Kirk**	95	95
11	Halvorson	99	99
12	Costello	95	95
13	**Biggert**	99	99
14	Foster	99	99
15	**Johnson**	92	92

KEY	**Republicans**	Democrats

	1	2
16 **Manzullo**	99	99
17 Hare	99	99
18 **Schock**	95	95
19 **Shimkus**	97	98
INDIANA		
1 Visclosky	99	99
2 Donnelly	99	99
3 **Souder**	95	95
4 **Buyer**	94	94
5 **Burton**	99	99
6 **Pence**	94	94
7 Carson	99	99
8 Ellsworth	99	99
9 Hill	97	97
IOWA		
1 Braley	93	93
2 Loebsack	97	97
3 Boswell	97	97
4 **Latham**	98	98
5 **King**	98	98
KANSAS		
1 **Moran**	97	97
2 **Jenkins**	100	100
3 Moore	99	99
4 **Tiahrt**	97	97
KENTUCKY		
1 **Whitfield**	97	97
2 **Guthrie**	99	99
3 Yarmuth	97	97
4 **Davis**	99	99
5 **Rogers**	98	98
6 Chandler	96	96
LOUISIANA		
1 **Scalise**	98	98
2 **Cao**	93	93
3 Melancon	92	92
4 **Fleming**	99	99
5 **Alexander**	95	95
6 **Cassidy**	95	95
7 **Boustany**	96	96
MAINE		
1 Pingree	97	98
2 Michaud	99	99
MARYLAND		
1 Kratovil	99	99
2 Ruppersberger	95	94
3 Sarbanes	98	98
4 Edwards	99	99
5 Hoyer	96	96
6 **Bartlett**	99	99
7 Cummings	98	98
8 Van Hollen	98	98
MASSACHUSETTS		
1 Olver	97	97
2 Neal	94	94
3 McGovern	97	97
4 Frank	96	96
5 Tsongas	96	96
6 Tierney	97	97
7 Markey	98	98
8 Capuano	83	83
9 Lynch	97	97
10 Delahunt	91	91
MICHIGAN		
1 Stupak	92	92
2 **Hoekstra**	93	93
3 **Ehlers**	96	96
4 **Camp**	98	99
5 Kildee	99	99
6 **Upton**	99	99
7 Schauer	99	99
8 **Rogers**	95	95
9 Peters	99	99
10 **Miller**	99	99
11 **McCotter**	99	99
12 Levin	99	99
13 Kilpatrick	96	96
14 Conyers	87	87
15 Dingell	96	96
MINNESOTA		
1 Walz	99	99
2 **Kline**	98	98
3 **Paulsen**	99	99
4 McCollum	97	97

	1	2
5 Ellison	91	91
6 **Bachmann**	89	89
7 Peterson	98	98
8 Oberstar	98	98
MISSISSIPPI		
1 Childers	99	99
2 Thompson	97	97
3 **Harper**	97	97
4 Taylor	96	96
MISSOURI		
1 Clay	96	96
2 **Akin**	99	99
3 Carnahan	98	98
4 Skelton	97	97
5 Cleaver	98	98
6 **Graves**	94	94
7 **Blunt**	93	93
8 **Emerson**	97	98
9 **Luetkemeyer**	99	99
MONTANA		
AL **Rehberg**	99	99
NEBRASKA		
1 **Fortenberry**	98	98
2 **Terry**	99	99
3 **Smith**	99	99
NEVADA		
1 Berkley	96	96
2 **Heller**	97	97
3 Titus	99	99
NEW HAMPSHIRE		
1 Shea-Porter	96	96
2 Hodes	98	98
NEW JERSEY		
1 Andrews	98	98
2 **LoBiondo**	100	100
3 Adler	98	98
4 **Smith**	96	96
5 **Garrett**	98	98
6 Pallone	97	97
7 **Lance**	99	99
8 Pascrell	92	92
9 Rothman	97	97
10 Payne	94	94
11 **Frelinghuysen**	99	99
12 Holt	98	98
13 Sires	96	96
NEW MEXICO		
1 Heinrich	99	99
2 Teague	98	98
3 Lujan	99	99
NEW YORK		
1 Bishop	99	99
2 Israel	95	95
3 **King**	99	99
4 McCarthy	87	87
5 Ackerman	93	93
6 Meeks	95	95
7 Crowley	96	96
8 Nadler	98	98
9 Weiner	96	96
10 Towns	95	95
11 Clarke	97	97
12 Velázquez	94	94
13 McMahon	98	98
14 Maloney	91	91
15 Rangel	94	94
16 Serrano	98	98
17 Engel	94	94
18 Lowey	98	98
19 Hall	95	95
20 Gillibrand[6]	100	100
20 Murphy[6]	95	95
21 Tonko	99	99
22 Hinchey	95	95
23 **McHugh**[7]	93	93
23 Owens[7]	99	99
24 Arcuri	99	99
25 Maffei	98	98
26 **Lee**	99	99
27 Higgins	97	97
28 Slaughter	93	93
29 Massa	99	99
NORTH CAROLINA		
1 Butterfield	94	94
2 Etheridge	98	98
3 **Jones**	99	99
4 Price	99	99

	1	2
5 **Foxx**	99	99
6 **Coble**	97	97
7 McIntyre	99	99
8 Kissell	98	98
9 **Myrick**	97	97
10 **McHenry**	98	98
11 Shuler	96	96
12 Watt	98	98
13 Miller	99	99
NORTH DAKOTA		
AL Pomeroy	97	97
OHIO		
1 Driehaus	99	99
2 **Schmidt**	95	95
3 **Turner**	98	99
4 **Jordan**	98	98
5 **Latta**	100	100
6 Wilson	96	96
7 **Austria**	99	99
8 **Boehner**	93	93
9 Kaptur	95	95
10 Kucinich	99	99
11 Fudge	95	95
12 **Tiberi**	94	94
13 Sutton	97	97
14 **LaTourette**	97	97
15 Kilroy	98	98
16 Boccieri	99	99
17 Ryan	96	96
18 Space	98	98
OKLAHOMA		
1 **Sullivan**	77	77
2 Boren	99	99
3 **Lucas**	91	92
4 **Cole**	98	98
5 **Fallin**	98	98
OREGON		
1 Wu	97	97
2 **Walden**	96	96
3 Blumenauer	98	98
4 DeFazio	97	97
5 Schrader	95	95
PENNSYLVANIA		
1 Brady	97	97
2 Fattah	98	98
3 Dahlkemper	99	99
4 Altmire	100	100
5 **Thompson**	99	99
6 **Gerlach**	93	93
7 Sestak	87	87
8 Murphy, P.	93	93
9 **Shuster**	96	97
10 Carney	91	91
11 Kanjorski	98	98
12 Murtha	90	90
13 Schwartz	98	98
14 Doyle	93	93
15 **Dent**	98	98
16 **Pitts**	98	98
17 Holden	98	98
18 **Murphy, T.**	96	96
19 **Platts**	97	97
RHODE ISLAND		
1 Kennedy	80	79
2 Langevin	99	99
SOUTH CAROLINA		
1 **Brown**	97	97
2 **Wilson**	99	99
3 **Barrett**	63	63
4 **Inglis**	99	99
5 Spratt	98	98
6 Clyburn	98	98
SOUTH DAKOTA		
AL Herseth Sandlin	97	97
TENNESSEE		
1 **Roe**	99	99
2 **Duncan**	99	99
3 **Wamp**	92	92
4 Davis	95	95
5 Cooper	97	97
6 Gordon	96	96
7 **Blackburn**	98	98
8 Tanner	91	91
9 Cohen	99	99

	1	2
TEXAS		
1 **Gohmert**	90	91
2 **Poe**	96	96
3 **Johnson, S.**	93	93
4 **Hall**	97	97
5 **Hensarling**	97	97
6 **Barton**	97	97
7 **Culberson**	97	97
8 **Brady**	96	96
9 Green, A.	99	99
10 **McCaul**	95	95
11 **Conaway**	95	95
12 **Granger**	89	89
13 **Thornberry**	99	99
14 **Paul**	91	91
15 Hinojosa	91	91
16 Reyes	96	96
17 Edwards	97	97
18 Jackson Lee	95	96
19 **Neugebauer**	95	95
20 Gonzalez	96	97
21 **Smith**	96	96
22 **Olson**	96	96
23 Rodriguez	98	98
24 **Marchant**	94	94
25 Doggett	99	99
26 **Burgess**	95	96
27 Ortiz	99	99
28 Cuellar	99	99
29 Green, G.	97	97
30 Johnson, E.	96	96
31 **Carter**	94	94
32 **Sessions**	95	96
UTAH		
1 **Bishop**	89	89
2 **Matheson**	99	99
3 **Chaffetz**	99	99
VERMONT		
AL Welch	95	95
VIRGINIA		
1 **Wittman**	99	99
2 Nye	99	99
3 Scott	97	97
4 **Forbes**	97	98
5 Perriello	95	95
6 **Goodlatte**	99	99
7 **Cantor**	96	96
8 Moran	86	86
9 Boucher	93	93
10 **Wolf**	99	99
11 Connolly	99	99
WASHINGTON		
1 Inslee	98	98
2 Larsen	96	96
3 Baird	97	97
4 Hastings	96	96
5 McMorris Rodgers	98	98
6 Dicks	97	97
7 McDermott	98	98
8 **Reichert**	99	99
9 Smith	95	95
WEST VIRGINIA		
1 Mollohan	96	96
2 **Capito**	99	99
3 Rahall	99	99
WISCONSIN		
1 **Ryan**	99	99
2 Baldwin	96	96
3 Kind	97	97
4 Moore	97	97
5 **Sensenbrenner**	100	100
6 **Petri**	99	99
7 Obey	98	98
8 Kagen	97	97
WYOMING		
AL **Lummis**	99	99
DELEGATES		
Faleomavaega (A.S.)	74	74
Norton (D.C.)	87	87
Bordallo (Guam)	79	79
Sablan (N. Marianas)[8]	93	93
Pierluisi (P.R.)	87	87
Christensen (V.I.)	90	90

KEY VOTES

Democrats Prevail on Top Issues, Struggle to Keep Troops in Line

WHAT BEGAN AS a promising year for congressional Democrats, thanks to their greater voting strength in both chambers and an ally in the White House, tightened over months of bitter partisanship into an endurance contest that lasted into Christmas Eve. In January, as Barack Obama was about to assume the presidency, Democrats had some Republican support in clearing legislation (S 181) that overturned a Supreme Court wage discrimination ruling. But by December, Senate Democratic leaders could just barely scrape together enough votes — all from their own caucus — to pass a historic health care overhaul bill (HR 3590).

In addition to the Senate health care vote, several other votes illustrated the precarious nature of what had once seemed an overwhelming Democratic majority. They included:

• A Senate vote in February to shut off debate on a compromise version of an economic stimulus bill (HR 1) that President Obama supported. Three Republicans voted with a unanimous Democratic caucus to invoke cloture on the bill, which called for $838.2 billion in tax cuts and spending for infrastructure and other projects to boost a sluggish economy.

• An April vote to reject an amendment by Republican Jeff Sessions of Alabama to the Senate's budget resolution. Just one Democrat, Evan Bayh of Indiana, supported the amendment, which would have frozen non-defense discretionary spending for two years.

• A June vote in the House on climate change legislation (HR 2454), which passed by a seven-vote margin. The bill drew eight GOP supporters, as dozens of Democrats, many representing heavy-manufacturing regions, balked at provisions to reward alternative sources of energy, possibly at the expense of energy producers that pollute but provide jobs. Similar tensions existed in the Senate, where its version had reached only the committee markup stage.

• A House vote in November on the health care legislation (HR 3962), which passed by a five-vote margin. Just one Republican — Anh "Joseph" Cao of Louisiana — voted with the majority. As with the House climate change vote, many Democrats from marginal or GOP-leaning districts spurned their leadership. And passage became possible only after abortion opponents were able to bring to the floor and approve an amendment barring direct or indirect federal funding of the procedure through health insurance, another key House vote.

Democratic voting strength in the Senate grew during the year, theoretically allowing the party a slight leeway on key votes. Arlen Specter of Pennsylvania, one of the three Republicans who supported cloture on the February stimulus bill, switched parties in late April and brought the Democratic caucus to 59. In July it grew to 60 — the

How CQ Picks Key Votes

Since its founding in 1945, Congressional Quarterly has selected a series of key votes for both the House and Senate on major issues of the year.

A vote is judged to be key by the extent to which it represents:

- a matter of major controversy.
- a matter of presidential or political power.
- a matter of potentially great impact on the nation and lives of Americans.

For each group of related votes in each chamber on an issue, one key vote is usually chosen — one that, in the opinion of CQ editors, was the most important in determining the outcome of the issue for the year or best reflected the views of the individual members of that issue.

number needed to end debate if Republicans threatened a filibuster — when Minnesota officials certified Democrat Al Franken the winner of a long and bitterly contested 2008 Senate race, unseating GOP incumbent Norm Coleman. But the increase from 58 to 60 scarcely helped Democratic leaders, who had plenty of dissenters within their own ranks on major legislation.

By year's end, Majority Leader Harry Reid of Nevada was forced to placate every single Democrat and independent holdout to win passage of the health care bill, as the 40-member Republican caucus stood united in a series of procedural votes. The key vote came very early on the morning of Dec. 21, when Reid rounded up just enough support to invoke cloture on the bill. The vote — 60 Democrats and independents for, 40 Republicans against — was the most significant partisan divide of the year.

Although health care was Obama's top priority both in his 2008 campaign and as 2009 progressed, his early focus was the staggering economic tumble, and the need to secure the second half of the $700 billion provided in 2009 for the unpopular Troubled Asset Relief Program set up to bail out banks. Five days before Obama took office, eight Democrats joined a majority of Senate Republicans in an attempt to withhold the funds. Democrats were able to block the joint resolution, sticking by the incoming president.

Democrats in Congress were also interested in enhancing their own power, and in a key vote, the House voted in June along partisan lines for a rule that sharply limited floor amendments as a way to expedite passage of an appropriations bill, setting a pattern for other legislation.

Besides votes on health care and climate change bills, other key votes chosen for historic reasons included:

• Passage in the House of a food safety bill. It, like the health care legislation, was a legacy of the dean of the House, Michigan Democrat John D. Dingell, who had long sought a comprehensive federal system to curb food-borne illnesses.

• In the Senate, a vote that cleared legislation expanding hate crimes covered by federal law, which supporters successfully attached to a popular defense bill. The significant civil rights legislation broadened federal statutes to extend hate crime protections to crimes based on sexual orientation, gender identity or disability.

• Votes in both chambers to allow the Food and Drug Administration to regulate tobacco. As health concerns grew, the influence of the tobacco lobby and its Capitol Hill backers had waned.

Following are the 13 key votes for the Senate and 11 for the House chosen by Congressional Quarterly editors.

HOUSE VOTES

50 Children's Health Insurance Program

Clearance by the House of an expansion of the Children's Health Insurance Program (CHIP).

The vote marked a landmark for Democrats in their new status controlling both the White House and Congress, allowing them to boast of their first victory among several major social policy programs that had been stymied by President George W. Bush.

The bill provides $32.8 billion in extra funding over 4½ years for CHIP. Lawmakers estimated at the time that it would allow coverage of an additional 4.1 million children. The program covered about 7 million in 2008.

Following easy Senate passage of the bill, only two House Democrats voted against it, and 40 House Republicans voted for it. President Obama signed the bill into law (PL 111-3) the same day.

HOUSE CLEARED HR 2 on Feb. 4, **290-135:** R 40-133; D 250-2. *(House vote 50, p. C-16; Senate vote 31, p. C-13, children's health insurance, p. 13-15)*

70 Economic Stimulus Conference Report

Passage of a $787 billion bill to help stimulate the economy through a combination of spending and tax cuts.

Enactment of the bill was an early and major legislative victory for President Obama, although the economy and high jobless numbers continued to dog the new administration during its first year in office.

Obama took office with the economy in recession and some politicians and economists warning of a possible second Great Depression. Against this backdrop, the presidential transition team and congressional Democratic leaders got to work quickly after the election on assembling the package, and it was signed into law less than a month after the new president was sworn in.

But the path to enactment was bumpy, and the effort required to get a final bill signed was an indicator of the political dynamic that has played out over the past year. There was little bipartisan support for the bill. No House Republicans voted for the conference report, and only three Senate Republicans did — one of whom, Arlen Specter of Pennsylvania, soon switched parties. The other two were Maine Republicans, Olympia J. Snowe and Susan Collins.

At first both parties expressed support for working together on the package, but, as has happened on bill after bill, Democratic and GOP leaders quickly drew battle lines with Republicans believing they had little to gain by compromising with Obama.

In another indicator of what was to come for the year, Senate moderates such as Ben Nelson, D-Neb., were also able to flex their dealmaking muscles, knowing that party leaders needed 60 votes to get around GOP filibuster attempts.

The role Senate moderates played was particularly irksome to House Democrats, who argued that Senate leaders watered down the bill by cutting back on such things as school construction funds in order to placate a few senators.

Similar tensions have played out in other areas, including how to construct a health care overhaul bill moving its way through Congress.

With regard to the stimulus, Senate Majority Leader Harry Reid, D-Nev., had little choice but to make compromises with a group led by Nelson and Collins, and House Democrats agreed to support a compromise in order to get something quickly into law. On the final vote only seven House Democrats voted against the bill.

HOUSE ADOPTED the conference report on HR 1 on Feb. 13, **246-183:** R 0-176; D 246-7. *(House vote 70, p. C-16; Senate vote 59, p. C-13; stimulus package, p. 7-3)*

104 Mortgage Loan Modification

Passage of a bill that would allow bankruptcy judges to write down the principal and interest rates of existing loans to a home's current market value for individuals whose mortgages were larger than the value of their homes or who met other requirements.

For House Democrats, the vote marked at least a temporary victory in a long-running battle. The financial industry had lobbied fiercely against the issue for years, and the industry appeared to gain enough traction the week of Feb. 23 to tamp down the populist-driven momentum when Democratic leaders were forced to pull the bill (HR 1106) from the floor amid last-minute concerns about whether it had enough votes to pass.

A group of centrist and conservative Democrats — mainly from the New Democrat and "Blue Dog" coalitions — had expressed concern that there would be a backlash from constituents already wary of trillions of dollars in bank bailouts.

Speaker Nancy Pelosi, D-Calif., who initially said the bill would be brought back to the floor unchanged, instead worked with dissidents to hammer out compromise language. The bill was put back onto the House floor — and passed — on March 5. But the difficulty Democratic leaders had getting their own members on board turned out to be a prescient glimpse into the difficulties the legislation and its bankruptcy provision would eventually face in the Senate, where the bankruptcy language was rejected.

HOUSE PASSED HR 1106 on March 5, **234-191:** R 7-167; D 227-24. *(House vote 104, p. C-16; Senate vote 174, p. C-14; mortgage relief package, p. 3-9)*

335 Tobacco Regulation

House clearing of a bill to authorize the Food and Drug Administration to regulate tobacco products.

The vote signified the first time that Congress granted the Food and Drug Administration (FDA) the power to regulate tobacco products, demonstrating the muscle of the Democrats' expanded congressional majority.

House and Senate Democrats had tried to pass the tobacco leg-

islation for years, but the House had traditionally been an obstacle until the 2006 midterm elections, which gave the party control of the chamber. The bill (HR 1256) gave the FDA the power to regulate the marketing, advertising and content of cigarettes. It is funded with user fees on tobacco products.

After Senate passage, the House cleared it overwhelmingly, with 70 Republicans joining almost all Democrats.

Some House Republicans who had opposed the bill maintained that it was essentially a new tax and that the FDA was the wrong agency to regulate tobacco. But many joined with Democrats to pass the legislation because of its potential public health effects, in a sign of the diminished influence of the tobacco industry on Congress.

HOUSE CLEARED HR 1256 on June 12, **307-97:** R 70-90; D 237-7. *(House vote 335, p. C-18; Senate vote 207, p. C-10; tobacco regulation, p. 17-4)*

352 Rule for Appropriations Floor Debate

Adoption of a rule governing debate on the fiscal 2010 Commerce-Justice-Science appropriations bill that restricted the number of amendments to the bill that could be offered.

This vote signaled a decision by House Democrats to fight back against what they regarded as Republican efforts to disrupt the appropriations process on the first of the 12 regular spending bills to come to the floor. GOP lawmakers had initially tried to offer 103 amendments to the relatively non-controversial Commerce-Justice-Science measure. After debate had already begun on the bill June 16, the Democrats returned to the Rules Committee and obtained a new rule for floor debate that allowed only 33 amendments.

House Majority Leader Steny H. Hoyer, D-Md., explained that the leadership was concerned that Republicans would offer scores of amendments to all the appropriations measures and delay action to an unacceptable degree. "We would like to proceed in a fashion that is reasonable and that provides for opportunities for amendments to be offered," Hoyer said. "But we also believe it is our responsibility to ensure that the appropriations process is completed."

The new, restrictive rule was adopted June 17, and action on amendments to the bill proceeded for a time. But Republicans eventually used parliamentary procedures to disrupt floor action, forcing 53 separate roll call votes on June 18, a modern record. The spending bill was passed that evening by a 259-157 vote, with 24 Republicans voting in favor. Democrats used restrictive rules to keep the appropriations process moving for the rest of the year.

HOUSE ADOPTED H Res 552 on June 17, **221-201:** R 0-174; D 221-27. *(House vote 352, p. C-18; Commerce-Justice-Science appropriations, p. 2-17)*

477 Climate Change Mitigation

House passage of a bill that would create a cap-and-trade system to limit emissions of greenhouse gases that cause global warming and require electric utilities to produce a percentage of their power from renewable sources such as wind, solar and geothermal.

In a dramatic vote that turned on the defection of eight Republicans who provided the slender margin of victory, the House passed legislation designed to address global warming by capping emissions of greenhouse gases and boosting the production of electricity from renewable sources. The vote marked the first time either chamber of Congress had passed an emissions cap, and it handed President Obama a hard-fought victory on one of his legislative priorities.

The legislation would cap greenhouse gas emissions at 17 percent below current levels by 2020, 42 percent below current levels by 2030 and 83 percent below current levels by 2050. Utilities, refineries and factories would have to hold government-issued emissions allowances, but the credits could be traded as commodities in the marketplace. Utilities would be required to generate a growing share of electricity from renewable sources while improving efficiency.

The bill that came to the floor was the product of months of negotiations between Energy and Commerce Chairman Henry A. Waxman, D-Calif., and moderate Democrats from industrial, rural and coal-producing districts, who feared that a cap on carbon emissions could harm their states' economies. In his efforts to win votes, Waxman agreed to concessions that included slowing the phase-in of emissions caps, providing some free emissions allowances to hard-hit industries and allowing farmers to earn money for agricultural practices that offset carbon emissions.

Even with the concessions, the fate of the bill remained in doubt in the hours leading up to the vote. Waxman and Democratic leaders spent the last 24 hours furiously lobbying fence-sitters. The White House also stepped in, calling on senior advisers Carol Browner, Rahm Emanuel and David Axelrod to press members for support, while Obama met with wavering Democrats. The night before the vote, Obama took advantage of a Hawaiian-style luau at the White House for lawmakers and their families to lobby undecided members.

Waxman's 300-page substitute amendment, incorporating a host of new provisions to win over a crucial handful of moderate Democrats, was filed in the early hours of June 26.

When the bill came to the floor that day, Minority Leader John A. Boehner, R-Ohio, mounted a last-ditch attempt to stall it with what amounted to a House equivalent of a filibuster. Using his unlimited leadership time to circumvent the time limit for debate, Boehner spent about an hour going almost line by line through the substitute amendment, questioning individual provisions.

The bill passed, 219-212, with 44 Democrats voting against the bill and eight Republican "yes" votes tipping the balance. While Boehner and Majority Leader Steny H. Hoyer, D-Md., were at odds on the merits of the bill, both agreed on its significance. Hoyer called the measure "historic," while Boehner described it as the "most profound piece of legislation to come to this floor in 100 years."

A similar measure (S 1733) stalled in the Senate, but bipartisan talks were aimed at devising a compromise bill that could come to the floor in the first half of 2010. The Obama administration has stepped up the pressure on senators by issuing an EPA order that would trigger the regulation of greenhouse gases under clean-air laws if Congress fails to act.

HOUSE PASSED HR 2454 on June 26, **219-212:** R 8-168, D 211-44. *(House vote 477, p. C-18; climate change bill, p. 10-3)*

680 Food Safety

Passage of a comprehensive food safety bill, after a string of food-borne illnesses shook the public's confidence and left key industry players searching for ways to reassure consumers.

The House vote signified passage of the first major food safety bill in decades.

Deaths from tainted spinach, jalapeño peppers and peanuts — all regulated by the Food and Drug Administration — provided the impetus for lawmakers to pass the Food Safety Enhancement Act (HR 2749). The Centers for Disease Control and Prevention estimate that each year food pathogens sicken 76 million people, sending 325,000 to the hospital and killing 5,000.

The bill had strong bipartisan support, despite fears expressed by GOP leaders and some farm-state Democrats that the legislation would impose burdensome regulations on small farms and food production operations.

Opponents said they still had concerns despite concessions by Michigan Democrat John D. Dingell, the No. 2 Democrat on the Energy and Commerce Committee. Dingell, who shepherded the bill through the House, negotiated with Agriculture Committee Chairman Collin C. Peterson, D-Minn., to exempt livestock, poultry and feed grain producers from most new FDA rules and continue regulation by the U.S. Agriculture Department.

Peterson won the concessions after threatening to have his committee issue an unfavorable recommendation on the bill — a symbolic act, because his panel did not have jurisdiction, but problematic if Democrats wanted to maintain a largely unified front on the bill.

Dingell also compromised on annual registration or user fees for food facilities to satisfy GOP objections. Fees were reduced to $500 per facility, from $1,000, with fees for companies with multiple facilities not to exceed $175,000.

HOUSE PASSED HR 2749 on July 30, **283-142:** R 54-122; D 229-20. *(House vote 680, p. C-18; food safety, p. 17-3)*

682 Cash for Clunkers

A bill to replenish a federal fund that offered as much as $4,500 to car owners who traded in fuel-inefficient vehicles for newer, more fuel-efficient vehicles.

With unusual alacrity, the House voted to replenish, with $2 billion, a popular auto trade-in program that nearly ran out of money only a week after it was implemented by the Transportation Department. The vote, taken just before the House recessed for August, demonstrated Democrats' continued support for the domestic auto industry and their pleasant surprise with an economic measure that actually stimulated quick demand — but also put on display GOP concerns that the government was picking winners and losers in its economic interventions of the past two years.

Designed to bolster the struggling auto industry while taking gas-guzzling vehicles off of the road, the program — known as "cash for clunkers" — was enacted as part of the war supplemental funding bill (PL 111-32) and implemented by the Transportation Department in late July.

The program offered up to $4,500 in cash rebates to help people who traded in cars or SUVs with a combined fuel economy of 18 miles per gallon or less to buy newer, more fuel-efficient vehicles. Congress appropriated $1 billion for the program, which was set to expire Nov. 1, or whenever the money ran out. Unlike some other economic measures enacted since the recession started, the program, touted by automakers and car dealers, fueled a huge consumer response, rapidly depleting the funds. Without action, funding appeared set to run out during the summer break.

After the Transportation Department notified congressional leaders July 30 that the funding was almost gone, Appropriations Chairman David R. Obey, D-Wis., quickly wrote legislation adding $2 billion to the program, designed to take it into the autumn as lawmakers prepared to leave town for the August recess. The funding was offset by taking $2 billion from Title 17 renewable-energy loan guarantees, which Democrats promised to replenish later. House leaders brought the bill to the House floor July 31, under suspension of the rules.

Even some skeptics of the program acknowledged its success, though conservatives called it an unfair handout to the auto industry. "'Cash for clunkers' is another example of the government picking winners and losers and enshrines us as a bailout nation," said Rep. Jeb Hensarling, R-Texas.

The Senate followed suit, clearing the bill the next week.

HOUSE PASSED HR 3435 on July 31, **316-109:** R 77-95, D 239-14. *(House vote 682, p. C-20; "cash for clunkers," p. 7-9)*

719 Student Loan Overhaul

Passage of a bill to establish the government as the sole provider of student loans and provide billions of dollars in savings toward various scholarship and education programs.

With this vote, the House took the first step toward a significant overhaul of the provision of student loans, one that would remove private companies from originating loans but preserve their role as servicers.

The bill passed by the House largely reflected the proposal put forth by the Obama administration to convert the private lending system to government loans and put the savings into education programs such as Pell grants, early-childhood education and community colleges.

But Democrats first had to defeat a series of amendments offered by Republicans, who said the bill overestimated the likely savings and threatened to wipe out tens of thousands of jobs. Republicans proposed preserving existing subsidies for private lenders through 2014 and creating a commission to develop a new private sector model for student lending.

In order to ease passage, bill sponsor George Miller, D-Calif., chairman of the Education and Labor Committee, encouraged members to vote for a GOP motion to recommit the bill to committee with instructions to report it back with language prohibiting the use of federal funds for the Association of Community Organizations for Reform Now (ACORN). Miller said ACORN would not receive funding under the bill, anyway.

The House passed the legislation as a reconciliation bill, leaving the option open in the Senate of avoiding a filibuster. But the Senate did not take up the measure at all in 2009.

HOUSE PASSED HR 3221 on Sept. 17, **253-171:** R 6-167; D 247-4. *(House vote 719, p. C-20; student loans, p. 8-3)*

884 Abortion Funding

In order to secure enough votes to pass their health care overhaul, House Democratic leaders allowed anti-abortion members of their caucus a vote on an amendment that would restrict insurance coverage for abortions.

With this vote, anti-abortion House Democrats and Republicans showed they were a force to be reckoned with, even though the Democratic majority was made up mostly of pro-choice members.

Lawmakers on either side of the abortion issue had observed an uneasy truce for years, essentially agreeing not to alter longstanding federal policy that prevents taxpayer dollars from being used to pay for the procedure. That truce was shattered during debate on Democratic health care overhaul legislation, leading to what abortion opponents considered the most important vote on the issue in more than a decade.

As the health care legislation was developed, Democrats had struggled to maintain the principle that taxpayer dollars would not pay for abortions. The bill would create a huge new subsidy program to help people buy health insurance and would also offer a new government-run insurance plan as an option to private insurance. In what liberals considered a compromise, the bill included language that would require insurance plans covering abortions — including the "public option" — to pay for the procedure using only revenue from premiums paid by their customers, not federal subsidies. But many abortion opponents, including the influential U.S. Conference of Catholic Bishops, considered that language nothing more than an accounting gimmick; the bill, they said, would lead to a huge increase in elective abortions.

Democrats won the House majority in large part by seeking candidates in 2006 and 2008 who could win conservative districts. These candidates were often opposed to abortion. On the health care bill, liberals reaped the sour fruits of the party's electoral strategy.

A group of about 40 anti-abortion Democrats led by Bart Stupak of Michigan told Democratic leaders they would not support the health care bill unless it included greater restrictions on abortion coverage. In a key point of dispute, Stupak and his allies demanded that the public option be forbidden from covering abortions altogether, arguing that by definition it would be a government program like Medicaid, the entitlement for the poor.

By law, Medicaid covers only abortions that result from rape or incest, or when a pregnancy threatens a woman's life. Democratic leaders negotiated directly with Stupak and the Catholic bishops up until hours before the vote, trying to find a compromise. In the end, they failed and instead agreed to allow a vote on a Stupak amendment that abortion rights supporters opposed.

HOUSE ADOPTED the Stupak amendment Nov. 7, **240-194:** R 176-0; D 64-194. (*House vote 884, p. C-20; health care overhaul, p. 13-3; abortion, p. 13-13*)

887 Health Care Overhaul

The House passed sweeping health care legislation aimed at insuring most Americans and paid for with a controversial combination of reductions in Medicare spending and tax increases.

Votes in Congress are too often described as historic, but the House's passage of health care overhaul legislation deserves the moniker. With the possible exception of the introduction of Medicare in 1965, never before had a chamber of Congress passed legislation that would so dramatically restructure the health care system; according to the Congressional Budget Office, the overhaul bill would ensure access to affordable health insurance for nearly every American.

Despite its lofty aims, Democrats had considerable trouble securing the votes for the bill, their top domestic priority of the year. Moderates and liberals in the caucus had clashed for months over controversial issues in the legislation, including a government-run insurance plan called the "public option," insurance coverage for abortion and whether the bill would sufficiently slow the rise of health care costs.

Democratic leaders didn't lock down support for the bill until the evening before the vote, when they agreed to allow a group of anti-abortion Democrats led by Michigan's Bart Stupak to offer an amendment restricting coverage for the procedure. The amendment was adopted, angering abortion rights supporters but securing passage of the legislation.

In a surprise, Democrats also won the support of a single Republican — freshman Anh "Joseph" Cao of Louisiana. Cao defeated Democrat William J. Jefferson (1991-2009) in 2008 after Jefferson came under criminal investigation for accepting bribes (he was later convicted and imprisoned). His district overwhelmingly supported President Obama's election, and Cao said Obama had promised additional federal assistance in the area's ongoing recovery from Hurricane Katrina in exchange for his vote.

In the vote's signature scene, Minority Whip Eric Cantor, R-Va., aware of Cao's possible defection, sat next to him as the roll was called, quietly lobbying him to stick with his party. Cao voted only after it became clear Democrats would win regardless.

HOUSE PASSED HR 3962 on Nov. 7, **220-215:** R 1-176; D 219-39. (*House vote 887, p. C-20; Senate vote 385, p. C-15, health care overhaul, p. 13-3*)

SENATE VOTES

5 Release of TARP Money

A joint resolution that would prevent the release of the second half of the $700 billion included in the 2008 financial industry bailout law.

In a solid opening win for the Obama administration before it even took office, the Senate on Jan. 15 easily voted down a measure that would have withheld the remaining half of the Troubled Asset Relief Fund (TARP).

The chamber voted down the resolution of disapproval by a vote of 42-52 after a week of intense lobbying from the Obama team as it began its efforts to address the nation's financial troubles.

It was a crucial first victory for an administration that would shortly thereafter begin the push for economic stimulus legislation that would approach $800 billion.

The outcome remained in doubt until the afternoon of the vote. Just a few hours before the roll call took place, leaders on both sides of the aisle received a letter from President-elect Obama providing more details about the conditions he proposed attaching to the remaining $350 billion of bailout money. Several senators credited other parts of the letter with tipping the scales for the vote. Obama also proposed directing a minimum of $50 billion toward foreclosure mitigation, increased transparency in the financial system and stronger reporting requirements for companies receiving bailout funds.

SENATE REJECTED S J Res 5 on Jan. 15, **42-52:** R 33-6; D 8-45; I 1-1. *(Senate vote 5, p. C-13; TARP funding, p. 7-12)*

14 Wage Discrimination

Senate passage of legislation designed to make it easier for victims of wage discrimination to seek remedies in court.

The vote marked an early victory for the newly enlarged Democratic majority in the Senate and paved the way for enactment of legislation designed to roll back a 2007 Supreme Court ruling that supporters said made recovery in wage discrimination suits more difficult.

Democrats immediately called for a legislative response after the Supreme Court ruled against Lilly Ledbetter, an Alabama tire plant employee who discovered she had been paid less than her male colleagues. The measure was designed to ensure that the statute of limitations begins to toll with the date of the most recent paycheck for which a disparity exists, rather than at the time the discrimination began, which is often years earlier.

Sponsors brought the measure to the Senate floor in January 2009 in far better position than a year earlier, when they could not find enough votes to invoke cloture or overcome a potential veto by President George W. Bush.

That changed with the election of Barack Obama, and Democrats teed the measure up for an early labor victory. Hoping to advance the bill quickly in the early months of the new administration, Senate Democrats bypassed committee consideration and took up a narrower version than that passed by the House two weeks earlier.

Republicans abandoned efforts to hold up the bill after Democrats agreed to a series of votes on GOP amendments, including one designed to start the clock running on the statute of limitations at the point at which a plaintiff "should be expected to have enough information" to realize that he or she was the victim of employment discrimination.

Democrats easily defeated those amendments, and five Republicans — including all four women in the GOP caucus — joined with Democrats to vote in favor of the underlying bill.

The House subsequently cleared the Senate bill, and it became the first piece of substantive legislation signed by President Obama.

SENATE PASSED S 181 (PL 111-2) on Jan. 22, **61-36:** R 5-36; D 54-0; I 2-0. *(Senate vote 14, p. C-13; wage discrimination, p. 9-4)*

31 Children's Health Insurance Program

Passage of a bill to expand the Children's Health Insurance Program.

While a handful of Republicans joined Democrats to move forward with one of the majority party's most important domestic priorities, notable were some of the Senate Republicans who voted against the $32.8 billion expansion of health care coverage to 4.1 million previously uninsured children.

Several supporters of the policy in previous Congresses, notably Finance Committee ranking GOP member Charles E. Grassley of Iowa, declined to vote yes this time, saying Democrats had gone beyond the deal made in the past Congress to expand the program. In all, nine Republicans voted for the bill, with Grassley and Orrin G. Hatch of Utah the notable exceptions among previous backers.

The Senate passage vote set up the House's vote to clear the bill for the president a week later.

SENATE PASSED HR 2 (PL 111-3) on Jan. 29, **66-32:** R 9-32; D 55-0; I 2-0. *(Senate vote 31, p. C-13; House vote 50, p. C-16; children's health insurance, p. 13-15)*

59 Stimulus Compromise

A motion to invoke cloture and thus limit debate on the economic stimulus bill (HR 1).

The vote illustrated the limits that Senate leaders would have in moving forward on the Democrats' agenda, as party moderates were able to scale back the size of the package for it to proceed.

While the Democrats gained seats in the 2008 elections, with GOP threats to filibuster major initiatives, 60 votes were needed to move most legislation. This dynamic was on display on this vote.

Senate Democratic leaders brought to the floor a bill whose 11-year cost grew to more than $900 billion, but moderates in both parties balked at the expense as well as some specific provisions.

A group led by Ben Nelson, D-Neb., and Susan Collins, R-Maine, which sometimes grew to as many as 20 centrist senators, began meeting to come up with ways to change the bill. Nelson and Collins, primarily, then began meeting with Senate Democratic leaders and White House officials to come up with a compromise.

In order to get the needed 60 votes to shut off a filibuster,

Senate leaders agreed to cut the bill's spending down to $838.1 billion, primarily by scaling back funds for state governments and school construction. Some Democratic senators were not happy with the compromise, but for leaders it was the price to pay for the votes.

In the end, three Republicans — Collins, Arlen Specter of Pennsylvania and Olympia J. Snowe of Maine — joined all Democrats to shut off debate and move the bill forward.

In April, Specter switched parties, citing the harsh reaction among Republican voters to his role in the stimulus debate as a factor in his decision.

SENATE AGREED to motion Feb. 9, **61-36:** R 3-36; D 56-0; I 2-0. *(Senate vote 59, p. C-13; House vote 70, p. C-16; stimulus law, p. 7-3)*

72 Gun Rights

Amended a District of Columbia voting rights bill with language that would bar the District from prohibiting firearms possession and repeal the city's registration laws.

The vote demonstrated the continued power of gun rights advocates, despite lopsided Democratic majorities in the Senate and House as well as a Democratic administration. Offered by Sen. John Ensign, R-Nev., the amendment was one of several initiatives by Republicans during the year to strengthen gun rights.

Most Senate Republicans opposed legislation to grant full House representation to residents of the capital city. The bill, by independent Joseph I. Lieberman of Connecticut, would add a full voting House member from the staunchly Democratic District, and, in the interests of partisan balance, another initially from conservative Utah.

The amendment would bar the District from prohibiting firearms possession, repeal most District firearms registration mandates, and repeal the city's requirement that firearms in homes had to be disassembled or secured with a trigger lock or other device. It was similar to legislation the House overwhelmingly passed in 2008.

"This really is about restoring Second Amendment rights to the residents who live here in the District of Columbia," Ensign said.

But opponents of Ensign's amendment said it was a mistake to roll back District of Columbia gun regulations.

"I believe the amendment is reckless. I believe it is irresponsible," California Democrat Dianne Feinstein said. "I believe it will lead to more weapons and more violence on the streets of our nation's capital."

Nearly two dozen Democrats — mostly from the South and West, where gun control is unpopular — joined all but one Republican in adopting the amendment.

The success of the amendment also derailed the underlying D.C. voting rights legislation in the House, which was slated to consider its version the week after the Senate acted. House Democratic leaders pulled the measure after moderate and conservative Democrats teamed with Republicans to push for a vote on a gun amendment.

SENATE ADOPTED a gun rights amendment to a D.C. voting rights bill (S 160) on Feb. 26, **62-36:** R 40-1; D 22-33; I 0-2. *(Senate vote 72, p. C-14; D.C. voting, p. 5-10)*

120 Limit on Discretionary Spending

Amendment to the Senate budget resolution (S Con Res 13) that would freeze non-defense discretionary spending for two years.

In bringing the vote to the floor, Senate Republicans tried to draw a clear contrast with Democrats over discretionary spending.

Jeff Sessions of Alabama offered the amendment during debate on the fiscal 2010 budget resolution as the GOP attempted to paint Democrats as profligate. He and other Republicans argued that the recently enacted $787 billion economic stimulus bill had showered domestic agencies and programs with funding and that deficit concerns should be heeded during debate on the budget.

But Democrats dismissed the GOP premise, saying many agencies had not received adequate resources during the George W. Bush presidency and needed more funding.

The amendment would have adjusted the totals in the budget resolution to set non-defense discretionary spending at fiscal 2009 levels for fiscal 2010 and fiscal 2011, then increase them by 1 percent in fiscal 2012 through fiscal 2014. Its only real effect would have been in fiscal 2010, since Congress writes a new budget resolution each year.

The amendment did draw the support of one Democrat: Evan Bayh of Indiana. Among Republicans, it was rejected by Susan Collins of Maine and Mel Martinez of Florida.

SENATE REJECTED the amendment to S Con Res 13 on April 1, **40-58:** R 39-2; D 1-54; I 0-2. *(Senate vote 120, p. C-14; budget resolution, p. 4-9)*

174 Mortgage Loan Modification

A proposed amendment to a foreclosure relief bill (S 896) would have allowed bankruptcy judges to write down the principal and interest rates of certain mortgages on primary homes if the homeowner and creditor had not been able to reach agreement on a reasonable loan modification.

The Senate vote on a so-called cramdown provision demonstrated the limits to which Congress would go to use government policy to try to stem home foreclosures.

Practically cursing at a lobbying juggernaut that he "frankly can't match," Richard J. Durbin, D-Ill., watched as his amendment to give bankruptcy judges the option of changing the terms of a mortgage fell to a united Republican caucus and a few steadfast Democrats.

Even with the support of the Obama administration, the Senate defeated the amendment, which Durbin tried to attach to a broader housing bill. Twelve Democrats joined Republicans to defeat the measure. The House had already passed a bill that included the provision.

Durbin blamed the defeat on the lobbying efforts of the banking industry, considered by most to be politically battered after six months of federal bailouts and economic disaster. But as the Senate vote demonstrated, the industry was far from being politically neutered.

"The big banks, J.P. Morgan Chase, you see them all over the United States — they were at the [negotiating] table until last week, and they decided, 'No, we will walk away, we are not interested in this conversation,'" Durbin said. "Wells Fargo, Bank of America, the list goes on and on. If any of the names sound familiar, it is that they are surviving today because of our taxpayer dollars."

But Minority Whip Jon Kyl, R-Ariz., had another view.

"'Cramdown' will not fix the recent downturn in the housing market but only prolong it, prolong the recovery, by increasing interest rates," he said. "Instead of encouraging homeowners who are at risk of foreclosure to file for bankruptcy, the federal government should encourage lenders to work with owners to modify loans where it is economically viable for the homeowners to remain in their homes."

SENATE REJECTED the Durbin amendment to S 896 on April 30, **45-51**: R 0-39; D 43-12; I 2-0. *(Senate vote 174, p. C-14; House vote 104, p. C-16; mortgage modification, p. 3-9)*

194 Credit Card Regulation

Senate passage of a bill that would impose restrictions on credit card company lending practices, including barring retroactive increases on annual percentage interest rates and requiring companies to give at least 45 days' notice before increasing such rates.

In a rare moment of bipartisanship on a major issue during the session, the vote marked a successful compromise on sweeping legislation designed to protect consumers from arbitrary increases in credit card interest rates and fees.

The top Democrat and Republican on the Senate Banking, Housing and Urban Affairs Committee — Chairman Christopher J. Dodd of Connecticut and ranking Republican Richard C. Shelby of Alabama — reached a deal in May that cleared the way for passage. They struck the deal on substitute language to a House-passed bill after months of discussions and a final weekend of legislative drafting by minority and majority staffs.

The compromise allowed for easy passage by the Senate. The issue was propelled by consumer anger, along with almost-daily calls from the Obama administration for Congress to act.

"This issue has finally reached a tipping point," Dodd said. "A lot of times we get in a discussion, and we're informing the public for the first time about a problem. In this case, the public is more aware than many are that serve in the halls of Congress."

SENATE PASSED HR 627 on May 19, **90-5**: R 35-4; D 53-1; I 2-0. *(Senate vote 194, p. C-14; credit card restrictions, p. 3-3)*

207 Tobacco Regulation

Senate passage of legislation giving the Food and Drug Administration (FDA) the power to regulate tobacco.

The vote, uniting all but one Senate Democrat with many Republicans against a handful of tobacco-state lawmakers who fought the bill, highlighted a more prominent influence among health advocates and the weakened state of the tobacco lobby.

Led by Richard M. Burr, R-N.C., and Kay Hagan, D-N.C., the opposition did not have the numbers to block a longtime priority for Democrats and Republicans, who saw the legislation as a major public health win. The bill (HR 1256) gave the FDA the right to regulate the marketing, advertising and content of cigarettes. The regulation is funded with user fees on tobacco products.

Its biggest champion, Edward M. Kennedy, D-Mass. (1962-2009), was absent from the vote, however, because of his battle with brain cancer, which eventually claimed his life later in the year. But broad support for the legislation, even from traditional Kennedy political foes such as John Cornyn, R-Texas, ensured its passage and eventual enactment (PL 111-31).

SENATE PASSED HR 1256 on June 11, **79-17**: R 23-16; D 54-1; I 2-0. *(Senate vote 207, p. C-15; House vote 335, p. C-18; tobacco rules, p. 17-4)*

233 Hate Crimes Expansion

Vote on motion to invoke cloture, and thus limit debate, on an amendment to the fiscal 2010 defense authorization measure aimed at expanding federal hate crimes law to cover crimes based on sexual orientation, gender identity or disability.

Backers of legislation to expand hate crimes law, which had been sought for years by gay rights and civil rights groups, had folded it into the annual defense authorization measure before, in order to try to get it enacted. In 2007, a similar hate crimes expansion was dropped from the conference report on the fiscal 2008 authorization bill at the insistence of the House.

Most Senate Republicans opposed the attachment of the hate crimes language — as an amendment by Judiciary Chairman Patrick J. Leahy, D-Vt. — to the defense authorization bill. South Carolina Republican Jim DeMint criticized Senate Democrats for engineering a vote on the provisions "in the middle of a defense authorization debate which should be bipartisan, should be focused on the defense of our country, a clear constitutional responsibility."

Senate Armed Services Chairman Carl Levin, D-Mich., defended the effort to attach the crime measure to the defense bill. "This bill is an available vehicle for an important subject. We've done this before on this bill," Levin said. "And one other thing that I feel keenly about as chairman of the Armed Services Committee: This bill embodies values of diversity and freedom that our men and women in uniform fight to defend."

With the House in Democratic hands and the Obama administration strongly supporting the hate crimes bill, senators cast their votes late at night July 16 knowing that if the provisions were written into the underlying measure in the Senate, there was a very good chance they would survive in the enacted legislation. Five Republicans joined 56 Democrats and two independents in voting to invoke cloture on the amendment. The Senate then adopted the amendment by unanimous consent. The underlying bill was eventually cleared and signed.

"The Senate has made it very clear how we hold in abhorrence hate crimes," Leahy said after the vote.

SENATE AGREED to the motion July 16, **63-28**: R 5-28; D 56-0; I 2-0. *(Senate vote 233, p. C-15; hate crimes expansion, p. 15-6)*

235 F-22 Funding

Adoption of an amendment to the fiscal 2010 defense authorization bill (S 1390) that terminated production of the F-22 Raptor fighter jet.

The vote was a significant victory for President Obama, who had threatened to veto any legislation that approved the purchase of additional F-22s. He argued that the Air Force had already purchased

enough of the planes, when combined with other assets, to combat likely threats in the future. While a broad swath of the Senate disagreed with him on that point, enough senators reversed themselves on this vote to give the White House the win.

Obama exerted considerable lobbying resources to gain those reversals and achieve a rarity: Congress terminating a major defense industrial program, no less one that had survived repeated attempts on its life in previous Congresses.

The amendment, by Armed Services Chairman Carl Levin, D-Mich., and ranking Republican John McCain of Arizona, took $1.75 billion that the panel's bill had dedicated to buy seven F-22s and instead dispersed it to various broad spending categories within the bill. It was unclear right up to the vote how it would turn out, and few predicted that Obama would win, as he did — hands down. Most Republicans were wary of ending production of a premier weapon in a period of uncertain security. Many Democrats, particularly those with jobs in their states reliant on the project, agreed.

But a critical group of senators from both parties, most of whom had no direct interest in the program, sided with the president out of loyalty or because they thought his decision was correct. Among the group were some Republicans who typically voted against the president on security issues, such as Jon Kyl of Arizona, and a Democrat, John Kerry, in whose state of Massachusetts some of the F-22 work is done.

To be sure, another big factor was the decision by the F-22's lead contractor, Lockheed Martin Corp., not to lobby publicly for the F-22 against the president's wishes (although the company could afford to stand above the fray because it makes the other top new warplane, the F-35).

After the vote, defense appropriators who had supported continued production of the F-22 relented and said they would not fund it because the Senate had spoken. And when the House and Senate conference committee met to hammer out the final version of the defense authorization bill, the House conferees, whose bill had backed more F-22 production, also gave way.

SENATE ADOPTED the amendment to S 1390 on July 21, **58-40:** R 15-25; D 42-14; I 1-1. *(Senate vote 235, p. C-15; defense authorization, p. 6-3)*

262 Confirmation of Sonia Sotomayor

Senate vote to confirm Sonia Sotomayor as an associate justice of the Supreme Court.

The vote enabled Sotomayor to replace David H. Souter on the Supreme Court and become the first Hispanic and third female associate justice. It demonstrated the strength of the 60-vote Senate Democratic caucus in preventing successful GOP filibusters of judicial nominations.

The outcome had been foretold for weeks. Besides the Democrats' solid majority in the Senate, Sotomayor's quietly competent performance during her Senate Judiciary Committee confirmation hearing in July had ensured her eventual confirmation.

The nominee had effectively rebutted GOP attacks against her and given Republican opponents nothing they could use to build momentum for a rejection of her candidacy. Jeff Sessions of Alabama, ranking Republican on the panel, ended any suspense about an attempt at a filibuster on the last day of the confirmation hearing. "I will not support and I don't think any member of this side will sup-

port a filibuster or any attempt to block a vote on your nomination," Sessions told Sotomayor.

The most inflammatory rhetoric during the floor debate came on its first day, when Oklahoma Republican James M. Inhofe branded as "racist" Sotomayor's much-debated past comment that a "wise Latina" judge often could reach a better conclusion than a white male counterpart.

Senate Judiciary Chairman Patrick J. Leahy, D-Vt., cast Sotomayor's nomination as akin to the evolution of civil rights and voting rights in American history — such as the 19th and 26th Amendments — and major legislation pertaining to those rights that was enacted during the 1960s. "These actions have marked progress along the path of inclusion. They recognize the great diversity that is the strength of our nation," Leahy said. "Judge Sotomayor's journey to this nomination is truly an American story."

By the time the Senate gathered Aug. 6 to vote on the nomination, it was easy to predict the final tally, because every Republican had already announced how he or she would vote.

George V. Voinovich of Ohio, who voted in favor of the nomination, was the last uncommitted Republican to announce his support in advance of the vote. "Judge Sotomayor is not the nominee I would have selected if I were president, but making a nomination is not my role here today," Voinovich said.

Unlike during most Senate votes, senators sat at their desks through the roll call, rising to cast their votes as their names were called. Nearly every senator participated, including Democrat Robert C. Byrd, who had been absent from Senate votes because of illness. The only absentee was Massachusetts Democrat Edward M. Kennedy, D-Mass., who was ailing from a brain tumor. The longtime liberal senator's absence from the historic vote was an unmistakable sign of his debilitation; Kennedy died a little more than two weeks later.

SENATE CONFIRMED Sotomayor on Aug. 6, **68-31:** R 9-31; D 57-0; I 2-0. *(Senate vote 262, p. C-15; Sotomayor nomination, p. 15-3)*

385 Health Care Overhaul/Cloture

Senate cloture vote to shut off debate on a health care overhaul bill (HR 3590) that would introduce fundamental changes in insurance coverage.

The vote was a perfect manifestation of the partisan gridlock that marked the first session of the 111th Congress, as the Senate by the barest possible margin stepped over the final obstacle to passage of the historic legislation. Majority Leader Harry Reid, D-Nev., needed the votes of all 60 members of the Democratic caucus (including two independents), as all 40 Republicans voted no.

The bill includes mandates on employers, establishment of insurance "exchanges" to serve as marketplaces where the uninsured could buy coverage, and, to pay for its implementation, new taxes on drugmakers, medical device makers, insurance companies and wealthy individuals.

But it also contains a number of compromise deals, without which Reid might not have won 60 votes. It bars direct or indirect federal support of abortions, a prohibition that secured the vote of the last remaining Democratic holdout, Ben Nelson of Nebraska. In another concession to independent Joseph I. Lieberman of Connecticut, a "public option" alternative from a group of 10 liberal and centrist Democrats was dropped from the bill. It would have allowed 55- to

64-year-olds to "buy in" to some form of Medicare coverage.

Three days later, the Senate passed the underlying bill, 60-39; the only change from the cloture vote tally being the absence of Jim Bunning, R-Ky. Passage sets up a January conference with the House, which passed its version in November.

Senate Republicans agreed with Reid that, in advancing the bill, Democrats were "reshaping the nation," although they said the out-come would mean higher costs and taxes and fewer health services. Minority Leader Mitch McConnell of Kentucky said that "Americans have already issued their verdict — they don't want it."

SENATE INVOKED CLOTURE on HR 3590 on Dec. 21, **60-40:** R 0-40; D 58-0; I 2-0. *(Senate vote 385, p. C-15; House vote 887, p. C-20; health care overhaul, p. 13-3)* ■

IN THE HOUSE | By Vote Number

50. HR 2. Children's Health Insurance/Motion to Concur.

Waxman, D-Calif., motion to concur in the Senate amendment to the bill that would reauthorize the State Children's Health Insurance Program over four and a half years and increase funding by $32.8 billion. To offset the cost of the expansion, it would increase the federal tax on cigarettes by 62 cents per pack and raise taxes on other tobacco products. It would remove a five-year waiting period for new, legal immigrants, including pregnant women, and loosen citizenship and eligibility documentation requirements. The bill would limit program eligibility to families earning three times the federal poverty level or less and would require states to phase out coverage of childless adults. Motion agreed to (thus clearing the bill for the president), 290-135: R 40-133; D 250-2. Feb. 4, 2009. *(Story, p. C-4)*

70. HR 1. Economic Stimulus/Conference Report.

Adoption of the conference report on the bill that would provide an estimated $787.2 billion in tax cuts and spending increases to stimulate the economy. It would prevent the alternative minimum tax from applying to millions of additional taxpayers in 2009 and increase the ceiling on federal borrowing by $789 billion to $12.104 trillion. The tax provisions, estimated to cost $211.8 billion through 2019, include extending current accelerated depreciation allowances for businesses, suspending taxes on the first $2,400 of unemployment benefits for 2009 and expanding a number of individual tax credits. Mandatory spending increases, expected to cost $267 billion through 2019, include an extension of unemployment and welfare benefits, Medicaid payments to states, and grants for health information technology. Discretionary spending, estimated at $308.3 billion through 2019, includes grants for state and local schools and funds for public housing, transportation and nutrition assistance. Adopted (thus sent to the Senate) 246-183: R 0-176; D 246-7. A "yea" was a vote in support of the president's position. Feb. 13, 2009. *(Story, p. C-4)*

104. HR 1106. Mortgage Loans Modification/Passage.

Passage of the bill that would allow bankruptcy judges to write down the principal and interest rates of loans issued before the bill's enactment to a home's current market value, for individuals whose mortgages are larger than the value of their homes or who meet other requirements. It would allow the government to reimburse mortgage lenders for reduced principal, interest rates or fees if the mortgage was guaranteed by the Federal Housing Administration, the Veterans Affairs Department or other federal mortgage guarantors. It also would modify the Hope for Homeowners program and would permanently increase, to $250,000, Federal Deposit Insurance Corporation and National Credit Union Administration deposit insurance coverage on individual bank accounts. The amount would be indexed to inflation from 2015 on. Passed 234-191: R 7-167; D 227-24. March 5, 2009. *(Story, p. C-4)*

[1] The Speaker votes only at her discretion.

[2] Rep. Hilda L. Solis, D-Calif., resigned Feb. 24, 2009, to become secretary of Labor. The last vote for which she was eligible was vote 79.

[3] Rep. Rahm Emanuel, D-Ill., resigned Jan. 2, 2009, to become President Obama's chief of staff. Emanuel was not eligible for any votes in 2009.

[4] Rep. Kirsten Gillibrand, D-N.Y., resigned Jan. 26, 2009, to fill the Senate seat vacated by fellow Democrat Hillary Rodham Clinton, who resigned Jan. 21, 2009, to become secretary of State. The last vote for which Gillibrand was eligible was vote 29.

[5] Del. Gregorio Kilili Camacho Sablan of the Northern Mariana Islands, who was elected in 2008 as an independent, informed the Speaker on Feb. 23, 2009, that he wished to list his party affiliation as Democrat. The first vote in the Committee of the Whole for which he asked to be counted with the Democrats is vote 100.

	50	70	104
ALABAMA			
1 **Bonner**	N	N	N
2 Bright	N	N	N
3 **Rogers**	Y	N	N
4 **Aderholt**	?	N	N
5 Griffith	Y	N	N
6 **Bachus**	N	N	N
7 Davis	Y	Y	Y
ALASKA			
AL **Young**	Y	N	N
ARIZONA			
1 Kirkpatrick	Y	Y	Y
2 **Franks**	N	N	N
3 **Shadegg**	N	N	N
4 Pastor	Y	Y	Y
5 Mitchell	Y	Y	Y
6 **Flake**	?	N	N
7 Grijalva	Y	Y	Y
8 Giffords	Y	Y	Y
ARKANSAS			
1 Berry	Y	Y	N
2 Snyder	Y	Y	Y
3 **Boozman**	N	N	N
4 Ross	Y	Y	Y
CALIFORNIA			
1 Thompson	Y	Y	Y
2 **Herger**	N	N	N
3 **Lungren**	N	N	N
4 **McClintock**	N	N	N
5 Matsui	Y	Y	Y
6 Woolsey	Y	Y	Y
7 Miller, George	Y	Y	Y
8 Pelosi[1]	Y	Y	Y
9 Lee	Y	Y	Y
10 Tauscher	Y	Y	Y
11 McNerney	Y	Y	Y
12 Speier	Y	Y	Y
13 Stark	?	Y	?
14 Eshoo	Y	Y	Y
15 Honda	Y	Y	Y
16 Lofgren	Y	Y	Y
17 Farr	Y	Y	Y
18 Cardoza	Y	Y	Y
19 **Radanovich**	N	N	N
20 Costa	Y	Y	Y
21 **Nunes**	N	N	N
22 **McCarthy**	N	N	N
23 Capps	Y	Y	Y
24 **Gallegly**	N	N	N
25 **McKeon**	N	N	N
26 **Dreier**	N	N	N
27 Sherman	Y	Y	Y
28 Berman	Y	Y	Y
29 Schiff	Y	Y	Y
30 Waxman	Y	Y	Y
31 Becerra	Y	Y	Y
32 Solis[2]	Y	Y	
33 Watson	Y	Y	Y
34 Roybal-Allard	Y	Y	Y
35 Waters	Y	Y	Y
36 Harman	Y	Y	Y
37 Richardson	Y	Y	Y
38 Napolitano	Y	Y	Y
39 Sánchez, Linda	Y	Y	Y
40 **Royce**	N	N	N
41 **Lewis**	N	N	N
42 **Miller, Gary**	N	N	?
43 Baca	Y	Y	Y
44 **Calvert**	N	N	N
45 **Bono Mack**	N	N	N
46 **Rohrabacher**	N	N	N
47 Sanchez, Loretta	Y	Y	Y
48 **Campbell**	–	–	N
49 **Issa**	N	N	N
50 **Bilbray**	N	N	N
51 Filner	Y	Y	Y
52 **Hunter**	N	N	N
53 Davis	Y	Y	Y

	50	70	104
COLORADO			
1 DeGette	Y	Y	Y
2 Polis	Y	Y	Y
3 Salazar	Y	Y	Y
4 Markey	Y	Y	N
5 **Lamborn**	N	N	N
6 **Coffman**	N	N	–
7 Perlmutter	Y	Y	Y
CONNECTICUT			
1 Larson	Y	Y	Y
2 Courtney	Y	Y	Y
3 DeLauro	Y	Y	Y
4 Himes	Y	Y	Y
5 Murphy	Y	Y	Y
DELAWARE			
AL **Castle**	Y	N	Y
FLORIDA			
1 **Miller**	N	N	N
2 Boyd	Y	Y	Y
3 Brown	Y	Y	Y
4 **Crenshaw**	N	N	N
5 **Brown-Waite**	N	N	N
6 **Stearns**	N	N	N
7 **Mica**	N	N	N
8 Grayson	Y	Y	Y
9 **Bilirakis**	N	N	N
10 **Young**	Y	N	N
11 Castor	Y	Y	Y
12 **Putnam**	N	N	N
13 **Buchanan**	N	N	N
14 **Mack**	N	N	N
15 **Posey**	N	N	N
16 **Rooney**	N	N	N
17 Meek	Y	Y	Y
18 **Ros-Lehtinen**	Y	N	Y
19 Wexler	Y	Y	Y
20 Wasserman Schultz	Y	Y	Y
21 **Diaz-Balart, L.**	Y	N	Y
22 Klein	Y	Y	Y
23 Hastings	Y	Y	Y
24 Kosmas	Y	Y	Y
25 **Diaz-Balart, M.**	Y	N	Y
GEORGIA			
1 **Kingston**	N	N	N
2 Bishop	Y	Y	Y
3 **Westmoreland**	N	N	N
4 Johnson	Y	Y	Y
5 Lewis	Y	Y	Y
6 **Price**	N	N	N
7 **Linder**	N	N	N
8 Marshall	N	Y	Y
9 **Deal**	N	N	N
10 **Broun**	N	N	N
11 **Gingrey**	N	N	N
12 Barrow	Y	Y	Y
13 Scott	Y	Y	Y
HAWAII			
1 Abercrombie	Y	Y	Y
2 Hirono	Y	Y	Y
IDAHO			
1 Minnick	Y	N	Y
2 **Simpson**	Y	N	N
ILLINOIS			
1 Rush	Y	Y	Y
2 Jackson	Y	Y	Y
3 Lipinski	Y	P	Y
4 Gutierrez	Y	Y	Y
5 Vacant[3]			
6 **Roskam**	N	N	N
7 Davis	Y	Y	Y
8 Bean	+	Y	Y
9 Schakowsky	Y	Y	Y
10 **Kirk**	Y	N	N
11 Halvorson	Y	Y	Y
12 Costello	Y	Y	Y
13 **Biggert**	N	N	N
14 Foster	Y	Y	Y
15 **Johnson**	N	N	N

KEY	**Republicans**	Democrats			
Y	Voted for (yea)		X Paired against		C Voted "present" to avoid possible conflict of interest
#	Paired for		– Announced against		
+	Announced for		P Voted "present"		? Did not vote or otherwise make a position known
N	Voted against (nay)				

	50	70	104
16 Manzullo	N	N	N
17 Hare	Y	Y	Y
18 Schock	N	N	N
19 Shimkus	N	N	N
INDIANA			
1 Visclosky	Y	Y	Y
2 Donnelly	Y	Y	Y
3 Souder	N	N	N
4 Buyer	N	N	N
5 Burton	N	N	N
6 Pence	N	N	N
7 Carson	Y	Y	Y
8 Ellsworth	Y	Y	N
9 Hill	Y	Y	N
IOWA			
1 Braley	Y	Y	Y
2 Loebsack	Y	Y	Y
3 Boswell	Y	Y	Y
4 Latham	N	N	N
5 King	N	N	N
KANSAS			
1 Moran	Y	N	N
2 Jenkins	N	N	N
3 Moore	Y	Y	Y
4 Tiahrt	N	N	N
KENTUCKY			
1 Whitfield	N	N	N
2 Guthrie	N	N	N
3 Yarmuth	Y	Y	Y
4 Davis	N	N	N
5 Rogers	N	N	N
6 Chandler	Y	Y	Y
LOUISIANA			
1 Scalise	N	N	N
2 Cao	Y	N	?
3 Melancon	Y	Y	?
4 Fleming	N	N	N
5 Alexander	N	N	N
6 Cassidy	N	N	N
7 Boustany	N	N	N
MAINE			
1 Pingree	Y	Y	Y
2 Michaud	Y	Y	Y
MARYLAND			
1 Kratovil	Y	Y	N
2 Ruppersberger	Y	Y	Y
3 Sarbanes	Y	Y	Y
4 Edwards	Y	Y	Y
5 Hoyer	Y	Y	Y
6 Bartlett	N	N	N
7 Cummings	Y	Y	Y
8 Van Hollen	Y	Y	Y
MASSACHUSETTS			
1 Olver	Y	Y	Y
2 Neal	Y	Y	Y
3 McGovern	Y	Y	Y
4 Frank	Y	Y	Y
5 Tsongas	Y	Y	Y
6 Tierney	Y	Y	Y
7 Markey	Y	Y	Y
8 Capuano	Y	Y	Y
9 Lynch	Y	Y	Y
10 Delahunt	Y	Y	Y
MICHIGAN			
1 Stupak	Y	Y	N
2 Hoekstra	N	N	N
3 Ehlers	Y	N	–
4 Camp	N	N	N
5 Kildee	Y	Y	Y
6 Upton	Y	N	N
7 Schauer	Y	Y	Y
8 Rogers	N	N	N
9 Peters	Y	Y	Y
10 Miller	Y	N	N
11 McCotter	Y	N	N
12 Levin	Y	Y	Y
13 Kilpatrick	Y	Y	Y
14 Conyers	Y	Y	Y
15 Dingell	Y	Y	Y
MINNESOTA			
1 Walz	Y	Y	Y
2 Kline	N	N	N
3 Paulsen	Y	N	N
4 McCollum	Y	Y	Y

	50	70	104
5 Ellison	Y	Y	Y
6 Bachmann	N	N	N
7 Peterson	Y	N	Y
8 Oberstar	Y	Y	Y
MISSISSIPPI			
1 Childers	Y	Y	N
2 Thompson	Y	Y	Y
3 Harper	N	N	N
4 Taylor	Y	N	N
MISSOURI			
1 Clay	Y	Y	Y
2 Akin	N	N	N
3 Carnahan	Y	Y	Y
4 Skelton	Y	Y	Y
5 Cleaver	Y	Y	Y
6 Graves	N	N	N
7 Blunt	N	N	N
8 Emerson	Y	N	N
9 Luetkemeyer	N	N	N
MONTANA			
AL Rehberg	Y	N	N
NEBRASKA			
1 Fortenberry	N	N	N
2 Terry	N	N	N
3 Smith	N	N	N
NEVADA			
1 Berkley	Y	Y	Y
2 Heller	N	N	N
3 Titus	Y	Y	Y
NEW HAMPSHIRE			
1 Shea-Porter	Y	Y	Y
2 Hodes	Y	Y	Y
NEW JERSEY			
1 Andrews	Y	Y	Y
2 LoBiondo	Y	N	N
3 Adler	Y	Y	Y
4 Smith	Y	N	N
5 Garrett	N	N	N
6 Pallone	Y	Y	Y
7 Lance	Y	N	N
8 Pascrell	Y	Y	Y
9 Rothman	Y	Y	Y
10 Payne	Y	Y	Y
11 Frelinghuysen	Y	N	N
12 Holt	Y	Y	Y
13 Sires	Y	Y	Y
NEW MEXICO			
1 Heinrich	Y	Y	Y
2 Teague	Y	Y	N
3 Lujan	Y	Y	Y
NEW YORK			
1 Bishop	Y	Y	Y
2 Israel	Y	Y	Y
3 King	Y	N	N
4 McCarthy	Y	Y	Y
5 Ackerman	Y	Y	Y
6 Meeks	Y	Y	Y
7 Crowley	Y	Y	Y
8 Nadler	Y	Y	Y
9 Weiner	Y	Y	Y
10 Towns	Y	Y	Y
11 Clarke	Y	Y	Y
12 Velázquez	Y	Y	Y
13 McMahon	Y	Y	Y
14 Maloney	Y	Y	Y
15 Rangel	Y	Y	Y
16 Serrano	Y	Y	Y
17 Engel	Y	Y	Y
18 Lowey	Y	Y	Y
19 Hall	Y	Y	Y
20 Vacant [4]			
21 Tonko	Y	Y	Y
22 Hinchey	Y	Y	Y
23 McHugh	Y	Y	Y
24 Arcuri	Y	Y	N
25 Maffei	Y	Y	Y
26 Lee	Y	–	N
27 Higgins	Y	Y	Y
28 Slaughter	Y	Y	Y
29 Massa	Y	Y	N
NORTH CAROLINA			
1 Butterfield	Y	Y	Y
2 Etheridge	Y	Y	Y
3 Jones	N	N	Y
4 Price	Y	Y	Y

	50	70	104
5 Foxx	N	N	N
6 Coble	N	N	N
7 McIntyre	Y	Y	Y
8 Kissell	?	Y	N
9 Myrick	N	N	N
10 McHenry	N	N	N
11 Shuler	Y	N	Y
12 Watt	Y	Y	Y
13 Miller	Y	Y	Y
NORTH DAKOTA			
AL Pomeroy	Y	Y	Y
OHIO			
1 Driehaus	Y	Y	Y
2 Schmidt	N	N	N
3 Turner	Y	N	Y
4 Jordan	N	N	N
5 Latta	N	N	N
6 Wilson	Y	Y	Y
7 Austria	Y	N	N
8 Boehner	N	N	N
9 Kaptur	Y	Y	Y
10 Kucinich	Y	Y	Y
11 Fudge	Y	Y	Y
12 Tiberi	Y	N	N
13 Sutton	Y	Y	Y
14 LaTourette	Y	N	N
15 Kilroy	Y	Y	Y
16 Boccieri	Y	Y	N
17 Ryan	Y	Y	Y
18 Space	Y	Y	Y
OKLAHOMA			
1 Sullivan	N	N	N
2 Boren	Y	Y	N
3 Lucas	N	N	N
4 Cole	N	N	N
5 Fallin	N	N	N
OREGON			
1 Wu	Y	Y	Y
2 Walden	N	N	N
3 Blumenauer	Y	Y	Y
4 DeFazio	Y	N	Y
5 Schrader	Y	Y	Y
PENNSYLVANIA			
1 Brady	Y	Y	Y
2 Fattah	Y	Y	Y
3 Dahlkemper	Y	Y	N
4 Altmire	Y	Y	Y
5 Thompson	Y	N	N
6 Gerlach	Y	N	N
7 Sestak	Y	Y	Y
8 Murphy, P.	Y	Y	Y
9 Shuster	N	N	N
10 Carney	Y	Y	N
11 Kanjorski	Y	Y	Y
12 Murtha	Y	Y	Y
13 Schwartz	Y	Y	Y
14 Doyle	Y	Y	Y
15 Dent	Y	N	N
16 Pitts	N	N	N
17 Holden	Y	N	N
18 Murphy, T.	Y	N	N
19 Platts	Y	N	N
RHODE ISLAND			
1 Kennedy	Y	Y	Y
2 Langevin	Y	Y	Y
SOUTH CAROLINA			
1 Brown	N	N	N
2 Wilson	N	N	N
3 Barrett	N	N	N
4 Inglis	N	N	N
5 Spratt	Y	Y	Y
6 Clyburn	Y	?	Y
SOUTH DAKOTA			
AL Herseth Sandlin	Y	Y	Y
TENNESSEE			
1 Roe	N	N	N
2 Duncan	N	N	N
3 Wamp	–	N	N
4 Davis	Y	Y	N
5 Cooper	Y	Y	Y
6 Gordon	Y	Y	N
7 Blackburn	N	N	N
8 Tanner	Y	Y	Y
9 Cohen	Y	Y	Y

	50	70	104
TEXAS			
1 Gohmert	N	N	N
2 Poe	?	N	N
3 Johnson, S.	N	N	N
4 Hall	N	N	N
5 Hensarling	N	N	N
6 Barton	N	N	N
7 Culberson	N	N	N
8 Brady	N	N	N
9 Green, A.	Y	Y	Y
10 McCaul	N	N	N
11 Conaway	N	N	N
12 Granger	N	N	N
13 Thornberry	N	N	N
14 Paul	N	N	N
15 Hinojosa	Y	Y	Y
16 Reyes	Y	Y	Y
17 Edwards	Y	Y	Y
18 Jackson Lee	Y	Y	Y
19 Neugebauer	N	N	N
20 Gonzalez	Y	Y	Y
21 Smith	N	N	N
22 Olson	N	N	N
23 Rodriguez	Y	Y	Y
24 Marchant	N	N	N
25 Doggett	Y	Y	Y
26 Burgess	N	N	N
27 Ortiz	Y	Y	Y
28 Cuellar	Y	Y	Y
29 Green, G.	Y	Y	Y
30 Johnson, E.	Y	Y	Y
31 Carter	N	N	N
32 Sessions	N	N	N
UTAH			
1 Bishop	N	N	N
2 Matheson	Y	Y	N
3 Chaffetz	N	N	N
VERMONT			
AL Welch	Y	Y	Y
VIRGINIA			
1 Wittman	N	N	N
2 Nye	Y	Y	Y
3 Scott	Y	Y	Y
4 Forbes	N	N	N
5 Perriello	Y	Y	?
6 Goodlatte	N	N	N
7 Cantor	N	N	N
8 Moran	Y	Y	Y
9 Boucher	Y	Y	Y
10 Wolf	Y	N	N
11 Connolly	Y	Y	Y
WASHINGTON			
1 Inslee	Y	Y	Y
2 Larsen	Y	Y	Y
3 Baird	Y	Y	Y
4 Hastings	N	N	N
5 McMorris Rodgers	N	N	N
6 Dicks	Y	Y	Y
7 McDermott	Y	Y	Y
8 Reichert	Y	N	N
9 Smith	Y	Y	Y
WEST VIRGINIA			
1 Mollohan	Y	Y	Y
2 Capito	Y	N	N
3 Rahall	Y	Y	Y
WISCONSIN			
1 Ryan	N	N	N
2 Baldwin	Y	Y	Y
3 Kind	Y	Y	N
4 Moore	Y	Y	Y
5 Sensenbrenner	N	N	N
6 Petri	Y	N	N
7 Obey	Y	Y	Y
8 Kagen	Y	Y	Y
WYOMING			
AL Lummis	N	N	N
DELEGATES			
Faleomavaega (A.S.)			
Norton (D.C.)			
Bordallo (Guam)			
Sablan (N. Marianas) [5]			
Pierluisi (P.R.)			
Christensen (V.I.)			

IN THE HOUSE | By Vote Number

335. HR 1256. **Tobacco Regulation/Motion to Concur.** Waxman, D-Calif., motion to concur in the Senate amendment to the bill that allows the Food and Drug Administration (FDA) to regulate the manufacture, sale and promotion of tobacco products. It would require new, larger labels warning consumers of the health risks associated with tobacco products and clarify that the FDA does not endorse the safety of such products. It would establish standards for tobacco products marketed as lower in health risks. The FDA could regulate the amount of nicotine but not ban any class of tobacco products or eliminate nicotine levels completely. The bill would restrict the additives that can be included in cigarettes and ban flavors except for menthol. It would require tobacco manufacturers and importers to pay quarterly user fees to help cover the cost of the regulation. Motion agreed to (thus clearing the bill for the president), 307-97: R 70-90; D 237-7. A "yea" was a vote in support of the president's position. June 12, 2009. *(Story, p. C-4)*

352. HR 2847. **Fiscal 2010 Commerce-Justice-Science Appropriations/Rule.** Adoption of the rule (H Res 552) that would provide for further House floor consideration of the bill that would appropriate $64.4 billion in fiscal 2010 for the departments of Commerce and Justice and other federal agencies, including NASA and the National Science Foundation. Adopted 221-201: R 0-174; D 221-27. June 17, 2009. *(Story, p. C-5)*

477. HR 2454. **Greenhouse Gas Emissions/Passage.** Passage of the bill that would create a cap-and-trade system to limit greenhouse gas emissions and set new requirements for electric utilities. Emission allowances would permit buyers to emit a certain amount of greenhouse gases. Most of the allowances initially would be provided free of charge. By 2030, most would be auctioned to polluters. The bill would set emissions limits at 17 percent below current levels in 2020, expanding to 83 percent in 2050. It would require utilities to produce 15 percent of the nation's electricity from renewable sources by 2020. It would establish programs to assist energy consumers with higher utility bills resulting from the new system. Passed 219-212: R 8-168; D 211-44. A "yea" was a vote in support of the president's position. June 26, 2009. *(Story, p. C-5)*

680. HR 2749. **Food Safety Overhaul/Passage.** Passage of the bill that would revise food safety laws, including establishing a risk-based inspection schedule for food facilities and imposing criminal and civil penalties for violations. The bill would require facilities that serve U.S. customers to register with the Food and Drug Administration (FDA) and pay a registration fee. Farms, grocery stores and restaurants would be exempt. Frequency of inspections would range from every six months to every five years, depending on the level of risk at the facility. The bill would also authorize the FDA to impose mandatory food quarantines and require facilities to implement written food safety plans. Passed 283-142: R 54-122; D 229-20. A "yea" was a vote in support of the president's position. July 30, 2009. *(Story, p. C-6)*

[1] The Speaker votes only at her discretion.

[2] Rep. Ellen O. Tauscher, D-Calif., resigned June 26, 2009, to become an undersecretary of State. The last vote for which she was eligible was vote 477.

[3] Rep. Judy Chu, D-Calif., was sworn in July 16, 2009, to fill the seat vacated by fellow Democrat Hilda L. Solis, who resigned Feb. 24, 2009, to become secretary of Labor. The first vote for which Chu was eligible was vote 549; the last vote for which Solis was eligible was vote 79.

[4] Rep. Mike Quigley, D-Ill., was sworn in April 21, 2009, to fill the seat vacated by fellow Democrat Rahm Emanuel, who resigned Jan. 2, 2009, to become President Obama's chief of staff. The first vote for which Quigley was eligible was vote 194; Emanuel was not eligible for any votes in 2009.

[5] Rep. Scott Murphy, D-N.Y., was sworn in April 29, 2009, to fill the seat vacated by fellow Democrat Kirsten Gillibrand, who resigned Jan. 26, 2009, to become a senator. The first vote for which Murphy was eligible was vote 221; the last vote for which Gillibrand was eligible was vote 29.

	335	352	477	680
ALABAMA				
1 Bonner	N	N	N	N
2 Bright	N	N	N	N
3 Rogers	Y	N	N	N
4 Aderholt	N	N	N	N
5 Griffith	Y	Y	N	N
6 Bachus	Y	N	N	N
7 Davis	Y	?	N	Y
ALASKA				
AL Young	Y	N	N	N
ARIZONA				
1 Kirkpatrick	N	Y	N	Y
2 Franks	N	N	N	N
3 Shadegg	N	N	N	N
4 Pastor	Y	Y	Y	Y
5 Mitchell	Y	N	N	Y
6 Flake	N	N	?	N
7 Grijalva	Y	Y	Y	Y
8 Giffords	Y	Y	Y	Y
ARKANSAS				
1 Berry	Y	Y	N	Y
2 Snyder	Y	Y	Y	Y
3 Boozman	N	N	N	N
4 Ross	Y	Y	N	Y
CALIFORNIA				
1 Thompson	Y	N	Y	Y
2 Herger	N	N	N	N
3 Lungren	Y	N	N	N
4 McClintock	N	N	N	N
5 Matsui	Y	Y	Y	Y
6 Woolsey	Y	N	Y	N
7 Miller, George	Y	N	Y	Y
8 Pelosi[1]	Y		Y	
9 Lee	Y	Y	Y	Y
10 Tauscher[2]	Y	Y	Y	
11 McNerney	Y	Y	Y	Y
12 Speier	Y	N	Y	Y
13 Stark	Y	Y	N	Y
14 Eshoo	?	N	Y	Y
15 Honda	Y	N	Y	Y
16 Lofgren	Y	Y	Y	Y
17 Farr	Y	N	Y	Y
18 Cardoza	Y	Y	Y	Y
19 Radanovich	N	N	N	N
20 Costa	Y	Y	N	Y
21 Nunes	?	N	N	N
22 McCarthy	N	N	N	N
23 Capps	Y	N	Y	Y
24 Gallegly	?	N	N	N
25 McKeon	Y	N	N	N
26 Dreier	N	N	N	N
27 Sherman	Y	Y	Y	Y
28 Berman	Y	Y	Y	Y
29 Schiff	Y	Y	Y	Y
30 Waxman	Y	Y	Y	Y
31 Becerra	Y	Y	Y	Y
32 Chu[3]				Y
33 Watson	Y	Y	Y	Y
34 Roybal-Allard	Y	Y	Y	Y
35 Waters	Y	N	Y	Y
36 Harman	Y	?	Y	Y
37 Richardson	Y	Y	Y	Y
38 Napolitano	Y	Y	Y	Y
39 Sánchez, Linda	Y	Y	Y	Y
40 Royce	N	N	N	N
41 Lewis	N	N	N	N
42 Miller, Gary	?	N	N	N
43 Baca	?	Y	Y	Y
44 Calvert	N	N	N	N
45 Bono Mack	Y	N	Y	N
46 Rohrabacher	N	N	N	N
47 Sanchez, Loretta	?	Y	Y	?
48 Campbell	N	N	N	N
49 Issa	N	N	N	N
50 Bilbray	Y	N	N	N
51 Filner	Y	Y	Y	Y
52 Hunter	N	N	N	N
53 Davis	Y	Y	Y	Y

	335	352	477	680
COLORADO				
1 DeGette	Y	Y	Y	Y
2 Polis	Y	Y	Y	Y
3 Salazar	Y	Y	N	?
4 Markey	Y	Y	N	Y
5 Lamborn	N	N	N	N
6 Coffman	N	N	N	N
7 Perlmutter	Y	Y	Y	Y
CONNECTICUT				
1 Larson	Y	+	Y	Y
2 Courtney	Y	Y	Y	Y
3 DeLauro	Y	Y	Y	Y
4 Himes	Y	Y	Y	Y
5 Murphy	Y	Y	Y	Y
DELAWARE				
AL Castle	Y	N	Y	Y
FLORIDA				
1 Miller	N	N	N	N
2 Boyd	Y	Y	Y	Y
3 Brown	?	Y	Y	Y
4 Crenshaw	Y	N	N	N
5 Brown-Waite	Y	N	N	Y
6 Stearns	Y	N	N	N
7 Mica	N	N	N	N
8 Grayson	Y	Y	Y	+
9 Bilirakis	Y	N	N	Y
10 Young	Y	?	N	Y
11 Castor	Y	Y	Y	Y
12 Putnam	Y	N	N	Y
13 Buchanan	?	N	N	Y
14 Mack	N	N	N	N
15 Posey	N	N	N	N
16 Rooney	Y	N	Y	N
17 Meek	Y	N	Y	Y
18 Ros-Lehtinen	Y	N	Y	Y
19 Wexler	Y	Y	Y	Y
20 Wasserman Schultz	Y	Y	Y	Y
21 Diaz-Balart, L.	N	N	N	Y
22 Klein	Y	N	Y	Y
23 Hastings	Y	Y	?	Y
24 Kosmas	Y	N	Y	Y
25 Diaz-Balart, M.	N	N	N	Y
GEORGIA				
1 Kingston	N	N	N	N
2 Bishop	Y	Y	Y	Y
3 Westmoreland	N	N	N	N
4 Johnson	Y	Y	Y	Y
5 Lewis	?	?	Y	Y
6 Price	N	N	N	N
7 Linder	N	N	N	?
8 Marshall	Y	N	N	Y
9 Deal	?	N	N	Y
10 Broun	N	N	N	N
11 Gingrey	?	N	Y	N
12 Barrow	Y	N	N	Y
13 Scott	Y	Y	Y	Y
HAWAII				
1 Abercrombie	Y	Y	Y	Y
2 Hirono	Y	Y	Y	Y
IDAHO				
1 Minnick	Y	N	N	N
2 Simpson	Y	N	N	N
ILLINOIS				
1 Rush	Y	Y	Y	Y
2 Jackson	Y	Y	Y	Y
3 Lipinski	Y	Y	Y	Y
4 Gutierrez	Y	Y	Y	Y
5 Quigley[4]	Y	Y	Y	Y
6 Roskam	Y	N	N	Y
7 Davis	Y	Y	Y	Y
8 Bean	Y	Y	Y	Y
9 Schakowsky	Y	Y	Y	Y
10 Kirk	Y	N	Y	Y
11 Halvorson	Y	Y	Y	Y
12 Costello	Y	Y	N	Y
13 Biggert	Y	N	N	Y
14 Foster	Y	Y	N	Y
15 Johnson	Y	N	N	N

KEY Republicans Democrats

Y Voted for (yea)	X Paired against
# Paired for	- Announced against
+ Announced for	P Voted "present"
N Voted against (nay)	C Voted "present" to avoid possible conflict of interest
	? Did not vote or otherwise make a position known

	335	352	477	680
16 Manzullo	Y	N	N	N
17 Hare	Y	Y	Y	Y
18 Schock	Y	N	N	N
19 Shimkus	Y	N	N	Y
INDIANA				
1 Visclosky	Y	Y	N	Y
2 Donnelly	Y	N	N	Y
3 Souder	N	N	N	N
4 Buyer	N	N	N	Y
5 Burton	Y	N	N	N
6 Pence	N	N	N	N
7 Carson	Y	Y	Y	Y
8 Ellsworth	Y	Y	N	Y
9 Hill	Y	N	Y	Y
IOWA				
1 Braley	Y	Y	Y	Y
2 Loebsack	Y	Y	Y	Y
3 Boswell	Y	Y	Y	Y
4 Latham	N	N	N	N
5 King	N	N	N	N
KANSAS				
1 Moran	N	N	N	N
2 Jenkins	N	N	N	N
3 Moore	Y	Y	Y	Y
4 Tiahrt	N	N	N	N
KENTUCKY				
1 Whitfield	N	N	N	Y
2 Guthrie	N	N	N	Y
3 Yarmuth	Y	Y	Y	Y
4 Davis	N	N	N	N
5 Rogers	N	N	N	Y
6 Chandler	Y	Y	Y	Y
LOUISIANA				
1 Scalise	N	N	N	Y
2 Cao	Y	N	N	Y
3 Melancon	Y	Y	Y	Y
4 Fleming	Y	N	N	N
5 Alexander	N	?	N	N
6 Cassidy	Y	N	N	Y
7 Boustany	N	N	N	N
MAINE				
1 Pingree	Y	Y	Y	N
2 Michaud	Y	Y	Y	Y
MARYLAND				
1 Kratovil	Y	N	Y	N
2 Ruppersberger	?	Y	Y	Y
3 Sarbanes	Y	Y	Y	Y
4 Edwards	Y	Y	Y	Y
5 Hoyer	Y	Y	Y	Y
6 Bartlett	Y	N	N	N
7 Cummings	Y	Y	Y	Y
8 Van Hollen	Y	Y	Y	Y
MASSACHUSETTS				
1 Olver	Y	Y	Y	Y
2 Neal	Y	Y	Y	Y
3 McGovern	Y	Y	Y	Y
4 Frank	Y	Y	Y	Y
5 Tsongas	Y	Y	Y	Y
6 Tierney	Y	Y	Y	Y
7 Markey	Y	Y	Y	Y
8 Capuano	Y	Y	Y	Y
9 Lynch	Y	Y	Y	Y
10 Delahunt	Y	Y	Y	Y
MICHIGAN				
1 Stupak	Y	Y	Y	Y
2 Hoekstra	N	N	N	N
3 Ehlers	?	N	N	Y
4 Camp	Y	N	N	Y
5 Kildee	Y	Y	Y	Y
6 Upton	Y	N	N	Y
7 Schauer	Y	Y	Y	Y
8 Rogers	?	N	N	Y
9 Peters	Y	Y	Y	Y
10 Miller	Y	N	N	Y
11 McCotter	N	N	N	Y
12 Levin	Y	Y	Y	Y
13 Kilpatrick	Y	Y	Y	Y
14 Conyers	Y	Y	Y	Y
15 Dingell	Y	Y	Y	Y
MINNESOTA				
1 Walz	Y	Y	Y	Y
2 Kline	?	N	N	Y
3 Paulsen	Y	N	N	Y
4 McCollum	Y	Y	Y	Y

	335	352	477	680
5 Ellison	Y	Y	Y	Y
6 Bachmann	N	?	N	Y
7 Peterson	Y	?	N	Y
8 Oberstar	Y	Y	Y	Y
MISSISSIPPI				
1 Childers	?	Y	N	N
2 Thompson	Y	Y	Y	Y
3 Harper	Y	N	N	N
4 Taylor	Y	Y	N	Y
MISSOURI				
1 Clay	Y	Y	Y	Y
2 Akin	N	N	N	–
3 Carnahan	Y	Y	Y	Y
4 Skelton	Y	Y	Y	Y
5 Cleaver	Y	Y	Y	Y
6 Graves	N	N	N	N
7 Blunt	?	N	N	N
8 Emerson	Y	N	N	N
9 Luetkemeyer	–	N	N	N
MONTANA				
AL Rehberg	Y	N	N	N
NEBRASKA				
1 Fortenberry	Y	N	N	Y
2 Terry	Y	N	N	Y
3 Smith	N	N	N	N
NEVADA				
1 Berkley	Y	Y	Y	Y
2 Heller	N	N	N	N
3 Titus	Y	Y	Y	Y
NEW HAMPSHIRE				
1 Shea-Porter	Y	Y	Y	Y
2 Hodes	Y	Y	Y	Y
NEW JERSEY				
1 Andrews	Y	Y	Y	Y
2 LoBiondo	Y	N	Y	Y
3 Adler	+	?	Y	+
4 Smith	Y	N	Y	Y
5 Garrett	N	N	N	N
6 Pallone	Y	Y	Y	Y
7 Lance	Y	N	Y	Y
8 Pascrell	Y	Y	Y	Y
9 Rothman	Y	Y	Y	Y
10 Payne	Y	Y	Y	Y
11 Frelinghuysen	Y	N	N	Y
12 Holt	+	Y	Y	Y
13 Sires	Y	Y	Y	Y
NEW MEXICO				
1 Heinrich	Y	Y	Y	N
2 Teague	Y	Y	Y	N
3 Lujan	Y	Y	Y	N
NEW YORK				
1 Bishop	Y	Y	Y	Y
2 Israel	Y	Y	Y	Y
3 King	Y	N	N	Y
4 McCarthy	Y	Y	Y	?
5 Ackerman	?	Y	Y	Y
6 Meeks	Y	Y	Y	Y
7 Crowley	Y	Y	Y	Y
8 Nadler	Y	Y	Y	Y
9 Weiner	Y	Y	Y	Y
10 Towns	Y	Y	Y	Y
11 Clarke	Y	Y	Y	Y
12 Velázquez	Y	Y	Y	Y
13 McMahon	Y	Y	Y	Y
14 Maloney	Y	Y	Y	Y
15 Rangel	Y	Y	Y	Y
16 Serrano	Y	Y	Y	Y
17 Engel	Y	Y	Y	Y
18 Lowey	Y	Y	Y	Y
19 Hall	Y	Y	Y	Y
20 Murphy[5]	Y	N	Y	Y
21 Tonko	Y	Y	Y	Y
22 Hinchey	Y	Y	Y	Y
23 McHugh	N	N	Y	Y
24 Arcuri	Y	N	Y	Y
25 Maffei	Y	Y	Y	Y
26 Lee	Y	N	N	Y
27 Higgins	Y	Y	Y	Y
28 Slaughter	Y	Y	Y	Y
29 Massa	Y	Y	N	Y
NORTH CAROLINA				
1 Butterfield	Y	Y	Y	Y
2 Etheridge	Y	Y	Y	Y
3 Jones	?	N	N	N
4 Price	Y	Y	Y	Y

	335	352	477	680
5 Foxx	N	N	N	N
6 Coble	N	N	N	N
7 McIntyre	N	Y	N	Y
8 Kissell	N	Y	N	Y
9 Myrick	N	N	N	N
10 McHenry	N	N	N	N
11 Shuler	N	N	Y	N
12 Watt	Y	Y	Y	Y
13 Miller	Y	Y	Y	Y
NORTH DAKOTA				
AL Pomeroy	Y	Y	N	Y
OHIO				
1 Driehaus	Y	Y	Y	Y
2 Schmidt	N	N	N	N
3 Turner	Y	N	N	Y
4 Jordan	N	N	N	N
5 Latta	N	N	N	N
6 Wilson	?	Y	N	Y
7 Austria	Y	N	N	N
8 Boehner	N	N	N	N
9 Kaptur	Y	Y	Y	Y
10 Kucinich	Y	Y	N	Y
11 Fudge	Y	Y	Y	Y
12 Tiberi	Y	N	N	Y
13 Sutton	Y	Y	Y	Y
14 LaTourette	Y	N	N	Y
15 Kilroy	Y	Y	Y	Y
16 Boccieri	Y	Y	Y	Y
17 Ryan	Y	Y	Y	Y
18 Space	Y	Y	Y	Y
OKLAHOMA				
1 Sullivan	?	?	–	N
2 Boren	Y	Y	N	Y
3 Lucas	N	N	N	N
4 Cole	N	N	N	N
5 Fallin	Y	N	N	N
OREGON				
1 Wu	Y	N	Y	Y
2 Walden	Y	N	Y	N
3 Blumenauer	Y	N	Y	Y
4 DeFazio	Y	N	N	Y
5 Schrader	Y	Y	Y	Y
PENNSYLVANIA				
1 Brady	Y	Y	Y	Y
2 Fattah	Y	Y	Y	Y
3 Dahlkemper	Y	Y	N	Y
4 Altmire	Y	Y	N	Y
5 Thompson	N	N	N	N
6 Gerlach	Y	N	N	Y
7 Sestak	Y	Y	Y	Y
8 Murphy, P.	Y	Y	Y	Y
9 Shuster	N	N	N	N
10 Carney	Y	N	N	Y
11 Kanjorski	Y	Y	Y	Y
12 Murtha	Y	Y	Y	?
13 Schwartz	Y	Y	Y	Y
14 Doyle	Y	Y	Y	Y
15 Dent	Y	N	N	Y
16 Pitts	N	N	N	N
17 Holden	Y	Y	N	Y
18 Murphy, T.	Y	N	N	Y
19 Platts	Y	N	N	Y
RHODE ISLAND				
1 Kennedy	?	?	Y	Y
2 Langevin	Y	Y	Y	Y
SOUTH CAROLINA				
1 Brown	Y	N	N	N
2 Wilson	N	N	N	N
3 Barrett	–	N	N	N
4 Inglis	N	N	N	N
5 Spratt	Y	Y	Y	Y
6 Clyburn	Y	Y	Y	Y
SOUTH DAKOTA				
AL Herseth Sandlin	Y	Y	N	Y
TENNESSEE				
1 Roe	N	N	N	N
2 Duncan	Y	N	N	N
3 Wamp	Y	N	N	N
4 Davis	N	Y	N	N
5 Cooper	Y	Y	Y	Y
6 Gordon	Y	Y	Y	Y
7 Blackburn	?	N	N	N
8 Tanner	Y	N	N	Y
9 Cohen	Y	Y	Y	Y

	335	352	477	680
TEXAS				
1 Gohmert	?	N	N	N
2 Poe	Y	N	N	N
3 Johnson, S.	N	N	N	N
4 Hall	Y	N	N	N
5 Hensarling	N	N	N	N
6 Barton	N	N	N	Y
7 Culberson	N	N	N	N
8 Brady	Y	N	N	N
9 Green, A.	Y	Y	Y	Y
10 McCaul	Y	N	N	N
11 Conaway	N	N	N	N
12 Granger	Y	N	N	N
13 Thornberry	N	N	N	N
14 Paul	N	N	N	N
15 Hinojosa	Y	Y	Y	Y
16 Reyes	Y	Y	Y	Y
17 Edwards	Y	Y	N	Y
18 Jackson Lee	Y	Y	Y	Y
19 Neugebauer	N	N	N	N
20 Gonzalez	Y	Y	Y	Y
21 Smith	Y	N	N	N
22 Olson	N	N	N	N
23 Rodriguez	Y	Y	N	Y
24 Marchant	?	N	N	N
25 Doggett	Y	Y	Y	Y
26 Burgess	N	N	N	N
27 Ortiz	Y	Y	Y	Y
28 Cuellar	Y	Y	Y	Y
29 Green, G.	Y	Y	Y	Y
30 Johnson, E.	Y	Y	Y	Y
31 Carter	N	N	N	N
32 Sessions	N	N	N	N
UTAH				
1 Bishop	N	N	N	N
2 Matheson	Y	Y	N	Y
3 Chaffetz	N	N	N	N
VERMONT				
AL Welch	Y	Y	Y	N
VIRGINIA				
1 Wittman	Y	N	N	N
2 Nye	Y	Y	N	Y
3 Scott	Y	Y	Y	Y
4 Forbes	N	N	N	N
5 Perriello	N	N	Y	N
6 Goodlatte	N	N	N	N
7 Cantor	Y	N	N	N
8 Moran	Y	Y	Y	Y
9 Boucher	Y	Y	Y	Y
10 Wolf	Y	N	N	Y
11 Connolly	Y	Y	Y	Y
WASHINGTON				
1 Inslee	Y	Y	Y	Y
2 Larsen	Y	Y	Y	Y
3 Baird	Y	Y	Y	Y
4 Hastings	?	N	N	N
5 McMorris Rodgers	Y	N	N	N
6 Dicks	Y	Y	Y	Y
7 McDermott	Y	Y	Y	Y
8 Reichert	Y	N	Y	Y
9 Smith	Y	Y	Y	Y
WEST VIRGINIA				
1 Mollohan	Y	Y	N	Y
2 Capito	Y	N	N	Y
3 Rahall	Y	N	N	Y
WISCONSIN				
1 Ryan	N	N	N	N
2 Baldwin	Y	Y	Y	Y
3 Kind	Y	Y	Y	N
4 Moore	Y	Y	Y	Y
5 Sensenbrenner	N	N	N	N
6 Petri	N	N	N	N
7 Obey	Y	Y	Y	Y
8 Kagen	Y	Y	Y	Y
WYOMING				
AL Lummis	N	N	N	N
DELEGATES				
Faleomavaega (A.S.)				
Norton (D.C.)				
Bordallo (Guam)				
Sablan (N. Marianas)				
Pierluisi (P.R.)				
Christensen (V.I.)				

IN THE HOUSE | By Vote Number

682. **HR 3435. Car Voucher Program Funding/Passage.** Obey, D-Wis., motion to suspend the rules and pass the bill that would provide $2 billion for the "cash for clunkers" vehicle trade-in program, which offers vouchers worth up to $4,500 toward the purchase of new vehicles to consumers who trade in their older, less efficient models. The funds would be transferred from the Energy Department's innovative technologies loan-guarantee program. Motion agreed to 316-109: R 77-95; D 239-14. A two-thirds majority of those present and voting (284 in this case) is required for passage under suspension of the rules. A "yea" was a vote in support of the president's position. July 31, 2009. *(Story, p. C-6)*

719. **HR 3221. Student Loan Overhaul/Passage.** Passage of the bill that would terminate the authority of the Federal Family Education Loan program to make or insure new loans after June 30, 2010, and direct the federal government to originate student loans. The legislation would provide for a competitive bidding process for entities to service the loans. The bill would make several modifications to education programs, including increasing funding for Pell grants, early-childhood education and community colleges. As amended, it would bar federal agreements from being entered into with certain organizations, including the Association of Community Organizations for Reform Now (ACORN). Passed 253-171: R 6-167; D 247-4. A "yea" was a vote in support of the president's position. Sept. 17, 2009. *(Story, p. C-6)*

884. **HR 3962. Health Care Overhaul/Abortion Funding Ban.** Stupak, D-Mich., amendment that would bar the use of federal funds authorized in the bill to pay for abortion or to cover any part of the costs of any health plan that includes abortion coverage, unless the pregnancy is the result of rape or incest or would endanger the woman's life. Individuals with subsidized policies who also want abortion coverage would have to purchase it separately, using their own money. The amendment would prohibit individuals from using affordability credits to purchase a plan that provides for elective abortions. Adopted 240-194: D 64-194; R 176-0. Nov. 7, 2009. *(Story, p. C-7)*

887. **HR 3962. Health Care Overhaul/Passage.** Passage of the bill that would overhaul the nation's health insurance system and require most individuals to buy health insurance by 2013. It would create an agency tasked with establishing a federal health insurance exchange, including a government-run "public option," to allow individuals without coverage to purchase insurance. Those who do not obtain coverage would be subject to an excise tax, with hardship waivers. Employers would be required to offer health insurance or contribute to a fund for coverage; non-compliance could bring penalties of up to 8 percent of their payrolls. It would provide tax credits to certain small businesses for providing coverage and provide subsidies to individuals making up to four times the federal poverty level, excluding illegal immigrants. The bill would bar the use of federal funds to provide abortions, except in cases of rape or incest or if the woman's life is in danger. Insurance companies could not deny or reduce coverage based on pre-existing medical conditions. Passed 220-215: D 219-39; R 1-176. A "yea" was a vote in support of the president's position. Nov. 7, 2009. *(Story, p. C-7)*

[1] The Speaker votes only at her discretion.

[2] Rep. John Garamendi, D-Calif., was sworn in Nov. 5, 2009, to fill the seat vacated by fellow Democrat Ellen O. Tauscher, who resigned June 26, 2009, to become an undersecretary of State. The first vote for which Garamendi was eligible was vote 858; the last vote for which Tauscher was eligible was vote 477.

[3] Rep. Bill Owens, D-N.Y., was sworn in Nov. 6, 2009, to fill the seat vacated by Republican John M. McHugh, who resigned Sept. 21, 2009, to become secretary of the Army. The first vote for which Owens was eligible was vote 867; the last vote for which McHugh was eligible was vote 719.

		682	719	884	887
ALABAMA					
1	**Bonner**	N	N	Y	N
2	Bright	Y	Y	Y	N
3	**Rogers**	Y	N	Y	N
4	**Aderholt**	Y	N	Y	N
5	Griffith	Y	Y	Y	N
6	**Bachus**	Y	N	Y	N
7	Davis	Y	Y	Y	N
ALASKA					
AL	**Young**	N	N	Y	N
ARIZONA					
1	Kirkpatrick	N	Y	N	Y
2	**Franks**	N	N	Y	N
3	**Shadegg**	N	N	P	N
4	Pastor	Y	Y	N	Y
5	Mitchell	N	Y	N	Y
6	**Flake**	N	N	Y	N
7	Grijalva	Y	Y	N	Y
8	Giffords	N	Y	N	Y
ARKANSAS					
1	Berry	Y	Y	Y	Y
2	Snyder	Y	Y	Y	Y
3	**Boozman**	N	N	Y	N
4	Ross	Y	Y	Y	Y
CALIFORNIA					
1	Thompson	Y	Y	N	Y
2	**Herger**	N	N	Y	N
3	**Lungren**	N	N	Y	N
4	**McClintock**	N	N	Y	N
5	Matsui	Y	Y	N	Y
6	Woolsey	Y	Y	N	Y
7	Miller, George	Y	Y	N	Y
8	Pelosi [1]		Y	N	Y
9	Lee		Y	N	Y
10	Garamendi [2]			N	Y
11	McNerney	Y	Y	N	Y
12	Speier	Y	Y	N	Y
13	Stark	Y	Y	N	Y
14	Eshoo	Y	Y	N	Y
15	Honda	Y	Y	N	Y
16	Lofgren	Y	Y	N	Y
17	Farr	Y	Y	N	Y
18	Cardoza	Y	Y	Y	Y
19	**Radanovich**	N	?	Y	N
20	Costa	Y	?	Y	N
21	**Nunes**	N	–	Y	N
22	**McCarthy**	N	N	Y	N
23	Capps	Y	Y	N	Y
24	**Gallegly**	N	N	Y	N
25	**McKeon**	Y	N	Y	N
26	**Dreier**	Y	N	Y	N
27	Sherman	Y	Y	N	Y
28	Berman	Y	Y	N	Y
29	Schiff	Y	Y	N	Y
30	Waxman	Y	Y	N	Y
31	Becerra	Y	Y	N	Y
32	Chu	Y	Y	N	Y
33	Watson	Y	Y	N	Y
34	Roybal-Allard	Y	Y	N	Y
35	Waters	Y	Y	N	Y
36	Harman	Y	Y	N	Y
37	Richardson	Y	Y	N	Y
38	Napolitano	Y	Y	N	Y
39	Sánchez, Linda	Y	Y	N	Y
40	**Royce**	N	N	Y	N
41	**Lewis**	N	N	Y	N
42	**Miller, Gary**	Y	N	Y	N
43	Baca	Y	Y	Y	Y
44	**Calvert**	Y	N	Y	N
45	**Bono Mack**	Y	N	Y	N
46	**Rohrabacher**	N	N	Y	N
47	Sanchez, Loretta	Y	Y	N	Y
48	**Campbell**	Y	N	Y	N
49	**Issa**	Y	N	Y	N
50	**Bilbray**	Y	N	Y	N
51	Filner	Y	Y	N	Y
52	**Hunter**	N	N	Y	N
53	Davis	Y	Y	N	Y
COLORADO					
1	DeGette	Y	Y	N	Y
2	Polis	N	Y	N	Y
3	Salazar	?	Y	N	Y
4	Markey	Y	Y	N	Y
5	**Lamborn**	N	N	Y	N
6	**Coffman**	N	N	Y	N
7	Perlmutter	Y	Y	N	Y
CONNECTICUT					
1	Larson	Y	Y	N	Y
2	Courtney	Y	Y	N	Y
3	DeLauro	Y	Y	N	Y
4	Himes	Y	Y	N	Y
5	Murphy	Y	Y	N	Y
DELAWARE					
AL	**Castle**	Y	N	Y	N
FLORIDA					
1	**Miller**	N	N	Y	N
2	Boyd	N	N	N	N
3	Brown	Y	Y	N	Y
4	**Crenshaw**	N	N	Y	N
5	**Brown-Waite**	N	N	Y	N
6	**Stearns**	N	N	Y	N
7	**Mica**	N	N	Y	N
8	Grayson	Y	Y	N	Y
9	**Bilirakis**	N	N	Y	N
10	**Young**	N	N	Y	N
11	Castor	Y	Y	N	Y
12	**Putnam**	N	N	Y	N
13	**Buchanan**	P	N	Y	N
14	**Mack**	N	N	Y	N
15	**Posey**	N	N	Y	N
16	**Rooney**	N	N	Y	N
17	Meek	Y	Y	N	Y
18	**Ros-Lehtinen**	Y	Y	N	Y
19	Wexler	Y	Y	N	Y
20	Wasserman Schultz	Y	Y	N	Y
21	**Diaz-Balart, L.**	Y	N	Y	N
22	Klein	Y	Y	N	Y
23	Hastings	Y	Y	N	Y
24	Kosmas	Y	Y	N	N
25	**Diaz-Balart, M.**	Y	N	Y	N
GEORGIA					
1	**Kingston**	Y	N	Y	N
2	Bishop	Y	Y	Y	Y
3	**Westmoreland**	N	N	Y	N
4	Johnson	Y	Y	N	Y
5	Lewis	Y	Y	N	Y
6	**Price**	N	N	Y	N
7	**Linder**	?	N	Y	N
8	Marshall	N	Y	N	Y
9	**Deal**	P	N	Y	N
10	**Broun**	N	N	Y	N
11	**Gingrey**	Y	N	Y	N
12	Barrow	Y	Y	Y	Y
13	Scott	Y	Y	N	Y
HAWAII					
1	Abercrombie	Y	+	N	Y
2	Hirono	Y	Y	N	Y
IDAHO					
1	Minnick	Y	Y	N	N
2	**Simpson**	Y	N	Y	N
ILLINOIS					
1	Rush	Y	Y	N	Y
2	Jackson	Y	Y	N	Y
3	Lipinski	Y	Y	Y	Y
4	Gutierrez	Y	Y	N	Y
5	Quigley	Y	Y	N	Y
6	**Roskam**	N	N	Y	N
7	Davis	Y	Y	N	Y
8	Bean	Y	Y	N	Y
9	Schakowsky	Y	Y	N	Y
10	**Kirk**	Y	N	Y	N
11	Halvorson	Y	Y	N	Y
12	Costello	Y	Y	Y	Y
13	**Biggert**	Y	N	Y	N
14	Foster	Y	Y	N	Y
15	**Johnson**	N	Y	N	Y

	682	719	884	887
16 Manzullo	Y	N	Y	N
17 Hare	Y	Y	N	Y
18 Schock	N	N	Y	N
19 Shimkus	Y	N	Y	N
INDIANA				
1 Visclosky	Y	Y	N	Y
2 Donnelly	Y	Y	Y	Y
3 Souder	Y	N	Y	N
4 Buyer	Y	N	Y	N
5 Burton	Y	N	Y	N
6 Pence	N	N	Y	N
7 Carson	Y	Y	N	Y
8 Ellsworth	Y	Y	Y	Y
9 Hill	Y	Y	Y	Y
IOWA				
1 Braley	Y	Y	N	Y
2 Loebsack	Y	Y	N	Y
3 Boswell	Y	Y	N	Y
4 Latham	Y	N	Y	N
5 King	N	N	Y	N
KANSAS				
1 Moran	N	N	Y	N
2 Jenkins	N	N	Y	N
3 Moore	Y	Y	N	Y
4 Tiahrt	Y	N	Y	N
KENTUCKY				
1 Whitfield	N	N	Y	N
2 Guthrie	Y	N	Y	N
3 Yarmuth	Y	Y	N	Y
4 Davis	Y	N	Y	N
5 Rogers	N	N	Y	N
6 Chandler	Y	Y	N	Y
LOUISIANA				
1 Scalise	N	N	Y	N
2 Cao	Y	Y	Y	Y
3 Melancon	Y	Y	Y	Y
4 Fleming	N	N	Y	N
5 Alexander	N	N	Y	N
6 Cassidy	Y	N	Y	N
7 Boustany	Y	N	Y	N
MAINE				
1 Pingree	Y	Y	N	Y
2 Michaud	Y	Y	Y	Y
MARYLAND				
1 Kratovil	Y	Y	N	N
2 Ruppersberger	Y	Y	N	Y
3 Sarbanes	Y	Y	N	Y
4 Edwards	Y	Y	N	Y
5 Hoyer	Y	Y	N	Y
6 Bartlett	N	N	Y	N
7 Cummings	Y	Y	N	Y
8 Van Hollen	Y	Y	N	Y
MASSACHUSETTS				
1 Olver	Y	Y	N	Y
2 Neal	Y	Y	Y	Y
3 McGovern	Y	Y	N	Y
4 Frank	Y	?	N	Y
5 Tsongas	Y	Y	N	Y
6 Tierney	N	Y	N	Y
7 Markey	Y	Y	N	Y
8 Capuano	Y	Y	Y	Y
9 Lynch	Y	Y	Y	Y
10 Delahunt	Y	Y	N	Y
MICHIGAN				
1 Stupak	Y	Y	Y	Y
2 Hoekstra	Y	N	Y	N
3 Ehlers	Y	N	Y	N
4 Camp	Y	Y	Y	Y
5 Kildee	Y	Y	Y	Y
6 Upton	Y	N	Y	N
7 Schauer	Y	Y	N	Y
8 Rogers	Y	N	Y	N
9 Peters	Y	Y	N	Y
10 Miller	Y	N	Y	N
11 McCotter	Y	Y	N	Y
12 Levin	Y	Y	N	Y
13 Kilpatrick	Y	Y	N	Y
14 Conyers	Y	+	N	Y
15 Dingell	Y	Y	N	Y
MINNESOTA				
1 Walz	Y	Y	N	Y
2 Kline	Y	N	Y	N
3 Paulsen	N	N	Y	N
4 McCollum	Y	Y	N	Y

	682	719	884	887
5 Ellison	Y	Y	N	Y
6 Bachmann	N	N	Y	N
7 Peterson	N	Y	Y	N
8 Oberstar	Y	Y	Y	Y
MISSISSIPPI				
1 Childers	Y	Y	Y	N
2 Thompson	Y	Y	N	Y
3 Harper	?	N	Y	N
4 Taylor	Y	Y	Y	N
MISSOURI				
1 Clay	Y	Y	N	Y
2 Akin	N	N	Y	N
3 Carnahan	Y	Y	N	Y
4 Skelton	Y	Y	Y	N
5 Cleaver	Y	Y	N	Y
6 Graves	N	N	Y	N
7 Blunt	Y	N	Y	N
8 Emerson	Y	N	Y	N
9 Luetkemeyer	N	N	Y	N
MONTANA				
AL Rehberg	Y	N	Y	N
NEBRASKA				
1 Fortenberry	N	N	Y	N
2 Terry	Y	N	Y	N
3 Smith	N	N	Y	N
NEVADA				
1 Berkley	Y	Y	N	Y
2 Heller	N	N	Y	N
3 Titus	Y	Y	N	Y
NEW HAMPSHIRE				
1 Shea-Porter	Y	Y	N	Y
2 Hodes	Y	Y	N	Y
NEW JERSEY				
1 Andrews	Y	Y	N	Y
2 LoBiondo	Y	N	Y	N
3 Adler	Y	Y	N	N
4 Smith	Y	N	Y	N
5 Garrett	N	N	Y	N
6 Pallone	Y	Y	N	Y
7 Lance	Y	N	Y	N
8 Pascrell	Y	Y	N	Y
9 Rothman	Y	Y	N	Y
10 Payne	Y	Y	N	Y
11 Frelinghuysen	N	N	Y	N
12 Holt	Y	Y	N	Y
13 Sires	Y	Y	N	Y
NEW MEXICO				
1 Heinrich	Y	Y	N	Y
2 Teague	Y	Y	Y	N
3 Lujan	Y	Y	N	Y
NEW YORK				
1 Bishop	Y	Y	N	Y
2 Israel	Y	Y	N	Y
3 King	Y	N	Y	N
4 McCarthy	+	Y	N	Y
5 Ackerman	Y	Y	N	Y
6 Meeks	Y	Y	N	Y
7 Crowley	Y	Y	N	Y
8 Nadler	Y	Y	N	Y
9 Weiner	Y	Y	N	Y
10 Towns	Y	Y	N	Y
11 Clarke	Y	Y	N	Y
12 Velázquez	Y	Y	N	Y
13 McMahon	Y	N	N	N
14 Maloney	Y	Y	N	Y
15 Rangel	Y	Y	N	Y
16 Serrano	Y	Y	N	Y
17 Engel	Y	Y	N	Y
18 Lowey	Y	Y	N	Y
19 Hall	Y	Y	N	Y
20 Murphy	N	Y	N	N
21 Tonko	Y	Y	N	Y
22 Hinchey	Y	Y	N	Y
23 McHugh[3]	Y	?		
23 Owens[3]			N	Y
24 Arcuri	Y	Y	N	Y
25 Maffei	Y	Y	N	Y
26 Lee	Y	N	Y	N
27 Higgins	Y	Y	N	Y
28 Slaughter	Y	Y	N	Y
29 Massa	Y	Y	N	N
NORTH CAROLINA				
1 Butterfield	Y	Y	N	Y
2 Etheridge	Y	Y	Y	Y
3 Jones	Y	N	Y	N
4 Price	Y	Y	N	Y

	682	719	884	887
5 Foxx	N	N	Y	N
6 Coble	Y	N	Y	N
7 McIntyre	Y	Y	Y	N
8 Kissell	Y	Y	N	N
9 Myrick	N	N	Y	N
10 McHenry	N	N	Y	N
11 Shuler	Y	Y	Y	N
12 Watt	Y	Y	N	Y
13 Miller	Y	Y	N	Y
NORTH DAKOTA				
AL Pomeroy	Y	Y	Y	Y
OHIO				
1 Driehaus	Y	Y	Y	Y
2 Schmidt	N	N	Y	N
3 Turner	Y	N	Y	N
4 Jordan	N	N	Y	N
5 Latta	N	N	Y	N
6 Wilson	Y	Y	Y	Y
7 Austria	Y	N	Y	N
8 Boehner	N	N	Y	N
9 Kaptur	Y	Y	Y	Y
10 Kucinich	Y	Y	N	Y
11 Fudge	Y	Y	N	Y
12 Tiberi	Y	N	Y	N
13 Sutton	Y	Y	N	Y
14 LaTourette	Y	N	Y	N
15 Kilroy	Y	Y	N	Y
16 Boccieri	Y	Y	Y	N
17 Ryan	Y	Y	Y	Y
18 Space	Y	Y	Y	Y
OKLAHOMA				
1 Sullivan	N	N	Y	N
2 Boren	Y	Y	N	Y
3 Lucas	N	N	Y	N
4 Cole	N	N	Y	N
5 Fallin	N	N	Y	N
OREGON				
1 Wu	Y	Y	N	Y
2 Walden	Y	N	Y	N
3 Blumenauer	N	Y	N	Y
4 DeFazio	Y	Y	N	Y
5 Schrader	N	Y	N	Y
PENNSYLVANIA				
1 Brady	Y	Y	N	Y
2 Fattah	Y	Y	N	Y
3 Dahlkemper	Y	Y	Y	Y
4 Altmire	Y	Y	Y	N
5 Thompson	N	Y	N	N
6 Gerlach	Y	N	Y	N
7 Sestak	Y	Y	N	Y
8 Murphy, P.	Y	Y	N	Y
9 Shuster	N	Y	N	N
10 Carney	Y	Y	Y	Y
11 Kanjorski	Y	N	Y	N
12 Murtha	Y	Y	Y	Y
13 Schwartz	Y	Y	N	Y
14 Doyle	Y	Y	Y	Y
15 Dent	N	N	Y	N
16 Pitts	Y	N	Y	N
17 Holden	Y	Y	N	N
18 Murphy, T.	Y	N	Y	N
19 Platts	Y	Y	Y	N
RHODE ISLAND				
1 Kennedy	Y	Y	N	Y
2 Langevin	Y	Y	Y	Y
SOUTH CAROLINA				
1 Brown	N	N	Y	N
2 Wilson	N	N	Y	N
3 Barrett	N	?	Y	N
4 Inglis	N	N	Y	N
5 Spratt	Y	Y	Y	Y
6 Clyburn	Y	Y	N	Y
SOUTH DAKOTA				
AL Herseth Sandlin	N	N	N	N
TENNESSEE				
1 Roe	Y	N	Y	N
2 Duncan	Y	N	Y	N
3 Wamp	Y	N	Y	N
4 Davis	Y	Y	N	Y
5 Cooper	Y	Y	Y	Y
6 Gordon	Y	Y	Y	Y
7 Blackburn	N	N	Y	N
8 Tanner	Y	?	Y	N
9 Cohen	Y	Y	N	Y

	682	719	884	887
TEXAS				
1 Gohmert	?	N	Y	N
2 Poe	Y	N	Y	N
3 Johnson, S.	N	N	Y	N
4 Hall	Y	N	Y	N
5 Hensarling	N	N	Y	N
6 Barton	Y	N	Y	N
7 Culberson	N	N	Y	N
8 Brady	N	N	Y	N
9 Green, A.	Y	Y	N	Y
10 McCaul	?	N	Y	N
11 Conaway	N	N	Y	N
12 Granger	N	N	Y	N
13 Thornberry	N	N	Y	N
14 Paul	N	?	Y	N
15 Hinojosa	Y	Y	N	Y
16 Reyes	Y	Y	Y	Y
17 Edwards	Y	Y	N	Y
18 Jackson Lee	Y	Y	N	Y
19 Neugebauer	N	N	Y	N
20 Gonzalez	Y	Y	N	Y
21 Smith	N	N	Y	N
22 Olson	N	N	Y	N
23 Rodriguez	Y	Y	Y	Y
24 Marchant	N	N	Y	N
25 Doggett	N	Y	N	Y
26 Burgess	N	N	Y	N
27 Ortiz	Y	Y	Y	Y
28 Cuellar	Y	Y	Y	Y
29 Green, G.	Y	Y	N	Y
30 Johnson, E.	Y	Y	N	Y
31 Carter	N	N	Y	N
32 Sessions	N	N	Y	N
UTAH				
1 Bishop	N	N	Y	N
2 Matheson	Y	Y	Y	N
3 Chaffetz	N	N	Y	N
VERMONT				
AL Welch	Y	Y	N	Y
VIRGINIA				
1 Wittman	N	N	Y	N
2 Nye	Y	Y	N	N
3 Scott	Y	Y	N	Y
4 Forbes	N	N	Y	N
5 Perriello	Y	Y	Y	Y
6 Goodlatte	N	N	Y	N
7 Cantor	N	N	Y	N
8 Moran	Y	Y	N	Y
9 Boucher	Y	Y	N	N
10 Wolf	N	N	Y	N
11 Connolly	Y	Y	N	Y
WASHINGTON				
1 Inslee	Y	Y	N	Y
2 Larsen	Y	Y	N	Y
3 Baird	N	N	Y	N
4 Hastings	N	N	Y	N
5 McMorris Rodgers	N	N	Y	N
6 Dicks	Y	Y	N	Y
7 McDermott	Y	Y	N	Y
8 Reichert	Y	N	Y	N
9 Smith	Y	Y	N	Y
WEST VIRGINIA				
1 Mollohan	Y	Y	Y	Y
2 Capito	Y	N	Y	N
3 Rahall	Y	Y	Y	Y
WISCONSIN				
1 Ryan	N	N	Y	N
2 Baldwin	Y	Y	N	Y
3 Kind	Y	Y	N	Y
4 Moore	Y	Y	N	Y
5 Sensenbrenner	N	N	Y	N
6 Petri	Y	Y	N	Y
7 Obey	Y	Y	N	Y
8 Kagen	Y	Y	N	Y
WYOMING				
AL Lummis	N	N	Y	N
DELEGATES				
Faleomavaega (A.S.)				
Norton (D.C.)				
Bordallo (Guam)				
Sablan (N. Marianas)				
Pierluisi (P.R.)				
Christensen (V.I.)				

IN THE SENATE | By Vote Number

5. S J Res 5. Troubled Asset Relief Program Disapproval/Passage.
Passage of the joint resolution that would prevent the release of the second half of the $700 billion provided under the 2008 financial industry bailout law. Rejected 42-52: R 33-6; D 8-45; I 1-1. Jan. 15, 2009. *(Story, p. C-8)*

14. S 181. Wage Discrimination/Passage.
Passage of the bill that would amend the 1964 Civil Rights Act to clarify time limits for workers to file employment discrimination lawsuits. The bill would allow workers who allege discrimination based on race, gender, national origin, religion, age or disability to file charges of pay discrimination within 180 days of the last received paycheck affected by the alleged discriminatory decision. The bill would renew the statute of limitations with each act of discrimination. Passed 61-36: R 5-36; D 54-0; I 2-0. (By unanimous consent, the Senate agreed to raise the majority requirement for passage of the bill to 59 votes.) Jan. 22, 2009. *(Story, p. C-8)*

31. HR 2. Children's Health Insurance/Passage.
Passage of the bill that would reauthorize the State Children's Health Insurance Program for four and a half years and increase funding by $32.8 billion. To offset the cost of the expansion, it would increase the federal tax on cigarettes to 62 cents per pack and raise taxes on other tobacco products. It would remove a five-year waiting period for new legal immigrants, including pregnant women, and loosen citizenship and eligibility documentation requirements. The bill would limit program eligibility to families earning three times the federal poverty level or less and would require states to phase out coverage of childless adults. Passed 66-32: R 9-32; D 55-0; I 2-0. Jan. 29, 2009. *(Story, p. C-8)*

59. HR 1. Economic Stimulus/Cloture.
Motion to invoke cloture (thus limiting debate) on the Reid, D-Nev. (for Nelson, D-Neb., and Collins, R-Maine), substitute amendment that would provide approximately $838 billion in tax cuts and additional spending to stimulate the economy, including a provision to exempt additional taxpayers from paying the alternative minimum tax in 2009. It would provide funds for a state fiscal stabilization fund and a one-time payment to seniors, disabled veterans and those who receive disability payments. The amendment would expand bonus depreciation for 2009, increase weekly unemployment benefits and provide an additional 20 weeks of unemployment benefits (an additional 33 weeks in states with high unemployment rates). It would suspend federal income tax on the first $2,400 of unemployment benefits for 2009. It would also expand the current homeownership tax credit by up to $15,000 and allow the credit for purchases of a primary residence. It would temporarily increase federal Medicaid matching payments for states by an estimated $87 billion. Motion agreed to 61-36: R 3-36; D 56-0; I 2-0. Three-fifths of the total Senate (60) is required to invoke cloture. Feb. 9, 2009. *(Story, p. C-8)*

[1] Sen. Michael Bennet, D-Colo., was sworn in Jan. 22, 2009, to fill the seat vacated by fellow Democrat Ken Salazar, who resigned Jan. 20, 2009, to become secretary of Interior. The first vote for which Bennet was eligible was vote 11; the last vote for which Salazar was eligible was vote 5.

[2] Sen. Ted Kaufman, D-Del., was sworn in Jan. 16, 2009, to fill the seat vacated by fellow Democrat Joseph R. Biden Jr., who resigned Jan. 15, 2009, to become vice president. The first vote for which Kaufman was eligible was vote 6; the last vote for which Biden was eligible was vote 5.

[3] Sen. Roland W. Burris, D-Ill., was sworn in Jan. 15, 2009, to fill the seat vacated by fellow Democrat Barack Obama, who resigned Nov. 16, 2008, to become president. The first vote for which Burris was eligible was vote 5; Obama was not eligible for any votes in 2009.

[4] Sen. Al Franken, D-Minn., was sworn in July 7, 2009, after he was certified the winner of that state's contested election. The first vote for which he was eligible was vote 218.

[5] Sen. Kirsten Gillibrand, D-N.Y., was sworn in Jan. 27, 2009, to fill the seat vacated by fellow Democrat Hillary Rodham Clinton, who resigned Jan. 21, 2009, to become secretary of State. The first vote for which Gillibrand was eligible was vote 16; the last vote for which Clinton was eligible was vote 6.

	5	14	31	59		5	14	31	59
ALABAMA					**MONTANA**				
Shelby	Y	N	N	N	Baucus	N	Y	Y	Y
Sessions	Y	N	N	N	Tester	#	Y	Y	Y
ALASKA					**NEBRASKA**				
Murkowski	Y	Y	Y	N	Nelson	Y	Y	Y	Y
Begich	N	Y	Y	Y	**Johanns**	Y	N	N	N
ARIZONA					**NEVADA**				
McCain	Y	N	N	N	Reid	N	Y	Y	Y
Kyl	N	N	N	N	**Ensign**	Y	N	N	N
ARKANSAS					**NEW HAMPSHIRE**				
Lincoln	Y	Y	Y	Y	**Gregg**	N	N	N	?
Pryor	N	Y	Y	Y	Shaheen	Y	Y	Y	Y
CALIFORNIA					**NEW JERSEY**				
Feinstein	N	Y	Y	Y	Lautenberg	N	Y	Y	Y
Boxer	N	Y	Y	Y	Menendez	N	Y	Y	Y
COLORADO					**NEW MEXICO**				
Udall	N	Y	Y	Y	Bingaman	N	Y	Y	Y
Salazar[1]	N				Udall	N	Y	Y	Y
Bennet[1]		Y	Y	Y	**NEW YORK**				
CONNECTICUT					Schumer	N	Y	Y	Y
Dodd	N	Y	Y	Y	Clinton[5]	N			
Lieberman	N	Y	Y	Y	Gillibrand[5]			Y	Y
DELAWARE					**NORTH CAROLINA**				
Biden[2]	N				**Burr**	Y	N	N	N
Carper	N	Y	Y	Y	Hagan	N	Y	Y	Y
Kaufman[2]		Y	Y	Y	**NORTH DAKOTA**				
FLORIDA					Conrad	N	Y	Y	Y
Nelson	N	Y	Y	Y	Dorgan	Y	Y	Y	Y
Martinez	Y	N	Y	N	**OHIO**				
GEORGIA					**Voinovich**	N	N	N	N
Chambliss	Y	N	N	N	Brown	X	Y	Y	Y
Isakson	Y	N	N	N	**OKLAHOMA**				
HAWAII					**Inhofe**	Y	N	N	N
Inouye	N	Y	Y	Y	**Coburn**	Y	N	N	N
Akaka	N	Y	Y	Y	**OREGON**				
IDAHO					Wyden	Y	Y	Y	Y
Crapo	Y	N	N	N	Merkley	N	Y	Y	Y
Risch	Y	N	N	N	**PENNSYLVANIA**				
ILLINOIS					**Specter**	Y	Y	Y	Y
Durbin	N	Y	Y	Y	Casey	N	Y	Y	Y
Burris[3]	N	Y	Y	Y	**RHODE ISLAND**				
INDIANA					Reed	N	Y	Y	Y
Lugar	N	N	Y	N	Whitehouse	N	Y	Y	Y
Bayh	Y	Y	Y	Y	**SOUTH CAROLINA**				
IOWA					**Graham**	Y	N	N	N
Grassley	Y	N	N	N	**DeMint**	Y	N	N	N
Harkin	N	Y	Y	Y	**SOUTH DAKOTA**				
KANSAS					Johnson	N	Y	Y	Y
Brownback	Y	N	N	N	**Thune**	Y	N	N	N
Roberts	Y	N	N	N	**TENNESSEE**				
KENTUCKY					**Alexander**	N	N	Y	N
McConnell	Y	N	N	N	**Corker**	Y	N	Y	N
Bunning	+	N	N	N	**TEXAS**				
LOUISIANA					**Hutchison**	Y	Y	Y	Y
Landrieu	N	Y	Y	Y	**Cornyn**	Y	N	N	–
Vitter	Y	N	N	N	**UTAH**				
MAINE					**Hatch**	#	N	N	N
Snowe	N	Y	Y	Y	**Bennett**	Y	N	N	N
Collins	Y	Y	Y	Y	**VERMONT**				
MARYLAND					Leahy	N	Y	Y	Y
Mikulski	N	Y	Y	Y	*Sanders*	Y	Y	Y	Y
Cardin	N	Y	Y	Y	**VIRGINIA**				
MASSACHUSETTS					Webb	N	Y	Y	Y
Kennedy	X	?	?	Y	Warner	N	Y	Y	Y
Kerry	N	Y	Y	Y	**WASHINGTON**				
MICHIGAN					Murray	N	Y	Y	Y
Levin	N	Y	Y	Y	Cantwell	Y	Y	Y	Y
Stabenow	N	Y	Y	Y	**WEST VIRGINIA**				
MINNESOTA					Byrd	N	Y	Y	Y
Klobuchar	N	Y	Y	Y	Rockefeller	N	Y	Y	Y
Vacant[4]					**WISCONSIN**				
MISSISSIPPI					Kohl	N	Y	Y	Y
Cochran	Y	N	N	N	Feingold	Y	Y	Y	Y
Wicker	Y	N	N	N	**WYOMING**				
MISSOURI					**Enzi**	Y	N	N	N
Bond	Y	N	N	N	**Barrasso**	Y	N	N	N
McCaskill	N	Y	Y	Y					

KEY **Republicans** Democrats *Independents*

Y Voted for (yea)	X Paired against	C Voted "present" to avoid possible conflict of interest
# Paired for	– Announced against	
+ Announced for	P Voted "present"	? Did not vote or otherwise make a position known
N Voted against (nay)		

IN THE SENATE | By Vote Number

72. **S 160. District of Columbia Voting Rights/District Gun Laws.**
Ensign, R-Nev., amendment that would ban the District of Columbia from prohibiting an individual from possessing firearms and repeal District laws barring possession of semiautomatic firearms. It would repeal the District's mandates for firearm registration and the requirement that firearms be disassembled or secured with a trigger lock in the home. District residents would be allowed to purchase firearms in Maryland and Virginia. Adopted 62-36: R 40-1; D 22-33; I 0-2. Feb. 26, 2009. *(Story, p. C-9)*

120. **S Con Res 13. Fiscal 2010 Budget Resolution/Non-Defense Discretionary Spending.** Sessions, R-Ala., amendment that would adjust the resolution to allow non-defense discretionary spending to be set at fiscal 2009 levels for fiscal 2010 and 2011, and allow it to increase by 1 percent annually in fiscal 2012 through 2014. Rejected 40-58: R 39-2; D 1-54; I 0-2. A "nay" was a vote in support of the president's position. April 1, 2009. *(Story, p. C-9)*

174. **S 896. Housing Loans Modification/'Cramdown' Provision.**
Durbin, D-Ill., amendment that would allow bankruptcy judges to write down the principal and interest rates of certain mortgages on primary homes if the homeowner and creditor have not been able to reach agreement on a reasonable modification of the loan. The amendment would apply only to borrowers who are at least 60 days delinquent on payments for loans originated before Jan. 1, 2009, and would set the maximum value of loans that qualify at $729,000. Rejected 45-51: R 0-39; D 43-12; I 2-0. (By unanimous consent, the Senate agreed to raise the majority requirement for adoption of the amendment to 60 votes.) April 30, 2009. *(Story, p. C-9)*

194. **HR 627. Credit Card Company Regulations/Passage.** Passage of the bill that would impose restrictions on credit card company lending practices. The bill would restrict when companies could increase the annual percentage interest rate retroactively on existing balances, require companies to give at least 45 days' notice before increasing an annual percentage rate or changing an open-ended contract, and restrict companies from computing interest charges based on balances from more than one billing cycle. The term "fixed rate" could only be used for a rate that will not change over a set period. Credit cards could not be issued to consumers under age 21 without a co-signer's acceptance of financial liability or a demonstrated ability to repay the credit extension. The bill's provisions would take effect nine months after enactment. Passed 90-5: R 35-4; D 53-1; I 2-0. A "yea" was a vote in support of the president's position. May 19, 2009. *(Story, p. C-10)*

	72	120	174	194			72	120	174	194
ALABAMA						**MONTANA**				
Shelby	Y	Y	N	Y		Baucus	Y	N	N	Y
Sessions	Y	Y	?	Y		Tester	Y	N	N	Y
ALASKA						**NEBRASKA**				
Murkowski	Y	Y	N	Y		Nelson	Y	N	N	Y
Begich	Y	N	Y	Y		**Johanns**	Y	Y	N	Y
ARIZONA						**NEVADA**				
McCain	Y	Y	N	Y		Reid	Y	N	Y	Y
Kyl	Y	Y	N	N		**Ensign**	Y	Y	N	+
ARKANSAS						**NEW HAMPSHIRE**				
Lincoln	Y	N	N	Y		**Gregg**	Y	Y	N	Y
Pryor	Y	N	N	Y		Shaheen	N	N	Y	Y
CALIFORNIA						**NEW JERSEY**				
Feinstein	N	N	Y	Y		Lautenberg	N	N	Y	Y
Boxer	N	N	Y	Y		Menendez	N	N	Y	Y
COLORADO						**NEW MEXICO**				
Udall	Y	N	Y	Y		Bingaman	N	N	Y	Y
Bennet	Y	N	N	Y		Udall	Y	N	Y	Y
CONNECTICUT						**NEW YORK**				
Dodd	N	N	Y	Y		Schumer	N	N	Y	Y
Lieberman	N	N	Y	Y		Gillibrand	N	N	Y	Y
DELAWARE						**NORTH CAROLINA**				
Carper	N	N	N	Y		**Burr**	Y	Y	N	Y
Kaufman	N	N	Y	Y		Hagan	Y	N	Y	Y
FLORIDA						**NORTH DAKOTA**				
Nelson	N	N	Y	Y		Conrad	Y	N	Y	Y
Martinez	Y	N	N	Y		Dorgan	Y	N	N	Y
GEORGIA						**OHIO**				
Chambliss	Y	Y	N	Y		**Voinovich**	Y	Y	N	Y
Isakson	Y	Y	N	Y		Brown	N	N	Y	Y
HAWAII						**OKLAHOMA**				
Inouye	N	N	Y	Y		**Inhofe**	Y	Y	N	Y
Akaka	N	N	Y	Y		**Coburn**	Y	Y	N	Y
IDAHO						**OREGON**				
Crapo	Y	Y	N	Y		Wyden	N	N	Y	Y
Risch	Y	Y	N	Y		Merkley	N	N	Y	Y
ILLINOIS						**PENNSYLVANIA**				
Durbin	N	N	Y	Y		Specter[2]	Y	Y	N	Y
Burris	N	N	Y	Y		Casey	Y	N	Y	Y
INDIANA						**RHODE ISLAND**				
Lugar	N	Y	N	Y		Reed	N	N	Y	Y
Bayh	Y	Y	Y	Y		Whitehouse	N	N	Y	Y
IOWA						**SOUTH CAROLINA**				
Grassley	Y	Y	N	Y		**Graham**	Y	Y	N	Y
Harkin	N	N	Y	Y		**DeMint**	Y	Y	N	Y
KANSAS						**SOUTH DAKOTA**				
Brownback	Y	Y	N	Y		Johnson	Y	N	N	N
Roberts	Y	Y	N	Y		**Thune**	Y	Y	N	Y
KENTUCKY						**TENNESSEE**				
McConnell	Y	Y	N	Y		**Alexander**	Y	Y	N	N
Bunning	Y	Y	N	Y		**Corker**	Y	Y	N	Y
LOUISIANA						**TEXAS**				
Landrieu	Y	N	N	Y		**Hutchison**	Y	Y	N	Y
Vitter	Y	Y	N	Y		**Cornyn**	Y	Y	N	Y
MAINE						**UTAH**				
Snowe	Y	Y	N	Y		**Hatch**	Y	Y	N	Y
Collins	Y	N	N	Y		**Bennett**	Y	Y	N	N
MARYLAND						**VERMONT**				
Mikulski	N	N	Y	Y		Leahy	N	N	Y	Y
Cardin	N	N	Y	Y		*Sanders*	N	N	Y	Y
MASSACHUSETTS						**VIRGINIA**				
Kennedy	?	?	?	?		Webb	Y	N	Y	Y
Kerry	N	N	Y	Y		Warner	Y	N	Y	Y
MICHIGAN						**WASHINGTON**				
Levin	N	N	Y	Y		Murray	N	N	Y	Y
Stabenow	N	N	Y	Y		Cantwell	N	N	Y	Y
MINNESOTA						**WEST VIRGINIA**				
Klobuchar	N	N	Y	Y		Byrd	Y	N	N	?
Vacant[1]						Rockefeller	N	N	?	+
MISSISSIPPI						**WISCONSIN**				
Cochran	Y	Y	N	Y		Kohl	N	N	Y	Y
Wicker	Y	Y	N	Y		Feingold	Y	N	Y	Y
MISSOURI						**WYOMING**				
Bond	Y	Y	N	Y		**Enzi**	Y	Y	N	Y
McCaskill	N	N	Y	Y		**Barrasso**	Y	Y	N	Y

KEY	**Republicans**	Democrats	*Independents*			
Y	Voted for (yea)		X	Paired against		C	Voted "present" to avoid possible conflict of interest
#	Paired for		–	Announced against		
+	Announced for		P	Voted "present"		?	Did not vote or otherwise make a position known
N	Voted against (nay)					

[1] Sen. Al Franken, D-Minn., was sworn in July 7, 2009, after he was certified the winner of that state's contested election. The first vote for which he was eligible was vote 218.

[2] Pennsylvania Sen. Arlen Specter switched party affiliation from Republican to Democrat, effective April 30, 2009. The first vote he cast as a Democrat was vote 174.

IN THE SENATE | By Vote Number

207. **HR 1256. Tobacco Regulation/Passage.** Passage of the bill that would allow the Food and Drug Administration (FDA) to regulate the manufacture, sale and promotion of tobacco products. It would require new, larger labels warning consumers of the health risks associated with tobacco products and clarify that the FDA does not endorse the safety of such products. It would establish standards for tobacco products marketed as lower in health risks. The FDA could regulate the amount of nicotine but not ban any class of tobacco products or eliminate nicotine levels completely. The bill would restrict the additives that can be included in cigarettes and ban flavors, except for menthol. It would require tobacco manufacturers and importers to pay quarterly user fees to help cover the cost of the regulation. Passed 79-17: R 23-16; D 54-1; I 2-0. A "yea" was a vote in support of the president's position. June 11, 2009. *(Story, p. C-10)*

233. **S 1390. Fiscal 2010 Defense Authorization/Cloture.** Motion to invoke cloture (thus limiting debate) on the Leahy, D-Vt., amendment, which would expand federal hate crimes law to cover crimes based on sexual orientation, gender identity or disability. Motion agreed to 63-28: R 5-28; D 56-0; I 2-0. Three-fifths of the total Senate (60) is required to invoke cloture. (Subsequently, the Leahy amendment was adopted by voice vote.) July 16, 2009. *(Story, p. C-10)*

235. **S 1390. Fiscal 2010 Defense Authorization/F-22 Aircraft.** Levin, D-Mich., amendment that would strike $1.75 billion for the procurement of F-22A aircraft. It would increase the authorization for operations and maintenance by $350 million for the Army, $100 million for the Navy, $250 million for the Air Force and $150 million defensewide. It would increase the authorization for military personnel by $400 million and general Defense Department activities by $500 million. Adopted 58-40: R 15-25; D 42-14; I 1-1. A "yea" was a vote in support of the president's position. July 21, 2009. *(Story, p. C-10)*

262. **Sotomayor Nomination/Confirmation.** Confirmation of President Obama's nomination of Sonia Sotomayor of New York to be an associate justice of the U.S. Supreme Court. Confirmed 68-31: R 9-31; D 57-0; I 2-0. A "yea" was a vote in support of the president's position. Aug. 6, 2009. *(Story, p. C-11)*

385. **HR 3590. Health Care Overhaul/Cloture.** Motion to invoke cloture (thus limiting debate) on the Reid, D-Nev., manager's amendment to the Reid substitute amendment. The manager's amendment would create a system of national private insurance plans known as exchanges that would be supervised by the Office of Personnel Management. The amendment would strike provisions in the substitute that would create a public health insurance option. It would increase the percentage of revenue that insurers covering employees of large businesses must spend on medical claims and further expand Medicaid coverage. It would require every exchange to offer at least one plan that does not cover abortion and would lay out a financial structure for insurance plans to cover abortion if they do not use federal subsidies to pay for the procedure. Motion agreed to 60-40: D 58-0; R 0-40; I 2-0. Three-fifths of the total Senate (60) is required to invoke cloture. A "yea" was a vote in support of the president's position. Dec. 21, 2009. *(Story, p. C-11)*

[1] Sen. George LeMieux, R-Fla., was sworn in Sept. 10, 2009, to fill the seat vacated by fellow Republican Mel Martinez, who resigned Sept. 9, 2009. The first vote for which LeMieux was eligible was vote 274; the last vote for which Martinez was eligible was vote 272.

[2] Sen. Paul G. Kirk Jr., D-Mass., was sworn in Sept. 25, 2009, to temporarily fill the seat vacated by fellow Democrat Edward M. Kennedy, who died Aug. 25, 2009. The first vote for which Kirk was eligible was vote 299; the last vote for which Kennedy was eligible was vote 270.

[3] Sen. Al Franken, D-Minn., was sworn in July 7, 2009, after he was certified the winner of that state's contested election. The first vote for which he is eligible was vote 218.

	207	233	235	262	385
ALABAMA					
Shelby	Y	N	Y	N	N
Sessions	Y	N	N	N	N
ALASKA					
Murkowski	Y	Y	N	N	N
Begich	Y	Y	N	Y	N
ARIZONA					
McCain	Y	N	N	N	N
Kyl	N	N	Y	N	N
ARKANSAS					
Lincoln	Y	Y	Y	Y	Y
Pryor	Y	Y	Y	Y	Y
CALIFORNIA					
Feinstein	Y	Y	N	N	Y
Boxer	Y	Y	N	Y	Y
COLORADO					
Udall	Y	Y	Y	Y	Y
Bennet	Y	Y	Y	Y	Y
CONNECTICUT					
Dodd	Y	Y	Y	Y	Y
Lieberman	Y	Y	N	Y	Y
DELAWARE					
Carper	Y	Y	Y	Y	Y
Kaufman	Y	Y	Y	Y	Y
FLORIDA					
Nelson	Y	Y	Y	Y	Y
Martinez[1]	Y	?	N	Y	
LeMieux[1]					N
GEORGIA					
Chambliss	N	N	N	N	N
Isakson	N	N	N	N	N
HAWAII					
Inouye	Y	Y	N	Y	Y
Akaka	Y	Y	N	Y	Y
IDAHO					
Crapo	Y	N	N	N	N
Risch	Y	N	N	N	N
ILLINOIS					
Durbin	Y	Y	Y	Y	Y
Burris	Y	Y	Y	Y	Y
INDIANA					
Lugar	Y	Y	Y	Y	N
Bayh	Y	Y	Y	Y	Y
IOWA					
Grassley	Y	N	N	N	N
Harkin	Y	Y	Y	Y	Y
KANSAS					
Brownback	N	N	N	N	N
Roberts	N	N	N	N	N
KENTUCKY					
McConnell	N	N	N	N	N
Bunning	N	?	N	N	N
LOUISIANA					
Landrieu	Y	Y	Y	Y	Y
Vitter	Y	N	N	N	N
MAINE					
Snowe	Y	Y	N	Y	N
Collins	Y	Y	N	Y	N
MARYLAND					
Mikulski	Y	Y	?	Y	Y
Cardin	Y	Y	Y	Y	Y
MASSACHUSETTS					
Kennedy[2]	?	?	?	?	
Kerry	Y	Y	Y	Y	Y
Kirk[2]					Y
MICHIGAN					
Levin	Y	Y	Y	Y	Y
Stabenow	Y	Y	Y	Y	Y
MINNESOTA					
Klobuchar	Y	Y	Y	Y	Y
Franken[3]		Y	Y	Y	Y
MISSISSIPPI					
Cochran	Y	N	N	N	N
Wicker	Y	N	N	N	N
MISSOURI					
Bond	-	?	Y	Y	N
McCaskill	Y	Y	Y	Y	Y

	207	233	235	262	385
MONTANA					
Baucus	Y	Y	N	Y	Y
Tester	Y	Y	N	Y	Y
NEBRASKA					
Nelson	Y	Y	Y	Y	Y
Johanns	Y	N	N	N	N
NEVADA					
Reid	Y	Y	Y	Y	Y
Ensign	N	N	Y	N	N
NEW HAMPSHIRE					
Gregg	Y	?	Y	Y	N
Shaheen	Y	Y	N	Y	Y
NEW JERSEY					
Lautenberg	Y	Y	Y	Y	Y
Menendez	Y	Y	Y	Y	Y
NEW MEXICO					
Bingaman	Y	Y	Y	Y	Y
Udall	Y	Y	N	Y	Y
NEW YORK					
Schumer	Y	Y	Y	Y	Y
Gillibrand	Y	Y	Y	Y	Y
NORTH CAROLINA					
Burr	N	N	N	N	N
Hagan	N	Y	Y	Y	Y
NORTH DAKOTA					
Conrad	Y	Y	Y	Y	Y
Dorgan	Y	Y	Y	Y	Y
OHIO					
Voinovich	Y	Y	Y	Y	N
Brown	Y	Y	Y	Y	Y
OKLAHOMA					
Inhofe	N	N	N	N	N
Coburn	N	N	Y	N	N
OREGON					
Wyden	Y	Y	Y	Y	Y
Merkley	Y	Y	Y	Y	Y
PENNSYLVANIA					
Specter	Y	Y	Y	Y	Y
Casey	Y	Y	Y	Y	Y
RHODE ISLAND					
Reed	Y	Y	Y	Y	Y
Whitehouse	Y	Y	Y	Y	Y
SOUTH CAROLINA					
Graham	N	?	Y	Y	N
DeMint	N	N	N	N	N
SOUTH DAKOTA					
Johnson	Y	Y	Y	Y	Y
Thune	Y	N	N	N	N
TENNESSEE					
Alexander	N	?	Y	Y	N
Corker	Y	?	Y	N	N
TEXAS					
Hutchison	Y	N	N	N	N
Cornyn	Y	N	N	N	N
UTAH					
Hatch	N	N	N	N	N
Bennett	N	N	N	N	N
VERMONT					
Leahy	Y	Y	Y	Y	Y
Sanders	Y	Y	Y	Y	Y
VIRGINIA					
Webb	Y	Y	Y	Y	Y
Warner	Y	Y	Y	Y	Y
WASHINGTON					
Murray	Y	Y	N	Y	Y
Cantwell	Y	Y	N	Y	Y
WEST VIRGINIA					
Byrd	?	?	N	Y	Y
Rockefeller	Y	Y	Y	Y	Y
WISCONSIN					
Kohl	Y	Y	Y	Y	Y
Feingold	Y	Y	Y	Y	Y
WYOMING					
Enzi	Y	N	N	N	N
Barrasso	Y	N	N	N	N

KEY	**Republicans**	Democrats	*Independents*
Y Voted for (yea)		**X** Paired against	**C** Voted "present" to avoid possible conflict of interest
# Paired for		**-** Announced against	
+ Announced for		**P** Voted "present"	**?** Did not vote or otherwise make a position known
N Voted against (nay)			

House
Roll Call
Votes

House Roll Call Index
By Bill Number

HR 35, H-4
HR 36, H-4
HR 44, H-28
HR 46, H-80
HR 80, H-28
HR 86, H-320
HR 129, H-184
HR 131, H-42
HR 146, H-34, H-54, H-56
HR 151, H-62
HR 310, H-228
HR 324, H-228, H-240, H-242
HR 347, H-96
HR 384, H-8, H-10, H-12
HR 388, H-70
HR 402, H-180
HR 403, H-124
HR 409, H-184
HR 411, H-70
HR 448, H-24
HR 479, H-60
HR 509, H-216
HR 515, H-312
HR 548, H-36
HR 556, H-216
HR 559, H-20
HR 577, H-62
HR 586, H-70
HR 601, H-28
HR 626, H-112
HR 627, H-82, H-100, H-102
HR 628, H-48
HR 637, H-30
HR 729, H-122
HR 730, H-54
HR 738, H-20
HR 762, H-182
HR 780, H-122
HR 813, H-44
HR 842, H-44
HR 905, H-246
HR 911, H-28
HR 915, H-102, H-104
HR 918, H-54
HR 934, H-182
HR 957, H-72
HR 965, H-230
HR 987, H-48
HR 1016, H-146, H-258
HR 1018, H-192
HR 1035, H-254
HR 1037, H-180
HR 1044, H-182
HR 1053, H-248
HR 1089, H-98
HR 1105, H-32
HR 1106, H-34, H-38, H-40
HR 1110, H-332
HR 1121, H-214
HR 1129, H-164
HR 1139, H-74
HR 1145, H-72, H-74
HR 1168, H-282

HR 1172, H-146
HR 1211, H-146
HR 1217, H-48
HR 1218, H-54
HR 1219, H-70
HR 1242, H-312
HR 1243, H-76
HR 1253, H-62
HR 1256, H-66, H-68, H-120
HR 1259, H-60
HR 1262, H-46
HR 1275, H-164
HR 1284, H-48
HR 1293, H-214
HR 1299, H-64
HR 1327, H-260
HR 1376, H-214
HR 1385, H-106
HR 1388, H-48, H-50, H-52,
  H-60, H-62
HR 1404, H-56, H-58
HR 1442, H-184
HR 1517, H-328
HR 1575, H-64
HR 1586, H-52
HR 1595, H-78
HR 1617, H-54
HR 1622, H-198
HR 1664, H-64, H-66
HR 1665, H-218
HR 1675, H-200
HR 1676, H-104
HR 1679, H-70
HR 1687, H-120
HR 1709, H-114
HR 1728, H-86, H-88
HR 1736, H-114
HR 1741, H-114
HR 1746, H-76
HR 1752, H-224
HR 1771, H-248
HR 1777, H-148
HR 1834, H-308
HR 1838, H-296
HR 1845, H-298
HR 1849, H-292
HR 1886, H-114, H-120
HR 1913, H-80
HR 1933, H-200
HR 1945, H-164
HR 2097, H-228
HR 2162, H-90
HR 2187, H-90, H-92, H-94
HR 2188, H-184
HR 2194, H-330
HR 2200, H-108, H-110, H-112
HR 2215, H-240
HR 2245, H-198
HR 2247, H-124
HR 2278, H-316
HR 2325, H-122
HR 2346, H-94, H-96, H-118,
  H-124

HR 2352, H-100, H-102
HR 2410, H-114, H-116, H-118
HR 2423, H-264
HR 2442, H-248, H-264
HR 2454, H-160, H-162
HR 2470, H-122
HR 2489, H-276
HR 2598, H-230
HR 2632, H-200
HR 2647, H-156, H-158, H-252,
  H-256, H-258
HR 2728, H-224
HR 2729, H-198
HR 2749, H-216, H-224
HR 2751, H-114
HR 2781, H-306
HR 2847, H-124, H-126, H-128,
  H-130, H-132, H-134, H-136,
  H-138, H-140, H-142, H-334
HR 2868, H-290, H-294, H-296
HR 2892, H-148, H-150, H-152,
  H-154, H-248, H-262, H-264
HR 2918, H-144, H-244, H-246
HR 2920, H-200, H-202
HR 2938, H-202
HR 2965, H-164, H-166
HR 2971, H-240
HR 2972, H-204
HR 2996, H-158, H-160, H-162,
  H-274, H-278
HR 2997, H-166, H-168, H-170,
  H-172, H-246, H-252, H-254
HR 3029, H-310
HR 3081, H-172, H-174, H-176
HR 3082, H-178
HR 3119, H-202
HR 3123, H-228
HR 3137, H-234
HR 3157, H-284
HR 3170, H-184, H-186, H-188,
  H-190
HR 3183, H-180, H-182, H-184,
  H-192, H-194, H-196, H-250
HR 3221, H-234, H-236, H-238
HR 3246, H-234, H-236
HR 3269, H-226
HR 3276, H-292
HR 3288, H-204, H-206, H-208,
  H-210, H-316, H-320, H-322
HR 3293, H-212, H-214
HR 3319, H-266
HR 3326, H-216, H-218, H-220,
  H-222, H-332
HR 3357, H-218
HR 3360, H-302
HR 3371, H-262
HR 3435, H-226
HR 3476, H-260
HR 3539, H-302
HR 3548, H-240, H-290
HR 3570, H-314
HR 3585, H-268, H-270, H-272
HR 3590, H-258

HR 3603, H-320
HR 3614, H-242
HR 3617, H-242
HR 3619, H-272, H-274
HR 3631, H-244
HR 3634, H-312
HR 3639, H-284, H-286, H-288
HR 3667, H-310
HR 3689, H-260
HR 3714, H-334
HR 3737, H-296
HR 3763, H-266
HR 3767, H-302
HR 3788, H-294
HR 3791, H-304, H-306
HR 3854, H-280
HR 3949, H-282
HR 3951, H-318
HR 3961, H-308
HR 3962, H-298, H-300
HR 3978, H-328
HR 3980, H-312
HR 4017, H-322
HR 4154, H-312, H-314
HR 4173, H-320, H-322, H-324,
  H-326, H-328
HR 4213, H-318, H-320
HR 4314, H-334

SENATE BILLS

S 22, H-44
S 181, H-14, H-16
S 234, H-30
S 328, H-18
S 352, H-20
S 383, H-56
S 386, H-86, H-98
S 407, H-146
S 454, H-92, H-104
S 509, H-282
S 896, H-98
S 1211, H-294
S 1314, H-302
S 1472, H-330
S 1599, H-306
S 1694, H-276
S 1793, H-266

S Con Res 13, H-72, H-76, H-78
S Con Res 30, H-200
S Con Res 31, H-160
S Con Res 43, H-268
S Con Res 45, H-278

IN THE HOUSE | By Vote Number

1. Quorum Call.* A quorum was present with 428 members responding (six members did not respond). Jan. 6, 2009.

2. Election of the Speaker. Nomination of Nancy Pelosi, D-Calif., and John A. Boehner, R-Ohio, for Speaker of the House of Representatives for the 111th Congress. Pelosi elected 255-174: R 0-174; D 255-0. [A "Y" on the chart represents a vote for Pelosi; an "N" represents a vote for Boehner. A majority of the votes cast for a person by name (215 in this case) is needed for election. All members-elect are eligible to vote on the election of the Speaker.] Jan. 6, 2009.

3. H Res 5. House Organizing Resolution/Motion to Commit. Dreier, R-Calif., motion to commit the resolution that would set the rules for the 111th Congress to a select committee comprised of the majority and minority leaders with instructions that it be reported back after striking language that would allow a motion to recommit with instructions to be offered only if the motion directs a committee to report the measure back "forthwith" and language that would remove six-year term limits on committee chairmanships. Motion rejected 174-249: R 174-0; D 0-249. Jan. 6, 2009.

4. H Res 5. House Organizing Resolution/Adoption. Adoption of the resolution that would set the rules for the 111th Congress. The rules would allow a motion to recommit with instructions to be offered only if the motion directs a committee to report the measure back "forthwith." It also would remove six-year term limits on committee chairmanships, allow exceptions to pay-as-you-go rules for provisions designated as emergency spending and allow bills that do not meet pay-as-you-go requirements to be combined with other bills that have the offsets. Adopted 242-181: R 0-175; D 242-6. Jan. 6, 2009.

5. HR 35. Presidential Records/Passage. Towns, D-N.Y., motion to suspend the rules and pass the bill that would allow a former president to request that the current president claim executive privilege over the release of the past president's records, but not require the current president to assert the privilege. Motion agreed to 359-58: R 114-58; D 245-0. A two-thirds majority of those present and voting (278 in this case) is required for passage under suspension of the rules. Jan. 7, 2009.

6. HR 36. Presidential Libraries/Passage. Towns, D-N.Y., motion to suspend the rules and pass the bill that would require fundraising organizations to report contributors whose donations to presidential libraries total $200 or more in a quarter. The report would go to the House Oversight and Government Reform Committee and the Senate Homeland Security and Governmental Affairs Committee. The measure would require the National Archives and Records Administration to post the information on a searchable public Web site. Motion agreed to 388-31: R 141-31; D 247-0. A two-thirds majority of those present and voting (280 in this case) is required for passage under suspension of the rules. Jan. 7, 2009.

	2	3	4	5	6
ALABAMA					
1 Bonner	N	Y	N	?	?
2 Bright	Y	N	Y	N	Y
3 Rogers	N	Y	N	N	N
4 Aderholt	N	Y	N	N	Y
5 Griffith	Y	N	Y	Y	Y
6 Bachus	N	Y	N	Y	Y
7 Davis	Y	N	Y	Y	Y
ALASKA					
AL Young	N	Y	N	Y	Y
ARIZONA					
1 Kirkpatrick	Y	N	Y	Y	Y
2 Franks	N	Y	N	N	N
3 Shadegg	N	Y	N	N	N
4 Pastor	Y	N	Y	Y	Y
5 Mitchell	Y	N	Y	Y	Y
6 Flake	N	Y	N	N	N
7 Grijalva	Y	N	Y	Y	Y
8 Giffords	Y	N	Y	Y	Y
ARKANSAS					
1 Berry	Y	N	Y	Y	Y
2 Snyder	Y	N	Y	?	?
3 Boozman	N	Y	N	Y	Y
4 Ross	Y	N	Y	Y	Y
CALIFORNIA					
1 Thompson	Y	N	Y	Y	Y
2 Herger	N	Y	N	Y	Y
3 Lungren	N	Y	N	N	Y
4 McClintock	N	Y	N	Y	Y
5 Matsui	Y	N	Y	Y	Y
6 Woolsey	Y	N	Y	Y	Y
7 Miller, George	Y	N	Y	Y	Y
8 Pelosi	Y		Y		
9 Lee	Y	N	Y	Y	Y
10 Tauscher	Y	N	Y	Y	Y
11 McNerney	Y	N	Y	Y	Y
12 Speier	Y	N	Y	Y	Y
13 Stark	Y	N	Y	Y	Y
14 Eshoo	Y	N	Y	Y	Y
15 Honda	Y	N	Y	Y	Y
16 Lofgren	Y	N	Y	Y	Y
17 Farr	Y	N	Y	Y	Y
18 Cardoza	Y	N	Y	Y	Y
19 Radanovich	N	Y	N	Y	Y
20 Costa	Y	N	Y	Y	Y
21 Nunes	N	Y	N	Y	+
22 McCarthy	N	Y	N	Y	Y
23 Capps	Y	N	Y	Y	Y
24 Gallegly	N	Y	N	?	?
25 McKeon	N	Y	N	Y	Y
26 Dreier	N	Y	N	Y	Y
27 Sherman	Y	N	Y	Y	Y
28 Berman	Y	N	Y	Y	Y
29 Schiff	Y	N	Y	Y	Y
30 Waxman	Y	N	Y	Y	Y
31 Becerra	Y	N	Y	Y	Y
32 Solis	Y	?	?	?	?
33 Watson	Y	N	Y	Y	Y
34 Roybal-Allard	Y	N	Y	Y	Y
35 Waters	Y	N	N	?	?
36 Harman	Y	N	Y	Y	Y
37 Richardson	Y	N	Y	Y	Y
38 Napolitano	Y	N	Y	Y	Y
39 Sánchez, Linda	Y	N	Y	Y	Y
40 Royce	N	Y	N	Y	Y
41 Lewis	N	Y	N	Y	Y
42 Miller, Gary	?	?	?	?	?
43 Baca	Y	N	Y	Y	Y
44 Calvert	N	Y	N	Y	Y
45 Bono Mack	N	Y	N	Y	Y
46 Rohrabacher	N	Y	N	Y	Y
47 Sanchez, Loretta	Y	N	?	Y	Y
48 Campbell	N	Y	N	N	N
49 Issa	N	Y	N	Y	Y
50 Bilbray	N	Y	N	Y	Y
51 Filner	Y	N	Y	Y	Y
52 Hunter	N	Y	N	Y	Y
53 Davis	Y	N	Y	Y	Y

	2	3	4	5	6
COLORADO					
1 DeGette	Y	N	Y	Y	Y
2 Polis	Y	N	Y	Y	Y
3 Salazar	Y	N	Y	Y	?
4 Markey	Y	N	Y	Y	Y
5 Lamborn	N	Y	N	N	N
6 Coffman	N	Y	N	Y	Y
7 Perlmutter	Y	N	Y	Y	Y
CONNECTICUT					
1 Larson	Y	N	Y	Y	Y
2 Courtney	Y	N	Y	Y	Y
3 DeLauro	Y	N	Y	Y	Y
4 Himes	Y	N	Y	Y	Y
5 Murphy	Y	N	Y	Y	Y
DELAWARE					
AL Castle	N	Y	N	Y	Y
FLORIDA					
1 Miller	N	Y	N	Y	Y
2 Boyd	Y	N	Y	Y	Y
3 Brown	Y	N	Y	Y	Y
4 Crenshaw	N	Y	N	Y	Y
5 Brown-Waite	N	Y	N	Y	Y
6 Stearns	N	Y	N	Y	Y
7 Mica	N	Y	N	Y	Y
8 Grayson	Y	N	Y	Y	Y
9 Bilirakis	N	Y	N	Y	Y
10 Young	N	Y	N	Y	Y
11 Castor	Y	N	Y	Y	Y
12 Putnam	N	Y	N	Y	Y
13 Buchanan	N	Y	N	Y	Y
14 Mack	N	Y	N	N	Y
15 Posey	N	?	N	Y	Y
16 Rooney	N	Y	N	N	Y
17 Meek	Y	N	Y	Y	Y
18 Ros-Lehtinen	N	Y	N	Y	Y
19 Wexler	Y	N	Y	Y	Y
20 Wasserman Schultz	Y	N	Y	Y	Y
21 Diaz-Balart, L.	N	Y	N	Y	Y
22 Klein	Y	N	Y	Y	Y
23 Hastings	Y	N	Y	Y	Y
24 Kosmas	Y	N	Y	Y	Y
25 Diaz-Balart, M.	N	Y	N	Y	Y
GEORGIA					
1 Kingston	N	Y	N	N	N
2 Bishop	Y	N	Y	Y	Y
3 Westmoreland	N	Y	N	N	N
4 Johnson	Y	N	Y	Y	Y
5 Lewis	Y	N	Y	Y	Y
6 Price	N	Y	N	N	Y
7 Linder	N	Y	N	N	Y
8 Marshall	Y	N	Y	Y	Y
9 Deal	N	Y	N	N	N
10 Broun	N	Y	N	N	N
11 Gingrey	N	Y	N	N	N
12 Barrow	Y	N	Y	Y	Y
13 Scott	Y	N	Y	Y	Y
HAWAII					
1 Abercrombie	Y	N	Y	Y	Y
2 Hirono	Y	N	Y	Y	Y
IDAHO					
1 Minnick	Y	N	N	Y	Y
2 Simpson	N	Y	N	Y	Y
ILLINOIS					
1 Rush	Y	N	Y	Y	Y
2 Jackson	Y	N	Y	Y	Y
3 Lipinski	Y	N	Y	Y	Y
4 Gutierrez	+	-	+	?	Y
5 Vacant					
6 Roskam	N	Y	N	Y	Y
7 Davis	Y	N	Y	Y	Y
8 Bean	Y	N	Y	Y	Y
9 Schakowsky	Y	N	Y	Y	Y
10 Kirk	N	Y	N	Y	Y
11 Halvorson	Y	N	Y	Y	Y
12 Costello	Y	N	Y	Y	Y
13 Biggert	N	Y	N	Y	Y
14 Foster	Y	N	Y	Y	Y
15 Johnson	N	Y	N	Y	Y

KEY   **Republicans**   Democrats

Y Voted for (yea)	X Paired against	C Voted "present" to avoid possible conflict of interest
# Paired for	– Announced against	
+ Announced for	P Voted "present"	? Did not vote or otherwise make a position known
N Voted against (nay)		

* CQ does not include quorum calls in its vote charts.

	2	3	4	5	6
16 Manzullo	N	Y	N	N	Y
17 Hare	Y	N	Y	Y	Y
18 Schock	N	Y	N	Y	Y
19 Shimkus	N	Y	N	Y	Y
INDIANA					
1 Visclosky	Y	N	Y	Y	Y
2 Donnelly	Y	N	Y	Y	Y
3 Souder	N	Y	N	Y	Y
4 Buyer	N	Y	N	Y	Y
5 Burton	N	Y	N	Y	Y
6 Pence	N	Y	N	N	Y
7 Carson	Y	N	Y	Y	Y
8 Ellsworth	Y	N	Y	Y	Y
9 Hill	Y	N	Y	Y	Y
IOWA					
1 Braley	Y	N	Y	Y	Y
2 Loebsack	Y	N	Y	Y	Y
3 Boswell	Y	N	Y	Y	Y
4 Latham	N	Y	N	Y	Y
5 King	N	Y	N	N	N
KANSAS					
1 Moran	N	Y	N	Y	Y
2 Jenkins	N	Y	N	Y	Y
3 Moore	Y	N	Y	Y	Y
4 Tiahrt	N	Y	N	Y	Y
KENTUCKY					
1 Whitfield	N	Y	N	Y	Y
2 Guthrie	N	Y	N	Y	Y
3 Yarmuth	Y	N	Y	Y	Y
4 Davis	N	Y	N	N	N
5 Rogers	N	Y	N	Y	Y
6 Chandler	Y	N	Y	Y	Y
LOUISIANA					
1 Scalise	N	Y	N	Y	Y
2 Cao	N	Y	N	Y	Y
3 Melancon	Y	N	?	Y	Y
4 Fleming	N	Y	N	N	Y
5 Alexander	N	Y	N	Y	Y
6 Cassidy	N	Y	N	N	Y
7 Boustany	N	Y	N	N	Y
MAINE					
1 Pingree	Y	N	Y	Y	Y
2 Michaud	Y	N	N	Y	Y
MARYLAND					
1 Kratovil	Y	N	Y	Y	Y
2 Ruppersberger	Y	N	Y	Y	Y
3 Sarbanes	Y	N	Y	Y	Y
4 Edwards	Y	N	Y	Y	Y
5 Hoyer	Y	N	Y	Y	Y
6 Bartlett	N	Y	N	Y	N
7 Cummings	Y	N	Y	Y	Y
8 Van Hollen	Y	N	Y	Y	Y
MASSACHUSETTS					
1 Olver	Y	N	Y	Y	Y
2 Neal	Y	N	Y	Y	Y
3 McGovern	Y	N	Y	Y	Y
4 Frank	Y	N	Y	Y	Y
5 Tsongas	Y	N	Y	Y	Y
6 Tierney	Y	N	Y	Y	Y
7 Markey	Y	N	Y	Y	Y
8 Capuano	Y	?	?	Y	Y
9 Lynch	Y	N	Y	Y	Y
10 Delahunt	Y	N	Y	Y	Y
MICHIGAN					
1 Stupak	Y	N	Y	Y	Y
2 Hoekstra	N	Y	N	Y	N
3 Ehlers	N	Y	N	Y	Y
4 Camp	N	Y	N	Y	Y
5 Kildee	Y	N	Y	Y	Y
6 Upton	N	Y	N	Y	Y
7 Schauer	Y	N	Y	Y	Y
8 Rogers	?	?	?	?	Y
9 Peters	Y	N	Y	Y	Y
10 Miller	N	Y	N	Y	Y
11 McCotter	N	Y	N	Y	Y
12 Levin	Y	N	Y	Y	Y
13 Kilpatrick	Y	N	Y	Y	Y
14 Conyers	Y	N	Y	Y	Y
15 Dingell	Y	N	Y	Y	Y
MINNESOTA					
1 Walz	Y	N	Y	Y	Y
2 Kline	N	Y	N	N	Y
3 Paulsen	N	Y	N	Y	Y
4 McCollum	Y	N	Y	Y	Y

	2	3	4	5	6
5 Ellison	Y	N	Y	Y	Y
6 Bachmann	N	Y	N	N	Y
7 Peterson	Y	N	Y	Y	Y
8 Oberstar	Y	N	Y	Y	Y
MISSISSIPPI					
1 Childers	Y	N	Y	Y	Y
2 Thompson	Y	N	Y	Y	Y
3 Harper	N	Y	N	Y	Y
4 Taylor	Y	N	Y	Y	Y
MISSOURI					
1 Clay	Y	N	Y	Y	Y
2 Akin	N	Y	N	N	N
3 Carnahan	Y	N	Y	Y	Y
4 Skelton	Y	N	Y	Y	Y
5 Cleaver	Y	N	Y	Y	Y
6 Graves	N	Y	N	?	?
7 Blunt	N	Y	N	Y	?
8 Emerson	N	Y	N	Y	Y
9 Luetkemeyer	N	Y	N	Y	Y
MONTANA					
AL Rehberg	N	Y	N	N	Y
NEBRASKA					
1 Fortenberry	N	Y	N	Y	Y
2 Terry	N	Y	N	Y	Y
3 Smith	N	Y	N	Y	Y
NEVADA					
1 Berkley	Y	N	Y	Y	Y
2 Heller	N	Y	N	Y	Y
3 Titus	Y	N	Y	Y	Y
NEW HAMPSHIRE					
1 Shea-Porter	Y	N	Y	Y	Y
2 Hodes	Y	N	Y	Y	Y
NEW JERSEY					
1 Andrews	Y	N	Y	Y	Y
2 LoBiondo	N	Y	N	Y	Y
3 Adler	Y	N	Y	Y	Y
4 Smith	N	Y	N	Y	Y
5 Garrett	N	Y	N	N	N
6 Pallone	Y	N	Y	Y	Y
7 Lance	N	Y	N	Y	Y
8 Pascrell	Y	N	Y	Y	Y
9 Rothman	Y	N	Y	Y	Y
10 Payne	Y	N	Y	Y	Y
11 Frelinghuysen	N	Y	N	Y	Y
12 Holt	Y	N	Y	Y	Y
13 Sires	Y	N	Y	Y	Y
NEW MEXICO					
1 Heinrich	Y	N	Y	Y	Y
2 Teague	Y	N	Y	Y	Y
3 Lujan	Y	N	Y	Y	Y
NEW YORK					
1 Bishop	Y	N	Y	Y	Y
2 Israel	Y	N	Y	Y	Y
3 King	N	Y	N	N	Y
4 McCarthy	Y	N	Y	Y	Y
5 Ackerman	Y	N	Y	Y	Y
6 Meeks	Y	N	Y	Y	Y
7 Crowley	Y	N	Y	Y	Y
8 Nadler	Y	N	Y	?	?
9 Weiner	Y	N	Y	Y	Y
10 Towns	Y	?	?	Y	Y
11 Clarke	Y	N	Y	Y	Y
12 Velázquez	Y	N	Y	Y	Y
13 McMahon	Y	N	Y	Y	Y
14 Maloney	Y	N	Y	Y	Y
15 Rangel	Y	N	Y	?	Y
16 Serrano	Y	N	Y	Y	Y
17 Engel	Y	N	Y	Y	Y
18 Lowey	Y	N	Y	Y	Y
19 Hall	Y	N	Y	Y	Y
20 Gillibrand	Y	N	Y	Y	Y
21 Tonko	Y	N	Y	Y	Y
22 Hinchey	Y	N	Y	Y	Y
23 McHugh	N	Y	N	Y	Y
24 Arcuri	Y	N	Y	Y	Y
25 Maffei	Y	N	Y	Y	Y
26 Lee	N	Y	N	Y	Y
27 Higgins	Y	N	Y	Y	Y
28 Slaughter	Y	N	Y	Y	Y
29 Massa	Y	N	Y	Y	Y
NORTH CAROLINA					
1 Butterfield	Y	N	Y	Y	?
2 Etheridge	Y	N	Y	Y	Y
3 Jones	N	Y	N	Y	Y
4 Price	Y	N	Y	Y	Y

	2	3	4	5	6
5 Foxx	N	Y	N	N	N
6 Coble	N	Y	N	Y	Y
7 McIntyre	Y	N	Y	Y	Y
8 Kissell	Y	N	Y	Y	Y
9 Myrick	N	Y	N	N	N
10 McHenry	N	Y	N	N	N
11 Shuler	Y	N	Y	Y	Y
12 Watt	Y	N	Y	Y	Y
13 Miller	Y	N	Y	Y	Y
NORTH DAKOTA					
AL Pomeroy	Y	N	?	Y	Y
OHIO					
1 Driehaus	Y	N	Y	Y	Y
2 Schmidt	N	Y	N	Y	Y
3 Turner	N	Y	N	Y	Y
4 Jordan	N	Y	N	N	Y
5 Latta	N	Y	N	Y	Y
6 Wilson	Y	N	Y	Y	Y
7 Austria	N	Y	N	Y	Y
8 Boehner	?	Y	N	N	Y
9 Kaptur	Y	N	Y	Y	Y
10 Kucinich	Y	N	Y	Y	Y
11 Fudge	Y	N	Y	Y	Y
12 Tiberi	N	Y	N	Y	Y
13 Sutton	Y	N	Y	Y	Y
14 LaTourette	N	Y	N	Y	Y
15 Kilroy	Y	N	Y	Y	Y
16 Boccieri	Y	N	Y	Y	Y
17 Ryan	Y	N	Y	Y	Y
18 Space	Y	N	Y	Y	Y
OKLAHOMA					
1 Sullivan	N	Y	N	Y	Y
2 Boren	Y	N	Y	Y	Y
3 Lucas	N	Y	N	Y	Y
4 Cole	N	Y	N	Y	Y
5 Fallin	N	Y	N	N	Y
OREGON					
1 Wu	Y	N	Y	Y	Y
2 Walden	N	Y	N	Y	Y
3 Blumenauer	Y	N	Y	?	Y
4 DeFazio	Y	N	Y	Y	Y
5 Schrader	Y	N	Y	Y	Y
PENNSYLVANIA					
1 Brady	Y	N	Y	Y	Y
2 Fattah	Y	N	Y	Y	Y
3 Dahlkemper	Y	N	Y	Y	Y
4 Altmire	Y	N	Y	Y	Y
5 Thompson	N	Y	N	Y	Y
6 Gerlach	N	Y	N	Y	Y
7 Sestak	Y	N	Y	Y	Y
8 Murphy, P.	Y	N	Y	Y	Y
9 Shuster	N	Y	N	N	Y
10 Carney	Y	N	Y	Y	Y
11 Kanjorski	Y	N	Y	Y	Y
12 Murtha	Y	N	Y	Y	Y
13 Schwartz	Y	N	Y	Y	Y
14 Doyle	Y	N	Y	Y	Y
15 Dent	N	Y	N	Y	Y
16 Pitts	N	Y	N	N	Y
17 Holden	Y	N	Y	Y	Y
18 Murphy, T.	N	Y	N	Y	Y
19 Platts	N	Y	N	Y	Y
RHODE ISLAND					
1 Kennedy	Y	N	Y	Y	Y
2 Langevin	Y	N	Y	Y	Y
SOUTH CAROLINA					
1 Brown	N	Y	N	Y	Y
2 Wilson	N	Y	N	Y	Y
3 Barrett	N	Y	N	N	Y
4 Inglis	N	Y	N	N	Y
5 Spratt	Y	N	Y	Y	Y
6 Clyburn	Y	N	Y	Y	Y
SOUTH DAKOTA					
AL Herseth Sandlin	Y	?	Y	+	+
TENNESSEE					
1 Roe	N	Y	N	Y	Y
2 Duncan	N	Y	N	Y	Y
3 Wamp	N	Y	N	Y	Y
4 Davis, L.	Y	N	Y	Y	Y
5 Cooper	Y	N	Y	Y	Y
6 Gordon	Y	N	Y	Y	Y
7 Blackburn	N	Y	N	N	Y
8 Tanner	Y	N	Y	Y	Y
9 Cohen	Y	N	Y	Y	Y

	2	3	4	5	6
TEXAS					
1 Gohmert	N	Y	N	Y	N
2 Poe	N	Y	N	N	N
3 Johnson, S.	N	Y	N	N	N
4 Hall	N	Y	N	N	Y
5 Hensarling	N	Y	N	N	N
6 Barton	N	Y	N	N	N
7 Culberson	N	Y	N	N	N
8 Brady	N	Y	N	Y	Y
9 Green, A.	Y	N	Y	Y	Y
10 McCaul	N	Y	N	Y	Y
11 Conaway	N	Y	N	N	N
12 Granger	N	Y	N	N	Y
13 Thornberry	N	Y	N	N	Y
14 Paul	N	Y	N	N	N
15 Hinojosa	Y	N	Y	Y	Y
16 Reyes	Y	N	Y	Y	Y
17 Edwards	Y	N	Y	Y	Y
18 Jackson Lee	Y	N	Y	Y	Y
19 Neugebauer	N	Y	N	N	Y
20 Gonzalez	Y	N	Y	Y	Y
21 Smith	N	Y	N	N	Y
22 Olson	N	Y	N	N	Y
23 Rodriguez	Y	N	Y	Y	Y
24 Marchant	N	Y	N	Y	Y
25 Doggett	Y	N	Y	Y	Y
26 Burgess	N	Y	N	Y	N
27 Ortiz	Y	N	Y	Y	Y
28 Cuellar	Y	N	Y	Y	Y
29 Green, G.	Y	N	Y	Y	Y
30 Johnson, E.	Y	N	Y	Y	Y
31 Carter	N	Y	N	N	N
32 Sessions	N	Y	N	N	Y
UTAH					
1 Bishop	N	Y	N	Y	Y
2 Matheson	Y	N	Y	Y	Y
3 Chaffetz	N	Y	N	N	Y
VERMONT					
AL Welch	Y	N	Y	Y	Y
VIRGINIA					
1 Wittman	Y	N	N	Y	Y
2 Nye	Y	N	Y	Y	Y
3 Scott	Y	N	Y	Y	Y
4 Forbes	N	Y	N	N	N
5 Perriello	Y	N	Y	Y	Y
6 Goodlatte	N	Y	N	Y	Y
7 Cantor	N	Y	N	N	Y
8 Moran	Y	N	Y	Y	Y
9 Boucher	Y	?	?	?	?
10 Wolf	N	Y	N	Y	Y
11 Connolly	Y	N	Y	Y	Y
WASHINGTON					
1 Inslee	Y	N	Y	Y	Y
2 Larsen	Y	N	Y	Y	Y
3 Baird	Y	N	N	Y	Y
4 Hastings	?	?	?	?	Y
5 McMorris Rodgers	N	Y	N	Y	Y
6 Dicks	Y	N	Y	Y	Y
7 McDermott	Y	N	Y	Y	Y
8 Reichert	N	Y	N	Y	Y
9 Smith	Y	N	Y	Y	Y
WEST VIRGINIA					
1 Mollohan	Y	N	Y	Y	Y
2 Capito	N	Y	N	Y	Y
3 Rahall	Y	N	Y	Y	Y
WISCONSIN					
1 Ryan	N	Y	N	Y	Y
2 Baldwin	Y	N	Y	Y	Y
3 Kind	Y	N	Y	?	Y
4 Moore	Y	N	Y	Y	Y
5 Sensenbrenner	N	Y	N	Y	Y
6 Petri	N	Y	N	Y	Y
7 Obey	Y	N	Y	Y	Y
8 Kagen	Y	N	Y	Y	Y
WYOMING					
AL Lummis	N	Y	N	Y	N
DELEGATES					
Faleomavaega (A.S.)					
Norton (D.C.)					
Bordallo (Guam)					
Sablan (N. Marianas)					
Pierluisi (P.R.)					
Christensen (V.I.)					

IN THE HOUSE | By Vote Number

7. HR 12. Paycheck Equality/Recommit. Price, R-Ga., motion to recommit the bill to the Education and Labor Committee with instructions that it be reported back forthwith with an amendment stipulating that employers found liable would not be required to compensate for expert fees in excess of $2,000 per hour in discrimination cases described in the measure. Motion rejected 178-240: R 169-1; D 9-239. Jan. 9, 2009.

8. HR 12. Paycheck Equality/Passage. Passage of the bill that would require employers seeking to justify unequal pay for male and female workers to prove that such disparities are job-related and required by a business necessity. It would bar retaliation by employers against employees who share salary information with their co-workers. Workers who won wage discrimination cases could collect compensatory and punitive damages. Passed 256-163: R 10-160; D 246-3. Jan. 9, 2009.

9. HR 11. Wage Discrimination/Passage. Passage of the bill that would amend the 1964 Civil Rights Act to allow employees to file charges of pay discrimination within 180 days of the last paycheck that is affected by the alleged discrimination. The bill would clarify that an employee is entitled to up to two years of back pay if it is determined that discrimination occurred. Passed 247-171: R 3-166; D 244-5. Jan. 9, 2009.

10. H Res 34. Israeli-Palestinian Conflict/Adoption. Berman, D-Calif., motion to suspend the rules and adopt the resolution that would express support and a commitment for the security of Israel, express that Hamas must end attacks against Israel, and reiterate support for a resolution of Israeli-Palestinian conflict achieved through negotiations. Motion agreed to 390-5: R 168-1; D 222-4. A two-thirds majority of those present and voting (264 in this case) is required for adoption under suspension of the rules. Jan. 9, 2009.

11. H Res 41. National Mentoring Month/Adoption. Hinojosa, D-Texas, motion to suspend the rules and adopt the resolution that would support the goals and ideals of a National Mentoring Month, recognize those who volunteer to mentor children and encourage more people to volunteer as mentors. Motion agreed to 411-0: R 167-0; D 244-0. A two-thirds majority of those present and voting (274 in this case) is required for adoption under suspension of the rules. Jan. 13, 2009.

12. H Res 50. Claiborne Pell Tribute/Adoption. Hinojosa, D-Texas, motion to suspend the rules and adopt the resolution that would honor the life of former Rhode Island Democratic Sen. Claiborne Pell (1961-97), who died Jan. 1, 2009, at age 90. Pell was the original sponsor of the legislation that created the Pell grant, a program that provides financial aid to college students. Motion agreed to 415-0: R 170-0; D 245-0. A two-thirds majority of those present and voting (277 in this case) is required for adoption under suspension of the rules. Jan. 13, 2009.

13. H Res 43. Martin Luther King Jr. Tribute/Adoption. Hinojosa, D-Texas, motion to suspend the rules and adopt the resolution that would encourage Americans to pay tribute to Dr. Martin Luther King Jr. through community service projects on Martin Luther King Day. Motion agreed to 415-0: R 169-0; D 246-0. A two-thirds majority of those present and voting (277 in this case) is required for adoption under suspension of the rules. Jan. 13, 2009.

	7	8	9	10	11	12	13
ALABAMA							
1 **Bonner**	Y	N	N	Y	Y	Y	Y
2 **Bright**	Y	N	N	Y	Y	Y	Y
3 **Rogers**	Y	N	N	Y	Y	Y	Y
4 **Aderholt**	Y	N	N	Y	Y	Y	Y
5 Griffith	N	N	N	Y	Y	Y	Y
6 **Bachus**	Y	N	–	Y	Y	Y	Y
7 Davis	N	Y	Y	Y	Y	Y	Y
ALASKA							
AL **Young**	Y	N	Y	Y	Y	Y	Y
ARIZONA							
1 Kirkpatrick	N	Y	Y	Y	Y	Y	Y
2 **Franks**	Y	N	N	Y	Y	Y	Y
3 **Shadegg**	?	?	?	?	Y	Y	Y
4 Pastor	N	Y	Y	Y	Y	Y	Y
5 Mitchell	Y	Y	Y	Y	Y	Y	Y
6 **Flake**	Y	N	N	Y	Y	Y	Y
7 Grijalva	N	Y	Y	P	?	?	?
8 Giffords	N	Y	Y	Y	Y	Y	Y
ARKANSAS							
1 Berry	?	?	?	?	Y	Y	Y
2 Snyder	?	?	?	?	?	?	?
3 **Boozman**	Y	N	N	Y	Y	Y	Y
4 Ross	N	Y	Y	Y	Y	Y	Y
CALIFORNIA							
1 Thompson	N	Y	Y	Y	Y	Y	Y
2 **Herger**	Y	N	N	Y	Y	Y	Y
3 **Lungren**	Y	N	N	Y	Y	Y	Y
4 **McClintock**	Y	N	N	Y	Y	Y	Y
5 Matsui	N	Y	Y	Y	Y	Y	Y
6 Woolsey	N	Y	Y	P	Y	Y	Y
7 Miller, George	N	Y	Y	P	Y	Y	Y
8 Pelosi		Y	Y	Y			
9 Lee	N	Y	Y	P	Y	Y	Y
10 Tauscher	N	Y	Y	Y	Y	Y	Y
11 McNerney	N	Y	Y	Y	Y	Y	Y
12 Speier	N	Y	Y	Y	Y	Y	Y
13 Stark	N	Y	Y	P	Y	Y	Y
14 Eshoo	N	Y	Y	Y	Y	Y	Y
15 Honda	N	Y	Y	Y	+	Y	Y
16 Lofgren	N	Y	Y	Y	Y	Y	Y
17 Farr	N	Y	Y	P	Y	Y	Y
18 Cardoza	N	Y	Y	Y	Y	Y	Y
19 **Radanovich**	Y	N	N	Y	Y	Y	Y
20 Costa	N	Y	Y	Y	Y	Y	Y
21 **Nunes**	Y	N	N	Y	Y	Y	Y
22 **McCarthy**	Y	N	N	Y	Y	Y	Y
23 Capps	N	Y	Y	Y	Y	Y	Y
24 **Gallegly**	?	?	?	?	?	?	?
25 **McKeon**	Y	N	N	Y	Y	Y	Y
26 **Dreier**	Y	N	N	Y	Y	Y	Y
27 Sherman	N	Y	Y	Y	Y	Y	Y
28 Berman	N	Y	Y	?	Y	Y	Y
29 Schiff	N	Y	Y	Y	Y	Y	Y
30 Waxman	N	Y	Y	Y	Y	Y	Y
31 Becerra	N	Y	Y	Y	Y	Y	Y
32 Solis	?	Y	Y	?	?	?	?
33 Watson	N	Y	Y	P	?	Y	Y
34 Roybal-Allard	N	Y	Y	Y	Y	Y	Y
35 Waters	N	Y	Y	N	Y	Y	Y
36 Harman	N	Y	Y	Y	Y	Y	Y
37 Richardson	N	Y	Y	Y	Y	Y	Y
38 Napolitano	N	Y	Y	Y	Y	Y	Y
39 Sánchez, Linda	N	Y	Y	Y	Y	Y	Y
40 **Royce**	Y	N	N	Y	Y	Y	Y
41 **Lewis**	Y	N	N	Y	Y	Y	Y
42 **Miller, Gary**	?	?	?	?	?	Y	Y
43 Baca	N	Y	Y	Y	Y	Y	Y
44 **Calvert**	Y	N	N	Y	Y	Y	Y
45 **Bono Mack**	Y	N	N	Y	Y	Y	Y
46 **Rohrabacher**	Y	N	N	Y	?	?	?
47 Sanchez, Loretta	N	Y	Y	P	Y	Y	Y
48 **Campbell**	Y	N	N	Y	Y	Y	Y
49 **Issa**	Y	N	N	Y	Y	Y	Y
50 **Bilbray**	Y	N	N	Y	Y	Y	Y
51 Filner	N	Y	Y	Y	Y	Y	Y
52 **Hunter**	Y	N	N	Y	Y	Y	Y
53 Davis	N	Y	Y	Y	Y	Y	Y

	7	8	9	10	11	12	13
COLORADO							
1 DeGette	N	Y	Y	Y	Y	Y	Y
2 Polis	N	Y	Y	Y	Y	Y	Y
3 Salazar	N	Y	Y	Y	Y	Y	Y
4 Markey	N	Y	Y	Y	Y	Y	Y
5 **Lamborn**	Y	N	N	Y	Y	Y	Y
6 **Coffman**	Y	N	N	Y	Y	Y	Y
7 Perlmutter	N	Y	Y	Y	Y	Y	Y
CONNECTICUT							
1 Larson	N	Y	Y	Y	Y	Y	Y
2 Courtney	N	Y	Y	Y	Y	Y	Y
3 DeLauro	N	Y	Y	Y	Y	Y	Y
4 Himes	N	Y	Y	Y	Y	Y	Y
5 Murphy	N	Y	Y	Y	Y	Y	Y
DELAWARE							
AL **Castle**	Y	Y	N	Y	Y	Y	Y
FLORIDA							
1 **Miller**	Y	N	N	Y	Y	Y	Y
2 Boyd	N	Y	N	Y	Y	Y	Y
3 Brown	N	Y	Y	Y	Y	Y	Y
4 **Crenshaw**	Y	N	N	Y	Y	Y	Y
5 **Brown-Waite**	Y	N	N	Y	Y	Y	Y
6 **Stearns**	Y	N	N	Y	Y	Y	Y
7 **Mica**	Y	N	N	Y	Y	Y	Y
8 Grayson	N	Y	Y	Y	Y	Y	Y
9 **Bilirakis**	Y	N	N	Y	Y	Y	Y
10 **Young**	Y	N	N	Y	Y	Y	Y
11 Castor	N	Y	Y	Y	Y	Y	Y
12 **Putnam**	Y	N	N	Y	Y	Y	Y
13 **Buchanan**	Y	N	N	Y	Y	Y	Y
14 **Mack**	Y	N	N	Y	Y	Y	Y
15 **Posey**	Y	N	N	Y	Y	Y	Y
16 **Rooney**	Y	N	N	Y	Y	Y	Y
17 Meek	N	Y	Y	Y	Y	Y	Y
18 **Ros-Lehtinen**	Y	N	N	Y	Y	Y	Y
19 Wexler	N	Y	Y	Y	Y	Y	Y
20 Wasserman Schultz	N	Y	Y	Y	Y	Y	Y
21 **Diaz-Balart, L.**	Y	N	Y	Y	Y	Y	Y
22 Klein	N	Y	Y	Y	Y	Y	Y
23 Hastings	N	Y	Y	Y	Y	Y	Y
24 Kosmas	N	Y	Y	Y	Y	Y	Y
25 **Diaz-Balart, M.**	Y	Y	N	Y	Y	Y	Y
GEORGIA							
1 **Kingston**	Y	N	N	Y	Y	Y	Y
2 Bishop	N	Y	Y	Y	Y	Y	Y
3 **Westmoreland**	Y	N	N	Y	Y	Y	Y
4 Johnson	N	Y	Y	P	Y	Y	Y
5 Lewis	N	Y	Y	Y	Y	Y	Y
6 **Price**	Y	N	N	Y	Y	Y	Y
7 **Linder**	Y	N	N	Y	Y	Y	Y
8 Marshall	Y	Y	Y	Y	Y	Y	Y
9 **Deal**	Y	N	N	Y	Y	Y	Y
10 **Broun**	Y	N	N	Y	Y	Y	Y
11 **Gingrey**	Y	N	N	Y	Y	Y	Y
12 Barrow	N	Y	Y	Y	Y	Y	Y
13 Scott	N	Y	Y	Y	Y	Y	Y
HAWAII							
1 Abercrombie	N	Y	Y	P	Y	Y	Y
2 Hirono	N	Y	Y	Y	Y	Y	Y
IDAHO							
1 Minnick	Y	N	Y	Y	Y	Y	Y
2 **Simpson**	Y	N	N	Y	Y	Y	Y
ILLINOIS							
1 Rush	N	Y	Y	Y	Y	Y	Y
2 Jackson	N	Y	Y	Y	Y	Y	Y
3 Lipinski	N	Y	Y	Y	Y	Y	Y
4 Gutierrez	N	Y	Y	Y	Y	Y	Y
5 Vacant							
6 **Roskam**	Y	N	N	Y	Y	Y	Y
7 Davis	N	Y	Y	Y	Y	Y	Y
8 Bean	N	Y	Y	Y	Y	Y	Y
9 Schakowsky	N	Y	Y	Y	Y	Y	Y
10 **Kirk**	Y	N	N	Y	Y	Y	Y
11 Halvorson	N	Y	Y	Y	Y	Y	Y
12 Costello	N	Y	Y	Y	Y	Y	Y
13 **Biggert**	Y	N	N	Y	Y	Y	Y
14 Foster	N	Y	Y	Y	Y	Y	Y
15 **Johnson**	N	Y	N	Y	Y	Y	Y

KEY | **Republicans** | Democrats

Y Voted for (yea)	X Paired against	C Voted "present" to avoid possible conflict of interest
# Paired for	– Announced against	
+ Announced for	P Voted "present"	? Did not vote or otherwise make a position known
N Voted against (nay)		

	7	8	9	10	11	12	13
16 **Manzullo**	Y	N	N	Y	Y	Y	Y
17 Hare	N	Y	Y	Y	Y	Y	Y
18 **Schock**	Y	N	N	Y	Y	Y	Y
19 **Shimkus**	Y	N	N	Y	Y	Y	Y
INDIANA							
1 Visclosky	N	Y	Y	Y	?	?	?
2 Donnelly	N	Y	Y	Y	Y	Y	Y
3 **Souder**	Y	N	N	Y	?	?	?
4 **Buyer**	Y	N	N	Y	Y	Y	Y
5 **Burton**	Y	N	N	Y	Y	Y	Y
6 **Pence**	Y	N	N	Y	Y	Y	Y
7 Carson	N	Y	Y	Y	Y	Y	Y
8 Ellsworth	N	Y	Y	Y	Y	Y	Y
9 Hill	N	Y	Y	Y	Y	Y	Y
IOWA							
1 Braley	N	Y	Y	Y	Y	Y	Y
2 Loebsack	N	Y	Y	Y	Y	Y	Y
3 Boswell	N	Y	Y	Y	Y	Y	Y
4 **Latham**	Y	N	N	Y	Y	Y	Y
5 **King**	Y	N	N	Y	Y	Y	Y
KANSAS							
1 **Moran**	Y	N	N	Y	?	?	?
2 **Jenkins**	Y	N	N	Y	Y	Y	Y
3 Moore	N	Y	Y	Y	Y	Y	Y
4 **Tiahrt**	?	?	?	?	Y	Y	Y
KENTUCKY							
1 **Whitfield**	Y	N	Y	Y	Y	Y	Y
2 **Guthrie**	Y	N	N	Y	Y	Y	Y
3 Yarmuth	N	Y	Y	Y	Y	Y	Y
4 **Davis**	Y	N	N	Y	Y	Y	Y
5 **Rogers**	Y	N	N	Y	Y	Y	Y
6 Chandler	N	Y	Y	Y	Y	Y	Y
LOUISIANA							
1 **Scalise**	Y	N	N	Y	Y	Y	Y
2 **Cao**	Y	Y	N	Y	Y	Y	Y
3 Melancon	N	Y	Y	Y	Y	Y	Y
4 **Fleming**	Y	N	N	Y	Y	Y	Y
5 **Alexander**	Y	N	N	Y	?	Y	Y
6 **Cassidy**	Y	N	N	Y	Y	Y	Y
7 **Boustany**	Y	N	N	Y	Y	Y	Y
MAINE							
1 Pingree	N	Y	Y	Y	Y	Y	Y
2 Michaud	N	Y	Y	Y	Y	Y	Y
MARYLAND							
1 Kratovil	N	Y	Y	Y	Y	Y	Y
2 Ruppersberger	N	Y	Y	Y	Y	Y	Y
3 Sarbanes	N	Y	Y	Y	Y	Y	Y
4 Edwards	N	Y	Y	P	Y	Y	Y
5 Hoyer	N	Y	Y	Y	Y	Y	Y
6 **Bartlett**	Y	N	N	Y	Y	Y	Y
7 Cummings	N	Y	Y	Y	Y	Y	Y
8 Van Hollen	N	Y	Y	Y	Y	Y	Y
MASSACHUSETTS							
1 Olver	N	Y	Y	P	Y	Y	Y
2 Neal	N	Y	Y	Y	Y	Y	Y
3 McGovern	N	Y	Y	Y	Y	Y	Y
4 Frank	N	Y	Y	Y	Y	Y	Y
5 Tsongas	N	Y	Y	Y	Y	Y	Y
6 Tierney	N	Y	Y	Y	Y	Y	Y
7 Markey	N	Y	Y	Y	Y	Y	Y
8 Capuano	N	Y	Y	Y	Y	Y	Y
9 Lynch	N	Y	Y	Y	Y	Y	Y
10 Delahunt	N	Y	Y	?	Y	Y	Y
MICHIGAN							
1 Stupak	N	Y	Y	Y	Y	Y	Y
2 **Hoekstra**	Y	N	N	Y	Y	Y	Y
3 **Ehlers**	Y	N	N	Y	Y	Y	Y
4 **Camp**	Y	N	N	Y	Y	Y	Y
5 Kildee	N	Y	Y	Y	Y	Y	Y
6 **Upton**	Y	N	N	Y	Y	Y	Y
7 Schauer	N	Y	Y	Y	Y	Y	Y
8 **Rogers**	Y	N	N	Y	Y	Y	Y
9 Peters	N	Y	Y	Y	Y	Y	Y
10 **Miller**	Y	N	N	Y	Y	Y	Y
11 **McCotter**	Y	N	N	Y	Y	Y	Y
12 Levin	N	Y	Y	Y	Y	Y	Y
13 Kilpatrick	N	Y	Y	P	Y	Y	Y
14 Conyers	N	Y	Y	Y	Y	Y	Y
15 Dingell	N	Y	Y	P	Y	Y	Y
MINNESOTA							
1 Walz	N	Y	Y	Y	Y	Y	Y
2 **Kline**	Y	N	N	Y	Y	Y	Y
3 **Paulsen**	Y	N	N	Y	Y	Y	Y
4 McCollum	N	Y	Y	P	Y	Y	Y

	7	8	9	10	11	12	13
5 Ellison	N	Y	Y	P	Y	Y	Y
6 **Bachmann**	Y	N	N	Y	Y	Y	Y
7 Peterson	N	Y	Y	Y	Y	Y	Y
8 Oberstar	N	Y	Y	Y	Y	Y	Y
MISSISSIPPI							
1 Childers	Y	Y	N	Y	Y	Y	Y
2 Thompson	N	Y	Y	Y	Y	Y	Y
3 **Harper**	Y	N	N	Y	Y	Y	Y
4 Taylor	Y	Y	Y	Y	Y	Y	Y
MISSOURI							
1 Clay	N	Y	Y	Y	Y	Y	Y
2 **Akin**	Y	N	N	Y	Y	Y	Y
3 Carnahan	N	Y	Y	Y	Y	Y	Y
4 Skelton	N	Y	Y	Y	Y	Y	Y
5 Cleaver	N	Y	Y	Y	Y	Y	Y
6 **Graves**	+	–	–	+	Y	Y	Y
7 **Blunt**	Y	N	N	Y	Y	Y	Y
8 **Emerson**	Y	N	N	Y	Y	Y	Y
9 **Luetkemeyer**	Y	N	N	Y	Y	Y	Y
MONTANA							
AL **Rehberg**	Y	N	N	Y	Y	Y	Y
NEBRASKA							
1 **Fortenberry**	Y	N	N	Y	Y	Y	Y
2 **Terry**	Y	N	N	Y	Y	Y	Y
3 **Smith**	Y	N	N	Y	Y	Y	Y
NEVADA							
1 Berkley	N	Y	Y	Y	Y	Y	Y
2 **Heller**	Y	N	N	Y	Y	Y	Y
3 Titus	N	Y	Y	Y	Y	Y	Y
NEW HAMPSHIRE							
1 Shea-Porter	N	Y	Y	Y	Y	Y	Y
2 Hodes	N	Y	Y	Y	Y	Y	Y
NEW JERSEY							
1 Andrews	N	Y	Y	Y	Y	Y	Y
2 **LoBiondo**	Y	N	N	Y	Y	Y	Y
3 Adler	N	Y	Y	Y	Y	Y	Y
4 **Smith**	Y	Y	Y	Y	Y	Y	Y
5 **Garrett**	Y	N	N	Y	Y	Y	Y
6 Pallone	N	Y	Y	Y	Y	Y	Y
7 **Lance**	Y	N	N	Y	Y	Y	Y
8 Pascrell	N	Y	Y	Y	Y	Y	Y
9 Rothman	N	Y	Y	Y	Y	Y	Y
10 Payne	N	Y	Y	P	Y	Y	Y
11 **Frelinghuysen**	Y	N	N	Y	Y	Y	Y
12 Holt	N	Y	Y	Y	Y	Y	Y
13 Sires	N	Y	Y	Y	Y	Y	Y
NEW MEXICO							
1 Heinrich	N	Y	Y	Y	Y	Y	Y
2 Teague	N	Y	Y	Y	Y	Y	Y
3 Lujan	N	Y	Y	Y	Y	Y	Y
NEW YORK							
1 Bishop	N	Y	Y	Y	Y	Y	Y
2 Israel	N	Y	Y	Y	Y	Y	Y
3 **King**	Y	N	N	Y	Y	Y	Y
4 McCarthy	N	Y	Y	Y	Y	Y	Y
5 Ackerman	N	Y	Y	Y	Y	Y	Y
6 Meeks	N	Y	Y	Y	Y	?	Y
7 Crowley	N	Y	Y	Y	Y	Y	Y
8 Nadler	N	+	Y	Y	Y	Y	Y
9 Weiner	N	Y	Y	Y	Y	Y	Y
10 Towns	N	Y	Y	Y	Y	Y	Y
11 Clarke	N	Y	Y	Y	Y	Y	Y
12 Velázquez	N	Y	Y	Y	Y	Y	Y
13 McMahon	N	Y	Y	Y	Y	Y	Y
14 Maloney	N	Y	Y	Y	Y	Y	Y
15 Rangel	N	Y	Y	Y	Y	Y	Y
16 Serrano	N	Y	Y	Y	Y	Y	Y
17 Engel	N	Y	Y	Y	Y	Y	Y
18 Lowey	N	Y	Y	Y	Y	Y	Y
19 Hall	N	Y	Y	Y	Y	Y	Y
20 Gillibrand	N	Y	Y	Y	Y	Y	Y
21 Tonko	N	Y	Y	Y	Y	Y	Y
22 Hinchey	N	Y	Y	P	Y	Y	Y
23 **McHugh**	Y	N	N	Y	Y	Y	Y
24 Arcuri	N	Y	Y	Y	Y	Y	Y
25 Maffei	N	Y	Y	Y	Y	Y	Y
26 **Lee**	Y	N	N	Y	Y	Y	Y
27 Higgins	N	Y	Y	Y	Y	Y	Y
28 Slaughter	N	Y	Y	Y	Y	Y	Y
29 Massa	N	Y	Y	Y	?	?	?
NORTH CAROLINA							
1 Butterfield	N	Y	Y	Y	Y	Y	Y
2 Etheridge	N	Y	Y	Y	Y	Y	Y
3 **Jones**	?	?	?	?	Y	Y	Y
4 Price	N	Y	Y	Y	Y	Y	Y

	7	8	9	10	11	12	13
5 **Foxx**	Y	N	N	Y	Y	Y	Y
6 **Coble**	Y	N	N	Y	Y	Y	Y
7 McIntyre	N	Y	Y	Y	Y	Y	Y
8 Kissell	N	Y	Y	Y	Y	Y	Y
9 **Myrick**	Y	N	N	Y	Y	Y	Y
10 **McHenry**	Y	N	N	Y	Y	Y	Y
11 Shuler	Y	Y	Y	Y	Y	Y	Y
12 Watt	N	Y	Y	Y	Y	Y	Y
13 Miller	N	Y	Y	Y	Y	Y	Y
NORTH DAKOTA							
AL Pomeroy	N	Y	Y	Y	Y	Y	Y
OHIO							
1 Driehaus	N	Y	Y	Y	Y	Y	Y
2 **Schmidt**	Y	N	N	Y	Y	Y	Y
3 **Turner**	Y	N	N	Y	Y	Y	Y
4 **Jordan**	Y	N	N	Y	Y	Y	Y
5 **Latta**	Y	N	N	Y	Y	Y	Y
6 Wilson	N	Y	Y	Y	Y	Y	Y
7 **Austria**	Y	N	N	Y	Y	Y	Y
8 **Boehner**	Y	N	N	Y	Y	Y	Y
9 Kaptur	N	Y	Y	Y	Y	Y	Y
10 Kucinich	N	Y	Y	N	Y	Y	Y
11 Fudge	N	Y	Y	Y	Y	Y	Y
12 **Tiberi**	Y	N	N	Y	Y	Y	Y
13 Sutton	N	Y	Y	Y	Y	Y	Y
14 **LaTourette**	Y	N	N	Y	Y	Y	Y
15 Kilroy	N	Y	Y	Y	Y	Y	Y
16 Boccieri	N	Y	Y	Y	Y	Y	Y
17 Ryan	N	Y	Y	Y	Y	Y	Y
18 Space	N	Y	Y	Y	Y	Y	Y
OKLAHOMA							
1 **Sullivan**	Y	N	N	Y	?	?	?
2 Boren	N	Y	N	Y	Y	Y	Y
3 **Lucas**	Y	N	N	Y	Y	Y	Y
4 **Cole**	Y	N	N	Y	Y	Y	Y
5 **Fallin**	Y	N	N	Y	Y	Y	Y
OREGON							
1 Wu	N	Y	Y	Y	Y	Y	Y
2 **Walden**	Y	N	N	Y	Y	Y	Y
3 Blumenauer	N	Y	Y	P	?	?	?
4 DeFazio	N	Y	Y	P	Y	Y	Y
5 Schrader	N	Y	Y	Y	Y	Y	Y
PENNSYLVANIA							
1 Brady	N	Y	Y	Y	Y	Y	Y
2 Fattah	N	Y	Y	Y	Y	Y	Y
3 Dahlkemper	N	Y	Y	Y	Y	Y	Y
4 Altmire	N	Y	Y	Y	Y	Y	Y
5 **Thompson**	Y	N	N	Y	Y	Y	Y
6 **Gerlach**	Y	Y	N	Y	Y	Y	Y
7 Sestak	N	Y	Y	Y	Y	Y	Y
8 Murphy, P.	N	Y	Y	Y	Y	Y	Y
9 **Shuster**	Y	N	N	Y	Y	Y	Y
10 Carney	Y	Y	Y	Y	Y	Y	Y
11 Kanjorski	N	Y	Y	Y	Y	Y	Y
12 Murtha	N	Y	Y	Y	Y	Y	Y
13 Schwartz	N	Y	Y	Y	Y	Y	Y
14 Doyle	N	Y	Y	Y	Y	Y	Y
15 **Dent**	Y	Y	N	Y	Y	Y	Y
16 **Pitts**	Y	N	N	Y	Y	Y	Y
17 Holden	N	Y	Y	Y	Y	Y	Y
18 **Murphy, T.**	Y	N	N	Y	Y	Y	Y
19 **Platts**	Y	N	N	Y	Y	Y	Y
RHODE ISLAND							
1 Kennedy	N	Y	Y	Y	Y	Y	Y
2 Langevin	N	Y	Y	Y	Y	Y	Y
SOUTH CAROLINA							
1 **Brown**	+	–	?	?	Y	Y	Y
2 **Wilson**	Y	N	N	Y	Y	Y	Y
3 **Barrett**	Y	N	N	Y	+	+	–
4 **Inglis**	Y	N	N	Y	Y	Y	Y
5 Spratt	N	Y	Y	Y	Y	Y	Y
6 Clyburn	N	Y	Y	Y	Y	Y	Y
SOUTH DAKOTA							
AL Herseth Sandlin	?	?	+	+	+	+	+
TENNESSEE							
1 **Roe**	Y	N	N	Y	Y	Y	Y
2 **Duncan**	Y	N	N	Y	Y	Y	Y
3 **Wamp**	Y	N	N	Y	?	?	?
4 Davis, L.	N	Y	Y	Y	Y	Y	Y
5 Cooper	N	Y	Y	Y	Y	Y	Y
6 Gordon	N	Y	Y	Y	Y	Y	Y
7 **Blackburn**	Y	N	N	Y	Y	Y	Y
8 Tanner	N	Y	Y	Y	Y	Y	Y
9 Cohen	N	Y	Y	Y	Y	Y	Y

	7	8	9	10	11	12	13
TEXAS							
1 **Gohmert**	Y	N	N	Y	?	Y	Y
2 **Poe**	Y	N	N	Y	Y	Y	Y
3 **Johnson, S.**	Y	N	N	Y	Y	Y	?
4 **Hall**	Y	N	N	Y	Y	Y	Y
5 **Hensarling**	Y	N	N	?	Y	Y	Y
6 **Barton**	Y	N	N	Y	Y	Y	Y
7 **Culberson**	Y	N	N	Y	Y	Y	Y
8 **Brady**	Y	N	N	Y	Y	Y	Y
9 Green, A.	N	Y	Y	Y	Y	Y	Y
10 **McCaul**	Y	N	N	Y	Y	Y	Y
11 **Conaway**	Y	N	N	Y	Y	Y	Y
12 **Granger**	+	–	–	+	Y	Y	Y
13 **Thornberry**	Y	N	N	Y	Y	Y	Y
14 **Paul**	Y	N	N	N	Y	Y	Y
15 Hinojosa	N	Y	Y	Y	Y	Y	Y
16 Reyes	N	Y	Y	Y	Y	Y	Y
17 Edwards	N	Y	Y	Y	Y	Y	Y
18 Jackson Lee	N	Y	Y	Y	Y	Y	Y
19 **Neugebauer**	Y	N	N	Y	Y	Y	Y
20 Gonzalez	N	Y	Y	Y	Y	Y	Y
21 **Smith**	Y	N	N	Y	Y	Y	Y
22 **Olson**	Y	N	N	Y	Y	Y	Y
23 Rodriguez	N	Y	Y	Y	Y	Y	Y
24 **Marchant**	Y	N	N	Y	Y	Y	Y
25 Doggett	N	Y	Y	Y	Y	Y	Y
26 **Burgess**	Y	N	N	Y	Y	Y	Y
27 Ortiz	N	Y	Y	Y	Y	Y	Y
28 Cuellar	N	Y	Y	Y	Y	Y	Y
29 Green, G.	N	Y	Y	Y	+	+	+
30 Johnson, E.	N	Y	Y	Y	Y	Y	Y
31 **Carter**	Y	N	N	Y	Y	Y	Y
32 **Sessions**	Y	N	N	Y	Y	Y	Y
UTAH							
1 **Bishop**	Y	N	N	Y	?	?	?
2 Matheson	Y	Y	Y	Y	Y	Y	Y
3 **Chaffetz**	Y	N	N	Y	Y	Y	Y
VERMONT							
AL Welch	N	Y	Y	Y	Y	Y	Y
VIRGINIA							
1 **Wittman**	Y	N	N	Y	Y	Y	Y
2 Nye	N	Y	Y	Y	Y	Y	Y
3 Scott	N	Y	Y	Y	Y	Y	Y
4 **Forbes**	Y	N	N	Y	Y	Y	Y
5 Perriello	N	Y	Y	Y	Y	Y	Y
6 **Goodlatte**	Y	N	N	Y	Y	Y	Y
7 **Cantor**	Y	N	N	Y	Y	Y	Y
8 Moran	N	Y	Y	P	Y	Y	Y
9 Boucher	?	?	?	?	Y	Y	?
10 **Wolf**	Y	N	N	Y	Y	Y	Y
11 Connolly	N	Y	Y	Y	Y	Y	Y
WASHINGTON							
1 Inslee	N	Y	Y	Y	Y	Y	Y
2 Larsen	N	Y	Y	Y	Y	Y	Y
3 Baird	?	+	+	?	Y	Y	Y
4 **Hastings**	Y	N	N	Y	Y	Y	Y
5 **McMorris Rodgers**	Y	N	N	Y	Y	Y	Y
6 Dicks	N	Y	Y	Y	Y	Y	Y
7 McDermott	N	Y	Y	P	Y	Y	Y
8 **Reichert**	Y	Y	N	Y	Y	Y	Y
9 Smith	N	Y	Y	Y	Y	Y	Y
WEST VIRGINIA							
1 Mollohan	N	Y	Y	Y	Y	Y	Y
2 **Capito**	Y	N	N	Y	Y	Y	Y
3 Rahall	N	Y	Y	N	Y	Y	Y
WISCONSIN							
1 **Ryan**	Y	N	N	Y	Y	Y	Y
2 Baldwin	N	Y	Y	Y	Y	Y	Y
3 Kind	N	Y	Y	Y	Y	Y	Y
4 Moore	N	Y	?	N	Y	Y	Y
5 **Sensenbrenner**	Y	N	N	Y	Y	Y	Y
6 **Petri**	Y	N	N	Y	Y	Y	Y
7 Obey	N	Y	Y	Y	Y	Y	Y
8 Kagen	–	+	+	+	Y	Y	Y
WYOMING							
AL **Lummis**	Y	N	N	Y	Y	Y	Y
DELEGATES							
Faleomavaega (A.S.)							
Norton (D.C.)							
Bordallo (Guam)							
Sablan (N. Marianas)							
Pierluisi (P.R.)							
Christensen (V.I.)							

IN THE HOUSE | By Vote Number

14. **HR 2. Children's Health Insurance/Rule.** Adoption of the rule (H Res 52) to provide for House floor consideration of a bill that would reauthorize the State Children's Health Insurance Program at nearly $60 billion over four and a half years. Adopted 244-178: R 0-175; D 244-3. Jan. 14, 2009.

15. **HR 2. Children's Health Insurance/Recommit.** Deal, R-Ga., motion to recommit the bill to the Energy and Commerce Committee with instructions that it be reported back forthwith after replacing the text with language that would reauthorize the State Children's Health Insurance Program for seven years, require states to insure at least 90 percent of children from families with incomes below 200 percent of the poverty level before expanding the program to higher income levels, increase restrictions on the eligibility of legal and illegal immigrants for the program, and pay for the expansion with changes to the corporate tax code. Motion rejected 179-247: R 174-3; D 5-244. Jan. 14, 2009.

16. **HR 2. Children's Health Insurance/Passage.** Passage of the bill that would reauthorize the State Children's Health Insurance Program at nearly $60 billion over four and a half years, expanding the program by $35 billion. To offset the cost of the expansion, it would increase the federal tax on cigarettes by 61 cents to $1 per pack and raise taxes on other tobacco products. The measure would allow states to provide pregnant women and children of legal immigrants with coverage under the program. The bill would limit program eligibility to families earning three times the federal poverty level or less and would require states to phase out coverage of childless adults by October 2010. Passed 289-139: R 40-137; D 249-2. Jan. 14, 2009.

17. **HR 384. Troubled Asset Relief Program/Rule.** Adoption of the rule (H Res 53) to provide for House floor consideration of a bill that would set new conditions on the use of funds provided under the 2008 financial industry bailout law. Adopted 235-191: R 0-176; D 235-15. Jan. 14, 2009.

18. **H Res 40. Committee Program Oversight/Adoption.** Cardoza, D-Calif., motion to suspend the rules and adopt the resolution that would amend House rules to require congressional committees to hold at least one meeting every 120 days on waste, fraud, abuse and mismanagement in government programs under the committees' jurisdiction. It also would require committees to hold hearings if they received information indicating the programs are at high risk for abuse. Motion agreed to 423-0: R 174-0; D 249-0. A two-thirds majority of those present and voting (282 in this case) is required for adoption under suspension of the rules. Jan. 14, 2009.

	14	15	16	17	18
ALABAMA					
1 Bonner	N	Y	N	N	Y
2 Bright	Y	Y	N	N	Y
3 Rogers	N	Y	Y	N	Y
4 Aderholt	N	Y	N	N	Y
5 Griffith	Y	N	Y	Y	Y
6 Bachus	N	Y	N	N	Y
7 Davis	Y	N	Y	Y	Y
ALASKA					
AL Young	N	Y	Y	N	Y
ARIZONA					
1 Kirkpatrick	Y	N	Y	Y	Y
2 Franks	N	Y	N	N	Y
3 Shadegg	N	Y	N	N	Y
4 Pastor	Y	N	Y	Y	Y
5 Mitchell	Y	N	Y	Y	Y
6 Flake	N	Y	N	N	Y
7 Grijalva	Y	N	Y	Y	Y
8 Giffords	Y	N	Y	N	Y
ARKANSAS					
1 Berry	Y	N	Y	Y	Y
2 Snyder	?	?	?	?	?
3 Boozman	N	Y	N	N	Y
4 Ross	Y	N	Y	Y	Y
CALIFORNIA					
1 Thompson	Y	N	Y	Y	Y
2 Herger	N	Y	N	N	Y
3 Lungren	N	Y	N	N	Y
4 McClintock	N	Y	N	N	Y
5 Matsui	Y	N	Y	Y	Y
6 Woolsey	Y	N	Y	Y	Y
7 Miller, George	Y	N	Y	Y	Y
8 Pelosi			Y		
9 Lee	Y	N	Y	Y	Y
10 Tauscher	Y	N	Y	Y	Y
11 McNerney	Y	N	Y	Y	Y
12 Speier	Y	N	Y	Y	Y
13 Stark	Y	N	Y	Y	Y
14 Eshoo	Y	N	Y	Y	Y
15 Honda	Y	N	Y	Y	Y
16 Lofgren	Y	N	Y	Y	Y
17 Farr	Y	N	Y	Y	Y
18 Cardoza	Y	N	Y	Y	Y
19 Radanovich	N	Y	N	N	Y
20 Costa	Y	N	Y	Y	Y
21 Nunes	N	Y	N	N	Y
22 McCarthy	N	Y	N	N	Y
23 Capps	Y	N	Y	Y	Y
24 Gallegly	N	Y	N	N	Y
25 McKeon	N	Y	N	N	Y
26 Dreier	N	Y	N	N	Y
27 Sherman	+	-	+	+	+
28 Berman	Y	N	Y	Y	Y
29 Schiff	Y	N	Y	Y	Y
30 Waxman	Y	N	Y	Y	Y
31 Becerra	Y	N	Y	Y	Y
32 Solis	?	?	?	?	?
33 Watson	Y	N	Y	Y	Y
34 Roybal-Allard	Y	N	Y	Y	Y
35 Waters	?	N	Y	Y	Y
36 Harman	Y	N	Y	Y	Y
37 Richardson	Y	N	Y	Y	Y
38 Napolitano	Y	N	Y	Y	Y
39 Sánchez, Linda	Y	N	Y	Y	Y
40 Royce	N	Y	N	N	Y
41 Lewis	N	Y	N	N	Y
42 Miller, Gary	N	Y	N	N	Y
43 Baca	Y	N	Y	Y	Y
44 Calvert	N	Y	N	N	Y
45 Bono Mack	N	Y	N	N	Y
46 Rohrabacher	N	Y	N	N	Y
47 Sanchez, Loretta	Y	N	Y	N	Y
48 Campbell	N	Y	N	N	Y
49 Issa	N	Y	N	N	Y
50 Bilbray	N	Y	N	N	Y
51 Filner	Y	N	Y	Y	Y
52 Hunter	N	Y	N	N	Y
53 Davis	Y	N	Y	Y	Y

	14	15	16	17	18
COLORADO					
1 DeGette	Y	N	Y	Y	Y
2 Polis	Y	N	Y	Y	Y
3 Salazar	Y	N	Y	Y	Y
4 Markey	Y	N	Y	Y	Y
5 Lamborn	N	Y	N	N	Y
6 Coffman	N	Y	N	N	Y
7 Perlmutter	Y	N	Y	Y	Y
CONNECTICUT					
1 Larson	Y	N	Y	Y	Y
2 Courtney	Y	N	Y	Y	Y
3 DeLauro	Y	N	Y	Y	Y
4 Himes	Y	N	Y	Y	Y
5 Murphy	Y	N	Y	Y	Y
DELAWARE					
AL Castle	N	Y	Y	N	Y
FLORIDA					
1 Miller	N	Y	N	N	Y
2 Boyd	Y	N	Y	Y	Y
3 Brown	Y	N	Y	Y	Y
4 Crenshaw	N	Y	N	N	Y
5 Brown-Waite	N	Y	N	N	Y
6 Stearns	N	Y	N	N	Y
7 Mica	N	Y	N	N	Y
8 Grayson	Y	N	Y	Y	Y
9 Bilirakis	N	Y	N	N	Y
10 Young	?	Y	N	Y	Y
11 Castor	Y	N	Y	Y	Y
12 Putnam	N	Y	N	N	Y
13 Buchanan	N	N	Y	N	Y
14 Mack	N	Y	N	N	Y
15 Posey	N	Y	N	N	Y
16 Rooney	N	Y	N	N	Y
17 Meek	Y	N	Y	Y	Y
18 Ros-Lehtinen	N	Y	N	N	Y
19 Wexler	Y	N	Y	Y	Y
20 Wasserman Schultz	Y	N	Y	Y	Y
21 Diaz-Balart, L.	Y	N	Y	Y	Y
22 Klein	Y	N	Y	Y	Y
23 Hastings	Y	N	Y	Y	Y
24 Kosmas	Y	N	Y	Y	Y
25 Diaz-Balart, M.	N	Y	Y	N	Y
GEORGIA					
1 Kingston	N	Y	N	N	Y
2 Bishop	Y	N	Y	Y	Y
3 Westmoreland	N	Y	N	N	Y
4 Johnson	Y	N	Y	Y	Y
5 Lewis	Y	N	Y	Y	Y
6 Price	N	Y	N	N	Y
7 Linder	N	Y	N	N	Y
8 Marshall	Y	Y	N	Y	Y
9 Deal	N	Y	N	N	Y
10 Broun	N	Y	N	N	Y
11 Gingrey	N	Y	N	N	Y
12 Barrow	Y	N	Y	Y	Y
13 Scott	Y	N	Y	Y	Y
HAWAII					
1 Abercrombie	Y	N	Y	Y	Y
2 Hirono	Y	N	Y	Y	Y
IDAHO					
1 Minnick	N	Y	Y	N	Y
2 Simpson	N	Y	Y	N	Y
ILLINOIS					
1 Rush	Y	N	Y	Y	Y
2 Jackson	Y	N	Y	Y	Y
3 Lipinski	Y	N	Y	Y	Y
4 Gutierrez	Y	N	Y	Y	Y
5 Vacant					
6 Roskam	N	Y	N	N	Y
7 Davis	Y	N	Y	Y	Y
8 Bean	Y	N	Y	Y	Y
9 Schakowsky	Y	N	Y	Y	Y
10 Kirk	N	Y	N	N	Y
11 Halvorson	Y	N	Y	Y	Y
12 Costello	Y	N	Y	Y	Y
13 Biggert	N	Y	N	N	Y
14 Foster	Y	N	Y	Y	Y
15 Johnson	N	Y	N	N	Y

KEY — **Republicans** Democrats

Y Voted for (yea)	X Paired against	C Voted "present" to avoid possible conflict of interest
# Paired for	- Announced against	? Did not vote or otherwise make a position known
+ Announced for	P Voted "present"	
N Voted against (nay)		

	14	15	16	17	18
16 Manzullo	N	Y	N	–	+
17 Hare	Y	N	Y	Y	Y
18 Schock	N	Y	N	N	?
19 Shimkus	N	Y	N	N	Y
INDIANA					
1 Visclosky	?	N	Y	Y	Y
2 Donnelly	Y	N	Y	Y	Y
3 Souder	N	Y	N	N	Y
4 Buyer	N	Y	N	N	?
5 Burton	N	Y	N	N	Y
6 Pence	N	Y	N	N	Y
7 Carson	Y	N	Y	Y	Y
8 Ellsworth	Y	N	Y	Y	Y
9 Hill	N	N	Y	N	Y
IOWA					
1 Braley	Y	N	Y	Y	Y
2 Loebsack	Y	N	Y	Y	Y
3 Boswell	Y	N	Y	Y	Y
4 Latham	N	Y	N	Y	Y
5 King	N	Y	N	N	Y
KANSAS					
1 Moran	N	Y	Y	N	Y
2 Jenkins	N	Y	N	N	Y
3 Moore	Y	N	Y	Y	Y
4 Tiahrt	N	Y	N	N	Y
KENTUCKY					
1 Whitfield	N	Y	N	N	Y
2 Guthrie	N	Y	N	N	Y
3 Yarmuth	Y	N	Y	Y	Y
4 Davis	N	Y	N	N	Y
5 Rogers	N	Y	N	N	Y
6 Chandler	Y	N	Y	Y	Y
LOUISIANA					
1 Scalise	N	Y	N	N	Y
2 Cao	N	Y	Y	N	Y
3 Melancon	Y	N	Y	N	Y
4 Fleming	N	Y	N	N	Y
5 Alexander	N	Y	N	N	Y
6 Cassidy	N	Y	N	N	Y
7 Boustany	N	Y	N	N	Y
MAINE					
1 Pingree	Y	N	Y	Y	Y
2 Michaud	Y	N	Y	Y	Y
MARYLAND					
1 Kratovil	Y	N	Y	N	Y
2 Ruppersberger	Y	N	Y	Y	Y
3 Sarbanes	Y	N	Y	Y	Y
4 Edwards	Y	N	Y	Y	Y
5 Hoyer	Y	N	Y	Y	Y
6 Bartlett	N	Y	N	N	Y
7 Cummings	Y	N	Y	Y	Y
8 Van Hollen	Y	N	Y	Y	Y
MASSACHUSETTS					
1 Olver	Y	N	Y	Y	Y
2 Neal	Y	N	Y	Y	Y
3 McGovern	Y	N	Y	Y	Y
4 Frank	Y	N	Y	Y	Y
5 Tsongas	Y	N	Y	Y	Y
6 Tierney	Y	N	Y	Y	Y
7 Markey	Y	N	Y	Y	Y
8 Capuano	Y	N	Y	Y	Y
9 Lynch	Y	N	Y	Y	Y
10 Delahunt	Y	N	Y	Y	Y
MICHIGAN					
1 Stupak	Y	N	Y	Y	Y
2 Hoekstra	N	Y	N	N	Y
3 Ehlers	N	Y	N	N	Y
4 Camp	N	Y	N	N	Y
5 Kildee	Y	N	Y	Y	Y
6 Upton	N	Y	Y	N	Y
7 Schauer	Y	N	Y	Y	Y
8 Rogers	N	Y	N	N	Y
9 Peters	Y	N	Y	Y	Y
10 Miller	N	Y	Y	N	Y
11 McCotter	N	Y	Y	N	Y
12 Levin	Y	N	Y	Y	Y
13 Kilpatrick	Y	N	Y	Y	Y
14 Conyers	Y	?	Y	Y	Y
15 Dingell	Y	N	Y	Y	Y
MINNESOTA					
1 Walz	Y	N	Y	Y	Y
2 Kline	N	Y	N	N	Y
3 Paulsen	N	Y	Y	N	Y
4 McCollum	Y	N	Y	Y	Y

	14	15	16	17	18
5 Ellison	Y	N	Y	Y	+
6 Bachmann	N	Y	N	N	Y
7 Peterson	Y	N	Y	Y	Y
8 Oberstar	Y	N	Y	Y	Y
MISSISSIPPI					
1 Childers	Y	N	Y	N	Y
2 Thompson	Y	N	Y	Y	Y
3 Harper	N	Y	N	N	Y
4 Taylor	Y	Y	Y	N	Y
MISSOURI					
1 Clay	Y	N	Y	Y	Y
2 Akin	N	Y	N	N	Y
3 Carnahan	Y	N	Y	Y	Y
4 Skelton	Y	N	Y	Y	Y
5 Cleaver	Y	N	Y	Y	Y
6 Graves	N	Y	N	N	Y
7 Blunt	N	Y	N	N	Y
8 Emerson	N	Y	N	N	Y
9 Luetkemeyer	N	Y	N	N	Y
MONTANA					
AL Rehberg	N	Y	Y	N	Y
NEBRASKA					
1 Fortenberry	N	Y	N	N	Y
2 Terry	N	Y	N	N	Y
3 Smith	N	Y	N	N	Y
NEVADA					
1 Berkley	Y	N	Y	Y	Y
2 Heller	N	Y	N	N	Y
3 Titus	Y	N	Y	Y	Y
NEW HAMPSHIRE					
1 Shea-Porter	Y	N	Y	Y	Y
2 Hodes	Y	N	Y	Y	Y
NEW JERSEY					
1 Andrews	Y	N	Y	Y	Y
2 LoBiondo	N	N	Y	N	Y
3 Adler	Y	N	Y	Y	Y
4 Smith	N	N	Y	N	Y
5 Garrett	N	Y	N	N	Y
6 Pallone	Y	N	Y	Y	Y
7 Lance	N	Y	Y	N	Y
8 Pascrell	Y	N	Y	Y	Y
9 Rothman	Y	N	Y	Y	Y
10 Payne	Y	N	Y	Y	Y
11 Frelinghuysen	N	Y	Y	N	Y
12 Holt	Y	N	Y	Y	Y
13 Sires	Y	N	Y	Y	Y
NEW MEXICO					
1 Heinrich	Y	N	Y	Y	Y
2 Teague	Y	N	Y	Y	Y
3 Lujan	Y	N	Y	Y	Y
NEW YORK					
1 Bishop	Y	N	Y	Y	Y
2 Israel	Y	N	Y	Y	Y
3 King	N	Y	Y	N	Y
4 McCarthy	Y	N	Y	Y	Y
5 Ackerman	Y	N	Y	Y	Y
6 Meeks	Y	N	+	Y	Y
7 Crowley	Y	N	Y	Y	Y
8 Nadler	Y	N	Y	Y	Y
9 Weiner	Y	N	Y	Y	Y
10 Towns	Y	N	Y	Y	Y
11 Clarke	Y	N	Y	Y	Y
12 Velázquez	Y	N	Y	Y	Y
13 McMahon	Y	N	Y	Y	Y
14 Maloney	?	N	Y	Y	Y
15 Rangel	Y	N	Y	Y	Y
16 Serrano	Y	N	Y	Y	Y
17 Engel	Y	N	Y	Y	Y
18 Lowey	Y	N	Y	Y	Y
19 Hall	Y	N	Y	Y	Y
20 Gillibrand	Y	N	Y	Y	Y
21 Tonko	Y	N	Y	Y	Y
22 Hinchey	Y	N	Y	Y	Y
23 McHugh	N	Y	Y	N	Y
24 Arcuri	Y	N	Y	Y	Y
25 Maffei	Y	N	Y	Y	Y
26 Lee	N	Y	Y	N	Y
27 Higgins	Y	N	Y	Y	Y
28 Slaughter	Y	N	Y	Y	Y
29 Massa	Y	N	Y	Y	Y
NORTH CAROLINA					
1 Butterfield	Y	N	Y	Y	Y
2 Etheridge	Y	N	Y	Y	Y
3 Jones	N	Y	N	N	Y
4 Price	Y	N	Y	Y	Y

	14	15	16	17	18
5 Foxx	N	Y	N	N	Y
6 Coble	N	Y	N	N	Y
7 McIntyre	Y	Y	Y	Y	Y
8 Kissell	Y	N	Y	Y	Y
9 Myrick	N	Y	N	N	Y
10 McHenry	N	Y	N	N	Y
11 Shuler	N	N	Y	N	Y
12 Watt	Y	N	Y	Y	Y
13 Miller	Y	N	Y	Y	Y
NORTH DAKOTA					
AL Pomeroy	Y	N	Y	Y	Y
OHIO					
1 Driehaus	Y	N	Y	Y	Y
2 Schmidt	N	Y	N	N	Y
3 Turner	N	Y	N	N	Y
4 Jordan	N	Y	N	N	Y
5 Latta	N	Y	N	N	Y
6 Wilson	Y	N	Y	Y	Y
7 Austria	N	Y	N	N	Y
8 Boehner	?	Y	N	N	Y
9 Kaptur	Y	N	Y	Y	Y
10 Kucinich	Y	N	Y	Y	Y
11 Fudge	Y	N	Y	Y	Y
12 Tiberi	N	Y	N	N	Y
13 Sutton	Y	N	Y	Y	Y
14 LaTourette	Y	N	Y	Y	Y
15 Kilroy	Y	N	Y	Y	Y
16 Boccieri	Y	N	Y	Y	Y
17 Ryan	Y	N	Y	Y	Y
18 Space	Y	N	Y	Y	Y
OKLAHOMA					
1 Sullivan	?	?	?	?	?
2 Boren	Y	N	Y	Y	Y
3 Lucas	N	Y	N	N	Y
4 Cole	N	Y	N	N	Y
5 Fallin	N	Y	N	N	Y
OREGON					
1 Wu	Y	N	Y	Y	Y
2 Walden	N	Y	N	N	Y
3 Blumenauer	Y	N	Y	Y	Y
4 DeFazio	Y	N	Y	Y	Y
5 Schrader	Y	N	Y	Y	Y
PENNSYLVANIA					
1 Brady	Y	N	Y	Y	Y
2 Fattah	Y	N	Y	Y	Y
3 Dahlkemper	Y	N	Y	Y	Y
4 Altmire	Y	N	Y	Y	Y
5 Thompson	N	Y	N	N	Y
6 Gerlach	N	Y	N	N	Y
7 Sestak	Y	N	Y	Y	Y
8 Murphy, P.	Y	N	Y	Y	Y
9 Shuster	N	Y	N	N	Y
10 Carney	Y	N	Y	Y	Y
11 Kanjorski	Y	N	Y	Y	Y
12 Murtha	Y	N	Y	Y	Y
13 Schwartz	Y	N	Y	Y	Y
14 Doyle	Y	N	Y	Y	Y
15 Dent	N	Y	Y	N	Y
16 Pitts	N	Y	N	N	Y
17 Holden	Y	N	Y	Y	Y
18 Murphy, T.	N	Y	Y	N	Y
19 Platts	N	Y	Y	N	Y
RHODE ISLAND					
1 Kennedy	Y	N	Y	Y	Y
2 Langevin	Y	N	Y	Y	Y
SOUTH CAROLINA					
1 Brown	N	Y	N	N	Y
2 Wilson	N	Y	N	N	Y
3 Barrett	N	Y	N	N	Y
4 Inglis	N	Y	N	N	Y
5 Spratt	Y	N	Y	Y	Y
6 Clyburn	Y	N	Y	Y	Y
SOUTH DAKOTA					
AL Herseth Sandlin	?	?	Y	?	+
TENNESSEE					
1 Roe	N	Y	N	N	Y
2 Duncan	N	Y	N	N	Y
3 Wamp	N	Y	N	N	Y
4 Davis, L.	Y	N	Y	Y	Y
5 Cooper	Y	N	Y	Y	Y
6 Gordon	Y	N	Y	Y	Y
7 Blackburn	N	Y	N	N	Y
8 Tanner	Y	N	Y	Y	Y
9 Cohen	Y	N	Y	Y	Y

	14	15	16	17	18
TEXAS					
1 Gohmert	N	Y	N	N	Y
2 Poe	N	Y	N	N	Y
3 Johnson, S.	N	Y	N	N	Y
4 Hall	N	Y	N	N	Y
5 Hensarling	N	Y	N	N	Y
6 Barton	N	Y	N	N	Y
7 Culberson	N	Y	N	N	Y
8 Brady	N	Y	N	N	Y
9 Green, A.	Y	N	Y	Y	Y
10 McCaul	N	Y	N	N	Y
11 Conaway	N	Y	N	N	Y
12 Granger	N	Y	N	N	Y
13 Thornberry	N	Y	N	N	Y
14 Paul	N	Y	N	N	Y
15 Hinojosa	Y	N	Y	Y	Y
16 Reyes	Y	N	Y	Y	Y
17 Edwards	Y	N	Y	Y	Y
18 Jackson Lee	Y	N	Y	Y	Y
19 Neugebauer	N	Y	N	N	Y
20 Gonzalez	Y	N	Y	Y	Y
21 Smith	N	Y	N	N	Y
22 Olson	N	Y	N	N	Y
23 Rodriguez	Y	N	Y	Y	Y
24 Marchant	N	Y	N	N	Y
25 Doggett	Y	N	Y	Y	Y
26 Burgess	N	Y	N	N	Y
27 Ortiz	Y	N	Y	Y	Y
28 Cuellar	Y	N	Y	Y	Y
29 Green, G.	Y	N	Y	Y	Y
30 Johnson, E.	Y	N	Y	Y	?
31 Carter	N	Y	N	N	Y
32 Sessions	N	Y	N	N	Y
UTAH					
1 Bishop	N	Y	N	N	Y
2 Matheson	Y	N	Y	Y	Y
3 Chaffetz	N	Y	N	N	Y
VERMONT					
AL Welch	Y	N	Y	Y	Y
VIRGINIA					
1 Wittman	N	Y	N	N	Y
2 Nye	Y	N	Y	Y	Y
3 Scott	Y	N	Y	Y	Y
4 Forbes	N	Y	N	N	Y
5 Perriello	Y	N	Y	Y	Y
6 Goodlatte	N	Y	N	N	Y
7 Cantor	N	Y	N	N	Y
8 Moran	Y	N	Y	Y	Y
9 Boucher	?	?	?	?	?
10 Wolf	N	Y	N	N	Y
11 Connolly	Y	N	Y	Y	Y
WASHINGTON					
1 Inslee	Y	N	Y	Y	Y
2 Larsen	Y	N	Y	Y	Y
3 Baird	Y	N	Y	Y	Y
4 Hastings	N	Y	N	N	Y
5 McMorris Rodgers	N	Y	N	N	Y
6 Dicks	Y	N	Y	Y	Y
7 McDermott	Y	N	Y	Y	Y
8 Reichert	N	Y	N	N	Y
9 Smith	Y	N	Y	Y	Y
WEST VIRGINIA					
1 Mollohan	Y	N	Y	Y	Y
2 Capito	N	Y	N	N	Y
3 Rahall	Y	N	Y	Y	Y
WISCONSIN					
1 Ryan	N	Y	N	N	Y
2 Baldwin	Y	N	Y	Y	Y
3 Kind	Y	N	Y	Y	Y
4 Moore	Y	N	Y	Y	Y
5 Sensenbrenner	N	Y	N	N	Y
6 Petri	N	Y	Y	N	Y
7 Obey	Y	N	Y	Y	Y
8 Kagen	Y	N	Y	Y	Y
WYOMING					
AL Lummis	N	Y	N	N	Y
DELEGATES					
Faleomavaega (A.S.)					
Norton (D.C.)					
Bordallo (Guam)					
Sablan (N. Marianas)					
Pierluisi (P.R.)					
Christensen (V.I.)					

IN THE HOUSE | By Vote Number

19. HR 384. **Troubled Asset Relief Program/Foreclosure Mitigation.** Frank, D-Mass., amendment that would add new conditions on the use of funds under the 2008 financial industry bailout law. It would require the Treasury to use between $40 billion and $100 billion for foreclosure mitigation and set other conditions related to housing, minorities and small business. The conditions would affect the second $350 billion provided under the 2008 financial services bailout law. The amendment would also allow the Treasury to apply the measure's executive compensation restrictions retroactively to institutions that have already received assistance under the program. Adopted in Committee of the Whole 275-152: R 33-142; D 242-10; I 0-0. Jan. 15, 2009.

20. HR 384. **Troubled Asset Relief Program/Meeting Observers.** Hensarling, R-Texas, amendment that would remove the Treasury secretary's authority to delegate an observer to attend meetings of the board of directors of institutions the program assists. Rejected in Committee of the Whole 151-274: R 148-25; D 3-249; I 0-0. Jan. 15, 2009.

21. HR 384. **Troubled Asset Relief Program/HOPE for Homeowners.** Bachmann, R-Minn., amendment that would eliminate certain changes and additional funding for the HOPE for Homeowners program. Rejected in Committee of the Whole 142-282: R 142-31; D 0-250; I 0-1. Jan. 15, 2009.

22. HR 384. **Troubled Asset Relief Program/Federal Reserve Disclosures.** Murphy, D-Pa., amendment that would require the Federal Reserve to disclose information regarding its mortgage-backed securities purchase program. Adopted in Committee of the Whole 426-0: R 173-0; D 252-0; I 1-0. Jan. 15, 2009.

23. HR 384. **Troubled Asset Relief Program/Previous Fund Usage Analysis.** Hinchey, D-N.Y., amendment that would require the Treasury Department to obtain information from the program's recipients on use of funds allocated in 2008 under the $700 billion 2008 financial industry bailout law and require the Treasury to conduct analysis of those funds within 30 days of the bill's enactment. Adopted in Committee of the Whole 427-1: R 174-0; D 253-0; I 0-1. Jan. 21, 2009.

24. HR 384. **Troubled Asset Relief Program/Motion to Table.** Frank, D-Mass., motion to table (kill) the Gohmert, R-Texas, appeal of the ruling of the chair with respect to the Frank point of order that the Gohmert motion to recommit the bill to the Financial Services Committee was not germane. The Gohmert motion would recommit the bill with instructions that it be reported back forthwith with language that would transfer funds to the Social Security trust funds. Motion agreed to 251-176: R 0-175; D 251-1. Jan. 21, 2009.

	19	20	21	22	23	24
ALABAMA						
1 **Bonner**	N	Y	Y	Y	Y	N
2 **Bright**	Y	N	N	Y	Y	Y
3 **Rogers**	N	Y	Y	Y	Y	N
4 **Aderholt**	N	Y	Y	Y	Y	N
5 Griffith	N	N	N	Y	Y	Y
6 **Bachus**	N	Y	Y	Y	Y	N
7 Davis	Y	N	N	Y	Y	Y
ALASKA						
AL **Young**	N	N	N	Y	?	?
ARIZONA						
1 Kirkpatrick	N	N	N	Y	Y	Y
2 **Franks**	N	Y	Y	Y	Y	N
3 **Shadegg**	N	Y	Y	Y	Y	N
4 Pastor	Y	N	N	Y	Y	Y
5 Mitchell	Y	N	N	Y	Y	Y
6 **Flake**	N	Y	Y	Y	Y	N
7 Grijalva	Y	N	N	Y	Y	Y
8 Giffords	Y	N	N	Y	Y	Y
ARKANSAS						
1 Berry	Y	N	N	Y	Y	Y
2 Snyder	?	?	?	?	Y	Y
3 **Boozman**	N	Y	Y	Y	Y	N
4 Ross	Y	N	N	Y	Y	Y
CALIFORNIA						
1 Thompson	Y	N	N	Y	Y	Y
2 **Herger**	N	Y	Y	Y	Y	N
3 **Lungren**	N	Y	Y	Y	Y	N
4 **McClintock**	N	Y	Y	Y	Y	N
5 Matsui	Y	N	N	Y	Y	Y
6 Woolsey	Y	N	N	Y	Y	Y
7 Miller, George	Y	N	N	Y	Y	Y
8 Pelosi						
9 Lee	Y	N	N	Y	Y	Y
10 Tauscher	Y	N	N	Y	Y	Y
11 McNerney	Y	N	N	Y	Y	Y
12 Speier	Y	N	N	Y	Y	Y
13 Stark	Y	N	N	Y	Y	Y
14 Eshoo	Y	N	N	Y	Y	Y
15 Honda	Y	N	N	Y	Y	Y
16 Lofgren	Y	N	N	Y	Y	Y
17 Farr	Y	N	N	Y	Y	Y
18 Cardoza	Y	N	N	Y	Y	Y
19 **Radanovich**	N	Y	Y	Y	Y	N
20 Costa	Y	N	N	Y	Y	Y
21 **Nunes**	N	Y	Y	Y	Y	N
22 **McCarthy**	N	Y	Y	Y	Y	N
23 Capps	Y	N	N	Y	Y	Y
24 **Gallegly**	N	Y	Y	Y	Y	N
25 **McKeon**	N	Y	Y	Y	Y	N
26 **Dreier**	N	Y	Y	Y	Y	N
27 Sherman	Y	N	N	Y	Y	Y
28 Berman	Y	N	N	Y	Y	Y
29 Schiff	Y	N	N	Y	Y	Y
30 Waxman	Y	N	N	Y	Y	Y
31 Becerra	Y	N	N	Y	Y	Y
32 Solis	?	?	?	?	?	?
33 Watson	Y	N	N	Y	?	Y
34 Roybal-Allard	Y	N	N	Y	Y	Y
35 Waters	Y	N	N	Y	Y	Y
36 Harman	Y	N	N	Y	?	Y
37 Richardson	Y	N	N	Y	Y	Y
38 Napolitano	Y	N	N	Y	Y	Y
39 Sánchez, Linda	Y	N	N	Y	Y	Y
40 **Royce**	N	Y	Y	Y	Y	N
41 **Lewis**	N	Y	Y	Y	Y	N
42 **Miller, Gary**	N	Y	Y	Y	Y	N
43 Baca	Y	N	N	Y	Y	Y
44 **Calvert**	N	Y	Y	Y	Y	N
45 **Bono Mack**	Y	Y	Y	Y	Y	N
46 **Rohrabacher**	N	N	N	Y	Y	N
47 Sanchez, Loretta	Y	N	N	Y	Y	Y
48 **Campbell**	Y	Y	Y	Y	Y	N
49 **Issa**	N	Y	Y	Y	Y	N
50 **Bilbray**	N	Y	Y	Y	Y	N
51 Filner	Y	N	N	Y	Y	Y
52 **Hunter**	N	Y	Y	Y	Y	N
53 Davis	Y	N	N	Y	Y	Y

	19	20	21	22	23	24
COLORADO						
1 DeGette	Y	N	N	Y	Y	Y
2 Polis	Y	N	N	Y	Y	Y
3 Salazar	Y	N	N	Y	Y	Y
4 Markey	Y	N	N	Y	Y	Y
5 **Lamborn**	N	Y	Y	Y	Y	N
6 **Coffman**	N	Y	Y	Y	Y	N
7 Perlmutter	Y	N	N	Y	Y	Y
CONNECTICUT						
1 Larson	Y	N	N	Y	Y	Y
2 Courtney	Y	N	N	Y	Y	Y
3 DeLauro	Y	N	N	Y	Y	Y
4 Himes	Y	N	N	Y	Y	Y
5 Murphy	Y	N	N	Y	Y	Y
DELAWARE						
AL **Castle**	Y	Y	N	Y	Y	N
FLORIDA						
1 **Miller**	N	Y	Y	Y	Y	N
2 Boyd	Y	N	N	Y	Y	Y
3 Brown	Y	N	N	Y	Y	Y
4 **Crenshaw**	N	N	Y	Y	Y	N
5 **Brown-Waite**	N	Y	Y	Y	Y	N
6 **Stearns**	Y	Y	Y	Y	Y	N
7 **Mica**	N	Y	Y	Y	Y	N
8 Grayson	Y	N	N	Y	Y	Y
9 **Bilirakis**	N	Y	Y	Y	Y	N
10 **Young**	N	Y	Y	Y	Y	N
11 Castor	Y	N	N	Y	Y	Y
12 **Putnam**	N	N	Y	Y	Y	N
13 **Buchanan**	N	Y	Y	Y	Y	N
14 **Mack**	N	Y	Y	Y	Y	N
15 **Posey**	N	Y	Y	Y	Y	N
16 **Rooney**	N	Y	Y	Y	Y	N
17 Meek	Y	N	N	Y	Y	Y
18 **Ros-Lehtinen**	Y	N	N	Y	Y	Y
19 Wexler	Y	N	N	Y	Y	Y
20 Wasserman Schultz	Y	N	N	Y	Y	Y
21 **Diaz-Balart, L.**	?	?	?	?	Y	Y
22 Klein	Y	N	N	Y	Y	Y
23 Hastings	Y	N	N	Y	Y	Y
24 Kosmas	Y	N	N	Y	Y	Y
25 **Diaz-Balart, M.**	Y	Y	N	Y	Y	N
GEORGIA						
1 **Kingston**	N	N	Y	Y	Y	N
2 Bishop	Y	N	N	Y	Y	Y
3 **Westmoreland**	N	Y	Y	Y	Y	N
4 Johnson	Y	N	N	Y	Y	Y
5 Lewis	Y	N	N	Y	Y	Y
6 **Price**	N	Y	Y	Y	Y	N
7 **Linder**	N	Y	Y	Y	Y	N
8 Marshall	Y	N	N	Y	Y	Y
9 **Deal**	N	?	?	?	Y	N
10 **Broun**	N	Y	Y	Y	Y	N
11 **Gingrey**	N	Y	Y	Y	Y	N
12 Barrow	Y	N	N	Y	Y	Y
13 Scott	Y	N	N	Y	Y	Y
HAWAII						
1 Abercrombie	Y	N	N	Y	Y	Y
2 Hirono	Y	N	N	Y	Y	Y
IDAHO						
1 Minnick	N	Y	N	Y	Y	Y
2 **Simpson**	N	Y	Y	Y	Y	N
ILLINOIS						
1 Rush	Y	?	?	?	Y	Y
2 Jackson	Y	N	N	Y	Y	Y
3 Lipinski	Y	N	N	Y	Y	Y
4 Gutierrez	Y	N	N	Y	Y	Y
5 Vacant						
6 **Roskam**	N	N	Y	Y	Y	N
7 Davis	Y	N	N	Y	Y	Y
8 Bean	Y	N	N	Y	Y	Y
9 Schakowsky	Y	N	N	Y	Y	Y
10 **Kirk**	N	N	Y	Y	Y	N
11 Halvorson	Y	N	N	Y	Y	Y
12 Costello	Y	N	N	Y	Y	Y
13 **Biggert**	Y	Y	Y	Y	Y	N
14 Foster	Y	N	N	Y	Y	Y
15 **Johnson**	N	N	Y	Y	Y	N

	19	20	21	22	23	24
16 **Manzullo**	N	Y	Y	Y	Y	N
17 Hare	Y	N	N	Y	Y	Y
18 **Schock**	Y	Y	N	Y	Y	N
19 **Shimkus**	N	N	Y	Y	Y	N
INDIANA						
1 Visclosky	Y	N	N	Y	Y	Y
2 Donnelly	Y	N	N	Y	Y	Y
3 **Souder**	Y	Y	N	Y	Y	N
4 **Buyer**	N	Y	Y	Y	Y	N
5 **Burton**	N	Y	Y	Y	Y	N
6 **Pence**	N	Y	Y	Y	Y	N
7 Carson	Y	N	N	Y	Y	Y
8 Ellsworth	Y	Y	N	Y	Y	Y
9 Hill	Y	N	N	Y	Y	Y
IOWA						
1 Braley	Y	N	N	Y	Y	Y
2 Loebsack	Y	N	N	Y	Y	Y
3 Boswell	Y	N	N	Y	Y	Y
4 **Latham**	N	Y	Y	Y	Y	N
5 **King**	N	Y	Y	Y	Y	N
KANSAS						
1 **Moran**	Y	N	Y	Y	Y	N
2 **Jenkins**	Y	Y	Y	Y	Y	N
3 Moore	Y	N	N	Y	Y	Y
4 **Tiahrt**	Y	Y	Y	Y	Y	N
KENTUCKY						
1 **Whitfield**	N	N	Y	Y	Y	N
2 **Guthrie**	N	Y	Y	Y	Y	N
3 Yarmuth	Y	N	N	Y	Y	Y
4 **Davis**	N	Y	Y	Y	Y	N
5 **Rogers**	N	Y	Y	Y	Y	N
6 Chandler	Y	N	N	Y	Y	Y
LOUISIANA						
1 **Scalise**	N	Y	Y	Y	Y	N
2 **Cao**	N	Y	Y	Y	Y	N
3 Melancon	Y	N	N	Y	Y	Y
4 **Fleming**	N	Y	Y	Y	Y	N
5 **Alexander**	N	Y	Y	Y	Y	N
6 **Cassidy**	N	Y	Y	Y	Y	N
7 **Boustany**	N	Y	Y	Y	Y	N
MAINE						
1 Pingree	Y	N	N	Y	Y	Y
2 Michaud	Y	N	N	Y	Y	Y
MARYLAND						
1 Kratovil	Y	N	N	Y	Y	Y
2 Ruppersberger	Y	N	N	Y	Y	Y
3 Sarbanes	Y	N	N	Y	Y	Y
4 Edwards	Y	N	N	Y	Y	Y
5 Hoyer	Y	N	N	Y	Y	Y
6 **Bartlett**	N	Y	Y	Y	Y	N
7 Cummings	Y	Y	N	Y	Y	Y
8 Van Hollen	Y	N	N	Y	Y	Y
MASSACHUSETTS						
1 Olver	Y	N	N	Y	Y	Y
2 Neal	Y	N	N	Y	Y	Y
3 McGovern	Y	N	N	Y	Y	Y
4 Frank	Y	N	N	Y	Y	Y
5 Tsongas	Y	N	N	Y	Y	Y
6 Tierney	Y	N	N	Y	Y	Y
7 Markey	Y	N	N	Y	Y	Y
8 Capuano	Y	N	N	Y	Y	Y
9 Lynch	Y	N	N	Y	Y	Y
10 Delahunt	Y	N	N	Y	Y	Y
MICHIGAN						
1 Stupak	Y	N	N	Y	Y	Y
2 **Hoekstra**	Y	Y	Y	Y	Y	N
3 **Ehlers**	Y	N	N	Y	Y	N
4 **Camp**	Y	Y	Y	Y	Y	N
5 Kildee	Y	N	N	Y	Y	Y
6 **Upton**	Y	N	N	Y	Y	N
7 Schauer	Y	N	N	Y	Y	Y
8 **Rogers**	N	Y	Y	Y	Y	N
9 Peters	Y	N	N	Y	Y	Y
10 **Miller**	Y	N	N	Y	Y	N
11 **McCotter**	Y	Y	Y	Y	Y	N
12 Levin	Y	N	N	Y	Y	Y
13 Kilpatrick	Y	N	N	Y	Y	Y
14 Conyers	Y	N	N	Y	Y	Y
15 Dingell	Y	N	N	Y	Y	Y
MINNESOTA						
1 Walz	Y	N	N	Y	Y	Y
2 **Kline**	N	Y	Y	Y	Y	N
3 **Paulsen**	N	Y	Y	Y	Y	N
4 McCollum	Y	N	N	Y	Y	Y

	19	20	21	22	23	24
5 Ellison	Y	N	N	Y	Y	Y
6 **Bachmann**	N	Y	Y	Y	Y	N
7 Peterson	N	N	N	Y	Y	Y
8 Oberstar	Y	N	N	Y	Y	Y
MISSISSIPPI						
1 Childers	Y	N	N	Y	Y	Y
2 Thompson	Y	N	N	Y	Y	Y
3 **Harper**	N	Y	Y	Y	Y	N
4 Taylor	N	N	N	Y	Y	Y
MISSOURI						
1 Clay	Y	N	N	Y	Y	Y
2 **Akin**	N	Y	Y	Y	Y	N
3 Carnahan	Y	N	N	Y	Y	Y
4 Skelton	Y	N	N	Y	Y	Y
5 Cleaver	Y	N	N	Y	Y	Y
6 **Graves**	N	Y	Y	Y	Y	N
7 **Blunt**	N	Y	Y	Y	Y	N
8 **Emerson**	N	N	Y	Y	Y	N
9 **Luetkemeyer**	N	Y	Y	Y	Y	N
MONTANA						
AL **Rehberg**	N	Y	Y	Y	Y	N
NEBRASKA						
1 **Fortenberry**	N	N	N	Y	Y	N
2 **Terry**	N	?	?	?	Y	N
3 **Smith**	N	Y	Y	Y	Y	N
NEVADA						
1 Berkley	Y	N	N	Y	Y	Y
2 **Heller**	N	N	N	Y	Y	N
3 Titus	Y	N	N	Y	Y	Y
NEW HAMPSHIRE						
1 Shea-Porter	Y	N	N	Y	Y	Y
2 Hodes	Y	N	N	Y	Y	Y
NEW JERSEY						
1 Andrews	Y	N	N	Y	Y	Y
2 **LoBiondo**	Y	Y	Y	Y	Y	N
3 Adler	Y	N	N	Y	Y	Y
4 **Smith**	Y	Y	N	Y	Y	N
5 **Garrett**	N	Y	Y	Y	Y	N
6 Pallone	Y	N	N	Y	Y	Y
7 **Lance**	Y	Y	Y	Y	Y	N
8 Pascrell	Y	N	N	Y	Y	Y
9 Rothman	Y	N	N	Y	Y	Y
10 Payne	Y	N	N	Y	Y	Y
11 **Frelinghuysen**	N	Y	Y	Y	Y	N
12 Holt	Y	N	N	Y	Y	Y
13 Sires	Y	N	N	Y	Y	Y
NEW MEXICO						
1 Heinrich	Y	N	N	Y	Y	Y
2 Teague	Y	N	N	Y	Y	Y
3 Lujan	Y	N	N	Y	Y	Y
NEW YORK						
1 Bishop	Y	N	N	Y	Y	Y
2 Israel	Y	N	N	Y	Y	Y
3 **King**	Y	Y	N	Y	Y	N
4 McCarthy	Y	N	N	Y	Y	Y
5 Ackerman	Y	N	N	Y	Y	Y
6 Meeks	Y	N	N	Y	Y	Y
7 Crowley	Y	N	N	Y	?	Y
8 Nadler	Y	N	N	Y	Y	Y
9 Weiner	Y	N	N	Y	Y	Y
10 Towns	Y	N	N	Y	Y	Y
11 Clarke	Y	N	N	Y	Y	Y
12 Velázquez	Y	N	N	Y	Y	Y
13 McMahon	Y	N	N	Y	Y	Y
14 Maloney	Y	N	N	Y	Y	Y
15 Rangel	Y	N	N	Y	Y	Y
16 Serrano	Y	N	N	Y	Y	Y
17 Engel	Y	N	N	Y	Y	Y
18 Lowey	Y	N	N	Y	Y	Y
19 Hall	Y	N	N	Y	Y	Y
20 Gillibrand	Y	N	N	Y	Y	Y
21 Tonko	Y	N	–	Y	Y	Y
22 Hinchey	Y	N	N	Y	Y	Y
23 **McHugh**	Y	Y	N	Y	Y	N
24 Arcuri	Y	N	N	Y	Y	Y
25 Maffei	Y	N	N	Y	Y	Y
26 **Lee**	N	Y	Y	Y	Y	N
27 Higgins	Y	N	N	Y	Y	Y
28 Slaughter	Y	N	N	Y	Y	Y
29 Massa	Y	N	N	Y	Y	Y
NORTH CAROLINA						
1 Butterfield	Y	N	N	Y	Y	Y
2 Etheridge	Y	N	N	Y	Y	Y
3 **Jones**	N	N	N	Y	Y	N
4 Price	Y	N	N	Y	Y	Y

	19	20	21	22	23	24
5 **Foxx**	N	Y	Y	Y	Y	N
6 **Coble**	N	N	Y	Y	Y	N
7 McIntyre	N	N	N	Y	Y	Y
8 Kissell	Y	N	N	Y	Y	Y
9 **Myrick**	N	Y	Y	Y	Y	N
10 **McHenry**	N	Y	Y	Y	Y	N
11 Shuler	?	?	?	?	Y	Y
12 Watt	Y	N	N	Y	Y	Y
13 Miller	Y	N	N	Y	Y	Y
NORTH DAKOTA						
AL Pomeroy	Y	N	N	Y	Y	Y
OHIO						
1 Driehaus	Y	N	N	Y	Y	Y
2 **Schmidt**	Y	Y	N	Y	Y	N
3 **Turner**	Y	N	N	Y	Y	N
4 **Jordan**	N	Y	Y	Y	Y	N
5 **Latta**	N	Y	Y	Y	Y	N
6 Wilson	Y	N	N	Y	Y	Y
7 **Austria**	N	Y	Y	Y	Y	N
8 **Boehner**	N	Y	Y	Y	Y	N
9 Kaptur	Y	N	N	Y	Y	Y
10 Kucinich	Y	N	N	Y	Y	Y
11 Fudge	Y	N	N	Y	Y	Y
12 **Tiberi**	Y	Y	N	Y	?	?
13 Sutton	Y	N	N	Y	Y	Y
14 **LaTourette**	Y	Y	N	Y	Y	N
15 Kilroy	Y	N	N	Y	Y	Y
16 Boccieri	Y	N	N	Y	Y	Y
17 Ryan	Y	N	N	Y	Y	Y
18 Space	Y	N	N	Y	Y	Y
OKLAHOMA						
1 **Sullivan**	?	?	?	?	Y	N
2 Boren	Y	N	N	Y	Y	Y
3 **Lucas**	N	Y	Y	Y	Y	N
4 **Cole**	N	Y	Y	Y	Y	N
5 **Fallin**	N	Y	Y	Y	Y	N
OREGON						
1 Wu	Y	N	N	Y	Y	Y
2 **Walden**	N	Y	N	Y	Y	N
3 Blumenauer	Y	N	N	Y	Y	Y
4 DeFazio	Y	N	N	Y	Y	Y
5 Schrader	Y	N	N	Y	Y	Y
PENNSYLVANIA						
1 Brady	Y	N	N	Y	Y	Y
2 Fattah	Y	N	N	Y	Y	Y
3 Dahlkemper	Y	N	N	Y	Y	Y
4 Altmire	N	N	N	Y	Y	Y
5 **Thompson**	N	Y	Y	Y	Y	N
6 **Gerlach**	Y	N	N	Y	Y	N
7 Sestak	?	?	?	?	Y	Y
8 Murphy, P.	Y	N	N	Y	Y	Y
9 **Shuster**	N	Y	Y	Y	Y	N
10 Carney	N	N	N	Y	Y	Y
11 Kanjorski	Y	N	N	Y	Y	Y
12 Murtha	Y	N	N	Y	Y	Y
13 Schwartz	Y	N	N	Y	Y	Y
14 Doyle	Y	N	N	Y	Y	Y
15 **Dent**	Y	N	N	Y	Y	N
16 **Pitts**	N	Y	N	Y	Y	N
17 Holden	N	N	N	Y	Y	Y
18 **Murphy, T.**	N	Y	N	Y	Y	N
19 **Platts**	N	N	N	Y	+	N
RHODE ISLAND						
1 Kennedy	Y	N	N	Y	Y	Y
2 Langevin	Y	N	N	Y	Y	Y
SOUTH CAROLINA						
1 **Brown**	N	Y	Y	Y	Y	N
2 **Wilson**	N	Y	Y	Y	Y	N
3 **Barrett**	N	Y	Y	Y	Y	N
4 **Inglis**	N	Y	Y	Y	Y	N
5 Spratt	Y	N	N	Y	Y	Y
6 Clyburn	Y	N	N	Y	Y	Y
SOUTH DAKOTA						
AL Herseth Sandlin	Y	N	N	Y	?	?
TENNESSEE						
1 **Roe**	N	N	Y	Y	Y	N
2 **Duncan**	N	Y	Y	Y	Y	N
3 **Wamp**	N	N	Y	Y	Y	N
4 Davis	Y	N	N	Y	Y	Y
5 Cooper	Y	N	N	Y	Y	Y
6 Gordon	Y	N	N	Y	Y	Y
7 **Blackburn**	N	Y	Y	Y	Y	N
8 Tanner	Y	N	N	Y	Y	Y
9 Cohen	Y	N	N	Y	Y	Y

	19	20	21	22	23	24
TEXAS						
1 **Gohmert**	N	Y	Y	Y	Y	N
2 **Poe**	N	Y	Y	Y	Y	N
3 **Johnson, S.**	N	Y	Y	Y	Y	N
4 **Hall**	N	Y	Y	Y	Y	N
5 **Hensarling**	N	Y	Y	Y	Y	N
6 **Barton**	Y	Y	N	Y	Y	N
7 **Culberson**	N	Y	Y	Y	Y	N
8 **Brady**	N	Y	Y	Y	Y	N
9 Green, A.	Y	N	N	Y	Y	Y
10 **McCaul**	N	Y	Y	Y	Y	N
11 **Conaway**	N	Y	Y	Y	Y	N
12 **Granger**	N	Y	Y	Y	Y	N
13 **Thornberry**	N	Y	Y	Y	Y	N
14 **Paul**	N	Y	Y	Y	Y	N
15 Hinojosa	Y	N	N	Y	Y	Y
16 Reyes	Y	N	N	Y	Y	Y
17 Edwards	Y	N	N	Y	Y	Y
18 Jackson Lee	Y	N	N	Y	Y	Y
19 **Neugebauer**	N	Y	Y	Y	+	–
20 Gonzalez	Y	N	N	Y	Y	Y
21 **Smith**	N	Y	Y	Y	Y	N
22 **Olson**	N	Y	Y	Y	Y	N
23 Rodriguez	Y	N	N	Y	Y	Y
24 **Marchant**	N	Y	Y	Y	Y	N
25 Doggett	N	N	N	Y	Y	Y
26 **Burgess**	N	Y	N	Y	Y	N
27 Ortiz	Y	N	N	Y	Y	Y
28 Cuellar	Y	N	N	Y	Y	N
29 Green, G.	Y	N	N	Y	Y	Y
30 Johnson, E.	Y	N	N	Y	Y	Y
31 **Carter**	N	Y	Y	Y	Y	N
32 **Sessions**	?	?	?	?	Y	N
UTAH						
1 **Bishop**	N	Y	Y	Y	Y	N
2 Matheson	Y	N	N	Y	Y	Y
3 **Chaffetz**	N	Y	Y	Y	Y	N
VERMONT						
AL Welch	Y	N	N	Y	Y	Y
VIRGINIA						
1 **Wittman**	N	Y	Y	Y	Y	N
2 Nye	Y	N	N	Y	Y	Y
3 Scott	Y	N	N	Y	Y	Y
4 **Forbes**	N	Y	Y	Y	Y	N
5 Perriello	Y	N	N	Y	Y	Y
6 **Goodlatte**	N	Y	Y	Y	Y	N
7 **Cantor**	N	Y	Y	Y	Y	N
8 Moran	Y	N	N	Y	Y	Y
9 Boucher	?	?	?	?	?	?
10 **Wolf**	N	Y	N	Y	Y	N
11 Connolly	Y	N	N	Y	Y	Y
WASHINGTON						
1 Inslee	Y	N	N	Y	Y	Y
2 Larsen	Y	N	N	Y	Y	Y
3 Baird	Y	N	N	Y	Y	Y
4 **Hastings**	N	Y	Y	Y	Y	N
5 **McMorris Rodgers**	N	Y	Y	Y	Y	N
6 Dicks	Y	N	N	Y	Y	Y
7 McDermott	Y	N	N	Y	Y	Y
8 **Reichert**	Y	Y	N	Y	Y	N
9 Smith	Y	N	N	Y	Y	Y
WEST VIRGINIA						
1 Mollohan	Y	N	N	Y	Y	Y
2 **Capito**	Y	Y	Y	Y	Y	N
3 Rahall	Y	N	N	Y	Y	Y
WISCONSIN						
1 **Ryan**	N	Y	Y	Y	Y	N
2 Baldwin	Y	N	N	Y	Y	Y
3 Kind	Y	N	N	Y	Y	Y
4 Moore	Y	N	?	Y	Y	Y
5 **Sensenbrenner**	N	Y	Y	Y	Y	N
6 **Petri**	Y	Y	Y	Y	Y	N
7 Obey	Y	N	N	Y	Y	Y
8 Kagen	Y	N	N	Y	Y	Y
WYOMING						
AL **Lummis**	N	Y	Y	Y	Y	N
DELEGATES						
Faleomavaega (A.S.)	?	?	?	?	Y	
Norton (D.C.)	Y	N	N	Y	Y	
Bordallo (Guam)	?	N	N	Y	+	
Sablan (N. Marianas)	?	?	N	Y	N	
Pierluisi (P.R.)	Y	N	N	Y	Y	
Christensen (V.I.)	?	?	?	?	Y	

IN THE HOUSE | By Vote Number

25. **HR 384. Troubled Asset Relief Program/Recommit.** Barrett, R-S.C., motion to recommit the bill to the Financial Services Committee with instructions that it be reported back forthwith with language that would require the Treasury Department to develop a plan for repayment of all assistance provided under the $700 billion 2008 financial industry bailout law and repeal authority to spend the final $350 billion. Motion rejected 199-228: R 172-2; D 27-226. Jan. 21, 2009.

26. **HR 384. Troubled Asset Relief Program/Passage.** Passage of the bill that would set conditions on the use of the second $350 billion provided under the 2008 financial industry bailout law. It would require the Treasury to commit between $40 billion and $100 billion for foreclosure mitigation and authorize the Treasury to provide assistance to domestic automobile manufacturers under the program. The bill's executive-compensation restrictions could be applied retroactively to institutions that have already received assistance under the program. Passed 260-166: R 18-156; D 242-10. Jan. 21, 2009.

27. **H J Res 3. Troubled Asset Relief Program Disapproval/Passage.** Passage of the joint resolution that would prevent the release of the second half of the $700 billion provided under the 2008 financial industry bailout law. Passed 270-155: R 171-4; D 99-151. A "nay" was a vote in support of the president's position. Jan. 22, 2009.

28. **H Res 56. National School Counseling Week/Adoption.** Loebsack, D-Iowa, motion to suspend the rules and adopt the resolution that would honor the contributions of school counselors in elementary and secondary schools, and encourage the observation of "National School Counseling Week" with activities that promote awareness of the role school counselors play in students' lives. Motion agreed to 417-0: R 172-0; D 245-0. A two-thirds majority of those present and voting (278 in this case) is required for adoption under suspension of the rules. Jan. 22, 2009.

29. **H Res 58. University of Florida Football Team Tribute/Adoption.** Loebsack, D-Iowa, motion to suspend the rules and adopt the resolution that would commend the University of Florida football team for winning the Bowl Championship Series National Championship. Motion agreed to 399-5: R 161-3; D 238-2. A two-thirds majority of those present and voting (270 in this case) is required for adoption under suspension of the rules. Jan. 22, 2009.

	25	26	27	28	29
ALABAMA					
1 Bonner	Y	N	Y	Y	Y
2 Bright	Y	N	Y	Y	P
3 Rogers	Y	N	Y	Y	?
4 Aderholt	Y	N	Y	Y	Y
5 Griffith	Y	Y	Y	Y	Y
6 Bachus	Y	N	Y	Y	Y
7 Davis	N	Y	Y	Y	Y
ALASKA					
AL Young	?	?	?	?	?
ARIZONA					
1 Kirkpatrick	N	N	Y	Y	Y
2 Franks	Y	N	Y	Y	Y
3 Shadegg	Y	N	Y	Y	Y
4 Pastor	N	Y	N	Y	Y
5 Mitchell	Y	Y	Y	Y	Y
6 Flake	Y	N	Y	Y	N
7 Grijalva	N	Y	N	Y	Y
8 Giffords	N	Y	N	Y	Y
ARKANSAS					
1 Berry	N	Y	Y	Y	N
2 Snyder	N	Y	N	Y	?
3 Boozman	Y	N	Y	Y	Y
4 Ross	N	Y	Y	Y	Y
CALIFORNIA					
1 Thompson	N	Y	N	Y	Y
2 Herger	Y	N	Y	Y	Y
3 Lungren	Y	N	Y	Y	Y
4 McClintock	Y	N	Y	Y	Y
5 Matsui	N	Y	N	Y	Y
6 Woolsey	N	Y	N	Y	Y
7 Miller, George	N	Y	N	Y	Y
8 Pelosi			N		
9 Lee	N	Y	N	Y	Y
10 Tauscher	N	Y	N	Y	Y
11 McNerney	N	Y	Y	Y	Y
12 Speier	N	Y	Y	Y	?
13 Stark	N	Y	N	Y	Y
14 Eshoo	N	Y	N	Y	Y
15 Honda	N	Y	N	Y	Y
16 Lofgren	N	Y	N	Y	Y
17 Farr	N	Y	N	Y	Y
18 Cardoza	N	Y	Y	Y	Y
19 Radanovich	Y	N	Y	Y	Y
20 Costa	N	Y	Y	Y	Y
21 Nunes	Y	N	Y	Y	Y
22 McCarthy	Y	N	Y	Y	Y
23 Capps	N	Y	N	Y	Y
24 Gallegly	Y	N	Y	?	?
25 McKeon	Y	N	Y	Y	Y
26 Dreier	Y	N	Y	Y	Y
27 Sherman	N	Y	N	Y	Y
28 Berman	N	Y	N	Y	Y
29 Schiff	N	Y	N	Y	Y
30 Waxman	N	Y	N	Y	Y
31 Becerra	N	Y	N	Y	Y
32 Solis	?	?	?	?	?
33 Watson	N	Y	N	Y	Y
34 Roybal-Allard	N	Y	N	Y	Y
35 Waters	N	Y	N	Y	Y
36 Harman	N	Y	Y	Y	Y
37 Richardson	N	Y	Y	Y	Y
38 Napolitano	N	Y	Y	Y	Y
39 Sánchez, Linda	N	Y	Y	Y	Y
40 Royce	Y	N	Y	Y	Y
41 Lewis	Y	N	Y	Y	Y
42 Miller, Gary	Y	N	Y	Y	Y
43 Baca	N	Y	N	Y	Y
44 Calvert	Y	N	Y	Y	Y
45 Bono Mack	Y	N	Y	Y	Y
46 Rohrabacher	Y	N	Y	Y	Y
47 Sanchez, Loretta	N	Y	Y	Y	Y
48 Campbell	N	Y	Y	Y	Y
49 Issa	Y	N	Y	Y	Y
50 Bilbray	Y	N	Y	Y	Y
51 Filner	N	Y	Y	Y	Y
52 Hunter	Y	N	Y	Y	Y
53 Davis	N	Y	N	Y	Y

	25	26	27	28	29
COLORADO					
1 DeGette	N	Y	N	Y	Y
2 Polis	N	Y	N	Y	Y
3 Salazar	N	Y	Y	Y	Y
4 Markey	N	Y	Y	+	Y
5 Lamborn	Y	N	Y	Y	Y
6 Coffman	Y	N	Y	Y	Y
7 Perlmutter	N	Y	N	Y	Y
CONNECTICUT					
1 Larson	N	Y	N	Y	Y
2 Courtney	N	Y	Y	Y	Y
3 DeLauro	N	Y	N	Y	Y
4 Himes	N	Y	N	Y	Y
5 Murphy	N	Y	N	Y	Y
DELAWARE					
AL Castle	Y	Y	Y	Y	Y
FLORIDA					
1 Miller	Y	N	Y	Y	Y
2 Boyd	N	Y	Y	Y	Y
3 Brown	N	Y	N	Y	Y
4 Crenshaw	Y	N	Y	Y	Y
5 Brown-Waite	Y	N	Y	Y	Y
6 Stearns	Y	N	Y	Y	Y
7 Mica	Y	N	Y	Y	Y
8 Grayson	N	Y	N	Y	Y
9 Bilirakis	Y	N	Y	Y	Y
10 Young	Y	N	Y	Y	Y
11 Castor	N	Y	N	Y	Y
12 Putnam	Y	N	Y	Y	Y
13 Buchanan	Y	N	Y	Y	Y
14 Mack	Y	N	Y	Y	Y
15 Posey	Y	N	Y	Y	Y
16 Rooney	Y	N	Y	Y	Y
17 Meek	N	Y	Y	Y	Y
18 Ros-Lehtinen	Y	N	Y	Y	Y
19 Wexler	N	Y	N	Y	Y
20 Wasserman Schultz	N	Y	N	Y	Y
21 Diaz-Balart, L.	Y	Y	Y	Y	Y
22 Klein	N	Y	N	Y	Y
23 Hastings	N	Y	N	Y	Y
24 Kosmas	N	Y	Y	Y	Y
25 Diaz-Balart, M.	Y	Y	Y	Y	Y
GEORGIA					
1 Kingston	Y	N	Y	Y	N
2 Bishop	N	Y	N	Y	Y
3 Westmoreland	Y	N	Y	Y	Y
4 Johnson	N	Y	N	Y	Y
5 Lewis	N	Y	N	Y	Y
6 Price	Y	N	Y	Y	Y
7 Linder	Y	N	Y	Y	Y
8 Marshall	N	N	N	Y	Y
9 Deal	Y	N	Y	Y	Y
10 Broun	Y	N	Y	Y	Y
11 Gingrey	Y	N	Y	Y	Y
12 Barrow	Y	Y	Y	Y	Y
13 Scott	N	Y	N	Y	Y
HAWAII					
1 Abercrombie	N	Y	N	Y	Y
2 Hirono	N	Y	N	Y	Y
IDAHO					
1 Minnick	Y	N	Y	Y	Y
2 Simpson	Y	N	Y	Y	Y
ILLINOIS					
1 Rush	N	Y	N	Y	Y
2 Jackson	N	Y	N	Y	Y
3 Lipinski	N	Y	Y	Y	Y
4 Gutierrez	N	Y	N	Y	Y
5 Vacant					
6 Roskam	Y	N	Y	Y	Y
7 Davis	N	Y	N	Y	Y
8 Bean	N	Y	N	Y	Y
9 Schakowsky	N	Y	N	Y	Y
10 Kirk	Y	N	Y	Y	Y
11 Halvorson	Y	Y	Y	Y	Y
12 Costello	N	Y	N	Y	Y
13 Biggert	Y	N	Y	Y	Y
14 Foster	N	Y	N	Y	Y
15 Johnson	Y	N	Y	Y	P

KEY   **Republicans**   Democrats

Y Voted for (yea)	X Paired against	C Voted "present" to avoid possible conflict of interest
# Paired for	− Announced against	
+ Announced for	P Voted "present"	? Did not vote or otherwise make a position known
N Voted against (nay)		

	25	26	27	28	29
16 Manzullo	Y	N	Y	Y	?
17 Hare	N	Y	Y	Y	Y
18 Schock	Y	Y	Y	Y	Y
19 Shimkus	Y	N	Y	Y	Y
INDIANA					
1 Visclosky	N	Y	Y	Y	Y
2 Donnelly	N	Y	N	Y	Y
3 Souder	?	Y	N	Y	Y
4 Buyer	Y	N	Y	Y	Y
5 Burton	Y	N	Y	Y	Y
6 Pence	Y	N	Y	Y	Y
7 Carson	N	Y	N	Y	Y
8 Ellsworth	Y	Y	Y	Y	Y
9 Hill	Y	Y	Y	Y	Y
IOWA					
1 Braley	N	Y	N	Y	Y
2 Loebsack	N	Y	N	Y	Y
3 Boswell	N	Y	N	Y	Y
4 Latham	Y	N	Y	Y	Y
5 King	Y	N	Y	Y	Y
KANSAS					
1 Moran	Y	N	Y	Y	Y
2 Jenkins	Y	N	Y	Y	Y
3 Moore	N	Y	N	Y	Y
4 Tiahrt	Y	N	Y	Y	Y
KENTUCKY					
1 Whitfield	Y	N	Y	Y	Y
2 Guthrie	Y	N	Y	Y	Y
3 Yarmuth	N	Y	N	Y	Y
4 Davis	Y	N	Y	Y	Y
5 Rogers	Y	N	Y	Y	Y
6 Chandler	Y	Y	Y	Y	Y
LOUISIANA					
1 Scalise	Y	N	Y	Y	Y
2 Cao	Y	N	Y	Y	Y
3 Melancon	Y	Y	Y	Y	Y
4 Fleming	Y	N	Y	Y	Y
5 Alexander	Y	N	Y	Y	Y
6 Cassidy	Y	N	Y	Y	Y
7 Boustany	Y	N	Y	Y	Y
MAINE					
1 Pingree	N	Y	Y	?	?
2 Michaud	Y	Y	Y	?	?
MARYLAND					
1 Kratovil	Y	Y	Y	Y	Y
2 Ruppersberger	N	Y	Y	Y	Y
3 Sarbanes	N	Y	N	Y	Y
4 Edwards	N	Y	N	Y	Y
5 Hoyer	N	Y	N	Y	Y
6 Bartlett	Y	N	Y	Y	Y
7 Cummings	N	Y	N	Y	Y
8 Van Hollen	N	Y	N	Y	Y
MASSACHUSETTS					
1 Olver	N	Y	N	Y	Y
2 Neal	N	Y	N	Y	Y
3 McGovern	N	Y	N	Y	Y
4 Frank	N	Y	N	Y	Y
5 Tsongas	N	Y	N	Y	Y
6 Tierney	N	Y	N	Y	Y
7 Markey	N	Y	N	Y	Y
8 Capuano	N	Y	Y	Y	Y
9 Lynch	N	Y	Y	Y	Y
10 Delahunt	N	Y	Y	Y	Y
MICHIGAN					
1 Stupak	N	Y	Y	Y	Y
2 Hoekstra	Y	Y	Y	Y	Y
3 Ehlers	Y	Y	Y	Y	Y
4 Camp	Y	Y	Y	Y	Y
5 Kildee	N	Y	N	Y	Y
6 Upton	Y	Y	Y	Y	Y
7 Schauer	N	Y	Y	Y	Y
8 Rogers	Y	Y	Y	Y	Y
9 Peters	N	Y	N	Y	Y
10 Miller	Y	Y	Y	Y	Y
11 McCotter	Y	Y	Y	Y	Y
12 Levin	N	Y	N	Y	Y
13 Kilpatrick	N	Y	N	Y	Y
14 Conyers	N	+	N	Y	Y
15 Dingell	N	Y	N	Y	Y
MINNESOTA					
1 Walz	N	Y	Y	Y	Y
2 Kline	Y	N	Y	Y	Y
3 Paulsen	Y	N	Y	Y	Y
4 McCollum	N	Y	Y	Y	Y

	25	26	27	28	29
5 Ellison	N	Y	N	Y	Y
6 Bachmann	Y	N	Y	Y	Y
7 Peterson	N	N	Y	Y	Y
8 Oberstar	N	Y	N	Y	Y
MISSISSIPPI					
1 Childers	Y	Y	Y	Y	Y
2 Thompson	N	Y	N	Y	Y
3 Harper	Y	N	Y	Y	Y
4 Taylor	Y	N	Y	Y	Y
MISSOURI					
1 Clay	N	Y	N	Y	Y
2 Akin	Y	N	Y	Y	Y
3 Carnahan	N	Y	N	Y	Y
4 Skelton	N	Y	?	?	?
5 Cleaver	N	Y	N	Y	Y
6 Graves	Y	N	Y	Y	Y
7 Blunt	Y	N	Y	Y	Y
8 Emerson	Y	N	Y	Y	Y
9 Luetkemeyer	Y	N	Y	Y	Y
MONTANA					
AL Rehberg	Y	N	Y	Y	Y
NEBRASKA					
1 Fortenberry	Y	N	Y	Y	Y
2 Terry	Y	N	Y	Y	Y
3 Smith	Y	N	Y	Y	Y
NEVADA					
1 Berkley	N	Y	Y	Y	Y
2 Heller	Y	N	Y	Y	Y
3 Titus	N	Y	Y	Y	Y
NEW HAMPSHIRE					
1 Shea-Porter	N	Y	Y	Y	Y
2 Hodes	Y	Y	Y	Y	Y
NEW JERSEY					
1 Andrews	N	Y	N	Y	Y
2 LoBiondo	Y	N	Y	Y	Y
3 Adler	N	Y	Y	Y	Y
4 Smith	Y	N	Y	Y	Y
5 Garrett	Y	N	Y	?	?
6 Pallone	N	Y	N	Y	Y
7 Lance	Y	Y	Y	Y	Y
8 Pascrell	N	Y	N	Y	Y
9 Rothman	N	Y	N	Y	Y
10 Payne	N	Y	N	Y	Y
11 Frelinghuysen	Y	N	Y	Y	Y
12 Holt	N	Y	N	Y	Y
13 Sires	N	Y	N	Y	Y
NEW MEXICO					
1 Heinrich	N	Y	Y	Y	Y
2 Teague	Y	Y	Y	Y	Y
3 Lujan	N	Y	Y	Y	Y
NEW YORK					
1 Bishop	N	Y	N	Y	Y
2 Israel	N	Y	N	Y	Y
3 King	Y	N	Y	Y	Y
4 McCarthy	N	Y	N	Y	Y
5 Ackerman	N	Y	N	Y	?
6 Meeks	N	Y	N	Y	Y
7 Crowley	N	Y	N	Y	Y
8 Nadler	N	Y	N	Y	Y
9 Weiner	N	Y	N	Y	Y
10 Towns	N	Y	N	Y	Y
11 Clarke	N	Y	N	Y	Y
12 Velázquez	N	Y	N	Y	Y
13 McMahon	N	Y	Y	Y	Y
14 Maloney	N	Y	N	Y	Y
15 Rangel	N	Y	N	Y	Y
16 Serrano	N	Y	N	Y	Y
17 Engel	N	Y	N	Y	Y
18 Lowey	N	Y	N	Y	Y
19 Hall	N	Y	N	Y	Y
20 Gillibrand	N	Y	N	Y	Y
21 Tonko	N	Y	N	Y	Y
22 Hinchey	N	Y	N	Y	Y
23 McHugh	Y	N	Y	Y	Y
24 Arcuri	Y	Y	Y	Y	Y
25 Maffei	N	Y	Y	Y	Y
26 Lee	Y	N	Y	Y	Y
27 Higgins	N	Y	N	Y	Y
28 Slaughter	N	Y	Y	?	Y
29 Massa	N	Y	Y	Y	Y
NORTH CAROLINA					
1 Butterfield	N	Y	N	Y	Y
2 Etheridge	N	Y	N	Y	Y
3 Jones	Y	N	Y	Y	Y
4 Price	N	Y	N	Y	Y

	25	26	27	28	29
5 Foxx	Y	N	Y	Y	Y
6 Coble	Y	N	Y	Y	Y
7 McIntyre	Y	N	Y	Y	Y
8 Kissell	N	Y	N	Y	Y
9 Myrick	Y	N	Y	Y	Y
10 McHenry	Y	N	Y	Y	Y
11 Shuler	Y	N	Y	Y	Y
12 Watt	N	Y	N	Y	Y
13 Miller	N	Y	N	Y	Y
NORTH DAKOTA					
AL Pomeroy	N	Y	N	Y	Y
OHIO					
1 Driehaus	N	Y	Y	Y	Y
2 Schmidt	Y	N	Y	Y	Y
3 Turner	Y	Y	Y	Y	Y
4 Jordan	Y	N	Y	Y	Y
5 Latta	Y	N	Y	Y	Y
6 Wilson	N	Y	N	Y	Y
7 Austria	Y	N	Y	Y	Y
8 Boehner	Y	N	Y	Y	Y
9 Kaptur	Y	Y	Y	Y	Y
10 Kucinich	N	Y	Y	Y	Y
11 Fudge	N	Y	N	Y	Y
12 Tiberi	?	?	?	?	?
13 Sutton	N	Y	N	Y	Y
14 LaTourette	Y	Y	Y	Y	Y
15 Kilroy	N	Y	Y	Y	Y
16 Boccieri	N	Y	N	Y	Y
17 Ryan	N	Y	N	Y	Y
18 Space	N	Y	Y	Y	Y
OKLAHOMA					
1 Sullivan	Y	N	Y	Y	Y
2 Boren	N	Y	Y	Y	Y
3 Lucas	Y	N	Y	Y	Y
4 Cole	Y	N	Y	Y	Y
5 Fallin	Y	N	Y	Y	Y
OREGON					
1 Wu	N	Y	N	Y	Y
2 Walden	Y	N	Y	Y	Y
3 Blumenauer	N	Y	N	Y	Y
4 DeFazio	Y	Y	Y	Y	Y
5 Schrader	N	Y	Y	Y	Y
PENNSYLVANIA					
1 Brady	N	Y	N	Y	Y
2 Fattah	N	Y	N	Y	Y
3 Dahlkemper	Y	Y	Y	Y	Y
4 Altmire	Y	N	Y	Y	N
5 Thompson	Y	N	Y	Y	Y
6 Gerlach	Y	Y	Y	Y	Y
7 Sestak	N	Y	N	Y	Y
8 Murphy, P.	N	Y	N	Y	Y
9 Shuster	Y	N	Y	Y	Y
10 Carney	Y	Y	Y	Y	?
11 Kanjorski	N	Y	N	Y	Y
12 Murtha	N	Y	N	Y	Y
13 Schwartz	N	Y	N	Y	Y
14 Doyle	N	Y	N	Y	Y
15 Dent	Y	N	Y	Y	Y
16 Pitts	Y	N	Y	Y	Y
17 Holden	N	N	Y	Y	Y
18 Murphy, T.	Y	N	Y	Y	Y
19 Platts	Y	N	Y	Y	Y
RHODE ISLAND					
1 Kennedy	N	Y	N	Y	Y
2 Langevin	N	Y	N	Y	Y
SOUTH CAROLINA					
1 Brown	Y	N	Y	Y	Y
2 Wilson	Y	N	Y	Y	Y
3 Barrett	Y	N	Y	Y	Y
4 Inglis	N	N	N	Y	Y
5 Spratt	N	Y	N	Y	Y
6 Clyburn	N	Y	N	Y	Y
SOUTH DAKOTA					
AL Herseth Sandlin	Y	Y	Y	Y	Y
TENNESSEE					
1 Roe	Y	N	Y	Y	Y
2 Duncan	Y	N	Y	Y	Y
3 Wamp	Y	N	Y	Y	?
4 Davis	N	Y	Y	Y	Y
5 Cooper	N	Y	N	Y	Y
6 Gordon	N	Y	N	Y	Y
7 Blackburn	Y	N	Y	Y	Y
8 Tanner	N	Y	?	?	?
9 Cohen	N	Y	N	Y	Y

	25	26	27	28	29
TEXAS					
1 Gohmert	Y	N	Y	Y	Y
2 Poe	Y	–	Y	Y	P
3 Johnson, S.	Y	N	Y	Y	Y
4 Hall	Y	N	Y	Y	Y
5 Hensarling	Y	N	Y	Y	Y
6 Barton	Y	N	Y	Y	N
7 Culberson	Y	N	Y	Y	P
8 Brady	Y	N	Y	Y	Y
9 Green, A.	N	Y	N	Y	Y
10 McCaul	Y	N	Y	Y	Y
11 Conaway	Y	N	Y	Y	Y
12 Granger	Y	N	Y	Y	Y
13 Thornberry	Y	N	Y	Y	Y
14 Paul	Y	N	Y	Y	Y
15 Hinojosa	N	Y	N	Y	Y
16 Reyes	N	Y	N	Y	Y
17 Edwards	N	Y	N	Y	Y
18 Jackson Lee	N	Y	N	Y	Y
19 Neugebauer	+	–	+	+	+
20 Gonzalez	N	Y	N	Y	Y
21 Smith	Y	N	Y	Y	Y
22 Olson	Y	N	Y	Y	Y
23 Rodriguez	Y	Y	Y	Y	Y
24 Marchant	Y	N	Y	?	?
25 Doggett	N	Y	N	Y	Y
26 Burgess	Y	N	Y	Y	Y
27 Ortiz	N	Y	N	Y	Y
28 Cuellar	N	Y	Y	Y	Y
29 Green, G.	N	Y	Y	Y	Y
30 Johnson, E.	N	Y	–	?	+
31 Carter	Y	N	Y	Y	Y
32 Sessions	Y	N	Y	Y	Y
UTAH					
1 Bishop	Y	N	Y	Y	P
2 Matheson	Y	Y	Y	Y	P
3 Chaffetz	Y	N	Y	Y	P
VERMONT					
AL Welch	N	Y	Y	Y	Y
VIRGINIA					
1 Wittman	Y	N	Y	Y	Y
2 Nye	Y	Y	Y	Y	Y
3 Scott	N	Y	N	Y	Y
4 Forbes	Y	N	Y	Y	Y
5 Perriello	N	Y	Y	Y	Y
6 Goodlatte	Y	N	Y	Y	Y
7 Cantor	Y	N	Y	Y	Y
8 Moran	N	Y	N	Y	Y
9 Boucher	?	?	?	?	?
10 Wolf	Y	N	Y	Y	Y
11 Connolly	N	Y	Y	Y	Y
WASHINGTON					
1 Inslee	N	Y	Y	Y	Y
2 Larsen	N	Y	N	Y	?
3 Baird	N	Y	N	Y	Y
4 Hastings	Y	N	Y	Y	Y
5 McMorris Rodgers	Y	N	Y	Y	P
6 Dicks	N	Y	N	Y	Y
7 McDermott	N	Y	Y	Y	Y
8 Reichert	Y	N	Y	Y	Y
9 Smith	N	Y	N	Y	Y
WEST VIRGINIA					
1 Mollohan	N	Y	?	?	?
2 Capito	Y	N	Y	Y	Y
3 Rahall	N	Y	N	Y	Y
WISCONSIN					
1 Ryan	Y	N	Y	Y	Y
2 Baldwin	N	Y	N	Y	Y
3 Kind	N	Y	N	Y	Y
4 Moore	N	Y	N	Y	Y
5 Sensenbrenner	Y	N	Y	Y	Y
6 Petri	Y	N	Y	Y	Y
7 Obey	N	Y	N	Y	Y
8 Kagen	N	Y	N	Y	Y
WYOMING					
AL Lummis	Y	N	Y	Y	Y
DELEGATES					
Faleomavaega (A.S.)					
Norton (D.C.)					
Bordallo (Guam)					
Sablan (N. Marianas)					
Pierluisi (P.R.)					
Christensen (V.I.)					

IN THE HOUSE | By Vote Number

30. H Res 31. National Data Privacy Day/Adoption. Welch, D-Vt., motion to suspend the rules and adopt the resolution that would support the designation of a "National Data Privacy Day." Motion agreed to 402-0: R 164-0; D 238-0. A two-thirds majority of those present and voting (268 in this case) is required for adoption under suspension of the rules. Jan. 26, 2009.

31. H Res 84. Tribute to Flight 1549/Adoption. Costello, D-Ill., motion to suspend the rules and adopt the resolution that would honor the actions of the pilot, crew and rescuers of the US Airways Flight 1549 that landed in the Hudson River on Jan. 15, 2009, shortly after departing LaGuardia Airport in New York. Motion agreed to 402-0: R 164-0; D 238-0. A two-thirds majority of those present and voting (268 in this case) is required for adoption under suspension of the rules. Jan. 26, 2009.

32. S 181. Wage Discrimination/Previous Question. Pingree, D-Maine, motion to order the previous question (thus ending debate and possibility of amendment) on adoption of the rule (H Res 87) to provide for further House floor consideration of the bill that would amend the 1964 Civil Rights Act to clarify time limits for workers to file employment discrimination lawsuits. Motion agreed to 252-175: R 0-175; D 252-0. Jan. 27, 2009.

33. S 181. Wage Discrimination/Rule. Adoption of the rule (H Res 87) to provide for consideration of the bill that would amend the 1964 Civil Rights Act to clarify time limits for workers to file employment discrimination lawsuits. Adopted 252-174: R 0-174; D 252-0. Jan. 27, 2009.

34. HR 1. Economic Stimulus/Previous Question. Slaughter, D-N.Y., motion to order the previous question (thus ending debate and possibility of amendment) on adoption of the rule (H Res 88) to provide for House floor consideration of the bill that would provide $815.8 billion for tax cuts and new spending to stimulate the economy. Motion agreed to 244-183: R 0-175; D 244-8. Jan. 27, 2009.

35. HR 1. Economic Stimulus/Rule. Adoption of the rule (H Res 88) to provide for House floor consideration of the bill that would provide $815.8 billion for tax cuts and new spending to stimulate the economy. Adopted 235-191: R 0-175; D 235-16. Jan. 27, 2009.

	30	31	32	33	34	35
ALABAMA						
1 **Bonner**	Y	Y	N	N	N	N
2 Bright	Y	Y	Y	Y	Y	N
3 **Rogers**	Y	Y	N	N	N	N
4 **Aderholt**	Y	Y	N	N	N	N
5 Griffith	Y	Y	Y	Y	Y	Y
6 **Bachus**	Y	Y	N	N	N	N
7 Davis	Y	Y	Y	Y	Y	Y
ALASKA						
AL **Young**	?	?	?	?	?	?
ARIZONA						
1 Kirkpatrick	Y	Y	Y	Y	Y	Y
2 **Franks**	Y	Y	N	N	N	N
3 **Shadegg**	Y	Y	N	N	N	N
4 Pastor	Y	Y	Y	Y	Y	Y
5 Mitchell	Y	Y	Y	Y	Y	Y
6 **Flake**	Y	Y	N	N	N	N
7 Grijalva	?	?	Y	Y	Y	Y
8 Giffords	Y	Y	Y	Y	Y	Y
ARKANSAS						
1 Berry	Y	Y	Y	Y	N	N
2 Snyder	Y	Y	Y	Y	Y	Y
3 **Boozman**	Y	Y	N	N	N	N
4 Ross	Y	Y	Y	Y	Y	Y
CALIFORNIA						
1 Thompson	Y	Y	Y	Y	Y	Y
2 **Herger**	Y	Y	N	N	N	N
3 **Lungren**	Y	Y	N	N	N	N
4 **McClintock**	Y	Y	N	N	N	N
5 Matsui	Y	Y	Y	Y	Y	Y
6 Woolsey	Y	Y	Y	Y	Y	Y
7 Miller, George	Y	Y	Y	Y	Y	Y
8 Pelosi						
9 Lee	Y	Y	Y	Y	Y	Y
10 Tauscher	Y	Y	Y	Y	Y	Y
11 McNerney	Y	Y	Y	Y	Y	Y
12 Speier	Y	Y	Y	Y	Y	Y
13 Stark	?	?	Y	Y	Y	Y
14 Eshoo	Y	Y	Y	Y	Y	Y
15 Honda	Y	Y	Y	Y	Y	Y
16 Lofgren	Y	Y	Y	Y	Y	Y
17 Farr	Y	Y	Y	Y	Y	Y
18 Cardoza	?	?	Y	Y	Y	Y
19 **Radanovich**	Y	Y	N	N	N	N
20 Costa	Y	Y	Y	Y	Y	Y
21 **Nunes**	Y	Y	N	N	N	N
22 **McCarthy**	Y	Y	N	N	N	N
23 Capps	Y	Y	Y	Y	Y	Y
24 **Gallegly**	Y	Y	N	N	N	N
25 **McKeon**	Y	Y	N	N	N	N
26 **Dreier**	Y	Y	N	N	N	N
27 Sherman	Y	Y	Y	Y	Y	Y
28 Berman	Y	Y	Y	Y	Y	Y
29 Schiff	Y	Y	Y	Y	Y	Y
30 Waxman	Y	Y	Y	Y	Y	?
31 Becerra	Y	Y	Y	Y	Y	Y
32 Solis	?	?	?	?	?	?
33 Watson	Y	Y	Y	Y	Y	Y
34 Roybal-Allard	Y	Y	Y	Y	Y	Y
35 Waters	Y	Y	Y	Y	Y	Y
36 Harman	Y	Y	Y	Y	Y	Y
37 Richardson	Y	Y	Y	Y	Y	Y
38 Napolitano	Y	Y	Y	Y	Y	Y
39 Sánchez, Linda	Y	Y	Y	Y	Y	Y
40 **Royce**	Y	Y	N	N	N	N
41 **Lewis**	Y	N	N	N	N	N
42 **Miller, Gary**	Y	Y	N	N	N	N
43 Baca	Y	Y	Y	Y	Y	Y
44 **Calvert**	Y	Y	N	N	N	N
45 **Bono Mack**	Y	Y	N	N	N	N
46 **Rohrabacher**	?	?	N	N	N	N
47 Sanchez, Loretta	Y	Y	Y	Y	Y	Y
48 **Campbell**	Y	Y	N	N	N	N
49 **Issa**	Y	N	N	N	N	N
50 **Bilbray**	Y	Y	N	N	N	N
51 Filner	Y	Y	Y	Y	Y	Y
52 **Hunter**	Y	Y	N	N	N	N
53 Davis	Y	Y	Y	Y	Y	Y

	30	31	32	33	34	35
COLORADO						
1 DeGette	Y	Y	Y	Y	Y	Y
2 Polis	Y	Y	Y	Y	Y	Y
3 Salazar	Y	Y	Y	Y	Y	Y
4 Markey	Y	Y	Y	Y	Y	Y
5 **Lamborn**	Y	Y	N	N	N	N
6 **Coffman**	Y	Y	N	N	N	N
7 Perlmutter	Y	Y	Y	Y	Y	Y
CONNECTICUT						
1 Larson	Y	Y	Y	Y	Y	Y
2 Courtney	Y	Y	Y	Y	Y	Y
3 DeLauro	Y	Y	Y	Y	Y	Y
4 Himes	Y	Y	Y	Y	Y	Y
5 Murphy	?	?	Y	Y	Y	Y
DELAWARE						
AL **Castle**	Y	Y	N	N	N	N
FLORIDA						
1 **Miller**	+	+	N	N	N	N
2 Boyd	Y	Y	Y	Y	N	N
3 Brown	Y	Y	Y	Y	Y	Y
4 **Crenshaw**	Y	Y	N	N	N	N
5 **Brown-Waite**	Y	Y	?	?	?	?
6 **Stearns**	Y	Y	N	N	N	N
7 **Mica**	Y	Y	N	N	N	N
8 Grayson	Y	Y	Y	Y	Y	Y
9 **Bilirakis**	Y	Y	N	N	N	N
10 **Young**	?	?	N	N	N	N
11 Castor	Y	Y	Y	Y	Y	Y
12 **Putnam**	Y	Y	N	N	N	N
13 **Buchanan**	Y	Y	N	N	N	N
14 **Mack**	Y	Y	N	N	N	N
15 **Posey**	Y	Y	N	N	N	N
16 **Rooney**	Y	Y	N	N	N	N
17 Meek	Y	Y	Y	Y	Y	Y
18 **Ros-Lehtinen**	Y	Y	N	N	N	N
19 Wexler	Y	Y	Y	Y	Y	Y
20 Wasserman Schultz	Y	Y	Y	Y	Y	Y
21 **Diaz-Balart, L.**	Y	Y	N	N	N	N
22 Klein	Y	Y	Y	Y	Y	Y
23 Hastings	Y	Y	Y	Y	Y	Y
24 Kosmas	Y	Y	Y	Y	Y	Y
25 **Diaz-Balart, M.**	Y	Y	N	N	N	N
GEORGIA						
1 **Kingston**	Y	Y	N	N	N	N
2 Bishop	Y	Y	Y	Y	Y	Y
3 **Westmoreland**	Y	Y	N	N	N	N
4 Johnson	Y	Y	Y	Y	Y	Y
5 Lewis	Y	Y	Y	Y	Y	Y
6 **Price**	Y	Y	N	N	N	N
7 **Linder**	Y	Y	N	N	N	N
8 Marshall	Y	Y	Y	Y	Y	Y
9 **Deal**	Y	Y	N	N	N	N
10 **Broun**	Y	Y	N	N	N	N
11 **Gingrey**	Y	Y	N	N	N	N
12 Barrow	Y	Y	Y	Y	Y	Y
13 Scott	Y	Y	Y	Y	Y	Y
HAWAII						
1 Abercrombie	Y	Y	Y	Y	Y	Y
2 Hirono	Y	Y	Y	Y	Y	Y
IDAHO						
1 Minnick	Y	Y	Y	Y	N	N
2 **Simpson**	?	?	N	N	N	N
ILLINOIS						
1 Rush	Y	Y	Y	Y	Y	Y
2 Jackson	Y	Y	Y	Y	Y	Y
3 Lipinski	Y	Y	Y	Y	Y	Y
4 Gutierrez	+	+	Y	Y	Y	Y
5 Vacant						
6 **Roskam**	Y	Y	N	N	N	N
7 Davis	Y	Y	Y	Y	Y	Y
8 Bean	Y	Y	Y	Y	Y	Y
9 Schakowsky	Y	Y	Y	Y	Y	Y
10 **Kirk**	Y	Y	N	N	N	N
11 Halvorson	Y	Y	Y	Y	Y	Y
12 Costello	Y	Y	Y	Y	Y	Y
13 **Biggert**	Y	Y	N	N	N	N
14 Foster	Y	Y	Y	Y	Y	Y
15 **Johnson**	Y	Y	N	N	N	N

KEY **Republicans** Democrats

Y Voted for (yea)	X Paired against	C Voted "present" to avoid possible conflict of interest
# Paired for	– Announced against	
+ Announced for	P Voted "present"	? Did not vote or otherwise make a position known
N Voted against (nay)		

	30	31	32	33	34	35
16 **Manzullo**	Y	Y	N	N	N	N
17 Hare	Y	Y	Y	Y	Y	Y
18 **Schock**	Y	Y	N	N	N	N
19 **Shimkus**	Y	Y	N	N	N	N
INDIANA						
1 Visclosky	Y	Y	Y	Y	Y	Y
2 Donnelly	Y	Y	Y	Y	Y	N
3 **Souder**	?	?	N	N	N	N
4 **Buyer**	Y	Y	N	N	N	N
5 **Burton**	Y	Y	N	N	N	N
6 **Pence**	Y	Y	N	N	N	N
7 Carson	Y	Y	Y	Y	Y	Y
8 Ellsworth	Y	Y	Y	Y	Y	Y
9 Hill	Y	Y	Y	Y	N	N
IOWA						
1 Braley	Y	Y	Y	Y	Y	Y
2 Loebsack	Y	Y	Y	Y	Y	Y
3 Boswell	Y	Y	Y	Y	N	N
4 **Latham**	Y	Y	N	N	N	N
5 **King**	Y	Y	N	N	N	N
KANSAS						
1 **Moran**	Y	Y	N	N	N	N
2 **Jenkins**	Y	Y	N	N	N	N
3 Moore	Y	Y	Y	Y	Y	Y
4 **Tiahrt**	Y	Y	N	N	N	N
KENTUCKY						
1 **Whitfield**	Y	Y	N	N	N	N
2 **Guthrie**	Y	Y	N	N	N	N
3 Yarmuth	Y	Y	Y	Y	Y	Y
4 **Davis**	Y	Y	N	N	N	N
5 **Rogers**	Y	Y	N	N	N	N
6 Chandler	Y	Y	Y	Y	Y	Y
LOUISIANA						
1 **Scalise**	Y	Y	N	N	N	N
2 **Cao**	?	?	N	N	N	N
3 Melancon	Y	Y	Y	Y	?	Y
4 **Fleming**	Y	Y	N	N	N	N
5 **Alexander**	Y	Y	N	N	N	N
6 **Cassidy**	Y	Y	N	N	N	N
7 **Boustany**	Y	Y	N	N	N	N
MAINE						
1 Pingree	Y	Y	Y	Y	Y	Y
2 Michaud	Y	Y	Y	Y	Y	N
MARYLAND						
1 Kratovil	Y	Y	Y	Y	Y	N
2 Ruppersberger	?	?	Y	?	Y	Y
3 Sarbanes	Y	Y	Y	Y	Y	Y
4 Edwards	Y	Y	Y	Y	Y	Y
5 Hoyer	Y	Y	Y	Y	Y	Y
6 **Bartlett**	Y	Y	N	N	N	N
7 Cummings	Y	Y	Y	Y	Y	Y
8 Van Hollen	Y	Y	Y	Y	Y	Y
MASSACHUSETTS						
1 Olver	Y	Y	Y	Y	Y	Y
2 Neal	?	?	Y	Y	Y	Y
3 McGovern	Y	Y	Y	Y	Y	Y
4 Frank	Y	Y	Y	Y	Y	Y
5 Tsongas	Y	Y	Y	Y	Y	Y
6 Tierney	Y	Y	Y	Y	Y	Y
7 Markey	Y	Y	Y	Y	Y	Y
8 Capuano	Y	Y	Y	Y	Y	Y
9 Lynch	Y	Y	Y	Y	Y	Y
10 Delahunt	Y	Y	Y	Y	Y	Y
MICHIGAN						
1 Stupak	Y	Y	Y	Y	Y	Y
2 **Hoekstra**	Y	Y	N	N	N	N
3 **Ehlers**	Y	Y	N	N	N	N
4 **Camp**	Y	Y	N	N	N	N
5 Kildee	Y	Y	Y	Y	Y	Y
6 **Upton**	Y	Y	N	N	N	N
7 Schauer	Y	Y	Y	Y	Y	Y
8 **Rogers**	Y	Y	N	N	N	N
9 Peters	Y	Y	Y	Y	Y	Y
10 **Miller**	Y	Y	N	N	N	N
11 **McCotter**	Y	Y	N	N	N	N
12 Levin	Y	Y	Y	Y	Y	Y
13 Kilpatrick	Y	Y	Y	Y	Y	Y
14 Conyers	Y	Y	Y	Y	Y	Y
15 Dingell	Y	Y	Y	Y	Y	Y
MINNESOTA						
1 Walz	Y	Y	Y	Y	Y	Y
2 **Kline**	Y	Y	N	N	N	N
3 **Paulsen**	Y	Y	N	N	N	N
4 McCollum	Y	Y	?	Y	Y	Y

	30	31	32	33	34	35
5 Ellison	Y	Y	Y	Y	Y	Y
6 **Bachmann**	Y	Y	N	N	N	N
7 Peterson	Y	Y	Y	Y	N	Y
8 Oberstar	Y	Y	Y	Y	Y	Y
MISSISSIPPI						
1 Childers	Y	Y	Y	Y	Y	Y
2 Thompson	Y	Y	Y	Y	Y	Y
3 **Harper**	Y	Y	N	N	N	N
4 Taylor	Y	Y	Y	Y	N	N
MISSOURI						
1 Clay	?	?	Y	Y	Y	Y
2 **Akin**	Y	Y	N	N	N	N
3 Carnahan	?	?	Y	Y	Y	Y
4 Skelton	Y	Y	Y	Y	Y	Y
5 Cleaver	Y	Y	Y	Y	Y	Y
6 **Graves**	+	+	N	N	N	N
7 **Blunt**	Y	Y	N	N	N	N
8 **Emerson**	?	?	N	N	N	N
9 **Luetkemeyer**	+	+	N	N	N	N
MONTANA						
AL **Rehberg**	Y	Y	N	N	N	N
NEBRASKA						
1 **Fortenberry**	Y	Y	N	N	N	N
2 **Terry**	Y	Y	N	N	N	N
3 **Smith**	Y	Y	N	N	N	N
NEVADA						
1 Berkley	Y	Y	Y	Y	Y	Y
2 **Heller**	Y	Y	N	N	N	N
3 Titus	Y	Y	Y	Y	Y	Y
NEW HAMPSHIRE						
1 Shea-Porter	Y	Y	Y	Y	Y	Y
2 Hodes	Y	Y	Y	Y	Y	Y
NEW JERSEY						
1 Andrews	Y	Y	Y	Y	Y	Y
2 **LoBiondo**	Y	Y	N	N	N	N
3 Adler	Y	Y	Y	Y	Y	Y
4 **Smith**	Y	Y	N	N	N	N
5 **Garrett**	Y	Y	N	N	N	N
6 Pallone	Y	Y	Y	Y	Y	Y
7 **Lance**	Y	Y	N	N	N	N
8 Pascrell	Y	Y	Y	Y	Y	Y
9 Rothman	Y	Y	Y	Y	Y	Y
10 Payne	?	?	Y	Y	Y	Y
11 **Frelinghuysen**	Y	Y	N	N	N	N
12 Holt	Y	Y	Y	Y	Y	Y
13 Sires	Y	Y	Y	Y	Y	Y
NEW MEXICO						
1 Heinrich	Y	Y	Y	Y	Y	Y
2 Teague	Y	Y	Y	Y	Y	Y
3 Lujan	Y	Y	Y	Y	Y	Y
NEW YORK						
1 Bishop	Y	Y	Y	Y	Y	Y
2 Israel	Y	Y	Y	Y	Y	Y
3 **King**	Y	Y	N	N	N	N
4 McCarthy	Y	Y	Y	Y	Y	Y
5 Ackerman	Y	Y	Y	Y	Y	Y
6 Meeks	Y	Y	Y	Y	Y	Y
7 Crowley	Y	Y	Y	Y	Y	Y
8 Nadler	Y	Y	Y	Y	Y	Y
9 Weiner	Y	Y	Y	Y	Y	Y
10 Towns	Y	Y	Y	Y	Y	Y
11 Clarke	Y	Y	Y	Y	Y	Y
12 Velázquez	Y	Y	Y	Y	Y	Y
13 McMahon	Y	Y	Y	Y	Y	Y
14 Maloney	Y	Y	Y	Y	Y	Y
15 Rangel	Y	Y	Y	Y	Y	Y
16 Serrano	Y	Y	Y	Y	Y	Y
17 Engel	Y	Y	Y	Y	Y	Y
18 Lowey	Y	Y	Y	Y	Y	Y
19 Hall	Y	Y	Y	Y	Y	Y
20 Vacant						
21 Tonko	Y	Y	Y	Y	Y	Y
22 Hinchey	Y	Y	Y	Y	Y	Y
23 **McHugh**	Y	Y	N	N	N	N
24 Arcuri	Y	Y	Y	Y	Y	Y
25 Maffei	Y	Y	Y	Y	Y	Y
26 **Lee**	Y	Y	N	N	N	N
27 Higgins	Y	Y	Y	Y	Y	Y
28 Slaughter	Y	Y	Y	Y	Y	Y
29 Massa	Y	Y	Y	Y	Y	?
NORTH CAROLINA						
1 Butterfield	Y	Y	Y	Y	Y	Y
2 Etheridge	Y	Y	Y	Y	Y	Y
3 **Jones**	Y	Y	N	N	N	N
4 Price	Y	Y	Y	Y	Y	Y

	30	31	32	33	34	35
5 **Foxx**	Y	Y	N	N	N	N
6 **Coble**	Y	Y	N	N	N	N
7 McIntyre	Y	Y	Y	Y	Y	Y
8 Kissell	Y	Y	Y	Y	Y	Y
9 **Myrick**	Y	Y	N	N	N	N
10 **McHenry**	Y	Y	N	N	N	N
11 Shuler	Y	Y	Y	Y	N	N
12 Watt	Y	Y	Y	Y	Y	Y
13 Miller	Y	Y	Y	Y	Y	Y
NORTH DAKOTA						
AL Pomeroy	Y	Y	Y	Y	Y	Y
OHIO						
1 Driehaus	Y	Y	Y	Y	Y	Y
2 **Schmidt**	Y	Y	N	N	N	N
3 **Turner**	Y	Y	N	N	N	N
4 **Jordan**	Y	Y	N	N	N	N
5 **Latta**	Y	Y	N	N	N	N
6 Wilson	Y	Y	Y	Y	Y	Y
7 **Austria**	Y	Y	N	N	N	N
8 **Boehner**	Y	Y	N	N	N	N
9 Kaptur	Y	Y	Y	Y	Y	Y
10 Kucinich	Y	Y	Y	Y	Y	Y
11 Fudge	Y	Y	Y	Y	Y	Y
12 **Tiberi**	?	?	?	?	?	?
13 Sutton	Y	Y	Y	Y	Y	Y
14 **LaTourette**	Y	Y	N	N	N	N
15 Kilroy	Y	Y	Y	Y	Y	Y
16 Boccieri	Y	Y	Y	Y	Y	Y
17 Ryan	Y	Y	Y	Y	Y	Y
18 Space	Y	Y	Y	Y	Y	Y
OKLAHOMA						
1 **Sullivan**	Y	Y	N	N	N	N
2 Boren	Y	Y	Y	Y	Y	Y
3 **Lucas**	Y	Y	N	N	N	N
4 **Cole**	Y	Y	N	N	N	N
5 **Fallin**	Y	Y	N	N	N	N
OREGON						
1 Wu	Y	Y	Y	Y	Y	Y
2 **Walden**	Y	Y	N	N	N	N
3 Blumenauer	?	?	Y	Y	Y	Y
4 DeFazio	Y	Y	Y	Y	Y	Y
5 Schrader	Y	Y	Y	Y	Y	Y
PENNSYLVANIA						
1 Brady	Y	Y	Y	Y	Y	Y
2 Fattah	Y	Y	Y	Y	Y	Y
3 Dahlkemper	Y	Y	Y	Y	Y	Y
4 Altmire	Y	Y	Y	Y	Y	Y
5 **Thompson**	Y	Y	N	N	N	N
6 **Gerlach**	Y	Y	N	N	N	N
7 Sestak	Y	Y	Y	Y	Y	Y
8 Murphy, P.	Y	Y	Y	Y	Y	Y
9 **Shuster**	Y	Y	N	N	N	N
10 Carney	Y	Y	Y	Y	Y	N
11 Kanjorski	Y	Y	Y	Y	Y	N
12 Murtha	Y	Y	Y	Y	Y	Y
13 Schwartz	Y	Y	Y	Y	Y	Y
14 Doyle	?	?	Y	Y	Y	Y
15 **Dent**	Y	Y	N	N	N	N
16 **Pitts**	Y	Y	N	N	N	N
17 Holden	Y	Y	Y	Y	Y	Y
18 **Murphy, T.**	Y	Y	N	N	N	N
19 **Platts**	Y	Y	N	N	N	N
RHODE ISLAND						
1 Kennedy	Y	Y	Y	Y	Y	Y
2 Langevin	Y	Y	Y	Y	Y	Y
SOUTH CAROLINA						
1 **Brown**	Y	Y	N	N	N	N
2 **Wilson**	Y	Y	N	N	N	N
3 **Barrett**	Y	Y	N	N	N	N
4 **Inglis**	Y	Y	N	N	N	N
5 Spratt	Y	Y	Y	Y	Y	Y
6 Clyburn	Y	Y	Y	Y	Y	Y
SOUTH DAKOTA						
AL Herseth Sandlin	Y	Y	Y	Y	Y	Y
TENNESSEE						
1 **Roe**	Y	Y	N	N	N	N
2 **Duncan**	Y	Y	N	N	N	N
3 **Wamp**	Y	Y	N	N	N	N
4 Davis, L.	Y	Y	Y	Y	Y	Y
5 Cooper	Y	Y	Y	Y	Y	N
6 Gordon	Y	Y	Y	Y	Y	Y
7 **Blackburn**	Y	Y	N	N	N	N
8 Tanner	Y	Y	Y	Y	Y	Y
9 Cohen	Y	Y	Y	Y	Y	Y

	30	31	32	33	34	35
TEXAS						
1 **Gohmert**	Y	Y	N	N	N	N
2 **Poe**	Y	Y	N	N	N	N
3 **Johnson, S.**	Y	Y	N	N	N	N
4 **Hall**	Y	Y	N	N	N	N
5 **Hensarling**	Y	Y	N	N	N	N
6 **Barton**	Y	Y	N	N	N	N
7 **Culberson**	Y	Y	N	N	N	N
8 **Brady**	Y	Y	N	N	N	N
9 Green, A.	Y	Y	Y	Y	Y	Y
10 **McCaul**	Y	Y	N	N	N	N
11 **Conaway**	Y	Y	N	N	N	N
12 **Granger**	Y	Y	N	N	N	N
13 **Thornberry**	Y	Y	N	N	N	N
14 **Paul**	Y	Y	N	N	N	N
15 Hinojosa	Y	Y	Y	Y	Y	Y
16 Reyes	Y	Y	Y	Y	Y	Y
17 Edwards	?	?	Y	Y	Y	Y
18 Jackson Lee	Y	Y	Y	Y	Y	Y
19 **Neugebauer**	Y	Y	N	N	N	N
20 Gonzalez	Y	Y	Y	Y	Y	Y
21 **Smith**	Y	Y	N	N	N	N
22 **Olson**	Y	Y	N	N	N	N
23 Rodriguez	?	?	Y	Y	Y	Y
24 **Marchant**	?	?	N	?	N	N
25 Doggett	Y	Y	Y	Y	Y	Y
26 **Burgess**	Y	Y	N	N	N	N
27 Ortiz	Y	Y	Y	Y	Y	Y
28 Cuellar	Y	Y	Y	Y	Y	Y
29 Green, G.	+	+	Y	Y	Y	Y
30 Johnson, E.	Y	Y	Y	Y	Y	Y
31 **Carter**	Y	Y	N	N	N	N
32 **Sessions**	Y	Y	N	N	N	N
UTAH						
1 **Bishop**	?	?	N	N	N	N
2 Matheson	Y	Y	Y	Y	Y	Y
3 **Chaffetz**	Y	Y	N	N	N	N
VERMONT						
AL Welch	Y	Y	Y	Y	Y	Y
VIRGINIA						
1 **Wittman**	Y	Y	N	N	N	N
2 Nye	Y	Y	Y	Y	Y	Y
3 Scott	Y	Y	Y	Y	Y	Y
4 **Forbes**	Y	Y	N	N	N	N
5 Perriello	Y	Y	Y	Y	Y	Y
6 **Goodlatte**	Y	Y	N	N	N	N
7 **Cantor**	?	?	N	N	N	N
8 Moran	Y	Y	Y	Y	Y	N
9 Boucher	Y	Y	Y	Y	Y	Y
10 **Wolf**	Y	Y	N	N	N	N
11 Connolly	Y	Y	Y	Y	Y	Y
WASHINGTON						
1 Inslee	Y	Y	Y	Y	Y	Y
2 Larsen	Y	Y	Y	Y	Y	Y
3 Baird	Y	Y	Y	Y	Y	Y
4 **Hastings**	Y	Y	N	N	N	N
5 **McMorris Rodgers**	Y	Y	N	N	N	N
6 Dicks	Y	Y	Y	Y	Y	Y
7 McDermott	Y	Y	Y	Y	Y	Y
8 **Reichert**	Y	Y	N	N	N	N
9 Smith	Y	Y	Y	Y	Y	Y
WEST VIRGINIA						
1 Mollohan	Y	Y	Y	Y	Y	Y
2 **Capito**	Y	Y	N	N	N	N
3 Rahall	Y	Y	Y	Y	Y	Y
WISCONSIN						
1 **Ryan**	Y	Y	N	N	N	N
2 Baldwin	Y	Y	Y	Y	Y	Y
3 Kind	Y	Y	Y	Y	Y	Y
4 Moore	Y	Y	Y	Y	Y	Y
5 **Sensenbrenner**	Y	Y	N	N	N	N
6 **Petri**	Y	Y	N	N	N	N
7 Obey	Y	Y	Y	Y	Y	Y
8 Kagen	Y	Y	Y	Y	Y	Y
WYOMING						
AL **Lummis**	Y	Y	N	N	N	N
DELEGATES						
Faleomavaega (A.S.)						
Norton (D.C.)						
Bordallo (Guam)						
Sablan (N. Marianas)						
Pierluisi (P.R.)						
Christensen (V.I.)						

IN THE HOUSE | By Vote Number

36. **S 181. Wage Discrimination/Commit.** McKeon, R-Calif., motion to commit the bill to the Education and Labor Committee. Motion rejected 176-250: R 174-1; D 2-249. Jan. 27, 2009.

37. **S 181. Wage Discrimination/Passage.** Passage of the bill that would amend the 1964 Civil Rights Act to clarify time limits for workers to file employment discrimination lawsuits. The bill would allow workers who allege discrimination based on race, gender, national origin, religion, age or disability to file charges of pay discrimination within 180 days of the last received paycheck affected by the alleged discriminatory decision. The bill would renew the statute of limitations with each act of discrimination. Passed 250-177: R 3-172; D 247-5. Jan. 27, 2009.

38. **HR 1. Economic Stimulus/Question of Consideration.** Question of whether the House should consider the bill that would provide $815.8 billion in tax cuts and new spending to stimulate the economy. Agreed to consider 224-199: R 0-172; D 224-27. Jan. 27, 2009.

39. **HR 1. Economic Stimulus/Question of Consideration.** Question of whether the House should consider the rule (H Res 92) to provide for House floor consideration of the bill that would provide $815.8 billion in tax cuts and new spending to stimulate the economy. Agreed to consider 240-174: R 0-169; D 240-5. (Stearns, R-Fla., had raised a point of order that the rule contained provisions that violated the Congressional Budget Act.) Jan. 28, 2009.

40. **HR 1. Economic Stimulus/Rule.** Adoption of the rule (H Res 92) to provide for further House floor consideration of the bill that would provide $815.8 billion for tax cuts and new spending to stimulate the economy. Adopted 243-185: R 0-176; D 243-9. Jan. 28, 2009.

	36	37	38	39	40
ALABAMA					
1 **Bonner**	Y	N	N	N	N
2 Bright	N	N	N	Y	Y
3 **Rogers**	Y	N	N	N	N
4 **Aderholt**	Y	N	N	?	N
5 Griffith	Y	N	N	Y	Y
6 **Bachus**	Y	N	N	N	N
7 Davis	N	Y	Y	Y	Y
ALASKA					
AL **Young**	?	?	?	?	N
ARIZONA					
1 Kirkpatrick	N	Y	Y	Y	Y
2 **Franks**	Y	N	N	N	N
3 **Shadegg**	Y	N	N	N	N
4 Pastor	N	Y	Y	Y	Y
5 Mitchell	N	Y	Y	Y	Y
6 **Flake**	Y	N	N	N	N
7 Grijalva	N	Y	Y	Y	Y
8 Giffords	N	Y	N	N	Y
ARKANSAS					
1 Berry	N	Y	N	N	N
2 Snyder	N	Y	Y	Y	Y
3 **Boozman**	Y	N	N	N	N
4 Ross	N	Y	Y	Y	Y
CALIFORNIA					
1 Thompson	N	Y	Y	Y	Y
2 **Herger**	Y	N	N	N	N
3 **Lungren**	Y	N	N	N	N
4 **McClintock**	Y	N	N	N	N
5 Matsui	N	Y	Y	Y	Y
6 Woolsey	N	Y	Y	Y	Y
7 Miller, George	N	Y	Y	Y	Y
8 Pelosi		Y	Y		
9 Lee	N	Y	Y	Y	Y
10 Tauscher	N	Y	Y	Y	Y
11 McNerney	N	Y	Y	Y	Y
12 Speier	N	Y	Y	Y	Y
13 Stark	N	Y	?	Y	Y
14 Eshoo	N	Y	Y	Y	Y
15 Honda	N	Y	Y	Y	Y
16 Lofgren	N	Y	Y	Y	Y
17 Farr	N	Y	Y	Y	Y
18 Cardoza	N	Y	Y	Y	Y
19 **Radanovich**	Y	N	N	N	N
20 Costa	N	Y	Y	Y	Y
21 **Nunes**	Y	N	N	N	N
22 **McCarthy**	Y	N	N	N	N
23 Capps	N	Y	Y	Y	Y
24 **Gallegly**	Y	N	N	N	N
25 **McKeon**	Y	N	N	N	N
26 **Dreier**	Y	N	N	N	N
27 Sherman	N	Y	Y	Y	Y
28 Berman	N	Y	Y	Y	Y
29 Schiff	N	Y	Y	Y	Y
30 Waxman	N	Y	Y	Y	Y
31 Becerra	N	Y	Y	Y	Y
32 Solis	N	Y	Y	?	?
33 Watson	N	Y	Y	Y	Y
34 Roybal-Allard	N	Y	Y	Y	Y
35 Waters	N	Y	Y	Y	Y
36 Harman	N	Y	Y	Y	Y
37 Richardson	N	Y	Y	Y	Y
38 Napolitano	N	Y	Y	Y	Y
39 Sánchez, Linda	N	Y	Y	Y	Y
40 **Royce**	Y	N	N	N	N
41 **Lewis**	Y	N	N	N	N
42 **Miller, Gary**	Y	N	N	N	N
43 Baca	N	Y	Y	Y	Y
44 **Calvert**	Y	N	N	N	N
45 **Bono Mack**	Y	N	N	N	N
46 **Rohrabacher**	Y	N	N	N	N
47 Sanchez, Loretta	N	Y	N	N	N
48 **Campbell**	Y	N	N	N	N
49 **Issa**	Y	N	N	N	N
50 **Bilbray**	Y	N	N	N	N
51 Filner	N	Y	Y	Y	Y
52 **Hunter**	Y	N	N	N	N
53 Davis	N	Y	Y	Y	Y

	36	37	38	39	40
COLORADO					
1 DeGette	N	Y	Y	Y	N
2 Polis	N	Y	Y	Y	Y
3 Salazar	N	Y	Y	Y	Y
4 Markey	N	Y	Y	Y	Y
5 **Lamborn**	Y	N	N	N	N
6 **Coffman**	Y	N	N	N	N
7 Perlmutter	N	Y	Y	Y	Y
CONNECTICUT					
1 Larson	N	Y	Y	Y	Y
2 Courtney	N	Y	Y	Y	Y
3 DeLauro	N	Y	Y	Y	Y
4 Himes	N	Y	Y	Y	Y
5 Murphy	N	Y	Y	Y	Y
DELAWARE					
AL **Castle**	Y	N	N	N	N
FLORIDA					
1 **Miller**	Y	N	N	N	N
2 Boyd	N	N	N	Y	N
3 Brown	N	Y	Y	Y	Y
4 **Crenshaw**	Y	N	N	?	N
5 **Brown-Waite**	?	?	?	?	?
6 **Stearns**	Y	N	N	N	N
7 **Mica**	Y	N	N	N	N
8 Grayson	N	Y	Y	Y	Y
9 **Bilirakis**	Y	N	N	N	N
10 **Young**	Y	N	N	?	N
11 Castor	N	Y	Y	Y	Y
12 **Putnam**	Y	N	N	N	N
13 **Buchanan**	Y	N	N	N	N
14 **Mack**	Y	N	N	N	N
15 **Posey**	Y	N	N	N	N
16 **Rooney**	Y	N	N	N	N
17 Meek	N	Y	Y	Y	Y
18 **Ros-Lehtinen**	Y	N	N	N	N
19 Wexler	N	Y	Y	?	Y
20 Wasserman Schultz	N	Y	Y	Y	Y
21 **Diaz-Balart, L.**	Y	N	N	N	N
22 Klein	N	Y	Y	Y	Y
23 Hastings	N	Y	Y	Y	Y
24 Kosmas	N	Y	Y	Y	Y
25 **Diaz-Balart, M.**	Y	N	N	N	N
GEORGIA					
1 **Kingston**	Y	N	?	N	N
2 Bishop	N	Y	Y	Y	Y
3 **Westmoreland**	Y	N	N	N	N
4 Johnson	N	Y	Y	Y	Y
5 Lewis	N	Y	Y	Y	Y
6 **Price**	Y	N	N	N	N
7 **Linder**	Y	N	?	N	N
8 Marshall	N	Y	N	Y	Y
9 **Deal**	Y	N	N	N	N
10 **Broun**	Y	N	N	N	N
11 **Gingrey**	Y	N	N	N	N
12 Barrow	N	Y	N	Y	Y
13 Scott	N	Y	Y	Y	Y
HAWAII					
1 Abercrombie	N	Y	Y	Y	Y
2 Hirono	N	Y	Y	Y	Y
IDAHO					
1 Minnick	N	Y	N	N	Y
2 **Simpson**	Y	N	N	?	N
ILLINOIS					
1 Rush	?	Y	Y	Y	Y
2 Jackson	N	Y	Y	Y	Y
3 Lipinski	N	Y	Y	Y	Y
4 Gutierrez	N	Y	Y	Y	Y
5 Vacant					
6 **Roskam**	Y	N	N	N	N
7 Davis	N	Y	Y	Y	Y
8 Bean	N	Y	Y	Y	Y
9 Schakowsky	N	Y	Y	Y	Y
10 **Kirk**	Y	N	N	N	N
11 Halvorson	N	Y	Y	Y	Y
12 Costello	N	Y	Y	Y	Y
13 **Biggert**	Y	N	N	N	N
14 Foster	N	Y	Y	Y	Y
15 **Johnson**	Y	N	N	N	N

KEY	**Republicans**	Democrats

Y	Voted for (yea)	X	Paired against	C	Voted "present" to avoid possible conflict of interest
#	Paired for	–	Announced against		
+	Announced for	P	Voted "present"	?	Did not vote or otherwise make a position known
N	Voted against (nay)				

	36	37	38	39	40
16 Manzullo	Y	N	N	N	N
17 Hare	N	Y	Y	Y	Y
18 Schock	Y	N	N	N	N
19 Shimkus	Y	N	N	N	N
INDIANA					
1 Visclosky	N	Y	Y	Y	Y
2 Donnelly	N	Y	N	Y	Y
3 Souder	Y	N	N	N	N
4 Buyer	Y	N	N	N	N
5 Burton	Y	N	N	N	N
6 Pence	Y	N	N	N	N
7 Carson	N	Y	Y	Y	Y
8 Ellsworth	N	Y	N	Y	Y
9 Hill	N	Y	Y	Y	N
IOWA					
1 Braley	N	Y	Y	Y	Y
2 Loebsack	N	Y	Y	Y	Y
3 Boswell	N	Y	Y	Y	Y
4 Latham	Y	N	N	N	N
5 King	Y	N	N	N	N
KANSAS					
1 Moran	Y	N	N	N	N
2 Jenkins	Y	N	N	N	N
3 Moore	N	Y	Y	Y	Y
4 Tiahrt	Y	N	N	N	N
KENTUCKY					
1 Whitfield	Y	Y	N	?	N
2 Guthrie	Y	N	N	N	N
3 Yarmuth	N	Y	Y	Y	Y
4 Davis	Y	N	N	N	N
5 Rogers	Y	N	N	N	N
6 Chandler	N	Y	Y	Y	Y
LOUISIANA					
1 Scalise	Y	N	N	N	N
2 Cao	Y	N	N	N	N
3 Melancon	N	Y	N	Y	Y
4 Fleming	Y	N	N	N	N
5 Alexander	Y	N	N	N	N
6 Cassidy	N	N	N	N	?
7 Boustany	Y	N	N	N	N
MAINE					
1 Pingree	N	Y	Y	Y	Y
2 Michaud	N	Y	N	Y	Y
MARYLAND					
1 Kratovil	N	Y	N	Y	Y
2 Ruppersberger	N	Y	Y	?	Y
3 Sarbanes	N	Y	Y	Y	Y
4 Edwards	N	Y	Y	Y	Y
5 Hoyer	N	Y	Y	Y	Y
6 Bartlett	Y	N	N	N	N
7 Cummings	N	Y	Y	Y	Y
8 Van Hollen	N	Y	Y	Y	Y
MASSACHUSETTS					
1 Olver	N	Y	Y	Y	Y
2 Neal	N	Y	Y	Y	Y
3 McGovern	N	Y	Y	Y	Y
4 Frank	N	Y	Y	Y	Y
5 Tsongas	N	Y	Y	Y	Y
6 Tierney	N	Y	Y	Y	Y
7 Markey	N	Y	Y	Y	Y
8 Capuano	N	Y	Y	Y	Y
9 Lynch	?	?	?	Y	Y
10 Delahunt	N	Y	Y	Y	?
MICHIGAN					
1 Stupak	N	Y	Y	Y	Y
2 Hoekstra	Y	N	N	N	N
3 Ehlers	Y	N	N	N	N
4 Camp	Y	N	N	N	N
5 Kildee	N	Y	Y	Y	Y
6 Upton	Y	N	N	N	N
7 Schauer	N	Y	Y	Y	Y
8 Rogers	Y	N	N	N	N
9 Peters	N	Y	Y	Y	Y
10 Miller	Y	N	N	N	N
11 McCotter	Y	N	N	N	N
12 Levin	N	Y	Y	Y	Y
13 Kilpatrick	N	Y	Y	Y	Y
14 Conyers	N	Y	Y	Y	Y
15 Dingell	N	Y	Y	?	Y
MINNESOTA					
1 Walz	N	Y	Y	Y	Y
2 Kline	Y	N	N	N	N
3 Paulsen	Y	N	N	N	N
4 McCollum	N	Y	Y	Y	Y

	36	37	38	39	40
5 Ellison	N	Y	Y	Y	Y
6 Bachmann	Y	N	N	N	N
7 Peterson	N	Y	N	Y	Y
8 Oberstar	N	Y	Y	Y	Y
MISSISSIPPI					
1 Childers	Y	N	N	Y	Y
2 Thompson	N	Y	Y	Y	Y
3 Harper	Y	N	N	N	N
4 Taylor	N	Y	N	N	N
MISSOURI					
1 Clay	N	Y	Y	?	Y
2 Akin	Y	N	N	N	N
3 Carnahan	N	Y	Y	Y	Y
4 Skelton	N	Y	Y	Y	Y
5 Cleaver	N	Y	Y	Y	Y
6 Graves	Y	N	N	N	N
7 Blunt	Y	N	N	N	N
8 Emerson	Y	N	N	N	N
9 Luetkemeyer	Y	N	N	N	N
MONTANA					
AL Rehberg	Y	N	N	N	N
NEBRASKA					
1 Fortenberry	Y	N	N	N	N
2 Terry	Y	N	N	N	N
3 Smith	Y	N	N	N	N
NEVADA					
1 Berkley	N	Y	Y	Y	Y
2 Heller	Y	N	N	N	N
3 Titus	N	Y	Y	Y	Y
NEW HAMPSHIRE					
1 Shea-Porter	N	Y	Y	Y	Y
2 Hodes	N	Y	Y	Y	Y
NEW JERSEY					
1 Andrews	N	Y	Y	Y	Y
2 LoBiondo	Y	N	N	N	N
3 Adler	N	Y	Y	Y	N
4 Smith	Y	Y	N	Y	Y
5 Garrett	Y	N	N	N	N
6 Pallone	N	?	Y	Y	Y
7 Lance	Y	Y	N	N	N
8 Pascrell	N	Y	Y	Y	Y
9 Rothman	N	Y	Y	Y	Y
10 Payne	N	Y	Y	Y	Y
11 Frelinghuysen	Y	N	N	N	N
12 Holt	N	Y	Y	Y	Y
13 Sires	N	Y	Y	Y	Y
NEW MEXICO					
1 Heinrich	N	Y	Y	Y	Y
2 Teague	N	Y	Y	Y	Y
3 Lujan	N	Y	Y	Y	Y
NEW YORK					
1 Bishop	N	Y	Y	Y	N
2 Israel	N	Y	Y	Y	Y
3 King	Y	N	N	N	N
4 McCarthy	N	Y	+	Y	Y
5 Ackerman	N	Y	Y	Y	Y
6 Meeks	N	Y	Y	Y	Y
7 Crowley	N	Y	Y	Y	Y
8 Nadler	N	Y	Y	Y	Y
9 Weiner	N	Y	Y	Y	Y
10 Towns	N	Y	Y	Y	Y
11 Clarke	N	Y	Y	Y	Y
12 Velázquez	N	Y	Y	Y	Y
13 McMahon	N	Y	Y	Y	Y
14 Maloney	N	Y	Y	Y	Y
15 Rangel	N	Y	Y	Y	Y
16 Serrano	N	Y	Y	Y	Y
17 Engel	N	Y	Y	Y	Y
18 Lowey	N	Y	Y	Y	Y
19 Hall	N	Y	Y	Y	Y
20 Vacant					
21 Tonko	N	Y	Y	Y	Y
22 Hinchey	N	Y	Y	Y	Y
23 McHugh	Y	N	N	N	N
24 Arcuri	N	Y	N	Y	Y
25 Maffei	N	Y	Y	Y	Y
26 Lee	Y	N	N	N	N
27 Higgins	N	Y	Y	?	Y
28 Slaughter	N	Y	Y	Y	Y
29 Massa	N	Y	Y	Y	Y
NORTH CAROLINA					
1 Butterfield	N	Y	Y	Y	Y
2 Etheridge	?	?	?	Y	Y
3 Jones	Y	N	N	N	N
4 Price	N	Y	Y	Y	Y

	36	37	38	39	40
5 Foxx	Y	N	N	N	N
6 Coble	Y	N	N	N	N
7 McIntyre	N	Y	N	Y	Y
8 Kissell	N	Y	Y	Y	Y
9 Myrick	Y	N	N	N	N
10 McHenry	Y	N	N	N	N
11 Shuler	N	Y	N	Y	Y
12 Watt	N	Y	Y	Y	Y
13 Miller	N	Y	Y	Y	Y
NORTH DAKOTA					
AL Pomeroy	N	Y	Y	Y	Y
OHIO					
1 Driehaus	N	Y	Y	Y	Y
2 Schmidt	Y	N	N	N	N
3 Turner	Y	N	N	N	N
4 Jordan	Y	N	N	N	N
5 Latta	Y	N	N	N	N
6 Wilson	N	Y	Y	Y	Y
7 Austria	Y	N	N	N	N
8 Boehner	Y	N	N	N	N
9 Kaptur	N	Y	N	Y	Y
10 Kucinich	N	Y	Y	Y	Y
11 Fudge	N	Y	Y	Y	Y
12 Tiberi	?	?	?	N	N
13 Sutton	N	Y	Y	Y	Y
14 LaTourette	Y	N	N	N	N
15 Kilroy	N	Y	Y	Y	Y
16 Boccieri	N	Y	Y	Y	Y
17 Ryan	N	Y	Y	Y	Y
18 Space	N	Y	N	?	Y
OKLAHOMA					
1 Sullivan	Y	N	N	N	N
2 Boren	N	N	N	Y	Y
3 Lucas	Y	N	N	N	N
4 Cole	Y	N	N	N	N
5 Fallin	Y	N	N	N	N
OREGON					
1 Wu	N	Y	Y	Y	Y
2 Walden	Y	N	N	N	N
3 Blumenauer	N	Y	Y	Y	Y
4 DeFazio	N	Y	Y	Y	Y
5 Schrader	N	Y	Y	Y	Y
PENNSYLVANIA					
1 Brady	N	Y	Y	Y	Y
2 Fattah	N	Y	Y	Y	Y
3 Dahlkemper	N	Y	Y	Y	Y
4 Altmire	N	Y	Y	Y	Y
5 Thompson	Y	N	N	N	N
6 Gerlach	Y	N	N	N	N
7 Sestak	N	Y	Y	Y	Y
8 Murphy, P.	N	Y	Y	Y	Y
9 Shuster	Y	N	N	N	N
10 Carney	N	Y	N	Y	Y
11 Kanjorski	N	Y	Y	Y	Y
12 Murtha	N	Y	Y	Y	Y
13 Schwartz	N	Y	Y	Y	Y
14 Doyle	N	Y	Y	Y	Y
15 Dent	Y	N	N	N	N
16 Pitts	Y	N	?	N	N
17 Holden	N	Y	Y	Y	Y
18 Murphy, T.	Y	N	N	N	N
19 Platts	Y	N	N	?	N
RHODE ISLAND					
1 Kennedy	N	Y	Y	Y	Y
2 Langevin	N	Y	Y	Y	Y
SOUTH CAROLINA					
1 Brown	Y	N	N	N	N
2 Wilson	Y	N	N	N	N
3 Barrett	Y	N	N	N	N
4 Inglis	Y	N	N	N	N
5 Spratt	N	Y	Y	Y	Y
6 Clyburn	N	Y	Y	Y	Y
SOUTH DAKOTA					
AL Herseth Sandlin	N	Y	Y	Y	Y
TENNESSEE					
1 Roe	Y	N	N	N	N
2 Duncan	Y	N	N	N	N
3 Wamp	Y	N	N	N	N
4 Davis, L.	N	Y	N	Y	Y
5 Cooper	N	Y	N	?	Y
6 Gordon	N	Y	Y	Y	Y
7 Blackburn	Y	N	N	N	N
8 Tanner	N	Y	Y	Y	Y
9 Cohen	N	Y	Y	Y	Y

	36	37	38	39	40
TEXAS					
1 Gohmert	Y	N	N	N	N
2 Poe	Y	N	N	N	N
3 Johnson, S.	Y	N	N	N	N
4 Hall	Y	N	N	N	N
5 Hensarling	Y	N	N	N	N
6 Barton	Y	N	N	N	N
7 Culberson	Y	N	N	?	N
8 Brady	Y	N	N	N	N
9 Green, A.	N	Y	Y	Y	Y
10 McCaul	Y	N	N	N	N
11 Conaway	Y	N	N	N	N
12 Granger	Y	N	N	N	N
13 Thornberry	Y	N	N	N	N
14 Paul	Y	N	N	N	N
15 Hinojosa	N	Y	Y	?	Y
16 Reyes	N	Y	Y	Y	Y
17 Edwards	N	Y	Y	Y	Y
18 Jackson Lee	N	Y	Y	Y	Y
19 Neugebauer	Y	N	N	N	N
20 Gonzalez	N	Y	Y	Y	Y
21 Smith	Y	N	N	N	N
22 Olson	Y	N	N	N	N
23 Rodriguez	N	Y	Y	Y	Y
24 Marchant	Y	N	N	N	N
25 Doggett	N	Y	Y	Y	Y
26 Burgess	Y	N	N	N	N
27 Ortiz	N	Y	Y	Y	Y
28 Cuellar	N	Y	Y	Y	Y
29 Green, G.	N	Y	Y	Y	Y
30 Johnson, E.	N	Y	Y	Y	Y
31 Carter	Y	N	N	N	N
32 Sessions	Y	N	N	N	N
UTAH					
1 Bishop	Y	N	N	N	N
2 Matheson	N	Y	Y	Y	Y
3 Chaffetz	Y	N	N	N	N
VERMONT					
AL Welch	N	Y	Y	Y	Y
VIRGINIA					
1 Wittman	Y	N	N	N	N
2 Nye	N	Y	Y	Y	Y
3 Scott	N	Y	Y	Y	Y
4 Forbes	Y	N	N	N	N
5 Perriello	N	Y	Y	Y	Y
6 Goodlatte	Y	N	N	N	N
7 Cantor	Y	N	N	N	N
8 Moran	N	Y	Y	Y	Y
9 Boucher	N	Y	Y	Y	Y
10 Wolf	Y	N	N	N	N
11 Connolly	N	Y	Y	Y	Y
WASHINGTON					
1 Inslee	N	Y	Y	Y	Y
2 Larsen	N	Y	Y	Y	Y
3 Baird	N	Y	Y	Y	Y
4 Hastings	Y	N	N	N	N
5 McMorris Rodgers	Y	N	N	N	N
6 Dicks	N	Y	Y	Y	Y
7 McDermott	N	Y	Y	Y	Y
8 Reichert	Y	N	N	N	N
9 Smith	N	Y	Y	Y	Y
WEST VIRGINIA					
1 Mollohan	N	Y	Y	Y	Y
2 Capito	Y	N	N	N	N
3 Rahall	N	Y	Y	Y	Y
WISCONSIN					
1 Ryan	Y	N	N	N	N
2 Baldwin	N	Y	Y	Y	Y
3 Kind	N	Y	Y	Y	Y
4 Moore	N	Y	Y	Y	Y
5 Sensenbrenner	Y	N	N	N	N
6 Petri	Y	N	N	N	N
7 Obey	N	Y	Y	Y	Y
8 Kagen	N	Y	Y	Y	Y
WYOMING					
AL Lummis	Y	N	N	N	N
DELEGATES					
Faleomavaega (A.S.)					
Norton (D.C.)					
Bordallo (Guam)					
Sablan (N. Marianas)					
Pierluisi (P.R.)					
Christensen (V.I.)					

IN THE HOUSE | By Vote Number

41. **S 328. Digital Television Transition/Passage.** Boucher, D-Va., motion to suspend the rules and pass the bill that would postpone the date, from Feb. 17, 2009, to June 12, 2009, by which full-power television stations must cease analog broadcasts. It would extend, from March 31, 2009, to July 31, 2009, the period during which households can obtain coupons for converter boxes. Motion rejected 258-168: R 22-155; D 236-13. A two-thirds majority of those present and voting (284 in this case) is required for passage under suspension of the rules. Jan. 28, 2009.

42. **HR 1. Economic Stimulus/Elimination of Appropriations.** Neugebauer, R-Texas, amendment that would strike the appropriations section of the bill. Rejected in Committee of the Whole 134-302: R 134-43; D 0-258; I 0-1. Jan. 28, 2009.

43. **HR 1. Economic Stimulus/Amtrak Capital Grants.** Flake, R-Ariz., amendment that would strike language allowing the Transportation secretary to make certain capital grants to Amtrak. Rejected in Committee of the Whole 116-320: R 116-61; D 0-258; I 0-1. Jan. 28, 2009.

44. **HR 1. Economic Stimulus/Substitute.** Camp, R-Mich., substitute amendment that would replace the text of the bill with language that would lower the bottom two income tax brackets for two years from 10 percent to 5 percent and from 15 percent to 10 percent, and exempt additional taxpayers from the alternative minimum tax for two years. It would allow businesses to carry back operating losses in 2008 and 2009 for five years, excluding companies that received funds under the Troubled Asset Relief Program; extend federal unemployment insurance through 2009; and temporarily exempt it from taxes. Rejected in Committee of the Whole 170-266: R 168-9; D 2-256; I 0-1. A "nay" was a vote in support of the president's position. Jan. 28, 2009.

45. **HR 1. Economic Stimulus/Recommit.** Lewis, R-Calif., motion to recommit the bill to the Appropriations Committee with instructions that it be reported back forthwith with language that would provide $36 billion for highway infrastructure and $24 billion for the Army Corps of Engineers, and strike more than $100 billion in funding for new or unauthorized programs. Motion rejected 159-270: R 146-31; D 13-239. Jan. 28, 2009.

46. **HR 1. Economic Stimulus/Passage.** Passage of the bill that would provide $819.5 billion in tax cuts and new spending through fiscal 2019 to stimulate the economy. Appropriations and other spending in the bill would yield estimated outlays of $637.3 billion. The total includes upgrades to transportation, infrastructure, construction, health care programs, education and housing assistance, and energy efficiency projects. The bill also includes $274.6 billion in tax benefits for individuals and businesses. Passed 244-188: R 0-177; D 244-11. A "yea" was a vote in support of the president's position. Jan. 28, 2009.

	41	42	43	44	45	46
ALABAMA						
1 Bonner	N	Y	N	Y	Y	N
2 Bright	Y	N	N	N	Y	N
3 Rogers	Y	N	N	Y	Y	N
4 Aderholt	Y	Y	N	Y	Y	N
5 Griffith	Y	N	N	N	Y	N
6 Bachus	N	Y	N	Y	Y	N
7 Davis	Y	N	N	N	N	Y
ALASKA						
AL Young	N	N	N	Y	Y	N
ARIZONA						
1 Kirkpatrick	Y	N	N	N	N	Y
2 Franks	N	Y	Y	Y	N	N
3 Shadegg	N	Y	Y	Y	Y	N
4 Pastor	Y	N	N	N	N	Y
5 Mitchell	Y	N	N	N	Y	Y
6 Flake	N	Y	Y	Y	Y	N
7 Grijalva	Y	N	N	N	N	Y
8 Giffords	Y	N	N	N	N	Y
ARKANSAS						
1 Berry	Y	N	N	N	N	Y
2 Snyder	Y	N	N	N	N	Y
3 Boozman	N	Y	N	Y	Y	N
4 Ross	Y	N	N	N	N	Y
CALIFORNIA						
1 Thompson	N	N	N	N	Y	Y
2 Herger	N	Y	Y	Y	Y	N
3 Lungren	N	Y	Y	Y	Y	N
4 McClintock	N	Y	Y	Y	Y	N
5 Matsui	Y	N	N	N	N	Y
6 Woolsey	Y	N	N	N	N	Y
7 Miller, George	Y	N	N	N	N	Y
8 Pelosi						Y
9 Lee	Y	N	N	N	N	Y
10 Tauscher	Y	N	N	N	N	Y
11 McNerney	Y	N	N	N	N	Y
12 Speier	Y	N	N	N	N	Y
13 Stark	Y	N	N	N	N	Y
14 Eshoo	Y	N	N	N	N	Y
15 Honda	Y	N	N	N	N	Y
16 Lofgren	Y	N	N	N	N	Y
17 Farr	Y	N	N	N	N	Y
18 Cardoza	Y	N	N	N	N	Y
19 Radanovich	N	Y	Y	Y	Y	N
20 Costa	Y	N	N	N	N	Y
21 Nunes	N	Y	Y	Y	Y	N
22 McCarthy	N	Y	Y	Y	Y	N
23 Capps	Y	N	N	N	N	Y
24 Gallegly	N	Y	Y	Y	Y	N
25 McKeon	N	Y	Y	Y	Y	N
26 Dreier	N	Y	Y	Y	Y	N
27 Sherman	Y	N	N	N	N	Y
28 Berman	Y	N	N	N	N	Y
29 Schiff	Y	N	N	N	N	Y
30 Waxman	Y	N	N	N	N	Y
31 Becerra	Y	N	N	N	N	Y
32 Solis	?	?	?	?	?	Y
33 Watson	Y	N	N	N	N	Y
34 Roybal-Allard	Y	N	N	N	N	Y
35 Waters	Y	N	N	N	N	Y
36 Harman	Y	N	N	N	N	Y
37 Richardson	Y	N	N	N	N	Y
38 Napolitano	Y	N	N	N	N	Y
39 Sánchez, Linda	Y	N	N	N	N	Y
40 Royce	N	Y	Y	Y	Y	N
41 Lewis	N	Y	Y	Y	Y	N
42 Miller, Gary	N	Y	Y	Y	Y	N
43 Baca	Y	N	N	N	N	Y
44 Calvert	N	Y	Y	Y	Y	N
45 Bono Mack	N	Y	N	Y	Y	N
46 Rohrabacher	N	Y	Y	Y	Y	N
47 Sanchez, Loretta	Y	N	N	N	N	Y
48 Campbell	N	Y	Y	Y	Y	N
49 Issa	N	Y	Y	Y	Y	N
50 Bilbray	N	Y	Y	Y	Y	N
51 Filner	Y	N	N	N	N	Y
52 Hunter	N	Y	Y	Y	Y	N
53 Davis	Y	N	N	N	N	Y

	41	42	43	44	45	46
COLORADO						
1 DeGette	Y	N	N	N	N	Y
2 Polis	Y	N	N	N	N	Y
3 Salazar	Y	N	N	N	N	Y
4 Markey	Y	N	N	N	N	Y
5 Lamborn	N	Y	Y	Y	N	N
6 Coffman	N	Y	Y	Y	N	N
7 Perlmutter	N	N	N	N	N	Y
CONNECTICUT						
1 Larson	Y	N	N	N	N	Y
2 Courtney	Y	N	N	N	N	Y
3 DeLauro	Y	N	N	N	N	Y
4 Himes	Y	N	N	N	N	Y
5 Murphy	Y	N	N	N	N	Y
DELAWARE						
AL Castle	N	N	N	N	Y	N
FLORIDA						
1 Miller	N	Y	Y	Y	N	N
2 Boyd	Y	N	N	N	N	N
3 Brown	Y	N	N	N	N	Y
4 Crenshaw	N	Y	N	Y	Y	N
5 Brown-Waite	?	?	?	?	?	?
6 Stearns	N	Y	Y	Y	Y	N
7 Mica	N	N	Y	Y	Y	N
8 Grayson	Y	N	N	N	N	Y
9 Bilirakis	Y	N	Y	Y	Y	N
10 Young	N	N	Y	Y	Y	N
11 Castor	Y	N	N	N	N	Y
12 Putnam	N	Y	Y	Y	Y	N
13 Buchanan	Y	N	Y	Y	Y	N
14 Mack	N	Y	Y	Y	N	N
15 Posey	Y	Y	Y	Y	Y	N
16 Rooney	N	N	Y	Y	Y	N
17 Meek	Y	N	N	N	N	Y
18 Ros-Lehtinen	Y	N	Y	Y	N	N
19 Wexler	Y	N	N	N	N	Y
20 Wasserman Schultz	Y	N	N	N	N	Y
21 Diaz-Balart, L.	Y	N	Y	Y	Y	N
22 Klein	Y	N	N	N	N	Y
23 Hastings	Y	N	N	N	N	Y
24 Kosmas	Y	N	N	N	N	Y
25 Diaz-Balart, M.	Y	N	Y	Y	Y	N
GEORGIA						
1 Kingston	N	Y	Y	Y	N	N
2 Bishop	Y	N	N	N	N	Y
3 Westmoreland	N	Y	Y	Y	N	N
4 Johnson	Y	N	N	N	N	Y
5 Lewis	Y	N	N	N	N	Y
6 Price	N	Y	Y	Y	N	N
7 Linder	N	Y	Y	Y	N	N
8 Marshall	Y	N	N	N	N	Y
9 Deal	N	Y	Y	Y	N	N
10 Broun	N	Y	Y	Y	N	N
11 Gingrey	N	Y	Y	Y	N	N
12 Barrow	Y	N	N	N	N	Y
13 Scott	Y	N	N	N	N	Y
HAWAII						
1 Abercrombie	Y	N	N	N	N	Y
2 Hirono	Y	N	N	N	N	Y
IDAHO						
1 Minnick	Y	N	N	Y	Y	N
2 Simpson	N	N	N	Y	Y	N
ILLINOIS						
1 Rush	Y	N	N	N	N	Y
2 Jackson	Y	N	N	N	N	Y
3 Lipinski	Y	N	N	N	N	Y
4 Gutierrez	Y	N	N	N	N	Y
5 Vacant						
6 Roskam	N	Y	N	Y	Y	N
7 Davis	Y	N	N	N	N	Y
8 Bean	Y	N	N	N	N	Y
9 Schakowsky	Y	N	N	N	N	Y
10 Kirk	N	N	Y	Y	Y	N
11 Halvorson	Y	N	N	N	N	Y
12 Costello	Y	N	N	N	N	Y
13 Biggert	N	Y	Y	Y	Y	N
14 Foster	Y	N	N	N	N	Y
15 Johnson	N	Y	N	Y	Y	N

KEY	Republicans	Democrats			
Y Voted for (yea)		X Paired against		C	Voted "present" to avoid possible conflict of interest
# Paired for		– Announced against			
+ Announced for		P Voted "present"		?	Did not vote or otherwise make a position known
N Voted against (nay)					

	41	42	43	44	45	46
16 **Manzullo**	N	Y	N	Y	N	N
17 Hare	Y	N	N	N	Y	N
18 **Schock**	N	N	N	Y	Y	N
19 **Shimkus**	N	Y	N	Y	Y	N
INDIANA						
1 Visclosky	Y	N	N	N	N	Y
2 Donnelly	Y	N	N	N	Y	Y
3 **Souder**	N	Y	N	Y	Y	N
4 **Buyer**	N	Y	Y	Y	Y	N
5 **Burton**	N	Y	Y	Y	Y	N
6 **Pence**	N	Y	Y	Y	Y	N
7 Carson	Y	N	N	N	N	Y
8 Ellsworth	Y	N	N	N	Y	N
9 Hill	Y	N	N	N	N	Y
IOWA						
1 Braley	Y	N	N	N	N	Y
2 Loebsack	Y	N	N	N	N	Y
3 Boswell	Y	N	N	N	N	Y
4 **Latham**	N	Y	N	Y	Y	N
5 **King**	N	Y	Y	Y	Y	N
KANSAS						
1 **Moran**	N	Y	Y	Y	N	N
2 **Jenkins**	N	Y	Y	Y	Y	N
3 Moore	Y	N	N	N	N	Y
4 **Tiahrt**	N	Y	Y	Y	Y	N
KENTUCKY						
1 **Whitfield**	N	N	N	Y	Y	N
2 **Guthrie**	N	Y	Y	Y	Y	N
3 Yarmuth	Y	N	N	N	N	Y
4 **Davis**	N	Y	Y	Y	Y	N
5 **Rogers**	Y	Y	Y	Y	Y	N
6 Chandler	Y	N	N	N	N	Y
LOUISIANA						
1 **Scalise**	N	Y	Y	Y	Y	N
2 **Cao**	N	N	N	Y	Y	N
3 Melancon	N	N	N	N	Y	Y
4 **Fleming**	N	Y	Y	Y	Y	N
5 **Alexander**	N	Y	N	Y	Y	N
6 **Cassidy**	N	Y	N	Y	Y	N
7 **Boustany**	N	Y	Y	Y	Y	N
MAINE						
1 Pingree	Y	N	N	N	N	Y
2 Michaud	Y	N	N	N	N	Y
MARYLAND						
1 Kratovil	Y	N	N	N	Y	N
2 Ruppersberger	Y	N	N	N	N	Y
3 Sarbanes	Y	N	N	N	N	Y
4 Edwards	Y	N	N	N	N	Y
5 Hoyer	Y	N	N	N	N	Y
6 **Bartlett**	N	Y	Y	Y	Y	N
7 Cummings	Y	N	N	N	N	Y
8 Van Hollen	Y	N	N	N	N	Y
MASSACHUSETTS						
1 Olver	Y	N	N	N	N	Y
2 Neal	Y	N	N	N	N	Y
3 McGovern	Y	N	N	N	N	Y
4 Frank	Y	N	N	N	N	Y
5 Tsongas	Y	N	N	N	N	Y
6 Tierney	Y	N	N	N	N	Y
7 Markey	Y	N	N	N	N	Y
8 Capuano	Y	N	N	N	N	Y
9 Lynch	Y	N	N	N	N	Y
10 Delahunt	?	N	N	N	N	Y
MICHIGAN						
1 Stupak	Y	N	N	N	N	Y
2 **Hoekstra**	N	Y	N	Y	N	N
3 **Ehlers**	N	N	N	Y	Y	N
4 **Camp**	N	Y	Y	Y	Y	N
5 Kildee	Y	N	N	N	N	Y
6 **Upton**	N	N	N	N	Y	N
7 Schauer	Y	N	N	N	N	Y
8 **Rogers**	N	Y	Y	Y	N	N
9 Peters	Y	N	N	N	N	Y
10 **Miller**	N	N	N	Y	Y	N
11 **McCotter**	N	N	N	Y	Y	N
12 Levin	Y	N	N	N	N	Y
13 Kilpatrick	Y	N	N	N	N	Y
14 Conyers	Y	N	N	N	N	Y
15 Dingell	Y	N	N	N	N	Y
MINNESOTA						
1 Walz	N	N	N	N	N	Y
2 **Kline**	N	Y	Y	Y	Y	N
3 **Paulsen**	N	N	Y	Y	Y	N
4 McCollum	Y	N	N	N	N	Y
5 Ellison	Y	N	N	N	N	Y
6 **Bachmann**	N	N	Y	Y	Y	N
7 Peterson	N	N	N	N	N	N
8 Oberstar	Y	N	N	N	N	Y
MISSISSIPPI						
1 Childers	Y	N	N	Y	Y	Y
2 Thompson	Y	N	N	N	N	Y
3 **Harper**	N	Y	Y	Y	Y	N
4 Taylor	Y	N	N	N	Y	N
MISSOURI						
1 Clay	Y	N	N	N	N	Y
2 **Akin**	N	Y	Y	Y	Y	N
3 Carnahan	Y	N	N	N	N	Y
4 Skelton	Y	N	N	N	N	Y
5 Cleaver	Y	N	N	N	N	Y
6 **Graves**	N	Y	Y	Y	Y	N
7 **Blunt**	N	Y	Y	Y	Y	N
8 **Emerson**	Y	N	N	Y	Y	N
9 **Luetkemeyer**	N	Y	Y	Y	Y	N
MONTANA						
AL **Rehberg**	N	N	N	Y	Y	N
NEBRASKA						
1 **Fortenberry**	Y	Y	N	Y	N	N
2 **Terry**	N	Y	Y	Y	Y	N
3 **Smith**	N	Y	Y	Y	Y	N
NEVADA						
1 Berkley	N	N	N	N	N	Y
2 **Heller**	N	N	Y	Y	Y	N
3 Titus	Y	N	N	N	N	Y
NEW HAMPSHIRE						
1 Shea-Porter	Y	N	N	N	N	Y
2 Hodes	Y	N	N	N	N	Y
NEW JERSEY						
1 Andrews	Y	N	N	N	N	Y
2 **LoBiondo**	Y	N	N	N	Y	N
3 Adler	N	N	N	N	N	Y
4 **Smith**	Y	N	N	N	Y	N
5 **Garrett**	N	Y	Y	Y	N	N
6 Pallone	Y	N	N	N	N	Y
7 **Lance**	N	N	N	Y	Y	N
8 Pascrell	Y	N	N	N	N	Y
9 Rothman	Y	N	N	N	N	Y
10 Payne	?	N	N	N	N	Y
11 **Frelinghuysen**	N	N	N	Y	Y	N
12 Holt	Y	N	N	N	N	Y
13 Sires	Y	N	N	N	N	Y
NEW MEXICO						
1 Heinrich	Y	N	N	N	N	Y
2 Teague	Y	N	N	N	N	Y
3 Lujan	Y	N	N	N	N	Y
NEW YORK						
1 Bishop	Y	N	N	N	N	Y
2 Israel	Y	N	N	N	N	Y
3 **King**	N	N	N	N	Y	N
4 McCarthy	Y	N	N	N	N	Y
5 Ackerman	Y	N	N	N	N	Y
6 Meeks	Y	N	N	N	N	Y
7 Crowley	Y	N	N	N	N	Y
8 Nadler	Y	N	N	N	N	Y
9 Weiner	Y	N	N	N	N	Y
10 Towns	?	N	N	N	N	Y
11 Clarke	Y	N	N	N	N	Y
12 Velázquez	Y	N	N	N	N	Y
13 McMahon	Y	N	N	N	N	Y
14 Maloney	Y	N	N	N	N	Y
15 Rangel	Y	N	N	N	N	Y
16 Serrano	Y	N	N	N	N	Y
17 Engel	Y	N	N	N	N	Y
18 Lowey	Y	N	N	N	N	Y
19 Hall	Y	N	N	N	N	Y
20 Vacant						
21 Tonko	Y	N	N	N	N	Y
22 Hinchey	Y	N	N	N	N	Y
23 **McHugh**	Y	N	N	N	Y	N
24 Arcuri	Y	N	N	N	Y	Y
25 Maffei	Y	N	N	N	N	Y
26 **Lee**	N	N	N	Y	Y	N
27 Higgins	Y	N	N	N	N	Y
28 Slaughter	Y	N	N	N	N	Y
29 Massa	Y	N	N	N	N	Y
NORTH CAROLINA						
1 Butterfield	Y	N	N	N	N	Y
2 Etheridge	Y	N	N	N	N	Y
3 **Jones**	N	N	N	Y	Y	N
4 Price	Y	N	N	N	N	Y
5 **Foxx**	N	Y	Y	Y	Y	N
6 **Coble**	N	N	Y	Y	Y	N
7 McIntyre	Y	N	N	N	N	Y
8 Kissell	Y	N	N	N	N	Y
9 **Myrick**	N	Y	Y	Y	Y	N
10 **McHenry**	N	Y	Y	Y	Y	N
11 Shuler	N	N	N	N	Y	N
12 Watt	Y	N	N	N	N	Y
13 Miller	Y	N	N	N	N	Y
NORTH DAKOTA						
AL Pomeroy	Y	N	N	N	N	Y
OHIO						
1 Driehaus	Y	N	N	N	N	Y
2 **Schmidt**	N	Y	N	Y	Y	N
3 **Turner**	Y	N	N	Y	Y	N
4 **Jordan**	N	Y	Y	Y	N	N
5 **Latta**	N	Y	Y	Y	Y	N
6 Wilson	?	N	N	N	N	Y
7 **Austria**	N	Y	Y	Y	Y	N
8 **Boehner**	N	Y	Y	Y	Y	N
9 Kaptur	Y	N	N	N	N	Y
10 Kucinich	Y	N	N	N	N	Y
11 Fudge	Y	N	N	N	N	Y
12 **Tiberi**	N	Y	Y	Y	Y	N
13 Sutton	Y	N	N	N	N	Y
14 **LaTourette**	Y	N	N	Y	Y	N
15 Kilroy	Y	N	N	N	N	Y
16 Boccieri	Y	N	N	N	N	Y
17 Ryan	Y	N	N	N	N	Y
18 Space	Y	N	N	N	N	Y
OKLAHOMA						
1 **Sullivan**	N	Y	N	Y	N	N
2 Boren	Y	N	N	N	N	Y
3 **Lucas**	N	Y	N	Y	Y	N
4 **Cole**	N	Y	N	Y	Y	N
5 **Fallin**	N	Y	N	Y	Y	N
OREGON						
1 Wu	Y	N	N	N	N	Y
2 **Walden**	N	N	N	Y	Y	N
3 Blumenauer	Y	N	N	N	N	Y
4 DeFazio	Y	N	N	N	N	Y
5 Schrader	Y	N	N	N	N	Y
PENNSYLVANIA						
1 Brady	Y	N	N	N	N	Y
2 Fattah	Y	N	N	N	N	Y
3 Dahlkemper	Y	N	N	N	N	Y
4 Altmire	N	N	N	N	Y	Y
5 **Thompson**	N	Y	Y	Y	Y	N
6 **Gerlach**	N	N	N	Y	Y	N
7 Sestak	Y	N	N	N	N	Y
8 Murphy, P.	Y	N	N	N	N	Y
9 **Shuster**	N	Y	N	Y	Y	N
10 Carney	Y	N	N	N	Y	Y
11 Kanjorski	Y	N	N	N	N	N
12 Murtha	Y	N	N	N	N	Y
13 Schwartz	Y	N	N	N	N	Y
14 Doyle	Y	N	N	N	N	Y
15 **Dent**	N	N	N	Y	Y	N
16 **Pitts**	N	Y	Y	Y	Y	N
17 Holden	N	N	N	N	N	Y
18 **Murphy, T.**	N	N	N	N	Y	N
19 **Platts**	N	N	N	Y	Y	N
RHODE ISLAND						
1 Kennedy	Y	N	N	N	N	Y
2 Langevin	Y	N	N	N	N	Y
SOUTH CAROLINA						
1 **Brown**	N	Y	Y	Y	Y	N
2 **Wilson**	N	Y	Y	Y	Y	N
3 **Barrett**	N	Y	Y	Y	N	N
4 **Inglis**	N	Y	Y	Y	Y	N
5 Spratt	Y	N	N	N	N	Y
6 Clyburn	Y	N	N	N	N	Y
SOUTH DAKOTA						
AL Herseth Sandlin	Y	N	N	N	N	Y
TENNESSEE						
1 **Roe**	Y	Y	Y	Y	Y	N
2 **Duncan**	N	Y	Y	Y	Y	N
3 **Wamp**	N	Y	Y	Y	Y	N
4 Davis, L.	Y	N	N	N	N	Y
5 Cooper	Y	N	N	N	N	N
6 Gordon	Y	N	N	N	N	Y
7 **Blackburn**	N	Y	Y	Y	N	N
8 Tanner	Y	N	N	N	N	Y
9 Cohen	Y	N	N	N	N	Y
TEXAS						
1 **Gohmert**	N	Y	Y	Y	Y	N
2 **Poe**	N	Y	Y	Y	N	N
3 **Johnson, S.**	N	Y	Y	Y	Y	N
4 **Hall**	N	Y	Y	Y	Y	N
5 **Hensarling**	N	Y	Y	Y	Y	N
6 **Barton**	N	Y	Y	Y	Y	N
7 **Culberson**	N	Y	Y	Y	N	N
8 **Brady**	N	Y	Y	Y	Y	N
9 Green, A.	Y	N	N	N	N	Y
10 **McCaul**	N	Y	Y	Y	Y	N
11 **Conaway**	N	Y	Y	Y	Y	N
12 **Granger**	N	Y	Y	Y	Y	N
13 **Thornberry**	N	Y	Y	Y	Y	N
14 **Paul**	N	Y	Y	Y	Y	N
15 Hinojosa	Y	N	N	N	N	Y
16 Reyes	Y	N	N	N	N	Y
17 Edwards	Y	N	N	N	N	Y
18 Jackson Lee	Y	N	N	N	N	Y
19 **Neugebauer**	N	Y	Y	Y	Y	N
20 Gonzalez	Y	N	N	N	N	Y
21 **Smith**	N	Y	Y	Y	Y	N
22 **Olson**	N	Y	Y	Y	Y	N
23 Rodriguez	Y	N	N	N	N	Y
24 **Marchant**	N	Y	Y	Y	Y	N
25 Doggett	N	N	N	N	?	Y
26 **Burgess**	N	Y	Y	Y	Y	N
27 Ortiz	Y	N	N	N	N	Y
28 Cuellar	Y	N	N	N	N	Y
29 Green, G.	Y	N	N	N	N	Y
30 Johnson, E.	Y	N	N	N	N	Y
31 **Carter**	N	Y	Y	Y	Y	N
32 **Sessions**	N	Y	Y	Y	Y	N
UTAH						
1 **Bishop**	N	Y	Y	Y	N	N
2 Matheson	Y	N	N	N	N	Y
3 **Chaffetz**	N	Y	Y	Y	N	N
VERMONT						
AL Welch	Y	N	N	N	N	Y
VIRGINIA						
1 **Wittman**	N	Y	N	Y	Y	N
2 Nye	Y	N	N	N	N	Y
3 Scott	Y	N	N	N	N	Y
4 **Forbes**	N	Y	Y	Y	N	N
5 Perriello	Y	N	N	N	N	Y
6 **Goodlatte**	N	Y	N	Y	Y	N
7 **Cantor**	N	Y	Y	Y	Y	N
8 Moran	Y	N	N	N	N	Y
9 Boucher	Y	N	N	N	N	Y
10 **Wolf**	N	Y	N	N	N	N
11 Connolly	Y	N	N	N	N	Y
WASHINGTON						
1 Inslee	Y	N	N	N	N	Y
2 Larsen	N	N	N	N	N	Y
3 Baird	Y	N	N	N	N	Y
4 **Hastings**	N	Y	Y	Y	Y	N
5 **McMorris Rodgers**	N	N	Y	Y	Y	N
6 Dicks	Y	N	N	N	N	Y
7 McDermott	Y	N	N	N	N	Y
8 **Reichert**	N	N	Y	Y	Y	N
9 Smith	Y	N	N	N	N	Y
WEST VIRGINIA						
1 Mollohan	Y	N	N	N	N	Y
2 **Capito**	N	N	N	Y	Y	N
3 Rahall	Y	N	N	N	N	Y
WISCONSIN						
1 **Ryan**	N	Y	Y	Y	Y	N
2 Baldwin	Y	N	N	N	N	Y
3 Kind	N	N	N	N	N	Y
4 Moore	Y	N	N	N	N	Y
5 **Sensenbrenner**	Y	Y	Y	Y	Y	N
6 **Petri**	Y	Y	N	Y	Y	N
7 Obey	Y	N	N	N	N	Y
8 Kagen	Y	N	N	N	N	Y
WYOMING						
AL **Lummis**	N	Y	Y	Y	Y	N
DELEGATES						
Faleomavaega (A.S.)		N	N	N		
Norton (D.C.)		N	N	N		
Bordallo (Guam)		N	N	N		
Sablan (N. Marianas)		N	N	N		
Pierluisi (P.R.)		N	N	N		
Christensen (V.I.)		N	N	N		

IN THE HOUSE | By Vote Number

47. **H Res 82. Stalking Awareness/Adoption.** Scott, D-Va., motion to suspend the rules and adopt the resolution that would express the sense of the House in support of National Stalking Awareness Month. Motion agreed to 417-0: R 170-0; D 247-0. A two-thirds majority of those present and voting (278 in this case) is required for adoption under suspension of the rules. Feb. 3, 2009.

48. **H Res 103. Teen Violence Awareness/Adoption.** Scott, D-Va., motion to suspend the rules and adopt the resolution that would support the goals and ideals of National Teen Dating Violence Awareness and Prevention Week. Motion agreed to 419-0: R 171-0; D 248-0. A two-thirds majority of those present and voting (280 in this case) is required for adoption under suspension of the rules. Feb. 3, 2009.

49. **HR 559. Terrorist Watch List Appeals/Passage.** Thompson, D-Miss., motion to suspend the rules and pass the bill that would require the Homeland Security Department to establish an office to redress claims for individuals barred from boarding an aircraft or who believe they were wrongly placed on a terrorist watch list and to establish a list of those wrongly identified. Motion agreed to 413-3: R 168-3; D 245-0. A two-thirds majority of those present and voting (278 in this case) is required for passage under suspension of the rules. Feb. 3, 2009.

50. **HR 2. Children's Health Insurance/Motion to Concur.** Waxman, D-Calif., motion to concur in the Senate amendment to the bill that would reauthorize the State Children's Health Insurance Program (SCHIP) over four and a half years and increase funding by $32.8 billion. To offset the cost of the expansion, it would increase the federal tax on cigarettes by 62 cents per pack and raise taxes on other tobacco products. It would remove a five-year waiting period for new, legal immigrants, including pregnant women, and loosen citizenship and eligibility documentation requirements. The bill would limit program eligibility to families earning three times the federal poverty level or less and would require states to phase out coverage of childless adults. Motion agreed to (thus clearing the bill for the president), 290-135: R 40-133; D 250-2. Feb. 4, 2009.

51. **S 352. Digital Television Transition/Commit.** Barton, R-Texas, motion to commit the bill to the Energy and Commerce Committee with instructions that it be reported back forthwith with language that would require analog television stations with spectrums to be used by emergency services providers to switch to digital by Feb. 17, 2009. Motion rejected 180-242: R 165-6; D 15-236. Feb. 4, 2009.

52. **S 352. Digital Television Transition/Passage.** Passage of the bill that would postpone, from Feb. 17, 2009, to June 12, 2009, the date by which full-power television stations must cease analog broadcasts. It would extend, from March 31, 2009, to July 31, 2009, the period that households can obtain coupons for converter boxes. It also would allow low-power stations to submit compensation requests for the cost of purchasing conversion devices. Passed, (thus clearing the bill for the president), 264-158: R 23-148; D 241-10. Feb. 4, 2009.

53. **HR 738. Prisoner Death Reporting/Passage.** Scott, D-Va., motion to suspend the rules and pass the bill that would require states receiving federal law enforcement grants to report information on prisoner deaths to the attorney general or forgo 10 percent of their federal law enforcement grant funds, and it would require the federal government to release information on prisoner deaths in federal facilities. Motion agreed to 407-1: R 165-0; D 242-1. A two-thirds majority of those present and voting (272 in this case) is required for passage under suspension of the rules. Feb. 4, 2009.

	47	48	49	50	51	52	53
ALABAMA							
1 **Bonner**	Y	Y	Y	N	Y	N	Y
2 **Bright**	Y	Y	Y	N	N	Y	Y
3 **Rogers**	Y	Y	Y	Y	Y	Y	Y
4 **Aderholt**	Y	Y	Y	?	?	?	?
5 Griffith	Y	Y	Y	Y	N	Y	Y
6 **Bachus**	Y	Y	Y	N	Y	N	Y
7 Davis	Y	Y	Y	Y	N	Y	Y
ALASKA							
AL **Young**	Y	Y	Y	Y	Y	N	Y
ARIZONA							
1 Kirkpatrick	Y	Y	Y	Y	N	Y	Y
2 **Franks**	Y	Y	Y	N	Y	N	Y
3 **Shadegg**	Y	Y	Y	N	Y	N	Y
4 Pastor	Y	Y	Y	Y	N	Y	Y
5 Mitchell	Y	Y	Y	Y	Y	Y	Y
6 **Flake**	?	?	?	?	?	?	?
7 Grijalva	Y	Y	Y	Y	N	Y	Y
8 Giffords	Y	Y	Y	Y	Y	Y	Y
ARKANSAS							
1 Berry	Y	Y	Y	Y	N	Y	Y
2 Snyder	Y	Y	Y	Y	N	Y	Y
3 **Boozman**	Y	Y	Y	N	Y	N	Y
4 Ross	Y	Y	Y	Y	N	Y	Y
CALIFORNIA							
1 Thompson	Y	Y	Y	Y	N	Y	Y
2 **Herger**	+	Y	Y	N	Y	N	Y
3 **Lungren**	Y	Y	Y	N	Y	N	Y
4 **McClintock**	Y	Y	Y	N	Y	N	Y
5 Matsui	Y	Y	Y	Y	N	Y	Y
6 Woolsey	Y	Y	Y	Y	N	Y	Y
7 Miller, George	Y	Y	Y	Y	N	Y	Y
8 Pelosi				Y			
9 Lee	Y	Y	Y	Y	N	Y	Y
10 Tauscher	Y	Y	Y	Y	N	Y	Y
11 McNerney	Y	Y	Y	Y	N	Y	Y
12 Speier	Y	Y	Y	Y	N	Y	Y
13 Stark	?	?	?	?	?	?	?
14 Eshoo	Y	Y	Y	Y	N	Y	Y
15 Honda	Y	Y	Y	Y	N	Y	Y
16 Lofgren	Y	Y	Y	Y	N	Y	Y
17 Farr	Y	Y	Y	Y	N	Y	Y
18 Cardoza	Y	Y	Y	Y	N	Y	Y
19 **Radanovich**	Y	Y	Y	N	Y	N	?
20 Costa	Y	Y	Y	Y	N	Y	Y
21 **Nunes**	Y	Y	Y	N	Y	N	Y
22 **McCarthy**	Y	Y	Y	N	Y	N	Y
23 Capps	Y	Y	Y	Y	N	Y	Y
24 **Gallegly**	Y	Y	Y	N	Y	N	?
25 **McKeon**	Y	Y	Y	?	?	?	?
26 **Dreier**	Y	Y	Y	N	Y	N	Y
27 Sherman	Y	Y	Y	Y	N	Y	Y
28 Berman	Y	Y	Y	Y	N	Y	Y
29 Schiff	Y	Y	Y	Y	N	Y	Y
30 Waxman	Y	Y	Y	Y	N	Y	Y
31 Becerra	Y	Y	Y	Y	N	Y	Y
32 Solis	?	?	?	Y	N	Y	Y
33 Watson	Y	Y	Y	Y	N	Y	Y
34 Roybal-Allard	Y	Y	Y	Y	N	Y	Y
35 Waters	Y	Y	Y	Y	N	Y	Y
36 Harman	Y	Y	Y	Y	N	Y	Y
37 Richardson	Y	Y	Y	Y	N	Y	Y
38 Napolitano	Y	Y	?	Y	N	Y	Y
39 Sánchez, Linda	Y	Y	Y	Y	N	Y	Y
40 **Royce**	Y	Y	Y	N	Y	N	Y
41 **Lewis**	Y	Y	Y	N	Y	N	Y
42 **Miller, Gary**	Y	Y	Y	N	Y	N	?
43 Baca	Y	Y	Y	Y	N	Y	Y
44 **Calvert**	Y	Y	Y	N	Y	N	?
45 **Bono Mack**	Y	Y	Y	N	Y	N	Y
46 **Rohrabacher**	Y	Y	Y	N	Y	N	Y
47 Sanchez, Loretta	Y	Y	Y	N	Y	Y	Y
48 **Campbell**	?	?	?	?	?	?	?
49 **Issa**	Y	Y	Y	N	Y	N	Y
50 **Bilbray**	Y	Y	Y	N	Y	N	Y
51 Filner	Y	Y	Y	Y	N	Y	Y
52 **Hunter**	Y	Y	Y	N	Y	N	Y
53 Davis	Y	Y	Y	Y	N	Y	Y
COLORADO							
1 DeGette	Y	Y	Y	Y	N	Y	Y
2 Polis	Y	Y	Y	Y	N	Y	Y
3 Salazar	Y	Y	Y	Y	N	Y	Y
4 Markey	Y	Y	Y	Y	N	Y	Y
5 **Lamborn**	Y	Y	Y	N	Y	N	Y
6 **Coffman**	Y	Y	Y	N	Y	N	Y
7 Perlmutter	Y	Y	Y	Y	N	N	Y
CONNECTICUT							
1 Larson	Y	Y	Y	Y	N	Y	?
2 Courtney	Y	Y	Y	Y	N	Y	Y
3 DeLauro	Y	Y	Y	Y	N	Y	Y
4 Himes	Y	Y	Y	Y	Y	Y	Y
5 Murphy	Y	Y	Y	Y	N	Y	Y
DELAWARE							
AL **Castle**	Y	Y	Y	Y	Y	N	Y
FLORIDA							
1 **Miller**	Y	Y	Y	N	Y	N	Y
2 Boyd	Y	Y	Y	Y	N	Y	Y
3 Brown	Y	Y	Y	Y	N	Y	Y
4 **Crenshaw**	Y	Y	Y	N	Y	N	Y
5 **Brown-Waite**	Y	Y	Y	N	Y	N	Y
6 **Stearns**	Y	Y	Y	N	Y	N	Y
7 **Mica**	Y	Y	Y	N	Y	N	Y
8 Grayson	Y	Y	Y	Y	N	Y	Y
9 **Bilirakis**	Y	Y	Y	N	Y	N	Y
10 **Young**	Y	Y	Y	N	Y	N	Y
11 Castor	Y	Y	Y	?	?	?	?
12 **Putnam**	Y	Y	Y	N	Y	N	Y
13 **Buchanan**	Y	Y	Y	Y	Y	N	Y
14 **Mack**	Y	Y	Y	N	Y	N	Y
15 **Posey**	Y	Y	Y	N	Y	N	Y
16 **Rooney**	Y	Y	Y	N	Y	N	Y
17 Meek	Y	Y	Y	Y	N	Y	Y
18 **Ros-Lehtinen**	Y	Y	Y	N	Y	N	Y
19 Wexler	Y	Y	Y	Y	N	Y	Y
20 Wasserman Schultz	Y	Y	Y	Y	N	Y	Y
21 **Diaz-Balart, L.**	Y	Y	Y	Y	Y	N	Y
22 Klein	Y	Y	Y	Y	N	Y	Y
23 Hastings	Y	Y	Y	Y	N	Y	Y
24 Kosmas	Y	Y	Y	Y	N	Y	Y
25 **Diaz-Balart, M.**	Y	Y	Y	Y	Y	Y	Y
GEORGIA							
1 **Kingston**	Y	Y	Y	N	Y	N	Y
2 Bishop	Y	Y	Y	N	Y	Y	Y
3 **Westmoreland**	Y	Y	N	N	Y	N	Y
4 Johnson	Y	Y	Y	Y	N	Y	Y
5 Lewis	Y	Y	Y	N	Y	Y	Y
6 **Price**	Y	Y	Y	N	Y	N	Y
7 **Linder**	Y	Y	Y	N	Y	N	Y
8 Marshall	Y	Y	Y	N	Y	Y	Y
9 **Deal**	Y	Y	Y	N	Y	N	Y
10 **Broun**	Y	Y	N	N	Y	N	?
11 **Gingrey**	Y	Y	Y	N	Y	N	Y
12 Barrow	Y	Y	Y	Y	N	Y	Y
13 Scott	Y	Y	Y	Y	N	Y	Y
HAWAII							
1 Abercrombie	Y	Y	Y	Y	N	Y	Y
2 Hirono	Y	Y	Y	Y	N	Y	Y
IDAHO							
1 Minnick	Y	Y	Y	Y	Y	Y	Y
2 **Simpson**	Y	Y	Y	+	–	+	Y
ILLINOIS							
1 Rush	Y	Y	Y	Y	N	Y	Y
2 Jackson	Y	Y	Y	Y	N	Y	Y
3 Lipinski	Y	Y	Y	Y	N	Y	Y
4 Gutierrez	Y	Y	Y	Y	N	Y	Y
5 Vacant							
6 **Roskam**	Y	Y	Y	N	Y	N	Y
7 Davis	Y	Y	Y	Y	N	Y	Y
8 Bean	Y	Y	Y	+	N	Y	Y
9 Schakowsky	Y	Y	Y	Y	N	Y	Y
10 **Kirk**	Y	Y	Y	Y	Y	N	Y
11 Halvorson	Y	Y	Y	Y	N	Y	Y
12 Costello	Y	Y	Y	Y	N	Y	Y
13 **Biggert**	Y	Y	Y	N	Y	N	Y
14 Foster	Y	Y	Y	Y	N	Y	Y
15 **Johnson**	Y	Y	Y	N	Y	N	Y

	47	48	49	50	51	52	53
16 **Manzullo**	Y	Y	Y	N	Y	N	Y
17 Hare	Y	Y	Y	Y	N	Y	Y
18 **Schock**	Y	Y	Y	N	?	N	Y
19 **Shimkus**	Y	Y	Y	N	Y	N	Y
INDIANA							
1 Visclosky	Y	Y	Y	Y	N	Y	Y
2 Donnelly	Y	Y	Y	Y	N	Y	Y
3 **Souder**	Y	Y	Y	N	Y	N	Y
4 **Buyer**	?	?	?	N	Y	N	Y
5 **Burton**	Y	Y	Y	N	Y	N	Y
6 **Pence**	Y	Y	Y	N	Y	N	Y
7 Carson	Y	Y	Y	Y	N	Y	Y
8 Ellsworth	Y	Y	Y	Y	N	Y	N
9 Hill	Y	Y	Y	Y	N	Y	Y
IOWA							
1 Braley	Y	Y	Y	Y	N	Y	Y
2 Loebsack	Y	Y	Y	Y	N	Y	Y
3 Boswell	Y	Y	Y	Y	N	Y	Y
4 **Latham**	Y	Y	Y	N	Y	N	Y
5 **King**	Y	Y	Y	N	Y	N	Y
KANSAS							
1 **Moran**	?	?	?	Y	Y	N	Y
2 **Jenkins**	Y	Y	Y	N	Y	N	Y
3 Moore	Y	Y	Y	Y	N	Y	Y
4 **Tiahrt**	?	?	?	N	Y	N	?
KENTUCKY							
1 **Whitfield**	Y	Y	Y	N	Y	N	Y
2 **Guthrie**	Y	Y	Y	N	Y	N	Y
3 Yarmuth	Y	Y	Y	Y	N	Y	Y
4 **Davis**	Y	Y	Y	N	Y	N	Y
5 **Rogers**	Y	Y	Y	N	Y	Y	Y
6 Chandler	Y	Y	Y	Y	N	Y	Y
LOUISIANA							
1 **Scalise**	Y	Y	Y	N	Y	N	Y
2 **Cao**	Y	Y	Y	Y	N	Y	Y
3 Melancon	Y	Y	Y	Y	N	N	Y
4 **Fleming**	Y	Y	Y	N	Y	N	Y
5 **Alexander**	Y	Y	Y	N	?	?	?
6 **Cassidy**	Y	Y	Y	N	Y	N	Y
7 **Boustany**	Y	Y	Y	N	Y	N	Y
MAINE							
1 Pingree	Y	Y	Y	Y	N	Y	Y
2 Michaud	Y	Y	Y	Y	N	Y	Y
MARYLAND							
1 Kratovil	Y	Y	Y	Y	N	Y	Y
2 Ruppersberger	Y	Y	Y	Y	N	Y	Y
3 Sarbanes	Y	Y	Y	Y	N	Y	Y
4 Edwards	Y	Y	Y	Y	N	Y	Y
5 Hoyer	Y	Y	Y	Y	N	Y	Y
6 **Bartlett**	Y	Y	Y	N	Y	N	Y
7 Cummings	Y	Y	Y	Y	N	Y	Y
8 Van Hollen	Y	Y	Y	Y	N	Y	Y
MASSACHUSETTS							
1 Olver	Y	Y	Y	Y	N	Y	Y
2 Neal	Y	Y	Y	Y	N	Y	Y
3 McGovern	Y	Y	Y	Y	N	Y	Y
4 Frank	Y	Y	?	Y	N	Y	Y
5 Tsongas	Y	Y	Y	Y	N	Y	Y
6 Tierney	Y	Y	Y	Y	N	Y	Y
7 Markey	Y	Y	Y	Y	N	Y	Y
8 Capuano	Y	Y	Y	Y	N	Y	Y
9 Lynch	Y	Y	Y	Y	N	Y	Y
10 Delahunt	Y	Y	Y	Y	N	Y	Y
MICHIGAN							
1 Stupak	?	?	Y	Y	N	Y	Y
2 **Hoekstra**	Y	Y	Y	N	Y	N	Y
3 **Ehlers**	Y	Y	Y	Y	Y	N	Y
4 **Camp**	Y	Y	Y	N	Y	N	Y
5 Kildee	Y	Y	Y	Y	N	Y	Y
6 **Upton**	Y	Y	Y	Y	Y	N	Y
7 Schauer	Y	Y	Y	Y	N	Y	Y
8 **Rogers**	Y	Y	Y	N	Y	N	Y
9 Peters	Y	Y	Y	Y	Y	Y	Y
10 **Miller**	Y	Y	Y	Y	Y	N	Y
11 **McCotter**	Y	Y	Y	Y	Y	N	Y
12 Levin	Y	Y	Y	Y	N	Y	Y
13 Kilpatrick	+	+	+	Y	N	Y	Y
14 Conyers	?	Y	Y	Y	N	Y	Y
15 Dingell	Y	Y	Y	Y	N	Y	Y
MINNESOTA							
1 Walz	Y	Y	Y	Y	Y	N	Y
2 **Kline**	Y	Y	Y	N	Y	N	Y
3 **Paulsen**	Y	Y	Y	Y	Y	N	Y
4 McCollum	Y	Y	Y	Y	N	Y	Y

	47	48	49	50	51	52	53
5 Ellison	Y	Y	Y	Y	N	Y	Y
6 **Bachmann**	Y	Y	Y	N	Y	N	Y
7 Peterson	Y	Y	Y	Y	N	Y	?
8 Oberstar	Y	Y	Y	Y	N	Y	Y
MISSISSIPPI							
1 Childers	Y	Y	Y	Y	N	Y	Y
2 Thompson	Y	Y	Y	Y	N	Y	Y
3 **Harper**	Y	Y	Y	N	Y	N	Y
4 Taylor	Y	Y	Y	Y	N	Y	Y
MISSOURI							
1 Clay	Y	Y	Y	Y	N	Y	Y
2 **Akin**	Y	Y	Y	N	Y	N	Y
3 Carnahan	Y	Y	Y	Y	N	Y	Y
4 Skelton	Y	Y	Y	Y	N	Y	Y
5 Cleaver	Y	Y	Y	Y	N	Y	Y
6 **Graves**	Y	Y	Y	N	Y	N	Y
7 **Blunt**	Y	Y	Y	N	Y	N	Y
8 **Emerson**	Y	Y	Y	Y	Y	Y	Y
9 **Luetkemeyer**	Y	Y	Y	N	Y	N	Y
MONTANA							
AL **Rehberg**	Y	Y	Y	Y	Y	N	Y
NEBRASKA							
1 **Fortenberry**	Y	Y	Y	N	Y	N	Y
2 **Terry**	Y	Y	Y	N	Y	N	Y
3 **Smith**	Y	Y	Y	N	Y	N	Y
NEVADA							
1 Berkley	Y	Y	Y	Y	N	N	Y
2 **Heller**	Y	Y	Y	N	Y	N	Y
3 Titus	Y	Y	Y	Y	N	Y	Y
NEW HAMPSHIRE							
1 Shea-Porter	Y	Y	Y	Y	N	Y	Y
2 Hodes	Y	Y	Y	Y	N	Y	Y
NEW JERSEY							
1 Andrews	Y	Y	Y	Y	N	Y	Y
2 **LoBiondo**	Y	Y	Y	Y	Y	Y	Y
3 Adler	Y	Y	Y	Y	N	N	Y
4 **Smith**	Y	Y	Y	Y	Y	Y	Y
5 **Garrett**	Y	Y	Y	N	Y	N	Y
6 Pallone	Y	Y	Y	Y	N	Y	Y
7 **Lance**	Y	Y	Y	Y	Y	N	Y
8 Pascrell	Y	Y	Y	Y	N	Y	Y
9 Rothman	Y	Y	Y	Y	N	Y	Y
10 Payne	?	?	?	Y	N	Y	Y
11 **Frelinghuysen**	Y	Y	Y	Y	Y	N	Y
12 Holt	Y	Y	Y	Y	N	Y	Y
13 Sires	Y	Y	Y	Y	N	Y	Y
NEW MEXICO							
1 Heinrich	Y	Y	Y	Y	N	Y	Y
2 Teague	Y	Y	Y	Y	Y	Y	Y
3 Lujan	Y	Y	Y	Y	N	Y	Y
NEW YORK							
1 Bishop	Y	Y	Y	Y	N	Y	Y
2 Israel	Y	Y	Y	Y	N	Y	Y
3 **King**	Y	Y	Y	Y	Y	N	Y
4 McCarthy	Y	Y	Y	Y	N	Y	Y
5 Ackerman	Y	Y	Y	Y	N	Y	Y
6 Meeks	Y	Y	Y	Y	N	Y	Y
7 Crowley	+	+	+	Y	N	Y	Y
8 Nadler	Y	Y	Y	Y	N	Y	Y
9 Weiner	Y	Y	Y	Y	N	Y	Y
10 Towns	Y	Y	Y	Y	N	Y	Y
11 Clarke	Y	Y	Y	Y	N	Y	Y
12 Velázquez	Y	Y	?	Y	N	Y	Y
13 McMahon	Y	Y	Y	Y	N	Y	Y
14 Maloney	Y	Y	Y	Y	N	Y	Y
15 Rangel	Y	Y	Y	Y	N	Y	?
16 Serrano	Y	Y	Y	Y	N	Y	Y
17 Engel	Y	Y	Y	Y	N	Y	Y
18 Lowey	Y	Y	Y	Y	N	Y	Y
19 Hall	Y	Y	Y	Y	N	Y	Y
20 Vacant							
21 Tonko	Y	Y	Y	Y	N	Y	Y
22 Hinchey	Y	Y	Y	Y	N	Y	Y
23 **McHugh**	Y	Y	Y	Y	Y	Y	Y
24 Arcuri	Y	Y	Y	Y	N	Y	Y
25 Maffei	Y	Y	Y	Y	N	Y	Y
26 **Lee**	Y	Y	Y	Y	Y	N	Y
27 Higgins	Y	Y	Y	Y	N	Y	Y
28 Slaughter	Y	Y	Y	Y	N	Y	?
29 Massa	Y	Y	Y	Y	N	Y	Y
NORTH CAROLINA							
1 Butterfield	Y	Y	Y	Y	N	Y	Y
2 Etheridge	Y	Y	Y	Y	N	Y	Y
3 **Jones**	Y	Y	Y	N	Y	Y	Y
4 Price	Y	Y	Y	Y	N	Y	Y

	47	48	49	50	51	52	53
5 **Foxx**	Y	Y	Y	N	Y	N	Y
6 **Coble**	Y	Y	Y	N	Y	N	Y
7 McIntyre	Y	Y	Y	Y	Y	Y	Y
8 Kissell	Y	Y	Y	?	?	?	?
9 **Myrick**	Y	Y	Y	N	Y	N	Y
10 **McHenry**	Y	Y	Y	N	Y	N	Y
11 Shuler	Y	Y	Y	Y	N	N	Y
12 Watt	Y	Y	Y	Y	N	Y	Y
13 Miller	Y	Y	Y	Y	N	Y	Y
NORTH DAKOTA							
AL Pomeroy	Y	Y	Y	Y	N	Y	Y
OHIO							
1 Driehaus	Y	Y	Y	Y	N	Y	Y
2 **Schmidt**	Y	Y	Y	N	Y	N	Y
3 **Turner**	Y	Y	Y	Y	Y	Y	Y
4 **Jordan**	Y	Y	Y	N	Y	N	Y
5 **Latta**	Y	Y	Y	N	Y	N	Y
6 Wilson	Y	Y	Y	Y	N	Y	Y
7 **Austria**	Y	Y	Y	Y	Y	N	Y
8 **Boehner**	Y	Y	Y	N	Y	N	Y
9 Kaptur	Y	Y	Y	Y	N	Y	Y
10 Kucinich	Y	Y	Y	Y	N	Y	Y
11 Fudge	Y	Y	Y	Y	N	Y	Y
12 **Tiberi**	Y	Y	Y	Y	Y	N	Y
13 Sutton	Y	Y	Y	Y	N	Y	Y
14 **LaTourette**	Y	Y	Y	Y	Y	Y	Y
15 Kilroy	Y	Y	Y	Y	N	Y	Y
16 Boccieri	Y	Y	Y	Y	N	Y	Y
17 Ryan	Y	Y	Y	Y	N	Y	Y
18 Space	Y	Y	Y	Y	N	Y	Y
OKLAHOMA							
1 **Sullivan**	Y	Y	Y	N	Y	Y	Y
2 Boren	Y	Y	Y	Y	N	Y	Y
3 **Lucas**	Y	Y	Y	N	Y	N	Y
4 **Cole**	Y	Y	Y	N	Y	N	Y
5 **Fallin**	Y	Y	Y	N	Y	N	Y
OREGON							
1 Wu	Y	Y	Y	Y	N	Y	Y
2 **Walden**	Y	Y	Y	N	Y	N	Y
3 Blumenauer	Y	Y	Y	Y	N	Y	Y
4 DeFazio	Y	Y	Y	Y	N	Y	Y
5 Schrader	Y	Y	Y	Y	N	Y	Y
PENNSYLVANIA							
1 Brady	Y	Y	Y	Y	N	Y	Y
2 Fattah	Y	Y	Y	Y	N	Y	Y
3 Dahlkemper	Y	Y	Y	Y	Y	Y	Y
4 Altmire	Y	Y	Y	Y	Y	N	Y
5 **Thompson**	Y	Y	Y	Y	Y	N	Y
6 **Gerlach**	Y	Y	Y	Y	Y	N	Y
7 Sestak	Y	Y	Y	Y	N	Y	Y
8 Murphy, P.	Y	Y	Y	Y	N	Y	Y
9 **Shuster**	Y	Y	Y	N	Y	Y	Y
10 Carney	Y	Y	Y	Y	Y	Y	Y
11 Kanjorski	Y	Y	Y	Y	N	Y	Y
12 Murtha	Y	Y	Y	Y	N	Y	Y
13 Schwartz	Y	Y	Y	Y	N	Y	?
14 Doyle	Y	Y	Y	Y	N	Y	Y
15 **Dent**	Y	Y	Y	Y	Y	N	Y
16 **Pitts**	Y	Y	Y	N	Y	N	Y
17 Holden	Y	Y	Y	Y	N	N	Y
18 **Murphy, T.**	Y	Y	Y	Y	Y	N	Y
19 **Platts**	Y	Y	Y	Y	Y	N	Y
RHODE ISLAND							
1 Kennedy	Y	Y	Y	Y	N	Y	Y
2 Langevin	Y	Y	Y	Y	N	Y	Y
SOUTH CAROLINA							
1 **Brown**	Y	Y	Y	N	Y	N	Y
2 **Wilson**	Y	Y	Y	N	Y	N	Y
3 **Barrett**	+	+	+	N	Y	N	Y
4 **Inglis**	Y	Y	Y	N	Y	N	Y
5 Spratt	Y	Y	Y	Y	N	Y	Y
6 Clyburn	Y	Y	Y	Y	N	Y	Y
SOUTH DAKOTA							
AL Herseth Sandlin	Y	Y	Y	Y	N	Y	Y
TENNESSEE							
1 **Roe**	Y	Y	Y	N	N	Y	Y
2 **Duncan**	Y	Y	Y	N	Y	Y	Y
3 **Wamp**	Y	Y	Y	–	Y	N	Y
4 Davis, L.	Y	Y	Y	Y	N	Y	Y
5 Cooper	Y	Y	Y	Y	N	Y	Y
6 Gordon	Y	Y	Y	Y	N	Y	Y
7 **Blackburn**	Y	Y	Y	N	Y	N	Y
8 Tanner	Y	Y	Y	Y	N	Y	Y
9 Cohen	Y	Y	Y	Y	N	Y	Y

	47	48	49	50	51	52	53
TEXAS							
1 **Gohmert**	Y	Y	Y	N	Y	N	Y
2 **Poe**	Y	Y	N	?	Y	N	Y
3 **Johnson, S.**	Y	Y	Y	N	Y	N	Y
4 **Hall**	Y	Y	Y	N	Y	N	Y
5 **Hensarling**	Y	Y	Y	N	Y	N	Y
6 **Barton**	Y	Y	Y	N	Y	N	Y
7 **Culberson**	Y	Y	Y	N	Y	N	Y
8 **Brady**	Y	Y	Y	N	Y	N	Y
9 Green, A.	Y	Y	Y	Y	N	Y	Y
10 **McCaul**	Y	Y	Y	N	Y	N	Y
11 **Conaway**	Y	Y	Y	N	Y	N	Y
12 **Granger**	Y	Y	Y	N	Y	N	Y
13 **Thornberry**	Y	Y	Y	N	Y	N	Y
14 **Paul**	Y	Y	Y	N	Y	?	?
15 Hinojosa	Y	Y	Y	Y	N	Y	Y
16 Reyes	Y	Y	Y	Y	N	Y	?
17 Edwards	Y	Y	Y	Y	N	Y	Y
18 Jackson Lee	Y	Y	Y	Y	N	Y	Y
19 **Neugebauer**	Y	Y	Y	N	Y	N	Y
20 Gonzalez	Y	Y	Y	Y	N	Y	Y
21 **Smith**	Y	Y	Y	N	Y	N	Y
22 **Olson**	Y	Y	Y	N	Y	N	Y
23 Rodriguez	Y	Y	Y	Y	N	Y	Y
24 **Marchant**	Y	Y	Y	N	Y	N	Y
25 Doggett	Y	Y	Y	Y	N	Y	Y
26 **Burgess**	Y	Y	Y	N	Y	N	Y
27 Ortiz	Y	Y	Y	Y	N	Y	Y
28 Cuellar	Y	Y	Y	Y	N	Y	Y
29 Green, G.	Y	Y	Y	Y	N	Y	Y
30 Johnson, E.	Y	Y	Y	Y	N	Y	Y
31 **Carter**	Y	Y	Y	N	Y	N	Y
32 **Sessions**	Y	Y	Y	N	Y	N	Y
UTAH							
1 **Bishop**	Y	Y	Y	N	Y	N	Y
2 Matheson	Y	Y	Y	Y	N	Y	Y
3 **Chaffetz**	Y	Y	Y	N	Y	N	Y
VERMONT							
AL Welch	Y	Y	Y	Y	N	Y	Y
VIRGINIA							
1 **Wittman**	Y	Y	Y	N	Y	N	Y
2 Nye	Y	Y	Y	Y	Y	Y	Y
3 Scott	Y	Y	Y	Y	N	Y	Y
4 **Forbes**	Y	Y	Y	N	Y	N	Y
5 Perriello	Y	Y	?	Y	Y	Y	Y
6 **Goodlatte**	Y	Y	Y	N	Y	N	Y
7 **Cantor**	Y	Y	Y	N	Y	N	Y
8 Moran	Y	Y	Y	Y	N	Y	Y
9 Boucher	Y	Y	Y	Y	N	Y	Y
10 **Wolf**	Y	Y	Y	Y	Y	N	Y
11 Connolly	Y	Y	Y	Y	N	Y	Y
WASHINGTON							
1 Inslee	Y	Y	Y	Y	N	Y	Y
2 Larsen	Y	Y	Y	Y	N	N	Y
3 Baird	Y	Y	Y	Y	N	Y	Y
4 **Hastings**	Y	Y	Y	N	Y	N	Y
5 **McMorris Rodgers**	?	?	?	N	Y	N	Y
6 Dicks	Y	Y	Y	Y	N	Y	Y
7 McDermott	Y	Y	Y	Y	N	Y	Y
8 **Reichert**	Y	Y	Y	Y	Y	N	Y
9 Smith	Y	Y	Y	Y	N	Y	?
WEST VIRGINIA							
1 Mollohan	Y	Y	Y	Y	N	Y	?
2 **Capito**	Y	Y	Y	Y	Y	N	Y
3 Rahall	Y	Y	Y	Y	N	Y	Y
WISCONSIN							
1 **Ryan**	Y	Y	Y	N	Y	N	Y
2 Baldwin	Y	Y	Y	Y	N	Y	Y
3 Kind	Y	Y	Y	Y	Y	N	Y
4 Moore	Y	Y	Y	Y	N	Y	Y
5 **Sensenbrenner**	Y	Y	Y	N	N	Y	Y
6 **Petri**	Y	Y	Y	Y	N	N	Y
7 Obey	Y	Y	Y	Y	N	Y	Y
8 Kagen	Y	Y	Y	Y	N	Y	Y
WYOMING							
AL **Lummis**	Y	Y	Y	N	Y	N	Y
DELEGATES							
Faleomavaega (A.S.)							
Norton (D.C.)							
Bordallo (Guam)							
Sablan (N. Marianas)							
Pierluisi (P.R.)							
Christensen (V.I.)							

IN THE HOUSE | By Vote Number

54. HR 1. Economic Stimulus/Motion to Instruct.
Lewis, R-Calif., motion to instruct House conferees not to vote on approval of the final conference agreement unless the text of the agreement has been available in an electronic, searchable and downloadable form for at least 48 hours. Motion agreed to 403-0: R 167-0; D 236-0. Feb. 10, 2009.

55. H Res 114. Girls and Women in Sports Day/Adoption.
Sablan, I-N. Marianas, motion to suspend the rules and adopt the resolution that would support the goals and ideals of "National Girls and Women in Sports Day" and encourage schools to continue to provide sports opportunities for girls and women. Motion agreed to 398-0: R 162-0; D 236-0. A two-thirds majority of those present and voting (266 in this case) is required for adoption under suspension of the rules. Feb. 10, 2009.

56. H Res 60. Quarterback Sam Bradford Tribute/Adoption.
Sablan, I-N. Marianas, motion to suspend the rules and adopt the resolution that would commend University of Oklahoma quarterback Sam Bradford for his academic accomplishments and congratulate him for winning the 2008 Heisman Trophy. Motion agreed to 394-0: R 162-0; D 232-0. A two-thirds majority of those present and voting (263 in this case) is required for adoption under suspension of the rules. Feb. 10, 2009.

57. H Res 143. Rep. Rangel Removal From Chairmanship/Motion to Table.
Crowley, D-N.Y., motion to table (kill) the Carter, R-Texas, privileged resolution that would remove Charles B. Rangel, D-N.Y., from his chairmanship of the House Ways and Means Committee. Motion agreed to 242-157: R 5-157; D 237-0. Feb. 10, 2009.

58. H Res 128. Miami University 200th Anniversary/Adoption.
Fudge, D-Ohio, motion to suspend the rules and adopt the resolution that would congratulate Miami University in Ohio on its 200th anniversary. Motion agreed to 413-0: R 170-0; D 243-0. A two-thirds majority of those present and voting (276 in this case) is required for adoption under suspension of the rules. Feb. 10, 2009.

59. H Res 134. Martin Luther King Jr. India Trip Anniversary/Adoption.
Johnson, D-Ga., motion to suspend the rules and adopt the resolution that would encourage Americans to remember the 50th anniversary of Dr. Martin Luther King Jr.'s visit to India and the impact that the trip and King's study of Mahatma Gandhi's philosophy had on the civil rights movement. Motion agreed to 406-0: R 165-0; D 241-0. A two-thirds majority of those present and voting (271 in this case) is required for adoption under suspension of the rules. Feb. 10, 2009.

60. H Con Res 47. Adjournment/Adoption.
Adoption of the concurrent resolution that would provide for adjournment of the House and Senate until 2 p.m., Monday, Feb. 23, 2009. Adopted 238-181: R 1-173; D 237-8. Feb. 11, 2009.

	54	55	56	57	58	59	60
ALABAMA							
1 **Bonner**	Y	?	Y	P	Y	Y	N
2 Bright	Y	Y	Y	Y	Y	Y	Y
3 **Rogers**	Y	Y	Y	N	Y	Y	N
4 **Aderholt**	Y	Y	Y	N	Y	Y	N
5 Griffith	Y	Y	Y	Y	Y	Y	Y
6 **Bachus**	Y	Y	?	N	Y	Y	N
7 Davis	Y	Y	Y	Y	Y	Y	Y
ALASKA							
AL **Young**	Y	Y	Y	Y	Y	Y	N
ARIZONA							
1 Kirkpatrick	Y	Y	Y	Y	Y	Y	Y
2 **Franks**	Y	Y	Y	N	Y	Y	N
3 **Shadegg**	Y	Y	Y	N	Y	N	N
4 Pastor	Y	Y	Y	Y	Y	Y	Y
5 Mitchell	Y	Y	Y	Y	Y	Y	Y
6 **Flake**	Y	Y	Y	N	Y	N	N
7 Grijalva	Y	Y	?	?	?	?	Y
8 Giffords	Y	Y	Y	Y	Y	Y	Y
ARKANSAS							
1 Berry	Y	Y	Y	Y	Y	Y	Y
2 Snyder	Y	Y	Y	Y	Y	Y	Y
3 **Boozman**	Y	Y	Y	N	Y	Y	N
4 Ross	Y	Y	Y	Y	Y	Y	Y
CALIFORNIA							
1 Thompson	Y	Y	Y	Y	Y	Y	Y
2 **Herger**	Y	Y	?	N	Y	Y	N
3 **Lungren**	Y	Y	Y	N	Y	Y	N
4 **McClintock**	Y	Y	Y	N	Y	N	N
5 Matsui	Y	Y	Y	Y	Y	Y	Y
6 Woolsey	+	+	+	Y	Y	Y	Y
7 Miller, George	Y	Y	Y	Y	Y	Y	Y
8 Pelosi							
9 Lee	Y	Y	Y	Y	Y	Y	Y
10 Tauscher	Y	Y	Y	Y	Y	Y	Y
11 McNerney	Y	Y	Y	Y	Y	Y	Y
12 Speier	Y	Y	Y	Y	Y	Y	Y
13 Stark	?	?	?	?	?	?	?
14 Eshoo	Y	Y	Y	Y	Y	Y	Y
15 Honda	Y	Y	Y	Y	Y	Y	Y
16 Lofgren	Y	Y	Y	P	Y	Y	Y
17 Farr	Y	Y	Y	Y	Y	Y	Y
18 Cardoza	Y	Y	Y	Y	Y	Y	Y
19 **Radanovich**	Y	Y	Y	N	Y	Y	N
20 Costa	Y	Y	Y	Y	Y	Y	Y
21 **Nunes**	Y	Y	Y	N	Y	Y	N
22 **McCarthy**	Y	Y	Y	N	Y	Y	N
23 Capps	Y	Y	Y	Y	Y	Y	Y
24 **Gallegly**	?	?	?	N	Y	Y	N
25 **McKeon**	Y	Y	Y	N	Y	Y	N
26 **Dreier**	Y	Y	Y	N	Y	Y	N
27 Sherman	Y	Y	Y	Y	Y	Y	Y
28 Berman	Y	Y	Y	Y	Y	Y	Y
29 Schiff	Y	Y	Y	Y	Y	Y	Y
30 Waxman	Y	Y	Y	Y	Y	Y	Y
31 Becerra	Y	Y	Y	Y	Y	Y	Y
32 Solis	Y	Y	Y	?	?	?	?
33 Watson	Y	Y	Y	Y	Y	Y	Y
34 Roybal-Allard	Y	Y	Y	Y	Y	Y	Y
35 Waters	Y	Y	Y	Y	Y	Y	Y
36 Harman	?	?	?	?	?	?	?
37 Richardson	Y	Y	Y	Y	Y	Y	Y
38 Napolitano	Y	Y	Y	Y	Y	Y	Y
39 Sánchez, Linda	Y	Y	Y	Y	Y	Y	Y
40 **Royce**	Y	Y	Y	N	Y	Y	N
41 **Lewis**	Y	Y	Y	N	Y	Y	N
42 **Miller, Gary**	?	?	?	N	Y	Y	N
43 Baca	Y	Y	Y	Y	Y	Y	Y
44 **Calvert**	Y	Y	Y	N	Y	Y	N
45 **Bono Mack**	Y	Y	Y	N	Y	Y	N
46 **Rohrabacher**	Y	Y	Y	N	Y	Y	N
47 Sanchez, Loretta	Y	Y	Y	Y	Y	Y	Y
48 **Campbell**	?	?	?	?	?	?	?
49 **Issa**	Y	Y	Y	N	Y	Y	N
50 **Bilbray**	?	?	?	N	Y	Y	N
51 Filner	Y	Y	Y	Y	Y	Y	Y
52 **Hunter**	Y	Y	Y	N	Y	Y	N
53 Davis	Y	Y	Y	Y	Y	Y	Y

	54	55	56	57	58	59	60
COLORADO							
1 DeGette	?	?	?	Y	Y	Y	Y
2 Polis	Y	Y	Y	Y	Y	Y	Y
3 Salazar	Y	Y	Y	Y	Y	Y	Y
4 Markey	Y	Y	Y	Y	Y	Y	Y
5 **Lamborn**	Y	Y	Y	N	Y	N	N
6 **Coffman**	Y	Y	Y	N	Y	Y	N
7 Perlmutter	Y	Y	Y	Y	Y	Y	Y
CONNECTICUT							
1 Larson	Y	Y	Y	Y	Y	Y	Y
2 Courtney	Y	Y	Y	Y	Y	Y	Y
3 DeLauro	Y	Y	Y	Y	Y	Y	Y
4 Himes	Y	Y	Y	Y	Y	Y	Y
5 Murphy	Y	Y	Y	Y	Y	Y	Y
DELAWARE							
AL Castle	Y	Y	Y	N	Y	Y	N
FLORIDA							
1 **Miller**	Y	Y	Y	N	Y	Y	N
2 Boyd	?	?	?	Y	Y	Y	Y
3 Brown	?	?	?	Y	Y	Y	Y
4 **Crenshaw**	Y	Y	Y	N	Y	Y	N
5 **Brown-Waite**	Y	Y	Y	N	Y	Y	N
6 **Stearns**	Y	Y	Y	N	Y	Y	N
7 **Mica**	Y	Y	Y	N	Y	Y	N
8 Grayson	?	?	?	Y	Y	Y	Y
9 **Bilirakis**	Y	Y	Y	N	Y	Y	N
10 **Young**	Y	Y	Y	N	Y	Y	N
11 Castor	?	?	?	P	Y	Y	Y
12 **Putnam**	+	+	+	−	+	+	N
13 **Buchanan**	Y	Y	Y	N	Y	Y	N
14 **Mack**	Y	Y	Y	N	Y	Y	N
15 **Posey**	Y	Y	Y	N	Y	Y	N
16 **Rooney**	Y	Y	Y	N	Y	Y	N
17 Meek	+	+	+	Y	Y	Y	Y
18 **Ros-Lehtinen**	Y	Y	Y	N	Y	Y	N
19 Wexler	?	?	?	?	?	?	Y
20 Wasserman Schultz	?	?	?	?	?	?	?
21 **Diaz-Balart, L.**	?	?	?	?	?	?	?
22 Klein	?	?	?	Y	Y	Y	Y
23 Hastings	Y	Y	Y	Y	Y	Y	Y
24 Kosmas	?	?	?	Y	Y	Y	Y
25 **Diaz-Balart, M.**	Y	Y	Y	N	Y	N	N
GEORGIA							
1 **Kingston**	Y	Y	Y	N	Y	Y	N
2 Bishop	Y	Y	Y	Y	Y	Y	Y
3 **Westmoreland**	Y	Y	Y	N	Y	Y	N
4 Johnson	Y	Y	Y	Y	Y	Y	Y
5 Lewis	Y	Y	?	Y	Y	Y	Y
6 **Price**	Y	Y	Y	N	Y	Y	N
7 **Linder**	Y	?	?	N	Y	Y	N
8 Marshall	Y	Y	Y	Y	Y	Y	Y
9 **Deal**	Y	Y	Y	N	Y	Y	N
10 **Broun**	Y	Y	Y	N	Y	N	N
11 **Gingrey**	Y	Y	Y	N	Y	Y	N
12 Barrow	Y	Y	Y	Y	Y	Y	Y
13 Scott	Y	Y	Y	Y	Y	Y	Y
HAWAII							
1 Abercrombie	Y	Y	Y	Y	Y	Y	Y
2 Hirono	Y	Y	Y	Y	Y	Y	Y
IDAHO							
1 Minnick	Y	Y	Y	Y	Y	Y	N
2 **Simpson**	Y	Y	Y	N	Y	Y	N
ILLINOIS							
1 Rush	?	?	?	Y	Y	Y	Y
2 Jackson	Y	Y	Y	Y	Y	Y	Y
3 Lipinski	Y	Y	Y	Y	Y	Y	Y
4 Gutierrez	Y	Y	Y	Y	Y	Y	Y
5 Vacant							
6 **Roskam**	Y	Y	Y	N	Y	Y	N
7 Davis	+	+	+	Y	Y	Y	Y
8 Bean	Y	Y	Y	Y	Y	?	Y
9 Schakowsky	Y	Y	Y	?	Y	Y	Y
10 **Kirk**	Y	Y	Y	N	Y	Y	N
11 Halvorson	Y	Y	Y	Y	Y	Y	Y
12 Costello	Y	Y	Y	Y	Y	Y	Y
13 **Biggert**	Y	Y	Y	N	Y	Y	N
14 Foster	Y	Y	Y	Y	Y	Y	Y
15 Johnson	+	+	+	−	+	+	+

	54	55	56	57	58	59	60
16 **Manzullo**	Y	Y	Y	N	Y	Y	N
17 Hare	Y	Y	Y	Y	Y	Y	Y
18 **Schock**	?	?	?	N	Y	Y	N
19 **Shimkus**	Y	Y	Y	N	Y	Y	N
INDIANA							
1 Visclosky	Y	Y	Y	Y	Y	Y	Y
2 Donnelly	Y	Y	Y	Y	Y	Y	N
3 **Souder**	?	?	?	N	Y	Y	N
4 **Buyer**	Y	Y	Y	N	Y	Y	N
5 **Burton**	Y	Y	Y	P	Y	Y	N
6 **Pence**	Y	Y	Y	N	?	?	N
7 Carson	Y	Y	Y	Y	Y	Y	Y
8 Ellsworth	Y	Y	Y	Y	Y	Y	N
9 Hill	Y	Y	Y	Y	Y	?	Y
IOWA							
1 Braley	Y	Y	Y	Y	Y	Y	Y
2 Loebsack	Y	Y	Y	Y	Y	Y	Y
3 Boswell	Y	Y	Y	Y	Y	Y	Y
4 **Latham**	Y	Y	Y	N	Y	Y	N
5 **King**	Y	Y	Y	N	Y	Y	N
KANSAS							
1 **Moran**	Y	Y	Y	N	Y	Y	N
2 **Jenkins**	Y	Y	Y	N	Y	Y	N
3 Moore	Y	Y	Y	Y	Y	Y	Y
4 **Tiahrt**	Y	Y	Y	N	Y	Y	N
KENTUCKY							
1 **Whitfield**	Y	Y	Y	N	Y	Y	N
2 **Guthrie**	Y	Y	Y	N	Y	Y	N
3 Yarmuth	Y	Y	Y	Y	Y	Y	Y
4 **Davis**	Y	Y	Y	N	Y	?	N
5 **Rogers**	Y	Y	Y	N	Y	Y	N
6 Chandler	Y	Y	Y	P	Y	Y	Y
LOUISIANA							
1 **Scalise**	Y	Y	Y	N	Y	Y	N
2 **Cao**	Y	Y	Y	N	Y	Y	N
3 Melancon	Y	Y	Y	Y	Y	Y	Y
4 **Fleming**	Y	Y	Y	N	Y	Y	N
5 **Alexander**	Y	Y	Y	N	Y	Y	?
6 **Cassidy**	Y	Y	Y	N	Y	Y	N
7 **Boustany**	Y	?	?	N	Y	Y	N
MAINE							
1 Pingree	Y	Y	Y	Y	Y	Y	Y
2 Michaud	Y	Y	Y	Y	Y	Y	Y
MARYLAND							
1 Kratovil	Y	Y	Y	Y	Y	Y	Y
2 Ruppersberger	Y	Y	Y	Y	Y	Y	Y
3 Sarbanes	Y	Y	Y	Y	Y	Y	Y
4 Edwards	Y	Y	Y	Y	Y	Y	Y
5 Hoyer	Y	Y	Y	Y	Y	Y	Y
6 **Bartlett**	Y	Y	Y	P	Y	Y	N
7 Cummings	Y	Y	Y	Y	Y	Y	Y
8 Van Hollen	Y	Y	Y	Y	Y	Y	?
MASSACHUSETTS							
1 Olver	Y	Y	Y	Y	Y	Y	Y
2 Neal	Y	Y	Y	Y	Y	Y	Y
3 McGovern	Y	Y	Y	Y	?	?	Y
4 Frank	Y	Y	Y	?	?	?	Y
5 Tsongas	Y	Y	Y	Y	Y	Y	Y
6 Tierney	Y	Y	Y	Y	Y	Y	Y
7 Markey	Y	Y	?	Y	Y	Y	Y
8 Capuano	Y	Y	Y	Y	Y	Y	Y
9 Lynch	Y	Y	Y	Y	Y	Y	Y
10 Delahunt	Y	Y	Y	Y	Y	Y	Y
MICHIGAN							
1 Stupak	Y	Y	Y	Y	Y	Y	Y
2 **Hoekstra**	Y	Y	Y	N	Y	Y	N
3 **Ehlers**	Y	Y	Y	N	Y	Y	N
4 **Camp**	Y	Y	Y	N	Y	Y	N
5 Kildee	Y	Y	Y	Y	Y	Y	Y
6 **Upton**	Y	Y	Y	N	Y	Y	N
7 Schauer	Y	Y	Y	Y	Y	Y	Y
8 **Rogers**	Y	Y	Y	N	Y	Y	N
9 Peters	Y	Y	Y	Y	Y	Y	Y
10 **Miller**	Y	Y	?	N	Y	Y	N
11 **McCotter**	Y	Y	Y	N	Y	Y	N
12 Levin	Y	Y	Y	Y	Y	Y	Y
13 Kilpatrick	Y	Y	Y	Y	Y	Y	Y
14 Conyers	Y	Y	Y	Y	Y	Y	Y
15 Dingell	Y	Y	Y	Y	Y	Y	Y
MINNESOTA							
1 Walz	Y	Y	Y	Y	Y	Y	Y
2 **Kline**	Y	Y	Y	P	Y	Y	N
3 **Paulsen**	Y	Y	Y	N	Y	Y	N
4 McCollum	Y	Y	Y	Y	Y	Y	Y

	54	55	56	57	58	59	60
5 Ellison	Y	Y	Y	Y	Y	Y	Y
6 **Bachmann**	Y	Y	Y	–	Y	Y	N
7 Peterson	Y	Y	Y	Y	Y	Y	Y
8 Oberstar	Y	Y	Y	Y	Y	Y	Y
MISSISSIPPI							
1 Childers	Y	Y	Y	Y	Y	Y	Y
2 Thompson	Y	Y	Y	Y	Y	Y	Y
3 **Harper**	Y	Y	Y	N	Y	Y	N
4 Taylor	Y	Y	Y	Y	Y	Y	Y
MISSOURI							
1 Clay	Y	Y	Y	Y	Y	Y	Y
2 **Akin**	Y	Y	Y	N	Y	Y	N
3 Carnahan	Y	Y	Y	Y	Y	Y	Y
4 Skelton	Y	Y	Y	Y	Y	Y	Y
5 Cleaver	Y	Y	Y	Y	Y	Y	Y
6 **Graves**	Y	Y	Y	N	Y	Y	N
7 **Blunt**	Y	Y	Y	?	?	?	N
8 **Emerson**	Y	Y	Y	N	Y	Y	N
9 **Luetkemeyer**	Y	Y	Y	N	Y	Y	N
MONTANA							
AL **Rehberg**	Y	Y	Y	N	Y	Y	N
NEBRASKA							
1 **Fortenberry**	Y	Y	Y	N	Y	Y	N
2 **Terry**	Y	Y	Y	N	Y	Y	N
3 **Smith**	Y	Y	Y	N	Y	Y	N
NEVADA							
1 Berkley	+	+	+	+	+	+	Y
2 **Heller**	Y	Y	Y	N	Y	Y	N
3 Titus	Y	Y	Y	Y	Y	Y	Y
NEW HAMPSHIRE							
1 Shea-Porter	Y	Y	Y	Y	Y	Y	Y
2 Hodes	Y	Y	Y	Y	Y	Y	Y
NEW JERSEY							
1 Andrews	Y	Y	Y	Y	Y	Y	Y
2 **LoBiondo**	Y	Y	Y	N	Y	Y	N
3 Adler	Y	Y	Y	Y	Y	Y	N
4 **Smith**	Y	Y	Y	N	Y	Y	N
5 **Garrett**	Y	Y	Y	N	?	?	N
6 Pallone	Y	Y	Y	Y	Y	Y	Y
7 **Lance**	Y	Y	Y	N	Y	Y	N
8 Pascrell	Y	Y	Y	Y	Y	Y	Y
9 Rothman	Y	Y	Y	Y	Y	Y	Y
10 Payne	Y	Y	Y	Y	Y	Y	Y
11 **Frelinghuysen**	Y	Y	Y	N	Y	?	N
12 Holt	Y	Y	Y	Y	Y	Y	Y
13 Sires	Y	Y	Y	Y	Y	Y	Y
NEW MEXICO							
1 Heinrich	Y	Y	Y	Y	Y	Y	Y
2 Teague	Y	Y	Y	Y	Y	Y	Y
3 Lujan	Y	Y	Y	Y	Y	Y	Y
NEW YORK							
1 Bishop	Y	Y	Y	Y	Y	Y	Y
2 Israel	Y	Y	Y	Y	Y	Y	Y
3 **King**	Y	Y	Y	Y	Y	Y	N
4 McCarthy	Y	Y	Y	Y	Y	Y	Y
5 Ackerman	Y	Y	Y	Y	Y	Y	Y
6 Meeks	Y	Y	Y	Y	Y	Y	?
7 Crowley	Y	Y	Y	Y	Y	Y	Y
8 Nadler	Y	Y	Y	Y	Y	Y	Y
9 Weiner	Y	Y	Y	Y	Y	Y	Y
10 Towns	Y	Y	Y	Y	Y	Y	Y
11 Clarke	Y	Y	Y	Y	Y	Y	Y
12 Velázquez	Y	Y	?	Y	Y	Y	Y
13 McMahon	Y	Y	Y	Y	Y	Y	Y
14 Maloney	Y	Y	Y	Y	Y	Y	Y
15 Rangel	Y	Y	Y	Y	Y	Y	Y
16 Serrano	Y	Y	Y	Y	Y	Y	Y
17 Engel	Y	Y	Y	Y	Y	Y	Y
18 Lowey	Y	Y	Y	Y	Y	Y	Y
19 Hall	Y	Y	?	Y	Y	Y	Y
20 Vacant							
21 Tonko	Y	Y	Y	Y	Y	Y	Y
22 Hinchey	?	Y	Y	Y	Y	Y	Y
23 **McHugh**	Y	Y	Y	N	Y	Y	N
24 Arcuri	Y	Y	Y	Y	Y	Y	Y
25 Maffei	Y	Y	Y	Y	Y	Y	Y
26 **Lee**	Y	Y	Y	N	Y	Y	N
27 Higgins	Y	Y	Y	Y	Y	Y	Y
28 Slaughter	Y	Y	Y	Y	Y	Y	Y
29 Massa	Y	Y	Y	Y	Y	Y	Y
NORTH CAROLINA							
1 Butterfield	Y	Y	Y	P	Y	Y	Y
2 Etheridge	Y	Y	Y	Y	Y	Y	Y
3 **Jones**	Y	Y	Y	Y	Y	Y	Y
4 Price	Y	Y	Y	Y	Y	Y	Y

	54	55	56	57	58	59	60
5 **Foxx**	Y	Y	Y	N	Y	Y	N
6 **Coble**	Y	Y	Y	N	Y	Y	N
7 McIntyre	Y	Y	Y	Y	Y	Y	Y
8 Kissell	Y	Y	Y	Y	Y	Y	Y
9 **Myrick**	Y	Y	Y	N	Y	Y	N
10 **McHenry**	Y	Y	Y	N	Y	Y	N
11 Shuler	Y	Y	Y	Y	Y	Y	N
12 Watt	Y	Y	Y	Y	Y	Y	Y
13 Miller	Y	Y	Y	Y	Y	Y	Y
NORTH DAKOTA							
AL Pomeroy	Y	Y	Y	Y	Y	Y	Y
OHIO							
1 Driehaus	Y	Y	Y	Y	Y	Y	Y
2 **Schmidt**	Y	Y	Y	N	Y	Y	N
3 **Turner**	Y	Y	Y	N	Y	Y	N
4 **Jordan**	Y	Y	Y	N	Y	Y	N
5 **Latta**	Y	Y	Y	N	Y	Y	N
6 Wilson	Y	Y	Y	Y	Y	Y	Y
7 **Austria**	Y	Y	Y	N	Y	Y	N
8 **Boehner**	Y	Y	Y	N	Y	Y	N
9 Kaptur	Y	Y	Y	Y	Y	Y	Y
10 Kucinich	Y	Y	Y	Y	Y	Y	Y
11 Fudge	Y	Y	Y	Y	Y	Y	Y
12 **Tiberi**	?	?	?	?	?	?	?
13 Sutton	Y	Y	Y	?	Y	Y	Y
14 **LaTourette**	Y	Y	Y	N	Y	Y	N
15 Kilroy	Y	Y	Y	Y	Y	Y	Y
16 Boccieri	Y	Y	Y	Y	Y	Y	Y
17 Ryan	Y	Y	Y	Y	?	?	Y
18 Space	Y	Y	Y	Y	Y	Y	Y
OKLAHOMA							
1 **Sullivan**	Y	Y	Y	N	Y	Y	N
2 Boren	Y	Y	Y	Y	Y	Y	Y
3 **Lucas**	Y	Y	Y	N	Y	Y	N
4 **Cole**	Y	Y	Y	N	Y	Y	N
5 **Fallin**	Y	Y	Y	N	Y	Y	N
OREGON							
1 Wu	Y	Y	Y	Y	Y	Y	Y
2 **Walden**	Y	Y	Y	N	Y	Y	N
3 Blumenauer	Y	Y	Y	Y	Y	Y	Y
4 DeFazio	Y	Y	Y	Y	Y	Y	Y
5 Schrader	Y	Y	Y	Y	Y	Y	Y
PENNSYLVANIA							
1 Brady	Y	Y	Y	Y	Y	Y	Y
2 Fattah	Y	Y	Y	Y	Y	Y	?
3 Dahlkemper	Y	Y	Y	Y	Y	Y	Y
4 Altmire	Y	Y	Y	Y	Y	Y	Y
5 **Thompson**	Y	Y	Y	N	Y	Y	N
6 **Gerlach**	Y	Y	Y	N	Y	Y	N
7 Sestak	Y	Y	Y	Y	Y	Y	Y
8 Murphy, P.	Y	Y	Y	Y	Y	Y	N
9 **Shuster**	Y	Y	Y	N	Y	Y	N
10 Carney	Y	Y	Y	Y	Y	Y	Y
11 Kanjorski	Y	Y	Y	Y	Y	Y	Y
12 Murtha	Y	Y	Y	Y	Y	Y	Y
13 Schwartz	Y	Y	Y	Y	Y	Y	Y
14 Doyle	Y	Y	Y	Y	Y	Y	Y
15 **Dent**	Y	Y	Y	P	Y	Y	N
16 **Pitts**	Y	?	Y	N	Y	Y	N
17 Holden	Y	Y	Y	Y	Y	Y	?
18 **Murphy, T.**	Y	Y	Y	N	Y	Y	N
19 **Platts**	Y	Y	Y	N	Y	Y	N
RHODE ISLAND							
1 Kennedy	Y	Y	Y	Y	Y	Y	Y
2 Langevin	Y	Y	Y	Y	Y	Y	Y
SOUTH CAROLINA							
1 **Brown**	Y	Y	Y	N	Y	Y	N
2 **Wilson**	Y	Y	Y	N	Y	Y	N
3 **Barrett**	Y	Y	Y	P	Y	Y	N
4 **Inglis**	Y	Y	Y	N	Y	Y	N
5 Spratt	Y	Y	Y	Y	Y	Y	Y
6 Clyburn	Y	Y	Y	Y	Y	Y	Y
SOUTH DAKOTA							
AL Herseth Sandlin	Y	Y	Y	Y	Y	Y	Y
TENNESSEE							
1 **Roe**	Y	Y	Y	N	Y	Y	N
2 **Duncan**	Y	Y	Y	N	Y	Y	N
3 **Wamp**	Y	Y	Y	N	Y	Y	N
4 Davis	Y	Y	Y	Y	Y	Y	Y
5 Cooper	Y	Y	Y	Y	Y	Y	Y
6 Gordon	Y	Y	Y	Y	Y	Y	Y
7 **Blackburn**	Y	Y	Y	N	Y	Y	N
8 Tanner	Y	Y	Y	Y	Y	Y	Y
9 Cohen	Y	Y	Y	Y	Y	Y	Y

	54	55	56	57	58	59	60
TEXAS							
1 **Gohmert**	Y	Y	Y	N	Y	Y	N
2 **Poe**	Y	Y	Y	P	Y	Y	N
3 **Johnson, S.**	Y	Y	Y	N	Y	Y	N
4 **Hall**	Y	Y	Y	N	Y	Y	N
5 **Hensarling**	Y	Y	Y	N	Y	Y	N
6 **Barton**	Y	Y	Y	N	Y	Y	N
7 **Culberson**	Y	Y	Y	N	Y	Y	N
8 **Brady**	Y	Y	Y	N	Y	Y	N
9 Green, A.	Y	Y	Y	Y	Y	Y	Y
10 **McCaul**	Y	Y	Y	N	Y	Y	N
11 **Conaway**	Y	Y	Y	P	Y	Y	N
12 **Granger**	?	?	?	?	?	?	N
13 **Thornberry**	Y	Y	Y	N	Y	Y	N
14 **Paul**	Y	Y	Y	Y	Y	Y	N
15 Hinojosa	Y	Y	Y	+	+	+	Y
16 Reyes	Y	Y	Y	Y	Y	Y	Y
17 Edwards	Y	Y	Y	Y	Y	Y	Y
18 Jackson Lee	Y	Y	Y	Y	Y	Y	Y
19 **Neugebauer**	Y	Y	Y	N	Y	Y	N
20 Gonzalez	Y	Y	Y	Y	Y	Y	Y
21 **Smith**	Y	Y	Y	N	Y	Y	N
22 **Olson**	Y	Y	Y	N	Y	?	N
23 Rodriguez	Y	Y	Y	Y	Y	Y	Y
24 **Marchant**	Y	Y	Y	N	Y	Y	N
25 Doggett	Y	Y	Y	Y	Y	Y	Y
26 **Burgess**	Y	Y	Y	N	Y	Y	N
27 Ortiz	Y	Y	Y	Y	Y	Y	Y
28 Cuellar	Y	Y	Y	Y	Y	Y	Y
29 Green, G.	Y	Y	Y	P	Y	Y	Y
30 Johnson, E.	Y	Y	Y	Y	Y	Y	Y
31 **Carter**	Y	Y	Y	N	Y	?	N
32 **Sessions**	?	?	?	N	Y	Y	N
UTAH							
1 **Bishop**	Y	Y	Y	N	Y	Y	N
2 Matheson	Y	Y	Y	Y	Y	Y	Y
3 **Chaffetz**	Y	Y	Y	N	Y	Y	N
VERMONT							
AL Welch	Y	Y	Y	P	Y	Y	?
VIRGINIA							
1 **Wittman**	Y	Y	Y	N	Y	Y	N
2 Nye	Y	Y	Y	Y	Y	Y	Y
3 Scott	Y	Y	Y	P	Y	Y	Y
4 **Forbes**	Y	Y	Y	N	Y	?	N
5 Perriello	Y	Y	Y	Y	Y	Y	Y
6 **Goodlatte**	Y	Y	Y	N	Y	Y	N
7 **Cantor**	Y	Y	Y	N	Y	Y	N
8 Moran	Y	Y	Y	Y	Y	Y	Y
9 Boucher	Y	Y	Y	Y	Y	Y	Y
10 **Wolf**	Y	Y	Y	N	Y	Y	N
11 Connolly	Y	Y	Y	Y	Y	Y	Y
WASHINGTON							
1 Inslee	Y	Y	Y	Y	Y	Y	Y
2 Larsen	Y	Y	?	Y	Y	Y	Y
3 Baird	Y	Y	Y	Y	?	?	Y
4 **Hastings**	Y	Y	Y	P	Y	Y	N
5 **McMorris Rodgers**	Y	Y	Y	N	Y	Y	N
6 Dicks	Y	Y	Y	Y	Y	Y	Y
7 McDermott	Y	Y	Y	Y	Y	Y	Y
8 **Reichert**	Y	Y	Y	N	Y	Y	N
9 Smith	Y	Y	Y	Y	Y	Y	Y
WEST VIRGINIA							
1 Mollohan	Y	Y	Y	Y	Y	Y	Y
2 **Capito**	Y	Y	Y	N	Y	Y	N
3 Rahall	Y	Y	Y	Y	Y	Y	Y
WISCONSIN							
1 **Ryan**	Y	Y	Y	N	Y	Y	N
2 Baldwin	Y	Y	Y	Y	Y	Y	Y
3 Kind	?	?	Y	Y	Y	Y	Y
4 Moore	Y	?	Y	Y	Y	Y	P
5 **Sensenbrenner**	Y	Y	Y	N	Y	Y	N
6 **Petri**	Y	Y	Y	N	Y	Y	N
7 Obey	Y	Y	Y	Y	Y	Y	Y
8 Kagen	Y	Y	Y	Y	Y	Y	Y
WYOMING							
AL **Lummis**	Y	Y	Y	N	Y	Y	N
DELEGATES							
Faleomavaega (A.S.)							
Norton (D.C.)							
Bordallo (Guam)							
Sablan (N. Marianas)							
Pierluisi (P.R.)							
Christensen (V.I.)							

IN THE HOUSE | By Vote Number

61. **H Res 154. Tribute to Rep. Dingell/Adoption.** Kildee, D-Mich., motion to suspend the rules and adopt the resolution that would honor Rep. John D. Dingell, D-Mich., for holding the record as the longest-serving member of the House. Motion agreed to 423-0: R 174-0; D 249-0. A two-thirds majority of those present and voting (282 in this case) is required for adoption under suspension of the rules. Feb. 11, 2009.

62. **HR 448. Elder Abuse Prevention/Passage.** Johnson, D-Ga., motion to suspend the rules and pass the bill that would authorize $220 million between fiscal 2009 and 2015 for grants for local law enforcement training regarding abuse of the elderly, assist state and local prosecutors in handling such cases, and assist abuse victims advocacy groups. The bill would authorize about $42 million to conduct a study of elder abuse laws and recommend policies. Motion agreed to 397-25: R 149-25; D 248-0. A two-thirds majority of those present and voting (282 in this case) is required for passage under suspension of the rules. Feb. 11, 2009.

63. **H Res 157. Suspension Motions/Rule.** Adoption of the rule to provide for House floor consideration of bills under suspension of the rules through the legislative day of Friday, Feb. 13, 2009, and amend a resolution (H Res 10) that set the daily hour of House meetings to stipulate the chamber would meet at 9 a.m. when it is in session on Fridays and Saturdays. Adopted 248-174: R 0-172; D 248-2. Feb. 12, 2009.

64. **H Res 117. National Engineers Week/Adoption.** Gordon, D-Tenn., motion to suspend the rules and adopt the resolution that would support the goals and ideals of National Engineers Week and pledge that the House work to ensure that the contributions of the engineering community are expressed through research and innovation. Motion agreed to 422-0: R 172-0; D 250-0. A two-thirds majority of those present and voting (282 in this case) is required for adoption under suspension of the rules. Feb. 12, 2009.

65. **H Con Res 35. NAACP 100th Anniversary/Adoption.** Johnson, D-Ga., motion to suspend the rules and adopt the resolution that would recognize the 100th anniversary of the NAACP and honor the association for its work. Motion agreed to 424-0: R 173-0; D 251-0. A two-thirds majority of those present and voting (283 in this case) is required for adoption under suspension of the rules. Feb. 12, 2009.

	61	62	63	64	65
ALABAMA					
1 Bonner	Y	Y	N	Y	Y
2 Bright	Y	Y	Y	Y	Y
3 **Rogers**	Y	Y	N	Y	Y
4 **Aderholt**	Y	Y	N	?	Y
5 Griffith	Y	Y	Y	Y	Y
6 **Bachus**	Y	Y	N	Y	Y
7 Davis	Y	Y	Y	Y	Y
ALASKA					
AL **Young**	Y	Y	N	Y	Y
ARIZONA					
1 Kirkpatrick	Y	Y	N	Y	Y
2 **Franks**	Y	N	N	Y	Y
3 **Shadegg**	Y	N	N	Y	Y
4 Pastor	Y	Y	Y	Y	Y
5 Mitchell	Y	Y	Y	Y	Y
6 **Flake**	Y	N	N	Y	Y
7 Grijalva	Y	Y	Y	Y	Y
8 Giffords	Y	Y	Y	Y	Y
ARKANSAS					
1 Berry	Y	Y	Y	Y	Y
2 Snyder	Y	Y	Y	Y	Y
3 **Boozman**	Y	Y	N	Y	Y
4 Ross	Y	Y	Y	Y	Y
CALIFORNIA					
1 Thompson	Y	Y	Y	Y	Y
2 **Herger**	Y	Y	N	Y	Y
3 **Lungren**	Y	Y	N	Y	Y
4 **McClintock**	Y	N	N	Y	Y
5 Matsui	Y	Y	Y	Y	Y
6 Woolsey	Y	Y	Y	Y	Y
7 Miller, George	Y	Y	Y	Y	Y
8 Pelosi	Y				
9 Lee	Y	Y	Y	Y	Y
10 Tauscher	Y	Y	Y	Y	Y
11 McNerney	Y	Y	Y	Y	Y
12 Speier	Y	Y	Y	Y	Y
13 Stark	?	?	?	?	?
14 Eshoo	Y	Y	Y	Y	Y
15 Honda	Y	Y	Y	Y	Y
16 Lofgren	Y	Y	Y	Y	Y
17 Farr	Y	Y	Y	Y	Y
18 Cardoza	Y	Y	Y	Y	Y
19 **Radanovich**	Y	Y	N	Y	Y
20 Costa	Y	Y	Y	Y	Y
21 **Nunes**	Y	Y	N	Y	Y
22 **McCarthy**	Y	Y	N	Y	Y
23 Capps	Y	Y	Y	Y	Y
24 **Gallegly**	Y	Y	N	Y	Y
25 **McKeon**	Y	Y	N	Y	Y
26 **Dreier**	Y	Y	N	Y	Y
27 Sherman	Y	Y	Y	Y	Y
28 Berman	Y	Y	Y	Y	Y
29 Schiff	Y	Y	Y	Y	Y
30 Waxman	Y	Y	Y	Y	Y
31 Becerra	Y	Y	Y	Y	Y
32 Solis	?	?	?	?	?
33 Watson	Y	Y	Y	Y	Y
34 Roybal-Allard	Y	Y	Y	Y	Y
35 Waters	Y	Y	Y	Y	Y
36 Harman	?	?	Y	Y	Y
37 Richardson	Y	Y	Y	Y	Y
38 Napolitano	Y	Y	Y	Y	Y
39 Sánchez, Linda	Y	Y	Y	Y	Y
40 **Royce**	Y	Y	N	Y	Y
41 **Lewis**	Y	Y	N	Y	Y
42 **Miller, Gary**	Y	Y	N	Y	Y
43 Baca	Y	Y	Y	Y	Y
44 **Calvert**	Y	Y	N	Y	Y
45 **Bono Mack**	Y	Y	N	Y	Y
46 **Rohrabacher**	Y	N	N	Y	Y
47 Sanchez, Loretta	Y	Y	Y	Y	Y
48 **Campbell**	?	?	?	?	?
49 **Issa**	Y	Y	N	Y	Y
50 **Bilbray**	Y	Y	N	Y	Y
51 Filner	Y	Y	Y	Y	Y
52 **Hunter**	Y	Y	N	Y	Y
53 Davis	Y	Y	Y	Y	Y

	61	62	63	64	65
COLORADO					
1 DeGette	Y	Y	Y	Y	Y
2 Polis	Y	Y	Y	Y	Y
3 Salazar	Y	Y	Y	Y	Y
4 Markey	Y	Y	Y	Y	Y
5 **Lamborn**	Y	Y	N	Y	Y
6 **Coffman**	Y	Y	N	Y	Y
7 Perlmutter	Y	Y	Y	Y	Y
CONNECTICUT					
1 Larson	Y	Y	Y	Y	Y
2 Courtney	Y	Y	Y	Y	Y
3 DeLauro	Y	Y	Y	Y	Y
4 Himes	Y	Y	Y	Y	Y
5 Murphy	Y	Y	Y	Y	Y
DELAWARE					
AL **Castle**	Y	Y	N	Y	Y
FLORIDA					
1 **Miller**	Y	Y	N	Y	Y
2 Boyd	Y	Y	Y	Y	Y
3 Brown	Y	Y	Y	Y	Y
4 **Crenshaw**	Y	Y	N	Y	Y
5 **Brown-Waite**	Y	Y	N	Y	Y
6 **Stearns**	Y	Y	N	Y	Y
7 **Mica**	Y	Y	N	Y	Y
8 Grayson	Y	Y	Y	Y	Y
9 **Bilirakis**	Y	Y	N	Y	Y
10 **Young**	Y	Y	N	Y	Y
11 Castor	Y	Y	Y	Y	Y
12 **Putnam**	Y	Y	N	Y	Y
13 **Buchanan**	Y	Y	N	Y	Y
14 **Mack**	Y	Y	N	Y	Y
15 **Posey**	Y	Y	N	Y	Y
16 **Rooney**	Y	Y	N	Y	Y
17 Meek	Y	Y	Y	Y	Y
18 **Ros-Lehtinen**	Y	Y	N	Y	Y
19 Wexler	?	?	Y	Y	Y
20 Wasserman Schultz	Y	Y	Y	Y	Y
21 **Diaz-Balart, L.**	Y	Y	N	Y	Y
22 Klein	Y	Y	Y	Y	Y
23 Hastings	Y	Y	Y	Y	Y
24 Kosmas	Y	Y	Y	Y	Y
25 **Diaz-Balart, M.**	Y	Y	N	Y	Y
GEORGIA					
1 **Kingston**	Y	N	N	Y	Y
2 Bishop	Y	Y	Y	Y	Y
3 **Westmoreland**	Y	N	N	Y	Y
4 Johnson	Y	Y	Y	Y	Y
5 Lewis	Y	Y	Y	Y	Y
6 **Price**	Y	N	N	Y	Y
7 **Linder**	Y	N	N	Y	Y
8 Marshall	Y	Y	Y	Y	Y
9 **Deal**	Y	N	N	Y	Y
10 **Broun**	Y	N	N	Y	Y
11 **Gingrey**	Y	Y	N	Y	Y
12 Barrow	Y	Y	Y	Y	Y
13 Scott	Y	Y	Y	Y	Y
HAWAII					
1 Abercrombie	Y	Y	Y	Y	Y
2 Hirono	Y	Y	Y	Y	Y
IDAHO					
1 Minnick	Y	Y	Y	Y	Y
2 **Simpson**	Y	Y	N	Y	Y
ILLINOIS					
1 Rush	Y	Y	Y	Y	Y
2 Jackson	Y	Y	Y	Y	Y
3 Lipinski	Y	Y	Y	Y	Y
4 Gutierrez	Y	Y	Y	Y	Y
5 Vacant					
6 **Roskam**	Y	Y	N	?	?
7 Davis	Y	Y	Y	Y	Y
8 Bean	Y	Y	Y	Y	Y
9 Schakowsky	Y	Y	Y	Y	Y
10 **Kirk**	Y	Y	N	Y	Y
11 Halvorson	Y	Y	Y	Y	Y
12 Costello	Y	Y	Y	Y	Y
13 **Biggert**	Y	Y	N	Y	Y
14 Foster	Y	Y	Y	Y	Y
15 **Johnson**	+	+	N	Y	Y

KEY **Republicans** Democrats

Y	Voted for (yea)
#	Paired for
+	Announced for
N	Voted against (nay)
X	Paired against
–	Announced against
P	Voted "present"
C	Voted "present" to avoid possible conflict of interest
?	Did not vote or otherwise make a position known

	61	62	63	64	65
16 Manzullo	Y	Y	N	Y	Y
17 Hare	Y	Y	Y	Y	Y
18 Schock	Y	Y	?	?	?
19 Shimkus	Y	N	N	Y	Y
INDIANA					
1 Visclosky	Y	Y	Y	Y	Y
2 Donnelly	Y	Y	Y	Y	Y
3 Souder	Y	Y	N	Y	Y
4 Buyer	Y	Y	?	Y	Y
5 Burton	Y	Y	N	Y	Y
6 Pence	Y	Y	N	Y	Y
7 Carson	Y	Y	Y	Y	Y
8 Ellsworth	Y	Y	Y	Y	Y
9 Hill	Y	Y	Y	Y	Y
IOWA					
1 Braley	Y	Y	Y	Y	Y
2 Loebsack	Y	Y	Y	Y	Y
3 Boswell	Y	Y	Y	Y	Y
4 Latham	Y	Y	N	Y	Y
5 King	Y	N	N	Y	Y
KANSAS					
1 Moran	Y	Y	N	Y	Y
2 Jenkins	Y	Y	N	Y	Y
3 Moore	Y	Y	Y	Y	Y
4 Tiahrt	Y	Y	N	Y	Y
KENTUCKY					
1 Whitfield	Y	Y	N	Y	Y
2 Guthrie	Y	Y	N	Y	Y
3 Yarmuth	Y	Y	Y	Y	Y
4 Davis	Y	Y	N	Y	Y
5 Rogers	Y	Y	N	Y	Y
6 Chandler	Y	Y	Y	Y	Y
LOUISIANA					
1 Scalise	Y	Y	N	Y	Y
2 Cao	Y	Y	N	Y	Y
3 Melancon	Y	Y	Y	Y	Y
4 Fleming	Y	Y	N	Y	Y
5 Alexander	?	?	N	Y	Y
6 Cassidy	Y	Y	N	Y	Y
7 Boustany	Y	Y	N	Y	Y
MAINE					
1 Pingree	Y	Y	?	?	Y
2 Michaud	Y	Y	Y	Y	Y
MARYLAND					
1 Kratovil	Y	Y	Y	Y	Y
2 Ruppersberger	Y	Y	Y	Y	Y
3 Sarbanes	Y	Y	Y	Y	Y
4 Edwards	Y	Y	Y	Y	Y
5 Hoyer	Y	Y	Y	Y	Y
6 Bartlett	Y	Y	N	Y	Y
7 Cummings	Y	Y	Y	Y	Y
8 Van Hollen	Y	Y	Y	Y	Y
MASSACHUSETTS					
1 Olver	Y	Y	Y	Y	Y
2 Neal	Y	Y	Y	Y	Y
3 McGovern	Y	Y	Y	Y	Y
4 Frank	Y	Y	Y	Y	Y
5 Tsongas	Y	Y	Y	Y	Y
6 Tierney	Y	Y	Y	Y	Y
7 Markey	Y	Y	Y	Y	Y
8 Capuano	Y	Y	Y	Y	Y
9 Lynch	Y	Y	Y	Y	Y
10 Delahunt	Y	Y	Y	Y	Y
MICHIGAN					
1 Stupak	Y	Y	Y	Y	Y
2 Hoekstra	Y	Y	N	Y	Y
3 Ehlers	Y	Y	N	Y	Y
4 Camp	Y	Y	N	Y	Y
5 Kildee	Y	Y	Y	Y	Y
6 Upton	Y	Y	N	Y	Y
7 Schauer	Y	Y	Y	Y	Y
8 Rogers	Y	Y	N	Y	Y
9 Peters	Y	Y	Y	Y	Y
10 Miller	Y	Y	N	Y	Y
11 McCotter	Y	Y	Y	Y	Y
12 Levin	Y	Y	Y	Y	Y
13 Kilpatrick	Y	Y	Y	Y	Y
14 Conyers	Y	Y	Y	Y	Y
15 Dingell	P	Y	Y	Y	Y
MINNESOTA					
1 Walz	Y	Y	Y	Y	Y
2 Kline	Y	Y	N	Y	Y
3 Paulsen	Y	Y	N	Y	Y
4 McCollum	Y	Y	Y	Y	Y

	61	62	63	64	65
5 Ellison	Y	Y	Y	Y	Y
6 Bachmann	Y	Y	N	Y	Y
7 Peterson	Y	Y	Y	Y	Y
8 Oberstar	Y	Y	Y	Y	Y
MISSISSIPPI					
1 Childers	Y	Y	Y	Y	Y
2 Thompson	Y	Y	Y	Y	Y
3 Harper	Y	Y	N	Y	Y
4 Taylor	Y	Y	Y	Y	Y
MISSOURI					
1 Clay	Y	Y	Y	Y	Y
2 Akin	Y	N	N	Y	Y
3 Carnahan	Y	Y	Y	Y	Y
4 Skelton	Y	Y	Y	Y	Y
5 Cleaver	Y	Y	Y	Y	Y
6 Graves	Y	Y	N	Y	Y
7 Blunt	Y	Y	?	?	?
8 Emerson	Y	Y	N	Y	Y
9 Luetkemeyer	Y	Y	N	Y	Y
MONTANA					
AL Rehberg	Y	Y	N	Y	Y
NEBRASKA					
1 Fortenberry	Y	Y	N	Y	Y
2 Terry	Y	Y	N	Y	Y
3 Smith	Y	Y	N	Y	Y
NEVADA					
1 Berkley	Y	Y	Y	Y	Y
2 Heller	Y	Y	N	Y	Y
3 Titus	Y	Y	Y	Y	Y
NEW HAMPSHIRE					
1 Shea-Porter	Y	Y	Y	Y	Y
2 Hodes	Y	Y	Y	Y	Y
NEW JERSEY					
1 Andrews	Y	Y	Y	Y	Y
2 LoBiondo	Y	Y	N	Y	Y
3 Adler	Y	Y	Y	Y	Y
4 Smith	Y	Y	N	Y	Y
5 Garrett	Y	N	N	Y	Y
6 Pallone	Y	Y	Y	Y	Y
7 Lance	Y	Y	N	Y	Y
8 Pascrell	Y	Y	Y	Y	Y
9 Rothman	Y	Y	Y	Y	Y
10 Payne	Y	Y	Y	Y	Y
11 Frelinghuysen	Y	Y	N	Y	Y
12 Holt	Y	Y	Y	Y	Y
13 Sires	Y	Y	Y	Y	Y
NEW MEXICO					
1 Heinrich	Y	Y	Y	Y	Y
2 Teague	Y	Y	Y	Y	Y
3 Lujan	Y	Y	Y	Y	Y
NEW YORK					
1 Bishop	Y	Y	Y	Y	Y
2 Israel	Y	Y	Y	Y	Y
3 King	Y	Y	N	Y	Y
4 McCarthy	Y	Y	Y	Y	Y
5 Ackerman	Y	Y	Y	Y	Y
6 Meeks	Y	Y	Y	Y	Y
7 Crowley	Y	Y	Y	Y	Y
8 Nadler	Y	Y	Y	Y	Y
9 Weiner	Y	Y	Y	Y	Y
10 Towns	Y	Y	Y	Y	Y
11 Clarke	Y	?	Y	Y	Y
12 Velázquez	Y	Y	Y	Y	Y
13 McMahon	Y	Y	Y	Y	Y
14 Maloney	Y	Y	Y	Y	Y
15 Rangel	Y	Y	Y	Y	Y
16 Serrano	Y	Y	Y	Y	Y
17 Engel	Y	Y	Y	Y	Y
18 Lowey	Y	Y	Y	Y	Y
19 Hall	Y	Y	Y	Y	Y
20 Vacant					
21 Tonko	Y	Y	Y	Y	Y
22 Hinchey	Y	Y	Y	Y	Y
23 McHugh	Y	Y	N	Y	Y
24 Arcuri	Y	Y	Y	Y	Y
25 Maffei	Y	Y	Y	Y	Y
26 Lee	Y	Y	N	Y	Y
27 Higgins	Y	Y	Y	Y	Y
28 Slaughter	Y	Y	Y	Y	Y
29 Massa	Y	Y	Y	Y	Y
NORTH CAROLINA					
1 Butterfield	Y	Y	Y	Y	Y
2 Etheridge	Y	Y	Y	Y	Y
3 Jones	Y	Y	N	Y	Y
4 Price	Y	Y	Y	Y	Y

	61	62	63	64	65
5 Foxx	Y	N	N	Y	Y
6 Coble	Y	Y	N	Y	Y
7 McIntyre	Y	Y	Y	Y	Y
8 Kissell	Y	Y	Y	Y	Y
9 Myrick	Y	Y	N	Y	Y
10 McHenry	Y	Y	N	Y	Y
11 Shuler	Y	Y	Y	Y	Y
12 Watt	Y	Y	Y	Y	Y
13 Miller	Y	Y	Y	Y	Y
NORTH DAKOTA					
AL Pomeroy	Y	Y	Y	Y	Y
OHIO					
1 Driehaus	Y	Y	Y	Y	Y
2 Schmidt	Y	Y	N	Y	Y
3 Turner	Y	Y	N	Y	Y
4 Jordan	Y	Y	N	Y	Y
5 Latta	Y	Y	N	Y	Y
6 Wilson	Y	Y	Y	Y	Y
7 Austria	Y	Y	N	Y	Y
8 Boehner	Y	Y	?	Y	Y
9 Kaptur	Y	Y	Y	Y	Y
10 Kucinich	Y	Y	Y	Y	Y
11 Fudge	Y	Y	Y	Y	Y
12 Tiberi	?	?	?	?	?
13 Sutton	Y	Y	Y	Y	Y
14 LaTourette	Y	Y	N	Y	Y
15 Kilroy	Y	Y	Y	Y	Y
16 Boccieri	Y	Y	Y	Y	Y
17 Ryan	Y	Y	Y	?	?
18 Space	Y	Y	Y	Y	Y
OKLAHOMA					
1 Sullivan	Y	Y	N	Y	Y
2 Boren	Y	Y	Y	Y	Y
3 Lucas	Y	Y	N	Y	Y
4 Cole	Y	Y	N	Y	Y
5 Fallin	Y	Y	N	Y	Y
OREGON					
1 Wu	Y	Y	Y	Y	Y
2 Walden	Y	Y	N	Y	Y
3 Blumenauer	Y	Y	Y	Y	Y
4 DeFazio	Y	Y	Y	Y	Y
5 Schrader	Y	Y	Y	Y	Y
PENNSYLVANIA					
1 Brady	Y	Y	Y	Y	Y
2 Fattah	Y	Y	Y	Y	Y
3 Dahlkemper	Y	Y	Y	Y	Y
4 Altmire	Y	Y	Y	Y	Y
5 Thompson	Y	Y	N	Y	Y
6 Gerlach	Y	Y	N	Y	Y
7 Sestak	Y	Y	Y	Y	Y
8 Murphy, P.	Y	Y	Y	Y	Y
9 Shuster	Y	Y	N	Y	Y
10 Carney	Y	Y	Y	Y	Y
11 Kanjorski	Y	Y	Y	Y	Y
12 Murtha	Y	Y	Y	Y	Y
13 Schwartz	Y	Y	Y	Y	Y
14 Doyle	Y	Y	Y	Y	Y
15 Dent	Y	Y	N	Y	Y
16 Pitts	Y	Y	N	Y	Y
17 Holden	?	?	Y	Y	Y
18 Murphy, T.	Y	Y	N	Y	Y
19 Platts	Y	Y	N	Y	Y
RHODE ISLAND					
1 Kennedy	Y	Y	Y	Y	Y
2 Langevin	Y	Y	Y	Y	Y
SOUTH CAROLINA					
1 Brown	Y	Y	N	Y	Y
2 Wilson	Y	Y	N	Y	Y
3 Barrett	Y	N	N	Y	Y
4 Inglis	Y	N	N	Y	Y
5 Spratt	Y	Y	Y	Y	Y
6 Clyburn	Y	Y	Y	Y	Y
SOUTH DAKOTA					
AL Herseth Sandlin	Y	Y	Y	Y	Y
TENNESSEE					
1 Roe	Y	Y	N	Y	Y
2 Duncan	Y	Y	N	Y	Y
3 Wamp	Y	Y	N	Y	Y
4 Davis, L.	Y	Y	Y	Y	Y
5 Cooper	Y	Y	Y	Y	Y
6 Gordon	Y	Y	Y	Y	Y
7 Blackburn	Y	Y	N	Y	Y
8 Tanner	Y	Y	Y	Y	Y
9 Cohen	Y	Y	Y	Y	Y

	61	62	63	64	65
TEXAS					
1 Gohmert	Y	Y	N	Y	Y
2 Poe	Y	Y	N	Y	Y
3 Johnson, S.	Y	Y	N	Y	Y
4 Hall	Y	Y	N	Y	Y
5 Hensarling	Y	N	N	Y	Y
6 Barton	Y	Y	N	Y	Y
7 Culberson	Y	Y	N	Y	Y
8 Brady	Y	N	N	Y	Y
9 Green, A.	Y	Y	Y	Y	Y
10 McCaul	Y	Y	N	Y	Y
11 Conaway	Y	N	N	Y	Y
12 Granger	Y	Y	N	Y	Y
13 Thornberry	Y	N	N	Y	Y
14 Paul	Y	N	N	Y	Y
15 Hinojosa	Y	Y	Y	Y	Y
16 Reyes	Y	Y	Y	Y	Y
17 Edwards	Y	Y	Y	Y	Y
18 Jackson Lee	Y	Y	Y	Y	Y
19 Neugebauer	Y	N	N	Y	Y
20 Gonzalez	Y	Y	Y	Y	Y
21 Smith	Y	Y	N	Y	Y
22 Olson	Y	Y	N	Y	Y
23 Rodriguez	Y	Y	Y	Y	Y
24 Marchant	Y	Y	N	Y	Y
25 Doggett	Y	Y	Y	Y	Y
26 Burgess	Y	Y	N	Y	Y
27 Ortiz	Y	Y	Y	Y	Y
28 Cuellar	Y	Y	Y	Y	Y
29 Green, G.	Y	Y	Y	Y	Y
30 Johnson, E.	Y	Y	Y	Y	Y
31 Carter	Y	N	N	Y	Y
32 Sessions	Y	Y	N	Y	Y
UTAH					
1 Bishop	Y	Y	N	Y	Y
2 Matheson	Y	Y	Y	Y	Y
3 Chaffetz	Y	Y	N	Y	Y
VERMONT					
AL Welch	Y	Y	Y	Y	Y
VIRGINIA					
1 Wittman	Y	Y	N	Y	Y
2 Nye	Y	Y	Y	Y	Y
3 Scott	Y	Y	Y	Y	Y
4 Forbes	Y	Y	N	Y	Y
5 Perriello	Y	Y	Y	Y	Y
6 Goodlatte	Y	Y	N	Y	Y
7 Cantor	Y	Y	N	Y	Y
8 Moran	Y	Y	Y	Y	Y
9 Boucher	Y	Y	Y	Y	Y
10 Wolf	Y	Y	N	Y	Y
11 Connolly	Y	Y	Y	Y	Y
WASHINGTON					
1 Inslee	Y	Y	Y	Y	Y
2 Larsen	Y	Y	Y	Y	Y
3 Baird	Y	Y	Y	Y	Y
4 Hastings	Y	Y	N	Y	Y
5 McMorris Rodgers	Y	Y	N	Y	Y
6 Dicks	Y	Y	Y	Y	Y
7 McDermott	Y	Y	Y	Y	Y
8 Reichert	Y	Y	N	Y	Y
9 Smith	Y	Y	Y	Y	Y
WEST VIRGINIA					
1 Mollohan	Y	Y	Y	Y	Y
2 Capito	Y	Y	N	Y	Y
3 Rahall	Y	Y	Y	Y	Y
WISCONSIN					
1 Ryan	Y	Y	N	Y	Y
2 Baldwin	Y	Y	Y	Y	Y
3 Kind	Y	Y	?	Y	Y
4 Moore	Y	Y	Y	Y	Y
5 Sensenbrenner	Y	N	N	Y	Y
6 Petri	Y	Y	N	Y	Y
7 Obey	Y	Y	Y	Y	Y
8 Kagen	Y	Y	Y	Y	Y
WYOMING					
AL Lummis	Y	N	N	Y	Y
DELEGATES					
Faleomavaega (A.S.)					
Norton (D.C.)					
Bordallo (Guam)					
Sablan (N. Marianas)					
Pierluisi (P.R.)					
Christensen (V.I.)					

IN THE HOUSE | By Vote Number

66. **HR 1. Economic Stimulus/Previous Question.** McGovern, D-Mass., motion to order the previous question (thus ending debate and possibility of amendment) on adoption of the rule (H Res 168) that would provide for House floor consideration of the conference report on the bill that would provide $787.2 billion in tax cuts and additional spending to stimulate the economy. Motion agreed to 234-194: R 0-176; D 234-18. Feb. 13, 2009.

67. **HR 1. Economic Stimulus/Rule.** Adoption of the rule (H Res 168) that would provide for House floor consideration of the conference report on the bill that would provide $787.2 billion in tax cuts and additional spending to stimulate the economy. Adopted 231-194: R 0-173; D 231-21. Feb. 13, 2009.

68. **HR 1. Economic Stimulus/Question of Consideration.** Question of whether the House should consider the conference report on the bill that would provide $787.2 billion in tax cuts and additional spending to stimulate the economy. Agreed to consider 232-195: R 0-176; D 232-19. Feb. 13, 2009.

69. **HR 1. Economic Stimulus/Recommit.** Miller, R-Mich., motion to recommit the bill to the conference committee with instructions that it be reported back with language that would provide a tax deduction equal to the cost of car loan interest and state sales tax on new car purchases in 2009. Motion rejected 186-244: R 172-4; D 14-240. Feb. 13, 2009.

70. **HR 1. Economic Stimulus/Conference Report.** Adoption of the conference report on the bill that would provide an estimated $787.2 billion in tax cuts and spending increases to stimulate the economy. It would prevent the alternative minimum tax from applying to millions of additional taxpayers in 2009 and increase the ceiling on federal borrowing by $789 billion to $12.104 trillion. The tax provisions, estimated to cost $211.8 billion through 2019, include extending current accelerated depreciation allowances for businesses, suspending taxes on the first $2,400 of unemployment benefits for 2009 and expanding a number of individual tax credits. Mandatory spending increases, expected to cost $267 billion through 2019, include an extension of unemployment and welfare benefits, Medicaid payments to states and grants for health information technology. Discretionary spending, estimated at $308.3 billion through 2019, includes grants for state and local schools and funds for public housing, transportation and nutrition assistance. Adopted (thus sent to the Senate) 246-183: R 0-176; D 246-7. A "yea" was a vote in support of the president's position. Feb. 13, 2009.

71. **H Res 139. Abraham Lincoln's Bicentennial/Adoption.** Lynch, D-Mass., motion to suspend the rules and adopt the resolution that would commemorate the bicentennial of President Abraham Lincoln's birth, recognize his commitment to unity in the United States and encourage Americans to fulfill his vision of equal rights for all. Motion agreed to 403-0: R 161-0; D 242-0. A two-thirds majority of those present and voting (269 in this case) is required for adoption under suspension of the rules. Feb. 13, 2009.

	66	67	68	69	70	71
ALABAMA						
1 Bonner	N	N	N	Y	N	Y
2 Bright	N	N	N	Y	N	Y
3 **Rogers**	N	N	N	Y	N	Y
4 **Aderholt**	N	N	N	Y	N	Y
5 Griffith	N	N	N	Y	N	Y
6 **Bachus**	N	N	N	Y	N	Y
7 Davis	Y	Y	Y	N	Y	Y
ALASKA						
AL **Young**	N	N	N	Y	N	Y
ARIZONA						
1 Kirkpatrick	Y	N	N	N	Y	Y
2 **Franks**	N	N	N	Y	N	Y
3 **Shadegg**	N	N	N	Y	N	+
4 Pastor	Y	Y	Y	N	Y	Y
5 Mitchell	N	N	Y	N	Y	Y
6 **Flake**	N	N	N	N	N	Y
7 Grijalva	Y	Y	Y	N	Y	Y
8 Giffords	Y	N	N	N	Y	Y
ARKANSAS						
1 Berry	Y	Y	Y	N	Y	Y
2 Snyder	Y	Y	Y	N	Y	Y
3 **Boozman**	N	N	N	Y	N	Y
4 Ross	Y	Y	Y	N	Y	Y
CALIFORNIA						
1 Thompson	Y	Y	Y	N	Y	Y
2 **Herger**	N	N	N	Y	N	Y
3 **Lungren**	N	N	N	Y	N	Y
4 **McClintock**	N	N	N	Y	N	Y
5 Matsui	Y	Y	Y	N	Y	Y
6 Woolsey	Y	Y	Y	N	Y	Y
7 Miller, George	Y	Y	Y	N	Y	Y
8 Pelosi				N	Y	
9 Lee	Y	Y	Y	N	Y	Y
10 Tauscher	Y	Y	Y	N	Y	Y
11 McNerney	Y	Y	Y	N	Y	Y
12 Speier	Y	Y	Y	N	Y	Y
13 Stark	?	?	?	N	Y	Y
14 Eshoo	Y	Y	Y	N	Y	Y
15 Honda	Y	Y	Y	N	Y	Y
16 Lofgren	Y	Y	Y	N	Y	Y
17 Farr	Y	Y	Y	N	Y	Y
18 Cardoza	Y	Y	Y	N	Y	Y
19 **Radanovich**	N	?	N	Y	N	Y
20 Costa	Y	Y	Y	N	Y	Y
21 **Nunes**	N	N	N	Y	N	+
22 **McCarthy**	N	N	N	Y	N	Y
23 Capps	Y	Y	Y	N	Y	Y
24 **Gallegly**	N	N	N	Y	N	Y
25 **McKeon**	N	N	N	Y	N	Y
26 **Dreier**	N	N	N	Y	N	Y
27 Sherman	Y	Y	Y	N	Y	Y
28 Berman	Y	Y	Y	N	Y	?
29 Schiff	Y	Y	Y	N	Y	Y
30 Waxman	Y	Y	Y	N	Y	Y
31 Becerra	Y	Y	Y	N	Y	Y
32 Solis	?	Y	Y	N	Y	Y
33 Watson	Y	Y	Y	N	Y	Y
34 Roybal-Allard	Y	Y	Y	N	Y	Y
35 Waters	Y	Y	Y	N	Y	Y
36 Harman	Y	Y	Y	N	Y	Y
37 Richardson	Y	Y	Y	N	Y	Y
38 Napolitano	Y	Y	Y	N	Y	Y
39 Sánchez, Linda	Y	Y	Y	N	Y	Y
40 **Royce**	N	N	N	Y	N	Y
41 **Lewis**	N	N	N	Y	N	Y
42 **Miller, Gary**	Y	Y	Y	N	Y	Y
43 Baca	Y	Y	Y	N	Y	Y
44 **Calvert**	N	N	N	Y	N	Y
45 **Bono Mack**	N	N	N	Y	N	Y
46 **Rohrabacher**	N	N	N	Y	N	Y
47 Sanchez, Loretta	Y	Y	Y	N	Y	Y
48 **Campbell**	?	?	?	?	?	?
49 **Issa**	N	N	N	Y	N	Y
50 **Bilbray**	N	N	N	Y	N	Y
51 Filner	Y	Y	Y	N	Y	Y
52 **Hunter**	N	N	N	Y	N	Y
53 Davis	Y	Y	Y	N	Y	Y

	66	67	68	69	70	71
COLORADO						
1 DeGette	Y	Y	Y	N	Y	Y
2 Polis	Y	Y	Y	N	Y	Y
3 Salazar	Y	Y	Y	N	Y	Y
4 Markey	Y	Y	Y	N	Y	Y
5 **Lamborn**	N	?	N	Y	N	Y
6 **Coffman**	N	N	N	Y	N	Y
7 Perlmutter	Y	Y	Y	N	Y	Y
CONNECTICUT						
1 Larson	Y	Y	Y	N	Y	Y
2 Courtney	Y	Y	Y	N	Y	Y
3 DeLauro	Y	Y	Y	N	Y	Y
4 Himes	Y	Y	Y	N	Y	Y
5 Murphy	Y	Y	Y	N	Y	Y
DELAWARE						
AL **Castle**	N	N	N	Y	N	Y
FLORIDA						
1 **Miller**	N	N	N	Y	N	Y
2 Boyd	N	N	Y	N	Y	Y
3 Brown	Y	Y	Y	N	Y	Y
4 **Crenshaw**	N	N	N	Y	N	Y
5 **Brown-Waite**	N	N	N	Y	N	?
6 **Stearns**	N	N	N	Y	N	Y
7 **Mica**	N	N	N	Y	N	Y
8 Grayson	Y	Y	Y	N	Y	Y
9 **Bilirakis**	N	N	N	Y	N	Y
10 **Young**	N	N	N	Y	N	Y
11 Castor	Y	Y	Y	N	Y	Y
12 **Putnam**	N	N	N	Y	N	Y
13 **Buchanan**	N	N	N	N	N	Y
14 **Mack**	N	N	N	Y	N	Y
15 **Posey**	N	N	N	Y	N	Y
16 **Rooney**	N	N	N	Y	N	Y
17 Meek	Y	Y	Y	N	Y	Y
18 **Ros-Lehtinen**	N	N	N	Y	N	Y
19 Wexler	Y	Y	Y	N	Y	Y
20 Wasserman Schultz	Y	Y	Y	N	Y	Y
21 **Diaz-Balart, L.**	N	N	N	Y	N	Y
22 Klein	Y	Y	Y	N	Y	Y
23 Hastings	Y	Y	Y	N	Y	Y
24 Kosmas	Y	Y	Y	N	Y	Y
25 **Diaz-Balart, M.**	N	N	N	Y	N	?
GEORGIA						
1 **Kingston**	N	N	N	Y	N	Y
2 Bishop	Y	Y	Y	N	Y	Y
3 **Westmoreland**	N	N	N	Y	N	Y
4 Johnson	Y	Y	Y	N	Y	Y
5 Lewis	Y	Y	Y	N	Y	Y
6 **Price**	N	N	N	Y	N	Y
7 **Linder**	N	N	N	Y	N	Y
8 Marshall	N	N	N	Y	N	Y
9 **Deal**	N	N	N	Y	N	?
10 **Broun**	N	N	N	Y	N	Y
11 **Gingrey**	N	N	N	Y	N	Y
12 Barrow	Y	Y	Y	Y	Y	Y
13 Scott	Y	Y	Y	N	Y	Y
HAWAII						
1 Abercrombie	H	H	H	N	Y	Y
2 Hirono	Y	Y	Y	N	Y	Y
IDAHO						
1 Minnick	N	N	N	N	N	Y
2 **Simpson**	N	N	N	Y	N	Y
ILLINOIS						
1 Rush	Y	Y	Y	N	Y	Y
2 Jackson	Y	Y	Y	N	Y	Y
3 Lipinski	Y	Y	Y	N	P	Y
4 Gutierrez	Y	Y	Y	N	Y	Y
5 Vacant						
6 **Roskam**	N	N	N	Y	N	Y
7 Davis	Y	Y	Y	N	Y	Y
8 Bean	Y	Y	Y	N	Y	Y
9 Schakowsky	Y	Y	Y	N	Y	Y
10 **Kirk**	N	N	N	Y	N	Y
11 Halvorson	Y	Y	Y	N	Y	Y
12 Costello	Y	Y	Y	N	Y	?
13 **Biggert**	N	N	N	Y	N	Y
14 Foster	Y	Y	Y	N	Y	Y
15 **Johnson**	N	N	N	Y	N	Y

KEY **Republicans** Democrats

Y Voted for (yea)	X Paired against
# Paired for	− Announced against
+ Announced for	P Voted "present"
N Voted against (nay)	

C Voted "present" to avoid possible conflict of interest

? Did not vote or otherwise make a position known

	66	67	68	69	70	71
16 **Manzullo**	N	N	N	Y	N	Y
17 Hare	Y	Y	Y	N	Y	Y
18 **Schock**	N	N	N	Y	N	Y
19 **Shimkus**	N	N	N	Y	N	Y
INDIANA						
1 Visclosky	Y	Y	Y	N	Y	Y
2 Donnelly	Y	Y	Y	N	Y	Y
3 **Souder**	N	N	N	Y	N	Y
4 **Buyer**	N	N	N	Y	N	Y
5 **Burton**	N	N	N	Y	N	Y
6 **Pence**	N	N	N	Y	N	Y
7 Carson	Y	Y	Y	N	Y	Y
8 Ellsworth	Y	N	Y	N	Y	Y
9 Hill	N	N	Y	N	Y	Y
IOWA						
1 Braley	Y	Y	Y	N	Y	Y
2 Loebsack	Y	Y	Y	N	Y	Y
3 Boswell	Y	Y	Y	N	Y	Y
4 **Latham**	N	N	N	Y	N	Y
5 **King**	N	N	N	Y	N	Y
KANSAS						
1 **Moran**	N	N	N	Y	N	Y
2 **Jenkins**	N	N	N	Y	N	Y
3 Moore	Y	Y	Y	N	Y	Y
4 **Tiahrt**	N	N	N	Y	N	Y
KENTUCKY						
1 **Whitfield**	N	N	N	Y	N	Y
2 **Guthrie**	N	N	N	Y	N	Y
3 Yarmuth	Y	Y	Y	N	Y	Y
4 **Davis**	N	N	N	Y	N	Y
5 **Rogers**	N	N	N	Y	N	Y
6 Chandler	Y	Y	Y	Y	Y	Y
LOUISIANA						
1 **Scalise**	N	N	N	Y	N	Y
2 **Cao**	N	–	N	Y	N	Y
3 Melancon	Y	N	Y	N	Y	Y
4 **Fleming**	N	N	N	Y	N	Y
5 **Alexander**	N	N	N	Y	N	Y
6 **Cassidy**	N	N	N	Y	N	Y
7 **Boustany**	N	N	N	Y	N	?
MAINE						
1 Pingree	Y	Y	Y	N	Y	Y
2 Michaud	Y	N	N	N	Y	Y
MARYLAND						
1 Kratovil	N	N	N	Y	Y	Y
2 Ruppersberger	Y	Y	Y	N	Y	Y
3 Sarbanes	Y	Y	Y	N	Y	Y
4 Edwards	Y	Y	Y	N	Y	Y
5 Hoyer	Y	Y	Y	N	Y	Y
6 **Bartlett**	N	N	N	Y	N	Y
7 Cummings	Y	Y	Y	N	Y	Y
8 Van Hollen	Y	Y	Y	N	Y	Y
MASSACHUSETTS						
1 Olver	Y	Y	Y	N	Y	Y
2 Neal	Y	Y	Y	N	Y	Y
3 McGovern	Y	Y	Y	N	Y	Y
4 Frank	Y	Y	Y	N	Y	Y
5 Tsongas	Y	Y	Y	N	Y	Y
6 Tierney	Y	Y	Y	N	Y	Y
7 Markey	Y	Y	Y	N	Y	Y
8 Capuano	Y	Y	Y	N	Y	Y
9 Lynch	Y	Y	Y	N	Y	Y
10 Delahunt	Y	Y	Y	N	Y	Y
MICHIGAN						
1 Stupak	Y	Y	Y	N	Y	Y
2 **Hoekstra**	N	N	N	Y	N	Y
3 **Ehlers**	N	N	N	Y	N	Y
4 **Camp**	N	N	N	Y	N	Y
5 Kildee	Y	Y	Y	N	Y	Y
6 **Upton**	N	N	N	Y	N	Y
7 Schauer	Y	Y	Y	Y	Y	Y
8 **Rogers**	N	N	N	Y	N	Y
9 Peters	Y	Y	Y	Y	Y	Y
10 **Miller**	N	N	N	Y	N	Y
11 **McCotter**	N	N	N	Y	N	Y
12 Levin	Y	Y	Y	N	Y	Y
13 Kilpatrick	Y	Y	Y	N	Y	Y
14 Conyers	Y	Y	Y	N	Y	Y
15 Dingell	Y	Y	Y	N	Y	Y
MINNESOTA						
1 Walz	Y	Y	Y	N	Y	Y
2 **Kline**	N	N	N	Y	N	Y
3 **Paulsen**	N	N	N	Y	N	Y
4 McCollum	Y	Y	Y	N	Y	Y

	66	67	68	69	70	71
5 Ellison	Y	Y	Y	N	Y	Y
6 **Bachmann**	N	N	N	Y	N	Y
7 Peterson	Y	Y	Y	N	N	Y
8 Oberstar	Y	Y	Y	N	Y	Y
MISSISSIPPI						
1 Childers	N	N	Y	Y	Y	Y
2 Thompson	Y	Y	Y	N	Y	Y
3 **Harper**	N	N	N	Y	N	Y
4 Taylor	N	N	N	N	N	?
MISSOURI						
1 Clay	Y	Y	Y	N	Y	?
2 **Akin**	N	N	N	Y	N	Y
3 Carnahan	Y	Y	Y	N	Y	Y
4 Skelton	Y	Y	Y	N	Y	Y
5 Cleaver	Y	Y	Y	N	Y	Y
6 **Graves**	N	N	N	Y	N	Y
7 **Blunt**	N	N	N	Y	N	?
8 **Emerson**	N	N	N	Y	N	Y
9 **Luetkemeyer**	N	N	N	Y	N	Y
MONTANA						
AL **Rehberg**	N	N	N	Y	N	Y
NEBRASKA						
1 **Fortenberry**	N	N	N	Y	N	Y
2 **Terry**	N	N	N	Y	N	Y
3 **Smith**	N	N	N	Y	N	Y
NEVADA						
1 Berkley	Y	Y	Y	N	Y	Y
2 **Heller**	N	N	N	Y	N	Y
3 Titus	Y	Y	Y	N	Y	Y
NEW HAMPSHIRE						
1 Shea-Porter	Y	Y	Y	N	Y	Y
2 Hodes	Y	Y	Y	N	Y	Y
NEW JERSEY						
1 Andrews	Y	Y	Y	N	Y	Y
2 **LoBiondo**	N	N	N	Y	N	Y
3 Adler	Y	Y	Y	N	Y	Y
4 **Smith**	N	N	N	Y	N	Y
5 **Garrett**	N	N	N	N	N	Y
6 Pallone	Y	Y	Y	N	Y	Y
7 **Lance**	N	N	N	Y	N	Y
8 Pascrell	Y	Y	Y	N	Y	Y
9 Rothman	Y	Y	Y	N	Y	Y
10 Payne	Y	Y	Y	N	Y	Y
11 **Frelinghuysen**	N	N	N	Y	N	Y
12 Holt	Y	Y	Y	N	Y	Y
13 Sires	Y	Y	Y	N	Y	Y
NEW MEXICO						
1 Heinrich	Y	Y	Y	N	Y	Y
2 Teague	Y	Y	Y	N	Y	Y
3 Lujan	Y	Y	Y	N	Y	Y
NEW YORK						
1 Bishop	Y	Y	Y	N	Y	Y
2 Israel	Y	?	Y	N	Y	Y
3 **King**	N	N	N	Y	N	Y
4 McCarthy	Y	Y	Y	N	Y	Y
5 Ackerman	Y	Y	Y	N	Y	?
6 Meeks	Y	Y	Y	N	Y	Y
7 Crowley	Y	Y	Y	N	Y	Y
8 Nadler	Y	Y	Y	N	Y	Y
9 Weiner	Y	Y	Y	N	Y	Y
10 Towns	Y	Y	Y	N	Y	Y
11 Clarke	Y	Y	Y	N	Y	Y
12 Velázquez	Y	Y	Y	N	Y	Y
13 McMahon	Y	Y	Y	N	Y	Y
14 Maloney	Y	Y	Y	N	Y	Y
15 Rangel	Y	Y	Y	N	Y	Y
16 Serrano	Y	Y	Y	N	Y	Y
17 Engel	Y	Y	Y	N	Y	Y
18 Lowey	Y	Y	Y	N	Y	Y
19 Hall	Y	Y	Y	N	Y	Y
20 Vacant						
21 Tonko	Y	Y	Y	N	Y	Y
22 Hinchey	Y	Y	Y	N	Y	?
23 **McHugh**	N	N	N	Y	N	Y
24 Arcuri	Y	Y	Y	Y	Y	Y
25 Maffei	Y	Y	Y	N	Y	Y
26 **Lee**	?	?	?	?	–	?
27 Higgins	Y	Y	Y	N	Y	Y
28 Slaughter	Y	Y	Y	N	Y	Y
29 Massa	Y	Y	Y	N	Y	Y
NORTH CAROLINA						
1 Butterfield	Y	Y	Y	N	Y	Y
2 Etheridge	Y	Y	Y	N	Y	Y
3 **Jones**	N	N	N	Y	N	Y
4 Price	Y	Y	Y	N	Y	Y

	66	67	68	69	70	71
5 **Foxx**	N	N	N	Y	N	Y
6 **Coble**	N	N	N	Y	N	Y
7 McIntyre	N	Y	Y	N	Y	Y
8 Kissell	Y	Y	Y	N	Y	Y
9 **Myrick**	N	N	N	Y	N	Y
10 **McHenry**	N	N	N	Y	N	Y
11 Shuler	N	N	N	N	N	Y
12 Watt	Y	Y	Y	N	Y	Y
13 Miller	Y	Y	Y	N	Y	Y
NORTH DAKOTA						
AL Pomeroy	Y	Y	Y	N	Y	Y
OHIO						
1 Driehaus	Y	Y	Y	N	Y	Y
2 **Schmidt**	N	N	N	Y	N	Y
3 **Turner**	N	N	N	Y	N	Y
4 **Jordan**	N	N	N	Y	N	Y
5 **Latta**	N	N	N	Y	N	Y
6 Wilson	Y	Y	Y	N	Y	Y
7 **Austria**	N	N	N	Y	N	Y
8 **Boehner**	N	N	N	Y	N	Y
9 Kaptur	Y	Y	Y	N	Y	Y
10 Kucinich	Y	Y	Y	N	Y	Y
11 Fudge	Y	Y	Y	N	Y	Y
12 **Tiberi**	N	N	N	Y	N	Y
13 Sutton	Y	Y	Y	N	Y	Y
14 **LaTourette**	N	N	N	Y	N	Y
15 Kilroy	N	Y	Y	N	Y	Y
16 Boccieri	Y	Y	Y	N	Y	Y
17 Ryan	Y	Y	Y	N	Y	?
18 Space	N	Y	Y	N	Y	Y
OKLAHOMA						
1 **Sullivan**	N	N	N	Y	N	?
2 Boren	Y	Y	Y	N	Y	Y
3 **Lucas**	N	N	N	Y	N	Y
4 **Cole**	N	N	N	Y	N	Y
5 **Fallin**	N	N	N	Y	N	Y
OREGON						
1 Wu	Y	Y	Y	N	Y	Y
2 **Walden**	N	N	N	Y	N	Y
3 Blumenauer	Y	Y	Y	N	Y	Y
4 DeFazio	Y	N	N	N	N	Y
5 Schrader	Y	Y	Y	N	Y	Y
PENNSYLVANIA						
1 Brady	Y	Y	Y	N	Y	Y
2 Fattah	Y	Y	Y	N	Y	Y
3 Dahlkemper	Y	Y	Y	N	Y	Y
4 Altmire	N	Y	Y	N	Y	Y
5 **Thompson**	N	N	N	Y	N	Y
6 **Gerlach**	N	N	N	Y	N	Y
7 Sestak	Y	Y	Y	N	Y	Y
8 Murphy, P.	Y	Y	Y	N	Y	Y
9 **Shuster**	N	N	N	Y	N	Y
10 Carney	N	N	N	Y	Y	Y
11 Kanjorski	Y	Y	Y	N	Y	Y
12 Murtha	Y	Y	Y	N	Y	Y
13 Schwartz	Y	Y	Y	N	Y	Y
14 Doyle	Y	Y	Y	N	Y	?
15 **Dent**	N	N	N	Y	N	Y
16 **Pitts**	N	N	N	Y	N	Y
17 Holden	Y	Y	Y	N	Y	Y
18 **Murphy, T.**	N	N	N	Y	N	?
19 **Platts**	N	N	N	Y	N	Y
RHODE ISLAND						
1 Kennedy	Y	Y	Y	N	Y	Y
2 Langevin	Y	Y	Y	N	Y	Y
SOUTH CAROLINA						
1 **Brown**	N	N	N	Y	N	Y
2 **Wilson**	N	N	N	Y	N	Y
3 **Barrett**	N	N	N	Y	N	Y
4 **Inglis**	N	N	N	Y	N	Y
5 Spratt	Y	Y	Y	N	Y	Y
6 Clyburn	Y	Y	Y	?	?	?
SOUTH DAKOTA						
AL Herseth Sandlin	Y	Y	Y	N	Y	Y
TENNESSEE						
1 **Roe**	N	N	N	Y	N	Y
2 **Duncan**	N	N	N	Y	N	Y
3 **Wamp**	N	N	N	Y	N	Y
4 Davis	Y	Y	?	N	Y	Y
5 Cooper	Y	Y	N	N	Y	Y
6 Gordon	Y	Y	?	N	Y	Y
7 **Blackburn**	N	N	N	Y	N	Y
8 Tanner	Y	N	Y	N	Y	Y
9 Cohen	Y	Y	N	N	Y	Y

	66	67	68	69	70	71
TEXAS						
1 **Gohmert**	N	N	N	Y	N	?
2 **Poe**	N	N	N	Y	N	Y
3 **Johnson, S.**	N	N	N	Y	N	Y
4 **Hall**	N	N	N	Y	N	Y
5 **Hensarling**	N	N	N	Y	N	Y
6 **Barton**	N	N	N	Y	N	Y
7 **Culberson**	N	N	N	Y	N	Y
8 **Brady**	N	N	N	Y	N	Y
9 Green, A.	Y	Y	Y	N	Y	Y
10 **McCaul**	N	N	N	Y	N	Y
11 **Conaway**	N	N	N	Y	N	Y
12 **Granger**	N	N	N	Y	N	Y
13 **Thornberry**	N	N	N	Y	N	Y
14 **Paul**	N	N	N	Y	N	?
15 Hinojosa	Y	Y	Y	N	Y	Y
16 Reyes	Y	Y	Y	N	Y	Y
17 Edwards	Y	Y	Y	N	Y	Y
18 Jackson Lee	Y	Y	Y	N	Y	Y
19 **Neugebauer**	N	N	N	Y	N	Y
20 Gonzalez	Y	Y	Y	N	Y	Y
21 **Smith**	N	N	N	Y	N	?
22 **Olson**	N	N	N	Y	N	Y
23 Rodriguez	Y	Y	Y	N	Y	Y
24 **Marchant**	N	N	N	Y	N	?
25 Doggett	Y	Y	N	N	Y	?
26 **Burgess**	N	N	N	Y	N	Y
27 Ortiz	Y	Y	Y	N	Y	Y
28 Cuellar	Y	Y	Y	Y	Y	Y
29 Green, G.	Y	Y	Y	N	Y	Y
30 Johnson, E.	Y	Y	Y	N	Y	?
31 **Carter**	N	N	N	Y	N	Y
32 **Sessions**	N	N	N	Y	N	Y
UTAH						
1 **Bishop**	N	N	N	Y	N	?
2 Matheson	Y	Y	Y	Y	Y	Y
3 **Chaffetz**	N	N	N	Y	N	Y
VERMONT						
AL Welch	Y	Y	Y	N	Y	Y
VIRGINIA						
1 **Wittman**	N	N	N	Y	N	Y
2 Nye	N	N	Y	Y	Y	Y
3 Scott	Y	Y	Y	N	Y	Y
4 **Forbes**	N	N	N	Y	N	Y
5 Perriello	N	Y	N	N	Y	Y
6 **Goodlatte**	N	N	N	Y	N	Y
7 **Cantor**	N	N	N	Y	N	Y
8 Moran	Y	Y	Y	N	Y	Y
9 Boucher	Y	Y	Y	N	Y	Y
10 **Wolf**	N	N	N	Y	N	Y
11 Connolly	Y	Y	Y	N	Y	Y
WASHINGTON						
1 Inslee	Y	Y	Y	N	Y	Y
2 Larsen	Y	Y	Y	N	Y	Y
3 Baird	Y	N	N	N	Y	Y
4 **Hastings**	N	N	N	Y	N	Y
5 **McMorris Rodgers**	N	N	N	Y	N	Y
6 Dicks	Y	Y	Y	N	Y	Y
7 McDermott	Y	Y	Y	N	Y	Y
8 **Reichert**	N	N	N	Y	N	Y
9 Smith	Y	Y	N	N	Y	Y
WEST VIRGINIA						
1 Mollohan	Y	Y	Y	N	Y	Y
2 **Capito**	N	N	N	Y	N	Y
3 Rahall	Y	Y	Y	N	Y	Y
WISCONSIN						
1 **Ryan**	N	N	N	N	N	Y
2 Baldwin	Y	Y	Y	N	Y	Y
3 Kind	Y	Y	Y	N	Y	Y
4 Moore	Y	Y	Y	N	Y	Y
5 **Sensenbrenner**	N	N	N	N	N	Y
6 **Petri**	N	N	N	Y	N	?
7 Obey	Y	Y	Y	N	Y	?
8 Kagen	Y	Y	Y	N	Y	Y
WYOMING						
AL **Lummis**	N	N	N	Y	N	Y
DELEGATES						
Faleomavaega (A.S.)						
Norton (D.C.)						
Bordallo (Guam)						
Sablan (N. Marianas)						
Pierluisi (P.R.)						
Christensen (V.I.)						

IN THE HOUSE | By Vote Number

72. HR 911. Child Abuse in Residential Programs/Passage.

McCarthy, D-N.Y., motion to suspend the rules and pass the bill that would require the Department of Health and Human Services to enforce health and safety standards for residential programs for children. It would require criminal background checks for staff, the creation of a child abuse and neglect hotline, and a public Web site with information about program ownership and compliance with state child abuse licensing requirements. Motion agreed to 295-102: R 64-101; D 231-1. A two-thirds majority of those present and voting (265 in this case) is required for passage under suspension of the rules. Feb. 23, 2009.

73. HR 44. Guam World War II Loyalty Recognition/Passage.

Bordallo, D-Guam, motion to suspend the rules and pass the bill that would recognize the suffering and loyalty of Guam residents during World War II and direct the Treasury Department to make payments to those who were killed, injured or otherwise abused or to their survivors. Motion agreed to 299-99: R 68-97; D 231-2. A two-thirds majority of those present and voting (266 in this case) is required for passage under suspension of the rules. Feb. 23, 2009.

74. HR 601. Utah Land Conveyance/Passage.

Bordallo, D-Guam, motion to suspend the rules and pass the bill that would direct the Agriculture Department to convey 31.5 acres that belong to the National Forest System in the Wasatch-Chache National Forest to the town of Mantua, Utah. Motion agreed to 396-1: R 165-0; D 231-1. A two-thirds majority of those present and voting (265 in this case) is required for passage under suspension of the rules. Feb. 23, 2009.

75. Procedural Motion/Journal.

Approval of the House Journal of Monday, Feb. 23, 2009. Approved 242-163: R 14-149; D 228-14. Feb. 24, 2009.

76. HR 80. Captive Primate Sale and Importation/Passage.

Bordallo, D-Guam, motion to suspend the rules and pass the bill that would amend the Lacey Act Amendments of 1981 to treat non-human primates as prohibited wildlife species, banning their interstate sale or importation. Motion agreed to 323-95: R 76-93; D 247-2. A two-thirds majority of those present and voting (279 in this case) is required for passage under suspension of the rules. Feb. 24, 2009.

	72	73	74	75	76
ALABAMA					
1 **Bonner**	N	N	Y	N	N
2 Bright	?	Y	Y	Y	Y
3 **Rogers**	N	Y	Y	N	Y
4 **Aderholt**	N	Y	Y	N	N
5 Griffith	Y	Y	Y	Y	Y
6 **Bachus**	N	Y	Y	N	Y
7 Davis	Y	Y	Y	Y	Y
ALASKA					
AL **Young**	Y	Y	Y	N	N
ARIZONA					
1 Kirkpatrick	Y	Y	Y	N	Y
2 **Franks**	N	N	Y	N	N
3 **Shadegg**	N	N	Y	N	N
4 Pastor	Y	Y	Y	Y	Y
5 Mitchell	Y	Y	Y	N	Y
6 **Flake**	N	N	Y	N	N
7 Grijalva	Y	Y	?	Y	Y
8 Giffords	Y	Y	Y	N	Y
ARKANSAS					
1 Berry	Y	Y	Y	Y	Y
2 Snyder	Y	Y	Y	Y	Y
3 **Boozman**	N	Y	Y	N	Y
4 Ross	Y	Y	Y	Y	Y
CALIFORNIA					
1 Thompson	Y	Y	Y	Y	Y
2 **Herger**	N	N	Y	N	N
3 **Lungren**	N	Y	Y	N	N
4 **McClintock**	N	N	Y	Y	N
5 Matsui	Y	Y	Y	Y	Y
6 Woolsey	Y	Y	Y	Y	Y
7 Miller, George	Y	Y	Y	Y	Y
8 Pelosi					
9 Lee	Y	Y	Y	Y	Y
10 Tauscher	Y	Y	Y	Y	Y
11 McNerney	Y	Y	Y	Y	Y
12 Speier	?	?	?	Y	Y
13 Stark	?	?	?	?	?
14 Eshoo	Y	Y	Y	Y	Y
15 Honda	Y	Y	Y	Y	Y
16 Lofgren	Y	Y	Y	Y	Y
17 Farr	Y	Y	Y	?	Y
18 Cardoza	Y	Y	Y	Y	Y
19 **Radanovich**	?	?	?	N	N
20 Costa	Y	Y	Y	Y	Y
21 **Nunes**	Y	N	Y	N	Y
22 **McCarthy**	N	N	Y	N	Y
23 Capps	Y	Y	Y	Y	Y
24 **Gallegly**	N	N	Y	N	Y
25 **McKeon**	Y	Y	Y	N	Y
26 **Dreier**	N	Y	Y	N	N
27 Sherman	Y	Y	Y	Y	Y
28 Berman	Y	Y	Y	Y	Y
29 Schiff	Y	Y	Y	Y	Y
30 Waxman	Y	Y	Y	Y	Y
31 Becerra	Y	Y	Y	Y	Y
32 Solis	?	?	?	?	?
33 Watson	?	?	?	?	?
34 Roybal-Allard	Y	Y	Y	Y	Y
35 Waters	Y	Y	Y	Y	Y
36 Harman	Y	Y	Y	Y	Y
37 Richardson	Y	Y	Y	Y	Y
38 Napolitano	Y	Y	Y	Y	Y
39 Sánchez, Linda	Y	Y	Y	Y	Y
40 **Royce**	N	N	Y	N	N
41 **Lewis**	?	?	?	N	Y
42 **Miller, Gary**	?	?	?	?	?
43 Baca	Y	Y	Y	Y	Y
44 **Calvert**	N	N	Y	N	Y
45 **Bono Mack**	Y	Y	Y	N	Y
46 **Rohrabacher**	?	?	?	N	N
47 Sanchez, Loretta	Y	Y	Y	Y	Y
48 **Campbell**	?	?	?	?	?
49 **Issa**	N	N	Y	N	N
50 **Bilbray**	N	N	Y	Y	Y
51 Filner	Y	Y	Y	Y	Y
52 **Hunter**	N	N	Y	N	N
53 Davis	Y	Y	Y	Y	Y

	72	73	74	75	76
COLORADO					
1 DeGette	Y	Y	Y	Y	Y
2 Polis	Y	Y	Y	Y	Y
3 Salazar	Y	Y	Y	Y	Y
4 Markey	Y	Y	Y	Y	Y
5 **Lamborn**	N	N	Y	N	N
6 **Coffman**	N	N	Y	N	N
7 Perlmutter	Y	Y	Y	Y	Y
CONNECTICUT					
1 Larson	Y	Y	Y	Y	Y
2 Courtney	Y	Y	Y	Y	Y
3 DeLauro	Y	Y	Y	Y	Y
4 Himes	Y	Y	Y	Y	Y
5 Murphy	Y	Y	Y	Y	Y
DELAWARE					
AL **Castle**	Y	N	Y	N	Y
FLORIDA					
1 **Miller**	N	Y	Y	N	N
2 Boyd	Y	Y	Y	Y	Y
3 Brown	Y	Y	Y	Y	Y
4 **Crenshaw**	?	?	?	N	N
5 **Brown-Waite**	Y	N	Y	N	N
6 **Stearns**	N	N	Y	N	Y
7 **Mica**	N	Y	Y	N	Y
8 Grayson	Y	Y	Y	Y	Y
9 **Bilirakis**	Y	Y	Y	N	Y
10 **Young**	Y	Y	Y	N	Y
11 Castor	Y	Y	Y	Y	Y
12 **Putnam**	Y	Y	Y	N	N
13 **Buchanan**	Y	N	Y	N	Y
14 **Mack**	N	N	Y	N	N
15 **Posey**	N	N	Y	N	N
16 **Rooney**	Y	N	Y	N	Y
17 Meek	Y	Y	Y	Y	Y
18 **Ros-Lehtinen**	Y	Y	Y	N	Y
19 Wexler	Y	Y	Y	Y	Y
20 Wasserman Schultz	Y	Y	N	?	Y
21 **Diaz-Balart, L.**	Y	Y	Y	N	Y
22 Klein	Y	Y	Y	Y	Y
23 Hastings	Y	Y	Y	Y	Y
24 Kosmas	Y	Y	Y	Y	Y
25 **Diaz-Balart, M.**	Y	Y	Y	N	Y
GEORGIA					
1 **Kingston**	N	N	Y	Y	N
2 Bishop	Y	Y	Y	?	Y
3 **Westmoreland**	N	N	Y	N	N
4 Johnson	Y	Y	Y	Y	Y
5 Lewis	Y	Y	Y	Y	Y
6 **Price**	N	N	Y	N	N
7 **Linder**	N	N	Y	N	Y
8 Marshall	Y	Y	Y	Y	Y
9 **Deal**	N	N	Y	N	N
10 **Broun**	N	N	Y	N	N
11 **Gingrey**	?	?	?	N	N
12 Barrow	Y	Y	Y	Y	Y
13 Scott	Y	Y	Y	Y	Y
HAWAII					
1 Abercrombie	Y	Y	Y	Y	Y
2 Hirono	Y	Y	Y	Y	Y
IDAHO					
1 Minnick	N	Y	Y	Y	Y
2 **Simpson**	Y	Y	Y	N	Y
ILLINOIS					
1 Rush	Y	Y	Y	Y	Y
2 Jackson	Y	Y	Y	Y	Y
3 Lipinski	Y	Y	Y	Y	Y
4 Gutierrez	?	?	?	Y	Y
5 Vacant					
6 **Roskam**	Y	N	Y	N	N
7 Davis	Y	Y	Y	Y	Y
8 Bean	?	?	?	Y	Y
9 Schakowsky	Y	Y	Y	Y	Y
10 **Kirk**	Y	Y	Y	N	Y
11 Halvorson	Y	Y	Y	Y	Y
12 Costello	Y	Y	Y	Y	Y
13 **Biggert**	Y	Y	Y	N	Y
14 Foster	Y	Y	Y	Y	Y
15 **Johnson**	Y	N	Y	N	Y

	72	73	74	75	76
16 Manzullo	N	Y	Y	N	N
17 Hare	Y	Y	Y	Y	Y
18 **Schock**	N	Y	Y	N	Y
19 **Shimkus**	Y	Y	Y	N	Y
INDIANA					
1 Visclosky	Y	Y	Y	Y	Y
2 Donnelly	Y	Y	Y	N	Y
3 **Souder**	N	Y	Y	?	?
4 **Buyer**	Y	Y	Y	N	Y
5 **Burton**	N	Y	Y	N	N
6 **Pence**	N	N	Y	N	N
7 Carson	Y	Y	Y	Y	Y
8 Ellsworth	Y	Y	Y	N	Y
9 Hill	Y	Y	Y	Y	Y
IOWA					
1 Braley	Y	Y	Y	Y	Y
2 Loebsack	Y	Y	Y	Y	Y
3 Boswell	Y	Y	Y	Y	Y
4 Latham	Y	N	Y	N	Y
5 King	N	N	Y	N	N
KANSAS					
1 **Moran**	N	Y	Y	N	N
2 **Jenkins**	N	Y	Y	N	N
3 Moore	Y	Y	Y	Y	Y
4 **Tiahrt**	N	N	Y	N	–
KENTUCKY					
1 **Whitfield**	Y	N	Y	Y	Y
2 **Guthrie**	Y	N	Y	N	N
3 Yarmuth	+	+	+	Y	Y
4 **Davis**	N	N	Y	N	N
5 **Rogers**	Y	N	Y	N	Y
6 Chandler	Y	Y	Y	Y	Y
LOUISIANA					
1 **Scalise**	Y	N	Y	N	N
2 **Cao**	?	?	?	?	?
3 Melancon	Y	Y	Y	Y	Y
4 **Fleming**	N	N	Y	N	Y
5 **Alexander**	N	Y	Y	N	Y
6 **Cassidy**	?	?	?	?	?
7 **Boustany**	N	N	Y	N	Y
MAINE					
1 Pingree	Y	Y	Y	Y	Y
2 Michaud	Y	Y	Y	Y	Y
MARYLAND					
1 Kratovil	Y	Y	Y	Y	Y
2 Ruppersberger	Y	Y	Y	Y	Y
3 Sarbanes	Y	Y	Y	Y	Y
4 Edwards	Y	Y	Y	Y	Y
5 Hoyer	Y	Y	Y	Y	Y
6 **Bartlett**	Y	Y	Y	N	Y
7 Cummings	Y	Y	Y	Y	Y
8 Van Hollen	Y	Y	Y	Y	Y
MASSACHUSETTS					
1 Olver	Y	Y	Y	Y	Y
2 Neal	?	?	?	Y	Y
3 McGovern	Y	Y	Y	Y	Y
4 Frank	Y	Y	Y	Y	Y
5 Tsongas	Y	Y	Y	Y	Y
6 Tierney	?	?	?	Y	Y
7 Markey	Y	Y	Y	Y	Y
8 Capuano	Y	Y	Y	Y	Y
9 Lynch	Y	Y	Y	Y	Y
10 Delahunt	Y	Y	Y	Y	Y
MICHIGAN					
1 Stupak	Y	Y	Y	Y	Y
2 **Hoekstra**	?	?	?	Y	N
3 **Ehlers**	Y	Y	Y	N	Y
4 **Camp**	N	N	Y	N	Y
5 Kildee	Y	Y	Y	Y	Y
6 **Upton**	Y	N	Y	N	Y
7 Schauer	Y	Y	Y	N	Y
8 **Rogers**	N	Y	Y	N	Y
9 Peters	Y	Y	Y	Y	Y
10 **Miller**	Y	N	Y	N	Y
11 **McCotter**	Y	Y	Y	N	Y
12 Levin	Y	Y	Y	Y	Y
13 Kilpatrick	+	+	+	Y	Y
14 Conyers	+	+	+	Y	Y
15 Dingell	Y	Y	Y	Y	Y
MINNESOTA					
1 Walz	Y	Y	Y	Y	N
2 **Kline**	N	Y	Y	N	N
3 **Paulsen**	Y	Y	Y	N	Y
4 McCollum	Y	Y	Y	Y	Y

	72	73	74	75	76
5 Ellison	Y	Y	Y	Y	Y
6 **Bachmann**	N	N	Y	?	?
7 Peterson	Y	Y	Y	N	N
8 Oberstar	Y	Y	Y	Y	Y
MISSISSIPPI					
1 Childers	Y	Y	Y	N	Y
2 Thompson	Y	Y	Y	Y	Y
3 **Harper**	N	N	Y	N	N
4 Taylor	?	?	?	Y	Y
MISSOURI					
1 Clay	Y	Y	Y	Y	Y
2 **Akin**	N	N	Y	N	N
3 Carnahan	Y	Y	Y	Y	Y
4 Skelton	Y	Y	Y	?	Y
5 Cleaver	Y	Y	Y	Y	Y
6 **Graves**	Y	N	Y	N	N
7 **Blunt**	N	N	Y	?	N
8 **Emerson**	Y	N	Y	N	Y
9 **Luetkemeyer**	Y	N	Y	N	N
MONTANA					
AL **Rehberg**	Y	Y	Y	N	Y
NEBRASKA					
1 **Fortenberry**	Y	N	Y	N	Y
2 **Terry**	Y	N	Y	N	N
3 **Smith**	N	N	Y	N	N
NEVADA					
1 Berkley	Y	Y	Y	Y	Y
2 **Heller**	Y	N	Y	N	Y
3 Titus	Y	Y	Y	Y	Y
NEW HAMPSHIRE					
1 Shea-Porter	?	?	?	Y	Y
2 Hodes	Y	Y	Y	Y	Y
NEW JERSEY					
1 Andrews	Y	Y	Y	Y	Y
2 **LoBiondo**	Y	Y	Y	N	Y
3 Adler	Y	Y	Y	Y	Y
4 **Smith**	Y	Y	Y	N	Y
5 **Garrett**	N	N	Y	N	N
6 Pallone	Y	Y	Y	Y	Y
7 **Lance**	Y	Y	Y	N	N
8 Pascrell	?	?	?	Y	Y
9 Rothman	Y	Y	Y	Y	Y
10 Payne	Y	Y	Y	Y	Y
11 **Frelinghuysen**	Y	Y	Y	N	Y
12 Holt	+	+	+	Y	Y
13 Sires	Y	Y	Y	Y	Y
NEW MEXICO					
1 Heinrich	Y	Y	Y	Y	Y
2 Teague	Y	Y	Y	?	Y
3 Lujan	Y	Y	Y	Y	Y
NEW YORK					
1 Bishop	Y	Y	Y	Y	Y
2 Israel	?	?	?	Y	Y
3 **King**	Y	Y	Y	N	Y
4 McCarthy	Y	Y	Y	Y	Y
5 Ackerman	Y	Y	Y	Y	Y
6 Meeks	Y	Y	Y	Y	Y
7 Crowley	Y	Y	Y	Y	Y
8 Nadler	Y	Y	Y	Y	Y
9 Weiner	?	?	?	Y	Y
10 Towns	Y	Y	Y	Y	Y
11 Clarke	Y	Y	Y	Y	Y
12 Velázquez	Y	Y	Y	Y	Y
13 McMahon	Y	Y	Y	Y	Y
14 Maloney	Y	Y	Y	Y	Y
15 Rangel	Y	Y	Y	Y	Y
16 Serrano	Y	Y	Y	Y	Y
17 Engel	Y	Y	Y	Y	Y
18 Lowey	Y	Y	Y	?	Y
19 Hall	Y	Y	Y	Y	Y
20 Vacant					
21 Tonko	Y	Y	Y	Y	Y
22 Hinchey	Y	Y	Y	Y	Y
23 **McHugh**	Y	Y	Y	?	Y
24 Arcuri	Y	Y	Y	N	Y
25 Maffei	Y	Y	Y	Y	Y
26 **Lee**	N	N	Y	N	Y
27 Higgins	Y	Y	Y	Y	Y
28 Slaughter	Y	Y	Y	Y	Y
29 Massa	Y	Y	Y	Y	Y
NORTH CAROLINA					
1 Butterfield	Y	Y	Y	Y	Y
2 Etheridge	Y	Y	Y	Y	Y
3 **Jones**	Y	Y	Y	N	Y
4 Price	Y	Y	Y	Y	Y

	72	73	74	75	76
5 **Foxx**	N	N	Y	N	N
6 **Coble**	N	N	Y	N	N
7 McIntyre	Y	Y	Y	Y	Y
8 Kissell	Y	Y	Y	Y	Y
9 **Myrick**	N	N	Y	N	N
10 **McHenry**	N	N	Y	N	N
11 Shuler	Y	Y	Y	N	Y
12 Watt	Y	Y	Y	Y	Y
13 Miller	Y	Y	Y	Y	Y
NORTH DAKOTA					
AL Pomeroy	Y	Y	Y	Y	Y
OHIO					
1 Driehaus	Y	Y	Y	Y	Y
2 **Schmidt**	N	N	Y	N	Y
3 **Turner**	Y	Y	Y	N	Y
4 **Jordan**	N	N	Y	N	N
5 **Latta**	N	N	Y	N	N
6 Wilson	Y	Y	Y	Y	Y
7 **Austria**	Y	N	Y	N	Y
8 **Boehner**	N	N	Y	?	N
9 Kaptur	Y	Y	Y	Y	Y
10 Kucinich	Y	Y	Y	Y	Y
11 Fudge	Y	Y	Y	Y	Y
12 **Tiberi**	?	?	?	N	Y
13 Sutton	Y	Y	Y	?	Y
14 **LaTourette**	Y	N	Y	N	Y
15 Kilroy	Y	Y	Y	Y	Y
16 Boccieri	Y	N	Y	Y	Y
17 Ryan	Y	Y	Y	Y	Y
18 Space	?	?	?	N	Y
OKLAHOMA					
1 **Sullivan**	N	N	Y	?	N
2 Boren	Y	Y	Y	Y	Y
3 **Lucas**	N	Y	Y	N	N
4 **Cole**	N	Y	Y	N	N
5 **Fallin**	N	Y	Y	N	N
OREGON					
1 Wu	Y	Y	Y	N	Y
2 **Walden**	Y	Y	Y	N	N
3 Blumenauer	Y	Y	Y	Y	Y
4 DeFazio	Y	Y	Y	Y	Y
5 Schrader	Y	Y	Y	Y	Y
PENNSYLVANIA					
1 Brady	Y	Y	Y	Y	Y
2 Fattah	Y	Y	Y	Y	Y
3 Dahlkemper	Y	Y	Y	Y	Y
4 Altmire	Y	N	Y	N	Y
5 **Thompson**	Y	N	Y	?	?
6 **Gerlach**	Y	Y	Y	Y	Y
7 Sestak	Y	Y	Y	Y	Y
8 Murphy, P.	Y	Y	Y	Y	Y
9 **Shuster**	N	N	Y	?	Y
10 Carney	Y	Y	Y	N	Y
11 Kanjorski	Y	Y	Y	Y	Y
12 Murtha	Y	Y	Y	Y	Y
13 Schwartz	Y	Y	Y	Y	Y
14 Doyle	Y	Y	Y	Y	Y
15 **Dent**	Y	Y	Y	Y	Y
16 **Pitts**	N	Y	Y	N	N
17 Holden	Y	Y	Y	?	Y
18 **Murphy, T.**	Y	Y	Y	N	Y
19 **Platts**	Y	Y	Y	N	Y
RHODE ISLAND					
1 Kennedy	Y	Y	Y	Y	Y
2 Langevin	Y	Y	Y	Y	Y
SOUTH CAROLINA					
1 **Brown**	Y	Y	Y	N	Y
2 **Wilson**	N	Y	Y	N	N
3 **Barrett**	N	N	Y	N	N
4 **Inglis**	N	N	Y	N	N
5 Spratt	Y	Y	Y	Y	Y
6 Clyburn	Y	Y	Y	Y	Y
SOUTH DAKOTA					
AL Herseth Sandlin	Y	Y	Y	Y	Y
TENNESSEE					
1 **Roe**	Y	N	Y	N	Y
2 **Duncan**	N	N	Y	N	N
3 **Wamp**	N	N	Y	N	N
4 Davis	Y	Y	Y	Y	Y
5 Cooper	Y	Y	Y	Y	Y
6 Gordon	Y	Y	Y	Y	Y
7 **Blackburn**	?	?	?	N	N
8 Tanner	Y	Y	Y	Y	Y
9 Cohen	Y	Y	Y	Y	?

	72	73	74	75	76
TEXAS					
1 **Gohmert**	N	Y	Y	?	N
2 **Poe**	N	N	Y	N	N
3 **Johnson, S.**	N	N	Y	N	N
4 **Hall**	N	N	Y	N	N
5 **Hensarling**	N	N	Y	N	N
6 **Barton**	N	N	Y	N	N
7 **Culberson**	Y	N	Y	N	N
8 **Brady**	N	N	Y	N	N
9 Green, A.	Y	Y	Y	Y	Y
10 **McCaul**	Y	Y	Y	N	N
11 **Conaway**	Y	Y	Y	N	N
12 **Granger**	N	N	Y	N	N
13 **Thornberry**	N	N	Y	N	N
14 **Paul**	N	N	Y	N	N
15 Hinojosa	Y	Y	Y	Y	Y
16 Reyes	Y	Y	Y	Y	Y
17 Edwards	Y	Y	Y	Y	Y
18 Jackson Lee	Y	Y	Y	Y	Y
19 **Neugebauer**	N	N	Y	N	N
20 Gonzalez	Y	Y	Y	Y	Y
21 **Smith**	N	N	Y	N	?
22 **Olson**	N	N	Y	N	N
23 Rodriguez	Y	Y	Y	Y	Y
24 **Marchant**	N	N	Y	N	N
25 Doggett	Y	Y	Y	Y	Y
26 **Burgess**	Y	Y	Y	?	Y
27 Ortiz	Y	Y	Y	Y	Y
28 Cuellar	Y	Y	Y	Y	Y
29 Green, G.	Y	Y	Y	Y	Y
30 Johnson, E.	?	?	?	N	Y
31 **Carter**	?	?	?	N	N
32 **Sessions**	N	N	Y	?	N
UTAH					
1 **Bishop**	N	Y	Y	N	N
2 Matheson	Y	Y	Y	Y	Y
3 **Chaffetz**	N	N	Y	N	N
VERMONT					
AL Welch	Y	Y	Y	Y	Y
VIRGINIA					
1 **Wittman**	N	N	Y	N	Y
2 Nye	Y	Y	Y	N	Y
3 Scott	Y	Y	Y	Y	Y
4 **Forbes**	N	Y	Y	N	Y
5 **Perriello**	?	?	?	?	?
6 **Goodlatte**	N	N	Y	N	N
7 **Cantor**	N	N	Y	N	N
8 **Moran**	?	?	?	Y	Y
9 Boucher	Y	Y	Y	Y	Y
10 **Wolf**	N	Y	Y	N	Y
11 Connolly	Y	Y	Y	Y	Y
WASHINGTON					
1 Inslee	Y	Y	Y	Y	Y
2 Larsen	Y	Y	Y	Y	Y
3 Baird	Y	Y	Y	Y	Y
4 **Hastings**	N	N	Y	N	N
5 **McMorris Rodgers**	N	N	Y	N	Y
6 Dicks	Y	Y	Y	Y	Y
7 McDermott	Y	Y	Y	Y	Y
8 **Reichert**	Y	Y	Y	Y	Y
9 Smith	Y	Y	Y	Y	Y
WEST VIRGINIA					
1 Mollohan	Y	Y	Y	Y	Y
2 **Capito**	Y	Y	Y	N	Y
3 Rahall	Y	Y	Y	Y	Y
WISCONSIN					
1 **Ryan**	N	Y	Y	N	N
2 Baldwin	Y	Y	Y	Y	Y
3 Kind	Y	Y	Y	Y	Y
4 Moore	Y	Y	Y	Y	Y
5 **Sensenbrenner**	N	Y	Y	N	Y
6 **Petri**	Y	Y	Y	N	Y
7 Obey	Y	Y	Y	Y	Y
8 Kagen	Y	Y	Y	Y	Y
WYOMING					
AL **Lummis**	N	N	Y	Y	N
DELEGATES					
Faleomavaega (A.S.)					
Norton (D.C.)					
Bordallo (Guam)					
Sablan (N. Marianas)					
Pierluisi (P.R.)					
Christensen (V.I.)					

IN THE HOUSE | By Vote Number

77. **HR 637. Orange County Water Projects/Passage.** Bordallo, D-Guam, motion to suspend the rules and pass the bill that would authorize $23.5 million for the Interior Department to assist San Juan Capistrano and San Clemente, Calif., with water projects. Motion agreed to 402-16: R 153-16; D 249-0. A two-thirds majority of those present and voting (279 in this case) is required for passage under suspension of the rules. Feb. 24, 2009.

78. **H Res 83. Black History Month/Adoption.** Lynch, D-Mass., motion to suspend the rules and adopt the resolution that would recognize the significance of Black History Month as a time to honor the contributions of African-Americans and that ethnic and racial diversity strengthens the United States. Motion agreed to 420-0: R 171-0; D 249-0. A two-thirds majority of those present and voting (280 in this case) is required for adoption under suspension of the rules. Feb. 24, 2009.

79. **S 234. Wilson Post Office/Passage.** Lynch, D-Mass., motion to suspend the rules and pass the bill that would designate a post office in Springfield, Ill., as the "Col. John H. Wilson Jr. Post Office Building." A World War II veteran from Springfield, Wilson worked in the Postal Service for 57 years. Motion agreed to 417-0: R 168-0; D 249-0. A two-thirds majority of those present and voting (278 in this case) is required for passage under suspension of the rules. Feb. 24, 2009.

80. **Procedural Motion/Journal.** Approval of the House Journal of Tuesday, Feb. 24, 2009. Approved 246-169: R 20-151; D 226-18. Feb. 25, 2009.

81. **H Res 47. Peace Officers Memorial Day/Adoption.** Lynch, D-Mass., motion to suspend the rules and adopt the resolution that would support the goals and ideals of Peace Officers Memorial Day to honor federal, state and local peace officers killed or disabled in the line of duty. Motion agreed to 421-0: R 174-0; D 247-0. A two-thirds majority of those present and voting (281 in this case) is required for adoption under suspension of the rules. Feb. 25, 2009.

	77	78	79	80	81
ALABAMA					
1 **Bonner**	Y	Y	Y	N	Y
2 **Bright**	Y	Y	Y	Y	Y
3 **Rogers**	Y	Y	Y	N	Y
4 **Aderholt**	Y	Y	Y	N	Y
5 Griffith	Y	Y	Y	Y	Y
6 **Bachus**	Y	Y	Y	N	Y
7 Davis	Y	Y	Y	Y	Y
ALASKA					
AL **Young**	Y	Y	Y	N	Y
ARIZONA					
1 Kirkpatrick	Y	Y	Y	N	Y
2 **Franks**	N	Y	Y	N	Y
3 **Shadegg**	N	Y	Y	N	Y
4 Pastor	Y	Y	Y	Y	Y
5 Mitchell	Y	Y	Y	Y	Y
6 **Flake**	N	Y	Y	N	Y
7 Grijalva	Y	Y	Y	Y	Y
8 Giffords	Y	Y	Y	N	Y
ARKANSAS					
1 Berry	Y	Y	Y	Y	Y
2 Snyder	Y	Y	Y	Y	Y
3 **Boozman**	Y	Y	Y	N	Y
4 Ross	Y	Y	Y	?	Y
CALIFORNIA					
1 Thompson	Y	Y	Y	N	Y
2 **Herger**	Y	Y	Y	N	Y
3 **Lungren**	Y	Y	Y	N	Y
4 **McClintock**	N	Y	Y	N	Y
5 Matsui	Y	Y	Y	Y	Y
6 Woolsey	Y	Y	Y	Y	Y
7 Miller, George	Y	Y	Y	Y	Y
8 Pelosi					
9 Lee	Y	Y	Y	Y	Y
10 Tauscher	Y	Y	Y	Y	Y
11 McNerney	Y	Y	Y	Y	Y
12 Speier	Y	Y	Y	Y	Y
13 Stark	?	?	?	?	?
14 Eshoo	Y	Y	Y	Y	Y
15 Honda	Y	Y	Y	Y	Y
16 Lofgren	Y	Y	Y	Y	Y
17 Farr	Y	Y	Y	Y	Y
18 Cardoza	Y	Y	Y	Y	Y
19 **Radanovich**	Y	Y	Y	N	Y
20 Costa	Y	Y	Y	Y	Y
21 **Nunes**	Y	Y	Y	N	Y
22 **McCarthy**	Y	Y	Y	N	Y
23 Capps	Y	Y	Y	Y	Y
24 **Gallegly**	Y	Y	Y	N	Y
25 **McKeon**	Y	Y	Y	N	Y
26 **Dreier**	Y	Y	Y	N	Y
27 Sherman	Y	Y	Y	Y	Y
28 Berman	Y	Y	Y	Y	Y
29 Schiff	Y	Y	Y	Y	Y
30 Waxman	Y	Y	Y	Y	Y
31 Becerra	Y	Y	Y	Y	Y
32 Solis*	?	?	?		
33 Watson	?	?	?	Y	Y
34 Roybal-Allard	Y	Y	Y	Y	Y
35 Waters	Y	Y	Y	Y	Y
36 Harman	Y	Y	Y	Y	Y
37 Richardson	Y	Y	Y	Y	Y
38 Napolitano	Y	Y	Y	Y	Y
39 Sánchez, Linda	Y	Y	Y	Y	Y
40 **Royce**	Y	Y	Y	N	Y
41 **Lewis**	Y	Y	Y	N	Y
42 **Miller, Gary**	?	?	?	?	?
43 Baca	Y	Y	Y	Y	Y
44 **Calvert**	Y	Y	Y	N	Y
45 **Bono Mack**	Y	Y	Y	N	Y
46 **Rohrabacher**	Y	Y	Y	N	Y
47 Sanchez, Loretta	Y	Y	Y	Y	Y
48 **Campbell**	?	?	?	?	?
49 **Issa**	Y	Y	Y	N	Y
50 **Bilbray**	Y	Y	Y	N	Y
51 Filner	Y	Y	Y	Y	Y
52 **Hunter**	Y	Y	Y	N	Y
53 Davis	Y	Y	Y	Y	Y

	77	78	79	80	81
COLORADO					
1 DeGette	Y	Y	Y	Y	Y
2 Polis	Y	Y	Y	Y	Y
3 Salazar	Y	Y	Y	Y	Y
4 Markey	Y	Y	Y	Y	Y
5 **Lamborn**	Y	Y	Y	N	Y
6 **Coffman**	Y	Y	Y	N	Y
7 Perlmutter	Y	Y	Y	N	Y
CONNECTICUT					
1 Larson	Y	Y	Y	Y	Y
2 Courtney	Y	Y	Y	Y	Y
3 DeLauro	Y	Y	Y	Y	Y
4 Himes	Y	Y	Y	Y	Y
5 Murphy	Y	Y	Y	Y	Y
DELAWARE					
AL **Castle**	Y	Y	Y	N	Y
FLORIDA					
1 **Miller**	Y	Y	Y	N	Y
2 Boyd	Y	Y	Y	Y	Y
3 Brown	Y	Y	Y	Y	Y
4 **Crenshaw**	Y	Y	Y	N	Y
5 **Brown-Waite**	Y	Y	Y	Y	Y
6 **Stearns**	N	Y	Y	N	Y
7 **Mica**	Y	Y	Y	N	Y
8 Grayson	Y	Y	Y	Y	Y
9 **Bilirakis**	Y	Y	Y	N	Y
10 **Young**	Y	Y	Y	N	Y
11 Castor	Y	Y	Y	Y	Y
12 **Putnam**	Y	Y	Y	N	Y
13 **Buchanan**	Y	Y	Y	N	Y
14 **Mack**	Y	Y	Y	N	Y
15 **Posey**	Y	Y	Y	N	Y
16 **Rooney**	Y	Y	Y	N	Y
17 Meek	Y	Y	Y	Y	Y
18 **Ros-Lehtinen**	Y	Y	Y	Y	Y
19 Wexler	Y	Y	Y	Y	Y
20 Wasserman Schultz	Y	Y	Y	Y	Y
21 **Diaz-Balart, L.**	Y	Y	Y	N	Y
22 Klein	Y	Y	Y	Y	Y
23 Hastings	Y	Y	Y	Y	Y
24 Kosmas	Y	Y	Y	Y	Y
25 **Diaz-Balart, M.**	Y	Y	Y	N	Y
GEORGIA					
1 **Kingston**	Y	Y	Y	N	Y
2 Bishop	Y	Y	Y	Y	Y
3 **Westmoreland**	Y	Y	Y	N	Y
4 Johnson	Y	Y	Y	Y	Y
5 Lewis	Y	Y	Y	Y	Y
6 **Price**	Y	Y	Y	N	Y
7 **Linder**	Y	Y	Y	N	Y
8 Marshall	Y	Y	Y	Y	Y
9 **Deal**	Y	Y	Y	N	Y
10 **Broun**	N	Y	Y	N	Y
11 **Gingrey**	Y	Y	Y	N	Y
12 Barrow	Y	Y	Y	Y	Y
13 Scott	Y	Y	Y	Y	Y
HAWAII					
1 Abercrombie	Y	Y	Y	Y	Y
2 Hirono	+	Y	Y	+	Y
IDAHO					
1 Minnick	Y	Y	Y	N	Y
2 **Simpson**	Y	Y	Y	Y	Y
ILLINOIS					
1 Rush	Y	Y	Y	?	?
2 Jackson	Y	Y	Y	Y	Y
3 Lipinski	Y	Y	Y	Y	Y
4 Gutierrez	Y	Y	Y	?	Y
5 Vacant					
6 **Roskam**	Y	Y	Y	N	Y
7 Davis	Y	Y	Y	Y	Y
8 Bean	Y	Y	Y	?	Y
9 Schakowsky	Y	Y	Y	Y	Y
10 **Kirk**	?	Y	Y	Y	Y
11 Halvorson	Y	Y	Y	Y	Y
12 Costello	Y	Y	Y	Y	Y
13 **Biggert**	Y	Y	Y	N	Y
14 Foster	Y	Y	Y	Y	Y
15 **Johnson**	Y	Y	Y	Y	Y

KEY	**Republicans**	Democrats		
Y Voted for (yea)		X Paired against		C Voted "present" to avoid possible conflict of interest
# Paired for		– Announced against		
+ Announced for		P Voted "present"		? Did not vote or otherwise make a position known
N Voted against (nay)				

*Rep. Hilda L. Solis, D-Calif., resigned Feb. 24 to become secretary of Labor. The last vote for which she was eligible was 79.

	77	78	79	80	81
16 Manzullo	Y	Y	Y	N	Y
17 Hare	Y	Y	Y	Y	Y
18 Schock	Y	Y	Y	N	Y
19 Shimkus	Y	Y	Y	N	Y
INDIANA					
1 Visclosky	Y	Y	Y	Y	Y
2 Donnelly	Y	Y	Y	N	Y
3 Souder	?	?	?	N	Y
4 Buyer	Y	Y	Y	N	Y
5 Burton	Y	Y	Y	N	Y
6 Pence	Y	Y	Y	N	Y
7 Carson	Y	Y	Y	Y	Y
8 Ellsworth	Y	Y	Y	N	Y
9 Hill	Y	Y	Y	Y	Y
IOWA					
1 Braley	Y	Y	Y	Y	Y
2 Loebsack	Y	Y	Y	Y	Y
3 Boswell	Y	Y	Y	Y	Y
4 Latham	Y	Y	Y	Y	Y
5 King	Y	Y	Y	N	Y
KANSAS					
1 Moran	Y	Y	Y	N	Y
2 Jenkins	Y	Y	Y	N	Y
3 Moore	Y	Y	Y	Y	Y
4 Tiahrt	Y	Y	Y	N	Y
KENTUCKY					
1 Whitfield	Y	Y	Y	Y	Y
2 Guthrie	Y	Y	Y	N	Y
3 Yarmuth	Y	Y	Y	Y	Y
4 Davis	Y	Y	Y	N	Y
5 Rogers	Y	Y	Y	N	Y
6 Chandler	Y	Y	Y	Y	Y
LOUISIANA					
1 Scalise	Y	Y	Y	N	Y
2 Cao	?	?	?	Y	Y
3 Melancon	Y	Y	Y	Y	Y
4 Fleming	Y	Y	Y	N	Y
5 Alexander	Y	Y	Y	N	Y
6 Cassidy	?	?	?	?	?
7 Boustany	Y	Y	Y	N	Y
MAINE					
1 Pingree	Y	Y	Y	Y	Y
2 Michaud	Y	Y	Y	Y	Y
MARYLAND					
1 Kratovil	Y	Y	Y	Y	Y
2 Ruppersberger	Y	Y	Y	Y	Y
3 Sarbanes	Y	Y	Y	Y	Y
4 Edwards	Y	Y	Y	Y	Y
5 Hoyer	Y	Y	Y	Y	Y
6 Bartlett	Y	Y	Y	N	Y
7 Cummings	Y	Y	Y	Y	Y
8 Van Hollen	Y	Y	Y	Y	Y
MASSACHUSETTS					
1 Olver	Y	Y	Y	Y	Y
2 Neal	Y	Y	Y	Y	Y
3 McGovern	Y	Y	Y	Y	Y
4 Frank	Y	Y	Y	Y	Y
5 Tsongas	Y	Y	Y	Y	Y
6 Tierney	Y	Y	Y	Y	Y
7 Markey	Y	Y	Y	Y	Y
8 Capuano	Y	Y	Y	Y	Y
9 Lynch	Y	Y	Y	Y	Y
10 Delahunt	Y	Y	Y	Y	Y
MICHIGAN					
1 Stupak	Y	Y	Y	N	Y
2 Hoekstra	Y	Y	Y	N	Y
3 Ehlers	N	Y	Y	N	Y
4 Camp	Y	Y	Y	N	Y
5 Kildee	Y	Y	Y	Y	Y
6 Upton	Y	Y	Y	N	Y
7 Schauer	Y	Y	Y	Y	Y
8 Rogers	Y	Y	Y	N	Y
9 Peters	Y	Y	Y	Y	Y
10 Miller	Y	Y	Y	N	Y
11 McCotter	Y	Y	Y	Y	Y
12 Levin	Y	Y	Y	Y	Y
13 Kilpatrick	Y	Y	Y	Y	Y
14 Conyers	Y	Y	Y	Y	Y
15 Dingell	Y	Y	Y	Y	Y
MINNESOTA					
1 Walz	Y	Y	Y	Y	Y
2 Kline	Y	Y	Y	N	Y
3 Paulsen	Y	Y	Y	N	Y
4 McCollum	Y	Y	Y	Y	Y

	77	78	79	80	81
5 Ellison	Y	Y	Y	Y	Y
6 Bachmann	?	?	?	Y	Y
7 Peterson	Y	Y	?	N	Y
8 Oberstar	Y	Y	Y	Y	Y
MISSISSIPPI					
1 Childers	Y	Y	Y	N	Y
2 Thompson	Y	Y	Y	Y	Y
3 Harper	Y	Y	Y	N	Y
4 Taylor	Y	Y	Y	Y	Y
MISSOURI					
1 Clay	Y	Y	Y	?	?
2 Akin	Y	Y	Y	N	Y
3 Carnahan	Y	Y	Y	Y	Y
4 Skelton	Y	Y	Y	Y	Y
5 Cleaver	Y	Y	Y	Y	Y
6 Graves	Y	Y	Y	N	Y
7 Blunt	Y	Y	Y	N	Y
8 Emerson	Y	Y	Y	N	Y
9 Luetkemeyer	Y	Y	Y	N	Y
MONTANA					
AL Rehberg	Y	Y	Y	N	Y
NEBRASKA					
1 Fortenberry	Y	Y	Y	N	Y
2 Terry	Y	Y	Y	N	Y
3 Smith	Y	Y	Y	N	Y
NEVADA					
1 Berkley	Y	Y	Y	Y	Y
2 Heller	Y	Y	Y	Y	Y
3 Titus	Y	Y	Y	Y	Y
NEW HAMPSHIRE					
1 Shea-Porter	Y	Y	Y	Y	Y
2 Hodes	Y	Y	Y	Y	Y
NEW JERSEY					
1 Andrews	Y	Y	Y	Y	Y
2 LoBiondo	Y	Y	Y	N	Y
3 Adler	Y	Y	Y	Y	Y
4 Smith	Y	Y	Y	N	Y
5 Garrett	N	Y	?	N	Y
6 Pallone	Y	Y	Y	Y	Y
7 Lance	Y	Y	Y	Y	Y
8 Pascrell	Y	Y	Y	Y	Y
9 Rothman	Y	Y	Y	Y	Y
10 Payne	Y	Y	Y	Y	Y
11 Frelinghuysen	Y	Y	Y	N	Y
12 Holt	Y	Y	Y	N	Y
13 Sires	Y	Y	Y	Y	Y
NEW MEXICO					
1 Heinrich	Y	Y	Y	Y	Y
2 Teague	Y	Y	Y	Y	Y
3 Lujan	Y	Y	Y	Y	Y
NEW YORK					
1 Bishop	Y	Y	Y	Y	Y
2 Israel	Y	Y	Y	Y	Y
3 King	Y	Y	Y	N	Y
4 McCarthy	Y	Y	Y	Y	Y
5 Ackerman	Y	?	Y	Y	Y
6 Meeks	Y	Y	Y	Y	Y
7 Crowley	Y	Y	Y	Y	Y
8 Nadler	Y	Y	Y	Y	Y
9 Weiner	Y	Y	Y	Y	Y
10 Towns	Y	Y	Y	Y	Y
11 Clarke	Y	Y	Y	Y	Y
12 Velázquez	Y	Y	Y	Y	Y
13 McMahon	Y	Y	Y	Y	Y
14 Maloney	Y	Y	Y	Y	Y
15 Rangel	Y	Y	Y	Y	Y
16 Serrano	Y	Y	Y	Y	Y
17 Engel	Y	Y	Y	Y	Y
18 Lowey	Y	Y	Y	Y	Y
19 Hall	Y	Y	Y	Y	Y
20 Vacant					
21 Tonko	Y	Y	Y	Y	Y
22 Hinchey	Y	Y	Y	Y	Y
23 McHugh	Y	Y	Y	N	Y
24 Arcuri	Y	Y	Y	N	Y
25 Maffei	Y	Y	Y	Y	Y
26 Lee	Y	Y	Y	N	Y
27 Higgins	Y	Y	Y	Y	Y
28 Slaughter	Y	Y	Y	Y	Y
29 Massa	Y	Y	Y	Y	Y
NORTH CAROLINA					
1 Butterfield	Y	Y	Y	Y	Y
2 Etheridge	Y	Y	Y	Y	Y
3 Jones	Y	Y	Y	N	Y
4 Price	Y	Y	Y	Y	Y

	77	78	79	80	81
5 Foxx	Y	Y	Y	N	Y
6 Coble	N	Y	Y	N	Y
7 McIntyre	Y	Y	Y	Y	Y
8 Kissell	Y	Y	Y	Y	Y
9 Myrick	Y	Y	Y	N	Y
10 McHenry	Y	Y	Y	?	Y
11 Shuler	Y	Y	Y	Y	Y
12 Watt	Y	Y	Y	Y	Y
13 Miller	Y	Y	Y	N	Y
NORTH DAKOTA					
AL Pomeroy	Y	Y	Y	Y	Y
OHIO					
1 Driehaus	Y	Y	Y	Y	Y
2 Schmidt	Y	Y	Y	N	Y
3 Turner	Y	Y	Y	N	Y
4 Jordan	N	Y	Y	N	Y
5 Latta	Y	Y	Y	N	Y
6 Wilson	Y	Y	Y	Y	Y
7 Austria	Y	Y	Y	N	Y
8 Boehner	Y	Y	Y	N	Y
9 Kaptur	Y	Y	Y	Y	Y
10 Kucinich	Y	Y	Y	Y	Y
11 Fudge	Y	Y	Y	Y	Y
12 Tiberi	Y	Y	Y	N	Y
13 Sutton	Y	Y	Y	Y	Y
14 LaTourette	?	Y	Y	N	Y
15 Kilroy	Y	Y	Y	Y	Y
16 Boccieri	Y	Y	Y	Y	Y
17 Ryan	Y	Y	Y	Y	?
18 Space	Y	Y	Y	N	Y
OKLAHOMA					
1 Sullivan	Y	Y	Y	N	Y
2 Boren	Y	Y	Y	N	Y
3 Lucas	Y	Y	Y	N	Y
4 Cole	Y	Y	Y	N	Y
5 Fallin	Y	Y	Y	N	Y
OREGON					
1 Wu	Y	Y	Y	?	?
2 Walden	Y	Y	Y	N	Y
3 Blumenauer	Y	Y	Y	Y	Y
4 DeFazio	Y	Y	Y	Y	Y
5 Schrader	Y	Y	Y	Y	Y
PENNSYLVANIA					
1 Brady	Y	Y	Y	Y	Y
2 Fattah	Y	Y	Y	Y	Y
3 Dahlkemper	Y	Y	Y	Y	Y
4 Altmire	Y	Y	Y	N	Y
5 Thompson	?	Y	Y	Y	Y
6 Gerlach	Y	Y	Y	Y	Y
7 Sestak	Y	Y	Y	Y	Y
8 Murphy, P.	Y	Y	Y	Y	Y
9 Shuster	Y	Y	Y	Y	Y
10 Carney	Y	Y	Y	N	Y
11 Kanjorski	Y	Y	Y	Y	Y
12 Murtha	Y	Y	Y	Y	Y
13 Schwartz	Y	Y	Y	Y	Y
14 Doyle	Y	Y	Y	Y	Y
15 Dent	Y	Y	Y	Y	Y
16 Pitts	Y	Y	Y	Y	Y
17 Holden	Y	Y	Y	?	Y
18 Murphy, T.	Y	Y	Y	N	Y
19 Platts	Y	Y	Y	?	?
RHODE ISLAND					
1 Kennedy	Y	Y	Y	Y	Y
2 Langevin	Y	Y	Y	Y	Y
SOUTH CAROLINA					
1 Brown	Y	Y	Y	N	Y
2 Wilson	Y	Y	Y	N	Y
3 Barrett	Y	Y	Y	N	Y
4 Inglis	Y	Y	Y	N	Y
5 Spratt	Y	Y	Y	Y	Y
6 Clyburn	Y	Y	Y	Y	Y
SOUTH DAKOTA					
AL Herseth Sandlin	Y	Y	Y	Y	Y
TENNESSEE					
1 Roe	Y	Y	Y	N	Y
2 Duncan	N	Y	Y	N	Y
3 Wamp	Y	Y	Y	N	Y
4 Davis	Y	Y	Y	Y	Y
5 Cooper	Y	Y	Y	Y	Y
6 Gordon	Y	Y	Y	Y	Y
7 Blackburn	Y	Y	Y	N	Y
8 Tanner	Y	Y	Y	Y	Y
9 Cohen	Y	Y	Y	Y	Y

	77	78	79	80	81
TEXAS					
1 Gohmert	Y	Y	Y	?	Y
2 Poe	N	Y	Y	N	Y
3 Johnson, S.	Y	Y	Y	N	Y
4 Hall	Y	Y	Y	N	Y
5 Hensarling	N	Y	Y	N	Y
6 Barton	Y	Y	Y	N	Y
7 Culberson	Y	Y	Y	N	Y
8 Brady	Y	Y	Y	N	Y
9 Green, A.	Y	Y	Y	Y	Y
10 McCaul	Y	?	Y	N	Y
11 Conaway	Y	Y	Y	N	Y
12 Granger	Y	Y	Y	N	Y
13 Thornberry	Y	Y	Y	N	Y
14 Paul	N	Y	Y	N	Y
15 Hinojosa	Y	Y	Y	Y	Y
16 Reyes	Y	Y	Y	Y	Y
17 Edwards	Y	Y	Y	Y	Y
18 Jackson Lee	Y	Y	Y	Y	Y
19 Neugebauer	N	Y	Y	N	Y
20 Gonzalez	Y	Y	Y	Y	Y
21 Smith	Y	Y	Y	N	Y
22 Olson	Y	Y	Y	N	Y
23 Rodriguez	Y	Y	Y	Y	Y
24 Marchant	Y	Y	Y	N	Y
25 Doggett	Y	Y	Y	Y	Y
26 Burgess	Y	Y	Y	N	Y
27 Ortiz	Y	Y	Y	Y	Y
28 Cuellar	Y	Y	Y	Y	Y
29 Green, G.	Y	Y	Y	Y	Y
30 Johnson, E.	Y	Y	Y	Y	Y
31 Carter	Y	Y	Y	N	Y
32 Sessions	Y	Y	?	N	Y
UTAH					
1 Bishop	Y	Y	Y	N	Y
2 Matheson	Y	Y	Y	Y	Y
3 Chaffetz	Y	Y	Y	N	Y
VERMONT					
AL Welch	Y	Y	Y	Y	Y
VIRGINIA					
1 Wittman	Y	Y	Y	N	Y
2 Nye	Y	Y	Y	N	Y
3 Scott	Y	Y	Y	Y	Y
4 Forbes	Y	Y	Y	N	Y
5 Perriello	?	?	?	?	?
6 Goodlatte	Y	Y	Y	N	Y
7 Cantor	Y	Y	Y	N	Y
8 Moran	Y	Y	Y	Y	Y
9 Boucher	Y	Y	Y	Y	Y
10 Wolf	Y	Y	Y	N	Y
11 Connolly	Y	Y	Y	Y	Y
WASHINGTON					
1 Inslee	Y	Y	Y	Y	Y
2 Larsen	Y	Y	Y	Y	Y
3 Baird	Y	Y	Y	Y	Y
4 Hastings	Y	Y	Y	N	Y
5 McMorris Rodgers	Y	Y	?	N	Y
6 Dicks	Y	Y	Y	Y	Y
7 McDermott	Y	Y	Y	Y	Y
8 Reichert	Y	Y	Y	N	Y
9 Smith	Y	Y	Y	Y	Y
WEST VIRGINIA					
1 Mollohan	Y	Y	Y	Y	Y
2 Capito	Y	Y	Y	N	Y
3 Rahall	Y	Y	Y	Y	Y
WISCONSIN					
1 Ryan	Y	Y	Y	N	Y
2 Baldwin	Y	Y	Y	Y	Y
3 Kind	Y	Y	Y	Y	Y
4 Moore	Y	Y	Y	Y	Y
5 Sensenbrenner	Y	Y	Y	N	Y
6 Petri	Y	Y	Y	N	Y
7 Obey	Y	Y	Y	Y	Y
8 Kagen	Y	Y	Y	Y	Y
WYOMING					
AL Lummis	N	Y	Y	?	Y
DELEGATES					
Faleomavaega (A.S.)					
Norton (D.C.)					
Bordallo (Guam)					
Sablan (N. Marianas)					
Pierluisi (P.R.)					
Christensen (V.I.)					

IN THE HOUSE | By Vote Number

82. H Res 180. America Saves Week/Adoption. Hinojosa, D-Texas, motion to suspend the rules and adopt the resolution that would support the goals and ideals of America Saves Week and acknowledge the efforts of the late Democratic Rep. Stephanie Tubbs Jones of Ohio to eliminate predatory lending and increase the nation's savings rate. Motion agreed to 415-2: R 171-2; D 244-0. A two-thirds majority of those present and voting (278 in this case) is required for adoption under suspension of the rules. Feb. 25, 2009.

83. HR 1105. Fiscal 2009 Omnibus Appropriations/Question of Consideration. Question of whether the House should consider the rule (H Res 184) to provide for House floor consideration of the bill that would provide fiscal 2009 appropriations for federal departments and agencies covered by nine unfinished fiscal 2009 spending bills. Agreed to consider 234-177: R 1-169; D 233-8. (Flake, R-Ariz., had raised a point of order that the rule contained a provision in violation of the Congressional Budget Act.) Feb. 25, 2009.

84. HR 1105. Fiscal 2009 Omnibus Appropriations/Previous Question. McGovern, D-Mass., motion to order the previous question (thus ending debate and possibility of amendment) on adoption of the rule (H Res 184) that would provide for House floor consideration of the bill that would provide fiscal 2009 appropriations for federal departments and agencies covered by nine unfinished fiscal 2009 spending bills. Motion agreed to 393-25: R 155-18; D 238-7. Feb. 25, 2009.

85. HR 1105. Fiscal 2009 Omnibus Appropriations/Rule. Adoption of the rule (H Res 184) that would provide for House floor consideration of the bill that would provide fiscal 2009 appropriations for federal departments and agencies covered by nine unfinished fiscal 2009 spending bills. Upon adoption, the rule would incorporate a provision to block the automatic cost-of-living adjustment for members of Congress in 2010. Adopted 398-24: R 153-21; D 245-3. Feb. 25, 2009.

86. HR 1105. Fiscal 2009 Omnibus Appropriations/Passage. Passage of the bill that would provide $410 billion in discretionary spending in fiscal 2009 for federal departments and agencies covered by nine unfinished fiscal 2009 spending bills. Those bills are Agriculture, Commerce-Justice-Science, Energy-Water, Financial Services, Interior-Environment, Labor-HHS-Education, Legislative Branch, State-Foreign Operations and Transportation-HUD. It also would provide $100 million for the U.S. Secret Service and block an automatic cost-of-living adjustment for members of Congress in 2010. Passed 245-178: R 16-158; D 229-20. Feb. 25, 2009.

	82	83	84	85	86
ALABAMA					
1 Bonner	Y	N	Y	Y	N
2 Bright	Y	Y	Y	Y	Y
3 Rogers	Y	N	Y	Y	N
4 Aderholt	Y	N	Y	Y	N
5 Griffith	Y	Y	Y	Y	Y
6 Bachus	Y	N	Y	Y	-
7 Davis	Y	Y	Y	Y	Y
ALASKA					
AL Young	Y	N	N	Y	Y
ARIZONA					
1 Kirkpatrick	Y	N	Y	Y	Y
2 Franks	Y	N	N	N	N
3 Shadegg	Y	N	Y	N	Y
4 Pastor	Y	Y	Y	Y	Y
5 Mitchell	Y	Y	Y	Y	N
6 Flake	N	N	N	N	N
7 Grijalva	Y	Y	Y	Y	Y
8 Giffords	Y	Y	Y	Y	N
ARKANSAS					
1 Berry	Y	Y	Y	Y	Y
2 Snyder	Y	Y	Y	Y	Y
3 Boozman	Y	N	Y	Y	N
4 Ross	Y	Y	Y	Y	Y
CALIFORNIA					
1 Thompson	Y	Y	Y	Y	Y
2 Herger	Y	N	Y	Y	N
3 Lungren	Y	N	Y	Y	N
4 McClintock	Y	N	Y	Y	N
5 Matsui	Y	Y	Y	Y	Y
6 Woolsey	Y	Y	Y	Y	Y
7 Miller, George	Y	Y	Y	Y	Y
8 Pelosi					
9 Lee	Y	Y	Y	Y	Y
10 Tauscher	Y	Y	Y	Y	Y
11 McNerney	Y	Y	Y	Y	Y
12 Speier	Y	Y	Y	Y	N
13 Stark	?	?	?	?	?
14 Eshoo	Y	Y	Y	Y	Y
15 Honda	Y	Y	Y	Y	Y
16 Lofgren	Y	Y	Y	Y	Y
17 Farr	Y	Y	Y	Y	Y
18 Cardoza	Y	Y	Y	Y	N
19 Radanovich	Y	N	Y	Y	N
20 Costa	Y	Y	Y	Y	N
21 Nunes	Y	N	Y	Y	N
22 McCarthy	Y	N	Y	Y	N
23 Capps	Y	Y	Y	Y	Y
24 Gallegly	Y	N	Y	Y	N
25 McKeon	Y	N	Y	Y	N
26 Dreier	Y	N	Y	Y	N
27 Sherman	Y	Y	Y	Y	Y
28 Berman	?	Y	Y	Y	Y
29 Schiff	Y	Y	Y	Y	Y
30 Waxman	Y	Y	Y	Y	Y
31 Becerra	Y	Y	Y	Y	Y
32 Vacant*					
33 Watson	Y	Y	Y	Y	Y
34 Roybal-Allard	Y	Y	Y	Y	Y
35 Waters	Y	Y	Y	Y	Y
36 Harman	Y	Y	Y	Y	Y
37 Richardson	Y	Y	Y	Y	Y
38 Napolitano	Y	Y	Y	Y	Y
39 Sánchez, Linda	Y	Y	Y	Y	Y
40 Royce	Y	N	Y	Y	N
41 Lewis	Y	N	Y	N	N
42 Miller, Gary	?	?	?	?	?
43 Baca	Y	Y	Y	Y	Y
44 Calvert	Y	N	Y	Y	N
45 Bono Mack	Y	N	Y	Y	N
46 Rohrabacher	Y	N	N	N	N
47 Sanchez, Loretta	Y	Y	Y	Y	Y
48 Campbell	?	?	?	?	?
49 Issa	?	N	Y	N	N
50 Bilbray	Y	N	Y	Y	N
51 Filner	Y	Y	Y	Y	Y
52 Hunter	Y	N	Y	N	N
53 Davis	Y	Y	Y	Y	Y

	82	83	84	85	86
COLORADO					
1 DeGette	Y	Y	Y	Y	Y
2 Polis	Y	Y	Y	Y	Y
3 Salazar	Y	Y	Y	Y	Y
4 Markey	Y	Y	Y	Y	Y
5 Lamborn	Y	N	N	N	N
6 Coffman	Y	N	Y	Y	N
7 Perlmutter	Y	Y	Y	Y	Y
CONNECTICUT					
1 Larson	Y	Y	+	+	Y
2 Courtney	Y	Y	Y	Y	Y
3 DeLauro	Y	Y	Y	Y	Y
4 Himes	?	Y	Y	Y	Y
5 Murphy	Y	Y	Y	Y	Y
DELAWARE					
AL Castle	Y	N	Y	Y	Y
FLORIDA					
1 Miller	Y	N	Y	Y	N
2 Boyd	Y	N	Y	Y	Y
3 Brown	Y	Y	Y	Y	Y
4 Crenshaw	Y	N	Y	Y	N
5 Brown-Waite	Y	N	Y	Y	N
6 Stearns	Y	N	Y	Y	N
7 Mica	Y	N	Y	N	N
8 Grayson	Y	Y	Y	Y	Y
9 Bilirakis	Y	N	Y	Y	N
10 Young	Y	N	Y	Y	N
11 Castor	Y	Y	Y	Y	Y
12 Putnam	Y	N	Y	Y	N
13 Buchanan	Y	N	Y	Y	N
14 Mack	Y	N	Y	Y	N
15 Posey	Y	N	Y	Y	N
16 Rooney	Y	N	Y	Y	N
17 Meek	Y	Y	Y	Y	Y
18 Ros-Lehtinen	Y	N	Y	Y	N
19 Wexler	Y	Y	Y	Y	Y
20 Wasserman Schultz	Y	Y	Y	Y	Y
21 Diaz-Balart, L.	Y	N	Y	Y	N
22 Klein	Y	Y	Y	Y	Y
23 Hastings	Y	Y	Y	Y	Y
24 Kosmas	Y	Y	Y	Y	Y
25 Diaz-Balart, M.	Y	N	Y	Y	N
GEORGIA					
1 Kingston	Y	N	Y	N	N
2 Bishop	Y	Y	Y	Y	Y
3 Westmoreland	Y	N	N	N	N
4 Johnson	Y	Y	Y	Y	Y
5 Lewis	Y	Y	Y	Y	Y
6 Price	Y	N	N	N	N
7 Linder	Y	N	Y	N	N
8 Marshall	Y	Y	Y	Y	Y
9 Deal	Y	N	N	N	N
10 Broun	Y	N	N	N	N
11 Gingrey	Y	N	Y	N	N
12 Barrow	Y	Y	Y	Y	Y
13 Scott	Y	Y	Y	Y	Y
HAWAII					
1 Abercrombie	Y	Y	Y	Y	Y
2 Hirono	Y	Y	Y	Y	Y
IDAHO					
1 Minnick	Y	N	N	Y	N
2 Simpson	Y	N	N	N	N
ILLINOIS					
1 Rush	?	?	?	?	?
2 Jackson	Y	Y	Y	Y	Y
3 Lipinski	Y	Y	Y	Y	Y
4 Gutierrez	Y	Y	Y	Y	Y
5 Vacant					
6 Roskam	Y	N	Y	N	N
7 Davis	Y	Y	?	?	Y
8 Bean	Y	Y	Y	Y	N
9 Schakowsky	Y	Y	Y	Y	Y
10 Kirk	Y	N	Y	N	N
11 Halvorson	Y	Y	Y	Y	Y
12 Costello	Y	N	Y	Y	Y
13 Biggert	Y	N	Y	Y	N
14 Foster	Y	Y	Y	Y	Y
15 Johnson	Y	N	Y	Y	N

KEY   Republicans   Democrats

Y Voted for (yea)	X Paired against	C Voted "present" to avoid possible conflict of interest
# Paired for	– Announced against	
+ Announced for	P Voted "present"	? Did not vote or otherwise make a position known
N Voted against (nay)		

Member	82	83	84	85	86
16 Manzullo	Y	N	Y	Y	N
17 Hare	Y	Y	Y	Y	Y
18 Schock	Y	N	Y	Y	N
19 Shimkus	Y	N	Y	Y	N
INDIANA					
1 Visclosky	Y	Y	Y	Y	Y
2 Donnelly	Y	Y	Y	Y	N
3 Souder	Y	N	Y	Y	N
4 Buyer	Y	?	Y	Y	N
5 Burton	Y	N	Y	Y	N
6 Pence	Y	N	Y	Y	N
7 Carson	Y	Y	Y	Y	Y
8 Ellsworth	Y	Y	Y	Y	Y
9 Hill	Y	Y	Y	Y	N
IOWA					
1 Braley	Y	Y	Y	Y	Y
2 Loebsack	Y	Y	Y	Y	Y
3 Boswell	Y	Y	Y	Y	Y
4 Latham	Y	N	Y	Y	N
5 King	Y	N	N	N	N
KANSAS					
1 Moran	Y	N	Y	Y	N
2 Jenkins	Y	N	Y	Y	N
3 Moore	Y	Y	Y	Y	Y
4 Tiahrt	Y	N	Y	Y	N
KENTUCKY					
1 Whitfield	Y	N	Y	Y	Y
2 Guthrie	Y	N	Y	Y	N
3 Yarmuth	Y	Y	Y	Y	Y
4 Davis	Y	N	Y	Y	N
5 Rogers	Y	N	Y	Y	N
6 Chandler	Y	Y	Y	Y	Y
LOUISIANA					
1 Scalise	Y	N	N	Y	N
2 Cao	Y	N	Y	Y	Y
3 Melancon	Y	Y	Y	Y	Y
4 Fleming	Y	N	Y	Y	N
5 Alexander	Y	N	Y	Y	N
6 Cassidy	?	?	?	?	?
7 Boustany	Y	N	Y	Y	N
MAINE					
1 Pingree	Y	Y	Y	Y	Y
2 Michaud	Y	Y	Y	Y	Y
MARYLAND					
1 Kratovil	Y	N	Y	Y	N
2 Ruppersberger	Y	Y	Y	Y	Y
3 Sarbanes	Y	Y	Y	Y	Y
4 Edwards	Y	Y	Y	Y	Y
5 Hoyer	Y	Y	?	Y	Y
6 Bartlett	Y	N	Y	Y	N
7 Cummings	Y	Y	Y	Y	Y
8 Van Hollen	Y	?	Y	Y	Y
MASSACHUSETTS					
1 Olver	Y	Y	Y	Y	Y
2 Neal	Y	Y	Y	Y	Y
3 McGovern	Y	Y	Y	Y	Y
4 Frank	Y	?	Y	Y	?
5 Tsongas	Y	Y	Y	Y	Y
6 Tierney	Y	Y	Y	Y	Y
7 Markey	Y	Y	Y	Y	Y
8 Capuano	Y	?	Y	Y	Y
9 Lynch	Y	Y	Y	Y	Y
10 Delahunt	Y	Y	Y	Y	Y
MICHIGAN					
1 Stupak	Y	Y	N	N	Y
2 Hoekstra	Y	N	Y	Y	N
3 Ehlers	Y	N	N	N	N
4 Camp	Y	N	Y	Y	N
5 Kildee	Y	Y	Y	Y	Y
6 Upton	Y	N	Y	Y	Y
7 Schauer	Y	Y	Y	Y	Y
8 Rogers	Y	N	Y	Y	N
9 Peters	Y	Y	Y	Y	Y
10 Miller	Y	N	Y	Y	N
11 McCotter	Y				
12 Levin	Y	Y	Y	Y	Y
13 Kilpatrick	Y	Y	Y	Y	Y
14 Conyers	Y	Y	Y	Y	Y
15 Dingell	Y	Y	Y	Y	Y
MINNESOTA					
1 Walz	Y	Y	Y	Y	Y
2 Kline	Y	N	Y	Y	N
3 Paulsen	Y	N	Y	Y	N
4 McCollum	Y	Y	Y	Y	Y
5 Ellison	Y	Y	Y	Y	Y
6 Bachmann	Y	N	Y	Y	N
7 Peterson	Y	Y	N	Y	N
8 Oberstar	Y	Y	Y	Y	Y
MISSISSIPPI					
1 Childers	Y	Y	Y	Y	Y
2 Thompson	Y	?	Y	Y	Y
3 Harper	Y	N	Y	Y	N
4 Taylor	Y	N	N	Y	N
MISSOURI					
1 Clay	?	Y	Y	Y	Y
2 Akin	Y	N	Y	Y	N
3 Carnahan	Y	Y	Y	Y	Y
4 Skelton	Y	Y	Y	Y	Y
5 Cleaver	Y	Y	Y	Y	Y
6 Graves	Y	N	Y	Y	N
7 Blunt	Y	N	N	N	N
8 Emerson	Y	N	Y	Y	Y
9 Luetkemeyer	Y	N	Y	Y	N
MONTANA					
AL Rehberg	Y	N	Y	Y	N
NEBRASKA					
1 Fortenberry	Y	N	Y	Y	N
2 Terry	Y	N	Y	Y	N
3 Smith	Y	N	Y	Y	N
NEVADA					
1 Berkley	Y	Y	Y	Y	Y
2 Heller	Y	Y	Y	Y	N
3 Titus	Y	Y	Y	Y	Y
NEW HAMPSHIRE					
1 Shea-Porter	Y	Y	Y	Y	Y
2 Hodes	Y	Y	Y	Y	Y
NEW JERSEY					
1 Andrews	Y	Y	Y	Y	Y
2 LoBiondo	Y	N	Y	Y	Y
3 Adler	Y	Y	Y	Y	Y
4 Smith	Y	N	N	N	N
5 Garrett	Y	N	Y	Y	N
6 Pallone	Y	Y	Y	Y	Y
7 Lance	Y	N	Y	Y	N
8 Pascrell	Y	Y	Y	Y	Y
9 Rothman	Y	Y	Y	Y	Y
10 Payne	Y	Y	Y	Y	Y
11 Frelinghuysen	Y	N	Y	Y	N
12 Holt	Y	Y	Y	Y	Y
13 Sires	Y	Y	Y	Y	Y
NEW MEXICO					
1 Heinrich	Y	Y	Y	Y	Y
2 Teague	Y	Y	Y	Y	Y
3 Lujan	Y	Y	Y	Y	Y
NEW YORK					
1 Bishop	Y	Y	Y	Y	Y
2 Israel	Y	Y	Y	Y	Y
3 King	Y	N	Y	Y	N
4 McCarthy	Y	Y	Y	Y	Y
5 Ackerman	Y	Y	Y	Y	Y
6 Meeks	Y	Y	Y	Y	Y
7 Crowley	Y	Y	Y	Y	Y
8 Nadler	Y	Y	Y	Y	Y
9 Weiner	Y	Y	Y	Y	Y
10 Towns	Y	Y	Y	Y	Y
11 Clarke	Y	Y	Y	Y	Y
12 Velázquez	Y	Y	Y	Y	Y
13 McMahon	Y	Y	Y	Y	Y
14 Maloney	Y	Y	Y	Y	Y
15 Rangel	Y	?	Y	Y	Y
16 Serrano	Y	Y	Y	Y	Y
17 Engel	Y	Y	Y	Y	Y
18 Lowey	Y	Y	Y	Y	Y
19 Hall	Y	Y	Y	Y	Y
20 Vacant					
21 Tonko	Y	Y	Y	Y	Y
22 Hinchey	Y	Y	Y	Y	Y
23 McHugh	Y	N	Y	Y	Y
24 Arcuri	Y	Y	Y	Y	Y
25 Maffei	Y	Y	Y	Y	Y
26 Lee	Y	?	Y	Y	N
27 Higgins	Y	Y	Y	Y	Y
28 Slaughter	Y	Y	Y	Y	Y
29 Massa	Y	Y	Y	Y	Y
NORTH CAROLINA					
1 Butterfield	Y	Y	?	Y	Y
2 Etheridge	Y	Y	Y	Y	Y
3 Jones	Y	N	Y	Y	N
4 Price	Y	Y	Y	Y	Y
5 Foxx	Y	N	Y	Y	N
6 Coble	Y	N	Y	Y	N
7 McIntyre	Y	N	Y	Y	Y
8 Kissell	Y	Y	Y	Y	Y
9 Myrick	Y	N	Y	Y	N
10 McHenry	Y	N	Y	Y	N
11 Shuler	Y	N	N	Y	N
12 Watt	Y	Y	Y	Y	Y
13 Miller	Y	Y	Y	Y	Y
NORTH DAKOTA					
AL Pomeroy	Y	Y	Y	Y	Y
OHIO					
1 Driehaus	Y	Y	Y	Y	N
2 Schmidt	Y	N	Y	Y	N
3 Turner	Y	N	Y	Y	N
4 Jordan	Y	N	N	N	N
5 Latta	Y	N	Y	Y	N
6 Wilson	Y	Y	Y	Y	Y
7 Austria	Y	N	Y	Y	N
8 Boehner	Y	?	Y	Y	N
9 Kaptur	Y	Y	Y	Y	Y
10 Kucinich	Y	N	N	N	Y
11 Fudge	Y	Y	Y	Y	Y
12 Tiberi	Y	N	Y	Y	N
13 Sutton	Y	Y	Y	Y	Y
14 LaTourette	Y	N	Y	Y	N
15 Kilroy	Y	Y	Y	Y	Y
16 Boccieri	Y	Y	Y	Y	Y
17 Ryan	?	Y	Y	Y	Y
18 Space	Y	Y	Y	Y	Y
OKLAHOMA					
1 Sullivan	Y	N	Y	Y	N
2 Boren	Y	Y	N	Y	Y
3 Lucas	Y	N	Y	Y	N
4 Cole	Y	N	Y	Y	N
5 Fallin	Y	N	Y	Y	N
OREGON					
1 Wu	?	?	Y	Y	Y
2 Walden	Y	N	Y	Y	N
3 Blumenauer	Y	Y	Y	Y	Y
4 DeFazio	Y	Y	Y	Y	Y
5 Schrader	Y	Y	Y	Y	Y
PENNSYLVANIA					
1 Brady	Y	Y	Y	Y	Y
2 Fattah	Y	Y	Y	Y	Y
3 Dahlkemper	Y	Y	Y	Y	Y
4 Altmire	Y	Y	Y	Y	Y
5 Thompson	Y	N	Y	Y	N
6 Gerlach	Y	N	Y	Y	N
7 Sestak	Y	?	Y	Y	Y
8 Murphy, P.	Y	Y	Y	Y	Y
9 Shuster	Y	N	Y	Y	N
10 Carney	Y	Y	Y	Y	Y
11 Kanjorski	Y	Y	Y	Y	Y
12 Murtha	Y	Y	Y	Y	Y
13 Schwartz	Y	+	Y	Y	Y
14 Doyle	Y	Y	Y	Y	Y
15 Dent	Y	N	Y	Y	Y
16 Pitts	Y	N	Y	Y	N
17 Holden	Y	Y	Y	Y	Y
18 Murphy, T.	Y	N	Y	Y	Y
19 Platts	?	?	?	?	N
RHODE ISLAND					
1 Kennedy	Y	Y	Y	Y	Y
2 Langevin	Y	Y	Y	Y	Y
SOUTH CAROLINA					
1 Brown	Y	N	Y	Y	N
2 Wilson	Y	N	Y	Y	N
3 Barrett	Y	N	?	Y	N
4 Inglis	Y	N	Y	Y	N
5 Spratt	Y	Y	Y	Y	Y
6 Clyburn	Y	Y	?	Y	Y
SOUTH DAKOTA					
AL Herseth Sandlin	Y	Y	Y	Y	Y
TENNESSEE					
1 Roe	Y	N	Y	Y	N
2 Duncan	Y	N	Y	Y	N
3 Wamp	Y	N	Y	Y	N
4 Davis	Y	?	Y	Y	Y
5 Cooper	Y	Y	Y	Y	Y
6 Gordon	Y	Y	Y	Y	Y
7 Blackburn	Y	N	Y	Y	N
8 Tanner	Y	Y	Y	Y	N
9 Cohen	Y	Y	Y	Y	Y
TEXAS					
1 Gohmert	Y	N	Y	Y	N
2 Poe	Y	N	N	Y	N
3 Johnson, S.	Y	N	Y	Y	N
4 Hall	Y	N	Y	Y	N
5 Hensarling	Y	N	Y	Y	N
6 Barton	Y	?	Y	N	N
7 Culberson	Y	N	Y	Y	N
8 Brady	Y	N	Y	Y	N
9 Green, A.	Y	Y	Y	Y	Y
10 McCaul	Y	N	Y	Y	N
11 Conaway	Y	N	Y	Y	N
12 Granger	Y	N	Y	Y	N
13 Thornberry	Y	N	Y	Y	N
14 Paul	N	N	N	N	N
15 Hinojosa	Y	Y	Y	Y	Y
16 Reyes	Y	Y	Y	Y	Y
17 Edwards	Y	Y	Y	Y	Y
18 Jackson Lee	Y	Y	Y	Y	Y
19 Neugebauer	Y	N	Y	Y	N
20 Gonzalez	Y	Y	Y	Y	Y
21 Smith	Y	N	Y	Y	N
22 Olson	Y	N	Y	Y	N
23 Rodriguez	Y	Y	Y	Y	Y
24 Marchant	Y	N	Y	Y	N
25 Doggett	Y	Y	Y	Y	Y
26 Burgess	Y	N	N	N	N
27 Ortiz	Y	Y	Y	Y	Y
28 Cuellar	Y	Y	Y	Y	Y
29 Green, G.	Y	Y	Y	Y	Y
30 Johnson, E.	Y	Y	Y	Y	Y
31 Carter	Y	N	Y	Y	N
32 Sessions	Y	N	Y	Y	N
UTAH					
1 Bishop	Y	N	Y	Y	N
2 Matheson	Y	Y	Y	Y	N
3 Chaffetz	Y	N	Y	Y	N
VERMONT					
AL Welch	Y	Y	Y	Y	Y
VIRGINIA					
1 Wittman	Y	N	Y	Y	N
2 Nye	Y	Y	Y	Y	N
3 Scott	Y	Y	Y	Y	Y
4 Forbes	Y	N	Y	Y	N
5 Perriello	?	?	?	?	?
6 Goodlatte	Y	N	Y	Y	N
7 Cantor	Y	N	Y	Y	N
8 Moran	Y	Y	Y	Y	Y
9 Boucher	Y	Y	Y	Y	Y
10 Wolf	Y	N	Y	Y	N
11 Connolly	Y	Y	Y	Y	Y
WASHINGTON					
1 Inslee	?	Y	Y	Y	Y
2 Larsen	Y	Y	Y	Y	Y
3 Baird	Y	Y	Y	Y	Y
4 Hastings	Y	N	Y	Y	N
5 McMorris Rodgers	Y	N	Y	Y	N
6 Dicks	Y	Y	Y	Y	Y
7 McDermott	Y	Y	Y	Y	Y
8 Reichert	Y	N	Y	Y	N
9 Smith	Y	Y	Y	Y	Y
WEST VIRGINIA					
1 Mollohan	Y	Y	Y	Y	Y
2 Capito	Y	N	Y	Y	N
3 Rahall	Y	Y	Y	Y	Y
WISCONSIN					
1 Ryan	Y	N	Y	Y	N
2 Baldwin	Y	Y	Y	Y	Y
3 Kind	Y	Y	Y	Y	N
4 Moore	Y	Y	Y	Y	Y
5 Sensenbrenner	Y	N	Y	Y	N
6 Petri	Y	N	Y	Y	N
7 Obey	Y	Y	Y	Y	Y
8 Kagen	Y	Y	Y	Y	Y
WYOMING					
AL Lummis	Y	N	Y	Y	N

DELEGATES

Faleomavaega (A.S.)
Norton (D.C.)
Bordallo (Guam)
Sablan (N. Marianas)
Pierluisi (P.R.)
Christensen (V.I.)

IN THE HOUSE | By Vote Number

87. **H Res 189. Earmark Investigation/Motion to Table.** Hoyer, D-Md., motion to table (kill) the Flake, R-Ariz., privileged resolution that would instruct the Committee on Standards of Official Conduct to investigate and report on the relationship between earmarks made by members of Congress and the details of past campaign contributions. Motion agreed to 226-182: R 2-165; D 224-17. Feb. 25, 2009.

88. **HR 1106. Mortgage Loans Modification/Previous Question.** Hastings, D-Fla., motion to order the previous question (thus ending debate and possibility of amendment) on adoption of the rule (H Res 190) that would provide for House floor consideration of the bill that would allow bankruptcy judges to order lenders to write down the principal and interest rates of loans for people whose mortgages are larger than the value of their homes. Motion agreed to 238-183: R 0-172; D 238-11. Feb. 26, 2009.

89. **HR 1106. Mortgage Loans Modification/Rule.** Adoption of the rule (H Res 190) that would provide for House floor consideration of the bill that would allow bankruptcy judges to order lenders to write down the principal and interest rates of loans for people whose mortgages are larger than the value of their homes. Adopted 224-198: R 0-172; D 224-26. Feb. 26, 2009.

90. **H Res 183. Continental Flight 3407/Adoption.** Arcuri, D-N.Y., motion to suspend the rules and adopt the resolution that would express condolences to the families and friends of those who died in the crash of Continental Connection Flight 3407 and commend those who responded to the emergency. Motion agreed to 399-0: R 161-0; D 238-0. A two-thirds majority of those present and voting (266 in this case) is required for adoption under suspension of the rules. Feb. 26, 2009.

91. **HR 146. Battlefields Grant Program/Passage.** Holt, D-N.J., motion to suspend the rules and pass the bill that would authorize $10 million annually in fiscal 2010-14 to provide matching grants to states and localities to acquire and protect significant battlefields and sites related to the Revolutionary War and the War of 1812. Motion agreed to 394-13: R 157-13; D 237-0. A two-thirds majority of those present and voting (272 in this case) is required for passage under suspension of the rules. March 3, 2009.

	87	88	89	90	91
ALABAMA					
1 Bonner	P	N	N	Y	Y
2 Bright	Y	Y	N	Y	Y
3 **Rogers**	N	N	N	Y	Y
4 **Aderholt**	N	N	N	Y	Y
5 Griffith	Y	Y	Y	Y	Y
6 **Bachus**	–	N	N	Y	Y
7 Davis	Y	Y	Y	Y	Y
ALASKA					
AL **Young**	N	N	N	Y	Y
ARIZONA					
1 Kirkpatrick	N	Y	N	Y	Y
2 **Franks**	N	N	N	Y	N
3 **Shadegg**	N	N	N	Y	N
4 Pastor	Y	Y	Y	Y	Y
5 Mitchell	N	Y	Y	Y	Y
6 **Flake**	N	N	N	Y	N
7 Grijalva	Y	Y	Y	?	Y
8 Giffords	N	Y	N	Y	Y
ARKANSAS					
1 Berry	Y	N	N	Y	Y
2 Snyder	Y	Y	Y	?	?
3 **Boozman**	N	N	N	Y	Y
4 Ross	Y	N	N	Y	Y
CALIFORNIA					
1 Thompson	Y	Y	Y	Y	Y
2 **Herger**	N	N	N	Y	Y
3 **Lungren**	N	N	N	Y	Y
4 **McClintock**	N	N	N	Y	Y
5 Matsui	Y	Y	Y	Y	Y
6 Woolsey	Y	Y	Y	Y	Y
7 Miller, George	Y	Y	Y	Y	Y
8 Pelosi					
9 Lee	Y	Y	Y	Y	?
10 Tauscher	Y	Y	Y	Y	Y
11 McNerney	N	Y	Y	Y	Y
12 Speier	Y	Y	Y	Y	?
13 Stark	?	?	?	?	?
14 Eshoo	Y	Y	Y	Y	Y
15 Honda	Y	Y	Y	Y	Y
16 Lofgren	P	Y	Y	Y	Y
17 Farr	Y	Y	Y	Y	Y
18 Cardoza	Y	Y	Y	Y	Y
19 **Radanovich**	N	N	N	Y	Y
20 Costa	Y	Y	Y	Y	Y
21 **Nunes**	N	N	N	Y	Y
22 **McCarthy**	N	N	N	Y	Y
23 Capps	Y	Y	Y	Y	Y
24 **Gallegly**	N	N	N	Y	Y
25 **McKeon**	N	N	N	Y	Y
26 **Dreier**	N	N	N	Y	Y
27 Sherman	Y	Y	Y	Y	Y
28 Berman	Y	Y	Y	?	Y
29 Schiff	Y	Y	Y	Y	Y
30 Waxman	Y	Y	Y	Y	Y
31 Becerra	Y	Y	Y	+	Y
32 Vacant					
33 Watson	Y	Y	Y	Y	Y
34 Roybal-Allard	Y	Y	Y	Y	Y
35 Waters	Y	Y	Y	Y	?
36 Harman	Y	Y	Y	Y	Y
37 Richardson	Y	Y	Y	Y	?
38 Napolitano	Y	Y	Y	Y	Y
39 Sánchez, Linda	Y	Y	Y	Y	Y
40 **Royce**	N	N	N	Y	N
41 **Lewis**	N	N	N	Y	Y
42 **Miller, Gary**	?	?	?	?	?
43 Baca	Y	Y	Y	Y	?
44 **Calvert**	N	N	N	Y	Y
45 **Bono Mack**	N	N	N	Y	Y
46 **Rohrabacher**	N	N	N	Y	N
47 Sanchez, Loretta	Y	Y	Y	?	Y
48 **Campbell**	–	–	–	+	+
49 **Issa**	N	N	N	Y	Y
50 **Bilbray**	N	N	N	Y	Y
51 Filner	Y	Y	Y	Y	Y
52 **Hunter**	N	N	N	Y	Y
53 Davis	Y	Y	Y	Y	Y

	87	88	89	90	91
COLORADO					
1 DeGette	Y	Y	Y	Y	Y
2 Polis	Y	Y	Y	Y	Y
3 Salazar	Y	Y	Y	Y	Y
4 Markey	Y	Y	Y	Y	Y
5 **Lamborn**	N	N	N	Y	Y
6 **Coffman**	N	N	N	Y	Y
7 Perlmutter	Y	Y	Y	Y	Y
CONNECTICUT					
1 Larson	Y	Y	Y	?	Y
2 Courtney	Y	Y	Y	Y	Y
3 DeLauro	Y	Y	Y	Y	Y
4 Himes	N	Y	Y	Y	Y
5 Murphy	Y	Y	Y	Y	Y
DELAWARE					
AL **Castle**	N	N	N	Y	Y
FLORIDA					
1 **Miller**	N	N	N	Y	Y
2 Boyd	Y	Y	Y	Y	Y
3 Brown	Y	Y	Y	Y	?
4 **Crenshaw**	N	N	N	Y	Y
5 **Brown-Waite**	N	N	N	Y	Y
6 **Stearns**	N	N	N	Y	Y
7 **Mica**	N	N	N	Y	Y
8 Grayson	Y	Y	Y	Y	Y
9 **Bilirakis**	N	N	N	Y	Y
10 **Young**	N	N	N	Y	?
11 Castor	P	Y	Y	Y	Y
12 **Putnam**	N	N	N	Y	+
13 **Buchanan**	N	N	N	Y	?
14 **Mack**	N	N	N	Y	Y
15 **Posey**	N	N	N	Y	Y
16 **Rooney**	N	N	N	Y	Y
17 Meek	Y	Y	Y	Y	Y
18 **Ros-Lehtinen**	N	N	N	Y	?
19 Wexler	Y	Y	Y	Y	Y
20 Wasserman Schultz	Y	Y	Y	Y	Y
21 **Diaz-Balart, L.**	N	N	N	Y	Y
22 Klein	Y	Y	Y	Y	Y
23 Hastings	Y	Y	Y	Y	Y
24 Kosmas	Y	N	Y	Y	Y
25 **Diaz-Balart, M.**	N	N	N	Y	Y
GEORGIA					
1 **Kingston**	N	N	N	Y	Y
2 Bishop	Y	Y	Y	Y	Y
3 **Westmoreland**	N	N	N	Y	Y
4 Johnson	Y	Y	Y	Y	?
5 Lewis	Y	Y	Y	Y	?
6 **Price**	N	N	N	Y	Y
7 **Linder**	N	N	N	?	Y
8 Marshall	Y	Y	Y	Y	Y
9 **Deal**	N	N	N	?	Y
10 **Broun**	N	N	N	Y	N
11 **Gingrey**	N	N	N	Y	Y
12 Barrow	Y	N	N	Y	Y
13 Scott	Y	Y	Y	Y	Y
HAWAII					
1 Abercrombie	Y	Y	Y	Y	Y
2 Hirono	Y	Y	Y	Y	Y
IDAHO					
1 Minnick	Y	N	N	Y	Y
2 **Simpson**	N	N	N	Y	Y
ILLINOIS					
1 Rush	?	Y	Y	Y	Y
2 Jackson	Y	Y	Y	Y	Y
3 Lipinski	Y	Y	Y	Y	Y
4 Gutierrez	Y	Y	Y	Y	Y
5 Vacant					
6 **Roskam**	N	N	N	Y	Y
7 Davis	Y	Y	Y	Y	Y
8 Bean	N	Y	Y	Y	Y
9 Schakowsky	Y	Y	Y	Y	Y
10 **Kirk**	N	N	N	?	Y
11 Halvorson	N	Y	Y	Y	Y
12 Costello	Y	Y	Y	Y	Y
13 **Biggert**	N	N	N	Y	Y
14 Foster	Y	Y	Y	Y	Y
15 **Johnson**	N	N	N	Y	Y

KEY **Republicans** Democrats

Y Voted for (yea)	X Paired against	C Voted "present" to avoid possible conflict of interest
# Paired for	– Announced against	
+ Announced for	P Voted "present"	? Did not vote or otherwise make a position known
N Voted against (nay)		

Member	87	88	89	90	91
16 Manzullo	N	N	N	Y	N
17 Hare	Y	Y	Y	Y	Y
18 Schock	N	N	N	Y	Y
19 Shimkus	N	N	N	Y	Y
INDIANA					
1 Visclosky	Y	Y	Y	Y	Y
2 Donnelly	N	N	N	Y	Y
3 Souder	N	N	N	Y	Y
4 Buyer	N	N	N	Y	Y
5 Burton	N	N	N	Y	Y
6 Pence	N	?	N	?	Y
7 Carson	Y	Y	Y	Y	Y
8 Ellsworth	N	Y	N	Y	Y
9 Hill	Y	N	N	?	Y
IOWA					
1 Braley	Y	Y	Y	Y	Y
2 Loebsack	N	Y	Y	Y	Y
3 Boswell	Y	Y	N	Y	Y
4 Latham	N	N	N	Y	Y
5 King	N	N	–	Y	+
KANSAS					
1 Moran	N	N	N	Y	Y
2 Jenkins	N	N	N	Y	N
3 Moore	Y	Y	Y	Y	Y
4 Tiahrt	N	N	N	Y	N
KENTUCKY					
1 Whitfield	P	N	N	Y	Y
2 Guthrie	N	N	N	Y	Y
3 Yarmuth	Y	Y	Y	Y	Y
4 Davis	N	N	N	Y	Y
5 Rogers	N	N	N	Y	Y
6 Chandler	P	Y	N	Y	Y
LOUISIANA					
1 Scalise	N	N	N	Y	Y
2 Cao	N	?	?	?	Y
3 Melancon	Y	Y	Y	Y	Y
4 Fleming	N	N	N	Y	Y
5 Alexander	N	N	N	Y	Y
6 Cassidy	?	?	?	?	Y
7 Boustany	N	N	N	Y	Y
MAINE					
1 Pingree	Y	Y	Y	Y	Y
2 Michaud	Y	Y	N	Y	Y
MARYLAND					
1 Kratovil	Y	Y	N	Y	Y
2 Ruppersberger	Y	Y	Y	Y	Y
3 Sarbanes	Y	Y	Y	Y	Y
4 Edwards	Y	Y	Y	Y	?
5 Hoyer	Y	Y	Y	Y	Y
6 Bartlett	N	N	N	Y	Y
7 Cummings	Y	Y	Y	Y	Y
8 Van Hollen	Y	Y	Y	Y	Y
MASSACHUSETTS					
1 Olver	Y	Y	Y	Y	Y
2 Neal	Y	Y	Y	Y	Y
3 McGovern	Y	Y	Y	Y	Y
4 Frank	?	Y	Y	Y	Y
5 Tsongas	Y	Y	Y	Y	Y
6 Tierney	Y	Y	Y	Y	Y
7 Markey	Y	Y	Y	Y	Y
8 Capuano	Y	Y	Y	Y	Y
9 Lynch	Y	Y	Y	Y	Y
10 Delahunt	Y	Y	Y	Y	Y
MICHIGAN					
1 Stupak	Y	Y	Y	Y	Y
2 Hoekstra	N	N	N	Y	Y
3 Ehlers	N	N	N	Y	+
4 Camp	N	N	N	Y	Y
5 Kildee	Y	Y	Y	Y	Y
6 Upton	N	N	N	Y	Y
7 Schauer	Y	Y	Y	Y	Y
8 Rogers	N	N	N	Y	Y
9 Peters	Y	Y	Y	Y	Y
10 Miller	N	N	N	?	Y
11 McCotter	N	N	N	Y	Y
12 Levin	Y	Y	Y	Y	Y
13 Kilpatrick	Y	Y	Y	?	Y
14 Conyers	Y	Y	Y	?	Y
15 Dingell	Y	Y	Y	Y	Y
MINNESOTA					
1 Walz	N	Y	Y	Y	Y
2 Kline	?	?	?	?	Y
3 Paulsen	N	N	N	Y	Y
4 McCollum	Y	Y	Y	Y	Y
5 Ellison	Y	Y	Y	Y	?
6 Bachmann	N	N	N	Y	Y
7 Peterson	Y	Y	N	Y	Y
8 Oberstar	Y	Y	Y	Y	Y
MISSISSIPPI					
1 Childers	Y	N	N	Y	Y
2 Thompson	Y	Y	Y	Y	Y
3 Harper	N	N	N	Y	Y
4 Taylor	Y	N	N	Y	Y
MISSOURI					
1 Clay	P	Y	Y	Y	Y
2 Akin	N	N	N	Y	Y
3 Carnahan	Y	Y	Y	Y	Y
4 Skelton	Y	Y	Y	Y	Y
5 Cleaver	Y	Y	Y	Y	Y
6 Graves	N	N	N	Y	Y
7 Blunt	N	N	N	Y	Y
8 Emerson	N	N	N	Y	Y
9 Luetkemeyer	N	N	N	Y	Y
MONTANA					
AL Rehberg	N	N	N	Y	Y
NEBRASKA					
1 Fortenberry	N	N	N	Y	Y
2 Terry	N	N	?	Y	Y
3 Smith	N	N	N	Y	Y
NEVADA					
1 Berkley	Y	Y	Y	Y	Y
2 Heller	N	N	N	Y	Y
3 Titus	Y	Y	Y	Y	Y
NEW HAMPSHIRE					
1 Shea-Porter	Y	Y	Y	Y	Y
2 Hodes	N	Y	Y	Y	Y
NEW JERSEY					
1 Andrews	Y	Y	Y	Y	Y
2 LoBiondo	N	N	N	Y	Y
3 Adler	Y	Y	Y	Y	Y
4 Smith	N	N	N	Y	Y
5 Garrett	N	N	N	Y	Y
6 Pallone	Y	Y	Y	Y	Y
7 Lance	N	N	N	Y	Y
8 Pascrell	Y	Y	Y	Y	Y
9 Rothman	Y	Y	Y	Y	Y
10 Payne	Y	Y	Y	Y	Y
11 Frelinghuysen	N	N	N	Y	Y
12 Holt	Y	Y	Y	Y	Y
13 Sires	Y	Y	Y	Y	Y
NEW MEXICO					
1 Heinrich	Y	Y	Y	Y	Y
2 Teague	N	N	N	Y	Y
3 Lujan	Y	Y	Y	Y	Y
NEW YORK					
1 Bishop	Y	Y	Y	Y	Y
2 Israel	Y	Y	Y	Y	Y
3 King	N	N	N	Y	Y
4 McCarthy	Y	Y	Y	Y	Y
5 Ackerman	Y	Y	Y	Y	Y
6 Meeks	Y	Y	Y	Y	Y
7 Crowley	Y	Y	Y	Y	Y
8 Nadler	Y	Y	Y	Y	Y
9 Weiner	Y	Y	Y	Y	Y
10 Towns	Y	Y	Y	Y	Y
11 Clarke	Y	Y	Y	Y	?
12 Velázquez	Y	Y	Y	?	Y
13 McMahon	Y	Y	Y	Y	Y
14 Maloney	Y	Y	Y	Y	Y
15 Rangel	Y	Y	Y	Y	Y
16 Serrano	Y	Y	Y	Y	Y
17 Engel	Y	Y	Y	Y	Y
18 Lowey	Y	Y	Y	Y	Y
19 Hall	Y	Y	Y	Y	Y
20 Vacant					
21 Tonko	Y	Y	Y	Y	Y
22 Hinchey	Y	Y	Y	Y	Y
23 McHugh	N	N	N	Y	Y
24 Arcuri	Y	Y	Y	Y	Y
25 Maffei	Y	Y	Y	Y	Y
26 Lee	N	N	N	Y	Y
27 Higgins	Y	Y	Y	Y	Y
28 Slaughter	Y	Y	Y	Y	Y
29 Massa	Y	Y	Y	?	Y
NORTH CAROLINA					
1 Butterfield	P	Y	Y	Y	Y
2 Etheridge	Y	Y	Y	Y	Y
3 Jones	Y	N	N	Y	Y
4 Price	Y	Y	Y	Y	Y
5 Foxx	N	N	N	Y	Y
6 Coble	N	N	N	Y	Y
7 McIntyre	Y	Y	Y	Y	Y
8 Kissell	N	Y	Y	Y	Y
9 Myrick	N	N	N	Y	Y
10 McHenry	N	N	N	Y	Y
11 Shuler	Y	Y	N	Y	Y
12 Watt	Y	Y	Y	Y	Y
13 Miller	Y	Y	Y	Y	Y
NORTH DAKOTA					
AL Pomeroy	Y	Y	Y	Y	Y
OHIO					
1 Driehaus	Y	Y	Y	Y	Y
2 Schmidt	N	N	N	Y	Y
3 Turner	N	N	N	Y	Y
4 Jordan	N	N	N	Y	Y
5 Latta	N	N	N	Y	Y
6 Wilson	Y	Y	Y	Y	Y
7 Austria	N	N	N	Y	Y
8 Boehner	N	N	N	Y	Y
9 Kaptur	Y	N	Y	Y	?
10 Kucinich	Y	Y	Y	Y	?
11 Fudge	Y	Y	Y	Y	?
12 Tiberi	N	N	N	?	Y
13 Sutton	Y	Y	Y	Y	Y
14 LaTourette	N	N	N	Y	Y
15 Kilroy	Y	Y	Y	Y	Y
16 Boccieri	N	Y	Y	Y	Y
17 Ryan	Y	Y	Y	Y	Y
18 Space	Y	Y	Y	Y	Y
OKLAHOMA					
1 Sullivan	N	N	N	?	Y
2 Boren	Y	Y	Y	Y	Y
3 Lucas	N	N	N	?	Y
4 Cole	N	N	N	Y	Y
5 Fallin	N	N	N	Y	Y
OREGON					
1 Wu	Y	Y	Y	Y	Y
2 Walden	N	N	N	Y	Y
3 Blumenauer	Y	Y	Y	Y	Y
4 DeFazio	Y	Y	Y	Y	Y
5 Schrader	Y	Y	N	Y	Y
PENNSYLVANIA					
1 Brady	Y	Y	Y	Y	Y
2 Fattah	Y	Y	Y	Y	Y
3 Dahlkemper	Y	Y	Y	Y	Y
4 Altmire	N	N	N	Y	Y
5 Thompson	N	N	N	Y	Y
6 Gerlach	N	N	N	Y	Y
7 Sestak	Y	Y	Y	Y	Y
8 Murphy, P.	Y	Y	Y	?	Y
9 Shuster	N	N	N	Y	Y
10 Carney	Y	Y	Y	Y	Y
11 Kanjorski	Y	Y	Y	Y	Y
12 Murtha	Y	Y	Y	Y	Y
13 Schwartz	Y	Y	Y	Y	Y
14 Doyle	Y	Y	Y	?	Y
15 Dent	P	N	N	Y	Y
16 Pitts	N	N	N	Y	Y
17 Holden	Y	Y	Y	Y	Y
18 Murphy, T.	Y	N	Y	Y	Y
19 Platts	N	N	N	Y	Y
RHODE ISLAND					
1 Kennedy	Y	Y	Y	Y	Y
2 Langevin	Y	Y	Y	Y	Y
SOUTH CAROLINA					
1 Brown	N	N	N	Y	Y
2 Wilson	N	N	N	Y	Y
3 Barrett	P	N	N	Y	Y
4 Inglis	N	N	N	Y	Y
5 Spratt	Y	Y	Y	Y	Y
6 Clyburn	Y	Y	Y	Y	Y
SOUTH DAKOTA					
AL Herseth Sandlin	Y	Y	Y	Y	Y
TENNESSEE					
1 Roe	N	N	N	Y	Y
2 Duncan	N	N	N	?	N
3 Wamp	N	N	N	?	Y
4 Davis	Y	Y	Y	Y	Y
5 Cooper	?	Y	Y	Y	Y
6 Gordon	Y	Y	Y	Y	Y
7 Blackburn	N	N	N	Y	Y
8 Tanner	Y	Y	Y	Y	Y
9 Cohen	Y	Y	Y	Y	Y
TEXAS					
1 Gohmert	N	N	N	Y	Y
2 Poe	N	N	N	Y	Y
3 Johnson, S.	N	N	N	Y	Y
4 Hall	N	N	N	Y	Y
5 Hensarling	N	N	N	Y	Y
6 Barton	N	N	N	Y	Y
7 Culberson	N	N	N	Y	Y
8 Brady	N	N	N	Y	Y
9 Green, A.	Y	Y	Y	Y	Y
10 McCaul	N	N	N	Y	Y
11 Conaway	P	N	N	Y	Y
12 Granger	N	N	N	Y	Y
13 Thornberry	N	N	N	Y	Y
14 Paul	N	N	N	Y	N
15 Hinojosa	Y	Y	Y	Y	Y
16 Reyes	Y	Y	Y	Y	Y
17 Edwards	Y	Y	Y	Y	Y
18 Jackson Lee	Y	Y	Y	Y	Y
19 Neugebauer	N	N	N	Y	Y
20 Gonzalez	Y	Y	Y	Y	Y
21 Smith	N	N	N	Y	Y
22 Olson	N	N	N	Y	Y
23 Rodriguez	Y	Y	Y	Y	Y
24 Marchant	N	N	N	Y	Y
25 Doggett	Y	Y	Y	Y	Y
26 Burgess	N	N	N	Y	Y
27 Ortiz	Y	Y	Y	Y	Y
28 Cuellar	Y	Y	Y	Y	Y
29 Green, G.	Y	Y	Y	Y	Y
30 Johnson, E.	Y	Y	Y	Y	Y
31 Carter	N	N	N	?	Y
32 Sessions	N	N	N	Y	Y
UTAH					
1 Bishop	N	N	N	Y	Y
2 Matheson	Y	N	N	Y	Y
3 Chaffetz	N	N	N	Y	N
VERMONT					
AL Welch	P	Y	Y	Y	Y
VIRGINIA					
1 Wittman	N	N	N	Y	Y
2 Nye	Y	?	Y	Y	Y
3 Scott	Y	Y	Y	Y	Y
4 Forbes	N	N	N	Y	Y
5 Perriello	?	?	?	?	?
6 Goodlatte	N	N	N	Y	Y
7 Cantor	N	N	N	Y	Y
8 Moran	Y	Y	Y	Y	Y
9 Boucher	?	?	?	?	Y
10 Wolf	N	N	N	Y	Y
11 Connolly	Y	Y	Y	Y	Y
WASHINGTON					
1 Inslee	Y	Y	Y	Y	Y
2 Larsen	Y	Y	Y	Y	Y
3 Baird	Y	Y	Y	Y	Y
4 Hastings	P	N	N	Y	Y
5 McMorris Rodgers	N	N	N	Y	Y
6 Dicks	Y	Y	Y	Y	Y
7 McDermott	Y	Y	Y	Y	Y
8 Reichert	N	N	N	Y	Y
9 Smith	Y	Y	Y	Y	Y
WEST VIRGINIA					
1 Mollohan	Y	Y	Y	Y	Y
2 Capito	N	N	N	Y	Y
3 Rahall	Y	Y	Y	Y	Y
WISCONSIN					
1 Ryan	N	N	N	Y	Y
2 Baldwin	Y	Y	Y	Y	Y
3 Kind	N	Y	Y	Y	Y
4 Moore	Y	Y	Y	Y	Y
5 Sensenbrenner	N	N	N	Y	Y
6 Petri	N	N	N	Y	Y
7 Obey	Y	Y	Y	Y	Y
8 Kagen	Y	Y	Y	Y	Y
WYOMING					
AL Lummis	N	N	N	Y	N
DELEGATES					
Faleomavaega (A.S.)					
Norton (D.C.)					
Bordallo (Guam)					
Sablan (N. Marianas)					
Pierluisi (P.R.)					
Christensen (V.I.)					

IN THE HOUSE | By Vote Number

92. HR 548. Civil War Battlefields Grant Program/Passage.
Holt, D-N.J., motion to suspend the rules and pass the bill that would authorize $10 million annually in fiscal 2009-13 for matching grants to aid states and localities in acquiring lands to preserve Civil War battlefields. Motion agreed to 402-13: R 157-13; D 245-0. A two-thirds majority of those present and voting (277 in this case) is required for passage under suspension of the rules. March 3, 2009.

93. H Res 77. University of Mary Washington Tribute/Adoption.
Polis, D-Colo., motion to suspend the rules and adopt the resolution that would congratulate the University of Mary Washington in Fredericksburg, Va., for more than 100 years of leadership and service. Motion agreed to 414-0: R 169-0; D 245-0. A two-thirds majority of those present and voting (276 in this case) is required for adoption under suspension of the rules. March 3, 2009.

94. H Res 201. Tribute to Beverly Eckert/Adoption.
Pascrell, D-N.J., motion to suspend the rules and adopt the resolution that would recognize Beverly Eckert's service to the nation and particularly to survivors and families of those who died in the Sept. 11, 2001, terrorist attacks. Eckert died in the February crash of Continental Connection Flight 3407 near Buffalo, N.Y. Motion agreed to 419-0: R 173-0; D 246-0. A two-thirds majority of those present and voting (280 in this case) is required for adoption under suspension of the rules. March 4, 2009.

95. H Res 195. Tribute to Homeland Security Employees/Adoption.
Carney, D-Pa., motion to suspend the rules and adopt the resolution that would honor the employees of the Department of Homeland Security on the agency's sixth anniversary for their efforts to keep the United States safe. Motion agreed to 418-0: R 173-0; D 245-0. A two-thirds majority of those present and voting (279 in this case) is required for adoption under suspension of the rules. March 4, 2009.

96. H Res 45. Criminal Justice Month/Adoption.
Lofgren, D-Calif., motion to suspend the rules and adopt the resolution that would express the sense of the House that National Criminal Justice Month provides an opportunity to educate Americans about the criminal justice system. Motion agreed to 415-0: R 172-0; D 243-0. A two-thirds majority of those present and voting (277 in this case) is required for adoption under suspension of the rules. March 4, 2009.

	92	93	94	95	96
ALABAMA					
1 **Bonner**	Y	Y	Y	Y	Y
2 Bright	Y	Y	Y	Y	Y
3 **Rogers**	Y	Y	Y	Y	Y
4 **Aderholt**	Y	Y	Y	Y	Y
5 Griffith	Y	Y	Y	Y	Y
6 **Bachus**	Y	Y	Y	Y	Y
7 Davis	Y	Y	Y	Y	Y
ALASKA					
AL **Young**	Y	Y	Y	Y	Y
ARIZONA					
1 Kirkpatrick	Y	Y	Y	Y	Y
2 **Franks**	N	Y	Y	Y	Y
3 **Shadegg**	N	Y	Y	Y	Y
4 Pastor	Y	Y	Y	Y	Y
5 Mitchell	Y	Y	Y	Y	Y
6 **Flake**	N	Y	Y	Y	Y
7 Grijalva	Y	Y	Y	Y	Y
8 Giffords	Y	Y	Y	Y	Y
ARKANSAS					
1 Berry	Y	Y	Y	Y	Y
2 Snyder	?	?	Y	Y	Y
3 **Boozman**	Y	Y	Y	Y	Y
4 Ross	Y	Y	Y	Y	Y
CALIFORNIA					
1 Thompson	Y	Y	Y	Y	Y
2 **Herger**	Y	Y	Y	Y	Y
3 **Lungren**	Y	Y	Y	Y	Y
4 **McClintock**	Y	Y	Y	Y	Y
5 Matsui	Y	Y	Y	Y	Y
6 Woolsey	Y	Y	Y	Y	Y
7 Miller, George	Y	Y	Y	Y	Y
8 Pelosi					
9 Lee	Y	Y	Y	Y	Y
10 Tauscher	Y	Y	Y	Y	Y
11 McNerney	Y	Y	Y	Y	Y
12 Speier	?	?	?	?	?
13 Stark	?	?	?	?	?
14 Eshoo	Y	Y	Y	Y	Y
15 Honda	Y	Y	Y	Y	Y
16 Lofgren	Y	Y	Y	Y	Y
17 Farr	Y	Y	Y	Y	Y
18 Cardoza	Y	Y	Y	Y	Y
19 **Radanovich**	Y	Y	Y	Y	Y
20 Costa	Y	Y	Y	Y	Y
21 **Nunes**	Y	Y	Y	Y	Y
22 **McCarthy**	Y	Y	Y	Y	Y
23 Capps	Y	Y	Y	Y	Y
24 **Gallegly**	Y	Y	Y	Y	Y
25 **McKeon**	Y	Y	Y	Y	Y
26 **Dreier**	Y	Y	Y	Y	Y
27 Sherman	Y	Y	Y	Y	Y
28 Berman	Y	Y	Y	Y	Y
29 Schiff	Y	Y	Y	Y	Y
30 Waxman	Y	Y	Y	Y	Y
31 Becerra	Y	Y	Y	Y	Y
32 Vacant					
33 Watson	Y	Y	Y	Y	Y
34 Roybal-Allard	Y	Y	Y	Y	Y
35 Waters	Y	Y	Y	Y	Y
36 Harman	Y	Y	Y	Y	Y
37 Richardson	Y	Y	Y	Y	Y
38 Napolitano	Y	Y	Y	Y	Y
39 Sánchez, Linda	Y	Y	Y	Y	Y
40 **Royce**	N	Y	Y	Y	Y
41 **Lewis**	Y	Y	Y	Y	Y
42 **Miller, Gary**	?	?	?	?	?
43 Baca	?	?	Y	Y	Y
44 **Calvert**	Y	Y	Y	Y	Y
45 **Bono Mack**	Y	Y	Y	Y	Y
46 **Rohrabacher**	N	Y	Y	Y	Y
47 Sanchez, Loretta	Y	Y	Y	Y	Y
48 **Campbell**	+	+	+	+	+
49 **Issa**	Y	Y	Y	Y	Y
50 **Bilbray**	Y	Y	Y	Y	Y
51 Filner	Y	Y	Y	Y	Y
52 **Hunter**	Y	Y	Y	Y	Y
53 Davis	Y	Y	Y	Y	Y

	92	93	94	95	96
COLORADO					
1 DeGette	Y	Y	Y	Y	Y
2 Polis	Y	Y	Y	Y	Y
3 Salazar	Y	Y	Y	Y	Y
4 Markey	Y	Y	Y	Y	Y
5 **Lamborn**	Y	Y	Y	Y	Y
6 **Coffman**	Y	Y	Y	Y	Y
7 Perlmutter	+	Y	Y	Y	Y
CONNECTICUT					
1 Larson	Y	Y	Y	+	+
2 Courtney	Y	Y	Y	Y	Y
3 DeLauro	Y	Y	Y	Y	Y
4 Himes	Y	Y	Y	Y	Y
5 Murphy	Y	Y	Y	Y	Y
DELAWARE					
AL **Castle**	Y	Y	Y	Y	Y
FLORIDA					
1 **Miller**	Y	Y	Y	Y	Y
2 Boyd	Y	Y	+	+	+
3 Brown	?	?	Y	Y	Y
4 **Crenshaw**	Y	Y	Y	Y	Y
5 **Brown-Waite**	Y	Y	Y	Y	Y
6 **Stearns**	Y	Y	Y	Y	Y
7 **Mica**	Y	Y	Y	Y	Y
8 Grayson	Y	Y	Y	Y	Y
9 **Bilirakis**	Y	Y	Y	Y	Y
10 **Young**	?	?	Y	Y	Y
11 Castor	Y	Y	Y	Y	Y
12 **Putnam**	+	+	+	+	+
13 **Buchanan**	?	?	Y	Y	Y
14 **Mack**	Y	Y	Y	Y	Y
15 **Posey**	Y	Y	Y	Y	Y
16 **Rooney**	Y	Y	Y	Y	Y
17 Meek	Y	Y	Y	Y	Y
18 **Ros-Lehtinen**	?	?	Y	Y	Y
19 Wexler	Y	Y	Y	Y	Y
20 Wasserman Schultz	Y	Y	Y	Y	Y
21 **Diaz-Balart, L.**	Y	Y	Y	Y	Y
22 Klein	Y	Y	Y	Y	Y
23 Hastings	Y	Y	Y	Y	Y
24 Kosmas	Y	Y	Y	Y	Y
25 **Diaz-Balart, M.**	Y	Y	Y	Y	Y
GEORGIA					
1 **Kingston**	Y	Y	Y	Y	Y
2 Bishop	Y	Y	Y	Y	Y
3 **Westmoreland**	Y	Y	Y	Y	Y
4 Johnson	Y	Y	Y	Y	Y
5 Lewis	Y	Y	Y	Y	Y
6 **Price**	Y	Y	Y	Y	Y
7 **Linder**	Y	Y	Y	Y	Y
8 Marshall	Y	Y	Y	Y	Y
9 **Deal**	Y	Y	Y	Y	Y
10 **Broun**	N	Y	Y	Y	Y
11 **Gingrey**	Y	Y	Y	Y	Y
12 Barrow	Y	Y	Y	Y	Y
13 Scott	Y	Y	Y	Y	Y
HAWAII					
1 Abercrombie	Y	Y	Y	Y	Y
2 Hirono	Y	Y	Y	Y	Y
IDAHO					
1 Minnick	Y	Y	Y	Y	Y
2 **Simpson**	Y	Y	Y	Y	Y
ILLINOIS					
1 Rush	Y	Y	Y	Y	Y
2 Jackson	Y	Y	Y	Y	Y
3 Lipinski	Y	Y	Y	Y	Y
4 Gutierrez	Y	Y	Y	Y	Y
5 Vacant					
6 **Roskam**	Y	Y	Y	Y	Y
7 Davis	Y	Y	?	?	?
8 Bean	Y	Y	Y	Y	Y
9 Schakowsky	Y	Y	Y	Y	Y
10 **Kirk**	Y	Y	Y	Y	Y
11 Halvorson	Y	Y	Y	Y	Y
12 Costello	Y	Y	Y	Y	Y
13 **Biggert**	Y	Y	Y	Y	Y
14 Foster	Y	Y	Y	Y	Y
15 Johnson	Y	Y	Y	Y	Y

	92	93	94	95	96
16 Manzullo	N	Y	Y	Y	Y
17 Hare	Y	Y	Y	Y	Y
18 **Schock**	Y	Y	Y	Y	Y
19 **Shimkus**	Y	Y	Y	Y	Y
INDIANA					
1 Visclosky	Y	Y	Y	Y	Y
2 Donnelly	Y	Y	Y	Y	Y
3 **Souder**	Y	Y	Y	Y	Y
4 **Buyer**	Y	Y	Y	Y	Y
5 **Burton**	Y	Y	Y	Y	Y
6 **Pence**	Y	Y	Y	Y	Y
7 Carson	Y	Y	Y	Y	Y
8 Ellsworth	Y	Y	Y	Y	Y
9 Hill	Y	Y	Y	Y	Y
IOWA					
1 Braley	Y	Y	Y	Y	Y
2 Loebsack	Y	Y	Y	Y	Y
3 Boswell	Y	Y	Y	Y	Y
4 **Latham**	Y	Y	Y	Y	Y
5 **King**	+	+	Y	Y	Y
KANSAS					
1 **Moran**	Y	Y	Y	Y	Y
2 **Jenkins**	N	Y	Y	Y	Y
3 Moore	Y	Y	Y	Y	Y
4 **Tiahrt**	N	Y	Y	Y	Y
KENTUCKY					
1 **Whitfield**	Y	Y	Y	Y	Y
2 **Guthrie**	Y	Y	Y	Y	Y
3 Yarmuth	Y	Y	Y	Y	Y
4 **Davis**	Y	Y	Y	Y	Y
5 **Rogers**	Y	Y	Y	Y	Y
6 Chandler	Y	Y	Y	Y	Y
LOUISIANA					
1 **Scalise**	Y	Y	Y	Y	Y
2 **Cao**	Y	Y	Y	Y	Y
3 Melancon	Y	Y	Y	Y	Y
4 **Fleming**	Y	Y	Y	Y	Y
5 **Alexander**	Y	Y	Y	Y	Y
6 **Cassidy**	Y	Y	Y	Y	Y
7 **Boustany**	Y	Y	Y	Y	Y
MAINE					
1 Pingree	Y	Y	Y	Y	Y
2 Michaud	Y	Y	Y	Y	Y
MARYLAND					
1 Kratovil	Y	Y	Y	Y	Y
2 Ruppersberger	Y	Y	Y	Y	Y
3 Sarbanes	Y	Y	Y	Y	Y
4 Edwards	Y	Y	Y	Y	Y
5 Hoyer	Y	Y	Y	Y	Y
6 **Bartlett**	Y	Y	Y	Y	Y
7 Cummings	Y	Y	Y	Y	Y
8 Van Hollen	Y	Y	Y	Y	Y
MASSACHUSETTS					
1 Olver	Y	Y	Y	Y	Y
2 Neal	Y	Y	Y	Y	Y
3 McGovern	Y	Y	Y	Y	Y
4 Frank	Y	Y	Y	Y	Y
5 Tsongas	Y	Y	Y	Y	Y
6 Tierney	Y	Y	Y	Y	Y
7 Markey	Y	Y	Y	Y	Y
8 Capuano	Y	Y	Y	Y	?
9 Lynch	Y	Y	Y	Y	Y
10 Delahunt	Y	Y	Y	Y	Y
MICHIGAN					
1 Stupak	Y	Y	Y	Y	Y
2 **Hoekstra**	Y	Y	Y	Y	Y
3 **Ehlers**	+	+	+	+	+
4 **Camp**	Y	Y	Y	Y	Y
5 Kildee	Y	Y	Y	Y	Y
6 **Upton**	Y	Y	Y	Y	Y
7 Schauer	Y	Y	Y	Y	Y
8 **Rogers**	Y	Y	Y	Y	?
9 Peters	Y	Y	Y	Y	Y
10 **Miller**	Y	Y	Y	Y	Y
11 **McCotter**	Y	Y	Y	Y	Y
12 Levin	Y	Y	Y	Y	Y
13 Kilpatrick	Y	Y	Y	Y	Y
14 Conyers	Y	Y	Y	Y	Y
15 Dingell	Y	Y	Y	Y	Y
MINNESOTA					
1 Walz	Y	Y	Y	Y	Y
2 **Kline**	Y	Y	Y	Y	Y
3 **Paulsen**	Y	Y	?	?	?
4 McCollum	Y	Y	?	?	?

	92	93	94	95	96
5 Ellison	?	?	Y	Y	Y
6 **Bachmann**	Y	Y	Y	Y	Y
7 Peterson	Y	Y	Y	Y	Y
8 Oberstar	Y	Y	Y	Y	Y
MISSISSIPPI					
1 Childers	Y	Y	Y	Y	Y
2 Thompson	Y	Y	Y	Y	Y
3 **Harper**	Y	Y	Y	Y	Y
4 Taylor	Y	Y	Y	Y	Y
MISSOURI					
1 Clay	Y	Y	Y	Y	Y
2 **Akin**	Y	Y	Y	Y	Y
3 Carnahan	Y	Y	Y	Y	Y
4 Skelton	Y	Y	Y	Y	Y
5 Cleaver	Y	Y	Y	Y	Y
6 **Graves**	Y	Y	Y	Y	Y
7 **Blunt**	Y	Y	Y	Y	Y
8 **Emerson**	Y	Y	Y	Y	Y
9 **Luetkemeyer**	Y	Y	Y	Y	Y
MONTANA					
AL **Rehberg**	Y	Y	Y	Y	Y
NEBRASKA					
1 **Fortenberry**	Y	Y	Y	Y	Y
2 **Terry**	Y	Y	Y	Y	Y
3 **Smith**	Y	Y	Y	Y	Y
NEVADA					
1 Berkley	Y	Y	Y	Y	Y
2 **Heller**	Y	Y	Y	Y	Y
3 Titus	Y	Y	Y	Y	Y
NEW HAMPSHIRE					
1 Shea-Porter	Y	Y	Y	Y	Y
2 Hodes	Y	Y	Y	Y	Y
NEW JERSEY					
1 Andrews	Y	Y	Y	Y	Y
2 **LoBiondo**	Y	Y	Y	Y	Y
3 Adler	Y	Y	Y	Y	Y
4 **Smith**	Y	Y	Y	Y	Y
5 **Garrett**	Y	Y	?	?	?
6 Pallone	Y	Y	Y	Y	Y
7 **Lance**	Y	Y	Y	Y	Y
8 Pascrell	Y	Y	Y	Y	Y
9 Rothman	Y	Y	Y	Y	Y
10 Payne	Y	Y	Y	Y	Y
11 **Frelinghuysen**	Y	Y	Y	Y	Y
12 Holt	Y	Y	Y	Y	Y
13 Sires	Y	Y	Y	Y	Y
NEW MEXICO					
1 Heinrich	Y	Y	Y	Y	Y
2 Teague	Y	Y	Y	Y	Y
3 Lujan	Y	Y	Y	Y	Y
NEW YORK					
1 Bishop	Y	Y	Y	Y	Y
2 Israel	Y	Y	Y	Y	Y
3 **King**	Y	Y	Y	Y	Y
4 McCarthy	Y	Y	Y	Y	Y
5 Ackerman	Y	Y	Y	Y	Y
6 Meeks	Y	Y	Y	Y	Y
7 Crowley	Y	Y	Y	Y	Y
8 Nadler	Y	Y	Y	Y	Y
9 Weiner	Y	Y	Y	Y	Y
10 Towns	Y	Y	Y	Y	Y
11 Clarke	Y	Y	Y	Y	Y
12 Velázquez	Y	Y	Y	Y	Y
13 McMahon	Y	Y	Y	Y	Y
14 Maloney	Y	Y	Y	Y	Y
15 Rangel	Y	Y	Y	Y	?
16 Serrano	Y	Y	Y	Y	Y
17 Engel	Y	Y	Y	Y	Y
18 Lowey	Y	Y	Y	Y	Y
19 Hall	Y	Y	+	+	+
20 Vacant					
21 Tonko	Y	Y	Y	Y	Y
22 Hinchey	Y	Y	Y	Y	Y
23 **McHugh**	Y	Y	Y	Y	Y
24 Arcuri	Y	Y	Y	Y	Y
25 Maffei	Y	Y	Y	Y	Y
26 **Lee**	Y	Y	Y	Y	Y
27 Higgins	Y	Y	Y	Y	Y
28 Slaughter	Y	Y	Y	Y	Y
29 Massa	Y	Y	Y	Y	Y
NORTH CAROLINA					
1 Butterfield	Y	Y	Y	Y	Y
2 Etheridge	Y	Y	Y	Y	Y
3 **Jones**	Y	Y	Y	Y	Y
4 Price	Y	Y	Y	Y	Y

	92	93	94	95	96
5 **Foxx**	Y	Y	Y	Y	Y
6 **Coble**	Y	Y	Y	Y	Y
7 McIntyre	Y	Y	Y	Y	Y
8 Kissell	Y	Y	Y	Y	Y
9 **Myrick**	Y	Y	Y	Y	Y
10 **McHenry**	Y	?	Y	Y	Y
11 Shuler	Y	Y	Y	Y	Y
12 Watt	Y	Y	Y	Y	Y
13 Miller	Y	Y	Y	Y	Y
NORTH DAKOTA					
AL Pomeroy	Y	Y	Y	Y	Y
OHIO					
1 Driehaus	Y	Y	Y	Y	Y
2 **Schmidt**	Y	Y	Y	Y	Y
3 **Turner**	Y	Y	Y	Y	Y
4 **Jordan**	Y	Y	Y	Y	Y
5 **Latta**	Y	Y	Y	Y	Y
6 Wilson	Y	?	Y	Y	Y
7 **Austria**	Y	Y	Y	Y	Y
8 **Boehner**	Y	Y	Y	Y	Y
9 Kaptur	Y	Y	Y	Y	Y
10 Kucinich	Y	Y	Y	Y	Y
11 Fudge	Y	Y	Y	Y	Y
12 **Tiberi**	Y	Y	Y	Y	Y
13 Sutton	Y	Y	Y	Y	Y
14 **LaTourette**	Y	Y	Y	Y	Y
15 Kilroy	Y	Y	Y	Y	Y
16 Boccieri	Y	Y	Y	Y	Y
17 Ryan	Y	Y	Y	Y	Y
18 Space	Y	Y	Y	Y	Y
OKLAHOMA					
1 **Sullivan**	Y	Y	Y	Y	Y
2 Boren	Y	Y	Y	Y	Y
3 **Lucas**	Y	Y	Y	Y	Y
4 **Cole**	Y	Y	Y	Y	Y
5 **Fallin**	Y	Y	Y	Y	Y
OREGON					
1 Wu	Y	Y	Y	Y	Y
2 **Walden**	Y	Y	Y	Y	Y
3 Blumenauer	Y	Y	Y	Y	Y
4 DeFazio	Y	Y	Y	Y	Y
5 Schrader	Y	Y	Y	Y	Y
PENNSYLVANIA					
1 Brady	Y	Y	Y	Y	Y
2 Fattah	Y	Y	Y	Y	Y
3 Dahlkemper	Y	Y	Y	Y	Y
4 Altmire	Y	Y	Y	Y	Y
5 **Thompson**	Y	Y	Y	Y	Y
6 **Gerlach**	Y	Y	Y	Y	Y
7 Sestak	Y	Y	Y	Y	Y
8 Murphy, P.	Y	Y	Y	Y	Y
9 **Shuster**	Y	Y	Y	Y	Y
10 Carney	Y	Y	Y	Y	Y
11 Kanjorski	Y	Y	Y	Y	Y
12 Murtha	Y	Y	Y	Y	Y
13 Schwartz	Y	Y	Y	Y	Y
14 Doyle	Y	Y	Y	Y	Y
15 **Dent**	Y	Y	Y	Y	Y
16 **Pitts**	Y	Y	Y	Y	Y
17 Holden	Y	Y	Y	Y	Y
18 **Murphy, T.**	Y	Y	Y	Y	Y
19 **Platts**	Y	Y	Y	Y	Y
RHODE ISLAND					
1 Kennedy	Y	Y	Y	Y	Y
2 Langevin	Y	Y	Y	Y	Y
SOUTH CAROLINA					
1 **Brown**	Y	Y	Y	Y	Y
2 **Wilson**	Y	Y	Y	Y	Y
3 **Barrett**	Y	Y	Y	Y	Y
4 **Inglis**	Y	Y	Y	Y	Y
5 Spratt	Y	Y	Y	Y	Y
6 Clyburn	Y	Y	Y	Y	Y
SOUTH DAKOTA					
AL Herseth Sandlin	Y	Y	Y	Y	Y
TENNESSEE					
1 **Roe**	Y	Y	Y	Y	Y
2 **Duncan**	N	Y	Y	Y	Y
3 **Wamp**	Y	Y	Y	Y	Y
4 Davis	Y	Y	Y	Y	Y
5 Cooper	Y	Y	Y	Y	Y
6 Gordon	Y	Y	Y	Y	Y
7 **Blackburn**	Y	Y	Y	Y	Y
8 Tanner	Y	Y	Y	Y	Y
9 Cohen	Y	Y	Y	Y	Y

	92	93	94	95	96
TEXAS					
1 **Gohmert**	Y	Y	Y	Y	Y
2 **Poe**	Y	Y	Y	Y	Y
3 **Johnson, S.**	Y	Y	Y	Y	Y
4 **Hall**	Y	Y	Y	Y	Y
5 **Hensarling**	Y	Y	Y	Y	Y
6 **Barton**	Y	Y	Y	Y	Y
7 **Culberson**	Y	Y	Y	Y	Y
8 **Brady**	Y	Y	Y	Y	Y
9 Green, A.	Y	Y	Y	Y	Y
10 **McCaul**	Y	Y	Y	Y	Y
11 **Conaway**	Y	Y	Y	Y	Y
12 **Granger**	Y	Y	Y	Y	Y
13 **Thornberry**	Y	Y	Y	Y	Y
14 **Paul**	N	Y	Y	Y	Y
15 Hinojosa	Y	Y	Y	Y	Y
16 Reyes	Y	Y	Y	Y	Y
17 Edwards	Y	Y	Y	Y	Y
18 Jackson Lee	Y	Y	Y	Y	Y
19 **Neugebauer**	Y	Y	Y	Y	Y
20 Gonzalez	Y	Y	Y	Y	Y
21 **Smith**	Y	Y	Y	Y	Y
22 **Olson**	Y	Y	Y	Y	Y
23 Rodriguez	Y	Y	Y	Y	Y
24 **Marchant**	Y	Y	Y	Y	Y
25 Doggett	Y	Y	Y	Y	Y
26 **Burgess**	Y	Y	Y	Y	Y
27 Ortiz	Y	Y	Y	Y	Y
28 Cuellar	Y	Y	Y	Y	Y
29 Green, G.	Y	Y	Y	Y	Y
30 Johnson, E.	Y	Y	Y	Y	Y
31 **Carter**	Y	Y	Y	Y	Y
32 **Sessions**	Y	Y	Y	Y	Y
UTAH					
1 **Bishop**	Y	Y	Y	Y	Y
2 Matheson	Y	Y	Y	Y	Y
3 **Chaffetz**	N	Y	Y	Y	Y
VERMONT					
AL Welch	Y	Y	Y	Y	Y
VIRGINIA					
1 **Wittman**	Y	Y	Y	Y	Y
2 Nye	Y	Y	Y	Y	Y
3 Scott	Y	Y	Y	Y	Y
4 **Forbes**	Y	Y	Y	Y	Y
5 Perriello	?	?	?	?	?
6 **Goodlatte**	Y	Y	Y	Y	Y
7 **Cantor**	Y	Y	Y	Y	Y
8 Moran	Y	Y	Y	Y	Y
9 Boucher	Y	Y	Y	Y	Y
10 **Wolf**	Y	Y	Y	Y	Y
11 Connolly	Y	Y	Y	Y	Y
WASHINGTON					
1 Inslee	Y	Y	Y	Y	Y
2 Larsen	Y	Y	Y	Y	Y
3 Baird	Y	Y	Y	Y	Y
4 **Hastings**	Y	Y	Y	Y	Y
5 **McMorris Rodgers**	Y	Y	Y	Y	Y
6 Dicks	Y	Y	Y	Y	Y
7 McDermott	Y	Y	Y	Y	Y
8 **Reichert**	Y	Y	Y	Y	Y
9 Smith	Y	Y	Y	Y	Y
WEST VIRGINIA					
1 Mollohan	Y	Y	Y	Y	Y
2 **Capito**	Y	Y	Y	Y	Y
3 Rahall	Y	Y	Y	Y	Y
WISCONSIN					
1 **Ryan**	Y	Y	Y	Y	Y
2 Baldwin	Y	Y	Y	Y	Y
3 Kind	Y	Y	Y	Y	Y
4 Moore	Y	Y	Y	Y	Y
5 **Sensenbrenner**	Y	Y	Y	Y	Y
6 **Petri**	Y	Y	Y	Y	Y
7 Obey	Y	Y	Y	Y	Y
8 Kagen	Y	Y	Y	Y	Y
WYOMING					
AL **Lummis**	N	Y	Y	Y	Y
DELEGATES					
Faleomavaega (A.S.)					
Norton (D.C.)					
Bordallo (Guam)					
Sablan (N. Marianas)					
Pierluisi (P.R.)					
Christensen (V.I.)					

IN THE HOUSE | By Vote Number

97. HR 1106. Mortgage Loans Modification/Rule.
Adoption of the rule (H Res 205) that would provide for House floor consideration of the bill that would allow bankruptcy judges to write down the principal and interest rates of loans for people whose mortgages are larger than the value of their homes. The rule contains self-executing language that upon adoption would modify the amendment made by a previously adopted rule. Adopted 239-181: R 0-174; D 239-7. March 5, 2009.

98. H Res 146. Read Across America Day/Adoption.
Polis, D-Colo., motion to suspend the rules and adopt the resolution that would honor Theodor Geisel, also known as Dr. Seuss, for his success in encouraging children to discover the joy of reading. The resolution also would commemorate the 12th anniversary of Read Across America Day on March 2. Motion agreed to 417-0: R 174-0; D 243-0. A two-thirds majority of those present and voting (278 in this case) is required for adoption under suspension of the rules. March 5, 2009.

99. H Con Res 14. Multiple Sclerosis Awareness Week/Adoption.
Capps, D-Calif., motion to suspend the rules and adopt the concurrent resolution that would support the goals and ideals of Multiple Sclerosis Awareness Week and recognize Americans who have multiple sclerosis. Motion agreed to 416-0: R 174-0; D 242-0. A two-thirds majority of those present and voting (278 in this case) is required for adoption under suspension of the rules. March 5, 2009.

100. HR 1106. Mortgage Loans Modification/Eligibility Standards.
Lofgren, D-Calif., amendment that would make individuals who can afford to repay their mortgages without judicial modification ineligible for loan relief, allow a bank to recover a higher percentage of funds if the homeowner sells the home for a profit, and require debtors to certify that they contacted a lender, provided proper statements and sought an agreement on a qualified loan modification. It would also require bankruptcy courts to use Federal Housing Administration appraisal guidelines when the fair-market value of a home is disputed and allow courts to lower an individual's interest rate instead of reducing mortgage principal. Adopted in Committee of the Whole 263-164: R 10-164; D 253-0. March 5, 2009.

101. HR 1106. Mortgage Loans Modification/Loss Recapture.
Price, R-Ga., amendment that would allow lenders to recapture funds up to the amount of principal lost in a mortgage modification if a homeowner sells the home at a profit. Rejected in Committee of the Whole 211-218: R 174-0; D 37-218. March 5, 2009.

	97	98	99	100	101
ALABAMA					
1 **Bonner**	N	Y	Y	N	Y
2 Bright	Y	Y	Y	Y	N
3 **Rogers**	N	Y	Y	N	Y
4 **Aderholt**	N	Y	Y	N	Y
5 Griffith	Y	Y	Y	Y	Y
6 **Bachus**	N	Y	Y	N	Y
7 Davis	Y	Y	Y	Y	Y
ALASKA					
AL **Young**	N	Y	Y	N	Y
ARIZONA					
1 Kirkpatrick	Y	Y	Y	Y	N
2 **Franks**	N	Y	Y	N	Y
3 **Shadegg**	N	Y	Y	N	Y
4 Pastor	Y	Y	Y	Y	N
5 Mitchell	Y	Y	Y	Y	Y
6 **Flake**	N	Y	Y	N	Y
7 Grijalva	Y	Y	Y	Y	N
8 Giffords	Y	Y	Y	Y	Y
ARKANSAS					
1 Berry	N	Y	Y	Y	Y
2 Snyder	Y	Y	Y	Y	N
3 **Boozman**	N	Y	Y	N	Y
4 Ross	Y	Y	Y	Y	N
CALIFORNIA					
1 Thompson	Y	Y	Y	Y	N
2 **Herger**	N	Y	Y	N	Y
3 **Lungren**	N	Y	Y	N	Y
4 **McClintock**	N	Y	Y	N	Y
5 Matsui	Y	Y	Y	Y	N
6 Woolsey	Y	Y	Y	Y	N
7 Miller, George	Y	+	+	Y	N
8 Pelosi					
9 Lee	Y	Y	Y	Y	N
10 Tauscher	Y	Y	Y	Y	N
11 McNerney	Y	Y	Y	Y	N
12 Speier	?	?	?	Y	N
13 Stark	?	?	?	?	?
14 Eshoo	Y	Y	Y	Y	N
15 Honda	Y	Y	Y	Y	N
16 Lofgren	Y	Y	Y	Y	N
17 Farr	Y	Y	Y	Y	N
18 Cardoza	Y	Y	Y	Y	N
19 **Radanovich**	N	Y	Y	N	Y
20 Costa	Y	Y	Y	Y	N
21 **Nunes**	N	Y	Y	N	Y
22 **McCarthy**	N	Y	Y	N	Y
23 Capps	Y	Y	Y	Y	N
24 **Gallegly**	N	Y	Y	N	Y
25 **McKeon**	N	?	?	N	Y
26 **Dreier**	N	Y	Y	N	Y
27 Sherman	Y	Y	Y	Y	N
28 Berman	Y	Y	Y	Y	N
29 Schiff	Y	Y	Y	Y	N
30 Waxman	Y	Y	Y	Y	N
31 Becerra	Y	Y	Y	Y	N
32 Vacant					
33 Watson	Y	Y	Y	Y	N
34 Roybal-Allard	Y	Y	Y	Y	N
35 Waters	Y	Y	Y	Y	N
36 Harman	Y	Y	Y	Y	N
37 Richardson	Y	Y	Y	Y	N
38 Napolitano	Y	Y	Y	Y	N
39 Sánchez, Linda	Y	Y	Y	Y	N
40 **Royce**	N	Y	Y	N	Y
41 **Lewis**	N	Y	Y	N	Y
42 **Miller, Gary**	?	?	?	?	?
43 Baca	Y	Y	Y	Y	N
44 **Calvert**	N	Y	Y	N	Y
45 **Bono Mack**	N	Y	Y	N	Y
46 **Rohrabacher**	N	Y	Y	N	Y
47 Sanchez, Loretta	Y	Y	Y	Y	N
48 **Campbell**	N	Y	Y	N	Y
49 **Issa**	N	Y	Y	N	Y
50 **Bilbray**	N	Y	Y	N	Y
51 Filner	Y	Y	Y	Y	N
52 **Hunter**	N	Y	Y	N	Y
53 Davis	Y	Y	Y	Y	N

	97	98	99	100	101
COLORADO					
1 DeGette	Y	Y	Y	Y	N
2 Polis	Y	Y	Y	Y	N
3 Salazar	Y	Y	Y	Y	N
4 Markey	Y	Y	Y	Y	N
5 **Lamborn**	N	Y	Y	N	Y
6 **Coffman**	N	Y	Y	?	?
7 Perlmutter	Y	Y	Y	Y	N
CONNECTICUT					
1 Larson	Y	Y	Y	Y	N
2 Courtney	Y	Y	Y	Y	N
3 DeLauro	Y	Y	Y	Y	N
4 Himes	Y	Y	Y	Y	Y
5 Murphy	Y	Y	Y	Y	Y
DELAWARE					
AL **Castle**	N	Y	Y	Y	Y
FLORIDA					
1 **Miller**	N	Y	Y	N	Y
2 Boyd	Y	Y	Y	Y	N
3 Brown	Y	Y	Y	Y	N
4 **Crenshaw**	N	Y	Y	N	Y
5 **Brown-Waite**	N	Y	Y	N	Y
6 **Stearns**	N	Y	Y	N	Y
7 **Mica**	N	Y	Y	N	Y
8 Grayson	Y	Y	Y	Y	N
9 **Bilirakis**	N	Y	Y	N	Y
10 **Young**	N	Y	Y	N	Y
11 Castor	Y	Y	Y	Y	N
12 **Putnam**	N	Y	Y	N	Y
13 **Buchanan**	N	Y	Y	N	Y
14 **Mack**	N	Y	Y	N	Y
15 **Posey**	N	Y	Y	N	Y
16 **Rooney**	N	Y	Y	N	Y
17 Meek	Y	Y	Y	Y	N
18 **Ros-Lehtinen**	N	Y	Y	Y	N
19 Wexler	Y	Y	Y	Y	N
20 Wasserman Schultz	Y	Y	Y	Y	N
21 **Diaz-Balart, L.**	N	Y	Y	Y	Y
22 Klein	Y	Y	Y	Y	N
23 Hastings	Y	Y	Y	Y	N
24 Kosmas	Y	Y	Y	Y	N
25 **Diaz-Balart, M.**	N	Y	Y	N	Y
GEORGIA					
1 **Kingston**	N	Y	Y	N	Y
2 Bishop	Y	Y	Y	Y	N
3 **Westmoreland**	N	Y	Y	N	Y
4 Johnson	Y	Y	Y	Y	N
5 Lewis	Y	Y	Y	Y	N
6 **Price**	N	Y	Y	N	Y
7 **Linder**	N	Y	Y	N	Y
8 Marshall	Y	Y	Y	Y	N
9 **Deal**	N	Y	Y	N	Y
10 **Broun**	N	Y	Y	N	Y
11 **Gingrey**	N	Y	Y	N	Y
12 Barrow	Y	Y	Y	Y	Y
13 Scott	Y	Y	Y	Y	N
HAWAII					
1 Abercrombie	Y	Y	Y	Y	N
2 Hirono	Y	Y	Y	Y	N
IDAHO					
1 Minnick	N	Y	Y	Y	Y
2 **Simpson**	N	Y	Y	N	Y
ILLINOIS					
1 Rush	Y	?	Y	Y	N
2 Jackson	Y	Y	Y	Y	N
3 Lipinski	Y	Y	Y	Y	N
4 Gutierrez	Y	Y	?	Y	N
5 Vacant					
6 **Roskam**	N	Y	Y	N	Y
7 Davis	?	?	?	Y	N
8 Bean	Y	Y	Y	Y	Y
9 Schakowsky	Y	Y	Y	Y	N
10 **Kirk**	N	Y	Y	N	Y
11 Halvorson	Y	Y	Y	Y	N
12 Costello	Y	Y	Y	Y	N
13 **Biggert**	N	Y	Y	N	Y
14 Foster	Y	Y	Y	Y	Y
15 **Johnson**	N	Y	Y	N	Y

KEY	Republicans	Democrats		
Y Voted for (yea)		**X** Paired against		**C** Voted "present" to avoid possible conflict of interest
# Paired for		**–** Announced against		
+ Announced for		**P** Voted "present"		**?** Did not vote or otherwise make a position known
N Voted against (nay)				

* Del. Gregorio Kilili Camacho Sablan of the Northern Mariana Islands, who was elected in 2008 as an independent, informed the Speaker on Feb. 23 that he wished to list his party affiliation as Democrat. The first vote in the Committee of the Whole for which he asked to be counted with the Democrats is vote 100.

	97	98	99	100	101
16 Manzullo	N	Y	Y	N	Y
17 Hare	Y	Y	Y	Y	N
18 Schock	–	Y	Y	N	Y
19 Shimkus	N	Y	Y	N	Y
INDIANA					
1 Visclosky	Y	Y	Y	Y	N
2 Donnelly	Y	Y	Y	Y	Y
3 Souder	N	Y	Y	N	Y
4 Buyer	N	Y	Y	N	Y
5 Burton	N	Y	Y	N	Y
6 Pence	N	Y	Y	N	Y
7 Carson	Y	Y	Y	Y	N
8 Ellsworth	Y	Y	Y	Y	Y
9 Hill	N	Y	Y	Y	N
IOWA					
1 Braley	Y	Y	Y	Y	N
2 Loebsack	Y	Y	Y	Y	N
3 Boswell	Y	Y	Y	Y	N
4 Latham	N	Y	Y	N	Y
5 King	N	Y	Y	N	Y
KANSAS					
1 Moran	N	Y	Y	N	Y
2 Jenkins	N	Y	Y	N	Y
3 Moore	Y	Y	Y	Y	N
4 Tiahrt	N	Y	Y	N	Y
KENTUCKY					
1 Whitfield	N	Y	Y	N	Y
2 Guthrie	N	Y	Y	N	Y
3 Yarmuth	Y	Y	Y	Y	N
4 Davis	N	Y	Y	N	Y
5 Rogers	N	Y	Y	N	Y
6 Chandler	Y	Y	Y	Y	Y
LOUISIANA					
1 Scalise	N	Y	Y	N	Y
2 Cao	?	?	?	?	?
3 Melancon	?	?	?	?	?
4 Fleming	N	Y	Y	N	Y
5 Alexander	N	Y	Y	N	Y
6 Cassidy	N	Y	Y	N	Y
7 Boustany	N	Y	Y	N	Y
MAINE					
1 Pingree	Y	Y	Y	Y	N
2 Michaud	Y	Y	Y	Y	Y
MARYLAND					
1 Kratovil	Y	Y	Y	Y	Y
2 Ruppersberger	Y	Y	Y	Y	N
3 Sarbanes	Y	Y	Y	Y	N
4 Edwards	Y	Y	Y	Y	N
5 Hoyer	Y	Y	Y	Y	N
6 Bartlett	N	Y	Y	N	Y
7 Cummings	Y	Y	Y	Y	N
8 Van Hollen	Y	Y	Y	Y	N
MASSACHUSETTS					
1 Olver	Y	Y	Y	Y	N
2 Neal	Y	Y	Y	Y	N
3 McGovern	Y	Y	Y	Y	N
4 Frank	Y	Y	Y	Y	N
5 Tsongas	Y	Y	Y	Y	N
6 Tierney	Y	Y	Y	Y	N
7 Markey	Y	Y	Y	Y	N
8 Capuano	Y	Y	Y	Y	N
9 Lynch	Y	Y	Y	Y	N
10 Delahunt	Y	Y	Y	Y	N
MICHIGAN					
1 Stupak	Y	Y	Y	Y	N
2 Hoekstra	N	Y	Y	N	Y
3 Ehlers	?	?	?	?	?
4 Camp	N	Y	Y	N	Y
5 Kildee	Y	Y	Y	Y	N
6 Upton	N	Y	Y	Y	Y
7 Schauer	Y	Y	Y	Y	N
8 Rogers	N	Y	Y	N	Y
9 Peters	Y	Y	Y	Y	N
10 Miller	N	Y	Y	N	Y
11 McCotter	N	Y	Y	N	Y
12 Levin	Y	Y	Y	Y	N
13 Kilpatrick	Y	Y	Y	?	N
14 Conyers	Y	Y	Y	?	N
15 Dingell	Y	Y	Y	?	N
MINNESOTA					
1 Walz	Y	Y	Y	Y	N
2 Kline	N	Y	Y	N	Y
3 Paulsen	N	Y	Y	N	Y
4 McCollum	Y	Y	Y	Y	N

	97	98	99	100	101
5 Ellison	Y	Y	Y	Y	N
6 Bachmann	N	Y	Y	N	Y
7 Peterson	Y	Y	Y	Y	Y
8 Oberstar	Y	Y	Y	Y	N
MISSISSIPPI					
1 Childers	N	Y	Y	Y	Y
2 Thompson	Y	Y	Y	Y	N
3 Harper	N	Y	Y	N	Y
4 Taylor	Y	Y	Y	Y	Y
MISSOURI					
1 Clay	Y	Y	Y	Y	N
2 Akin	N	Y	Y	N	Y
3 Carnahan	Y	Y	Y	Y	N
4 Skelton	Y	Y	Y	Y	N
5 Cleaver	Y	?	Y	Y	N
6 Graves	N	Y	Y	N	Y
7 Blunt	N	Y	Y	N	Y
8 Emerson	N	Y	Y	N	Y
9 Luetkemeyer	N	Y	Y	N	Y
MONTANA					
AL Rehberg	N	Y	Y	N	Y
NEBRASKA					
1 Fortenberry	N	Y	Y	N	Y
2 Terry	N	Y	Y	N	Y
3 Smith	N	Y	Y	N	Y
NEVADA					
1 Berkley	Y	Y	Y	Y	N
2 Heller	N	Y	Y	N	Y
3 Titus	Y	Y	Y	Y	N
NEW HAMPSHIRE					
1 Shea-Porter	Y	Y	Y	Y	Y
2 Hodes	Y	Y	Y	Y	Y
NEW JERSEY					
1 Andrews	Y	Y	Y	Y	N
2 LoBiondo	N	Y	Y	N	Y
3 Adler	Y	Y	Y	Y	N
4 Smith	N	Y	Y	N	Y
5 Garrett	N	Y	Y	N	Y
6 Pallone	Y	Y	Y	Y	N
7 Lance	N	Y	Y	Y	Y
8 Pascrell	Y	Y	Y	Y	N
9 Rothman	Y	Y	Y	Y	N
10 Payne	Y	Y	Y	Y	N
11 Frelinghuysen	N	Y	Y	N	Y
12 Holt	Y	Y	Y	Y	N
13 Sires	Y	Y	Y	Y	N
NEW MEXICO					
1 Heinrich	Y	Y	Y	Y	Y
2 Teague	N	Y	Y	Y	Y
3 Lujan	Y	Y	Y	Y	N
NEW YORK					
1 Bishop	Y	Y	Y	Y	N
2 Israel	Y	Y	Y	Y	N
3 King	N	Y	Y	N	Y
4 McCarthy	Y	Y	Y	Y	N
5 Ackerman	Y	Y	Y	Y	N
6 Meeks	Y	Y	Y	Y	N
7 Crowley	Y	Y	Y	Y	N
8 Nadler	Y	Y	Y	Y	N
9 Weiner	Y	Y	Y	Y	N
10 Towns	Y	Y	Y	Y	N
11 Clarke	Y	Y	Y	Y	N
12 Velázquez	Y	Y	Y	Y	N
13 McMahon	Y	Y	Y	Y	N
14 Maloney	Y	Y	Y	Y	N
15 Rangel	Y	Y	Y	Y	N
16 Serrano	Y	Y	Y	Y	N
17 Engel	Y	Y	Y	Y	N
18 Lowey	Y	Y	Y	Y	N
19 Hall	Y	?	?	Y	N
20 Vacant					
21 Tonko	Y	Y	Y	Y	N
22 Hinchey	Y	Y	Y	Y	N
23 McHugh	N	Y	Y	Y	Y
24 Arcuri	Y	Y	Y	Y	Y
25 Maffei	Y	Y	Y	Y	N
26 Lee	N	Y	Y	N	Y
27 Higgins	Y	Y	Y	Y	N
28 Slaughter	Y	Y	Y	Y	N
29 Massa	Y	Y	Y	Y	N
NORTH CAROLINA					
1 Butterfield	Y	Y	Y	Y	N
2 Etheridge	Y	Y	Y	Y	N
3 Jones	N	Y	Y	Y	Y
4 Price	Y	Y	Y	Y	N

	97	98	99	100	101
5 Foxx	N	Y	Y	Y	Y
6 Coble	N	Y	Y	N	Y
7 McIntyre	Y	Y	Y	Y	Y
8 Kissell	Y	Y	Y	Y	N
9 Myrick	N	Y	Y	N	Y
10 McHenry	N	Y	Y	N	Y
11 Shuler	Y	Y	Y	Y	N
12 Watt	Y	Y	Y	Y	N
13 Miller	Y	Y	Y	Y	N
NORTH DAKOTA					
AL Pomeroy	Y	Y	Y	Y	N
OHIO					
1 Driehaus	Y	Y	Y	Y	N
2 Schmidt	N	Y	Y	N	Y
3 Turner	N	Y	Y	Y	Y
4 Jordan	N	Y	Y	N	Y
5 Latta	N	Y	Y	N	Y
6 Wilson	Y	Y	Y	Y	N
7 Austria	N	Y	Y	N	Y
8 Boehner	N	Y	Y	N	Y
9 Kaptur	P	Y	Y	Y	N
10 Kucinich	N	Y	Y	Y	N
11 Fudge	Y	Y	Y	Y	N
12 Tiberi	N	Y	Y	N	Y
13 Sutton	Y	Y	Y	Y	N
14 LaTourette	N	Y	Y	N	Y
15 Kilroy	Y	Y	Y	Y	N
16 Boccieri	Y	Y	Y	Y	N
17 Ryan	Y	Y	Y	Y	N
18 Space	Y	Y	Y	Y	N
OKLAHOMA					
1 Sullivan	N	Y	Y	N	Y
2 Boren	Y	Y	Y	Y	Y
3 Lucas	N	Y	Y	N	Y
4 Cole	N	Y	Y	N	Y
5 Fallin	N	Y	Y	N	Y
OREGON					
1 Wu	Y	Y	Y	Y	N
2 Walden	N	Y	Y	N	Y
3 Blumenauer	Y	Y	Y	Y	N
4 DeFazio	Y	Y	Y	Y	N
5 Schrader	Y	Y	Y	Y	N
PENNSYLVANIA					
1 Brady	Y	Y	Y	Y	N
2 Fattah	Y	Y	Y	Y	N
3 Dahlkemper	Y	Y	Y	Y	Y
4 Altmire	Y	Y	Y	Y	Y
5 Thompson	N	Y	Y	N	Y
6 Gerlach	N	Y	Y	N	Y
7 Sestak	Y	Y	Y	Y	N
8 Murphy, P.	Y	Y	Y	Y	N
9 Shuster	N	Y	Y	N	Y
10 Carney	Y	Y	Y	Y	N
11 Kanjorski	Y	Y	Y	Y	N
12 Murtha	Y	Y	Y	Y	N
13 Schwartz	Y	Y	Y	Y	N
14 Doyle	Y	Y	Y	Y	N
15 Dent	N	Y	Y	N	Y
16 Pitts	N	Y	Y	N	Y
17 Holden	Y	Y	Y	Y	N
18 Murphy, T.	N	Y	Y	N	Y
19 Platts	N	Y	Y	N	Y
RHODE ISLAND					
1 Kennedy	Y	Y	Y	Y	N
2 Langevin	Y	Y	Y	Y	N
SOUTH CAROLINA					
1 Brown	N	Y	Y	N	Y
2 Wilson	N	Y	Y	N	Y
3 Barrett	N	Y	Y	N	Y
4 Inglis	N	Y	Y	N	Y
5 Spratt	Y	Y	Y	Y	N
6 Clyburn	Y	Y	Y	Y	N
SOUTH DAKOTA					
AL Herseth Sandlin	Y	Y	Y	Y	N
TENNESSEE					
1 Roe	N	Y	Y	N	Y
2 Duncan	N	Y	Y	N	Y
3 Wamp	N	Y	Y	N	Y
4 Davis	Y	Y	Y	Y	N
5 Cooper	Y	Y	Y	Y	N
6 Gordon	Y	Y	Y	Y	N
7 Blackburn	N	Y	Y	N	Y
8 Tanner	Y	Y	Y	Y	N
9 Cohen	Y	Y	Y	Y	N

	97	98	99	100	101
TEXAS					
1 Gohmert	N	Y	Y	N	Y
2 Poe	N	Y	Y	N	Y
3 Johnson, S.	N	Y	Y	N	Y
4 Hall	N	Y	Y	N	Y
5 Hensarling	N	Y	Y	N	Y
6 Barton	N	Y	Y	N	Y
7 Culberson	N	Y	Y	N	Y
8 Brady	N	Y	Y	N	Y
9 Green, A.	Y	Y	Y	Y	N
10 McCaul	N	Y	Y	N	Y
11 Conaway	N	Y	Y	N	Y
12 Granger	N	Y	Y	N	Y
13 Thornberry	N	Y	Y	N	Y
14 Paul	N	Y	Y	N	Y
15 Hinojosa	?	?	?	Y	N
16 Reyes	Y	Y	Y	Y	N
17 Edwards	Y	Y	Y	Y	Y
18 Jackson Lee	Y	Y	Y	Y	N
19 Neugebauer	N	Y	Y	N	Y
20 Gonzalez	Y	Y	Y	Y	N
21 Smith	N	Y	Y	N	Y
22 Olson	N	Y	Y	N	Y
23 Rodriguez	Y	Y	?	Y	N
24 Marchant	N	Y	Y	N	Y
25 Doggett	Y	Y	Y	Y	N
26 Burgess	N	Y	Y	N	Y
27 Ortiz	Y	Y	Y	Y	N
28 Cuellar	Y	Y	Y	Y	N
29 Green, G.	Y	Y	+	Y	N
30 Johnson, E.	Y	Y	Y	Y	N
31 Carter	N	Y	Y	N	Y
32 Sessions	N	Y	Y	N	Y
UTAH					
1 Bishop	N	Y	Y	N	Y
2 Matheson	N	Y	Y	Y	Y
3 Chaffetz	N	Y	Y	N	Y
VERMONT					
AL Welch	Y	Y	Y	Y	N
VIRGINIA					
1 Wittman	N	Y	Y	N	Y
2 Nye	Y	Y	Y	Y	N
3 Scott	Y	Y	Y	Y	N
4 Forbes	N	Y	Y	N	Y
5 Perriello	?	?	?	?	?
6 Goodlatte	N	Y	Y	N	Y
7 Cantor	N	Y	Y	N	Y
8 Moran	Y	Y	Y	Y	N
9 Boucher	Y	Y	Y	Y	N
10 Wolf	N	Y	Y	N	Y
11 Connolly	Y	Y	Y	Y	Y
WASHINGTON					
1 Inslee	Y	Y	Y	Y	N
2 Larsen	Y	Y	Y	Y	N
3 Baird	Y	Y	Y	Y	N
4 Hastings	N	Y	Y	N	Y
5 McMorris Rodgers	N	Y	Y	N	Y
6 Dicks	Y	Y	Y	Y	N
7 McDermott	Y	Y	Y	Y	N
8 Reichert	N	Y	Y	N	Y
9 Smith	Y	Y	Y	Y	N
WEST VIRGINIA					
1 Mollohan	Y	Y	Y	Y	N
2 Capito	N	Y	Y	N	Y
3 Rahall	Y	Y	Y	Y	N
WISCONSIN					
1 Ryan	N	Y	Y	N	Y
2 Baldwin	Y	Y	Y	Y	N
3 Kind	Y	Y	Y	Y	Y
4 Moore	Y	Y	Y	Y	N
5 Sensenbrenner	N	Y	Y	N	Y
6 Petri	N	Y	Y	N	Y
7 Obey	Y	Y	Y	Y	N
8 Kagen	Y	Y	Y	Y	N
WYOMING					
AL Lummis	N	Y	Y	N	Y
DELEGATES					
Faleomavaega (A.S.)				?	?
Norton (D.C.)				Y	N
Bordallo (Guam)				Y	N
Sablan (N. Marianas)*				Y	N
Pierluisi (P.R.)				Y	N
Christensen (V.I.)				Y	N

IN THE HOUSE | By Vote Number

102. **HR 1106. Mortgage Loans Modification/Credit Counseling.** Peters, D-Mich., amendment that would allow a debtor whose home is in foreclosure to meet the credit counseling requirement by receiving counseling before or up to 30 days after the filing. Adopted in Committee of the Whole 423-2: R 169-2; D 254-0. March 5, 2009.

103. **HR 1106. Mortgage Loans Modification/Recommit.** Price, R-Ga., motion to recommit the bill to the Judiciary and Financial Services committees with instructions that it be reported back forthwith using language that would bar the use of funds from the Troubled Asset Relief Program for foreclosure prevention or mitigation unless a plan for the use of the funds is submitted to Congress. Motion rejected 182-242: R 174-0; D 8-242. March 5, 2009.

104. **HR 1106. Mortgage Loans Modification/Passage.** Passage of the bill that would allow bankruptcy judges to write down the principal and interest rates of loans issued before the bill's enactment, to a home's current market value, for individuals whose mortgages are larger than the value of their homes or who meet other requirements. It would allow the government to reimburse mortgage lenders for reduced principal, interest rates or fees if the mortgage was guaranteed by the Federal Housing Administration, the Veterans Affairs Department or other federal mortgage guarantors. It also would modify the Hope for Homeowners program and would permanently increase, to $250,000, Federal Deposit Insurance Corporation and National Credit Union Administration deposit insurance coverage on individual bank accounts. The amount would be indexed to inflation from 2015 on. Passed 234-191: R 7-167; D 227-24. March 5, 2009.

105. **H Res 212. Earmark Investigation/Motion to Table.** Clyburn, D-S.C., motion to table (kill) the Flake, R-Ariz., privileged resolution that would instruct the Committee on Standards of Official Conduct to investigate and report on the relationship between earmark requests made by members on behalf of clients of an unnamed defense lobbying firm, as well as the source and timing of past campaign contributions related to those requests. Motion agreed to 222-181: R 4-160; D 218-21. March 5, 2009.

106. **H Res 153. Tribute to USC Football/Adoption.** Polis, D-Colo., motion to suspend the rules and adopt the resolution that would commend the University of Southern California's football team for winning the 2009 Rose Bowl and applaud the team's coach, Pete Carroll, for his leadership in the community. Motion agreed to 362-15: R 154-5; D 208-10. A two-thirds majority of those present and voting (252 in this case) is required for adoption under suspension of the rules. March 5, 2009.

	102	103	104	105	106
ALABAMA					
1 Bonner	Y	Y	N	P	Y
2 Bright	Y	Y	N	N	Y
3 **Rogers**	Y	Y	N	N	Y
4 **Aderholt**	Y	Y	N	N	Y
5 Griffith	Y	N	Y	Y	Y
6 **Bachus**	Y	Y	N	N	Y
7 Davis	Y	N	Y	?	?
ALASKA					
AL **Young**	Y	Y	N	Y	Y
ARIZONA					
1 Kirkpatrick	Y	N	Y	N	Y
2 **Franks**	Y	Y	N	N	Y
3 **Shadegg**	Y	Y	N	N	Y
4 Pastor	Y	N	Y	Y	Y
5 Mitchell	Y	N	Y	N	Y
6 **Flake**	N	N	N	N	Y
7 Grijalva	Y	N	Y	Y	?
8 Giffords	Y	N	Y	N	Y
ARKANSAS					
1 Berry	Y	N	N	Y	N
2 Snyder	Y	N	Y	Y	Y
3 **Boozman**	Y	Y	N	N	Y
4 Ross	Y	N	Y	Y	Y
CALIFORNIA					
1 Thompson	Y	N	Y	Y	Y
2 **Herger**	Y	Y	N	N	Y
3 **Lungren**	Y	Y	N	N	Y
4 **McClintock**	Y	Y	N	N	Y
5 Matsui	Y	N	Y	Y	Y
6 Woolsey	Y	N	Y	Y	Y
7 Miller, George	Y	N	Y	Y	Y
8 Pelosi		Y			
9 Lee	Y	N	Y	Y	Y
10 Tauscher	Y	N	Y	Y	Y
11 McNerney	Y	N	Y	N	Y
12 Speier	Y	N	Y	Y	Y
13 Stark	?	?	?	?	?
14 Eshoo	Y	N	Y	Y	Y
15 Honda	Y	N	Y	Y	Y
16 Lofgren	Y	N	Y	P	?
17 Farr	Y	N	Y	Y	Y
18 Cardoza	Y	N	Y	Y	Y
19 **Radanovich**	Y	Y	N	N	Y
20 Costa	Y	N	Y	Y	Y
21 **Nunes**	Y	Y	N	N	Y
22 **McCarthy**	Y	Y	N	N	Y
23 Capps	Y	N	Y	Y	Y
24 **Gallegly**	Y	Y	N	N	?
25 **McKeon**	Y	Y	N	N	Y
26 **Dreier**	Y	Y	N	N	Y
27 Sherman	Y	N	Y	Y	Y
28 Berman	Y	N	Y	Y	Y
29 Schiff	Y	N	Y	Y	Y
30 Waxman	Y	N	Y	Y	Y
31 Becerra	Y	N	Y	Y	Y
32 Vacant					
33 Watson	Y	N	Y	Y	Y
34 Roybal-Allard	Y	N	Y	Y	Y
35 Waters	Y	N	Y	Y	Y
36 Harman	Y	N	Y	Y	?
37 Richardson	Y	N	Y	Y	Y
38 Napolitano	Y	N	Y	Y	Y
39 Sánchez, Linda	Y	N	Y	Y	Y
40 **Royce**	Y	Y	N	N	Y
41 **Lewis**	N	Y	N	N	Y
42 **Miller, Gary**	?	?	?	?	?
43 Baca	Y	N	Y	Y	Y
44 **Calvert**	Y	Y	N	?	?
45 **Bono Mack**	Y	Y	N	N	Y
46 **Rohrabacher**	Y	Y	N	Y	Y
47 Sanchez, Loretta	Y	N	Y	Y	Y
48 **Campbell**	Y	Y	N	N	Y
49 **Issa**	Y	Y	N	N	Y
50 **Bilbray**	?	Y	N	N	Y
51 Filner	Y	N	Y	Y	Y
52 **Hunter**	Y	Y	N	N	Y
53 Davis	Y	N	Y	Y	?

	102	103	104	105	106
COLORADO					
1 DeGette	Y	N	Y	Y	?
2 Polis	Y	N	Y	Y	Y
3 Salazar	Y	N	Y	Y	Y
4 Markey	Y	N	N	Y	Y
5 **Lamborn**	Y	Y	N	N	Y
6 **Coffman**	?	?	?	?	?
7 Perlmutter	Y	N	Y	Y	Y
CONNECTICUT					
1 Larson	Y	N	Y	Y	Y
2 Courtney	Y	N	Y	Y	Y
3 DeLauro	Y	N	Y	Y	Y
4 Himes	Y	N	Y	N	Y
5 Murphy	Y	N	Y	Y	Y
DELAWARE					
AL **Castle**	Y	Y	Y	N	Y
FLORIDA					
1 **Miller**	Y	Y	N	N	Y
2 Boyd	Y	N	Y	Y	Y
3 Brown	Y	N	Y	Y	Y
4 **Crenshaw**	Y	Y	N	N	Y
5 **Brown-Waite**	Y	Y	N	N	?
6 **Stearns**	Y	Y	N	N	Y
7 **Mica**	Y	Y	N	N	Y
8 Grayson	Y	N	Y	Y	Y
9 **Bilirakis**	Y	Y	N	N	Y
10 **Young**	Y	Y	N	N	Y
11 Castor	Y	N	Y	P	Y
12 **Putnam**	Y	Y	N	N	?
13 **Buchanan**	Y	Y	N	N	Y
14 **Mack**	Y	Y	N	N	Y
15 **Posey**	Y	Y	N	N	Y
16 **Rooney**	Y	Y	N	N	Y
17 Meek	Y	N	Y	Y	Y
18 **Ros-Lehtinen**	Y	Y	N	Y	Y
19 Wexler	Y	N	Y	Y	Y
20 Wasserman Schultz	Y	N	Y	Y	Y
21 **Diaz-Balart, L.**	Y	Y	N	Y	Y
22 Klein	Y	N	Y	Y	Y
23 Hastings	Y	N	Y	Y	?
24 Kosmas	Y	N	Y	N	Y
25 **Diaz-Balart, M.**	Y	Y	Y	N	Y
GEORGIA					
1 **Kingston**	Y	Y	N	N	Y
2 Bishop	Y	N	Y	Y	Y
3 **Westmoreland**	Y	Y	N	N	Y
4 Johnson	Y	N	Y	Y	Y
5 Lewis	Y	N	Y	Y	Y
6 **Price**	Y	Y	N	N	Y
7 **Linder**	Y	Y	N	N	?
8 Marshall	Y	Y	Y	Y	Y
9 **Deal**	Y	Y	N	N	Y
10 **Broun**	Y	Y	N	Y	Y
11 **Gingrey**	Y	Y	N	N	Y
12 Barrow	Y	Y	Y	Y	Y
13 Scott	Y	N	Y	Y	Y
HAWAII					
1 Abercrombie	Y	N	Y	Y	Y
2 Hirono	Y	N	Y	Y	Y
IDAHO					
1 **Minnick**	Y	Y	N	N	Y
2 **Simpson**	Y	Y	N	N	Y
ILLINOIS					
1 Rush	Y	N	Y	Y	Y
2 Jackson	Y	N	Y	Y	Y
3 Lipinski	Y	N	Y	Y	Y
4 Gutierrez	Y	N	Y	Y	?
5 Vacant					
6 **Roskam**	Y	Y	N	N	Y
7 Davis	Y	N	Y	Y	Y
8 Bean	Y	N	Y	Y	Y
9 Schakowsky	Y	N	Y	Y	?
10 **Kirk**	Y	Y	N	N	Y
11 Halvorson	Y	N	Y	N	Y
12 Costello	Y	N	Y	Y	Y
13 **Biggert**	Y	Y	N	N	Y
14 Foster	Y	N	Y	N	Y
15 **Johnson**	Y	Y	N	N	Y

	102	103	104	105	106
16 **Manzullo**	Y	Y	N	N	Y
17 Hare	Y	N	Y	Y	P
18 **Schock**	Y	Y	N	N	Y
19 **Shimkus**	Y	Y	N	N	Y
INDIANA					
1 Visclosky	Y	N	Y	N	Y
2 Donnelly	Y	Y	Y	N	P
3 **Souder**	Y	Y	N	N	N
4 **Buyer**	Y	Y	N	N	?
5 **Burton**	Y	Y	N	N	Y
6 **Pence**	Y	Y	N	N	Y
7 Carson	Y	N	Y	Y	Y
8 Ellsworth	Y	N	Y	N	Y
9 Hill	Y	N	N	Y	Y
IOWA					
1 Braley	Y	N	Y	Y	Y
2 Loebsack	Y	N	Y	N	Y
3 Boswell	Y	N	Y	Y	Y
4 **Latham**	Y	Y	N	P	Y
5 **King**	Y	Y	N	N	Y
KANSAS					
1 **Moran**	Y	Y	N	N	Y
2 **Jenkins**	Y	Y	N	N	Y
3 Moore	Y	N	Y	Y	Y
4 **Tiahrt**	Y	Y	N	N	Y
KENTUCKY					
1 **Whitfield**	Y	Y	N	N	?
2 **Guthrie**	Y	Y	N	N	Y
3 Yarmuth	Y	N	Y	Y	?
4 **Davis**	Y	Y	N	N	Y
5 **Rogers**	Y	Y	N	N	Y
6 Chandler	Y	N	Y	P	Y
LOUISIANA					
1 **Scalise**	Y	Y	N	N	Y
2 **Cao**	?	?	?	?	?
3 Melancon	?	?	?	?	?
4 **Fleming**	Y	Y	N	N	?
5 **Alexander**	Y	Y	N	N	?
6 **Cassidy**	Y	Y	N	N	P
7 **Boustany**	Y	Y	N	N	Y
MAINE					
1 Pingree	Y	N	Y	Y	Y
2 Michaud	Y	N	Y	Y	Y
MARYLAND					
1 Kratovil	Y	N	Y	N	Y
2 Ruppersberger	Y	N	Y	Y	Y
3 Sarbanes	Y	N	Y	Y	Y
4 Edwards	Y	N	Y	Y	Y
5 Hoyer	Y	N	Y	Y	Y
6 **Bartlett**	Y	Y	N	N	Y
7 Cummings	Y	N	Y	Y	Y
8 Van Hollen	Y	N	Y	Y	Y
MASSACHUSETTS					
1 Olver	Y	N	Y	Y	Y
2 Neal	Y	N	Y	Y	Y
3 McGovern	Y	N	Y	Y	Y
4 Frank	Y	N	Y	Y	Y
5 Tsongas	Y	N	Y	Y	Y
6 Tierney	Y	N	Y	Y	Y
7 Markey	Y	N	Y	Y	Y
8 Capuano	Y	N	Y	Y	Y
9 Lynch	Y	N	Y	Y	Y
10 Delahunt	Y	N	Y	Y	Y
MICHIGAN					
1 Stupak	Y	N	N	Y	Y
2 **Hoekstra**	Y	Y	N	N	Y
3 **Ehlers**	?	?	?	?	?
4 **Camp**	Y	Y	N	N	Y
5 Kildee	Y	N	Y	Y	Y
6 **Upton**	Y	Y	N	N	Y
7 Schauer	Y	N	Y	Y	Y
8 **Rogers**	Y	Y	N	N	Y
9 Peters	Y	N	Y	Y	Y
10 **Miller**	Y	Y	N	N	Y
11 **McCotter**	Y	Y	N	N	Y
12 Levin	Y	N	Y	Y	Y
13 Kilpatrick	Y	N	Y	Y	Y
14 Conyers	Y	N	Y	Y	?
15 Dingell	Y	N	Y	Y	Y
MINNESOTA					
1 Walz	Y	N	Y	N	Y
2 **Kline**	Y	Y	N	P	Y
3 **Paulsen**	Y	Y	N	N	Y
4 McCollum	Y	N	Y	Y	Y

	102	103	104	105	106
5 Ellison	Y	N	Y	Y	Y
6 **Bachmann**	Y	Y	N	N	Y
7 Peterson	Y	N	Y	Y	Y
8 Oberstar	Y	N	Y	Y	Y
MISSISSIPPI					
1 Childers	Y	Y	N	Y	Y
2 Thompson	Y	N	Y	Y	Y
3 **Harper**	Y	Y	N	N	Y
4 Taylor	Y	N	N	Y	Y
MISSOURI					
1 Clay	Y	N	Y	Y	Y
2 **Akin**	?	Y	N	N	Y
3 Carnahan	Y	N	Y	Y	Y
4 Skelton	Y	N	Y	Y	Y
5 Cleaver	Y	N	Y	Y	Y
6 **Graves**	Y	Y	N	N	Y
7 **Blunt**	Y	Y	N	N	Y
8 **Emerson**	Y	Y	N	N	Y
9 **Luetkemeyer**	Y	Y	N	N	Y
MONTANA					
AL **Rehberg**	Y	Y	N	N	Y
NEBRASKA					
1 **Fortenberry**	Y	Y	N	N	Y
2 **Terry**	Y	Y	N	N	N
3 **Smith**	Y	Y	N	N	Y
NEVADA					
1 Berkley	Y	N	Y	Y	Y
2 **Heller**	Y	Y	N	N	Y
3 Titus	Y	N	Y	Y	Y
NEW HAMPSHIRE					
1 Shea-Porter	Y	N	Y	Y	Y
2 Hodes	Y	N	Y	N	Y
NEW JERSEY					
1 Andrews	Y	N	Y	Y	Y
2 **LoBiondo**	Y	Y	N	N	Y
3 Adler	Y	N	Y	Y	Y
4 **Smith**	Y	N	N	Y	Y
5 **Garrett**	Y	Y	N	N	Y
6 Pallone	Y	N	Y	Y	Y
7 **Lance**	Y	N	N	Y	Y
8 Pascrell	Y	N	Y	Y	?
9 Rothman	Y	N	Y	Y	Y
10 Payne	Y	N	Y	Y	Y
11 **Frelinghuysen**	Y	Y	N	N	Y
12 Holt	Y	N	Y	Y	Y
13 Sires	Y	N	Y	Y	Y
NEW MEXICO					
1 Heinrich	Y	N	Y	Y	Y
2 Teague	Y	Y	N	N	Y
3 Lujan	Y	N	Y	Y	Y
NEW YORK					
1 Bishop	Y	N	Y	Y	Y
2 Israel	Y	N	Y	Y	Y
3 **King**	Y	Y	N	N	N
4 McCarthy	Y	N	Y	Y	?
5 Ackerman	Y	N	Y	?	?
6 Meeks	Y	N	Y	Y	Y
7 Crowley	Y	N	Y	Y	Y
8 Nadler	Y	N	Y	Y	Y
9 Weiner	Y	N	Y	Y	Y
10 Towns	Y	N	Y	Y	Y
11 Clarke	Y	N	Y	Y	Y
12 Velázquez	Y	N	Y	Y	Y
13 McMahon	Y	N	Y	Y	Y
14 Maloney	Y	N	Y	Y	Y
15 Rangel	Y	N	Y	Y	Y
16 Serrano	Y	N	Y	Y	Y
17 Engel	Y	N	Y	Y	Y
18 Lowey	Y	N	Y	Y	Y
19 Hall	Y	N	Y	?	?
20 Vacant					
21 Tonko	Y	N	Y	Y	Y
22 Hinchey	Y	N	Y	Y	?
23 **McHugh**	Y	Y	Y	N	Y
24 Arcuri	Y	N	N	Y	Y
25 Maffei	Y	N	Y	Y	Y
26 **Lee**	Y	Y	N	N	Y
27 Higgins	Y	N	Y	Y	Y
28 Slaughter	Y	N	Y	Y	Y
29 Massa	Y	N	N	Y	Y
NORTH CAROLINA					
1 Butterfield	Y	N	Y	P	Y
2 Etheridge	Y	N	Y	Y	Y
3 **Jones**	Y	Y	Y	Y	Y
4 Price	Y	N	Y	Y	?

	102	103	104	105	106
5 **Foxx**	Y	Y	N	N	Y
6 **Coble**	Y	Y	N	N	Y
7 McIntyre	Y	Y	Y	Y	Y
8 Kissell	Y	N	N	N	Y
9 **Myrick**	Y	Y	N	P	Y
10 **McHenry**	Y	Y	N	N	Y
11 Shuler	Y	N	Y	Y	?
12 Watt	Y	N	Y	Y	Y
13 Miller	Y	N	Y	Y	Y
NORTH DAKOTA					
AL Pomeroy	Y	N	Y	Y	Y
OHIO					
1 Driehaus	Y	N	Y	Y	Y
2 **Schmidt**	Y	Y	N	N	Y
3 **Turner**	Y	Y	N	Y	?
4 **Jordan**	Y	Y	N	N	Y
5 **Latta**	Y	Y	N	N	Y
6 Wilson	Y	N	Y	Y	Y
7 **Austria**	Y	Y	N	N	Y
8 **Boehner**	Y	Y	N	N	?
9 Kaptur	?	N	Y	Y	Y
10 Kucinich	Y	N	Y	Y	Y
11 Fudge	Y	N	Y	Y	Y
12 **Tiberi**	Y	Y	N	N	Y
13 Sutton	Y	N	Y	Y	Y
14 **LaTourette**	Y	Y	N	Y	Y
15 Kilroy	Y	N	Y	Y	Y
16 Boccieri	Y	N	Y	N	N
17 Ryan	Y	N	Y	Y	Y
18 Space	Y	N	Y	Y	Y
OKLAHOMA					
1 **Sullivan**	Y	Y	N	N	?
2 Boren	Y	N	N	Y	Y
3 **Lucas**	Y	Y	N	N	Y
4 **Cole**	Y	Y	N	N	Y
5 **Fallin**	Y	Y	N	N	Y
OREGON					
1 Wu	Y	N	Y	Y	?
2 **Walden**	Y	Y	N	P	Y
3 Blumenauer	Y	N	Y	Y	Y
4 DeFazio	Y	N	Y	Y	Y
5 Schrader	Y	N	Y	Y	Y
PENNSYLVANIA					
1 Brady	Y	N	Y	Y	Y
2 Fattah	Y	N	Y	Y	Y
3 Dahlkemper	Y	N	N	Y	N
4 Altmire	Y	N	Y	Y	N
5 **Thompson**	Y	Y	N	N	Y
6 **Gerlach**	Y	Y	N	N	Y
7 Sestak	Y	N	Y	Y	Y
8 Murphy, P.	Y	N	Y	Y	Y
9 **Shuster**	Y	Y	N	N	Y
10 Carney	Y	N	Y	N	N
11 Kanjorski	Y	N	?	N	N
12 Murtha	Y	N	Y	Y	Y
13 Schwartz	Y	N	Y	Y	Y
14 Doyle	Y	N	Y	Y	N
15 **Dent**	Y	N	P	Y	Y
16 **Pitts**	Y	Y	N	N	Y
17 Holden	Y	N	N	Y	?
18 **Murphy, T.**	Y	Y	N	N	Y
19 **Platts**	Y	Y	N	N	Y
RHODE ISLAND					
1 Kennedy	Y	N	Y	?	Y
2 Langevin	Y	N	Y	Y	Y
SOUTH CAROLINA					
1 **Brown**	Y	Y	N	N	Y
2 **Wilson**	Y	Y	N	N	Y
3 **Barrett**	Y	Y	N	P	?
4 **Inglis**	Y	Y	N	N	Y
5 Spratt	Y	N	Y	Y	Y
6 Clyburn	Y	N	Y	Y	Y
SOUTH DAKOTA					
AL Herseth Sandlin	Y	N	Y	Y	Y
TENNESSEE					
1 **Roe**	Y	Y	N	N	Y
2 **Duncan**	Y	Y	N	N	Y
3 **Wamp**	Y	Y	N	N	Y
4 Davis	Y	N	Y	Y	Y
5 Cooper	Y	N	Y	Y	Y
6 Gordon	Y	N	Y	Y	Y
7 **Blackburn**	Y	Y	N	N	Y
8 Tanner	Y	N	Y	Y	Y
9 Cohen	Y	N	Y	Y	Y

	102	103	104	105	106
TEXAS					
1 **Gohmert**	Y	Y	N	N	?
2 **Poe**	Y	Y	N	N	Y
3 **Johnson, S.**	Y	Y	N	N	Y
4 **Hall**	Y	Y	N	N	Y
5 **Hensarling**	Y	Y	N	N	Y
6 **Barton**	Y	Y	N	N	Y
7 **Culberson**	Y	Y	N	N	Y
8 **Brady**	Y	Y	N	N	Y
9 Green, A.	Y	N	Y	Y	Y
10 **McCaul**	Y	Y	N	N	Y
11 **Conaway**	Y	Y	N	P	Y
12 **Granger**	Y	Y	N	N	Y
13 **Thornberry**	Y	Y	N	N	Y
14 **Paul**	Y	Y	N	N	Y
15 Hinojosa	Y	N	Y	Y	Y
16 Reyes	Y	N	Y	Y	Y
17 Edwards	Y	N	N	Y	?
18 Jackson Lee	Y	N	Y	Y	?
19 **Neugebauer**	Y	Y	N	N	Y
20 Gonzalez	Y	N	Y	Y	Y
21 **Smith**	Y	Y	N	N	Y
22 **Olson**	Y	Y	N	N	Y
23 Rodriguez	Y	N	Y	Y	Y
24 **Marchant**	Y	Y	N	N	Y
25 Doggett	Y	N	Y	Y	Y
26 **Burgess**	Y	Y	N	N	?
27 Ortiz	Y	N	Y	Y	Y
28 Cuellar	Y	N	Y	Y	Y
29 Green, G.	Y	N	Y	Y	?
30 Johnson, E.	Y	N	Y	Y	Y
31 **Carter**	Y	Y	N	N	Y
32 **Sessions**	Y	Y	N	N	Y
UTAH					
1 **Bishop**	Y	Y	N	N	Y
2 Matheson	Y	N	N	Y	Y
3 **Chaffetz**	Y	Y	N	N	Y
VERMONT					
AL Welch	Y	N	Y	P	Y
VIRGINIA					
1 **Wittman**	Y	Y	N	N	Y
2 Nye	Y	N	Y	Y	Y
3 Scott	Y	N	Y	Y	Y
4 **Forbes**	Y	Y	N	N	Y
5 Perriello	?	?	?	?	?
6 **Goodlatte**	Y	Y	N	N	Y
7 **Cantor**	Y	Y	N	N	Y
8 Moran	Y	N	Y	?	?
9 Boucher	Y	N	Y	Y	Y
10 **Wolf**	Y	Y	N	N	Y
11 Connolly	Y	N	Y	Y	Y
WASHINGTON					
1 Inslee	Y	N	Y	Y	Y
2 Larsen	Y	N	Y	Y	?
3 Baird	Y	N	Y	Y	P
4 **Hastings**	Y	Y	N	P	Y
5 **McMorris Rodgers**	?	Y	N	N	Y
6 Dicks	Y	N	Y	Y	?
7 McDermott	Y	N	Y	Y	Y
8 **Reichert**	Y	Y	N	N	Y
9 Smith	Y	N	Y	Y	Y
WEST VIRGINIA					
1 Mollohan	Y	N	Y	Y	Y
2 **Capito**	Y	Y	N	N	Y
3 Rahall	Y	N	Y	Y	N
WISCONSIN					
1 **Ryan**	Y	Y	N	N	N
2 Baldwin	Y	N	Y	Y	Y
3 Kind	Y	N	N	N	?
4 Moore	Y	N	Y	Y	Y
5 **Sensenbrenner**	Y	Y	N	N	N
6 **Petri**	Y	Y	N	N	Y
7 Obey	Y	N	Y	Y	?
8 Kagen	Y	N	Y	Y	N
WYOMING					
AL **Lummis**	Y	Y	N	N	Y
DELEGATES					
Faleomavaega (A.S.)	?				
Norton (D.C.)	Y				
Bordallo (Guam)	Y				
Sablan (N. Marianas)	Y				
Pierluisi (P.R.)	Y				
Christensen (V.I.)	Y				

IN THE HOUSE | By Vote Number

107. **Procedural Motion/Journal.** Approval of the House Journal of Thursday, March 5, 2009. Approved 220-142: R 19-128; D 201-14. March 6, 2009.

108. **H J Res 38. Fiscal 2009 Continuing Resolution/Recommit.** Lewis, R-Calif., motion to recommit the bill to the Appropriations Committee with instructions that it be immediately reported back with language that would continue federal spending for most departments and agencies covered in the nine unfinished fiscal 2009 appropriations bills at fiscal 2008 levels for the remainder of this fiscal year. Motion rejected 160-218: R 152-0; D 8-218. March 6, 2009.

109. **H J Res 38. Fiscal 2009 Continuing Resolution/Passage.** Passage of the joint resolution that would provide continuing appropriations until March 11, 2009, for all federal departments and agencies whose fiscal 2009 appropriations bills have not been enacted. Funding would mostly be set at fiscal 2008 levels. Passed 328-50: R 104-48; D 224-2. March 6, 2009.

110. **H Res 210. School Breakfast Program/Adoption.** Woolsey, D-Calif., motion to suspend the rules and adopt the resolution that would recognize the importance of the National School Breakfast Program and its effect on the lives of low-income children and families, encourage states to strengthen such programs and recognize the need to provide states with resources to increase availability of breakfasts. Motion agreed to 383-11: R 152-11; D 231-0. A two-thirds majority of those present and voting (263 in this case) is required for adoption under suspension of the rules. March 9, 2009.

111. **H Res 222. National Assessment Governing Board/Adoption.** Woolsey, D-Calif., motion to suspend the rules and adopt the resolution that would congratulate the National Assessment Governing Board on its 20th anniversary in measuring student academic achievement. Motion agreed to 388-9: R 156-9; D 232-0. A two-thirds majority of those present and voting (265 in this case) is required for adoption under suspension of the rules. March 9, 2009.

112. **HR 131. Ronald Reagan Commission/Passage.** Lynch, D-Mass., motion to suspend the rules and pass the bill that would create a commission to develop a commemoration of the 100th anniversary, in 2011, of the birth of President Ronald Reagan. Commission members would be unpaid but would be reimbursed for travel expenses. Motion agreed to 371-19: R 160-2; D 211-17. A two-thirds majority of those present and voting (260 in this case) is required for passage under suspension of the rules. March 9, 2009.

	107	108	109	110	111	112
ALABAMA						
1 **Bonner**	N	Y	N	Y	Y	Y
2 Bright	Y	N	Y	Y	Y	Y
3 **Rogers**	N	Y	Y	Y	Y	Y
4 **Aderholt**	N	Y	Y	Y	Y	Y
5 Griffith	Y	N	Y	Y	Y	Y
6 **Bachus**	N	Y	N	Y	Y	Y
7 Davis	?	?	?	Y	Y	Y
ALASKA						
AL **Young**	?	Y	Y	Y	Y	Y
ARIZONA						
1 Kirkpatrick	N	N	Y	?	?	?
2 **Franks**	Y	Y	N	Y	N	Y
3 **Shadegg**	N	Y	N	N	Y	Y
4 Pastor	Y	N	Y	Y	Y	Y
5 Mitchell	N	Y	Y	Y	Y	Y
6 **Flake**	N	Y	N	N	N	N
7 Grijalva	?	N	Y	?	?	?
8 Giffords	Y	Y	Y	Y	Y	Y
ARKANSAS						
1 Berry	N	N	Y	Y	Y	Y
2 Snyder	Y	N	Y	Y	Y	Y
3 **Boozman**	N	Y	Y	Y	Y	Y
4 Ross	Y	N	Y	Y	Y	Y
CALIFORNIA						
1 Thompson	N	N	Y	Y	Y	Y
2 **Herger**	N	Y	N	Y	Y	Y
3 **Lungren**	N	Y	N	Y	Y	Y
4 **McClintock**	Y	Y	Y	Y	Y	Y
5 Matsui	Y	N	Y	Y	Y	Y
6 Woolsey	Y	N	Y	Y	Y	N
7 Miller, George	Y	N	Y	Y	Y	N
8 Pelosi						
9 Lee	Y	N	Y	Y	Y	N
10 Tauscher	Y	N	Y	Y	Y	Y
11 McNerney	Y	N	Y	Y	Y	Y
12 Speier	?	N	Y	Y	Y	Y
13 Stark	?	?	?	?	?	?
14 Eshoo	Y	N	Y	Y	Y	Y
15 Honda	Y	N	Y	Y	Y	Y
16 Lofgren	?	?	?	Y	Y	Y
17 Farr	Y	N	Y	Y	Y	Y
18 Cardoza	Y	N	Y	Y	Y	Y
19 **Radanovich**	?	Y	N	Y	?	Y
20 Costa	Y	N	Y	Y	Y	Y
21 **Nunes**	N	Y	Y	Y	Y	Y
22 **McCarthy**	Y	N	Y	Y	Y	Y
23 Capps	Y	N	Y	Y	Y	Y
24 **Gallegly**	?	?	?	Y	Y	Y
25 **McKeon**	N	Y	?	Y	Y	Y
26 **Dreier**	N	Y	Y	Y	Y	Y
27 Sherman	Y	N	Y	Y	Y	Y
28 Berman	?	?	?	Y	Y	Y
29 Schiff	Y	N	Y	Y	Y	Y
30 Waxman	Y	N	Y	Y	Y	Y
31 Becerra	?	N	Y	Y	Y	Y
32 Vacant						
33 Watson	Y	N	Y	Y	Y	Y
34 Roybal-Allard	Y	N	Y	Y	Y	Y
35 Waters	Y	N	Y	Y	Y	Y
36 Harman	?	?	?	Y	Y	Y
37 Richardson	Y	N	Y	?	?	?
38 Napolitano	Y	N	Y	Y	Y	Y
39 Sánchez, Linda	Y	N	Y	Y	Y	Y
40 **Royce**	N	Y	N	Y	Y	Y
41 **Lewis**	N	Y	N	Y	Y	Y
42 **Miller, Gary**	?	?	?	?	?	Y
43 Baca	Y	N	Y	Y	Y	Y
44 **Calvert**	?	?	?	Y	Y	Y
45 **Bono Mack**	?	?	?	Y	Y	Y
46 **Rohrabacher**	N	Y	Y	?	?	?
47 Sanchez, Loretta	Y	N	Y	Y	Y	Y
48 **Campbell**	N	Y	Y	N	N	Y
49 **Issa**	?	?	?	Y	Y	Y
50 **Bilbray**	Y	Y	Y	Y	Y	Y
51 Filner	Y	N	Y	Y	Y	N
52 **Hunter**	N	Y	N	Y	Y	Y
53 Davis	Y	N	Y	Y	Y	Y

	107	108	109	110	111	112
COLORADO						
1 DeGette	Y	N	Y	Y	Y	Y
2 Polis	Y	N	Y	Y	Y	Y
3 Salazar	Y	N	Y	Y	Y	Y
4 Markey	Y	N	Y	Y	Y	Y
5 **Lamborn**	N	Y	Y	Y	Y	Y
6 **Coffman**	–	+	+	Y	Y	Y
7 Perlmutter	Y	N	Y	Y	Y	Y
CONNECTICUT						
1 Larson	Y	N	Y	Y	Y	Y
2 Courtney	Y	N	Y	Y	Y	Y
3 DeLauro	Y	N	Y	Y	Y	Y
4 Himes	Y	N	Y	Y	Y	Y
5 Murphy	Y	N	Y	Y	Y	Y
DELAWARE						
AL **Castle**	N	Y	Y	Y	Y	Y
FLORIDA						
1 **Miller**	N	Y	Y	Y	Y	Y
2 Boyd	Y	N	Y	Y	Y	Y
3 Brown	Y	N	Y	?	?	?
4 **Crenshaw**	N	Y	Y	Y	Y	Y
5 **Brown-Waite**	?	?	?	Y	Y	Y
6 **Stearns**	N	Y	N	Y	Y	Y
7 **Mica**	N	Y	Y	Y	Y	Y
8 Grayson	Y	N	Y	Y	Y	P
9 **Bilirakis**	N	Y	Y	Y	Y	Y
10 **Young**	N	Y	Y	?	?	?
11 Castor	Y	N	Y	Y	Y	Y
12 **Putnam**	–	+	+	+	+	+
13 **Buchanan**	Y	Y	Y	?	?	?
14 **Mack**	N	Y	N	N	Y	Y
15 **Posey**	Y	Y	Y	Y	Y	Y
16 **Rooney**	Y	Y	Y	Y	Y	?
17 Meek	Y	N	Y	Y	Y	Y
18 **Ros-Lehtinen**	?	?	?	Y	Y	Y
19 Wexler	Y	N	Y	Y	Y	Y
20 Wasserman Schultz	Y	N	Y	Y	Y	Y
21 **Diaz-Balart, L.**	N	Y	Y	Y	Y	Y
22 Klein	Y	N	Y	+	+	+
23 Hastings	Y	N	Y	Y	Y	Y
24 Kosmas	Y	N	Y	Y	Y	Y
25 **Diaz-Balart, M.**	N	Y	Y	Y	Y	Y
GEORGIA						
1 **Kingston**	Y	Y	N	Y	Y	Y
2 Bishop	?	?	?	Y	Y	Y
3 **Westmoreland**	N	Y	N	Y	Y	Y
4 Johnson	Y	N	Y	?	Y	N
5 Lewis	Y	N	Y	Y	Y	Y
6 **Price**	N	Y	N	Y	Y	Y
7 **Linder**	N	Y	N	Y	Y	Y
8 Marshall	Y	N	Y	Y	Y	Y
9 **Deal**	?	?	?	Y	Y	Y
10 **Broun**	N	Y	N	N	N	Y
11 **Gingrey**	N	Y	N	Y	Y	Y
12 Barrow	Y	N	Y	Y	Y	Y
13 Scott	Y	N	Y	Y	Y	Y
HAWAII						
1 Abercrombie	?	?	?	?	?	?
2 Hirono	?	N	Y	Y	Y	N
IDAHO						
1 Minnick	?	Y	Y	Y	Y	Y
2 **Simpson**	N	Y	Y	Y	Y	Y
ILLINOIS						
1 Rush	Y	N	Y	?	?	?
2 Jackson	Y	N	Y	Y	Y	Y
3 Lipinski	?	?	?	Y	Y	Y
4 Gutierrez	Y	N	Y	?	+	+
5 Vacant						
6 **Roskam**	?	?	?	Y	Y	Y
7 Davis	Y	N	Y	Y	Y	Y
8 Bean	Y	N	Y	Y	Y	Y
9 Schakowsky	Y	N	Y	Y	Y	Y
10 **Kirk**	N	Y	Y	Y	Y	Y
11 Halvorson	Y	N	Y	Y	Y	Y
12 Costello	Y	N	Y	Y	Y	Y
13 **Biggert**	Y	Y	Y	Y	Y	Y
14 Foster	Y	N	Y	Y	?	Y
15 **Johnson**	+	+	–	?	+	+

KEY   **Republicans**   Democrats

Y Voted for (yea)	X Paired against	C Voted "present" to avoid possible conflict of interest
# Paired for	– Announced against	
+ Announced for	P Voted "present"	? Did not vote or otherwise make a position known
N Voted against (nay)		

	107	108	109	110	111	112
16 **Manzullo**	N	Y	N	Y	Y	Y
17 Hare	Y	N	Y	Y	Y	Y
18 **Schock**	N	Y	Y	Y	Y	Y
19 **Shimkus**	?	?	?	Y	Y	Y
INDIANA						
1 Visclosky	Y	N	Y	Y	Y	Y
2 Donnelly	N	Y	Y	Y	Y	Y
3 **Souder**	N	Y	Y	Y	N	Y
4 **Buyer**	?	?	?	Y	Y	Y
5 **Burton**	N	Y	N	Y	Y	Y
6 **Pence**	N	Y	Y	Y	Y	Y
7 Carson	Y	N	Y	Y	Y	Y
8 Ellsworth	N	Y	Y	Y	Y	Y
9 Hill	Y	N	Y	Y	Y	Y
IOWA						
1 Braley	Y	N	Y	Y	Y	Y
2 Loebsack	Y	N	Y	Y	Y	Y
3 Boswell	Y	N	Y	Y	Y	Y
4 **Latham**	Y	Y	Y	Y	Y	Y
5 **King**	N	Y	N	N	Y	Y
KANSAS						
1 **Moran**	N	Y	N	Y	Y	Y
2 **Jenkins**	N	Y	Y	Y	Y	Y
3 Moore	Y	N	Y	Y	Y	Y
4 **Tiahrt**	?	Y	N	+	Y	Y
KENTUCKY						
1 **Whitfield**	N	Y	Y	Y	Y	Y
2 **Guthrie**	N	Y	Y	Y	Y	Y
3 Yarmuth	Y	N	Y	Y	Y	Y
4 **Davis**	N	Y	N	Y	Y	Y
5 **Rogers**	?	?	?	Y	Y	Y
6 Chandler	Y	N	Y	Y	Y	Y
LOUISIANA						
1 **Scalise**	N	Y	Y	Y	Y	Y
2 **Cao**	?	?	?	Y	Y	Y
3 Melancon	?	?	?	Y	Y	Y
4 **Fleming**	N	Y	Y	Y	Y	Y
5 **Alexander**	N	Y	Y	Y	Y	Y
6 **Cassidy**	Y	Y	Y	?	?	?
7 **Boustany**	N	Y	Y	Y	Y	Y
MAINE						
1 Pingree	Y	N	Y	Y	Y	Y
2 Michaud	Y	N	Y	Y	Y	Y
MARYLAND						
1 Kratovil	Y	N	Y	Y	Y	Y
2 Ruppersberger	Y	N	Y	Y	Y	Y
3 Sarbanes	Y	N	Y	Y	Y	Y
4 Edwards	Y	N	Y	Y	Y	N
5 Hoyer	Y	N	Y	Y	Y	Y
6 **Bartlett**	N	Y	N	Y	Y	Y
7 Cummings	Y	N	Y	Y	Y	Y
8 Van Hollen	Y	N	Y	Y	Y	Y
MASSACHUSETTS						
1 Olver	Y	N	Y	Y	Y	N
2 Neal	?	?	?	?	?	?
3 McGovern	Y	N	Y	Y	Y	Y
4 Frank	Y	N	Y	Y	Y	Y
5 Tsongas	Y	N	Y	Y	Y	Y
6 Tierney	Y	N	Y	Y	Y	?
7 Markey	Y	N	Y	Y	Y	Y
8 Capuano	Y	N	Y	Y	Y	Y
9 Lynch	Y	N	Y	Y	Y	Y
10 Delahunt	Y	N	Y	Y	Y	Y
MICHIGAN						
1 Stupak	N	N	N	Y	Y	Y
2 **Hoekstra**	Y	Y	Y	?	?	?
3 **Ehlers**	–	+	+	Y	Y	Y
4 **Camp**	?	?	?	Y	Y	Y
5 Kildee	Y	N	Y	Y	Y	Y
6 **Upton**	N	Y	Y	Y	Y	Y
7 Schauer	Y	N	Y	Y	Y	Y
8 **Rogers**	N	Y	Y	Y	Y	Y
9 Peters	Y	N	Y	Y	Y	Y
10 **Miller**	N	Y	Y	Y	Y	Y
11 **McCotter**	?	Y	Y	?	?	?
12 Levin	Y	N	Y	Y	Y	Y
13 Kilpatrick	Y	N	Y	Y	Y	Y
14 Conyers	Y	N	Y	Y	Y	Y
15 Dingell	?	?	?	Y	Y	Y
MINNESOTA						
1 Walz	Y	N	Y	Y	Y	Y
2 **Kline**	N	Y	Y	Y	Y	Y
3 **Paulsen**	N	Y	Y	Y	Y	Y
4 McCollum	Y	N	Y	Y	Y	Y

	107	108	109	110	111	112
5 Ellison	Y	N	Y	?	?	?
6 **Bachmann**	N	Y	N	Y	Y	Y
7 Peterson	N	N	Y	Y	Y	Y
8 Oberstar	?	N	Y	Y	Y	N
MISSISSIPPI						
1 Childers	Y	Y	Y	Y	Y	Y
2 Thompson	?	N	Y	Y	Y	Y
3 **Harper**	N	Y	Y	Y	Y	Y
4 Taylor	Y	N	Y	Y	Y	Y
MISSOURI						
1 Clay	Y	N	Y	Y	Y	Y
2 **Akin**	N	Y	N	N	N	Y
3 Carnahan	Y	N	Y	Y	Y	Y
4 Skelton	Y	N	Y	Y	Y	Y
5 Cleaver	Y	N	Y	Y	Y	Y
6 **Graves**	N	Y	Y	?	?	?
7 **Blunt**	N	Y	N	Y	Y	Y
8 **Emerson**	N	Y	Y	Y	Y	Y
9 **Luetkemeyer**	N	Y	Y	Y	Y	Y
MONTANA						
AL **Rehberg**	N	Y	Y	Y	Y	Y
NEBRASKA						
1 **Fortenberry**	Y	Y	Y	Y	Y	Y
2 **Terry**	N	Y	Y	Y	Y	Y
3 **Smith**	N	Y	Y	Y	Y	Y
NEVADA						
1 Berkley	Y	N	Y	+	?	?
2 **Heller**	Y	Y	Y	Y	Y	Y
3 Titus	Y	N	Y	Y	Y	Y
NEW HAMPSHIRE						
1 Shea-Porter	Y	N	Y	Y	Y	Y
2 Hodes	Y	N	Y	Y	Y	Y
NEW JERSEY						
1 Andrews	Y	N	Y	Y	Y	Y
2 **LoBiondo**	N	Y	Y	Y	Y	Y
3 Adler	Y	N	Y	Y	Y	Y
4 **Smith**	N	Y	Y	Y	Y	Y
5 **Garrett**	N	Y	N	Y	N	Y
6 Pallone	Y	N	Y	Y	Y	Y
7 **Lance**	Y	Y	Y	Y	Y	Y
8 Pascrell	Y	N	N	Y	Y	Y
9 Rothman	Y	N	Y	Y	Y	Y
10 Payne	Y	N	Y	Y	Y	N
11 **Frelinghuysen**	N	Y	Y	Y	Y	Y
12 Holt	Y	N	Y	Y	Y	Y
13 Sires	Y	N	Y	Y	Y	Y
NEW MEXICO						
1 Heinrich	Y	N	Y	Y	Y	Y
2 Teague	Y	N	Y	Y	Y	Y
3 Lujan	Y	N	Y	Y	Y	Y
NEW YORK						
1 Bishop	Y	N	Y	Y	Y	Y
2 Israel	Y	N	Y	Y	Y	Y
3 **King**	N	Y	Y	Y	Y	Y
4 McCarthy	Y	N	Y	Y	Y	Y
5 Ackerman	Y	N	Y	Y	Y	Y
6 Meeks	Y	?	Y	?	?	?
7 Crowley	Y	N	+	Y	Y	Y
8 Nadler	Y	N	Y	Y	Y	N
9 Weiner	Y	N	Y	Y	Y	Y
10 Towns	Y	N	Y	Y	Y	Y
11 Clarke	Y	N	Y	Y	Y	Y
12 Velázquez	Y	N	Y	Y	Y	Y
13 McMahon	Y	N	Y	Y	Y	Y
14 Maloney	Y	N	Y	?	Y	Y
15 Rangel	?	?	?	Y	Y	?
16 Serrano	Y	N	Y	Y	Y	Y
17 Engel	?	N	Y	?	?	?
18 Lowey	Y	N	Y	Y	Y	Y
19 Hall	?	?	?	Y	Y	?
20 Vacant						
21 Tonko	Y	N	Y	Y	Y	Y
22 Hinchey	Y	N	Y	Y	Y	N
23 **McHugh**	N	?	Y	Y	Y	Y
24 Arcuri	N	N	Y	Y	Y	Y
25 Maffei	Y	N	Y	Y	Y	Y
26 **Lee**	N	Y	Y	Y	Y	Y
27 Higgins	Y	N	Y	Y	Y	Y
28 Slaughter	Y	N	Y	Y	Y	N
29 Massa	Y	N	Y	Y	Y	Y
NORTH CAROLINA						
1 Butterfield	?	N	Y	Y	Y	Y
2 Etheridge	Y	N	Y	Y	Y	Y
3 **Jones**	N	Y	Y	Y	Y	Y
4 Price	Y	N	Y	Y	Y	Y

	107	108	109	110	111	112
5 **Foxx**	N	Y	N	Y	Y	Y
6 **Coble**	N	Y	Y	Y	Y	Y
7 McIntyre	Y	N	Y	Y	Y	Y
8 Kissell	Y	N	Y	Y	P	Y
9 **Myrick**	N	Y	Y	Y	Y	Y
10 **McHenry**	N	Y	N	Y	Y	Y
11 Shuler	?	?	?	Y	Y	Y
12 Watt	Y	N	Y	Y	Y	Y
13 Miller	Y	N	Y	Y	Y	Y
NORTH DAKOTA						
AL Pomeroy	Y	N	Y	Y	Y	Y
OHIO						
1 Driehaus	Y	N	Y	Y	Y	Y
2 **Schmidt**	N	Y	Y	Y	Y	Y
3 **Turner**	N	Y	Y	Y	Y	Y
4 **Jordan**	?	?	?	Y	Y	Y
5 **Latta**	N	Y	N	Y	Y	Y
6 Wilson	?	?	?	Y	Y	Y
7 **Austria**	N	Y	Y	Y	Y	Y
8 **Boehner**	N	Y	Y	Y	Y	Y
9 Kaptur	?	?	?	Y	Y	Y
10 Kucinich	Y	N	Y	?	?	?
11 Fudge	Y	N	Y	Y	Y	N
12 **Tiberi**	?	?	?	Y	Y	Y
13 Sutton	Y	N	Y	Y	Y	Y
14 **LaTourette**	?	Y	Y	Y	Y	Y
15 Kilroy	?	?	?	Y	Y	Y
16 Boccieri	?	?	?	Y	Y	Y
17 Ryan	Y	N	Y	Y	Y	Y
18 Space	?	?	?	?	?	?
OKLAHOMA						
1 **Sullivan**	?	?	?	Y	Y	Y
2 Boren	Y	N	Y	Y	Y	Y
3 **Lucas**	N	Y	Y	?	?	?
4 **Cole**	N	Y	N	Y	Y	Y
5 **Fallin**	N	Y	N	Y	Y	Y
OREGON						
1 Wu	Y	N	Y	Y	Y	Y
2 **Walden**	N	Y	Y	Y	Y	Y
3 Blumenauer	Y	N	Y	Y	Y	Y
4 DeFazio	?	?	?	Y	Y	Y
5 Schrader	?	N	Y	Y	Y	Y
PENNSYLVANIA						
1 Brady	Y	N	Y	Y	Y	Y
2 Fattah	?	?	?	Y	Y	Y
3 Dahlkemper	Y	N	Y	Y	Y	Y
4 Altmire	N	Y	Y	Y	Y	Y
5 **Thompson**	N	Y	Y	Y	Y	Y
6 **Gerlach**	Y	Y	Y	Y	Y	Y
7 Sestak	Y	N	Y	Y	Y	Y
8 Murphy, P.	Y	N	Y	Y	Y	Y
9 **Shuster**	N	Y	Y	Y	Y	Y
10 Carney	N	N	Y	Y	Y	Y
11 Kanjorski	Y	N	Y	Y	Y	Y
12 Murtha	Y	N	Y	?	?	?
13 Schwartz	Y	N	Y	Y	Y	Y
14 Doyle	Y	N	Y	Y	Y	Y
15 **Dent**	Y	Y	Y	Y	Y	Y
16 **Pitts**	?	?	?	Y	Y	Y
17 Holden	Y	N	Y	Y	Y	Y
18 **Murphy, T.**	N	Y	Y	Y	Y	Y
19 **Platts**	N	Y	Y	Y	Y	Y
RHODE ISLAND						
1 Kennedy	Y	N	Y	Y	Y	Y
2 Langevin	?	N	Y	Y	Y	Y
SOUTH CAROLINA						
1 **Brown**	?	?	?	Y	Y	Y
2 **Wilson**	N	Y	Y	Y	Y	Y
3 **Barrett**	–	+	–	Y	Y	Y
4 **Inglis**	N	Y	Y	Y	Y	Y
5 Spratt	Y	N	Y	Y	Y	Y
6 Clyburn	Y	N	Y	Y	Y	Y
SOUTH DAKOTA						
AL Herseth Sandlin	Y	N	Y	Y	Y	Y
TENNESSEE						
1 **Roe**	N	Y	Y	?	?	?
2 **Duncan**	?	?	?	N	Y	Y
3 **Wamp**	N	Y	Y	Y	Y	Y
4 Davis	Y	N	Y	Y	Y	Y
5 Cooper	Y	N	Y	?	?	?
6 Gordon	N	N	Y	Y	Y	Y
7 **Blackburn**	N	Y	N	Y	Y	Y
8 Tanner	Y	N	Y	Y	Y	Y
9 Cohen	Y	N	Y	Y	Y	N

	107	108	109	110	111	112
TEXAS						
1 **Gohmert**	?	Y	Y	?	Y	?
2 **Poe**	N	Y	N	N	N	Y
3 **Johnson, S.**	N	Y	N	Y	Y	Y
4 **Hall**	N	Y	Y	Y	Y	Y
5 **Hensarling**	N	Y	Y	Y	Y	Y
6 **Barton**	Y	Y	N	Y	Y	Y
7 **Culberson**	N	Y	Y	Y	Y	Y
8 **Brady**	N	Y	Y	Y	Y	Y
9 Green, A.	Y	N	Y	Y	Y	Y
10 **McCaul**	N	Y	Y	Y	Y	Y
11 **Conaway**	N	Y	Y	Y	Y	Y
12 **Granger**	N	Y	Y	Y	Y	Y
13 **Thornberry**	N	Y	N	Y	Y	Y
14 **Paul**	N	Y	N	N	N	N
15 Hinojosa	Y	N	Y	Y	Y	Y
16 Reyes	Y	N	Y	Y	Y	Y
17 Edwards	?	N	Y	Y	Y	Y
18 Jackson Lee	?	?	?	Y	Y	Y
19 **Neugebauer**	N	Y	N	Y	Y	Y
20 Gonzalez	Y	N	Y	Y	Y	Y
21 **Smith**	N	Y	N	Y	Y	Y
22 **Olson**	N	Y	Y	Y	Y	Y
23 Rodriguez	Y	N	Y	?	?	?
24 **Marchant**	N	Y	Y	?	Y	Y
25 Doggett	?	N	Y	Y	Y	?
26 **Burgess**	N	Y	N	Y	Y	Y
27 Ortiz	Y	N	Y	Y	Y	Y
28 Cuellar	?	?	?	Y	Y	Y
29 Green, G.	+	+	+	Y	Y	Y
30 Johnson, E.	Y	N	Y	Y	Y	N
31 **Carter**	N	Y	N	Y	Y	Y
32 **Sessions**	N	Y	N	Y	Y	Y
UTAH						
1 **Bishop**	N	Y	Y	Y	Y	Y
2 Matheson	N	N	Y	Y	Y	Y
3 **Chaffetz**	N	Y	N	N	Y	Y
VERMONT						
AL Welch	Y	N	Y	Y	Y	Y
VIRGINIA						
1 **Wittman**	N	Y	Y	Y	Y	Y
2 Nye	N	Y	Y	Y	Y	Y
3 Scott	Y	N	Y	Y	Y	Y
4 **Forbes**	Y	Y	Y	Y	Y	Y
5 Perriello	?	?	?	Y	Y	Y
6 **Goodlatte**	Y	Y	Y	Y	Y	Y
7 **Cantor**	N	Y	Y	Y	Y	Y
8 Moran	Y	N	Y	Y	Y	Y
9 Boucher	Y	N	Y	Y	Y	Y
10 **Wolf**	N	Y	Y	Y	Y	Y
11 Connolly	Y	N	Y	Y	Y	Y
WASHINGTON						
1 Inslee	Y	N	Y	Y	Y	Y
2 Larsen	Y	N	Y	?	?	?
3 Baird	Y	N	Y	Y	Y	Y
4 **Hastings**	N	Y	Y	Y	Y	Y
5 **McMorris Rodgers**	N	Y	Y	Y	Y	?
6 Dicks	Y	N	Y	Y	Y	Y
7 McDermott	Y	–	–	Y	Y	N
8 **Reichert**	N	Y	Y	Y	Y	Y
9 Smith	Y	N	Y	Y	Y	Y
WEST VIRGINIA						
1 Mollohan	Y	N	Y	Y	Y	Y
2 **Capito**	N	Y	Y	Y	Y	Y
3 Rahall	Y	N	Y	Y	Y	Y
WISCONSIN						
1 **Ryan**	N	Y	Y	Y	Y	Y
2 Baldwin	Y	N	Y	Y	Y	Y
3 Kind	Y	N	Y	Y	Y	Y
4 Moore	Y	N	Y	Y	Y	Y
5 **Sensenbrenner**	N	Y	N	Y	Y	Y
6 **Petri**	N	Y	N	Y	Y	Y
7 Obey	Y	N	Y	Y	Y	Y
8 Kagen	Y	N	Y	Y	Y	Y
WYOMING						
AL **Lummis**	N	Y	Y	N	Y	Y
DELEGATES						
Faleomavaega (A.S.)						
Norton (D.C.)						
Bordallo (Guam)						
Sablan (N. Marianas)						
Pierluisi (P.R.)						
Christensen (V.I.)						

IN THE HOUSE | By Vote Number

113. **H Res 228. Earmark Investigation/Motion to Table.** Clyburn, D-S.C., motion to table (kill) the Flake, R-Ariz., privileged resolution that would instruct the Committee on Standards of Official Conduct to investigate and report on the relationship between earmarks made by members of Congress and the details of past campaign contributions. Motion agreed to 228-184: R 4-162; D 224-22. March 10, 2009.

114. **HR 813. J. Herbert W. Small Courthouse/Passage.** Edwards, D-Md., motion to suspend the rules and pass the bill that would designate the federal building and U.S. courthouse in Elizabeth City, N.C., as the "J. Herbert W. Small Federal Building and United States Courthouse." Motion agreed to 427-0: R 176-0; D 251-0. A two-thirds majority of those present and voting (285 in this case) is required for passage under suspension of the rules. March 10, 2009.

115. **HR 842. R. Jess Brown Courthouse/Passage.** Edwards, D-Md., motion to suspend the rules and pass the bill that would designate a U.S. courthouse to be constructed in Jackson, Miss., as the "R. Jess Brown United States Courthouse." Motion agreed to 424-0: R 174-0; D 250-0. A two-thirds majority of those present and voting (283 in this case) is required for passage under suspension of the rules. March 10, 2009.

116. **H Res 67. Mars Exploration Rovers/Adoption.** Davis, D-Tenn., motion to suspend the rules and adopt the resolution that would recognize the scientific contributions of NASA's Mars exploration rovers and commend the staff of the Jet Propulsion Laboratory and Cornell University for successfully operating the rovers. Motion agreed to 421-0: R 173-0; D 248-0. A two-thirds majority of those present and voting (281 in this case) is required for adoption under suspension of the rules. March 11, 2009.

117. **S 22. Public Lands Designation/Passage.** Rahall, D-W.Va., motion to suspend the rules and pass the bill that would designate more than 2 million acres of new protected wilderness areas nationwide, in addition to wild and scenic rivers, historic sites and expansions of national parks. It would authorize new water projects and allow water settlements in Western states. The bill also would codify a National Landscape Conservation System to improve management of protected federal land. Motion rejected 282-144: R 34-141; D 248-3. A two-thirds majority of those present and voting (284 in this case) is required for passage under suspension of the rules. March 11, 2009.

118. **H Con Res 38. Peace Officers' Memorial Service/Adoption.** Edwards, D-Md., motion to suspend the rules and adopt the resolution that would allow the U.S. Capitol grounds to be used May 15, 2009, for the 28th annual National Peace Officers' Memorial Service, honoring law enforcement officers who died in the line of duty in 2008. Motion agreed to 417-0: R 173-0; D 244-0. A two-thirds majority of those present and voting (278 in this case) is required for adoption under suspension of the rules. March 11, 2009.

	113	114	115	116	117	118
ALABAMA						
1 Bonner	P	Y	Y	Y	N	Y
2 Bright	N	Y	Y	?	?	?
3 Rogers	N	Y	Y	Y	N	Y
4 Aderholt	N	Y	Y	Y	N	Y
5 Griffith	Y	Y	Y	Y	Y	Y
6 Bachus	N	Y	Y	Y	N	Y
7 Davis	Y	Y	Y	Y	Y	Y
ALASKA						
AL Young	Y	Y	Y	Y	Y	Y
ARIZONA						
1 Kirkpatrick	N	Y	Y	Y	Y	Y
2 Franks	N	Y	Y	Y	N	Y
3 Shadegg	N	Y	Y	Y	N	Y
4 Pastor	Y	Y	Y	Y	Y	Y
5 Mitchell	N	Y	Y	Y	Y	Y
6 Flake	N	Y	Y	Y	N	Y
7 Grijalva	Y	Y	Y	Y	Y	Y
8 Giffords	N	Y	Y	Y	Y	Y
ARKANSAS						
1 Berry	Y	Y	Y	Y	Y	Y
2 Snyder	Y	Y	Y	Y	Y	Y
3 Boozman	N	Y	Y	Y	N	Y
4 Ross	Y	Y	Y	Y	Y	Y
CALIFORNIA						
1 Thompson	Y	Y	Y	Y	Y	Y
2 Herger	N	Y	Y	Y	N	Y
3 Lungren	N	Y	Y	Y	N	Y
4 McClintock	N	Y	Y	Y	N	Y
5 Matsui	Y	Y	Y	Y	Y	Y
6 Woolsey	Y	Y	Y	Y	Y	Y
7 Miller, George	Y	Y	Y	Y	Y	Y
8 Pelosi					Y	
9 Lee	Y	Y	Y	Y	Y	Y
10 Tauscher	Y	Y	Y	Y	Y	Y
11 McNerney	N	Y	Y	Y	Y	Y
12 Speier	Y	Y	Y	Y	Y	Y
13 Stark	Y	Y	Y	Y	Y	Y
14 Eshoo	Y	Y	Y	Y	Y	Y
15 Honda	Y	Y	Y	Y	Y	Y
16 Lofgren	P	Y	Y	Y	Y	Y
17 Farr	Y	Y	Y	Y	Y	Y
18 Cardoza	Y	Y	Y	Y	Y	Y
19 Radanovich	N	Y	Y	?	?	Y
20 Costa	Y	Y	Y	Y	Y	Y
21 Nunes	N	Y	Y	Y	N	Y
22 McCarthy	N	Y	Y	Y	N	Y
23 Capps	Y	Y	Y	Y	Y	?
24 Gallegly	N	Y	Y	Y	Y	Y
25 McKeon	N	Y	Y	Y	Y	Y
26 Dreier	N	Y	Y	Y	Y	Y
27 Sherman	Y	Y	Y	Y	Y	Y
28 Berman	Y	Y	Y	Y	Y	Y
29 Schiff	Y	Y	Y	Y	Y	Y
30 Waxman	Y	Y	Y	Y	Y	Y
31 Becerra	Y	Y	Y	Y	Y	Y
32 Vacant						
33 Watson	Y	Y	Y	Y	Y	?
34 Roybal-Allard	Y	Y	Y	Y	Y	Y
35 Waters	Y	Y	Y	Y	Y	Y
36 Harman	Y	Y	Y	Y	Y	Y
37 Richardson	Y	Y	Y	Y	Y	Y
38 Napolitano	Y	Y	Y	Y	Y	Y
39 Sánchez, Linda	Y	Y	Y	Y	Y	Y
40 Royce	N	Y	Y	Y	N	Y
41 Lewis	N	Y	Y	Y	Y	Y
42 Miller, Gary	?	?	?	?	?	?
43 Baca	Y	Y	Y	Y	Y	Y
44 Calvert	N	Y	Y	Y	N	Y
45 Bono Mack	N	Y	Y	Y	Y	Y
46 Rohrabacher	Y	Y	Y	Y	N	?
47 Sanchez, Loretta	Y	Y	Y	Y	Y	Y
48 Campbell	N	Y	Y	Y	N	Y
49 Issa	N	Y	Y	Y	N	Y
50 Bilbray	N	Y	Y	Y	N	Y
51 Filner	Y	Y	Y	Y	Y	Y
52 Hunter	N	Y	Y	Y	N	Y
53 Davis	Y	Y	Y	Y	Y	Y

	113	114	115	116	117	118
COLORADO						
1 DeGette	Y	Y	Y	Y	Y	Y
2 Polis	Y	Y	Y	Y	Y	Y
3 Salazar	Y	Y	Y	Y	Y	Y
4 Markey	Y	Y	Y	Y	Y	Y
5 Lamborn	N	Y	Y	Y	N	Y
6 Coffman	N	Y	Y	Y	N	Y
7 Perlmutter	Y	Y	Y	Y	Y	Y
CONNECTICUT						
1 Larson	Y	Y	Y	Y	Y	Y
2 Courtney	Y	Y	Y	Y	Y	Y
3 DeLauro	Y	Y	Y	Y	Y	Y
4 Himes	N	Y	Y	Y	Y	Y
5 Murphy	Y	Y	Y	Y	Y	Y
DELAWARE						
AL Castle	N	Y	Y	Y	Y	Y
FLORIDA						
1 Miller	N	Y	Y	Y	N	Y
2 Boyd	Y	Y	Y	Y	Y	Y
3 Brown	Y	Y	Y	Y	Y	Y
4 Crenshaw	N	Y	Y	Y	N	Y
5 Brown-Waite	N	Y	Y	Y	N	Y
6 Stearns	N	Y	Y	Y	N	Y
7 Mica	N	Y	Y	Y	N	Y
8 Grayson	Y	Y	Y	Y	Y	Y
9 Bilirakis	N	Y	Y	Y	N	Y
10 Young	N	Y	Y	Y	N	Y
11 Castor	P	Y	Y	Y	Y	Y
12 Putnam	−	+	+	Y	N	Y
13 Buchanan	N	Y	Y	Y	N	Y
14 Mack	N	Y	Y	Y	N	Y
15 Posey	N	Y	Y	Y	N	Y
16 Rooney	N	Y	+	Y	N	Y
17 Meek	Y	Y	Y	Y	Y	Y
18 Ros-Lehtinen	N	Y	Y	Y	Y	Y
19 Wexler	Y	Y	Y	Y	Y	Y
20 Wasserman Schultz	Y	Y	Y	Y	Y	Y
21 Diaz-Balart, L.	N	Y	Y	Y	N	Y
22 Klein	Y	Y	Y	Y	Y	Y
23 Hastings	Y	Y	Y	Y	Y	Y
24 Kosmas	N	Y	Y	?	?	?
25 Diaz-Balart, M.	N	Y	Y	Y	N	Y
GEORGIA						
1 Kingston	N	Y	Y	Y	N	Y
2 Bishop	Y	Y	Y	Y	Y	Y
3 Westmoreland	N	Y	Y	Y	N	Y
4 Johnson	Y	Y	Y	Y	Y	Y
5 Lewis	Y	Y	Y	Y	Y	Y
6 Price	N	Y	Y	Y	N	Y
7 Linder	N	Y	Y	Y	N	Y
8 Marshall	Y	Y	Y	Y	Y	Y
9 Deal	N	Y	Y	Y	N	Y
10 Broun	N	Y	Y	Y	N	Y
11 Gingrey	N	Y	Y	Y	N	Y
12 Barrow	Y	Y	Y	Y	Y	Y
13 Scott	Y	Y	Y	Y	Y	Y
HAWAII						
1 Abercrombie	?	?	?	Y	Y	Y
2 Hirono	Y	Y	Y	Y	Y	Y
IDAHO						
1 Minnick	N	Y	Y	Y	Y	Y
2 Simpson	N	Y	Y	Y	Y	Y
ILLINOIS						
1 Rush	Y	Y	Y	Y	Y	?
2 Jackson	Y	Y	Y	Y	Y	Y
3 Lipinski	Y	Y	Y	Y	Y	Y
4 Gutierrez	Y	Y	Y	Y	Y	?
5 Vacant						
6 Roskam	N	Y	Y	Y	N	Y
7 Davis	Y	Y	Y	Y	Y	Y
8 Bean	Y	Y	Y	Y	Y	Y
9 Schakowsky	Y	Y	Y	Y	Y	Y
10 Kirk	N	Y	Y	Y	Y	?
11 Halvorson	N	Y	Y	Y	Y	Y
12 Costello	Y	Y	Y	Y	Y	Y
13 Biggert	N	Y	Y	Y	N	Y
14 Foster	N	Y	Y	Y	Y	Y
15 Johnson	N	Y	Y	Y	Y	Y

KEY   **Republicans**   Democrats

Y Voted for (yea)	X Paired against	C Voted "present" to avoid possible conflict of interest
# Paired for	− Announced against	
+ Announced for	P Voted "present"	? Did not vote or otherwise make a position known
N Voted against (nay)		

	113	114	115	116	117	118
16 **Manzullo**	N	Y	Y	Y	N	Y
17 Hare	Y	Y	Y	Y	Y	Y
18 **Schock**	N	Y	Y	?	N	Y
19 **Shimkus**	N	Y	Y	Y	N	Y
INDIANA						
1 Visclosky	N	Y	Y	Y	Y	Y
2 Donnelly	N	Y	Y	Y	Y	Y
3 **Souder**	N	Y	Y	Y	N	Y
4 **Buyer**	N	Y	Y	?	N	Y
5 **Burton**	N	Y	Y	Y	N	Y
6 **Pence**	N	Y	Y	Y	N	Y
7 Carson	Y	Y	Y	Y	Y	Y
8 Ellsworth	N	Y	Y	Y	Y	Y
9 Hill	Y	Y	Y	Y	Y	Y
IOWA						
1 Braley	Y	Y	Y	Y	Y	Y
2 Loebsack	N	Y	Y	Y	Y	Y
3 Boswell	Y	Y	Y	Y	Y	Y
4 **Latham**	P	Y	Y	Y	N	Y
5 **King**	N	Y	Y	Y	N	Y
KANSAS						
1 **Moran**	N	Y	Y	Y	N	Y
2 **Jenkins**	N	Y	Y	Y	N	Y
3 Moore	Y	Y	Y	Y	Y	Y
4 **Tiahrt**	N	Y	Y	Y	N	Y
KENTUCKY						
1 **Whitfield**	N	Y	Y	Y	Y	Y
2 **Guthrie**	N	Y	Y	Y	N	Y
3 Yarmuth	Y	Y	Y	Y	Y	Y
4 **Davis**	N	Y	Y	Y	N	Y
5 **Rogers**	N	Y	Y	Y	N	Y
6 Chandler	P	Y	Y	Y	Y	Y
LOUISIANA						
1 **Scalise**	N	Y	Y	Y	N	Y
2 **Cao**	N	Y	Y	Y	N	Y
3 Melancon	Y	Y	Y	Y	Y	Y
4 **Fleming**	N	Y	Y	Y	N	Y
5 **Alexander**	N	Y	Y	?	?	?
6 **Cassidy**	N	Y	Y	Y	N	Y
7 **Boustany**	N	Y	Y	Y	N	Y
MAINE						
1 Pingree	Y	Y	Y	Y	Y	Y
2 Michaud	Y	Y	Y	Y	Y	Y
MARYLAND						
1 Kratovil	Y	Y	Y	Y	Y	Y
2 Ruppersberger	Y	Y	Y	Y	Y	Y
3 Sarbanes	Y	Y	Y	Y	Y	Y
4 Edwards	Y	Y	Y	Y	Y	?
5 Hoyer	Y	Y	Y	Y	Y	Y
6 **Bartlett**	N	Y	Y	Y	N	Y
7 Cummings	Y	Y	Y	Y	Y	Y
8 Van Hollen	Y	Y	Y	Y	Y	Y
MASSACHUSETTS						
1 Olver	Y	Y	Y	Y	Y	Y
2 Neal	Y	Y	Y	Y	Y	Y
3 McGovern	Y	Y	Y	Y	Y	Y
4 Frank	Y	Y	Y	Y	Y	Y
5 Tsongas	Y	Y	Y	Y	Y	Y
6 Tierney	Y	Y	Y	Y	Y	Y
7 Markey	Y	Y	Y	Y	Y	Y
8 Capuano	Y	Y	Y	Y	Y	Y
9 Lynch	Y	Y	Y	Y	Y	Y
10 Delahunt	Y	Y	Y	Y	Y	Y
MICHIGAN						
1 Stupak	Y	Y	Y	Y	Y	Y
2 **Hoekstra**	N	Y	Y	Y	N	Y
3 **Ehlers**	N	Y	Y	Y	Y	Y
4 **Camp**	N	Y	Y	Y	N	Y
5 Kildee	Y	Y	Y	Y	Y	Y
6 **Upton**	N	Y	Y	Y	Y	Y
7 Schauer	Y	Y	Y	Y	Y	Y
8 **Rogers**	N	Y	Y	Y	N	Y
9 Peters	Y	Y	Y	Y	Y	Y
10 **Miller**	N	Y	Y	Y	Y	Y
11 **McCotter**	N	Y	Y	Y	N	Y
12 Levin	Y	Y	Y	Y	Y	Y
13 Kilpatrick	Y	Y	Y	Y	Y	Y
14 Conyers	Y	Y	Y	Y	Y	Y
15 Dingell	Y	Y	Y	Y	Y	?
MINNESOTA						
1 Walz	N	Y	Y	Y	Y	Y
2 **Kline**	P	Y	Y	Y	N	Y
3 **Paulsen**	N	Y	Y	Y	Y	Y
4 McCollum	Y	Y	Y	Y	Y	Y

	113	114	115	116	117	118
5 Ellison	Y	Y	Y	Y	Y	Y
6 **Bachmann**	N	Y	Y	Y	N	Y
7 Peterson	Y	Y	Y	Y	N	Y
8 Oberstar	Y	Y	?	Y	Y	Y
MISSISSIPPI						
1 Childers	Y	Y	Y	Y	Y	Y
2 Thompson	Y	Y	Y	Y	Y	Y
3 **Harper**	N	Y	Y	Y	N	Y
4 Taylor	Y	Y	Y	Y	Y	Y
MISSOURI						
1 Clay	Y	Y	Y	Y	Y	Y
2 **Akin**	N	Y	Y	Y	N	Y
3 Carnahan	Y	Y	Y	Y	Y	Y
4 Skelton	Y	Y	Y	Y	Y	Y
5 Cleaver	Y	Y	Y	Y	Y	Y
6 **Graves**	N	Y	Y	Y	N	Y
7 **Blunt**	?	Y	Y	Y	N	Y
8 **Emerson**	N	Y	Y	Y	N	Y
9 **Luetkemeyer**	N	Y	Y	Y	N	Y
MONTANA						
AL **Rehberg**	N	Y	Y	Y	N	Y
NEBRASKA						
1 **Fortenberry**	N	Y	Y	Y	Y	Y
2 **Terry**	N	Y	Y	Y	N	Y
3 **Smith**	N	Y	Y	Y	N	Y
NEVADA						
1 Berkley	Y	Y	Y	Y	Y	Y
2 **Heller**	N	Y	Y	Y	N	Y
3 Titus	Y	Y	Y	Y	Y	Y
NEW HAMPSHIRE						
1 Shea-Porter	Y	Y	Y	Y	Y	Y
2 Hodes	N	Y	Y	Y	Y	Y
NEW JERSEY						
1 Andrews	Y	Y	Y	Y	Y	Y
2 **LoBiondo**	N	Y	Y	Y	Y	Y
3 Adler	Y	Y	Y	Y	Y	Y
4 **Smith**	N	Y	Y	Y	Y	Y
5 **Garrett**	N	Y	Y	Y	N	Y
6 Pallone	Y	Y	Y	Y	Y	Y
7 **Lance**	N	Y	Y	Y	Y	Y
8 Pascrell	Y	Y	Y	Y	Y	Y
9 Rothman	Y	Y	Y	Y	Y	Y
10 Payne	Y	Y	Y	Y	Y	Y
11 **Frelinghuysen**	N	Y	Y	Y	Y	Y
12 Holt	Y	Y	Y	Y	Y	Y
13 Sires	Y	Y	Y	Y	Y	Y
NEW MEXICO						
1 Heinrich	Y	Y	Y	Y	Y	Y
2 Teague	N	Y	Y	Y	Y	Y
3 Lujan	Y	Y	Y	Y	Y	Y
NEW YORK						
1 Bishop	Y	Y	Y	Y	Y	Y
2 Israel	Y	Y	Y	Y	Y	Y
3 **King**	N	Y	Y	Y	N	Y
4 McCarthy	Y	Y	Y	+	Y	Y
5 Ackerman	Y	Y	Y	Y	Y	Y
6 Meeks	Y	Y	Y	Y	Y	Y
7 Crowley	Y	Y	Y	Y	Y	Y
8 Nadler	Y	Y	Y	Y	Y	Y
9 Weiner	Y	Y	Y	Y	Y	Y
10 Towns	Y	Y	Y	Y	Y	Y
11 Clarke	Y	Y	Y	Y	Y	Y
12 Velázquez	Y	Y	Y	Y	Y	Y
13 McMahon	Y	Y	Y	Y	Y	Y
14 Maloney	Y	Y	Y	?	Y	Y
15 Rangel	Y	Y	Y	Y	Y	Y
16 Serrano	Y	Y	Y	Y	Y	Y
17 Engel	Y	Y	Y	Y	Y	Y
18 Lowey	Y	Y	Y	Y	Y	Y
19 Hall	Y	Y	Y	?	?	?
20 Vacant						
21 Tonko	Y	Y	Y	Y	Y	Y
22 Hinchey	Y	Y	Y	Y	Y	Y
23 **McHugh**	N	Y	Y	Y	N	Y
24 Arcuri	Y	Y	Y	Y	Y	Y
25 Maffei	Y	Y	Y	Y	Y	Y
26 **Lee**	N	Y	Y	Y	N	Y
27 Higgins	Y	Y	Y	Y	Y	Y
28 Slaughter	Y	Y	Y	Y	Y	Y
29 Massa	Y	Y	Y	Y	Y	Y
NORTH CAROLINA						
1 Butterfield	P	Y	Y	Y	Y	Y
2 Etheridge	Y	Y	Y	Y	Y	Y
3 **Jones**	Y	Y	Y	Y	Y	Y
4 Price	Y	Y	Y	Y	Y	Y

	113	114	115	116	117	118
5 **Foxx**	N	Y	Y	Y	N	Y
6 **Coble**	N	Y	Y	Y	N	Y
7 McIntyre	Y	Y	Y	Y	Y	Y
8 Kissell	N	Y	Y	Y	Y	Y
9 **Myrick**	N	Y	Y	Y	N	Y
10 **McHenry**	N	Y	Y	Y	N	Y
11 Shuler	Y	Y	Y	Y	Y	Y
12 Watt	Y	Y	Y	Y	Y	Y
13 Miller	Y	Y	Y	Y	Y	Y
NORTH DAKOTA						
AL Pomeroy	Y	Y	Y	Y	Y	Y
OHIO						
1 Driehaus	Y	Y	Y	Y	Y	Y
2 **Schmidt**	N	Y	Y	Y	N	Y
3 **Turner**	N	Y	Y	Y	Y	Y
4 **Jordan**	N	Y	Y	Y	N	Y
5 **Latta**	N	Y	Y	Y	N	Y
6 Wilson	Y	Y	Y	Y	Y	Y
7 **Austria**	N	Y	Y	Y	N	Y
8 **Boehner**	N	Y	Y	Y	N	Y
9 Kaptur	Y	Y	Y	Y	Y	Y
10 Kucinich	Y	Y	Y	Y	Y	Y
11 Fudge	Y	Y	Y	Y	Y	Y
12 **Tiberi**	N	Y	Y	Y	N	Y
13 Sutton	Y	Y	Y	Y	Y	Y
14 **LaTourette**	N	Y	Y	Y	Y	Y
15 Kilroy	Y	Y	Y	Y	Y	Y
16 Boccieri	N	Y	Y	Y	Y	Y
17 Ryan	Y	Y	Y	Y	Y	Y
18 Space	Y	Y	Y	Y	Y	Y
OKLAHOMA						
1 **Sullivan**	N	Y	Y	Y	N	Y
2 Boren	Y	Y	Y	Y	N	Y
3 **Lucas**	N	Y	Y	Y	N	Y
4 **Cole**	N	Y	Y	Y	N	Y
5 **Fallin**	N	Y	Y	Y	N	Y
OREGON						
1 Wu	Y	Y	Y	Y	Y	Y
2 **Walden**	P	Y	Y	Y	Y	Y
3 Blumenauer	Y	Y	Y	Y	Y	Y
4 DeFazio	Y	Y	Y	Y	Y	Y
5 Schrader	Y	Y	Y	Y	Y	Y
PENNSYLVANIA						
1 Brady	Y	Y	Y	Y	Y	Y
2 Fattah	Y	Y	Y	Y	Y	Y
3 Dahlkemper	Y	Y	Y	Y	Y	Y
4 Altmire	Y	Y	Y	Y	Y	Y
5 **Thompson**	N	Y	Y	Y	N	Y
6 **Gerlach**	N	Y	Y	Y	Y	Y
7 Sestak	Y	Y	Y	Y	Y	Y
8 Murphy, P.	Y	Y	Y	Y	Y	Y
9 **Shuster**	N	Y	Y	Y	N	Y
10 Carney	Y	Y	Y	Y	Y	Y
11 Kanjorski	Y	Y	Y	Y	Y	Y
12 Murtha	Y	Y	Y	Y	Y	Y
13 Schwartz	Y	Y	Y	Y	Y	Y
14 Doyle	Y	Y	Y	Y	Y	Y
15 **Dent**	P	Y	Y	Y	Y	Y
16 **Pitts**	N	Y	Y	Y	N	Y
17 Holden	Y	Y	Y	Y	Y	Y
18 **Murphy, T.**	Y	Y	Y	Y	N	Y
19 **Platts**	N	Y	Y	Y	Y	Y
RHODE ISLAND						
1 Kennedy	Y	Y	Y	Y	Y	Y
2 Langevin	Y	Y	Y	Y	Y	Y
SOUTH CAROLINA						
1 **Brown**	N	Y	Y	Y	N	Y
2 **Wilson**	N	Y	Y	Y	N	Y
3 **Barrett**	P	Y	Y	Y	N	Y
4 **Inglis**	N	Y	Y	Y	N	Y
5 Spratt	Y	Y	Y	Y	Y	Y
6 Clyburn	Y	Y	Y	Y	Y	Y
SOUTH DAKOTA						
AL Herseth Sandlin	Y	Y	Y	Y	Y	Y
TENNESSEE						
1 **Roe**	N	Y	Y	Y	N	Y
2 **Duncan**	N	Y	Y	Y	N	Y
3 **Wamp**	N	Y	Y	Y	Y	Y
4 Davis	Y	Y	Y	Y	Y	Y
5 Cooper	?	?	?	Y	Y	Y
6 Gordon	Y	Y	Y	Y	Y	Y
7 **Blackburn**	N	Y	Y	Y	N	Y
8 Tanner	Y	Y	Y	Y	Y	Y
9 Cohen	Y	Y	Y	Y	Y	Y

	113	114	115	116	117	118
TEXAS						
1 **Gohmert**	N	Y	?	Y	N	Y
2 **Poe**	P	Y	Y	Y	N	Y
3 **Johnson, S.**	N	Y	Y	Y	N	Y
4 **Hall**	N	Y	Y	Y	N	Y
5 **Hensarling**	N	Y	Y	Y	N	Y
6 **Barton**	N	Y	Y	Y	N	Y
7 **Culberson**	N	Y	Y	Y	N	Y
8 **Brady**	N	Y	Y	Y	N	Y
9 Green, A.	Y	Y	Y	Y	Y	Y
10 **McCaul**	N	Y	Y	Y	N	Y
11 **Conaway**	P	Y	Y	Y	N	Y
12 **Granger**	N	Y	Y	Y	N	Y
13 **Thornberry**	N	Y	Y	Y	N	Y
14 **Paul**	N	Y	Y	Y	N	Y
15 Hinojosa	Y	Y	Y	Y	Y	Y
16 Reyes	Y	Y	Y	Y	Y	Y
17 Edwards	Y	Y	Y	Y	Y	Y
18 Jackson Lee	Y	Y	Y	Y	Y	Y
19 **Neugebauer**	N	Y	Y	Y	N	Y
20 Gonzalez	Y	Y	Y	Y	Y	Y
21 **Smith**	N	Y	Y	Y	N	Y
22 **Olson**	N	Y	Y	Y	N	Y
23 Rodriguez	Y	Y	Y	Y	Y	Y
24 **Marchant**	N	Y	Y	Y	N	Y
25 Doggett	Y	Y	Y	Y	Y	Y
26 **Burgess**	N	Y	Y	Y	N	Y
27 Ortiz	Y	Y	Y	Y	Y	Y
28 Cuellar	Y	Y	Y	Y	Y	Y
29 Green, G.	Y	Y	Y	Y	Y	Y
30 Johnson, E.	Y	Y	Y	Y	Y	Y
31 **Carter**	N	Y	Y	Y	N	Y
32 **Sessions**	N	Y	Y	Y	N	Y
UTAH						
1 **Bishop**	N	Y	Y	Y	N	Y
2 Matheson	Y	Y	Y	Y	Y	Y
3 **Chaffetz**	N	Y	Y	Y	N	Y
VERMONT						
AL Welch	P	Y	Y	Y	Y	Y
VIRGINIA						
1 **Wittman**	N	Y	Y	Y	Y	Y
2 Nye	Y	Y	Y	Y	Y	Y
3 Scott	Y	Y	Y	Y	Y	Y
4 **Forbes**	N	Y	Y	Y	N	Y
5 Perriello	N	Y	Y	Y	Y	Y
6 **Goodlatte**	N	Y	Y	Y	N	Y
7 **Cantor**	N	Y	Y	Y	N	Y
8 Moran	Y	Y	Y	Y	Y	Y
9 Boucher	Y	Y	Y	Y	Y	Y
10 **Wolf**	N	Y	Y	Y	Y	Y
11 Connolly	Y	Y	Y	Y	Y	Y
WASHINGTON						
1 Inslee	Y	Y	Y	Y	Y	Y
2 Larsen	Y	Y	Y	Y	Y	Y
3 Baird	Y	Y	Y	Y	Y	Y
4 **Hastings**	P	Y	Y	Y	N	Y
5 **McMorris Rodgers**	N	Y	Y	Y	N	Y
6 Dicks	Y	Y	Y	Y	Y	Y
7 McDermott	Y	Y	Y	Y	Y	Y
8 **Reichert**	N	Y	Y	Y	Y	Y
9 Smith	Y	Y	Y	Y	Y	Y
WEST VIRGINIA						
1 Mollohan	Y	Y	Y	Y	Y	Y
2 **Capito**	N	Y	Y	Y	Y	Y
3 Rahall	Y	Y	Y	Y	Y	Y
WISCONSIN						
1 **Ryan**	N	Y	Y	Y	N	Y
2 Baldwin	Y	Y	Y	Y	Y	Y
3 Kind	N	Y	Y	Y	Y	Y
4 Moore	Y	Y	Y	Y	Y	Y
5 **Sensenbrenner**	N	Y	Y	Y	N	Y
6 **Petri**	N	Y	Y	Y	Y	Y
7 Obey	Y	Y	Y	Y	Y	Y
8 Kagen	Y	Y	Y	Y	Y	Y
WYOMING						
AL **Lummis**	N	Y	Y	Y	N	Y
DELEGATES						
Faleomavaega (A.S.)						
Norton (D.C.)						
Bordallo (Guam)						
Sablan (N. Marianas)						
Pierluisi (P.R.)						
Christensen (V.I.)						

IN THE HOUSE | By Vote Number

119. **H Con Res 64. Tribute to Military Families/Adoption.** Skelton, D-Mo., motion to suspend the rules and adopt the concurrent resolution that would express appreciation to the families of members of the armed forces and urge the president to designate 2009 as "Year of the Military Family." Motion agreed to 422-0: R 174-0; D 248-0. A two-thirds majority of those present and voting (282 in this case) is required for adoption under suspension of the rules. March 11, 2009.

120. **H Res 125. Return of Sean Goldman/Adoption.** Berman, D-Calif., motion to suspend the rules and adopt the resolution that would call on the central authority of Brazil to immediately return Sean Goldman to his father, David Goldman, in the United States and request the Brazilian government to fulfill its obligation under international law to follow the guidelines of the Hague Convention. Motion agreed to 418-0: R 173-0; D 245-0. A two-thirds majority of those present and voting (279 in this case) is required for adoption under suspension of the rules. March 11, 2009.

121. **H Res 226. Recognition of Tibetans/Adoption.** Berman, D-Calif., motion to suspend the rules and adopt the resolution that would call on the People's Republic of China to immediately lift harsh policies imposed on Tibetans. It would also recognize the people of India for their generosity toward the Tibetan refugee population and recognize the Tibetan people for perseverance in the face of hardship. Motion agreed to 422-1: R 174-1; D 248-0. A two-thirds majority of those present and voting (282 in this case) is required for adoption under suspension of the rules. March 11, 2009.

122. **HR 1262. Clean Water Revolving Fund/Davis-Bacon Requirements.** Mack, R-Fla., amendment that would remove the Davis-Bacon Act provisions in the bill, which require contractors for projects that receive federal funds to pay the prevailing local wages and benefits to employees. Rejected in Committee of the Whole 140-284: R 139-35; D 1-249. March 12, 2009.

123. **HR 1262. Clean Water Revolving Fund/Passage.** Passage of the bill that would authorize $13.8 billion in fiscal 2010-14 for the Clean Water State Revolving Fund and more than $3 billion for other EPA projects related to water pollution and sewage control. The bill would expand the scope of water projects eligible to receive funding through state loan programs and apply Davis-Bacon rules, which require contractors for federally funded projects to pay the prevailing local wages and benefits to employees, to projects receiving grants or loans through the revolving fund. The bill's costs would be offset by an increase on the vessel tonnage duties on ships entering from foreign ports. Passed 317-101: R 73-101; D 244-0. March 12, 2009.

124. **H Res 224. Pi Day/Adoption.** Davis, D-Tenn., motion to suspend the rules and adopt the resolution that would support the designation of "Pi Day" and encourage schools to observe the day with activities that teach students about Pi and engage them in the study of math. Motion agreed to 391-10: R 162-10; D 229-0. A two-thirds majority of those present and voting (268 in this case) is required for adoption under suspension of the rules. March 12, 2009.

	119	120	121	122	123	124
ALABAMA						
1 Bonner	Y	?	Y	Y	N	Y
2 Bright	?	?	?	?	?	?
3 Rogers	Y	Y	Y	Y	N	Y
4 Aderholt	Y	Y	Y	N	N	Y
5 Griffith	Y	Y	Y	N	Y	Y
6 Bachus	Y	Y	Y	Y	N	Y
7 Davis	Y	Y	Y	N	Y	Y
ALASKA						
AL Young	Y	Y	Y	N	Y	Y
ARIZONA						
1 Kirkpatrick	Y	Y	Y	N	Y	Y
2 Franks	Y	Y	Y	Y	N	Y
3 Shadegg	Y	Y	Y	Y	N	Y
4 Pastor	Y	Y	Y	N	Y	Y
5 Mitchell	Y	Y	Y	N	Y	Y
6 Flake	Y	Y	Y	Y	N	N
7 Grijalva	Y	Y	Y	N	Y	Y
8 Giffords	Y	Y	Y	N	Y	?
ARKANSAS						
1 Berry	Y	Y	Y	N	Y	Y
2 Snyder	Y	Y	Y	N	Y	Y
3 Boozman	Y	Y	Y	Y	Y	Y
4 Ross	Y	Y	Y	N	Y	Y
CALIFORNIA						
1 Thompson	Y	Y	Y	N	Y	?
2 Herger	Y	Y	Y	Y	N	Y
3 Lungren	Y	Y	Y	Y	N	Y
4 McClintock	Y	Y	Y	Y	N	Y
5 Matsui	Y	Y	Y	N	Y	Y
6 Woolsey	Y	Y	Y	N	Y	Y
7 Miller, George	Y	Y	Y	N	Y	Y
8 Pelosi		Y				
9 Lee	Y	Y	Y	N	Y	Y
10 Tauscher	Y	Y	Y	N	Y	Y
11 McNerney	Y	Y	Y	N	Y	Y
12 Speier	Y	Y	Y	?	?	?
13 Stark	?	?	?	N	Y	Y
14 Eshoo	Y	Y	Y	N	Y	Y
15 Honda	Y	Y	Y	N	Y	Y
16 Lofgren	Y	?	Y	N	Y	Y
17 Farr	Y	Y	Y	N	Y	Y
18 Cardoza	Y	Y	Y	N	Y	Y
19 Radanovich	?	?	?	?	?	?
20 Costa	Y	Y	Y	N	Y	Y
21 Nunes	Y	Y	Y	Y	N	
22 McCarthy	Y	Y	Y	Y	N	Y
23 Capps	Y	Y	Y	N	Y	Y
24 Gallegly	Y	Y	Y	Y	N	Y
25 McKeon	Y	Y	Y	Y	N	Y
26 Dreier	Y	Y	Y	Y	N	Y
27 Sherman	Y	Y	Y	N	Y	Y
28 Berman	Y	Y	Y	N	Y	Y
29 Schiff	Y	Y	Y	N	Y	Y
30 Waxman	Y	Y	Y	N	Y	Y
31 Becerra	Y	Y	Y	N	Y	Y
32 Vacant						
33 Watson	Y	Y	Y	N	Y	Y
34 Roybal-Allard	Y	Y	Y	-	?	?
35 Waters	Y	Y	Y	N	Y	Y
36 Harman	Y	Y	Y	N	Y	Y
37 Richardson	Y	Y	Y	N	Y	Y
38 Napolitano	Y	Y	Y	N	Y	Y
39 Sánchez, Linda	Y	Y	Y	N	Y	Y
40 Royce	Y	Y	Y	Y	N	Y
41 Lewis	Y	Y	Y	Y	N	Y
42 Miller, Gary	?	?	?	?	?	?
43 Baca	Y	Y	Y	N	Y	Y
44 Calvert	Y	Y	Y	Y	Y	Y
45 Bono Mack	Y	Y	Y	Y	N	Y
46 Rohrabacher	Y	Y	Y	Y	N	Y
47 Sanchez, Loretta	Y	Y	Y	N	Y	Y
48 Campbell	Y	Y	Y	Y	N	Y
49 Issa	Y	Y	Y	Y	Y	Y
50 Bilbray	Y	Y	Y	Y	Y	Y
51 Filner	Y	Y	Y	N	Y	Y
52 Hunter	Y	Y	Y	Y	N	Y
53 Davis	Y	Y	Y	N	Y	Y

	119	120	121	122	123	124
COLORADO						
1 DeGette	Y	Y	Y	N	Y	Y
2 Polis	Y	Y	Y	Y	Y	Y
3 Salazar	Y	Y	Y	N	Y	Y
4 Markey	Y	Y	Y	N	Y	Y
5 Lamborn	Y	Y	Y	Y	N	Y
6 Coffman	Y	Y	Y	Y	N	Y
7 Perlmutter	Y	Y	Y	N	Y	?
CONNECTICUT						
1 Larson	Y	Y	Y	N	Y	?
2 Courtney	Y	Y	Y	N	Y	Y
3 DeLauro	Y	Y	Y	N	Y	Y
4 Himes	Y	Y	Y	N	Y	Y
5 Murphy	Y	Y	Y	N	Y	Y
DELAWARE						
AL Castle	Y	Y	Y	N	Y	Y
FLORIDA						
1 Miller	Y	Y	Y	Y	N	N
2 Boyd	Y	Y	Y	N	Y	Y
3 Brown	Y	Y	Y	N	Y	Y
4 Crenshaw	Y	Y	Y	Y	N	Y
5 Brown-Waite	Y	Y	Y	Y	N	Y
6 Stearns	Y	Y	Y	Y	N	Y
7 Mica	Y	Y	Y	Y	N	Y
8 Grayson	Y	Y	Y	N	Y	Y
9 Bilirakis	Y	Y	Y	Y	Y	Y
10 Young	Y	Y	Y	Y	Y	Y
11 Castor	Y	Y	Y	N	Y	?
12 Putnam	Y	Y	Y	Y	N	Y
13 Buchanan	Y	Y	Y	Y	N	Y
14 Mack	Y	Y	Y	Y	N	Y
15 Posey	Y	Y	Y	Y	N	Y
16 Rooney	Y	Y	Y	Y	N	Y
17 Meek	Y	Y	Y	N	Y	Y
18 Ros-Lehtinen	Y	Y	Y	N	Y	Y
19 Wexler	Y	Y	Y	N	Y	Y
20 Wasserman Schultz	Y	Y	N	?	?	
21 Diaz-Balart, L.	Y	Y	Y	N	Y	Y
22 Klein	Y	Y	Y	N	Y	Y
23 Hastings	Y	Y	Y	N	Y	Y
24 Kosmas	?	?	?	N	Y	Y
25 Diaz-Balart, M.	Y	Y	Y	N	Y	Y
GEORGIA						
1 Kingston	Y	Y	Y	Y	N	Y
2 Bishop	Y	Y	Y	N	Y	Y
3 Westmoreland	?	Y	Y	Y	N	Y
4 Johnson	Y	Y	Y	N	Y	Y
5 Lewis	Y	Y	Y	N	Y	Y
6 Price	Y	Y	Y	Y	N	Y
7 Linder	Y	Y	Y	Y	N	?
8 Marshall	Y	Y	Y	N	Y	Y
9 Deal	Y	Y	Y	Y	N	Y
10 Broun	Y	Y	Y	Y	N	Y
11 Gingrey	Y	Y	Y	Y	N	Y
12 Barrow	Y	Y	Y	N	Y	Y
13 Scott	Y	Y	Y	N	Y	Y
HAWAII						
1 Abercrombie	Y	Y	Y	N	Y	Y
2 Hirono	Y	Y	Y	N	Y	Y
IDAHO						
1 Minnick	Y	Y	Y	N	Y	Y
2 Simpson	Y	Y	Y	Y	N	Y
ILLINOIS						
1 Rush	Y	Y	Y	N	Y	Y
2 Jackson	Y	Y	Y	N	Y	Y
3 Lipinski	Y	Y	Y	N	Y	Y
4 Gutierrez	Y	Y	Y	N	Y	Y
5 Vacant						
6 Roskam	Y	Y	Y	Y	N	Y
7 Davis	Y	Y	Y	N	Y	Y
8 Bean	Y	Y	Y	N	Y	Y
9 Schakowsky	Y	Y	Y	N	Y	Y
10 Kirk	Y	Y	Y	Y	N	Y
11 Halvorson	Y	Y	Y	N	Y	Y
12 Costello	Y	Y	Y	N	Y	Y
13 Biggert	Y	Y	Y	Y	N	Y
14 Foster	Y	Y	Y	N	Y	Y
15 Johnson	Y	Y	Y	Y	N	N

KEY | **Republicans** | Democrats

Y Voted for (yea)	X Paired against	C Voted "present" to avoid possible conflict of interest
# Paired for	- Announced against	
+ Announced for	P Voted "present"	? Did not vote or otherwise make a position known
N Voted against (nay)		

	119	120	121	122	123	124
16 **Manzullo**	Y	Y	Y	Y	N	Y
17 Hare	Y	Y	Y	N	Y	Y
18 **Schock**	Y	Y	Y	N	Y	Y
19 **Shimkus**	Y	Y	Y	N	Y	Y
INDIANA						
1 Visclosky	Y	Y	Y	N	Y	Y
2 Donnelly	Y	Y	Y	N	Y	Y
3 **Souder**	Y	Y	Y	Y	N	Y
4 **Buyer**	Y	Y	Y	Y	Y	Y
5 **Burton**	Y	Y	Y	Y	N	Y
6 **Pence**	Y	Y	Y	Y	N	N
7 Carson	Y	Y	Y	N	Y	Y
8 Ellsworth	Y	Y	Y	N	Y	Y
9 Hill	Y	Y	Y	N	Y	Y
IOWA						
1 Braley	+	Y	Y	N	Y	Y
2 Loebsack	Y	Y	Y	N	Y	Y
3 Boswell	Y	Y	Y	N	Y	Y
4 **Latham**	Y	Y	Y	Y	N	Y
5 **King**	Y	Y	Y	Y	N	Y
KANSAS						
1 **Moran**	Y	Y	Y	Y	N	Y
2 **Jenkins**	Y	Y	Y	Y	N	Y
3 Moore	Y	Y	?	N	Y	Y
4 **Tiahrt**	Y	Y	Y	Y	N	Y
KENTUCKY						
1 **Whitfield**	Y	Y	Y	Y	Y	Y
2 **Guthrie**	Y	Y	Y	Y	Y	Y
3 Yarmuth	Y	Y	Y	N	Y	Y
4 **Davis**	Y	Y	Y	Y	Y	Y
5 **Rogers**	Y	Y	Y	Y	Y	Y
6 Chandler	Y	Y	Y	N	Y	Y
LOUISIANA						
1 **Scalise**	Y	Y	Y	Y	N	Y
2 **Cao**	Y	Y	Y	Y	Y	Y
3 Melancon	Y	Y	Y	N	Y	Y
4 **Fleming**	Y	Y	Y	Y	N	Y
5 **Alexander**	?	?	?	N	Y	Y
6 **Cassidy**	Y	Y	Y	Y	Y	Y
7 **Boustany**	Y	Y	Y	Y	N	Y
MAINE						
1 Pingree	Y	Y	Y	N	Y	Y
2 Michaud	Y	Y	Y	N	Y	Y
MARYLAND						
1 Kratovil	Y	Y	Y	N	Y	Y
2 Ruppersberger	Y	Y	Y	N	Y	Y
3 Sarbanes	Y	Y	Y	N	Y	Y
4 Edwards	Y	Y	Y	N	Y	Y
5 Hoyer	Y	?	Y	N	Y	Y
6 **Bartlett**	Y	Y	Y	Y	N	Y
7 Cummings	Y	Y	Y	N	Y	Y
8 Van Hollen	Y	Y	Y	N	Y	Y
MASSACHUSETTS						
1 Olver	Y	Y	Y	N	Y	Y
2 Neal	Y	Y	Y	N	Y	Y
3 McGovern	Y	Y	Y	N	Y	Y
4 Frank	Y	Y	Y	N	Y	Y
5 Tsongas	Y	Y	Y	N	Y	Y
6 Tierney	Y	Y	Y	N	Y	Y
7 Markey	Y	Y	Y	N	Y	Y
8 Capuano	Y	Y	Y	N	Y	Y
9 Lynch	Y	Y	Y	N	Y	Y
10 Delahunt	Y	Y	Y	N	Y	Y
MICHIGAN						
1 Stupak	Y	Y	Y	N	Y	Y
2 **Hoekstra**	Y	Y	Y	Y	Y	Y
3 **Ehlers**	Y	Y	Y	Y	Y	Y
4 **Camp**	Y	Y	Y	Y	Y	Y
5 Kildee	Y	Y	Y	N	Y	Y
6 **Upton**	Y	Y	Y	N	Y	Y
7 Schauer	Y	Y	Y	N	Y	Y
8 **Rogers**	Y	Y	Y	Y	Y	Y
9 Peters	Y	Y	Y	N	Y	Y
10 **Miller**	Y	Y	Y	N	Y	Y
11 **McCotter**	Y	Y	Y	N	Y	Y
12 Levin	Y	Y	Y	N	Y	Y
13 Kilpatrick	Y	Y	Y	N	Y	Y
14 Conyers	Y	Y	Y	–	+	+
15 Dingell	Y	Y	Y	?	?	?
MINNESOTA						
1 Walz	Y	Y	Y	N	Y	Y
2 **Kline**	Y	Y	Y	Y	N	Y
3 **Paulsen**	Y	Y	Y	Y	Y	Y
4 McCollum	Y	Y	Y	N	Y	Y

	119	120	121	122	123	124
5 Ellison	Y	?	Y	N	Y	Y
6 **Bachmann**	Y	Y	Y	Y	N	Y
7 Peterson	Y	Y	Y	N	Y	Y
8 Oberstar	Y	Y	Y	N	Y	Y
MISSISSIPPI						
1 Childers	Y	Y	Y	N	Y	Y
2 Thompson	Y	Y	Y	N	Y	Y
3 **Harper**	Y	Y	Y	Y	Y	Y
4 Taylor	Y	Y	Y	N	Y	Y
MISSOURI						
1 Clay	Y	Y	Y	N	Y	Y
2 **Akin**	Y	Y	Y	Y	N	Y
3 Carnahan	Y	Y	Y	N	Y	Y
4 Skelton	Y	Y	Y	N	Y	Y
5 Cleaver	Y	Y	Y	N	Y	Y
6 **Graves**	Y	Y	Y	Y	Y	Y
7 **Blunt**	Y	Y	Y	Y	N	Y
8 **Emerson**	Y	Y	Y	N	Y	Y
9 **Luetkemeyer**	Y	Y	Y	Y	Y	Y
MONTANA						
AL **Rehberg**	Y	Y	Y	N	Y	Y
NEBRASKA						
1 **Fortenberry**	Y	Y	Y	Y	Y	Y
2 **Terry**	Y	Y	Y	Y	Y	Y
3 **Smith**	Y	Y	Y	Y	N	Y
NEVADA						
1 Berkley	Y	Y	Y	N	Y	Y
2 **Heller**	Y	Y	Y	Y	N	N
3 Titus	Y	Y	Y	N	Y	Y
NEW HAMPSHIRE						
1 Shea-Porter	Y	Y	Y	N	Y	Y
2 Hodes	Y	Y	Y	N	Y	Y
NEW JERSEY						
1 Andrews	Y	Y	Y	N	Y	Y
2 **LoBiondo**	Y	Y	Y	N	Y	Y
3 Adler	Y	Y	Y	N	Y	Y
4 **Smith**	Y	Y	Y	N	Y	Y
5 **Garrett**	Y	Y	Y	Y	N	Y
6 Pallone	Y	Y	Y	N	Y	Y
7 **Lance**	Y	Y	Y	N	Y	Y
8 Pascrell	Y	Y	Y	N	Y	Y
9 Rothman	Y	Y	Y	N	Y	Y
10 Payne	Y	Y	Y	N	Y	Y
11 **Frelinghuysen**	Y	Y	Y	Y	N	Y
12 Holt	Y	Y	Y	N	Y	Y
13 Sires	Y	Y	Y	N	Y	Y
NEW MEXICO						
1 Heinrich	Y	Y	Y	N	Y	Y
2 Teague	Y	Y	Y	N	Y	Y
3 Lujan	Y	Y	Y	N	Y	Y
NEW YORK						
1 Bishop	Y	Y	Y	N	Y	?
2 Israel	Y	Y	Y	N	Y	?
3 **King**	Y	Y	Y	N	Y	Y
4 McCarthy	Y	Y	Y	N	Y	Y
5 Ackerman	Y	Y	?	N	Y	?
6 Meeks	Y	Y	Y	N	Y	Y
7 Crowley	Y	Y	Y	N	Y	?
8 Nadler	Y	Y	Y	N	Y	Y
9 Weiner	Y	Y	Y	N	Y	Y
10 Towns	Y	Y	Y	N	Y	Y
11 Clarke	Y	Y	Y	N	Y	Y
12 Velázquez	Y	Y	Y	N	Y	Y
13 McMahon	Y	Y	Y	N	Y	Y
14 Maloney	Y	Y	Y	N	Y	Y
15 Rangel	Y	Y	Y	N	Y	?
16 Serrano	Y	Y	Y	N	Y	Y
17 Engel	Y	Y	Y	N	Y	Y
18 Lowey	Y	Y	Y	N	Y	Y
19 Hall	?	?	?	N	Y	Y
20 Vacant						
21 Tonko	Y	Y	Y	N	Y	Y
22 Hinchey	Y	Y	Y	N	Y	Y
23 **McHugh**	Y	Y	Y	N	Y	Y
24 Arcuri	Y	Y	Y	N	Y	Y
25 Maffei	Y	Y	Y	N	Y	?
26 **Lee**	Y	Y	Y	Y	Y	Y
27 Higgins	Y	Y	Y	N	Y	?
28 Slaughter	Y	Y	Y	N	Y	?
29 Massa	Y	Y	Y	N	Y	Y
NORTH CAROLINA						
1 Butterfield	Y	?	Y	N	Y	Y
2 Etheridge	Y	Y	Y	?	?	?
3 **Jones**	Y	Y	Y	Y	Y	Y
4 Price	Y	Y	Y	N	Y	Y

	119	120	121	122	123	124
5 **Foxx**	Y	Y	Y	Y	N	Y
6 **Coble**	Y	Y	Y	Y	N	Y
7 McIntyre	Y	Y	Y	N	Y	Y
8 Kissell	Y	Y	Y	N	Y	Y
9 **Myrick**	Y	Y	Y	Y	N	Y
10 **McHenry**	Y	Y	Y	Y	N	Y
11 Shuler	Y	Y	Y	N	Y	Y
12 Watt	Y	Y	Y	N	Y	Y
13 Miller	Y	Y	Y	N	Y	Y
NORTH DAKOTA						
AL Pomeroy	Y	Y	Y	N	Y	Y
OHIO						
1 Driehaus	Y	Y	Y	N	Y	Y
2 **Schmidt**	Y	Y	Y	N	Y	Y
3 **Turner**	Y	Y	Y	N	Y	Y
4 **Jordan**	Y	Y	Y	Y	N	Y
5 **Latta**	Y	Y	Y	Y	N	Y
6 Wilson	Y	Y	Y	N	Y	Y
7 **Austria**	Y	Y	Y	Y	N	Y
8 **Boehner**	Y	+	Y	Y	N	Y
9 Kaptur	Y	Y	Y	N	Y	Y
10 Kucinich	Y	Y	Y	N	Y	Y
11 Fudge	Y	Y	Y	N	Y	Y
12 **Tiberi**	Y	Y	Y	N	Y	Y
13 Sutton	Y	Y	Y	N	Y	Y
14 **LaTourette**	Y	Y	Y	N	Y	Y
15 Kilroy	Y	Y	Y	N	Y	Y
16 Boccieri	Y	Y	Y	N	Y	Y
17 Ryan	Y	Y	Y	N	Y	Y
18 Space	Y	Y	Y	N	Y	Y
OKLAHOMA						
1 **Sullivan**	Y	Y	Y	Y	N	Y
2 Boren	Y	Y	Y	N	Y	Y
3 **Lucas**	Y	Y	Y	Y	N	Y
4 **Cole**	Y	Y	Y	Y	N	Y
5 **Fallin**	Y	Y	Y	Y	N	Y
OREGON						
1 Wu	Y	Y	Y	N	Y	Y
2 **Walden**	Y	Y	Y	N	Y	Y
3 Blumenauer	Y	Y	Y	N	Y	Y
4 DeFazio	Y	Y	Y	N	Y	Y
5 Schrader	Y	Y	Y	N	Y	Y
PENNSYLVANIA						
1 Brady	Y	Y	Y	N	Y	Y
2 Fattah	Y	Y	Y	N	Y	Y
3 Dahlkemper	Y	Y	Y	N	Y	Y
4 Altmire	Y	Y	Y	N	Y	Y
5 **Thompson**	Y	Y	Y	Y	N	Y
6 **Gerlach**	Y	Y	Y	N	Y	Y
7 Sestak	Y	Y	Y	?	?	?
8 Murphy, P.	Y	Y	Y	N	Y	Y
9 **Shuster**	Y	Y	Y	Y	Y	N
10 Carney	Y	Y	Y	N	Y	Y
11 Kanjorski	Y	Y	Y	N	Y	Y
12 Murtha	Y	Y	Y	N	Y	Y
13 Schwartz	Y	Y	Y	N	Y	Y
14 Doyle	Y	Y	Y	N	Y	?
15 **Dent**	Y	Y	Y	Y	Y	Y
16 **Pitts**	Y	Y	Y	Y	N	Y
17 Holden	Y	Y	Y	N	Y	Y
18 **Murphy, T.**	Y	Y	Y	N	Y	Y
19 **Platts**	Y	Y	Y	Y	Y	Y
RHODE ISLAND						
1 Kennedy	Y	Y	Y	N	Y	Y
2 Langevin	Y	Y	Y	N	Y	Y
SOUTH CAROLINA						
1 **Brown**	Y	Y	Y	Y	N	Y
2 **Wilson**	Y	Y	Y	Y	N	Y
3 **Barrett**	Y	Y	Y	Y	N	Y
4 **Inglis**	Y	Y	Y	Y	N	Y
5 Spratt	Y	Y	Y	N	Y	Y
6 Clyburn	Y	Y	Y	N	Y	Y
SOUTH DAKOTA						
AL Herseth Sandlin	Y	Y	Y	N	Y	Y
TENNESSEE						
1 **Roe**	Y	Y	Y	Y	Y	Y
2 **Duncan**	Y	Y	Y	Y	Y	Y
3 **Wamp**	Y	Y	Y	Y	Y	Y
4 Davis	Y	Y	Y	N	Y	Y
5 Cooper	Y	Y	Y	N	Y	Y
6 Gordon	Y	Y	Y	N	Y	Y
7 **Blackburn**	Y	Y	Y	Y	N	Y
8 Tanner	Y	Y	Y	?	?	?
9 Cohen	Y	Y	Y	N	Y	Y

	119	120	121	122	123	124
TEXAS						
1 **Gohmert**	Y	Y	Y	Y	N	Y
2 **Poe**	Y	Y	Y	Y	N	N
3 **Johnson, S.**	Y	Y	Y	Y	N	Y
4 **Hall**	Y	Y	Y	Y	N	Y
5 **Hensarling**	Y	Y	Y	?	?	?
6 **Barton**	Y	Y	Y	Y	N	Y
7 **Culberson**	Y	Y	Y	Y	N	Y
8 **Brady**	Y	Y	Y	Y	N	Y
9 Green, A.	Y	Y	Y	N	Y	Y
10 **McCaul**	Y	Y	Y	Y	N	Y
11 **Conaway**	Y	Y	Y	Y	N	Y
12 **Granger**	Y	Y	Y	Y	N	Y
13 **Thornberry**	Y	Y	Y	Y	N	Y
14 **Paul**	Y	Y	N	Y	N	N
15 Hinojosa	Y	Y	Y	N	Y	Y
16 Reyes	Y	Y	Y	N	Y	Y
17 Edwards	Y	Y	Y	N	Y	Y
18 Jackson Lee	Y	Y	Y	N	Y	Y
19 **Neugebauer**	Y	Y	Y	Y	N	N
20 Gonzalez	Y	Y	Y	N	Y	Y
21 **Smith**	Y	Y	Y	Y	N	Y
22 **Olson**	Y	Y	Y	?	?	?
23 Rodriguez	Y	Y	Y	N	Y	Y
24 **Marchant**	Y	Y	Y	Y	N	Y
25 Doggett	Y	Y	Y	N	Y	Y
26 **Burgess**	Y	Y	Y	Y	N	Y
27 Ortiz	Y	Y	Y	N	Y	Y
28 Cuellar	Y	Y	Y	N	Y	Y
29 Green, G.	Y	Y	Y	N	Y	Y
30 Johnson, E.	Y	Y	Y	N	Y	Y
31 **Carter**	Y	Y	Y	Y	N	Y
32 **Sessions**	Y	Y	Y	Y	N	Y
UTAH						
1 **Bishop**	Y	Y	Y	Y	N	Y
2 Matheson	Y	Y	Y	N	Y	Y
3 **Chaffetz**	Y	Y	Y	Y	N	N
VERMONT						
AL Welch	Y	Y	Y	N	Y	?
VIRGINIA						
1 **Wittman**	Y	Y	Y	Y	Y	Y
2 Nye	Y	Y	Y	N	Y	Y
3 Scott	Y	Y	Y	N	Y	Y
4 **Forbes**	Y	Y	Y	Y	Y	Y
5 Perriello	Y	Y	Y	N	Y	Y
6 **Goodlatte**	Y	Y	Y	Y	Y	Y
7 **Cantor**	Y	Y	Y	Y	N	Y
8 Moran	Y	Y	Y	N	Y	Y
9 Boucher	Y	Y	Y	N	Y	Y
10 **Wolf**	Y	Y	Y	Y	N	Y
11 Connolly	Y	Y	Y	N	Y	Y
WASHINGTON						
1 Inslee	Y	Y	Y	N	Y	Y
2 Larsen	Y	Y	Y	N	Y	Y
3 Baird	Y	Y	Y	N	Y	Y
4 **Hastings**	Y	Y	Y	Y	N	?
5 **McMorris Rodgers**	Y	Y	Y	Y	N	Y
6 Dicks	Y	Y	Y	N	Y	Y
7 McDermott	Y	Y	Y	N	Y	Y
8 **Reichert**	Y	Y	Y	N	Y	Y
9 Smith	Y	Y	Y	N	Y	Y
WEST VIRGINIA						
1 Mollohan	Y	Y	Y	N	Y	Y
2 **Capito**	Y	Y	Y	N	Y	Y
3 Rahall	Y	Y	Y	N	Y	Y
WISCONSIN						
1 **Ryan**	Y	Y	Y	N	N	Y
2 Baldwin	Y	Y	Y	N	Y	Y
3 Kind	Y	Y	Y	N	Y	Y
4 Moore	Y	Y	Y	N	Y	Y
5 **Sensenbrenner**	Y	Y	Y	Y	N	Y
6 **Petri**	Y	Y	Y	N	Y	Y
7 Obey	Y	Y	Y	N	Y	Y
8 Kagen	Y	Y	Y	N	Y	Y
WYOMING						
AL **Lummis**	Y	Y	Y	Y	N	Y
DELEGATES						
Faleomavaega (A.S.)				?		
Norton (D.C.)				N		
Bordallo (Guam)				N		
Sablan (N. Marianas)				N		
Pierluisi (P.R.)				N		
Christensen (V.I.)				N		

IN THE HOUSE | By Vote Number

125. **HR 987. John Challis Post Office/Passage.** Lynch, D-Mass., motion to suspend the rules and pass the bill that would designate a post office in Freedom, Pa., as the "John Scott Challis Jr. Post Office." Motion agreed to 384-0: R 151-0; D 233-0. A two-thirds majority of those present and voting (256 in this case) is required for passage under suspension of the rules. March 16, 2009.

126. **HR 1217. Peter Navarro Post Office/Passage.** Lynch, D-Mass., motion to suspend the rules and pass the bill that would designate a post office in Ballwin, Mo., as the "Spc. Peter J. Navarro Post Office Building." Motion agreed to 384-0: R 150-0; D 234-0. A two-thirds majority of those present and voting (256 in this case) is required for passage under suspension of the rules. March 16, 2009.

127. **HR 1284. Ed Freeman Post Office/Passage.** Lynch, D-Mass., motion to suspend the rules and pass the bill that would designate a post office in McLain, Miss., as the "Maj. Ed W. Freeman Post Office." Motion agreed to 418-0: R 171-0; D 247-0. A two-thirds majority of those present and voting (256 in this case) is required for passage under suspension of the rules. March 16, 2009.

128. **H Res 240. Social Work Day and Month/Adoption.** Polis, D-Colo., motion to suspend the rules and adopt the resolution that would support the goals and ideals of Professional Social Work Month and World Social Work Day, recognize the contributions of social workers and encourage young people to enter the profession. Motion agreed to 421-0: R 172-0; D 249-0. A two-thirds majority of those present and voting (281 in this case) is required for adoption under suspension of the rules. March 17, 2009.

129. **H Res 211. National Women's History Month/Adoption.** Clay, D-Mo., motion to suspend the rules and adopt the resolution that would support the goals and ideals of National Women's History Month, as well as recognize and honor women and organizations in the United States that promote teaching women's history. Motion agreed to 418-0: R 171-0; D 247-0. A two-thirds majority of those present and voting (279 in this case) is required for adoption under suspension of the rules. March 17, 2009.

130. **HR 628. Patent Law Pilot Program/Passage.** Johnson, D-Ga., motion to suspend the rules and pass the bill that would authorize $5 million annually over 10 years for a pilot program to increase expertise among judges in selected districts on cases involving patent law and plant variety protection. Motion agreed to 409-7: R 163-7; D 246-0. A two-thirds majority of those present and voting (278 in this case) is required for passage under suspension of the rules. March 17, 2009.

131. **HR 1388. National Service Programs/Previous Question.** Matsui, D-Calif., motion to order the previous question (thus ending debate and possibility of amendment) on adoption of the rule (H Res 250) that would provide for House floor consideration of the bill that would reauthorize Corporation for National Community Service programs through fiscal 2014 and increase the education reward for full-time service volunteers. Motion agreed to 221-182: R 0-174; D 221-8. March 18, 2009.

	125	126	127	128	129	130	131
ALABAMA							
1 **Bonner**	Y	Y	Y	Y	Y	Y	N
2 Bright	Y	Y	Y	Y	Y	Y	Y
3 **Rogers**	Y	Y	Y	Y	Y	Y	N
4 **Aderholt**	Y	Y	Y	Y	Y	Y	N
5 Griffith	Y	Y	Y	Y	Y	Y	Y
6 **Bachus**	Y	Y	Y	Y	Y	Y	N
7 Davis	Y	Y	Y	Y	Y	Y	Y
ALASKA							
AL **Young**	Y	Y	Y	Y	Y	Y	N
ARIZONA							
1 Kirkpatrick	Y	Y	Y	Y	Y	Y	Y
2 **Franks**	Y	Y	Y	Y	Y	Y	N
3 **Shadegg**	Y	Y	Y	Y	Y	Y	N
4 Pastor	Y	Y	Y	Y	Y	Y	?
5 Mitchell	Y	Y	Y	Y	Y	Y	Y
6 **Flake**	?	?	?	Y	Y	N	N
7 Grijalva	?	?	?	Y	Y	Y	?
8 Giffords	Y	Y	Y	Y	Y	Y	Y
ARKANSAS							
1 Berry	Y	Y	Y	Y	Y	Y	Y
2 Snyder	Y	Y	Y	Y	Y	Y	Y
3 **Boozman**	Y	Y	Y	Y	Y	Y	N
4 Ross	Y	Y	Y	Y	Y	Y	Y
CALIFORNIA							
1 Thompson	Y	Y	Y	Y	Y	Y	Y
2 **Herger**	Y	Y	Y	Y	Y	Y	N
3 **Lungren**	Y	Y	Y	Y	Y	Y	N
4 **McClintock**	Y	Y	Y	Y	Y	Y	N
5 Matsui	Y	Y	Y	Y	Y	Y	Y
6 Woolsey	Y	Y	Y	Y	Y	Y	Y
7 Miller, George	Y	Y	Y	Y	Y	Y	Y
8 Pelosi							
9 Lee	Y	Y	Y	Y	Y	Y	Y
10 Tauscher	Y	Y	Y	Y	Y	Y	Y
11 McNerney	Y	Y	Y	Y	Y	Y	N
12 Speier	?	?	?	Y	Y	Y	Y
13 Stark	?	?	?	Y	Y	Y	Y
14 Eshoo	Y	Y	Y	Y	Y	Y	Y
15 Honda	Y	Y	Y	Y	Y	Y	Y
16 Lofgren	Y	Y	Y	Y	Y	Y	Y
17 Farr	Y	Y	Y	Y	Y	Y	Y
18 Cardoza	Y	Y	Y	Y	Y	Y	?
19 **Radanovich**	?	?	?	Y	Y	Y	N
20 Costa	Y	Y	Y	Y	Y	Y	?
21 **Nunes**	Y	Y	Y	Y	Y	Y	N
22 **McCarthy**	Y	Y	Y	Y	Y	Y	N
23 Capps	Y	Y	Y	Y	Y	Y	Y
24 **Gallegly**	?	?	?	Y	Y	Y	N
25 **McKeon**	Y	Y	Y	Y	Y	Y	N
26 **Dreier**	?	?	?	?	?	?	N
27 Sherman	Y	Y	Y	Y	Y	Y	Y
28 Berman	Y	Y	Y	Y	Y	Y	?
29 Schiff	Y	Y	Y	Y	Y	Y	Y
30 Waxman	Y	Y	Y	Y	Y	Y	Y
31 Becerra	Y	Y	Y	Y	Y	Y	?
32 Vacant							
33 Watson	Y	Y	Y	Y	Y	Y	Y
34 Roybal-Allard	Y	Y	Y	Y	Y	Y	+
35 Waters	Y	Y	Y	Y	Y	Y	Y
36 Harman	Y	Y	Y	Y	Y	Y	Y
37 Richardson	Y	Y	Y	Y	Y	Y	Y
38 Napolitano	Y	Y	Y	Y	Y	Y	?
39 Sánchez, Linda	+	+	+	Y	Y	Y	+
40 **Royce**	Y	Y	Y	Y	Y	Y	N
41 **Lewis**	Y	Y	Y	Y	Y	Y	N
42 **Miller, Gary**	?	?	?	?	?	?	?
43 Baca	Y	Y	Y	Y	Y	Y	?
44 **Calvert**	Y	Y	Y	Y	Y	Y	N
45 **Bono Mack**	Y	Y	Y	Y	Y	Y	N
46 **Rohrabacher**	?	?	?	Y	Y	Y	N
47 Sanchez, Loretta	Y	Y	Y	Y	Y	Y	?
48 **Campbell**	Y	Y	Y	Y	Y	Y	N
49 **Issa**	Y	Y	Y	Y	Y	Y	N
50 **Bilbray**	Y	Y	Y	Y	Y	Y	N
51 Filner	Y	Y	Y	Y	Y	Y	Y
52 **Hunter**	Y	Y	Y	Y	Y	Y	N
53 Davis	Y	Y	Y	Y	Y	Y	Y

	125	126	127	128	129	130	131
COLORADO							
1 DeGette	Y	Y	Y	Y	Y	Y	Y
2 Polis	Y	Y	Y	Y	Y	Y	Y
3 Salazar	Y	Y	Y	Y	Y	Y	?
4 Markey	Y	Y	Y	Y	Y	Y	Y
5 **Lamborn**	Y	Y	Y	Y	Y	Y	N
6 **Coffman**	Y	Y	Y	Y	Y	Y	N
7 Perlmutter	Y	Y	Y	Y	Y	Y	Y
CONNECTICUT							
1 Larson	Y	Y	Y	Y	Y	Y	Y
2 Courtney	Y	Y	Y	Y	Y	Y	Y
3 DeLauro	Y	Y	Y	Y	Y	Y	Y
4 Himes	Y	Y	Y	Y	Y	Y	Y
5 Murphy	Y	Y	Y	Y	Y	Y	Y
DELAWARE							
AL **Castle**	Y	Y	Y	Y	Y	Y	N
FLORIDA							
1 **Miller**	Y	Y	Y	Y	Y	Y	N
2 Boyd	Y	Y	Y	Y	Y	Y	Y
3 Brown	?	?	?	Y	Y	Y	Y
4 **Crenshaw**	Y	Y	Y	Y	Y	Y	N
5 **Brown-Waite**	Y	Y	Y	Y	Y	Y	N
6 **Stearns**	Y	Y	Y	Y	Y	Y	N
7 **Mica**	Y	Y	Y	Y	Y	Y	N
8 Grayson	Y	Y	Y	Y	Y	Y	Y
9 **Bilirakis**	Y	?	Y	Y	Y	Y	N
10 **Young**	Y	Y	Y	Y	Y	Y	N
11 Castor	Y	Y	Y	Y	Y	Y	Y
12 **Putnam**	+	+	+	+	+	+	N
13 **Buchanan**	Y	Y	Y	Y	Y	Y	N
14 **Mack**	Y	Y	Y	Y	Y	Y	N
15 **Posey**	Y	Y	Y	Y	Y	Y	N
16 **Rooney**	Y	Y	Y	Y	Y	Y	N
17 Meek	Y	Y	Y	Y	Y	Y	Y
18 **Ros-Lehtinen**	Y	Y	Y	Y	Y	Y	N
19 Wexler	Y	Y	Y	Y	Y	Y	Y
20 Wasserman Schultz	Y	Y	Y	Y	Y	Y	Y
21 **Diaz-Balart, L.**	Y	Y	Y	Y	Y	Y	N
22 Klein	Y	Y	Y	Y	Y	Y	Y
23 Hastings	Y	Y	Y	Y	Y	Y	Y
24 Kosmas	Y	Y	Y	Y	Y	Y	Y
25 **Diaz-Balart, M.**	Y	Y	Y	Y	Y	Y	N
GEORGIA							
1 **Kingston**	Y	Y	Y	Y	Y	Y	N
2 Bishop	Y	Y	Y	Y	Y	Y	Y
3 **Westmoreland**	Y	Y	Y	Y	Y	Y	N
4 Johnson	Y	Y	Y	Y	Y	Y	Y
5 Lewis	Y	Y	Y	Y	Y	Y	Y
6 **Price**	Y	Y	Y	Y	Y	Y	N
7 **Linder**	Y	Y	Y	Y	Y	Y	N
8 Marshall	Y	Y	Y	Y	Y	Y	Y
9 **Deal**	Y	Y	Y	Y	Y	Y	N
10 **Broun**	Y	Y	Y	Y	Y	Y	N
11 **Gingrey**	?	?	?	Y	Y	Y	N
12 Barrow	Y	Y	Y	Y	Y	Y	Y
13 Scott	Y	Y	?	Y	Y	Y	Y
HAWAII							
1 Abercrombie	Y	Y	Y	+	+	+	Y
2 Hirono	Y	Y	Y	Y	Y	Y	Y
IDAHO							
1 Minnick	Y	Y	Y	Y	Y	Y	Y
2 **Simpson**	Y	Y	Y	Y	Y	Y	N
ILLINOIS							
1 Rush	Y	Y	Y	Y	Y	Y	Y
2 Jackson	Y	Y	Y	Y	Y	Y	Y
3 Lipinski	Y	Y	Y	Y	Y	Y	Y
4 Gutierrez	+	+	+	Y	Y	?	?
5 Vacant							
6 **Roskam**	?	?	?	Y	Y	Y	Y
7 Davis	Y	Y	Y	Y	Y	Y	Y
8 Bean	Y	Y	Y	Y	Y	Y	Y
9 Schakowsky	Y	Y	Y	Y	Y	Y	Y
10 **Kirk**	?	?	?	Y	Y	Y	Y
11 Halvorson	Y	Y	Y	Y	Y	Y	Y
12 Costello	Y	Y	Y	Y	Y	Y	Y
13 **Biggert**	Y	Y	Y	Y	Y	Y	N
14 Foster	Y	Y	Y	Y	Y	Y	Y
15 **Johnson**	+	+	+	Y	Y	N	N

KEY	**Republicans**	Democrats		
Y	Voted for (yea)	X	Paired against	C Voted "present" to avoid possible conflict of interest
#	Paired for	–	Announced against	
+	Announced for	P	Voted "present"	? Did not vote or otherwise make a position known
N	Voted against (nay)			

	125	126	127	128	129	130	131
16 **Manzullo**	Y	Y	Y	Y	Y	N	N
17 Hare	Y	Y	Y	Y	Y	Y	N
18 **Schock**	Y	Y	?	Y	Y	Y	N
19 **Shimkus**	?	Y	Y	Y	Y	Y	N
INDIANA							
1 Visclosky	Y	Y	Y	Y	Y	Y	Y
2 Donnelly	Y	Y	Y	Y	Y	Y	Y
3 **Souder**	Y	Y	Y	Y	Y	Y	N
4 **Buyer**	Y	Y	Y	Y	Y	Y	N
5 **Burton**	Y	Y	Y	Y	Y	Y	N
6 **Pence**	+	+	+	Y	Y	Y	N
7 Carson	Y	Y	Y	Y	Y	Y	Y
8 Ellsworth	Y	Y	Y	Y	Y	Y	Y
9 Hill	Y	Y	Y	Y	Y	Y	Y
IOWA							
1 Braley	Y	Y	Y	Y	Y	Y	Y
2 Loebsack	Y	Y	Y	Y	Y	Y	Y
3 Boswell	Y	Y	Y	Y	Y	Y	Y
4 **Latham**	Y	Y	Y	Y	Y	Y	N
5 **King**	Y	Y	Y	Y	Y	Y	N
KANSAS							
1 **Moran**	Y	Y	Y	Y	Y	Y	N
2 **Jenkins**	Y	Y	Y	Y	Y	Y	N
3 Moore	Y	Y	Y	Y	Y	Y	Y
4 **Tiahrt**	Y	Y	Y	Y	Y	Y	N
KENTUCKY							
1 **Whitfield**	Y	Y	Y	Y	Y	Y	N
2 **Guthrie**	Y	Y	Y	Y	Y	Y	N
3 Yarmuth	Y	Y	Y	Y	Y	Y	Y
4 **Davis**	Y	Y	Y	Y	Y	Y	N
5 **Rogers**	?	?	?	Y	Y	Y	N
6 Chandler	Y	Y	Y	Y	Y	Y	Y
LOUISIANA							
1 **Scalise**	Y	Y	Y	Y	Y	Y	N
2 **Cao**	?	?	?	Y	Y	Y	N
3 Melancon	Y	Y	Y	Y	Y	Y	Y
4 **Fleming**	Y	Y	Y	Y	Y	Y	N
5 **Alexander**	Y	Y	Y	Y	Y	Y	N
6 **Cassidy**	Y	Y	Y	Y	Y	Y	N
7 **Boustany**	?	?	?	?	?	?	?
MAINE							
1 Pingree	Y	Y	Y	Y	Y	Y	Y
2 Michaud	Y	Y	Y	Y	Y	Y	Y
MARYLAND							
1 Kratovil	Y	Y	Y	Y	Y	Y	Y
2 Ruppersberger	Y	Y	Y	Y	Y	Y	Y
3 Sarbanes	Y	Y	Y	Y	Y	Y	Y
4 Edwards	Y	Y	Y	Y	Y	Y	Y
5 Hoyer	Y	Y	Y	Y	Y	Y	Y
6 **Bartlett**	Y	Y	Y	Y	Y	Y	N
7 Cummings	Y	Y	Y	Y	Y	Y	Y
8 Van Hollen	Y	Y	Y	Y	Y	Y	Y
MASSACHUSETTS							
1 Olver	Y	Y	Y	Y	Y	Y	Y
2 Neal	Y	Y	Y	Y	Y	Y	Y
3 McGovern	Y	Y	Y	Y	Y	Y	Y
4 Frank	Y	Y	Y	Y	Y	Y	Y
5 Tsongas	Y	Y	Y	Y	Y	Y	Y
6 Tierney	Y	Y	Y	Y	Y	Y	Y
7 Markey	Y	Y	Y	Y	Y	Y	Y
8 Capuano	Y	Y	Y	Y	Y	Y	Y
9 Lynch	Y	Y	Y	Y	Y	Y	Y
10 Delahunt	?	?	?	Y	Y	Y	Y
MICHIGAN							
1 Stupak	Y	Y	Y	Y	Y	Y	Y
2 **Hoekstra**	Y	Y	Y	Y	Y	Y	N
3 **Ehlers**	Y	Y	Y	Y	Y	Y	N
4 **Camp**	Y	Y	Y	Y	Y	Y	N
5 Kildee	Y	Y	Y	Y	Y	Y	Y
6 **Upton**	Y	Y	Y	Y	Y	Y	N
7 Schauer	Y	Y	Y	Y	Y	Y	Y
8 **Rogers**	Y	Y	Y	Y	Y	Y	N
9 Peters	Y	Y	Y	Y	Y	Y	Y
10 **Miller**	Y	Y	Y	Y	Y	Y	N
11 **McCotter**	Y	Y	Y	Y	Y	Y	N
12 Levin	Y	Y	Y	Y	Y	Y	Y
13 Kilpatrick	Y	Y	Y	Y	Y	Y	Y
14 Conyers	?	Y	Y	Y	Y	Y	Y
15 Dingell	Y	Y	Y	Y	Y	Y	Y
MINNESOTA							
1 Walz	?	?	?	Y	Y	Y	Y
2 **Kline**	Y	Y	Y	Y	Y	Y	N
3 **Paulsen**	Y	Y	Y	Y	Y	Y	N
4 McCollum	Y	Y	Y	Y	Y	Y	Y

	125	126	127	128	129	130	131
5 Ellison	Y	Y	Y	Y	Y	Y	Y
6 **Bachmann**	Y	Y	Y	Y	Y	Y	N
7 Peterson	Y	Y	Y	Y	Y	Y	Y
8 Oberstar	Y	Y	Y	Y	Y	Y	Y
MISSISSIPPI							
1 Childers	Y	Y	Y	Y	Y	Y	N
2 Thompson	Y	Y	Y	Y	Y	Y	Y
3 **Harper**	Y	Y	Y	Y	Y	Y	N
4 Taylor	Y	Y	Y	Y	Y	Y	N
MISSOURI							
1 Clay	Y	Y	Y	Y	Y	Y	Y
2 **Akin**	Y	Y	Y	Y	Y	Y	N
3 Carnahan	Y	Y	Y	Y	Y	Y	Y
4 Skelton	Y	Y	Y	Y	Y	Y	Y
5 Cleaver	Y	Y	Y	Y	Y	Y	Y
6 **Graves**	Y	Y	Y	Y	Y	Y	N
7 **Blunt**	Y	Y	Y	Y	Y	Y	N
8 **Emerson**	?	?	?	Y	Y	Y	N
9 **Luetkemeyer**	+	+	+	Y	Y	Y	N
MONTANA							
AL **Rehberg**	Y	Y	Y	Y	Y	Y	N
NEBRASKA							
1 **Fortenberry**	Y	Y	Y	Y	Y	Y	N
2 **Terry**	Y	Y	Y	Y	Y	Y	N
3 **Smith**	Y	Y	Y	Y	Y	Y	N
NEVADA							
1 Berkley	Y	Y	Y	Y	Y	Y	Y
2 **Heller**	Y	Y	Y	Y	Y	Y	N
3 Titus	Y	Y	Y	Y	Y	Y	Y
NEW HAMPSHIRE							
1 Shea-Porter	?	?	?	?	?	?	Y
2 Hodes	Y	Y	Y	Y	Y	Y	Y
NEW JERSEY							
1 Andrews	Y	Y	Y	Y	Y	Y	Y
2 **LoBiondo**	Y	Y	Y	Y	Y	Y	N
3 Adler	Y	Y	Y	Y	Y	Y	Y
4 **Smith**	Y	Y	Y	Y	Y	Y	N
5 **Garrett**	Y	Y	Y	Y	Y	Y	N
6 Pallone	Y	Y	Y	Y	Y	Y	Y
7 **Lance**	Y	Y	Y	Y	Y	Y	N
8 Pascrell	+	+	+	Y	Y	Y	Y
9 Rothman	Y	Y	Y	Y	Y	Y	Y
10 Payne	Y	Y	Y	Y	Y	Y	Y
11 **Frelinghuysen**	Y	Y	Y	Y	Y	Y	N
12 Holt	Y	Y	Y	Y	Y	Y	Y
13 Sires	Y	Y	Y	Y	Y	Y	?
NEW MEXICO							
1 Heinrich	Y	Y	Y	Y	Y	Y	Y
2 Teague	Y	Y	Y	Y	Y	Y	Y
3 Lujan	Y	Y	Y	Y	Y	Y	?
NEW YORK							
1 Bishop	Y	Y	Y	Y	Y	Y	Y
2 Israel	Y	Y	Y	Y	Y	Y	Y
3 **King**	Y	Y	Y	Y	Y	Y	N
4 McCarthy	Y	Y	Y	Y	Y	Y	Y
5 Ackerman	Y	Y	Y	Y	Y	Y	Y
6 Meeks	Y	Y	Y	Y	Y	Y	Y
7 Crowley	Y	Y	Y	Y	Y	?	Y
8 Nadler	Y	Y	Y	Y	Y	Y	Y
9 Weiner	Y	Y	Y	Y	Y	Y	Y
10 Towns	Y	Y	Y	Y	Y	Y	Y
11 Clarke	Y	Y	Y	Y	Y	Y	Y
12 Velázquez	Y	Y	Y	Y	Y	?	?
13 McMahon	Y	Y	Y	Y	Y	Y	Y
14 Maloney	Y	Y	Y	Y	Y	Y	Y
15 Rangel	Y	Y	Y	Y	?	Y	Y
16 Serrano	Y	Y	Y	Y	Y	Y	?
17 Engel	Y	Y	Y	Y	Y	Y	Y
18 Lowey	Y	Y	Y	Y	Y	Y	Y
19 Hall	?	?	?	Y	Y	Y	Y
20 Vacant							
21 Tonko	Y	Y	Y	Y	Y	Y	Y
22 Hinchey	?	?	?	?	?	?	?
23 **McHugh**	Y	Y	Y	Y	Y	Y	N
24 Arcuri	Y	Y	Y	Y	Y	Y	Y
25 Maffei	Y	Y	Y	Y	Y	Y	Y
26 **Lee**	Y	Y	Y	Y	Y	Y	N
27 Higgins	Y	Y	Y	Y	Y	Y	Y
28 Slaughter	Y	Y	Y	Y	Y	Y	Y
29 Massa	Y	Y	Y	Y	Y	Y	Y
NORTH CAROLINA							
1 Butterfield	Y	Y	Y	Y	Y	Y	Y
2 Etheridge	Y	Y	Y	Y	Y	Y	Y
3 **Jones**	Y	Y	Y	Y	Y	Y	N
4 Price	Y	Y	Y	Y	Y	Y	Y

	125	126	127	128	129	130	131
5 **Foxx**	Y	Y	Y	Y	Y	N	N
6 **Coble**	Y	Y	Y	Y	Y	Y	N
7 McIntyre	Y	Y	Y	Y	Y	Y	Y
8 Kissell	Y	Y	Y	Y	Y	Y	Y
9 **Myrick**	+	+	+	Y	Y	Y	N
10 **McHenry**	Y	Y	Y	Y	Y	Y	N
11 Shuler	Y	Y	Y	Y	Y	Y	Y
12 Watt	Y	Y	Y	Y	Y	Y	Y
13 Miller	Y	Y	Y	Y	Y	Y	Y
NORTH DAKOTA							
AL Pomeroy	Y	Y	Y	Y	Y	Y	Y
OHIO							
1 Driehaus	Y	Y	Y	Y	Y	Y	Y
2 **Schmidt**	Y	Y	Y	Y	Y	Y	N
3 **Turner**	?	?	?	Y	Y	Y	N
4 **Jordan**	?	?	?	Y	Y	Y	N
5 **Latta**	Y	Y	Y	Y	Y	Y	N
6 Wilson	Y	Y	Y	Y	Y	Y	Y
7 **Austria**	Y	Y	Y	Y	Y	Y	N
8 **Boehner**	Y	Y	Y	Y	Y	Y	N
9 Kaptur	Y	Y	Y	Y	Y	Y	Y
10 Kucinich	Y	Y	Y	Y	Y	Y	Y
11 Fudge	Y	Y	Y	Y	Y	Y	Y
12 **Tiberi**	Y	Y	Y	Y	Y	Y	N
13 Sutton	Y	Y	Y	Y	Y	Y	Y
14 **LaTourette**	Y	Y	Y	Y	Y	Y	N
15 Kilroy	Y	Y	Y	Y	Y	Y	Y
16 Boccieri	Y	Y	Y	Y	Y	Y	Y
17 Ryan	Y	Y	Y	Y	?	Y	Y
18 Space	Y	Y	Y	Y	Y	Y	Y
OKLAHOMA							
1 **Sullivan**	Y	Y	Y	Y	Y	Y	N
2 Boren	?	?	?	Y	Y	Y	Y
3 **Lucas**	?	?	?	?	?	?	?
4 **Cole**	Y	Y	Y	Y	Y	Y	N
5 **Fallin**	Y	Y	Y	Y	Y	Y	N
OREGON							
1 Wu	Y	Y	Y	Y	Y	Y	Y
2 **Walden**	Y	Y	Y	Y	Y	Y	N
3 Blumenauer	Y	Y	Y	Y	Y	Y	Y
4 DeFazio	Y	Y	Y	Y	Y	Y	Y
5 Schrader	Y	Y	Y	Y	Y	Y	Y
PENNSYLVANIA							
1 Brady	Y	Y	Y	Y	Y	Y	Y
2 Fattah	Y	Y	Y	Y	Y	Y	Y
3 Dahlkemper	Y	Y	Y	Y	Y	Y	Y
4 Altmire	Y	Y	Y	Y	Y	Y	Y
5 **Thompson**	?	?	?	Y	Y	Y	N
6 **Gerlach**	Y	Y	Y	Y	Y	Y	N
7 Sestak	Y	Y	Y	Y	Y	Y	Y
8 Murphy, P.	Y	Y	Y	Y	Y	Y	Y
9 **Shuster**	Y	Y	Y	Y	Y	?	N
10 Carney	Y	Y	Y	Y	Y	Y	Y
11 Kanjorski	Y	Y	Y	Y	Y	Y	Y
12 Murtha	Y	Y	Y	Y	Y	Y	Y
13 Schwartz	Y	Y	Y	Y	Y	Y	Y
14 Doyle	?	?	?	Y	Y	Y	Y
15 **Dent**	Y	Y	Y	Y	Y	Y	N
16 **Pitts**	Y	Y	Y	Y	Y	Y	N
17 Holden	Y	Y	Y	Y	Y	Y	Y
18 **Murphy, T.**	Y	Y	Y	Y	Y	Y	N
19 **Platts**	Y	Y	Y	Y	Y	Y	N
RHODE ISLAND							
1 Kennedy	?	?	?	Y	Y	Y	Y
2 Langevin	Y	Y	Y	Y	Y	Y	Y
SOUTH CAROLINA							
1 **Brown**	Y	Y	Y	Y	Y	Y	N
2 **Wilson**	Y	Y	Y	Y	Y	Y	N
3 **Barrett**	Y	Y	Y	Y	Y	Y	N
4 **Inglis**	Y	Y	Y	Y	Y	+	N
5 Spratt	Y	Y	Y	Y	Y	Y	Y
6 Clyburn	Y	Y	Y	Y	Y	Y	Y
SOUTH DAKOTA							
AL Herseth Sandlin	Y	Y	Y	Y	Y	Y	Y
TENNESSEE							
1 **Roe**	Y	Y	Y	Y	Y	Y	N
2 **Duncan**	Y	Y	Y	Y	Y	N	N
3 **Wamp**	?	?	?	Y	Y	Y	N
4 Davis	Y	Y	Y	Y	Y	Y	Y
5 Cooper	Y	Y	Y	Y	Y	Y	Y
6 Gordon	Y	Y	Y	Y	Y	Y	Y
7 **Blackburn**	Y	Y	Y	Y	Y	Y	N
8 Tanner	Y	Y	Y	Y	Y	Y	Y
9 Cohen	Y	Y	Y	Y	Y	Y	Y

	125	126	127	128	129	130	131
TEXAS							
1 **Gohmert**	?	?	?	Y	?	Y	N
2 **Poe**	Y	Y	Y	Y	Y	Y	N
3 **Johnson, S.**	Y	Y	Y	Y	Y	Y	N
4 **Hall**	Y	Y	Y	Y	Y	Y	N
5 **Hensarling**	Y	Y	Y	Y	Y	Y	N
6 **Barton**	Y	Y	Y	Y	Y	Y	N
7 **Culberson**	Y	Y	Y	Y	Y	Y	N
8 **Brady**	Y	Y	Y	Y	Y	Y	N
9 Green, A.	Y	Y	Y	Y	Y	Y	Y
10 **McCaul**	?	?	?	Y	Y	Y	N
11 **Conaway**	Y	Y	Y	Y	Y	Y	N
12 **Granger**	Y	Y	Y	Y	Y	Y	N
13 **Thornberry**	Y	Y	Y	Y	Y	Y	N
14 **Paul**	Y	Y	Y	Y	Y	N	N
15 Hinojosa	Y	Y	Y	Y	Y	Y	?
16 Reyes	Y	Y	Y	Y	Y	Y	?
17 Edwards	Y	Y	Y	Y	Y	Y	Y
18 Jackson Lee	Y	Y	Y	Y	Y	Y	Y
19 **Neugebauer**	Y	Y	Y	Y	Y	Y	N
20 Gonzalez	Y	Y	Y	Y	Y	Y	?
21 **Smith**	Y	Y	Y	Y	Y	Y	N
22 **Olson**	?	?	?	?	?	?	?
23 Rodriguez	Y	Y	Y	Y	Y	Y	?
24 **Marchant**	Y	?	Y	Y	Y	Y	N
25 Doggett	Y	Y	Y	Y	Y	Y	Y
26 **Burgess**	Y	Y	Y	Y	Y	Y	N
27 Ortiz	Y	Y	Y	Y	Y	Y	?
28 Cuellar	Y	Y	Y	Y	Y	Y	?
29 Green, G.	Y	Y	Y	Y	Y	Y	Y
30 Johnson, E.	Y	Y	Y	Y	Y	Y	Y
31 **Carter**	Y	Y	Y	Y	Y	Y	N
32 **Sessions**	Y	Y	Y	Y	Y	Y	N
UTAH							
1 **Bishop**	Y	Y	Y	Y	Y	Y	N
2 Matheson	Y	Y	Y	Y	Y	Y	Y
3 **Chaffetz**	Y	Y	Y	Y	Y	Y	N
VERMONT							
AL Welch	?	?	?	?	?	?	Y
VIRGINIA							
1 **Wittman**	Y	Y	Y	Y	Y	Y	N
2 Nye	Y	Y	Y	Y	Y	Y	N
3 Scott	Y	Y	Y	Y	Y	Y	Y
4 **Forbes**	Y	Y	Y	Y	Y	Y	N
5 Perriello	Y	Y	Y	Y	Y	Y	N
6 **Goodlatte**	Y	Y	Y	Y	Y	Y	N
7 **Cantor**	Y	Y	Y	Y	Y	Y	N
8 Moran	?	?	?	Y	Y	Y	Y
9 Boucher	?	?	?	Y	Y	Y	Y
10 **Wolf**	Y	Y	Y	Y	Y	Y	N
11 Connolly	Y	Y	Y	Y	Y	Y	Y
WASHINGTON							
1 Inslee	Y	Y	Y	Y	Y	Y	Y
2 Larsen	Y	Y	Y	Y	Y	Y	Y
3 Baird	Y	Y	Y	Y	Y	Y	Y
4 **Hastings**	Y	Y	Y	Y	Y	Y	N
5 **McMorris Rodgers**	Y	Y	Y	Y	Y	Y	N
6 Dicks	Y	Y	Y	Y	Y	Y	Y
7 McDermott	Y	Y	Y	Y	Y	Y	Y
8 **Reichert**	Y	Y	Y	Y	Y	Y	N
9 Smith	?	?	?	Y	Y	Y	Y
WEST VIRGINIA							
1 Mollohan	Y	Y	Y	Y	Y	Y	Y
2 **Capito**	Y	Y	Y	Y	Y	Y	N
3 Rahall	Y	Y	Y	Y	Y	Y	Y
WISCONSIN							
1 **Ryan**	Y	Y	Y	Y	Y	Y	N
2 Baldwin	Y	Y	Y	Y	Y	Y	Y
3 Kind	Y	Y	Y	Y	Y	Y	Y
4 Moore	Y	Y	Y	Y	Y	Y	Y
5 **Sensenbrenner**	Y	Y	Y	Y	Y	Y	N
6 **Petri**	Y	Y	Y	Y	Y	Y	N
7 Obey	Y	Y	Y	Y	Y	Y	Y
8 Kagen	Y	Y	Y	Y	Y	Y	Y
WYOMING							
AL **Lummis**	Y	Y	Y	Y	Y	N	N
DELEGATES							
Faleomavaega (A.S.)							
Norton (D.C.)							
Bordallo (Guam)							
Sablan (N. Marianas)							
Pierluisi (P.R.)							
Christensen (V.I.)							

IN THE HOUSE | By Vote Number

132. **HR 1388. National Service Programs/Rule.** Adoption of the rule (H Res 205) that would provide for House floor consideration of the bill that would reauthorize Corporation for National Community Service programs through fiscal 2014 and increase the education reward for full-time service volunteers. Adopted 248-174: R 1-172; D 247-2. March 18, 2009.

133. **HR 1388. National Service Programs/Clean Energy Programs.** Pingree, D-Maine, amendment that would add development of clean energy programs designed to meet the needs of rural communities to the list of approved Clean Energy Corps activities. Adopted in Committee of the Whole 388-36: R 135-36; D 253-0. March 18, 2009.

134. **HR 1388. National Service Programs/Volunteer Generation Fund.** Loebsack, D-Iowa, amendment that would authorize funding for the Corporation for National and Community Service to administer a new grant program called the Volunteer Generation Fund, to assist non-profit, faith-based and other civic organizations to develop and carry out volunteer programs. Adopted in Committee of the Whole 261-168: R 11-163; D 250-5. March 18, 2009.

135. **HR 1388. National Service Programs/Authorization Levels.** Roe, R-Tenn., amendment that would set authorization levels for service programs in the bill at $405 million for fiscal 2010 and such sums as necessary for fiscal 2011-14. Rejected in Committee of the Whole 175-256: R 171-3; D 4-253. March 18, 2009.

136. **HR 1388. National Service Programs/Student and Elderly Assistance.** Kilroy, D-Ohio, amendment that would allow the bill's grant funds to be used for volunteers in physical education classes at elementary and secondary schools and after-school activities, and for student nutrition education, as well as for food delivery, home legal and medical services, and transportation for the elderly. Adopted in Committee of the Whole 372-57: R 118-56; D 254-1. March 18, 2009.

137. **HR 1388. National Service Programs/Operational Support Increase.** Markey, D-Colo., amendment that would increase the authorization for operational grants to approved national service programs from $600 to $800 per full-time volunteer and from $800 to $1,000 per volunteer if the program supports at least 50 percent disadvantaged youth. Adopted in Committee of the Whole 283-147: R 30-145; D 253-2. March 18, 2009.

138. **HR 1388. National Service Programs/National Service Reserve Corps.** Titus, D-Nev., amendment that would create a National Service Reserve Corps to respond to national disasters and other emergencies and require corps volunteers to contribute at least 10 hours annually. Adopted in Committee of the Whole 339-93: R 83-92; D 256-1. March 18, 2009.

	132	133	134	135	136	137	138
ALABAMA							
1 Bonner	N	Y	N	Y	N	N	N
2 Bright	Y	Y	Y	Y	Y	Y	Y
3 Rogers	N	Y	N	Y	N	N	N
4 Aderholt	N	Y	N	Y	N	N	N
5 Griffith	Y	Y	Y	N	Y	Y	Y
6 Bachus	N	Y	N	Y	N	Y	N
7 Davis	Y	Y	Y	N	Y	Y	Y
ALASKA							
AL Young	N	Y	N	Y	Y	N	Y
ARIZONA							
1 Kirkpatrick	Y	Y	Y	N	Y	Y	Y
2 Franks	N	N	N	Y	N	N	N
3 Shadegg	N	N	N	Y	N	N	N
4 Pastor	Y	Y	Y	N	Y	Y	Y
5 Mitchell	N	Y	Y	N	Y	Y	Y
6 Flake	N	N	N	Y	N	N	N
7 Grijalva	Y	Y	Y	N	Y	Y	Y
8 Giffords	Y	Y	N	N	Y	Y	Y
ARKANSAS							
1 Berry	Y	Y	N	N	N	N	N
2 Snyder	Y	Y	Y	N	Y	Y	Y
3 Boozman	N	Y	N	Y	N	N	N
4 Ross	Y	Y	Y	N	Y	Y	Y
CALIFORNIA							
1 Thompson	Y	Y	Y	N	Y	Y	Y
2 Herger	N	Y	N	Y	N	N	N
3 Lungren	N	Y	N	Y	Y	N	Y
4 McClintock	N	Y	N	Y	N	N	N
5 Matsui	Y	Y	Y	N	Y	Y	Y
6 Woolsey	Y	Y	Y	N	Y	Y	Y
7 Miller, George	Y	Y	Y	N	Y	Y	Y
8 Pelosi							
9 Lee	Y	Y	Y	N	Y	Y	Y
10 Tauscher	Y	Y	Y	N	Y	Y	Y
11 McNerney	Y	Y	Y	N	Y	?	Y
12 Speier	Y	Y	Y	N	Y	Y	Y
13 Stark	Y	Y	Y	N	Y	Y	Y
14 Eshoo	Y	Y	Y	N	Y	Y	Y
15 Honda	Y	?	Y	N	Y	Y	Y
16 Lofgren	Y	Y	Y	N	Y	Y	Y
17 Farr	Y	Y	Y	N	Y	Y	Y
18 Cardoza	?	Y	Y	N	Y	Y	Y
19 Radanovich	N	N	N	Y	N	N	N
20 Costa	?	Y	Y	N	Y	Y	Y
21 Nunes	N	N	N	Y	N	N	N
22 McCarthy	N	Y	N	Y	N	N	N
23 Capps	Y	Y	Y	N	Y	Y	Y
24 Gallegly	?	Y	N	Y	Y	N	Y
25 McKeon	N	Y	N	Y	N	N	Y
26 Dreier	N	Y	N	Y	Y	N	Y
27 Sherman	Y	Y	Y	N	Y	Y	Y
28 Berman	Y	Y	Y	N	Y	Y	Y
29 Schiff	Y	Y	Y	N	Y	Y	Y
30 Waxman	Y	Y	Y	N	Y	Y	Y
31 Becerra	Y	Y	Y	N	Y	Y	Y
32 Vacant							
33 Watson	Y	Y	Y	N	Y	Y	Y
34 Roybal-Allard	Y	Y	Y	N	Y	Y	Y
35 Waters	Y	Y	Y	N	Y	Y	Y
36 Harman	Y	Y	Y	N	Y	Y	Y
37 Richardson	Y	Y	Y	N	Y	Y	Y
38 Napolitano	Y	Y	Y	N	Y	Y	Y
39 Sánchez, Linda	Y	Y	Y	N	Y	Y	Y
40 Royce	N	N	N	Y	N	N	N
41 Lewis	N	Y	N	Y	Y	N	Y
42 Miller, Gary	?	?	?	?	?	?	?
43 Baca	Y	Y	Y	N	Y	Y	Y
44 Calvert	N	Y	N	Y	N	Y	Y
45 Bono Mack	N	Y	N	Y	Y	N	Y
46 Rohrabacher	N	N	N	Y	N	N	N
47 Sanchez, Loretta	?	?	?	?	?	?	?
48 Campbell	N	N	N	Y	N	N	N
49 Issa	N	Y	N	Y	N	N	N
50 Bilbray	N	Y	N	Y	Y	N	N
51 Filner	Y	Y	Y	N	Y	Y	Y
52 Hunter	N	Y	N	Y	N	N	N
53 Davis	Y	Y	Y	N	Y	Y	Y

	132	133	134	135	136	137	138
COLORADO							
1 DeGette	Y	Y	Y	N	Y	Y	Y
2 Polis	Y	Y	Y	N	Y	Y	Y
3 Salazar	Y	Y	Y	N	Y	Y	Y
4 Markey	Y	Y	Y	N	Y	Y	Y
5 Lamborn	N	N	N	Y	N	N	N
6 Coffman	N	Y	N	Y	N	Y	N
7 Perlmutter	Y	Y	Y	N	Y	Y	Y
CONNECTICUT							
1 Larson	Y	Y	?	N	Y	Y	Y
2 Courtney	Y	Y	Y	N	Y	Y	Y
3 DeLauro	Y	Y	Y	N	Y	Y	Y
4 Himes	Y	Y	Y	N	Y	Y	Y
5 Murphy	Y	Y	Y	N	Y	Y	Y
DELAWARE							
AL Castle	N	Y	N	Y	Y	Y	Y
FLORIDA							
1 Miller	N	N	N	Y	Y	N	N
2 Boyd	Y	Y	Y	N	Y	Y	Y
3 Brown	Y	Y	Y	N	Y	Y	Y
4 Crenshaw	N	Y	N	Y	Y	N	Y
5 Brown-Waite	N	Y	N	Y	Y	N	Y
6 Stearns	N	N	N	Y	Y	N	N
7 Mica	N	Y	N	Y	N	N	N
8 Grayson	Y	Y	Y	N	Y	Y	Y
9 Bilirakis	N	Y	Y	Y	Y	N	Y
10 Young	N	Y	N	Y	N	N	N
11 Castor	Y	Y	Y	N	Y	Y	Y
12 Putnam	N	Y	N	Y	N	Y	Y
13 Buchanan	N	Y	N	Y	Y	N	Y
14 Mack	N	N	N	Y	N	N	N
15 Posey	N	Y	N	Y	Y	N	N
16 Rooney	N	Y	N	Y	Y	N	Y
17 Meek	Y	Y	Y	N	Y	Y	Y
18 Ros-Lehtinen	N	Y	Y	Y	Y	Y	Y
19 Wexler	Y	Y	Y	N	Y	Y	Y
20 Wasserman Schultz	Y	Y	Y	N	Y	Y	Y
21 Diaz-Balart, L.	N	Y	N	Y	Y	Y	Y
22 Klein	Y	Y	Y	N	Y	Y	Y
23 Hastings	Y	Y	Y	N	Y	Y	Y
24 Kosmas	Y	Y	Y	N	Y	Y	Y
25 Diaz-Balart, M.	N	Y	N	Y	Y	Y	Y
GEORGIA							
1 Kingston	N	N	N	Y	N	N	N
2 Bishop	Y	Y	Y	N	Y	Y	Y
3 Westmoreland	N	N	N	Y	N	N	N
4 Johnson	Y	Y	Y	N	Y	Y	Y
5 Lewis	Y	Y	Y	N	Y	Y	Y
6 Price	N	Y	N	Y	Y	N	N
7 Linder	N	N	N	Y	N	N	N
8 Marshall	Y	Y	Y	N	Y	Y	Y
9 Deal	N	N	N	Y	N	N	N
10 Broun	N	N	N	Y	N	N	N
11 Gingrey	N	Y	N	Y	N	N	N
12 Barrow	Y	Y	Y	N	Y	Y	Y
13 Scott	Y	Y	Y	N	Y	Y	Y
HAWAII							
1 Abercrombie	Y	Y	Y	N	Y	Y	Y
2 Hirono	Y	Y	Y	N	Y	Y	Y
IDAHO							
1 Minnick	Y	Y	N	Y	Y	?	Y
2 Simpson	N	Y	N	Y	N	N	N
ILLINOIS							
1 Rush	Y	Y	Y	N	Y	Y	Y
2 Jackson	Y	Y	Y	N	Y	Y	Y
3 Lipinski	Y	Y	Y	N	Y	Y	Y
4 Gutierrez	Y	Y	Y	N	Y	Y	Y
5 Vacant							
6 Roskam	N	N	N	Y	N	N	Y
7 Davis	Y	Y	Y	N	Y	Y	Y
8 Bean	Y	Y	Y	N	Y	Y	Y
9 Schakowsky	Y	Y	Y	N	?	Y	Y
10 Kirk	N	Y	N	Y	N	N	N
11 Halvorson	Y	Y	Y	N	Y	Y	Y
12 Costello	Y	Y	Y	N	Y	Y	Y
13 Biggert	N	Y	N	Y	Y	Y	Y
14 Foster	Y	Y	Y	N	Y	Y	Y
15 Johnson	N	Y	N	Y	Y	Y	Y

KEY **Republicans** Democrats

Y	Voted for (yea)	X	Paired against	C	Voted "present" to avoid possible conflict of interest
#	Paired for	–	Announced against		
+	Announced for	P	Voted "present"	?	Did not vote or otherwise make a position known
N	Voted against (nay)				

	132	133	134	135	136	137	138
16 **Manzullo**	N	Y	N	Y	Y	N	N
17 Hare	Y	Y	Y	N	Y	Y	Y
18 **Schock**	N	Y	N	Y	Y	N	Y
19 **Shimkus**	N	Y	N	Y	Y	N	Y
INDIANA							
1 Visclosky	Y	Y	Y	N	Y	Y	Y
2 Donnelly	Y	Y	Y	N	Y	Y	Y
3 **Souder**	N	Y	N	Y	N	N	N
4 **Buyer**	N	Y	N	Y	Y	N	N
5 **Burton**	N	N	N	Y	Y	N	N
6 **Pence**	N	N	N	Y	N	N	Y
7 Carson	Y	Y	Y	N	Y	Y	Y
8 Ellsworth	Y	Y	Y	N	Y	Y	Y
9 Hill	Y	Y	Y	N	Y	Y	Y
IOWA							
1 Braley	Y	Y	Y	N	Y	Y	Y
2 Loebsack	Y	Y	Y	N	Y	Y	Y
3 Boswell	Y	Y	Y	N	Y	Y	Y
4 **Latham**	N	Y	N	Y	Y	N	N
5 **King**	N	N	N	Y	N	N	N
KANSAS							
1 **Moran**	N	Y	N	Y	Y	N	N
2 **Jenkins**	N	Y	N	Y	Y	N	N
3 Moore	Y	Y	Y	N	Y	Y	Y
4 **Tiahrt**	N	+	N	Y	Y	N	N
KENTUCKY							
1 **Whitfield**	N	Y	N	Y	Y	N	Y
2 **Guthrie**	N	Y	N	Y	Y	Y	Y
3 Yarmuth	Y	Y	Y	N	Y	Y	Y
4 **Davis**	N	Y	N	Y	N	N	N
5 **Rogers**	N	Y	N	Y	Y	N	Y
6 Chandler	Y	Y	Y	N	Y	Y	Y
LOUISIANA							
1 **Scalise**	N	N	N	Y	N	N	Y
2 **Cao**	N	Y	N	Y	Y	N	Y
3 Melancon	Y	Y	Y	N	Y	Y	Y
4 **Fleming**	N	Y	N	Y	N	N	N
5 **Alexander**	N	?	N	Y	N	N	N
6 **Cassidy**	N	Y	N	Y	Y	N	Y
7 **Boustany**	?	?	?	?	?	?	?
MAINE							
1 Pingree	Y	Y	Y	N	Y	Y	Y
2 Michaud	Y	Y	Y	N	Y	Y	Y
MARYLAND							
1 Kratovil	Y	Y	Y	N	Y	Y	Y
2 Ruppersberger	Y	Y	Y	N	Y	Y	Y
3 Sarbanes	Y	Y	Y	N	Y	Y	Y
4 Edwards	Y	Y	Y	N	Y	Y	Y
5 Hoyer	Y	Y	Y	N	Y	Y	Y
6 **Bartlett**	N	Y	N	Y	Y	N	N
7 Cummings	Y	Y	Y	N	Y	Y	Y
8 Van Hollen	Y	Y	Y	N	Y	Y	Y
MASSACHUSETTS							
1 Olver	Y	Y	Y	N	Y	Y	Y
2 Neal	Y	Y	Y	N	Y	Y	Y
3 McGovern	Y	Y	Y	N	Y	Y	Y
4 Frank	Y	Y	Y	N	Y	Y	Y
5 Tsongas	Y	Y	Y	N	Y	Y	Y
6 Tierney	Y	Y	Y	N	Y	Y	Y
7 Markey	Y	Y	Y	N	Y	Y	Y
8 Capuano	Y	?	Y	N	Y	Y	Y
9 Lynch	Y	Y	Y	N	Y	Y	Y
10 Delahunt	Y	Y	Y	N	Y	Y	Y
MICHIGAN							
1 Stupak	Y	Y	Y	N	Y	Y	Y
2 **Hoekstra**	N	Y	N	Y	Y	N	N
3 **Ehlers**	N	Y	Y	Y	Y	Y	Y
4 **Camp**	N	Y	N	Y	Y	N	Y
5 Kildee	Y	Y	Y	N	Y	Y	Y
6 **Upton**	N	Y	N	Y	Y	Y	Y
7 Schauer	Y	Y	Y	N	Y	Y	Y
8 **Rogers**	N	Y	N	Y	Y	N	Y
9 Peters	Y	Y	Y	N	Y	Y	Y
10 **Miller**	N	Y	N	Y	Y	Y	Y
11 **McCotter**	N	Y	N	Y	Y	N	Y
12 Levin	Y	Y	Y	N	Y	Y	Y
13 Kilpatrick	Y	Y	Y	N	Y	Y	Y
14 Conyers	Y	Y	Y	N	Y	Y	Y
15 Dingell	Y	Y	Y	N	Y	Y	Y
MINNESOTA							
1 Walz	Y	Y	Y	N	Y	Y	Y
2 **Kline**	N	Y	N	Y	Y	N	N
3 **Paulsen**	N	Y	N	Y	Y	N	Y
4 McCollum	Y	Y	Y	N	Y	Y	Y

	132	133	134	135	136	137	138
5 Ellison	Y	Y	Y	N	Y	Y	Y
6 **Bachmann**	N	Y	N	Y	N	N	N
7 Peterson	Y	Y	Y	N	Y	Y	Y
8 Oberstar	Y	Y	Y	N	Y	Y	Y
MISSISSIPPI							
1 Childers	Y	Y	Y	Y	Y	Y	Y
2 Thompson	Y	Y	Y	N	Y	Y	Y
3 **Harper**	N	Y	N	Y	N	N	N
4 Taylor	N	Y	Y	N	Y	Y	Y
MISSOURI							
1 Clay	Y	Y	Y	N	Y	Y	Y
2 **Akin**	N	N	N	Y	N	N	N
3 Carnahan	Y	Y	Y	N	Y	Y	Y
4 Skelton	Y	Y	Y	N	?	Y	Y
5 Cleaver	Y	Y	Y	N	Y	Y	Y
6 **Graves**	N	Y	N	Y	Y	N	N
7 **Blunt**	N	N	N	Y	N	N	N
8 **Emerson**	N	Y	N	Y	Y	N	Y
9 **Luetkemeyer**	N	Y	N	Y	Y	N	Y
MONTANA							
AL **Rehberg**	N	Y	N	Y	Y	N	Y
NEBRASKA							
1 **Fortenberry**	N	Y	N	Y	Y	Y	Y
2 **Terry**	N	Y	N	Y	Y	Y	Y
3 **Smith**	N	Y	N	Y	Y	Y	Y
NEVADA							
1 Berkley	Y	Y	Y	N	Y	Y	Y
2 **Heller**	N	Y	N	Y	Y	Y	Y
3 Titus	Y	Y	Y	N	Y	Y	Y
NEW HAMPSHIRE							
1 Shea-Porter	Y	Y	Y	N	Y	Y	Y
2 Hodes	Y	Y	Y	N	Y	Y	Y
NEW JERSEY							
1 Andrews	Y	Y	Y	N	Y	Y	Y
2 **LoBiondo**	N	Y	N	Y	Y	Y	Y
3 Adler	Y	Y	Y	N	Y	Y	Y
4 **Smith**	N	Y	N	Y	Y	Y	Y
5 **Garrett**	N	N	N	Y	Y	N	N
6 Pallone	Y	Y	Y	N	Y	Y	Y
7 **Lance**	N	Y	Y	Y	Y	Y	Y
8 Pascrell	Y	Y	Y	N	Y	Y	Y
9 Rothman	Y	Y	Y	N	Y	Y	Y
10 Payne	Y	Y	Y	N	Y	Y	Y
11 **Frelinghuysen**	N	Y	N	Y	Y	Y	Y
12 Holt	Y	Y	Y	N	Y	Y	Y
13 Sires	Y	Y	Y	N	Y	Y	Y
NEW MEXICO							
1 Heinrich	Y	Y	Y	N	Y	Y	Y
2 Teague	Y	Y	Y	N	Y	Y	Y
3 Lujan	Y	Y	Y	N	Y	Y	Y
NEW YORK							
1 Bishop	Y	Y	Y	N	Y	Y	Y
2 Israel	Y	Y	Y	N	Y	Y	Y
3 **King**	N	Y	N	Y	Y	Y	Y
4 McCarthy	Y	Y	Y	N	Y	Y	Y
5 Ackerman	Y	Y	Y	N	Y	Y	Y
6 Meeks	Y	Y	Y	N	Y	Y	Y
7 Crowley	Y	Y	Y	N	Y	Y	Y
8 Nadler	Y	Y	Y	N	Y	Y	Y
9 Weiner	Y	Y	Y	N	Y	Y	Y
10 Towns	Y	Y	Y	N	Y	Y	Y
11 Clarke	Y	Y	Y	N	Y	Y	Y
12 Velázquez	Y	Y	Y	N	Y	Y	Y
13 McMahon	Y	Y	Y	N	Y	Y	Y
14 Maloney	Y	Y	Y	N	Y	Y	Y
15 Rangel	Y	Y	Y	N	Y	Y	Y
16 Serrano	Y	Y	Y	N	Y	Y	Y
17 Engel	Y	Y	Y	N	Y	Y	Y
18 Lowey	Y	Y	Y	N	Y	Y	Y
19 Hall	Y	Y	Y	N	Y	Y	Y
20 Vacant							
21 Tonko	Y	Y	Y	N	Y	Y	Y
22 Hinchey	?	?	?	?	?	?	?
23 **McHugh**	N	Y	N	Y	Y	Y	Y
24 Arcuri	Y	Y	Y	N	Y	Y	Y
25 Maffei	Y	Y	Y	N	Y	Y	Y
26 **Lee**	N	Y	N	Y	Y	Y	Y
27 Higgins	Y	Y	Y	N	Y	Y	Y
28 Slaughter	Y	Y	Y	N	Y	Y	Y
29 Massa	Y	Y	Y	N	Y	Y	Y
NORTH CAROLINA							
1 Butterfield	Y	Y	Y	N	Y	Y	Y
2 Etheridge	Y	Y	Y	N	Y	Y	Y
3 **Jones**	N	Y	N	Y	Y	N	N
4 Price	Y	Y	Y	N	Y	Y	Y

	132	133	134	135	136	137	138
5 **Foxx**	N	N	N	Y	N	N	N
6 **Coble**	N	Y	N	Y	N	N	N
7 McIntyre	Y	Y	Y	N	Y	Y	Y
8 Kissell	Y	Y	Y	N	Y	Y	Y
9 **Myrick**	N	Y	N	Y	Y	N	Y
10 **McHenry**	N	Y	N	Y	Y	N	Y
11 Shuler	Y	Y	Y	N	Y	Y	Y
12 Watt	Y	Y	Y	N	Y	Y	Y
13 Miller	Y	Y	Y	N	Y	Y	Y
NORTH DAKOTA							
AL Pomeroy	Y	Y	Y	N	Y	Y	Y
OHIO							
1 Driehaus	Y	Y	Y	N	Y	Y	Y
2 **Schmidt**	N	Y	N	Y	Y	N	N
3 **Turner**	N	Y	Y	Y	Y	Y	Y
4 **Jordan**	N	N	N	Y	N	N	N
5 **Latta**	N	N	N	Y	N	N	N
6 Wilson	Y	Y	Y	N	Y	Y	Y
7 **Austria**	N	Y	N	Y	Y	N	Y
8 **Boehner**	N	Y	N	Y	N	N	N
9 Kaptur	Y	Y	Y	N	Y	Y	Y
10 Kucinich	Y	Y	Y	N	Y	Y	Y
11 Fudge	Y	Y	Y	N	Y	Y	Y
12 **Tiberi**	N	Y	N	Y	Y	N	Y
13 Sutton	Y	Y	Y	N	Y	Y	Y
14 **LaTourette**	N	Y	N	N	Y	N	Y
15 Kilroy	Y	Y	Y	N	Y	Y	Y
16 Boccieri	Y	Y	Y	N	Y	Y	Y
17 Ryan	Y	Y	Y	N	Y	Y	Y
18 Space	Y	Y	Y	N	Y	Y	Y
OKLAHOMA							
1 **Sullivan**	N	Y	N	Y	Y	N	N
2 Boren	Y	Y	Y	N	Y	Y	Y
3 **Lucas**	?	?	?	?	?	N	Y
4 **Cole**	N	Y	N	Y	Y	N	Y
5 **Fallin**	N	Y	N	Y	Y	N	Y
OREGON							
1 Wu	Y	Y	Y	N	Y	Y	Y
2 **Walden**	N	Y	N	Y	Y	N	Y
3 Blumenauer	Y	Y	Y	N	Y	Y	Y
4 DeFazio	Y	Y	Y	N	Y	Y	Y
5 Schrader	Y	Y	Y	N	Y	Y	Y
PENNSYLVANIA							
1 Brady	Y	Y	Y	N	Y	Y	Y
2 Fattah	Y	Y	Y	N	Y	Y	Y
3 Dahlkemper	Y	Y	Y	N	Y	Y	Y
4 Altmire	Y	Y	N	N	Y	N	Y
5 **Thompson**	N	Y	N	Y	Y	N	Y
6 **Gerlach**	N	Y	Y	Y	Y	Y	Y
7 Sestak	Y	Y	Y	N	Y	Y	Y
8 Murphy, P.	Y	Y	Y	N	Y	Y	Y
9 **Shuster**	N	Y	N	Y	N	N	N
10 Carney	Y	Y	Y	N	Y	Y	Y
11 Kanjorski	Y	Y	Y	N	Y	Y	Y
12 Murtha	Y	Y	Y	N	Y	Y	Y
13 Schwartz	Y	Y	Y	N	Y	Y	Y
14 Doyle	Y	Y	Y	N	Y	Y	Y
15 **Dent**	N	Y	Y	Y	Y	Y	Y
16 **Pitts**	N	Y	N	Y	Y	N	Y
17 Holden	Y	Y	N	N	Y	Y	Y
18 **Murphy, T.**	N	Y	N	Y	Y	Y	Y
19 **Platts**	Y	Y	Y	N	Y	Y	Y
RHODE ISLAND							
1 Kennedy	Y	Y	Y	N	Y	Y	Y
2 Langevin	Y	Y	Y	N	Y	Y	Y
SOUTH CAROLINA							
1 **Brown**	N	Y	N	Y	Y	N	Y
2 **Wilson**	N	Y	N	Y	Y	N	N
3 **Barrett**	N	N	N	Y	N	N	N
4 **Inglis**	N	Y	N	Y	N	N	N
5 Spratt	Y	Y	Y	N	Y	Y	Y
6 Clyburn	Y	Y	Y	N	Y	Y	Y
SOUTH DAKOTA							
AL Herseth Sandlin	Y	Y	Y	N	Y	Y	Y
TENNESSEE							
1 **Roe**	N	Y	N	Y	Y	N	Y
2 **Duncan**	N	Y	N	Y	Y	N	N
3 **Wamp**	N	Y	N	Y	Y	N	Y
4 Davis	Y	?	?	N	Y	Y	Y
5 Cooper	Y	Y	Y	N	Y	Y	Y
6 Gordon	Y	Y	Y	N	Y	Y	Y
7 **Blackburn**	N	Y	N	Y	Y	N	N
8 Tanner	Y	Y	Y	Y	Y	Y	Y
9 Cohen	Y	Y	Y	N	Y	Y	Y

	132	133	134	135	136	137	138
TEXAS							
1 **Gohmert**	N	Y	N	Y	N	N	N
2 **Poe**	N	N	N	Y	N	N	N
3 **Johnson, S.**	N	N	N	Y	N	N	N
4 **Hall**	N	Y	N	Y	N	N	N
5 **Hensarling**	N	N	N	Y	N	N	N
6 **Barton**	N	N	N	Y	Y	N	Y
7 **Culberson**	N	Y	N	Y	N	N	N
8 **Brady**	N	Y	N	Y	N	N	N
9 Green, A.	Y	Y	Y	N	Y	Y	Y
10 **McCaul**	N	Y	N	Y	Y	N	Y
11 **Conaway**	N	Y	N	Y	Y	N	N
12 **Granger**	N	Y	N	Y	N	N	N
13 **Thornberry**	N	Y	N	Y	N	N	N
14 **Paul**	N	N	N	Y	Y	N	N
15 Hinojosa	Y	Y	Y	N	Y	Y	Y
16 Reyes	Y	Y	Y	N	Y	Y	Y
17 Edwards	Y	Y	Y	N	Y	Y	Y
18 Jackson Lee	Y	Y	Y	N	Y	Y	Y
19 **Neugebauer**	N	Y	N	Y	N	N	N
20 Gonzalez	Y	Y	Y	N	Y	Y	Y
21 **Smith**	N	Y	N	Y	Y	N	Y
22 **Olson**	?	?	?	?	?	?	?
23 Rodriguez	Y	Y	Y	N	Y	Y	Y
24 **Marchant**	N	N	N	Y	N	N	N
25 Doggett	Y	Y	Y	N	Y	Y	Y
26 **Burgess**	N	Y	N	Y	Y	N	Y
27 Ortiz	Y	Y	Y	N	Y	Y	Y
28 Cuellar	Y	Y	Y	N	Y	Y	Y
29 Green, G.	Y	Y	Y	N	Y	Y	Y
30 Johnson, E.	Y	Y	Y	N	Y	Y	Y
31 **Carter**	N	N	N	Y	N	N	N
32 **Sessions**	N	N	N	Y	N	N	N
UTAH							
1 **Bishop**	N	?	N	Y	N	N	N
2 Matheson	Y	Y	Y	N	Y	Y	Y
3 **Chaffetz**	N	Y	N	Y	Y	N	Y
VERMONT							
AL Welch	Y	Y	Y	N	Y	Y	Y
VIRGINIA							
1 **Wittman**	N	Y	N	Y	Y	Y	Y
2 Nye	Y	Y	Y	N	Y	Y	Y
3 Scott	Y	Y	Y	N	Y	Y	Y
4 **Forbes**	N	Y	N	Y	Y	N	N
5 Perriello	Y	Y	Y	N	Y	Y	Y
6 **Goodlatte**	N	Y	N	Y	Y	N	N
7 **Cantor**	N	Y	N	Y	N	N	N
8 Moran	Y	Y	Y	N	Y	Y	Y
9 Boucher	Y	Y	Y	N	Y	Y	Y
10 **Wolf**	N	Y	N	Y	Y	N	Y
11 Connolly	Y	Y	Y	N	Y	Y	Y
WASHINGTON							
1 Inslee	Y	Y	Y	N	Y	Y	Y
2 Larsen	Y	Y	Y	N	Y	Y	Y
3 Baird	Y	Y	Y	N	Y	Y	Y
4 **Hastings**	N	N	N	Y	N	N	N
5 **McMorris Rodgers**	N	Y	N	Y	Y	N	Y
6 Dicks	Y	Y	Y	N	Y	Y	Y
7 McDermott	Y	Y	Y	N	Y	Y	Y
8 **Reichert**	N	Y	N	Y	Y	Y	Y
9 Smith	Y	Y	Y	N	Y	Y	Y
WEST VIRGINIA							
1 Mollohan	Y	Y	Y	N	Y	Y	Y
2 **Capito**	N	Y	N	Y	Y	Y	Y
3 Rahall	Y	Y	Y	N	Y	Y	Y
WISCONSIN							
1 **Ryan**	N	Y	N	Y	Y	N	N
2 Baldwin	Y	Y	Y	N	Y	Y	Y
3 Kind	Y	Y	Y	N	Y	Y	Y
4 Moore	Y	Y	Y	N	Y	Y	Y
5 **Sensenbrenner**	N	Y	N	Y	Y	N	N
6 **Petri**	N	Y	Y	Y	Y	N	Y
7 Obey	Y	?	Y	N	Y	Y	Y
8 Kagen	Y	Y	Y	N	Y	Y	Y
WYOMING							
AL **Lummis**	N	N	N	Y	N	N	N
DELEGATES							
Faleomavaega (A.S.)		Y	Y	N	Y	Y	Y
Norton (D.C.)		Y	Y	N	Y	Y	Y
Bordallo (Guam)		Y	Y	N	Y	Y	Y
Sablan (N. Marianas)		Y	Y	N	Y	Y	Y
Pierluisi (P.R.)		Y	Y	N	Y	Y	Y
Christensen (V.I.)		Y	Y	N	Y	Y	Y

IN THE HOUSE | By Vote Number

139. **HR 1388. National Service Programs/Recommit.** Foxx, R-N.C., motion to recommit the bill to the Education and Labor Committee with instructions that it be reported back immediately with language that would bar participants in approved national service positions from attempting to influence legislation; organizing or engaging in protests, petitions, boycotts or strikes; assisting, promoting or deterring union organizing; or engaging in religious instruction, as well as other activities. Motion agreed to 318-105: R 174-0; D 144-105. March 18, 2009.

140. **HR 1388. National Service Programs/Passage.** Passage of the bill that would reauthorize Corporation for National and Community Service programs through fiscal 2014, increase the education reward for full-time service volunteers from $4,725 to $5,350 in fiscal 2010 and make the reward equal to the maximum annual Pell grant thereafter. It would authorize funding for fiscal 2010-14 for AmeriCorps, Volunteers in Service to America program, Learn and Serve America, the Retired and Senior Volunteer Program, the Foster Grandparent Program, and the Senior Companion Program. It also would bar participants in approved national service positions from taking part in certain political activities, such as attempting to influence legislation or engaging in protests or strikes. Passed 321-105: R 70-104; D 251-1. A "yea" was a vote in support of the president's position. March 18, 2009.

141. **H Res 265. Earmark Investigation/Motion to Table.** Becerra, D-Calif., motion to table (kill) the Flake, R-Ariz., privileged resolution that would instruct the Committee on Standards of Official Conduct to investigate and report on the relationship between earmarks made by members of Congress and the details of past campaign contributions. Motion agreed to 226-180: R 4-158; D 222-22. March 19, 2009.

142. **H Res 257. Suspension Motions/Previous Question.** Pingree, D-Maine, motion to order the previous question (thus ending debate and possibility of amendment) on adoption of the resolution that would provide for House floor consideration of bills under suspension of the rules on the legislative day March, 19, 2009. Motion agreed to 242-180: R 0-172; D 242-8. (Subsequently, the rule was adopted by voice vote.) March 19, 2009.

143. **HR 1586. Bonus Tax for Federally Assisted Companies/Passage.** Rangel, D-N.Y., motion to suspend the rules and pass the bill that would impose a 90 percent tax on bonuses given after Dec. 31, 2008, to certain employees of companies that received more than $5 billion from the Troubled Asset Relief Program, to employees of Fannie Mae and Freddie Mac, and to members of affiliated groups or partnerships in which more than 50 percent of the capital or profits is owned by the above parties. It would apply to bonus recipients with adjusted gross incomes of more than $125,000 per year ($250,000 for joint filers). Motion agreed to 328-93: R 85-87; D 243-6. A two-thirds majority of those present and voting (281 in this case) is required for passage under suspension of the rules. March 19, 2009.

144. **H Con Res 76. Bonus Payment Disapproval/Adoption.** Frank, D-Mass., motion to suspend the rules and adopt the concurrent resolution that would express the sense of Congress that the president is appropriately exercising all of the authorities granted by Congress under the 2008 financial bailout law by taking action to ensure that American International Group repay taxpayer money given in retention bonuses and that companies that receive money from the law limit base salaries to $500,000 per year and do not give excessive compensation payments or so-called golden parachutes going forward. Motion rejected 255-160: R 12-159; D 243-1. A two-thirds majority of those present and voting (277 in this case) is required for adoption under suspension of the rules. March 19, 2009.

	139	140	141	142	143	144
ALABAMA						
1 Bonner	Y	N	P	N	N	N
2 Bright	Y	Y	N	N	Y	N
3 Rogers	Y	N	N	N	Y	N
4 Aderholt	Y	N	N	N	Y	N
5 Griffith	Y	Y	Y	Y	Y	Y
6 Bachus	Y	Y	N	N	N	N
7 Davis	Y	Y	Y	Y	Y	Y
ALASKA						
AL Young	Y	Y	Y	N	Y	N
ARIZONA						
1 Kirkpatrick	Y	Y	N	Y	Y	Y
2 Franks	Y	N	N	N	N	N
3 Shadegg	Y	N	N	N	N	N
4 Pastor	Y	Y	Y	Y	Y	Y
5 Mitchell	Y	Y	N	N	Y	Y
6 Flake	Y	N	N	N	N	N
7 Grijalva	N	Y	Y	Y	Y	Y
8 Giffords	Y	Y	N	Y	Y	Y
ARKANSAS						
1 Berry	N	N	Y	Y	Y	Y
2 Snyder	Y	Y	Y	N	Y	Y
3 Boozman	Y	N	N	N	Y	N
4 Ross	Y	Y	Y	Y	Y	Y
CALIFORNIA						
1 Thompson	Y	Y	Y	Y	Y	Y
2 Herger	Y	N	N	N	Y	N
3 Lungren	Y	N	N	N	Y	N
4 McClintock	Y	N	N	N	N	N
5 Matsui	N	Y	Y	Y	Y	Y
6 Woolsey	N	Y	Y	Y	Y	Y
7 Miller, George	Y	Y	Y	Y	Y	Y
8 Pelosi	?	Y				
9 Lee		N	Y	Y	Y	Y
10 Tauscher	Y	Y	Y	Y	Y	Y
11 McNerney	Y	Y	N	N	Y	+
12 Speier	N	Y	Y	Y	Y	Y
13 Stark	N	Y	Y	Y	Y	Y
14 Eshoo	Y	Y	Y	Y	Y	Y
15 Honda	Y	Y	Y	Y	Y	Y
16 Lofgren	N	Y	P	Y	Y	Y
17 Farr	Y	Y	Y	Y	Y	Y
18 Cardoza	N	Y	Y	Y	Y	Y
19 Radanovich	Y	N	?	?	?	?
20 Costa	?	Y	Y	Y	Y	Y
21 Nunes	Y	N	N	N	N	N
22 McCarthy	Y	N	N	N	N	N
23 Capps	N	Y	Y	Y	Y	Y
24 Gallegly	Y	Y	N	N	Y	Y
25 McKeon	Y	Y	N	N	Y	N
26 Dreier	Y	N	N	N	N	N
27 Sherman	N	Y	Y	Y	Y	Y
28 Berman	N	Y	Y	Y	Y	Y
29 Schiff	Y	Y	Y	Y	Y	Y
30 Waxman	Y	Y	Y	Y	Y	Y
31 Becerra	N	Y	Y	Y	Y	Y
32 Vacant						
33 Watson	N	Y	Y	Y	Y	Y
34 Roybal-Allard	N	Y	Y	Y	Y	Y
35 Waters	N	Y	Y	Y	Y	Y
36 Harman	Y	Y	Y	Y	Y	Y
37 Richardson	N	Y	Y	Y	Y	Y
38 Napolitano	N	Y	+	+	+	+
39 Sánchez, Linda	N	Y	Y	Y	Y	Y
40 Royce	Y	N	N	N	Y	N
41 Lewis	Y	N	N	N	N	N
42 Miller, Gary	?	?	?	?	?	?
43 Baca	N	Y	Y	Y	Y	Y
44 Calvert	Y	N	N	N	Y	N
45 Bono Mack	Y	N	N	N	Y	N
46 Rohrabacher	Y	N	N	Y	N	Y
47 Sanchez, Loretta	?	?	Y	Y	Y	Y
48 Campbell	Y	N	N	N	N	N
49 Issa	Y	N	N	N	N	N
50 Bilbray	Y	Y	N	N	Y	N
51 Filner	N	Y	Y	Y	Y	Y
52 Hunter	Y	N	N	N	N	N
53 Davis	N	Y	Y	Y	Y	Y

	139	140	141	142	143	144
COLORADO						
1 DeGette	N	Y	Y	Y	Y	Y
2 Polis	N	Y	Y	Y	Y	Y
3 Salazar	Y	Y	Y	Y	Y	Y
4 Markey	Y	Y	Y	Y	Y	Y
5 Lamborn	Y	N	N	N	N	N
6 Coffman	Y	N	N	N	N	N
7 Perlmutter	N	Y	Y	Y	Y	Y
CONNECTICUT						
1 Larson	N	Y	Y	Y	Y	Y
2 Courtney	N	Y	Y	Y	Y	Y
3 DeLauro	N	Y	Y	Y	Y	Y
4 Himes	Y	Y	N	Y	Y	Y
5 Murphy	Y	Y	Y	Y	Y	Y
DELAWARE						
AL Castle	Y	Y	N	N	Y	N
FLORIDA						
1 Miller	Y	N	N	N	N	N
2 Boyd	Y	Y	Y	Y	Y	Y
3 Brown	N	Y	Y	Y	Y	Y
4 Crenshaw	Y	N	N	N	Y	N
5 Brown-Waite	Y	N	N	N	Y	N
6 Stearns	Y	N	N	N	N	N
7 Mica	Y	N	N	N	N	N
8 Grayson	Y	Y	Y	Y	Y	Y
9 Bilirakis	Y	Y	N	N	Y	N
10 Young	Y	Y	N	N	N	N
11 Castor	N	Y	P	Y	Y	Y
12 Putnam	Y	Y	N	N	Y	N
13 Buchanan	Y	Y	N	N	Y	N
14 Mack	Y	N	N	N	N	N
15 Posey	Y	N	N	N	Y	N
16 Rooney	Y	N	N	N	Y	N
17 Meek	N	Y	Y	Y	Y	Y
18 Ros-Lehtinen	Y	Y	N	N	Y	Y
19 Wexler	Y	Y	Y	Y	Y	Y
20 Wasserman Schultz	Y	Y	Y	Y	Y	?
21 Diaz-Balart, L.	Y	Y	P	N	Y	N
22 Klein	Y	Y	Y	Y	Y	Y
23 Hastings	N	Y	Y	Y	Y	Y
24 Kosmas	Y	Y	N	Y	Y	Y
25 Diaz-Balart, M.	Y	Y	N	N	Y	N
GEORGIA						
1 Kingston	Y	N	N	N	N	N
2 Bishop	Y	Y	Y	Y	Y	Y
3 Westmoreland	?	N	N	N	N	N
4 Johnson	Y	Y	Y	Y	Y	Y
5 Lewis	N	Y	Y	Y	Y	Y
6 Price	Y	N	N	N	N	N
7 Linder	Y	N	N	N	N	?
8 Marshall	Y	Y	Y	Y	Y	Y
9 Deal	Y	N	N	N	N	N
10 Broun	Y	N	N	N	N	N
11 Gingrey	Y	N	N	N	N	N
12 Barrow	Y	Y	N	Y	Y	Y
13 Scott	Y	Y	Y	Y	Y	Y
HAWAII						
1 Abercrombie	N	Y	Y	Y	Y	Y
2 Hirono	N	Y	Y	Y	Y	Y
IDAHO						
1 Minnick	Y	Y	N	N	N	Y
2 Simpson	Y	Y	N	N	N	Y
ILLINOIS						
1 Rush	N	Y	Y	Y	Y	Y
2 Jackson	N	Y	Y	Y	Y	Y
3 Lipinski	Y	Y	Y	Y	Y	Y
4 Gutierrez	N	Y	Y	Y	Y	Y
5 Vacant						
6 Roskam	Y	N	N	Y	N	N
7 Davis	Y	Y	Y	Y	Y	Y
8 Bean	N	Y	Y	Y	N	Y
9 Schakowsky	N	Y	Y	Y	Y	Y
10 Kirk	Y	Y	N	Y	N	Y
11 Halvorson	Y	Y	Y	Y	Y	Y
12 Costello	Y	Y	Y	Y	Y	Y
13 Biggert	Y	Y	N	Y	N	N
14 Foster	Y	Y	Y	Y	N	Y
15 Johnson	Y	Y	N	Y	N	Y

KEY   Republicans   Democrats

Y	Voted for (yea)	X	Paired against
#	Paired for	–	Announced against
+	Announced for	P	Voted "present"
N	Voted against (nay)		
C	Voted "present" to avoid possible conflict of interest		
?	Did not vote or otherwise make a position known		

	139	140	141	142	143	144
16 **Manzullo**	Y	N	N	N	Y	Y
17 Hare	N	Y	Y	Y	Y	Y
18 **Schock**	Y	Y	N	N	Y	N
19 **Shimkus**	Y	Y	N	N	Y	N
INDIANA						
1 Visclosky	Y	Y	N	Y	Y	Y
2 Donnelly	Y	Y	N	Y	Y	Y
3 **Souder**	Y	Y	?	?	?	?
4 **Buyer**	Y	N	N	N	N	N
5 **Burton**	Y	N	N	N	N	N
6 **Pence**	Y	N	N	N	N	N
7 Carson	N	Y	Y	Y	Y	Y
8 Ellsworth	Y	Y	N	Y	Y	Y
9 Hill	Y	Y	P	Y	Y	Y
IOWA						
1 Braley	N	Y	Y	Y	Y	Y
2 Loebsack	Y	Y	N	Y	Y	Y
3 Boswell	Y	Y	Y	Y	Y	Y
4 **Latham**	Y	Y	N	N	Y	N
5 **King**	Y	N	N	N	N	N
KANSAS						
1 **Moran**	Y	N	N	N	Y	N
2 **Jenkins**	Y	N	N	N	N	N
3 Moore	Y	Y	Y	Y	Y	Y
4 **Tiahrt**	Y	N	N	N	N	N
KENTUCKY						
1 **Whitfield**	Y	N	N	N	Y	N
2 **Guthrie**	Y	Y	N	N	Y	N
3 Yarmuth	Y	Y	Y	Y	Y	Y
4 **Davis**	Y	N	N	N	Y	N
5 **Rogers**	Y	Y	N	N	Y	N
6 Chandler	Y	Y	P	Y	Y	Y
LOUISIANA						
1 **Scalise**	Y	N	N	N	N	N
2 **Cao**	Y	Y	N	N	Y	Y
3 Melancon	Y	Y	Y	Y	Y	Y
4 **Fleming**	Y	N	N	N	Y	N
5 **Alexander**	Y	N	N	N	Y	N
6 **Cassidy**	Y	Y	N	N	Y	N
7 **Boustany**	?	?	?	?	?	?
MAINE						
1 Pingree	N	Y	Y	Y	Y	Y
2 Michaud	Y	Y	Y	Y	Y	Y
MARYLAND						
1 Kratovil	Y	Y	Y	Y	Y	Y
2 Ruppersberger	Y	Y	Y	Y	Y	Y
3 Sarbanes	N	Y	Y	Y	Y	Y
4 Edwards	N	Y	Y	Y	Y	Y
5 Hoyer	Y	Y	Y	Y	Y	Y
6 **Bartlett**	Y	N	N	N	N	N
7 Cummings	Y	Y	Y	Y	Y	Y
8 Van Hollen	Y	Y	Y	Y	Y	Y
MASSACHUSETTS						
1 Olver	N	Y	Y	Y	Y	Y
2 Neal	Y	Y	Y	Y	Y	Y
3 McGovern	N	Y	Y	Y	Y	Y
4 Frank	N	Y	Y	Y	Y	Y
5 Tsongas	N	Y	Y	Y	Y	Y
6 Tierney	N	Y	Y	Y	Y	Y
7 Markey	Y	Y	Y	Y	Y	Y
8 Capuano	N	Y	Y	Y	Y	Y
9 Lynch	Y	Y	Y	Y	Y	Y
10 Delahunt	N	Y	?	?	?	?
MICHIGAN						
1 Stupak	Y	Y	Y	Y	Y	Y
2 **Hoekstra**	Y	N	N	N	Y	N
3 **Ehlers**	Y	Y	N	N	Y	N
4 **Camp**	Y	Y	N	N	Y	N
5 Kildee	Y	Y	Y	Y	Y	Y
6 **Upton**	Y	Y	N	N	Y	N
7 Schauer	Y	Y	Y	Y	Y	Y
8 **Rogers**	Y	Y	N	N	Y	N
9 Peters	Y	Y	Y	Y	Y	Y
10 **Miller**	Y	Y	N	N	Y	N
11 **McCotter**	Y	Y	N	N	N	N
12 Levin	N	Y	Y	Y	Y	Y
13 Kilpatrick	N	Y	Y	Y	Y	Y
14 Conyers	Y	Y	Y	Y	Y	Y
15 Dingell	Y	Y	Y	Y	Y	Y
MINNESOTA						
1 Walz	Y	Y	N	Y	Y	Y
2 **Kline**	Y	N	P	N	N	N
3 **Paulsen**	Y	Y	N	N	N	N
4 McCollum	N	Y	Y	Y	Y	Y

	139	140	141	142	143	144
5 Ellison	N	Y	Y	Y	Y	Y
6 **Bachmann**	Y	N	N	N	N	N
7 Peterson	Y	Y	Y	Y	Y	Y
8 Oberstar	Y	Y	Y	Y	Y	Y
MISSISSIPPI						
1 Childers	Y	Y	Y	N	Y	Y
2 Thompson	N	Y	Y	Y	Y	Y
3 **Harper**	Y	N	N	N	N	N
4 Taylor	Y	Y	Y	Y	Y	N
MISSOURI						
1 Clay	N	Y	Y	Y	Y	Y
2 **Akin**	Y	N	N	N	N	N
3 Carnahan	Y	Y	Y	Y	Y	Y
4 Skelton	Y	Y	Y	Y	Y	Y
5 Cleaver	N	Y	Y	Y	Y	Y
6 **Graves**	Y	N	N	N	N	N
7 **Blunt**	Y	N	N	N	Y	N
8 **Emerson**	Y	Y	N	N	Y	N
9 **Luetkemeyer**	Y	N	N	N	N	N
MONTANA						
AL **Rehberg**	Y	Y	N	N	Y	N
NEBRASKA						
1 **Fortenberry**	Y	Y	N	N	Y	N
2 **Terry**	Y	Y	N	N	N	N
3 **Smith**	Y	N	N	N	N	N
NEVADA						
1 Berkley	Y	Y	Y	Y	Y	Y
2 **Heller**	Y	Y	N	N	Y	N
3 Titus	Y	Y	Y	Y	Y	Y
NEW HAMPSHIRE						
1 Shea-Porter	Y	Y	Y	Y	Y	Y
2 Hodes	Y	Y	N	Y	Y	Y
NEW JERSEY						
1 Andrews	Y	Y	Y	Y	Y	Y
2 **LoBiondo**	Y	Y	N	N	Y	N
3 Adler	Y	Y	Y	Y	Y	Y
4 **Smith**	Y	Y	N	N	Y	N
5 **Garrett**	Y	N	N	N	N	N
6 Pallone	Y	Y	Y	Y	Y	Y
7 **Lance**	Y	Y	N	N	Y	N
8 Pascrell	Y	Y	Y	Y	Y	?
9 Rothman	Y	Y	Y	Y	Y	Y
10 Payne	N	Y	Y	Y	Y	Y
11 **Frelinghuysen**	Y	Y	N	N	Y	N
12 Holt	N	Y	Y	Y	Y	Y
13 Sires	Y	Y	Y	Y	Y	Y
NEW MEXICO						
1 Heinrich	Y	Y	Y	Y	Y	Y
2 Teague	Y	Y	N	Y	Y	Y
3 Lujan	N	Y	Y	Y	Y	Y
NEW YORK						
1 Bishop	N	Y	Y	Y	Y	Y
2 Israel	Y	Y	Y	Y	Y	Y
3 **King**	Y	Y	N	N	N	N
4 McCarthy	Y	Y	Y	Y	Y	Y
5 Ackerman	N	Y	Y	Y	Y	Y
6 Meeks	Y	Y	Y	Y	Y	Y
7 Crowley	N	Y	Y	Y	Y	Y
8 Nadler	N	Y	Y	Y	Y	Y
9 Weiner	N	Y	Y	Y	Y	Y
10 Towns	Y	Y	Y	Y	Y	Y
11 Clarke	N	Y	Y	Y	Y	Y
12 Velázquez	N	Y	Y	Y	Y	Y
13 McMahon	Y	Y	Y	Y	N	Y
14 Maloney	Y	Y	Y	Y	Y	Y
15 Rangel	Y	Y	Y	Y	Y	Y
16 Serrano	N	Y	Y	Y	Y	Y
17 Engel	N	Y	Y	Y	Y	Y
18 Lowey	N	Y	Y	Y	Y	Y
19 Hall	N	Y	Y	Y	Y	Y
20 Vacant						
21 Tonko	N	Y	Y	Y	Y	Y
22 Hinchey	?	?	?	?	?	?
23 **McHugh**	Y	Y	N	N	Y	N
24 Arcuri	Y	Y	Y	Y	Y	Y
25 Maffei	Y	Y	Y	Y	Y	Y
26 **Lee**	Y	Y	N	N	Y	N
27 Higgins	N	Y	Y	Y	Y	Y
28 Slaughter	N	Y	Y	Y	Y	+
29 Massa	Y	Y	Y	Y	Y	Y
NORTH CAROLINA						
1 Butterfield	Y	Y	P	Y	Y	Y
2 Etheridge	Y	Y	Y	Y	Y	Y
3 **Jones**	Y	N	Y	N	Y	Y
4 Price	Y	Y	Y	Y	Y	Y

	139	140	141	142	143	144
5 **Foxx**	Y	N	N	N	N	N
6 **Coble**	Y	N	N	N	N	N
7 McIntyre	Y	Y	N	Y	Y	Y
8 Kissell	N	Y	Y	Y	N	Y
9 **Myrick**	Y	N	N	N	N	N
10 **McHenry**	Y	N	N	N	N	N
11 Shuler	Y	Y	Y	Y	Y	Y
12 Watt	N	Y	Y	Y	Y	Y
13 Miller	Y	Y	Y	Y	Y	Y
NORTH DAKOTA						
AL Pomeroy	Y	Y	Y	Y	Y	Y
OHIO						
1 Driehaus	Y	Y	Y	Y	Y	Y
2 **Schmidt**	Y	N	N	N	Y	N
3 **Turner**	Y	Y	N	N	Y	N
4 **Jordan**	Y	N	N	N	N	N
5 **Latta**	Y	N	N	N	N	N
6 Wilson	Y	Y	Y	Y	Y	Y
7 **Austria**	Y	Y	N	N	N	N
8 **Boehner**	Y	N	N	N	N	N
9 Kaptur	Y	Y	Y	Y	Y	Y
10 Kucinich	N	Y	Y	Y	Y	Y
11 Fudge	N	Y	Y	Y	Y	Y
12 **Tiberi**	Y	Y	N	N	Y	N
13 Sutton	N	Y	Y	Y	Y	Y
14 **LaTourette**	Y	Y	N	N	N	N
15 Kilroy	Y	Y	Y	Y	Y	Y
16 Boccieri	Y	Y	N	Y	Y	Y
17 Ryan	Y	Y	Y	Y	Y	Y
18 Space	Y	Y	Y	Y	Y	Y
OKLAHOMA						
1 **Sullivan**	Y	Y	N	N	N	N
2 Boren	Y	Y	Y	Y	Y	Y
3 **Lucas**	Y	Y	N	N	N	N
4 **Cole**	Y	Y	N	N	N	N
5 **Fallin**	Y	N	N	N	N	N
OREGON						
1 Wu	N	Y	Y	Y	Y	Y
2 **Walden**	Y	Y	P	N	Y	Y
3 Blumenauer	Y	Y	Y	Y	Y	Y
4 DeFazio	Y	Y	Y	Y	Y	Y
5 Schrader	Y	Y	Y	Y	Y	Y
PENNSYLVANIA						
1 Brady	N	Y	Y	Y	Y	Y
2 Fattah	N	Y	Y	Y	Y	Y
3 Dahlkemper	Y	Y	Y	Y	Y	Y
4 Altmire	Y	Y	Y	Y	Y	Y
5 **Thompson**	Y	Y	N	N	N	N
6 **Gerlach**	Y	Y	N	N	Y	N
7 Sestak	Y	Y	Y	Y	Y	Y
8 Murphy, P.	Y	Y	Y	Y	Y	Y
9 **Shuster**	Y	N	?	N	N	N
10 Carney	Y	Y	Y	Y	Y	Y
11 Kanjorski	N	Y	Y	Y	Y	Y
12 Murtha	N	Y	Y	Y	Y	Y
13 Schwartz	N	Y	Y	Y	Y	Y
14 Doyle	N	Y	Y	Y	Y	?
15 **Dent**	Y	Y	P	N	Y	N
16 **Pitts**	Y	N	N	N	N	N
17 Holden	Y	Y	Y	Y	Y	Y
18 **Murphy, T.**	Y	Y	Y	N	N	N
19 **Platts**	Y	Y	N	N	Y	N
RHODE ISLAND						
1 Kennedy	Y	Y	Y	Y	Y	Y
2 Langevin	Y	Y	Y	Y	Y	Y
SOUTH CAROLINA						
1 **Brown**	Y	N	N	N	Y	N
2 **Wilson**	Y	N	N	N	N	N
3 **Barrett**	Y	N	P	N	N	N
4 **Inglis**	Y	N	N	N	N	N
5 Spratt	Y	Y	Y	Y	Y	Y
6 Clyburn	N	Y	Y	Y	Y	Y
SOUTH DAKOTA						
AL Herseth Sandlin	Y	Y	Y	Y	Y	Y
TENNESSEE						
1 **Roe**	Y	Y	N	N	Y	N
2 **Duncan**	Y	N	N	N	Y	N
3 **Wamp**	Y	N	N	N	Y	N
4 Davis	Y	Y	Y	Y	+	+
5 Cooper	Y	Y	Y	Y	Y	Y
6 Gordon	Y	Y	Y	Y	Y	Y
7 **Blackburn**	Y	N	N	N	N	N
8 Tanner	Y	Y	Y	Y	Y	Y
9 Cohen	N	Y	Y	Y	Y	Y

	139	140	141	142	143	144
TEXAS						
1 **Gohmert**	Y	?	N	N	N	N
2 **Poe**	Y	N	P	N	N	N
3 **Johnson, S.**	Y	N	N	N	N	N
4 **Hall**	Y	N	N	N	N	N
5 **Hensarling**	Y	N	N	N	N	N
6 **Barton**	Y	N	N	N	Y	N
7 **Culberson**	Y	N	?	?	?	?
8 **Brady**	Y	N	N	N	N	N
9 Green, A.	N	Y	Y	Y	Y	Y
10 **McCaul**	Y	N	N	N	Y	N
11 **Conaway**	Y	N	P	N	N	N
12 **Granger**	Y	N	N	N	N	N
13 **Thornberry**	Y	N	N	N	N	N
14 **Paul**	Y	N	N	N	N	N
15 Hinojosa	Y	Y	Y	Y	Y	Y
16 Reyes	Y	Y	Y	Y	Y	Y
17 Edwards	?	Y	Y	Y	Y	Y
18 Jackson Lee	N	Y	Y	Y	Y	Y
19 **Neugebauer**	Y	N	N	N	N	N
20 Gonzalez	Y	Y	Y	Y	Y	Y
21 **Smith**	Y	N	N	N	Y	N
22 **Olson**	?	?	?	?	?	?
23 Rodriguez	Y	Y	Y	Y	Y	Y
24 **Marchant**	Y	N	N	N	N	N
25 Doggett	N	Y	Y	Y	Y	Y
26 **Burgess**	Y	N	N	N	N	N
27 Ortiz	Y	Y	Y	Y	Y	Y
28 Cuellar	Y	Y	Y	Y	Y	Y
29 Green, G.	N	Y	Y	Y	Y	Y
30 Johnson, E.	N	Y	Y	Y	Y	Y
31 **Carter**	Y	N	N	N	N	N
32 **Sessions**	Y	N	N	N	N	N
UTAH						
1 **Bishop**	Y	N	N	N	N	N
2 Matheson	Y	Y	Y	Y	Y	Y
3 **Chaffetz**	Y	N	N	N	N	N
VERMONT						
AL Welch	N	Y	P	Y	Y	Y
VIRGINIA						
1 **Wittman**	Y	Y	N	N	Y	Y
2 Nye	Y	Y	Y	N	Y	Y
3 Scott	N	Y	Y	Y	Y	Y
4 **Forbes**	Y	N	N	N	Y	N
5 Perriello	Y	Y	N	Y	Y	Y
6 **Goodlatte**	Y	N	N	N	Y	N
7 **Cantor**	Y	N	N	N	Y	Y
8 Moran	Y	Y	Y	Y	Y	Y
9 Boucher	Y	Y	Y	Y	Y	Y
10 **Wolf**	Y	Y	N	N	Y	N
11 Connolly	Y	Y	Y	Y	Y	Y
WASHINGTON						
1 Inslee	N	Y	Y	Y	Y	Y
2 Larsen	N	Y	Y	Y	Y	Y
3 Baird	N	Y	Y	Y	Y	Y
4 **Hastings**	Y	N	P	N	N	N
5 **McMorris Rodgers**	Y	Y	N	N	Y	N
6 Dicks	Y	Y	Y	Y	Y	Y
7 McDermott	N	Y	Y	Y	Y	Y
8 **Reichert**	Y	Y	N	N	Y	N
9 Smith	Y	Y	Y	Y	Y	Y
WEST VIRGINIA						
1 Mollohan	Y	Y	Y	Y	Y	Y
2 **Capito**	Y	Y	N	N	Y	N
3 Rahall	Y	Y	Y	Y	Y	Y
WISCONSIN						
1 **Ryan**	Y	N	N	N	Y	N
2 Baldwin	N	Y	Y	Y	Y	Y
3 Kind	Y	Y	N	Y	Y	Y
4 Moore	N	Y	Y	Y	Y	Y
5 **Sensenbrenner**	Y	N	N	N	N	N
6 **Petri**	Y	Y	N	N	Y	N
7 Obey	Y	Y	Y	Y	Y	Y
8 Kagen	Y	Y	Y	Y	Y	Y
WYOMING						
AL **Lummis**	Y	N	N	N	N	N
DELEGATES						
Faleomavaega (A.S.)						
Norton (D.C.)						
Bordallo (Guam)						
Sablan (N. Marianas)						
Pierluisi (P.R.)						
Christensen (V.I.)						

IN THE HOUSE | By Vote Number

145. **HR 918. Stan Lundine Post Office/Passage.** Lynch, D-Mass., motion to suspend the rules and pass the bill that would designate a post office in Jamestown, N.Y., as the "Stan Lundine Post Office Building." Motion agreed to 396-0: R 168-0; D 228-0. A two-thirds majority of those present and voting (264 in this case) is required for passage under suspension of the rules. March 23, 2009.

146. **HR 1218. Drew Weaver Post Office/Passage.** Lynch, D-Mass., motion to suspend the rules and pass the bill that would designate a post office in St. Charles, Mo., as the "Lance Cpl. Drew W. Weaver Post Office Building." Motion agreed to 399-0: R 168-0; D 231-0. A two-thirds majority of those present and voting (266 in this case) is required for passage under suspension of the rules. March 23, 2009.

147. **HR 1617. Homeland Security Privacy Officials/Passage.** Carney, D-Pa., motion to suspend the rules and pass the bill that would require the Homeland Security Department to designate full-time privacy officials for certain components of the department. Officials would advise on privacy considerations for new laws or regulations, and monitor privacy training and compliance with privacy laws. Motion agreed to 412-3: R 167-3; D 245-0. A two-thirds majority of those present and voting (277 in this case) is required for passage under suspension of the rules. March 24, 2009.

148. **HR 730. Technical Nuclear Forensics/Passage.** Carney, D-Pa., motion to suspend the rules and pass the bill that would authorize $30 million annually in fiscal 2009-11 for the Department of Homeland Security to develop the capacity to trace nuclear and radiological material back to its source, establish a national technical nuclear forensics center, and promote continued study of nuclear forensics. Motion agreed to 402-16: R 156-16; D 246-0. A two-thirds majority of those present and voting (279 in this case) is required for passage under suspension of the rules. March 24, 2009.

149. **H Res 182. School Social Work Week/Adoption.** Woolsey, D-Calif., motion to suspend the rules and adopt the resolution that would support the designation of School Social Work Week and honor the contributions of school social workers. Motion agreed to 415-0: R 171-0; D 244-0. A two-thirds majority of those present and voting (277 in this case) is required for adoption under suspension of the rules. March 24, 2009.

150. **HR 146. Public Lands Designation/Previous Question.** Pingree, D-Maine, motion to order the previous question (thus ending debate and possibility of amendment) on adoption of the rule (H Res 280) that would provide for House floor consideration of the Senate amendment to the bill that would designate more than 2 million new acres of protected wilderness areas nationwide, in addition to wild and scenic rivers, historic sites, and expansions of national parks. Motion agreed to 242-180: R 1-171; D 241-9. March 25, 2009.

	145	146	147	148	149	150
ALABAMA						
1 **Bonner**	Y	Y	Y	Y	Y	N
2 Bright	Y	Y	Y	Y	Y	Y
3 **Rogers**	Y	Y	Y	Y	Y	N
4 **Aderholt**	Y	Y	Y	Y	Y	N
5 Griffith	Y	Y	Y	Y	Y	N
6 **Bachus**	Y	Y	Y	Y	Y	N
7 Davis	?	?	Y	Y	Y	Y
ALASKA						
AL **Young**	Y	Y	Y	Y	Y	N
ARIZONA						
1 Kirkpatrick	Y	Y	Y	Y	Y	N
2 **Franks**	Y	Y	Y	Y	Y	N
3 **Shadegg**	Y	Y	Y	Y	Y	N
4 Pastor	Y	Y	Y	Y	Y	Y
5 Mitchell	Y	Y	Y	Y	Y	Y
6 **Flake**	Y	Y	Y	N	Y	N
7 Grijalva	?	?	Y	Y	Y	Y
8 Giffords	Y	Y	Y	Y	Y	Y
ARKANSAS						
1 Berry	Y	Y	Y	Y	Y	Y
2 Snyder	Y	Y	Y	Y	Y	Y
3 **Boozman**	Y	Y	Y	Y	Y	N
4 Ross	Y	Y	Y	Y	Y	Y
CALIFORNIA						
1 Thompson	Y	Y	Y	Y	?	Y
2 **Herger**	Y	Y	Y	Y	Y	N
3 **Lungren**	Y	Y	Y	Y	Y	N
4 **McClintock**	Y	Y	Y	Y	Y	N
5 Matsui	Y	Y	Y	Y	Y	Y
6 Woolsey	Y	Y	Y	Y	Y	Y
7 Miller, George	Y	Y	Y	Y	Y	Y
8 Pelosi						
9 Lee	Y	Y	Y	Y	Y	Y
10 Tauscher	Y	Y	Y	Y	Y	Y
11 McNerney	Y	Y	Y	Y	Y	Y
12 Speier	Y	Y	Y	Y	Y	Y
13 Stark	?	?	Y	Y	Y	Y
14 Eshoo	Y	Y	Y	Y	Y	Y
15 Honda	Y	Y	Y	Y	Y	Y
16 Lofgren	Y	Y	Y	Y	Y	Y
17 Farr	?	?	Y	Y	Y	Y
18 Cardoza	Y	Y	Y	Y	Y	Y
19 **Radanovich**	Y	Y	?	?	?	Y
20 Costa	Y	Y	Y	Y	Y	Y
21 **Nunes**	Y	Y	Y	Y	Y	N
22 **McCarthy**	Y	Y	Y	Y	Y	N
23 Capps	Y	Y	Y	Y	Y	Y
24 **Gallegly**	Y	Y	Y	Y	Y	N
25 **McKeon**	Y	Y	Y	Y	Y	N
26 **Dreier**	Y	Y	Y	Y	Y	N
27 Sherman	Y	Y	Y	Y	Y	Y
28 Berman	Y	Y	Y	Y	Y	Y
29 Schiff	Y	Y	Y	Y	Y	Y
30 Waxman	Y	Y	Y	Y	Y	Y
31 Becerra	Y	Y	Y	Y	Y	Y
32 Vacant						
33 Watson	Y	Y	Y	Y	Y	Y
34 Roybal-Allard	Y	Y	Y	Y	Y	Y
35 Waters	Y	Y	Y	Y	Y	Y
36 Harman	Y	Y	Y	Y	Y	Y
37 Richardson	Y	Y	Y	Y	Y	Y
38 Napolitano	Y	Y	Y	Y	Y	Y
39 Sánchez, Linda	Y	Y	Y	Y	Y	Y
40 **Royce**	Y	Y	Y	Y	Y	N
41 **Lewis**	Y	Y	Y	Y	Y	N
42 **Miller, Gary**	?	?	?	?	?	?
43 Baca	Y	Y	Y	Y	Y	Y
44 **Calvert**	Y	Y	Y	Y	Y	N
45 **Bono Mack**	Y	Y	Y	Y	Y	N
46 **Rohrabacher**	?	?	Y	Y	Y	N
47 Sanchez, Loretta	Y	Y	Y	Y	Y	Y
48 **Campbell**	Y	Y	Y	Y	Y	N
49 **Issa**	Y	Y	Y	Y	Y	N
50 **Bilbray**	Y	Y	Y	Y	Y	N
51 Filner	Y	Y	Y	Y	Y	Y
52 **Hunter**	Y	Y	Y	Y	Y	N
53 Davis	Y	Y	Y	Y	Y	Y

	145	146	147	148	149	150
COLORADO						
1 DeGette	Y	Y	Y	Y	Y	Y
2 Polis	Y	Y	Y	Y	Y	Y
3 Salazar	Y	Y	Y	Y	Y	Y
4 Markey	Y	Y	Y	Y	Y	Y
5 **Lamborn**	Y	Y	Y	Y	Y	N
6 **Coffman**	Y	Y	Y	Y	Y	–
7 Perlmutter	Y	Y	Y	Y	Y	Y
CONNECTICUT						
1 Larson	Y	Y	Y	Y	Y	?
2 Courtney	Y	Y	Y	Y	Y	Y
3 DeLauro	Y	Y	Y	Y	Y	Y
4 Himes	Y	Y	Y	Y	Y	Y
5 Murphy	Y	Y	Y	Y	Y	Y
DELAWARE						
AL **Castle**	Y	Y	Y	Y	Y	N
FLORIDA						
1 **Miller**	Y	Y	Y	Y	Y	N
2 Boyd	Y	Y	Y	Y	Y	Y
3 Brown	?	?	Y	Y	Y	Y
4 **Crenshaw**	Y	Y	Y	Y	Y	N
5 **Brown-Waite**	Y	Y	Y	Y	Y	N
6 **Stearns**	Y	Y	Y	Y	Y	N
7 **Mica**	Y	Y	Y	Y	Y	N
8 Grayson	Y	Y	Y	Y	Y	Y
9 **Bilirakis**	Y	Y	Y	Y	Y	N
10 **Young**	Y	Y	Y	Y	Y	N
11 Castor	Y	Y	Y	Y	Y	Y
12 **Putnam**	Y	Y	Y	Y	Y	N
13 **Buchanan**	Y	Y	Y	Y	Y	N
14 **Mack**	Y	Y	Y	Y	Y	N
15 **Posey**	Y	Y	Y	Y	Y	N
16 **Rooney**	Y	Y	Y	Y	Y	N
17 Meek	Y	Y	Y	Y	Y	Y
18 **Ros-Lehtinen**	Y	Y	Y	Y	Y	N
19 Wexler	Y	Y	Y	Y	Y	Y
20 Wasserman Schultz	Y	Y	Y	Y	Y	Y
21 **Diaz-Balart, L.**	Y	Y	Y	Y	Y	N
22 Klein	Y	Y	Y	Y	Y	Y
23 Hastings	Y	Y	Y	Y	Y	Y
24 Kosmas	?	?	Y	Y	Y	N
25 **Diaz-Balart, M.**	Y	Y	Y	Y	Y	N
GEORGIA						
1 **Kingston**	Y	Y	Y	N	Y	N
2 Bishop	Y	Y	Y	Y	Y	Y
3 **Westmoreland**	?	?	?	?	?	?
4 Johnson	Y	Y	Y	Y	Y	Y
5 Lewis	?	Y	Y	Y	Y	Y
6 **Price**	Y	Y	Y	Y	Y	N
7 **Linder**	Y	Y	Y	N	Y	N
8 Marshall	Y	Y	Y	Y	Y	Y
9 **Deal**	Y	Y	Y	N	Y	N
10 **Broun**	Y	Y	Y	N	Y	N
11 **Gingrey**	Y	Y	Y	N	Y	N
12 Barrow	Y	Y	Y	Y	Y	N
13 Scott	Y	Y	Y	Y	Y	Y
HAWAII						
1 Abercrombie	Y	Y	Y	Y	Y	Y
2 Hirono	Y	Y	Y	Y	Y	Y
IDAHO						
1 Minnick	Y	Y	Y	Y	Y	N
2 **Simpson**	Y	Y	Y	Y	Y	N
ILLINOIS						
1 Rush	Y	Y	Y	Y	Y	Y
2 Jackson	Y	Y	Y	Y	Y	Y
3 Lipinski	Y	Y	Y	Y	Y	Y
4 Gutierrez	?	?	Y	Y	Y	Y
5 Vacant						
6 **Roskam**	Y	Y	Y	Y	Y	N
7 Davis	Y	Y	Y	Y	Y	Y
8 Bean	Y	Y	Y	Y	Y	Y
9 Schakowsky	Y	Y	Y	Y	Y	Y
10 **Kirk**	Y	Y	Y	Y	Y	N
11 Halvorson	Y	Y	Y	Y	Y	Y
12 Costello	?	?	?	?	?	Y
13 **Biggert**	Y	Y	Y	Y	Y	N
14 Foster	Y	Y	Y	Y	Y	Y
15 Johnson	?	?	Y	Y	Y	Y

KEY | **Republicans** | Democrats

Y	Voted for (yea)	X	Paired against	C	Voted "present" to avoid possible conflict of interest
#	Paired for	–	Announced against		
+	Announced for	P	Voted "present"	?	Did not vote or otherwise make a position known
N	Voted against (nay)				

	145	146	147	148	149	150
16 **Manzullo**	Y	Y	Y	N	Y	N
17 Hare	Y	Y	Y	Y	Y	Y
18 **Schock**	?	?	Y	Y	Y	N
19 **Shimkus**	Y	Y	Y	Y	Y	N
INDIANA						
1 Visclosky	Y	Y	Y	Y	Y	Y
2 Donnelly	Y	Y	Y	Y	Y	Y
3 **Souder**	Y	Y	Y	Y	Y	N
4 **Buyer**	Y	Y	Y	Y	Y	N
5 **Burton**	Y	Y	Y	Y	Y	N
6 **Pence**	Y	Y	Y	Y	Y	N
7 Carson	Y	Y	Y	Y	Y	Y
8 Ellsworth	Y	Y	Y	Y	Y	Y
9 Hill	Y	Y	?	?	?	Y
IOWA						
1 Braley	?	Y	?	?	Y	Y
2 Loebsack	Y	Y	Y	Y	Y	Y
3 Boswell	?	?	Y	Y	Y	Y
4 **Latham**	Y	Y	Y	Y	Y	N
5 **King**	Y	Y	Y	Y	Y	N
KANSAS						
1 **Moran**	Y	Y	Y	Y	Y	N
2 **Jenkins**	Y	Y	Y	Y	Y	N
3 Moore	Y	Y	Y	Y	Y	Y
4 **Tiahrt**	Y	Y	Y	Y	Y	N
KENTUCKY						
1 **Whitfield**	Y	Y	Y	Y	Y	N
2 **Guthrie**	Y	Y	Y	Y	Y	N
3 Yarmuth	?	?	Y	Y	Y	Y
4 **Davis**	Y	Y	Y	Y	Y	N
5 **Rogers**	Y	Y	Y	Y	Y	N
6 Chandler	Y	Y	Y	Y	Y	Y
LOUISIANA						
1 **Scalise**	Y	Y	Y	Y	Y	N
2 **Cao**	Y	Y	Y	Y	Y	N
3 Melancon	Y	Y	Y	Y	Y	Y
4 **Fleming**	Y	Y	Y	Y	Y	N
5 **Alexander**	Y	Y	Y	Y	Y	N
6 **Cassidy**	Y	Y	Y	Y	Y	?
7 **Boustany**	Y	Y	Y	Y	Y	N
MAINE						
1 Pingree	Y	Y	Y	Y	Y	Y
2 Michaud	Y	Y	Y	Y	Y	Y
MARYLAND						
1 Kratovil	Y	Y	Y	Y	Y	Y
2 Ruppersberger	Y	Y	Y	Y	Y	Y
3 Sarbanes	?	?	Y	Y	Y	?
4 Edwards	Y	Y	Y	Y	Y	Y
5 Hoyer	Y	Y	Y	Y	Y	Y
6 **Bartlett**	Y	Y	Y	Y	Y	N
7 Cummings	Y	Y	Y	Y	Y	Y
8 Van Hollen	Y	Y	Y	Y	Y	Y
MASSACHUSETTS						
1 Olver	Y	Y	Y	Y	Y	Y
2 Neal	?	?	Y	Y	Y	Y
3 McGovern	Y	Y	Y	Y	Y	Y
4 Frank	Y	Y	Y	Y	Y	Y
5 Tsongas	?	?	Y	Y	Y	Y
6 Tierney	Y	Y	Y	Y	Y	Y
7 Markey	Y	Y	Y	Y	Y	Y
8 Capuano	Y	Y	Y	Y	Y	Y
9 Lynch	Y	Y	Y	Y	Y	Y
10 Delahunt	Y	Y	Y	Y	Y	Y
MICHIGAN						
1 Stupak	Y	Y	Y	Y	Y	Y
2 **Hoekstra**	?	?	Y	Y	Y	N
3 **Ehlers**	Y	Y	Y	Y	Y	N
4 **Camp**	Y	Y	Y	Y	Y	N
5 Kildee	Y	Y	Y	Y	Y	Y
6 **Upton**	Y	Y	Y	Y	Y	N
7 Schauer	Y	Y	Y	Y	Y	Y
8 **Rogers**	Y	Y	Y	Y	Y	N
9 Peters	Y	Y	Y	Y	Y	Y
10 **Miller**	Y	Y	Y	Y	Y	N
11 **McCotter**	Y	Y	?	?	?	N
12 Levin	Y	Y	Y	Y	Y	Y
13 Kilpatrick	Y	Y	Y	Y	Y	Y
14 Conyers	Y	Y	Y	Y	Y	Y
15 Dingell	?	?	Y	Y	Y	Y
MINNESOTA						
1 Walz	Y	Y	Y	Y	Y	Y
2 **Kline**	Y	Y	Y	Y	Y	N
3 **Paulsen**	Y	Y	Y	Y	Y	N
4 McCollum	Y	Y	Y	Y	Y	Y

	145	146	147	148	149	150
5 Ellison	?	?	Y	Y	Y	Y
6 **Bachmann**	Y	Y	Y	Y	Y	N
7 Peterson	Y	Y	Y	Y	Y	Y
8 Oberstar	Y	Y	Y	Y	Y	Y
MISSISSIPPI						
1 Childers	Y	Y	Y	Y	Y	Y
2 Thompson	Y	Y	Y	Y	Y	Y
3 **Harper**	Y	Y	Y	Y	Y	N
4 Taylor	Y	Y	?	?	?	Y
MISSOURI						
1 Clay	Y	Y	Y	Y	Y	Y
2 **Akin**	Y	Y	Y	N	Y	N
3 Carnahan	Y	Y	Y	Y	Y	Y
4 Skelton	Y	Y	Y	Y	Y	Y
5 Cleaver	?	?	?	Y	Y	Y
6 **Graves**	Y	Y	Y	Y	Y	N
7 **Blunt**	Y	Y	?	Y	Y	N
8 **Emerson**	Y	Y	Y	Y	Y	N
9 **Luetkemeyer**	Y	Y	Y	Y	Y	N
MONTANA						
AL **Rehberg**	Y	Y	Y	Y	Y	N
NEBRASKA						
1 **Fortenberry**	Y	Y	Y	Y	Y	N
2 **Terry**	Y	Y	Y	Y	Y	N
3 **Smith**	Y	Y	Y	Y	Y	N
NEVADA						
1 Berkley	Y	Y	Y	Y	Y	Y
2 **Heller**	Y	Y	Y	Y	Y	N
3 Titus	Y	Y	Y	Y	Y	Y
NEW HAMPSHIRE						
1 Shea-Porter	Y	Y	Y	Y	Y	Y
2 Hodes	Y	Y	Y	Y	Y	Y
NEW JERSEY						
1 Andrews	Y	Y	Y	Y	Y	Y
2 **LoBiondo**	Y	Y	Y	Y	Y	N
3 Adler	?	Y	Y	Y	Y	Y
4 **Smith**	?	?	?	?	?	N
5 **Garrett**	Y	Y	Y	Y	Y	N
6 Pallone	Y	Y	Y	Y	Y	Y
7 **Lance**	Y	Y	Y	Y	Y	N
8 Pascrell	?	?	+	+	+	Y
9 Rothman	Y	Y	Y	Y	Y	Y
10 Payne	Y	Y	Y	Y	Y	Y
11 **Frelinghuysen**	Y	Y	Y	Y	Y	N
12 Holt	Y	Y	Y	Y	Y	Y
13 Sires	Y	Y	Y	Y	Y	Y
NEW MEXICO						
1 Heinrich	Y	Y	Y	Y	Y	Y
2 Teague	Y	Y	Y	Y	Y	Y
3 Lujan	Y	Y	Y	Y	Y	Y
NEW YORK						
1 Bishop	Y	Y	Y	Y	Y	Y
2 Israel	Y	Y	Y	Y	Y	Y
3 **King**	Y	Y	Y	Y	Y	N
4 McCarthy	Y	Y	Y	Y	Y	Y
5 Ackerman	Y	Y	Y	Y	Y	Y
6 Meeks	Y	Y	Y	Y	Y	Y
7 Crowley	Y	Y	Y	Y	Y	Y
8 Nadler	Y	Y	Y	Y	Y	Y
9 Weiner	Y	Y	Y	Y	Y	Y
10 Towns	Y	Y	Y	Y	Y	Y
11 Clarke	+	+	Y	Y	Y	Y
12 Velázquez	Y	Y	Y	Y	Y	Y
13 McMahon	Y	Y	Y	Y	Y	Y
14 Maloney	Y	Y	Y	Y	Y	Y
15 Rangel	Y	Y	Y	Y	Y	Y
16 Serrano	Y	Y	Y	Y	Y	Y
17 Engel	?	?	?	?	?	?
18 Lowey	Y	Y	Y	Y	Y	Y
19 Hall	Y	Y	Y	Y	Y	Y
20 Vacant						
21 Tonko	Y	Y	Y	Y	Y	Y
22 Hinchey	Y	Y	Y	Y	Y	Y
23 **McHugh**	Y	Y	Y	Y	Y	N
24 Arcuri	Y	Y	Y	Y	Y	Y
25 Maffei	Y	Y	Y	Y	Y	Y
26 **Lee**	Y	Y	Y	Y	Y	N
27 Higgins	Y	Y	Y	Y	Y	Y
28 Slaughter	Y	+	Y	Y	Y	Y
29 Massa	Y	Y	Y	Y	Y	Y
NORTH CAROLINA						
1 Butterfield	Y	Y	Y	Y	Y	Y
2 Etheridge	Y	Y	Y	Y	Y	Y
3 **Jones**	Y	Y	Y	Y	Y	N
4 Price	Y	Y	Y	Y	Y	Y

	145	146	147	148	149	150
5 **Foxx**	Y	Y	Y	Y	Y	N
6 **Coble**	Y	Y	Y	N	Y	N
7 McIntyre	Y	Y	Y	Y	Y	Y
8 Kissell	Y	Y	Y	Y	Y	Y
9 **Myrick**	Y	Y	Y	Y	Y	N
10 **McHenry**	Y	Y	Y	Y	Y	N
11 Shuler	Y	Y	Y	Y	Y	Y
12 Watt	Y	Y	Y	Y	Y	Y
13 Miller	Y	Y	Y	Y	Y	Y
NORTH DAKOTA						
AL Pomeroy	?	?	?	?	?	Y
OHIO						
1 Driehaus	Y	Y	Y	Y	Y	Y
2 **Schmidt**	Y	Y	Y	Y	Y	N
3 **Turner**	Y	Y	Y	Y	?	N
4 **Jordan**	Y	Y	Y	Y	Y	N
5 **Latta**	Y	Y	Y	Y	Y	N
6 Wilson	Y	Y	Y	Y	Y	Y
7 **Austria**	Y	Y	Y	Y	Y	N
8 **Boehner**	Y	Y	Y	Y	Y	N
9 Kaptur	Y	Y	Y	Y	Y	Y
10 Kucinich	Y	Y	Y	Y	Y	Y
11 Fudge	Y	Y	Y	Y	Y	Y
12 **Tiberi**	Y	Y	Y	Y	Y	N
13 Sutton	Y	Y	Y	Y	Y	Y
14 **LaTourette**	Y	Y	Y	Y	Y	N
15 Kilroy	Y	Y	Y	Y	Y	Y
16 Boccieri	Y	Y	Y	Y	Y	Y
17 Ryan	Y	Y	Y	Y	Y	Y
18 Space	Y	Y	Y	Y	Y	Y
OKLAHOMA						
1 **Sullivan**	?	?	Y	Y	Y	?
2 Boren	Y	Y	Y	Y	Y	Y
3 **Lucas**	Y	Y	Y	Y	Y	N
4 **Cole**	Y	Y	Y	Y	Y	N
5 **Fallin**	Y	Y	Y	Y	Y	N
OREGON						
1 Wu	Y	Y	Y	Y	?	Y
2 **Walden**	Y	Y	Y	Y	Y	N
3 Blumenauer	Y	Y	Y	Y	Y	Y
4 DeFazio	Y	Y	Y	Y	Y	Y
5 Schrader	Y	Y	Y	Y	Y	Y
PENNSYLVANIA						
1 Brady	?	?	Y	Y	Y	Y
2 Fattah	Y	Y	Y	Y	Y	Y
3 Dahlkemper	Y	Y	Y	Y	Y	N
4 Altmire	Y	Y	Y	Y	Y	Y
5 **Thompson**	Y	Y	Y	Y	Y	N
6 **Gerlach**	Y	Y	Y	Y	Y	N
7 Sestak	Y	Y	Y	Y	Y	Y
8 Murphy, P.	Y	Y	Y	Y	Y	Y
9 **Shuster**	Y	Y	Y	Y	Y	N
10 Carney	Y	Y	Y	Y	Y	N
11 Kanjorski	Y	Y	Y	Y	Y	Y
12 Murtha	Y	Y	Y	Y	Y	Y
13 Schwartz	Y	Y	Y	Y	Y	Y
14 Doyle	Y	Y	Y	Y	Y	Y
15 **Dent**	Y	Y	Y	Y	Y	N
16 **Pitts**	Y	Y	Y	Y	Y	N
17 Holden	Y	Y	Y	Y	Y	Y
18 **Murphy, T.**	Y	Y	Y	Y	Y	N
19 **Platts**	Y	Y	Y	Y	Y	N
RHODE ISLAND						
1 Kennedy	Y	Y	Y	Y	Y	Y
2 Langevin	Y	Y	Y	Y	Y	Y
SOUTH CAROLINA						
1 **Brown**	Y	Y	Y	Y	Y	N
2 **Wilson**	Y	Y	Y	Y	Y	N
3 **Barrett**	Y	Y	Y	Y	Y	N
4 **Inglis**	Y	Y	Y	Y	Y	N
5 Spratt	Y	Y	Y	Y	Y	Y
6 Clyburn	Y	Y	Y	Y	Y	Y
SOUTH DAKOTA						
AL Herseth Sandlin	Y	Y	Y	Y	?	Y
TENNESSEE						
1 **Roe**	Y	Y	Y	Y	Y	N
2 **Duncan**	Y	Y	Y	N	Y	N
3 **Wamp**	Y	Y	Y	Y	Y	N
4 Davis	Y	Y	Y	Y	Y	Y
5 Cooper	Y	Y	Y	Y	Y	Y
6 Gordon	Y	Y	Y	Y	Y	Y
7 **Blackburn**	Y	Y	Y	Y	Y	N
8 Tanner	Y	Y	Y	Y	Y	Y
9 Cohen	Y	Y	Y	Y	Y	Y

	145	146	147	148	149	150
TEXAS						
1 **Gohmert**	Y	Y	N	N	Y	?
2 **Poe**	Y	Y	Y	N	Y	N
3 **Johnson, S.**	?	?	?	Y	Y	N
4 **Hall**	Y	Y	Y	Y	Y	N
5 **Hensarling**	Y	Y	Y	Y	Y	N
6 **Barton**	Y	Y	Y	Y	Y	N
7 **Culberson**	Y	Y	Y	Y	Y	N
8 **Brady**	Y	Y	Y	Y	Y	N
9 Green, A.	Y	Y	Y	Y	Y	Y
10 **McCaul**	Y	Y	Y	Y	Y	N
11 **Conaway**	Y	Y	Y	Y	Y	N
12 **Granger**	Y	Y	Y	Y	Y	N
13 **Thornberry**	Y	Y	Y	Y	Y	N
14 **Paul**	Y	Y	N	N	Y	N
15 Hinojosa	Y	Y	Y	Y	Y	Y
16 Reyes	Y	Y	Y	Y	Y	Y
17 Edwards	Y	Y	Y	Y	Y	Y
18 Jackson Lee	Y	Y	Y	Y	Y	Y
19 **Neugebauer**	Y	Y	Y	Y	Y	N
20 Gonzalez	Y	Y	Y	Y	Y	Y
21 **Smith**	Y	Y	Y	Y	Y	N
22 **Olson**	Y	Y	Y	Y	Y	N
23 Rodriguez	Y	Y	Y	Y	Y	Y
24 **Marchant**	?	?	Y	Y	Y	N
25 Doggett	Y	Y	Y	Y	Y	Y
26 **Burgess**	Y	Y	Y	N	Y	N
27 Ortiz	Y	Y	Y	Y	Y	Y
28 Cuellar	Y	Y	Y	Y	Y	Y
29 Green, G.	Y	Y	Y	Y	Y	Y
30 Johnson, E.	Y	Y	Y	Y	Y	Y
31 **Carter**	Y	Y	Y	Y	Y	N
32 **Sessions**	Y	Y	?	?	?	N
UTAH						
1 **Bishop**	Y	Y	Y	Y	Y	N
2 Matheson	Y	Y	Y	Y	Y	Y
3 **Chaffetz**	Y	Y	Y	Y	Y	N
VERMONT						
AL Welch	Y	Y	Y	Y	Y	Y
VIRGINIA						
1 **Wittman**	Y	Y	Y	Y	Y	N
2 Nye	Y	Y	Y	Y	Y	N
3 Scott	Y	Y	Y	Y	Y	Y
4 **Forbes**	Y	Y	Y	Y	Y	N
5 Perriello	Y	Y	Y	Y	Y	N
6 **Goodlatte**	Y	Y	Y	Y	Y	N
7 **Cantor**	Y	Y	Y	Y	Y	N
8 Moran	Y	Y	Y	Y	Y	Y
9 Boucher	?	Y	Y	Y	Y	Y
10 **Wolf**	Y	Y	Y	Y	Y	N
11 Connolly	Y	Y	Y	Y	Y	Y
WASHINGTON						
1 Inslee	Y	Y	Y	Y	Y	Y
2 Larsen	Y	Y	Y	Y	Y	Y
3 Baird	Y	Y	Y	Y	Y	Y
4 **Hastings**	Y	Y	Y	Y	Y	N
5 **McMorris Rodgers**	Y	Y	Y	Y	Y	N
6 Dicks	Y	Y	Y	Y	Y	Y
7 McDermott	Y	Y	Y	Y	Y	Y
8 **Reichert**	Y	Y	Y	Y	Y	Y
9 Smith	Y	Y	Y	Y	Y	Y
WEST VIRGINIA						
1 Mollohan	Y	Y	Y	Y	Y	Y
2 **Capito**	Y	Y	Y	Y	Y	N
3 Rahall	Y	Y	Y	Y	Y	Y
WISCONSIN						
1 **Ryan**	Y	Y	Y	Y	Y	N
2 Baldwin	Y	Y	Y	Y	Y	Y
3 Kind	Y	Y	Y	Y	Y	Y
4 Moore	Y	Y	Y	Y	Y	Y
5 **Sensenbrenner**	Y	Y	Y	N	Y	N
6 **Petri**	Y	Y	Y	Y	Y	N
7 Obey	Y	Y	Y	Y	Y	Y
8 Kagen	Y	Y	Y	Y	Y	Y
WYOMING						
AL **Lummis**	Y	Y	N	N	Y	N
DELEGATES						
Faleomavaega (A.S.)						
Norton (D.C.)						
Bordallo (Guam)						
Sablan (N. Marianas)						
Pierluisi (P.R.)						
Christensen (V.I.)						

IN THE HOUSE | By Vote Number

151. **HR 146. Public Lands Designation/Rule.** Adoption of the rule (H Res 280) that would provide for House floor consideration of the Senate amendment to the bill that would designate more than 2 million new acres of protected wilderness areas nationwide, in addition to wild and scenic rivers, historic sites and expansions of national parks. Adopted 247-177: R 1-174; D 246-3. March 25, 2009.

152. **S 383. TARP Inspector General Authority/Passage.** Moore, D-Kan., motion to suspend the rules and pass the bill that would give the inspector general of the Troubled Asset Relief Program more flexibility in hiring auditors and investigators, and require the inspector general to submit a report to Congress by Sept. 1 on recipients' use of the program's funds. Motion agreed to 423-0: R 174-0; D 249-0. A two-thirds majority of those present and voting (282 in this case) is required for passage under suspension of the rules. March 25, 2009.

153. **HR 146. Public Lands Designation/Motion to Concur.** Rahall, D-W.Va., motion to concur in the Senate amendment to the bill that would designate more than 2 million new acres of protected wilderness areas nationwide, in addition to wild and scenic rivers, historic sites and expansions of national parks. It would authorize new water projects and allow water settlement rights in Western states. It would codify a system to improve management of protected federal land. It would specify that bill provisions would not restrict access for hunting, fishing or trapping activities otherwise allowed by law and would not affect state authority to regulate these activities. Motion agreed to (thus clearing the bill for the president) 285-140: R 38-136; D 247-4. March 25, 2009.

154. **H Res 273. Greece's Anniversary of Independence/Adoption.** Berman, D-Calif., motion to suspend the rules and adopt the resolution that would congratulate the people of Greece as they celebrate the 188th anniversary of the independence of their country. Motion agreed to 423-0: R 173-0; D 250-0. A two-thirds majority of those present and voting (282 in this case) is required for adoption under suspension of the rules. March 25, 2009.

155. **H Res 286. Earmark Investigation/Motion to Table.** Miller, D-Calif., motion to table (kill) the Flake, R-Ariz., privileged resolution that would instruct the Committee on Standards of Official Conduct to investigate and report on the relationship between earmarks made by members of Congress and the details of past campaign contributions. Motion agreed to 223-182: R 4-157; D 219-25. March 25, 2009.

156. **HR 1404. Federal Lands Wildfire Fund/Rule.** Adoption of the rule (H Res 281) that would provide for House floor consideration of the bill that would authorize a fund to help pay the costs of responding to catastrophic wildfires on federal lands. Adopted 248-175: R 0-173; D 248-2. March 25, 2009.

	151	152	153	154	155	156
ALABAMA						
1 Bonner	N	Y	N	Y	P	N
2 Bright	Y	Y	Y	Y	N	Y
3 Rogers	N	Y	N	Y	N	N
4 Aderholt	N	Y	N	Y	N	N
5 Griffith	Y	Y	Y	Y	Y	Y
6 Bachus	N	Y	N	Y	N	N
7 Davis	Y	Y	Y	Y	Y	Y
ALASKA						
AL Young	N	Y	Y	Y	Y	N
ARIZONA						
1 Kirkpatrick	N	Y	Y	Y	N	Y
2 Franks	N	Y	N	Y	N	N
3 Shadegg	N	Y	N	Y	N	N
4 Pastor	Y	Y	Y	Y	Y	Y
5 Mitchell	Y	Y	Y	Y	N	Y
6 Flake	N	Y	N	Y	N	N
7 Grijalva	Y	Y	Y	Y	Y	Y
8 Giffords	Y	Y	Y	Y	N	Y
ARKANSAS						
1 Berry	Y	Y	Y	Y	Y	Y
2 Snyder	Y	Y	Y	Y	Y	Y
3 Boozman	N	Y	N	Y	N	N
4 Ross	Y	Y	Y	Y	Y	Y
CALIFORNIA						
1 Thompson	Y	Y	Y	Y	Y	Y
2 Herger	N	Y	N	Y	N	N
3 Lungren	N	Y	N	Y	N	N
4 McClintock	N	Y	N	Y	N	N
5 Matsui	Y	Y	Y	Y	Y	Y
6 Woolsey	+	Y	Y	Y	Y	Y
7 Miller, George	Y	Y	Y	Y	Y	Y
8 Pelosi						
9 Lee	Y	Y	Y	Y	Y	Y
10 Tauscher	Y	Y	Y	Y	P	Y
11 McNerney	Y	Y	Y	Y	N	Y
12 Speier	Y	Y	Y	Y	Y	Y
13 Stark	Y	Y	Y	Y	Y	Y
14 Eshoo	Y	?	Y	Y	Y	Y
15 Honda	Y	Y	Y	Y	Y	Y
16 Lofgren	Y	Y	Y	Y	P	Y
17 Farr	Y	Y	Y	Y	Y	Y
18 Cardoza	Y	Y	Y	Y	Y	Y
19 Radanovich	N	Y	N	Y	N	N
20 Costa	Y	Y	Y	Y	Y	Y
21 Nunes	N	Y	N	Y	N	N
22 McCarthy	N	Y	N	Y	N	N
23 Capps	Y	Y	Y	Y	Y	Y
24 Gallegly	N	Y	N	Y	N	N
25 McKeon	N	Y	Y	Y	N	N
26 Dreier	N	Y	N	Y	N	N
27 Sherman	Y	Y	Y	Y	Y	Y
28 Berman	Y	Y	Y	Y	Y	Y
29 Schiff	Y	Y	Y	Y	Y	Y
30 Waxman	Y	Y	Y	Y	Y	Y
31 Becerra	Y	Y	Y	Y	Y	Y
32 Vacant						
33 Watson	Y	Y	Y	Y	Y	Y
34 Roybal-Allard	Y	Y	Y	Y	Y	Y
35 Waters	Y	Y	Y	Y	?	Y
36 Harman	Y	Y	Y	Y	Y	Y
37 Richardson	Y	Y	Y	Y	Y	Y
38 Napolitano	Y	Y	Y	Y	Y	Y
39 Sánchez, Linda	Y	Y	Y	Y	Y	Y
40 Royce	N	Y	N	Y	N	N
41 Lewis	N	Y	N	Y	N	N
42 Miller, Gary	?	?	?	?	?	?
43 Baca	Y	Y	Y	Y	Y	Y
44 Calvert	N	Y	N	Y	N	N
45 Bono Mack	N	Y	Y	Y	N	N
46 Rohrabacher	N	?	N	Y	N	N
47 Sanchez, Loretta	Y	Y	Y	Y	Y	Y
48 Campbell	N	Y	N	Y	N	N
49 Issa	N	Y	N	Y	N	N
50 Bilbray	N	Y	N	Y	N	N
51 Filner	Y	Y	Y	Y	Y	Y
52 Hunter	N	Y	N	Y	N	N
53 Davis	Y	Y	Y	Y	Y	Y

	151	152	153	154	155	156
COLORADO						
1 DeGette	Y	Y	Y	Y	Y	Y
2 Polis	Y	Y	Y	Y	Y	Y
3 Salazar	Y	Y	Y	Y	Y	Y
4 Markey	Y	Y	Y	Y	Y	Y
5 Lamborn	N	Y	N	Y	N	N
6 Coffman	N	Y	N	Y	N	N
7 Perlmutter	Y	Y	Y	Y	Y	Y
CONNECTICUT						
1 Larson	Y	Y	Y	Y	Y	Y
2 Courtney	Y	Y	Y	Y	Y	Y
3 DeLauro	Y	Y	Y	Y	Y	Y
4 Himes	Y	Y	Y	Y	N	Y
5 Murphy	Y	Y	Y	Y	Y	Y
DELAWARE						
AL Castle	N	Y	Y	Y	N	N
FLORIDA						
1 Miller	N	Y	N	Y	N	N
2 Boyd	Y	Y	Y	Y	Y	Y
3 Brown	Y	Y	Y	Y	Y	Y
4 Crenshaw	N	Y	N	Y	N	N
5 Brown-Waite	N	Y	N	Y	N	N
6 Stearns	N	Y	N	Y	N	N
7 Mica	N	Y	N	Y	N	N
8 Grayson	Y	Y	Y	Y	Y	Y
9 Bilirakis	N	Y	N	Y	N	N
10 Young	N	Y	Y	Y	N	N
11 Castor	Y	Y	Y	Y	P	Y
12 Putnam	N	Y	N	Y	N	N
13 Buchanan	N	Y	N	Y	N	N
14 Mack	N	Y	N	Y	N	N
15 Posey	N	Y	N	?	N	N
16 Rooney	N	Y	N	Y	N	N
17 Meek	Y	Y	Y	Y	Y	Y
18 Ros-Lehtinen	N	Y	Y	Y	N	N
19 Wexler	Y	Y	Y	Y	Y	Y
20 Wasserman Schultz	Y	Y	Y	Y	Y	Y
21 Diaz-Balart, L.	N	Y	N	Y	P	N
22 Klein	Y	Y	Y	Y	Y	Y
23 Hastings	Y	Y	Y	Y	Y	Y
24 Kosmas	Y	Y	Y	Y	N	Y
25 Diaz-Balart, M.	N	Y	N	Y	N	N
GEORGIA						
1 Kingston	N	Y	N	Y	N	N
2 Bishop	Y	Y	Y	Y	Y	Y
3 Westmoreland	?	?	?	?	?	?
4 Johnson	Y	Y	Y	Y	Y	Y
5 Lewis	Y	Y	Y	Y	Y	Y
6 Price	–	+	N	Y	N	N
7 Linder	N	Y	N	Y	N	N
8 Marshall	Y	Y	N	Y	Y	Y
9 Deal	N	Y	N	Y	?	?
10 Broun	N	Y	N	Y	N	N
11 Gingrey	N	Y	N	Y	N	N
12 Barrow	Y	Y	Y	Y	Y	Y
13 Scott	Y	Y	Y	Y	Y	Y
HAWAII						
1 Abercrombie	Y	Y	Y	Y	Y	Y
2 Hirono	Y	Y	Y	Y	Y	Y
IDAHO						
1 Minnick	Y	Y	Y	Y	N	Y
2 Simpson	N	Y	Y	Y	N	N
ILLINOIS						
1 Rush	Y	Y	Y	Y	Y	Y
2 Jackson	Y	Y	Y	Y	Y	Y
3 Lipinski	Y	Y	Y	Y	Y	Y
4 Gutierrez	Y	Y	Y	Y	Y	Y
5 Vacant						
6 Roskam	N	Y	N	Y	N	N
7 Davis	Y	Y	Y	Y	Y	Y
8 Bean	Y	Y	Y	Y	N	Y
9 Schakowsky	Y	Y	Y	Y	Y	Y
10 Kirk	N	Y	Y	Y	N	N
11 Halvorson	Y	Y	Y	Y	Y	Y
12 Costello	Y	Y	Y	Y	Y	Y
13 Biggert	N	Y	N	Y	N	N
14 Foster	Y	Y	Y	Y	N	Y
15 Johnson	N	Y	Y	Y	N	N

KEY	**Republicans**	Democrats		
Y Voted for (yea)		X Paired against		C Voted "present" to avoid possible conflict of interest
# Paired for		– Announced against		? Did not vote or otherwise make a position known
+ Announced for		P Voted "present"		
N Voted against (nay)				

	151	152	153	154	155	156
16 **Manzullo**	N	Y	N	Y	N	N
17 Hare	Y	Y	Y	Y	Y	Y
18 **Schock**	N	Y	N	Y	N	N
19 **Shimkus**	N	Y	N	Y	N	N
INDIANA						
1 Visclosky	Y	Y	Y	Y	N	Y
2 Donnelly	N	Y	Y	Y	N	N
3 **Souder**	N	Y	?	?	?	?
4 **Buyer**	N	Y	N	Y	N	N
5 **Burton**	N	Y	N	Y	N	N
6 **Pence**	N	Y	N	Y	N	N
7 Carson	Y	Y	Y	Y	Y	Y
8 Ellsworth	Y	Y	Y	Y	N	Y
9 Hill	Y	Y	Y	Y	N	N
IOWA						
1 Braley	Y	Y	Y	Y	Y	Y
2 Loebsack	Y	Y	Y	Y	N	Y
3 Boswell	Y	Y	Y	Y	Y	Y
4 **Latham**	N	Y	N	Y	P	N
5 **King**	N	Y	N	Y	N	N
KANSAS						
1 **Moran**	N	Y	N	Y	N	N
2 **Jenkins**	N	Y	N	Y	N	N
3 Moore	Y	Y	Y	Y	Y	Y
4 **Tiahrt**	N	Y	N	Y	N	N
KENTUCKY						
1 **Whitfield**	N	Y	Y	Y	N	N
2 **Guthrie**	N	Y	N	Y	N	N
3 Yarmuth	Y	?	Y	Y	Y	Y
4 **Davis**	N	Y	N	Y	N	N
5 **Rogers**	N	Y	N	Y	N	N
6 Chandler	Y	Y	Y	Y	P	Y
LOUISIANA						
1 **Scalise**	N	Y	N	Y	N	N
2 **Cao**	N	Y	N	Y	N	N
3 Melancon	Y	Y	Y	Y	?	Y
4 **Fleming**	N	Y	N	Y	N	N
5 **Alexander**	N	Y	N	Y	N	N
6 **Cassidy**	N	Y	Y	Y	N	N
7 **Boustany**	N	Y	N	Y	N	N
MAINE						
1 Pingree	Y	Y	Y	Y	Y	Y
2 Michaud	Y	Y	Y	Y	Y	Y
MARYLAND						
1 Kratovil	Y	Y	Y	?	Y	Y
2 Ruppersberger	Y	Y	Y	Y	Y	Y
3 Sarbanes	?	?	Y	Y	Y	Y
4 Edwards	Y	Y	Y	Y	Y	Y
5 Hoyer	Y	Y	Y	Y	Y	Y
6 **Bartlett**	N	Y	N	Y	N	N
7 Cummings	Y	Y	Y	Y	Y	Y
8 Van Hollen	Y	Y	Y	Y	Y	Y
MASSACHUSETTS						
1 Olver	Y	Y	Y	Y	?	?
2 Neal	Y	Y	Y	Y	Y	Y
3 McGovern	Y	Y	Y	Y	Y	Y
4 Frank	Y	Y	Y	Y	Y	Y
5 Tsongas	Y	Y	Y	Y	Y	Y
6 Tierney	Y	Y	Y	Y	Y	Y
7 Markey	Y	Y	Y	Y	Y	Y
8 Capuano	Y	Y	Y	Y	Y	Y
9 Lynch	Y	Y	Y	Y	Y	Y
10 Delahunt	Y	Y	Y	Y	Y	Y
MICHIGAN						
1 Stupak	N	Y	N	Y	Y	Y
2 **Hoekstra**	N	Y	N	Y	N	N
3 **Ehlers**	N	Y	Y	Y	N	N
4 **Camp**	N	Y	N	Y	N	N
5 Kildee	Y	Y	Y	Y	Y	Y
6 **Upton**	N	Y	Y	Y	N	N
7 Schauer	Y	Y	Y	Y	Y	Y
8 **Rogers**	N	Y	N	Y	N	N
9 Peters	Y	Y	Y	Y	Y	Y
10 **Miller**	N	Y	Y	Y	N	N
11 **McCotter**	N	Y	N	Y	N	N
12 Levin	Y	Y	Y	Y	Y	Y
13 Kilpatrick	Y	Y	Y	Y	Y	Y
14 Conyers	Y	Y	Y	Y	Y	Y
15 Dingell	Y	Y	Y	Y	Y	Y
MINNESOTA						
1 Walz	Y	Y	Y	Y	N	Y
2 **Kline**	N	Y	N	Y	P	N
3 **Paulsen**	N	Y	Y	Y	N	N
4 McCollum	Y	Y	Y	Y	Y	Y

	151	152	153	154	155	156
5 Ellison	Y	Y	Y	Y	Y	Y
6 **Bachmann**	N	Y	N	Y	N	N
7 Peterson	Y	Y	N	Y	Y	Y
8 Oberstar	Y	Y	Y	Y	Y	Y
MISSISSIPPI						
1 Childers	?	Y	Y	Y	Y	Y
2 Thompson	Y	Y	Y	Y	Y	Y
3 **Harper**	N	Y	N	Y	N	N
4 Taylor	Y	Y	Y	Y	Y	Y
MISSOURI						
1 Clay	Y	Y	Y	Y	Y	Y
2 **Akin**	N	Y	N	Y	N	N
3 Carnahan	Y	Y	Y	Y	Y	Y
4 Skelton	Y	Y	Y	Y	Y	Y
5 Cleaver	Y	Y	Y	Y	Y	Y
6 **Graves**	N	Y	N	Y	N	N
7 **Blunt**	N	Y	N	Y	N	N
8 **Emerson**	N	Y	N	Y	N	N
9 **Luetkemeyer**	N	Y	N	Y	N	N
MONTANA						
AL **Rehberg**	N	Y	N	Y	N	N
NEBRASKA						
1 **Fortenberry**	N	Y	Y	Y	N	N
2 **Terry**	N	Y	N	Y	N	N
3 **Smith**	N	Y	N	Y	N	N
NEVADA						
1 Berkley	Y	Y	Y	Y	Y	Y
2 **Heller**	N	Y	N	Y	N	N
3 Titus	Y	Y	Y	Y	Y	Y
NEW HAMPSHIRE						
1 Shea-Porter	Y	Y	Y	Y	Y	Y
2 Hodes	Y	Y	Y	Y	N	Y
NEW JERSEY						
1 Andrews	Y	Y	Y	Y	Y	Y
2 **LoBiondo**	N	Y	Y	Y	N	N
3 Adler	Y	Y	Y	Y	Y	Y
4 **Smith**	N	Y	Y	Y	N	N
5 **Garrett**	N	Y	N	Y	N	N
6 Pallone	Y	Y	Y	Y	Y	Y
7 **Lance**	N	Y	Y	Y	N	N
8 Pascrell	Y	Y	Y	Y	Y	Y
9 Rothman	Y	Y	Y	Y	Y	Y
10 Payne	Y	Y	Y	Y	Y	Y
11 **Frelinghuysen**	N	Y	Y	Y	N	N
12 Holt	Y	Y	Y	Y	Y	Y
13 Sires	Y	Y	Y	Y	Y	Y
NEW MEXICO						
1 Heinrich	Y	Y	Y	Y	Y	Y
2 Teague	Y	Y	Y	Y	N	Y
3 Lujan	Y	Y	Y	Y	Y	Y
NEW YORK						
1 Bishop	Y	Y	Y	Y	Y	Y
2 Israel	Y	Y	Y	Y	Y	?
3 **King**	N	Y	N	Y	N	N
4 McCarthy	Y	Y	Y	Y	Y	Y
5 Ackerman	Y	Y	Y	Y	Y	Y
6 Meeks	Y	Y	Y	Y	Y	Y
7 Crowley	Y	Y	Y	Y	Y	Y
8 Nadler	Y	Y	Y	Y	Y	Y
9 Weiner	Y	Y	Y	Y	Y	Y
10 Towns	Y	Y	Y	Y	Y	Y
11 Clarke	Y	Y	Y	Y	Y	Y
12 Velázquez	Y	Y	Y	Y	Y	Y
13 McMahon	Y	Y	Y	Y	Y	Y
14 Maloney	Y	Y	Y	Y	Y	Y
15 Rangel	Y	Y	Y	Y	Y	Y
16 Serrano	Y	Y	Y	Y	Y	Y
17 Engel	?	?	?	?	?	?
18 Lowey	Y	Y	Y	Y	Y	Y
19 Hall	Y	Y	Y	Y	Y	Y
20 Vacant						
21 Tonko	Y	Y	Y	Y	Y	Y
22 Hinchey	Y	Y	Y	Y	Y	Y
23 **McHugh**	N	Y	N	Y	N	N
24 Arcuri	Y	Y	Y	Y	Y	Y
25 Maffei	Y	Y	Y	Y	Y	Y
26 **Lee**	N	Y	Y	Y	N	N
27 Higgins	Y	Y	Y	Y	Y	Y
28 Slaughter	Y	Y	Y	Y	Y	Y
29 Massa	Y	Y	Y	Y	Y	Y
NORTH CAROLINA						
1 Butterfield	Y	Y	Y	Y	P	Y
2 Etheridge	Y	Y	Y	Y	Y	Y
3 **Jones**	N	Y	Y	Y	Y	N
4 Price	Y	Y	Y	Y	Y	Y

	151	152	153	154	155	156
5 **Foxx**	N	Y	N	Y	N	N
6 **Coble**	N	Y	N	Y	N	N
7 McIntyre	Y	Y	Y	Y	N	Y
8 Kissell	Y	Y	Y	Y	Y	Y
9 **Myrick**	N	Y	N	Y	P	N
10 **McHenry**	N	Y	N	Y	N	N
11 Shuler	Y	Y	Y	Y	Y	Y
12 Watt	Y	Y	Y	Y	Y	Y
13 Miller	Y	Y	Y	Y	Y	Y
NORTH DAKOTA						
AL Pomeroy	Y	Y	Y	Y	Y	Y
OHIO						
1 Driehaus	Y	Y	Y	Y	Y	Y
2 **Schmidt**	N	Y	N	Y	N	N
3 **Turner**	N	Y	Y	Y	N	N
4 **Jordan**	N	Y	N	Y	N	N
5 **Latta**	N	Y	N	Y	N	N
6 Wilson	Y	Y	Y	Y	Y	Y
7 **Austria**	N	Y	N	Y	N	N
8 **Boehner**	N	Y	N	Y	N	N
9 Kaptur	Y	Y	Y	Y	Y	Y
10 Kucinich	Y	Y	Y	Y	Y	Y
11 Fudge	Y	Y	?	?	Y	Y
12 **Tiberi**	N	Y	N	Y	N	N
13 Sutton	Y	Y	Y	Y	Y	Y
14 **LaTourette**	N	Y	Y	Y	N	N
15 Kilroy	Y	Y	Y	Y	Y	Y
16 Boccieri	Y	Y	Y	Y	N	Y
17 Ryan	Y	Y	Y	Y	Y	Y
18 Space	Y	Y	Y	Y	Y	Y
OKLAHOMA						
1 **Sullivan**	N	Y	N	Y	N	N
2 Boren	Y	Y	N	Y	Y	Y
3 **Lucas**	N	Y	N	Y	N	N
4 **Cole**	N	Y	N	Y	N	N
5 **Fallin**	N	Y	N	Y	N	N
OREGON						
1 Wu	Y	Y	Y	Y	Y	Y
2 **Walden**	N	Y	Y	Y	P	N
3 Blumenauer	Y	Y	Y	Y	Y	Y
4 DeFazio	Y	Y	Y	Y	Y	Y
5 Schrader	Y	Y	Y	Y	Y	Y
PENNSYLVANIA						
1 Brady	Y	Y	Y	Y	Y	Y
2 Fattah	Y	Y	Y	Y	Y	Y
3 Dahlkemper	Y	Y	Y	Y	Y	Y
4 Altmire	Y	Y	Y	Y	Y	Y
5 **Thompson**	N	Y	N	Y	N	N
6 **Gerlach**	N	Y	Y	Y	N	N
7 Sestak	Y	Y	Y	Y	Y	Y
8 Murphy, P.	Y	Y	Y	Y	Y	Y
9 **Shuster**	N	Y	N	Y	?	N
10 Carney	Y	Y	Y	Y	Y	Y
11 Kanjorski	Y	Y	Y	Y	Y	Y
12 Murtha	Y	Y	Y	Y	Y	Y
13 Schwartz	Y	Y	Y	Y	Y	Y
14 Doyle	Y	Y	Y	Y	Y	Y
15 **Dent**	N	Y	Y	Y	P	N
16 **Pitts**	N	Y	N	Y	N	N
17 Holden	Y	Y	Y	Y	Y	Y
18 **Murphy, T.**	N	Y	N	Y	Y	N
19 **Platts**	N	Y	Y	Y	N	N
RHODE ISLAND						
1 Kennedy	Y	Y	Y	Y	Y	Y
2 Langevin	Y	Y	Y	Y	Y	Y
SOUTH CAROLINA						
1 **Brown**	N	Y	N	Y	N	N
2 **Wilson**	N	Y	N	Y	N	N
3 **Barrett**	N	Y	N	Y	P	N
4 **Inglis**	N	Y	Y	Y	N	N
5 Spratt	Y	Y	Y	Y	Y	Y
6 Clyburn	Y	Y	Y	Y	Y	Y
SOUTH DAKOTA						
AL Herseth Sandlin	Y	Y	Y	Y	N	Y
TENNESSEE						
1 **Roe**	N	Y	N	Y	N	N
2 **Duncan**	N	Y	N	Y	N	N
3 **Wamp**	N	Y	Y	Y	N	N
4 Davis	Y	Y	Y	Y	Y	Y
5 Cooper	Y	Y	Y	Y	Y	Y
6 Gordon	Y	Y	Y	Y	Y	Y
7 **Blackburn**	N	Y	N	Y	N	N
8 Tanner	Y	Y	Y	Y	Y	Y
9 Cohen	Y	Y	Y	Y	Y	Y

	151	152	153	154	155	156
TEXAS						
1 **Gohmert**	N	Y	N	Y	N	N
2 **Poe**	N	Y	N	Y	P	N
3 **Johnson, S.**	N	Y	N	Y	N	N
4 **Hall**	N	Y	N	Y	N	N
5 **Hensarling**	N	Y	N	Y	N	N
6 **Barton**	N	Y	N	Y	N	N
7 **Culberson**	N	Y	N	Y	N	N
8 **Brady**	N	Y	N	Y	N	N
9 Green, A.	Y	Y	Y	Y	Y	Y
10 **McCaul**	N	Y	N	Y	N	N
11 **Conaway**	N	Y	N	Y	P	N
12 **Granger**	N	Y	?	?	N	N
13 **Thornberry**	N	Y	N	Y	N	N
14 **Paul**	N	Y	N	Y	N	N
15 Hinojosa	Y	Y	Y	Y	Y	Y
16 Reyes	Y	Y	Y	Y	Y	Y
17 Edwards	Y	Y	Y	Y	Y	Y
18 Jackson Lee	Y	Y	Y	Y	Y	Y
19 **Neugebauer**	N	Y	N	Y	N	N
20 Gonzalez	Y	Y	Y	Y	Y	Y
21 **Smith**	N	Y	Y	Y	N	N
22 **Olson**	N	Y	N	Y	N	N
23 Rodriguez	Y	Y	Y	Y	Y	Y
24 **Marchant**	N	Y	N	Y	N	N
25 Doggett	Y	Y	Y	Y	Y	Y
26 **Burgess**	N	Y	N	Y	N	N
27 Ortiz	Y	Y	Y	Y	Y	Y
28 Cuellar	Y	Y	Y	Y	Y	Y
29 Green, G.	Y	Y	Y	Y	Y	Y
30 Johnson, E.	Y	Y	Y	Y	Y	Y
31 **Carter**	N	Y	N	Y	N	N
32 **Sessions**	N	Y	N	Y	N	N
UTAH						
1 **Bishop**	N	Y	N	Y	N	N
2 Matheson	Y	Y	Y	Y	Y	Y
3 **Chaffetz**	N	Y	N	Y	N	N
VERMONT						
AL Welch	Y	Y	Y	Y	P	Y
VIRGINIA						
1 **Wittman**	N	Y	Y	Y	N	N
2 Nye	Y	Y	Y	Y	Y	Y
3 Scott	Y	Y	Y	Y	Y	Y
4 **Forbes**	N	Y	N	Y	N	N
5 Perriello	Y	Y	Y	Y	N	Y
6 **Goodlatte**	N	Y	N	Y	N	N
7 **Cantor**	N	Y	N	Y	?	?
8 Moran	Y	Y	Y	Y	Y	Y
9 Boucher	Y	Y	Y	Y	Y	Y
10 **Wolf**	N	Y	Y	Y	N	N
11 Connolly	Y	Y	Y	Y	Y	Y
WASHINGTON						
1 Inslee	Y	Y	Y	Y	Y	Y
2 Larsen	Y	Y	Y	Y	Y	Y
3 Baird	Y	Y	Y	Y	Y	Y
4 **Hastings**	N	Y	N	Y	P	N
5 **McMorris Rodgers**	N	Y	N	Y	N	N
6 Dicks	Y	Y	Y	Y	Y	Y
7 McDermott	Y	Y	Y	Y	Y	Y
8 **Reichert**	Y	Y	Y	Y	N	N
9 Smith	Y	Y	Y	Y	N	Y
WEST VIRGINIA						
1 Mollohan	Y	Y	Y	Y	Y	Y
2 **Capito**	N	Y	Y	Y	N	N
3 Rahall	Y	Y	Y	Y	Y	Y
WISCONSIN						
1 **Ryan**	N	Y	N	Y	N	N
2 Baldwin	Y	Y	Y	Y	Y	Y
3 Kind	Y	Y	Y	Y	N	Y
4 Moore	Y	Y	Y	Y	Y	Y
5 **Sensenbrenner**	N	Y	N	Y	N	N
6 **Petri**	N	Y	Y	Y	N	N
7 Obey	Y	Y	Y	Y	Y	Y
8 Kagen	Y	Y	Y	Y	Y	Y
WYOMING						
AL **Lummis**	N	Y	N	Y	N	N
DELEGATES						
Faleomavaega (A.S.)						
Norton (D.C.)						
Bordallo (Guam)						
Sablan (N. Marianas)						
Pierluisi (P.R.)						
Christensen (V.I.)						

IN THE HOUSE | By Vote Number

157. HR 1404. Federal Lands Wildfire Fund/Insect Infestation **Containment.** Perlmutter, D-Colo., amendment that would allow funds authorized in the bill to be used to contain insect infestations. Adopted in Committee of the Whole 420-0: R 171-0; D 249-0. March 26, 2009.

158. HR 1404. Federal Lands Wildfire Fund/Property Owner **Notification.** Hastings, R-Wash., amendment that would require the Department of Agriculture to provide advance written notice to individuals who own adjacent land before setting fires on National Forest System property. Adopted in Committee of the Whole 420-0: R 171-0; D 249-0. March 26, 2009.

159. HR 1404. Federal Lands Wildfire Fund/Insect Infestation **Assessment.** Minnick, D-Idaho, amendment that would require the Interior and Agriculture departments to take into account the effect of insect infestation on the risk for wildfires when assessing eligibility for use of funds authorized by the bill. Adopted in Committee of the Whole 422-0: R 172-0; D 250-0. March 26, 2009.

160. HR 1404. Federal Lands Wildfire Fund/Shared Cost Grants. Kirkpatrick, D-Ariz., amendment that would allow the Interior and Agriculture departments to provide shared cost grants to communities included in a map of fire-risk priority areas and that meet two of the bill's four criteria for the grants. Adopted in Committee of the Whole 418-2: R 171-1; D 247-1. March 26, 2009.

161. HR 1404. Federal Lands Wildfire Fund/Hazardous Fuels **Reduction.** Goodlatte, R-Va., amendment that would allow the Agriculture Department to enter into contracts with a state forester to implement hazardous fuels reduction projects on National Forest System lands to prevent or reduce the severity of wildfires. Rejected in Committee of the Whole 148-272: R 140-32; D 8-240. March 26, 2009.

162. HR 1404. Federal Lands Wildfire Fund/Passage. Passage of the bill that would authorize a fund to help pay the costs of responding to catastrophic wildfires on federal lands, require the Interior and Agriculture departments to develop wildfire management strategies, and establish a grant program within each department to award funds to state, local and tribal governments to develop wildfire response plans. Passed 412-3: R 169-3; D 243-0. March 26, 2009.

	157	158	159	160	161	162
ALABAMA						
1 Bonner	Y	Y	Y	Y	Y	Y
2 Bright	Y	Y	Y	Y	Y	Y
3 Rogers	Y	Y	Y	Y	Y	Y
4 Aderholt	Y	Y	Y	Y	Y	Y
5 Griffith	?	?	?	?	?	?
6 Bachus	Y	Y	Y	Y	Y	Y
7 Davis	Y	Y	Y	Y	N	Y
ALASKA						
AL Young	Y	Y	Y	Y	N	Y
ARIZONA						
1 Kirkpatrick	Y	Y	Y	N	N	Y
2 Franks	Y	Y	Y	Y	Y	Y
3 Shadegg	Y	Y	Y	Y	Y	Y
4 Pastor	Y	Y	Y	N	N	Y
5 Mitchell	Y	Y	Y	N	N	Y
6 Flake	Y	Y	Y	Y	Y	N
7 Grijalva	Y	Y	Y	N	N	Y
8 Giffords	Y	Y	Y	N	N	Y
ARKANSAS						
1 Berry	Y	Y	Y	N	N	Y
2 Snyder	Y	Y	Y	N	N	Y
3 Boozman	Y	Y	Y	Y	Y	Y
4 Ross	Y	Y	Y	N	N	Y
CALIFORNIA						
1 Thompson	Y	Y	Y	N	N	Y
2 Herger	Y	Y	Y	Y	Y	Y
3 Lungren	Y	Y	Y	Y	Y	Y
4 McClintock	Y	Y	Y	Y	Y	Y
5 Matsui	Y	Y	Y	N	N	Y
6 Woolsey	Y	Y	Y	N	N	Y
7 Miller, George	Y	Y	Y	?	N	Y
8 Pelosi						
9 Lee	Y	Y	Y	N	N	Y
10 Tauscher	Y	Y	Y	N	N	Y
11 McNerney	Y	Y	Y	N	N	Y
12 Speier	Y	Y	Y	N	N	Y
13 Stark	Y	Y	Y	N	N	Y
14 Eshoo	Y	Y	Y	N	N	Y
15 Honda	Y	Y	Y	N	N	Y
16 Lofgren	Y	Y	Y	N	N	Y
17 Farr	Y	Y	Y	N	N	Y
18 Cardoza	Y	Y	Y	N	N	Y
19 Radanovich	Y	Y	Y	Y	Y	Y
20 Costa	Y	Y	Y	N	N	Y
21 Nunes	Y	Y	Y	Y	Y	Y
22 McCarthy	Y	Y	Y	Y	Y	Y
23 Capps	Y	Y	Y	N	N	Y
24 Gallegly	Y	Y	Y	Y	Y	Y
25 McKeon	Y	Y	Y	Y	Y	Y
26 Dreier	Y	Y	Y	Y	Y	Y
27 Sherman	Y	Y	Y	N	N	Y
28 Berman	Y	Y	Y	N	N	Y
29 Schiff	Y	Y	Y	N	N	Y
30 Waxman	Y	Y	Y	N	N	Y
31 Becerra	Y	Y	Y	N	N	Y
32 Vacant						
33 Watson	Y	Y	Y	N	N	Y
34 Roybal-Allard	Y	Y	Y	N	N	Y
35 Waters	Y	Y	Y	N	N	Y
36 Harman	Y	Y	Y	N	N	Y
37 Richardson	Y	Y	Y	N	N	Y
38 Napolitano	Y	Y	Y	N	N	Y
39 Sánchez, Linda	Y	Y	Y	N	N	Y
40 Royce	Y	Y	Y	Y	Y	Y
41 Lewis	Y	Y	Y	Y	Y	Y
42 Miller, Gary	?	?	?	?	?	?
43 Baca	Y	Y	Y	N	N	Y
44 Calvert	Y	Y	Y	Y	Y	Y
45 Bono Mack	Y	Y	Y	Y	Y	Y
46 Rohrabacher	Y	Y	Y	Y	Y	Y
47 Sanchez, Loretta	Y	Y	Y	N	N	Y
48 Campbell	Y	Y	Y	Y	Y	Y
49 Issa	Y	Y	Y	N	Y	Y
50 Bilbray	Y	Y	Y	Y	Y	Y
51 Filner	Y	Y	Y	N	N	Y
52 Hunter	Y	Y	Y	Y	Y	Y
53 Davis	+	+	+	+	–	+

	157	158	159	160	161	162
COLORADO						
1 DeGette	Y	Y	Y	Y	N	Y
2 Polis	Y	Y	Y	Y	N	Y
3 Salazar	Y	Y	Y	Y	N	Y
4 Markey	Y	Y	Y	Y	N	Y
5 Lamborn	Y	Y	Y	Y	Y	Y
6 Coffman	Y	Y	Y	Y	Y	Y
7 Perlmutter	Y	Y	Y	Y	N	Y
CONNECTICUT						
1 Larson	Y	Y	Y	Y	N	Y
2 Courtney	Y	Y	Y	Y	N	Y
3 DeLauro	Y	Y	Y	Y	N	Y
4 Himes	Y	Y	Y	Y	N	Y
5 Murphy	Y	Y	Y	Y	N	Y
DELAWARE						
AL Castle	Y	Y	Y	Y	N	Y
FLORIDA						
1 Miller	Y	Y	Y	Y	Y	Y
2 Boyd	Y	Y	Y	Y	N	Y
3 Brown	Y	Y	Y	Y	N	Y
4 Crenshaw	Y	Y	Y	Y	Y	Y
5 Brown-Waite	Y	Y	Y	Y	Y	Y
6 Stearns	Y	Y	Y	Y	Y	Y
7 Mica	Y	Y	Y	Y	Y	Y
8 Grayson	Y	Y	Y	Y	N	Y
9 Bilirakis	Y	Y	Y	Y	Y	Y
10 Young	Y	Y	Y	Y	Y	Y
11 Castor	Y	Y	Y	Y	N	?
12 Putnam	Y	Y	Y	Y	Y	Y
13 Buchanan	Y	Y	Y	Y	Y	Y
14 Mack	Y	Y	Y	Y	Y	Y
15 Posey	Y	Y	Y	Y	Y	Y
16 Rooney	Y	Y	Y	Y	Y	Y
17 Meek	Y	Y	Y	Y	N	Y
18 Ros-Lehtinen	Y	Y	Y	Y	N	Y
19 Wexler	Y	Y	Y	Y	N	Y
20 Wasserman Schultz	Y	Y	Y	Y	N	Y
21 Diaz-Balart, L.	Y	Y	Y	Y	N	Y
22 Klein	Y	Y	Y	Y	N	Y
23 Hastings	Y	Y	Y	Y	N	Y
24 Kosmas	Y	Y	Y	Y	N	Y
25 Diaz-Balart, M.	Y	Y	Y	Y	N	Y
GEORGIA						
1 Kingston	Y	Y	Y	Y	Y	Y
2 Bishop	Y	Y	Y	Y	N	Y
3 Westmoreland	Y	Y	Y	Y	Y	Y
4 Johnson	Y	Y	Y	Y	N	Y
5 Lewis	Y	Y	Y	Y	N	Y
6 Price	Y	Y	Y	Y	Y	Y
7 Linder	?	?	?	?	?	?
8 Marshall	Y	Y	Y	Y	N	Y
9 Deal	?	?	?	?	?	?
10 Broun	Y	Y	Y	Y	Y	Y
11 Gingrey	Y	Y	Y	Y	Y	Y
12 Barrow	Y	Y	Y	Y	N	Y
13 Scott	Y	Y	Y	Y	N	Y
HAWAII						
1 Abercrombie	Y	Y	Y	Y	N	Y
2 Hirono	Y	Y	Y	Y	N	Y
IDAHO						
1 Minnick	Y	Y	Y	Y	Y	Y
2 Simpson	Y	Y	Y	Y	Y	Y
ILLINOIS						
1 Rush	Y	Y	Y	Y	N	Y
2 Jackson	Y	Y	Y	Y	N	Y
3 Lipinski	Y	Y	Y	Y	N	Y
4 Gutierrez	Y	Y	Y	Y	N	Y
5 Vacant						
6 Roskam	Y	Y	Y	Y	N	Y
7 Davis	Y	Y	Y	Y	N	Y
8 Bean	Y	Y	Y	Y	N	Y
9 Schakowsky	Y	Y	Y	Y	N	Y
10 Kirk	Y	Y	Y	Y	N	Y
11 Halvorson	Y	Y	Y	Y	N	Y
12 Costello	Y	Y	Y	Y	N	Y
13 Biggert	Y	Y	Y	Y	N	Y
14 Foster	Y	Y	Y	Y	Y	Y
15 Johnson	Y	Y	Y	Y	Y	Y

KEY **Republicans** Democrats

Y Voted for (yea)	X Paired against	C Voted "present" to avoid possible conflict of interest
# Paired for	– Announced against	
+ Announced for	P Voted "present"	? Did not vote or otherwise make a position known
N Voted against (nay)		

	157	158	159	160	161	162
16 **Manzullo**	Y	Y	Y	Y	Y	Y
17 Hare	Y	Y	Y	Y	N	Y
18 **Schock**	Y	Y	Y	Y	N	Y
19 **Shimkus**	Y	Y	Y	Y	Y	Y
INDIANA						
1 Visclosky	Y	Y	Y	Y	N	Y
2 Donnelly	Y	Y	Y	Y	N	Y
3 **Souder**	?	?	?	?	?	?
4 **Buyer**	Y	Y	Y	Y	Y	Y
5 **Burton**	Y	Y	Y	Y	Y	Y
6 **Pence**	Y	Y	Y	Y	Y	Y
7 Carson	Y	Y	Y	Y	N	Y
8 Ellsworth	Y	Y	Y	Y	N	Y
9 Hill	Y	Y	Y	Y	N	Y
IOWA						
1 Braley	Y	Y	Y	Y	N	Y
2 Loebsack	Y	Y	Y	Y	N	Y
3 Boswell	Y	Y	Y	Y	N	Y
4 **Latham**	Y	Y	Y	Y	Y	Y
5 **King**	Y	Y	Y	Y	Y	Y
KANSAS						
1 **Moran**	Y	Y	Y	Y	Y	Y
2 **Jenkins**	Y	Y	Y	Y	Y	Y
3 Moore	Y	Y	Y	Y	N	Y
4 **Tiahrt**	Y	Y	Y	Y	Y	Y
KENTUCKY						
1 **Whitfield**	Y	Y	Y	Y	Y	Y
2 **Guthrie**	Y	Y	Y	Y	Y	Y
3 Yarmuth	Y	Y	Y	Y	N	Y
4 **Davis**	Y	Y	Y	Y	Y	Y
5 **Rogers**	Y	Y	Y	Y	Y	Y
6 Chandler	Y	Y	Y	Y	N	Y
LOUISIANA						
1 **Scalise**	Y	Y	Y	Y	Y	Y
2 **Cao**	Y	Y	Y	Y	N	Y
3 Melancon	Y	Y	Y	Y	N	Y
4 **Fleming**	Y	Y	Y	Y	Y	Y
5 **Alexander**	?	Y	Y	Y	N	Y
6 **Cassidy**	Y	Y	Y	Y	Y	Y
7 **Boustany**	Y	Y	Y	Y	Y	Y
MAINE						
1 Pingree	Y	Y	Y	Y	N	Y
2 Michaud	Y	Y	Y	Y	N	Y
MARYLAND						
1 Kratovil	Y	Y	Y	Y	N	Y
2 Ruppersberger	Y	Y	Y	Y	Y	Y
3 Sarbanes	?	Y	Y	Y	N	Y
4 Edwards	Y	Y	Y	Y	N	Y
5 Hoyer	?	?	?	?	?	?
6 **Bartlett**	Y	Y	Y	Y	Y	Y
7 Cummings	Y	Y	Y	Y	N	Y
8 Van Hollen	Y	Y	Y	Y	N	Y
MASSACHUSETTS						
1 Olver	Y	Y	Y	Y	N	Y
2 Neal	Y	Y	Y	Y	N	Y
3 McGovern	Y	Y	Y	Y	N	Y
4 Frank	Y	Y	Y	Y	N	Y
5 Tsongas	Y	Y	Y	Y	N	Y
6 Tierney	Y	Y	Y	Y	N	Y
7 Markey	Y	Y	Y	Y	N	Y
8 Capuano	Y	Y	Y	Y	N	Y
9 Lynch	Y	Y	Y	Y	N	Y
10 Delahunt	Y	Y	Y	Y	N	Y
MICHIGAN						
1 Stupak	Y	Y	Y	Y	N	Y
2 **Hoekstra**	Y	Y	Y	Y	Y	Y
3 **Ehlers**	Y	Y	Y	Y	Y	Y
4 **Camp**	Y	Y	Y	Y	Y	Y
5 Kildee	Y	Y	Y	Y	N	Y
6 **Upton**	Y	Y	Y	Y	N	Y
7 Schauer	Y	Y	Y	Y	N	Y
8 **Rogers**	Y	Y	Y	Y	Y	Y
9 Peters	Y	Y	Y	Y	N	Y
10 **Miller**	Y	Y	Y	Y	N	Y
11 **McCotter**	Y	Y	Y	Y	N	Y
12 Levin	Y	Y	Y	Y	N	Y
13 Kilpatrick	Y	Y	Y	Y	N	Y
14 Conyers	Y	Y	Y	Y	N	Y
15 Dingell	Y	Y	Y	Y	N	Y
MINNESOTA						
1 Walz	Y	Y	Y	Y	N	Y
2 **Kline**	Y	Y	Y	Y	Y	Y
3 **Paulsen**	Y	Y	Y	Y	Y	Y
4 McCollum	Y	Y	Y	Y	N	Y

	157	158	159	160	161	162
5 Ellison	Y	Y	Y	Y	N	Y
6 **Bachmann**	Y	Y	Y	Y	Y	Y
7 Peterson	Y	Y	Y	Y	N	Y
8 Oberstar	Y	Y	Y	Y	N	Y
MISSISSIPPI						
1 Childers	Y	Y	Y	Y	N	Y
2 Thompson	Y	Y	Y	Y	N	Y
3 **Harper**	Y	Y	Y	Y	Y	Y
4 Taylor	Y	Y	Y	Y	N	Y
MISSOURI						
1 Clay	Y	Y	Y	Y	N	Y
2 **Akin**	Y	Y	Y	Y	Y	Y
3 Carnahan	Y	Y	Y	Y	N	Y
4 Skelton	Y	Y	Y	Y	N	Y
5 Cleaver	Y	Y	Y	Y	N	Y
6 **Graves**	Y	Y	Y	Y	Y	Y
7 **Blunt**	Y	Y	Y	Y	Y	Y
8 **Emerson**	Y	Y	Y	Y	N	Y
9 **Luetkemeyer**	Y	Y	Y	Y	Y	Y
MONTANA						
AL **Rehberg**	Y	Y	Y	Y	Y	Y
NEBRASKA						
1 **Fortenberry**	Y	Y	Y	Y	Y	Y
2 **Terry**	Y	Y	Y	Y	Y	Y
3 **Smith**	Y	Y	Y	Y	Y	Y
NEVADA						
1 Berkley	Y	?	Y	Y	N	Y
2 **Heller**	Y	Y	Y	Y	Y	Y
3 Titus	Y	Y	Y	Y	N	Y
NEW HAMPSHIRE						
1 Shea-Porter	Y	Y	Y	Y	N	Y
2 Hodes	Y	Y	Y	Y	N	Y
NEW JERSEY						
1 Andrews	Y	Y	Y	Y	N	Y
2 **LoBiondo**	Y	Y	Y	Y	N	Y
3 Adler	Y	Y	Y	Y	N	Y
4 **Smith**	Y	Y	Y	Y	N	Y
5 **Garrett**	Y	Y	Y	Y	Y	Y
6 Pallone	Y	Y	Y	Y	N	Y
7 **Lance**	Y	Y	Y	Y	N	Y
8 Pascrell	+	+	+	+	–	+
9 Rothman	Y	Y	Y	Y	N	Y
10 Payne	Y	Y	Y	Y	N	Y
11 **Frelinghuysen**	Y	Y	Y	Y	Y	Y
12 Holt	Y	Y	Y	Y	N	Y
13 Sires	Y	Y	Y	Y	Y	Y
NEW MEXICO						
1 Heinrich	Y	Y	Y	Y	N	Y
2 Teague	Y	Y	Y	Y	N	Y
3 Lujan	Y	Y	Y	Y	N	Y
NEW YORK						
1 Bishop	Y	Y	Y	Y	N	Y
2 Israel	Y	Y	Y	Y	N	Y
3 **King**	Y	Y	Y	Y	N	Y
4 McCarthy	Y	Y	Y	Y	Y	Y
5 Ackerman	Y	Y	Y	Y	N	Y
6 Meeks	Y	Y	Y	Y	N	Y
7 Crowley	Y	Y	Y	Y	N	Y
8 Nadler	Y	Y	Y	Y	N	Y
9 Weiner	Y	Y	Y	Y	N	Y
10 Towns	Y	Y	Y	Y	N	Y
11 Clarke	Y	Y	Y	Y	N	Y
12 Velázquez	Y	Y	Y	Y	N	Y
13 McMahon	Y	Y	Y	Y	N	Y
14 Maloney	Y	Y	Y	Y	N	Y
15 Rangel	Y	Y	Y	Y	N	Y
16 Serrano	Y	Y	Y	Y	N	Y
17 Engel	Y	Y	Y	Y	N	Y
18 Lowey	Y	Y	Y	Y	N	Y
19 Hall	Y	Y	Y	Y	N	Y
20 Vacant						
21 Tonko	Y	Y	Y	Y	N	Y
22 Hinchey	Y	Y	Y	Y	N	Y
23 **McHugh**	Y	Y	Y	Y	N	Y
24 Arcuri	Y	Y	Y	Y	N	Y
25 Maffei	Y	Y	Y	Y	N	Y
26 **Lee**	Y	Y	Y	Y	Y	Y
27 Higgins	Y	Y	Y	Y	N	Y
28 Slaughter	Y	Y	Y	Y	N	Y
29 Massa	Y	Y	Y	Y	N	Y
NORTH CAROLINA						
1 Butterfield	Y	Y	Y	Y	N	Y
2 Etheridge	Y	Y	Y	Y	N	Y
3 **Jones**	Y	Y	Y	Y	Y	Y
4 Price	Y	Y	Y	Y	N	Y

	157	158	159	160	161	162
5 **Foxx**	Y	Y	Y	Y	Y	Y
6 **Coble**	Y	Y	Y	Y	Y	Y
7 McIntyre	Y	Y	Y	Y	N	Y
8 Kissell	Y	Y	Y	Y	N	Y
9 **Myrick**	Y	Y	Y	Y	Y	Y
10 **McHenry**	Y	Y	Y	Y	Y	Y
11 Shuler	Y	Y	Y	Y	N	Y
12 Watt	Y	Y	Y	Y	N	Y
13 Miller	Y	Y	Y	Y	N	Y
NORTH DAKOTA						
AL Pomeroy	?	?	?	?	?	?
OHIO						
1 Driehaus	Y	Y	Y	Y	N	Y
2 **Schmidt**	Y	Y	Y	Y	N	Y
3 **Turner**	Y	Y	Y	Y	N	Y
4 **Jordan**	Y	Y	Y	Y	Y	Y
5 **Latta**	Y	Y	Y	Y	Y	Y
6 Wilson	Y	Y	Y	Y	N	Y
7 **Austria**	Y	Y	Y	Y	Y	Y
8 **Boehner**	Y	Y	Y	Y	Y	Y
9 Kaptur	Y	Y	Y	Y	N	Y
10 Kucinich	Y	Y	Y	N	N	Y
11 Fudge	Y	Y	Y	Y	N	Y
12 **Tiberi**	Y	Y	Y	Y	N	Y
13 Sutton	Y	Y	Y	Y	N	Y
14 **LaTourette**	Y	Y	Y	Y	N	Y
15 Kilroy	Y	Y	Y	Y	N	Y
16 Boccieri	Y	Y	Y	Y	N	Y
17 Ryan	Y	Y	Y	Y	N	Y
18 Space	Y	Y	Y	Y	N	Y
OKLAHOMA						
1 **Sullivan**	Y	Y	Y	Y	Y	Y
2 Boren	Y	Y	Y	?	N	Y
3 **Lucas**	Y	Y	Y	Y	Y	Y
4 **Cole**	Y	Y	Y	Y	Y	Y
5 **Fallin**	Y	Y	Y	Y	Y	Y
OREGON						
1 Wu	Y	Y	Y	Y	N	Y
2 **Walden**	Y	Y	Y	Y	N	Y
3 Blumenauer	Y	Y	Y	Y	N	Y
4 DeFazio	Y	Y	Y	Y	N	Y
5 Schrader	Y	Y	Y	Y	Y	Y
PENNSYLVANIA						
1 Brady	Y	Y	Y	Y	N	Y
2 Fattah	Y	Y	Y	Y	N	Y
3 Dahlkemper	Y	Y	Y	Y	N	Y
4 Altmire	Y	Y	Y	Y	N	Y
5 **Thompson**	Y	Y	Y	Y	Y	Y
6 **Gerlach**	Y	Y	Y	Y	N	Y
7 Sestak	Y	Y	Y	Y	N	Y
8 Murphy, P.	Y	Y	Y	Y	N	Y
9 **Shuster**	Y	Y	Y	Y	Y	Y
10 Carney	Y	Y	Y	Y	N	Y
11 Kanjorski	Y	Y	Y	Y	N	Y
12 Murtha	Y	Y	Y	Y	N	Y
13 Schwartz	Y	Y	Y	Y	N	Y
14 Doyle	?	?	?	?	?	?
15 **Dent**	Y	Y	Y	Y	Y	Y
16 **Pitts**	Y	Y	Y	Y	Y	Y
17 Holden	Y	Y	Y	Y	N	Y
18 **Murphy, T.**	?	?	?	?	?	?
19 **Platts**	Y	Y	Y	Y	Y	Y
RHODE ISLAND						
1 Kennedy	Y	Y	Y	Y	N	Y
2 Langevin	Y	Y	Y	Y	N	Y
SOUTH CAROLINA						
1 **Brown**	Y	Y	Y	Y	Y	Y
2 **Wilson**	Y	Y	Y	Y	Y	Y
3 **Barrett**	Y	Y	Y	Y	Y	Y
4 **Inglis**	Y	Y	Y	Y	Y	Y
5 Spratt	Y	Y	Y	Y	N	Y
6 Clyburn	Y	Y	Y	Y	N	Y
SOUTH DAKOTA						
AL Herseth Sandlin	Y	Y	Y	Y	Y	Y
TENNESSEE						
1 **Roe**	Y	Y	Y	Y	Y	Y
2 **Duncan**	Y	Y	Y	Y	Y	Y
3 **Wamp**	Y	Y	Y	Y	Y	Y
4 Davis	?	?	?	?	?	?
5 Cooper	Y	Y	Y	Y	N	Y
6 Gordon	Y	Y	Y	Y	N	Y
7 **Blackburn**	Y	?	Y	Y	Y	Y
8 Tanner	Y	Y	Y	Y	N	Y
9 Cohen	Y	Y	Y	Y	N	Y

	157	158	159	160	161	162
TEXAS						
1 **Gohmert**	Y	Y	Y	Y	Y	Y
2 **Poe**	?	?	?	?	?	?
3 **Johnson, S.**	Y	Y	Y	Y	Y	Y
4 **Hall**	Y	Y	Y	Y	Y	Y
5 **Hensarling**	Y	Y	Y	Y	Y	Y
6 **Barton**	Y	Y	Y	Y	Y	Y
7 **Culberson**	Y	Y	Y	Y	Y	Y
8 **Brady**	Y	Y	Y	Y	Y	Y
9 Green, A.	Y	Y	Y	Y	N	Y
10 **McCaul**	Y	Y	Y	Y	Y	Y
11 **Conaway**	Y	Y	Y	Y	Y	Y
12 **Granger**	Y	Y	Y	Y	Y	Y
13 **Thornberry**	Y	Y	Y	Y	Y	Y
14 **Paul**	Y	Y	Y	Y	Y	N
15 Hinojosa	?	?	?	?	?	?
16 Reyes	Y	Y	Y	Y	N	Y
17 Edwards	Y	Y	Y	Y	N	Y
18 Jackson Lee	Y	Y	Y	Y	N	Y
19 **Neugebauer**	Y	Y	Y	Y	Y	Y
20 Gonzalez	Y	Y	Y	Y	N	Y
21 **Smith**	Y	Y	Y	Y	Y	Y
22 **Olson**	Y	Y	Y	Y	Y	Y
23 Rodriguez	Y	Y	Y	Y	N	Y
24 **Marchant**	Y	Y	Y	Y	Y	Y
25 Doggett	Y	Y	Y	Y	N	Y
26 **Burgess**	Y	Y	Y	Y	Y	Y
27 Ortiz	Y	Y	Y	Y	N	Y
28 Cuellar	Y	Y	Y	Y	N	Y
29 Green, G.	Y	Y	Y	Y	N	Y
30 Johnson, E.	Y	Y	Y	Y	N	Y
31 **Carter**	Y	Y	Y	Y	Y	Y
32 **Sessions**	Y	Y	Y	Y	Y	Y
UTAH						
1 **Bishop**	Y	Y	Y	Y	Y	Y
2 Matheson	Y	Y	Y	Y	N	Y
3 **Chaffetz**	Y	Y	Y	Y	Y	Y
VERMONT						
AL Welch	Y	Y	Y	?	?	Y
VIRGINIA						
1 **Wittman**	Y	Y	Y	Y	Y	Y
2 Nye	Y	Y	Y	Y	N	Y
3 Scott	Y	Y	Y	Y	N	Y
4 **Forbes**	Y	Y	Y	Y	Y	Y
5 Perriello	Y	Y	Y	Y	N	Y
6 **Goodlatte**	Y	Y	Y	Y	Y	Y
7 **Cantor**	Y	Y	Y	Y	Y	Y
8 Moran	Y	Y	Y	Y	N	Y
9 Boucher	Y	Y	Y	Y	N	Y
10 **Wolf**	Y	Y	Y	Y	Y	Y
11 Connolly	Y	Y	Y	Y	N	Y
WASHINGTON						
1 Inslee	Y	Y	Y	Y	N	Y
2 Larsen	Y	Y	Y	Y	N	Y
3 Baird	Y	Y	Y	Y	N	Y
4 **Hastings**	Y	Y	Y	Y	Y	Y
5 **McMorris Rodgers**	Y	Y	Y	Y	Y	Y
6 Dicks	Y	Y	Y	Y	N	Y
7 McDermott	Y	Y	Y	Y	N	Y
8 **Reichert**	Y	Y	Y	Y	N	Y
9 Smith	Y	Y	Y	Y	N	?
WEST VIRGINIA						
1 Mollohan	Y	Y	Y	Y	N	Y
2 **Capito**	Y	Y	Y	Y	N	Y
3 Rahall	Y	Y	Y	Y	N	Y
WISCONSIN						
1 **Ryan**	Y	Y	Y	Y	N	Y
2 Baldwin	Y	Y	Y	Y	N	Y
3 Kind	Y	Y	Y	Y	N	Y
4 Moore	Y	Y	Y	Y	N	Y
5 **Sensenbrenner**	Y	Y	Y	Y	N	N
6 **Petri**	Y	Y	Y	Y	N	Y
7 Obey	Y	Y	Y	Y	N	Y
8 Kagen	Y	Y	Y	Y	N	Y
WYOMING						
AL **Lummis**	Y	Y	Y	Y	Y	Y
DELEGATES						
Faleomavaega (A.S.)	?	?	?	?	?	
Norton (D.C.)	Y	Y	Y	Y	N	
Bordallo (Guam)	Y	Y	Y	Y	N	
Sablan (N. Marianas)	Y	Y	Y	Y	N	
Pierluisi (P.R.)	Y	Y	Y	Y	N	
Christensen (V.I.)	Y	Y	Y	Y	N	

IN THE HOUSE | By Vote Number

163. **H Res 295. Earmark Investigation/Motion to Table.** Miller, D-Calif., motion to table (kill) the Flake, R-Ariz., privileged resolution that would instruct the Committee on Standards of Official Conduct to investigate and report on the relationship between earmark requests made by members of Congress and the details of past campaign contributions. Motion agreed to 210-173: R 4-148; D 206-25. March 30, 2009.

164. **HR 20. Postpartum Depression Assistance/Passage.** Pallone, D-N.J., motion to suspend the rules and pass the bill that would authorize funding in fiscal years 2010 through 2012 for the Health and Human Services Department to conduct research on postpartum depression. It would allow the department to develop improved diagnostic techniques, establish education programs, and give grants for services to individuals and their families. Motion agreed to 391-8: R 153-8; D 238-0. A two-thirds majority of those present and voting (266 in this case) is required for passage under suspension of the rules. March 30, 2009.

165. **HR 479. Emergency Medicaid Services for Children/Passage.** Pallone, D-N.J., motion to suspend the rules and pass the bill that would authorize about $138 million for the Emergency Medicaid Services for Children program for fiscal years 2010 through 2014. Motion agreed to 390-6: R 155-6; D 235-0. A two-thirds majority of those present and voting (264 in this case) is required for passage under suspension of the rules. March 30, 2009.

166. **HR 1388. National Service Programs/Rule.** Adoption of the rule (H Res 296) that would provide for House floor consideration of the Senate amendments to the bill that would reauthorize Corporation for National and Community Service programs through fiscal 2014 and increase the education award for full-time service volunteers. Adopted 240-173: R 0-173; D 240-0. March 31, 2009.

167. **HR 1259. Dextromethorphan Restrictions/Passage.** Pallone, D-N.J., motion to suspend the rules and pass the bill that would make it illegal to distribute or possess an unfinished form of the drug dextromethorphan. The restrictions would not apply to employees of the Health and Human Services Department registered to handle such drugs, to individuals approved for pharmaceutical practices or to carriers distributing the drug to individuals licensed to handle it. Motion agreed to 407-8: R 164-8; D 243-0. A two-thirds majority of those present and voting (277 in this case) is required for passage under suspension of the rules. March 31, 2009.

168. **H Res 282. Egypt-Israel Peace Treaty/Adoption.** Connolly, D-Va., motion to suspend the rules and adopt the resolution that would recognize the 30th anniversary of the peace treaty between Egypt and Israel, urge the countries to strengthen their relationship and encourage continued U.S. efforts to foster initiatives to resolve conflicts in the Middle East. Motion agreed to 418-1: R 174-1; D 244-0. A two-thirds majority of those present and voting (280 in this case) is required for adoption under suspension of the rules. March 31, 2009.

	163	164	165	166	167	168
ALABAMA						
1 Bonner	P	Y	Y	N	Y	Y
2 Bright	N	Y	Y	Y	Y	Y
3 Rogers	N	Y	Y	N	Y	Y
4 Aderholt	N	Y	Y	N	Y	Y
5 Griffith	Y	Y	Y	Y	Y	Y
6 Bachus	N	Y	Y	N	Y	Y
7 Davis	Y	Y	Y	Y	Y	Y
ALASKA						
AL Young	Y	Y	Y	N	Y	Y
ARIZONA						
1 Kirkpatrick	N	Y	Y	Y	Y	Y
2 Franks	N	Y	Y	N	?	Y
3 Shadegg	N	N	Y	N	Y	Y
4 Pastor	Y	Y	Y	Y	Y	Y
5 Mitchell	N	Y	Y	Y	Y	Y
6 Flake	N	N	N	N	N	Y
7 Grijalva	Y	Y	?	Y	Y	Y
8 Giffords	N	Y	Y	Y	Y	Y
ARKANSAS						
1 Berry	Y	Y	Y	Y	Y	Y
2 Snyder	Y	Y	Y	Y	Y	Y
3 Boozman	N	Y	Y	N	Y	Y
4 Ross	Y	Y	Y	Y	Y	Y
CALIFORNIA						
1 Thompson	Y	Y	Y	Y	Y	Y
2 Herger	N	Y	Y	N	Y	Y
3 Lungren	N	Y	Y	N	Y	Y
4 McClintock	N	N	N	N	N	Y
5 Matsui	Y	Y	Y	Y	Y	Y
6 Woolsey	Y	Y	Y	Y	Y	Y
7 Miller, George	Y	Y	Y	Y	Y	Y
8 Pelosi						
9 Lee	Y	Y	Y	Y	Y	Y
10 Tauscher	Y	Y	Y	Y	Y	Y
11 McNerney	N	Y	Y	Y	Y	Y
12 Speier	?	?	?	Y	Y	Y
13 Stark	Y	Y	Y	Y	Y	Y
14 Eshoo	Y	Y	Y	Y	Y	Y
15 Honda	Y	Y	Y	Y	Y	Y
16 Lofgren	P	Y	Y	Y	Y	Y
17 Farr	Y	Y	Y	Y	Y	Y
18 Cardoza	Y	Y	Y	Y	Y	Y
19 Radanovich	N	Y	Y	N	Y	Y
20 Costa	Y	Y	Y	Y	Y	Y
21 Nunes	N	Y	Y	N	Y	Y
22 McCarthy	N	Y	Y	N	Y	Y
23 Capps	Y	Y	Y	Y	Y	Y
24 Gallegly	N	Y	Y	N	Y	Y
25 McKeon	N	Y	Y	N	Y	Y
26 Dreier	N	Y	Y	N	Y	Y
27 Sherman	Y	Y	Y	Y	Y	Y
28 Berman	Y	Y	Y	Y	Y	Y
29 Schiff	Y	Y	Y	Y	Y	Y
30 Waxman	Y	Y	Y	Y	Y	Y
31 Becerra	Y	Y	Y	Y	Y	Y
32 Vacant						
33 Watson	Y	Y	Y	?	Y	?
34 Roybal-Allard	Y	Y	Y	Y	Y	Y
35 Waters	Y	Y	Y	Y	Y	Y
36 Harman	Y	Y	Y	Y	Y	Y
37 Richardson	Y	Y	Y	Y	Y	Y
38 Napolitano	Y	Y	Y	Y	Y	Y
39 Sánchez, Linda	Y	Y	Y	Y	Y	Y
40 Royce	N	Y	Y	N	N	Y
41 Lewis	N	Y	Y	N	Y	Y
42 Miller, Gary	?	?	?	?	?	?
43 Baca	Y	Y	Y	Y	Y	Y
44 Calvert	N	Y	Y	N	Y	Y
45 Bono Mack	Y	Y	Y	N	Y	Y
46 Rohrabacher	Y	Y	Y	N	N	Y
47 Sanchez, Loretta	Y	Y	Y	Y	Y	Y
48 Campbell	?	?	?	N	N	Y
49 Issa	N	Y	Y	N	Y	Y
50 Bilbray	N	Y	Y	N	Y	Y
51 Filner	Y	Y	Y	Y	Y	Y
52 Hunter	N	Y	Y	N	Y	Y
53 Davis	Y	Y	Y	Y	Y	Y

	163	164	165	166	167	168
COLORADO						
1 DeGette	?	?	?	Y	Y	Y
2 Polis	Y	Y	Y	Y	Y	Y
3 Salazar	Y	Y	Y	Y	Y	Y
4 Markey	Y	Y	Y	Y	Y	Y
5 Lamborn	N	Y	Y	N	Y	Y
6 Coffman	N	Y	Y	N	Y	Y
7 Perlmutter	Y	Y	Y	Y	Y	Y
CONNECTICUT						
1 Larson	Y	Y	Y	Y	Y	Y
2 Courtney	Y	Y	Y	Y	Y	Y
3 DeLauro	Y	Y	Y	Y	Y	Y
4 Himes	N	Y	Y	Y	Y	Y
5 Murphy	Y	Y	Y	Y	Y	?
DELAWARE						
AL Castle	N	Y	Y	N	Y	Y
FLORIDA						
1 Miller	N	Y	Y	N	Y	Y
2 Boyd	Y	Y	Y	Y	Y	Y
3 Brown	?	?	?	?	?	?
4 Crenshaw	N	Y	Y	N	Y	Y
5 Brown-Waite	N	Y	Y	N	Y	Y
6 Stearns	N	Y	Y	N	Y	Y
7 Mica	N	Y	Y	N	Y	Y
8 Grayson	?	?	?	Y	Y	Y
9 Bilirakis	N	Y	Y	N	Y	Y
10 Young	N	Y	Y	N	Y	Y
11 Castor	P	Y	Y	Y	Y	Y
12 Putnam	N	Y	Y	N	Y	Y
13 Buchanan	N	Y	Y	N	Y	Y
14 Mack	N	Y	Y	N	Y	Y
15 Posey	N	Y	Y	N	Y	Y
16 Rooney	N	Y	Y	N	Y	Y
17 Meek	Y	Y	Y	Y	Y	Y
18 Ros-Lehtinen	Y	Y	Y	Y	Y	Y
19 Wexler	Y	Y	Y	Y	Y	Y
20 Wasserman Schultz	Y	Y	Y	Y	Y	Y
21 Diaz-Balart, L.	P	Y	Y	N	Y	Y
22 Klein	Y	Y	Y	Y	Y	Y
23 Hastings	Y	Y	Y	Y	Y	Y
24 Kosmas	N	Y	Y	Y	Y	Y
25 Diaz-Balart, M.	N	Y	Y	N	Y	Y
GEORGIA						
1 Kingston	?	?	?	N	Y	Y
2 Bishop	Y	Y	Y	Y	Y	Y
3 Westmoreland	?	?	?	?	?	?
4 Johnson	Y	Y	Y	Y	Y	Y
5 Lewis	Y	Y	Y	?	?	?
6 Price	N	Y	Y	N	Y	Y
7 Linder	?	?	?	N	Y	Y
8 Marshall	Y	Y	Y	Y	Y	Y
9 Deal	N	Y	Y	N	Y	Y
10 Broun	N	N	N	N	N	Y
11 Gingrey	N	Y	Y	N	Y	Y
12 Barrow	Y	Y	Y	Y	Y	Y
13 Scott	Y	Y	Y	Y	Y	Y
HAWAII						
1 Abercrombie	Y	Y	Y	Y	Y	Y
2 Hirono	Y	Y	Y	Y	Y	Y
IDAHO						
1 Minnick	N	Y	Y	?	Y	Y
2 Simpson	N	Y	Y	N	Y	Y
ILLINOIS						
1 Rush	Y	Y	Y	Y	Y	Y
2 Jackson	Y	Y	Y	Y	Y	Y
3 Lipinski	Y	Y	Y	Y	Y	Y
4 Gutierrez	Y	Y	Y	Y	Y	Y
5 Vacant						
6 Roskam	N	Y	Y	N	Y	Y
7 Davis	Y	Y	Y	Y	Y	Y
8 Bean	N	Y	Y	Y	Y	Y
9 Schakowsky	Y	Y	Y	Y	Y	Y
10 Kirk	N	Y	Y	N	Y	Y
11 Halvorson	N	Y	Y	Y	Y	Y
12 Costello	Y	Y	Y	Y	Y	Y
13 Biggert	N	Y	Y	N	Y	Y
14 Foster	N	Y	Y	Y	Y	Y
15 Johnson	+	+	+	N	Y	Y

KEY	**Republicans**	Democrats			
Y Voted for (yea)		X Paired against		C Voted "present" to avoid possible conflict of interest	
# Paired for		– Announced against			
+ Announced for		P Voted "present"		? Did not vote or otherwise make a position known	
N Voted against (nay)					

	163	164	165	166	167	168
16 **Manzullo**	N	Y	Y	N	Y	Y
17 Hare	Y	Y	Y	Y	Y	Y
18 **Schock**	N	Y	Y	N	Y	Y
19 **Shimkus**	N	Y	Y	N	Y	Y
INDIANA						
1 Visclosky	N	Y	Y	Y	Y	Y
2 Donnelly	N	Y	Y	Y	Y	Y
3 **Souder**	N	Y	Y	N	Y	Y
4 **Buyer**	N	Y	Y	N	Y	Y
5 **Burton**	N	Y	Y	N	Y	Y
6 **Pence**	N	Y	Y	N	Y	Y
7 Carson	Y	Y	Y	Y	Y	Y
8 Ellsworth	N	Y	Y	Y	Y	Y
9 Hill	N	Y	Y	Y	Y	Y
IOWA						
1 Braley	Y	Y	Y	Y	Y	Y
2 Loebsack	N	Y	Y	Y	Y	Y
3 Boswell	Y	Y	Y	Y	Y	Y
4 **Latham**	P	Y	Y	N	Y	Y
5 **King**	N	Y	Y	N	Y	Y
KANSAS						
1 **Moran**	?	?	?	N	Y	Y
2 **Jenkins**	N	Y	Y	N	Y	Y
3 Moore	Y	Y	Y	?	Y	Y
4 **Tiahrt**	N	Y	Y	N	Y	Y
KENTUCKY						
1 **Whitfield**	N	Y	Y	N	Y	Y
2 **Guthrie**	N	Y	Y	N	Y	Y
3 Yarmuth	Y	Y	Y	Y	Y	Y
4 **Davis**	N	Y	Y	N	Y	Y
5 **Rogers**	N	Y	Y	N	Y	Y
6 Chandler	P	Y	?	Y	Y	Y
LOUISIANA						
1 **Scalise**	N	Y	Y	N	Y	Y
2 **Cao**	N	Y	Y	N	Y	Y
3 Melancon	?	?	?	Y	Y	Y
4 **Fleming**	N	Y	Y	N	Y	Y
5 **Alexander**	N	Y	Y	N	Y	Y
6 **Cassidy**	N	Y	Y	N	Y	Y
7 **Boustany**	N	Y	Y	N	Y	Y
MAINE						
1 Pingree	Y	Y	Y	Y	Y	Y
2 Michaud	Y	Y	Y	Y	Y	Y
MARYLAND						
1 Kratovil	Y	Y	Y	Y	Y	Y
2 Ruppersberger	Y	Y	Y	Y	Y	Y
3 Sarbanes	Y	Y	Y	Y	Y	Y
4 Edwards	Y	Y	Y	Y	Y	Y
5 Hoyer	Y	Y	Y	Y	Y	Y
6 **Bartlett**	N	Y	Y	N	Y	Y
7 Cummings	Y	Y	Y	Y	Y	Y
8 Van Hollen	Y	Y	Y	Y	Y	Y
MASSACHUSETTS						
1 Olver	Y	Y	Y	?	Y	Y
2 Neal	?	?	?	Y	Y	Y
3 McGovern	Y	Y	Y	Y	Y	Y
4 Frank	?	Y	Y	Y	Y	Y
5 Tsongas	Y	Y	Y	Y	Y	Y
6 Tierney	Y	Y	Y	Y	Y	Y
7 Markey	Y	Y	Y	Y	Y	Y
8 Capuano	Y	Y	Y	Y	Y	Y
9 Lynch	Y	Y	Y	Y	Y	Y
10 Delahunt	Y	Y	Y	Y	Y	Y
MICHIGAN						
1 Stupak	Y	Y	Y	Y	Y	Y
2 **Hoekstra**	?	?	?	N	Y	Y
3 **Ehlers**	N	Y	Y	N	Y	Y
4 **Camp**	N	Y	Y	N	Y	Y
5 Kildee	Y	Y	Y	Y	Y	Y
6 **Upton**	N	Y	Y	N	Y	Y
7 Schauer	Y	Y	Y	Y	Y	Y
8 **Rogers**	N	Y	Y	N	Y	Y
9 Peters	Y	Y	Y	Y	Y	Y
10 **Miller**	N	Y	Y	N	Y	Y
11 **McCotter**	N	Y	Y	N	Y	Y
12 Levin	Y	Y	Y	Y	Y	Y
13 Kilpatrick	Y	Y	Y	Y	Y	Y
14 Conyers	Y	Y	Y	?	Y	Y
15 Dingell	Y	Y	Y	Y	Y	Y
MINNESOTA						
1 Walz	N	Y	Y	Y	Y	Y
2 **Kline**	P	Y	Y	N	Y	Y
3 **Paulsen**	N	Y	Y	N	Y	Y
4 McCollum	?	Y	Y	Y	Y	Y

	163	164	165	166	167	168
5 Ellison	Y	Y	Y	Y	Y	Y
6 **Bachmann**	N	Y	Y	N	Y	Y
7 Peterson	Y	Y	Y	Y	Y	Y
8 Oberstar	Y	Y	Y	Y	Y	Y
MISSISSIPPI						
1 Childers	Y	Y	Y	Y	Y	Y
2 Thompson	Y	Y	Y	Y	Y	Y
3 **Harper**	N	Y	Y	N	Y	Y
4 Taylor	Y	Y	Y	Y	Y	Y
MISSOURI						
1 Clay	Y	Y	Y	Y	Y	Y
2 **Akin**	N	Y	Y	N	Y	Y
3 Carnahan	Y	Y	Y	Y	Y	Y
4 Skelton	Y	Y	Y	Y	Y	Y
5 Cleaver	Y	Y	Y	Y	Y	Y
6 **Graves**	N	Y	Y	N	Y	Y
7 **Blunt**	?	?	?	N	Y	Y
8 **Emerson**	N	Y	Y	N	Y	Y
9 **Luetkemeyer**	N	Y	Y	N	Y	Y
MONTANA						
AL **Rehberg**	N	Y	Y	N	Y	Y
NEBRASKA						
1 **Fortenberry**	N	Y	Y	N	Y	Y
2 **Terry**	N	Y	Y	N	Y	Y
3 **Smith**	N	Y	Y	N	Y	Y
NEVADA						
1 Berkley	+	+	+	Y	Y	Y
2 **Heller**	?	?	?	N	Y	Y
3 Titus	Y	Y	Y	Y	Y	Y
NEW HAMPSHIRE						
1 Shea-Porter	Y	Y	Y	Y	Y	Y
2 Hodes	N	Y	Y	Y	Y	Y
NEW JERSEY						
1 Andrews	Y	Y	Y	Y	Y	Y
2 **LoBiondo**	N	Y	Y	N	Y	Y
3 Adler	Y	Y	Y	Y	Y	Y
4 **Smith**	N	Y	Y	N	Y	Y
5 **Garrett**	N	Y	Y	N	Y	Y
6 Pallone	Y	Y	Y	Y	Y	Y
7 **Lance**	N	Y	Y	N	Y	Y
8 Pascrell	+	+	+	+	+	+
9 Rothman	Y	Y	Y	Y	Y	Y
10 Payne	Y	Y	Y	Y	Y	Y
11 **Frelinghuysen**	N	Y	Y	N	Y	Y
12 Holt	Y	Y	Y	Y	Y	Y
13 Sires	Y	Y	Y	Y	Y	Y
NEW MEXICO						
1 Heinrich	Y	Y	Y	Y	Y	Y
2 Teague	N	Y	Y	Y	Y	Y
3 Lujan	Y	Y	Y	Y	Y	Y
NEW YORK						
1 Bishop	Y	Y	Y	Y	Y	Y
2 Israel	Y	Y	Y	Y	Y	Y
3 **King**	N	Y	Y	N	Y	Y
4 McCarthy	Y	Y	Y	Y	Y	Y
5 Ackerman	Y	Y	Y	Y	Y	Y
6 Meeks	Y	Y	Y	Y	Y	Y
7 Crowley	Y	Y	Y	Y	Y	Y
8 Nadler	Y	Y	Y	Y	Y	Y
9 Weiner	Y	Y	Y	Y	Y	Y
10 Towns	Y	Y	Y	Y	Y	Y
11 Clarke	Y	Y	Y	Y	Y	Y
12 Velázquez	Y	Y	Y	Y	Y	Y
13 McMahon	Y	Y	Y	Y	Y	Y
14 Maloney	?	?	?	Y	Y	Y
15 Rangel	Y	Y	Y	Y	?	Y
16 Serrano	Y	Y	Y	Y	Y	Y
17 Engel	Y	Y	Y	Y	Y	Y
18 Lowey	Y	Y	Y	Y	Y	Y
19 Hall	Y	Y	Y	Y	Y	Y
20 Vacant						
21 Tonko	Y	Y	Y	Y	Y	Y
22 Hinchey	?	?	?	Y	Y	Y
23 **McHugh**	N	Y	Y	N	Y	Y
24 Arcuri	Y	Y	Y	Y	Y	Y
25 Maffei	Y	Y	Y	Y	Y	Y
26 **Lee**	N	Y	Y	N	Y	Y
27 Higgins	Y	Y	Y	Y	Y	Y
28 Slaughter	Y	Y	Y	Y	Y	Y
29 Massa	Y	Y	Y	Y	Y	Y
NORTH CAROLINA						
1 Butterfield	?	?	?	Y	Y	Y
2 Etheridge	Y	Y	Y	Y	Y	Y
3 **Jones**	Y	Y	Y	N	Y	Y
4 Price	Y	Y	Y	Y	Y	Y

	163	164	165	166	167	168
5 **Foxx**	N	Y	Y	N	Y	Y
6 **Coble**	N	Y	Y	N	Y	Y
7 McIntyre	N	Y	Y	Y	Y	Y
8 Kissell	Y	Y	Y	Y	Y	Y
9 **Myrick**	P	Y	Y	N	Y	Y
10 **McHenry**	N	Y	Y	N	Y	Y
11 Shuler	Y	Y	Y	Y	Y	Y
12 Watt	Y	Y	Y	?	?	?
13 Miller	Y	Y	Y	Y	Y	Y
NORTH DAKOTA						
AL Pomeroy	?	?	?	?	?	?
OHIO						
1 Driehaus	Y	Y	Y	Y	Y	Y
2 **Schmidt**	N	Y	Y	N	Y	Y
3 **Turner**	N	Y	Y	N	Y	Y
4 **Jordan**	N	Y	Y	N	Y	Y
5 **Latta**	N	Y	Y	N	Y	Y
6 Wilson	Y	Y	Y	Y	Y	Y
7 **Austria**	N	Y	Y	N	Y	Y
8 **Boehner**	N	Y	Y	N	Y	Y
9 Kaptur	Y	Y	Y	Y	Y	Y
10 Kucinich	Y	Y	Y	Y	Y	Y
11 Fudge	Y	Y	Y	Y	Y	Y
12 **Tiberi**	N	Y	Y	N	Y	Y
13 Sutton	Y	Y	Y	Y	Y	Y
14 **LaTourette**	N	Y	Y	N	Y	Y
15 Kilroy	Y	Y	Y	?	Y	Y
16 Boccieri	N	Y	Y	Y	Y	Y
17 Ryan	?	Y	Y	Y	Y	Y
18 Space	Y	Y	Y	Y	Y	Y
OKLAHOMA						
1 **Sullivan**	N	Y	Y	N	Y	Y
2 Boren	Y	Y	Y	Y	Y	Y
3 **Lucas**	N	Y	Y	N	Y	Y
4 **Cole**	N	Y	Y	N	Y	Y
5 **Fallin**	N	Y	Y	N	Y	Y
OREGON						
1 Wu	Y	Y	Y	Y	Y	Y
2 **Walden**	P	Y	Y	N	Y	Y
3 Blumenauer	Y	Y	Y	Y	Y	Y
4 DeFazio	Y	Y	Y	Y	Y	Y
5 Schrader	Y	Y	Y	Y	Y	Y
PENNSYLVANIA						
1 Brady	Y	Y	Y	Y	Y	Y
2 Fattah	Y	Y	Y	?	Y	Y
3 Dahlkemper	Y	Y	Y	Y	Y	Y
4 Altmire	Y	Y	Y	Y	Y	Y
5 **Thompson**	N	Y	Y	N	Y	Y
6 **Gerlach**	N	Y	Y	N	Y	Y
7 Sestak	Y	Y	Y	Y	Y	Y
8 Murphy, P.	Y	Y	Y	Y	Y	Y
9 **Shuster**	N	Y	Y	N	Y	Y
10 Carney	Y	Y	Y	Y	Y	Y
11 Kanjorski	Y	Y	Y	Y	Y	Y
12 Murtha	Y	Y	Y	Y	Y	Y
13 Schwartz	Y	Y	Y	Y	Y	Y
14 Doyle	Y	Y	Y	Y	Y	Y
15 **Dent**	P	Y	Y	N	Y	Y
16 **Pitts**	N	Y	Y	N	Y	Y
17 Holden	Y	Y	Y	Y	Y	Y
18 **Murphy, T.**	Y	Y	Y	N	Y	Y
19 **Platts**	N	Y	Y	N	Y	Y
RHODE ISLAND						
1 Kennedy	Y	Y	Y	Y	Y	Y
2 Langevin	Y	Y	Y	Y	Y	Y
SOUTH CAROLINA						
1 **Brown**	N	Y	Y	N	Y	Y
2 **Wilson**	N	Y	Y	N	Y	Y
3 **Barrett**	+	+	+	N	Y	Y
4 **Inglis**	N	Y	Y	N	Y	Y
5 Spratt	Y	Y	Y	Y	Y	Y
6 Clyburn	Y	Y	Y	Y	Y	Y
SOUTH DAKOTA						
AL Herseth Sandlin	N	Y	Y	Y	Y	Y
TENNESSEE						
1 **Roe**	N	Y	Y	N	Y	Y
2 **Duncan**	N	Y	Y	N	Y	Y
3 **Wamp**	N	Y	Y	N	Y	Y
4 Davis	Y	Y	Y	Y	Y	?
5 Cooper	Y	Y	Y	Y	Y	Y
6 Gordon	Y	Y	?	Y	Y	Y
7 **Blackburn**	N	Y	Y	N	Y	Y
8 Tanner	Y	Y	Y	Y	Y	Y
9 Cohen	Y	Y	Y	Y	Y	Y

	163	164	165	166	167	168
TEXAS						
1 **Gohmert**	?	?	?	N	Y	Y
2 **Poe**	P	N	Y	N	N	Y
3 **Johnson, S.**	N	Y	Y	N	Y	Y
4 **Hall**	N	Y	Y	N	Y	Y
5 **Hensarling**	?	?	?	?	?	?
6 **Barton**	N	Y	Y	N	Y	Y
7 **Culberson**	N	N	Y	N	Y	Y
8 **Brady**	N	Y	Y	N	?	Y
9 Green, A.	Y	Y	Y	Y	Y	Y
10 **McCaul**	N	Y	Y	N	Y	Y
11 **Conaway**	P	Y	Y	N	Y	Y
12 **Granger**	N	Y	Y	N	Y	Y
13 **Thornberry**	N	Y	Y	N	Y	Y
14 **Paul**	N	N	N	N	N	N
15 Hinojosa	Y	Y	Y	Y	Y	Y
16 Reyes	?	?	?	Y	Y	Y
17 Edwards	Y	Y	Y	Y	Y	Y
18 Jackson Lee	Y	Y	Y	Y	Y	Y
19 **Neugebauer**	N	Y	Y	N	Y	Y
20 Gonzalez	Y	Y	Y	Y	Y	Y
21 **Smith**	N	Y	Y	?	Y	Y
22 **Olson**	N	Y	Y	N	+	Y
23 Rodriguez	Y	Y	Y	Y	Y	Y
24 **Marchant**	?	?	?	N	Y	Y
25 Doggett	Y	Y	Y	Y	Y	Y
26 **Burgess**	N	Y	Y	N	Y	Y
27 Ortiz	Y	Y	Y	Y	Y	Y
28 Cuellar	Y	Y	Y	Y	Y	Y
29 Green, G.	Y	Y	Y	Y	+	Y
30 Johnson, E.	Y	Y	Y	Y	Y	Y
31 **Carter**	?	?	?	N	Y	Y
32 **Sessions**	?	?	?	N	Y	Y
UTAH						
1 **Bishop**	N	Y	Y	N	Y	Y
2 Matheson	Y	Y	Y	Y	Y	Y
3 **Chaffetz**	N	Y	Y	N	Y	Y
VERMONT						
AL Welch	P	Y	Y	Y	?	?
VIRGINIA						
1 **Wittman**	N	Y	Y	N	Y	Y
2 Nye	Y	Y	Y	Y	Y	Y
3 Scott	Y	Y	Y	Y	Y	Y
4 **Forbes**	N	Y	Y	N	Y	Y
5 Perriello	N	Y	Y	Y	Y	Y
6 **Goodlatte**	N	Y	Y	–	Y	Y
7 **Cantor**	N	Y	Y	N	Y	Y
8 Moran	?	?	?	Y	Y	Y
9 Boucher	Y	Y	Y	?	Y	Y
10 **Wolf**	N	Y	Y	N	Y	Y
11 Connolly	Y	Y	Y	Y	Y	Y
WASHINGTON						
1 Inslee	Y	Y	Y	Y	Y	Y
2 Larsen	?	?	?	Y	Y	Y
3 Baird	Y	Y	Y	Y	Y	Y
4 **Hastings**	?	?	?	N	Y	Y
5 **McMorris Rodgers**	N	Y	Y	N	Y	Y
6 Dicks	Y	Y	Y	Y	Y	Y
7 McDermott	Y	Y	Y	Y	Y	Y
8 **Reichert**	N	Y	Y	N	Y	Y
9 Smith	N	Y	Y	Y	Y	Y
WEST VIRGINIA						
1 Mollohan	Y	Y	Y	Y	Y	Y
2 **Capito**	N	Y	Y	N	Y	Y
3 Rahall	Y	Y	Y	Y	Y	Y
WISCONSIN						
1 **Ryan**	N	Y	Y	N	Y	Y
2 Baldwin	Y	Y	Y	Y	Y	Y
3 Kind	N	Y	Y	Y	Y	Y
4 Moore	Y	Y	Y	Y	Y	Y
5 **Sensenbrenner**	N	N	N	N	Y	Y
6 **Petri**	N	Y	Y	N	Y	Y
7 Obey	Y	Y	Y	Y	Y	Y
8 Kagen	Y	Y	Y	Y	Y	Y
WYOMING						
AL **Lummis**	N	Y	N	N	Y	Y
DELEGATES						
Faleomavaega (A.S.)						
Norton (D.C.)						
Bordallo (Guam)						
Sablan (N. Marianas)						
Pierluisi (P.R.)						
Christensen (V.I.)						

IN THE HOUSE | By Vote Number

169. **HR 1388. National Service Programs/Motion to Concur.** Miller, D-Calif., motion to concur in the Senate amendments to the bill that would reauthorize Corporation for National and Community Service programs through fiscal 2014, increase the education award for full-time service volunteers from $4,725 to $5,350 and make the award equal to the maximum annual Pell grant thereafter. States would be required to match corporation service funds for state commissions on national service. It also would bar participants in national service programs from engaging in certain activities, such as lobbying or providing abortion services or referrals, as part of their program duties. Motion agreed to (thus clearing the bill for the president), 275-149: R 26-149; D 249-0. A "yea" was a vote in support of the president's position. March 31, 2009.

170. **HR 577. Children's Vision Care Grants/Passage.** Pallone, D-N.J., motion to suspend the rules and pass the bill that would authorize $65 million in fiscal 2010-14 for the Centers for Disease Control and Prevention to award matching-fund grants to states for children's vision care. Motion agreed to 404-17: R 155-17; D 249-0. A two-thirds majority of those present and voting (281 in this case) is required for passage under suspension of the rules. March 31, 2009.

171. **HR 1253. Health Coverage Limitation Conditions/Passage.** Pallone, D-N.J., motion to suspend the rules and pass the bill that would require group health plan providers to meet certain conditions in order to limit coverage to beneficiaries. Providers would have to make their limitations and restrictions explicit and clear, disclose them to plan sponsors in writing in advance of the point of sale, and give the information to beneficiaries upon enrollment. Motion agreed to 422-3: R 173-2; D 249-1. A two-thirds majority of those present and voting (284 in this case) is required for passage under suspension of the rules. March 31, 2009.

172. **H Res 279. Committee Funding/Adoption.** Adoption of the resolution that would provide $304.5 million in the 111th Congress for 19 standing committees of the House, the Permanent Select Committee on Intelligence, and the Select Committee on Energy Independence and Global Warming. The resolution would specify that about $150 million would be for the first session and about $155 million for the second session, and it would prohibit committees from spending 2009 money in 2010 unless the chairmen and ranking members justify the expenses to the House Administration Committee. Adopted 288-136: R 43-130; D 245-6. March 31, 2009.

173. **HR 151. Congressional Clerkship Program/Passage.** Brady, D-Pa., motion to suspend the rules and pass the bill that would authorize unspecified funds to establish the Daniel Webster Congressional Clerkship program to allow graduates of accredited law schools to serve as clerks in the Senate or House for one-year terms. Clerks would be appointed to majority and minority offices equally. Motion agreed to 381-42: R 130-42; D 251-0. A two-thirds majority of those present and voting (282 in this case) is required for passage under suspension of the rules. March 31, 2009.

	169	170	171	172	173
ALABAMA					
1 Bonner	N	Y	Y	Y	Y
2 Bright	Y	Y	Y	N	Y
3 Rogers	N	Y	Y	Y	Y
4 Aderholt	N	Y	Y	Y	Y
5 Griffith	Y	Y	Y	Y	Y
6 Bachus	N	Y	Y	Y	Y
7 Davis	Y	Y	Y	Y	Y
ALASKA					
AL Young	N	Y	Y	Y	N
ARIZONA					
1 Kirkpatrick	Y	Y	Y	Y	Y
2 Franks	N	Y	Y	N	N
3 Shadegg	N	N	Y	N	N
4 Pastor	Y	Y	Y	Y	Y
5 Mitchell	Y	Y	Y	N	Y
6 Flake	N	N	Y	N	N
7 Grijalva	Y	Y	Y	Y	Y
8 Giffords	Y	Y	Y	Y	Y
ARKANSAS					
1 Berry	Y	Y	Y	Y	Y
2 Snyder	Y	Y	Y	Y	Y
3 Boozman	N	Y	Y	N	Y
4 Ross	Y	+	Y	Y	Y
CALIFORNIA					
1 Thompson	Y	Y	Y	Y	Y
2 Herger	N	Y	Y	N	Y
3 Lungren	N	Y	Y	Y	Y
4 McClintock	N	N	Y	N	N
5 Matsui	Y	Y	Y	Y	Y
6 Woolsey	Y	Y	Y	Y	Y
7 Miller, George	Y	Y	Y	Y	Y
8 Pelosi	Y				
9 Lee	Y	Y	Y	Y	Y
10 Tauscher	Y	Y	Y	Y	Y
11 McNerney	Y	Y	Y	Y	Y
12 Speier	Y	Y	Y	Y	Y
13 Stark	Y	Y	Y	Y	Y
14 Eshoo	Y	Y	Y	Y	Y
15 Honda	Y	Y	Y	Y	Y
16 Lofgren	Y	Y	Y	Y	Y
17 Farr	Y	Y	Y	Y	Y
18 Cardoza	Y	Y	Y	Y	Y
19 Radanovich	N	Y	Y	N	Y
20 Costa	Y	Y	Y	Y	Y
21 Nunes	N	Y	Y	N	N
22 McCarthy	N	Y	Y	Y	Y
23 Capps	Y	Y	Y	Y	Y
24 Gallegly	N	Y	Y	N	Y
25 McKeon	Y	Y	Y	Y	Y
26 Dreier	N	Y	Y	Y	Y
27 Sherman	Y	Y	Y	Y	Y
28 Berman	Y	Y	Y	Y	Y
29 Schiff	Y	Y	Y	Y	Y
30 Waxman	Y	Y	Y	Y	Y
31 Becerra	Y	Y	Y	Y	Y
32 Vacant					
33 Watson	Y	Y	Y	Y	Y
34 Roybal-Allard	Y	Y	Y	Y	Y
35 Waters	Y	Y	Y	Y	Y
36 Harman	Y	Y	Y	Y	Y
37 Richardson	Y	Y	Y	Y	Y
38 Napolitano	Y	Y	Y	Y	Y
39 Sánchez, Linda	Y	Y	Y	Y	Y
40 Royce	N	N	Y	N	N
41 Lewis	Y	Y	Y	Y	Y
42 Miller, Gary	?	?	?	?	?
43 Baca	Y	Y	Y	Y	Y
44 Calvert	N	Y	Y	N	Y
45 Bono Mack	Y	Y	Y	Y	Y
46 Rohrabacher	N	Y	Y	N	N
47 Sanchez, Loretta	Y	Y	Y	Y	?
48 Campbell	N	N	Y	N	Y
49 Issa	N	Y	Y	N	N
50 Bilbray	N	Y	Y	N	Y
51 Filner	Y	Y	Y	Y	Y
52 Hunter	N	Y	Y	N	N
53 Davis	Y	Y	Y	Y	Y

	169	170	171	172	173
COLORADO					
1 DeGette	Y	Y	Y	Y	Y
2 Polis	Y	Y	Y	Y	Y
3 Salazar	Y	Y	Y	Y	Y
4 Markey	Y	Y	Y	Y	Y
5 Lamborn	N	Y	Y	N	N
6 Coffman	N	Y	Y	N	Y
7 Perlmutter	Y	Y	Y	Y	Y
CONNECTICUT					
1 Larson	Y	Y	Y	Y	Y
2 Courtney	Y	Y	Y	Y	Y
3 DeLauro	Y	Y	Y	Y	Y
4 Himes	Y	Y	Y	Y	Y
5 Murphy	Y	Y	Y	Y	Y
DELAWARE					
AL Castle	Y	Y	Y	N	Y
FLORIDA					
1 Miller	N	Y	Y	N	Y
2 Boyd	Y	Y	Y	Y	Y
3 Brown	Y	Y	Y	Y	Y
4 Crenshaw	N	Y	Y	Y	Y
5 Brown-Waite	N	Y	Y	N	Y
6 Stearns	N	N	Y	N	N
7 Mica	N	Y	Y	N	Y
8 Grayson	Y	Y	Y	Y	Y
9 Bilirakis	N	Y	Y	N	Y
10 Young	N	Y	Y	Y	N
11 Castor	Y	Y	Y	Y	Y
12 Putnam	N	Y	Y	N	Y
13 Buchanan	Y	Y	Y	Y	Y
14 Mack	N	Y	Y	N	N
15 Posey	N	Y	Y	N	Y
16 Rooney	N	Y	Y	N	N
17 Meek	Y	Y	Y	Y	Y
18 Ros-Lehtinen	N	Y	Y	Y	Y
19 Wexler	Y	Y	Y	Y	Y
20 Wasserman Schultz	Y	Y	Y	Y	Y
21 Diaz-Balart, L.	N	Y	Y	Y	Y
22 Klein	Y	Y	Y	Y	Y
23 Hastings	Y	Y	Y	Y	Y
24 Kosmas	Y	Y	Y	Y	Y
25 Diaz-Balart, M.	N	Y	Y	N	Y
GEORGIA					
1 Kingston	N	N	Y	N	N
2 Bishop	Y	Y	Y	Y	Y
3 Westmoreland	?	?	?	?	?
4 Johnson	Y	Y	Y	Y	Y
5 Lewis	+	Y	Y	Y	Y
6 Price	N	Y	Y	N	N
7 Linder	N	Y	Y	N	N
8 Marshall	Y	Y	Y	Y	Y
9 Deal	N	Y	Y	N	N
10 Broun	N	N	N	N	N
11 Gingrey	N	Y	Y	N	N
12 Barrow	Y	Y	Y	Y	Y
13 Scott	Y	Y	Y	Y	Y
HAWAII					
1 Abercrombie	Y	Y	Y	Y	Y
2 Hirono	Y	Y	Y	Y	Y
IDAHO					
1 Minnick	Y	Y	Y	N	Y
2 Simpson	N	Y	Y	Y	?
ILLINOIS					
1 Rush	Y	Y	?	Y	Y
2 Jackson	Y	Y	Y	Y	Y
3 Lipinski	Y	Y	Y	Y	Y
4 Gutierrez	Y	Y	Y	Y	Y
5 Vacant					
6 Roskam	N	Y	Y	Y	Y
7 Davis	Y	Y	Y	Y	Y
8 Bean	Y	Y	Y	Y	Y
9 Schakowsky	Y	Y	Y	Y	Y
10 Kirk	Y	Y	Y	N	Y
11 Halvorson	Y	Y	Y	Y	Y
12 Costello	Y	Y	Y	Y	Y
13 Biggert	Y	Y	Y	N	Y
14 Foster	Y	Y	Y	Y	Y
15 Johnson	N	Y	Y	N	Y

	169	170	171	172	173
16 Manzullo	N	Y	Y	N	N
17 Hare	+	+	Y	Y	Y
18 Schock	N	Y	Y	N	Y
19 Shimkus	N	Y	Y	N	Y
INDIANA					
1 Visclosky	Y	Y	Y	Y	Y
2 Donnelly	Y	Y	Y	Y	Y
3 Souder	Y	Y	Y	N	Y
4 Buyer	N	Y	Y	Y	Y
5 Burton	N	Y	Y	N	Y
6 Pence	N	Y	Y	N	Y
7 Carson	Y	Y	Y	Y	Y
8 Ellsworth	Y	Y	Y	Y	Y
9 Hill	Y	Y	Y	Y	Y
IOWA					
1 Braley	Y	Y	Y	Y	Y
2 Loebsack	Y	Y	Y	Y	Y
3 Boswell	Y	Y	Y	Y	Y
4 Latham	N	Y	Y	N	Y
5 King	N	N	Y	N	Y
KANSAS					
1 Moran	N	Y	Y	N	Y
2 Jenkins	N	Y	Y	N	Y
3 Moore	Y	Y	Y	Y	Y
4 Tiahrt	N	+	Y	N	Y
KENTUCKY					
1 Whitfield	N	Y	Y	Y	Y
2 Guthrie	N	Y	Y	N	Y
3 Yarmuth	Y	Y	Y	Y	Y
4 Davis	N	Y	Y	N	Y
5 Rogers	N	Y	Y	N	Y
6 Chandler	Y	Y	Y	Y	Y
LOUISIANA					
1 Scalise	N	Y	Y	N	N
2 Cao	Y	Y	Y	N	Y
3 Melancon	Y	Y	Y	Y	Y
4 Fleming	N	Y	Y	Y	Y
5 Alexander	N	Y	Y	N	Y
6 Cassidy	Y	Y	Y	N	N
7 Boustany	N	Y	Y	Y	Y
MAINE					
1 Pingree	Y	Y	Y	Y	Y
2 Michaud	Y	Y	Y	Y	Y
MARYLAND					
1 Kratovil	Y	Y	Y	N	Y
2 Ruppersberger	Y	Y	Y	Y	Y
3 Sarbanes	Y	Y	Y	Y	Y
4 Edwards	Y	Y	Y	Y	Y
5 Hoyer	Y	Y	Y	Y	Y
6 Bartlett	N	Y	Y	N	N
7 Cummings	Y	Y	Y	Y	Y
8 Van Hollen	Y	Y	Y	Y	Y
MASSACHUSETTS					
1 Olver	Y	Y	Y	Y	Y
2 Neal	Y	Y	Y	Y	Y
3 McGovern	+	Y	Y	Y	Y
4 Frank	Y	Y	Y	Y	Y
5 Tsongas	Y	Y	Y	Y	Y
6 Tierney	Y	Y	Y	Y	Y
7 Markey	Y	Y	Y	Y	Y
8 Capuano	Y	Y	Y	Y	Y
9 Lynch	Y	Y	Y	Y	Y
10 Delahunt	Y	Y	Y	Y	Y
MICHIGAN					
1 Stupak	Y	Y	Y	Y	Y
2 Hoekstra	N	Y	Y	N	N
3 Ehlers	Y	Y	Y	Y	Y
4 Camp	Y	Y	Y	Y	Y
5 Kildee	Y	Y	Y	Y	Y
6 Upton	Y	Y	Y	N	Y
7 Schauer	Y	Y	Y	Y	Y
8 Rogers	N	Y	Y	N	Y
9 Peters	Y	Y	Y	Y	Y
10 Miller	Y	Y	Y	N	Y
11 McCotter	N	Y	Y	N	Y
12 Levin	Y	Y	Y	Y	Y
13 Kilpatrick	Y	Y	Y	Y	Y
14 Conyers	Y	Y	Y	Y	Y
15 Dingell	Y	Y	Y	Y	Y
MINNESOTA					
1 Walz	Y	Y	Y	Y	Y
2 Kline	N	Y	Y	N	Y
3 Paulsen	N	Y	Y	N	Y
4 McCollum	Y	Y	Y	Y	Y

	169	170	171	172	173
5 Ellison	Y	Y	Y	Y	Y
6 Bachmann	N	Y	Y	N	Y
7 Peterson	Y	Y	Y	Y	Y
8 Oberstar	Y	Y	Y	Y	Y
MISSISSIPPI					
1 Childers	Y	Y	Y	Y	Y
2 Thompson	Y	Y	Y	Y	Y
3 Harper	N	Y	Y	Y	Y
4 Taylor	Y	Y	Y	N	Y
MISSOURI					
1 Clay	Y	Y	Y	Y	Y
2 Akin	N	N	Y	N	N
3 Carnahan	Y	Y	Y	Y	Y
4 Skelton	Y	Y	Y	Y	Y
5 Cleaver	Y	Y	Y	Y	Y
6 Graves	N	Y	Y	N	Y
7 Blunt	N	Y	Y	N	Y
8 Emerson	N	Y	Y	N	Y
9 Luetkemeyer	N	Y	Y	N	Y
MONTANA					
AL Rehberg	N	Y	Y	N	Y
NEBRASKA					
1 Fortenberry	N	Y	Y	N	Y
2 Terry	Y	Y	Y	Y	Y
3 Smith	N	Y	Y	Y	Y
NEVADA					
1 Berkley	Y	Y	Y	Y	Y
2 Heller	N	Y	Y	Y	Y
3 Titus	Y	Y	Y	Y	Y
NEW HAMPSHIRE					
1 Shea-Porter	Y	Y	Y	Y	Y
2 Hodes	Y	Y	Y	Y	Y
NEW JERSEY					
1 Andrews	Y	Y	Y	Y	Y
2 LoBiondo	Y	Y	Y	N	Y
3 Adler	Y	Y	Y	Y	Y
4 Smith	Y	Y	Y	Y	Y
5 Garrett	N	Y	Y	N	N
6 Pallone	Y	Y	Y	Y	Y
7 Lance	Y	Y	Y	Y	Y
8 Pascrell	+	+	+	+	+
9 Rothman	Y	Y	Y	Y	Y
10 Payne	Y	Y	Y	Y	Y
11 Frelinghuysen	N	Y	Y	N	Y
12 Holt	Y	Y	Y	Y	Y
13 Sires	Y	Y	Y	Y	Y
NEW MEXICO					
1 Heinrich	Y	Y	Y	Y	Y
2 Teague	Y	Y	Y	Y	Y
3 Lujan	Y	Y	Y	Y	Y
NEW YORK					
1 Bishop	Y	Y	Y	Y	Y
2 Israel	?	Y	Y	Y	Y
3 King	Y	Y	Y	Y	Y
4 McCarthy	Y	Y	Y	Y	Y
5 Ackerman	Y	Y	Y	Y	Y
6 Meeks	Y	Y	Y	Y	Y
7 Crowley	Y	Y	Y	Y	Y
8 Nadler	Y	Y	Y	Y	Y
9 Weiner	Y	Y	Y	Y	Y
10 Towns	Y	Y	Y	Y	Y
11 Clarke	Y	Y	Y	Y	Y
12 Velázquez	Y	Y	Y	Y	Y
13 McMahon	Y	Y	Y	Y	Y
14 Maloney	Y	Y	Y	Y	Y
15 Rangel	Y	Y	Y	Y	Y
16 Serrano	Y	Y	Y	Y	Y
17 Engel	Y	Y	Y	Y	Y
18 Lowey	Y	Y	Y	Y	Y
19 Hall	Y	Y	Y	Y	Y
20 Vacant					
21 Tonko	Y	Y	Y	Y	Y
22 Hinchey	Y	Y	Y	Y	Y
23 McHugh	Y	Y	Y	Y	Y
24 Arcuri	Y	Y	Y	Y	Y
25 Maffei	Y	Y	Y	Y	Y
26 Lee	Y	Y	Y	N	Y
27 Higgins	Y	Y	Y	Y	Y
28 Slaughter	Y	Y	Y	Y	Y
29 Massa	Y	Y	Y	Y	Y
NORTH CAROLINA					
1 Butterfield	Y	Y	Y	Y	Y
2 Etheridge	Y	Y	Y	Y	Y
3 Jones	N	Y	Y	N	N
4 Price	Y	Y	Y	Y	Y

	169	170	171	172	173
5 Foxx	N	N	Y	N	N
6 Coble	N	Y	Y	N	N
7 McIntyre	Y	Y	Y	Y	Y
8 Kissell	Y	Y	Y	Y	Y
9 Myrick	N	Y	Y	N	Y
10 McHenry	N	Y	Y	N	Y
11 Shuler	Y	Y	Y	Y	Y
12 Watt	Y	Y	Y	Y	Y
13 Miller	Y	Y	Y	Y	Y
NORTH DAKOTA					
AL Pomeroy	Y	Y	Y	Y	Y
OHIO					
1 Driehaus	Y	Y	Y	Y	Y
2 Schmidt	N	Y	Y	N	N
3 Turner	Y	Y	Y	Y	Y
4 Jordan	N	Y	Y	N	N
5 Latta	N	Y	Y	N	Y
6 Wilson	Y	Y	Y	Y	Y
7 Austria	N	Y	Y	N	Y
8 Boehner	N	Y	Y	N	Y
9 Kaptur	Y	Y	Y	Y	Y
10 Kucinich	Y	Y	Y	Y	Y
11 Fudge	Y	Y	Y	Y	Y
12 Tiberi	N	Y	Y	N	N
13 Sutton	Y	Y	Y	Y	Y
14 LaTourette	N	Y	Y	Y	Y
15 Kilroy	Y	Y	Y	Y	Y
16 Boccieri	Y	Y	Y	Y	Y
17 Ryan	Y	Y	Y	Y	Y
18 Space	Y	Y	Y	Y	Y
OKLAHOMA					
1 Sullivan	N	Y	Y	N	Y
2 Boren	Y	Y	Y	Y	Y
3 Lucas	N	Y	Y	Y	Y
4 Cole	N	Y	Y	-	Y
5 Fallin	N	Y	Y	N	Y
OREGON					
1 Wu	Y	Y	Y	?	Y
2 Walden	N	Y	Y	N	Y
3 Blumenauer	Y	Y	Y	Y	Y
4 DeFazio	Y	Y	Y	Y	Y
5 Schrader	Y	Y	Y	Y	Y
PENNSYLVANIA					
1 Brady	Y	Y	Y	Y	Y
2 Fattah	Y	Y	Y	Y	Y
3 Dahlkemper	Y	Y	Y	Y	Y
4 Altmire	Y	Y	Y	Y	Y
5 Thompson	Y	Y	Y	Y	Y
6 Gerlach	N	Y	Y	N	Y
7 Sestak	Y	Y	Y	Y	Y
8 Murphy, P.	Y	Y	Y	Y	Y
9 Shuster	N	Y	Y	Y	N
10 Carney	Y	Y	Y	Y	Y
11 Kanjorski	Y	Y	Y	Y	Y
12 Murtha	Y	Y	Y	Y	Y
13 Schwartz	Y	Y	Y	Y	Y
14 Doyle	Y	Y	Y	Y	Y
15 Dent	N	Y	Y	N	Y
16 Pitts	N	?	Y	Y	Y
17 Holden	Y	Y	Y	Y	Y
18 Murphy, T.	N	Y	Y	N	Y
19 Platts	Y	Y	Y	N	Y
RHODE ISLAND					
1 Kennedy	Y	Y	Y	Y	Y
2 Langevin	Y	Y	Y	Y	Y
SOUTH CAROLINA					
1 Brown	N	Y	Y	N	Y
2 Wilson	N	Y	Y	N	Y
3 Barrett	N	Y	Y	N	Y
4 Inglis	N	N	Y	N	N
5 Spratt	Y	Y	Y	Y	Y
6 Clyburn	Y	Y	Y	Y	Y
SOUTH DAKOTA					
AL Herseth Sandlin	Y	Y	Y	Y	Y
TENNESSEE					
1 Roe	N	Y	Y	N	Y
2 Duncan	N	Y	Y	N	Y
3 Wamp	N	Y	Y	N	Y
4 Davis	Y	Y	Y	Y	Y
5 Cooper	Y	Y	Y	Y	Y
6 Gordon	Y	Y	Y	Y	Y
7 Blackburn	N	Y	Y	N	?
8 Tanner	Y	Y	Y	Y	Y
9 Cohen	Y	Y	Y	Y	Y

	169	170	171	172	173
TEXAS					
1 Gohmert	N	Y	Y	N	N
2 Poe	N	N	Y	N	N
3 Johnson, S.	N	Y	Y	N	Y
4 Hall	N	Y	Y	Y	Y
5 Hensarling	?	?	?	?	?
6 Barton	N	Y	Y	Y	Y
7 Culberson	N	Y	Y	N	Y
8 Brady	N	Y	Y	N	Y
9 Green, A.	Y	Y	Y	Y	Y
10 McCaul	N	Y	Y	N	Y
11 Conaway	N	Y	Y	N	N
12 Granger	N	Y	Y	N	Y
13 Thornberry	N	Y	Y	N	Y
14 Paul	N	N	N	N	N
15 Hinojosa	Y	Y	?	Y	Y
16 Reyes	Y	Y	Y	Y	Y
17 Edwards	Y	Y	Y	Y	Y
18 Jackson Lee	Y	Y	Y	Y	Y
19 Neugebauer	N	Y	Y	N	N
20 Gonzalez	Y	Y	Y	Y	Y
21 Smith	N	Y	Y	N	Y
22 Olson	N	Y	Y	N	Y
23 Rodriguez	Y	Y	Y	Y	Y
24 Marchant	N	?	Y	N	Y
25 Doggett	Y	Y	Y	Y	Y
26 Burgess	N	Y	Y	N	Y
27 Ortiz	Y	Y	Y	Y	Y
28 Cuellar	Y	Y	Y	Y	Y
29 Green, G.	Y	Y	Y	Y	Y
30 Johnson, E.	Y	Y	Y	Y	Y
31 Carter	N	Y	Y	N	Y
32 Sessions	N	Y	Y	N	Y
UTAH					
1 Bishop	N	Y	Y	N	Y
2 Matheson	Y	Y	Y	Y	Y
3 Chaffetz	N	N	Y	N	N
VERMONT					
AL Welch	Y	Y	Y	Y	Y
VIRGINIA					
1 Wittman	N	Y	Y	N	Y
2 Nye	Y	Y	Y	Y	Y
3 Scott	Y	Y	Y	Y	Y
4 Forbes	N	Y	Y	N	Y
5 Perriello	Y	Y	Y	Y	Y
6 Goodlatte	N	Y	Y	N	Y
7 Cantor	N	Y	Y	N	Y
8 Moran	+	Y	Y	Y	Y
9 Boucher	Y	Y	Y	Y	Y
10 Wolf	N	Y	Y	N	Y
11 Connolly	Y	Y	Y	Y	Y
WASHINGTON					
1 Inslee	Y	Y	Y	Y	Y
2 Larsen	Y	Y	Y	Y	Y
3 Baird	Y	Y	Y	Y	Y
4 Hastings	N	Y	Y	?	?
5 McMorris Rodgers	N	Y	Y	N	Y
6 Dicks	Y	Y	Y	Y	Y
7 McDermott	Y	Y	Y	Y	Y
8 Reichert	Y	Y	Y	Y	Y
9 Smith	Y	Y	Y	Y	Y
WEST VIRGINIA					
1 Mollohan	Y	Y	Y	Y	Y
2 Capito	Y	Y	Y	Y	Y
3 Rahall	Y	Y	Y	Y	Y
WISCONSIN					
1 Ryan	N	Y	Y	N	Y
2 Baldwin	Y	Y	Y	Y	Y
3 Kind	Y	Y	Y	N	Y
4 Moore	Y	Y	Y	Y	Y
5 Sensenbrenner	N	N	Y	N	Y
6 Petri	N	Y	Y	N	Y
7 Obey	Y	?	Y	Y	Y
8 Kagen	Y	Y	N	Y	Y
WYOMING					
AL **Lummis**	N	N	Y	Y	N
DELEGATES					
Faleomavaega (A.S.)					
Norton (D.C.)					
Bordallo (Guam)					
Sablan (N. Marianas)					
Pierluisi (P.R.)					
Christensen (V.I.)					

IN THE HOUSE | By Vote Number

174. **HR 1299. Capitol Police Administration/Passage.** Brady, D-Pa., motion to suspend the rules and pass the bill that would clarify the administrative authorities within the Capitol Police. It would specify that the pay for the chief administrative officer be $1,000 less than the annual rate of pay for the chief of the Capitol Police, require the police chief to give notice to certain congressional committees prior to changes in employment positions and repeal rules requiring Capitol Police officers to purchase their own uniforms. Motion agreed to 416-1: R 170-0; D 246-1. A two-thirds majority of those present and voting (278 in this case) is required for passage under suspension of the rules. March 31, 2009.

175. **H Res 312. Earmark Investigation/Motion to Table.** Hall, D-N.Y., motion to table (kill) the Flake, R-Ariz., privileged resolution that would instruct the Committee on Standards of Official Conduct to investigate and report on the relationship between earmark requests made by members of Congress and the details of past campaign contributions. Motion agreed to 217-185: R 5-158; D 212-27. April 1, 2009.

176. **H Con Res 85. Fiscal 2010 Budget Resolution/Rule.** Adoption of the rule (H Res 305) that would provide for House floor consideration of the concurrent resolution that would set broad spending and revenue targets for the next five years. Adopted 234-179: R 0-174; D 234-5. April 1, 2009.

177. **HR 1664. Executive Compensation Standards/Rule.** Adoption of the rule (H Res 306) that would provide for House floor consideration of the bill that would prohibit certain entities that received federal bailout funds from paying compensation that the Treasury Department deems excessive. Adopted 236-175: R 0-171; D 236-4. April 1, 2009.

178. **HR 1575. Compensation Payments/Passage.** Conyers, D-Mich., motion to suspend the rules and pass the bill that would allow the attorney general to recover certain compensation payments given on or after Sept. 1, 2008, to employees of companies that received more than $10 billion in assistance on or after that date. Excessive employee compensation would be deemed a fraudulent transfer of funds, allowing the Justice Department to file civil actions to force return of the payments. Companies could also be liable for civil action if future payments were greater than 10 times the amount of the mean compensation paid to non-management employees. Motion rejected 223-196: R 9-165; D 214-31. A two-thirds majority of those present and voting (280 in this case) is required for passage under suspension of the rules. April 1, 2009.

179. **H Res 290. Oakland Police Officers/Adoption.** Conyers, D-Mich., motion to suspend the rules and adopt the resolution that would extend condolences to the families of Sgts. Mark Dunakin, Ervin Romans and Daniel Sakai and Officer John Hege of the Oakland Police Department in Oakland, Calif., who died in the line of duty on March 21. Motion agreed to 417-0: R 173-0; D 244-0. A two-thirds majority of those present and voting (278 in this case) is required for adoption under suspension of the rules. April 1, 2009.

	174	175	176	177	178	179
ALABAMA						
1 **Bonner**	Y	P	N	N	N	Y
2 Bright	Y	N	Y	Y	N	Y
3 **Rogers**	Y	N	N	N	N	Y
4 **Aderholt**	Y	N	N	N	N	Y
5 Griffith	Y	Y	Y	Y	N	Y
6 **Bachus**	Y	N	N	N	N	Y
7 Davis	Y	Y	Y	Y	Y	Y
ALASKA						
AL **Young**	Y	Y	N	N	N	Y
ARIZONA						
1 Kirkpatrick	Y	N	Y	N	N	Y
2 **Franks**	Y	N	N	N	N	Y
3 **Shadegg**	Y	N	N	N	N	Y
4 Pastor	Y	Y	Y	Y	Y	Y
5 Mitchell	Y	N	Y	Y	N	Y
6 **Flake**	Y	N	N	N	N	Y
7 Grijalva	Y	Y	Y	Y	Y	Y
8 Giffords	Y	N	Y	Y	Y	Y
ARKANSAS						
1 Berry	Y	Y	Y	Y	Y	Y
2 Snyder	Y	Y	Y	Y	N	Y
3 **Boozman**	Y	N	N	N	N	Y
4 Ross	Y	Y	Y	Y	Y	Y
CALIFORNIA						
1 Thompson	Y	Y	Y	Y	Y	Y
2 **Herger**	Y	N	N	N	N	Y
3 **Lungren**	Y	N	N	N	N	Y
4 **McClintock**	Y	N	N	N	N	Y
5 Matsui	Y	Y	Y	Y	Y	Y
6 Woolsey	Y	Y	Y	Y	Y	Y
7 Miller, George	Y	Y	Y	Y	Y	Y
8 Pelosi						Y
9 Lee	Y	Y	Y	Y	Y	Y
10 Tauscher	Y	Y	Y	Y	N	Y
11 McNerney	Y	N	Y	Y	Y	Y
12 Speier	Y	Y	Y	Y	Y	Y
13 Stark	Y	Y	Y	Y	Y	Y
14 Eshoo	Y	Y	Y	Y	Y	Y
15 Honda	Y	Y	?	Y	Y	Y
16 Lofgren	Y	P	Y	?	Y	Y
17 Farr	Y	Y	Y	Y	Y	Y
18 Cardoza	?	Y	Y	Y	N	Y
19 **Radanovich**	Y	N	N	N	N	Y
20 Costa	Y	Y	Y	Y	Y	Y
21 **Nunes**	Y	N	N	N	N	Y
22 **McCarthy**	Y	N	N	N	N	Y
23 Capps	Y	Y	Y	Y	Y	Y
24 **Gallegly**	Y	N	N	N	N	Y
25 **McKeon**	Y	N	N	N	N	Y
26 **Dreier**	Y	N	N	N	N	Y
27 Sherman	Y	Y	?	Y	Y	Y
28 Berman	Y	Y	Y	?	Y	Y
29 Schiff	Y	Y	Y	Y	Y	Y
30 Waxman	Y	Y	Y	Y	Y	Y
31 Becerra	Y	+	Y	Y	Y	Y
32 Vacant						
33 Watson	Y	Y	Y	Y	Y	Y
34 Roybal-Allard	Y	Y	Y	Y	Y	Y
35 Waters	Y	Y	?	Y	Y	Y
36 Harman	Y	Y	Y	Y	Y	Y
37 Richardson	Y	Y	Y	Y	Y	Y
38 Napolitano	Y	Y	Y	Y	Y	Y
39 Sánchez, Linda	Y	Y	Y	Y	Y	Y
40 **Royce**	Y	N	N	N	N	Y
41 **Lewis**	Y	N	N	N	N	Y
42 **Miller, Gary**	?	?	?	?	?	?
43 Baca	Y	Y	Y	Y	Y	Y
44 **Calvert**	Y	N	N	N	N	Y
45 **Bono Mack**	Y	Y	N	N	N	Y
46 **Rohrabacher**	Y	Y	N	N	Y	Y
47 Sanchez, Loretta	?	?	?	?	?	?
48 **Campbell**	Y	N	N	N	N	Y
49 **Issa**	Y	N	N	N	N	Y
50 **Bilbray**	Y	N	N	N	N	Y
51 Filner	Y	Y	Y	Y	Y	Y
52 **Hunter**	Y	N	N	N	N	Y
53 Davis	Y	Y	Y	Y	Y	Y

	174	175	176	177	178	179
COLORADO						
1 DeGette	Y	Y	Y	Y	Y	Y
2 Polis	Y	Y	Y	Y	Y	Y
3 Salazar	Y	Y	Y	Y	Y	Y
4 Markey	Y	Y	Y	Y	Y	Y
5 **Lamborn**	Y	N	N	N	N	Y
6 **Coffman**	Y	N	N	N	N	Y
7 Perlmutter	Y	Y	Y	Y	Y	Y
CONNECTICUT						
1 Larson	Y	+	+	+	+	Y
2 Courtney	Y	Y	Y	Y	Y	Y
3 DeLauro	Y	Y	Y	Y	Y	Y
4 Himes	Y	N	Y	N	Y	Y
5 Murphy	Y	Y	Y	Y	Y	Y
DELAWARE						
AL Castle	Y	N	N	N	N	Y
FLORIDA						
1 **Miller**	Y	N	N	N	N	Y
2 Boyd	Y	Y	Y	Y	Y	Y
3 Brown	Y	Y	Y	?	Y	Y
4 **Crenshaw**	Y	N	N	N	N	Y
5 **Brown-Waite**	Y	N	N	N	N	Y
6 **Stearns**	Y	N	N	N	N	Y
7 **Mica**	Y	N	N	N	N	Y
8 Grayson	Y	Y	Y	Y	Y	Y
9 **Bilirakis**	Y	N	N	N	N	Y
10 **Young**	Y	N	N	N	N	Y
11 Castor	?	P	Y	Y	Y	Y
12 **Putnam**	Y	N	N	N	N	Y
13 **Buchanan**	Y	N	N	N	N	Y
14 **Mack**	Y	N	N	N	N	Y
15 **Posey**	Y	N	N	N	N	Y
16 **Rooney**	Y	N	N	N	N	Y
17 Meek	Y	Y	Y	Y	Y	Y
18 **Ros-Lehtinen**	Y	N	N	N	N	Y
19 Wexler	Y	Y	Y	Y	Y	Y
20 Wasserman Schultz	Y	Y	Y	Y	Y	Y
21 **Diaz-Balart, L.**	Y	P	N	N	Y	Y
22 Klein	Y	Y	Y	?	Y	Y
23 Hastings	Y	Y	Y	Y	Y	Y
24 Kosmas	Y	Y	Y	Y	Y	Y
25 **Diaz-Balart, M.**	Y	N	N	N	Y	Y
GEORGIA						
1 **Kingston**	Y	N	N	?	N	Y
2 Bishop	Y	Y	Y	Y	Y	Y
3 **Westmoreland**	?	?	?	?	?	?
4 Johnson	Y	Y	Y	Y	Y	Y
5 Lewis	Y	Y	Y	Y	Y	Y
6 **Price**	Y	N	N	N	N	Y
7 **Linder**	Y	N	N	N	N	Y
8 Marshall	Y	Y	Y	Y	N	Y
9 **Deal**	Y	N	N	N	N	Y
10 **Broun**	Y	N	N	N	N	Y
11 **Gingrey**	Y	N	N	N	N	Y
12 Barrow	Y	Y	N	Y	N	Y
13 Scott	Y	Y	Y	Y	Y	Y
HAWAII						
1 Abercrombie	Y	Y	Y	Y	Y	Y
2 Hirono	Y	Y	Y	Y	Y	Y
IDAHO						
1 Minnick	N	N	N	N	N	Y
2 **Simpson**	?	N	N	N	N	Y
ILLINOIS						
1 Rush	Y	Y	Y	Y	Y	Y
2 Jackson	Y	Y	Y	Y	Y	Y
3 Lipinski	Y	Y	Y	Y	Y	Y
4 Gutierrez	Y	Y	Y	Y	Y	Y
5 Vacant						
6 **Roskam**	Y	N	N	N	N	Y
7 Davis	Y	Y	Y	Y	Y	Y
8 Bean	Y	N	Y	N	Y	Y
9 Schakowsky	Y	Y	Y	Y	Y	Y
10 **Kirk**	Y	N	N	N	N	Y
11 Halvorson	Y	N	Y	Y	Y	Y
12 Costello	Y	Y	Y	Y	Y	Y
13 **Biggert**	Y	N	N	N	N	Y
14 Foster	Y	N	Y	N	N	Y
15 **Johnson**	Y	N	N	N	N	Y

KEY   **Republicans**   Democrats

Y Voted for (yea)	X Paired against
# Paired for	− Announced against
+ Announced for	P Voted "present"
N Voted against (nay)	

C Voted "present" to avoid possible conflict of interest

? Did not vote or otherwise make a position known

	174	175	176	177	178	179
16 **Manzullo**	Y	N	N	N	N	Y
17 Hare	Y	Y	Y	Y	Y	Y
18 **Schock**	Y	N	N	N	N	Y
19 **Shimkus**	Y	N	N	N	N	Y
INDIANA						
1 Visclosky	Y	N	Y	Y	Y	Y
2 Donnelly	Y	N	Y	Y	Y	Y
3 **Souder**	Y	N	N	N	N	Y
4 **Buyer**	Y	N	N	N	N	Y
5 **Burton**	Y	N	N	N	N	Y
6 **Pence**	Y	N	N	N	N	Y
7 Carson	Y	Y	Y	Y	Y	Y
8 Ellsworth	Y	N	Y	Y	N	Y
9 Hill	?	N	Y	N	Y	Y
IOWA						
1 Braley	Y	Y	Y	N	Y	Y
2 Loebsack	Y	N	Y	Y	Y	Y
3 Boswell	Y	Y	Y	Y	Y	Y
4 **Latham**	Y	P	N	N	N	Y
5 **King**	Y	N	N	N	N	Y
KANSAS						
1 **Moran**	Y	N	N	N	N	Y
2 **Jenkins**	Y	N	N	N	N	Y
3 Moore	Y	Y	Y	Y	Y	Y
4 **Tiahrt**	Y	N	N	N	N	Y
KENTUCKY						
1 **Whitfield**	Y	N	N	N	N	Y
2 **Guthrie**	Y	N	N	N	N	Y
3 Yarmuth	Y	Y	Y	Y	Y	Y
4 **Davis**	Y	N	N	N	N	Y
5 **Rogers**	Y	N	N	N	Y	Y
6 Chandler	Y	P	Y	Y	Y	Y
LOUISIANA						
1 **Scalise**	Y	N	N	N	N	Y
2 **Cao**	Y	N	N	N	Y	Y
3 Melancon	Y	Y	Y	Y	Y	Y
4 **Fleming**	Y	N	N	N	N	Y
5 **Alexander**	Y	N	N	N	N	Y
6 **Cassidy**	Y	N	N	N	N	Y
7 **Boustany**	Y	N	N	N	N	Y
MAINE						
1 Pingree	Y	Y	Y	Y	Y	Y
2 Michaud	Y	Y	Y	Y	Y	Y
MARYLAND						
1 Kratovil	Y	Y	Y	Y	Y	Y
2 Ruppersberger	Y	Y	Y	Y	Y	Y
3 Sarbanes	Y	Y	Y	Y	Y	Y
4 Edwards	Y	Y	Y	Y	Y	Y
5 Hoyer	Y	Y	Y	Y	Y	Y
6 **Bartlett**	Y	N	N	N	N	Y
7 Cummings	Y	Y	Y	Y	Y	Y
8 Van Hollen	Y	Y	Y	Y	Y	Y
MASSACHUSETTS						
1 Olver	Y	Y	Y	Y	Y	Y
2 Neal	Y	Y	Y	Y	Y	Y
3 McGovern	Y	Y	Y	Y	Y	Y
4 Frank	Y	Y	?	Y	Y	Y
5 Tsongas	Y	Y	Y	Y	N	Y
6 Tierney	Y	Y	?	Y	Y	Y
7 Markey	Y	Y	Y	Y	Y	Y
8 Capuano	Y	Y	Y	Y	Y	Y
9 Lynch	Y	Y	Y	Y	Y	Y
10 Delahunt	Y	Y	Y	Y	Y	Y
MICHIGAN						
1 Stupak	Y	Y	Y	Y	Y	Y
2 **Hoekstra**	Y	N	N	N	N	Y
3 **Ehlers**	Y	N	N	N	N	Y
4 **Camp**	Y	N	N	N	N	Y
5 Kildee	Y	Y	Y	Y	Y	Y
6 **Upton**	Y	N	N	N	N	Y
7 Schauer	Y	?	?	?	?	?
8 **Rogers**	Y	N	N	N	N	Y
9 Peters	Y	Y	Y	Y	Y	Y
10 **Miller**	Y	N	N	N	N	Y
11 **McCotter**	Y	N	N	N	N	Y
12 Levin	Y	+	+	+	+	+
13 Kilpatrick	Y	Y	Y	Y	?	?
14 Conyers	Y	Y	Y	Y	Y	Y
15 Dingell	Y	Y	Y	Y	Y	Y
MINNESOTA						
1 Walz	Y	N	Y	Y	Y	Y
2 **Kline**	Y	P	N	N	N	Y
3 **Paulsen**	Y	N	N	N	N	Y
4 McCollum	Y	Y	Y	Y	N	Y

	174	175	176	177	178	179
5 Ellison	Y	Y	Y	Y	Y	Y
6 **Bachmann**	Y	N	N	N	N	Y
7 Peterson	Y	Y	Y	Y	Y	Y
8 Oberstar	Y	Y	Y	?	Y	Y
MISSISSIPPI						
1 Childers	Y	N	N	Y	N	Y
2 Thompson	Y	?	?	?	?	?
3 **Harper**	Y	N	N	N	N	Y
4 Taylor	Y	Y	N	Y	Y	Y
MISSOURI						
1 Clay	Y	Y	Y	Y	Y	Y
2 **Akin**	Y	N	N	N	N	Y
3 Carnahan	Y	Y	Y	Y	Y	Y
4 Skelton	Y	Y	Y	Y	Y	Y
5 Cleaver	Y	Y	Y	Y	Y	Y
6 **Graves**	Y	N	N	N	N	Y
7 **Blunt**	Y	N	N	N	N	Y
8 **Emerson**	Y	N	N	N	N	Y
9 **Luetkemeyer**	Y	N	N	N	N	Y
MONTANA						
AL **Rehberg**	Y	N	N	N	N	Y
NEBRASKA						
1 **Fortenberry**	Y	N	N	N	N	Y
2 **Terry**	Y	N	N	N	N	Y
3 **Smith**	Y	N	N	N	N	Y
NEVADA						
1 Berkley	Y	Y	Y	Y	Y	Y
2 **Heller**	Y	N	N	N	N	Y
3 Titus	Y	Y	Y	Y	Y	Y
NEW HAMPSHIRE						
1 Shea-Porter	Y	Y	Y	Y	Y	Y
2 Hodes	Y	N	Y	Y	Y	Y
NEW JERSEY						
1 Andrews	Y	Y	Y	Y	Y	Y
2 **LoBiondo**	Y	N	N	N	N	Y
3 Adler	Y	Y	Y	Y	Y	Y
4 **Smith**	Y	N	N	N	N	Y
5 **Garrett**	Y	N	N	N	N	Y
6 Pallone	Y	?	?	?	?	?
7 **Lance**	Y	N	N	N	N	Y
8 Pascrell	+	+	+	+	+	+
9 Rothman	Y	Y	Y	Y	Y	Y
10 Payne	Y	Y	Y	Y	Y	Y
11 **Frelinghuysen**	Y	N	N	N	N	Y
12 Holt	Y	Y	Y	Y	Y	Y
13 Sires	Y	Y	Y	Y	Y	Y
NEW MEXICO						
1 Heinrich	Y	Y	Y	Y	Y	Y
2 Teague	Y	N	Y	Y	Y	Y
3 Lujan	Y	Y	Y	Y	Y	Y
NEW YORK						
1 Bishop	Y	Y	Y	Y	Y	Y
2 Israel	Y	Y	Y	Y	Y	Y
3 **King**	Y	N	N	N	N	Y
4 McCarthy	Y	Y	Y	Y	N	Y
5 Ackerman	Y	Y	Y	Y	N	Y
6 Meeks	Y	Y	Y	Y	N	Y
7 Crowley	Y	Y	Y	Y	N	Y
8 Nadler	Y	Y	Y	Y	N	Y
9 Weiner	Y	Y	Y	Y	Y	Y
10 Towns	Y	Y	Y	Y	Y	Y
11 Clarke	Y	Y	Y	Y	Y	?
12 Velázquez	Y	Y	Y	Y	Y	Y
13 McMahon	Y	Y	Y	Y	N	Y
14 Maloney	Y	Y	Y	Y	Y	Y
15 Rangel	Y	Y	Y	?	Y	Y
16 Serrano	Y	Y	Y	Y	Y	Y
17 Engel	Y	Y	Y	Y	Y	Y
18 Lowey	Y	Y	Y	Y	Y	Y
19 Hall	Y	Y	Y	Y	Y	Y
20 Vacant						
21 Tonko	Y	Y	Y	Y	Y	Y
22 Hinchey	Y	Y	Y	Y	Y	Y
23 **McHugh**	Y	N	N	N	N	Y
24 Arcuri	Y	Y	Y	Y	Y	Y
25 Maffei	Y	Y	Y	Y	Y	Y
26 **Lee**	Y	N	N	N	N	Y
27 Higgins	Y	Y	Y	Y	Y	Y
28 Slaughter	Y	Y	Y	Y	Y	Y
29 Massa	Y	Y	Y	Y	Y	Y
NORTH CAROLINA						
1 Butterfield	Y	P	Y	Y	Y	Y
2 Etheridge	Y	Y	Y	Y	Y	Y
3 **Jones**	Y	Y	N	N	Y	Y
4 Price	Y	Y	Y	Y	Y	Y

	174	175	176	177	178	179
5 **Foxx**	Y	N	N	N	N	Y
6 **Coble**	Y	Y	N	N	N	Y
7 McIntyre	Y	N	Y	Y	Y	Y
8 Kissell	Y	Y	Y	Y	Y	Y
9 **Myrick**	Y	P	N	N	N	Y
10 **McHenry**	Y	N	N	N	N	Y
11 Shuler	Y	Y	Y	Y	Y	Y
12 Watt	Y	Y	Y	Y	Y	Y
13 Miller	Y	Y	Y	Y	Y	Y
NORTH DAKOTA						
AL Pomeroy	Y	Y	Y	Y	Y	Y
OHIO						
1 Driehaus	Y	Y	Y	Y	Y	Y
2 **Schmidt**	Y	N	?	?	?	?
3 **Turner**	Y	N	N	N	N	Y
4 **Jordan**	Y	N	N	N	N	Y
5 **Latta**	Y	N	N	N	N	Y
6 Wilson	Y	Y	Y	Y	Y	Y
7 **Austria**	Y	N	N	N	N	Y
8 **Boehner**	Y	N	N	N	N	Y
9 Kaptur	Y	?	Y	Y	Y	Y
10 Kucinich	Y	Y	N	Y	Y	Y
11 Fudge	Y	Y	Y	Y	Y	Y
12 **Tiberi**	Y	N	N	N	N	Y
13 Sutton	Y	Y	Y	Y	Y	Y
14 **LaTourette**	Y	N	N	N	N	?
15 Kilroy	Y	Y	Y	Y	Y	Y
16 Boccieri	Y	N	Y	Y	Y	Y
17 Ryan	Y	Y	Y	Y	Y	Y
18 Space	Y	Y	Y	Y	Y	Y
OKLAHOMA						
1 **Sullivan**	Y	N	N	N	N	Y
2 Boren	Y	Y	Y	Y	N	Y
3 **Lucas**	Y	N	N	N	N	Y
4 **Cole**	Y	N	N	N	N	Y
5 **Fallin**	Y	N	N	N	N	Y
OREGON						
1 Wu	Y	Y	Y	Y	N	Y
2 **Walden**	Y	P	N	N	N	Y
3 Blumenauer	Y	Y	Y	Y	Y	Y
4 DeFazio	Y	Y	Y	Y	Y	Y
5 Schrader	Y	Y	Y	Y	N	Y
PENNSYLVANIA						
1 Brady	Y	Y	Y	Y	Y	Y
2 Fattah	Y	Y	Y	Y	Y	Y
3 Dahlkemper	Y	Y	Y	Y	Y	Y
4 Altmire	Y	Y	Y	Y	Y	Y
5 **Thompson**	Y	N	N	N	N	Y
6 **Gerlach**	Y	N	N	N	N	Y
7 Sestak	Y	Y	Y	Y	N	Y
8 Murphy, P.	Y	Y	Y	Y	Y	Y
9 **Shuster**	Y	?	N	N	N	Y
10 Carney	Y	Y	Y	Y	Y	Y
11 Kanjorski	Y	Y	Y	Y	N	Y
12 Murtha	Y	Y	Y	Y	Y	Y
13 Schwartz	Y	Y	Y	Y	Y	Y
14 Doyle	Y	Y	Y	Y	Y	Y
15 **Dent**	Y	P	N	N	N	Y
16 **Pitts**	Y	N	N	N	N	Y
17 Holden	Y	Y	Y	Y	Y	Y
18 **Murphy, T.**	Y	N	N	N	N	Y
19 **Platts**	Y	N	N	N	N	Y
RHODE ISLAND						
1 Kennedy	Y	Y	Y	Y	Y	Y
2 Langevin	Y	Y	Y	Y	Y	Y
SOUTH CAROLINA						
1 **Brown**	Y	N	N	N	N	Y
2 **Wilson**	Y	N	N	N	N	Y
3 **Barrett**	?	P	N	N	N	Y
4 **Inglis**	Y	N	N	N	N	Y
5 Spratt	Y	Y	Y	Y	Y	Y
6 Clyburn	Y	Y	Y	Y	Y	Y
SOUTH DAKOTA						
AL Herseth Sandlin	Y	N	Y	Y	Y	Y
TENNESSEE						
1 **Roe**	Y	N	N	N	N	Y
2 **Duncan**	Y	N	N	N	Y	Y
3 **Wamp**	Y	N	N	N	N	Y
4 Davis	Y	Y	Y	Y	Y	Y
5 Cooper	Y	Y	Y	Y	Y	Y
6 Gordon	Y	Y	Y	Y	Y	Y
7 **Blackburn**	?	N	N	N	N	Y
8 Tanner	Y	Y	Y	Y	Y	Y
9 Cohen	Y	Y	Y	Y	Y	Y

	174	175	176	177	178	179
TEXAS						
1 **Gohmert**	Y	N	N	N	N	Y
2 **Poe**	Y	P	N	N	N	Y
3 **Johnson, S.**	Y	N	N	N	N	Y
4 **Hall**	Y	N	N	N	Y	Y
5 **Hensarling**	?	N	N	N	N	Y
6 **Barton**	Y	?	?	?	?	?
7 **Culberson**	Y	N	N	N	N	Y
8 **Brady**	Y	N	N	N	N	Y
9 Green, A.	Y	Y	Y	Y	Y	Y
10 **McCaul**	Y	N	N	N	N	Y
11 **Conaway**	Y	P	N	N	N	Y
12 **Granger**	Y	N	N	N	N	Y
13 **Thornberry**	Y	N	N	N	N	Y
14 **Paul**	Y	N	N	N	N	Y
15 Hinojosa	Y	Y	Y	Y	Y	Y
16 Reyes	Y	Y	Y	Y	Y	Y
17 Edwards	Y	Y	Y	Y	Y	Y
18 Jackson Lee	Y	Y	Y	Y	Y	Y
19 **Neugebauer**	Y	N	N	N	N	Y
20 Gonzalez	Y	Y	Y	Y	Y	Y
21 **Smith**	+	N	N	N	N	Y
22 **Olson**	Y	N	N	N	N	Y
23 Rodriguez	Y	Y	Y	Y	Y	Y
24 **Marchant**	Y	N	N	N	N	Y
25 Doggett	Y	Y	?	Y	Y	Y
26 **Burgess**	Y	N	N	?	N	Y
27 Ortiz	Y	Y	Y	Y	Y	Y
28 Cuellar	Y	Y	Y	Y	N	Y
29 Green, G.	Y	Y	Y	Y	Y	?
30 Johnson, E.	Y	Y	Y	Y	Y	Y
31 **Carter**	Y	N	N	N	N	Y
32 **Sessions**	Y	N	N	N	N	Y
UTAH						
1 **Bishop**	Y	N	N	N	N	Y
2 Matheson	Y	N	Y	Y	N	Y
3 **Chaffetz**	Y	N	N	N	N	Y
VERMONT						
AL Welch	Y	P	?	Y	Y	Y
VIRGINIA						
1 **Wittman**	Y	N	N	N	N	Y
2 Nye	Y	Y	Y	Y	Y	Y
3 Scott	Y	Y	Y	Y	Y	Y
4 **Forbes**	Y	N	N	N	N	Y
5 Perriello	Y	N	Y	Y	Y	Y
6 **Goodlatte**	Y	N	N	N	N	Y
7 **Cantor**	Y	N	N	P	N	Y
8 Moran	Y	Y	Y	Y	Y	?
9 Boucher	Y	Y	Y	Y	Y	Y
10 **Wolf**	Y	N	N	N	N	Y
11 Connolly	Y	Y	Y	Y	Y	Y
WASHINGTON						
1 Inslee	Y	Y	Y	Y	Y	Y
2 Larsen	Y	Y	Y	Y	Y	Y
3 Baird	Y	Y	Y	Y	Y	Y
4 **Hastings**	?	P	N	N	N	Y
5 **McMorris Rodgers**	Y	N	N	N	N	Y
6 Dicks	Y	Y	Y	Y	Y	Y
7 McDermott	?	Y	Y	Y	Y	Y
8 **Reichert**	Y	N	N	N	N	Y
9 Smith	Y	N	Y	Y	Y	Y
WEST VIRGINIA						
1 Mollohan	Y	Y	Y	Y	Y	Y
2 **Capito**	Y	N	N	N	N	Y
3 Rahall	Y	Y	Y	Y	Y	Y
WISCONSIN						
1 **Ryan**	Y	N	N	N	N	Y
2 Baldwin	Y	Y	Y	Y	Y	Y
3 Kind	Y	N	Y	Y	N	Y
4 Moore	Y	Y	Y	Y	Y	Y
5 **Sensenbrenner**	Y	N	N	N	N	Y
6 **Petri**	Y	N	N	N	N	Y
7 Obey	Y	Y	Y	Y	Y	Y
8 Kagen	Y	Y	Y	Y	Y	Y
WYOMING						
AL **Lummis**	Y	N	N	N	N	Y
DELEGATES						
Faleomavaega (A.S.)						
Norton (D.C.)						
Bordallo (Guam)						
Sablan (N. Marianas)						
Pierluisi (P.R.)						
Christensen (V.I.)						

IN THE HOUSE | By Vote Number

180. HR 1664. Executive Compensation Standards/Payment Schedule. Bean, D-Ill., amendment that would allow entities that enter into a repayment schedule established by the Treasury Department and do not default to be exempt from the compensation restrictions in the bill. Adopted in Committee of the Whole 228-198: R 165-8; D 63-190. April 1, 2009.

181. HR 1664. Executive Compensation Standards/Compensation Definition. Dahlkemper, D-Pa., amendment that would clarify the definition of compensation in the bill to include payments made before, during and after employment, including payments of money, transfers of property or provision of services. Adopted in Committee of the Whole 246-180: R 6-167; D 240-13. April 1, 2009.

182. HR 1664. Executive Compensation Standards/Passage. Passage of the bill that would prohibit firms that received funds under the Troubled Asset Relief Program, as well as Fannie Mae, Freddie Mac and the Federal Home Loan Bank System, from paying compensation deemed excessive by the Treasury Department. The covered institutions that enter into a repayment schedule established by the Treasury and do not default would be exempt. The institutions would be required to report to the department within 90 days of enactment, and yearly thereafter, on the number of employees who receive compensation of more than $500,000, $1 million, $2 million, $3 million and $5 million. The restrictions would be lifted when an institution repays the borrowed funds. Passed 247-171: R 10-163; D 237-8. April 1, 2009.

183. H Con Res 93. Adjournment/Rule. Adoption of the concurrent resolution that would provide for adjournment of the House until 2 p.m., Tuesday, April 21, 2009, and the Senate until 12 p.m., Monday, April 20, 2009. Adopted 244-177: R 7-167; D 237-10. April 2, 2009.

184. H Con Res 85. Fiscal 2010 Budget Resolution/Rule. Adoption of the rule (H Res 316) that would provide for further House floor consideration of the concurrent resolution that would set broad spending and revenue targets for the next five years. Adopted 242-182: R 0-176; D 242-6. April 2, 2009.

185. HR 1256. Tobacco Regulation/Substitute. Buyer, R-Ind., substitute amendment that would create a center within the Health and Human Services Department to regulate tobacco products. It would require the center to report to Congress on the benefits of restricting the marketing and advertising of tobacco products, including the free speech implications. It would eliminate the proposed user fees on tobacco manufacturers and importers, prohibit restrictions on raw tobacco growers, and prohibit tobacco or nicotine products from being regulated as a food, drug, or device under the Federal Food, Drug and Cosmetic Act, except for those marketed for use as a medical treatment. Rejected 142-284: R 124-51; D 18-233. April 2, 2009.

186. HR 1256. Tobacco Regulation/Recommit. Rogers, R-Mich., motion to recommit the bill to the Energy and Commerce Committee with instructions that it be immediately reported back with language that would bar the use of funds other than the user fees collected from tobacco manufacturers and importers to pay for the regulations authorized under the bill. Motion rejected 169-256: R 157-18; D 12-238. April 2, 2009.

	180	181	182	183	184	185	186
ALABAMA							
1 **Bonner**	Y	N	N	N	Y	Y	Y
2 Bright	N	Y	Y	Y	Y	Y	Y
3 **Rogers**	Y	N	N	N	Y	N	Y
4 **Aderholt**	Y	N	N	N	Y	Y	Y
5 Griffith	Y	Y	Y	?	Y	N	N
6 **Bachus**	Y	N	N	N	N	Y	Y
7 Davis	N	Y	Y	Y	Y	N	N
ALASKA							
AL **Young**	Y	N	N	N	Y	N	Y
ARIZONA							
1 Kirkpatrick	Y	N	N	Y	Y	N	Y
2 **Franks**	Y	N	N	N	N	Y	Y
3 **Shadegg**	Y	N	N	N	N	Y	Y
4 Pastor	N	Y	Y	Y	Y	N	N
5 Mitchell	N	Y	N	N	Y	N	N
6 **Flake**	Y	N	N	N	N	N	Y
7 Grijalva	N	Y	Y	Y	Y	N	N
8 Giffords	Y	Y	Y	Y	Y	N	N
ARKANSAS							
1 Berry	N	Y	Y	Y	Y	N	N
2 Snyder	Y	N	N	Y	Y	N	N
3 **Boozman**	Y	N	N	N	N	Y	Y
4 Ross	Y	Y	Y	Y	Y	N	N
CALIFORNIA							
1 Thompson	N	Y	Y	Y	Y	N	N
2 **Herger**	Y	N	N	N	N	N	Y
3 **Lungren**	Y	N	N	N	N	Y	Y
4 **McClintock**	Y	N	N	N	N	Y	Y
5 Matsui	N	Y	Y	Y	Y	N	N
6 Woolsey	N	Y	Y	Y	Y	N	N
7 Miller, George	N	Y	Y	Y	Y	N	N
8 Pelosi							
9 Lee	N	Y	Y	Y	Y	N	N
10 Tauscher	N	Y	Y	Y	Y	N	N
11 McNerney	N	Y	Y	Y	Y	N	N
12 Speier	N	Y	Y	Y	Y	N	N
13 Stark	N	Y	Y	Y	Y	N	N
14 Eshoo	N	Y	Y	Y	Y	N	N
15 Honda	N	Y	Y	Y	Y	N	N
16 Lofgren	N	Y	Y	Y	Y	N	N
17 Farr	N	Y	Y	Y	Y	N	N
18 Cardoza	N	Y	Y	Y	Y	N	N
19 **Radanovich**	Y	N	N	N	N	Y	Y
20 Costa	N	Y	Y	Y	Y	N	N
21 **Nunes**	Y	N	N	N	N	Y	Y
22 **McCarthy**	Y	N	N	N	N	Y	Y
23 Capps	N	Y	Y	Y	Y	N	N
24 **Gallegly**	Y	N	N	N	N	Y	Y
25 **McKeon**	Y	N	N	N	N	Y	Y
26 **Dreier**	Y	N	N	N	N	Y	Y
27 Sherman	N	Y	Y	Y	Y	N	N
28 Berman	N	Y	Y	Y	Y	N	N
29 Schiff	N	Y	Y	Y	Y	N	N
30 Waxman	N	Y	Y	Y	Y	N	N
31 Becerra	N	Y	Y	Y	Y	N	N
32 Vacant							
33 Watson	N	Y	Y	Y	Y	N	N
34 Roybal-Allard	N	Y	Y	Y	Y	N	N
35 Waters	N	Y	Y	Y	Y	N	N
36 Harman	Y	Y	Y	Y	Y	N	N
37 Richardson	N	Y	Y	?	Y	N	N
38 Napolitano	N	Y	Y	Y	Y	N	N
39 Sánchez, Linda	N	Y	Y	Y	Y	N	N
40 **Royce**	Y	N	N	N	N	Y	N
41 **Lewis**	Y	N	N	N	N	Y	Y
42 **Miller, Gary**	?	?	?	?	?	?	?
43 Baca	N	Y	Y	Y	Y	N	N
44 **Calvert**	Y	N	N	N	N	Y	Y
45 **Bono Mack**	Y	N	N	N	N	N	Y
46 **Rohrabacher**	N	N	Y	N	N	N	Y
47 Sanchez, Loretta	?	?	?	Y	Y	N	N
48 **Campbell**	Y	N	N	N	N	Y	Y
49 **Issa**	Y	N	N	N	N	Y	Y
50 **Bilbray**	Y	N	N	N	N	N	Y
51 Filner	N	Y	Y	Y	Y	N	N
52 **Hunter**	Y	N	N	N	N	Y	Y
53 Davis	N	Y	Y	Y	Y	N	N

	180	181	182	183	184	185	186
COLORADO							
1 DeGette	N	Y	Y	Y	Y	N	N
2 Polis	Y	Y	Y	Y	Y	N	N
3 Salazar	Y	Y	Y	Y	Y	N	N
4 Markey	Y	Y	Y	Y	Y	N	N
5 **Lamborn**	Y	N	N	N	N	N	Y
6 **Coffman**	N	N	N	N	N	Y	Y
7 Perlmutter	Y	Y	Y	Y	Y	N	N
CONNECTICUT							
1 Larson	N	Y	Y	Y	Y	N	N
2 Courtney	N	Y	Y	Y	Y	N	N
3 DeLauro	N	Y	Y	Y	Y	N	N
4 Himes	Y	Y	Y	Y	Y	N	N
5 Murphy	N	Y	Y	Y	Y	N	N
DELAWARE							
AL **Castle**	Y	N	N	N	N	N	N
FLORIDA							
1 **Miller**	Y	N	N	N	N	Y	Y
2 Boyd	N	Y	Y	Y	Y	Y	N
3 Brown	N	Y	Y	Y	Y	N	N
4 **Crenshaw**	Y	N	N	N	N	Y	Y
5 **Brown-Waite**	Y	Y	N	N	N	N	Y
6 **Stearns**	Y	N	N	N	N	Y	Y
7 **Mica**	Y	N	N	N	N	Y	Y
8 Grayson	N	Y	Y	Y	Y	N	N
9 **Bilirakis**	Y	N	N	N	N	Y	Y
10 **Young**	Y	N	N	N	N	Y	Y
11 Castor	N	Y	Y	Y	Y	N	N
12 **Putnam**	Y	N	N	N	N	Y	Y
13 **Buchanan**	N	N	N	N	N	Y	Y
14 **Mack**	Y	N	N	N	N	N	N
15 **Posey**	Y	Y	N	N	N	Y	Y
16 **Rooney**	Y	Y	N	N	N	Y	Y
17 Meek	N	Y	Y	Y	Y	N	N
18 **Ros-Lehtinen**	N	Y	N	N	N	Y	N
19 Wexler	N	Y	Y	Y	Y	N	N
20 Wasserman Schultz	N	Y	Y	Y	Y	N	N
21 **Diaz-Balart, L.**	Y	Y	Y	N	N	Y	N
22 Klein	N	Y	Y	?	Y	N	N
23 Hastings	N	Y	Y	Y	Y	N	N
24 Kosmas	N	Y	N	Y	Y	N	N
25 **Diaz-Balart, M.**	Y	Y	Y	N	N	Y	N
GEORGIA							
1 **Kingston**	Y	N	N	N	N	Y	Y
2 Bishop	N	Y	Y	Y	Y	Y	N
3 **Westmoreland**	?	?	?	?	?	?	?
4 Johnson	N	Y	Y	Y	Y	N	N
5 Lewis	N	Y	Y	Y	Y	N	N
6 **Price**	Y	N	N	N	N	N	Y
7 **Linder**	N	N	N	N	N	N	Y
8 Marshall	Y	N	Y	Y	Y	N	N
9 **Deal**	Y	N	N	N	N	Y	Y
10 **Broun**	Y	N	N	N	N	N	Y
11 **Gingrey**	Y	N	N	N	N	N	Y
12 Barrow	N	Y	Y	Y	Y	N	N
13 Scott	N	Y	Y	Y	Y	N	N
HAWAII							
1 Abercrombie	N	Y	Y	Y	Y	N	N
2 Hirono	N	Y	Y	Y	Y	N	N
IDAHO							
1 **Minnick**	Y	N	N	Y	Y	Y	N
2 **Simpson**	Y	N	N	N	N	N	Y
ILLINOIS							
1 Rush	Y	Y	Y	Y	Y	N	N
2 Jackson	N	Y	Y	Y	Y	N	N
3 Lipinski	N	Y	Y	Y	Y	N	N
4 Gutierrez	N	Y	Y	Y	Y	N	N
5 Vacant							
6 **Roskam**	Y	N	N	N	N	Y	Y
7 Davis	N	Y	Y	Y	Y	N	N
8 Bean	Y	Y	Y	Y	Y	N	N
9 Schakowsky	N	Y	Y	Y	Y	N	N
10 **Kirk**	Y	N	N	N	N	N	Y
11 Halvorson	N	Y	Y	Y	Y	N	N
12 Costello	N	Y	Y	Y	Y	N	N
13 **Biggert**	Y	N	N	N	N	N	N
14 Foster	Y	Y	Y	Y	Y	N	N
15 **Johnson**	Y	N	Y	N	Y	N	Y

	180	181	182	183	184	185	186
16 **Manzullo**	Y	N	N	N	N	Y	Y
17 Hare	N	Y	Y	Y	Y	N	N
18 **Schock**	Y	N	N	N	N	Y	Y
19 **Shimkus**	Y	N	N	N	N	Y	Y
INDIANA							
1 Visclosky	N	Y	Y	Y	Y	N	N
2 Donnelly	N	Y	Y	N	Y	N	Y
3 **Souder**	Y	N	N	N	N	Y	Y
4 **Buyer**	Y	N	N	N	N	Y	Y
5 **Burton**	Y	N	N	N	N	Y	Y
6 **Pence**	Y	N	N	N	N	Y	Y
7 Carson	N	Y	Y	Y	Y	N	N
8 Ellsworth	N	Y	Y	N	Y	N	Y
9 Hill	N	Y	Y	Y	Y	Y	N
IOWA							
1 Braley	N	Y	N	Y	Y	N	N
2 Loebsack	N	Y	?	Y	Y	N	N
3 Boswell	N	Y	Y	Y	Y	N	N
4 **Latham**	Y	N	N	N	N	Y	Y
5 **King**	Y	N	N	N	N	Y	Y
KANSAS							
1 **Moran**	Y	N	N	N	N	Y	Y
2 **Jenkins**	Y	N	N	N	N	N	Y
3 Moore	N	Y	Y	Y	Y	N	N
4 **Tiahrt**	Y	N	N	N	N	Y	Y
KENTUCKY							
1 **Whitfield**	Y	N	N	N	N	Y	Y
2 **Guthrie**	Y	N	N	N	N	Y	Y
3 Yarmuth	Y	Y	Y	Y	Y	N	N
4 **Davis**	Y	N	N	N	N	Y	Y
5 **Rogers**	Y	N	N	N	N	Y	Y
6 Chandler	N	Y	Y	Y	Y	N	Y
LOUISIANA							
1 **Scalise**	Y	N	N	N	N	Y	Y
2 **Cao**	Y	N	Y	N	N	N	Y
3 Melancon	N	N	Y	Y	N	N	N
4 **Fleming**	Y	N	N	N	N	Y	Y
5 **Alexander**	Y	N	N	N	N	Y	Y
6 **Cassidy**	Y	N	N	N	N	Y	Y
7 **Boustany**	Y	N	N	N	N	Y	Y
MAINE							
1 Pingree	N	Y	Y	Y	Y	N	N
2 Michaud	N	Y	Y	Y	Y	N	N
MARYLAND							
1 Kratovil	Y	Y	Y	N	N	N	N
2 Ruppersberger	Y	Y	Y	Y	Y	N	N
3 Sarbanes	N	Y	Y	Y	Y	N	N
4 Edwards	N	Y	Y	Y	Y	N	N
5 Hoyer	N	Y	Y	Y	Y	N	N
6 **Bartlett**	Y	N	N	N	N	N	Y
7 Cummings	N	Y	Y	Y	Y	N	N
8 Van Hollen	N	Y	Y	Y	Y	N	N
MASSACHUSETTS							
1 Olver	N	Y	Y	Y	Y	N	N
2 Neal	Y	N	Y	Y	Y	N	N
3 McGovern	N	Y	Y	Y	Y	N	N
4 Frank	N	Y	Y	Y	Y	N	N
5 Tsongas	N	Y	Y	Y	Y	N	N
6 Tierney	N	Y	Y	Y	Y	N	N
7 Markey	Y	Y	Y	Y	Y	N	N
8 Capuano	N	Y	Y	Y	Y	N	N
9 Lynch	N	Y	Y	Y	Y	N	N
10 Delahunt	N	Y	Y	Y	Y	N	N
MICHIGAN							
1 Stupak	N	Y	Y	Y	Y	N	N
2 **Hoekstra**	Y	N	N	N	N	Y	Y
3 **Ehlers**	Y	N	N	Y	N	N	N
4 **Camp**	Y	N	N	N	N	Y	Y
5 Kildee	N	Y	Y	Y	Y	N	N
6 **Upton**	Y	N	N	N	N	N	N
7 Schauer	N	Y	Y	Y	Y	N	N
8 **Rogers**	Y	N	N	N	N	Y	Y
9 Peters	N	Y	Y	Y	Y	N	N
10 **Miller**	Y	N	N	N	N	N	N
11 **McCotter**	Y	N	N	N	N	Y	Y
12 Levin	–	?	+	Y	Y	N	N
13 Kilpatrick	N	Y	Y	Y	Y	N	N
14 Conyers	N	Y	Y	Y	Y	N	N
15 Dingell	N	Y	Y	Y	Y	N	N
MINNESOTA							
1 Walz	N	Y	Y	Y	Y	N	N
2 **Kline**	Y	N	N	N	N	Y	Y
3 **Paulsen**	Y	N	N	N	N	Y	Y
4 McCollum	Y	Y	Y	Y	Y	N	N

	180	181	182	183	184	185	186
5 Ellison	N	Y	Y	Y	Y	N	N
6 **Bachmann**	Y	N	N	?	N	Y	Y
7 Peterson	Y	Y	Y	Y	Y	Y	N
8 Oberstar	Y	Y	Y	Y	Y	N	N
MISSISSIPPI							
1 Childers	Y	N	Y	Y	N	N	N
2 Thompson	?	?	?	Y	Y	N	N
3 **Harper**	Y	N	N	N	N	Y	Y
4 Taylor	N	Y	Y	Y	N	N	N
MISSOURI							
1 Clay	N	Y	Y	Y	Y	N	N
2 **Akin**	Y	N	N	N	N	Y	Y
3 Carnahan	N	Y	Y	Y	Y	N	N
4 Skelton	N	Y	Y	Y	Y	N	N
5 Cleaver	N	Y	Y	Y	Y	N	N
6 **Graves**	Y	N	N	N	N	Y	Y
7 **Blunt**	Y	N	N	?	N	?	?
8 **Emerson**	Y	N	N	N	N	N	Y
9 **Luetkemeyer**	Y	N	N	N	N	Y	Y
MONTANA							
AL **Rehberg**	Y	N	N	N	N	N	Y
NEBRASKA							
1 **Fortenberry**	Y	N	N	N	N	N	Y
2 **Terry**	Y	N	N	N	N	Y	Y
3 **Smith**	Y	N	N	N	N	Y	Y
NEVADA							
1 Berkley	N	Y	Y	Y	Y	N	N
2 **Heller**	Y	N	N	N	N	Y	Y
3 Titus	N	Y	Y	Y	Y	N	N
NEW HAMPSHIRE							
1 Shea-Porter	N	Y	Y	Y	Y	N	N
2 Hodes	N	Y	Y	Y	Y	N	N
NEW JERSEY							
1 Andrews	N	Y	Y	Y	Y	N	N
2 **LoBiondo**	Y	N	N	N	N	N	N
3 Adler	Y	Y	Y	N	Y	N	N
4 **Smith**	Y	N	N	N	Y	N	N
5 **Garrett**	Y	N	N	N	N	Y	Y
6 Pallone	?	?	?	Y	Y	N	N
7 **Lance**	Y	N	N	N	N	N	N
8 Pascrell	–	+	+	+	+	–	–
9 Rothman	N	Y	Y	Y	Y	N	N
10 Payne	N	Y	Y	Y	Y	N	N
11 **Frelinghuysen**	Y	N	N	N	N	N	Y
12 Holt	N	Y	Y	Y	Y	N	N
13 Sires	N	Y	Y	Y	Y	N	N
NEW MEXICO							
1 Heinrich	N	Y	Y	Y	Y	N	N
2 Teague	N	Y	Y	Y	Y	N	N
3 Lujan	N	Y	Y	Y	Y	N	N
NEW YORK							
1 Bishop	Y	Y	Y	Y	Y	N	N
2 Israel	Y	Y	Y	Y	Y	N	N
3 **King**	Y	N	N	N	N	Y	N
4 McCarthy	N	Y	Y	Y	Y	N	N
5 Ackerman	Y	Y	Y	Y	Y	N	N
6 Meeks	Y	Y	Y	Y	Y	N	N
7 Crowley	Y	Y	Y	Y	Y	N	N
8 Nadler	Y	Y	Y	Y	Y	N	N
9 Weiner	Y	Y	Y	Y	Y	N	N
10 Towns	N	Y	Y	Y	Y	N	N
11 Clarke	Y	Y	Y	Y	Y	N	N
12 Velázquez	N	Y	Y	Y	Y	N	N
13 McMahon	Y	N	Y	Y	Y	N	N
14 Maloney	Y	Y	Y	Y	Y	N	N
15 Rangel	Y	Y	Y	Y	Y	N	N
16 Serrano	N	Y	Y	Y	Y	N	N
17 Engel	Y	Y	Y	Y	Y	N	N
18 Lowey	Y	Y	Y	Y	Y	N	N
19 Hall	N	Y	Y	Y	Y	N	N
20 Vacant							
21 Tonko	N	Y	Y	Y	Y	N	N
22 Hinchey	N	Y	Y	Y	Y	N	N
23 **McHugh**	Y	N	N	N	N	N	N
24 Arcuri	N	Y	Y	Y	Y	N	N
25 Maffei	Y	Y	Y	N	Y	N	N
26 **Lee**	Y	N	N	N	N	N	Y
27 Higgins	N	Y	Y	Y	Y	N	N
28 Slaughter	N	Y	Y	Y	Y	N	N
29 Massa	Y	Y	Y	Y	Y	N	N
NORTH CAROLINA							
1 Butterfield	N	Y	Y	Y	Y	Y	N
2 Etheridge	Y	Y	Y	Y	Y	Y	Y
3 **Jones**	Y	N	Y	N	N	N	Y
4 Price	N	Y	Y	Y	Y	N	N

	180	181	182	183	184	185	186
5 **Foxx**	Y	N	N	N	N	Y	Y
6 **Coble**	Y	N	N	N	N	Y	Y
7 McIntyre	Y	Y	Y	Y	Y	Y	Y
8 Kissell	N	Y	Y	Y	Y	Y	Y
9 **Myrick**	Y	N	N	N	N	Y	Y
10 **McHenry**	Y	N	N	N	N	Y	Y
11 Shuler	Y	Y	Y	Y	?	Y	Y
12 Watt	N	Y	?	Y	Y	N	N
13 Miller	N	Y	Y	Y	Y	Y	N
NORTH DAKOTA							
AL Pomeroy	Y	Y	Y	Y	Y	N	N
OHIO							
1 Driehaus	N	Y	Y	Y	Y	N	N
2 **Schmidt**	?	?	?	N	N	Y	Y
3 **Turner**	Y	N	N	N	N	Y	Y
4 **Jordan**	Y	N	N	N	N	N	Y
5 **Latta**	Y	N	N	N	N	N	Y
6 Wilson	N	Y	Y	Y	Y	N	N
7 **Austria**	Y	N	N	N	N	Y	Y
8 **Boehner**	Y	N	N	N	N	Y	Y
9 Kaptur	N	Y	Y	Y	Y	N	?
10 Kucinich	N	Y	Y	Y	Y	N	N
11 Fudge	N	Y	Y	Y	Y	N	N
12 **Tiberi**	Y	N	N	N	N	Y	Y
13 Sutton	N	Y	Y	Y	Y	N	N
14 **LaTourette**	Y	N	N	N	N	Y	Y
15 Kilroy	N	Y	Y	Y	Y	N	N
16 Boccieri	Y	Y	Y	Y	Y	N	N
17 Ryan	N	Y	Y	Y	Y	N	N
18 Space	N	Y	Y	Y	Y	N	N
OKLAHOMA							
1 **Sullivan**	N	N	N	N	N	Y	Y
2 Boren	N	Y	Y	Y	Y	N	N
3 **Lucas**	Y	N	N	N	N	N	Y
4 **Cole**	Y	N	N	N	N	N	Y
5 **Fallin**	Y	N	N	N	N	N	Y
OREGON							
1 Wu	Y	Y	Y	Y	Y	N	N
2 **Walden**	Y	N	N	N	N	N	Y
3 Blumenauer	N	Y	Y	Y	Y	N	N
4 DeFazio	N	Y	Y	Y	Y	N	N
5 Schrader	N	Y	Y	Y	Y	N	N
PENNSYLVANIA							
1 Brady	N	Y	Y	Y	Y	N	N
2 Fattah	N	Y	Y	Y	Y	N	N
3 Dahlkemper	N	Y	Y	Y	Y	N	N
4 Altmire	Y	Y	Y	Y	Y	N	N
5 **Thompson**	Y	N	N	N	N	N	Y
6 **Gerlach**	Y	N	N	Y	N	N	Y
7 Sestak	Y	N	N	Y	Y	N	N
8 Murphy, P.	Y	Y	Y	Y	Y	N	N
9 **Shuster**	N	N	N	N	N	Y	Y
10 Carney	N	Y	Y	Y	N	N	N
11 Kanjorski	Y	Y	Y	Y	Y	N	N
12 Murtha	N	Y	Y	Y	Y	N	N
13 Schwartz	Y	Y	Y	Y	Y	N	N
14 Doyle	N	Y	Y	Y	Y	N	N
15 **Dent**	Y	N	N	Y	N	N	Y
16 **Pitts**	Y	N	N	N	N	Y	Y
17 Holden	N	Y	Y	Y	Y	N	N
18 **Murphy, T.**	Y	N	N	N	N	N	Y
19 **Platts**	Y	N	N	N	N	N	N
RHODE ISLAND							
1 Kennedy	–	+	+	Y	Y	N	N
2 Langevin	N	Y	Y	Y	Y	N	N
SOUTH CAROLINA							
1 **Brown**	Y	N	N	N	N	Y	Y
2 **Wilson**	Y	N	N	N	N	Y	Y
3 **Barrett**	Y	N	N	N	N	Y	Y
4 **Inglis**	Y	N	N	N	N	Y	Y
5 Spratt	N	Y	Y	Y	Y	Y	N
6 Clyburn	N	Y	Y	Y	Y	N	N
SOUTH DAKOTA							
AL Herseth Sandlin	N	Y	Y	Y	Y	N	N
TENNESSEE							
1 **Roe**	Y	N	N	N	N	N	Y
2 **Duncan**	Y	N	Y	N	N	Y	Y
3 **Wamp**	Y	N	N	N	N	Y	Y
4 Davis	Y	Y	Y	Y	Y	N	N
5 Cooper	Y	Y	Y	Y	Y	N	N
6 Gordon	N	Y	Y	Y	Y	N	N
7 **Blackburn**	Y	N	N	N	N	Y	Y
8 Tanner	Y	N	Y	Y	Y	Y	N
9 Cohen	Y	Y	Y	Y	Y	N	N

	180	181	182	183	184	185	186
TEXAS							
1 **Gohmert**	Y	N	N	N	N	Y	Y
2 **Poe**	Y	N	N	N	N	N	N
3 **Johnson, S.**	Y	N	N	N	N	Y	Y
4 **Hall**	Y	N	N	N	N	Y	Y
5 **Hensarling**	Y	N	N	N	N	Y	Y
6 **Barton**	?	?	?	N	N	Y	Y
7 **Culberson**	Y	N	N	N	N	Y	Y
8 **Brady**	Y	N	N	N	N	Y	Y
9 Green, A.	N	Y	Y	Y	Y	N	N
10 **McCaul**	Y	N	N	N	N	Y	Y
11 **Conaway**	Y	N	N	N	N	N	Y
12 **Granger**	Y	N	N	N	N	Y	Y
13 **Thornberry**	Y	N	N	N	N	Y	Y
14 **Paul**	Y	N	N	N	N	N	Y
15 Hinojosa	N	Y	Y	?	?	?	?
16 Reyes	N	Y	Y	Y	Y	N	N
17 Edwards	N	Y	Y	Y	Y	N	N
18 Jackson Lee	N	Y	Y	Y	Y	N	N
19 **Neugebauer**	Y	N	N	N	N	Y	Y
20 Gonzalez	N	Y	Y	Y	Y	N	N
21 **Smith**	Y	N	N	N	N	Y	Y
22 **Olson**	Y	N	N	N	N	Y	Y
23 Rodriguez	N	Y	Y	Y	Y	N	N
24 **Marchant**	Y	N	N	N	N	Y	Y
25 Doggett	N	Y	Y	Y	Y	N	N
26 **Burgess**	Y	N	N	N	N	Y	Y
27 Ortiz	N	Y	Y	Y	Y	N	N
28 Cuellar	Y	Y	Y	Y	Y	N	Y
29 Green, G.	N	Y	Y	Y	Y	N	N
30 Johnson, E.	N	Y	Y	Y	Y	N	N
31 **Carter**	N	N	N	N	N	Y	Y
32 **Sessions**	Y	N	N	N	N	Y	Y
UTAH							
1 **Bishop**	Y	N	N	N	N	Y	Y
2 Matheson	Y	Y	N	Y	Y	N	N
3 **Chaffetz**	Y	N	N	N	N	N	Y
VERMONT							
AL Welch	N	Y	Y	Y	Y	N	N
VIRGINIA							
1 **Wittman**	Y	N	N	N	N	Y	Y
2 Nye	Y	Y	Y	Y	Y	Y	Y
3 Scott	N	Y	Y	Y	Y	N	N
4 **Forbes**	Y	N	N	N	N	Y	Y
5 Perriello	N	Y	Y	Y	Y	Y	Y
6 **Goodlatte**	Y	N	N	N	N	Y	Y
7 **Cantor**	P	P	P	N	N	Y	Y
8 Moran	N	N	N	Y	Y	N	N
9 Boucher	Y	N	Y	Y	Y	N	N
10 **Wolf**	Y	N	N	N	N	N	Y
11 Connolly	N	Y	Y	Y	Y	N	N
WASHINGTON							
1 Inslee	N	Y	Y	Y	Y	N	N
2 Larsen	Y	Y	Y	Y	Y	N	N
3 Baird	N	Y	Y	Y	?	N	N
4 **Hastings**	Y	N	N	N	N	Y	Y
5 **McMorris Rodgers**	Y	N	N	N	N	Y	Y
6 Dicks	N	Y	Y	Y	Y	N	N
7 McDermott	N	Y	Y	Y	Y	N	N
8 **Reichert**	Y	N	N	Y	N	N	N
9 Smith	Y	Y	Y	Y	Y	N	N
WEST VIRGINIA							
1 Mollohan	N	Y	Y	Y	Y	N	N
2 **Capito**	Y	N	N	N	N	N	Y
3 Rahall	N	Y	Y	Y	Y	Y	N
WISCONSIN							
1 **Ryan**	Y	N	N	N	N	Y	Y
2 Baldwin	N	Y	Y	Y	Y	N	N
3 Kind	Y	Y	Y	Y	Y	N	N
4 Moore	N	Y	Y	?	?	N	N
5 **Sensenbrenner**	Y	N	N	N	N	Y	Y
6 **Petri**	Y	N	N	N	N	Y	Y
7 Obey	N	Y	Y	Y	Y	N	N
8 Kagen	N	Y	Y	Y	Y	N	N
WYOMING							
AL **Lummis**	Y	N	N	N	N	N	Y
DELEGATES							
Faleomavaega (A.S.)	N	Y					
Norton (D.C.)	N	Y					
Bordallo (Guam)	N	Y					
Sablan (N. Marianas)	N	Y					
Pierluisi (P.R.)	N	Y					
Christensen (V.I.)	N	Y					

IN THE HOUSE | By Vote Number

187. **HR 1256. Tobacco Regulation/Passage.** Passage of the bill that would authorize the Food and Drug Administration (FDA) to regulate the manufacturing, sale and promotion of tobacco products. The agency would be required to establish tobacco product standards for labeling, nicotine yields and other harmful components if it determines it is necessary to protect public health. The FDA could not ban any class of tobacco products or require the elimination of nicotine. It would impose user fees on tobacco manufacturers and importers to help pay for the regulation. Passed 298-112: R 70-104; D 228-8. A "yea" was a vote in support of the president's position. April 2, 2009.

188. **H Con Res 85. Fiscal 2010 Budget Resolution/Congressional Progressive Caucus Substitute.** Woolsey, D-Calif., substitute amendment that would cap non-defense, domestic discretionary spending at $991 billion for fiscal 2010. It would cap defense spending at $479 billion and accelerate the redeployment of soldiers and military contractors in Iraq. It would assume a repeal of the 2001 and 2003 tax cuts for the top 1 percent of households and the elimination of certain corporate tax provisions. It would call for priority funding for health care, education, veterans, poverty reduction, foreign assistance, combating global warming and renewable energy. Rejected in Committee of the Whole 84-348: R 0-176; D 84-172. April 2, 2009.

189. **H Con Res 85. Fiscal 2010 Budget Resolution/Republican Study Committee Substitute.** Jordan, R-Ohio, substitute amendment that would set total outlays at $2.59 trillion for fiscal 2010 and project a budget surplus within 10 years. It would assume an extension of the 2001 and 2003 tax cuts and provide for reconciliation legislation to cut taxes by $1.2 trillion and reduce mandatory spending by $482 billion over five years. It would call on House committees to identify savings by June 15 that amount to 1 percent of total mandatory spending under their jurisdictions from activities determined to be wasteful, unnecessary or lower priority. Rejected in Committee of the Whole 111-322: R 111-65; D 0-257. April 2, 2009.

190. **H Con Res 85. Fiscal 2010 Budget Resolution/Congressional Black Caucus Substitute.** Lee, D-Calif., substitute amendment that would set total outlays at $3.02 trillion in fiscal 2010. It would assume increased federal revenue by a repeal of the 2001 and 2003 tax cuts on the top 1 percent of U.S. households. It also would call for a 0.6 percent surtax on adjustable gross income exceeding $500,000 for individuals ($1 million for joint filers) as well as more funding than in the underlying resolution for health care, education, veterans, foreign assistance, job training, justice and transportation. Rejected in Committee of the Whole 113-318: R 0-175; D 113-143. April 2, 2009.

191. **H Con Res 85. Fiscal 2010 Budget Resolution/Republican Substitute.** Ryan, R-Wis., substitute amendment that would set total outlays at $2.73 trillion in fiscal 2010 and freeze funding levels in all areas except defense and veterans' programs. It would assume an extension of the 2001 and 2003 tax cuts for the top 1 percent of U.S. households, provide for reconciliation legislation to reduce mandatory spending by $1.38 trillion over 10 years and place a moratorium on earmarks for the year. Rejected in Committee of the Whole 137-293: R 137-38; D 0-255. April 2, 2009.

192. **H Con Res 85. Fiscal 2010 Budget Resolution/Adoption.** Adoption of the concurrent resolution that would allow up to $1.09 trillion in non-emergency discretionary spending for fiscal 2010, plus $130 billion in fiscal 2010 for operations in Iraq and Afghanistan. It would create 17 reserve funds, each with a specific purpose to allow for increases in spending or changes in tax policy, provided the increase is offset. It would call on the Energy and Commerce, Ways and Means, and Education and Labor committees to report reconciliation bills that would reduce the deficit by $1 billion in fiscal 2009-14 and provide for health care and education investments. It would assume a reduction of the deficit to $598 billion by fiscal 2014. Adopted 233-196: R 0-176; D 233-20. April 2, 2009.

	187	188	189	190	191	192
ALABAMA						
1 Bonner	N	N	Y	N	Y	N
2 Bright	N	N	N	N	N	N
3 Rogers	Y	N	N	N	N	N
4 Aderholt	N	N	N	Y	N	N
5 Griffith	Y	N	N	N	N	N
6 Bachus	N	N	Y	N	Y	N
7 Davis	Y	N	N	P	N	Y
ALASKA						
AL Young	Y	N	Y	N	Y	N
ARIZONA						
1 Kirkpatrick	N	N	N	N	N	Y
2 Franks	N	N	Y	N	?	N
3 Shadegg	N	N	Y	N	Y	N
4 Pastor	Y	Y	N	Y	N	Y
5 Mitchell	Y	N	N	N	N	Y
6 Flake	N	N	Y	N	Y	N
7 Grijalva	+	Y	N	Y	N	Y
8 Giffords	Y	N	N	N	N	Y
ARKANSAS						
1 Berry	Y	N	N	N	N	Y
2 Snyder	Y	N	N	N	N	Y
3 Boozman	N	N	Y	N	Y	N
4 Ross	Y	N	N	N	N	Y
CALIFORNIA						
1 Thompson	Y	N	N	N	N	Y
2 Herger	N	N	Y	N	Y	N
3 Lungren	N	N	Y	N	Y	N
4 McClintock	N	N	Y	N	Y	N
5 Matsui	Y	N	N	Y	N	Y
6 Woolsey	Y	Y	N	Y	N	Y
7 Miller, George	Y	Y	N	Y	N	Y
8 Pelosi		?				Y
9 Lee	Y	Y	N	Y	N	Y
10 Tauscher	Y	N	N	N	N	Y
11 McNerney	Y	N	N	N	N	Y
12 Speier	Y	N	N	Y	N	Y
13 Stark	Y	Y	N	Y	N	Y
14 Eshoo	Y	N	N	N	N	Y
15 Honda	Y	Y	N	Y	N	Y
16 Lofgren	Y	N	N	Y	N	Y
17 Farr	Y	Y	N	Y	N	Y
18 Cardoza	?	N	N	N	N	Y
19 Radanovich	N	N	Y	N	Y	N
20 Costa	N	N	N	N	?	Y
21 Nunes	N	N	N	N	Y	N
22 McCarthy	N	N	Y	N	Y	N
23 Capps	Y	N	N	Y	N	Y
24 Gallegly	Y	N	Y	N	Y	N
25 McKeon	Y	N	N	Y	N	N
26 Dreier	Y	N	N	N	Y	N
27 Sherman	Y	N	N	Y	N	Y
28 Berman	Y	N	N	Y	N	Y
29 Schiff	Y	N	N	N	N	Y
30 Waxman	Y	Y	N	Y	N	Y
31 Becerra	+	Y	N	Y	N	Y
32 Vacant						
33 Watson	Y	Y	N	Y	N	Y
34 Roybal-Allard	+	Y	N	Y	N	Y
35 Waters	Y	Y	N	Y	N	Y
36 Harman	Y	N	N	N	N	Y
37 Richardson	Y	Y	N	Y	N	Y
38 Napolitano	+	Y	N	Y	N	Y
39 Sánchez, Linda	Y	Y	N	Y	N	Y
40 Royce	N	N	Y	N	Y	N
41 Lewis	Y	N	N	N	Y	N
42 Miller, Gary	?	?	?	?	?	?
43 Baca	Y	N	N	N	N	Y
44 Calvert	N	N	N	N	Y	N
45 Bono Mack	Y	N	N	N	Y	N
46 Rohrabacher	N	N	Y	N	Y	N
47 Sanchez, Loretta	Y	N	N	N	N	Y
48 Campbell	N	N	Y	N	Y	N
49 Issa	N	N	Y	N	Y	N
50 Bilbray	Y	N	N	N	Y	N
51 Filner	Y	Y	N	Y	N	Y
52 Hunter	N	N	N	N	Y	N
53 Davis	Y	N	N	N	N	Y

	187	188	189	190	191	192
COLORADO						
1 DeGette	Y	N	N	N	N	Y
2 Polis	Y	Y	N	N	N	Y
3 Salazar	+	N	N	N	N	Y
4 Markey	Y	N	N	N	N	N
5 Lamborn	N	N	Y	N	Y	N
6 Coffman	N	N	Y	N	Y	N
7 Perlmutter	Y	N	N	N	N	Y
CONNECTICUT						
1 Larson	+	N	N	Y	N	Y
2 Courtney	Y	N	N	N	N	Y
3 DeLauro	Y	N	N	Y	N	Y
4 Himes	Y	N	N	N	N	Y
5 Murphy	Y	N	N	N	N	Y
DELAWARE						
AL Castle	Y	N	N	N	N	N
FLORIDA						
1 Miller	N	N	Y	N	Y	N
2 Boyd	Y	N	N	N	N	Y
3 Brown	Y	N	N	Y	N	Y
4 Crenshaw	N	N	N	N	Y	N
5 Brown-Waite	Y	N	N	N	N	N
6 Stearns	N	N	Y	N	Y	N
7 Mica	N	N	Y	N	Y	N
8 Grayson	Y	N	N	N	N	Y
9 Bilirakis	Y	N	Y	N	Y	N
10 Young	Y	N	Y	N	Y	N
11 Castor	Y	N	N	Y	N	Y
12 Putnam	Y	N	N	N	Y	N
13 Buchanan	Y	N	N	N	N	N
14 Mack	N	N	N	N	Y	N
15 Posey	N	N	Y	N	Y	N
16 Rooney	N	N	N	N	Y	N
17 Meek	Y	N	N	Y	N	Y
18 Ros-Lehtinen	Y	N	N	N	N	N
19 Wexler	Y	Y	N	Y	N	Y
20 Wasserman Schultz	Y	N	N	N	N	Y
21 Diaz-Balart, L.	N	N	N	N	N	N
22 Klein	Y	N	N	N	N	Y
23 Hastings	Y	Y	N	Y	N	Y
24 Kosmas	Y	N	N	N	N	Y
25 Diaz-Balart, M.	N	N	N	N	N	N
GEORGIA						
1 Kingston	N	N	Y	N	Y	N
2 Bishop	+	N	N	Y	N	Y
3 Westmoreland	?	?	?	?	?	?
4 Johnson	Y	Y	N	Y	N	Y
5 Lewis	Y	?	N	Y	N	Y
6 Price	N	N	Y	N	Y	N
7 Linder	N	N	Y	N	Y	N
8 Marshall	Y	N	N	N	N	Y
9 Deal	N	N	Y	N	Y	N
10 Broun	?	N	Y	N	Y	N
11 Gingrey	N	N	Y	N	Y	N
12 Barrow	Y	N	N	N	N	Y
13 Scott	Y	N	N	Y	N	Y
HAWAII						
1 Abercrombie	Y	Y	N	Y	N	Y
2 Hirono	Y	Y	N	Y	N	Y
IDAHO						
1 Minnick	Y	N	N	N	N	N
2 Simpson	Y	N	Y	N	Y	N
ILLINOIS						
1 Rush	Y	N	Y	N	Y	N
2 Jackson	Y	Y	N	Y	N	Y
3 Lipinski	Y	N	N	N	N	Y
4 Gutierrez	+	Y	N	Y	N	Y
5 Vacant						
6 Roskam	Y	N	Y	N	Y	N
7 Davis	Y	Y	N	Y	N	Y
8 Bean	Y	N	N	N	N	Y
9 Schakowsky	Y	Y	N	Y	N	Y
10 Kirk	Y	N	N	N	N	N
11 Halvorson	Y	N	N	N	N	Y
12 Costello	Y	N	N	N	N	Y
13 Biggert	Y	N	N	N	N	N
14 Foster	Y	N	N	N	N	Y
15 Johnson	Y	N	N	N	N	Y

KEY   **Republicans**   Democrats

Y Voted for (yea)	X Paired against	C Voted "present" to avoid possible conflict of interest
# Paired for	– Announced against	
+ Announced for	P Voted "present"	? Did not vote or otherwise make a position known
N Voted against (nay)		

	187	188	189	190	191	192
16 **Manzullo**	Y	N	Y	N	Y	N
17 Hare	Y	Y	N	Y	N	Y
18 **Schock**	Y	N	N	N	Y	N
19 **Shimkus**	Y	N	Y	N	Y	N
INDIANA						
1 Visclosky	Y	N	N	N	N	Y
2 Donnelly	Y	N	N	N	N	N
3 **Souder**	N	N	N	N	N	N
4 **Buyer**	N	N	N	?	Y	N
5 **Burton**	N	N	Y	N	Y	N
6 **Pence**	N	N	Y	N	Y	N
7 Carson	Y	Y	N	Y	N	Y
8 Ellsworth	Y	N	N	N	N	Y
9 Hill	Y	N	N	N	N	Y
IOWA						
1 Braley	Y	N	N	Y	N	Y
2 Loebsack	Y	N	N	Y	N	Y
3 Boswell	Y	N	N	N	N	Y
4 **Latham**	N	N	N	N	N	N
5 **King**	N	N	Y	N	Y	N
KANSAS						
1 **Moran**	N	N	Y	N	Y	N
2 **Jenkins**	N	N	N	N	N	N
3 Moore	Y	N	N	N	N	Y
4 **Tiahrt**	N	N	Y	N	Y	N
KENTUCKY						
1 **Whitfield**	N	N	Y	N	Y	N
2 **Guthrie**	N	N	N	N	Y	N
3 Yarmuth	Y	N	N	N	N	Y
4 **Davis**	N	N	N	N	Y	N
5 **Rogers**	N	N	N	N	Y	N
6 Chandler	Y	N	N	N	N	Y
LOUISIANA						
1 **Scalise**	N	N	Y	N	Y	N
2 **Cao**	Y	N	N	N	N	N
3 Melancon	Y	N	N	N	N	Y
4 **Fleming**	Y	N	Y	N	Y	N
5 **Alexander**	N	N	Y	N	Y	N
6 **Cassidy**	Y	N	Y	N	Y	N
7 **Boustany**	N	N	Y	N	Y	N
MAINE						
1 Pingree	Y	Y	N	Y	N	Y
2 Michaud	Y	N	N	N	N	Y
MARYLAND						
1 Kratovil	Y	N	N	N	N	N
2 Ruppersberger	Y	N	N	N	N	Y
3 Sarbanes	Y	N	N	Y	N	Y
4 Edwards	Y	Y	N	Y	N	Y
5 Hoyer	Y	N	N	Y	N	Y
6 **Bartlett**	Y	N	Y	N	Y	N
7 Cummings	Y	Y	N	Y	N	Y
8 Van Hollen	Y	N	N	Y	N	Y
MASSACHUSETTS						
1 Olver	Y	Y	N	Y	N	Y
2 Neal	Y	N	N	N	N	Y
3 McGovern	Y	Y	N	Y	N	Y
4 Frank	Y	Y	N	Y	N	Y
5 Tsongas	Y	N	N	N	N	Y
6 Tierney	Y	Y	N	N	N	Y
7 Markey	Y	Y	N	Y	N	Y
8 Capuano	Y	Y	N	Y	N	Y
9 Lynch	Y	N	N	Y	N	Y
10 Delahunt	Y	N	N	Y	N	Y
MICHIGAN						
1 Stupak	Y	N	N	N	N	Y
2 **Hoekstra**	N	N	Y	N	Y	N
3 **Ehlers**	Y	N	N	N	Y	N
4 **Camp**	Y	N	N	N	Y	N
5 Kildee	Y	N	N	N	N	Y
6 **Upton**	Y	N	N	N	N	N
7 Schauer	Y	N	N	N	N	Y
8 **Rogers**	N	N	Y	N	Y	N
9 Peters	Y	N	N	N	N	Y
10 **Miller**	Y	N	N	N	N	N
11 **McCotter**	N	N	N	N	N	N
12 Levin	+	N	N	N	N	Y
13 Kilpatrick	Y	N	N	Y	N	Y
14 Conyers	Y	Y	N	Y	N	Y
15 Dingell	Y	N	N	N	N	Y
MINNESOTA						
1 Walz	Y	N	N	N	N	Y
2 **Kline**	N	N	Y	N	Y	N
3 **Paulsen**	Y	N	N	N	Y	N
4 McCollum	Y	Y	N	Y	N	Y

	187	188	189	190	191	192
5 Ellison	Y	Y	N	Y	N	Y
6 **Bachmann**	N	N	Y	N	Y	N
7 Peterson	N	N	N	N	N	Y
8 Oberstar	Y	Y	N	Y	N	Y
MISSISSIPPI						
1 Childers	Y	N	N	N	N	N
2 Thompson	Y	Y	N	Y	N	Y
3 **Harper**	Y	N	Y	N	Y	N
4 Taylor	Y	N	N	N	N	N
MISSOURI						
1 Clay	Y	Y	N	Y	N	Y
2 **Akin**	N	N	Y	N	Y	N
3 Carnahan	Y	N	N	N	N	Y
4 Skelton	Y	N	N	N	N	Y
5 Cleaver	Y	Y	N	Y	N	Y
6 **Graves**	N	N	Y	N	Y	N
7 **Blunt**	?	N	Y	N	Y	N
8 **Emerson**	Y	N	N	N	N	N
9 **Luetkemeyer**	N	N	Y	N	Y	N
MONTANA						
AL **Rehberg**	Y	N	Y	N	Y	N
NEBRASKA						
1 **Fortenberry**	Y	N	N	N	Y	N
2 **Terry**	Y	N	N	N	Y	N
3 **Smith**	N	N	Y	N	Y	N
NEVADA						
1 Berkley	Y	N	N	N	N	Y
2 **Heller**	N	N	N	N	N	N
3 Titus	Y	N	N	N	N	Y
NEW HAMPSHIRE						
1 Shea-Porter	Y	N	N	N	N	Y
2 Hodes	Y	N	N	N	N	Y
NEW JERSEY						
1 Andrews	Y	N	N	Y	N	Y
2 **LoBiondo**	Y	N	N	N	N	N
3 Adler	Y	N	N	N	N	Y
4 **Smith**	Y	N	N	N	N	N
5 **Garrett**	N	N	Y	N	Y	N
6 Pallone	Y	Y	N	Y	N	Y
7 **Lance**	Y	N	N	N	N	N
8 Pascrell	?	N	N	Y	N	Y
9 Rothman	Y	N	N	Y	N	Y
10 Payne	Y	Y	N	Y	N	Y
11 **Frelinghuysen**	Y	N	N	N	Y	N
12 Holt	Y	Y	N	Y	N	Y
13 Sires	Y	N	N	N	N	Y
NEW MEXICO						
1 Heinrich	Y	N	N	N	N	Y
2 Teague	Y	N	N	N	N	N
3 Lujan	+	N	N	N	N	Y
NEW YORK						
1 Bishop	Y	N	N	N	N	Y
2 Israel	Y	N	N	N	N	Y
3 **King**	Y	N	N	N	N	N
4 McCarthy	Y	N	N	N	N	Y
5 Ackerman	Y	N	N	N	N	Y
6 Meeks	Y	N	N	Y	N	Y
7 Crowley	Y	N	N	Y	N	Y
8 Nadler	Y	Y	N	Y	N	Y
9 Weiner	Y	N	N	Y	N	Y
10 Towns	Y	Y	N	Y	N	Y
11 Clarke	Y	Y	N	Y	N	Y
12 Velázquez	+	Y	N	Y	N	Y
13 McMahon	Y	N	N	N	N	Y
14 Maloney	Y	N	N	Y	N	Y
15 Rangel	Y	Y	N	Y	N	Y
16 Serrano	Y	Y	N	Y	N	Y
17 Engel	Y	Y	N	Y	N	Y
18 Lowey	Y	N	N	Y	N	Y
19 Hall	Y	N	N	N	N	Y
20 Vacant						
21 Tonko	Y	N	N	N	N	Y
22 Hinchey	Y	Y	N	Y	N	Y
23 **McHugh**	Y	N	N	N	N	N
24 Arcuri	Y	N	N	N	N	Y
25 Maffei	Y	N	N	N	N	Y
26 **Lee**	Y	N	N	N	N	N
27 Higgins	Y	N	N	N	N	Y
28 Slaughter	Y	Y	N	Y	N	Y
29 Massa	Y	N	N	N	N	Y
NORTH CAROLINA						
1 Butterfield	Y	N	N	Y	N	Y
2 Etheridge	Y	N	N	N	N	Y
3 **Jones**	N	N	Y	N	Y	N
4 Price	Y	N	N	Y	N	Y

	187	188	189	190	191	192
5 **Foxx**	N	N	Y	N	Y	N
6 **Coble**	N	N	Y	N	Y	N
7 McIntyre	N	N	N	N	N	N
8 Kissell	N	N	N	N	N	Y
9 **Myrick**	N	N	Y	N	Y	N
10 **McHenry**	N	N	Y	N	Y	N
11 Shuler	N	N	N	N	N	Y
12 Watt	Y	Y	N	Y	N	Y
13 Miller	Y	N	N	N	N	Y
NORTH DAKOTA						
AL Pomeroy	Y	N	N	N	N	Y
OHIO						
1 Driehaus	Y	N	N	N	N	Y
2 **Schmidt**	N	N	Y	N	Y	N
3 **Turner**	Y	N	N	N	Y	N
4 **Jordan**	N	N	Y	N	Y	N
5 **Latta**	N	N	Y	N	Y	N
6 Wilson	Y	N	N	N	N	Y
7 **Austria**	Y	N	N	N	Y	N
8 **Boehner**	N	N	N	N	Y	N
9 Kaptur	Y	N	N	N	N	Y
10 Kucinich	Y	Y	N	N	N	N
11 Fudge	Y	Y	N	Y	N	Y
12 **Tiberi**	Y	N	N	N	Y	N
13 Sutton	Y	N	N	Y	N	Y
14 **LaTourette**	Y	N	N	N	N	N
15 Kilroy	Y	N	N	N	N	Y
16 Boccieri	Y	N	N	N	N	Y
17 Ryan	Y	N	N	N	N	Y
18 Space	Y	N	N	N	N	Y
OKLAHOMA						
1 **Sullivan**	N	N	Y	N	Y	N
2 Boren	Y	N	N	N	N	N
3 **Lucas**	N	N	N	N	Y	N
4 **Cole**	N	N	Y	N	Y	N
5 **Fallin**	Y	N	Y	N	Y	N
OREGON						
1 Wu	+	Y	N	Y	N	Y
2 **Walden**	Y	N	N	N	N	N
3 Blumenauer	Y	Y	N	Y	N	Y
4 DeFazio	Y	Y	N	Y	N	Y
5 Schrader	Y	N	N	N	N	Y
PENNSYLVANIA						
1 Brady	Y	Y	N	Y	N	Y
2 Fattah	Y	Y	N	Y	N	Y
3 Dahlkemper	Y	N	N	N	N	Y
4 Altmire	Y	N	N	N	N	Y
5 **Thompson**	N	N	Y	N	Y	N
6 **Gerlach**	Y	N	N	N	N	N
7 Sestak	Y	N	N	N	N	Y
8 Murphy, P.	Y	N	N	N	N	Y
9 **Shuster**	N	N	N	N	Y	N
10 Carney	?	N	N	N	N	Y
11 Kanjorski	Y	N	N	N	N	Y
12 Murtha	Y	N	N	N	N	Y
13 Schwartz	Y	N	N	N	N	Y
14 Doyle	Y	Y	N	Y	N	Y
15 **Dent**	Y	N	N	N	Y	N
16 **Pitts**	N	N	Y	N	Y	N
17 Holden	Y	N	N	N	N	Y
18 **Murphy, T.**	Y	N	N	N	N	N
19 **Platts**	Y	N	N	N	N	N
RHODE ISLAND						
1 Kennedy	Y	N	N	Y	N	Y
2 Langevin	Y	N	N	N	N	Y
SOUTH CAROLINA						
1 **Brown**	Y	N	Y	N	Y	N
2 **Wilson**	N	N	Y	N	Y	N
3 **Barrett**	N	N	Y	N	Y	N
4 **Inglis**	N	N	Y	N	Y	N
5 Spratt	Y	N	N	N	N	Y
6 Clyburn	Y	Y	N	Y	N	Y
SOUTH DAKOTA						
AL Herseth Sandlin	Y	N	N	N	N	Y
TENNESSEE						
1 **Roe**	N	N	Y	N	Y	N
2 **Duncan**	Y	N	N	N	N	N
3 **Wamp**	Y	N	Y	N	Y	N
4 Davis	N	N	N	N	N	Y
5 Cooper	Y	N	N	N	N	Y
6 Gordon	Y	N	N	N	N	Y
7 **Blackburn**	N	N	Y	N	Y	N
8 Tanner	Y	N	N	N	N	Y
9 Cohen	Y	Y	N	Y	N	Y

	187	188	189	190	191	192
TEXAS						
1 **Gohmert**	N	N	Y	N	Y	N
2 **Poe**	N	N	Y	N	Y	N
3 **Johnson, S.**	N	N	Y	N	Y	N
4 **Hall**	Y	N	Y	N	Y	N
5 **Hensarling**	N	N	Y	N	Y	N
6 **Barton**	N	N	Y	N	N	N
7 **Culberson**	N	N	Y	N	Y	N
8 **Brady**	Y	N	Y	N	Y	N
9 Green, A.	Y	N	N	Y	N	Y
10 **McCaul**	Y	N	Y	N	Y	N
11 **Conaway**	N	N	Y	N	Y	N
12 **Granger**	N	N	N	N	Y	N
13 **Thornberry**	N	N	Y	N	Y	N
14 **Paul**	N	N	Y	N	N	N
15 Hinojosa	?	?	?	?	?	?
16 Reyes	Y	N	N	N	N	Y
17 Edwards	Y	N	N	N	N	Y
18 Jackson Lee	Y	Y	N	Y	N	Y
19 **Neugebauer**	N	N	Y	N	Y	N
20 Gonzalez	?	N	N	N	N	Y
21 **Smith**	Y	N	Y	N	Y	N
22 **Olson**	N	N	Y	N	Y	N
23 Rodriguez	Y	Y	N	N	N	Y
24 **Marchant**	N	N	Y	N	Y	N
25 Doggett	Y	N	N	N	N	Y
26 **Burgess**	N	N	Y	N	N	N
27 Ortiz	Y	N	N	N	N	Y
28 Cuellar	Y	N	N	N	N	Y
29 Green, G.	Y	N	N	Y	N	Y
30 Johnson, E.	Y	Y	N	Y	N	Y
31 **Carter**	N	N	Y	N	Y	N
32 **Sessions**	N	N	Y	N	Y	N
UTAH						
1 **Bishop**	N	N	Y	N	Y	N
2 Matheson	Y	N	N	N	N	N
3 **Chaffetz**	N	N	Y	N	Y	N
VERMONT						
AL Welch	Y	Y	N	Y	N	Y
VIRGINIA						
1 **Wittman**	Y	N	N	N	Y	N
2 Nye	Y	N	N	N	N	N
3 Scott	Y	N	N	Y	N	Y
4 **Forbes**	N	N	N	N	Y	N
5 Perriello	N	N	N	N	N	N
6 **Goodlatte**	N	N	Y	N	Y	N
7 **Cantor**	Y	N	Y	N	Y	N
8 Moran	Y	Y	N	Y	N	Y
9 Boucher	Y	N	N	N	N	Y
10 **Wolf**	Y	N	N	N	Y	N
11 Connolly	Y	N	N	N	N	Y
WASHINGTON						
1 Inslee	Y	N	N	N	N	Y
2 Larsen	Y	N	N	N	N	Y
3 Baird	Y	N	N	N	N	Y
4 **Hastings**	Y	N	Y	N	Y	N
5 **McMorris Rodgers**	Y	N	Y	N	Y	N
6 Dicks	Y	N	N	N	N	Y
7 McDermott	Y	Y	N	Y	N	Y
8 **Reichert**	Y	N	N	N	N	N
9 Smith	Y	N	N	N	N	Y
WEST VIRGINIA						
1 Mollohan	Y	N	N	N	N	Y
2 **Capito**	Y	N	N	N	N	N
3 Rahall	Y	Y	N	N	N	Y
WISCONSIN						
1 **Ryan**	N	N	N	N	Y	N
2 Baldwin	Y	Y	N	Y	N	Y
3 Kind	Y	N	N	N	N	Y
4 Moore	Y	Y	N	Y	N	Y
5 **Sensenbrenner**	N	N	Y	N	Y	N
6 **Petri**	N	N	Y	N	Y	N
7 Obey	Y	Y	N	Y	N	Y
8 Kagen	Y	N	N	N	N	Y
WYOMING						
AL **Lummis**	N	N	Y	N	Y	N
DELEGATES						
Faleomavaega (A.S.)		Y	N	Y	N	
Norton (D.C.)		Y	N	Y	–	
Bordallo (Guam)		N	N	Y	N	
Sablan (N. Marianas)		?	?	?	?	
Pierluisi (P.R.)		N	N	N	N	
Christensen (V.I.)		Y	N	Y	N	

IN THE HOUSE | By Vote Number

193. **HR 388. Crane Conservation/Passage.** Christensen, D-V.I., motion to suspend the rules and pass the bill that would establish a grant program to protect crane populations and authorize $5 million annually in fiscal 2010-14 for the program. Motion agreed to 288-116: R 52-115; D 236-1. A two-thirds majority of those present and voting (270 in this case) is required for passage under suspension of the rules. April 21, 2009.

194. **HR 411. Rare Cat and Dog Conservation Programs/Passage.** Christensen, D-V.I., motion to suspend the rules and pass the bill that would authorize $5 million annually in fiscal 2010-14 for a grant program for international rare cat and dog conservation. Motion agreed to 290-118: R 52-117; D 238-1. A two-thirds majority of those present and voting (272 in this case) is required for passage under suspension of the rules. April 21, 2009.

195. **HR 1219. Lake Hodges Water Projects/Passage.** Christensen, D-V.I., motion to suspend the rules and pass the bill that would allow the Interior Department to work with the Olivenhain Municipal Water District on projects to improve surface water from Lake Hodges in San Diego County, Calif. Motion agreed to 362-43: R 124-43; D 238-0. A two-thirds majority of those present and voting (270 in this case) is required for passage under suspension of the rules. April 21, 2009.

196. **HR 1679. House Reservists Pay Adjustment/Passage.** Brady, D-Pa., motion to suspend the rules and pass the bill that would require the House of Representatives to provide supplemental income to House employees involuntarily called to active duty as armed forces reservists by paying the difference between employees' military compensation and House salaries. Individuals would have to be House employees for at least 90 days before military activation to receive the supplemental pay. Motion agreed to 423-0: R 173-0; D 250-0. A two-thirds majority of those present and voting (282 in this case) is required for passage under suspension of the rules. April 22, 2009.

197. **HR 586. Civil Rights History Project/Passage.** Brady, D-Pa., motion to suspend the rules and pass the bill that would authorize $500,000 in fiscal 2010 and further sums in fiscal 2011-14 for the Library of Congress and the Smithsonian Institution to gather testimonials of participants in the civil rights movement. Motion agreed to 422-0: R 172-0; D 250-0. A two-thirds majority of those present and voting (282 in this case) is required for passage under suspension of the rules. April 22, 2009.

	193	194	195	196	197
ALABAMA					
1 Bonner	N	N	Y	Y	Y
2 Bright	N	N	Y	Y	Y
3 Rogers	N	N	Y	Y	Y
4 Aderholt	N	N	Y	Y	Y
5 Griffith	Y	Y	Y	Y	Y
6 Bachus	?	?	?	Y	Y
7 Davis	Y	Y	Y	Y	Y
ALASKA					
AL Young	N	N	Y	Y	Y
ARIZONA					
1 Kirkpatrick	Y	Y	Y	Y	Y
2 Franks	N	N	N	Y	Y
3 Shadegg	N	N	N	Y	Y
4 Pastor	Y	Y	Y	Y	Y
5 Mitchell	Y	Y	Y	Y	Y
6 Flake	N	N	N	Y	Y
7 Grijalva	Y	Y	Y	Y	Y
8 Giffords	Y	Y	Y	Y	Y
ARKANSAS					
1 Berry	Y	Y	Y	Y	Y
2 Snyder	Y	Y	Y	Y	Y
3 Boozman	N	N	Y	Y	Y
4 Ross	Y	Y	Y	Y	Y
CALIFORNIA					
1 Thompson	Y	Y	Y	Y	Y
2 Herger	N	N	Y	Y	Y
3 Lungren	?	?	?	?	?
4 McClintock	N	N	N	Y	Y
5 Matsui	Y	Y	Y	Y	Y
6 Woolsey	Y	Y	Y	Y	Y
7 Miller, George	Y	Y	Y	Y	Y
8 Pelosi					
9 Lee	Y	Y	Y	Y	Y
10 Tauscher	Y	Y	Y	Y	Y
11 McNerney	Y	Y	?	Y	Y
12 Speier	Y	Y	Y	Y	Y
13 Stark	Y	Y	Y	Y	Y
14 Eshoo	Y	Y	Y	Y	Y
15 Honda	Y	Y	Y	Y	Y
16 Lofgren	Y	Y	Y	Y	Y
17 Farr	Y	Y	Y	Y	Y
18 Cardoza	Y	Y	Y	Y	Y
19 Radanovich	?	?	?	Y	Y
20 Costa	Y	Y	Y	Y	Y
21 Nunes	N	Y	Y	Y	Y
22 McCarthy	N	N	Y	Y	Y
23 Capps	Y	Y	Y	Y	Y
24 Gallegly	Y	Y	Y	Y	Y
25 McKeon	N	Y	Y	Y	Y
26 Dreier	N	N	Y	Y	Y
27 Sherman	Y	Y	Y	Y	Y
28 Berman	Y	Y	Y	Y	Y
29 Schiff	Y	Y	Y	Y	Y
30 Waxman	Y	Y	Y	Y	Y
31 Becerra	Y	Y	Y	Y	Y
32 Vacant					
33 Watson	Y	Y	Y	Y	Y
34 Roybal-Allard	Y	Y	Y	Y	Y
35 Waters	Y	Y	Y	Y	Y
36 Harman	Y	Y	Y	Y	Y
37 Richardson	Y	Y	Y	Y	Y
38 Napolitano	Y	Y	Y	Y	Y
39 Sánchez, Linda	Y	Y	Y	Y	Y
40 Royce	N	Y	Y	Y	Y
41 Lewis	N	N	Y	Y	Y
42 Miller, Gary	N	N	Y	Y	Y
43 Baca	Y	Y	Y	Y	Y
44 Calvert	N	N	Y	Y	Y
45 Bono Mack	Y	Y	Y	Y	Y
46 Rohrabacher	N	N	Y	Y	Y
47 Sanchez, Loretta	Y	Y	Y	Y	Y
48 Campbell	?	?	?	?	?
49 Issa	N	N	?	Y	Y
50 Bilbray	N	Y	Y	Y	Y
51 Filner	Y	Y	Y	Y	Y
52 Hunter	N	N	Y	Y	Y
53 Davis	Y	Y	Y	Y	Y

	193	194	195	196	197
COLORADO					
1 DeGette	Y	Y	Y	Y	Y
2 Polis	Y	Y	Y	Y	Y
3 Salazar	Y	Y	Y	Y	Y
4 Markey	Y	Y	Y	Y	Y
5 Lamborn	N	N	N	Y	Y
6 Coffman	N	N	Y	Y	Y
7 Perlmutter	Y	Y	Y	Y	Y
CONNECTICUT					
1 Larson	Y	Y	Y	Y	Y
2 Courtney	Y	Y	Y	Y	Y
3 DeLauro	Y	Y	Y	Y	Y
4 Himes	Y	Y	Y	Y	Y
5 Murphy	Y	Y	Y	Y	Y
DELAWARE					
AL Castle	Y	Y	Y	Y	Y
FLORIDA					
1 Miller	N	N	N	Y	Y
2 Boyd	Y	Y	Y	Y	Y
3 Brown	?	?	?	Y	Y
4 Crenshaw	?	?	?	Y	Y
5 Brown-Waite	Y	N	Y	Y	Y
6 Stearns	N	N	N	Y	Y
7 Mica	N	Y	Y	Y	Y
8 Grayson	Y	Y	Y	Y	Y
9 Bilirakis	Y	Y	Y	Y	Y
10 Young	Y	Y	Y	Y	Y
11 Castor	Y	Y	Y	Y	Y
12 Putnam	Y	N	Y	Y	Y
13 Buchanan	Y	Y	Y	Y	Y
14 Mack	N	Y	Y	Y	Y
15 Posey	Y	N	Y	Y	Y
16 Rooney	N	N	Y	Y	Y
17 Meek	Y	Y	Y	Y	Y
18 Ros-Lehtinen	Y	Y	Y	Y	Y
19 Wexler	Y	Y	Y	Y	Y
20 Wasserman Schultz	Y	Y	Y	Y	Y
21 Diaz-Balart, L.	Y	Y	Y	Y	Y
22 Klein	Y	Y	Y	Y	Y
23 Hastings	Y	Y	Y	Y	Y
24 Kosmas	Y	Y	Y	Y	Y
25 Diaz-Balart, M.	Y	Y	Y	Y	Y
GEORGIA					
1 Kingston	N	N	N	?	?
2 Bishop	Y	Y	Y	Y	Y
3 Westmoreland	N	N	N	Y	Y
4 Johnson	Y	Y	Y	Y	Y
5 Lewis	Y	Y	Y	Y	Y
6 Price	N	N	Y	Y	Y
7 Linder	N	N	N	Y	Y
8 Marshall	Y	Y	Y	Y	Y
9 Deal	N	N	Y	Y	Y
10 Broun	?	?	?	Y	Y
11 Gingrey	N	N	N	?	?
12 Barrow	Y	Y	Y	Y	Y
13 Scott	Y	Y	Y	Y	Y
HAWAII					
1 Abercrombie	Y	Y	Y	Y	Y
2 Hirono	Y	Y	Y	Y	Y
IDAHO					
1 Minnick	Y	Y	Y	Y	Y
2 Simpson	Y	N	Y	Y	Y
ILLINOIS					
1 Rush	Y	Y	Y	Y	Y
2 Jackson	?	?	?	?	?
3 Lipinski	Y	Y	Y	Y	Y
4 Gutierrez	Y	Y	Y	Y	Y
5 Quigley*		Y	Y	Y	Y
6 Roskam	Y	Y	Y	Y	Y
7 Davis	Y	Y	Y	Y	Y
8 Bean	Y	Y	Y	Y	Y
9 Schakowsky	Y	Y	Y	Y	Y
10 Kirk	Y	Y	Y	Y	Y
11 Halvorson	Y	Y	Y	Y	Y
12 Costello	Y	Y	Y	Y	Y
13 Biggert	Y	Y	Y	Y	Y
14 Foster	Y	Y	Y	Y	Y
15 Johnson	Y	Y	Y	Y	Y

*Rep. Mike Quigley, D-Ill., was sworn in April 21, 2009, to fill the seat vacated by fellow Democrat Rahm Emanuel, who resigned Jan. 2, 2009, to become President Obama's chief of staff. The first vote for which Quigley was eligible was vote 194.

	193	194	195	196	197
16 Manzullo	N	N	Y	Y	Y
17 Hare	Y	Y	Y	Y	Y
18 Schock	Y	Y	Y	Y	Y
19 Shimkus	N	N	Y	Y	Y
INDIANA					
1 Visclosky	Y	Y	Y	Y	Y
2 Donnelly	Y	Y	Y	Y	Y
3 Souder	N	N	N	Y	Y
4 Buyer	N	N	N	Y	Y
5 Burton	N	N	N	Y	Y
6 Pence	N	N	N	Y	Y
7 Carson	Y	Y	Y	Y	Y
8 Ellsworth	Y	Y	Y	Y	Y
9 Hill	Y	Y	Y	Y	Y
IOWA					
1 Braley	Y	Y	Y	Y	Y
2 Loebsack	Y	Y	Y	Y	Y
3 Boswell	+	+	+	+	+
4 Latham	N	N	Y	Y	Y
5 King	N	N	N	Y	Y
KANSAS					
1 Moran	N	N	N	Y	Y
2 Jenkins	N	N	Y	Y	Y
3 Moore	Y	Y	Y	Y	Y
4 Tiahrt	N	N	Y	Y	Y
KENTUCKY					
1 Whitfield	Y	Y	Y	Y	Y
2 Guthrie	N	N	Y	Y	Y
3 Yarmuth	Y	Y	Y	Y	Y
4 Davis	N	N	Y	Y	Y
5 Rogers	N	Y	Y	Y	Y
6 Chandler	Y	Y	Y	Y	Y
LOUISIANA					
1 Scalise	N	N	Y	Y	Y
2 Cao	Y	Y	Y	Y	Y
3 Melancon	Y	Y	Y	Y	Y
4 Fleming	N	N	Y	Y	Y
5 Alexander	N	N	N	Y	Y
6 Cassidy	Y	N	N	Y	Y
7 Boustany	Y	Y	Y	Y	Y
MAINE					
1 Pingree	Y	Y	Y	Y	Y
2 Michaud	Y	Y	Y	Y	Y
MARYLAND					
1 Kratovil	Y	Y	Y	Y	Y
2 Ruppersberger	Y	Y	Y	Y	Y
3 Sarbanes	Y	Y	Y	Y	Y
4 Edwards	Y	Y	Y	Y	Y
5 Hoyer	Y	Y	Y	Y	Y
6 Bartlett	?	Y	Y	Y	Y
7 Cummings	Y	Y	Y	Y	Y
8 Van Hollen	Y	Y	Y	Y	Y
MASSACHUSETTS					
1 Olver	Y	Y	Y	Y	Y
2 Neal	?	?	?	Y	Y
3 McGovern	Y	Y	Y	Y	Y
4 Frank	Y	Y	Y	Y	Y
5 Tsongas	Y	Y	Y	Y	Y
6 Tierney	Y	Y	Y	Y	Y
7 Markey	Y	Y	Y	Y	Y
8 Capuano	Y	Y	Y	Y	Y
9 Lynch	Y	Y	Y	Y	Y
10 Delahunt	Y	Y	Y	Y	Y
MICHIGAN					
1 Stupak	Y	Y	Y	Y	Y
2 Hoekstra	N	N	Y	Y	Y
3 Ehlers	Y	Y	Y	Y	Y
4 Camp	Y	Y	Y	Y	Y
5 Kildee	Y	Y	Y	Y	Y
6 Upton	Y	Y	Y	Y	Y
7 Schauer	Y	Y	Y	Y	Y
8 Rogers	Y	Y	Y	Y	Y
9 Peters	Y	Y	Y	Y	Y
10 Miller	Y	Y	Y	Y	Y
11 McCotter	Y	Y	Y	Y	Y
12 Levin	Y	Y	Y	Y	Y
13 Kilpatrick	Y	Y	Y	Y	Y
14 Conyers	Y	Y	Y	Y	Y
15 Dingell	Y	Y	Y	Y	Y
MINNESOTA					
1 Walz	Y	Y	Y	Y	Y
2 Kline	N	N	Y	Y	Y
3 Paulsen	N	N	Y	Y	Y
4 McCollum	Y	Y	Y	Y	Y

	193	194	195	196	197
5 Ellison	Y	Y	Y	Y	Y
6 Bachmann	N	N	Y	Y	Y
7 Peterson	Y	Y	Y	Y	Y
8 Oberstar	Y	Y	Y	Y	Y
MISSISSIPPI					
1 Childers	Y	Y	Y	Y	Y
2 Thompson	Y	Y	Y	Y	Y
3 Harper	N	N	N	Y	Y
4 Taylor	Y	Y	Y	Y	Y
MISSOURI					
1 Clay	Y	Y	Y	Y	Y
2 Akin	N	N	N	Y	Y
3 Carnahan	Y	Y	Y	Y	Y
4 Skelton	Y	Y	Y	Y	Y
5 Cleaver	Y	Y	Y	Y	Y
6 Graves	N	N	Y	Y	Y
7 Blunt	N	N	N	Y	Y
8 Emerson	Y	N	Y	Y	Y
9 Luetkemeyer	N	N	N	Y	Y
MONTANA					
AL Rehberg	N	N	Y	Y	Y
NEBRASKA					
1 Fortenberry	Y	Y	Y	Y	Y
2 Terry	Y	N	Y	Y	Y
3 Smith	Y	N	Y	Y	Y
NEVADA					
1 Berkley	Y	Y	Y	Y	Y
2 Heller	N	N	N	Y	Y
3 Titus	Y	Y	Y	Y	Y
NEW HAMPSHIRE					
1 Shea-Porter	Y	Y	Y	Y	Y
2 Hodes	Y	Y	Y	Y	Y
NEW JERSEY					
1 Andrews	Y	Y	Y	Y	Y
2 LoBiondo	Y	Y	Y	Y	Y
3 Adler	Y	Y	Y	Y	Y
4 Smith	Y	Y	Y	Y	Y
5 Garrett	N	N	N	Y	Y
6 Pallone	Y	Y	Y	Y	Y
7 Lance	Y	Y	Y	Y	Y
8 Pascrell	Y	Y	Y	Y	Y
9 Rothman	Y	Y	Y	Y	Y
10 Payne	Y	Y	Y	Y	Y
11 Frelinghuysen	?	?	?	Y	Y
12 Holt	Y	Y	Y	Y	Y
13 Sires	Y	Y	Y	Y	Y
NEW MEXICO					
1 Heinrich	Y	Y	Y	Y	Y
2 Teague	Y	Y	Y	Y	Y
3 Lujan	Y	Y	Y	Y	Y
NEW YORK					
1 Bishop	Y	Y	Y	Y	Y
2 Israel	Y	Y	Y	Y	Y
3 King	Y	Y	Y	Y	Y
4 McCarthy	Y	Y	Y	Y	Y
5 Ackerman	Y	Y	Y	Y	Y
6 Meeks	Y	Y	Y	Y	Y
7 Crowley	Y	Y	Y	Y	Y
8 Nadler	Y	Y	Y	Y	Y
9 Weiner	Y	?	?	Y	Y
10 Towns	Y	Y	Y	Y	Y
11 Clarke	Y	Y	Y	Y	Y
12 Velázquez	Y	Y	Y	Y	Y
13 McMahon	Y	Y	Y	Y	Y
14 Maloney	Y	Y	Y	Y	Y
15 Rangel	Y	Y	Y	Y	Y
16 Serrano	Y	Y	Y	Y	Y
17 Engel	Y	Y	Y	Y	Y
18 Lowey	Y	Y	Y	Y	Y
19 Hall	Y	Y	Y	Y	Y
20 Vacant					
21 Tonko	Y	Y	Y	Y	Y
22 Hinchey	Y	Y	Y	Y	Y
23 McHugh	Y	Y	Y	Y	Y
24 Arcuri	Y	Y	Y	Y	Y
25 Maffei	Y	Y	Y	Y	Y
26 Lee	N	Y	Y	Y	Y
27 Higgins	Y	Y	Y	Y	Y
28 Slaughter	Y	Y	Y	Y	Y
29 Massa	Y	Y	Y	Y	Y
NORTH CAROLINA					
1 Butterfield	?	?	?	?	?
2 Etheridge	Y	Y	Y	Y	Y
3 Jones	Y	Y	Y	Y	Y
4 Price	Y	Y	Y	Y	Y

	193	194	195	196	197
5 Foxx	N	N	N	Y	Y
6 Coble	N	N	N	Y	Y
7 McIntyre	Y	Y	Y	Y	Y
8 Kissell	?	?	?	Y	Y
9 Myrick	N	N	N	Y	Y
10 McHenry	N	N	Y	Y	Y
11 Shuler	?	?	?	Y	Y
12 Watt	Y	Y	Y	Y	Y
13 Miller	Y	Y	Y	Y	Y
NORTH DAKOTA					
AL Pomeroy	?	?	?	Y	Y
OHIO					
1 Driehaus	Y	Y	Y	Y	Y
2 Schmidt	Y	Y	Y	Y	Y
3 Turner	Y	Y	Y	Y	Y
4 Jordan	N	N	N	Y	Y
5 Latta	N	N	Y	Y	Y
6 Wilson	Y	Y	Y	Y	Y
7 Austria	Y	Y	Y	Y	Y
8 Boehner	N	N	Y	Y	Y
9 Kaptur	Y	Y	Y	Y	Y
10 Kucinich	Y	Y	Y	Y	Y
11 Fudge	Y	Y	Y	Y	Y
12 Tiberi	N	Y	Y	Y	Y
13 Sutton	Y	Y	Y	Y	Y
14 LaTourette	Y	N	Y	Y	Y
15 Kilroy	Y	Y	Y	Y	Y
16 Boccieri	Y	Y	Y	Y	Y
17 Ryan	Y	Y	Y	Y	Y
18 Space	Y	Y	Y	Y	Y
OKLAHOMA					
1 Sullivan	N	N	N	Y	Y
2 Boren	Y	Y	Y	Y	Y
3 Lucas	N	N	Y	Y	Y
4 Cole	N	N	Y	Y	Y
5 Fallin	N	N	Y	Y	Y
OREGON					
1 Wu	Y	Y	Y	Y	Y
2 Walden	N	N	Y	Y	Y
3 Blumenauer	Y	Y	Y	Y	Y
4 DeFazio	Y	Y	Y	Y	Y
5 Schrader	Y	Y	Y	Y	Y
PENNSYLVANIA					
1 Brady	Y	Y	Y	Y	Y
2 Fattah	Y	Y	Y	Y	Y
3 Dahlkemper	Y	Y	Y	Y	Y
4 Altmire	Y	Y	Y	Y	Y
5 Thompson	N	N	Y	Y	Y
6 Gerlach	Y	Y	Y	Y	Y
7 Sestak	Y	Y	Y	Y	Y
8 Murphy, P.	Y	Y	Y	Y	Y
9 Shuster	N	N	Y	Y	Y
10 Carney	+	+	+	Y	Y
11 Kanjorski	Y	Y	Y	Y	Y
12 Murtha	?	?	?	Y	Y
13 Schwartz	Y	Y	Y	Y	Y
14 Doyle	Y	Y	Y	Y	Y
15 Dent	Y	Y	Y	Y	Y
16 Pitts	N	N	Y	Y	Y
17 Holden	Y	Y	Y	Y	Y
18 Murphy, T.	Y	Y	Y	Y	Y
19 Platts	Y	Y	Y	Y	Y
RHODE ISLAND					
1 Kennedy	+	+	+	Y	Y
2 Langevin	Y	Y	Y	Y	Y
SOUTH CAROLINA					
1 Brown	Y	Y	Y	Y	Y
2 Wilson	N	N	N	Y	Y
3 Barrett	+	−	+	Y	Y
4 Inglis	N	N	Y	Y	Y
5 Spratt	Y	Y	Y	Y	Y
6 Clyburn	Y	Y	Y	Y	Y
SOUTH DAKOTA					
AL Herseth Sandlin	Y	Y	Y	Y	Y
TENNESSEE					
1 Roe	N	N	Y	Y	Y
2 Duncan	N	N	N	Y	Y
3 Wamp	N	N	N	Y	Y
4 Davis	Y	Y	Y	Y	Y
5 Cooper	Y	Y	Y	Y	Y
6 Gordon	Y	Y	Y	Y	Y
7 Blackburn	N	N	Y	Y	Y
8 Tanner	Y	Y	Y	Y	Y
9 Cohen	Y	Y	Y	Y	Y

	193	194	195	196	197
TEXAS					
1 Gohmert	N	N	?	Y	Y
2 Poe	N	N	N	Y	Y
3 Johnson, S.	?	?	?	Y	Y
4 Hall	N	N	Y	Y	Y
5 Hensarling	N	N	N	Y	Y
6 Barton	Y	N	Y	Y	Y
7 Culberson	N	N	N	Y	Y
8 Brady	N	N	Y	Y	Y
9 Green, A.	Y	Y	Y	Y	Y
10 McCaul	N	Y	Y	Y	Y
11 Conaway	N	N	N	Y	Y
12 Granger	N	N	Y	Y	Y
13 Thornberry	N	N	Y	Y	Y
14 Paul	N	N	Y	Y	?
15 Hinojosa	?	?	?	?	?
16 Reyes	?	?	?	?	?
17 Edwards	Y	Y	Y	Y	Y
18 Jackson Lee	Y	Y	Y	Y	Y
19 Neugebauer	N	N	N	Y	Y
20 Gonzalez	Y	Y	Y	Y	Y
21 Smith	N	N	Y	?	?
22 Olson	N	N	Y	Y	Y
23 Rodriguez	Y	Y	Y	Y	Y
24 Marchant	N	N	N	Y	Y
25 Doggett	Y	Y	Y	Y	Y
26 Burgess	N	N	N	Y	Y
27 Ortiz	Y	Y	Y	Y	Y
28 Cuellar	Y	Y	Y	Y	Y
29 Green, G.	Y	Y	Y	Y	Y
30 Johnson, E.	+	Y	Y	Y	Y
31 Carter	N	N	Y	Y	Y
32 Sessions	?	N	N	Y	Y
UTAH					
1 Bishop	N	N	Y	Y	Y
2 Matheson	Y	Y	Y	Y	Y
3 Chaffetz	N	N	Y	Y	Y
VERMONT					
AL Welch	Y	Y	Y	Y	Y
VIRGINIA					
1 Wittman	N	N	Y	Y	Y
2 Nye	Y	Y	Y	Y	Y
3 Scott	Y	Y	Y	Y	Y
4 Forbes	N	N	Y	Y	Y
5 Perriello	Y	Y	Y	Y	Y
6 Goodlatte	N	N	Y	Y	Y
7 Cantor	N	N	Y	Y	Y
8 Moran	?	?	?	Y	Y
9 Boucher	Y	Y	Y	Y	Y
10 Wolf	Y	Y	Y	Y	Y
11 Connolly	Y	Y	Y	Y	Y
WASHINGTON					
1 Inslee	Y	Y	Y	Y	Y
2 Larsen	Y	Y	Y	Y	Y
3 Baird	?	Y	Y	Y	Y
4 Hastings	N	N	Y	Y	Y
5 McMorris Rodgers	N	N	N	Y	Y
6 Dicks	Y	Y	Y	Y	Y
7 McDermott	Y	Y	Y	Y	Y
8 Reichert	N	N	Y	Y	Y
9 Smith	Y	Y	Y	Y	Y
WEST VIRGINIA					
1 Mollohan	Y	Y	Y	Y	Y
2 Capito	Y	Y	Y	Y	Y
3 Rahall	Y	Y	Y	Y	Y
WISCONSIN					
1 Ryan	Y	N	Y	Y	Y
2 Baldwin	Y	Y	Y	Y	Y
3 Kind	Y	Y	Y	Y	Y
4 Moore	Y	Y	Y	Y	Y
5 Sensenbrenner	N	N	N	Y	Y
6 Petri	Y	Y	Y	Y	Y
7 Obey	Y	Y	Y	Y	Y
8 Kagen	Y	Y	Y	Y	Y
WYOMING					
AL Lummis	N	N	Y	Y	Y
DELEGATES					
Faleomavaega (A.S.)					
Norton (D.C.)					
Bordallo (Guam)					
Sablan (N. Marianas)					
Pierluisi (P.R.)					
Christensen (V.I.)					

IN THE HOUSE | By Vote Number

198. **S Con Res 13. Fiscal 2010 Budget Resolution/Motion to Instruct.** Ryan, R-Wis., motion to instruct conferees to strike provisions in the resolution that would provide reconciliation instructions on health care and student loans. It would instruct conferees to insist on points of order against legislation that would prohibit individuals from keeping their health plans or choice of doctors or that would increase revenue above levels established in the budget resolution. It would also instruct them to recede to Senate language that would prevent clean energy and climate change legislation from being considered under the reconciliation process. Motion rejected 196-227: R 173-0; D 23-227. April 22, 2009.

199. **HR 957. Higher Education Energy Programs/Passage.** Gordon, D-Tenn., motion to suspend the rules and pass the bill that would authorize the Energy Department to provide funds to the National Science Foundation for graduate education and curriculum development in advanced energy and "green" building technologies. Motion agreed to 411-6: R 165-6; D 246-0. A two-thirds majority of those present and voting (278 in this case) is required for passage under suspension of the rules. April 22, 2009.

200. **HR 1145. National Water Quality and Development/Natural Disaster Impact.** Kosmas, D-Fla., amendment that would require the interagency committee established by the bill to assess the impact of natural disasters on water resources. Adopted in Committee of the Whole 424-0: R 174-0; D 250-0. April 23, 2009.

201. **HR 1145. National Water Quality and Development/Renewable-Energy Analysis.** Teague, D-N.M., amendment that would require the national water research and assessment plan to include analysis of the amount, proximity and type of water required for the production of alternative and renewable-energy resources. Adopted in Committee of the Whole 423-1: R 170-1; D 253-0. April 23, 2009.

202. **HR 1145. National Water Quality and Development/GAO Duplication Study.** Roskam, R-Ill., amendment that would require the Government Accountability Office to study and report on whether any of the requirements of the bill duplicate responsibilities of existing programs and, if so, whether the bill's provisions should be implemented. Rejected in Committee of the Whole 194-236: R 175-0; D 19-236. April 23, 2009.

	198	199	200	201	202
ALABAMA					
1 Bonner	Y	Y	Y	Y	Y
2 Bright	Y	Y	Y	Y	N
3 Rogers	Y	Y	Y	Y	Y
4 Aderholt	Y	Y	Y	Y	Y
5 Griffith	Y	Y	Y	Y	N
6 Bachus	Y	Y	Y	Y	Y
7 Davis	N	Y	Y	Y	N
ALASKA					
AL Young	Y	N	Y	Y	Y
ARIZONA					
1 Kirkpatrick	N	Y	Y	Y	N
2 Franks	Y	Y	Y	Y	Y
3 Shadegg	Y	N	Y	Y	Y
4 Pastor	N	Y	Y	Y	N
5 Mitchell	Y	Y	Y	Y	N
6 Flake	Y	N	Y	Y	Y
7 Grijalva	N	Y	Y	Y	N
8 Giffords	N	Y	Y	Y	N
ARKANSAS					
1 Berry	N	Y	Y	Y	N
2 Snyder	N	Y	Y	Y	N
3 Boozman	Y	Y	Y	Y	Y
4 Ross	N	Y	Y	Y	N
CALIFORNIA					
1 Thompson	N	Y	Y	Y	N
2 Herger	Y	Y	Y	Y	Y
3 Lungren	?	?	Y	Y	Y
4 McClintock	Y	N	Y	N	Y
5 Matsui	N	Y	Y	Y	N
6 Woolsey	N	Y	Y	Y	N
7 Miller, George	N	Y	Y	Y	N
8 Pelosi					
9 Lee	N	Y	Y	Y	N
10 Tauscher	N	Y	Y	Y	N
11 McNerney	N	Y	Y	Y	N
12 Speier	N	Y	Y	Y	N
13 Stark	N	Y	Y	Y	N
14 Eshoo	N	Y	Y	Y	N
15 Honda	N	Y	Y	Y	N
16 Lofgren	N	Y	Y	Y	N
17 Farr	N	Y	Y	Y	N
18 Cardoza	N	Y	Y	Y	N
19 Radanovich	Y	?	Y	Y	Y
20 Costa	N	Y	?	Y	N
21 Nunes	Y	Y	Y	Y	Y
22 McCarthy	Y	Y	Y	Y	Y
23 Capps	N	Y	Y	Y	N
24 Gallegly	Y	Y	Y	Y	Y
25 McKeon	Y	Y	Y	Y	Y
26 Dreier	Y	Y	Y	Y	Y
27 Sherman	N	Y	Y	Y	N
28 Berman	N	Y	Y	?	N
29 Schiff	N	Y	Y	Y	N
30 Waxman	N	Y	Y	Y	N
31 Becerra	N	Y	Y	Y	N
32 Vacant					
33 Watson	N	Y	Y	Y	N
34 Roybal-Allard	N	Y	Y	Y	N
35 Waters	N	Y	Y	Y	Y
36 Harman	N	Y	Y	Y	N
37 Richardson	N	Y	Y	Y	N
38 Napolitano	N	Y	Y	Y	N
39 Sánchez, Linda	N	Y	Y	Y	N
40 Royce	Y	Y	Y	Y	Y
41 Lewis	Y	Y	Y	Y	Y
42 Miller, Gary	Y	Y	Y	Y	Y
43 Baca	N	Y	Y	Y	N
44 Calvert	Y	Y	Y	Y	Y
45 Bono Mack	Y	Y	Y	Y	Y
46 Rohrabacher	Y	Y	Y	Y	Y
47 Sanchez, Loretta	N	Y	Y	Y	N
48 Campbell	?	?	Y	Y	Y
49 Issa	Y	Y	Y	Y	Y
50 Bilbray	Y	Y	Y	Y	Y
51 Filner	N	Y	Y	Y	N
52 Hunter	Y	Y	Y	Y	Y
53 Davis	N	Y	Y	Y	N

	198	199	200	201	202
COLORADO					
1 DeGette	N	Y	Y	Y	N
2 Polis	N	Y	Y	Y	N
3 Salazar	N	Y	Y	Y	N
4 Markey	Y	Y	Y	Y	Y
5 Lamborn	Y	Y	Y	Y	Y
6 Coffman	Y	Y	Y	Y	Y
7 Perlmutter	N	Y	Y	Y	N
CONNECTICUT					
1 Larson	N	Y	Y	Y	N
2 Courtney	N	Y	Y	Y	N
3 DeLauro	N	Y	Y	Y	N
4 Himes	N	Y	Y	Y	N
5 Murphy	N	Y	Y	Y	N
DELAWARE					
AL Castle	Y	Y	Y	Y	Y
FLORIDA					
1 Miller	Y	Y	Y	Y	Y
2 Boyd	N	Y	Y	Y	N
3 Brown	N	Y	Y	Y	N
4 Crenshaw	Y	Y	Y	Y	Y
5 Brown-Waite	Y	Y	Y	Y	Y
6 Stearns	Y	Y	+	+	Y
7 Mica	Y	Y	Y	Y	Y
8 Grayson	N	Y	Y	Y	N
9 Bilirakis	Y	Y	Y	Y	Y
10 Young	Y	Y	Y	Y	Y
11 Castor	N	Y	Y	Y	N
12 Putnam	Y	Y	?	?	Y
13 Buchanan	Y	Y	Y	Y	Y
14 Mack	Y	Y	Y	Y	Y
15 Posey	Y	Y	Y	Y	Y
16 Rooney	Y	Y	Y	Y	Y
17 Meek	N	Y	Y	Y	N
18 Ros-Lehtinen	Y	Y	Y	Y	Y
19 Wexler	N	Y	Y	Y	N
20 Wasserman Schultz	N	Y	?	?	N
21 Diaz-Balart, L.	Y	Y	Y	Y	Y
22 Klein	N	Y	?	Y	N
23 Hastings	N	Y	Y	Y	N
24 Kosmas	Y	Y	Y	Y	Y
25 Diaz-Balart, M.	Y	Y	Y	Y	Y
GEORGIA					
1 Kingston	?	?	Y	Y	Y
2 Bishop	N	Y	Y	Y	N
3 Westmoreland	Y	Y	Y	Y	Y
4 Johnson	N	Y	Y	Y	N
5 Lewis	N	Y	Y	Y	N
6 Price	Y	Y	Y	Y	Y
7 Linder	Y	Y	Y	Y	Y
8 Marshall	Y	Y	Y	Y	N
9 Deal	Y	Y	Y	Y	Y
10 Broun	Y	N	Y	Y	Y
11 Gingrey	?	?	Y	Y	Y
12 Barrow	Y	Y	Y	Y	N
13 Scott	N	Y	Y	Y	N
HAWAII					
1 Abercrombie	N	Y	Y	Y	N
2 Hirono	N	Y	Y	Y	N
IDAHO					
1 Minnick	Y	Y	Y	Y	Y
2 Simpson	Y	Y	Y	Y	Y
ILLINOIS					
1 Rush	N	?	?	Y	N
2 Jackson	?	?	?	?	?
3 Lipinski	N	Y	Y	Y	N
4 Gutierrez	N	Y	Y	Y	N
5 Quigley	N	Y	Y	Y	N
6 Roskam	Y	Y	Y	Y	Y
7 Davis	N	Y	Y	Y	N
8 Bean	N	Y	Y	Y	N
9 Schakowsky	N	Y	Y	Y	N
10 Kirk	Y	Y	Y	Y	Y
11 Halvorson	N	Y	Y	Y	N
12 Costello	N	Y	Y	Y	N
13 Biggert	Y	Y	Y	Y	Y
14 Foster	N	Y	Y	Y	N
15 Johnson	Y	Y	Y	Y	Y

KEY	Republicans	Democrats		
Y Voted for (yea)		X Paired against		C Voted "present" to avoid possible conflict of interest
# Paired for		– Announced against		
+ Announced for		P Voted "present"		? Did not vote or otherwise make a position known
N Voted against (nay)				

	198	199	200	201	202
16 Manzullo	Y	Y	Y	Y	Y
17 Hare	N	Y	Y	Y	N
18 Schock	Y	Y	Y	Y	Y
19 Shimkus	Y	Y	Y	Y	Y
INDIANA					
1 Visclosky	N	Y	Y	Y	N
2 Donnelly	Y	Y	Y	Y	N
3 Souder	Y	Y	Y	Y	Y
4 Buyer	Y	Y	Y	Y	Y
5 Burton	Y	Y	Y	Y	Y
6 Pence	Y	Y	Y	Y	Y
7 Carson	N	Y	Y	Y	N
8 Ellsworth	Y	Y	Y	Y	N
9 Hill	Y	Y	Y	Y	N
IOWA					
1 Braley	N	Y	Y	Y	N
2 Loebsack	N	Y	Y	Y	N
3 Boswell	−	+	Y	Y	N
4 Latham	Y	Y	Y	Y	Y
5 King	Y	Y	Y	Y	Y
KANSAS					
1 Moran	Y	Y	?	?	?
2 Jenkins	Y	Y	Y	Y	Y
3 Moore	N	Y	Y	Y	N
4 Tiahrt	Y	Y	Y	Y	Y
KENTUCKY					
1 Whitfield	Y	Y	Y	Y	Y
2 Guthrie	Y	Y	Y	Y	Y
3 Yarmuth	N	Y	Y	Y	Y
4 Davis	Y	Y	Y	Y	Y
5 Rogers	Y	Y	Y	Y	Y
6 Chandler	N	Y	Y	Y	N
LOUISIANA					
1 Scalise	Y	Y	Y	Y	Y
2 Cao	Y	Y	Y	Y	Y
3 Melancon	N	Y	Y	Y	N
4 Fleming	Y	Y	Y	Y	Y
5 Alexander	Y	Y	Y	Y	Y
6 Cassidy	Y	Y	Y	Y	Y
7 Boustany	Y	Y	Y	Y	Y
MAINE					
1 Pingree	N	Y	Y	Y	N
2 Michaud	N	Y	Y	Y	N
MARYLAND					
1 Kratovil	N	Y	Y	Y	N
2 Ruppersberger	N	Y	Y	Y	N
3 Sarbanes	N	Y	Y	Y	N
4 Edwards	N	Y	Y	Y	N
5 Hoyer	N	Y	Y	Y	N
6 Bartlett	Y	Y	Y	Y	Y
7 Cummings	N	Y	Y	Y	N
8 Van Hollen	N	Y	Y	Y	N
MASSACHUSETTS					
1 Olver	N	Y	Y	Y	N
2 Neal	N	Y	Y	Y	N
3 McGovern	N	Y	Y	Y	N
4 Frank	N	Y	Y	Y	N
5 Tsongas	N	Y	Y	Y	N
6 Tierney	N	Y	Y	Y	N
7 Markey	N	Y	Y	Y	N
8 Capuano	N	Y	Y	Y	N
9 Lynch	N	?	Y	Y	Y
10 Delahunt	N	Y	Y	Y	N
MICHIGAN					
1 Stupak	N	Y	Y	Y	N
2 Hoekstra	Y	Y	Y	Y	Y
3 Ehlers	Y	Y	Y	Y	Y
4 Camp	Y	Y	Y	Y	Y
5 Kildee	N	Y	Y	Y	N
6 Upton	Y	Y	Y	Y	Y
7 Schauer	N	Y	Y	Y	N
8 Rogers	Y	Y	Y	Y	Y
9 Peters	N	Y	Y	Y	N
10 Miller	Y	Y	Y	Y	Y
11 McCotter	Y	Y	Y	Y	Y
12 Levin	N	Y	Y	Y	N
13 Kilpatrick	N	Y	Y	Y	N
14 Conyers	N	Y	Y	Y	N
15 Dingell	N	Y	Y	Y	N
MINNESOTA					
1 Walz	N	Y	Y	Y	N
2 Kline	Y	Y	Y	Y	Y
3 Paulsen	Y	Y	Y	Y	Y
4 McCollum	N	Y	Y	Y	N

	198	199	200	201	202
5 Ellison	N	Y	Y	Y	N
6 Bachmann	Y	Y	Y	Y	Y
7 Peterson	N	Y	Y	Y	N
8 Oberstar	N	Y	Y	Y	N
MISSISSIPPI					
1 Childers	Y	Y	Y	Y	Y
2 Thompson	N	Y	Y	Y	N
3 Harper	Y	Y	Y	Y	Y
4 Taylor	Y	Y	Y	Y	Y
MISSOURI					
1 Clay	N	Y	Y	Y	N
2 Akin	Y	Y	Y	Y	Y
3 Carnahan	N	Y	Y	Y	N
4 Skelton	N	Y	Y	Y	N
5 Cleaver	N	Y	Y	Y	N
6 Graves	Y	Y	Y	Y	Y
7 Blunt	Y	Y	Y	Y	Y
8 Emerson	Y	Y	Y	Y	Y
9 Luetkemeyer	Y	Y	Y	Y	Y
MONTANA					
AL Rehberg	Y	Y	Y	Y	Y
NEBRASKA					
1 Fortenberry	Y	Y	Y	?	?
2 Terry	Y	Y	Y	Y	Y
3 Smith	Y	Y	Y	Y	Y
NEVADA					
1 Berkley	N	Y	Y	Y	N
2 Heller	Y	Y	Y	Y	Y
3 Titus	N	Y	Y	Y	N
NEW HAMPSHIRE					
1 Shea-Porter	N	Y	Y	Y	N
2 Hodes	N	Y	Y	Y	N
NEW JERSEY					
1 Andrews	N	Y	Y	Y	N
2 LoBiondo	Y	Y	Y	Y	Y
3 Adler	N	Y	Y	Y	N
4 Smith	Y	Y	Y	Y	Y
5 Garrett	Y	Y	Y	Y	Y
6 Pallone	N	Y	Y	Y	N
7 Lance	Y	Y	Y	Y	Y
8 Pascrell	N	Y	Y	Y	N
9 Rothman	N	Y	Y	Y	N
10 Payne	N	Y	Y	Y	N
11 Frelinghuysen	Y	Y	Y	Y	Y
12 Holt	N	Y	Y	Y	N
13 Sires	N	Y	Y	Y	N
NEW MEXICO					
1 Heinrich	N	Y	Y	Y	Y
2 Teague	Y	Y	Y	Y	N
3 Lujan	N	Y	Y	Y	N
NEW YORK					
1 Bishop	N	Y	Y	Y	N
2 Israel	N	Y	?	Y	N
3 King	Y	Y	Y	Y	Y
4 McCarthy	N	Y	Y	Y	N
5 Ackerman	N	Y	Y	Y	N
6 Meeks	N	Y	?	?	?
7 Crowley	N	Y	Y	Y	N
8 Nadler	N	Y	Y	Y	N
9 Weiner	N	Y	Y	Y	N
10 Towns	N	Y	?	?	N
11 Clarke	N	Y	Y	Y	N
12 Velázquez	N	Y	Y	Y	N
13 McMahon	N	Y	Y	Y	N
14 Maloney	N	Y	Y	Y	N
15 Rangel	N	Y	Y	Y	N
16 Serrano	N	Y	Y	Y	N
17 Engel	N	Y	Y	Y	N
18 Lowey	N	Y	Y	Y	N
19 Hall	N	Y	Y	Y	N
20 Vacant					
21 Tonko	N	Y	Y	Y	N
22 Hinchey	N	Y	Y	Y	N
23 McHugh	Y	Y	Y	Y	Y
24 Arcuri	N	Y	Y	Y	Y
25 Maffei	N	Y	Y	Y	Y
26 Lee	Y	Y	Y	Y	Y
27 Higgins	N	?	Y	Y	Y
28 Slaughter	N	Y	Y	Y	N
29 Massa	N	Y	Y	Y	N
NORTH CAROLINA					
1 Butterfield	?	?	Y	Y	N
2 Etheridge	N	Y	Y	Y	N
3 Jones	Y	Y	Y	Y	Y
4 Price	N	Y	Y	Y	N

	198	199	200	201	202
5 Foxx	Y	Y	Y	Y	Y
6 Coble	Y	Y	Y	Y	Y
7 McIntyre	Y	Y	Y	Y	N
8 Kissell	N	Y	Y	Y	N
9 Myrick	Y	Y	Y	Y	Y
10 McHenry	Y	Y	Y	Y	Y
11 Shuler	Y	Y	Y	Y	Y
12 Watt	N	Y	Y	Y	N
13 Miller	N	Y	Y	Y	N
NORTH DAKOTA					
AL Pomeroy	Y	Y	Y	Y	N
OHIO					
1 Driehaus	N	Y	Y	Y	Y
2 Schmidt	Y	Y	Y	Y	Y
3 Turner	Y	Y	Y	Y	Y
4 Jordan	Y	Y	Y	Y	Y
5 Latta	Y	Y	Y	Y	Y
6 Wilson	N	Y	Y	Y	N
7 Austria	Y	Y	Y	Y	Y
8 Boehner	Y	Y	Y	Y	Y
9 Kaptur	N	Y	Y	Y	N
10 Kucinich	N	Y	Y	Y	N
11 Fudge	N	Y	Y	Y	N
12 Tiberi	Y	Y	Y	Y	Y
13 Sutton	N	Y	Y	Y	N
14 LaTourette	N	Y	Y	Y	Y
15 Kilroy	N	Y	Y	Y	N
16 Boccieri	N	Y	Y	Y	N
17 Ryan	N	Y	Y	Y	N
18 Space	Y	Y	Y	Y	N
OKLAHOMA					
1 Sullivan	Y	Y	Y	?	Y
2 Boren	Y	Y	Y	Y	Y
3 Lucas	Y	Y	Y	Y	Y
4 Cole	Y	Y	Y	Y	Y
5 Fallin	Y	Y	Y	Y	Y
OREGON					
1 Wu	N	Y	Y	Y	N
2 Walden	Y	Y	Y	Y	Y
3 Blumenauer	N	Y	Y	Y	N
4 DeFazio	N	Y	Y	Y	N
5 Schrader	N	Y	Y	Y	Y
PENNSYLVANIA					
1 Brady	N	Y	Y	Y	N
2 Fattah	N	Y	Y	Y	N
3 Dahlkemper	N	Y	Y	Y	Y
4 Altmire	N	Y	Y	Y	N
5 Thompson	Y	Y	Y	Y	Y
6 Gerlach	Y	Y	Y	Y	Y
7 Sestak	N	Y	Y	Y	N
8 Murphy, P.	N	Y	Y	Y	N
9 Shuster	Y	Y	Y	Y	Y
10 Carney	N	Y	Y	Y	N
11 Kanjorski	N	Y	Y	Y	N
12 Murtha	N	Y	Y	Y	N
13 Schwartz	N	Y	Y	Y	N
14 Doyle	N	Y	Y	Y	N
15 Dent	Y	Y	Y	Y	Y
16 Pitts	Y	Y	Y	Y	Y
17 Holden	N	Y	Y	Y	N
18 Murphy, T.	Y	Y	Y	Y	Y
19 Platts	Y	Y	Y	Y	Y
RHODE ISLAND					
1 Kennedy	N	Y	Y	Y	N
2 Langevin	N	Y	Y	Y	N
SOUTH CAROLINA					
1 Brown	Y	Y	Y	Y	Y
2 Wilson	Y	Y	Y	Y	Y
3 Barrett	Y	Y	Y	Y	Y
4 Inglis	Y	Y	Y	Y	Y
5 Spratt	N	Y	Y	Y	N
6 Clyburn	N	Y	Y	Y	N
SOUTH DAKOTA					
AL Herseth Sandlin	N	Y	Y	Y	N
TENNESSEE					
1 Roe	Y	?	Y	Y	Y
2 Duncan	Y	Y	Y	Y	Y
3 Wamp	Y	Y	Y	Y	Y
4 Davis	N	Y	Y	Y	N
5 Cooper	N	Y	Y	Y	N
6 Gordon	N	Y	Y	Y	N
7 Blackburn	Y	Y	Y	Y	Y
8 Tanner	N	Y	Y	Y	N
9 Cohen	N	Y	Y	Y	N

	198	199	200	201	202
TEXAS					
1 Gohmert	Y	Y	Y	Y	Y
2 Poe	Y	Y	Y	Y	Y
3 Johnson, S.	Y	Y	Y	Y	Y
4 Hall	Y	Y	Y	Y	Y
5 Hensarling	Y	Y	Y	Y	Y
6 Barton	Y	Y	Y	Y	Y
7 Culberson	Y	Y	Y	Y	Y
8 Brady	Y	Y	Y	Y	Y
9 Green, A.	N	Y	Y	Y	N
10 McCaul	Y	Y	Y	Y	Y
11 Conaway	Y	Y	Y	Y	Y
12 Granger	Y	Y	Y	Y	Y
13 Thornberry	Y	Y	Y	Y	Y
14 Paul	Y	N	Y	Y	Y
15 Hinojosa	N	Y	Y	Y	N
16 Reyes	?	?	?	?	?
17 Edwards	N	Y	Y	Y	N
18 Jackson Lee	N	Y	Y	Y	N
19 Neugebauer	Y	Y	Y	Y	Y
20 Gonzalez	N	Y	Y	Y	N
21 Smith	?	?	?	?	?
22 Olson	Y	Y	Y	Y	Y
23 Rodriguez	N	Y	Y	Y	N
24 Marchant	Y	Y	Y	Y	Y
25 Doggett	N	Y	Y	Y	N
26 Burgess	N	Y	Y	Y	N
27 Ortiz	N	Y	Y	Y	N
28 Cuellar	N	Y	Y	Y	N
29 Green, G.	N	Y	Y	Y	N
30 Johnson, E.	N	Y	Y	Y	N
31 Carter	Y	Y	Y	Y	Y
32 Sessions	Y	Y	Y	Y	Y
UTAH					
1 Bishop	Y	Y	Y	?	Y
2 Matheson	Y	Y	Y	Y	N
3 Chaffetz	Y	Y	Y	Y	Y
VERMONT					
AL Welch	N	Y	Y	Y	N
VIRGINIA					
1 Wittman	Y	Y	Y	Y	Y
2 Nye	Y	Y	Y	Y	N
3 Scott	N	Y	Y	Y	N
4 Forbes	Y	Y	Y	Y	Y
5 Perriello	Y	Y	Y	Y	Y
6 Goodlatte	Y	Y	Y	Y	Y
7 Cantor	Y	Y	Y	Y	Y
8 Moran	N	Y	Y	Y	N
9 Boucher	N	Y	Y	Y	N
10 Wolf	Y	Y	Y	Y	Y
11 Connolly	N	Y	Y	Y	N
WASHINGTON					
1 Inslee	N	Y	Y	Y	Y
2 Larsen	N	Y	Y	Y	N
3 Baird	N	Y	Y	Y	N
4 Hastings	Y	Y	Y	Y	Y
5 McMorris Rodgers	Y	Y	Y	Y	Y
6 Dicks	N	Y	Y	Y	N
7 McDermott	N	?	Y	Y	N
8 Reichert	Y	Y	Y	Y	Y
9 Smith	N	Y	Y	Y	N
WEST VIRGINIA					
1 Mollohan	N	Y	Y	Y	N
2 Capito	Y	Y	Y	Y	Y
3 Rahall	N	Y	Y	Y	N
WISCONSIN					
1 Ryan	Y	Y	Y	Y	Y
2 Baldwin	N	Y	Y	Y	N
3 Kind	N	Y	Y	Y	N
4 Moore	N	Y	Y	Y	N
5 Sensenbrenner	Y	Y	Y	Y	Y
6 Petri	Y	Y	Y	Y	Y
7 Obey	N	Y	Y	Y	N
8 Kagen	N	Y	Y	Y	N
WYOMING					
AL Lummis	Y	Y	Y	Y	Y
DELEGATES					
Faleomavaega (A.S.)			Y	Y	N
Norton (D.C.)			+	+	−
Bordallo (Guam)			Y	Y	N
Sablan (N. Marianas)			Y	Y	N
Pierluisi (P.R.)			Y	Y	?
Christensen (V.I.)			Y	Y	N

IN THE HOUSE | By Vote Number

203. **HR 1145. National Water Quality and Development/ Interagency Duplication Study.** Shadegg, R-Ariz., amendment that would require the interagency committee created in the bill to identify duplicated federal water-related activities and recommend how to avoid such duplication. It would require the president to ensure that federal agencies participating in the national water quality and development initiative do not request appropriations for duplicated activities. Rejected in Committee of the Whole 160-271: R 154-19; D 6-252. April 23, 2009.

204. **HR 1145. National Water Quality and Development/Recommit.** Nunes, R-Calif., motion to recommit the bill to the Science and Technology Committee with instructions that it be immediately reported back with language requiring the president to submit a report to Congress within 90 days identifying the statutory or regulatory barriers that contribute to job loss in rural or agricultural areas by preventing the use of technology, technique, data collection method or model. It would require the president to recommend steps to mitigate those impacts. Motion agreed to 392-28: R 172-1; D 220-27. April 23, 2009.

205. **HR 1145. National Water Quality and Development/Passage.** Passage of the bill that would authorize $2 million annually in fiscal 2010-14 for a National Oceanic and Atmospheric Administration initiative to improve national water research and development. The bill would require the creation of an interagency committee to develop a national water research and assessment plan that includes a national water census, methods to resolve resource conflicts, forecasting models and technology developments to increase water supplies and quality. Passed 413-10: R 162-10; D 251-0. April 23, 2009.

206. **HR 1139. Community Oriented Policing Services/Passage.** Weiner, D-N.Y., motion to suspend the rules and pass the bill that would authorize $1.8 billion a year in fiscal 2009-14 for the Justice Department's Community Oriented Policing Services program and expand types of activities eligible for program grants. The bill would increase from 3 percent to 5 percent the amount of funding used to provide technical assistance to states and localities, and require that individuals recruited through the Troops to Cops program be honorably discharged members of the military. Motion agreed to 342-78: R 94-78; D 248-0. A two-thirds majority of those present and voting (280 in this case) is required for passage under suspension of the rules. April 23, 2009.

	203	204	205	206
ALABAMA				
1 **Bonner**	Y	+	Y	Y
2 Bright	N	Y	Y	Y
3 **Rogers**	Y	Y	Y	Y
4 **Aderholt**	Y	Y	Y	Y
5 Griffith	N	Y	Y	Y
6 **Bachus**	Y	Y	Y	N
7 Davis	N	Y	Y	Y
ALASKA				
AL **Young**	Y	Y	Y	Y
ARIZONA				
1 Kirkpatrick	Y	Y	Y	Y
2 **Franks**	Y	Y	N	N
3 **Shadegg**	Y	Y	N	N
4 Pastor	N	Y	Y	Y
5 Mitchell	Y	Y	Y	Y
6 **Flake**	Y	Y	N	N
7 Grijalva	N	Y	Y	Y
8 Giffords	N	Y	Y	Y
ARKANSAS				
1 Berry	N	Y	Y	Y
2 Snyder	N	Y	Y	Y
3 **Boozman**	Y	Y	Y	Y
4 Ross	N	Y	Y	Y
CALIFORNIA				
1 Thompson	N	Y	Y	Y
2 **Herger**	Y	Y	Y	N
3 **Lungren**	N	Y	Y	N
4 **McClintock**	N	Y	N	N
5 Matsui	N	Y	Y	Y
6 Woolsey	N	N	Y	Y
7 Miller, George	N	Y	Y	Y
8 Pelosi				
9 Lee	N	N	Y	Y
10 Tauscher	N	Y	Y	Y
11 McNerney	N	Y	Y	Y
12 Speier	N	Y	Y	Y
13 Stark	N	N	Y	?
14 Eshoo	N	Y	Y	Y
15 Honda	N	N	Y	Y
16 Lofgren	N	Y	Y	Y
17 Farr	N	Y	Y	Y
18 Cardoza	N	Y	Y	Y
19 **Radanovich**	Y	Y	Y	N
20 Costa	N	Y	Y	Y
21 **Nunes**	N	Y	Y	N
22 **McCarthy**	N	Y	Y	N
23 Capps	N	Y	Y	Y
24 **Gallegly**	N	Y	Y	N
25 **McKeon**	N	Y	Y	N
26 **Dreier**	Y	Y	N	N
27 Sherman	N	Y	Y	Y
28 Berman	N	Y	Y	Y
29 Schiff	N	Y	Y	Y
30 Waxman	N	N	Y	Y
31 Becerra	N	Y	Y	Y
32 Vacant				
33 Watson	N	N	Y	Y
34 Roybal-Allard	N	Y	Y	Y
35 Waters	N	N	Y	Y
36 Harman	N	Y	Y	Y
37 Richardson	N	Y	Y	Y
38 Napolitano	N	Y	Y	Y
39 Sánchez, Linda	N	Y	Y	Y
40 **Royce**	N	Y	Y	N
41 **Lewis**	N	Y	Y	Y
42 **Miller, Gary**	N	Y	Y	N
43 Baca	N	Y	Y	Y
44 **Calvert**	N	Y	Y	Y
45 **Bono Mack**	N	Y	Y	Y
46 **Rohrabacher**	N	Y	Y	N
47 Sanchez, Loretta	N	Y	Y	Y
48 **Campbell**	N	Y	Y	N
49 **Issa**	Y	Y	N	N
50 **Bilbray**	N	Y	Y	Y
51 Filner	N	Y	Y	Y
52 **Hunter**	Y	Y	Y	Y
53 Davis	N	Y	Y	Y

	203	204	205	206
COLORADO				
1 DeGette	N	Y	Y	Y
2 Polis	N	Y	Y	Y
3 Salazar	N	Y	Y	Y
4 Markey	N	Y	Y	Y
5 **Lamborn**	Y	Y	Y	N
6 **Coffman**	Y	Y	Y	Y
7 Perlmutter	N	Y	Y	Y
CONNECTICUT				
1 Larson	N	Y	Y	Y
2 Courtney	N	Y	Y	Y
3 DeLauro	N	Y	Y	Y
4 Himes	N	Y	Y	Y
5 Murphy	N	Y	Y	Y
DELAWARE				
AL **Castle**	Y	Y	Y	Y
FLORIDA				
1 **Miller**	Y	Y	Y	N
2 Boyd	N	Y	Y	Y
3 Brown	N	Y	Y	Y
4 **Crenshaw**	Y	Y	Y	Y
5 **Brown-Waite**	Y	Y	Y	N
6 **Stearns**	Y	Y	Y	Y
7 **Mica**	Y	Y	Y	Y
8 Grayson	N	Y	Y	Y
9 **Bilirakis**	Y	Y	Y	Y
10 **Young**	Y	Y	Y	Y
11 Castor	N	Y	Y	Y
12 **Putnam**	Y	Y	Y	Y
13 **Buchanan**	Y	Y	Y	Y
14 **Mack**	Y	Y	Y	N
15 **Posey**	Y	Y	Y	Y
16 **Rooney**	Y	Y	Y	Y
17 Meek	N	Y	Y	Y
18 **Ros-Lehtinen**	Y	Y	Y	Y
19 Wexler	N	Y	Y	Y
20 Wasserman Schultz	N	?	Y	Y
21 **Diaz-Balart, L.**	Y	Y	Y	Y
22 Klein	N	Y	Y	Y
23 Hastings	N	Y	Y	Y
24 Kosmas	N	Y	Y	Y
25 **Diaz-Balart, M.**	Y	Y	Y	Y
GEORGIA				
1 **Kingston**	Y	Y	Y	Y
2 Bishop	N	Y	Y	Y
3 **Westmoreland**	Y	Y	Y	N
4 Johnson	N	Y	Y	Y
5 Lewis	N	Y	Y	Y
6 **Price**	Y	Y	Y	N
7 **Linder**	Y	Y	?	?
8 Marshall	N	Y	Y	Y
9 **Deal**	Y	Y	Y	N
10 **Broun**	Y	Y	N	N
11 **Gingrey**	Y	Y	Y	Y
12 Barrow	N	Y	Y	Y
13 Scott	N	+	Y	Y
HAWAII				
1 Abercrombie	N	Y	Y	Y
2 Hirono	N	N	Y	Y
IDAHO				
1 **Minnick**	Y	Y	Y	Y
2 **Simpson**	Y	Y	Y	Y
ILLINOIS				
1 Rush	N	Y	Y	Y
2 Jackson	?	?	?	?
3 Lipinski	N	Y	Y	Y
4 Gutierrez	N	Y	Y	Y
5 Quigley	N	Y	Y	Y
6 **Roskam**	Y	Y	Y	Y
7 Davis	N	Y	Y	Y
8 Bean	N	Y	Y	Y
9 Schakowsky	N	N	Y	Y
10 **Kirk**	Y	Y	Y	Y
11 Halvorson	N	Y	Y	Y
12 Costello	N	Y	Y	Y
13 **Biggert**	Y	Y	Y	Y
14 Foster	N	Y	Y	Y
15 **Johnson**	Y	Y	Y	Y

	203	204	205	206
16 Manzullo	Y	Y	Y	N
17 Hare	N	Y	Y	Y
18 Schock	Y	Y	Y	Y
19 Shimkus	Y	Y	Y	?
INDIANA				
1 Visclosky	N	Y	Y	Y
2 Donnelly	N	Y	Y	Y
3 Souder	Y	Y	Y	Y
4 Buyer	Y	Y	Y	N
5 Burton	Y	Y	Y	N
6 Pence	Y	Y	Y	N
7 Carson	N	N	Y	Y
8 Ellsworth	N	Y	Y	Y
9 Hill	N	Y	Y	Y
IOWA				
1 Braley	N	N	Y	Y
2 Loebsack	N	Y	Y	Y
3 Boswell	N	Y	Y	Y
4 Latham	Y	Y	Y	Y
5 King	Y	Y	Y	N
KANSAS				
1 Moran	?	?	?	?
2 Jenkins	Y	Y	Y	N
3 Moore	N	Y	Y	Y
4 Tiahrt	Y	Y	Y	Y
KENTUCKY				
1 Whitfield	Y	Y	Y	Y
2 Guthrie	Y	Y	Y	Y
3 Yarmuth	N	Y	Y	Y
4 Davis	Y	Y	Y	Y
5 Rogers	Y	Y	Y	Y
6 Chandler	N	Y	Y	Y
LOUISIANA				
1 Scalise	Y	Y	Y	Y
2 Cao	N	Y	Y	Y
3 Melancon	N	Y	Y	Y
4 Fleming	Y	Y	Y	Y
5 Alexander	Y	Y	Y	Y
6 Cassidy	Y	Y	Y	Y
7 Boustany	Y	Y	Y	Y
MAINE				
1 Pingree	N	Y	Y	Y
2 Michaud	N	Y	Y	Y
MARYLAND				
1 Kratovil	N	Y	Y	Y
2 Ruppersberger	N	Y	Y	Y
3 Sarbanes	N	Y	Y	Y
4 Edwards	N	N	Y	Y
5 Hoyer	N	Y	Y	Y
6 Bartlett	Y	Y	Y	N
7 Cummings	N	Y	Y	Y
8 Van Hollen	N	Y	Y	Y
MASSACHUSETTS				
1 Olver	N	Y	Y	Y
2 Neal	N	Y	Y	Y
3 McGovern	N	Y	Y	Y
4 Frank	N	Y	Y	Y
5 Tsongas	N	N	Y	Y
6 Tierney	N	Y	Y	Y
7 Markey	N	Y	Y	Y
8 Capuano	N	Y	Y	Y
9 Lynch	N	Y	Y	Y
10 Delahunt	N	Y	Y	Y
MICHIGAN				
1 Stupak	N	Y	Y	Y
2 Hoekstra	Y	Y	Y	Y
3 Ehlers	N	Y	Y	N
4 Camp	Y	Y	Y	N
5 Kildee	N	Y	Y	Y
6 Upton	Y	Y	Y	Y
7 Schauer	N	Y	Y	Y
8 Rogers	Y	Y	Y	Y
9 Peters	N	Y	Y	Y
10 Miller	Y	N	N	Y
11 McCotter	Y	Y	Y	Y
12 Levin	N	Y	Y	Y
13 Kilpatrick	N	N	Y	Y
14 Conyers	N	N	Y	Y
15 Dingell	N	Y	Y	Y
MINNESOTA				
1 Walz	N	Y	Y	Y
2 Kline	Y	Y	Y	N
3 Paulsen	Y	Y	Y	Y
4 McCollum	N	Y	Y	Y

	203	204	205	206
5 Ellison	N	Y	Y	Y
6 Bachmann	Y	Y	Y	N
7 Peterson	N	Y	Y	Y
8 Oberstar	N	Y	Y	Y
MISSISSIPPI				
1 Childers	Y	Y	Y	Y
2 Thompson	N	Y	Y	Y
3 Harper	?	?	?	?
4 Taylor	N	Y	Y	Y
MISSOURI				
1 Clay	N	N	Y	Y
2 Akin	Y	Y	Y	N
3 Carnahan	N	Y	Y	Y
4 Skelton	N	Y	Y	Y
5 Cleaver	N	Y	Y	Y
6 Graves	Y	Y	Y	Y
7 Blunt	Y	Y	Y	N
8 Emerson	Y	Y	Y	Y
9 Luetkemeyer	Y	Y	Y	Y
MONTANA				
AL Rehberg	Y	Y	Y	Y
NEBRASKA				
1 Fortenberry	Y	Y	Y	Y
2 Terry	Y	Y	Y	Y
3 Smith	Y	Y	Y	N
NEVADA				
1 Berkley	N	Y	Y	Y
2 Heller	Y	Y	Y	Y
3 Titus	N	Y	Y	Y
NEW HAMPSHIRE				
1 Shea-Porter	N	Y	Y	Y
2 Hodes	N	Y	Y	Y
NEW JERSEY				
1 Andrews	N	Y	Y	Y
2 LoBiondo	Y	Y	Y	Y
3 Adler	N	Y	Y	Y
4 Smith	N	Y	Y	Y
5 Garrett	Y	Y	N	N
6 Pallone	N	Y	Y	Y
7 Lance	Y	Y	Y	Y
8 Pascrell	N	Y	Y	Y
9 Rothman	N	Y	Y	Y
10 Payne	N	Y	Y	Y
11 Frelinghuysen	Y	Y	Y	Y
12 Holt	N	N	Y	Y
13 Sires	N	Y	Y	Y
NEW MEXICO				
1 Heinrich	N	Y	Y	Y
2 Teague	N	Y	Y	Y
3 Lujan	N	Y	Y	Y
NEW YORK				
1 Bishop	N	Y	Y	Y
2 Israel	N	Y	Y	Y
3 King	N	Y	Y	Y
4 McCarthy	N	Y	Y	Y
5 Ackerman	N	Y	Y	Y
6 Meeks	N	Y	Y	Y
7 Crowley	N	Y	Y	Y
8 Nadler	N	N	Y	Y
9 Weiner	N	Y	Y	Y
10 Towns	N	Y	Y	Y
11 Clarke	N	N	Y	Y
12 Velázquez	N	N	Y	Y
13 McMahon	N	Y	Y	Y
14 Maloney	N	Y	Y	Y
15 Rangel	N	Y	Y	Y
16 Serrano	N	Y	Y	Y
17 Engel	N	?	Y	Y
18 Lowey	N	Y	Y	Y
19 Hall	N	Y	Y	Y
20 Vacant				
21 Tonko	N	Y	Y	Y
22 Hinchey	N	N	Y	Y
23 McHugh	N	Y	Y	Y
24 Arcuri	N	Y	Y	Y
25 Maffei	N	Y	Y	?
26 Lee	Y	Y	Y	Y
27 Higgins	N	Y	Y	Y
28 Slaughter	N	+	Y	Y
29 Massa	N	Y	Y	Y
NORTH CAROLINA				
1 Butterfield	N	Y	Y	Y
2 Etheridge	N	Y	Y	Y
3 Jones	Y	Y	Y	Y
4 Price	N	Y	Y	Y

	203	204	205	206
5 Foxx	Y	Y	N	N
6 Coble	Y	Y	N	N
7 McIntyre	N	Y	Y	Y
8 Kissell	N	Y	Y	Y
9 Myrick	Y	Y	Y	N
10 McHenry	Y	Y	Y	N
11 Shuler	Y	Y	Y	Y
12 Watt	N	Y	Y	Y
13 Miller	N	Y	Y	Y
NORTH DAKOTA				
AL Pomeroy	N	Y	Y	Y
OHIO				
1 Driehaus	N	Y	Y	Y
2 Schmidt	Y	Y	Y	Y
3 Turner	Y	Y	Y	Y
4 Jordan	Y	Y	Y	N
5 Latta	Y	Y	Y	Y
6 Wilson	N	Y	Y	Y
7 Austria	Y	Y	Y	Y
8 Boehner	Y	Y	?	?
9 Kaptur	N	Y	Y	Y
10 Kucinich	N	N	Y	Y
11 Fudge	N	Y	Y	Y
12 Tiberi	?	Y	Y	Y
13 Sutton	N	Y	Y	Y
14 LaTourette	?	Y	Y	Y
15 Kilroy	N	Y	Y	Y
16 Boccieri	N	Y	Y	Y
17 Ryan	N	Y	Y	Y
18 Space	N	Y	Y	Y
OKLAHOMA				
1 Sullivan	Y	Y	Y	N
2 Boren	N	Y	Y	Y
3 Lucas	Y	Y	Y	N
4 Cole	Y	Y	Y	N
5 Fallin	Y	Y	Y	N
OREGON				
1 Wu	N	N	Y	Y
2 Walden	Y	Y	Y	Y
3 Blumenauer	N	Y	Y	Y
4 DeFazio	N	Y	Y	Y
5 Schrader	N	Y	Y	Y
PENNSYLVANIA				
1 Brady	N	Y	Y	Y
2 Fattah	N	N	Y	Y
3 Dahlkemper	N	Y	Y	Y
4 Altmire	N	N	Y	Y
5 Thompson	Y	Y	Y	Y
6 Gerlach	Y	Y	Y	Y
7 Sestak	N	Y	Y	Y
8 Murphy, P.	N	Y	Y	Y
9 Shuster	Y	Y	Y	Y
10 Carney	N	Y	Y	Y
11 Kanjorski	N	Y	Y	Y
12 Murtha	N	Y	Y	Y
13 Schwartz	N	Y	Y	Y
14 Doyle	N	Y	Y	?
15 Dent	Y	Y	Y	Y
16 Pitts	Y	Y	Y	N
17 Holden	N	Y	Y	Y
18 Murphy, T.	Y	Y	Y	Y
19 Platts	Y	Y	Y	Y
RHODE ISLAND				
1 Kennedy	N	Y	Y	Y
2 Langevin	N	Y	Y	Y
SOUTH CAROLINA				
1 Brown	Y	Y	Y	N
2 Wilson	Y	Y	Y	N
3 Barrett	Y	Y	Y	N
4 Inglis	Y	Y	Y	N
5 Spratt	N	Y	Y	Y
6 Clyburn	N	Y	Y	?
SOUTH DAKOTA				
AL Herseth Sandlin	N	Y	Y	Y
TENNESSEE				
1 Roe	Y	Y	Y	Y
2 Duncan	Y	Y	Y	N
3 Wamp	Y	Y	Y	Y
4 Davis	N	Y	Y	Y
5 Cooper	N	Y	Y	Y
6 Gordon	N	Y	Y	Y
7 Blackburn	Y	Y	Y	N
8 Tanner	N	Y	Y	Y
9 Cohen	N	Y	Y	Y

	203	204	205	206
TEXAS				
1 Gohmert	Y	Y	Y	N
2 Poe	Y	Y	N	Y
3 Johnson, S.	Y	Y	Y	Y
4 Hall	Y	Y	Y	Y
5 Hensarling	Y	Y	N	N
6 Barton	Y	Y	Y	N
7 Culberson	Y	Y	N	N
8 Brady	Y	Y	Y	N
9 Green, A.	N	Y	Y	Y
10 McCaul	Y	Y	Y	Y
11 Conaway	Y	Y	Y	N
12 Granger	Y	Y	Y	N
13 Thornberry	Y	Y	Y	N
14 Paul	Y	Y	?	Y
15 Hinojosa	N	Y	Y	Y
16 Reyes	?	?	?	?
17 Edwards	N	Y	Y	Y
18 Jackson Lee	N	Y	Y	Y
19 Neugebauer	Y	Y	Y	N
20 Gonzalez	N	Y	Y	Y
21 Smith	?	?	?	?
22 Olson	Y	Y	Y	N
23 Rodriguez	N	Y	Y	Y
24 Marchant	Y	Y	Y	N
25 Doggett	N	Y	Y	Y
26 Burgess	Y	Y	Y	Y
27 Ortiz	N	Y	Y	Y
28 Cuellar	Y	Y	Y	Y
29 Green, G.	N	+	Y	Y
30 Johnson, E.	N	Y	Y	Y
31 Carter	Y	Y	Y	N
32 Sessions	Y	Y	Y	N
UTAH				
1 Bishop	Y	Y	Y	N
2 Matheson	N	Y	Y	Y
3 Chaffetz	Y	Y	Y	Y
VERMONT				
AL Welch	N	Y	Y	Y
VIRGINIA				
1 Wittman	Y	Y	Y	Y
2 Nye	N	Y	Y	Y
3 Scott	N	Y	Y	Y
4 Forbes	Y	Y	Y	Y
5 Perriello	N	Y	Y	Y
6 Goodlatte	Y	Y	Y	N
7 Cantor	Y	Y	Y	N
8 Moran	N	Y	Y	Y
9 Boucher	N	Y	Y	Y
10 Wolf	Y	Y	Y	Y
11 Connolly	N	Y	Y	Y
WASHINGTON				
1 Inslee	N	Y	Y	Y
2 Larsen	N	Y	Y	Y
3 Baird	N	Y	?	Y
4 Hastings	Y	+	Y	N
5 McMorris Rodgers	Y	Y	Y	Y
6 Dicks	N	Y	Y	Y
7 McDermott	N	Y	Y	Y
8 Reichert	Y	Y	Y	Y
9 Smith	N	Y	Y	Y
WEST VIRGINIA				
1 Mollohan	N	Y	Y	Y
2 Capito	Y	Y	Y	Y
3 Rahall	N	Y	Y	Y
WISCONSIN				
1 Ryan	Y	Y	Y	N
2 Baldwin	N	N	Y	Y
3 Kind	N	Y	Y	Y
4 Moore	N	Y	Y	Y
5 Sensenbrenner	Y	Y	Y	N
6 Petri	Y	Y	Y	Y
7 Obey	N	Y	Y	Y
8 Kagen	N	Y	Y	Y
WYOMING				
AL Lummis	Y	Y	Y	N
DELEGATES				
Faleomavaega (A.S.)	N			
Norton (D.C.)	N			
Bordallo (Guam)	N			
Sablan (N. Marianas)	N			
Pierluisi (P.R.)	N			
Christensen (V.I.)	N			

IN THE HOUSE | By Vote Number

207. **H Res 329. Steamboat Accident Anniversary/Adoption.** Snyder, D-Ark., motion to suspend the rules and adopt the resolution that would recognize the 144-year anniversary of the accident of the steamboat ship SS *Sultana*. Motion agreed to 393-0: R 163-0; D 230-0. A two-thirds majority of those present and voting (262 in this case) is required for adoption under suspension of the rules. April 27, 2009.

208. **HR 1746. Pre-Disaster Mitigation Program/Passage.** Oberstar, D-Minn., motion to suspend the rules and pass the bill that would authorize $250 million annually in fiscal 2010-12 for the Federal Emergency Management Agency's pre-disaster mitigation program. The bill would increase the minimum amount a state can receive to $575,000 but would maintain an existing requirement that states receive the lesser of that amount or 1 percent of the annual funds appropriated for the program. Motion agreed to 339-56: R 107-56; D 232-0. A two-thirds majority of those present and voting (264 in this case) is required for passage under suspension of the rules. April 27, 2009.

209. **H Res 335. National Volunteer Week/Adoption.** Sablan, D-N. Marianas, motion to suspend the rules and adopt the resolution that would support the goals and ideals of National Volunteer Week, recognize the critical role of service programs and honor the contributions of American volunteers. Motion agreed to 396-0: R 163-0; D 233-0. A two-thirds majority of those present and voting (264 in this case) is required for adoption under suspension of the rules. April 27, 2009.

210. **HR 1243. Arnold Palmer Gold Medal/Passage.** Baca, D-Calif., motion to suspend the rules and pass the bill that would authorize $30,000 to create a gold medal to recognize Arnold Palmer's service in promoting excellence and good sportsmanship, and allow the Treasury Department to sell duplicates to cover the production costs. Motion agreed to 422-1: R 175-1; D 247-0. A two-thirds majority of those present and voting (282 in this case) is required for passage under suspension of the rules. April 28, 2009.

211. **H Res 344. University of Connecticut Women's Basketball/ Adoption.** Sablan, D-N. Marianas, motion to suspend the rules and adopt the resolution that would commend the University of Connecticut for winning the 2009 National Collegiate Athletic Association Division I women's basketball tournament. Motion agreed to 425-0: R 176-0; D 249-0. A two-thirds majority of those present and voting (284 in this case) is required for adoption under suspension of the rules. April 28, 2009.

212. **S Con Res 13. Fiscal 2010 Budget Resolution/Same-Day Consideration.** Adoption of the rule (H Res 365) that would waive the two-thirds majority vote requirement for same-day consideration of a rule for the conference report on the concurrent resolution that would allow up to $1.086 trillion in non-emergency discretionary spending for fiscal 2010, plus $130 billion in fiscal 2010 for operations in Iraq and Afghanistan. Adopted 233-191: R 1-174; D 232-17. April 28, 2009.

	207	208	209	210	211	212
ALABAMA						
1 Bonner	Y	Y	Y	Y	Y	N
2 Bright	Y	Y	Y	Y	Y	N
3 Rogers	Y	Y	Y	Y	Y	N
4 Aderholt	Y	Y	Y	Y	Y	N
5 Griffith	Y	Y	Y	Y	Y	N
6 Bachus	Y	Y	Y	Y	Y	N
7 Davis	Y	Y	Y	Y	Y	Y
ALASKA						
AL Young	Y	Y	Y	Y	Y	N
ARIZONA						
1 Kirkpatrick	Y	Y	Y	Y	Y	N
2 Franks	Y	N	Y	Y	Y	N
3 Shadegg	Y	N	Y	Y	Y	N
4 Pastor	Y	Y	Y	Y	Y	Y
5 Mitchell	Y	Y	Y	Y	Y	N
6 Flake	Y	N	Y	Y	Y	N
7 Grijalva	?	?	?	Y	Y	Y
8 Giffords	Y	Y	Y	Y	Y	Y
ARKANSAS						
1 Berry	Y	Y	Y	Y	Y	Y
2 Snyder	Y	Y	Y	Y	Y	Y
3 Boozman	Y	Y	Y	Y	Y	N
4 Ross	Y	Y	Y	Y	Y	Y
CALIFORNIA						
1 Thompson	Y	Y	Y	Y	Y	Y
2 Herger	Y	Y	Y	Y	Y	N
3 Lungren	Y	Y	Y	Y	Y	N
4 McClintock	Y	N	Y	Y	Y	N
5 Matsui	Y	Y	Y	Y	Y	Y
6 Woolsey	Y	Y	Y	Y	Y	Y
7 Miller, George	Y	Y	Y	Y	Y	Y
8 Pelosi						
9 Lee	Y	Y	Y	Y	Y	Y
10 Tauscher	Y	Y	Y	Y	Y	Y
11 McNerney	Y	Y	Y	Y	Y	Y
12 Speier	Y	Y	Y	Y	Y	Y
13 Stark	?	?	?	?	?	?
14 Eshoo	Y	Y	Y	Y	Y	Y
15 Honda	Y	Y	Y	Y	Y	Y
16 Lofgren	Y	Y	Y	?	Y	Y
17 Farr	Y	Y	Y	Y	Y	Y
18 Cardoza	Y	Y	Y	Y	Y	Y
19 Radanovich	Y	N	Y	Y	Y	N
20 Costa	Y	Y	Y	Y	Y	Y
21 Nunes	Y	Y	Y	Y	Y	N
22 McCarthy	Y	Y	Y	Y	Y	N
23 Capps	Y	Y	Y	Y	Y	Y
24 Gallegly	Y	Y	Y	Y	Y	N
25 McKeon	Y	Y	Y	Y	Y	N
26 Dreier	?	?	?	Y	Y	N
27 Sherman	Y	Y	Y	Y	Y	Y
28 Berman	Y	Y	Y	Y	Y	Y
29 Schiff	Y	Y	Y	Y	Y	Y
30 Waxman	?	?	?	Y	Y	Y
31 Becerra	Y	Y	Y	Y	Y	Y
32 Vacant						
33 Watson	Y	Y	Y	Y	Y	Y
34 Roybal-Allard	Y	Y	Y	Y	Y	Y
35 Waters	Y	Y	Y	Y	Y	Y
36 Harman	Y	Y	Y	Y	Y	Y
37 Richardson	Y	Y	Y	Y	Y	Y
38 Napolitano	Y	Y	Y	Y	Y	Y
39 Sánchez, Linda	Y	Y	Y	Y	Y	Y
40 Royce	Y	N	Y	Y	Y	N
41 Lewis	Y	Y	Y	Y	Y	N
42 Miller, Gary	Y	Y	Y	Y	Y	N
43 Baca	Y	Y	Y	Y	Y	Y
44 Calvert	Y	Y	Y	Y	Y	N
45 Bono Mack	Y	Y	Y	Y	Y	N
46 Rohrabacher	?	?	?	Y	Y	N
47 Sanchez, Loretta	Y	Y	Y	Y	Y	Y
48 Campbell	Y	N	Y	Y	Y	N
49 Issa	Y	N	Y	Y	Y	N
50 Bilbray	Y	Y	Y	Y	Y	N
51 Filner	Y	Y	Y	Y	Y	Y
52 Hunter	Y	Y	Y	Y	Y	N
53 Davis	Y	Y	Y	Y	Y	Y

	207	208	209	210	211	212
COLORADO						
1 DeGette	Y	Y	Y	Y	Y	Y
2 Polis	Y	Y	Y	Y	Y	Y
3 Salazar	Y	Y	Y	Y	Y	Y
4 Markey	Y	Y	Y	Y	Y	Y
5 Lamborn	Y	N	Y	Y	Y	N
6 Coffman	Y	N	Y	Y	Y	N
7 Perlmutter	Y	Y	Y	Y	Y	Y
CONNECTICUT						
1 Larson	Y	Y	Y	Y	Y	Y
2 Courtney	Y	Y	Y	Y	Y	Y
3 DeLauro	Y	Y	Y	Y	Y	Y
4 Himes	Y	Y	Y	Y	Y	Y
5 Murphy	Y	Y	Y	Y	Y	Y
DELAWARE						
AL Castle	Y	Y	Y	Y	Y	N
FLORIDA						
1 Miller	Y	N	Y	Y	Y	N
2 Boyd	Y	Y	Y	Y	Y	Y
3 Brown	?	?	?	?	?	?
4 Crenshaw	Y	Y	Y	Y	Y	N
5 Brown-Waite	Y	Y	Y	Y	Y	N
6 Stearns	Y	N	Y	Y	Y	N
7 Mica	Y	Y	Y	Y	Y	N
8 Grayson	Y	Y	Y	Y	Y	Y
9 Bilirakis	Y	Y	Y	Y	Y	N
10 Young	?	?	?	Y	Y	N
11 Castor	Y	Y	Y	Y	Y	Y
12 Putnam	Y	Y	Y	Y	Y	N
13 Buchanan	Y	Y	Y	Y	Y	N
14 Mack	Y	Y	Y	Y	Y	N
15 Posey	Y	Y	Y	Y	Y	N
16 Rooney	Y	Y	Y	Y	Y	N
17 Meek	Y	Y	Y	Y	Y	Y
18 Ros-Lehtinen	Y	Y	Y	Y	Y	N
19 Wexler	Y	Y	Y	Y	Y	Y
20 Wasserman Schultz	Y	Y	Y	Y	Y	Y
21 Diaz-Balart, L.	Y	Y	Y	Y	Y	N
22 Klein	Y	Y	Y	Y	Y	Y
23 Hastings	Y	Y	Y	Y	Y	Y
24 Kosmas	Y	Y	Y	Y	Y	Y
25 Diaz-Balart, M.	Y	Y	Y	Y	Y	N
GEORGIA						
1 Kingston	?	?	?	Y	Y	N
2 Bishop	Y	Y	Y	Y	Y	Y
3 Westmoreland	Y	N	Y	Y	Y	N
4 Johnson	Y	?	Y	Y	Y	Y
5 Lewis	Y	Y	Y	Y	Y	Y
6 Price	Y	N	Y	Y	Y	N
7 Linder	Y	N	Y	Y	Y	N
8 Marshall	Y	Y	Y	Y	Y	Y
9 Deal	Y	N	?	Y	Y	N
10 Broun	Y	N	Y	Y	Y	N
11 Gingrey	Y	N	Y	Y	Y	N
12 Barrow	Y	Y	Y	Y	Y	Y
13 Scott	Y	Y	Y	Y	Y	Y
HAWAII						
1 Abercrombie	Y	Y	Y	Y	Y	Y
2 Hirono	Y	Y	Y	Y	Y	Y
IDAHO						
1 Minnick	Y	Y	Y	Y	Y	N
2 Simpson	Y	Y	Y	Y	Y	N
ILLINOIS						
1 Rush	Y	Y	Y	Y	Y	Y
2 Jackson	?	?	?	?	?	?
3 Lipinski	?	?	?	Y	Y	Y
4 Gutierrez	+	+	+	Y	Y	Y
5 Quigley	Y	Y	Y	Y	Y	Y
6 Roskam	Y	Y	Y	Y	Y	N
7 Davis	Y	Y	Y	Y	Y	Y
8 Bean	Y	Y	Y	Y	Y	Y
9 Schakowsky	Y	Y	Y	Y	Y	Y
10 Kirk	Y	?	Y	Y	Y	N
11 Halvorson	Y	Y	Y	Y	Y	Y
12 Costello	?	?	?	Y	Y	Y
13 Biggert	Y	Y	Y	Y	Y	N
14 Foster	Y	Y	Y	Y	Y	Y
15 Johnson	+	+	+	Y	Y	N

KEY

Republicans	Democrats		

Y Voted for (yea)

\# Paired for

\+ Announced for

N Voted against (nay)

X Paired against

– Announced against

P Voted "present"

C Voted "present" to avoid possible conflict of interest

? Did not vote or otherwise make a position known

	207	208	209	210	211	212
16 **Manzullo**	Y	N	Y	Y	Y	N
17 Hare	Y	Y	Y	Y	Y	Y
18 **Schock**	Y	Y	Y	Y	Y	N
19 **Shimkus**	Y	Y	Y	Y	Y	N
INDIANA						
1 Visclosky	Y	Y	Y	Y	Y	Y
2 Donnelly	Y	Y	Y	Y	Y	Y
3 **Souder**	Y	Y	Y	Y	Y	N
4 **Buyer**	Y	N	Y	Y	Y	N
5 **Burton**	Y	N	Y	Y	Y	N
6 **Pence**	Y	N	Y	Y	Y	N
7 Carson	Y	Y	Y	Y	Y	Y
8 Ellsworth	Y	Y	Y	Y	Y	Y
9 Hill	Y	Y	Y	Y	Y	N
IOWA						
1 Braley	?	Y	Y	Y	Y	Y
2 Loebsack	Y	Y	Y	Y	Y	Y
3 Boswell	Y	Y	Y	Y	Y	Y
4 **Latham**	Y	Y	Y	Y	Y	N
5 **King**	Y	Y	Y	Y	Y	N
KANSAS						
1 **Moran**	Y	Y	Y	Y	Y	N
2 **Jenkins**	Y	Y	Y	Y	Y	N
3 Moore	Y	Y	Y	Y	Y	Y
4 **Tiahrt**	Y	N	Y	Y	Y	N
KENTUCKY						
1 **Whitfield**	Y	Y	Y	Y	Y	N
2 **Guthrie**	Y	Y	Y	Y	Y	N
3 Yarmuth	Y	Y	Y	Y	Y	Y
4 **Davis**	Y	Y	Y	Y	Y	N
5 **Rogers**	Y	Y	Y	Y	Y	N
6 Chandler	Y	Y	Y	Y	Y	Y
LOUISIANA						
1 **Scalise**	Y	Y	Y	Y	Y	N
2 **Cao**	Y	Y	Y	Y	Y	N
3 Melancon	Y	Y	Y	Y	Y	Y
4 **Fleming**	Y	Y	Y	Y	Y	N
5 **Alexander**	Y	Y	Y	Y	Y	N
6 **Cassidy**	Y	Y	Y	Y	Y	N
7 **Boustany**	Y	Y	Y	Y	Y	N
MAINE						
1 Pingree	Y	Y	Y	Y	Y	Y
2 Michaud	Y	Y	Y	Y	Y	N
MARYLAND						
1 Kratovil	Y	Y	Y	Y	Y	N
2 Ruppersberger	Y	Y	Y	Y	Y	Y
3 Sarbanes	Y	Y	Y	Y	Y	Y
4 Edwards	Y	Y	Y	Y	Y	Y
5 Hoyer	Y	Y	Y	Y	Y	Y
6 **Bartlett**	Y	N	Y	Y	Y	Y
7 Cummings	Y	Y	Y	Y	Y	Y
8 Van Hollen	Y	Y	Y	Y	Y	Y
MASSACHUSETTS						
1 Olver	Y	Y	Y	Y	Y	Y
2 Neal	?	?	?	Y	Y	Y
3 McGovern	Y	Y	Y	Y	Y	Y
4 Frank	Y	Y	Y	Y	Y	Y
5 Tsongas	Y	Y	Y	Y	Y	Y
6 Tierney	Y	Y	Y	Y	Y	Y
7 Markey	Y	Y	Y	Y	Y	Y
8 Capuano	Y	Y	Y	Y	Y	Y
9 Lynch	Y	Y	Y	Y	Y	Y
10 Delahunt	Y	Y	Y	Y	Y	Y
MICHIGAN						
1 Stupak	Y	Y	Y	Y	Y	Y
2 **Hoekstra**	Y	Y	Y	Y	Y	N
3 **Ehlers**	Y	Y	Y	Y	Y	N
4 **Camp**	Y	Y	Y	Y	Y	N
5 Kildee	Y	Y	Y	Y	Y	Y
6 **Upton***	Y	Y	Y	Y	Y	N
7 Schauer	Y	Y	Y	Y	Y	Y
8 **Rogers**	Y	Y	Y	Y	Y	?
9 Peters	Y	Y	Y	Y	Y	Y
10 **Miller**	Y	Y	Y	Y	Y	N
11 **McCotter**	Y	Y	Y	Y	Y	N
12 Levin	Y	Y	Y	Y	Y	Y
13 Kilpatrick	Y	Y	Y	Y	Y	Y
14 Conyers	?	Y	Y	Y	Y	Y
15 Dingell	Y	Y	Y	Y	Y	Y
MINNESOTA						
1 Walz	Y	Y	Y	Y	Y	Y
2 **Kline**	Y	N	Y	Y	Y	N
3 **Paulsen**	Y	Y	Y	Y	Y	N
4 McCollum	Y	Y	Y	Y	Y	Y
5 Ellison	Y	Y	Y	Y	Y	Y
6 **Bachmann**	Y	N	Y	Y	Y	N
7 Peterson	Y	Y	Y	Y	Y	Y
8 Oberstar	Y	Y	Y	Y	Y	Y
MISSISSIPPI						
1 Childers	Y	Y	Y	Y	Y	N
2 Thompson	Y	Y	Y	Y	Y	Y
3 **Harper**	Y	N	Y	Y	Y	N
4 Taylor	Y	Y	Y	Y	Y	N
MISSOURI						
1 Clay	Y	Y	Y	?	?	?
2 **Akin**	Y	N	Y	Y	Y	N
3 Carnahan	Y	Y	Y	Y	Y	Y
4 Skelton	Y	Y	Y	Y	Y	Y
5 Cleaver	Y	Y	Y	Y	Y	Y
6 **Graves**	Y	Y	Y	Y	Y	N
7 **Blunt**	Y	Y	Y	Y	Y	N
8 **Emerson**	Y	Y	Y	Y	Y	N
9 **Luetkemeyer**	Y	Y	Y	Y	Y	N
MONTANA						
AL **Rehberg**	Y	Y	Y	Y	Y	N
NEBRASKA						
1 **Fortenberry**	+	+	+	Y	Y	N
2 **Terry**	?	?	?	Y	Y	N
3 **Smith**	Y	Y	Y	Y	Y	N
NEVADA						
1 Berkley	Y	Y	Y	Y	Y	Y
2 **Heller**	Y	Y	Y	Y	Y	N
3 Titus	Y	Y	Y	Y	Y	Y
NEW HAMPSHIRE						
1 Shea-Porter	Y	Y	Y	Y	Y	Y
2 Hodes	Y	Y	Y	Y	Y	Y
NEW JERSEY						
1 Andrews	Y	Y	Y	Y	Y	Y
2 **LoBiondo**	Y	Y	Y	Y	Y	N
3 Adler	Y	Y	Y	Y	Y	Y
4 **Smith**	Y	Y	Y	Y	Y	N
5 **Garrett**	?	N	Y	Y	Y	N
6 Pallone	?	?	?	Y	Y	Y
7 **Lance**	Y	Y	Y	Y	Y	N
8 Pascrell	Y	Y	Y	Y	Y	Y
9 Rothman	Y	Y	Y	Y	Y	Y
10 Payne	Y	Y	Y	Y	Y	Y
11 **Frelinghuysen**	Y	Y	Y	Y	Y	N
12 Holt	Y	Y	Y	Y	Y	Y
13 Sires	?	?	?	Y	Y	Y
NEW MEXICO						
1 Heinrich	Y	Y	Y	Y	Y	Y
2 Teague	Y	Y	Y	Y	Y	Y
3 Lujan	Y	Y	Y	Y	Y	Y
NEW YORK						
1 Bishop	Y	Y	Y	Y	Y	Y
2 Israel	Y	Y	Y	Y	Y	Y
3 **King**	?	?	?	Y	Y	N
4 McCarthy	Y	Y	Y	Y	Y	Y
5 Ackerman	Y	Y	Y	Y	Y	Y
6 Meeks	Y	Y	Y	Y	Y	Y
7 Crowley	Y	Y	Y	Y	Y	Y
8 Nadler	Y	Y	Y	Y	Y	Y
9 Weiner	?	?	?	Y	Y	Y
10 Towns	Y	Y	Y	Y	Y	Y
11 Clarke	+	+	+	Y	Y	Y
12 Velázquez	Y	Y	Y	Y	Y	Y
13 McMahon	Y	Y	Y	Y	Y	Y
14 Maloney	Y	Y	Y	Y	Y	Y
15 Rangel	Y	Y	Y	Y	Y	Y
16 Serrano	Y	Y	Y	Y	Y	Y
17 Engel	Y	Y	Y	Y	Y	Y
18 Lowey	Y	Y	Y	Y	Y	Y
19 Hall	Y	Y	Y	Y	Y	Y
20 Vacant*						
21 Tonko	Y	Y	Y	Y	Y	Y
22 Hinchey	Y	Y	Y	Y	Y	Y
23 **McHugh**	Y	Y	Y	Y	Y	N
24 Arcuri	Y	Y	Y	Y	Y	Y
25 Maffei	Y	Y	Y	Y	Y	Y
26 **Lee**	Y	Y	Y	Y	Y	N
27 Higgins	Y	Y	Y	Y	Y	Y
28 Slaughter	Y	Y	Y	Y	Y	Y
29 Massa	Y	Y	Y	P	Y	Y
NORTH CAROLINA						
1 Butterfield	Y	Y	Y	Y	Y	Y
2 Etheridge	Y	Y	Y	Y	Y	Y
3 **Jones**	Y	Y	Y	Y	Y	N
4 Price	Y	Y	Y	Y	Y	Y
5 **Foxx**	Y	N	Y	Y	Y	N
6 **Coble**	Y	N	Y	Y	Y	N
7 McIntyre	Y	Y	Y	Y	Y	Y
8 Kissell	Y	Y	Y	Y	Y	Y
9 **Myrick**	Y	Y	Y	Y	Y	N
10 **McHenry**	Y	N	Y	Y	Y	N
11 Shuler	?	?	?	Y	Y	N
12 Watt	Y	Y	Y	Y	Y	Y
13 Miller	Y	Y	Y	Y	Y	Y
NORTH DAKOTA						
AL Pomeroy	Y	Y	Y	Y	Y	Y
OHIO						
1 Driehaus	Y	Y	Y	Y	Y	N
2 **Schmidt**	Y	Y	Y	Y	Y	N
3 **Turner**	Y	Y	Y	Y	Y	N
4 **Jordan**	Y	N	Y	Y	Y	N
5 **Latta**	Y	Y	Y	Y	Y	N
6 Wilson	Y	Y	Y	Y	Y	Y
7 **Austria**	Y	Y	Y	Y	Y	N
8 **Boehner**	Y	N	Y	Y	Y	N
9 Kaptur	Y	Y	Y	Y	Y	Y
10 Kucinich	Y	Y	Y	Y	Y	Y
11 Fudge	Y	Y	Y	Y	Y	Y
12 **Tiberi**	?	?	?	Y	Y	N
13 Sutton	Y	Y	Y	Y	Y	Y
14 **LaTourette**	Y	Y	Y	Y	Y	N
15 Kilroy	?	?	?	Y	Y	N
16 Boccieri	Y	Y	Y	Y	Y	Y
17 Ryan	Y	Y	Y	Y	Y	Y
18 Space	Y	Y	Y	Y	Y	Y
OKLAHOMA						
1 **Sullivan**	Y	N	Y	Y	Y	N
2 Boren	Y	Y	Y	Y	Y	Y
3 **Lucas**	Y	Y	Y	Y	Y	N
4 **Cole**	Y	Y	Y	Y	Y	N
5 **Fallin**	Y	Y	Y	Y	Y	N
OREGON						
1 Wu	?	?	?	?	?	?
2 **Walden**	Y	Y	Y	Y	Y	N
3 Blumenauer	Y	Y	Y	Y	Y	Y
4 DeFazio	Y	Y	Y	Y	Y	Y
5 Schrader	Y	Y	Y	Y	Y	Y
PENNSYLVANIA						
1 Brady	Y	Y	Y	Y	Y	Y
2 Fattah	Y	Y	Y	Y	Y	Y
3 Dahlkemper	Y	Y	Y	Y	Y	Y
4 Altmire	Y	Y	Y	Y	Y	Y
5 **Thompson**	?	?	?	Y	Y	N
6 **Gerlach**	Y	Y	Y	Y	Y	N
7 Sestak	Y	Y	Y	Y	Y	Y
8 Murphy, P.	Y	Y	Y	Y	Y	Y
9 **Shuster**	Y	Y	Y	Y	Y	N
10 Carney	+	+	+	Y	Y	N
11 Kanjorski	Y	Y	Y	Y	Y	Y
12 Murtha	Y	Y	Y	Y	Y	Y
13 Schwartz	Y	Y	Y	Y	Y	Y
14 Doyle	Y	Y	Y	Y	Y	Y
15 **Dent**	Y	Y	Y	Y	Y	N
16 **Pitts**	Y	N	Y	Y	Y	N
17 Holden	Y	Y	Y	Y	Y	Y
18 **Murphy, T.**	Y	Y	Y	Y	Y	N
19 **Platts**	Y	Y	Y	Y	Y	N
RHODE ISLAND						
1 Kennedy	Y	Y	Y	Y	Y	Y
2 Langevin	Y	Y	Y	Y	Y	Y
SOUTH CAROLINA						
1 **Brown**	Y	Y	Y	Y	Y	N
2 **Wilson**	Y	N	Y	Y	Y	N
3 **Barrett**	+	−	+	Y	Y	N
4 **Inglis**	Y	N	Y	Y	Y	N
5 Spratt	Y	Y	Y	Y	Y	Y
6 Clyburn	Y	Y	Y	Y	Y	Y
SOUTH DAKOTA						
AL Herseth Sandlin	Y	Y	Y	Y	Y	Y
TENNESSEE						
1 **Roe**	Y	Y	Y	Y	Y	N
2 **Duncan**	Y	N	Y	Y	Y	N
3 **Wamp**	?	?	?	Y	Y	N
4 Davis	Y	Y	Y	Y	Y	Y
5 Cooper	Y	Y	Y	Y	Y	Y
6 Gordon	Y	Y	Y	Y	Y	Y
7 **Blackburn**	Y	N	Y	Y	Y	N
8 Tanner	Y	Y	Y	Y	Y	Y
9 Cohen	Y	Y	Y	Y	Y	Y
TEXAS						
1 **Gohmert**	Y	Y	Y	Y	Y	N
2 **Poe**	Y	Y	Y	Y	Y	N
3 **Johnson, S.**	?	?	?	?	?	?
4 **Hall**	Y	Y	Y	Y	Y	N
5 **Hensarling**	Y	N	Y	Y	Y	N
6 **Barton**	Y	N	Y	Y	Y	N
7 **Culberson**	Y	N	Y	Y	Y	N
8 **Brady**	Y	Y	Y	Y	Y	N
9 Green, A.	Y	Y	Y	Y	Y	Y
10 **McCaul**	Y	Y	Y	Y	Y	N
11 **Conaway**	Y	N	Y	Y	Y	N
12 **Granger**	Y	Y	Y	Y	Y	N
13 **Thornberry**	Y	Y	Y	Y	Y	N
14 **Paul**	Y	N	Y	N	Y	N
15 Hinojosa	Y	Y	Y	Y	Y	Y
16 Reyes	?	?	?	Y	Y	Y
17 Edwards	Y	Y	Y	Y	Y	Y
18 Jackson Lee	+	+	+	Y	Y	Y
19 **Neugebauer**	Y	N	Y	Y	Y	N
20 Gonzalez	Y	Y	Y	Y	Y	Y
21 **Smith**	Y	Y	Y	Y	Y	N
22 **Olson**	Y	Y	Y	Y	Y	N
23 Rodriguez	Y	Y	Y	Y	Y	Y
24 **Marchant**	Y	N	Y	Y	Y	N
25 Doggett	Y	Y	Y	Y	Y	Y
26 **Burgess**	?	?	?	?	?	?
27 Ortiz	Y	Y	Y	Y	Y	Y
28 Cuellar	Y	Y	Y	Y	Y	Y
29 Green, G.	Y	Y	Y	Y	Y	Y
30 Johnson, E.	Y	Y	Y	Y	Y	Y
31 **Carter**	Y	N	Y	Y	Y	N
32 **Sessions**	Y	Y	Y	Y	Y	N
UTAH						
1 **Bishop**	Y	N	Y	Y	Y	N
2 Matheson	Y	Y	Y	Y	Y	Y
3 **Chaffetz**	Y	N	Y	Y	Y	N
VERMONT						
AL Welch	Y	Y	Y	Y	Y	Y
VIRGINIA						
1 **Wittman**	Y	Y	Y	Y	Y	N
2 Nye	Y	Y	Y	Y	Y	Y
3 Scott	Y	Y	Y	Y	Y	Y
4 **Forbes**	Y	Y	Y	Y	Y	N
5 Perriello	Y	Y	Y	Y	Y	Y
6 **Goodlatte**	Y	N	Y	Y	Y	N
7 **Cantor**	Y	N	Y	Y	Y	N
8 Moran	?	?	?	Y	Y	Y
9 Boucher	Y	Y	Y	Y	Y	Y
10 **Wolf**	Y	Y	Y	Y	Y	N
11 Connolly	Y	Y	Y	Y	Y	Y
WASHINGTON						
1 Inslee	Y	Y	Y	Y	Y	Y
2 Larsen	?	?	?	Y	Y	Y
3 Baird	Y	Y	Y	Y	Y	N
4 **Hastings**	Y	N	Y	Y	Y	N
5 **McMorris Rodgers**	Y	Y	Y	Y	Y	N
6 Dicks	Y	Y	Y	Y	Y	Y
7 McDermott	Y	Y	Y	Y	Y	Y
8 **Reichert**	Y	Y	Y	Y	Y	N
9 Smith	Y	Y	Y	Y	Y	Y
WEST VIRGINIA						
1 Mollohan	?	Y	Y	Y	Y	Y
2 **Capito**	Y	Y	Y	Y	Y	N
3 Rahall	Y	Y	Y	Y	Y	Y
WISCONSIN						
1 **Ryan**	Y	Y	Y	Y	Y	N
2 Baldwin	Y	Y	Y	Y	Y	Y
3 Kind	Y	Y	Y	Y	Y	Y
4 Moore	Y	Y	Y	Y	Y	Y
5 **Sensenbrenner**	Y	N	Y	Y	Y	N
6 **Petri**	Y	N	Y	Y	Y	N
7 Obey	Y	Y	Y	Y	Y	Y
8 Kagen	Y	Y	Y	Y	Y	Y
WYOMING						
AL **Lummis**	Y	N	Y	Y	Y	N
DELEGATES						
Faleomavaega (A.S.)						
Norton (D.C.)						
Bordallo (Guam)						
Sablan (N. Marianas)						
Pierluisi (P.R.)						
Christensen (V.I.)						

IN THE HOUSE | By Vote Number

213. S Con Res 13. Fiscal 2010 Budget Resolution/Two-Day Debate.
McGovern, D-Mass., amendment to the rule (H Res 371) that would provide for House floor consideration of the conference report on the concurrent resolution that would allow up to $1.086 trillion in non-emergency discretionary spending for fiscal 2010, plus $130 billion in fiscal 2010 for operations in Iraq and Afghanistan. The amendment would allow the chair to postpone further consideration of the conference report to such time as designated by the Speaker, allowing for debate to take place over a two-day period. Adopted 240-179: R 0-173; D 240-6. April 28, 2009.

214. S Con Res 13. Fiscal 2010 Budget Resolution/Rule.
Adoption of the rule (H Res 371) that would provide for House floor consideration of the conference report on the concurrent resolution that would allow up to $1.086 trillion in non-emergency discretionary spending for fiscal 2010, plus $130 billion in fiscal 2010 for operations in Iraq and Afghanistan. Adopted 234-185: R 0-174; D 234-11. April 28, 2009.

215. HR 1595. Brian Schramm Post Office/Passage.
Lynch, D-Mass., motion to suspend the rules and pass the bill that would designate a post office in Rochester, N.Y., as the "Brian K. Schramm Post Office Building." Motion agreed to 420-0: R 173-0; D 247-0. A two-thirds majority of those present and voting (280 in this case) is required for passage under suspension of the rules. April 28, 2009.

216. S Con Res 13. Fiscal 2010 Budget Resolution/Conference Report.
Adoption of the conference report on the concurrent resolution that would allow up to $1.086 trillion in non-emergency discretionary spending for fiscal 2010, plus $130 billion in fiscal 2010 for operations in Iraq and Afghanistan. It would assume $764 billion in tax cuts over five years, including an extension of the 2001 and 2003 tax cuts for households earning less than $250,000 annually, a three-year adjustment to prevent additional taxpayers from paying the alternative minimum tax, and a permanent extension of the 2009 estate tax levels. It includes reconciliation instructions to House and Senate committees to report a total of $2 billion in savings, presumably from health care and student loan programs, by Oct. 15. It would create a deficit-neutral reserve fund for health care and climate change legislation. Adopted (thus sent to the Senate) 233-193: R 0-176; D 233-17. April 29, 2009.

217. H Res 357. Financial Literacy Month/Adoption.
Moore, D-Kan., motion to suspend the rules and adopt the resolution that would support the goals and ideals of Financial Literacy Month and recognize the importance of managing personal finances, increasing savings and reducing debt. Motion agreed to 419-3: R 172-3; D 247-0. A two-thirds majority of those present and voting (282 in this case) is required for adoption under suspension of the rules. April 29, 2009.

218. H Res 109. National Crime Victims' Rights Week/Adoption.
Scott, D-Va., motion to suspend the rules and adopt the resolution that would support the mission and goals of 2009 National Crime Victims' Rights Week and recognize the 25th anniversary of the enactment of the Victims of Crime Act of 1984. Motion agreed to 422-0: R 174-0; D 248-0. A two-thirds majority of those present and voting (282 in this case) is required for adoption under suspension of the rules. April 29, 2009.

	213	214	215	216	217	218
ALABAMA						
1 Bonner	N	N	Y	N	Y	Y
2 Bright	Y	Y	Y	N	Y	Y
3 Rogers	N	N	Y	N	Y	Y
4 Aderholt	N	N	Y	N	Y	Y
5 Griffith	Y	Y	Y	N	Y	Y
6 Bachus	N	N	Y	N	Y	Y
7 Davis	Y	Y	Y	Y	Y	Y
ALASKA						
AL Young	N	N	Y	N	Y	Y
ARIZONA						
1 Kirkpatrick	Y	Y	Y	Y	Y	Y
2 Franks	N	N	Y	N	Y	Y
3 Shadegg	N	N	Y	N	Y	Y
4 Pastor	Y	Y	Y	Y	Y	Y
5 Mitchell	Y	Y	Y	N	Y	Y
6 Flake	N	N	Y	N	N	Y
7 Grijalva	Y	Y	Y	Y	Y	Y
8 Giffords	Y	Y	Y	Y	Y	Y
ARKANSAS						
1 Berry	Y	Y	Y	Y	Y	Y
2 Snyder	Y	Y	Y	Y	Y	Y
3 Boozman	N	N	Y	N	Y	Y
4 Ross	Y	Y	Y	Y	Y	Y
CALIFORNIA						
1 Thompson	Y	Y	Y	Y	Y	Y
2 Herger	N	N	Y	N	Y	Y
3 Lungren	N	N	Y	N	Y	Y
4 McClintock	N	N	Y	N	Y	Y
5 Matsui	Y	Y	Y	Y	Y	Y
6 Woolsey	Y	Y	Y	Y	Y	Y
7 Miller, George	Y	Y	Y	Y	Y	Y
8 Pelosi				Y		
9 Lee	Y	Y	Y	Y		Y
10 Tauscher	Y	Y	Y	Y	Y	Y
11 McNerney	Y	Y	Y	Y	Y	Y
12 Speier	Y	Y	Y	Y	Y	Y
13 Stark	?	?	?	?	?	Y
14 Eshoo	Y	Y	Y	Y	Y	Y
15 Honda	Y	Y	Y	Y	Y	Y
16 Lofgren	Y	Y	Y	Y	Y	Y
17 Farr	Y	Y	Y	Y	Y	Y
18 Cardoza	Y	Y	Y	Y	Y	Y
19 Radanovich	N	N	Y	N	Y	Y
20 Costa	Y	Y	Y	Y	Y	Y
21 Nunes	N	N	Y	N	Y	Y
22 McCarthy	N	N	Y	N	Y	Y
23 Capps	Y	Y	Y	Y	Y	Y
24 Gallegly	N	N	Y	N	Y	Y
25 McKeon	?	?	?	N	Y	Y
26 Dreier	N	N	Y	N	Y	Y
27 Sherman	Y	Y	Y	Y	Y	Y
28 Berman	Y	Y	Y	Y	Y	Y
29 Schiff	Y	Y	Y	Y	Y	Y
30 Waxman	Y	Y	Y	Y	Y	Y
31 Becerra	Y	Y	Y	Y	Y	Y
32 Vacant						
33 Watson	Y	Y	Y	Y	Y	Y
34 Roybal-Allard	Y	Y	Y	Y	Y	Y
35 Waters	Y	Y	Y	Y	Y	Y
36 Harman	Y	Y	Y	Y	Y	Y
37 Richardson	Y	Y	Y	Y	Y	Y
38 Napolitano	Y	Y	Y	Y	Y	Y
39 Sánchez, Linda	Y	Y	Y	Y	Y	Y
40 Royce	N	N	Y	N	Y	Y
41 Lewis	N	N	Y	N	Y	Y
42 Miller, Gary	N	N	Y	N	Y	Y
43 Baca	Y	Y	Y	Y	Y	Y
44 Calvert	N	N	Y	N	Y	Y
45 Bono Mack	N	N	Y	N	Y	Y
46 Rohrabacher	N	N	Y	N	Y	Y
47 Sanchez, Loretta	Y	Y	?	?	Y	?
48 Campbell	N	N	Y	N	Y	Y
49 Issa	N	N	Y	N	Y	Y
50 Bilbray	N	N	Y	N	Y	Y
51 Filner	Y	Y	Y	Y	Y	Y
52 Hunter	N	N	Y	N	Y	Y
53 Davis	Y	Y	Y	Y	Y	Y
COLORADO						
1 DeGette	Y	Y	Y	Y	Y	Y
2 Polis	Y	Y	Y	Y	Y	Y
3 Salazar	Y	Y	Y	Y	Y	Y
4 Markey	Y	Y	Y	N	Y	Y
5 Lamborn	N	N	Y	N	Y	Y
6 Coffman	N	N	Y	N	Y	Y
7 Perlmutter	Y	Y	Y	Y	Y	Y
CONNECTICUT						
1 Larson	Y	Y	Y	Y	Y	Y
2 Courtney	Y	Y	Y	Y	Y	Y
3 DeLauro	Y	Y	Y	Y	Y	Y
4 Himes	Y	Y	Y	Y	Y	Y
5 Murphy	Y	Y	Y	Y	Y	Y
DELAWARE						
AL Castle	N	N	Y	N	Y	Y
FLORIDA						
1 Miller	N	N	Y	N	Y	Y
2 Boyd	Y	Y	Y	Y	Y	Y
3 Brown	?	?	?	Y	Y	Y
4 Crenshaw	N	N	Y	N	Y	Y
5 Brown-Waite	N	N	Y	N	Y	Y
6 Stearns	N	N	Y	N	Y	Y
7 Mica	N	N	Y	N	Y	Y
8 Grayson	Y	Y	Y	Y	Y	Y
9 Bilirakis	N	N	Y	N	Y	Y
10 Young	N	N	Y	N	Y	Y
11 Castor	Y	Y	Y	Y	Y	Y
12 Putnam	N	N	Y	N	Y	Y
13 Buchanan	N	N	Y	N	Y	Y
14 Mack	N	N	Y	N	Y	Y
15 Posey	N	N	Y	N	Y	Y
16 Rooney	N	N	Y	N	Y	Y
17 Meek	Y	Y	Y	Y	Y	Y
18 Ros-Lehtinen	N	N	Y	N	Y	Y
19 Wexler	Y	Y	Y	Y	Y	Y
20 Wasserman Schultz	Y	Y	Y	Y	Y	Y
21 Diaz-Balart, L.	N	N	Y	N	Y	Y
22 Klein	Y	Y	Y	Y	Y	Y
23 Hastings	Y	Y	Y	Y	Y	Y
24 Kosmas	Y	Y	Y	Y	Y	Y
25 Diaz-Balart, M.	N	N	Y	N	Y	Y
GEORGIA						
1 Kingston	N	N	Y	N	Y	Y
2 Bishop	Y	Y	Y	Y	Y	Y
3 Westmoreland	N	N	Y	N	Y	Y
4 Johnson	Y	Y	Y	Y	Y	Y
5 Lewis	Y	Y	Y	?	?	Y
6 Price	N	N	Y	N	Y	Y
7 Linder	N	N	Y	N	Y	Y
8 Marshall	N	N	Y	N	Y	Y
9 Deal	N	N	Y	N	Y	Y
10 Broun	N	N	Y	N	Y	Y
11 Gingrey	N	N	Y	N	Y	Y
12 Barrow	Y	N	Y	N	Y	Y
13 Scott	Y	Y	Y	Y	Y	Y
HAWAII						
1 Abercrombie	Y	Y	Y	Y	Y	Y
2 Hirono	Y	Y	Y	Y	Y	Y
IDAHO						
1 Minnick	N	N	Y	N	Y	Y
2 Simpson	N	N	Y	N	Y	Y
ILLINOIS						
1 Rush	Y	Y	Y	Y	Y	Y
2 Jackson	?	?	?	?	?	?
3 Lipinski	Y	Y	Y	Y	Y	Y
4 Gutierrez	Y	Y	Y	Y	Y	Y
5 Quigley	Y	Y	Y	Y	Y	Y
6 Roskam	N	N	Y	N	Y	Y
7 Davis	Y	Y	Y	Y	Y	Y
8 Bean	Y	Y	Y	Y	Y	Y
9 Schakowsky	Y	Y	Y	Y	Y	Y
10 Kirk	N	N	Y	N	Y	?
11 Halvorson	Y	Y	Y	Y	Y	Y
12 Costello	Y	Y	Y	Y	Y	Y
13 Biggert	N	N	Y	N	Y	Y
14 Foster	Y	Y	Y	N	Y	Y
15 Johnson	N	N	Y	N	Y	Y

	213	214	215	216	217	218
16 **Manzullo**	N	N	Y	N	Y	Y
17 Hare	Y	Y	Y	Y	Y	Y
18 **Schock**	N	N	Y	N	Y	Y
19 **Shimkus**	N	N	Y	N	Y	Y
INDIANA						
1 Visclosky	Y	Y	Y	Y	Y	Y
2 Donnelly	Y	Y	Y	Y	Y	Y
3 **Souder**	N	N	Y	N	Y	Y
4 **Buyer**	N	N	Y	N	Y	Y
5 **Burton**	N	N	Y	N	Y	Y
6 **Pence**	N	N	Y	N	Y	Y
7 Carson	Y	Y	Y	Y	Y	Y
8 Ellsworth	Y	Y	Y	Y	Y	Y
9 Hill	Y	Y	Y	Y	Y	Y
IOWA						
1 Braley	Y	Y	Y	Y	Y	Y
2 Loebsack	Y	Y	Y	Y	Y	Y
3 Boswell	Y	Y	Y	Y	Y	Y
4 **Latham**	N	N	Y	N	Y	Y
5 **King**	N	N	Y	N	Y	Y
KANSAS						
1 **Moran**	N	N	Y	N	Y	Y
2 **Jenkins**	N	N	Y	N	Y	Y
3 Moore	Y	Y	Y	Y	Y	Y
4 **Tiahrt**	N	N	Y	N	Y	Y
KENTUCKY						
1 **Whitfield**	N	N	Y	N	Y	Y
2 **Guthrie**	N	N	Y	N	Y	Y
3 Yarmuth	Y	Y	Y	Y	Y	Y
4 **Davis**	N	N	Y	N	Y	Y
5 **Rogers**	N	N	Y	N	Y	Y
6 Chandler	Y	Y	Y	Y	Y	Y
LOUISIANA						
1 **Scalise**	N	N	Y	N	Y	Y
2 **Cao**	N	N	Y	N	Y	Y
3 Melancon	Y	?	Y	Y	Y	Y
4 **Fleming**	N	N	Y	N	Y	Y
5 **Alexander**	N	N	Y	N	Y	Y
6 **Cassidy**	N	N	Y	N	Y	Y
7 **Boustany**	N	N	Y	N	Y	Y
MAINE						
1 Pingree	Y	Y	Y	Y	Y	Y
2 Michaud	N	N	Y	Y	Y	Y
MARYLAND						
1 Kratovil	N	N	Y	N	Y	Y
2 Ruppersberger	Y	Y	Y	Y	Y	Y
3 Sarbanes	Y	Y	Y	Y	Y	Y
4 Edwards	Y	Y	Y	Y	Y	Y
5 Hoyer	Y	Y	Y	Y	Y	Y
6 **Bartlett**	N	N	Y	N	Y	Y
7 Cummings	Y	Y	Y	Y	Y	Y
8 Van Hollen	Y	Y	Y	Y	?	Y
MASSACHUSETTS						
1 Olver	Y	Y	Y	Y	Y	Y
2 Neal	Y	Y	Y	Y	Y	Y
3 McGovern	Y	Y	Y	Y	Y	Y
4 Frank	Y	Y	Y	Y	Y	Y
5 Tsongas	Y	Y	Y	Y	Y	Y
6 Tierney	Y	Y	Y	Y	Y	Y
7 Markey	Y	Y	Y	Y	Y	Y
8 Capuano	Y	Y	Y	Y	Y	Y
9 Lynch	Y	Y	Y	Y	Y	Y
10 Delahunt	Y	Y	Y	Y	Y	Y
MICHIGAN						
1 Stupak	Y	Y	Y	Y	Y	Y
2 **Hoekstra**	N	N	Y	N	Y	Y
3 **Ehlers**	N	N	Y	N	Y	Y
4 **Camp**	N	N	Y	N	Y	Y
5 Kildee	Y	Y	Y	Y	Y	Y
6 **Upton**	N	N	Y	N	Y	Y
7 Schauer	Y	Y	Y	Y	Y	Y
8 **Rogers**	N	N	Y	N	Y	Y
9 Peters	Y	Y	Y	Y	Y	Y
10 **Miller**	N	N	Y	N	Y	Y
11 **McCotter**	N	N	Y	N	Y	Y
12 Levin	Y	Y	Y	Y	Y	Y
13 Kilpatrick	Y	Y	Y	Y	Y	?
14 Conyers	Y	Y	Y	Y	Y	Y
15 Dingell	Y	Y	Y	Y	Y	Y
MINNESOTA						
1 Walz	Y	Y	Y	Y	Y	Y
2 **Kline**	N	N	Y	N	Y	Y
3 **Paulsen**	N	N	Y	N	Y	Y
4 McCollum	Y	Y	Y	Y	Y	Y

	213	214	215	216	217	218
5 Ellison	Y	Y	Y	Y	Y	Y
6 **Bachmann**	N	N	Y	N	Y	Y
7 Peterson	Y	Y	Y	Y	Y	Y
8 Oberstar	Y	Y	Y	Y	Y	Y
MISSISSIPPI						
1 Childers	Y	N	Y	N	Y	Y
2 Thompson	Y	Y	Y	Y	Y	Y
3 **Harper**	N	N	Y	N	Y	Y
4 Taylor	N	N	Y	N	Y	Y
MISSOURI						
1 Clay	?	?	?	Y	Y	Y
2 **Akin**	N	N	Y	N	Y	Y
3 Carnahan	Y	Y	Y	Y	Y	Y
4 Skelton	Y	Y	Y	Y	Y	Y
5 Cleaver	Y	Y	Y	Y	Y	Y
6 **Graves**	N	N	Y	N	Y	Y
7 **Blunt**	N	N	Y	N	Y	Y
8 **Emerson**	N	N	Y	N	Y	Y
9 **Luetkemeyer**	N	N	Y	N	Y	Y
MONTANA						
AL **Rehberg**	N	N	Y	N	Y	Y
NEBRASKA						
1 **Fortenberry**	N	N	Y	N	Y	Y
2 **Terry**	N	N	Y	N	Y	Y
3 **Smith**	N	N	Y	N	Y	Y
NEVADA						
1 Berkley	Y	Y	Y	Y	Y	Y
2 **Heller**	N	N	Y	N	Y	Y
3 Titus	Y	Y	Y	Y	Y	Y
NEW HAMPSHIRE						
1 Shea-Porter	Y	Y	Y	Y	Y	Y
2 Hodes	Y	Y	Y	Y	Y	Y
NEW JERSEY						
1 Andrews	Y	Y	Y	Y	Y	Y
2 **LoBiondo**	N	N	Y	N	Y	Y
3 Adler	Y	Y	Y	Y	Y	Y
4 **Smith**	N	N	Y	N	Y	Y
5 **Garrett**	N	N	Y	N	Y	Y
6 Pallone	Y	Y	Y	Y	Y	Y
7 **Lance**	N	N	Y	N	Y	Y
8 Pascrell	Y	Y	Y	Y	Y	Y
9 Rothman	Y	Y	Y	Y	Y	Y
10 Payne	Y	Y	Y	Y	Y	Y
11 **Frelinghuysen**	N	N	Y	N	Y	Y
12 Holt	Y	Y	Y	Y	Y	Y
13 Sires	Y	Y	Y	Y	Y	Y
NEW MEXICO						
1 Heinrich	Y	Y	Y	Y	Y	Y
2 Teague	Y	Y	Y	N	Y	Y
3 Lujan	Y	Y	Y	Y	Y	Y
NEW YORK						
1 Bishop	Y	Y	Y	Y	Y	Y
2 Israel	Y	Y	Y	Y	Y	Y
3 **King**	N	N	Y	N	Y	Y
4 McCarthy	Y	Y	Y	Y	Y	Y
5 Ackerman	Y	Y	Y	Y	Y	Y
6 Meeks	?	Y	Y	Y	Y	Y
7 Crowley	Y	Y	Y	Y	Y	Y
8 Nadler	Y	Y	Y	Y	Y	Y
9 Weiner	Y	Y	Y	Y	Y	Y
10 Towns	Y	Y	Y	Y	Y	Y
11 Clarke	Y	Y	Y	Y	Y	Y
12 Velázquez	Y	Y	Y	Y	Y	Y
13 McMahon	Y	Y	Y	Y	Y	Y
14 Maloney	Y	Y	Y	Y	Y	Y
15 Rangel	Y	Y	Y	Y	Y	Y
16 Serrano	Y	Y	Y	Y	Y	Y
17 Engel	Y	Y	Y	Y	Y	Y
18 Lowey	Y	Y	Y	Y	Y	Y
19 Hall	Y	Y	Y	Y	Y	Y
20 Murphy*						
21 Tonko	Y	Y	Y	Y	Y	Y
22 Hinchey	Y	Y	Y	Y	Y	Y
23 **McHugh**	N	N	Y	N	Y	Y
24 Arcuri	Y	Y	Y	Y	Y	Y
25 Maffei	Y	Y	Y	Y	Y	Y
26 **Lee**	N	N	Y	N	Y	Y
27 Higgins	Y	Y	Y	Y	Y	Y
28 Slaughter	Y	Y	Y	Y	Y	Y
29 Massa	?	?	?	Y	Y	Y
NORTH CAROLINA						
1 Butterfield	Y	Y	Y	Y	?	?
2 Etheridge	Y	Y	Y	Y	Y	Y
3 **Jones**	N	N	Y	N	Y	Y
4 Price	Y	Y	Y	Y	Y	Y

	213	214	215	216	217	218
5 **Foxx**	N	N	Y	N	Y	Y
6 **Coble**	N	N	Y	N	Y	Y
7 McIntyre	Y	Y	Y	N	Y	Y
8 Kissell	Y	Y	Y	Y	Y	Y
9 **Myrick**	N	N	Y	N	Y	Y
10 **McHenry**	N	N	Y	N	Y	Y
11 Shuler	Y	N	Y	Y	Y	Y
12 Watt	Y	?	Y	Y	Y	Y
13 Miller	Y	Y	Y	Y	Y	Y
NORTH DAKOTA						
AL Pomeroy	Y	Y	Y	Y	Y	Y
OHIO						
1 Driehaus	Y	Y	Y	Y	Y	Y
2 **Schmidt**	N	N	Y	N	Y	Y
3 **Turner**	N	N	Y	N	Y	Y
4 **Jordan**	N	N	Y	N	Y	Y
5 **Latta**	N	N	Y	N	Y	Y
6 Wilson	Y	Y	Y	Y	Y	Y
7 **Austria**	N	N	Y	N	Y	Y
8 **Boehner**	N	N	Y	N	?	?
9 Kaptur	Y	Y	Y	Y	Y	Y
10 Kucinich	Y	N	Y	N	Y	Y
11 Fudge	Y	Y	Y	Y	Y	Y
12 **Tiberi**	N	N	Y	N	Y	Y
13 Sutton	Y	Y	Y	Y	Y	Y
14 **LaTourette**	N	N	Y	N	Y	Y
15 Kilroy	Y	Y	Y	Y	Y	Y
16 Boccieri	Y	Y	Y	Y	Y	Y
17 Ryan	Y	Y	Y	Y	Y	Y
18 Space	Y	Y	Y	Y	Y	Y
OKLAHOMA						
1 **Sullivan**	N	N	Y	N	Y	Y
2 Boren	Y	Y	Y	N	Y	Y
3 **Lucas**	N	N	Y	N	Y	Y
4 **Cole**	N	N	Y	N	Y	Y
5 **Fallin**	–	N	Y	N	Y	Y
OREGON						
1 Wu	?	?	?	Y	Y	Y
2 **Walden**	N	N	Y	N	Y	Y
3 Blumenauer	Y	Y	Y	Y	Y	Y
4 DeFazio	Y	Y	Y	Y	Y	Y
5 Schrader	Y	Y	Y	Y	Y	Y
PENNSYLVANIA						
1 Brady	Y	Y	Y	Y	Y	Y
2 Fattah	Y	Y	Y	Y	Y	Y
3 Dahlkemper	Y	Y	Y	Y	Y	Y
4 Altmire	Y	Y	Y	Y	Y	Y
5 **Thompson**	N	N	Y	N	Y	Y
6 **Gerlach**	N	N	Y	N	Y	Y
7 Sestak	Y	Y	Y	Y	Y	Y
8 Murphy, P.	Y	Y	Y	Y	Y	Y
9 **Shuster**	N	N	Y	N	Y	Y
10 Carney	Y	Y	Y	Y	Y	Y
11 Kanjorski	Y	Y	Y	Y	Y	Y
12 Murtha	Y	Y	Y	Y	Y	Y
13 Schwartz	Y	Y	Y	Y	Y	Y
14 Doyle	Y	Y	Y	Y	Y	Y
15 **Dent**	N	N	Y	N	Y	Y
16 **Pitts**	N	N	Y	N	Y	Y
17 Holden	Y	Y	Y	Y	Y	Y
18 **Murphy, T.**	N	N	Y	N	Y	Y
19 **Platts**	N	N	Y	N	Y	Y
RHODE ISLAND						
1 Kennedy	Y	Y	Y	Y	Y	Y
2 Langevin	Y	Y	Y	Y	Y	Y
SOUTH CAROLINA						
1 **Brown**	N	N	Y	N	Y	Y
2 **Wilson**	N	N	Y	N	Y	Y
3 **Barrett**	N	N	Y	N	Y	Y
4 **Inglis**	N	N	Y	N	Y	Y
5 Spratt	Y	Y	Y	Y	Y	Y
6 Clyburn	Y	Y	Y	Y	Y	Y
SOUTH DAKOTA						
AL Herseth Sandlin	Y	Y	Y	Y	Y	Y
TENNESSEE						
1 **Roe**	N	N	Y	N	Y	Y
2 **Duncan**	N	N	Y	N	Y	Y
3 **Wamp**	N	N	Y	N	Y	Y
4 Davis	Y	Y	Y	Y	Y	Y
5 Cooper	Y	Y	Y	Y	Y	Y
6 Gordon	Y	Y	Y	Y	Y	Y
7 **Blackburn**	N	N	Y	N	Y	Y
8 Tanner	Y	Y	Y	Y	Y	Y
9 Cohen	Y	Y	Y	Y	Y	Y

	213	214	215	216	217	218
TEXAS						
1 **Gohmert**	N	N	Y	N	Y	Y
2 **Poe**	N	N	Y	N	Y	Y
3 **Johnson, S.**	?	?	?	N	Y	Y
4 **Hall**	N	N	Y	N	Y	Y
5 **Hensarling**	N	N	Y	N	Y	Y
6 **Barton**	N	N	Y	N	Y	Y
7 **Culberson**	N	N	Y	N	Y	Y
8 **Brady**	N	N	Y	N	Y	Y
9 Green, A.	Y	Y	Y	Y	Y	Y
10 **McCaul**	N	N	Y	N	Y	Y
11 **Conaway**	N	N	Y	N	Y	Y
12 **Granger**	?	?	?	?	?	?
13 **Thornberry**	N	N	Y	N	Y	Y
14 **Paul**	N	N	Y	N	N	Y
15 Hinojosa	Y	Y	Y	+	+	+
16 Reyes	Y	Y	Y	Y	Y	Y
17 Edwards	?	?	?	Y	Y	Y
18 Jackson Lee	Y	Y	Y	Y	Y	Y
19 **Neugebauer**	N	N	Y	N	Y	Y
20 Gonzalez	Y	Y	Y	Y	Y	Y
21 **Smith**	N	N	Y	N	Y	Y
22 **Olson**	N	N	Y	N	Y	Y
23 Rodriguez	Y	Y	Y	Y	Y	Y
24 **Marchant**	N	N	?	N	Y	Y
25 Doggett	Y	Y	Y	Y	Y	Y
26 **Burgess**	?	?	?	–	?	?
27 Ortiz	Y	Y	Y	Y	Y	Y
28 Cuellar	Y	Y	Y	Y	Y	Y
29 Green, G.	Y	Y	Y	Y	Y	Y
30 Johnson, E.	Y	Y	Y	Y	Y	Y
31 **Carter**	N	N	Y	N	Y	Y
32 **Sessions**	N	N	Y	N	Y	Y
UTAH						
1 **Bishop**	N	N	Y	N	Y	Y
2 Matheson	Y	N	Y	N	Y	Y
3 **Chaffetz**	N	N	Y	N	N	Y
VERMONT						
AL Welch	Y	Y	Y	Y	Y	Y
VIRGINIA						
1 **Wittman**	N	N	Y	N	Y	Y
2 Nye	N	N	Y	N	Y	Y
3 Scott	Y	Y	Y	Y	Y	Y
4 **Forbes**	N	N	Y	N	Y	Y
5 Perriello	Y	Y	Y	?	?	?
6 **Goodlatte**	N	N	Y	N	Y	Y
7 **Cantor**	N	N	Y	N	Y	Y
8 Moran	Y	Y	Y	Y	Y	Y
9 Boucher	Y	Y	Y	Y	Y	Y
10 **Wolf**	N	N	Y	N	Y	Y
11 Connolly	Y	Y	Y	Y	Y	Y
WASHINGTON						
1 Inslee	Y	Y	Y	Y	Y	Y
2 Larsen	Y	Y	Y	Y	Y	Y
3 Baird	Y	Y	Y	Y	Y	Y
4 **Hastings**	N	N	Y	N	Y	Y
5 **McMorris Rodgers**	N	N	Y	N	Y	Y
6 Dicks	Y	Y	Y	Y	Y	Y
7 McDermott	Y	Y	Y	Y	Y	Y
8 **Reichert**	N	N	Y	N	Y	Y
9 Smith	Y	Y	Y	Y	Y	Y
WEST VIRGINIA						
1 Mollohan	Y	Y	Y	Y	Y	Y
2 **Capito**	N	N	Y	N	Y	Y
3 Rahall	Y	Y	Y	Y	Y	Y
WISCONSIN						
1 **Ryan**	N	N	Y	N	Y	Y
2 Baldwin	Y	Y	Y	Y	Y	Y
3 Kind	Y	Y	Y	Y	Y	Y
4 Moore	Y	Y	Y	Y	Y	Y
5 **Sensenbrenner**	N	N	Y	N	Y	Y
6 **Petri**	N	N	Y	N	Y	Y
7 Obey	Y	Y	Y	Y	Y	Y
8 Kagen	Y	Y	Y	Y	Y	Y
WYOMING						
AL **Lummis**	N	N	Y	N	Y	Y
DELEGATES						
Faleomavaega (A.S.)						
Norton (D.C.)						
Bordallo (Guam)						
Sablan (N. Marianas)						
Pierluisi (P.R.)						
Christensen (V.I.)						

IN THE HOUSE | By Vote Number

219. **HR 1913. Hate Crimes Prosecution/Previous Question.** Hastings, D-Fla., motion to order the previous question (thus ending debate and possibility of amendment) on adoption of the rule (H Res 372) that would provide for House floor consideration of the bill that would expand the definition of federal hate crimes and authorize funding for the hiring of additional personnel and the allocation of grants for the investigation and prosecution of such crimes. Motion agreed to 234-181: R 0-173; D 234-8. April 29, 2009.

220. **HR 1913. Hate Crimes Prosecution/Rule.** Adoption of the rule (H Res 372) that would provide for House floor consideration of the bill that would expand the definition of federal hate crimes and authorize funding for the hiring of additional personnel and the allocation of grants for the investigation and prosecution of such crimes. Adopted 234-190: R 0-175; D 234-15. April 29, 2009.

221. **HR 46. Family Self-Sufficiency Program/Passage.** Baca, D-Calif., motion to suspend the rules and pass the bill that would provide new incentives for agencies that participate in the Housing and Urban Development Department's family self-sufficiency program. It would require HUD to charge all local public housing agencies a fee to cover the costs of the program. Motion agreed to 397-19: R 151-19; D 246-0. A two-thirds majority of those present and voting (278 in this case) is required for passage under suspension of the rules. April 29, 2009.

222. **HR 1913. Hate Crimes Prosecution/Recommit.** Gohmert, R-Texas, motion to recommit the bill to the Judiciary Committee with instructions that it be reported back immediately with language that would authorize the death penalty for certain violent hate crimes and expand federal hate crimes law to cover acts committed against individuals based on their age, armed forces or law enforcement status. Motion rejected 185-241: R 160-16; D 25-225. April 29, 2009.

223. **HR 1913. Hate Crimes Prosecution/Passage.** Passage of the bill that would expand federal hate crimes law to cover those based on sexual orientation, gender or disability. Crimes motivated by gender identity or sexual orientation in which fire, a gun or a bomb is used would be punishable by a fine and up to 10 years in prison. Crimes involving kidnapping or murder would be punishable by life in prison. The bill would authorize funds in fiscal 2010-11 for grants to law enforcement agencies to investigate and prosecute hate crimes and funds through fiscal 2012 for additional Justice Department personnel to address hate crimes. Passed 249-175: R 18-158; D 231-17. April 29, 2009.

	219	220	221	222	223
ALABAMA					
1 **Bonner**	N	N	Y	Y	N
2 Bright	N	Y	Y	N	N
3 **Rogers**	N	N	Y	Y	N
4 **Aderholt**	N	N	Y	Y	N
5 Griffith	Y	N	Y	Y	N
6 **Bachus**	N	N	?	Y	N
7 Davis	Y	Y	Y	Y	N
ALASKA					
AL **Young**	N	N	Y	Y	N
ARIZONA					
1 Kirkpatrick	Y	Y	Y	N	Y
2 **Franks**	N	N	Y	Y	N
3 **Shadegg**	N	N	N	Y	N
4 Pastor	Y	Y	Y	N	Y
5 Mitchell	Y	Y	Y	Y	Y
6 **Flake**	N	N	N	Y	N
7 Grijalva	Y	Y	Y	N	Y
8 Giffords	Y	Y	Y	N	Y
ARKANSAS					
1 Berry	Y	Y	Y	?	?
2 Snyder	Y	Y	Y	N	Y
3 **Boozman**	N	N	Y	Y	N
4 Ross	N	N	Y	N	N
CALIFORNIA					
1 Thompson	Y	Y	Y	N	Y
2 **Herger**	N	N	Y	Y	N
3 **Lungren**	N	N	Y	Y	N
4 **McClintock**	N	N	Y	Y	N
5 Matsui	Y	Y	Y	N	Y
6 Woolsey	Y	Y	Y	N	Y
7 Miller, George	Y	Y	Y	N	+
8 Pelosi					Y
9 Lee	Y	Y	Y	N	Y
10 Tauscher	Y	Y	Y	N	Y
11 McNerney	Y	Y	Y	N	Y
12 Speier	Y	Y	Y	N	Y
13 Stark	?	?	?	?	?
14 Eshoo	Y	Y	Y	N	Y
15 Honda	Y	Y	Y	N	Y
16 Lofgren	Y	Y	Y	N	Y
17 Farr	Y	Y	Y	N	Y
18 Cardoza	Y	Y	Y	N	Y
19 **Radanovich**	N	N	Y	Y	N
20 Costa	Y	Y	Y	Y	Y
21 **Nunes**	N	N	Y	Y	N
22 **McCarthy**	?	N	Y	Y	N
23 Capps	Y	Y	Y	N	Y
24 **Gallegly**	N	N	Y	Y	N
25 **McKeon**	N	N	Y	Y	N
26 **Dreier**	N	N	Y	Y	N
27 Sherman	Y	Y	Y	N	Y
28 Berman	Y	Y	Y	N	Y
29 Schiff	Y	Y	Y	N	Y
30 Waxman	?	?	Y	N	Y
31 Becerra	+	Y	Y	N	Y
32 Vacant					
33 Watson	Y	Y	Y	N	Y
34 Roybal-Allard	Y	Y	Y	N	Y
35 Waters	Y	Y	Y	N	Y
36 Harman	Y	Y	Y	N	Y
37 Richardson	Y	Y	Y	Y	Y
38 Napolitano	Y	Y	Y	N	Y
39 Sánchez, Linda	Y	Y	Y	N	Y
40 **Royce**	N	N	Y	Y	N
41 **Lewis**	N	N	Y	Y	N
42 **Miller, Gary**	N	N	Y	Y	N
43 Baca	Y	Y	Y	N	Y
44 **Calvert**	N	N	Y	Y	N
45 **Bono Mack**	N	N	Y	N	Y
46 **Rohrabacher**	N	N	Y	Y	N
47 Sanchez, Loretta	Y	Y	Y	N	Y
48 **Campbell**	N	N	N	Y	N
49 **Issa**	N	N	Y	Y	N
50 **Bilbray**	N	N	Y	N	N
51 Filner	Y	Y	Y	N	Y
52 **Hunter**	N	N	Y	Y	N
53 Davis	Y	Y	Y	N	Y

	219	220	221	222	223
COLORADO					
1 DeGette	Y	Y	Y	N	Y
2 Polis	Y	Y	Y	N	Y
3 Salazar	Y	Y	Y	N	Y
4 Markey	Y	Y	Y	N	Y
5 **Lamborn**	N	N	Y	Y	N
6 **Coffman**	N	N	Y	Y	N
7 Perlmutter	Y	?	Y	N	Y
CONNECTICUT					
1 Larson	+	Y	Y	N	Y
2 Courtney	Y	Y	Y	N	Y
3 DeLauro	Y	Y	Y	N	Y
4 Himes	Y	Y	Y	N	Y
5 Murphy	Y	Y	Y	N	Y
DELAWARE					
AL **Castle**	N	N	Y	Y	Y
FLORIDA					
1 **Miller**	N	N	Y	Y	N
2 Boyd	Y	Y	Y	N	Y
3 Brown	Y	Y	Y	N	Y
4 **Crenshaw**	N	N	Y	Y	N
5 **Brown-Waite**	N	N	Y	Y	N
6 **Stearns**	N	N	N	Y	N
7 **Mica**	N	N	Y	Y	N
8 Grayson	Y	Y	Y	N	Y
9 **Bilirakis**	N	N	Y	Y	N
10 **Young**	N	N	Y	Y	N
11 Castor	Y	Y	Y	N	Y
12 **Putnam**	N	N	Y	N	N
13 **Buchanan**	N	N	Y	Y	N
14 **Mack**	N	N	Y	N	N
15 **Posey**	N	N	Y	Y	N
16 **Rooney**	N	N	Y	Y	N
17 Meek	Y	Y	Y	N	Y
18 **Ros-Lehtinen**	N	N	Y	N	Y
19 Wexler	Y	Y	Y	N	Y
20 Wasserman Schultz	Y	Y	Y	N	Y
21 **Diaz-Balart, L.**	N	N	?	Y	Y
22 Klein	Y	Y	Y	Y	Y
23 Hastings	Y	Y	Y	N	Y
24 Kosmas	?	Y	Y	N	Y
25 **Diaz-Balart, M.**	N	N	Y	Y	Y
GEORGIA					
1 **Kingston**	N	N	N	Y	N
2 Bishop	Y	Y	?	N	Y
3 **Westmoreland**	N	N	N	Y	N
4 Johnson	Y	Y	Y	N	Y
5 Lewis	Y	Y	Y	N	Y
6 **Price**	N	N	N	Y	N
7 **Linder**	N	N	?	Y	N
8 Marshall	Y	Y	Y	Y	Y
9 **Deal**	N	N	Y	Y	N
10 **Broun**	N	N	N	Y	N
11 **Gingrey**	N	N	Y	Y	N
12 Barrow	Y	Y	Y	Y	Y
13 Scott	Y	Y	Y	N	Y
HAWAII					
1 Abercrombie	Y	Y	Y	N	Y
2 Hirono	Y	Y	Y	N	Y
IDAHO					
1 Minnick	N	N	Y	Y	Y
2 **Simpson**	N	N	Y	Y	N
ILLINOIS					
1 Rush	Y	Y	Y	N	Y
2 Jackson	Y	Y	Y	N	Y
3 Lipinski	Y	Y	Y	N	Y
4 Gutierrez	?	Y	Y	N	Y
5 Quigley	Y	Y	Y	N	Y
6 **Roskam**	N	N	Y	Y	N
7 Davis	Y	Y	Y	N	Y
8 Bean	Y	Y	Y	N	Y
9 Schakowsky	Y	Y	Y	N	Y
10 **Kirk**	N	N	Y	Y	Y
11 Halvorson	Y	Y	Y	N	Y
12 Costello	Y	Y	Y	N	Y
13 **Biggert**	N	N	Y	N	Y
14 Foster	Y	Y	Y	N	Y
15 **Johnson**	N	N	Y	Y	N

	219	220	221	222	223
16 Manzullo	N	N	Y	Y	N
17 Hare	Y	Y	Y	N	Y
18 Schock	N	N	Y	Y	N
19 Shimkus	N	N	Y	Y	N
INDIANA					
1 Visclosky	Y	Y	Y	N	Y
2 Donnelly	Y	N	Y	N	N
3 Souder	N	N	Y	Y	N
4 Buyer	N	N	Y	Y	N
5 Burton	N	N	Y	Y	N
6 Pence	N	N	Y	Y	N
7 Carson	Y	Y	Y	N	Y
8 Ellsworth	Y	N	Y	N	N
9 Hill	N	N	Y	N	Y
IOWA					
1 Braley	Y	Y	Y	N	Y
2 Loebsack	Y	Y	Y	N	Y
3 Boswell	Y	Y	Y	N	Y
4 Latham	N	N	Y	Y	N
5 King	N	N	Y	Y	N
KANSAS					
1 Moran	N	N	Y	Y	N
2 Jenkins	N	N	Y	N	N
3 Moore	Y	Y	Y	N	Y
4 Tiahrt	N	N	Y	Y	N
KENTUCKY					
1 Whitfield	N	N	Y	Y	N
2 Guthrie	N	N	Y	Y	N
3 Yarmuth	Y	Y	Y	N	Y
4 Davis	N	N	Y	Y	N
5 Rogers	N	N	Y	Y	N
6 Chandler	Y	Y	Y	N	Y
LOUISIANA					
1 Scalise	N	N	N	Y	N
2 Cao	N	N	Y	N	Y
3 Melancon	Y	N	Y	N	Y
4 Fleming	N	N	Y	Y	N
5 Alexander	N	N	Y	Y	N
6 Cassidy	N	N	N	Y	Y
7 Boustany	N	N	Y	Y	N
MAINE					
1 Pingree	Y	Y	Y	N	Y
2 Michaud	Y	Y	Y	N	Y
MARYLAND					
1 Kratovil	Y	N	Y	N	Y
2 Ruppersberger	Y	Y	Y	N	+
3 Sarbanes	Y	Y	Y	N	Y
4 Edwards	Y	Y	Y	N	Y
5 Hoyer	Y	Y	Y	N	Y
6 Bartlett	N	N	Y	Y	N
7 Cummings	Y	Y	?	N	Y
8 Van Hollen	Y	Y	Y	N	Y
MASSACHUSETTS					
1 Olver	Y	Y	Y	N	Y
2 Neal	Y	Y	Y	N	Y
3 McGovern	Y	Y	Y	N	Y
4 Frank	Y	Y	Y	N	Y
5 Tsongas	Y	Y	Y	N	Y
6 Tierney	Y	Y	Y	N	Y
7 Markey	Y	Y	Y	N	Y
8 Capuano	Y	Y	Y	N	Y
9 Lynch	Y	Y	Y	N	Y
10 Delahunt	Y	Y	Y	N	Y
MICHIGAN					
1 Stupak	Y	Y	Y	N	Y
2 Hoekstra	N	N	Y	N	N
3 Ehlers	-	N	Y	N	N
4 Camp	N	N	N	Y	N
5 Kildee	Y	Y	Y	N	Y
6 Upton	N	N	Y	Y	N
7 Schauer	Y	Y	Y	N	Y
8 Rogers	N	N	Y	Y	N
9 Peters	Y	Y	Y	N	Y
10 Miller	N	N	Y	Y	N
11 McCotter	N	N	Y	Y	N
12 Levin	Y	Y	Y	N	Y
13 Kilpatrick	Y	Y	Y	N	Y
14 Conyers	Y	Y	Y	N	Y
15 Dingell	Y	Y	Y	N	Y
MINNESOTA					
1 Walz	Y	Y	Y	N	Y
2 Kline	N	N	Y	Y	N
3 Paulsen	N	N	Y	Y	N
4 McCollum	Y	Y	Y	N	Y

	219	220	221	222	223
5 Ellison	Y	Y	Y	N	Y
6 Bachmann	N	N	Y	Y	N
7 Peterson	Y	Y	Y	N	N
8 Oberstar	Y	Y	Y	N	Y
MISSISSIPPI					
1 Childers	N	N	Y	Y	N
2 Thompson	?	Y	Y	N	Y
3 Harper	N	N	Y	Y	N
4 Taylor	N	N	Y	Y	N
MISSOURI					
1 Clay	Y	Y	Y	N	Y
2 Akin	N	N	Y	Y	N
3 Carnahan	Y	Y	Y	N	Y
4 Skelton	Y	Y	Y	N	Y
5 Cleaver	Y	Y	Y	N	Y
6 Graves	N	N	N	Y	N
7 Blunt	N	N	N	Y	N
8 Emerson	N	N	Y	Y	N
9 Luetkemeyer	N	N	Y	Y	N
MONTANA					
AL Rehberg	N	N	Y	Y	N
NEBRASKA					
1 Fortenberry	N	N	Y	Y	N
2 Terry	N	N	Y	Y	N
3 Smith	N	N	?	Y	N
NEVADA					
1 Berkley	Y	Y	Y	N	Y
2 Heller	N	N	Y	Y	N
3 Titus	Y	Y	Y	N	Y
NEW HAMPSHIRE					
1 Shea-Porter	Y	Y	Y	N	Y
2 Hodes	Y	Y	Y	N	Y
NEW JERSEY					
1 Andrews	Y	Y	Y	N	Y
2 LoBiondo	N	N	Y	Y	Y
3 Adler	Y	Y	Y	N	Y
4 Smith	N	N	Y	N	N
5 Garrett	N	N	Y	Y	N
6 Pallone	Y	Y	Y	N	Y
7 Lance	N	N	Y	Y	Y
8 Pascrell	Y	Y	Y	N	Y
9 Rothman	Y	Y	Y	N	Y
10 Payne	Y	Y	Y	N	Y
11 Frelinghuysen	N	N	Y	Y	Y
12 Holt	Y	Y	Y	N	Y
13 Sires	Y	Y	Y	N	Y
NEW MEXICO					
1 Heinrich	Y	Y	Y	N	Y
2 Teague	Y	Y	Y	?	?
3 Lujan	Y	Y	Y	N	Y
NEW YORK					
1 Bishop	Y	Y	Y	N	Y
2 Israel	Y	Y	Y	N	Y
3 King	N	N	Y	Y	N
4 McCarthy	Y	Y	Y	N	Y
5 Ackerman	Y	Y	Y	N	Y
6 Meeks	Y	Y	Y	N	Y
7 Crowley	Y	Y	Y	N	Y
8 Nadler	Y	Y	Y	N	Y
9 Weiner	Y	Y	Y	N	Y
10 Towns	Y	Y	Y	N	Y
11 Clarke	Y	Y	Y	N	Y
12 Velázquez	Y	Y	Y	N	Y
13 McMahon	Y	Y	Y	N	Y
14 Maloney	Y	Y	Y	N	Y
15 Rangel	Y	Y	Y	N	Y
16 Serrano	Y	Y	Y	N	Y
17 Engel	Y	Y	Y	N	Y
18 Lowey	Y	Y	Y	N	Y
19 Hall	Y	Y	Y	N	Y
20 Murphy*			Y	N	Y
21 Tonko	Y	Y	Y	N	Y
22 Hinchey	Y	Y	Y	N	Y
23 McHugh	N	N	Y	Y	N
24 Arcuri	Y	Y	Y	Y	Y
25 Maffei	Y	Y	Y	N	Y
26 Lee	N	Y	Y	Y	N
27 Higgins	Y	Y	Y	N	Y
28 Slaughter	Y	Y	Y	N	Y
29 Massa	Y	Y	Y	N	Y
NORTH CAROLINA					
1 Butterfield	?	?	?	?	?
2 Etheridge	Y	Y	Y	N	Y
3 Jones	N	N	Y	Y	N
4 Price	Y	Y	Y	N	Y

	219	220	221	222	223
5 Foxx	N	N	Y	Y	N
6 Coble	N	N	Y	Y	N
7 McIntyre	N	N	Y	N	N
8 Kissell	Y	Y	Y	N	Y
9 Myrick	N	N	Y	Y	N
10 McHenry	N	N	Y	Y	N
11 Shuler	Y	N	Y	N	N
12 Watt	Y	Y	Y	N	Y
13 Miller	Y	Y	Y	Y	Y
NORTH DAKOTA					
AL Pomeroy	Y	Y	Y	N	Y
OHIO					
1 Driehaus	Y	Y	Y	N	Y
2 Schmidt	N	N	Y	Y	N
3 Turner	N	N	Y	Y	N
4 Jordan	N	N	Y	Y	N
5 Latta	N	N	Y	Y	N
6 Wilson	Y	Y	Y	N	Y
7 Austria	N	N	Y	Y	N
8 Boehner	?	?	Y	Y	N
9 Kaptur	Y	Y	Y	N	Y
10 Kucinich	Y	Y	Y	N	Y
11 Fudge	Y	Y	Y	N	Y
12 Tiberi	N	N	Y	Y	N
13 Sutton	Y	Y	Y	N	Y
14 LaTourette	N	N	Y	Y	N
15 Kilroy	?	Y	Y	N	Y
16 Boccieri	Y	Y	Y	Y	Y
17 Ryan	Y	Y	Y	N	Y
18 Space	Y	Y	Y	Y	Y
OKLAHOMA					
1 Sullivan	N	N	Y	Y	N
2 Boren	Y	N	Y	N	N
3 Lucas	N	N	Y	Y	N
4 Cole	N	N	Y	Y	N
5 Fallin	N	N	Y	Y	N
OREGON					
1 Wu	Y	Y	Y	N	Y
2 Walden	N	N	Y	Y	Y
3 Blumenauer	Y	Y	Y	N	Y
4 DeFazio	Y	Y	Y	N	Y
5 Schrader	Y	Y	Y	N	Y
PENNSYLVANIA					
1 Brady	Y	Y	Y	N	Y
2 Fattah	Y	Y	Y	N	Y
3 Dahlkemper	Y	Y	Y	N	Y
4 Altmire	Y	Y	Y	Y	Y
5 Thompson	N	N	Y	Y	N
6 Gerlach	N	N	Y	Y	Y
7 Sestak	Y	Y	Y	N	Y
8 Murphy, P.	Y	Y	Y	N	Y
9 Shuster	N	N	Y	Y	N
10 Carney	N	N	Y	N	N
11 Kanjorski	Y	Y	Y	N	Y
12 Murtha	Y	Y	Y	N	?
13 Schwartz	Y	Y	Y	N	Y
14 Doyle	Y	Y	?	N	Y
15 Dent	N	N	Y	Y	N
16 Pitts	N	N	N	Y	N
17 Holden	Y	Y	Y	N	Y
18 Murphy, T.	N	N	Y	Y	N
19 Platts	N	N	Y	N	Y
RHODE ISLAND					
1 Kennedy	Y	Y	Y	N	Y
2 Langevin	Y	Y	Y	N	Y
SOUTH CAROLINA					
1 Brown	N	N	Y	Y	N
2 Wilson	N	N	Y	Y	N
3 Barrett	N	N	Y	Y	N
4 Inglis	N	N	Y	Y	N
5 Spratt	Y	Y	Y	N	Y
6 Clyburn	Y	Y	Y	N	Y
SOUTH DAKOTA					
AL Herseth Sandlin	Y	Y	Y	Y	Y
TENNESSEE					
1 Roe	N	N	Y	Y	N
2 Duncan	N	N	N	Y	N
3 Wamp	N	N	Y	Y	N
4 Davis	Y	Y	Y	N	Y
5 Cooper	Y	Y	Y	N	Y
6 Gordon	Y	Y	Y	N	N
7 Blackburn	N	N	Y	Y	N
8 Tanner	Y	Y	Y	N	N
9 Cohen	Y	Y	Y	N	Y

	219	220	221	222	223
TEXAS					
1 Gohmert	N	N	N	Y	N
2 Poe	N	N	Y	Y	N
3 Johnson, S.	N	N	Y	Y	N
4 Hall	N	N	Y	Y	N
5 Hensarling	N	N	Y	Y	N
6 Barton	N	N	Y	Y	N
7 Culberson	N	N	N	Y	N
8 Brady	N	N	Y	Y	N
9 Green, A.	Y	Y	Y	N	Y
10 McCaul	N	N	Y	Y	N
11 Conaway	N	N	Y	Y	N
12 Granger	?	?	?	?	?
13 Thornberry	N	N	Y	Y	N
14 Paul	N	N	?	N	N
15 Hinojosa	Y	Y	Y	N	Y
16 Reyes	Y	Y	Y	N	Y
17 Edwards	Y	Y	Y	N	Y
18 Jackson Lee	Y	Y	Y	N	Y
19 Neugebauer	N	N	Y	Y	N
20 Gonzalez	Y	Y	Y	N	Y
21 Smith	N	N	Y	Y	N
22 Olson	N	N	Y	Y	N
23 Rodriguez	Y	Y	Y	N	Y
24 Marchant	N	N	Y	Y	N
25 Doggett	Y	Y	Y	N	Y
26 Burgess	?	?	?	?	-
27 Ortiz	Y	Y	Y	N	Y
28 Cuellar	Y	Y	Y	N	Y
29 Green, G.	Y	Y	Y	N	Y
30 Johnson, E.	Y	Y	Y	N	Y
31 Carter	N	N	Y	Y	N
32 Sessions	N	N	?	Y	N
UTAH					
1 Bishop	N	N	Y	Y	N
2 Matheson	Y	Y	Y	Y	Y
3 Chaffetz	N	N	Y	Y	N
VERMONT					
AL Welch	Y	Y	Y	N	Y
VIRGINIA					
1 Wittman	N	N	Y	Y	N
2 Nye	Y	Y	?	Y	Y
3 Scott	Y	Y	Y	N	Y
4 Forbes	N	N	Y	Y	N
5 Perriello	?	?	?	?	?
6 Goodlatte	N	N	N	Y	N
7 Cantor	N	N	Y	Y	N
8 Moran	Y	Y	Y	N	Y
9 Boucher	?	?	Y	N	Y
10 Wolf	N	N	Y	Y	N
11 Connolly	Y	Y	Y	N	Y
WASHINGTON					
1 Inslee	?	Y	Y	N	Y
2 Larsen	Y	Y	?	N	Y
3 Baird	Y	Y	Y	N	Y
4 Hastings	N	N	Y	Y	N
5 McMorris Rodgers	N	N	Y	Y	N
6 Dicks	Y	Y	?	N	Y
7 McDermott	Y	Y	Y	N	Y
8 Reichert	N	N	Y	Y	N
9 Smith	Y	Y	Y	N	Y
WEST VIRGINIA					
1 Mollohan	Y	Y	Y	N	Y
2 Capito	N	N	Y	Y	N
3 Rahall	Y	Y	Y	N	Y
WISCONSIN					
1 Ryan	N	N	Y	Y	N
2 Baldwin	Y	Y	Y	N	Y
3 Kind	Y	Y	Y	N	Y
4 Moore	Y	Y	Y	N	Y
5 Sensenbrenner	N	N	Y	Y	N
6 Petri	N	N	Y	Y	N
7 Obey	Y	Y	Y	N	Y
8 Kagen	Y	Y	Y	N	Y
WYOMING					
AL Lummis	N	N	Y	Y	N
DELEGATES					
Faleomavaega (A.S.)					
Norton (D.C.)					
Bordallo (Guam)					
Sablan (N. Marianas)					
Pierluisi (P.R.)					
Christensen (V.I.)					

IN THE HOUSE | By Vote Number

224. HR 627. **Credit Card Company Regulations/Rule.** Adoption of the rule (H Res 379) that would provide for House floor consideration of the bill that would set regulations for credit card company practices. Adopted 249-175: R 0-174; D 249-1. April 30, 2009.

225. HR 627. **Credit Card Company Regulations/College Student Credit Limit.** Slaughter, D-N.Y., amendment that would limit credit lines for full-time college students ages 18 to 20 to the greater of $500 or 20 percent of a student's annual income if there is no co-signer on the account. It would prohibit companies from issuing cards to a student who already has one. It would require creditors to obtain proof of income, as well as credit and income histories from college students before issuing them credit cards. Adopted in Committee of the Whole 276-154: R 46-129; D 230-25. April 30, 2009.

226. HR 627. **Credit Card Company Regulations/Over Limit Fees.** Maloney, D-N.Y., amendment that would prohibit credit card companies from charging fees when individuals spend beyond their credit limits unless a cardholder has opted verbally or in writing for the ability to do so. Adopted in Committee of the Whole 284-149: R 43-133; D 241-16. April 30, 2009.

227. HR 627. **Credit Card Company Regulations/Recommit.** Roskam, R-Ill., motion to recommit the bill to the Financial Services Committee with instructions that it be immediately reported back with language that would prevent the bill's provisions from taking effect until the Federal Reserve Board completes a study determining whether the bill would reduce available credit to small businesses. Motion rejected 164-263: R 159-16; D 5-247. April 30, 2009.

228. HR 627. **Credit Card Company Regulations/Passage.** Passage of the bill that would impose restrictions on credit card company lending practices. It would restrict when companies can increase annual percentage interest rates retroactively on existing balances, require companies to give at least 45 days' notice before increasing an annual percentage rate or adding fees, and restrict companies from computing interest charges on balances from more than one billing cycle. Credit companies could not use the term "fixed rate" except when referring to a rate that will not change for any reason over a set period or the term "prime rate" except when referring to the rate published by the Federal Reserve Board. It would require the Federal Reserve to establish standards for payment workouts under an open-ended consumer credit plan, collect information on the lending practices of credit card companies and report to Congress annually on its findings. Passed 357-70: R 105-69; D 252-1. A "yea" was a vote in support of the president's position. April 30, 2009.

	224	225	226	227	228
ALABAMA					
1 Bonner	N	N	N	Y	N
2 Bright	Y	N	Y	N	Y
3 Rogers	N	N	N	Y	Y
4 Aderholt	N	N	Y	Y	Y
5 Griffith	Y	N	Y	N	Y
6 Bachus	N	N	N	Y	N
7 Davis	Y	Y	Y	N	Y
ALASKA					
AL Young	N	N	N	Y	Y
ARIZONA					
1 Kirkpatrick	Y	Y	Y	Y	Y
2 Franks	N	N	N	Y	N
3 Shadegg	N	N	N	Y	N
4 Pastor	Y	Y	Y	N	Y
5 Mitchell	Y	N	Y	N	Y
6 Flake	N	N	N	Y	N
7 Grijalva	Y	Y	Y	N	Y
8 Giffords	Y	N	Y	Y	Y
ARKANSAS					
1 Berry	?	?	?	?	?
2 Snyder	Y	N	Y	N	Y
3 Boozman	N	N	N	Y	Y
4 Ross	Y	Y	Y	N	Y
CALIFORNIA					
1 Thompson	Y	Y	Y	N	Y
2 Herger	N	N	N	Y	N
3 Lungren	N	Y	N	Y	N
4 McClintock	N	N	N	Y	N
5 Matsui	Y	Y	Y	N	Y
6 Woolsey	Y	Y	Y	N	Y
7 Miller, George	Y	Y	Y	N	Y
8 Pelosi					Y
9 Lee	Y	Y	Y	N	Y
10 Tauscher	Y	Y	Y	N	Y
11 McNerney	Y	Y	Y	Y	Y
12 Speier	Y	Y	Y	N	Y
13 Stark	?	?	?	?	?
14 Eshoo	Y	Y	Y	N	Y
15 Honda	Y	Y	Y	N	Y
16 Lofgren	Y	Y	Y	N	Y
17 Farr	Y	Y	Y	N	Y
18 Cardoza	Y	Y	Y	N	Y
19 Radanovich	N	Y	N	Y	Y
20 Costa	Y	Y	N	N	Y
21 Nunes	N	N	N	Y	N
22 McCarthy	N	N	N	Y	N
23 Capps	Y	Y	Y	N	Y
24 Gallegly	N	N	N	N	Y
25 McKeon	N	N	N	Y	N
26 Dreier	N	N	N	Y	N
27 Sherman	Y	Y	Y	N	Y
28 Berman	Y	Y	Y	N	Y
29 Schiff	Y	Y	Y	N	Y
30 Waxman	Y	Y	Y	N	Y
31 Becerra	Y	Y	Y	N	Y
32 Vacant					
33 Watson	Y	Y	Y	N	Y
34 Roybal-Allard	Y	Y	Y	N	Y
35 Waters	Y	Y	Y	N	Y
36 Harman	Y	Y	Y	N	Y
37 Richardson	Y	Y	Y	N	Y
38 Napolitano	Y	Y	Y	N	Y
39 Sánchez, Linda	Y	Y	Y	N	Y
40 Royce	N	N	N	Y	N
41 Lewis	N	N	N	Y	Y
42 Miller, Gary	N	N	N	Y	N
43 Baca	Y	Y	Y	N	Y
44 Calvert	N	N	N	Y	Y
45 Bono Mack	N	Y	N	Y	Y
46 Rohrabacher	N	N	Y	N	Y
47 Sanchez, Loretta	Y	Y	Y	N	Y
48 Campbell	N	N	Y	Y	Y
49 Issa	N	N	N	Y	Y
50 Bilbray	N	N	Y	Y	Y
51 Filner	Y	Y	Y	N	Y
52 Hunter	N	N	N	Y	Y
53 Davis	Y	Y	Y	N	Y

	224	225	226	227	228
COLORADO					
1 DeGette	Y	Y	Y	N	Y
2 Polis	Y	N	Y	N	Y
3 Salazar	Y	N	N	N	Y
4 Markey	Y	Y	N	N	Y
5 Lamborn	N	N	N	Y	N
6 Coffman	N	N	N	Y	Y
7 Perlmutter	Y	N	Y	N	Y
CONNECTICUT					
1 Larson	Y	Y	Y	N	Y
2 Courtney	Y	Y	Y	N	Y
3 DeLauro	Y	Y	Y	N	Y
4 Himes	Y	N	Y	N	Y
5 Murphy	Y	Y	Y	N	Y
DELAWARE					
AL Castle	N	N	N	Y	Y
FLORIDA					
1 Miller	N	N	N	Y	N
2 Boyd	Y	N	N	N	Y
3 Brown	Y	Y	Y	N	Y
4 Crenshaw	N	Y	Y	Y	Y
5 Brown-Waite	N	Y	N	Y	Y
6 Stearns	N	Y	Y	Y	Y
7 Mica	N	N	N	Y	Y
8 Grayson	Y	Y	Y	N	Y
9 Bilirakis	N	N	Y	Y	Y
10 Young	N	Y	N	Y	Y
11 Castor	Y	Y	Y	N	Y
12 Putnam	N	N	Y	Y	Y
13 Buchanan	N	Y	Y	Y	Y
14 Mack	N	N	N	Y	N
15 Posey	N	N	N	Y	Y
16 Rooney	N	N	Y	Y	Y
17 Meek	Y	Y	Y	N	Y
18 Ros-Lehtinen	N	Y	Y	N	Y
19 Wexler	Y	Y	Y	N	Y
20 Wasserman Schultz	Y	Y	Y	N	Y
21 Diaz-Balart, L.	N	N	Y	Y	Y
22 Klein	Y	Y	Y	N	Y
23 Hastings	?	?	?	?	?
24 Kosmas	Y	N	Y	N	Y
25 Diaz-Balart, M.	N	N	Y	Y	Y
GEORGIA					
1 Kingston	N	N	Y	Y	Y
2 Bishop	Y	Y	Y	N	Y
3 Westmoreland	N	N	N	Y	N
4 Johnson	Y	?	Y	N	Y
5 Lewis	Y	Y	Y	N	Y
6 Price	N	N	N	Y	N
7 Linder	N	N	N	Y	N
8 Marshall	Y	Y	Y	N	Y
9 Deal	N	Y	N	Y	N
10 Broun	N	N	N	Y	N
11 Gingrey	N	Y	N	Y	N
12 Barrow	Y	Y	Y	N	Y
13 Scott	Y	Y	Y	N	Y
HAWAII					
1 Abercrombie	Y	Y	Y	N	Y
2 Hirono	Y	Y	Y	N	Y
IDAHO					
1 Minnick	Y	Y	N	Y	Y
2 Simpson	N	N	N	Y	Y
ILLINOIS					
1 Rush	Y	+	Y	N	Y
2 Jackson	Y	Y	Y	N	Y
3 Lipinski	Y	Y	Y	N	Y
4 Gutierrez	Y	Y	Y	N	Y
5 Quigley	Y	Y	Y	N	Y
6 Roskam	N	Y	N	Y	N
7 Davis	Y	Y	Y	N	Y
8 Bean	Y	N	N	N	Y
9 Schakowsky	Y	Y	Y	N	Y
10 Kirk	N	Y	N	Y	Y
11 Halvorson	Y	Y	Y	N	Y
12 Costello	Y	Y	Y	N	Y
13 Biggert	N	N	N	Y	Y
14 Foster	Y	N	Y	N	Y
15 Johnson	N	N	N	Y	Y

KEY   **Republicans**   Democrats

Y Voted for (yea)	X Paired against	C Voted "present" to avoid possible conflict of interest
# Paired for	– Announced against	
+ Announced for	P Voted "present"	? Did not vote or otherwise make a position known
N Voted against (nay)		

	224	225	226	227	228
16 Manzullo	N	N	N	Y	N
17 Hare	Y	Y	Y	N	Y
18 Schock	N	N	N	Y	Y
19 Shimkus	N	Y	N	Y	Y
INDIANA					
1 Visclosky	Y	Y	Y	N	Y
2 Donnelly	Y	Y	Y	N	Y
3 Souder	N	N	N	Y	Y
4 Buyer	N	Y	Y	Y	Y
5 Burton	N	N	N	Y	Y
6 Pence	N	N	N	Y	?
7 Carson	Y	Y	Y	N	Y
8 Ellsworth	Y	Y	Y	N	Y
9 Hill	N	Y	Y	N	Y
IOWA					
1 Braley	Y	Y	Y	N	Y
2 Loebsack	Y	Y	Y	N	Y
3 Boswell	Y	Y	Y	N	Y
4 Latham	N	N	Y	Y	Y
5 King	N	N	N	Y	N
KANSAS					
1 Moran	N	N	N	Y	Y
2 Jenkins	N	N	N	Y	N
3 Moore	Y	Y	Y	N	Y
4 Tiahrt	N	N	Y	Y	N
KENTUCKY					
1 Whitfield	N	N	N	Y	Y
2 Guthrie	N	Y	N	Y	Y
3 Yarmuth	Y	Y	Y	N	Y
4 Davis	N	N	N	Y	N
5 Rogers	N	Y	Y	Y	Y
6 Chandler	Y	Y	Y	N	Y
LOUISIANA					
1 Scalise	N	N	N	Y	N
2 Cao	N	Y	Y	Y	Y
3 Melancon	Y	Y	Y	N	Y
4 Fleming	N	Y	Y	Y	Y
5 Alexander	N	N	N	Y	Y
6 Cassidy	N	N	Y	Y	Y
7 Boustany	N	N	N	Y	Y
MAINE					
1 Pingree	Y	Y	Y	N	Y
2 Michaud	Y	Y	Y	N	Y
MARYLAND					
1 Kratovil	Y	Y	Y	N	Y
2 Ruppersberger	?	Y	Y	N	Y
3 Sarbanes	Y	Y	Y	N	Y
4 Edwards	Y	Y	Y	N	Y
5 Hoyer	Y	Y	Y	N	Y
6 Bartlett	N	N	N	Y	Y
7 Cummings	Y	Y	Y	N	Y
8 Van Hollen	Y	Y	Y	N	Y
MASSACHUSETTS					
1 Olver	Y	N	Y	N	Y
2 Neal	Y	Y	Y	N	Y
3 McGovern	Y	Y	Y	N	Y
4 Frank	Y	Y	Y	N	Y
5 Tsongas	Y	Y	Y	N	Y
6 Tierney	Y	Y	Y	N	Y
7 Markey	Y	Y	Y	N	Y
8 Capuano	Y	Y	Y	N	Y
9 Lynch	Y	Y	Y	N	Y
10 Delahunt	Y	Y	Y	N	Y
MICHIGAN					
1 Stupak	Y	Y	Y	N	Y
2 Hoekstra	N	N	N	Y	Y
3 Ehlers	N	Y	N	N	Y
4 Camp	N	Y	N	Y	Y
5 Kildee	Y	Y	Y	N	Y
6 Upton	N	N	N	N	Y
7 Schauer	Y	Y	Y	N	Y
8 Rogers	N	Y	Y	Y	Y
9 Peters	Y	Y	Y	N	Y
10 Miller	N	Y	N	Y	Y
11 McCotter	N	Y	N	Y	Y
12 Levin	Y	Y	Y	N	Y
13 Kilpatrick	Y	Y	Y	N	Y
14 Conyers	Y	Y	Y	N	Y
15 Dingell	?	Y	Y	N	Y
MINNESOTA					
1 Walz	Y	Y	Y	N	Y
2 Kline	N	N	N	Y	N
3 Paulsen	N	Y	N	Y	Y
4 McCollum	Y	Y	Y	N	Y

	224	225	226	227	228
5 Ellison	Y	Y	Y	N	Y
6 Bachmann	N	N	N	Y	N
7 Peterson	Y	Y	Y	N	Y
8 Oberstar	Y	Y	Y	N	Y
MISSISSIPPI					
1 Childers	Y	N	N	N	Y
2 Thompson	Y	Y	Y	N	Y
3 Harper	N	N	N	Y	Y
4 Taylor	Y	Y	Y	N	Y
MISSOURI					
1 Clay	Y	Y	Y	N	Y
2 Akin	N	N	N	Y	Y
3 Carnahan	Y	Y	Y	N	Y
4 Skelton	Y	Y	N	N	Y
5 Cleaver	Y	Y	Y	N	Y
6 Graves	N	N	N	Y	Y
7 Blunt	N	N	N	Y	Y
8 Emerson	N	N	N	Y	Y
9 Luetkemeyer	N	N	N	Y	Y
MONTANA					
AL Rehberg	N	N	N	Y	Y
NEBRASKA					
1 Fortenberry	N	Y	Y	N	Y
2 Terry	N	N	Y	Y	Y
3 Smith	N	N	N	Y	N
NEVADA					
1 Berkley	Y	Y	Y	N	Y
2 Heller	N	N	N	Y	N
3 Titus	Y	Y	Y	N	Y
NEW HAMPSHIRE					
1 Shea-Porter	Y	Y	Y	N	Y
2 Hodes	Y	Y	Y	N	Y
NEW JERSEY					
1 Andrews	Y	Y	Y	N	Y
2 LoBiondo	N	Y	Y	N	Y
3 Adler	Y	Y	Y	N	Y
4 Smith	N	Y	N	N	Y
5 Garrett	N	N	N	Y	N
6 Pallone	Y	Y	Y	N	Y
7 Lance	N	N	N	Y	Y
8 Pascrell	Y	Y	Y	N	Y
9 Rothman	Y	Y	Y	N	Y
10 Payne	Y	Y	Y	N	Y
11 Frelinghuysen	N	N	N	N	Y
12 Holt	Y	Y	Y	N	Y
13 Sires	Y	Y	Y	N	Y
NEW MEXICO					
1 Heinrich	Y	Y	Y	N	Y
2 Teague	Y	Y	Y	N	Y
3 Lujan	Y	Y	Y	N	Y
NEW YORK					
1 Bishop	Y	Y	Y	N	Y
2 Israel	Y	Y	Y	N	Y
3 King	N	N	Y	Y	Y
4 McCarthy	Y	Y	Y	N	Y
5 Ackerman	Y	Y	Y	N	Y
6 Meeks	Y	Y	Y	N	Y
7 Crowley	Y	Y	Y	N	Y
8 Nadler	Y	Y	Y	N	Y
9 Weiner	Y	Y	Y	N	Y
10 Towns	Y	Y	Y	N	Y
11 Clarke	Y	Y	Y	N	Y
12 Velázquez	Y	Y	Y	N	Y
13 McMahon	Y	N	Y	N	Y
14 Maloney	Y	Y	Y	N	Y
15 Rangel	Y	Y	Y	N	Y
16 Serrano	Y	Y	Y	N	Y
17 Engel	Y	Y	Y	N	Y
18 Lowey	Y	Y	Y	N	Y
19 Hall	Y	Y	Y	N	Y
20 Murphy*	Y	Y	Y	N	Y
21 Tonko	Y	Y	Y	N	Y
22 Hinchey	Y	Y	Y	N	Y
23 McHugh	N	N	Y	N	Y
24 Arcuri	Y	Y	N	N	Y
25 Maffei	Y	Y	Y	N	Y
26 Lee	N	Y	N	Y	Y
27 Higgins	Y	Y	Y	N	Y
28 Slaughter	Y	Y	Y	N	Y
29 Massa	Y	Y	Y	N	Y
NORTH CAROLINA					
1 Butterfield	Y	Y	Y	N	Y
2 Etheridge	Y	Y	Y	N	Y
3 Jones	N	Y	Y	N	Y
4 Price	Y	Y	Y	N	Y

	224	225	226	227	228
5 Foxx	N	N	N	Y	N
6 Coble	N	N	N	Y	N
7 McIntyre	Y	N	Y	N	Y
8 Kissell	Y	Y	Y	N	Y
9 Myrick	N	Y	N	Y	N
10 McHenry	N	N	N	Y	N
11 Shuler	Y	Y	N	N	Y
12 Watt	Y	Y	Y	N	Y
13 Miller	Y	Y	Y	N	Y
NORTH DAKOTA					
AL Pomeroy	Y	Y	Y	N	Y
OHIO					
1 Driehaus	Y	Y	Y	N	Y
2 Schmidt	N	N	N	Y	N
3 Turner	N	Y	Y	Y	Y
4 Jordan	N	N	N	Y	N
5 Latta	N	N	N	Y	N
6 Wilson	Y	Y	Y	N	Y
7 Austria	N	N	N	Y	Y
8 Boehner	N	N	N	Y	N
9 Kaptur	Y	Y	Y	N	Y
10 Kucinich	Y	Y	Y	N	Y
11 Fudge	Y	Y	Y	N	Y
12 Tiberi	N	N	N	Y	Y
13 Sutton	Y	Y	Y	N	Y
14 LaTourette	N	N	Y	Y	Y
15 Kilroy	Y	Y	Y	N	Y
16 Boccieri	Y	Y	Y	N	Y
17 Ryan	Y	Y	Y	N	Y
18 Space	Y	Y	N	N	Y
OKLAHOMA					
1 Sullivan	N	N	N	Y	Y
2 Boren	Y	Y	Y	N	Y
3 Lucas	N	N	N	Y	N
4 Cole	N	Y	Y	Y	Y
5 Fallin	N	N	N	Y	Y
OREGON					
1 Wu	Y	Y	Y	N	Y
2 Walden	N	N	N	Y	Y
3 Blumenauer	Y	Y	Y	N	Y
4 DeFazio	Y	Y	Y	N	Y
5 Schrader	Y	Y	Y	N	Y
PENNSYLVANIA					
1 Brady	Y	Y	Y	N	Y
2 Fattah	Y	Y	Y	N	Y
3 Dahlkemper	Y	Y	Y	N	Y
4 Altmire	Y	N	Y	N	Y
5 Thompson	N	N	N	Y	Y
6 Gerlach	N	Y	Y	N	Y
7 Sestak	Y	Y	Y	N	Y
8 Murphy, P.	Y	Y	Y	N	Y
9 Shuster	N	N	N	Y	Y
10 Carney	Y	Y	Y	N	Y
11 Kanjorski	Y	Y	Y	N	Y
12 Murtha	Y	Y	Y	N	Y
13 Schwartz	Y	Y	Y	N	Y
14 Doyle	Y	Y	Y	N	Y
15 Dent	N	Y	Y	Y	Y
16 Pitts	N	N	N	Y	N
17 Holden	Y	Y	Y	N	Y
18 Murphy, T.	N	N	N	N	Y
19 Platts	Y	Y	Y	N	Y
RHODE ISLAND					
1 Kennedy	Y	Y	Y	N	Y
2 Langevin	Y	Y	Y	N	Y
SOUTH CAROLINA					
1 Brown	N	N	Y	Y	Y
2 Wilson	N	N	N	Y	Y
3 Barrett	N	N	N	Y	Y
4 Inglis	N	N	N	Y	N
5 Spratt	Y	Y	Y	N	Y
6 Clyburn	Y	Y	Y	N	Y
SOUTH DAKOTA					
AL Herseth Sandlin	Y	N	Y	N	N
TENNESSEE					
1 Roe	N	N	N	Y	Y
2 Duncan	N	Y	Y	N	Y
3 Wamp	N	Y	Y	Y	Y
4 Davis	Y	Y	Y	N	Y
5 Cooper	Y	Y	Y	N	Y
6 Gordon	Y	Y	Y	N	Y
7 Blackburn	N	N	N	Y	N
8 Tanner	Y	N	N	N	Y
9 Cohen	Y	Y	Y	N	Y

	224	225	226	227	228
TEXAS					
1 Gohmert	N	Y	Y	Y	N
2 Poe	N	N	N	Y	N
3 Johnson, S.	N	N	N	Y	N
4 Hall	N	N	N	Y	Y
5 Hensarling	N	N	N	Y	N
6 Barton	N	Y	N	Y	Y
7 Culberson	N	N	Y	Y	Y
8 Brady	?	N	Y	Y	N
9 Green, A.	Y	Y	Y	N	Y
10 McCaul	N	N	Y	Y	Y
11 Conaway	N	N	N	Y	N
12 Granger	?	?	?	?	?
13 Thornberry	N	N	N	Y	N
14 Paul	N	N	N	Y	N
15 Hinojosa	Y	Y	Y	N	Y
16 Reyes	Y	Y	Y	N	Y
17 Edwards	Y	Y	Y	N	Y
18 Jackson Lee	Y	Y	Y	N	Y
19 Neugebauer	N	N	N	Y	N
20 Gonzalez	Y	Y	Y	N	Y
21 Smith	N	N	N	Y	N
22 Olson	N	N	N	Y	N
23 Rodriguez	Y	Y	Y	N	Y
24 Marchant	N	N	N	Y	N
25 Doggett	Y	N	Y	N	Y
26 Burgess	?	?	?	?	?
27 Ortiz	Y	Y	Y	N	Y
28 Cuellar	Y	Y	Y	N	Y
29 Green, G.	Y	Y	Y	N	Y
30 Johnson, E.	Y	Y	Y	N	Y
31 Carter	N	N	N	Y	N
32 Sessions	N	N	N	Y	N
UTAH					
1 Bishop	N	?	N	Y	N
2 Matheson	Y	N	N	N	Y
3 Chaffetz	N	N	N	Y	N
VERMONT					
AL Welch	Y	Y	Y	N	Y
VIRGINIA					
1 Wittman	N	Y	N	Y	Y
2 Nye	Y	Y	Y	N	Y
3 Scott	Y	Y	Y	N	Y
4 Forbes	N	Y	N	Y	Y
5 Perriello	Y	Y	Y	N	Y
6 Goodlatte	N	N	N	Y	N
7 Cantor	N	N	N	Y	N
8 Moran	Y	Y	Y	N	Y
9 Boucher	Y	Y	Y	N	Y
10 Wolf	N	Y	N	Y	Y
11 Connolly	Y	Y	Y	N	Y
WASHINGTON					
1 Inslee	Y	Y	Y	N	Y
2 Larsen	Y	Y	Y	N	Y
3 Baird	Y	Y	Y	N	Y
4 Hastings	N	N	N	?	?
5 McMorris Rodgers	?	N	N	Y	N
6 Dicks	Y	Y	Y	N	Y
7 McDermott	Y	Y	Y	N	Y
8 Reichert	N	N	N	Y	Y
9 Smith	Y	Y	Y	N	Y
WEST VIRGINIA					
1 Mollohan	Y	Y	Y	N	Y
2 Capito	N	Y	N	Y	Y
3 Rahall	Y	Y	Y	N	Y
WISCONSIN					
1 Ryan	N	N	N	Y	N
2 Baldwin	Y	Y	Y	N	Y
3 Kind	Y	Y	Y	N	Y
4 Moore	Y	Y	Y	N	Y
5 Sensenbrenner	N	N	N	Y	N
6 Petri	N	Y	Y	N	Y
7 Obey	Y	N	Y	N	Y
8 Kagen	Y	Y	Y	N	Y
WYOMING					
AL Lummis	N	N	N	Y	N
DELEGATES					
Faleomavaega (A.S.)	Y	Y			
Norton (D.C.)	Y	Y			
Bordallo (Guam)	-	+			
Sablan (N. Marianas)	Y	Y			
Pierluisi (P.R.)	Y	Y			
Christensen (V.I.)	Y	Y			

IN THE HOUSE | By Vote Number

229. **H Res 230. Cinco de Mayo/Adoption.** Payne, D-N.J., motion to suspend the rules and adopt the resolution that would request that the president issue a proclamation recognizing the Mexican people's struggle for freedom and the importance of Cinco de Mayo with appropriate activities. Motion agreed to 395-0: R 166-0; D 229-0. A two-thirds majority of those present and voting (264 in this case) is required for adoption under suspension of the rules. May 4, 2009.

230. **H Con Res 111. Anniversary of Israeli Independence/Adoption.** Payne, D-N.J., motion to suspend the rules and adopt the resolution that would congratulate the people of Israel on the 61st anniversary of the country's independence, recognize the country for providing refuge and a national homeland for the Jewish people, and commend the commitment of the United States to support Israel. Motion agreed to 394-0: R 165-0; D 229-0. A two-thirds majority of those present and voting (263 in this case) is required for adoption under suspension of the rules. May 4, 2009.

231. **H Res 299. Public Service Recognition Week/Adoption.** Lynch, D-Mass., motion to suspend the rules and adopt the resolution that would commend public servants for their contributions to the United States during Public Service Recognition Week and throughout the year. Motion agreed to 419-0: R 171-0; D 248-0. A two-thirds majority of those present and voting (280 in this case) is required for adoption under suspension of the rules. May 5, 2009.

232. **H Res 338. Community College Month/Adoption.** Polis, D-Colo., motion to suspend the rules and adopt the resolution that would support the goals and ideals of National Community College Month and congratulate community colleges for their contributions to education and workforce development. Motion agreed to 424-0: R 175-0; D 249-0. A two-thirds majority of those present and voting (283 in this case) is required for adoption under suspension of the rules. May 5, 2009.

233. **H Res 353. Global Youth Services Days/Adoption.** Polis, D-Colo., motion to suspend the rules and adopt the resolution that would support the goals and ideals of Global Youth Services Days 2009 and commend U.S. youth volunteers. Motion agreed to 424-0: R 175-0; D 249-0. A two-thirds majority of those present and voting (283 in this case) is required for adoption under suspension of the rules. May 5, 2009.

	229	230	231	232	233
ALABAMA					
1 **Bonner**	Y	Y	Y	Y	Y
2 Bright	Y	Y	Y	Y	Y
3 **Rogers**	Y	Y	Y	Y	Y
4 **Aderholt**	Y	Y	Y	Y	Y
5 Griffith	Y	Y	Y	Y	Y
6 **Bachus**	Y	Y	Y	Y	Y
7 Davis	Y	Y	Y	Y	Y
ALASKA					
AL **Young**	Y	Y	Y	Y	Y
ARIZONA					
1 Kirkpatrick	Y	Y	Y	Y	Y
2 **Franks**	Y	Y	Y	Y	Y
3 **Shadegg**	Y	Y	Y	Y	Y
4 Pastor	Y	Y	Y	Y	Y
5 Mitchell	Y	Y	Y	Y	Y
6 **Flake**	Y	Y	Y	Y	Y
7 Grijalva	?	?	Y	Y	Y
8 Giffords	Y	Y	Y	Y	Y
ARKANSAS					
1 Berry	Y	Y	Y	Y	Y
2 Snyder	Y	Y	Y	Y	Y
3 **Boozman**	Y	Y	Y	Y	Y
4 Ross	Y	Y	Y	Y	Y
CALIFORNIA					
1 Thompson	Y	Y	Y	Y	Y
2 **Herger**	Y	Y	Y	Y	Y
3 **Lungren**	Y	Y	Y	Y	Y
4 **McClintock**	Y	Y	Y	Y	Y
5 Matsui	Y	Y	Y	Y	Y
6 Woolsey	Y	Y	Y	Y	Y
7 Miller, George	Y	Y	Y	Y	Y
8 Pelosi					
9 Lee	Y	Y	Y	Y	Y
10 Tauscher	Y	Y	Y	Y	Y
11 McNerney	Y	Y	Y	Y	Y
12 Speier	Y	Y	Y	Y	Y
13 Stark	?	?	?	?	?
14 Eshoo	Y	Y	Y	Y	Y
15 Honda	Y	Y	Y	Y	Y
16 Lofgren	Y	Y	Y	Y	Y
17 Farr	Y	Y	Y	Y	Y
18 Cardoza	Y	Y	Y	Y	Y
19 **Radanovich**	Y	Y	Y	Y	Y
20 Costa	Y	Y	Y	Y	Y
21 **Nunes**	Y	Y	Y	Y	Y
22 **McCarthy**	Y	Y	Y	Y	Y
23 Capps	Y	Y	Y	Y	Y
24 **Gallegly**	?	?	Y	Y	Y
25 **McKeon**	Y	Y	Y	Y	Y
26 **Dreier**	Y	Y	Y	Y	Y
27 Sherman	Y	Y	Y	Y	Y
28 Berman	Y	Y	Y	Y	Y
29 Schiff	Y	Y	Y	Y	Y
30 Waxman	Y	Y	Y	Y	Y
31 Becerra	Y	Y	Y	Y	Y
32 Vacant					
33 Watson	Y	Y	Y	Y	Y
34 Roybal-Allard	Y	Y	Y	Y	Y
35 Waters	?	?	Y	Y	Y
36 Harman	Y	Y	Y	Y	Y
37 Richardson	Y	Y	Y	Y	Y
38 Napolitano	+	?	Y	Y	Y
39 Sánchez, Linda	+	+	Y	Y	Y
40 **Royce**	Y	Y	Y	Y	Y
41 **Lewis**	Y	Y	Y	Y	Y
42 **Miller, Gary**	Y	Y	Y	Y	Y
43 Baca	Y	Y	Y	Y	Y
44 **Calvert**	Y	Y	Y	Y	Y
45 **Bono Mack**	Y	Y	Y	Y	Y
46 **Rohrabacher**	?	?	Y	Y	Y
47 Sanchez, Loretta	Y	Y	Y	Y	Y
48 **Campbell**	Y	Y	P	Y	Y
49 **Issa**	Y	Y	Y	Y	Y
50 **Bilbray**	Y	Y	Y	Y	Y
51 Filner	Y	Y	Y	Y	Y
52 **Hunter**	Y	Y	Y	Y	Y
53 Davis	Y	Y	Y	Y	Y

	229	230	231	232	233
COLORADO					
1 DeGette	Y	Y	Y	Y	Y
2 Polis	Y	Y	Y	Y	Y
3 Salazar	Y	Y	Y	Y	Y
4 Markey	Y	Y	Y	Y	Y
5 **Lamborn**	Y	Y	Y	Y	Y
6 **Coffman**	Y	Y	Y	Y	Y
7 Perlmutter	Y	Y	Y	Y	Y
CONNECTICUT					
1 Larson	Y	Y	Y	Y	Y
2 Courtney	Y	Y	Y	Y	Y
3 DeLauro	Y	Y	Y	Y	Y
4 Himes	Y	Y	Y	Y	Y
5 Murphy	Y	Y	Y	Y	Y
DELAWARE					
AL **Castle**	Y	Y	Y	Y	Y
FLORIDA					
1 **Miller**	Y	Y	Y	Y	Y
2 Boyd	Y	Y	Y	Y	Y
3 Brown	?	?	Y	Y	Y
4 **Crenshaw**	Y	Y	Y	Y	Y
5 **Brown-Waite**	Y	Y	Y	Y	Y
6 **Stearns**	Y	Y	Y	Y	Y
7 **Mica**	Y	Y	Y	Y	Y
8 Grayson	Y	Y	Y	Y	Y
9 **Bilirakis**	Y	Y	Y	Y	Y
10 **Young**	Y	Y	Y	Y	Y
11 Castor	Y	Y	Y	Y	Y
12 **Putnam**	Y	Y	Y	Y	Y
13 **Buchanan**	Y	Y	Y	Y	Y
14 **Mack**	Y	Y	Y	Y	Y
15 **Posey**	Y	Y	Y	Y	Y
16 **Rooney**	Y	Y	Y	Y	Y
17 Meek	Y	Y	Y	Y	Y
18 **Ros-Lehtinen**	Y	Y	Y	Y	Y
19 Wexler	Y	Y	Y	Y	Y
20 Wasserman Schultz	Y	Y	Y	Y	Y
21 **Diaz-Balart, L.**	Y	Y	Y	Y	Y
22 Klein	Y	Y	Y	Y	Y
23 Hastings	Y	Y	Y	Y	Y
24 Kosmas	Y	Y	Y	Y	Y
25 **Diaz-Balart, M.**	Y	Y	Y	Y	Y
GEORGIA					
1 **Kingston**	Y	Y	Y	Y	Y
2 Bishop	Y	Y	Y	Y	Y
3 **Westmoreland**	+	+	Y	Y	Y
4 Johnson	Y	Y	Y	Y	Y
5 Lewis	Y	Y	Y	Y	Y
6 **Price**	Y	Y	Y	Y	Y
7 **Linder**	Y	Y	Y	Y	Y
8 Marshall	Y	?	Y	Y	Y
9 **Deal**	?	?	?	?	?
10 **Broun**	Y	Y	Y	Y	Y
11 **Gingrey**	Y	Y	Y	Y	Y
12 Barrow	Y	Y	Y	Y	Y
13 Scott	Y	Y	Y	Y	Y
HAWAII					
1 Abercrombie	Y	Y	Y	Y	Y
2 Hirono	Y	Y	Y	Y	Y
IDAHO					
1 Minnick	Y	Y	Y	Y	Y
2 **Simpson**	Y	Y	Y	Y	Y
ILLINOIS					
1 Rush	Y	Y	Y	Y	Y
2 Jackson	Y	Y	Y	Y	Y
3 Lipinski	?	?	Y	Y	Y
4 Gutierrez	Y	Y	Y	Y	Y
5 Vacant					
5 Quigley	Y	Y	Y	Y	Y
6 **Roskam**	Y	Y	Y	Y	Y
7 Davis	Y	Y	Y	Y	Y
8 Bean	?	?	Y	Y	Y
9 Schakowsky	Y	Y	Y	Y	Y
10 **Kirk**	Y	Y	Y	Y	Y
11 Halvorson	Y	Y	Y	Y	Y
12 Costello	Y	Y	Y	Y	Y
13 **Biggert**	Y	Y	Y	Y	Y
14 Foster	Y	Y	Y	Y	Y
15 **Johnson**	+	+	Y	Y	Y

KEY	**Republicans**	Democrats
Y	Voted for (yea)	
#	Paired for	
+	Announced for	
N	Voted against (nay)	

X	Paired against
–	Announced against
P	Voted "present"

C	Voted "present" to avoid possible conflict of interest
?	Did not vote or otherwise make a position known

	229	230	231	232	233
16 Manzullo	Y	Y	Y	Y	Y
17 Hare	Y	Y	Y	Y	Y
18 Schock	Y	Y	Y	Y	Y
19 Shimkus	Y	Y	Y	Y	Y
INDIANA					
1 Visclosky	Y	Y	Y	Y	Y
2 Donnelly	Y	Y	Y	Y	Y
3 Souder	Y	Y	Y	Y	Y
4 Buyer	Y	Y	Y	Y	Y
5 Burton	Y	Y	Y	Y	Y
6 Pence	Y	Y	Y	Y	Y
7 Carson	Y	Y	Y	Y	Y
8 Ellsworth	Y	Y	Y	Y	Y
9 Hill	Y	Y	Y	Y	?
IOWA					
1 Braley	+	+	Y	Y	Y
2 Loebsack	Y	Y	Y	Y	Y
3 Boswell	Y	Y	Y	Y	Y
4 Latham	Y	Y	Y	Y	Y
5 King	Y	Y	Y	Y	Y
KANSAS					
1 Moran	Y	Y	Y	Y	Y
2 Jenkins	Y	Y	Y	Y	Y
3 Moore	Y	Y	Y	Y	Y
4 Tiahrt	Y	Y	Y	Y	Y
KENTUCKY					
1 Whitfield	?	?	Y	Y	Y
2 Guthrie	Y	Y	Y	Y	Y
3 Yarmuth	Y	Y	Y	Y	Y
4 Davis	Y	Y	Y	Y	Y
5 Rogers	Y	Y	Y	Y	Y
6 Chandler	Y	Y	Y	Y	Y
LOUISIANA					
1 Scalise	Y	Y	Y	Y	Y
2 Cao	Y	Y	Y	Y	Y
3 Melancon	Y	Y	Y	Y	Y
4 Fleming	Y	Y	Y	Y	Y
5 Alexander	Y	Y	Y	Y	Y
6 Cassidy	Y	Y	Y	Y	Y
7 Boustany	Y	Y	Y	Y	Y
MAINE					
1 Pingree	Y	Y	Y	Y	Y
2 Michaud	Y	Y	Y	Y	Y
MARYLAND					
1 Kratovil	Y	Y	Y	Y	Y
2 Ruppersberger	Y	Y	Y	Y	Y
3 Sarbanes	Y	Y	Y	Y	Y
4 Edwards	Y	Y	Y	Y	Y
5 Hoyer	Y	Y	Y	Y	Y
6 Bartlett	Y	Y	Y	Y	Y
7 Cummings	Y	Y	Y	Y	Y
8 Van Hollen	Y	Y	Y	Y	Y
MASSACHUSETTS					
1 Olver	Y	Y	Y	Y	Y
2 Neal	?	?	Y	Y	Y
3 McGovern	Y	Y	Y	Y	Y
4 Frank	Y	Y	Y	Y	Y
5 Tsongas	Y	Y	Y	Y	Y
6 Tierney	Y	Y	Y	Y	Y
7 Markey	Y	Y	Y	Y	Y
8 Capuano	+	+	+	+	+
9 Lynch	Y	Y	Y	Y	Y
10 Delahunt	Y	Y	Y	Y	Y
MICHIGAN					
1 Stupak	Y	Y	Y	Y	Y
2 Hoekstra	Y	Y	Y	Y	Y
3 Ehlers	Y	Y	Y	Y	Y
4 Camp	Y	Y	Y	Y	Y
5 Kildee	Y	Y	Y	Y	Y
6 Upton	Y	Y	Y	Y	Y
7 Schauer	Y	Y	Y	Y	Y
8 Rogers	Y	Y	Y	Y	Y
9 Peters	Y	Y	Y	Y	Y
10 Miller	Y	Y	Y	Y	Y
11 McCotter	Y	Y	Y	Y	Y
12 Levin	Y	Y	Y	Y	Y
13 Kilpatrick	?	Y	Y	Y	Y
14 Conyers	+	+	+	+	+
15 Dingell	Y	Y	?	Y	Y
MINNESOTA					
1 Walz	Y	Y	Y	Y	Y
2 Kline	Y	Y	Y	Y	Y
3 Paulsen	Y	Y	Y	Y	Y
4 McCollum	Y	Y	Y	Y	Y

	229	230	231	232	233
5 Ellison	Y	Y	Y	Y	Y
6 Bachmann	Y	Y	Y	Y	Y
7 Peterson	Y	Y	Y	Y	Y
8 Oberstar	Y	Y	Y	Y	Y
MISSISSIPPI					
1 Childers	?	?	Y	Y	Y
2 Thompson	Y	Y	Y	Y	Y
3 Harper	Y	Y	Y	Y	Y
4 Taylor	Y	Y	Y	Y	Y
MISSOURI					
1 Clay	Y	Y	Y	Y	Y
2 Akin	Y	Y	Y	Y	Y
3 Carnahan	Y	Y	Y	Y	Y
4 Skelton	Y	Y	Y	Y	Y
5 Cleaver	Y	Y	Y	Y	Y
6 Graves	Y	Y	Y	Y	Y
7 Blunt	Y	Y	Y	Y	Y
8 Emerson	Y	Y	Y	Y	Y
9 Luetkemeyer	Y	Y	Y	Y	Y
MONTANA					
AL Rehberg	Y	Y	Y	Y	Y
NEBRASKA					
1 Fortenberry	Y	Y	?	?	?
2 Terry	Y	Y	Y	Y	Y
3 Smith	Y	Y	Y	Y	Y
NEVADA					
1 Berkley	Y	Y	Y	Y	Y
2 Heller	Y	Y	Y	Y	Y
3 Titus	Y	Y	Y	Y	Y
NEW HAMPSHIRE					
1 Shea-Porter	Y	Y	Y	Y	Y
2 Hodes	Y	Y	Y	Y	Y
NEW JERSEY					
1 Andrews	Y	Y	Y	Y	Y
2 LoBiondo	Y	Y	Y	Y	Y
3 Adler	Y	Y	Y	Y	Y
4 Smith	Y	Y	Y	Y	Y
5 Garrett	Y	Y	Y	Y	Y
6 Pallone	Y	Y	Y	Y	Y
7 Lance	Y	Y	Y	Y	Y
8 Pascrell	+	+	+	+	+
9 Rothman	Y	Y	Y	Y	Y
10 Payne	Y	Y	Y	Y	Y
11 Frelinghuysen	Y	Y	Y	Y	Y
12 Holt	Y	Y	Y	Y	Y
13 Sires	Y	Y	Y	Y	Y
NEW MEXICO					
1 Heinrich	Y	Y	Y	Y	Y
2 Teague	Y	Y	Y	Y	Y
3 Lujan	Y	Y	Y	Y	Y
NEW YORK					
1 Bishop	Y	Y	Y	Y	Y
2 Israel	?	Y	Y	?	Y
3 King	Y	Y	Y	Y	Y
4 McCarthy	Y	Y	Y	Y	Y
5 Ackerman	Y	Y	Y	Y	Y
6 Meeks	Y	Y	Y	Y	Y
7 Crowley	Y	Y	Y	Y	Y
8 Nadler	Y	Y	Y	Y	Y
9 Weiner	Y	Y	Y	Y	Y
10 Towns	?	?	Y	Y	Y
11 Clarke	Y	Y	Y	Y	Y
12 Velázquez	Y	Y	Y	Y	Y
13 McMahon	Y	Y	Y	Y	Y
14 Maloney	?	?	Y	Y	Y
15 Rangel	Y	Y	Y	Y	Y
16 Serrano	Y	Y	Y	Y	Y
17 Engel	Y	Y	Y	Y	Y
18 Lowey	Y	Y	Y	Y	Y
19 Hall	Y	Y	Y	Y	Y
20 Murphy	Y	Y	Y	Y	Y
21 Tonko	Y	Y	Y	Y	Y
22 Hinchey	Y	Y	Y	Y	Y
23 McHugh	Y	Y	Y	Y	Y
24 Arcuri	Y	Y	Y	Y	Y
25 Maffei	Y	Y	Y	Y	Y
26 Lee	Y	Y	Y	Y	Y
27 Higgins	Y	Y	Y	Y	Y
28 Slaughter	Y	Y	Y	Y	Y
29 Massa	Y	Y	Y	Y	Y
NORTH CAROLINA					
1 Butterfield	Y	Y	Y	Y	Y
2 Etheridge	Y	Y	Y	Y	Y
3 Jones	Y	Y	Y	Y	Y
4 Price	?	?	Y	Y	Y

	229	230	231	232	233
5 Foxx	Y	Y	Y	Y	Y
6 Coble	Y	Y	Y	Y	Y
7 McIntyre	Y	Y	Y	Y	Y
8 Kissell	Y	Y	Y	Y	Y
9 Myrick	Y	Y	Y	Y	Y
10 McHenry	Y	Y	Y	Y	Y
11 Shuler	?	?	Y	Y	Y
12 Watt	Y	Y	Y	Y	Y
13 Miller	Y	Y	Y	Y	Y
NORTH DAKOTA					
AL Pomeroy	Y	Y	Y	Y	Y
OHIO					
1 Driehaus	Y	Y	Y	Y	Y
2 Schmidt	Y	Y	Y	Y	Y
3 Turner	Y	Y	Y	Y	Y
4 Jordan	Y	Y	Y	Y	Y
5 Latta	Y	Y	Y	Y	Y
6 Wilson	Y	Y	Y	Y	Y
7 Austria	Y	Y	Y	Y	Y
8 Boehner	Y	Y	Y	Y	Y
9 Kaptur	Y	Y	Y	Y	Y
10 Kucinich	Y	Y	Y	Y	Y
11 Fudge	Y	Y	Y	Y	Y
12 Tiberi	?	?	Y	Y	Y
13 Sutton	Y	Y	Y	Y	Y
14 LaTourette	Y	Y	Y	Y	Y
15 Kilroy	Y	Y	Y	Y	Y
16 Boccieri	Y	Y	Y	Y	Y
17 Ryan	Y	Y	Y	Y	Y
18 Space	Y	Y	Y	Y	Y
OKLAHOMA					
1 Sullivan	Y	Y	Y	Y	Y
2 Boren	Y	Y	Y	Y	Y
3 Lucas	?	?	Y	Y	Y
4 Cole	Y	Y	Y	Y	Y
5 Fallin	Y	Y	Y	Y	Y
OREGON					
1 Wu	Y	Y	Y	Y	Y
2 Walden	Y	Y	Y	Y	Y
3 Blumenauer	Y	Y	Y	Y	Y
4 DeFazio	?	?	Y	Y	Y
5 Schrader	Y	Y	Y	Y	Y
PENNSYLVANIA					
1 Brady	?	?	Y	Y	Y
2 Fattah	Y	Y	Y	Y	Y
3 Dahlkemper	Y	Y	Y	Y	Y
4 Altmire	Y	Y	Y	Y	Y
5 Thompson	Y	Y	Y	Y	Y
6 Gerlach	?	?	Y	Y	Y
7 Sestak	Y	Y	Y	Y	Y
8 Murphy, P.	Y	Y	Y	Y	Y
9 Shuster	Y	Y	Y	Y	Y
10 Carney	Y	Y	Y	Y	Y
11 Kanjorski	Y	Y	Y	Y	Y
12 Murtha	?	?	?	?	?
13 Schwartz	Y	Y	Y	Y	Y
14 Doyle	Y	Y	Y	Y	Y
15 Dent	Y	Y	Y	Y	Y
16 Pitts	Y	Y	Y	Y	Y
17 Holden	Y	Y	Y	Y	Y
18 Murphy, T.	Y	Y	Y	Y	Y
19 Platts	Y	Y	Y	Y	Y
RHODE ISLAND					
1 Kennedy	Y	Y	Y	Y	Y
2 Langevin	Y	Y	Y	Y	Y
SOUTH CAROLINA					
1 Brown	Y	Y	Y	Y	Y
2 Wilson	Y	Y	Y	Y	Y
3 Barrett	+	+	Y	Y	Y
4 Inglis	?	?	Y	Y	Y
5 Spratt	Y	Y	Y	Y	Y
6 Clyburn	Y	Y	Y	Y	Y
SOUTH DAKOTA					
AL Herseth Sandlin	Y	Y	Y	Y	Y
TENNESSEE					
1 Roe	Y	Y	Y	Y	Y
2 Duncan	Y	Y	Y	Y	Y
3 Wamp	Y	Y	Y	Y	Y
4 Davis	Y	Y	Y	Y	Y
5 Cooper	Y	Y	Y	Y	Y
6 Gordon	Y	Y	Y	Y	Y
7 Blackburn	Y	Y	P	Y	Y
8 Tanner	Y	Y	Y	Y	Y
9 Cohen	Y	Y	Y	Y	Y

	229	230	231	232	233
TEXAS					
1 Gohmert	Y	Y	Y	Y	Y
2 Poe	Y	Y	Y	Y	Y
3 Johnson, S.	Y	Y	Y	Y	Y
4 Hall	Y	Y	Y	Y	Y
5 Hensarling	Y	Y	Y	Y	Y
6 Barton	Y	Y	Y	Y	Y
7 Culberson	Y	Y	Y	Y	Y
8 Brady	Y	Y	Y	Y	Y
9 Green, A.	Y	Y	Y	Y	Y
10 McCaul	Y	Y	Y	Y	Y
11 Conaway	Y	Y	P	Y	Y
12 Granger	Y	Y	Y	Y	Y
13 Thornberry	?	?	Y	Y	Y
14 Paul	Y	?	Y	Y	Y
15 Hinojosa	Y	Y	Y	Y	Y
16 Reyes	Y	Y	Y	Y	Y
17 Edwards	Y	Y	Y	Y	Y
18 Jackson Lee	Y	Y	Y	Y	Y
19 Neugebauer	Y	Y	P	Y	Y
20 Gonzalez	Y	Y	Y	Y	Y
21 Smith	Y	Y	Y	Y	Y
22 Olson	Y	Y	Y	Y	Y
23 Rodriguez	Y	Y	Y	Y	Y
24 Marchant	Y	Y	Y	Y	Y
25 Doggett	Y	Y	Y	Y	Y
26 Burgess	Y	Y	Y	Y	Y
27 Ortiz	Y	Y	Y	Y	Y
28 Cuellar	Y	Y	Y	Y	Y
29 Green, G.	Y	Y	Y	Y	Y
30 Johnson, E.	Y	Y	Y	Y	Y
31 Carter	Y	Y	Y	Y	Y
32 Sessions	Y	Y	Y	Y	Y
UTAH					
1 Bishop	Y	Y	Y	Y	Y
2 Matheson	Y	?	Y	Y	Y
3 Chaffetz	Y	Y	Y	Y	Y
VERMONT					
AL Welch	Y	Y	Y	Y	Y
VIRGINIA					
1 Wittman	Y	Y	Y	Y	Y
2 Nye	Y	Y	Y	Y	Y
3 Scott	Y	Y	Y	Y	Y
4 Forbes	Y	Y	Y	Y	Y
5 Perriello	Y	Y	Y	Y	Y
6 Goodlatte	Y	Y	Y	Y	Y
7 Cantor	Y	Y	Y	Y	Y
8 Moran	?	?	Y	Y	Y
9 Boucher	?	?	?	Y	Y
10 Wolf	Y	Y	Y	Y	Y
11 Connolly	Y	Y	Y	Y	Y
WASHINGTON					
1 Inslee	Y	Y	Y	Y	Y
2 Larsen	Y	Y	Y	Y	Y
3 Baird	Y	Y	Y	Y	Y
4 Hastings	Y	Y	Y	Y	Y
5 McMorris Rodgers	Y	Y	Y	Y	Y
6 Dicks	Y	Y	Y	Y	Y
7 McDermott	Y	Y	Y	Y	Y
8 Reichert	Y	Y	Y	Y	Y
9 Smith	?	?	Y	Y	Y
WEST VIRGINIA					
1 Mollohan	Y	Y	Y	Y	Y
2 Capito	Y	Y	?	?	?
3 Rahall	Y	Y	Y	Y	Y
WISCONSIN					
1 Ryan	Y	Y	Y	Y	Y
2 Baldwin	Y	Y	Y	Y	Y
3 Kind	Y	Y	Y	Y	Y
4 Moore	Y	Y	Y	Y	Y
5 Sensenbrenner	Y	Y	Y	Y	Y
6 Petri	Y	Y	Y	Y	Y
7 Obey	Y	Y	Y	Y	Y
8 Kagen	Y	Y	Y	Y	Y
WYOMING					
AL Lummis	Y	Y	Y	Y	Y
DELEGATES					
Faleomavaega (A.S.)					
Norton (D.C.)					
Bordallo (Guam)					
Sablan (N. Marianas)					
Pierluisi (P.R.)					
Christensen (V.I.)					

IN THE HOUSE | By Vote Number

234. **H Res 367. National Train Day/Adoption.** Brown, D-Fla., motion to suspend the rules and adopt the resolution that would support the goals and ideals of National Train Day as designated by Amtrak and recognize the contributions of trains to the national transportation system. Motion agreed to 426-0: R 176-0; D 250-0. A two-thirds majority of those present and voting (284 in this case) is required for adoption under suspension of the rules. May 6, 2009.

235. **S 386. Financial Fraud/Passage.** Scott, D-Va., motion to suspend the rules and pass the bill, as amended, that would expand federal fraud laws to cover funds paid under the economic stimulus package and the Troubled Asset Relief Program, as well as to mortgage lenders not directly regulated or insured by the federal government. It would authorize additional funds in fiscal 2010-11 for the Justice Department and other federal agencies as well as for state and local law enforcement investigations. Motion agreed to 367-59: R 117-59; D 250-0. A two-thirds majority of those present and voting (284 in this case) is required for passage under suspension of the rules. A "yea" was a vote in support of the president's position. May 6, 2009.

236. **H Res 348. University of North Carolina Basketball/Adoption.** Polis, D-Colo., motion to suspend the rules and adopt the resolution that would congratulate the University of North Carolina for winning the 2009 National Collegiate Athletic Association Division I Men's Basketball Championship. Motion agreed to 423-0: R 176-0; D 247-0. A two-thirds majority of those present and voting (282 in this case) is required for adoption under suspension of the rules. May 6, 2009.

237. **HR 1728. Mortgage Lending Standards/Rule.** Adoption of the rule (H Res 406) that would provide for House floor consideration of the bill that would impose restrictions and set standards for mortgage lenders. Adopted 247-174: R 0-173; D 247-1. May 7, 2009.

238. **HR 1728. Mortgage Lending Standards/Elected Office Crimes.** Frank, D-Mass., amendment that would bar the use of funds in the bill for legal assistance or housing counseling grants to organizations that have been convicted of federal crimes related to elected office or that employ individuals who have been convicted of such crimes. Adopted in Committee of the Whole 245-176: R 0-172; D 245-4. May 7, 2009.

	234	235	236	237	238
ALABAMA					
1 **Bonner**	Y	Y	Y	N	N
2 **Bright**	Y	Y	Y	Y	N
3 **Rogers**	Y	Y	Y	N	N
4 **Aderholt**	Y	Y	Y	N	N
5 Griffith	Y	Y	Y	Y	Y
6 **Bachus**	Y	Y	Y	N	N
7 Davis	Y	Y	Y	Y	Y
ALASKA					
AL **Young**	Y	N	Y	N	N
ARIZONA					
1 Kirkpatrick	Y	Y	Y	Y	Y
2 **Franks**	Y	N	Y	N	N
3 **Shadegg**	Y	N	Y	N	N
4 Pastor	Y	Y	Y	Y	Y
5 Mitchell	Y	Y	Y	Y	N
6 **Flake**	Y	N	Y	N	N
7 Grijalva	Y	Y	Y	Y	Y
8 Giffords	Y	Y	Y	Y	N
ARKANSAS					
1 Berry	?	?	?	?	?
2 Snyder	Y	Y	Y	Y	Y
3 **Boozman**	Y	Y	Y	N	N
4 Ross	Y	Y	Y	Y	Y
CALIFORNIA					
1 Thompson	Y	Y	Y	Y	Y
2 **Herger**	Y	Y	Y	N	N
3 **Lungren**	Y	Y	Y	N	N
4 **McClintock**	Y	Y	Y	N	N
5 Matsui	Y	Y	Y	Y	Y
6 Woolsey	Y	Y	Y	Y	Y
7 Miller, George	Y	Y	Y	?	Y
8 Pelosi					
9 Lee	Y	Y	Y	Y	Y
10 Tauscher	Y	Y	Y	Y	Y
11 McNerney	Y	Y	Y	Y	Y
12 Speier	?	?	?	Y	Y
13 Stark	?	?	?	?	?
14 Eshoo	Y	Y	Y	Y	Y
15 Honda	Y	Y	Y	Y	Y
16 Lofgren	Y	Y	Y	Y	Y
17 Farr	Y	Y	Y	Y	Y
18 Cardoza	Y	Y	Y	Y	Y
19 **Radanovich**	Y	Y	Y	N	N
20 Costa	Y	Y	Y	Y	Y
21 **Nunes**	Y	Y	Y	N	N
22 **McCarthy**	Y	Y	Y	N	N
23 Capps	Y	Y	Y	+	+
24 **Gallegly**	Y	Y	Y	N	N
25 **McKeon**	Y	Y	Y	N	N
26 **Dreier**	Y	N	Y	N	N
27 Sherman	Y	Y	Y	Y	Y
28 Berman	Y	Y	Y	Y	Y
29 Schiff	Y	Y	Y	Y	Y
30 Waxman	Y	Y	Y	Y	Y
31 Becerra	Y	Y	Y	Y	Y
32 Vacant					
33 Watson	Y	Y	Y	Y	Y
34 Roybal-Allard	Y	Y	Y	Y	Y
35 Waters	Y	Y	Y	Y	Y
36 Harman	Y	Y	Y	Y	Y
37 Richardson	Y	Y	Y	Y	Y
38 Napolitano	Y	Y	Y	Y	Y
39 Sánchez, Linda	Y	Y	?	Y	Y
40 **Royce**	Y	Y	Y	N	N
41 **Lewis**	Y	Y	Y	N	N
42 **Miller, Gary**	Y	Y	Y	N	N
43 Baca	Y	Y	Y	Y	Y
44 **Calvert**	Y	Y	Y	N	N
45 **Bono Mack**	Y	Y	Y	N	N
46 **Rohrabacher**	Y	Y	Y	N	N
47 Sanchez, Loretta	Y	Y	Y	Y	Y
48 **Campbell**	Y	N	Y	N	N
49 **Issa**	Y	Y	Y	N	N
50 **Bilbray**	Y	Y	Y	N	N
51 Filner	Y	Y	Y	Y	Y
52 **Hunter**	Y	Y	Y	N	N
53 Davis	Y	Y	Y	Y	Y

	234	235	236	237	238
COLORADO					
1 DeGette	Y	Y	Y	Y	Y
2 Polis	Y	Y	Y	Y	Y
3 Salazar	Y	Y	Y	Y	Y
4 Markey	Y	Y	Y	Y	Y
5 **Lamborn**	Y	N	Y	N	N
6 **Coffman**	Y	Y	Y	N	N
7 Perlmutter	Y	Y	Y	Y	Y
CONNECTICUT					
1 Larson	Y	Y	Y	Y	Y
2 Courtney	Y	Y	Y	Y	Y
3 DeLauro	Y	Y	Y	Y	Y
4 Himes	Y	Y	Y	Y	Y
5 Murphy	Y	Y	Y	Y	Y
DELAWARE					
AL **Castle**	Y	Y	Y	N	N
FLORIDA					
1 **Miller**	Y	N	Y	N	N
2 Boyd	Y	Y	Y	Y	Y
3 Brown	Y	Y	Y	Y	Y
4 **Crenshaw**	Y	Y	Y	N	N
5 **Brown-Waite**	Y	Y	Y	N	N
6 **Stearns**	Y	Y	Y	N	N
7 **Mica**	Y	Y	Y	N	N
8 Grayson	Y	P	Y	Y	Y
9 **Bilirakis**	Y	Y	Y	N	N
10 **Young**	Y	Y	Y	N	N
11 Castor	Y	Y	Y	Y	Y
12 **Putnam**	Y	Y	Y	N	N
13 **Buchanan**	Y	Y	Y	N	N
14 **Mack**	Y	N	Y	N	N
15 **Posey**	Y	Y	Y	N	N
16 **Rooney**	Y	Y	Y	N	N
17 Meek	Y	Y	Y	Y	Y
18 **Ros-Lehtinen**	Y	Y	Y	N	N
19 Wexler	Y	Y	Y	Y	Y
20 Wasserman Schultz	Y	Y	Y	Y	Y
21 **Diaz-Balart, L.**	Y	Y	Y	N	N
22 Klein	Y	Y	Y	Y	Y
23 Hastings	Y	Y	Y	Y	Y
24 Kosmas	Y	Y	Y	Y	Y
25 **Diaz-Balart, M.**	Y	Y	Y	N	N
GEORGIA					
1 **Kingston**	Y	N	Y	N	N
2 Bishop	Y	Y	Y	Y	Y
3 **Westmoreland**	Y	N	Y	N	N
4 Johnson	Y	Y	Y	Y	?
5 Lewis	Y	Y	Y	Y	Y
6 **Price**	Y	N	Y	N	N
7 **Linder**	Y	N	Y	N	N
8 Marshall	Y	Y	Y	Y	Y
9 **Deal**	Y	N	Y	N	N
10 **Broun**	Y	N	Y	N	N
11 **Gingrey**	Y	N	Y	N	N
12 Barrow	Y	Y	Y	Y	Y
13 Scott	Y	Y	Y	Y	Y
HAWAII					
1 Abercrombie	Y	Y	Y	Y	Y
2 Hirono	Y	Y	?	Y	Y
IDAHO					
1 **Minnick**	Y	Y	Y	Y	N
2 **Simpson**	Y	Y	Y	N	N
ILLINOIS					
1 Rush	Y	Y	Y	Y	Y
2 Jackson	Y	Y	Y	Y	Y
3 Lipinski	Y	Y	Y	Y	Y
4 Gutierrez	Y	Y	Y	Y	Y
5 Vacant					
5 Quigley	Y	Y	Y	Y	Y
6 **Roskam**	Y	Y	Y	N	N
7 Davis	Y	Y	Y	Y	Y
8 Bean	Y	Y	Y	Y	Y
9 Schakowsky	Y	Y	Y	Y	Y
10 **Kirk**	Y	Y	Y	N	N
11 Halvorson	Y	Y	Y	Y	Y
12 Costello	Y	Y	Y	Y	Y
13 **Biggert**	Y	Y	Y	N	N
14 Foster	Y	Y	Y	Y	Y
15 Johnson	Y	Y	Y	N	N

KEY **Republicans** Democrats

Y Voted for (yea)	X Paired against	C Voted "present" to avoid possible conflict of interest
# Paired for	– Announced against	
+ Announced for	P Voted "present"	? Did not vote or otherwise make a position known
N Voted against (nay)		

	234	235	236	237	238
16 Manzullo	Y	N	Y	N	N
17 Hare	Y	Y	Y	Y	Y
18 Schock	Y	Y	Y	N	N
19 Shimkus	Y	Y	Y	N	N
INDIANA					
1 Visclosky	Y	Y	Y	Y	Y
2 Donnelly	Y	Y	Y	Y	Y
3 Souder	Y	Y	Y	N	N
4 Buyer	Y	Y	Y	N	N
5 Burton	Y	N	Y	N	N
6 Pence	Y	N	Y	N	N
7 Carson	Y	Y	Y	Y	Y
8 Ellsworth	Y	Y	Y	Y	Y
9 Hill	Y	Y	Y	N	Y
IOWA					
1 Braley	Y	Y	Y	Y	Y
2 Loebsack	Y	Y	Y	Y	Y
3 Boswell	Y	Y	Y	Y	Y
4 Latham	Y	Y	Y	N	N
5 King	Y	N	Y	–	N
KANSAS					
1 Moran	Y	Y	Y	N	N
2 Jenkins	Y	Y	Y	N	N
3 Moore	Y	Y	Y	Y	?
4 Tiahrt	Y	Y	Y	N	N
KENTUCKY					
1 Whitfield	Y	Y	Y	N	N
2 Guthrie	Y	Y	Y	N	N
3 Yarmuth	Y	Y	Y	Y	Y
4 Davis	Y	N	Y	N	N
5 Rogers	Y	Y	Y	N	N
6 Chandler	Y	Y	Y	Y	Y
LOUISIANA					
1 Scalise	Y	Y	Y	?	?
2 Cao	Y	Y	Y	N	N
3 Melancon	Y	Y	Y	Y	Y
4 Fleming	Y	Y	Y	N	N
5 Alexander	Y	Y	Y	N	N
6 Cassidy	Y	Y	Y	N	N
7 Boustany	Y	N	Y	N	N
MAINE					
1 Pingree	Y	Y	Y	Y	Y
2 Michaud	Y	Y	Y	Y	Y
MARYLAND					
1 Kratovil	Y	Y	Y	Y	Y
2 Ruppersberger	Y	Y	Y	Y	Y
3 Sarbanes	Y	Y	Y	Y	Y
4 Edwards	Y	Y	Y	Y	Y
5 Hoyer	Y	Y	Y	Y	Y
6 Bartlett	Y	Y	Y	N	N
7 Cummings	Y	Y	Y	Y	Y
8 Van Hollen	Y	Y	Y	Y	Y
MASSACHUSETTS					
1 Olver	Y	Y	Y	Y	Y
2 Neal	Y	Y	Y	Y	Y
3 McGovern	Y	Y	Y	Y	Y
4 Frank	Y	Y	Y	Y	Y
5 Tsongas	Y	Y	Y	Y	Y
6 Tierney	Y	Y	Y	Y	Y
7 Markey	Y	Y	Y	Y	Y
8 Capuano	Y	Y	Y	Y	Y
9 Lynch	Y	Y	Y	Y	Y
10 Delahunt	Y	Y	Y	Y	Y
MICHIGAN					
1 Stupak	Y	Y	Y	Y	Y
2 Hoekstra	Y	Y	Y	N	N
3 Ehlers	Y	N	Y	N	N
4 Camp	Y	Y	Y	N	N
5 Kildee	Y	Y	Y	Y	Y
6 Upton	Y	Y	Y	N	N
7 Schauer	Y	Y	Y	Y	Y
8 Rogers	Y	Y	Y	N	N
9 Peters	Y	Y	Y	Y	Y
10 Miller	Y	Y	Y	N	N
11 McCotter	Y	Y	Y	N	N
12 Levin	Y	Y	Y	Y	Y
13 Kilpatrick	Y	Y	Y	Y	Y
14 Conyers	Y	Y	Y	Y	Y
15 Dingell	Y	Y	Y	Y	Y
MINNESOTA					
1 Walz	Y	Y	Y	Y	Y
2 Kline	Y	N	Y	N	N
3 Paulsen	Y	Y	Y	N	N
4 McCollum	Y	Y	Y	Y	Y

	234	235	236	237	238
5 Ellison	Y	Y	Y	Y	Y
6 Bachmann	Y	N	Y	N	N
7 Peterson	Y	Y	Y	Y	Y
8 Oberstar	Y	Y	Y	Y	Y
MISSISSIPPI					
1 Childers	Y	Y	Y	Y	Y
2 Thompson	Y	Y	Y	Y	?
3 Harper	Y	Y	Y	N	N
4 Taylor	Y	Y	Y	Y	Y
MISSOURI					
1 Clay	Y	Y	Y	Y	Y
2 Akin	Y	N	Y	N	N
3 Carnahan	Y	Y	Y	Y	Y
4 Skelton	?	?	?	Y	Y
5 Cleaver	Y	Y	Y	Y	Y
6 Graves	Y	Y	Y	N	N
7 Blunt	Y	Y	Y	N	?
8 Emerson	Y	Y	Y	N	N
9 Luetkemeyer	Y	Y	Y	N	N
MONTANA					
AL Rehberg	Y	Y	Y	N	N
NEBRASKA					
1 Fortenberry	?	?	?	?	?
2 Terry	Y	Y	Y	N	N
3 Smith	Y	N	Y	N	N
NEVADA					
1 Berkley	Y	Y	Y	Y	Y
2 Heller	Y	Y	Y	–	–
3 Titus	Y	Y	Y	Y	Y
NEW HAMPSHIRE					
1 Shea-Porter	Y	Y	Y	Y	Y
2 Hodes	Y	Y	Y	Y	Y
NEW JERSEY					
1 Andrews	Y	Y	Y	Y	Y
2 LoBiondo	Y	Y	Y	N	N
3 Adler	Y	Y	Y	Y	Y
4 Smith	Y	Y	Y	N	N
5 Garrett	Y	N	Y	N	N
6 Pallone	Y	Y	Y	Y	Y
7 Lance	Y	Y	Y	N	N
8 Pascrell	Y	Y	Y	Y	Y
9 Rothman	Y	Y	Y	Y	Y
10 Payne	Y	Y	Y	Y	Y
11 Frelinghuysen	Y	Y	Y	N	N
12 Holt	Y	Y	Y	?	?
13 Sires	Y	Y	Y	Y	Y
NEW MEXICO					
1 Heinrich	Y	Y	Y	Y	Y
2 Teague	Y	Y	Y	Y	Y
3 Lujan	Y	Y	Y	Y	Y
NEW YORK					
1 Bishop	Y	Y	Y	Y	Y
2 Israel	Y	Y	Y	Y	Y
3 King	Y	Y	Y	N	N
4 McCarthy	Y	Y	Y	Y	Y
5 Ackerman	Y	Y	Y	Y	Y
6 Meeks	Y	Y	Y	Y	Y
7 Crowley	Y	Y	Y	Y	Y
8 Nadler	Y	Y	Y	?	?
9 Weiner	Y	Y	Y	Y	Y
10 Towns	Y	Y	Y	Y	Y
11 Clarke	Y	Y	Y	Y	Y
12 Velázquez	Y	Y	Y	Y	Y
13 McMahon	Y	Y	Y	Y	Y
14 Maloney	Y	Y	Y	Y	Y
15 Rangel	Y	Y	Y	Y	Y
16 Serrano	Y	Y	Y	Y	Y
17 Engel	Y	Y	Y	?	Y
18 Lowey	Y	Y	Y	Y	Y
19 Hall	Y	Y	Y	Y	Y
20 Murphy	Y	Y	Y	Y	Y
21 Tonko	Y	Y	Y	Y	Y
22 Hinchey	Y	Y	Y	Y	Y
23 McHugh	Y	Y	Y	N	N
24 Arcuri	Y	Y	Y	Y	Y
25 Maffei	Y	Y	Y	Y	Y
26 Lee	Y	Y	Y	N	N
27 Higgins	Y	Y	Y	?	Y
28 Slaughter	Y	Y	Y	Y	Y
29 Massa	Y	Y	Y	Y	Y
NORTH CAROLINA					
1 Butterfield	Y	Y	Y	Y	Y
2 Etheridge	Y	Y	Y	Y	Y
3 Jones	Y	Y	Y	N	N
4 Price	Y	Y	Y	Y	Y

	234	235	236	237	238
5 Foxx	Y	N	Y	N	N
6 Coble	Y	Y	Y	N	N
7 McIntyre	Y	Y	Y	Y	?
8 Kissell	Y	Y	Y	Y	Y
9 Myrick	Y	N	Y	N	N
10 McHenry	Y	N	Y	N	N
11 Shuler	Y	Y	Y	Y	Y
12 Watt	Y	Y	Y	Y	Y
13 Miller	Y	Y	Y	Y	Y
NORTH DAKOTA					
AL Pomeroy	Y	Y	Y	Y	Y
OHIO					
1 Driehaus	Y	Y	Y	Y	Y
2 Schmidt	Y	Y	Y	N	N
3 Turner	Y	Y	Y	N	N
4 Jordan	Y	N	Y	N	N
5 Latta	Y	N	Y	N	N
6 Wilson	Y	Y	Y	Y	Y
7 Austria	Y	Y	Y	N	N
8 Boehner	Y	N	Y	N	N
9 Kaptur	Y	Y	?	Y	Y
10 Kucinich	Y	Y	Y	Y	Y
11 Fudge	Y	Y	Y	Y	Y
12 Tiberi	Y	Y	Y	N	N
13 Sutton	Y	Y	Y	Y	Y
14 LaTourette	Y	Y	Y	N	N
15 Kilroy	Y	Y	Y	Y	Y
16 Boccieri	Y	Y	Y	Y	Y
17 Ryan	Y	Y	Y	Y	Y
18 Space	Y	Y	Y	Y	Y
OKLAHOMA					
1 Sullivan	Y	N	Y	N	N
2 Boren	Y	Y	Y	Y	Y
3 Lucas	Y	N	Y	N	N
4 Cole	Y	N	Y	N	N
5 Fallin	Y	Y	Y	N	N
OREGON					
1 Wu	Y	Y	Y	Y	Y
2 Walden	Y	Y	Y	N	N
3 Blumenauer	?	Y	Y	Y	Y
4 DeFazio	Y	Y	Y	Y	Y
5 Schrader	Y	Y	Y	Y	Y
PENNSYLVANIA					
1 Brady	Y	Y	Y	Y	Y
2 Fattah	Y	Y	Y	Y	Y
3 Dahlkemper	Y	Y	Y	Y	Y
4 Altmire	Y	Y	Y	Y	Y
5 Thompson	Y	Y	Y	N	N
6 Gerlach	Y	Y	Y	N	N
7 Sestak	Y	Y	Y	Y	Y
8 Murphy, P.	Y	Y	Y	Y	Y
9 Shuster	Y	Y	Y	N	N
10 Carney	Y	Y	Y	Y	Y
11 Kanjorski	Y	Y	Y	Y	Y
12 Murtha	Y	Y	Y	Y	Y
13 Schwartz	Y	Y	Y	Y	Y
14 Doyle	Y	Y	Y	Y	Y
15 Dent	Y	Y	Y	N	N
16 Pitts	Y	Y	Y	N	N
17 Holden	Y	Y	Y	Y	Y
18 Murphy, T.	Y	Y	Y	N	N
19 Platts	Y	Y	Y	N	N
RHODE ISLAND					
1 Kennedy	Y	Y	Y	Y	Y
2 Langevin	Y	Y	Y	Y	Y
SOUTH CAROLINA					
1 Brown	Y	Y	Y	N	N
2 Wilson	Y	Y	Y	N	N
3 Barrett	Y	N	Y	N	N
4 Inglis	Y	Y	Y	N	N
5 Spratt	Y	Y	Y	Y	Y
6 Clyburn	Y	Y	Y	Y	Y
SOUTH DAKOTA					
AL Herseth Sandlin	Y	Y	Y	Y	Y
TENNESSEE					
1 Roe	Y	Y	Y	N	N
2 Duncan	Y	N	Y	N	N
3 Wamp	?	?	?	?	?
4 Davis	Y	Y	Y	Y	Y
5 Cooper	Y	Y	Y	Y	Y
6 Gordon	Y	Y	Y	Y	Y
7 Blackburn	Y	N	Y	N	N
8 Tanner	Y	Y	Y	Y	Y
9 Cohen	Y	Y	Y	Y	Y

	234	235	236	237	238
TEXAS					
1 Gohmert	Y	Y	Y	N	N
2 Poe	Y	N	Y	N	N
3 Johnson, S.	Y	N	Y	N	N
4 Hall	Y	Y	Y	N	N
5 Hensarling	Y	N	Y	N	N
6 Barton	Y	Y	Y	N	N
7 Culberson	Y	N	Y	N	?
8 Brady	Y	N	Y	N	N
9 Green, A.	Y	Y	Y	Y	Y
10 McCaul	Y	Y	Y	N	N
11 Conaway	Y	N	Y	N	N
12 Granger	Y	Y	Y	N	N
13 Thornberry	Y	Y	Y	N	N
14 Paul	Y	N	Y	N	N
15 Hinojosa	Y	Y	Y	Y	?
16 Reyes	Y	Y	Y	Y	Y
17 Edwards	Y	Y	Y	Y	Y
18 Jackson Lee	Y	Y	Y	Y	Y
19 Neugebauer	Y	N	Y	N	N
20 Gonzalez	Y	Y	Y	Y	Y
21 Smith	Y	Y	Y	N	N
22 Olson	Y	N	Y	N	N
23 Rodriguez	Y	Y	Y	Y	Y
24 Marchant	Y	N	Y	N	N
25 Doggett	Y	Y	Y	Y	Y
26 Burgess	Y	Y	Y	N	N
27 Ortiz	Y	Y	Y	Y	Y
28 Cuellar	Y	Y	Y	Y	Y
29 Green, G.	Y	Y	Y	Y	Y
30 Johnson, E.	Y	Y	Y	Y	Y
31 Carter	Y	N	Y	N	N
32 Sessions	Y	N	Y	N	N
UTAH					
1 Bishop	Y	N	Y	N	N
2 Matheson	Y	Y	Y	Y	Y
3 Chaffetz	Y	N	Y	N	N
VERMONT					
AL Welch	Y	Y	Y	Y	Y
VIRGINIA					
1 Wittman	Y	Y	Y	N	N
2 Nye	Y	Y	Y	Y	Y
3 Scott	Y	Y	Y	Y	Y
4 Forbes	Y	Y	Y	N	N
5 Perriello	Y	Y	Y	Y	Y
6 Goodlatte	Y	Y	Y	N	N
7 Cantor	Y	Y	Y	N	N
8 Moran	Y	Y	Y	Y	Y
9 Boucher	Y	Y	Y	Y	Y
10 Wolf	Y	Y	Y	N	N
11 Connolly	Y	Y	Y	Y	Y
WASHINGTON					
1 Inslee	Y	Y	Y	Y	Y
2 Larsen	Y	Y	Y	Y	Y
3 Baird	Y	Y	Y	Y	Y
4 Hastings	Y	N	Y	N	N
5 McMorris Rodgers	Y	Y	Y	N	N
6 Dicks	Y	Y	Y	Y	Y
7 McDermott	Y	Y	Y	Y	Y
8 Reichert	Y	Y	Y	N	N
9 Smith	Y	Y	Y	Y	Y
WEST VIRGINIA					
1 Mollohan	Y	Y	Y	Y	?
2 Capito	Y	Y	Y	N	N
3 Rahall	Y	Y	Y	Y	Y
WISCONSIN					
1 Ryan	Y	Y	Y	N	N
2 Baldwin	Y	Y	Y	Y	Y
3 Kind	Y	Y	Y	Y	Y
4 Moore	Y	Y	Y	Y	Y
5 Sensenbrenner	Y	Y	Y	N	N
6 Petri	Y	Y	Y	N	N
7 Obey	Y	Y	Y	Y	Y
8 Kagen	Y	Y	Y	Y	Y
WYOMING					
AL Lummis	Y	N	Y	N	N
DELEGATES					
Faleomavaega (A.S.)				Y	
Norton (D.C.)				Y	
Bordallo (Guam)				Y	
Sablan (N. Marianas)				Y	
Pierluisi (P.R.)				?	
Christensen (V.I.)				Y	

IN THE HOUSE | By Vote Number

239. **HR 1728. Mortgage Lending Standards/Assignee and Securitizer Liability.** Hensarling, R-Texas, amendment that would strike provisions related to liability of assignees and securitizers in the bill. Rejected in Committee of the Whole 171-252: R 167-6; D 4-246. May 7, 2009.

240. **HR 1728. Mortgage Lending Standards/Federal Reserve Certification.** Price, R-Ga., amendment that would delay mortgage lending standards provisions in the bill for 90 days after the Federal Reserve Board of Governors certifies that the provisions would not reduce the availability or increase the price of credit for qualified mortgages. Rejected in Committee of the Whole 167-259: R 163-10; D 4-249. May 7, 2009.

241. **HR 1728. Mortgage Lending Standards/Loan Restrictions.** McHenry, R-N.C., amendment that would strike language in the bill that would set restrictions for high-cost mortgages, such as those with annual percentage rates that exceed prime by 6.5 percent, including provisions that would prohibit creditors from extending credit to borrowers with such mortgages without certification from a mortgage counselor approved by the Housing and Urban Development Department. Rejected in Committee of the Whole 171-255: R 169-4; D 2-251. May 7, 2009.

242. **HR 1728. Mortgage Lending Standards/Passage.** Passage of the bill that would impose restrictions and set standards for mortgage lenders. Creditors would have to retain at least 5 percent of the credit risk on any non-qualified mortgage that is transferred, sold or conveyed. It would require lenders to be licensed and registered when required under state or federal law and would prohibit compensation structures that could cause loan originators to steer applicants toward mortgages that they lack a reasonable ability to repay or are based on loan terms other than principal. Lenders would be required to obtain proof of a borrower's ability to repay a home loan and barred from providing refinancing credit unless the lender reasonably determines refinancing would provide tangible benefit to the borrower. Passed 300-114: R 60-111; D 240-3. May 7, 2009.

	239	240	241	242
ALABAMA				
1 Bonner	Y	Y	Y	N
2 Bright	Y	Y	Y	N
3 Rogers	Y	Y	Y	Y
4 Aderholt	Y	Y	Y	N
5 Griffith	N	N	N	Y
6 Bachus	Y	Y	Y	N
7 Davis	N	N	N	Y
ALASKA				
AL Young	Y	Y	Y	N
ARIZONA				
1 Kirkpatrick	Y	Y	Y	N
2 Franks	Y	Y	Y	N
3 Shadegg	N	Y	Y	N
4 Pastor	N	N	N	Y
5 Mitchell	N	N	N	Y
6 Flake	Y	Y	Y	N
7 Grijalva	N	N	N	Y
8 Giffords	N	N	N	Y
ARKANSAS				
1 Berry	?	?	?	?
2 Snyder	N	N	N	Y
3 Boozman	Y	Y	Y	N
4 Ross	N	N	N	Y
CALIFORNIA				
1 Thompson	N	N	N	Y
2 Herger	Y	Y	Y	N
3 Lungren	Y	Y	Y	Y
4 McClintock	Y	Y	Y	N
5 Matsui	N	N	N	Y
6 Woolsey	N	N	N	Y
7 Miller, George	N	N	N	Y
8 Pelosi				
9 Lee	N	N	N	Y
10 Tauscher	N	N	N	Y
11 McNerney	N	N	N	Y
12 Speier	N	N	N	Y
13 Stark	?	?	?	?
14 Eshoo	N	N	N	Y
15 Honda	N	N	N	Y
16 Lofgren	N	N	N	Y
17 Farr	N	N	N	Y
18 Cardoza	N	N	N	Y
19 Radanovich	Y	Y	Y	N
20 Costa	N	N	N	Y
21 Nunes	Y	Y	Y	N
22 McCarthy	Y	Y	Y	N
23 Capps	?	–	–	+
24 Gallegly	Y	Y	Y	N
25 McKeon	Y	Y	Y	N
26 Dreier	Y	Y	Y	Y
27 Sherman	N	N	N	Y
28 Berman	N	N	N	Y
29 Schiff	N	N	N	Y
30 Waxman	N	N	N	Y
31 Becerra	N	N	N	Y
32 Vacant				
33 Watson	N	N	N	Y
34 Roybal-Allard	N	N	N	Y
35 Waters	N	N	N	Y
36 Harman	N	N	N	Y
37 Richardson	N	N	N	Y
38 Napolitano	N	N	N	Y
39 Sánchez, Linda	N	N	N	Y
40 Royce	Y	Y	Y	N
41 Lewis	Y	Y	Y	N
42 Miller, Gary	Y	Y	Y	N
43 Baca	N	N	N	?
44 Calvert	Y	Y	Y	Y
45 Bono Mack	Y	Y	Y	Y
46 Rohrabacher	Y	Y	Y	Y
47 Sanchez, Loretta	N	N	N	Y
48 Campbell	Y	Y	Y	?
49 Issa	Y	Y	Y	N
50 Bilbray	Y	Y	Y	Y
51 Filner	N	N	N	Y
52 Hunter	Y	Y	Y	N
53 Davis	N	N	N	Y

	239	240	241	242
COLORADO				
1 DeGette	N	N	N	Y
2 Polis	N	N	N	Y
3 Salazar	N	N	N	Y
4 Markey	N	N	N	Y
5 Lamborn	Y	Y	Y	N
6 Coffman	Y	Y	Y	N
7 Perlmutter	N	N	N	Y
CONNECTICUT				
1 Larson	N	N	N	Y
2 Courtney	N	N	N	Y
3 DeLauro	N	N	N	Y
4 Himes	N	N	N	Y
5 Murphy	N	N	N	Y
DELAWARE				
AL Castle	Y	Y	Y	Y
FLORIDA				
1 Miller	Y	Y	Y	N
2 Boyd	N	N	N	+
3 Brown	N	N	N	Y
4 Crenshaw	Y	Y	Y	N
5 Brown-Waite	Y	N	Y	Y
6 Stearns	N	Y	Y	N
7 Mica	Y	Y	Y	N
8 Grayson	N	N	N	Y
9 Bilirakis	Y	Y	Y	Y
10 Young	Y	Y	Y	N
11 Castor	N	N	N	Y
12 Putnam	Y	Y	Y	N
13 Buchanan	Y	Y	Y	Y
14 Mack	Y	Y	Y	N
15 Posey	Y	Y	Y	N
16 Rooney	Y	Y	Y	Y
17 Meek	N	N	N	Y
18 Ros-Lehtinen	Y	Y	Y	Y
19 Wexler	N	N	N	Y
20 Wasserman Schultz	N	N	N	Y
21 Diaz-Balart, L.	Y	Y	Y	Y
22 Klein	N	N	N	Y
23 Hastings	N	N	N	Y
24 Kosmas	N	N	N	Y
25 Diaz-Balart, M.	Y	Y	Y	Y
GEORGIA				
1 Kingston	Y	Y	Y	N
2 Bishop	N	N	N	Y
3 Westmoreland	Y	Y	Y	N
4 Johnson	N	N	N	Y
5 Lewis	N	N	N	Y
6 Price	Y	Y	Y	N
7 Linder	Y	Y	Y	?
8 Marshall	N	N	N	Y
9 Deal	Y	Y	Y	N
10 Broun	Y	Y	Y	N
11 Gingrey	Y	Y	Y	N
12 Barrow	N	N	N	Y
13 Scott	N	N	N	Y
HAWAII				
1 Abercrombie	N	N	N	Y
2 Hirono	N	N	N	Y
IDAHO				
1 Minnick	N	N	N	Y
2 Simpson	Y	Y	Y	Y
ILLINOIS				
1 Rush	N	N	N	Y
2 Jackson	N	N	N	Y
3 Lipinski	N	N	N	Y
4 Gutierrez	N	N	N	Y
5 Vacant				
5 Quigley	N	N	N	Y
6 Roskam	Y	Y	Y	N
7 Davis	N	N	N	Y
8 Bean	N	N	N	Y
9 Schakowsky	N	N	N	Y
10 Kirk	Y	Y	Y	Y
11 Halvorson	N	N	N	Y
12 Costello	N	N	N	Y
13 Biggert	Y	Y	Y	Y
14 Foster	N	N	N	Y
15 Johnson	N	Y	Y	Y

Member	239	240	241	242
16 Manzullo	Y	Y	Y	N
17 Hare	N	N	N	Y
18 Schock	Y	Y	Y	Y
19 Shimkus	Y	Y	Y	Y
INDIANA				
1 Visclosky	N	N	N	Y
2 Donnelly	N	N	N	Y
3 Souder	Y	Y	Y	Y
4 Buyer	Y	Y	Y	Y
5 Burton	Y	Y	Y	Y
6 Pence	Y	Y	Y	N
7 Carson	N	N	N	Y
8 Ellsworth	N	N	N	Y
9 Hill	N	N	N	Y
IOWA				
1 Braley	N	N	N	Y
2 Loebsack	N	N	N	Y
3 Boswell	N	N	N	Y
4 Latham	Y	Y	Y	Y
5 King	Y	Y	Y	N
KANSAS				
1 Moran	Y	Y	Y	N
2 Jenkins	Y	Y	Y	N
3 Moore	N	N	N	Y
4 Tiahrt	Y	Y	Y	N
KENTUCKY				
1 Whitfield	Y	Y	Y	N
2 Guthrie	Y	Y	Y	N
3 Yarmuth	N	N	N	Y
4 Davis	Y	Y	Y	N
5 Rogers	Y	Y	Y	N
6 Chandler	N	N	N	Y
LOUISIANA				
1 Scalise	?	?	?	?
2 Cao	Y	Y	Y	N
3 Melancon	N	N	N	Y
4 Fleming	Y	Y	Y	N
5 Alexander	Y	Y	Y	N
6 Cassidy	Y	Y	Y	N
7 Boustany	Y	Y	Y	N
MAINE				
1 Pingree	N	N	N	Y
2 Michaud	N	N	N	Y
MARYLAND				
1 Kratovil	Y	N	N	Y
2 Ruppersberger	N	N	N	Y
3 Sarbanes	N	N	N	Y
4 Edwards	N	N	N	Y
5 Hoyer	N	N	N	Y
6 Bartlett	Y	Y	Y	Y
7 Cummings	N	N	N	Y
8 Van Hollen	N	N	N	Y
MASSACHUSETTS				
1 Olver	N	N	N	Y
2 Neal	N	N	N	Y
3 McGovern	N	N	N	Y
4 Frank	N	N	N	Y
5 Tsongas	N	N	N	Y
6 Tierney	N	N	N	Y
7 Markey	N	N	N	Y
8 Capuano	N	N	N	Y
9 Lynch	N	N	N	Y
10 Delahunt	N	N	N	Y
MICHIGAN				
1 Stupak	N	N	N	Y
2 Hoekstra	Y	Y	Y	N
3 Ehlers	N	N	Y	Y
4 Camp	Y	Y	Y	N
5 Kildee	N	N	N	Y
6 Upton	Y	Y	Y	Y
7 Schauer	N	N	N	Y
8 Rogers	Y	Y	Y	Y
9 Peters	N	N	N	Y
10 Miller	Y	Y	Y	Y
11 McCotter	Y	Y	Y	Y
12 Levin	N	N	N	Y
13 Kilpatrick	N	N	N	Y
14 Conyers	N	N	N	Y
15 Dingell	N	N	N	Y
MINNESOTA				
1 Walz	N	N	N	Y
2 Kline	Y	Y	Y	N
3 Paulsen	Y	Y	Y	N
4 McCollum	N	N	N	Y

Member	239	240	241	242
5 Ellison	N	N	N	Y
6 Bachmann	Y	Y	Y	N
7 Peterson	N	N	N	Y
8 Oberstar	N	N	N	Y
MISSISSIPPI				
1 Childers	N	N	N	Y
2 Thompson	?	?	?	?
3 Harper	Y	Y	Y	N
4 Taylor	N	N	N	Y
MISSOURI				
1 Clay	N	N	N	Y
2 Akin	Y	Y	Y	N
3 Carnahan	N	N	N	Y
4 Skelton	N	N	N	Y
5 Cleaver	N	N	N	Y
6 Graves	Y	Y	Y	N
7 Blunt	?	?	?	?
8 Emerson	Y	Y	Y	Y
9 Luetkemeyer	Y	Y	Y	N
MONTANA				
AL Rehberg	Y	Y	Y	N
NEBRASKA				
1 Fortenberry	?	?	?	?
2 Terry	Y	Y	Y	Y
3 Smith	Y	Y	Y	N
NEVADA				
1 Berkley	N	N	N	Y
2 Heller	+	+	+	+
3 Titus	N	N	N	Y
NEW HAMPSHIRE				
1 Shea-Porter	N	N	N	Y
2 Hodes	N	N	N	Y
NEW JERSEY				
1 Andrews	N	N	N	Y
2 LoBiondo	Y	N	Y	Y
3 Adler	N	N	N	Y
4 Smith	Y	N	Y	Y
5 Garrett	Y	Y	Y	N
6 Pallone	N	N	N	Y
7 Lance	Y	N	Y	Y
8 Pascrell	N	N	N	Y
9 Rothman	N	N	N	Y
10 Payne	N	N	N	Y
11 Frelinghuysen	Y	Y	Y	N
12 Holt	?	?	?	?
13 Sires	N	N	N	Y
NEW MEXICO				
1 Heinrich	N	N	N	Y
2 Teague	N	N	N	Y
3 Lujan	N	N	N	Y
NEW YORK				
1 Bishop	N	N	N	Y
2 Israel	N	N	N	Y
3 King	Y	Y	Y	Y
4 McCarthy	N	N	N	Y
5 Ackerman	N	N	N	Y
6 Meeks	N	N	N	Y
7 Crowley	N	N	N	Y
8 Nadler	?	?	?	?
9 Weiner	N	N	N	Y
10 Towns	N	N	N	Y
11 Clarke	N	N	N	Y
12 Velázquez	?	N	N	Y
13 McMahon	Y	N	N	Y
14 Maloney	N	N	N	Y
15 Rangel	N	N	N	Y
16 Serrano	N	N	N	Y
17 Engel	N	N	N	Y
18 Lowey	N	N	N	Y
19 Hall	N	N	N	Y
20 Murphy	N	Y	N	Y
21 Tonko	N	N	N	Y
22 Hinchey	N	N	N	Y
23 McHugh	Y	Y	Y	Y
24 Arcuri	N	Y	N	Y
25 Maffei	N	N	N	Y
26 Lee	Y	Y	Y	N
27 Higgins	N	N	N	Y
28 Slaughter	N	N	N	+
29 Massa	N	N	N	Y
NORTH CAROLINA				
1 Butterfield	N	N	N	Y
2 Etheridge	N	N	N	Y
3 Jones	N	N	N	Y
4 Price	N	N	N	Y

Member	239	240	241	242
5 Foxx	Y	Y	Y	N
6 Coble	Y	Y	Y	N
7 McIntyre	N	N	N	Y
8 Kissell	N	N	N	Y
9 Myrick	Y	Y	Y	N
10 McHenry	Y	Y	Y	N
11 Shuler	N	N	N	Y
12 Watt	N	N	N	Y
13 Miller	N	N	N	Y
NORTH DAKOTA				
AL Pomeroy	N	N	N	Y
OHIO				
1 Driehaus	N	N	N	Y
2 Schmidt	Y	Y	Y	N
3 Turner	N	Y	N	Y
4 Jordan	Y	Y	Y	N
5 Latta	Y	Y	Y	N
6 Wilson	N	N	N	Y
7 Austria	Y	Y	Y	N
8 Boehner	Y	Y	Y	N
9 Kaptur	N	N	N	Y
10 Kucinich	N	N	N	Y
11 Fudge	N	N	N	Y
12 Tiberi	Y	Y	Y	Y
13 Sutton	N	N	N	Y
14 LaTourette	Y	Y	Y	Y
15 Kilroy	N	N	N	Y
16 Boccieri	N	N	N	Y
17 Ryan	N	N	N	Y
18 Space	N	N	N	Y
OKLAHOMA				
1 Sullivan	Y	Y	Y	N
2 Boren	N	N	N	Y
3 Lucas	Y	Y	Y	N
4 Cole	Y	Y	Y	N
5 Fallin	Y	Y	Y	N
OREGON				
1 Wu	N	N	N	Y
2 Walden	Y	Y	Y	Y
3 Blumenauer	N	N	N	Y
4 DeFazio	?	N	N	Y
5 Schrader	N	N	N	N
PENNSYLVANIA				
1 Brady	N	N	N	Y
2 Fattah	N	N	N	Y
3 Dahlkemper	N	N	N	Y
4 Altmire	N	N	N	Y
5 Thompson	Y	Y	Y	N
6 Gerlach	Y	N	Y	Y
7 Sestak	N	N	N	Y
8 Murphy, P.	N	N	N	Y
9 Shuster	Y	Y	Y	N
10 Carney	N	N	N	Y
11 Kanjorski	N	N	N	Y
12 Murtha	N	N	N	Y
13 Schwartz	N	N	N	Y
14 Doyle	N	N	N	Y
15 Dent	Y	N	Y	Y
16 Pitts	Y	Y	Y	N
17 Holden	N	N	N	Y
18 Murphy, T.	Y	N	N	Y
19 Platts	Y	N	Y	Y
RHODE ISLAND				
1 Kennedy	N	N	N	Y
2 Langevin	N	N	N	Y
SOUTH CAROLINA				
1 Brown	Y	Y	Y	N
2 Wilson	Y	Y	Y	N
3 Barrett	Y	Y	Y	N
4 Inglis	Y	Y	Y	N
5 Spratt	N	N	N	Y
6 Clyburn	N	N	N	Y
SOUTH DAKOTA				
AL Herseth Sandlin	N	N	N	Y
TENNESSEE				
1 Roe	Y	Y	Y	N
2 Duncan	Y	Y	Y	N
3 Wamp	?	?	?	?
4 Davis	N	N	N	Y
5 Cooper	N	N	N	Y
6 Gordon	N	N	N	Y
7 Blackburn	Y	Y	Y	N
8 Tanner	N	N	N	Y
9 Cohen	N	N	N	Y

Member	239	240	241	242
TEXAS				
1 Gohmert	Y	Y	Y	N
2 Poe	Y	Y	Y	N
3 Johnson, S.	Y	Y	Y	N
4 Hall	Y	Y	Y	N
5 Hensarling	Y	Y	Y	N
6 Barton	Y	Y	Y	N
7 Culberson	Y	Y	Y	Y
8 Brady	Y	Y	Y	N
9 Green, A.	N	N	N	Y
10 McCaul	Y	Y	Y	N
11 Conaway	Y	Y	Y	N
12 Granger	Y	Y	Y	N
13 Thornberry	Y	Y	Y	N
14 Paul	Y	Y	Y	N
15 Hinojosa	?	?	?	?
16 Reyes	N	N	N	Y
17 Edwards	?	N	N	Y
18 Jackson Lee	N	N	N	Y
19 Neugebauer	Y	Y	Y	N
20 Gonzalez	N	N	N	Y
21 Smith	Y	Y	Y	N
22 Olson	Y	Y	Y	N
23 Rodriguez	N	N	N	Y
24 Marchant	Y	Y	Y	N
25 Doggett	N	N	N	Y
26 Burgess	Y	Y	Y	N
27 Ortiz	N	N	N	Y
28 Cuellar	N	N	N	Y
29 Green, G.	N	N	N	?
30 Johnson, E.	N	N	N	Y
31 Carter	Y	Y	Y	N
32 Sessions	Y	Y	Y	N
UTAH				
1 Bishop	Y	Y	Y	N
2 Matheson	N	N	N	Y
3 Chaffetz	Y	Y	Y	N
VERMONT				
AL Welch	N	N	N	Y
VIRGINIA				
1 Wittman	Y	Y	Y	Y
2 Nye	N	N	N	Y
3 Scott	N	N	N	Y
4 Forbes	Y	Y	Y	N
5 Perriello	N	N	N	Y
6 Goodlatte	Y	Y	Y	N
7 Cantor	Y	Y	Y	N
8 Moran	N	N	N	Y
9 Boucher	N	N	N	Y
10 Wolf	Y	Y	Y	Y
11 Connolly	N	N	N	Y
WASHINGTON				
1 Inslee	N	N	N	Y
2 Larsen	N	N	N	Y
3 Baird	N	N	N	Y
4 Hastings	Y	Y	Y	N
5 McMorris Rodgers	Y	Y	Y	N
6 Dicks	N	N	N	Y
7 McDermott	N	N	N	Y
8 Reichert	Y	Y	N	Y
9 Smith	N	N	N	Y
WEST VIRGINIA				
1 Mollohan	N	N	N	Y
2 Capito	Y	Y	Y	Y
3 Rahall	N	N	N	Y
WISCONSIN				
1 Ryan	Y	Y	Y	N
2 Baldwin	N	N	N	Y
3 Kind	N	N	N	?
4 Moore	N	N	N	Y
5 Sensenbrenner	Y	Y	Y	N
6 Petri	Y	Y	Y	N
7 Obey	N	N	N	Y
8 Kagen	N	N	N	Y
WYOMING				
AL Lummis	Y	Y	Y	N
DELEGATES				
Faleomavaega (A.S.)	N	N	N	
Norton (D.C.)	N	N	N	
Bordallo (Guam)	N	N	N	
Sablan (N. Marianas)	N	N	N	
Pierluisi (P.R.)	?	?	?	
Christensen (V.I.)	N	N	N	

IN THE HOUSE | By Vote Number

243. **H Res 425. Earmark Investigation/Motion to Table.** Slaughter, D-N.Y., motion to table (kill) the Flake, R-Ariz., privileged resolution that would instruct the Committee on Standards of Official Conduct to investigate and report on the relationship between earmarks made by members of Congress and the details of past campaign contributions. Motion agreed to 215-182: R 4-153; D 211-29. May 12, 2009.

244. **H Res 413. IEEE Engineering the Future Day/Adoption.** Gordon, D-Tenn., motion to suspend the rules and adopt the resolution that would support the goals and ideals of the IEEE Engineering the Future Day, and recognize the importance of engineering and technology to meeting the nation's most pressing challenges. Motion agreed to 409-0: R 168-0; D 241-0. A two-thirds majority of those present and voting (273 in this case) is required for adoption under suspension of the rules. May 12, 2009.

245. **H Res 378. Margaret Thatcher Tribute/Adoption.** Berman, D-Calif., motion to suspend the rules and adopt the resolution that would recognize the 30th anniversary of the election of Margaret Thatcher as the first female prime minister of Great Britain, recognize her work in promoting individual rights and free markets around the world, and acknowledge the strong diplomatic relationship she fostered between the United States and Great Britain. Motion agreed to 339-64: R 165-0; D 174-64. A two-thirds majority of those present and voting (269 in this case) is required for adoption under suspension of the rules. May 12, 2009.

246. **HR 2187. Energy Efficient School Construction/Rule.** Adoption of the rule (H Res 427) that would provide for House floor consideration of the bill that would authorize funding for school renovation and modernization projects, with an emphasis on high-performing schools that meet environmental or energy efficiency standards. Adopted 248-175: R 1-173; D 247-2. May 13, 2009.

247. **H Con Res 84. National Military Appreciation Month/Adoption.** Lynch, D-Mass., motion to suspend the rules and adopt the concurrent resolution that would support the goals and objectives of National Military Appreciation Month and urge the president to issue a proclamation calling on the American people to observe the month annually. Motion agreed to 421-0: R 172-0; D 249-0. A two-thirds majority of those present and voting (281 in this case) is required for adoption under suspension of the rules. May 13, 2009.

248. **HR 2162. Herbert A. Littleton Post Office/Passage.** Lynch, D-Mass., motion to suspend the rules and pass the bill that would designate a post office in Nampa, Idaho, as the "Herbert A. Littleton Postal Station." Motion agreed to 420-0: R 171-0; D 249-0. A two-thirds majority of those present and voting (280 in this case) is required for passage under suspension of the rules. May 13, 2009.

249. **HR 2187. Energy Efficient School Construction/Advisory Council.** Titus, D-Nev., amendment that would require the Education Department to establish an advisory council on the impact of energy efficient and environmental schools on teaching and learning, health energy costs, and the environment. The council would also recommend federal policies to increase the number of energy efficient schools. Adopted in Committee of the Whole 270-160: R 19-158; D 251-2. May 13, 2009.

	243	244	245	246	247	248	249
ALABAMA							
1 Bonner	?	?	?	N	Y	Y	N
2 Bright	N	Y	Y	Y	Y	Y	Y
3 Rogers	N	Y	Y	N	Y	Y	N
4 Aderholt	N	Y	Y	N	Y	Y	N
5 Griffith	Y	Y	Y	Y	Y	Y	Y
6 Bachus	N	Y	Y	N	Y	Y	N
7 Davis	Y	Y	Y	Y	Y	Y	Y
ALASKA							
AL Young	Y	Y	Y	N	Y	Y	N
ARIZONA							
1 Kirkpatrick	N	Y	Y	Y	Y	Y	Y
2 Franks	N	Y	Y	N	Y	Y	N
3 Shadegg	N	Y	Y	N	Y	Y	N
4 Pastor	Y	Y	Y	Y	Y	Y	Y
5 Mitchell	N	Y	Y	Y	Y	Y	Y
6 Flake	N	Y	Y	N	Y	Y	N
7 Grijalva	Y	?	?	Y	Y	Y	Y
8 Giffords	N	Y	Y	Y	Y	Y	Y
ARKANSAS							
1 Berry	Y	Y	Y	Y	Y	Y	Y
2 Snyder	Y	Y	Y	Y	Y	Y	Y
3 Boozman	N	Y	Y	N	Y	Y	N
4 Ross	Y	Y	Y	Y	Y	Y	Y
CALIFORNIA							
1 Thompson	Y	Y	Y	Y	Y	Y	Y
2 Herger	N	Y	Y	N	Y	Y	N
3 Lungren	N	Y	Y	N	Y	Y	N
4 McClintock	N	Y	Y	N	Y	Y	N
5 Matsui	Y	Y	Y	Y	Y	Y	Y
6 Woolsey	Y	Y	N	Y	Y	Y	+
7 Miller, George	Y	Y	N	Y	Y	Y	Y
8 Pelosi							
9 Lee	Y	Y	N	Y	Y	Y	Y
10 Tauscher	Y	Y	Y	Y	Y	Y	Y
11 McNerney	N	Y	N	Y	Y	Y	Y
12 Speier	Y	Y	Y	Y	Y	Y	Y
13 Stark	?	?	?	?	?	?	?
14 Eshoo	Y	Y	Y	Y	Y	Y	Y
15 Honda	Y	Y	Y	Y	Y	Y	Y
16 Lofgren	P	Y	Y	Y	Y	Y	Y
17 Farr	Y	Y	Y	Y	Y	Y	Y
18 Cardoza	Y	Y	N	?	?	Y	Y
19 Radanovich	N	Y	Y	N	?	?	N
20 Costa	Y	Y	Y	Y	Y	Y	Y
21 Nunes	N	Y	Y	N	Y	Y	N
22 McCarthy	N	Y	Y	N	Y	Y	N
23 Capps	Y	Y	Y	Y	Y	Y	Y
24 Gallegly	N	Y	Y	N	Y	Y	N
25 McKeon	N	Y	Y	N	Y	Y	N
26 Dreier	N	Y	Y	N	Y	Y	N
27 Sherman	Y	Y	Y	Y	Y	Y	Y
28 Berman	Y	Y	Y	Y	Y	Y	Y
29 Schiff	Y	Y	Y	Y	Y	Y	Y
30 Waxman	Y	Y	Y	Y	Y	Y	Y
31 Becerra	Y	Y	Y	Y	Y	Y	Y
32 Vacant							
33 Watson	Y	Y	N	Y	Y	Y	Y
34 Roybal-Allard	Y	Y	Y	Y	Y	Y	Y
35 Waters	Y	Y	N	Y	Y	Y	Y
36 Harman	Y	Y	Y	Y	Y	Y	Y
37 Richardson	Y	Y	Y	Y	Y	Y	Y
38 Napolitano	Y	Y	Y	Y	Y	Y	Y
39 Sánchez, Linda	Y	Y	N	?	?	?	Y
40 Royce	N	Y	Y	N	Y	Y	N
41 Lewis	N	Y	Y	N	Y	Y	N
42 Miller, Gary	N	Y	Y	N	Y	Y	N
43 Baca	Y	Y	Y	Y	Y	Y	Y
44 Calvert	N	Y	Y	N	Y	Y	N
45 Bono Mack	N	Y	Y	N	Y	Y	N
46 Rohrabacher	?	?	?	N	Y	Y	N
47 Sanchez, Loretta	Y	Y	Y	Y	Y	Y	Y
48 Campbell	?	?	Y	N	Y	Y	N
49 Issa	N	Y	Y	N	Y	Y	N
50 Bilbray	Y	Y	Y	Y	Y	Y	Y
51 Filner	Y	Y	N	Y	Y	Y	Y
52 Hunter	N	Y	Y	N	Y	Y	N
53 Davis	Y	Y	Y	Y	Y	Y	Y

	243	244	245	246	247	248	249
COLORADO							
1 DeGette	Y	Y	Y	Y	Y	Y	Y
2 Polis	Y	Y	Y	Y	Y	Y	Y
3 Salazar	Y	Y	Y	Y	Y	Y	Y
4 Markey	Y	Y	Y	Y	Y	Y	Y
5 Lamborn	N	Y	Y	N	Y	?	N
6 Coffman	N	Y	Y	N	Y	Y	N
7 Perlmutter	Y	Y	Y	Y	Y	Y	Y
CONNECTICUT							
1 Larson	Y	Y	N	Y	Y	Y	Y
2 Courtney	Y	Y	N	Y	Y	Y	Y
3 DeLauro	Y	Y	N	Y	Y	Y	Y
4 Himes	N	Y	Y	?	?	?	?
5 Murphy	Y	Y	N	Y	Y	Y	Y
DELAWARE							
AL Castle	N	Y	Y	N	Y	Y	Y
FLORIDA							
1 Miller	N	Y	Y	N	Y	Y	N
2 Boyd	Y	Y	Y	Y	Y	Y	Y
3 Brown	Y	Y	Y	Y	Y	Y	Y
4 Crenshaw	N	Y	Y	N	Y	Y	N
5 Brown-Waite	N	Y	Y	N	Y	Y	N
6 Stearns	–	Y	Y	N	Y	Y	N
7 Mica	N	Y	Y	N	Y	Y	N
8 Grayson	Y	Y	Y	Y	Y	Y	Y
9 Bilirakis	N	Y	Y	N	Y	Y	N
10 Young	N	Y	Y	N	Y	Y	N
11 Castor	P	Y	Y	Y	Y	Y	Y
12 Putnam	N	Y	Y	N	Y	Y	N
13 Buchanan	N	Y	Y	N	Y	Y	N
14 Mack	N	Y	Y	N	Y	Y	N
15 Posey	N	Y	Y	N	Y	Y	N
16 Rooney	N	Y	Y	N	Y	Y	N
17 Meek	Y	Y	Y	Y	Y	Y	Y
18 Ros-Lehtinen	N	Y	Y	N	Y	Y	N
19 Wexler	Y	Y	Y	Y	Y	Y	Y
20 Wasserman Schultz	Y	Y	Y	Y	Y	Y	Y
21 Diaz-Balart, L.	P	Y	N	Y	Y	Y	N
22 Klein	Y	Y	Y	Y	Y	Y	Y
23 Hastings	Y	Y	Y	Y	Y	Y	Y
24 Kosmas	N	Y	Y	Y	Y	Y	Y
25 Diaz-Balart, M.	N	Y	Y	N	Y	Y	N
GEORGIA							
1 Kingston	N	Y	Y	N	Y	Y	N
2 Bishop	Y	Y	Y	Y	Y	Y	Y
3 Westmoreland	N	Y	Y	N	Y	Y	N
4 Johnson	N	Y	Y	Y	Y	Y	?
5 Lewis	Y	Y	N	Y	Y	Y	Y
6 Price	N	Y	Y	N	?	Y	N
7 Linder	N	Y	Y	N	Y	Y	N
8 Marshall	Y	Y	Y	Y	Y	Y	Y
9 Deal	N	Y	Y	N	?	Y	N
10 Broun	N	Y	Y	N	Y	Y	N
11 Gingrey	N	Y	Y	N	Y	Y	N
12 Barrow	Y	Y	Y	Y	Y	Y	Y
13 Scott	Y	Y	Y	Y	Y	Y	Y
HAWAII							
1 Abercrombie	Y	Y	N	Y	Y	Y	Y
2 Hirono	Y	Y	Y	Y	Y	Y	Y
IDAHO							
1 Minnick	N	Y	Y	N	Y	Y	Y
2 Simpson	N	Y	Y	N	Y	Y	Y
ILLINOIS							
1 Rush	Y	Y	Y	Y	Y	Y	Y
2 Jackson	Y	Y	Y	Y	Y	Y	Y
3 Lipinski	Y	Y	Y	Y	Y	Y	Y
4 Gutierrez	Y	?	Y	Y	Y	Y	Y
5 Quigley	N	Y	Y	Y	Y	Y	Y
6 Roskam	N	Y	Y	N	Y	Y	N
7 Davis	Y	Y	Y	Y	Y	Y	Y
8 Bean	Y	Y	Y	Y	Y	Y	Y
9 Schakowsky	Y	Y	Y	Y	Y	Y	Y
10 Kirk	N	?	Y	N	Y	Y	Y
11 Halvorson	N	Y	Y	Y	Y	Y	Y
12 Costello	Y	Y	N	Y	Y	Y	Y
13 Biggert	N	Y	Y	N	Y	Y	N
14 Foster	N	Y	Y	Y	Y	Y	Y
15 Johnson	–	+	+	–	+	+	Y

	243	244	245	246	247	248	249
16 **Manzullo**	N	Y	?	N	Y	Y	N
17 Hare	Y	Y	N	Y	Y	Y	Y
18 **Schock**	N	Y	Y	?	Y	Y	N
19 **Shimkus**	N	Y	Y	N	Y	Y	N
INDIANA							
1 Visclosky	N	Y	Y	Y	Y	Y	Y
2 Donnelly	N	Y	P	Y	Y	Y	Y
3 **Souder**	N	Y	Y	N	Y	Y	N
4 **Buyer**	N	Y	Y	N	Y	?	N
5 **Burton**	N	Y	Y	N	Y	Y	N
6 **Pence**	N	Y	Y	N	Y	Y	N
7 Carson	Y	Y	Y	Y	Y	Y	Y
8 Ellsworth	N	Y	Y	Y	Y	Y	Y
9 Hill	N	Y	Y	N	Y	Y	Y
IOWA							
1 Braley	Y	Y	N	Y	Y	Y	Y
2 Loebsack	N	Y	Y	Y	Y	Y	Y
3 Boswell	Y	Y	Y	Y	Y	Y	Y
4 **Latham**	P	Y	Y	N	Y	Y	N
5 **King**	N	Y	Y	N	Y	Y	N
KANSAS							
1 **Moran**	N	Y	Y	N	Y	Y	N
2 **Jenkins**	N	Y	Y	N	Y	Y	N
3 Moore	Y	?	Y	Y	Y	Y	Y
4 **Tiahrt**	N	Y	Y	N	Y	Y	N
KENTUCKY							
1 **Whitfield**	N	Y	Y	N	Y	Y	N
2 **Guthrie**	N	Y	Y	N	Y	Y	N
3 Yarmuth	Y	Y	N	Y	Y	Y	Y
4 **Davis**	N	Y	Y	N	Y	Y	N
5 **Rogers**	?	?	?	N	Y	Y	N
6 Chandler	P	Y	Y	Y	Y	Y	Y
LOUISIANA							
1 **Scalise**	N	Y	Y	N	Y	Y	N
2 **Cao**	?	?	?	Y	Y	Y	Y
3 Melancon	Y	Y	Y	Y	Y	Y	Y
4 **Fleming**	N	Y	Y	N	Y	Y	N
5 **Alexander**	N	Y	Y	N	Y	Y	N
6 **Cassidy**	N	Y	Y	N	Y	Y	N
7 **Boustany**	N	Y	Y	N	Y	Y	N
MAINE							
1 Pingree	Y	Y	N	?	Y	Y	Y
2 Michaud	Y	Y	Y	Y	Y	Y	Y
MARYLAND							
1 Kratovil	Y	Y	Y	Y	Y	Y	Y
2 Ruppersberger	Y	Y	Y	Y	Y	Y	Y
3 Sarbanes	Y	Y	N	Y	Y	Y	Y
4 Edwards	Y	Y	N	Y	Y	Y	Y
5 Hoyer	Y	Y	Y	Y	Y	Y	Y
6 **Bartlett**	N	Y	Y	N	Y	Y	N
7 Cummings	+	+	+	Y	Y	Y	Y
8 Van Hollen	Y	Y	Y	Y	Y	Y	Y
MASSACHUSETTS							
1 Olver	Y	Y	N	Y	Y	Y	Y
2 Neal	Y	Y	N	Y	Y	Y	Y
3 McGovern	Y	Y	N	Y	Y	Y	Y
4 Frank	Y	Y	N	Y	Y	Y	Y
5 Tsongas	Y	Y	Y	Y	Y	Y	Y
6 Tierney	Y	Y	N	Y	Y	Y	Y
7 Markey	Y	Y	N	Y	Y	Y	Y
8 Capuano	Y	Y	N	Y	Y	Y	Y
9 Lynch	Y	Y	N	Y	Y	Y	Y
10 Delahunt	Y	Y	N	Y	Y	Y	Y
MICHIGAN							
1 Stupak	Y	Y	Y	Y	Y	Y	Y
2 **Hoekstra**	?	?	?	N	Y	Y	N
3 **Ehlers**	N	Y	Y	N	Y	Y	Y
4 **Camp**	N	Y	Y	N	Y	Y	N
5 Kildee	Y	Y	Y	Y	Y	Y	Y
6 **Upton**	N	Y	Y	N	Y	Y	Y
7 Schauer	Y	Y	Y	Y	Y	?	Y
8 **Rogers**	N	Y	Y	N	Y	Y	N
9 Peters	Y	Y	Y	Y	Y	Y	Y
10 **Miller**	N	Y	Y	N	Y	Y	N
11 **McCotter**	N	Y	Y	N	Y	Y	N
12 Levin	Y	Y	N	Y	Y	Y	Y
13 Kilpatrick	?	+	+	Y	Y	Y	Y
14 Conyers	Y	Y	N	Y	Y	Y	Y
15 Dingell	Y	Y	Y	Y	Y	Y	Y
MINNESOTA							
1 Walz	N	Y	Y	Y	Y	Y	Y
2 **Kline**	P	Y	Y	N	Y	Y	N
3 **Paulsen**	N	Y	Y	N	Y	Y	N
4 McCollum	Y	Y	Y	Y	Y	Y	Y

	243	244	245	246	247	248	249
5 Ellison	Y	Y	Y	Y	Y	Y	Y
6 **Bachmann**	N	Y	Y	N	Y	Y	N
7 Peterson	Y	Y	Y	Y	Y	Y	Y
8 Oberstar	Y	Y	Y	Y	Y	Y	Y
MISSISSIPPI							
1 Childers	N	Y	Y	Y	Y	Y	Y
2 Thompson	Y	Y	Y	Y	Y	Y	Y
3 **Harper**	N	Y	Y	N	Y	Y	N
4 Taylor	Y	Y	Y	Y	Y	Y	Y
MISSOURI							
1 Clay	Y	Y	Y	Y	Y	Y	Y
2 **Akin**	N	Y	Y	N	Y	Y	N
3 Carnahan	Y	Y	Y	Y	Y	Y	Y
4 Skelton	Y	Y	Y	Y	Y	Y	Y
5 Cleaver	Y	Y	Y	Y	Y	Y	Y
6 **Graves**	N	Y	Y	N	Y	Y	N
7 **Blunt**	N	Y	Y	N	Y	Y	N
8 **Emerson**	N	Y	Y	N	Y	Y	N
9 **Luetkemeyer**	N	Y	Y	N	Y	Y	N
MONTANA							
AL **Rehberg**	N	Y	Y	N	Y	Y	N
NEBRASKA							
1 **Fortenberry**	N	Y	Y	N	Y	Y	Y
2 **Terry**	N	Y	Y	N	Y	Y	N
3 **Smith**	N	Y	Y	N	Y	Y	N
NEVADA							
1 Berkley	Y	Y	Y	Y	Y	Y	Y
2 **Heller**	N	Y	Y	N	Y	Y	N
3 Titus	Y	Y	Y	Y	Y	Y	Y
NEW HAMPSHIRE							
1 Shea-Porter	Y	Y	Y	Y	Y	Y	Y
2 Hodes	N	Y	N	Y	Y	Y	Y
NEW JERSEY							
1 Andrews	Y	Y	Y	Y	Y	Y	Y
2 **LoBiondo**	N	Y	Y	N	Y	Y	Y
3 Adler	Y	Y	Y	Y	Y	Y	N
4 **Smith**	N	Y	?	N	Y	Y	Y
5 **Garrett**	N	Y	Y	N	Y	Y	?
6 Pallone	Y	Y	Y	Y	Y	Y	Y
7 **Lance**	N	Y	Y	N	Y	Y	Y
8 Pascrell	Y	Y	N	Y	Y	Y	Y
9 Rothman	Y	Y	P	Y	Y	Y	Y
10 Payne	Y	Y	N	Y	Y	Y	Y
11 **Frelinghuysen**	N	Y	Y	N	Y	Y	N
12 Holt	Y	Y	Y	Y	Y	Y	Y
13 Sires	+	+	+	Y	Y	Y	Y
NEW MEXICO							
1 Heinrich	Y	Y	Y	Y	Y	Y	Y
2 Teague	N	Y	Y	Y	Y	Y	Y
3 Lujan	Y	Y	Y	Y	Y	Y	Y
NEW YORK							
1 Bishop	Y	Y	Y	Y	Y	Y	Y
2 Israel	?	?	?	Y	Y	Y	Y
3 **King**	N	Y	P	N	Y	Y	N
4 McCarthy	Y	Y	P	Y	Y	Y	Y
5 Ackerman	Y	Y	N	Y	Y	Y	Y
6 Meeks	Y	Y	N	Y	?	Y	Y
7 Crowley	Y	Y	N	Y	Y	Y	Y
8 Nadler	Y	Y	Y	Y	Y	Y	Y
9 Weiner	Y	Y	N	Y	Y	Y	Y
10 Towns	Y	Y	Y	Y	Y	Y	?
11 Clarke	Y	Y	N	Y	Y	Y	Y
12 Velázquez	Y	Y	N	Y	Y	Y	Y
13 McMahon	Y	Y	N	Y	Y	Y	Y
14 Maloney	Y	Y	P	Y	Y	Y	Y
15 Rangel	Y	Y	Y	Y	Y	Y	Y
16 Serrano	Y	Y	N	Y	Y	Y	Y
17 Engel	Y	Y	Y	Y	Y	Y	Y
18 Lowey	Y	Y	Y	Y	Y	Y	Y
19 Hall	Y	Y	Y	Y	Y	Y	Y
20 Murphy	N	Y	N	Y	Y	Y	Y
21 Tonko	Y	Y	Y	Y	Y	Y	Y
22 Hinchey	?	?	?	Y	Y	Y	Y
23 **McHugh**	N	Y	Y	N	Y	Y	Y
24 Arcuri	Y	Y	N	Y	Y	Y	Y
25 Maffei	Y	Y	Y	Y	Y	Y	Y
26 **Lee**	N	Y	Y	N	Y	Y	N
27 Higgins	Y	Y	N	Y	Y	Y	Y
28 Slaughter	Y	Y	Y	Y	Y	Y	Y
29 Massa	Y	Y	Y	Y	Y	Y	Y
NORTH CAROLINA							
1 Butterfield	P	Y	Y	Y	Y	Y	Y
2 Etheridge	Y	Y	Y	Y	Y	Y	Y
3 **Jones**	Y	Y	Y	N	Y	Y	N
4 Price	Y	Y	Y	Y	Y	Y	Y

	243	244	245	246	247	248	249
5 **Foxx**	N	Y	Y	N	Y	Y	N
6 **Coble**	Y	Y	Y	N	Y	Y	N
7 McIntyre	N	Y	Y	Y	Y	Y	Y
8 Kissell	Y	Y	Y	Y	Y	Y	Y
9 **Myrick**	P	Y	Y	–	+	+	N
10 **McHenry**	N	Y	Y	N	Y	Y	N
11 Shuler	Y	Y	Y	Y	Y	Y	Y
12 Watt	Y	Y	Y	Y	Y	Y	Y
13 Miller	Y	Y	Y	Y	Y	Y	Y
NORTH DAKOTA							
AL Pomeroy	Y	Y	Y	Y	Y	Y	Y
OHIO							
1 Driehaus	Y	Y	Y	Y	Y	Y	Y
2 **Schmidt**	N	Y	Y	N	Y	Y	N
3 **Turner**	N	Y	Y	N	Y	Y	N
4 **Jordan**	–	?	+	N	Y	Y	N
5 **Latta**	N	Y	Y	N	Y	Y	N
6 Wilson	Y	Y	Y	Y	Y	Y	Y
7 **Austria**	N	Y	Y	N	Y	Y	N
8 **Boehner**	N	Y	?	N	Y	Y	N
9 Kaptur	Y	Y	P	Y	Y	Y	?
10 Kucinich	Y	Y	Y	Y	Y	Y	Y
11 Fudge	Y	Y	Y	Y	Y	Y	Y
12 **Tiberi**	N	Y	Y	N	Y	Y	N
13 Sutton	Y	Y	N	Y	Y	Y	Y
14 **LaTourette**	N	Y	Y	N	Y	Y	N
15 Kilroy	Y	Y	N	Y	Y	Y	Y
16 Boccieri	N	Y	Y	Y	Y	Y	Y
17 Ryan	Y	Y	N	Y	Y	Y	Y
18 Space	Y	Y	Y	Y	Y	Y	Y
OKLAHOMA							
1 **Sullivan**	N	Y	Y	N	Y	Y	N
2 Boren	Y	Y	Y	Y	Y	Y	Y
3 **Lucas**	N	Y	Y	N	Y	Y	N
4 **Cole**	N	Y	Y	N	Y	Y	N
5 **Fallin**	N	Y	Y	N	Y	Y	N
OREGON							
1 Wu	Y	Y	N	Y	Y	Y	Y
2 **Walden**	P	Y	Y	N	Y	Y	N
3 Blumenauer	Y	Y	N	Y	Y	Y	Y
4 DeFazio	Y	Y	N	Y	Y	Y	Y
5 Schrader	Y	Y	Y	Y	Y	Y	Y
PENNSYLVANIA							
1 Brady	Y	Y	N	Y	Y	Y	Y
2 Fattah	Y	Y	Y	Y	Y	Y	Y
3 Dahlkemper	Y	Y	Y	Y	Y	Y	Y
4 Altmire	Y	Y	Y	Y	Y	Y	Y
5 **Thompson**	N	Y	Y	N	Y	Y	N
6 **Gerlach**	N	Y	Y	N	Y	Y	Y
7 Sestak	Y	Y	Y	Y	Y	Y	Y
8 Murphy, P.	Y	Y	N	Y	Y	Y	Y
9 **Shuster**	?	Y	Y	N	Y	Y	N
10 Carney	Y	Y	N	Y	Y	Y	Y
11 Kanjorski	Y	Y	Y	Y	Y	Y	Y
12 Murtha	Y	?	?	Y	Y	Y	Y
13 Schwartz	Y	Y	Y	Y	Y	?	Y
14 Doyle	Y	Y	N	Y	Y	Y	Y
15 **Dent**	P	Y	Y	N	Y	Y	Y
16 **Pitts**	N	Y	Y	N	Y	Y	N
17 Holden	Y	Y	N	Y	Y	Y	Y
18 **Murphy, T.**	Y	Y	Y	N	Y	Y	N
19 **Platts**	N	Y	Y	N	Y	Y	Y
RHODE ISLAND							
1 Kennedy	Y	Y	Y	Y	Y	Y	Y
2 Langevin	Y	Y	N	Y	Y	Y	Y
SOUTH CAROLINA							
1 **Brown**	N	Y	Y	N	Y	Y	N
2 **Wilson**	N	Y	Y	N	Y	Y	N
3 **Barrett**	P	Y	?	N	Y	Y	N
4 **Inglis**	N	Y	Y	N	Y	Y	N
5 Spratt	Y	Y	Y	Y	Y	Y	Y
6 Clyburn	Y	Y	Y	Y	Y	Y	Y
SOUTH DAKOTA							
AL Herseth Sandlin	N	Y	Y	Y	Y	Y	Y
TENNESSEE							
1 **Roe**	N	Y	Y	N	Y	Y	N
2 **Duncan**	N	Y	Y	N	Y	Y	N
3 **Wamp**	N	Y	Y	N	Y	Y	N
4 Davis	Y	Y	Y	Y	Y	Y	Y
5 Cooper	Y	Y	Y	Y	Y	Y	Y
6 Gordon	Y	Y	Y	Y	Y	Y	Y
7 **Blackburn**	N	Y	Y	N	Y	Y	N
8 Tanner	?	?	?	?	?	?	?
9 Cohen	Y	Y	N	Y	Y	Y	Y

	243	244	245	246	247	248	249
TEXAS							
1 **Gohmert**	N	Y	Y	N	Y	Y	N
2 **Poe**	P	Y	Y	N	Y	Y	N
3 **Johnson, S.**	N	Y	Y	N	Y	Y	N
4 **Hall**	N	Y	Y	N	Y	Y	N
5 **Hensarling**	N	Y	Y	N	Y	Y	N
6 **Barton**	N	Y	Y	N	Y	Y	N
7 **Culberson**	?	?	?	N	Y	Y	N
8 **Brady**	N	Y	Y	N	Y	Y	N
9 Green, A.	Y	Y	Y	Y	Y	Y	Y
10 **McCaul**	N	Y	Y	N	Y	?	Y
11 **Conaway**	P	Y	Y	N	Y	Y	N
12 **Granger**	N	Y	Y	N	Y	Y	N
13 **Thornberry**	N	Y	Y	N	Y	Y	N
14 **Paul**	N	Y	Y	?	?	?	N
15 Hinojosa	Y	Y	Y	Y	Y	Y	Y
16 Reyes	Y	Y	Y	Y	Y	Y	Y
17 Edwards	Y	Y	Y	Y	Y	Y	Y
18 Jackson Lee	Y	Y	Y	Y	Y	Y	Y
19 **Neugebauer**	N	Y	Y	N	Y	Y	N
20 Gonzalez	Y	Y	Y	Y	Y	Y	Y
21 **Smith**	N	Y	Y	N	Y	Y	N
22 **Olson**	N	Y	Y	N	Y	Y	N
23 Rodriguez	Y	Y	Y	Y	Y	Y	Y
24 **Marchant**	N	Y	Y	N	Y	Y	N
25 Doggett	Y	Y	Y	Y	Y	Y	Y
26 **Burgess**	N	Y	Y	N	Y	Y	N
27 Ortiz	Y	Y	Y	Y	Y	Y	Y
28 Cuellar	Y	Y	Y	Y	Y	Y	Y
29 Green, G.	Y	Y	Y	Y	Y	Y	Y
30 Johnson, E.	Y	Y	N	Y	Y	Y	Y
31 **Carter**	N	Y	Y	N	Y	Y	N
32 **Sessions**	N	Y	Y	N	Y	Y	N
UTAH							
1 **Bishop**	N	Y	Y	N	Y	Y	N
2 Matheson	N	Y	Y	Y	Y	Y	Y
3 **Chaffetz**	N	Y	Y	N	Y	Y	N
VERMONT							
AL Welch	P	Y	N	Y	Y	Y	Y
VIRGINIA							
1 **Wittman**	N	Y	Y	N	Y	Y	N
2 Nye	Y	Y	Y	Y	Y	Y	Y
3 Scott	Y	Y	Y	Y	Y	Y	Y
4 **Forbes**	N	Y	Y	N	Y	Y	N
5 Perriello	N	Y	Y	Y	Y	Y	Y
6 **Goodlatte**	N	Y	Y	N	Y	Y	N
7 **Cantor**	N	Y	Y	N	Y	Y	N
8 Moran	?	?	?	Y	Y	Y	Y
9 Boucher	Y	Y	Y	Y	Y	Y	Y
10 **Wolf**	N	Y	Y	N	Y	Y	N
11 Connolly	Y	Y	N	Y	Y	Y	Y
WASHINGTON							
1 Inslee	Y	Y	Y	Y	Y	Y	Y
2 Larsen	Y	Y	Y	Y	Y	Y	Y
3 Baird	?	?	?	Y	Y	Y	Y
4 **Hastings**	P	Y	Y	N	Y	Y	N
5 **McMorris Rodgers**	N	Y	Y	N	Y	Y	N
6 Dicks	Y	Y	Y	Y	Y	Y	Y
7 McDermott	Y	Y	Y	Y	Y	Y	Y
8 **Reichert**	N	Y	Y	N	Y	Y	N
9 Smith	N	Y	Y	Y	Y	Y	N
WEST VIRGINIA							
1 Mollohan	?	?	?	Y	Y	Y	Y
2 **Capito**	N	Y	Y	N	Y	Y	N
3 Rahall	Y	Y	Y	Y	Y	Y	Y
WISCONSIN							
1 **Ryan**	N	Y	Y	N	Y	Y	N
2 Baldwin	Y	Y	Y	Y	Y	Y	Y
3 Kind	N	Y	Y	Y	Y	Y	Y
4 Moore	Y	Y	Y	Y	Y	Y	Y
5 **Sensenbrenner**	N	Y	Y	N	Y	Y	N
6 **Petri**	N	Y	Y	N	Y	Y	N
7 Obey	Y	Y	N	Y	Y	Y	Y
8 Kagen	Y	Y	Y	Y	Y	Y	Y
WYOMING							
AL **Lummis**	N	Y	Y	N	Y	Y	N
DELEGATES							
Faleomavaega (A.S.)							Y
Norton (D.C.)							Y
Bordallo (Guam)							Y
Sablan (N. Marianas)							Y
Pierluisi (P.R.)							Y
Christensen (V.I.)							Y

IN THE HOUSE | By Vote Number

250. **HR 2187. Energy Efficient School Construction/Project Impact Evaluation.** Roe, R-Tenn., amendment that would require the Education Department to evaluate the impact of funds authorized under the bill on student academic achievement and to submit a report to Congress on its findings after 2015. Adopted in Committee of the Whole 432-2: R 177-1; D 255-1. May 13, 2009.

251. **HR 2187. Energy Efficient School Construction/Domestic Hardwood.** Ellsworth, D-Ind., amendment that would allow local educational agencies to use sustainable, domestic hardwood lumber that is certified as renewable by the Department of Agriculture Forest Service for public school construction. It would require agencies receiving funds to disclose whether installed flooring was made from renewable sources. Adopted in Committee of the Whole 425-7: R 170-7; D 255-0. May 13, 2009.

252. **S 454. HR 2101. Weapons Acquisition Overhaul/Adoption.** Skelton, D-Mo., motion to suspend the rules and adopt the resolution (H Res 432) that would pass HR 2101, take up S 454 and amend it with the text of HR 2101, and pass S 454 as amended and request a conference with the Senate. The House amendment would require the Defense secretary to designate officials in the office for oversight to oversee cost estimation, systems engineering and performance assessment of major weapons acquisitions programs; include an assessment of technological maturity; and require input from combat force commanders. It would require the Defense secretary to ensure that the acquisition strategy includes measures to foster competition. Motion agreed to 428-0: R 177-0; D 251-0. A two-thirds majority of those present and voting (286 in this case) is required for adoption under suspension of the rules. A "yea" was a vote in support of the president's position. May 13, 2009.

253. **H Res 204. American Dental Association Anniversary/Adoption.** Christensen, D-V.I., motion to suspend the rules and adopt the resolution that would congratulate the American Dental Association on its 150th anniversary, commend the group's work to improve the oral health care of low-income children and recognize dentists who volunteer to provide care to Americans. Motion agreed to 424-0: R 176-0; D 248-0. A two-thirds majority of those present and voting (283 in this case) is required for adoption under suspension of the rules. May 13, 2009.

254. **S 454. Weapons Acquisition Overhaul/Motion to Close Conference.** Skelton, D-Mo., motion to close portions of the conference on the bill that would overhaul major elements of the Defense Department's weapons acquisition process. Motion agreed to 409-11: R 175-1; D 234-10. May 13, 2009.

255. **HR 2187. Energy Efficient School Construction/Project Education.** Giffords, D-Ariz., amendment that would allow local education agencies to encourage schools to teach students about projects authorized under the bill, including the energy efficiency and environmental benefits of the projects. Adopted in Committee of the Whole 334-97: R 80-96; D 254-1. May 14, 2009.

256. **HR 2187. Energy Efficient School Construction/Reserved Funding.** Bright, D-Ala., amendment that would require the Department of Education to reserve 5 percent of the bill's authorized funding for grants to local educational agencies that serve areas with significant economic distress or that are recovering from natural disasters. Adopted in Committee of the Whole 433-0: R 176-0; D 257-0. May 14, 2009.

	250	251	252	253	254	255	256
ALABAMA							
1 **Bonner**	Y	Y	Y	Y	Y	N	Y
2 Bright	Y	Y	Y	Y	Y	Y	Y
3 **Rogers**	Y	Y	Y	Y	Y	Y	Y
4 **Aderholt**	Y	Y	Y	Y	Y	N	Y
5 Griffith	Y	Y	Y	Y	Y	Y	Y
6 **Bachus**	Y	Y	Y	Y	Y	Y	Y
7 Davis	Y	Y	Y	Y	Y	Y	Y
ALASKA							
AL **Young**	Y	Y	Y	Y	Y	Y	Y
ARIZONA							
1 Kirkpatrick	Y	Y	Y	Y	Y	Y	Y
2 **Franks**	Y	Y	Y	Y	Y	N	Y
3 **Shadegg**	Y	N	Y	Y	Y	N	Y
4 Pastor	Y	Y	Y	Y	Y	Y	Y
5 Mitchell	Y	Y	Y	Y	Y	Y	Y
6 **Flake**	Y	N	Y	Y	Y	N	Y
7 Grijalva	Y	Y	Y	Y	Y	Y	Y
8 Giffords	Y	Y	Y	Y	Y	Y	Y
ARKANSAS							
1 Berry	Y	Y	Y	Y	Y	Y	Y
2 Snyder	Y	Y	Y	Y	Y	Y	Y
3 **Boozman**	Y	Y	Y	Y	Y	N	Y
4 Ross	Y	Y	Y	Y	Y	Y	Y
CALIFORNIA							
1 Thompson	Y	Y	Y	Y	Y	Y	Y
2 **Herger**	Y	Y	Y	Y	Y	N	Y
3 **Lungren**	Y	Y	Y	Y	Y	N	Y
4 **McClintock**	Y	Y	Y	Y	Y	N	Y
5 Matsui	Y	Y	Y	Y	Y	Y	Y
6 Woolsey	Y	Y	Y	Y	N	Y	Y
7 Miller, George	Y	Y	Y	Y	?	Y	Y
8 Pelosi							
9 Lee	Y	Y	Y	Y	N	Y	Y
10 Tauscher	Y	Y	Y	Y	Y	Y	Y
11 McNerney	Y	Y	Y	Y	Y	Y	Y
12 Speier	Y	Y	Y	Y	N	Y	Y
13 Stark	?	?	?	?	?	?	?
14 Eshoo	Y	Y	Y	Y	Y	Y	Y
15 Honda	N	Y	Y	Y	N	Y	Y
16 Lofgren	Y	Y	Y	Y	Y	Y	Y
17 Farr	Y	Y	Y	Y	?	Y	Y
18 Cardoza	Y	Y	Y	Y	Y	Y	Y
19 **Radanovich**	Y	Y	Y	Y	?	Y	?
20 Costa	Y	Y	Y	Y	Y	Y	Y
21 **Nunes**	Y	Y	Y	Y	Y	N	Y
22 **McCarthy**	Y	Y	Y	Y	Y	N	Y
23 Capps	Y	Y	Y	Y	Y	Y	Y
24 **Gallegly**	Y	Y	Y	Y	Y	Y	Y
25 **McKeon**	Y	Y	Y	Y	Y	Y	Y
26 **Dreier**	Y	Y	Y	Y	Y	Y	Y
27 Sherman	Y	Y	Y	Y	Y	Y	Y
28 Berman	Y	Y	Y	Y	Y	Y	Y
29 Schiff	Y	Y	Y	Y	Y	Y	Y
30 Waxman	Y	Y	Y	Y	?	Y	Y
31 Becerra	Y	Y	Y	Y	Y	Y	Y
32 Vacant							
33 Watson	Y	Y	Y	Y	Y	Y	Y
34 Roybal-Allard	Y	Y	Y	Y	Y	Y	Y
35 Waters	Y	Y	Y	Y	N	Y	Y
36 Harman	Y	Y	Y	Y	Y	Y	Y
37 Richardson	Y	Y	Y	Y	Y	Y	Y
38 Napolitano	Y	Y	Y	Y	Y	Y	Y
39 Sánchez, Linda	?	?	?	?	?	?	?
40 **Royce**	Y	N	Y	Y	Y	N	Y
41 **Lewis**	Y	?	Y	Y	Y	Y	Y
42 **Miller, Gary**	Y	Y	Y	Y	Y	Y	Y
43 Baca	Y	Y	Y	Y	Y	Y	Y
44 **Calvert**	Y	Y	Y	Y	Y	Y	Y
45 **Bono Mack**	Y	Y	Y	Y	Y	Y	Y
46 **Rohrabacher**	Y	Y	Y	Y	Y	N	Y
47 Sanchez, Loretta	Y	Y	Y	Y	Y	Y	Y
48 **Campbell**	Y	N	Y	Y	Y	N	Y
49 **Issa**	Y	Y	Y	Y	Y	Y	Y
50 **Bilbray**	Y	Y	Y	Y	Y	N	Y
51 Filner	Y	Y	Y	Y	N	Y	Y
52 **Hunter**	Y	Y	Y	Y	Y	N	Y
53 Davis	Y	Y	Y	Y	Y	Y	Y

	250	251	252	253	254	255	256
COLORADO							
1 DeGette	Y	Y	Y	Y	Y	Y	Y
2 Polis	Y	Y	Y	Y	Y	Y	Y
3 Salazar	Y	Y	Y	Y	Y	Y	Y
4 Markey	Y	Y	Y	Y	Y	Y	Y
5 **Lamborn**	Y	Y	Y	Y	Y	N	Y
6 **Coffman**	Y	Y	Y	Y	Y	N	Y
7 Perlmutter	Y	Y	Y	Y	Y	Y	Y
CONNECTICUT							
1 Larson	Y	Y	Y	Y	Y	Y	Y
2 Courtney	Y	Y	Y	Y	Y	Y	Y
3 DeLauro	Y	Y	Y	Y	Y	Y	Y
4 Himes	?	?	Y	Y	Y	Y	Y
5 Murphy	Y	Y	Y	Y	Y	Y	Y
DELAWARE							
AL **Castle**	Y	Y	Y	Y	Y	Y	Y
FLORIDA							
1 **Miller**	Y	Y	Y	Y	Y	N	Y
2 Boyd	Y	Y	Y	Y	Y	Y	Y
3 Brown	Y	Y	Y	Y	Y	Y	Y
4 **Crenshaw**	Y	Y	Y	Y	Y	Y	Y
5 **Brown-Waite**	Y	Y	Y	Y	Y	Y	Y
6 **Stearns**	Y	Y	Y	Y	Y	N	Y
7 **Mica**	Y	Y	Y	Y	Y	N	Y
8 Grayson	Y	Y	Y	Y	Y	Y	Y
9 **Bilirakis**	Y	Y	Y	Y	Y	Y	Y
10 **Young**	Y	Y	Y	Y	Y	Y	Y
11 Castor	Y	Y	Y	Y	Y	Y	Y
12 **Putnam**	Y	Y	Y	Y	Y	Y	Y
13 **Buchanan**	Y	Y	Y	Y	Y	Y	Y
14 **Mack**	Y	Y	Y	Y	Y	Y	Y
15 **Posey**	Y	Y	Y	Y	Y	N	Y
16 **Rooney**	Y	Y	Y	Y	Y	N	Y
17 Meek	Y	Y	Y	Y	Y	Y	Y
18 **Ros-Lehtinen**	Y	Y	Y	Y	Y	Y	Y
19 Wexler	Y	Y	Y	Y	Y	Y	Y
20 Wasserman Schultz	Y	Y	Y	Y	Y	Y	Y
21 **Diaz-Balart, L.**	Y	Y	Y	?	?	Y	Y
22 Klein	Y	Y	Y	Y	Y	Y	Y
23 Hastings	Y	Y	Y	Y	Y	Y	Y
24 Kosmas	Y	Y	Y	Y	Y	Y	Y
25 **Diaz-Balart, M.**	Y	Y	Y	?	?	Y	Y
GEORGIA							
1 **Kingston**	Y	Y	Y	Y	Y	N	Y
2 Bishop	Y	Y	Y	Y	Y	Y	Y
3 **Westmoreland**	Y	Y	Y	Y	Y	Y	Y
4 Johnson	Y	Y	Y	Y	Y	Y	Y
5 Lewis	Y	Y	Y	Y	Y	Y	Y
6 **Price**	Y	Y	Y	Y	Y	N	Y
7 **Linder**	Y	Y	Y	Y	Y	Y	Y
8 Marshall	Y	Y	Y	Y	Y	Y	Y
9 **Deal**	Y	Y	Y	Y	Y	N	Y
10 **Broun**	Y	Y	Y	Y	N	N	Y
11 **Gingrey**	Y	Y	Y	Y	Y	N	Y
12 Barrow	Y	Y	Y	Y	Y	Y	Y
13 Scott	Y	Y	Y	Y	Y	Y	Y
HAWAII							
1 Abercrombie	Y	Y	Y	Y	Y	Y	Y
2 Hirono	Y	Y	Y	Y	Y	Y	Y
IDAHO							
1 Minnick	Y	Y	Y	Y	Y	Y	Y
2 **Simpson**	Y	Y	Y	Y	Y	N	Y
ILLINOIS							
1 Rush	Y	Y	Y	Y	Y	Y	Y
2 Jackson	Y	Y	Y	Y	Y	Y	Y
3 Lipinski	Y	Y	Y	Y	Y	Y	Y
4 Gutierrez	Y	Y	Y	Y	Y	Y	Y
5 Quigley	Y	Y	Y	Y	Y	Y	Y
6 **Roskam**	Y	Y	Y	Y	Y	N	Y
7 Davis	Y	Y	Y	Y	Y	Y	Y
8 Bean	Y	Y	Y	Y	Y	Y	Y
9 Schakowsky	Y	Y	Y	Y	Y	Y	Y
10 **Kirk**	Y	Y	Y	Y	Y	Y	Y
11 Halvorson	Y	Y	Y	Y	Y	Y	Y
12 Costello	Y	Y	Y	Y	Y	Y	Y
13 **Biggert**	Y	Y	Y	Y	Y	Y	Y
14 Foster	Y	Y	Y	Y	Y	Y	Y
15 **Johnson**	Y	Y	Y	Y	N	Y	Y

	250	251	252	253	254	255	256
16 **Manzullo**	Y	Y	Y	Y	Y	Y	Y
17 Hare	Y	Y	Y	Y	Y	Y	Y
18 **Schock**	Y	Y	Y	Y	Y	N	Y
19 **Shimkus**	Y	Y	Y	Y	Y	N	Y
INDIANA							
1 Visclosky	Y	Y	Y	Y	Y	Y	Y
2 Donnelly	Y	Y	Y	Y	Y	Y	Y
3 **Souder**	Y	Y	Y	Y	Y	N	Y
4 **Buyer**	Y	Y	Y	Y	Y	N	Y
5 **Burton**	Y	Y	Y	Y	Y	N	Y
6 **Pence**	Y	Y	Y	Y	Y	N	Y
7 Carson	Y	Y	Y	Y	Y	Y	Y
8 Ellsworth	Y	Y	Y	Y	Y	Y	Y
9 Hill	Y	Y	Y	Y	Y	Y	Y
IOWA							
1 Braley	Y	Y	Y	Y	Y	Y	Y
2 Loebsack	Y	Y	Y	Y	Y	Y	Y
3 Boswell	Y	Y	Y	Y	Y	Y	Y
4 **Latham**	Y	Y	Y	Y	Y	Y	Y
5 **King**	Y	N	Y	Y	Y	N	Y
KANSAS							
1 **Moran**	Y	Y	Y	Y	Y	N	Y
2 **Jenkins**	Y	Y	Y	Y	Y	N	Y
3 Moore	Y	Y	Y	Y	Y	Y	Y
4 **Tiahrt**	Y	Y	Y	Y	Y	N	Y
KENTUCKY							
1 **Whitfield**	Y	Y	Y	Y	Y	N	?
2 **Guthrie**	Y	Y	Y	Y	Y	Y	Y
3 Yarmuth	Y	Y	Y	Y	Y	Y	Y
4 **Davis**	Y	Y	Y	Y	Y	Y	Y
5 **Rogers**	Y	Y	Y	Y	Y	Y	Y
6 Chandler	Y	Y	Y	Y	Y	Y	Y
LOUISIANA							
1 **Scalise**	Y	Y	Y	Y	Y	N	Y
2 **Cao**	Y	Y	Y	Y	Y	Y	Y
3 Melancon	Y	Y	Y	Y	Y	Y	Y
4 **Fleming**	Y	Y	Y	Y	Y	Y	Y
5 **Alexander**	Y	Y	Y	Y	Y	Y	Y
6 **Cassidy**	Y	Y	Y	Y	Y	N	Y
7 **Boustany**	Y	Y	Y	Y	Y	Y	Y
MAINE							
1 Pingree	Y	Y	Y	Y	Y	Y	Y
2 Michaud	Y	Y	Y	Y	Y	Y	Y
MARYLAND							
1 Kratovil	Y	Y	Y	Y	Y	Y	Y
2 Ruppersberger	Y	Y	Y	Y	Y	Y	Y
3 Sarbanes	Y	Y	Y	Y	Y	Y	Y
4 Edwards	Y	Y	Y	Y	Y	Y	Y
5 Hoyer	Y	Y	Y	Y	Y	Y	Y
6 **Bartlett**	Y	Y	Y	Y	Y	Y	Y
7 Cummings	Y	Y	Y	Y	Y	Y	Y
8 Van Hollen	Y	Y	Y	Y	Y	Y	Y
MASSACHUSETTS							
1 Olver	Y	Y	Y	Y	?	Y	Y
2 Neal	Y	Y	Y	Y	Y	Y	Y
3 McGovern	Y	Y	Y	Y	Y	Y	Y
4 Frank	Y	Y	Y	Y	Y	Y	Y
5 Tsongas	Y	Y	Y	Y	Y	Y	Y
6 Tierney	Y	Y	Y	Y	Y	N	Y
7 Markey	Y	Y	Y	Y	Y	Y	Y
8 Capuano	Y	Y	Y	Y	Y	Y	Y
9 Lynch	Y	Y	Y	Y	Y	Y	Y
10 Delahunt	Y	Y	Y	Y	Y	Y	Y
MICHIGAN							
1 Stupak	Y	Y	Y	Y	Y	Y	Y
2 **Hoekstra**	Y	Y	Y	Y	Y	N	Y
3 **Ehlers**	Y	Y	Y	Y	Y	Y	Y
4 **Camp**	Y	Y	Y	Y	Y	N	Y
5 Kildee	Y	Y	Y	Y	Y	Y	Y
6 **Upton**	Y	Y	Y	Y	Y	Y	Y
7 Schauer	Y	Y	Y	Y	Y	Y	Y
8 **Rogers**	Y	Y	Y	Y	Y	N	Y
9 Peters	Y	Y	Y	Y	Y	Y	Y
10 **Miller**	Y	Y	Y	Y	Y	Y	Y
11 **McCotter**	Y	Y	Y	Y	Y	N	Y
12 Levin	Y	Y	Y	Y	Y	Y	Y
13 Kilpatrick	Y	Y	Y	Y	Y	Y	Y
14 Conyers	Y	Y	Y	Y	Y	Y	Y
15 Dingell	Y	Y	Y	Y	Y	Y	Y
MINNESOTA							
1 Walz	Y	Y	Y	Y	Y	Y	Y
2 **Kline**	Y	Y	Y	Y	Y	Y	Y
3 **Paulsen**	Y	Y	Y	Y	Y	Y	Y
4 McCollum	Y	Y	Y	Y	Y	Y	Y

	250	251	252	253	254	255	256
5 Ellison	Y	Y	Y	Y	N	Y	Y
6 **Bachmann**	Y	Y	?	Y	Y	N	Y
7 Peterson	Y	Y	Y	Y	Y	Y	Y
8 Oberstar	Y	Y	Y	Y	Y	Y	Y
MISSISSIPPI							
1 Childers	Y	Y	Y	Y	Y	Y	Y
2 Thompson	Y	Y	Y	Y	Y	Y	Y
3 **Harper**	Y	Y	Y	Y	Y	N	Y
4 Taylor	Y	Y	Y	Y	Y	Y	Y
MISSOURI							
1 Clay	Y	Y	Y	Y	Y	Y	Y
2 **Akin**	Y	Y	Y	Y	Y	N	Y
3 Carnahan	Y	Y	Y	Y	Y	Y	Y
4 Skelton	Y	Y	Y	Y	Y	Y	Y
5 Cleaver	Y	Y	Y	Y	Y	Y	Y
6 **Graves**	Y	Y	Y	Y	Y	N	Y
7 **Blunt**	Y	Y	Y	Y	Y	N	Y
8 **Emerson**	Y	Y	Y	Y	Y	Y	Y
9 **Luetkemeyer**	Y	Y	Y	Y	Y	N	Y
MONTANA							
AL **Rehberg**	Y	Y	Y	Y	Y	Y	Y
NEBRASKA							
1 **Fortenberry**	Y	Y	Y	Y	Y	Y	Y
2 **Terry**	Y	Y	Y	Y	Y	Y	Y
3 **Smith**	Y	Y	Y	Y	Y	Y	Y
NEVADA							
1 Berkley	Y	Y	Y	Y	Y	Y	Y
2 **Heller**	Y	Y	Y	Y	Y	N	Y
3 Titus	Y	Y	Y	Y	Y	Y	Y
NEW HAMPSHIRE							
1 Shea-Porter	Y	Y	Y	Y	Y	Y	Y
2 Hodes	Y	Y	Y	Y	Y	Y	Y
NEW JERSEY							
1 Andrews	Y	Y	Y	Y	Y	Y	Y
2 **LoBiondo**	Y	Y	Y	Y	Y	Y	Y
3 Adler	Y	Y	Y	Y	Y	Y	Y
4 **Smith**	Y	Y	Y	Y	Y	Y	Y
5 **Garrett**	Y	Y	Y	Y	Y	N	Y
6 Pallone	Y	Y	Y	Y	Y	Y	Y
7 **Lance**	Y	Y	Y	Y	Y	Y	Y
8 Pascrell	Y	Y	Y	Y	Y	Y	Y
9 Rothman	Y	Y	Y	Y	Y	Y	Y
10 Payne	Y	Y	Y	Y	Y	Y	Y
11 **Frelinghuysen**	Y	Y	Y	Y	Y	Y	Y
12 Holt	Y	Y	Y	Y	Y	Y	Y
13 Sires	Y	Y	Y	Y	Y	Y	Y
NEW MEXICO							
1 Heinrich	Y	Y	Y	Y	Y	Y	Y
2 Teague	Y	Y	Y	Y	Y	Y	Y
3 Lujan	Y	Y	Y	Y	Y	Y	Y
NEW YORK							
1 Bishop	Y	Y	Y	Y	Y	Y	Y
2 Israel	Y	Y	Y	?	?	Y	Y
3 **King**	Y	Y	Y	Y	Y	Y	Y
4 McCarthy	Y	Y	Y	Y	Y	Y	Y
5 Ackerman	Y	Y	Y	Y	Y	Y	Y
6 Meeks	Y	Y	Y	Y	Y	Y	Y
7 Crowley	Y	Y	Y	Y	Y	Y	Y
8 Nadler	Y	Y	Y	Y	Y	Y	Y
9 Weiner	Y	Y	Y	Y	Y	Y	Y
10 Towns	Y	Y	Y	Y	Y	Y	Y
11 Clarke	Y	Y	Y	Y	Y	Y	Y
12 Velázquez	Y	Y	Y	Y	?	Y	Y
13 McMahon	Y	Y	Y	Y	Y	Y	Y
14 Maloney	Y	Y	Y	Y	Y	Y	Y
15 Rangel	Y	Y	Y	Y	Y	Y	Y
16 Serrano	Y	Y	Y	Y	Y	Y	Y
17 Engel	Y	Y	Y	Y	Y	?	Y
18 Lowey	Y	Y	Y	Y	Y	Y	Y
19 Hall	Y	Y	Y	Y	Y	Y	Y
20 Murphy	Y	Y	Y	Y	Y	Y	Y
21 Tonko	Y	Y	Y	Y	Y	Y	Y
22 Hinchey	Y	Y	Y	Y	Y	Y	Y
23 **McHugh**	Y	Y	Y	Y	Y	Y	Y
24 Arcuri	Y	Y	Y	Y	Y	Y	Y
25 Maffei	Y	Y	Y	Y	Y	Y	Y
26 **Lee**	Y	Y	Y	Y	Y	Y	Y
27 Higgins	Y	Y	Y	Y	Y	Y	Y
28 Slaughter	Y	Y	Y	?	Y	Y	Y
29 Massa	Y	Y	Y	Y	Y	Y	Y
NORTH CAROLINA							
1 Butterfield	Y	Y	Y	Y	Y	Y	Y
2 Etheridge	Y	Y	Y	Y	Y	Y	Y
3 **Jones**	Y	Y	Y	Y	Y	Y	Y
4 Price	Y	Y	Y	Y	Y	Y	Y

	250	251	252	253	254	255	256
5 **Foxx**	Y	Y	Y	Y	Y	N	Y
6 **Coble**	Y	Y	Y	Y	Y	Y	Y
7 McIntyre	Y	Y	Y	Y	Y	Y	Y
8 Kissell	Y	Y	Y	Y	Y	Y	Y
9 **Myrick**	Y	Y	Y	Y	Y	Y	Y
10 **McHenry**	Y	Y	Y	Y	Y	Y	Y
11 Shuler	Y	Y	Y	Y	Y	Y	Y
12 Watt	Y	Y	Y	Y	Y	Y	Y
13 Miller	Y	Y	Y	Y	Y	Y	Y
NORTH DAKOTA							
AL Pomeroy	Y	Y	Y	Y	Y	Y	Y
OHIO							
1 Driehaus	Y	Y	Y	Y	Y	Y	Y
2 **Schmidt**	Y	Y	Y	Y	Y	Y	Y
3 **Turner**	Y	Y	Y	Y	Y	Y	Y
4 **Jordan**	Y	Y	Y	Y	Y	N	Y
5 **Latta**	Y	Y	Y	Y	Y	N	Y
6 Wilson	Y	Y	Y	Y	Y	Y	Y
7 **Austria**	Y	Y	Y	Y	Y	Y	Y
8 **Boehner**	Y	Y	Y	Y	Y	N	Y
9 Kaptur	Y	Y	Y	Y	Y	Y	Y
10 Kucinich	Y	Y	Y	Y	N	Y	Y
11 Fudge	Y	Y	Y	Y	Y	Y	Y
12 **Tiberi**	Y	Y	Y	Y	Y	Y	Y
13 Sutton	Y	Y	Y	Y	Y	Y	Y
14 **LaTourette**	Y	Y	Y	Y	Y	Y	Y
15 Kilroy	Y	Y	Y	Y	Y	Y	Y
16 Boccieri	Y	Y	Y	Y	Y	Y	Y
17 Ryan	Y	Y	Y	Y	Y	Y	Y
18 Space	Y	Y	Y	Y	Y	Y	Y
OKLAHOMA							
1 **Sullivan**	Y	Y	Y	Y	Y	N	Y
2 Boren	Y	Y	Y	Y	Y	Y	Y
3 **Lucas**	Y	Y	Y	Y	Y	N	Y
4 **Cole**	Y	Y	Y	Y	Y	N	Y
5 **Fallin**	Y	Y	Y	Y	Y	N	Y
OREGON							
1 Wu	Y	Y	Y	Y	Y	Y	Y
2 **Walden**	N	Y	Y	Y	Y	N	Y
3 Blumenauer	Y	Y	Y	Y	N	Y	Y
4 DeFazio	Y	Y	Y	Y	Y	Y	Y
5 Schrader	Y	Y	Y	Y	Y	Y	Y
PENNSYLVANIA							
1 Brady	Y	Y	Y	Y	Y	Y	Y
2 Fattah	Y	Y	Y	Y	Y	Y	Y
3 Dahlkemper	Y	Y	Y	Y	Y	Y	Y
4 Altmire	Y	Y	Y	Y	Y	Y	Y
5 **Thompson**	Y	Y	Y	Y	Y	N	Y
6 **Gerlach**	Y	Y	Y	Y	Y	Y	Y
7 Sestak	Y	Y	Y	Y	Y	Y	Y
8 Murphy, P.	Y	Y	Y	Y	Y	Y	Y
9 **Shuster**	Y	Y	Y	Y	Y	N	Y
10 Carney	Y	Y	Y	Y	Y	Y	Y
11 Kanjorski	Y	Y	Y	Y	Y	Y	Y
12 Murtha	Y	Y	?	?	?	Y	Y
13 Schwartz	Y	Y	Y	Y	Y	Y	Y
14 Doyle	Y	Y	Y	Y	Y	Y	Y
15 **Dent**	Y	Y	Y	Y	Y	Y	Y
16 **Pitts**	Y	Y	Y	Y	Y	Y	Y
17 Holden	Y	Y	Y	Y	Y	Y	Y
18 **Murphy, T.**	Y	Y	Y	Y	Y	Y	Y
19 **Platts**	Y	Y	Y	Y	Y	Y	Y
RHODE ISLAND							
1 Kennedy	Y	Y	Y	Y	Y	Y	Y
2 Langevin	Y	Y	Y	Y	Y	Y	Y
SOUTH CAROLINA							
1 **Brown**	Y	Y	Y	Y	Y	Y	Y
2 **Wilson**	Y	Y	Y	Y	Y	N	Y
3 **Barrett**	Y	Y	Y	Y	Y	N	Y
4 **Inglis**	Y	Y	Y	Y	Y	Y	Y
5 Spratt	Y	Y	Y	Y	Y	Y	Y
6 Clyburn	Y	Y	Y	Y	Y	Y	Y
SOUTH DAKOTA							
AL Herseth Sandlin	Y	Y	Y	Y	Y	Y	Y
TENNESSEE							
1 **Roe**	Y	Y	Y	Y	Y	Y	Y
2 **Duncan**	Y	Y	Y	Y	Y	N	Y
3 **Wamp**	Y	Y	Y	Y	Y	Y	Y
4 Davis	Y	Y	Y	Y	Y	Y	Y
5 Cooper	Y	Y	Y	Y	Y	Y	Y
6 Gordon	Y	Y	Y	Y	Y	Y	Y
7 **Blackburn**	Y	Y	Y	Y	Y	N	Y
8 Tanner	?	?	?	?	?	?	?
9 Cohen	Y	Y	Y	Y	Y	Y	Y

	250	251	252	253	254	255	256
TEXAS							
1 **Gohmert**	Y	Y	Y	Y	Y	N	Y
2 **Poe**	Y	Y	Y	Y	Y	N	Y
3 **Johnson, S.**	Y	Y	Y	Y	Y	N	Y
4 **Hall**	Y	Y	Y	Y	Y	Y	Y
5 **Hensarling**	Y	Y	Y	Y	Y	N	Y
6 **Barton**	Y	Y	Y	Y	Y	N	Y
7 **Culberson**	Y	Y	Y	Y	Y	Y	Y
8 **Brady**	Y	Y	Y	Y	Y	N	Y
9 Green, A.	Y	Y	Y	Y	Y	Y	Y
10 **McCaul**	Y	Y	Y	Y	Y	Y	Y
11 **Conaway**	Y	Y	Y	Y	Y	N	Y
12 **Granger**	Y	Y	Y	Y	Y	N	Y
13 **Thornberry**	Y	Y	Y	Y	Y	N	Y
14 **Paul**	Y	Y	Y	Y	Y	N	Y
15 Hinojosa	Y	Y	Y	Y	Y	Y	Y
16 Reyes	Y	Y	Y	Y	Y	Y	Y
17 Edwards	Y	Y	Y	?	?	Y	Y
18 Jackson Lee	Y	Y	Y	Y	Y	Y	Y
19 **Neugebauer**	Y	Y	Y	Y	Y	N	Y
20 Gonzalez	Y	Y	Y	Y	Y	Y	Y
21 **Smith**	Y	Y	Y	Y	Y	Y	Y
22 **Olson**	Y	Y	Y	Y	Y	Y	Y
23 Rodriguez	Y	Y	Y	Y	Y	Y	Y
24 **Marchant**	Y	Y	Y	Y	Y	N	Y
25 Doggett	Y	Y	Y	Y	Y	Y	Y
26 **Burgess**	Y	Y	Y	Y	Y	N	Y
27 Ortiz	Y	Y	Y	Y	Y	Y	Y
28 Cuellar	Y	Y	Y	Y	Y	Y	Y
29 Green, G.	Y	Y	Y	Y	Y	Y	Y
30 Johnson, E.	Y	?	Y	Y	Y	Y	Y
31 **Carter**	Y	Y	Y	Y	Y	N	Y
32 **Sessions**	Y	Y	Y	Y	Y	N	Y
UTAH							
1 **Bishop**	Y	Y	Y	Y	Y	?	Y
2 Matheson	Y	Y	Y	Y	Y	Y	Y
3 **Chaffetz**	Y	Y	Y	Y	Y	N	Y
VERMONT							
AL Welch	Y	Y	Y	Y	Y	?	Y
VIRGINIA							
1 **Wittman**	Y	Y	Y	Y	Y	Y	Y
2 Nye	Y	Y	Y	Y	Y	Y	Y
3 Scott	Y	Y	Y	Y	Y	Y	Y
4 **Forbes**	Y	Y	Y	Y	Y	Y	Y
5 Perriello	Y	Y	Y	Y	Y	Y	Y
6 **Goodlatte**	Y	Y	Y	Y	Y	Y	Y
7 **Cantor**	Y	Y	Y	Y	Y	N	Y
8 Moran	Y	Y	Y	Y	Y	Y	Y
9 Boucher	Y	Y	Y	Y	Y	Y	Y
10 **Wolf**	Y	Y	Y	Y	Y	Y	Y
11 Connolly	?	Y	Y	Y	Y	Y	Y
WASHINGTON							
1 Inslee	Y	Y	Y	Y	Y	Y	Y
2 Larsen	Y	Y	Y	Y	Y	Y	Y
3 Baird	Y	Y	Y	Y	Y	Y	Y
4 **Hastings**	Y	Y	Y	Y	Y	N	Y
5 **McMorris Rodgers**	Y	Y	Y	Y	Y	N	Y
6 Dicks	Y	Y	Y	Y	Y	Y	Y
7 McDermott	Y	Y	Y	Y	N	Y	Y
8 **Reichert**	Y	Y	Y	Y	Y	Y	Y
9 Smith	Y	Y	Y	Y	Y	Y	Y
WEST VIRGINIA							
1 Mollohan	Y	Y	Y	Y	Y	Y	Y
2 **Capito**	Y	Y	Y	Y	Y	Y	Y
3 Rahall	Y	Y	Y	Y	Y	Y	Y
WISCONSIN							
1 **Ryan**	Y	Y	Y	Y	Y	N	Y
2 Baldwin	Y	Y	Y	Y	Y	Y	Y
3 Kind	Y	Y	Y	Y	Y	Y	Y
4 Moore	Y	Y	Y	Y	Y	Y	Y
5 **Sensenbrenner**	Y	N	Y	Y	Y	N	Y
6 **Petri**	Y	N	Y	Y	Y	N	Y
7 Obey	Y	?	Y	Y	Y	Y	Y
8 Kagen	Y	Y	Y	Y	Y	Y	Y
WYOMING							
AL **Lummis**	Y	Y	Y	Y	Y	Y	Y
DELEGATES							
Faleomavaega (A.S.)	Y	Y				Y	Y
Norton (D.C.)	Y	Y				Y	Y
Bordallo (Guam)	Y	Y				?	?
Sablan (N. Marianas)	Y	Y				Y	Y
Pierluisi (P.R.)	Y	Y				Y	Y
Christensen (V.I.)	Y	Y				Y	Y

IN THE HOUSE | By Vote Number

257. **HR 2187. Energy Efficient School Construction/Respiratory Illness Reduction.** Griffith, D-Ala., amendment that would allow grants authorized in the bill to be used for reducing airborne particles such as dust, sand and pollens in schools to reduce the incidence of asthma and other respiratory illnesses among students and staff. Adopted in Committee of the Whole 433-0: R 176-0; D 257-0. May 14, 2009.

258. **HR 2187. Energy Efficient School Construction/Recommit.** Thompson, R-Pa., motion to recommit the bill to the Education and Labor Committee with instructions that it be immediately reported back with language that would prevent any funds to be authorized under the bill in a fiscal year following any year that the federal deficit is in excess of $500 billion. Motion rejected 182-247: R 176-1; D 6-246. May 14, 2009.

259. **HR 2187. Energy Efficient School Construction/Passage.** Passage of the bill that would authorize $6.4 billion for school construction projects in fiscal 2010 and unspecified sums in fiscal 2011-15, and require that certain percentages of the funds be used for construction that meets environmental or energy efficiency standards. It would also authorize funds for the repair of public schools damaged by hurricanes Katrina and Rita, apply Davis-Bacon wage requirements to the projects, and bar states from taking into account funds authorized under the bill when determining a school's eligibility for other aid. Passed 275-155: R 24-154; D 251-1. May 14, 2009.

260. **HR 2187. Energy Efficient School Construction/Amend Title.** Kline, R-Minn., amendment that would change the title of the bill to "A bill to saddle future generations with billions in debt and for other purposes." Rejected 149-257: R 149-25; D 0-232. May 14, 2009.

261. **HR 2346. Fiscal 2009 Supplemental/Previous Question.** Perlmutter, D-Colo., motion to order the previous question (thus ending debate and possibility of amendment) on adoption of the rule (H Res 434) that would provide for House floor consideration of the bill that would appropriate $96.7 billion in emergency supplemental funds for fiscal 2009, including funding for the wars in Iraq and Afghanistan and for pandemic flu preparations. Motion agreed to 240-188: R 0-178; D 240-10. May 14, 2009.

262. **HR 2346. Fiscal 2009 Supplemental/Rule.** Adoption of the rule (H Res 434) to provide for House floor consideration of a bill that would appropriate $96.7 billion in emergency supplemental funds for fiscal 2009, including funding for the wars in Iraq and Afghanistan and for pandemic flu preparations. Adopted 247-178: R 5-170; D 242-8. May 14, 2009.

	257	258	259	260	261	262
ALABAMA						
1 Bonner	Y	Y	N	Y	N	N
2 Bright	Y	N	Y	N	Y	Y
3 Rogers	Y	Y	N	Y	N	N
4 Aderholt	Y	Y	N	Y	N	N
5 Griffith	Y	N	Y	N	Y	Y
6 Bachus	Y	Y	N	Y	N	N
7 Davis	Y	N	Y	N	Y	Y
ALASKA						
AL Young	Y	Y	N	Y	N	N
ARIZONA						
1 Kirkpatrick	Y	N	Y	N	Y	Y
2 Franks	Y	Y	N	Y	N	N
3 Shadegg	Y	Y	N	Y	N	N
4 Pastor	Y	N	Y	N	Y	Y
5 Mitchell	Y	N	Y	N	Y	Y
6 Flake	Y	Y	N	Y	N	N
7 Grijalva	Y	N	Y	N	Y	Y
8 Giffords	Y	N	Y	N	Y	Y
ARKANSAS						
1 Berry	Y	N	Y	N	Y	Y
2 Snyder	Y	N	Y	N	Y	Y
3 Boozman	Y	Y	N	Y	N	N
4 Ross	Y	N	Y	N	Y	Y
CALIFORNIA						
1 Thompson	Y	N	Y	N	Y	Y
2 Herger	Y	Y	N	Y	N	N
3 Lungren	Y	Y	N	Y	N	N
4 McClintock	Y	Y	N	Y	N	N
5 Matsui	Y	N	Y	?	Y	Y
6 Woolsey	Y	N	Y	N	Y	Y
7 Miller, George	Y	N	Y	N	Y	Y
8 Pelosi						
9 Lee	Y	N	Y	N	Y	Y
10 Tauscher	Y	N	Y	N	Y	Y
11 McNerney	Y	N	Y	N	Y	N
12 Speier	Y	N	Y	N	Y	Y
13 Stark	?	?	?	?	?	?
14 Eshoo	Y	N	Y	N	Y	Y
15 Honda	Y	N	Y	N	Y	+
16 Lofgren	Y	N	Y	N	Y	Y
17 Farr	Y	N	Y	N	Y	Y
18 Cardoza	Y	N	Y	N	Y	Y
19 Radanovich	?	Y	N	Y	N	N
20 Costa	Y	N	Y	N	Y	Y
21 Nunes	Y	Y	N	Y	N	N
22 McCarthy	Y	Y	N	Y	N	N
23 Capps	Y	N	Y	N	Y	Y
24 Gallegly	Y	Y	N	Y	N	N
25 McKeon	Y	Y	N	Y	N	N
26 Dreier	Y	Y	N	Y	N	N
27 Sherman	Y	N	Y	N	Y	Y
28 Berman	Y	N	Y	N	Y	Y
29 Schiff	Y	N	Y	N	Y	Y
30 Waxman	Y	N	Y	N	Y	Y
31 Becerra	Y	N	Y	N	Y	Y
32 Vacant						
33 Watson	Y	N	Y	N	Y	Y
34 Roybal-Allard	Y	N	Y	N	Y	Y
35 Waters	Y	N	Y	N	Y	Y
36 Harman	Y	N	Y	N	Y	Y
37 Richardson	Y	N	Y	N	Y	Y
38 Napolitano	Y	N	Y	N	Y	Y
39 Sánchez, Linda	?	?	?	?	?	?
40 Royce	Y	Y	N	N	N	N
41 Lewis	Y	Y	N	N	N	N
42 Miller, Gary	Y	Y	N	Y	N	N
43 Baca	Y	N	Y	N	Y	Y
44 Calvert	Y	Y	N	Y	N	N
45 Bono Mack	Y	Y	N	Y	N	N
46 Rohrabacher	Y	Y	N	Y	N	N
47 Sanchez, Loretta	Y	N	Y	N	Y	Y
48 Campbell	Y	Y	N	Y	N	N
49 Issa	Y	Y	N	Y	N	N
50 Bilbray	Y	Y	N	Y	N	N
51 Filner	Y	N	Y	N	N	N
52 Hunter	Y	Y	N	Y	N	N
53 Davis	Y	N	Y	N	Y	Y

	257	258	259	260	261	262
COLORADO						
1 DeGette	Y	N	Y	?	Y	Y
2 Polis	Y	N	Y	N	Y	Y
3 Salazar	Y	N	Y	N	Y	Y
4 Markey	Y	N	Y	N	Y	Y
5 Lamborn	Y	Y	N	Y	N	N
6 Coffman	Y	Y	N	Y	N	N
7 Perlmutter	Y	N	Y	N	Y	Y
CONNECTICUT						
1 Larson	Y	N	Y	N	Y	Y
2 Courtney	Y	N	Y	N	Y	Y
3 DeLauro	Y	N	Y	N	Y	Y
4 Himes	Y	N	Y	N	Y	Y
5 Murphy	Y	N	Y	N	Y	Y
DELAWARE						
AL Castle	Y	Y	N	N	N	N
FLORIDA						
1 Miller	Y	Y	N	Y	N	N
2 Boyd	Y	N	Y	N	Y	Y
3 Brown	Y	N	Y	N	Y	Y
4 Crenshaw	Y	Y	N	Y	N	N
5 Brown-Waite	Y	Y	N	Y	N	N
6 Stearns	Y	Y	N	Y	N	N
7 Mica	Y	Y	N	N	N	N
8 Grayson	Y	N	Y	N	Y	Y
9 Bilirakis	Y	Y	N	Y	N	N
10 Young	Y	Y	N	N	N	N
11 Castor	Y	N	Y	N	Y	Y
12 Putnam	+	Y	N	Y	N	N
13 Buchanan	Y	Y	N	Y	N	?
14 Mack	Y	Y	N	N	N	N
15 Posey	Y	Y	Y	N	N	N
16 Rooney	Y	Y	N	Y	N	N
17 Meek	Y	N	Y	N	Y	Y
18 Ros-Lehtinen	Y	Y	Y	N	N	N
19 Wexler	Y	N	Y	?	Y	Y
20 Wasserman Schultz	Y	N	Y	N	Y	Y
21 Diaz-Balart, L.	Y	Y	Y	?	N	N
22 Klein	Y	N	Y	N	Y	Y
23 Hastings	Y	N	Y	N	Y	Y
24 Kosmas	Y	N	Y	N	Y	Y
25 Diaz-Balart, M.	Y	Y	Y	?	N	N
GEORGIA						
1 Kingston	Y	Y	N	Y	N	N
2 Bishop	Y	N	Y	N	Y	Y
3 Westmoreland	Y	Y	N	Y	N	N
4 Johnson	Y	N	Y	N	?	Y
5 Lewis	Y	N	Y	N	Y	N
6 Price	Y	Y	N	Y	N	N
7 Linder	Y	Y	N	Y	N	N
8 Marshall	Y	N	Y	N	Y	Y
9 Deal	Y	Y	N	Y	N	N
10 Broun	Y	Y	N	Y	N	N
11 Gingrey	Y	Y	N	Y	N	N
12 Barrow	Y	N	Y	N	Y	Y
13 Scott	Y	N	Y	N	Y	Y
HAWAII						
1 Abercrombie	Y	N	Y	N	Y	Y
2 Hirono	Y	N	Y	N	Y	Y
IDAHO						
1 Minnick	Y	N	Y	N	N	Y
2 Simpson	Y	Y	N	Y	N	N
ILLINOIS						
1 Rush	Y	N	Y	?	Y	Y
2 Jackson	Y	N	Y	N	Y	Y
3 Lipinski	Y	N	Y	N	Y	Y
4 Gutierrez	Y	N	Y	N	Y	Y
5 Quigley	Y	N	Y	N	Y	Y
6 Roskam	Y	Y	N	Y	N	N
7 Davis	Y	N	Y	N	Y	Y
8 Bean	Y	N	Y	N	Y	Y
9 Schakowsky	Y	N	Y	N	Y	Y
10 Kirk	Y	Y	N	N	N	N
11 Halvorson	Y	N	Y	N	Y	Y
12 Costello	Y	N	Y	N	Y	Y
13 Biggert	Y	Y	N	Y	N	N
14 Foster	Y	N	Y	N	Y	Y
15 Johnson	Y	Y	N	Y	N	N

KEY	**Republicans**	Democrats
Y	Voted for (yea)	X Paired against	C Voted "present" to avoid possible conflict of interest
#	Paired for	– Announced against	
+	Announced for	P Voted "present"	? Did not vote or otherwise make a position known
N	Voted against (nay)		

	257	258	259	260	261	262
16 **Manzullo**	Y	Y	N	Y	N	N
17 Hare	Y	N	Y	N	Y	Y
18 **Schock**	Y	Y	N	Y	N	N
19 **Shimkus**	Y	Y	N	Y	N	N
INDIANA						
1 Visclosky	Y	N	Y	N	Y	Y
2 Donnelly	Y	N	Y	N	Y	Y
3 **Souder**	Y	Y	N	Y	N	N
4 **Buyer**	Y	Y	N	Y	N	N
5 **Burton**	Y	Y	N	Y	N	N
6 **Pence**	Y	Y	N	?	N	N
7 Carson	Y	N	Y	N	Y	Y
8 Ellsworth	Y	N	Y	N	Y	Y
9 Hill	Y	N	Y	N	N	N
IOWA						
1 Braley	Y	N	Y	N	Y	Y
2 Loebsack	Y	N	Y	N	Y	Y
3 Boswell	Y	N	Y	N	Y	Y
4 **Latham**	Y	Y	N	Y	N	N
5 **King**	Y	Y	N	Y	N	N
KANSAS						
1 **Moran**	Y	Y	N	Y	N	N
2 **Jenkins**	Y	Y	N	Y	N	N
3 Moore	Y	N	Y	?	Y	Y
4 **Tiahrt**	Y	Y	N	Y	N	N
KENTUCKY						
1 **Whitfield**	Y	Y	N	Y	N	N
2 **Guthrie**	Y	Y	N	Y	N	N
3 Yarmuth	Y	N	Y	N	Y	Y
4 **Davis**	Y	Y	N	Y	N	N
5 **Rogers**	Y	Y	N	Y	N	N
6 Chandler	Y	N	Y	N	Y	Y
LOUISIANA						
1 **Scalise**	Y	Y	N	Y	N	N
2 **Cao**	Y	Y	Y	N	N	N
3 Melancon	Y	N	Y	N	Y	Y
4 **Fleming**	Y	Y	N	Y	N	N
5 **Alexander**	Y	Y	N	Y	N	N
6 **Cassidy**	Y	+	N	Y	N	N
7 **Boustany**	Y	Y	N	Y	N	N
MAINE						
1 Pingree	Y	N	Y	N	Y	Y
2 Michaud	Y	N	Y	N	Y	N
MARYLAND						
1 Kratovil	Y	N	Y	N	N	N
2 Ruppersberger	Y	N	Y	N	Y	Y
3 Sarbanes	Y	N	Y	?	Y	Y
4 Edwards	Y	N	Y	N	Y	Y
5 Hoyer	Y	N	Y	N	Y	Y
6 **Bartlett**	Y	Y	N	Y	N	N
7 Cummings	Y	N	Y	N	Y	Y
8 Van Hollen	Y	N	Y	?	Y	Y
MASSACHUSETTS						
1 Olver	Y	N	Y	N	Y	Y
2 Neal	Y	N	Y	N	Y	Y
3 McGovern	Y	N	Y	N	Y	Y
4 Frank	Y	N	Y	N	Y	Y
5 Tsongas	Y	N	Y	N	Y	Y
6 Tierney	Y	N	Y	N	Y	Y
7 Markey	Y	N	Y	N	Y	Y
8 Capuano	Y	N	Y	N	Y	Y
9 Lynch	Y	N	Y	N	Y	Y
10 Delahunt	Y	N	Y	N	N	?
MICHIGAN						
1 Stupak	Y	N	Y	N	Y	Y
2 **Hoekstra**	Y	Y	N	Y	N	N
3 **Ehlers**	Y	Y	Y	N	N	N
4 **Camp**	Y	Y	N	Y	N	?
5 Kildee	Y	N	Y	N	Y	Y
6 **Upton**	Y	Y	N	Y	N	N
7 Schauer	Y	N	Y	N	Y	Y
8 **Rogers**	Y	Y	N	N	N	N
9 Peters	Y	N	Y	N	Y	Y
10 **Miller**	Y	Y	Y	N	N	N
11 **McCotter**	Y	Y	Y	N	N	N
12 Levin	Y	N	Y	N	Y	Y
13 Kilpatrick	Y	N	Y	?	Y	Y
14 Conyers	Y	N	Y	N	Y	Y
15 Dingell	Y	N	Y	N	Y	Y
MINNESOTA						
1 Walz	Y	N	Y	N	Y	Y
2 **Kline**	Y	Y	N	Y	N	N
3 **Paulsen**	Y	Y	N	Y	N	N
4 McCollum	Y	N	Y	N	Y	Y

	257	258	259	260	261	262
5 Ellison	Y	N	Y	N	Y	Y
6 **Bachmann**	Y	Y	N	Y	N	N
7 Peterson	Y	N	Y	N	Y	Y
8 Oberstar	Y	N	Y	N	Y	Y
MISSISSIPPI						
1 Childers	Y	Y	Y	N	N	Y
2 Thompson	Y	N	Y	N	Y	Y
3 **Harper**	Y	Y	N	Y	N	N
4 Taylor	Y	Y	N	N	N	Y
MISSOURI						
1 Clay	Y	N	Y	N	Y	Y
2 **Akin**	Y	Y	N	Y	N	N
3 Carnahan	Y	N	Y	N	Y	Y
4 Skelton	Y	N	Y	N	Y	Y
5 Cleaver	Y	N	Y	N	Y	Y
6 **Graves**	Y	Y	N	Y	N	N
7 **Blunt**	Y	Y	N	Y	N	N
8 **Emerson**	Y	Y	N	Y	N	N
9 **Luetkemeyer**	Y	Y	N	Y	N	N
MONTANA						
AL **Rehberg**	Y	Y	N	Y	N	N
NEBRASKA						
1 **Fortenberry**	Y	Y	N	Y	N	N
2 **Terry**	Y	Y	N	Y	N	N
3 **Smith**	Y	Y	N	Y	N	N
NEVADA						
1 Berkley	Y	N	Y	N	Y	Y
2 **Heller**	Y	Y	N	Y	N	Y
3 Titus	Y	N	Y	N	Y	Y
NEW HAMPSHIRE						
1 Shea-Porter	Y	N	Y	N	Y	Y
2 Hodes	Y	N	Y	N	Y	Y
NEW JERSEY						
1 Andrews	Y	N	Y	N	Y	Y
2 **LoBiondo**	Y	Y	Y	N	N	N
3 Adler	Y	Y	Y	N	Y	Y
4 **Smith**	Y	Y	Y	N	N	N
5 **Garrett**	Y	Y	N	Y	N	N
6 Pallone	Y	N	Y	N	Y	Y
7 **Lance**	Y	Y	Y	N	N	Y
8 Pascrell	Y	N	Y	N	Y	Y
9 Rothman	Y	N	Y	N	Y	Y
10 Payne	Y	N	Y	N	Y	Y
11 **Frelinghuysen**	Y	Y	N	Y	N	N
12 Holt	Y	N	Y	N	Y	Y
13 Sires	Y	N	Y	N	Y	Y
NEW MEXICO						
1 Heinrich	Y	N	Y	N	Y	Y
2 Teague	Y	N	Y	N	Y	Y
3 Lujan	Y	N	Y	N	Y	Y
NEW YORK						
1 Bishop	Y	N	Y	N	Y	Y
2 Israel	Y	N	Y	N	Y	Y
3 **King**	Y	Y	Y	N	N	N
4 McCarthy	Y	N	Y	N	Y	Y
5 Ackerman	Y	N	Y	N	Y	Y
6 Meeks	Y	N	Y	N	Y	Y
7 Crowley	Y	N	Y	N	Y	Y
8 Nadler	Y	N	Y	N	Y	Y
9 Weiner	Y	N	Y	N	Y	Y
10 Towns	Y	N	Y	N	Y	Y
11 Clarke	Y	N	Y	N	Y	Y
12 Velázquez	Y	N	Y	?	Y	Y
13 McMahon	Y	N	Y	N	Y	Y
14 Maloney	Y	N	Y	N	Y	Y
15 Rangel	Y	N	Y	N	Y	Y
16 Serrano	Y	N	Y	?	Y	Y
17 Engel	Y	N	Y	N	Y	Y
18 Lowey	Y	N	Y	N	Y	Y
19 Hall	Y	N	Y	?	Y	Y
20 Murphy	Y	N	Y	N	Y	Y
21 Tonko	Y	N	Y	N	Y	Y
22 Hinchey	Y	N	Y	N	Y	Y
23 **McHugh**	Y	Y	Y	N	N	Y
24 Arcuri	Y	Y	Y	N	N	Y
25 Maffei	Y	N	Y	N	Y	Y
26 **Lee**	Y	Y	N	Y	N	N
27 Higgins	Y	N	Y	N	Y	Y
28 Slaughter	Y	N	Y	N	Y	Y
29 Massa	Y	N	Y	N	Y	Y
NORTH CAROLINA						
1 Butterfield	Y	N	Y	N	Y	Y
2 Etheridge	Y	N	Y	N	Y	Y
3 **Jones**	Y	Y	N	N	N	N
4 Price	Y	N	Y	N	Y	Y

	257	258	259	260	261	262
5 **Foxx**	Y	Y	N	Y	N	N
6 **Coble**	Y	Y	N	Y	N	N
7 McIntyre	Y	N	Y	N	Y	Y
8 Kissell	Y	N	Y	N	Y	Y
9 **Myrick**	Y	Y	N	Y	N	N
10 **McHenry**	Y	Y	N	Y	N	N
11 Shuler	Y	N	Y	N	Y	Y
12 Watt	Y	N	Y	N	Y	Y
13 Miller	Y	N	Y	N	Y	Y
NORTH DAKOTA						
AL Pomeroy	Y	N	Y	N	Y	Y
OHIO						
1 Driehaus	Y	N	Y	N	Y	Y
2 **Schmidt**	Y	Y	N	Y	N	Y
3 **Turner**	Y	Y	N	Y	N	N
4 **Jordan**	Y	Y	N	Y	N	N
5 **Latta**	Y	Y	N	Y	N	N
6 Wilson	Y	N	Y	N	Y	Y
7 **Austria**	Y	Y	N	Y	N	N
8 **Boehner**	Y	Y	N	Y	N	N
9 Kaptur	Y	N	Y	N	Y	Y
10 Kucinich	Y	N	Y	N	Y	N
11 Fudge	Y	N	Y	N	Y	Y
12 **Tiberi**	Y	Y	N	Y	N	N
13 Sutton	Y	N	Y	N	Y	Y
14 **LaTourette**	Y	Y	Y	N	N	N
15 Kilroy	Y	N	Y	N	Y	Y
16 Boccieri	Y	N	Y	N	Y	Y
17 Ryan	Y	N	Y	N	Y	Y
18 Space	Y	N	Y	N	Y	Y
OKLAHOMA						
1 **Sullivan**	Y	Y	N	Y	N	N
2 Boren	Y	N	Y	N	Y	Y
3 **Lucas**	Y	Y	N	Y	N	N
4 **Cole**	Y	Y	N	Y	N	N
5 **Fallin**	Y	Y	N	Y	N	N
OREGON						
1 Wu	Y	N	Y	N	Y	Y
2 **Walden**	Y	Y	N	Y	N	N
3 Blumenauer	Y	N	Y	N	Y	Y
4 DeFazio	Y	N	Y	N	Y	Y
5 Schrader	Y	N	Y	N	Y	Y
PENNSYLVANIA						
1 Brady	Y	N	Y	N	Y	Y
2 Fattah	Y	N	Y	N	Y	Y
3 Dahlkemper	Y	N	Y	?	Y	Y
4 Altmire	Y	N	Y	N	Y	Y
5 **Thompson**	Y	Y	N	Y	N	N
6 **Gerlach**	Y	Y	Y	Y	N	N
7 Sestak	Y	N	Y	N	Y	Y
8 Murphy, P.	Y	N	Y	N	Y	Y
9 **Shuster**	Y	Y	N	Y	N	N
10 Carney	Y	N	Y	?	Y	Y
11 Kanjorski	Y	N	Y	N	Y	Y
12 Murtha	Y	N	Y	N	Y	Y
13 Schwartz	Y	N	Y	N	Y	Y
14 Doyle	Y	N	Y	?	Y	Y
15 **Dent**	Y	Y	Y	N	N	N
16 **Pitts**	Y	Y	N	Y	N	N
17 Holden	Y	N	Y	N	Y	Y
18 **Murphy, T.**	Y	Y	Y	N	N	N
19 **Platts**	Y	Y	Y	N	N	Y
RHODE ISLAND						
1 Kennedy	Y	N	Y	N	Y	Y
2 Langevin	Y	N	Y	N	Y	Y
SOUTH CAROLINA						
1 **Brown**	Y	Y	N	Y	N	N
2 **Wilson**	Y	Y	N	Y	N	N
3 **Barrett**	Y	Y	N	Y	N	N
4 **Inglis**	Y	Y	N	Y	N	N
5 Spratt	Y	N	Y	N	Y	Y
6 Clyburn	Y	N	Y	N	Y	Y
SOUTH DAKOTA						
AL Herseth Sandlin	Y	N	Y	N	Y	Y
TENNESSEE						
1 **Roe**	Y	Y	N	Y	N	N
2 **Duncan**	Y	Y	N	Y	N	N
3 **Wamp**	Y	Y	N	Y	N	N
4 Davis	Y	N	Y	N	Y	Y
5 Cooper	Y	N	Y	N	Y	Y
6 Gordon	Y	N	Y	?	Y	Y
7 **Blackburn**	Y	Y	N	Y	N	N
8 Tanner	?	?	?	?	?	?
9 Cohen	Y	N	Y	N	Y	Y

	257	258	259	260	261	262
TEXAS						
1 **Gohmert**	Y	Y	N	Y	N	N
2 **Poe**	Y	Y	N	Y	N	N
3 **Johnson, S.**	Y	Y	N	Y	N	N
4 **Hall**	Y	Y	N	Y	N	N
5 **Hensarling**	Y	Y	N	Y	N	N
6 **Barton**	Y	Y	N	Y	N	N
7 **Culberson**	Y	Y	N	Y	N	N
8 **Brady**	Y	Y	N	N	N	N
9 Green, A.	Y	N	Y	N	Y	Y
10 **McCaul**	Y	Y	Y	N	N	N
11 **Conaway**	Y	Y	N	Y	N	N
12 **Granger**	Y	Y	N	Y	N	N
13 **Thornberry**	Y	Y	N	Y	N	N
14 **Paul**	Y	Y	N	Y	N	N
15 Hinojosa	Y	N	Y	N	Y	Y
16 Reyes	Y	N	Y	N	Y	Y
17 Edwards	Y	N	Y	N	Y	Y
18 Jackson Lee	Y	N	Y	N	Y	Y
19 **Neugebauer**	Y	Y	N	Y	N	N
20 Gonzalez	Y	N	Y	N	Y	Y
21 **Smith**	Y	Y	N	Y	N	N
22 **Olson**	Y	Y	N	Y	N	N
23 Rodriguez	Y	N	Y	N	Y	Y
24 **Marchant**	Y	Y	N	Y	N	N
25 Doggett	Y	N	Y	N	Y	Y
26 **Burgess**	Y	Y	N	Y	N	N
27 Ortiz	Y	N	Y	N	Y	Y
28 Cuellar	Y	N	Y	N	Y	Y
29 Green, G.	Y	N	Y	N	Y	Y
30 Johnson, E.	Y	N	Y	N	Y	Y
31 **Carter**	Y	Y	N	?	N	N
32 **Sessions**	Y	Y	N	Y	N	N
UTAH						
1 **Bishop**	Y	Y	N	Y	N	N
2 Matheson	Y	N	Y	N	Y	Y
3 **Chaffetz**	Y	Y	N	Y	N	N
VERMONT						
AL Welch	Y	N	Y	N	Y	Y
VIRGINIA						
1 **Wittman**	Y	Y	N	Y	N	–
2 Nye	Y	Y	Y	N	N	Y
3 Scott	Y	N	Y	N	Y	Y
4 **Forbes**	Y	Y	N	Y	N	N
5 Perriello	Y	Y	Y	N	Y	Y
6 **Goodlatte**	Y	Y	N	Y	N	N
7 **Cantor**	Y	Y	N	Y	N	N
8 Moran	Y	N	Y	?	Y	Y
9 Boucher	Y	Y	Y	N	?	Y
10 **Wolf**	Y	Y	N	Y	N	N
11 Connolly	Y	N	Y	N	Y	Y
WASHINGTON						
1 Inslee	Y	N	Y	N	Y	Y
2 Larsen	Y	N	Y	N	Y	Y
3 Baird	Y	N	Y	N	Y	Y
4 **Hastings**	Y	Y	N	Y	N	N
5 **McMorris Rodgers**	Y	Y	N	Y	N	N
6 Dicks	Y	N	Y	N	Y	Y
7 McDermott	Y	N	Y	?	Y	Y
8 **Reichert**	Y	Y	Y	N	N	N
9 Smith	Y	N	Y	?	Y	Y
WEST VIRGINIA						
1 Mollohan	Y	N	Y	N	Y	Y
2 **Capito**	Y	Y	N	Y	N	N
3 Rahall	Y	N	Y	N	Y	Y
WISCONSIN						
1 **Ryan**	Y	Y	N	Y	N	N
2 Baldwin	Y	N	Y	N	Y	Y
3 Kind	Y	N	Y	N	Y	Y
4 Moore	Y	N	Y	–	Y	Y
5 **Sensenbrenner**	Y	Y	N	Y	N	N
6 **Petri**	Y	Y	N	Y	N	N
7 Obey	Y	N	Y	N	Y	Y
8 Kagen	Y	N	Y	?	Y	Y
WYOMING						
AL **Lummis**	Y	Y	N	Y	N	N
DELEGATES						
Faleomavaega (A.S.)	?					
Norton (D.C.)	Y					
Bordallo (Guam)	Y					
Sablan (N. Marianas)	Y					
Pierluisi (P.R.)	Y					
Christensen (V.I.)	Y					

IN THE HOUSE | By Vote Number

263. **H Res 377. Armed Forces Appreciation/Adoption.** Massa, D-N.Y., motion to suspend the rules and adopt the resolution that would honor members of the armed forces and their families for their service and sacrifice, state that the House remains committed to supporting the military, and encourage Americans to show appreciation on Armed Forces Day 2009. Motion agreed to 420-0: R 172-0; D 248-0. A two-thirds majority of those present and voting (280 in this case) is required for adoption under suspension of the rules. May 14, 2009.

264. **HR 2346. Fiscal 2009 Supplemental/Recommit.** Rogers, R-Ky., motion to recommit the bill to the Appropriations Committee with instructions that it be immediately reported back with language that would strike provisions that would move funding for the Pakistan Counterinsurgency Capability Fund from the Defense Department to the State Department and provisions that would move funding from certain military operations accounts. It would shift money in the bill for developing countries affected by global warming to counternarcotics and law enforcement operations on the U.S. border. Motion rejected 191-237: R 174-4; D 17-233. May 14, 2009.

265. **HR 2346. Fiscal 2009 Supplemental/Passage.** Passage of the bill that would appropriate $96.7 billion in emergency supplemental funds for fiscal 2009, including funding for the wars in Iraq and Afghanistan and for pandemic flu preparations. It would provide $47.7 billion for ongoing military operations, $10.1 billion for foreign aid and stabilization programs, and $2 billion to address potential pandemic flu. The bill would provide for additional pay to military personnel who have had their enlistments involuntarily extended. It also would prohibit funds appropriated in the bill from being used to release detainees held at Guantánamo Bay, Cuba, into the United States. Passed 368-60: R 168-9; D 200-51. A "yea" was a vote in support of the president's position. May 14, 2009.

266. **HR 347. World War II Gold Medal/Passage.** Watt, D-N.C., motion to suspend the rules and pass the bill that would authorize $30,000 to create a gold medal to recognize the 100th Infantry Battalion and the 442nd Regimental Combat Team of the U.S. Army for their dedicated service during World War II. It would allow the Treasury Department to create duplicate medals to be sold to cover production costs. Motion agreed to 411-0: R 173-0; D 238-0. A two-thirds majority of those present and voting (274 in this case) is required for passage under suspension of the rules. May 14, 2009.

	263	264	265	266
ALABAMA				
1 **Bonner**	Y	Y	Y	Y
2 Bright	Y	N	Y	Y
3 **Rogers**	Y	Y	Y	Y
4 **Aderholt**	Y	Y	Y	Y
5 Griffith	Y	Y	Y	Y
6 **Bachus**	Y	Y	Y	Y
7 Davis	Y	N	Y	Y
ALASKA				
AL **Young**	Y	Y	Y	Y
ARIZONA				
1 Kirkpatrick	Y	Y	Y	Y
2 **Franks**	?	Y	Y	?
3 **Shadegg**	Y	Y	Y	Y
4 Pastor	Y	N	Y	Y
5 Mitchell	Y	Y	Y	Y
6 **Flake**	Y	N	N	?
7 Grijalva	Y	N	N	Y
8 Giffords	Y	Y	Y	Y
ARKANSAS				
1 Berry	Y	N	Y	Y
2 Snyder	Y	N	Y	Y
3 **Boozman**	Y	Y	Y	Y
4 Ross	Y	N	Y	Y
CALIFORNIA				
1 Thompson	Y	N	N	Y
2 **Herger**	Y	Y	Y	Y
3 **Lungren**	Y	Y	Y	Y
4 **McClintock**	Y	Y	Y	Y
5 Matsui	Y	N	N	Y
6 Woolsey	Y	N	N	Y
7 Miller, George	Y	N	N	Y
8 Pelosi				
9 Lee	Y	N	N	Y
10 Tauscher	Y	N	Y	Y
11 McNerney	Y	Y	Y	?
12 Speier	Y	N	N	Y
13 Stark	?	?	?	?
14 Eshoo	Y	N	Y	Y
15 Honda	Y	N	N	Y
16 Lofgren	Y	N	N	Y
17 Farr	Y	N	N	Y
18 Cardoza	Y	N	Y	Y
19 **Radanovich**	Y	Y	Y	Y
20 Costa	Y	N	Y	Y
21 **Nunes**	Y	Y	Y	Y
22 **McCarthy**	Y	Y	Y	Y
23 Capps	Y	N	Y	Y
24 **Gallegly**	Y	Y	Y	Y
25 **McKeon**	Y	Y	Y	Y
26 **Dreier**	Y	Y	Y	Y
27 Sherman	Y	N	Y	Y
28 Berman	Y	N	Y	Y
29 Schiff	Y	N	Y	Y
30 Waxman	Y	N	Y	Y
31 Becerra	Y	N	Y	Y
32 Vacant				
33 Watson	Y	N	N	Y
34 Roybal-Allard	Y	N	Y	Y
35 Waters	Y	N	N	Y
36 Harman	Y	N	Y	?
37 Richardson	Y	N	Y	Y
38 Napolitano	Y	N	N	Y
39 Sánchez, Linda	?	?	?	?
40 **Royce**	Y	Y	N	Y
41 **Lewis**	Y	Y	Y	Y
42 **Miller, Gary**	Y	Y	Y	Y
43 Baca	Y	N	Y	Y
44 **Calvert**	Y	Y	Y	Y
45 **Bono Mack**	Y	Y	Y	Y
46 **Rohrabacher**	Y	Y	Y	Y
47 Sanchez, Loretta	Y	N	Y	Y
48 **Campbell**	Y	N	N	?
49 **Issa**	Y	Y	Y	Y
50 **Bilbray**	Y	Y	Y	Y
51 Filner	Y	N	N	Y
52 **Hunter**	Y	Y	Y	Y
53 Davis	Y	N	Y	Y

	263	264	265	266
COLORADO				
1 DeGette	Y	N	Y	Y
2 Polis	Y	N	N	Y
3 Salazar	Y	N	Y	Y
4 Markey	Y	N	Y	Y
5 **Lamborn**	Y	Y	Y	Y
6 **Coffman**	Y	Y	Y	Y
7 Perlmutter	Y	N	Y	Y
CONNECTICUT				
1 Larson	Y	N	Y	Y
2 Courtney	Y	N	Y	Y
3 DeLauro	Y	N	Y	Y
4 Himes	Y	N	Y	Y
5 Murphy	Y	N	Y	Y
DELAWARE				
AL **Castle**	Y	Y	Y	Y
FLORIDA				
1 **Miller**	Y	Y	Y	Y
2 Boyd	Y	N	Y	?
3 Brown	Y	N	Y	Y
4 **Crenshaw**	Y	Y	Y	Y
5 **Brown-Waite**	Y	Y	Y	Y
6 **Stearns**	Y	Y	Y	Y
7 **Mica**	Y	Y	Y	Y
8 Grayson	Y	N	N	Y
9 **Bilirakis**	Y	Y	Y	Y
10 **Young**	Y	Y	Y	Y
11 Castor	Y	N	Y	Y
12 **Putnam**	Y	Y	Y	Y
13 **Buchanan**	Y	Y	Y	Y
14 **Mack**	Y	Y	Y	Y
15 **Posey**	Y	Y	Y	Y
16 **Rooney**	Y	Y	Y	Y
17 Meek	Y	N	Y	Y
18 **Ros-Lehtinen**	Y	Y	Y	Y
19 Wexler	Y	N	Y	Y
20 Wasserman Schultz	Y	N	Y	Y
21 **Diaz-Balart, L.**	Y	Y	Y	Y
22 Klein	Y	N	Y	Y
23 Hastings	Y	N	Y	Y
24 Kosmas	Y	N	Y	?
25 **Diaz-Balart, M.**	Y	Y	Y	Y
GEORGIA				
1 **Kingston**	Y	Y	Y	Y
2 Bishop	Y	N	Y	Y
3 **Westmoreland**	Y	Y	Y	Y
4 Johnson	Y	?	Y	Y
5 Lewis	Y	N	N	Y
6 **Price**	Y	Y	Y	Y
7 **Linder**	Y	Y	Y	?
8 Marshall	Y	Y	Y	?
9 **Deal**	Y	Y	Y	Y
10 **Broun**	Y	Y	Y	Y
11 **Gingrey**	Y	Y	Y	Y
12 Barrow	Y	Y	Y	Y
13 Scott	Y	N	Y	Y
HAWAII				
1 Abercrombie	Y	N	Y	?
2 Hirono	Y	N	Y	Y
IDAHO				
1 Minnick	Y	Y	Y	Y
2 **Simpson**	Y	Y	Y	Y
ILLINOIS				
1 Rush	Y	N	Y	Y
2 Jackson	Y	N	Y	Y
3 Lipinski	Y	N	Y	Y
4 Gutierrez	Y	N	N	Y
5 Quigley	Y	N	Y	Y
6 **Roskam**	Y	Y	Y	Y
7 Davis	Y	N	Y	Y
8 Bean	Y	N	Y	Y
9 Schakowsky	Y	N	N	Y
10 **Kirk**	Y	Y	Y	Y
11 Halvorson	Y	N	Y	Y
12 Costello	Y	N	N	?
13 **Biggert**	Y	Y	Y	Y
14 Foster	Y	N	Y	Y
15 **Johnson**	Y	Y	N	Y

	263	264	265	266
16 **Manzullo**	Y	Y	Y	Y
17 Hare	Y	N	Y	Y
18 **Schock**	Y	Y	Y	Y
19 **Shimkus**	Y	Y	Y	Y
INDIANA				
1 Visclosky	Y	N	Y	Y
2 Donnelly	Y	N	Y	Y
3 **Souder**	Y	Y	Y	Y
4 **Buyer**	Y	Y	Y	Y
5 **Burton**	Y	Y	Y	Y
6 **Pence**	Y	Y	Y	Y
7 Carson	Y	N	Y	Y
8 Ellsworth	Y	N	Y	Y
9 Hill	Y	N	Y	Y
IOWA				
1 Braley	Y	N	Y	Y
2 Loebsack	Y	N	Y	Y
3 Boswell	Y	N	Y	?
4 **Latham**	Y	Y	Y	Y
5 **King**	Y	Y	Y	Y
KANSAS				
1 **Moran**	Y	Y	Y	Y
2 **Jenkins**	Y	Y	Y	Y
3 Moore	Y	N	Y	Y
4 **Tiahrt**	Y	Y	Y	Y
KENTUCKY				
1 **Whitfield**	Y	Y	Y	Y
2 **Guthrie**	Y	Y	Y	Y
3 Yarmuth	Y	N	Y	Y
4 **Davis**	Y	Y	Y	?
5 **Rogers**	Y	Y	Y	Y
6 Chandler	Y	N	Y	Y
LOUISIANA				
1 **Scalise**	Y	Y	Y	Y
2 **Cao**	Y	Y	Y	Y
3 Melancon	Y	N	Y	Y
4 **Fleming**	Y	Y	Y	Y
5 **Alexander**	Y	Y	Y	Y
6 **Cassidy**	Y	Y	Y	Y
7 **Boustany**	?	Y	Y	Y
MAINE				
1 Pingree	Y	N	N	Y
2 Michaud	Y	N	N	Y
MARYLAND				
1 Kratovil	Y	Y	Y	Y
2 Ruppersberger	Y	N	Y	Y
3 Sarbanes	Y	N	Y	Y
4 Edwards	Y	N	N	Y
5 Hoyer	Y	N	Y	Y
6 **Bartlett**	Y	Y	Y	Y
7 Cummings	Y	N	Y	Y
8 Van Hollen	Y	N	Y	Y
MASSACHUSETTS				
1 Olver	Y	N	Y	Y
2 Neal	Y	N	N	Y
3 McGovern	Y	N	N	Y
4 Frank	Y	N	N	Y
5 Tsongas	Y	N	N	?
6 Tierney	Y	N	N	Y
7 Markey	Y	N	N	Y
8 Capuano	Y	N	Y	Y
9 Lynch	Y	N	Y	Y
10 Delahunt	?	?	?	?
MICHIGAN				
1 Stupak	Y	N	Y	Y
2 **Hoekstra**	Y	Y	Y	Y
3 **Ehlers**	Y	Y	N	Y
4 **Camp**	Y	Y	Y	Y
5 Kildee	Y	N	Y	Y
6 **Upton**	Y	Y	Y	Y
7 Schauer	Y	Y	Y	Y
8 **Rogers**	Y	Y	Y	Y
9 Peters	Y	Y	Y	Y
10 **Miller**	?	Y	Y	Y
11 **McCotter**	Y	Y	Y	Y
12 Levin	Y	N	Y	Y
13 Kilpatrick	Y	N	Y	Y
14 Conyers	Y	N	N	Y
15 Dingell	Y	N	Y	Y
MINNESOTA				
1 Walz	Y	N	Y	Y
2 **Kline**	Y	Y	Y	Y
3 **Paulsen**	Y	Y	Y	Y
4 McCollum	Y	N	Y	Y

	263	264	265	266
5 Ellison	Y	N	N	Y
6 **Bachmann**	Y	Y	Y	Y
7 Peterson	Y	N	Y	Y
8 Oberstar	Y	N	N	Y
MISSISSIPPI				
1 Childers	Y	Y	Y	Y
2 Thompson	Y	N	Y	Y
3 **Harper**	Y	Y	Y	Y
4 Taylor	Y	Y	Y	Y
MISSOURI				
1 Clay	Y	N	Y	Y
2 **Akin**	Y	Y	Y	Y
3 Carnahan	Y	N	Y	Y
4 Skelton	Y	N	Y	Y
5 Cleaver	Y	N	Y	Y
6 **Graves**	Y	Y	Y	Y
7 **Blunt**	Y	Y	Y	Y
8 **Emerson**	Y	Y	Y	Y
9 **Luetkemeyer**	Y	Y	Y	Y
MONTANA				
AL **Rehberg**	Y	Y	Y	Y
NEBRASKA				
1 **Fortenberry**	Y	Y	Y	Y
2 **Terry**	Y	Y	Y	Y
3 **Smith**	Y	Y	Y	Y
NEVADA				
1 Berkley	Y	N	Y	Y
2 **Heller**	Y	Y	Y	Y
3 Titus	Y	N	Y	Y
NEW HAMPSHIRE				
1 Shea-Porter	Y	N	N	Y
2 Hodes	Y	N	Y	Y
NEW JERSEY				
1 Andrews	Y	N	Y	Y
2 **LoBiondo**	Y	Y	Y	Y
3 Adler	Y	Y	Y	Y
4 **Smith**	Y	Y	Y	Y
5 **Garrett**	Y	Y	Y	Y
6 Pallone	Y	N	Y	Y
7 **Lance**	Y	Y	Y	Y
8 Pascrell	Y	N	Y	?
9 Rothman	Y	N	Y	Y
10 Payne	Y	N	N	Y
11 **Frelinghuysen**	Y	Y	Y	Y
12 Holt	Y	N	Y	Y
13 Sires	Y	N	Y	Y
NEW MEXICO				
1 Heinrich	Y	N	Y	Y
2 Teague	Y	Y	Y	Y
3 Lujan	Y	N	Y	Y
NEW YORK				
1 Bishop	Y	N	Y	Y
2 Israel	Y	N	Y	Y
3 **King**	Y	Y	Y	Y
4 McCarthy	Y	N	Y	Y
5 Ackerman	Y	N	Y	Y
6 Meeks	Y	N	Y	Y
7 Crowley	Y	N	Y	Y
8 Nadler	Y	N	Y	Y
9 Weiner	Y	N	N	Y
10 Towns	Y	N	Y	Y
11 Clarke	Y	N	N	Y
12 Velázquez	Y	N	N	Y
13 McMahon	Y	N	Y	Y
14 Maloney	Y	N	Y	Y
15 Rangel	Y	N	Y	Y
16 Serrano	?	N	N	Y
17 Engel	Y	N	Y	Y
18 Lowey	Y	N	Y	Y
19 Hall	Y	N	Y	Y
20 Murphy	Y	N	Y	Y
21 Tonko	Y	N	Y	Y
22 Hinchey	Y	N	Y	Y
23 **McHugh**	Y	Y	Y	Y
24 Arcuri	Y	Y	Y	Y
25 Maffei	Y	N	Y	Y
26 **Lee**	Y	Y	Y	Y
27 Higgins	Y	N	Y	Y
28 Slaughter	Y	N	Y	Y
29 Massa	Y	N	N	Y
NORTH CAROLINA				
1 Butterfield	Y	N	Y	Y
2 Etheridge	Y	N	Y	Y
3 **Jones**	Y	Y	Y	Y
4 Price	Y	N	Y	Y

	263	264	265	266
5 **Foxx**	Y	Y	Y	Y
6 **Coble**	Y	Y	Y	Y
7 McIntyre	Y	Y	Y	Y
8 Kissell	Y	N	Y	Y
9 **Myrick**	Y	Y	Y	Y
10 **McHenry**	Y	Y	Y	Y
11 Shuler	Y	N	Y	Y
12 Watt	Y	N	Y	Y
13 Miller	Y	N	Y	Y
NORTH DAKOTA				
AL Pomeroy	Y	N	Y	Y
OHIO				
1 Driehaus	Y	N	Y	Y
2 **Schmidt**	Y	Y	Y	Y
3 Turner	Y	Y	Y	Y
4 **Jordan**	?	Y	Y	Y
5 **Latta**	Y	Y	Y	Y
6 Wilson	Y	N	Y	Y
7 **Austria**	Y	Y	Y	Y
8 **Boehner**	Y	Y	Y	Y
9 Kaptur	Y	N	N	Y
10 Kucinich	Y	N	N	Y
11 Fudge	Y	N	Y	Y
12 **Tiberi**	Y	Y	Y	Y
13 Sutton	Y	N	Y	Y
14 **LaTourette**	Y	Y	Y	Y
15 Kilroy	Y	N	Y	Y
16 Boccieri	Y	N	Y	Y
17 Ryan	Y	N	Y	Y
18 Space	Y	N	Y	Y
OKLAHOMA				
1 **Sullivan**	Y	Y	Y	Y
2 Boren	Y	N	Y	Y
3 **Lucas**	Y	Y	Y	Y
4 **Cole**	Y	Y	Y	Y
5 **Fallin**	Y	Y	Y	Y
OREGON				
1 Wu	Y	N	Y	Y
2 **Walden**	Y	Y	Y	Y
3 Blumenauer	Y	N	Y	Y
4 DeFazio	Y	N	Y	Y
5 Schrader	Y	N	Y	Y
PENNSYLVANIA				
1 Brady	Y	N	Y	Y
2 Fattah	Y	N	Y	Y
3 Dahlkemper	Y	N	Y	Y
4 Altmire	Y	N	Y	Y
5 **Thompson**	Y	Y	Y	Y
6 **Gerlach**	Y	Y	Y	Y
7 Sestak	Y	N	Y	Y
8 Murphy, P.	Y	N	Y	Y
9 **Shuster**	Y	Y	Y	Y
10 Carney	Y	N	Y	Y
11 Kanjorski	Y	N	Y	Y
12 Murtha	Y	N	Y	Y
13 Schwartz	Y	N	Y	Y
14 Doyle	Y	N	Y	Y
15 **Dent**	Y	Y	Y	Y
16 **Pitts**	Y	Y	Y	Y
17 Holden	Y	N	Y	Y
18 **Murphy, T.**	Y	Y	Y	Y
19 **Platts**	Y	Y	Y	Y
RHODE ISLAND				
1 Kennedy	Y	N	Y	Y
2 Langevin	+	N	Y	Y
SOUTH CAROLINA				
1 **Brown**	Y	Y	Y	Y
2 **Wilson**	Y	Y	Y	Y
3 **Barrett**	Y	Y	Y	Y
4 **Inglis**	Y	Y	Y	Y
5 Spratt	Y	N	Y	Y
6 Clyburn	Y	N	Y	Y
SOUTH DAKOTA				
AL Herseth Sandlin	Y	N	Y	Y
TENNESSEE				
1 **Roe**	Y	Y	Y	Y
2 **Duncan**	Y	N	N	Y
3 **Wamp**	Y	Y	Y	Y
4 Davis	Y	N	Y	Y
5 Cooper	?	N	N	Y
6 Gordon	Y	N	Y	Y
7 **Blackburn**	Y	Y	Y	Y
8 Tanner	?	?	?	?
9 Cohen	Y	N	N	Y

	263	264	265	266
TEXAS				
1 **Gohmert**	Y	Y	Y	Y
2 **Poe**	Y	Y	Y	Y
3 **Johnson, S.**	Y	Y	Y	Y
4 **Hall**	Y	Y	Y	Y
5 **Hensarling**	Y	Y	Y	Y
6 **Barton**	Y	Y	Y	Y
7 **Culberson**	Y	Y	Y	Y
8 **Brady**	Y	Y	Y	Y
9 Green, A.	Y	N	Y	Y
10 **McCaul**	Y	Y	Y	Y
11 **Conaway**	Y	Y	Y	Y
12 **Granger**	Y	Y	Y	Y
13 **Thornberry**	Y	Y	Y	Y
14 **Paul**	Y	N	N	Y
15 Hinojosa	Y	N	Y	Y
16 Reyes	Y	N	Y	Y
17 Edwards	Y	N	Y	Y
18 Jackson Lee	Y	N	Y	Y
19 **Neugebauer**	Y	Y	Y	Y
20 Gonzalez	Y	N	Y	Y
21 **Smith**	Y	Y	Y	Y
22 **Olson**	Y	Y	Y	Y
23 Rodriguez	Y	N	Y	Y
24 **Marchant**	Y	Y	Y	Y
25 Doggett	Y	N	N	Y
26 **Burgess**	Y	Y	Y	Y
27 Ortiz	Y	N	Y	Y
28 Cuellar	Y	N	Y	Y
29 Green, G.	Y	N	Y	Y
30 Johnson, E.	Y	N	Y	Y
31 **Carter**	Y	Y	Y	Y
32 **Sessions**	Y	Y	Y	Y
UTAH				
1 **Bishop**	Y	Y	Y	Y
2 Matheson	Y	N	Y	Y
3 **Chaffetz**	Y	Y	Y	Y
VERMONT				
AL Welch	Y	N	N	Y
VIRGINIA				
1 **Wittman**	Y	Y	Y	Y
2 Nye	Y	Y	Y	Y
3 Scott	Y	N	Y	Y
4 **Forbes**	Y	Y	Y	Y
5 Perriello	Y	N	Y	Y
6 **Goodlatte**	Y	Y	Y	Y
7 **Cantor**	?	Y	Y	Y
8 Moran	Y	N	Y	Y
9 Boucher	Y	N	Y	Y
10 **Wolf**	Y	Y	Y	Y
11 Connolly	Y	N	Y	Y
WASHINGTON				
1 Inslee	Y	N	N	Y
2 Larsen	Y	N	Y	Y
3 Baird	Y	N	Y	Y
4 **Hastings**	Y	Y	Y	Y
5 **McMorris Rodgers**	Y	Y	?	Y
6 Dicks	Y	N	Y	Y
7 McDermott	Y	N	N	Y
8 **Reichert**	?	Y	Y	Y
9 Smith	Y	N	Y	Y
WEST VIRGINIA				
1 Mollohan	Y	N	Y	Y
2 **Capito**	Y	Y	Y	Y
3 Rahall	Y	N	Y	Y
WISCONSIN				
1 **Ryan**	Y	Y	Y	Y
2 Baldwin	Y	N	N	Y
3 Kind	Y	N	Y	Y
4 Moore	Y	N	Y	?
5 **Sensenbrenner**	Y	Y	Y	Y
6 **Petri**	Y	Y	N	Y
7 Obey	Y	N	Y	?
8 Kagen	Y	N	N	Y
WYOMING				
AL **Lummis**	Y	Y	Y	Y
DELEGATES				
Faleomavaega (A.S.)				
Norton (D.C.)				
Bordallo (Guam)				
Sablan (N. Marianas)				
Pierluisi (P.R.)				
Christensen (V.I.)				

IN THE HOUSE | By Vote Number

267. **H Res 300. Camp Dudley YMCA Anniversary/Adoption.** Tonko, D-N.Y., motion to suspend the rules and adopt the resolution that would congratulate Camp Dudley YMCA of Westport, N.Y., on its 125th anniversary and recognize the camp's staff, campers and alumni for their contributions to their community. Motion agreed to 388-0: R 165-0; D 223-0. A two-thirds majority of those present and voting (259 in this case) is required for adoption under suspension of the rules. May 18, 2009.

268. **S 386. Financial Fraud/Passage.** Scott, D-Va., motion to suspend the rules and concur in the Senate amendment to the House amendments to the bill that would expand federal fraud laws to cover funds paid under the economic stimulus package and the Troubled Asset Relief Program, as well as to mortgage lenders not directly regulated or insured by the federal government. It would authorize additional funds in fiscal 2010-11 for the Justice Department, state and local law enforcement investigations, the Secret Service, the FBI, the Securities and Exchange Commission, and other purposes. It would create a 10-member independent commission to study the financial markets and make regulatory recommendations. Motion agreed to (thus clearing the bill for the president) 338-52: R 114-52; D 224-0. A two-thirds majority of those present and voting (260 in this case) is required for passage under suspension of the rules. A "yea" was a vote in support of the president's position. May 18, 2009.

269. **H Res 442. Child and Adult Care Food Program/Adoption.** Tonko, D-N.Y., motion to suspend the rules and adopt the resolution that would recognize the importance of the Child and Adult Care Food Program and its effect on low-income children and families, encourage states to better coordinate the use of funding across early-learning and child development programs, and recognize the need to provide adequate resources to improve food that the program serves. Motion agreed to 377-10: R 155-10; D 222-0. A two-thirds majority of those present and voting (258 in this case) is required for adoption under suspension of the rules. May 18, 2009.

270. **HR 1089. Armed Forces Employment Rights Oversight/Passage.** Filner, D-Calif., motion to suspend the rules and pass the bill that would grant the Office of Special Counsel jurisdiction in enforcing employment rights of veterans and members of the armed forces employed by federal executive agencies. It would also allow individuals to file complaints with the special counsel. Motion agreed to 423-0: R 176-0; D 247-0. A two-thirds majority of those present and voting (282 in this case) is required for passage under suspension of the rules. May 19, 2009.

271. **S 896. Housing Loans Modification/Passage.** Frank, D-Mass., motion to suspend the rules and pass the bill that would ease the application and eligibility requirements for the Hope for Homeowners Program. It would extend a temporary increase to $250,000 of Federal Deposit Insurance Corporation (FDIC) and National Credit Union Administration deposit insurance on individual bank accounts until Dec. 31, 2013. It would increase the FDIC's borrowing authority to $100 billion and provide temporary authority for further increases to $500 billion if deemed necessary. The bill would protect lenders from legal liability if certain criteria are met during the loan modification process. It would authorize $2.2 billion for programs to reduce homelessness nationwide. Motion agreed to 367-54: R 123-51; D 244-3. A two-thirds majority of those present and voting (281 in this case) is required for passage under suspension of the rules. A "yea" was a vote in support of the president's position. May 19, 2009.

	267	268	269	270	271
ALABAMA					
1 Bonner	Y	Y	Y	Y	Y
2 Bright	Y	Y	Y	Y	Y
3 Rogers	Y	Y	Y	Y	Y
4 Aderholt	Y	Y	Y	Y	Y
5 Griffith	Y	Y	Y	Y	Y
6 Bachus	Y	Y	Y	Y	Y
7 Davis	?	?	?	Y	Y
ALASKA					
AL Young	Y	Y	Y	Y	Y
ARIZONA					
1 Kirkpatrick	Y	Y	Y	Y	Y
2 Franks	Y	N	Y	Y	N
3 Shadegg	Y	N	N	Y	N
4 Pastor	Y	Y	Y	Y	Y
5 Mitchell	Y	Y	Y	Y	Y
6 Flake	Y	N	N	Y	N
7 Grijalva	?	?	?	Y	Y
8 Giffords	Y	Y	Y	Y	Y
ARKANSAS					
1 Berry	Y	Y	Y	Y	Y
2 Snyder	?	Y	Y	Y	Y
3 Boozman	Y	Y	Y	Y	Y
4 Ross	Y	Y	Y	Y	Y
CALIFORNIA					
1 Thompson	Y	Y	Y	Y	Y
2 Herger	Y	Y	Y	Y	Y
3 Lungren	Y	Y	Y	Y	Y
4 McClintock	Y	Y	N	Y	N
5 Matsui	Y	Y	Y	Y	Y
6 Woolsey	Y	Y	Y	Y	Y
7 Miller, George	Y	Y	Y	Y	Y
8 Pelosi					
9 Lee	Y	Y	Y	Y	Y
10 Tauscher	Y	Y	Y	Y	Y
11 McNerney	Y	Y	Y	Y	Y
12 Speier	?	?	?	?	?
13 Stark	?	?	?	?	?
14 Eshoo	Y	Y	Y	Y	Y
15 Honda	Y	Y	Y	+	+
16 Lofgren	Y	Y	Y	Y	N
17 Farr	Y	Y	Y	Y	Y
18 Cardoza	Y	Y	Y	?	Y
19 Radanovich	Y	Y	Y	Y	N
20 Costa	Y	Y	Y	Y	Y
21 Nunes	Y	Y	Y	Y	Y
22 McCarthy	Y	Y	Y	Y	Y
23 Capps	Y	Y	?	Y	Y
24 Gallegly	Y	Y	Y	Y	Y
25 McKeon	Y	Y	Y	Y	Y
26 Dreier	Y	Y	Y	Y	Y
27 Sherman	Y	Y	Y	Y	Y
28 Berman	Y	Y	Y	Y	Y
29 Schiff	Y	Y	Y	Y	Y
30 Waxman	Y	Y	Y	Y	Y
31 Becerra	Y	Y	Y	Y	Y
32 Vacant					
33 Watson	Y	Y	Y	Y	Y
34 Roybal-Allard	Y	Y	Y	Y	Y
35 Waters	?	?	?	Y	Y
36 Harman	?	?	?	Y	Y
37 Richardson	Y	Y	Y	Y	Y
38 Napolitano	Y	Y	Y	Y	Y
39 Sánchez, Linda	?	?	?	?	?
40 Royce	Y	Y	Y	Y	N
41 Lewis	Y	Y	Y	Y	Y
42 Miller, Gary	Y	Y	Y	Y	Y
43 Baca	Y	Y	Y	Y	Y
44 Calvert	Y	Y	Y	Y	Y
45 Bono Mack	Y	Y	Y	Y	Y
46 Rohrabacher	?	?	?	Y	N
47 Sanchez, Loretta	?	?	?	Y	Y
48 Campbell	Y	N	N	Y	N
49 Issa	Y	Y	Y	Y	N
50 Bilbray	Y	Y	Y	Y	Y
51 Filner	Y	Y	Y	Y	Y
52 Hunter	Y	Y	Y	Y	Y
53 Davis	Y	Y	Y	Y	Y

	267	268	269	270	271
COLORADO					
1 DeGette	Y	Y	Y	Y	Y
2 Polis	Y	Y	Y	Y	Y
3 Salazar	Y	Y	Y	Y	Y
4 Markey	Y	Y	Y	Y	Y
5 Lamborn	Y	N	Y	Y	N
6 Coffman	Y	Y	Y	Y	Y
7 Perlmutter	Y	Y	Y	Y	Y
CONNECTICUT					
1 Larson	Y	Y	Y	Y	Y
2 Courtney	Y	Y	Y	Y	Y
3 DeLauro	Y	Y	Y	Y	Y
4 Himes	Y	Y	Y	Y	Y
5 Murphy	Y	Y	Y	Y	Y
DELAWARE					
AL Castle	Y	Y	Y	Y	Y
FLORIDA					
1 Miller	Y	N	Y	Y	N
2 Boyd	Y	Y	Y	Y	Y
3 Brown	?	?	?	Y	Y
4 Crenshaw	Y	Y	Y	Y	Y
5 Brown-Waite	Y	Y	Y	Y	Y
6 Stearns	Y	Y	Y	Y	Y
7 Mica	+	+	+	Y	Y
8 Grayson	?	?	?	Y	Y
9 Bilirakis	Y	Y	Y	Y	Y
10 Young	Y	Y	Y	Y	Y
11 Castor	Y	Y	?	Y	Y
12 Putnam	Y	Y	Y	Y	Y
13 Buchanan	Y	Y	Y	Y	Y
14 Mack	Y	N	Y	Y	N
15 Posey	Y	Y	Y	Y	Y
16 Rooney	Y	Y	Y	Y	Y
17 Meek	Y	Y	Y	Y	Y
18 Ros-Lehtinen	Y	Y	Y	Y	Y
19 Wexler	Y	Y	Y	Y	Y
20 Wasserman Schultz	Y	Y	Y	Y	Y
21 Diaz-Balart, L.	Y	Y	Y	Y	Y
22 Klein	Y	Y	Y	Y	Y
23 Hastings	Y	Y	Y	Y	Y
24 Kosmas	?	?	?	Y	Y
25 Diaz-Balart, M.	Y	Y	Y	Y	?
GEORGIA					
1 Kingston	Y	N	N	Y	N
2 Bishop	Y	Y	Y	Y	Y
3 Westmoreland	Y	N	Y	Y	N
4 Johnson	Y	Y	Y	Y	Y
5 Lewis	?	?	?	Y	Y
6 Price	Y	N	Y	Y	N
7 Linder	Y	Y	Y	Y	N
8 Marshall	Y	Y	Y	Y	Y
9 Deal	?	?	?	Y	N
10 Broun	Y	N	N	Y	N
11 Gingrey	Y	Y	Y	Y	N
12 Barrow	Y	Y	Y	Y	Y
13 Scott	Y	Y	Y	Y	Y
HAWAII					
1 Abercrombie	Y	Y	Y	Y	Y
2 Hirono	Y	Y	Y	Y	Y
IDAHO					
1 Minnick	Y	Y	Y	Y	Y
2 Simpson	Y	Y	Y	Y	Y
ILLINOIS					
1 Rush	Y	Y	Y	Y	Y
2 Jackson	Y	Y	Y	Y	Y
3 Lipinski	Y	Y	Y	Y	Y
4 Gutierrez	+	?	+	Y	Y
5 Quigley	Y	Y	Y	Y	Y
6 Roskam	Y	Y	Y	Y	Y
7 Davis	Y	Y	Y	Y	Y
8 Bean	Y	Y	Y	Y	Y
9 Schakowsky	Y	Y	Y	Y	Y
10 Kirk	Y	Y	Y	Y	Y
11 Halvorson	Y	Y	Y	Y	Y
12 Costello	?	?	?	Y	Y
13 Biggert	?	?	?	Y	Y
14 Foster	Y	Y	Y	Y	Y
15 Johnson	+	+	+	Y	Y

KEY	**Republicans**	Democrats			
Y	Voted for (yea)		X	Paired against		C	Voted "present" to avoid possible conflict of interest
#	Paired for		–	Announced against	
+	Announced for		P	Voted "present"		?	Did not vote or otherwise make a position known
N	Voted against (nay)				

	267	268	269	270	271
16 Manzullo	Y	N	Y	Y	Y
17 Hare	Y	Y	Y	Y	Y
18 **Schock**	Y	Y	Y	?	Y
19 **Shimkus**	Y	Y	Y	Y	Y
INDIANA					
1 Visclosky	Y	Y	Y	Y	Y
2 Donnelly	Y	Y	Y	Y	Y
3 **Souder**	?	?	?	Y	Y
4 **Buyer**	Y	Y	Y	Y	?
5 **Burton**	Y	N	Y	Y	N
6 **Pence**	Y	N	Y	Y	N
7 Carson	Y	Y	Y	Y	Y
8 Ellsworth	Y	Y	Y	Y	Y
9 Hill	Y	Y	Y	Y	Y
IOWA					
1 Braley	Y	Y	Y	Y	Y
2 Loebsack	Y	Y	Y	Y	Y
3 Boswell	Y	Y	Y	Y	Y
4 **Latham**	Y	Y	Y	Y	Y
5 **King**	Y	N	N	Y	N
KANSAS					
1 **Moran**	Y	Y	Y	Y	Y
2 **Jenkins**	Y	Y	Y	Y	Y
3 Moore	Y	Y	Y	Y	Y
4 **Tiahrt**	Y	Y	Y	Y	Y
KENTUCKY					
1 **Whitfield**	Y	Y	Y	Y	N
2 **Guthrie**	Y	Y	Y	Y	Y
3 Yarmuth	Y	Y	Y	Y	Y
4 **Davis**	Y	N	Y	Y	Y
5 **Rogers**	Y	Y	Y	Y	Y
6 Chandler	Y	Y	Y	Y	Y
LOUISIANA					
1 **Scalise**	Y	Y	Y	Y	Y
2 **Cao**	Y	Y	Y	Y	Y
3 Melancon	Y	Y	Y	Y	Y
4 **Fleming**	Y	Y	Y	Y	Y
5 **Alexander**	Y	Y	Y	Y	Y
6 **Cassidy**	Y	Y	Y	Y	Y
7 **Boustany**	Y	N	Y	Y	Y
MAINE					
1 Pingree	Y	Y	Y	Y	Y
2 Michaud	Y	Y	Y	Y	Y
MARYLAND					
1 Kratovil	Y	Y	Y	Y	Y
2 Ruppersberger	Y	Y	Y	Y	Y
3 Sarbanes	Y	Y	Y	Y	Y
4 Edwards	Y	Y	Y	Y	Y
5 Hoyer	Y	Y	Y	Y	Y
6 **Bartlett**	Y	N	Y	Y	N
7 Cummings	Y	Y	Y	Y	Y
8 Van Hollen	Y	Y	Y	Y	Y
MASSACHUSETTS					
1 Olver	Y	Y	Y	Y	Y
2 Neal	Y	Y	Y	Y	Y
3 McGovern	Y	Y	Y	Y	Y
4 Frank	Y	Y	Y	Y	Y
5 Tsongas	Y	Y	Y	Y	Y
6 Tierney	Y	Y	Y	Y	Y
7 Markey	Y	Y	Y	Y	Y
8 Capuano	Y	Y	Y	Y	Y
9 Lynch	Y	Y	Y	Y	Y
10 Delahunt	?	?	?	?	?
MICHIGAN					
1 Stupak	?	?	?	Y	N
2 **Hoekstra**	Y	Y	Y	Y	Y
3 **Ehlers**	Y	N	Y	Y	Y
4 **Camp**	Y	N	Y	Y	Y
5 Kildee	Y	Y	Y	Y	Y
6 **Upton**	Y	Y	Y	Y	Y
7 Schauer	Y	Y	Y	Y	Y
8 **Rogers**	Y	Y	Y	Y	Y
9 Peters	Y	Y	Y	Y	Y
10 **Miller**	Y	Y	Y	Y	Y
11 **McCotter**	Y	Y	Y	Y	Y
12 Levin	Y	Y	Y	Y	Y
13 Kilpatrick	Y	Y	Y	Y	Y
14 Conyers	Y	Y	Y	Y	Y
15 Dingell	Y	Y	Y	Y	Y
MINNESOTA					
1 Walz	Y	Y	Y	Y	Y
2 **Kline**	Y	N	Y	Y	Y
3 **Paulsen**	Y	Y	Y	Y	Y
4 McCollum	+	+	+	Y	Y

	267	268	269	270	271
5 Ellison	?	?	?	Y	Y
6 **Bachmann**	Y	N	Y	Y	N
7 Peterson	Y	Y	Y	Y	Y
8 Oberstar	Y	Y	Y	Y	Y
MISSISSIPPI					
1 Childers	Y	Y	Y	Y	Y
2 Thompson	Y	Y	Y	Y	Y
3 **Harper**	Y	Y	Y	Y	N
4 Taylor	Y	Y	Y	Y	N
MISSOURI					
1 Clay	Y	Y	Y	Y	Y
2 **Akin**	Y	N	N	Y	N
3 Carnahan	Y	Y	Y	Y	Y
4 Skelton	Y	Y	Y	Y	Y
5 Cleaver	Y	Y	Y	Y	Y
6 **Graves**	+	+	+	Y	Y
7 **Blunt**	Y	Y	Y	Y	Y
8 **Emerson**	Y	Y	Y	Y	Y
9 **Luetkemeyer**	Y	Y	Y	Y	Y
MONTANA					
AL **Rehberg**	Y	Y	Y	Y	Y
NEBRASKA					
1 **Fortenberry**	Y	Y	Y	Y	Y
2 **Terry**	Y	Y	Y	Y	Y
3 **Smith**	Y	N	Y	Y	Y
NEVADA					
1 Berkley	Y	Y	Y	Y	Y
2 **Heller**	Y	Y	Y	Y	Y
3 Titus	Y	Y	Y	Y	Y
NEW HAMPSHIRE					
1 Shea-Porter	Y	Y	Y	Y	Y
2 Hodes	Y	Y	Y	Y	Y
NEW JERSEY					
1 Andrews	Y	Y	Y	Y	Y
2 **LoBiondo**	Y	N	Y	Y	Y
3 Adler	Y	Y	Y	Y	Y
4 **Smith**	Y	Y	Y	Y	Y
5 **Garrett**	?	N	Y	Y	N
6 Pallone	Y	Y	Y	Y	Y
7 **Lance**	Y	Y	Y	Y	Y
8 Pascrell	Y	Y	Y	Y	Y
9 Rothman	Y	Y	Y	Y	Y
10 Payne	Y	Y	Y	Y	Y
11 **Frelinghuysen**	Y	Y	Y	Y	Y
12 Holt	Y	Y	Y	Y	Y
13 Sires	Y	Y	Y	Y	Y
NEW MEXICO					
1 Heinrich	Y	Y	Y	Y	Y
2 Teague	Y	Y	Y	Y	Y
3 Lujan	Y	Y	Y	Y	Y
NEW YORK					
1 Bishop	Y	Y	Y	Y	Y
2 Israel	Y	Y	Y	Y	Y
3 **King**	Y	Y	Y	Y	Y
4 McCarthy	Y	Y	Y	Y	Y
5 Ackerman	Y	Y	Y	Y	Y
6 Meeks	Y	Y	Y	?	Y
7 Crowley	Y	Y	Y	Y	Y
8 Nadler	Y	Y	Y	Y	Y
9 Weiner	Y	Y	Y	Y	Y
10 Towns	?	?	?	Y	Y
11 Clarke	Y	Y	Y	Y	Y
12 Velázquez	Y	Y	Y	Y	Y
13 McMahon	Y	Y	Y	Y	Y
14 Maloney	+	+	+	Y	Y
15 Rangel	Y	Y	Y	Y	Y
16 Serrano	Y	Y	Y	Y	Y
17 Engel	Y	Y	Y	Y	Y
18 Lowey	Y	Y	Y	Y	Y
19 Hall	Y	Y	Y	Y	Y
20 Murphy	Y	Y	Y	Y	Y
21 Tonko	Y	Y	Y	Y	Y
22 Hinchey	Y	Y	Y	Y	Y
23 **McHugh**	Y	Y	Y	Y	Y
24 Arcuri	Y	Y	Y	Y	Y
25 Maffei	Y	Y	Y	Y	Y
26 **Lee**	Y	Y	Y	Y	Y
27 Higgins	Y	Y	Y	Y	Y
28 Slaughter	Y	Y	Y	Y	Y
29 Massa	Y	Y	Y	Y	Y
NORTH CAROLINA					
1 Butterfield	Y	Y	Y	Y	Y
2 Etheridge	Y	Y	Y	Y	Y
3 **Jones**	Y	Y	Y	Y	Y
4 Price	Y	Y	Y	Y	Y

	267	268	269	270	271
5 **Foxx**	Y	N	Y	Y	N
6 **Coble**	Y	Y	Y	Y	Y
7 McIntyre	Y	Y	Y	Y	Y
8 Kissell	+	+	+	Y	Y
9 **Myrick**	Y	N	Y	Y	Y
10 **McHenry**	Y	N	Y	Y	N
11 Shuler	?	?	?	Y	Y
12 Watt	?	?	?	Y	Y
13 Miller	Y	Y	Y	Y	Y
NORTH DAKOTA					
AL Pomeroy	Y	Y	Y	Y	Y
OHIO					
1 Driehaus	Y	Y	Y	Y	Y
2 **Schmidt**	Y	Y	Y	Y	Y
3 **Turner**	Y	Y	Y	Y	Y
4 **Jordan**	Y	N	Y	Y	N
5 **Latta**	Y	N	Y	Y	Y
6 Wilson	Y	Y	Y	Y	Y
7 **Austria**	Y	Y	Y	Y	Y
8 **Boehner**	Y	N	Y	Y	Y
9 Kaptur	Y	Y	Y	Y	P
10 Kucinich	Y	Y	Y	Y	Y
11 Fudge	Y	Y	Y	Y	Y
12 **Tiberi**	Y	Y	Y	Y	Y
13 Sutton	Y	Y	Y	Y	Y
14 **LaTourette**	Y	Y	Y	Y	Y
15 Kilroy	Y	Y	Y	Y	Y
16 Boccieri	Y	Y	Y	Y	Y
17 Ryan	+	+	+	Y	Y
18 Space	Y	Y	Y	Y	Y
OKLAHOMA					
1 **Sullivan**	?	?	?	Y	Y
2 Boren	Y	Y	Y	Y	Y
3 **Lucas**	Y	N	Y	Y	Y
4 **Cole**	Y	N	Y	Y	Y
5 **Fallin**	Y	Y	Y	Y	Y
OREGON					
1 Wu	Y	Y	Y	Y	Y
2 **Walden**	Y	Y	Y	Y	Y
3 Blumenauer	Y	Y	Y	Y	Y
4 DeFazio	Y	Y	Y	Y	Y
5 Schrader	Y	Y	Y	Y	Y
PENNSYLVANIA					
1 Brady	Y	Y	Y	?	?
2 Fattah	Y	Y	Y	Y	Y
3 Dahlkemper	Y	Y	Y	Y	Y
4 Altmire	Y	Y	Y	Y	Y
5 **Thompson**	Y	Y	Y	Y	Y
6 **Gerlach**	?	?	?	Y	Y
7 Sestak	Y	Y	Y	Y	Y
8 Murphy, P.	Y	Y	Y	Y	Y
9 **Shuster**	Y	Y	Y	Y	Y
10 Carney	+	+	+	Y	Y
11 Kanjorski	?	?	?	Y	Y
12 Murtha	Y	Y	Y	Y	Y
13 Schwartz	Y	Y	Y	Y	Y
14 Doyle	Y	Y	Y	Y	Y
15 **Dent**	Y	Y	Y	Y	Y
16 **Pitts**	Y	Y	Y	Y	Y
17 Holden	?	?	?	Y	Y
18 **Murphy, T.**	Y	Y	Y	Y	Y
19 **Platts**	Y	Y	Y	Y	Y
RHODE ISLAND					
1 Kennedy	?	?	?	Y	Y
2 Langevin	Y	Y	Y	Y	Y
SOUTH CAROLINA					
1 **Brown**	Y	Y	Y	Y	Y
2 **Wilson**	Y	Y	Y	Y	Y
3 **Barrett**	+	-	+	+	-
4 **Inglis**	Y	Y	Y	Y	N
5 Spratt	Y	Y	Y	Y	Y
6 Clyburn	Y	Y	Y	Y	Y
SOUTH DAKOTA					
AL Herseth Sandlin	Y	Y	Y	Y	Y
TENNESSEE					
1 **Roe**	Y	Y	Y	Y	Y
2 **Duncan**	Y	N	Y	Y	N
3 **Wamp**	?	?	?	Y	Y
4 Davis	Y	Y	Y	Y	Y
5 Cooper	Y	Y	Y	Y	Y
6 Gordon	Y	Y	Y	Y	Y
7 **Blackburn**	Y	N	Y	Y	N
8 Tanner	?	?	?	Y	Y
9 Cohen	Y	Y	Y	Y	Y

	267	268	269	270	271
TEXAS					
1 **Gohmert**	Y	Y	?	Y	N
2 **Poe**	Y	Y	Y	Y	N
3 **Johnson, S.**	Y	N	Y	Y	N
4 **Hall**	Y	Y	Y	Y	N
5 **Hensarling**	Y	N	Y	Y	N
6 **Barton**	Y	N	Y	Y	N
7 **Culberson**	Y	N	Y	Y	N
8 **Brady**	Y	N	Y	Y	N
9 Green, A.	Y	Y	Y	Y	Y
10 **McCaul**	Y	Y	Y	Y	Y
11 **Conaway**	Y	N	Y	Y	N
12 **Granger**	Y	N	Y	Y	N
13 **Thornberry**	Y	N	Y	Y	N
14 **Paul**	Y	N	N	Y	N
15 Hinojosa	Y	Y	Y	Y	Y
16 Reyes	Y	Y	Y	Y	Y
17 Edwards	Y	Y	Y	Y	Y
18 Jackson Lee	Y	Y	Y	Y	Y
19 **Neugebauer**	Y	N	Y	Y	N
20 Gonzalez	Y	Y	Y	Y	Y
21 **Smith**	Y	Y	Y	Y	Y
22 **Olson**	Y	N	Y	Y	N
23 Rodriguez	Y	Y	Y	Y	Y
24 **Marchant**	?	?	?	Y	N
25 Doggett	Y	Y	Y	Y	Y
26 **Burgess**	Y	N	Y	Y	N
27 Ortiz	Y	Y	Y	Y	Y
28 Cuellar	Y	Y	Y	Y	Y
29 Green, G.	Y	Y	Y	Y	Y
30 Johnson, E.	Y	Y	Y	Y	Y
31 **Carter**	Y	N	Y	Y	N
32 **Sessions**	Y	N	Y	Y	N
UTAH					
1 **Bishop**	Y	N	Y	Y	Y
2 Matheson	Y	Y	Y	Y	Y
3 **Chaffetz**	Y	N	N	Y	Y
VERMONT					
AL Welch	Y	Y	Y	Y	Y
VIRGINIA					
1 **Wittman**	Y	Y	Y	Y	Y
2 Nye	Y	Y	Y	Y	Y
3 Scott	Y	Y	Y	Y	Y
4 **Forbes**	Y	Y	Y	Y	Y
5 Perriello	Y	Y	Y	Y	Y
6 **Goodlatte**	Y	Y	Y	Y	Y
7 **Cantor**	Y	Y	Y	Y	Y
8 **Moran**	?	?	?	Y	Y
9 Boucher	Y	Y	Y	Y	Y
10 **Wolf**	Y	Y	Y	Y	Y
11 Connolly	Y	Y	Y	Y	Y
WASHINGTON					
1 Inslee	Y	Y	Y	Y	Y
2 Larsen	Y	Y	Y	Y	Y
3 Baird	Y	Y	Y	Y	Y
4 **Hastings**	Y	Y	Y	Y	Y
5 **McMorris Rodgers**	Y	Y	Y	Y	Y
6 Dicks	Y	Y	Y	Y	Y
7 McDermott	Y	Y	Y	Y	Y
8 **Reichert**	Y	Y	Y	Y	Y
9 Smith	?	?	?	Y	Y
WEST VIRGINIA					
1 Mollohan	Y	Y	Y	Y	Y
2 **Capito**	Y	Y	Y	Y	Y
3 Rahall	Y	Y	Y	Y	Y
WISCONSIN					
1 **Ryan**	Y	Y	Y	Y	—
2 Baldwin	Y	Y	Y	Y	Y
3 Kind	Y	Y	Y	Y	Y
4 Moore	Y	Y	Y	Y	Y
5 **Sensenbrenner**	Y	Y	Y	Y	N
6 **Petri**	Y	Y	Y	Y	Y
7 Obey	Y	Y	Y	Y	Y
8 Kagen	Y	Y	Y	Y	Y
WYOMING					
AL **Lummis**	Y	N	Y	Y	Y
DELEGATES					
Faleomavaega (A.S.)					
Norton (D.C.)					
Bordallo (Guam)					
Sablan (N. Marianas)					
Pierluisi (P.R.)					
Christensen (V.I.)					

IN THE HOUSE | By Vote Number

272. **H Res 360. Memorial Day/Adoption.** Filner, D-Calif., motion to suspend the rules and adopt the resolution that would urge people to visit national cemeteries, memorials and markers on Memorial Day. Motion agreed to 422-0: R 176-0; D 246-0. A two-thirds majority of those present and voting (282 in this case) is required for adoption under suspension of the rules. May 19, 2009.

273. **HR 627. Credit Card Company Regulations/Rule.** Adoption of the rule (H Res 456) that would provide for House floor consideration of the Senate amendment to the bill that would impose restrictions on credit card company lending practices. The rule would provide for a motion to concur in the Senate amendment, with a separate vote on concurring with a section that would bar the Interior Department from prohibiting an individual from possessing a firearm in a national park or wildlife refuge. If either vote failed, the House would not be considered to have acted on the Senate amendment. Adopted 247-180: R 2-174; D 245-6. May 20, 2009.

274. **HR 2352. Small Business Entrepreneurial Programs/Previous Question.** Polis, D-Colo., motion to order the previous question (thus ending debate and possibility of amendment) on adoption of the rule (H Res 457) that would provide for House floor consideration of the bill that would reauthorize Small Business Administration entrepreneurial development programs in fiscal 2010 and 2011. Motion agreed to 244-175: R 0-172; D 244-3. May 20, 2009.

275. **HR 2352. Small Business Entrepreneurial Programs/Rule.** Adoption of the rule (H Res 457) to provide for House floor consideration of a bill that would reauthorize Small Business Administration entrepreneurial development programs in fiscal 2010 and 2011. Adopted 247-175: R 0-173; D 247-2. May 20, 2009.

276. **HR 627. Credit Card Company Regulations/Motion to Concur.** Frank, D-Mass., motion to concur in certain provisions of the Senate amendment to the bill that would impose restrictions on credit card company lending practices. The bill would restrict when companies could increase the annual percentage interest rate retroactively on existing balances, require companies to give at least 45 days' notice before increasing an annual percentage rate or changing an open-ended contract, and restrict companies from computing interest charges based on balances from more than one billing cycle. The term "fixed rate" could be used only for a rate that will not change over a set period. Credit cards could not be issued to consumers under age 21 without a cosigner's acceptance of financial liability or a demonstrated ability to repay the credit extension. The bill's provisions would take effect nine months after enactment. Motion agreed to 361-64: R 113-63; D 248-1. A "yea" was a vote in support of the president's position. May 20, 2009.

277. **HR 627. Credit Card Company Regulations/Motion to Concur.** Frank, D-Mass., motion to concur in section 512 of the Senate amendment to the bill that would impose restrictions on credit card company lending practices. Section 512 would bar the Interior Department from prohibiting an individual from possessing a firearm in national parks or wildlife refuges in compliance with state laws. Motion agreed to (thus clearing the measure for the president) 279-147: R 174-2; D 105-145. May 20, 2009.

	272	273	274	275	276	277
ALABAMA						
1 **Bonner**	Y	N	N	N	N	Y
2 Bright	Y	Y	Y	Y	Y	Y
3 **Rogers**	Y	N	N	N	Y	Y
4 **Aderholt**	Y	N	N	N	Y	Y
5 Griffith	Y	Y	Y	Y	Y	Y
6 **Bachus**	Y	N	?	N	N	Y
7 Davis	Y	Y	Y	Y	Y	Y
ALASKA						
AL **Young**	Y	N	N	N	Y	Y
ARIZONA						
1 Kirkpatrick	Y	Y	Y	Y	Y	Y
2 **Franks**	Y	N	N	N	N	Y
3 **Shadegg**	Y	N	N	N	N	Y
4 Pastor	Y	Y	Y	Y	Y	N
5 Mitchell	Y	Y	Y	Y	Y	Y
6 **Flake**	Y	N	N	N	N	Y
7 Grijalva	Y	N	Y	Y	Y	Y
8 Giffords	Y	Y	Y	Y	Y	Y
ARKANSAS						
1 Berry	Y	Y	Y	Y	Y	Y
2 Snyder	Y	Y	Y	Y	Y	N
3 **Boozman**	Y	N	N	N	Y	Y
4 Ross	Y	Y	Y	Y	Y	Y
CALIFORNIA						
1 Thompson	Y	Y	Y	Y	Y	N
2 **Herger**	Y	N	N	N	N	Y
3 **Lungren**	Y	N	N	N	Y	Y
4 **McClintock**	Y	N	N	N	N	Y
5 Matsui	Y	Y	Y	Y	Y	N
6 Woolsey	Y	Y	Y	Y	Y	N
7 Miller, George	Y	Y	Y	Y	Y	N
8 Pelosi						
9 Lee	Y	Y	Y	Y	Y	N
10 Tauscher	Y	Y	Y	Y	Y	N
11 McNerney	Y	Y	Y	Y	Y	N
12 Speier	?	?	?	?	?	?
13 Stark	?	?	?	?	?	?
14 Eshoo	Y	Y	Y	Y	Y	N
15 Honda	Y	Y	Y	Y	Y	N
16 Lofgren	Y	Y	Y	Y	Y	N
17 Farr	Y	Y	Y	Y	Y	N
18 Cardoza	?	Y	Y	Y	Y	N
19 **Radanovich**	Y	N	N	?	Y	Y
20 Costa	Y	Y	Y	Y	Y	Y
21 **Nunes**	Y	N	N	N	N	Y
22 **McCarthy**	Y	N	N	N	N	Y
23 Capps	+	Y	Y	Y	Y	N
24 **Gallegly**	Y	N	N	N	Y	Y
25 **McKeon**	Y	N	N	N	Y	Y
26 **Dreier**	Y	N	N	N	Y	Y
27 Sherman	Y	Y	Y	Y	Y	N
28 Berman	Y	Y	?	Y	Y	N
29 Schiff	Y	Y	Y	Y	Y	N
30 Waxman	Y	Y	Y	Y	Y	N
31 Becerra	Y	Y	Y	Y	Y	N
32 Vacant						
33 Watson	Y	Y	Y	Y	Y	N
34 Roybal-Allard	Y	Y	Y	Y	Y	N
35 Waters	Y	Y	Y	?	Y	N
36 Harman	Y	Y	Y	Y	Y	N
37 Richardson	Y	Y	Y	Y	Y	N
38 Napolitano	Y	Y	Y	Y	Y	N
39 Sánchez, Linda	?	?	?	?	?	?
40 **Royce**	Y	N	N	N	N	Y
41 **Lewis**	Y	N	N	N	Y	Y
42 **Miller, Gary**	Y	N	N	N	N	Y
43 Baca	Y	Y	Y	Y	Y	Y
44 **Calvert**	Y	N	N	N	Y	Y
45 **Bono Mack**	Y	N	N	N	Y	Y
46 **Rohrabacher**	Y	N	N	N	Y	Y
47 Sanchez, Loretta	Y	Y	Y	Y	Y	N
48 **Campbell**	Y	N	N	N	Y	Y
49 **Issa**	Y	N	N	N	N	Y
50 **Bilbray**	Y	N	N	N	Y	Y
51 Filner	Y	Y	Y	Y	Y	N
52 **Hunter**	Y	N	N	N	Y	Y
53 Davis	Y	Y	Y	Y	Y	N

	272	273	274	275	276	277
COLORADO						
1 DeGette	Y	Y	Y	Y	Y	Y
2 Polis	Y	Y	Y	Y	+	+
3 Salazar	Y	Y	Y	Y	Y	Y
4 Markey	Y	Y	Y	Y	Y	Y
5 **Lamborn**	Y	N	N	N	N	Y
6 **Coffman**	Y	N	N	N	N	Y
7 Perlmutter	Y	Y	Y	Y	Y	Y
CONNECTICUT						
1 Larson	Y	Y	Y	Y	Y	N
2 Courtney	Y	Y	Y	Y	Y	Y
3 DeLauro	Y	Y	Y	Y	Y	N
4 Himes	Y	Y	Y	Y	Y	N
5 Murphy	Y	Y	Y	Y	Y	N
DELAWARE						
AL **Castle**	Y	N	N	N	Y	N
FLORIDA						
1 **Miller**	Y	N	N	N	N	Y
2 Boyd	Y	Y	Y	Y	Y	Y
3 Brown	Y	Y	Y	Y	Y	N
4 **Crenshaw**	Y	N	N	N	Y	Y
5 **Brown-Waite**	Y	N	N	N	Y	Y
6 **Stearns**	Y	N	N	N	Y	Y
7 **Mica**	Y	N	N	N	Y	Y
8 Grayson	Y	Y	Y	Y	Y	N
9 **Bilirakis**	Y	N	N	N	N	Y
10 **Young**	Y	N	N	N	Y	Y
11 Castor	Y	Y	Y	Y	Y	N
12 **Putnam**	Y	N	N	N	Y	Y
13 **Buchanan**	Y	N	P	N	Y	Y
14 **Mack**	Y	N	N	N	N	Y
15 **Posey**	Y	N	N	N	N	Y
16 **Rooney**	Y	N	N	N	Y	Y
17 Meek	Y	Y	Y	Y	Y	Y
18 **Ros-Lehtinen**	Y	N	N	N	Y	Y
19 Wexler	Y	Y	Y	Y	Y	N
20 Wasserman Schultz	Y	Y	Y	Y	Y	N
21 **Diaz-Balart, L.**	Y	N	N	N	Y	Y
22 Klein	Y	Y	+	+	Y	N
23 Hastings	Y	Y	Y	Y	Y	N
24 Kosmas	Y	Y	Y	Y	Y	N
25 **Diaz-Balart, M.**	Y	N	N	N	Y	Y
GEORGIA						
1 **Kingston**	Y	N	N	N	Y	Y
2 Bishop	Y	Y	Y	Y	Y	Y
3 **Westmoreland**	Y	N	N	N	N	Y
4 Johnson	Y	Y	Y	Y	Y	Y
5 Lewis	Y	Y	Y	Y	Y	N
6 **Price**	Y	N	N	N	N	Y
7 **Linder**	Y	N	N	N	N	Y
8 Marshall	Y	Y	Y	Y	Y	Y
9 **Deal**	Y	N	N	N	N	Y
10 **Broun**	Y	N	N	N	N	Y
11 **Gingrey**	Y	N	N	N	N	Y
12 Barrow	Y	Y	Y	Y	Y	Y
13 Scott	Y	Y	Y	Y	Y	N
HAWAII						
1 Abercrombie	Y	Y	Y	Y	Y	N
2 Hirono	Y	Y	Y	Y	Y	N
IDAHO						
1 Minnick	Y	N	N	N	Y	Y
2 **Simpson**	Y	N	N	N	Y	Y
ILLINOIS						
1 Rush	Y	Y	Y	Y	Y	N
2 Jackson	Y	Y	Y	Y	Y	N
3 Lipinski	Y	Y	Y	Y	Y	Y
4 Gutierrez	Y	Y	Y	Y	Y	N
5 Quigley	Y	Y	Y	Y	Y	N
6 **Roskam**	Y	N	N	N	N	Y
7 Davis	Y	Y	Y	Y	Y	N
8 Bean	Y	Y	Y	Y	Y	Y
9 Schakowsky	Y	Y	Y	Y	Y	N
10 **Kirk**	Y	N	N	N	Y	N
11 Halvorson	Y	Y	Y	Y	Y	Y
12 Costello	Y	Y	Y	Y	Y	Y
13 **Biggert**	Y	N	N	N	N	Y
14 Foster	Y	Y	Y	Y	Y	Y
15 Johnson	Y	N	N	N	Y	Y

KEY	Republicans	Democrats			
Y Voted for (yea)		X Paired against		C Voted "present" to avoid possible conflict of interest	
# Paired for		– Announced against			
+ Announced for		P Voted "present"		? Did not vote or otherwise make a position known	
N Voted against (nay)					

	272	273	274	275	276	277
16 **Manzullo**	Y	N	N	N	Y	Y
17 Hare	Y	Y	Y	Y	Y	N
18 **Schock**	Y	N	N	N	Y	Y
19 **Shimkus**	Y	N	N	N	Y	Y
INDIANA						
1 Visclosky	Y	Y	Y	Y	Y	N
2 Donnelly	Y	Y	Y	Y	Y	Y
3 **Souder**	Y	N	N	N	Y	Y
4 **Buyer**	Y	N	N	N	Y	Y
5 **Burton**	Y	N	N	N	N	Y
6 **Pence**	Y	N	N	N	N	Y
7 Carson	Y	Y	Y	Y	Y	N
8 Ellsworth	Y	Y	Y	Y	Y	Y
9 Hill	Y	N	N	N	Y	Y
IOWA						
1 Braley	Y	+	+	+	+	–
2 Loebsack	Y	Y	Y	Y	Y	N
3 Boswell	Y	Y	Y	Y	Y	Y
4 **Latham**	Y	N	N	N	Y	Y
5 **King**	Y	N	N	N	N	Y
KANSAS						
1 **Moran**	Y	N	N	N	Y	Y
2 **Jenkins**	Y	N	N	N	N	Y
3 Moore	Y	Y	Y	Y	Y	N
4 **Tiahrt**	Y	N	N	N	N	Y
KENTUCKY						
1 **Whitfield**	Y	N	N	N	Y	Y
2 **Guthrie**	Y	N	N	N	Y	Y
3 Yarmuth	Y	Y	Y	Y	Y	N
4 **Davis**	Y	N	N	N	N	Y
5 **Rogers**	Y	N	N	N	Y	Y
6 Chandler	Y	Y	Y	Y	Y	Y
LOUISIANA						
1 **Scalise**	Y	N	N	N	N	Y
2 **Cao**	Y	N	N	N	Y	Y
3 Melancon	Y	Y	Y	Y	Y	Y
4 **Fleming**	Y	N	N	N	N	Y
5 **Alexander**	Y	N	N	N	Y	Y
6 **Cassidy**	Y	N	N	N	Y	Y
7 **Boustany**	Y	N	N	N	Y	Y
MAINE						
1 Pingree	Y	Y	Y	Y	Y	N
2 Michaud	Y	Y	Y	Y	Y	Y
MARYLAND						
1 Kratovil	Y	Y	Y	Y	Y	Y
2 Ruppersberger	Y	Y	Y	Y	Y	N
3 Sarbanes	Y	Y	Y	Y	Y	N
4 Edwards	Y	Y	Y	Y	Y	N
5 Hoyer	Y	Y	Y	Y	Y	N
6 **Bartlett**	Y	N	N	N	Y	Y
7 Cummings	Y	Y	Y	Y	Y	N
8 Van Hollen	Y	Y	?	Y	Y	N
MASSACHUSETTS						
1 Olver	Y	Y	Y	Y	Y	N
2 Neal	Y	Y	Y	Y	Y	N
3 McGovern	Y	Y	Y	Y	Y	N
4 Frank	Y	Y	Y	Y	Y	N
5 Tsongas	Y	Y	Y	Y	Y	N
6 Tierney	Y	Y	Y	Y	Y	N
7 Markey	Y	Y	Y	Y	Y	N
8 Capuano	Y	Y	Y	Y	Y	N
9 Lynch	Y	Y	Y	Y	Y	N
10 Delahunt	?	Y	Y	Y	Y	N
MICHIGAN						
1 Stupak	Y	Y	Y	Y	Y	Y
2 **Hoekstra**	Y	N	N	N	Y	Y
3 **Ehlers**	Y	N	N	N	Y	Y
4 **Camp**	Y	N	N	N	Y	Y
5 Kildee	Y	Y	Y	Y	Y	N
6 **Upton**	Y	N	N	N	Y	Y
7 Schauer	Y	Y	Y	Y	Y	Y
8 **Rogers**	Y	N	N	N	Y	Y
9 Peters	Y	Y	N	Y	Y	N
10 **Miller**	Y	N	N	N	Y	Y
11 **McCotter**	Y	N	N	N	Y	Y
12 Levin	Y	Y	Y	Y	Y	N
13 Kilpatrick	Y	Y	Y	Y	Y	N
14 Conyers	Y	Y	Y	Y	Y	N
15 Dingell	Y	Y	Y	Y	Y	Y
MINNESOTA						
1 Walz	Y	Y	Y	Y	Y	Y
2 **Kline**	Y	N	N	N	N	Y
3 **Paulsen**	Y	N	N	N	Y	Y
4 McCollum	Y	Y	Y	Y	Y	N

	272	273	274	275	276	277
5 Ellison	Y	Y	Y	Y	Y	N
6 **Bachmann**	Y	?	?	?	?	?
7 Peterson	Y	Y	Y	Y	Y	Y
8 Oberstar	Y	Y	Y	Y	Y	Y
MISSISSIPPI						
1 Childers	Y	Y	Y	Y	Y	Y
2 Thompson	Y	Y	Y	Y	Y	Y
3 **Harper**	Y	N	N	N	Y	Y
4 Taylor	Y	Y	Y	Y	Y	Y
MISSOURI						
1 Clay	Y	Y	Y	Y	Y	N
2 **Akin**	Y	N	N	N	Y	Y
3 Carnahan	Y	Y	Y	Y	Y	N
4 Skelton	Y	Y	Y	Y	Y	Y
5 Cleaver	Y	Y	Y	Y	Y	N
6 **Graves**	Y	N	N	N	Y	Y
7 **Blunt**	Y	N	N	N	Y	Y
8 **Emerson**	Y	N	N	N	Y	Y
9 **Luetkemeyer**	Y	N	N	N	Y	Y
MONTANA						
AL **Rehberg**	Y	N	N	N	Y	Y
NEBRASKA						
1 **Fortenberry**	Y	N	N	N	Y	Y
2 **Terry**	Y	N	N	N	Y	Y
3 **Smith**	Y	N	N	N	N	Y
NEVADA						
1 Berkley	Y	Y	?	Y	Y	Y
2 **Heller**	?	N	N	N	N	Y
3 Titus	Y	Y	Y	Y	Y	Y
NEW HAMPSHIRE						
1 Shea-Porter	Y	Y	Y	Y	Y	N
2 Hodes	Y	Y	Y	Y	Y	Y
NEW JERSEY						
1 Andrews	Y	Y	Y	Y	Y	N
2 **LoBiondo**	Y	N	N	N	Y	Y
3 Adler	Y	Y	Y	Y	Y	Y
4 **Smith**	Y	N	N	N	Y	Y
5 **Garrett**	Y	N	N	N	N	Y
6 Pallone	Y	Y	Y	Y	Y	Y
7 **Lance**	Y	N	N	N	Y	Y
8 Pascrell	Y	Y	Y	Y	Y	N
9 Rothman	Y	Y	Y	Y	Y	N
10 Payne	Y	Y	Y	Y	Y	N
11 **Frelinghuysen**	Y	N	N	N	Y	Y
12 Holt	Y	Y	Y	Y	Y	N
13 Sires	Y	Y	Y	Y	Y	Y
NEW MEXICO						
1 Heinrich	Y	Y	Y	Y	Y	Y
2 Teague	Y	Y	Y	Y	Y	Y
3 Lujan	Y	Y	Y	Y	Y	N
NEW YORK						
1 Bishop	Y	Y	Y	Y	Y	N
2 Israel	Y	Y	Y	Y	Y	N
3 **King**	Y	N	N	N	Y	Y
4 McCarthy	Y	N	Y	Y	Y	N
5 Ackerman	Y	Y	Y	Y	Y	N
6 Meeks	Y	Y	Y	Y	Y	Y
7 Crowley	Y	Y	Y	Y	Y	N
8 Nadler	Y	Y	Y	Y	Y	N
9 Weiner	Y	Y	Y	Y	Y	N
10 Towns	Y	Y	Y	Y	Y	N
11 Clarke	Y	Y	Y	Y	Y	N
12 Velázquez	?	Y	Y	Y	Y	N
13 McMahon	Y	Y	Y	Y	Y	N
14 Maloney	Y	Y	Y	Y	Y	N
15 Rangel	Y	Y	Y	Y	Y	N
16 Serrano	Y	Y	Y	Y	Y	N
17 Engel	Y	Y	Y	Y	Y	N
18 Lowey	Y	Y	Y	Y	Y	N
19 Hall	Y	Y	Y	Y	Y	N
20 Murphy	Y	Y	Y	Y	Y	Y
21 Tonko	Y	Y	Y	Y	Y	N
22 Hinchey	Y	Y	Y	Y	Y	Y
23 **McHugh**	Y	N	N	N	Y	Y
24 Arcuri	Y	Y	Y	Y	Y	Y
25 Maffei	Y	Y	Y	Y	Y	N
26 **Lee**	Y	N	N	N	Y	Y
27 Higgins	Y	Y	Y	Y	Y	Y
28 Slaughter	Y	Y	Y	Y	Y	N
29 Massa	Y	Y	Y	Y	Y	Y
NORTH CAROLINA						
1 Butterfield	Y	Y	Y	Y	Y	N
2 Etheridge	Y	Y	Y	Y	Y	Y
3 **Jones**	Y	Y	N	N	Y	Y
4 Price	Y	Y	Y	Y	Y	N

	272	273	274	275	276	277
5 **Foxx**	Y	N	N	N	N	Y
6 **Coble**	Y	N	N	N	N	Y
7 McIntyre	Y	Y	Y	Y	Y	Y
8 Kissell	Y	Y	Y	Y	Y	Y
9 **Myrick**	Y	N	N	N	N	Y
10 **McHenry**	Y	N	N	N	N	Y
11 Shuler	Y	Y	Y	Y	Y	Y
12 Watt	Y	Y	Y	Y	Y	N
13 Miller	Y	Y	Y	Y	Y	N
NORTH DAKOTA						
AL Pomeroy	Y	Y	Y	Y	Y	Y
OHIO						
1 Driehaus	Y	Y	Y	Y	Y	Y
2 **Schmidt**	Y	N	N	N	Y	Y
3 **Turner**	Y	N	N	N	Y	Y
4 **Jordan**	Y	N	N	N	N	Y
5 **Latta**	Y	N	N	N	N	Y
6 Wilson	Y	Y	Y	Y	Y	Y
7 **Austria**	Y	N	N	N	Y	Y
8 **Boehner**	Y	N	N	N	N	Y
9 Kaptur	Y	Y	Y	Y	Y	N
10 Kucinich	Y	Y	Y	Y	Y	N
11 Fudge	Y	Y	Y	Y	Y	N
12 **Tiberi**	Y	N	N	N	Y	Y
13 Sutton	Y	Y	Y	Y	Y	N
14 **LaTourette**	Y	N	N	N	Y	Y
15 Kilroy	Y	Y	Y	Y	Y	N
16 Boccieri	Y	Y	Y	Y	Y	Y
17 Ryan	Y	Y	Y	Y	Y	Y
18 Space	Y	Y	Y	Y	Y	Y
OKLAHOMA						
1 **Sullivan**	Y	N	N	N	N	Y
2 Boren	Y	Y	Y	Y	Y	Y
3 **Lucas**	Y	N	N	N	N	Y
4 **Cole**	Y	N	N	N	Y	Y
5 **Fallin**	Y	N	N	N	Y	Y
OREGON						
1 Wu	Y	Y	Y	Y	Y	N
2 **Walden**	Y	N	N	N	Y	Y
3 Blumenauer	Y	Y	Y	Y	Y	N
4 DeFazio	Y	Y	Y	Y	Y	Y
5 Schrader	Y	Y	Y	Y	Y	Y
PENNSYLVANIA						
1 Brady	?	Y	Y	Y	Y	N
2 Fattah	Y	Y	Y	Y	Y	N
3 Dahlkemper	Y	Y	Y	Y	Y	Y
4 Altmire	Y	N	Y	Y	Y	Y
5 **Thompson**	Y	N	N	N	N	Y
6 **Gerlach**	Y	N	N	N	Y	Y
7 Sestak	Y	Y	Y	Y	Y	N
8 Murphy, P.	Y	Y	Y	Y	Y	Y
9 **Shuster**	Y	N	N	N	Y	Y
10 Carney	Y	Y	Y	Y	Y	Y
11 Kanjorski	Y	Y	Y	Y	Y	Y
12 Murtha	Y	Y	Y	Y	Y	Y
13 Schwartz	Y	Y	Y	Y	Y	N
14 Doyle	Y	Y	Y	Y	Y	N
15 **Dent**	Y	N	N	N	Y	Y
16 **Pitts**	Y	N	N	N	Y	Y
17 Holden	Y	Y	Y	Y	Y	Y
18 **Murphy, T.**	Y	N	N	N	Y	Y
19 **Platts**	Y	N	N	N	Y	Y
RHODE ISLAND						
1 Kennedy	Y	Y	Y	Y	Y	Y
2 Langevin	Y	Y	Y	Y	Y	N
SOUTH CAROLINA						
1 **Brown**	Y	N	N	N	Y	Y
2 **Wilson**	Y	N	N	N	Y	Y
3 **Barrett**	+	?	?	?	?	?
4 **Inglis**	Y	N	N	N	N	Y
5 Spratt	Y	Y	Y	Y	Y	Y
6 Clyburn	Y	Y	Y	Y	Y	N
SOUTH DAKOTA						
AL Herseth Sandlin	Y	Y	Y	Y	N	Y
TENNESSEE						
1 **Roe**	Y	N	N	N	Y	Y
2 **Duncan**	Y	N	N	N	Y	Y
3 **Wamp**	Y	N	N	N	Y	Y
4 Davis	?	Y	Y	Y	Y	Y
5 Cooper	Y	Y	Y	Y	Y	N
6 Gordon	Y	Y	Y	Y	Y	Y
7 **Blackburn**	Y	N	N	N	N	Y
8 Tanner	Y	Y	Y	Y	Y	Y
9 Cohen	Y	Y	Y	Y	Y	N

	272	273	274	275	276	277
TEXAS						
1 **Gohmert**	Y	N	N	N	Y	Y
2 **Poe**	Y	N	N	N	N	Y
3 **Johnson, S.**	Y	N	N	N	N	Y
4 **Hall**	Y	N	N	N	Y	Y
5 **Hensarling**	Y	N	N	N	N	Y
6 **Barton**	Y	N	?	?	Y	Y
7 **Culberson**	Y	N	N	N	Y	Y
8 **Brady**	Y	N	N	N	N	Y
9 Green, A.	Y	Y	Y	Y	Y	N
10 **McCaul**	Y	N	N	N	Y	Y
11 **Conaway**	Y	N	N	N	N	Y
12 **Granger**	Y	N	N	N	Y	Y
13 **Thornberry**	Y	N	N	N	N	Y
14 **Paul**	Y	N	N	N	N	Y
15 Hinojosa	Y	Y	Y	Y	+	N
16 Reyes	Y	Y	Y	Y	Y	Y
17 Edwards	Y	Y	Y	Y	Y	Y
18 Jackson Lee	Y	Y	Y	Y	Y	N
19 **Neugebauer**	Y	N	N	N	N	Y
20 Gonzalez	Y	Y	Y	Y	Y	N
21 **Smith**	Y	N	N	N	Y	Y
22 **Olson**	Y	N	N	N	N	Y
23 Rodriguez	Y	Y	Y	Y	Y	Y
24 **Marchant**	Y	N	N	N	N	Y
25 Doggett	Y	Y	Y	Y	Y	N
26 **Burgess**	Y	N	N	N	Y	Y
27 Ortiz	Y	Y	Y	Y	Y	Y
28 Cuellar	Y	Y	Y	Y	Y	Y
29 Green, G.	Y	Y	Y	Y	Y	Y
30 Johnson, E.	Y	Y	Y	Y	Y	N
31 **Carter**	Y	N	N	N	N	Y
32 **Sessions**	Y	N	N	N	N	Y
UTAH						
1 **Bishop**	Y	N	?	?	N	Y
2 Matheson	Y	Y	Y	Y	Y	Y
3 **Chaffetz**	Y	N	N	N	N	Y
VERMONT						
AL Welch	Y	Y	Y	Y	Y	Y
VIRGINIA						
1 **Wittman**	Y	N	N	N	Y	Y
2 Nye	Y	Y	Y	Y	Y	Y
3 Scott	Y	Y	Y	Y	Y	N
4 **Forbes**	Y	N	N	N	Y	Y
5 Perriello	Y	Y	Y	Y	Y	Y
6 **Goodlatte**	Y	N	N	N	N	Y
7 **Cantor**	Y	N	N	N	N	Y
8 Moran	Y	Y	Y	Y	Y	N
9 Boucher	Y	Y	Y	Y	Y	Y
10 **Wolf**	Y	N	N	N	Y	Y
11 Connolly	Y	Y	Y	Y	Y	N
WASHINGTON						
1 Inslee	Y	Y	Y	Y	Y	N
2 Larsen	Y	Y	Y	Y	Y	N
3 Baird	Y	Y	Y	Y	Y	N
4 **Hastings**	Y	N	N	N	N	Y
5 **McMorris Rodgers**	Y	N	N	N	N	Y
6 Dicks	Y	Y	Y	Y	Y	N
7 McDermott	Y	Y	Y	Y	Y	N
8 **Reichert**	Y	N	N	N	Y	Y
9 Smith	Y	Y	Y	Y	Y	Y
WEST VIRGINIA						
1 Mollohan	Y	Y	Y	Y	Y	Y
2 **Capito**	Y	N	N	N	Y	Y
3 Rahall	Y	Y	Y	Y	Y	Y
WISCONSIN						
1 **Ryan**	Y	N	N	N	N	Y
2 Baldwin	Y	Y	Y	Y	Y	N
3 Kind	Y	Y	Y	Y	Y	Y
4 Moore	Y	Y	Y	Y	Y	N
5 **Sensenbrenner**	Y	N	N	N	Y	Y
6 **Petri**	Y	N	N	N	Y	Y
7 Obey	Y	Y	Y	Y	Y	Y
8 Kagen	Y	Y	Y	Y	Y	Y
WYOMING						
AL **Lummis**	Y	N	N	N	Y	Y
DELEGATES						
Faleomavaega (A.S.)						
Norton (D.C.)						
Bordallo (Guam)						
Sablan (N. Marianas)						
Pierluisi (P.R.)						
Christensen (V.I.)						

IN THE HOUSE | By Vote Number

278. **H Res 297. National Missing Children's Day/Adoption.** Tonko, D-N.Y., motion to suspend the rules and adopt the resolution that would recognize National Missing Children's Day and encourage Americans to raise public awareness about the issue of missing children. Motion agreed to 423-0: R 175-0; D 248-0. A two-thirds majority of those present and voting (282 in this case) is required for adoption under suspension of the rules. May 20, 2009.

279. **HR 2352. Small Business Entrepreneurial Programs/Rural Entrepreneurship Council.** Kratovil, D-Md., amendment that would require the Small Business Administration to create an advisory council made up of government officials and volunteers from the academic, small-business, agriculture and technology fields. The council would provide a report to Congress on rural entrepreneurship as well as ongoing advice and recommendations on policies to foster entrepreneurship in rural communities. Adopted in Committee of the Whole 427-0: R 173-0; D 254-0. May 20, 2009.

280. **HR 2352. Small Business Entrepreneurial Programs/Recommit.** Capito, R-W.Va., motion to recommit the bill to the House Small Business Committee with instructions that it be reported back immediately with language that would require small-business development centers to provide information and technical assistance to any small-business owner whose costs increased as a result of a tax on carbon emissions. Motion agreed to 385-41: R 175-0; D 210-41. May 20, 2009.

281. **HR 2352. Small Business Entrepreneurial Programs/Passage.** Passage of the bill that would reauthorize the Small Business Administration's entrepreneurial development programs. It would authorize funding for fiscal 2010-11 for small-business development centers, as well as funds to establish business center programs for veterans and women, to support distance learning projects and for other small-business programs. Passed 406-15: R 159-15; D 247-0. May 20, 2009.

282. **H Con Res 133. Adjournment/Adoption.** Adoption of the concurrent resolution that would provide for adjournment of the House until 2 p.m., Tuesday, June 2, 2009, and the Senate until 12 p.m., Monday, June 1, 2009. Adopted 237-184: R 5-169; D 232-15. May 21, 2009.

283. **Review of House Speaker's Statements/Motion to Table.** Hoyer, D-Md., motion to table (kill) the Bishop, R-Utah, appeal of the ruling of the chair that the draft resolution does not constitute a point of privilege under Rule IX of the House. The draft resolution would require the House to establish a Select Intelligence Committee select subcommittee to review and verify the accuracy of House Speaker Nancy Pelosi's public statements regarding the CIA deceiving Congress and report to the House on its findings no later than 60 days after the adoption of the resolution. The committee would be made up of four members of the full committee, two appointed by the chairman and two appointed by the ranking minority member. Motion agreed to 252-172: R 2-172; D 250-0. May 21, 2009.

284. **HR 915. FAA Reauthorization/Previous Question.** Arcuri, D-N.Y., motion to order the previous question (thus ending debate and possibility of amendment) on adoption of the rule (H Res 464) that would provide for House floor consideration of a bill that would reauthorize the Federal Aviation Administration (FAA). Motion agreed to 246-175: R 0-172; D 246-3. May 21, 2009.

	278	279	280	281	282	283	284
ALABAMA							
1 **Bonner**	Y	Y	Y	Y	N	N	N
2 Bright	Y	Y	Y	Y	Y	Y	Y
3 **Rogers**	Y	Y	Y	Y	N	N	N
4 **Aderholt**	Y	Y	Y	Y	N	N	N
5 Griffith	Y	Y	Y	Y	Y	Y	Y
6 **Bachus**	Y	Y	Y	Y	N	N	N
7 Davis	Y	Y	Y	Y	Y	Y	Y
ALASKA							
AL **Young**	Y	Y	Y	N	N	N	N
ARIZONA							
1 Kirkpatrick	Y	Y	Y	Y	Y	Y	Y
2 **Franks**	Y	Y	Y	N	N	N	N
3 **Shadegg**	Y	Y	Y	N	N	N	N
4 Pastor	Y	Y	Y	Y	Y	Y	Y
5 Mitchell	Y	Y	Y	Y	Y	Y	Y
6 **Flake**	Y	Y	Y	N	?	?	?
7 Grijalva	Y	Y	Y	Y	Y	Y	Y
8 Giffords	Y	Y	Y	Y	Y	Y	Y
ARKANSAS							
1 Berry	Y	Y	Y	Y	Y	Y	Y
2 Snyder	Y	Y	Y	Y	Y	Y	Y
3 **Boozman**	Y	Y	Y	Y	N	N	N
4 Ross	Y	Y	Y	Y	Y	Y	Y
CALIFORNIA							
1 Thompson	Y	Y	Y	Y	Y	Y	Y
2 **Herger**	Y	Y	Y	N	N	N	N
3 **Lungren**	Y	Y	Y	N	N	N	N
4 **McClintock**	Y	Y	Y	N	N	N	N
5 Matsui	Y	N	Y	Y	Y	Y	Y
6 Woolsey	Y	N	Y	Y	Y	Y	Y
7 Miller, George	Y	Y	Y	Y	Y	Y	Y
8 Pelosi							
9 Lee	Y	Y	N	Y	Y	Y	Y
10 Tauscher	Y	Y	Y	Y	Y	Y	Y
11 McNerney	Y	Y	Y	Y	Y	Y	Y
12 Speier	?	?	?	?	?	?	?
13 Stark	?	?	?	?	?	?	?
14 Eshoo	Y	Y	N	Y	Y	Y	Y
15 Honda	Y	N	Y	Y	Y	Y	Y
16 Lofgren	Y	N	Y	Y	Y	Y	Y
17 Farr	Y	Y	N	Y	Y	Y	Y
18 Cardoza	Y	Y	Y	Y	Y	Y	Y
19 **Radanovich**	Y	Y	Y	Y	N	N	N
20 Costa	Y	Y	Y	Y	Y	Y	Y
21 **Nunes**	Y	Y	Y	Y	N	N	N
22 **McCarthy**	Y	Y	Y	Y	N	N	N
23 Capps	Y	Y	Y	Y	Y	Y	Y
24 **Gallegly**	Y	Y	Y	Y	N	N	N
25 **McKeon**	Y	Y	Y	Y	N	N	N
26 **Dreier**	Y	Y	Y	N	N	N	N
27 Sherman	Y	Y	N	Y	Y	Y	Y
28 Berman	Y	Y	Y	Y	Y	Y	Y
29 Schiff	Y	Y	Y	Y	Y	Y	Y
30 Waxman	Y	Y	Y	Y	Y	Y	Y
31 Becerra	Y	+	Y	Y	Y	Y	Y
32 Vacant							
33 Watson	Y	Y	Y	Y	Y	Y	Y
34 Roybal-Allard	Y	Y	Y	Y	Y	Y	Y
35 Waters	Y	N	Y	Y	Y	Y	Y
36 Harman	Y	N	Y	Y	Y	Y	Y
37 Richardson	Y	Y	Y	Y	Y	Y	Y
38 Napolitano	Y	Y	Y	Y	Y	Y	Y
39 Sánchez, Linda	?	?	?	?	?	?	?
40 **Royce**	Y	Y	Y	N	N	N	N
41 **Lewis**	Y	Y	Y	Y	N	N	N
42 **Miller, Gary**	Y	Y	Y	Y	N	N	N
43 Baca	Y	Y	Y	Y	Y	Y	Y
44 **Calvert**	Y	Y	Y	Y	N	N	N
45 **Bono Mack**	Y	Y	Y	Y	N	N	N
46 **Rohrabacher**	Y	Y	Y	Y	N	N	N
47 Sanchez, Loretta	Y	Y	Y	Y	Y	Y	Y
48 **Campbell**	Y	Y	Y	N	N	N	N
49 **Issa**	Y	Y	Y	N	N	N	N
50 **Bilbray**	Y	Y	Y	Y	N	N	N
51 Filner	Y	Y	Y	Y	Y	Y	Y
52 **Hunter**	Y	Y	Y	Y	N	N	N
53 Davis	Y	Y	Y	Y	Y	Y	Y

	278	279	280	281	282	283	284
COLORADO							
1 DeGette	Y	Y	Y	Y	Y	Y	Y
2 Polis	+	Y	N	Y	Y	Y	Y
3 Salazar	Y	Y	Y	Y	Y	Y	Y
4 Markey	Y	Y	Y	Y	?	?	?
5 **Lamborn**	Y	Y	Y	N	N	N	N
6 **Coffman**	Y	Y	Y	N	N	N	N
7 Perlmutter	Y	Y	Y	Y	Y	Y	Y
CONNECTICUT							
1 Larson	Y	Y	Y	Y	Y	Y	Y
2 Courtney	Y	Y	Y	Y	Y	Y	Y
3 DeLauro	Y	Y	Y	Y	Y	Y	Y
4 Himes	Y	Y	Y	Y	Y	Y	Y
5 Murphy	Y	Y	Y	Y	Y	Y	Y
DELAWARE							
AL Castle	Y	Y	Y	N	N	N	N
FLORIDA							
1 **Miller**	Y	Y	Y	N	N	N	N
2 Boyd	Y	Y	Y	?	Y	Y	Y
3 Brown	Y	Y	Y	Y	Y	Y	Y
4 **Crenshaw**	Y	Y	Y	N	N	N	N
5 **Brown-Waite**	Y	Y	Y	Y	N	N	N
6 **Stearns**	Y	Y	Y	Y	N	N	N
7 **Mica**	Y	Y	Y	N	N	N	N
8 Grayson	Y	Y	Y	Y	Y	Y	Y
9 **Bilirakis**	Y	Y	Y	Y	N	N	N
10 **Young**	Y	Y	Y	Y	N	N	N
11 Castor	Y	?	Y	Y	Y	Y	Y
12 **Putnam**	Y	Y	Y	Y	N	N	N
13 **Buchanan**	Y	Y	Y	Y	N	N	N
14 **Mack**	Y	Y	Y	N	N	N	N
15 **Posey**	Y	Y	Y	N	N	N	N
16 **Rooney**	Y	Y	Y	N	N	N	–
17 Meek	Y	Y	Y	Y	Y	Y	Y
18 **Ros-Lehtinen**	Y	Y	Y	N	N	N	N
19 Wexler	Y	Y	Y	Y	Y	Y	Y
20 Wasserman Schultz	Y	Y	Y	Y	Y	Y	Y
21 **Diaz-Balart, L.**	Y	Y	Y	N	N	N	N
22 Klein	Y	Y	?	Y	Y	Y	Y
23 Hastings	Y	Y	Y	Y	Y	Y	Y
24 Kosmas	Y	Y	Y	Y	Y	Y	Y
25 **Diaz-Balart, M.**	Y	Y	Y	N	N	N	N
GEORGIA							
1 **Kingston**	Y	Y	Y	N	N	N	N
2 Bishop	Y	N	Y	Y	Y	Y	Y
3 **Westmoreland**	Y	Y	Y	N	N	N	N
4 Johnson	Y	N	?	Y	Y	Y	Y
5 Lewis	Y	N	Y	Y	Y	Y	Y
6 **Price**	Y	Y	Y	N	N	N	N
7 **Linder**	Y	?	Y	N	N	N	N
8 Marshall	Y	Y	Y	Y	Y	Y	Y
9 **Deal**	Y	Y	Y	N	N	N	N
10 **Broun**	Y	Y	N	N	N	N	N
11 **Gingrey**	Y	Y	Y	N	N	N	N
12 Barrow	Y	Y	Y	Y	Y	Y	Y
13 Scott	Y	Y	Y	Y	Y	Y	Y
HAWAII							
1 Abercrombie	Y	Y	N	Y	Y	Y	Y
2 Hirono	Y	Y	N	Y	Y	Y	Y
IDAHO							
1 Minnick	Y	Y	Y	N	N	Y	N
2 **Simpson**	Y	Y	Y	N	N	N	N
ILLINOIS							
1 Rush	?	Y	Y	Y	Y	Y	Y
2 Jackson	Y	Y	Y	Y	Y	Y	Y
3 Lipinski	Y	Y	Y	Y	Y	Y	Y
4 Gutierrez	Y	Y	Y	Y	Y	Y	Y
5 Quigley	Y	Y	Y	Y	Y	Y	Y
6 **Roskam**	Y	Y	Y	Y	N	N	N
7 Davis	Y	Y	Y	Y	Y	Y	Y
8 Bean	Y	Y	Y	Y	?	Y	Y
9 Schakowsky	Y	Y	Y	Y	Y	Y	Y
10 **Kirk**	Y	Y	Y	N	N	N	N
11 Halvorson	Y	Y	Y	Y	Y	Y	Y
12 Costello	Y	Y	Y	Y	Y	Y	Y
13 **Biggert**	Y	Y	Y	N	N	N	N
14 Foster	Y	Y	Y	Y	Y	Y	Y
15 **Johnson**	Y	Y	Y	N	N	N	N

KEY   **Republicans**   Democrats

Y Voted for (yea)
\# Paired for
\+ Announced for
N Voted against (nay)

X Paired against
– Announced against
P Voted "present"

C Voted "present" to avoid possible conflict of interest
? Did not vote or otherwise make a position known

	278	279	280	281	282	283	284
16 **Manzullo**	Y	Y	Y	Y	N	N	N
17 Hare	Y	Y	Y	Y	Y	Y	Y
18 **Schock**	Y	Y	Y	Y	N	N	N
19 **Shimkus**	Y	Y	Y	Y	N	N	N
INDIANA							
1 Visclosky	Y	Y	Y	Y	Y	Y	Y
2 Donnelly	Y	Y	Y	Y	N	Y	Y
3 **Souder**	Y	Y	Y	Y	N	N	N
4 **Buyer**	Y	Y	Y	Y	N	N	N
5 **Burton**	Y	Y	Y	Y	N	N	N
6 **Pence**	Y	Y	Y	Y	N	N	N
7 Carson	Y	Y	Y	Y	Y	Y	Y
8 Ellsworth	Y	Y	Y	Y	N	Y	Y
9 Hill	Y	Y	Y	Y	Y	Y	N
IOWA							
1 Braley	+	+	+	+	Y	Y	Y
2 Loebsack	Y	Y	Y	Y	Y	Y	Y
3 Boswell	Y	Y	Y	Y	Y	Y	Y
4 **Latham**	Y	Y	Y	Y	N	N	N
5 **King**	Y	Y	Y	?	N	N	N
KANSAS							
1 **Moran**	Y	Y	Y	N	N	N	N
2 **Jenkins**	Y	Y	Y	Y	N	N	N
3 Moore	Y	Y	Y	Y	Y	Y	Y
4 **Tiahrt**	Y	Y	Y	Y	N	N	N
KENTUCKY							
1 **Whitfield**	Y	Y	Y	Y	N	N	N
2 **Guthrie**	Y	Y	Y	Y	N	N	N
3 Yarmuth	Y	Y	Y	Y	Y	Y	Y
4 **Davis**	Y	Y	Y	Y	N	N	N
5 **Rogers**	Y	Y	Y	Y	N	N	N
6 Chandler	Y	Y	Y	Y	Y	Y	Y
LOUISIANA							
1 **Scalise**	Y	Y	Y	Y	N	N	–
2 **Cao**	Y	Y	Y	Y	N	N	N
3 Melancon	Y	Y	Y	Y	Y	Y	Y
4 **Fleming**	Y	Y	Y	Y	N	N	N
5 **Alexander**	Y	Y	Y	Y	N	N	N
6 **Cassidy**	Y	Y	Y	Y	N	N	N
7 **Boustany**	Y	Y	Y	Y	N	N	N
MAINE							
1 Pingree	Y	Y	Y	Y	Y	Y	Y
2 Michaud	Y	Y	Y	Y	Y	Y	Y
MARYLAND							
1 Kratovil	Y	Y	Y	Y	N	Y	Y
2 Ruppersberger	Y	Y	Y	Y	Y	Y	Y
3 Sarbanes	Y	Y	Y	Y	Y	Y	Y
4 Edwards	Y	Y	N	Y	Y	Y	Y
5 Hoyer	Y	Y	Y	Y	Y	Y	Y
6 **Bartlett**	Y	Y	Y	Y	N	N	N
7 Cummings	Y	Y	Y	Y	Y	Y	Y
8 Van Hollen	Y	Y	Y	Y	Y	Y	Y
MASSACHUSETTS							
1 Olver	Y	Y	N	Y	Y	Y	Y
2 Neal	Y	Y	Y	Y	Y	Y	Y
3 McGovern	Y	Y	N	Y	Y	Y	Y
4 Frank	Y	Y	N	Y	Y	Y	Y
5 Tsongas	Y	Y	N	Y	Y	Y	Y
6 Tierney	Y	Y	N	Y	Y	Y	Y
7 Markey	Y	Y	N	Y	Y	Y	Y
8 Capuano	Y	Y	N	Y	Y	Y	Y
9 Lynch	Y	Y	Y	Y	Y	Y	Y
10 Delahunt	Y	Y	Y	Y	Y	Y	Y
MICHIGAN							
1 Stupak	Y	Y	Y	Y	Y	Y	Y
2 **Hoekstra**	Y	Y	Y	Y	N	N	N
3 **Ehlers**	Y	Y	Y	Y	Y	N	N
4 **Camp**	Y	Y	Y	Y	N	N	N
5 Kildee	Y	Y	Y	Y	Y	Y	Y
6 **Upton**	Y	Y	Y	Y	N	N	N
7 Schauer	Y	Y	Y	Y	Y	Y	Y
8 **Rogers**	Y	Y	Y	Y	N	N	N
9 Peters	Y	Y	Y	Y	Y	Y	Y
10 **Miller**	Y	Y	Y	Y	N	N	N
11 **McCotter**	Y	Y	Y	Y	N	N	N
12 Levin	Y	Y	Y	Y	Y	Y	Y
13 Kilpatrick	Y	Y	Y	Y	Y	Y	Y
14 Conyers	Y	Y	N	?	Y	Y	Y
15 Dingell	Y	Y	N	Y	Y	Y	Y
MINNESOTA							
1 Walz	Y	Y	Y	Y	Y	Y	Y
2 **Kline**	Y	Y	Y	Y	N	N	N
3 **Paulsen**	Y	Y	Y	Y	N	N	N
4 McCollum	Y	Y	Y	Y	Y	Y	Y

	278	279	280	281	282	283	284
5 Ellison	Y	Y	Y	Y	Y	Y	Y
6 **Bachmann**	?	?	?	?	?	?	?
7 Peterson	Y	Y	Y	Y	Y	Y	Y
8 Oberstar	Y	Y	Y	Y	Y	Y	Y
MISSISSIPPI							
1 Childers	Y	Y	Y	Y	N	Y	Y
2 Thompson	Y	Y	Y	Y	Y	Y	Y
3 **Harper**	Y	Y	Y	?	N	N	N
4 Taylor	Y	Y	Y	Y	Y	Y	Y
MISSOURI							
1 Clay	Y	Y	N	Y	Y	Y	Y
2 **Akin**	Y	Y	Y	Y	N	N	N
3 Carnahan	Y	Y	Y	Y	Y	Y	Y
4 Skelton	Y	Y	Y	Y	Y	Y	Y
5 Cleaver	Y	Y	N	Y	Y	Y	Y
6 **Graves**	Y	Y	Y	Y	N	N	N
7 **Blunt**	Y	Y	Y	Y	N	N	N
8 **Emerson**	Y	Y	Y	Y	N	N	N
9 **Luetkemeyer**	Y	Y	Y	Y	N	N	N
MONTANA							
AL **Rehberg**	Y	Y	Y	Y	N	N	N
NEBRASKA							
1 **Fortenberry**	Y	Y	Y	Y	N	N	N
2 **Terry**	Y	Y	Y	Y	N	N	N
3 **Smith**	Y	Y	Y	Y	N	N	N
NEVADA							
1 Berkley	Y	Y	Y	Y	Y	Y	Y
2 **Heller**	Y	Y	Y	Y	N	N	N
3 Titus	Y	Y	Y	Y	Y	Y	Y
NEW HAMPSHIRE							
1 Shea-Porter	Y	Y	Y	Y	Y	Y	Y
2 Hodes	Y	Y	Y	Y	Y	Y	Y
NEW JERSEY							
1 Andrews	Y	Y	Y	Y	Y	Y	Y
2 **LoBiondo**	Y	Y	Y	Y	N	N	N
3 Adler	Y	Y	Y	Y	N	Y	Y
4 **Smith**	Y	Y	Y	Y	N	N	N
5 **Garrett**	Y	Y	Y	Y	N	N	N
6 Pallone	Y	Y	Y	Y	Y	Y	Y
7 **Lance**	Y	Y	Y	Y	N	N	N
8 Pascrell	Y	Y	Y	Y	Y	Y	Y
9 Rothman	Y	Y	Y	Y	Y	Y	Y
10 Payne	Y	Y	Y	Y	Y	Y	Y
11 **Frelinghuysen**	?	Y	Y	Y	N	N	N
12 Holt	Y	Y	N	Y	Y	Y	Y
13 Sires	Y	Y	Y	Y	Y	Y	Y
NEW MEXICO							
1 Heinrich	Y	Y	Y	Y	Y	Y	Y
2 Teague	Y	Y	Y	Y	Y	Y	Y
3 Lujan	Y	Y	Y	Y	Y	Y	Y
NEW YORK							
1 Bishop	Y	Y	Y	Y	Y	Y	Y
2 Israel	Y	Y	Y	Y	Y	Y	Y
3 **King**	Y	Y	Y	Y	N	N	N
4 McCarthy	Y	Y	Y	Y	Y	Y	Y
5 Ackerman	Y	Y	Y	Y	Y	Y	Y
6 Meeks	Y	Y	Y	Y	Y	Y	Y
7 Crowley	Y	Y	N	Y	Y	Y	Y
8 Nadler	Y	Y	Y	Y	Y	Y	Y
9 Weiner	Y	Y	Y	Y	Y	Y	Y
10 Towns	Y	Y	N	Y	Y	Y	Y
11 Clarke	Y	Y	N	Y	Y	Y	Y
12 Velázquez	Y	Y	Y	Y	Y	Y	Y
13 McMahon	Y	Y	Y	Y	Y	Y	Y
14 Maloney	Y	Y	Y	Y	Y	Y	Y
15 Rangel	Y	Y	Y	Y	Y	Y	Y
16 Serrano	Y	Y	Y	Y	Y	Y	Y
17 Engel	Y	Y	Y	Y	?	Y	Y
18 Lowey	Y	Y	Y	Y	Y	Y	Y
19 Hall	Y	Y	Y	Y	Y	Y	Y
20 Murphy	Y	Y	Y	Y	N	Y	Y
21 Tonko	Y	Y	Y	Y	Y	Y	Y
22 Hinchey	Y	Y	Y	Y	Y	Y	Y
23 **McHugh**	Y	Y	Y	Y	N	N	N
24 Arcuri	Y	Y	Y	Y	N	Y	Y
25 Maffei	Y	Y	Y	Y	N	Y	Y
26 **Lee**	Y	Y	Y	Y	N	N	N
27 Higgins	Y	Y	Y	Y	Y	Y	Y
28 Slaughter	Y	Y	Y	Y	Y	Y	Y
29 Massa	Y	Y	Y	Y	Y	Y	Y
NORTH CAROLINA							
1 Butterfield	Y	Y	Y	Y	Y	Y	Y
2 Etheridge	Y	Y	Y	Y	Y	Y	Y
3 **Jones**	Y	Y	Y	Y	N	Y	N
4 Price	Y	Y	Y	Y	Y	Y	Y

	278	279	280	281	282	283	284
5 **Foxx**	Y	Y	Y	N	N	N	N
6 **Coble**	Y	Y	Y	Y	N	N	N
7 McIntyre	Y	Y	Y	Y	Y	Y	Y
8 Kissell	Y	Y	Y	Y	Y	Y	Y
9 **Myrick**	Y	Y	Y	Y	N	N	N
10 **McHenry**	Y	Y	Y	Y	N	N	N
11 Shuler	Y	Y	Y	Y	Y	Y	Y
12 Watt	Y	Y	Y	Y	Y	Y	Y
13 Miller	Y	Y	Y	Y	Y	Y	Y
NORTH DAKOTA							
AL Pomeroy	Y	Y	Y	Y	Y	Y	Y
OHIO							
1 Driehaus	Y	Y	Y	Y	Y	Y	Y
2 **Schmidt**	Y	Y	Y	Y	N	N	N
3 **Turner**	Y	Y	Y	Y	N	N	N
4 **Jordan**	Y	Y	Y	Y	N	N	N
5 **Latta**	Y	Y	Y	Y	N	N	N
6 Wilson	Y	Y	Y	Y	Y	Y	Y
7 **Austria**	Y	Y	Y	Y	N	N	N
8 **Boehner**	Y	Y	Y	Y	N	N	N
9 Kaptur	Y	Y	Y	Y	?	?	?
10 Kucinich	Y	Y	Y	Y	N	Y	Y
11 Fudge	Y	Y	N	Y	Y	Y	Y
12 **Tiberi**	Y	Y	Y	Y	N	N	N
13 Sutton	Y	Y	Y	Y	Y	Y	Y
14 **LaTourette**	Y	Y	?	Y	N	N	N
15 Kilroy	Y	Y	Y	Y	Y	Y	Y
16 Boccieri	Y	Y	Y	Y	Y	Y	Y
17 Ryan	Y	Y	N	Y	Y	Y	Y
18 Space	Y	Y	Y	Y	Y	Y	Y
OKLAHOMA							
1 **Sullivan**	Y	Y	Y	Y	N	N	N
2 Boren	Y	Y	Y	Y	Y	Y	Y
3 **Lucas**	Y	Y	Y	Y	N	N	N
4 **Cole**	Y	Y	Y	Y	N	N	N
5 **Fallin**	Y	Y	Y	Y	N	N	N
OREGON							
1 Wu	Y	Y	Y	Y	Y	Y	Y
2 **Walden**	Y	Y	Y	Y	N	N	N
3 Blumenauer	Y	Y	Y	Y	Y	Y	Y
4 DeFazio	Y	Y	Y	Y	Y	Y	Y
5 Schrader	Y	Y	Y	Y	Y	Y	Y
PENNSYLVANIA							
1 Brady	Y	Y	Y	Y	Y	Y	Y
2 Fattah	Y	Y	Y	Y	Y	Y	Y
3 Dahlkemper	Y	Y	Y	Y	N	Y	Y
4 Altmire	Y	Y	Y	Y	N	Y	Y
5 **Thompson**	Y	?	Y	Y	N	N	N
6 **Gerlach**	Y	Y	Y	Y	N	N	N
7 Sestak	Y	Y	Y	Y	Y	Y	N
8 Murphy, P.	Y	Y	Y	Y	Y	Y	Y
9 **Shuster**	Y	Y	Y	Y	N	N	N
10 Carney	Y	Y	Y	Y	N	Y	Y
11 Kanjorski	Y	Y	Y	Y	Y	Y	Y
12 Murtha	?	Y	Y	Y	Y	Y	Y
13 Schwartz	Y	Y	Y	Y	Y	Y	Y
14 Doyle	Y	Y	Y	Y	Y	Y	?
15 **Dent**	Y	Y	Y	Y	N	N	N
16 **Pitts**	Y	Y	Y	Y	N	N	N
17 Holden	Y	Y	Y	Y	Y	Y	Y
18 **Murphy, T.**	Y	Y	Y	Y	N	?	?
19 **Platts**	Y	Y	Y	Y	N	N	N
RHODE ISLAND							
1 Kennedy	Y	Y	Y	Y	Y	Y	Y
2 Langevin	Y	Y	Y	Y	Y	Y	Y
SOUTH CAROLINA							
1 **Brown**	Y	Y	Y	Y	N	N	N
2 **Wilson**	Y	Y	Y	Y	N	N	N
3 **Barrett**	?	?	?	?	?	?	?
4 **Inglis**	Y	Y	Y	Y	N	N	N
5 Spratt	Y	Y	Y	Y	Y	Y	Y
6 Clyburn	Y	Y	Y	Y	Y	Y	Y
SOUTH DAKOTA							
AL Herseth Sandlin	Y	Y	Y	Y	Y	Y	Y
TENNESSEE							
1 **Roe**	Y	Y	Y	Y	N	N	N
2 **Duncan**	Y	Y	Y	N	N	N	N
3 **Wamp**	Y	Y	Y	Y	N	N	N
4 Davis	Y	Y	Y	Y	Y	Y	Y
5 Cooper	Y	Y	Y	Y	Y	Y	Y
6 Gordon	Y	Y	Y	Y	Y	Y	Y
7 **Blackburn**	Y	Y	Y	Y	N	N	N
8 Tanner	Y	Y	Y	Y	Y	Y	Y
9 Cohen	Y	Y	Y	Y	Y	Y	Y

	278	279	280	281	282	283	284
TEXAS							
1 **Gohmert**	Y	Y	Y	Y	?	N	N
2 **Poe**	Y	Y	Y	Y	N	N	N
3 **Johnson, S.**	Y	Y	Y	Y	N	N	N
4 **Hall**	Y	Y	Y	Y	N	N	N
5 **Hensarling**	Y	Y	Y	N	N	N	N
6 **Barton**	Y	Y	Y	Y	N	N	N
7 **Culberson**	Y	Y	Y	N	N	N	N
8 **Brady**	Y	Y	Y	Y	N	N	N
9 Green, A.	Y	Y	Y	Y	Y	Y	Y
10 **McCaul**	Y	Y	Y	Y	N	N	N
11 **Conaway**	Y	Y	Y	Y	N	N	N
12 **Granger**	Y	Y	Y	Y	N	N	N
13 **Thornberry**	Y	Y	Y	Y	N	N	N
14 **Paul**	Y	Y	Y	N	Y	Y	N
15 Hinojosa	Y	Y	Y	Y	+	Y	Y
16 Reyes	Y	Y	Y	Y	Y	Y	Y
17 Edwards	Y	Y	Y	Y	Y	Y	Y
18 Jackson Lee	Y	Y	Y	Y	Y	Y	Y
19 **Neugebauer**	Y	Y	Y	Y	N	N	N
20 Gonzalez	Y	Y	Y	Y	Y	Y	Y
21 **Smith**	Y	Y	Y	Y	N	N	N
22 **Olson**	Y	Y	Y	Y	N	N	N
23 Rodriguez	Y	Y	Y	Y	Y	Y	Y
24 **Marchant**	Y	Y	Y	Y	N	N	N
25 Doggett	Y	Y	Y	Y	Y	Y	Y
26 **Burgess**	Y	Y	Y	Y	N	N	N
27 Ortiz	Y	Y	Y	Y	Y	Y	Y
28 Cuellar	Y	Y	Y	Y	Y	Y	Y
29 Green, G.	Y	Y	Y	Y	Y	Y	Y
30 Johnson, E.	Y	Y	N	Y	Y	Y	Y
31 **Carter**	Y	Y	Y	Y	N	N	N
32 **Sessions**	Y	Y	Y	Y	N	N	N
UTAH							
1 **Bishop**	Y	?	Y	Y	N	N	N
2 Matheson	Y	Y	Y	Y	Y	Y	Y
3 **Chaffetz**	Y	Y	Y	N	Y	N	N
VERMONT							
AL Welch	Y	Y	Y	Y	Y	Y	Y
VIRGINIA							
1 **Wittman**	Y	Y	Y	Y	N	N	N
2 Nye	Y	Y	Y	Y	Y	Y	Y
3 Scott	Y	Y	Y	Y	Y	Y	Y
4 **Forbes**	Y	Y	Y	Y	N	N	N
5 Perriello	Y	Y	Y	Y	N	Y	Y
6 **Goodlatte**	Y	Y	Y	Y	N	N	N
7 **Cantor**	Y	Y	Y	Y	N	N	N
8 Moran	Y	Y	Y	Y	Y	Y	Y
9 Boucher	Y	Y	Y	Y	Y	Y	Y
10 **Wolf**	Y	Y	Y	Y	N	N	N
11 Connolly	Y	Y	N	Y	Y	Y	Y
WASHINGTON							
1 Inslee	Y	Y	Y	Y	Y	Y	Y
2 Larsen	Y	Y	Y	Y	Y	Y	Y
3 Baird	Y	Y	Y	Y	Y	Y	Y
4 **Hastings**	Y	Y	Y	Y	N	N	N
5 **McMorris Rodgers**	Y	Y	Y	Y	N	N	N
6 Dicks	Y	Y	Y	Y	Y	Y	Y
7 McDermott	Y	Y	N	Y	Y	Y	Y
8 **Reichert**	Y	Y	Y	Y	N	N	N
9 Smith	Y	Y	Y	Y	Y	Y	Y
WEST VIRGINIA							
1 Mollohan	Y	Y	Y	Y	Y	Y	Y
2 **Capito**	Y	Y	Y	Y	N	N	N
3 Rahall	Y	Y	Y	Y	Y	Y	Y
WISCONSIN							
1 **Ryan**	Y	Y	Y	Y	N	N	N
2 Baldwin	Y	Y	N	Y	Y	Y	Y
3 Kind	Y	Y	Y	Y	Y	Y	Y
4 Moore	Y	Y	N	Y	Y	Y	Y
5 **Sensenbrenner**	Y	Y	Y	Y	N	N	N
6 **Petri**	Y	Y	Y	Y	N	N	N
7 Obey	Y	Y	Y	Y	N	Y	Y
8 Kagen	Y	Y	Y	Y	Y	Y	Y
WYOMING							
AL **Lummis**	Y	Y	Y	Y	Y	N	N
DELEGATES							
Faleomavaega (A.S.)		Y					
Norton (D.C.)		Y					
Bordallo (Guam)		Y					
Sablan (N. Marianas)		Y					
Pierluisi (P.R.)		?					
Christensen (V.I.)		Y					

IN THE HOUSE | By Vote Number

285. **HR 915. FAA Reauthorization/Rule.** Adoption of the rule (H Res 464) to provide for House floor consideration of a bill that would reauthorize the Federal Aviation Administration (FAA). Adopted 234-178: R 0-169; D 234-9. May 21, 2009.

286. **S 454. Weapons Acquisition Overhaul/Conference Report.** Adoption of the conference report on the bill that would overhaul major elements of the Defense Department's weapons acquisition process. The Pentagon would have to require competition and revise regulations regarding conflicts of interest for major acquisitions programs. It would establish the position of director of cost assessment and program evaluation. It would also require the Defense secretary to designate a director to oversee developmental test and evaluation, and a director to oversee systems engineering. It would require the Pentagon to ensure that cost, performance and schedule objectives are balanced. Adopted (thus cleared for the president) 411-0: R 165-0; D 246-0. A "yea" was a vote in support of the president's position. May 21, 2009.

287. **HR 1676. Tobacco Shipping Restrictions/Passage.** Weiner, D-N.Y., motion to suspend the rules and pass the bill that would prohibit the U.S. Postal Service from transporting tobacco products, excluding cigars, to consumers in the continental United States and require tobacco sellers to use shipping methods that verify that recipients are of legal age. Sellers would have to register with the Justice Department, and the agency would keep lists of those that fail to register or comply with shipping rules. Motion agreed to 397-11: R 159-9; D 238-2. A two-thirds majority of those present and voting (272 in this case) is required for passage under suspension of the rules. May 21, 2009.

288. **HR 915. FAA Reauthorization/Whistleblower Protection.** Burgess, R-Texas, amendment that would express the sense of Congress that whistleblowers at the FAA be granted the full protection of the law. Adopted in Committee of the Whole 420-0: R 172-0; D 248-0. May 21, 2009.

289. **HR 915. FAA Reauthorization/Project Naming.** McCaul, R-Texas, amendment that would bar the use of funds in the bill to name any project or program for an individual serving as a member, delegate, resident commissioner or senator of the U.S. Congress. Adopted in Committee of the Whole 417-2: R 171-0; D 246-2. May 21, 2009.

290. **HR 915. FAA Reauthorization/Recommit.** Campbell, R-Calif., motion to recommit the bill to the Transportation and Infrastructure Committee with instructions that it be reported back immediately with language that would bar the use of the funds in the bill for subsidizing a public airport located three miles northeast of Johnstown, Pa., that offers scheduled commercial air carrier service and general aviation service and has a joint military control tower. Motion rejected 154-263: R 143-28; D 11-235. May 21, 2009.

291. **HR 915. FAA Reauthorization/Passage.** Passage of the bill that would authorize $53.5 billion through fiscal 2012 for the FAA. It would require airlines and airports to develop contingency plans for stranded passengers, prohibit passengers from talking on mobile devices while a plane is in flight and increase the number of daily long-distance flights permitted from Ronald Reagan Washington National Airport. The bill would require the FAA to establish fees for aircraft registration and certification, impose a $130 fee for registering an aircraft, and increase to $7, from $4.50, the maximum passenger facility charge. It would require maintenance inspectors who oversee airlines to be rotated every five years, establish a new labor dispute system for air traffic controllers and require additional inspections at aviation repair stations overseas. Passed 277-136: R 37-132; D 240-4. May 21, 2009.

	285	286	287	288	289	290	291
ALABAMA							
1 **Bonner**	N	Y	Y	Y	Y	N	N
2 Bright	N	Y	+	Y	Y	Y	N
3 **Rogers**	N	Y	Y	Y	Y	Y	N
4 **Aderholt**	N	?	Y	Y	Y	N	N
5 Griffith	Y	Y	Y	Y	Y	N	Y
6 **Bachus**	N	Y	Y	Y	Y	Y	N
7 Davis	Y	Y	Y	Y	Y	N	Y
ALASKA							
AL **Young**	N	?	Y	Y	Y	N	Y
ARIZONA							
1 Kirkpatrick	N	Y	Y	Y	Y	Y	Y
2 **Franks**	N	Y	Y	Y	Y	Y	N
3 **Shadegg**	N	Y	Y	Y	Y	Y	N
4 Pastor	Y	Y	Y	Y	Y	N	Y
5 Mitchell	Y	Y	Y	Y	Y	N	Y
6 **Flake**	?	?	?	?	?	?	?
7 Grijalva	Y	?	Y	Y	Y	N	Y
8 Giffords	Y	Y	Y	Y	Y	N	Y
ARKANSAS							
1 Berry	Y	Y	Y	Y	Y	N	Y
2 Snyder	Y	Y	Y	Y	Y	N	Y
3 **Boozman**	N	Y	Y	Y	Y	Y	N
4 Ross	Y	Y	Y	Y	Y	N	Y
CALIFORNIA							
1 Thompson	Y	Y	Y	Y	Y	N	Y
2 **Herger**	N	?	Y	Y	Y	Y	N
3 **Lungren**	N	Y	Y	Y	Y	Y	N
4 **McClintock**	N	Y	N	Y	Y	Y	N
5 Matsui	Y	Y	Y	Y	Y	N	Y
6 Woolsey	Y	Y	?	Y	Y	N	Y
7 Miller, George	Y	Y	Y	Y	Y	N	Y
8 Pelosi							
9 Lee	Y	Y	Y	Y	Y	N	Y
10 Tauscher	Y	Y	Y	Y	Y	N	Y
11 McNerney	Y	Y	Y	Y	Y	N	Y
12 Speier	?	?	?	?	?	N	Y
13 Stark	?	?	?	?	?	?	?
14 Eshoo	Y	Y	Y	Y	Y	N	Y
15 Honda	Y	Y	Y	Y	Y	N	Y
16 Lofgren	Y	Y	Y	?	?	N	Y
17 Farr	Y	Y	Y	Y	Y	N	Y
18 Cardoza	Y	Y	Y	Y	Y	N	Y
19 **Radanovich**	N	Y	Y	Y	Y	Y	N
20 Costa	Y	Y	Y	Y	Y	N	Y
21 **Nunes**	N	Y	Y	Y	?	?	?
22 **McCarthy**	N	Y	Y	Y	Y	Y	N
23 Capps	Y	Y	Y	Y	Y	N	Y
24 **Gallegly**	N	Y	Y	Y	Y	Y	N
25 **McKeon**	N	Y	Y	Y	Y	Y	N
26 **Dreier**	N	Y	Y	Y	Y	Y	N
27 Sherman	Y	Y	Y	Y	Y	N	Y
28 Berman	Y	Y	Y	Y	Y	N	Y
29 Schiff	Y	Y	Y	Y	Y	N	Y
30 Waxman	Y	Y	Y	Y	Y	N	Y
31 Becerra	Y	Y	Y	Y	Y	N	Y
32 Vacant							
33 Watson	Y	Y	Y	Y	Y	N	Y
34 Roybal-Allard	Y	Y	Y	Y	Y	N	Y
35 Waters	Y	Y	Y	Y	Y	N	Y
36 Harman	Y	Y	Y	Y	Y	N	Y
37 Richardson	Y	Y	Y	Y	Y	N	Y
38 Napolitano	?	Y	Y	Y	Y	N	Y
39 Sánchez, Linda	?	?	?	?	?	?	?
40 **Royce**	N	Y	Y	Y	Y	Y	N
41 **Lewis**	N	Y	Y	Y	Y	N	Y
42 **Miller, Gary**	N	Y	Y	Y	Y	N	Y
43 Baca	Y	Y	Y	Y	Y	N	Y
44 **Calvert**	N	Y	Y	Y	Y	N	N
45 **Bono Mack**	N	Y	Y	Y	Y	Y	N
46 **Rohrabacher**	N	Y	N	Y	Y	N	N
47 Sanchez, Loretta	Y	Y	Y	Y	Y	N	Y
48 **Campbell**	N	Y	N	Y	Y	N	N
49 **Issa**	N	Y	Y	Y	Y	N	N
50 **Bilbray**	N	Y	Y	Y	Y	N	Y
51 Filner	Y	Y	Y	Y	Y	N	Y
52 **Hunter**	N	Y	Y	Y	Y	Y	N
53 Davis	Y	Y	Y	Y	Y	N	Y

	285	286	287	288	289	290	291
COLORADO							
1 DeGette	Y	Y	Y	Y	Y	N	Y
2 Polis	Y	Y	Y	Y	Y	N	Y
3 Salazar	Y	Y	Y	Y	Y	N	Y
4 Markey	?	+	?	?	?	?	?
5 **Lamborn**	N	Y	Y	Y	Y	Y	N
6 **Coffman**	N	Y	Y	Y	Y	Y	N
7 Perlmutter	Y	Y	Y	?	?	?	?
CONNECTICUT							
1 Larson	Y	Y	Y	Y	Y	N	Y
2 Courtney	Y	Y	Y	Y	Y	N	Y
3 DeLauro	Y	Y	Y	Y	Y	N	Y
4 Himes	Y	Y	Y	Y	Y	N	Y
5 Murphy	Y	Y	Y	Y	Y	N	Y
DELAWARE							
AL **Castle**	N	Y	Y	Y	Y	Y	Y
FLORIDA							
1 **Miller**	N	Y	Y	Y	Y	Y	N
2 Boyd	Y	Y	Y	?	?	?	+
3 Brown	Y	Y	Y	Y	Y	N	Y
4 **Crenshaw**	N	Y	Y	Y	Y	N	N
5 **Brown-Waite**	N	Y	Y	Y	Y	N	N
6 **Stearns**	–	Y	Y	Y	Y	N	N
7 **Mica**	N	Y	Y	Y	Y	N	Y
8 Grayson	Y	Y	Y	Y	Y	N	Y
9 **Bilirakis**	N	Y	Y	Y	Y	N	N
10 **Young**	N	Y	Y	Y	Y	N	N
11 Castor	Y	Y	Y	Y	Y	N	Y
12 **Putnam**	N	Y	Y	Y	Y	N	N
13 **Buchanan**	N	Y	Y	Y	Y	N	N
14 **Mack**	N	Y	Y	Y	Y	N	N
15 **Posey**	N	Y	Y	Y	Y	N	N
16 **Rooney**	–	+	+	Y	Y	N	N
17 Meek	Y	Y	Y	Y	Y	N	Y
18 **Ros-Lehtinen**	N	Y	Y	Y	Y	Y	Y
19 Wexler	Y	Y	Y	Y	Y	N	Y
20 Wasserman Schultz	Y	Y	Y	Y	Y	N	Y
21 **Diaz-Balart, L.**	N	Y	Y	Y	Y	N	Y
22 Klein	Y	Y	Y	Y	Y	N	Y
23 Hastings	Y	Y	Y	Y	Y	N	Y
24 Kosmas	Y	Y	Y	Y	Y	Y	Y
25 **Diaz-Balart, M.**	N	Y	Y	Y	Y	Y	Y
GEORGIA							
1 **Kingston**	N	Y	N	?	?	?	?
2 Bishop	Y	Y	Y	Y	Y	N	Y
3 **Westmoreland**	N	Y	N	Y	Y	Y	N
4 Johnson	Y	Y	Y	?	Y	N	Y
5 Lewis	Y	Y	Y	Y	Y	N	Y
6 **Price**	N	+	Y	Y	Y	Y	N
7 **Linder**	N	Y	Y	Y	Y	Y	N
8 Marshall	?	Y	Y	Y	Y	N	Y
9 **Deal**	N	?	?	?	?	?	?
10 **Broun**	N	Y	N	Y	Y	Y	N
11 **Gingrey**	N	Y	Y	Y	Y	Y	N
12 Barrow	Y	Y	Y	Y	Y	N	Y
13 Scott	Y	Y	Y	Y	Y	N	Y
HAWAII							
1 Abercrombie	Y	Y	Y	Y	Y	N	Y
2 Hirono	Y	Y	Y	Y	Y	N	Y
IDAHO							
1 **Minnick**	N	Y	Y	Y	Y	N	Y
2 **Simpson**	N	Y	Y	Y	Y	N	N
ILLINOIS							
1 Rush	Y	Y	Y	Y	Y	N	Y
2 Jackson	Y	Y	Y	Y	Y	N	Y
3 Lipinski	Y	Y	Y	Y	Y	N	Y
4 Gutierrez	Y	Y	?	Y	Y	N	Y
5 Quigley	Y	Y	Y	Y	Y	N	Y
6 **Roskam**	N	Y	Y	Y	Y	Y	N
7 Davis	?	Y	Y	Y	Y	N	Y
8 Bean	Y	Y	Y	Y	Y	N	Y
9 Schakowsky	Y	Y	Y	Y	Y	N	Y
10 **Kirk**	N	Y	Y	Y	Y	Y	Y
11 Halvorson	Y	Y	N	Y	Y	N	Y
12 Costello	Y	Y	Y	Y	Y	N	Y
13 **Biggert**	N	Y	Y	Y	Y	N	Y
14 Foster	Y	Y	Y	Y	Y	N	Y
15 **Johnson**	N	Y	Y	Y	Y	N	Y

	285	286	287	288	289	290	291
16 **Manzullo**	N	Y	Y	Y	Y	Y	N
17 Hare	Y	Y	?	Y	Y	N	Y
18 **Schock**	?	Y	Y	Y	Y	Y	?
19 **Shimkus**	N	Y	Y	Y	Y	Y	Y
INDIANA							
1 Visclosky	Y	Y	Y	Y	Y	N	Y
2 Donnelly	Y	Y	Y	Y	Y	N	Y
3 **Souder**	N	Y	Y	Y	Y	Y	N
4 **Buyer**	N	Y	Y	Y	Y	Y	Y
5 **Burton**	N	Y	Y	Y	Y	Y	N
6 **Pence**	N	Y	Y	Y	Y	Y	N
7 Carson	Y	Y	Y	Y	Y	N	Y
8 Ellsworth	Y	Y	N	Y	Y	N	Y
9 Hill	N	Y	?	Y	Y	N	Y
IOWA							
1 Braley	Y	Y	Y	Y	Y	N	Y
2 Loebsack	Y	Y	Y	Y	Y	N	Y
3 Boswell	Y	Y	Y	Y	Y	N	Y
4 **Latham**	N	Y	Y	Y	Y	Y	N
5 **King**	N	Y	Y	Y	Y	Y	N
KANSAS							
1 **Moran**	N	Y	Y	Y	Y	Y	Y
2 **Jenkins**	N	Y	Y	Y	Y	Y	Y
3 Moore	Y	Y	Y	Y	Y	N	Y
4 **Tiahrt**	N	Y	Y	Y	Y	N	Y
KENTUCKY							
1 **Whitfield**	N	Y	?	Y	Y	N	N
2 **Guthrie**	N	Y	Y	Y	Y	Y	N
3 Yarmuth	Y	Y	Y	Y	Y	N	Y
4 **Davis**	N	Y	Y	Y	Y	Y	Y
5 **Rogers**	N	Y	Y	Y	Y	N	Y
6 Chandler	Y	Y	Y	Y	Y	N	Y
LOUISIANA							
1 **Scalise**	N	Y	Y	Y	Y	Y	N
2 **Cao**	N	Y	Y	Y	Y	N	Y
3 Melancon	Y	Y	Y	Y	Y	N	Y
4 **Fleming**	N	Y	Y	Y	Y	Y	N
5 **Alexander**	N	Y	Y	Y	Y	N	N
6 **Cassidy**	?	Y	Y	Y	Y	Y	N
7 **Boustany**	N	Y	Y	Y	Y	Y	N
MAINE							
1 Pingree	Y	Y	Y	Y	Y	N	Y
2 Michaud	Y	Y	Y	Y	Y	N	Y
MARYLAND							
1 Kratovil	Y	Y	Y	Y	Y	N	Y
2 Ruppersberger	Y	Y	Y	Y	Y	N	Y
3 Sarbanes	Y	Y	Y	Y	Y	N	Y
4 Edwards	Y	Y	Y	Y	Y	N	Y
5 Hoyer	Y	Y	Y	Y	Y	N	Y
6 **Bartlett**	N	Y	Y	Y	Y	N	N
7 Cummings	Y	Y	Y	Y	Y	N	Y
8 Van Hollen	Y	Y	Y	Y	Y	N	Y
MASSACHUSETTS							
1 Olver	Y	Y	Y	Y	Y	N	Y
2 Neal	Y	Y	Y	Y	Y	N	Y
3 McGovern	Y	Y	Y	Y	Y	N	Y
4 Frank	Y	Y	Y	Y	Y	N	Y
5 Tsongas	Y	Y	Y	Y	Y	N	Y
6 Tierney	Y	Y	Y	Y	Y	N	Y
7 Markey	Y	Y	Y	Y	Y	N	Y
8 Capuano	Y	Y	Y	Y	Y	N	Y
9 Lynch	Y	Y	Y	Y	Y	N	Y
10 Delahunt	Y	Y	Y	Y	Y	N	Y
MICHIGAN							
1 Stupak	Y	Y	Y	Y	Y	N	Y
2 **Hoekstra**	N	Y	Y	Y	Y	Y	N
3 **Ehlers**	N	Y	Y	Y	Y	Y	N
4 **Camp**	N	Y	Y	Y	Y	Y	N
5 Kildee	Y	Y	Y	Y	Y	N	Y
6 **Upton**	N	Y	Y	Y	Y	Y	N
7 Schauer	Y	Y	Y	Y	Y	N	?
8 **Rogers**	N	Y	Y	Y	Y	Y	N
9 Peters	Y	Y	Y	Y	Y	N	Y
10 **Miller**	N	Y	Y	Y	Y	Y	Y
11 **McCotter**	N	Y	Y	Y	Y	Y	Y
12 Levin	Y	Y	Y	Y	Y	N	Y
13 Kilpatrick	Y	Y	Y	Y	Y	N	Y
14 Conyers	Y	Y	Y	Y	Y	N	Y
15 Dingell	Y	Y	Y	Y	Y	N	Y
MINNESOTA							
1 Walz	Y	Y	Y	Y	Y	N	Y
2 **Kline**	N	Y	Y	Y	Y	Y	N
3 **Paulsen**	N	Y	Y	Y	Y	Y	N
4 McCollum	Y	Y	Y	Y	Y	N	Y

	285	286	287	288	289	290	291
5 Ellison	Y	Y	Y	Y	Y	N	Y
6 **Bachmann**	?	?	?	?	?	?	?
7 Peterson	Y	Y	Y	Y	Y	N	Y
8 Oberstar	Y	Y	Y	Y	Y	N	Y
MISSISSIPPI							
1 Childers	N	Y	Y	Y	Y	N	Y
2 Thompson	Y	Y	Y	Y	Y	N	Y
3 **Harper**	N	Y	Y	Y	Y	Y	N
4 Taylor	Y	Y	Y	Y	Y	N	Y
MISSOURI							
1 Clay	Y	Y	Y	Y	?	N	Y
2 **Akin**	N	Y	Y	Y	Y	Y	N
3 Carnahan	Y	Y	Y	Y	Y	N	Y
4 Skelton	Y	Y	Y	Y	Y	N	Y
5 Cleaver	?	Y	Y	Y	Y	N	Y
6 **Graves**	N	Y	Y	Y	Y	Y	N
7 **Blunt**	N	Y	Y	Y	Y	Y	N
8 **Emerson**	N	Y	Y	Y	Y	N	N
9 **Luetkemeyer**	N	Y	Y	Y	Y	Y	N
MONTANA							
AL **Rehberg**	N	Y	Y	Y	Y	N	N
NEBRASKA							
1 **Fortenberry**	N	Y	Y	Y	Y	Y	N
2 **Terry**	N	Y	Y	Y	Y	Y	N
3 **Smith**	N	Y	Y	Y	Y	Y	N
NEVADA							
1 Berkley	Y	Y	Y	?	?	?	?
2 **Heller**	N	Y	Y	Y	Y	Y	N
3 Titus	Y	Y	Y	Y	Y	Y	Y
NEW HAMPSHIRE							
1 Shea-Porter	Y	Y	Y	Y	Y	N	Y
2 Hodes	Y	Y	Y	Y	Y	N	Y
NEW JERSEY							
1 Andrews	Y	Y	Y	?	Y	N	Y
2 **LoBiondo**	N	Y	Y	Y	Y	N	Y
3 Adler	Y	Y	Y	Y	Y	N	Y
4 **Smith**	N	Y	Y	Y	Y	N	Y
5 **Garrett**	N	Y	Y	Y	Y	Y	N
6 Pallone	Y	Y	Y	Y	Y	N	Y
7 **Lance**	N	Y	Y	Y	Y	Y	Y
8 Pascrell	Y	Y	Y	Y	Y	N	Y
9 Rothman	Y	Y	Y	Y	Y	N	Y
10 Payne	Y	Y	Y	Y	Y	N	Y
11 **Frelinghuysen**	N	Y	Y	Y	Y	N	N
12 Holt	Y	Y	Y	Y	Y	N	Y
13 Sires	Y	Y	Y	Y	Y	N	Y
NEW MEXICO							
1 Heinrich	Y	Y	Y	Y	Y	N	Y
2 Teague	Y	Y	Y	Y	Y	N	Y
3 Lujan	Y	Y	Y	Y	Y	N	Y
NEW YORK							
1 Bishop	Y	Y	Y	Y	Y	N	Y
2 Israel	Y	Y	Y	Y	Y	N	Y
3 **King**	N	Y	Y	Y	Y	Y	Y
4 McCarthy	Y	Y	Y	Y	Y	N	Y
5 Ackerman	Y	Y	Y	Y	Y	N	Y
6 Meeks	Y	Y	Y	Y	Y	N	Y
7 Crowley	Y	Y	Y	Y	Y	N	Y
8 Nadler	Y	Y	Y	Y	Y	N	Y
9 Weiner	Y	Y	Y	Y	Y	N	Y
10 Towns	Y	Y	Y	Y	Y	N	Y
11 Clarke	Y	Y	Y	Y	Y	N	Y
12 Velázquez	Y	Y	Y	Y	Y	N	Y
13 McMahon	Y	Y	Y	Y	Y	N	Y
14 Maloney	Y	Y	Y	Y	Y	N	Y
15 Rangel	Y	Y	Y	Y	Y	N	Y
16 Serrano	Y	Y	Y	Y	Y	N	Y
17 Engel	Y	Y	Y	Y	Y	N	Y
18 Lowey	Y	Y	Y	Y	Y	N	Y
19 Hall	Y	Y	Y	Y	Y	N	Y
20 Murphy	Y	Y	Y	Y	Y	N	Y
21 Tonko	Y	Y	Y	Y	Y	N	Y
22 Hinchey	Y	Y	Y	Y	Y	N	Y
23 **McHugh**	N	Y	Y	?	?	?	?
24 Arcuri	Y	Y	Y	Y	Y	N	Y
25 Maffei	Y	Y	Y	Y	Y	N	Y
26 **Lee**	N	Y	Y	Y	Y	Y	Y
27 Higgins	Y	Y	Y	Y	?	N	Y
28 Slaughter	Y	Y	Y	Y	Y	N	Y
29 Massa	Y	Y	Y	Y	Y	N	Y
NORTH CAROLINA							
1 Butterfield	Y	Y	Y	Y	Y	N	Y
2 Etheridge	Y	Y	Y	Y	Y	N	Y
3 **Jones**	N	Y	Y	Y	Y	N	N
4 Price	Y	Y	Y	Y	Y	N	Y

	285	286	287	288	289	290	291
5 **Foxx**	N	Y	Y	Y	Y	Y	N
6 **Coble**	N	Y	Y	Y	Y	Y	N
7 McIntyre	Y	Y	Y	Y	Y	N	Y
8 Kissell	Y	Y	Y	Y	Y	Y	Y
9 **Myrick**	N	Y	Y	Y	Y	Y	N
10 **McHenry**	N	Y	Y	Y	Y	Y	N
11 Shuler	N	Y	Y	Y	Y	N	Y
12 Watt	Y	Y	Y	Y	Y	N	Y
13 Miller	Y	Y	Y	Y	Y	N	Y
NORTH DAKOTA							
AL Pomeroy	Y	Y	Y	Y	Y	N	?
OHIO							
1 Driehaus	Y	+	+	+	+	–	+
2 **Schmidt**	N	Y	Y	Y	Y	Y	N
3 **Turner**	N	Y	Y	Y	Y	Y	N
4 **Jordan**	N	Y	Y	Y	Y	Y	N
5 **Latta**	N	Y	Y	Y	Y	Y	N
6 Wilson	Y	?	?	Y	Y	N	Y
7 **Austria**	N	Y	Y	Y	Y	Y	N
8 **Boehner**	N	Y	?	Y	Y	Y	N
9 Kaptur	?	?	?	?	?	?	?
10 Kucinich	Y	Y	Y	Y	Y	N	Y
11 Fudge	Y	Y	Y	Y	Y	N	Y
12 **Tiberi**	N	Y	Y	Y	Y	Y	N
13 Sutton	?	Y	Y	Y	Y	N	Y
14 **LaTourette**	?	Y	Y	Y	Y	N	Y
15 Kilroy	Y	Y	Y	Y	Y	Y	Y
16 Boccieri	Y	Y	Y	Y	Y	N	Y
17 Ryan	Y	Y	Y	Y	Y	N	Y
18 Space	Y	Y	Y	Y	Y	N	Y
OKLAHOMA							
1 **Sullivan**	N	Y	Y	Y	Y	Y	N
2 Boren	Y	Y	Y	Y	Y	N	Y
3 **Lucas**	N	Y	Y	Y	Y	Y	N
4 **Cole**	N	Y	Y	Y	Y	Y	N
5 **Fallin**	N	Y	Y	Y	Y	Y	N
OREGON							
1 Wu	Y	Y	Y	Y	Y	N	Y
2 **Walden**	N	Y	Y	Y	Y	Y	?
3 Blumenauer	Y	Y	Y	Y	Y	N	Y
4 DeFazio	Y	Y	Y	Y	Y	N	Y
5 Schrader	Y	Y	Y	Y	Y	N	Y
PENNSYLVANIA							
1 Brady	Y	Y	Y	Y	Y	N	Y
2 Fattah	Y	Y	Y	Y	Y	N	Y
3 Dahlkemper	Y	Y	Y	Y	Y	N	Y
4 Altmire	Y	Y	Y	Y	Y	N	Y
5 **Thompson**	N	?	?	Y	Y	N	Y
6 **Gerlach**	N	Y	Y	Y	Y	Y	Y
7 Sestak	N	Y	Y	Y	Y	N	N
8 Murphy, P.	Y	Y	Y	Y	Y	N	Y
9 **Shuster**	N	Y	Y	Y	Y	N	N
10 Carney	Y	Y	Y	Y	Y	N	Y
11 Kanjorski	Y	Y	Y	Y	Y	N	Y
12 Murtha	Y	Y	Y	Y	Y	N	Y
13 Schwartz	Y	Y	Y	Y	Y	N	Y
14 Doyle	?	?	?	Y	Y	N	Y
15 **Dent**	N	Y	Y	Y	Y	N	Y
16 **Pitts**	N	Y	Y	Y	Y	Y	N
17 Holden	Y	Y	Y	Y	Y	N	Y
18 **Murphy, T.**	?	?	?	Y	Y	N	Y
19 **Platts**	N	Y	Y	Y	Y	N	Y
RHODE ISLAND							
1 Kennedy	Y	Y	Y	Y	Y	N	Y
2 Langevin	Y	Y	Y	Y	Y	N	Y
SOUTH CAROLINA							
1 **Brown**	N	Y	Y	Y	Y	N	N
2 **Wilson**	N	Y	Y	Y	Y	Y	N
3 **Barrett**	?	?	?	?	?	?	?
4 **Inglis**	N	Y	Y	Y	Y	Y	N
5 Spratt	Y	Y	Y	Y	Y	N	Y
6 Clyburn	Y	Y	Y	Y	Y	N	Y
SOUTH DAKOTA							
AL Herseth Sandlin	Y	Y	Y	Y	Y	N	Y
TENNESSEE							
1 **Roe**	N	Y	Y	Y	Y	Y	N
2 **Duncan**	N	Y	Y	Y	Y	Y	Y
3 **Wamp**	N	Y	Y	Y	Y	Y	N
4 Davis	Y	Y	Y	Y	Y	N	Y
5 Cooper	Y	Y	Y	Y	Y	Y	Y
6 Gordon	Y	Y	Y	Y	Y	N	Y
7 **Blackburn**	N	Y	N	Y	Y	Y	N
8 Tanner	N	Y	Y	Y	Y	N	Y
9 Cohen	Y	Y	Y	Y	Y	N	N

	285	286	287	288	289	290	291
TEXAS							
1 **Gohmert**	N	Y	Y	Y	Y	Y	N
2 **Poe**	N	Y	Y	Y	Y	Y	N
3 **Johnson, S.**	N	Y	Y	Y	Y	Y	N
4 **Hall**	N	Y	Y	Y	Y	N	N
5 **Hensarling**	N	Y	?	Y	Y	Y	N
6 **Barton**	N	Y	Y	Y	Y	Y	N
7 **Culberson**	N	Y	Y	Y	Y	Y	N
8 **Brady**	N	Y	Y	Y	Y	Y	N
9 Green, A.	Y	Y	Y	Y	Y	N	Y
10 **McCaul**	N	Y	Y	Y	Y	Y	N
11 **Conaway**	N	Y	Y	Y	Y	Y	N
12 **Granger**	N	Y	Y	Y	Y	Y	N
13 **Thornberry**	N	Y	Y	Y	Y	Y	N
14 **Paul**	N	Y	N	Y	Y	N	N
15 Hinojosa	Y	Y	Y	Y	Y	N	Y
16 Reyes	Y	Y	Y	Y	Y	N	Y
17 Edwards	Y	Y	Y	Y	Y	N	Y
18 Jackson Lee	Y	Y	Y	Y	Y	N	Y
19 **Neugebauer**	N	Y	Y	Y	Y	Y	N
20 Gonzalez	Y	Y	Y	Y	Y	N	Y
21 **Smith**	N	Y	Y	Y	Y	Y	N
22 **Olson**	N	Y	Y	Y	Y	Y	N
23 Rodriguez	Y	Y	?	Y	Y	N	Y
24 **Marchant**	N	Y	N	Y	Y	Y	N
25 Doggett	Y	Y	Y	Y	Y	N	Y
26 **Burgess**	N	Y	Y	Y	Y	Y	N
27 Ortiz	Y	Y	Y	Y	Y	N	Y
28 Cuellar	Y	Y	Y	Y	Y	N	Y
29 Green, G.	Y	Y	Y	Y	Y	N	Y
30 Johnson, E.	Y	Y	Y	Y	Y	N	Y
31 **Carter**	N	Y	Y	Y	Y	Y	N
32 **Sessions**	N	Y	Y	Y	Y	Y	N
UTAH							
1 **Bishop**	N	?	Y	Y	Y	Y	N
2 Matheson	Y	Y	Y	Y	Y	N	Y
3 **Chaffetz**	N	Y	Y	Y	Y	Y	N
VERMONT							
AL Welch	Y	Y	Y	Y	Y	N	Y
VIRGINIA							
1 **Wittman**	N	Y	Y	Y	Y	Y	Y
2 Nye	Y	Y	Y	Y	Y	N	Y
3 Scott	Y	Y	Y	Y	Y	N	Y
4 **Forbes**	N	Y	Y	Y	Y	Y	N
5 Perriello	Y	Y	Y	Y	Y	Y	Y
6 **Goodlatte**	N	Y	Y	Y	Y	Y	N
7 **Cantor**	N	Y	Y	Y	Y	Y	N
8 Moran	Y	Y	Y	Y	N	N	Y
9 Boucher	Y	Y	Y	Y	Y	N	Y
10 **Wolf**	N	Y	Y	Y	Y	Y	Y
11 Connolly	Y	Y	Y	Y	Y	N	Y
WASHINGTON							
1 Inslee	Y	Y	Y	Y	Y	N	Y
2 Larsen	Y	Y	Y	Y	Y	N	Y
3 Baird	Y	Y	Y	Y	Y	N	Y
4 **Hastings**	N	Y	Y	Y	Y	Y	N
5 **McMorris Rodgers**	N	Y	Y	Y	Y	Y	N
6 Dicks	Y	Y	Y	Y	Y	N	Y
7 McDermott	Y	Y	Y	Y	Y	N	Y
8 **Reichert**	N	Y	Y	Y	Y	Y	Y
9 Smith	?	Y	Y	Y	Y	N	Y
WEST VIRGINIA							
1 Mollohan	Y	Y	Y	Y	Y	N	Y
2 **Capito**	N	Y	Y	Y	Y	Y	Y
3 Rahall	Y	Y	Y	Y	N	N	Y
WISCONSIN							
1 **Ryan**	N	Y	Y	Y	Y	Y	N
2 Baldwin	Y	Y	Y	Y	Y	N	Y
3 Kind	Y	Y	Y	Y	Y	N	Y
4 Moore	Y	Y	Y	Y	Y	N	Y
5 **Sensenbrenner**	N	Y	Y	Y	Y	Y	N
6 **Petri**	N	Y	Y	Y	Y	Y	N
7 Obey	Y	Y	?	Y	Y	N	Y
8 Kagen	Y	Y	Y	Y	Y	N	Y
WYOMING							
AL **Lummis**	N	?	Y	Y	Y	Y	N
DELEGATES							
Faleomavaega (A.S.)				Y	Y		
Norton (D.C.)				Y	Y		
Bordallo (Guam)				Y	Y		
Sablan (N. Marianas)				?	?		
Pierluisi (P.R.)				Y	Y		
Christensen (V.I.)				Y	Y		

IN THE HOUSE | By Vote Number

292. **H Res 421. Great Smoky Mountains National Park Anniversary/Adoption.** Christensen, D-V.I., motion to suspend the rules and adopt the resolution that would congratulate the Great Smoky Mountains National Park on its 75th anniversary. Motion agreed to 392-1: R 166-0; D 226-1. A two-thirds majority of those present and voting (262 in this case) is required for adoption under suspension of the rules. June 2, 2009.

293. **H J Res 40. Native American Heritage Day/Passage.** Christensen, D-V.I., motion to suspend the rules and pass the joint resolution that would encourage Americans to observe Native American Heritage Day by performing activities related to the cultures, traditions and languages of Native Americans. Motion agreed to 385-0: R 160-0; D 225-0. A two-thirds majority of those present and voting (257 in this case) is required for passage under suspension of the rules. June 2, 2009.

294. **H Res 489. Anniversary of Tiananmen Square Protests/Adoption.** Levin, D-Mich., motion to suspend the rules and adopt the resolution that would recognize the 20th anniversary of the 1989 Tiananmen Square protests and express sympathy for the families of those killed, tortured and imprisoned for their participation in the protests. Motion agreed to 396-1: R 164-1; D 232-0. A two-thirds majority of those present and voting (265 in this case) is required for adoption under suspension of the rules. June 2, 2009.

295. **HR 31. HR 1385. Federal Recognition for Indian Tribes/Rule.** Adoption of the rule (H Res 490) to provide for House floor consideration of a bill (HR 31) that would provide federal recognition to the Lumbee Tribe in North Carolina and prohibit the tribe from running gambling businesses, and a bill (HR 1385) that would provide federal recognition to six Virginia American Indian tribes and prohibit them from running gambling businesses. Adopted 231-174: R 2-166; D 229-8. June 3, 2009.

296. **HR 31. Federal Recognition for Lumbee Tribe/Recommit.** Hastings, R-Wash., motion to recommit the bill to the Natural Resources Committee with instructions that it be immediately reported back with language that would require the Interior secretary to verify that individuals enrolled in the Lumbee Tribe are descendants of Cheraw or other coastal North Carolina Indian tribes for purposes of the delivery of federal services. Motion rejected 197-224: R 160-12; D 37-212. June 3, 2009.

	292	293	294	295	296
ALABAMA					
1 Bonner	Y	Y	Y	N	N
2 Bright	Y	Y	Y	Y	Y
3 Rogers	Y	Y	Y	N	?
4 Aderholt	Y	Y	Y	N	N
5 Griffith	?	?	?	N	N
6 Bachus	Y	Y	Y	N	Y
7 Davis	Y	Y	Y	Y	Y
ALASKA					
AL Young	Y	Y	Y	N	N
ARIZONA					
1 Kirkpatrick	Y	?	Y	Y	N
2 Franks	+	+	+	N	Y
3 Shadegg	Y	Y	Y	N	Y
4 Pastor	Y	Y	Y	Y	N
5 Mitchell	Y	Y	Y	Y	N
6 Flake	Y	Y	Y	N	Y
7 Grijalva	Y	Y	Y	Y	N
8 Giffords	Y	Y	Y	Y	N
ARKANSAS					
1 Berry	N	Y	Y	Y	N
2 Snyder	Y	Y	Y	Y	N
3 Boozman	Y	Y	Y	N	Y
4 Ross	Y	Y	Y	Y	N
CALIFORNIA					
1 Thompson	Y	Y	Y	Y	N
2 Herger	Y	Y	Y	N	Y
3 Lungren	Y	Y	Y	N	N
4 McClintock	Y	Y	Y	N	Y
5 Matsui	Y	Y	Y	Y	N
6 Woolsey	Y	Y	Y	Y	N
7 Miller, George	Y	Y	Y	Y	N
8 Pelosi		Y			
9 Lee	Y	Y	Y	Y	N
10 Tauscher	Y	Y	Y	Y	N
11 McNerney	Y	Y	Y	Y	N
12 Speier	?	?	?	Y	N
13 Stark	Y	Y	Y	Y	N
14 Eshoo	Y	Y	Y	Y	N
15 Honda	Y	Y	Y	Y	N
16 Lofgren	Y	Y	Y	Y	N
17 Farr	Y	Y	Y	Y	N
18 Cardoza	Y	Y	Y	Y	N
19 Radanovich	?	Y	Y	N	Y
20 Costa	Y	Y	Y	Y	N
21 Nunes	Y	Y	Y	N	Y
22 McCarthy	Y	Y	Y	N	Y
23 Capps	Y	Y	Y	Y	N
24 Gallegly	Y	Y	Y	N	Y
25 McKeon	Y	Y	Y	N	Y
26 Dreier	Y	Y	Y	N	Y
27 Sherman	Y	Y	Y	Y	N
28 Berman	Y	Y	Y	Y	N
29 Schiff	Y	Y	Y	Y	N
30 Waxman	Y	Y	Y	Y	N
31 Becerra	Y	Y	Y	+	–
32 Vacant					
33 Watson	Y	Y	Y	Y	N
34 Roybal-Allard	Y	Y	Y	Y	N
35 Waters	?	?	?	Y	N
36 Harman	Y	?	Y	Y	N
37 Richardson	Y	Y	Y	Y	N
38 Napolitano	Y	Y	Y	Y	N
39 Sánchez, Linda	Y	Y	Y	?	?
40 Royce	Y	Y	Y	N	Y
41 Lewis	Y	Y	Y	N	Y
42 Miller, Gary	Y	Y	Y	N	Y
43 Baca	Y	Y	Y	Y	N
44 Calvert	Y	Y	Y	N	Y
45 Bono Mack	Y	Y	Y	N	Y
46 Rohrabacher	Y	Y	Y	N	Y
47 Sanchez, Loretta	?	?	?	?	?
48 Campbell	Y	Y	Y	N	Y
49 Issa	Y	Y	Y	N	Y
50 Bilbray	Y	Y	Y	N	Y
51 Filner	Y	Y	Y	Y	N
52 Hunter	Y	Y	Y	N	Y
53 Davis	Y	Y	Y	Y	N

	292	293	294	295	296
COLORADO					
1 DeGette	Y	Y	Y	Y	N
2 Polis	Y	Y	Y	Y	N
3 Salazar	?	?	?	Y	N
4 Markey	Y	Y	Y	Y	N
5 Lamborn	Y	Y	Y	N	Y
6 Coffman	Y	Y	Y	N	Y
7 Perlmutter	Y	Y	Y	Y	N
CONNECTICUT					
1 Larson	Y	Y	Y	Y	N
2 Courtney	Y	Y	Y	Y	Y
3 DeLauro	Y	Y	Y	Y	Y
4 Himes	Y	Y	Y	Y	N
5 Murphy	Y	Y	Y	Y	Y
DELAWARE					
AL Castle	Y	Y	Y	N	Y
FLORIDA					
1 Miller	Y	Y	Y	N	Y
2 Boyd	Y	Y	Y	Y	Y
3 Brown	?	?	?	?	N
4 Crenshaw	Y	Y	Y	N	Y
5 Brown-Waite	Y	Y	Y	N	Y
6 Stearns	Y	Y	?	N	Y
7 Mica	Y	Y	Y	N	Y
8 Grayson	Y	Y	Y	?	N
9 Bilirakis	Y	Y	Y	N	Y
10 Young	Y	Y	Y	N	Y
11 Castor	Y	Y	Y	Y	N
12 Putnam	Y	Y	Y	N	Y
13 Buchanan	Y	Y	Y	N	Y
14 Mack	Y	Y	Y	N	Y
15 Posey	Y	Y	Y	N	Y
16 Rooney	Y	Y	Y	N	Y
17 Meek	Y	Y	Y	?	N
18 Ros-Lehtinen	?	?	?	?	?
19 Wexler	Y	Y	Y	Y	N
20 Wasserman Schultz	Y	Y	Y	Y	N
21 Diaz-Balart, L.	Y	Y	Y	N	N
22 Klein	Y	Y	Y	Y	N
23 Hastings	Y	Y	Y	Y	N
24 Kosmas	Y	Y	Y	Y	N
25 Diaz-Balart, M.	Y	Y	Y	N	N
GEORGIA					
1 Kingston	Y	Y	Y	N	Y
2 Bishop	Y	Y	Y	Y	N
3 Westmoreland	Y	Y	Y	–	Y
4 Johnson	?	?	?	Y	N
5 Lewis	Y	Y	Y	Y	N
6 Price	Y	Y	Y	N	Y
7 Linder	Y	Y	Y	N	Y
8 Marshall	Y	Y	Y	Y	N
9 Deal	Y	Y	Y	N	Y
10 Broun	+	+	+	–	+
11 Gingrey	Y	Y	Y	N	Y
12 Barrow	Y	Y	Y	Y	N
13 Scott	Y	Y	Y	Y	N
HAWAII					
1 Abercrombie	Y	Y	Y	Y	N
2 Hirono	Y	Y	Y	Y	N
IDAHO					
1 Minnick	Y	Y	Y	N	Y
2 Simpson	Y	Y	Y	N	Y
ILLINOIS					
1 Rush	Y	Y	Y	Y	N
2 Jackson	Y	Y	Y	Y	N
3 Lipinski	?	?	?	Y	N
4 Gutierrez	Y	Y	Y	?	N
5 Quigley	Y	Y	Y	Y	Y
6 Roskam	Y	Y	Y	N	Y
7 Davis	Y	Y	Y	?	?
8 Bean	Y	Y	Y	?	N
9 Schakowsky	Y	Y	Y	Y	N
10 Kirk	Y	Y	Y	N	Y
11 Halvorson	Y	Y	Y	Y	N
12 Costello	Y	Y	Y	Y	N
13 Biggert	Y	Y	Y	N	N
14 Foster	Y	Y	Y	N	N
15 Johnson	+	+	+	N	Y

KEY	**Republicans**	Democrats		
Y Voted for (yea)		X Paired against		C Voted "present" to avoid possible conflict of interest
# Paired for		– Announced against		
+ Announced for		P Voted "present"		? Did not vote or otherwise make a position known
N Voted against (nay)				

	292	293	294	295	296
16 **Manzullo**	Y	Y	Y	N	Y
17 Hare	Y	Y	Y	Y	N
18 **Schock**	Y	Y	Y	?	Y
19 **Shimkus**	Y	Y	Y	N	Y
INDIANA					
1 Visclosky	Y	Y	Y	Y	N
2 Donnelly	Y	Y	Y	Y	Y
3 **Souder**	Y	Y	Y	N	Y
4 **Buyer**	Y	Y	Y	N	Y
5 **Burton**	Y	Y	Y	N	Y
6 **Pence**	Y	Y	Y	–	Y
7 Carson	Y	Y	Y	Y	N
8 Ellsworth	Y	Y	Y	N	Y
9 Hill	Y	Y	Y	N	Y
IOWA					
1 Braley	Y	Y	Y	Y	N
2 Loebsack	Y	Y	Y	Y	N
3 Boswell	Y	Y	Y	Y	N
4 Latham	Y	Y	Y	N	Y
5 **King**	Y	Y	Y	N	Y
KANSAS					
1 **Moran**	Y	Y	Y	N	Y
2 **Jenkins**	Y	Y	Y	N	Y
3 Moore	Y	Y	Y	Y	N
4 **Tiahrt**	Y	Y	Y	N	Y
KENTUCKY					
1 **Whitfield**	Y	Y	Y	N	Y
2 **Guthrie**	Y	Y	Y	N	Y
3 Yarmuth	Y	+	Y	Y	N
4 **Davis**	Y	Y	Y	N	Y
5 **Rogers**	Y	Y	Y	N	Y
6 Chandler	Y	Y	Y	Y	Y
LOUISIANA					
1 **Scalise**	Y	Y	Y	N	Y
2 **Cao**	Y	Y	Y	N	Y
3 Melancon	Y	Y	Y	?	N
4 **Fleming**	Y	Y	Y	N	Y
5 **Alexander**	Y	Y	Y	N	Y
6 **Cassidy**	Y	Y	Y	N	Y
7 **Boustany**	Y	Y	Y	N	Y
MAINE					
1 Pingree	Y	Y	Y	?	N
2 Michaud	Y	Y	Y	Y	N
MARYLAND					
1 Kratovil	Y	Y	Y	Y	N
2 Ruppersberger	?	?	?	?	?
3 Sarbanes	Y	Y	Y	Y	N
4 Edwards	Y	Y	Y	Y	N
5 Hoyer	Y	Y	Y	Y	N
6 **Bartlett**	Y	Y	Y	N	Y
7 Cummings	Y	Y	Y	Y	N
8 Van Hollen	Y	Y	Y	Y	N
MASSACHUSETTS					
1 Olver	Y	Y	Y	Y	N
2 Neal	Y	Y	Y	Y	N
3 McGovern	Y	Y	Y	Y	N
4 Frank	Y	Y	Y	Y	N
5 Tsongas	Y	Y	Y	Y	N
6 Tierney	Y	Y	Y	Y	N
7 Markey	Y	Y	Y	Y	N
8 Capuano	Y	Y	Y	Y	N
9 Lynch	Y	Y	Y	Y	N
10 Delahunt	?	?	?	Y	N
MICHIGAN					
1 Stupak	Y	Y	Y	N	Y
2 **Hoekstra**	Y	Y	Y	N	Y
3 **Ehlers**	Y	Y	Y	N	Y
4 **Camp**	Y	Y	Y	N	Y
5 Kildee	Y	Y	Y	Y	N
6 **Upton**	Y	Y	Y	N	Y
7 Schauer	Y	Y	Y	Y	N
8 **Rogers**	Y	Y	Y	N	Y
9 Peters	?	?	Y	Y	N
10 **Miller**	Y	Y	Y	N	Y
11 **McCotter**	Y	Y	Y	N	Y
12 Levin	Y	Y	Y	Y	N
13 Kilpatrick	Y	Y	Y	Y	N
14 Conyers	+	+	+	Y	N
15 Dingell	Y	Y	Y	?	N
MINNESOTA					
1 Walz	Y	Y	Y	Y	N
2 **Kline**	Y	Y	Y	N	Y
3 **Paulsen**	Y	Y	Y	N	Y
4 McCollum	?	Y	Y	Y	N

	292	293	294	295	296
5 Ellison	Y	Y	Y	Y	N
6 **Bachmann**	Y	Y	Y	N	Y
7 Peterson	Y	Y	Y	N	Y
8 Oberstar	Y	Y	Y	Y	N
MISSISSIPPI					
1 Childers	Y	Y	Y	Y	Y
2 Thompson	Y	Y	Y	Y	N
3 **Harper**	+	+	+	N	Y
4 Taylor	Y	Y	Y	Y	Y
MISSOURI					
1 Clay	Y	Y	Y	Y	N
2 **Akin**	Y	Y	Y	N	Y
3 Carnahan	Y	Y	Y	Y	N
4 Skelton	Y	?	Y	Y	N
5 Cleaver	Y	Y	Y	Y	N
6 **Graves**	Y	Y	Y	N	Y
7 **Blunt**	Y	Y	Y	?	Y
8 **Emerson**	Y	Y	Y	N	Y
9 **Luetkemeyer**	Y	Y	Y	N	Y
MONTANA					
AL **Rehberg**	Y	Y	Y	N	Y
NEBRASKA					
1 **Fortenberry**	Y	Y	Y	N	Y
2 **Terry**	Y	Y	Y	N	Y
3 **Smith**	Y	Y	Y	N	Y
NEVADA					
1 Berkley	Y	Y	Y	Y	N
2 **Heller**	Y	Y	Y	N	Y
3 Titus	Y	Y	Y	Y	N
NEW HAMPSHIRE					
1 Shea-Porter	Y	Y	Y	Y	Y
2 Hodes	Y	Y	Y	Y	N
NEW JERSEY					
1 Andrews	Y	Y	Y	Y	N
2 **LoBiondo**	Y	Y	Y	N	Y
3 Adler	Y	Y	Y	Y	N
4 **Smith**	?	?	?	N	Y
5 **Garrett**	Y	Y	Y	N	Y
6 Pallone	?	?	?	Y	N
7 **Lance**	Y	Y	Y	N	Y
8 Pascrell	Y	Y	Y	Y	N
9 Rothman	?	?	?	Y	N
10 Payne	?	?	?	Y	N
11 **Frelinghuysen**	Y	Y	Y	N	Y
12 Holt	Y	Y	Y	Y	N
13 Sires	Y	Y	Y	Y	Y
NEW MEXICO					
1 Heinrich	Y	Y	Y	Y	N
2 Teague	Y	Y	Y	Y	Y
3 Lujan	Y	Y	Y	Y	N
NEW YORK					
1 Bishop	Y	Y	Y	Y	N
2 Israel	Y	Y	Y	Y	N
3 **King**	Y	Y	Y	N	Y
4 McCarthy	Y	Y	Y	Y	N
5 Ackerman	Y	Y	Y	Y	N
6 Meeks	?	?	?	Y	N
7 Crowley	Y	Y	Y	Y	N
8 Nadler	Y	Y	Y	Y	N
9 Weiner	Y	Y	?	Y	N
10 Towns	Y	Y	Y	Y	N
11 Clarke	?	Y	Y	Y	N
12 Velázquez	Y	Y	Y	Y	N
13 McMahon	?	?	?	Y	N
14 Maloney	?	?	Y	Y	N
15 Rangel	Y	?	Y	Y	Y
16 Serrano	Y	Y	Y	Y	N
17 Engel	?	?	?	?	N
18 Lowey	Y	Y	Y	+	N
19 Hall	Y	Y	Y	Y	Y
20 Murphy	Y	Y	Y	Y	N
21 Tonko	Y	Y	Y	Y	N
22 Hinchey	Y	Y	Y	Y	N
23 **McHugh**	Y	Y	Y	N	Y
24 Arcuri	Y	Y	Y	Y	Y
25 Maffei	Y	Y	Y	Y	Y
26 Lee	Y	Y	Y	N	Y
27 Higgins	Y	Y	Y	Y	N
28 Slaughter	Y	Y	Y	Y	N
29 Massa	Y	Y	Y	Y	N
NORTH CAROLINA					
1 Butterfield	Y	Y	Y	Y	N
2 Etheridge	+	+	+	Y	N
3 **Jones**	Y	Y	Y	N	Y
4 Price	Y	Y	Y	Y	N

	292	293	294	295	296
5 **Foxx**	Y	Y	Y	N	Y
6 **Coble**	+	+	+	N	Y
7 McIntyre	Y	Y	Y	N	Y
8 Kissell	Y	Y	Y	Y	Y
9 **Myrick**	Y	Y	Y	N	Y
10 **McHenry**	Y	Y	Y	N	Y
11 Shuler	?	?	?	N	Y
12 Watt	Y	Y	Y	Y	N
13 Miller	Y	Y	Y	Y	N
NORTH DAKOTA					
AL Pomeroy	Y	Y	Y	Y	N
OHIO					
1 Driehaus	Y	Y	Y	Y	N
2 **Schmidt**	Y	Y	Y	N	Y
3 Turner	Y	Y	Y	N	Y
4 **Jordan**	Y	Y	Y	N	Y
5 **Latta**	Y	Y	Y	N	Y
6 Wilson	?	?	?	?	?
7 Austria	Y	Y	Y	N	Y
8 **Boehner**	Y	Y	Y	N	Y
9 Kaptur	Y	Y	Y	Y	N
10 Kucinich	Y	Y	Y	Y	N
11 Fudge	Y	Y	Y	Y	N
12 **Tiberi**	Y	?	Y	N	Y
13 Sutton	?	Y	Y	Y	N
14 **LaTourette**	Y	Y	Y	N	Y
15 Kilroy	Y	Y	Y	Y	N
16 Boccieri	Y	Y	Y	Y	N
17 Ryan	Y	Y	Y	Y	N
18 Space	Y	Y	Y	Y	Y
OKLAHOMA					
1 **Sullivan**	?	?	?	?	?
2 Boren	Y	Y	Y	Y	Y
3 **Lucas**	Y	?	Y	N	Y
4 **Cole**	Y	Y	Y	N	Y
5 **Fallin**	Y	Y	Y	N	Y
OREGON					
1 Wu	Y	Y	Y	Y	N
2 **Walden**	Y	Y	Y	N	Y
3 Blumenauer	Y	Y	Y	Y	N
4 DeFazio	Y	Y	Y	Y	N
5 Schrader	Y	Y	Y	Y	N
PENNSYLVANIA					
1 Brady	Y	Y	Y	Y	N
2 Fattah	Y	Y	Y	Y	N
3 Dahlkemper	Y	Y	Y	Y	N
4 Altmire	Y	Y	Y	N	Y
5 **Thompson**	Y	Y	Y	N	Y
6 **Gerlach**	Y	Y	Y	N	Y
7 Sestak	?	?	?	Y	N
8 Murphy, P.	Y	Y	Y	Y	N
9 **Shuster**	Y	?	Y	N	Y
10 Carney	Y	Y	Y	Y	Y
11 Kanjorski	Y	Y	Y	Y	N
12 Murtha	Y	Y	Y	Y	N
13 Schwartz	Y	Y	Y	Y	N
14 Doyle	?	?	?	Y	N
15 **Dent**	Y	Y	Y	N	Y
16 **Pitts**	Y	Y	Y	N	Y
17 Holden	Y	Y	Y	N	Y
18 **Murphy, T.**	Y	Y	Y	N	Y
19 **Platts**	Y	Y	Y	N	Y
RHODE ISLAND					
1 Kennedy	Y	Y	Y	?	N
2 Langevin	Y	Y	Y	Y	N
SOUTH CAROLINA					
1 **Brown**	Y	Y	Y	N	N
2 **Wilson**	+	+	+	N	Y
3 **Barrett**	+	+	+	N	Y
4 **Inglis**	Y	Y	Y	N	Y
5 Spratt	Y	Y	Y	Y	N
6 Clyburn	Y	Y	Y	Y	N
SOUTH DAKOTA					
AL Herseth Sandlin	Y	Y	Y	Y	N
TENNESSEE					
1 Roe	Y	Y	Y	N	Y
2 **Duncan**	Y	Y	Y	N	Y
3 **Wamp**	Y	Y	Y	N	Y
4 Davis	Y	Y	Y	?	Y
5 Cooper	Y	Y	Y	Y	N
6 Gordon	Y	Y	Y	Y	N
7 **Blackburn**	Y	Y	Y	N	Y
8 Tanner	Y	Y	Y	N	Y
9 Cohen	Y	Y	Y	Y	N

	292	293	294	295	296
TEXAS					
1 **Gohmert**	Y	Y	Y	N	Y
2 **Poe**	Y	Y	Y	N	Y
3 **Johnson, S.**	?	?	?	?	?
4 **Hall**	Y	Y	Y	N	Y
5 **Hensarling**	Y	Y	Y	N	Y
6 **Barton**	Y	Y	Y	N	Y
7 **Culberson**	Y	Y	Y	N	Y
8 **Brady**	Y	?	Y	N	Y
9 Green, A.	Y	Y	Y	Y	N
10 **McCaul**	Y	?	Y	N	Y
11 **Conaway**	Y	Y	Y	N	Y
12 **Granger**	Y	Y	Y	N	Y
13 **Thornberry**	Y	Y	Y	N	Y
14 **Paul**	Y	Y	N	N	Y
15 Hinojosa	Y	Y	Y	Y	N
16 Reyes	Y	Y	Y	Y	N
17 Edwards	Y	Y	Y	Y	N
18 Jackson Lee	+	+	+	Y	N
19 **Neugebauer**	Y	Y	Y	N	Y
20 Gonzalez	Y	Y	Y	Y	N
21 **Smith**	Y	Y	Y	N	N
22 **Olson**	Y	Y	Y	N	Y
23 Rodriguez	Y	Y	Y	Y	N
24 **Marchant**	Y	Y	Y	Y	Y
25 Doggett	Y	Y	Y	Y	N
26 **Burgess**	Y	?	?	N	Y
27 Ortiz	Y	Y	Y	Y	N
28 Cuellar	Y	Y	Y	Y	N
29 Green, G.	Y	Y	Y	Y	N
30 Johnson, E.	Y	Y	Y	Y	N
31 **Carter**	Y	Y	Y	N	Y
32 **Sessions**	Y	Y	Y	N	Y
UTAH					
1 **Bishop**	Y	Y	Y	?	?
2 Matheson	Y	Y	Y	Y	N
3 **Chaffetz**	Y	Y	Y	N	Y
VERMONT					
AL Welch	Y	Y	Y	?	N
VIRGINIA					
1 **Wittman**	Y	Y	Y	N	Y
2 Nye	Y	Y	Y	Y	Y
3 Scott	Y	Y	Y	Y	N
4 **Forbes**	Y	Y	Y	N	Y
5 Perriello	Y	Y	Y	Y	N
6 **Goodlatte**	Y	Y	Y	N	Y
7 **Cantor**	Y	Y	Y	N	Y
8 Moran	Y	Y	Y	Y	N
9 Boucher	Y	Y	Y	Y	N
10 **Wolf**	Y	Y	Y	N	Y
11 Connolly	Y	Y	Y	Y	N
WASHINGTON					
1 Inslee	Y	Y	Y	Y	N
2 Larsen	Y	Y	Y	Y	N
3 Baird	Y	Y	Y	Y	Y
4 **Hastings**	Y	Y	Y	N	Y
5 **McMorris Rodgers**	Y	Y	Y	–	Y
6 Dicks	Y	Y	Y	Y	N
7 McDermott	Y	Y	Y	Y	N
8 **Reichert**	Y	Y	Y	N	Y
9 Smith	Y	Y	Y	Y	N
WEST VIRGINIA					
1 Mollohan	Y	Y	Y	Y	N
2 **Capito**	Y	Y	Y	N	Y
3 Rahall	Y	Y	Y	Y	N
WISCONSIN					
1 **Ryan**	Y	Y	Y	N	Y
2 Baldwin	Y	Y	Y	Y	N
3 Kind	Y	Y	Y	Y	N
4 Moore	Y	Y	Y	Y	N
5 **Sensenbrenner**	Y	Y	Y	N	Y
6 **Petri**	Y	Y	Y	N	Y
7 Obey	Y	Y	Y	Y	N
8 Kagen	Y	Y	Y	Y	N
WYOMING					
AL **Lummis**	Y	?	Y	N	Y
DELEGATES					
Faleomavaega (A.S.)					
Norton (D.C.)					
Bordallo (Guam)					
Sablan (N. Marianas)					
Pierluisi (P.R.)					
Christensen (V.I.)					

IN THE HOUSE | By Vote Number

297. **HR 31. Federal Recognition for Lumbee Tribe/Passage.**
Passage of the bill that would provide federal recognition to the Lumbee Tribe in North Carolina and prohibit the tribe from running gambling businesses. It would repeal a 1956 law that denied tribe members federal assistance based on their status as American Indians. It would authorize unspecified sums to conduct activities relating to federal recognition and assistance. Passed 240-179: R 28-144; D 212-35. June 3, 2009.

298. **H Con Res 109. Breast Cancer Race for the Cure/Adoption.**
Capps, D-Calif., motion to suspend the rules and adopt the concurrent resolution that would remember the lives of those who have died from breast cancer, express support for survivors and congratulate participants in the Susan G. Komen Global Race for the Cure. Motion agreed to 417-0: R 169-0; D 248-0. A two-thirds majority of those present and voting (278 in this case) is required for adoption under suspension of the rules. June 3, 2009.

299. **H Res 471. Camp Liberty Shooting/Adoption.** Kratovil, D-Md., motion to suspend the rules and adopt the resolution that would express condolences to the families and friends of victims of the May 11, 2009, shooting at the combat stress clinic at Camp Liberty, Iraq, convey gratitude to armed forces members and commit to focusing on the mental health of U.S. military members. Motion agreed to 416-0: R 170-0; D 246-0. A two-thirds majority of those present and voting (278 in this case) is required for adoption under suspension of the rules. June 3, 2009.

300. **H Res 500. PMA Group Misconduct/Motion to Refer.**
McGovern, D-Mass., motion to refer the Hoyer, D-Md., privileged resolution to the Committee on Standards of Official Conduct. The Hoyer resolution would require the committee to report to the House, within 45 days of the resolution's adoption, on actions it has taken concerning any misconduct of members and employees of the House in connection with activities of the PMA Group. Motion agreed to 270-134: R 28-134; D 242-0. June 3, 2009.

301. **HR 2200. TSA Authorization/Rule.** Adoption of the rule (H Res 474) to provide for House floor consideration of a bill that would authorize $7.6 billion in fiscal 2010 and $8.1 billion in fiscal 2011 for the Transportation Security Administration (TSA). Adopted 243-179: R 0-176; D 243-3. June 4, 2009.

	297	298	299	300	301
ALABAMA					
1 Bonner	Y	Y	Y	P	N
2 Bright	N	Y	Y	P	Y
3 **Rogers**	?	Y	Y	N	N
4 **Aderholt**	Y	Y	Y	N	N
5 Griffith	N	Y	Y	Y	Y
6 **Bachus**	N	Y	Y	N	N
7 Davis	Y	Y	Y	Y	Y
ALASKA					
AL **Young**	Y	Y	Y	Y	N
ARIZONA					
1 Kirkpatrick	Y	Y	Y	Y	Y
2 **Franks**	N	Y	Y	N	N
3 **Shadegg**	N	Y	Y	N	N
4 Pastor	Y	Y	Y	Y	Y
5 Mitchell	Y	Y	Y	Y	Y
6 **Flake**	N	Y	Y	N	N
7 Grijalva	Y	Y	Y	Y	Y
8 Giffords	Y	Y	Y	Y	Y
ARKANSAS					
1 Berry	Y	Y	Y	Y	Y
2 Snyder	Y	Y	Y	Y	N
3 **Boozman**	N	Y	Y	N	N
4 Ross	Y	Y	Y	Y	Y
CALIFORNIA					
1 Thompson	Y	Y	Y	Y	Y
2 **Herger**	N	Y	Y	N	N
3 **Lungren**	N	Y	Y	N	N
4 **McClintock**	N	Y	Y	N	N
5 Matsui	Y	Y	Y	Y	Y
6 Woolsey	Y	Y	Y	Y	Y
7 Miller, George	Y	Y	Y	Y	Y
8 Pelosi					
9 Lee	Y	Y	Y	Y	Y
10 Tauscher	Y	Y	Y	Y	Y
11 McNerney	Y	Y	Y	Y	Y
12 Speier	Y	Y	Y	Y	Y
13 Stark	Y	Y	Y	Y	?
14 Eshoo	Y	Y	Y	Y	Y
15 Honda	Y	Y	Y	Y	Y
16 Lofgren	Y	Y	Y	P	Y
17 Farr	Y	Y	Y	Y	Y
18 Cardoza	Y	Y	Y	Y	Y
19 **Radanovich**	N	Y	Y	N	N
20 Costa	Y	Y	Y	Y	Y
21 **Nunes**	Y	Y	Y	N	N
22 **McCarthy**	Y	Y	Y	N	N
23 Capps	Y	Y	Y	Y	Y
24 **Gallegly**	N	Y	Y	N	N
25 **McKeon**	Y	Y	Y	N	N
26 **Dreier**	N	Y	Y	N	N
27 Sherman	Y	Y	Y	Y	Y
28 Berman	Y	Y	?	Y	Y
29 Schiff	Y	Y	Y	Y	Y
30 Waxman	Y	Y	Y	Y	Y
31 Becerra	+	+	+	+	Y
32 Vacant					
33 Watson	Y	Y	Y	Y	Y
34 Roybal-Allard	Y	Y	Y	Y	Y
35 Waters	Y	Y	Y	Y	Y
36 Harman	Y	Y	Y	Y	Y
37 Richardson	Y	Y	Y	Y	Y
38 Napolitano	Y	Y	Y	Y	Y
39 Sánchez, Linda	?	?	?	?	?
40 **Royce**	N	Y	Y	N	N
41 **Lewis**	N	Y	Y	N	N
42 **Miller, Gary**	N	Y	Y	N	N
43 Baca	N	Y	Y	N	N
44 **Calvert**	N	Y	Y	N	N
45 **Bono Mack**	N	Y	Y	N	N
46 **Rohrabacher**	N	Y	Y	N	N
47 Sanchez, Loretta	?	?	?	?	Y
48 **Campbell**	N	Y	Y	N	N
49 **Issa**	N	Y	Y	N	N
50 **Bilbray**	N	Y	?	N	N
51 Filner	Y	Y	Y	Y	Y
52 **Hunter**	N	Y	Y	N	N
53 Davis	Y	Y	Y	Y	Y
COLORADO					
1 DeGette	Y	Y	Y	Y	Y
2 Polis	Y	Y	Y	Y	Y
3 Salazar	Y	Y	Y	Y	Y
4 Markey	Y	Y	Y	Y	Y
5 **Lamborn**	N	Y	Y	N	N
6 **Coffman**	N	Y	Y	N	N
7 Perlmutter	Y	Y	Y	Y	Y
CONNECTICUT					
1 Larson	Y	Y	Y	Y	Y
2 Courtney	N	Y	Y	Y	Y
3 DeLauro	N	Y	Y	Y	Y
4 Himes	N	Y	Y	Y	Y
5 Murphy	N	Y	Y	Y	Y
DELAWARE					
AL **Castle**	N	Y	Y	Y	N
FLORIDA					
1 **Miller**	N	Y	Y	N	N
2 Boyd	Y	Y	Y	Y	Y
3 Brown	Y	Y	Y	Y	Y
4 **Crenshaw**	N	Y	Y	N	N
5 **Brown-Waite**	N	Y	Y	N	N
6 **Stearns**	N	Y	Y	N	N
7 **Mica**	N	Y	Y	N	N
8 **Grayson**	Y	Y	Y	Y	Y
9 **Bilirakis**	N	Y	Y	N	N
10 **Young**	N	Y	Y	N	N
11 Castor	Y	Y	Y	P	Y
12 **Putnam**	N	Y	Y	N	N
13 **Buchanan**	N	Y	Y	N	N
14 **Mack**	N	Y	Y	N	N
15 **Posey**	N	Y	Y	N	N
16 **Rooney**	N	Y	Y	N	N
17 Meek	Y	Y	Y	Y	Y
18 **Ros-Lehtinen**	?	?	?	?	Y
19 Wexler	Y	Y	Y	Y	Y
20 Wasserman Schultz	N	Y	Y	Y	Y
21 **Diaz-Balart, L.**	Y	Y	Y	P	N
22 Klein	Y	Y	Y	Y	Y
23 Hastings	Y	Y	Y	Y	Y
24 Kosmas	Y	Y	Y	Y	Y
25 **Diaz-Balart, M.**	Y	Y	Y	N	N
GEORGIA					
1 **Kingston**	N	Y	Y	N	N
2 Bishop	Y	Y	Y	Y	Y
3 **Westmoreland**	N	Y	Y	N	N
4 Johnson	Y	Y	Y	Y	Y
5 Lewis	Y	Y	Y	Y	Y
6 **Price**	N	Y	Y	N	N
7 **Linder**	N	Y	Y	N	N
8 Marshall	Y	Y	Y	Y	Y
9 **Deal**	N	Y	Y	N	N
10 **Broun**	-	+	+	-	N
11 **Gingrey**	N	Y	Y	N	N
12 Barrow	Y	Y	Y	Y	Y
13 Scott	Y	Y	Y	Y	Y
HAWAII					
1 Abercrombie	?	Y	Y	Y	Y
2 Hirono	Y	Y	Y	Y	Y
IDAHO					
1 Minnick	N	Y	Y	N	N
2 **Simpson**	Y	Y	Y	N	N
ILLINOIS					
1 Rush	Y	Y	Y	Y	Y
2 Jackson	Y	Y	Y	Y	Y
3 Lipinski	Y	Y	Y	Y	Y
4 Gutierrez	Y	Y	Y	Y	Y
5 Quigley	N	Y	Y	Y	Y
6 **Roskam**	N	Y	Y	N	N
7 Davis	?	?	?	?	Y
8 Bean	Y	Y	Y	Y	Y
9 Schakowsky	Y	Y	Y	Y	Y
10 **Kirk**	N	Y	?	N	N
11 Halvorson	Y	Y	Y	Y	Y
12 Costello	Y	Y	Y	Y	Y
13 **Biggert**	Y	Y	Y	N	Y
14 Foster	Y	Y	Y	Y	Y
15 **Johnson**	N	Y	Y	N	N

	297	298	299	300	301
16 Manzullo	N	Y	Y	N	N
17 Hare	Y	Y	Y	Y	Y
18 Schock	N	Y	Y	N	N
19 Shimkus	Y	Y	Y	N	N
INDIANA					
1 Visclosky	Y	Y	Y	Y	Y
2 Donnelly	Y	Y	Y	Y	Y
3 Souder	Y	Y	Y	N	N
4 Buyer	N	Y	Y	Y	N
5 Burton	N	Y	Y	N	N
6 Pence	N	?	Y	N	N
7 Carson	Y	Y	Y	Y	Y
8 Ellsworth	N	Y	Y	Y	Y
9 Hill	N	Y	Y	Y	N
IOWA					
1 Braley	Y	Y	Y	Y	?
2 Loebsack	Y	Y	Y	Y	Y
3 Boswell	Y	Y	Y	Y	Y
4 Latham	N	Y	Y	P	N
5 King	N	Y	Y	N	N
KANSAS					
1 Moran	N	Y	Y	N	N
2 Jenkins	N	Y	Y	N	N
3 Moore	Y	Y	Y	Y	Y
4 Tiahrt	N	Y	Y	N	N
KENTUCKY					
1 Whitfield	N	Y	Y	N	N
2 Guthrie	N	Y	Y	N	N
3 Yarmuth	Y	Y	Y	Y	Y
4 Davis	Y	Y	Y	N	N
5 Rogers	N	Y	Y	N	N
6 Chandler	Y	Y	Y	P	Y
LOUISIANA					
1 Scalise	N	Y	Y	N	N
2 Cao	N	Y	Y	N	N
3 Melancon	Y	Y	Y	Y	Y
4 Fleming	N	Y	Y	N	N
5 Alexander	N	Y	Y	N	N
6 Cassidy	N	Y	Y	N	N
7 Boustany	N	Y	Y	N	N
MAINE					
1 Pingree	Y	Y	Y	Y	Y
2 Michaud	Y	Y	Y	Y	Y
MARYLAND					
1 Kratovil	Y	Y	Y	Y	Y
2 Ruppersberger	?	?	?	?	?
3 Sarbanes	Y	Y	Y	Y	Y
4 Edwards	Y	Y	Y	Y	Y
5 Hoyer	Y	Y	Y	Y	Y
6 Bartlett	N	Y	Y	N	N
7 Cummings	Y	Y	Y	Y	Y
8 Van Hollen	Y	Y	Y	Y	Y
MASSACHUSETTS					
1 Olver	Y	Y	Y	Y	Y
2 Neal	Y	Y	Y	Y	Y
3 McGovern	Y	Y	Y	Y	Y
4 Frank	Y	Y	Y	Y	Y
5 Tsongas	Y	Y	Y	Y	Y
6 Tierney	Y	Y	Y	Y	Y
7 Markey	Y	Y	Y	Y	Y
8 Capuano	Y	Y	Y	Y	Y
9 Lynch	Y	Y	Y	Y	Y
10 Delahunt	N	Y	Y	Y	Y
MICHIGAN					
1 Stupak	N	Y	Y	Y	Y
2 Hoekstra	N	Y	Y	N	N
3 Ehlers	N	Y	Y	Y	N
4 Camp	N	Y	Y	N	N
5 Kildee	Y	Y	Y	Y	Y
6 Upton	N	Y	Y	Y	N
7 Schauer	N	Y	Y	Y	Y
8 Rogers	N	Y	Y	N	N
9 Peters	Y	Y	Y	Y	Y
10 Miller	N	Y	Y	N	N
11 McCotter	N	Y	Y	N	N
12 Levin	Y	Y	Y	Y	Y
13 Kilpatrick	Y	Y	Y	Y	Y
14 Conyers	Y	Y	Y	Y	Y
15 Dingell	Y	Y	Y	Y	Y
MINNESOTA					
1 Walz	Y	Y	Y	Y	Y
2 Kline	N	Y	Y	P	N
3 Paulsen	N	Y	Y	N	N
4 McCollum	Y	Y	Y	Y	Y

	297	298	299	300	301
5 Ellison	Y	Y	Y	Y	Y
6 Bachmann	N	Y	Y	N	N
7 Peterson	Y	Y	Y	Y	Y
8 Oberstar	Y	Y	Y	Y	Y
MISSISSIPPI					
1 Childers	N	Y	Y	Y	Y
2 Thompson	Y	Y	Y	Y	Y
3 Harper	N	Y	Y	N	N
4 Taylor	N	Y	Y	Y	Y
MISSOURI					
1 Clay	Y	Y	Y	Y	Y
2 Akin	N	Y	Y	N	N
3 Carnahan	Y	Y	Y	Y	Y
4 Skelton	Y	Y	Y	Y	Y
5 Cleaver	Y	Y	Y	Y	Y
6 Graves	N	Y	Y	N	N
7 Blunt	N	Y	Y	N	N
8 Emerson	N	Y	Y	N	N
9 Luetkemeyer	N	Y	Y	N	N
MONTANA					
AL Rehberg	N	Y	Y	N	N
NEBRASKA					
1 Fortenberry	N	Y	Y	N	N
2 Terry	Y	Y	Y	?	N
3 Smith	N	Y	Y	N	N
NEVADA					
1 Berkley	Y	Y	Y	Y	Y
2 Heller	Y	Y	Y	N	N
3 Titus	Y	Y	Y	Y	Y
NEW HAMPSHIRE					
1 Shea-Porter	Y	Y	Y	Y	Y
2 Hodes	Y	Y	Y	Y	Y
NEW JERSEY					
1 Andrews	Y	Y	Y	Y	Y
2 LoBiondo	N	Y	Y	Y	N
3 Adler	N	Y	Y	Y	Y
4 Smith	N	Y	Y	Y	N
5 Garrett	N	Y	Y	N	N
6 Pallone	Y	Y	Y	Y	Y
7 Lance	N	Y	Y	Y	N
8 Pascrell	Y	Y	Y	Y	Y
9 Rothman	Y	Y	Y	Y	Y
10 Payne	Y	Y	Y	Y	Y
11 Frelinghuysen	N	Y	Y	N	N
12 Holt	Y	Y	Y	Y	Y
13 Sires	N	Y	Y	Y	Y
NEW MEXICO					
1 Heinrich	Y	Y	Y	Y	Y
2 Teague	N	Y	Y	Y	Y
3 Lujan	Y	Y	Y	Y	Y
NEW YORK					
1 Bishop	Y	Y	Y	Y	Y
2 Israel	Y	Y	Y	Y	Y
3 King	Y	Y	Y	N	N
4 McCarthy	Y	Y	Y	Y	Y
5 Ackerman	Y	Y	Y	Y	Y
6 Meeks	Y	Y	Y	Y	Y
7 Crowley	Y	Y	Y	Y	Y
8 Nadler	Y	Y	Y	Y	Y
9 Weiner	Y	Y	Y	Y	Y
10 Towns	Y	Y	Y	Y	Y
11 Clarke	Y	Y	Y	Y	Y
12 Velázquez	Y	Y	Y	Y	Y
13 McMahon	Y	Y	Y	Y	Y
14 Maloney	Y	Y	Y	Y	Y
15 Rangel	?	Y	Y	Y	Y
16 Serrano	Y	Y	Y	Y	Y
17 Engel	Y	Y	Y	Y	Y
18 Lowey	Y	Y	Y	Y	Y
19 Hall	N	Y	Y	Y	Y
20 Murphy	Y	Y	Y	Y	Y
21 Tonko	Y	Y	Y	Y	Y
22 Hinchey	Y	Y	Y	Y	Y
23 McHugh	Y	Y	Y	N	N
24 Arcuri	N	Y	Y	Y	Y
25 Maffei	N	Y	Y	Y	Y
26 Lee	N	Y	Y	N	N
27 Higgins	Y	Y	Y	Y	Y
28 Slaughter	Y	Y	Y	Y	Y
29 Massa	Y	Y	Y	Y	Y
NORTH CAROLINA					
1 Butterfield	Y	Y	Y	P	Y
2 Etheridge	Y	Y	Y	Y	Y
3 Jones	N	Y	Y	Y	Y
4 Price	Y	Y	Y	Y	Y

	297	298	299	300	301
5 Foxx	N	Y	Y	N	N
6 Coble	Y	Y	Y	N	N
7 McIntyre	Y	Y	Y	Y	Y
8 Kissell	Y	Y	Y	Y	Y
9 Myrick	N	+	+	P	N
10 McHenry	N	Y	Y	N	N
11 Shuler	N	Y	Y	N	N
12 Watt	Y	?	Y	Y	Y
13 Miller	Y	Y	Y	Y	Y
NORTH DAKOTA					
AL Pomeroy	N	Y	Y	Y	Y
OHIO					
1 Driehaus	Y	Y	Y	Y	Y
2 Schmidt	N	?	Y	Y	N
3 Turner	N	Y	Y	Y	N
4 Jordan	N	Y	Y	N	N
5 Latta	N	Y	Y	N	N
6 Wilson	?	?	?	?	?
7 Austria	N	Y	Y	N	N
8 Boehner	N	Y	Y	N	N
9 Kaptur	Y	Y	Y	Y	Y
10 Kucinich	Y	Y	Y	Y	Y
11 Fudge	Y	Y	Y	Y	Y
12 Tiberi	N	Y	Y	N	N
13 Sutton	Y	Y	Y	Y	Y
14 LaTourette	Y	Y	Y	Y	Y
15 Kilroy	Y	Y	Y	Y	Y
16 Boccieri	Y	Y	Y	Y	Y
17 Ryan	Y	Y	Y	Y	Y
18 Space	Y	Y	Y	Y	Y
OKLAHOMA					
1 Sullivan	?	?	?	?	?
2 Boren	N	Y	Y	Y	Y
3 Lucas	N	Y	Y	N	N
4 Cole	N	Y	Y	N	N
5 Fallin	N	Y	Y	N	N
OREGON					
1 Wu	Y	Y	Y	Y	Y
2 Walden	Y	Y	Y	P	N
3 Blumenauer	Y	Y	Y	Y	Y
4 DeFazio	Y	Y	Y	Y	Y
5 Schrader	Y	Y	Y	Y	Y
PENNSYLVANIA					
1 Brady	Y	Y	Y	Y	Y
2 Fattah	Y	Y	Y	Y	Y
3 Dahlkemper	Y	Y	Y	Y	Y
4 Altmire	N	Y	Y	Y	Y
5 Thompson	N	Y	Y	N	N
6 Gerlach	N	Y	Y	Y	N
7 Sestak	Y	Y	Y	Y	?
8 Murphy, P.	N	Y	Y	Y	Y
9 Shuster	N	Y	Y	N	N
10 Carney	N	Y	Y	Y	Y
11 Kanjorski	Y	Y	Y	Y	Y
12 Murtha	Y	Y	Y	Y	Y
13 Schwartz	Y	Y	Y	Y	Y
14 Doyle	Y	Y	Y	Y	Y
15 Dent	N	Y	Y	P	N
16 Pitts	N	?	Y	N	N
17 Holden	Y	Y	Y	Y	Y
18 Murphy, T.	N	Y	Y	N	N
19 Platts	Y	Y	Y	N	N
RHODE ISLAND					
1 Kennedy	Y	Y	Y	Y	?
2 Langevin	Y	Y	Y	Y	Y
SOUTH CAROLINA					
1 Brown	Y	Y	Y	N	N
2 Wilson	N	Y	Y	N	N
3 Barrett	N	Y	Y	P	N
4 Inglis	N	Y	Y	N	N
5 Spratt	Y	Y	Y	Y	Y
6 Clyburn	Y	Y	Y	Y	Y
SOUTH DAKOTA					
AL Herseth Sandlin	N	Y	Y	Y	Y
TENNESSEE					
1 Roe	N	Y	Y	N	N
2 Duncan	N	Y	Y	N	N
3 Wamp	N	Y	Y	N	N
4 Davis	N	Y	Y	Y	Y
5 Cooper	Y	Y	Y	Y	?
6 Gordon	Y	Y	Y	?	?
7 Blackburn	N	Y	Y	N	N
8 Tanner	N	Y	Y	Y	Y
9 Cohen	Y	Y	Y	Y	Y

	297	298	299	300	301
TEXAS					
1 Gohmert	Y	Y	Y	Y	N
2 Poe	N	Y	Y	P	N
3 Johnson, S.	?	?	?	?	N
4 Hall	N	Y	Y	Y	N
5 Hensarling	N	Y	Y	N	N
6 Barton	N	Y	Y	N	?
7 Culberson	N	Y	Y	N	N
8 Brady	Y	Y	Y	N	N
9 Green, A.	Y	Y	Y	Y	Y
10 McCaul	N	Y	Y	N	N
11 Conaway	N	Y	Y	P	N
12 Granger	N	Y	Y	N	N
13 Thornberry	Y	Y	Y	N	N
14 Paul	N	Y	Y	N	N
15 Hinojosa	Y	Y	Y	Y	+
16 Reyes	Y	Y	Y	Y	Y
17 Edwards	Y	Y	Y	Y	Y
18 Jackson Lee	Y	Y	Y	Y	Y
19 Neugebauer	N	Y	Y	N	N
20 Gonzalez	Y	Y	Y	Y	Y
21 Smith	Y	Y	Y	N	N
22 Olson	N	Y	Y	N	N
23 Rodriguez	Y	Y	Y	Y	Y
24 Marchant	N	Y	Y	N	N
25 Doggett	Y	Y	Y	Y	Y
26 Burgess	N	Y	Y	N	N
27 Ortiz	Y	Y	Y	Y	Y
28 Cuellar	Y	Y	Y	Y	Y
29 Green, G.	Y	Y	Y	Y	Y
30 Johnson, E.	Y	Y	Y	Y	Y
31 Carter	N	Y	Y	N	N
32 Sessions	N	Y	Y	N	N
UTAH					
1 Bishop	?	?	?	N	N
2 Matheson	Y	Y	Y	Y	Y
3 Chaffetz	N	Y	Y	N	N
VERMONT					
AL Welch	Y	Y	Y	P	Y
VIRGINIA					
1 Wittman	N	Y	Y	Y	N
2 Nye	N	Y	Y	Y	Y
3 Scott	Y	Y	Y	Y	Y
4 Forbes	N	Y	Y	Y	N
5 Perriello	N	Y	Y	Y	Y
6 Goodlatte	N	Y	Y	Y	N
7 Cantor	N	Y	Y	N	N
8 Moran	Y	Y	Y	Y	Y
9 Boucher	Y	Y	Y	Y	Y
10 Wolf	N	Y	Y	Y	N
11 Connolly	Y	Y	Y	Y	Y
WASHINGTON					
1 Inslee	Y	Y	Y	Y	Y
2 Larsen	Y	Y	Y	Y	Y
3 Baird	Y	Y	Y	Y	Y
4 Hastings	N	Y	Y	P	N
5 McMorris Rodgers	N	Y	Y	N	N
6 Dicks	Y	Y	Y	Y	Y
7 McDermott	Y	Y	Y	Y	Y
8 Reichert	N	Y	Y	N	N
9 Smith	Y	Y	Y	Y	Y
WEST VIRGINIA					
1 Mollohan	Y	Y	?	Y	Y
2 Capito	Y	Y	Y	N	N
3 Rahall	Y	Y	Y	Y	Y
WISCONSIN					
1 Ryan	N	Y	Y	N	N
2 Baldwin	Y	Y	Y	Y	Y
3 Kind	Y	Y	Y	Y	Y
4 Moore	Y	Y	Y	Y	Y
5 Sensenbrenner	N	Y	Y	N	N
6 Petri	N	Y	Y	Y	N
7 Obey	Y	Y	Y	Y	Y
8 Kagen	Y	Y	Y	Y	Y
WYOMING					
AL Lummis	N	Y	Y	N	N
DELEGATES					
Faleomavaega (A.S.)					
Norton (D.C.)					
Bordallo (Guam)					
Sablan (N. Marianas)					
Pierluisi (P.R.)					
Christensen (V.I.)					

IN THE HOUSE | By Vote Number

302. **HR 1817. John Wilder Post Office/Passage.** Lynch, D-Mass., motion to suspend the rules and pass the bill that would designate a post office in Somerville, Tenn., as the "John S. Wilder Post Office Building." Motion agreed to 420-0: R 176-0; D 244-0. A two-thirds majority of those present and voting (280 in this case) is required for passage under suspension of the rules. June 4, 2009.

303. **H Res 196. University of Tennessee Women's Basketball/Adoption.** Tonko, D-N.Y., motion to suspend the rules and adopt the resolution that would congratulate the head coach of the University of Tennessee women's basketball team, Pat Summitt, on her 1,000th victory and recognize the players, coaches and alumni who have contributed to the success of the women's basketball program. Motion agreed to 417-0: R 176-0; D 241-0. A two-thirds majority of those present and voting (278 in this case) is required for adoption under suspension of the rules. June 4, 2009.

304. **HR 2200. TSA Authorization/Imminent Threat Security Directives.** Mica, R-Fla., amendment that would allow the TSA to issue a regulation or security directive to respond to an imminent threat of finite duration and require the TSA to comply with rule-making requirements when a security directive or emergency order has been in place for more than 180 days. Adopted in Committee of the Whole 219-211: R 177-0; D 42-211. June 4, 2009.

305. **HR 2200. TSA Authorization/Body Imaging Screening.** Chaffetz, R-Utah, amendment that would bar the use of whole-body imaging technology as the primary method of airport security screening. Whole-body imaging could be used if a passenger is not allowed to board a plane based on another screening method. Passengers would have the option of a pat-down search as an alternative. It would also prohibit whole-body screening images from being stored, transferred, shared or copied after a boarding determination has been made. Adopted in Committee of the Whole 310-118: R 119-57; D 191-61. June 4, 2009.

306. **HR 2200. TSA Authorization/Detainee No-Fly Status.** Thompson, D-Miss., amendment that would require the names of all detainees at the detention facility at Guantánamo Bay, Cuba, be added to the no-fly list unless the president certifies that the detainee does not pose a threat to the United States. Adopted 412-12: R 176-1; D 236-11. (The amendment was made in order pursuant to the voice vote adoption of the King, R-N.Y., motion to recommit the bill with instructions.) June 4, 2009.

	302	303	304	305	306
ALABAMA					
1 Bonner	Y	Y	Y	N	Y
2 Bright	Y	Y	Y	N	Y
3 Rogers	Y	Y	Y	N	Y
4 Aderholt	Y	Y	Y	N	Y
5 Griffith	Y	Y	Y	Y	Y
6 Bachus	Y	Y	Y	Y	Y
7 Davis	Y	Y	N	Y	Y
ALASKA					
AL Young	Y	Y	Y	N	Y
ARIZONA					
1 Kirkpatrick	Y	Y	N	Y	Y
2 Franks	Y	Y	Y	N	Y
3 Shadegg	Y	Y	Y	N	Y
4 Pastor	Y	Y	N	Y	Y
5 Mitchell	Y	Y	Y	Y	Y
6 Flake	Y	Y	Y	Y	Y
7 Grijalva	Y	Y	N	Y	Y
8 Giffords	Y	Y	Y	Y	Y
ARKANSAS					
1 Berry	Y	Y	N	N	Y
2 Snyder	Y	Y	N	N	Y
3 Boozman	Y	Y	Y	Y	Y
4 Ross	Y	Y	Y	Y	Y
CALIFORNIA					
1 Thompson	Y	Y	N	N	Y
2 Herger	Y	Y	Y	N	Y
3 Lungren	Y	Y	Y	N	Y
4 McClintock	Y	Y	Y	Y	Y
5 Matsui	Y	Y	N	N	Y
6 Woolsey	Y	Y	N	Y	Y
7 Miller, George	Y	Y	N	Y	Y
8 Pelosi					
9 Lee	Y	Y	N	Y	N
10 Tauscher	Y	Y	N	Y	Y
11 McNerney	Y	Y	N	Y	Y
12 Speier	Y	Y	N	Y	Y
13 Stark	?	?	N	Y	?
14 Eshoo	Y	Y	N	N	Y
15 Honda	?	?	N	N	Y
16 Lofgren	Y	Y	N	Y	Y
17 Farr	Y	Y	N	Y	Y
18 Cardoza	Y	Y	N	Y	Y
19 Radanovich	Y	Y	Y	Y	Y
20 Costa	Y	Y	N	Y	Y
21 Nunes	Y	Y	Y	N	Y
22 McCarthy	Y	Y	Y	Y	Y
23 Capps	Y	Y	N	Y	Y
24 Gallegly	Y	Y	Y	N	Y
25 McKeon	Y	Y	Y	Y	Y
26 Dreier	Y	Y	Y	Y	Y
27 Sherman	Y	Y	N	Y	Y
28 Berman	Y	Y	N	Y	Y
29 Schiff	Y	Y	N	Y	Y
30 Waxman	Y	Y	N	Y	Y
31 Becerra	Y	Y	N	Y	Y
32 Vacant					
33 Watson	Y	Y	N	Y	Y
34 Roybal-Allard	Y	Y	N	Y	Y
35 Waters	Y	Y	N	N	N
36 Harman	Y	Y	N	N	Y
37 Richardson	Y	Y	N	Y	Y
38 Napolitano	Y	Y	N	Y	Y
39 Sánchez, Linda	?	?	?	?	?
40 Royce	Y	Y	Y	N	Y
41 Lewis	Y	Y	Y	Y	Y
42 Miller, Gary	Y	Y	Y	Y	Y
43 Baca	Y	Y	N	Y	Y
44 Calvert	Y	Y	Y	Y	Y
45 Bono Mack	Y	Y	Y	N	Y
46 Rohrabacher	Y	Y	Y	N	Y
47 Sanchez, Loretta	Y	Y	Y	Y	Y
48 Campbell	Y	Y	Y	Y	Y
49 Issa	Y	Y	Y	Y	Y
50 Bilbray	Y	Y	Y	N	Y
51 Filner	Y	Y	N	N	Y
52 Hunter	Y	Y	Y	Y	Y
53 Davis	Y	Y	N	Y	Y

	302	303	304	305	306
COLORADO					
1 DeGette	Y	Y	N	N	Y
2 Polis	Y	?	N	Y	Y
3 Salazar	Y	Y	Y	Y	Y
4 Markey	Y	Y	Y	N	Y
5 Lamborn	Y	Y	Y	Y	Y
6 Coffman	Y	Y	Y	N	Y
7 Perlmutter	Y	Y	N	Y	Y
CONNECTICUT					
1 Larson	Y	Y	N	Y	Y
2 Courtney	Y	Y	?	?	?
3 DeLauro	Y	Y	N	N	Y
4 Himes	Y	Y	N	N	Y
5 Murphy	Y	Y	N	Y	Y
DELAWARE					
AL Castle	Y	Y	Y	N	Y
FLORIDA					
1 Miller	Y	Y	Y	N	Y
2 Boyd	Y	Y	N	N	Y
3 Brown	Y	Y	N	N	Y
4 Crenshaw	Y	Y	Y	Y	Y
5 Brown-Waite	Y	Y	Y	Y	Y
6 Stearns	Y	Y	Y	Y	Y
7 Mica	Y	Y	Y	N	Y
8 Grayson	Y	Y	N	Y	Y
9 Bilirakis	Y	Y	Y	N	Y
10 Young	Y	Y	Y	N	Y
11 Castor	Y	Y	N	Y	Y
12 Putnam	Y	Y	Y	Y	Y
13 Buchanan	Y	Y	Y	Y	Y
14 Mack	Y	Y	Y	Y	Y
15 Posey	Y	Y	Y	Y	Y
16 Rooney	Y	Y	Y	Y	Y
17 Meek	Y	Y	N	Y	Y
18 Ros-Lehtinen	Y	Y	Y	N	Y
19 Wexler	Y	Y	N	Y	Y
20 Wasserman Schultz	Y	Y	N	Y	Y
21 Diaz-Balart, L.	Y	Y	Y	Y	Y
22 Klein	Y	Y	Y	N	Y
23 Hastings	Y	Y	N	Y	Y
24 Kosmas	Y	Y	N	Y	Y
25 Diaz-Balart, M.	Y	Y	Y	Y	Y
GEORGIA					
1 Kingston	Y	Y	Y	Y	Y
2 Bishop	Y	Y	N	Y	Y
3 Westmoreland	Y	Y	Y	Y	Y
4 Johnson	Y	?	N	Y	Y
5 Lewis	Y	Y	N	Y	Y
6 Price	Y	Y	Y	Y	Y
7 Linder	Y	Y	Y	Y	Y
8 Marshall	Y	Y	N	Y	Y
9 Deal	Y	Y	Y	Y	Y
10 Broun	Y	Y	Y	Y	Y
11 Gingrey	Y	Y	Y	Y	Y
12 Barrow	Y	Y	Y	Y	Y
13 Scott	Y	Y	N	Y	Y
HAWAII					
1 Abercrombie	Y	Y	Y	Y	Y
2 Hirono	Y	Y	Y	Y	Y
IDAHO					
1 Minnick	Y	Y	Y	N	Y
2 Simpson	Y	Y	Y	N	Y
ILLINOIS					
1 Rush	Y	Y	N	Y	Y
2 Jackson	Y	Y	N	Y	Y
3 Lipinski	Y	Y	N	Y	Y
4 Gutierrez	Y	Y	N	Y	Y
5 Quigley	Y	Y	N	Y	Y
6 Roskam	Y	Y	Y	Y	Y
7 Davis	Y	Y	N	Y	Y
8 Bean	Y	Y	N	N	Y
9 Schakowsky	Y	Y	N	N	Y
10 Kirk	Y	Y	Y	N	Y
11 Halvorson	Y	Y	N	N	Y
12 Costello	Y	Y	N	Y	Y
13 Biggert	Y	Y	Y	N	Y
14 Foster	Y	Y	N	N	Y
15 Johnson	Y	Y	Y	Y	Y

KEY   **Republicans**   Democrats

Y Voted for (yea)	X Paired against	C Voted "present" to avoid possible conflict of interest
# Paired for	– Announced against	
+ Announced for	P Voted "present"	? Did not vote or otherwise make a position known
N Voted against (nay)		

	302	303	304	305	306
16 **Manzullo**	Y	Y	Y	Y	Y
17 Hare	Y	Y	N	Y	Y
18 **Schock**	Y	Y	Y	Y	Y
19 **Shimkus**	Y	Y	Y	Y	Y
INDIANA					
1 Visclosky	Y	Y	N	N	Y
2 Donnelly	Y	Y	Y	Y	Y
3 **Souder**	Y	Y	Y	N	Y
4 **Buyer**	Y	Y	Y	Y	Y
5 **Burton**	Y	Y	Y	N	Y
6 **Pence**	?	Y	Y	Y	Y
7 Carson	Y	Y	N	Y	Y
8 Ellsworth	Y	Y	Y	Y	Y
9 Hill	Y	Y	Y	Y	Y
IOWA					
1 Braley	Y	?	N	Y	Y
2 Loebsack	Y	Y	Y	Y	Y
3 Boswell	Y	Y	?	?	?
4 **Latham**	Y	Y	Y	N	Y
5 **King**	Y	Y	Y	Y	Y
KANSAS					
1 **Moran**	Y	Y	Y	Y	Y
2 **Jenkins**	Y	Y	Y	Y	Y
3 Moore	Y	Y	N	Y	Y
4 **Tiahrt**	Y	Y	Y	Y	Y
KENTUCKY					
1 **Whitfield**	Y	Y	Y	Y	Y
2 **Guthrie**	Y	Y	Y	Y	Y
3 Yarmuth	Y	Y	N	Y	Y
4 **Davis**	Y	Y	Y	Y	Y
5 **Rogers**	Y	Y	Y	N	Y
6 Chandler	Y	Y	Y	Y	Y
LOUISIANA					
1 **Scalise**	Y	Y	Y	Y	Y
2 **Cao**	Y	Y	Y	Y	Y
3 Melancon	Y	Y	Y	Y	Y
4 **Fleming**	Y	Y	Y	N	Y
5 **Alexander**	Y	?	Y	Y	Y
6 **Cassidy**	Y	Y	Y	Y	Y
7 **Boustany**	Y	Y	Y	N	Y
MAINE					
1 Pingree	Y	Y	N	Y	Y
2 Michaud	Y	Y	N	Y	Y
MARYLAND					
1 Kratovil	Y	Y	Y	N	Y
2 Ruppersberger	?	?	?	?	?
3 Sarbanes	Y	Y	N	Y	Y
4 Edwards	Y	Y	N	Y	Y
5 Hoyer	Y	Y	N	Y	Y
6 **Bartlett**	Y	Y	Y	Y	Y
7 Cummings	Y	Y	N	Y	Y
8 Van Hollen	Y	Y	N	Y	Y
MASSACHUSETTS					
1 Olver	Y	Y	N	N	Y
2 Neal	Y	Y	N	Y	Y
3 McGovern	Y	Y	N	Y	Y
4 Frank	Y	Y	N	N	Y
5 Tsongas	Y	Y	N	Y	Y
6 Tierney	Y	Y	N	Y	Y
7 Markey	Y	Y	N	Y	Y
8 Capuano	Y	Y	N	Y	Y
9 Lynch	Y	Y	N	Y	Y
10 Delahunt	Y	Y	N	Y	Y
MICHIGAN					
1 Stupak	Y	Y	N	Y	Y
2 **Hoekstra**	Y	Y	Y	N	Y
3 **Ehlers**	Y	Y	Y	N	Y
4 **Camp**	Y	Y	Y	Y	Y
5 Kildee	Y	Y	N	Y	Y
6 **Upton**	Y	Y	Y	Y	Y
7 Schauer	Y	Y	N	N	Y
8 **Rogers**	Y	Y	Y	N	Y
9 Peters	Y	Y	N	Y	Y
10 **Miller**	Y	Y	Y	N	Y
11 **McCotter**	Y	Y	Y	Y	Y
12 Levin	Y	Y	N	Y	Y
13 Kilpatrick	Y	Y	N	Y	Y
14 Conyers	Y	?	N	Y	N
15 Dingell	Y	Y	N	Y	Y
MINNESOTA					
1 Walz	Y	Y	Y	Y	Y
2 **Kline**	Y	Y	Y	Y	Y
3 **Paulsen**	Y	Y	Y	N	Y
4 McCollum	Y	Y	N	Y	Y
5 Ellison	Y	Y	N	Y	Y
6 **Bachmann**	Y	Y	Y	Y	Y
7 Peterson	Y	Y	Y	N	Y
8 Oberstar	Y	Y	Y	N	Y
MISSISSIPPI					
1 Childers	Y	Y	N	Y	Y
2 Thompson	Y	Y	N	N	Y
3 **Harper**	Y	Y	Y	Y	Y
4 Taylor	Y	Y	Y	Y	Y
MISSOURI					
1 Clay	Y	Y	N	Y	N
2 **Akin**	Y	Y	Y	N	Y
3 Carnahan	Y	Y	N	N	Y
4 Skelton	Y	Y	N	N	Y
5 Cleaver	Y	Y	N	Y	N
6 **Graves**	Y	Y	Y	N	Y
7 **Blunt**	Y	Y	Y	Y	Y
8 **Emerson**	Y	Y	Y	Y	Y
9 **Luetkemeyer**	Y	Y	Y	Y	Y
MONTANA					
AL **Rehberg**	Y	Y	Y	Y	Y
NEBRASKA					
1 **Fortenberry**	Y	Y	Y	Y	Y
2 **Terry**	Y	Y	Y	Y	Y
3 **Smith**	Y	Y	Y	Y	Y
NEVADA					
1 Berkley	Y	Y	Y	Y	Y
2 **Heller**	Y	Y	Y	Y	Y
3 Titus	Y	Y	N	Y	Y
NEW HAMPSHIRE					
1 Shea-Porter	Y	Y	N	Y	Y
2 Hodes	Y	Y	N	Y	Y
NEW JERSEY					
1 Andrews	Y	Y	N	N	Y
2 **LoBiondo**	Y	Y	Y	N	Y
3 Adler	?	Y	N	Y	Y
4 **Smith**	Y	Y	Y	Y	Y
5 **Garrett**	Y	Y	Y	Y	Y
6 Pallone	Y	?	N	Y	Y
7 **Lance**	Y	Y	Y	N	Y
8 Pascrell	Y	Y	N	Y	Y
9 Rothman	Y	Y	N	Y	Y
10 Payne	Y	Y	N	Y	Y
11 **Frelinghuysen**	Y	Y	Y	N	Y
12 Holt	Y	Y	N	Y	Y
13 Sires	Y	Y	N	Y	Y
NEW MEXICO					
1 Heinrich	Y	Y	Y	Y	Y
2 Teague	Y	Y	N	Y	Y
3 Lujan	Y	Y	N	Y	Y
NEW YORK					
1 Bishop	Y	Y	N	N	Y
2 Israel	Y	Y	N	Y	Y
3 **King**	Y	Y	Y	N	Y
4 McCarthy	Y	Y	N	N	Y
5 Ackerman	Y	Y	N	N	Y
6 Meeks	Y	Y	N	Y	Y
7 Crowley	Y	Y	N	Y	Y
8 Nadler	Y	Y	N	Y	N
9 Weiner	Y	Y	N	Y	Y
10 Towns	Y	Y	N	N	Y
11 Clarke	Y	Y	N	Y	N
12 Velázquez	Y	Y	N	Y	Y
13 McMahon	Y	Y	N	+	Y
14 Maloney	Y	Y	N	Y	Y
15 Rangel	Y	Y	N	Y	Y
16 Serrano	?	Y	N	Y	Y
17 Engel	Y	Y	N	Y	Y
18 Lowey	Y	Y	N	N	Y
19 Hall	Y	Y	N	Y	Y
20 Murphy	Y	Y	Y	Y	Y
21 Tonko	Y	Y	N	Y	Y
22 Hinchey	Y	Y	N	Y	Y
23 **McHugh**	Y	Y	Y	Y	Y
24 Arcuri	Y	Y	Y	Y	Y
25 Maffei	Y	Y	N	Y	Y
26 **Lee**	Y	Y	Y	N	Y
27 Higgins	Y	Y	N	Y	Y
28 Slaughter	Y	Y	?	N	Y
29 Massa	Y	Y	N	Y	Y
NORTH CAROLINA					
1 Butterfield	Y	Y	N	N	Y
2 Etheridge	Y	Y	N	Y	Y
3 **Jones**	Y	Y	Y	Y	Y
4 Price	Y	?	N	N	Y
5 **Foxx**	Y	Y	Y	N	Y
6 **Coble**	Y	Y	Y	Y	Y
7 McIntyre	Y	Y	Y	Y	Y
8 Kissell	Y	Y	Y	Y	Y
9 **Myrick**	Y	Y	Y	Y	Y
10 **McHenry**	Y	Y	Y	Y	Y
11 Shuler	Y	Y	Y	Y	Y
12 Watt	Y	Y	N	Y	Y
13 Miller	Y	Y	N	Y	Y
NORTH DAKOTA					
AL Pomeroy	Y	Y	N	Y	Y
OHIO					
1 Driehaus	+	Y	Y	Y	Y
2 **Schmidt**	Y	Y	Y	Y	Y
3 **Turner**	Y	Y	Y	Y	Y
4 **Jordan**	Y	Y	Y	Y	Y
5 **Latta**	Y	Y	Y	Y	Y
6 Wilson	?	?	?	?	?
7 **Austria**	Y	Y	Y	Y	Y
8 **Boehner**	Y	Y	Y	Y	Y
9 Kaptur	Y	Y	N	Y	Y
10 Kucinich	Y	Y	N	Y	Y
11 Fudge	Y	Y	N	Y	Y
12 **Tiberi**	Y	Y	Y	Y	Y
13 Sutton	Y	Y	N	Y	Y
14 **LaTourette**	Y	Y	Y	N	Y
15 Kilroy	Y	Y	N	Y	Y
16 Boccieri	Y	Y	Y	Y	Y
17 Ryan	Y	Y	N	N	Y
18 Space	Y	Y	N	Y	?
OKLAHOMA					
1 **Sullivan**	?	?	?	?	?
2 Boren	Y	Y	N	N	Y
3 **Lucas**	Y	Y	Y	N	Y
4 **Cole**	Y	Y	Y	N	Y
5 **Fallin**	Y	Y	Y	Y	Y
OREGON					
1 Wu	Y	Y	N	N	Y
2 **Walden**	Y	Y	Y	N	Y
3 Blumenauer	Y	Y	N	N	Y
4 DeFazio	Y	Y	N	N	Y
5 Schrader	Y	Y	N	N	Y
PENNSYLVANIA					
1 Brady	Y	Y	N	Y	Y
2 Fattah	Y	Y	N	Y	Y
3 Dahlkemper	Y	Y	Y	Y	Y
4 Altmire	Y	Y	Y	Y	Y
5 **Thompson**	Y	Y	Y	Y	Y
6 **Gerlach**	Y	Y	Y	N	Y
7 Sestak	?	?	N	N	Y
8 Murphy, P.	Y	Y	N	N	Y
9 **Shuster**	Y	Y	Y	Y	Y
10 Carney	Y	Y	N	N	Y
11 Kanjorski	Y	Y	N	Y	Y
12 Murtha	Y	Y	N	Y	Y
13 Schwartz	Y	Y	N	N	Y
14 Doyle	Y	Y	N	Y	Y
15 **Dent**	Y	Y	Y	N	Y
16 **Pitts**	Y	Y	Y	Y	Y
17 Holden	Y	Y	N	N	Y
18 **Murphy, T.**	Y	Y	Y	Y	Y
19 **Platts**	Y	Y	Y	N	Y
RHODE ISLAND					
1 Kennedy	Y	Y	N	+	Y
2 Langevin	Y	Y	N	Y	Y
SOUTH CAROLINA					
1 **Brown**	Y	Y	Y	Y	Y
2 **Wilson**	Y	Y	Y	Y	Y
3 **Barrett**	Y	Y	Y	N	Y
4 **Inglis**	Y	Y	Y	Y	Y
5 Spratt	Y	Y	N	N	Y
6 Clyburn	Y	Y	N	N	Y
SOUTH DAKOTA					
AL Herseth Sandlin	Y	Y	N	Y	Y
TENNESSEE					
1 **Roe**	Y	Y	Y	Y	Y
2 **Duncan**	Y	Y	Y	Y	Y
3 **Wamp**	Y	Y	Y	Y	Y
4 Davis	Y	Y	N	N	Y
5 Cooper	?	?	Y	Y	Y
6 Gordon	Y	Y	N	N	Y
7 **Blackburn**	Y	Y	Y	N	Y
8 Tanner	Y	Y	Y	Y	Y
9 Cohen	Y	Y	N	Y	Y
TEXAS					
1 **Gohmert**	Y	Y	Y	Y	Y
2 **Poe**	Y	Y	Y	Y	Y
3 **Johnson, S.**	Y	Y	Y	Y	Y
4 **Hall**	Y	Y	Y	Y	Y
5 **Hensarling**	Y	Y	Y	Y	Y
6 **Barton**	Y	Y	Y	Y	Y
7 **Culberson**	Y	Y	Y	Y	Y
8 **Brady**	Y	Y	Y	Y	Y
9 Green, A.	Y	Y	N	Y	Y
10 **McCaul**	Y	Y	Y	Y	Y
11 **Conaway**	Y	Y	Y	Y	Y
12 **Granger**	Y	Y	Y	N	Y
13 **Thornberry**	Y	Y	Y	Y	Y
14 **Paul**	Y	Y	Y	Y	N
15 Hinojosa	Y	Y	N	Y	Y
16 Reyes	Y	Y	N	Y	Y
17 Edwards	?	?	N	N	Y
18 Jackson Lee	Y	Y	?	?	?
19 **Neugebauer**	Y	Y	Y	Y	Y
20 Gonzalez	Y	Y	N	Y	Y
21 **Smith**	Y	Y	Y	Y	Y
22 **Olson**	Y	Y	Y	Y	Y
23 Rodriguez	Y	Y	N	Y	Y
24 **Marchant**	Y	Y	Y	Y	Y
25 Doggett	Y	Y	N	Y	Y
26 **Burgess**	Y	Y	Y	Y	Y
27 Ortiz	Y	Y	N	Y	Y
28 Cuellar	Y	Y	N	Y	Y
29 Green, G.	Y	Y	N	Y	Y
30 Johnson, E.	Y	Y	N	Y	Y
31 **Carter**	Y	Y	Y	Y	Y
32 **Sessions**	Y	Y	Y	Y	Y
UTAH					
1 **Bishop**	Y	Y	Y	?	Y
2 Matheson	Y	Y	Y	Y	Y
3 **Chaffetz**	Y	Y	Y	Y	Y
VERMONT					
AL Welch	Y	Y	N	Y	Y
VIRGINIA					
1 **Wittman**	Y	Y	Y	N	Y
2 Nye	Y	Y	Y	N	Y
3 Scott	Y	Y	N	Y	Y
4 **Forbes**	Y	Y	Y	Y	Y
5 Perriello	Y	Y	N	Y	Y
6 **Goodlatte**	Y	Y	Y	Y	Y
7 **Cantor**	Y	Y	Y	N	Y
8 Moran	Y	Y	N	Y	N
9 Boucher	Y	Y	N	Y	Y
10 **Wolf**	Y	Y	Y	Y	Y
11 Connolly	Y	Y	N	Y	Y
WASHINGTON					
1 Inslee	Y	Y	Y	Y	Y
2 Larsen	Y	Y	N	Y	Y
3 Baird	Y	Y	N	Y	Y
4 **Hastings**	Y	Y	Y	N	Y
5 **McMorris Rodgers**	Y	Y	Y	Y	Y
6 Dicks	Y	Y	N	N	Y
7 McDermott	Y	Y	N	Y	Y
8 **Reichert**	Y	Y	Y	Y	Y
9 Smith	Y	Y	N	Y	N
WEST VIRGINIA					
1 Mollohan	Y	Y	N	N	Y
2 **Capito**	Y	Y	Y	N	Y
3 Rahall	Y	Y	N	N	Y
WISCONSIN					
1 **Ryan**	Y	Y	Y	Y	Y
2 Baldwin	Y	Y	N	Y	Y
3 Kind	Y	Y	N	Y	Y
4 Moore	Y	Y	N	Y	N
5 **Sensenbrenner**	Y	Y	Y	N	Y
6 **Petri**	Y	Y	Y	Y	Y
7 Obey	Y	Y	N	N	Y
8 Kagen	Y	Y	N	Y	Y
WYOMING					
AL **Lummis**	Y	Y	Y	Y	Y
DELEGATES					
Faleomavaega (A.S.)			N	Y	
Norton (D.C.)			N	N	
Bordallo (Guam)			N	Y	
Sablan (N. Marianas)			?	?	
Pierluisi (P.R.)			N	Y	
Christensen (V.I.)			N	Y	

IN THE HOUSE | By Vote Number

307. **HR 2200. TSA Authorization/Passage.** Passage of the bill that would authorize $7.6 billion in fiscal 2010 and $8.1 billion in fiscal 2011 for the TSA. It would require the TSA to ensure that at least 250 explosives detection canine teams are devoted to surface security and direct the agency to establish a system to verify all air cargo screening on inbound foreign passenger flights within two years. It would authorize the hiring of 200 additional surface transportation security inspectors in fiscal 2010 and 100 in fiscal 2011. The names of all detainees at the detention facility at Guantánamo Bay, Cuba, would be added to the no-fly list unless the president certified that a detainee does not pose a threat to the United States. Passed 397-25: R 157-20; D 240-5. June 4, 2009.

308. **HR 626. Federal Employee Paid Parental Leave/Accrued Leave Use Requirements.** Issa, R-Calif., amendment that would require federal employees to use all accrued leave before receiving additional paid parental leave. Additional paid parental leave granted under the bill would be treated as an advance with a repayment requirement. Rejected in Committee of the Whole 157-258: R 154-17; D 3-241. June 4, 2009.

309. **HR 626. Federal Employee Paid Parental Leave/Recommit.** Issa, R-Calif., motion to recommit the bill to the Oversight and Government Reform Committee with instructions that it be immediately reported back with language that would terminate the provisions of the bill on the 30th day following a fiscal year in which the federal deficit exceeds $500 billion. Motion rejected 171-241: R 163-10; D 8-231. June 4, 2009.

310. **HR 626. Federal Employee Paid Parental Leave/Passage.** Passage of the bill that would grant federal employees paid leave for up to four weeks to care for newborn and newly adopted or foster children. Employees could use accrued annual or sick leave for parental leave. It would clarify that employees would not be required to first use annual or sick leave before paid parental leave is available. The bill would also extend paid family leave benefits to employees of Congress, the Government Accountability Office and the Library of Congress. Passed 258-154: R 24-149; D 234-5. June 4, 2009.

	307	308	309	310
ALABAMA				
1 Bonner	Y	Y	Y	N
2 Bright	Y	N	Y	N
3 Rogers	Y	Y	Y	N
4 Aderholt	Y	Y	Y	N
5 Griffith	Y	N	Y	N
6 Bachus	Y	Y	Y	N
7 Davis	Y	N	N	Y
ALASKA				
AL Young	Y	Y	Y	N
ARIZONA				
1 Kirkpatrick	Y	N	N	Y
2 Franks	Y	Y	Y	N
3 Shadegg	Y	Y	Y	N
4 Pastor	Y	N	N	Y
5 Mitchell	Y	N	N	Y
6 Flake	N	Y	Y	N
7 Grijalva	Y	N	N	Y
8 Giffords	Y	–	N	Y
ARKANSAS				
1 Berry	Y	N	N	Y
2 Snyder	Y	N	N	Y
3 Boozman	Y	Y	Y	N
4 Ross	Y	N	N	Y
CALIFORNIA				
1 Thompson	Y	N	N	Y
2 Herger	Y	Y	Y	N
3 Lungren	Y	Y	Y	N
4 McClintock	N	Y	Y	N
5 Matsui	Y	N	N	Y
6 Woolsey	Y	N	N	Y
7 Miller, George	Y	N	N	Y
8 Pelosi				
9 Lee	Y	N	N	Y
10 Tauscher	Y	N	N	Y
11 McNerney	Y	N	N	Y
12 Speier	Y	N	N	Y
13 Stark	N	N	N	Y
14 Eshoo	Y	N	N	Y
15 Honda	Y	N	N	Y
16 Lofgren	Y	N	N	Y
17 Farr	Y	N	N	Y
18 Cardoza	Y	N	N	Y
19 Radanovich	Y	Y	Y	N
20 Costa	Y	N	N	Y
21 Nunes	N	Y	Y	N
22 McCarthy	Y	Y	Y	N
23 Capps	Y	N	N	Y
24 Gallegly	Y	Y	Y	N
25 McKeon	Y	Y	Y	N
26 Dreier	Y	Y	Y	N
27 Sherman	Y	N	N	Y
28 Berman	Y	N	N	Y
29 Schiff	Y	N	N	Y
30 Waxman	Y	N	N	Y
31 Becerra	Y	N	N	Y
32 Vacant				
33 Watson	Y	N	N	Y
34 Roybal-Allard	Y	N	N	Y
35 Waters	Y	N	N	?
36 Harman	Y	N	N	Y
37 Richardson	Y	N	N	Y
38 Napolitano	Y	N	N	Y
39 Sánchez, Linda	?	?	?	?
40 Royce	N	Y	Y	N
41 Lewis	Y	Y	Y	N
42 Miller, Gary	Y	Y	Y	N
43 Baca	Y	?	?	?
44 Calvert	Y	Y	Y	N
45 Bono Mack	Y	Y	Y	N
46 Rohrabacher	Y	Y	Y	N
47 Sanchez, Loretta	Y	N	N	Y
48 Campbell	N	Y	Y	N
49 Issa	Y	Y	Y	N
50 Bilbray	Y	Y	Y	N
51 Filner	Y	N	N	Y
52 Hunter	Y	Y	Y	N
53 Davis	Y	N	N	Y
COLORADO				
1 DeGette	Y	N	N	Y
2 Polis	Y	N	N	Y
3 Salazar	Y	N	N	Y
4 Markey	Y	N	N	Y
5 Lamborn	Y	Y	Y	N
6 Coffman	Y	Y	Y	N
7 Perlmutter	Y	N	N	Y
CONNECTICUT				
1 Larson	Y	N	N	Y
2 Courtney	?	?	?	?
3 DeLauro	Y	N	N	Y
4 Himes	Y	N	N	Y
5 Murphy	Y	N	N	Y
DELAWARE				
AL Castle	Y	Y	Y	Y
FLORIDA				
1 Miller	Y	Y	Y	N
2 Boyd	Y	?	?	?
3 Brown	Y	N	N	Y
4 Crenshaw	Y	Y	Y	N
5 Brown-Waite	Y	Y	Y	N
6 Stearns	Y	+	Y	N
7 Mica	Y	Y	Y	N
8 Grayson	Y	N	N	Y
9 Bilirakis	Y	Y	Y	N
10 Young	Y	Y	Y	N
11 Castor	Y	N	N	Y
12 Putnam	Y	Y	Y	N
13 Buchanan	Y	Y	Y	N
14 Mack	Y	Y	Y	N
15 Posey	Y	Y	Y	N
16 Rooney	Y	Y	Y	N
17 Meek	Y	N	N	Y
18 Ros-Lehtinen	Y	N	N	Y
19 Wexler	Y	N	N	Y
20 Wasserman Schultz	Y	N	N	Y
21 Diaz-Balart, L.	Y	N	N	Y
22 Klein	Y	N	N	Y
23 Hastings	Y	N	N	Y
24 Kosmas	Y	N	N	Y
25 Diaz-Balart, M.	Y	Y	Y	Y
GEORGIA				
1 Kingston	N	Y	Y	N
2 Bishop	Y	N	N	Y
3 Westmoreland	Y	Y	Y	N
4 Johnson	Y	?	?	?
5 Lewis	Y	N	N	Y
6 Price	N	Y	Y	N
7 Linder	N	Y	Y	N
8 Marshall	Y	N	N	Y
9 Deal	N	Y	Y	N
10 Broun	N	Y	Y	N
11 Gingrey	Y	Y	Y	N
12 Barrow	Y	N	N	Y
13 Scott	Y	N	N	Y
HAWAII				
1 Abercrombie	Y	N	N	Y
2 Hirono	Y	N	N	Y
IDAHO				
1 Minnick	Y	Y	Y	N
2 Simpson	Y	Y	Y	N
ILLINOIS				
1 Rush	Y	N	N	Y
2 Jackson	Y	N	N	Y
3 Lipinski	Y	N	N	Y
4 Gutierrez	Y	N	N	Y
5 Quigley	Y	N	N	Y
6 Roskam	Y	Y	Y	N
7 Davis	Y	?	?	?
8 Bean	Y	N	N	Y
9 Schakowsky	Y	N	N	Y
10 Kirk	Y	N	Y	Y
11 Halvorson	Y	N	N	Y
12 Costello	Y	N	N	Y
13 Biggert	Y	Y	Y	N
14 Foster	Y	N	N	Y
15 Johnson	Y	N	Y	Y

KEY   **Republicans**   Democrats

Y Voted for (yea)	X Paired against	C Voted "present" to avoid possible conflict of interest
# Paired for	– Announced against	
+ Announced for	P Voted "present"	? Did not vote or otherwise make a position known
N Voted against (nay)		

	307	308	309	310
16 Manzullo	Y	Y	Y	N
17 Hare	Y	N	N	Y
18 Schock	Y	Y	Y	N
19 Shimkus	Y	Y	Y	N
INDIANA				
1 Visclosky	Y	N	N	Y
2 Donnelly	Y	N	N	Y
3 Souder	Y	Y	Y	N
4 Buyer	Y	Y	Y	Y
5 Burton	Y	Y	Y	N
6 Pence	Y	Y	Y	N
7 Carson	Y	N	N	Y
8 Ellsworth	Y	N	N	Y
9 Hill	Y	N	N	Y
IOWA				
1 Braley	Y	N	N	Y
2 Loebsack	Y	N	N	Y
3 Boswell	?	?	?	?
4 Latham	Y	Y	Y	N
5 King	N	Y	Y	N
KANSAS				
1 Moran	Y	Y	Y	N
2 Jenkins	Y	Y	Y	N
3 Moore	Y	N	N	Y
4 Tiahrt	Y	Y	Y	N
KENTUCKY				
1 Whitfield	Y	Y	Y	N
2 Guthrie	Y	Y	Y	N
3 Yarmuth	Y	N	N	Y
4 Davis	Y	Y	Y	N
5 Rogers	Y	Y	Y	N
6 Chandler	Y	N	N	Y
LOUISIANA				
1 Scalise	Y	Y	Y	N
2 Cao	Y	N	N	Y
3 Melancon	Y	N	N	Y
4 Fleming	Y	Y	Y	N
5 Alexander	Y	Y	Y	N
6 Cassidy	Y	Y	Y	N
7 Boustany	Y	Y	Y	N
MAINE				
1 Pingree	Y	N	N	Y
2 Michaud	Y	N	N	Y
MARYLAND				
1 Kratovil	Y	N	N	Y
2 Ruppersberger	?	?	?	?
3 Sarbanes	Y	N	N	Y
4 Edwards	Y	N	N	Y
5 Hoyer	Y	N	N	Y
6 Bartlett	Y	Y	Y	N
7 Cummings	Y	N	N	Y
8 Van Hollen	Y	N	N	Y
MASSACHUSETTS				
1 Olver	Y	N	N	Y
2 Neal	Y	N	N	Y
3 McGovern	Y	N	N	Y
4 Frank	Y	N	N	Y
5 Tsongas	Y	N	N	Y
6 Tierney	Y	N	N	Y
7 Markey	N	N	N	Y
8 Capuano	Y	–	–	+
9 Lynch	Y	N	N	Y
10 Delahunt	Y	N	N	Y
MICHIGAN				
1 Stupak	Y	N	N	N
2 Hoekstra	Y	Y	Y	N
3 Ehlers	Y	Y	Y	N
4 Camp	Y	Y	?	?
5 Kildee	Y	N	N	Y
6 Upton	Y	N	Y	Y
7 Schauer	Y	?	?	?
8 Rogers	Y	?	?	?
9 Peters	Y	N	N	Y
10 Miller	Y	Y	Y	N
11 McCotter	Y	N	N	Y
12 Levin	Y	N	N	Y
13 Kilpatrick	Y	N	N	Y
14 Conyers	N	N	?	Y
15 Dingell	Y	N	N	Y
MINNESOTA				
1 Walz	Y	N	N	Y
2 Kline	Y	Y	Y	N
3 Paulsen	Y	Y	Y	N
4 McCollum	Y	N	N	Y

	307	308	309	310
5 Ellison	Y	N	N	Y
6 Bachmann	Y	+	Y	N
7 Peterson	Y	N	N	Y
8 Oberstar	Y	N	N	Y
MISSISSIPPI				
1 Childers	Y	Y	Y	Y
2 Thompson	Y	N	N	Y
3 Harper	Y	Y	Y	N
4 Taylor	Y	N	N	Y
MISSOURI				
1 Clay	Y	N	N	Y
2 Akin	Y	Y	Y	N
3 Carnahan	Y	N	N	Y
4 Skelton	Y	?	?	?
5 Cleaver	Y	N	N	Y
6 Graves	Y	Y	Y	N
7 Blunt	Y	Y	Y	N
8 Emerson	Y	N	N	Y
9 Luetkemeyer	Y	Y	Y	N
MONTANA				
AL Rehberg	Y	Y	Y	N
NEBRASKA				
1 Fortenberry	Y	Y	Y	N
2 Terry	Y	Y	Y	N
3 Smith	Y	Y	Y	N
NEVADA				
1 Berkley	Y	N	N	Y
2 Heller	Y	Y	Y	N
3 Titus	Y	N	N	Y
NEW HAMPSHIRE				
1 Shea-Porter	Y	N	N	Y
2 Hodes	Y	N	N	Y
NEW JERSEY				
1 Andrews	Y	N	N	Y
2 LoBiondo	Y	N	N	Y
3 Adler	?	N	Y	Y
4 Smith	Y	N	N	Y
5 Garrett	Y	Y	Y	N
6 Pallone	Y	N	N	Y
7 Lance	Y	N	N	Y
8 Pascrell	Y	N	N	Y
9 Rothman	Y	N	N	Y
10 Payne	Y	N	N	Y
11 Frelinghuysen	Y	Y	Y	N
12 Holt	N	N	N	Y
13 Sires	Y	N	N	Y
NEW MEXICO				
1 Heinrich	Y	N	N	Y
2 Teague	Y	N	N	Y
3 Lujan	Y	N	N	Y
NEW YORK				
1 Bishop	Y	N	N	Y
2 Israel	Y	N	N	Y
3 King	Y	Y	Y	N
4 McCarthy	Y	N	N	Y
5 Ackerman	Y	N	N	Y
6 Meeks	Y	N	N	Y
7 Crowley	Y	N	N	Y
8 Nadler	N	N	N	Y
9 Weiner	Y	N	N	Y
10 Towns	Y	N	N	Y
11 Clarke	Y	N	N	Y
12 Velázquez	Y	N	N	Y
13 McMahon	Y	N	N	Y
14 Maloney	Y	N	N	Y
15 Rangel	Y	N	N	Y
16 Serrano	Y	N	N	Y
17 Engel	Y	N	N	Y
18 Lowey	Y	N	N	Y
19 Hall	Y	N	N	Y
20 Murphy	Y	N	N	Y
21 Tonko	Y	N	N	Y
22 Hinchey	Y	N	N	Y
23 McHugh	Y	N	N	Y
24 Arcuri	Y	N	N	Y
25 Maffei	Y	N	N	Y
26 Lee	Y	Y	Y	N
27 Higgins	Y	N	N	Y
28 Slaughter	Y	N	N	Y
29 Massa	Y	N	N	Y
NORTH CAROLINA				
1 Butterfield	Y	N	N	Y
2 Etheridge	Y	N	N	Y
3 Jones	Y	Y	Y	N
4 Price	Y	N	N	Y

	307	308	309	310
5 Foxx	N	Y	Y	N
6 Coble	Y	Y	Y	N
7 McIntyre	Y	N	N	Y
8 Kissell	Y	N	N	Y
9 Myrick	Y	Y	Y	N
10 McHenry	N	Y	Y	N
11 Shuler	Y	N	N	Y
12 Watt	Y	N	N	Y
13 Miller	Y	N	N	Y
NORTH DAKOTA				
AL Pomeroy	Y	N	N	Y
OHIO				
1 Driehaus	Y	N	N	Y
2 Schmidt	Y	Y	Y	N
3 Turner	Y	Y	Y	N
4 Jordan	Y	Y	Y	N
5 Latta	Y	Y	Y	N
6 Wilson	?	?	?	?
7 Austria	Y	Y	Y	N
8 Boehner	Y	Y	Y	N
9 Kaptur	Y	N	N	P
10 Kucinich	Y	N	N	Y
11 Fudge	Y	N	N	Y
12 Tiberi	Y	Y	Y	N
13 Sutton	Y	N	N	Y
14 LaTourette	Y	N	N	Y
15 Kilroy	Y	N	N	Y
16 Boccieri	Y	N	N	Y
17 Ryan	Y	N	N	Y
18 Space	Y	N	N	Y
OKLAHOMA				
1 Sullivan	?	?	?	?
2 Boren	Y	N	N	Y
3 Lucas	Y	Y	Y	N
4 Cole	Y	Y	Y	N
5 Fallin	Y	Y	Y	N
OREGON				
1 Wu	Y	N	N	Y
2 Walden	Y	Y	Y	N
3 Blumenauer	?	?	?	?
4 DeFazio	Y	N	N	Y
5 Schrader	Y	N	N	N
PENNSYLVANIA				
1 Brady	Y	N	N	Y
2 Fattah	?	N	N	Y
3 Dahlkemper	Y	N	N	Y
4 Altmire	Y	N	N	Y
5 Thompson	Y	Y	Y	N
6 Gerlach	Y	Y	Y	N
7 Sestak	Y	N	N	Y
8 Murphy, P.	Y	N	N	Y
9 Shuster	N	Y	Y	N
10 Carney	Y	N	N	Y
11 Kanjorski	Y	N	N	N
12 Murtha	Y	N	N	Y
13 Schwartz	Y	N	N	Y
14 Doyle	Y	N	N	Y
15 Dent	Y	Y	Y	N
16 Pitts	Y	Y	Y	N
17 Holden	Y	N	N	Y
18 Murphy, T.	Y	N	N	Y
19 Platts	Y	Y	Y	Y
RHODE ISLAND				
1 Kennedy	?	N	?	Y
2 Langevin	Y	N	N	Y
SOUTH CAROLINA				
1 Brown	Y	Y	Y	N
2 Wilson	Y	Y	Y	N
3 Barrett	Y	?	Y	N
4 Inglis	Y	Y	Y	N
5 Spratt	Y	N	N	Y
6 Clyburn	Y	N	N	Y
SOUTH DAKOTA				
AL Herseth Sandlin	Y	N	N	Y
TENNESSEE				
1 Roe	Y	Y	Y	N
2 Duncan	N	Y	Y	N
3 Wamp	Y	Y	Y	N
4 Davis	Y	N	N	Y
5 Cooper	Y	N	N	Y
6 Gordon	Y	N	N	Y
7 Blackburn	N	Y	Y	N
8 Tanner	Y	N	N	Y
9 Cohen	Y	N	N	Y

	307	308	309	310
TEXAS				
1 Gohmert	Y	Y	Y	N
2 Poe	Y	Y	Y	N
3 Johnson, S.	N	Y	Y	N
4 Hall	Y	Y	Y	N
5 Hensarling	Y	Y	Y	N
6 Barton	Y	Y	Y	N
7 Culberson	Y	Y	Y	N
8 Brady	N	Y	Y	N
9 Green, A.	Y	N	N	Y
10 McCaul	Y	Y	Y	N
11 Conaway	N	Y	Y	N
12 Granger	Y	Y	Y	N
13 Thornberry	Y	Y	Y	N
14 Paul	N	Y	Y	N
15 Hinojosa	Y	?	?	?
16 Reyes	Y	N	N	Y
17 Edwards	Y	N	N	Y
18 Jackson Lee	?	?	?	?
19 Neugebauer	Y	Y	Y	N
20 Gonzalez	Y	N	N	Y
21 Smith	Y	Y	Y	N
22 Olson	Y	Y	Y	N
23 Rodriguez	Y	N	N	Y
24 Marchant	Y	?	?	?
25 Doggett	Y	N	N	Y
26 Burgess	Y	Y	Y	N
27 Ortiz	Y	N	N	Y
28 Cuellar	Y	N	N	Y
29 Green, G.	Y	N	N	Y
30 Johnson, E.	Y	N	N	Y
31 Carter	Y	?	?	?
32 Sessions	Y	Y	Y	N
UTAH				
1 Bishop	Y	Y	Y	N
2 Matheson	Y	N	N	Y
3 Chaffetz	Y	Y	Y	N
VERMONT				
AL Welch	Y	N	N	Y
VIRGINIA				
1 Wittman	Y	N	N	Y
2 Nye	Y	N	Y	Y
3 Scott	Y	N	N	Y
4 Forbes	Y	Y	Y	N
5 Perriello	Y	N	Y	Y
6 Goodlatte	Y	Y	Y	N
7 Cantor	Y	Y	Y	N
8 Moran	Y	N	N	Y
9 Boucher	Y	N	N	Y
10 Wolf	Y	Y	Y	N
11 Connolly	Y	N	N	Y
WASHINGTON				
1 Inslee	Y	N	N	Y
2 Larsen	Y	N	N	Y
3 Baird	Y	N	N	Y
4 Hastings	Y	Y	Y	N
5 McMorris Rodgers	Y	Y	Y	N
6 Dicks	Y	N	N	Y
7 McDermott	Y	N	N	Y
8 Reichert	Y	N	N	Y
9 Smith	Y	N	N	Y
WEST VIRGINIA				
1 Mollohan	Y	N	N	Y
2 Capito	Y	Y	Y	Y
3 Rahall	Y	N	N	Y
WISCONSIN				
1 Ryan	Y	Y	Y	N
2 Baldwin	Y	N	N	Y
3 Kind	Y	N	N	Y
4 Moore	Y	N	N	Y
5 Sensenbrenner	Y	Y	Y	N
6 Petri	Y	Y	Y	N
7 Obey	Y	N	N	Y
8 Kagen	Y	N	N	Y
WYOMING				
AL Lummis	Y	Y	Y	N
DELEGATES				
Faleomavaega (A.S.)		N		
Norton (D.C.)		N		
Bordallo (Guam)		?		
Sablan (N. Marianas)		?		
Pierluisi (P.R.)		N		
Christensen (V.I.)		N		

IN THE HOUSE | By Vote Number

311. **HR 1736. International Science and Technology/Passage.** Baird, D-Wash., motion to suspend the rules and pass the bill that would require the director of the Office of Science and Technology Policy to establish a committee to coordinate international science and technology cooperative research and training activities supported by federal agencies. Motion agreed to 341-52: R 110-52; D 231-0. A two-thirds majority of those present and voting (262 in this case) is required for passage under suspension of the rules. June 8, 2009.

312. **HR 1709. Science and Math Education/Passage.** Baird, D-Wash., motion to suspend the rules and pass the bill that would require the Office of Science and Technology Policy to establish a committee to coordinate federal programs and activities in support of science, technology, engineering and mathematics education. Motion agreed to 353-39: R 124-39; D 229-0. A two-thirds majority of those present and voting (262 in this case) is required for passage under suspension of the rules. June 8, 2009.

313. **H Res 420. Flag Day/Adoption.** Lynch, D-Mass., motion to suspend the rules and adopt the resolution that would support the goals and ideals of Flag Day. Motion agreed to 391-0: R 162-0; D 229-0. A two-thirds majority of those present and voting (261 in this case) is required for adoption under suspension of the rules. June 8, 2009.

314. **HR 2751. Fuel-Efficient Car Voucher Program/Passage.** Sutton, D-Ohio, motion to suspend the rules and pass the bill that would authorize $4 billion for the Transportation Department to establish a one-year program to allow individuals to turn certain vehicles with low fuel economy ratings over to the government in exchange for vouchers of up to $4,500 for more fuel-efficient vehicles. Motion agreed to 298-119: R 59-110; D 239-9. A two-thirds majority of those present and voting (278 in this case) is required for passage under suspension of the rules. A "yea" was a vote in support of the president's position. June 9, 2009.

315. **HR 1741. Witness Protection Grants/Passage.** Johnson, D-Ga., motion to suspend the rules and pass the bill that would authorize $30 million annually from fiscal 2010 to 2014 for the Justice Department to make competitive grants to state, local and tribal governments to establish and maintain short-term witness protection programs. Motion agreed to 412-11: R 163-11; D 249-0. A two-thirds majority of those present and voting (282 in this case) is required for passage under suspension of the rules. June 9, 2009.

316. **H Res 505. Condolences for George Tiller/Adoption.** Nadler, D-N.Y., motion to suspend the rules and adopt the resolution that would offer condolences to the family of George Tiller, a doctor who was killed in Wichita, Kan., on May 31, 2009, and commit to the principles of tolerance and the message that violence is not the appropriate response to differences in beliefs. Motion agreed to 423-0: R 174-0; D 249-0. A two-thirds majority of those present and voting (282 in this case) is required for adoption under suspension of the rules. June 9, 2009.

317. **HR 1886. HR 2410. Pakistan Aid and State Department Reauthorization/Rule.** Adoption of the rule (H Res 522) to provide for House floor consideration of a bill (HR 2410) that would authorize $18 billion in fiscal 2010 and unspecified sums in fiscal 2011 for the State Department, the United Nations and other diplomatic programs, and a bill (HR 1886) that would authorize non-military and military aid to Pakistan through fiscal 2013. Adopted 238-183: R 1-172; D 237-11. June 10, 2009.

	311	312	313	314	315	316	317
ALABAMA							
1 **Bonner**	Y	Y	Y	N	Y	Y	N
2 Bright	Y	Y	Y	Y	Y	Y	N
3 **Rogers**	Y	Y	Y	N	Y	Y	N
4 **Aderholt**	Y	Y	Y	N	Y	Y	N
5 Griffith	Y	Y	Y	Y	Y	Y	Y
6 **Bachus**	N	Y	Y	N	Y	Y	N
7 Davis	Y	Y	Y	Y	Y	Y	Y
ALASKA							
AL **Young**	Y	Y	Y	N	Y	Y	N
ARIZONA							
1 Kirkpatrick	Y	Y	Y	N	Y	Y	Y
2 **Franks**	N	N	Y	N	Y	Y	N
3 **Shadegg**	N	N	Y	N	N	Y	N
4 Pastor	Y	Y	Y	Y	Y	Y	Y
5 Mitchell	Y	Y	Y	Y	Y	Y	Y
6 **Flake**	N	N	Y	N	N	Y	N
7 Grijalva	?	?	?	Y	Y	Y	Y
8 Giffords	Y	Y	Y	N	Y	Y	Y
ARKANSAS							
1 Berry	Y	Y	Y	Y	Y	Y	Y
2 Snyder	?	?	?	Y	Y	Y	Y
3 **Boozman**	Y	Y	Y	N	Y	Y	N
4 Ross	Y	Y	Y	Y	Y	Y	Y
CALIFORNIA							
1 Thompson	Y	Y	Y	Y	Y	Y	Y
2 **Herger**	Y	Y	Y	N	Y	Y	N
3 **Lungren**	N	Y	Y	N	Y	Y	N
4 **McClintock**	N	N	Y	N	N	Y	N
5 Matsui	Y	Y	Y	Y	Y	Y	Y
6 Woolsey	Y	Y	Y	Y	Y	Y	+
7 Miller, George	+	+	?	Y	Y	Y	Y
8 Pelosi				Y			
9 Lee	Y	Y	Y	Y	Y	Y	Y
10 Tauscher	Y	Y	Y	Y	Y	Y	Y
11 McNerney	Y	Y	Y	Y	Y	Y	Y
12 Speier	Y	Y	?	Y	Y	Y	Y
13 Stark	Y	Y	Y	Y	Y	Y	Y
14 Eshoo	Y	Y	Y	Y	Y	Y	Y
15 Honda	Y	Y	Y	Y	Y	Y	Y
16 Lofgren	Y	Y	Y	Y	Y	Y	Y
17 Farr	Y	Y	Y	Y	Y	Y	Y
18 Cardoza	Y	Y	Y	Y	Y	Y	Y
19 **Radanovich**	Y	Y	Y	N	Y	Y	N
20 Costa	Y	Y	Y	Y	Y	Y	Y
21 **Nunes**	N	N	Y	N	Y	Y	N
22 **McCarthy**	Y	Y	Y	N	Y	Y	N
23 Capps	Y	Y	Y	Y	Y	Y	Y
24 **Gallegly**	Y	Y	Y	N	Y	Y	N
25 **McKeon**	Y	Y	Y	Y	Y	Y	N
26 **Dreier**	Y	Y	Y	Y	Y	Y	N
27 Sherman	Y	Y	Y	Y	Y	Y	Y
28 Berman	Y	Y	Y	Y	Y	Y	Y
29 Schiff	Y	Y	Y	Y	Y	Y	Y
30 Waxman	Y	Y	Y	Y	Y	Y	Y
31 Becerra	Y	Y	Y	Y	Y	Y	Y
32 Vacant							
33 Watson	Y	Y	Y	Y	Y	Y	Y
34 Roybal-Allard	Y	Y	Y	Y	Y	Y	Y
35 Waters	?	?	?	Y	Y	Y	Y
36 Harman	Y	Y	Y	Y	Y	Y	Y
37 Richardson	Y	Y	Y	Y	Y	Y	Y
38 Napolitano	Y	Y	Y	Y	Y	Y	Y
39 Sánchez, Linda	Y	Y	Y	?	?	?	?
40 **Royce**	N	Y	Y	N	Y	Y	N
41 **Lewis**	Y	Y	Y	N	Y	Y	N
42 **Miller, Gary**	?	?	?	Y	Y	Y	N
43 Baca	Y	Y	Y	Y	Y	Y	Y
44 **Calvert**	Y	Y	Y	N	Y	Y	N
45 **Bono Mack**	?	?	?	?	?	?	?
46 **Rohrabacher**	?	?	?	N	Y	Y	N
47 Sanchez, Loretta	Y	Y	Y	Y	Y	Y	Y
48 **Campbell**	N	N	Y	N	Y	Y	N
49 **Issa**	N	N	Y	N	Y	Y	N
50 **Bilbray**	Y	Y	Y	Y	Y	Y	N
51 Filner	Y	Y	Y	Y	Y	Y	Y
52 **Hunter**	N	Y	?	N	Y	Y	N
53 Davis	Y	Y	Y	Y	Y	Y	Y

	311	312	313	314	315	316	317
COLORADO							
1 DeGette	?	?	?	Y	Y	Y	Y
2 Polis	Y	Y	Y	N	Y	Y	Y
3 Salazar	Y	Y	Y	Y	Y	Y	Y
4 Markey	Y	Y	Y	Y	Y	Y	Y
5 **Lamborn**	N	N	Y	N	Y	Y	N
6 **Coffman**	N	Y	Y	N	Y	Y	N
7 Perlmutter	Y	Y	Y	Y	Y	Y	Y
CONNECTICUT							
1 Larson	Y	Y	Y	Y	Y	Y	Y
2 Courtney	?	?	?	Y	Y	Y	Y
3 DeLauro	Y	Y	Y	Y	Y	Y	Y
4 Himes	Y	Y	Y	Y	Y	Y	Y
5 Murphy	Y	Y	Y	Y	Y	Y	Y
DELAWARE							
AL **Castle**	Y	Y	Y	Y	Y	Y	Y
FLORIDA							
1 **Miller**	N	Y	Y	N	Y	Y	N
2 Boyd	?	?	?	N	Y	Y	Y
3 Brown	Y	Y	Y	Y	Y	Y	Y
4 **Crenshaw**	Y	Y	Y	N	Y	Y	N
5 **Brown-Waite**	Y	Y	Y	Y	Y	Y	N
6 **Stearns**	N	N	Y	Y	Y	Y	N
7 **Mica**	Y	Y	Y	N	Y	Y	N
8 Grayson	Y	Y	Y	Y	Y	Y	Y
9 **Bilirakis**	Y	Y	Y	N	Y	Y	N
10 **Young**	Y	Y	Y	N	Y	Y	N
11 Castor	Y	Y	Y	Y	Y	Y	Y
12 **Putnam**	+	+	+	?	Y	Y	N
13 **Buchanan**	Y	Y	Y	P	Y	Y	N
14 **Mack**	?	?	?	?	?	?	?
15 **Posey**	Y	Y	Y	N	Y	Y	N
16 **Rooney**	Y	Y	Y	N	N	Y	N
17 Meek	Y	Y	Y	Y	Y	Y	Y
18 **Ros-Lehtinen**	Y	Y	Y	Y	Y	Y	Y
19 Wexler	?	?	?	Y	Y	Y	Y
20 Wasserman Schultz	Y	Y	Y	Y	Y	Y	Y
21 **Diaz-Balart, L.**	Y	Y	Y	Y	Y	Y	Y
22 Klein	Y	Y	Y	Y	Y	Y	Y
23 Hastings	Y	Y	Y	Y	Y	Y	Y
24 Kosmas	Y	Y	Y	Y	Y	Y	Y
25 **Diaz-Balart, M.**	Y	Y	Y	Y	Y	Y	Y
GEORGIA							
1 **Kingston**	N	N	Y	N	Y	Y	N
2 Bishop	Y	Y	Y	Y	Y	Y	Y
3 **Westmoreland**	N	N	Y	N	Y	Y	N
4 Johnson	Y	Y	Y	Y	Y	Y	Y
5 Lewis	?	?	?	?	?	?	?
6 **Price**	N	Y	Y	N	Y	Y	N
7 **Linder**	N	N	Y	N	Y	Y	N
8 Marshall	Y	Y	Y	Y	Y	Y	Y
9 **Deal**	?	?	?	P	Y	Y	N
10 **Broun**	N	N	Y	N	N	Y	N
11 **Gingrey**	N	Y	Y	N	Y	Y	N
12 Barrow	Y	Y	Y	Y	Y	Y	Y
13 Scott	Y	Y	Y	Y	Y	Y	Y
HAWAII							
1 Abercrombie	Y	Y	Y	Y	Y	Y	Y
2 Hirono	Y	Y	Y	Y	Y	Y	Y
IDAHO							
1 Minnick	Y	Y	Y	Y	Y	Y	N
2 **Simpson**	Y	Y	Y	N	Y	Y	N
ILLINOIS							
1 Rush	Y	Y	Y	Y	Y	Y	Y
2 Jackson	Y	Y	Y	Y	Y	Y	Y
3 Lipinski	Y	Y	Y	Y	Y	Y	Y
4 Gutierrez	Y	Y	Y	Y	Y	Y	Y
5 Quigley	Y	Y	Y	Y	Y	Y	Y
6 **Roskam**	Y	Y	Y	N	Y	Y	N
7 Davis	Y	Y	Y	Y	Y	Y	Y
8 Bean	Y	Y	Y	Y	Y	Y	Y
9 Schakowsky	Y	Y	Y	Y	Y	Y	Y
10 **Kirk**	Y	Y	Y	N	Y	Y	N
11 Halvorson	Y	Y	Y	Y	Y	Y	Y
12 Costello	?	?	?	Y	Y	Y	Y
13 **Biggert**	Y	Y	Y	N	Y	Y	N
14 Foster	Y	Y	Y	Y	Y	Y	Y
15 Johnson	+	+	+	Y	Y	Y	N

KEY   **Republicans**   Democrats

Y Voted for (yea)	**X** Paired against	**C** Voted "present" to avoid possible conflict of interest
# Paired for	**–** Announced against	
+ Announced for	**P** Voted "present"	**?** Did not vote or otherwise make a position known
N Voted against (nay)		

	311	312	313	314	315	316	317
16 **Manzullo**	Y	Y	Y	Y	Y	Y	N
17 Hare	Y	Y	Y	Y	Y	Y	Y
18 **Schock**	?	?	?	N	Y	Y	?
19 **Shimkus**	Y	Y	Y	Y	Y	Y	N
INDIANA							
1 Visclosky	Y	Y	Y	Y	Y	Y	Y
2 Donnelly	Y	Y	Y	Y	Y	Y	N
3 **Souder**	Y	Y	Y	Y	Y	Y	N
4 **Buyer**	Y	Y	Y	Y	Y	?	N
5 **Burton**	Y	Y	Y	Y	Y	Y	N
6 **Pence**	N	N	Y	N	Y	Y	N
7 Carson	Y	Y	Y	Y	Y	Y	Y
8 Ellsworth	Y	Y	Y	Y	Y	Y	N
9 Hill	Y	Y	Y	Y	Y	Y	Y
IOWA							
1 Braley	Y	Y	Y	+	Y	Y	Y
2 Loebsack	Y	Y	Y	?	?	?	?
3 Boswell	Y	Y	Y	Y	Y	Y	Y
4 **Latham**	Y	Y	Y	Y	Y	Y	N
5 **King**	N	N	Y	Y	Y	Y	N
KANSAS							
1 **Moran**	N	Y	Y	N	Y	Y	N
2 **Jenkins**	Y	Y	Y	N	Y	Y	N
3 Moore	Y	Y	Y	Y	Y	Y	Y
4 **Tiahrt**	+	Y	Y	N	Y	Y	N
KENTUCKY							
1 **Whitfield**	N	Y	Y	?	?	Y	N
2 **Guthrie**	Y	Y	Y	Y	Y	Y	N
3 Yarmuth	Y	Y	Y	Y	Y	Y	Y
4 **Davis**	Y	Y	Y	N	Y	Y	N
5 **Rogers**	Y	Y	Y	N	Y	Y	N
6 Chandler	Y	Y	Y	Y	Y	Y	Y
LOUISIANA							
1 **Scalise**	N	N	Y	N	Y	Y	N
2 **Cao**	Y	Y	Y	Y	Y	Y	N
3 Melancon	Y	Y	?	Y	Y	Y	Y
4 **Fleming**	Y	Y	Y	N	Y	Y	N
5 **Alexander**	Y	Y	Y	N	Y	Y	N
6 **Cassidy**	Y	Y	Y	Y	Y	Y	N
7 **Boustany**	N	N	Y	N	Y	Y	N
MAINE							
1 Pingree	Y	Y	Y	Y	Y	Y	Y
2 Michaud	Y	Y	Y	Y	Y	Y	N
MARYLAND							
1 Kratovil	Y	Y	Y	Y	Y	Y	Y
2 Ruppersberger	?	?	?	?	?	?	Y
3 Sarbanes	Y	Y	Y	Y	Y	Y	Y
4 Edwards	Y	Y	Y	Y	Y	Y	Y
5 Hoyer	Y	Y	Y	Y	Y	Y	Y
6 **Bartlett**	Y	Y	Y	N	Y	Y	N
7 Cummings	Y	Y	Y	Y	Y	Y	Y
8 Van Hollen	Y	Y	Y	Y	Y	Y	Y
MASSACHUSETTS							
1 Olver	Y	Y	Y	Y	Y	Y	Y
2 Neal	Y	Y	Y	Y	Y	Y	Y
3 McGovern	?	?	?	Y	Y	Y	Y
4 Frank	Y	Y	Y	Y	Y	Y	Y
5 Tsongas	Y	Y	Y	Y	Y	Y	Y
6 Tierney	Y	?	Y	Y	Y	Y	Y
7 Markey	Y	Y	Y	Y	Y	Y	Y
8 Capuano	Y	Y	Y	Y	Y	Y	Y
9 Lynch	Y	Y	Y	Y	Y	Y	Y
10 Delahunt	Y	Y	Y	Y	Y	Y	Y
MICHIGAN							
1 Stupak	Y	Y	Y	Y	Y	Y	Y
2 **Hoekstra**	?	?	?	Y	Y	Y	N
3 **Ehlers**	Y	Y	Y	Y	Y	Y	N
4 **Camp**	Y	Y	Y	Y	Y	Y	N
5 Kildee	Y	Y	Y	Y	Y	Y	Y
6 **Upton**	Y	Y	Y	Y	Y	Y	N
7 Schauer	Y	Y	Y	Y	Y	Y	Y
8 **Rogers**	Y	Y	Y	Y	Y	Y	N
9 Peters	Y	Y	Y	Y	Y	Y	Y
10 **Miller**	Y	Y	Y	Y	Y	Y	N
11 **McCotter**	Y	Y	Y	Y	Y	Y	N
12 Levin	Y	Y	Y	Y	Y	Y	Y
13 Kilpatrick	Y	Y	Y	Y	Y	Y	Y
14 Conyers	Y	Y	Y	?	Y	Y	Y
15 Dingell	Y	Y	Y	Y	Y	Y	Y
MINNESOTA							
1 Walz	Y	Y	Y	Y	Y	Y	Y
2 **Kline**	Y	Y	Y	N	Y	Y	N
3 **Paulsen**	Y	Y	Y	N	Y	Y	N
4 McCollum	Y	Y	Y	Y	Y	Y	Y

	311	312	313	314	315	316	317
5 Ellison	Y	Y	Y	Y	Y	Y	+
6 **Bachmann**	N	N	Y	N	Y	Y	N
7 Peterson	Y	Y	Y	Y	Y	Y	Y
8 Oberstar	Y	Y	Y	Y	Y	Y	Y
MISSISSIPPI							
1 Childers	Y	Y	Y	Y	Y	Y	N
2 Thompson	Y	Y	Y	Y	Y	Y	Y
3 **Harper**	Y	Y	Y	N	Y	Y	N
4 Taylor	Y	Y	Y	N	Y	Y	N
MISSOURI							
1 Clay	Y	Y	Y	Y	Y	Y	Y
2 **Akin**	N	N	Y	N	Y	Y	N
3 Carnahan	Y	Y	Y	Y	Y	Y	Y
4 Skelton	Y	Y	Y	Y	Y	Y	Y
5 Cleaver	?	?	?	Y	Y	Y	Y
6 **Graves**	Y	Y	Y	N	Y	Y	N
7 **Blunt**	N	Y	Y	Y	Y	Y	N
8 **Emerson**	Y	Y	Y	Y	Y	Y	N
9 **Luetkemeyer**	Y	Y	Y	N	Y	Y	N
MONTANA							
AL **Rehberg**	Y	Y	Y	N	Y	Y	N
NEBRASKA							
1 **Fortenberry**	Y	Y	Y	N	Y	Y	N
2 **Terry**	Y	Y	Y	Y	Y	Y	N
3 **Smith**	Y	Y	Y	N	Y	Y	N
NEVADA							
1 Berkley	Y	Y	Y	Y	Y	Y	Y
2 **Heller**	Y	Y	Y	N	Y	Y	N
3 Titus	Y	Y	Y	Y	Y	Y	Y
NEW HAMPSHIRE							
1 Shea-Porter	Y	Y	Y	Y	Y	Y	Y
2 Hodes	+	+	+	Y	Y	Y	Y
NEW JERSEY							
1 Andrews	Y	Y	Y	Y	Y	Y	Y
2 **LoBiondo**	Y	Y	Y	Y	Y	Y	N
3 Adler	Y	Y	Y	Y	Y	Y	Y
4 **Smith**	Y	Y	Y	Y	Y	Y	Y
5 **Garrett**	N	N	Y	N	Y	Y	N
6 Pallone	Y	Y	Y	Y	Y	Y	Y
7 **Lance**	Y	Y	Y	Y	Y	Y	N
8 Pascrell	Y	Y	Y	Y	Y	Y	Y
9 Rothman	?	?	?	Y	Y	Y	Y
10 Payne	Y	Y	Y	Y	Y	Y	Y
11 **Frelinghuysen**	Y	Y	Y	Y	Y	Y	N
12 Holt	Y	Y	Y	Y	Y	Y	Y
13 Sires	Y	Y	Y	Y	Y	Y	Y
NEW MEXICO							
1 Heinrich	Y	Y	Y	Y	Y	Y	Y
2 Teague	Y	Y	Y	Y	Y	Y	Y
3 Lujan	Y	Y	Y	Y	Y	Y	Y
NEW YORK							
1 Bishop	Y	Y	Y	Y	Y	Y	Y
2 Israel	Y	Y	Y	Y	Y	Y	Y
3 **King**	Y	Y	Y	N	Y	Y	N
4 McCarthy	+	+	+	Y	Y	Y	Y
5 Ackerman	Y	Y	Y	Y	Y	Y	Y
6 Meeks	Y	Y	Y	Y	Y	Y	Y
7 Crowley	Y	Y	Y	Y	Y	Y	Y
8 Nadler	Y	Y	Y	Y	Y	Y	Y
9 Weiner	Y	Y	Y	Y	Y	Y	Y
10 Towns	Y	Y	Y	Y	Y	Y	Y
11 Clarke	Y	Y	Y	Y	Y	Y	Y
12 Velázquez	Y	Y	Y	Y	Y	Y	Y
13 McMahon	Y	Y	Y	Y	Y	Y	Y
14 Maloney	?	?	?	Y	Y	Y	Y
15 Rangel	Y	Y	Y	Y	Y	Y	Y
16 Serrano	Y	Y	Y	Y	Y	Y	Y
17 Engel	Y	Y	Y	Y	Y	Y	Y
18 Lowey	Y	Y	Y	Y	Y	Y	Y
19 Hall	Y	Y	Y	Y	Y	Y	Y
20 Murphy	Y	Y	Y	Y	Y	Y	Y
21 Tonko	Y	Y	Y	Y	Y	Y	Y
22 Hinchey	Y	Y	Y	Y	Y	Y	Y
23 **McHugh**	Y	Y	Y	Y	Y	Y	N
24 Arcuri	Y	Y	Y	Y	Y	Y	Y
25 Maffei	Y	Y	Y	Y	Y	Y	Y
26 **Lee**	Y	Y	Y	Y	Y	Y	N
27 Higgins	Y	Y	Y	Y	Y	Y	Y
28 Slaughter	Y	Y	Y	Y	Y	Y	Y
29 Massa	Y	Y	Y	Y	Y	Y	Y
NORTH CAROLINA							
1 Butterfield	?	?	?	Y	Y	Y	Y
2 Etheridge	Y	Y	Y	Y	Y	Y	Y
3 **Jones**	Y	Y	Y	N	Y	Y	N
4 Price	Y	Y	Y	Y	Y	Y	Y

	311	312	313	314	315	316	317
5 **Foxx**	N	N	Y	N	N	Y	N
6 **Coble**	N	N	Y	Y	Y	Y	N
7 McIntyre	Y	Y	Y	Y	Y	Y	Y
8 Kissell	Y	Y	Y	Y	Y	Y	Y
9 **Myrick**	Y	Y	Y	Y	Y	Y	N
10 **McHenry**	N	N	Y	N	Y	Y	N
11 Shuler	Y	Y	Y	Y	Y	Y	Y
12 Watt	Y	Y	Y	Y	Y	Y	Y
13 Miller	Y	Y	Y	Y	Y	Y	Y
NORTH DAKOTA							
AL Pomeroy	Y	Y	Y	Y	Y	Y	Y
OHIO							
1 Driehaus	Y	Y	Y	Y	Y	Y	N
2 **Schmidt**	Y	Y	Y	N	Y	Y	N
3 **Turner**	Y	Y	Y	Y	Y	Y	N
4 **Jordan**	N	N	Y	N	Y	Y	N
5 **Latta**	Y	Y	Y	N	Y	Y	N
6 Wilson	Y	Y	Y	Y	Y	Y	Y
7 **Austria**	Y	Y	Y	Y	Y	Y	N
8 **Boehner**	Y	N	Y	N	Y	Y	N
9 Kaptur	Y	?	Y	Y	Y	Y	Y
10 Kucinich	Y	Y	Y	Y	Y	Y	Y
11 Fudge	Y	Y	Y	Y	Y	Y	Y
12 **Tiberi**	Y	Y	Y	Y	Y	Y	N
13 Sutton	Y	Y	Y	Y	Y	Y	Y
14 **LaTourette**	Y	Y	Y	Y	Y	Y	N
15 Kilroy	Y	Y	Y	Y	Y	Y	Y
16 Boccieri	Y	Y	Y	Y	Y	Y	Y
17 Ryan	Y	Y	Y	Y	Y	Y	Y
18 Space	Y	Y	Y	Y	Y	Y	Y
OKLAHOMA							
1 **Sullivan**	?	?	?	?	?	?	?
2 Boren	Y	Y	Y	Y	Y	Y	Y
3 **Lucas**	Y	Y	Y	N	Y	Y	N
4 **Cole**	Y	Y	Y	N	Y	Y	N
5 **Fallin**	Y	Y	Y	N	Y	Y	N
OREGON							
1 Wu	Y	Y	Y	Y	Y	Y	Y
2 **Walden**	Y	Y	Y	Y	Y	Y	N
3 Blumenauer	Y	Y	Y	Y	Y	Y	Y
4 DeFazio	Y	Y	Y	Y	Y	Y	Y
5 Schrader	+	+	+	Y	Y	Y	Y
PENNSYLVANIA							
1 Brady	Y	Y	Y	Y	Y	Y	Y
2 Fattah	Y	Y	Y	Y	Y	Y	Y
3 Dahlkemper	Y	Y	Y	Y	Y	Y	N
4 Altmire	Y	Y	Y	Y	Y	Y	Y
5 **Thompson**	Y	Y	Y	N	Y	Y	N
6 **Gerlach**	Y	Y	Y	Y	Y	Y	N
7 Sestak	?	?	?	Y	Y	Y	Y
8 Murphy, P.	Y	Y	Y	Y	Y	Y	Y
9 **Shuster**	N	Y	Y	N	Y	Y	N
10 Carney	Y	Y	Y	Y	Y	Y	Y
11 Kanjorski	Y	Y	Y	Y	Y	Y	Y
12 Murtha	Y	Y	Y	Y	Y	Y	Y
13 Schwartz	Y	Y	Y	Y	Y	Y	Y
14 Doyle	Y	Y	Y	Y	Y	Y	Y
15 **Dent**	Y	Y	Y	N	Y	Y	N
16 **Pitts**	N	Y	Y	Y	Y	Y	N
17 Holden	Y	Y	Y	Y	Y	Y	Y
18 **Murphy, T.**	Y	Y	Y	Y	Y	Y	N
19 **Platts**	Y	Y	Y	N	Y	Y	N
RHODE ISLAND							
1 Kennedy	?	?	?	?	?	?	?
2 Langevin	Y	Y	Y	Y	Y	Y	Y
SOUTH CAROLINA							
1 **Brown**	Y	Y	Y	N	Y	Y	N
2 **Wilson**	Y	Y	Y	N	Y	Y	N
3 **Barrett**	–	–	+	N	Y	Y	N
4 **Inglis**	Y	Y	Y	N	N	Y	N
5 Spratt	Y	Y	Y	Y	Y	Y	Y
6 Clyburn	Y	Y	Y	Y	Y	Y	Y
SOUTH DAKOTA							
AL Herseth Sandlin	Y	Y	Y	N	Y	Y	Y
TENNESSEE							
1 **Roe**	Y	Y	Y	Y	Y	Y	N
2 **Duncan**	N	N	Y	N	N	Y	N
3 **Wamp**	?	?	?	N	Y	Y	N
4 Davis	Y	Y	Y	Y	Y	Y	?
5 Cooper	Y	Y	Y	Y	Y	Y	Y
6 Gordon	Y	Y	Y	Y	Y	Y	Y
7 **Blackburn**	Y	Y	Y	N	Y	Y	N
8 Tanner	Y	Y	Y	Y	Y	Y	Y
9 Cohen	Y	Y	Y	Y	Y	Y	Y

	311	312	313	314	315	316	317
TEXAS							
1 **Gohmert**	N	N	Y	N	Y	Y	N
2 **Poe**	N	N	Y	Y	Y	Y	N
3 **Johnson, S.**	N	Y	Y	N	Y	Y	N
4 **Hall**	Y	Y	Y	Y	Y	Y	N
5 **Hensarling**	N	N	Y	N	Y	Y	N
6 **Barton**	Y	Y	Y	Y	Y	Y	N
7 **Culberson**	N	N	Y	N	Y	Y	N
8 **Brady**	Y	Y	Y	N	Y	Y	N
9 Green, A.	Y	Y	Y	Y	Y	Y	Y
10 **McCaul**	Y	Y	Y	N	Y	Y	N
11 **Conaway**	N	N	Y	N	Y	Y	N
12 **Granger**	Y	Y	Y	N	Y	Y	?
13 **Thornberry**	Y	N	Y	N	Y	Y	N
14 **Paul**	N	N	Y	N	N	Y	N
15 Hinojosa	Y	Y	Y	Y	Y	Y	Y
16 Reyes	Y	Y	Y	Y	Y	Y	Y
17 Edwards	Y	Y	Y	Y	Y	Y	Y
18 Jackson Lee	Y	Y	Y	Y	Y	Y	Y
19 **Neugebauer**	N	N	Y	N	Y	Y	N
20 Gonzalez	?	?	?	?	?	?	Y
21 **Smith**	Y	Y	Y	N	Y	Y	N
22 **Olson**	Y	Y	Y	N	Y	Y	N
23 Rodriguez	Y	Y	Y	Y	Y	Y	Y
24 **Marchant**	N	N	Y	N	Y	Y	N
25 Doggett	Y	Y	Y	N	Y	Y	Y
26 **Burgess**	N	Y	Y	N	N	Y	N
27 Ortiz	Y	Y	Y	Y	Y	Y	Y
28 Cuellar	Y	Y	Y	Y	Y	Y	Y
29 Green, G.	Y	Y	Y	Y	Y	Y	Y
30 Johnson, E.	Y	Y	Y	Y	Y	Y	Y
31 **Carter**	N	N	Y	N	Y	Y	N
32 **Sessions**	?	?	?	?	Y	Y	N
UTAH							
1 **Bishop**	?	?	?	?	Y	Y	N
2 Matheson	Y	Y	Y	Y	Y	Y	Y
3 **Chaffetz**	N	N	Y	N	Y	Y	N
VERMONT							
AL Welch	Y	Y	Y	Y	Y	Y	Y
VIRGINIA							
1 **Wittman**	Y	Y	Y	N	Y	Y	N
2 Nye	Y	Y	Y	Y	Y	Y	Y
3 Scott	Y	Y	Y	Y	Y	Y	Y
4 **Forbes**	Y	Y	Y	N	Y	Y	N
5 Perriello	Y	Y	Y	Y	Y	Y	Y
6 **Goodlatte**	Y	Y	Y	N	Y	Y	N
7 **Cantor**	Y	Y	Y	N	Y	Y	N
8 Moran	?	?	?	Y	Y	Y	Y
9 Boucher	Y	Y	Y	Y	Y	Y	Y
10 **Wolf**	Y	Y	Y	N	Y	Y	N
11 Connolly	Y	Y	Y	Y	Y	Y	Y
WASHINGTON							
1 Inslee	Y	Y	Y	Y	Y	Y	Y
2 Larsen	Y	Y	Y	Y	Y	Y	Y
3 Baird	Y	Y	Y	N	Y	Y	Y
4 **Hastings**	?	?	?	N	Y	Y	N
5 **McMorris Rodgers**	Y	Y	Y	N	Y	Y	N
6 Dicks	Y	Y	Y	Y	Y	Y	Y
7 McDermott	Y	Y	Y	Y	Y	Y	Y
8 **Reichert**	Y	Y	Y	Y	Y	Y	N
9 Smith	Y	Y	Y	Y	Y	Y	Y
WEST VIRGINIA							
1 Mollohan	Y	Y	Y	Y	Y	Y	Y
2 **Capito**	Y	Y	Y	Y	Y	Y	N
3 Rahall	Y	Y	Y	Y	Y	Y	Y
WISCONSIN							
1 **Ryan**	Y	Y	Y	N	Y	Y	N
2 Baldwin	Y	Y	Y	Y	Y	Y	Y
3 Kind	?	?	+	Y	Y	Y	Y
4 Moore	Y	Y	Y	Y	Y	Y	Y
5 **Sensenbrenner**	N	N	Y	N	Y	Y	N
6 **Petri**	Y	Y	Y	Y	Y	Y	N
7 Obey	Y	Y	Y	Y	Y	Y	Y
8 Kagen	Y	Y	Y	Y	Y	Y	Y
WYOMING							
AL **Lummis**	N	N	Y	N	N	Y	N
DELEGATES							
Faleomavaega (A.S.)							
Norton (D.C.)							
Bordallo (Guam)							
Sablan (N. Marianas)							
Pierluisi (P.R.)							
Christensen (V.I.)							

IN THE HOUSE | By Vote Number

318. **H Res 453. Tribute to AmeriCorps/Adoption.** Tonko, D-N.Y., motion to suspend the rules and adopt the resolution that would acknowledge the accomplishments of AmeriCorps members, alumni and community partners and encourage Americans to consider serving in AmeriCorps. Motion agreed to 359-60: R 112-60; D 247-0. A two-thirds majority of those present and voting (280 in this case) is required for adoption under suspension of the rules. June 10, 2009.

319. **H Res 454. Center for Missing and Exploited Children/ Adoption.** Tonko, D-N.Y., motion to suspend the rules and adopt the resolution that would recognize the 25th anniversary of the National Center for Missing and Exploited Children. Motion agreed to 419-0: R 174-0; D 245-0. A two-thirds majority of those present and voting (280 in this case) is required for adoption under suspension of the rules. June 10, 2009.

320. **HR 2410. State Department Authorization/Manager's Amendment.** Berman, D-Calif., amendment that would authorize payment in addition to a death gratuity to surviving dependents of Foreign Service or executive branch employees who are victims of international terrorism. It also would require the president to report to Congress on plans to streamline U.S. export controls and processes to better serve the needs of the U.S. scientific and research community. It would stipulate that nothing in the bill regarding the establishment of an office for global women's issues should be construed as affecting existing statutory prohibitions related to abortion. Adopted in Committee of the Whole 257-171: R 7-169; D 250-2. June 10, 2009.

321. **HR 2410. State Department Authorization/International Atomic Energy Agency Contributions.** Ros-Lehtinen, R-Fla., amendment that would require the State Department to withhold $4.5 million from its contributions to the International Atomic Energy Agency, an amount equal to the monetary value of nuclear technical cooperation the agency provided to Iran, Syria, Sudan and Cuba in 2007. Rejected in Committee of the Whole 205-224: R 174-1; D 31-223. June 10, 2009.

322. **HR 2410. State Department Authorization/Sudan Crisis Plan.** McCaul, R-Texas, amendment that would require the president to develop a plan to address the crisis in Sudan, advance U.S. national security and humanitarian interests in the country, resolve the conflict in Darfur and combat Islamist extremism. Adopted in Committee of the Whole 429-0: R 177-0; D 252-0. June 10, 2009.

323. **HR 2410. State Department Authorization/Technology Intellectual Property Rights.** Larsen, D-Wash., amendment that would specify that it is U.S. policy to ensure robust compliance with international property rights protections related to energy and environmental technologies, with respect to the United Nations Framework Convention on Climate Change. Adopted in Committee of the Whole 432-0: R 177-0; D 255-0. June 10, 2009.

	318	319	320	321	322	323
ALABAMA						
1 **Bonner**	Y	Y	N	Y	Y	Y
2 Bright	Y	Y	Y	Y	Y	Y
3 **Rogers**	Y	Y	N	Y	Y	Y
4 **Aderholt**	N	Y	N	Y	Y	Y
5 Griffith	Y	Y	Y	N	Y	Y
6 **Bachus**	Y	Y	N	Y	Y	Y
7 Davis	Y	Y	Y	Y	Y	Y
ALASKA						
AL **Young**	Y	Y	N	Y	Y	Y
ARIZONA						
1 Kirkpatrick	Y	Y	Y	Y	Y	Y
2 **Franks**	N	Y	N	Y	Y	Y
3 **Shadegg**	N	Y	N	Y	Y	Y
4 Pastor	Y	Y	Y	N	Y	Y
5 Mitchell	Y	Y	Y	Y	Y	Y
6 **Flake**	N	Y	?	?	Y	Y
7 Grijalva	Y	Y	Y	N	Y	Y
8 Giffords	Y	Y	Y	Y	Y	Y
ARKANSAS						
1 Berry	Y	Y	Y	N	Y	Y
2 Snyder	Y	Y	Y	N	Y	Y
3 **Boozman**	Y	Y	N	Y	Y	Y
4 Ross	Y	Y	Y	N	Y	Y
CALIFORNIA						
1 Thompson	Y	Y	Y	N	Y	Y
2 **Herger**	N	Y	N	Y	Y	Y
3 **Lungren**	Y	Y	N	Y	Y	Y
4 **McClintock**	N	Y	N	Y	Y	Y
5 Matsui	Y	Y	Y	N	Y	Y
6 Woolsey	Y	Y	Y	N	Y	Y
7 Miller, George	Y	Y	Y	N	Y	Y
8 Pelosi						
9 Lee	Y	Y	Y	N	Y	Y
10 Tauscher	Y	Y	Y	N	Y	Y
11 McNerney	Y	Y	Y	Y	Y	Y
12 Speier	Y	Y	Y	N	Y	Y
13 Stark	Y	Y	?	N	Y	Y
14 Eshoo	Y	Y	Y	N	Y	Y
15 Honda	Y	Y	Y	N	Y	Y
16 Lofgren	Y	Y	Y	N	Y	Y
17 Farr	Y	Y	Y	N	Y	Y
18 Cardoza	Y	Y	Y	N	Y	Y
19 **Radanovich**	N	Y	N	Y	Y	Y
20 Costa	Y	Y	Y	N	Y	Y
21 **Nunes**	Y	Y	N	Y	Y	Y
22 **McCarthy**	Y	Y	N	Y	Y	Y
23 Capps	Y	Y	Y	N	Y	Y
24 **Gallegly**	Y	Y	N	Y	Y	Y
25 **McKeon**	Y	Y	N	Y	Y	Y
26 **Dreier**	N	Y	N	Y	Y	Y
27 Sherman	Y	Y	Y	Y	Y	Y
28 Berman	Y	Y	Y	N	Y	Y
29 Schiff	Y	Y	Y	N	Y	Y
30 Waxman	Y	Y	Y	N	Y	Y
31 Becerra	Y	Y	Y	N	Y	Y
32 Vacant						
33 Watson	Y	Y	Y	N	Y	Y
34 Roybal-Allard	Y	Y	Y	N	Y	Y
35 Waters	Y	Y	Y	N	Y	Y
36 Harman	Y	Y	Y	N	Y	Y
37 Richardson	Y	Y	Y	N	Y	Y
38 Napolitano	Y	Y	Y	N	Y	Y
39 Sánchez, Linda	?	?	?	?	?	?
40 **Royce**	N	Y	N	Y	Y	Y
41 **Lewis**	Y	Y	N	Y	Y	Y
42 **Miller, Gary**	N	Y	N	Y	Y	Y
43 Baca	Y	Y	Y	N	Y	Y
44 **Calvert**	Y	Y	N	Y	Y	Y
45 **Bono Mack**	?	?	Y	Y	Y	Y
46 **Rohrabacher**	N	Y	N	Y	Y	Y
47 Sanchez, Loretta	Y	Y	Y	N	Y	Y
48 **Campbell**	N	Y	N	Y	Y	Y
49 **Issa**	N	Y	N	Y	Y	Y
50 **Bilbray**	Y	Y	N	Y	Y	Y
51 Filner	Y	Y	Y	N	Y	Y
52 **Hunter**	N	Y	N	Y	Y	Y
53 Davis	Y	Y	Y	N	Y	Y

	318	319	320	321	322	323
COLORADO						
1 DeGette	Y	Y	Y	N	Y	Y
2 Polis	Y	Y	Y	N	Y	Y
3 Salazar	Y	Y	Y	N	Y	Y
4 Markey	Y	Y	Y	N	Y	Y
5 **Lamborn**	N	Y	N	Y	Y	Y
6 **Coffman**	N	Y	N	Y	Y	Y
7 Perlmutter	Y	Y	Y	N	Y	Y
CONNECTICUT						
1 Larson	Y	Y	Y	N	Y	Y
2 Courtney	Y	Y	Y	N	Y	Y
3 DeLauro	Y	Y	Y	N	Y	Y
4 Himes	Y	Y	Y	N	Y	Y
5 Murphy	Y	Y	Y	N	Y	Y
DELAWARE						
AL **Castle**	Y	Y	Y	Y	Y	Y
FLORIDA						
1 **Miller**	Y	Y	N	Y	Y	Y
2 Boyd	Y	Y	Y	N	Y	Y
3 Brown	Y	Y	Y	N	Y	Y
4 **Crenshaw**	Y	Y	N	Y	Y	Y
5 **Brown-Waite**	Y	Y	N	Y	Y	Y
6 **Stearns**	N	Y	N	Y	Y	Y
7 **Mica**	Y	Y	N	Y	Y	Y
8 Grayson	Y	Y	Y	N	Y	Y
9 **Bilirakis**	Y	Y	N	Y	Y	Y
10 **Young**	Y	Y	Y	N	Y	Y
11 Castor	Y	Y	Y	N	Y	Y
12 **Putnam**	Y	Y	N	Y	Y	Y
13 **Buchanan**	Y	Y	N	Y	Y	Y
14 **Mack**	?	?	N	Y	Y	Y
15 **Posey**	N	Y	N	Y	Y	Y
16 **Rooney**	N	Y	N	Y	Y	Y
17 Meek	Y	Y	Y	N	Y	Y
18 **Ros-Lehtinen**	Y	Y	Y	N	Y	Y
19 Wexler	Y	Y	Y	N	Y	Y
20 Wasserman Schultz	Y	Y	Y	N	Y	Y
21 **Diaz-Balart, L.**	Y	Y	N	Y	Y	Y
22 Klein	Y	Y	Y	N	Y	Y
23 Hastings	Y	Y	Y	N	Y	Y
24 Kosmas	Y	Y	Y	N	Y	Y
25 **Diaz-Balart, M.**	Y	Y	N	Y	Y	Y
GEORGIA						
1 **Kingston**	N	Y	N	Y	Y	Y
2 Bishop	Y	Y	Y	N	Y	Y
3 **Westmoreland**	N	Y	N	Y	Y	Y
4 Johnson	Y	Y	Y	N	Y	Y
5 Lewis	?	?	?	?	?	?
6 **Price**	Y	Y	N	Y	Y	Y
7 **Linder**	N	Y	N	Y	Y	Y
8 Marshall	Y	Y	Y	Y	Y	Y
9 **Deal**	N	Y	N	Y	Y	Y
10 **Broun**	N	Y	N	Y	Y	Y
11 **Gingrey**	N	Y	N	Y	Y	Y
12 Barrow	Y	Y	Y	Y	Y	Y
13 Scott	Y	Y	Y	N	Y	Y
HAWAII						
1 Abercrombie	Y	Y	Y	?	Y	Y
2 Hirono	Y	Y	Y	N	Y	Y
IDAHO						
1 Minnick	Y	Y	Y	N	Y	Y
2 **Simpson**	Y	Y	N	Y	Y	Y
ILLINOIS						
1 Rush	Y	Y	Y	N	Y	Y
2 Jackson	Y	Y	Y	N	Y	Y
3 Lipinski	Y	Y	Y	N	Y	Y
4 Gutierrez	Y	Y	Y	N	?	Y
5 Quigley	Y	Y	Y	N	Y	Y
6 **Roskam**	N	Y	N	Y	Y	Y
7 Davis	Y	Y	Y	N	Y	Y
8 Bean	Y	Y	Y	Y	Y	Y
9 Schakowsky	Y	Y	Y	N	Y	Y
10 **Kirk**	Y	Y	Y	N	Y	Y
11 Halvorson	Y	Y	Y	N	Y	Y
12 Costello	Y	Y	Y	N	Y	Y
13 **Biggert**	Y	Y	Y	Y	Y	Y
14 Foster	Y	Y	Y	N	Y	Y
15 **Johnson**	N	Y	N	Y	Y	Y

KEY   **Republicans**   Democrats

Y Voted for (yea)	X Paired against
# Paired for	− Announced against
+ Announced for	P Voted "present"
N Voted against (nay)	

C Voted "present" to avoid possible conflict of interest

? Did not vote or otherwise make a position known

	318	319	320	321	322	323
16 **Manzullo**	Y	Y	N	Y	Y	Y
17 Hare	Y	Y	Y	N	Y	Y
18 **Schock**	Y	Y	N	Y	Y	Y
19 **Shimkus**	Y	Y	N	Y	Y	Y
INDIANA						
1 Visclosky	Y	Y	Y	N	Y	Y
2 Donnelly	Y	Y	Y	Y	Y	Y
3 **Souder**	Y	Y	N	Y	Y	Y
4 **Buyer**	N	Y	N	Y	Y	Y
5 **Burton**	N	Y	N	Y	Y	Y
6 **Pence**	N	Y	N	Y	Y	Y
7 Carson	Y	Y	Y	N	Y	Y
8 Ellsworth	Y	Y	Y	Y	Y	Y
9 Hill	?	?	?	?	?	?
IOWA						
1 Braley	Y	Y	Y	N	Y	Y
2 Loebsack	?	?	?	?	?	?
3 Boswell	Y	Y	Y	N	?	Y
4 **Latham**	Y	Y	N	Y	Y	Y
5 **King**	N	Y	N	Y	Y	Y
KANSAS						
1 **Moran**	Y	Y	N	Y	Y	Y
2 **Jenkins**	Y	Y	N	Y	Y	Y
3 Moore	Y	Y	Y	N	Y	Y
4 **Tiahrt**	N	Y	N	Y	Y	Y
KENTUCKY						
1 **Whitfield**	Y	Y	N	Y	Y	Y
2 **Guthrie**	Y	Y	N	Y	Y	Y
3 Yarmuth	Y	Y	Y	N	Y	Y
4 **Davis**	Y	Y	N	Y	Y	Y
5 **Rogers**	Y	Y	N	Y	Y	Y
6 Chandler	Y	Y	Y	N	Y	Y
LOUISIANA						
1 **Scalise**	Y	Y	N	Y	Y	Y
2 **Cao**	Y	Y	N	Y	Y	Y
3 Melancon	Y	Y	Y	N	Y	Y
4 **Fleming**	Y	Y	N	Y	Y	Y
5 **Alexander**	Y	Y	N	Y	Y	Y
6 **Cassidy**	Y	Y	N	Y	Y	Y
7 **Boustany**	Y	Y	N	Y	Y	Y
MAINE						
1 Pingree	Y	Y	Y	N	Y	Y
2 Michaud	Y	Y	Y	N	Y	Y
MARYLAND						
1 Kratovil	Y	Y	Y	N	Y	Y
2 Ruppersberger	Y	Y	?	?	?	?
3 Sarbanes	Y	Y	Y	N	Y	Y
4 Edwards	Y	Y	Y	N	Y	Y
5 Hoyer	?	?	Y	N	Y	Y
6 **Bartlett**	?	?	N	Y	Y	Y
7 Cummings	Y	Y	Y	N	Y	Y
8 Van Hollen	Y	Y	Y	N	Y	Y
MASSACHUSETTS						
1 Olver	Y	Y	Y	N	Y	Y
2 Neal	Y	Y	Y	N	Y	Y
3 McGovern	Y	Y	Y	N	Y	Y
4 Frank	Y	Y	Y	N	Y	Y
5 Tsongas	Y	Y	Y	N	Y	Y
6 Tierney	Y	Y	Y	N	Y	Y
7 Markey	Y	Y	Y	N	Y	Y
8 Capuano	Y	Y	Y	N	Y	Y
9 Lynch	Y	Y	Y	N	Y	Y
10 Delahunt	Y	Y	Y	N	Y	Y
MICHIGAN						
1 Stupak	Y	Y	Y	N	Y	Y
2 **Hoekstra**	Y	Y	N	Y	Y	Y
3 **Ehlers**	Y	Y	N	Y	Y	Y
4 **Camp**	Y	Y	N	Y	Y	Y
5 Kildee	Y	Y	Y	N	Y	Y
6 **Upton**	Y	Y	N	Y	Y	Y
7 Schauer	Y	Y	Y	N	Y	Y
8 **Rogers**	Y	Y	N	Y	Y	Y
9 Peters	Y	Y	Y	N	Y	Y
10 **Miller**	Y	Y	N	Y	Y	Y
11 **McCotter**	Y	Y	N	Y	Y	Y
12 Levin	Y	Y	Y	N	Y	Y
13 Kilpatrick	Y	Y	Y	Y	Y	Y
14 Conyers	Y	Y	Y	N	Y	Y
15 Dingell	Y	Y	Y	N	Y	Y
MINNESOTA						
1 Walz	Y	Y	Y	N	Y	Y
2 **Kline**	N	Y	N	Y	Y	Y
3 **Paulsen**	Y	Y	N	Y	Y	Y
4 McCollum	Y	Y	Y	N	Y	Y

	318	319	320	321	322	323
5 Ellison	Y	Y	Y	N	Y	Y
6 **Bachmann**	N	Y	N	Y	Y	Y
7 Peterson	?	Y	N	N	Y	Y
8 Oberstar	Y	Y	Y	N	Y	Y
MISSISSIPPI						
1 Childers	Y	Y	Y	Y	Y	Y
2 Thompson	Y	Y	Y	N	Y	Y
3 **Harper**	Y	Y	N	Y	Y	Y
4 Taylor	Y	Y	Y	Y	Y	Y
MISSOURI						
1 Clay	Y	Y	Y	N	Y	Y
2 **Akin**	N	Y	N	Y	Y	Y
3 Carnahan	Y	?	Y	N	Y	Y
4 Skelton	Y	Y	Y	N	Y	Y
5 Cleaver	Y	Y	Y	N	Y	Y
6 **Graves**	Y	Y	N	Y	Y	Y
7 **Blunt**	Y	Y	N	Y	Y	Y
8 **Emerson**	Y	Y	Y	Y	Y	Y
9 **Luetkemeyer**	N	Y	N	Y	Y	Y
MONTANA						
AL **Rehberg**	Y	Y	N	Y	Y	Y
NEBRASKA						
1 **Fortenberry**	Y	Y	N	Y	Y	Y
2 **Terry**	Y	Y	N	Y	Y	Y
3 **Smith**	Y	Y	N	Y	Y	Y
NEVADA						
1 Berkley	Y	Y	Y	N	Y	Y
2 **Heller**	Y	Y	N	Y	Y	Y
3 Titus	Y	Y	Y	N	Y	Y
NEW HAMPSHIRE						
1 Shea-Porter	Y	Y	Y	N	Y	Y
2 Hodes	Y	Y	Y	N	Y	Y
NEW JERSEY						
1 Andrews	Y	Y	Y	N	Y	Y
2 **LoBiondo**	Y	Y	N	Y	Y	Y
3 Adler	Y	Y	Y	Y	Y	Y
4 **Smith**	Y	Y	N	Y	Y	Y
5 **Garrett**	N	Y	N	Y	Y	Y
6 Pallone	Y	Y	Y	N	Y	Y
7 **Lance**	Y	Y	Y	Y	Y	Y
8 Pascrell	Y	Y	Y	N	Y	Y
9 Rothman	Y	Y	Y	N	Y	Y
10 Payne	Y	Y	Y	N	Y	Y
11 **Frelinghuysen**	Y	Y	N	Y	Y	Y
12 Holt	Y	Y	Y	N	Y	Y
13 Sires	Y	Y	Y	N	Y	Y
NEW MEXICO						
1 Heinrich	Y	Y	Y	N	Y	Y
2 Teague	Y	Y	Y	N	Y	Y
3 Lujan	Y	Y	Y	N	Y	Y
NEW YORK						
1 Bishop	Y	Y	Y	N	Y	Y
2 Israel	Y	Y	Y	N	Y	Y
3 **King**	Y	Y	N	Y	Y	Y
4 McCarthy	Y	Y	Y	N	Y	Y
5 Ackerman	Y	Y	Y	N	Y	Y
6 Meeks	Y	Y	Y	N	Y	Y
7 Crowley	Y	Y	Y	N	Y	Y
8 Nadler	Y	Y	Y	N	Y	Y
9 Weiner	Y	Y	Y	N	Y	Y
10 Towns	Y	Y	Y	N	Y	Y
11 Clarke	Y	Y	Y	N	Y	Y
12 Velázquez	Y	Y	Y	N	Y	Y
13 McMahon	Y	Y	Y	Y	Y	Y
14 Maloney	Y	Y	Y	N	Y	Y
15 Rangel	Y	?	Y	N	Y	Y
16 Serrano	Y	Y	Y	N	Y	Y
17 Engel	Y	Y	Y	Y	Y	Y
18 Lowey	Y	Y	Y	N	Y	Y
19 Hall	Y	Y	Y	Y	Y	Y
20 Murphy	Y	Y	Y	N	Y	Y
21 Tonko	Y	Y	Y	N	Y	Y
22 Hinchey	Y	Y	Y	N	Y	Y
23 **McHugh**	Y	Y	Y	Y	Y	Y
24 Arcuri	Y	Y	Y	Y	Y	Y
25 Maffei	Y	Y	Y	N	Y	Y
26 **Lee**	Y	Y	N	Y	Y	Y
27 Higgins	Y	Y	Y	N	Y	Y
28 Slaughter	Y	Y	Y	N	Y	Y
29 Massa	Y	Y	Y	N	Y	Y
NORTH CAROLINA						
1 Butterfield	Y	Y	Y	N	Y	Y
2 Etheridge	Y	Y	Y	N	Y	Y
3 **Jones**	N	Y	N	Y	Y	Y
4 Price	Y	Y	Y	N	Y	Y

	318	319	320	321	322	323
5 **Foxx**	N	Y	N	Y	Y	Y
6 **Coble**	N	Y	N	Y	Y	Y
7 McIntyre	Y	Y	Y	N	Y	Y
8 Kissell	Y	Y	Y	N	Y	Y
9 **Myrick**	N	Y	N	Y	Y	Y
10 **McHenry**	N	Y	N	Y	Y	Y
11 Shuler	Y	Y	Y	N	Y	Y
12 Watt	Y	Y	Y	N	Y	Y
13 Miller	Y	Y	Y	N	Y	Y
NORTH DAKOTA						
AL Pomeroy	Y	Y	Y	N	Y	Y
OHIO						
1 Driehaus	Y	Y	Y	N	Y	Y
2 **Schmidt**	Y	Y	N	Y	Y	Y
3 **Turner**	Y	Y	N	Y	Y	Y
4 **Jordan**	N	Y	N	Y	Y	Y
5 **Latta**	N	Y	N	Y	Y	Y
6 Wilson	Y	Y	Y	N	Y	Y
7 **Austria**	Y	Y	N	Y	Y	Y
8 **Boehner**	Y	Y	N	Y	Y	Y
9 Kaptur	Y	Y	Y	N	Y	Y
10 Kucinich	Y	Y	Y	N	Y	Y
11 Fudge	Y	Y	Y	N	Y	Y
12 **Tiberi**	Y	Y	N	Y	Y	Y
13 Sutton	Y	Y	Y	N	Y	Y
14 **LaTourette**	Y	Y	N	Y	Y	Y
15 Kilroy	Y	Y	Y	N	Y	Y
16 Boccieri	Y	Y	Y	Y	Y	Y
17 Ryan	Y	Y	Y	N	Y	Y
18 Space	Y	Y	Y	Y	Y	Y
OKLAHOMA						
1 **Sullivan**	?	?	?	?	?	?
2 Boren	Y	Y	Y	Y	Y	Y
3 **Lucas**	?	Y	N	Y	Y	Y
4 **Cole**	Y	Y	N	Y	Y	Y
5 **Fallin**	Y	Y	N	Y	Y	Y
OREGON						
1 Wu	Y	Y	Y	N	Y	Y
2 **Walden**	Y	Y	N	Y	Y	Y
3 Blumenauer	Y	Y	Y	N	Y	Y
4 DeFazio	Y	?	Y	N	Y	Y
5 Schrader	Y	Y	Y	N	Y	Y
PENNSYLVANIA						
1 Brady	Y	Y	Y	N	Y	Y
2 Fattah	Y	Y	Y	N	Y	Y
3 Dahlkemper	Y	Y	N	Y	Y	Y
4 Altmire	Y	Y	Y	N	Y	Y
5 **Thompson**	Y	Y	N	Y	Y	Y
6 **Gerlach**	Y	Y	N	Y	Y	Y
7 Sestak	Y	Y	Y	N	Y	Y
8 Murphy, P.	Y	Y	Y	N	Y	Y
9 **Shuster**	Y	Y	N	Y	Y	Y
10 Carney	Y	Y	Y	N	Y	Y
11 Kanjorski	Y	Y	Y	N	Y	Y
12 Murtha	Y	Y	Y	N	Y	Y
13 Schwartz	Y	Y	Y	N	Y	Y
14 Doyle	Y	Y	Y	N	Y	Y
15 **Dent**	Y	Y	Y	Y	Y	Y
16 **Pitts**	N	Y	N	Y	Y	Y
17 Holden	Y	Y	Y	N	Y	Y
18 **Murphy, T.**	Y	Y	N	Y	Y	Y
19 **Platts**	Y	Y	N	Y	Y	Y
RHODE ISLAND						
1 Kennedy	?	?	?	?	?	?
2 Langevin	Y	Y	Y	N	Y	Y
SOUTH CAROLINA						
1 **Brown**	Y	Y	N	Y	Y	Y
2 **Wilson**	Y	Y	N	Y	Y	Y
3 **Barrett**	Y	Y	N	Y	Y	Y
4 **Inglis**	N	Y	N	Y	Y	Y
5 Spratt	Y	Y	Y	N	Y	Y
6 Clyburn	Y	Y	Y	N	Y	Y
SOUTH DAKOTA						
AL Herseth Sandlin	Y	Y	Y	Y	Y	Y
TENNESSEE						
1 **Roe**	Y	Y	N	Y	Y	Y
2 **Duncan**	N	Y	N	Y	Y	Y
3 **Wamp**	Y	Y	N	Y	Y	Y
4 Davis	?	?	Y	Y	Y	Y
5 Cooper	Y	Y	Y	N	Y	Y
6 Gordon	Y	Y	Y	Y	Y	Y
7 **Blackburn**	Y	Y	N	Y	Y	Y
8 Tanner	Y	Y	Y	N	Y	Y
9 Cohen	Y	Y	Y	Y	Y	Y

	318	319	320	321	322	323
TEXAS						
1 **Gohmert**	?	Y	N	Y	Y	Y
2 **Poe**	N	Y	N	Y	Y	Y
3 **Johnson, S.**	N	Y	N	Y	Y	Y
4 **Hall**	Y	Y	N	Y	Y	Y
5 **Hensarling**	N	Y	N	Y	Y	Y
6 **Barton**	Y	Y	N	Y	Y	Y
7 **Culberson**	N	Y	N	Y	Y	Y
8 **Brady**	N	Y	N	Y	Y	Y
9 Green, A.	Y	Y	Y	N	Y	Y
10 **McCaul**	Y	Y	N	Y	Y	Y
11 **Conaway**	N	Y	N	Y	Y	Y
12 **Granger**	Y	Y	N	Y	Y	Y
13 **Thornberry**	N	Y	N	Y	Y	Y
14 **Paul**	N	Y	N	N	Y	Y
15 Hinojosa	Y	Y	+	N	Y	Y
16 Reyes	Y	Y	Y	N	Y	Y
17 Edwards	Y	Y	Y	N	Y	Y
18 Jackson Lee	Y	Y	Y	N	Y	Y
19 **Neugebauer**	N	Y	N	Y	Y	Y
20 Gonzalez	Y	Y	Y	N	Y	Y
21 **Smith**	Y	Y	N	?	Y	Y
22 **Olson**	N	Y	N	Y	Y	Y
23 Rodriguez	Y	Y	Y	N	Y	Y
24 **Marchant**	Y	Y	N	Y	Y	Y
25 Doggett	Y	Y	Y	N	Y	Y
26 **Burgess**	N	Y	N	Y	Y	Y
27 Ortiz	Y	Y	Y	N	Y	Y
28 Cuellar	Y	Y	Y	Y	Y	Y
29 Green, G.	Y	Y	Y	N	Y	Y
30 Johnson, E.	Y	Y	Y	N	Y	Y
31 **Carter**	N	Y	N	Y	Y	Y
32 **Sessions**	Y	Y	N	Y	Y	Y
UTAH						
1 **Bishop**	Y	Y	N	Y	Y	Y
2 Matheson	Y	Y	Y	N	Y	Y
3 **Chaffetz**	Y	Y	N	Y	Y	Y
VERMONT						
AL Welch	Y	Y	Y	N	Y	Y
VIRGINIA						
1 **Wittman**	Y	Y	N	Y	Y	Y
2 Nye	Y	Y	Y	N	Y	Y
3 Scott	Y	Y	Y	N	Y	Y
4 **Forbes**	Y	Y	N	Y	Y	Y
5 Perriello	Y	Y	Y	N	Y	Y
6 **Goodlatte**	N	Y	N	Y	Y	Y
7 **Cantor**	Y	Y	N	Y	Y	Y
8 Moran	Y	Y	?	N	Y	Y
9 Boucher	Y	Y	Y	Y	Y	Y
10 **Wolf**	Y	Y	N	Y	Y	Y
11 Connolly	Y	Y	Y	N	Y	Y
WASHINGTON						
1 Inslee	Y	Y	Y	N	Y	Y
2 Larsen	Y	Y	Y	N	Y	Y
3 Baird	Y	Y	Y	N	Y	Y
4 **Hastings**	Y	Y	N	Y	Y	Y
5 **McMorris Rodgers**	Y	Y	N	Y	Y	Y
6 Dicks	Y	Y	Y	N	Y	Y
7 McDermott	Y	Y	Y	N	Y	Y
8 **Reichert**	Y	Y	N	Y	Y	Y
9 Smith	Y	Y	Y	N	Y	Y
WEST VIRGINIA						
1 Mollohan	Y	Y	Y	N	Y	Y
2 **Capito**	Y	Y	N	Y	Y	Y
3 Rahall	Y	Y	Y	N	Y	Y
WISCONSIN						
1 **Ryan**	Y	Y	N	Y	Y	Y
2 Baldwin	Y	Y	Y	N	Y	Y
3 Kind	Y	Y	Y	N	Y	Y
4 Moore	Y	Y	Y	N	Y	Y
5 **Sensenbrenner**	N	Y	N	Y	Y	Y
6 **Petri**	Y	Y	N	Y	Y	Y
7 Obey	Y	Y	Y	N	Y	Y
8 Kagen	Y	Y	Y	N	Y	Y
WYOMING						
AL **Lummis**	Y	Y	N	Y	Y	Y
DELEGATES						
Faleomavaega (A.S.)			Y	N	Y	Y
Norton (D.C.)			Y	N	+	Y
Bordallo (Guam)			Y	Y	Y	Y
Sablan (N. Marianas)			Y	N	Y	Y
Pierluisi (P.R.)			Y	N	Y	Y
Christensen (V.I.)			Y	N	Y	Y

IN THE HOUSE | By Vote Number

324. **HR 2410. State Department Authorization/Film Release.** Brown-Waite, R-Fla., amendment that would strike the bill's provision providing for the domestic release of the Voice of America film "A Fateful Harvest." Rejected in Committee of the Whole 178-254: R 166-11; D 12-243. June 10, 2009.

325. **HR 2410. State Department Authorization/Sanction of Eritrea.** Royce, R-Calif., amendment that would express a sense of Congress that Eritrea's support for armed insurgents in Somalia poses a significant threat to the United States and to East African nations, urge the secretary of State to designate Eritrea as a state sponsor of terrorism, and urge the U.N. Security Council to impose sanctions on the country. Rejected in Committee of the Whole 183-245: R 169-6; D 14-239. June 10, 2009.

326. **HR 2410. State Department Authorization/Reward for Terrorist Information.** Kirk, R-Ill., amendment that would allow the State Department to make payments from the Rewards for Justice program to foreign government officers or employees who provide information leading to the capture of high-profile terrorists. Adopted in Committee of the Whole 428-3: R 176-1; D 252-2. June 10, 2009.

327. **HR 2410. State Department Authorization/Recommit.** Burton, R-Ind., motion to recommit the bill to the Foreign Affairs Committee with instructions that it immediately be reported back with language that strikes the text of the bill and substitutes provisions that would require the president to impose sanctions on any entity that provides Iran with refined petroleum resources or that contributes to the enhancement of Iran's ability to import refined petroleum. Motion rejected 174-250: R 169-8; D 5-242. June 10, 2009.

328. **HR 2410. State Department Authorization/Passage.** Passage of the bill that would authorize $18 billion in fiscal 2010 and unspecified sums in 2011 for programs at the State Department and Peace Corps, for U.N. peacekeeping dues, and for other diplomatic programs. The fiscal 2010 total includes $7.3 billion for the State Department's operating budget; $2.3 billion for U.S.-assessed contributions to the United Nations and international peacekeeping activities; $1.8 billion for embassy security, construction and maintenance; $1.8 billion for assessed contributions to international organizations; and $1.6 billion for general migration and refugee assistance. It would allow the State Department to hire more than 1,500 additional entry-level Foreign Service officers and require the president to conduct a review of the U.S. arms export controls system. Passed 235-187: R 7-169; D 228-18. June 10, 2009.

329. **HR 2346. Fiscal 2009 Supplemental/Motion to Instruct.** Lewis, R-Calif., motion to instruct conferees to insist on funding levels that will not result in total funding that exceeds the total in the Senate amendment, insist on House funding levels related to defense and military construction, recede to the Senate on provisions related to protecting detainee photo records, and withhold their approval of the conference agreement unless the text has been available in an electronic, searchable and downloadable form for at least 48 hours. Motion agreed to 267-152: R 172-4; D 95-148. June 11, 2009.

	324	325	326	327	328	329
ALABAMA						
1 **Bonner**	Y	Y	Y	Y	N	Y
2 **Bright**	Y	Y	Y	Y	N	Y
3 **Rogers**	Y	Y	Y	Y	N	Y
4 **Aderholt**	Y	Y	Y	Y	N	Y
5 Griffith	N	N	Y	N	Y	N
6 **Bachus**	Y	Y	Y	Y	?	Y
7 Davis	Y	Y	Y	N	Y	Y
ALASKA						
AL **Young**	Y	Y	Y	Y	N	Y
ARIZONA						
1 Kirkpatrick	N	N	Y	N	Y	Y
2 **Franks**	Y	Y	Y	Y	N	Y
3 **Shadegg**	Y	Y	Y	Y	N	Y
4 Pastor	N	N	Y	N	Y	N
5 Mitchell	N	N	Y	Y	Y	Y
6 **Flake**	Y	N	Y	N	N	Y
7 Grijalva	N	N	Y	N	Y	N
8 Giffords	N	N	Y	N	Y	Y
ARKANSAS						
1 Berry	N	N	Y	N	Y	Y
2 Snyder	N	N	Y	N	Y	N
3 **Boozman**	Y	Y	Y	Y	N	Y
4 Ross	N	N	Y	N	Y	Y
CALIFORNIA						
1 Thompson	N	N	Y	N	Y	N
2 **Herger**	Y	?	Y	Y	N	Y
3 **Lungren**	Y	Y	Y	Y	N	Y
4 **McClintock**	Y	Y	Y	Y	N	Y
5 Matsui	N	N	Y	N	Y	N
6 Woolsey	N	N	Y	N	Y	N
7 Miller, George	N	N	Y	N	Y	N
8 Pelosi						
9 Lee	N	N	Y	N	Y	N
10 Tauscher	N	N	Y	N	Y	N
11 McNerney	Y	N	Y	?	Y	Y
12 Speier	N	N	Y	N	Y	N
13 Stark	N	?	N	N	Y	?
14 Eshoo	N	N	Y	N	Y	N
15 Honda	N	N	Y	N	Y	N
16 Lofgren	N	N	Y	N	Y	N
17 Farr	N	N	Y	N	Y	N
18 Cardoza	N	N	Y	N	Y	Y
19 **Radanovich**	Y	Y	Y	Y	N	Y
20 Costa	N	N	Y	N	Y	Y
21 **Nunes**	Y	Y	Y	Y	N	Y
22 **McCarthy**	Y	Y	Y	Y	N	Y
23 Capps	N	N	Y	N	Y	N
24 **Gallegly**	Y	Y	Y	Y	N	Y
25 **McKeon**	Y	Y	Y	Y	N	Y
26 **Dreier**	Y	Y	Y	Y	N	Y
27 Sherman	N	Y	Y	N	Y	N
28 Berman	N	?	Y	N	Y	N
29 Schiff	N	N	Y	N	Y	N
30 Waxman	N	N	Y	N	Y	N
31 Becerra	N	N	Y	N	Y	N
32 Vacant						
33 Watson	N	N	Y	N	Y	N
34 Roybal-Allard	N	N	Y	N	Y	N
35 Waters	N	N	Y	N	Y	N
36 Harman	N	N	Y	N	Y	N
37 Richardson	N	N	Y	N	Y	?
38 Napolitano	N	N	Y	N	Y	N
39 Sánchez, Linda	?	?	?	?	?	?
40 **Royce**	Y	Y	Y	Y	N	Y
41 **Lewis**	Y	Y	Y	Y	N	Y
42 **Miller, Gary**	Y	Y	Y	Y	N	Y
43 Baca	N	N	Y	N	Y	?
44 **Calvert**	Y	Y	Y	Y	N	Y
45 **Bono Mack**	Y	Y	Y	Y	N	Y
46 **Rohrabacher**	Y	N	Y	Y	N	Y
47 Sanchez, Loretta	N	N	Y	N	Y	N
48 **Campbell**	Y	Y	Y	Y	N	Y
49 **Issa**	Y	Y	Y	Y	N	Y
50 **Bilbray**	Y	Y	Y	Y	N	Y
51 Filner	N	N	Y	N	Y	N
52 **Hunter**	Y	Y	Y	Y	N	Y
53 Davis	N	N	Y	N	Y	N

	324	325	326	327	328	329
COLORADO						
1 DeGette	N	N	Y	N	Y	N
2 Polis	N	N	Y	N	Y	N
3 Salazar	N	N	Y	N	Y	Y
4 Markey	Y	N	Y	N	Y	Y
5 **Lamborn**	Y	Y	Y	Y	N	Y
6 **Coffman**	N	Y	Y	Y	N	Y
7 Perlmutter	Y	N	Y	N	Y	Y
CONNECTICUT						
1 Larson	N	N	Y	N	Y	N
2 Courtney	N	N	Y	N	Y	Y
3 DeLauro	N	N	Y	N	Y	N
4 Himes	N	N	Y	N	Y	?
5 Murphy	N	N	Y	N	Y	Y
DELAWARE						
AL Castle	N	N	Y	N	Y	Y
FLORIDA						
1 **Miller**	Y	Y	Y	Y	N	Y
2 Boyd	N	N	Y	N	Y	Y
3 Brown	N	N	Y	N	Y	N
4 **Crenshaw**	Y	Y	Y	Y	N	Y
5 **Brown-Waite**	Y	Y	Y	Y	N	Y
6 **Stearns**	Y	Y	Y	Y	N	Y
7 **Mica**	Y	Y	Y	N	N	Y
8 Grayson	N	N	Y	N	Y	N
9 **Bilirakis**	Y	Y	Y	Y	N	Y
10 **Young**	Y	Y	Y	Y	N	Y
11 Castor	N	N	Y	N	Y	N
12 **Putnam**	Y	Y	Y	Y	N	Y
13 **Buchanan**	Y	Y	Y	Y	N	Y
14 **Mack**	Y	Y	Y	Y	N	Y
15 **Posey**	Y	Y	Y	Y	N	Y
16 **Rooney**	Y	Y	Y	Y	N	Y
17 Meek	N	N	Y	N	Y	N
18 **Ros-Lehtinen**	Y	Y	Y	Y	N	Y
19 Wexler	N	N	Y	N	Y	N
20 Wasserman Schultz	N	N	Y	N	Y	N
21 **Diaz-Balart, L.**	Y	Y	Y	Y	N	Y
22 Klein	N	N	Y	N	Y	N
23 Hastings	N	N	Y	N	Y	N
24 Kosmas	N	N	Y	N	Y	Y
25 **Diaz-Balart, M.**	Y	Y	Y	Y	N	Y
GEORGIA						
1 **Kingston**	Y	Y	Y	Y	N	Y
2 Bishop	N	N	Y	N	Y	Y
3 **Westmoreland**	Y	Y	Y	Y	N	Y
4 Johnson	N	N	Y	N	Y	N
5 Lewis	?	?	?	?	?	?
6 **Price**	Y	Y	Y	Y	N	Y
7 **Linder**	Y	Y	Y	Y	N	Y
8 Marshall	N	N	Y	N	Y	Y
9 **Deal**	Y	Y	Y	Y	N	Y
10 **Broun**	Y	Y	Y	Y	N	Y
11 **Gingrey**	Y	Y	Y	Y	N	Y
12 Barrow	N	Y	Y	Y	Y	Y
13 Scott	N	N	Y	N	Y	N
HAWAII						
1 Abercrombie	N	N	Y	N	Y	Y
2 Hirono	N	N	Y	N	Y	N
IDAHO						
1 Minnick	Y	N	Y	N	Y	Y
2 **Simpson**	Y	Y	Y	Y	N	Y
ILLINOIS						
1 Rush	N	N	Y	N	Y	N
2 Jackson	N	N	Y	N	Y	N
3 Lipinski	N	N	Y	N	Y	Y
4 Gutierrez	N	N	Y	N	Y	N
5 Quigley	N	N	Y	N	Y	N
6 **Roskam**	Y	Y	Y	Y	N	Y
7 Davis	N	N	Y	N	Y	N
8 Bean	N	N	Y	N	Y	Y
9 Schakowsky	N	N	Y	N	Y	Y
10 **Kirk**	N	Y	Y	Y	Y	Y
11 Halvorson	N	N	Y	N	Y	Y
12 Costello	N	N	Y	N	N	Y
13 **Biggert**	N	?	Y	N	Y	Y
14 Foster	N	N	Y	N	Y	N
15 **Johnson**	Y	Y	Y	N	N	N

	324	325	326	327	328	329
16 **Manzullo**	Y	Y	Y	Y	N	Y
17 Hare	N	N	Y	N	Y	N
18 **Schock**	N	Y	Y	Y	N	Y
19 **Shimkus**	Y	Y	Y	Y	N	Y
INDIANA						
1 Visclosky	N	N	Y	N	Y	N
2 Donnelly	N	N	Y	N	N	Y
3 **Souder**	Y	Y	Y	Y	N	Y
4 **Buyer**	Y	Y	Y	Y	N	Y
5 **Burton**	Y	Y	Y	Y	N	Y
6 **Pence**	Y	Y	Y	Y	N	Y
7 Carson	N	N	Y	N	Y	N
8 Ellsworth	N	N	Y	N	N	Y
9 Hill	?	?	?	?	?	?
IOWA						
1 Braley	N	N	Y	N	Y	N
2 Loebsack	?	?	?	?	?	N
3 Boswell	N	N	Y	N	Y	?
4 **Latham**	Y	Y	Y	Y	N	Y
5 **King**	Y	Y	Y	Y	N	Y
KANSAS						
1 **Moran**	Y	Y	Y	Y	N	Y
2 **Jenkins**	Y	Y	Y	Y	N	Y
3 Moore	N	N	Y	N	Y	Y
4 **Tiahrt**	Y	Y	Y	Y	N	Y
KENTUCKY						
1 **Whitfield**	Y	Y	Y	Y	N	Y
2 **Guthrie**	Y	Y	Y	Y	N	Y
3 Yarmuth	N	N	Y	N	Y	N
4 **Davis**	Y	Y	Y	Y	N	Y
5 **Rogers**	Y	Y	Y	Y	N	Y
6 Chandler	N	N	Y	N	Y	Y
LOUISIANA						
1 **Scalise**	Y	Y	Y	Y	N	Y
2 **Cao**	Y	Y	Y	Y	N	Y
3 Melancon	N	N	Y	N	N	Y
4 **Fleming**	Y	Y	Y	Y	N	Y
5 **Alexander**	Y	Y	Y	Y	N	Y
6 **Cassidy**	Y	Y	Y	Y	N	Y
7 **Boustany**	Y	Y	Y	Y	N	Y
MAINE						
1 Pingree	N	N	Y	N	Y	N
2 Michaud	N	N	Y	N	Y	N
MARYLAND						
1 Kratovil	N	N	Y	N	Y	Y
2 Ruppersberger	?	?	?	?	?	N
3 Sarbanes	N	N	Y	N	Y	N
4 Edwards	N	N	Y	N	Y	N
5 Hoyer	N	N	Y	N	Y	N
6 **Bartlett**	Y	Y	Y	Y	N	Y
7 Cummings	N	N	Y	N	Y	N
8 Van Hollen	N	N	Y	N	Y	N
MASSACHUSETTS						
1 Olver	N	N	Y	N	Y	N
2 Neal	N	N	Y	N	Y	N
3 McGovern	N	N	Y	N	Y	N
4 Frank	Y	N	Y	N	Y	N
5 Tsongas	N	N	Y	N	Y	N
6 Tierney	N	N	Y	N	Y	N
7 Markey	N	N	Y	N	Y	N
8 Capuano	N	N	Y	N	Y	N
9 Lynch	N	Y	Y	N	Y	N
10 Delahunt	N	N	Y	N	?	?
MICHIGAN						
1 Stupak	N	N	Y	N	Y	N
2 **Hoekstra**	Y	Y	Y	Y	N	Y
3 **Ehlers**	Y	Y	Y	Y	N	Y
4 **Camp**	Y	Y	Y	Y	N	Y
5 Kildee	N	N	Y	N	Y	N
6 **Upton**	Y	Y	Y	Y	N	Y
7 Schauer	N	N	Y	N	Y	Y
8 **Rogers**	Y	Y	Y	Y	N	Y
9 Peters	N	N	Y	N	Y	Y
10 **Miller**	Y	Y	Y	Y	N	Y
11 **McCotter**	Y	Y	Y	Y	N	Y
12 Levin	N	N	Y	N	Y	N
13 Kilpatrick	N	N	Y	N	Y	N
14 Conyers	N	N	Y	N	Y	N
15 Dingell	N	N	Y	N	Y	N
MINNESOTA						
1 Walz	N	N	Y	N	Y	Y
2 **Kline**	Y	Y	Y	Y	N	Y
3 **Paulsen**	Y	Y	Y	Y	N	Y
4 McCollum	N	N	N	N	Y	N

	324	325	326	327	328	329
5 Ellison	N	N	Y	N	?	?
6 **Bachmann**	Y	Y	Y	Y	N	Y
7 Peterson	N	N	Y	N	N	Y
8 Oberstar	N	N	Y	N	Y	N
MISSISSIPPI						
1 Childers	N	N	Y	N	N	Y
2 Thompson	N	N	Y	N	Y	Y
3 **Harper**	Y	Y	Y	Y	N	Y
4 Taylor	N	N	Y	N	N	Y
MISSOURI						
1 Clay	N	N	Y	N	Y	N
2 **Akin**	Y	Y	Y	Y	N	Y
3 Carnahan	N	N	Y	N	Y	N
4 Skelton	N	N	Y	N	Y	Y
5 Cleaver	N	N	Y	N	Y	N
6 **Graves**	Y	Y	Y	Y	N	Y
7 **Blunt**	N	Y	Y	Y	N	Y
8 **Emerson**	Y	Y	Y	Y	N	Y
9 **Luetkemeyer**	Y	Y	Y	Y	N	Y
MONTANA						
AL **Rehberg**	Y	Y	Y	Y	N	Y
NEBRASKA						
1 **Fortenberry**	Y	N	Y	Y	N	Y
2 **Terry**	Y	Y	Y	Y	N	Y
3 **Smith**	Y	Y	Y	Y	N	Y
NEVADA						
1 Berkley	N	N	Y	N	Y	N
2 **Heller**	Y	Y	Y	Y	N	Y
3 Titus	N	N	Y	N	Y	Y
NEW HAMPSHIRE						
1 Shea-Porter	N	N	Y	N	Y	Y
2 Hodes	N	N	Y	N	Y	Y
NEW JERSEY						
1 Andrews	N	N	Y	N	Y	N
2 **LoBiondo**	Y	Y	Y	Y	N	Y
3 Adler	N	N	Y	N	Y	Y
4 **Smith**	Y	Y	Y	Y	N	Y
5 **Garrett**	Y	Y	Y	Y	N	Y
6 Pallone	N	N	Y	N	Y	N
7 **Lance**	Y	Y	Y	Y	Y	Y
8 Pascrell	N	N	Y	N	Y	N
9 Rothman	N	N	Y	N	Y	N
10 Payne	N	N	Y	N	Y	N
11 **Frelinghuysen**	Y	Y	Y	Y	N	Y
12 Holt	N	N	+	N	Y	N
13 Sires	N	N	Y	N	Y	N
NEW MEXICO						
1 Heinrich	N	Y	Y	N	Y	N
2 Teague	N	N	Y	N	Y	Y
3 Lujan	N	N	Y	N	Y	N
NEW YORK						
1 Bishop	N	N	Y	N	Y	Y
2 Israel	N	N	Y	N	Y	N
3 **King**	Y	Y	Y	Y	N	Y
4 McCarthy	N	N	Y	N	Y	Y
5 Ackerman	N	N	Y	N	Y	N
6 Meeks	N	N	Y	N	Y	N
7 Crowley	N	N	Y	N	Y	N
8 Nadler	N	N	Y	N	Y	N
9 Weiner	N	N	Y	N	Y	N
10 Towns	N	N	Y	N	Y	N
11 Clarke	N	N	Y	N	Y	N
12 Velázquez	N	N	Y	N	Y	N
13 McMahon	N	Y	Y	N	Y	Y
14 Maloney	Y	N	Y	N	Y	N
15 Rangel	N	N	Y	N	Y	N
16 Serrano	N	N	Y	N	Y	N
17 Engel	N	N	Y	N	Y	N
18 Lowey	N	N	Y	N	Y	N
19 Hall	N	Y	Y	N	Y	Y
20 Murphy	Y	N	Y	N	Y	Y
21 Tonko	N	N	Y	N	Y	N
22 Hinchey	N	N	Y	N	Y	N
23 **McHugh**	N	Y	Y	N	Y	Y
24 Arcuri	N	N	Y	N	Y	Y
25 Maffei	N	N	Y	N	Y	Y
26 **Lee**	N	Y	Y	Y	N	Y
27 Higgins	N	N	Y	N	Y	N
28 Slaughter	N	N	Y	N	Y	N
29 Massa	N	N	Y	N	N	Y
NORTH CAROLINA						
1 Butterfield	N	N	Y	N	Y	N
2 Etheridge	N	N	Y	N	Y	N
3 **Jones**	N	N	Y	N	N	N
4 Price	N	N	Y	N	Y	N

	324	325	326	327	328	329
5 **Foxx**	Y	Y	Y	Y	N	Y
6 **Coble**	Y	Y	Y	Y	N	Y
7 McIntyre	N	Y	Y	N	N	Y
8 Kissell	N	N	Y	N	Y	Y
9 **Myrick**	Y	Y	Y	Y	N	Y
10 **McHenry**	Y	Y	Y	Y	N	Y
11 Shuler	N	N	Y	N	Y	Y
12 Watt	N	N	Y	N	Y	N
13 Miller	N	N	Y	N	Y	Y
NORTH DAKOTA						
AL Pomeroy	N	N	Y	N	Y	N
OHIO						
1 Driehaus	N	N	Y	N	Y	Y
2 **Schmidt**	Y	Y	Y	Y	N	Y
3 **Turner**	Y	Y	Y	Y	N	Y
4 **Jordan**	Y	Y	Y	Y	N	Y
5 **Latta**	Y	Y	Y	Y	N	Y
6 Wilson	N	N	Y	N	Y	Y
7 **Austria**	Y	Y	Y	Y	N	Y
8 **Boehner**	Y	Y	Y	Y	N	Y
9 Kaptur	N	N	Y	N	Y	Y
10 Kucinich	N	N	Y	N	N	N
11 Fudge	N	N	Y	N	Y	N
12 **Tiberi**	Y	Y	Y	Y	N	Y
13 Sutton	N	N	Y	N	Y	N
14 **LaTourette**	N	Y	Y	N	Y	Y
15 Kilroy	N	N	Y	N	Y	N
16 Boccieri	N	N	Y	N	Y	Y
17 Ryan	N	N	Y	N	Y	Y
18 Space	N	N	Y	N	Y	Y
OKLAHOMA						
1 **Sullivan**	?	?	?	?	?	?
2 Boren	N	N	Y	N	N	Y
3 **Lucas**	Y	Y	Y	Y	N	Y
4 **Cole**	Y	Y	Y	Y	N	Y
5 **Fallin**	Y	Y	Y	Y	N	Y
OREGON						
1 Wu	N	N	Y	N	Y	N
2 **Walden**	Y	Y	Y	Y	N	Y
3 Blumenauer	N	N	Y	N	Y	N
4 DeFazio	N	N	Y	N	Y	N
5 Schrader	Y	N	Y	N	Y	N
PENNSYLVANIA						
1 Brady	N	N	Y	N	Y	N
2 Fattah	N	N	Y	N	Y	N
3 Dahlkemper	N	N	Y	N	N	Y
4 Altmire	Y	N	Y	N	Y	Y
5 **Thompson**	Y	Y	Y	Y	N	Y
6 **Gerlach**	Y	Y	Y	Y	N	Y
7 Sestak	N	N	Y	N	Y	N
8 Murphy, P.	N	N	Y	N	Y	Y
9 **Shuster**	Y	Y	Y	Y	N	Y
10 Carney	N	Y	Y	N	Y	Y
11 Kanjorski	N	Y	Y	N	Y	N
12 Murtha	N	N	Y	N	Y	Y
13 Schwartz	N	N	Y	N	Y	N
14 Doyle	N	N	Y	N	Y	N
15 **Dent**	N	Y	Y	Y	Y	Y
16 **Pitts**	Y	Y	Y	Y	N	Y
17 Holden	N	N	Y	N	Y	Y
18 **Murphy, T.**	Y	Y	Y	Y	N	Y
19 **Platts**	Y	Y	Y	Y	N	Y
RHODE ISLAND						
1 Kennedy	?	?	?	?	?	?
2 Langevin	N	N	Y	N	Y	N
SOUTH CAROLINA						
1 **Brown**	Y	Y	Y	Y	N	Y
2 **Wilson**	Y	Y	Y	Y	N	Y
3 **Barrett**	Y	Y	Y	Y	N	Y
4 **Inglis**	Y	Y	Y	Y	N	Y
5 Spratt	N	N	Y	N	Y	Y
6 Clyburn	N	N	Y	N	Y	N
SOUTH DAKOTA						
AL Herseth Sandlin	N	N	Y	N	Y	Y
TENNESSEE						
1 **Roe**	Y	Y	Y	Y	N	Y
2 **Duncan**	Y	Y	Y	N	N	N
3 **Wamp**	Y	Y	Y	Y	N	Y
4 Davis	N	N	Y	N	Y	Y
5 Cooper	N	N	Y	N	Y	Y
6 Gordon	Y	N	Y	N	Y	Y
7 **Blackburn**	Y	Y	Y	Y	N	Y
8 Tanner	N	N	Y	N	Y	Y
9 Cohen	N	N	Y	N	Y	N

	324	325	326	327	328	329
TEXAS						
1 **Gohmert**	Y	Y	Y	Y	N	Y
2 **Poe**	Y	Y	Y	Y	N	Y
3 **Johnson, S.**	Y	Y	Y	Y	N	Y
4 **Hall**	Y	Y	Y	Y	N	Y
5 **Hensarling**	Y	Y	Y	Y	N	Y
6 **Barton**	Y	Y	Y	Y	N	Y
7 **Culberson**	Y	Y	Y	Y	N	Y
8 **Brady**	Y	Y	Y	Y	N	Y
9 Green, A.	N	N	Y	N	Y	N
10 **McCaul**	Y	Y	Y	Y	N	Y
11 **Conaway**	Y	Y	Y	Y	N	Y
12 **Granger**	Y	Y	Y	Y	N	Y
13 **Thornberry**	Y	Y	Y	Y	N	Y
14 **Paul**	Y	N	N	N	N	N
15 Hinojosa	N	N	Y	N	Y	Y
16 Reyes	N	N	Y	N	Y	Y
17 Edwards	N	N	Y	N	Y	Y
18 Jackson Lee	N	N	Y	N	Y	N
19 **Neugebauer**	Y	Y	Y	Y	N	Y
20 Gonzalez	N	N	Y	N	Y	N
21 **Smith**	Y	Y	Y	Y	N	Y
22 **Olson**	Y	Y	Y	Y	N	Y
23 Rodriguez	N	N	Y	N	Y	Y
24 **Marchant**	Y	Y	Y	Y	N	Y
25 Doggett	N	N	Y	N	Y	N
26 **Burgess**	Y	Y	Y	Y	N	Y
27 Ortiz	N	N	Y	N	Y	Y
28 Cuellar	N	N	Y	N	Y	Y
29 Green, G.	N	N	Y	N	Y	N
30 Johnson, E.	N	N	Y	N	Y	N
31 **Carter**	Y	Y	Y	Y	N	Y
32 **Sessions**	Y	Y	Y	Y	N	Y
UTAH						
1 **Bishop**	Y	Y	Y	Y	N	Y
2 Matheson	N	N	Y	N	Y	Y
3 **Chaffetz**	Y	Y	Y	Y	N	Y
VERMONT						
AL Welch	N	N	Y	N	Y	N
VIRGINIA						
1 **Wittman**	Y	Y	Y	Y	N	Y
2 Nye	N	Y	Y	N	Y	Y
3 Scott	N	N	Y	N	Y	N
4 **Forbes**	Y	Y	Y	Y	N	Y
5 Perriello	N	Y	Y	N	Y	Y
6 **Goodlatte**	Y	Y	Y	Y	N	Y
7 **Cantor**	Y	Y	Y	Y	N	Y
8 Moran	N	N	Y	N	Y	N
9 Boucher	N	N	Y	N	Y	Y
10 **Wolf**	Y	Y	Y	Y	N	Y
11 Connolly	N	N	Y	N	Y	N
WASHINGTON						
1 Inslee	N	N	Y	N	Y	N
2 Larsen	N	N	Y	N	Y	N
3 Baird	N	N	Y	N	Y	N
4 **Hastings**	Y	Y	Y	Y	N	Y
5 **McMorris Rodgers**	Y	Y	Y	Y	N	Y
6 Dicks	N	N	Y	N	Y	N
7 McDermott	N	N	Y	N	Y	N
8 **Reichert**	Y	Y	Y	Y	Y	Y
9 Smith	N	N	Y	N	Y	Y
WEST VIRGINIA						
1 Mollohan	N	N	Y	N	N	N
2 **Capito**	Y	Y	Y	Y	N	Y
3 Rahall	N	N	Y	N	N	Y
WISCONSIN						
1 **Ryan**	Y	Y	Y	Y	N	Y
2 Baldwin	N	N	Y	N	Y	N
3 Kind	N	N	Y	N	Y	N
4 Moore	N	N	Y	N	Y	N
5 **Sensenbrenner**	Y	Y	Y	Y	N	Y
6 **Petri**	Y	Y	Y	Y	N	Y
7 Obey	N	N	Y	N	Y	N
8 Kagen	N	N	Y	?	?	?
WYOMING						
AL **Lummis**	Y	Y	Y	Y	N	Y
DELEGATES						
Faleomavaega (A.S.)	N	N	Y			
Norton (D.C.)	N	N	Y			
Bordallo (Guam)	N	N	Y			
Sablan (N. Marianas)	N	N	Y			
Pierluisi (P.R.)	N	N	Y			
Christensen (V.I.)	N	N	Y			

IN THE HOUSE | By Vote Number

330. **HR 1687. Ralph Regula Courthouse/Passage.** Boccieri, D-Ohio, motion to suspend the rules and pass the bill that would designate a U.S. courthouse in Canton, Ohio, as the "Ralph Regula Federal Building and United States Courthouse." Motion agreed to 416-0: R 173-0; D 243-0. A two-thirds majority of those present and voting (278 in this case) is required for passage under suspension of the rules. June 11, 2009.

331. **HR 1886. Pakistan Aid Authorization/Republican Substitute.** Ros-Lehtinen, R-Fla., substitute amendment that would authorize $1.5 billion in non-military aid for Pakistan in fiscal 2010 and unspecified amounts through 2013, with no additional requirements on the use of the funds. It would require an interagency strategy and implementation plan for Pakistan's long-term security, quarterly briefings on developments in Pakistan and written notification to Congress of adjustments in strategy and changes in allocations and expenditures of Pakistan aid. Rejected 173-246: R 172-2; D 1-244. June 11, 2009.

332. **HR 1886. Pakistan Aid Authorization/Recommit.** Rogers, R-Mich., motion to recommit the bill to the Foreign Affairs Committee with instructions that it be immediately reported back with language that would strike the text of the bill and insert provisions that would authorize $2.8 billion annually in aid for Afghanistan and $1.5 billion annually in aid for Pakistan in fiscal 2010 through 2013, with no additional requirements on the use of the funds. The provisions also would authorize up to $700 million for a Pakistan counterinsurgency fund in 2010 and require the president to submit interagency strategies and implementation plans for the long-term security of Pakistan and Afghanistan. Motion rejected 164-245: R 162-8; D 2-237. June 11, 2009.

333. **HR 1886. Pakistan Aid Authorization/Passage.** Passage of the bill that would authorize $1.5 billion annually in non-military aid for Pakistan in fiscal 2010 through 2013 and $400 million in military assistance in fiscal 2010. It would bar military aid to Pakistan unless the president determines the country is cooperating in dismantling nuclear supply networks and fighting terrorist groups. The bill would authorize $300 million in fiscal 2010 for a State Department-managed Pakistani counterinsurgency fund, with stipulations that the money could not be used to purchase F-16 fighter aircraft without a presidential waiver. It would also authorize reconstruction opportunity zones to allow for duty-free imports from Pakistan and Afghanistan, under certain conditions. Passed 234-185: R 8-167; D 226-18. June 11, 2009.

334. **H Res 529. Holocaust Museum Attack/Adoption.** Rahall, D-W.Va., motion to suspend the rules and adopt the resolution that would condemn the attack at the U.S. Holocaust Memorial Museum on June 10, 2009, and honor the bravery of the museum's employees and security personnel. A two-thirds majority of those present and voting (276 in this case) is required for adoption under suspension of the rules. Motion agreed to 413-0: R 171-0; D 242-0. June 11, 2009.

335. **HR 1256. Tobacco Regulation/Motion to Concur.** Waxman, D-Calif., motion to concur in the Senate amendment to the bill that allows the Food and Drug Administration to regulate the manufacture, sale and promotion of tobacco products. It would require new, larger labels warning consumers of the health risks associated with tobacco products and clarify that the FDA does not endorse the safety of such products. It would establish standards for tobacco products marketed as lower in health risks. The FDA could regulate the amount of nicotine but not ban any class of tobacco products or eliminate nicotine levels completely. The bill would restrict the additives that can be included in cigarettes and ban flavors except for menthol. It would require tobacco manufacturers and importers to pay quarterly user fees to help cover the cost of the regulation. Motion agreed to (thus clearing the bill for the president), 307-97: R 70-90; D 237-7. A "yea" was a vote in support of the president's position. June 12, 2009.

	330	331	332	333	334	335
ALABAMA						
1 Bonner	Y	Y	Y	N	Y	N
2 Bright	Y	N	N	N	Y	N
3 Rogers	Y	Y	Y	N	Y	Y
4 Aderholt	Y	Y	Y	N	Y	N
5 Griffith	Y	N	Y	Y	Y	Y
6 Bachus	Y	Y	Y	N	Y	Y
7 Davis	Y	N	N	Y	Y	Y
ALASKA						
AL Young	Y	Y	Y	N	Y	Y
ARIZONA						
1 Kirkpatrick	Y	N	N	Y	Y	N
2 Franks	Y	Y	Y	N	Y	N
3 Shadegg	Y	Y	Y	N	Y	N
4 Pastor	Y	N	N	Y	Y	Y
5 Mitchell	Y	N	N	Y	Y	Y
6 Flake	Y	Y	Y	N	Y	N
7 Grijalva	Y	N	N	Y	Y	Y
8 Giffords	Y	N	N	Y	Y	Y
ARKANSAS						
1 Berry	Y	N	N	Y	Y	Y
2 Snyder	Y	N	N	Y	Y	Y
3 Boozman	Y	Y	Y	N	Y	N
4 Ross	Y	N	N	Y	Y	Y
CALIFORNIA						
1 Thompson	Y	N	N	Y	Y	Y
2 Herger	Y	Y	Y	N	Y	N
3 Lungren	Y	Y	N	Y	Y	Y
4 McClintock	Y	Y	Y	N	Y	N
5 Matsui	Y	N	N	Y	Y	Y
6 Woolsey	Y	N	N	Y	Y	Y
7 Miller, George	Y	N	N	Y	Y	Y
8 Pelosi	Y			Y		Y
9 Lee	Y	N	N	Y	Y	Y
10 Tauscher	Y	N	N	Y	Y	Y
11 McNerney	Y	N	N	Y	Y	Y
12 Speier	Y	N	N	Y	Y	Y
13 Stark	Y	N	N	N	Y	Y
14 Eshoo	Y	N	N	Y	Y	?
15 Honda	Y	N	N	Y	Y	Y
16 Lofgren	Y	N	N	Y	Y	Y
17 Farr	Y	N	N	Y	Y	Y
18 Cardoza	Y	N	N	Y	Y	Y
19 Radanovich	?	Y	Y	N	Y	N
20 Costa	Y	N	N	Y	Y	Y
21 Nunes	Y	Y	Y	N	?	?
22 McCarthy	Y	Y	Y	N	Y	Y
23 Capps	Y	N	N	Y	Y	Y
24 Gallegly	Y	Y	Y	N	Y	?
25 McKeon	Y	Y	Y	N	Y	Y
26 Dreier	Y	Y	Y	N	Y	Y
27 Sherman	?	N	N	Y	Y	Y
28 Berman	Y	N	N	Y	Y	Y
29 Schiff	Y	N	N	Y	Y	Y
30 Waxman	Y	N	N	Y	Y	Y
31 Becerra	Y	N	–	Y	Y	Y
32 Vacant						
33 Watson	Y	N	N	N	Y	Y
34 Roybal-Allard	Y	N	N	Y	Y	Y
35 Waters	Y	N	N	N	Y	Y
36 Harman	Y	N	N	Y	Y	Y
37 Richardson	?	?	?	N	?	Y
38 Napolitano	Y	N	N	?	Y	Y
39 Sánchez, Linda	?	?	?	?	?	Y
40 Royce	Y	Y	Y	Y	Y	N
41 Lewis	Y	Y	Y	N	Y	Y
42 Miller, Gary	Y	Y	Y	N	Y	?
43 Baca	+	?	?	+	+	?
44 Calvert	Y	Y	Y	N	Y	N
45 Bono Mack	Y	Y	Y	N	Y	Y
46 Rohrabacher	Y	N	N	N	Y	N
47 Sanchez, Loretta	Y	N	N	Y	Y	?
48 Campbell	Y	Y	Y	N	Y	N
49 Issa	Y	Y	Y	N	Y	N
50 Bilbray	Y	Y	Y	N	Y	Y
51 Filner	Y	N	N	Y	Y	Y
52 Hunter	Y	Y	Y	N	Y	N
53 Davis	Y	N	N	Y	Y	Y
COLORADO						
1 DeGette	Y	N	Y	Y	Y	Y
2 Polis	Y	N	N	Y	Y	Y
3 Salazar	Y	N	N	Y	Y	Y
4 Markey	Y	N	N	Y	Y	Y
5 Lamborn	Y	Y	Y	N	Y	N
6 Coffman	Y	Y	Y	N	Y	N
7 Perlmutter	Y	N	N	Y	Y	Y
CONNECTICUT						
1 Larson	Y	N	N	Y	Y	Y
2 Courtney	Y	N	N	Y	Y	Y
3 DeLauro	Y	N	N	Y	Y	Y
4 Himes	?	?	?	?	?	?
5 Murphy	Y	N	N	?	Y	Y
DELAWARE						
AL Castle	Y	Y	Y	N	Y	Y
FLORIDA						
1 Miller	Y	Y	Y	N	Y	N
2 Boyd	Y	N	N	Y	Y	Y
3 Brown	Y	?	?	?	?	?
4 Crenshaw	Y	Y	Y	N	Y	Y
5 Brown-Waite	Y	Y	Y	N	Y	Y
6 Stearns	Y	Y	Y	N	Y	Y
7 Mica	Y	Y	Y	N	Y	N
8 Grayson	Y	N	N	Y	Y	Y
9 Bilirakis	Y	Y	Y	N	Y	Y
10 Young	Y	Y	Y	N	Y	Y
11 Castor	Y	N	N	Y	Y	Y
12 Putnam	Y	Y	Y	N	Y	Y
13 Buchanan	Y	Y	Y	N	Y	?
14 Mack	Y	Y	Y	N	Y	N
15 Posey	Y	Y	Y	N	Y	N
16 Rooney	Y	Y	Y	N	Y	N
17 Meek	Y	N	N	Y	Y	Y
18 Ros-Lehtinen	Y	N	N	Y	Y	Y
19 Wexler	Y	N	N	Y	Y	Y
20 Wasserman Schultz	Y	N	N	Y	Y	Y
21 Diaz-Balart, L.	Y	Y	Y	N	Y	N
22 Klein	Y	N	N	Y	Y	Y
23 Hastings	Y	N	N	Y	Y	Y
24 Kosmas	Y	N	N	Y	Y	Y
25 Diaz-Balart, M.	Y	Y	Y	N	Y	N
GEORGIA						
1 Kingston	Y	Y	Y	N	Y	N
2 Bishop	Y	N	N	Y	Y	Y
3 Westmoreland	Y	Y	Y	N	Y	N
4 Johnson	Y	N	N	Y	Y	Y
5 Lewis	?	?	?	?	?	?
6 Price	Y	Y	Y	N	Y	N
7 Linder	Y	Y	Y	N	?	N
8 Marshall	Y	N	Y	Y	Y	Y
9 Deal	Y	Y	Y	N	Y	?
10 Broun	Y	Y	Y	N	Y	N
11 Gingrey	Y	Y	Y	N	Y	?
12 Barrow	Y	N	N	Y	Y	Y
13 Scott	Y	N	N	Y	Y	Y
HAWAII						
1 Abercrombie	Y	N	N	N	Y	Y
2 Hirono	Y	N	N	Y	+	Y
IDAHO						
1 Minnick	Y	N	?	N	Y	Y
2 Simpson	Y	Y	Y	N	Y	Y
ILLINOIS						
1 Rush	Y	N	N	Y	Y	Y
2 Jackson	Y	N	N	Y	Y	Y
3 Lipinski	Y	N	N	N	Y	Y
4 Gutierrez	Y	N	N	Y	Y	Y
5 Quigley	Y	N	N	Y	Y	Y
6 Roskam	Y	Y	Y	N	Y	Y
7 Davis	Y	N	N	Y	Y	Y
8 Bean	Y	N	N	Y	Y	Y
9 Schakowsky	Y	N	N	Y	Y	Y
10 Kirk	Y	Y	Y	Y	Y	Y
11 Halvorson	Y	N	N	Y	Y	Y
12 Costello	Y	N	N	Y	Y	Y
13 Biggert	Y	Y	Y	N	Y	Y
14 Foster	Y	N	N	Y	Y	Y
15 Johnson	Y	Y	N	?	Y	Y

KEY   Republicans   Democrats

Y Voted for (yea)	**X** Paired against
# Paired for	**–** Announced against
+ Announced for	**P** Voted "present"
N Voted against (nay)	

C Voted "present" to avoid possible conflict of interest

? Did not vote or otherwise make a position known

	330	331	332	333	334	335
16 **Manzullo**	Y	Y	Y	N	Y	Y
17 Hare	Y	N	N	Y	Y	Y
18 **Schock**	Y	Y	Y	N	Y	Y
19 **Shimkus**	Y	Y	Y	N	Y	Y
INDIANA						
1 Visclosky	Y	N	?	Y	Y	Y
2 Donnelly	Y	N	N	Y	Y	Y
3 **Souder**	Y	Y	Y	N	Y	N
4 **Buyer**	Y	Y	Y	N	Y	N
5 **Burton**	Y	Y	Y	N	Y	Y
6 **Pence**	Y	Y	Y	N	Y	N
7 Carson	Y	N	N	Y	Y	Y
8 Ellsworth	Y	N	N	Y	Y	Y
9 Hill	?	N	N	Y	Y	Y
IOWA						
1 Braley	?	N	N	Y	Y	Y
2 Loebsack	Y	N	N	Y	Y	Y
3 Boswell	?	N	N	Y	Y	Y
4 **Latham**	Y	Y	Y	N	Y	N
5 **King**	Y	Y	+	N	Y	N
KANSAS						
1 **Moran**	Y	Y	Y	N	Y	N
2 **Jenkins**	Y	Y	Y	N	Y	N
3 Moore	Y	N	N	Y	Y	Y
4 **Tiahrt**	Y	Y	Y	N	Y	N
KENTUCKY						
1 **Whitfield**	Y	Y	Y	N	Y	N
2 **Guthrie**	Y	Y	Y	N	Y	N
3 Yarmuth	Y	N	N	Y	Y	Y
4 **Davis**	Y	Y	Y	N	Y	N
5 **Rogers**	Y	Y	Y	N	Y	N
6 Chandler	Y	N	N	Y	Y	Y
LOUISIANA						
1 **Scalise**	Y	Y	Y	N	Y	N
2 **Cao**	Y	Y	Y	Y	Y	Y
3 Melancon	Y	N	Y	Y	Y	Y
4 **Fleming**	Y	Y	Y	N	Y	Y
5 **Alexander**	Y	Y	Y	N	Y	N
6 **Cassidy**	Y	Y	+	N	Y	Y
7 **Boustany**	Y	Y	Y	N	Y	N
MAINE						
1 Pingree	Y	N	N	Y	Y	Y
2 Michaud	Y	N	N	N	Y	Y
MARYLAND						
1 Kratovil	Y	N	N	Y	Y	Y
2 Ruppersberger	Y	N	N	Y	?	?
3 Sarbanes	Y	N	N	Y	Y	Y
4 Edwards	Y	N	N	Y	Y	Y
5 Hoyer	Y	N	N	Y	Y	Y
6 **Bartlett**	Y	Y	Y	N	Y	Y
7 Cummings	Y	N	N	Y	Y	Y
8 Van Hollen	Y	N	N	Y	Y	Y
MASSACHUSETTS						
1 Olver	Y	N	N	Y	Y	Y
2 Neal	Y	N	N	Y	Y	Y
3 McGovern	Y	N	N	Y	Y	Y
4 Frank	Y	N	N	Y	Y	Y
5 Tsongas	Y	N	N	Y	Y	Y
6 Tierney	Y	N	N	Y	Y	Y
7 Markey	Y	N	N	Y	Y	Y
8 Capuano	Y	N	N	Y	Y	Y
9 Lynch	Y	N	N	Y	Y	Y
10 Delahunt	?	?	?	?	?	Y
MICHIGAN						
1 Stupak	Y	N	N	Y	Y	Y
2 **Hoekstra**	Y	Y	Y	N	Y	N
3 **Ehlers**	Y	Y	Y	Y	Y	?
4 **Camp**	Y	Y	Y	N	Y	Y
5 Kildee	Y	N	N	Y	Y	Y
6 **Upton**	Y	Y	Y	Y	Y	Y
7 Schauer	Y	N	N	Y	Y	Y
8 **Rogers**	Y	Y	Y	N	Y	?
9 Peters	Y	N	N	Y	Y	Y
10 **Miller**	Y	Y	Y	N	Y	Y
11 **McCotter**	Y	Y	Y	N	Y	N
12 Levin	Y	N	N	Y	Y	Y
13 Kilpatrick	Y	N	N	Y	Y	Y
14 Conyers	Y	N	N	N	Y	Y
15 Dingell	Y	N	N	Y	Y	Y
MINNESOTA						
1 Walz	Y	N	N	Y	Y	Y
2 **Kline**	Y	Y	Y	N	Y	?
3 **Paulsen**	Y	Y	Y	N	Y	Y
4 McCollum	Y	N	N	Y	Y	Y
5 Ellison	Y	N	N	Y	Y	Y
6 **Bachmann**	Y	Y	Y	N	Y	N
7 Peterson	Y	N	?	Y	Y	Y
8 Oberstar	Y	?	N	Y	Y	Y
MISSISSIPPI						
1 Childers	Y	N	N	Y	?	?
2 Thompson	Y	N	N	Y	Y	Y
3 **Harper**	Y	Y	Y	N	Y	Y
4 Taylor	Y	N	N	Y	Y	Y
MISSOURI						
1 Clay	Y	N	N	Y	Y	Y
2 **Akin**	Y	Y	Y	N	Y	N
3 Carnahan	Y	N	N	Y	Y	Y
4 Skelton	Y	N	N	Y	Y	Y
5 Cleaver	Y	N	N	Y	Y	Y
6 **Graves**	Y	Y	Y	N	Y	N
7 **Blunt**	Y	?	?	?	?	?
8 **Emerson**	Y	Y	Y	N	Y	Y
9 **Luetkemeyer**	Y	Y	?	N	Y	?
MONTANA						
AL **Rehberg**	Y	Y	Y	N	Y	Y
NEBRASKA						
1 **Fortenberry**	Y	Y	Y	N	Y	Y
2 **Terry**	Y	Y	Y	N	Y	Y
3 **Smith**	Y	Y	Y	N	Y	N
NEVADA						
1 Berkley	Y	N	N	Y	Y	Y
2 **Heller**	Y	N	N	N	Y	N
3 Titus	Y	N	N	Y	Y	Y
NEW HAMPSHIRE						
1 Shea-Porter	Y	N	N	Y	Y	Y
2 Hodes	Y	N	N	Y	Y	Y
NEW JERSEY						
1 Andrews	Y	N	N	Y	Y	Y
2 **LoBiondo**	Y	Y	Y	N	Y	Y
3 Adler	Y	N	N	Y	Y	?
4 **Smith**	Y	Y	Y	N	Y	Y
5 **Garrett**	?	Y	Y	N	Y	N
6 Pallone	Y	N	N	Y	Y	Y
7 **Lance**	Y	Y	Y	N	Y	Y
8 Pascrell	Y	N	N	Y	Y	Y
9 Rothman	Y	N	N	Y	Y	Y
10 Payne	Y	N	N	Y	Y	Y
11 **Frelinghuysen**	Y	Y	Y	N	Y	Y
12 Holt	Y	N	N	Y	Y	?
13 Sires	Y	N	N	Y	Y	Y
NEW MEXICO						
1 Heinrich	Y	N	N	Y	Y	Y
2 Teague	Y	N	N	Y	Y	Y
3 Lujan	Y	N	N	Y	Y	Y
NEW YORK						
1 Bishop	Y	N	N	Y	Y	Y
2 Israel	Y	N	N	Y	Y	Y
3 **King**	Y	Y	Y	N	Y	Y
4 McCarthy	Y	N	N	Y	Y	Y
5 Ackerman	Y	N	N	Y	?	?
6 Meeks	Y	N	N	Y	Y	Y
7 Crowley	Y	N	N	Y	Y	Y
8 Nadler	Y	N	N	Y	Y	Y
9 Weiner	Y	N	N	Y	Y	Y
10 Towns	Y	N	N	Y	Y	Y
11 Clarke	Y	N	N	Y	Y	Y
12 Velázquez	Y	N	N	Y	Y	Y
13 McMahon	Y	N	N	Y	Y	Y
14 Maloney	Y	N	N	Y	Y	Y
15 Rangel	Y	N	N	Y	Y	Y
16 Serrano	Y	N	N	Y	Y	Y
17 Engel	Y	N	N	Y	Y	Y
18 Lowey	Y	N	N	Y	Y	Y
19 Hall	Y	N	N	Y	Y	Y
20 Murphy	Y	N	N	Y	Y	Y
21 Tonko	Y	N	–	Y	Y	Y
22 Hinchey	Y	N	N	Y	Y	Y
23 **McHugh**	Y	Y	Y	Y	Y	N
24 Arcuri	Y	N	N	N	Y	Y
25 Maffei	Y	N	N	Y	Y	Y
26 **Lee**	Y	Y	Y	N	Y	Y
27 Higgins	Y	N	N	Y	Y	Y
28 Slaughter	?	N	–	Y	Y	Y
29 Massa	Y	N	N	N	Y	Y
NORTH CAROLINA						
1 Butterfield	Y	N	N	Y	Y	Y
2 Etheridge	Y	N	N	Y	Y	Y
3 **Jones**	Y	Y	N	N	Y	?
4 Price	Y	N	N	Y	Y	Y
5 **Foxx**	Y	Y	Y	N	Y	N
6 **Coble**	Y	Y	Y	N	Y	N
7 McIntyre	Y	N	?	Y	Y	N
8 Kissell	Y	N	N	N	Y	N
9 **Myrick**	Y	Y	Y	N	Y	N
10 **McHenry**	?	Y	Y	N	Y	N
11 Shuler	Y	N	N	N	Y	N
12 Watt	Y	N	N	Y	Y	Y
13 Miller	Y	N	N	Y	Y	Y
NORTH DAKOTA						
AL Pomeroy	Y	N	N	Y	Y	Y
OHIO						
1 Driehaus	Y	N	N	Y	Y	Y
2 **Schmidt**	Y	Y	?	N	Y	N
3 **Turner**	Y	Y	Y	N	Y	Y
4 **Jordan**	Y	Y	Y	N	Y	N
5 **Latta**	Y	Y	Y	N	Y	N
6 Wilson	Y	N	N	Y	Y	?
7 **Austria**	Y	Y	Y	N	Y	Y
8 **Boehner**	Y	Y	Y	N	Y	N
9 Kaptur	Y	N	N	N	Y	Y
10 Kucinich	Y	N	N	N	Y	Y
11 Fudge	Y	N	N	Y	Y	Y
12 **Tiberi**	Y	Y	Y	N	Y	Y
13 Sutton	Y	N	N	Y	Y	Y
14 **LaTourette**	Y	Y	Y	N	Y	Y
15 Kilroy	Y	N	N	Y	Y	Y
16 Boccieri	Y	N	N	Y	Y	Y
17 Ryan	Y	N	N	Y	Y	Y
18 Space	Y	N	N	Y	Y	Y
OKLAHOMA						
1 **Sullivan**	?	?	?	?	?	?
2 Boren	Y	N	N	Y	Y	Y
3 **Lucas**	Y	?	?	N	Y	N
4 **Cole**	Y	Y	Y	N	Y	N
5 **Fallin**	Y	Y	Y	N	Y	Y
OREGON						
1 Wu	Y	N	N	Y	Y	Y
2 **Walden**	Y	Y	Y	N	Y	Y
3 Blumenauer	Y	N	N	Y	Y	Y
4 DeFazio	Y	N	N	Y	Y	Y
5 Schrader	Y	N	N	Y	Y	Y
PENNSYLVANIA						
1 Brady	Y	N	N	Y	Y	Y
2 Fattah	Y	N	N	Y	Y	Y
3 Dahlkemper	Y	N	N	Y	Y	Y
4 Altmire	Y	N	N	Y	Y	Y
5 **Thompson**	Y	Y	Y	N	Y	N
6 **Gerlach**	Y	Y	Y	N	Y	Y
7 Sestak	Y	N	N	Y	Y	Y
8 Murphy, P.	Y	N	N	Y	Y	Y
9 **Shuster**	Y	Y	Y	N	Y	N
10 Carney	Y	N	N	Y	Y	Y
11 Kanjorski	Y	N	N	Y	Y	Y
12 Murtha	Y	N	N	Y	Y	Y
13 Schwartz	Y	N	N	Y	Y	Y
14 Doyle	Y	N	N	Y	Y	Y
15 **Dent**	Y	Y	Y	N	Y	Y
16 **Pitts**	Y	Y	Y	N	Y	N
17 Holden	Y	N	N	Y	Y	Y
18 **Murphy, T.**	Y	Y	Y	N	Y	Y
19 **Platts**	Y	Y	Y	N	Y	Y
RHODE ISLAND						
1 Kennedy	?	?	?	?	?	?
2 Langevin	Y	N	N	Y	Y	Y
SOUTH CAROLINA						
1 **Brown**	Y	Y	Y	N	Y	Y
2 **Wilson**	Y	Y	Y	N	Y	N
3 **Barrett**	Y	Y	Y	N	?	?
4 **Inglis**	Y	Y	Y	N	Y	N
5 Spratt	Y	N	N	Y	Y	Y
6 Clyburn	Y	N	N	Y	Y	Y
SOUTH DAKOTA						
AL Herseth Sandlin	Y	N	N	Y	Y	Y
TENNESSEE						
1 **Roe**	Y	Y	Y	N	Y	N
2 **Duncan**	Y	Y	N	N	Y	Y
3 **Wamp**	Y	Y	Y	N	Y	Y
4 Davis	Y	N	N	Y	Y	N
5 Cooper	Y	N	N	Y	Y	Y
6 Gordon	Y	N	N	Y	Y	Y
7 **Blackburn**	Y	Y	Y	N	?	?
8 Tanner	Y	N	N	Y	Y	Y
9 Cohen	Y	N	N	Y	Y	Y
TEXAS						
1 **Gohmert**	Y	Y	Y	N	Y	?
2 **Poe**	Y	Y	Y	N	?	Y
3 **Johnson, S.**	Y	Y	Y	N	Y	N
4 **Hall**	Y	Y	Y	N	Y	Y
5 **Hensarling**	?	Y	Y	N	Y	N
6 **Barton**	Y	Y	Y	N	Y	N
7 **Culberson**	Y	Y	Y	N	Y	N
8 **Brady**	Y	Y	Y	N	Y	Y
9 Green, A.	Y	N	N	Y	Y	Y
10 **McCaul**	Y	Y	Y	N	Y	Y
11 **Conaway**	Y	Y	Y	N	Y	N
12 **Granger**	Y	Y	Y	N	Y	Y
13 **Thornberry**	Y	Y	Y	N	Y	N
14 **Paul**	Y	Y	N	N	Y	N
15 Hinojosa	Y	N	N	Y	Y	Y
16 Reyes	Y	N	N	Y	Y	Y
17 Edwards	Y	N	N	Y	Y	Y
18 Jackson Lee	Y	N	N	Y	Y	Y
19 **Neugebauer**	Y	Y	Y	N	Y	N
20 Gonzalez	Y	N	N	Y	Y	Y
21 **Smith**	Y	Y	Y	N	Y	Y
22 **Olson**	Y	Y	Y	N	Y	N
23 Rodriguez	Y	N	N	Y	Y	Y
24 **Marchant**	Y	Y	Y	N	Y	?
25 Doggett	Y	N	N	N	Y	Y
26 **Burgess**	Y	Y	Y	N	Y	N
27 Ortiz	Y	N	N	Y	Y	Y
28 Cuellar	Y	N	N	Y	Y	Y
29 Green, G.	Y	N	N	Y	Y	Y
30 Johnson, E.	Y	N	N	Y	Y	Y
31 **Carter**	Y	Y	Y	N	Y	N
32 **Sessions**	Y	Y	Y	N	Y	N
UTAH						
1 **Bishop**	Y	?	Y	N	Y	N
2 Matheson	Y	N	N	Y	Y	Y
3 **Chaffetz**	Y	Y	N	N	Y	N
VERMONT						
AL Welch	Y	N	N	Y	Y	Y
VIRGINIA						
1 **Wittman**	Y	Y	Y	N	Y	Y
2 Nye	Y	N	N	Y	Y	Y
3 Scott	Y	N	N	Y	Y	Y
4 **Forbes**	Y	Y	Y	N	Y	N
5 Perriello	Y	N	N	N	Y	N
6 **Goodlatte**	Y	Y	+	N	Y	N
7 **Cantor**	Y	Y	Y	N	Y	Y
8 Moran	Y	N	N	Y	?	Y
9 Boucher	Y	N	N	Y	Y	Y
10 **Wolf**	Y	Y	Y	N	Y	Y
11 Connolly	Y	N	N	Y	Y	Y
WASHINGTON						
1 Inslee	Y	N	N	Y	Y	Y
2 Larsen	Y	N	N	Y	Y	Y
3 Baird	Y	N	N	Y	Y	Y
4 **Hastings**	Y	Y	Y	N	Y	?
5 **McMorris Rodgers**	Y	Y	Y	N	Y	Y
6 Dicks	Y	N	N	Y	Y	Y
7 McDermott	Y	N	N	N	Y	Y
8 **Reichert**	Y	Y	Y	Y	Y	Y
9 Smith	Y	N	N	Y	Y	Y
WEST VIRGINIA						
1 Mollohan	Y	N	N	Y	Y	Y
2 **Capito**	Y	Y	Y	N	Y	Y
3 Rahall	Y	N	N	Y	Y	Y
WISCONSIN						
1 **Ryan**	Y	Y	Y	N	Y	N
2 Baldwin	Y	N	N	Y	Y	Y
3 Kind	Y	N	N	Y	Y	Y
4 Moore	Y	N	N	Y	Y	Y
5 **Sensenbrenner**	Y	Y	Y	N	Y	N
6 **Petri**	Y	Y	Y	N	Y	N
7 Obey	Y	N	N	Y	Y	Y
8 Kagen	?	?	?	?	?	Y
WYOMING						
AL **Lummis**	Y	Y	Y	N	Y	N
DELEGATES						
Faleomavaega (A.S.)						
Norton (D.C.)						
Bordallo (Guam)						
Sablan (N. Marianas)						
Pierluisi (P.R.)						
Christensen (V.I.)						

IN THE HOUSE | By Vote Number

336. **H Res 430. Abruzzo Earthquake/Adoption.** Faleomavaega, D-A.S., motion to suspend the rules and adopt the resolution that would express condolences to the families of those killed and injured in the April 6, 2009, earthquake that struck the Abruzzo region of central Italy, applaud the response of rescue workers, and urge Americans to support humanitarian aid efforts. Motion agreed to 381-0: R 151-0; D 230-0. A two-thirds majority of those present and voting (254 in this case) is required for adoption under suspension of the rules. June 15, 2009.

337. **HR 2325. Laredo Veterans Post Office/Passage.** Lynch, D-Mass., motion to suspend the rules and pass the bill that would designate a post office in Laredo, Texas, as the "Laredo Veterans Post Office." Motion agreed to 374-0: R 149-0; D 225-0. A two-thirds majority of those present and voting (250 in this case) is required for passage under suspension of the rules. June 15, 2009.

338. **HR 729. School Overnight Trip Plans/Passage.** Sablan, D-N. Marianas, motion to suspend the rules and pass the bill that would require local education agencies receiving funds under the Safe and Drug-Free Schools and Communities program to require schools sponsoring off-campus overnight field trips to develop written safety plans. Motion agreed to 319-60: R 92-60; D 227-0. A two-thirds majority of those present and voting (253 in this case) is required for passage under suspension of the rules. June 15, 2009.

339. **H Res 540. ConAgra Explosion Victims/Adoption.** Scott, D-Va., motion to suspend the rules and adopt the resolution that would express condolences to the families and friends of the victims of the explosion on June 9, 2009, at the ConAgra Foods plant in Garner, N.C., honor those who died or were injured, and commend the response of emergency personnel. Motion agreed to 381-0: R 153-0; D 228-0. A two-thirds majority of those present and voting (254 in this case) is required for adoption under suspension of the rules. June 15, 2009.

340. **HR 2470. Roy Boehm Post Office/Passage.** Lynch, D-Mass., motion to suspend the rules and pass the bill that would designate a post office in Port Charlotte, Fla., as the "Lt. Cmdr. Roy H. Boehm Post Office Building." Motion agreed to 417-0: R 172-0; D 245-0. A two-thirds majority of those present and voting (278 in this case) is required for passage under suspension of the rules. June 16, 2009.

341. **HR 780. Student Internet Safety/Passage.** Sablan, D-N. Marianas, motion to suspend the rules and pass the bill that would allow local education agencies to use certain education grants for programs to protect students against Internet predators and inappropriate material, educate students about appropriate Internet behavior, and promote parental involvement in children's Internet use. Motion agreed to 416-0: R 173-0; D 243-0. A two-thirds majority of those present and voting (278 in this case) is required for passage under suspension of the rules. June 16, 2009.

342. **Review of House Speaker's Statements/Motion to Table.** Hastings, D-Fla., motion to table (kill) the Bishop, R-Utah, appeal of the ruling of the chair that the draft resolution does not constitute a point of privilege under Rule IX of the House. The draft resolution would require the House to establish a Select Intelligence subcommittee to review and verify the accuracy of House Speaker Nancy Pelosi's public statements regarding the CIA deceiving Congress, and report to the House on its findings no later than 60 days after the adoption of the resolution. The committee would be made up of four members of the full committee — two appointed by the chairman and two by the ranking minority member. Motion agreed to 247-171: R 2-171; D 245-0. June 16, 2009.

	336	337	338	339	340	341	342
ALABAMA							
1 **Bonner**	?	?	?	?	?	?	?
2 Bright	Y	Y	Y	Y	Y	Y	Y
3 **Rogers**	Y	Y	Y	Y	Y	Y	N
4 **Aderholt**	Y	Y	Y	Y	Y	Y	N
5 Griffith	Y	Y	Y	Y	Y	Y	Y
6 **Bachus**	Y	Y	Y	Y	Y	Y	N
7 Davis	Y	Y	Y	Y	Y	Y	Y
ALASKA							
AL **Young**	Y	Y	N	Y	Y	Y	N
ARIZONA							
1 Kirkpatrick	Y	Y	Y	Y	Y	Y	Y
2 **Franks**	Y	Y	Y	Y	Y	Y	N
3 **Shadegg**	?	?	?	?	Y	Y	N
4 Pastor	Y	Y	Y	Y	Y	Y	Y
5 Mitchell	Y	Y	Y	Y	Y	Y	Y
6 **Flake**	Y	N	Y	N	Y	Y	N
7 Grijalva	?	?	?	?	Y	Y	Y
8 Giffords	Y	Y	Y	Y	Y	Y	Y
ARKANSAS							
1 Berry	?	Y	Y	Y	Y	Y	Y
2 Snyder	Y	Y	Y	Y	Y	Y	Y
3 **Boozman**	Y	Y	Y	Y	Y	Y	N
4 Ross	Y	Y	Y	Y	Y	Y	Y
CALIFORNIA							
1 Thompson	Y	Y	Y	Y	Y	Y	Y
2 **Herger**	Y	Y	Y	Y	Y	Y	N
3 **Lungren**	Y	N	Y	N	Y	Y	N
4 **McClintock**	Y	N	Y	N	Y	Y	N
5 Matsui	Y	Y	Y	Y	Y	Y	Y
6 Woolsey	Y	Y	Y	Y	Y	Y	Y
7 Miller, George	Y	Y	Y	Y	Y	Y	Y
8 Pelosi	Y						
9 Lee	Y	Y	Y	Y	Y	Y	Y
10 Tauscher	Y	Y	Y	Y	Y	Y	Y
11 McNerney	Y	Y	Y	Y	Y	Y	Y
12 Speier	Y	Y	Y	Y	Y	Y	Y
13 Stark	Y	Y	Y	Y	Y	Y	Y
14 Eshoo	Y	Y	Y	Y	Y	Y	Y
15 Honda	Y	Y	Y	Y	Y	Y	Y
16 Lofgren	Y	Y	Y	Y	Y	Y	Y
17 Farr	Y	Y	Y	Y	Y	Y	Y
18 Cardoza	Y	Y	Y	Y	Y	Y	Y
19 **Radanovich**	Y	Y	N	Y	Y	Y	N
20 Costa	Y	Y	Y	Y	Y	Y	Y
21 **Nunes**	Y	Y	Y	Y	Y	Y	N
22 **McCarthy**	Y	Y	Y	Y	Y	Y	N
23 Capps	Y	Y	Y	Y	Y	Y	Y
24 **Gallegly**	Y	Y	N	Y	Y	Y	N
25 **McKeon**	Y	Y	N	Y	Y	Y	N
26 **Dreier**	Y	Y	N	Y	Y	Y	N
27 Sherman	Y	Y	Y	Y	Y	Y	Y
28 Berman	Y	Y	?	Y	Y	Y	Y
29 Schiff	Y	Y	Y	Y	Y	Y	Y
30 Waxman	Y	Y	Y	Y	Y	Y	Y
31 Becerra	Y	Y	Y	Y	Y	Y	Y
32 Vacant							
33 Watson	Y	Y	Y	Y	Y	Y	Y
34 Roybal-Allard	Y	Y	Y	Y	Y	Y	Y
35 Waters	?	?	?	?	?	?	Y
36 Harman	Y	Y	Y	Y	Y	Y	Y
37 Richardson	Y	Y	Y	Y	Y	Y	Y
38 Napolitano	Y	Y	Y	Y	Y	Y	Y
39 Sánchez, Linda	Y	Y	Y	Y	?	?	?
40 **Royce**	Y	Y	N	Y	Y	Y	N
41 **Lewis**	Y	?	?	Y	Y	Y	N
42 **Miller, Gary**	Y	Y	N	Y	Y	Y	N
43 Baca	Y	Y	Y	Y	Y	Y	Y
44 **Calvert**	Y	Y	Y	Y	Y	Y	N
45 **Bono Mack**	Y	Y	Y	Y	Y	Y	N
46 **Rohrabacher**	?	?	?	?	Y	Y	N
47 Sanchez, Loretta	Y	Y	Y	Y	Y	Y	Y
48 **Campbell**	Y	Y	N	Y	Y	Y	N
49 **Issa**	Y	Y	N	Y	Y	Y	N
50 **Bilbray**	Y	Y	Y	Y	Y	Y	N
51 Filner	Y	Y	Y	Y	Y	Y	Y
52 **Hunter**	Y	Y	Y	Y	Y	Y	N
53 Davis	Y	Y	Y	Y	Y	Y	Y

	336	337	338	339	340	341	342
COLORADO							
1 DeGette	Y	Y	Y	Y	Y	Y	Y
2 Polis	Y	Y	Y	Y	Y	Y	Y
3 Salazar	Y	Y	Y	Y	Y	Y	Y
4 Markey	Y	Y	Y	Y	Y	Y	Y
5 **Lamborn**	Y	N	N	Y	Y	Y	N
6 **Coffman**	+	Y	Y	Y	Y	Y	N
7 Perlmutter	Y	Y	+	Y	Y	Y	Y
CONNECTICUT							
1 Larson	Y	?	Y	Y	+	+	+
2 Courtney	Y	Y	Y	Y	Y	Y	Y
3 DeLauro	Y	Y	Y	Y	Y	Y	Y
4 Himes	Y	Y	Y	Y	Y	Y	Y
5 Murphy	Y	Y	Y	Y	Y	Y	Y
DELAWARE							
AL **Castle**	Y	Y	Y	Y	Y	Y	N
FLORIDA							
1 **Miller**	Y	N	N	Y	Y	Y	N
2 Boyd	Y	Y	Y	Y	Y	Y	Y
3 Brown	?	?	?	?	Y	Y	Y
4 **Crenshaw**	Y	Y	Y	Y	Y	Y	N
5 **Brown-Waite**	Y	Y	Y	Y	Y	Y	N
6 **Stearns**	Y	Y	Y	Y	Y	Y	N
7 **Mica**	Y	Y	Y	Y	Y	Y	N
8 Grayson	Y	Y	Y	Y	Y	Y	Y
9 **Bilirakis**	Y	Y	Y	Y	Y	Y	N
10 **Young**	?	?	?	?	?	?	?
11 Castor	Y	Y	Y	Y	Y	Y	Y
12 **Putnam**	?	+	+	+	?	Y	N
13 **Buchanan**	Y	Y	Y	Y	Y	Y	N
14 **Mack**	Y	Y	Y	Y	Y	Y	N
15 **Posey**	Y	Y	Y	Y	Y	Y	N
16 **Rooney**	Y	Y	Y	Y	Y	Y	N
17 Meek	Y	Y	Y	Y	Y	Y	Y
18 **Ros-Lehtinen**	Y	Y	Y	Y	Y	Y	N
19 Wexler	Y	Y	Y	Y	Y	Y	Y
20 Wasserman Schultz	Y	Y	Y	Y	Y	Y	Y
21 **Diaz-Balart, L.**	Y	Y	Y	Y	Y	Y	N
22 Klein	Y	Y	Y	Y	Y	Y	Y
23 Hastings	Y	Y	Y	Y	Y	Y	Y
24 Kosmas	Y	Y	Y	Y	Y	Y	Y
25 **Diaz-Balart, M.**	Y	Y	Y	Y	Y	Y	N
GEORGIA							
1 **Kingston**	Y	Y	N	Y	Y	Y	N
2 Bishop	Y	Y	Y	Y	Y	Y	Y
3 **Westmoreland**	Y	Y	N	Y	Y	Y	N
4 Johnson	Y	Y	Y	Y	Y	Y	Y
5 Lewis	?	?	?	?	?	?	?
6 **Price**	Y	Y	N	Y	Y	Y	N
7 **Linder**	Y	Y	Y	Y	Y	Y	N
8 Marshall	?	?	?	Y	Y	Y	Y
9 **Deal**	?	?	?	?	Y	Y	N
10 **Broun**	+	+	−	+	Y	Y	N
11 **Gingrey**	?	?	?	?	Y	Y	N
12 Barrow	Y	Y	Y	Y	Y	Y	Y
13 Scott	Y	Y	Y	Y	Y	Y	Y
HAWAII							
1 Abercrombie	Y	Y	Y	Y	Y	Y	Y
2 Hirono	Y	Y	Y	Y	Y	Y	Y
IDAHO							
1 Minnick	Y	Y	Y	Y	Y	Y	Y
2 **Simpson**	?	?	?	?	Y	Y	N
ILLINOIS							
1 Rush	?	?	?	?	Y	Y	Y
2 Jackson	Y	Y	Y	Y	Y	Y	Y
3 Lipinski	Y	Y	Y	Y	Y	Y	Y
4 Gutierrez	Y	Y	Y	Y	Y	Y	Y
5 Quigley	Y	Y	Y	Y	Y	Y	Y
6 **Roskam**	Y	Y	Y	Y	Y	Y	N
7 Davis	Y	Y	Y	Y	Y	Y	Y
8 Bean	Y	Y	Y	Y	Y	Y	Y
9 Schakowsky	Y	Y	Y	Y	Y	Y	Y
10 **Kirk**	Y	Y	Y	Y	Y	Y	Y
11 Halvorson	Y	Y	Y	Y	Y	Y	Y
12 Costello	?	?	?	?	?	?	?
13 **Biggert**	Y	N	Y	Y	Y	Y	N
14 Foster	Y	Y	Y	Y	Y	Y	Y
15 **Johnson**	?	?	?	?	Y	Y	N

	336	337	338	339	340	341	342
16 **Manzullo**	+	+	–	?	Y	Y	N
17 Hare	Y	Y	Y	Y	Y	Y	Y
18 **Schock**	Y	Y	Y	Y	Y	Y	N
19 **Shimkus**	Y	Y	N	Y	Y	Y	N
INDIANA							
1 Visclosky	Y	Y	Y	Y	Y	Y	Y
2 Donnelly	+	+	–	+	Y	Y	Y
3 **Souder**	Y	Y	N	Y	Y	Y	N
4 **Buyer**	Y	Y	N	Y	Y	Y	N
5 **Burton**	Y	Y	N	Y	Y	Y	N
6 **Pence**	Y	Y	N	Y	Y	Y	N
7 Carson	Y	Y	Y	Y	Y	Y	Y
8 Ellsworth	Y	Y	Y	Y	Y	Y	Y
9 Hill	Y	Y	Y	Y	Y	Y	Y
IOWA							
1 Braley	Y	Y	+	Y	Y	Y	Y
2 Loebsack	?	?	?	?	Y	Y	Y
3 Boswell	Y	Y	Y	Y	Y	Y	Y
4 **Latham**	Y	Y	Y	Y	Y	Y	N
5 **King**	Y	Y	N	Y	Y	Y	N
KANSAS							
1 **Moran**	Y	Y	N	Y	Y	Y	N
2 **Jenkins**	Y	Y	Y	Y	Y	Y	N
3 Moore	Y	Y	Y	Y	Y	Y	Y
4 **Tiahrt**	Y	Y	N	Y	Y	Y	N
KENTUCKY							
1 **Whitfield**	Y	Y	Y	Y	Y	Y	N
2 **Guthrie**	Y	Y	Y	Y	Y	Y	N
3 Yarmuth	Y	Y	Y	Y	Y	Y	Y
4 **Davis**	Y	Y	N	Y	Y	Y	N
5 **Rogers**	Y	Y	Y	Y	Y	Y	N
6 Chandler	Y	Y	Y	Y	Y	Y	Y
LOUISIANA							
1 **Scalise**	Y	Y	Y	Y	Y	Y	N
2 **Cao**	Y	Y	Y	Y	Y	Y	N
3 Melancon	Y	Y	Y	Y	Y	Y	Y
4 **Fleming**	Y	Y	Y	Y	Y	Y	N
5 **Alexander**	?	?	?	?	?	?	?
6 **Cassidy**	Y	Y	N	Y	Y	Y	N
7 **Boustany**	Y	?	Y	Y	Y	Y	N
MAINE							
1 Pingree	?	?	?	?	Y	Y	Y
2 Michaud	?	+	+	+	Y	Y	Y
MARYLAND							
1 Kratovil	Y	Y	Y	Y	Y	Y	Y
2 Ruppersberger	Y	Y	Y	Y	Y	Y	Y
3 Sarbanes	Y	Y	Y	Y	Y	Y	Y
4 Edwards	Y	Y	Y	Y	Y	Y	Y
5 Hoyer	Y	Y	Y	Y	?	?	Y
6 **Bartlett**	Y	Y	N	Y	Y	Y	N
7 Cummings	Y	Y	Y	Y	Y	Y	Y
8 Van Hollen	Y	Y	Y	Y	Y	Y	Y
MASSACHUSETTS							
1 Olver	Y	?	Y	Y	Y	Y	Y
2 Neal	Y	Y	Y	Y	Y	Y	Y
3 McGovern	Y	Y	Y	Y	Y	Y	Y
4 Frank	?	?	?	?	Y	Y	Y
5 Tsongas	Y	Y	Y	Y	Y	Y	Y
6 Tierney	Y	Y	Y	Y	Y	Y	Y
7 Markey	Y	Y	Y	Y	Y	Y	Y
8 Capuano	Y	?	Y	Y	Y	Y	Y
9 Lynch	Y	Y	Y	Y	Y	Y	Y
10 Delahunt	Y	Y	Y	Y	Y	Y	Y
MICHIGAN							
1 Stupak	Y	Y	Y	Y	Y	Y	Y
2 **Hoekstra**	?	?	?	?	Y	Y	N
3 **Ehlers**	Y	Y	Y	Y	Y	Y	N
4 **Camp**	Y	Y	Y	Y	Y	Y	N
5 Kildee	Y	Y	Y	Y	Y	Y	Y
6 **Upton**	Y	Y	Y	Y	Y	Y	N
7 Schauer	Y	Y	Y	Y	Y	Y	Y
8 **Rogers**	?	?	?	?	Y	Y	N
9 Peters	Y	Y	Y	Y	Y	Y	Y
10 **Miller**	Y	Y	Y	Y	Y	Y	N
11 **McCotter**	Y	Y	Y	Y	Y	Y	N
12 Levin	Y	Y	Y	Y	Y	Y	Y
13 Kilpatrick	Y	Y	Y	Y	Y	Y	Y
14 Conyers	Y	Y	Y	Y	Y	Y	Y
15 Dingell	Y	Y	Y	Y	Y	Y	Y
MINNESOTA							
1 Walz	Y	Y	Y	Y	Y	Y	Y
2 **Kline**	Y	Y	N	Y	Y	Y	N
3 **Paulsen**	Y	Y	Y	Y	Y	Y	N
4 McCollum	Y	Y	Y	Y	Y	Y	Y
5 Ellison	Y	Y	Y	Y	Y	Y	Y
6 **Bachmann**	?	?	?	?	Y	Y	N
7 Peterson	Y	Y	Y	Y	Y	Y	Y
8 Oberstar	Y	Y	Y	Y	Y	Y	Y
MISSISSIPPI							
1 Childers	Y	Y	Y	Y	Y	Y	Y
2 Thompson	Y	Y	Y	Y	Y	Y	Y
3 **Harper**	Y	Y	N	Y	Y	Y	N
4 Taylor	Y	Y	Y	Y	Y	Y	Y
MISSOURI							
1 Clay	Y	Y	Y	Y	Y	Y	Y
2 **Akin**	Y	Y	N	Y	Y	Y	N
3 Carnahan	Y	Y	Y	Y	Y	Y	Y
4 Skelton	Y	Y	Y	Y	Y	Y	Y
5 Cleaver	Y	Y	Y	Y	Y	Y	Y
6 **Graves**	?	?	?	?	Y	Y	N
7 **Blunt**	?	?	?	?	Y	Y	?
8 **Emerson**	Y	Y	Y	Y	Y	Y	N
9 **Luetkemeyer**	Y	Y	Y	Y	Y	Y	N
MONTANA							
AL **Rehberg**	Y	Y	Y	Y	Y	Y	N
NEBRASKA							
1 **Fortenberry**	Y	Y	Y	Y	Y	Y	N
2 **Terry**	Y	Y	Y	Y	Y	Y	N
3 **Smith**	Y	Y	Y	Y	Y	Y	N
NEVADA							
1 Berkley	Y	Y	Y	Y	+	+	+
2 **Heller**	Y	Y	Y	Y	Y	Y	N
3 Titus	Y	Y	Y	Y	Y	Y	Y
NEW HAMPSHIRE							
1 Shea-Porter	Y	Y	Y	Y	Y	Y	Y
2 Hodes	Y	Y	Y	Y	Y	Y	Y
NEW JERSEY							
1 Andrews	Y	Y	Y	Y	Y	Y	Y
2 **LoBiondo**	Y	Y	Y	Y	Y	Y	N
3 Adler	Y	Y	Y	Y	Y	Y	Y
4 **Smith**	Y	Y	Y	Y	Y	Y	N
5 **Garrett**	Y	Y	N	Y	Y	Y	N
6 Pallone	Y	Y	Y	Y	Y	Y	Y
7 **Lance**	Y	Y	Y	Y	Y	Y	N
8 Pascrell	Y	?	Y	?	Y	Y	Y
9 Rothman	Y	Y	Y	Y	Y	Y	Y
10 Payne	Y	Y	Y	Y	Y	Y	Y
11 **Frelinghuysen**	Y	Y	Y	Y	Y	Y	N
12 Holt	Y	Y	Y	Y	Y	Y	Y
13 Sires	+	+	+	?	Y	Y	Y
NEW MEXICO							
1 Heinrich	Y	Y	Y	Y	Y	Y	Y
2 Teague	Y	Y	Y	Y	Y	Y	Y
3 Lujan	Y	Y	Y	Y	Y	Y	Y
NEW YORK							
1 Bishop	Y	Y	Y	Y	Y	Y	Y
2 Israel	Y	Y	Y	Y	Y	Y	Y
3 **King**	Y	Y	Y	Y	Y	Y	N
4 McCarthy	Y	?	Y	Y	Y	Y	Y
5 Ackerman	Y	Y	Y	Y	Y	Y	Y
6 Meeks	Y	Y	Y	Y	Y	Y	Y
7 Crowley	Y	Y	Y	Y	Y	Y	Y
8 Nadler	Y	Y	Y	Y	Y	Y	Y
9 Weiner	Y	Y	Y	Y	Y	Y	Y
10 Towns	?	?	?	?	Y	Y	Y
11 Clarke	Y	Y	Y	Y	Y	Y	Y
12 Velázquez	Y	Y	Y	Y	Y	Y	Y
13 McMahon	?	Y	Y	Y	Y	Y	Y
14 Maloney	+	+	+	+	Y	Y	Y
15 Rangel	Y	Y	Y	Y	Y	Y	Y
16 Serrano	Y	Y	Y	Y	Y	Y	Y
17 Engel	?	?	?	?	Y	Y	Y
18 Lowey	Y	Y	Y	Y	Y	Y	Y
19 Hall	Y	Y	Y	Y	Y	Y	Y
20 Murphy	Y	Y	Y	Y	Y	Y	Y
21 Tonko	Y	Y	Y	Y	Y	Y	Y
22 Hinchey	Y	Y	Y	Y	Y	Y	Y
23 **McHugh**	Y	Y	Y	Y	Y	Y	N
24 Arcuri	Y	Y	Y	Y	Y	Y	Y
25 Maffei	Y	Y	Y	Y	Y	Y	Y
26 **Lee**	Y	Y	Y	Y	Y	Y	N
27 Higgins	Y	Y	Y	Y	Y	Y	Y
28 Slaughter	Y	Y	Y	Y	Y	Y	Y
29 Massa	Y	Y	Y	Y	Y	Y	Y
NORTH CAROLINA							
1 Butterfield	Y	Y	Y	Y	Y	Y	Y
2 Etheridge	Y	Y	Y	Y	Y	Y	Y
3 **Jones**	Y	Y	Y	Y	Y	Y	Y
4 Price	Y	Y	Y	Y	Y	Y	Y
5 **Foxx**	Y	Y	N	Y	Y	Y	N
6 **Coble**	+	+	–	+	Y	Y	N
7 McIntyre	Y	Y	Y	Y	Y	Y	Y
8 Kissell	Y	Y	Y	Y	Y	Y	Y
9 **Myrick**	Y	Y	N	Y	Y	Y	N
10 **McHenry**	Y	Y	N	Y	Y	Y	N
11 Shuler	?	?	?	?	Y	Y	Y
12 Watt	Y	Y	Y	Y	Y	Y	Y
13 Miller	Y	Y	Y	Y	Y	Y	Y
NORTH DAKOTA							
AL Pomeroy	Y	Y	Y	Y	Y	Y	Y
OHIO							
1 Driehaus	Y	Y	Y	Y	Y	Y	Y
2 **Schmidt**	Y	Y	Y	Y	Y	Y	N
3 **Turner**	Y	Y	Y	Y	Y	Y	N
4 **Jordan**	Y	Y	N	Y	Y	Y	N
5 **Latta**	Y	Y	Y	Y	Y	Y	N
6 Wilson	Y	Y	Y	Y	?	?	?
7 **Austria**	Y	Y	Y	Y	Y	Y	N
8 **Boehner**	Y	Y	N	Y	Y	Y	N
9 Kaptur	Y	Y	?	Y	Y	Y	Y
10 Kucinich	Y	Y	Y	Y	Y	Y	Y
11 Fudge	Y	Y	Y	Y	Y	Y	Y
12 **Tiberi**	Y	?	Y	Y	Y	Y	N
13 Sutton	Y	Y	Y	Y	Y	Y	Y
14 **LaTourette**	Y	Y	Y	Y	Y	Y	N
15 Kilroy	+	+	+	+	Y	Y	Y
16 Boccieri	Y	Y	Y	Y	Y	Y	Y
17 Ryan	Y	Y	Y	Y	Y	Y	Y
18 Space	Y	?	Y	Y	Y	Y	Y
OKLAHOMA							
1 **Sullivan**	?	?	?	?	?	?	?
2 Boren	Y	Y	Y	Y	Y	Y	Y
3 **Lucas**	Y	Y	Y	Y	Y	Y	N
4 **Cole**	Y	Y	Y	Y	Y	Y	N
5 **Fallin**	Y	Y	Y	Y	Y	Y	N
OREGON							
1 Wu	Y	Y	Y	Y	Y	Y	Y
2 **Walden**	Y	Y	N	Y	Y	Y	N
3 Blumenauer	Y	Y	Y	Y	Y	Y	Y
4 DeFazio	Y	Y	Y	Y	Y	Y	Y
5 Schrader	Y	Y	Y	Y	Y	Y	Y
PENNSYLVANIA							
1 Brady	Y	Y	Y	Y	Y	Y	Y
2 Fattah	Y	Y	Y	Y	Y	Y	Y
3 Dahlkemper	Y	Y	Y	Y	Y	Y	Y
4 Altmire	Y	Y	Y	Y	Y	Y	Y
5 **Thompson**	Y	Y	Y	Y	Y	Y	N
6 **Gerlach**	Y	Y	Y	Y	Y	Y	N
7 Sestak	?	?	?	?	Y	Y	Y
8 Murphy, P.	Y	Y	Y	Y	Y	Y	Y
9 **Shuster**	Y	Y	Y	Y	Y	Y	N
10 Carney	Y	Y	Y	Y	Y	Y	Y
11 Kanjorski	Y	Y	Y	Y	Y	Y	Y
12 Murtha	Y	Y	Y	Y	Y	Y	Y
13 Schwartz	Y	Y	Y	Y	Y	Y	Y
14 Doyle	Y	Y	Y	Y	Y	Y	Y
15 **Dent**	Y	Y	Y	Y	Y	Y	N
16 **Pitts**	Y	Y	Y	Y	Y	Y	N
17 Holden	Y	Y	Y	Y	Y	Y	Y
18 **Murphy, T.**	Y	Y	Y	Y	Y	Y	N
19 **Platts**	Y	Y	Y	Y	Y	Y	N
RHODE ISLAND							
1 Kennedy	?	?	?	?	?	?	?
2 Langevin	Y	Y	Y	Y	Y	Y	Y
SOUTH CAROLINA							
1 **Brown**	Y	Y	Y	Y	Y	Y	N
2 **Wilson**	Y	Y	Y	Y	Y	Y	N
3 **Barrett**	+	+	–	?	Y	Y	N
4 **Inglis**	Y	Y	N	Y	Y	Y	N
5 Spratt	Y	Y	Y	Y	Y	Y	Y
6 Clyburn	Y	Y	Y	Y	Y	Y	Y
SOUTH DAKOTA							
AL Herseth Sandlin	Y	Y	Y	Y	Y	Y	Y
TENNESSEE							
1 **Roe**	Y	Y	Y	Y	Y	?	N
2 **Duncan**	?	?	?	?	Y	Y	N
3 **Wamp**	Y	Y	Y	Y	Y	Y	N
4 Davis	Y	Y	Y	Y	Y	Y	Y
5 Cooper	?	?	?	?	Y	Y	Y
6 Gordon	Y	Y	Y	Y	Y	Y	Y
7 **Blackburn**	?	?	?	?	Y	Y	N
8 Tanner	Y	Y	Y	Y	Y	Y	Y
9 Cohen	Y	Y	Y	Y	Y	Y	Y
TEXAS							
1 **Gohmert**	Y	Y	N	Y	Y	Y	N
2 **Poe**	Y	Y	N	Y	Y	Y	N
3 **Johnson, S.**	Y	Y	N	Y	Y	Y	N
4 **Hall**	Y	Y	Y	Y	Y	Y	N
5 **Hensarling**	?	?	?	?	Y	Y	N
6 **Barton**	Y	Y	N	Y	Y	Y	N
7 **Culberson**	Y	Y	Y	Y	Y	Y	N
8 **Brady**	?	?	?	?	Y	Y	N
9 Green, A.	Y	Y	Y	Y	Y	Y	Y
10 **McCaul**	Y	Y	Y	Y	Y	Y	N
11 **Conaway**	Y	Y	N	Y	Y	Y	N
12 **Granger**	Y	Y	N	Y	Y	Y	N
13 **Thornberry**	Y	Y	N	Y	Y	Y	N
14 **Paul**	Y	Y	N	Y	Y	Y	Y
15 Hinojosa	Y	Y	Y	Y	Y	Y	Y
16 Reyes	Y	Y	Y	?	Y	Y	Y
17 Edwards	Y	Y	Y	Y	Y	Y	Y
18 Jackson Lee	Y	Y	Y	Y	Y	Y	Y
19 **Neugebauer**	Y	Y	N	Y	Y	Y	N
20 Gonzalez	Y	Y	Y	Y	Y	Y	Y
21 **Smith**	Y	?	Y	Y	Y	Y	N
22 **Olson**	Y	Y	Y	Y	Y	Y	N
23 Rodriguez	Y	Y	Y	Y	Y	Y	Y
24 **Marchant**	+	?	?	?	Y	Y	N
25 Doggett	Y	Y	Y	Y	Y	Y	Y
26 **Burgess**	Y	Y	N	Y	Y	Y	N
27 Ortiz	Y	Y	Y	?	Y	Y	Y
28 Cuellar	Y	Y	Y	Y	Y	Y	Y
29 Green, G.	Y	Y	Y	Y	Y	Y	Y
30 Johnson, E.	?	?	?	?	Y	Y	Y
31 **Carter**	?	Y	N	Y	Y	Y	N
32 **Sessions**	Y	Y	N	Y	Y	Y	N
UTAH							
1 **Bishop**	Y	Y	N	Y	Y	Y	N
2 Matheson	Y	Y	Y	Y	Y	Y	Y
3 **Chaffetz**	Y	Y	N	Y	Y	Y	N
VERMONT							
AL Welch	Y	Y	Y	Y	Y	Y	Y
VIRGINIA							
1 **Wittman**	Y	Y	Y	Y	Y	Y	N
2 Nye	Y	Y	Y	Y	Y	Y	Y
3 Scott	Y	Y	Y	Y	Y	Y	Y
4 **Forbes**	Y	Y	Y	Y	Y	Y	N
5 Perriello	Y	Y	Y	Y	Y	Y	Y
6 **Goodlatte**	Y	Y	Y	Y	Y	Y	N
7 **Cantor**	Y	Y	N	Y	Y	Y	N
8 Moran	?	?	?	?	Y	Y	Y
9 Boucher	?	?	?	?	Y	Y	Y
10 **Wolf**	Y	Y	Y	Y	Y	Y	N
11 Connolly	Y	Y	Y	Y	?	?	?
WASHINGTON							
1 Inslee	Y	Y	Y	Y	Y	Y	Y
2 Larsen	Y	Y	Y	Y	Y	Y	Y
3 Baird	Y	Y	Y	Y	Y	Y	Y
4 **Hastings**	Y	Y	N	Y	Y	Y	N
5 **McMorris Rodgers**	Y	Y	Y	Y	Y	Y	N
6 Dicks	Y	Y	Y	Y	Y	Y	Y
7 McDermott	Y	Y	Y	Y	Y	Y	Y
8 **Reichert**	Y	Y	Y	Y	Y	Y	N
9 Smith	Y	Y	Y	Y	Y	Y	Y
WEST VIRGINIA							
1 Mollohan	Y	Y	Y	Y	Y	Y	Y
2 **Capito**	Y	Y	Y	Y	Y	Y	N
3 Rahall	Y	Y	Y	Y	Y	Y	Y
WISCONSIN							
1 **Ryan**	Y	Y	N	Y	Y	Y	N
2 Baldwin	Y	Y	Y	Y	Y	?	Y
3 Kind	Y	Y	Y	Y	Y	Y	Y
4 Moore	Y	Y	Y	Y	Y	Y	?
5 **Sensenbrenner**	Y	Y	Y	Y	Y	Y	N
6 **Petri**	Y	Y	Y	Y	Y	Y	N
7 Obey	Y	Y	Y	Y	Y	?	Y
8 Kagen	Y	Y	Y	Y	Y	Y	Y
WYOMING							
AL **Lummis**	Y	Y	N	Y	?	Y	N
DELEGATES							
Faleomavaega (A.S.)							
Norton (D.C.)							
Bordallo (Guam)							
Sablan (N. Marianas)							
Pierluisi (P.R.)							
Christensen (V.I.)							

IN THE HOUSE | By Vote Number

343. **HR 2247. Congressional Rules and Reports/Passage.** Cohen, D-Tenn., motion to suspend the rules and pass the bill that would repeal the requirement that agencies submit rules and reports to the House and Senate that are published in the Federal Register. Instead, the Government Accountability Office would be required to submit a weekly report to the House and Senate listing all rules received since the last report. Motion agreed to 414-0: R 170-0; D 244-0. A two-thirds majority of those present and voting (276 in this case) is required for passage under suspension of the rules. June 16, 2009.

344. **HR 403. Low-Income Veterans' Housing/Passage.** A. Green, D-Texas, motion to suspend the rules and pass the bill that would authorize $200 million for the Department of Housing and Urban Development (HUD) to assist private nonprofit organizations and consumer cooperatives in expanding the supply of permanent housing and support services for veterans' families with incomes of less than 50 percent of the median income for their area of residence. It would require HUD to provide at least 20,000 housing rental vouchers to qualifying veterans' families. Motion agreed to 417-2: R 172-2; D 245-0. A two-thirds majority of those present and voting (280 in this case) is required for passage under suspension of the rules. June 16, 2009.

345. **HR 2346. Fiscal 2009 Supplemental/Rule.** Adoption of the rule (H Res 545) that would provide for House floor consideration of the conference report on the bill that would appropriate $105.9 billion in emergency supplemental funds for fiscal 2009, including funding for the wars in Iraq and Afghanistan and pandemic flu preparations. Adopted 238-183: R 0-173; D 238-10. June 16, 2009.

346. **HR 2847. Fiscal 2010 Commerce-Justice-Science Appropriations/Previous Question.** Arcuri, D-N.Y., motion to order the previous question (thus ending debate and possibility of amendment) on adoption of the rule (H Res 544) to provide for House floor consideration of the bill that would appropriate $64.4 billion in fiscal 2010 for the departments of Commerce and Justice and other federal agencies, including NASA and the National Science Foundation. Motion agreed to 247-176: R 0-175; D 247-1. June 16, 2009.

347. **HR 2847. Fiscal 2010 Commerce-Justice-Science Appropriations/Rule.** Adoption of the rule (H Res 544) that would provide for House floor consideration of the bill that would appropriate $64.4 billion in fiscal 2010 for the departments of Commerce and Justice and other federal agencies, including NASA and the National Science Foundation. Adopted 247-174: R 1-173; D 246-1. June 16, 2009.

348. **HR 2346. Fiscal 2009 Supplemental/Conference Report.** Adoption of the conference report on the bill that would appropriate $105.9 billion in emergency supplemental funds for fiscal 2009, including funding for the wars in Iraq and Afghanistan and pandemic flu preparations. It would provide $79.9 billion for defense funding, $10.4 billion for foreign aid and stabilization programs, and $7.7 billion to address potential pandemic flu. It would appropriate $5 billion related to International Monetary Fund activities and $1 billion for a program to encourage consumers to trade in their cars for new, more fuel-efficient vehicles. It also would bar the use of funds in the bill to release detainees at Guantánamo Bay, Cuba, into the United States. Adopted (thus sent to the Senate) 226-202: R 5-170; D 221-32. A "yea" was a vote in support of the president's position. June 16, 2009.

	343	344	345	346	347	348
ALABAMA						
1 Bonner	?	?	N	N	N	N
2 Bright	Y	Y	Y	Y	Y	Y
3 Rogers	Y	Y	N	N	N	N
4 Aderholt	Y	Y	N	N	N	N
5 Griffith	Y	Y	Y	Y	Y	Y
6 Bachus	Y	Y	N	N	N	N
7 Davis	Y	Y	Y	Y	Y	Y
ALASKA						
AL Young	Y	Y	N	N	N	N
ARIZONA						
1 Kirkpatrick	Y	Y	Y	Y	Y	Y
2 Franks	Y	Y	N	N	N	N
3 Shadegg	Y	Y	N	N	N	N
4 Pastor	Y	Y	Y	Y	Y	Y
5 Mitchell	Y	Y	Y	Y	Y	Y
6 Flake	Y	N	N	N	N	N
7 Grijalva	Y	Y	Y	Y	Y	N
8 Giffords	Y	Y	Y	Y	Y	Y
ARKANSAS						
1 Berry	Y	Y	Y	Y	Y	Y
2 Snyder	Y	Y	Y	Y	Y	Y
3 Boozman	Y	Y	N	N	?	N
4 Ross	Y	Y	Y	Y	Y	Y
CALIFORNIA						
1 Thompson	Y	Y	Y	Y	Y	Y
2 Herger	Y	Y	N	N	N	N
3 Lungren	Y	Y	N	N	N	N
4 McClintock	Y	Y	N	N	N	N
5 Matsui	Y	Y	Y	Y	Y	Y
6 Woolsey	Y	Y	Y	Y	Y	N
7 Miller, George	Y	Y	Y	Y	Y	Y
8 Pelosi						Y
9 Lee	Y	Y	Y	Y	Y	Y
10 Tauscher	Y	Y	Y	Y	Y	Y
11 McNerney	Y	Y	Y	Y	Y	Y
12 Speier	Y	Y	Y	Y	Y	Y
13 Stark	Y	Y	Y	Y	Y	Y
14 Eshoo	Y	Y	Y	Y	Y	Y
15 Honda	Y	Y	Y	Y	Y	Y
16 Lofgren	Y	Y	Y	Y	Y	Y
17 Farr	Y	Y	Y	Y	Y	Y
18 Cardoza	Y	Y	Y	Y	Y	Y
19 Radanovich	Y	Y	N	N	N	N
20 Costa	Y	Y	Y	Y	Y	Y
21 Nunes	Y	Y	N	N	N	N
22 McCarthy	Y	Y	N	N	N	N
23 Capps	Y	Y	Y	Y	Y	Y
24 Gallegly	Y	Y	N	N	N	N
25 McKeon	Y	Y	N	N	N	N
26 Dreier	Y	N	N	N	N	N
27 Sherman	Y	Y	Y	Y	Y	Y
28 Berman	Y	Y	Y	Y	Y	Y
29 Schiff	Y	Y	Y	Y	Y	Y
30 Waxman	Y	Y	Y	Y	Y	Y
31 Becerra	Y	Y	Y	Y	Y	Y
32 Vacant						
33 Watson	Y	Y	Y	Y	Y	N
34 Roybal-Allard	Y	Y	Y	Y	Y	Y
35 Waters	Y	Y	N	Y	Y	N
36 Harman	Y	Y	Y	Y	Y	Y
37 Richardson	Y	Y	Y	Y	Y	Y
38 Napolitano	Y	Y	Y	Y	Y	Y
39 Sánchez, Linda	?	?	?	?	?	?
40 Royce	Y	Y	N	N	N	N
41 Lewis	Y	Y	N	N	N	N
42 Miller, Gary	Y	Y	N	N	N	N
43 Baca	Y	Y	Y	Y	Y	Y
44 Calvert	Y	Y	N	N	N	N
45 Bono Mack	Y	Y	N	N	N	N
46 Rohrabacher	Y	Y	N	N	N	N
47 Sanchez, Loretta	Y	Y	Y	Y	Y	Y
48 Campbell	Y	N	N	N	N	N
49 Issa	Y	Y	N	N	N	N
50 Bilbray	Y	Y	N	N	N	N
51 Filner	Y	Y	N	Y	Y	N
52 Hunter	Y	Y	N	N	N	N
53 Davis	Y	Y	Y	Y	Y	Y

	343	344	345	346	347	348
COLORADO						
1 DeGette	Y	Y	Y	Y	Y	Y
2 Polis	Y	Y	Y	Y	Y	N
3 Salazar	Y	Y	Y	Y	Y	Y
4 Markey	Y	Y	Y	Y	Y	Y
5 Lamborn	Y	Y	N	N	N	N
6 Coffman	Y	Y	N	N	N	N
7 Perlmutter	Y	Y	Y	Y	Y	Y
CONNECTICUT						
1 Larson	+	+	+	+	+	Y
2 Courtney	Y	Y	Y	Y	Y	Y
3 DeLauro	Y	Y	Y	Y	Y	Y
4 Himes	Y	Y	Y	Y	Y	Y
5 Murphy	Y	Y	Y	Y	Y	Y
DELAWARE						
AL Castle	Y	Y	N	N	N	N
FLORIDA						
1 Miller	Y	Y	N	N	N	N
2 Boyd	Y	Y	Y	Y	Y	Y
3 Brown	Y	Y	Y	Y	Y	Y
4 Crenshaw	Y	Y	N	N	N	N
5 Brown-Waite	Y	Y	N	N	N	N
6 Stearns	Y	Y	N	N	N	N
7 Mica	Y	Y	N	N	N	N
8 Grayson	Y	Y	Y	Y	Y	Y
9 Bilirakis	Y	Y	N	N	N	N
10 Young	?	?	?	?	?	?
11 Castor	Y	Y	Y	Y	Y	Y
12 Putnam	Y	Y	Y	Y	Y	N
13 Buchanan	Y	Y	N	N	N	N
14 Mack	Y	Y	N	N	N	N
15 Posey	Y	Y	N	N	N	N
16 Rooney	Y	Y	N	N	N	N
17 Meek	Y	Y	Y	Y	Y	Y
18 Ros-Lehtinen	Y	Y	N	N	N	N
19 Wexler	Y	Y	Y	Y	Y	Y
20 Wasserman Schultz	Y	Y	Y	Y	Y	Y
21 Diaz-Balart, L.	Y	Y	N	N	N	N
22 Klein	Y	Y	Y	Y	Y	Y
23 Hastings	Y	Y	Y	Y	Y	Y
24 Kosmas	Y	Y	Y	Y	Y	Y
25 Diaz-Balart, M.	?	Y	N	N	N	N
GEORGIA						
1 Kingston	Y	Y	N	N	N	N
2 Bishop	Y	Y	Y	Y	Y	Y
3 Westmoreland	Y	Y	N	N	N	N
4 Johnson	Y	Y	Y	Y	Y	Y
5 Lewis	?	?	?	?	?	?
6 Price	Y	Y	N	N	N	N
7 Linder	Y	Y	N	N	N	N
8 Marshall	Y	Y	Y	Y	Y	Y
9 Deal	Y	Y	N	N	N	N
10 Broun	?	Y	N	N	N	N
11 Gingrey	Y	Y	N	N	N	N
12 Barrow	Y	Y	Y	Y	Y	Y
13 Scott	Y	Y	Y	Y	Y	Y
HAWAII						
1 Abercrombie	Y	Y	Y	Y	Y	Y
2 Hirono	Y	Y	Y	Y	Y	Y
IDAHO						
1 Minnick	Y	Y	N	N	N	Y
2 Simpson	Y	Y	N	N	N	N
ILLINOIS						
1 Rush	Y	Y	N	Y	Y	Y
2 Jackson	Y	Y	Y	Y	Y	Y
3 Lipinski	Y	Y	Y	Y	Y	Y
4 Gutierrez	Y	Y	Y	Y	Y	Y
5 Quigley	Y	Y	Y	Y	Y	Y
6 Roskam	Y	Y	N	N	N	N
7 Davis	Y	Y	Y	Y	Y	Y
8 Bean	Y	Y	+	Y	Y	Y
9 Schakowsky	Y	Y	Y	Y	Y	Y
10 Kirk	Y	Y	N	N	Y	N
11 Halvorson	Y	Y	Y	Y	Y	Y
12 Costello	?	?	Y	Y	Y	Y
13 Biggert	Y	Y	N	N	N	N
14 Foster	Y	Y	Y	Y	Y	N
15 Johnson	Y	Y	N	N	Y	N

	343	344	345	346	347	348
16 **Manzullo**	Y	Y	N	N	N	N
17 Hare	Y	Y	Y	Y	Y	Y
18 **Schock**	Y	Y	N	N	N	N
19 **Shimkus**	Y	Y	N	N	N	N
INDIANA						
1 Visclosky	Y	Y	Y	Y	Y	Y
2 Donnelly	Y	Y	Y	Y	Y	Y
3 **Souder**	Y	Y	N	N	N	N
4 **Buyer**	Y	Y	N	N	N	N
5 **Burton**	Y	Y	N	N	N	N
6 **Pence**	Y	Y	?	N	N	N
7 Carson	Y	Y	Y	Y	Y	Y
8 Ellsworth	Y	Y	Y	Y	Y	Y
9 Hill	Y	Y	Y	Y	Y	Y
IOWA						
1 Braley	Y	Y	Y	Y	Y	Y
2 Loebsack	Y	Y	Y	Y	Y	Y
3 Boswell	Y	Y	Y	Y	Y	Y
4 **Latham**	Y	Y	N	N	N	N
5 **King**	+	Y	N	N	N	N
KANSAS						
1 **Moran**	Y	Y	N	N	N	N
2 **Jenkins**	Y	Y	N	N	N	N
3 Moore	Y	Y	Y	Y	Y	Y
4 **Tiahrt**	Y	Y	N	N	N	N
KENTUCKY						
1 **Whitfield**	Y	Y	N	N	N	N
2 **Guthrie**	Y	Y	N	N	N	N
3 Yarmuth	Y	Y	Y	Y	Y	Y
4 **Davis**	Y	Y	N	N	N	N
5 **Rogers**	Y	Y	N	N	N	N
6 Chandler	Y	Y	Y	Y	Y	Y
LOUISIANA						
1 **Scalise**	Y	Y	N	N	N	N
2 **Cao**	Y	Y	N	N	N	Y
3 Melancon	Y	Y	Y	Y	Y	Y
4 **Fleming**	Y	Y	N	N	N	N
5 **Alexander**	?	?	?	?	?	?
6 **Cassidy**	Y	Y	N	N	N	N
7 **Boustany**	Y	Y	N	N	N	N
MAINE						
1 Pingree	Y	Y	Y	Y	Y	N
2 Michaud	Y	Y	N	Y	Y	N
MARYLAND						
1 Kratovil	Y	Y	N	Y	Y	Y
2 Ruppersberger	Y	Y	Y	Y	Y	Y
3 Sarbanes	?	Y	Y	Y	Y	Y
4 Edwards	Y	Y	Y	Y	Y	N
5 Hoyer	Y	Y	Y	Y	Y	Y
6 **Bartlett**	Y	Y	N	N	N	N
7 Cummings	Y	Y	Y	Y	Y	Y
8 Van Hollen	Y	Y	Y	Y	Y	Y
MASSACHUSETTS						
1 Olver	Y	Y	Y	Y	Y	Y
2 Neal	Y	Y	Y	Y	Y	Y
3 McGovern	Y	Y	Y	Y	Y	N
4 Frank	Y	Y	Y	Y	Y	Y
5 Tsongas	Y	Y	Y	Y	Y	N
6 Tierney	Y	Y	Y	Y	Y	N
7 Markey	Y	Y	Y	Y	Y	Y
8 Capuano	Y	Y	Y	Y	Y	N
9 Lynch	Y	Y	Y	Y	Y	Y
10 Delahunt	Y	Y	Y	Y	Y	Y
MICHIGAN						
1 Stupak	Y	Y	Y	Y	Y	Y
2 **Hoekstra**	Y	Y	N	N	N	N
3 **Ehlers**	Y	Y	N	N	N	N
4 **Camp**	Y	Y	N	N	N	N
5 Kildee	Y	Y	Y	Y	Y	Y
6 **Upton**	Y	Y	N	N	N	N
7 Schauer	Y	Y	Y	Y	Y	Y
8 **Rogers**	Y	Y	N	N	N	N
9 Peters	Y	Y	Y	Y	Y	Y
10 **Miller**	Y	Y	N	N	N	Y
11 **McCotter**	Y	Y	N	N	N	N
12 Levin	Y	Y	Y	Y	Y	Y
13 Kilpatrick	Y	Y	Y	Y	Y	Y
14 Conyers	Y	Y	Y	Y	Y	N
15 Dingell	Y	Y	Y	Y	Y	Y
MINNESOTA						
1 Walz	Y	Y	Y	Y	?	Y
2 **Kline**	Y	Y	N	N	N	N
3 **Paulsen**	Y	Y	N	N	N	N
4 McCollum	Y	Y	Y	Y	Y	Y
5 Ellison	Y	Y	Y	Y	Y	N
6 **Bachmann**	Y	Y	N	N	N	N
7 Peterson	Y	?	Y	Y	Y	Y
8 Oberstar	Y	Y	Y	Y	Y	Y
MISSISSIPPI						
1 Childers	Y	Y	Y	Y	Y	Y
2 Thompson	Y	Y	Y	Y	Y	Y
3 **Harper**	Y	Y	N	N	N	N
4 Taylor	Y	Y	Y	Y	Y	Y
MISSOURI						
1 Clay	Y	Y	Y	Y	Y	Y
2 **Akin**	Y	Y	N	N	N	N
3 Carnahan	Y	Y	Y	Y	?	Y
4 Skelton	Y	Y	Y	Y	Y	Y
5 Cleaver	Y	Y	Y	Y	Y	Y
6 **Graves**	Y	Y	N	N	N	N
7 **Blunt**	Y	Y	N	N	N	N
8 **Emerson**	Y	Y	N	N	N	N
9 **Luetkemeyer**	Y	Y	N	N	N	N
MONTANA						
AL **Rehberg**	Y	Y	N	N	N	N
NEBRASKA						
1 **Fortenberry**	Y	Y	N	N	N	N
2 **Terry**	Y	Y	N	N	N	N
3 **Smith**	Y	Y	N	N	N	N
NEVADA						
1 Berkley	+	+	+	+	+	+
2 **Heller**	Y	Y	N	N	N	N
3 Titus	Y	Y	Y	Y	Y	Y
NEW HAMPSHIRE						
1 Shea-Porter	Y	Y	Y	Y	Y	N
2 Hodes	Y	Y	Y	Y	Y	Y
NEW JERSEY						
1 Andrews	Y	Y	Y	Y	Y	Y
2 **LoBiondo**	Y	Y	N	N	N	N
3 Adler	Y	Y	Y	Y	Y	Y
4 **Smith**	Y	Y	N	N	N	N
5 **Garrett**	Y	Y	N	N	N	N
6 Pallone	Y	Y	Y	Y	Y	Y
7 **Lance**	Y	Y	N	N	N	N
8 Pascrell	Y	Y	Y	Y	Y	Y
9 Rothman	Y	Y	Y	Y	Y	Y
10 Payne	Y	Y	Y	Y	Y	N
11 **Frelinghuysen**	Y	Y	N	N	N	N
12 Holt	Y	Y	Y	Y	Y	Y
13 Sires	Y	Y	Y	Y	Y	Y
NEW MEXICO						
1 Heinrich	Y	Y	N	Y	Y	Y
2 Teague	Y	Y	Y	Y	Y	Y
3 Lujan	Y	Y	Y	Y	Y	Y
NEW YORK						
1 Bishop	Y	Y	Y	Y	Y	Y
2 Israel	Y	Y	Y	Y	Y	Y
3 **King**	Y	Y	N	N	N	Y
4 McCarthy	?	Y	Y	Y	Y	Y
5 Ackerman	Y	Y	Y	Y	Y	Y
6 Meeks	Y	Y	Y	Y	Y	Y
7 Crowley	Y	Y	Y	Y	Y	Y
8 Nadler	Y	Y	Y	Y	Y	Y
9 Weiner	Y	Y	Y	Y	Y	Y
10 Towns	Y	Y	Y	Y	Y	Y
11 Clarke	Y	Y	Y	Y	Y	Y
12 Velázquez	Y	Y	Y	Y	Y	Y
13 McMahon	Y	Y	Y	Y	Y	Y
14 Maloney	Y	Y	Y	Y	Y	Y
15 Rangel	?	Y	Y	Y	Y	Y
16 Serrano	Y	Y	Y	Y	Y	N
17 Engel	Y	Y	Y	Y	Y	Y
18 Lowey	Y	Y	Y	Y	Y	Y
19 Hall	Y	Y	Y	Y	Y	Y
20 Murphy	Y	Y	Y	Y	Y	Y
21 Tonko	Y	Y	Y	Y	Y	Y
22 Hinchey	Y	Y	Y	Y	Y	Y
23 **McHugh**	Y	Y	N	N	N	Y
24 Arcuri	Y	Y	Y	Y	Y	Y
25 Maffei	Y	Y	Y	Y	Y	Y
26 **Lee**	Y	Y	N	N	N	N
27 Higgins	Y	Y	Y	Y	Y	Y
28 Slaughter	Y	Y	Y	Y	Y	Y
29 Massa	Y	Y	Y	Y	Y	N
NORTH CAROLINA						
1 Butterfield	Y	Y	Y	Y	Y	Y
2 Etheridge	Y	Y	Y	Y	Y	Y
3 **Jones**	Y	Y	N	N	N	N
4 Price	Y	Y	Y	Y	Y	Y
5 **Foxx**	Y	Y	N	N	N	N
6 **Coble**	Y	Y	N	N	N	N
7 McIntyre	Y	Y	Y	Y	Y	Y
8 Kissell	Y	Y	Y	Y	Y	Y
9 **Myrick**	Y	Y	N	N	N	N
10 **McHenry**	Y	Y	N	N	N	N
11 Shuler	Y	Y	Y	Y	Y	Y
12 Watt	Y	Y	Y	Y	Y	Y
13 Miller	Y	Y	Y	Y	Y	Y
NORTH DAKOTA						
AL Pomeroy	Y	Y	Y	Y	Y	Y
OHIO						
1 Driehaus	Y	Y	Y	Y	Y	Y
2 **Schmidt**	Y	Y	N	N	N	N
3 **Turner**	Y	Y	N	N	N	N
4 **Jordan**	Y	Y	N	N	N	N
5 **Latta**	Y	Y	N	N	N	N
6 Wilson	?	?	Y	Y	Y	Y
7 **Austria**	Y	Y	N	N	N	N
8 **Boehner**	Y	Y	N	N	N	N
9 Kaptur	Y	Y	N	Y	Y	N
10 Kucinich	Y	Y	N	Y	Y	N
11 Fudge	Y	Y	Y	Y	Y	Y
12 **Tiberi**	Y	Y	N	N	N	N
13 Sutton	Y	Y	Y	Y	Y	Y
14 **LaTourette**	Y	Y	N	N	N	N
15 Kilroy	Y	Y	Y	Y	Y	Y
16 Boccieri	Y	Y	Y	Y	Y	Y
17 Ryan	Y	Y	Y	Y	Y	Y
18 Space	Y	Y	Y	Y	Y	Y
OKLAHOMA						
1 **Sullivan**	?	?	?	?	?	?
2 Boren	Y	Y	Y	Y	Y	Y
3 **Lucas**	Y	Y	N	N	N	N
4 **Cole**	Y	Y	N	N	N	N
5 **Fallin**	Y	Y	N	N	N	N
OREGON						
1 Wu	Y	Y	Y	Y	Y	Y
2 **Walden**	Y	Y	N	N	N	N
3 Blumenauer	Y	Y	Y	Y	Y	Y
4 DeFazio	Y	Y	Y	Y	Y	Y
5 Schrader	Y	Y	Y	Y	Y	Y
PENNSYLVANIA						
1 Brady	Y	Y	Y	Y	Y	Y
2 Fattah	Y	Y	Y	Y	Y	Y
3 Dahlkemper	Y	Y	Y	Y	Y	Y
4 Altmire	Y	Y	Y	Y	Y	Y
5 **Thompson**	Y	Y	N	N	N	N
6 **Gerlach**	Y	Y	N	N	N	N
7 Sestak	Y	Y	Y	Y	Y	Y
8 Murphy, P.	Y	Y	Y	Y	Y	Y
9 **Shuster**	Y	Y	N	N	N	N
10 Carney	Y	Y	Y	Y	Y	Y
11 Kanjorski	Y	Y	Y	Y	Y	Y
12 Murtha	Y	Y	Y	Y	Y	Y
13 Schwartz	Y	Y	Y	Y	Y	Y
14 Doyle	Y	Y	Y	Y	Y	Y
15 **Dent**	Y	Y	N	N	N	N
16 **Pitts**	Y	Y	N	N	N	N
17 Holden	Y	Y	Y	Y	Y	Y
18 **Murphy, T.**	Y	Y	N	N	N	N
19 **Platts**	Y	Y	N	N	N	N
RHODE ISLAND						
1 Kennedy	?	?	?	?	?	?
2 Langevin	Y	Y	Y	Y	Y	Y
SOUTH CAROLINA						
1 **Brown**	Y	Y	N	N	N	N
2 **Wilson**	Y	Y	N	N	N	N
3 **Barrett**	Y	Y	N	N	N	N
4 **Inglis**	Y	Y	N	N	N	N
5 Spratt	Y	Y	Y	Y	Y	Y
6 Clyburn	Y	Y	Y	Y	Y	Y
SOUTH DAKOTA						
AL Herseth Sandlin	Y	Y	Y	Y	Y	Y
TENNESSEE						
1 **Roe**	Y	Y	N	N	N	N
2 **Duncan**	Y	Y	N	N	N	N
3 **Wamp**	Y	Y	N	N	N	N
4 Davis	Y	Y	Y	Y	Y	Y
5 Cooper	Y	Y	Y	Y	Y	Y
6 Gordon	Y	Y	Y	Y	Y	Y
7 **Blackburn**	Y	Y	N	N	N	N
8 Tanner	Y	Y	Y	Y	Y	Y
9 Cohen	Y	Y	Y	Y	Y	Y
TEXAS						
1 **Gohmert**	Y	Y	N	N	N	N
2 **Poe**	Y	Y	N	N	N	N
3 **Johnson, S.**	Y	Y	N	N	N	N
4 **Hall**	Y	Y	?	N	N	N
5 **Hensarling**	Y	Y	N	N	N	N
6 **Barton**	?	Y	N	N	N	N
7 **Culberson**	Y	Y	N	N	N	N
8 **Brady**	Y	Y	N	N	N	N
9 Green, A.	Y	Y	Y	Y	Y	Y
10 **McCaul**	Y	Y	N	N	N	N
11 **Conaway**	Y	Y	N	N	N	N
12 **Granger**	Y	Y	N	N	N	N
13 **Thornberry**	Y	Y	N	N	N	N
14 **Paul**	Y	N	N	N	N	N
15 Hinojosa	Y	Y	Y	Y	Y	Y
16 Reyes	Y	Y	Y	?	Y	Y
17 Edwards	Y	Y	Y	Y	Y	Y
18 Jackson Lee	Y	Y	Y	Y	Y	Y
19 **Neugebauer**	Y	Y	N	N	N	N
20 Gonzalez	Y	Y	Y	Y	Y	Y
21 **Smith**	Y	Y	N	N	N	N
22 **Olson**	Y	Y	N	N	N	N
23 Rodriguez	Y	Y	Y	Y	Y	Y
24 **Marchant**	Y	Y	N	N	N	N
25 Doggett	Y	Y	Y	Y	Y	N
26 **Burgess**	Y	Y	N	N	N	N
27 Ortiz	Y	Y	Y	Y	Y	Y
28 Cuellar	Y	Y	Y	?	Y	Y
29 Green, G.	Y	+	Y	Y	+	Y
30 Johnson, E.	Y	Y	Y	Y	Y	Y
31 **Carter**	Y	Y	N	N	N	N
32 **Sessions**	Y	Y	N	N	N	N
UTAH						
1 **Bishop**	Y	Y	N	N	N	N
2 Matheson	Y	Y	Y	Y	Y	Y
3 **Chaffetz**	Y	Y	N	N	N	N
VERMONT						
AL Welch	Y	Y	Y	Y	Y	N
VIRGINIA						
1 **Wittman**	Y	Y	N	N	N	N
2 Nye	Y	Y	Y	Y	Y	Y
3 Scott	Y	Y	Y	Y	Y	Y
4 **Forbes**	Y	Y	N	N	N	N
5 Perriello	Y	Y	Y	Y	Y	Y
6 **Goodlatte**	Y	Y	N	N	N	N
7 **Cantor**	Y	Y	N	N	N	N
8 Moran	Y	Y	Y	Y	Y	Y
9 Boucher	Y	Y	Y	Y	Y	Y
10 **Wolf**	Y	Y	N	N	N	N
11 Connolly	?	?	Y	Y	Y	Y
WASHINGTON						
1 Inslee	Y	Y	Y	Y	Y	Y
2 Larsen	Y	Y	Y	Y	Y	Y
3 Baird	Y	Y	Y	Y	Y	Y
4 **Hastings**	Y	Y	N	N	N	N
5 **McMorris Rodgers**	Y	Y	N	N	N	N
6 Dicks	Y	Y	Y	Y	Y	Y
7 McDermott	Y	Y	?	Y	Y	Y
8 **Reichert**	Y	Y	N	N	N	N
9 Smith	Y	Y	Y	Y	Y	Y
WEST VIRGINIA						
1 Mollohan	Y	Y	Y	Y	Y	Y
2 **Capito**	Y	Y	N	N	N	N
3 Rahall	Y	Y	Y	Y	Y	Y
WISCONSIN						
1 **Ryan**	Y	Y	N	N	N	N
2 Baldwin	Y	Y	Y	Y	Y	N
3 Kind	Y	Y	Y	Y	Y	Y
4 Moore	Y	Y	Y	Y	Y	Y
5 **Sensenbrenner**	Y	Y	N	N	N	N
6 **Petri**	Y	Y	N	N	N	N
7 Obey	Y	Y	Y	Y	Y	Y
8 Kagen	Y	Y	Y	Y	Y	Y
WYOMING						
AL **Lummis**	Y	Y	N	N	N	N
DELEGATES						
Faleomavaega (A.S.)						
Norton (D.C.)						
Bordallo (Guam)						
Sablan (N. Marianas)						
Pierluisi (P.R.)						
Christensen (V.I.)						

IN THE HOUSE | By Vote Number

349. H Res 366. National Eye Institute Anniversary/Adoption.
Baldwin, D-Wis., motion to suspend the rules and adopt the resolution that would recognize the 40th anniversary of the National Eye Institute and urge federal support to prevent, treat and research vision impairment and eye disease. Motion agreed to 411-0: R 170-0; D 241-0. A two-thirds majority of those present and voting (274 in this case) is required for adoption under suspension of the rules. June 16, 2009.

350. HR 2847. Fiscal 2010 Commerce-Justice-Science Appropriations/Motion to Rise. Mollohan, D-W.Va., motion to rise from the Committee of the Whole. Motion agreed to 179-124: R 0-123; D 179-1. June 16, 2009.

351. HR 2847. Fiscal 2010 Commerce-Justice-Science Appropriations/Previous Question. Slaughter, D-N.Y., motion to order the previous question (thus ending debate and possibility of amendment) on adoption of the rule (H Res 552) to provide for further House floor consideration of the bill that would appropriate $64.4 billion in fiscal 2010 for the departments of Commerce and Justice and other federal agencies, including NASA and the National Science Foundation. Motion agreed to 238-180: R 0-171; D 238-9. June 17, 2009.

352. HR 2847. Fiscal 2010 Commerce-Justice-Science Appropriations/Rule. Adoption of the rule (H Res 552) that would provide for further House floor consideration of the bill that would appropriate $64.4 billion in fiscal 2010 for the departments of Commerce and Justice and other federal agencies, including NASA and the National Science Foundation. Adopted 221-201: R 0-174; D 221-27. June 17, 2009.

353. HR 2847. Fiscal 2010 Commerce-Justice-Science Appropriations/National Oceanic and Atmospheric Administration.
Bordallo, D-Guam, amendment that would increase the amount provided for the National Oceanic and Atmospheric Administration operations, research and facilities account by $500,000, offset by a reduction of the same amount for the Commerce Department's management salaries and expenses account. Adopted in Committee of the Whole 411-14: R 173-2; D 238-12. June 17, 2009.

354. HR 2847. Fiscal 2010 Commerce-Justice-Science Appropriations/Office on Violence Against Women. Moore, D-Wis., amendment that would increase the amount provided for the Office on Violence Against Women for legal assistance to domestic violence victims by $4 million, offset by a reduction of the same amount for the Commerce Department's management salaries and expenses account. Adopted in Committee of the Whole 425-4: R 172-3; D 253-1. June 17, 2009.

355. HR 2847. Fiscal 2010 Commerce-Justice-Science Appropriations/National Criminal History Improvement Program.
Boswell, D-Iowa, amendment that would increase funding for the National Criminal History Improvement Program, which funds infrastructure development for a national criminal records database, by $2.5 million, offset by a reduction of the same amount for the Justice Department's general administration salaries and expenses account. Adopted in Committee of the Whole 422-2: R 169-2; D 253-0. June 17, 2009.

	349	350	351	352	353	354	355
ALABAMA							
1 Bonner	Y	?	N	N	Y	Y	Y
2 Bright	Y	Y	?	N	Y	Y	Y
3 Rogers	Y	N	N	N	Y	Y	Y
4 Aderholt	Y	?	N	N	Y	Y	Y
5 Griffith	Y	Y	Y	Y	Y	Y	Y
6 Bachus	Y	N	N	N	Y	Y	Y
7 Davis	Y	Y	Y	?	Y	Y	Y
ALASKA							
AL Young	Y	?	N	N	Y	Y	?
ARIZONA							
1 Kirkpatrick	Y	Y	Y	Y	Y	Y	Y
2 Franks	Y	N	N	N	Y	Y	Y
3 Shadegg	Y	?	N	N	Y	Y	Y
4 Pastor	Y	Y	Y	Y	Y	Y	Y
5 Mitchell	Y	Y	N	N	Y	Y	Y
6 Flake	Y	N	N	N	Y	Y	Y
7 Grijalva	?	?	Y	Y	Y	Y	Y
8 Giffords	Y	Y	Y	Y	?	Y	Y
ARKANSAS							
1 Berry	Y	Y	Y	Y	Y	Y	Y
2 Snyder	Y	Y	Y	Y	Y	Y	Y
3 Boozman	Y	N	N	N	Y	Y	Y
4 Ross	Y	Y	Y	Y	Y	Y	Y
CALIFORNIA							
1 Thompson	Y	Y	Y	N	Y	Y	Y
2 Herger	Y	N	+	N	Y	Y	Y
3 Lungren	Y	?	N	N	Y	Y	Y
4 McClintock	Y	?	N	N	Y	Y	Y
5 Matsui	Y	?	Y	N	Y	Y	Y
6 Woolsey	Y	+	Y	N	Y	Y	Y
7 Miller, George	Y	?	Y	N	Y	Y	Y
8 Pelosi							
9 Lee	Y	Y	Y	Y	Y	Y	Y
10 Tauscher	Y	Y	Y	Y	Y	Y	Y
11 McNerney	Y	Y	Y	Y	Y	Y	Y
12 Speier	Y	?	Y	N	Y	Y	Y
13 Stark	?	?	Y	N	Y	Y	Y
14 Eshoo	Y	?	Y	N	Y	Y	Y
15 Honda	?	?	Y	N	Y	?	Y
16 Lofgren	Y	Y	Y	N	Y	Y	Y
17 Farr	Y	Y	Y	N	Y	Y	Y
18 Cardoza	Y	Y	Y	Y	Y	Y	Y
19 Radanovich	Y	?	N	N	Y	Y	Y
20 Costa	Y	Y	Y	Y	Y	Y	Y
21 Nunes	Y	N	N	N	Y	Y	Y
22 McCarthy	Y	N	N	N	Y	Y	Y
23 Capps	Y	Y	Y	Y	Y	Y	Y
24 Gallegly	Y	?	N	N	Y	Y	Y
25 McKeon	Y	N	N	N	Y	Y	Y
26 Dreier	Y	N	N	N	Y	Y	Y
27 Sherman	Y	?	Y	Y	Y	Y	Y
28 Berman	?	?	Y	Y	Y	Y	Y
29 Schiff	Y	?	Y	Y	Y	Y	Y
30 Waxman	Y	?	Y	Y	Y	Y	Y
31 Becerra	Y	+	Y	Y	Y	Y	Y
32 Vacant							
33 Watson	Y	Y	Y	Y	Y	Y	Y
34 Roybal-Allard	Y	Y	Y	Y	Y	Y	Y
35 Waters	Y	Y	Y	N	Y	Y	Y
36 Harman	?	?	?	?	?	?	?
37 Richardson	Y	Y	Y	Y	Y	Y	Y
38 Napolitano	Y	+	Y	Y	Y	Y	Y
39 Sánchez, Linda	Y	?	Y	Y	?	?	Y
40 Royce	Y	?	N	N	Y	Y	Y
41 Lewis	Y	N	N	N	Y	Y	Y
42 Miller, Gary	Y	?	N	N	Y	Y	Y
43 Baca	Y	Y	Y	Y	Y	Y	Y
44 Calvert	Y	N	N	N	Y	Y	Y
45 Bono Mack	Y	?	N	N	Y	Y	Y
46 Rohrabacher	Y	?	N	N	Y	Y	Y
47 Sanchez, Loretta	Y	Y	Y	Y	Y	Y	Y
48 Campbell	Y	N	N	N	Y	Y	Y
49 Issa	Y	N	N	N	Y	Y	Y
50 Bilbray	Y	N	N	N	Y	Y	Y
51 Filner	Y	Y	Y	Y	Y	Y	Y
52 Hunter	Y	N	N	N	Y	Y	Y
53 Davis	Y	Y	Y	Y	Y	Y	Y

	349	350	351	352	353	354	355
COLORADO							
1 DeGette	Y	?	Y	Y	Y	Y	Y
2 Polis	Y	Y	Y	Y	Y	Y	Y
3 Salazar	Y	Y	Y	Y	Y	Y	Y
4 Markey	Y	Y	Y	Y	N	Y	Y
5 Lamborn	Y	N	N	N	Y	Y	Y
6 Coffman	Y	N	N	N	Y	Y	Y
7 Perlmutter	Y	Y	Y	Y	N	Y	Y
CONNECTICUT							
1 Larson	+	+	+	+	+	+	+
2 Courtney	Y	Y	Y	Y	Y	Y	Y
3 DeLauro	Y	Y	Y	Y	Y	Y	Y
4 Himes	Y	Y	Y	Y	Y	Y	Y
5 Murphy	Y	Y	Y	Y	Y	Y	?
DELAWARE							
AL Castle	Y	N	N	N	Y	Y	Y
FLORIDA							
1 Miller	Y	N	N	N	Y	Y	Y
2 Boyd	Y	?	Y	Y	Y	Y	Y
3 Brown	Y	Y	Y	Y	Y	Y	Y
4 Crenshaw	Y	?	N	N	Y	Y	Y
5 Brown-Waite	Y	N	N	N	Y	Y	Y
6 Stearns	Y	N	N	N	Y	Y	Y
7 Mica	Y	N	N	N	Y	Y	Y
8 Grayson	Y	Y	Y	Y	Y	Y	Y
9 Bilirakis	Y	?	N	N	Y	Y	Y
10 Young	?	?	?	?	Y	Y	Y
11 Castor	Y	Y	Y	Y	Y	Y	Y
12 Putnam	Y	N	N	N	Y	Y	Y
13 Buchanan	Y	N	N	N	Y	Y	Y
14 Mack	Y	?	N	N	Y	Y	Y
15 Posey	Y	N	N	N	Y	Y	Y
16 Rooney	Y	N	N	N	Y	Y	Y
17 Meek	Y	Y	Y	N	Y	Y	Y
18 Ros-Lehtinen	Y	N	N	N	Y	Y	Y
19 Wexler	Y	?	Y	Y	Y	Y	Y
20 Wasserman Schultz	Y	Y	Y	Y	Y	Y	Y
21 Diaz-Balart, L.	Y	?	N	N	Y	Y	Y
22 Klein	Y	Y	Y	N	Y	Y	Y
23 Hastings	Y	Y	Y	N	Y	Y	Y
24 Kosmas	Y	Y	N	Y	Y	Y	Y
25 Diaz-Balart, M.	Y	N	N	N	Y	Y	Y
GEORGIA							
1 Kingston	Y	?	N	N	Y	Y	Y
2 Bishop	Y	Y	Y	Y	Y	Y	Y
3 Westmoreland	Y	?	N	N	Y	Y	Y
4 Johnson	Y	Y	Y	Y	Y	Y	Y
5 Lewis	?	?	?	?	?	?	?
6 Price	Y	N	N	N	N	Y	Y
7 Linder	Y	?	N	N	Y	Y	Y
8 Marshall	Y	Y	Y	Y	Y	Y	Y
9 Deal	Y	N	N	N	Y	Y	Y
10 Broun	Y	N	N	N	Y	Y	Y
11 Gingrey	Y	N	N	N	Y	Y	Y
12 Barrow	Y	Y	Y	Y	Y	Y	Y
13 Scott	Y	Y	Y	Y	Y	Y	Y
HAWAII							
1 Abercrombie	Y	Y	Y	Y	Y	Y	Y
2 Hirono	Y	Y	Y	Y	Y	Y	Y
IDAHO							
1 Minnick	Y	Y	N	N	Y	Y	Y
2 Simpson	Y	?	N	N	Y	Y	Y
ILLINOIS							
1 Rush	Y	Y	Y	Y	Y	Y	Y
2 Jackson	Y	Y	Y	Y	Y	Y	Y
3 Lipinski	Y	Y	Y	Y	Y	Y	Y
4 Gutierrez	Y	Y	Y	Y	Y	Y	Y
5 Quigley	Y	Y	Y	Y	Y	Y	Y
6 Roskam	Y	?	N	N	Y	Y	Y
7 Davis	Y	?	Y	Y	Y	Y	Y
8 Bean	Y	?	Y	Y	N	Y	Y
9 Schakowsky	Y	Y	Y	Y	Y	Y	Y
10 Kirk	Y	N	N	N	Y	Y	Y
11 Halvorson	Y	Y	Y	Y	Y	Y	Y
12 Costello	Y	?	Y	Y	Y	Y	Y
13 Biggert	Y	N	N	N	Y	Y	Y
14 Foster	Y	Y	Y	N	Y	Y	Y
15 Johnson	Y	N	N	N	Y	Y	Y

KEY   **Republicans**   Democrats

Y Voted for (yea)	X Paired against	C Voted "present" to avoid possible conflict of interest
# Paired for	– Announced against	
+ Announced for	P Voted "present"	? Did not vote or otherwise make a position known
N Voted against (nay)		

	349	350	351	352	353	354	355
16 **Manzullo**	Y	?	N	N	Y	Y	Y
17 Hare	Y	?	Y	Y	Y	Y	Y
18 **Schock**	Y	N	N	N	Y	Y	Y
19 **Shimkus**	Y	N	N	N	Y	Y	Y
INDIANA							
1 Visclosky	Y	Y	Y	Y	Y	Y	Y
2 Donnelly	Y	Y	Y	N	Y	Y	Y
3 **Souder**	Y	?	N	N	Y	Y	Y
4 **Buyer**	Y	N	N	N	Y	Y	Y
5 **Burton**	Y	N	N	N	Y	Y	Y
6 **Pence**	Y	N	N	N	Y	Y	Y
7 Carson	Y	Y	Y	Y	Y	Y	Y
8 Ellsworth	Y	Y	Y	Y	Y	Y	Y
9 Hill	Y	?	N	N	Y	Y	Y
IOWA							
1 Braley	Y	?	Y	Y	Y	Y	Y
2 Loebsack	Y	Y	Y	Y	Y	Y	Y
3 Boswell	Y	Y	Y	Y	Y	Y	Y
4 **Latham**	Y	N	N	N	Y	Y	Y
5 **King**	Y	N	N	N	Y	N	Y
KANSAS							
1 **Moran**	Y	?	N	N	Y	Y	Y
2 **Jenkins**	Y	N	N	N	N	Y	N
3 Moore	Y	Y	Y	Y	Y	Y	Y
4 **Tiahrt**	Y	N	N	N	Y	Y	Y
KENTUCKY							
1 **Whitfield**	Y	?	N	N	Y	Y	Y
2 **Guthrie**	Y	N	N	N	Y	Y	Y
3 Yarmuth	Y	Y	Y	Y	Y	Y	Y
4 **Davis**	Y	N	N	N	Y	Y	Y
5 **Rogers**	Y	?	N	N	Y	Y	Y
6 Chandler	Y	Y	Y	Y	Y	Y	Y
LOUISIANA							
1 **Scalise**	Y	N	N	N	Y	Y	Y
2 **Cao**	Y	?	N	N	Y	Y	Y
3 Melancon	Y	Y	Y	Y	Y	Y	Y
4 **Fleming**	Y	N	N	N	Y	Y	Y
5 **Alexander**	?	?	?	?	?	?	?
6 **Cassidy**	Y	N	N	N	Y	Y	Y
7 **Boustany**	Y	N	N	N	Y	Y	Y
MAINE							
1 Pingree	Y	Y	Y	Y	Y	Y	Y
2 Michaud	Y	Y	Y	Y	Y	Y	Y
MARYLAND							
1 Kratovil	Y	Y	N	N	Y	Y	Y
2 Ruppersberger	Y	?	Y	Y	Y	Y	Y
3 Sarbanes	Y	?	Y	Y	Y	Y	Y
4 Edwards	Y	?	Y	Y	Y	Y	Y
5 Hoyer	Y	Y	Y	Y	Y	Y	Y
6 **Bartlett**	Y	N	N	N	Y	Y	Y
7 Cummings	Y	?	Y	Y	?	Y	Y
8 Van Hollen	Y	Y	Y	Y	Y	Y	Y
MASSACHUSETTS							
1 Olver	Y	?	Y	Y	Y	Y	Y
2 Neal	?	?	Y	Y	Y	Y	Y
3 McGovern	Y	Y	Y	Y	Y	Y	Y
4 Frank	?	Y	Y	Y	N	Y	Y
5 Tsongas	Y	Y	Y	Y	Y	Y	Y
6 Tierney	Y	?	Y	Y	Y	Y	Y
7 Markey	Y	?	Y	Y	Y	Y	Y
8 Capuano	Y	Y	Y	Y	?	Y	Y
9 Lynch	Y	Y	Y	Y	Y	Y	Y
10 Delahunt	Y	Y	Y	Y	Y	Y	Y
MICHIGAN							
1 Stupak	Y	?	Y	Y	Y	Y	Y
2 **Hoekstra**	Y	N	N	N	Y	Y	Y
3 **Ehlers**	Y	N	N	N	Y	Y	Y
4 **Camp**	Y	N	N	N	Y	Y	Y
5 Kildee	Y	Y	Y	Y	Y	Y	Y
6 **Upton**	Y	N	N	N	Y	Y	Y
7 Schauer	Y	Y	Y	Y	N	Y	Y
8 **Rogers**	Y	N	N	N	Y	Y	Y
9 Peters	Y	Y	Y	Y	Y	Y	Y
10 **Miller**	Y	N	N	N	Y	Y	Y
11 **McCotter**	Y	N	N	N	Y	Y	Y
12 Levin	Y	Y	Y	Y	Y	Y	Y
13 Kilpatrick	Y	?	Y	Y	Y	Y	Y
14 Conyers	Y	?	Y	N	Y	Y	Y
15 Dingell	Y	?	Y	Y	Y	Y	Y
MINNESOTA							
1 Walz	Y	Y	Y	Y	N	Y	Y
2 **Kline**	Y	N	N	N	Y	Y	Y
3 **Paulsen**	Y	N	N	N	Y	Y	Y
4 McCollum	Y	?	Y	Y	Y	Y	Y

	349	350	351	352	353	354	355
5 Ellison	Y	Y	Y	Y	Y	Y	Y
6 **Bachmann**	Y	N	?	?	?	?	?
7 Peterson	Y	?	Y	?	Y	Y	Y
8 Oberstar	Y	?	Y	Y	Y	Y	Y
MISSISSIPPI							
1 Childers	Y	Y	N	Y	Y	Y	Y
2 Thompson	Y	Y	Y	Y	Y	Y	Y
3 **Harper**	Y	N	N	N	Y	Y	Y
4 Taylor	Y	Y	Y	Y	Y	Y	Y
MISSOURI							
1 Clay	Y	?	Y	Y	Y	Y	Y
2 **Akin**	Y	N	N	N	Y	Y	Y
3 Carnahan	Y	Y	Y	Y	Y	Y	Y
4 Skelton	Y	Y	Y	Y	Y	Y	Y
5 Cleaver	Y	Y	Y	Y	Y	Y	Y
6 **Graves**	Y	N	N	N	Y	Y	Y
7 **Blunt**	Y	?	N	N	Y	Y	Y
8 **Emerson**	Y	?	N	N	Y	Y	Y
9 **Luetkemeyer**	Y	?	N	N	Y	Y	Y
MONTANA							
AL **Rehberg**	Y	N	N	N	Y	Y	Y
NEBRASKA							
1 **Fortenberry**	Y	N	N	N	Y	Y	Y
2 **Terry**	Y	N	N	N	Y	Y	Y
3 **Smith**	Y	N	N	N	Y	Y	Y
NEVADA							
1 Berkley	+	+	Y	Y	Y	Y	Y
2 **Heller**	Y	N	N	N	Y	Y	Y
3 Titus	Y	Y	Y	Y	Y	Y	Y
NEW HAMPSHIRE							
1 Shea-Porter	Y	Y	Y	Y	Y	Y	Y
2 Hodes	Y	Y	Y	Y	N	Y	Y
NEW JERSEY							
1 Andrews	Y	Y	Y	Y	Y	Y	Y
2 **LoBiondo**	Y	N	N	N	Y	Y	Y
3 Adler	Y	Y	?	?	?	?	?
4 **Smith**	Y	?	N	N	Y	Y	Y
5 **Garrett**	Y	N	N	N	Y	Y	Y
6 Pallone	Y	?	Y	Y	Y	Y	Y
7 **Lance**	Y	N	N	N	Y	Y	Y
8 Pascrell	Y	Y	Y	Y	Y	Y	Y
9 Rothman	Y	?	Y	Y	Y	Y	Y
10 Payne	Y	Y	Y	Y	Y	Y	Y
11 **Frelinghuysen**	Y	?	N	N	Y	Y	Y
12 Holt	Y	Y	Y	Y	Y	Y	Y
13 Sires	Y	?	Y	Y	Y	Y	Y
NEW MEXICO							
1 Heinrich	Y	Y	Y	Y	Y	Y	Y
2 Teague	Y	Y	Y	Y	Y	Y	Y
3 Lujan	Y	Y	Y	Y	Y	Y	Y
NEW YORK							
1 Bishop	Y	Y	Y	Y	N	Y	Y
2 Israel	Y	Y	Y	Y	Y	Y	Y
3 **King**	Y	?	N	N	Y	Y	Y
4 McCarthy	Y	Y	Y	Y	Y	Y	Y
5 Ackerman	Y	Y	Y	Y	Y	Y	Y
6 Meeks	Y	?	Y	Y	Y	Y	Y
7 Crowley	Y	?	Y	Y	Y	Y	Y
8 Nadler	Y	?	Y	Y	Y	Y	Y
9 Weiner	Y	?	Y	Y	Y	Y	Y
10 Towns	Y	Y	Y	Y	Y	Y	Y
11 Clarke	Y	Y	Y	Y	Y	Y	Y
12 Velázquez	Y	?	Y	Y	Y	Y	Y
13 McMahon	Y	Y	Y	Y	Y	Y	Y
14 Maloney	?	Y	Y	Y	Y	Y	Y
15 Rangel	Y	?	Y	Y	Y	Y	Y
16 Serrano	Y	?	Y	Y	Y	Y	Y
17 Engel	Y	Y	Y	Y	Y	Y	Y
18 Lowey	Y	Y	Y	Y	Y	Y	Y
19 Hall	Y	Y	Y	Y	Y	Y	Y
20 Murphy	Y	Y	Y	N	Y	Y	Y
21 Tonko	Y	Y	Y	Y	Y	Y	Y
22 Hinchey	Y	Y	Y	Y	Y	Y	Y
23 **McHugh**	Y	?	N	N	Y	Y	Y
24 Arcuri	Y	Y	N	N	N	Y	Y
25 Maffei	Y	?	Y	Y	Y	Y	Y
26 **Lee**	Y	N	N	N	Y	Y	Y
27 Higgins	Y	?	Y	Y	Y	Y	Y
28 Slaughter	Y	Y	Y	Y	Y	Y	Y
29 Massa	Y	Y	Y	Y	Y	Y	Y
NORTH CAROLINA							
1 Butterfield	Y	Y	Y	Y	Y	Y	Y
2 Etheridge	Y	Y	Y	Y	Y	Y	Y
3 **Jones**	Y	N	N	N	Y	Y	Y
4 Price	Y	Y	Y	Y	Y	Y	Y

	349	350	351	352	353	354	355
5 **Foxx**	Y	N	N	N	Y	Y	Y
6 **Coble**	Y	N	N	N	Y	Y	Y
7 McIntyre	Y	Y	Y	Y	Y	Y	Y
8 Kissell	Y	Y	Y	Y	Y	Y	Y
9 **Myrick**	Y	?	N	N	Y	Y	Y
10 **McHenry**	?	N	N	N	Y	Y	Y
11 Shuler	Y	Y	N	N	Y	Y	Y
12 Watt	Y	Y	Y	Y	Y	Y	Y
13 Miller	Y	Y	Y	Y	Y	Y	Y
NORTH DAKOTA							
AL Pomeroy	Y	Y	Y	Y	Y	Y	Y
OHIO							
1 Driehaus	Y	Y	Y	Y	Y	Y	Y
2 **Schmidt**	Y	N	N	N	Y	Y	Y
3 **Turner**	Y	N	N	N	Y	Y	Y
4 **Jordan**	Y	N	N	N	Y	Y	Y
5 **Latta**	Y	N	N	N	Y	Y	Y
6 Wilson	Y	Y	Y	Y	Y	Y	Y
7 **Austria**	Y	N	N	N	Y	Y	Y
8 **Boehner**	Y	N	N	N	Y	Y	Y
9 Kaptur	Y	?	Y	Y	Y	Y	Y
10 Kucinich	Y	Y	Y	Y	Y	Y	Y
11 Fudge	Y	Y	Y	Y	Y	Y	Y
12 **Tiberi**	Y	N	N	N	Y	Y	Y
13 Sutton	Y	?	Y	Y	Y	Y	Y
14 **LaTourette**	Y	?	N	N	Y	Y	Y
15 Kilroy	Y	Y	Y	Y	Y	Y	Y
16 Boccieri	Y	Y	Y	Y	Y	Y	Y
17 Ryan	Y	Y	Y	Y	Y	Y	Y
18 Space	Y	?	Y	Y	Y	Y	Y
OKLAHOMA							
1 **Sullivan**	?	?	?	?	?	?	?
2 Boren	Y	Y	Y	Y	Y	Y	Y
3 **Lucas**	Y	?	N	N	Y	Y	Y
4 **Cole**	Y	N	N	N	Y	N	Y
5 **Fallin**	Y	N	N	N	Y	Y	Y
OREGON							
1 Wu	Y	N	Y	N	Y	Y	Y
2 **Walden**	Y	N	N	N	Y	Y	Y
3 Blumenauer	Y	Y	Y	N	Y	Y	Y
4 DeFazio	Y	Y	Y	N	Y	Y	Y
5 Schrader	Y	?	Y	Y	Y	Y	?
PENNSYLVANIA							
1 Brady	Y	Y	Y	Y	Y	Y	Y
2 Fattah	Y	Y	Y	Y	Y	Y	Y
3 Dahlkemper	Y	Y	Y	Y	Y	Y	Y
4 Altmire	Y	Y	Y	Y	Y	Y	Y
5 **Thompson**	Y	N	N	N	Y	Y	Y
6 **Gerlach**	Y	N	N	N	Y	Y	Y
7 Sestak	Y	Y	Y	Y	Y	Y	Y
8 Murphy, P.	Y	Y	Y	Y	Y	Y	Y
9 **Shuster**	Y	N	N	N	Y	Y	?
10 Carney	Y	?	Y	N	N	Y	Y
11 Kanjorski	Y	Y	Y	Y	Y	Y	Y
12 Murtha	Y	?	Y	Y	Y	Y	Y
13 Schwartz	Y	Y	Y	Y	Y	Y	Y
14 Doyle	Y	?	Y	Y	Y	Y	Y
15 **Dent**	Y	N	N	N	Y	Y	Y
16 **Pitts**	Y	?	N	N	Y	Y	Y
17 Holden	Y	?	Y	Y	Y	Y	Y
18 **Murphy, T.**	Y	N	N	N	Y	Y	Y
19 **Platts**	Y	N	N	N	Y	Y	Y
RHODE ISLAND							
1 Kennedy	?	?	?	?	?	?	?
2 Langevin	Y	Y	+	Y	Y	Y	Y
SOUTH CAROLINA							
1 **Brown**	Y	N	N	N	Y	Y	Y
2 **Wilson**	Y	N	N	N	Y	Y	Y
3 **Barrett**	Y	N	N	N	Y	Y	Y
4 **Inglis**	Y	N	N	N	Y	Y	Y
5 Spratt	Y	Y	Y	Y	Y	Y	Y
6 Clyburn	Y	Y	Y	Y	Y	Y	Y
SOUTH DAKOTA							
AL Herseth Sandlin	Y	Y	Y	Y	Y	Y	Y
TENNESSEE							
1 **Roe**	Y	N	N	N	Y	Y	Y
2 **Duncan**	Y	?	N	N	Y	Y	Y
3 **Wamp**	Y	?	N	N	Y	Y	Y
4 Davis	Y	Y	Y	Y	?	Y	Y
5 Cooper	Y	Y	Y	Y	Y	Y	Y
6 Gordon	Y	?	Y	Y	Y	Y	Y
7 **Blackburn**	Y	N	N	N	Y	Y	Y
8 Tanner	Y	?	Y	Y	Y	Y	Y
9 Cohen	Y	Y	Y	Y	Y	Y	Y

	349	350	351	352	353	354	355
TEXAS							
1 **Gohmert**	Y	N	N	N	Y	Y	Y
2 **Poe**	+	–	N	N	Y	Y	Y
3 **Johnson, S.**	Y	?	N	N	Y	Y	Y
4 **Hall**	Y	N	N	N	Y	Y	Y
5 **Hensarling**	Y	?	N	N	Y	Y	Y
6 **Barton**	?	N	N	N	Y	N	N
7 **Culberson**	Y	?	N	N	Y	Y	Y
8 **Brady**	Y	?	N	N	Y	Y	Y
9 Green, A.	Y	Y	Y	Y	Y	Y	Y
10 **McCaul**	Y	?	N	N	Y	Y	Y
11 **Conaway**	Y	N	N	N	Y	Y	Y
12 **Granger**	Y	?	N	N	Y	Y	Y
13 **Thornberry**	Y	N	N	N	Y	Y	Y
14 **Paul**	Y	?	N	N	Y	Y	?
15 Hinojosa	Y	?	Y	Y	Y	Y	Y
16 Reyes	Y	Y	Y	Y	Y	Y	Y
17 Edwards	?	?	Y	Y	?	Y	Y
18 Jackson Lee	Y	Y	Y	Y	Y	Y	Y
19 **Neugebauer**	Y	N	N	N	Y	Y	?
20 Gonzalez	Y	Y	Y	Y	Y	Y	Y
21 **Smith**	?	N	N	N	Y	Y	Y
22 **Olson**	Y	?	N	N	Y	Y	Y
23 Rodriguez	Y	Y	Y	Y	Y	Y	Y
24 **Marchant**	Y	?	N	N	Y	Y	Y
25 Doggett	Y	Y	Y	Y	Y	Y	Y
26 **Burgess**	Y	N	N	N	Y	Y	Y
27 Ortiz	Y	Y	Y	Y	Y	Y	Y
28 Cuellar	Y	Y	Y	Y	Y	Y	Y
29 Green, G.	Y	?	Y	Y	Y	Y	Y
30 Johnson, E.	Y	?	Y	Y	Y	Y	Y
31 **Carter**	?	N	N	N	Y	Y	Y
32 **Sessions**	Y	N	N	N	Y	Y	Y
UTAH							
1 **Bishop**	Y	N	?	N	Y	Y	Y
2 Matheson	Y	?	?	Y	Y	Y	Y
3 **Chaffetz**	Y	N	N	N	Y	Y	Y
VERMONT							
AL Welch	Y	Y	Y	Y	Y	Y	Y
VIRGINIA							
1 **Wittman**	Y	N	N	N	Y	Y	Y
2 Nye	Y	Y	Y	Y	Y	Y	Y
3 Scott	Y	?	Y	Y	Y	Y	Y
4 **Forbes**	Y	N	N	N	Y	Y	Y
5 Perriello	Y	Y	N	N	Y	Y	Y
6 **Goodlatte**	Y	N	N	N	Y	Y	Y
7 **Cantor**	Y	N	?	N	Y	Y	Y
8 Moran	Y	?	Y	Y	Y	Y	Y
9 Boucher	Y	?	Y	Y	Y	Y	Y
10 **Wolf**	Y	N	N	N	Y	Y	Y
11 Connolly	Y	Y	Y	Y	N	Y	Y
WASHINGTON							
1 Inslee	Y	Y	Y	Y	Y	Y	Y
2 Larsen	Y	Y	Y	Y	Y	Y	Y
3 Baird	Y	?	Y	Y	Y	N	Y
4 **Hastings**	Y	N	N	N	Y	Y	Y
5 **McMorris Rodgers**	Y	N	N	N	Y	Y	Y
6 Dicks	Y	?	Y	Y	Y	Y	Y
7 McDermott	Y	?	Y	Y	Y	Y	Y
8 **Reichert**	Y	?	N	N	Y	Y	Y
9 Smith	Y	Y	Y	Y	Y	Y	Y
WEST VIRGINIA							
1 Mollohan	Y	Y	Y	Y	Y	Y	Y
2 **Capito**	Y	N	N	N	Y	Y	Y
3 Rahall	Y	Y	Y	Y	Y	Y	Y
WISCONSIN							
1 **Ryan**	Y	N	N	N	Y	Y	Y
2 Baldwin	Y	Y	Y	Y	Y	Y	Y
3 Kind	Y	?	Y	Y	Y	Y	Y
4 Moore	Y	Y	Y	Y	Y	Y	Y
5 **Sensenbrenner**	Y	N	N	N	Y	Y	Y
6 **Petri**	Y	?	N	N	Y	Y	Y
7 Obey	Y	Y	Y	Y	Y	Y	Y
8 Kagen	?	Y	Y	Y	Y	Y	Y
WYOMING							
AL **Lummis**	Y	N	N	N	Y	Y	Y
DELEGATES							
Faleomavaega (A.S.)		Y			Y	Y	Y
Norton (D.C.)		?			Y	Y	Y
Bordallo (Guam)		Y			Y	Y	Y
Sablan (N. Marianas)		Y			Y	Y	Y
Pierluisi (P.R.)		?			Y	Y	Y
Christensen (V.I.)		?			Y	Y	Y

IN THE HOUSE | By Vote Number

356. HR 2847. Fiscal 2010 Commerce-Justice-Science Appropriations/Federal Prison System. Roe, R-Tenn., amendment that would reduce funding by $97.4 million for the federal prison system's salaries and expenses account. Rejected in Committee of the Whole 140-283: R 125-49; D 15-234. June 18, 2009.

357. HR 2847. Fiscal 2010 Commerce-Justice-Science Appropriations/DNA Collection and Analysis Systems. Nadler, D-N.Y., amendment that would increase the amount provided for grants to state and local government DNA collection and analysis systems by $5 million, offset by a reduction of the same amount to Office of Justice programs. Adopted in Committee of the Whole 418-3: R 169-3; D 249-0. June 18, 2009.

358. HR 2847. Fiscal 2010 Commerce-Justice-Science Appropriations/Historically Black Colleges and Universities. Johnson, D-Texas, amendment that would require at least $32 million of the $863 million provided for National Science Foundation math and science education programs to be available for historically black colleges' and universities' undergraduate programs. Adopted in Committee of the Whole 389-35: R 138-35; D 251-0. June 18, 2009.

359. HR 2847. Fiscal 2010 Commerce-Justice-Science Appropriations/Legal Services Corporation. Hensarling, R-Texas, amendment that would strike language from the bill providing for $440 million for the Legal Services Corporation, which provides legal assistance to low-income people. Rejected in Committee of the Whole 105-323: R 104-71; D 1-252. A "nay" was a vote in support of the president's position. June 18, 2009.

360. HR 2847. Fiscal 2010 Commerce-Justice-Science Appropriations/Closure of Guantánamo Bay Prison. Lewis, R-Calif., amendment that would bar the use of funds in the bill to close the detention facility at Guantánamo Bay, Cuba. Rejected in Committee of the Whole 212-216: R 172-3; D 40-213. June 18, 2009.

361. HR 2847. Fiscal 2010 Commerce-Justice-Science Appropriations/Revote on Closure of Guantánamo Bay Prison. Revote on the Lewis, R-Calif., amendment. Under House rules, an automatic revote in the full House is required on any vote in the Committee of the Whole in which the delegates' votes provide the winning margin. Previously, the Lewis amendment was rejected in the Committee of the Whole, 212-216, triggering the separate vote in the full House. Delegates may not vote in the full House. Rejected 212-213: R 173-2; D 39-211. A "nay" was a vote in support of the president's position. June 18, 2009.

362. HR 2847. Fiscal 2010 Commerce-Justice-Science Appropriations/Economic Development and Technology Programs. Tiahrt, R-Kan., amendment that would bar the use of funds in the bill for the Economic Development Administration's economic development assistance programs, the National Telecommunications and Information Administration's digital-to-analog converter box program, and the National Institute of Standards and Technology's research facilities construction account. Rejected in Committee of the Whole 161-270: R 156-19; D 5-251. June 18, 2009.

	356	357	358	359	360	361	362
ALABAMA							
1 **Bonner**	N	Y	Y	N	Y	Y	Y
2 Bright	Y	Y	Y	N	Y	Y	N
3 **Rogers**	N	Y	Y	N	Y	Y	N
4 **Aderholt**	N	Y	Y	N	Y	Y	Y
5 Griffith	N	Y	Y	N	Y	Y	N
6 **Bachus**	Y	Y	Y	N	Y	Y	Y
7 Davis	N	Y	Y	N	Y	N	N
ALASKA							
AL **Young**	N	N	?	Y	Y	Y	Y
ARIZONA							
1 Kirkpatrick	N	Y	Y	N	Y	Y	N
2 **Franks**	N	Y	N	Y	Y	Y	Y
3 **Shadegg**	Y	Y	Y	Y	Y	Y	Y
4 Pastor	N	Y	Y	N	N	N	N
5 Mitchell	Y	Y	Y	N	Y	Y	N
6 **Flake**	Y	Y	N	Y	Y	Y	Y
7 Grijalva	N	Y	Y	N	N	N	N
8 Giffords	N	Y	Y	N	N	N	N
ARKANSAS							
1 Berry	N	Y	Y	N	N	N	N
2 Snyder	N	Y	Y	N	N	N	N
3 **Boozman**	Y	Y	Y	N	Y	Y	Y
4 Ross	N	Y	Y	N	Y	Y	N
CALIFORNIA							
1 Thompson	N	Y	Y	N	N	N	N
2 **Herger**	Y	Y	N	Y	Y	Y	N
3 **Lungren**	Y	Y	Y	Y	Y	Y	Y
4 **McClintock**	Y	Y	N	Y	Y	Y	Y
5 Matsui	N	Y	Y	N	N	N	N
6 Woolsey	N	Y	Y	N	N	N	N
7 Miller, George	N	Y	Y	N	N	N	N
8 Pelosi					N		
9 Lee	N	Y	Y	N	N	N	N
10 Tauscher	?	?	?	?	?	?	?
11 McNerney	N	Y	Y	N	N	N	N
12 Speier	N	Y	Y	N	N	N	N
13 Stark	N	Y	Y	N	N	N	N
14 Eshoo	N	Y	Y	N	N	N	N
15 Honda	N	Y	Y	N	N	N	N
16 Lofgren	N	Y	Y	N	N	N	N
17 Farr	N	Y	Y	N	N	N	N
18 Cardoza	N	Y	Y	N	N	N	N
19 **Radanovich**	Y	Y	Y	Y	Y	Y	Y
20 Costa	Y	Y	?	N	N	N	N
21 **Nunes**	Y	Y	Y	Y	Y	Y	Y
22 **McCarthy**	Y	Y	Y	Y	Y	Y	Y
23 Capps	N	Y	Y	N	N	N	N
24 **Gallegly**	Y	Y	Y	N	Y	Y	Y
25 **McKeon**	N	Y	Y	Y	Y	Y	Y
26 **Dreier**	Y	Y	Y	Y	Y	Y	Y
27 Sherman	N	Y	Y	N	N	N	N
28 Berman	N	Y	Y	N	N	N	N
29 Schiff	N	Y	Y	N	N	N	N
30 Waxman	N	Y	Y	N	N	N	N
31 Becerra	N	Y	Y	N	N	N	N
32 Vacant							
33 Watson	N	Y	Y	N	N	N	N
34 Roybal-Allard	N	Y	Y	N	N	N	N
35 Waters	N	Y	Y	N	N	N	N
36 Harman	?	?	?	?	?	?	?
37 Richardson	N	Y	Y	N	N	N	N
38 Napolitano	N	Y	Y	N	N	N	N
39 Sánchez, Linda	?	?	?	?	?	N	N
40 **Royce**	Y	Y	Y	Y	Y	Y	Y
41 **Lewis**	Y	Y	Y	Y	Y	Y	Y
42 **Miller, Gary**	Y	Y	Y	N	Y	Y	Y
43 Baca	N	Y	Y	N	N	N	N
44 **Calvert**	Y	Y	Y	Y	Y	Y	Y
45 **Bono Mack**	Y	Y	Y	Y	Y	Y	Y
46 **Rohrabacher**	Y	Y	Y	N	Y	Y	Y
47 Sanchez, Loretta	N	Y	Y	N	Y	N	N
48 **Campbell**	Y	Y	N	Y	Y	Y	Y
49 **Issa**	Y	Y	Y	Y	Y	Y	Y
50 **Bilbray**	N	Y	N	Y	Y	Y	Y
51 Filner	N	Y	Y	N	N	N	N
52 **Hunter**	Y	Y	Y	Y	Y	Y	Y
53 Davis	N	Y	Y	N	N	N	N

	356	357	358	359	360	361	362
COLORADO							
1 DeGette	N	Y	Y	N	N	N	N
2 Polis	N	Y	Y	N	N	N	N
3 Salazar	N	Y	Y	N	N	N	N
4 Markey	Y	Y	Y	N	N	N	N
5 **Lamborn**	N	Y	N	Y	Y	Y	Y
6 **Coffman**	Y	Y	Y	N	Y	Y	Y
7 Perlmutter	N	Y	Y	N	N	N	N
CONNECTICUT							
1 Larson	N	Y	Y	N	N	N	N
2 Courtney	N	Y	Y	N	N	N	N
3 DeLauro	N	Y	Y	N	N	N	N
4 Himes	Y	Y	Y	N	N	N	N
5 Murphy	N	Y	Y	N	N	N	N
DELAWARE							
AL **Castle**	Y	Y	Y	N	Y	Y	Y
FLORIDA							
1 **Miller**	Y	Y	N	Y	Y	Y	Y
2 Boyd	N	Y	Y	N	N	N	N
3 Brown	N	Y	Y	N	N	N	N
4 **Crenshaw**	Y	Y	Y	Y	Y	Y	Y
5 **Brown-Waite**	Y	Y	N	Y	Y	Y	Y
6 **Stearns**	N	Y	Y	N	Y	Y	Y
7 **Mica**	Y	Y	Y	Y	Y	Y	Y
8 Grayson	N	Y	Y	N	Y	N	N
9 **Bilirakis**	Y	Y	Y	Y	Y	Y	Y
10 **Young**	N	Y	Y	Y	Y	Y	Y
11 Castor	N	Y	Y	N	N	N	N
12 **Putnam**	Y	Y	Y	Y	Y	Y	Y
13 **Buchanan**	Y	Y	N	Y	Y	Y	Y
14 **Mack**	Y	Y	Y	Y	Y	Y	Y
15 **Posey**	Y	Y	Y	Y	Y	Y	Y
16 **Rooney**	Y	Y	Y	Y	Y	Y	Y
17 Meek	N	Y	Y	N	Y	N	N
18 **Ros-Lehtinen**	Y	Y	Y	N	Y	Y	Y
19 Wexler	N	Y	Y	N	N	N	N
20 Wasserman Schultz	N	Y	Y	N	N	N	N
21 **Diaz-Balart, L.**	N	Y	Y	N	Y	N	N
22 Klein	N	Y	Y	N	Y	N	N
23 Hastings	N	Y	Y	N	N	N	N
24 Kosmas	N	Y	Y	N	Y	N	N
25 **Diaz-Balart, M.**	Y	Y	Y	N	Y	Y	N
GEORGIA							
1 **Kingston**	Y	Y	Y	N	Y	Y	Y
2 Bishop	N	Y	Y	N	N	N	N
3 **Westmoreland**	?	Y	N	Y	Y	Y	Y
4 Johnson	?	Y	Y	N	N	N	N
5 Lewis	?	?	?	?	?	?	?
6 **Price**	Y	Y	Y	Y	Y	Y	Y
7 **Linder**	Y	N	Y	Y	Y	Y	Y
8 Marshall	N	Y	Y	N	N	N	N
9 **Deal**	Y	Y	Y	Y	Y	Y	Y
10 **Broun**	Y	Y	Y	Y	Y	Y	Y
11 **Gingrey**	Y	Y	Y	Y	Y	Y	Y
12 Barrow	N	Y	Y	N	Y	Y	N
13 Scott	N	Y	Y	N	Y	Y	N
HAWAII							
1 Abercrombie	N	Y	Y	N	N	N	N
2 Hirono	N	Y	Y	N	N	N	N
IDAHO							
1 **Minnick**	Y	Y	Y	N	N	N	N
2 **Simpson**	Y	Y	Y	Y	Y	Y	Y
ILLINOIS							
1 Rush	N	Y	Y	N	N	N	N
2 Jackson	N	Y	Y	N	N	N	N
3 Lipinski	N	Y	Y	N	N	N	N
4 Gutierrez	N	Y	N	N	N	N	N
5 Quigley	N	Y	Y	N	N	N	N
6 **Roskam**	Y	Y	Y	Y	Y	Y	Y
7 Davis	?	?	?	N	N	N	N
8 Bean	N	Y	Y	N	Y	Y	N
9 Schakowsky	N	Y	Y	N	N	N	N
10 **Kirk**	N	Y	Y	N	Y	Y	Y
11 Halvorson	N	Y	Y	N	Y	Y	N
12 Costello	N	Y	Y	N	N	N	N
13 **Biggert**	N	Y	Y	N	Y	Y	Y
14 Foster	N	Y	Y	N	Y	Y	N
15 **Johnson**	Y	Y	Y	N	N	N	N

	356	357	358	359	360	361	362
16 **Manzullo**	Y	Y	Y	Y	Y	Y	Y
17 Hare	N	Y	Y	N	N	N	N
18 **Schock**	Y	Y	Y	N	Y	Y	Y
19 **Shimkus**	N	Y	Y	N	Y	Y	Y
INDIANA							
1 Visclosky	N	Y	Y	N	N	N	N
2 Donnelly	N	Y	Y	N	Y	Y	N
3 **Souder**	Y	Y	Y	Y	Y	Y	Y
4 **Buyer**	Y	Y	Y	Y	Y	Y	Y
5 **Burton**	Y	Y	Y	Y	Y	Y	Y
6 **Pence**	Y	Y	N	Y	Y	Y	Y
7 Carson	N	Y	Y	N	N	N	N
8 Ellsworth	N	Y	Y	N	N	N	N
9 Hill	N	Y	Y	N	N	N	N
IOWA							
1 Braley	N	Y	Y	N	N	N	N
2 Loebsack	N	Y	Y	N	N	N	N
3 Boswell	N	Y	Y	N	N	N	N
4 **Latham**	N	Y	Y	N	Y	Y	Y
5 **King**	Y	Y	N	Y	Y	Y	Y
KANSAS							
1 **Moran**	N	Y	Y	Y	Y	Y	Y
2 **Jenkins**	N	Y	Y	Y	Y	Y	Y
3 Moore	N	Y	Y	N	N	N	N
4 **Tiahrt**	N	Y	Y	Y	Y	Y	Y
KENTUCKY							
1 **Whitfield**	Y	Y	N	Y	Y	Y	Y
2 **Guthrie**	Y	Y	Y	N	Y	Y	Y
3 Yarmuth	N	Y	Y	N	N	N	N
4 **Davis**	Y	Y	N	N	Y	Y	Y
5 **Rogers**	N	Y	Y	N	Y	Y	Y
6 Chandler	N	Y	Y	N	N	N	N
LOUISIANA							
1 **Scalise**	Y	Y	N	Y	Y	Y	Y
2 **Cao**	N	Y	Y	N	Y	Y	Y
3 Melancon	N	Y	Y	N	Y	Y	N
4 **Fleming**	N	Y	Y	Y	Y	Y	Y
5 **Alexander**	Y	Y	Y	N	Y	Y	Y
6 **Cassidy**	N	Y	Y	N	Y	Y	N
7 **Boustany**	Y	Y	Y	N	Y	Y	N
MAINE							
1 Pingree	N	Y	Y	N	N	N	N
2 Michaud	N	Y	Y	N	N	Y	N
MARYLAND							
1 Kratovil	?	?	Y	N	Y	Y	N
2 Ruppersberger	N	Y	Y	N	N	N	N
3 Sarbanes	N	Y	Y	N	N	N	N
4 Edwards	N	Y	Y	N	N	N	N
5 Hoyer	N	?	Y	N	N	N	N
6 **Bartlett**	Y	Y	Y	Y	N	Y	Y
7 Cummings	N	Y	Y	N	N	N	N
8 Van Hollen	N	Y	Y	N	N	N	N
MASSACHUSETTS							
1 Olver	N	Y	Y	N	N	N	N
2 Neal	N	Y	Y	N	N	N	N
3 McGovern	N	Y	Y	N	N	N	N
4 Frank	N	Y	Y	N	N	N	N
5 Tsongas	N	Y	Y	N	N	N	N
6 Tierney	N	Y	Y	N	N	N	N
7 Markey	N	Y	Y	N	N	N	N
8 Capuano	N	Y	Y	N	N	N	N
9 Lynch	N	Y	Y	N	N	N	N
10 Delahunt	N	Y	Y	N	N	N	N
MICHIGAN							
1 Stupak	N	Y	Y	N	N	N	N
2 **Hoekstra**	Y	Y	Y	Y	Y	Y	Y
3 **Ehlers**	Y	Y	Y	N	Y	Y	N
4 **Camp**	Y	Y	Y	N	Y	Y	Y
5 Kildee	N	Y	Y	N	N	N	N
6 **Upton**	Y	Y	Y	N	Y	Y	Y
7 Schauer	N	Y	Y	N	N	N	N
8 **Rogers**	Y	?	N	N	Y	Y	Y
9 Peters	N	Y	Y	N	N	N	N
10 **Miller**	N	Y	Y	N	Y	Y	Y
11 **McCotter**	N	Y	Y	N	Y	Y	Y
12 Levin	N	Y	Y	N	N	N	N
13 Kilpatrick	N	Y	Y	N	N	N	N
14 Conyers	Y	Y	Y	N	?	N	N
15 Dingell	N	Y	Y	N	N	N	N
MINNESOTA							
1 Walz	N	Y	Y	N	N	N	N
2 **Kline**	Y	Y	Y	Y	Y	Y	Y
3 **Paulsen**	Y	Y	Y	N	Y	Y	Y
4 McCollum	N	Y	Y	N	N	N	N

	356	357	358	359	360	361	362
5 Ellison	?	?	?	?	?	?	?
6 **Bachmann**	?	?	?	?	?	?	?
7 Peterson	N	Y	Y	N	N	N	N
8 Oberstar	N	Y	Y	N	N	N	N
MISSISSIPPI							
1 Childers	N	Y	Y	N	Y	Y	N
2 Thompson	N	Y	Y	N	N	N	N
3 **Harper**	Y	Y	N	N	Y	Y	Y
4 Taylor	Y	Y	Y	N	Y	Y	Y
MISSOURI							
1 Clay	N	Y	Y	N	N	N	N
2 **Akin**	Y	Y	Y	Y	Y	Y	Y
3 Carnahan	N	Y	Y	N	N	N	N
4 Skelton	N	Y	Y	N	N	N	N
5 Cleaver	N	Y	Y	N	N	N	N
6 **Graves**	Y	Y	Y	N	Y	Y	Y
7 **Blunt**	N	Y	Y	N	Y	Y	Y
8 **Emerson**	Y	Y	Y	N	Y	Y	Y
9 **Luetkemeyer**	Y	Y	Y	N	Y	Y	Y
MONTANA							
AL **Rehberg**	Y	Y	Y	Y	Y	Y	Y
NEBRASKA							
1 **Fortenberry**	N	Y	Y	N	Y	Y	N
2 **Terry**	Y	Y	Y	N	Y	Y	Y
3 **Smith**	Y	Y	Y	Y	Y	Y	Y
NEVADA							
1 Berkley	N	Y	Y	N	N	N	N
2 **Heller**	Y	Y	Y	Y	Y	Y	N
3 Titus	N	Y	Y	N	Y	Y	N
NEW HAMPSHIRE							
1 Shea-Porter	N	Y	Y	N	Y	?	N
2 Hodes	N	Y	Y	N	N	N	N
NEW JERSEY							
1 Andrews	N	Y	Y	N	N	N	N
2 **LoBiondo**	N	Y	Y	N	Y	Y	Y
3 Adler	Y	Y	Y	N	Y	Y	Y
4 **Smith**	N	Y	Y	N	Y	Y	Y
5 **Garrett**	Y	Y	N	Y	Y	Y	Y
6 Pallone	N	Y	Y	N	N	N	N
7 **Lance**	N	Y	Y	N	Y	Y	Y
8 Pascrell	N	Y	Y	N	N	N	N
9 Rothman	N	Y	Y	N	N	N	N
10 Payne	?	?	?	?	N	N	N
11 **Frelinghuysen**	N	Y	Y	N	Y	Y	N
12 Holt	N	Y	Y	N	N	N	N
13 Sires	N	Y	Y	N	N	N	N
NEW MEXICO							
1 Heinrich	N	Y	Y	N	N	N	N
2 Teague	N	Y	Y	N	Y	Y	N
3 Lujan	N	Y	Y	N	N	N	N
NEW YORK							
1 Bishop	N	Y	Y	N	N	N	N
2 Israel	N	Y	Y	N	N	N	N
3 **King**	Y	Y	Y	N	Y	Y	N
4 McCarthy	N	Y	Y	N	N	N	N
5 Ackerman	N	Y	Y	N	N	N	N
6 Meeks	N	Y	Y	N	N	N	N
7 Crowley	N	Y	Y	N	N	N	N
8 Nadler	Y	Y	Y	N	N	N	N
9 Weiner	N	Y	Y	N	N	N	N
10 Towns	N	Y	Y	N	N	N	N
11 Clarke	N	Y	Y	N	N	N	N
12 Velázquez	N	Y	Y	N	N	N	N
13 McMahon	N	Y	Y	N	N	N	N
14 Maloney	N	Y	Y	N	N	N	N
15 Rangel	?	?	Y	N	N	N	N
16 Serrano	N	Y	Y	N	N	N	N
17 Engel	N	Y	Y	N	N	N	N
18 Lowey	N	Y	Y	N	N	N	N
19 Hall	N	Y	Y	N	N	N	N
20 Murphy	Y	Y	Y	N	Y	Y	N
21 Tonko	N	Y	Y	N	N	N	N
22 Hinchey	Y	Y	Y	N	N	N	N
23 **McHugh**	N	Y	Y	N	Y	Y	N
24 Arcuri	N	Y	Y	N	N	N	N
25 Maffei	N	Y	Y	N	N	N	N
26 **Lee**	N	Y	Y	Y	Y	Y	Y
27 Higgins	N	Y	Y	N	N	N	N
28 Slaughter	N	+	+	N	N	N	N
29 Massa	N	Y	Y	N	N	N	N
NORTH CAROLINA							
1 Butterfield	N	Y	Y	N	N	N	N
2 Etheridge	N	Y	Y	N	N	N	N
3 **Jones**	N	Y	Y	N	Y	Y	Y
4 Price	N	Y	Y	N	N	N	N

	356	357	358	359	360	361	362
5 **Foxx**	Y	Y	N	Y	Y	Y	Y
6 **Coble**	Y	Y	N	Y	Y	Y	Y
7 McIntyre	N	Y	Y	N	Y	Y	N
8 Kissell	N	Y	Y	N	Y	Y	N
9 **Myrick**	N	Y	Y	Y	Y	Y	Y
10 **McHenry**	Y	Y	Y	Y	Y	Y	Y
11 Shuler	N	Y	Y	N	N	N	N
12 Watt	N	Y	Y	N	N	N	N
13 Miller	N	Y	Y	N	N	N	N
NORTH DAKOTA							
AL Pomeroy	N	Y	Y	N	N	N	N
OHIO							
1 Driehaus	N	Y	Y	N	N	N	N
2 **Schmidt**	?	?	?	?	?	?	?
3 **Turner**	N	Y	Y	N	Y	Y	N
4 **Jordan**	Y	Y	Y	Y	Y	Y	Y
5 **Latta**	Y	Y	Y	Y	Y	Y	Y
6 Wilson	N	Y	Y	N	N	N	N
7 **Austria**	Y	Y	Y	Y	Y	Y	Y
8 **Boehner**	Y	Y	Y	Y	Y	Y	Y
9 Kaptur	N	Y	Y	N	N	N	N
10 Kucinich	N	Y	Y	N	N	N	N
11 Fudge	N	Y	Y	N	N	N	N
12 **Tiberi**	Y	Y	Y	N	Y	Y	Y
13 Sutton	N	Y	Y	N	N	N	N
14 **LaTourette**	N	Y	Y	N	Y	Y	N
15 Kilroy	N	Y	Y	N	N	N	N
16 Boccieri	N	Y	Y	N	Y	Y	N
17 Ryan	N	Y	Y	N	N	N	N
18 Space	N	Y	Y	N	N	N	N
OKLAHOMA							
1 **Sullivan**	?	?	?	?	?	?	?
2 Boren	N	Y	Y	N	Y	Y	N
3 **Lucas**	N	Y	Y	N	Y	Y	Y
4 **Cole**	N	Y	Y	N	Y	Y	Y
5 **Fallin**	N	Y	Y	N	Y	Y	Y
OREGON							
1 Wu	N	Y	Y	N	N	N	N
2 **Walden**	N	Y	Y	N	Y	Y	Y
3 Blumenauer	N	Y	Y	N	N	N	N
4 DeFazio	N	Y	Y	N	N	N	N
5 Schrader	N	Y	Y	N	N	N	Y
PENNSYLVANIA							
1 Brady	N	Y	Y	N	N	N	N
2 Fattah	N	Y	Y	N	N	N	N
3 Dahlkemper	N	Y	Y	N	N	N	N
4 Altmire	N	Y	Y	N	Y	Y	N
5 **Thompson**	N	Y	N	N	Y	Y	N
6 **Gerlach**	N	Y	Y	N	Y	Y	Y
7 Sestak	N	Y	Y	N	N	N	N
8 Murphy, P.	N	Y	Y	N	N	N	N
9 **Shuster**	N	Y	N	N	Y	Y	Y
10 Carney	N	Y	Y	N	Y	Y	N
11 Kanjorski	N	Y	Y	N	N	N	N
12 Murtha	N	Y	Y	N	N	N	N
13 Schwartz	N	Y	Y	N	N	N	N
14 Doyle	?	Y	Y	N	N	N	N
15 **Dent**	N	Y	Y	N	Y	Y	Y
16 **Pitts**	Y	Y	Y	Y	Y	Y	Y
17 Holden	N	Y	Y	N	N	N	N
18 **Murphy, T.**	Y	Y	Y	N	Y	Y	Y
19 **Platts**	N	Y	Y	N	Y	Y	Y
RHODE ISLAND							
1 Kennedy	?	?	?	?	?	?	?
2 Langevin	N	Y	Y	N	N	N	N
SOUTH CAROLINA							
1 **Brown**	Y	Y	Y	Y	Y	Y	Y
2 **Wilson**	Y	Y	Y	Y	Y	Y	Y
3 **Barrett**	Y	Y	Y	Y	Y	Y	Y
4 **Inglis**	Y	Y	Y	N	Y	Y	Y
5 Spratt	N	Y	Y	N	N	N	N
6 Clyburn	N	Y	Y	N	N	N	N
SOUTH DAKOTA							
AL Herseth Sandlin	N	Y	Y	N	Y	Y	N
TENNESSEE							
1 **Roe**	Y	Y	Y	N	Y	Y	Y
2 **Duncan**	Y	Y	Y	Y	Y	Y	Y
3 **Wamp**	Y	Y	Y	Y	Y	Y	Y
4 Davis	N	Y	Y	N	Y	Y	N
5 Cooper	Y	Y	Y	N	N	N	N
6 Gordon	N	Y	Y	N	Y	Y	N
7 **Blackburn**	Y	Y	N	Y	Y	Y	Y
8 Tanner	Y	Y	Y	N	Y	Y	N
9 Cohen	N	Y	Y	N	N	N	N

	356	357	358	359	360	361	362
TEXAS							
1 **Gohmert**	Y	Y	Y	Y	Y	Y	Y
2 **Poe**	Y	Y	Y	N	Y	Y	Y
3 **Johnson, S.**	Y	Y	N	Y	Y	Y	Y
4 **Hall**	Y	N	Y	Y	Y	Y	Y
5 **Hensarling**	Y	Y	N	Y	Y	Y	Y
6 **Barton**	Y	Y	Y	Y	Y	Y	Y
7 **Culberson**	Y	Y	N	Y	Y	Y	Y
8 **Brady**	Y	Y	N	Y	Y	Y	Y
9 Green, A.	N	Y	Y	N	N	N	N
10 **McCaul**	Y	Y	Y	N	Y	Y	Y
11 **Conaway**	Y	Y	N	Y	Y	Y	Y
12 **Granger**	Y	Y	Y	Y	Y	Y	Y
13 **Thornberry**	Y	Y	N	Y	Y	Y	Y
14 **Paul**	Y	?	?	Y	N	N	Y
15 Hinojosa	N	Y	Y	N	N	N	N
16 Reyes	N	Y	Y	N	N	N	N
17 Edwards	N	Y	Y	N	N	N	N
18 Jackson Lee	N	Y	Y	N	N	N	N
19 **Neugebauer**	Y	Y	N	Y	Y	Y	Y
20 Gonzalez	N	Y	Y	N	N	N	N
21 **Smith**	N	Y	Y	Y	Y	Y	Y
22 **Olson**	Y	Y	N	Y	Y	Y	Y
23 Rodriguez	N	Y	Y	N	N	N	N
24 **Marchant**	Y	Y	Y	Y	Y	Y	Y
25 Doggett	N	Y	Y	N	N	N	N
26 **Burgess**	Y	Y	Y	Y	Y	Y	Y
27 Ortiz	N	Y	Y	N	N	N	N
28 Cuellar	N	Y	Y	N	Y	Y	N
29 Green, G.	N	Y	Y	N	N	N	N
30 Johnson, E.	N	Y	Y	N	N	N	N
31 **Carter**	Y	Y	Y	Y	Y	Y	Y
32 **Sessions**	Y	Y	N	Y	Y	Y	Y
UTAH							
1 **Bishop**	Y	Y	Y	Y	Y	Y	Y
2 Matheson	N	Y	Y	N	Y	Y	N
3 **Chaffetz**	Y	Y	Y	Y	Y	Y	Y
VERMONT							
AL Welch	Y	Y	Y	N	?	N	N
VIRGINIA							
1 **Wittman**	Y	Y	Y	Y	Y	Y	N
2 Nye	N	Y	Y	N	Y	Y	N
3 Scott	N	Y	Y	N	N	N	N
4 **Forbes**	N	Y	Y	Y	Y	Y	Y
5 Perriello	N	Y	Y	N	N	N	N
6 **Goodlatte**	Y	Y	Y	Y	Y	Y	Y
7 **Cantor**	Y	Y	Y	Y	Y	Y	Y
8 Moran	N	Y	Y	N	N	N	N
9 Boucher	N	Y	Y	N	N	N	N
10 **Wolf**	N	Y	Y	N	Y	Y	Y
11 Connolly	N	Y	Y	N	N	N	N
WASHINGTON							
1 Inslee	N	Y	Y	?	N	N	N
2 Larsen	N	Y	Y	N	N	N	N
3 Baird	N	Y	Y	N	N	N	N
4 **Hastings**	Y	Y	Y	Y	Y	Y	Y
5 **McMorris Rodgers**	Y	?	Y	Y	Y	Y	Y
6 Dicks	N	Y	Y	N	N	N	N
7 McDermott	N	Y	Y	N	N	N	N
8 **Reichert**	N	Y	Y	N	Y	Y	Y
9 Smith	N	Y	Y	N	N	N	Y
WEST VIRGINIA							
1 Mollohan	N	Y	Y	N	N	N	N
2 **Capito**	Y	Y	Y	N	Y	Y	Y
3 Rahall	N	Y	Y	N	N	N	N
WISCONSIN							
1 **Ryan**	Y	Y	Y	Y	Y	Y	Y
2 Baldwin	N	Y	Y	N	N	N	N
3 Kind	N	Y	Y	N	N	N	N
4 Moore	N	Y	Y	N	N	N	N
5 **Sensenbrenner**	Y	Y	Y	Y	Y	Y	Y
6 **Petri**	Y	Y	Y	Y	Y	Y	Y
7 Obey	N	Y	Y	N	N	N	N
8 Kagen	N	Y	Y	N	N	N	N
WYOMING							
AL **Lummis**	Y	Y	N	Y	Y	Y	Y
DELEGATES							
Faleomavaega (A.S.)	N	Y	Y	N	N		N
Norton (D.C.)	N	Y	Y	N	N		N
Bordallo (Guam)	N	Y	Y	N	N		N
Sablan (N. Marianas)	N	Y	Y	N	N		N
Pierluisi (P.R.)	N	Y	Y	N	N		N
Christensen (V.I.)	N	Y	Y	N	N		N

IN THE HOUSE | By Vote Number

363. **HR 2847. Fiscal 2010 Commerce-Justice-Science Appropriations/Energy Star Designation.** Cuellar, D-Texas, amendment that would bar the use of funds in the bill to purchase light bulbs that do not have an "Energy Star" or "Federal Energy Management Program" designation. Adopted in Committee of the Whole 343-87: R 88-86; D 255-1. June 18, 2009.

364. **HR 2847. Fiscal 2010 Commerce-Justice-Science Appropriations/Justice Department Funds Reduction.** Price, R-Ga., amendment that would reduce funds in the bill for the Justice Department by $100 million. Rejected in Committee of the Whole 165-257: R 153-21; D 12-236. June 18, 2009.

365. **HR 2847. Fiscal 2010 Commerce-Justice-Science Appropriations/Expired Grant Accounts' Undisbursed Balances.** Hodes, D-N.H., amendment that would require the Office of Management and Budget to instruct any department or agency receiving funds under the bill to track undisbursed balances in expired grant accounts and require the office to include in its annual performance reports the findings and details of actions taken to resolve the balances. Adopted in Committee of the Whole 422-0: R 173-0; D 249-0. June 18, 2009.

366. **HR 2847. Fiscal 2010 Commerce-Justice-Science Appropriations/Reallocation of California's Water.** Nunes, R-Calif., amendment that would bar the use of funds in the bill to implement a biological assessment in the National Marine Fisheries Service's report on the long-term operations of California's Central Valley Project and State Water Project, which calls for reallocating state water supplies. Rejected in Committee of the Whole 208-218: R 171-3; D 37-215. June 18, 2009.

367. **HR 2847. Fiscal 2010 Commerce-Justice-Science Appropriations/Reduction of Discretionary Funds.** Blackburn, R-Tenn., amendment that would reduce discretionary spending in the bill by 5 percent. Rejected in Committee of the Whole 177-248: R 158-16; D 19-232. A "nay" was a vote in support of the president's position. June 18, 2009.

368. **HR 2847. Fiscal 2010 Commerce-Justice-Science Appropriations/Office of the Census and Commerce Department Relocation.** Burton, R-Ind., amendment that would bar the use of funds in the bill to relocate the Office of the Census or employees from the Commerce Department to the jurisdiction of the Executive Office of the President. Adopted in Committee of the Whole 262-162: R 173-0; D 89-162. June 18, 2009.

369. **HR 2847. Fiscal 2010 Commerce-Justice-Science Appropriations/Reduction of Discretionary Funds.** Price, R-Ga., amendment that would cut discretionary spending in the bill by $644 million, or 1 percent. Rejected in Committee of the Whole 188-236: R 159-12; D 29-224. June 18, 2009.

	363	364	365	366	367	368	369
ALABAMA							
1 **Bonner**	N	Y	Y	Y	Y	Y	Y
2 Bright	Y	Y	Y	N	Y	Y	Y
3 **Rogers**	Y	N	Y	Y	Y	Y	Y
4 **Aderholt**	N	Y	Y	Y	Y	Y	Y
5 Griffith	Y	?	Y	N	N	Y	N
6 **Bachus**	N	Y	Y	Y	Y	Y	Y
7 Davis	Y	N	Y	N	N	Y	N
ALASKA							
AL **Young**	N	Y	Y	Y	N	?	N
ARIZONA							
1 Kirkpatrick	Y	N	Y	N	Y	Y	Y
2 **Franks**	N	Y	Y	Y	Y	Y	Y
3 **Shadegg**	N	Y	Y	Y	Y	Y	Y
4 Pastor	Y	N	Y	N	N	Y	N
5 Mitchell	Y	Y	Y	N	Y	Y	Y
6 **Flake**	N	Y	Y	Y	Y	Y	Y
7 Grijalva	Y	N	Y	N	N	N	N
8 Giffords	Y	N	Y	N	N	N	Y
ARKANSAS							
1 Berry	Y	N	Y	N	N	N	N
2 Snyder	Y	N	Y	N	N	N	N
3 **Boozman**	N	Y	Y	Y	Y	Y	Y
4 Ross	Y	N	Y	N	Y	N	N
CALIFORNIA							
1 Thompson	Y	N	Y	N	N	N	N
2 **Herger**	Y	Y	?	Y	Y	Y	Y
3 **Lungren**	Y	Y	Y	Y	Y	Y	Y
4 **McClintock**	N	Y	Y	Y	Y	Y	Y
5 Matsui	Y	N	Y	N	N	N	N
6 Woolsey	Y	?	Y	N	N	N	N
7 Miller, George	Y	N	Y	N	N	N	N
8 Pelosi							
9 Lee	Y	N	Y	N	N	N	N
10 Tauscher	?	?	?	?	?	?	?
11 McNerney	Y	N	Y	N	N	N	N
12 Speier	Y	N	?	N	N	N	N
13 Stark	Y	N	Y	N	N	N	N
14 Eshoo	Y	N	Y	N	N	N	N
15 Honda	Y	N	Y	N	N	N	N
16 Lofgren	Y	N	Y	N	N	N	N
17 Farr	Y	N	Y	N	N	N	N
18 Cardoza	Y	N	Y	N	N	?	N
19 **Radanovich**	N	Y	Y	Y	Y	Y	Y
20 Costa	Y	N	Y	N	N	N	N
21 **Nunes**	N	Y	Y	Y	Y	Y	Y
22 **McCarthy**	N	Y	Y	Y	Y	Y	Y
23 Capps	Y	N	Y	N	N	N	N
24 **Gallegly**	N	Y	Y	Y	Y	Y	Y
25 **McKeon**	N	Y	Y	Y	Y	Y	Y
26 **Dreier**	Y	Y	Y	Y	Y	Y	Y
27 Sherman	Y	N	Y	N	N	N	N
28 Berman	Y	N	Y	N	N	N	N
29 Schiff	Y	N	Y	N	N	N	N
30 Waxman	Y	N	Y	N	N	N	N
31 Becerra	Y	N	Y	N	N	N	N
32 Vacant							
33 Watson	Y	N	Y	N	N	?	N
34 Roybal-Allard	Y	N	Y	N	N	N	N
35 Waters	Y	N	Y	N	N	N	N
36 Harman	?	?	?	?	?	?	?
37 Richardson	Y	N	Y	N	N	N	N
38 Napolitano	Y	N	Y	N	N	N	N
39 Sánchez, Linda	Y	?	?	?	?	?	?
40 **Royce**	Y	Y	Y	Y	Y	Y	Y
41 **Lewis**	Y	Y	Y	Y	Y	Y	Y
42 **Miller, Gary**	N	Y	Y	Y	Y	Y	Y
43 Baca	Y	N	Y	N	N	N	N
44 **Calvert**	Y	Y	Y	Y	Y	Y	Y
45 **Bono Mack**	Y	Y	Y	Y	Y	Y	Y
46 **Rohrabacher**	Y	Y	Y	Y	Y	Y	Y
47 Sanchez, Loretta	Y	N	Y	N	N	N	N
48 **Campbell**	N	Y	Y	Y	Y	Y	Y
49 **Issa**	N	Y	Y	?	Y	Y	Y
50 **Bilbray**	Y	N	Y	Y	Y	Y	Y
51 Filner	Y	N	Y	N	N	N	N
52 **Hunter**	N	Y	Y	Y	Y	Y	Y
53 Davis	Y	N	Y	N	N	N	N

	363	364	365	366	367	368	369
COLORADO							
1 DeGette	Y	N	Y	N	N	N	N
2 Polis	Y	N	Y	N	N	N	N
3 Salazar	Y	N	Y	N	N	N	N
4 Markey	Y	N	Y	N	N	N	N
5 **Lamborn**	N	Y	Y	Y	Y	Y	Y
6 **Coffman**	N	Y	Y	Y	Y	Y	Y
7 Perlmutter	Y	N	Y	N	N	N	N
CONNECTICUT							
1 Larson	Y	N	Y	N	N	N	N
2 Courtney	Y	N	Y	N	N	N	N
3 DeLauro	Y	N	Y	N	N	N	N
4 Himes	Y	N	?	N	Y	Y	Y
5 Murphy	Y	?	Y	N	N	Y	N
DELAWARE							
AL **Castle**	Y	Y	Y	Y	Y	Y	Y
FLORIDA							
1 **Miller**	N	Y	Y	Y	Y	Y	Y
2 Boyd	Y	N	Y	N	N	N	N
3 Brown	Y	N	Y	N	N	N	N
4 **Crenshaw**	Y	Y	Y	Y	Y	Y	Y
5 **Brown-Waite**	Y	Y	Y	Y	Y	Y	Y
6 **Stearns**	N	Y	Y	Y	Y	Y	Y
7 **Mica**	N	Y	Y	Y	Y	Y	Y
8 Grayson	Y	N	Y	N	N	N	N
9 **Bilirakis**	Y	Y	Y	Y	Y	Y	Y
10 **Young**	Y	N	Y	Y	Y	Y	Y
11 Castor	Y	N	Y	N	N	N	N
12 **Putnam**	Y	Y	Y	Y	Y	Y	Y
13 **Buchanan**	Y	Y	Y	Y	Y	Y	Y
14 **Mack**	N	Y	Y	Y	Y	Y	Y
15 **Posey**	N	Y	Y	Y	N	Y	Y
16 **Rooney**	N	Y	Y	Y	Y	Y	Y
17 Meek	Y	N	Y	N	N	N	N
18 **Ros-Lehtinen**	Y	Y	Y	Y	Y	Y	Y
19 Wexler	Y	N	Y	N	N	N	N
20 Wasserman Schultz	Y	N	Y	N	N	N	N
21 **Diaz-Balart, L.**	Y	Y	Y	Y	Y	Y	Y
22 Klein	Y	N	Y	N	N	N	N
23 Hastings	Y	N	Y	N	N	N	N
24 Kosmas	Y	N	Y	N	N	Y	N
25 **Diaz-Balart, M.**	Y	Y	Y	Y	Y	Y	Y
GEORGIA							
1 **Kingston**	N	Y	Y	Y	Y	Y	Y
2 Bishop	Y	N	Y	N	Y	N	N
3 **Westmoreland**	N	Y	Y	Y	Y	Y	Y
4 Johnson	Y	N	Y	N	N	N	N
5 Lewis	?	?	?	?	?	?	?
6 **Price**	N	Y	Y	Y	Y	Y	Y
7 **Linder**	N	Y	Y	Y	Y	Y	Y
8 Marshall	Y	Y	Y	Y	N	Y	Y
9 **Deal**	N	Y	Y	Y	Y	Y	Y
10 **Broun**	N	Y	Y	Y	Y	Y	Y
11 **Gingrey**	N	Y	Y	Y	Y	Y	Y
12 Barrow	Y	N	Y	N	Y	N	N
13 Scott	Y	N	Y	N	N	N	N
HAWAII							
1 Abercrombie	Y	N	Y	N	N	N	N
2 Hirono	Y	N	Y	N	N	N	N
IDAHO							
1 Minnick	Y	Y	Y	Y	Y	Y	Y
2 **Simpson**	N	Y	Y	Y	Y	Y	Y
ILLINOIS							
1 Rush	Y	N	Y	N	?	N	N
2 Jackson	Y	N	Y	N	N	N	N
3 Lipinski	Y	N	Y	N	Y	N	N
4 Gutierrez	Y	N	Y	N	N	N	N
5 Quigley	Y	N	Y	N	N	N	N
6 **Roskam**	N	Y	Y	Y	Y	Y	Y
7 Davis	Y	N	Y	N	?	N	N
8 Bean	Y	?	Y	N	N	Y	N
9 Schakowsky	Y	N	Y	N	N	N	N
10 **Kirk**	Y	N	Y	Y	Y	Y	Y
11 Halvorson	Y	N	Y	N	N	N	N
12 Costello	Y	N	Y	N	N	N	N
13 **Biggert**	Y	N	Y	Y	Y	Y	Y
14 Foster	Y	N	Y	Y	Y	Y	N
15 **Johnson**	Y	Y	Y	Y	Y	Y	Y

KEY   **Republicans**   Democrats

Y Voted for (yea)	X Paired against	C Voted "present" to avoid possible conflict of interest
# Paired for	– Announced against	
+ Announced for	P Voted "present"	? Did not vote or otherwise make a position known
N Voted against (nay)		

	363	364	365	366	367	368	369
16 **Manzullo**	Y	Y	Y	Y	Y	Y	Y
17 Hare	Y	N	Y	N	N	N	N
18 **Schock**	Y	Y	Y	Y	Y	Y	Y
19 **Shimkus**	N	Y	Y	Y	Y	Y	Y
INDIANA							
1 Visclosky	Y	N	Y	N	N	N	N
2 Donnelly	Y	N	Y	N	N	Y	Y
3 **Souder**	N	Y	Y	Y	Y	Y	Y
4 **Buyer**	Y	Y	Y	Y	Y	Y	Y
5 **Burton**	N	Y	Y	Y	Y	Y	Y
6 **Pence**	N	Y	Y	Y	Y	Y	Y
7 Carson	Y	N	Y	N	N	N	N
8 Ellsworth	Y	N	Y	N	N	N	Y
9 Hill	Y	N	Y	Y	N	Y	Y
IOWA							
1 Braley	Y	N	Y	N	N	N	N
2 Loebsack	Y	N	Y	N	N	Y	N
3 Boswell	Y	N	Y	N	N	Y	N
4 **Latham**	Y	Y	Y	Y	Y	Y	Y
5 **King**	N	Y	Y	Y	Y	Y	Y
KANSAS							
1 **Moran**	Y	Y	Y	Y	Y	Y	Y
2 **Jenkins**	N	Y	Y	Y	Y	Y	Y
3 Moore	Y	N	Y	Y	N	N	N
4 **Tiahrt**	N	Y	Y	Y	Y	Y	Y
KENTUCKY							
1 **Whitfield**	Y	Y	Y	Y	Y	Y	Y
2 **Guthrie**	Y	Y	Y	Y	Y	Y	Y
3 Yarmuth	Y	N	?	N	N	Y	N
4 **Davis**	Y	Y	Y	Y	Y	Y	Y
5 **Rogers**	Y	Y	Y	Y	Y	Y	Y
6 Chandler	Y	N	Y	N	N	Y	N
LOUISIANA							
1 **Scalise**	N	Y	Y	Y	Y	Y	Y
2 **Cao**	Y	N	Y	Y	Y	Y	N
3 Melancon	Y	N	Y	?	N	Y	Y
4 **Fleming**	N	Y	Y	Y	Y	Y	Y
5 **Alexander**	N	Y	Y	Y	Y	Y	Y
6 **Cassidy**	Y	Y	Y	Y	Y	Y	Y
7 **Boustany**	N	Y	Y	Y	Y	Y	Y
MAINE							
1 Pingree	Y	N	Y	N	N	N	N
2 Michaud	Y	N	Y	N	N	Y	N
MARYLAND							
1 Kratovil	Y	N	Y	Y	Y	Y	Y
2 Ruppersberger	Y	N	Y	Y	N	N	N
3 Sarbanes	Y	N	Y	N	N	Y	N
4 Edwards	Y	N	Y	N	N	N	N
5 Hoyer	Y	N	Y	Y	N	N	N
6 **Bartlett**	Y	Y	Y	Y	Y	Y	Y
7 Cummings	Y	N	Y	N	N	Y	N
8 Van Hollen	Y	N	Y	N	N	?	N
MASSACHUSETTS							
1 Olver	Y	N	Y	N	N	N	N
2 Neal	Y	N	Y	N	N	N	N
3 McGovern	Y	N	Y	N	N	N	N
4 Frank	Y	N	Y	N	N	N	N
5 Tsongas	Y	N	Y	N	N	N	N
6 Tierney	Y	N	Y	N	N	N	N
7 Markey	Y	N	Y	N	N	N	N
8 Capuano	Y	N	Y	N	N	N	N
9 Lynch	Y	N	Y	Y	N	N	N
10 Delahunt	Y	N	Y	N	?	N	N
MICHIGAN							
1 Stupak	Y	N	Y	N	N	N	N
2 **Hoekstra**	N	Y	Y	Y	Y	Y	Y
3 **Ehlers**	Y	?	Y	Y	N	Y	N
4 **Camp**	Y	Y	Y	Y	Y	Y	Y
5 Kildee	Y	N	Y	N	N	Y	N
6 **Upton**	Y	Y	Y	Y	Y	Y	Y
7 Schauer	Y	N	Y	N	N	Y	N
8 **Rogers**	N	Y	Y	Y	Y	Y	Y
9 Peters	Y	N	Y	N	N	Y	Y
10 **Miller**	Y	Y	Y	Y	Y	Y	Y
11 **McCotter**	N	Y	Y	Y	Y	Y	Y
12 Levin	Y	N	Y	N	N	N	N
13 Kilpatrick	Y	N	Y	N	N	N	N
14 Conyers	Y	N	Y	N	N	?	N
15 Dingell	Y	N	Y	N	N	N	N
MINNESOTA							
1 Walz	Y	N	Y	Y	N	Y	N
2 **Kline**	N	Y	Y	Y	Y	Y	Y
3 **Paulsen**	Y	Y	Y	Y	Y	Y	Y
4 McCollum	Y	N	Y	N	N	N	N

	363	364	365	366	367	368	369
5 Ellison	?	?	?	?	?	?	?
6 **Bachmann**	?	?	?	?	?	?	?
7 Peterson	Y	N	Y	Y	N	Y	N
8 Oberstar	Y	N	Y	N	N	Y	N
MISSISSIPPI							
1 Childers	Y	Y	Y	Y	N	Y	Y
2 Thompson	Y	N	Y	N	N	N	N
3 **Harper**	Y	Y	Y	Y	Y	Y	Y
4 Taylor	Y	Y	Y	Y	Y	Y	Y
MISSOURI							
1 Clay	Y	N	Y	N	N	N	N
2 **Akin**	N	Y	Y	Y	Y	Y	Y
3 Carnahan	Y	N	Y	N	N	N	N
4 Skelton	Y	N	Y	N	N	Y	N
5 Cleaver	Y	N	Y	N	N	N	N
6 **Graves**	Y	Y	Y	Y	Y	Y	Y
7 **Blunt**	N	Y	Y	Y	Y	Y	Y
8 **Emerson**	Y	Y	Y	Y	Y	Y	Y
9 **Luetkemeyer**	Y	Y	Y	Y	Y	Y	Y
MONTANA							
AL **Rehberg**	N	Y	Y	Y	Y	Y	Y
NEBRASKA							
1 **Fortenberry**	Y	Y	Y	Y	Y	Y	Y
2 **Terry**	Y	Y	Y	Y	Y	Y	Y
3 **Smith**	Y	Y	Y	Y	Y	Y	Y
NEVADA							
1 Berkley	Y	N	Y	?	N	Y	N
2 **Heller**	Y	Y	Y	Y	Y	Y	Y
3 Titus	Y	N	Y	N	N	Y	N
NEW HAMPSHIRE							
1 Shea-Porter	Y	N	Y	N	N	Y	N
2 Hodes	Y	N	Y	N	N	Y	N
NEW JERSEY							
1 Andrews	Y	N	Y	N	N	N	N
2 **LoBiondo**	Y	N	Y	N	N	Y	N
3 Adler	Y	N	Y	Y	Y	Y	Y
4 **Smith**	Y	N	Y	N	N	Y	N
5 **Garrett**	N	Y	Y	Y	N	?	Y
6 Pallone	Y	N	Y	N	?	N	N
7 **Lance**	Y	N	Y	Y	N	Y	N
8 Pascrell	Y	N	Y	N	N	N	N
9 Rothman	Y	N	Y	N	N	N	N
10 Payne	Y	N	Y	N	N	N	N
11 **Frelinghuysen**	Y	N	Y	Y	N	Y	N
12 Holt	Y	N	Y	N	N	N	N
13 Sires	Y	N	Y	Y	N	N	N
NEW MEXICO							
1 Heinrich	Y	N	Y	N	Y	Y	Y
2 Teague	Y	N	Y	N	N	N	N
3 Lujan	Y	N	Y	N	N	N	N
NEW YORK							
1 Bishop	Y	N	Y	N	N	Y	N
2 Israel	Y	N	Y	N	N	Y	N
3 **King**	Y	N	Y	Y	N	Y	N
4 McCarthy	Y	N	?	N	N	N	N
5 Ackerman	Y	N	Y	N	N	N	N
6 Meeks	Y	N	Y	N	N	N	N
7 Crowley	Y	?	Y	N	N	Y	N
8 Nadler	Y	N	Y	N	N	Y	N
9 Weiner	Y	N	Y	?	N	N	N
10 Towns	Y	N	Y	N	N	N	N
11 Clarke	Y	N	Y	N	N	N	N
12 Velázquez	Y	N	Y	N	N	N	N
13 McMahon	Y	N	Y	N	N	N	Y
14 Maloney	Y	N	Y	N	N	N	N
15 Rangel	Y	N	Y	N	N	N	?
16 Serrano	Y	N	Y	N	N	N	N
17 Engel	Y	N	Y	N	N	N	N
18 Lowey	Y	N	Y	N	N	N	N
19 Hall	Y	N	Y	N	N	N	N
20 Murphy	Y	Y	?	Y	Y	Y	Y
21 Tonko	Y	N	Y	N	N	N	N
22 Hinchey	Y	N	Y	N	N	N	N
23 **McHugh**	Y	N	Y	Y	N	Y	N
24 Arcuri	Y	N	Y	N	Y	Y	Y
25 Maffei	Y	N	Y	N	N	N	N
26 **Lee**	Y	Y	Y	Y	Y	Y	Y
27 Higgins	Y	N	Y	N	N	N	N
28 Slaughter	N	N	Y	N	N	N	N
29 Massa	Y	N	Y	N	N	Y	N
NORTH CAROLINA							
1 Butterfield	Y	N	Y	N	N	N	?
2 Etheridge	Y	N	Y	N	N	Y	N
3 **Jones**	N	Y	Y	Y	Y	Y	Y
4 Price	Y	N	Y	N	N	N	N

	363	364	365	366	367	368	369
5 **Foxx**	N	Y	Y	Y	Y	Y	Y
6 **Coble**	N	Y	Y	Y	Y	Y	Y
7 McIntyre	Y	N	Y	N	N	Y	N
8 Kissell	Y	N	Y	N	N	N	N
9 **Myrick**	N	Y	Y	Y	Y	Y	Y
10 **McHenry**	N	Y	Y	Y	Y	Y	Y
11 Shuler	Y	Y	Y	N	Y	N	Y
12 Watt	Y	N	Y	N	N	N	N
13 Miller	Y	N	Y	N	N	N	N
NORTH DAKOTA							
AL Pomeroy	Y	N	Y	N	N	Y	N
OHIO							
1 Driehaus	Y	N	Y	N	Y	Y	Y
2 **Schmidt**	?	?	?	?	?	?	?
3 **Turner**	Y	N	Y	Y	N	Y	N
4 **Jordan**	N	Y	Y	Y	Y	Y	Y
5 **Latta**	N	Y	Y	Y	Y	Y	Y
6 Wilson	Y	N	Y	N	N	Y	N
7 **Austria**	N	Y	Y	Y	Y	Y	Y
8 **Boehner**	N	Y	Y	Y	Y	Y	Y
9 Kaptur	Y	N	Y	N	N	Y	N
10 Kucinich	Y	N	Y	N	N	N	N
11 Fudge	Y	N	Y	N	N	N	N
12 **Tiberi**	N	Y	Y	Y	Y	Y	Y
13 Sutton	Y	N	Y	N	N	N	N
14 **LaTourette**	Y	N	Y	Y	N	Y	N
15 Kilroy	Y	N	Y	N	N	N	N
16 Boccieri	Y	N	Y	N	N	Y	N
17 Ryan	Y	N	Y	N	N	Y	N
18 Space	Y	N	Y	N	N	Y	N
OKLAHOMA							
1 **Sullivan**	?	?	?	?	?	?	?
2 Boren	Y	N	Y	Y	Y	Y	Y
3 **Lucas**	Y	Y	Y	Y	Y	Y	?
4 **Cole**	N	Y	Y	Y	Y	Y	Y
5 **Fallin**	Y	Y	Y	Y	Y	Y	Y
OREGON							
1 Wu	Y	N	Y	N	N	Y	N
2 **Walden**	Y	N	Y	Y	Y	Y	Y
3 Blumenauer	Y	N	Y	N	N	N	N
4 DeFazio	Y	N	Y	N	N	Y	N
5 Schrader	Y	N	Y	N	N	Y	N
PENNSYLVANIA							
1 Brady	Y	N	Y	N	N	N	N
2 Fattah	Y	N	Y	N	N	N	N
3 Dahlkemper	Y	Y	Y	N	N	Y	N
4 Altmire	Y	Y	Y	Y	Y	Y	Y
5 **Thompson**	N	Y	Y	Y	Y	Y	Y
6 **Gerlach**	Y	N	Y	Y	N	Y	Y
7 Sestak	Y	N	Y	N	N	N	N
8 Murphy, P.	Y	N	Y	N	N	Y	N
9 **Shuster**	Y	Y	?	Y	?	Y	Y
10 Carney	Y	N	Y	N	N	Y	N
11 Kanjorski	Y	N	Y	N	N	N	N
12 Murtha	Y	N	Y	N	N	N	N
13 Schwartz	Y	N	?	N	N	Y	N
14 Doyle	Y	N	Y	N	N	N	N
15 **Dent**	Y	N	Y	Y	N	Y	Y
16 **Pitts**	?	Y	Y	Y	Y	Y	Y
17 Holden	Y	N	Y	N	N	Y	N
18 **Murphy, T.**	Y	Y	Y	Y	Y	Y	Y
19 **Platts**	Y	N	Y	Y	N	Y	Y
RHODE ISLAND							
1 Kennedy	?	?	?	?	?	?	?
2 Langevin	Y	N	Y	N	N	N	N
SOUTH CAROLINA							
1 **Brown**	Y	Y	Y	Y	Y	Y	Y
2 **Wilson**	Y	Y	Y	Y	Y	Y	Y
3 **Barrett**	Y	Y	Y	Y	Y	Y	Y
4 **Inglis**	Y	Y	Y	Y	Y	Y	Y
5 Spratt	Y	N	Y	N	N	N	N
6 Clyburn	Y	N	Y	N	N	N	N
SOUTH DAKOTA							
AL Herseth Sandlin	Y	N	Y	Y	N	Y	N
TENNESSEE							
1 **Roe**	Y	Y	Y	Y	Y	Y	Y
2 **Duncan**	N	Y	Y	Y	Y	Y	Y
3 **Wamp**	Y	Y	Y	Y	Y	Y	Y
4 Davis	Y	N	Y	Y	N	Y	N
5 Cooper	Y	Y	Y	Y	Y	Y	Y
6 Gordon	Y	N	Y	N	N	N	N
7 **Blackburn**	N	Y	Y	Y	Y	Y	Y
8 Tanner	Y	N	Y	Y	N	Y	N
9 Cohen	Y	N	Y	N	N	N	N

	363	364	365	366	367	368	369
TEXAS							
1 **Gohmert**	N	Y	Y	Y	Y	Y	Y
2 **Poe**	N	Y	Y	Y	Y	Y	Y
3 **Johnson, S.**	N	Y	Y	Y	Y	Y	Y
4 **Hall**	N	Y	Y	Y	Y	Y	?
5 **Hensarling**	Y	Y	Y	Y	Y	Y	Y
6 **Barton**	Y	Y	Y	Y	Y	Y	Y
7 **Culberson**	Y	Y	Y	Y	Y	Y	Y
8 **Brady**	N	Y	Y	Y	Y	Y	Y
9 Green, A.	Y	N	Y	N	N	N	N
10 **McCaul**	Y	N	Y	Y	Y	Y	Y
11 **Conaway**	N	Y	Y	Y	Y	Y	Y
12 **Granger**	Y	Y	Y	Y	Y	Y	Y
13 **Thornberry**	N	Y	Y	Y	Y	Y	Y
14 **Paul**	N	Y	Y	Y	Y	Y	Y
15 Hinojosa	Y	?	Y	N	N	N	N
16 Reyes	Y	?	Y	N	N	N	N
17 Edwards	Y	N	Y	Y	N	Y	N
18 Jackson Lee	Y	N	Y	N	N	N	N
19 **Neugebauer**	Y	Y	Y	Y	Y	Y	?
20 Gonzalez	Y	N	Y	N	N	N	N
21 **Smith**	Y	Y	Y	Y	Y	Y	Y
22 **Olson**	N	Y	Y	Y	Y	Y	N
23 Rodriguez	Y	N	Y	N	N	Y	N
24 **Marchant**	N	Y	Y	Y	Y	Y	Y
25 Doggett	Y	N	Y	N	N	Y	N
26 **Burgess**	Y	Y	Y	Y	Y	Y	Y
27 Ortiz	Y	N	Y	N	N	N	N
28 Cuellar	Y	N	Y	N	N	N	N
29 Green, G.	Y	N	Y	N	N	N	N
30 Johnson, E.	Y	N	Y	N	N	N	N
31 **Carter**	N	Y	Y	Y	Y	Y	Y
32 **Sessions**	Y	Y	Y	Y	Y	Y	Y
UTAH							
1 **Bishop**	N	Y	Y	Y	Y	Y	Y
2 Matheson	Y	N	Y	Y	N	Y	Y
3 **Chaffetz**	Y	Y	Y	Y	Y	Y	Y
VERMONT							
AL Welch	Y	N	Y	N	N	N	N
VIRGINIA							
1 **Wittman**	Y	Y	Y	Y	Y	Y	+
2 Nye	Y	N	Y	Y	Y	Y	Y
3 Scott	Y	N	Y	N	N	N	N
4 **Forbes**	N	Y	Y	Y	Y	Y	Y
5 Perriello	Y	N	Y	Y	N	Y	N
6 **Goodlatte**	Y	Y	Y	Y	Y	Y	Y
7 **Cantor**	Y	Y	Y	Y	Y	Y	Y
8 Moran	Y	N	Y	N	N	Y	N
9 Boucher	Y	N	Y	N	N	N	N
10 **Wolf**	Y	Y	Y	Y	N	Y	Y
11 Connolly	Y	N	Y	N	N	N	N
WASHINGTON							
1 Inslee	Y	N	Y	N	N	Y	N
2 Larsen	Y	N	Y	N	N	N	N
3 Baird	Y	N	Y	Y	N	N	N
4 **Hastings**	N	Y	Y	Y	Y	Y	Y
5 **McMorris Rodgers**	N	Y	Y	Y	Y	Y	Y
6 Dicks	Y	N	Y	N	N	Y	N
7 McDermott	Y	N	Y	N	N	N	N
8 **Reichert**	Y	N	Y	Y	N	N	N
9 Smith	Y	N	Y	N	N	Y	Y
WEST VIRGINIA							
1 Mollohan	Y	N	Y	N	N	Y	N
2 **Capito**	Y	Y	Y	Y	Y	Y	N
3 Rahall	Y	N	Y	N	N	N	N
WISCONSIN							
1 **Ryan**	N	Y	Y	Y	Y	Y	Y
2 Baldwin	Y	N	Y	N	N	N	N
3 Kind	Y	N	Y	N	N	N	N
4 Moore	Y	N	Y	N	N	N	N
5 **Sensenbrenner**	N	Y	Y	Y	Y	Y	Y
6 **Petri**	Y	Y	Y	Y	Y	Y	Y
7 Obey	Y	N	Y	N	N	N	N
8 Kagen	Y	N	Y	N	N	N	N
WYOMING							
AL **Lummis**	N	Y	Y	Y	Y	Y	Y
DELEGATES							
Faleomavaega (A.S.)	Y	N	Y	N	N	N	N
Norton (D.C.)	Y	N	Y	N	N	N	N
Bordallo (Guam)	Y	N	Y	N	N	Y	N
Sablan (N. Marianas)	Y	N	Y	N	N	N	N
Pierluisi (P.R.)	Y	N	Y	N	N	N	N
Christensen (V.I.)	Y	N	Y	N	N	N	N

IN THE HOUSE | By Vote Number

370. **HR 2847. Fiscal 2010 Commerce-Justice-Science Appropriations/Appropriations Reduction.** Jordan, R-Ohio, amendment that would reduce funds appropriated in the bill by $12.5 billion. Rejected in Committee of the Whole 147-275: R 140-33; D 7-242. June 18, 2009.

371. **HR 2847. Fiscal 2010 Commerce-Justice-Science Appropriations/Office on Violence Against Women.** Reichert, R-Wash., amendment that would increase the amount provided for the Office on Violence Against Women by $2.5 million for a program supporting teens through education, offset by a reduction of the same amount for the Commerce Department's management salaries and expenses account. Adopted in Committee of the Whole 417-1: R 170-0; D 247-1. June 18, 2009.

372. **HR 2847. Fiscal 2010 Commerce-Justice-Science Appropriations/National Climate Service.** Broun, R-Ga., amendment that would bar the use of funds in the bill to establish or implement a National Climate Service, a partnership between federal agencies to collaborate with universities, agencies and organizations on climate issues. Rejected in Committee of the Whole 161-262: R 154-19; D 7-243. June 18, 2009.

373. **HR 2847. Fiscal 2010 Commerce-Justice-Science Appropriations/Grand Prairie Arts Initiative.** Hensarling, R-Texas, amendment that would bar the use of funds appropriated in the bill for the Art Center of the Grand Prairie in Stuttgart, Ark., for the Grand Prairie Arts Initiative. Rejected in Committee of the Whole 134-294: R 128-46; D 6-248. June 18, 2009.

374. **HR 2847. Fiscal 2010 Commerce-Justice-Science Appropriations/Maine Lobster Research.** Hensarling, R-Texas, amendment that would bar the use of funds appropriated in the bill for the Maine Department of Marine Resources in Augusta for Maine Lobster Research and the Inshore Trawling Survey. Rejected in Committee of the Whole 115-311: R 108-65; D 7-246. June 18, 2009.

375. **HR 2847. Fiscal 2010 Commerce-Justice-Science Appropriations/Future Forecasters Project.** Campbell, R-Calif., amendment that would bar the use of funds appropriated in the bill for the National Oceanic and Atmospheric Administration (NOAA) for San José State University's Training for the Next Generation of Weather Forecasters project. It would also reduce funding for NOAA by $180,000. Rejected in Committee of the Whole 123-303: R 117-57; D 6-246. June 18, 2009.

376. **HR 2847. Fiscal 2010 Commerce-Justice-Science Appropriations/Jamaica Export Center.** Campbell, R-Calif., amendment that would bar the use of funds appropriated in the bill for the Minority Business Development Agency for the Jamaica Export Center at the Jamaica Chamber of Commerce in Jamaica, N.Y. It would also reduce funding for the Minority Business Development Agency by $100,000. Rejected in Committee of the Whole 129-295: R 123-48; D 6-247. June 18, 2009.

	370	371	372	373	374	375	376
ALABAMA							
1 **Bonner**	Y	Y	Y	N	N	N	N
2 Bright	Y	Y	Y	N	?	Y	Y
3 **Rogers**	Y	Y	Y	N	N	N	N
4 **Aderholt**	Y	Y	Y	N	N	N	N
5 Griffith	N	Y	N	N	N	N	N
6 **Bachus**	Y	Y	Y	N	N	N	N
7 Davis	N	Y	N	N	N	N	N
ALASKA							
AL **Young**	N	Y	Y	N	N	N	Y
ARIZONA							
1 Kirkpatrick	Y	Y	N	N	N	N	N
2 **Franks**	Y	Y	Y	Y	Y	Y	Y
3 **Shadegg**	Y	Y	Y	Y	?	Y	Y
4 Pastor	N	Y	N	N	N	N	N
5 Mitchell	Y	Y	Y	Y	Y	N	N
6 **Flake**	Y	Y	Y	Y	Y	Y	Y
7 Grijalva	N	Y	N	N	N	N	N
8 Giffords	N	Y	N	N	N	N	N
ARKANSAS							
1 Berry	N	Y	N	N	N	N	N
2 Snyder	N	Y	N	N	N	N	N
3 **Boozman**	Y	Y	Y	N	Y	Y	Y
4 Ross	N	Y	N	N	N	N	N
CALIFORNIA							
1 Thompson	N	N	N	N	N	N	N
2 **Herger**	Y	Y	Y	Y	Y	Y	Y
3 **Lungren**	Y	Y	Y	Y	Y	Y	Y
4 **McClintock**	Y	Y	Y	Y	Y	Y	Y
5 Matsui	N	Y	N	N	N	N	N
6 Woolsey	N	Y	N	N	N	N	N
7 Miller, George	?	Y	N	N	N	N	N
8 Pelosi							
9 Lee	N	Y	N	N	N	N	N
10 Tauscher	?	?	?	?	?	?	?
11 McNerney	N	Y	N	N	N	N	N
12 Speier	N	Y	N	N	N	N	N
13 Stark	N	Y	N	N	?	N	Y
14 Eshoo	N	Y	N	N	N	N	N
15 Honda	N	Y	N	N	N	N	N
16 Lofgren	N	Y	N	N	N	N	N
17 Farr	N	Y	?	N	N	N	N
18 Cardoza	N	Y	N	N	N	N	N
19 **Radanovich**	Y	Y	Y	Y	Y	Y	Y
20 Costa	N	Y	N	N	N	N	N
21 **Nunes**	Y	Y	Y	Y	Y	Y	Y
22 **McCarthy**	Y	Y	Y	Y	Y	Y	Y
23 Capps	N	Y	N	N	N	N	N
24 **Gallegly**	Y	Y	Y	Y	Y	Y	Y
25 **McKeon**	Y	Y	Y	N	N	N	N
26 **Dreier**	N	Y	Y	N	N	N	N
27 Sherman	N	Y	N	N	N	N	N
28 Berman	N	?	N	N	N	N	N
29 Schiff	N	Y	N	N	N	N	N
30 Waxman	N	Y	?	N	N	N	N
31 Becerra	N	Y	N	N	N	N	N
32 Vacant							
33 Watson	N	?	N	N	N	N	N
34 Roybal-Allard	N	Y	N	N	N	N	N
35 Waters	N	Y	N	N	N	N	N
36 Harman	?	?	?	?	?	?	?
37 Richardson	N	Y	N	N	N	N	N
38 Napolitano	N	Y	N	N	N	N	N
39 Sánchez, Linda	?	?	?	N	N	N	N
40 **Royce**	Y	Y	Y	Y	Y	Y	Y
41 **Lewis**	Y	Y	Y	N	N	N	N
42 **Miller, Gary**	Y	Y	Y	N	N	N	N
43 Baca	N	Y	N	N	N	N	N
44 **Calvert**	Y	Y	Y	Y	N	N	Y
45 **Bono Mack**	Y	Y	Y	Y	Y	Y	Y
46 **Rohrabacher**	Y	?	Y	Y	N	Y	Y
47 Sanchez, Loretta	N	Y	N	N	N	N	N
48 **Campbell**	Y	Y	Y	Y	Y	Y	Y
49 **Issa**	Y	Y	Y	Y	Y	Y	Y
50 **Bilbray**	Y	Y	Y	Y	Y	N	Y
51 Filner	N	Y	N	N	N	N	N
52 **Hunter**	Y	Y	Y	Y	N	Y	Y
53 Davis	N	Y	N	N	N	N	N

	370	371	372	373	374	375	376
COLORADO							
1 DeGette	N	Y	N	N	N	N	N
2 Polis	N	Y	N	N	N	N	N
3 Salazar	N	Y	N	N	N	N	N
4 Markey	N	Y	N	N	N	N	N
5 **Lamborn**	Y	Y	Y	Y	Y	Y	Y
6 **Coffman**	Y	Y	Y	Y	Y	Y	Y
7 Perlmutter	N	Y	N	N	N	N	N
CONNECTICUT							
1 Larson	N	Y	N	N	N	N	N
2 Courtney	N	Y	N	N	N	N	N
3 DeLauro	N	Y	N	N	N	N	N
4 Himes	N	Y	N	N	N	N	N
5 Murphy	N	Y	?	N	N	N	N
DELAWARE							
AL **Castle**	N	Y	N	Y	Y	Y	Y
FLORIDA							
1 **Miller**	Y	Y	Y	Y	Y	Y	Y
2 Boyd	N	Y	N	N	N	N	N
3 Brown	N	Y	N	N	N	N	N
4 **Crenshaw**	Y	Y	Y	N	N	N	N
5 **Brown-Waite**	Y	Y	Y	Y	N	N	Y
6 **Stearns**	Y	Y	Y	Y	Y	Y	Y
7 **Mica**	Y	Y	Y	Y	Y	Y	Y
8 Grayson	N	Y	N	N	N	N	N
9 **Bilirakis**	N	Y	Y	Y	Y	Y	Y
10 **Young**	N	Y	Y	N	N	N	Y
11 Castor	N	Y	N	N	N	N	N
12 **Putnam**	Y	Y	Y	N	N	N	Y
13 **Buchanan**	Y	Y	N	Y	N	N	N
14 **Mack**	Y	Y	Y	Y	Y	Y	Y
15 **Posey**	N	Y	Y	Y	Y	Y	Y
16 **Rooney**	Y	Y	Y	Y	Y	Y	Y
17 Meek	N	Y	N	N	N	N	N
18 **Ros-Lehtinen**	Y	Y	N	N	N	N	N
19 Wexler	N	Y	N	N	N	N	N
20 Wasserman Schultz	N	Y	N	N	N	N	N
21 **Diaz-Balart, L.**	Y	Y	N	N	N	N	N
22 Klein	N	Y	N	N	N	N	N
23 Hastings	N	Y	N	N	N	N	N
24 Kosmas	N	Y	N	N	N	N	N
25 **Diaz-Balart, M.**	Y	Y	N	N	N	N	N
GEORGIA							
1 **Kingston**	Y	Y	Y	Y	Y	Y	Y
2 Bishop	N	Y	N	N	N	N	N
3 **Westmoreland**	Y	Y	Y	Y	Y	Y	Y
4 Johnson	N	Y	N	N	N	N	N
5 Lewis	?	?	?	?	?	?	?
6 **Price**	Y	Y	Y	Y	Y	Y	Y
7 **Linder**	Y	Y	Y	Y	Y	Y	Y
8 Marshall	N	Y	N	Y	N	N	N
9 **Deal**	Y	?	?	?	?	?	?
10 **Broun**	Y	Y	Y	Y	Y	Y	Y
11 **Gingrey**	Y	Y	Y	Y	Y	Y	Y
12 Barrow	N	Y	N	N	N	N	N
13 Scott	N	Y	N	N	N	N	N
HAWAII							
1 Abercrombie	N	Y	N	N	N	N	N
2 Hirono	N	Y	N	N	N	N	N
IDAHO							
1 Minnick	Y	Y	Y	Y	Y	Y	Y
2 **Simpson**	N	Y	Y	N	N	N	N
ILLINOIS							
1 Rush	N	Y	N	N	N	N	N
2 Jackson	N	Y	N	N	N	N	N
3 Lipinski	N	Y	N	N	N	N	N
4 Gutierrez	N	Y	N	N	N	N	N
5 Quigley	N	Y	N	N	N	N	N
6 **Roskam**	Y	Y	Y	Y	Y	Y	Y
7 Davis	N	Y	N	N	N	N	N
8 Bean	N	Y	N	Y	?	N	N
9 Schakowsky	N	Y	N	N	N	N	N
10 **Kirk**	?	Y	N	Y	Y	Y	Y
11 Halvorson	N	Y	N	N	N	N	N
12 Costello	N	Y	N	N	N	N	N
13 **Biggert**	N	Y	N	Y	N	N	Y
14 Foster	N	Y	N	Y	N	Y	N
15 **Johnson**	Y	Y	Y	Y	Y	N	Y

KEY **Republicans** Democrats

	370	371	372	373	374	375	376
16 **Manzullo**	Y	Y	Y	Y	N	Y	Y
17 Hare	N	Y	N	N	N	N	N
18 **Schock**	N	Y	Y	Y	N	N	N
19 **Shimkus**	Y	Y	Y	Y	Y	Y	Y
INDIANA							
1 Visclosky	N	Y	N	N	N	N	N
2 Donnelly	N	Y	N	N	N	N	N
3 **Souder**	Y	Y	Y	Y	N	Y	Y
4 **Buyer**	Y	Y	Y	Y	Y	Y	?
5 **Burton**	Y	Y	Y	Y	Y	Y	Y
6 **Pence**	Y	Y	Y	Y	Y	Y	Y
7 Carson	N	Y	N	N	N	N	N
8 Ellsworth	N	Y	N	N	N	N	N
9 Hill	N	Y	N	N	N	N	N
IOWA							
1 Braley	N	Y	N	N	N	N	N
2 Loebsack	N	Y	N	N	N	N	N
3 Boswell	N	Y	N	N	N	N	N
4 **Latham**	N	Y	Y	N	N	N	N
5 **King**	Y	Y	Y	Y	Y	Y	Y
KANSAS							
1 **Moran**	Y	Y	Y	Y	Y	Y	Y
2 **Jenkins**	Y	Y	Y	Y	Y	Y	Y
3 Moore	N	Y	N	N	N	N	N
4 **Tiahrt**	Y	Y	Y	Y	Y	Y	Y
KENTUCKY							
1 **Whitfield**	N	Y	Y	N	N	N	Y
2 **Guthrie**	Y	Y	Y	N	N	N	N
3 Yarmuth	N	Y	N	N	N	N	N
4 **Davis**	Y	Y	Y	Y	N	Y	Y
5 **Rogers**	N	Y	Y	N	N	N	?
6 Chandler	N	Y	N	N	N	N	N
LOUISIANA							
1 **Scalise**	Y	Y	Y	Y	Y	Y	Y
2 **Cao**	N	Y	N	N	N	N	N
3 Melancon	N	Y	N	N	N	N	N
4 **Fleming**	Y	Y	Y	Y	Y	Y	Y
5 **Alexander**	Y	Y	Y	N	N	N	Y
6 **Cassidy**	Y	Y	N	Y	Y	Y	Y
7 **Boustany**	Y	Y	Y	Y	Y	Y	Y
MAINE							
1 Pingree	N	Y	N	N	N	N	N
2 Michaud	N	Y	N	N	N	N	N
MARYLAND							
1 Kratovil	N	Y	N	N	N	N	N
2 Ruppersberger	N	Y	N	N	N	N	N
3 Sarbanes	N	Y	N	N	N	N	N
4 Edwards	N	Y	N	N	N	N	N
5 Hoyer	N	Y	N	N	N	N	N
6 **Bartlett**	Y	Y	Y	Y	N	Y	N
7 Cummings	N	Y	N	N	N	N	N
8 Van Hollen	N	Y	N	N	N	N	N
MASSACHUSETTS							
1 Olver	N	Y	N	N	N	N	N
2 Neal	N	Y	N	N	N	N	N
3 McGovern	N	Y	N	N	N	N	?
4 Frank	N	Y	N	N	N	N	N
5 Tsongas	N	Y	N	N	N	N	N
6 Tierney	?	Y	N	N	N	N	N
7 Markey	N	Y	N	N	N	N	N
8 Capuano	N	Y	N	N	N	N	N
9 Lynch	N	Y	N	N	N	N	N
10 Delahunt	N	Y	N	N	N	N	?
MICHIGAN							
1 Stupak	N	Y	N	N	N	N	N
2 **Hoekstra**	Y	Y	Y	Y	Y	Y	Y
3 **Ehlers**	N	Y	N	Y	N	Y	Y
4 **Camp**	N	Y	Y	Y	N	Y	Y
5 Kildee	N	Y	N	N	N	N	N
6 **Upton**	N	Y	Y	Y	N	Y	Y
7 Schauer	N	Y	N	Y	Y	Y	Y
8 **Rogers**	Y	Y	Y	Y	N	Y	Y
9 Peters	N	Y	N	N	N	N	N
10 **Miller**	N	Y	Y	Y	Y	N	Y
11 **McCotter**	Y	Y	Y	Y	Y	Y	Y
12 Levin	N	Y	N	N	N	N	N
13 Kilpatrick	N	Y	N	?	N	N	N
14 Conyers	N	?	?	N	N	N	N
15 Dingell	N	Y	N	N	N	N	N
MINNESOTA							
1 Walz	N	Y	N	N	N	N	N
2 **Kline**	Y	Y	Y	Y	Y	Y	Y
3 **Paulsen**	Y	Y	Y	Y	Y	Y	Y
4 McCollum	N	Y	N	N	N	?	N

	370	371	372	373	374	375	376
5 Ellison	?	?	?	?	?	?	?
6 **Bachmann**	?	?	?	?	?	?	?
7 Peterson	N	Y	N	N	N	N	N
8 Oberstar	N	Y	N	N	N	N	N
MISSISSIPPI							
1 Childers	Y	Y	Y	N	N	N	N
2 Thompson	N	Y	N	N	N	N	N
3 **Harper**	Y	Y	Y	Y	Y	Y	Y
4 Taylor	Y	Y	Y	N	N	N	N
MISSOURI							
1 Clay	N	Y	N	N	N	N	N
2 **Akin**	Y	Y	Y	Y	Y	Y	Y
3 Carnahan	N	Y	N	N	N	N	N
4 Skelton	N	Y	N	N	N	N	N
5 Cleaver	N	Y	N	N	N	N	N
6 **Graves**	Y	Y	Y	Y	Y	Y	Y
7 **Blunt**	Y	Y	Y	Y	Y	Y	N
8 **Emerson**	Y	Y	Y	N	N	N	N
9 **Luetkemeyer**	Y	Y	Y	Y	Y	Y	Y
MONTANA							
AL **Rehberg**	Y	Y	Y	N	N	N	Y
NEBRASKA							
1 **Fortenberry**	Y	Y	N	Y	N	N	Y
2 **Terry**	Y	Y	Y	Y	Y	Y	Y
3 **Smith**	Y	Y	Y	Y	Y	Y	N
NEVADA							
1 Berkley	N	Y	N	N	N	N	N
2 **Heller**	Y	Y	Y	Y	Y	Y	Y
3 Titus	N	Y	N	N	N	N	N
NEW HAMPSHIRE							
1 Shea-Porter	N	Y	N	N	N	N	N
2 Hodes	N	Y	N	N	N	N	N
NEW JERSEY							
1 Andrews	N	Y	N	N	N	N	N
2 **LoBiondo**	N	Y	N	N	N	N	N
3 Adler	N	Y	N	N	N	N	N
4 **Smith**	N	Y	N	N	N	N	N
5 **Garrett**	Y	Y	Y	Y	Y	Y	Y
6 Pallone	N	Y	N	N	N	N	N
7 **Lance**	N	Y	N	Y	N	Y	Y
8 Pascrell	N	Y	N	N	N	N	N
9 Rothman	N	Y	N	N	N	N	N
10 Payne	N	Y	N	N	N	N	N
11 **Frelinghuysen**	N	Y	Y	N	N	N	N
12 Holt	N	Y	N	N	N	N	N
13 Sires	N	Y	N	N	N	N	N
NEW MEXICO							
1 Heinrich	N	Y	N	N	N	N	N
2 Teague	N	Y	N	N	N	N	N
3 Lujan	N	Y	N	N	N	N	N
NEW YORK							
1 Bishop	N	Y	N	N	N	N	N
2 Israel	N	Y	N	N	N	N	N
3 **King**	N	Y	Y	N	N	N	N
4 McCarthy	N	Y	N	N	N	N	N
5 Ackerman	N	?	N	N	N	?	N
6 Meeks	N	Y	N	N	N	N	N
7 Crowley	N	Y	N	N	N	N	N
8 Nadler	N	Y	N	N	N	N	N
9 Weiner	N	Y	N	N	N	N	N
10 Towns	N	Y	N	N	N	N	N
11 Clarke	N	Y	N	N	N	N	N
12 Velázquez	N	Y	N	N	N	N	N
13 McMahon	N	Y	N	N	N	N	N
14 Maloney	N	Y	N	N	N	N	N
15 Rangel	N	Y	N	N	N	N	N
16 Serrano	N	Y	N	N	N	N	N
17 Engel	N	Y	N	N	N	N	N
18 Lowey	N	Y	N	N	N	N	N
19 Hall	N	Y	N	N	N	N	N
20 Murphy	N	?	N	N	N	N	N
21 Tonko	N	Y	N	N	N	N	N
22 Hinchey	N	Y	N	N	N	N	N
23 **McHugh**	N	Y	N	N	N	N	N
24 Arcuri	N	Y	N	N	N	N	N
25 Maffei	N	Y	N	N	N	N	N
26 **Lee**	Y	Y	Y	Y	N	Y	N
27 Higgins	N	Y	N	N	N	N	N
28 Slaughter	N	+	N	N	N	N	N
29 Massa	N	Y	?	Y	Y	Y	Y
NORTH CAROLINA							
1 Butterfield	N	Y	N	N	N	N	N
2 Etheridge	N	Y	N	N	N	N	N
3 **Jones**	Y	Y	Y	N	N	Y	N
4 Price	N	Y	N	N	N	N	N

	370	371	372	373	374	375	376
5 **Foxx**	Y	Y	Y	Y	Y	Y	Y
6 **Coble**	Y	Y	Y	Y	Y	Y	Y
7 McIntyre	N	Y	N	N	N	N	N
8 Kissell	N	Y	N	N	N	N	N
9 **Myrick**	Y	Y	Y	Y	Y	Y	Y
10 **McHenry**	Y	Y	Y	Y	Y	Y	Y
11 Shuler	N	Y	N	N	N	N	N
12 Watt	?	Y	N	N	N	N	N
13 Miller	N	Y	N	N	N	N	N
NORTH DAKOTA							
AL Pomeroy	N	Y	N	N	N	N	N
OHIO							
1 Driehaus	N	Y	N	N	N	N	N
2 **Schmidt**	?	?	?	?	?	?	?
3 **Turner**	N	Y	Y	N	N	N	N
4 **Jordan**	Y	Y	Y	Y	Y	Y	Y
5 **Latta**	Y	Y	Y	Y	Y	Y	Y
6 Wilson	N	Y	N	N	N	N	N
7 **Austria**	Y	Y	Y	Y	Y	Y	Y
8 **Boehner**	Y	Y	Y	Y	Y	Y	Y
9 Kaptur	N	Y	N	N	N	N	N
10 Kucinich	N	Y	N	N	N	N	N
11 Fudge	N	Y	N	N	N	N	N
12 **Tiberi**	Y	Y	Y	Y	Y	Y	Y
13 Sutton	N	Y	N	N	N	N	N
14 **LaTourette**	N	Y	Y	N	N	N	N
15 Kilroy	N	Y	N	N	N	N	N
16 Boccieri	N	Y	N	N	N	N	N
17 Ryan	N	Y	N	N	N	N	N
18 Space	N	Y	N	N	N	N	N
OKLAHOMA							
1 **Sullivan**	?	?	?	?	?	?	?
2 Boren	N	Y	Y	N	N	N	N
3 **Lucas**	Y	Y	Y	N	N	N	N
4 **Cole**	Y	?	?	N	N	N	N
5 **Fallin**	Y	Y	Y	Y	Y	Y	Y
OREGON							
1 Wu	N	Y	N	N	N	N	N
2 **Walden**	N	Y	Y	Y	N	N	Y
3 Blumenauer	N	Y	N	N	N	N	N
4 DeFazio	N	Y	N	N	N	N	N
5 Schrader	N	Y	N	N	N	N	N
PENNSYLVANIA							
1 Brady	N	Y	N	N	N	N	N
2 Fattah	N	Y	N	N	N	N	N
3 Dahlkemper	N	Y	N	N	N	N	N
4 Altmire	N	Y	N	N	N	N	N
5 **Thompson**	Y	Y	Y	N	N	N	N
6 **Gerlach**	N	Y	Y	N	N	N	N
7 Sestak	N	Y	N	N	N	N	N
8 Murphy, P.	N	Y	N	N	N	N	N
9 **Shuster**	Y	?	Y	Y	N	N	N
10 Carney	N	Y	N	N	N	N	N
11 Kanjorski	N	Y	N	N	N	N	N
12 Murtha	N	Y	N	N	N	N	N
13 Schwartz	N	Y	N	N	N	N	N
14 Doyle	N	Y	N	N	N	N	N
15 **Dent**	N	Y	Y	N	Y	Y	N
16 **Pitts**	Y	Y	Y	Y	Y	Y	?
17 Holden	N	Y	N	N	N	N	N
18 **Murphy, T.**	N	?	N	N	N	N	N
19 **Platts**	N	Y	Y	N	Y	Y	N
RHODE ISLAND							
1 Kennedy	?	?	?	?	?	?	?
2 Langevin	N	Y	N	N	N	N	N
SOUTH CAROLINA							
1 **Brown**	Y	Y	Y	N	N	N	N
2 **Wilson**	Y	Y	Y	Y	Y	Y	Y
3 **Barrett**	Y	Y	Y	Y	Y	Y	Y
4 **Inglis**	Y	Y	N	Y	Y	Y	Y
5 Spratt	N	Y	N	N	N	N	?
6 Clyburn	N	Y	N	N	N	N	N
SOUTH DAKOTA							
AL Herseth Sandlin	N	Y	N	N	N	N	N
TENNESSEE							
1 **Roe**	Y	Y	Y	Y	Y	Y	Y
2 **Duncan**	Y	Y	Y	Y	Y	Y	Y
3 **Wamp**	Y	Y	N	Y	Y	Y	Y
4 Davis	N	Y	N	N	N	N	N
5 Cooper	N	Y	N	Y	Y	Y	Y
6 Gordon	N	Y	N	N	N	N	N
7 **Blackburn**	Y	Y	Y	Y	Y	Y	Y
8 Tanner	N	Y	N	N	N	N	N
9 Cohen	N	Y	N	N	N	N	N

	370	371	372	373	374	375	376
TEXAS							
1 **Gohmert**	Y	Y	Y	Y	Y	Y	Y
2 **Poe**	Y	Y	Y	Y	Y	N	Y
3 **Johnson, S.**	Y	Y	Y	Y	Y	Y	Y
4 **Hall**	Y	Y	Y	Y	Y	Y	Y
5 **Hensarling**	Y	Y	Y	Y	Y	Y	Y
6 **Barton**	Y	Y	Y	Y	Y	Y	N
7 **Culberson**	Y	Y	Y	Y	Y	N	N
8 **Brady**	Y	Y	Y	Y	Y	Y	Y
9 Green, A.	N	Y	N	N	N	N	N
10 **McCaul**	Y	Y	Y	Y	Y	Y	Y
11 **Conaway**	Y	Y	Y	Y	Y	Y	Y
12 **Granger**	Y	Y	Y	N	N	N	N
13 **Thornberry**	Y	Y	Y	Y	Y	Y	Y
14 **Paul**	Y	Y	Y	N	N	Y	Y
15 Hinojosa	N	Y	N	N	N	N	N
16 Reyes	N	Y	N	N	N	N	N
17 Edwards	N	Y	N	N	N	N	N
18 Jackson Lee	N	Y	N	N	N	N	N
19 **Neugebauer**	Y	Y	Y	Y	Y	Y	Y
20 Gonzalez	N	Y	N	N	N	N	N
21 **Smith**	+	Y	Y	N	N	N	N
22 **Olson**	N	Y	Y	Y	Y	Y	Y
23 Rodriguez	N	Y	N	N	N	N	N
24 **Marchant**	Y	Y	Y	Y	Y	Y	Y
25 Doggett	N	Y	N	N	N	N	N
26 **Burgess**	Y	Y	Y	Y	Y	Y	Y
27 Ortiz	N	Y	N	N	N	N	N
28 Cuellar	N	Y	N	N	N	N	N
29 Green, G.	N	Y	N	–	N	N	N
30 Johnson, E.	N	Y	N	N	N	N	N
31 **Carter**	Y	Y	Y	Y	Y	N	N
32 **Sessions**	Y	Y	Y	Y	Y	Y	Y
UTAH							
1 **Bishop**	Y	Y	Y	Y	Y	Y	Y
2 Matheson	N	Y	N	N	N	N	N
3 **Chaffetz**	Y	Y	Y	Y	Y	Y	Y
VERMONT							
AL Welch	N	Y	N	N	?	N	N
VIRGINIA							
1 **Wittman**	Y	Y	Y	Y	N	Y	Y
2 Nye	Y	Y	N	N	N	N	N
3 Scott	N	Y	N	N	N	N	N
4 **Forbes**	Y	Y	Y	Y	Y	N	Y
5 Perriello	N	Y	N	N	N	N	N
6 **Goodlatte**	Y	Y	Y	Y	Y	Y	Y
7 **Cantor**	Y	Y	Y	Y	Y	Y	Y
8 Moran	N	Y	N	N	N	N	N
9 Boucher	N	Y	N	N	N	N	N
10 **Wolf**	N	Y	Y	N	Y	N	N
11 Connolly	N	Y	N	N	N	N	N
WASHINGTON							
1 Inslee	N	Y	N	N	N	N	N
2 Larsen	N	Y	N	N	N	N	N
3 Baird	N	N	N	N	N	N	N
4 **Hastings**	Y	Y	Y	N	N	N	N
5 **McMorris Rodgers**	Y	Y	Y	Y	Y	Y	Y
6 Dicks	N	Y	N	N	N	N	N
7 McDermott	?	Y	N	N	N	N	N
8 **Reichert**	N	Y	N	N	N	N	N
9 Smith	N	Y	N	N	N	N	N
WEST VIRGINIA							
1 Mollohan	N	Y	N	N	N	N	N
2 **Capito**	Y	Y	Y	N	N	N	N
3 Rahall	N	Y	N	N	N	N	N
WISCONSIN							
1 **Ryan**	Y	Y	Y	Y	Y	Y	Y
2 Baldwin	N	Y	N	N	N	N	N
3 Kind	N	Y	N	N	N	N	N
4 Moore	N	Y	N	N	N	N	N
5 **Sensenbrenner**	Y	Y	Y	Y	Y	Y	Y
6 **Petri**	Y	Y	N	Y	Y	Y	Y
7 Obey	N	Y	N	N	N	N	N
8 Kagen	N	Y	N	N	N	N	N
WYOMING							
AL **Lummis**	Y	Y	Y	Y	Y	Y	Y
DELEGATES							
Faleomavaega (A.S.)	?	Y	N	N	N	N	N
Norton (D.C.)	N	?	N	N	N	N	N
Bordallo (Guam)	N	Y	N	N	N	N	N
Sablan (N. Marianas)	?	Y	N	N	N	?	N
Pierluisi (P.R.)	N	Y	N	N	N	N	N
Christensen (V.I.)	N	Y	N	N	N	N	N

IN THE HOUSE | By Vote Number

377. **HR 2847. Fiscal 2010 Commerce-Justice-Science Appropriations/Summer Flounder and Black Sea Initiative.** Campbell, R-Calif., amendment that would bar the use of funds appropriated in the bill for the National Oceanic and Atmospheric Administration (NOAA) for the Summer Flounder and Black Sea Initiative of the Partnership for Mid-Atlantic Fisheries in Point Pleasant Beach, N.J. It would also reduce funding for NOAA by $600,000. Rejected in Committee of the Whole 102-317: R 95-76; D 7-241. June 18, 2009.

378. **HR 2847. Fiscal 2010 Commerce-Justice-Science Appropriations/National Drug Intelligence Center.** Flake, R-Ariz., amendment that would bar the use of funds appropriated in the bill for operations of the National Drug Intelligence Center. It would also reduce funding for the Justice Department's general administration account by $44 million. Rejected in Committee of the Whole 130-295: R 124-50; D 6-245. June 18, 2009.

379. **HR 2847. Fiscal 2010 Commerce-Justice-Science Appropriations/Innovative Science Learning Center.** Flake, R-Ariz., amendment that would bar the use of funds appropriated in the bill for the Innovative Science Learning Center at ScienceSouth in Florence, S.C. It would reduce funding for NASA by $500,000. Rejected in Committee of the Whole 107-320: R 104-68; D 3-252. June 18, 2009.

380. **HR 2847. Fiscal 2010 Commerce-Justice-Science Appropriations/Environmental Science Initiative.** Flake, R-Ariz., amendment that would bar the use of funds appropriated in the bill for the Environmental Science Initiative at Drew University in Madison, N.J. It would reduce funding for NASA by $1 million. Rejected in Committee of the Whole 100-318: R 92-80; D 8-238. June 18, 2009.

381. **HR 2847. Fiscal 2010 Commerce-Justice-Science Appropriations/JASON Project.** Flake, R-Ariz., amendment that would bar the use of funds appropriated in the bill for the Science Education Through Exploration project of the JASON Project in Ashburn, Va. It also would reduce funding for the National Oceanic and Atmospheric Administration by $4 million. Rejected in Committee of the Whole 119-306: R 115-59; D 4-247. June 18, 2009.

382. **HR 2847. Fiscal 2010 Commerce-Justice-Science Appropriations/Institute for Seafood Studies.** Flake, R-Ariz., amendment that would bar the use of funds appropriated in the bill for the Institute of Seafood Studies at Nicholls State University in Thibodaux, La. It would also reduce funding for the National Oceanic and Atmospheric Administration by $325,000. Rejected in Committee of the Whole 124-303: R 116-59; D 8-244. June 18, 2009.

383. **HR 2847. Fiscal 2010 Commerce-Justice-Science Appropriations/Revote on Office of the Census and Commerce Department Relocation.** Revote on Burton, R-Ind., amendment (vote 368). Under House rules, any member (in this case Westmoreland, R-Ga.) may demand a revote in the full House on an amendment adopted in the Committee of the Whole. Delegates may not vote in the full House. Adopted 251-168: R 173-0; D 78-168. June 18, 2009.

	377	378	379	380	381	382	383
ALABAMA							
1 Bonner	N	N	N	N	N	N	Y
2 Bright	N	N	N	Y	N	N	Y
3 Rogers	N	N	N	N	N	N	Y
4 Aderholt	N	N	N	N	N	N	Y
5 Griffith	N	N	N	N	N	N	Y
6 Bachus	?	N	N	N	N	N	Y
7 Davis	N	N	N	N	N	N	?
ALASKA							
AL Young	N	N	Y	N	N	N	Y
ARIZONA							
1 Kirkpatrick	N	N	N	N	N	N	Y
2 Franks	Y	Y	Y	Y	Y	Y	Y
3 Shadegg	Y	Y	Y	Y	Y	Y	Y
4 Pastor	N	N	N	N	N	N	Y
5 Mitchell	Y	Y	N	N	Y	Y	Y
6 Flake	Y	Y	Y	Y	Y	Y	Y
7 Grijalva	N	N	N	Y	N	N	N
8 Giffords	N	N	N	N	N	N	N
ARKANSAS							
1 Berry	N	N	N	N	N	N	Y
2 Snyder	N	N	N	N	N	N	Y
3 Boozman	N	Y	Y	N	Y	Y	Y
4 Ross	N	N	N	N	N	N	Y
CALIFORNIA							
1 Thompson	?	N	N	N	N	N	N
2 Herger	?	Y	Y	Y	Y	Y	Y
3 Lungren	N	Y	Y	Y	Y	Y	Y
4 McClintock	Y	Y	Y	Y	Y	Y	Y
5 Matsui	N	N	N	N	N	N	N
6 Woolsey	N	N	N	N	N	N	N
7 Miller, George	N	N	N	N	N	N	N
8 Pelosi							
9 Lee	N	N	N	N	N	N	N
10 Tauscher	?	?	?	?	?	?	?
11 McNerney	?	N	N	N	N	N	N
12 Speier	Y	N	N	Y	Y	N	N
13 Stark	N	N	N	N	N	N	N
14 Eshoo	N	N	N	N	N	N	N
15 Honda	N	N	N	N	N	N	N
16 Lofgren	N	N	N	N	N	N	N
17 Farr	N	N	N	N	N	N	N
18 Cardoza	N	N	N	?	N	N	N
19 Radanovich	Y	Y	?	Y	Y	Y	Y
20 Costa	N	N	N	N	N	N	N
21 Nunes	Y	Y	Y	Y	Y	Y	Y
22 McCarthy	Y	Y	Y	Y	Y	Y	Y
23 Capps	N	N	N	N	N	N	N
24 Gallegly	Y	Y	N	N	Y	Y	N
25 McKeon	N	Y	N	N	Y	N	Y
26 Dreier	N	Y	N	N	N	N	Y
27 Sherman	N	N	N	N	N	N	N
28 Berman	N	N	N	N	N	N	N
29 Schiff	N	N	N	N	N	N	N
30 Waxman	N	N	N	?	N	N	N
31 Becerra	N	N	N	N	N	N	N
32 Vacant							
33 Watson	N	N	N	N	N	N	N
34 Roybal-Allard	N	N	N	N	N	N	N
35 Waters	N	N	N	N	N	N	N
36 Harman	?	?	?	?	?	?	?
37 Richardson	N	N	N	N	N	N	N
38 Napolitano	N	N	N	N	N	N	N
39 Sánchez, Linda	N	N	N	N	N	N	N
40 Royce	Y	Y	Y	N	Y	Y	Y
41 Lewis	N	N	N	N	N	N	Y
42 Miller, Gary	N	N	N	N	N	N	Y
43 Baca	N	N	N	N	N	N	N
44 Calvert	N	Y	N	N	N	N	Y
45 Bono Mack	N	Y	Y	Y	Y	Y	Y
46 Rohrabacher	Y	Y	Y	Y	Y	Y	Y
47 Sanchez, Loretta	?	N	N	N	N	N	N
48 Campbell	Y	Y	Y	Y	Y	Y	Y
49 Issa	Y	Y	Y	Y	Y	Y	Y
50 Bilbray	Y	N	Y	Y	Y	Y	Y
51 Filner	N	N	N	N	N	N	N
52 Hunter	N	Y	Y	Y	N	N	Y
53 Davis	N	N	N	N	N	N	N
COLORADO							
1 DeGette	N	?	N	N	N	N	N
2 Polis	N	N	N	N	N	N	N
3 Salazar	N	N	N	N	N	N	N
4 Markey	N	N	N	N	N	N	N
5 Lamborn	Y	Y	Y	Y	Y	Y	Y
6 Coffman	Y	Y	Y	Y	Y	Y	Y
7 Perlmutter	N	N	N	N	N	N	N
CONNECTICUT							
1 Larson	–	–	–	?	N	N	N
2 Courtney	N	N	N	N	N	?	?
3 DeLauro	N	N	N	N	N	Y	N
4 Himes	N	N	N	N	N	N	Y
5 Murphy	N	N	N	N	N	N	Y
DELAWARE							
AL Castle	N	Y	Y	N	Y	Y	Y
FLORIDA							
1 Miller	Y	Y	Y	Y	Y	Y	Y
2 Boyd	N	N	N	N	N	N	Y
3 Brown	N	N	N	N	N	N	N
4 Crenshaw	N	N	N	N	N	N	N
5 Brown-Waite	N	Y	Y	N	Y	N	Y
6 Stearns	Y	Y	+	Y	Y	Y	Y
7 Mica	N	Y	Y	N	Y	Y	Y
8 Grayson	N	N	N	N	N	N	N
9 Bilirakis	Y	Y	Y	N	Y	N	Y
10 Young	N	N	N	N	N	N	N
11 Castor	N	N	N	N	N	N	N
12 Putnam	N	Y	Y	N	N	N	Y
13 Buchanan	N	Y	N	Y	Y	Y	Y
14 Mack	Y	Y	Y	Y	Y	Y	Y
15 Posey	Y	Y	Y	Y	Y	Y	Y
16 Rooney	N	Y	N	Y	Y	Y	Y
17 Meek	N	N	N	N	N	N	N
18 Ros-Lehtinen	N	N	N	N	N	N	N
19 Wexler	N	N	N	N	N	N	N
20 Wasserman Schultz	N	N	N	N	N	N	N
21 Diaz-Balart, L.	N	N	N	N	N	N	Y
22 Klein	N	N	N	N	N	N	?
23 Hastings	N	N	N	N	N	N	N
24 Kosmas	N	N	N	N	N	N	Y
25 Diaz-Balart, M.	N	N	N	N	N	N	N
GEORGIA							
1 Kingston	N	Y	Y	N	Y	Y	Y
2 Bishop	N	N	N	N	N	N	N
3 Westmoreland	Y	Y	Y	Y	Y	Y	Y
4 Johnson	N	N	N	N	N	N	N
5 Lewis	?	?	?	?	?	?	?
6 Price	Y	Y	Y	Y	Y	Y	Y
7 Linder	Y	Y	Y	Y	Y	Y	Y
8 Marshall	Y	N	N	N	N	Y	N
9 Deal	?	?	?	?	?	?	?
10 Broun	Y	Y	Y	Y	Y	Y	?
11 Gingrey	Y	Y	Y	Y	Y	Y	Y
12 Barrow	N	N	N	N	N	N	Y
13 Scott	N	N	N	N	N	N	N
HAWAII							
1 Abercrombie	N	N	N	N	N	N	N
2 Hirono	N	N	N	N	N	N	N
IDAHO							
1 Minnick	Y	Y	Y	Y	Y	Y	Y
2 Simpson	N	N	N	N	Y	N	Y
ILLINOIS							
1 Rush	?	N	N	N	N	N	N
2 Jackson	N	N	N	N	N	N	N
3 Lipinski	N	N	N	N	N	N	N
4 Gutierrez	N	N	N	N	N	N	N
5 Quigley	N	N	N	N	N	N	N
6 Roskam	Y	Y	Y	Y	Y	Y	Y
7 Davis	N	N	N	N	N	N	N
8 Bean	N	?	N	Y	N	Y	N
9 Schakowsky	N	N	N	N	N	N	N
10 Kirk	Y	Y	?	Y	Y	Y	Y
11 Halvorson	N	N	N	N	N	N	Y
12 Costello	N	N	N	N	N	N	N
13 Biggert	N	Y	N	N	N	N	Y
14 Foster	Y	Y	N	N	N	N	Y
15 Johnson	Y	Y	Y	?	Y	Y	Y

KEY   **Republicans**   Democrats

Y Voted for (yea)	**X** Paired against	**C** Voted "present" to avoid possible conflict of interest
# Paired for	**–** Announced against	
+ Announced for	**P** Voted "present"	**?** Did not vote or otherwise make a position known
N Voted against (nay)		

	377	378	379	380	381	382	383
16 **Manzullo**	N	Y	Y	Y	Y	Y	Y
17 Hare	N	N	N	N	N	N	N
18 **Schock**	N	Y	N	N	Y	Y	Y
19 **Shimkus**	N	Y	Y	Y	Y	Y	Y
INDIANA							
1 Visclosky	N	N	N	N	N	N	Y
2 Donnelly	N	N	N	N	N	N	Y
3 **Souder**	Y	N	Y	N	Y	Y	Y
4 **Buyer**	Y	?	Y	Y	Y	Y	Y
5 **Burton**	Y	Y	Y	Y	Y	Y	Y
6 **Pence**	Y	Y	Y	Y	Y	Y	Y
7 Carson	N	N	N	N	N	N	N
8 Ellsworth	N	N	N	N	N	N	N
9 Hill	N	N	N	N	N	N	Y
IOWA							
1 Braley	N	N	N	N	N	N	N
2 Loebsack	N	N	N	N	N	N	Y
3 Boswell	N	N	N	N	N	N	N
4 **Latham**	N	Y	N	N	N	N	Y
5 **King**	Y	Y	Y	Y	Y	Y	?
KANSAS							
1 **Moran**	Y	Y	Y	Y	Y	Y	Y
2 **Jenkins**	Y	Y	Y	Y	Y	Y	Y
3 Moore	N	N	N	N	N	N	Y
4 **Tiahrt**	Y	N	Y	N	N	Y	Y
KENTUCKY							
1 **Whitfield**	N	Y	N	N	N	N	Y
2 **Guthrie**	N	N	N	N	N	N	Y
3 Yarmuth	N	N	N	N	N	N	Y
4 **Davis**	N	Y	Y	N	N	N	Y
5 **Rogers**	N	N	N	N	N	N	Y
6 Chandler	N	N	N	N	N	N	Y
LOUISIANA							
1 **Scalise**	Y	Y	Y	Y	Y	N	Y
2 **Cao**	N	N	N	N	N	N	Y
3 Melancon	N	N	N	N	N	N	Y
4 **Fleming**	Y	Y	Y	Y	Y	Y	Y
5 **Alexander**	N	N	N	N	N	N	Y
6 **Cassidy**	Y	Y	Y	Y	Y	Y	Y
7 **Boustany**	Y	Y	Y	Y	Y	Y	Y
MAINE							
1 Pingree	N	N	N	N	N	N	N
2 Michaud	N	N	N	N	N	N	Y
MARYLAND							
1 Kratovil	N	N	N	N	N	N	Y
2 Ruppersberger	N	N	N	N	N	N	N
3 Sarbanes	N	N	N	N	N	N	Y
4 Edwards	N	N	N	N	N	N	N
5 Hoyer	N	N	N	N	N	N	N
6 **Bartlett**	N	Y	N	N	N	Y	Y
7 Cummings	N	N	N	N	N	N	N
8 Van Hollen	N	N	N	N	N	N	N
MASSACHUSETTS							
1 Olver	N	N	N	N	N	N	N
2 Neal	N	N	N	N	N	N	N
3 McGovern	N	N	N	N	N	N	N
4 Frank	N	N	N	N	N	N	N
5 Tsongas	N	N	N	N	N	N	N
6 Tierney	N	N	N	N	?	N	N
7 Markey	N	N	N	N	N	N	N
8 Capuano	N	N	N	N	N	N	N
9 Lynch	N	N	N	N	N	N	N
10 Delahunt	N	N	N	N	N	N	N
MICHIGAN							
1 Stupak	N	N	N	N	N	N	N
2 **Hoekstra**	Y	Y	Y	Y	Y	Y	Y
3 **Ehlers**	N	N	N	N	N	N	Y
4 **Camp**	N	Y	N	N	N	N	Y
5 Kildee	N	N	N	N	N	N	N
6 **Upton**	N	Y	N	N	Y	N	Y
7 Schauer	Y	N	N	Y	N	Y	Y
8 **Rogers**	Y	Y	N	N	N	Y	Y
9 Peters	N	N	N	N	N	N	Y
10 **Miller**	N	Y	N	Y	Y	Y	Y
11 **McCotter**	Y	Y	Y	Y	Y	Y	Y
12 Levin	N	N	N	N	N	N	N
13 Kilpatrick	N	?	N	N	N	N	N
14 Conyers	N	N	N	N	N	N	N
15 Dingell	?	N	N	N	N	N	N
MINNESOTA							
1 Walz	N	N	N	N	N	N	Y
2 **Kline**	Y	Y	Y	Y	Y	Y	Y
3 **Paulsen**	Y	N	Y	Y	Y	Y	Y
4 McCollum	N	N	N	N	N	N	N

	377	378	379	380	381	382	383
5 Ellison	?	?	?	?	?	?	?
6 **Bachmann**	?	?	?	?	?	?	?
7 Peterson	N	N	N	N	N	N	N
8 Oberstar	N	N	N	N	N	N	N
MISSISSIPPI							
1 Childers	N	N	N	N	N	N	Y
2 Thompson	N	N	N	N	N	N	N
3 **Harper**	Y	Y	Y	Y	Y	Y	Y
4 Taylor	N	N	N	N	N	N	Y
MISSOURI							
1 Clay	N	N	N	N	N	N	N
2 **Akin**	Y	Y	Y	Y	Y	Y	Y
3 Carnahan	N	N	N	N	N	N	N
4 Skelton	N	N	N	N	N	N	Y
5 Cleaver	N	N	N	N	N	N	N
6 **Graves**	Y	Y	Y	Y	Y	Y	Y
7 **Blunt**	Y	Y	N	N	Y	Y	Y
8 **Emerson**	N	N	N	N	N	N	Y
9 **Luetkemeyer**	Y	Y	Y	Y	Y	Y	Y
MONTANA							
AL **Rehberg**	N	Y	N	N	N	N	Y
NEBRASKA							
1 **Fortenberry**	N	Y	N	Y	N	N	Y
2 **Terry**	Y	Y	Y	N	Y	Y	Y
3 **Smith**	Y	Y	Y	Y	Y	Y	Y
NEVADA							
1 Berkley	N	N	N	N	N	N	Y
2 **Heller**	Y	Y	Y	Y	Y	Y	Y
3 Titus	N	N	N	N	N	N	Y
NEW HAMPSHIRE							
1 Shea-Porter	N	N	N	N	N	N	Y
2 Hodes	N	N	N	N	?	Y	Y
NEW JERSEY							
1 Andrews	N	N	N	N	N	N	N
2 **LoBiondo**	N	N	N	N	N	N	Y
3 Adler	N	N	N	N	N	N	Y
4 **Smith**	N	N	N	N	N	N	Y
5 **Garrett**	Y	Y	Y	Y	Y	Y	Y
6 Pallone	N	N	N	N	N	N	N
7 **Lance**	N	Y	N	N	Y	Y	Y
8 Pascrell	N	N	N	N	N	N	N
9 Rothman	N	N	N	N	N	N	N
10 Payne	N	N	N	N	N	N	N
11 **Frelinghuysen**	N	N	N	N	N	N	Y
12 Holt	N	N	N	N	N	N	N
13 Sires	N	N	N	N	N	N	N
NEW MEXICO							
1 Heinrich	N	N	N	N	N	N	Y
2 Teague	N	N	N	N	N	N	N
3 Lujan	N	N	N	N	N	N	N
NEW YORK							
1 Bishop	N	N	N	N	N	N	Y
2 Israel	N	N	N	N	N	N	N
3 **King**	N	N	N	N	N	N	Y
4 McCarthy	N	N	N	N	N	N	N
5 Ackerman	N	N	N	N	N	N	N
6 Meeks	N	N	N	N	N	N	N
7 Crowley	N	N	N	N	N	N	N
8 Nadler	N	N	N	N	N	N	Y
9 Weiner	N	N	N	N	N	N	N
10 Towns	N	N	N	N	N	N	N
11 Clarke	N	N	N	N	N	N	N
12 Velázquez	N	N	N	N	N	N	N
13 McMahon	N	N	N	N	N	N	N
14 Maloney	N	N	N	N	N	N	N
15 Rangel	N	N	N	?	N	N	N
16 Serrano	N	N	N	N	N	N	N
17 Engel	N	N	N	N	N	N	N
18 Lowey	N	N	N	N	N	N	N
19 Hall	N	N	N	N	N	N	N
20 Murphy	N	N	N	N	N	N	Y
21 Tonko	N	N	N	N	N	N	N
22 Hinchey	N	N	N	N	N	N	N
23 **McHugh**	N	N	N	Y	N	N	Y
24 Arcuri	N	N	N	N	N	N	Y
25 Maffei	N	N	N	N	N	N	Y
26 **Lee**	N	Y	N	N	N	N	Y
27 Higgins	N	N	N	N	N	N	N
28 Slaughter	N	N	N	N	N	N	N
29 Massa	N	N	Y	N	N	N	Y
NORTH CAROLINA							
1 Butterfield	N	N	N	N	N	N	N
2 Etheridge	N	N	N	N	N	N	Y
3 **Jones**	Y	Y	Y	Y	Y	Y	Y
4 Price	N	N	N	N	N	N	N

	377	378	379	380	381	382	383
5 **Foxx**	Y	Y	Y	Y	Y	Y	Y
6 **Coble**	N	Y	Y	N	Y	Y	Y
7 McIntyre	N	N	N	N	N	N	Y
8 Kissell	N	N	N	N	N	N	N
9 **Myrick**	Y	Y	Y	Y	Y	Y	Y
10 **McHenry**	N	Y	Y	Y	Y	Y	Y
11 Shuler	N	N	N	N	N	N	N
12 Watt	N	N	N	N	N	N	N
13 Miller	N	N	N	N	N	N	N
NORTH DAKOTA							
AL Pomeroy	N	N	N	N	N	N	N
OHIO							
1 Driehaus	N	N	N	N	N	N	Y
2 **Schmidt**	Y	Y	Y	Y	Y	Y	Y
3 **Turner**	N	N	N	N	N	N	Y
4 **Jordan**	Y	Y	Y	Y	Y	Y	Y
5 **Latta**	Y	Y	Y	Y	Y	Y	Y
6 Wilson	N	N	N	N	N	N	N
7 **Austria**	Y	Y	Y	Y	Y	Y	Y
8 **Boehner**	?	Y	Y	?	Y	Y	Y
9 Kaptur	N	N	N	N	?	N	N
10 Kucinich	N	N	N	N	N	N	N
11 Fudge	N	N	N	N	N	N	N
12 **Tiberi**	Y	Y	Y	N	Y	Y	Y
13 Sutton	N	N	N	?	N	N	N
14 **LaTourette**	N	N	N	N	N	N	Y
15 Kilroy	N	N	N	N	N	N	N
16 Boccieri	N	N	N	N	?	N	Y
17 Ryan	N	N	N	N	N	N	N
18 Space	N	N	N	N	N	N	Y
OKLAHOMA							
1 **Sullivan**	?	?	?	?	?	?	?
2 Boren	N	N	N	N	N	N	Y
3 **Lucas**	N	N	N	N	N	N	Y
4 **Cole**	N	N	N	N	N	N	Y
5 **Fallin**	Y	Y	Y	Y	Y	Y	Y
OREGON							
1 Wu	N	N	N	N	N	N	Y
2 **Walden**	N	Y	N	N	Y	Y	Y
3 Blumenauer	N	N	N	N	N	N	N
4 DeFazio	N	N	N	N	N	N	N
5 Schrader	?	N	N	N	N	N	Y
PENNSYLVANIA							
1 Brady	N	N	N	N	N	N	N
2 Fattah	N	N	N	N	N	N	N
3 Dahlkemper	N	N	N	N	N	N	Y
4 Altmire	N	N	N	N	N	N	Y
5 **Thompson**	N	N	N	N	N	N	Y
6 **Gerlach**	N	N	N	N	Y	Y	Y
7 Sestak	N	N	N	N	N	N	N
8 Murphy, P.	N	N	N	N	N	N	N
9 **Shuster**	N	N	N	N	N	N	Y
10 Carney	N	N	N	N	N	N	Y
11 Kanjorski	N	N	N	N	N	N	N
12 Murtha	N	N	N	?	N	N	N
13 Schwartz	N	?	N	N	N	N	Y
14 Doyle	N	N	N	N	N	N	N
15 **Dent**	N	N	N	N	Y	Y	Y
16 **Pitts**	Y	Y	Y	Y	Y	Y	Y
17 Holden	N	N	N	?	N	N	Y
18 **Murphy, T.**	N	N	N	N	N	N	Y
19 **Platts**	N	N	N	N	Y	Y	Y
RHODE ISLAND							
1 Kennedy	?	?	?	?	?	?	?
2 Langevin	N	N	N	N	N	N	N
SOUTH CAROLINA							
1 **Brown**	N	Y	N	N	N	N	Y
2 **Wilson**	Y	Y	N	Y	Y	Y	Y
3 **Barrett**	Y	Y	N	Y	Y	Y	Y
4 **Inglis**	Y	Y	N	Y	Y	Y	Y
5 Spratt	N	N	N	N	N	N	N
6 Clyburn	N	N	N	?	N	N	N
SOUTH DAKOTA							
AL Herseth Sandlin	N	N	N	N	N	N	Y
TENNESSEE							
1 **Roe**	Y	Y	Y	Y	Y	Y	Y
2 **Duncan**	Y	Y	Y	?	Y	Y	Y
3 **Wamp**	Y	Y	Y	Y	Y	Y	Y
4 Davis	?	N	N	N	N	N	Y
5 Cooper	Y	Y	Y	Y	Y	Y	Y
6 Gordon	N	N	N	N	N	N	Y
7 **Blackburn**	Y	Y	Y	Y	Y	Y	Y
8 Tanner	N	N	N	N	N	N	Y
9 Cohen	N	N	N	N	N	?	?

	377	378	379	380	381	382	383
TEXAS							
1 **Gohmert**	Y	Y	Y	N	Y	N	Y
2 **Poe**	Y	N	Y	N	Y	N	Y
3 **Johnson, S.**	Y	Y	Y	Y	Y	Y	Y
4 **Hall**	Y	Y	Y	N	Y	Y	Y
5 **Hensarling**	Y	Y	Y	Y	Y	Y	Y
6 **Barton**	N	N	Y	N	N	N	Y
7 **Culberson**	N	N	N	N	N	Y	Y
8 **Brady**	Y	Y	Y	Y	Y	Y	Y
9 Green, A.	N	N	N	N	N	N	N
10 **McCaul**	Y	Y	Y	Y	Y	Y	Y
11 **Conaway**	Y	Y	Y	Y	Y	Y	Y
12 **Granger**	N	N	N	N	N	N	Y
13 **Thornberry**	Y	Y	Y	Y	Y	Y	Y
14 **Paul**	Y	Y	Y	Y	Y	Y	Y
15 Hinojosa	N	N	N	N	N	N	N
16 Reyes	N	N	N	N	N	N	N
17 Edwards	N	N	N	?	N	N	Y
18 Jackson Lee	N	N	N	N	N	N	Y
19 **Neugebauer**	Y	Y	Y	Y	Y	Y	Y
20 Gonzalez	N	N	N	N	N	N	N
21 **Smith**	N	N	N	N	N	N	Y
22 **Olson**	Y	Y	Y	Y	Y	Y	Y
23 Rodriguez	N	N	N	N	N	N	Y
24 **Marchant**	?	Y	Y	Y	Y	Y	Y
25 Doggett	N	N	N	N	?	N	Y
26 **Burgess**	Y	Y	Y	Y	Y	Y	Y
27 Ortiz	N	N	N	N	N	N	N
28 Cuellar	N	N	N	N	N	N	N
29 Green, G.	N	N	N	N	N	N	N
30 Johnson, E.	N	N	N	N	N	N	N
31 **Carter**	N	N	N	N	N	N	Y
32 **Sessions**	Y	Y	Y	Y	Y	Y	Y
UTAH							
1 **Bishop**	N	N	Y	N	Y	Y	Y
2 Matheson	N	N	N	N	N	N	Y
3 **Chaffetz**	Y	Y	Y	Y	Y	Y	Y
VERMONT							
AL Welch	N	N	N	N	N	N	N
VIRGINIA							
1 **Wittman**	N	Y	Y	Y	N	Y	Y
2 Nye	N	N	N	Y	N	N	Y
3 Scott	N	N	N	N	N	?	N
4 **Forbes**	Y	Y	N	N	N	N	Y
5 Perriello	N	Y	N	N	N	N	Y
6 **Goodlatte**	Y	Y	Y	Y	Y	Y	Y
7 **Cantor**	Y	Y	Y	Y	?	Y	Y
8 Moran	N	N	N	N	N	N	N
9 Boucher	N	N	N	N	N	N	N
10 **Wolf**	N	Y	N	N	N	N	Y
11 Connolly	N	N	N	N	N	N	N
WASHINGTON							
1 Inslee	N	N	N	N	N	N	Y
2 Larsen	N	N	N	N	N	N	N
3 Baird	N	N	N	N	N	N	N
4 **Hastings**	N	N	N	N	N	N	Y
5 **McMorris Rodgers**	Y	N	Y	Y	Y	Y	Y
6 Dicks	N	N	N	N	N	N	Y
7 McDermott	N	N	N	N	N	N	N
8 **Reichert**	N	Y	N	N	N	N	Y
9 Smith	N	N	N	N	N	N	Y
WEST VIRGINIA							
1 Mollohan	N	N	N	N	N	N	Y
2 **Capito**	N	N	N	N	N	N	Y
3 Rahall	N	N	N	N	N	N	N
WISCONSIN							
1 **Ryan**	Y	Y	Y	Y	Y	Y	Y
2 Baldwin	N	N	N	N	N	N	N
3 Kind	N	N	N	N	N	N	N
4 Moore	N	N	N	N	N	N	N
5 **Sensenbrenner**	Y	Y	Y	Y	Y	Y	Y
6 **Petri**	Y	Y	Y	Y	Y	Y	Y
7 Obey	N	N	N	N	N	N	N
8 Kagen	N	N	N	N	N	N	N
WYOMING							
AL **Lummis**	Y	Y	Y	Y	Y	Y	Y
DELEGATES							
Faleomavaega (A.S.)	N	N	N	N	N	N	
Norton (D.C.)	N	N	N	N	N	N	
Bordallo (Guam)	N	N	N	N	N	N	
Sablan (N. Marianas)	N	N	N	N	N	?	
Pierluisi (P.R.)	N	N	N	N	N	N	
Christensen (V.I.)	N	N	N	N	N	N	

IN THE HOUSE | By Vote Number

384. **HR 2847. Fiscal 2010 Commerce-Justice-Science Appropriations/Revote on State Criminal Alien Assistance Program.** Revote on the Mollohan, D-W.Va., amendment that would increase the amount provided for the Justice Department's State Criminal Alien Assistance Program by $100 million. It would be offset by Justice Department reductions of $21 million to the sharing technology Unified Financial Management System and $79 million to Office of Justice programs. Under House rules, any member (in this case Westmoreland, R-Ga.) may demand a revote in the full House on an amendment adopted in the Committee of the Whole. Previously the Mollohan amendment was adopted by voice vote in the Committee of the Whole. Delegates may not vote in the full House. Adopted 405-1: R 171-0; D 234-1. June 18, 2009.

385. **HR 2847. Fiscal 2010 Commerce-Justice-Science Appropriations/Motion to Reconsider State Criminal Alien Assistance Program.** Price, R-Ga., motion to reconsider the vote on the Mollohan, D-W.Va., amendment. Motion rejected 172-245: R 169-4; D 3-241. June 18, 2009.

386. **HR 2847. Fiscal 2010 Commerce-Justice-Science Appropriations/Revote on International Trade Administration.** Revote on the Schock, R-Ill., amendment that would increase the amount provided for the International Trade Administration by $500,000, offset by a reduction of the same amount for the Census Bureau. Under House rules, any member (in this case Westmoreland, R-Ga.) may demand a revote in the full House on an amendment adopted in the Committee of the Whole. Previously, the Schock amendment was adopted by voice vote in the Committee of the Whole. Delegates may not vote in the full House. Rejected 179-236: R 168-3; D 11-233. June 18, 2009.

387. **HR 2847. Fiscal 2010 Commerce-Justice-Science Appropriations/Motion to Reconsider International Trade Administration.** Boehner, R-Ohio, motion to reconsider the vote on the Schock, R-Ill., amendment. Motion rejected 177-241: R 171-2; D 6-239. June 18, 2009.

388. **HR 2847. Fiscal 2010 Commerce-Justice-Science Appropriations/Revote on National Oceanic and Atmospheric Administration.** Revote on the Bordallo, D-Guam, amendment (vote 353). Under House rules, any member (in this case Westmoreland, R-Ga.) may demand a revote in the full House on an amendment adopted in the Committee of the Whole. Delegates may not vote in the full House. Adopted 405-12: R 172-1; D 233-11. June 18, 2009.

389. **HR 2847. Fiscal 2010 Commerce-Justice-Science Appropriations/Motion to Reconsider National Oceanic and Atmospheric Administration.** King, R-Iowa, motion to reconsider the vote on the Bordallo, D-Guam, amendment. Motion rejected 172-239: R 169-3; D 3-236. June 18, 2009.

390. **HR 2847. Fiscal 2010 Commerce-Justice-Science Appropriations/Revote on Office on Violence Against Women.** Revote on the Moore, D-Wis., amendment (vote 354). Under House rules, any member (in this case Westmoreland, R-Ga.) may demand a revote in the full House on an amendment adopted in the Committee of the Whole. Delegates may not vote in the full House. Adopted 414-0: R 173-0; D 241-0. June 18, 2009.

	384	385	386	387	388	389	390
ALABAMA							
1 **Bonner**	Y	Y	Y	Y	Y	Y	Y
2 Bright	Y	N	N	N	Y	N	Y
3 **Rogers**	Y	Y	Y	Y	Y	Y	Y
4 **Aderholt**	Y	Y	Y	Y	Y	Y	Y
5 Griffith	Y	N	N	N	Y	?	Y
6 **Bachus**	Y	Y	Y	Y	Y	Y	Y
7 Davis	?	?	?	?	?	?	?
ALASKA							
AL **Young**	Y	Y	N	N	Y	N	Y
ARIZONA							
1 Kirkpatrick	Y	N	Y	N	Y	N	Y
2 **Franks**	Y	Y	Y	Y	Y	Y	Y
3 **Shadegg**	Y	Y	Y	Y	Y	Y	Y
4 Pastor	Y	N	N	N	Y	N	Y
5 Mitchell	Y	N	Y	N	Y	N	Y
6 **Flake**	Y	Y	Y	Y	Y	Y	Y
7 Grijalva	Y	N	N	N	Y	N	Y
8 Giffords	Y	N	N	N	Y	N	Y
ARKANSAS							
1 Berry	Y	N	N	N	Y	N	Y
2 Snyder	Y	N	Y	N	Y	N	Y
3 **Boozman**	Y	Y	Y	Y	Y	Y	Y
4 Ross	Y	N	N	N	Y	N	Y
CALIFORNIA							
1 Thompson	Y	N	N	N	Y	N	Y
2 **Herger**	Y	Y	Y	Y	Y	Y	Y
3 **Lungren**	Y	Y	Y	Y	Y	Y	Y
4 **McClintock**	Y	Y	Y	Y	Y	Y	Y
5 Matsui	?	N	N	N	Y	N	Y
6 Woolsey	?	N	N	N	Y	N	Y
7 Miller, George	Y	N	N	N	Y	N	Y
8 Pelosi							
9 Lee	Y	N	N	N	Y	N	Y
10 Tauscher	?	?	?	?	?	?	?
11 McNerney	Y	N	N	N	Y	N	Y
12 Speier	Y	N	N	N	Y	N	Y
13 Stark	Y	N	N	N	Y	N	Y
14 Eshoo	Y	N	N	N	Y	N	Y
15 Honda	Y	N	N	N	Y	N	Y
16 Lofgren	Y	N	N	N	Y	N	Y
17 Farr	?	N	N	N	Y	N	Y
18 Cardoza	Y	N	N	N	Y	N	Y
19 **Radanovich**	Y	Y	Y	Y	Y	Y	Y
20 Costa	Y	N	N	N	Y	N	Y
21 **Nunes**	Y	Y	Y	Y	Y	Y	Y
22 **McCarthy**	Y	Y	Y	Y	Y	Y	Y
23 Capps	Y	N	N	N	Y	N	Y
24 **Gallegly**	Y	Y	Y	Y	Y	Y	Y
25 **McKeon**	Y	Y	Y	Y	Y	Y	Y
26 **Dreier**	Y	Y	Y	Y	Y	Y	Y
27 Sherman	Y	N	N	N	Y	N	Y
28 Berman	Y	N	N	N	Y	N	Y
29 Schiff	Y	N	N	N	Y	N	Y
30 Waxman	Y	N	N	N	Y	N	Y
31 Becerra	Y	N	N	N	Y	N	Y
32 Vacant							
33 Watson	Y	N	N	N	Y	N	Y
34 Roybal-Allard	Y	N	N	N	Y	N	Y
35 Waters	Y	N	N	N	Y	N	Y
36 Harman	?	?	?	?	?	?	?
37 Richardson	Y	N	N	N	Y	N	Y
38 Napolitano	Y	N	N	N	Y	N	Y
39 Sánchez, Linda	?	?	?	?	?	?	?
40 **Royce**	Y	Y	Y	Y	Y	Y	Y
41 **Lewis**	Y	Y	Y	Y	Y	Y	Y
42 **Miller, Gary**	Y	Y	Y	Y	Y	Y	Y
43 **Baca**	Y	N	N	N	Y	N	Y
44 **Calvert**	Y	Y	Y	Y	Y	Y	Y
45 **Bono Mack**	Y	Y	Y	Y	Y	Y	Y
46 **Rohrabacher**	Y	Y	Y	Y	Y	Y	Y
47 Sanchez, Loretta	Y	N	N	N	Y	N	Y
48 **Campbell**	Y	Y	Y	Y	Y	Y	Y
49 **Issa**	Y	Y	Y	Y	Y	Y	Y
50 **Bilbray**	Y	Y	Y	Y	Y	Y	Y
51 Filner	Y	N	N	N	Y	N	Y
52 **Hunter**	Y	Y	Y	Y	Y	Y	Y
53 Davis	Y	N	N	N	Y	N	Y
COLORADO							
1 DeGette	Y	N	N	N	Y	N	Y
2 Polis	Y	N	N	N	Y	N	Y
3 Salazar	Y	N	N	N	Y	N	Y
4 Markey	?	N	N	N	Y	N	Y
5 **Lamborn**	Y	Y	Y	Y	Y	Y	Y
6 **Coffman**	Y	Y	Y	Y	Y	Y	Y
7 Perlmutter	Y	N	N	N	N	N	Y
CONNECTICUT							
1 Larson	Y	N	N	N	Y	N	?
2 Courtney	?	?	?	N	Y	N	Y
3 DeLauro	Y	N	N	N	Y	N	Y
4 Himes	Y	N	N	N	Y	N	Y
5 Murphy	?	N	N	N	Y	N	Y
DELAWARE							
AL **Castle**	Y	Y	Y	Y	Y	Y	Y
FLORIDA							
1 **Miller**	Y	Y	Y	Y	Y	Y	Y
2 Boyd	Y	N	N	N	Y	N	Y
3 Brown	Y	?	N	?	Y	N	Y
4 **Crenshaw**	Y	Y	Y	Y	Y	Y	Y
5 **Brown-Waite**	Y	Y	Y	Y	Y	Y	Y
6 **Stearns**	+	Y	Y	Y	Y	Y	Y
7 **Mica**	+	N	Y	Y	Y	Y	Y
8 Grayson	Y	N	N	N	Y	N	Y
9 **Bilirakis**	Y	Y	Y	Y	Y	Y	Y
10 **Young**	Y	Y	Y	Y	Y	Y	Y
11 Castor	Y	N	N	N	Y	N	Y
12 **Putnam**	Y	Y	Y	Y	Y	Y	Y
13 **Buchanan**	Y	Y	Y	Y	Y	Y	Y
14 **Mack**	Y	Y	Y	Y	Y	Y	Y
15 **Posey**	Y	Y	Y	Y	Y	Y	Y
16 **Rooney**	Y	Y	Y	Y	Y	Y	Y
17 Meek	Y	N	N	N	Y	N	Y
18 **Ros-Lehtinen**	Y	Y	Y	Y	Y	?	Y
19 Wexler	Y	N	N	N	Y	N	Y
20 Wasserman Schultz	Y	N	N	N	Y	N	Y
21 **Diaz-Balart, L.**	Y	Y	Y	Y	Y	Y	Y
22 Klein	Y	N	N	N	Y	N	Y
23 Hastings	Y	N	N	N	Y	N	?
24 Kosmas	Y	N	N	N	Y	N	Y
25 **Diaz-Balart, M.**	Y	Y	Y	Y	Y	Y	Y
GEORGIA							
1 **Kingston**	Y	Y	Y	Y	Y	Y	Y
2 Bishop	Y	N	?	N	Y	N	Y
3 **Westmoreland**	Y	Y	Y	Y	Y	Y	Y
4 Johnson	Y	N	N	N	Y	N	Y
5 Lewis	?	?	?	?	?	?	?
6 **Price**	Y	Y	Y	Y	Y	Y	Y
7 **Linder**	Y	Y	Y	Y	Y	Y	Y
8 Marshall	Y	N	N	N	Y	N	Y
9 **Deal**	?	?	?	?	?	?	?
10 **Broun**	Y	Y	Y	Y	Y	Y	Y
11 **Gingrey**	Y	Y	Y	Y	Y	Y	Y
12 Barrow	Y	N	Y	N	Y	N	Y
13 Scott	Y	N	N	N	Y	N	Y
HAWAII							
1 Abercrombie	Y	N	N	N	Y	?	Y
2 Hirono	Y	N	N	N	Y	N	Y
IDAHO							
1 Minnick	Y	N	Y	N	Y	N	Y
2 **Simpson**	Y	Y	Y	Y	Y	Y	Y
ILLINOIS							
1 Rush	Y	N	N	N	Y	N	Y
2 Jackson	Y	N	N	N	Y	N	Y
3 Lipinski	Y	N	N	N	Y	N	Y
4 Gutierrez	Y	N	N	N	Y	N	Y
5 Quigley	Y	N	N	N	Y	N	Y
6 **Roskam**	Y	Y	Y	Y	Y	Y	Y
7 Davis	Y	N	N	N	Y	N	Y
8 Bean	Y	?	N	N	N	N	Y
9 Schakowsky	Y	N	N	N	Y	N	Y
10 **Kirk**	Y	Y	Y	Y	Y	?	Y
11 Halvorson	Y	N	N	N	Y	N	Y
12 Costello	Y	N	N	N	Y	N	Y
13 **Biggert**	Y	Y	Y	Y	Y	Y	Y
14 Foster	Y	N	N	N	N	N	Y
15 Johnson	Y	N	Y	N	Y	N	Y

KEY **Republicans** Democrats

Y Voted for (yea)	X Paired against	C Voted "present" to avoid possible conflict of interest
# Paired for	– Announced against	
+ Announced for	P Voted "present"	? Did not vote or otherwise make a position known
N Voted against (nay)		

	384	385	386	387	388	389	390
16 **Manzullo**	Y	Y	Y	Y	Y	Y	Y
17 Hare	Y	N	N	N	Y	N	Y
18 **Schock**	Y	Y	Y	Y	Y	Y	Y
19 **Shimkus**	Y	Y	Y	Y	Y	Y	Y
INDIANA							
1 Visclosky	Y	N	N	N	Y	N	Y
2 Donnelly	Y	N	N	N	Y	N	Y
3 **Souder**	Y	Y	Y	Y	Y	Y	Y
4 **Buyer**	Y	Y	Y	Y	Y	Y	Y
5 **Burton**	Y	Y	Y	Y	Y	Y	Y
6 **Pence**	Y	Y	Y	Y	Y	Y	Y
7 Carson	Y	N	N	N	Y	N	Y
8 Ellsworth	Y	N	N	N	Y	N	Y
9 Hill	Y	N	N	N	Y	N	Y
IOWA							
1 Braley	Y	N	N	N	Y	N	Y
2 Loebsack	Y	N	N	N	Y	N	Y
3 Boswell	Y	N	N	N	Y	N	Y
4 **Latham**	Y	Y	Y	Y	Y	Y	Y
5 **King**	Y	Y	Y	Y	Y	Y	Y
KANSAS							
1 **Moran**	Y	Y	Y	Y	Y	Y	Y
2 **Jenkins**	Y	Y	Y	Y	N	Y	Y
3 Moore	Y	N	N	N	Y	N	Y
4 **Tiahrt**	Y	Y	Y	Y	Y	Y	Y
KENTUCKY							
1 **Whitfield**	Y	Y	Y	Y	Y	Y	Y
2 **Guthrie**	Y	Y	Y	Y	Y	Y	Y
3 Yarmuth	Y	N	N	N	Y	N	Y
4 **Davis**	Y	Y	Y	Y	Y	Y	Y
5 **Rogers**	Y	Y	Y	Y	Y	Y	Y
6 Chandler	Y	N	N	N	Y	?	Y
LOUISIANA							
1 **Scalise**	Y	Y	Y	Y	Y	Y	Y
2 **Cao**	Y	N	Y	Y	Y	N	Y
3 Melancon	Y	N	N	N	Y	N	Y
4 **Fleming**	Y	Y	Y	Y	Y	Y	Y
5 **Alexander**	?	Y	Y	Y	Y	Y	Y
6 **Cassidy**	Y	Y	Y	Y	Y	Y	Y
7 **Boustany**	Y	Y	Y	Y	Y	Y	Y
MAINE							
1 Pingree	Y	N	N	N	Y	N	Y
2 Michaud	Y	N	N	N	Y	N	Y
MARYLAND							
1 Kratovil	Y	N	N	N	Y	N	Y
2 Ruppersberger	Y	N	N	N	Y	?	Y
3 Sarbanes	Y	N	N	N	Y	N	Y
4 Edwards	Y	N	N	N	Y	N	Y
5 Hoyer	Y	N	N	N	?	N	Y
6 **Bartlett**	Y	Y	Y	Y	Y	Y	Y
7 Cummings	Y	N	N	N	Y	N	Y
8 Van Hollen	Y	N	N	N	Y	N	Y
MASSACHUSETTS							
1 Olver	Y	N	N	N	Y	N	?
2 Neal	Y	N	N	N	Y	N	Y
3 McGovern	Y	N	N	N	Y	N	Y
4 Frank	Y	N	N	N	Y	?	Y
5 Tsongas	Y	N	N	N	Y	N	Y
6 Tierney	Y	N	N	N	Y	N	Y
7 Markey	Y	N	N	N	Y	N	Y
8 Capuano	Y	N	N	N	Y	N	Y
9 Lynch	?	N	N	N	Y	N	Y
10 Delahunt	Y	N	N	N	Y	N	Y
MICHIGAN							
1 Stupak	Y	N	N	N	Y	N	Y
2 **Hoekstra**	Y	Y	Y	Y	Y	Y	Y
3 **Ehlers**	Y	Y	Y	Y	Y	Y	Y
4 **Camp**	Y	Y	Y	Y	Y	Y	Y
5 Kildee	Y	N	N	N	Y	N	Y
6 **Upton**	Y	Y	Y	Y	Y	Y	Y
7 Schauer	Y	N	N	N	N	N	Y
8 **Rogers**	Y	Y	Y	Y	Y	Y	Y
9 Peters	Y	N	N	N	Y	N	Y
10 **Miller**	Y	Y	Y	Y	Y	Y	Y
11 **McCotter**	Y	Y	Y	Y	Y	Y	Y
12 Levin	Y	N	N	N	Y	N	Y
13 Kilpatrick	?	N	N	Y	Y	N	Y
14 Conyers	?	N	N	N	Y	N	Y
15 Dingell	N	N	N	N	Y	N	Y
MINNESOTA							
1 Walz	Y	N	N	N	N	N	Y
2 **Kline**	Y	Y	Y	Y	Y	Y	Y
3 **Paulsen**	Y	Y	Y	Y	Y	Y	Y
4 McCollum	Y	N	N	N	Y	N	Y

	384	385	386	387	388	389	390
5 Ellison	?	?	?	?	?	?	?
6 **Bachmann**	?	?	?	?	?	?	?
7 Peterson	?	N	N	N	Y	N	Y
8 Oberstar	?	Y	N	N	Y	N	Y
MISSISSIPPI							
1 Childers	Y	N	N	Y	Y	Y	Y
2 Thompson	Y	N	N	N	Y	N	Y
3 **Harper**	Y	Y	Y	Y	Y	Y	Y
4 Taylor	Y	N	N	N	Y	N	Y
MISSOURI							
1 Clay	Y	N	N	N	Y	N	Y
2 **Akin**	Y	Y	Y	Y	Y	Y	Y
3 Carnahan	Y	N	N	N	Y	N	Y
4 Skelton	Y	N	N	N	Y	?	Y
5 Cleaver	Y	N	N	N	Y	N	Y
6 **Graves**	Y	Y	?	Y	Y	Y	Y
7 **Blunt**	Y	Y	Y	Y	Y	Y	Y
8 **Emerson**	Y	Y	Y	Y	Y	Y	Y
9 **Luetkemeyer**	Y	Y	Y	Y	Y	Y	Y
MONTANA							
AL **Rehberg**	Y	Y	Y	Y	Y	Y	Y
NEBRASKA							
1 **Fortenberry**	Y	Y	Y	Y	Y	Y	Y
2 **Terry**	Y	Y	Y	Y	Y	Y	Y
3 **Smith**	Y	Y	Y	Y	Y	Y	Y
NEVADA							
1 Berkley	Y	N	N	N	Y	N	Y
2 **Heller**	Y	Y	Y	Y	Y	Y	Y
3 Titus	Y	N	N	N	Y	N	Y
NEW HAMPSHIRE							
1 Shea-Porter	Y	N	N	N	Y	N	Y
2 Hodes	Y	N	N	N	N	N	Y
NEW JERSEY							
1 Andrews	Y	N	N	N	Y	N	Y
2 **LoBiondo**	Y	Y	Y	Y	Y	Y	Y
3 Adler	Y	N	N	N	N	N	Y
4 **Smith**	?	N	Y	Y	Y	Y	Y
5 **Garrett**	Y	Y	Y	?	Y	Y	Y
6 Pallone	Y	N	N	N	Y	N	Y
7 **Lance**	Y	Y	Y	Y	Y	Y	Y
8 Pascrell	Y	Y	N	Y	Y	Y	Y
9 Rothman	Y	N	N	N	Y	N	Y
10 Payne	Y	N	N	N	Y	N	Y
11 **Frelinghuysen**	Y	Y	Y	Y	Y	Y	Y
12 Holt	Y	N	N	N	Y	N	Y
13 Sires	Y	N	N	N	Y	N	Y
NEW MEXICO							
1 Heinrich	Y	N	N	N	Y	N	Y
2 Teague	Y	N	N	N	Y	N	Y
3 Lujan	Y	N	N	N	Y	N	Y
NEW YORK							
1 Bishop	Y	N	N	N	N	N	Y
2 Israel	Y	N	N	N	Y	N	Y
3 **King**	Y	Y	Y	Y	Y	Y	Y
4 McCarthy	Y	N	N	N	Y	N	Y
5 Ackerman	Y	N	N	N	Y	N	Y
6 Meeks	Y	N	N	N	Y	N	Y
7 Crowley	Y	N	N	N	Y	N	Y
8 Nadler	Y	N	N	N	Y	N	Y
9 Weiner	Y	N	N	N	Y	N	Y
10 Towns	Y	N	N	N	Y	N	Y
11 Clarke	Y	N	N	N	Y	N	Y
12 Velázquez	Y	N	N	N	Y	N	?
13 McMahon	Y	N	N	N	N	N	Y
14 Maloney	Y	N	N	N	Y	N	Y
15 Rangel	Y	N	?	N	?	N	Y
16 Serrano	Y	N	N	N	Y	N	Y
17 Engel	Y	N	N	N	Y	?	Y
18 Lowey	Y	N	N	N	Y	N	Y
19 Hall	Y	N	N	N	Y	N	Y
20 Murphy	Y	N	N	N	Y	N	Y
21 Tonko	Y	N	N	N	Y	N	Y
22 Hinchey	Y	N	N	N	Y	N	Y
23 **McHugh**	Y	Y	N	Y	Y	Y	Y
24 Arcuri	Y	N	N	N	N	N	Y
25 Maffei	Y	N	N	N	Y	N	Y
26 **Lee**	Y	Y	Y	Y	Y	Y	Y
27 Higgins	Y	N	N	N	Y	N	Y
28 Slaughter	Y	N	N	N	Y	N	Y
29 Massa	Y	N	N	N	Y	N	Y
NORTH CAROLINA							
1 Butterfield	?	N	N	N	Y	N	Y
2 Etheridge	Y	N	N	N	Y	N	Y
3 **Jones**	Y	Y	Y	Y	Y	Y	Y
4 Price	Y	N	N	N	Y	N	Y

	384	385	386	387	388	389	390
5 **Foxx**	Y	Y	Y	Y	Y	Y	Y
6 **Coble**	Y	Y	Y	Y	Y	?	Y
7 McIntyre	Y	N	Y	N	Y	N	Y
8 Kissell	Y	N	N	N	Y	N	Y
9 **Myrick**	Y	Y	Y	Y	Y	Y	Y
10 **McHenry**	Y	Y	Y	Y	Y	Y	Y
11 Shuler	Y	N	N	Y	Y	Y	Y
12 Watt	Y	N	N	N	Y	N	Y
13 Miller	Y	N	N	N	Y	N	Y
NORTH DAKOTA							
AL Pomeroy	Y	N	N	N	Y	N	Y
OHIO							
1 Driehaus	Y	N	N	N	Y	N	Y
2 **Schmidt**	Y	Y	Y	Y	Y	Y	Y
3 **Turner**	Y	?	Y	Y	Y	Y	Y
4 **Jordan**	Y	Y	Y	Y	Y	Y	Y
5 **Latta**	Y	Y	Y	Y	Y	Y	Y
6 Wilson	Y	N	N	N	Y	N	Y
7 **Austria**	Y	Y	Y	Y	Y	Y	Y
8 **Boehner**	Y	Y	N	Y	Y	Y	Y
9 Kaptur	Y	N	N	N	Y	N	Y
10 Kucinich	Y	N	N	N	Y	N	Y
11 Fudge	Y	N	N	N	Y	N	Y
12 **Tiberi**	Y	Y	Y	Y	Y	Y	Y
13 Sutton	Y	N	N	N	Y	N	Y
14 **LaTourette**	Y	Y	Y	Y	Y	Y	Y
15 Kilroy	Y	N	N	N	Y	N	Y
16 Boccieri	Y	N	N	N	Y	N	Y
17 Ryan	Y	N	N	N	Y	N	Y
18 Space	Y	N	N	N	Y	N	Y
OKLAHOMA							
1 **Sullivan**	?	?	?	?	?	?	?
2 Boren	Y	N	N	N	Y	N	Y
3 **Lucas**	Y	Y	Y	Y	Y	Y	Y
4 **Cole**	Y	Y	Y	Y	Y	Y	Y
5 **Fallin**	Y	Y	Y	Y	Y	Y	Y
OREGON							
1 Wu	Y	N	N	N	Y	N	Y
2 **Walden**	Y	Y	Y	Y	Y	Y	Y
3 Blumenauer	Y	N	N	N	Y	N	Y
4 DeFazio	Y	N	N	?	Y	N	Y
5 Schrader	Y	N	N	N	Y	N	Y
PENNSYLVANIA							
1 Brady	Y	N	N	N	Y	N	Y
2 Fattah	Y	N	N	N	Y	N	Y
3 Dahlkemper	Y	N	N	N	Y	N	Y
4 Altmire	Y	N	Y	N	Y	N	Y
5 **Thompson**	Y	Y	Y	Y	Y	Y	Y
6 **Gerlach**	Y	Y	Y	Y	Y	Y	Y
7 Sestak	Y	N	N	N	Y	?	?
8 Murphy, P.	Y	N	N	N	Y	N	Y
9 **Shuster**	Y	Y	?	Y	Y	Y	?
10 Carney	Y	N	N	N	Y	N	Y
11 Kanjorski	Y	N	N	N	Y	N	Y
12 Murtha	Y	N	N	N	Y	N	Y
13 Schwartz	Y	N	N	N	?	N	Y
14 Doyle	Y	N	N	N	Y	N	Y
15 **Dent**	Y	Y	Y	Y	Y	Y	Y
16 **Pitts**	Y	Y	Y	Y	?	Y	Y
17 Holden	Y	N	N	N	Y	N	Y
18 **Murphy, T.**	Y	Y	Y	Y	Y	Y	Y
19 **Platts**	Y	Y	?	Y	Y	Y	Y
RHODE ISLAND							
1 Kennedy	?	?	?	?	?	?	?
2 Langevin	Y	N	N	N	Y	N	Y
SOUTH CAROLINA							
1 **Brown**	Y	Y	Y	Y	Y	Y	Y
2 **Wilson**	Y	Y	Y	Y	Y	Y	Y
3 **Barrett**	Y	Y	Y	Y	Y	Y	Y
4 **Inglis**	Y	Y	Y	Y	Y	Y	Y
5 Spratt	Y	N	N	N	Y	N	Y
6 Clyburn	Y	N	N	N	Y	N	Y
SOUTH DAKOTA							
AL Herseth Sandlin	Y	N	N	N	Y	N	Y
TENNESSEE							
1 **Roe**	Y	Y	Y	Y	Y	Y	Y
2 **Duncan**	Y	Y	Y	Y	Y	Y	Y
3 **Wamp**	Y	Y	Y	Y	Y	Y	Y
4 Davis	Y	N	N	N	Y	N	Y
5 Cooper	Y	N	N	N	Y	N	Y
6 Gordon	Y	N	N	N	Y	N	Y
7 **Blackburn**	Y	Y	Y	Y	Y	Y	Y
8 Tanner	Y	N	Y	N	Y	N	Y
9 Cohen	Y	N	N	N	Y	N	Y

	384	385	386	387	388	389	390
TEXAS							
1 **Gohmert**	Y	Y	Y	Y	Y	Y	Y
2 **Poe**	Y	Y	Y	Y	Y	Y	Y
3 **Johnson, S.**	Y	Y	Y	Y	Y	Y	Y
4 **Hall**	Y	Y	Y	Y	Y	Y	Y
5 **Hensarling**	Y	Y	Y	Y	Y	Y	Y
6 **Barton**	Y	Y	Y	Y	Y	Y	Y
7 **Culberson**	Y	Y	Y	Y	Y	Y	Y
8 **Brady**	Y	Y	Y	Y	Y	Y	Y
9 Green, A.	Y	N	N	N	Y	N	Y
10 **McCaul**	Y	Y	Y	Y	Y	Y	Y
11 **Conaway**	Y	Y	Y	Y	Y	Y	Y
12 **Granger**	Y	Y	Y	Y	Y	Y	Y
13 **Thornberry**	Y	Y	Y	Y	Y	Y	Y
14 **Paul**	Y	Y	Y	Y	Y	Y	Y
15 Hinojosa	Y	N	N	N	Y	N	Y
16 Reyes	Y	N	N	N	Y	N	Y
17 Edwards	Y	N	N	N	Y	N	Y
18 Jackson Lee	Y	N	N	N	Y	N	Y
19 **Neugebauer**	Y	Y	Y	Y	Y	Y	Y
20 Gonzalez	Y	N	N	N	Y	N	Y
21 **Smith**	Y	Y	Y	Y	Y	Y	Y
22 **Olson**	Y	Y	Y	Y	Y	Y	Y
23 Rodriguez	Y	N	N	N	Y	N	Y
24 **Marchant**	Y	Y	Y	Y	Y	Y	Y
25 Doggett	Y	N	N	N	Y	N	?
26 **Burgess**	Y	Y	Y	Y	Y	Y	Y
27 Ortiz	Y	N	N	N	Y	N	Y
28 Cuellar	Y	N	N	N	Y	N	Y
29 Green, G.	Y	N	N	N	Y	?	Y
30 Johnson, E.	Y	N	N	N	Y	N	Y
31 **Carter**	Y	Y	Y	Y	Y	Y	Y
32 **Sessions**	Y	Y	Y	Y	Y	Y	Y
UTAH							
1 **Bishop**	Y	?	Y	Y	Y	Y	Y
2 Matheson	Y	N	N	N	Y	N	Y
3 **Chaffetz**	Y	Y	Y	Y	Y	Y	Y
VERMONT							
AL Welch	Y	N	N	N	Y	N	Y
VIRGINIA							
1 **Wittman**	Y	Y	Y	Y	Y	Y	Y
2 Nye	Y	N	Y	N	Y	N	Y
3 Scott	Y	N	N	N	Y	N	Y
4 **Forbes**	Y	Y	Y	Y	Y	Y	Y
5 Perriello	Y	N	N	N	Y	N	Y
6 **Goodlatte**	Y	Y	Y	Y	Y	Y	Y
7 **Cantor**	Y	Y	?	?	?	Y	Y
8 Moran	Y	N	N	N	Y	N	Y
9 Boucher	Y	N	N	N	Y	N	Y
10 **Wolf**	Y	Y	Y	Y	Y	Y	Y
11 Connolly	Y	N	N	N	N	N	Y
WASHINGTON							
1 Inslee	Y	N	N	N	Y	N	Y
2 Larsen	Y	N	N	N	Y	N	Y
3 Baird	?	?	?	?	Y	N	Y
4 **Hastings**	Y	Y	Y	Y	Y	Y	Y
5 **McMorris Rodgers**	Y	Y	Y	Y	Y	Y	Y
6 Dicks	Y	N	N	N	Y	N	Y
7 McDermott	Y	N	N	N	Y	N	Y
8 **Reichert**	Y	Y	Y	Y	Y	Y	Y
9 Smith	Y	N	N	N	Y	N	Y
WEST VIRGINIA							
1 Mollohan	Y	N	N	N	Y	N	Y
2 **Capito**	Y	Y	Y	Y	Y	Y	Y
3 Rahall	Y	N	N	N	Y	N	Y
WISCONSIN							
1 **Ryan**	Y	Y	Y	Y	Y	Y	Y
2 Baldwin	Y	N	N	N	Y	N	Y
3 Kind	Y	N	N	N	Y	N	Y
4 Moore	Y	N	N	N	?	N	Y
5 **Sensenbrenner**	Y	Y	Y	Y	Y	Y	Y
6 **Petri**	Y	Y	Y	Y	Y	Y	Y
7 Obey	Y	N	N	N	Y	N	Y
8 Kagen	Y	N	N	N	Y	N	Y
WYOMING							
AL **Lummis**	Y	Y	Y	Y	Y	Y	Y
DELEGATES							
Faleomavaega (A.S.)							
Norton (D.C.)							
Bordallo (Guam)							
Sablan (N. Marianas)							
Pierluisi (P.R.)							
Christensen (V.I.)							

IN THE HOUSE | By Vote Number

391. HR 2847. Fiscal 2010 Commerce-Justice-Science Appropriations/Motion to Reconsider Office on Violence Against Women. King, R-Iowa, motion to reconsider the vote on the Moore, D-Wis., amendment. Motion rejected 170-248: R 168-6; D 2-242. June 18, 2009.

392. HR 2847. Fiscal 2010 Commerce-Science-Justice Appropriations/Revote on National Criminal History Improvement Program. Revote on the Boswell, D-Iowa, amendment (vote 355). Under House rules, any member (in this case Westmoreland, R-Ga.) may demand a revote in the full House on an amendment adopted in the Committee of the Whole. Delegates may not vote in the full House. Adopted 416-1: R 174-1; D 242-0. June 18, 2009.

393. HR 2847. Fiscal 2010 Commerce-Science-Justice Appropriations/Motion to Reconsider National Criminal History Improvement Program. King, R-Iowa, motion to reconsider the vote on the Boswell, D-Iowa, amendment. Motion rejected 125-295: R 122-53; D 3-242. June 18, 2009.

394. HR 2847. Fiscal 2010 Commerce-Justice-Science Appropriations/Revote on DNA Collection and Analysis Systems. Revote on the Nadler, D-N.Y., amendment (vote 357). Under House rules, any member (in this case Westmoreland, R-Ga.) may demand a revote in the full House on an amendment adopted in the Committee of the Whole. Delegates may not vote in the full House. Adopted 411-1: R 171-0; D 240-1. June 18, 2009.

395. HR 2847. Fiscal 2010 Commerce-Justice-Science Appropriations/Motion to Reconsider DNA Collection and Analysis Systems. King, R-Iowa, motion to reconsider the vote on the Nadler, D-N.Y., amendment. Motion rejected 163-246: R 160-9; D 3-237. June 18, 2009.

396. HR 2847. Fiscal 2010 Commerce-Justice-Science Appropriations/Revote on Historically Black Colleges and Universities. Revote on the Johnson, D-Texas, amendment (vote 358). Under House rules, any member (in this case Westmoreland, R-Ga.) may demand a revote in the full House on an amendment adopted in the Committee of the Whole. Delegates may not vote in the full House. Adopted 387-31: R 144-29; D 243-2. June 18, 2009.

397. HR 2847. Fiscal 2010 Commerce-Justice-Science Appropriations/Motion to Reconsider Historically Black Colleges and Universities. Broun, R-Ga., motion to reconsider the vote on the Johnson, D-Texas, amendment. Motion rejected 166-250: R 162-11; D 4-239. June 18, 2009.

	391	392	393	394	395	396	397
ALABAMA							
1 **Bonner**	Y	Y	N	Y	Y	Y	Y
2 Bright	N	Y	N	Y	N	Y	Y
3 **Rogers**	Y	Y	N	Y	Y	Y	Y
4 **Aderholt**	Y	Y	Y	Y	Y	Y	Y
5 Griffith	N	Y	N	Y	?	Y	N
6 **Bachus**	Y	Y	Y	Y	Y	Y	Y
7 Davis	?	?	?	?	?	?	?
ALASKA							
AL **Young**	N	Y	N	Y	N	Y	N
ARIZONA							
1 Kirkpatrick	N	Y	N	Y	N	Y	N
2 **Franks**	Y	Y	Y	Y	Y	N	Y
3 **Shadegg**	Y	Y	N	Y	Y	Y	Y
4 Pastor	N	Y	N	Y	N	Y	N
5 Mitchell	N	Y	N	Y	N	Y	N
6 **Flake**	Y	Y	N	Y	Y	N	Y
7 Grijalva	N	Y	N	Y	N	Y	N
8 Giffords	N	Y	N	Y	N	Y	N
ARKANSAS							
1 Berry	N	Y	N	Y	N	Y	N
2 Snyder	N	Y	N	Y	N	Y	N
3 **Boozman**	Y	Y	N	Y	Y	Y	Y
4 Ross	N	Y	N	Y	N	Y	N
CALIFORNIA							
1 Thompson	N	Y	N	Y	N	Y	N
2 **Herger**	Y	Y	Y	Y	Y	N	Y
3 **Lungren**	Y	Y	Y	Y	Y	Y	Y
4 **McClintock**	Y	Y	Y	Y	Y	N	Y
5 Matsui	N	Y	N	Y	N	Y	N
6 Woolsey	N	Y	N	Y	N	Y	N
7 Miller, George	N	Y	N	Y	N	Y	N
8 Pelosi							
9 Lee	N	Y	N	Y	N	Y	N
10 Tauscher	?	?	?	?	?	?	?
11 McNerney	N	Y	N	Y	N	Y	N
12 Speier	N	Y	N	Y	N	Y	N
13 Stark	N	Y	N	Y	N	Y	N
14 Eshoo	N	Y	N	Y	N	Y	N
15 Honda	N	Y	N	Y	N	Y	N
16 Lofgren	N	Y	N	Y	N	Y	N
17 Farr	N	Y	N	Y	N	Y	N
18 Cardoza	N	?	N	?	N	Y	N
19 **Radanovich**	Y	Y	Y	Y	Y	Y	Y
20 Costa	N	Y	N	Y	N	Y	N
21 **Nunes**	Y	Y	Y	Y	Y	Y	Y
22 **McCarthy**	Y	Y	Y	Y	Y	Y	Y
23 Capps	N	Y	N	Y	N	Y	N
24 **Gallegly**	Y	Y	Y	Y	Y	Y	Y
25 **McKeon**	Y	Y	N	Y	Y	Y	Y
26 **Dreier**	Y	Y	Y	Y	Y	Y	Y
27 Sherman	N	Y	N	Y	N	Y	N
28 Berman	N	Y	N	Y	N	Y	N
29 Schiff	N	Y	N	Y	N	Y	N
30 Waxman	N	Y	N	Y	N	Y	N
31 Becerra	N	Y	N	Y	N	Y	N
32 Vacant							
33 Watson	N	Y	N	Y	N	Y	N
34 Roybal-Allard	N	Y	N	Y	N	Y	N
35 Waters	N	Y	N	Y	N	Y	N
36 Harman	?	?	?	?	?	?	?
37 Richardson	N	Y	N	Y	N	Y	N
38 Napolitano	N	Y	N	Y	N	Y	N
39 Sánchez, Linda	?	?	?	?	?	?	?
40 **Royce**	Y	Y	Y	Y	Y	Y	Y
41 **Lewis**	Y	Y	Y	Y	Y	Y	Y
42 **Miller, Gary**	Y	Y	Y	Y	Y	Y	Y
43 Baca	N	Y	N	Y	N	Y	N
44 **Calvert**	Y	Y	Y	Y	Y	Y	Y
45 **Bono Mack**	Y	Y	Y	Y	Y	Y	Y
46 **Rohrabacher**	Y	Y	Y	Y	Y	Y	Y
47 Sanchez, Loretta	N	Y	N	Y	N	Y	N
48 **Campbell**	Y	Y	Y	Y	Y	N	Y
49 **Issa**	Y	Y	Y	Y	Y	Y	Y
50 **Bilbray**	Y	Y	Y	Y	Y	N	Y
51 Filner	N	Y	N	Y	N	Y	N
52 **Hunter**	Y	Y	Y	Y	Y	Y	Y
53 Davis	N	Y	N	Y	N	Y	N

	391	392	393	394	395	396	397
COLORADO							
1 DeGette	N	Y	N	Y	N	Y	N
2 Polis	N	Y	N	Y	?	Y	N
3 Salazar	N	Y	N	Y	N	Y	N
4 Markey	N	Y	N	Y	N	Y	N
5 **Lamborn**	Y	Y	Y	Y	Y	N	Y
6 **Coffman**	Y	Y	Y	Y	Y	N	Y
7 Perlmutter	N	Y	N	Y	N	?	N
CONNECTICUT							
1 Larson	N	Y	N	Y	N	Y	N
2 Courtney	N	Y	N	Y	N	Y	N
3 DeLauro	N	Y	N	Y	N	Y	N
4 Himes	N	Y	N	Y	N	Y	N
5 Murphy	N	Y	N	Y	?	Y	N
DELAWARE							
AL **Castle**	Y	Y	Y	Y	Y	Y	Y
FLORIDA							
1 **Miller**	Y	Y	N	Y	Y	N	Y
2 Boyd	N	Y	N	Y	N	Y	N
3 Brown	N	Y	N	Y	N	Y	N
4 **Crenshaw**	Y	Y	Y	Y	Y	Y	Y
5 **Brown-Waite**	Y	Y	Y	Y	N	Y	Y
6 **Stearns**	Y	Y	Y	Y	Y	Y	Y
7 **Mica**	Y	Y	Y	Y	Y	Y	Y
8 Grayson	N	Y	N	Y	N	Y	N
9 **Bilirakis**	Y	Y	Y	Y	Y	Y	Y
10 **Young**	N	Y	N	Y	Y	Y	N
11 Castor	N	Y	N	Y	N	Y	N
12 **Putnam**	Y	Y	Y	Y	Y	Y	Y
13 **Buchanan**	Y	Y	Y	Y	Y	Y	Y
14 **Mack**	Y	Y	Y	Y	Y	Y	Y
15 **Posey**	Y	Y	Y	Y	Y	Y	Y
16 **Rooney**	Y	Y	Y	Y	Y	Y	Y
17 Meek	N	Y	N	?	N	Y	N
18 **Ros-Lehtinen**	Y	Y	Y	Y	Y	Y	Y
19 Wexler	N	Y	N	Y	N	Y	N
20 Wasserman Schultz	N	Y	N	Y	N	Y	N
21 **Diaz-Balart, L.**	Y	Y	Y	Y	?	Y	Y
22 Klein	N	Y	N	Y	N	Y	N
23 Hastings	N	Y	N	Y	N	Y	N
24 Kosmas	N	Y	N	Y	N	Y	N
25 **Diaz-Balart, M.**	Y	Y	N	Y	Y	Y	Y
GEORGIA							
1 **Kingston**	Y	Y	N	Y	Y	Y	Y
2 Bishop	N	Y	N	Y	N	Y	N
3 **Westmoreland**	Y	Y	Y	Y	Y	N	Y
4 Johnson	N	Y	N	Y	N	Y	N
5 Lewis	?	?	?	?	?	?	?
6 **Price**	Y	Y	Y	Y	Y	Y	Y
7 **Linder**	Y	Y	Y	Y	Y	N	Y
8 Marshall	N	?	N	Y	N	Y	N
9 **Deal**	?	?	?	?	?	?	?
10 **Broun**	Y	Y	Y	Y	Y	Y	Y
11 **Gingrey**	Y	Y	Y	Y	Y	Y	Y
12 Barrow	N	Y	N	Y	N	Y	N
13 Scott	N	Y	N	Y	N	Y	N
HAWAII							
1 Abercrombie	N	?	N	?	N	Y	N
2 Hirono	N	Y	N	Y	N	Y	N
IDAHO							
1 Minnick	N	Y	N	Y	N	Y	N
2 **Simpson**	Y	Y	N	Y	Y	Y	Y
ILLINOIS							
1 Rush	N	Y	N	Y	N	Y	N
2 Jackson	N	Y	N	Y	N	Y	N
3 Lipinski	N	Y	N	Y	N	Y	N
4 Gutierrez	?	Y	N	Y	N	Y	N
5 Quigley	N	Y	N	Y	N	Y	N
6 **Roskam**	Y	Y	Y	Y	Y	Y	Y
7 Davis	N	Y	N	Y	N	Y	N
8 Bean	N	Y	N	Y	N	Y	N
9 Schakowsky	N	Y	N	Y	N	Y	N
10 **Kirk**	Y	Y	N	Y	N	Y	?
11 Halvorson	N	Y	N	Y	N	Y	N
12 Costello	N	Y	N	Y	N	Y	N
13 **Biggert**	Y	Y	N	Y	Y	Y	Y
14 Foster	N	Y	N	Y	N	Y	N
15 **Johnson**	N	Y	N	Y	N	Y	N

	391	392	393	394	395	396	397
16 **Manzullo**	Y	Y	N	Y	Y	Y	Y
17 Hare	N	Y	N	Y	N	Y	N
18 **Schock**	Y	Y	Y	Y	Y	Y	Y
19 **Shimkus**	Y	Y	Y	Y	Y	Y	Y
INDIANA							
1 Visclosky	N	Y	N	Y	N	Y	N
2 Donnelly	N	Y	N	Y	N	Y	N
3 **Souder**	Y	Y	Y	Y	Y	Y	Y
4 **Buyer**	Y	Y	Y	Y	Y	Y	Y
5 **Burton**	Y	Y	N	Y	Y	Y	Y
6 **Pence**	Y	Y	Y	Y	Y	N	Y
7 Carson	N	Y	N	Y	N	Y	N
8 Ellsworth	N	Y	N	Y	N	Y	N
9 Hill	N	Y	N	Y	N	Y	N
IOWA							
1 Braley	N	Y	N	Y	N	Y	N
2 Loebsack	N	Y	N	Y	N	Y	N
3 Boswell	N	Y	N	Y	N	Y	N
4 **Latham**	Y	Y	Y	Y	Y	Y	Y
5 **King**	Y	Y	Y	Y	Y	N	Y
KANSAS							
1 **Moran**	Y	Y	Y	Y	Y	Y	Y
2 **Jenkins**	Y	N	Y	Y	Y	Y	Y
3 Moore	N	Y	N	Y	N	Y	N
4 **Tiahrt**	Y	Y	Y	Y	Y	Y	Y
KENTUCKY							
1 **Whitfield**	Y	Y	Y	Y	Y	Y	Y
2 **Guthrie**	Y	Y	Y	Y	Y	Y	Y
3 Yarmuth	N	Y	?	?	?	?	?
4 **Davis**	Y	Y	Y	Y	Y	N	Y
5 **Rogers**	Y	Y	Y	Y	Y	Y	Y
6 Chandler	N	Y	N	Y	N	Y	N
LOUISIANA							
1 **Scalise**	Y	Y	Y	Y	Y	N	Y
2 **Cao**	N	Y	N	Y	N	Y	N
3 Melancon	N	Y	N	Y	N	Y	N
4 **Fleming**	Y	Y	N	Y	Y	Y	Y
5 **Alexander**	Y	Y	N	Y	Y	Y	Y
6 **Cassidy**	Y	Y	Y	Y	Y	Y	Y
7 **Boustany**	Y	Y	Y	Y	Y	Y	Y
MAINE							
1 Pingree	N	Y	N	Y	N	Y	N
2 Michaud	N	Y	N	Y	N	Y	N
MARYLAND							
1 Kratovil	N	Y	N	Y	N	Y	N
2 Ruppersberger	N	Y	N	Y	N	Y	N
3 Sarbanes	N	Y	N	Y	N	Y	N
4 Edwards	N	Y	N	Y	N	Y	N
5 Hoyer	N	Y	N	Y	N	Y	N
6 **Bartlett**	Y	Y	Y	Y	Y	Y	Y
7 Cummings	N	Y	N	Y	N	Y	N
8 Van Hollen	N	Y	N	Y	?	Y	?
MASSACHUSETTS							
1 Olver	?	?	N	Y	N	Y	N
2 Neal	N	Y	N	Y	N	Y	N
3 McGovern	N	Y	N	Y	N	Y	N
4 Frank	N	Y	N	Y	N	Y	N
5 Tsongas	N	Y	N	Y	N	Y	N
6 Tierney	N	Y	N	Y	N	Y	N
7 Markey	N	Y	?	?	N	Y	N
8 Capuano	N	Y	N	Y	N	Y	N
9 Lynch	N	Y	N	Y	N	Y	N
10 Delahunt	N	Y	N	Y	N	Y	N
MICHIGAN							
1 Stupak	N	Y	N	Y	N	Y	N
2 **Hoekstra**	Y	Y	Y	Y	Y	Y	Y
3 **Ehlers**	Y	Y	Y	?	Y	Y	Y
4 **Camp**	Y	Y	Y	Y	Y	Y	Y
5 Kildee	N	Y	N	Y	N	Y	N
6 **Upton**	Y	Y	Y	Y	Y	Y	Y
7 Schauer	N	Y	N	Y	N	Y	N
8 **Rogers**	Y	Y	N	Y	Y	Y	Y
9 Peters	N	Y	N	Y	N	Y	N
10 **Miller**	Y	Y	N	Y	Y	Y	Y
11 **McCotter**	Y	Y	Y	Y	Y	Y	Y
12 Levin	N	Y	N	Y	N	N	N
13 Kilpatrick	N	Y	N	Y	N	Y	N
14 Conyers	N	Y	N	Y	N	Y	N
15 Dingell	N	Y	N	Y	N	Y	N
MINNESOTA							
1 Walz	N	Y	N	Y	N	Y	N
2 **Kline**	Y	Y	Y	Y	Y	Y	Y
3 **Paulsen**	Y	Y	Y	Y	Y	Y	Y
4 McCollum	N	Y	N	Y	N	Y	N

	391	392	393	394	395	396	397
5 Ellison	?	?	?	?	?	?	?
6 **Bachmann**	?	?	?	?	?	?	?
7 Peterson	N	Y	N	Y	N	Y	N
8 Oberstar	N	Y	N	Y	N	Y	N
MISSISSIPPI							
1 Childers	N	Y	N	Y	Y	Y	Y
2 Thompson	N	Y	N	Y	N	Y	N
3 **Harper**	Y	Y	Y	Y	Y	N	Y
4 Taylor	N	Y	N	Y	N	Y	N
MISSOURI							
1 Clay	N	Y	N	Y	N	Y	N
2 **Akin**	Y	Y	Y	Y	Y	Y	Y
3 Carnahan	N	Y	N	Y	N	Y	N
4 Skelton	N	Y	N	Y	N	Y	N
5 Cleaver	N	Y	Y	Y	N	N	N
6 **Graves**	Y	Y	Y	Y	Y	Y	Y
7 **Blunt**	Y	Y	Y	Y	?	Y	Y
8 **Emerson**	Y	Y	Y	Y	Y	Y	Y
9 **Luetkemeyer**	Y	Y	Y	Y	Y	Y	Y
MONTANA							
AL **Rehberg**	Y	Y	N	Y	Y	Y	Y
NEBRASKA							
1 **Fortenberry**	Y	Y	N	Y	Y	Y	Y
2 **Terry**	Y	Y	N	Y	Y	Y	Y
3 **Smith**	Y	Y	Y	Y	Y	Y	Y
NEVADA							
1 Berkley	N	Y	N	Y	N	Y	N
2 **Heller**	Y	Y	N	Y	Y	Y	Y
3 Titus	N	Y	N	Y	N	Y	N
NEW HAMPSHIRE							
1 Shea-Porter	N	Y	N	Y	N	Y	N
2 Hodes	N	Y	N	Y	N	Y	N
NEW JERSEY							
1 Andrews	N	Y	N	Y	N	Y	N
2 **LoBiondo**	Y	Y	N	Y	N	Y	N
3 Adler	N	Y	N	Y	N	Y	N
4 **Smith**	?	Y	N	Y	Y	Y	Y
5 **Garrett**	Y	Y	N	Y	Y	Y	Y
6 Pallone	N	Y	N	Y	N	Y	N
7 **Lance**	Y	Y	Y	Y	Y	Y	Y
8 Pascrell	Y	Y	Y	Y	Y	Y	Y
9 Rothman	N	Y	N	Y	N	Y	N
10 Payne	N	Y	N	Y	N	Y	N
11 **Frelinghuysen**	Y	Y	Y	Y	?	Y	Y
12 Holt	N	Y	N	Y	N	Y	N
13 Sires	N	Y	N	Y	N	Y	N
NEW MEXICO							
1 Heinrich	N	Y	N	Y	N	Y	N
2 Teague	N	Y	N	Y	N	Y	N
3 Lujan	N	Y	N	Y	N	Y	N
NEW YORK							
1 Bishop	N	Y	N	Y	N	Y	N
2 Israel	N	Y	N	Y	N	Y	N
3 **King**	Y	Y	Y	Y	Y	Y	Y
4 McCarthy	N	Y	N	Y	N	Y	N
5 Ackerman	N	Y	N	Y	N	Y	N
6 Meeks	N	Y	N	Y	N	Y	N
7 Crowley	N	Y	N	Y	N	Y	N
8 Nadler	N	Y	N	Y	N	Y	N
9 Weiner	N	Y	N	Y	N	Y	N
10 Towns	N	Y	N	Y	N	Y	N
11 Clarke	N	Y	N	Y	N	Y	N
12 Velázquez	N	Y	N	Y	N	Y	N
13 McMahon	N	Y	N	Y	N	Y	N
14 Maloney	N	Y	N	Y	N	Y	N
15 Rangel	N	Y	N	Y	N	Y	N
16 Serrano	N	?	N	Y	N	Y	N
17 Engel	N	Y	N	Y	N	Y	N
18 Lowey	N	Y	N	Y	N	Y	N
19 Hall	N	Y	N	Y	N	Y	N
20 Murphy	N	Y	N	Y	N	Y	N
21 Tonko	N	Y	N	Y	N	Y	N
22 Hinchey	N	Y	N	Y	N	Y	N
23 **McHugh**	Y	Y	Y	Y	Y	Y	Y
24 Arcuri	N	Y	N	Y	N	Y	N
25 Maffei	N	Y	N	Y	N	Y	N
26 **Lee**	Y	Y	N	Y	Y	Y	Y
27 Higgins	N	Y	N	Y	N	Y	N
28 Slaughter	N	Y	N	Y	N	Y	N
29 Massa	N	Y	N	Y	N	Y	N
NORTH CAROLINA							
1 Butterfield	N	Y	N	Y	N	Y	N
2 Etheridge	N	Y	N	Y	N	Y	N
3 **Jones**	N	Y	N	Y	N	Y	N
4 Price	N	Y	N	Y	N	Y	N

	391	392	393	394	395	396	397
5 **Foxx**	Y	Y	N	Y	Y	N	Y
6 **Coble**	Y	Y	Y	Y	Y	N	Y
7 McIntyre	N	Y	N	Y	N	Y	N
8 Kissell	N	Y	N	Y	N	Y	N
9 **Myrick**	Y	Y	Y	Y	Y	Y	Y
10 **McHenry**	Y	Y	Y	Y	Y	Y	Y
11 Shuler	Y	Y	Y	Y	Y	Y	Y
12 Watt	N	Y	N	Y	N	Y	N
13 Miller	N	Y	N	Y	N	Y	N
NORTH DAKOTA							
AL Pomeroy	N	Y	N	Y	N	Y	N
OHIO							
1 Driehaus	N	Y	N	Y	N	Y	N
2 **Schmidt**	Y	Y	Y	Y	Y	Y	Y
3 **Turner**	Y	Y	Y	Y	Y	Y	Y
4 **Jordan**	Y	Y	N	Y	Y	Y	Y
5 **Latta**	Y	Y	N	Y	Y	Y	Y
6 Wilson	N	Y	N	Y	N	Y	N
7 **Austria**	Y	Y	Y	Y	Y	Y	Y
8 **Boehner**	Y	Y	N	Y	Y	Y	?
9 Kaptur	?	Y	N	Y	N	Y	N
10 Kucinich	N	Y	N	Y	N	Y	N
11 Fudge	N	Y	N	Y	N	Y	N
12 **Tiberi**	Y	Y	N	Y	Y	Y	N
13 Sutton	N	Y	N	Y	N	Y	N
14 **LaTourette**	Y	Y	Y	Y	Y	Y	Y
15 Kilroy	N	Y	N	Y	N	Y	N
16 Boccieri	N	Y	N	Y	N	Y	N
17 Ryan	N	Y	N	Y	N	Y	N
18 Space	N	Y	N	Y	N	Y	N
OKLAHOMA							
1 **Sullivan**	?	?	?	?	?	?	?
2 Boren	N	Y	N	Y	N	Y	N
3 **Lucas**	Y	Y	Y	Y	Y	Y	Y
4 **Cole**	Y	Y	Y	Y	Y	Y	Y
5 **Fallin**	Y	Y	Y	Y	Y	Y	Y
OREGON							
1 Wu	N	Y	N	Y	N	Y	N
2 **Walden**	Y	Y	N	Y	N	Y	N
3 Blumenauer	N	Y	N	Y	N	Y	N
4 DeFazio	N	Y	N	Y	N	Y	N
5 Schrader	N	Y	N	Y	N	Y	N
PENNSYLVANIA							
1 Brady	N	Y	N	Y	N	Y	N
2 Fattah	N	Y	N	Y	N	Y	N
3 Dahlkemper	N	Y	N	Y	N	Y	N
4 Altmire	N	Y	N	Y	N	Y	N
5 **Thompson**	Y	Y	Y	Y	Y	N	Y
6 **Gerlach**	Y	Y	Y	Y	Y	Y	Y
7 Sestak	?	?	?	?	?	?	?
8 Murphy, P.	N	Y	N	Y	?	Y	N
9 **Shuster**	Y	Y	Y	Y	Y	Y	Y
10 Carney	N	Y	N	Y	N	Y	N
11 Kanjorski	N	Y	N	Y	N	Y	N
12 Murtha	N	Y	N	Y	N	Y	N
13 Schwartz	N	Y	N	Y	?	Y	N
14 Doyle	N	Y	N	Y	N	Y	N
15 **Dent**	Y	Y	N	Y	Y	Y	Y
16 **Pitts**	Y	Y	N	Y	Y	Y	Y
17 Holden	N	Y	N	Y	N	Y	N
18 **Murphy, T.**	Y	Y	Y	Y	Y	Y	Y
19 **Platts**	Y	Y	Y	Y	Y	Y	Y
RHODE ISLAND							
1 Kennedy	?	?	?	?	?	?	?
2 Langevin	N	Y	N	Y	N	Y	N
SOUTH CAROLINA							
1 **Brown**	Y	Y	N	Y	Y	Y	Y
2 **Wilson**	Y	Y	Y	Y	Y	Y	Y
3 **Barrett**	Y	Y	Y	Y	Y	Y	Y
4 **Inglis**	Y	Y	Y	Y	Y	Y	Y
5 Spratt	N	Y	N	Y	N	Y	N
6 Clyburn	N	Y	N	Y	N	Y	N
SOUTH DAKOTA							
AL Herseth Sandlin	N	Y	N	Y	N	Y	N
TENNESSEE							
1 **Roe**	Y	Y	Y	Y	Y	Y	Y
2 **Duncan**	Y	Y	N	Y	Y	Y	Y
3 **Wamp**	Y	Y	Y	Y	Y	Y	Y
4 Davis	N	Y	N	Y	N	Y	N
5 Cooper	N	Y	N	?	N	Y	N
6 Gordon	N	Y	N	N	N	Y	?
7 **Blackburn**	Y	Y	Y	Y	Y	N	Y
8 Tanner	N	Y	N	Y	N	Y	N
9 Cohen	N	Y	N	Y	N	Y	N

	391	392	393	394	395	396	397
TEXAS							
1 **Gohmert**	Y	Y	Y	Y	Y	?	Y
2 **Poe**	Y	Y	Y	Y	Y	Y	Y
3 **Johnson, S.**	Y	Y	Y	Y	Y	Y	Y
4 **Hall**	Y	Y	Y	Y	Y	Y	Y
5 **Hensarling**	Y	Y	Y	Y	Y	N	Y
6 **Barton**	Y	Y	Y	Y	Y	Y	Y
7 **Culberson**	Y	Y	Y	Y	Y	N	Y
8 **Brady**	Y	Y	N	Y	?	N	Y
9 Green, A.	N	Y	N	Y	N	Y	N
10 **McCaul**	Y	Y	N	Y	Y	Y	Y
11 **Conaway**	Y	Y	N	Y	Y	N	Y
12 **Granger**	Y	Y	Y	Y	Y	Y	Y
13 **Thornberry**	Y	Y	Y	Y	Y	N	Y
14 **Paul**	Y	Y	Y	?	?	?	N
15 Hinojosa	N	Y	N	Y	N	Y	N
16 Reyes	N	Y	N	Y	N	Y	N
17 Edwards	N	Y	N	Y	N	Y	N
18 Jackson Lee	N	Y	N	Y	N	Y	N
19 **Neugebauer**	Y	Y	Y	Y	Y	N	Y
20 Gonzalez	N	Y	N	Y	N	Y	N
21 **Smith**	Y	Y	Y	?	Y	Y	Y
22 **Olson**	Y	Y	Y	Y	Y	N	Y
23 Rodriguez	N	Y	N	Y	N	Y	N
24 **Marchant**	Y	Y	N	Y	Y	Y	Y
25 Doggett	N	Y	N	Y	N	Y	N
26 **Burgess**	Y	Y	Y	Y	Y	Y	Y
27 Ortiz	N	Y	N	Y	N	Y	N
28 Cuellar	N	Y	N	Y	N	Y	N
29 Green, G.	N	Y	N	Y	N	Y	?
30 Johnson, E.	N	Y	N	Y	N	Y	N
31 **Carter**	Y	Y	N	Y	Y	Y	Y
32 **Sessions**	Y	Y	Y	Y	Y	N	Y
UTAH							
1 **Bishop**	Y	Y	Y	P	Y	Y	Y
2 Matheson	N	Y	N	Y	N	Y	N
3 **Chaffetz**	Y	Y	Y	Y	Y	Y	Y
VERMONT							
AL Welch	N	Y	N	Y	N	Y	N
VIRGINIA							
1 **Wittman**	Y	Y	Y	Y	Y	Y	Y
2 Nye	N	Y	N	Y	N	Y	N
3 Scott	N	Y	N	Y	N	Y	N
4 **Forbes**	Y	Y	N	Y	Y	Y	Y
5 Perriello	N	Y	N	Y	N	Y	N
6 **Goodlatte**	Y	Y	N	Y	Y	Y	Y
7 **Cantor**	Y	Y	N	Y	?	Y	Y
8 Moran	N	Y	N	Y	N	Y	N
9 Boucher	N	Y	N	Y	N	Y	N
10 **Wolf**	Y	Y	Y	Y	Y	Y	Y
11 Connolly	N	Y	N	Y	N	Y	N
WASHINGTON							
1 Inslee	N	Y	N	Y	N	Y	N
2 Larsen	N	Y	N	Y	N	Y	N
3 Baird	N	Y	N	Y	N	Y	N
4 **Hastings**	Y	Y	Y	Y	Y	Y	Y
5 **McMorris Rodgers**	Y	Y	Y	Y	Y	Y	Y
6 Dicks	N	Y	N	Y	N	Y	N
7 McDermott	N	Y	N	Y	N	Y	N
8 **Reichert**	Y	Y	Y	Y	Y	Y	Y
9 Smith	N	Y	N	Y	N	Y	N
WEST VIRGINIA							
1 Mollohan	N	Y	N	Y	N	Y	N
2 **Capito**	Y	Y	Y	Y	Y	Y	Y
3 Rahall	N	Y	N	Y	N	Y	N
WISCONSIN							
1 **Ryan**	Y	Y	Y	Y	Y	Y	Y
2 Baldwin	N	Y	N	Y	N	Y	N
3 Kind	N	Y	N	Y	N	Y	N
4 Moore	N	Y	N	Y	N	Y	N
5 **Sensenbrenner**	Y	Y	Y	Y	Y	Y	Y
6 **Petri**	Y	Y	Y	Y	Y	Y	Y
7 Obey	N	Y	N	Y	N	Y	N
8 Kagen	N	Y	N	Y	N	Y	N
WYOMING							
AL **Lummis**	Y	Y	Y	Y	Y	N	Y
DELEGATES							
Faleomavaega (A.S.)							
Norton (D.C.)							
Bordallo (Guam)							
Sablan (N. Marianas)							
Pierluisi (P.R.)							
Christensen (V.I.)							

IN THE HOUSE | By Vote Number

398. **HR 2847. Fiscal 2010 Commerce-Justice-Science Appropriations/Revote on Energy Star Designation.** Revote on the Cuellar, D-Texas, amendment (vote 363). Under House rules, any member (in this case Westmoreland, R-Ga.) may demand a revote in the full House on an amendment adopted in the Committee of the Whole. Delegates may not vote in the full House. Adopted 338-74: R 97-74; D 241-0. June 18, 2009.

399. **HR 2847. Fiscal 2010 Commerce-Justice-Science Appropriations/Motion to Reconsider Energy Star Designation.** Hensarling, R-Texas, motion to reconsider the vote on the Cuellar, D-Texas, amendment. Motion rejected 165-245: R 160-9; D 5-236. June 18, 2009.

400. **HR 2847. Fiscal 2010 Commerce-Justice-Science Appropriations/Revote on Expired Grant Accounts' Undisbursed Balances.** Revote on the Hodes, D-N.H., amendment (vote 365). Under House rules, any member (in this case Westmoreland, R-Ga.) may demand a revote in the full House on an amendment adopted in the Committee of the Whole. Delegates may not vote in the full House. Adopted 413-0: R 171-0; D 242-0. June 18, 2009.

401. **HR 2847. Fiscal 2010 Commerce-Justice-Science Appropriations/Motion to Reconsider Expired Grant Accounts' Undisbursed Balances.** King, R-Iowa, motion to reconsider the vote on the Hodes, D-N.H., amendment. Motion rejected 165-247: R 161-11; D 4-236. June 18, 2009.

402. **HR 2847. Fiscal 2010 Commerce-Justice-Science Appropriations/Motion to Table.** Obey, D-Wis., motion to table (kill) the Rogers, R-Mich., appeal of the ruling of the chair with respect to the Obey point of order that the Lewis, R-Calif., motion to recommit the bill contained provisions not specifically contained or authorized in existing law. The motion would recommit the bill to the Appropriations Committee with instructions that it be immediately reported back with language that would bar the use of funds in the bill by the Justice Department to provide Miranda rights to detainees in the custody of the U.S. military in Afghanistan. Motion agreed to 246-171: R 2-166; D 244-5. June 18, 2009.

403. **HR 2847. Fiscal 2010 Commerce-Justice-Science Appropriations/Motion to Reconsider Tabling of Appeal.** Rogers, R-Mich., motion to reconsider the vote on the Obey, D-Wis., motion to table (kill) the Rogers appeal of the ruling of the chair with respect to the Obey point of order that the Lewis, R-Calif., motion to recommit the bill contained provisions not specifically contained or authorized in existing law. Motion rejected 168-243: R 162-9; D 6-234. June 18, 2009.

	398	399	400	401	402	403
ALABAMA						
1 Bonner	N	Y	Y	Y	N	Y
2 Bright	Y	Y	Y	Y	N	Y
3 Rogers	Y	Y	Y	Y	N	Y
4 Aderholt	N	Y	Y	Y	N	?
5 Griffith	Y	N	Y	N	N	N
6 Bachus	N	Y	Y	Y	N	Y
7 Davis	?	?	?	?	Y	N
ALASKA						
AL Young	Y	N	Y	N	N	N
ARIZONA						
1 Kirkpatrick	Y	N	Y	N	Y	N
2 Franks	N	Y	Y	Y	N	Y
3 Shadegg	N	Y	Y	Y	N	Y
4 Pastor	Y	N	Y	N	Y	N
5 Mitchell	Y	N	Y	N	Y	N
6 Flake	N	Y	Y	Y	N	Y
7 Grijalva	Y	N	Y	N	Y	N
8 Giffords	Y	N	Y	N	Y	N
ARKANSAS						
1 Berry	Y	N	Y	N	Y	N
2 Snyder	Y	N	Y	N	Y	N
3 Boozman	N	Y	Y	Y	N	Y
4 Ross	Y	N	Y	N	Y	N
CALIFORNIA						
1 Thompson	Y	N	Y	N	Y	N
2 Herger	Y	Y	Y	Y	N	Y
3 Lungren	Y	Y	Y	Y	N	Y
4 McClintock	N	Y	Y	Y	N	Y
5 Matsui	Y	N	Y	N	Y	N
6 Woolsey	Y	N	Y	N	Y	N
7 Miller, George	Y	N	Y	N	Y	N
8 Pelosi						
9 Lee	Y	N	Y	N	Y	?
10 Tauscher	?	?	?	?	?	?
11 McNerney	Y	N	Y	N	Y	?
12 Speier	Y	N	Y	N	Y	N
13 Stark	Y	N	Y	N	Y	N
14 Eshoo	Y	N	Y	N	Y	N
15 Honda	Y	N	Y	N	Y	N
16 Lofgren	Y	N	Y	N	Y	N
17 Farr	?	N	Y	N	Y	N
18 Cardoza	Y	N	Y	N	Y	N
19 Radanovich	Y	Y	Y	Y	N	Y
20 Costa	Y	N	Y	N	Y	N
21 Nunes	N	Y	Y	Y	N	Y
22 McCarthy	N	Y	Y	Y	N	Y
23 Capps	Y	N	Y	N	Y	N
24 Gallegly	Y	Y	Y	Y	N	Y
25 McKeon	N	Y	Y	Y	N	Y
26 Dreier	Y	Y	Y	Y	N	?
27 Sherman	Y	N	Y	N	Y	N
28 Berman	Y	N	Y	N	Y	N
29 Schiff	Y	N	Y	N	Y	N
30 Waxman	?	N	Y	N	Y	N
31 Becerra	Y	N	Y	N	Y	N
32 Vacant						
33 Watson	Y	N	Y	N	Y	N
34 Roybal-Allard	Y	N	Y	N	Y	N
35 Waters	Y	N	Y	N	Y	N
36 Harman	?	?	?	?	?	?
37 Richardson	Y	N	Y	N	Y	N
38 Napolitano	Y	N	Y	N	Y	N
39 Sánchez, Linda	?	?	?	?	Y	N
40 Royce	Y	Y	Y	Y	N	Y
41 Lewis	Y	Y	?	Y	N	Y
42 Miller, Gary	Y	Y	Y	Y	N	Y
43 Baca	Y	N	Y	N	Y	N
44 Calvert	Y	Y	Y	Y	N	N
45 Bono Mack	Y	Y	Y	Y	N	Y
46 Rohrabacher	Y	Y	Y	Y	N	Y
47 Sanchez, Loretta	Y	N	Y	N	Y	N
48 Campbell	N	Y	Y	Y	N	Y
49 Issa	N	Y	Y	Y	?	Y
50 Bilbray	N	Y	Y	N	N	Y
51 Filner	Y	N	Y	N	Y	N
52 Hunter	N	Y	Y	Y	N	Y
53 Davis	Y	N	Y	N	Y	N

	398	399	400	401	402	403
COLORADO						
1 DeGette	Y	N	Y	N	Y	N
2 Polis	Y	N	Y	N	Y	N
3 Salazar	Y	N	Y	N	Y	N
4 Markey	Y	N	Y	N	Y	N
5 Lamborn	N	Y	Y	Y	N	Y
6 Coffman	N	Y	Y	Y	N	Y
7 Perlmutter	Y	N	Y	N	Y	N
CONNECTICUT						
1 Larson	Y	N	Y	N	Y	N
2 Courtney	Y	N	Y	N	Y	N
3 DeLauro	Y	N	Y	N	Y	?
4 Himes	Y	N	Y	N	Y	N
5 Murphy	Y	N	Y	N	Y	N
DELAWARE						
AL Castle	Y	Y	Y	Y	N	Y
FLORIDA						
1 Miller	N	Y	Y	Y	N	Y
2 Boyd	Y	N	Y	N	Y	N
3 Brown	Y	N	Y	N	Y	N
4 Crenshaw	Y	Y	Y	Y	N	Y
5 Brown-Waite	Y	Y	Y	Y	N	Y
6 Stearns	N	N	Y	N	N	Y
7 Mica	Y	Y	Y	Y	N	Y
8 Grayson	Y	N	Y	N	Y	N
9 Bilirakis	Y	Y	Y	Y	N	Y
10 Young	N	Y	Y	Y	N	Y
11 Castor	Y	N	Y	N	Y	N
12 Putnam	Y	Y	Y	Y	N	Y
13 Buchanan	Y	Y	Y	Y	N	Y
14 Mack	N	Y	Y	Y	N	Y
15 Posey	N	Y	Y	Y	N	Y
16 Rooney	N	Y	Y	Y	N	Y
17 Meek	Y	N	Y	N	Y	N
18 Ros-Lehtinen	Y	Y	Y	Y	N	Y
19 Wexler	Y	N	Y	N	Y	N
20 Wasserman Schultz	Y	N	Y	N	Y	N
21 Diaz-Balart, L.	Y	Y	Y	Y	N	Y
22 Klein	Y	N	?	N	Y	N
23 Hastings	Y	N	Y	N	Y	N
24 Kosmas	Y	N	Y	N	Y	N
25 Diaz-Balart, M.	Y	Y	Y	Y	N	Y
GEORGIA						
1 Kingston	N	Y	Y	Y	N	Y
2 Bishop	Y	N	Y	N	Y	N
3 Westmoreland	N	Y	Y	Y	?	Y
4 Johnson	Y	N	Y	N	Y	N
5 Lewis	?	?	?	?	?	?
6 Price	N	Y	Y	Y	N	Y
7 Linder	N	Y	Y	Y	N	Y
8 Marshall	Y	N	Y	?	Y	N
9 Deal	?	?	?	?	?	?
10 Broun	N	Y	Y	Y	N	Y
11 Gingrey	N	Y	Y	Y	N	Y
12 Barrow	Y	N	Y	N	Y	N
13 Scott	Y	N	Y	N	Y	N
HAWAII						
1 Abercrombie	Y	N	Y	N	Y	N
2 Hirono	Y	?	Y	N	Y	N
IDAHO						
1 Minnick	Y	N	Y	N	Y	N
2 Simpson	N	Y	Y	Y	N	Y
ILLINOIS						
1 Rush	Y	N	Y	N	Y	?
2 Jackson	Y	N	Y	N	Y	N
3 Lipinski	Y	N	Y	N	Y	N
4 Gutierrez	Y	N	Y	?	Y	N
5 Quigley	Y	N	Y	N	Y	N
6 Roskam	N	Y	Y	Y	N	Y
7 Davis	Y	N	Y	N	Y	N
8 Bean	Y	N	Y	N	Y	N
9 Schakowsky	Y	N	Y	N	Y	N
10 Kirk	Y	?	?	Y	N	Y
11 Halvorson	Y	N	Y	N	Y	N
12 Costello	Y	N	Y	N	Y	N
13 Biggert	Y	Y	Y	Y	N	Y
14 Foster	Y	N	Y	N	Y	N
15 Johnson	Y	N	Y	Y	Y	N

KEY   **Republicans**   Democrats

Y	Voted for (yea)
#	Paired for
+	Announced for
N	Voted against (nay)
X	Paired against
–	Announced against
P	Voted "present"
C	Voted "present" to avoid possible conflict of interest
?	Did not vote or otherwise make a position known

	398	399	400	401	402	403
16 **Manzullo**	Y	Y	Y	Y	N	Y
17 Hare	Y	N	Y	N	Y	N
18 **Schock**	Y	Y	Y	Y	N	Y
19 **Shimkus**	N	Y	Y	Y	N	Y
INDIANA						
1 Visclosky	Y	N	Y	N	Y	N
2 Donnelly	Y	N	Y	N	Y	N
3 **Souder**	Y	Y	Y	Y	N	Y
4 **Buyer**	Y	Y	Y	Y	N	Y
5 **Burton**	N	Y	Y	Y	N	Y
6 **Pence**	N	Y	Y	Y	N	Y
7 Carson	Y	N	Y	N	Y	N
8 Ellsworth	Y	N	Y	N	Y	N
9 Hill	Y	N	Y	N	Y	Y
IOWA						
1 Braley	Y	N	Y	N	Y	N
2 Loebsack	Y	N	Y	N	Y	N
3 Boswell	Y	N	Y	N	Y	N
4 **Latham**	Y	Y	Y	Y	N	Y
5 **King**	N	Y	Y	Y	N	Y
KANSAS						
1 **Moran**	Y	Y	Y	Y	N	Y
2 **Jenkins**	N	Y	Y	Y	N	Y
3 Moore	Y	N	Y	N	Y	N
4 **Tiahrt**	N	Y	Y	Y	N	?
KENTUCKY						
1 **Whitfield**	Y	Y	Y	Y	N	Y
2 **Guthrie**	Y	Y	Y	Y	N	Y
3 Yarmuth	?	Y	Y	N	Y	N
4 **Davis**	Y	Y	Y	Y	N	Y
5 **Rogers**	Y	Y	Y	Y	N	Y
6 Chandler	Y	N	Y	N	Y	N
LOUISIANA						
1 **Scalise**	N	Y	Y	Y	N	Y
2 **Cao**	Y	N	Y	N	N	N
3 Melancon	Y	N	Y	N	Y	N
4 **Fleming**	N	Y	Y	Y	N	Y
5 **Alexander**	N	?	?	?	N	Y
6 **Cassidy**	Y	Y	Y	Y	N	Y
7 **Boustany**	N	Y	Y	Y	N	Y
MAINE						
1 Pingree	Y	N	Y	N	Y	N
2 Michaud	Y	N	Y	N	Y	N
MARYLAND						
1 Kratovil	Y	N	Y	N	Y	N
2 Ruppersberger	Y	N	Y	N	Y	N
3 Sarbanes	Y	N	Y	N	Y	N
4 Edwards	Y	N	Y	N	Y	N
5 Hoyer	Y	N	?	N	Y	N
6 **Bartlett**	Y	Y	Y	Y	N	Y
7 Cummings	Y	N	Y	N	N	N
8 Van Hollen	Y	N	Y	N	Y	N
MASSACHUSETTS						
1 Olver	Y	N	Y	N	Y	N
2 Neal	Y	N	Y	N	Y	N
3 McGovern	Y	N	Y	N	Y	N
4 Frank	Y	N	Y	N	Y	N
5 Tsongas	Y	N	Y	N	Y	N
6 Tierney	Y	N	Y	N	Y	N
7 Markey	Y	N	Y	N	Y	N
8 Capuano	Y	N	Y	N	Y	N
9 Lynch	Y	N	Y	N	Y	N
10 Delahunt	Y	N	Y	N	Y	N
MICHIGAN						
1 Stupak	Y	N	Y	N	Y	N
2 **Hoekstra**	Y	Y	Y	Y	N	Y
3 **Ehlers**	Y	Y	Y	Y	N	Y
4 **Camp**	Y	Y	Y	Y	N	Y
5 Kildee	Y	N	Y	N	Y	N
6 **Upton**	Y	Y	Y	Y	N	Y
7 Schauer	Y	N	Y	N	Y	N
8 **Rogers**	N	Y	Y	?	Y	Y
9 Peters	Y	N	Y	N	Y	N
10 **Miller**	Y	Y	Y	Y	N	Y
11 **McCotter**	N	Y	Y	Y	N	Y
12 Levin	Y	N	Y	N	Y	N
13 Kilpatrick	Y	N	Y	N	Y	N
14 Conyers	?	?	?	?	Y	N
15 Dingell	Y	N	Y	N	Y	N
MINNESOTA						
1 Walz	Y	N	Y	N	Y	N
2 **Kline**	N	Y	Y	Y	N	Y
3 **Paulsen**	Y	Y	Y	Y	N	Y
4 McCollum	Y	N	Y	N	Y	N

	398	399	400	401	402	403
5 Ellison	?	?	?	?	?	?
6 **Bachmann**	?	?	?	?	?	?
7 Peterson	Y	N	Y	N	Y	N
8 Oberstar	Y	N	Y	N	Y	N
MISSISSIPPI						
1 Childers	Y	Y	Y	Y	N	Y
2 Thompson	Y	N	Y	N	Y	N
3 **Harper**	Y	Y	Y	Y	N	Y
4 Taylor	Y	N	Y	N	Y	N
MISSOURI						
1 Clay	Y	N	Y	N	Y	N
2 **Akin**	Y	Y	Y	Y	N	Y
3 Carnahan	Y	N	Y	N	Y	N
4 Skelton	Y	N	Y	N	Y	N
5 Cleaver	Y	N	Y	N	Y	N
6 **Graves**	Y	Y	Y	Y	N	Y
7 **Blunt**	N	Y	Y	Y	N	Y
8 **Emerson**	Y	Y	Y	Y	N	Y
9 **Luetkemeyer**	Y	Y	Y	Y	N	Y
MONTANA						
AL **Rehberg**	N	Y	Y	Y	N	Y
NEBRASKA						
1 **Fortenberry**	Y	Y	Y	Y	N	Y
2 **Terry**	Y	Y	Y	Y	N	Y
3 **Smith**	Y	Y	Y	Y	N	Y
NEVADA						
1 Berkley	Y	N	Y	N	Y	N
2 **Heller**	Y	Y	Y	Y	N	Y
3 Titus	Y	N	Y	N	Y	N
NEW HAMPSHIRE						
1 Shea-Porter	Y	N	Y	N	Y	N
2 Hodes	Y	N	Y	N	Y	N
NEW JERSEY						
1 Andrews	Y	N	Y	N	Y	N
2 **LoBiondo**	Y	N	Y	N	N	Y
3 Adler	Y	N	Y	N	Y	N
4 **Smith**	?	Y	Y	Y	N	Y
5 **Garrett**	Y	Y	Y	Y	N	Y
6 Pallone	Y	N	Y	N	Y	N
7 **Lance**	Y	Y	Y	Y	N	Y
8 Pascrell	Y	Y	Y	Y	Y	Y
9 Rothman	Y	N	Y	N	Y	?
10 Payne	Y	N	Y	N	Y	N
11 **Frelinghuysen**	Y	N	Y	Y	N	Y
12 Holt	Y	N	Y	N	Y	N
13 Sires	Y	N	Y	N	Y	N
NEW MEXICO						
1 Heinrich	Y	N	Y	N	Y	N
2 Teague	Y	N	Y	N	Y	N
3 Lujan	Y	N	Y	N	Y	N
NEW YORK						
1 Bishop	Y	N	Y	N	Y	N
2 Israel	Y	N	Y	N	Y	N
3 **King**	Y	Y	Y	Y	N	Y
4 McCarthy	Y	N	Y	N	Y	N
5 Ackerman	Y	N	Y	N	Y	N
6 Meeks	Y	N	Y	N	Y	N
7 Crowley	Y	N	Y	N	Y	N
8 Nadler	Y	N	Y	N	Y	N
9 Weiner	Y	N	Y	N	Y	N
10 Towns	Y	N	Y	N	Y	N
11 Clarke	Y	N	Y	N	Y	N
12 Velázquez	Y	N	Y	N	Y	N
13 McMahon	Y	N	Y	N	Y	N
14 Maloney	Y	N	Y	?	Y	N
15 Rangel	?	?	?	?	Y	N
16 Serrano	Y	?	Y	N	Y	N
17 Engel	Y	N	Y	N	Y	N
18 Lowey	Y	N	Y	N	Y	?
19 Hall	Y	N	Y	N	Y	N
20 Murphy	Y	N	Y	N	Y	N
21 Tonko	Y	N	Y	N	Y	N
22 Hinchey	Y	N	Y	N	Y	N
23 **McHugh**	Y	Y	Y	Y	N	Y
24 Arcuri	Y	N	Y	N	Y	N
25 Maffei	Y	N	Y	N	Y	N
26 **Lee**	Y	Y	Y	Y	N	Y
27 Higgins	Y	N	Y	N	Y	N
28 Slaughter	Y	N	Y	N	Y	N
29 Massa	Y	N	Y	N	Y	N
NORTH CAROLINA						
1 Butterfield	Y	N	Y	N	Y	N
2 Etheridge	Y	N	Y	N	Y	N
3 **Jones**	N	N	Y	N	N	N
4 Price	Y	N	Y	N	Y	N

	398	399	400	401	402	403
5 **Foxx**	N	Y	Y	Y	N	Y
6 **Coble**	N	Y	Y	Y	N	Y
7 McIntyre	Y	N	Y	N	Y	N
8 Kissell	Y	N	Y	N	Y	N
9 **Myrick**	N	Y	Y	Y	N	Y
10 **McHenry**	N	Y	Y	Y	N	Y
11 Shuler	Y	Y	Y	Y	Y	Y
12 Watt	Y	N	Y	N	Y	N
13 Miller	Y	N	Y	N	Y	N
NORTH DAKOTA						
AL Pomeroy	Y	?	Y	N	Y	N
OHIO						
1 Driehaus	Y	N	Y	N	Y	N
2 **Schmidt**	Y	Y	?	?	?	?
3 **Turner**	Y	Y	Y	Y	N	Y
4 **Jordan**	N	Y	Y	Y	N	Y
5 **Latta**	N	Y	Y	Y	N	Y
6 Wilson	Y	N	Y	N	Y	N
7 **Austria**	Y	?	Y	Y	N	Y
8 **Boehner**	?	?	Y	Y	?	Y
9 Kaptur	?	N	Y	N	Y	N
10 Kucinich	Y	N	Y	N	Y	N
11 Fudge	Y	N	Y	N	Y	N
12 **Tiberi**	N	Y	Y	Y	N	Y
13 Sutton	Y	N	Y	N	Y	N
14 **LaTourette**	Y	Y	Y	Y	N	Y
15 Kilroy	Y	N	Y	N	Y	N
16 Boccieri	Y	N	Y	N	Y	N
17 Ryan	Y	N	Y	?	Y	?
18 Space	Y	N	Y	N	Y	N
OKLAHOMA						
1 **Sullivan**	?	?	?	?	?	?
2 Boren	Y	N	Y	N	Y	N
3 **Lucas**	Y	Y	Y	Y	N	Y
4 **Cole**	N	Y	Y	Y	N	Y
5 **Fallin**	Y	Y	Y	Y	N	Y
OREGON						
1 Wu	Y	N	Y	N	Y	N
2 **Walden**	Y	Y	Y	N	N	N
3 Blumenauer	Y	N	Y	N	N	N
4 DeFazio	Y	N	Y	N	Y	N
5 Schrader	Y	N	Y	N	Y	N
PENNSYLVANIA						
1 Brady	Y	N	Y	N	Y	N
2 Fattah	Y	N	Y	N	Y	N
3 Dahlkemper	Y	N	Y	N	Y	N
4 Altmire	Y	N	Y	N	Y	N
5 **Thompson**	N	Y	Y	Y	N	Y
6 **Gerlach**	Y	Y	Y	Y	N	Y
7 Sestak	?	?	?	?	?	?
8 Murphy, P.	Y	N	Y	N	Y	N
9 **Shuster**	Y	Y	Y	Y	N	Y
10 Carney	Y	N	Y	N	N	Y
11 Kanjorski	Y	N	Y	N	Y	N
12 Murtha	Y	N	Y	N	Y	N
13 Schwartz	Y	N	Y	N	Y	N
14 Doyle	Y	N	Y	N	Y	N
15 **Dent**	Y	Y	Y	Y	N	N
16 **Pitts**	N	Y	Y	Y	N	Y
17 Holden	Y	N	Y	N	Y	N
18 **Murphy, T.**	Y	Y	Y	Y	?	Y
19 **Platts**	Y	Y	Y	Y	N	Y
RHODE ISLAND						
1 Kennedy	?	?	?	?	?	?
2 Langevin	Y	N	Y	N	Y	?
SOUTH CAROLINA						
1 **Brown**	Y	Y	Y	Y	N	Y
2 **Wilson**	Y	Y	Y	Y	N	Y
3 **Barrett**	Y	Y	Y	Y	N	Y
4 **Inglis**	Y	Y	Y	Y	N	Y
5 Spratt	Y	N	Y	N	Y	N
6 Clyburn	Y	N	Y	N	Y	N
SOUTH DAKOTA						
AL Herseth Sandlin	Y	N	Y	N	Y	?
TENNESSEE						
1 **Roe**	Y	Y	Y	Y	N	Y
2 **Duncan**	N	Y	Y	Y	N	Y
3 **Wamp**	Y	Y	Y	Y	N	Y
4 Davis	Y	N	Y	N	Y	N
5 Cooper	Y	N	Y	N	Y	N
6 Gordon	Y	?	Y	N	Y	N
7 **Blackburn**	N	Y	Y	Y	N	Y
8 Tanner	Y	N	Y	N	Y	N
9 Cohen	Y	N	Y	N	Y	N

	398	399	400	401	402	403
TEXAS						
1 **Gohmert**	N	Y	Y	Y	N	Y
2 **Poe**	N	Y	Y	Y	N	Y
3 **Johnson, S.**	N	Y	Y	Y	N	Y
4 **Hall**	Y	?	Y	Y	N	Y
5 **Hensarling**	Y	Y	Y	Y	N	Y
6 **Barton**	Y	Y	Y	Y	N	Y
7 **Culberson**	Y	Y	Y	Y	N	Y
8 **Brady**	N	Y	Y	Y	N	Y
9 Green, A.	Y	N	Y	N	Y	N
10 **McCaul**	Y	Y	Y	Y	N	Y
11 **Conaway**	N	Y	Y	Y	N	Y
12 **Granger**	Y	Y	Y	Y	N	Y
13 **Thornberry**	N	Y	Y	Y	N	Y
14 **Paul**	N	N	Y	N	N	N
15 Hinojosa	Y	N	Y	N	Y	N
16 Reyes	Y	N	Y	N	Y	N
17 Edwards	Y	N	Y	N	Y	N
18 Jackson Lee	Y	N	Y	N	Y	N
19 **Neugebauer**	N	Y	Y	Y	N	Y
20 Gonzalez	Y	N	Y	N	Y	N
21 **Smith**	Y	Y	Y	Y	N	Y
22 **Olson**	N	Y	Y	Y	N	Y
23 Rodriguez	Y	N	Y	N	Y	N
24 **Marchant**	N	Y	Y	Y	N	Y
25 Doggett	Y	N	Y	N	Y	N
26 **Burgess**	Y	Y	Y	Y	N	Y
27 Ortiz	Y	N	Y	N	Y	N
28 Cuellar	Y	N	Y	N	Y	N
29 Green, G.	Y	N	Y	N	Y	N
30 Johnson, E.	Y	N	Y	N	Y	N
31 **Carter**	Y	Y	Y	Y	?	Y
32 **Sessions**	N	Y	Y	Y	N	Y
UTAH						
1 **Bishop**	N	Y	Y	Y	N	Y
2 Matheson	Y	N	Y	N	Y	N
3 **Chaffetz**	Y	?	Y	Y	N	Y
VERMONT						
AL Welch	Y	N	Y	N	Y	N
VIRGINIA						
1 **Wittman**	Y	Y	Y	Y	N	Y
2 Nye	Y	N	Y	N	Y	N
3 Scott	Y	N	Y	N	Y	N
4 **Forbes**	N	Y	Y	Y	N	Y
5 Perriello	Y	N	Y	N	Y	N
6 **Goodlatte**	Y	Y	Y	Y	N	Y
7 **Cantor**	?	Y	Y	Y	?	Y
8 Moran	Y	N	Y	N	Y	N
9 Boucher	Y	N	Y	N	Y	N
10 **Wolf**	Y	Y	Y	Y	N	Y
11 Connolly	Y	N	Y	N	Y	N
WASHINGTON						
1 Inslee	Y	N	Y	N	Y	N
2 Larsen	Y	N	Y	N	Y	N
3 Baird	Y	N	Y	N	Y	N
4 **Hastings**	N	Y	Y	Y	N	Y
5 **McMorris Rodgers**	N	Y	Y	Y	N	Y
6 Dicks	Y	N	Y	N	Y	N
7 McDermott	Y	N	Y	N	Y	N
8 **Reichert**	Y	Y	Y	Y	N	Y
9 Smith	Y	N	?	N	Y	N
WEST VIRGINIA						
1 Mollohan	Y	N	Y	N	Y	N
2 **Capito**	Y	Y	Y	Y	N	Y
3 Rahall	Y	N	Y	N	Y	N
WISCONSIN						
1 **Ryan**	?	Y	Y	Y	N	Y
2 Baldwin	Y	N	Y	N	Y	N
3 Kind	Y	N	Y	N	Y	N
4 Moore	Y	N	Y	?	Y	N
5 **Sensenbrenner**	Y	Y	Y	Y	N	Y
6 **Petri**	Y	Y	Y	Y	N	Y
7 Obey	Y	N	Y	N	Y	N
8 Kagen	Y	N	Y	N	Y	N
WYOMING						
AL **Lummis**	N	Y	Y	Y	N	Y
DELEGATES						
Faleomavaega (A.S.)						
Norton (D.C.)						
Bordallo (Guam)						
Sablan (N. Marianas)						
Pierluisi (P.R.)						
Christensen (V.I.)						

IN THE HOUSE | By Vote Number

404. HR 2847. Fiscal 2010 Commerce-Justice-Science Appropriations/Motion to Recommit. Lewis, R-Calif., motion to recommit the bill to the Appropriations Committee with instructions that it be reported back immediately with language that would increase the amount provided for Justice Department salaries and expenses for department leadership by $1 million and immediately decrease that funding by $1 million. It would increase the amount provided for the FBI's salaries and expenses for overseas deployments and other activities by $1 million and immediately decrease that funding by $1 million. Motion agreed to 312-103: R 172-1; D 140-102. June 18, 2009.

405. HR 2847. Fiscal 2010 Commerce-Justice-Science Appropriations/Motion to Reconsider Recommit. Broun, R-Ga., motion to reconsider the vote on the Lewis, R-Calif., motion to recommit the bill with instructions on Justice Department and FBI salaries and expenses (vote 404). Motion rejected 139-266: R 134-32; D 5-234. June 18, 2009.

406. HR 2847. Fiscal 2010 Commerce-Justice-Science Appropriations/Justice Department and FBI Funding. Obey, D-Wis., amendment that would increase the amount provided for the Justice Department's salaries and expenses for department leadership by $1 million and immediately decrease that funding by $1 million. It would increase the amount provided for the FBI's salaries and expenses for overseas deployments and other activities by $1 million and immediately decrease that funding by $1 million. Adopted 402-13: R 174-1; D 228-12. (The amendment was made in order pursuant to the adoption of the Lewis, R-Calif., motion to recommit the bill with instructions.) June 18, 2009.

407. HR 2847. Fiscal 2010 Commerce-Justice-Science Appropriations/Motion to Reconsider Justice Department and FBI Funding. Broun, R-Ga., motion to reconsider the vote on the Obey, D-Wis., amendment (vote 406). Motion rejected 149-267: R 143-27; D 6-240. June 18, 2009.

408. HR 2847. Fiscal 2010 Commerce-Justice-Science Appropriations/Passage. Passage of the bill that would appropriate $64.3 billion in fiscal 2010 for the departments of Commerce and Justice, NASA and several other science agencies. It would provide $27.7 billion for the Justice Department and $13.8 billion for the Commerce Department. It would provide $7.9 billion for the FBI, $18.2 billion for NASA, $6.9 billion for the National Science Foundation and $4.6 billion for the National Oceanic and Atmospheric Administration. It would prohibit funds appropriated in the bill from being used to release detainees at Guantánamo Bay, Cuba, into the United States. The bill also would require the Justice Department to clarify its policy on the use of federal law enforcement against medical marijuana programs. Passed 259-157: R 24-149; D 235-8. A "yea" was a vote in support of the president's position. June 18, 2009.

	404	405	406	407	408
ALABAMA					
1 **Bonner**	Y	Y	Y	Y	N
2 **Bright**	Y	Y	Y	Y	N
3 **Rogers**	Y	Y	Y	Y	N
4 **Aderholt**	Y	Y	Y	Y	N
5 Griffith	Y	N	Y	N	N
6 **Bachus**	Y	Y	Y	Y	N
7 Davis	Y	N	Y	N	N
ALASKA					
AL **Young**	Y	N	Y	N	N
ARIZONA					
1 **Kirkpatrick**	Y	N	Y	N	Y
2 **Franks**	Y	Y	Y	Y	N
3 **Shadegg**	Y	Y	Y	Y	N
4 Pastor	N	N	Y	N	Y
5 Mitchell	Y	N	Y	N	Y
6 **Flake**	Y	Y	Y	Y	N
7 Grijalva	N	N	Y	N	Y
8 **Giffords**	Y	N	Y	N	Y
ARKANSAS					
1 Berry	Y	N	Y	N	Y
2 Snyder	Y	N	Y	N	Y
3 **Boozman**	Y	Y	Y	Y	N
4 Ross	Y	N	Y	Y	Y
CALIFORNIA					
1 Thompson	N	N	Y	N	Y
2 **Herger**	Y	Y	Y	Y	N
3 **Lungren**	Y	?	Y	Y	N
4 **McClintock**	Y	N	N	N	N
5 Matsui	N	N	Y	N	Y
6 Woolsey	N	N	?	N	Y
7 Miller, George	N	N	Y	N	Y
8 Pelosi					
9 Lee	N	N	Y	N	Y
10 Tauscher	?	?	?	?	?
11 McNerney	Y	N	Y	N	Y
12 Speier	Y	N	Y	N	Y
13 Stark	N	N	Y	N	Y
14 Eshoo	N	N	Y	N	Y
15 Honda	N	N	Y	N	Y
16 Lofgren	N	N	Y	N	Y
17 Farr	N	N	Y	N	Y
18 Cardoza	Y	N	Y	N	Y
19 **Radanovich**	?	Y	Y	Y	N
20 Costa	Y	N	Y	N	Y
21 **Nunes**	Y	Y	Y	Y	N
22 **McCarthy**	Y	?	Y	Y	N
23 Capps	Y	?	Y	N	Y
24 **Gallegly**	Y	Y	Y	Y	N
25 **McKeon**	Y	Y	Y	Y	N
26 **Dreier**	Y	Y	Y	Y	N
27 Sherman	N	N	Y	N	Y
28 Berman	N	N	Y	N	Y
29 Schiff	Y	N	Y	N	Y
30 Waxman	N	N	N	N	Y
31 Becerra	N	N	Y	N	Y
32 Vacant					
33 Watson	N	N	Y	N	Y
34 Roybal-Allard	N	N	Y	N	Y
35 Waters	?	N	Y	N	Y
36 Harman	?	?	?	?	?
37 Richardson	Y	N	Y	N	Y
38 Napolitano	N	N	Y	N	Y
39 Sánchez, Linda	N	?	?	?	?
40 **Royce**	Y	?	Y	Y	N
41 **Lewis**	Y	Y	Y	Y	N
42 **Miller, Gary**	Y	Y	Y	Y	N
43 Baca	Y	N	Y	N	Y
44 **Calvert**	Y	Y	Y	Y	N
45 **Bono Mack**	Y	Y	Y	Y	N
46 **Rohrabacher**	Y	Y	Y	Y	N
47 Sanchez, Loretta	Y	N	Y	N	Y
48 **Campbell**	Y	Y	Y	Y	N
49 **Issa**	Y	Y	Y	Y	N
50 **Bilbray**	Y	N	Y	Y	N
51 Filner	N	Y	N	N	Y
52 **Hunter**	Y	Y	Y	Y	N
53 Davis	Y	N	Y	N	Y

	404	405	406	407	408
COLORADO					
1 DeGette	Y	N	Y	N	Y
2 Polis	N	N	Y	N	?
3 Salazar	Y	N	Y	N	Y
4 Markey	Y	N	Y	N	Y
5 **Lamborn**	Y	Y	Y	Y	N
6 **Coffman**	Y	Y	Y	Y	N
7 Perlmutter	Y	N	Y	N	Y
CONNECTICUT					
1 Larson	Y	N	Y	N	Y
2 Courtney	Y	N	Y	N	Y
3 DeLauro	Y	N	Y	N	Y
4 Himes	Y	N	Y	N	Y
5 Murphy	Y	N	Y	N	Y
DELAWARE					
AL **Castle**	Y	N	Y	N	N
FLORIDA					
1 **Miller**	Y	Y	Y	Y	N
2 Boyd	Y	N	Y	N	Y
3 Brown	Y	N	Y	N	Y
4 **Crenshaw**	Y	Y	Y	Y	N
5 **Brown-Waite**	Y	Y	Y	Y	N
6 **Stearns**	Y	Y	Y	Y	N
7 **Mica**	Y	N	Y	?	N
8 Grayson	Y	N	Y	Y	Y
9 **Bilirakis**	Y	N	Y	N	–
10 **Young**	Y	N	Y	N	N
11 Castor	N	N	Y	N	Y
12 **Putnam**	Y	Y	Y	Y	N
13 **Buchanan**	Y	N	N	N	N
14 **Mack**	Y	Y	Y	Y	N
15 **Posey**	Y	N	Y	Y	N
16 **Rooney**	Y	Y	Y	Y	N
17 Meek	Y	N	Y	N	Y
18 **Ros-Lehtinen**	Y	Y	Y	Y	Y
19 Wexler	N	N	Y	N	Y
20 Wasserman Schultz	Y	N	Y	N	Y
21 **Diaz-Balart, L.**	Y	Y	Y	Y	Y
22 Klein	Y	N	?	N	Y
23 Hastings	N	N	Y	N	Y
24 Kosmas	Y	N	Y	N	Y
25 **Diaz-Balart, M.**	Y	Y	Y	Y	Y
GEORGIA					
1 **Kingston**	Y	Y	Y	Y	N
2 Bishop	N	N	Y	N	Y
3 **Westmoreland**	Y	Y	Y	Y	N
4 Johnson	N	N	Y	N	Y
5 Lewis	?	?	?	?	?
6 **Price**	Y	Y	Y	Y	N
7 **Linder**	Y	N	Y	N	N
8 Marshall	Y	N	Y	N	Y
9 **Deal**	?	?	?	?	?
10 **Broun**	Y	Y	Y	Y	N
11 **Gingrey**	Y	?	Y	Y	N
12 Barrow	Y	N	Y	N	Y
13 Scott	Y	N	Y	N	Y
HAWAII					
1 Abercrombie	Y	?	Y	N	Y
2 Hirono	N	N	Y	N	Y
IDAHO					
1 Minnick	Y	N	Y	N	?
2 **Simpson**	Y	Y	Y	Y	N
ILLINOIS					
1 Rush	?	N	Y	N	Y
2 Jackson	N	N	N	N	Y
3 Lipinski	Y	N	Y	N	Y
4 Gutierrez	N	N	?	N	Y
5 Quigley	Y	N	Y	N	Y
6 **Roskam**	Y	Y	Y	Y	N
7 Davis	N	N	Y	N	Y
8 Bean	N	N	?	N	Y
9 Schakowsky	N	N	Y	N	Y
10 **Kirk**	Y	Y	Y	Y	N
11 Halvorson	Y	N	Y	N	Y
12 Costello	Y	N	Y	N	Y
13 **Biggert**	Y	N	Y	N	Y
14 Foster	Y	N	Y	N	Y
15 Johnson	Y	Y	N	Y	N

KEY   **Republicans**   Democrats

Y Voted for (yea)	X Paired against
# Paired for	– Announced against
+ Announced for	P Voted "present"
N Voted against (nay)	

C Voted "present" to avoid possible conflict of interest

? Did not vote or otherwise make a position known

	404	405	406	407	408
16 Manzullo	Y	Y	Y	Y	N
17 Hare	Y	N	Y	N	Y
18 Schock	Y	Y	Y	Y	N
19 Shimkus	Y	Y	Y	Y	N
INDIANA					
1 Visclosky	Y	N	Y	N	Y
2 Donnelly	Y	N	Y	N	Y
3 Souder	Y	Y	Y	Y	N
4 Buyer	Y	Y	Y	Y	N
5 Burton	Y	Y	Y	Y	N
6 Pence	Y	Y	Y	Y	N
7 Carson	Y	N	Y	N	Y
8 Ellsworth	Y	N	Y	N	Y
9 Hill	Y	N	Y	N	Y
IOWA					
1 Braley	N	N	Y	N	Y
2 Loebsack	?	N	Y	N	Y
3 Boswell	Y	N	Y	N	Y
4 Latham	Y	Y	Y	Y	N
5 King	Y	Y	Y	?	N
KANSAS					
1 Moran	Y	Y	Y	Y	N
2 Jenkins	Y	Y	Y	Y	N
3 Moore	?	N	Y	N	Y
4 Tiahrt	Y	Y	Y	Y	N
KENTUCKY					
1 Whitfield	Y	Y	Y	Y	N
2 Guthrie	Y	Y	Y	Y	N
3 Yarmuth	Y	N	Y	N	Y
4 Davis	Y	Y	Y	Y	N
5 Rogers	Y	Y	Y	Y	Y
6 Chandler	Y	N	Y	N	Y
LOUISIANA					
1 Scalise	Y	Y	Y	Y	N
2 Cao	Y	N	Y	N	Y
3 Melancon	Y	N	Y	N	Y
4 Fleming	Y	Y	Y	Y	N
5 Alexander	Y	Y	Y	Y	N
6 Cassidy	Y	N	Y	N	Y
7 Boustany	Y	Y	Y	Y	N
MAINE					
1 Pingree	N	N	Y	N	Y
2 Michaud	N	N	N	N	Y
MARYLAND					
1 Kratovil	Y	N	Y	N	Y
2 Ruppersberger	Y	N	Y	N	Y
3 Sarbanes	N	N	N	N	Y
4 Edwards	N	N	N	N	Y
5 Hoyer	Y	N	Y	N	Y
6 Bartlett	Y	Y	Y	Y	N
7 Cummings	N	N	Y	N	Y
8 Van Hollen	Y	N	Y	N	Y
MASSACHUSETTS					
1 Olver	N	N	Y	?	Y
2 Neal	Y	N	?	N	Y
3 McGovern	N	N	N	N	Y
4 Frank	N	N	N	N	Y
5 Tsongas	N	N	N	N	Y
6 Tierney	N	N	N	N	Y
7 Markey	Y	N	Y	N	Y
8 Capuano	Y	N	Y	N	Y
9 Lynch	Y	N	Y	N	Y
10 Delahunt	N	N	Y	N	Y
MICHIGAN					
1 Stupak	Y	N	Y	N	Y
2 Hoekstra	Y	Y	Y	Y	N
3 Ehlers	Y	Y	Y	?	Y
4 Camp	Y	Y	Y	Y	N
5 Kildee	N	N	Y	N	Y
6 Upton	Y	Y	Y	Y	N
7 Schauer	N	N	Y	N	Y
8 Rogers	Y	N	Y	N	Y
9 Peters	Y	N	Y	N	Y
10 Miller	Y	Y	Y	Y	N
11 McCotter	Y	Y	Y	Y	N
12 Levin	Y	N	Y	N	Y
13 Kilpatrick	N	N	Y	N	Y
14 Conyers	N	N	Y	N	Y
15 Dingell	Y	N	Y	N	Y
MINNESOTA					
1 Walz	Y	N	Y	N	Y
2 Kline	Y	N	Y	N	N
3 Paulsen	Y	N	Y	N	N
4 McCollum	Y	N	Y	N	Y

	404	405	406	407	408
5 Ellison	?	?	?	?	?
6 Bachmann	?	?	?	?	?
7 Peterson	Y	N	?	N	Y
8 Oberstar	N	N	Y	N	Y
MISSISSIPPI					
1 Childers	Y	Y	Y	Y	Y
2 Thompson	N	N	Y	N	Y
3 Harper	Y	Y	Y	Y	N
4 Taylor	Y	N	Y	N	N
MISSOURI					
1 Clay	Y	N	Y	N	Y
2 Akin	Y	Y	Y	Y	N
3 Carnahan	Y	N	Y	N	Y
4 Skelton	Y	N	Y	N	Y
5 Cleaver	N	N	Y	N	Y
6 Graves	Y	Y	Y	Y	N
7 Blunt	Y	N	Y	N	N
8 Emerson	Y	?	Y	N	Y
9 Luetkemeyer	Y	Y	Y	Y	N
MONTANA					
AL Rehberg	Y	Y	Y	Y	N
NEBRASKA					
1 Fortenberry	Y	Y	Y	Y	N
2 Terry	Y	Y	Y	N	N
3 Smith	Y	Y	Y	Y	N
NEVADA					
1 Berkley	N	N	Y	N	Y
2 Heller	Y	?	Y	Y	N
3 Titus	Y	N	Y	N	Y
NEW HAMPSHIRE					
1 Shea-Porter	Y	N	Y	N	Y
2 Hodes	Y	N	Y	N	Y
NEW JERSEY					
1 Andrews	Y	N	Y	N	Y
2 LoBiondo	Y	Y	Y	N	Y
3 Adler	Y	N	Y	N	Y
4 Smith	Y	N	Y	Y	Y
5 Garrett	Y	Y	Y	Y	N
6 Pallone	Y	N	Y	N	Y
7 Lance	Y	Y	Y	N	Y
8 Pascrell	Y	N	Y	N	Y
9 Rothman	Y	?	Y	N	Y
10 Payne	Y	N	Y	N	Y
11 Frelinghuysen	Y	Y	Y	Y	Y
12 Holt	N	N	Y	N	Y
13 Sires	Y	N	Y	N	Y
NEW MEXICO					
1 Heinrich	Y	N	Y	N	Y
2 Teague	Y	?	Y	N	Y
3 Lujan	Y	N	Y	N	Y
NEW YORK					
1 Bishop	N	N	Y	N	Y
2 Israel	N	N	N	N	Y
3 King	Y	N	Y	Y	?
4 McCarthy	N	N	Y	N	Y
5 Ackerman	N	N	Y	N	Y
6 Meeks	Y	N	Y	N	Y
7 Crowley	N	N	Y	N	Y
8 Nadler	N	N	Y	N	Y
9 Weiner	Y	?	Y	N	Y
10 Towns	N	N	Y	N	Y
11 Clarke	N	?	Y	N	Y
12 Velázquez	N	N	Y	N	Y
13 McMahon	Y	N	Y	N	Y
14 Maloney	Y	N	Y	N	Y
15 Rangel	?	?	?	?	?
16 Serrano	N	N	Y	N	Y
17 Engel	N	N	Y	N	Y
18 Lowey	N	N	Y	N	Y
19 Hall	Y	N	Y	N	Y
20 Murphy	Y	N	Y	N	Y
21 Tonko	Y	N	Y	N	Y
22 Hinchey	N	N	Y	N	Y
23 McHugh	Y	Y	Y	Y	Y
24 Arcuri	Y	Y	Y	Y	Y
25 Maffei	Y	N	Y	N	Y
26 Lee	Y	Y	Y	Y	N
27 Higgins	Y	N	Y	N	Y
28 Slaughter	?	N	N	N	Y
29 Massa	Y	N	Y	N	Y
NORTH CAROLINA					
1 Butterfield	N	?	Y	N	Y
2 Etheridge	Y	N	Y	N	Y
3 Jones	Y	N	Y	N	Y
4 Price	N	N	Y	N	Y

	404	405	406	407	408
5 Foxx	Y	Y	Y	Y	N
6 Coble	Y	Y	Y	Y	N
7 McIntyre	Y	N	Y	N	Y
8 Kissell	Y	N	Y	N	Y
9 Myrick	Y	Y	Y	Y	Y
10 McHenry	Y	Y	Y	Y	N
11 Shuler	Y	Y	Y	Y	Y
12 Watt	N	N	N	N	Y
13 Miller	N	N	Y	N	Y
NORTH DAKOTA					
AL Pomeroy	Y	N	Y	N	?
OHIO					
1 Driehaus	Y	N	Y	N	Y
2 Schmidt	Y	Y	Y	Y	N
3 Turner	Y	Y	Y	Y	N
4 Jordan	Y	Y	Y	Y	N
5 Latta	Y	Y	Y	Y	N
6 Wilson	N	N	Y	N	Y
7 Austria	Y	Y	Y	Y	N
8 Boehner	Y	N	Y	N	N
9 Kaptur	Y	N	Y	N	Y
10 Kucinich	N	N	Y	N	Y
11 Fudge	N	N	Y	N	Y
12 Tiberi	Y	Y	Y	Y	N
13 Sutton	N	N	Y	N	?
14 LaTourette	Y	Y	Y	Y	Y
15 Kilroy	Y	N	Y	N	Y
16 Boccieri	Y	N	Y	N	Y
17 Ryan	N	N	Y	N	Y
18 Space	Y	N	Y	N	Y
OKLAHOMA					
1 Sullivan	?	?	?	?	?
2 Boren	Y	N	Y	N	Y
3 Lucas	Y	Y	Y	Y	N
4 Cole	Y	Y	Y	?	N
5 Fallin	Y	Y	Y	Y	Y
OREGON					
1 Wu	N	N	Y	N	Y
2 Walden	Y	N	Y	N	N
3 Blumenauer	N	N	Y	N	Y
4 DeFazio	Y	N	Y	N	Y
5 Schrader	Y	N	Y	N	Y
PENNSYLVANIA					
1 Brady	Y	N	Y	N	Y
2 Fattah	N	N	Y	N	Y
3 Dahlkemper	Y	N	Y	N	Y
4 Altmire	Y	N	Y	N	Y
5 Thompson	Y	Y	Y	Y	N
6 Gerlach	Y	Y	Y	N	Y
7 Sestak	?	?	?	?	?
8 Murphy, P.	Y	N	Y	N	Y
9 Shuster	Y	Y	Y	Y	N
10 Carney	Y	N	Y	N	Y
11 Kanjorski	N	N	Y	N	Y
12 Murtha	N	N	Y	N	Y
13 Schwartz	N	N	Y	N	Y
14 Doyle	Y	N	Y	N	Y
15 Dent	Y	Y	Y	Y	Y
16 Pitts	Y	Y	Y	Y	N
17 Holden	Y	N	Y	N	Y
18 Murphy, T.	Y	Y	Y	Y	Y
19 Platts	Y	N	Y	N	Y
RHODE ISLAND					
1 Kennedy	?	?	?	?	?
2 Langevin	Y	N	Y	N	Y
SOUTH CAROLINA					
1 Brown	Y	Y	Y	Y	N
2 Wilson	Y	Y	Y	Y	N
3 Barrett	Y	Y	Y	Y	N
4 Inglis	Y	N	Y	N	Y
5 Spratt	Y	N	Y	N	Y
6 Clyburn	N	N	Y	N	Y
SOUTH DAKOTA					
AL Herseth Sandlin	Y	N	Y	N	Y
TENNESSEE					
1 Roe	Y	Y	Y	Y	N
2 Duncan	Y	Y	Y	Y	N
3 Wamp	Y	Y	Y	Y	N
4 Davis	Y	N	Y	N	Y
5 Cooper	Y	N	Y	N	Y
6 Gordon	N	N	Y	N	Y
7 Blackburn	Y	?	Y	Y	N
8 Tanner	Y	N	Y	N	Y
9 Cohen	N	N	Y	N	Y

	404	405	406	407	408
TEXAS					
1 Gohmert	Y	?	Y	Y	N
2 Poe	?	Y	Y	Y	N
3 Johnson, S.	Y	N	Y	N	N
4 Hall	Y	Y	Y	Y	N
5 Hensarling	Y	?	Y	Y	N
6 Barton	Y	Y	Y	Y	N
7 Culberson	Y	Y	Y	Y	N
8 Brady	Y	Y	Y	Y	N
9 Green, A.	N	N	Y	N	Y
10 McCaul	Y	N	Y	N	Y
11 Conaway	Y	Y	Y	Y	N
12 Granger	Y	Y	Y	Y	N
13 Thornberry	Y	Y	Y	Y	N
14 Paul	N	N	N	N	N
15 Hinojosa	Y	N	Y	N	Y
16 Reyes	Y	N	Y	N	Y
17 Edwards	Y	N	Y	N	Y
18 Jackson Lee	N	N	Y	N	Y
19 Neugebauer	Y	Y	Y	Y	N
20 Gonzalez	N	N	Y	N	Y
21 Smith	Y	Y	Y	Y	N
22 Olson	Y	Y	Y	Y	N
23 Rodriguez	Y	N	Y	N	Y
24 Marchant	Y	Y	Y	Y	N
25 Doggett	?	N	Y	N	Y
26 Burgess	Y	N	Y	N	Y
27 Ortiz	Y	N	Y	N	Y
28 Cuellar	Y	N	Y	N	Y
29 Green, G.	Y	N	Y	N	Y
30 Johnson, E.	N	N	Y	N	Y
31 Carter	Y	Y	Y	Y	N
32 Sessions	Y	Y	Y	Y	N
UTAH					
1 Bishop	Y	Y	Y	?	N
2 Matheson	Y	N	Y	N	N
3 Chaffetz	Y	Y	Y	Y	N
VERMONT					
AL Welch	N	N	Y	N	Y
VIRGINIA					
1 Wittman	Y	N	Y	N	N
2 Nye	Y	N	Y	N	Y
3 Scott	N	N	Y	N	Y
4 Forbes	Y	Y	Y	Y	N
5 Perriello	Y	N	Y	N	Y
6 Goodlatte	Y	Y	Y	Y	N
7 Cantor	Y	Y	Y	Y	N
8 Moran	N	?	Y	N	Y
9 Boucher	Y	N	Y	N	Y
10 Wolf	Y	Y	Y	Y	Y
11 Connolly	N	N	Y	N	Y
WASHINGTON					
1 Inslee	Y	N	Y	N	Y
2 Larsen	N	N	Y	N	Y
3 Baird	N	N	Y	N	Y
4 Hastings	Y	Y	Y	Y	N
5 McMorris Rodgers	Y	Y	Y	Y	N
6 Dicks	Y	N	Y	N	Y
7 McDermott	N	N	Y	N	Y
8 Reichert	Y	Y	Y	Y	N
9 Smith	N	N	N	N	Y
WEST VIRGINIA					
1 Mollohan	N	N	Y	N	Y
2 Capito	Y	Y	Y	Y	N
3 Rahall	Y	N	Y	N	Y
WISCONSIN					
1 Ryan	Y	Y	Y	Y	N
2 Baldwin	N	N	Y	N	Y
3 Kind	N	N	Y	N	Y
4 Moore	N	N	Y	N	Y
5 Sensenbrenner	Y	Y	Y	Y	N
6 Petri	Y	Y	Y	Y	N
7 Obey	Y	N	?	N	Y
8 Kagen	N	N	N	N	Y
WYOMING					
AL Lummis	Y	Y	Y	N	N
DELEGATES					
Faleomavaega (A.S.)					
Norton (D.C.)					
Bordallo (Guam)					
Sablan (N. Marianas)					
Pierluisi (P.R.)					
Christensen (V.I.)					

IN THE HOUSE | By Vote Number

409. **HR 2918. Fiscal 2010 Legislative Branch Appropriations/ Previous Question.** Hastings, D-Fla., motion to order the previous question (thus ending debate and possibility of amendment) on adoption of the rule (H Res 559) that would provide for House floor consideration of the bill that would appropriate $3.7 billion in fiscal 2010 for legislative branch operations, excluding Senate operations. Motion agreed to 230-177: R 0-171; D 230-6. June 19, 2009.

410. **HR 2918. Fiscal 2010 Legislative Branch Appropriations/Rule.** Adoption of the rule (H Res 559) that would provide for House floor consideration of the bill that would appropriate $3.7 billion in fiscal 2010 for legislative branch operations, excluding Senate operations. Adopted 226-179: R 0-168; D 226-11. June 19, 2009.

411. **H Res 560. Condemn Iran Violence/Adoption.** Berman, D-Calif., motion to suspend the rules and adopt the resolution that would condemn the ongoing violence against demonstrators by the government of Iran, affirm the importance of democratic and fair elections, and express support for all Iranian citizens who struggle for freedom, human rights, civil liberties and protection of the rule of law. Motion agreed to 405-1: R 170-1; D 235-0. A two-thirds majority of those present and voting (271 in this case) is required for adoption under suspension of the rules. June 19, 2009.

412. **HR 2918. Fiscal 2010 Legislative Branch Appropriations/ Recommit.** Kingston, R-Ga., motion to recommit the bill to the Appropriations Committee with instructions that it be reported back forthwith with language that would reduce the amount for House of Representatives employee benefits by $100,000. Motion agreed to 374-34: R 169-0; D 205-34. June 19, 2009.

413. **HR 2918. Fiscal 2010 Legislative Branch Appropriations/ Passage.** Passage of the bill that would appropriate $3.7 billion in fiscal 2010 for legislative branch operations, excluding Senate operations. The total would include $1.4 billion for operations of the House, $647 million for the Library of Congress, $559 million for the Government Accountability Office, $325 million for the Capitol Police and $146 million for the Government Printing Office. Passed 232-178: R 18-151; D 214-27. June 19, 2009.

414. **Procedural Matter/Quorum Call.** * A quorum was present with 395 members responding (38 members did not respond). June 19, 2009.

415. **H Res 520. Impeachment of Judge Kent/Violation of Trust.** Adoption of Article I of the resolution, which would impeach Judge Samuel B. Kent, of the U.S. District Court for the Southern District of Texas, for engaging in conduct "incompatible with the trust and confidence placed in him as a judge" by making unwanted sexual contact with an employee between 2003 and 2007. Adopted 389-0: R 163-0; D 226-0. June 19, 2009.

416. **H Res 520. Impeachment of Judge Kent/Violation of Trust.** Adoption of Article II of the resolution, which would impeach Judge Samuel B. Kent, of the U.S. District Court for the Southern District of Texas, for engaging in conduct "incompatible with the trust and confidence placed in him as a judge" by making unwanted sexual contact with an employee between 2001 and 2007. Adopted 385-0: R 160-0; D 225-0. June 19, 2009.

*CQ does not include quorum calls in its vote charts.

	409	410	411	412	413	415	416
ALABAMA							
1 **Bonner**	N	N	Y	Y	N	Y	Y
2 Bright	Y	N	Y	Y	N	Y	Y
3 **Rogers**	N	N	Y	Y	N	Y	Y
4 **Aderholt**	N	N	Y	Y	Y	Y	Y
5 Griffith	Y	Y	Y	Y	Y	Y	Y
6 **Bachus**	N	N	Y	Y	N	Y	Y
7 Davis	Y	Y	Y	?	?	?	?
ALASKA							
AL **Young**	N	N	Y	Y	Y	Y	Y
ARIZONA							
1 Kirkpatrick	Y	N	Y	Y	N	Y	Y
2 **Franks**	N	N	Y	Y	N	Y	Y
3 **Shadegg**	?	?	?	?	?	?	?
4 Pastor	Y	Y	Y	Y	N	Y	Y
5 Mitchell	N	N	Y	Y	N	Y	Y
6 **Flake**	N	N	Y	Y	N	Y	Y
7 Grijalva	Y	Y	Y	Y	Y	Y	Y
8 Giffords	Y	N	Y	Y	N	Y	Y
ARKANSAS							
1 Berry	Y	Y	Y	Y	Y	Y	Y
2 Snyder	Y	Y	Y	Y	Y	Y	Y
3 **Boozman**	N	N	Y	Y	N	Y	Y
4 Ross	Y	Y	Y	Y	Y	Y	Y
CALIFORNIA							
1 Thompson	Y	Y	Y	Y	Y	Y	Y
2 **Herger**	N	N	Y	Y	N	Y	Y
3 **Lungren**	N	N	Y	Y	N	Y	Y
4 **McClintock**	N	N	Y	Y	N	Y	Y
5 Matsui	Y	Y	Y	Y	N	Y	Y
6 Woolsey	Y	+	Y	Y	Y	Y	Y
7 Miller, George	Y	Y	Y	Y	Y	Y	Y
8 Pelosi							
9 Lee	Y	Y	Y	N	Y	Y	Y
10 Tauscher	Y	Y	Y	Y	Y	Y	Y
11 McNerney	Y	Y	Y	Y	N	Y	Y
12 Speier	Y	Y	Y	Y	Y	?	?
13 Stark	?	Y	Y	Y	Y	Y	Y
14 Eshoo	Y	Y	Y	Y	Y	+	+
15 Honda	Y	Y	Y	Y	Y	Y	Y
16 Lofgren	Y	Y	Y	Y	Y	Y	Y
17 Farr	Y	Y	Y	Y	Y	?	?
18 Cardoza	Y	Y	Y	Y	Y	Y	Y
19 **Radanovich**	N	N	Y	Y	N	Y	Y
20 Costa	Y	Y	Y	Y	Y	?	Y
21 **Nunes**	N	N	Y	Y	N	Y	Y
22 **McCarthy**	N	?	Y	Y	N	Y	Y
23 Capps	Y	Y	Y	Y	Y	Y	Y
24 **Gallegly**	N	N	Y	Y	N	Y	Y
25 **McKeon**	N	N	Y	Y	N	Y	Y
26 **Dreier**	N	N	Y	Y	N	Y	Y
27 Sherman	Y	Y	Y	N	Y	Y	Y
28 Berman	Y	Y	Y	Y	Y	Y	Y
29 Schiff	Y	Y	Y	Y	Y	Y	Y
30 Waxman	Y	Y	Y	Y	Y	Y	Y
31 Becerra	Y	Y	Y	Y	Y	Y	Y
32 Vacant							
33 Watson	Y	Y	Y	N	Y	Y	Y
34 Roybal-Allard	Y	Y	Y	Y	Y	Y	Y
35 Waters	Y	?	Y	N	Y	Y	Y
36 Harman	?	?	?	?	?	?	?
37 Richardson	Y	Y	Y	Y	Y	Y	Y
38 Napolitano	Y	Y	Y	N	Y	Y	Y
39 Sánchez, Linda	?	?	?	?	?	?	?
40 **Royce**	N	N	Y	N	Y	Y	Y
41 **Lewis**	N	N	Y	Y	N	Y	Y
42 **Miller, Gary**	N	N	Y	N	Y	Y	Y
43 Baca	Y	Y	Y	Y	Y	Y	Y
44 **Calvert**	N	N	Y	Y	N	Y	Y
45 **Bono Mack**	N	N	Y	Y	N	Y	Y
46 **Rohrabacher**	N	N	Y	N	Y	Y	Y
47 Sanchez, Loretta	Y	Y	Y	Y	Y	Y	Y
48 **Campbell**	N	N	Y	Y	N	Y	Y
49 **Issa**	N	N	Y	Y	N	Y	Y
50 **Bilbray**	N	N	Y	Y	N	Y	Y
51 Filner	Y	Y	Y	N	Y	Y	Y
52 **Hunter**	N	N	Y	Y	N	Y	Y
53 Davis	Y	Y	Y	Y	Y	Y	Y

	409	410	411	412	413	415	416
COLORADO							
1 DeGette	Y	Y	Y	Y	Y	Y	Y
2 Polis	Y	Y	Y	Y	Y	Y	Y
3 Salazar	Y	Y	Y	Y	Y	Y	Y
4 Markey	Y	Y	Y	Y	N	Y	Y
5 **Lamborn**	N	N	Y	Y	N	Y	Y
6 **Coffman**	N	N	Y	Y	N	Y	Y
7 Perlmutter	Y	Y	Y	Y	Y	Y	Y
CONNECTICUT							
1 Larson	Y	Y	Y	Y	Y	Y	Y
2 Courtney	Y	Y	Y	Y	Y	Y	Y
3 DeLauro	Y	Y	Y	Y	Y	Y	Y
4 Himes	Y	Y	Y	Y	Y	Y	Y
5 Murphy	Y	Y	Y	Y	Y	Y	Y
DELAWARE							
AL **Castle**	N	N	Y	Y	N	Y	Y
FLORIDA							
1 **Miller**	N	N	Y	Y	?	Y	Y
2 Boyd	Y	Y	Y	Y	Y	Y	Y
3 Brown	Y	Y	Y	Y	Y	Y	Y
4 **Crenshaw**	N	N	Y	Y	Y	?	?
5 **Brown-Waite**	N	N	Y	Y	N	Y	Y
6 **Stearns**	N	N	Y	N	+	+	
7 **Mica**	N	N	Y	Y	N	Y	Y
8 Grayson	Y	Y	Y	Y	Y	Y	Y
9 **Bilirakis**	N	N	Y	Y	N	Y	Y
10 **Young**	N	N	Y	Y	N	Y	Y
11 Castor	Y	Y	Y	Y	Y	Y	Y
12 **Putnam**	N	N	Y	Y	N	Y	Y
13 **Buchanan**	N	N	Y	Y	N	Y	Y
14 **Mack**	N	N	Y	Y	N	Y	Y
15 **Posey**	N	N	Y	Y	N	?	?
16 **Rooney**	N	N	Y	Y	N	Y	Y
17 Meek	Y	Y	Y	Y	Y	Y	Y
18 **Ros-Lehtinen**	N	N	Y	Y	N	Y	Y
19 Wexler	Y	Y	Y	Y	Y	Y	Y
20 Wasserman Schultz	Y	Y	Y	Y	Y	Y	Y
21 **Diaz-Balart, L.**	N	N	Y	Y	N	Y	Y
22 Klein	Y	Y	Y	Y	Y	Y	Y
23 Hastings	Y	Y	Y	Y	Y	Y	Y
24 Kosmas	Y	Y	Y	Y	Y	Y	Y
25 **Diaz-Balart, M.**	N	N	Y	Y	Y	Y	Y
GEORGIA							
1 **Kingston**	N	N	Y	Y	N	Y	Y
2 Bishop	+	+	+	+	+	+	+
3 **Westmoreland**	−	−	+	−	−	+	+
4 Johnson	Y	?	Y	?	Y	Y	Y
5 Lewis	?	?	?	?	?	?	?
6 **Price**	N	N	Y	N	Y	Y	Y
7 **Linder**	N	N	Y	Y	N	Y	Y
8 Marshall	Y	Y	Y	Y	N	Y	Y
9 **Deal**	?	?	?	?	?	?	?
10 **Broun**	N	?	Y	Y	N	Y	Y
11 **Gingrey**	N	N	Y	Y	N	Y	Y
12 Barrow	Y	Y	Y	Y	Y	Y	Y
13 Scott	Y	Y	Y	Y	Y	Y	Y
HAWAII							
1 Abercrombie	Y	?	Y	Y	Y	Y	Y
2 Hirono	Y	Y	Y	N	Y	Y	Y
IDAHO							
1 Minnick	N	N	Y	Y	N	Y	Y
2 **Simpson**	N	N	Y	Y	Y	Y	Y
ILLINOIS							
1 Rush	Y	Y	Y	Y	Y	Y	Y
2 Jackson	Y	Y	Y	Y	Y	Y	Y
3 Lipinski	Y	Y	Y	Y	Y	Y	Y
4 Gutierrez	Y	Y	Y	Y	Y	Y	Y
5 Quigley	Y	Y	Y	Y	Y	Y	Y
6 **Roskam**	N	N	Y	Y	N	Y	Y
7 Davis	Y	Y	Y	N	Y	Y	Y
8 Bean	Y	Y	Y	Y	N	Y	Y
9 Schakowsky	Y	Y	Y	Y	Y	Y	Y
10 **Kirk**	N	N	Y	Y	Y	Y	Y
11 Halvorson	Y	Y	Y	Y	Y	Y	Y
12 Costello	Y	Y	Y	N	N	?	?
13 **Biggert**	N	N	Y	Y	N	Y	Y
14 Foster	Y	Y	Y	Y	Y	Y	Y
15 **Johnson**	N	N	Y	Y	N	Y	Y

KEY **Republicans** Democrats

Y Voted for (yea)	X Paired against
# Paired for	− Announced against
+ Announced for	P Voted "present"
N Voted against (nay)	C Voted "present" to avoid possible conflict of interest
	? Did not vote or otherwise make a position known

	409	410	411	412	413	415	416
16 Manzullo	N	N	Y	Y	N	Y	Y
17 Hare	Y	Y	Y	Y	Y	Y	Y
18 **Schock**	N	N	Y	Y	N	Y	Y
19 **Shimkus**	N	N	Y	Y	N	Y	Y
INDIANA							
1 Visclosky	Y	Y	Y	Y	Y	Y	Y
2 Donnelly	Y	Y	Y	Y	N	Y	Y
3 **Souder**	N	N	Y	Y	N	Y	Y
4 **Buyer**	N	N	Y	Y	N	Y	Y
5 **Burton**	N	N	Y	Y	N	Y	Y
6 **Pence**	N	N	Y	Y	N	Y	Y
7 Carson	Y	Y	Y	Y	Y	Y	Y
8 Ellsworth	Y	Y	P	Y	Y	Y	Y
9 Hill	N	N	Y	Y	Y	Y	Y
IOWA							
1 Braley	Y	Y	Y	Y	Y	Y	Y
2 Loebsack	Y	Y	P	Y	Y	Y	Y
3 Boswell	Y	Y	Y	Y	Y	Y	Y
4 **Latham**	N	?	Y	Y	Y	Y	Y
5 **King**	N	N	Y	Y	N	Y	Y
KANSAS							
1 **Moran**	N	N	Y	Y	N	Y	Y
2 **Jenkins**	N	N	Y	Y	N	Y	Y
3 Moore	Y	Y	Y	Y	Y	Y	Y
4 **Tiahrt**	N	N	Y	Y	N	+	+
KENTUCKY							
1 **Whitfield**	N	N	Y	Y	N	Y	Y
2 **Guthrie**	N	N	Y	Y	N	Y	Y
3 Yarmuth	Y	Y	Y	Y	Y	Y	?
4 **Davis**	N	N	Y	Y	N	Y	Y
5 **Rogers**	N	N	Y	Y	N	Y	Y
6 Chandler	Y	Y	Y	Y	Y	Y	Y
LOUISIANA							
1 **Scalise**	N	N	Y	Y	N	Y	Y
2 **Cao**	N	N	Y	Y	Y	Y	Y
3 Melancon	Y	Y	Y	Y	Y	?	?
4 **Fleming**	N	N	Y	Y	N	Y	Y
5 **Alexander**	N	N	Y	Y	N	Y	Y
6 **Cassidy**	N	N	Y	Y	N	Y	?
7 **Boustany**	N	N	Y	Y	N	Y	Y
MAINE							
1 Pingree	Y	Y	Y	N	Y	Y	Y
2 Michaud	Y	Y	Y	Y	Y	Y	Y
MARYLAND							
1 Kratovil	N	N	Y	Y	N	Y	Y
2 Ruppersberger	?	?	?	Y	Y	Y	Y
3 Sarbanes	Y	Y	Y	Y	Y	Y	Y
4 Edwards	Y	Y	Y	N	Y	Y	Y
5 Hoyer	Y	Y	Y	Y	Y	Y	Y
6 **Bartlett**	N	N	Y	Y	N	Y	Y
7 Cummings	Y	Y	Y	N	Y	Y	Y
8 Van Hollen	Y	Y	Y	Y	Y	Y	Y
MASSACHUSETTS							
1 Olver	Y	Y	Y	Y	Y	Y	Y
2 Neal	Y	Y	Y	Y	Y	?	?
3 McGovern	Y	Y	Y	N	Y	?	?
4 Frank	Y	Y	Y	Y	Y	Y	Y
5 Tsongas	Y	Y	Y	N	Y	Y	Y
6 Tierney	Y	Y	Y	Y	Y	?	?
7 Markey	Y	Y	Y	Y	Y	Y	Y
8 Capuano	?	?	?	?	?	?	?
9 Lynch	Y	Y	Y	Y	Y	Y	Y
10 Delahunt	Y	Y	Y	Y	Y	Y	Y
MICHIGAN							
1 Stupak	Y	Y	Y	Y	Y	Y	Y
2 **Hoekstra**	N	N	Y	?	N	Y	Y
3 **Ehlers**	N	N	Y	Y	N	Y	Y
4 **Camp**	N	N	Y	Y	N	Y	Y
5 Kildee	Y	Y	Y	Y	Y	Y	Y
6 **Upton**	N	N	Y	Y	N	Y	Y
7 Schauer	Y	Y	Y	Y	Y	Y	Y
8 **Rogers**	N	N	Y	Y	N	Y	Y
9 Peters	Y	Y	Y	Y	Y	Y	Y
10 **Miller**	N	N	Y	Y	N	Y	Y
11 **McCotter**	N	N	Y	Y	N	Y	Y
12 Levin	Y	Y	Y	Y	Y	Y	Y
13 Kilpatrick	Y	Y	Y	+	+	+	+
14 Conyers	?	Y	Y	N	Y	Y	Y
15 Dingell	Y	Y	Y	Y	Y	Y	Y
MINNESOTA							
1 Walz	Y	Y	Y	Y	Y	Y	Y
2 **Kline**	N	N	Y	Y	N	?	?
3 **Paulsen**	N	N	Y	Y	N	Y	Y
4 McCollum	Y	Y	Y	Y	Y	Y	Y

	409	410	411	412	413	415	416
5 Ellison	Y	Y	Y	N	Y	Y	Y
6 **Bachmann**	?	?	?	?	?	?	?
7 Peterson	Y	Y	Y	Y	Y	Y	Y
8 Oberstar	Y	Y	Y	N	Y	Y	Y
MISSISSIPPI							
1 Childers	Y	Y	Y	Y	Y	Y	Y
2 Thompson	Y	Y	Y	Y	Y	Y	Y
3 **Harper**	N	N	Y	Y	N	Y	Y
4 Taylor	Y	Y	Y	Y	N	Y	Y
MISSOURI							
1 Clay	Y	Y	Y	N	Y	Y	Y
2 **Akin**	N	N	Y	Y	N	Y	Y
3 Carnahan	Y	Y	Y	Y	Y	Y	Y
4 Skelton	?	?	?	Y	Y	Y	Y
5 Cleaver	N	Y	Y	Y	Y	Y	Y
6 **Graves**	N	N	Y	Y	N	Y	Y
7 **Blunt**	N	N	Y	Y	N	?	?
8 **Emerson**	N	N	Y	Y	Y	Y	Y
9 **Luetkemeyer**	N	N	Y	Y	N	Y	Y
MONTANA							
AL **Rehberg**	N	N	Y	Y	N	Y	Y
NEBRASKA							
1 **Fortenberry**	N	N	Y	Y	N	Y	Y
2 **Terry**	N	N	Y	Y	N	Y	Y
3 **Smith**	N	N	Y	Y	N	Y	Y
NEVADA							
1 Berkley	Y	Y	Y	Y	Y	Y	Y
2 **Heller**	–	N	Y	Y	N	Y	Y
3 Titus	Y	Y	Y	Y	Y	Y	Y
NEW HAMPSHIRE							
1 Shea-Porter	Y	Y	Y	Y	Y	Y	Y
2 Hodes	Y	Y	Y	Y	Y	Y	Y
NEW JERSEY							
1 Andrews	Y	Y	Y	Y	Y	Y	Y
2 **LoBiondo**	N	N	Y	Y	N	Y	Y
3 Adler	?	?	?	Y	N	Y	Y
4 **Smith**	N	N	Y	Y	N	Y	Y
5 **Garrett**	N	N	Y	Y	N	Y	Y
6 Pallone	Y	Y	Y	Y	Y	Y	Y
7 **Lance**	N	N	Y	Y	Y	Y	Y
8 Pascrell	Y	Y	Y	?	Y	Y	Y
9 Rothman	Y	Y	Y	Y	Y	Y	Y
10 Payne	Y	Y	Y	N	Y	Y	Y
11 **Frelinghuysen**	N	N	Y	Y	N	Y	Y
12 Holt	Y	Y	Y	N	Y	Y	Y
13 Sires	Y	Y	Y	Y	Y	Y	Y
NEW MEXICO							
1 Heinrich	Y	Y	Y	Y	Y	Y	Y
2 Teague	Y	Y	Y	Y	N	Y	Y
3 Lujan	Y	Y	Y	Y	Y	Y	Y
NEW YORK							
1 Bishop	?	?	?	?	?	?	?
2 Israel	Y	Y	Y	Y	Y	Y	Y
3 **King**	N	N	Y	Y	N	Y	Y
4 McCarthy	Y	Y	Y	Y	Y	Y	Y
5 Ackerman	Y	Y	Y	Y	Y	?	?
6 Meeks	Y	Y	Y	Y	Y	Y	Y
7 Crowley	Y	Y	+	N	Y	Y	Y
8 Nadler	Y	Y	Y	N	Y	Y	Y
9 Weiner	Y	Y	Y	N	Y	Y	Y
10 Towns	Y	Y	Y	Y	Y	Y	Y
11 Clarke	Y	Y	Y	N	Y	Y	Y
12 Velázquez	?	?	?	?	?	?	?
13 McMahon	Y	Y	Y	Y	Y	Y	Y
14 Maloney	Y	Y	Y	Y	Y	Y	Y
15 Rangel	Y	Y	Y	Y	Y	Y	Y
16 Serrano	Y	Y	Y	N	Y	Y	Y
17 Engel	Y	Y	Y	Y	Y	Y	Y
18 Lowey	Y	Y	Y	Y	Y	Y	Y
19 Hall	Y	Y	Y	Y	Y	Y	Y
20 Murphy	Y	N	Y	Y	N	Y	Y
21 Tonko	Y	Y	Y	Y	Y	Y	Y
22 Hinchey	Y	Y	Y	Y	Y	Y	Y
23 **McHugh**	N	N	Y	Y	N	Y	Y
24 Arcuri	Y	Y	Y	Y	N	Y	Y
25 Maffei	Y	Y	Y	Y	Y	Y	Y
26 **Lee**	N	N	Y	Y	N	Y	Y
27 Higgins	Y	Y	Y	Y	Y	?	?
28 Slaughter	Y	Y	Y	Y	Y	?	?
29 Massa	Y	Y	Y	Y	N	Y	Y
NORTH CAROLINA							
1 Butterfield	Y	Y	Y	Y	Y	Y	Y
2 Etheridge	Y	Y	Y	Y	Y	Y	Y
3 **Jones**	N	N	Y	Y	N	Y	Y
4 Price	Y	Y	Y	Y	Y	Y	Y

	409	410	411	412	413	415	416
5 **Foxx**	N	N	Y	Y	N	Y	Y
6 **Coble**	N	N	Y	Y	N	Y	Y
7 McIntyre	Y	Y	Y	Y	Y	Y	Y
8 Kissell	Y	Y	Y	Y	Y	Y	Y
9 **Myrick**	N	N	Y	Y	N	Y	Y
10 **McHenry**	N	N	Y	Y	N	Y	Y
11 Shuler	N	N	Y	Y	Y	Y	Y
12 Watt	Y	Y	Y	N	Y	Y	Y
13 Miller	Y	Y	Y	Y	Y	Y	Y
NORTH DAKOTA							
AL Pomeroy	Y	Y	Y	Y	Y	Y	Y
OHIO							
1 Driehaus	Y	Y	Y	Y	N	Y	Y
2 **Schmidt**	N	N	Y	Y	N	Y	Y
3 **Turner**	N	N	Y	Y	N	Y	Y
4 **Jordan**	N	N	Y	Y	N	Y	Y
5 **Latta**	N	N	Y	Y	N	Y	Y
6 Wilson	Y	Y	Y	Y	Y	Y	Y
7 **Austria**	N	N	Y	Y	N	Y	Y
8 **Boehner**	N	N	Y	Y	N	?	?
9 Kaptur	?	Y	Y	Y	Y	Y	Y
10 Kucinich	Y	Y	Y	N	Y	Y	Y
11 Fudge	Y	Y	Y	N	Y	Y	Y
12 **Tiberi**	N	N	Y	Y	N	Y	Y
13 Sutton	Y	Y	Y	Y	Y	Y	Y
14 **LaTourette**	N	N	Y	?	?	?	?
15 Kilroy	Y	Y	Y	Y	Y	Y	Y
16 Boccieri	Y	Y	Y	Y	Y	Y	Y
17 Ryan	Y	?	Y	Y	Y	Y	Y
18 Space	Y	Y	Y	Y	Y	Y	Y
OKLAHOMA							
1 **Sullivan**	?	?	?	?	?	?	?
2 Boren	Y	Y	Y	Y	Y	Y	Y
3 **Lucas**	N	N	Y	Y	N	Y	Y
4 **Cole**	N	N	Y	Y	Y	Y	Y
5 **Fallin**	N	N	Y	Y	N	Y	Y
OREGON							
1 Wu	Y	Y	Y	Y	Y	Y	Y
2 **Walden**	N	N	Y	Y	N	Y	Y
3 Blumenauer	?	Y	Y	Y	Y	Y	Y
4 DeFazio	?	?	?	?	?	?	?
5 Schrader	Y	Y	Y	Y	Y	Y	Y
PENNSYLVANIA							
1 Brady	Y	Y	Y	Y	Y	Y	Y
2 Fattah	?	?	?	?	?	?	?
3 Dahlkemper	Y	Y	Y	Y	Y	Y	Y
4 Altmire	Y	Y	Y	Y	N	Y	Y
5 **Thompson**	N	N	Y	Y	N	Y	Y
6 **Gerlach**	N	N	Y	Y	N	Y	Y
7 Sestak	?	?	?	?	?	?	?
8 Murphy, P.	Y	Y	Y	Y	N	Y	Y
9 **Shuster**	N	N	Y	Y	N	Y	Y
10 Carney	Y	N	Y	Y	Y	Y	Y
11 Kanjorski	Y	Y	Y	?	?	?	?
12 Murtha	Y	Y	Y	Y	Y	Y	Y
13 Schwartz	Y	Y	Y	Y	Y	Y	Y
14 Doyle	Y	Y	?	Y	Y	?	?
15 **Dent**	N	N	Y	Y	N	Y	Y
16 **Pitts**	N	N	Y	Y	N	Y	Y
17 Holden	Y	Y	Y	Y	Y	Y	Y
18 **Murphy, T.**	N	N	Y	Y	N	Y	+
19 **Platts**	N	N	Y	Y	N	Y	Y
RHODE ISLAND							
1 Kennedy	?	?	?	?	?	?	?
2 Langevin	Y	Y	Y	Y	Y	Y	Y
SOUTH CAROLINA							
1 **Brown**	N	N	Y	Y	N	Y	Y
2 **Wilson**	N	N	Y	Y	N	Y	Y
3 **Barrett**	–	–	+	+	–	+	+
4 **Inglis**	N	N	Y	Y	N	Y	Y
5 Spratt	?	Y	Y	Y	Y	Y	Y
6 Clyburn	Y	Y	Y	N	Y	Y	Y
SOUTH DAKOTA							
AL Herseth Sandlin	Y	Y	Y	Y	Y	Y	Y
TENNESSEE							
1 **Roe**	N	N	Y	Y	N	Y	Y
2 **Duncan**	N	N	Y	Y	N	Y	Y
3 **Wamp**	N	N	Y	Y	Y	Y	Y
4 Davis	Y	Y	Y	Y	Y	Y	Y
5 Cooper	Y	Y	Y	Y	Y	Y	Y
6 Gordon	Y	Y	?	Y	Y	Y	Y
7 **Blackburn**	N	N	Y	Y	N	Y	Y
8 Tanner	Y	Y	Y	Y	Y	Y	Y
9 Cohen	Y	Y	Y	Y	N	Y	Y

	409	410	411	412	413	415	416
TEXAS							
1 **Gohmert**	N	N	Y	Y	N	Y	Y
2 **Poe**	N	N	Y	Y	N	Y	Y
3 **Johnson, S.**	N	N	Y	Y	N	Y	Y
4 **Hall**	N	N	Y	Y	N	Y	Y
5 **Hensarling**	N	N	Y	Y	N	Y	Y
6 **Barton**	N	?	Y	Y	N	Y	Y
7 **Culberson**	N	N	Y	Y	N	Y	Y
8 **Brady**	N	N	Y	Y	N	Y	Y
9 Green, A.	Y	Y	Y	Y	Y	Y	Y
10 **McCaul**	N	N	Y	Y	N	Y	Y
11 **Conaway**	N	N	Y	Y	N	Y	Y
12 **Granger**	N	N	Y	Y	N	Y	Y
13 **Thornberry**	N	N	Y	Y	N	Y	Y
14 **Paul**	N	N	N	Y	N	Y	?
15 Hinojosa	Y	Y	Y	Y	Y	Y	Y
16 Reyes	Y	Y	Y	Y	Y	Y	Y
17 Edwards	Y	Y	Y	Y	Y	Y	Y
18 Jackson Lee	Y	Y	Y	N	Y	Y	Y
19 **Neugebauer**	N	N	Y	Y	N	Y	Y
20 Gonzalez	Y	Y	Y	Y	Y	?	?
21 **Smith**	N	N	Y	Y	N	Y	Y
22 **Olson**	N	N	Y	Y	N	Y	Y
23 Rodriguez	Y	Y	Y	Y	Y	Y	Y
24 **Marchant**	N	N	Y	Y	N	Y	Y
25 Doggett	Y	Y	Y	Y	Y	Y	Y
26 **Burgess**	N	N	Y	Y	N	Y	Y
27 Ortiz	Y	Y	Y	Y	Y	Y	Y
28 Cuellar	Y	Y	Y	Y	Y	Y	Y
29 Green, G.	Y	Y	Y	Y	N	Y	Y
30 Johnson, E.	Y	Y	Y	Y	Y	Y	Y
31 **Carter**	N	N	?	Y	Y	Y	Y
32 **Sessions**	N	N	Y	?	?	?	?
UTAH							
1 **Bishop**	N	N	Y	Y	N	Y	Y
2 Matheson	Y	Y	Y	Y	N	Y	Y
3 **Chaffetz**	N	N	Y	Y	N	Y	Y
VERMONT							
AL Welch	Y	Y	Y	N	Y	?	?
VIRGINIA							
1 **Wittman**	N	N	Y	Y	N	Y	Y
2 Nye	Y	N	Y	Y	N	Y	Y
3 Scott	Y	Y	Y	Y	Y	Y	?
4 **Forbes**	N	N	Y	Y	N	Y	Y
5 Perriello	Y	Y	Y	Y	N	Y	Y
6 **Goodlatte**	N	N	Y	Y	N	Y	Y
7 **Cantor**	N	N	Y	Y	N	Y	Y
8 Moran	Y	Y	Y	Y	Y	Y	Y
9 Boucher	Y	Y	Y	Y	Y	Y	Y
10 **Wolf**	N	N	Y	Y	N	Y	Y
11 Connolly	Y	Y	Y	N	Y	Y	Y
WASHINGTON							
1 Inslee	Y	Y	Y	Y	Y	Y	Y
2 Larsen	Y	Y	Y	Y	Y	Y	Y
3 Baird	Y	Y	Y	Y	Y	Y	Y
4 **Hastings**	N	N	Y	Y	N	Y	Y
5 **McMorris Rodgers**	N	N	Y	Y	N	Y	Y
6 Dicks	Y	Y	Y	Y	Y	Y	Y
7 McDermott	Y	Y	Y	Y	Y	Y	Y
8 **Reichert**	N	N	Y	Y	N	Y	Y
9 Smith	Y	Y	Y	Y	Y	Y	Y
WEST VIRGINIA							
1 Mollohan	Y	Y	Y	N	Y	Y	Y
2 **Capito**	N	N	Y	Y	Y	Y	Y
3 Rahall	Y	Y	Y	Y	Y	Y	Y
WISCONSIN							
1 **Ryan**	N	N	Y	Y	N	Y	Y
2 Baldwin	Y	Y	Y	Y	N	Y	Y
3 Kind	Y	Y	Y	Y	N	Y	Y
4 Moore	Y	Y	Y	Y	Y	Y	Y
5 **Sensenbrenner**	N	N	Y	Y	N	Y	Y
6 **Petri**	N	N	Y	Y	N	Y	Y
7 Obey	Y	Y	Y	Y	Y	Y	Y
8 Kagen	Y	Y	Y	Y	Y	Y	Y
WYOMING							
AL **Lummis**	N	N	Y	Y	N	Y	Y
DELEGATES							
Faleomavaega (A.S.)							
Norton (D.C.)							
Bordallo (Guam)							
Sablan (N. Marianas)							
Pierluisi (P.R.)							
Christensen (V.I.)							

IN THE HOUSE | By Vote Number

417. **H Res 520. Impeachment of Judge Kent/Obstruction of Justice.** Adoption of Article III of the resolution, which would impeach Judge Samuel B. Kent, of the U.S. District Court for the Southern District of Texas, for obstruction of justice for making false statements regarding allegations of sexual assault in June 2007 to a 5th Circuit Court of Appeals special investigative committee. Adopted 381-0: R 158-0; D 223-0. June 19, 2009.

418. **H Res 520. Impeachment of Judge Kent/False Statements.** Adoption of Article IV of the resolution, which would impeach Judge Samuel B. Kent, of the U.S. District Court for the Southern District of Texas, for making false statements regarding allegations of sexual assault to FBI agents in November 2007 and Justice Department representatives in August 2008. Adopted 372-0: R 155-0; D 217-0. June 19, 2009.

419. **S 407. Veterans' Cost-of-Living Adjustment/Passage.** Filner, D-Calif., motion to suspend the rules and pass the bill that would require the Veterans Affairs Department to increase payments to veterans and their dependents for disability and indemnity compensation by the same cost-of-living adjustment used for Social Security recipients. The increase would take effect Dec. 1, 2009, with adjustments rounded to the next-lowest dollar. Motion agreed to 403-0: R 167-0; D 236-0. A two-thirds majority of those present and voting (269 in this case) is required for passage under suspension of the rules. June 23, 2009.

420. **HR 1016. VA Health Care Advance Appropriations/Passage.** Filner, D-Calif., motion to suspend the rules and pass the bill that would provide authority for Congress to provide one year of advance appropriations for certain medical accounts in the annual Veterans Affairs (VA) appropriations bill, beginning in fiscal 2011. The accounts include prosthetic research and information technology. It would require that the president's annual budget include estimates of the funding needed in the following year for the specified VA accounts. The bill would require the Government Accountability Office to study the adequacy and accuracy of the budget projections for VA health care expenditures. Motion agreed to 409-1: R 167-1; D 242-0. A two-thirds majority of those present and voting (274 in this case) is required for passage under suspension of the rules. A "yea" was a vote in support of the president's position. June 23, 2009.

421. **HR 1211. Health Care for Women Veterans/Passage.** Filner, D-Calif., motion to suspend the rules and pass the bill that would authorize $10.5 million to expand women's health care in the Veterans Affairs Department (VA) to study potential barriers to health care, assess whether current VA programs meet the needs of women veterans and provide child care assistance to certain veterans. It would also require training and certification for VA mental health care providers treating veterans suffering from sexual trauma and post-traumatic stress disorder. Motion agreed to 408-0: R 166-0; D 242-0. A two-thirds majority of those present and voting (272 in this case) is required for passage under suspension of the rules. June 23, 2009.

422. **HR 1172. Veteran Scholarship List/Passage.** Filner, D-Calif., motion to suspend the rules and pass the bill that would require the Veterans Affairs Department to post a list of organizations providing scholarships to veterans and their survivors on the department's Web site by June 1, 2010. Motion agreed to 411-0: R 168-0; D 243-0. A two-thirds majority of those present and voting (274 in this case) is required for passage under suspension of the rules. June 23, 2009.

	417	418	419	420	421	422
ALABAMA						
1 **Bonner**	Y	Y	Y	Y	Y	Y
2 Bright	Y	Y	Y	Y	Y	Y
3 **Rogers**	Y	Y	Y	Y	Y	Y
4 **Aderholt**	Y	Y	Y	Y	Y	Y
5 Griffith	Y	Y	Y	Y	Y	Y
6 **Bachus**	Y	Y	Y	Y	Y	Y
7 Davis	?	?	?	Y	Y	Y
ALASKA						
AL **Young**	Y	Y	Y	Y	Y	Y
ARIZONA						
1 Kirkpatrick	Y	Y	Y	Y	Y	Y
2 **Franks**	Y	Y	Y	Y	Y	Y
3 **Shadegg**	?	?	?	?	?	?
4 Pastor	Y	Y	Y	Y	Y	Y
5 Mitchell	Y	Y	Y	Y	Y	Y
6 **Flake**	Y	Y	Y	Y	Y	Y
7 Grijalva	Y	Y	?	Y	Y	Y
8 Giffords	Y	Y	Y	Y	Y	Y
ARKANSAS						
1 Berry	Y	Y	Y	Y	Y	Y
2 Snyder	Y	Y	Y	Y	Y	Y
3 **Boozman**	Y	Y	Y	Y	Y	Y
4 Ross	Y	Y	Y	Y	Y	Y
CALIFORNIA						
1 Thompson	Y	+	Y	Y	Y	Y
2 **Herger**	Y	Y	Y	Y	Y	Y
3 **Lungren**	Y	Y	Y	Y	Y	Y
4 **McClintock**	Y	Y	Y	Y	Y	Y
5 Matsui	Y	Y	Y	Y	Y	Y
6 Woolsey	Y	+	+	+	+	+
7 Miller, George	Y	Y	Y	Y	Y	Y
8 Pelosi						
9 Lee	Y	Y	Y	Y	Y	Y
10 Tauscher	Y	Y	Y	Y	Y	Y
11 McNerney	Y	Y	Y	Y	Y	Y
12 Speier	?	?	Y	Y	Y	Y
13 Stark	Y	Y	Y	Y	Y	Y
14 Eshoo	+	+	Y	Y	Y	Y
15 Honda	Y	Y	Y	Y	Y	Y
16 Lofgren	Y	Y	Y	Y	Y	Y
17 Farr	?	?	Y	Y	Y	Y
18 Cardoza	Y	Y	Y	Y	Y	Y
19 **Radanovich**	Y	Y	?	?	?	?
20 Costa	Y	Y	?	?	?	?
21 **Nunes**	Y	Y	Y	Y	Y	Y
22 **McCarthy**	Y	Y	Y	Y	Y	Y
23 Capps	Y	Y	Y	Y	Y	Y
24 **Gallegly**	Y	Y	Y	Y	Y	Y
25 **McKeon**	Y	Y	Y	Y	Y	Y
26 **Dreier**	Y	Y	Y	Y	Y	Y
27 Sherman	Y	Y	Y	Y	Y	Y
28 Berman	Y	Y	Y	Y	Y	Y
29 Schiff	Y	Y	Y	Y	Y	Y
30 Waxman	Y	Y	Y	Y	Y	Y
31 Becerra	Y	Y	Y	Y	Y	
32 Vacant						
33 Watson	Y	Y	Y	Y	Y	Y
34 Roybal-Allard	Y	Y	Y	Y	Y	Y
35 Waters	Y	Y	Y	Y	Y	Y
36 Harman	?	?	Y	Y	Y	Y
37 Richardson	Y	Y	Y	Y	Y	Y
38 Napolitano	Y	Y	Y	Y	Y	Y
39 Sánchez, Linda	?	?	Y	Y	Y	Y
40 **Royce**	Y	Y	Y	Y	Y	Y
41 **Lewis**	Y	Y	Y	Y	Y	Y
42 **Miller, Gary**	Y	Y	Y	Y	Y	Y
43 Baca	Y	+	Y	Y	Y	Y
44 **Calvert**	Y	Y	Y	Y	Y	Y
45 **Bono Mack**	Y	Y	Y	Y	Y	Y
46 **Rohrabacher**	Y	Y	Y	Y	Y	Y
47 Sanchez, Loretta	Y	Y	Y	Y	Y	Y
48 **Campbell**	Y	Y	?	?	?	Y
49 **Issa**	Y	Y	Y	Y	Y	Y
50 **Bilbray**	Y	Y	Y	Y	Y	Y
51 Filner	Y	Y	Y	Y	Y	Y
52 **Hunter**	Y	Y	Y	Y	Y	Y
53 Davis	Y	Y	Y	Y	Y	Y

	417	418	419	420	421	422
COLORADO						
1 DeGette	Y	Y	?	Y	Y	Y
2 Polis	Y	Y	Y	Y	Y	Y
3 Salazar	Y	Y	Y	Y	Y	Y
4 Markey	Y	Y	Y	Y	Y	Y
5 **Lamborn**	Y	Y	Y	Y	Y	Y
6 **Coffman**	Y	Y	Y	Y	+	Y
7 Perlmutter	Y	Y	Y	Y	Y	Y
CONNECTICUT						
1 Larson	Y	Y	Y	Y	Y	Y
2 Courtney	Y	Y	Y	Y	Y	Y
3 DeLauro	Y	Y	Y	Y	Y	Y
4 Himes	Y	Y	Y	Y	Y	Y
5 Murphy	Y	?	Y	Y	Y	Y
DELAWARE						
AL **Castle**	Y	Y	Y	Y	Y	Y
FLORIDA						
1 **Miller**	Y	Y	Y	Y	Y	Y
2 Boyd	Y	Y	?	Y	Y	Y
3 Brown	Y	Y	Y	Y	Y	Y
4 **Crenshaw**	?	?	Y	Y	Y	Y
5 **Brown-Waite**	Y	Y	Y	Y	Y	Y
6 **Stearns**	+	+	Y	Y	Y	Y
7 **Mica**	Y	Y	Y	Y	Y	Y
8 Grayson	Y	Y	Y	Y	Y	Y
9 **Bilirakis**	Y	Y	Y	Y	Y	Y
10 **Young**	Y	Y	Y	Y	Y	Y
11 Castor	Y	?	Y	Y	Y	Y
12 **Putnam**	Y	Y	Y	Y	Y	Y
13 **Buchanan**	Y	Y	Y	Y	Y	Y
14 **Mack**	Y	Y	Y	Y	Y	Y
15 **Posey**	?	?	Y	Y	Y	Y
16 **Rooney**	?	Y	Y	Y	Y	Y
17 Meek	Y	Y	Y	Y	Y	Y
18 **Ros-Lehtinen**	Y	Y	Y	Y	Y	Y
19 Wexler	Y	Y	Y	Y	Y	Y
20 Wasserman Schultz	Y	Y	Y	Y	Y	Y
21 **Diaz-Balart, L.**	Y	Y	Y	Y	Y	Y
22 Klein	Y	Y	Y	Y	Y	Y
23 Hastings	Y	Y	Y	Y	Y	Y
24 Kosmas	Y	Y	Y	Y	Y	Y
25 **Diaz-Balart, M.**	Y	Y	Y	Y	Y	Y
GEORGIA						
1 **Kingston**	Y	Y	Y	Y	Y	Y
2 Bishop	+	+	Y	Y	Y	Y
3 **Westmoreland**	+	+	Y	Y	Y	Y
4 Johnson	Y	Y	Y	Y	Y	Y
5 Lewis	?	?	?	?	?	?
6 **Price**	Y	Y	Y	Y	Y	Y
7 **Linder**	Y	Y	Y	Y	Y	Y
8 Marshall	Y	Y	Y	Y	Y	Y
9 **Deal**	?	?	Y	Y	Y	Y
10 **Broun**	Y	Y	Y	Y	Y	Y
11 **Gingrey**	Y	Y	Y	Y	Y	Y
12 Barrow	Y	Y	Y	Y	Y	Y
13 Scott	Y	Y	Y	Y	Y	Y
HAWAII						
1 Abercrombie	Y	Y	Y	Y	Y	Y
2 Hirono	Y	Y	Y	Y	Y	Y
IDAHO						
1 Minnick	Y	Y	Y	Y	Y	Y
2 **Simpson**	Y	Y	Y	Y	Y	Y
ILLINOIS						
1 Rush	Y	Y	Y	Y	Y	Y
2 Jackson	Y	Y	Y	Y	Y	Y
3 Lipinski	Y	Y	Y	Y	Y	Y
4 Gutierrez	Y	Y	?	?	?	?
5 Quigley	Y	Y	Y	Y	Y	Y
6 **Roskam**	Y	?	Y	Y	Y	Y
7 Davis	Y	Y	Y	Y	Y	Y
8 Bean	Y	Y	Y	Y	Y	Y
9 Schakowsky	Y	Y	Y	Y	Y	Y
10 **Kirk**	Y	Y	Y	Y	Y	Y
11 Halvorson	Y	Y	Y	Y	Y	Y
12 Costello	?	?	Y	Y	Y	Y
13 **Biggert**	Y	Y	Y	Y	Y	Y
14 Foster	Y	Y	Y	Y	Y	Y
15 **Johnson**	Y	Y	Y	Y	Y	Y

	417	418	419	420	421	422
16 **Manzullo**	Y	Y	Y	Y	Y	Y
17 Hare	Y	Y	Y	Y	Y	Y
18 **Schock**	Y	Y	?	?	?	?
19 **Shimkus**	Y	Y	Y	Y	Y	Y
INDIANA						
1 Visclosky	Y	Y	Y	Y	Y	Y
2 Donnelly	Y	Y	Y	Y	Y	Y
3 **Souder**	Y	Y	Y	Y	Y	Y
4 **Buyer**	Y	Y	Y	N	Y	Y
5 **Burton**	Y	Y	Y	Y	Y	Y
6 **Pence**	Y	Y	Y	Y	Y	Y
7 Carson	Y	Y	Y	Y	Y	Y
8 Ellsworth	Y	Y	Y	Y	Y	Y
9 Hill	Y	Y	Y	Y	Y	Y
IOWA						
1 Braley	Y	Y	+	+	+	+
2 Loebsack	Y	Y	Y	Y	Y	Y
3 Boswell	Y	Y	Y	Y	Y	Y
4 **Latham**	Y	Y	Y	Y	Y	Y
5 **King**	Y	Y	Y	Y	?	Y
KANSAS						
1 **Moran**	Y	Y	Y	Y	Y	Y
2 **Jenkins**	Y	Y	Y	Y	Y	Y
3 Moore	Y	Y	Y	Y	Y	Y
4 **Tiahrt**	+	+	Y	Y	Y	Y
KENTUCKY						
1 **Whitfield**	Y	Y	Y	Y	Y	Y
2 **Guthrie**	Y	Y	Y	Y	Y	Y
3 Yarmuth	?	?	Y	Y	Y	Y
4 **Davis**	Y	Y	Y	Y	Y	Y
5 **Rogers**	Y	Y	Y	Y	Y	Y
6 Chandler	Y	Y	Y	Y	Y	Y
LOUISIANA						
1 **Scalise**	Y	Y	Y	Y	Y	Y
2 **Cao**	Y	Y	Y	Y	Y	Y
3 Melancon	?	?	Y	Y	Y	Y
4 **Fleming**	Y	Y	Y	Y	Y	Y
5 **Alexander**	Y	Y	Y	Y	Y	Y
6 **Cassidy**	?	?	Y	Y	Y	Y
7 **Boustany**	Y	Y	Y	Y	Y	Y
MAINE						
1 Pingree	Y	Y	Y	Y	Y	Y
2 Michaud	Y	Y	Y	Y	Y	Y
MARYLAND						
1 Kratovil	Y	Y	Y	Y	Y	Y
2 Ruppersberger	Y	Y	Y	Y	Y	Y
3 Sarbanes	Y	Y	Y	Y	Y	Y
4 Edwards	Y	Y	Y	Y	Y	Y
5 Hoyer	Y	Y	Y	Y	Y	Y
6 **Bartlett**	Y	Y	Y	Y	Y	Y
7 Cummings	Y	Y	Y	?	Y	Y
8 Van Hollen	Y	Y	Y	Y	Y	Y
MASSACHUSETTS						
1 Olver	Y	Y	Y	Y	Y	Y
2 Neal	?	?	Y	Y	Y	Y
3 McGovern	?	?	Y	Y	Y	Y
4 Frank	Y	Y	Y	Y	Y	Y
5 Tsongas	Y	Y	Y	Y	Y	Y
6 Tierney	?	?	Y	Y	Y	Y
7 Markey	Y	Y	Y	Y	Y	Y
8 Capuano	?	?	Y	Y	Y	Y
9 Lynch	Y	Y	Y	Y	Y	Y
10 Delahunt	Y	Y	Y	Y	Y	Y
MICHIGAN						
1 Stupak	Y	Y	Y	Y	Y	Y
2 **Hoekstra**	Y	Y	Y	Y	Y	Y
3 **Ehlers**	Y	Y	Y	Y	Y	Y
4 **Camp**	Y	?	Y	Y	Y	Y
5 Kildee	Y	Y	Y	Y	Y	Y
6 **Upton**	Y	Y	Y	Y	Y	Y
7 Schauer	Y	Y	Y	Y	Y	Y
8 **Rogers**	Y	?	Y	Y	Y	Y
9 Peters	Y	Y	Y	Y	Y	Y
10 **Miller**	Y	Y	Y	Y	Y	Y
11 **McCotter**	Y	Y	Y	Y	Y	Y
12 Levin	Y	Y	Y	Y	Y	Y
13 Kilpatrick	+	+	Y	Y	Y	Y
14 Conyers	Y	Y	?	?	?	?
15 Dingell	Y	Y	Y	Y	Y	Y
MINNESOTA						
1 Walz	Y	Y	Y	Y	Y	Y
2 **Kline**	?	?	Y	Y	Y	Y
3 **Paulsen**	Y	Y	+	+	+	+
4 McCollum	Y	Y	Y	Y	Y	Y

	417	418	419	420	421	422
5 Ellison	Y	Y	Y	Y	Y	Y
6 **Bachmann**	?	?	Y	Y	Y	Y
7 Peterson	?	Y	Y	Y	Y	Y
8 Oberstar	Y	Y	Y	Y	Y	Y
MISSISSIPPI						
1 Childers	Y	Y	Y	Y	Y	Y
2 Thompson	Y	Y	Y	Y	Y	Y
3 **Harper**	Y	Y	Y	Y	Y	Y
4 Taylor	Y	Y	Y	Y	Y	Y
MISSOURI						
1 Clay	Y	Y	Y	Y	Y	Y
2 **Akin**	Y	Y	Y	Y	Y	Y
3 Carnahan	Y	Y	Y	Y	Y	Y
4 Skelton	Y	Y	Y	Y	Y	Y
5 Cleaver	Y	Y	Y	Y	Y	Y
6 **Graves**	Y	Y	Y	Y	Y	Y
7 **Blunt**	?	?	?	?	?	?
8 **Emerson**	Y	Y	Y	Y	Y	Y
9 **Luetkemeyer**	Y	Y	Y	Y	Y	Y
MONTANA						
AL **Rehberg**	Y	Y	Y	Y	Y	Y
NEBRASKA						
1 **Fortenberry**	Y	Y	Y	Y	Y	Y
2 **Terry**	Y	Y	Y	Y	Y	Y
3 **Smith**	Y	Y	Y	Y	Y	Y
NEVADA						
1 Berkley	Y	Y	Y	Y	Y	Y
2 **Heller**	+	+	Y	Y	Y	Y
3 Titus	Y	Y	Y	Y	Y	Y
NEW HAMPSHIRE						
1 Shea-Porter	Y	Y	?	?	?	?
2 Hodes	Y	Y	Y	Y	Y	Y
NEW JERSEY						
1 Andrews	Y	Y	Y	Y	Y	Y
2 **LoBiondo**	Y	Y	Y	Y	Y	Y
3 Adler	Y	Y	Y	Y	Y	Y
4 **Smith**	Y	Y	Y	Y	Y	Y
5 **Garrett**	Y	Y	Y	Y	Y	Y
6 Pallone	Y	Y	Y	Y	Y	Y
7 **Lance**	Y	Y	Y	Y	Y	Y
8 Pascrell	Y	Y	Y	Y	Y	Y
9 Rothman	Y	Y	Y	Y	Y	Y
10 Payne	Y	Y	?	?	?	?
11 **Frelinghuysen**	Y	Y	Y	Y	Y	Y
12 Holt	Y	Y	Y	Y	Y	Y
13 Sires	Y	Y	Y	Y	Y	Y
NEW MEXICO						
1 Heinrich	Y	Y	Y	Y	Y	Y
2 Teague	Y	Y	Y	Y	Y	Y
3 Lujan	Y	Y	Y	Y	Y	Y
NEW YORK						
1 Bishop	?	?	Y	Y	Y	Y
2 Israel	Y	Y	Y	Y	Y	Y
3 **King**	Y	Y	Y	Y	Y	Y
4 McCarthy	Y	Y	?	Y	Y	Y
5 Ackerman	?	?	Y	Y	Y	Y
6 Meeks	Y	Y	Y	Y	Y	Y
7 Crowley	Y	Y	Y	Y	Y	Y
8 Nadler	Y	Y	Y	Y	Y	Y
9 Weiner	Y	Y	Y	Y	Y	Y
10 Towns	Y	Y	Y	Y	Y	Y
11 Clarke	Y	Y	Y	Y	Y	Y
12 Velázquez	?	?	Y	Y	Y	Y
13 McMahon	Y	Y	Y	Y	Y	Y
14 Maloney	Y	Y	Y	Y	Y	Y
15 Rangel	Y	Y	Y	Y	Y	Y
16 Serrano	Y	Y	Y	Y	Y	Y
17 Engel	Y	Y	Y	Y	Y	Y
18 Lowey	Y	Y	Y	Y	Y	Y
19 Hall	Y	Y	Y	Y	Y	Y
20 Murphy	Y	Y	Y	Y	Y	Y
21 Tonko	Y	Y	Y	Y	Y	Y
22 Hinchey	Y	?	Y	Y	Y	Y
23 **McHugh**	Y	Y	Y	Y	Y	Y
24 Arcuri	Y	Y	Y	Y	Y	Y
25 Maffei	Y	Y	Y	Y	Y	Y
26 **Lee**	Y	Y	Y	Y	Y	Y
27 Higgins	?	?	?	Y	Y	Y
28 Slaughter	?	?	Y	Y	Y	Y
29 Massa	Y	Y	Y	Y	Y	Y
NORTH CAROLINA						
1 Butterfield	Y	Y	Y	Y	Y	Y
2 Etheridge	Y	Y	Y	Y	Y	Y
3 **Jones**	Y	?	Y	Y	Y	Y
4 Price	Y	Y	Y	Y	Y	Y

	417	418	419	420	421	422
5 **Foxx**	Y	Y	Y	Y	Y	Y
6 **Coble**	Y	Y	Y	Y	Y	Y
7 McIntyre	Y	Y	Y	Y	Y	Y
8 Kissell	Y	Y	Y	Y	Y	Y
9 **Myrick**	Y	Y	Y	Y	Y	Y
10 **McHenry**	Y	Y	+	+	+	+
11 Shuler	Y	Y	?	?	?	?
12 Watt	Y	P	Y	Y	Y	Y
13 Miller	Y	Y	Y	Y	Y	Y
NORTH DAKOTA						
AL Pomeroy	Y	Y	Y	Y	Y	Y
OHIO						
1 Driehaus	Y	Y	Y	Y	Y	Y
2 **Schmidt**	Y	Y	Y	Y	Y	Y
3 **Turner**	Y	Y	Y	Y	Y	Y
4 **Jordan**	Y	Y	Y	Y	Y	Y
5 **Latta**	Y	Y	Y	Y	Y	Y
6 Wilson	Y	Y	Y	Y	Y	Y
7 **Austria**	Y	Y	Y	Y	Y	Y
8 **Boehner**	?	?	Y	Y	Y	Y
9 Kaptur	Y	Y	Y	Y	Y	Y
10 Kucinich	Y	Y	Y	Y	Y	Y
11 Fudge	Y	Y	Y	Y	Y	Y
12 **Tiberi**	Y	Y	Y	Y	Y	Y
13 Sutton	Y	Y	Y	Y	Y	Y
14 **LaTourette**	?	?	Y	Y	Y	Y
15 Kilroy	Y	Y	Y	Y	Y	Y
16 Boccieri	Y	Y	Y	Y	Y	Y
17 Ryan	Y	Y	Y	Y	Y	Y
18 Space	Y	Y	Y	Y	Y	Y
OKLAHOMA						
1 **Sullivan**	?	?	?	?	?	?
2 Boren	Y	Y	Y	Y	Y	Y
3 **Lucas**	Y	Y	Y	Y	Y	Y
4 **Cole**	Y	Y	Y	Y	Y	Y
5 **Fallin**	Y	Y	Y	Y	Y	Y
OREGON						
1 Wu	Y	Y	?	Y	Y	Y
2 **Walden**	Y	Y	Y	Y	Y	Y
3 Blumenauer	Y	Y	Y	Y	Y	Y
4 DeFazio	?	?	Y	Y	Y	Y
5 Schrader	Y	Y	Y	Y	Y	Y
PENNSYLVANIA						
1 Brady	Y	Y	Y	Y	Y	Y
2 Fattah	?	?	Y	Y	Y	Y
3 Dahlkemper	Y	Y	Y	Y	Y	Y
4 Altmire	Y	Y	Y	Y	Y	Y
5 **Thompson**	Y	Y	Y	Y	Y	Y
6 **Gerlach**	Y	Y	Y	Y	Y	Y
7 Sestak	?	?	Y	Y	Y	Y
8 Murphy, P.	Y	Y	Y	Y	Y	Y
9 **Shuster**	Y	Y	Y	Y	Y	Y
10 Carney	Y	Y	Y	Y	Y	Y
11 Kanjorski	?	?	Y	Y	Y	Y
12 Murtha	Y	Y	Y	Y	Y	Y
13 Schwartz	Y	Y	Y	Y	Y	Y
14 Doyle	?	?	Y	Y	Y	Y
15 **Dent**	Y	Y	Y	Y	Y	Y
16 **Pitts**	Y	Y	Y	Y	Y	Y
17 Holden	Y	Y	Y	Y	Y	Y
18 **Murphy, T.**	+	+	Y	Y	Y	Y
19 **Platts**	Y	Y	Y	Y	Y	Y
RHODE ISLAND						
1 Kennedy	?	?	?	?	?	?
2 Langevin	Y	Y	Y	Y	Y	Y
SOUTH CAROLINA						
1 **Brown**	Y	Y	Y	Y	Y	Y
2 **Wilson**	Y	Y	Y	Y	Y	Y
3 **Barrett**	+	+	Y	Y	Y	Y
4 **Inglis**	Y	Y	Y	Y	Y	Y
5 Spratt	Y	Y	Y	Y	Y	Y
6 Clyburn	Y	Y	Y	Y	Y	Y
SOUTH DAKOTA						
AL Herseth Sandlin	Y	Y	Y	Y	Y	Y
TENNESSEE						
1 **Roe**	Y	Y	Y	Y	Y	Y
2 **Duncan**	Y	Y	Y	Y	Y	Y
3 **Wamp**	Y	Y	Y	Y	Y	Y
4 Davis	Y	Y	Y	Y	Y	Y
5 Cooper	Y	Y	Y	Y	Y	Y
6 Gordon	Y	Y	Y	Y	Y	Y
7 **Blackburn**	Y	Y	Y	Y	Y	Y
8 Tanner	Y	Y	Y	Y	Y	Y
9 Cohen	Y	Y	Y	Y	?	Y

	417	418	419	420	421	422
TEXAS						
1 **Gohmert**	Y	Y	Y	Y	Y	Y
2 **Poe**	Y	Y	Y	Y	Y	Y
3 **Johnson, S.**	Y	Y	Y	Y	Y	Y
4 **Hall**	Y	Y	Y	Y	Y	Y
5 **Hensarling**	Y	Y	Y	Y	Y	Y
6 **Barton**	Y	Y	Y	Y	Y	Y
7 **Culberson**	Y	Y	Y	Y	Y	Y
8 **Brady**	Y	Y	+	+	+	+
9 Green, A.	Y	Y	Y	Y	Y	Y
10 **McCaul**	Y	Y	Y	Y	Y	Y
11 **Conaway**	Y	Y	Y	Y	Y	Y
12 **Granger**	Y	Y	Y	Y	Y	Y
13 **Thornberry**	Y	Y	Y	Y	Y	Y
14 **Paul**	?	?	Y	Y	Y	Y
15 Hinojosa	Y	Y	Y	Y	Y	Y
16 Reyes	Y	Y	Y	Y	Y	Y
17 Edwards	Y	Y	Y	Y	Y	Y
18 Jackson Lee	Y	Y	Y	Y	Y	Y
19 **Neugebauer**	Y	Y	Y	Y	Y	Y
20 Gonzalez	?	?	Y	Y	Y	Y
21 **Smith**	Y	Y	Y	Y	Y	Y
22 **Olson**	Y	Y	Y	Y	Y	Y
23 Rodriguez	+	+	Y	Y	Y	Y
24 **Marchant**	Y	Y	Y	Y	Y	Y
25 Doggett	Y	Y	Y	Y	Y	Y
26 **Burgess**	Y	Y	Y	Y	Y	Y
27 Ortiz	Y	Y	Y	Y	Y	Y
28 Cuellar	Y	Y	Y	Y	Y	Y
29 Green, G.	+	+	Y	Y	Y	Y
30 Johnson, E.	Y	Y	Y	Y	Y	Y
31 **Carter**	Y	Y	Y	Y	Y	Y
32 **Sessions**	?	?	Y	Y	Y	Y
UTAH						
1 **Bishop**	Y	Y	Y	Y	Y	Y
2 Matheson	Y	Y	Y	Y	Y	Y
3 **Chaffetz**	Y	Y	Y	Y	Y	Y
VERMONT						
AL Welch	?	?	Y	Y	Y	Y
VIRGINIA						
1 **Wittman**	Y	Y	Y	Y	Y	Y
2 Nye	Y	Y	Y	Y	Y	Y
3 Scott	Y	Y	Y	Y	Y	Y
4 **Forbes**	Y	Y	Y	Y	Y	Y
5 Perriello	Y	Y	Y	Y	Y	Y
6 **Goodlatte**	Y	Y	Y	Y	Y	Y
7 **Cantor**	Y	Y	Y	Y	Y	Y
8 Moran	Y	Y	Y	Y	Y	Y
9 Boucher	Y	Y	Y	Y	Y	Y
10 **Wolf**	Y	Y	Y	Y	Y	Y
11 Connolly	Y	Y	Y	Y	Y	Y
WASHINGTON						
1 Inslee	Y	Y	Y	Y	Y	Y
2 Larsen	Y	Y	?	?	?	?
3 Baird	Y	Y	Y	Y	Y	Y
4 **Hastings**	Y	Y	?	Y	Y	Y
5 **McMorris Rodgers**	Y	Y	Y	Y	Y	Y
6 Dicks	Y	Y	Y	Y	Y	Y
7 McDermott	Y	Y	Y	Y	Y	Y
8 **Reichert**	Y	Y	Y	Y	Y	Y
9 Smith	Y	Y	Y	Y	Y	Y
WEST VIRGINIA						
1 Mollohan	Y	Y	?	?	?	?
2 **Capito**	Y	Y	Y	Y	Y	Y
3 Rahall	Y	Y	Y	Y	Y	Y
WISCONSIN						
1 **Ryan**	Y	Y	Y	Y	Y	Y
2 Baldwin	Y	Y	Y	Y	Y	Y
3 Kind	Y	Y	Y	Y	Y	Y
4 Moore	Y	Y	Y	Y	Y	Y
5 **Sensenbrenner**	Y	Y	Y	Y	Y	Y
6 **Petri**	Y	Y	Y	Y	Y	Y
7 Obey	Y	Y	Y	Y	Y	Y
8 Kagen	Y	Y	Y	Y	Y	Y
WYOMING						
AL **Lummis**	Y	Y	?	?	?	?
DELEGATES						
Faleomavaega (A.S.)						
Norton (D.C.)						
Bordallo (Guam)						
Sablan (N. Marianas)						
Pierluisi (P.R.)						
Christensen (V.I.)						

IN THE HOUSE | By Vote Number

423. **HR 1777. Student Financial Assistance Revisions/Passage.** Hinojosa, D-Texas, motion to suspend the rules and pass the bill that would make technical changes to the Higher Education Opportunity Act, including a clarification that assistance received under the Montgomery GI bill is exempt from federal financial aid calculations. It also would provide scholarships to students whose parent or guardian died in military service in Iraq or Afghanistan after Sept. 11, 2001. Motion agreed to 411-0: R 168-0; D 243-0. A two-thirds majority of those present and voting (274 in this case) is required for passage under suspension of the rules. June 23, 2009.

424. **Procedural Motion/Motion to Adjourn.** Boehner, R-Ohio, motion to adjourn. Motion rejected 96-308: R 93-75; D 3-233. June 24, 2009.

425. **Procedural Motion/Motion to Adjourn.** Broun, R-Ga., motion to adjourn. Motion rejected 73-316: R 70-96; D 3-220. June 24, 2009.

426. **Procedural Motion/Motion to Adjourn.** Wilson, R-S.C., motion to adjourn. Motion rejected 26-361: R 22-139; D 4-222. June 24, 2009.

427. **Procedural Motion/Motion to Adjourn.** Tiberi, R-Ohio, motion to adjourn. Motion rejected 25-366: R 21-144; D 4-222. June 24, 2009.

428. **HR 2892. Fiscal 2010 Homeland Security Appropriations/ Previous Question.** Perlmutter, D-Colo., motion to order the previous question (thus ending debate and possibility of amendment) on adoption of the rule (H Res 573) that would provide for House floor consideration of a bill that would appropriate $44 billion in fiscal 2010 for the Homeland Security Department. Motion agreed to 238-174: R 1-171; D 237-3. June 24, 2009.

429. **HR 2892. Fiscal 2010 Homeland Security Appropriations/ Motion to Reconsider.** Broun, R-Ga., motion to reconsider the vote on the Perlmutter, D-Colo., motion to order the previous question (thus ending debate and possibility of amendment) on adoption of the rule (H Res 573) that would provide for House floor consideration of the bill that would appropriate $44 billion in fiscal 2010 for the Homeland Security Department. Motion rejected 172-238: R 169-4; D 3-234. June 24, 2009.

	423	424	425	426	427	428	429
ALABAMA							
1 Bonner	Y	Y	N	N	N	N	Y
2 Bright	Y	N	N	Y	Y	?	?
3 Rogers	Y	Y	Y	?	N	N	Y
4 Aderholt	Y	Y	Y	N	N	N	Y
5 Griffith	Y	N	N	N	N	N	Y
6 Bachus	Y	Y	?	?	N	N	Y
7 Davis	Y	N	N	N	N	Y	N
ALASKA							
AL Young	Y	Y	Y	Y	Y	N	N
ARIZONA							
1 Kirkpatrick	Y	N	N	N	N	Y	N
2 Franks	Y	N	N	N	N	N	Y
3 Shadegg	?	?	Y	N	Y	N	Y
4 Pastor	Y	N	N	N	N	Y	N
5 Mitchell	Y	N	N	N	N	Y	N
6 Flake	Y	Y	Y	N	N	N	Y
7 Grijalva	Y	N	?	N	?	Y	N
8 Giffords	Y	N	N	N	N	Y	N
ARKANSAS							
1 Berry	Y	N	N	?	N	Y	N
2 Snyder	Y	N	N	N	?	?	?
3 Boozman	Y	N	N	N	N	N	Y
4 Ross	Y	N	N	?	?	Y	N
CALIFORNIA							
1 Thompson	Y	N	N	N	N	Y	N
2 Herger	Y	N	N	N	N	N	Y
3 Lungren	Y	Y	N	N	N	N	Y
4 McClintock	Y	N	N	N	N	N	Y
5 Matsui	Y	N	?	N	N	Y	N
6 Woolsey	+	N	N	N	N	Y	N
7 Miller, George	Y	N	N	N	N	Y	N
8 Pelosi							
9 Lee	Y	N	N	N	N	Y	N
10 Tauscher	Y	N	N	N	N	Y	N
11 McNerney	Y	N	N	N	N	Y	N
12 Speier	Y	N	N	?	N	?	N
13 Stark	Y	N	N	?	?	Y	N
14 Eshoo	Y	N	N	N	N	Y	N
15 Honda	Y	N	N	N	N	Y	N
16 Lofgren	Y	N	N	N	N	Y	N
17 Farr	Y	N	N	N	N	Y	N
18 Cardoza	Y	?	?	N	N	Y	N
19 Radanovich	?	Y	Y	N	N	N	Y
20 Costa	?	N	?	N	N	Y	N
21 Nunes	Y	Y	Y	N	N	N	Y
22 McCarthy	Y	N	N	N	N	N	Y
23 Capps	Y	N	N	N	N	Y	N
24 Gallegly	Y	Y	Y	N	N	N	Y
25 McKeon	Y	Y	Y	N	N	N	Y
26 Dreier	Y	N	N	N	N	N	Y
27 Sherman	Y	N	N	N	N	?	N
28 Berman	Y	?	?	N	N	Y	N
29 Schiff	Y	N	N	N	N	Y	N
30 Waxman	Y	?	?	N	N	Y	N
31 Becerra	Y	N	N	N	N	Y	N
32 Vacant							
33 Watson	Y	N	?	?	N	?	N
34 Roybal-Allard	Y	N	N	N	N	Y	N
35 Waters	Y	N	N	N	?	Y	N
36 Harman	Y	N	?	N	N	Y	N
37 Richardson	Y	N	N	N	N	Y	N
38 Napolitano	Y	N	N	N	N	Y	N
39 Sánchez, Linda	Y	N	N	?	?	Y	N
40 Royce	Y	N	N	N	N	N	Y
41 Lewis	Y	Y	Y	N	N	N	Y
42 Miller, Gary	Y	Y	Y	N	N	N	Y
43 Baca	Y	N	N	N	N	Y	N
44 Calvert	Y	N	N	N	N	N	Y
45 Bono Mack	Y	N	N	N	N	N	Y
46 Rohrabacher	Y	Y	N	N	N	N	Y
47 Sanchez, Loretta	Y	N	N	N	N	Y	N
48 Campbell	?	?	?	?	?	?	?
49 Issa	Y	N	Y	N	N	?	Y
50 Bilbray	Y	N	N	N	N	N	Y
51 Filner	Y	N	N	N	N	Y	N
52 Hunter	Y	Y	N	N	N	N	Y
53 Davis	Y	N	N	N	N	Y	N
COLORADO							
1 DeGette	Y	N	N	N	N	Y	N
2 Polis	Y	N	N	N	N	Y	N
3 Salazar	Y	N	N	N	N	Y	N
4 Markey	Y	N	N	N	N	?	?
5 Lamborn	Y	Y	Y	N	N	N	Y
6 Coffman	Y	Y	Y	Y	N	N	Y
7 Perlmutter	Y	N	N	N	N	Y	N
CONNECTICUT							
1 Larson	Y	N	N	N	N	Y	N
2 Courtney	Y	N	N	N	N	Y	N
3 DeLauro	Y	N	N	N	N	Y	N
4 Himes	Y	N	N	N	N	?	?
5 Murphy	Y	N	?	N	N	Y	N
DELAWARE							
AL Castle	Y	N	N	N	N	N	Y
FLORIDA							
1 Miller	Y	N	N	N	N	N	Y
2 Boyd	Y	N	N	N	?	Y	N
3 Brown	Y	N	N	N	N	Y	N
4 Crenshaw	Y	Y	N	N	N	N	Y
5 Brown-Waite	Y	Y	N	N	N	N	Y
6 Stearns	Y	Y	N	N	N	N	Y
7 Mica	Y	N	N	N	N	N	?
8 Grayson	Y	N	N	N	N	Y	N
9 Bilirakis	Y	N	N	N	N	N	Y
10 Young	Y	Y	Y	N	N	N	Y
11 Castor	Y	N	N	N	N	Y	N
12 Putnam	Y	N	N	N	N	N	Y
13 Buchanan	Y	N	N	?	N	N	Y
14 Mack	Y	N	N	N	N	N	Y
15 Posey	Y	N	N	-	N	N	Y
16 Rooney	Y	N	N	N	N	N	Y
17 Meek	Y	?	N	N	N	Y	N
18 Ros-Lehtinen	Y	N	N	?	N	Y	N
19 Wexler	Y	N	N	N	N	Y	N
20 Wasserman Schultz	Y	N	N	N	N	Y	N
21 Diaz-Balart, L.	Y	N	N	N	N	N	Y
22 Klein	Y	N	N	N	N	Y	N
23 Hastings	Y	N	N	N	N	Y	N
24 Kosmas	Y	N	N	N	N	Y	N
25 Diaz-Balart, M.	Y	N	N	N	N	N	Y
GEORGIA							
1 Kingston	Y	Y	Y	Y	Y	N	Y
2 Bishop	Y	N	N	N	N	Y	N
3 Westmoreland	Y	N	N	N	?	N	Y
4 Johnson	Y	N	N	N	N	Y	N
5 Lewis	?	?	?	?	?	?	?
6 Price	Y	N	N	N	N	N	Y
7 Linder	Y	N	N	N	N	N	Y
8 Marshall	Y	N	N	N	N	Y	N
9 Deal	Y	N	Y	N	N	Y	N
10 Broun	Y	Y	Y	N	Y	Y	Y
11 Gingrey	Y	Y	?	?	Y	N	Y
12 Barrow	Y	N	N	N	N	Y	N
13 Scott	Y	N	N	N	N	Y	N
HAWAII							
1 Abercrombie	Y	?	N	N	N	Y	?
2 Hirono	Y	N	N	N	N	Y	N
IDAHO							
1 Minnick	Y	N	N	N	N	Y	N
2 Simpson	Y	?	N	Y	N	N	Y
ILLINOIS							
1 Rush	Y	N	N	?	N	Y	N
2 Jackson	Y	N	N	N	N	Y	N
3 Lipinski	Y	N	N	N	N	Y	N
4 Gutierrez	?	N	N	N	?	Y	N
5 Quigley	Y	N	N	N	N	Y	N
6 Roskam	Y	N	N	N	N	N	Y
7 Davis	Y	N	N	?	N	Y	N
8 Bean	Y	N	N	N	N	Y	N
9 Schakowsky	Y	N	N	N	?	Y	N
10 Kirk	Y	N	N	N	N	N	Y
11 Halvorson	Y	N	N	?	N	Y	N
12 Costello	Y	N	N	N	N	Y	N
13 Biggert	Y	N	N	N	N	N	Y
14 Foster	Y	N	N	N	N	Y	N
15 Johnson	Y	Y	?	Y	Y	N	Y

	423	424	425	426	427	428	429
16 **Manzullo**	Y	N	N	N	?	N	Y
17 Hare	Y	N	N	N	N	Y	N
18 **Schock**	?	Y	Y	N	N	N	Y
19 **Shimkus**	Y	Y	Y	N	N	N	Y
INDIANA							
1 Visclosky	Y	N	N	N	N	Y	N
2 Donnelly	Y	N	N	N	N	Y	N
3 **Souder**	Y	Y	Y	Y	Y	?	Y
4 **Buyer**	Y	N	N	N	N	N	Y
5 **Burton**	Y	Y	Y	N	N	N	Y
6 **Pence**	Y	Y	Y	?	N	N	Y
7 Carson	Y	N	N	N	N	Y	N
8 Ellsworth	Y	?	N	N	N	Y	N
9 Hill	Y	N	N	N	?	N	N
IOWA							
1 Braley	Y	N	N	N	?	Y	N
2 Loebsack	Y	N	N	N	N	Y	N
3 Boswell	Y	N	N	N	N	Y	N
4 **Latham**	Y	Y	N	N	N	N	Y
5 **King**	Y	Y	Y	Y	Y	N	Y
KANSAS							
1 **Moran**	Y	N	N	N	N	N	Y
2 **Jenkins**	Y	Y	Y	N	N	N	Y
3 Moore	Y	N	N	N	N	Y	N
4 **Tiahrt**	Y	Y	Y	Y	Y	N	Y
KENTUCKY							
1 **Whitfield**	Y	Y	N	Y	N	N	Y
2 **Guthrie**	Y	N	N	N	N	N	Y
3 Yarmuth	Y	N	?	N	?	Y	N
4 **Davis**	Y	N	N	N	N	N	Y
5 **Rogers**	Y	N	N	N	N	N	Y
6 Chandler	Y	Y	N	N	N	Y	N
LOUISIANA							
1 **Scalise**	Y	Y	N	N	N	N	Y
2 **Cao**	Y	Y	N	?	?	N	N
3 Melancon	Y	N	N	N	?	Y	N
4 **Fleming**	Y	Y	Y	?	?	N	Y
5 **Alexander**	Y	Y	Y	N	N	N	Y
6 **Cassidy**	Y	N	N	N	N	N	Y
7 **Boustany**	Y	N	N	N	N	?	Y
MAINE							
1 Pingree	Y	N	N	N	N	Y	N
2 Michaud	Y	N	N	N	N	Y	N
MARYLAND							
1 Kratovil	Y	N	N	N	N	Y	N
2 Ruppersberger	Y	?	N	N	N	Y	N
3 Sarbanes	Y	?	?	N	N	Y	N
4 Edwards	Y	N	N	N	N	Y	N
5 Hoyer	Y	?	?	?	N	Y	N
6 **Bartlett**	Y	Y	Y	Y	Y	N	Y
7 Cummings	Y	N	N	N	N	Y	N
8 Van Hollen	Y	N	N	?	N	Y	N
MASSACHUSETTS							
1 Olver	Y	N	?	N	N	Y	N
2 Neal	Y	N	N	N	N	Y	N
3 McGovern	Y	N	N	N	N	Y	N
4 Frank	Y	Y	?	?	N	Y	?
5 Tsongas	Y	N	N	N	N	Y	N
6 Tierney	Y	N	?	?	?	Y	N
7 Markey	Y	N	N	N	N	Y	Y
8 Capuano	Y	N	N	?	N	Y	N
9 Lynch	Y	N	N	N	N	Y	N
10 Delahunt	Y	N	?	N	N	Y	N
MICHIGAN							
1 Stupak	Y	?	?	?	?	?	?
2 **Hoekstra**	Y	N	N	N	N	N	Y
3 **Ehlers**	Y	N	N	N	N	N	Y
4 **Camp**	Y	Y	Y	N	N	N	Y
5 Kildee	Y	N	N	N	N	Y	N
6 **Upton**	Y	N	N	N	N	N	Y
7 Schauer	Y	N	N	N	N	?	N
8 **Rogers**	Y	Y	N	N	N	N	Y
9 Peters	Y	N	N	N	N	Y	N
10 **Miller**	Y	N	N	N	N	N	Y
11 **McCotter**	Y	N	N	?	N	N	Y
12 Levin	Y	N	N	N	N	Y	N
13 Kilpatrick	Y	N	N	N	N	N	N
14 Conyers	?	?	?	?	?	Y	N
15 Dingell	Y	N	N	?	?	Y	N
MINNESOTA							
1 Walz	Y	N	N	N	N	Y	N
2 **Kline**	Y	Y	Y	N	N	N	Y
3 **Paulsen**	Y	N	N	N	N	N	Y
4 McCollum	Y	N	N	N	N	Y	N

	423	424	425	426	427	428	429
5 Ellison	Y	N	N	N	N	Y	?
6 **Bachmann**	Y	N	N	N	N	N	Y
7 Peterson	Y	N	N	N	?	Y	N
8 Oberstar	Y	N	N	N	N	Y	N
MISSISSIPPI							
1 Childers	Y	N	Y	N	N	Y	N
2 Thompson	Y	N	?	N	N	Y	N
3 **Harper**	Y	Y	Y	N	N	N	Y
4 Taylor	Y	N	N	N	N	Y	N
MISSOURI							
1 Clay	Y	Y	Y	Y	Y	Y	N
2 **Akin**	Y	Y	Y	N	N	N	Y
3 Carnahan	Y	N	N	N	N	Y	N
4 Skelton	Y	N	N	N	N	Y	N
5 Cleaver	Y	N	N	N	N	Y	N
6 **Graves**	Y	N	N	N	N	N	Y
7 **Blunt**	?	N	N	N	N	N	Y
8 **Emerson**	Y	N	N	N	N	N	Y
9 **Luetkemeyer**	Y	N	N	N	N	N	Y
MONTANA							
AL **Rehberg**	Y	N	N	N	N	N	Y
NEBRASKA							
1 **Fortenberry**	Y	N	N	N	N	N	Y
2 **Terry**	Y	N	N	N	N	N	Y
3 **Smith**	Y	Y	Y	N	N	N	Y
NEVADA							
1 Berkley	Y	N	N	N	N	Y	?
2 **Heller**	Y	N	N	N	N	N	Y
3 Titus	Y	N	N	N	N	Y	N
NEW HAMPSHIRE							
1 Shea-Porter	?	?	?	?	?	?	?
2 Hodes	Y	N	N	N	N	Y	N
NEW JERSEY							
1 Andrews	?	N	N	N	N	Y	N
2 **LoBiondo**	Y	N	N	N	N	N	Y
3 Adler	Y	N	N	N	N	Y	N
4 **Smith**	Y	N	N	N	N	N	Y
5 **Garrett**	Y	Y	Y	Y	Y	N	Y
6 Pallone	Y	N	N	N	N	Y	N
7 **Lance**	Y	N	N	N	N	N	Y
8 Pascrell	Y	N	?	N	N	Y	N
9 Rothman	Y	N	N	N	N	Y	N
10 Payne	?	N	N	N	N	Y	N
11 **Frelinghuysen**	Y	Y	N	N	N	N	Y
12 Holt	Y	N	N	N	Y	Y	N
13 Sires	Y	N	N	N	N	Y	N
NEW MEXICO							
1 Heinrich	Y	N	N	N	N	Y	N
2 Teague	Y	N	Y	N	N	Y	N
3 Lujan	Y	N	N	N	N	Y	N
NEW YORK							
1 Bishop	Y	N	N	N	N	Y	N
2 Israel	Y	N	N	N	N	Y	N
3 **King**	Y	N	N	N	N	N	Y
4 McCarthy	Y	N	N	N	N	Y	N
5 Ackerman	Y	N	N	N	N	Y	N
6 Meeks	Y	N	N	?	N	Y	N
7 Crowley	Y	N	N	N	N	Y	N
8 Nadler	Y	N	N	N	N	Y	N
9 Weiner	Y	N	N	N	N	Y	N
10 Towns	Y	N	N	N	N	Y	N
11 Clarke	Y	N	?	N	N	Y	N
12 Velázquez	Y	N	N	N	N	Y	N
13 McMahon	Y	N	N	N	N	Y	N
14 Maloney	Y	N	?	N	N	Y	N
15 Rangel	Y	?	N	?	?	Y	?
16 Serrano	Y	N	N	N	N	Y	N
17 Engel	Y	N	N	?	N	Y	N
18 Lowey	Y	N	N	N	N	Y	N
19 Hall	Y	N	N	N	?	Y	N
20 Murphy	Y	N	N	N	N	Y	N
21 Tonko	Y	N	N	N	N	Y	N
22 Hinchey	Y	N	N	Y	N	Y	N
23 **McHugh**	Y	N	N	N	N	N	Y
24 Arcuri	Y	N	N	N	N	Y	N
25 Maffei	Y	N	N	N	N	Y	N
26 **Lee**	Y	N	N	N	N	N	Y
27 Higgins	Y	N	?	?	N	Y	N
28 Slaughter	Y	N	N	N	N	Y	N
29 Massa	Y	N	N	N	N	Y	N
NORTH CAROLINA							
1 Butterfield	Y	N	N	N	N	Y	N
2 Etheridge	Y	N	N	N	N	Y	N
3 **Jones**	Y	Y	N	N	N	N	N
4 Price	Y	N	N	N	N	Y	N

	423	424	425	426	427	428	429
5 **Foxx**	Y	Y	N	N	N	N	Y
6 **Coble**	Y	Y	N	N	N	N	Y
7 McIntyre	Y	N	N	N	N	Y	N
8 Kissell	Y	N	N	N	N	?	?
9 **Myrick**	Y	Y	N	N	N	N	Y
10 **McHenry**	+	?	?	?	?	?	?
11 Shuler	?	?	N	N	N	N	Y
12 Watt	Y	N	N	N	N	Y	N
13 Miller	Y	N	?	N	?	?	N
NORTH DAKOTA							
AL Pomeroy	Y	N	N	N	N	Y	N
OHIO							
1 Driehaus	Y	N	N	N	N	Y	N
2 **Schmidt**	Y	Y	Y	N	N	N	Y
3 **Turner**	Y	Y	Y	?	N	N	Y
4 **Jordan**	Y	N	N	N	N	N	Y
5 **Latta**	Y	N	N	N	N	N	Y
6 Wilson	Y	N	N	N	N	Y	Y
7 **Austria**	Y	Y	Y	N	N	N	Y
8 **Boehner**	Y	Y	Y	Y	?	N	Y
9 Kaptur	Y	N	N	N	N	Y	N
10 Kucinich	Y	N	N	N	N	Y	N
11 Fudge	Y	N	N	N	N	Y	N
12 **Tiberi**	Y	N	N	N	Y	N	Y
13 Sutton	Y	N	N	N	N	Y	N
14 **LaTourette**	Y	N	N	N	N	N	Y
15 Kilroy	Y	N	N	N	N	Y	N
16 Boccieri	Y	N	N	N	N	Y	N
17 Ryan	Y	N	N	N	N	Y	N
18 Space	Y	N	N	N	N	Y	N
OKLAHOMA							
1 **Sullivan**	?	?	?	?	?	?	?
2 Boren	Y	N	N	N	N	Y	N
3 **Lucas**	Y	N	?	N	N	N	Y
4 **Cole**	Y	Y	Y	?	N	N	Y
5 **Fallin**	Y	Y	Y	N	N	N	Y
OREGON							
1 Wu	Y	N	N	N	N	?	N
2 **Walden**	Y	N	N	N	N	N	Y
3 Blumenauer	Y	N	N	N	N	Y	N
4 DeFazio	Y	N	N	N	N	Y	N
5 Schrader	Y	N	N	?	N	Y	N
PENNSYLVANIA							
1 Brady	Y	N	N	N	N	Y	N
2 Fattah	Y	N	N	N	N	Y	N
3 Dahlkemper	Y	N	N	N	N	Y	N
4 Altmire	Y	N	N	N	N	Y	N
5 **Thompson**	Y	Y	Y	Y	N	N	Y
6 **Gerlach**	Y	?	N	N	N	N	N
7 Sestak	Y	N	N	N	N	Y	N
8 Murphy, P.	Y	N	N	N	N	Y	N
9 **Shuster**	Y	?	Y	N	N	N	Y
10 Carney	Y	N	N	N	N	Y	N
11 Kanjorski	Y	N	N	N	N	Y	N
12 Murtha	Y	N	N	N	N	Y	N
13 Schwartz	Y	N	N	?	N	Y	N
14 Doyle	Y	?	?	?	?	Y	?
15 **Dent**	Y	N	N	N	N	N	Y
16 **Pitts**	Y	Y	Y	Y	N	N	Y
17 Holden	Y	N	N	N	N	Y	N
18 **Murphy, T.**	Y	N	N	?	?	N	Y
19 **Platts**	Y	N	N	N	N	N	Y
RHODE ISLAND							
1 Kennedy	?	?	?	?	?	?	?
2 Langevin	Y	N	N	N	N	Y	N
SOUTH CAROLINA							
1 **Brown**	Y	N	N	N	N	N	Y
2 **Wilson**	Y	Y	N	Y	N	N	Y
3 **Barrett**	Y	Y	Y	N	N	N	Y
4 **Inglis**	Y	Y	Y	N	N	N	Y
5 Spratt	Y	N	N	N	N	Y	N
6 Clyburn	Y	N	N	N	N	Y	N
SOUTH DAKOTA							
AL Herseth Sandlin	Y	N	N	N	N	Y	N
TENNESSEE							
1 **Roe**	Y	Y	Y	N	N	N	Y
2 **Duncan**	Y	Y	N	N	N	N	Y
3 **Wamp**	Y	Y	Y	N	N	N	Y
4 Davis	Y	N	N	N	N	Y	?
5 Cooper	Y	N	N	N	N	Y	N
6 Gordon	Y	N	N	Y	N	Y	N
7 **Blackburn**	Y	Y	Y	N	N	N	Y
8 Tanner	Y	N	N	N	N	Y	N
9 Cohen	Y	N	N	N	N	Y	N

	423	424	425	426	427	428	429
TEXAS							
1 **Gohmert**	Y	Y	?	Y	Y	N	Y
2 **Poe**	Y	N	N	N	N	N	Y
3 **Johnson, S.**	Y	Y	Y	Y	Y	N	Y
4 **Hall**	Y	N	N	N	N	N	Y
5 **Hensarling**	Y	Y	Y	Y	Y	N	Y
6 **Barton**	Y	Y	Y	N	Y	N	Y
7 **Culberson**	Y	Y	N	N	N	N	Y
8 **Brady**	?	?	?	N	N	N	Y
9 Green, A.	Y	N	N	N	N	Y	N
10 **McCaul**	Y	Y	?	N	N	N	Y
11 **Conaway**	Y	N	N	N	N	N	Y
12 **Granger**	Y	Y	Y	N	N	N	Y
13 **Thornberry**	Y	Y	Y	N	N	N	Y
14 **Paul**	Y	Y	Y	?	?	N	?
15 Hinojosa	Y	N	N	N	?	Y	N
16 Reyes	Y	N	N	N	N	Y	N
17 Edwards	Y	?	?	N	N	Y	N
18 Jackson Lee	Y	N	N	N	N	Y	N
19 **Neugebauer**	Y	Y	Y	N	N	N	Y
20 Gonzalez	Y	N	N	N	N	Y	N
21 **Smith**	Y	Y	Y	N	N	N	Y
22 **Olson**	Y	Y	Y	N	N	N	Y
23 Rodriguez	Y	N	N	N	N	Y	N
24 **Marchant**	Y	?	?	N	N	N	Y
25 Doggett	Y	N	N	N	N	Y	N
26 **Burgess**	Y	N	?	N	N	N	Y
27 Ortiz	Y	N	N	N	N	Y	N
28 Cuellar	Y	N	N	N	N	Y	N
29 Green, G.	Y	N	N	N	N	Y	N
30 Johnson, E.	Y	N	N	N	N	Y	N
31 **Carter**	Y	Y	Y	Y	Y	N	Y
32 **Sessions**	Y	Y	Y	?	Y	N	Y
UTAH							
1 **Bishop**	Y	?	N	N	N	N	Y
2 Matheson	Y	N	N	?	N	Y	?
3 **Chaffetz**	Y	Y	Y	Y	Y	N	Y
VERMONT							
AL Welch	Y	N	N	N	N	Y	N
VIRGINIA							
1 **Wittman**	Y	Y	N	N	N	N	Y
2 Nye	Y	N	N	N	N	Y	N
3 Scott	Y	N	N	N	N	Y	N
4 **Forbes**	Y	Y	N	N	N	N	Y
5 Perriello	Y	N	N	N	N	Y	N
6 **Goodlatte**	Y	Y	Y	N	N	N	Y
7 **Cantor**	Y	Y	N	N	N	N	Y
8 Moran	Y	N	?	?	?	Y	N
9 Boucher	Y	N	?	N	N	Y	N
10 **Wolf**	Y	N	N	N	N	N	Y
11 Connolly	Y	N	N	N	Y	Y	N
WASHINGTON							
1 Inslee	Y	N	N	N	N	Y	N
2 Larsen	?	N	N	N	N	Y	N
3 Baird	Y	N	N	N	?	Y	N
4 **Hastings**	Y	Y	Y	Y	Y	N	Y
5 **McMorris Rodgers**	Y	Y	Y	N	N	N	Y
6 Dicks	Y	?	N	N	N	Y	N
7 McDermott	Y	N	N	N	N	Y	N
8 **Reichert**	?	N	N	N	N	N	Y
9 Smith	Y	N	N	N	N	Y	N
WEST VIRGINIA							
1 Mollohan	?	N	N	N	N	Y	N
2 **Capito**	Y	Y	Y	N	N	N	Y
3 Rahall	Y	N	N	N	N	Y	N
WISCONSIN							
1 **Ryan**	Y	Y	Y	N	N	N	Y
2 Baldwin	Y	N	N	N	N	Y	N
3 Kind	Y	N	N	N	N	Y	N
4 Moore	Y	N	?	N	N	Y	N
5 **Sensenbrenner**	Y	Y	Y	Y	Y	N	Y
6 **Petri**	Y	Y	Y	N	N	N	Y
7 Obey	Y	N	N	N	N	Y	N
8 Kagen	Y	N	N	N	?	Y	N
WYOMING							
AL **Lummis**	?	Y	N	N	N	N	Y
DELEGATES							
Faleomavaega (A.S.)							
Norton (D.C.)							
Bordallo (Guam)							
Sablan (N. Marianas)							
Pierluisi (P.R.)							
Christensen (V.I.)							

IN THE HOUSE | By Vote Number

430. **HR 2892. Fiscal 2010 Homeland Security Appropriations/Rule.** Adoption of the rule (H Res 573) to provide for House floor consideration of the bill that would appropriate $44 billion in fiscal 2010 for the Homeland Security Department. Adopted 239-184: R 1-174; D 238-10. June 24, 2009.

431. **HR 2892. Fiscal 2010 Homeland Security Appropriations/ Motion to Reconsider.** Westmoreland, R-Ga., motion to reconsider the vote on adoption of the rule (H Res 573) to provide for House floor consideration of the bill that would appropriate $44 billion in fiscal 2010 for the Homeland Security Department. Motion rejected 169-251: R 165-8; D 4-243. June 24, 2009.

432. **Procedural Motion/Motion to Adjourn.** Price, R-Ga., motion to adjourn. Motion rejected 31-393: R 29-147; D 2-246. June 24, 2009.

433. **HR 2990. Armed Forces Pay and Retirement Benefits/ Passage.** Skelton, D-Mo., motion to suspend the rules and pass the bill that would extend, through 2010, bonus and special pay for members of the armed forces, including members of the reserve forces, health care professionals and nuclear officers. The bill would entitle reservists to have their retirement pay computed again if they are recalled to active duty and serve for at least two years. It would make some disabled retirees eligible for one year of simultaneous military retirement and veterans disability payments. Motion agreed to 404-0: R 165-0; D 239-0. A two-thirds majority of those present and voting (270 in this case) is required for passage under suspension of the rules. June 24, 2009.

434. **Procedural Motion/Motion to Adjourn.** King, R-Iowa, motion to adjourn. Motion rejected 36-381: R 32-143; D 4-238. June 24, 2009.

435. **HR 2892. Fiscal 2010 Homeland Security Appropriations/ Manager's Amendment.** Price, D-N.C., amendment that would increase funding for firefighter assistance grants by $10 million, state and local programs by $7 million and U.S. Customs and Border Protection salaries and expenses by $4.9 million. It would reduce funds for various offices by an equal amount. It also would bar the use of funds in the bill for first-class travel or to close or transfer operations of the Federal Emergency Management Agency's Florida Long Term Recovery Office. Adopted in Committee of the Whole 345-85: R 91-85; D 254-0. June 24, 2009.

436. **HR 2892. Fiscal 2010 Homeland Security Appropriations. Customs and Border Protection.** Lewis, R-Calif., amendment that would increase the amount provided for Customs and Border Protection by $34 million, offset by cuts to the Office of the Secretary, the Office of the Under Secretary of Management, the Chief Financial Officer and the Chief Information Officer. Adopted in Committee of the Whole 375-55: R 177-0; D 198-55. June 24, 2009.

	430	431	432	433	434	435	436
ALABAMA							
1 Bonner	N	Y	N	Y	N	N	Y
2 Bright	N	N	N	Y	N	Y	Y
3 Rogers	N	Y	N	Y	N	N	Y
4 Aderholt	N	Y	N	?	N	N	Y
5 Griffith	Y	N	N	Y	N	Y	Y
6 Bachus	N	Y	N	?	N	N	Y
7 Davis	Y	N	N	Y	N	Y	Y
ALASKA							
AL Young	N	N	Y	?	Y	Y	Y
ARIZONA							
1 Kirkpatrick	Y	N	N	Y	N	Y	Y
2 Franks	N	Y	N	Y	N	N	Y
3 Shadegg	N	Y	Y	Y	Y	N	Y
4 Pastor	Y	N	N	Y	N	Y	Y
5 Mitchell	Y	N	N	Y	N	Y	Y
6 Flake	N	Y	N	Y	N	N	Y
7 Grijalva	Y	N	N	Y	N	Y	N
8 Giffords	Y	N	N	Y	N	Y	Y
ARKANSAS							
1 Berry	Y	N	N	Y	N	Y	N
2 Snyder	?	?	N	Y	N	Y	N
3 Boozman	N	Y	N	Y	N	Y	Y
4 Ross	Y	N	N	Y	N	Y	Y
CALIFORNIA							
1 Thompson	Y	N	N	Y	N	Y	Y
2 Herger	N	Y	N	Y	N	Y	Y
3 Lungren	N	Y	N	Y	N	N	Y
4 McClintock	N	Y	N	Y	N	N	Y
5 Matsui	Y	N	N	Y	N	Y	Y
6 Woolsey	Y	N	Y	Y	N	Y	N
7 Miller, George	Y	N	?	N	Y	N	N
8 Pelosi							
9 Lee	Y	N	N	Y	N	Y	N
10 Tauscher	Y	N	N	Y	N	Y	Y
11 McNerney	Y	N	N	Y	N	Y	Y
12 Speier	Y	N	N	Y	N	Y	Y
13 Stark	Y	N	N	Y	?	Y	N
14 Eshoo	Y	N	N	Y	N	Y	N
15 Honda	Y	N	N	Y	N	Y	Y
16 Lofgren	Y	N	N	Y	N	Y	Y
17 Farr	Y	N	N	Y	N	Y	N
18 Cardoza	Y	N	N	Y	N	Y	Y
19 Radanovich	N	Y	N	Y	N	N	Y
20 Costa	Y	N	N	Y	N	Y	Y
21 Nunes	N	Y	N	Y	N	N	Y
22 McCarthy	N	Y	N	Y	N	Y	Y
23 Capps	Y	N	N	Y	N	Y	Y
24 Gallegly	N	Y	N	Y	N	N	Y
25 McKeon	N	Y	N	Y	N	N	Y
26 Dreier	N	Y	N	Y	N	N	Y
27 Sherman	Y	N	N	Y	N	Y	Y
28 Berman	Y	N	N	Y	N	Y	Y
29 Schiff	Y	N	N	Y	N	Y	Y
30 Waxman	Y	N	N	Y	N	Y	Y
31 Becerra	Y	N	N	Y	N	Y	Y
32 Vacant							
33 Watson	Y	N	N	Y	N	Y	N
34 Roybal-Allard	Y	N	N	Y	N	Y	Y
35 Waters	Y	N	N	Y	N	Y	Y
36 Harman	Y	N	N	Y	N	Y	Y
37 Richardson	Y	N	N	Y	Y	Y	Y
38 Napolitano	Y	N	N	Y	N	Y	Y
39 Sánchez, Linda	Y	N	N	Y	N	Y	Y
40 Royce	N	Y	N	Y	N	Y	Y
41 Lewis	N	Y	N	Y	Y	N	Y
42 Miller, Gary	N	Y	Y	Y	N	N	Y
43 Baca	Y	N	N	Y	N	Y	Y
44 Calvert	N	Y	N	Y	N	N	Y
45 Bono Mack	N	Y	N	Y	N	Y	Y
46 Rohrabacher	N	N	N	Y	N	N	Y
47 Sanchez, Loretta	Y	N	N	Y	N	Y	Y
48 Campbell	?	?	?	?	?	N	Y
49 Issa	N	Y	Y	Y	Y	N	Y
50 Bilbray	N	Y	N	Y	N	Y	Y
51 Filner	Y	N	N	Y	N	Y	Y
52 Hunter	N	Y	N	Y	N	N	Y
53 Davis	Y	N	N	Y	N	Y	Y

	430	431	432	433	434	435	436
COLORADO							
1 DeGette	Y	N	N	Y	N	Y	N
2 Polis	Y	N	N	Y	N	Y	N
3 Salazar	Y	N	N	Y	N	Y	Y
4 Markey	Y	N	N	Y	N	Y	Y
5 Lamborn	N	Y	N	Y	N	N	Y
6 Coffman	N	Y	Y	Y	Y	N	Y
7 Perlmutter	Y	N	N	Y	N	Y	N
CONNECTICUT							
1 Larson	Y	N	N	Y	N	Y	Y
2 Courtney	Y	N	N	Y	N	Y	Y
3 DeLauro	Y	N	N	Y	N	Y	Y
4 Himes	Y	N	N	Y	N	Y	Y
5 Murphy	Y	N	N	Y	N	Y	Y
DELAWARE							
AL Castle	N	Y	N	Y	N	Y	Y
FLORIDA							
1 Miller	N	Y	N	Y	N	N	Y
2 Boyd	Y	N	N	Y	N	Y	Y
3 Brown	Y	N	N	Y	N	Y	Y
4 Crenshaw	N	Y	N	Y	N	N	Y
5 Brown-Waite	N	N	N	Y	Y	Y	Y
6 Stearns	N	Y	Y	Y	Y	Y	Y
7 Mica	N	Y	N	Y	N	N	Y
8 Grayson	Y	N	N	Y	N	Y	Y
9 Bilirakis	N	Y	N	Y	N	N	Y
10 Young	N	Y	N	Y	N	Y	Y
11 Castor	Y	N	N	Y	N	Y	Y
12 Putnam	N	Y	N	Y	N	Y	Y
13 Buchanan	N	Y	N	Y	N	N	Y
14 Mack	N	Y	N	Y	N	N	Y
15 Posey	N	Y	N	Y	N	N	Y
16 Rooney	N	Y	N	+	N	Y	Y
17 Meek	Y	N	N	Y	N	Y	Y
18 Ros-Lehtinen	N	Y	N	Y	N	N	Y
19 Wexler	Y	N	N	Y	N	Y	Y
20 Wasserman Schultz	Y	N	N	Y	N	Y	Y
21 Diaz-Balart, L.	N	Y	N	Y	N	Y	Y
22 Klein	Y	N	N	Y	N	Y	Y
23 Hastings	Y	N	N	Y	N	Y	N
24 Kosmas	Y	N	N	Y	N	Y	Y
25 Diaz-Balart, M.	N	Y	N	Y	N	Y	Y
GEORGIA							
1 Kingston	N	Y	Y	?	Y	N	Y
2 Bishop	Y	N	N	Y	N	Y	Y
3 Westmoreland	Y	Y	Y	Y	Y	Y	Y
4 Johnson	Y	N	N	Y	N	Y	Y
5 Lewis	?	?	?	?	?	?	?
6 Price	N	Y	Y	Y	Y	Y	Y
7 Linder	N	Y	N	?	?	N	Y
8 Marshall	Y	N	N	Y	N	Y	Y
9 Deal	N	Y	N	Y	N	N	Y
10 Broun	N	Y	Y	Y	Y	N	Y
11 Gingrey	N	Y	Y	Y	Y	N	Y
12 Barrow	Y	N	N	Y	N	Y	Y
13 Scott	Y	N	N	Y	N	Y	Y
HAWAII							
1 Abercrombie	Y	N	N	Y	N	Y	Y
2 Hirono	Y	N	N	Y	N	Y	N
IDAHO							
1 Minnick	N	N	N	Y	?	Y	Y
2 Simpson	N	Y	N	Y	N	N	Y
ILLINOIS							
1 Rush	Y	N	N	Y	?	Y	Y
2 Jackson	Y	N	N	Y	N	Y	N
3 Lipinski	Y	N	N	Y	N	Y	Y
4 Gutierrez	Y	N	N	Y	N	Y	Y
5 Quigley	Y	N	N	Y	N	Y	Y
6 Roskam	N	Y	N	Y	N	Y	Y
7 Davis	Y	N	N	Y	?	?	?
8 Bean	N	N	N	Y	N	Y	Y
9 Schakowsky	Y	N	N	Y	N	Y	Y
10 Kirk	N	Y	N	?	N	?	Y
11 Halvorson	Y	N	N	Y	N	Y	Y
12 Costello	Y	N	N	Y	N	Y	Y
13 Biggert	N	Y	N	Y	N	Y	Y
14 Foster	Y	N	N	Y	N	Y	Y
15 Johnson	N	N	Y	Y	Y	Y	Y

KEY Republicans   Democrats

Y Voted for (yea)	**X** Paired against	**C** Voted "present" to avoid possible conflict of interest
# Paired for	**–** Announced against	
+ Announced for	**P** Voted "present"	**?** Did not vote or otherwise make a position known
N Voted against (nay)		

	430	431	432	433	434	435	436
16 **Manzullo**	N	Y	N	Y	Y	Y	Y
17 Hare	Y	N	N	Y	N	Y	Y
18 **Schock**	N	Y	N	Y	N	Y	Y
19 **Shimkus**	N	Y	N	Y	N	N	Y
INDIANA							
1 Visclosky	Y	N	N	Y	N	Y	N
2 Donnelly	Y	N	N	Y	N	Y	Y
3 **Souder**	N	Y	Y	Y	Y	N	Y
4 **Buyer**	N	Y	N	Y	N	Y	Y
5 **Burton**	N	Y	N	Y	N	Y	Y
6 **Pence**	N	Y	N	Y	N	N	Y
7 Carson	Y	N	N	Y	N	Y	N
8 Ellsworth	Y	N	N	Y	N	Y	Y
9 Hill	N	N	N	Y	N	Y	Y
IOWA							
1 Braley	Y	N	N	Y	N	Y	Y
2 Loebsack	Y	N	N	Y	N	Y	Y
3 Boswell	?	N	N	Y	N	Y	Y
4 **Latham**	N	Y	N	Y	N	N	Y
5 **King**	N	Y	Y	Y	Y	N	Y
KANSAS							
1 **Moran**	N	Y	N	Y	N	Y	Y
2 **Jenkins**	N	Y	N	Y	N	Y	Y
3 Moore	Y	N	N	Y	N	Y	Y
4 **Tiahrt**	N	Y	Y	Y	Y	Y	Y
KENTUCKY							
1 **Whitfield**	N	Y	N	Y	N	Y	Y
2 **Guthrie**	N	Y	N	Y	N	N	Y
3 Yarmuth	Y	N	N	Y	N	Y	Y
4 **Davis**	N	Y	N	Y	N	N	Y
5 **Rogers**	N	Y	N	Y	N	N	Y
6 Chandler	Y	N	N	Y	N	Y	Y
LOUISIANA							
1 **Scalise**	N	Y	N	Y	N	N	Y
2 **Cao**	N	N	N	Y	N	Y	Y
3 Melancon	N	N	N	Y	N	Y	Y
4 **Fleming**	N	Y	N	Y	N	N	Y
5 **Alexander**	N	Y	N	Y	N	Y	Y
6 **Cassidy**	N	Y	N	Y	N	Y	Y
7 **Boustany**	N	Y	N	Y	N	N	Y
MAINE							
1 Pingree	Y	N	N	Y	N	Y	Y
2 Michaud	Y	N	N	Y	N	Y	Y
MARYLAND							
1 Kratovil	Y	N	N	Y	N	Y	Y
2 Ruppersberger	Y	N	N	Y	N	Y	Y
3 Sarbanes	Y	N	N	Y	N	Y	Y
4 Edwards	Y	N	N	Y	N	Y	N
5 Hoyer	Y	N	N	Y	N	Y	N
6 **Bartlett**	N	Y	Y	Y	Y	Y	Y
7 Cummings	Y	N	N	Y	N	Y	Y
8 Van Hollen	Y	N	N	Y	N	Y	Y
MASSACHUSETTS							
1 Olver	Y	N	N	Y	N	Y	N
2 Neal	Y	N	N	?	N	Y	Y
3 McGovern	Y	N	N	Y	N	Y	N
4 Frank	Y	N	N	Y	N	Y	?
5 Tsongas	Y	N	N	Y	N	Y	N
6 Tierney	Y	N	N	?	N	Y	Y
7 Markey	Y	N	N	?	N	Y	Y
8 Capuano	Y	N	N	Y	N	?	?
9 Lynch	Y	N	N	Y	N	Y	Y
10 Delahunt	Y	N	N	Y	N	Y	Y
MICHIGAN							
1 Stupak	?	?	?	?	?	?	?
2 **Hoekstra**	N	Y	N	Y	N	Y	Y
3 **Ehlers**	N	Y	N	?	N	N	Y
4 **Camp**	N	Y	N	Y	N	Y	Y
5 Kildee	Y	N	N	Y	N	Y	Y
6 **Upton**	N	Y	N	Y	N	Y	Y
7 Schauer	Y	N	N	Y	N	Y	Y
8 **Rogers**	N	Y	N	Y	N	N	Y
9 Peters	Y	N	N	Y	N	Y	Y
10 **Miller**	N	Y	N	Y	N	Y	Y
11 **McCotter**	N	Y	N	Y	N	Y	Y
12 Levin	Y	N	N	Y	N	Y	Y
13 Kilpatrick	Y	N	N	Y	N	Y	N
14 Conyers	Y	?	?	?	?	Y	N
15 Dingell	Y	N	N	Y	N	Y	Y
MINNESOTA							
1 Walz	Y	N	N	Y	N	Y	Y
2 **Kline**	N	Y	N	Y	N	N	Y
3 **Paulsen**	N	Y	N	Y	N	Y	Y
4 McCollum	Y	N	N	Y	N	Y	Y
5 Ellison	Y	N	N	Y	N	Y	N
6 **Bachmann**	N	Y	N	Y	N	N	Y
7 Peterson	Y	N	N	Y	N	Y	Y
8 Oberstar	Y	N	N	Y	N	Y	Y
MISSISSIPPI							
1 Childers	N	Y	N	Y	N	Y	Y
2 Thompson	Y	N	N	Y	N	Y	Y
3 **Harper**	N	Y	N	Y	N	N	Y
4 Taylor	N	N	N	Y	N	Y	Y
MISSOURI							
1 Clay	Y	N	N	Y	N	Y	Y
2 **Akin**	N	Y	N	Y	N	N	Y
3 Carnahan	Y	?	N	Y	N	Y	Y
4 Skelton	Y	N	N	Y	N	Y	Y
5 Cleaver	Y	N	N	Y	N	Y	Y
6 **Graves**	N	Y	N	Y	N	N	Y
7 **Blunt**	N	Y	N	Y	N	N	Y
8 **Emerson**	N	Y	N	Y	N	N	Y
9 **Luetkemeyer**	N	Y	N	Y	N	Y	Y
MONTANA							
AL **Rehberg**	N	Y	N	Y	N	Y	Y
NEBRASKA							
1 **Fortenberry**	N	Y	N	Y	N	Y	Y
2 **Terry**	N	Y	N	Y	N	Y	Y
3 **Smith**	N	Y	N	Y	N	Y	Y
NEVADA							
1 Berkley	Y	N	N	Y	N	Y	Y
2 **Heller**	N	Y	N	Y	N	Y	Y
3 Titus	Y	N	N	Y	N	Y	Y
NEW HAMPSHIRE							
1 Shea-Porter	?	?	?	?	?	Y	Y
2 Hodes	Y	N	N	Y	N	Y	Y
NEW JERSEY							
1 Andrews	Y	N	N	Y	N	Y	N
2 **LoBiondo**	N	Y	N	Y	N	Y	Y
3 Adler	Y	N	N	Y	N	Y	Y
4 **Smith**	N	Y	N	Y	N	Y	Y
5 **Garrett**	N	Y	Y	Y	Y	N	Y
6 Pallone	Y	N	N	Y	N	Y	Y
7 **Lance**	N	Y	N	Y	N	Y	Y
8 Pascrell	Y	N	N	Y	N	Y	Y
9 Rothman	Y	N	N	Y	N	Y	Y
10 Payne	Y	N	N	Y	?	Y	Y
11 **Frelinghuysen**	N	Y	N	Y	N	N	Y
12 Holt	Y	N	N	Y	N	Y	Y
13 Sires	Y	N	N	Y	N	Y	N
NEW MEXICO							
1 Heinrich	Y	N	N	Y	N	Y	Y
2 Teague	Y	N	N	Y	N	Y	Y
3 Lujan	Y	?	N	Y	N	Y	Y
NEW YORK							
1 Bishop	Y	N	N	Y	N	Y	Y
2 Israel	Y	N	N	Y	N	Y	Y
3 **King**	N	Y	N	Y	N	Y	Y
4 McCarthy	Y	N	N	Y	N	Y	Y
5 Ackerman	Y	N	N	Y	N	Y	N
6 Meeks	Y	N	N	Y	N	Y	Y
7 Crowley	Y	N	N	Y	N	Y	N
8 Nadler	Y	N	N	Y	N	Y	Y
9 Weiner	Y	N	N	Y	N	Y	Y
10 Towns	Y	N	N	Y	N	Y	Y
11 Clarke	Y	N	N	Y	N	Y	N
12 Velázquez	Y	N	N	?	N	Y	N
13 McMahon	Y	N	N	Y	N	Y	Y
14 Maloney	Y	N	N	Y	N	Y	Y
15 Rangel	Y	N	N	Y	N	Y	Y
16 Serrano	Y	N	N	Y	N	Y	N
17 Engel	Y	N	N	Y	N	Y	Y
18 Lowey	Y	N	N	Y	N	Y	Y
19 Hall	Y	N	N	Y	N	Y	Y
20 Murphy	N	N	N	Y	N	Y	Y
21 Tonko	Y	N	N	Y	N	Y	N
22 Hinchey	Y	N	N	Y	N	Y	N
23 **McHugh**	N	Y	N	Y	N	Y	Y
24 Arcuri	Y	N	N	?	N	Y	Y
25 Maffei	Y	N	N	Y	N	Y	Y
26 **Lee**	N	Y	N	Y	N	Y	Y
27 Higgins	Y	N	N	Y	N	Y	Y
28 Slaughter	Y	N	N	Y	N	Y	N
29 Massa	Y	N	N	Y	Y	Y	Y
NORTH CAROLINA							
1 Butterfield	Y	N	N	Y	N	Y	N
2 Etheridge	Y	N	N	Y	N	Y	Y
3 **Jones**	N	N	N	Y	N	Y	Y
4 Price	Y	N	N	Y	N	Y	N
5 **Foxx**	N	Y	N	Y	N	N	Y
6 **Coble**	N	Y	N	Y	N	N	Y
7 McIntyre	Y	N	N	+	N	Y	Y
8 Kissell	Y	N	N	Y	N	Y	Y
9 **Myrick**	N	Y	N	Y	N	N	Y
10 **McHenry**	?	?	N	Y	N	N	Y
11 Shuler	N	Y	N	Y	N	Y	Y
12 Watt	Y	N	N	Y	N	Y	N
13 Miller	Y	N	N	Y	N	Y	N
NORTH DAKOTA							
AL Pomeroy	Y	N	N	Y	N	Y	Y
OHIO							
1 Driehaus	Y	N	N	Y	N	Y	Y
2 **Schmidt**	N	Y	N	Y	N	Y	Y
3 **Turner**	N	Y	N	Y	N	Y	Y
4 **Jordan**	N	Y	N	Y	N	N	Y
5 **Latta**	N	Y	N	Y	N	N	Y
6 Wilson	Y	N	N	Y	N	Y	Y
7 **Austria**	N	Y	N	Y	N	Y	Y
8 **Boehner**	N	Y	Y	Y	Y	Y	Y
9 Kaptur	Y	N	N	Y	N	Y	Y
10 Kucinich	Y	N	N	Y	N	Y	Y
11 Fudge	Y	N	N	Y	N	Y	N
12 **Tiberi**	N	Y	N	Y	N	Y	Y
13 Sutton	Y	N	N	Y	N	Y	Y
14 **LaTourette**	N	Y	N	Y	N	Y	Y
15 Kilroy	Y	N	N	Y	N	Y	Y
16 Boccieri	Y	N	N	Y	N	Y	Y
17 Ryan	Y	N	N	Y	N	Y	Y
18 Space	Y	N	N	Y	N	Y	Y
OKLAHOMA							
1 **Sullivan**	?	?	?	?	?	?	?
2 Boren	N	N	N	Y	N	Y	Y
3 **Lucas**	N	Y	N	Y	N	Y	Y
4 **Cole**	N	Y	N	Y	N	Y	Y
5 **Fallin**	N	Y	N	?	N	Y	Y
OREGON							
1 Wu	Y	N	N	Y	N	Y	Y
2 **Walden**	N	Y	N	Y	N	Y	Y
3 Blumenauer	Y	N	N	Y	N	Y	N
4 DeFazio	Y	N	N	Y	N	Y	Y
5 Schrader	Y	N	N	Y	N	Y	Y
PENNSYLVANIA							
1 Brady	Y	N	N	Y	N	Y	Y
2 Fattah	Y	N	N	Y	N	Y	Y
3 Dahlkemper	Y	N	N	Y	N	Y	Y
4 Altmire	Y	N	N	Y	N	Y	Y
5 **Thompson**	N	Y	N	Y	N	Y	Y
6 **Gerlach**	N	N	N	Y	N	Y	Y
7 Sestak	Y	N	N	Y	N	Y	Y
8 Murphy, P.	Y	N	N	Y	N	Y	Y
9 **Shuster**	N	Y	N	Y	N	N	Y
10 Carney	Y	N	N	Y	N	Y	Y
11 Kanjorski	Y	N	N	Y	N	Y	Y
12 Murtha	Y	N	N	Y	N	Y	Y
13 Schwartz	Y	N	N	Y	N	Y	Y
14 Doyle	?	N	N	Y	N	Y	Y
15 **Dent**	N	N	N	Y	N	Y	Y
16 **Pitts**	N	Y	N	Y	N	Y	Y
17 Holden	Y	N	N	Y	N	Y	Y
18 **Murphy, T.**	N	Y	N	Y	N	Y	Y
19 **Platts**	N	Y	N	Y	N	Y	Y
RHODE ISLAND							
1 Kennedy	?	?	?	?	?	?	?
2 Langevin	Y	N	N	Y	N	Y	Y
SOUTH CAROLINA							
1 **Brown**	N	Y	N	Y	N	Y	Y
2 **Wilson**	N	Y	N	Y	N	N	Y
3 **Barrett**	N	Y	N	Y	N	N	Y
4 **Inglis**	N	Y	N	Y	N	N	Y
5 Spratt	Y	N	N	Y	Y	Y	Y
6 Clyburn	Y	N	N	Y	N	Y	Y
SOUTH DAKOTA							
AL Herseth Sandlin	Y	N	N	Y	N	Y	Y
TENNESSEE							
1 **Roe**	N	Y	N	Y	N	Y	Y
2 **Duncan**	N	Y	N	Y	N	N	Y
3 **Wamp**	N	Y	N	Y	N	N	Y
4 Davis	Y	N	N	Y	N	Y	Y
5 Cooper	Y	N	N	Y	N	Y	Y
6 Gordon	Y	N	N	Y	N	Y	Y
7 **Blackburn**	N	Y	Y	Y	Y	Y	Y
8 Tanner	Y	N	N	Y	N	Y	Y
9 Cohen	Y	Y	N	Y	N	Y	Y
TEXAS							
1 **Gohmert**	N	Y	Y	Y	Y	N	Y
2 **Poe**	N	Y	N	Y	N	Y	Y
3 **Johnson, S.**	N	Y	Y	Y	Y	Y	Y
4 **Hall**	N	Y	N	Y	N	N	Y
5 **Hensarling**	N	Y	Y	Y	Y	N	Y
6 **Barton**	N	Y	Y	Y	Y	N	Y
7 **Culberson**	N	Y	N	Y	N	N	Y
8 **Brady**	N	Y	N	Y	N	N	Y
9 Green, A.	Y	N	N	Y	N	Y	Y
10 **McCaul**	N	Y	N	Y	N	N	Y
11 **Conaway**	N	Y	N	+	N	N	Y
12 **Granger**	N	Y	N	Y	Y	N	Y
13 **Thornberry**	N	Y	N	Y	Y	N	Y
14 **Paul**	N	Y	N	Y	N	N	Y
15 Hinojosa	Y	N	N	Y	?	Y	Y
16 Reyes	Y	N	N	Y	N	Y	Y
17 Edwards	Y	N	N	Y	N	Y	Y
18 Jackson Lee	Y	N	N	Y	N	Y	Y
19 **Neugebauer**	N	Y	N	Y	N	N	Y
20 Gonzalez	Y	N	N	Y	N	Y	Y
21 **Smith**	N	Y	N	?	N	N	Y
22 **Olson**	N	Y	Y	Y	Y	N	Y
23 Rodriguez	Y	N	N	Y	N	Y	Y
24 **Marchant**	N	Y	Y	Y	Y	N	Y
25 Doggett	Y	N	N	Y	N	Y	Y
26 **Burgess**	N	?	N	Y	N	N	Y
27 Ortiz	Y	N	N	Y	N	Y	Y
28 Cuellar	Y	N	N	Y	N	Y	Y
29 Green, G.	Y	N	N	Y	N	Y	Y
30 Johnson, E.	Y	N	N	?	N	Y	Y
31 **Carter**	N	Y	Y	Y	Y	N	Y
32 **Sessions**	N	Y	Y	Y	Y	N	Y
UTAH							
1 **Bishop**	N	Y	N	Y	N	N	Y
2 Matheson	Y	N	N	Y	N	Y	Y
3 **Chaffetz**	N	Y	Y	Y	Y	N	Y
VERMONT							
AL Welch	Y	N	N	Y	N	Y	Y
VIRGINIA							
1 **Wittman**	N	Y	N	Y	N	Y	Y
2 Nye	Y	N	N	Y	N	Y	Y
3 Scott	Y	Y	N	Y	N	Y	N
4 **Forbes**	N	Y	N	Y	N	Y	Y
5 Perriello	Y	N	N	Y	N	Y	Y
6 **Goodlatte**	N	Y	N	Y	N	Y	Y
7 **Cantor**	N	Y	N	Y	N	Y	Y
8 Moran	Y	N	N	Y	N	Y	N
9 Boucher	Y	N	N	?	N	Y	Y
10 **Wolf**	N	Y	N	Y	N	Y	Y
11 Connolly	Y	N	Y	Y	Y	Y	Y
WASHINGTON							
1 Inslee	Y	N	N	Y	N	Y	Y
2 Larsen	Y	N	?	Y	N	Y	Y
3 Baird	Y	N	N	Y	N	Y	Y
4 **Hastings**	N	Y	Y	Y	Y	N	Y
5 **McMorris Rodgers**	N	Y	N	Y	N	Y	Y
6 Dicks	Y	N	N	Y	N	?	?
7 McDermott	Y	N	N	Y	?	Y	N
8 **Reichert**	N	Y	N	Y	N	Y	Y
9 Smith	Y	N	N	Y	N	Y	Y
WEST VIRGINIA							
1 Mollohan	Y	N	N	Y	N	Y	N
2 **Capito**	N	Y	N	Y	N	Y	Y
3 Rahall	Y	N	N	+	N	Y	Y
WISCONSIN							
1 **Ryan**	N	?	N	Y	N	N	Y
2 Baldwin	Y	N	N	Y	N	Y	N
3 Kind	Y	N	N	Y	N	Y	Y
4 Moore	Y	N	N	Y	N	Y	N
5 **Sensenbrenner**	N	Y	Y	Y	Y	N	Y
6 **Petri**	N	Y	N	Y	N	N	Y
7 Obey	Y	N	?	?	?	Y	Y
8 Kagen	Y	N	N	Y	N	Y	Y
WYOMING							
AL **Lummis**	N	Y	N	Y	N	N	Y
DELEGATES							
Faleomavaega (A.S.)						Y	Y
Norton (D.C.)						Y	N
Bordallo (Guam)						Y	N
Sablan (N. Marianas)						Y	N
Pierluisi (P.R.)						Y	Y
Christensen (V.I.)						?	?

IN THE HOUSE | By Vote Number

437. HR 2892. Fiscal 2010 Homeland Security Appropriations/ **Domestic Nuclear Detection Office.** King, R-N.Y., amendment that would increase the amount provided for the Domestic Nuclear Detection Office's research and operations by $50 million, offset by reductions for the Office of the Undersecretary of Management and the Office of the Secretary. Adopted in Committee of the Whole 282-148: R 168-9; D 114-139. June 24, 2009.

438. HR 2892. Fiscal 2010 Homeland Security Appropriations/Visa **Security Program.** Bilirakis, R-Fla., amendment that would increase the amount provided for the U.S. Immigration and Customs Enforcement Visa Security Program by $1.7 million, offset by a reduction of the same amount for the Office of the Secretary. Adopted in Committee of the Whole 423-6: R 176-0; D 247-6. June 24, 2009.

439. HR 2892. Fiscal 2010 Homeland Security Appropriations/ **Customs and Border Protection.** King, R-Iowa, amendment that would reduce the amount provided for U.S. Customs and Border Protection salaries and expenses by $1 million and immediately increase that funding by $1 million. Adopted in Committee of the Whole 240-187: R 175-2; D 65-185. June 24, 2009.

440. HR 2892. Fiscal 2010 Homeland Security Appropriations/ **Federal Air Marshals.** Duncan, R-Tenn., amendment that would reduce the amount provided for the Federal Air Marshal program from $860 million to $820 million. Rejected in Committee of the Whole 134-294: R 124-52; D 10-242. June 24, 2009.

441. HR 2892. Fiscal 2010 Homeland Security Appropriations/ **National Predisaster Mitigation Fund.** Poe, R-Texas, amendment that would increase the amount provided for the National Predisaster Mitigation Fund by $32 million, offset by a reduction of the same amount for the Federal Emergency Management Agency management and administration account. Rejected in Committee of the Whole 202-230: R 169-7; D 33-223. June 24, 2009.

442. HR 2892. Fiscal 2010 Homeland Security Appropriations/ **Illegal Workers.** King, R-Iowa, amendment that would bar the use of funds in the bill to employ illegal workers, as defined in the Immigration and Nationality Act. Adopted in Committee of the Whole 349-84: R 177-0; D 172-84. June 24, 2009.

443. HR 2892. Fiscal 2010 Homeland Security Appropriations/ **Funding Decreases.** Neugebauer, R-Texas, amendment that would reduce spending in the bill by $2.8 billion — cuts that include $1 billion from aviation security, $680 million from Customs and Border Protection and $610 million from the Federal Emergency Management Agency. Rejected in Committee of the Whole 113-318: R 109-68; D 4-250. A "nay" was a vote in support of the president's position. June 24, 2009.

	437	438	439	440	441	442	443
ALABAMA							
1 Bonner	Y	Y	Y	N	Y	Y	Y
2 Bright	N	Y	N	Y	N	Y	Y
3 Rogers	Y	Y	Y	N	Y	Y	N
4 Aderholt	Y	Y	Y	Y	Y	Y	N
5 Griffith	Y	Y	Y	N	Y	Y	N
6 Bachus	Y	Y	Y	N	Y	Y	N
7 Davis	Y	Y	Y	N	N	Y	N
ALASKA							
AL Young	Y	Y	Y	Y	Y	Y	N
ARIZONA							
1 Kirkpatrick	N	Y	Y	N	N	Y	N
2 Franks	Y	Y	Y	Y	Y	Y	Y
3 Shadegg	Y	Y	Y	Y	Y	Y	Y
4 Pastor	N	Y	N	Y	N	Y	N
5 Mitchell	Y	Y	Y	N	N	Y	Y
6 Flake	Y	Y	Y	Y	Y	Y	Y
7 Grijalva	N	N	N	N	N	N	N
8 Giffords	Y	Y	Y	N	N	Y	N
ARKANSAS							
1 Berry	N	Y	N	N	N	Y	N
2 Snyder	N	Y	N	N	N	Y	N
3 Boozman	Y	Y	Y	Y	Y	Y	Y
4 Ross	N	Y	N	N	N	Y	N
CALIFORNIA							
1 Thompson	N	Y	N	N	N	Y	N
2 Herger	Y	Y	Y	Y	Y	Y	Y
3 Lungren	Y	Y	Y	N	Y	Y	N
4 McClintock	Y	Y	Y	Y	Y	Y	Y
5 Matsui	N	Y	N	N	N	Y	N
6 Woolsey	N	N	N	N	N	N	N
7 Miller, George	N	Y	N	?	N	Y	N
8 Pelosi							
9 Lee	N	N	N	N	N	N	N
10 Tauscher	N	Y	N	N	N	N	N
11 McNerney	Y	Y	Y	N	Y	Y	N
12 Speier	N	Y	N	N	N	Y	N
13 Stark	N	Y	N	N	N	Y	N
14 Eshoo	N	Y	N	N	N	Y	N
15 Honda	N	Y	N	N	N	N	N
16 Lofgren	Y	Y	N	N	N	Y	N
17 Farr	N	Y	N	Y	N	Y	N
18 Cardoza	Y	Y	N	N	Y	Y	N
19 Radanovich	Y	Y	Y	Y	Y	Y	Y
20 Costa	N	Y	N	N	N	Y	N
21 Nunes	Y	Y	Y	Y	Y	Y	Y
22 McCarthy	Y	Y	Y	Y	Y	Y	N
23 Capps	Y	Y	N	N	N	N	N
24 Gallegly	Y	Y	Y	Y	Y	Y	Y
25 McKeon	Y	Y	Y	Y	Y	Y	Y
26 Dreier	Y	Y	Y	N	Y	Y	N
27 Sherman	Y	Y	N	N	N	Y	N
28 Berman	Y	Y	N	N	N	N	N
29 Schiff	Y	Y	N	N	N	Y	N
30 Waxman	Y	Y	N	N	N	Y	N
31 Becerra	N	Y	N	N	N	N	N
32 Vacant							
33 Watson	N	Y	N	N	N	N	N
34 Roybal-Allard	N	Y	N	N	N	N	N
35 Waters	N	Y	N	N	N	N	N
36 Harman	Y	Y	N	N	Y	Y	N
37 Richardson	Y	Y	N	N	N	Y	N
38 Napolitano	N	Y	N	N	N	N	N
39 Sánchez, Linda	N	Y	N	N	N	N	N
40 Royce	Y	Y	Y	Y	Y	Y	Y
41 Lewis	Y	Y	Y	N	Y	Y	N
42 Miller, Gary	Y	Y	Y	Y	Y	Y	Y
43 Baca	Y	Y	N	N	Y	Y	N
44 Calvert	Y	Y	Y	N	Y	Y	N
45 Bono Mack	Y	Y	Y	Y	Y	Y	Y
46 Rohrabacher	Y	Y	Y	Y	Y	Y	Y
47 Sanchez, Loretta	N	Y	N	Y	Y	N	N
48 Campbell	Y	Y	Y	Y	Y	Y	Y
49 Issa	Y	Y	Y	Y	Y	Y	Y
50 Bilbray	Y	Y	Y	Y	Y	Y	Y
51 Filner	N	Y	N	N	N	N	N
52 Hunter	Y	Y	Y	Y	Y	Y	Y
53 Davis	N	Y	N	N	N	Y	N

	437	438	439	440	441	442	443
COLORADO							
1 DeGette	N	Y	N	N	N	N	N
2 Polis	N	Y	N	Y	N	N	N
3 Salazar	N	Y	N	N	N	Y	N
4 Markey	N	Y	Y	N	N	Y	N
5 Lamborn	Y	Y	Y	Y	Y	Y	Y
6 Coffman	Y	Y	Y	N	Y	Y	N
7 Perlmutter	N	Y	N	N	N	Y	N
CONNECTICUT							
1 Larson	N	Y	N	N	N	Y	N
2 Courtney	N	Y	N	N	N	Y	N
3 DeLauro	N	Y	N	N	N	Y	N
4 Himes	Y	Y	N	N	N	Y	N
5 Murphy	Y	Y	N	N	N	Y	N
DELAWARE							
AL Castle	Y	Y	Y	Y	Y	Y	N
FLORIDA							
1 Miller	Y	Y	Y	Y	Y	Y	Y
2 Boyd	N	Y	N	N	N	Y	N
3 Brown	Y	Y	N	N	N	Y	N
4 Crenshaw	Y	Y	Y	N	Y	Y	N
5 Brown-Waite	Y	Y	Y	Y	Y	Y	Y
6 Stearns	Y	Y	Y	Y	Y	Y	N
7 Mica	Y	Y	Y	Y	Y	Y	N
8 Grayson	Y	Y	N	N	N	Y	N
9 Bilirakis	Y	Y	Y	N	Y	Y	N
10 Young	Y	Y	Y	N	Y	Y	Y
11 Castor	N	Y	N	N	N	N	N
12 Putnam	Y	Y	Y	Y	Y	Y	N
13 Buchanan	Y	Y	Y	Y	Y	Y	N
14 Mack	Y	Y	Y	Y	Y	Y	Y
15 Posey	Y	Y	Y	Y	Y	Y	Y
16 Rooney	Y	Y	Y	Y	Y	Y	N
17 Meek	Y	Y	N	N	N	N	N
18 Ros-Lehtinen	Y	Y	Y	N	Y	Y	N
19 Wexler	Y	Y	N	N	N	N	N
20 Wasserman Schultz	N	Y	N	N	N	N	N
21 Diaz-Balart, L.	Y	Y	Y	N	Y	Y	N
22 Klein	Y	Y	Y	N	N	Y	N
23 Hastings	Y	Y	N	N	N	Y	N
24 Kosmas	N	Y	N	N	N	Y	N
25 Diaz-Balart, M.	Y	Y	Y	N	Y	Y	N
GEORGIA							
1 Kingston	Y	Y	Y	Y	Y	Y	Y
2 Bishop	N	Y	N	N	Y	Y	N
3 Westmoreland	Y	Y	Y	Y	Y	Y	Y
4 Johnson	N	Y	N	N	N	N	N
5 Lewis	?	?	?	?	?	?	?
6 Price	Y	Y	Y	Y	Y	Y	Y
7 Linder	Y	Y	Y	Y	Y	Y	Y
8 Marshall	Y	Y	Y	N	N	Y	N
9 Deal	Y	Y	Y	Y	Y	Y	Y
10 Broun	Y	Y	Y	Y	Y	Y	Y
11 Gingrey	Y	Y	Y	Y	Y	Y	Y
12 Barrow	Y	Y	Y	N	N	Y	N
13 Scott	Y	Y	?	N	N	Y	N
HAWAII							
1 Abercrombie	Y	Y	N	N	N	Y	N
2 Hirono	N	Y	N	N	N	N	N
IDAHO							
1 Minnick	Y	Y	Y	Y	Y	Y	Y
2 Simpson	N	Y	N	N	Y	Y	Y
ILLINOIS							
1 Rush	N	N	N	N	N	N	N
2 Jackson	N	N	N	N	N	N	N
3 Lipinski	N	Y	N	N	N	Y	N
4 Gutierrez	N	N	N	N	N	N	N
5 Quigley	N	Y	N	N	Y	N	N
6 Roskam	Y	Y	Y	N	Y	Y	N
7 Davis	?	Y	N	N	N	N	N
8 Bean	Y	Y	Y	N	Y	Y	N
9 Schakowsky	N	Y	N	N	N	N	N
10 Kirk	Y	Y	Y	N	Y	Y	N
11 Halvorson	N	Y	N	N	N	Y	N
12 Costello	Y	Y	N	N	Y	Y	N
13 Biggert	Y	Y	Y	N	Y	Y	N
14 Foster	Y	Y	Y	N	N	Y	N
15 Johnson	Y	Y	Y	N	Y	Y	N

KEY **Republicans** Democrats

Y Voted for (yea)	X Paired against
# Paired for	− Announced against
+ Announced for	P Voted "present"
N Voted against (nay)	

C Voted "present" to avoid possible conflict of interest

? Did not vote or otherwise make a position known

	437	438	439	440	441	442	443
16 **Manzullo**	Y	Y	Y	N	Y	Y	Y
17 Hare	N	Y	N	N	N	N	N
18 **Schock**	Y	Y	Y	Y	N	Y	N
19 **Shimkus**	N	Y	Y	Y	Y	Y	N
INDIANA							
1 Visclosky	N	Y	N	N	N	Y	N
2 Donnelly	Y	Y	Y	N	Y	Y	N
3 **Souder**	Y	Y	Y	N	Y	Y	N
4 **Buyer**	Y	Y	Y	Y	Y	Y	Y
5 **Burton**	Y	Y	Y	Y	Y	Y	Y
6 **Pence**	Y	Y	Y	Y	Y	Y	Y
7 Carson	Y	Y	N	N	N	Y	N
8 Ellsworth	N	Y	Y	N	Y	Y	N
9 Hill	Y	Y	N	N	N	Y	N
IOWA							
1 Braley	N	Y	N	N	N	N	N
2 Loebsack	N	Y	Y	N	Y	Y	N
3 Boswell	N	Y	Y	N	N	Y	N
4 **Latham**	N	Y	Y	N	Y	Y	N
5 **King**	Y	Y	Y	Y	Y	Y	Y
KANSAS							
1 **Moran**	Y	Y	Y	Y	Y	Y	Y
2 **Jenkins**	Y	Y	Y	Y	Y	Y	Y
3 Moore	Y	Y	N	N	N	Y	N
4 **Tiahrt**	Y	Y	Y	N	Y	Y	Y
KENTUCKY							
1 **Whitfield**	Y	Y	Y	Y	Y	Y	Y
2 **Guthrie**	Y	Y	Y	N	Y	Y	Y
3 Yarmuth	N	Y	Y	N	N	Y	N
4 **Davis**	Y	Y	Y	Y	Y	Y	N
5 **Rogers**	N	Y	Y	N	Y	Y	N
6 Chandler	N	Y	Y	N	N	Y	N
LOUISIANA							
1 **Scalise**	Y	Y	Y	Y	Y	Y	Y
2 **Cao**	Y	Y	Y	Y	Y	Y	N
3 Melancon	Y	Y	Y	N	Y	Y	N
4 **Fleming**	Y	Y	Y	Y	Y	Y	Y
5 **Alexander**	Y	Y	Y	Y	Y	Y	Y
6 **Cassidy**	Y	Y	Y	Y	Y	Y	N
7 **Boustany**	Y	Y	Y	Y	Y	Y	Y
MAINE							
1 Pingree	N	Y	N	N	N	Y	N
2 Michaud	N	Y	Y	N	N	Y	N
MARYLAND							
1 Kratovil	N	Y	Y	N	N	Y	N
2 Ruppersberger	Y	Y	N	N	N	Y	N
3 Sarbanes	N	Y	N	N	N	N	N
4 Edwards	N	N	N	N	N	N	N
5 Hoyer	N	Y	N	N	N	N	N
6 **Bartlett**	Y	Y	Y	Y	Y	Y	Y
7 Cummings	Y	Y	N	N	N	N	N
8 Van Hollen	N	Y	N	N	N	Y	N
MASSACHUSETTS							
1 Olver	N	Y	N	N	N	N	N
2 Neal	Y	Y	N	N	N	Y	N
3 McGovern	N	Y	N	N	N	Y	N
4 Frank	?	?	?	?	N	Y	N
5 Tsongas	N	Y	N	N	N	N	N
6 Tierney	N	Y	N	N	N	Y	N
7 Markey	Y	Y	N	N	N	N	N
8 Capuano	?	?	?	?	?	?	?
9 Lynch	Y	Y	N	N	N	Y	N
10 Delahunt	Y	Y	N	N	N	Y	N
MICHIGAN							
1 Stupak	?	?	?	?	?	?	?
2 **Hoekstra**	Y	Y	Y	Y	Y	Y	Y
3 **Ehlers**	Y	Y	Y	Y	Y	Y	Y
4 **Camp**	Y	Y	Y	Y	Y	Y	N
5 Kildee	N	Y	N	N	N	Y	N
6 **Upton**	Y	Y	Y	Y	N	Y	N
7 Schauer	N	Y	Y	N	N	Y	N
8 **Rogers**	Y	Y	Y	Y	Y	Y	Y
9 Peters	N	Y	Y	N	N	Y	N
10 **Miller**	Y	Y	Y	N	N	Y	N
11 **McCotter**	Y	Y	Y	N	Y	Y	Y
12 Levin	N	Y	N	N	N	Y	N
13 Kilpatrick	N	Y	N	N	N	N	N
14 Conyers	N	N	N	N	N	N	N
15 Dingell	N	Y	N	N	N	Y	N
MINNESOTA							
1 Walz	N	Y	Y	N	N	Y	N
2 **Kline**	Y	Y	Y	N	Y	Y	Y
3 **Paulsen**	Y	Y	Y	N	Y	Y	Y
4 McCollum	N	Y	N	N	N	N	N
5 Ellison	Y	Y	N	N	N	N	N
6 **Bachmann**	Y	Y	Y	Y	Y	Y	Y
7 Peterson	N	Y	N	N	N	Y	N
8 Oberstar	N	Y	N	N	N	Y	N
MISSISSIPPI							
1 Childers	Y	Y	Y	N	Y	Y	N
2 Thompson	N	Y	N	N	N	N	N
3 **Harper**	Y	Y	Y	Y	Y	Y	N
4 Taylor	Y	Y	Y	N	Y	Y	N
MISSOURI							
1 Clay	Y	Y	N	N	N	N	N
2 **Akin**	Y	Y	Y	Y	Y	Y	Y
3 Carnahan	N	Y	N	N	N	Y	N
4 Skelton	N	Y	N	N	Y	Y	N
5 Cleaver	N	Y	N	N	N	N	N
6 **Graves**	Y	Y	Y	Y	Y	Y	Y
7 **Blunt**	Y	Y	Y	Y	Y	Y	Y
8 **Emerson**	Y	Y	Y	Y	Y	Y	N
9 **Luetkemeyer**	Y	Y	Y	Y	Y	Y	Y
MONTANA							
AL **Rehberg**	Y	Y	Y	Y	Y	Y	Y
NEBRASKA							
1 **Fortenberry**	Y	Y	Y	N	Y	Y	N
2 **Terry**	Y	Y	Y	Y	Y	Y	Y
3 **Smith**	Y	Y	Y	Y	Y	Y	Y
NEVADA							
1 Berkley	Y	Y	Y	N	N	Y	N
2 **Heller**	Y	Y	Y	Y	Y	Y	Y
3 Titus	N	Y	Y	N	N	Y	N
NEW HAMPSHIRE							
1 Shea-Porter	N	Y	Y	N	N	Y	N
2 Hodes	N	Y	N	N	N	Y	N
NEW JERSEY							
1 Andrews	N	Y	N	N	N	N	N
2 **LoBiondo**	Y	Y	Y	N	Y	Y	N
3 Adler	N	Y	N	N	N	Y	Y
4 **Smith**	Y	Y	Y	N	Y	Y	N
5 **Garrett**	Y	Y	Y	Y	Y	Y	Y
6 Pallone	Y	Y	N	N	N	Y	N
7 **Lance**	Y	Y	Y	N	Y	Y	N
8 Pascrell	Y	Y	N	N	N	Y	N
9 Rothman	Y	Y	N	N	N	Y	N
10 Payne	Y	Y	N	N	N	Y	N
11 **Frelinghuysen**	Y	Y	Y	N	Y	Y	N
12 Holt	Y	Y	N	N	N	N	N
13 Sires	Y	Y	N	N	N	N	N
NEW MEXICO							
1 Heinrich	Y	Y	N	N	N	Y	N
2 Teague	N	Y	Y	N	N	Y	N
3 Lujan	N	Y	N	N	N	N	N
NEW YORK							
1 Bishop	Y	Y	Y	N	Y	Y	N
2 Israel	Y	Y	N	N	Y	N	N
3 **King**	Y	Y	Y	N	Y	Y	N
4 McCarthy	Y	Y	Y	N	N	Y	N
5 Ackerman	Y	Y	N	N	N	N	N
6 Meeks	Y	Y	N	N	N	Y	N
7 Crowley	Y	Y	N	N	N	N	N
8 Nadler	Y	Y	N	N	N	N	N
9 Weiner	Y	Y	N	N	N	Y	N
10 Towns	Y	Y	N	N	N	N	?
11 Clarke	Y	N	N	N	N	N	N
12 Velázquez	Y	Y	N	N	N	N	N
13 McMahon	Y	Y	N	N	N	N	N
14 Maloney	Y	Y	N	N	N	Y	N
15 Rangel	Y	Y	N	N	N	N	N
16 Serrano	Y	Y	N	N	N	N	N
17 Engel	Y	Y	N	N	N	N	N
18 Lowey	Y	Y	N	N	N	Y	N
19 Hall	Y	Y	Y	N	N	Y	N
20 Murphy	Y	Y	Y	N	Y	Y	N
21 Tonko	Y	Y	N	N	N	N	N
22 Hinchey	Y	Y	N	N	N	Y	N
23 **McHugh**	Y	Y	Y	N	Y	Y	N
24 Arcuri	Y	Y	Y	N	Y	Y	N
25 Maffei	Y	Y	Y	N	N	Y	N
26 **Lee**	Y	Y	Y	Y	Y	Y	N
27 Higgins	Y	Y	Y	N	N	Y	N
28 Slaughter	N	Y	N	N	N	N	N
29 Massa	Y	Y	N	N	Y	Y	N
NORTH CAROLINA							
1 Butterfield	N	Y	N	?	N	Y	N
2 Etheridge	N	Y	N	N	N	Y	N
3 **Jones**	Y	Y	Y	Y	N	Y	Y
4 Price	N	Y	N	N	N	Y	N
5 **Foxx**	Y	Y	Y	Y	Y	Y	Y
6 **Coble**	Y	Y	Y	Y	Y	Y	Y
7 McIntyre	N	Y	Y	N	N	Y	N
8 Kissell	Y	Y	N	N	N	Y	N
9 **Myrick**	Y	Y	Y	Y	Y	Y	Y
10 **McHenry**	Y	Y	Y	Y	Y	Y	N
11 Shuler	Y	Y	Y	N	Y	Y	N
12 Watt	Y	Y	N	N	N	N	N
13 Miller	N	Y	N	N	N	Y	N
NORTH DAKOTA							
AL Pomeroy	Y	Y	N	N	Y	Y	N
OHIO							
1 Driehaus	Y	Y	Y	N	N	Y	N
2 **Schmidt**	Y	Y	Y	Y	Y	Y	N
3 **Turner**	Y	Y	Y	N	Y	Y	N
4 **Jordan**	Y	Y	Y	Y	Y	Y	Y
5 **Latta**	Y	Y	Y	Y	Y	Y	Y
6 Wilson	Y	Y	Y	N	N	Y	N
7 **Austria**	Y	Y	Y	N	Y	Y	N
8 **Boehner**	Y	Y	Y	?	?	Y	Y
9 Kaptur	Y	Y	N	N	Y	N	N
10 Kucinich	Y	Y	Y	N	N	N	N
11 Fudge	Y	Y	N	N	N	N	N
12 **Tiberi**	Y	Y	Y	Y	Y	Y	Y
13 Sutton	N	Y	N	N	N	N	N
14 **LaTourette**	Y	Y	Y	N	Y	Y	N
15 Kilroy	Y	Y	N	N	N	Y	N
16 Boccieri	Y	Y	Y	N	N	Y	N
17 Ryan	Y	Y	N	N	N	N	N
18 Space	Y	Y	Y	N	Y	Y	N
OKLAHOMA							
1 **Sullivan**	?	?	?	?	?	?	?
2 Boren	Y	Y	Y	N	Y	Y	N
3 **Lucas**	Y	Y	Y	N	Y	Y	Y
4 **Cole**	Y	Y	Y	Y	Y	Y	Y
5 **Fallin**	Y	Y	Y	Y	Y	Y	Y
OREGON							
1 Wu	N	Y	N	N	N	Y	N
2 **Walden**	Y	Y	Y	Y	Y	Y	N
3 Blumenauer	N	Y	N	N	N	N	N
4 DeFazio	N	Y	P	N	N	Y	N
5 Schrader	N	Y	N	N	N	Y	N
PENNSYLVANIA							
1 Brady	Y	Y	N	N	N	Y	N
2 Fattah	Y	Y	N	N	N	Y	N
3 Dahlkemper	N	+	Y	Y	Y	Y	N
4 Altmire	Y	Y	Y	N	N	Y	N
5 **Thompson**	Y	Y	Y	Y	Y	Y	N
6 **Gerlach**	Y	Y	Y	N	Y	Y	N
7 Sestak	Y	Y	Y	N	N	Y	N
8 Murphy, P.	Y	Y	Y	N	Y	Y	N
9 **Shuster**	Y	Y	Y	Y	Y	Y	Y
10 Carney	Y	Y	N	N	N	Y	N
11 Kanjorski	Y	Y	N	N	N	Y	N
12 Murtha	Y	Y	N	N	N	Y	N
13 Schwartz	Y	Y	N	N	N	Y	N
14 Doyle	N	Y	N	N	N	N	N
15 **Dent**	Y	Y	Y	N	Y	Y	N
16 **Pitts**	Y	Y	Y	Y	Y	Y	N
17 Holden	N	Y	N	N	N	Y	N
18 **Murphy, T.**	Y	Y	Y	Y	Y	Y	N
19 **Platts**	Y	Y	Y	N	Y	Y	N
RHODE ISLAND							
1 Kennedy	?	?	?	?	?	?	?
2 Langevin	N	Y	N	N	N	Y	N
SOUTH CAROLINA							
1 **Brown**	Y	Y	Y	N	Y	Y	N
2 **Wilson**	Y	Y	Y	Y	Y	Y	Y
3 **Barrett**	Y	Y	Y	Y	Y	Y	Y
4 **Inglis**	Y	Y	Y	Y	Y	Y	Y
5 Spratt	N	Y	?	N	N	Y	N
6 Clyburn	N	Y	N	N	N	N	N
SOUTH DAKOTA							
AL Herseth Sandlin	N	Y	Y	N	N	Y	N
TENNESSEE							
1 **Roe**	Y	Y	Y	Y	Y	Y	Y
2 **Duncan**	N	Y	Y	Y	Y	Y	Y
3 **Wamp**	Y	Y	Y	Y	Y	Y	N
4 Davis	N	Y	Y	N	N	Y	N
5 Cooper	N	Y	N	N	N	Y	N
6 Gordon	N	Y	Y	N	N	Y	N
7 **Blackburn**	Y	Y	Y	Y	Y	Y	Y
8 Tanner	N	Y	N	N	N	Y	N
9 Cohen	N	Y	N	N	N	Y	N
TEXAS							
1 **Gohmert**	Y	Y	Y	Y	Y	Y	Y
2 **Poe**	Y	Y	Y	Y	Y	Y	Y
3 **Johnson, S.**	Y	Y	Y	Y	Y	Y	Y
4 **Hall**	Y	Y	Y	Y	Y	Y	Y
5 **Hensarling**	Y	Y	Y	Y	Y	Y	Y
6 **Barton**	Y	Y	Y	Y	Y	Y	Y
7 **Culberson**	N	Y	Y	N	Y	Y	Y
8 **Brady**	Y	Y	Y	Y	Y	Y	Y
9 Green, A.	N	Y	N	N	N	Y	N
10 **McCaul**	Y	Y	Y	Y	Y	Y	N
11 **Conaway**	Y	?	Y	Y	Y	Y	Y
12 **Granger**	N	Y	Y	N	Y	Y	N
13 **Thornberry**	Y	Y	Y	Y	Y	Y	Y
14 **Paul**	Y	Y	N	Y	Y	Y	Y
15 Hinojosa	N	Y	N	N	N	Y	N
16 Reyes	Y	Y	N	N	N	Y	N
17 Edwards	N	Y	N	N	N	Y	?
18 Jackson Lee	N	Y	N	N	Y	N	N
19 **Neugebauer**	Y	Y	Y	Y	Y	Y	Y
20 Gonzalez	N	Y	N	N	N	Y	N
21 **Smith**	Y	Y	Y	Y	Y	Y	N
22 **Olson**	Y	Y	Y	Y	Y	Y	Y
23 Rodriguez	N	Y	N	N	N	Y	N
24 **Marchant**	Y	Y	Y	Y	Y	Y	Y
25 Doggett	N	Y	N	N	N	Y	N
26 **Burgess**	Y	Y	Y	Y	Y	Y	Y
27 Ortiz	Y	Y	N	N	Y	Y	N
28 Cuellar	Y	Y	N	N	Y	Y	N
29 Green, G.	Y	Y	N	N	Y	Y	N
30 Johnson, E.	N	Y	N	N	N	Y	N
31 **Carter**	N	Y	Y	N	Y	Y	N
32 **Sessions**	Y	Y	Y	Y	Y	Y	Y
UTAH							
1 **Bishop**	Y	Y	Y	N	Y	Y	Y
2 Matheson	Y	Y	Y	N	Y	Y	N
3 **Chaffetz**	Y	Y	Y	Y	Y	Y	Y
VERMONT							
AL Welch	N	Y	N	Y	N	Y	N
VIRGINIA							
1 **Wittman**	Y	Y	Y	Y	Y	Y	N
2 Nye	Y	Y	Y	N	Y	Y	N
3 Scott	Y	Y	N	N	N	N	N
4 **Forbes**	Y	Y	Y	N	Y	Y	N
5 Perriello	N	Y	Y	N	N	Y	N
6 **Goodlatte**	Y	Y	Y	Y	N	Y	Y
7 **Cantor**	Y	Y	Y	Y	Y	Y	Y
8 Moran	N	Y	N	N	N	N	N
9 Boucher	Y	Y	N	N	N	Y	N
10 **Wolf**	Y	Y	Y	N	Y	Y	N
11 Connolly	Y	Y	Y	N	N	Y	N
WASHINGTON							
1 Inslee	Y	Y	N	N	N	Y	N
2 Larsen	N	Y	N	N	N	Y	N
3 Baird	Y	Y	N	Y	N	Y	N
4 **Hastings**	N	Y	Y	Y	Y	Y	Y
5 **McMorris Rodgers**	Y	Y	Y	Y	Y	Y	Y
6 Dicks	?	?	?	?	N	Y	N
7 McDermott	N	Y	N	Y	N	N	N
8 **Reichert**	Y	Y	Y	N	Y	Y	Y
9 Smith	N	Y	Y	N	N	Y	N
WEST VIRGINIA							
1 Mollohan	N	Y	N	N	N	N	N
2 **Capito**	Y	Y	Y	N	Y	Y	N
3 Rahall	N	Y	N	N	N	N	N
WISCONSIN							
1 **Ryan**	Y	Y	Y	Y	Y	Y	Y
2 Baldwin	N	Y	N	N	N	N	N
3 Kind	N	Y	N	N	N	Y	N
4 Moore	N	Y	N	N	N	N	N
5 **Sensenbrenner**	Y	Y	Y	Y	Y	Y	Y
6 **Petri**	Y	Y	Y	Y	Y	Y	Y
7 Obey	N	Y	N	N	N	Y	N
8 Kagen	N	Y	N	N	N	Y	N
WYOMING							
AL **Lummis**	Y	Y	Y	Y	Y	Y	Y
DELEGATES							
Faleomavaega (A.S.)	Y	Y	Y	Y	N	Y	N
Norton (D.C.)	N	Y	N	N	Y	N	N
Bordallo (Guam)	N	Y	Y	N	N	Y	N
Sablan (N. Marianas)	N	Y	N	N	N	Y	N
Pierluisi (P.R.)	Y	Y	?	N	N	N	N
Christensen (V.I.)	?	?	?	?	?	?	?

IN THE HOUSE | By Vote Number

444. HR 2892. Fiscal 2010 Homeland Security Appropriations/ **Grant to Emeryville.** Flake, R-Ariz., amendment that would bar the use of funds appropriated in the bill for a grant to the city of Emeryville, Calif. Rejected in Committee of the Whole 110-322: R 107-69; D 3-253. June 24, 2009.

445. HR 2892. Fiscal 2010 Homeland Security Appropriations/ **Grant to Harris County Flood Control District.** Flake, R-Ariz., amendment that would bar the use of funds appropriated in the bill for a grant to the Harris County Flood Control District in Texas. Rejected in Committee of the Whole 82-348: R 77-99; D 5-249. June 24, 2009.

446. HR 2892. Fiscal 2010 Homeland Security Appropriations/ **National Institute for Hometown Security.** Flake, R-Ariz., amendment that would bar the use of funds appropriated in the bill for the National Institute for Hometown Security in Kentucky, and cut $10 million set aside for the project from the bill total. Rejected in Committee of the Whole 114-317: R 97-78; D 17-239. June 24, 2009.

447. HR 2892. Fiscal 2010 Homeland Security Appropriations/ **Global Solar.** Flake, R-Ariz., amendment that would bar the use of funds appropriated in the bill for an award to Global Solar in Arizona for portable solar-charging rechargeable battery systems, and would cut $800,000 set aside for the project from the bill total. Rejected in Committee of the Whole 110-318: R 102-73; D 8-245. June 24, 2009.

448. HR 2892. Fiscal 2010 Homeland Security Appropriations/ **Interoperable Communications.** Flake, R-Ariz., amendment that would bar the use of funds appropriated in the bill for SEARCH of Sacramento, Calif., for interoperable communications, technical assistance and outreach programs, and reduce the amount provided in the bill by $1 million. Rejected in Committee of the Whole 112-320: R 108-68; D 4-252. June 24, 2009.

449. HR 2892. Fiscal 2010 Homeland Security Appropriations/ **Recommit.** Rogers, R-Ky., motion to recommit the bill to the Appropriations Committee with instructions that it be reported back immediately with language that would increase the amount provided for the U.S. Citizenship and Immigration Service's E-Verify program by $50 million, offset by a reduction of the same amount for the Office of the Under Secretary for Management. Motion agreed to 234-193: R 173-3; D 61-190. June 24, 2009.

450. HR 2892. Fiscal 2010 Homeland Security Appropriations/ **Passage.** Passage of the bill that would provide $44 billion in fiscal 2010 for the Homeland Security Department and related activities. The total would include $10 billion for Customs and Border Protection; $7.7 billion for the Transportation Security Administration, including fees; $10 billion for the Coast Guard; $1.5 billion for the Secret Service; and $7.4 billion for the Federal Emergency Management Agency. It would require the department to conduct threat assessments of detainees at Guantánamo Bay, Cuba, put the detainees on the FBI "no-fly" list and deny them immigration benefits. Passed 389-37: R 139-37; D 250-0. A "yea" was a vote in support of the president's position. June 24, 2009.

	444	445	446	447	448	449	450
ALABAMA							
1 Bonner	N	N	N	N	N	Y	Y
2 Bright	N	N	Y	Y	N	Y	Y
3 Rogers	N	N	N	N	N	Y	Y
4 Aderholt	N	N	N	N	N	Y	Y
5 Griffith	N	N	N	N	N	Y	Y
6 Bachus	N	N	N	N	N	Y	Y
7 Davis	N	N	N	N	N	Y	Y
ALASKA							
AL Young	N	N	N	N	N	Y	Y
ARIZONA							
1 Kirkpatrick	N	N	N	N	N	Y	Y
2 Franks	Y	Y	Y	Y	Y	Y	N
3 Shadegg	Y	Y	Y	Y	Y	Y	Y
4 Pastor	N	N	N	N	N	N	Y
5 Mitchell	N	N	N	N	N	Y	Y
6 Flake	Y	Y	Y	Y	Y	N	N
7 Grijalva	N	N	N	N	N	N	Y
8 Giffords	N	N	N	N	N	Y	Y
ARKANSAS							
1 Berry	N	N	N	N	N	N	Y
2 Snyder	N	N	N	N	N	N	Y
3 Boozman	Y	N	Y	Y	Y	Y	Y
4 Ross	N	N	N	N	N	Y	Y
CALIFORNIA							
1 Thompson	N	N	N	N	N	N	Y
2 Herger	N	N	N	N	Y	Y	Y
3 Lungren	Y	N	Y	N	N	Y	Y
4 McClintock	Y	Y	Y	Y	Y	Y	N
5 Matsui	N	N	N	N	N	N	Y
6 Woolsey	N	N	N	N	N	N	Y
7 Miller, George	N	N	N	N	N	N	Y
8 Pelosi							
9 Lee	N	N	N	N	N	N	Y
10 Tauscher	N	N	N	N	N	N	Y
11 McNerney	N	N	N	N	N	Y	Y
12 Speier	N	N	Y	Y	N	Y	Y
13 Stark	N	N	N	N	N	N	Y
14 Eshoo	N	N	N	N	N	N	Y
15 Honda	N	N	N	N	N	N	Y
16 Lofgren	N	?	N	N	N	N	Y
17 Farr	N	N	N	N	N	N	Y
18 Cardoza	N	N	N	N	N	N	Y
19 Radanovich	Y	Y	Y	Y	Y	Y	Y
20 Costa	N	N	N	N	N	N	Y
21 Nunes	Y	N	N	N	Y	Y	Y
22 McCarthy	Y	N	Y	Y	Y	Y	Y
23 Capps	N	N	N	N	N	N	Y
24 Gallegly	N	N	N	Y	Y	Y	Y
25 McKeon	N	N	N	N	N	Y	Y
26 Dreier	Y	Y	Y	Y	Y	Y	Y
27 Sherman	N	N	N	N	N	N	Y
28 Berman	N	N	N	N	N	N	Y
29 Schiff	N	N	N	N	N	N	Y
30 Waxman	N	N	N	N	N	N	Y
31 Becerra	N	N	N	N	N	N	Y
32 Vacant							
33 Watson	N	N	N	N	N	N	Y
34 Roybal-Allard	N	N	N	?	N	N	Y
35 Waters	N	N	N	N	N	N	Y
36 Harman	N	N	N	N	N	N	Y
37 Richardson	N	N	N	N	N	N	Y
38 Napolitano	N	N	N	N	N	N	Y
39 Sánchez, Linda	N	N	N	N	N	N	Y
40 Royce	Y	Y	Y	Y	Y	Y	N
41 Lewis	N	N	N	N	N	Y	Y
42 Miller, Gary	Y	N	N	N	N	Y	Y
43 Baca	N	N	N	N	N	N	Y
44 Calvert	N	N	N	N	N	Y	Y
45 Bono Mack	Y	Y	Y	Y	Y	Y	Y
46 Rohrabacher	Y	Y	Y	N	Y	Y	Y
47 Sanchez, Loretta	N	N	N	N	N	N	Y
48 Campbell	Y	Y	Y	Y	Y	Y	N
49 Issa	Y	Y	Y	Y	Y	Y	Y
50 Bilbray	N	N	Y	N	Y	Y	Y
51 Filner	N	N	N	N	N	N	Y
52 Hunter	N	N	Y	N	Y	Y	Y
53 Davis	N	N	N	N	N	N	Y

	444	445	446	447	448	449	450
COLORADO							
1 DeGette	N	N	N	N	N	N	Y
2 Polis	N	N	N	N	N	N	Y
3 Salazar	N	N	N	N	N	N	Y
4 Markey	N	N	N	N	Y	Y	Y
5 Lamborn	Y	Y	Y	Y	Y	Y	Y
6 Coffman	Y	Y	Y	Y	Y	Y	Y
7 Perlmutter	N	N	N	N	N	N	Y
CONNECTICUT							
1 Larson	N	N	N	N	N	N	Y
2 Courtney	N	N	N	N	N	N	Y
3 DeLauro	N	N	N	N	N	N	Y
4 Himes	N	N	N	N	N	Y	Y
5 Murphy	N	N	N	N	N	N	?
DELAWARE							
AL Castle	N	N	Y	Y	Y	Y	N
FLORIDA							
1 Miller	Y	Y	Y	Y	Y	Y	Y
2 Boyd	N	N	N	N	N	N	Y
3 Brown	N	N	N	N	N	N	Y
4 Crenshaw	N	N	N	N	N	N	Y
5 Brown-Waite	N	N	N	N	N	N	Y
6 Stearns	Y	Y	Y	Y	Y	Y	Y
7 Mica	Y	N	N	N	Y	Y	Y
8 Grayson	N	N	N	N	N	N	Y
9 Bilirakis	N	N	N	Y	Y	Y	Y
10 Young	N	N	N	N	N	N	Y
11 Castor	N	N	N	N	N	N	Y
12 Putnam	Y	N	Y	N	Y	Y	Y
13 Buchanan	N	N	N	N	N	Y	Y
14 Mack	Y	Y	Y	Y	Y	Y	Y
15 Posey	Y	Y	N	Y	Y	Y	Y
16 Rooney	Y	N	Y	N	Y	Y	Y
17 Meek	N	N	N	N	N	N	Y
18 Ros-Lehtinen	N	N	N	N	N	N	Y
19 Wexler	N	N	N	N	N	N	Y
20 Wasserman Schultz	N	N	N	N	N	N	Y
21 Diaz-Balart, L.	N	N	N	N	N	Y	Y
22 Klein	N	N	N	N	N	N	Y
23 Hastings	N	N	N	N	N	N	Y
24 Kosmas	N	N	Y	Y	Y	N	Y
25 Diaz-Balart, M.	N	N	N	N	N	Y	Y
GEORGIA							
1 Kingston	Y	Y	N	Y	Y	Y	Y
2 Bishop	N	N	N	N	N	Y	Y
3 Westmoreland	Y	Y	Y	Y	Y	Y	N
4 Johnson	N	N	N	N	N	N	Y
5 Lewis	?	?	?	?	?	?	?
6 Price	Y	Y	Y	Y	Y	Y	Y
7 Linder	Y	Y	Y	Y	Y	Y	N
8 Marshall	N	N	N	N	N	Y	Y
9 Deal	Y	Y	Y	Y	Y	Y	N
10 Broun	Y	Y	Y	Y	Y	Y	N
11 Gingrey	Y	Y	Y	Y	Y	Y	N
12 Barrow	N	N	N	N	N	Y	Y
13 Scott	N	N	N	N	N	N	Y
HAWAII							
1 Abercrombie	N	N	N	N	N	N	Y
2 Hirono	N	N	N	N	N	N	Y
IDAHO							
1 Minnick	Y	Y	Y	Y	Y	Y	Y
2 Simpson	N	N	N	N	N	Y	Y
ILLINOIS							
1 Rush	N	N	N	N	N	N	Y
2 Jackson	N	N	N	N	N	N	Y
3 Lipinski	N	N	N	N	N	N	Y
4 Gutierrez	N	N	N	N	N	N	Y
5 Quigley	N	N	N	N	N	N	Y
6 Roskam	Y	N	Y	Y	Y	Y	Y
7 Davis	N	N	N	N	N	N	Y
8 Bean	N	N	N	N	N	Y	Y
9 Schakowsky	N	N	N	N	N	N	Y
10 Kirk	Y	N	Y	N	Y	Y	Y
11 Halvorson	N	N	Y	Y	Y	Y	Y
12 Costello	N	N	N	N	N	N	Y
13 Biggert	N	N	N	N	Y	Y	Y
14 Foster	N	N	N	N	Y	Y	Y
15 Johnson	Y	Y	Y	Y	Y	Y	Y

	444	445	446	447	448	449	450
16 **Manzullo**	N	N	N	Y	Y	Y	Y
17 Hare	N	N	N	N	N	N	Y
18 **Schock**	N	N	N	N	Y	Y	Y
19 **Shimkus**	N	N	Y	Y	N	Y	Y
INDIANA							
1 Visclosky	N	N	N	N	N	N	Y
2 Donnelly	N	N	N	N	N	Y	Y
3 **Souder**	Y	N	N	Y	Y	Y	Y
4 **Buyer**	?	Y	Y	Y	N	Y	Y
5 **Burton**	Y	Y	N	Y	Y	Y	Y
6 **Pence**	Y	Y	Y	Y	Y	Y	N
7 Carson	N	N	N	N	N	N	Y
8 Ellsworth	N	N	N	N	N	Y	Y
9 Hill	N	N	N	N	N	Y	Y
IOWA							
1 Braley	N	N	N	N	N	N	Y
2 Loebsack	N	N	N	N	N	Y	Y
3 Boswell	N	N	N	N	N	N	Y
4 **Latham**	N	N	N	N	N	Y	Y
5 **King**	Y	Y	Y	Y	Y	Y	Y
KANSAS							
1 **Moran**	Y	Y	Y	Y	Y	Y	Y
2 **Jenkins**	Y	Y	Y	Y	Y	Y	N
3 Moore	N	N	N	N	N	N	Y
4 **Tiahrt**	Y	N	N	Y	N	Y	Y
KENTUCKY							
1 **Whitfield**	N	N	N	N	N	Y	Y
2 **Guthrie**	N	N	N	N	N	Y	Y
3 Yarmuth	N	N	N	N	N	N	Y
4 **Davis**	N	N	N	N	N	Y	Y
5 **Rogers**	N	N	N	N	N	Y	Y
6 Chandler	N	N	N	N	N	N	Y
LOUISIANA							
1 **Scalise**	Y	N	Y	Y	N	Y	Y
2 **Cao**	N	N	N	N	N	Y	Y
3 Melancon	N	N	N	N	N	N	Y
4 **Fleming**	Y	Y	Y	Y	Y	Y	Y
5 **Alexander**	N	N	N	N	N	Y	Y
6 **Cassidy**	Y	Y	Y	Y	Y	Y	Y
7 **Boustany**	Y	Y	Y	Y	Y	Y	Y
MAINE							
1 Pingree	N	N	N	N	N	N	Y
2 Michaud	N	N	N	N	N	N	Y
MARYLAND							
1 Kratovil	N	N	N	N	N	Y	Y
2 Ruppersberger	N	N	N	N	N	Y	Y
3 Sarbanes	N	N	N	N	N	N	Y
4 Edwards	N	N	N	N	N	N	Y
5 Hoyer	N	N	N	N	N	N	Y
6 **Bartlett**	N	N	Y	Y	Y	Y	Y
7 Cummings	N	N	N	N	N	N	Y
8 Van Hollen	N	N	N	N	N	N	Y
MASSACHUSETTS							
1 Olver	N	N	N	N	N	N	Y
2 Neal	N	N	N	N	N	N	Y
3 McGovern	N	N	N	N	N	N	Y
4 Frank	N	N	Y	?	N	N	Y
5 Tsongas	N	N	N	N	N	N	Y
6 Tierney	N	N	Y	N	N	N	Y
7 Markey	N	N	N	N	N	N	Y
8 Capuano	?	?	?	?	?	?	?
9 Lynch	N	N	Y	N	N	N	Y
10 Delahunt	N	N	N	N	N	N	Y
MICHIGAN							
1 Stupak	?	?	?	?	?	?	?
2 **Hoekstra**	Y	Y	Y	Y	Y	Y	N
3 **Ehlers**	Y	Y	Y	Y	Y	Y	Y
4 **Camp**	N	N	N	N	N	Y	Y
5 Kildee	N	N	N	N	N	N	Y
6 **Upton**	Y	Y	Y	N	Y	Y	Y
7 Schauer	N	N	Y	N	N	Y	Y
8 **Rogers**	Y	Y	Y	Y	Y	Y	Y
9 Peters	N	N	N	N	N	Y	Y
10 **Miller**	N	N	N	Y	N	Y	Y
11 **McCotter**	Y	Y	Y	Y	Y	Y	Y
12 Levin	N	N	N	N	N	N	Y
13 Kilpatrick	N	N	N	N	N	N	Y
14 Conyers	N	N	N	N	N	N	Y
15 Dingell	N	N	N	N	N	N	Y
MINNESOTA							
1 Walz	N	N	N	N	N	Y	Y
2 **Kline**	Y	Y	Y	Y	Y	Y	Y
3 **Paulsen**	Y	Y	Y	Y	Y	Y	Y
4 McCollum	N	N	N	N	N	N	Y
5 Ellison	N	N	N	N	N	N	Y
6 **Bachmann**	Y	Y	Y	Y	Y	Y	Y
7 Peterson	N	N	N	N	N	N	Y
8 Oberstar	N	N	N	N	N	N	Y
MISSISSIPPI							
1 Childers	N	N	N	N	N	Y	Y
2 Thompson	N	N	N	N	N	N	Y
3 **Harper**	Y	Y	Y	Y	Y	Y	Y
4 Taylor	N	N	N	N	N	Y	Y
MISSOURI							
1 Clay	N	N	N	N	N	N	Y
2 **Akin**	Y	Y	Y	N	Y	Y	Y
3 Carnahan	N	N	N	N	N	N	Y
4 Skelton	N	N	N	N	N	Y	Y
5 Cleaver	N	N	N	N	N	N	Y
6 **Graves**	Y	Y	Y	Y	Y	Y	Y
7 **Blunt**	Y	N	Y	N	Y	Y	N
8 **Emerson**	N	N	N	N	N	Y	Y
9 **Luetkemeyer**	Y	Y	Y	Y	Y	Y	Y
MONTANA							
AL **Rehberg**	N	N	N	N	N	Y	Y
NEBRASKA							
1 **Fortenberry**	N	N	Y	N	Y	Y	Y
2 **Terry**	Y	Y	Y	Y	Y	Y	Y
3 **Smith**	Y	Y	Y	Y	Y	Y	Y
NEVADA							
1 Berkley	N	N	N	N	N	N	Y
2 **Heller**	Y	Y	Y	Y	Y	Y	Y
3 Titus	N	N	N	N	N	Y	Y
NEW HAMPSHIRE							
1 Shea-Porter	N	N	N	N	N	Y	Y
2 Hodes	N	N	N	N	N	Y	Y
NEW JERSEY							
1 Andrews	N	N	N	N	N	N	Y
2 **LoBiondo**	N	N	N	N	N	Y	Y
3 Adler	N	N	N	N	N	Y	Y
4 **Smith**	N	N	N	N	N	Y	Y
5 **Garrett**	Y	Y	Y	Y	Y	Y	N
6 Pallone	N	N	N	N	N	N	Y
7 **Lance**	Y	N	Y	Y	N	Y	Y
8 Pascrell	N	N	N	N	N	N	Y
9 Rothman	N	N	N	N	N	N	Y
10 Payne	N	N	N	N	N	N	Y
11 **Frelinghuysen**	N	N	N	N	N	Y	Y
12 Holt	N	N	N	N	N	N	Y
13 Sires	N	N	N	N	N	N	Y
NEW MEXICO							
1 Heinrich	N	N	N	N	N	N	Y
2 Teague	N	N	N	N	N	Y	Y
3 Lujan	N	N	N	N	N	N	Y
NEW YORK							
1 Bishop	N	N	N	N	N	N	Y
2 Israel	N	N	N	N	N	N	Y
3 **King**	N	N	N	N	N	Y	Y
4 McCarthy	N	N	N	N	N	N	Y
5 Ackerman	N	N	N	N	N	N	Y
6 Meeks	N	N	N	N	N	N	Y
7 Crowley	N	N	N	N	N	N	Y
8 Nadler	N	N	Y	N	N	N	Y
9 Weiner	N	N	N	N	N	N	Y
10 Towns	N	N	N	N	N	N	Y
11 Clarke	N	N	N	N	N	N	Y
12 Velázquez	N	N	N	N	N	N	Y
13 McMahon	N	N	N	N	N	Y	Y
14 Maloney	N	N	N	N	N	N	Y
15 Rangel	N	N	Y	N	N	N	Y
16 Serrano	N	N	N	N	N	N	Y
17 Engel	N	N	N	N	N	N	Y
18 Lowey	N	N	N	N	N	N	Y
19 Hall	N	N	N	N	N	Y	Y
20 Murphy	N	N	N	N	N	Y	Y
21 Tonko	N	N	N	N	N	N	Y
22 Hinchey	N	N	N	N	N	N	Y
23 **McHugh**	N	N	N	N	N	Y	Y
24 Arcuri	N	N	N	N	N	Y	Y
25 Maffei	N	N	N	N	N	Y	Y
26 **Lee**	N	N	N	N	N	Y	Y
27 Higgins	N	N	N	N	N	N	Y
28 Slaughter	N	N	N	N	N	N	Y
29 Massa	N	N	N	N	N	N	Y
NORTH CAROLINA							
1 Butterfield	N	N	N	N	N	N	Y
2 Etheridge	N	N	N	N	N	N	Y
3 **Jones**	N	N	N	N	N	Y	Y
4 Price	N	N	N	N	N	N	Y
5 **Foxx**	Y	Y	Y	Y	Y	Y	N
6 **Coble**	Y	Y	Y	Y	Y	Y	Y
7 McIntyre	N	N	N	N	N	Y	Y
8 Kissell	N	N	N	N	N	Y	Y
9 **Myrick**	Y	Y	Y	Y	Y	Y	Y
10 **McHenry**	Y	Y	Y	Y	Y	Y	Y
11 Shuler	N	N	N	N	N	Y	Y
12 Watt	N	N	N	N	N	N	Y
13 Miller	N	N	N	N	N	N	Y
NORTH DAKOTA							
AL Pomeroy	N	N	N	N	N	N	Y
OHIO							
1 Driehaus	N	N	N	N	N	Y	Y
2 **Schmidt**	Y	Y	Y	Y	Y	Y	Y
3 **Turner**	N	N	N	N	N	Y	Y
4 **Jordan**	Y	Y	Y	Y	Y	Y	Y
5 **Latta**	Y	N	N	Y	Y	Y	Y
6 Wilson	N	N	N	N	N	N	Y
7 **Austria**	Y	N	Y	Y	Y	Y	Y
8 **Boehner**	Y	?	?	?	?	Y	N
9 Kaptur	N	N	N	N	N	N	Y
10 Kucinich	N	N	N	N	N	N	Y
11 Fudge	N	N	N	N	N	N	Y
12 **Tiberi**	Y	Y	Y	Y	Y	Y	Y
13 Sutton	N	N	N	N	N	N	Y
14 **LaTourette**	N	N	N	N	N	Y	Y
15 Kilroy	N	N	N	N	N	N	Y
16 Boccieri	N	N	N	N	N	Y	Y
17 Ryan	N	N	N	N	N	N	Y
18 Space	N	N	N	N	N	Y	Y
OKLAHOMA							
1 **Sullivan**	?	?	?	?	?	?	?
2 Boren	N	N	N	N	N	Y	Y
3 **Lucas**	N	N	N	N	N	?	Y
4 **Cole**	N	N	N	N	N	Y	Y
5 **Fallin**	Y	Y	Y	Y	Y	Y	Y
OREGON							
1 Wu	N	N	N	N	N	N	Y
2 **Walden**	N	N	N	Y	Y	Y	Y
3 Blumenauer	N	N	N	N	N	N	Y
4 DeFazio	N	N	N	N	N	Y	Y
5 Schrader	N	N	N	?	N	N	Y
PENNSYLVANIA							
1 Brady	N	N	N	N	N	N	Y
2 Fattah	N	N	N	N	N	N	Y
3 Dahlkemper	N	N	N	N	N	Y	Y
4 Altmire	N	N	N	N	N	Y	Y
5 **Thompson**	N	N	N	N	N	Y	Y
6 **Gerlach**	N	N	N	Y	N	Y	Y
7 Sestak	N	N	N	N	N	N	Y
8 Murphy, P.	N	N	N	N	N	Y	Y
9 **Shuster**	N	N	N	N	N	Y	Y
10 Carney	N	N	N	N	N	Y	Y
11 Kanjorski	N	N	N	N	N	Y	Y
12 Murtha	N	N	N	N	N	N	Y
13 Schwartz	N	N	N	N	N	N	Y
14 Doyle	N	N	N	N	N	N	Y
15 **Dent**	N	N	N	Y	N	Y	Y
16 **Pitts**	Y	Y	Y	Y	Y	Y	Y
17 Holden	N	N	N	N	N	N	Y
18 **Murphy, T.**	N	N	N	N	N	Y	Y
19 **Platts**	Y	N	Y	Y	N	Y	Y
RHODE ISLAND							
1 Kennedy	?	?	?	?	?	?	?
2 Langevin	N	N	N	N	N	N	Y
SOUTH CAROLINA							
1 **Brown**	Y	N	N	N	Y	Y	Y
2 **Wilson**	Y	Y	Y	Y	Y	Y	Y
3 **Barrett**	Y	Y	Y	Y	Y	Y	N
4 **Inglis**	Y	Y	Y	Y	Y	Y	N
5 Spratt	N	N	N	N	N	N	Y
6 Clyburn	N	N	N	N	N	N	Y
SOUTH DAKOTA							
AL Herseth Sandlin	N	N	N	N	N	Y	Y
TENNESSEE							
1 **Roe**	Y	Y	Y	Y	Y	Y	Y
2 **Duncan**	Y	N	N	Y	Y	Y	N
3 **Wamp**	Y	Y	N	N	Y	Y	Y
4 Davis	N	N	N	N	N	Y	Y
5 Cooper	Y	Y	Y	Y	Y	N	Y
6 Gordon	N	N	N	N	N	N	Y
7 **Blackburn**	Y	Y	Y	Y	Y	Y	N
8 Tanner	N	N	N	N	N	Y	Y
9 Cohen	N	N	N	N	N	N	Y
TEXAS							
1 **Gohmert**	N	N	Y	?	Y	Y	N
2 **Poe**	N	N	Y	N	Y	Y	Y
3 **Johnson, S.**	Y	N	Y	N	Y	N	Y
4 **Hall**	N	N	?	Y	Y	Y	N
5 **Hensarling**	Y	Y	Y	Y	Y	Y	N
6 **Barton**	Y	N	N	Y	Y	Y	Y
7 **Culberson**	N	N	N	N	N	Y	Y
8 **Brady**	Y	N	Y	N	Y	Y	N
9 Green, A.	N	N	N	N	N	N	Y
10 **McCaul**	Y	Y	Y	Y	Y	Y	Y
11 **Conaway**	Y	Y	Y	Y	Y	Y	Y
12 **Granger**	N	N	N	N	N	Y	Y
13 **Thornberry**	Y	Y	Y	Y	Y	Y	Y
14 **Paul**	N	N	Y	Y	Y	N	N
15 Hinojosa	N	N	N	N	N	N	Y
16 Reyes	N	N	N	N	N	N	Y
17 Edwards	N	N	N	N	N	N	Y
18 Jackson Lee	N	N	N	N	N	N	Y
19 **Neugebauer**	Y	Y	Y	Y	Y	Y	N
20 Gonzalez	N	N	N	N	N	N	Y
21 **Smith**	N	N	N	N	N	Y	Y
22 **Olson**	N	N	Y	Y	Y	Y	Y
23 Rodriguez	N	N	N	N	N	N	Y
24 **Marchant**	Y	N	Y	Y	Y	Y	Y
25 Doggett	N	Y	Y	N	N	N	Y
26 **Burgess**	Y	Y	Y	Y	Y	Y	N
27 Ortiz	N	N	N	N	N	N	Y
28 Cuellar	N	N	N	N	N	N	Y
29 Green, G.	N	N	N	N	N	N	Y
30 Johnson, E.	N	N	N	N	N	N	Y
31 **Carter**	N	N	N	N	N	Y	Y
32 **Sessions**	Y	Y	Y	Y	Y	Y	?
UTAH							
1 **Bishop**	Y	N	Y	Y	N	Y	N
2 Matheson	N	N	N	N	N	Y	Y
3 **Chaffetz**	Y	Y	Y	Y	Y	Y	N
VERMONT							
AL Welch	N	N	N	N	N	N	Y
VIRGINIA							
1 **Wittman**	Y	N	N	N	Y	Y	Y
2 Nye	Y	Y	N	N	N	Y	Y
3 Scott	N	N	N	N	N	N	Y
4 **Forbes**	Y	N	N	N	Y	Y	Y
5 Perriello	N	N	N	N	N	Y	Y
6 **Goodlatte**	Y	Y	Y	Y	Y	Y	N
7 **Cantor**	Y	Y	Y	Y	Y	Y	Y
8 Moran	N	N	Y	N	N	N	Y
9 Boucher	N	N	N	N	N	N	Y
10 **Wolf**	Y	N	N	N	N	Y	Y
11 Connolly	N	N	N	N	N	N	Y
WASHINGTON							
1 Inslee	N	N	N	N	N	N	Y
2 Larsen	N	N	N	N	N	N	Y
3 Baird	N	N	Y	Y	N	N	Y
4 **Hastings**	N	N	N	N	N	Y	Y
5 **McMorris Rodgers**	Y	N	Y	Y	Y	Y	Y
6 Dicks	N	N	N	N	N	N	Y
7 McDermott	N	N	N	N	N	N	Y
8 **Reichert**	N	N	N	N	N	Y	Y
9 Smith	N	N	N	N	N	Y	Y
WEST VIRGINIA							
1 Mollohan	N	N	N	N	N	N	Y
2 **Capito**	N	N	N	N	N	Y	Y
3 Rahall	N	N	N	N	N	N	Y
WISCONSIN							
1 **Ryan**	Y	Y	Y	Y	Y	Y	N
2 Baldwin	N	N	N	N	N	N	Y
3 Kind	N	Y	Y	N	N	N	Y
4 Moore	N	N	N	N	N	N	Y
5 **Sensenbrenner**	Y	Y	Y	Y	Y	Y	N
6 **Petri**	Y	Y	Y	Y	Y	Y	N
7 Obey	N	N	N	N	N	N	Y
8 Kagen	N	?	N	N	N	N	Y
WYOMING							
AL **Lummis**	Y	Y	Y	Y	Y	Y	Y
DELEGATES							
Faleomavaega (A.S.)	N	N	N	N	N		
Norton (D.C.)	N	N	N	N	N		
Bordallo (Guam)	N	N	N	N	N		
Sablan (N. Marianas)	N	N	N	N	N		
Pierluisi (P.R.)	N	N	N	N	N		
Christensen (V.I.)	?	?	?	?	?		

IN THE HOUSE | By Vote Number

451. HR 2647. Fiscal 2010 Defense Authorization/Previous Question. Pingree, D-Maine, motion to order the previous question (thus ending debate and possibility of amendment) on adoption of the rule (H Res 572) to provide for House floor consideration of a bill that would authorize $680.4 billion for defense programs in fiscal 2010, including emergency funds for operations in Iraq and Afghanistan. Motion agreed to 245-181: R 0-175; D 245-6. June 24, 2009.

452. HR 2647. Fiscal 2010 Defense Authorization/Rule. Adoption of the rule (H Res 572) that would provide for House floor consideration of the bill that would authorize $680.4 billion for defense programs in fiscal 2010, including emergency funds for operations in Iraq and Afghanistan. Adopted 222-202: R 1-175; D 221-27. June 24, 2009.

453. HR 2647. Fiscal 2010 Defense Authorization/Afghanistan Exit Strategy. McGovern, D-Mass., amendment that would require the Defense Department to submit a report to Congress no later than Dec. 31, 2009, outlining an exit strategy for U.S. military forces involved in the war in Afghanistan. Rejected in Committee of the Whole 138-278: R 7-164; D 131-114. June 25, 2009.

454. HR 2647. Fiscal 2010 Defense Authorization/Western Hemisphere Institute for Security Cooperation. McGovern, D-Mass., amendment that would require the Defense Department to publicly release information on students and instructors at the Western Hemisphere Institute for Security Cooperation for fiscal 2005 and beyond. The information would have to include the full name, rank and country of origin of each student and instructor and the courses each took or taught. Adopted in Committee of the Whole 224-190: R 6-164; D 218-26. June 25, 2009.

455. HR 2647. Fiscal 2010 Defense Authorization/Missile Defense. Franks, R-Ariz., amendment that would increase the amount authorized for the Missile Defense Agency by $1.2 billion, offset by a reduction of the same amount for defense environmental cleanup. It would state that it is U.S. policy to continue development of systems to intercept missiles in the boost phase of flight as well as a layered missile defense system. Rejected in Committee of the Whole 171-244: R 159-13; D 12-231. June 25, 2009.

456. HR 2647. Fiscal 2010 Defense Authorization/Non-Disclosure Agreement Reports. Akin, R-Mo., amendment that would require the Defense Department to report to Congress within 14 days of requiring employees to sign non-disclosure agreements related to their official duties, not including agreements regarding security clearances. Reports would include descriptions of prohibited discussion topics, the number of signatories and the duration of each agreement. Rejected in Committee of the Whole 186-226: R 169-3; D 17-223. June 25, 2009.

457. HR 2647. Fiscal 2010 Defense Authorization/Interrogation Videotaping. Holt, D-N.J., amendment that would require the videotaping of all intelligence interrogations of detainees in the custody of the Defense Department, excluding tactical questioning as defined by the Army Field Manual on Human Intelligence Collector Operations. It would require the department to submit a report to Congress, no later than 30 days after the bill's enactment, containing guidelines for videotaping interrogations. Adopted in Committee of the Whole 224-193: R 10-162; D 214-31. June 25, 2009.

	451	452	453	454	455	456	457
ALABAMA							
1 **Bonner**	N	N	N	N	Y	Y	N
2 Bright	Y	Y	N	N	Y	N	N
3 **Rogers**	N	N	N	N	Y	Y	N
4 **Aderholt**	N	N	N	N	Y	Y	N
5 Griffith	Y	Y	N	Y	Y	Y	N
6 **Bachus**	N	N	N	N	Y	Y	N
7 Davis	Y	N	Y	N	Y	N	N
ALASKA							
AL **Young**	N	N	N	N	Y	Y	N
ARIZONA							
1 Kirkpatrick	Y	Y	N	N	Y	N	N
2 **Franks**	N	N	N	N	Y	Y	N
3 **Shadegg**	N	N	N	N	Y	Y	N
4 Pastor	Y	Y	Y	Y	N	N	Y
5 Mitchell	N	N	N	Y	N	N	Y
6 **Flake**	N	N	?	?	?	?	?
7 Grijalva	Y	Y	Y	Y	N	N	Y
8 Giffords	Y	Y	N	Y	N	N	Y
ARKANSAS							
1 Berry	Y	Y	N	Y	N	N	Y
2 Snyder	Y	Y	N	N	N	N	Y
3 **Boozman**	N	N	N	N	Y	Y	N
4 Ross	Y	Y	N	Y	N	N	N
CALIFORNIA							
1 Thompson	Y	Y	Y	Y	N	N	Y
2 **Herger**	N	N	N	N	Y	Y	N
3 **Lungren**	N	N	N	N	Y	Y	N
4 **McClintock**	N	N	N	N	Y	Y	N
5 Matsui	Y	Y	Y	Y	N	N	Y
6 Woolsey	Y	N	Y	Y	N	–	Y
7 Miller, George	Y	Y	Y	Y	N	N	Y
8 Pelosi							
9 Lee	Y	Y	Y	Y	N	N	Y
10 Tauscher	Y	Y	N	Y	N	N	Y
11 McNerney	Y	Y	N	Y	N	N	Y
12 Speier	Y	Y	Y	Y	N	N	Y
13 Stark	Y	N	Y	Y	N	?	Y
14 Eshoo	Y	Y	Y	Y	N	N	Y
15 Honda	Y	Y	Y	Y	N	N	Y
16 Lofgren	Y	Y	+	+	–	–	+
17 Farr	Y	N	Y	Y	N	N	Y
18 Cardoza	Y	Y	N	Y	N	N	N
19 **Radanovich**	N	N	N	N	Y	Y	N
20 Costa	Y	N	N	N	Y	N	N
21 **Nunes**	N	N	N	N	Y	Y	N
22 **McCarthy**	N	N	N	N	Y	Y	N
23 Capps	Y	Y	Y	Y	N	N	Y
24 **Gallegly**	N	N	N	N	Y	Y	N
25 **McKeon**	N	N	N	N	Y	Y	N
26 **Dreier**	N	N	N	N	Y	Y	N
27 Sherman	Y	Y	N	N	Y	N	Y
28 Berman	Y	N	–	+	–	–	+
29 Schiff	Y	Y	N	Y	N	N	Y
30 Waxman	Y	?	Y	Y	N	N	Y
31 Becerra	Y	Y	+	+	–	–	+
32 Vacant							
33 Watson	Y	Y	Y	Y	N	N	Y
34 Roybal-Allard	Y	Y	N	Y	N	N	Y
35 Waters	Y	Y	Y	Y	N	N	Y
36 Harman	Y	Y	Y	Y	N	N	Y
37 Richardson	Y	Y	Y	Y	N	N	Y
38 Napolitano	Y	Y	Y	Y	N	N	Y
39 Sánchez, Linda	Y	Y	Y	Y	N	N	Y
40 **Royce**	N	N	N	N	Y	Y	N
41 **Lewis**	N	N	N	N	Y	Y	N
42 **Miller, Gary**	N	N	N	N	Y	Y	N
43 Baca	Y	Y	Y	N	Y	N	Y
44 **Calvert**	N	N	N	N	Y	Y	N
45 **Bono Mack**	N	N	N	N	Y	Y	N
46 **Rohrabacher**	N	N	Y	N	Y	Y	Y
47 Sanchez, Loretta	Y	Y	?	?	?	?	?
48 **Campbell**	N	N	N	N	Y	Y	N
49 **Issa**	N	N	N	N	Y	Y	N
50 **Bilbray**	N	N	N	N	Y	Y	N
51 Filner	Y	Y	Y	Y	N	N	Y
52 **Hunter**	N	N	N	N	Y	Y	N
53 Davis	Y	Y	N	Y	N	N	Y

	451	452	453	454	455	456	457
COLORADO							
1 DeGette	Y	Y	Y	Y	N	N	Y
2 Polis	Y	Y	Y	Y	N	N	Y
3 Salazar	Y	Y	N	Y	N	N	Y
4 Markey	Y	Y	N	N	N	N	Y
5 **Lamborn**	N	N	N	N	Y	Y	N
6 **Coffman**	N	N	N	N	Y	Y	N
7 Perlmutter	Y	Y	Y	N	N	N	Y
CONNECTICUT							
1 Larson	Y	Y	Y	+	N	N	Y
2 Courtney	Y	Y	Y	Y	N	N	Y
3 DeLauro	Y	Y	Y	Y	N	N	Y
4 Himes	Y	Y	Y	Y	N	N	Y
5 Murphy	Y	Y	Y	Y	N	N	N
DELAWARE							
AL **Castle**	N	N	N	N	N	Y	Y
FLORIDA							
1 **Miller**	N	N	N	N	Y	Y	N
2 Boyd	Y	Y	N	Y	N	?	Y
3 Brown	Y	Y	Y	Y	N	N	Y
4 **Crenshaw**	N	N	N	N	Y	Y	N
5 **Brown-Waite**	N	N	N	N	Y	Y	N
6 **Stearns**	N	N	N	Y	Y	Y	N
7 **Mica**	N	N	N	Y	Y	Y	N
8 Grayson	Y	Y	Y	Y	N	Y	Y
9 **Bilirakis**	N	N	N	N	Y	Y	N
10 **Young**	N	N	N	N	Y	Y	N
11 Castor	Y	Y	Y	Y	N	N	Y
12 **Putnam**	N	N	?	?	?	?	?
13 **Buchanan**	N	N	N	N	Y	Y	N
14 **Mack**	N	N	N	N	Y	Y	N
15 **Posey**	N	N	N	N	Y	Y	N
16 **Rooney**	N	N	N	N	Y	Y	N
17 Meek	Y	Y	N	Y	N	?	Y
18 **Ros-Lehtinen**	N	N	N	N	Y	Y	N
19 Wexler	Y	Y	Y	Y	N	N	Y
20 Wasserman Schultz	Y	Y	Y	Y	N	N	Y
21 **Diaz-Balart, L.**	N	N	?	?	?	?	?
22 Klein	Y	Y	Y	Y	N	N	Y
23 Hastings	Y	Y	?	?	?	?	?
24 Kosmas	Y	Y	N	Y	N	N	N
25 **Diaz-Balart, M.**	N	N	N	N	Y	Y	N
GEORGIA							
1 **Kingston**	N	N	N	?	Y	Y	N
2 Bishop	Y	Y	N	Y	N	N	Y
3 **Westmoreland**	N	N	N	N	Y	Y	N
4 Johnson	Y	Y	Y	Y	N	N	Y
5 Lewis	?	?	?	?	?	?	?
6 **Price**	N	N	N	N	Y	Y	N
7 **Linder**	N	N	N	N	Y	Y	N
8 Marshall	Y	Y	N	Y	N	N	Y
9 **Deal**	N	N	N	N	Y	Y	N
10 **Broun**	N	N	N	N	Y	Y	N
11 **Gingrey**	N	N	N	N	Y	Y	N
12 Barrow	Y	Y	N	N	Y	N	N
13 Scott	Y	Y	N	Y	N	N	Y
HAWAII							
1 Abercrombie	Y	Y	Y	Y	N	N	Y
2 Hirono	Y	Y	Y	Y	N	N	Y
IDAHO							
1 Minnick	N	N	N	N	Y	Y	Y
2 **Simpson**	N	N	N	N	Y	Y	N
ILLINOIS							
1 Rush	Y	Y	N	Y	N	N	Y
2 Jackson	Y	Y	Y	Y	N	N	Y
3 Lipinski	Y	Y	N	Y	N	N	Y
4 Gutierrez	Y	Y	?	?	?	?	?
5 Quigley	Y	Y	Y	Y	N	N	Y
6 **Roskam**	N	N	N	N	Y	Y	N
7 Davis	Y	Y	Y	Y	N	?	Y
8 Bean	Y	Y	N	Y	N	N	Y
9 Schakowsky	Y	Y	Y	Y	N	N	Y
10 **Kirk**	N	N	N	N	Y	Y	N
11 Halvorson	Y	Y	N	Y	Y	Y	N
12 Costello	Y	Y	N	Y	N	N	Y
13 **Biggert**	N	N	N	N	Y	Y	N
14 Foster	Y	Y	N	Y	N	N	Y
15 **Johnson**	N	Y	N	Y	N	Y	Y

	451	452	453	454	455	456	457
16 **Manzullo**	N	N	N	N	Y	Y	N
17 Hare	Y	Y	Y	Y	N	N	Y
18 **Schock**	N	N	N	N	Y	Y	N
19 **Shimkus**	N	N	N	N	Y	Y	N
INDIANA							
1 Visclosky	Y	Y	Y	Y	N	N	Y
2 Donnelly	Y	N	N	Y	N	N	N
3 **Souder**	N	N	N	N	Y	Y	N
4 **Buyer**	?	N	N	N	Y	Y	N
5 **Burton**	N	N	N	N	Y	Y	N
6 **Pence**	N	N	N	N	Y	Y	N
7 Carson	Y	Y	Y	Y	N	N	Y
8 Ellsworth	Y	Y	N	Y	N	N	N
9 Hill	Y	N	Y	Y	N	N	Y
IOWA							
1 Braley	Y	Y	Y	Y	N	N	Y
2 Loebsack	Y	Y	Y	Y	N	N	Y
3 Boswell	Y	Y	Y	Y	N	N	Y
4 **Latham**	N	N	N	N	Y	Y	N
5 **King**	N	N	N	N	Y	Y	N
KANSAS							
1 **Moran**	N	N	N	N	Y	Y	N
2 **Jenkins**	N	N	N	N	Y	Y	N
3 Moore	Y	Y	N	Y	N	N	Y
4 **Tiahrt**	N	N	N	N	Y	Y	N
KENTUCKY							
1 **Whitfield**	N	N	Y	N	Y	Y	N
2 **Guthrie**	N	N	N	N	Y	Y	N
3 Yarmuth	Y	Y	Y	Y	N	N	Y
4 **Davis**	N	N	N	N	Y	Y	N
5 **Rogers**	N	N	N	N	Y	Y	N
6 Chandler	Y	Y	N	Y	N	N	N
LOUISIANA							
1 **Scalise**	N	N	N	N	Y	Y	N
2 **Cao**	N	N	?	?	?	?	?
3 Melancon	Y	N	N	N	N	N	Y
4 **Fleming**	N	N	N	N	Y	Y	N
5 **Alexander**	N	N	N	N	Y	Y	N
6 **Cassidy**	N	N	N	N	Y	Y	Y
7 **Boustany**	N	N	N	N	Y	Y	N
MAINE							
1 Pingree	Y	Y	Y	Y	N	N	Y
2 Michaud	Y	Y	Y	Y	N	N	Y
MARYLAND							
1 Kratovil	Y	N	N	Y	N	N	N
2 Ruppersberger	Y	Y	N	Y	N	N	Y
3 Sarbanes	Y	Y	Y	Y	N	N	Y
4 Edwards	Y	Y	Y	Y	N	N	Y
5 Hoyer	Y	Y	N	Y	N	N	Y
6 **Bartlett**	N	N	N	N	Y	Y	Y
7 Cummings	Y	Y	N	Y	N	N	Y
8 Van Hollen	Y	Y	N	Y	N	N	Y
MASSACHUSETTS							
1 Olver	Y	Y	Y	Y	N	N	Y
2 Neal	Y	Y	Y	Y	N	N	Y
3 McGovern	Y	Y	Y	Y	N	N	Y
4 Frank	Y	N	Y	Y	N	N	Y
5 Tsongas	Y	Y	Y	Y	N	N	Y
6 Tierney	Y	Y	Y	Y	N	N	Y
7 Markey	N	Y	Y	Y	N	N	Y
8 Capuano	?	?	+	+	–	–	+
9 Lynch	Y	Y	Y	Y	N	N	Y
10 Delahunt	Y	Y	Y	Y	N	N	Y
MICHIGAN							
1 Stupak	?	?	N	N	N	N	Y
2 **Hoekstra**	N	N	N	N	Y	Y	N
3 **Ehlers**	N	N	N	Y	N	N	Y
4 **Camp**	N	N	N	N	Y	Y	N
5 Kildee	Y	Y	N	Y	N	N	Y
6 **Upton**	N	N	N	N	Y	Y	N
7 Schauer	Y	Y	N	Y	N	N	Y
8 **Rogers**	N	N	N	N	Y	Y	N
9 Peters	Y	Y	Y	Y	Y	N	Y
10 **Miller**	N	N	N	N	Y	Y	N
11 **McCotter**	N	N	N	N	Y	Y	N
12 Levin	Y	Y	N	Y	N	N	Y
13 Kilpatrick	Y	Y	Y	Y	N	N	Y
14 Conyers	Y	Y	+	+	–	–	+
15 Dingell	Y	Y	N	Y	N	N	N
MINNESOTA							
1 Walz	Y	Y	Y	Y	N	N	Y
2 **Kline**	N	N	N	N	Y	Y	N
3 **Paulsen**	N	N	N	N	Y	Y	N
4 McCollum	Y	Y	Y	Y	N	N	Y

	451	452	453	454	455	456	457
5 Ellison	Y	Y	Y	Y	N	N	Y
6 **Bachmann**	N	N	N	N	Y	Y	N
7 Peterson	Y	Y	N	N	N	N	N
8 Oberstar	Y	Y	Y	Y	N	N	Y
MISSISSIPPI							
1 Childers	Y	N	N	N	N	Y	N
2 Thompson	Y	Y	N	Y	N	N	Y
3 **Harper**	N	N	N	N	Y	Y	N
4 Taylor	N	N	N	Y	N	Y	N
MISSOURI							
1 Clay	Y	Y	Y	Y	N	N	Y
2 **Akin**	N	N	N	N	Y	Y	N
3 Carnahan	Y	Y	N	Y	N	N	Y
4 Skelton	Y	Y	N	Y	N	N	Y
5 Cleaver	Y	Y	N	Y	N	N	Y
6 **Graves**	N	N	N	N	Y	Y	N
7 **Blunt**	N	N	N	N	Y	Y	N
8 **Emerson**	N	N	N	N	Y	Y	N
9 **Luetkemeyer**	N	N	N	N	Y	Y	N
MONTANA							
AL **Rehberg**	N	N	N	N	Y	Y	N
NEBRASKA							
1 **Fortenberry**	N	N	N	N	Y	Y	N
2 **Terry**	N	N	N	N	Y	Y	N
3 **Smith**	N	N	N	N	Y	Y	N
NEVADA							
1 Berkley	Y	Y	Y	Y	N	N	Y
2 **Heller**	N	N	N	N	Y	Y	N
3 Titus	Y	Y	N	Y	N	N	Y
NEW HAMPSHIRE							
1 Shea-Porter	Y	Y	Y	Y	N	N	Y
2 Hodes	Y	Y	Y	Y	N	Y	Y
NEW JERSEY							
1 Andrews	Y	Y	N	Y	N	N	Y
2 **LoBiondo**	N	N	N	N	Y	Y	N
3 Adler	Y	Y	N	N	N	N	Y
4 **Smith**	N	N	N	N	Y	Y	Y
5 **Garrett**	N	N	N	N	Y	Y	N
6 Pallone	Y	Y	Y	Y	N	N	Y
7 **Lance**	N	N	N	N	Y	Y	N
8 Pascrell	Y	Y	Y	Y	N	N	Y
9 Rothman	Y	Y	Y	Y	N	N	Y
10 Payne	Y	Y	Y	Y	N	N	Y
11 **Frelinghuysen**	N	N	N	N	Y	Y	N
12 Holt	Y	Y	Y	Y	N	N	Y
13 Sires	Y	Y	N	Y	N	N	Y
NEW MEXICO							
1 Heinrich	Y	N	Y	Y	N	N	Y
2 Teague	Y	Y	N	Y	N	N	N
3 Lujan	Y	Y	Y	Y	N	N	Y
NEW YORK							
1 Bishop	N	Y	Y	Y	N	N	Y
2 Israel	Y	Y	Y	Y	N	N	Y
3 **King**	N	N	N	N	Y	Y	N
4 McCarthy	Y	Y	N	Y	N	N	Y
5 Ackerman	Y	Y	N	Y	N	N	Y
6 Meeks	Y	Y	N	Y	N	N	Y
7 Crowley	Y	Y	+	+	–	–	+
8 Nadler	Y	Y	Y	Y	N	Y	Y
9 Weiner	Y	Y	+	?	–	–	+
10 Towns	Y	Y	Y	Y	N	N	Y
11 Clarke	Y	Y	Y	Y	N	N	Y
12 Velázquez	Y	Y	?	?	?	?	?
13 McMahon	Y	Y	N	N	Y	Y	Y
14 Maloney	Y	Y	Y	Y	N	N	Y
15 Rangel	Y	Y	N	Y	N	N	Y
16 Serrano	Y	Y	Y	Y	N	N	Y
17 Engel	Y	Y	N	Y	N	Y	Y
18 Lowey	Y	Y	N	Y	N	N	Y
19 Hall	Y	Y	Y	Y	N	N	Y
20 Murphy	Y	N	N	Y	N	N	Y
21 Tonko	Y	Y	N	Y	N	N	Y
22 Hinchey	Y	Y	Y	Y	N	N	Y
23 **McHugh**	N	N	N	Y	N	Y	N
24 Arcuri	Y	Y	N	Y	N	N	N
25 Maffei	Y	Y	Y	Y	N	N	Y
26 **Lee**	N	N	N	N	Y	Y	N
27 Higgins	Y	Y	N	Y	N	N	Y
28 Slaughter	Y	?	Y	Y	N	N	Y
29 Massa	Y	Y	Y	Y	N	N	Y
NORTH CAROLINA							
1 Butterfield	Y	Y	N	Y	N	N	Y
2 Etheridge	Y	Y	N	Y	N	N	Y
3 **Jones**	N	N	Y	Y	N	Y	Y
4 Price	Y	Y	Y	Y	N	N	Y

	451	452	453	454	455	456	457
5 **Foxx**	N	N	N	N	Y	Y	N
6 **Coble**	?	?	Y	N	Y	Y	N
7 McIntyre	Y	Y	N	Y	N	N	Y
8 Kissell	Y	Y	N	Y	N	N	Y
9 **Myrick**	N	N	N	N	Y	Y	N
10 **McHenry**	N	N	N	N	Y	Y	N
11 Shuler	N	N	N	N	N	N	N
12 Watt	Y	Y	Y	Y	N	N	Y
13 Miller	Y	Y	N	Y	N	N	Y
NORTH DAKOTA							
AL Pomeroy	Y	Y	N	Y	N	N	Y
OHIO							
1 Driehaus	Y	Y	Y	Y	N	N	Y
2 **Schmidt**	N	N	N	N	Y	Y	N
3 **Turner**	N	N	N	N	Y	Y	N
4 **Jordan**	N	N	N	N	Y	Y	N
5 **Latta**	N	N	N	N	Y	Y	N
6 Wilson	Y	Y	Y	Y	N	N	Y
7 **Austria**	N	N	N	N	Y	Y	N
8 **Boehner**	N	N	N	N	Y	Y	N
9 Kaptur	Y	Y	Y	Y	N	N	Y
10 Kucinich	Y	N	Y	Y	N	Y	Y
11 Fudge	Y	Y	Y	Y	N	N	Y
12 **Tiberi**	N	N	N	N	Y	Y	N
13 Sutton	Y	Y	Y	Y	N	N	Y
14 **LaTourette**	N	N	N	N	Y	Y	N
15 Kilroy	Y	Y	Y	Y	N	N	Y
16 Boccieri	Y	Y	N	Y	N	N	Y
17 Ryan	Y	Y	Y	Y	N	N	Y
18 Space	Y	Y	N	N	Y	N	N
OKLAHOMA							
1 **Sullivan**	?	?	?	?	?	?	?
2 Boren	Y	N	N	Y	N	Y	N
3 **Lucas**	N	N	N	N	Y	Y	N
4 **Cole**	N	N	N	N	Y	Y	N
5 **Fallin**	N	N	N	N	Y	Y	N
OREGON							
1 Wu	Y	Y	N	Y	N	Y	Y
2 **Walden**	N	N	N	N	Y	Y	N
3 Blumenauer	Y	N	Y	Y	N	N	Y
4 DeFazio	Y	Y	Y	Y	N	N	Y
5 Schrader	Y	Y	Y	Y	N	N	Y
PENNSYLVANIA							
1 Brady	Y	Y	Y	Y	N	N	Y
2 Fattah	Y	Y	Y	Y	N	N	Y
3 Dahlkemper	Y	Y	Y	N	N	N	Y
4 Altmire	Y	Y	N	Y	N	N	N
5 **Thompson**	N	N	N	N	Y	Y	N
6 **Gerlach**	N	N	N	N	Y	Y	N
7 Sestak	Y	Y	Y	Y	N	N	Y
8 Murphy, P.	Y	Y	N	Y	N	N	Y
9 **Shuster**	N	N	N	N	Y	Y	N
10 Carney	Y	Y	N	N	N	N	Y
11 Kanjorski	Y	Y	Y	Y	N	N	Y
12 Murtha	Y	Y	Y	Y	N	N	Y
13 Schwartz	Y	Y	N	Y	N	N	Y
14 Doyle	Y	Y	Y	Y	N	N	Y
15 **Dent**	N	N	N	N	Y	Y	N
16 **Pitts**	N	N	N	N	Y	Y	N
17 Holden	Y	Y	N	N	N	N	N
18 **Murphy, T.**	N	N	N	N	Y	Y	N
19 **Platts**	N	N	N	N	Y	Y	N
RHODE ISLAND							
1 Kennedy	?	?	?	?	?	?	?
2 Langevin	Y	Y	N	Y	N	N	Y
SOUTH CAROLINA							
1 **Brown**	N	N	N	N	Y	Y	N
2 **Wilson**	N	N	N	N	N	Y	N
3 **Barrett**	N	N	N	N	Y	Y	N
4 **Inglis**	N	N	N	N	Y	Y	Y
5 Spratt	Y	Y	N	Y	N	N	Y
6 Clyburn	Y	Y	?	?	?	?	?
SOUTH DAKOTA							
AL Herseth Sandlin	Y	Y	N	N	Y	N	Y
TENNESSEE							
1 **Roe**	N	N	N	N	Y	Y	N
2 **Duncan**	N	N	Y	Y	N	Y	N
3 **Wamp**	N	N	N	N	N	Y	N
4 Davis	Y	Y	N	Y	?	N	N
5 Cooper	Y	Y	N	N	N	N	Y
6 Gordon	Y	Y	Y	N	N	N	N
7 **Blackburn**	N	N	N	N	Y	Y	N
8 Tanner	Y	Y	N	N	N	N	Y
9 Cohen	Y	Y	Y	Y	N	N	Y

	451	452	453	454	455	456	457
TEXAS							
1 **Gohmert**	N	N	N	N	Y	Y	N
2 **Poe**	N	N	N	Y	Y	Y	N
3 **Johnson, S.**	N	N	N	N	Y	Y	N
4 **Hall**	N	N	N	N	Y	Y	N
5 **Hensarling**	N	N	N	N	Y	Y	N
6 **Barton**	N	N	N	N	Y	Y	N
7 **Culberson**	N	N	N	N	Y	Y	N
8 **Brady**	N	N	N	N	Y	Y	N
9 Green, A.	Y	Y	N	Y	N	N	Y
10 **McCaul**	N	N	N	N	Y	Y	N
11 **Conaway**	N	N	N	N	Y	Y	N
12 **Granger**	N	N	N	N	Y	Y	N
13 **Thornberry**	N	N	N	N	Y	Y	N
14 **Paul**	N	N	Y	N	Y	Y	Y
15 Hinojosa	Y	?	Y	Y	N	N	Y
16 Reyes	Y	Y	?	?	?	?	?
17 Edwards	Y	Y	N	Y	N	N	Y
18 Jackson Lee	Y	Y	+	+	–	–	+
19 **Neugebauer**	N	N	N	N	Y	Y	N
20 Gonzalez	Y	Y	Y	Y	N	N	Y
21 **Smith**	N	N	?	?	?	?	?
22 **Olson**	N	N	N	N	Y	Y	N
23 Rodriguez	Y	Y	N	Y	N	N	Y
24 **Marchant**	N	N	N	N	Y	Y	N
25 Doggett	Y	Y	Y	Y	N	Y	Y
26 **Burgess**	N	N	N	N	Y	Y	N
27 Ortiz	Y	Y	N	Y	N	N	Y
28 Cuellar	Y	Y	N	N	Y	N	N
29 Green, G.	Y	Y	N	Y	N	N	Y
30 Johnson, E.	Y	Y	N	Y	N	N	Y
31 **Carter**	N	N	N	N	Y	Y	N
32 **Sessions**	N	N	N	N	Y	Y	N
UTAH							
1 **Bishop**	N	N	N	N	Y	Y	N
2 Matheson	Y	Y	N	N	N	N	N
3 **Chaffetz**	N	N	N	N	Y	Y	N
VERMONT							
AL Welch	Y	Y	Y	Y	?	N	Y
VIRGINIA							
1 **Wittman**	N	N	N	N	Y	Y	N
2 Nye	Y	Y	N	Y	N	N	Y
3 Scott	Y	Y	Y	Y	N	N	Y
4 **Forbes**	N	N	N	N	Y	Y	N
5 Perriello	Y	Y	Y	Y	N	N	Y
6 **Goodlatte**	N	N	N	N	Y	Y	N
7 **Cantor**	N	N	?	?	Y	Y	N
8 Moran	Y	Y	Y	Y	N	N	Y
9 Boucher	Y	Y	N	Y	N	N	Y
10 **Wolf**	N	N	N	N	Y	Y	N
11 Connolly	Y	Y	N	Y	N	N	Y
WASHINGTON							
1 Inslee	Y	Y	Y	Y	N	N	Y
2 Larsen	Y	Y	N	Y	N	N	Y
3 Baird	Y	Y	N	Y	N	N	N
4 **Hastings**	N	N	N	N	N	Y	N
5 **McMorris Rodgers**	N	N	N	N	N	Y	N
6 Dicks	Y	Y	N	Y	N	N	Y
7 McDermott	Y	Y	Y	Y	N	N	Y
8 **Reichert**	N	N	N	N	N	N	N
9 Smith	Y	Y	N	Y	N	N	Y
WEST VIRGINIA							
1 Mollohan	Y	Y	Y	Y	N	N	Y
2 **Capito**	N	N	N	N	Y	Y	N
3 Rahall	Y	Y	N	Y	N	N	Y
WISCONSIN							
1 **Ryan**	N	N	N	N	Y	Y	N
2 Baldwin	N	Y	Y	Y	N	N	Y
3 Kind	Y	N	N	Y	N	N	Y
4 Moore	Y	N	Y	Y	N	N	Y
5 **Sensenbrenner**	N	N	N	N	Y	Y	N
6 **Petri**	N	N	Y	Y	Y	Y	N
7 Obey	Y	N	Y	Y	N	N	Y
8 Kagen	Y	Y	Y	Y	N	N	Y
WYOMING							
AL **Lummis**	N	N	N	N	Y	Y	N
DELEGATES							
Faleomavaega (A.S.)			Y	Y	N	N	Y
Norton (D.C.)			N	Y	N	N	Y
Bordallo (Guam)			N	Y	N	N	Y
Sablan (N. Marianas)			N	Y	N	N	Y
Pierluisi (P.R.)			N	Y	N	N	Y
Christensen (V.I.)			Y	Y	N	N	Y

IN THE HOUSE | By Vote Number

458. HR 2647. Fiscal 2010 Defense Authorization/Federal Agencies **Fuel Purchase.** Connolly, D-Va., amendment that would allow federal agencies to enter into contracts to purchase a generally available fuel that is not alternative or synthetic or predominantly produced from a non-conventional petroleum source, with some stipulations. Adopted in Committee of the Whole 416-0: R 172-0; D 244-0. June 25, 2009.

459. HR 2647. Fiscal 2010 Defense Authorization/**Recommit.** Forbes, R-Va., motion to recommit the bill to the Armed Services Committee with instructions that it be reported back immediately with language that would increase the amount authorized for missile defense by $1.2 billion, the Army's procurement of weapons and tracked combat vehicles by $798 million, the Air Force's procurement of aircraft by $510 million, and the Army's procurement of aircraft by $92 million. The increases would be offset by a reduction of the same amount for defense environmental cleanup. Motion rejected 170-244: R 157-16; D 13-228. June 25, 2009.

460. HR 2647. Fiscal 2010 Defense Authorization/**Passage.** Passage of the bill that would authorize $681 billion for defense programs in fiscal 2010, including about $130 billion for the wars in Iraq and Afghanistan and other operations. The total includes $185.6 billion for operations and maintenance; $23.3 billion for military construction; and $135.7 billion for military personnel. The overall total includes $27 billion for the Defense Health Program. The bill would authorize a 3.4 percent pay raise for military personnel. It would prohibit detainees at Guantánamo Bay, Cuba, from being transferred to U.S. soil until the president submits a plan to Congress and consults with the governors of affected states. It would require the videotaping of all intelligence interrogations of Defense Department detainees, excluding tactical questioning. Passed 389-22: R 168-2; D 221-20. A "nay" was a vote in support of the president's position. June 25, 2009.

461. **Open Rules for Appropriations Bills/Motion to Table.** Dicks, D-Wash., motion to table (kill) the Price, R-Ga., appeal of the ruling of the chair that the draft resolution by Price does not constitute a point of privilege under Rule IX of the House. The draft resolution would require the House Rules Committee to report open rules for all regular appropriations bills in the 111th Congress and call on the House to not require pre-printing of amendments. Motion agreed to 245-174: R 0-171; D 245-3. June 25, 2009.

462. HR 2996. Fiscal 2010 Interior-Environment Appropriations/**Previous Question.** Polis, D-Colo., motion to order the previous question (thus ending debate and possibility of amendment) on adoption of the rule (H Res 578) that would provide for House floor consideration of the bill that would appropriate $32.7 billion in fiscal 2010 for the Interior Department, EPA and related agencies. Motion agreed to 241-182: R 0-174; D 241-8. June 25, 2009.

463. HR 2996. Fiscal 2010 Interior-Environment Appropriations/**Rule.** Adoption of the rule (H Res 578) to provide for House floor consideration of the bill that would appropriate $32.7 billion in fiscal 2010 for the Interior Department, EPA and related agencies. Adopted 238-184: R 1-172; D 237-12. June 25, 2009.

	458	459	460	461	462	463
ALABAMA						
1 **Bonner**	Y	Y	Y	N	N	N
2 Bright	Y	Y	Y	Y	Y	N
3 **Rogers**	Y	Y	Y	N	N	N
4 **Aderholt**	Y	Y	?	N	N	N
5 Griffith	Y	Y	N	Y	Y	Y
6 **Bachus**	Y	Y	Y	N	N	N
7 Davis	Y	Y	Y	Y	Y	Y
ALASKA						
AL **Young**	Y	Y	Y	N	N	N
ARIZONA						
1 Kirkpatrick	Y	Y	Y	Y	Y	N
2 **Franks**	Y	Y	Y	N	N	N
3 **Shadegg**	Y	Y	Y	N	N	N
4 Pastor	Y	N	Y	Y	Y	Y
5 Mitchell	Y	N	Y	Y	N	N
6 **Flake**	?	?	?	?	?	?
7 Grijalva	Y	N	Y	Y	Y	Y
8 Giffords	Y	N	Y	Y	Y	Y
ARKANSAS						
1 Berry	Y	N	Y	Y	Y	Y
2 Snyder	Y	N	Y	Y	Y	Y
3 **Boozman**	Y	Y	Y	N	N	N
4 Ross	Y	N	Y	Y	Y	Y
CALIFORNIA						
1 Thompson	Y	N	Y	Y	Y	Y
2 **Herger**	Y	Y	?	N	N	N
3 **Lungren**	Y	Y	Y	N	N	N
4 **McClintock**	Y	Y	Y	N	N	N
5 Matsui	Y	N	Y	Y	Y	Y
6 Woolsey	Y	N	N	Y	Y	Y
7 Miller, George	Y	N	N	Y	Y	?
8 Pelosi						
9 Lee	Y	N	N	Y	Y	Y
10 Tauscher	Y	N	Y	Y	Y	Y
11 McNerney	Y	N	Y	Y	Y	Y
12 Speier	Y	N	Y	Y	Y	Y
13 Stark	Y	N	Y	Y	Y	Y
14 Eshoo	Y	N	Y	Y	Y	Y
15 Honda	Y	N	Y	Y	Y	Y
16 Lofgren	+	–	Y	Y	Y	Y
17 Farr	Y	N	Y	Y	Y	Y
18 Cardoza	Y	N	Y	Y	Y	Y
19 **Radanovich**	Y	Y	Y	N	N	N
20 Costa	Y	N	Y	N	Y	Y
21 **Nunes**	Y	Y	Y	N	N	N
22 **McCarthy**	Y	Y	Y	N	N	N
23 Capps	Y	N	Y	Y	Y	Y
24 **Gallegly**	Y	Y	Y	N	N	N
25 **McKeon**	Y	Y	Y	N	N	N
26 **Dreier**	Y	Y	Y	N	N	N
27 Sherman	Y	N	Y	Y	Y	Y
28 Berman	+	N	Y	Y	Y	Y
29 Schiff	Y	N	Y	Y	Y	Y
30 Waxman	Y	N	N	Y	Y	Y
31 Becerra	+	–	+	Y	Y	Y
32 Vacant						
33 Watson	Y	N	Y	Y	Y	Y
34 Roybal-Allard	Y	N	Y	Y	Y	Y
35 Waters	Y	N	N	Y	Y	Y
36 Harman	Y	N	Y	Y	Y	Y
37 Richardson	Y	N	Y	Y	Y	Y
38 Napolitano	Y	N	Y	Y	Y	Y
39 Sánchez, Linda	Y	N	Y	Y	Y	Y
40 **Royce**	Y	Y	Y	N	N	N
41 **Lewis**	Y	Y	Y	N	N	N
42 **Miller, Gary**	Y	Y	Y	N	N	N
43 Baca	Y	N	Y	Y	Y	Y
44 **Calvert**	Y	Y	Y	N	N	N
45 **Bono Mack**	Y	Y	Y	N	N	N
46 **Rohrabacher**	Y	Y	Y	N	N	N
47 Sanchez, Loretta	?	N	Y	Y	Y	Y
48 **Campbell**	Y	Y	Y	N	N	N
49 **Issa**	Y	Y	Y	N	N	N
50 **Bilbray**	Y	Y	Y	N	N	N
51 Filner	Y	N	N	Y	Y	Y
52 **Hunter**	Y	Y	Y	N	N	N
53 Davis	Y	N	Y	Y	Y	Y

	458	459	460	461	462	463
COLORADO						
1 DeGette	Y	N	Y	Y	Y	Y
2 Polis	Y	N	N	?	?	?
3 Salazar	Y	N	Y	Y	Y	Y
4 Markey	Y	N	Y	Y	Y	Y
5 **Lamborn**	Y	Y	N	N	N	N
6 **Coffman**	Y	Y	Y	N	N	N
7 Perlmutter	Y	N	Y	Y	Y	Y
CONNECTICUT						
1 Larson	Y	N	+	Y	Y	Y
2 Courtney	Y	N	Y	Y	Y	Y
3 DeLauro	Y	N	Y	Y	Y	Y
4 Himes	Y	N	Y	Y	Y	Y
5 Murphy	Y	N	Y	Y	Y	Y
DELAWARE						
AL **Castle**	Y	Y	Y	N	N	N
FLORIDA						
1 **Miller**	Y	Y	Y	N	N	N
2 Boyd	Y	N	Y	Y	Y	Y
3 Brown	Y	N	P	Y	Y	Y
4 **Crenshaw**	Y	Y	Y	N	N	N
5 **Brown-Waite**	Y	Y	Y	N	N	N
6 **Stearns**	Y	Y	N	N	N	N
7 **Mica**	Y	Y	Y	N	N	N
8 Grayson	Y	N	Y	Y	Y	Y
9 **Bilirakis**	Y	Y	Y	N	N	N
10 **Young**	Y	Y	Y	N	N	N
11 Castor	Y	N	Y	Y	Y	Y
12 **Putnam**	?	?	?	N	N	N
13 **Buchanan**	Y	Y	Y	N	N	N
14 **Mack**	Y	Y	N	N	N	N
15 **Posey**	Y	Y	Y	N	N	N
16 **Rooney**	Y	Y	N	N	N	N
17 Meek	Y	N	Y	Y	Y	Y
18 **Ros-Lehtinen**	Y	Y	Y	N	N	N
19 Wexler	Y	N	Y	Y	Y	Y
20 Wasserman Schultz	Y	N	Y	Y	Y	Y
21 **Diaz-Balart, L.**	?	?	?	N	N	N
22 Klein	Y	N	Y	Y	Y	Y
23 Hastings	?	?	?	?	?	?
24 Kosmas	Y	N	Y	Y	Y	?
25 **Diaz-Balart, M.**	Y	Y	Y	N	N	N
GEORGIA						
1 **Kingston**	Y	Y	Y	N	N	N
2 Bishop	Y	N	Y	Y	Y	Y
3 **Westmoreland**	Y	Y	Y	N	N	N
4 Johnson	Y	N	Y	Y	Y	Y
5 Lewis	?	?	?	?	?	?
6 **Price**	Y	Y	Y	N	N	N
7 **Linder**	Y	Y	N	N	N	N
8 Marshall	Y	Y	Y	Y	Y	Y
9 **Deal**	Y	N	Y	?	N	N
10 **Broun**	Y	Y	N	N	N	N
11 **Gingrey**	Y	Y	Y	N	N	N
12 Barrow	Y	N	Y	Y	Y	Y
13 Scott	Y	N	Y	Y	Y	Y
HAWAII						
1 Abercrombie	Y	N	Y	Y	Y	Y
2 Hirono	Y	N	Y	Y	Y	Y
IDAHO						
1 **Minnick**	Y	N	N	N	N	N
2 **Simpson**	Y	N	Y	N	N	N
ILLINOIS						
1 Rush	Y	N	Y	Y	Y	Y
2 Jackson	Y	N	N	Y	Y	Y
3 Lipinski	Y	N	Y	Y	Y	Y
4 Gutierrez	?	?	?	Y	Y	Y
5 Quigley	Y	N	Y	Y	Y	Y
6 **Roskam**	Y	Y	Y	N	N	N
7 Davis	Y	N	Y	Y	Y	Y
8 Bean	Y	N	Y	Y	Y	Y
9 Schakowsky	Y	N	Y	Y	Y	Y
10 **Kirk**	Y	Y	Y	?	N	N
11 Halvorson	Y	N	Y	Y	Y	Y
12 Costello	Y	N	Y	Y	Y	Y
13 **Biggert**	Y	Y	N	N	N	N
14 Foster	Y	N	Y	Y	Y	Y
15 **Johnson**	Y	Y	Y	N	N	N

	458	459	460	461	462	463
16 **Manzullo**	Y	Y	Y	N	N	N
17 Hare	Y	N	Y	Y	Y	Y
18 **Schock**	Y	Y	Y	N	N	N
19 **Shimkus**	Y	Y	Y	N	N	Y
INDIANA						
1 Visclosky	Y	N	Y	Y	Y	Y
2 Donnelly	Y	Y	Y	Y	Y	Y
3 **Souder**	Y	Y	Y	N	N	N
4 **Buyer**	Y	Y	?	N	N	N
5 **Burton**	Y	Y	Y	N	N	N
6 **Pence**	Y	Y	Y	N	N	N
7 Carson	Y	N	Y	Y	Y	Y
8 Ellsworth	Y	N	Y	Y	Y	Y
9 Hill	Y	N	Y	N	N	N
IOWA						
1 Braley	Y	N	Y	Y	Y	Y
2 Loebsack	Y	N	Y	Y	Y	Y
3 Boswell	Y	N	Y	Y	Y	Y
4 **Latham**	Y	Y	Y	N	N	N
5 **King**	Y	Y	Y	N	N	N
KANSAS						
1 **Moran**	Y	Y	Y	N	N	N
2 **Jenkins**	Y	Y	Y	N	N	N
3 Moore	Y	N	Y	Y	Y	Y
4 **Tiahrt**	Y	Y	Y	N	N	?
KENTUCKY						
1 **Whitfield**	Y	N	Y	N	N	N
2 **Guthrie**	Y	Y	Y	N	N	N
3 Yarmuth	Y	N	Y	Y	Y	Y
4 **Davis**	Y	Y	Y	N	N	N
5 **Rogers**	Y	Y	Y	N	N	N
6 Chandler	Y	N	Y	Y	Y	Y
LOUISIANA						
1 **Scalise**	Y	Y	Y	N	N	N
2 **Cao**	?	?	?	N	N	N
3 Melancon	Y	N	Y	Y	N	N
4 **Fleming**	Y	Y	Y	N	N	N
5 **Alexander**	Y	Y	Y	N	N	N
6 **Cassidy**	Y	Y	Y	N	N	N
7 **Boustany**	Y	Y	Y	N	N	N
MAINE						
1 Pingree	Y	N	Y	Y	Y	Y
2 Michaud	Y	N	N	Y	Y	Y
MARYLAND						
1 Kratovil	Y	N	Y	Y	Y	Y
2 Ruppersberger	Y	N	Y	Y	Y	Y
3 Sarbanes	Y	N	+	Y	Y	Y
4 Edwards	Y	N	Y	Y	Y	Y
5 Hoyer	Y	N	Y	Y	Y	Y
6 **Bartlett**	Y	Y	Y	N	N	N
7 Cummings	Y	N	Y	Y	Y	Y
8 Van Hollen	Y	N	Y	Y	Y	Y
MASSACHUSETTS						
1 Olver	Y	?	N	Y	Y	Y
2 Neal	Y	N	Y	Y	Y	Y
3 McGovern	Y	N	Y	Y	Y	Y
4 Frank	Y	N	N	Y	Y	Y
5 Tsongas	Y	N	Y	Y	Y	Y
6 Tierney	Y	N	N	Y	Y	Y
7 Markey	Y	N	?	Y	Y	Y
8 Capuano	+	−	+	Y	Y	Y
9 Lynch	Y	N	Y	Y	Y	Y
10 Delahunt	Y	N	Y	Y	Y	Y
MICHIGAN						
1 Stupak	Y	N	Y	Y	Y	Y
2 **Hoekstra**	Y	Y	Y	N	N	N
3 **Ehlers**	Y	Y	Y	?	N	N
4 **Camp**	Y	Y	Y	N	N	N
5 Kildee	Y	N	Y	Y	Y	Y
6 **Upton**	Y	Y	Y	N	N	N
7 Schauer	Y	N	Y	Y	Y	Y
8 **Rogers**	Y	Y	Y	N	N	N
9 Peters	Y	N	Y	Y	Y	Y
10 **Miller**	Y	Y	Y	N	N	N
11 **McCotter**	Y	Y	Y	N	N	N
12 Levin	Y	N	Y	Y	Y	Y
13 Kilpatrick	Y	N	Y	Y	Y	Y
14 Conyers	+	−	Y	?	?	Y
15 Dingell	Y	N	Y	Y	Y	Y
MINNESOTA						
1 Walz	Y	N	Y	Y	Y	Y
2 **Kline**	Y	Y	Y	N	N	N
3 **Paulsen**	Y	Y	Y	N	N	N
4 McCollum	Y	N	Y	Y	Y	Y

	458	459	460	461	462	463
5 Ellison	Y	N	N	Y	Y	Y
6 **Bachmann**	Y	Y	Y	N	?	N
7 Peterson	Y	N	Y	Y	Y	Y
8 Oberstar	Y	N	Y	Y	Y	Y
MISSISSIPPI						
1 Childers	Y	N	Y	Y	N	N
2 Thompson	Y	N	Y	Y	Y	Y
3 **Harper**	Y	Y	Y	N	N	N
4 Taylor	Y	N	Y	Y	N	N
MISSOURI						
1 Clay	Y	N	Y	Y	Y	Y
2 **Akin**	Y	Y	Y	N	N	N
3 Carnahan	Y	N	?	Y	Y	Y
4 Skelton	Y	N	Y	Y	Y	Y
5 Cleaver	Y	N	Y	Y	Y	Y
6 **Graves**	Y	Y	Y	N	N	N
7 **Blunt**	Y	Y	Y	?	N	N
8 **Emerson**	Y	Y	Y	N	N	N
9 **Luetkemeyer**	Y	Y	Y	N	N	N
MONTANA						
AL **Rehberg**	Y	Y	Y	N	N	N
NEBRASKA						
1 **Fortenberry**	Y	Y	Y	N	N	N
2 **Terry**	Y	Y	Y	?	N	N
3 **Smith**	Y	Y	Y	N	N	N
NEVADA						
1 Berkley	Y	N	Y	Y	Y	Y
2 **Heller**	Y	Y	Y	N	N	N
3 Titus	Y	N	Y	Y	Y	Y
NEW HAMPSHIRE						
1 Shea-Porter	Y	N	Y	Y	Y	Y
2 Hodes	Y	N	Y	Y	Y	Y
NEW JERSEY						
1 Andrews	Y	N	Y	Y	Y	Y
2 **LoBiondo**	Y	Y	Y	N	N	N
3 Adler	Y	Y	Y	Y	Y	Y
4 **Smith**	Y	Y	Y	N	N	N
5 **Garrett**	Y	Y	Y	N	N	N
6 Pallone	Y	N	Y	Y	Y	Y
7 **Lance**	Y	Y	Y	N	N	N
8 Pascrell	Y	N	Y	Y	Y	Y
9 Rothman	Y	N	Y	Y	Y	Y
10 Payne	Y	N	Y	Y	Y	Y
11 **Frelinghuysen**	Y	Y	Y	N	N	N
12 Holt	Y	N	Y	Y	Y	Y
13 Sires	Y	N	Y	Y	Y	Y
NEW MEXICO						
1 Heinrich	Y	N	Y	Y	Y	Y
2 Teague	Y	Y	Y	Y	Y	Y
3 Lujan	Y	N	Y	Y	Y	Y
NEW YORK						
1 Bishop	Y	N	Y	Y	Y	Y
2 Israel	Y	N	Y	Y	Y	Y
3 **King**	Y	Y	Y	N	N	N
4 McCarthy	Y	N	Y	Y	Y	Y
5 Ackerman	Y	N	Y	Y	Y	Y
6 Meeks	Y	N	Y	Y	Y	Y
7 Crowley	+	−	+	Y	Y	Y
8 Nadler	Y	N	Y	Y	Y	Y
9 Weiner	+	−	Y	Y	Y	Y
10 Towns	Y	N	Y	Y	Y	Y
11 Clarke	Y	N	Y	Y	Y	Y
12 Velázquez	?	?	?	Y	Y	Y
13 McMahon	Y	Y	Y	Y	Y	Y
14 Maloney	Y	N	Y	Y	Y	Y
15 Rangel	Y	N	Y	Y	Y	Y
16 Serrano	Y	N	N	Y	Y	Y
17 Engel	Y	N	Y	?	Y	Y
18 Lowey	Y	N	Y	Y	Y	Y
19 Hall	Y	N	Y	Y	Y	Y
20 Murphy	Y	N	Y	Y	Y	N
21 Tonko	Y	N	Y	Y	Y	Y
22 Hinchey	Y	N	Y	Y	Y	Y
23 **McHugh**	Y	Y	Y	N	N	N
24 Arcuri	Y	N	Y	Y	Y	Y
25 Maffei	?	N	Y	Y	Y	Y
26 **Lee**	Y	Y	Y	N	N	N
27 Higgins	Y	N	Y	Y	Y	Y
28 Slaughter	Y	N	Y	?	Y	Y
29 Massa	Y	N	Y	Y	Y	Y
NORTH CAROLINA						
1 Butterfield	Y	N	Y	Y	?	Y
2 Etheridge	Y	N	Y	Y	Y	Y
3 **Jones**	Y	N	Y	N	N	N
4 Price	Y	N	Y	Y	Y	Y

	458	459	460	461	462	463
5 **Foxx**	Y	Y	Y	N	N	N
6 **Coble**	Y	Y	Y	N	N	N
7 McIntyre	Y	N	Y	Y	Y	Y
8 Kissell	Y	N	Y	Y	Y	Y
9 **Myrick**	Y	Y	Y	N	N	N
10 **McHenry**	Y	Y	Y	N	N	N
11 Shuler	Y	N	Y	Y	N	N
12 Watt	Y	N	Y	Y	Y	Y
13 Miller	Y	N	Y	Y	Y	Y
NORTH DAKOTA						
AL Pomeroy	Y	N	Y	Y	Y	Y
OHIO						
1 Driehaus	Y	N	Y	Y	Y	Y
2 **Schmidt**	Y	N	Y	N	N	N
3 **Turner**	Y	Y	Y	N	N	N
4 **Jordan**	Y	Y	Y	N	N	N
5 **Latta**	Y	Y	Y	N	N	N
6 Wilson	Y	N	Y	Y	Y	Y
7 **Austria**	Y	Y	Y	N	N	N
8 **Boehner**	Y	Y	Y	N	N	N
9 Kaptur	Y	N	Y	Y	Y	Y
10 Kucinich	Y	N	N	Y	Y	Y
11 Fudge	Y	N	Y	Y	Y	Y
12 **Tiberi**	Y	Y	Y	N	N	N
13 Sutton	Y	N	Y	Y	Y	Y
14 **LaTourette**	Y	Y	Y	N	N	N
15 Kilroy	Y	N	Y	Y	Y	Y
16 Boccieri	Y	N	Y	Y	Y	Y
17 Ryan	Y	N	Y	Y	Y	Y
18 Space	Y	Y	Y	Y	Y	Y
OKLAHOMA						
1 **Sullivan**	?	?	?	?	?	?
2 Boren	Y	N	Y	Y	Y	Y
3 **Lucas**	Y	Y	Y	N	N	N
4 **Cole**	Y	Y	Y	N	N	N
5 **Fallin**	Y	Y	Y	N	N	N
OREGON						
1 Wu	Y	N	Y	Y	Y	Y
2 **Walden**	Y	Y	Y	N	N	N
3 Blumenauer	Y	N	Y	Y	Y	Y
4 DeFazio	Y	N	Y	Y	Y	Y
5 Schrader	Y	N	Y	Y	Y	Y
PENNSYLVANIA						
1 Brady	Y	N	Y	Y	Y	Y
2 Fattah	Y	N	Y	Y	Y	Y
3 Dahlkemper	Y	N	Y	Y	Y	Y
4 Altmire	Y	N	Y	Y	Y	Y
5 **Thompson**	Y	Y	Y	N	N	N
6 **Gerlach**	Y	Y	Y	N	?	?
7 Sestak	Y	N	Y	Y	Y	Y
8 Murphy, P.	Y	N	Y	Y	Y	Y
9 **Shuster**	Y	Y	Y	N	N	N
10 Carney	Y	Y	Y	Y	Y	Y
11 Kanjorski	Y	N	Y	Y	Y	Y
12 Murtha	Y	N	Y	Y	Y	Y
13 Schwartz	Y	N	Y	Y	Y	Y
14 Doyle	Y	N	Y	Y	Y	Y
15 **Dent**	Y	Y	Y	N	N	N
16 **Pitts**	Y	Y	Y	N	N	N
17 Holden	Y	N	Y	Y	Y	Y
18 **Murphy, T.**	Y	Y	Y	N	N	N
19 **Platts**	Y	Y	Y	N	N	N
RHODE ISLAND						
1 Kennedy	?	?	?	?	?	?
2 Langevin	Y	N	Y	Y	Y	Y
SOUTH CAROLINA						
1 **Brown**	Y	Y	Y	N	N	N
2 **Wilson**	Y	Y	Y	N	N	N
3 **Barrett**	Y	N	Y	N	N	N
4 **Inglis**	Y	Y	Y	N	N	N
5 Spratt	Y	N	Y	Y	Y	Y
6 Clyburn	?	N	Y	Y	Y	Y
SOUTH DAKOTA						
AL Herseth Sandlin	Y	Y	Y	Y	Y	Y
TENNESSEE						
1 **Roe**	Y	Y	Y	N	N	N
2 **Duncan**	Y	N	N	N	N	N
3 **Wamp**	Y	N	Y	N	N	N
4 Davis	Y	N	Y	Y	Y	Y
5 Cooper	Y	N	Y	Y	Y	Y
6 Gordon	Y	N	Y	Y	Y	Y
7 **Blackburn**	Y	Y	Y	N	N	N
8 Tanner	Y	N	Y	Y	Y	Y
9 Cohen	Y	N	Y	Y	Y	Y

	458	459	460	461	462	463
TEXAS						
1 **Gohmert**	Y	Y	Y	N	N	N
2 **Poe**	Y	Y	Y	N	N	N
3 **Johnson, S.**	Y	Y	Y	N	N	N
4 **Hall**	Y	Y	Y	N	N	N
5 **Hensarling**	Y	Y	Y	N	N	N
6 **Barton**	Y	Y	Y	N	N	N
7 **Culberson**	Y	Y	Y	N	N	N
8 **Brady**	Y	Y	Y	N	N	N
9 Green, A.	Y	N	Y	Y	Y	Y
10 **McCaul**	Y	Y	Y	N	N	N
11 **Conaway**	Y	Y	Y	N	N	N
12 **Granger**	Y	Y	Y	N	N	N
13 **Thornberry**	Y	Y	Y	N	N	N
14 **Paul**	Y	N	N	N	N	N
15 Hinojosa	Y	N	Y	Y	Y	Y
16 Reyes	?	?	?	Y	Y	Y
17 Edwards	Y	N	Y	Y	Y	Y
18 Jackson Lee	+	−	Y	Y	Y	Y
19 **Neugebauer**	Y	Y	Y	N	N	N
20 Gonzalez	Y	N	Y	Y	Y	Y
21 **Smith**	?	Y	Y	N	N	N
22 **Olson**	Y	Y	Y	N	N	N
23 Rodriguez	Y	N	Y	Y	Y	Y
24 **Marchant**	Y	Y	Y	N	N	N
25 Doggett	Y	N	Y	Y	Y	Y
26 **Burgess**	Y	Y	Y	N	N	N
27 Ortiz	Y	N	Y	Y	Y	Y
28 Cuellar	Y	N	Y	Y	Y	Y
29 Green, G.	Y	N	Y	Y	Y	Y
30 Johnson, E.	Y	N	Y	Y	Y	Y
31 **Carter**	Y	Y	Y	N	N	N
32 **Sessions**	Y	Y	Y	N	N	N
UTAH						
1 **Bishop**	Y	Y	Y	N	N	N
2 Matheson	Y	N	Y	Y	Y	Y
3 **Chaffetz**	Y	Y	Y	N	N	N
VERMONT						
AL Welch	Y	N	N	Y	Y	Y
VIRGINIA						
1 **Wittman**	Y	Y	Y	N	N	N
2 Nye	Y	N	Y	Y	N	N
3 Scott	Y	N	Y	Y	Y	Y
4 **Forbes**	Y	Y	Y	N	N	N
5 Perriello	Y	Y	Y	Y	Y	N
6 **Goodlatte**	Y	Y	Y	N	N	N
7 **Cantor**	Y	Y	Y	N	N	N
8 Moran	Y	N	Y	Y	Y	Y
9 Boucher	Y	N	Y	Y	Y	Y
10 **Wolf**	Y	Y	Y	N	N	N
11 Connolly	Y	N	Y	Y	Y	Y
WASHINGTON						
1 Inslee	Y	N	Y	Y	Y	Y
2 Larsen	Y	N	Y	Y	Y	Y
3 Baird	Y	N	Y	Y	Y	Y
4 **Hastings**	Y	N	Y	N	N	N
5 **McMorris Rodgers**	Y	N	Y	N	N	N
6 Dicks	Y	N	Y	Y	Y	Y
7 McDermott	Y	N	Y	Y	Y	Y
8 **Reichert**	Y	N	Y	N	N	?
9 Smith	Y	N	Y	Y	Y	Y
WEST VIRGINIA						
1 Mollohan	Y	N	Y	Y	Y	Y
2 **Capito**	Y	Y	Y	N	N	N
3 Rahall	Y	N	Y	Y	Y	Y
WISCONSIN						
1 **Ryan**	Y	Y	Y	N	N	N
2 Baldwin	Y	N	N	Y	Y	Y
3 Kind	Y	N	Y	Y	Y	Y
4 Moore	Y	N	N	Y	Y	Y
5 **Sensenbrenner**	Y	Y	Y	N	N	N
6 **Petri**	Y	Y	Y	N	N	N
7 Obey	Y	N	Y	Y	Y	Y
8 Kagen	Y	N	Y	Y	Y	Y
WYOMING						
AL **Lummis**	Y	N	Y	N	N	N
DELEGATES						
Faleomavaega (A.S.)	Y					
Norton (D.C.)	Y					
Bordallo (Guam)	Y					
Sablan (N. Marianas)	Y					
Pierluisi (P.R.)	Y					
Christensen (V.I.)	Y					

IN THE HOUSE | By Vote Number

464. **S Con Res 31. Adjournment/Adoption.** Adoption of the concurrent resolution that would provide for adjournment of the House until 2 p.m. Tuesday, July 7, 2009, and the Senate until 12 p.m. Monday, July 6, 2009. Adopted 243-180: R 4-169; D 239-11. June 26, 2009.

465. **HR 2454. Greenhouse Gas Emissions/Previous Question.** Matsui, D-Calif., motion to order the previous question (thus ending debate and possibility of amendment) on adoption of the rule (H Res 587) that would provide for House floor consideration of a bill that would establish a system in which greenhouse gases would be limited and allowances for emissions could be purchased. Motion agreed to 232-189: R 0-173; D 232-16. June 26, 2009.

466. **HR 2454. Greenhouse Gas Emissions/Rule.** Adoption of the rule (H Res 587) to provide for House floor consideration of a bill that would establish a system in which greenhouse gases would be limited and allowances for emissions could be purchased. Adopted 217-205: R 0-175; D 217-30. June 26, 2009.

467. **HR 2996. Fiscal 2010 Interior-Environment Appropriations/Carson City Fire Department.** Heller, R-Nev., amendment that would bar the use of funds appropriated in the bill for the construction of a fire facility on land managed by the Bureau of Land Management located east of the corner of South Edmonds Drive and Koontz Lane in Carson City, Nev. Rejected in Committee of the Whole 202-225: R 171-1; D 31-224. June 26, 2009.

468. **HR 2996. Fiscal 2010 Interior-Environment Appropriations/Funding Reduction.** Jordan, R-Ohio, amendment that would reduce overall spending in the bill by $5.75 billion. Rejected in Committee of the Whole 169-259: R 155-20; D 14-239. A "nay" was a vote in support of the president's position. June 26, 2009.

469. **HR 2996. Fiscal 2010 Interior-Environment Appropriations/EPA Funding Reduction.** Stearns, R-Fla., amendment that would reduce the amount provided for the EPA by 38 percent. Rejected in Committee of the Whole 170-261: R 162-14; D 8-247. A "nay" was a vote in support of the president's position. June 26, 2009.

470. **HR 2996. Fiscal 2010 Interior-Environment Appropriations/Good Fellow Lodge Restoration.** Flake, R-Ariz., amendment that would bar funds appropriated in the bill for National Park Service construction from being used for a project to restore Good Fellow Lodge at Indiana Dunes National Lakeshore in Porter, Ind. Rejected in Committee of the Whole 123-305: R 117-59; D 6-246. June 26, 2009.

	464	465	466	467	468	469	470
ALABAMA							
1 Bonner	N	N	N	Y	Y	Y	N
2 Bright	N	Y	N	Y	Y	Y	Y
3 Rogers	N	N	N	Y	Y	Y	N
4 Aderholt	N	N	N	Y	Y	Y	N
5 Griffith	N	N	N	Y	N	N	N
6 Bachus	N	N	N	Y	Y	Y	N
7 Davis	Y	Y	Y	N	N	N	N
ALASKA							
AL Young	N	N	N	Y	N	Y	N
ARIZONA							
1 Kirkpatrick	Y	Y	Y	N	Y	N	N
2 Franks	N	N	N	Y	Y	Y	Y
3 Shadegg	N	N	N	Y	Y	Y	Y
4 Pastor	Y	Y	Y	N	N	N	N
5 Mitchell	N	N	N	Y	Y	Y	N
6 Flake	?	?	?	?	?	?	?
7 Grijalva	Y	Y	Y	N	N	N	N
8 Giffords	Y	Y	Y	Y	Y	N	Y
ARKANSAS							
1 Berry	Y	Y	Y	N	N	N	N
2 Snyder	Y	Y	Y	N	N	N	N
3 Boozman	N	N	N	Y	Y	Y	N
4 Ross	Y	Y	N	N	N	N	N
CALIFORNIA							
1 Thompson	Y	Y	Y	N	N	N	N
2 Herger	N	N	Y	Y	Y	Y	Y
3 Lungren	N	N	N	Y	Y	Y	Y
4 McClintock	N	N	N	Y	Y	Y	Y
5 Matsui	Y	Y	Y	N	N	N	N
6 Woolsey	Y	+	Y	N	N	N	N
7 Miller, George	Y	Y	Y	N	N	N	N
8 Pelosi							
9 Lee	Y	Y	Y	N	N	N	N
10 Tauscher	Y	Y	Y	N	N	N	N
11 McNerney	Y	Y	Y	N	N	N	N
12 Speier	Y	Y	Y	N	N	N	N
13 Stark	Y	Y	N	N	N	N	N
14 Eshoo	Y	Y	Y	N	N	N	N
15 Honda	Y	Y	Y	N	N	N	N
16 Lofgren	Y	Y	Y	N	N	N	N
17 Farr	Y	Y	Y	N	?	N	N
18 Cardoza	Y	Y	Y	N	N	N	N
19 Radanovich	N	?	N	Y	Y	Y	Y
20 Costa	Y	Y	Y	N	N	N	N
21 Nunes	N	N	N	Y	Y	Y	Y
22 McCarthy	N	N	N	Y	Y	Y	Y
23 Capps	Y	Y	Y	N	N	N	N
24 Gallegly	N	N	N	Y	Y	Y	Y
25 McKeon	N	N	N	Y	Y	Y	Y
26 Dreier	N	N	N	Y	Y	Y	Y
27 Sherman	Y	Y	Y	N	N	N	N
28 Berman	Y	Y	Y	N	N	N	N
29 Schiff	Y	Y	Y	N	N	N	N
30 Waxman	Y	Y	?	N	N	N	?
31 Becerra	Y	Y	Y	N	N	N	N
32 Vacant							
33 Watson	Y	Y	Y	N	N	N	N
34 Roybal-Allard	Y	Y	Y	N	N	N	N
35 Waters	Y	Y	Y	N	N	N	N
36 Harman	Y	Y	Y	N	N	N	N
37 Richardson	Y	Y	Y	N	N	N	N
38 Napolitano	Y	Y	Y	N	N	N	N
39 Sánchez, Linda	Y	Y	Y	N	N	N	N
40 Royce	N	N	N	Y	Y	Y	Y
41 Lewis	N	N	N	Y	Y	Y	Y
42 Miller, Gary	N	N	N	?	Y	Y	N
43 Baca	Y	Y	Y	N	N	N	N
44 Calvert	N	N	N	Y	Y	Y	N
45 Bono Mack	N	N	N	Y	Y	Y	Y
46 Rohrabacher	N	N	N	Y	Y	Y	Y
47 Sanchez, Loretta	Y	Y	Y	N	N	N	N
48 Campbell	N	N	N	Y	Y	Y	Y
49 Issa	N	N	N	Y	Y	Y	Y
50 Bilbray	N	N	N	Y	Y	Y	Y
51 Filner	Y	Y	Y	N	N	N	N
52 Hunter	N	N	N	Y	Y	Y	Y
53 Davis	Y	Y	Y	N	N	N	N

	464	465	466	467	468	469	470
COLORADO							
1 DeGette	Y	Y	Y	N	N	N	N
2 Polis	Y	Y	Y	N	N	N	N
3 Salazar	Y	Y	N	N	N	N	N
4 Markey	Y	Y	Y	N	N	N	N
5 Lamborn	N	N	N	Y	Y	Y	Y
6 Coffman	N	N	N	Y	Y	Y	Y
7 Perlmutter	Y	Y	Y	N	N	N	N
CONNECTICUT							
1 Larson	Y	Y	Y	N	N	N	N
2 Courtney	Y	Y	Y	N	N	N	N
3 DeLauro	Y	Y	Y	N	N	N	N
4 Himes	Y	Y	Y	N	N	N	N
5 Murphy	Y	Y	Y	N	N	N	N
DELAWARE							
AL Castle	N	N	N	Y	N	Y	Y
FLORIDA							
1 Miller	N	N	N	Y	Y	Y	Y
2 Boyd	Y	Y	Y	N	N	N	N
3 Brown	Y	Y	Y	N	?	N	N
4 Crenshaw	N	N	N	Y	Y	Y	N
5 Brown-Waite	N	N	N	Y	Y	Y	Y
6 Stearns	N	N	N	Y	Y	Y	N
7 Mica	N	N	N	Y	Y	Y	N
8 Grayson	Y	Y	Y	N	N	N	N
9 Bilirakis	N	N	N	Y	Y	Y	Y
10 Young	N	N	N	Y	N	Y	N
11 Castor	Y	Y	Y	N	N	N	N
12 Putnam	N	N	N	Y	Y	Y	Y
13 Buchanan	N	N	N	?	Y	Y	N
14 Mack	N	N	N	Y	Y	Y	Y
15 Posey	N	N	N	Y	Y	Y	Y
16 Rooney	N	N	N	Y	Y	Y	N
17 Meek	Y	Y	Y	N	N	N	N
18 Ros-Lehtinen	Y	Y	Y	N	N	N	N
19 Wexler	Y	Y	Y	N	N	N	?
20 Wasserman Schultz	Y	Y	Y	N	N	N	N
21 Diaz-Balart, L.	N	N	N	?	Y	Y	N
22 Klein	Y	Y	Y	N	N	N	N
23 Hastings	?	?	?	?	?	?	?
24 Kosmas	Y	Y	Y	N	Y	N	N
25 Diaz-Balart, M.	N	N	N	Y	Y	Y	N
GEORGIA							
1 Kingston	N	N	N	Y	Y	Y	Y
2 Bishop	Y	Y	Y	N	N	N	N
3 Westmoreland	N	N	N	Y	Y	Y	Y
4 Johnson	Y	Y	Y	N	N	N	N
5 Lewis	+	+	?	?	?	?	?
6 Price	N	N	N	Y	Y	Y	Y
7 Linder	N	N	N	Y	Y	Y	Y
8 Marshall	Y	Y	Y	N	N	N	N
9 Deal	N	N	N	Y	Y	Y	Y
10 Broun	N	N	N	Y	Y	Y	Y
11 Gingrey	N	N	N	Y	Y	Y	Y
12 Barrow	Y	N	N	N	N	N	N
13 Scott	Y	Y	Y	N	N	N	N
HAWAII							
1 Abercrombie	Y	Y	Y	N	N	N	N
2 Hirono	Y	Y	Y	N	N	N	N
IDAHO							
1 Minnick	N	N	N	Y	?	N	Y
2 Simpson	N	N	N	Y	Y	Y	N
ILLINOIS							
1 Rush	Y	Y	Y	N	N	N	N
2 Jackson	Y	Y	Y	N	N	N	N
3 Lipinski	Y	Y	Y	N	N	N	N
4 Gutierrez	Y	Y	Y	N	N	N	N
5 Quigley	Y	Y	Y	N	N	N	N
6 Roskam	N	N	N	Y	Y	Y	Y
7 Davis	Y	Y	Y	N	N	N	N
8 Bean	Y	Y	Y	N	N	N	N
9 Schakowsky	Y	Y	Y	N	N	N	N
10 Kirk	N	N	N	Y	Y	Y	N
11 Halvorson	Y	Y	Y	N	N	N	N
12 Costello	Y	Y	Y	N	N	N	N
13 Biggert	N	N	N	Y	Y	Y	N
14 Foster	Y	Y	Y	N	N	N	N
15 Johnson	N	N	N	Y	Y	Y	N

	464	465	466	467	468	469	470
16 **Manzullo**	N	N	N	Y	Y	Y	Y
17 Hare	Y	Y	Y	N	N	N	N
18 **Schock**	N	N	N	Y	Y	Y	N
19 **Shimkus**	N	N	N	Y	Y	Y	N
INDIANA							
1 Visclosky	Y	Y	Y	N	N	N	N
2 Donnelly	Y	Y	Y	Y	N	N	N
3 **Souder**	N	N	N	Y	Y	Y	N
4 **Buyer**	N	N	N	Y	Y	Y	N
5 **Burton**	N	N	N	Y	Y	Y	Y
6 **Pence**	N	N	N	Y	Y	Y	Y
7 Carson	Y	Y	Y	N	N	N	N
8 Ellsworth	Y	Y	Y	Y	N	N	N
9 Hill	Y	N	N	N	N	N	N
IOWA							
1 Braley	Y	Y	Y	N	N	N	N
2 Loebsack	Y	Y	Y	N	N	N	N
3 Boswell	Y	Y	Y	N	N	N	N
4 **Latham**	N	N	N	Y	Y	Y	N
5 **King**	N	N	N	Y	Y	Y	Y
KANSAS							
1 **Moran**	N	N	N	Y	Y	Y	Y
2 **Jenkins**	N	N	N	Y	N	Y	Y
3 Moore	Y	Y	Y	N	N	N	N
4 **Tiahrt**	N	N	N	Y	Y	Y	Y
KENTUCKY							
1 **Whitfield**	N	N	N	Y	Y	Y	N
2 **Guthrie**	N	N	N	Y	Y	Y	N
3 Yarmuth	Y	Y	Y	N	N	N	N
4 **Davis**	N	N	N	Y	Y	Y	Y
5 **Rogers**	N	N	N	Y	Y	Y	N
6 Chandler	Y	Y	Y	N	N	N	N
LOUISIANA							
1 **Scalise**	N	N	N	Y	Y	Y	Y
2 **Cao**	N	N	N	Y	N	Y	N
3 Melancon	Y	N	N	N	N	N	N
4 **Fleming**	N	N	N	Y	Y	Y	N
5 **Alexander**	N	N	N	Y	Y	Y	Y
6 **Cassidy**	N	N	N	Y	Y	Y	Y
7 **Boustany**	N	N	N	Y	Y	Y	Y
MAINE							
1 Pingree	Y	Y	Y	N	N	N	N
2 Michaud	Y	Y	Y	Y	N	N	N
MARYLAND							
1 Kratovil	Y	Y	Y	N	N	Y	N
2 Ruppersberger	Y	Y	Y	N	N	N	N
3 Sarbanes	Y	Y	Y	N	N	N	N
4 Edwards	Y	Y	Y	N	N	N	N
5 Hoyer	Y	?	Y	N	N	N	N
6 **Bartlett**	N	N	N	Y	Y	Y	Y
7 Cummings	Y	Y	Y	Y	N	N	N
8 Van Hollen	Y	Y	Y	N	N	N	N
MASSACHUSETTS							
1 Olver	Y	Y	Y	N	N	N	N
2 Neal	Y	Y	Y	N	N	N	N
3 McGovern	Y	Y	Y	N	N	N	N
4 Frank	Y	Y	Y	N	N	N	N
5 Tsongas	Y	Y	Y	N	N	N	N
6 Tierney	Y	Y	Y	N	N	N	N
7 Markey	Y	Y	Y	N	N	N	?
8 Capuano	Y	Y	Y	N	N	N	N
9 Lynch	Y	Y	Y	N	N	N	N
10 Delahunt	Y	Y	Y	N	N	N	N
MICHIGAN							
1 Stupak	Y	Y	Y	N	N	N	N
2 **Hoekstra**	N	N	N	Y	Y	Y	Y
3 **Ehlers**	Y	N	N	Y	N	N	Y
4 **Camp**	N	N	N	Y	Y	Y	Y
5 Kildee	Y	Y	Y	N	N	N	N
6 **Upton**	Y	N	N	N	Y	N	Y
7 Schauer	Y	Y	Y	N	N	N	Y
8 **Rogers**	N	N	N	Y	Y	Y	Y
9 Peters	Y	Y	Y	N	N	N	N
10 **Miller**	N	N	N	Y	Y	Y	Y
11 **McCotter**	N	N	N	Y	Y	Y	Y
12 Levin	Y	Y	Y	N	N	N	N
13 Kilpatrick	Y	Y	Y	?	?	?	?
14 Conyers	Y	Y	Y	N	N	N	N
15 Dingell	Y	Y	Y	N	N	N	N
MINNESOTA							
1 Walz	Y	Y	+	N	N	N	N
2 **Kline**	N	N	N	?	Y	Y	Y
3 **Paulsen**	N	N	N	Y	Y	N	Y
4 McCollum	Y	Y	Y	N	N	N	N
5 Ellison	Y	Y	Y	N	N	N	N
6 **Bachmann**	N	N	N	Y	Y	Y	Y
7 Peterson	Y	Y	Y	N	N	N	N
8 Oberstar	Y	Y	Y	N	N	N	N
MISSISSIPPI							
1 Childers	N	N	N	N	N	Y	N
2 Thompson	Y	Y	Y	N	N	N	N
3 **Harper**	N	N	N	Y	Y	Y	Y
4 Taylor	N	N	N	Y	Y	Y	N
MISSOURI							
1 Clay	Y	Y	Y	N	N	N	N
2 **Akin**	N	N	N	Y	Y	Y	Y
3 Carnahan	Y	Y	Y	N	N	N	N
4 Skelton	Y	Y	Y	N	N	N	N
5 Cleaver	Y	Y	Y	N	N	N	N
6 **Graves**	N	N	N	Y	Y	Y	Y
7 **Blunt**	N	N	N	Y	Y	Y	Y
8 **Emerson**	N	N	N	Y	Y	Y	N
9 **Luetkemeyer**	N	N	N	Y	Y	Y	Y
MONTANA							
AL **Rehberg**	N	N	N	Y	Y	Y	N
NEBRASKA							
1 **Fortenberry**	N	N	N	Y	N	N	Y
2 **Terry**	N	N	N	Y	Y	N	Y
3 **Smith**	N	N	N	Y	Y	Y	Y
NEVADA							
1 Berkley	Y	Y	Y	Y	N	N	N
2 **Heller**	N	N	N	Y	Y	Y	Y
3 Titus	Y	Y	Y	Y	N	N	N
NEW HAMPSHIRE							
1 Shea-Porter	Y	Y	Y	N	N	N	N
2 Hodes	Y	Y	Y	Y	N	N	N
NEW JERSEY							
1 Andrews	Y	Y	Y	N	N	N	N
2 **LoBiondo**	N	N	N	Y	N	N	N
3 Adler	N	Y	Y	N	Y	N	N
4 **Smith**	N	N	N	N	N	N	N
5 **Garrett**	N	N	N	Y	Y	Y	Y
6 Pallone	Y	Y	Y	N	N	N	N
7 **Lance**	N	N	N	Y	Y	N	Y
8 Pascrell	Y	Y	Y	N	N	N	N
9 Rothman	Y	Y	Y	N	N	N	N
10 Payne	Y	Y	Y	N	N	N	N
11 **Frelinghuysen**	N	N	N	Y	N	Y	N
12 Holt	Y	Y	N	N	N	N	N
13 Sires	Y	Y	Y	N	N	N	N
NEW MEXICO							
1 Heinrich	Y	Y	Y	Y	N	N	N
2 Teague	Y	Y	Y	N	N	N	N
3 Lujan	Y	Y	Y	N	N	N	N
NEW YORK							
1 Bishop	Y	Y	Y	N	N	N	N
2 Israel	Y	Y	Y	N	N	N	N
3 **King**	N	N	N	Y	Y	Y	N
4 McCarthy	Y	Y	Y	N	N	N	N
5 Ackerman	?	?	?	N	N	N	N
6 Meeks	Y	Y	Y	N	N	N	N
7 Crowley	Y	Y	Y	N	N	N	N
8 Nadler	Y	Y	Y	Y	N	N	N
9 Weiner	Y	Y	Y	N	N	N	N
10 Towns	Y	Y	Y	N	N	N	N
11 Clarke	Y	Y	Y	N	N	N	N
12 Velázquez	Y	Y	Y	N	N	N	N
13 McMahon	Y	Y	Y	Y	N	N	N
14 Maloney	Y	Y	+	N	N	N	N
15 Rangel	Y	Y	Y	N	N	N	N
16 Serrano	Y	Y	Y	N	N	N	?
17 Engel	Y	Y	Y	N	N	N	N
18 Lowey	Y	Y	Y	N	N	N	N
19 Hall	Y	Y	Y	N	N	N	N
20 Murphy	Y	?	Y	N	N	N	N
21 Tonko	Y	Y	Y	N	N	N	N
22 Hinchey	Y	Y	Y	N	N	N	N
23 **McHugh**	N	N	N	Y	N	Y	N
24 Arcuri	N	Y	Y	Y	Y	N	N
25 Maffei	Y	Y	Y	N	N	N	N
26 **Lee**	N	N	N	Y	Y	Y	N
27 Higgins	Y	Y	Y	N	N	N	N
28 Slaughter	Y	Y	Y	N	N	N	N
29 Massa	Y	Y	Y	Y	N	Y	N
NORTH CAROLINA							
1 Butterfield	Y	Y	Y	N	N	N	N
2 Etheridge	Y	Y	Y	N	N	N	N
3 **Jones**	N	N	N	Y	Y	Y	Y
4 Price	Y	Y	Y	N	N	N	N
5 **Foxx**	N	N	N	Y	Y	Y	Y
6 **Coble**	N	N	N	Y	Y	Y	N
7 McIntyre	Y	Y	Y	N	N	N	N
8 Kissell	Y	Y	Y	N	N	N	N
9 **Myrick**	N	N	N	Y	Y	Y	Y
10 **McHenry**	?	N	N	Y	Y	Y	Y
11 Shuler	N	N	N	N	N	N	N
12 Watt	Y	Y	Y	N	N	N	N
13 Miller	Y	Y	Y	N	N	N	N
NORTH DAKOTA							
AL Pomeroy	Y	Y	Y	N	N	N	N
OHIO							
1 Driehaus	Y	Y	Y	N	N	N	N
2 **Schmidt**	N	N	N	Y	Y	Y	Y
3 **Turner**	N	N	N	Y	N	N	N
4 **Jordan**	N	N	N	Y	Y	Y	Y
5 **Latta**	N	N	N	Y	Y	Y	Y
6 Wilson	Y	Y	Y	N	N	N	N
7 **Austria**	N	N	N	Y	Y	Y	Y
8 **Boehner**	N	?	N	Y	?	Y	Y
9 Kaptur	Y	Y	Y	N	N	N	N
10 Kucinich	Y	N	N	Y	N	N	N
11 Fudge	Y	Y	Y	N	N	N	N
12 **Tiberi**	N	N	N	Y	Y	Y	N
13 Sutton	?	Y	Y	N	N	N	N
14 **LaTourette**	N	N	N	N	N	N	N
15 Kilroy	Y	Y	Y	N	N	N	N
16 Boccieri	Y	Y	Y	Y	N	N	N
17 Ryan	Y	Y	Y	N	N	N	N
18 Space	Y	Y	Y	N	N	N	N
OKLAHOMA							
1 **Sullivan**	?	?	?	?	?	?	?
2 Boren	Y	N	N	Y	N	N	N
3 **Lucas**	N	N	N	Y	Y	Y	N
4 **Cole**	N	N	N	Y	Y	Y	N
5 **Fallin**	N	N	N	Y	Y	Y	Y
OREGON							
1 Wu	Y	Y	Y	N	N	N	N
2 **Walden**	N	N	N	Y	N	Y	N
3 Blumenauer	Y	Y	Y	N	N	N	N
4 DeFazio	Y	Y	N	N	N	N	N
5 Schrader	Y	Y	Y	N	N	N	N
PENNSYLVANIA							
1 Brady	Y	Y	Y	N	N	N	N
2 Fattah	Y	Y	Y	N	N	N	N
3 Dahlkemper	Y	Y	N	N	N	N	N
4 Altmire	N	N	N	Y	Y	N	N
5 **Thompson**	N	N	N	Y	Y	Y	N
6 **Gerlach**	N	N	N	Y	N	N	Y
7 Sestak	Y	Y	Y	N	N	N	N
8 Murphy, P.	Y	Y	Y	N	Y	N	N
9 **Shuster**	N	N	N	Y	Y	Y	N
10 Carney	N	Y	N	N	N	N	N
11 Kanjorski	Y	Y	Y	N	N	N	N
12 Murtha	Y	Y	Y	N	N	N	N
13 Schwartz	Y	Y	Y	N	N	N	N
14 Doyle	Y	Y	Y	N	N	N	N
15 **Dent**	N	N	N	Y	Y	Y	Y
16 **Pitts**	N	N	N	Y	Y	Y	Y
17 Holden	Y	Y	Y	N	N	N	N
18 **Murphy, T.**	N	N	N	Y	N	N	N
19 **Platts**	N	N	N	Y	N	N	Y
RHODE ISLAND							
1 Kennedy	?	?	?	?	?	?	?
2 Langevin	Y	Y	Y	N	N	N	N
SOUTH CAROLINA							
1 **Brown**	N	N	N	Y	Y	Y	Y
2 **Wilson**	N	N	N	Y	Y	Y	Y
3 **Barrett**	N	N	N	Y	Y	Y	Y
4 **Inglis**	N	N	N	Y	Y	Y	Y
5 Spratt	Y	Y	Y	N	N	N	N
6 Clyburn	Y	Y	Y	N	N	N	N
SOUTH DAKOTA							
AL Herseth Sandlin	Y	Y	Y	Y	N	N	N
TENNESSEE							
1 **Roe**	N	N	N	Y	Y	Y	Y
2 **Duncan**	N	N	N	Y	Y	Y	Y
3 **Wamp**	N	N	N	Y	Y	Y	N
4 Davis	Y	Y	Y	N	N	N	N
5 Cooper	Y	Y	Y	N	N	N	Y
6 Gordon	Y	Y	Y	N	N	N	N
7 **Blackburn**	N	N	N	Y	Y	Y	Y
8 Tanner	Y	Y	Y	N	N	Y	N
9 Cohen	Y	Y	Y	N	N	N	N
TEXAS							
1 **Gohmert**	Y	N	N	Y	Y	Y	Y
2 **Poe**	N	N	N	Y	Y	Y	Y
3 **Johnson, S.**	N	N	N	Y	Y	Y	Y
4 **Hall**	?	N	N	Y	Y	Y	N
5 **Hensarling**	N	N	N	Y	Y	Y	Y
6 **Barton**	N	N	N	Y	Y	Y	N
7 **Culberson**	?	?	?	Y	Y	Y	N
8 **Brady**	N	N	N	Y	Y	Y	Y
9 Green, A.	Y	Y	Y	N	N	N	N
10 **McCaul**	N	N	N	Y	Y	Y	Y
11 **Conaway**	N	N	N	Y	Y	Y	Y
12 **Granger**	N	N	N	Y	Y	Y	N
13 **Thornberry**	N	N	N	Y	Y	Y	Y
14 **Paul**	N	N	N	Y	Y	Y	Y
15 Hinojosa	Y	Y	Y	N	N	N	N
16 Reyes	Y	Y	Y	Y	N	N	N
17 Edwards	Y	Y	Y	N	N	N	N
18 Jackson Lee	Y	Y	Y	N	N	N	N
19 **Neugebauer**	N	N	N	Y	Y	Y	Y
20 Gonzalez	Y	Y	Y	N	N	N	N
21 **Smith**	N	N	N	Y	Y	Y	N
22 **Olson**	N	N	N	Y	Y	Y	Y
23 Rodriguez	Y	Y	Y	N	N	N	N
24 **Marchant**	N	N	N	Y	Y	Y	N
25 Doggett	Y	Y	N	N	N	N	N
26 **Burgess**	N	N	N	Y	Y	Y	Y
27 Ortiz	Y	Y	Y	N	N	N	N
28 Cuellar	Y	Y	Y	N	N	N	N
29 Green, G.	Y	Y	Y	N	N	N	N
30 Johnson, E.	Y	Y	Y	N	N	N	N
31 **Carter**	N	N	N	Y	Y	Y	Y
32 **Sessions**	N	N	N	Y	Y	Y	Y
UTAH							
1 **Bishop**	N	N	N	Y	Y	Y	Y
2 Matheson	Y	N	N	Y	N	N	N
3 **Chaffetz**	Y	N	N	Y	Y	Y	Y
VERMONT							
AL Welch	Y	Y	Y	N	N	N	N
VIRGINIA							
1 **Wittman**	N	N	N	Y	Y	Y	Y
2 Nye	Y	N	N	N	Y	N	N
3 Scott	Y	Y	Y	N	N	N	N
4 **Forbes**	N	N	N	Y	Y	Y	Y
5 Perriello	Y	Y	Y	Y	N	N	N
6 **Goodlatte**	N	N	N	Y	Y	Y	Y
7 **Cantor**	N	N	N	Y	Y	Y	Y
8 Moran	Y	Y	Y	N	N	N	N
9 Boucher	Y	Y	Y	N	N	N	N
10 **Wolf**	N	N	N	Y	Y	Y	N
11 Connolly	Y	Y	Y	N	N	N	N
WASHINGTON							
1 Inslee	Y	Y	Y	N	N	N	N
2 Larsen	Y	Y	Y	N	N	N	N
3 Baird	Y	N	N	Y	N	N	N
4 **Hastings**	N	N	N	Y	Y	Y	N
5 **McMorris Rodgers**	N	N	N	Y	Y	Y	N
6 Dicks	Y	Y	Y	N	N	N	N
7 McDermott	Y	Y	Y	N	N	N	N
8 **Reichert**	N	N	N	Y	N	N	N
9 Smith	Y	Y	Y	N	N	N	N
WEST VIRGINIA							
1 Mollohan	Y	Y	?	N	N	N	N
2 **Capito**	N	N	N	Y	Y	Y	N
3 Rahall	Y	Y	N	N	N	N	N
WISCONSIN							
1 **Ryan**	N	N	N	Y	Y	Y	Y
2 Baldwin	Y	Y	Y	N	N	N	N
3 Kind	Y	Y	Y	N	N	N	?
4 Moore	Y	Y	Y	N	N	N	N
5 **Sensenbrenner**	N	N	N	Y	Y	Y	Y
6 **Petri**	N	N	N	Y	Y	Y	Y
7 Obey	Y	Y	Y	N	N	N	N
8 Kagen	Y	Y	Y	N	N	N	N
WYOMING							
AL **Lummis**	N	N	N	Y	Y	Y	Y
DELEGATES							
Faleomavaega (A.S.)				N	N	N	N
Norton (D.C.)				–	–	–	N
Bordallo (Guam)				+	N	N	N
Sablan (N. Marianas)				N	N	N	N
Pierluisi (P.R.)				N	N	N	N
Christensen (V.I.)				N	N	?	N

HOUSE VOTES

IN THE HOUSE | By Vote Number

471. **HR 2996. Fiscal 2010 Interior-Environment Appropriations/ Village Park Historic Preservation.** Campbell, R-Calif., amendment that would bar the use of funds appropriated in the bill for the Village Park Historic Preservation project at Traditional Arts in Canton, N.Y., and cut $150,000 set aside for the project from the bill total. Rejected in Committee of the Whole 122-309: R 112-63; D 10-246. June 26, 2009.

472. **HR 2996. Fiscal 2010 Interior-Environment Appropriations/ Tarrytown Music Hall Restoration.** Flake, R-Ariz., amendment that would bar the use of funds appropriated in the bill for the Tarrytown Music Hall Restoration project of The Friends of the Mozartina Musical Arts Conservatory in Tarrytown, N.Y., and cut $150,000 set aside for the project from the bill total. Rejected in Committee of the Whole 122-301: R 113-57; D 9-244. June 26, 2009.

473. **HR 2996. Fiscal 2010 Interior-Environment Appropriations/ Angel Island Hospital Rehabilitation.** Hensarling, R-Texas, amendment that would bar the use of funds appropriated in the bill for the Angel Island State Park Immigration Station Hospital Rehabilitation project of the Angel Island Immigration Station Foundation in San Francisco. It would cut $1 million set aside for the project from the bill total. Rejected in Committee of the Whole 131-296: R 125-48; D 6-248. June 26, 2009.

474. **HR 2996. Fiscal 2010 Interior-Environment Appropriations/ Historic Coal and Iron Building Rehabilitation.** Flake, R-Ariz., amendment that would bar the use of funds appropriated in the bill for the Historic Fort Payne Coal and Iron Building Rehabilitation project in Fort Payne, Ala. It would cut $150,000 set aside for the project from the bill total. Rejected in Committee of the Whole 114-317: R 104-71; D 10-246. June 26, 2009.

475. **HR 2996. Fiscal 2010 Interior-Environment Appropriations/ Passage.** Passage of the bill that would provide $32.4 billion in fiscal 2010 for the Interior Department, the EPA and related agencies, including $32.3 billion in discretionary funding. The bill would provide $11 billion for the Interior Department, $10.5 billion for the EPA, $5.4 billion for the Forest Service, $1.1 billion for the Bureau of Land Management and $4 billion for the Indian Health Service. It would prohibit funds appropriated in the bill from being used to release detainees at Guantánamo Bay, Cuba, into the United States. Passed 254-173: R 17-159; D 237-14. A "yea" was a vote in support of the president's position. June 26, 2009.

476. **HR 2454. Greenhouse Gas Emissions/Republican Substitute.** Forbes, R-Va., substitute amendment that would strike the text of the bill and insert provisions that would authorize $24 billion for fiscal 2010-19 and unspecified sums thereafter for the Energy Department to establish a grant program and prize system to provide awards to researchers, businesses, universities and others for work on sustainable fuel and energy-efficient technologies. It would establish a commission that would be required to submit a report with recommendations to Congress for the United States to achieve 50 percent energy independence within 10 years and 100 percent energy independence within 20 years. Rejected 172-256: R 165-11; D 7-245. A "nay" was a vote in support of the president's position. June 26, 2009.

477. **HR 2454. Greenhouse Gas Emissions/Passage.** Passage of the bill that would create a cap-and-trade system to limit greenhouse gas emissions and set new requirements for electric utilities. Emission allowances would permit buyers to emit a certain amount of greenhouse gases. Most of the allowances would initially be provided free of charge. By 2030, most would be auctioned to polluters. The bill would set emissions limits at 17 percent below current levels in 2020, expanding to 83 percent in 2050. It would require utilities to produce 15 percent of the nation's electricity from renewable sources by 2020. It would establish programs to assist energy consumers with higher utility bills resulting from the new system. Passed 219-212: R 8-168; D 211-44. A "yea" was a vote in support of the president's position. June 26, 2009.

	471	472	473	474	475	476	477
ALABAMA							
1 Bonner	N	N	N	N	N	Y	N
2 Bright	Y	Y	Y	Y	N	N	N
3 Rogers	N	N	N	N	N	Y	N
4 Aderholt	N	N	N	N	N	Y	N
5 Griffith	N	N	N	N	Y	N	N
6 Bachus	N	N	N	N	N	Y	N
7 Davis	N	N	N	N	Y	N	N
ALASKA							
AL Young	N	N	N	N	Y	Y	N
ARIZONA							
1 Kirkpatrick	N	N	N	N	Y	N	N
2 Franks	Y	Y	Y	Y	N	Y	N
3 Shadegg	Y	Y	Y	Y	N	Y	N
4 Pastor	N	N	N	N	Y	N	Y
5 Mitchell	Y	Y	Y	Y	N	N	N
6 Flake	?	?	?	?	?	?	?
7 Grijalva	N	N	N	N	Y	N	Y
8 Giffords	N	N	N	N	Y	N	Y
ARKANSAS							
1 Berry	N	N	N	N	Y	N	Y
2 Snyder	N	N	N	N	Y	N	Y
3 Boozman	Y	Y	Y	Y	N	Y	N
4 Ross	N	N	N	N	Y	N	N
CALIFORNIA							
1 Thompson	N	N	N	N	Y	N	Y
2 Herger	Y	Y	Y	Y	N	Y	N
3 Lungren	Y	Y	Y	Y	N	Y	N
4 McClintock	Y	Y	Y	Y	N	Y	N
5 Matsui	N	N	N	N	Y	N	Y
6 Woolsey	N	N	N	N	Y	N	Y
7 Miller, George	N	N	N	N	Y	N	Y
8 Pelosi							Y
9 Lee	N	N	N	N	Y	N	Y
10 Tauscher	N	N	N	N	Y	N	Y
11 McNerney	N	N	N	N	Y	N	Y
12 Speier	N	N	N	N	Y	N	Y
13 Stark	N	N	?	N	Y	N	Y
14 Eshoo	N	N	N	N	Y	N	Y
15 Honda	N	N	N	N	Y	N	Y
16 Lofgren	N	N	N	N	Y	N	Y
17 Farr	N	N	N	N	Y	N	Y
18 Cardoza	N	N	N	N	Y	N	Y
19 Radanovich	Y	Y	Y	Y	N	Y	N
20 Costa	N	N	N	N	Y	N	N
21 Nunes	Y	Y	Y	Y	N	Y	N
22 McCarthy	Y	Y	Y	Y	N	Y	N
23 Capps	N	N	N	N	Y	N	Y
24 Gallegly	N	Y	Y	N	N	Y	N
25 McKeon	N	N	Y	N	N	Y	N
26 Dreier	N	N	N	N	N	Y	N
27 Sherman	N	N	N	N	Y	N	Y
28 Berman	N	N	N	N	Y	N	Y
29 Schiff	N	N	N	N	Y	N	Y
30 Waxman	N	N	N	N	Y	N	Y
31 Becerra	N	N	N	N	Y	N	Y
32 Vacant							
33 Watson	N	N	N	N	Y	N	Y
34 Roybal-Allard	N	N	N	N	Y	N	Y
35 Waters	N	N	N	N	Y	Y	Y
36 Harman	N	N	N	N	Y	N	Y
37 Richardson	N	N	N	N	Y	N	Y
38 Napolitano	N	N	N	N	Y	N	Y
39 Sánchez, Linda	N	N	N	N	Y	N	Y
40 Royce	Y	Y	Y	Y	N	Y	N
41 Lewis	N	N	N	N	N	Y	N
42 Miller, Gary	N	Y	N	N	N	Y	N
43 Baca	N	N	N	N	Y	N	Y
44 Calvert	N	N	N	N	N	Y	N
45 Bono Mack	Y	Y	Y	Y	N	Y	N
46 Rohrabacher	Y	Y	Y	Y	N	Y	N
47 Sanchez, Loretta	N	N	N	N	Y	N	Y
48 Campbell	Y	Y	Y	Y	N	Y	N
49 Issa	Y	Y	Y	Y	N	Y	N
50 Bilbray	Y	?	Y	N	N	Y	N
51 Filner	N	N	N	N	Y	N	Y
52 Hunter	Y	Y	Y	Y	N	Y	N
53 Davis	N	N	N	N	Y	N	Y
COLORADO							
1 DeGette	N	N	N	N	Y	N	Y
2 Polis	N	N	N	N	Y	N	Y
3 Salazar	N	N	N	N	Y	N	N
4 Markey	N	N	N	N	N	Y	Y
5 Lamborn	Y	Y	Y	Y	N	Y	N
6 Coffman	Y	Y	Y	Y	N	Y	N
7 Perlmutter	N	N	N	N	Y	N	Y
CONNECTICUT							
1 Larson	N	N	N	N	Y	N	Y
2 Courtney	N	N	N	N	Y	N	Y
3 DeLauro	N	N	N	N	Y	N	Y
4 Himes	N	N	N	N	Y	N	Y
5 Murphy	N	N	N	N	Y	N	Y
DELAWARE							
AL Castle	N	N	Y	N	Y	N	Y
FLORIDA							
1 Miller	Y	Y	Y	Y	N	Y	N
2 Boyd	N	N	N	N	Y	N	Y
3 Brown	N	N	N	N	Y	N	Y
4 Crenshaw	N	N	N	N	N	Y	N
5 Brown-Waite	Y	Y	Y	Y	N	Y	N
6 Stearns	Y	Y	Y	Y	N	Y	N
7 Mica	N	N	N	N	N	Y	N
8 Grayson	N	N	N	N	Y	N	Y
9 Bilirakis	N	Y	Y	N	N	Y	N
10 Young	N	N	N	N	N	Y	N
11 Castor	N	N	N	N	Y	N	Y
12 Putnam	N	N	N	N	N	Y	N
13 Buchanan	N	N	Y	N	N	Y	N
14 Mack	Y	Y	Y	Y	N	Y	N
15 Posey	Y	Y	Y	Y	N	Y	N
16 Rooney	Y	Y	Y	Y	N	Y	N
17 Meek	N	N	N	N	Y	N	Y
18 Ros-Lehtinen	N	?	N	N	Y	N	Y
19 Wexler	N	N	N	N	Y	N	Y
20 Wasserman Schultz	N	N	N	N	Y	N	Y
21 Diaz-Balart, L.	N	N	N	N	N	Y	N
22 Klein	N	–	N	N	Y	N	Y
23 Hastings	?	?	?	?	?	?	?
24 Kosmas	N	N	N	N	Y	N	Y
25 Diaz-Balart, M.	N	N	N	N	N	Y	N
GEORGIA							
1 Kingston	Y	Y	Y	Y	N	Y	N
2 Bishop	N	?	N	N	Y	N	Y
3 Westmoreland	Y	Y	Y	Y	N	Y	N
4 Johnson	N	N	N	N	Y	N	Y
5 Lewis	?	?	?	?	?	?	Y
6 Price	Y	?	Y	Y	N	Y	N
7 Linder	Y	Y	Y	Y	N	Y	N
8 Marshall	N	N	N	N	Y	N	N
9 Deal	Y	Y	Y	Y	N	Y	N
10 Broun	Y	Y	Y	Y	N	Y	N
11 Gingrey	Y	N	N	Y	N	Y	N
12 Barrow	N	N	N	N	Y	N	N
13 Scott	N	N	N	N	Y	N	Y
HAWAII							
1 Abercrombie	N	N	N	N	Y	N	Y
2 Hirono	N	N	N	N	Y	N	Y
IDAHO							
1 Minnick	Y	Y	Y	Y	N	N	N
2 Simpson	N	N	N	N	N	Y	N
ILLINOIS							
1 Rush	N	?	?	N	Y	N	Y
2 Jackson	N	N	N	N	Y	N	Y
3 Lipinski	N	N	N	N	Y	N	Y
4 Gutierrez	N	N	N	N	Y	N	Y
5 Quigley	N	N	N	N	Y	N	Y
6 Roskam	Y	Y	Y	Y	N	Y	N
7 Davis	N	N	N	N	Y	N	Y
8 Bean	Y	Y	Y	N	N	Y	N
9 Schakowsky	N	N	N	N	Y	N	Y
10 Kirk	Y	Y	Y	Y	N	Y	Y
11 Halvorson	N	N	N	N	Y	N	Y
12 Costello	N	N	N	N	Y	N	N
13 Biggert	Y	N	N	N	N	Y	N
14 Foster	Y	N	Y	N	Y	N	Y
15 Johnson	Y	Y	Y	Y	N	Y	N

KEY **Republicans** Democrats

Y Voted for (yea)	X Paired against	C Voted "present" to avoid possible conflict of interest
# Paired for	– Announced against	
+ Announced for	P Voted "present"	? Did not vote or otherwise make a position known
N Voted against (nay)		

	471	472	473	474	475	476	477
16 **Manzullo**	Y	Y	N	Y	N	Y	N
17 Hare	N	N	N	N	Y	N	Y
18 **Schock**	N	N	Y	N	N	Y	N
19 **Shimkus**	Y	Y	Y	N	N	Y	N
INDIANA							
1 Visclosky	N	N	N	N	Y	N	N
2 Donnelly	N	N	N	N	N	N	N
3 **Souder**	N	N	N	N	N	Y	N
4 **Buyer**	Y	Y	Y	Y	N	Y	N
5 **Burton**	Y	Y	Y	Y	N	Y	N
6 **Pence**	Y	Y	Y	Y	N	Y	N
7 Carson	N	N	N	N	Y	N	Y
8 Ellsworth	N	N	N	N	Y	N	N
9 Hill	N	N	N	N	N	N	Y
IOWA							
1 Braley	N	N	N	N	Y	N	Y
2 Loebsack	N	N	N	N	Y	N	Y
3 Boswell	N	N	?	N	Y	N	Y
4 **Latham**	N	N	N	N	N	Y	N
5 **King**	Y	Y	Y	Y	N	Y	N
KANSAS							
1 **Moran**	Y	Y	Y	Y	N	Y	N
2 **Jenkins**	Y	Y	Y	Y	N	Y	N
3 Moore	N	N	N	N	Y	N	Y
4 **Tiahrt**	N	Y	Y	N	N	Y	N
KENTUCKY							
1 **Whitfield**	N	N	Y	N	N	Y	N
2 **Guthrie**	N	N	N	N	N	Y	N
3 Yarmuth	N	N	N	N	Y	N	Y
4 **Davis**	Y	Y	Y	Y	N	Y	N
5 **Rogers**	N	N	Y	N	N	Y	N
6 Chandler	?	N	N	N	Y	N	Y
LOUISIANA							
1 **Scalise**	Y	Y	Y	Y	N	Y	N
2 **Cao**	N	N	N	N	Y	Y	N
3 Melancon	N	N	N	N	?	N	N
4 **Fleming**	Y	Y	Y	Y	N	Y	N
5 **Alexander**	Y	Y	Y	Y	N	Y	N
6 **Cassidy**	Y	Y	Y	Y	N	Y	N
7 **Boustany**	Y	Y	Y	Y	N	Y	N
MAINE							
1 Pingree	N	N	N	N	Y	N	Y
2 Michaud	N	N	N	N	Y	N	Y
MARYLAND							
1 Kratovil	N	N	N	N	N	N	Y
2 Ruppersberger	N	N	N	N	Y	N	Y
3 Sarbanes	N	N	N	N	Y	N	Y
4 Edwards	N	N	N	N	Y	N	Y
5 Hoyer	N	N	N	N	Y	N	Y
6 **Bartlett**	Y	Y	Y	Y	N	Y	N
7 Cummings	N	N	N	N	Y	N	Y
8 Van Hollen	N	N	N	N	Y	N	Y
MASSACHUSETTS							
1 Olver	N	N	N	?	Y	N	Y
2 Neal	N	N	N	N	Y	N	Y
3 McGovern	N	N	N	N	Y	N	Y
4 Frank	N	N	N	N	Y	N	Y
5 Tsongas	N	N	N	N	Y	N	Y
6 Tierney	Y	N	N	Y	Y	N	Y
7 Markey	N	N	N	N	Y	N	Y
8 Capuano	N	N	N	N	Y	N	Y
9 Lynch	N	N	N	N	Y	N	Y
10 Delahunt	N	N	N	N	Y	N	Y
MICHIGAN							
1 Stupak	N	N	N	N	Y	N	Y
2 **Hoekstra**	Y	Y	Y	Y	N	Y	N
3 **Ehlers**	Y	Y	Y	Y	Y	Y	N
4 **Camp**	N	Y	N	N	N	Y	N
5 Kildee	N	N	N	N	Y	N	Y
6 **Upton**	N	Y	N	Y	N	Y	N
7 Schauer	Y	Y	N	Y	Y	N	Y
8 **Rogers**	N	N	Y	N	N	Y	N
9 Peters	N	N	N	N	Y	N	Y
10 **Miller**	Y	Y	Y	Y	Y	Y	N
11 **McCotter**	Y	Y	Y	Y	N	Y	N
12 Levin	N	N	N	N	Y	N	Y
13 Kilpatrick	N	N	N	N	Y	N	Y
14 Conyers	N	N	N	N	Y	N	Y
15 Dingell	N	N	N	N	Y	N	Y
MINNESOTA							
1 Walz	N	N	N	N	Y	N	Y
2 **Kline**	Y	Y	Y	Y	N	Y	N
3 **Paulsen**	Y	Y	Y	Y	N	Y	N
4 McCollum	N	N	N	N	Y	N	Y

	471	472	473	474	475	476	477
5 Ellison	N	N	N	N	Y	N	Y
6 **Bachmann**	Y	Y	Y	Y	N	Y	N
7 Peterson	N	N	N	N	Y	N	Y
8 Oberstar	N	N	N	N	Y	N	Y
MISSISSIPPI							
1 Childers	N	N	N	N	N	N	N
2 Thompson	N	N	N	N	Y	N	Y
3 **Harper**	Y	Y	Y	N	N	Y	N
4 Taylor	N	Y	N	N	N	N	N
MISSOURI							
1 Clay	N	N	N	N	Y	N	Y
2 **Akin**	Y	Y	Y	Y	N	Y	N
3 Carnahan	N	N	N	N	Y	N	Y
4 Skelton	N	N	N	N	Y	N	Y
5 Cleaver	N	N	N	N	Y	N	Y
6 **Graves**	Y	Y	Y	Y	N	Y	N
7 **Blunt**	N	Y	Y	N	N	Y	N
8 **Emerson**	N	N	N	N	N	Y	N
9 **Luetkemeyer**	Y	Y	Y	Y	N	Y	N
MONTANA							
AL **Rehberg**	N	N	N	N	N	Y	N
NEBRASKA							
1 **Fortenberry**	Y	Y	Y	N	N	Y	N
2 **Terry**	Y	Y	Y	Y	N	Y	N
3 **Smith**	Y	Y	Y	Y	N	Y	N
NEVADA							
1 Berkley	N	N	N	N	Y	N	Y
2 **Heller**	Y	Y	Y	Y	Y	N	N
3 Titus	N	N	N	N	Y	N	Y
NEW HAMPSHIRE							
1 Shea-Porter	N	N	N	N	Y	N	Y
2 Hodes	N	N	N	N	Y	N	Y
NEW JERSEY							
1 Andrews	N	N	N	N	Y	N	Y
2 **LoBiondo**	N	N	N	N	Y	N	Y
3 Adler	Y	N	N	N	Y	N	Y
4 **Smith**	N	N	N	N	Y	N	N
5 **Garrett**	Y	Y	Y	Y	N	N	N
6 Pallone	N	N	N	N	Y	N	Y
7 **Lance**	N	Y	Y	Y	Y	Y	Y
8 Pascrell	N	N	N	N	Y	N	Y
9 Rothman	N	N	N	N	Y	N	Y
10 Payne	N	N	N	N	Y	N	Y
11 **Frelinghuysen**	N	N	N	N	N	Y	N
12 Holt	N	N	N	N	Y	N	Y
13 Sires	N	N	N	N	Y	N	Y
NEW MEXICO							
1 Heinrich	N	N	N	N	Y	N	Y
2 Teague	N	N	N	N	Y	N	Y
3 Lujan	N	N	N	N	Y	N	Y
NEW YORK							
1 Bishop	N	N	N	N	Y	N	Y
2 Israel	?	N	N	?	Y	N	Y
3 **King**	N	N	N	N	N	Y	N
4 McCarthy	N	N	N	N	Y	N	Y
5 Ackerman	N	N	N	N	Y	N	Y
6 Meeks	N	N	N	N	Y	N	Y
7 Crowley	N	?	N	N	Y	N	Y
8 Nadler	N	N	N	N	Y	N	Y
9 Weiner	N	N	N	N	Y	N	Y
10 Towns	N	N	N	N	Y	N	Y
11 Clarke	N	N	N	N	Y	N	Y
12 Velázquez	N	N	N	N	Y	N	Y
13 McMahon	Y	Y	N	Y	Y	N	Y
14 Maloney	N	N	N	N	Y	N	Y
15 Rangel	N	N	N	N	Y	N	Y
16 Serrano	N	N	N	N	Y	N	Y
17 Engel	N	N	N	N	Y	N	Y
18 Lowey	N	N	N	N	Y	N	Y
19 Hall	N	N	N	N	Y	N	Y
20 Murphy	N	N	N	N	Y	N	Y
21 Tonko	N	N	N	N	Y	N	Y
22 Hinchey	N	N	N	N	Y	N	Y
23 **McHugh**	N	N	N	N	Y	Y	Y
24 Arcuri	N	N	N	N	Y	N	N
25 Maffei	N	N	N	N	Y	N	Y
26 **Lee**	Y	Y	Y	Y	N	Y	N
27 Higgins	N	N	N	N	Y	N	Y
28 Slaughter	N	N	N	N	Y	N	Y
29 Massa	N	N	N	N	Y	N	N
NORTH CAROLINA							
1 Butterfield	N	N	N	N	Y	N	Y
2 Etheridge	N	N	N	N	Y	N	Y
3 **Jones**	N	Y	Y	Y	N	Y	N
4 Price	N	N	N	N	Y	N	Y

	471	472	473	474	475	476	477
5 **Foxx**	Y	Y	Y	Y	N	N	N
6 **Coble**	Y	Y	Y	Y	N	Y	N
7 McIntyre	N	N	N	N	Y	N	N
8 Kissell	N	N	N	N	Y	N	N
9 **Myrick**	Y	Y	Y	Y	N	Y	N
10 **McHenry**	Y	Y	Y	Y	N	Y	N
11 Shuler	N	N	N	N	Y	N	Y
12 Watt	N	N	N	N	Y	N	Y
13 Miller	N	N	N	N	Y	N	Y
NORTH DAKOTA							
AL Pomeroy	N	N	N	N	Y	N	N
OHIO							
1 Driehaus	N	N	N	N	Y	N	Y
2 **Schmidt**	Y	Y	Y	Y	N	Y	N
3 **Turner**	N	N	N	N	Y	Y	N
4 **Jordan**	Y	Y	Y	Y	N	N	N
5 **Latta**	Y	Y	Y	Y	N	Y	N
6 Wilson	N	N	N	N	Y	N	N
7 **Austria**	Y	Y	Y	Y	N	Y	N
8 **Boehner**	N	Y	Y	N	N	Y	N
9 Kaptur	N	N	N	N	Y	N	Y
10 Kucinich	N	N	N	N	Y	N	N
11 Fudge	N	N	N	N	Y	N	Y
12 **Tiberi**	Y	Y	Y	Y	N	Y	N
13 Sutton	N	N	N	N	Y	N	Y
14 **LaTourette**	N	N	N	N	Y	Y	N
15 Kilroy	N	N	N	N	Y	N	Y
16 Boccieri	N	N	N	N	Y	N	Y
17 Ryan	N	N	N	N	Y	N	Y
18 Space	N	N	N	N	Y	N	Y
OKLAHOMA							
1 **Sullivan**	?	?	?	?	?	?	–
2 Boren	N	N	N	N	Y	Y	N
3 **Lucas**	N	N	N	N	N	Y	N
4 **Cole**	N	N	N	N	Y	Y	N
5 **Fallin**	Y	Y	Y	Y	N	Y	N
OREGON							
1 Wu	N	N	N	N	Y	?	Y
2 **Walden**	N	N	N	N	Y	Y	N
3 Blumenauer	N	N	N	N	Y	N	Y
4 DeFazio	N	N	N	N	Y	N	N
5 Schrader	N	N	N	N	Y	N	Y
PENNSYLVANIA							
1 Brady	N	N	N	N	Y	N	Y
2 Fattah	N	N	N	N	Y	N	Y
3 Dahlkemper	N	N	N	N	Y	N	N
4 Altmire	N	N	N	N	Y	Y	N
5 **Thompson**	N	N	N	N	N	Y	N
6 **Gerlach**	Y	N	Y	N	N	Y	N
7 Sestak	N	N	N	N	Y	N	Y
8 Murphy, P.	N	N	N	N	Y	N	Y
9 **Shuster**	N	N	N	N	N	Y	N
10 Carney	N	N	N	N	Y	Y	N
11 Kanjorski	N	N	N	N	Y	N	Y
12 Murtha	N	N	N	N	Y	N	Y
13 Schwartz	N	N	?	N	Y	N	Y
14 Doyle	N	N	N	N	Y	N	Y
15 **Dent**	N	N	Y	N	N	Y	N
16 **Pitts**	Y	Y	Y	Y	N	Y	N
17 Holden	N	N	N	N	Y	Y	N
18 **Murphy, T.**	N	N	N	N	Y	N	N
19 **Platts**	?	?	?	?	N	Y	N
RHODE ISLAND							
1 Kennedy	?	?	?	?	?	N	Y
2 Langevin	N	N	N	N	Y	N	Y
SOUTH CAROLINA							
1 **Brown**	N	N	N	N	N	Y	N
2 **Wilson**	Y	Y	Y	Y	N	Y	N
3 **Barrett**	Y	Y	Y	Y	N	Y	N
4 **Inglis**	Y	Y	Y	Y	N	Y	N
5 Spratt	N	N	N	N	Y	N	Y
6 Clyburn	N	?	N	N	Y	N	Y
SOUTH DAKOTA							
AL Herseth Sandlin	N	N	N	N	Y	N	N
TENNESSEE							
1 **Roe**	Y	Y	Y	Y	N	Y	N
2 **Duncan**	Y	Y	Y	Y	N	Y	N
3 **Wamp**	Y	Y	Y	N	N	Y	N
4 Davis	N	N	N	N	Y	N	N
5 Cooper	Y	Y	Y	Y	Y	N	Y
6 Gordon	N	N	N	N	Y	N	Y
7 **Blackburn**	Y	Y	Y	Y	N	Y	N
8 Tanner	N	N	N	N	N	N	N
9 Cohen	N	N	N	N	Y	N	Y

	471	472	473	474	475	476	477
TEXAS							
1 **Gohmert**	Y	?	Y	Y	N	Y	N
2 **Poe**	Y	Y	Y	N	N	Y	N
3 **Johnson, S.**	Y	Y	Y	Y	N	Y	N
4 **Hall**	Y	N	Y	Y	N	Y	N
5 **Hensarling**	Y	Y	Y	Y	N	Y	N
6 **Barton**	N	N	Y	Y	N	Y	N
7 **Culberson**	N	N	N	N	N	Y	N
8 **Brady**	Y	Y	Y	Y	N	Y	N
9 Green, A.	N	N	N	N	Y	N	Y
10 **McCaul**	Y	Y	Y	Y	N	Y	N
11 **Conaway**	Y	Y	Y	Y	N	Y	N
12 **Granger**	N	N	N	N	N	Y	N
13 **Thornberry**	Y	Y	Y	Y	N	Y	N
14 **Paul**	Y	Y	Y	Y	N	Y	N
15 Hinojosa	N	N	N	N	Y	N	Y
16 Reyes	N	N	N	N	Y	N	Y
17 Edwards	N	N	N	N	Y	N	N
18 Jackson Lee	N	N	N	N	Y	N	Y
19 **Neugebauer**	Y	Y	Y	Y	N	Y	N
20 Gonzalez	N	N	N	N	Y	N	Y
21 **Smith**	N	N	?	N	N	Y	N
22 **Olson**	Y	Y	Y	Y	N	Y	N
23 Rodriguez	N	N	N	N	Y	N	N
24 **Marchant**	Y	Y	Y	Y	N	Y	N
25 Doggett	N	N	N	N	Y	N	Y
26 **Burgess**	Y	Y	Y	Y	N	Y	N
27 Ortiz	N	N	N	N	Y	N	N
28 Cuellar	N	N	N	N	Y	N	Y
29 Green, G.	N	N	N	N	Y	N	Y
30 Johnson, E.	N	N	N	N	Y	N	Y
31 **Carter**	N	N	N	N	N	Y	N
32 **Sessions**	Y	Y	Y	Y	N	Y	N
UTAH							
1 **Bishop**	Y	Y	Y	N	N	Y	N
2 Matheson	N	Y	Y	N	N	N	N
3 **Chaffetz**	Y	Y	Y	Y	N	Y	N
VERMONT							
AL Welch	N	N	N	N	Y	N	Y
VIRGINIA							
1 **Wittman**	Y	Y	?	Y	N	Y	N
2 Nye	N	N	N	Y	N	N	N
3 Scott	N	N	N	N	Y	N	Y
4 **Forbes**	Y	Y	Y	Y	N	Y	N
5 Perriello	N	N	N	N	N	N	Y
6 **Goodlatte**	Y	Y	Y	Y	N	Y	N
7 **Cantor**	Y	Y	Y	N	N	Y	N
8 Moran	N	N	N	N	Y	?	Y
9 Boucher	N	N	N	N	Y	N	Y
10 **Wolf**	N	N	N	N	N	Y	N
11 Connolly	N	N	N	N	Y	N	Y
WASHINGTON							
1 Inslee	N	N	N	N	Y	N	Y
2 Larsen	N	N	N	N	Y	N	Y
3 Baird	N	N	N	N	Y	N	Y
4 **Hastings**	N	N	N	N	N	Y	N
5 **McMorris Rodgers**	Y	Y	Y	Y	N	Y	N
6 Dicks	N	N	N	N	Y	N	Y
7 McDermott	N	N	N	N	Y	N	Y
8 **Reichert**	N	N	N	N	Y	Y	Y
9 Smith	N	N	N	N	Y	N	Y
WEST VIRGINIA							
1 Mollohan	N	N	N	N	Y	N	N
2 **Capito**	N	N	N	N	N	Y	N
3 Rahall	N	N	N	N	Y	N	N
WISCONSIN							
1 **Ryan**	Y	Y	Y	Y	N	N	N
2 Baldwin	N	N	N	N	Y	N	Y
3 Kind	N	N	N	N	Y	N	Y
4 Moore	N	N	N	N	Y	N	Y
5 **Sensenbrenner**	Y	Y	Y	Y	N	Y	N
6 **Petri**	N	Y	Y	Y	N	Y	N
7 Obey	N	N	N	N	Y	N	Y
8 Kagen	N	N	N	N	Y	N	Y
WYOMING							
AL **Lummis**	Y	Y	Y	Y	N	Y	N
DELEGATES							
Faleomavaega (A.S.)	N	N	N	N			
Norton (D.C.)	N	N	N	N			
Bordallo (Guam)	N	N	N	N			
Sablan (N. Marianas)	N	N	N	N			
Pierluisi (P.R.)	N	N	N	N			
Christensen (V.I.)	N	N	N	N			

IN THE HOUSE | By Vote Number

478. **H Con Res 135. Slave Labor Marker/Adoption.** Johnson, D-Ga., motion to suspend the rules and adopt the concurrent resolution that would direct the Architect of the Capitol to design and place a marker in Emancipation Hall of the Capitol Visitor Center that recognizes the role slaves played in building the U.S. Capitol. Motion agreed to 399-1: R 162-1; D 237-0. A two-thirds majority of those present and voting (267 in this case) is required for adoption under suspension of the rules. July 7, 2009.

479. **HR 1129. Native American Iron-Working Program/Passage.** Bordallo, D-Guam, motion to suspend the rules and pass the bill that would authorize an Interior Department grant program for entities to provide an iron-working training program for Native Americans that includes classroom and on-the-job training, as well as job placement for those who complete the program. Motion agreed to 329-75: R 90-75; D 239-0. A two-thirds majority of those present and voting (270 in this case) is required for passage under suspension of the rules. July 7, 2009.

480. **HR 2965. Small-Business Programs Reauthorization/Rule.** Adoption of the rule (H Res 610) to provide for House floor consideration of the bill that would extend the authorization of the Small Business Innovation Research and Small Business Technology Transfer programs through fiscal 2011. Adopted 236-187: R 0-175; D 236-12. July 8, 2009.

481. **HR 1275. Utah Land Exchange/Passage.** Bordallo, D-Guam, motion to suspend the rules and pass the bill that would authorize unspecified sums for the Interior Department to exchange federal land for state trust land in Grand, San Juan and Uintah counties of Utah. Motion agreed to 423-0: R 175-0; D 248-0. A two-thirds majority of those present and voting (282 in this case) is required for passage under suspension of the rules. July 8, 2009.

482. **HR 1945. Tule River Tribe Water Study/Passage.** Bordallo, D-Guam, motion to suspend the rules and pass the bill that would authorize $3 million for the Interior Department to complete a study to evaluate water supply alternatives for the Tule River Indian Reservation in Tulare County, Calif., within two years. It would not allow the study to consider potential water usage for the tribe's casino and gaming activities. Motion agreed to 417-3: R 168-3; D 249-0. A two-thirds majority of those present and voting (280 in this case) is required for passage under suspension of the rules. July 8, 2009.

483. **HR 2965. Small-Business Programs Reauthorization/Space Shuttle Businesses.** Kosmas, D-Fla., amendment that would require commercialization programs established by agencies with space shuttle-related activities to include efforts to help small businesses affected by the termination of the space shuttle program. Adopted in Committee of the Whole 427-4: R 172-4; D 255-0. July 8, 2009.

484. **HR 2965. Small-Business Programs Reauthorization/Committee Substitute.** House Small Business Committee substitute amendment, as amended in the Committee of the Whole, that would reauthorize the Small Business Innovation Research and Small Business Technology Transfer programs through fiscal 2011. Adopted 411-15: R 162-15; D 249-0. (Pursuant to the rule, the House was previously considering the committee substitute as the original text of the bill for the purpose of amendment.) July 8, 2009.

	478	479	480	481	482	483	484
ALABAMA							
1 Bonner	Y	N	N	Y	Y	Y	Y
2 Bright	Y	Y	Y	Y	Y	Y	Y
3 Rogers	Y	Y	N	Y	Y	Y	Y
4 Aderholt	?	?	N	Y	Y	Y	Y
5 Griffith	Y	Y	?	Y	Y	Y	Y
6 Bachus	Y	Y	N	Y	Y	Y	Y
7 Davis	Y	Y	Y	Y	Y	Y	Y
ALASKA							
AL Young	Y	Y	N	Y	Y	Y	Y
ARIZONA							
1 Kirkpatrick	Y	Y	N	Y	Y	Y	Y
2 Franks	Y	N	N	Y	Y	Y	N
3 Shadegg	Y	N	N	Y	Y	Y	N
4 Pastor	Y	Y	Y	Y	Y	Y	Y
5 Mitchell	Y	Y	Y	Y	Y	Y	Y
6 Flake	Y	N	N	Y	Y	N	N
7 Grijalva	?	?	Y	Y	Y	Y	Y
8 Giffords	Y	Y	Y	Y	Y	Y	Y
ARKANSAS							
1 Berry	Y	Y	Y	Y	Y	Y	Y
2 Snyder	Y	Y	Y	Y	Y	Y	Y
3 Boozman	Y	N	N	Y	Y	Y	Y
4 Ross	Y	Y	Y	Y	Y	Y	Y
CALIFORNIA							
1 Thompson	Y	Y	Y	Y	Y	Y	Y
2 Herger	Y	N	N	Y	Y	Y	Y
3 Lungren	Y	Y	N	Y	Y	Y	Y
4 McClintock	Y	N	N	Y	Y	Y	N
5 Matsui	Y	Y	Y	Y	Y	Y	Y
6 Woolsey	Y	Y	Y	Y	Y	Y	Y
7 Miller, George	Y	Y	Y	Y	Y	Y	Y
8 Pelosi							
9 Lee	Y	Y	Y	Y	Y	Y	Y
10 Vacant*							
11 McNerney	Y	Y	Y	Y	Y	Y	Y
12 Speier	?	Y	Y	Y	Y	Y	Y
13 Stark	Y	Y	Y	Y	Y	Y	Y
14 Eshoo	Y	Y	Y	Y	Y	Y	Y
15 Honda	Y	Y	Y	Y	Y	Y	Y
16 Lofgren	Y	Y	Y	Y	Y	Y	Y
17 Farr	Y	Y	Y	Y	Y	Y	Y
18 Cardoza	Y	Y	+	+	Y	?	Y
19 Radanovich	Y	N	N	Y	Y	Y	Y
20 Costa	Y	Y	Y	Y	Y	Y	Y
21 Nunes	Y	Y	N	Y	Y	Y	Y
22 McCarthy	Y	N	N	Y	Y	Y	Y
23 Capps	Y	Y	Y	Y	Y	Y	Y
24 Gallegly	Y	Y	N	Y	Y	Y	Y
25 McKeon	Y	N	N	Y	Y	Y	Y
26 Dreier	Y	Y	N	Y	Y	Y	Y
27 Sherman	Y	Y	Y	Y	Y	Y	Y
28 Berman	Y	Y	Y	Y	Y	Y	Y
29 Schiff	Y	Y	Y	Y	Y	Y	Y
30 Waxman	Y	Y	Y	Y	Y	Y	?
31 Becerra	Y	Y	Y	Y	Y	Y	Y
32 Vacant							
33 Watson	Y	Y	Y	Y	Y	Y	Y
34 Roybal-Allard	Y	Y	Y	Y	Y	Y	Y
35 Waters	Y	Y	Y	Y	Y	Y	Y
36 Harman	Y	Y	Y	Y	Y	Y	Y
37 Richardson	Y	Y	Y	Y	Y	Y	Y
38 Napolitano	Y	Y	Y	Y	Y	Y	Y
39 Sánchez, Linda	Y	Y	Y	Y	Y	Y	Y
40 Royce	Y	N	N	Y	Y	Y	Y
41 Lewis	Y	N	N	Y	Y	Y	Y
42 Miller, Gary	Y	Y	N	Y	Y	Y	Y
43 Baca	Y	Y	Y	Y	Y	Y	Y
44 Calvert	Y	Y	N	Y	Y	Y	Y
45 Bono Mack	Y	Y	N	Y	Y	Y	Y
46 Rohrabacher	?	?	N	Y	Y	Y	Y
47 Sanchez, Loretta	Y	Y	Y	Y	Y	Y	Y
48 Campbell	Y	N	N	Y	Y	Y	Y
49 Issa	Y	N	N	Y	Y	Y	Y
50 Bilbray	Y	Y	N	Y	Y	Y	Y
51 Filner	Y	Y	Y	Y	Y	Y	Y
52 Hunter	Y	Y	N	Y	Y	Y	Y
53 Davis	Y	Y	Y	Y	Y	Y	Y

	478	479	480	481	482	483	484
COLORADO							
1 DeGette	Y	Y	Y	Y	Y	Y	Y
2 Polis	Y	Y	Y	Y	Y	Y	Y
3 Salazar	Y	Y	Y	Y	Y	Y	Y
4 Markey	Y	Y	Y	Y	Y	Y	Y
5 Lamborn	Y	N	N	Y	Y	Y	Y
6 Coffman	Y	N	N	Y	?	Y	Y
7 Perlmutter	Y	Y	Y	Y	Y	Y	Y
CONNECTICUT							
1 Larson	Y	Y	Y	Y	Y	Y	Y
2 Courtney	Y	Y	N	Y	Y	Y	Y
3 DeLauro	Y	Y	Y	Y	Y	Y	Y
4 Himes	Y	Y	Y	Y	Y	Y	Y
5 Murphy	Y	Y	Y	Y	Y	Y	Y
DELAWARE							
AL Castle	Y	Y	N	Y	Y	Y	Y
FLORIDA							
1 Miller	Y	N	N	Y	Y	Y	N
2 Boyd	Y	Y	Y	Y	Y	Y	Y
3 Brown	Y	Y	Y	Y	Y	Y	Y
4 Crenshaw	Y	N	N	Y	Y	Y	Y
5 Brown-Waite	Y	N	N	Y	Y	Y	Y
6 Stearns	Y	N	N	Y	Y	Y	Y
7 Mica	+	+	N	Y	Y	Y	Y
8 Grayson	Y	Y	Y	Y	Y	Y	Y
9 Bilirakis	Y	N	N	Y	Y	Y	Y
10 Young	Y	Y	N	Y	Y	Y	Y
11 Castor	Y	Y	Y	Y	Y	?	Y
12 Putnam	Y	Y	N	Y	Y	Y	Y
13 Buchanan	Y	N	N	Y	Y	Y	Y
14 Mack	Y	N	N	Y	Y	Y	Y
15 Posey	Y	N	N	Y	Y	Y	Y
16 Rooney	Y	N	N	Y	Y	Y	Y
17 Meek	Y	Y	Y	Y	Y	Y	Y
18 Ros-Lehtinen	Y	Y	N	Y	?	Y	Y
19 Wexler	?	?	Y	Y	Y	Y	Y
20 Wasserman Schultz	Y	Y	Y	Y	Y	Y	Y
21 Diaz-Balart, L.	Y	N	N	Y	Y	Y	Y
22 Klein	Y	Y	N	Y	Y	Y	Y
23 Hastings	Y	Y	Y	Y	Y	Y	Y
24 Kosmas	Y	Y	Y	Y	Y	Y	Y
25 Diaz-Balart, M.	Y	Y	N	Y	?	Y	Y
GEORGIA							
1 Kingston	Y	N	N	Y	Y	Y	Y
2 Bishop	Y	Y	Y	Y	Y	Y	Y
3 Westmoreland	?	?	N	Y	Y	Y	Y
4 Johnson	Y	Y	Y	Y	Y	Y	Y
5 Lewis	Y	Y	Y	Y	Y	Y	Y
6 Price	Y	N	N	Y	Y	N	Y
7 Linder	Y	N	N	Y	Y	Y	Y
8 Marshall	Y	Y	Y	Y	Y	Y	Y
9 Deal	?	?	N	Y	Y	Y	Y
10 Broun	+	-	-	+	-	-	-
11 Gingrey	Y	Y	N	Y	Y	Y	Y
12 Barrow	Y	Y	Y	Y	Y	Y	Y
13 Scott	Y	Y	Y	Y	Y	Y	Y
HAWAII							
1 Abercrombie	Y	Y	Y	Y	?	Y	Y
2 Hirono	Y	Y	Y	Y	Y	Y	Y
IDAHO							
1 Minnick	Y	Y	N	Y	Y	Y	Y
2 Simpson	Y	Y	N	Y	Y	Y	Y
ILLINOIS							
1 Rush	Y	Y	Y	Y	Y	Y	Y
2 Jackson	Y	Y	Y	Y	Y	Y	Y
3 Lipinski	Y	Y	Y	Y	Y	Y	Y
4 Gutierrez	?	?	Y	Y	Y	Y	Y
5 Quigley	Y	Y	Y	Y	Y	Y	Y
6 Roskam	Y	N	N	Y	Y	Y	Y
7 Davis	Y	Y	Y	Y	Y	Y	Y
8 Bean	?	?	Y	Y	Y	Y	Y
9 Schakowsky	Y	Y	Y	Y	Y	Y	Y
10 Kirk	Y	Y	N	Y	Y	Y	Y
11 Halvorson	Y	Y	Y	Y	Y	Y	Y
12 Costello	Y	Y	Y	Y	Y	Y	Y
13 Biggert	Y	Y	N	Y	Y	Y	Y
14 Foster	Y	Y	Y	Y	Y	Y	Y
15 Johnson	Y	N	N	Y	Y	Y	Y

KEY	**Republicans**	Democrats			
Y Voted for (yea)		X Paired against		C Voted "present" to avoid possible conflict of interest	
# Paired for		− Announced against			
+ Announced for		P Voted "present"		? Did not vote or otherwise make a position known	
N Voted against (nay)					

*Rep. Ellen O. Tauscher, D-Calif., resigned June 26 to become an undersecretary of State. The last vote for which she was eligible was vote 477.

Member	478	479	480	481	482	483	484
16 **Manzullo**	Y	N	N	Y	Y	Y	N
17 Hare	Y	Y	Y	Y	Y	Y	Y
18 **Schock**	Y	N	N	Y	Y	Y	Y
19 **Shimkus**	Y	N	N	Y	Y	Y	Y
INDIANA							
1 Visclosky	Y	Y	Y	Y	Y	Y	Y
2 Donnelly	Y	Y	Y	Y	Y	Y	Y
3 **Souder**	Y	N	N	Y	Y	Y	Y
4 **Buyer**	Y	Y	N	Y	Y	Y	Y
5 **Burton**	?	–	N	Y	Y	Y	Y
6 **Pence**	Y	N	N	Y	Y	Y	Y
7 Carson	Y	Y	Y	Y	Y	Y	Y
8 Ellsworth	+	+	+	+	+	+	+
9 Hill	Y	Y	N	Y	Y	Y	Y
IOWA							
1 Braley	Y	Y	Y	Y	Y	Y	Y
2 Loebsack	Y	Y	Y	Y	Y	Y	Y
3 Boswell	Y	Y	Y	Y	Y	Y	Y
4 **Latham**	Y	Y	N	Y	Y	Y	Y
5 **King**	N	N	N	Y	Y	N	Y
KANSAS							
1 **Moran**	Y	N	N	Y	Y	Y	Y
2 **Jenkins**	Y	Y	N	Y	Y	Y	Y
3 Moore	Y	Y	N	Y	Y	Y	Y
4 **Tiahrt**	Y	Y	N	Y	Y	Y	Y
KENTUCKY							
1 **Whitfield**	Y	Y	N	Y	Y	Y	Y
2 **Guthrie**	Y	Y	N	Y	Y	Y	Y
3 Yarmuth	Y	Y	Y	Y	Y	Y	Y
4 **Davis**	Y	Y	N	Y	Y	Y	Y
5 **Rogers**	?	?	N	Y	Y	Y	Y
6 Chandler	Y	Y	Y	Y	Y	Y	Y
LOUISIANA							
1 **Scalise**	Y	N	N	Y	Y	Y	Y
2 **Cao**	Y	Y	N	Y	Y	Y	Y
3 Melancon	?	?	Y	?	Y	Y	Y
4 **Fleming**	Y	N	N	Y	Y	Y	Y
5 **Alexander**	Y	Y	N	Y	Y	Y	Y
6 **Cassidy**	Y	N	N	Y	Y	Y	Y
7 **Boustany**	Y	N	N	Y	Y	Y	Y
MAINE							
1 Pingree	Y	Y	Y	Y	Y	Y	Y
2 Michaud	Y	Y	Y	Y	Y	Y	Y
MARYLAND							
1 Kratovil	Y	Y	Y	Y	Y	Y	Y
2 Ruppersberger	Y	Y	Y	Y	Y	Y	Y
3 Sarbanes	Y	Y	Y	Y	Y	Y	Y
4 Edwards	Y	Y	Y	Y	Y	Y	Y
5 Hoyer	Y	Y	Y	Y	Y	Y	Y
6 **Bartlett**	Y	Y	N	Y	Y	Y	Y
7 Cummings	Y	Y	Y	Y	Y	Y	Y
8 Van Hollen	Y	Y	Y	Y	Y	Y	Y
MASSACHUSETTS							
1 Olver	Y	Y	Y	Y	Y	Y	Y
2 Neal	Y	Y	Y	Y	Y	Y	Y
3 McGovern	Y	Y	Y	Y	Y	Y	Y
4 Frank	Y	Y	Y	Y	Y	Y	Y
5 Tsongas	Y	Y	N	Y	Y	Y	Y
6 Tierney	Y	Y	Y	Y	Y	Y	Y
7 Markey	Y	Y	N	Y	Y	Y	Y
8 Capuano	Y	Y	Y	Y	Y	Y	Y
9 Lynch	Y	Y	Y	Y	Y	Y	Y
10 Delahunt	?	?	Y	Y	Y	Y	Y
MICHIGAN							
1 Stupak	Y	Y	Y	Y	Y	Y	Y
2 **Hoekstra**	Y	N	N	Y	Y	Y	Y
3 **Ehlers**	Y	Y	N	Y	Y	Y	Y
4 **Camp**	Y	Y	N	Y	Y	Y	Y
5 Kildee	Y	Y	Y	Y	Y	Y	Y
6 **Upton**	Y	Y	N	Y	Y	Y	Y
7 Schauer	Y	Y	Y	Y	Y	Y	Y
8 **Rogers**	Y	Y	N	Y	Y	Y	Y
9 Peters	Y	Y	Y	Y	Y	Y	Y
10 **Miller**	Y	Y	N	Y	Y	Y	Y
11 **McCotter**	Y	Y	N	Y	Y	Y	Y
12 Levin	Y	Y	Y	Y	Y	Y	Y
13 Kilpatrick	Y	Y	Y	Y	Y	Y	Y
14 Conyers	?	Y	Y	Y	Y	Y	Y
15 Dingell	Y	Y	Y	?	?	Y	Y
MINNESOTA							
1 Walz	Y	Y	Y	Y	Y	Y	Y
2 **Kline**	Y	N	N	Y	Y	Y	Y
3 **Paulsen**	Y	Y	N	Y	Y	Y	Y
4 McCollum	Y	Y	Y	Y	Y	Y	Y
5 Ellison	Y	Y	Y	Y	Y	Y	Y
6 **Bachmann**	Y	N	N	Y	Y	Y	Y
7 Peterson	Y	Y	Y	Y	Y	Y	Y
8 Oberstar	Y	Y	Y	Y	Y	Y	Y
MISSISSIPPI							
1 Childers	+	+	Y	Y	Y	Y	Y
2 Thompson	Y	Y	Y	Y	Y	Y	Y
3 **Harper**	Y	N	N	Y	Y	Y	Y
4 Taylor	Y	Y	Y	Y	Y	Y	Y
MISSOURI							
1 Clay	Y	Y	Y	Y	Y	Y	Y
2 **Akin**	Y	N	N	Y	Y	Y	Y
3 Carnahan	Y	Y	Y	Y	Y	Y	Y
4 Skelton	Y	Y	Y	Y	Y	Y	Y
5 Cleaver	Y	Y	Y	Y	Y	Y	Y
6 **Graves**	Y	Y	N	Y	Y	Y	Y
7 **Blunt**	?	?	N	Y	Y	Y	Y
8 **Emerson**	Y	Y	N	Y	Y	Y	Y
9 **Luetkemeyer**	Y	N	N	Y	Y	Y	Y
MONTANA							
AL **Rehberg**	Y	Y	N	Y	Y	Y	Y
NEBRASKA							
1 **Fortenberry**	Y	Y	N	Y	Y	Y	Y
2 **Terry**	Y	Y	N	Y	Y	Y	Y
3 **Smith**	Y	Y	N	Y	Y	Y	Y
NEVADA							
1 Berkley	Y	Y	Y	Y	Y	Y	Y
2 **Heller**	Y	Y	N	Y	Y	Y	Y
3 Titus	Y	Y	Y	Y	Y	Y	Y
NEW HAMPSHIRE							
1 Shea-Porter	Y	Y	Y	Y	Y	Y	Y
2 Hodes	Y	Y	N	Y	Y	Y	Y
NEW JERSEY							
1 Andrews	Y	Y	?	Y	Y	Y	Y
2 **LoBiondo**	Y	Y	N	Y	Y	Y	Y
3 Adler	Y	Y	Y	Y	Y	Y	Y
4 **Smith**	Y	Y	N	Y	Y	Y	Y
5 **Garrett**	?	N	N	Y	Y	Y	Y
6 Pallone	Y	Y	Y	Y	Y	Y	Y
7 **Lance**	Y	Y	N	Y	Y	Y	Y
8 Pascrell	Y	Y	Y	Y	Y	Y	Y
9 Rothman	Y	Y	Y	Y	Y	Y	Y
10 Payne	?	?	Y	Y	Y	Y	Y
11 **Frelinghuysen**	Y	Y	N	Y	Y	Y	Y
12 Holt	Y	Y	Y	Y	Y	Y	Y
13 Sires	Y	Y	Y	Y	Y	Y	Y
NEW MEXICO							
1 Heinrich	Y	Y	N	Y	Y	Y	Y
2 Teague	Y	Y	Y	Y	Y	Y	Y
3 Lujan	Y	Y	Y	Y	Y	Y	Y
NEW YORK							
1 Bishop	Y	Y	Y	Y	Y	Y	Y
2 Israel	Y	Y	Y	Y	Y	Y	Y
3 **King**	Y	Y	N	Y	Y	Y	Y
4 McCarthy	Y	Y	Y	Y	Y	Y	Y
5 Ackerman	Y	Y	Y	Y	Y	Y	Y
6 Meeks	Y	Y	Y	Y	Y	Y	Y
7 Crowley	Y	Y	Y	Y	Y	Y	Y
8 Nadler	Y	Y	Y	Y	Y	Y	Y
9 Weiner	Y	Y	Y	Y	Y	Y	Y
10 Towns	Y	Y	Y	Y	Y	Y	Y
11 Clarke	Y	Y	Y	Y	Y	Y	Y
12 Velázquez	Y	Y	Y	Y	Y	Y	Y
13 McMahon	Y	Y	Y	Y	Y	Y	Y
14 Maloney	Y	Y	Y	Y	Y	Y	Y
15 Rangel	Y	Y	Y	Y	Y	Y	Y
16 Serrano	Y	Y	Y	Y	Y	Y	Y
17 Engel	Y	Y	Y	Y	Y	Y	Y
18 Lowey	Y	Y	Y	Y	Y	Y	Y
19 Hall	?	?	Y	Y	Y	Y	Y
20 Murphy	Y	Y	Y	Y	Y	Y	Y
21 Tonko	Y	Y	Y	Y	Y	Y	Y
22 Hinchey	Y	Y	Y	Y	Y	Y	Y
23 **McHugh**	Y	Y	N	Y	Y	Y	Y
24 Arcuri	Y	Y	Y	Y	Y	Y	Y
25 Maffei	Y	Y	Y	Y	Y	Y	Y
26 **Lee**	Y	Y	N	Y	?	Y	Y
27 Higgins	Y	Y	Y	Y	Y	Y	Y
28 Slaughter	Y	Y	Y	Y	Y	Y	Y
29 Massa	Y	Y	Y	Y	Y	Y	Y
NORTH CAROLINA							
1 Butterfield	Y	Y	Y	?	Y	Y	Y
2 Etheridge	Y	Y	Y	Y	Y	Y	Y
3 **Jones**	Y	Y	N	Y	Y	Y	Y
4 Price	Y	Y	Y	Y	Y	Y	Y
5 **Foxx**	Y	N	N	Y	Y	N	N
6 **Coble**	Y	N	N	Y	N	Y	Y
7 McIntyre	Y	Y	Y	Y	Y	Y	Y
8 Kissell	+	+	Y	Y	Y	Y	Y
9 **Myrick**	Y	N	N	Y	Y	Y	Y
10 **McHenry**	Y	Y	N	Y	Y	Y	Y
11 Shuler	Y	Y	N	Y	Y	Y	Y
12 Watt	Y	Y	Y	Y	Y	Y	Y
13 Miller	?	?	?	Y	Y	Y	Y
NORTH DAKOTA							
AL Pomeroy	Y	Y	Y	Y	Y	Y	Y
OHIO							
1 Driehaus	Y	Y	Y	Y	Y	Y	Y
2 **Schmidt**	Y	N	N	Y	Y	Y	Y
3 **Turner**	Y	Y	N	Y	Y	Y	Y
4 **Jordan**	Y	N	N	Y	Y	Y	Y
5 **Latta**	Y	N	N	Y	Y	Y	Y
6 Wilson	Y	Y	Y	Y	Y	Y	Y
7 **Austria**	Y	Y	N	Y	Y	Y	Y
8 **Boehner**	Y	N	N	Y	Y	Y	Y
9 Kaptur	Y	Y	Y	Y	Y	Y	Y
10 Kucinich	Y	Y	Y	Y	Y	Y	Y
11 Fudge	Y	Y	Y	Y	Y	Y	Y
12 **Tiberi**	Y	N	N	Y	Y	Y	Y
13 Sutton	Y	Y	Y	Y	Y	Y	Y
14 **LaTourette**	Y	Y	N	Y	Y	Y	Y
15 Kilroy	Y	Y	Y	Y	Y	Y	Y
16 Boccieri	Y	Y	Y	Y	Y	Y	Y
17 Ryan	Y	Y	Y	Y	Y	Y	Y
18 Space	Y	Y	Y	Y	Y	Y	Y
OKLAHOMA							
1 **Sullivan**	Y	Y	N	Y	Y	Y	Y
2 Boren	Y	Y	Y	Y	Y	Y	Y
3 **Lucas**	Y	Y	N	Y	Y	Y	Y
4 **Cole**	Y	Y	N	Y	Y	Y	Y
5 **Fallin**	?	?	N	Y	Y	Y	Y
OREGON							
1 Wu	Y	Y	Y	Y	Y	Y	Y
2 **Walden**	Y	Y	N	Y	Y	Y	Y
3 Blumenauer	Y	Y	Y	Y	Y	Y	Y
4 DeFazio	Y	Y	Y	Y	Y	Y	Y
5 Schrader	Y	Y	Y	Y	Y	Y	Y
PENNSYLVANIA							
1 Brady	Y	Y	Y	Y	Y	Y	Y
2 Fattah	Y	Y	Y	Y	Y	Y	Y
3 Dahlkemper	Y	Y	Y	Y	Y	Y	Y
4 Altmire	Y	Y	Y	Y	Y	Y	Y
5 **Thompson**	Y	N	N	Y	Y	Y	Y
6 **Gerlach**	Y	Y	N	Y	Y	Y	Y
7 Sestak	?	?	?	?	?	?	?
8 Murphy, P.	Y	Y	Y	Y	Y	Y	Y
9 **Shuster**	Y	N	N	Y	?	Y	Y
10 Carney	Y	Y	Y	Y	Y	Y	Y
11 Kanjorski	Y	Y	Y	Y	Y	Y	Y
12 Murtha	Y	Y	Y	Y	Y	Y	?
13 Schwartz	Y	Y	Y	Y	Y	Y	Y
14 Doyle	Y	Y	Y	Y	Y	Y	Y
15 **Dent**	Y	Y	N	Y	Y	Y	Y
16 **Pitts**	Y	N	N	Y	Y	Y	Y
17 Holden	Y	Y	Y	Y	Y	Y	Y
18 **Murphy, T.**	Y	Y	N	Y	Y	Y	Y
19 **Platts**	Y	Y	N	Y	Y	Y	Y
RHODE ISLAND							
1 Kennedy	Y	Y	Y	Y	Y	Y	Y
2 Langevin	Y	Y	Y	Y	Y	Y	Y
SOUTH CAROLINA							
1 **Brown**	Y	N	N	Y	Y	Y	Y
2 **Wilson**	Y	Y	N	Y	Y	Y	Y
3 **Barrett**	+	–	–	+	Y	Y	Y
4 **Inglis**	?	?	N	Y	Y	Y	Y
5 Spratt	Y	Y	Y	Y	Y	Y	Y
6 Clyburn	Y	Y	Y	Y	Y	Y	Y
SOUTH DAKOTA							
AL Herseth Sandlin	Y	Y	Y	Y	Y	Y	Y
TENNESSEE							
1 **Roe**	Y	N	N	Y	Y	Y	Y
2 **Duncan**	Y	N	N	Y	Y	Y	N
3 **Wamp**	Y	Y	N	Y	Y	Y	Y
4 Davis	Y	Y	Y	Y	Y	Y	Y
5 Cooper	Y	Y	Y	Y	Y	Y	Y
6 Gordon	Y	Y	Y	Y	Y	Y	Y
7 **Blackburn**	Y	Y	N	Y	Y	Y	Y
8 Tanner	Y	Y	Y	Y	Y	Y	Y
9 Cohen	Y	Y	Y	Y	Y	Y	Y
TEXAS							
1 **Gohmert**	?	N	N	Y	Y	Y	Y
2 **Poe**	Y	Y	N	Y	Y	Y	N
3 **Johnson, S.**	Y	N	N	Y	Y	Y	Y
4 **Hall**	Y	Y	N	Y	Y	Y	Y
5 **Hensarling**	?	?	?	?	?	Y	Y
6 **Barton**	Y	N	N	Y	Y	Y	Y
7 **Culberson**	Y	N	N	Y	Y	Y	Y
8 **Brady**	Y	N	N	Y	Y	Y	Y
9 Green, A.	Y	Y	Y	Y	Y	Y	Y
10 **McCaul**	Y	N	N	Y	Y	Y	Y
11 **Conaway**	Y	N	N	Y	Y	Y	Y
12 **Granger**	Y	N	N	Y	Y	Y	Y
13 **Thornberry**	Y	N	N	Y	Y	Y	Y
14 **Paul**	Y	N	N	Y	N	Y	N
15 Hinojosa	Y	Y	Y	Y	Y	Y	Y
16 Reyes	Y	Y	Y	Y	Y	Y	Y
17 Edwards	Y	Y	Y	Y	Y	Y	Y
18 Jackson Lee	?	?	Y	Y	Y	Y	Y
19 **Neugebauer**	Y	N	N	Y	Y	Y	Y
20 Gonzalez	Y	Y	Y	Y	Y	Y	Y
21 **Smith**	Y	Y	N	Y	Y	Y	Y
22 **Olson**	Y	N	N	Y	Y	Y	Y
23 Rodriguez	Y	Y	Y	Y	Y	Y	Y
24 **Marchant**	Y	N	N	Y	Y	Y	N
25 Doggett	Y	Y	Y	Y	Y	Y	Y
26 **Burgess**	Y	N	N	Y	Y	Y	Y
27 Ortiz	Y	Y	Y	Y	Y	Y	Y
28 Cuellar	Y	Y	Y	Y	Y	Y	Y
29 Green, G.	Y	Y	Y	Y	Y	Y	Y
30 Johnson, E.	?	?	Y	Y	Y	Y	Y
31 **Carter**	Y	N	N	Y	Y	Y	Y
32 **Sessions**	Y	Y	N	Y	Y	Y	Y
UTAH							
1 **Bishop**	Y	Y	N	Y	Y	Y	Y
2 Matheson	Y	Y	Y	Y	Y	Y	Y
3 **Chaffetz**	Y	N	N	Y	Y	Y	N
VERMONT							
AL Welch	Y	Y	Y	Y	Y	Y	Y
VIRGINIA							
1 **Wittman**	Y	Y	N	Y	Y	Y	Y
2 Nye	Y	Y	Y	Y	Y	Y	Y
3 Scott	Y	Y	Y	Y	Y	Y	Y
4 **Forbes**	Y	Y	N	Y	Y	Y	Y
5 Perriello	Y	Y	N	Y	Y	Y	Y
6 **Goodlatte**	Y	Y	N	Y	Y	Y	Y
7 **Cantor**	Y	N	N	Y	Y	Y	Y
8 Moran	Y	Y	Y	Y	Y	Y	Y
9 Boucher	Y	Y	Y	Y	Y	Y	Y
10 **Wolf**	Y	Y	N	Y	Y	Y	Y
11 Connolly	Y	Y	Y	Y	Y	Y	Y
WASHINGTON							
1 Inslee	Y	Y	Y	Y	Y	Y	Y
2 Larsen	Y	Y	Y	Y	Y	Y	Y
3 Baird	Y	Y	Y	Y	Y	Y	Y
4 **Hastings**	Y	N	N	Y	Y	Y	Y
5 **McMorris Rodgers**	Y	Y	N	Y	Y	Y	Y
6 Dicks	Y	Y	Y	Y	Y	Y	Y
7 McDermott	Y	Y	Y	Y	Y	Y	Y
8 **Reichert**	Y	Y	N	Y	Y	Y	Y
9 Smith	Y	Y	Y	Y	Y	Y	Y
WEST VIRGINIA							
1 Mollohan	Y	Y	Y	Y	Y	Y	Y
2 **Capito**	Y	Y	N	Y	Y	Y	Y
3 Rahall	Y	Y	Y	Y	Y	Y	Y
WISCONSIN							
1 **Ryan**	Y	Y	N	Y	Y	Y	N
2 Baldwin	Y	Y	Y	Y	Y	Y	Y
3 Kind	Y	Y	Y	Y	Y	Y	Y
4 Moore	Y	Y	Y	Y	Y	Y	Y
5 **Sensenbrenner**	Y	Y	N	Y	N	Y	N
6 **Petri**	Y	Y	N	Y	Y	Y	N
7 Obey	Y	Y	Y	Y	Y	Y	Y
8 Kagen	Y	Y	Y	Y	Y	Y	Y
WYOMING							
AL **Lummis**	Y	Y	N	Y	Y	Y	Y
DELEGATES							
Faleomavaega (A.S.)					?		
Norton (D.C.)					Y		
Bordallo (Guam)					Y		
Sablan (N. Marianas)					Y		
Pierluisi (P.R.)					Y		
Christensen (V.I.)					Y		

IN THE HOUSE | By Vote Number

485. **HR 2965. Small-Business Programs Reauthorization/Motion to Table.** Velázquez, D-N.Y., motion to table (kill) the Simpson, R-Idaho, appeal of the ruling of the chair with respect to the Velázquez point of order that the Simpson motion to recommit the bill was not germane. The motion would recommit the bill to the Small Business Committee with instructions that it be immediately reported back with language expressing the sense of Congress that the House should abide by regular order when considering appropriations bills. Motion agreed to 246-181: R 2-175; D 244-6. July 8, 2009.

486. **HR 2965. Small-Business Programs Reauthorization/Passage.** Passage of the bill that would reauthorize the Small Business Innovation Research and Small Business Technology Transfer programs through fiscal 2011. The bill would give preference in awarding grants under the programs to businesses owned by service-disabled veterans, women or minorities, or that are located in rural areas. It would increase the maximum grants for the initial stage of research and technology transfer projects to $250,000, and to $2 million for the second stage of such projects. Passed 386-41: R 149-28; D 237-13. July 8, 2009.

487. **Procedural Motion/Journal.** Approval of the House Journal of Tuesday, July 7, 2009. Approved 237-184: R 20-154; D 217-30. July 8, 2009.

488. **Procedural Motion/Motion to Adjourn.** Westmoreland, R-Ga., motion to adjourn. Motion rejected 36-364: R 33-135; D 3-229. July 8, 2009.

489. **HR 2997. Fiscal 2010 Agriculture Appropriations/Question of Consideration.** Question of whether the House should consider the rule (H Res 609) to provide for House floor consideration of the bill that would appropriate $123.8 billion in fiscal 2010 for the Department of Agriculture and related agencies, including the Food and Drug Administration. Agreed to consider 244-185: R 0-177; D 244-8. (Flake, R-Ariz., had raised a point of order that the rule contained a provision that violated the Budget Act.) July 8, 2009.

490. **Procedural Motion/Motion to Adjourn.** Foxx, R-N.C., motion to adjourn. Motion rejected 35-368: R 29-140; D 6-228. July 8, 2009.

491. **HR 2997. Fiscal 2010 Agriculture Appropriations/Previous Question.** McGovern, D-Mass., motion to order the previous question (thus ending debate and possibility of amendment) on adoption of the rule (H Res 609) that would provide for House floor consideration of a bill that would appropriate $123.8 billion in fiscal 2010 for the Department of Agriculture and related agencies, including the Food and Drug Administration. Motion agreed to 239-183: R 1-176; D 238-7. July 8, 2009.

	485	486	487	488	489	490	491
ALABAMA							
1 Bonner	N	Y	N	N	N	N	N
2 Bright	N	Y	?	N	N	N	Y
3 Rogers	N	N	N	N	N	N	N
4 Aderholt	N	Y	Y	N	N	N	N
5 Griffith	N	Y	N	N	Y	N	Y
6 Bachus	N	Y	N	N	N	N	N
7 Davis	Y	Y	Y	N	Y	N	Y
ALASKA							
AL Young	N	Y	N	N	N	Y	N
ARIZONA							
1 Kirkpatrick	Y	Y	N	N	Y	N	Y
2 Franks	N	N	N	N	N	?	N
3 Shadegg	N	N	N	Y	N	N	N
4 Pastor	Y	Y	Y	N	Y	N	Y
5 Mitchell	Y	Y	N	N	N	Y	N
6 Flake	N	N	N	Y	N	Y	N
7 Grijalva	Y	Y	Y	?	Y	N	Y
8 Giffords	Y	Y	N	N	Y	N	Y
ARKANSAS							
1 Berry	Y	Y	Y	N	Y	N	Y
2 Snyder	Y	Y	Y	N	Y	N	Y
3 Boozman	N	Y	N	N	N	N	N
4 Ross	Y	Y	Y	N	Y	N	Y
CALIFORNIA							
1 Thompson	Y	Y	N	N	Y	N	Y
2 Herger	N	Y	N	?	N	N	N
3 Lungren	N	Y	N	N	N	N	N
4 McClintock	N	N	Y	N	N	N	N
5 Matsui	Y	Y	Y	N	Y	N	Y
6 Woolsey	Y	Y	Y	N	Y	N	Y
7 Miller, George	Y	Y	Y	?	Y	N	Y
8 Pelosi							
9 Lee	Y	Y	Y	?	Y	N	Y
10 Vacant							
11 McNerney	Y	Y	Y	N	Y	N	Y
12 Speier	Y	Y	Y	N	Y	?	Y
13 Stark	Y	Y	Y	N	Y	N	Y
14 Eshoo	Y	Y	Y	N	Y	N	Y
15 Honda	Y	Y	Y	?	Y	N	Y
16 Lofgren	Y	Y	Y	N	Y	N	Y
17 Farr	Y	Y	Y	N	Y	N	Y
18 Cardoza	Y	Y	Y	N	Y	N	Y
19 Radanovich	N	Y	N	?	N	N	N
20 Costa	Y	Y	Y	N	Y	N	Y
21 Nunes	N	Y	N	N	N	N	N
22 McCarthy	N	Y	N	N	N	N	N
23 Capps	Y	Y	Y	N	Y	N	Y
24 Gallegly	N	Y	N	N	N	N	N
25 McKeon	N	Y	N	N	N	N	N
26 Dreier	N	Y	N	N	N	N	N
27 Sherman	Y	Y	Y	N	Y	N	Y
28 Berman	Y	Y	Y	N	Y	N	Y
29 Schiff	Y	Y	Y	N	Y	N	Y
30 Waxman	Y	Y	Y	N	Y	N	Y
31 Becerra	Y	Y	Y	N	Y	N	Y
32 Vacant							
33 Watson	Y	?	?	?	Y	N	Y
34 Roybal-Allard	Y	Y	Y	N	Y	N	Y
35 Waters	Y	Y	Y	Y	Y	N	Y
36 Harman	?	?	?	N	Y	N	Y
37 Richardson	Y	Y	Y	N	Y	N	Y
38 Napolitano	Y	Y	Y	?	Y	N	Y
39 Sánchez, Linda	Y	Y	Y	N	Y	?	Y
40 Royce	N	N	N	N	N	N	N
41 Lewis	N	Y	N	Y	N	N	Y
42 Miller, Gary	N	N	N	N	N	Y	?
43 Baca	Y	Y	Y	N	Y	N	Y
44 Calvert	N	Y	N	N	N	N	N
45 Bono Mack	N	N	N	N	N	N	N
46 Rohrabacher	N	N	N	N	N	N	N
47 Sanchez, Loretta	Y	Y	Y	?	Y	N	Y
48 Campbell	N	N	N	Y	N	Y	N
49 Issa	N	N	N	Y	N	N	N
50 Bilbray	N	Y	N	N	N	N	N
51 Filner	Y	Y	Y	N	Y	N	Y
52 Hunter	N	Y	N	N	N	N	N
53 Davis	Y	Y	Y	N	Y	N	Y

	485	486	487	488	489	490	491
COLORADO							
1 DeGette	Y	Y	Y	N	Y	N	Y
2 Polis	Y	Y	Y	N	Y	N	Y
3 Salazar	Y	Y	Y	N	Y	N	Y
4 Markey	Y	Y	N	N	Y	N	Y
5 Lamborn	N	Y	N	?	N	Y	N
6 Coffman	N	Y	N	Y	N	Y	N
7 Perlmutter	Y	Y	Y	N	Y	N	Y
CONNECTICUT							
1 Larson	Y	Y	Y	N	Y	N	Y
2 Courtney	Y	N	Y	N	Y	N	Y
3 DeLauro	Y	Y	Y	N	Y	N	Y
4 Himes	Y	Y	Y	N	Y	N	Y
5 Murphy	Y	N	Y	N	Y	N	Y
DELAWARE							
AL Castle	N	Y	N	N	N	N	N
FLORIDA							
1 Miller	N	Y	N	N	N	N	N
2 Boyd	Y	Y	Y	N	Y	N	Y
3 Brown	Y	Y	Y	N	Y	N	Y
4 Crenshaw	N	Y	N	N	N	N	N
5 Brown-Waite	N	Y	N	?	N	N	N
6 Stearns	N	Y	N	N	N	?	N
7 Mica	N	Y	N	N	N	N	N
8 Grayson	Y	Y	Y	N	Y	N	Y
9 Bilirakis	N	Y	N	?	N	N	N
10 Young	N	Y	N	N	N	N	N
11 Castor	Y	Y	Y	N	Y	N	Y
12 Putnam	N	Y	N	N	N	N	N
13 Buchanan	Y	Y	Y	N	N	N	N
14 Mack	N	Y	N	Y	N	N	N
15 Posey	N	N	Y	N	N	N	N
16 Rooney	N	Y	N	N	N	N	N
17 Meek	Y	Y	Y	N	Y	N	Y
18 Ros-Lehtinen	N	Y	?	N	N	N	N
19 Wexler	Y	Y	Y	?	Y	N	Y
20 Wasserman Schultz	Y	Y	Y	N	Y	?	Y
21 Diaz-Balart, L.	N	Y	N	N	N	N	N
22 Klein	Y	Y	Y	N	Y	N	Y
23 Hastings	Y	Y	Y	N	Y	N	Y
24 Kosmas	N	Y	Y	N	Y	N	Y
25 Diaz-Balart, M.	N	Y	N	N	N	N	N
GEORGIA							
1 Kingston	N	N	N	N	N	Y	N
2 Bishop	Y	Y	Y	N	Y	?	Y
3 Westmoreland	N	Y	N	Y	N	Y	N
4 Johnson	Y	Y	Y	N	Y	N	Y
5 Lewis	Y	Y	Y	N	Y	N	Y
6 Price	N	Y	N	Y	N	Y	N
7 Linder	N	N	N	?	N	N	N
8 Marshall	Y	Y	Y	N	Y	N	Y
9 Deal	N	Y	N	N	N	N	N
10 Broun	–	–	–	+	N	Y	N
11 Gingrey	N	Y	N	N	N	N	N
12 Barrow	Y	Y	Y	N	Y	N	Y
13 Scott	Y	Y	Y	N	Y	N	Y
HAWAII							
1 Abercrombie	Y	Y	Y	N	Y	N	Y
2 Hirono	Y	Y	Y	N	Y	N	Y
IDAHO							
1 Minnick	N	Y	N	N	N	N	Y
2 Simpson	N	Y	N	N	N	N	N
ILLINOIS							
1 Rush	Y	Y	Y	N	Y	?	Y
2 Jackson	Y	Y	Y	N	Y	N	Y
3 Lipinski	Y	Y	Y	N	Y	N	Y
4 Gutierrez	Y	Y	Y	N	Y	Y	Y
5 Quigley	Y	Y	Y	N	Y	N	Y
6 Roskam	N	Y	N	N	N	N	N
7 Davis	Y	Y	Y	N	Y	N	Y
8 Bean	Y	Y	Y	N	Y	?	Y
9 Schakowsky	Y	Y	Y	N	Y	N	Y
10 Kirk	N	Y	N	N	N	N	N
11 Halvorson	Y	Y	N	Y	Y	Y	Y
12 Costello	Y	Y	Y	N	Y	N	Y
13 Biggert	N	Y	N	N	N	N	N
14 Foster	Y	Y	Y	N	Y	N	Y
15 Johnson	Y	Y	Y	N	Y	N	Y

KEY   **Republicans**   Democrats

Y Voted for (yea)	X Paired against
# Paired for	– Announced against
+ Announced for	P Voted "present"
N Voted against (nay)	

C Voted "present" to avoid possible conflict of interest

? Did not vote or otherwise make a position known

	485	486	487	488	489	490	491
16 **Manzullo**	N	N	N	N	N	N	N
17 Hare	Y	Y	Y	N	Y	N	Y
18 **Schock**	N	Y	N	N	N	?	N
19 **Shimkus**	N	Y	N	?	N	Y	N
INDIANA							
1 Visclosky	Y	Y	Y	N	Y	N	Y
2 Donnelly	Y	Y	N	N	Y	N	Y
3 **Souder**	N	Y	N	Y	N	?	N
4 **Buyer**	N	Y	Y	N	N	N	N
5 **Burton**	N	Y	N	N	N	N	N
6 **Pence**	N	Y	N	Y	N	Y	N
7 Carson	Y	Y	Y	N	Y	N	Y
8 Ellsworth	Y	Y	N	–	Y	N	Y
9 Hill	Y	Y	N	N	Y	N	N
IOWA							
1 Braley	Y	Y	Y	N	Y	N	Y
2 Loebsack	Y	Y	Y	N	Y	N	Y
3 Boswell	Y	Y	N	N	Y	N	Y
4 **Latham**	N	Y	Y	N	N	N	N
5 **King**	N	Y	N	Y	N	Y	N
KANSAS							
1 **Moran**	N	Y	N	N	N	N	N
2 **Jenkins**	N	Y	N	N	N	N	N
3 Moore	Y	Y	N	N	Y	N	Y
4 **Tiahrt**	N	Y	N	Y	N	Y	N
KENTUCKY							
1 **Whitfield**	N	Y	Y	N	N	N	N
2 **Guthrie**	N	Y	N	N	N	N	N
3 Yarmuth	Y	Y	Y	N	Y	N	Y
4 **Davis**	N	Y	N	N	N	N	N
5 **Rogers**	N	Y	N	N	N	N	N
6 Chandler	Y	Y	Y	?	Y	N	Y
LOUISIANA							
1 **Scalise**	N	Y	N	N	N	N	N
2 **Cao**	N	Y	N	N	N	N	N
3 Melancon	?	Y	Y	N	Y	N	Y
4 **Fleming**	N	Y	N	N	N	N	N
5 **Alexander**	N	Y	N	N	N	N	N
6 **Cassidy**	N	Y	N	N	N	?	N
7 **Boustany**	N	Y	N	N	N	N	N
MAINE							
1 Pingree	Y	Y	Y	N	Y	N	Y
2 Michaud	Y	Y	Y	N	Y	N	Y
MARYLAND							
1 Kratovil	N	Y	N	N	Y	N	Y
2 Ruppersberger	Y	Y	Y	N	Y	N	Y
3 Sarbanes	Y	Y	Y	N	Y	N	Y
4 Edwards	Y	Y	Y	N	Y	N	Y
5 Hoyer	Y	Y	Y	N	Y	N	Y
6 **Bartlett**	N	Y	N	Y	N	Y	N
7 Cummings	Y	Y	Y	N	Y	?	Y
8 Van Hollen	Y	Y	Y	N	Y	N	Y
MASSACHUSETTS							
1 Olver	Y	Y	Y	N	Y	N	Y
2 Neal	Y	Y	Y	N	Y	N	Y
3 McGovern	Y	Y	Y	N	Y	N	Y
4 Frank	Y	Y	Y	?	Y	N	Y
5 Tsongas	Y	N	Y	N	Y	N	Y
6 Tierney	Y	Y	Y	N	Y	N	Y
7 Markey	Y	N	N	N	Y	N	Y
8 Capuano	Y	Y	Y	N	Y	N	Y
9 Lynch	Y	Y	Y	N	Y	N	Y
10 Delahunt	Y	Y	Y	?	Y	N	Y
MICHIGAN							
1 Stupak	Y	Y	N	N	Y	N	Y
2 **Hoekstra**	N	N	Y	N	N	N	N
3 **Ehlers**	N	Y	Y	N	N	N	N
4 **Camp**	N	Y	N	N	N	N	N
5 Kildee	Y	Y	Y	N	Y	N	Y
6 **Upton**	N	Y	N	N	N	N	N
7 Schauer	Y	N	Y	N	Y	N	Y
8 **Rogers**	N	Y	N	N	N	N	N
9 Peters	Y	Y	Y	N	Y	N	Y
10 **Miller**	N	Y	N	N	N	N	N
11 **McCotter**	N	Y	N	N	N	N	N
12 Levin	Y	Y	Y	N	Y	N	Y
13 Kilpatrick	Y	Y	Y	N	Y	N	Y
14 Conyers	Y	?	?	N	Y	N	Y
15 Dingell	Y	Y	Y	N	Y	N	Y
MINNESOTA							
1 Walz	Y	Y	Y	N	Y	N	Y
2 **Kline**	N	Y	N	N	N	N	N
3 **Paulsen**	N	Y	Y	N	N	N	N
4 McCollum	Y	Y	Y	N	Y	N	Y
5 Ellison	Y	N	Y	N	Y	N	Y
6 **Bachmann**	N	Y	N	N	N	N	N
7 Peterson	Y	Y	N	N	Y	N	Y
8 Oberstar	Y	Y	Y	N	Y	N	Y
MISSISSIPPI							
1 Childers	Y	Y	N	N	Y	?	Y
2 Thompson	Y	Y	Y	N	Y	N	Y
3 **Harper**	N	Y	N	N	N	N	N
4 Taylor	Y	N	N	N	N	Y	N
MISSOURI							
1 Clay	Y	Y	Y	N	Y	Y	Y
2 **Akin**	N	Y	N	N	N	N	N
3 Carnahan	Y	Y	Y	N	Y	N	Y
4 Skelton	Y	Y	Y	N	Y	N	Y
5 Cleaver	Y	Y	Y	N	Y	N	Y
6 **Graves**	N	Y	N	N	N	N	N
7 **Blunt**	N	Y	N	N	N	N	N
8 **Emerson**	N	Y	?	N	N	N	N
9 **Luetkemeyer**	N	Y	N	Y	N	N	N
MONTANA							
AL **Rehberg**	N	Y	N	N	N	N	N
NEBRASKA							
1 **Fortenberry**	N	Y	Y	N	N	N	N
2 **Terry**	N	Y	N	N	N	N	N
3 **Smith**	N	Y	N	N	N	N	N
NEVADA							
1 Berkley	Y	Y	Y	N	Y	N	Y
2 **Heller**	N	Y	Y	N	N	N	N
3 Titus	Y	Y	Y	N	Y	N	Y
NEW HAMPSHIRE							
1 Shea-Porter	Y	Y	Y	N	Y	N	Y
2 Hodes	Y	N	Y	N	Y	N	Y
NEW JERSEY							
1 Andrews	Y	Y	Y	N	Y	?	?
2 **LoBiondo**	N	Y	N	N	N	N	N
3 Adler	Y	Y	N	N	Y	N	Y
4 **Smith**	N	Y	N	?	N	N	N
5 **Garrett**	N	Y	N	Y	N	Y	N
6 Pallone	Y	Y	Y	N	Y	N	Y
7 **Lance**	N	Y	Y	N	N	N	N
8 Pascrell	Y	Y	Y	N	Y	N	Y
9 Rothman	Y	Y	Y	N	Y	N	Y
10 Payne	Y	Y	Y	N	Y	N	Y
11 **Frelinghuysen**	N	Y	N	N	N	N	N
12 Holt	Y	Y	Y	N	Y	N	Y
13 Sires	Y	Y	Y	N	Y	N	Y
NEW MEXICO							
1 Heinrich	Y	Y	Y	N	Y	N	Y
2 Teague	Y	N	Y	N	Y	N	Y
3 Lujan	Y	Y	Y	–	Y	N	Y
NEW YORK							
1 Bishop	Y	Y	Y	N	Y	N	Y
2 Israel	Y	Y	Y	N	Y	N	Y
3 **King**	N	Y	N	N	N	N	N
4 McCarthy	Y	Y	Y	N	Y	N	Y
5 Ackerman	Y	Y	Y	N	Y	?	Y
6 Meeks	Y	Y	Y	N	Y	N	Y
7 Crowley	Y	Y	Y	?	Y	N	Y
8 Nadler	Y	Y	Y	N	Y	N	Y
9 Weiner	Y	Y	Y	N	Y	?	Y
10 Towns	Y	Y	Y	N	Y	N	Y
11 Clarke	Y	Y	Y	?	Y	?	Y
12 Velázquez	Y	Y	Y	N	Y	N	Y
13 McMahon	Y	Y	?	N	Y	N	Y
14 Maloney	Y	Y	Y	N	Y	N	Y
15 Rangel	Y	Y	Y	N	Y	Y	Y
16 Serrano	Y	Y	Y	N	Y	N	Y
17 Engel	Y	Y	Y	?	Y	N	Y
18 Lowey	Y	Y	Y	N	Y	N	Y
19 Hall	Y	Y	Y	N	Y	N	Y
20 Murphy	Y	Y	N	N	N	N	Y
21 Tonko	Y	Y	Y	N	Y	N	Y
22 Hinchey	Y	Y	Y	N	Y	N	Y
23 **McHugh**	N	Y	N	N	N	N	N
24 Arcuri	Y	Y	N	N	Y	N	Y
25 Maffei	Y	Y	Y	N	Y	N	Y
26 **Lee**	N	N	N	N	N	N	N
27 Higgins	Y	Y	Y	N	Y	N	Y
28 Slaughter	Y	Y	Y	N	Y	N	Y
29 Massa	Y	Y	Y	N	Y	N	Y
NORTH CAROLINA							
1 Butterfield	Y	Y	Y	N	Y	N	Y
2 Etheridge	Y	Y	N	N	N	N	N
3 **Jones**	N	Y	N	N	N	N	N
4 Price	Y	Y	Y	N	Y	N	?
5 **Foxx**	N	N	N	Y	N	Y	N
6 **Coble**	N	Y	N	N	N	N	N
7 McIntyre	Y	Y	Y	N	Y	N	Y
8 Kissell	Y	Y	Y	N	Y	N	Y
9 **Myrick**	N	Y	N	N	N	N	N
10 **McHenry**	N	Y	N	N	N	Y	N
11 Shuler	Y	Y	N	N	Y	N	N
12 Watt	Y	Y	Y	N	Y	?	Y
13 Miller	Y	Y	Y	N	Y	N	Y
NORTH DAKOTA							
AL Pomeroy	Y	Y	Y	N	Y	N	Y
OHIO							
1 Driehaus	Y	Y	Y	N	Y	N	Y
2 **Schmidt**	N	Y	N	N	N	N	N
3 **Turner**	N	Y	N	Y	N	N	N
4 **Jordan**	N	N	N	N	N	N	N
5 **Latta**	N	Y	N	N	N	N	N
6 Wilson	Y	Y	Y	N	Y	N	Y
7 **Austria**	N	Y	N	N	N	N	N
8 **Boehner**	N	Y	N	Y	N	Y	N
9 Kaptur	Y	Y	Y	N	Y	N	Y
10 Kucinich	Y	N	Y	N	Y	N	Y
11 Fudge	Y	N	Y	N	Y	?	?
12 **Tiberi**	N	Y	N	Y	N	N	N
13 Sutton	Y	Y	Y	N	Y	?	Y
14 **LaTourette**	N	Y	N	N	N	N	N
15 Kilroy	Y	Y	Y	N	Y	N	Y
16 Boccieri	Y	Y	Y	N	Y	N	Y
17 Ryan	Y	Y	Y	N	Y	?	Y
18 Space	Y	Y	N	N	Y	N	Y
OKLAHOMA							
1 **Sullivan**	N	Y	N	N	N	?	N
2 Boren	Y	Y	N	N	Y	N	Y
3 **Lucas**	N	Y	N	N	N	N	N
4 **Cole**	N	Y	N	N	N	N	N
5 **Fallin**	N	Y	N	N	N	N	N
OREGON							
1 Wu	Y	Y	?	?	Y	N	Y
2 **Walden**	N	Y	N	N	N	N	N
3 Blumenauer	Y	Y	Y	N	Y	N	Y
4 DeFazio	Y	Y	Y	N	Y	N	Y
5 Schrader	Y	Y	Y	N	Y	N	Y
PENNSYLVANIA							
1 Brady	Y	Y	Y	N	Y	N	Y
2 Fattah	Y	Y	Y	N	Y	N	Y
3 Dahlkemper	Y	Y	Y	N	Y	N	Y
4 Altmire	Y	Y	Y	N	Y	N	Y
5 **Thompson**	N	Y	N	N	N	N	N
6 **Gerlach**	N	Y	N	N	N	N	N
7 Sestak	?	?	?	?	?	?	?
8 Murphy, P.	Y	Y	Y	N	Y	N	Y
9 **Shuster**	N	Y	N	N	N	N	N
10 Carney	Y	Y	N	N	Y	N	Y
11 Kanjorski	Y	Y	Y	N	Y	N	Y
12 Murtha	Y	Y	Y	N	Y	N	Y
13 Schwartz	Y	Y	Y	N	Y	N	N
14 Doyle	Y	Y	Y	N	Y	?	Y
15 **Dent**	N	Y	Y	N	N	N	N
16 **Pitts**	N	Y	Y	N	N	N	N
17 Holden	Y	Y	Y	N	Y	N	?
18 **Murphy, T.**	N	Y	N	N	N	N	N
19 **Platts**	N	Y	N	N	N	N	N
RHODE ISLAND							
1 Kennedy	Y	Y	Y	?	Y	N	Y
2 Langevin	Y	Y	Y	N	Y	N	Y
SOUTH CAROLINA							
1 **Brown**	N	Y	N	N	N	N	N
2 **Wilson**	N	Y	N	N	N	N	N
3 **Barrett**	N	Y	N	N	N	N	N
4 **Inglis**	N	Y	N	Y	N	Y	N
5 Spratt	Y	Y	Y	N	Y	N	Y
6 Clyburn	Y	Y	Y	N	Y	N	Y
SOUTH DAKOTA							
AL Herseth Sandlin	Y	N	Y	N	Y	N	Y
TENNESSEE							
1 **Roe**	N	Y	N	N	N	N	N
2 **Duncan**	N	N	N	N	N	N	N
3 **Wamp**	N	Y	N	N	N	N	N
4 Davis	Y	Y	Y	N	Y	N	Y
5 Cooper	Y	Y	Y	N	N	N	Y
6 Gordon	Y	Y	Y	N	Y	N	Y
7 **Blackburn**	N	N	N	Y	N	N	N
8 Tanner	Y	Y	Y	N	Y	N	Y
9 Cohen	Y	Y	Y	N	Y	N	Y
TEXAS							
1 **Gohmert**	N	Y	P	Y	N	?	N
2 **Poe**	N	N	N	N	N	N	N
3 **Johnson, S.**	N	Y	N	Y	N	Y	N
4 **Hall**	N	Y	N	N	N	N	N
5 **Hensarling**	N	N	N	Y	N	Y	N
6 **Barton**	N	Y	N	Y	N	?	N
7 **Culberson**	N	Y	N	N	N	N	N
8 **Brady**	N	Y	N	N	N	N	N
9 Green, A.	Y	Y	Y	N	Y	N	Y
10 **McCaul**	N	Y	Y	N	N	N	N
11 **Conaway**	N	Y	N	N	N	N	N
12 **Granger**	N	Y	N	N	N	?	N
13 **Thornberry**	N	N	N	Y	N	Y	N
14 **Paul**	N	N	N	Y	N	Y	N
15 Hinojosa	Y	Y	Y	N	Y	?	?
16 Reyes	Y	Y	Y	N	Y	N	Y
17 Edwards	Y	Y	Y	?	Y	N	Y
18 Jackson Lee	Y	Y	Y	?	Y	N	Y
19 **Neugebauer**	N	Y	N	N	N	N	N
20 Gonzalez	Y	Y	Y	N	Y	N	Y
21 **Smith**	N	Y	N	N	N	N	N
22 **Olson**	N	Y	N	Y	N	Y	N
23 Rodriguez	Y	Y	Y	N	Y	N	Y
24 **Marchant**	N	N	N	Y	N	Y	N
25 Doggett	Y	Y	Y	N	Y	N	Y
26 **Burgess**	N	Y	N	N	N	N	N
27 Ortiz	Y	Y	Y	N	Y	N	Y
28 Cuellar	Y	Y	Y	?	Y	N	Y
29 Green, G.	Y	Y	Y	N	Y	N	Y
30 Johnson, E.	Y	Y	Y	N	Y	N	Y
31 **Carter**	N	Y	N	N	N	N	N
32 **Sessions**	N	N	N	?	N	N	N
UTAH							
1 **Bishop**	N	Y	N	Y	N	N	N
2 Matheson	Y	Y	Y	N	Y	N	?
3 **Chaffetz**	N	N	Y	Y	N	Y	N
VERMONT							
AL Welch	Y	N	Y	N	Y	N	Y
VIRGINIA							
1 **Wittman**	N	Y	N	N	–	N	N
2 Nye	N	Y	N	N	N	N	N
3 Scott	Y	Y	Y	N	Y	N	Y
4 **Forbes**	N	Y	N	N	N	N	N
5 Perriello	Y	Y	Y	N	Y	N	Y
6 **Goodlatte**	N	Y	N	N	N	N	N
7 **Cantor**	N	Y	N	N	N	N	N
8 Moran	Y	Y	Y	N	Y	?	?
9 Boucher	Y	Y	Y	N	Y	N	Y
10 **Wolf**	N	Y	N	N	N	N	N
11 Connolly	Y	Y	N	Y	Y	Y	Y
WASHINGTON							
1 Inslee	Y	Y	Y	N	Y	N	Y
2 Larsen	Y	Y	Y	N	Y	N	Y
3 Baird	Y	Y	Y	N	Y	N	Y
4 **Hastings**	N	Y	N	N	N	N	N
5 **McMorris Rodgers**	N	Y	N	N	N	N	N
6 Dicks	?	Y	Y	N	Y	N	Y
7 McDermott	Y	Y	Y	N	Y	N	Y
8 **Reichert**	N	Y	N	N	N	N	N
9 Smith	Y	Y	Y	N	Y	N	Y
WEST VIRGINIA							
1 Mollohan	Y	Y	Y	N	Y	N	Y
2 **Capito**	N	Y	Y	N	N	N	N
3 Rahall	Y	Y	Y	N	Y	N	Y
WISCONSIN							
1 **Ryan**	N	Y	N	N	N	N	N
2 Baldwin	Y	Y	Y	N	Y	N	Y
3 Kind	Y	Y	Y	N	Y	N	Y
4 Moore	Y	Y	Y	N	Y	N	Y
5 **Sensenbrenner**	N	N	N	N	N	N	N
6 **Petri**	N	N	N	N	N	N	N
7 Obey	Y	Y	Y	N	Y	N	Y
8 Kagen	Y	Y	Y	N	Y	N	Y
WYOMING							
AL **Lummis**	N	Y	N	N	N	N	N
DELEGATES							
Faleomavaega (A.S.)							
Norton (D.C.)							
Bordallo (Guam)							
Sablan (N. Marianas)							
Pierluisi (P.R.)							
Christensen (V.I.)							

IN THE HOUSE | By Vote Number

492. HR 2997. Fiscal 2010 Agriculture Appropriations/Motion to Reconsider. Mica, R-Fla., motion to reconsider the vote on the McGovern, D-Mass., motion to order the previous question (thus ending debate and possibility of amendment) on adoption of the rule (H Res 609) that would provide for House floor consideration of the bill that would appropriate $123.8 billion in fiscal 2010 for the Department of Agriculture and related agencies, including the Food and Drug Administration. Motion rejected 175-251: R 168-9; D 7-242. July 8, 2009.

493. HR 2997. Fiscal 2010 Agriculture Appropriations/Rule. Adoption of the rule (H Res 609) to provide for House floor consideration of the bill that would appropriate $123.8 billion in fiscal 2010 for the Department of Agriculture and related agencies, including the Food and Drug Administration. Adopted 238-186: R 1-176; D 237-10. July 8, 2009.

494. HR 2997. Fiscal 2010 Agriculture Appropriations/Motion to Reconsider. Mica, R-Fla., motion to reconsider the vote on the adoption of the rule (H Res 609) that would provide for House floor consideration of the bill that would appropriate $123.8 billion in fiscal 2010 for the Department of Agriculture and related agencies, including the Food and Drug Administration. Motion rejected 170-254: R 166-11; D 4-243. July 8, 2009.

495. H Con Res 142. National Men's Health Week/Adoption. Lynch, D-Mass., motion to suspend the rules and adopt the concurrent resolution that would support the annual National Men's Health Week. Motion agreed to 417-3: R 174-3; D 243-0. A two-thirds majority of those present and voting (280 in this case) is required for adoption under suspension of the rules. July 8, 2009.

496. Procedural Motion/Motion to Adjourn. Mica, R-Fla., motion to adjourn. Motion rejected 41-369: R 36-138; D 5-231. July 8, 2009.

497. Procedural Motion/Motion to Adjourn. McMorris Rodgers, R-Wash., motion to adjourn. Motion rejected 31-385: R 27-147; D 4-238. July 9, 2009.

498. HR 2997. Fiscal 2010 Agriculture Appropriations/Manager's Amendment. DeLauro, D-Conn., amendment that would appropriate $235 million in tobacco product user fees for the Food and Drug Administration and make a number of small changes to increase or decrease funding for various accounts, including increasing funding for the Agriculture Department's Office of Inspector General by $500,000. Adopted in Committee of the Whole 266-161: R 19-157; D 247-4. July 9, 2009.

	492	493	494	495	496	497	498
ALABAMA							
1 Bonner	Y	N	Y	Y	N	N	N
2 Bright	Y	N	Y	Y	N	N	Y
3 Rogers	Y	N	Y	Y	N	N	N
4 Aderholt	Y	N	Y	Y	N	N	N
5 Griffith	N	Y	N	Y	N	N	Y
6 Bachus	Y	N	Y	Y	N	N	N
7 Davis	N	Y	N	Y	N	N	Y
ALASKA							
AL Young	Y	N	N	Y	Y	Y	N
ARIZONA							
1 Kirkpatrick	N	Y	N	Y	N	N	Y
2 Franks	Y	N	Y	Y	N	N	N
3 Shadegg	Y	N	Y	Y	Y	Y	N
4 Pastor	N	Y	N	Y	N	N	Y
5 Mitchell	N	N	N	Y	N	N	Y
6 Flake	Y	N	N	Y	N	N	N
7 Grijalva	N	Y	N	Y	N	N	Y
8 Giffords	Y	Y	N	Y	N	N	Y
ARKANSAS							
1 Berry	N	Y	N	Y	?	N	Y
2 Snyder	N	N	N	Y	N	N	Y
3 Boozman	Y	N	Y	Y	N	N	N
4 Ross	N	Y	N	Y	N	N	Y
CALIFORNIA							
1 Thompson	N	Y	N	Y	N	N	Y
2 Herger	N	N	Y	Y	N	N	N
3 Lungren	Y	N	Y	Y	N	N	N
4 McClintock	Y	N	Y	Y	N	N	N
5 Matsui	N	Y	N	Y	?	N	Y
6 Woolsey	N	Y	N	+	–	N	Y
7 Miller, George	N	Y	N	Y	Y	N	Y
8 Pelosi							
9 Lee	N	Y	N	Y	N	N	Y
10 Vacant							
11 McNerney	N	Y	N	Y	N	N	Y
12 Speier	N	Y	N	Y	N	N	Y
13 Stark	N	?	N	Y	N	N	Y
14 Eshoo	N	Y	N	Y	N	N	Y
15 Honda	N	Y	N	Y	N	N	Y
16 Lofgren	N	Y	N	Y	N	N	Y
17 Farr	N	Y	N	Y	N	N	Y
18 Cardoza	N	Y	N	Y	N	N	Y
19 Radanovich	Y	N	Y	Y	N	N	N
20 Costa	N	Y	N	Y	N	?	Y
21 Nunes	Y	N	Y	Y	N	N	N
22 McCarthy	Y	N	Y	Y	N	N	N
23 Capps	N	Y	N	Y	N	N	Y
24 Gallegly	Y	N	Y	Y	N	N	N
25 McKeon	Y	N	Y	Y	N	N	N
26 Dreier	Y	N	Y	Y	N	N	N
27 Sherman	N	Y	N	Y	N	N	Y
28 Berman	N	Y	N	Y	N	N	Y
29 Schiff	N	Y	N	Y	N	N	Y
30 Waxman	N	Y	N	Y	N	N	?
31 Becerra	N	Y	N	Y	N	N	Y
32 Vacant							
33 Watson	N	Y	N	Y	N	N	Y
34 Roybal-Allard	N	Y	N	Y	N	N	Y
35 Waters	N	Y	?	Y	N	N	Y
36 Harman	N	Y	?	Y	N	N	Y
37 Richardson	N	Y	N	Y	N	N	Y
38 Napolitano	N	Y	N	Y	N	N	Y
39 Sánchez, Linda	N	Y	N	Y	N	N	Y
40 Royce	Y	N	Y	Y	N	N	N
41 Lewis	Y	N	Y	Y	N	N	N
42 Miller, Gary	Y	N	Y	Y	N	N	N
43 Baca	N	Y	N	Y	N	N	Y
44 Calvert	Y	N	Y	Y	N	N	N
45 Bono Mack	Y	N	Y	Y	N	N	N
46 Rohrabacher	Y	N	Y	Y	N	N	N
47 Sanchez, Loretta	N	Y	N	Y	N	N	Y
48 Campbell	Y	N	Y	Y	Y	Y	N
49 Issa	Y	N	Y	Y	N	N	N
50 Bilbray	Y	N	Y	Y	N	N	N
51 Filner	N	Y	N	Y	N	N	Y
52 Hunter	Y	N	Y	Y	N	N	N
53 Davis	N	Y	N	Y	N	N	Y

	492	493	494	495	496	497	498
COLORADO							
1 DeGette	N	Y	N	Y	N	N	Y
2 Polis	N	Y	N	Y	N	N	Y
3 Salazar	N	Y	N	Y	N	N	Y
4 Markey	N	Y	N	Y	N	N	Y
5 Lamborn	Y	N	Y	Y	Y	Y	N
6 Coffman	Y	N	Y	Y	Y	Y	N
7 Perlmutter	N	Y	N	Y	N	N	Y
CONNECTICUT							
1 Larson	N	Y	N	Y	N	N	Y
2 Courtney	N	Y	N	Y	N	N	Y
3 DeLauro	N	Y	N	Y	N	N	Y
4 Himes	N	Y	N	Y	N	N	Y
5 Murphy	N	Y	N	Y	N	N	Y
DELAWARE							
AL Castle	Y	N	Y	Y	N	N	N
FLORIDA							
1 Miller	Y	N	Y	Y	N	N	N
2 Boyd	N	Y	N	Y	N	N	Y
3 Brown	N	Y	N	Y	N	N	Y
4 Crenshaw	Y	N	Y	Y	N	N	N
5 Brown-Waite	Y	N	Y	Y	N	N	N
6 Stearns	Y	N	Y	Y	N	N	N
7 Mica	Y	Y	Y	Y	Y	Y	N
8 Grayson	N	Y	N	Y	N	N	Y
9 Bilirakis	Y	N	Y	Y	N	N	N
10 Young	Y	N	Y	Y	Y	Y	N
11 Castor	N	Y	N	Y	N	N	Y
12 Putnam	Y	N	Y	Y	N	N	Y
13 Buchanan	Y	N	Y	Y	N	N	N
14 Mack	Y	N	Y	Y	N	N	N
15 Posey	Y	N	Y	Y	N	N	N
16 Rooney	Y	N	Y	Y	N	N	N
17 Meek	N	Y	N	Y	N	N	Y
18 Ros-Lehtinen	Y	N	Y	Y	N	N	N
19 Wexler	N	Y	N	Y	N	N	Y
20 Wasserman Schultz	N	Y	N	Y	N	N	Y
21 Diaz-Balart, L.	Y	N	Y	Y	N	N	N
22 Klein	N	Y	N	Y	N	N	Y
23 Hastings	N	Y	N	Y	N	N	Y
24 Kosmas	N	Y	N	Y	N	N	Y
25 Diaz-Balart, M.	Y	N	Y	Y	N	N	N
GEORGIA							
1 Kingston	Y	N	Y	N	N	N	N
2 Bishop	N	Y	N	Y	N	N	Y
3 Westmoreland	Y	N	Y	Y	Y	?	N
4 Johnson	N	Y	N	Y	N	N	Y
5 Lewis	N	Y	N	Y	N	N	Y
6 Price	Y	N	Y	Y	Y	Y	Y
7 Linder	N	N	Y	?	N	N	N
8 Marshall	N	Y	N	Y	N	N	Y
9 Deal	Y	N	Y	Y	N	N	N
10 Broun	Y	N	Y	Y	Y	Y	N
11 Gingrey	Y	N	Y	Y	Y	Y	N
12 Barrow	N	Y	N	Y	N	N	Y
13 Scott	N	Y	N	Y	N	N	Y
HAWAII							
1 Abercrombie	N	Y	N	Y	N	N	Y
2 Hirono	N	Y	N	Y	N	N	Y
IDAHO							
1 Minnick	N	Y	N	Y	N	N	Y
2 Simpson	Y	N	Y	Y	N	N	N
ILLINOIS							
1 Rush	N	Y	N	Y	N	N	Y
2 Jackson	N	Y	N	Y	N	N	Y
3 Lipinski	N	Y	N	Y	N	N	Y
4 Gutierrez	N	Y	N	Y	?	N	Y
5 Quigley	N	Y	N	Y	N	N	Y
6 Roskam	Y	N	Y	Y	N	N	N
7 Davis	N	Y	N	Y	N	N	Y
8 Bean	Y	N	Y	Y	N	N	N
9 Schakowsky	N	Y	N	Y	N	N	?
10 Kirk	Y	N	Y	Y	N	N	Y
11 Halvorson	N	Y	N	Y	N	Y	Y
12 Costello	N	Y	N	Y	N	N	Y
13 Biggert	Y	N	Y	Y	N	N	N
14 Foster	N	Y	N	Y	N	N	Y
15 Johnson	Y	N	Y	Y	Y	Y	N

KEY	**Republicans**	Democrats		
Y Voted for (yea)		X Paired against		C Voted "present" to avoid possible conflict of interest
# Paired for		– Announced against		
+ Announced for		P Voted "present"		? Did not vote or otherwise make a position known
N Voted against (nay)				

	492	493	494	495	496	497	498
16 **Manzullo**	Y	N	Y	Y	N	N	N
17 Hare	N	Y	N	Y	N	N	Y
18 **Schock**	Y	N	Y	Y	N	N	Y
19 **Shimkus**	Y	N	Y	Y	Y	N	N
INDIANA							
1 Visclosky	N	Y	N	Y	N	N	Y
2 Donnelly	N	Y	N	Y	N	N	Y
3 **Souder**	Y	N	Y	Y	Y	Y	N
4 **Buyer**	N	N	Y	Y	?	N	N
5 **Burton**	Y	N	Y	Y	N	N	N
6 **Pence**	Y	N	Y	Y	Y	N	N
7 Carson	N	Y	N	Y	N	N	Y
8 Ellsworth	N	Y	N	Y	N	N	Y
9 Hill	N	N	N	Y	N	N	Y
IOWA							
1 Braley	N	Y	N	Y	N	N	Y
2 Loebsack	N	Y	N	Y	N	N	Y
3 Boswell	N	Y	N	Y	N	N	Y
4 **Latham**	Y	N	Y	Y	N	N	N
5 **King**	Y	N	Y	Y	Y	Y	N
KANSAS							
1 **Moran**	Y	N	Y	Y	N	N	N
2 **Jenkins**	Y	N	Y	Y	N	N	N
3 Moore	N	Y	N	Y	N	N	Y
4 **Tiahrt**	Y	N	Y	Y	Y	Y	N
KENTUCKY							
1 **Whitfield**	Y	N	Y	Y	N	N	N
2 **Guthrie**	Y	N	Y	Y	N	N	N
3 Yarmuth	N	Y	N	Y	N	N	Y
4 **Davis**	Y	N	Y	Y	N	N	N
5 **Rogers**	Y	N	Y	Y	N	N	N
6 Chandler	N	Y	N	Y	N	N	Y
LOUISIANA							
1 **Scalise**	Y	N	Y	Y	N	N	N
2 **Cao**	Y	N	N	Y	N	N	Y
3 Melancon	N	Y	N	?	?	N	Y
4 **Fleming**	Y	N	Y	Y	N	Y	N
5 **Alexander**	Y	N	Y	Y	N	N	N
6 **Cassidy**	Y	N	Y	Y	N	N	N
7 **Boustany**	Y	N	Y	Y	N	N	N
MAINE							
1 Pingree	N	Y	N	Y	N	N	Y
2 Michaud	N	Y	N	Y	N	N	Y
MARYLAND							
1 Kratovil	N	Y	N	Y	N	N	N
2 Ruppersberger	N	Y	N	Y	N	?	Y
3 Sarbanes	N	Y	N	Y	N	N	Y
4 Edwards	N	Y	N	Y	N	N	Y
5 Hoyer	N	Y	N	Y	N	N	Y
6 **Bartlett**	Y	N	Y	Y	Y	Y	N
7 Cummings	N	Y	N	Y	N	N	Y
8 Van Hollen	N	Y	N	Y	N	N	Y
MASSACHUSETTS							
1 Olver	N	Y	N	Y	N	N	Y
2 Neal	N	Y	N	Y	N	N	Y
3 McGovern	N	Y	N	Y	N	N	Y
4 Frank	N	N	N	Y	N	N	Y
5 Tsongas	N	Y	N	Y	N	N	Y
6 Tierney	N	Y	N	Y	?	N	Y
7 Markey	N	Y	N	Y	N	N	Y
8 Capuano	N	Y	N	Y	N	N	Y
9 Lynch	N	Y	N	Y	N	N	Y
10 Delahunt	N	Y	N	Y	N	N	Y
MICHIGAN							
1 Stupak	N	Y	N	Y	N	N	?
2 **Hoekstra**	Y	N	Y	Y	N	N	N
3 **Ehlers**	Y	N	Y	Y	N	N	N
4 **Camp**	Y	N	Y	Y	N	N	N
5 Kildee	N	Y	N	Y	N	N	Y
6 **Upton**	Y	N	Y	Y	N	N	N
7 Schauer	N	Y	N	Y	N	N	Y
8 **Rogers**	Y	N	Y	Y	N	N	N
9 Peters	N	Y	N	Y	N	N	Y
10 **Miller**	N	N	Y	Y	N	N	N
11 **McCotter**	Y	N	Y	Y	N	N	N
12 Levin	N	Y	N	Y	N	N	Y
13 Kilpatrick	N	Y	N	Y	N	N	Y
14 Conyers	N	Y	N	Y	N	N	Y
15 Dingell	N	Y	N	Y	N	N	Y
MINNESOTA							
1 Walz	N	Y	N	Y	N	N	Y
2 **Kline**	Y	N	Y	Y	N	N	N
3 **Paulsen**	Y	N	Y	Y	N	N	Y
4 McCollum	N	Y	N	Y	N	N	Y
5 Ellison	N	Y	N	Y	N	N	Y
6 **Bachmann**	Y	N	Y	Y	N	N	N
7 Peterson	N	Y	N	Y	?	N	Y
8 Oberstar	N	Y	N	Y	N	N	Y
MISSISSIPPI							
1 Childers	N	Y	N	Y	?	N	Y
2 Thompson	N	Y	N	Y	N	N	Y
3 **Harper**	Y	N	Y	Y	N	N	N
4 Taylor	N	N	N	Y	N	N	Y
MISSOURI							
1 Clay	N	Y	N	Y	N	N	Y
2 **Akin**	Y	N	Y	Y	N	N	N
3 Carnahan	N	Y	N	Y	N	N	Y
4 Skelton	N	Y	N	Y	N	N	Y
5 Cleaver	N	Y	N	?	N	N	Y
6 **Graves**	Y	N	Y	Y	N	N	N
7 **Blunt**	Y	N	Y	Y	N	N	N
8 **Emerson**	N	N	Y	Y	N	N	N
9 **Luetkemeyer**	Y	N	Y	Y	N	N	N
MONTANA							
AL **Rehberg**	Y	N	Y	Y	N	N	N
NEBRASKA							
1 **Fortenberry**	Y	N	Y	Y	N	N	Y
2 **Terry**	Y	N	N	Y	N	N	Y
3 **Smith**	Y	N	Y	Y	Y	N	N
NEVADA							
1 Berkley	N	Y	N	Y	N	N	Y
2 **Heller**	Y	N	N	Y	N	N	Y
3 Titus	N	Y	N	Y	N	N	Y
NEW HAMPSHIRE							
1 Shea-Porter	N	Y	N	Y	N	N	Y
2 Hodes	N	Y	N	Y	N	N	Y
NEW JERSEY							
1 Andrews	?	?	?	?	?	?	Y
2 **LoBiondo**	Y	N	Y	Y	N	N	Y
3 Adler	N	Y	N	Y	N	N	Y
4 **Smith**	Y	N	Y	Y	N	N	Y
5 **Garrett**	Y	N	Y	Y	Y	Y	N
6 Pallone	N	Y	N	Y	N	N	Y
7 **Lance**	Y	N	Y	Y	N	N	N
8 Pascrell	N	Y	N	Y	N	Y	Y
9 Rothman	N	Y	N	Y	N	N	Y
10 Payne	N	Y	N	Y	N	N	Y
11 **Frelinghuysen**	Y	N	Y	Y	N	N	N
12 Holt	N	Y	N	Y	N	N	Y
13 Sires	N	Y	N	Y	?	N	Y
NEW MEXICO							
1 Heinrich	N	Y	N	Y	N	N	Y
2 Teague	N	Y	N	Y	N	N	Y
3 Lujan	N	Y	N	Y	N	N	Y
NEW YORK							
1 Bishop	N	Y	N	Y	N	N	Y
2 Israel	N	Y	N	Y	N	N	Y
3 **King**	Y	N	Y	Y	N	N	N
4 McCarthy	N	Y	N	Y	N	N	?
5 Ackerman	N	Y	N	Y	N	N	Y
6 Meeks	N	Y	?	Y	N	N	Y
7 Crowley	N	Y	N	Y	N	N	Y
8 Nadler	N	Y	N	Y	N	N	Y
9 Weiner	N	Y	N	?	?	N	Y
10 Towns	N	?	N	Y	N	N	Y
11 Clarke	N	Y	N	Y	N	N	Y
12 Velázquez	N	Y	N	Y	N	N	Y
13 McMahon	Y	Y	N	Y	N	N	Y
14 Maloney	N	Y	N	Y	?	N	Y
15 Rangel	N	Y	N	Y	N	N	Y
16 Serrano	N	Y	N	Y	N	N	Y
17 Engel	N	Y	N	Y	N	?	Y
18 Lowey	N	Y	N	Y	N	N	Y
19 Hall	N	Y	N	Y	N	N	Y
20 Murphy	N	N	N	Y	N	?	?
21 Tonko	N	Y	N	Y	N	N	+
22 Hinchey	N	Y	N	Y	N	N	Y
23 **McHugh**	Y	N	Y	Y	N	N	N
24 Arcuri	Y	Y	Y	Y	N	N	Y
25 Maffei	N	Y	N	Y	N	N	Y
26 **Lee**	Y	N	Y	Y	N	N	N
27 Higgins	N	Y	N	Y	N	N	Y
28 Slaughter	N	Y	N	Y	N	?	?
29 Massa	N	Y	N	Y	N	N	Y
NORTH CAROLINA							
1 Butterfield	N	Y	N	Y	N	N	Y
2 Etheridge	N	N	N	Y	N	N	N
3 **Jones**	N	N	N	Y	N	N	N
4 Price	N	Y	N	Y	N	N	Y
5 **Foxx**	Y	N	Y	Y	Y	Y	N
6 **Coble**	Y	N	Y	Y	N	N	N
7 McIntyre	N	Y	N	Y	N	N	N
8 Kissell	N	Y	N	Y	N	N	Y
9 **Myrick**	Y	N	N	Y	N	N	N
10 **McHenry**	Y	N	Y	Y	Y	Y	N
11 Shuler	Y	N	Y	Y	N	?	N
12 Watt	N	Y	N	Y	N	N	Y
13 Miller	N	Y	N	Y	N	N	Y
NORTH DAKOTA							
AL Pomeroy	N	Y	N	Y	N	N	Y
OHIO							
1 Driehaus	N	Y	N	Y	N	N	Y
2 **Schmidt**	Y	N	Y	Y	N	N	N
3 **Turner**	Y	N	Y	Y	N	N	N
4 **Jordan**	Y	N	Y	Y	N	N	N
5 **Latta**	Y	N	Y	Y	N	N	N
6 Wilson	N	Y	N	Y	N	N	Y
7 **Austria**	Y	N	Y	Y	N	N	N
8 **Boehner**	Y	N	Y	Y	Y	N	N
9 Kaptur	N	Y	N	Y	N	N	Y
10 Kucinich	N	Y	N	Y	N	N	Y
11 Fudge	?	?	?	?	?	?	?
12 **Tiberi**	Y	N	Y	Y	N	N	N
13 Sutton	N	Y	N	Y	N	N	Y
14 **LaTourette**	Y	N	Y	Y	Y	N	N
15 Kilroy	N	Y	N	Y	Y	N	Y
16 Boccieri	N	Y	N	Y	Y	N	Y
17 Ryan	N	Y	N	Y	N	N	Y
18 Space	N	Y	N	Y	N	N	Y
OKLAHOMA							
1 **Sullivan**	Y	N	Y	Y	?	N	N
2 Boren	N	Y	N	Y	N	N	Y
3 **Lucas**	Y	N	Y	Y	N	N	N
4 **Cole**	Y	N	Y	Y	N	N	N
5 **Fallin**	Y	N	Y	Y	N	N	N
OREGON							
1 Wu	N	Y	N	Y	N	N	Y
2 **Walden**	Y	N	N	Y	N	N	N
3 Blumenauer	N	Y	N	Y	N	N	Y
4 DeFazio	N	Y	N	?	N	N	Y
5 Schrader	N	Y	N	Y	N	N	Y
PENNSYLVANIA							
1 Brady	N	Y	N	Y	N	N	Y
2 Fattah	N	Y	N	Y	N	N	Y
3 Dahlkemper	N	Y	N	Y	N	N	Y
4 Altmire	N	Y	N	Y	N	N	Y
5 **Thompson**	Y	N	Y	Y	N	N	N
6 **Gerlach**	Y	N	N	Y	N	N	Y
7 Sestak	?	?	?	?	?	N	Y
8 Murphy, P.	N	Y	N	Y	N	?	Y
9 **Shuster**	Y	N	Y	Y	N	N	N
10 Carney	N	Y	N	Y	N	N	Y
11 Kanjorski	N	Y	N	Y	N	N	Y
12 Murtha	N	Y	N	?	?	Y	Y
13 Schwartz	–	Y	N	Y	N	N	Y
14 Doyle	N	Y	N	Y	N	?	Y
15 **Dent**	Y	N	Y	Y	N	N	Y
16 **Pitts**	Y	N	Y	Y	N	N	N
17 Holden	N	Y	N	Y	N	N	Y
18 **Murphy, T.**	Y	N	Y	Y	N	N	Y
19 **Platts**	Y	N	Y	Y	N	N	Y
RHODE ISLAND							
1 Kennedy	N	Y	N	Y	N	N	Y
2 Langevin	N	Y	N	Y	N	N	Y
SOUTH CAROLINA							
1 **Brown**	Y	N	Y	Y	N	N	N
2 **Wilson**	Y	N	Y	Y	N	N	N
3 **Barrett**	Y	N	Y	Y	N	N	N
4 **Inglis**	Y	N	Y	Y	N	N	?
5 Spratt	N	Y	N	Y	N	Y	Y
6 Clyburn	N	Y	N	Y	N	N	Y
SOUTH DAKOTA							
AL Herseth Sandlin	N	Y	N	Y	N	N	Y
TENNESSEE							
1 **Roe**	Y	N	Y	Y	N	N	N
2 **Duncan**	Y	N	Y	Y	N	N	N
3 **Wamp**	Y	N	Y	Y	N	N	N
4 Davis	N	Y	N	Y	N	N	Y
5 Cooper	N	Y	N	Y	N	N	Y
6 Gordon	N	Y	N	Y	N	N	Y
7 **Blackburn**	Y	N	Y	Y	Y	Y	N
8 Tanner	N	Y	N	?	?	N	Y
9 Cohen	N	Y	N	Y	N	N	Y
TEXAS							
1 **Gohmert**	Y	N	Y	Y	Y	Y	N
2 **Poe**	Y	N	Y	Y	N	N	N
3 **Johnson, S.**	Y	N	N	Y	Y	N	N
4 **Hall**	Y	N	Y	Y	N	N	N
5 **Hensarling**	Y	N	Y	Y	Y	Y	N
6 **Barton**	Y	N	Y	Y	Y	Y	N
7 **Culberson**	Y	N	Y	Y	N	N	N
8 **Brady**	Y	N	Y	Y	N	N	N
9 Green, A.	N	Y	N	Y	N	N	Y
10 **McCaul**	Y	N	Y	Y	N	N	N
11 **Conaway**	Y	N	Y	Y	N	N	N
12 **Granger**	?	?	?	?	?	?	?
13 **Thornberry**	Y	N	Y	Y	Y	Y	N
14 **Paul**	N	N	N	N	Y	Y	N
15 Hinojosa	?	?	?	?	?	N	Y
16 Reyes	N	Y	N	Y	N	N	Y
17 Edwards	N	Y	N	Y	N	N	Y
18 Jackson Lee	N	?	N	Y	N	N	Y
19 **Neugebauer**	Y	N	Y	Y	N	N	N
20 Gonzalez	N	Y	N	Y	N	N	Y
21 **Smith**	Y	N	Y	Y	N	N	N
22 **Olson**	Y	N	Y	Y	Y	Y	N
23 Rodriguez	N	Y	N	Y	N	N	Y
24 **Marchant**	Y	N	Y	Y	N	Y	N
25 Doggett	N	Y	N	Y	N	N	Y
26 **Burgess**	Y	N	N	Y	N	N	N
27 Ortiz	N	Y	N	Y	N	N	Y
28 Cuellar	N	Y	N	Y	N	N	Y
29 Green, G.	N	Y	N	Y	N	N	Y
30 Johnson, E.	N	Y	N	Y	N	N	Y
31 **Carter**	Y	N	Y	Y	N	N	N
32 **Sessions**	Y	N	Y	Y	Y	Y	N
UTAH							
1 **Bishop**	Y	N	Y	Y	N	P	N
2 Matheson	N	Y	N	Y	N	N	Y
3 **Chaffetz**	Y	N	Y	Y	Y	Y	N
VERMONT							
AL Welch	N	Y	N	Y	N	N	Y
VIRGINIA							
1 **Wittman**	Y	N	Y	Y	N	N	Y
2 Nye	Y	N	Y	Y	N	N	Y
3 Scott	N	Y	N	Y	N	N	Y
4 **Forbes**	Y	N	Y	Y	N	N	N
5 Perriello	N	Y	N	Y	N	N	Y
6 **Goodlatte**	Y	N	Y	Y	N	N	N
7 **Cantor**	Y	N	Y	Y	N	?	N
8 Moran	N	Y	N	Y	N	N	Y
9 Boucher	N	Y	N	Y	N	?	Y
10 **Wolf**	Y	N	Y	Y	N	N	N
11 Connolly	N	Y	N	Y	Y	Y	Y
WASHINGTON							
1 Inslee	N	Y	N	Y	N	N	Y
2 Larsen	N	Y	N	Y	N	N	Y
3 Baird	N	Y	N	Y	N	?	?
4 **Hastings**	Y	N	Y	Y	N	N	N
5 **McMorris Rodgers**	Y	N	Y	Y	N	N	Y
6 Dicks	N	Y	N	Y	?	N	Y
7 McDermott	N	Y	N	Y	N	N	Y
8 **Reichert**	Y	N	Y	Y	N	N	N
9 Smith	N	Y	N	Y	N	N	Y
WEST VIRGINIA							
1 Mollohan	N	Y	N	Y	N	N	Y
2 **Capito**	Y	N	Y	Y	N	N	N
3 Rahall	N	Y	N	Y	N	N	Y
WISCONSIN							
1 **Ryan**	N	N	Y	Y	N	N	N
2 Baldwin	N	Y	N	Y	N	N	Y
3 Kind	N	Y	N	Y	N	N	Y
4 Moore	N	Y	N	Y	N	N	Y
5 **Sensenbrenner**	Y	N	Y	Y	Y	N	N
6 **Petri**	N	N	Y	Y	N	N	N
7 Obey	N	Y	N	Y	N	N	Y
8 Kagen	N	Y	N	Y	N	N	Y
WYOMING							
AL **Lummis**	Y	N	Y	Y	N	N	N
DELEGATES							
Faleomavaega (A.S.)							Y
Norton (D.C.)							Y
Bordallo (Guam)							Y
Sablan (N. Marianas)							Y
Pierluisi (P.R.)							Y
Christensen (V.I.)							Y

IN THE HOUSE | By Vote Number

499. HR 2997. Fiscal 2010 Agriculture Appropriations/Economic Research Service. Brady, R-Texas, amendment that would increase the amount provided for the Economic Research Service by $50,000, offset by a reduction of the same amount for the Office of the Chief Economist. Adopted in Committee of the Whole 404-27: R 172-4; D 232-23. July 9, 2009.

500. HR 2997. Fiscal 2010 Agriculture Appropriations/Rural Water and Waste Disposal. Capito, R-W.Va., amendment that would increase the amount provided for the Rural Water and Waste Disposal Program by $10 million, offset by a reduction of the same amount for the department's Office of the Chief Information Officer. Adopted in Committee of the Whole 426-3: R 177-0; D 249-3. July 9, 2009.

501. HR 2997. Fiscal 2010 Agriculture Appropriations/Food and Drug Administration. Broun, R-Ga., amendment that would reduce the amount provided for Food and Drug Administration salaries and expenses by $373 million. Rejected in Committee of the Whole 135-292: R 132-44; D 3-248. July 9, 2009.

502. HR 2997. Fiscal 2010 Agriculture Appropriations/Discretionary Spending Reduction. Blackburn, R-Tenn., amendment that would reduce discretionary spending appropriated in the bill by 5 percent. Rejected in Committee of the Whole 185-248: R 163-13; D 22-235. A "nay" was a vote in support of the president's position. July 9, 2009.

503. HR 2997. Fiscal 2010 Agriculture Appropriations/National Biodiversity Conservation Project. Hensarling, R-Texas, amendment that would bar funds appropriated in the bill for the Animal and Plant Health Inspection Service's salaries and expenses account from being used for the National Biodiversity Conservation Strategy project in Kiski Basin, Pa., and cut $200,000 intended for the project from the account. Rejected in Committee of the Whole 122-307: R 114-62; D 8-245. July 9, 2009.

504. HR 2997. Fiscal 2010 Agriculture Appropriations/Indiana Specialty Crops. Campbell, R-Calif., amendment that would bar funds appropriated in the bill for the National Institute of Food and Agriculture's research and education account from being used for specialty crops in Indiana, and cut $235,000 intended for the project from the account. Rejected in Committee of the Whole 111-320: R 108-68; D 3-252. July 9, 2009.

505. HR 2997. Fiscal 2010 Agriculture Appropriations/Foundry Sand Byproducts Utilization. Flake, R-Ariz., amendment that would bar funds appropriated in the bill for the Agricultural Research Service's salaries and expenses account from being used for the Foundry Sand Byproducts Utilization project in Beltsville, Md., and cut $638,000 intended for the project from the account. Rejected in Committee of the Whole 115-319: R 112-65; D 3-254. July 9, 2009.

	499	500	501	502	503	504	505
ALABAMA							
1 Bonner	Y	Y	Y	Y	N	N	N
2 Bright	Y	Y	Y	Y	Y	N	N
3 Rogers	N	Y	N	N	N	N	N
4 Aderholt	Y	Y	?	Y	N	N	N
5 Griffith	Y	Y	N	Y	N	N	N
6 Bachus	Y	Y	Y	Y	Y	N	N
7 Davis	Y	Y	N	N	N	N	N
ALASKA							
AL Young	Y	Y	N	N	N	N	N
ARIZONA							
1 Kirkpatrick	Y	Y	N	Y	N	N	N
2 Franks	Y	Y	Y	Y	Y	Y	Y
3 Shadegg	Y	Y	Y	Y	Y	Y	Y
4 Pastor	Y	Y	N	N	N	N	N
5 Mitchell	Y	Y	N	Y	Y	Y	N
6 Flake	Y	Y	Y	Y	Y	Y	Y
7 Grijalva	Y	Y	N	N	N	N	N
8 Giffords	Y	Y	N	N	N	N	N
ARKANSAS							
1 Berry	Y	Y	N	N	N	N	N
2 Snyder	Y	Y	N	N	N	N	N
3 Boozman	Y	Y	Y	Y	Y	Y	Y
4 Ross	Y	Y	N	N	N	N	N
CALIFORNIA							
1 Thompson	Y	Y	N	N	N	N	N
2 Herger	Y	Y	Y	Y	Y	Y	Y
3 Lungren	Y	Y	Y	Y	Y	Y	Y
4 McClintock	Y	Y	Y	Y	Y	Y	Y
5 Matsui	Y	N	N	N	N	N	N
6 Woolsey	Y	Y	N	N	N	N	N
7 Miller, George	Y	Y	N	N	N	N	N
8 Pelosi							
9 Lee	Y	Y	N	N	N	N	N
10 Vacant							
11 McNerney	Y	Y	N	N	N	N	N
12 Speier	Y	Y	N	N	?	N	?
13 Stark	Y	Y	N	N	N	N	N
14 Eshoo	Y	Y	N	N	N	N	N
15 Honda	Y	?	N	N	N	N	N
16 Lofgren	Y	Y	N	N	N	N	N
17 Farr	Y	?	N	N	N	N	N
18 Cardoza	Y	Y	N	N	N	N	N
19 Radanovich	Y	Y	Y	Y	N	Y	Y
20 Costa	Y	Y	N	N	N	N	N
21 Nunes	Y	Y	Y	Y	Y	Y	Y
22 McCarthy	Y	Y	Y	Y	Y	Y	Y
23 Capps	Y	Y	N	N	N	N	N
24 Gallegly	Y	Y	Y	Y	N	N	N
25 McKeon	Y	Y	Y	Y	N	N	N
26 Dreier	Y	Y	Y	Y	N	N	N
27 Sherman	N	Y	N	N	N	N	N
28 Berman	Y	Y	N	N	N	N	N
29 Schiff	Y	Y	N	N	N	N	N
30 Waxman	Y	Y	N	N	N	N	N
31 Becerra	Y	Y	N	N	N	N	N
32 Vacant							
33 Watson	Y	Y	N	N	N	N	N
34 Roybal-Allard	Y	Y	N	N	N	N	N
35 Waters	Y	Y	N	?	N	N	N
36 Harman	Y	Y	N	N	N	N	N
37 Richardson	Y	Y	?	N	N	N	N
38 Napolitano	Y	Y	N	N	N	N	N
39 Sánchez, Linda	Y	Y	N	N	N	N	N
40 Royce	Y	Y	Y	Y	Y	Y	Y
41 Lewis	Y	Y	Y	Y	N	N	N
42 Miller, Gary	Y	Y	Y	Y	N	N	N
43 Baca	Y	Y	N	N	N	N	N
44 Calvert	Y	Y	Y	Y	N	N	N
45 Bono Mack	Y	Y	Y	Y	Y	Y	Y
46 Rohrabacher	Y	Y	Y	Y	Y	Y	Y
47 Sanchez, Loretta	Y	Y	N	N	N	N	N
48 Campbell	Y	Y	Y	Y	Y	Y	Y
49 Issa	Y	Y	Y	Y	Y	Y	Y
50 Bilbray	Y	Y	Y	Y	Y	Y	N
51 Filner	Y	Y	N	N	N	N	N
52 Hunter	Y	Y	Y	Y	N	Y	N
53 Davis	Y	Y	N	N	N	N	N

	499	500	501	502	503	504	505
COLORADO							
1 DeGette	Y	Y	N	N	N	N	N
2 Polis	Y	Y	N	N	N	N	N
3 Salazar	Y	Y	N	N	N	N	N
4 Markey	Y	Y	N	N	N	N	N
5 Lamborn	Y	Y	Y	Y	Y	Y	Y
6 Coffman	Y	Y	Y	Y	Y	Y	Y
7 Perlmutter	Y	Y	N	N	N	N	N
CONNECTICUT							
1 Larson	Y	Y	N	N	N	N	N
2 Courtney	N	Y	N	N	N	N	N
3 DeLauro	Y	Y	N	N	N	N	N
4 Himes	Y	Y	N	Y	N	N	N
5 Murphy	Y	Y	N	N	N	N	N
DELAWARE							
AL Castle	Y	Y	N	Y	Y	N	Y
FLORIDA							
1 Miller	Y	Y	Y	Y	Y	Y	Y
2 Boyd	Y	Y	N	N	N	N	N
3 Brown	Y	Y	N	N	N	N	N
4 Crenshaw	Y	Y	Y	Y	Y	Y	Y
5 Brown-Waite	Y	Y	Y	N	?	Y	N
6 Stearns	Y	Y	Y	Y	Y	Y	Y
7 Mica	Y	Y	Y	Y	Y	Y	Y
8 Grayson	Y	Y	N	N	N	N	N
9 Bilirakis	Y	Y	N	N	N	Y	Y
10 Young	Y	Y	N	N	N	N	N
11 Castor	Y	Y	N	N	N	N	N
12 Putnam	Y	Y	N	N	N	N	N
13 Buchanan	Y	Y	Y	Y	Y	Y	Y
14 Mack	Y	Y	Y	Y	Y	Y	Y
15 Posey	Y	Y	Y	Y	Y	Y	Y
16 Rooney	Y	Y	Y	Y	N	Y	Y
17 Meek	Y	Y	N	N	N	N	N
18 Ros-Lehtinen	Y	Y	N	Y	N	N	N
19 Wexler	Y	Y	N	N	N	N	N
20 Wasserman Schultz	Y	Y	N	N	N	N	N
21 Diaz-Balart, L.	Y	Y	Y	Y	N	N	N
22 Klein	Y	Y	N	N	N	N	N
23 Hastings	Y	Y	N	N	N	N	N
24 Kosmas	Y	Y	?	Y	?	N	N
25 Diaz-Balart, M.	Y	Y	Y	Y	N	N	N
GEORGIA							
1 Kingston	Y	Y	Y	Y	N	N	Y
2 Bishop	Y	Y	N	N	N	N	N
3 Westmoreland	Y	Y	Y	Y	Y	Y	Y
4 Johnson	Y	Y	N	N	N	N	N
5 Lewis	Y	Y	N	N	N	N	N
6 Price	Y	Y	Y	Y	Y	Y	Y
7 Linder	Y	Y	Y	Y	Y	Y	Y
8 Marshall	N	Y	N	N	N	N	N
9 Deal	Y	Y	N	Y	Y	Y	Y
10 Broun	Y	Y	Y	Y	Y	Y	Y
11 Gingrey	Y	Y	Y	Y	Y	Y	Y
12 Barrow	Y	Y	N	N	N	N	N
13 Scott	Y	Y	N	N	N	N	N
HAWAII							
1 Abercrombie	Y	Y	N	N	N	N	N
2 Hirono	Y	Y	N	N	N	N	N
IDAHO							
1 Minnick	Y	Y	N	Y	Y	Y	Y
2 Simpson	Y	Y	N	Y	N	N	N
ILLINOIS							
1 Rush	?	Y	N	N	N	N	N
2 Jackson	Y	Y	N	N	N	N	N
3 Lipinski	Y	Y	N	N	N	N	N
4 Gutierrez	Y	Y	?	N	?	N	N
5 Quigley	Y	Y	N	N	N	N	N
6 Roskam	Y	Y	N	Y	Y	Y	Y
7 Davis	Y	Y	N	N	N	N	N
8 Bean	Y	Y	N	N	N	N	N
9 Schakowsky	?	?	N	N	N	N	N
10 Kirk	Y	Y	N	Y	N	N	Y
11 Halvorson	N	Y	N	N	N	N	N
12 Costello	Y	Y	N	N	N	N	N
13 Biggert	Y	Y	N	Y	N	N	N
14 Foster	Y	Y	N	Y	N	N	N
15 Johnson	Y	Y	Y	Y	N	N	Y

	499	500	501	502	503	504	505
16 **Manzullo**	Y	Y	Y	Y	Y	Y	N
17 Hare	N	Y	N	N	N	N	N
18 **Schock**	Y	Y	Y	Y	Y	N	Y
19 **Shimkus**	Y	Y	N	Y	Y	N	Y
INDIANA							
1 Visclosky	Y	Y	N	N	N	N	N
2 Donnelly	Y	Y	N	Y	N	N	N
3 **Souder**	Y	Y	Y	Y	Y	N	N
4 **Buyer**	Y	Y	N	N	Y	N	Y
5 **Burton**	Y	Y	Y	Y	Y	Y	Y
6 **Pence**	Y	Y	Y	Y	Y	Y	Y
7 Carson	Y	Y	N	N	N	N	N
8 Ellsworth	Y	Y	N	N	N	N	N
9 Hill	Y	Y	N	N	N	N	N
IOWA							
1 Braley	N	Y	N	N	N	N	N
2 Loebsack	N	Y	N	N	N	N	N
3 Boswell	Y	Y	N	N	N	N	N
4 **Latham**	Y	Y	Y	Y	N	?	N
5 **King**	Y	Y	Y	Y	Y	Y	Y
KANSAS							
1 **Moran**	Y	Y	Y	Y	N	Y	Y
2 **Jenkins**	Y	Y	N	Y	Y	Y	Y
3 Moore	Y	Y	N	N	N	N	N
4 **Tiahrt**	Y	Y	Y	Y	N	Y	Y
KENTUCKY							
1 **Whitfield**	Y	Y	Y	Y	N	N	N
2 **Guthrie**	Y	Y	Y	Y	N	N	N
3 Yarmuth	Y	Y	N	N	N	N	N
4 **Davis**	Y	Y	N	Y	N	N	N
5 **Rogers**	Y	Y	Y	Y	N	N	N
6 Chandler	Y	Y	N	N	N	N	N
LOUISIANA							
1 **Scalise**	Y	Y	Y	Y	Y	Y	Y
2 **Cao**	Y	Y	N	N	N	N	N
3 Melancon	Y	Y	N	N	N	N	N
4 **Fleming**	Y	Y	Y	Y	Y	Y	Y
5 **Alexander**	Y	Y	Y	Y	N	N	N
6 **Cassidy**	Y	Y	N	Y	Y	Y	Y
7 **Boustany**	Y	Y	Y	Y	N	Y	Y
MAINE							
1 Pingree	N	Y	N	N	N	N	N
2 Michaud	N	Y	N	N	N	N	N
MARYLAND							
1 Kratovil	Y	Y	N	Y	N	N	N
2 Ruppersberger	Y	Y	N	N	N	N	N
3 Sarbanes	Y	Y	N	N	N	N	N
4 Edwards	Y	Y	N	N	N	N	N
5 Hoyer	Y	Y	N	N	N	N	N
6 **Bartlett**	Y	Y	Y	Y	N	N	N
7 Cummings	Y	Y	N	N	N	N	N
8 Van Hollen	Y	Y	N	N	N	N	N
MASSACHUSETTS							
1 Olver	Y	Y	N	N	N	N	N
2 Neal	Y	Y	N	N	N	N	N
3 McGovern	Y	Y	N	N	N	N	N
4 Frank	Y	Y	N	N	N	?	N
5 Tsongas	Y	Y	N	N	N	N	N
6 Tierney	Y	Y	N	N	N	N	N
7 Markey	Y	Y	N	N	N	N	N
8 Capuano	Y	Y	N	N	N	N	N
9 Lynch	Y	Y	N	N	N	N	N
10 Delahunt	Y	Y	N	N	N	?	?
MICHIGAN							
1 Stupak	Y	Y	N	N	N	N	N
2 **Hoekstra**	N	Y	N	Y	Y	Y	Y
3 **Ehlers**	Y	Y	Y	Y	N	Y	Y
4 **Camp**	Y	Y	N	Y	Y	N	N
5 Kildee	Y	Y	N	N	N	N	N
6 **Upton**	Y	Y	N	Y	Y	N	N
7 Schauer	N	Y	N	N	N	N	N
8 **Rogers**	Y	Y	N	Y	Y	Y	N
9 Peters	Y	Y	N	Y	N	N	N
10 **Miller**	Y	Y	Y	Y	Y	Y	Y
11 **McCotter**	N	Y	Y	Y	Y	Y	Y
12 Levin	Y	Y	N	N	N	N	N
13 Kilpatrick	Y	Y	N	N	N	N	N
14 Conyers	Y	Y	N	N	N	N	N
15 Dingell	Y	Y	N	N	N	N	N
MINNESOTA							
1 Walz	Y	Y	N	N	N	N	N
2 **Kline**	Y	Y	Y	Y	Y	Y	Y
3 **Paulsen**	Y	Y	Y	Y	Y	Y	Y
4 McCollum	Y	Y	N	N	N	N	N

	499	500	501	502	503	504	505
5 Ellison	Y	Y	N	N	N	N	N
6 **Bachmann**	Y	Y	Y	Y	Y	Y	Y
7 Peterson	Y	Y	N	N	N	N	N
8 Oberstar	Y	Y	N	N	N	N	N
MISSISSIPPI							
1 Childers	Y	Y	N	Y	N	N	N
2 Thompson	Y	Y	N	N	N	N	N
3 **Harper**	Y	Y	Y	Y	Y	N	N
4 Taylor	N	Y	N	Y	N	N	N
MISSOURI							
1 Clay	Y	Y	N	N	N	N	N
2 **Akin**	Y	Y	Y	Y	Y	Y	Y
3 Carnahan	Y	Y	N	N	?	N	N
4 Skelton	Y	Y	N	N	N	N	N
5 Cleaver	Y	Y	N	N	N	N	N
6 **Graves**	Y	Y	Y	Y	Y	Y	Y
7 **Blunt**	Y	Y	N	Y	Y	Y	N
8 **Emerson**	Y	Y	Y	Y	N	N	N
9 **Luetkemeyer**	Y	Y	Y	Y	Y	Y	Y
MONTANA							
AL **Rehberg**	Y	Y	Y	Y	N	N	N
NEBRASKA							
1 **Fortenberry**	Y	Y	N	N	N	N	N
2 **Terry**	Y	Y	Y	Y	Y	Y	Y
3 **Smith**	Y	Y	Y	Y	Y	Y	Y
NEVADA							
1 Berkley	Y	Y	Y	N	N	N	N
2 **Heller**	Y	Y	Y	Y	Y	Y	Y
3 Titus	Y	Y	N	N	N	N	N
NEW HAMPSHIRE							
1 Shea-Porter	Y	Y	N	N	N	N	N
2 Hodes	N	Y	N	N	N	N	N
NEW JERSEY							
1 Andrews	Y	Y	N	N	N	N	N
2 **LoBiondo**	Y	Y	N	N	N	N	N
3 Adler	Y	Y	Y	Y	N	N	N
4 **Smith**	Y	Y	N	N	N	N	N
5 **Garrett**	Y	Y	Y	Y	Y	Y	Y
6 Pallone	Y	Y	N	N	N	N	N
7 **Lance**	Y	Y	Y	Y	Y	Y	Y
8 Pascrell	Y	Y	N	N	N	N	N
9 Rothman	Y	Y	N	N	N	N	N
10 Payne	Y	Y	N	N	N	N	N
11 **Frelinghuysen**	Y	Y	N	Y	N	N	N
12 Holt	Y	Y	N	N	N	N	N
13 Sires	Y	Y	N	N	N	N	N
NEW MEXICO							
1 Heinrich	Y	Y	N	Y	N	N	N
2 Teague	N	Y	N	N	N	N	N
3 Lujan	Y	Y	N	N	N	N	N
NEW YORK							
1 Bishop	Y	Y	N	N	N	N	N
2 Israel	Y	Y	N	N	N	N	N
3 **King**	Y	Y	N	N	N	N	N
4 McCarthy	Y	Y	N	N	N	N	N
5 Ackerman	Y	Y	N	N	N	N	N
6 Meeks	Y	Y	N	N	N	N	N
7 Crowley	Y	Y	N	N	N	N	N
8 Nadler	N	Y	N	N	N	N	N
9 Weiner	Y	Y	N	N	N	N	N
10 Towns	Y	Y	?	N	N	N	N
11 Clarke	Y	Y	N	N	N	N	N
12 Velázquez	Y	Y	N	N	N	N	N
13 McMahon	Y	Y	N	N	N	N	N
14 Maloney	Y	Y	N	N	N	N	N
15 Rangel	Y	Y	N	N	N	N	N
16 Serrano	Y	Y	N	N	N	N	N
17 Engel	Y	Y	N	N	N	N	N
18 Lowey	Y	Y	N	N	N	N	N
19 Hall	Y	Y	N	N	N	N	N
20 Murphy	?	?	?	?	?	?	?
21 Tonko	Y	Y	N	N	N	N	N
22 Hinchey	Y	Y	N	N	N	N	N
23 **McHugh**	Y	Y	N	N	N	N	N
24 Arcuri	Y	Y	N	Y	N	N	N
25 Maffei	N	Y	N	N	N	N	N
26 **Lee**	Y	Y	Y	Y	N	N	N
27 Higgins	Y	Y	N	N	N	N	N
28 Slaughter	Y	Y	N	N	N	N	N
29 Massa	Y	Y	N	Y	N	N	N
NORTH CAROLINA							
1 Butterfield	Y	Y	N	N	N	N	N
2 Etheridge	Y	Y	N	N	N	N	N
3 **Jones**	N	Y	Y	Y	N	N	N
4 Price	Y	Y	N	N	N	N	N

	499	500	501	502	503	504	505
5 **Foxx**	Y	Y	Y	Y	Y	Y	Y
6 **Coble**	Y	Y	Y	Y	Y	Y	N
7 McIntyre	Y	Y	N	N	N	N	N
8 Kissell	N	Y	N	N	N	N	N
9 **Myrick**	Y	Y	Y	Y	Y	Y	Y
10 **McHenry**	Y	Y	Y	Y	Y	Y	Y
11 Shuler	Y	Y	N	N	N	N	N
12 Watt	Y	Y	N	N	N	N	N
13 Miller	Y	Y	N	N	N	N	N
NORTH DAKOTA							
AL Pomeroy	Y	Y	N	N	N	N	N
OHIO							
1 Driehaus	Y	Y	N	Y	N	N	N
2 **Schmidt**	Y	Y	Y	Y	Y	N	Y
3 **Turner**	Y	Y	Y	N	N	N	N
4 **Jordan**	Y	Y	Y	Y	Y	Y	Y
5 **Latta**	Y	Y	Y	Y	Y	Y	Y
6 Wilson	Y	Y	N	N	N	N	N
7 **Austria**	Y	Y	Y	Y	Y	Y	Y
8 **Boehner**	Y	Y	Y	Y	Y	Y	Y
9 Kaptur	N	Y	N	N	N	N	N
10 Kucinich	N	Y	N	N	Y	N	N
11 Fudge	?	?	?	?	?	?	?
12 **Tiberi**	Y	Y	N	N	Y	Y	Y
13 Sutton	N	Y	N	N	N	N	N
14 **LaTourette**	Y	Y	N	N	N	N	N
15 Kilroy	Y	Y	N	N	N	N	N
16 Boccieri	Y	Y	N	N	N	N	N
17 Ryan	?	Y	N	N	N	N	N
18 Space	Y	Y	N	N	N	N	N
OKLAHOMA							
1 **Sullivan**	Y	Y	N	Y	Y	Y	Y
2 Boren	Y	Y	N	Y	N	N	N
3 **Lucas**	Y	Y	Y	Y	N	N	N
4 **Cole**	Y	Y	Y	Y	N	N	N
5 **Fallin**	Y	Y	Y	Y	Y	Y	Y
OREGON							
1 Wu	Y	Y	N	N	N	N	N
2 **Walden**	Y	Y	N	Y	Y	N	Y
3 Blumenauer	N	Y	N	N	N	N	N
4 DeFazio	N	Y	N	N	N	N	N
5 Schrader	Y	Y	N	N	N	N	N
PENNSYLVANIA							
1 Brady	Y	Y	N	N	N	N	N
2 Fattah	Y	Y	N	N	N	N	N
3 Dahlkemper	Y	Y	N	N	N	N	N
4 Altmire	Y	Y	N	Y	N	N	N
5 **Thompson**	Y	Y	Y	Y	N	N	N
6 **Gerlach**	Y	Y	N	Y	N	Y	N
7 Sestak	Y	Y	N	N	N	N	N
8 Murphy, P.	Y	Y	N	Y	N	N	N
9 **Shuster**	Y	Y	Y	Y	Y	Y	N
10 Carney	Y	Y	N	N	N	N	N
11 Kanjorski	Y	Y	N	N	N	N	N
12 Murtha	Y	Y	N	N	N	N	N
13 Schwartz	Y	Y	N	N	N	N	N
14 Doyle	Y	Y	N	N	N	N	N
15 **Dent**	Y	Y	N	Y	N	N	N
16 **Pitts**	Y	Y	Y	Y	Y	Y	Y
17 Holden	Y	Y	N	N	N	N	N
18 **Murphy, T.**	Y	Y	N	N	N	N	N
19 **Platts**	Y	Y	N	Y	N	Y	N
RHODE ISLAND							
1 Kennedy	Y	Y	N	N	N	N	N
2 Langevin	Y	Y	N	N	N	N	N
SOUTH CAROLINA							
1 **Brown**	Y	Y	Y	Y	N	N	N
2 **Wilson**	Y	Y	Y	Y	Y	Y	Y
3 **Barrett**	Y	Y	Y	Y	Y	Y	Y
4 **Inglis**	Y	Y	N	Y	Y	Y	Y
5 Spratt	Y	Y	N	N	N	N	N
6 Clyburn	Y	Y	N	N	N	N	N
SOUTH DAKOTA							
AL Herseth Sandlin	Y	Y	N	N	N	N	N
TENNESSEE							
1 **Roe**	Y	Y	Y	Y	Y	Y	Y
2 **Duncan**	Y	Y	Y	Y	Y	Y	Y
3 **Wamp**	Y	Y	Y	Y	Y	Y	Y
4 Davis	N	Y	N	N	N	N	N
5 Cooper	Y	Y	N	Y	Y	Y	Y
6 Gordon	Y	Y	N	N	N	N	N
7 **Blackburn**	Y	Y	Y	Y	Y	Y	Y
8 Tanner	Y	Y	N	N	N	N	N
9 Cohen	Y	Y	N	N	N	N	N

	499	500	501	502	503	504	505
TEXAS							
1 **Gohmert**	Y	Y	Y	Y	Y	N	Y
2 **Poe**	Y	Y	Y	Y	Y	Y	N
3 **Johnson, S.**	Y	Y	Y	Y	Y	Y	Y
4 **Hall**	Y	Y	Y	Y	Y	Y	Y
5 **Hensarling**	Y	Y	Y	Y	Y	Y	Y
6 **Barton**	Y	Y	Y	Y	Y	Y	Y
7 **Culberson**	Y	Y	Y	Y	N	N	N
8 **Brady**	Y	Y	N	Y	Y	Y	Y
9 Green, A.	Y	Y	N	N	N	N	N
10 **McCaul**	Y	Y	N	Y	Y	Y	Y
11 **Conaway**	Y	Y	Y	Y	Y	Y	Y
12 **Granger**	?	?	?	?	?	?	?
13 **Thornberry**	Y	Y	Y	Y	Y	Y	Y
14 **Paul**	Y	Y	Y	Y	Y	Y	Y
15 Hinojosa	Y	Y	N	N	N	N	N
16 Reyes	Y	?	?	N	N	N	N
17 Edwards	Y	Y	N	N	N	N	N
18 Jackson Lee	Y	Y	?	N	N	N	N
19 **Neugebauer**	Y	Y	Y	Y	Y	Y	Y
20 Gonzalez	Y	Y	N	N	N	N	N
21 **Smith**	Y	Y	Y	Y	N	N	N
22 **Olson**	Y	Y	Y	Y	Y	Y	Y
23 Rodriguez	Y	Y	N	N	N	N	N
24 **Marchant**	Y	Y	Y	Y	Y	Y	Y
25 Doggett	Y	Y	N	N	N	N	N
26 **Burgess**	Y	Y	N	Y	Y	Y	Y
27 Ortiz	Y	Y	N	N	N	N	N
28 Cuellar	Y	Y	N	N	N	N	N
29 Green, G.	Y	Y	N	N	N	N	N
30 Johnson, E.	Y	Y	N	N	N	N	N
31 **Carter**	Y	Y	Y	Y	N	N	N
32 **Sessions**	Y	Y	Y	Y	Y	Y	Y
UTAH							
1 **Bishop**	?	Y	Y	?	Y	N	Y
2 Matheson	Y	Y	N	N	Y	N	N
3 **Chaffetz**	Y	Y	Y	Y	Y	Y	Y
VERMONT							
AL Welch	Y	Y	N	N	N	N	N
VIRGINIA							
1 **Wittman**	Y	Y	N	Y	Y	Y	Y
2 Nye	N	Y	N	Y	N	N	N
3 Scott	Y	Y	N	N	N	N	N
4 **Forbes**	Y	Y	N	Y	Y	Y	Y
5 Perriello	Y	Y	N	N	N	N	N
6 **Goodlatte**	Y	Y	Y	Y	Y	Y	Y
7 **Cantor**	Y	Y	Y	Y	Y	Y	Y
8 Moran	Y	N	N	N	N	N	N
9 Boucher	Y	Y	N	N	N	N	N
10 **Wolf**	Y	Y	Y	Y	Y	N	N
11 Connolly	Y	N	N	N	N	N	N
WASHINGTON							
1 Inslee	Y	Y	N	N	N	N	N
2 Larsen	Y	Y	N	N	N	N	N
3 Baird	Y	Y	N	N	N	N	N
4 **Hastings**	Y	Y	Y	Y	N	N	N
5 **McMorris Rodgers**	Y	Y	Y	Y	Y	N	Y
6 Dicks	Y	Y	N	N	N	N	N
7 McDermott	Y	?	N	N	N	N	N
8 **Reichert**	Y	Y	Y	Y	N	N	N
9 Smith	Y	Y	N	N	N	N	N
WEST VIRGINIA							
1 Mollohan	Y	Y	N	N	N	N	N
2 **Capito**	Y	Y	Y	Y	N	N	N
3 Rahall	Y	Y	N	N	N	N	N
WISCONSIN							
1 **Ryan**	Y	Y	Y	Y	Y	Y	Y
2 Baldwin	Y	Y	N	N	N	N	N
3 Kind	Y	Y	N	N	N	N	Y
4 Moore	Y	Y	N	N	N	N	N
5 **Sensenbrenner**	Y	Y	Y	Y	Y	Y	Y
6 **Petri**	Y	Y	Y	Y	Y	Y	Y
7 Obey	Y	Y	N	N	N	N	N
8 Kagen	Y	Y	N	N	N	N	N
WYOMING							
AL **Lummis**	Y	Y	Y	Y	Y	Y	Y
DELEGATES							
Faleomavaega (A.S.)	Y	Y	N	N	N	N	N
Norton (D.C.)	Y	Y	N	N	N	N	N
Bordallo (Guam)	Y	Y	N	N	N	N	N
Sablan (N. Marianas)	Y	Y	N	N	N	N	N
Pierluisi (P.R.)	Y	Y	N	N	N	N	N
Christensen (V.I.)	Y	?	?	?	N	N	N

IN THE HOUSE | By Vote Number

506. **HR 2997. Fiscal 2010 Agriculture Appropriations/Agriculture Energy Innovation Center.** Flake, R-Ariz., amendment that would bar funds appropriated in the bill for the National Institute of Food and Agriculture's research and education account from being available for a special grant for the Agriculture Energy Innovation Center in Georgia. It would cut $1 million intended for the project from the account. Rejected in Committee of the Whole 103-328: R 94-83; D 9-245. July 9, 2009.

507. **HR 2997. Fiscal 2010 Agriculture Appropriations/Potato Research.** Flake, R-Ariz., amendment that would bar funds appropriated in the bill for the National Institute of Food and Agriculture's research and education account from being available for potato research in Idaho, Oregon and Washington, and cut $1 million intended for the program from the account. Rejected in Committee of the Whole 97-333: R 86-87; D 11-246. July 9, 2009.

508. **HR 2997. Fiscal 2010 Agriculture Appropriations/Broadband Loan Guarantees.** Kingston, R-Ga., amendment that would bar the use of funds in the bill to pay employees who administer broadband loans or loan guarantees before Sept. 15, 2010, using authorities granted under the bill. Rejected in Committee of the Whole 140-292: R 138-39; D 2-253. July 9, 2009.

509. **HR 2997. Fiscal 2010 Agriculture Appropriations/Motion to Table.** DeLauro, D-Conn., motion to table (kill) the Kingston, R-Ga., appeal of the ruling of the chair with respect to the DeLauro point of order that the Kingston motion to recommit the bill constituted legislating on an appropriations bill. The motion would recommit the bill to the Appropriations Committee with instructions that it be immediately reported back with language that would state it is the policy of the House that the bill should be re-opened for amendment under regular order. Motion agreed to 246-179: R 0-174; D 246-5. July 9, 2009.

510. **HR 2997. Fiscal 2010 Agriculture Appropriations/Passage.** Passage of the bill that would appropriate $123.8 billion in fiscal 2010 for the Agriculture Department and related agencies, including $22.9 billion in discretionary funding. The bill would provide $20.4 billion for the Agriculture Department, $2.35 billion for the Food and Drug Administration and $7.5 billion for the Women, Infants and Children program. It would fund the food stamp program at $61.4 billion and the child nutrition program at $16.8 billion. Passed 266-160: R 27-150; D 239-10. A "yea" was a vote in support of the president's position. July 9, 2009.

511. **Open Rules for Appropriations Bills/Motion to Table.** Cardoza, D-Calif., motion to table (kill) the Price, R-Ga., appeal of the ruling of the chair that the draft resolution does not constitute a point of privilege under Rule IX of the House. The draft resolution would require the House Rules Committee to report open rules for all general appropriations bills in the 111th Congress and call on the House to not require preprinting of amendments. Motion agreed to 240-179: R 0-176; D 240-3. July 9, 2009.

512. **HR 3081. Fiscal 2010 State-Foreign Operations Appropriations/Previous Question.** Cardoza, D-Calif., motion to order the previous question (thus ending debate and possibility of amendment) on adoption of the rule (H Res 617) to provide for House floor consideration of the bill that would appropriate $49 billion in fiscal 2010 for the State Department, foreign assistance and other international activities. Motion agreed to 217-187: R 0-171; D 217-16. July 9, 2009.

	506	507	508	509	510	511	512
ALABAMA							
1 **Bonner**	N	N	Y	N	N	N	N
2 **Bright**	Y	Y	N	Y	Y	Y	N
3 **Rogers**	N	N	Y	N	Y	N	N
4 **Aderholt**	N	N	Y	N	N	N	?
5 Griffith	N	N	N	Y	Y	Y	N
6 **Bachus**	N	N	Y	N	N	N	N
7 Davis	N	N	N	Y	Y	Y	Y
ALASKA							
AL **Young**	N	N	N	N	N	N	N
ARIZONA							
1 Kirkpatrick	N	N	N	Y	Y	Y	Y
2 **Franks**	Y	Y	Y	N	N	N	N
3 **Shadegg**	Y	Y	Y	N	N	N	?
4 Pastor	N	N	N	Y	Y	Y	Y
5 Mitchell	Y	Y	N	Y	N	Y	Y
6 **Flake**	Y	Y	Y	N	N	N	N
7 Grijalva	N	N	N	Y	Y	Y	Y
8 Giffords	Y	Y	Y	Y	Y	Y	Y
ARKANSAS							
1 Berry	N	N	N	Y	Y	Y	Y
2 Snyder	N	N	N	Y	Y	Y	Y
3 **Boozman**	Y	Y	Y	N	N	N	N
4 Ross	N	N	N	Y	Y	Y	Y
CALIFORNIA							
1 Thompson	N	N	Y	Y	Y	Y	?
2 **Herger**	Y	Y	Y	N	N	N	N
3 **Lungren**	Y	Y	Y	N	N	N	N
4 **McClintock**	Y	Y	Y	N	N	N	N
5 Matsui	N	N	N	Y	Y	Y	Y
6 Woolsey	?	N	N	Y	Y	?	Y
7 Miller, George	N	N	N	Y	Y	Y	?
8 Pelosi							
9 Lee	N	N	N	Y	Y	Y	Y
10 Vacant							
11 McNerney	N	N	N	Y	Y	Y	Y
12 Speier	Y	Y	Y	Y	Y	Y	Y
13 Stark	N	N	N	Y	Y	Y	Y
14 Eshoo	N	N	N	Y	Y	Y	+
15 Honda	N	N	N	Y	Y	Y	?
16 Lofgren	Y	N	N	Y	Y	Y	Y
17 Farr	N	N	N	Y	Y	Y	Y
18 Cardoza	N	N	N	Y	Y	Y	?
19 **Radanovich**	Y	N	N	N	N	N	N
20 Costa	N	N	N	Y	Y	Y	?
21 **Nunes**	Y	N	Y	N	N	N	N
22 **McCarthy**	Y	N	Y	N	N	N	N
23 Capps	N	N	N	Y	Y	Y	Y
24 **Gallegly**	N	Y	N	N	N	N	N
25 **McKeon**	Y	Y	Y	N	N	N	N
26 **Dreier**	N	N	Y	N	N	N	N
27 Sherman	N	N	N	Y	Y	Y	Y
28 Berman	N	N	N	Y	Y	Y	Y
29 Schiff	N	N	N	Y	Y	Y	Y
30 Waxman	N	N	N	Y	Y	?	Y
31 Becerra	N	N	N	Y	Y	Y	Y
32 Vacant							
33 Watson	N	N	N	Y	Y	Y	Y
34 Roybal-Allard	N	N	N	Y	Y	Y	Y
35 Waters	N	N	N	Y	Y	Y	Y
36 Harman	N	N	N	Y	Y	Y	Y
37 Richardson	N	N	N	Y	Y	Y	Y
38 Napolitano	N	N	N	Y	Y	Y	?
39 Sánchez, Linda	N	N	N	Y	Y	Y	Y
40 **Royce**	Y	Y	Y	N	N	N	N
41 **Lewis**	N	N	Y	N	N	N	N
42 **Miller, Gary**	N	N	Y	N	N	N	N
43 Baca	N	N	N	Y	Y	Y	Y
44 **Calvert**	N	N	Y	N	N	N	N
45 **Bono Mack**	Y	Y	Y	N	N	N	N
46 **Rohrabacher**	N	Y	N	N	N	N	N
47 Sanchez, Loretta	N	N	N	Y	Y	Y	Y
48 **Campbell**	Y	Y	Y	N	N	N	N
49 **Issa**	Y	Y	Y	N	N	N	N
50 **Bilbray**	Y	N	Y	N	N	N	N
51 Filner	N	N	N	Y	Y	Y	Y
52 **Hunter**	N	N	N	Y	N	N	N
53 Davis	N	N	N	Y	Y	Y	Y
COLORADO							
1 DeGette	N	N	N	Y	Y	Y	Y
2 Polis	N	N	N	Y	Y	Y	Y
3 Salazar	N	N	N	Y	Y	Y	?
4 Markey	N	N	N	Y	+	Y	Y
5 **Lamborn**	Y	Y	Y	N	N	N	N
6 **Coffman**	Y	Y	Y	N	N	N	N
7 Perlmutter	N	N	N	Y	Y	Y	Y
CONNECTICUT							
1 Larson	N	N	N	Y	Y	Y	Y
2 Courtney	N	N	N	Y	Y	Y	Y
3 DeLauro	N	N	N	Y	Y	?	?
4 Himes	N	N	N	Y	Y	Y	Y
5 Murphy	?	N	N	Y	Y	Y	Y
DELAWARE							
AL **Castle**	Y	N	Y	N	N	N	N
FLORIDA							
1 **Miller**	Y	Y	Y	N	N	N	N
2 Boyd	N	N	N	Y	Y	Y	Y
3 Brown	N	N	N	Y	Y	Y	Y
4 **Crenshaw**	N	N	Y	N	N	N	N
5 **Brown-Waite**	N	N	N	Y	N	N	N
6 **Stearns**	Y	Y	Y	N	N	N	N
7 **Mica**	N	N	Y	N	N	N	N
8 Grayson	N	N	N	Y	Y	Y	Y
9 **Bilirakis**	N	N	N	Y	N	N	N
10 **Young**	N	N	Y	N	N	N	?
11 Castor	N	N	N	Y	Y	Y	Y
12 **Putnam**	N	Y	N	Y	Y	Y	Y
13 **Buchanan**	Y	?	Y	N	N	N	N
14 **Mack**	Y	Y	Y	N	N	N	N
15 **Posey**	Y	Y	Y	N	N	N	N
16 **Rooney**	N	N	N	Y	N	N	N
17 Meek	N	N	N	Y	Y	Y	Y
18 **Ros-Lehtinen**	N	N	N	Y	Y	Y	Y
19 Wexler	N	N	N	Y	Y	Y	Y
20 Wasserman Schultz	N	N	N	Y	Y	Y	Y
21 **Diaz-Balart, L.**	N	N	Y	N	N	N	N
22 Klein	N	N	N	Y	Y	Y	Y
23 Hastings	N	N	N	Y	Y	Y	Y
24 Kosmas	N	N	N	Y	Y	Y	Y
25 **Diaz-Balart, M.**	N	N	Y	N	N	N	N
GEORGIA							
1 **Kingston**	N	N	Y	N	N	N	N
2 Bishop	N	N	N	Y	Y	Y	Y
3 **Westmoreland**	Y	Y	Y	N	N	N	N
4 Johnson	N	N	N	Y	Y	?	Y
5 Lewis	N	N	N	Y	Y	Y	Y
6 **Price**	Y	Y	Y	N	N	N	N
7 **Linder**	Y	Y	Y	N	N	N	N
8 Marshall	N	N	N	Y	Y	Y	Y
9 **Deal**	N	Y	N	N	N	N	N
10 **Broun**	Y	Y	Y	N	N	N	N
11 **Gingrey**	N	Y	N	N	N	N	N
12 Barrow	N	N	N	Y	Y	Y	Y
13 Scott	N	N	N	Y	Y	Y	Y
HAWAII							
1 Abercrombie	N	N	N	Y	Y	Y	Y
2 Hirono	N	N	N	Y	Y	Y	+
IDAHO							
1 Minnick	Y	Y	Y	N	N	Y	N
2 **Simpson**	N	N	Y	N	N	N	N
ILLINOIS							
1 Rush	N	N	N	Y	Y	Y	Y
2 Jackson	N	N	N	Y	Y	Y	Y
3 Lipinski	N	N	N	Y	Y	Y	Y
4 Gutierrez	N	N	N	Y	Y	Y	Y
5 Quigley	N	N	N	Y	Y	Y	Y
6 **Roskam**	N	Y	N	N	N	N	N
7 Davis	N	N	N	Y	Y	Y	Y
8 Bean	N	Y	N	Y	N	Y	N
9 Schakowsky	N	N	N	Y	Y	?	Y
10 **Kirk**	N	N	Y	N	N	N	N
11 Halvorson	N	Y	N	Y	N	Y	N
12 Costello	N	?	N	Y	Y	Y	Y
13 **Biggert**	N	N	N	N	N	N	N
14 Foster	N	Y	N	Y	N	N	Y
15 **Johnson**	Y	Y	N	N	N	N	N

KEY	**Republicans**	Democrats		
Y Voted for (yea)		X Paired against		C Voted "present" to avoid possible conflict of interest
# Paired for		- Announced against		
+ Announced for		P Voted "present"		? Did not vote or otherwise make a position known
N Voted against (nay)				

	506	507	508	509	510	511	512
16 **Manzullo**	Y	Y	Y	N	N	N	N
17 Hare	N	N	N	Y	Y	Y	Y
18 **Schock**	N	N	Y	N	Y	N	N
19 **Shimkus**	N	N	Y	N	Y	N	N
INDIANA							
1 Visclosky	N	N	N	Y	Y	Y	Y
2 Donnelly	N	N	N	Y	Y	Y	N
3 **Souder**	Y	Y	N	N	Y	N	N
4 **Buyer**	N	N	Y	N	N	N	N
5 **Burton**	Y	Y	Y	N	N	N	N
6 **Pence**	Y	Y	Y	N	N	N	N
7 Carson	N	N	N	Y	Y	Y	Y
8 Ellsworth	N	N	N	Y	Y	Y	Y
9 Hill	N	N	N	Y	N	Y	N
IOWA							
1 Braley	N	N	N	Y	Y	Y	Y
2 Loebsack	N	N	N	Y	Y	Y	Y
3 Boswell	N	N	N	Y	Y	Y	Y
4 **Latham**	N	N	N	N	N	N	N
5 **King**	Y	?	Y	N	N	N	N
KANSAS							
1 **Moran**	Y	Y	N	N	N	N	N
2 **Jenkins**	Y	Y	N	N	Y	N	N
3 Moore	N	N	N	Y	Y	Y	Y
4 **Tiahrt**	N	N	N	N	N	N	N
KENTUCKY							
1 **Whitfield**	N	N	Y	N	N	N	N
2 **Guthrie**	N	N	Y	N	N	N	N
3 Yarmuth	N	N	N	Y	Y	Y	Y
4 **Davis**	N	N	Y	N	N	N	N
5 **Rogers**	N	N	Y	N	N	N	N
6 Chandler	N	N	N	Y	Y	Y	Y
LOUISIANA							
1 **Scalise**	Y	Y	Y	N	N	N	N
2 **Cao**	N	N	Y	N	Y	N	N
3 Melancon	N	N	N	Y	Y	Y	N
4 **Fleming**	Y	Y	Y	N	N	N	N
5 **Alexander**	N	N	N	N	N	N	N
6 **Cassidy**	Y	Y	N	N	N	N	N
7 **Boustany**	Y	Y	N	N	N	N	N
MAINE							
1 Pingree	N	N	N	?	Y	Y	Y
2 Michaud	N	N	N	Y	Y	Y	Y
MARYLAND							
1 Kratovil	N	N	N	N	Y	N	N
2 Ruppersberger	N	N	N	Y	Y	Y	Y
3 Sarbanes	N	N	N	Y	Y	Y	Y
4 Edwards	N	N	N	Y	Y	Y	Y
5 Hoyer	N	N	N	Y	Y	Y	Y
6 **Bartlett**	N	N	Y	N	N	N	N
7 Cummings	N	N	N	Y	Y	Y	Y
8 Van Hollen	N	N	N	Y	Y	Y	Y
MASSACHUSETTS							
1 Olver	N	N	N	Y	Y	Y	Y
2 Neal	N	N	N	Y	Y	Y	Y
3 McGovern	N	N	N	Y	Y	Y	Y
4 Frank	N	N	N	Y	Y	Y	Y
5 Tsongas	N	N	N	Y	Y	Y	Y
6 Tierney	N	N	N	Y	Y	Y	Y
7 Markey	N	N	N	Y	Y	Y	Y
8 Capuano	N	N	N	Y	Y	Y	Y
9 Lynch	N	N	N	Y	Y	Y	Y
10 Delahunt	N	N	N	Y	Y	Y	Y
MICHIGAN							
1 Stupak	N	N	N	Y	Y	Y	N
2 **Hoekstra**	Y	N	N	N	N	N	N
3 **Ehlers**	Y	Y	Y	N	N	N	N
4 **Camp**	N	N	N	N	N	N	N
5 Kildee	N	N	N	Y	Y	Y	Y
6 **Upton**	Y	N	Y	N	N	N	N
7 Schauer	N	N	N	Y	Y	Y	Y
8 **Rogers**	N	N	Y	N	N	N	?
9 Peters	N	N	N	Y	N	Y	Y
10 **Miller**	Y	Y	N	N	Y	N	N
11 **McCotter**	Y	Y	Y	N	N	N	N
12 Levin	N	N	N	Y	Y	Y	Y
13 Kilpatrick	N	N	N	Y	Y	Y	Y
14 Conyers	N	N	N	Y	Y	Y	Y
15 Dingell	N	N	N	Y	Y	Y	Y
MINNESOTA							
1 Walz	N	N	N	Y	Y	Y	Y
2 **Kline**	Y	Y	Y	N	N	N	N
3 **Paulsen**	Y	N	Y	N	N	N	N
4 McCollum	N	N	N	Y	Y	Y	Y

	506	507	508	509	510	511	512
5 Ellison	N	N	N	Y	Y	Y	?
6 **Bachmann**	Y	Y	Y	N	N	N	N
7 Peterson	N	N	N	Y	Y	Y	Y
8 Oberstar	N	N	N	Y	Y	Y	Y
MISSISSIPPI							
1 Childers	N	N	N	Y	Y	Y	N
2 Thompson	N	N	N	Y	Y	Y	Y
3 **Harper**	N	N	N	N	Y	N	N
4 Taylor	N	N	N	Y	N	?	?
MISSOURI							
1 Clay	N	N	N	Y	Y	Y	Y
2 **Akin**	Y	Y	Y	N	N	N	N
3 Carnahan	N	N	N	Y	Y	Y	Y
4 Skelton	N	N	N	Y	Y	Y	Y
5 Cleaver	N	N	N	Y	Y	Y	?
6 **Graves**	Y	Y	Y	N	N	N	N
7 **Blunt**	N	N	Y	N	N	N	N
8 **Emerson**	N	N	Y	N	Y	N	N
9 **Luetkemeyer**	Y	?	Y	N	Y	N	N
MONTANA							
AL **Rehberg**	N	N	N	N	N	N	N
NEBRASKA							
1 **Fortenberry**	N	N	Y	N	Y	N	N
2 **Terry**	N	N	N	N	N	N	N
3 **Smith**	Y	+	Y	N	N	N	N
NEVADA							
1 Berkley	N	N	N	Y	Y	Y	Y
2 **Heller**	Y	Y	Y	N	N	N	N
3 Titus	N	N	N	Y	Y	Y	Y
NEW HAMPSHIRE							
1 Shea-Porter	N	N	N	Y	Y	Y	Y
2 Hodes	N	Y	N	Y	Y	Y	Y
NEW JERSEY							
1 Andrews	N	N	N	Y	Y	Y	Y
2 **LoBiondo**	N	N	Y	N	Y	N	N
3 Adler	N	N	N	Y	N	Y	?
4 **Smith**	N	N	Y	N	Y	?	N
5 **Garrett**	Y	Y	Y	N	N	N	N
6 Pallone	N	N	N	Y	Y	Y	Y
7 **Lance**	Y	Y	Y	N	N	N	N
8 Pascrell	?	N	N	Y	Y	Y	Y
9 Rothman	N	N	N	Y	Y	Y	Y
10 Payne	N	N	N	Y	Y	Y	Y
11 **Frelinghuysen**	N	N	Y	N	N	N	N
12 Holt	N	N	N	Y	Y	Y	Y
13 Sires	N	N	N	Y	Y	Y	Y
NEW MEXICO							
1 Heinrich	N	N	N	Y	Y	Y	Y
2 Teague	N	N	N	Y	Y	Y	Y
3 Lujan	N	N	N	Y	Y	Y	Y
NEW YORK							
1 Bishop	N	N	N	Y	Y	Y	Y
2 Israel	N	N	N	Y	Y	Y	Y
3 **King**	N	N	Y	N	N	N	N
4 McCarthy	N	N	N	Y	Y	Y	Y
5 Ackerman	N	N	N	Y	Y	Y	Y
6 Meeks	N	N	N	Y	Y	Y	Y
7 Crowley	N	N	N	Y	Y	Y	Y
8 Nadler	N	N	N	Y	Y	Y	Y
9 Weiner	N	N	N	Y	Y	Y	Y
10 Towns	N	N	N	Y	Y	Y	Y
11 Clarke	N	N	N	Y	Y	Y	Y
12 Velázquez	N	N	N	Y	Y	Y	Y
13 McMahon	N	N	N	Y	Y	Y	Y
14 Maloney	N	N	N	Y	Y	Y	Y
15 Rangel	N	N	N	Y	Y	?	?
16 Serrano	N	N	N	Y	Y	Y	Y
17 Engel	N	N	N	Y	Y	Y	Y
18 Lowey	N	N	N	Y	Y	Y	Y
19 Hall	N	N	N	Y	Y	Y	Y
20 Murphy	?	?	?	?	?	?	?
21 Tonko	N	N	N	Y	Y	Y	Y
22 Hinchey	N	N	N	Y	Y	Y	Y
23 **McHugh**	N	N	N	N	Y	N	N
24 Arcuri	N	N	N	Y	Y	Y	Y
25 Maffei	N	N	N	Y	Y	Y	Y
26 **Lee**	N	N	N	N	N	N	N
27 Higgins	N	N	N	Y	Y	Y	Y
28 Slaughter	N	N	N	Y	Y	Y	Y
29 Massa	N	N	N	Y	Y	Y	Y
NORTH CAROLINA							
1 Butterfield	N	N	N	Y	Y	Y	Y
2 Etheridge	N	N	N	Y	Y	Y	Y
3 **Jones**	N	N	Y	N	Y	N	N
4 Price	N	N	N	Y	Y	Y	Y

	506	507	508	509	510	511	512
5 **Foxx**	Y	Y	Y	N	N	N	N
6 **Coble**	Y	Y	Y	N	N	N	N
7 McIntyre	N	N	N	Y	Y	Y	N
8 Kissell	N	N	N	Y	Y	Y	Y
9 **Myrick**	Y	Y	Y	N	N	N	N
10 **McHenry**	Y	Y	Y	N	N	N	N
11 Shuler	N	N	N	Y	Y	Y	N
12 Watt	N	N	N	Y	Y	Y	Y
13 Miller	N	N	N	Y	Y	Y	Y
NORTH DAKOTA							
AL Pomeroy	N	N	N	Y	Y	Y	?
OHIO							
1 Driehaus	N	N	N	N	Y	Y	N
2 **Schmidt**	N	N	Y	N	N	N	N
3 **Turner**	N	N	N	N	Y	N	N
4 **Jordan**	Y	Y	Y	N	N	N	N
5 **Latta**	Y	Y	Y	N	N	N	N
6 Wilson	N	N	N	Y	Y	Y	Y
7 **Austria**	N	N	Y	N	Y	N	N
8 **Boehner**	Y	Y	Y	?	N	N	?
9 Kaptur	N	N	N	Y	Y	Y	Y
10 Kucinich	N	N	N	Y	Y	Y	Y
11 Fudge	?	?	?	?	?	?	?
12 **Tiberi**	Y	N	Y	N	N	N	N
13 Sutton	N	N	N	Y	Y	Y	Y
14 **LaTourette**	N	N	N	N	Y	N	N
15 Kilroy	N	N	N	Y	Y	Y	Y
16 Boccieri	N	N	N	Y	Y	Y	Y
17 Ryan	N	N	?	Y	Y	Y	Y
18 Space	N	N	N	Y	Y	Y	Y
OKLAHOMA							
1 **Sullivan**	Y	Y	Y	N	N	N	N
2 Boren	N	N	N	Y	Y	Y	Y
3 **Lucas**	N	N	N	N	N	N	N
4 **Cole**	N	N	Y	N	N	N	N
5 **Fallin**	Y	Y	Y	N	N	N	N
OREGON							
1 Wu	N	N	N	Y	Y	Y	Y
2 **Walden**	N	N	Y	N	N	N	N
3 Blumenauer	N	N	N	Y	Y	Y	Y
4 DeFazio	N	N	N	Y	?	Y	Y
5 Schrader	N	N	N	Y	Y	Y	Y
PENNSYLVANIA							
1 Brady	N	N	N	Y	Y	Y	Y
2 Fattah	N	N	N	Y	Y	Y	Y
3 Dahlkemper	N	N	N	Y	Y	Y	Y
4 Altmire	N	N	N	Y	N	Y	Y
5 **Thompson**	N	N	Y	N	Y	N	N
6 **Gerlach**	N	N	N	N	N	N	N
7 Sestak	N	N	?	Y	Y	Y	Y
8 Murphy, P.	N	N	N	Y	Y	Y	Y
9 **Shuster**	N	N	N	N	N	N	N
10 Carney	N	N	N	Y	Y	Y	Y
11 Kanjorski	N	N	N	Y	Y	Y	?
12 Murtha	N	N	N	Y	Y	Y	Y
13 Schwartz	N	N	N	Y	Y	Y	Y
14 Doyle	N	N	N	Y	Y	Y	Y
15 **Dent**	N	N	N	N	N	N	N
16 **Pitts**	Y	Y	Y	N	N	N	N
17 Holden	N	N	N	Y	Y	Y	N
18 **Murphy, T.**	N	N	N	N	Y	N	N
19 **Platts**	N	N	N	N	N	N	N
RHODE ISLAND							
1 Kennedy	N	N	N	Y	Y	Y	Y
2 Langevin	N	N	N	Y	Y	Y	Y
SOUTH CAROLINA							
1 **Brown**	N	N	Y	N	N	N	N
2 **Wilson**	Y	Y	Y	N	N	N	N
3 **Barrett**	Y	Y	Y	N	N	N	N
4 **Inglis**	Y	Y	Y	N	N	N	N
5 Spratt	N	N	N	Y	Y	Y	Y
6 Clyburn	N	N	N	Y	Y	Y	Y
SOUTH DAKOTA							
AL Herseth Sandlin	N	N	N	Y	Y	Y	Y
TENNESSEE							
1 **Roe**	Y	Y	Y	N	N	N	N
2 **Duncan**	Y	Y	Y	N	N	N	N
3 **Wamp**	Y	Y	Y	N	N	N	N
4 Davis	N	N	N	Y	Y	Y	Y
5 Cooper	Y	Y	N	Y	Y	Y	Y
6 Gordon	N	N	N	Y	Y	?	Y
7 **Blackburn**	Y	Y	N	N	N	N	N
8 Tanner	N	N	N	Y	Y	Y	Y
9 Cohen	N	N	N	Y	Y	Y	Y

	506	507	508	509	510	511	512
TEXAS							
1 **Gohmert**	N	Y	Y	?	N	N	N
2 **Poe**	Y	N	N	N	N	N	N
3 **Johnson, S.**	Y	Y	Y	N	N	N	N
4 **Hall**	Y	Y	Y	N	Y	N	N
5 **Hensarling**	Y	Y	Y	N	N	N	N
6 **Barton**	N	N	Y	N	N	N	N
7 **Culberson**	N	N	Y	N	N	N	N
8 **Brady**	N	N	Y	N	N	N	N
9 Green, A.	N	N	N	Y	Y	Y	Y
10 **McCaul**	Y	Y	N	N	N	N	N
11 **Conaway**	Y	Y	Y	N	N	N	N
12 **Granger**	?	?	?	?	?	?	?
13 **Thornberry**	Y	Y	Y	N	N	N	N
14 **Paul**	Y	Y	Y	N	N	N	N
15 Hinojosa	N	N	N	Y	Y	Y	Y
16 Reyes	N	N	N	Y	Y	Y	Y
17 Edwards	N	N	N	Y	Y	Y	Y
18 Jackson Lee	N	N	N	Y	Y	Y	Y
19 **Neugebauer**	Y	Y	Y	N	N	N	N
20 Gonzalez	N	N	N	Y	Y	Y	Y
21 **Smith**	N	N	Y	N	N	N	N
22 **Olson**	Y	Y	Y	N	N	N	N
23 Rodriguez	N	N	N	Y	Y	Y	Y
24 **Marchant**	Y	Y	N	N	N	N	N
25 Doggett	N	N	N	Y	Y	Y	Y
26 **Burgess**	Y	Y	Y	N	N	N	N
27 Ortiz	N	N	N	Y	Y	Y	Y
28 Cuellar	N	N	N	Y	Y	Y	Y
29 Green, G.	N	N	N	Y	?	Y	Y
30 Johnson, E.	N	N	N	Y	Y	Y	Y
31 **Carter**	N	N	Y	?	N	N	N
32 **Sessions**	Y	Y	Y	N	N	N	N
UTAH							
1 **Bishop**	N	N	Y	N	N	N	N
2 Matheson	N	N	N	Y	N	Y	Y
3 **Chaffetz**	Y	Y	Y	N	N	N	N
VERMONT							
AL Welch	N	N	N	Y	Y	Y	Y
VIRGINIA							
1 **Wittman**	Y	Y	N	N	N	N	N
2 Nye	Y	N	N	N	N	N	Y
3 Scott	N	N	N	Y	Y	Y	Y
4 **Forbes**	Y	Y	Y	N	N	N	N
5 Perriello	N	N	N	Y	Y	Y	Y
6 **Goodlatte**	Y	Y	Y	N	N	N	N
7 **Cantor**	N	Y	Y	N	N	N	?
8 Moran	N	N	N	Y	Y	?	Y
9 Boucher	N	N	N	Y	Y	Y	Y
10 **Wolf**	N	N	Y	N	N	N	N
11 Connolly	N	N	N	Y	Y	Y	Y
WASHINGTON							
1 Inslee	N	N	N	Y	Y	Y	Y
2 Larsen	N	N	N	Y	Y	Y	Y
3 Baird	N	N	N	Y	Y	Y	Y
4 **Hastings**	N	N	Y	N	N	N	N
5 **McMorris Rodgers**	N	N	Y	N	N	N	N
6 Dicks	N	N	N	Y	Y	Y	?
7 McDermott	N	N	N	Y	Y	Y	Y
8 **Reichert**	N	N	Y	N	N	N	N
9 Smith	N	N	N	Y	Y	Y	Y
WEST VIRGINIA							
1 Mollohan	N	N	N	Y	Y	Y	Y
2 **Capito**	N	N	N	N	N	N	N
3 Rahall	N	N	N	Y	Y	Y	N
WISCONSIN							
1 **Ryan**	Y	Y	Y	N	N	N	N
2 Baldwin	N	N	N	Y	Y	Y	Y
3 Kind	Y	Y	N	Y	N	Y	Y
4 Moore	N	Y	N	Y	Y	Y	Y
5 **Sensenbrenner**	Y	Y	Y	N	N	N	N
6 **Petri**	Y	Y	N	N	N	N	N
7 Obey	N	N	N	Y	Y	Y	Y
8 Kagen	?	N	N	Y	Y	Y	?
WYOMING							
AL **Lummis**	Y	Y	Y	N	N	N	N
DELEGATES							
Faleomavaega (A.S.)	N	N	N				
Norton (D.C.)	N	N	N				
Bordallo (Guam)	N	N	?				
Sablan (N. Marianas)	N	N	N				
Pierluisi (P.R.)	N	N	N				
Christensen (V.I.)	N	N	N				

IN THE HOUSE | By Vote Number

513. H Res 617. Fiscal 2010 State-Foreign Operations **Appropriations/Rule.** Adoption of the rule to provide for House floor consideration of the bill (HR 3081) that would appropriate $49 billion in fiscal 2010 for the State Department, foreign assistance and other international activities. Adopted 223-200: R 0-176; D 223-24. July 9, 2009.

514. H Con Res 127. Caribbean-American Heritage Month/ **Adoption.** Lynch, D-Mass., motion to suspend the rules and adopt the concurrent resolution that would support the goals and ideals of Caribbean-American Heritage Month and affirm that the contributions of Caribbean-Americans are a significant part of the heritage of the United States. Motion agreed to 423-0: R 176-0; D 247-0. A two-thirds majority of those present and voting (282 in this case) is required for adoption under suspension of the rules. July 9, 2009.

515. H Con Res 131. Capitol Visitor Center Engraving/Adoption. Christensen, D-V.I., motion to suspend the rules and adopt the concurrent resolution that would require the Architect of the Capitol to engrave the Pledge of Allegiance and "In God we trust" in the Capitol Visitor Center with approval from the House Administration and Senate Rules and Administration committees. Motion agreed to 410-8: R 173-1; D 237-7. A two-thirds majority of those present and voting (279 in this case) is required for adoption under suspension of the rules. July 9, 2009.

516. HR 3081. Fiscal 2010 State-Foreign Operations **Appropriations/Manager's Amendment.** Lowey, D-N.Y., amendment that would make a variety of small funding changes, including increasing funding for the Office of the Inspector General by $8 million, global health activities by $10 million, water and sanitation supply projects by $25 million, and the Democracy Fund by $10 million. It would decrease funds for the department's capital investment fund by $25 million and the U.S. Agency for International Development (USAID) capital investment fund by $28 million. Adopted in Committee of the Whole 261-168: R 9-165; D 252-3. July 9, 2009.

517. HR 3081. Fiscal 2010 State-Foreign Operations **Appropriations/Diplomatic and Consular Programs.** Buyer, R-Ind., amendment that would reduce the amount provided for the State Department and Foreign Service diplomatic and consular programs by $1.2 billion, USAID by $330 million and global health activities by $670 million. Rejected in Committee of the Whole 156-271: R 150-25; D 6-246. A "nay" was a vote in support of the president's position. July 9, 2009.

518. HR 3081. Fiscal 2010 State-Foreign Operations **Appropriations/Peace Corps.** Stearns, R-Fla., amendment that would reduce the amount provided for the Peace Corps by $77 million. Rejected in Committee of the Whole 172-259: R 159-17; D 13-242. July 9, 2009.

519. HR 3081. Fiscal 2010 State-Foreign Operations **Appropriations/Saudi Arabia Waiver Authority.** Weiner, D-N.Y., amendment to strike language that would allow the president to overrule a ban on funds to Saudi Arabia if the country cooperates with efforts to combat international terrorism. Adopted in Committee of the Whole 297-135: R 139-37; D 158-98. July 9, 2009.

	513	514	515	516	517	518	519
ALABAMA							
1 **Bonner**	N	Y	Y	N	Y	Y	Y
2 **Bright**	N	Y	Y	Y	Y	Y	Y
3 **Rogers**	N	Y	Y	N	N	N	Y
4 **Aderholt**	N	Y	Y	N	Y	Y	N
5 Griffith	Y	Y	Y	Y	N	N	Y
6 **Bachus**	N	Y	Y	N	Y	Y	Y
7 Davis	Y	Y	Y	Y	N	N	Y
ALASKA							
AL **Young**	N	Y	Y	Y	Y	Y	Y
ARIZONA							
1 Kirkpatrick	Y	Y	Y	Y	Y	N	Y
2 **Franks**	N	Y	Y	N	Y	Y	Y
3 **Shadegg**	N	Y	Y	N	Y	Y	Y
4 Pastor	Y	Y	Y	Y	N	N	N
5 Mitchell	N	Y	Y	Y	N	N	Y
6 **Flake**	N	Y	Y	N	Y	Y	Y
7 Grijalva	Y	Y	Y	Y	N	N	N
8 Giffords	Y	Y	Y	Y	N	N	Y
ARKANSAS							
1 Berry	Y	Y	Y	Y	N	N	N
2 Snyder	N	Y	Y	Y	N	N	N
3 **Boozman**	N	Y	Y	N	Y	Y	Y
4 Ross	Y	Y	Y	Y	?	N	Y
CALIFORNIA							
1 Thompson	Y	Y	Y	Y	N	N	Y
2 **Herger**	N	Y	Y	N	Y	Y	Y
3 **Lungren**	N	Y	Y	N	Y	Y	Y
4 **McClintock**	N	Y	Y	N	Y	Y	Y
5 Matsui	Y	Y	Y	Y	N	N	N
6 Woolsey	Y	Y	Y	Y	N	N	N
7 Miller, George	Y	Y	Y	Y	N	N	N
8 Pelosi							
9 Lee	Y	Y	Y	Y	N	N	N
10 Vacant							
11 McNerney	Y	Y	Y	Y	N	N	N
12 Speier	Y	Y	Y	Y	N	N	Y
13 Stark	Y	Y	N	Y	N	N	N
14 Eshoo	Y	Y	Y	Y	N	N	N
15 Honda	Y	Y	N	Y	N	N	N
16 Lofgren	Y	Y	Y	Y	N	N	N
17 Farr	Y	Y	P	Y	N	N	N
18 Cardoza	Y	Y	Y	Y	?	N	Y
19 **Radanovich**	N	Y	Y	N	Y	Y	Y
20 Costa	Y	Y	Y	Y	N	N	N
21 **Nunes**	N	Y	Y	N	Y	Y	Y
22 **McCarthy**	N	Y	Y	N	Y	Y	Y
23 Capps	Y	Y	Y	Y	N	N	N
24 **Gallegly**	N	Y	Y	N	Y	Y	Y
25 **McKeon**	N	Y	Y	N	Y	Y	Y
26 **Dreier**	N	Y	Y	N	Y	Y	Y
27 Sherman	Y	Y	?	Y	N	N	Y
28 Berman	Y	Y	Y	Y	N	N	N
29 Schiff	Y	Y	Y	Y	N	N	N
30 Waxman	Y	Y	Y	Y	N	N	Y
31 Becerra	?	Y	Y	Y	N	N	N
32 Vacant							
33 Watson	Y	Y	Y	Y	N	N	Y
34 Roybal-Allard	Y	Y	Y	Y	N	N	N
35 Waters	Y	Y	Y	Y	N	N	Y
36 Harman	Y	Y	Y	Y	N	N	N
37 Richardson	Y	Y	Y	Y	N	N	N
38 Napolitano	Y	Y	Y	Y	N	N	N
39 Sánchez, Linda	Y	Y	Y	Y	N	N	Y
40 **Royce**	N	Y	Y	N	Y	Y	Y
41 **Lewis**	N	Y	Y	N	Y	Y	Y
42 **Miller, Gary**	N	Y	Y	N	Y	Y	Y
43 Baca	Y	Y	Y	Y	N	N	Y
44 **Calvert**	N	Y	Y	N	Y	Y	Y
45 **Bono Mack**	N	Y	Y	N	Y	Y	Y
46 **Rohrabacher**	N	Y	Y	N	Y	Y	Y
47 Sanchez, Loretta	Y	Y	Y	Y	N	N	Y
48 **Campbell**	N	Y	Y	N	Y	Y	Y
49 **Issa**	N	Y	Y	N	Y	Y	N
50 **Bilbray**	N	Y	Y	N	Y	Y	N
51 Filner	Y	Y	Y	Y	N	N	Y
52 **Hunter**	N	Y	Y	N	Y	Y	Y
53 Davis	Y	Y	Y	Y	N	N	Y
COLORADO							
1 DeGette	Y	Y	Y	Y	N	N	Y
2 Polis	Y	Y	Y	Y	N	N	Y
3 Salazar	Y	Y	Y	Y	N	N	Y
4 Markey	Y	Y	Y	Y	N	N	Y
5 **Lamborn**	N	Y	Y	N	Y	Y	Y
6 **Coffman**	N	Y	Y	N	Y	Y	Y
7 Perlmutter	Y	Y	Y	Y	N	N	Y
CONNECTICUT							
1 Larson	+	+	+	+	–	–	+
2 Courtney	Y	Y	Y	Y	N	N	Y
3 DeLauro	?	?	?	?	?	?	?
4 Himes	Y	Y	Y	Y	N	N	Y
5 Murphy	Y	Y	Y	Y	N	N	Y
DELAWARE							
AL **Castle**	N	Y	Y	N	N	Y	N
FLORIDA							
1 **Miller**	N	Y	Y	N	Y	Y	Y
2 Boyd	Y	Y	Y	Y	N	N	Y
3 Brown	Y	Y	Y	Y	N	N	N
4 **Crenshaw**	N	Y	Y	N	N	N	Y
5 **Brown-Waite**	N	Y	Y	N	Y	Y	Y
6 **Stearns**	N	Y	Y	Y	Y	Y	Y
7 **Mica**	N	Y	Y	N	Y	Y	Y
8 Grayson	Y	Y	Y	Y	N	N	Y
9 **Bilirakis**	N	Y	Y	N	Y	Y	Y
10 **Young**	N	Y	Y	N	Y	Y	Y
11 Castor	Y	Y	Y	Y	N	N	N
12 **Putnam**	N	Y	Y	N	Y	Y	Y
13 **Buchanan**	N	Y	Y	N	Y	Y	Y
14 **Mack**	N	Y	Y	N	Y	Y	Y
15 **Posey**	N	Y	Y	N	Y	Y	Y
16 **Rooney**	N	Y	Y	N	Y	Y	Y
17 Meek	Y	Y	Y	Y	N	N	Y
18 **Ros-Lehtinen**	N	Y	Y	N	Y	N	Y
19 Wexler	Y	Y	Y	Y	N	N	N
20 Wasserman Schultz	Y	Y	Y	Y	N	N	Y
21 **Diaz-Balart, L.**	N	Y	Y	N	Y	N	Y
22 Klein	Y	Y	Y	Y	N	N	Y
23 Hastings	Y	Y	Y	Y	N	N	N
24 Kosmas	Y	Y	Y	Y	N	N	Y
25 **Diaz-Balart, M.**	N	Y	Y	N	Y	Y	Y
GEORGIA							
1 **Kingston**	N	Y	Y	N	Y	N	Y
2 Bishop	Y	Y	Y	Y	N	N	Y
3 **Westmoreland**	N	Y	Y	N	Y	Y	Y
4 Johnson	Y	Y	Y	Y	N	N	N
5 Lewis	Y	Y	Y	Y	N	N	Y
6 **Price**	N	Y	Y	Y	Y	Y	Y
7 **Linder**	N	Y	?	N	Y	Y	Y
8 Marshall	Y	Y	Y	Y	N	N	N
9 **Deal**	N	Y	Y	N	Y	Y	Y
10 **Broun**	N	Y	Y	N	Y	Y	Y
11 **Gingrey**	N	Y	Y	N	Y	Y	Y
12 Barrow	Y	Y	Y	N	?	Y	Y
13 Scott	Y	Y	Y	Y	N	N	N
HAWAII							
1 Abercrombie	Y	Y	Y	Y	N	N	Y
2 Hirono	Y	Y	N	Y	N	N	N
IDAHO							
1 Minnick	N	Y	Y	Y	N	Y	N
2 **Simpson**	N	Y	Y	N	Y	Y	Y
ILLINOIS							
1 Rush	Y	Y	Y	Y	N	N	Y
2 Jackson	Y	Y	Y	Y	N	N	N
3 Lipinski	N	Y	Y	Y	N	N	Y
4 Gutierrez	Y	Y	Y	Y	N	N	Y
5 Quigley	Y	Y	Y	Y	N	N	Y
6 **Roskam**	N	Y	Y	N	Y	Y	Y
7 Davis	Y	Y	Y	Y	N	N	Y
8 Bean	Y	Y	Y	Y	N	N	Y
9 Schakowsky	Y	Y	Y	Y	N	N	N
10 **Kirk**	N	Y	Y	N	N	N	Y
11 Halvorson	Y	Y	Y	Y	N	N	Y
12 Costello	Y	Y	Y	Y	N	N	Y
13 **Biggert**	N	Y	Y	N	N	Y	Y
14 Foster	Y	Y	Y	Y	N	N	Y
15 **Johnson**	N	Y	Y	N	Y	Y	Y

KEY   **Republicans**   Democrats

Y Voted for (yea)	X Paired against
# Paired for	– Announced against
+ Announced for	P Voted "present"
N Voted against (nay)	

C Voted "present" to avoid possible conflict of interest

? Did not vote or otherwise make a position known

	513	514	515	516	517	518	519
16 **Manzullo**	N	Y	Y	N	Y	Y	Y
17 Hare	Y	Y	Y	Y	N	N	Y
18 **Schock**	N	Y	Y	Y	Y	Y	N
19 **Shimkus**	N	Y	Y	N	Y	Y	Y
INDIANA							
1 Visclosky	Y	Y	Y	Y	N	N	Y
2 Donnelly	N	Y	Y	Y	N	N	Y
3 **Souder**	N	Y	Y	N	Y	Y	Y
4 **Buyer**	N	Y	?	N	Y	Y	Y
5 **Burton**	N	Y	Y	N	Y	Y	Y
6 **Pence**	N	Y	Y	N	Y	Y	Y
7 Carson	Y	Y	Y	Y	N	N	N
8 Ellsworth	N	Y	Y	Y	N	Y	Y
9 Hill	N	Y	Y	Y	?	N	Y
IOWA							
1 Braley	Y	Y	Y	Y	N	N	N
2 Loebsack	Y	Y	Y	Y	N	N	N
3 Boswell	Y	Y	Y	Y	N	N	N
4 **Latham**	N	Y	Y	N	Y	Y	N
5 **King**	N	Y	Y	N	Y	Y	N
KANSAS							
1 **Moran**	N	Y	Y	N	Y	Y	Y
2 **Jenkins**	N	Y	Y	N	Y	Y	Y
3 Moore	Y	Y	Y	Y	N	N	Y
4 **Tiahrt**	N	Y	Y	N	Y	Y	Y
KENTUCKY							
1 **Whitfield**	N	Y	Y	N	N	N	Y
2 **Guthrie**	N	Y	Y	N	Y	Y	Y
3 Yarmuth	Y	Y	Y	Y	N	N	Y
4 **Davis**	N	Y	Y	N	N	N	N
5 **Rogers**	N	Y	Y	N	Y	Y	Y
6 Chandler	Y	Y	Y	Y	N	N	Y
LOUISIANA							
1 **Scalise**	N	Y	Y	N	Y	Y	Y
2 **Cao**	N	Y	Y	Y	N	Y	Y
3 Melancon	N	Y	Y	Y	N	N	Y
4 **Fleming**	N	Y	Y	N	Y	Y	N
5 **Alexander**	N	Y	Y	N	Y	N	Y
6 **Cassidy**	N	Y	Y	N	Y	Y	N
7 **Boustany**	N	Y	Y	N	Y	Y	N
MAINE							
1 Pingree	Y	Y	Y	Y	N	N	N
2 Michaud	Y	Y	Y	Y	N	N	N
MARYLAND							
1 Kratovil	N	Y	Y	Y	N	Y	Y
2 Ruppersberger	Y	Y	Y	Y	N	N	N
3 Sarbanes	Y	Y	Y	Y	N	N	N
4 Edwards	Y	Y	N	Y	N	N	N
5 Hoyer	Y	Y	Y	Y	N	N	Y
6 **Bartlett**	N	Y	Y	N	Y	Y	Y
7 Cummings	Y	Y	Y	Y	N	N	Y
8 Van Hollen	Y	Y	Y	Y	N	N	N
MASSACHUSETTS							
1 Olver	Y	Y	Y	Y	N	N	N
2 Neal	Y	Y	Y	Y	N	N	Y
3 McGovern	Y	Y	Y	Y	N	N	N
4 Frank	Y	Y	Y	Y	N	N	Y
5 Tsongas	Y	Y	Y	Y	N	N	N
6 Tierney	?	Y	Y	Y	N	N	Y
7 Markey	Y	Y	Y	Y	N	N	Y
8 Capuano	Y	Y	Y	Y	N	N	Y
9 Lynch	Y	Y	Y	Y	N	N	Y
10 Delahunt	Y	Y	Y	Y	N	N	N
MICHIGAN							
1 Stupak	N	Y	?	Y	N	N	N
2 **Hoekstra**	N	Y	Y	N	Y	Y	Y
3 **Ehlers**	N	Y	Y	N	N	N	N
4 **Camp**	N	Y	Y	N	Y	Y	Y
5 Kildee	Y	Y	Y	Y	N	N	Y
6 **Upton**	N	Y	Y	N	N	Y	Y
7 Schauer	Y	Y	Y	Y	N	N	Y
8 **Rogers**	N	Y	Y	N	Y	Y	N
9 Peters	Y	Y	Y	Y	N	N	Y
10 **Miller**	N	Y	Y	N	N	Y	Y
11 **McCotter**	N	Y	Y	N	Y	Y	Y
12 Levin	Y	Y	Y	Y	N	N	Y
13 Kilpatrick	Y	Y	Y	Y	N	N	N
14 Conyers	Y	Y	N	Y	N	N	N
15 Dingell	Y	Y	Y	Y	N	N	N
MINNESOTA							
1 Walz	Y	Y	Y	Y	N	N	N
2 **Kline**	N	Y	Y	N	Y	Y	N
3 **Paulsen**	N	Y	Y	N	Y	Y	Y
4 McCollum	Y	Y	Y	Y	N	N	N

	513	514	515	516	517	518	519
5 Ellison	Y	Y	Y	Y	N	N	N
6 **Bachmann**	N	?	Y	N	Y	Y	Y
7 Peterson	Y	Y	Y	Y	N	N	N
8 Oberstar	Y	Y	Y	Y	N	N	N
MISSISSIPPI							
1 Childers	N	Y	Y	Y	Y	Y	Y
2 Thompson	Y	Y	Y	Y	N	N	N
3 **Harper**	N	Y	Y	N	Y	Y	Y
4 Taylor	N	Y	Y	Y	Y	N	Y
MISSOURI							
1 Clay	Y	Y	Y	Y	N	N	N
2 **Akin**	N	Y	Y	N	Y	Y	Y
3 Carnahan	Y	Y	Y	Y	N	N	N
4 Skelton	N	Y	Y	Y	N	N	N
5 Cleaver	Y	Y	Y	Y	N	N	N
6 **Graves**	N	Y	Y	N	Y	Y	Y
7 **Blunt**	N	Y	Y	N	Y	Y	N
8 **Emerson**	N	Y	Y	Y	N	N	Y
9 **Luetkemeyer**	N	Y	Y	N	Y	Y	Y
MONTANA							
AL **Rehberg**	N	Y	Y	N	Y	Y	Y
NEBRASKA							
1 **Fortenberry**	N	Y	Y	N	N	Y	N
2 **Terry**	N	Y	Y	N	Y	N	Y
3 **Smith**	N	Y	Y	N	Y	Y	Y
NEVADA							
1 Berkley	Y	Y	Y	Y	N	N	Y
2 **Heller**	N	Y	Y	–	+	+	+
3 Titus	Y	Y	Y	Y	N	Y	Y
NEW HAMPSHIRE							
1 Shea-Porter	Y	Y	Y	Y	N	N	N
2 Hodes	Y	Y	Y	Y	N	N	Y
NEW JERSEY							
1 Andrews	Y	Y	Y	Y	N	N	Y
2 **LoBiondo**	N	Y	Y	Y	N	Y	Y
3 Adler	Y	Y	Y	Y	N	Y	Y
4 **Smith**	N	Y	Y	?	N	Y	Y
5 **Garrett**	N	Y	Y	N	Y	Y	Y
6 Pallone	Y	Y	Y	Y	N	N	Y
7 **Lance**	N	Y	Y	N	N	Y	Y
8 Pascrell	Y	Y	Y	Y	N	N	Y
9 Rothman	Y	Y	Y	Y	N	N	Y
10 Payne	Y	Y	Y	Y	N	N	N
11 **Frelinghuysen**	N	Y	Y	N	Y	Y	N
12 Holt	Y	Y	Y	Y	N	N	Y
13 Sires	Y	Y	Y	Y	N	N	Y
NEW MEXICO							
1 Heinrich	Y	Y	Y	Y	N	N	Y
2 Teague	Y	Y	Y	N	Y	Y	Y
3 Lujan	Y	Y	Y	Y	N	N	Y
NEW YORK							
1 Bishop	Y	Y	Y	Y	N	N	Y
2 Israel	Y	Y	Y	Y	N	N	Y
3 **King**	N	Y	Y	N	N	N	N
4 McCarthy	Y	Y	Y	Y	N	N	Y
5 Ackerman	Y	Y	Y	Y	N	N	N
6 Meeks	Y	Y	Y	Y	N	N	N
7 Crowley	Y	Y	Y	Y	N	N	Y
8 Nadler	Y	Y	Y	Y	N	N	N
9 Weiner	Y	Y	Y	Y	N	N	Y
10 Towns	Y	Y	Y	Y	N	N	Y
11 Clarke	Y	Y	Y	Y	N	N	Y
12 Velázquez	Y	Y	Y	Y	N	N	N
13 McMahon	Y	Y	Y	Y	N	N	Y
14 Maloney	Y	Y	Y	Y	N	N	Y
15 Rangel	Y	Y	Y	Y	N	N	Y
16 Serrano	Y	Y	Y	Y	N	N	N
17 Engel	Y	Y	Y	Y	N	N	Y
18 Lowey	Y	Y	Y	Y	N	N	Y
19 Hall	Y	Y	Y	Y	N	N	Y
20 Murphy	?	?	?	?	?	?	?
21 Tonko	Y	Y	Y	Y	N	N	Y
22 Hinchey	Y	Y	Y	Y	N	N	N
23 **McHugh**	N	Y	Y	Y	N	N	Y
24 Arcuri	Y	Y	Y	Y	N	N	Y
25 Maffei	Y	Y	Y	Y	N	N	Y
26 **Lee**	N	Y	Y	N	N	Y	Y
27 Higgins	Y	Y	Y	Y	N	N	Y
28 Slaughter	Y	Y	Y	Y	N	N	Y
29 Massa	Y	Y	Y	Y	N	N	Y
NORTH CAROLINA							
1 Butterfield	Y	Y	Y	Y	N	N	Y
2 Etheridge	Y	Y	Y	Y	N	N	N
3 **Jones**	N	Y	Y	N	Y	Y	Y
4 Price	Y	Y	Y	Y	N	N	N

	513	514	515	516	517	518	519
5 **Foxx**	N	Y	Y	N	Y	Y	Y
6 **Coble**	N	Y	Y	N	Y	Y	Y
7 McIntyre	N	Y	Y	Y	N	N	Y
8 Kissell	Y	Y	Y	Y	N	N	Y
9 **Myrick**	N	Y	Y	N	Y	Y	Y
10 **McHenry**	N	Y	?	N	Y	Y	Y
11 Shuler	N	Y	Y	N	N	Y	Y
12 Watt	Y	Y	Y	Y	N	N	N
13 Miller	Y	Y	Y	Y	N	N	N
NORTH DAKOTA							
AL Pomeroy	?	Y	Y	Y	N	N	Y
OHIO							
1 Driehaus	N	Y	Y	Y	N	N	Y
2 **Schmidt**	N	Y	Y	N	Y	Y	N
3 **Turner**	N	Y	Y	N	Y	N	Y
4 **Jordan**	N	Y	Y	?	Y	Y	Y
5 **Latta**	N	Y	Y	N	Y	Y	Y
6 Wilson	Y	Y	Y	Y	N	Y	Y
7 **Austria**	N	Y	Y	N	Y	Y	Y
8 **Boehner**	N	Y	Y	N	Y	Y	N
9 Kaptur	Y	Y	?	Y	N	N	Y
10 Kucinich	Y	Y	Y	Y	N	N	N
11 Fudge	?	?	?	?	?	?	?
12 **Tiberi**	N	Y	Y	N	Y	Y	Y
13 Sutton	Y	Y	Y	Y	N	N	Y
14 **LaTourette**	N	Y	Y	N	N	N	Y
15 Kilroy	Y	Y	Y	Y	N	N	Y
16 Boccieri	N	Y	Y	Y	N	N	Y
17 Ryan	Y	Y	Y	Y	N	N	Y
18 Space	Y	Y	Y	Y	N	N	Y
OKLAHOMA							
1 **Sullivan**	N	Y	Y	N	Y	Y	Y
2 Boren	Y	Y	Y	Y	N	N	Y
3 **Lucas**	N	Y	Y	N	Y	Y	Y
4 **Cole**	N	Y	Y	N	Y	Y	Y
5 **Fallin**	N	Y	Y	N	Y	Y	Y
OREGON							
1 Wu	Y	Y	Y	Y	N	N	Y
2 **Walden**	N	Y	Y	Y	Y	Y	Y
3 Blumenauer	Y	Y	Y	Y	N	N	N
4 DeFazio	Y	Y	Y	Y	N	N	Y
5 Schrader	Y	?	Y	Y	N	Y	Y
PENNSYLVANIA							
1 Brady	Y	Y	Y	Y	N	N	Y
2 Fattah	Y	?	Y	Y	N	N	N
3 Dahlkemper	N	Y	Y	Y	N	N	N
4 Altmire	N	Y	Y	Y	N	N	Y
5 **Thompson**	N	Y	Y	N	Y	Y	Y
6 **Gerlach**	N	Y	Y	N	Y	Y	Y
7 Sestak	Y	Y	Y	Y	N	N	N
8 Murphy, P.	Y	Y	Y	Y	N	N	Y
9 **Shuster**	N	Y	Y	N	Y	Y	Y
10 Carney	Y	Y	Y	Y	N	N	Y
11 Kanjorski	N	Y	Y	Y	N	N	N
12 Murtha	Y	?	?	Y	N	N	Y
13 Schwartz	Y	Y	Y	Y	Y	N	Y
14 Doyle	Y	Y	Y	Y	N	N	Y
15 **Dent**	N	Y	Y	N	Y	Y	Y
16 **Pitts**	N	Y	Y	N	Y	Y	Y
17 Holden	N	Y	Y	Y	N	N	Y
18 **Murphy, T.**	N	Y	Y	N	Y	N	Y
19 **Platts**	N	Y	Y	Y	N	Y	Y
RHODE ISLAND							
1 Kennedy	Y	Y	Y	Y	N	N	Y
2 Langevin	Y	Y	Y	Y	N	N	Y
SOUTH CAROLINA							
1 **Brown**	N	Y	Y	N	Y	Y	Y
2 **Wilson**	N	Y	Y	N	Y	Y	Y
3 **Barrett**	N	Y	Y	N	Y	Y	Y
4 **Inglis**	N	Y	Y	N	Y	Y	Y
5 Spratt	Y	Y	Y	Y	N	N	N
6 Clyburn	Y	Y	Y	Y	N	N	N
SOUTH DAKOTA							
AL Herseth Sandlin	N	Y	Y	Y	N	N	Y
TENNESSEE							
1 **Roe**	N	Y	Y	N	Y	Y	Y
2 **Duncan**	N	Y	Y	N	Y	Y	N
3 **Wamp**	N	Y	Y	N	Y	N	Y
4 Davis	Y	Y	Y	Y	N	N	Y
5 Cooper	Y	Y	Y	Y	N	N	Y
6 Gordon	Y	Y	Y	Y	N	N	Y
7 **Blackburn**	N	Y	Y	N	Y	Y	Y
8 Tanner	Y	Y	Y	Y	N	N	Y
9 Cohen	Y	Y	Y	Y	N	N	Y

	513	514	515	516	517	518	519
TEXAS							
1 **Gohmert**	N	Y	Y	N	?	Y	Y
2 **Poe**	N	Y	Y	N	Y	Y	Y
3 **Johnson, S.**	N	Y	Y	N	Y	Y	N
4 **Hall**	N	Y	Y	N	Y	Y	Y
5 **Hensarling**	N	Y	Y	N	Y	Y	Y
6 **Barton**	N	Y	Y	N	Y	Y	N
7 **Culberson**	N	Y	Y	N	Y	Y	Y
8 **Brady**	N	Y	Y	N	Y	Y	N
9 Green, A.	Y	Y	Y	Y	N	N	Y
10 **McCaul**	N	Y	Y	N	Y	Y	Y
11 **Conaway**	N	Y	Y	N	Y	Y	N
12 **Granger**	?	?	?	?	?	?	?
13 **Thornberry**	N	Y	Y	N	Y	Y	N
14 **Paul**	N	Y	N	N	Y	Y	Y
15 Hinojosa	Y	Y	Y	+	–	N	Y
16 Reyes	Y	Y	Y	Y	N	N	Y
17 Edwards	Y	Y	Y	Y	N	N	Y
18 Jackson Lee	Y	Y	Y	Y	N	N	N
19 **Neugebauer**	N	Y	Y	N	Y	Y	Y
20 Gonzalez	Y	Y	Y	Y	N	N	N
21 **Smith**	N	Y	Y	N	Y	Y	Y
22 **Olson**	N	Y	Y	N	Y	Y	Y
23 Rodriguez	Y	Y	Y	Y	N	N	Y
24 **Marchant**	N	Y	Y	N	Y	Y	Y
25 Doggett	Y	Y	Y	Y	N	N	Y
26 **Burgess**	N	Y	Y	N	Y	Y	Y
27 Ortiz	Y	Y	Y	Y	N	N	Y
28 Cuellar	Y	Y	Y	N	N	N	N
29 Green, G.	Y	Y	Y	Y	N	N	Y
30 Johnson, E.	Y	Y	Y	Y	N	N	N
31 **Carter**	N	Y	Y	N	Y	Y	Y
32 **Sessions**	N	Y	Y	N	Y	Y	Y
UTAH							
1 **Bishop**	N	Y	Y	N	Y	Y	N
2 Matheson	Y	Y	Y	Y	N	N	Y
3 **Chaffetz**	N	Y	Y	N	Y	Y	Y
VERMONT							
AL Welch	Y	Y	Y	Y	N	N	N
VIRGINIA							
1 **Wittman**	N	Y	Y	N	Y	Y	Y
2 Nye	Y	Y	Y	Y	N	N	Y
3 Scott	Y	Y	N	Y	N	N	Y
4 **Forbes**	N	Y	Y	N	Y	Y	Y
5 Perriello	Y	Y	Y	Y	N	N	Y
6 **Goodlatte**	N	Y	Y	N	Y	Y	Y
7 **Cantor**	N	Y	Y	N	Y	Y	Y
8 Moran	Y	Y	P	Y	N	N	N
9 Boucher	Y	Y	Y	Y	N	N	Y
10 **Wolf**	?	Y	Y	N	Y	Y	Y
11 Connolly	Y	Y	Y	Y	N	N	Y
WASHINGTON							
1 Inslee	Y	Y	Y	Y	N	N	N
2 Larsen	Y	Y	Y	Y	N	N	N
3 Baird	Y	Y	Y	Y	N	N	N
4 **Hastings**	N	Y	Y	N	Y	Y	Y
5 **McMorris Rodgers**	N	Y	Y	N	Y	Y	Y
6 Dicks	Y	Y	Y	Y	N	N	Y
7 McDermott	Y	Y	N	Y	N	N	N
8 **Reichert**	N	Y	Y	Y	N	N	N
9 Smith	Y	Y	Y	Y	N	N	Y
WEST VIRGINIA							
1 Mollohan	Y	Y	Y	Y	N	N	Y
2 **Capito**	N	Y	Y	N	N	Y	Y
3 Rahall	N	Y	Y	Y	N	N	N
WISCONSIN							
1 **Ryan**	N	Y	Y	N	Y	Y	N
2 Baldwin	Y	Y	Y	Y	N	N	N
3 Kind	Y	Y	Y	Y	N	N	N
4 Moore	Y	Y	Y	Y	N	N	N
5 **Sensenbrenner**	N	Y	Y	N	Y	Y	Y
6 **Petri**	N	Y	Y	N	Y	N	Y
7 Obey	Y	Y	Y	Y	N	N	N
8 Kagen	Y	Y	Y	Y	N	N	Y
WYOMING							
AL **Lummis**	N	Y	Y	N	Y	Y	Y
DELEGATES							
Faleomavaega (A.S.)				Y	N	N	Y
Norton (D.C.)				Y	N	N	N
Bordallo (Guam)				Y	N	N	N
Sablan (N. Marianas)				Y	N	N	Y
Pierluisi (P.R.)				Y	N	N	N
Christensen (V.I.)				Y	N	N	N

IN THE HOUSE | By Vote Number

520. HR 3081. Fiscal 2010 State-Foreign Operations Appropriations/Multilateral Assistance. Culberson, R-Texas, amendment that would reduce the amount provided for multilateral assistance by $506 million. Rejected in Committee of the Whole 174-256: R 164-12; D 10-244. A "nay" was a vote in support of the president's position. July 9, 2009.

521. HR 3081. Fiscal 2010 State-Foreign Operations Appropriations/Conditions on Funding for International Banks. Kirk, R-Ill., amendment that would bar the Treasury Department from using funds appropriated in the bill to negotiate an agreement in contravention of current law relating to U.S. participation in the International Monetary Fund and World Bank. Adopted in Committee of the Whole 429-2: R 176-0; D 253-2. A "nay" was a vote in support of the president's position. July 9, 2009.

522. HR 3081. Fiscal 2010 State-Foreign Operations Appropriations/One-Time Educational Program. Flake, R-Ariz., amendment that would bar the use of funds in the bill for a one-time special educational, professional and cultural exchange grants program. It also would reduce funds appropriated in the bill by $8 million. Rejected in Committee of the Whole 164-268: R 151-25; D 13-243. July 9, 2009.

523. HR 3081. Fiscal 2010 State-Foreign Operations Appropriations/Motion to Table. Lowey, D-N.Y., motion to table (kill) the Kirk, R-Ill., appeal of the ruling of the chair with respect to the Lowey point of order that the Kirk motion to recommit the bill constituted legislating on an appropriations bill. The motion would recommit the bill to the Appropriations Committee with instructions that it be immediately reported back with language that would state that it is the policy of the House that the bill should be re-opened for amendment under regular order. Motion agreed to 238-180: R 0-175; D 238-5. July 9, 2009.

524. HR 3081. Fiscal 2010 State-Foreign Operations Appropriations/Recommit. Kirk, R-Ill., motion to recommit the bill to the Appropriations Committee with instructions that it be immediately reported back with language that would increase the amount provided for grants to the National Endowment for Democracy by $15 million, offset by a reduction of the same amount for contributions to international organizations. Motion rejected 192-233: R 172-2; D 20-231. July 9, 2009.

525. HR 3081. Fiscal 2010 State-Foreign Operations Appropriations/Passage. Passage of the bill that would appropriate $49 billion in fiscal 2010 for the State Department, foreign assistance and other international activities. It would provide $16.1 billion for the State Department, $2.7 billion in assistance for Afghanistan, $2.2 billion for Israel, $1.5 billion for Pakistan and $1.3 billion for Egypt. It would appropriate $5.8 billion for programs to combat HIV/AIDS as well as $1.4 billion for the Millennium Challenge Corporation. Passed 318-106: R 76-97; D 242-9. A "yea" was a vote in support of the president's position. July 9, 2009.

	520	521	522	523	524	525
ALABAMA						
1 Bonner	Y	Y	Y	N	Y	Y
2 Bright	Y	Y	Y	Y	Y	Y
3 Rogers	N	Y	N	N	Y	Y
4 Aderholt	Y	Y	N	N	Y	Y
5 Griffith	N	Y	N	Y	Y	Y
6 Bachus	N	Y	N	N	Y	N
7 Davis	N	Y	N	Y	N	Y
ALASKA						
AL Young	Y	Y	Y	N	Y	Y
ARIZONA						
1 Kirkpatrick	Y	Y	Y	Y	N	Y
2 Franks	Y	Y	Y	N	Y	N
3 Shadegg	Y	Y	Y	N	Y	Y
4 Pastor	N	Y	N	Y	N	Y
5 Mitchell	N	Y	N	Y	N	Y
6 Flake	Y	Y	Y	N	N	N
7 Grijalva	N	Y	N	Y	N	Y
8 Giffords	N	Y	Y	N	Y	Y
ARKANSAS						
1 Berry	N	Y	N	Y	N	Y
2 Snyder	N	Y	N	Y	N	Y
3 Boozman	Y	Y	Y	N	Y	N
4 Ross	N	Y	N	Y	N	Y
CALIFORNIA						
1 Thompson	N	Y	N	Y	N	Y
2 Herger	Y	Y	Y	N	Y	N
3 Lungren	Y	Y	Y	N	Y	N
4 McClintock	Y	Y	Y	N	Y	N
5 Matsui	N	Y	N	Y	N	Y
6 Woolsey	N	Y	N	Y	N	Y
7 Miller, George	N	Y	N	?	N	Y
8 Pelosi						
9 Lee	N	Y	N	Y	N	Y
10 Vacant						
11 McNerney	N	Y	N	Y	N	Y
12 Speier	N	Y	N	Y	N	Y
13 Stark	N	N	N	?	N	N
14 Eshoo	N	Y	N	Y	N	Y
15 Honda	N	Y	N	Y	N	Y
16 Lofgren	N	Y	N	Y	N	Y
17 Farr	N	Y	N	Y	N	Y
18 Cardoza	N	Y	N	Y	N	Y
19 Radanovich	Y	Y	Y	N	Y	N
20 Costa	N	Y	N	Y	N	Y
21 Nunes	Y	Y	Y	N	Y	N
22 McCarthy	Y	Y	Y	N	Y	N
23 Capps	N	Y	N	Y	N	Y
24 Gallegly	Y	Y	Y	N	Y	N
25 McKeon	Y	Y	Y	N	Y	N
26 Dreier	Y	Y	Y	N	Y	N
27 Sherman	N	Y	N	Y	N	Y
28 Berman	N	Y	N	Y	N	Y
29 Schiff	N	Y	N	Y	N	Y
30 Waxman	N	Y	N	?	N	Y
31 Becerra	N	?	N	Y	N	Y
32 Vacant						
33 Watson	N	Y	N	Y	N	Y
34 Roybal-Allard	N	Y	N	Y	N	Y
35 Waters	N	Y	N	Y	N	Y
36 Harman	N	Y	N	Y	N	Y
37 Richardson	N	Y	N	Y	N	Y
38 Napolitano	N	Y	N	Y	N	Y
39 Sánchez, Linda	N	Y	N	Y	N	Y
40 Royce	Y	Y	Y	N	Y	N
41 Lewis	Y	Y	Y	N	Y	N
42 Miller, Gary	Y	Y	Y	N	Y	N
43 Baca	N	Y	N	Y	N	Y
44 Calvert	Y	Y	Y	N	Y	N
45 Bono Mack	Y	Y	Y	N	Y	Y
46 Rohrabacher	Y	Y	Y	N	Y	N
47 Sanchez, Loretta	N	Y	N	Y	N	Y
48 Campbell	Y	Y	Y	N	Y	N
49 Issa	Y	Y	Y	N	Y	N
50 Bilbray	Y	Y	Y	N	Y	N
51 Filner	N	Y	N	Y	N	Y
52 Hunter	Y	Y	Y	N	Y	N
53 Davis	N	Y	N	Y	N	Y

	520	521	522	523	524	525
COLORADO						
1 DeGette	N	Y	N	Y	N	Y
2 Polis	N	Y	N	Y	N	Y
3 Salazar	N	Y	N	Y	N	Y
4 Markey	N	Y	N	Y	N	Y
5 Lamborn	Y	Y	Y	N	Y	Y
6 Coffman	Y	Y	Y	N	Y	Y
7 Perlmutter	N	Y	N	Y	N	Y
CONNECTICUT						
1 Larson	–	+	–	+	–	+
2 Courtney	N	Y	N	Y	N	Y
3 DeLauro	?	?	?	?	?	?
4 Himes	N	Y	N	Y	N	Y
5 Murphy	?	Y	N	Y	N	Y
DELAWARE						
AL Castle	Y	Y	N	N	Y	Y
FLORIDA						
1 Miller	Y	Y	Y	N	Y	N
2 Boyd	N	Y	N	Y	N	Y
3 Brown	N	Y	N	Y	N	Y
4 Crenshaw	Y	Y	N	N	Y	Y
5 Brown-Waite	Y	Y	Y	N	Y	N
6 Stearns	Y	Y	Y	N	Y	Y
7 Mica	Y	Y	Y	N	Y	Y
8 Grayson	N	Y	N	Y	N	Y
9 Bilirakis	Y	Y	Y	N	Y	Y
10 Young	Y	Y	Y	N	Y	N
11 Castor	N	Y	N	Y	N	Y
12 Putnam	Y	Y	Y	N	Y	Y
13 Buchanan	Y	Y	Y	N	Y	Y
14 Mack	Y	Y	Y	N	Y	Y
15 Posey	Y	Y	Y	N	Y	N
16 Rooney	Y	Y	Y	N	Y	Y
17 Meek	N	Y	N	Y	N	Y
18 Ros-Lehtinen	N	Y	N	Y	N	Y
19 Wexler	N	Y	N	Y	N	Y
20 Wasserman Schultz	N	Y	N	Y	N	Y
21 Diaz-Balart, L.	Y	Y	N	N	Y	Y
22 Klein	N	Y	N	Y	N	Y
23 Hastings	N	Y	N	Y	N	Y
24 Kosmas	N	Y	N	Y	N	Y
25 Diaz-Balart, M.	Y	Y	N	N	Y	Y
GEORGIA						
1 Kingston	Y	Y	Y	N	Y	N
2 Bishop	N	Y	N	Y	N	Y
3 Westmoreland	Y	Y	Y	N	Y	N
4 Johnson	N	Y	N	Y	N	Y
5 Lewis	N	Y	N	Y	N	Y
6 Price	Y	Y	Y	N	Y	N
7 Linder	Y	Y	Y	N	Y	N
8 Marshall	N	Y	N	Y	N	Y
9 Deal	Y	Y	Y	N	Y	N
10 Broun	Y	Y	Y	N	Y	N
11 Gingrey	Y	Y	Y	N	Y	N
12 Barrow	N	Y	N	Y	N	Y
13 Scott	N	Y	N	Y	N	Y
HAWAII						
1 Abercrombie	N	Y	N	Y	N	Y
2 Hirono	N	Y	N	Y	N	Y
IDAHO						
1 Minnick	N	Y	Y	Y	N	Y
2 Simpson	Y	Y	N	N	Y	N
ILLINOIS						
1 Rush	N	Y	N	Y	N	Y
2 Jackson	N	Y	N	Y	N	Y
3 Lipinski	N	Y	N	Y	N	Y
4 Gutierrez	N	Y	N	Y	N	Y
5 Quigley	N	Y	N	Y	N	Y
6 Roskam	N	Y	Y	N	Y	Y
7 Davis	N	Y	N	Y	N	Y
8 Bean	N	Y	N	Y	N	Y
9 Schakowsky	N	Y	N	Y	N	Y
10 Kirk	Y	Y	Y	N	Y	Y
11 Halvorson	Y	Y	Y	N	Y	Y
12 Costello	N	Y	N	Y	N	Y
13 Biggert	N	Y	N	N	Y	Y
14 Foster	N	Y	N	Y	N	Y
15 Johnson	Y	Y	Y	N	Y	N

	520	521	522	523	524	525
16 **Manzullo**	Y	Y	Y	N	Y	N
17 Hare	N	Y	N	Y	N	Y
18 **Schock**	Y	Y	Y	N	Y	Y
19 **Shimkus**	Y	Y	N	N	Y	N
INDIANA						
1 Visclosky	N	Y	N	Y	N	Y
2 Donnelly	N	Y	N	Y	Y	Y
3 **Souder**	Y	Y	Y	N	Y	Y
4 **Buyer**	Y	Y	Y	N	Y	N
5 **Burton**	Y	Y	Y	N	Y	Y
6 **Pence**	Y	Y	Y	N	Y	Y
7 Carson	N	Y	N	Y	N	Y
8 Ellsworth	N	Y	N	N	N	Y
9 Hill	N	Y	N	?	N	Y
IOWA						
1 Braley	N	Y	N	Y	N	Y
2 Loebsack	N	Y	N	Y	N	Y
3 Boswell	N	Y	N	Y	N	Y
4 **Latham**	Y	Y	N	N	Y	N
5 **King**	Y	Y	Y	N	Y	N
KANSAS						
1 **Moran**	Y	Y	Y	N	Y	Y
2 **Jenkins**	Y	Y	Y	N	Y	Y
3 Moore	N	Y	N	Y	N	Y
4 **Tiahrt**	Y	Y	Y	N	Y	Y
KENTUCKY						
1 **Whitfield**	Y	Y	Y	N	Y	Y
2 **Guthrie**	Y	Y	Y	N	Y	Y
3 Yarmuth	N	Y	N	Y	N	Y
4 **Davis**	Y	Y	Y	N	Y	N
5 **Rogers**	Y	Y	Y	N	Y	N
6 Chandler	N	Y	N	Y	N	Y
LOUISIANA						
1 **Scalise**	Y	Y	Y	N	Y	Y
2 **Cao**	Y	Y	N	N	Y	Y
3 Melancon	N	Y	N	N	N	Y
4 **Fleming**	Y	Y	Y	N	Y	Y
5 **Alexander**	Y	Y	Y	N	Y	Y
6 **Cassidy**	Y	Y	Y	N	Y	Y
7 **Boustany**	Y	Y	Y	N	Y	N
MAINE						
1 Pingree	N	Y	N	Y	N	Y
2 Michaud	N	Y	N	Y	N	Y
MARYLAND						
1 Kratovil	N	Y	Y	Y	N	Y
2 Ruppersberger	N	Y	N	Y	N	Y
3 Sarbanes	N	Y	N	Y	N	Y
4 Edwards	N	Y	N	Y	N	Y
5 Hoyer	N	Y	N	Y	N	Y
6 **Bartlett**	Y	Y	Y	N	Y	N
7 Cummings	N	Y	N	Y	N	Y
8 Van Hollen	N	Y	N	Y	N	Y
MASSACHUSETTS						
1 Olver	N	Y	N	Y	N	Y
2 Neal	N	Y	N	Y	N	Y
3 McGovern	N	Y	N	Y	N	Y
4 Frank	N	Y	N	Y	N	Y
5 Tsongas	N	Y	N	Y	N	Y
6 Tierney	N	Y	N	Y	N	Y
7 Markey	N	Y	N	Y	N	Y
8 Capuano	N	Y	N	Y	N	Y
9 Lynch	N	Y	N	Y	N	Y
10 Delahunt	N	Y	N	Y	N	Y
MICHIGAN						
1 Stupak	N	Y	N	Y	N	N
2 **Hoekstra**	Y	Y	Y	N	Y	N
3 **Ehlers**	N	Y	Y	N	Y	N
4 **Camp**	Y	Y	Y	N	Y	N
5 Kildee	N	Y	N	Y	N	Y
6 **Upton**	Y	Y	N	N	Y	N
7 Schauer	N	Y	N	Y	Y	Y
8 **Rogers**	Y	Y	Y	N	Y	N
9 Peters	N	Y	N	Y	N	Y
10 **Miller**	Y	Y	Y	N	Y	Y
11 **McCotter**	Y	Y	Y	N	Y	Y
12 Levin	N	Y	N	Y	N	Y
13 Kilpatrick	N	Y	N	Y	N	Y
14 Conyers	N	Y	N	Y	N	Y
15 Dingell	N	Y	N	Y	N	Y
MINNESOTA						
1 Walz	N	Y	N	Y	N	Y
2 **Kline**	Y	Y	Y	N	Y	Y
3 **Paulsen**	Y	Y	Y	N	Y	Y
4 McCollum	N	Y	N	Y	N	Y

	520	521	522	523	524	525
5 Ellison	N	Y	N	Y	N	Y
6 **Bachmann**	Y	Y	Y	N	Y	Y
7 Peterson	N	Y	N	Y	N	N
8 Oberstar	N	Y	N	Y	N	Y
MISSISSIPPI						
1 Childers	Y	Y	N	Y	Y	Y
2 Thompson	N	Y	N	Y	N	Y
3 **Harper**	Y	Y	Y	N	Y	Y
4 Taylor	Y	Y	Y	Y	N	N
MISSOURI						
1 Clay	N	Y	N	Y	N	Y
2 **Akin**	Y	Y	Y	N	Y	–
3 Carnahan	N	Y	N	Y	N	Y
4 Skelton	N	Y	N	Y	N	Y
5 Cleaver	N	Y	N	Y	N	Y
6 **Graves**	Y	Y	Y	N	?	?
7 **Blunt**	N	Y	N	N	Y	N
8 **Emerson**	Y	Y	N	N	Y	N
9 **Luetkemeyer**	Y	Y	Y	N	Y	N
MONTANA						
AL **Rehberg**	Y	Y	Y	N	Y	N
NEBRASKA						
1 **Fortenberry**	Y	Y	N	N	Y	N
2 **Terry**	Y	Y	N	N	Y	Y
3 **Smith**	Y	Y	Y	N	Y	N
NEVADA						
1 Berkley	N	Y	N	Y	N	Y
2 **Heller**	+	+	+	–	+	–
3 Titus	N	Y	Y	Y	N	Y
NEW HAMPSHIRE						
1 Shea-Porter	N	Y	N	Y	N	Y
2 Hodes	N	Y	Y	Y	N	Y
NEW JERSEY						
1 Andrews	N	Y	N	?	N	Y
2 **LoBiondo**	Y	Y	Y	N	Y	Y
3 Adler	N	Y	N	Y	N	Y
4 **Smith**	Y	Y	N	N	Y	N
5 **Garrett**	Y	Y	Y	N	Y	Y
6 Pallone	N	Y	N	Y	N	Y
7 **Lance**	Y	Y	Y	N	Y	Y
8 Pascrell	N	Y	N	Y	N	Y
9 Rothman	N	Y	N	Y	N	Y
10 Payne	N	Y	N	Y	N	Y
11 **Frelinghuysen**	Y	Y	Y	N	Y	Y
12 Holt	N	Y	N	Y	N	Y
13 Sires	N	Y	N	Y	Y	Y
NEW MEXICO						
1 Heinrich	N	Y	N	Y	N	Y
2 Teague	Y	Y	N	Y	Y	N
3 Lujan	N	Y	N	Y	N	Y
NEW YORK						
1 Bishop	N	Y	N	Y	N	Y
2 Israel	N	Y	N	Y	N	Y
3 **King**	N	Y	N	N	Y	Y
4 McCarthy	N	Y	N	Y	N	Y
5 Ackerman	N	Y	N	Y	N	Y
6 Meeks	N	Y	N	Y	N	Y
7 Crowley	N	Y	N	Y	N	Y
8 Nadler	N	Y	N	Y	N	Y
9 Weiner	N	Y	N	Y	N	Y
10 Towns	N	Y	N	Y	N	Y
11 Clarke	N	Y	N	Y	N	Y
12 Velázquez	N	Y	N	Y	N	Y
13 McMahon	N	Y	N	Y	Y	Y
14 Maloney	N	Y	N	Y	N	Y
15 Rangel	N	Y	N	?	N	Y
16 Serrano	N	Y	N	Y	N	Y
17 Engel	N	Y	N	Y	N	Y
18 Lowey	N	Y	N	Y	N	Y
19 Hall	N	Y	N	Y	N	Y
20 Murphy	?	?	?	Y	Y	Y
21 Tonko	N	Y	N	Y	N	Y
22 Hinchey	N	Y	N	Y	N	Y
23 **McHugh**	N	Y	N	N	Y	Y
24 Arcuri	N	Y	N	N	Y	Y
25 Maffei	N	Y	N	Y	N	Y
26 **Lee**	Y	Y	Y	N	Y	Y
27 Higgins	N	Y	N	Y	N	Y
28 Slaughter	N	Y	N	?	N	Y
29 Massa	N	Y	N	Y	N	Y
NORTH CAROLINA						
1 Butterfield	N	Y	N	Y	N	Y
2 Etheridge	N	Y	N	Y	N	Y
3 **Jones**	Y	Y	Y	N	Y	N
4 Price	N	Y	N	Y	N	Y

	520	521	522	523	524	525
5 **Foxx**	Y	Y	Y	N	Y	N
6 **Coble**	Y	Y	Y	N	Y	N
7 McIntyre	N	Y	N	Y	N	N
8 Kissell	N	Y	N	Y	N	Y
9 **Myrick**	Y	Y	Y	N	Y	N
10 **McHenry**	Y	Y	Y	N	Y	N
11 Shuler	N	Y	Y	Y	Y	Y
12 Watt	N	Y	N	Y	N	Y
13 Miller	N	Y	N	Y	N	Y
NORTH DAKOTA						
AL Pomeroy	N	Y	N	Y	N	Y
OHIO						
1 Driehaus	N	Y	N	Y	N	Y
2 **Schmidt**	Y	Y	Y	N	Y	Y
3 **Turner**	Y	Y	N	N	Y	Y
4 **Jordan**	Y	Y	Y	N	Y	N
5 **Latta**	Y	Y	Y	N	Y	N
6 Wilson	N	Y	N	Y	N	Y
7 **Austria**	Y	Y	Y	N	Y	Y
8 **Boehner**	Y	Y	Y	?	?	?
9 Kaptur	N	Y	N	Y	N	Y
10 Kucinich	N	N	N	Y	N	N
11 Fudge	?	?	?	?	?	?
12 **Tiberi**	Y	Y	Y	N	Y	Y
13 Sutton	N	Y	N	Y	N	Y
14 **LaTourette**	Y	Y	N	N	Y	Y
15 Kilroy	N	Y	N	Y	N	Y
16 Boccieri	Y	Y	N	Y	N	Y
17 Ryan	N	Y	N	Y	N	Y
18 Space	N	Y	N	Y	Y	Y
OKLAHOMA						
1 **Sullivan**	Y	Y	Y	N	Y	Y
2 Boren	N	Y	N	Y	Y	Y
3 **Lucas**	Y	Y	Y	N	Y	N
4 **Cole**	Y	Y	Y	N	Y	Y
5 **Fallin**	Y	Y	Y	N	Y	N
OREGON						
1 Wu	N	Y	N	Y	N	Y
2 **Walden**	N	Y	Y	N	Y	N
3 Blumenauer	N	Y	N	Y	N	Y
4 DeFazio	Y	Y	N	Y	N	Y
5 Schrader	N	Y	N	Y	N	Y
PENNSYLVANIA						
1 Brady	N	Y	N	Y	N	Y
2 Fattah	N	Y	N	Y	N	Y
3 Dahlkemper	N	Y	Y	Y	Y	Y
4 Altmire	Y	Y	Y	Y	Y	Y
5 **Thompson**	Y	Y	N	N	Y	Y
6 **Gerlach**	Y	Y	Y	N	Y	Y
7 Sestak	N	Y	N	Y	N	Y
8 Murphy, P.	N	Y	N	Y	Y	Y
9 **Shuster**	Y	Y	Y	N	Y	Y
10 Carney	N	Y	N	N	Y	Y
11 Kanjorski	N	Y	N	Y	N	Y
12 Murtha	N	Y	N	Y	N	Y
13 Schwartz	N	Y	N	Y	N	Y
14 Doyle	N	Y	N	Y	N	Y
15 **Dent**	Y	Y	Y	N	Y	Y
16 **Pitts**	Y	Y	Y	N	Y	N
17 Holden	Y	Y	N	Y	N	Y
18 **Murphy, T.**	Y	Y	N	N	Y	Y
19 **Platts**	Y	Y	Y	N	Y	Y
RHODE ISLAND						
1 Kennedy	N	Y	N	Y	N	Y
2 Langevin	N	Y	N	Y	N	Y
SOUTH CAROLINA						
1 **Brown**	Y	Y	Y	N	Y	N
2 **Wilson**	Y	Y	Y	N	Y	Y
3 **Barrett**	Y	Y	Y	N	Y	N
4 **Inglis**	N	Y	Y	N	Y	Y
5 Spratt	N	Y	N	Y	N	Y
6 Clyburn	N	Y	N	Y	N	Y
SOUTH DAKOTA						
AL Herseth Sandlin	N	Y	N	Y	N	N
TENNESSEE						
1 **Roe**	Y	Y	Y	N	Y	Y
2 **Duncan**	Y	Y	Y	N	Y	N
3 **Wamp**	Y	Y	Y	N	Y	Y
4 Davis	N	Y	N	Y	N	Y
5 Cooper	N	Y	N	Y	N	Y
6 Gordon	N	Y	N	?	N	Y
7 **Blackburn**	Y	Y	Y	N	Y	N
8 Tanner	N	Y	N	Y	N	Y
9 Cohen	N	Y	Y	Y	N	Y

	520	521	522	523	524	525
TEXAS						
1 **Gohmert**	Y	Y	Y	N	Y	N
2 **Poe**	Y	Y	Y	N	Y	N
3 **Johnson, S.**	Y	Y	Y	N	Y	N
4 **Hall**	Y	Y	Y	N	Y	N
5 **Hensarling**	Y	Y	Y	N	Y	N
6 **Barton**	Y	Y	Y	N	Y	N
7 **Culberson**	Y	Y	Y	N	Y	N
8 **Brady**	N	Y	Y	N	Y	N
9 Green, A.	N	Y	N	Y	N	Y
10 **McCaul**	Y	Y	Y	N	Y	N
11 **Conaway**	Y	Y	Y	N	Y	N
12 **Granger**	?	?	?	?	?	?
13 **Thornberry**	Y	Y	Y	N	Y	N
14 **Paul**	Y	Y	Y	N	N	N
15 Hinojosa	N	Y	N	Y	N	Y
16 Reyes	N	Y	N	Y	N	Y
17 Edwards	?	Y	N	Y	N	Y
18 Jackson Lee	N	Y	N	Y	N	Y
19 **Neugebauer**	Y	Y	Y	N	Y	N
20 Gonzalez	N	Y	N	Y	N	Y
21 **Smith**	Y	Y	Y	N	Y	N
22 **Olson**	Y	Y	Y	N	Y	N
23 Rodriguez	N	Y	N	Y	N	Y
24 **Marchant**	Y	Y	Y	N	Y	N
25 Doggett	N	Y	N	Y	N	Y
26 **Burgess**	Y	Y	Y	N	Y	N
27 Ortiz	N	Y	N	Y	N	Y
28 Cuellar	N	Y	N	Y	N	Y
29 Green, G.	N	Y	N	Y	N	Y
30 Johnson, E.	N	Y	N	Y	N	Y
31 **Carter**	Y	Y	Y	N	Y	N
32 **Sessions**	Y	Y	Y	N	Y	Y
UTAH						
1 **Bishop**	Y	Y	Y	N	Y	N
2 Matheson	N	Y	N	Y	N	N
3 **Chaffetz**	Y	Y	Y	N	Y	N
VERMONT						
AL Welch	N	Y	N	Y	N	Y
VIRGINIA						
1 **Wittman**	Y	Y	Y	N	Y	N
2 Nye	N	Y	N	N	N	Y
3 Scott	N	Y	N	Y	N	Y
4 **Forbes**	Y	Y	Y	N	Y	N
5 Perriello	N	Y	N	Y	N	Y
6 **Goodlatte**	Y	Y	Y	N	Y	N
7 **Cantor**	Y	Y	Y	N	Y	Y
8 Moran	N	Y	N	Y	N	Y
9 Boucher	N	Y	N	Y	N	Y
10 **Wolf**	Y	Y	N	N	Y	N
11 Connolly	N	Y	N	Y	N	Y
WASHINGTON						
1 Inslee	N	Y	N	Y	N	Y
2 Larsen	N	Y	N	Y	N	Y
3 Baird	N	Y	N	Y	N	Y
4 **Hastings**	Y	Y	Y	N	Y	N
5 **McMorris Rodgers**	Y	Y	Y	N	Y	N
6 Dicks	N	Y	N	Y	N	Y
7 McDermott	N	Y	N	Y	N	Y
8 **Reichert**	N	Y	N	N	Y	Y
9 Smith	N	Y	N	Y	N	Y
WEST VIRGINIA						
1 Mollohan	N	Y	N	Y	N	Y
2 **Capito**	Y	Y	Y	N	Y	Y
3 Rahall	N	Y	N	Y	N	Y
WISCONSIN						
1 **Ryan**	Y	Y	Y	N	Y	N
2 Baldwin	N	Y	N	Y	N	Y
3 Kind	N	Y	N	Y	N	Y
4 Moore	N	Y	N	Y	N	Y
5 **Sensenbrenner**	Y	Y	Y	N	Y	N
6 **Petri**	Y	Y	Y	N	Y	N
7 Obey	N	Y	N	Y	N	Y
8 Kagen	N	Y	N	Y	N	Y
WYOMING						
AL **Lummis**	Y	Y	Y	N	Y	N
DELEGATES						
Faleomavaega (A.S.)	N	Y	N			
Norton (D.C.)	N	Y	N			
Bordallo (Guam)	N	Y	N			
Sablan (N. Marianas)	N	Y	N			
Pierluisi (P.R.)	N	Y	N			
Christensen (V.I.)	N	Y	N			

IN THE HOUSE | By Vote Number

526. **HR 3082. Fiscal 2010 Military Construction-VA Appropriations/Previous Question.** Pingree, D-Maine, motion to order the previous question (thus ending debate and possibility of amendment) on adoption of the rule (H Res 622) that would provide for House floor consideration of the bill that would appropriate $133.7 billion in fiscal 2010 for the Department of Veterans Affairs, military construction and military family housing. Motion agreed to 244-174: R 0-169; D 244-5. July 10, 2009.

527. **HR 3082. Fiscal 2010 Military Construction-VA Appropriations/Rule.** Adoption of the rule (H Res 622) to provide for House floor consideration of the bill that would appropriate $133.7 billion in fiscal 2010 for the Department of Veterans Affairs, military construction and military family housing. Adopted 241-179: R 0-171; D 241-8. July 10, 2009.

528. **HR 3082. Fiscal 2010 Military Construction-VA Appropriations/Military Construction Projects.** Flake, R-Ariz., amendment that would bar the use of funds in the bill for 109 member-requested military construction projects, including $26.4 million for a fitness center at Mayport Naval Station, Fla.; $21.2 million for the U.S. Air Forces Central Headquarters at Shaw Air Force Base, S.C.; and $21 million for a consolidated communications facility at MacDill Air Force Base, Fla. Rejected in Committee of the Whole 62-358: R 59-109; D 3-249. July 10, 2009.

529. **HR 3082. Fiscal 2010 Military Construction-VA Appropriations/Passage.** Passage of the bill that would provide $133.7 billion in fiscal 2010 for the Department of Veterans Affairs, military construction and military family housing, including $77.9 billion in discretionary funding. The bill would provide $108.9 billion for the Department of Veterans Affairs, including $45.1 billion for veterans' health programs. It would provide $14.2 billion for military construction, $2 billion for military family housing and $8 billion for base realignment and closure. In addition, the bill would provide $48.2 billion in advance appropriations for veterans' medical care in fiscal 2011. Passed 415-3: R 167-2; D 248-1. A "yea" was a vote in support of the president's position. July 10, 2009.

530. **Motion to Adjourn/Procedural Motion.** Hastings, D-Fla., motion to adjourn. Motion agreed to 208-172: R 9-149; D 199-23. July 13, 2009.

531. **Motion to Adjourn/Procedural Motion.** Broun, R-Ga., motion to adjourn. Motion rejected 22-380: R 22-145; D 0-235. July 14, 2009.

532. **Motion to Adjourn/Procedural Motion.** Broun, R-Ga., motion to adjourn. Motion rejected 23-377: R 21-145; D 2-232. July 14, 2009.

	526	527	528	529	530	531	532
ALABAMA							
1 **Bonner**	N	N	N	Y	N	N	N
2 Bright	Y	N	N	Y	N	N	N
3 **Rogers**	N	N	N	Y	N	N	N
4 **Aderholt**	N	N	N	?	N	N	N
5 Griffith	Y	Y	N	Y	Y	N	N
6 **Bachus**	N	N	N	Y	N	N	Y
7 Davis	Y	Y	N	Y	N	N	N
ALASKA							
AL **Young**	N	N	N	Y	Y	Y	?
ARIZONA							
1 Kirkpatrick	Y	Y	N	Y	Y	N	N
2 **Franks**	N	N	Y	Y	N	N	N
3 **Shadegg**	N	N	Y	Y	N	N	Y
4 Pastor	Y	Y	N	Y	Y	N	N
5 Mitchell	Y	Y	N	Y	N	N	N
6 **Flake**	N	N	Y	N	N	Y	Y
7 Grijalva	Y	Y	N	Y	?	?	?
8 Giffords	Y	Y	N	Y	N	N	N
ARKANSAS							
1 Berry	Y	Y	N	Y	N	N	N
2 Snyder	Y	N	N	Y	Y	N	N
3 **Boozman**	N	N	N	Y	N	N	N
4 Ross	Y	Y	N	Y	+	N	N
CALIFORNIA							
1 Thompson	Y	Y	N	Y	Y	N	N
2 **Herger**	N	N	Y	Y	N	N	N
3 **Lungren**	N	N	Y	Y	N	N	N
4 **McClintock**	N	N	Y	Y	N	N	N
5 Matsui	Y	Y	N	Y	Y	N	N
6 Woolsey	Y	Y	N	Y	Y	N	N
7 Miller, George	Y	Y	N	Y	Y	N	N
8 Pelosi							
9 Lee	Y	Y	N	Y	Y	N	N
10 Vacant							
11 McNerney	Y	Y	N	Y	N	N	N
12 Speier	Y	Y	N	Y	Y	N	?
13 Stark	Y	Y	N	N	Y	N	Y
14 Eshoo	Y	Y	N	Y	Y	N	N
15 Honda	Y	Y	N	Y	Y	N	N
16 Lofgren	Y	Y	N	Y	N	N	N
17 Farr	Y	?	N	Y	N	N	N
18 Cardoza	Y	Y	N	Y	Y	N	N
19 **Radanovich**	N	N	N	Y	N	N	N
20 Costa	Y	Y	N	Y	Y	N	N
21 **Nunes**	N	N	Y	Y	N	N	N
22 **McCarthy**	N	N	Y	Y	N	N	N
23 Capps	Y	Y	N	Y	Y	N	N
24 **Gallegly**	N	N	N	Y	N	N	N
25 **McKeon**	N	N	N	Y	N	N	N
26 **Dreier**	N	N	N	Y	N	N	N
27 Sherman	Y	Y	N	Y	Y	N	N
28 Berman	Y	Y	N	Y	Y	N	?
29 Schiff	Y	Y	N	Y	Y	N	N
30 Waxman	Y	Y	N	Y	Y	N	N
31 Becerra	Y	Y	N	Y	Y	N	N
32 Vacant*							
33 Watson	Y	Y	N	Y	?	N	N
34 Roybal-Allard	Y	Y	N	Y	Y	N	N
35 Waters	Y	Y	N	Y	?	N	N
36 Harman	Y	Y	N	Y	Y	N	N
37 Richardson	Y	Y	N	Y	Y	N	N
38 Napolitano	Y	Y	N	Y	Y	N	N
39 Sánchez, Linda	Y	Y	N	Y	Y	N	N
40 **Royce**	N	N	N	Y	N	N	N
41 **Lewis**	N	N	N	Y	Y	N	N
42 **Miller, Gary**	N	N	N	Y	N	N	N
43 Baca	Y	Y	N	Y	Y	N	N
44 **Calvert**	N	N	N	Y	Y	N	N
45 **Bono Mack**	N	N	N	Y	?	?	N
46 **Rohrabacher**	?	N	Y	Y	?	N	N
47 Sanchez, Loretta	Y	Y	N	Y	Y	N	N
48 **Campbell**	N	N	N	N	N	Y	Y
49 **Issa**	N	N	Y	N	N	Y	Y
50 **Bilbray**	N	N	N	Y	N	N	N
51 Filner	Y	Y	N	Y	Y	-	-
52 **Hunter**	N	N	N	Y	N	N	N
53 Davis	Y	Y	N	Y	Y	N	N

	526	527	528	529	530	531	532
COLORADO							
1 DeGette	Y	Y	N	Y	Y	N	N
2 Polis	Y	Y	N	Y	Y	N	N
3 Salazar	Y	Y	N	Y	Y	N	N
4 Markey	Y	Y	N	Y	Y	N	N
5 **Lamborn**	N	N	Y	Y	N	N	N
6 **Coffman**	N	N	Y	Y	N	N	N
7 Perlmutter	Y	Y	N	Y	Y	N	N
CONNECTICUT							
1 Larson	Y	Y	N	Y	Y	N	N
2 Courtney	Y	Y	N	Y	Y	N	N
3 DeLauro	Y	Y	N	Y	Y	N	N
4 Himes	Y	Y	N	Y	Y	N	N
5 Murphy	Y	Y	N	Y	Y	N	N
DELAWARE							
AL **Castle**	N	N	N	Y	N	N	N
FLORIDA							
1 **Miller**	N	N	N	Y	N	N	N
2 Boyd	Y	Y	N	Y	Y	N	N
3 Brown	Y	Y	N	Y	?	N	N
4 **Crenshaw**	N	N	N	Y	N	Y	N
5 **Brown-Waite**	N	N	N	Y	?	N	N
6 **Stearns**	N	N	Y	Y	?	-	N
7 **Mica**	N	N	N	Y	N	N	N
8 Grayson	Y	Y	N	Y	Y	N	N
9 **Bilirakis**	N	N	N	Y	N	N	N
10 **Young**	N	N	N	Y	?	?	?
11 Castor	Y	Y	N	Y	Y	N	N
12 **Putnam**	N	N	N	Y	N	N	N
13 **Buchanan**	N	N	N	Y	N	N	N
14 **Mack**	N	N	?	Y	?	?	?
15 **Posey**	N	N	N	Y	N	N	N
16 **Rooney**	N	N	N	Y	N	N	N
17 Meek	Y	Y	N	Y	Y	N	N
18 **Ros-Lehtinen**	N	N	N	Y	N	N	N
19 Wexler	Y	Y	N	Y	N	N	N
20 Wasserman Schultz	Y	Y	N	Y	Y	N	N
21 **Diaz-Balart, L.**	N	N	N	Y	N	N	N
22 Klein	+	+	-	+	Y	N	N
23 Hastings	Y	Y	N	Y	Y	N	N
24 Kosmas	Y	Y	N	Y	Y	N	N
25 **Diaz-Balart, M.**	N	N	N	Y	N	N	N
GEORGIA							
1 **Kingston**	N	N	N	Y	N	N	N
2 Bishop	Y	Y	N	Y	Y	?	N
3 **Westmoreland**	N	N	Y	Y	N	N	Y
4 Johnson	Y	Y	N	Y	Y	N	N
5 Lewis	Y	Y	N	Y	Y	N	N
6 **Price**	N	N	Y	Y	N	Y	Y
7 **Linder**	N	N	Y	Y	?	N	N
8 Marshall	Y	Y	Y	?	N	N	N
9 **Deal**	N	N	Y	Y	?	N	N
10 **Broun**	N	N	Y	Y	N	Y	Y
11 **Gingrey**	N	N	Y	Y	N	N	N
12 Barrow	Y	Y	N	Y	Y	N	N
13 Scott	Y	Y	N	Y	Y	N	N
HAWAII							
1 Abercrombie	Y	Y	N	Y	Y	N	N
2 Hirono	Y	Y	N	Y	Y	N	N
IDAHO							
1 Minnick	N	Y	N	Y	N	N	N
2 **Simpson**	N	N	N	Y	N	N	N
ILLINOIS							
1 Rush	Y	N	N	Y	Y	N	N
2 Jackson	Y	Y	N	Y	Y	N	N
3 Lipinski	Y	Y	N	Y	?	N	N
4 Gutierrez	Y	Y	N	Y	?	N	?
5 Quigley	Y	Y	N	Y	Y	N	N
6 **Roskam**	N	N	N	Y	N	N	N
7 Davis	Y	Y	N	Y	?	N	?
8 Bean	Y	Y	N	Y	Y	N	N
9 Schakowsky	Y	Y	N	Y	Y	N	?
10 **Kirk**	N	N	Y	N	Y	N	N
11 Halvorson	Y	Y	N	Y	Y	N	N
12 Costello	Y	Y	N	Y	?	N	N
13 **Biggert**	N	N	N	Y	N	N	N
14 Foster	Y	Y	N	Y	Y	N	N
15 **Johnson**	N	N	Y	Y	+	Y	Y

	526	527	528	529	530	531	532
16 **Manzullo**	N	N	N	Y	N	N	N
17 Hare	Y	Y	N	Y	Y	N	N
18 **Schock**	N	N	N	Y	N	N	N
19 **Shimkus**	N	N	N	Y	N	N	N
INDIANA							
1 Visclosky	Y	Y	N	Y	Y	N	N
2 Donnelly	Y	Y	N	Y	N	N	N
3 **Souder**	N	N	N	Y	N	Y	Y
4 **Buyer**	N	?	N	Y	N	N	N
5 **Burton**	N	N	N	Y	Y	N	N
6 **Pence**	N	N	Y	Y	N	Y	Y
7 Carson	Y	Y	N	Y	Y	N	N
8 Ellsworth	Y	Y	N	Y	N	N	N
9 Hill	N	N	N	Y	?	N	N
IOWA							
1 Braley	Y	Y	N	Y	Y	N	N
2 Loebsack	Y	Y	N	Y	Y	N	N
3 Boswell	Y	Y	N	Y	Y	N	N
4 **Latham**	N	N	N	Y	N	N	N
5 **King**	N	N	N	Y	N	Y	Y
KANSAS							
1 **Moran**	N	N	N	Y	N	N	N
2 **Jenkins**	N	N	Y	Y	N	N	N
3 Moore	N	N	N	Y	Y	N	N
4 **Tiahrt**	N	N	N	Y	N	Y	Y
KENTUCKY							
1 **Whitfield**	N	N	N	Y	N	N	N
2 **Guthrie**	N	N	N	Y	N	N	N
3 Yarmuth	Y	Y	N	Y	Y	N	N
4 **Davis**	N	N	N	Y	N	N	N
5 **Rogers**	N	N	N	Y	N	N	N
6 Chandler	Y	Y	N	Y	Y	N	N
LOUISIANA							
1 **Scalise**	N	N	N	Y	N	N	N
2 **Cao**	N	N	N	Y	N	N	N
3 Melancon	N	N	N	Y	Y	N	N
4 **Fleming**	N	N	N	Y	N	N	N
5 **Alexander**	N	N	N	Y	N	N	N
6 **Cassidy**	N	N	Y	Y	N	N	N
7 **Boustany**	N	N	Y	Y	N	N	N
MAINE							
1 Pingree	Y	Y	N	Y	Y	N	N
2 Michaud	Y	Y	N	Y	N	N	N
MARYLAND							
1 Kratovil	Y	Y	N	Y	Y	N	N
2 Ruppersberger	Y	Y	N	Y	Y	N	N
3 Sarbanes	Y	Y	N	Y	Y	?	N
4 Edwards	Y	Y	N	Y	Y	N	N
5 Hoyer	Y	Y	N	Y	Y	N	N
6 **Bartlett**	N	N	N	Y	N	Y	Y
7 Cummings	Y	Y	N	Y	Y	N	N
8 Van Hollen	Y	Y	N	Y	Y	N	N
MASSACHUSETTS							
1 Olver	Y	Y	N	Y	Y	?	N
2 Neal	Y	Y	N	Y	Y	N	N
3 McGovern	Y	Y	N	Y	Y	N	N
4 Frank	Y	Y	N	Y	?	N	N
5 Tsongas	Y	Y	N	Y	Y	N	N
6 Tierney	Y	Y	N	Y	?	N	N
7 Markey	Y	Y	N	Y	Y	N	N
8 Capuano	Y	Y	N	Y	Y	N	N
9 Lynch	Y	Y	N	Y	Y	N	N
10 Delahunt	?	Y	N	Y	Y	N	N
MICHIGAN							
1 Stupak	Y	Y	N	Y	Y	N	N
2 **Hoekstra**	?	?	?	?	?	N	N
3 **Ehlers**	N	N	Y	Y	N	N	N
4 **Camp**	N	N	N	Y	N	Y	N
5 Kildee	Y	Y	N	Y	Y	N	N
6 **Upton**	N	N	N	Y	?	N	N
7 Schauer	Y	Y	N	Y	?	N	N
8 **Rogers**	N	N	Y	Y	N	N	N
9 Peters	Y	Y	N	Y	N	N	N
10 **Miller**	N	N	N	Y	N	N	N
11 **McCotter**	N	N	Y	Y	N	N	N
12 Levin	Y	Y	N	Y	Y	N	N
13 Kilpatrick	Y	Y	N	?	Y	N	N
14 Conyers	Y	Y	N	Y	+	?	?
15 Dingell	Y	Y	N	Y	Y	?	N
MINNESOTA							
1 Walz	Y	Y	N	Y	Y	N	N
2 **Kline**	N	N	Y	Y	N	N	N
3 **Paulsen**	N	N	N	Y	N	N	N
4 McCollum	Y	Y	N	Y	Y	N	?

	526	527	528	529	530	531	532
5 Ellison	Y	Y	N	Y	Y	N	N
6 **Bachmann**	N	N	Y	Y	N	N	N
7 Peterson	Y	Y	N	Y	Y	N	N
8 Oberstar	Y	Y	N	Y	Y	N	N
MISSISSIPPI							
1 Childers	Y	Y	N	Y	Y	N	N
2 Thompson	Y	Y	N	Y	N	N	N
3 **Harper**	N	N	N	Y	N	N	N
4 Taylor	Y	Y	N	Y	Y	N	N
MISSOURI							
1 Clay	Y	Y	N	Y	Y	?	?
2 **Akin**	N	N	N	Y	?	N	N
3 Carnahan	Y	Y	N	Y	Y	?	?
4 Skelton	Y	Y	N	Y	Y	N	N
5 Cleaver	Y	Y	N	Y	Y	N	N
6 **Graves**	?	?	?	?	?	N	N
7 **Blunt**	N	N	?	Y	N	N	N
8 **Emerson**	N	N	N	Y	N	N	N
9 **Luetkemeyer**	N	N	Y	Y	?	N	N
MONTANA							
AL **Rehberg**	N	N	N	Y	N	N	N
NEBRASKA							
1 **Fortenberry**	N	N	N	Y	N	N	N
2 **Terry**	N	N	N	Y	N	N	N
3 **Smith**	N	N	N	Y	N	N	N
NEVADA							
1 Berkley	Y	Y	N	Y	Y	N	N
2 **Heller**	–	–	+	–	N	N	N
3 Titus	Y	Y	N	Y	Y	N	N
NEW HAMPSHIRE							
1 Shea-Porter	Y	Y	N	Y	Y	?	Y
2 Hodes	Y	Y	N	Y	Y	N	N
NEW JERSEY							
1 Andrews	Y	Y	N	Y	Y	N	N
2 **LoBiondo**	N	N	N	Y	N	N	N
3 Adler	Y	Y	N	Y	N	N	N
4 **Smith**	N	N	N	Y	N	N	N
5 **Garrett**	N	N	Y	Y	N	Y	N
6 Pallone	Y	Y	N	Y	Y	N	N
7 **Lance**	N	N	Y	Y	N	N	N
8 Pascrell	Y	Y	N	Y	Y	N	N
9 Rothman	Y	Y	N	Y	?	?	N
10 Payne	Y	Y	?	Y	Y	N	N
11 **Frelinghuysen**	N	N	N	Y	N	N	N
12 Holt	Y	Y	N	Y	Y	N	N
13 Sires	Y	Y	N	Y	+	N	N
NEW MEXICO							
1 Heinrich	Y	Y	N	Y	Y	N	N
2 Teague	Y	Y	N	Y	Y	N	N
3 Lujan	Y	Y	N	Y	Y	N	N
NEW YORK							
1 Bishop	Y	Y	N	Y	Y	N	N
2 Israel	Y	Y	N	Y	Y	N	N
3 **King**	N	N	N	Y	N	N	N
4 McCarthy	Y	Y	N	Y	Y	N	?
5 Ackerman	Y	Y	N	Y	Y	N	N
6 Meeks	Y	Y	N	Y	?	?	N
7 Crowley	Y	Y	N	Y	Y	N	N
8 Nadler	Y	Y	N	Y	Y	N	N
9 Weiner	Y	Y	N	Y	?	N	N
10 Towns	Y	Y	N	Y	Y	?	N
11 Clarke	Y	Y	N	Y	Y	N	N
12 Velázquez	Y	Y	N	Y	Y	N	N
13 McMahon	Y	Y	N	Y	N	N	N
14 Maloney	Y	Y	N	Y	?	N	N
15 Rangel	Y	?	N	Y	Y	N	?
16 Serrano	Y	Y	N	Y	Y	N	N
17 Engel	Y	Y	?	Y	?	N	N
18 Lowey	Y	Y	N	Y	Y	N	N
19 Hall	Y	Y	N	Y	Y	N	N
20 Murphy	Y	N	N	Y	?	N	N
21 Tonko	Y	Y	N	Y	Y	N	N
22 Hinchey	Y	Y	N	Y	?	N	N
23 **McHugh**	N	N	–	+	N	N	N
24 Arcuri	Y	Y	N	Y	N	N	N
25 Maffei	Y	Y	N	Y	Y	N	N
26 **Lee**	N	N	N	Y	N	N	N
27 Higgins	Y	Y	N	Y	Y	N	N
28 Slaughter	Y	Y	N	Y	Y	N	N
29 Massa	Y	Y	N	Y	N	N	N
NORTH CAROLINA							
1 Butterfield	Y	Y	N	Y	?	N	N
2 Etheridge	Y	Y	N	Y	Y	N	N
3 **Jones**	N	N	N	Y	Y	N	N
4 Price	Y	Y	N	Y	Y	N	N

	526	527	528	529	530	531	532
5 **Foxx**	N	N	Y	Y	N	N	N
6 **Coble**	N	N	N	Y	?	N	N
7 McIntyre	Y	Y	N	Y	Y	N	N
8 Kissell	Y	Y	N	Y	Y	N	N
9 **Myrick**	N	N	Y	Y	N	N	N
10 **McHenry**	N	N	Y	Y	N	N	N
11 Shuler	N	N	N	Y	N	N	N
12 Watt	Y	Y	N	Y	Y	N	N
13 Miller	Y	Y	N	Y	Y	N	?
NORTH DAKOTA							
AL Pomeroy	Y	Y	N	Y	Y	N	N
OHIO							
1 Driehaus	Y	Y	N	Y	Y	N	N
2 **Schmidt**	N	N	N	Y	N	N	N
3 **Turner**	N	N	N	Y	Y	N	N
4 **Jordan**	N	N	N	Y	N	N	N
5 **Latta**	N	N	N	Y	N	N	N
6 Wilson	Y	Y	N	Y	Y	N	N
7 **Austria**	N	N	N	Y	N	N	N
8 **Boehner**	N	N	N	Y	N	N	N
9 Kaptur	Y	Y	?	?	Y	N	N
10 Kucinich	Y	Y	N	Y	N	N	N
11 Fudge	?	?	?	+	Y	N	N
12 **Tiberi**	N	N	Y	Y	N	N	N
13 Sutton	Y	Y	N	Y	Y	?	?
14 **LaTourette**	N	N	N	Y	N	N	?
15 Kilroy	Y	Y	N	Y	Y	N	N
16 Boccieri	Y	Y	N	Y	N	N	N
17 Ryan	Y	Y	N	Y	Y	N	N
18 Space	Y	Y	N	Y	Y	N	N
OKLAHOMA							
1 **Sullivan**	N	N	Y	Y	N	?	Y
2 Boren	Y	Y	N	Y	Y	N	N
3 **Lucas**	N	N	N	Y	N	N	N
4 **Cole**	N	N	N	Y	N	N	N
5 **Fallin**	N	N	N	Y	N	N	N
OREGON							
1 Wu	Y	Y	N	Y	Y	N	N
2 **Walden**	N	N	N	Y	N	N	N
3 Blumenauer	Y	Y	N	Y	Y	N	N
4 DeFazio	Y	Y	N	Y	Y	N	N
5 Schrader	Y	Y	N	Y	?	?	?
PENNSYLVANIA							
1 Brady	Y	Y	N	Y	Y	N	N
2 Fattah	Y	Y	N	Y	Y	N	N
3 Dahlkemper	Y	Y	N	Y	Y	N	N
4 Altmire	Y	Y	N	Y	N	N	N
5 **Thompson**	N	N	N	Y	N	N	N
6 **Gerlach**	N	N	N	Y	?	N	?
7 Sestak	Y	Y	N	Y	?	?	?
8 Murphy, P.	?	?	N	Y	Y	N	N
9 **Shuster**	N	N	N	Y	N	N	N
10 Carney	Y	Y	N	Y	N	N	N
11 Kanjorski	Y	Y	N	Y	Y	N	N
12 Murtha	Y	Y	N	Y	?	N	N
13 Schwartz	Y	Y	N	Y	Y	N	N
14 Doyle	Y	Y	N	Y	Y	?	N
15 **Dent**	N	N	N	Y	N	N	N
16 **Pitts**	N	N	Y	Y	N	N	N
17 Holden	Y	Y	N	Y	Y	N	N
18 **Murphy, T.**	N	N	N	Y	N	N	N
19 **Platts**	?	N	N	Y	N	N	N
RHODE ISLAND							
1 Kennedy	Y	Y	N	Y	Y	N	N
2 Langevin	Y	Y	N	Y	Y	N	N
SOUTH CAROLINA							
1 **Brown**	N	N	Y	Y	N	N	N
2 **Wilson**	N	N	Y	Y	N	N	N
3 **Barrett**	–	–	+	+	–	–	–
4 **Inglis**	N	N	Y	Y	N	N	N
5 Spratt	Y	Y	N	Y	Y	N	N
6 Clyburn	Y	Y	N	Y	Y	N	N
SOUTH DAKOTA							
AL Herseth Sandlin	Y	Y	N	Y	?	N	N
TENNESSEE							
1 **Roe**	N	N	Y	Y	N	N	N
2 **Duncan**	N	N	Y	Y	N	N	N
3 **Wamp**	N	N	N	Y	N	N	N
4 Davis	Y	Y	N	Y	Y	N	N
5 Cooper	Y	Y	Y	Y	Y	N	N
6 Gordon	Y	Y	N	Y	?	N	N
7 **Blackburn**	N	N	N	Y	N	Y	Y
8 Tanner	Y	Y	N	Y	N	N	N
9 Cohen	Y	Y	N	Y	Y	N	N

	526	527	528	529	530	531	532
TEXAS							
1 **Gohmert**	N	N	Y	Y	N	Y	?
2 **Poe**	N	N	N	Y	N	N	N
3 **Johnson, S.**	N	N	N	Y	Y	Y	N
4 **Hall**	N	N	Y	Y	N	N	N
5 **Hensarling**	N	N	Y	Y	N	Y	Y
6 **Barton**	N	N	Y	Y	?	Y	Y
7 **Culberson**	N	N	N	Y	N	?	N
8 **Brady**	N	N	Y	Y	N	N	N
9 Green, A.	Y	Y	N	Y	Y	N	N
10 **McCaul**	N	N	Y	Y	N	N	?
11 **Conaway**	N	N	Y	Y	N	N	N
12 **Granger**	–	–	–	+	N	N	N
13 **Thornberry**	N	N	N	Y	N	N	N
14 **Paul**	?	?	?	?	Y	Y	Y
15 Hinojosa	Y	Y	N	Y	Y	N	N
16 Reyes	Y	Y	N	Y	?	N	N
17 Edwards	Y	Y	N	Y	Y	?	N
18 Jackson Lee	Y	Y	–	Y	Y	N	N
19 **Neugebauer**	N	N	Y	Y	–	N	N
20 Gonzalez	Y	Y	N	Y	Y	N	N
21 **Smith**	N	N	N	Y	N	N	?
22 **Olson**	N	N	N	Y	Y	Y	Y
23 Rodriguez	Y	Y	N	Y	Y	N	N
24 **Marchant**	N	N	Y	?	N	N	?
25 Doggett	Y	Y	N	Y	Y	N	N
26 **Burgess**	N	N	N	Y	N	N	N
27 Ortiz	Y	Y	N	Y	Y	N	N
28 Cuellar	Y	Y	N	Y	Y	N	N
29 Green, G.	Y	Y	N	Y	Y	N	N
30 Johnson, E.	Y	Y	N	Y	Y	N	N
31 **Carter**	N	N	N	Y	N	N	N
32 **Sessions**	N	N	Y	Y	N	N	Y
UTAH							
1 **Bishop**	?	N	?	Y	N	?	?
2 Matheson	Y	Y	N	Y	?	N	N
3 **Chaffetz**	N	N	Y	Y	Y	Y	Y
VERMONT							
AL Welch	Y	Y	N	Y	Y	N	N
VIRGINIA							
1 **Wittman**	N	N	N	Y	N	?	N
2 Nye	Y	Y	N	Y	Y	N	N
3 Scott	Y	Y	N	Y	?	N	N
4 **Forbes**	N	N	N	Y	N	N	N
5 Perriello	Y	Y	N	Y	N	N	?
6 **Goodlatte**	N	N	Y	Y	N	N	N
7 **Cantor**	N	N	Y	Y	?	?	N
8 Moran	Y	Y	N	Y	N	N	?
9 Boucher	?	Y	N	Y	Y	?	N
10 **Wolf**	N	N	N	Y	N	N	N
11 Connolly	Y	Y	N	Y	Y	N	N
WASHINGTON							
1 Inslee	Y	Y	N	Y	Y	N	N
2 Larsen	Y	Y	N	Y	Y	N	N
3 Baird	Y	Y	N	Y	Y	N	?
4 **Hastings**	N	N	N	Y	N	N	?
5 **McMorris Rodgers**	N	N	N	Y	N	N	N
6 Dicks	Y	Y	N	Y	Y	N	N
7 McDermott	Y	Y	N	Y	Y	N	N
8 **Reichert**	N	N	N	Y	N	N	N
9 Smith	Y	Y	N	Y	Y	N	N
WEST VIRGINIA							
1 Mollohan	Y	Y	N	Y	?	N	N
2 **Capito**	N	N	N	Y	N	N	N
3 Rahall	Y	Y	N	Y	N	N	N
WISCONSIN							
1 **Ryan**	N	N	Y	Y	N	N	N
2 Baldwin	Y	Y	N	Y	Y	N	N
3 Kind	Y	Y	N	Y	Y	N	N
4 Moore	Y	Y	N	Y	Y	N	N
5 **Sensenbrenner**	N	N	Y	Y	N	N	N
6 **Petri**	N	N	Y	Y	N	N	N
7 Obey	Y	Y	N	Y	Y	N	N
8 Kagen	Y	Y	N	Y	Y	N	N
WYOMING							
AL **Lummis**	N	N	Y	Y	N	N	N
DELEGATES							
Faleomavaega (A.S.)			?				
Norton (D.C.)			?				
Bordallo (Guam)			N				
Sablan (N. Marianas)			N				
Pierluisi (P.R.)			N				
Christensen (V.I.)			N				

IN THE HOUSE | By Vote Number

533. **H Res 612. Sympathies for Metrorail Victims/Adoption.**
Norton, D-D.C., motion to suspend the rules and adopt the resolution that would express the sympathies of the House for the victims of the Washington Metrorail accident on June 22, 2009, and for their families, friends and associates. Motion agreed to 421-0: R 175-0; D 246-0. A two-thirds majority of those present and voting (281 in this case) is required for adoption under suspension of the rules. July 14, 2009.

534. **H Res 469. Tribute to Wayman Lawrence Tisdale/Adoption.**
Norton, D-D.C., motion to suspend the rules and adopt the resolution that would express the sorrow of the House at the death of Wayman Lawrence Tisdale, the former professional basketball player and jazz musician, and extend condolences to his family, friends, colleagues and his home state of Oklahoma. Motion agreed to 418-0: R 174-0; D 244-0. A two-thirds majority of those present and voting (279 in this case) is required for adoption under suspension of the rules. July 14, 2009.

535. **HR 1037. Pilot Work-Study Programs for Veterans/Passage.**
Filner, D-Calif., motion to suspend the rules and pass the bill that would authorize $10 million per year in fiscal years 2010-14 for the Veterans Affairs Department to conduct a five-year pilot project to test the feasibility and advisability of expanding work-study activities for veterans. Motion agreed to 422-0: R 175-0; D 247-0. A two-thirds majority of those present and voting (282 in this case) is required for passage under suspension of the rules. July 14, 2009.

536. **HR 402. Tallent Veterans Affairs Clinic/Passage.** Filner, D-Calif., motion to suspend the rules and pass the bill that would designate the Veterans Affairs Department outpatient clinic in Knoxville, Tenn., as the "William C. Tallent Department of Veterans Affairs Outpatient Clinic." Motion agreed to 419-0: R 175-0; D 244-0. A two-thirds majority of those present and voting (280 in this case) is required for passage under suspension of the rules. July 14, 2009.

537. **Motion to Adjourn/Procedural Motion.** Gingrey, R-Ga., motion to adjourn. Motion rejected 23-361: R 22-142; D 1-219. July 15, 2009.

538. **HR 3183. Fiscal 2010 Energy-Water Appropriations/Previous Question.** Matsui, D-Calif., motion to order the previous question (thus ending debate and possibility of amendment) on adoption of the rule (H Res 645) that would provide for House floor consideration of a bill that would appropriate $33.3 billion in fiscal 2010 for energy and water development projects in the Energy Department, Army Corps of Engineers, Bureau of Reclamation and other agencies. Motion agreed to 237-177: R 1-172; D 236-5. July 15, 2009.

539. **HR 3183. Fiscal 2010 Energy-Water Appropriations/Rule.**
Adoption of the rule (H Res 645) to provide for House floor consideration of the bill that would appropriate $33.3 billion in fiscal 2010 for energy and water development projects for the Energy Department, Army Corps of Engineers, Bureau of Reclamation and other agencies. Adopted 238-185: R 0-176; D 238-9. July 15, 2009.

	533	534	535	536	537	538	539
ALABAMA							
1 **Bonner**	Y	Y	Y	Y	N	N	N
2 Bright	Y	Y	Y	Y	N	Y	N
3 **Rogers**	Y	Y	Y	Y	?	N	N
4 **Aderholt**	Y	Y	Y	Y	N	N	N
5 Griffith	Y	Y	Y	Y	N	Y	Y
6 **Bachus**	Y	Y	Y	Y	N	?	N
7 Davis	Y	Y	Y	Y	N	Y	Y
ALASKA							
AL **Young**	Y	Y	Y	Y	Y	N	N
ARIZONA							
1 Kirkpatrick	Y	Y	Y	Y	N	Y	Y
2 **Franks**	Y	Y	Y	Y	N	N	N
3 **Shadegg**	Y	Y	Y	Y	N	N	N
4 Pastor	Y	Y	Y	Y	N	Y	Y
5 Mitchell	Y	Y	Y	Y	N	Y	Y
6 **Flake**	Y	Y	Y	Y	Y	N	N
7 Grijalva	Y	Y	Y	Y	?	Y	Y
8 Giffords	Y	Y	Y	Y	N	Y	Y
ARKANSAS							
1 Berry	Y	Y	Y	Y	N	Y	Y
2 Snyder	Y	Y	Y	Y	N	Y	N
3 **Boozman**	Y	Y	Y	Y	N	N	N
4 Ross	Y	Y	Y	Y	?	Y	Y
CALIFORNIA							
1 Thompson	Y	Y	Y	Y	N	Y	Y
2 **Herger**	Y	Y	Y	Y	N	N	N
3 **Lungren**	Y	Y	Y	Y	N	N	N
4 **McClintock**	Y	Y	Y	Y	N	N	N
5 Matsui	Y	Y	Y	Y	N	Y	Y
6 Woolsey	Y	Y	Y	Y	N	Y	Y
7 Miller, George	Y	Y	Y	Y	N	Y	Y
8 Pelosi							
9 Lee	Y	Y	Y	Y	N	Y	Y
10 Vacant							
11 McNerney	Y	Y	Y	Y	N	Y	Y
12 Speier	Y	Y	Y	Y	N	Y	Y
13 Stark	Y	Y	Y	Y	?	Y	Y
14 Eshoo	Y	Y	Y	Y	N	Y	Y
15 Honda	Y	Y	Y	Y	N	Y	Y
16 Lofgren	Y	Y	Y	Y	N	Y	Y
17 Farr	Y	Y	Y	Y	N	Y	Y
18 Cardoza	Y	Y	Y	Y	?	Y	Y
19 **Radanovich**	Y	Y	Y	Y	N	N	N
20 Costa	Y	Y	Y	Y	N	Y	Y
21 **Nunes**	Y	Y	Y	Y	N	N	N
22 **McCarthy**	Y	Y	Y	Y	N	N	N
23 Capps	Y	Y	Y	Y	N	Y	Y
24 **Gallegly**	Y	Y	Y	Y	N	N	N
25 **McKeon**	?	Y	Y	Y	N	N	N
26 **Dreier**	Y	Y	Y	Y	N	N	N
27 Sherman	Y	Y	Y	Y	N	Y	Y
28 Berman	Y	Y	Y	Y	N	Y	Y
29 Schiff	Y	Y	Y	Y	N	Y	Y
30 Waxman	Y	Y	Y	Y	N	?	Y
31 Becerra	Y	Y	Y	Y	N	Y	Y
32 Vacant*							
33 Watson	Y	Y	Y	Y	N	Y	Y
34 Roybal-Allard	Y	Y	Y	Y	N	Y	Y
35 Waters	Y	Y	Y	Y	N	Y	Y
36 Harman	Y	Y	Y	Y	N	Y	Y
37 Richardson	Y	Y	Y	Y	N	Y	Y
38 Napolitano	Y	Y	Y	Y	N	Y	Y
39 Sánchez, Linda	Y	Y	Y	Y	?	Y	Y
40 **Royce**	Y	Y	Y	Y	N	N	N
41 **Lewis**	Y	Y	Y	Y	N	N	N
42 **Miller, Gary**	Y	Y	Y	Y	N	N	N
43 Baca	Y	Y	Y	Y	N	Y	Y
44 **Calvert**	Y	Y	Y	Y	N	N	N
45 **Bono Mack**	Y	Y	Y	Y	?	N	N
46 **Rohrabacher**	Y	Y	Y	Y	N	N	N
47 Sanchez, Loretta	Y	Y	Y	Y	N	Y	Y
48 **Campbell**	Y	Y	Y	Y	N	N	N
49 **Issa**	Y	Y	Y	Y	N	?	N
50 **Bilbray**	Y	Y	Y	Y	N	N	N
51 Filner	+	+	+	+	N	Y	Y
52 **Hunter**	Y	Y	Y	Y	N	N	N
53 Davis	Y	Y	Y	Y	N	Y	Y

	533	534	535	536	537	538	539
COLORADO							
1 DeGette	Y	Y	Y	Y	N	Y	Y
2 Polis	Y	Y	Y	Y	N	Y	Y
3 Salazar	Y	Y	Y	Y	N	Y	Y
4 Markey	Y	Y	Y	Y	N	Y	Y
5 **Lamborn**	Y	Y	Y	Y	N	N	N
6 **Coffman**	Y	Y	Y	Y	N	N	N
7 Perlmutter	Y	Y	Y	Y	N	Y	Y
CONNECTICUT							
1 Larson	Y	Y	Y	Y	N	Y	Y
2 Courtney	Y	Y	Y	Y	N	Y	Y
3 DeLauro	Y	Y	Y	Y	N	Y	Y
4 Himes	Y	Y	Y	Y	N	Y	Y
5 Murphy	Y	Y	Y	Y	N	Y	Y
DELAWARE							
AL **Castle**	Y	Y	Y	Y	N	N	N
FLORIDA							
1 **Miller**	Y	Y	Y	Y	N	N	N
2 Boyd	Y	Y	Y	Y	N	Y	Y
3 Brown	Y	Y	Y	Y	N	Y	Y
4 **Crenshaw**	Y	Y	Y	Y	N	N	N
5 **Brown-Waite**	Y	Y	Y	Y	N	N	N
6 **Stearns**	Y	Y	Y	Y	N	N	N
7 **Mica**	Y	Y	Y	Y	N	N	N
8 Grayson	Y	Y	Y	Y	N	Y	Y
9 **Bilirakis**	Y	Y	Y	Y	N	N	N
10 **Young**	?	?	?	?	?	?	?
11 Castor	Y	Y	Y	Y	N	Y	Y
12 **Putnam**	Y	Y	Y	Y	N	N	N
13 **Buchanan**	Y	Y	Y	Y	N	N	N
14 **Mack**	Y	Y	Y	Y	?	N	N
15 **Posey**	Y	Y	Y	Y	N	N	N
16 **Rooney**	Y	Y	Y	Y	N	N	N
17 Meek	Y	Y	Y	Y	N	Y	Y
18 **Ros-Lehtinen**	Y	Y	Y	Y	N	N	N
19 Wexler	Y	Y	Y	Y	N	Y	Y
20 Wasserman Schultz	Y	Y	Y	Y	?	Y	Y
21 **Diaz-Balart, L.**	Y	Y	Y	Y	N	N	N
22 Klein	Y	Y	Y	Y	N	Y	Y
23 Hastings	Y	Y	Y	Y	N	Y	Y
24 Kosmas	Y	Y	Y	Y	?	Y	Y
25 **Diaz-Balart, M.**	Y	Y	Y	Y	N	N	N
GEORGIA							
1 **Kingston**	Y	Y	Y	Y	N	N	N
2 Bishop	Y	Y	Y	Y	?	Y	Y
3 **Westmoreland**	Y	Y	Y	Y	N	N	N
4 Johnson	?	Y	Y	Y	N	Y	Y
5 Lewis	Y	Y	Y	Y	N	Y	Y
6 **Price**	Y	Y	Y	Y	N	N	N
7 **Linder**	Y	Y	Y	Y	N	N	N
8 Marshall	Y	Y	Y	Y	N	Y	Y
9 **Deal**	Y	Y	Y	Y	N	N	N
10 **Broun**	Y	Y	Y	Y	N	N	N
11 **Gingrey**	Y	Y	Y	Y	Y	N	N
12 Barrow	Y	Y	Y	Y	N	Y	Y
13 Scott	Y	Y	Y	Y	?	N	N
HAWAII							
1 Abercrombie	Y	Y	Y	Y	N	Y	Y
2 Hirono	Y	Y	Y	Y	N	Y	Y
IDAHO							
1 Minnick	Y	Y	Y	Y	N	N	N
2 **Simpson**	Y	Y	Y	Y	N	N	N
ILLINOIS							
1 Rush	Y	Y	Y	Y	?	Y	Y
2 Jackson	Y	Y	Y	Y	N	Y	Y
3 Lipinski	Y	Y	Y	Y	N	Y	Y
4 Gutierrez	Y	Y	Y	Y	?	Y	Y
5 Quigley	Y	Y	Y	Y	N	Y	Y
6 **Roskam**	Y	Y	Y	Y	N	N	N
7 Davis	Y	Y	Y	Y	N	Y	Y
8 Bean	Y	Y	Y	Y	N	Y	Y
9 Schakowsky	Y	Y	Y	Y	N	Y	Y
10 **Kirk**	Y	Y	?	Y	?	N	N
11 Halvorson	Y	Y	Y	Y	N	Y	Y
12 Costello	Y	Y	Y	Y	N	Y	Y
13 **Biggert**	Y	Y	Y	Y	N	N	N
14 Foster	Y	Y	Y	Y	N	Y	Y
15 **Johnson**	Y	Y	Y	Y	N	N	N

KEY   **Republicans**   Democrats

Y Voted for (yea)	**X** Paired against	**C** Voted "present" to avoid possible conflict of interest
# Paired for	**–** Announced against	
+ Announced for	**P** Voted "present"	**?** Did not vote or otherwise make a position known
N Voted against (nay)		

	533	534	535	536	537	538	539
16 **Manzullo**	Y	Y	Y	Y	N	N	N
17 Hare	Y	Y	Y	Y	N	Y	Y
18 **Schock**	Y	Y	Y	Y	?	N	N
19 **Shimkus**	Y	Y	Y	Y	N	N	N
INDIANA							
1 Visclosky	Y	Y	Y	Y	N	Y	Y
2 Donnelly	Y	Y	Y	Y	N	Y	Y
3 **Souder**	Y	Y	Y	Y	Y	N	N
4 **Buyer**	Y	Y	Y	Y	N	N	N
5 **Burton**	Y	Y	Y	Y	N	N	N
6 **Pence**	Y	?	Y	Y	Y	N	N
7 Carson	Y	Y	Y	Y	N	Y	Y
8 Ellsworth	Y	Y	Y	Y	N	Y	N
9 Hill	Y	Y	Y	Y	N	N	N
IOWA							
1 Braley	Y	Y	Y	Y	N	Y	Y
2 Loebsack	Y	Y	Y	Y	N	Y	Y
3 Boswell	Y	Y	Y	Y	N	Y	Y
4 **Latham**	Y	Y	Y	Y	N	N	N
5 **King**	Y	Y	Y	Y	Y	N	N
KANSAS							
1 **Moran**	Y	Y	Y	Y	N	N	N
2 **Jenkins**	Y	Y	Y	Y	N	N	N
3 Moore	Y	Y	Y	Y	N	Y	Y
4 **Tiahrt**	Y	Y	Y	Y	Y	N	N
KENTUCKY							
1 **Whitfield**	Y	Y	Y	Y	N	N	N
2 **Guthrie**	Y	Y	Y	Y	N	N	N
3 Yarmuth	Y	Y	Y	Y	N	Y	Y
4 **Davis**	Y	Y	Y	Y	N	N	N
5 **Rogers**	Y	Y	Y	Y	N	N	N
6 Chandler	Y	Y	Y	Y	N	Y	Y
LOUISIANA							
1 **Scalise**	Y	Y	Y	Y	N	N	N
2 **Cao**	Y	Y	Y	Y	N	N	N
3 Melancon	Y	Y	Y	Y	N	N	N
4 **Fleming**	Y	Y	Y	Y	N	N	N
5 **Alexander**	Y	Y	Y	Y	N	N	N
6 **Cassidy**	Y	Y	Y	Y	?	?	?
7 **Boustany**	Y	Y	Y	Y	N	N	N
MAINE							
1 Pingree	Y	Y	Y	Y	N	Y	Y
2 Michaud	Y	Y	Y	Y	N	Y	Y
MARYLAND							
1 Kratovil	Y	Y	Y	Y	N	Y	N
2 Ruppersberger	Y	Y	Y	?	?	Y	Y
3 Sarbanes	Y	Y	Y	Y	N	Y	Y
4 Edwards	Y	Y	Y	Y	N	Y	Y
5 Hoyer	Y	?	?	?	N	Y	Y
6 **Bartlett**	Y	Y	Y	Y	Y	N	N
7 Cummings	?	Y	Y	Y	?	Y	Y
8 Van Hollen	Y	Y	Y	Y	N	Y	Y
MASSACHUSETTS							
1 Olver	Y	Y	Y	Y	N	Y	Y
2 Neal	Y	Y	Y	Y	N	Y	Y
3 McGovern	Y	Y	Y	Y	?	?	Y
4 Frank	Y	Y	Y	Y	N	Y	Y
5 Tsongas	Y	Y	Y	Y	N	Y	Y
6 Tierney	Y	Y	Y	Y	N	Y	Y
7 Markey	Y	Y	Y	Y	N	Y	Y
8 Capuano	Y	Y	Y	Y	N	Y	Y
9 Lynch	Y	Y	Y	Y	N	?	Y
10 Delahunt	Y	?	Y	Y	N	Y	Y
MICHIGAN							
1 Stupak	Y	Y	Y	Y	N	Y	Y
2 **Hoekstra**	Y	Y	Y	Y	N	Y	N
3 **Ehlers**	Y	Y	Y	Y	?	N	N
4 **Camp**	Y	Y	Y	Y	N	N	N
5 Kildee	Y	Y	Y	Y	N	Y	Y
6 **Upton**	Y	Y	Y	Y	N	N	N
7 Schauer	Y	Y	Y	Y	N	Y	Y
8 **Rogers**	Y	Y	Y	Y	N	N	N
9 Peters	Y	Y	Y	Y	N	Y	Y
10 **Miller**	Y	Y	Y	Y	N	N	N
11 **McCotter**	Y	Y	Y	Y	N	N	N
12 Levin	Y	Y	Y	Y	N	+	+
13 Kilpatrick	Y	Y	Y	Y	N	Y	Y
14 Conyers	+	+	+	+	?	?	?
15 Dingell	Y	Y	Y	Y	N	Y	Y
MINNESOTA							
1 Walz	Y	Y	Y	Y	N	Y	Y
2 **Kline**	Y	Y	Y	Y	N	N	N
3 **Paulsen**	Y	Y	Y	Y	N	N	N
4 McCollum	Y	Y	Y	Y	N	Y	Y
5 Ellison	Y	Y	Y	Y	N	Y	Y
6 **Bachmann**	Y	Y	Y	Y	N	N	N
7 Peterson	Y	Y	Y	Y	N	Y	Y
8 Oberstar	Y	Y	Y	Y	N	Y	Y
MISSISSIPPI							
1 Childers	Y	Y	Y	Y	?	Y	Y
2 Thompson	Y	Y	Y	Y	N	Y	Y
3 **Harper**	Y	Y	Y	Y	N	N	N
4 Taylor	Y	Y	Y	Y	N	Y	Y
MISSOURI							
1 Clay	?	?	?	?	N	Y	Y
2 **Akin**	Y	Y	Y	Y	N	N	N
3 Carnahan	?	?	?	?	N	Y	Y
4 Skelton	Y	Y	Y	Y	N	Y	Y
5 Cleaver	Y	Y	Y	Y	N	Y	Y
6 **Graves**	Y	Y	Y	Y	N	N	N
7 **Blunt**	Y	Y	Y	Y	N	N	N
8 **Emerson**	Y	Y	Y	Y	N	N	N
9 **Luetkemeyer**	Y	Y	Y	Y	N	N	N
MONTANA							
AL **Rehberg**	Y	Y	Y	Y	N	N	N
NEBRASKA							
1 **Fortenberry**	Y	Y	Y	Y	N	N	N
2 **Terry**	Y	Y	Y	Y	N	N	N
3 **Smith**	Y	Y	Y	Y	N	N	N
NEVADA							
1 Berkley	Y	Y	Y	Y	N	Y	Y
2 **Heller**	Y	Y	Y	Y	N	N	N
3 Titus	Y	Y	Y	Y	N	Y	Y
NEW HAMPSHIRE							
1 Shea-Porter	Y	Y	Y	Y	N	Y	Y
2 Hodes	Y	Y	Y	Y	N	Y	Y
NEW JERSEY							
1 Andrews	Y	Y	Y	Y	?	Y	Y
2 **LoBiondo**	Y	Y	Y	Y	N	N	N
3 Adler	Y	Y	Y	Y	N	Y	Y
4 **Smith**	Y	Y	Y	Y	?	N	N
5 **Garrett**	Y	Y	Y	Y	Y	N	N
6 Pallone	Y	Y	Y	Y	N	Y	Y
7 **Lance**	Y	Y	Y	Y	N	N	N
8 Pascrell	Y	Y	Y	Y	N	Y	Y
9 Rothman	Y	Y	Y	Y	N	Y	Y
10 Payne	Y	Y	Y	Y	N	Y	Y
11 **Frelinghuysen**	Y	Y	Y	Y	N	N	N
12 Holt	Y	Y	Y	Y	N	Y	Y
13 Sires	Y	Y	Y	Y	N	Y	Y
NEW MEXICO							
1 Heinrich	Y	Y	Y	Y	N	Y	Y
2 Teague	Y	Y	Y	Y	N	Y	Y
3 Lujan	Y	Y	Y	Y	N	Y	Y
NEW YORK							
1 Bishop	Y	Y	Y	Y	N	Y	Y
2 Israel	Y	Y	Y	Y	?	Y	Y
3 **King**	Y	Y	Y	Y	N	N	N
4 McCarthy	Y	?	Y	Y	N	Y	Y
5 Ackerman	Y	Y	Y	Y	N	Y	Y
6 Meeks	Y	Y	Y	Y	N	Y	Y
7 Crowley	Y	Y	Y	Y	N	Y	Y
8 Nadler	Y	Y	Y	Y	N	Y	Y
9 Weiner	Y	Y	Y	Y	N	Y	Y
10 Towns	Y	Y	Y	Y	N	Y	Y
11 Clarke	Y	Y	Y	Y	N	Y	Y
12 Velázquez	Y	Y	Y	Y	N	Y	Y
13 McMahon	Y	Y	Y	Y	N	Y	Y
14 Maloney	Y	Y	Y	Y	N	Y	Y
15 Rangel	Y	Y	Y	Y	N	Y	Y
16 Serrano	Y	Y	Y	Y	?	Y	Y
17 Engel	Y	Y	Y	Y	?	?	?
18 Lowey	Y	Y	Y	Y	?	Y	Y
19 Hall	Y	Y	Y	Y	N	Y	Y
20 Murphy	Y	Y	Y	Y	N	Y	N
21 Tonko	Y	Y	Y	Y	N	Y	Y
22 Hinchey	Y	Y	Y	Y	N	Y	Y
23 **McHugh**	Y	Y	Y	Y	?	N	N
24 Arcuri	Y	Y	Y	Y	N	Y	Y
25 Maffei	Y	Y	Y	Y	N	Y	Y
26 **Lee**	Y	Y	Y	Y	N	N	N
27 Higgins	Y	Y	Y	Y	?	?	Y
28 Slaughter	Y	Y	Y	Y	N	Y	Y
29 Massa	Y	Y	Y	Y	N	Y	Y
NORTH CAROLINA							
1 Butterfield	Y	Y	Y	Y	?	Y	Y
2 Etheridge	Y	Y	Y	Y	N	Y	Y
3 **Jones**	Y	Y	Y	Y	N	N	N
4 Price	Y	Y	Y	Y	N	Y	Y
5 **Foxx**	Y	Y	Y	Y	N	N	N
6 **Coble**	Y	Y	Y	Y	N	N	N
7 McIntyre	Y	Y	Y	Y	N	+	Y
8 Kissell	Y	Y	Y	Y	N	Y	Y
9 **Myrick**	Y	Y	Y	Y	N	N	N
10 **McHenry**	Y	Y	Y	Y	N	N	N
11 Shuler	Y	Y	Y	Y	N	N	N
12 Watt	Y	Y	Y	Y	N	Y	Y
13 Miller	Y	Y	Y	Y	N	Y	Y
NORTH DAKOTA							
AL Pomeroy	Y	Y	Y	Y	N	Y	Y
OHIO							
1 Driehaus	Y	Y	Y	Y	N	Y	Y
2 **Schmidt**	Y	Y	Y	Y	N	N	N
3 **Turner**	Y	?	Y	Y	N	N	N
4 **Jordan**	Y	Y	Y	Y	N	N	N
5 **Latta**	Y	Y	Y	Y	N	N	N
6 Wilson	Y	Y	Y	Y	N	Y	Y
7 **Austria**	Y	Y	Y	Y	N	N	N
8 **Boehner**	Y	Y	Y	Y	N	N	N
9 Kaptur	Y	Y	Y	Y	N	Y	Y
10 Kucinich	Y	Y	Y	Y	N	Y	Y
11 Fudge	Y	Y	Y	Y	N	Y	Y
12 **Tiberi**	Y	Y	Y	Y	N	N	N
13 Sutton	Y	Y	Y	Y	?	Y	Y
14 **LaTourette**	Y	Y	Y	Y	N	N	N
15 Kilroy	Y	Y	Y	Y	N	Y	Y
16 Boccieri	Y	Y	Y	Y	N	Y	Y
17 Ryan	Y	Y	Y	Y	?	Y	Y
18 Space	Y	Y	Y	Y	N	Y	Y
OKLAHOMA							
1 **Sullivan**	Y	Y	Y	Y	N	N	N
2 Boren	Y	Y	Y	Y	N	Y	Y
3 **Lucas**	Y	Y	Y	Y	N	N	N
4 **Cole**	Y	Y	Y	Y	N	N	N
5 **Fallin**	Y	Y	Y	Y	N	N	N
OREGON							
1 Wu	Y	Y	Y	Y	N	Y	Y
2 **Walden**	Y	Y	Y	Y	N	N	N
3 Blumenauer	Y	Y	Y	Y	N	Y	Y
4 DeFazio	Y	Y	Y	Y	N	Y	Y
5 Schrader	?	?	?	?	?	?	?
PENNSYLVANIA							
1 Brady	Y	Y	Y	Y	N	Y	Y
2 Fattah	Y	Y	Y	Y	N	Y	Y
3 Dahlkemper	Y	Y	Y	Y	N	Y	Y
4 Altmire	Y	Y	Y	Y	N	Y	Y
5 **Thompson**	Y	Y	Y	Y	N	N	N
6 **Gerlach**	Y	Y	Y	Y	N	?	N
7 Sestak	?	?	?	?	?	?	?
8 Murphy, P.	Y	Y	Y	Y	N	Y	Y
9 **Shuster**	Y	Y	Y	Y	N	N	N
10 Carney	Y	Y	Y	Y	N	Y	Y
11 Kanjorski	Y	Y	Y	Y	N	Y	Y
12 Murtha	Y	Y	Y	Y	N	Y	Y
13 Schwartz	Y	Y	Y	Y	N	Y	Y
14 Doyle	Y	Y	Y	Y	?	Y	Y
15 **Dent**	Y	Y	Y	Y	N	N	N
16 **Pitts**	Y	Y	Y	Y	N	N	N
17 Holden	Y	Y	Y	Y	N	Y	Y
18 **Murphy, T.**	Y	Y	Y	Y	N	N	N
19 **Platts**	Y	Y	Y	Y	?	N	N
RHODE ISLAND							
1 Kennedy	Y	Y	Y	Y	N	Y	Y
2 Langevin	Y	Y	Y	Y	N	Y	Y
SOUTH CAROLINA							
1 **Brown**	Y	Y	Y	Y	N	N	N
2 **Wilson**	Y	Y	Y	?	N	N	N
3 **Barrett**	+	+	+	+	N	N	N
4 **Inglis**	Y	Y	Y	Y	N	N	N
5 Spratt	Y	Y	Y	Y	Y	Y	Y
6 Clyburn	Y	Y	Y	Y	N	Y	Y
SOUTH DAKOTA							
AL Herseth Sandlin	Y	Y	Y	Y	N	Y	Y
TENNESSEE							
1 **Roe**	Y	Y	Y	Y	N	N	N
2 **Duncan**	Y	Y	Y	Y	N	N	N
3 **Wamp**	Y	Y	Y	Y	N	N	N
4 Davis	Y	Y	Y	Y	?	Y	Y
5 Cooper	Y	Y	Y	Y	N	Y	Y
6 Gordon	Y	Y	Y	Y	?	?	?
7 **Blackburn**	Y	Y	Y	Y	Y	N	N
8 Tanner	Y	Y	Y	Y	N	Y	Y
9 Cohen	Y	Y	Y	Y	N	Y	Y
TEXAS							
1 **Gohmert**	Y	Y	Y	Y	Y	N	N
2 **Poe**	Y	Y	Y	Y	N	N	N
3 **Johnson, S.**	Y	Y	Y	Y	N	N	N
4 **Hall**	Y	Y	Y	Y	N	N	N
5 **Hensarling**	Y	Y	Y	Y	Y	N	N
6 **Barton**	Y	Y	Y	Y	Y	N	N
7 **Culberson**	Y	Y	Y	Y	N	N	N
8 **Brady**	Y	Y	Y	Y	N	N	N
9 Green, A.	Y	Y	Y	Y	N	+	Y
10 **McCaul**	Y	Y	Y	Y	?	N	N
11 **Conaway**	Y	Y	Y	Y	N	N	N
12 **Granger**	Y	Y	Y	Y	N	N	N
13 **Thornberry**	Y	Y	Y	Y	Y	N	N
14 **Paul**	Y	Y	Y	Y	?	N	N
15 Hinojosa	Y	?	Y	Y	N	?	Y
16 Reyes	Y	Y	Y	Y	N	Y	Y
17 Edwards	Y	Y	Y	Y	N	Y	Y
18 Jackson Lee	Y	Y	Y	Y	?	Y	Y
19 **Neugebauer**	Y	Y	Y	Y	N	N	N
20 Gonzalez	Y	Y	Y	Y	N	Y	Y
21 **Smith**	Y	Y	Y	Y	N	N	N
22 **Olson**	Y	Y	Y	Y	Y	N	N
23 Rodriguez	Y	Y	Y	Y	N	Y	Y
24 **Marchant**	Y	Y	Y	Y	?	N	N
25 Doggett	Y	Y	Y	Y	N	Y	Y
26 **Burgess**	Y	Y	Y	Y	N	N	N
27 Ortiz	Y	Y	Y	Y	N	Y	Y
28 Cuellar	Y	Y	Y	Y	N	Y	?
29 Green, G.	Y	Y	Y	Y	N	Y	Y
30 Johnson, E.	Y	Y	Y	Y	N	Y	Y
31 **Carter**	Y	Y	Y	Y	N	N	N
32 **Sessions**	Y	Y	Y	Y	N	N	N
UTAH							
1 **Bishop**	Y	Y	Y	Y	N	N	N
2 Matheson	Y	Y	Y	Y	N	Y	Y
3 **Chaffetz**	Y	Y	Y	Y	Y	N	N
VERMONT							
AL Welch	Y	Y	Y	Y	N	Y	Y
VIRGINIA							
1 **Wittman**	Y	Y	Y	Y	N	N	N
2 Nye	Y	Y	Y	Y	N	N	N
3 Scott	Y	Y	Y	Y	N	Y	Y
4 **Forbes**	Y	Y	Y	Y	N	N	N
5 Perriello	Y	Y	Y	Y	N	Y	Y
6 **Goodlatte**	Y	Y	Y	Y	N	N	N
7 **Cantor**	Y	Y	Y	Y	N	N	N
8 Moran	Y	Y	Y	Y	N	Y	Y
9 Boucher	Y	Y	Y	Y	N	Y	Y
10 **Wolf**	Y	Y	Y	Y	N	N	N
11 Connolly	Y	Y	Y	Y	N	Y	Y
WASHINGTON							
1 Inslee	Y	Y	Y	Y	?	Y	Y
2 Larsen	Y	Y	Y	Y	?	Y	Y
3 Baird	Y	Y	Y	Y	N	Y	Y
4 **Hastings**	Y	Y	Y	Y	N	N	N
5 **McMorris Rodgers**	Y	Y	Y	Y	N	N	N
6 Dicks	Y	Y	Y	Y	?	Y	Y
7 McDermott	Y	Y	Y	Y	?	Y	Y
8 **Reichert**	Y	Y	Y	Y	N	N	N
9 Smith	Y	Y	Y	Y	N	Y	Y
WEST VIRGINIA							
1 Mollohan	Y	Y	Y	Y	?	Y	Y
2 **Capito**	Y	Y	Y	Y	N	N	N
3 Rahall	Y	Y	Y	Y	N	Y	Y
WISCONSIN							
1 **Ryan**	Y	Y	Y	Y	N	N	N
2 Baldwin	Y	Y	Y	Y	N	Y	Y
3 Kind	Y	Y	Y	Y	N	Y	Y
4 Moore	Y	Y	Y	Y	N	Y	Y
5 **Sensenbrenner**	Y	Y	Y	Y	N	N	N
6 **Petri**	Y	Y	Y	Y	N	N	N
7 Obey	Y	Y	Y	Y	N	Y	Y
8 Kagen	Y	Y	Y	Y	N	Y	Y
WYOMING							
AL **Lummis**	Y	Y	Y	Y	N	N	N
DELEGATES							
Faleomavaega (A.S.)							
Norton (D.C.)							
Bordallo (Guam)							
Sablan (N. Marianas)							
Pierluisi (P.R.)							
Christensen (V.I.)							

IN THE HOUSE | By Vote Number

540. HR 1044. Port Chicago Naval Magazine National Memorial/ **Passage.** Bordallo, D-Guam, motion to suspend the rules and pass the bill that would require the Interior Department to administer the Port Chicago Naval Magazine National Memorial as a part of the National Park System. Motion agreed to 415-3: R 172-3; D 243-0. A two-thirds majority of those present and voting (279 in this case) is required for passage under suspension of the rules. July 15, 2009.

541. HR 934. Northern Mariana Islands Submerged Lands/ **Passage.** Bordallo, D-Guam, motion to suspend the rules and pass the bill that would place certain submerged lands within the jurisdiction of the government of the Commonwealth of the Northern Mariana Islands. Motion agreed to 416-0: R 176-0; D 240-0. A two-thirds majority of those present and voting (278 in this case) is required for passage under suspension of the rules. July 15, 2009.

542. HR 762. BLM Patent Affirmation/Passage. Bordallo, D-Guam, motion to suspend the rules and pass the bill that would affirm and validate land Patent No. 27-2005-0081 and its associated land reconfiguration, which was issued by the Bureau of Land Management on Feb. 18, 2005. Motion agreed to 413-0: R 173-0; D 240-0. A two-thirds majority of those present and voting (276 in this case) is required for passage under suspension of the rules. July 15, 2009.

543. HR 3183. Fiscal 2010 Energy-Water Appropriations/Manager's **Amendment.** Pastor, D-Ariz., amendment that would make increases and decreases in a number of programs funded in the bill. Funds in the bill could not be used to buy passenger motor vehicles unless they are purchased from Ford, GM or Chrysler. They also could not be used to buy light bulbs that are not Energy Star qualified or have the Federal Energy Management Program designation. Adopted in Committee of the Whole 261-172: R 25-152; D 236-20. July 15, 2009.

544. HR 3183. Fiscal 2010 Energy-Water Appropriations/Army **Corps of Engineers Construction.** Connolly, D-Va., amendment that would increase funding for Corps of Engineers construction by $7 million, offset by a reduction of the same amount for corps expenses. Adopted in Committee of the Whole 362-69: R 115-62; D 247-7. July 15, 2009.

545. HR 3183. Fiscal 2010 Energy-Water Appropriations/Power **Program Services.** Hastings, R-Wash., amendment that would make $5 million available for the Power Program Services to implement Bureau of Reclamation hydropower facilities installations. Adopted in Committee of the Whole 432-0: R 176-0; D 256-0. July 15, 2009.

546. HR 3183. Fiscal 2010 Energy-Water Appropriations/Energy **Efficiency and Renewable Activities.** Boren, D-Okla., amendment that would increase funding for Energy Department energy-efficiency and renewable-energy activities by $5 million, offset by an equal reduction in the department's administration expenses. Adopted in Committee of the Whole 429-4: R 173-4; D 256-0. July 15, 2009.

	540	541	542	543	544	545	546
ALABAMA							
1 Bonner	Y	Y	Y	N	N	Y	Y
2 Bright	Y	Y	Y	N	Y	Y	Y
3 Rogers	Y	Y	Y	N	Y	Y	Y
4 Aderholt	Y	Y	Y	N	Y	Y	Y
5 Griffith	Y	Y	Y	N	Y	Y	Y
6 Bachus	Y	Y	Y	N	Y	Y	Y
7 Davis	Y	Y	Y	Y	Y	Y	Y
ALASKA							
AL Young	Y	Y	Y	Y	N	Y	Y
ARIZONA							
1 Kirkpatrick	Y	Y	Y	Y	Y	Y	Y
2 Franks	Y	Y	Y	N	N	Y	Y
3 Shadegg	Y	Y	Y	N	N	Y	Y
4 Pastor	Y	Y	Y	Y	?	Y	Y
5 Mitchell	Y	Y	Y	Y	Y	Y	Y
6 Flake	N	Y	Y	N	N	Y	N
7 Grijalva	Y	Y	Y	Y	Y	Y	Y
8 Giffords	Y	Y	Y	Y	Y	Y	Y
ARKANSAS							
1 Berry	Y	Y	Y	Y	Y	Y	Y
2 Snyder	Y	Y	Y	N	Y	Y	Y
3 Boozman	Y	Y	Y	N	N	Y	Y
4 Ross	Y	Y	Y	Y	Y	Y	Y
CALIFORNIA							
1 Thompson	Y	Y	Y	Y	Y	Y	Y
2 Herger	Y	Y	Y	N	Y	Y	Y
3 Lungren	Y	Y	Y	N	N	Y	Y
4 McClintock	Y	Y	Y	N	N	Y	N
5 Matsui	Y	Y	Y	Y	Y	Y	Y
6 Woolsey	Y	Y	Y	Y	Y	Y	Y
7 Miller, George	Y	Y	?	Y	Y	Y	Y
8 Pelosi							
9 Lee	Y	Y	Y	Y	Y	Y	Y
10 Vacant							
11 McNerney	Y	Y	Y	N	Y	Y	Y
12 Speier	Y	Y	Y	Y	Y	Y	Y
13 Stark	Y	Y	Y	Y	Y	Y	Y
14 Eshoo	Y	Y	Y	N	Y	Y	Y
15 Honda	Y	?	Y	N	Y	Y	Y
16 Lofgren	Y	Y	Y	Y	Y	Y	Y
17 Farr	Y	Y	Y	Y	Y	Y	Y
18 Cardoza	Y	Y	Y	Y	Y	Y	Y
19 Radanovich	Y	Y	Y	N	Y	Y	Y
20 Costa	Y	Y	Y	Y	Y	Y	Y
21 Nunes	Y	Y	Y	N	Y	Y	Y
22 McCarthy	Y	Y	Y	N	Y	Y	Y
23 Capps	+	+	+	Y	Y	Y	Y
24 Gallegly	Y	Y	Y	N	Y	Y	Y
25 McKeon	Y	Y	Y	N	Y	Y	Y
26 Dreier	Y	Y	Y	N	Y	Y	Y
27 Sherman	Y	Y	Y	Y	Y	Y	Y
28 Berman	Y	?	Y	Y	Y	Y	Y
29 Schiff	Y	Y	Y	Y	Y	Y	Y
30 Waxman	Y	Y	Y	Y	Y	Y	Y
31 Becerra	Y	Y	Y	Y	Y	Y	Y
32 Vacant							
33 Watson	Y	Y	Y	Y	Y	Y	Y
34 Roybal-Allard	Y	Y	?	Y	Y	Y	Y
35 Waters	Y	Y	?	Y	Y	Y	Y
36 Harman	Y	Y	Y	N	Y	Y	Y
37 Richardson	Y	Y	Y	N	Y	Y	Y
38 Napolitano	Y	Y	Y	Y	Y	Y	Y
39 Sánchez, Linda	Y	Y	Y	Y	Y	Y	Y
40 Royce	Y	Y	Y	N	N	Y	Y
41 Lewis	Y	Y	Y	N	Y	Y	Y
42 Miller, Gary	Y	Y	Y	N	Y	Y	Y
43 Baca	Y	Y	Y	Y	Y	Y	Y
44 Calvert	Y	Y	Y	N	Y	Y	Y
45 Bono Mack	Y	Y	Y	N	Y	Y	Y
46 Rohrabacher	Y	Y	Y	N	N	Y	Y
47 Sanchez, Loretta	Y	Y	Y	Y	Y	Y	Y
48 Campbell	Y	Y	Y	N	N	Y	N
49 Issa	Y	Y	Y	N	Y	Y	Y
50 Bilbray	Y	Y	Y	Y	Y	Y	Y
51 Filner	Y	Y	Y	Y	Y	Y	Y
52 Hunter	Y	Y	Y	N	Y	Y	Y
53 Davis	Y	Y	Y	Y	Y	Y	Y

	540	541	542	543	544	545	546
COLORADO							
1 DeGette	Y	Y	Y	Y	Y	Y	Y
2 Polis	Y	Y	Y	Y	Y	Y	Y
3 Salazar	Y	Y	Y	Y	Y	Y	Y
4 Markey	Y	Y	Y	Y	Y	Y	Y
5 Lamborn	Y	Y	Y	N	N	Y	Y
6 Coffman	Y	Y	Y	N	N	Y	Y
7 Perlmutter	Y	Y	Y	Y	Y	Y	Y
CONNECTICUT							
1 Larson	Y	Y	Y	Y	Y	Y	Y
2 Courtney	Y	Y	Y	Y	Y	Y	Y
3 DeLauro	Y	Y	Y	Y	Y	Y	Y
4 Himes	Y	Y	Y	Y	Y	Y	Y
5 Murphy	Y	Y	Y	Y	Y	Y	Y
DELAWARE							
AL Castle	Y	Y	Y	Y	Y	Y	Y
FLORIDA							
1 Miller	Y	Y	Y	N	N	Y	Y
2 Boyd	Y	Y	Y	Y	Y	Y	Y
3 Brown	Y	Y	Y	Y	Y	Y	Y
4 Crenshaw	Y	Y	?	N	Y	Y	Y
5 Brown-Waite	Y	Y	?	N	Y	Y	Y
6 Stearns	Y	Y	Y	N	N	Y	Y
7 Mica	Y	Y	Y	N	Y	Y	Y
8 Grayson	Y	Y	Y	Y	Y	Y	Y
9 Bilirakis	Y	Y	Y	N	Y	Y	Y
10 Young	?	?	?	?	?	?	?
11 Castor	Y	Y	Y	Y	Y	Y	Y
12 Putnam	Y	Y	Y	N	Y	Y	Y
13 Buchanan	Y	Y	Y	N	Y	Y	Y
14 Mack	Y	Y	Y	N	Y	Y	Y
15 Posey	Y	Y	Y	N	Y	Y	Y
16 Rooney	Y	Y	Y	N	Y	Y	Y
17 Meek	Y	Y	Y	?	Y	Y	Y
18 Ros-Lehtinen	Y	Y	Y	Y	Y	Y	Y
19 Wexler	Y	Y	Y	Y	Y	Y	Y
20 Wasserman Schultz	Y	Y	Y	Y	Y	Y	Y
21 Diaz-Balart, L.	Y	Y	Y	Y	Y	Y	Y
22 Klein	Y	Y	Y	Y	Y	Y	Y
23 Hastings	Y	Y	Y	Y	Y	Y	Y
24 Kosmas	Y	Y	Y	Y	Y	Y	Y
25 Diaz-Balart, M.	Y	Y	Y	Y	Y	Y	Y
GEORGIA							
1 Kingston	Y	Y	Y	N	Y	Y	Y
2 Bishop	Y	Y	Y	Y	Y	Y	Y
3 Westmoreland	Y	Y	Y	N	N	Y	Y
4 Johnson	Y	Y	Y	Y	Y	Y	Y
5 Lewis	Y	Y	Y	Y	Y	Y	Y
6 Price	Y	Y	Y	N	N	Y	Y
7 Linder	Y	Y	Y	N	N	Y	Y
8 Marshall	Y	Y	Y	Y	Y	Y	Y
9 Deal	Y	Y	Y	N	N	Y	Y
10 Broun	N	Y	Y	N	N	Y	Y
11 Gingrey	Y	Y	Y	N	Y	Y	Y
12 Barrow	Y	Y	Y	Y	Y	Y	Y
13 Scott	Y	Y	Y	Y	Y	Y	Y
HAWAII							
1 Abercrombie	Y	Y	Y	Y	Y	Y	Y
2 Hirono	Y	Y	Y	Y	Y	Y	Y
IDAHO							
1 Minnick	Y	Y	Y	Y	Y	Y	Y
2 Simpson	Y	Y	Y	N	Y	Y	Y
ILLINOIS							
1 Rush	Y	Y	Y	Y	Y	Y	Y
2 Jackson	Y	Y	Y	Y	Y	Y	Y
3 Lipinski	Y	Y	Y	Y	Y	Y	Y
4 Gutierrez	Y	Y	Y	Y	Y	Y	Y
5 Quigley	Y	Y	Y	Y	Y	Y	Y
6 Roskam	Y	Y	Y	N	Y	Y	Y
7 Davis	Y	Y	?	Y	Y	Y	Y
8 Bean	Y	Y	Y	Y	Y	Y	Y
9 Schakowsky	Y	Y	Y	Y	Y	Y	Y
10 Kirk	Y	Y	Y	N	Y	Y	Y
11 Halvorson	Y	Y	Y	Y	Y	Y	Y
12 Costello	Y	Y	Y	Y	Y	Y	Y
13 Biggert	Y	Y	Y	N	Y	Y	Y
14 Foster	Y	Y	Y	Y	Y	Y	Y
15 Johnson	Y	Y	Y	N	N	Y	Y

KEY	**Republicans**	Democrats		
Y Voted for (yea)		X Paired against		C Voted "present" to avoid possible conflict of interest
# Paired for		– Announced against		
+ Announced for		P Voted "present"		? Did not vote or otherwise make a position known
N Voted against (nay)				

	540	541	542	543	544	545	546
16 **Manzullo**	Y	Y	Y	N	Y	Y	Y
17 Hare	Y	Y	Y	Y	Y	Y	Y
18 **Schock**	Y	Y	Y	N	Y	Y	Y
19 **Shimkus**	Y	Y	Y	N	Y	Y	Y
INDIANA							
1 Visclosky	Y	Y	Y	Y	Y	Y	Y
2 Donnelly	Y	Y	Y	Y	Y	Y	Y
3 **Souder**	Y	Y	Y	N	N	Y	Y
4 **Buyer**	Y	Y	Y	N	Y	Y	Y
5 **Burton**	Y	Y	Y	N	N	Y	Y
6 **Pence**	Y	Y	Y	N	Y	Y	Y
7 Carson	Y	Y	Y	Y	Y	Y	Y
8 Ellsworth	Y	Y	Y	N	Y	Y	Y
9 Hill	Y	Y	Y	N	Y	Y	Y
IOWA							
1 Braley	Y	Y	Y	Y	Y	Y	Y
2 Loebsack	Y	Y	Y	Y	Y	Y	Y
3 Boswell	Y	Y	Y	Y	Y	Y	Y
4 **Latham**	Y	Y	Y	N	Y	Y	Y
5 **King**	Y	Y	Y	N	N	Y	Y
KANSAS							
1 **Moran**	Y	Y	Y	N	N	Y	Y
2 **Jenkins**	Y	Y	Y	N	N	Y	Y
3 Moore	Y	Y	Y	Y	Y	Y	Y
4 **Tiahrt**	Y	Y	Y	N	N	Y	Y
KENTUCKY							
1 **Whitfield**	Y	Y	Y	N	N	Y	Y
2 **Guthrie**	Y	Y	Y	N	Y	Y	Y
3 Yarmuth	Y	Y	Y	Y	Y	Y	Y
4 **Davis**	Y	Y	Y	N	Y	Y	Y
5 **Rogers**	Y	Y	Y	N	Y	Y	Y
6 Chandler	Y	Y	Y	N	Y	Y	Y
LOUISIANA							
1 **Scalise**	Y	Y	Y	N	Y	Y	Y
2 **Cao**	Y	Y	Y	Y	Y	Y	Y
3 Melancon	Y	Y	Y	N	N	Y	Y
4 **Fleming**	Y	Y	Y	N	Y	Y	Y
5 **Alexander**	Y	Y	Y	N	Y	Y	Y
6 **Cassidy**	?	Y	Y	N	N	Y	Y
7 **Boustany**	Y	Y	Y	N	Y	Y	Y
MAINE							
1 Pingree	Y	Y	Y	Y	Y	Y	Y
2 Michaud	Y	Y	Y	Y	Y	Y	Y
MARYLAND							
1 Kratovil	Y	Y	Y	N	Y	Y	Y
2 Ruppersberger	Y	Y	Y	Y	Y	Y	Y
3 Sarbanes	Y	Y	Y	Y	Y	Y	Y
4 Edwards	Y	Y	Y	Y	Y	Y	Y
5 Hoyer	Y	Y	Y	Y	Y	Y	Y
6 **Bartlett**	Y	Y	Y	N	Y	Y	Y
7 Cummings	Y	Y	Y	Y	Y	Y	Y
8 Van Hollen	Y	Y	Y	Y	Y	Y	Y
MASSACHUSETTS							
1 Olver	Y	Y	Y	Y	Y	Y	Y
2 Neal	Y	Y	Y	Y	Y	Y	Y
3 McGovern	Y	Y	Y	Y	Y	Y	Y
4 Frank	Y	Y	Y	Y	Y	Y	Y
5 Tsongas	Y	Y	Y	Y	Y	Y	Y
6 Tierney	Y	Y	Y	Y	Y	Y	Y
7 Markey	Y	Y	Y	Y	Y	Y	Y
8 Capuano	Y	Y	Y	Y	Y	Y	Y
9 Lynch	Y	Y	Y	Y	Y	Y	Y
10 Delahunt	Y	Y	?	Y	Y	Y	Y
MICHIGAN							
1 Stupak	Y	Y	Y	Y	Y	Y	Y
2 **Hoekstra**	Y	Y	Y	N	Y	Y	Y
3 **Ehlers**	Y	Y	Y	Y	Y	Y	N
4 **Camp**	Y	Y	Y	Y	Y	Y	Y
5 Kildee	Y	Y	Y	Y	Y	Y	Y
6 **Upton**	Y	Y	Y	Y	Y	Y	Y
7 Schauer	Y	Y	Y	Y	N	Y	Y
8 **Rogers**	Y	Y	Y	N	Y	Y	Y
9 Peters	Y	Y	Y	Y	Y	Y	Y
10 **Miller**	Y	Y	Y	Y	Y	Y	Y
11 **McCotter**	Y	Y	Y	Y	Y	Y	Y
12 Levin	+	+	+	Y	Y	Y	Y
13 Kilpatrick	Y	Y	Y	Y	Y	Y	Y
14 Conyers	?	?	?	Y	Y	Y	Y
15 Dingell	Y	Y	Y	Y	Y	Y	Y
MINNESOTA							
1 Walz	Y	Y	Y	Y	Y	Y	Y
2 **Kline**	Y	Y	Y	N	N	Y	Y
3 **Paulsen**	Y	Y	Y	N	Y	Y	Y
4 McCollum	Y	Y	Y	Y	Y	Y	Y
5 Ellison	Y	Y	Y	Y	Y	Y	Y
6 **Bachmann**	Y	Y	Y	N	N	Y	Y
7 Peterson	Y	Y	Y	Y	Y	Y	Y
8 Oberstar	Y	Y	Y	Y	Y	Y	Y
MISSISSIPPI							
1 Childers	Y	Y	Y	Y	Y	Y	Y
2 Thompson	Y	Y	Y	Y	Y	Y	Y
3 **Harper**	Y	Y	Y	N	Y	Y	Y
4 Taylor	?	?	Y	Y	Y	Y	Y
MISSOURI							
1 Clay	Y	Y	Y	Y	Y	Y	Y
2 **Akin**	Y	Y	Y	N	N	Y	Y
3 Carnahan	Y	Y	Y	Y	Y	Y	Y
4 Skelton	Y	Y	Y	Y	Y	Y	Y
5 Cleaver	Y	Y	Y	Y	Y	Y	Y
6 **Graves**	Y	Y	Y	N	Y	Y	Y
7 **Blunt**	Y	Y	Y	N	Y	Y	Y
8 **Emerson**	Y	Y	Y	N	Y	Y	Y
9 **Luetkemeyer**	Y	Y	Y	N	N	Y	Y
MONTANA							
AL **Rehberg**	Y	Y	Y	N	Y	Y	Y
NEBRASKA							
1 **Fortenberry**	Y	Y	Y	N	Y	Y	Y
2 **Terry**	Y	Y	Y	N	Y	Y	Y
3 **Smith**	Y	Y	Y	N	Y	Y	Y
NEVADA							
1 Berkley	Y	?	Y	Y	Y	Y	Y
2 **Heller**	Y	Y	Y	Y	N	Y	Y
3 Titus	Y	Y	Y	Y	Y	Y	Y
NEW HAMPSHIRE							
1 Shea-Porter	Y	Y	Y	Y	Y	Y	Y
2 Hodes	Y	Y	Y	Y	Y	Y	Y
NEW JERSEY							
1 Andrews	Y	Y	Y	Y	Y	Y	Y
2 **LoBiondo**	Y	Y	Y	Y	Y	Y	Y
3 Adler	Y	Y	Y	Y	Y	Y	Y
4 **Smith**	Y	Y	Y	Y	Y	Y	Y
5 **Garrett**	Y	Y	Y	N	Y	Y	Y
6 Pallone	Y	Y	Y	Y	Y	Y	Y
7 **Lance**	Y	Y	Y	N	Y	Y	Y
8 Pascrell	Y	Y	Y	Y	Y	Y	Y
9 Rothman	Y	Y	Y	Y	Y	Y	Y
10 Payne	Y	Y	Y	Y	Y	Y	Y
11 **Frelinghuysen**	Y	Y	Y	N	Y	Y	Y
12 Holt	Y	Y	Y	Y	Y	Y	Y
13 Sires	Y	Y	Y	Y	Y	Y	Y
NEW MEXICO							
1 Heinrich	Y	Y	Y	Y	Y	Y	Y
2 Teague	Y	Y	Y	Y	N	Y	Y
3 Lujan	Y	Y	Y	Y	Y	Y	Y
NEW YORK							
1 Bishop	Y	Y	Y	Y	Y	Y	Y
2 Israel	Y	Y	Y	Y	Y	Y	Y
3 **King**	Y	Y	Y	N	Y	Y	Y
4 McCarthy	?	?	?	Y	Y	Y	Y
5 Ackerman	Y	Y	Y	Y	Y	Y	Y
6 Meeks	Y	Y	Y	Y	Y	Y	Y
7 Crowley	Y	Y	Y	Y	Y	Y	Y
8 Nadler	Y	Y	Y	Y	Y	Y	Y
9 Weiner	Y	Y	Y	Y	Y	Y	Y
10 Towns	Y	Y	Y	Y	Y	Y	Y
11 Clarke	Y	Y	Y	Y	Y	Y	Y
12 Velázquez	Y	Y	Y	Y	Y	Y	Y
13 McMahon	Y	Y	Y	Y	Y	Y	Y
14 Maloney	Y	Y	Y	Y	Y	Y	Y
15 Rangel	Y	Y	Y	Y	Y	Y	Y
16 Serrano	Y	Y	Y	Y	Y	Y	Y
17 Engel	?	?	?	Y	Y	Y	Y
18 Lowey	Y	Y	Y	Y	Y	Y	Y
19 Hall	Y	Y	Y	Y	Y	Y	Y
20 Murphy	Y	Y	Y	Y	Y	Y	Y
21 Tonko	Y	Y	Y	Y	Y	Y	Y
22 Hinchey	Y	Y	Y	Y	Y	Y	Y
23 **McHugh**	Y	Y	Y	Y	Y	Y	Y
24 Arcuri	Y	Y	Y	Y	Y	Y	Y
25 Maffei	Y	Y	Y	Y	Y	Y	Y
26 **Lee**	Y	Y	Y	N	N	Y	Y
27 Higgins	Y	Y	Y	Y	Y	Y	Y
28 Slaughter	Y	Y	Y	Y	Y	Y	Y
29 Massa	Y	Y	Y	Y	Y	Y	Y
NORTH CAROLINA							
1 Butterfield	Y	Y	Y	Y	Y	Y	Y
2 Etheridge	Y	Y	Y	Y	Y	Y	Y
3 **Jones**	Y	Y	Y	N	Y	Y	Y
4 Price	Y	Y	Y	Y	Y	Y	Y
5 **Foxx**	Y	Y	Y	N	N	Y	Y
6 **Coble**	Y	Y	Y	N	Y	Y	Y
7 McIntyre	Y	Y	Y	Y	Y	Y	Y
8 Kissell	Y	Y	Y	Y	Y	Y	Y
9 **Myrick**	Y	Y	Y	N	N	Y	Y
10 **McHenry**	Y	Y	Y	N	Y	Y	Y
11 Shuler	Y	Y	Y	Y	N	Y	Y
12 Watt	Y	Y	Y	Y	Y	Y	Y
13 Miller	Y	Y	Y	Y	Y	Y	Y
NORTH DAKOTA							
AL Pomeroy	Y	Y	Y	Y	Y	Y	Y
OHIO							
1 Driehaus	Y	Y	Y	Y	Y	Y	Y
2 **Schmidt**	Y	Y	Y	N	Y	Y	Y
3 **Turner**	Y	Y	Y	Y	Y	Y	Y
4 **Jordan**	Y	Y	Y	N	N	Y	Y
5 **Latta**	Y	Y	Y	N	N	Y	Y
6 Wilson	Y	Y	Y	Y	Y	Y	Y
7 **Austria**	Y	Y	Y	N	Y	Y	Y
8 **Boehner**	Y	Y	Y	N	Y	Y	Y
9 Kaptur	Y	Y	Y	Y	Y	Y	Y
10 Kucinich	Y	Y	Y	Y	Y	Y	Y
11 Fudge	Y	Y	Y	Y	Y	Y	Y
12 **Tiberi**	Y	Y	Y	N	N	Y	Y
13 Sutton	Y	Y	Y	Y	Y	Y	Y
14 **LaTourette**	Y	Y	Y	N	Y	Y	Y
15 Kilroy	Y	Y	Y	Y	Y	Y	Y
16 Boccieri	Y	Y	Y	Y	Y	Y	Y
17 Ryan	Y	?	Y	Y	Y	Y	Y
18 Space	Y	Y	Y	Y	N	Y	Y
OKLAHOMA							
1 **Sullivan**	Y	Y	Y	N	N	Y	Y
2 Boren	Y	Y	Y	Y	Y	Y	Y
3 **Lucas**	Y	Y	Y	Y	Y	Y	Y
4 **Cole**	Y	Y	Y	N	Y	Y	Y
5 **Fallin**	Y	Y	Y	N	Y	Y	Y
OREGON							
1 Wu	Y	Y	Y	Y	Y	Y	Y
2 **Walden**	Y	Y	Y	N	N	Y	Y
3 Blumenauer	Y	Y	Y	N	Y	Y	Y
4 DeFazio	Y	Y	Y	Y	Y	Y	Y
5 Schrader	?	?	?	?	?	?	?
PENNSYLVANIA							
1 Brady	Y	Y	Y	Y	Y	Y	Y
2 Fattah	Y	Y	Y	Y	Y	Y	Y
3 Dahlkemper	Y	Y	Y	Y	Y	Y	Y
4 Altmire	Y	Y	Y	Y	Y	Y	Y
5 **Thompson**	Y	Y	Y	N	Y	Y	Y
6 **Gerlach**	Y	Y	Y	Y	Y	Y	Y
7 Sestak	?	?	?	?	?	?	?
8 Murphy, P.	Y	Y	Y	Y	Y	Y	Y
9 **Shuster**	Y	Y	Y	N	Y	Y	Y
10 Carney	Y	Y	Y	Y	Y	Y	Y
11 Kanjorski	Y	Y	Y	Y	Y	Y	Y
12 Murtha	Y	Y	Y	Y	Y	Y	Y
13 Schwartz	Y	Y	Y	Y	Y	Y	Y
14 Doyle	Y	Y	Y	Y	Y	Y	Y
15 **Dent**	Y	Y	Y	Y	Y	Y	Y
16 **Pitts**	Y	Y	?	N	Y	Y	Y
17 Holden	Y	Y	Y	Y	Y	Y	Y
18 **Murphy, T.**	Y	Y	Y	Y	Y	Y	Y
19 **Platts**	Y	Y	Y	Y	Y	?	Y
RHODE ISLAND							
1 Kennedy	Y	Y	Y	Y	Y	Y	Y
2 Langevin	Y	Y	Y	Y	Y	Y	Y
SOUTH CAROLINA							
1 **Brown**	Y	Y	Y	N	Y	Y	Y
2 **Wilson**	Y	Y	Y	N	N	Y	Y
3 **Barrett**	Y	Y	Y	N	N	Y	Y
4 **Inglis**	Y	Y	Y	Y	N	Y	Y
5 Spratt	Y	Y	Y	Y	Y	Y	Y
6 Clyburn	Y	Y	Y	Y	Y	Y	Y
SOUTH DAKOTA							
AL Herseth Sandlin	Y	Y	Y	Y	?	Y	Y
TENNESSEE							
1 **Roe**	Y	Y	Y	N	Y	Y	Y
2 **Duncan**	Y	Y	Y	Y	N	Y	Y
3 **Wamp**	Y	Y	Y	N	Y	Y	Y
4 Davis	Y	Y	Y	Y	Y	Y	Y
5 Cooper	Y	Y	Y	Y	N	Y	Y
6 Gordon	?	?	?	N	Y	Y	Y
7 **Blackburn**	Y	Y	Y	N	Y	Y	Y
8 Tanner	Y	Y	Y	Y	Y	Y	Y
9 Cohen	Y	Y	Y	Y	Y	Y	Y
TEXAS							
1 **Gohmert**	Y	Y	Y	N	N	Y	Y
2 **Poe**	Y	Y	Y	N	Y	Y	Y
3 **Johnson, S.**	Y	Y	Y	N	N	Y	Y
4 **Hall**	Y	Y	Y	N	Y	Y	Y
5 **Hensarling**	Y	Y	Y	N	N	Y	Y
6 **Barton**	Y	Y	Y	Y	Y	Y	Y
7 **Culberson**	Y	Y	Y	N	Y	Y	Y
8 **Brady**	Y	Y	Y	N	N	Y	Y
9 Green, A.	Y	Y	Y	Y	Y	Y	Y
10 **McCaul**	?	?	?	N	Y	Y	Y
11 **Conaway**	Y	Y	Y	N	N	Y	Y
12 **Granger**	Y	Y	Y	N	Y	Y	Y
13 **Thornberry**	Y	Y	Y	N	N	Y	Y
14 **Paul**	N	Y	Y	N	Y	Y	Y
15 Hinojosa	Y	Y	Y	Y	Y	Y	Y
16 Reyes	Y	Y	Y	Y	Y	Y	Y
17 Edwards	Y	Y	Y	Y	Y	Y	Y
18 Jackson Lee	Y	Y	Y	Y	Y	Y	Y
19 **Neugebauer**	Y	Y	Y	N	N	Y	Y
20 Gonzalez	Y	Y	Y	N	Y	Y	Y
21 **Smith**	Y	Y	Y	N	Y	Y	Y
22 **Olson**	Y	Y	Y	N	N	Y	Y
23 Rodriguez	Y	Y	Y	N	Y	Y	Y
24 **Marchant**	Y	Y	Y	N	Y	Y	Y
25 Doggett	Y	Y	Y	Y	Y	Y	Y
26 **Burgess**	Y	Y	Y	N	N	Y	Y
27 Ortiz	Y	Y	Y	N	Y	Y	Y
28 Cuellar	Y	Y	Y	N	Y	Y	Y
29 Green, G.	Y	Y	Y	Y	Y	Y	Y
30 Johnson, E.	?	?	?	Y	Y	Y	Y
31 **Carter**	Y	Y	Y	N	Y	Y	Y
32 **Sessions**	Y	Y	Y	N	N	Y	Y
UTAH							
1 **Bishop**	Y	Y	Y	N	N	Y	Y
2 Matheson	Y	Y	Y	Y	Y	Y	Y
3 **Chaffetz**	Y	Y	Y	N	Y	Y	Y
VERMONT							
AL Welch	Y	Y	Y	Y	Y	Y	Y
VIRGINIA							
1 **Wittman**	Y	Y	Y	N	Y	Y	Y
2 Nye	Y	Y	Y	Y	Y	Y	Y
3 Scott	Y	Y	Y	Y	Y	Y	Y
4 **Forbes**	Y	Y	Y	N	Y	Y	Y
5 Perriello	Y	Y	Y	Y	Y	Y	Y
6 **Goodlatte**	Y	Y	Y	N	Y	Y	Y
7 **Cantor**	Y	Y	Y	N	Y	Y	Y
8 Moran	Y	Y	Y	Y	Y	Y	Y
9 Boucher	Y	Y	Y	Y	Y	Y	Y
10 **Wolf**	Y	Y	Y	N	Y	Y	Y
11 Connolly	Y	Y	Y	Y	Y	Y	Y
WASHINGTON							
1 Inslee	?	Y	Y	Y	Y	Y	Y
2 Larsen	Y	Y	Y	Y	Y	Y	Y
3 Baird	Y	Y	Y	Y	Y	Y	Y
4 **Hastings**	Y	Y	Y	N	N	Y	Y
5 **McMorris Rodgers**	Y	Y	Y	N	Y	Y	Y
6 Dicks	Y	Y	Y	Y	Y	Y	Y
7 McDermott	Y	Y	Y	Y	Y	Y	Y
8 **Reichert**	Y	Y	Y	N	Y	Y	Y
9 Smith	Y	Y	Y	Y	Y	Y	Y
WEST VIRGINIA							
1 Mollohan	Y	Y	Y	Y	Y	Y	Y
2 **Capito**	Y	Y	Y	N	Y	Y	Y
3 Rahall	Y	Y	Y	Y	Y	Y	Y
WISCONSIN							
1 **Ryan**	Y	Y	Y	N	N	Y	Y
2 Baldwin	Y	Y	Y	Y	Y	Y	Y
3 Kind	Y	Y	Y	Y	Y	Y	Y
4 Moore	Y	Y	Y	Y	Y	?	Y
5 **Sensenbrenner**	Y	Y	Y	N	N	Y	Y
6 **Petri**	Y	Y	Y	N	Y	Y	Y
7 Obey	Y	Y	Y	Y	Y	Y	Y
8 Kagen	Y	Y	Y	Y	Y	Y	Y
WYOMING							
AL **Lummis**	Y	Y	Y	N	Y	Y	Y
DELEGATES							
Faleomavaega (A.S.)				?	?	?	?
Norton (D.C.)				Y	Y	Y	Y
Bordallo (Guam)				?	Y	Y	Y
Sablan (N. Marianas)				Y	Y	Y	?
Pierluisi (P.R.)				Y	Y	Y	Y
Christensen (V.I.)				Y	Y	Y	Y

IN THE HOUSE | By Vote Number

547. **HR 3183. Fiscal 2010 Energy-Water Appropriations/Energy Efficiency and Renewable Activities.** Miller, R-Mich., amendment that would increase funding for Energy Department energy efficiency and renewable-energy activities by $10 million, offset by a reduction of the same amount for the department's administration expenses. Adopted in Committee of the Whole 431-1: R 177-0; D 254-1. July 15, 2009.

548. **HR 1442. Mount Olivet Cemetery Association Conveyance/Passage.** Bordallo, D-Guam, motion to suspend the rules and pass the bill that would require the Interior Department to convey to the Mount Olivet Cemetery Association of Salt Lake City the federal reversionary interest in 60 acres of land. Motion agreed to 422-0: R 173-0; D 249-0. A two-thirds majority of those present and voting (282 in this case) is required for passage under suspension of the rules. July 16, 2009.

549. **HR 129. Los Padres National Forest Land Conveyance/Passage.** Bordallo, D-Guam, motion to suspend the rules and pass the bill that would authorize the Agriculture Department to convey five acres within the Los Padres National Forest in Santa Barbara County, Calif., to the White Lotus Foundation. Motion agreed to 422-0: R 173-0; D 249-0. A two-thirds majority of those present and voting (282 in this case) is required for passage under suspension of the rules. July 16, 2009.

550. **HR 2188. Migratory Birds Conservation/Passage.** Bordallo, D-Guam, motion to suspend the rules and pass the bill that would establish a program coordinated among federal agencies and states to develop, implement and support conservation strategies to promote sustainable populations of migratory birds. Motion agreed to 400-0: R 165-0; D 235-0. A two-thirds majority of those present and voting (267 in this case) is required for passage under suspension of the rules. July 16, 2009.

551. **HR 409. Nevada Speedway Land Conveyance/Passage.** Baca, D-Calif., motion to suspend the rules and pass the bill that would require the Interior Department to sell 115 acres of Bureau of Land Management land to the Nevada Speedway for a parking lot expansion. Motion agreed to 406-0: R 161-0; D 245-0. A two-thirds majority of those present and voting (271 in this case) is required for passage under suspension of the rules. July 16, 2009.

552. **HR 3170. Fiscal 2010 Financial Services Appropriations/Previous Question.** Perlmutter, D-Colo., motion to order the previous question (thus ending debate and possibility of amendment) on adoption of the rule (H Res 644) that would provide for House floor consideration of the bill that would provide $46.2 billion in fiscal 2010 for the Treasury Department, the Office of Personnel Management and other agencies, and the District of Columbia. Motion agreed to 227-200: R 2-172; D 225-28. July 16, 2009.

553. **HR 3170. Fiscal 2010 Financial Services Appropriations/Rule.** Adoption of the rule (H Res 644) to provide for House floor consideration of the bill that would appropriate $46.2 billion in fiscal 2010 for the Treasury Department, the Office of Personnel Management and other agencies, and the District of Columbia. Adopted 216-213: R 0-174; D 216-39. July 16, 2009.

	547	548	549	550	551	552	553
ALABAMA							
1 Bonner	Y	Y	Y	Y	Y	N	N
2 Bright	Y	Y	Y	Y	Y	N	N
3 Rogers	Y	Y	Y	Y	Y	N	N
4 Aderholt	Y	Y	Y	Y	Y	N	N
5 Griffith	Y	Y	Y	Y	Y	N	N
6 Bachus	Y	Y	?	Y	Y	Y	N
7 Davis	Y	Y	Y	Y	Y	N	N
ALASKA							
AL Young	Y	Y	Y	Y	Y	N	N
ARIZONA							
1 Kirkpatrick	Y	Y	Y	Y	Y	Y	N
2 Franks	Y	Y	Y	Y	Y	N	N
3 Shadegg	Y	Y	Y	Y	Y	N	N
4 Pastor	Y	Y	Y	Y	Y	Y	Y
5 Mitchell	Y	Y	Y	Y	Y	Y	Y
6 Flake	Y	Y	Y	Y	Y	N	N
7 Grijalva	Y	Y	Y	Y	Y	Y	Y
8 Giffords	Y	Y	Y	Y	Y	Y	Y
ARKANSAS							
1 Berry	Y	Y	Y	Y	Y	N	Y
2 Snyder	Y	Y	Y	?	Y	Y	Y
3 Boozman	Y	Y	Y	Y	Y	N	N
4 Ross	Y	Y	Y	Y	Y	N	Y
CALIFORNIA							
1 Thompson	Y	Y	Y	Y	Y	Y	Y
2 Herger	Y	Y	Y	Y	Y	N	N
3 Lungren	Y	Y	Y	Y	Y	N	N
4 McClintock	Y	Y	Y	Y	Y	N	N
5 Matsui	Y	Y	Y	Y	Y	Y	Y
6 Woolsey	Y	Y	Y	Y	Y	Y	Y
7 Miller, George	Y	Y	Y	Y	Y	Y	Y
8 Pelosi							Y
9 Lee	Y	Y	Y	Y	Y	Y	Y
10 Vacant							
11 McNerney	Y	Y	Y	Y	Y	N	Y
12 Speier	Y	Y	Y	Y	Y	Y	Y
13 Stark	Y	Y	Y	Y	Y	Y	Y
14 Eshoo	Y	+	Y	Y	Y	Y	Y
15 Honda	Y	Y	Y	Y	Y	Y	Y
16 Lofgren	Y	Y	Y	Y	Y	Y	Y
17 Farr	?	Y	Y	Y	Y	Y	Y
18 Cardoza	Y	Y	Y	Y	Y	Y	Y
19 Radanovich	Y	Y	Y	Y	Y	N	N
20 Costa	Y	Y	Y	Y	Y	Y	Y
21 Nunes	Y	Y	Y	Y	Y	N	N
22 McCarthy	Y	Y	Y	Y	Y	N	N
23 Capps	Y	Y	Y	+	Y	Y	Y
24 Gallegly	Y	Y	Y	Y	Y	N	N
25 McKeon	Y	Y	Y	Y	Y	N	N
26 Dreier	Y	Y	Y	Y	Y	N	N
27 Sherman	Y	Y	Y	Y	Y	?	Y
28 Berman	Y	Y	Y	Y	Y	Y	Y
29 Schiff	Y	Y	Y	Y	Y	Y	Y
30 Waxman	Y	Y	Y	Y	?	Y	Y
31 Becerra	Y	Y	Y	Y	Y	Y	Y
32 Chu*			Y	Y	Y	Y	Y
33 Watson	Y	Y	Y	Y	Y	Y	Y
34 Roybal-Allard	Y	Y	Y	Y	Y	Y	Y
35 Waters	Y	Y	Y	Y	Y	Y	Y
36 Harman	Y	Y	Y	?	Y	Y	Y
37 Richardson	Y	Y	Y	Y	Y	Y	Y
38 Napolitano	Y	Y	Y	Y	Y	Y	Y
39 Sánchez, Linda	Y	Y	Y	Y	Y	Y	Y
40 Royce	Y	Y	Y	Y	Y	N	N
41 Lewis	Y	Y	Y	Y	Y	N	N
42 Miller, Gary	Y	Y	Y	Y	Y	N	N
43 Baca	Y	Y	Y	Y	Y	Y	Y
44 Calvert	Y	Y	Y	Y	Y	N	N
45 Bono Mack	Y	Y	Y	Y	Y	N	N
46 Rohrabacher	Y	Y	Y	Y	?	N	N
47 Sanchez, Loretta	Y	Y	Y	Y	Y	Y	Y
48 Campbell	Y	Y	Y	Y	Y	N	N
49 Issa	Y	Y	Y	Y	Y	N	N
50 Bilbray	Y	Y	Y	Y	Y	N	N
51 Filner	Y	Y	Y	Y	Y	Y	Y
52 Hunter	Y	Y	Y	Y	Y	N	N
53 Davis	Y	Y	Y	Y	Y	Y	Y

	547	548	549	550	551	552	553
COLORADO							
1 DeGette	Y	Y	Y	Y	Y	Y	Y
2 Polis	Y	Y	Y	Y	Y	Y	Y
3 Salazar	Y	Y	Y	Y	Y	Y	Y
4 Markey	Y	Y	Y	Y	Y	Y	Y
5 Lamborn	Y	Y	Y	Y	Y	N	N
6 Coffman	Y	+	Y	Y	Y	N	N
7 Perlmutter	Y	Y	Y	Y	Y	Y	Y
CONNECTICUT							
1 Larson	Y	Y	Y	Y	Y	Y	Y
2 Courtney	Y	Y	Y	Y	Y	Y	Y
3 DeLauro	Y	Y	Y	Y	Y	Y	Y
4 Himes	Y	Y	Y	Y	Y	Y	Y
5 Murphy	Y	Y	Y	Y	?	Y	Y
DELAWARE							
AL Castle	Y	Y	Y	Y	Y	Y	N
FLORIDA							
1 Miller	Y	Y	Y	Y	Y	N	N
2 Boyd	Y	Y	Y	Y	Y	Y	Y
3 Brown	Y	Y	Y	Y	Y	Y	Y
4 Crenshaw	Y	Y	Y	Y	Y	N	N
5 Brown-Waite	Y	Y	Y	Y	Y	N	N
6 Stearns	Y	Y	Y	Y	Y	N	N
7 Mica	Y	Y	Y	Y	Y	N	N
8 Grayson	Y	Y	Y	Y	Y	Y	Y
9 Bilirakis	Y	Y	Y	Y	Y	N	N
10 Young	?	?	?	?	?	?	?
11 Castor	Y	Y	Y	Y	Y	Y	Y
12 Putnam	Y	Y	Y	Y	Y	N	N
13 Buchanan	Y	Y	Y	Y	Y	N	N
14 Mack	Y	Y	Y	Y	Y	N	N
15 Posey	Y	Y	Y	Y	?	N	N
16 Rooney	Y	Y	Y	Y	Y	N	N
17 Meek	Y	Y	Y	Y	Y	Y	Y
18 Ros-Lehtinen	Y	Y	Y	Y	Y	N	N
19 Wexler	Y	Y	Y	Y	Y	Y	Y
20 Wasserman Schultz	Y	Y	Y	Y	Y	Y	Y
21 Diaz-Balart, L.	Y	Y	Y	Y	Y	N	N
22 Klein	Y	Y	Y	Y	Y	Y	Y
23 Hastings	Y	Y	Y	Y	Y	Y	Y
24 Kosmas	Y	Y	Y	?	Y	Y	Y
25 Diaz-Balart, M.	Y	Y	Y	Y	Y	N	N
GEORGIA							
1 Kingston	Y	Y	Y	Y	Y	N	N
2 Bishop	Y	Y	Y	Y	Y	Y	Y
3 Westmoreland	Y	Y	Y	Y	Y	N	N
4 Johnson	?	?	Y	Y	Y	Y	Y
5 Lewis	Y	Y	Y	Y	Y	Y	Y
6 Price	Y	Y	Y	Y	?	-	-
7 Linder	Y	Y	Y	Y	Y	N	N
8 Marshall	Y	Y	Y	Y	Y	N	N
9 Deal	Y	Y	Y	Y	Y	N	N
10 Broun	Y	Y	Y	Y	Y	N	N
11 Gingrey	Y	Y	Y	Y	Y	N	N
12 Barrow	Y	Y	Y	Y	Y	Y	Y
13 Scott	Y	Y	Y	Y	Y	Y	Y
HAWAII							
1 Abercrombie	Y	Y	Y	Y	Y	Y	Y
2 Hirono	Y	Y	Y	Y	Y	Y	Y
IDAHO							
1 Minnick	Y	Y	Y	Y	Y	N	N
2 Simpson	Y	Y	Y	?	Y	N	N
ILLINOIS							
1 Rush	Y	Y	?	Y	Y	Y	Y
2 Jackson	Y	Y	Y	Y	Y	Y	Y
3 Lipinski	Y	Y	Y	Y	Y	Y	N
4 Gutierrez	Y	Y	Y	?	?	Y	Y
5 Quigley	Y	Y	Y	Y	Y	Y	Y
6 Roskam	Y	Y	Y	Y	Y	N	N
7 Davis	Y	Y	Y	Y	Y	Y	Y
8 Bean	Y	Y	Y	?	Y	Y	Y
9 Schakowsky	Y	Y	Y	Y	Y	Y	Y
10 Kirk	Y	Y	Y	Y	Y	N	N
11 Halvorson	Y	Y	Y	+	Y	Y	Y
12 Costello	Y	Y	Y	Y	Y	N	N
13 Biggert	Y	Y	Y	Y	Y	N	N
14 Foster	Y	Y	Y	?	Y	Y	Y
15 Johnson	Y	Y	Y	Y	Y	N	N

KEY Republicans   Democrats

Y Voted for (yea)	X Paired against	C Voted "present" to avoid possible conflict of interest
# Paired for	– Announced against	
+ Announced for	P Voted "present"	? Did not vote or otherwise make a position known
N Voted against (nay)		

*Rep. Judy Chu, D-Calif., was sworn in July 16, 2009, to fill the seat vacated by Hilda L. Solis, who resigned to become secretary of Labor. The first vote for which Chu was eligible was vote 549.

	547	548	549	550	551	552	553
16 **Manzullo**	Y	Y	Y	Y	Y	N	N
17 Hare	Y	Y	Y	Y	Y	Y	Y
18 **Schock**	Y	Y	Y	Y	Y	N	N
19 **Shimkus**	Y	Y	Y	Y	Y	N	N
INDIANA							
1 Visclosky	Y	Y	Y	Y	Y	Y	Y
2 Donnelly	Y	Y	Y	Y	Y	N	N
3 **Souder**	Y	Y	Y	Y	Y	N	N
4 **Buyer**	Y	Y	Y	Y	Y	N	N
5 **Burton**	Y	Y	Y	Y	Y	N	N
6 **Pence**	Y	?	?	?	?	?	?
7 Carson	Y	Y	Y	Y	Y	Y	Y
8 Ellsworth	Y	Y	Y	Y	Y	N	N
9 Hill	Y	Y	Y	Y	Y	N	N
IOWA							
1 Braley	Y	Y	Y	Y	Y	Y	Y
2 Loebsack	Y	Y	Y	Y	Y	Y	Y
3 Boswell	Y	Y	Y	Y	Y	Y	Y
4 **Latham**	Y	Y	Y	Y	Y	N	N
5 **King**	Y	Y	Y	Y	Y	N	N
KANSAS							
1 **Moran**	Y	Y	Y	Y	Y	N	N
2 **Jenkins**	Y	Y	Y	Y	Y	N	N
3 Moore	Y	Y	Y	?	Y	Y	Y
4 **Tiahrt**	Y	Y	Y	Y	Y	N	N
KENTUCKY							
1 **Whitfield**	Y	Y	Y	Y	Y	N	N
2 **Guthrie**	Y	Y	Y	Y	Y	N	N
3 Yarmuth	Y	Y	Y	Y	Y	Y	Y
4 **Davis**	Y	Y	Y	Y	Y	N	N
5 **Rogers**	Y	Y	Y	Y	Y	N	N
6 Chandler	Y	Y	Y	Y	Y	Y	Y
LOUISIANA							
1 **Scalise**	Y	Y	Y	Y	Y	N	N
2 **Cao**	Y	Y	Y	Y	Y	N	N
3 Melancon	Y	Y	Y	Y	Y	N	N
4 **Fleming**	Y	Y	Y	Y	Y	N	N
5 **Alexander**	Y	Y	Y	Y	Y	N	N
6 **Cassidy**	Y	Y	Y	Y	Y	N	N
7 **Boustany**	Y	Y	Y	Y	Y	N	N
MAINE							
1 Pingree	Y	Y	Y	Y	Y	Y	Y
2 Michaud	Y	Y	Y	Y	Y	N	N
MARYLAND							
1 Kratovil	Y	Y	Y	Y	Y	Y	Y
2 Ruppersberger	Y	Y	Y	Y	Y	Y	Y
3 Sarbanes	Y	Y	Y	Y	Y	Y	Y
4 Edwards	Y	Y	Y	Y	Y	Y	Y
5 Hoyer	Y	Y	Y	Y	Y	Y	Y
6 **Bartlett**	Y	Y	Y	Y	Y	N	N
7 Cummings	Y	Y	Y	Y	Y	Y	Y
8 Van Hollen	Y	Y	Y	Y	Y	Y	Y
MASSACHUSETTS							
1 Olver	Y	Y	Y	Y	?	Y	Y
2 Neal	Y	Y	Y	Y	Y	Y	Y
3 McGovern	Y	Y	Y	Y	Y	Y	Y
4 Frank	Y	Y	Y	Y	Y	Y	Y
5 Tsongas	Y	Y	Y	Y	Y	Y	Y
6 Tierney	Y	Y	Y	Y	Y	Y	Y
7 Markey	Y	Y	Y	Y	Y	Y	Y
8 Capuano	Y	Y	Y	Y	Y	Y	Y
9 Lynch	Y	Y	Y	Y	Y	Y	Y
10 Delahunt	Y	Y	Y	Y	Y	Y	Y
MICHIGAN							
1 Stupak	Y	Y	Y	Y	Y	N	N
2 **Hoekstra**	Y	Y	Y	Y	Y	N	N
3 **Ehlers**	Y	Y	Y	Y	Y	N	N
4 **Camp**	Y	Y	Y	Y	Y	N	N
5 Kildee	Y	Y	Y	Y	Y	N	N
6 **Upton**	Y	Y	Y	Y	Y	N	N
7 Schauer	Y	Y	Y	Y	Y	Y	Y
8 **Rogers**	Y	Y	Y	Y	Y	N	N
9 Peters	Y	Y	Y	Y	Y	Y	Y
10 **Miller**	Y	Y	Y	Y	Y	N	N
11 **McCotter**	Y	Y	Y	Y	Y	N	N
12 Levin	Y	Y	Y	Y	Y	Y	Y
13 Kilpatrick	Y	Y	Y	Y	Y	Y	Y
14 Conyers	Y	Y	Y	Y	Y	Y	Y
15 Dingell	Y	?	Y	Y	Y	N	Y
MINNESOTA							
1 Walz	Y	Y	Y	Y	Y	Y	Y
2 **Kline**	Y	Y	Y	Y	Y	N	N
3 **Paulsen**	Y	Y	Y	Y	Y	N	N
4 McCollum	Y	Y	Y	Y	Y	Y	Y
5 Ellison	Y	Y	Y	Y	Y	Y	Y
6 **Bachmann**	Y	Y	Y	Y	Y	N	N
7 Peterson	Y	Y	Y	Y	Y	N	N
8 Oberstar	Y	?	Y	Y	Y	N	N
MISSISSIPPI							
1 Childers	Y	Y	Y	Y	Y	N	N
2 Thompson	Y	Y	Y	Y	Y	Y	Y
3 **Harper**	Y	Y	Y	Y	Y	N	N
4 Taylor	Y	Y	Y	Y	Y	N	N
MISSOURI							
1 Clay	Y	Y	?	Y	Y	Y	Y
2 **Akin**	Y	Y	Y	Y	Y	N	N
3 Carnahan	Y	Y	Y	Y	Y	Y	Y
4 Skelton	Y	Y	Y	Y	Y	N	N
5 Cleaver	Y	Y	Y	Y	Y	Y	Y
6 **Graves**	Y	Y	Y	Y	Y	N	N
7 **Blunt**	Y	Y	Y	Y	Y	N	N
8 **Emerson**	Y	Y	Y	Y	Y	N	N
9 **Luetkemeyer**	Y	Y	Y	Y	Y	N	N
MONTANA							
AL **Rehberg**	Y	Y	Y	Y	Y	N	N
NEBRASKA							
1 **Fortenberry**	Y	Y	Y	Y	Y	N	N
2 **Terry**	Y	Y	Y	Y	Y	N	N
3 **Smith**	Y	Y	Y	Y	Y	N	N
NEVADA							
1 Berkley	Y	Y	Y	Y	Y	Y	Y
2 **Heller**	Y	Y	Y	Y	Y	N	N
3 Titus	Y	Y	?	Y	Y	Y	Y
NEW HAMPSHIRE							
1 Shea-Porter	Y	Y	Y	Y	Y	Y	Y
2 Hodes	Y	Y	Y	Y	Y	Y	Y
NEW JERSEY							
1 Andrews	Y	Y	Y	Y	Y	Y	Y
2 **LoBiondo**	Y	Y	Y	Y	Y	N	N
3 Adler	Y	Y	Y	+	Y	Y	Y
4 **Smith**	Y	Y	Y	Y	Y	N	N
5 **Garrett**	Y	Y	Y	Y	Y	N	N
6 Pallone	Y	Y	Y	Y	Y	Y	Y
7 **Lance**	Y	Y	Y	Y	Y	N	N
8 Pascrell	Y	Y	Y	Y	Y	Y	Y
9 Rothman	Y	Y	Y	Y	Y	Y	Y
10 Payne	Y	Y	Y	Y	Y	Y	Y
11 **Frelinghuysen**	Y	Y	Y	Y	Y	N	N
12 Holt	Y	Y	Y	Y	Y	Y	Y
13 Sires	Y	Y	?	Y	Y	Y	Y
NEW MEXICO							
1 Heinrich	Y	Y	Y	?	Y	Y	Y
2 Teague	Y	Y	Y	Y	Y	Y	Y
3 Lujan	Y	Y	Y	Y	Y	Y	Y
NEW YORK							
1 Bishop	Y	Y	Y	Y	Y	Y	Y
2 Israel	Y	Y	Y	?	Y	Y	Y
3 **King**	Y	Y	Y	Y	Y	N	N
4 McCarthy	Y	Y	Y	Y	Y	Y	Y
5 Ackerman	Y	Y	Y	Y	Y	Y	Y
6 Meeks	Y	Y	Y	Y	Y	Y	Y
7 Crowley	Y	Y	Y	?	Y	Y	Y
8 Nadler	Y	Y	Y	Y	Y	Y	Y
9 Weiner	Y	Y	Y	Y	Y	Y	Y
10 Towns	Y	Y	Y	Y	Y	Y	Y
11 Clarke	Y	Y	Y	Y	Y	Y	Y
12 Velázquez	Y	Y	?	Y	Y	Y	Y
13 McMahon	Y	Y	Y	+	Y	Y	Y
14 Maloney	Y	Y	Y	Y	?	Y	Y
15 Rangel	Y	Y	Y	Y	Y	Y	Y
16 Serrano	Y	Y	Y	?	Y	Y	Y
17 Engel	Y	Y	Y	Y	Y	Y	Y
18 Lowey	Y	Y	Y	Y	Y	Y	Y
19 Hall	Y	Y	Y	Y	Y	Y	Y
20 Murphy	Y	Y	Y	?	Y	Y	Y
21 Tonko	Y	Y	Y	Y	Y	Y	Y
22 Hinchey	Y	Y	Y	Y	Y	Y	Y
23 **McHugh**	Y	Y	Y	Y	Y	N	N
24 Arcuri	Y	Y	Y	Y	Y	Y	Y
25 Maffei	Y	Y	Y	Y	Y	Y	Y
26 **Lee**	Y	Y	Y	Y	Y	N	N
27 Higgins	Y	Y	Y	Y	Y	Y	Y
28 Slaughter	Y	Y	Y	Y	Y	Y	Y
29 Massa	Y	Y	Y	Y	Y	Y	Y
NORTH CAROLINA							
1 Butterfield	Y	Y	Y	Y	Y	Y	Y
2 Etheridge	Y	Y	Y	Y	Y	Y	Y
3 **Jones**	Y	Y	Y	Y	Y	N	N
4 Price	Y	Y	Y	Y	Y	Y	Y
5 **Foxx**	Y	Y	Y	Y	Y	N	N
6 **Coble**	Y	Y	Y	Y	Y	N	N
7 McIntyre	Y	Y	Y	Y	?	N	N
8 Kissell	Y	Y	Y	Y	Y	Y	Y
9 **Myrick**	Y	Y	Y	Y	Y	N	N
10 **McHenry**	Y	Y	Y	Y	Y	N	N
11 Shuler	Y	Y	Y	Y	Y	N	N
12 Watt	Y	Y	Y	Y	Y	Y	Y
13 Miller	Y	Y	Y	Y	Y	Y	Y
NORTH DAKOTA							
AL Pomeroy	Y	Y	Y	Y	Y	Y	Y
OHIO							
1 Driehaus	Y	Y	Y	Y	Y	N	N
2 **Schmidt**	Y	Y	Y	Y	Y	N	N
3 **Turner**	Y	Y	Y	Y	Y	N	N
4 **Jordan**	Y	Y	Y	Y	Y	N	N
5 **Latta**	Y	Y	Y	Y	Y	N	N
6 Wilson	Y	Y	Y	Y	Y	Y	N
7 **Austria**	Y	Y	Y	Y	Y	N	N
8 **Boehner**	Y	Y	Y	Y	Y	N	N
9 Kaptur	Y	Y	Y	Y	Y	Y	Y
10 Kucinich	Y	Y	Y	Y	Y	Y	Y
11 Fudge	Y	Y	Y	Y	Y	Y	Y
12 **Tiberi**	Y	Y	Y	Y	Y	N	N
13 Sutton	Y	Y	Y	Y	Y	Y	Y
14 **LaTourette**	Y	Y	Y	Y	?	N	N
15 Kilroy	Y	Y	Y	Y	Y	Y	Y
16 Boccieri	Y	Y	Y	Y	Y	N	N
17 Ryan	Y	Y	Y	Y	Y	Y	Y
18 Space	Y	Y	Y	Y	Y	Y	Y
OKLAHOMA							
1 **Sullivan**	Y	Y	Y	Y	Y	N	N
2 Boren	Y	Y	Y	Y	Y	N	N
3 **Lucas**	Y	?	?	?	?	?	?
4 **Cole**	Y	Y	Y	?	Y	N	N
5 **Fallin**	Y	Y	Y	?	Y	N	N
OREGON							
1 Wu	Y	Y	Y	Y	Y	Y	Y
2 **Walden**	Y	Y	Y	Y	Y	N	N
3 Blumenauer	Y	Y	Y	Y	Y	Y	Y
4 DeFazio	Y	Y	Y	Y	Y	Y	Y
5 Schrader	?	?	?	?	?	?	?
PENNSYLVANIA							
1 Brady	Y	Y	Y	Y	Y	Y	Y
2 Fattah	Y	Y	Y	Y	Y	Y	Y
3 Dahlkemper	Y	Y	Y	Y	Y	N	N
4 Altmire	Y	Y	Y	Y	Y	Y	N
5 **Thompson**	Y	Y	Y	Y	Y	N	N
6 **Gerlach**	Y	Y	Y	Y	Y	N	N
7 Sestak	?	Y	Y	Y	?	Y	Y
8 Murphy, P.	Y	Y	Y	Y	Y	Y	Y
9 **Shuster**	Y	Y	Y	Y	Y	N	N
10 Carney	Y	Y	Y	Y	Y	Y	N
11 Kanjorski	Y	Y	Y	Y	Y	Y	N
12 Murtha	Y	Y	Y	Y	Y	Y	N
13 Schwartz	Y	Y	Y	?	Y	Y	Y
14 Doyle	Y	Y	Y	Y	Y	Y	N
15 **Dent**	Y	Y	Y	Y	Y	N	N
16 **Pitts**	Y	Y	Y	Y	Y	N	N
17 Holden	Y	Y	Y	Y	Y	Y	N
18 **Murphy, T.**	Y	Y	Y	Y	Y	N	N
19 **Platts**	Y	Y	Y	Y	Y	N	N
RHODE ISLAND							
1 Kennedy	Y	Y	Y	Y	?	Y	Y
2 Langevin	Y	Y	Y	Y	Y	Y	Y
SOUTH CAROLINA							
1 **Brown**	Y	Y	Y	Y	Y	N	N
2 **Wilson**	Y	Y	Y	Y	Y	N	N
3 **Barrett**	Y	Y	Y	Y	Y	N	N
4 **Inglis**	Y	Y	Y	Y	Y	N	N
5 Spratt	Y	Y	Y	Y	Y	Y	Y
6 Clyburn	Y	Y	Y	Y	Y	Y	Y
SOUTH DAKOTA							
AL Herseth Sandlin	Y	Y	Y	Y	Y	Y	Y
TENNESSEE							
1 **Roe**	Y	Y	Y	Y	Y	N	N
2 **Duncan**	Y	Y	Y	Y	Y	N	N
3 **Wamp**	Y	Y	Y	Y	Y	N	N
4 Davis	Y	Y	Y	Y	Y	Y	N
5 Cooper	Y	Y	Y	Y	Y	Y	Y
6 Gordon	Y	Y	Y	Y	Y	Y	Y
7 **Blackburn**	Y	Y	Y	Y	Y	N	N
8 Tanner	Y	Y	Y	Y	Y	Y	Y
9 Cohen	Y	Y	Y	Y	Y	Y	Y
TEXAS							
1 **Gohmert**	Y	?	Y	Y	Y	N	N
2 **Poe**	Y	Y	Y	Y	Y	N	N
3 **Johnson, S.**	Y	Y	Y	Y	Y	N	N
4 **Hall**	Y	Y	?	Y	Y	N	N
5 **Hensarling**	Y	Y	Y	Y	Y	N	N
6 **Barton**	Y	Y	Y	?	?	N	N
7 **Culberson**	Y	Y	Y	Y	?	N	N
8 **Brady**	Y	Y	Y	Y	Y	N	N
9 Green, A.	Y	Y	Y	Y	Y	Y	Y
10 **McCaul**	Y	Y	Y	Y	Y	N	N
11 **Conaway**	Y	Y	Y	?	?	N	N
12 **Granger**	Y	Y	Y	?	?	N	N
13 **Thornberry**	Y	Y	Y	?	?	N	N
14 **Paul**	Y	Y	Y	Y	Y	N	N
15 Hinojosa	Y	Y	Y	Y	Y	Y	Y
16 Reyes	Y	Y	Y	Y	Y	Y	Y
17 Edwards	Y	Y	Y	Y	Y	Y	Y
18 Jackson Lee	Y	Y	Y	Y	Y	Y	Y
19 **Neugebauer**	Y	Y	Y	Y	Y	N	N
20 Gonzalez	Y	Y	Y	Y	Y	Y	Y
21 **Smith**	Y	Y	Y	?	?	N	N
22 **Olson**	Y	Y	Y	?	?	N	N
23 Rodriguez	Y	Y	Y	Y	?	Y	Y
24 **Marchant**	Y	Y	Y	Y	Y	N	N
25 Doggett	Y	Y	Y	Y	Y	Y	Y
26 **Burgess**	Y	Y	Y	?	?	N	N
27 Ortiz	Y	Y	Y	Y	Y	N	Y
28 Cuellar	Y	Y	Y	Y	Y	Y	Y
29 Green, G.	Y	Y	Y	Y	Y	Y	Y
30 Johnson, E.	Y	Y	Y	Y	Y	Y	Y
31 **Carter**	Y	Y	Y	?	?	N	N
32 **Sessions**	Y	Y	Y	Y	Y	N	N
UTAH							
1 **Bishop**	Y	Y	Y	Y	Y	N	N
2 Matheson	Y	Y	Y	Y	Y	Y	Y
3 **Chaffetz**	Y	Y	Y	Y	Y	N	N
VERMONT							
AL Welch	Y	Y	Y	Y	Y	Y	Y
VIRGINIA							
1 **Wittman**	Y	Y	Y	Y	Y	N	N
2 Nye	Y	Y	Y	Y	Y	N	N
3 Scott	Y	Y	Y	Y	Y	Y	Y
4 **Forbes**	Y	Y	Y	Y	Y	N	N
5 Perriello	Y	Y	Y	Y	Y	Y	N
6 **Goodlatte**	Y	Y	Y	Y	Y	N	N
7 **Cantor**	Y	Y	Y	Y	Y	N	N
8 Moran	Y	Y	Y	Y	Y	Y	Y
9 Boucher	Y	Y	Y	Y	Y	Y	Y
10 **Wolf**	Y	Y	Y	Y	Y	N	N
11 Connolly	Y	Y	Y	Y	Y	Y	Y
WASHINGTON							
1 Inslee	Y	Y	Y	?	Y	Y	Y
2 Larsen	Y	Y	Y	Y	Y	Y	Y
3 Baird	N	Y	Y	Y	Y	Y	Y
4 **Hastings**	Y	Y	Y	Y	Y	N	N
5 **McMorris Rodgers**	Y	Y	Y	Y	Y	N	N
6 Dicks	Y	Y	Y	Y	Y	Y	Y
7 McDermott	Y	Y	Y	Y	Y	Y	Y
8 **Reichert**	Y	Y	Y	Y	Y	N	N
9 Smith	Y	Y	Y	Y	Y	Y	Y
WEST VIRGINIA							
1 Mollohan	Y	Y	Y	Y	Y	Y	N
2 **Capito**	Y	Y	Y	Y	Y	N	N
3 Rahall	Y	Y	Y	Y	Y	Y	N
WISCONSIN							
1 **Ryan**	Y	Y	Y	Y	Y	N	N
2 Baldwin	Y	Y	Y	Y	Y	Y	Y
3 Kind	Y	Y	Y	?	Y	Y	Y
4 Moore	Y	Y	Y	Y	Y	Y	Y
5 **Sensenbrenner**	Y	Y	Y	Y	Y	N	N
6 **Petri**	Y	Y	Y	Y	Y	N	N
7 Obey	Y	Y	Y	Y	Y	Y	Y
8 Kagen	Y	Y	Y	Y	Y	Y	Y
WYOMING							
AL **Lummis**	Y	Y	Y	Y	Y	N	N
DELEGATES							
Faleomavaega (A.S.)	?						
Norton (D.C.)	Y						
Bordallo (Guam)	Y						
Sablan (N. Marianas)	Y						
Pierluisi (P.R.)	Y						
Christensen (V.I.)	Y						

IN THE HOUSE | By Vote Number

554. **H Res 543. Home Safety Month/Adoption.** Halvorson, D-Ill., motion to suspend the rules and adopt the resolution that would express support for the designation of June as Home Safety Month. Motion agreed to 416-9: R 163-9; D 253-0. A two-thirds majority of those present and voting (284 in this case) is required for adoption under suspension of the rules. July 16, 2009.

555. **HR 3170. Fiscal 2010 Financial Services Appropriations/ Council of Economic Advisers.** Price, R-Ga., amendment that would strike $4 million in funding for the Council of Economic Advisers' salaries and expenses. Rejected in Committee of the Whole 146-279: R 139-34; D 7-245. A "nay" was a vote in support of the president's position. July 16, 2009.

556. **HR 3170. Fiscal 2010 Financial Services Appropriations/ Election Assistance Commission.** Emerson, R-Mo., amendment that would reduce the amount provided for the Election Assistance Commission for election reform programs by $50 million. Rejected in Committee of the Whole 172-250: R 157-15; D 15-235. July 16, 2009.

557. **HR 3170. Fiscal 2010 Financial Services Appropriations/ Discretionary Spending Reduction.** Blackburn, R-Tenn., amendment that would reduce discretionary spending in the bill by 5 percent. Rejected in Committee of the Whole 184-247: R 164-11; D 20-236. A "nay" was a vote in support of the president's position. July 16, 2009.

558. **HR 3170. Fiscal 2010 Financial Services Appropriations/ Council on Environmental Quality.** Broun, R-Ga., amendment that would bar the use of funds appropriated in the bill for salaries for the assistant to the president on energy and climate change, the deputy assistant to the president on energy and climate change, or any position in the Council on Environmental Quality. Rejected in Committee of the Whole 149-282: R 148-27; D 1-255. A "nay" was a vote in support of the president's position. July 16, 2009.

559. **HR 3170. Fiscal 2010 Financial Services Appropriations/ Small-Business Incubator Project.** Flake, R-Ariz., amendment that would bar the use of funds appropriated in the bill for a small-business incubator project at the University of West Georgia in Carrollton, Ga., and cut $100,000 intended for the project from the bill. Rejected in Committee of the Whole 89-342: R 80-95; D 9-247. July 16, 2009.

560. **HR 3170. Fiscal 2010 Financial Services Appropriations/ Commercial Driver Training Institute.** Flake, R-Ariz., amendment that would bar the use of funds appropriated in the bill for the Commercial Driver Training Institute project of Arkansas State University in Newport, Ark., and cut $200,000 intended for the project from the bill. Rejected in Committee of the Whole 115-314: R 109-65; D 6-249. July 16, 2009.

	554	555	556	557	558	559	560
ALABAMA							
1 **Bonner**	Y	Y	Y	Y	Y	N	N
2 Bright	Y	Y	Y	Y	N	Y	Y
3 **Rogers**	Y	Y	Y	Y	Y	N	N
4 **Aderholt**	Y	Y	Y	Y	Y	N	N
5 Griffith	Y	N	N	N	N	N	N
6 **Bachus**	Y	N	Y	Y	Y	N	N
7 Davis	Y	N	N	N	N	N	N
ALASKA							
AL **Young**	Y	Y	Y	N	Y	N	N
ARIZONA							
1 Kirkpatrick	Y	N	N	Y	N	N	N
2 **Franks**	Y	Y	Y	Y	Y	Y	Y
3 **Shadegg**	N	Y	Y	Y	Y	Y	Y
4 Pastor	Y	N	N	N	N	N	N
5 Mitchell	Y	N	N	Y	N	N	N
6 **Flake**	N	Y	Y	Y	Y	Y	Y
7 Grijalva	Y	N	N	N	N	N	N
8 Giffords	Y	N	N	Y	N	Y	N
ARKANSAS							
1 Berry	Y	N	N	N	N	N	N
2 Snyder	Y	N	N	N	N	N	N
3 **Boozman**	Y	Y	Y	Y	Y	N	N
4 Ross	Y	N	N	N	N	N	N
CALIFORNIA							
1 Thompson	Y	N	N	N	N	N	N
2 **Herger**	Y	Y	Y	Y	Y	Y	Y
3 **Lungren**	Y	N	Y	Y	Y	Y	Y
4 **McClintock**	Y	Y	Y	Y	Y	Y	Y
5 Matsui	Y	N	N	N	N	N	N
6 Woolsey	Y	N	N	N	N	N	N
7 Miller, George	Y	N	?	N	N	N	N
8 Pelosi							
9 Lee	Y	N	N	N	N	N	N
10 Vacant							
11 McNerney	Y	N	N	N	N	N	N
12 Speier	Y	N	N	N	N	Y	N
13 Stark	Y	N	N	N	N	N	N
14 Eshoo	Y	N	N	N	N	N	N
15 Honda	Y	N	N	N	N	N	N
16 Lofgren	Y	N	N	N	N	N	N
17 Farr	Y	N	N	N	N	N	N
18 Cardoza	Y	N	N	N	N	N	N
19 **Radanovich**	Y	N	Y	Y	Y	N	N
20 Costa	Y	?	N	N	N	N	N
21 **Nunes**	Y	Y	Y	Y	Y	Y	Y
22 **McCarthy**	Y	Y	Y	Y	Y	N	Y
23 Capps	Y	N	N	N	N	N	N
24 **Gallegly**	Y	Y	Y	Y	Y	N	N
25 **McKeon**	Y	Y	Y	Y	Y	N	N
26 **Dreier**	Y	Y	Y	Y	Y	Y	N
27 Sherman	Y	N	N	N	N	N	N
28 Berman	Y	N	N	N	N	N	N
29 Schiff	Y	N	N	N	N	N	N
30 Waxman	Y	N	N	N	N	N	N
31 Becerra	Y	N	N	N	N	N	N
32 Chu	Y	N	N	N	N	N	N
33 Watson	Y	N	N	N	N	N	N
34 Roybal-Allard	Y	N	N	N	N	N	N
35 Waters	Y	N	N	N	N	N	N
36 Harman	Y	N	N	N	N	N	N
37 Richardson	Y	N	N	N	N	N	N
38 Napolitano	Y	Y	N	N	N	N	N
39 Sánchez, Linda	Y	N	N	N	N	N	N
40 **Royce**	Y	Y	Y	Y	Y	Y	Y
41 **Lewis**	Y	N	?	N	Y	N	N
42 **Miller, Gary**	Y	N	Y	Y	Y	N	N
43 Baca	Y	N	N	N	N	N	N
44 **Calvert**	Y	Y	Y	Y	Y	N	N
45 **Bono Mack**	Y	Y	Y	N	N	N	N
46 **Rohrabacher**	Y	Y	Y	N	Y	Y	Y
47 Sanchez, Loretta	Y	N	N	N	N	N	N
48 **Campbell**	Y	Y	Y	Y	Y	Y	Y
49 **Issa**	P	Y	Y	Y	Y	Y	Y
50 **Bilbray**	Y	Y	Y	Y	N	Y	N
51 Filner	Y	N	N	N	N	N	N
52 **Hunter**	Y	Y	Y	Y	Y	N	N
53 Davis	Y	N	N	N	N	N	N

	554	555	556	557	558	559	560
COLORADO							
1 DeGette	Y	N	N	N	N	N	N
2 Polis	Y	N	N	N	N	N	N
3 Salazar	Y	N	?	N	N	N	N
4 Markey	Y	N	N	N	N	N	N
5 **Lamborn**	Y	Y	Y	Y	Y	Y	Y
6 **Coffman**	Y	Y	Y	Y	Y	Y	Y
7 Perlmutter	Y	N	N	N	N	N	N
CONNECTICUT							
1 Larson	Y	N	Y	N	N	N	N
2 Courtney	Y	N	N	N	N	N	N
3 DeLauro	Y	N	N	N	N	N	N
4 Himes	Y	N	N	N	N	N	N
5 Murphy	Y	N	N	N	N	N	N
DELAWARE							
AL **Castle**	Y	N	Y	Y	N	N	Y
FLORIDA							
1 **Miller**	Y	Y	Y	Y	Y	Y	Y
2 Boyd	Y	N	N	N	N	N	N
3 Brown	Y	N	N	N	N	N	N
4 **Crenshaw**	Y	Y	Y	N	N	N	N
5 **Brown-Waite**	Y	N	Y	N	Y	N	Y
6 **Stearns**	Y	Y	Y	Y	Y	Y	Y
7 **Mica**	Y	Y	Y	Y	Y	N	N
8 Grayson	Y	N	N	N	N	N	N
9 **Bilirakis**	Y	Y	Y	Y	Y	N	N
10 **Young**	?	Y	Y	Y	N	N	N
11 Castor	Y	N	N	N	N	N	N
12 **Putnam**	Y	N	Y	N	N	N	N
13 **Buchanan**	Y	N	Y	Y	N	N	Y
14 **Mack**	Y	Y	Y	Y	Y	Y	Y
15 **Posey**	Y	Y	Y	Y	Y	Y	Y
16 **Rooney**	N	Y	Y	Y	Y	N	N
17 Meek	Y	N	N	N	N	N	N
18 **Ros-Lehtinen**	Y	N	Y	N	N	N	N
19 Wexler	Y	N	N	N	N	N	N
20 Wasserman Schultz	Y	N	N	N	N	N	N
21 **Diaz-Balart, L.**	Y	N	Y	N	N	N	N
22 Klein	Y	N	N	N	N	N	N
23 Hastings	Y	N	N	N	N	N	N
24 Kosmas	Y	N	N	N	N	N	N
25 **Diaz-Balart, M.**	Y	N	Y	N	N	N	N
GEORGIA							
1 **Kingston**	N	Y	Y	Y	Y	Y	Y
2 Bishop	Y	N	N	N	N	N	N
3 **Westmoreland**	Y	Y	Y	Y	Y	Y	Y
4 Johnson	Y	N	N	N	N	N	N
5 Lewis	Y	N	N	N	N	N	N
6 **Price**	Y	Y	Y	Y	Y	Y	Y
7 **Linder**	Y	Y	Y	Y	Y	Y	Y
8 Marshall	Y	N	Y	N	N	N	N
9 **Deal**	Y	Y	Y	Y	Y	N	Y
10 **Broun**	Y	Y	Y	Y	Y	Y	Y
11 **Gingrey**	Y	Y	Y	Y	Y	Y	Y
12 Barrow	Y	N	N	N	N	N	N
13 Scott	Y	N	N	N	N	N	N
HAWAII							
1 Abercrombie	Y	N	N	N	N	N	N
2 Hirono	Y	N	N	N	N	N	N
IDAHO							
1 Minnick	Y	N	Y	N	N	Y	Y
2 **Simpson**	Y	N	Y	Y	N	N	N
ILLINOIS							
1 Rush	Y	N	N	N	N	N	N
2 Jackson	Y	N	N	N	N	N	N
3 Lipinski	Y	N	N	Y	N	N	N
4 Gutierrez	Y	N	N	Y	N	N	N
5 Quigley	Y	N	N	N	N	N	N
6 **Roskam**	Y	Y	Y	Y	Y	N	Y
7 Davis	Y	N	N	N	N	N	N
8 Bean	Y	N	N	N	N	N	N
9 Schakowsky	Y	N	N	N	Y	N	N
10 **Kirk**	Y	Y	N	N	N	N	N
11 Halvorson	Y	N	N	N	N	N	N
12 Costello	Y	N	Y	N	N	N	N
13 **Biggert**	Y	Y	Y	Y	Y	N	N
14 Foster	Y	N	N	N	N	N	N
15 **Johnson**	Y	Y	Y	Y	Y	Y	Y

KEY	**Republicans**		Democrats			
Y	Voted for (yea)		X	Paired against	C	Voted "present" to avoid possible conflict of interest
#	Paired for		–	Announced against		
+	Announced for		P	Voted "present"	?	Did not vote or otherwise make a position known
N	Voted against (nay)					

	554	555	556	557	558	559	560
16 **Manzullo**	Y	Y	Y	Y	Y	N	Y
17 Hare	Y	N	N	N	N	N	N
18 **Schock**	Y	Y	N	Y	Y	N	Y
19 **Shimkus**	Y	Y	Y	Y	Y	Y	Y
INDIANA							
1 Visclosky	Y	N	N	N	N	N	N
2 Donnelly	Y	N	N	N	N	N	N
3 **Souder**	Y	Y	Y	Y	Y	N	Y
4 **Buyer**	Y	Y	Y	Y	Y	Y	N
5 **Burton**	Y	Y	Y	Y	Y	N	Y
6 **Pence**	?	?	?	?	?	?	?
7 Carson	Y	N	N	N	N	N	N
8 Ellsworth	Y	N	N	N	N	N	N
9 Hill	Y	N	N	N	N	N	N
IOWA							
1 Braley	Y	N	–	N	N	N	N
2 Loebsack	Y	N	N	N	N	N	N
3 Boswell	Y	N	N	N	N	N	N
4 **Latham**	Y	Y	Y	Y	Y	N	N
5 **King**	Y	Y	Y	Y	Y	Y	Y
KANSAS							
1 **Moran**	Y	Y	N	Y	Y	Y	Y
2 **Jenkins**	Y	Y	Y	Y	N	Y	Y
3 Moore	Y	N	N	N	N	N	N
4 **Tiahrt**	Y	Y	Y	Y	Y	N	N
KENTUCKY							
1 **Whitfield**	Y	N	Y	Y	Y	N	N
2 **Guthrie**	Y	Y	Y	Y	Y	N	N
3 Yarmuth	Y	N	N	N	N	N	N
4 **Davis**	Y	Y	Y	Y	Y	N	N
5 **Rogers**	Y	Y	Y	N	Y	N	?
6 Chandler	Y	N	N	N	N	N	N
LOUISIANA							
1 **Scalise**	Y	Y	Y	Y	Y	Y	Y
2 **Cao**	Y	Y	Y	Y	N	N	N
3 Melancon	Y	N	N	Y	N	N	N
4 **Fleming**	Y	Y	Y	Y	Y	Y	Y
5 **Alexander**	Y	Y	Y	Y	Y	N	N
6 **Cassidy**	Y	Y	Y	Y	N	Y	Y
7 **Boustany**	Y	Y	Y	Y	Y	Y	Y
MAINE							
1 Pingree	Y	N	N	N	N	N	N
2 Michaud	Y	Y	N	N	N	N	N
MARYLAND							
1 Kratovil	Y	N	Y	Y	N	N	N
2 Ruppersberger	Y	N	N	N	N	N	N
3 Sarbanes	Y	N	N	N	N	N	N
4 Edwards	Y	N	N	N	N	N	N
5 Hoyer	Y	N	N	N	N	N	N
6 **Bartlett**	Y	Y	Y	Y	Y	N	N
7 Cummings	Y	N	N	N	N	N	N
8 Van Hollen	Y	N	N	N	N	N	N
MASSACHUSETTS							
1 Olver	Y	N	?	N	N	N	?
2 Neal	Y	N	N	N	N	N	N
3 McGovern	Y	N	?	N	N	N	N
4 Frank	Y	N	N	N	N	N	N
5 Tsongas	Y	N	N	N	N	N	N
6 Tierney	Y	N	N	N	N	N	N
7 Markey	Y	N	N	N	N	N	N
8 Capuano	Y	N	N	N	N	N	N
9 Lynch	Y	N	N	N	N	N	N
10 Delahunt	Y	N	N	N	N	N	N
MICHIGAN							
1 Stupak	Y	N	N	N	N	N	N
2 **Hoekstra**	Y	Y	Y	Y	Y	Y	Y
3 **Ehlers**	Y	N	Y	N	N	Y	Y
4 **Camp**	Y	Y	Y	Y	Y	N	N
5 Kildee	Y	N	N	N	N	N	N
6 **Upton**	Y	N	Y	Y	Y	N	Y
7 Schauer	Y	N	N	N	N	N	Y
8 **Rogers**	Y	?	Y	Y	Y	N	Y
9 Peters	Y	N	Y	N	N	N	N
10 **Miller**	Y	N	N	Y	Y	N	N
11 **McCotter**	Y	N	Y	Y	Y	Y	Y
12 Levin	Y	N	N	N	N	N	N
13 Kilpatrick	Y	N	N	N	N	N	N
14 Conyers	Y	N	N	N	N	N	N
15 Dingell	Y	N	N	N	N	N	N
MINNESOTA							
1 Walz	Y	N	N	N	N	N	N
2 **Kline**	Y	Y	Y	Y	Y	Y	Y
3 **Paulsen**	Y	Y	Y	Y	Y	N	Y
4 McCollum	Y	N	N	N	N	N	N

	554	555	556	557	558	559	560
5 Ellison	Y	N	N	N	N	N	N
6 **Bachmann**	Y	Y	Y	Y	Y	Y	Y
7 Peterson	Y	N	N	N	N	N	N
8 Oberstar	Y	N	N	N	N	N	N
MISSISSIPPI							
1 Childers	Y	N	Y	Y	N	N	N
2 Thompson	Y	N	N	N	N	N	N
3 **Harper**	Y	Y	Y	Y	Y	N	N
4 Taylor	Y	N	Y	Y	N	N	N
MISSOURI							
1 Clay	Y	N	N	N	N	N	N
2 **Akin**	Y	Y	Y	Y	Y	N	Y
3 Carnahan	Y	N	N	N	N	N	N
4 Skelton	Y	N	N	N	N	N	N
5 Cleaver	Y	Y	Y	N	N	N	N
6 **Graves**	Y	Y	Y	Y	Y	Y	Y
7 **Blunt**	Y	Y	Y	Y	Y	N	N
8 **Emerson**	Y	N	Y	N	Y	N	N
9 **Luetkemeyer**	Y	Y	Y	Y	Y	Y	Y
MONTANA							
AL **Rehberg**	Y	Y	Y	Y	Y	N	N
NEBRASKA							
1 **Fortenberry**	Y	N	N	Y	N	Y	Y
2 **Terry**	Y	Y	N	Y	Y	N	Y
3 **Smith**	Y	Y	Y	Y	Y	Y	Y
NEVADA							
1 Berkley	Y	N	N	N	N	N	N
2 **Heller**	Y	Y	Y	Y	Y	Y	Y
3 Titus	Y	N	N	N	N	N	N
NEW HAMPSHIRE							
1 Shea-Porter	Y	N	N	N	N	N	N
2 Hodes	Y	N	N	N	N	N	N
NEW JERSEY							
1 Andrews	Y	N	N	N	N	N	N
2 **LoBiondo**	Y	N	N	Y	N	N	N
3 Adler	Y	N	N	Y	N	N	N
4 **Smith**	Y	Y	N	Y	N	N	N
5 **Garrett**	Y	Y	Y	Y	Y	Y	Y
6 Pallone	Y	N	N	N	N	N	N
7 **Lance**	Y	N	Y	Y	N	N	Y
8 Pascrell	Y	N	N	N	N	N	N
9 Rothman	Y	N	N	N	N	N	N
10 Payne	Y	?	N	N	N	N	N
11 **Frelinghuysen**	Y	N	Y	Y	N	N	N
12 Holt	Y	N	N	N	N	N	N
13 Sires	Y	N	N	N	N	N	N
NEW MEXICO							
1 Heinrich	Y	N	N	Y	N	N	N
2 Teague	Y	N	N	N	N	N	N
3 Lujan	Y	N	N	N	N	N	N
NEW YORK							
1 Bishop	Y	N	N	N	N	Y	N
2 Israel	Y	N	N	N	N	N	N
3 **King**	Y	N	N	Y	N	N	N
4 McCarthy	Y	N	N	N	N	N	N
5 Ackerman	Y	N	N	N	N	N	N
6 Meeks	Y	N	N	N	N	N	N
7 Crowley	Y	N	N	N	N	N	N
8 Nadler	Y	N	N	N	N	N	N
9 Weiner	Y	N	N	N	N	N	N
10 Towns	Y	N	N	N	N	N	N
11 Clarke	Y	N	N	N	N	N	N
12 Velázquez	Y	?	?	?	?	?	?
13 McMahon	Y	N	N	N	N	Y	N
14 Maloney	Y	N	N	N	N	N	N
15 Rangel	?	N	?	N	N	N	N
16 Serrano	Y	N	N	N	N	N	N
17 Engel	Y	?	N	N	N	N	N
18 Lowey	Y	N	N	N	N	N	N
19 Hall	Y	N	N	N	N	N	N
20 Murphy	Y	N	N	N	N	N	N
21 Tonko	Y	N	N	N	N	N	N
22 Hinchey	Y	N	N	N	N	N	N
23 **McHugh**	Y	N	N	N	N	N	N
24 Arcuri	Y	N	Y	Y	N	N	N
25 Maffei	Y	N	N	N	N	N	N
26 **Lee**	N	Y	N	Y	Y	N	Y
27 Higgins	Y	N	N	N	N	N	N
28 Slaughter	Y	N	N	N	N	N	N
29 Massa	Y	N	N	N	N	N	N
NORTH CAROLINA							
1 Butterfield	Y	N	N	N	N	N	N
2 Etheridge	Y	N	N	N	N	N	N
3 **Jones**	Y	N	Y	Y	Y	N	N
4 Price	Y	N	N	N	N	N	N

	554	555	556	557	558	559	560
5 **Foxx**	Y	Y	Y	Y	Y	Y	Y
6 **Coble**	Y	Y	Y	Y	Y	Y	Y
7 McIntyre	Y	N	N	N	N	N	N
8 Kissell	Y	N	N	N	N	N	N
9 **Myrick**	Y	Y	Y	Y	Y	Y	Y
10 **McHenry**	Y	Y	Y	Y	Y	Y	Y
11 Shuler	Y	N	N	N	N	N	N
12 Watt	Y	N	N	N	N	N	N
13 Miller	Y	N	N	N	N	N	N
NORTH DAKOTA							
AL Pomeroy	Y	N	N	N	N	N	N
OHIO							
1 Driehaus	Y	N	N	Y	N	N	N
2 **Schmidt**	Y	Y	Y	Y	Y	Y	Y
3 **Turner**	Y	N	N	N	N	N	N
4 **Jordan**	Y	Y	Y	Y	Y	Y	Y
5 **Latta**	Y	Y	Y	Y	Y	Y	Y
6 Wilson	Y	N	N	N	N	N	N
7 **Austria**	Y	Y	Y	Y	Y	N	Y
8 **Boehner**	Y	Y	Y	Y	Y	Y	Y
9 Kaptur	Y	Y	N	N	N	N	N
10 Kucinich	Y	N	N	N	N	N	N
11 Fudge	Y	N	N	N	N	N	N
12 **Tiberi**	Y	Y	Y	Y	Y	Y	Y
13 Sutton	Y	N	N	N	N	N	N
14 **LaTourette**	Y	N	Y	N	Y	N	N
15 Kilroy	Y	N	N	N	N	N	N
16 Boccieri	Y	N	N	N	N	N	N
17 Ryan	Y	N	N	N	N	N	N
18 Space	Y	?	N	N	Y	N	N
OKLAHOMA							
1 **Sullivan**	Y	Y	Y	Y	Y	Y	Y
2 Boren	Y	N	Y	Y	N	N	N
3 **Lucas**	?	?	?	?	?	?	?
4 **Cole**	Y	Y	Y	Y	Y	N	N
5 **Fallin**	Y	Y	Y	Y	Y	Y	Y
OREGON							
1 Wu	Y	N	N	N	N	N	N
2 **Walden**	Y	N	Y	Y	N	N	Y
3 Blumenauer	Y	N	N	N	N	N	N
4 DeFazio	Y	Y	N	N	N	N	N
5 Schrader	?	N	N	N	N	N	N
PENNSYLVANIA							
1 Brady	Y	Y	N	N	N	N	N
2 Fattah	Y	N	N	N	N	N	N
3 Dahlkemper	Y	N	N	N	N	N	N
4 Altmire	Y	N	N	Y	N	N	N
5 **Thompson**	Y	Y	Y	Y	Y	N	N
6 **Gerlach**	Y	N	N	Y	Y	N	N
7 Sestak	Y	N	N	N	N	N	N
8 Murphy, P.	Y	N	N	Y	N	N	N
9 **Shuster**	Y	Y	Y	Y	Y	N	N
10 Carney	Y	N	N	N	N	N	N
11 Kanjorski	Y	N	N	N	N	N	N
12 Murtha	Y	N	N	N	N	N	N
13 Schwartz	Y	N	N	N	N	N	N
14 Doyle	Y	N	N	N	N	N	N
15 **Dent**	Y	N	Y	Y	Y	N	Y
16 **Pitts**	Y	Y	Y	Y	Y	Y	Y
17 Holden	Y	N	N	N	N	N	N
18 **Murphy, T.**	Y	N	N	Y	N	N	N
19 **Platts**	Y	Y	N	Y	Y	Y	Y
RHODE ISLAND							
1 Kennedy	Y	N	–	N	–	–	–
2 Langevin	Y	N	N	N	N	N	N
SOUTH CAROLINA							
1 **Brown**	Y	Y	Y	Y	Y	N	N
2 **Wilson**	Y	Y	Y	Y	Y	Y	Y
3 **Barrett**	Y	?	?	?	?	?	?
4 **Inglis**	Y	N	Y	N	N	Y	Y
5 Spratt	Y	N	N	N	N	N	N
6 Clyburn	Y	N	N	N	N	N	N
SOUTH DAKOTA							
AL Herseth Sandlin	Y	N	N	N	N	N	N
TENNESSEE							
1 **Roe**	Y	Y	Y	Y	Y	Y	Y
2 **Duncan**	Y	Y	Y	Y	Y	N	Y
3 **Wamp**	Y	Y	Y	Y	Y	Y	Y
4 Davis	Y	N	N	N	N	N	N
5 Cooper	Y	N	N	Y	N	Y	Y
6 Gordon	Y	N	N	N	N	N	N
7 **Blackburn**	N	Y	Y	Y	Y	Y	Y
8 Tanner	Y	N	N	N	N	N	N
9 Cohen	Y	N	N	N	N	N	N

	554	555	556	557	558	559	560
TEXAS							
1 **Gohmert**	P	Y	Y	Y	Y	Y	Y
2 **Poe**	P	Y	Y	Y	Y	N	Y
3 **Johnson, S.**	Y	Y	Y	Y	Y	Y	Y
4 **Hall**	Y	Y	Y	Y	Y	Y	Y
5 **Hensarling**	Y	Y	Y	Y	Y	Y	Y
6 **Barton**	Y	Y	Y	Y	Y	N	N
7 **Culberson**	Y	Y	Y	Y	Y	N	N
8 **Brady**	Y	Y	Y	Y	Y	Y	Y
9 Green, A.	Y	N	N	N	N	N	N
10 **McCaul**	Y	Y	Y	Y	Y	Y	Y
11 **Conaway**	Y	Y	Y	Y	Y	Y	Y
12 **Granger**	Y	Y	Y	Y	Y	N	N
13 **Thornberry**	Y	N	Y	Y	Y	Y	Y
14 **Paul**	N	Y	Y	Y	Y	Y	Y
15 Hinojosa	Y	N	N	N	N	N	N
16 Reyes	Y	N	N	N	N	N	N
17 Edwards	Y	N	N	N	N	N	N
18 Jackson Lee	Y	N	N	N	N	N	N
19 **Neugebauer**	Y	Y	Y	Y	Y	Y	Y
20 Gonzalez	Y	N	N	N	N	N	N
21 **Smith**	Y	Y	Y	Y	Y	N	N
22 **Olson**	Y	Y	Y	Y	Y	Y	Y
23 Rodriguez	Y	N	N	N	N	N	N
24 **Marchant**	Y	Y	Y	Y	Y	N	Y
25 Doggett	Y	N	N	N	N	N	N
26 **Burgess**	Y	?	Y	Y	Y	Y	Y
27 Ortiz	Y	N	N	N	N	N	N
28 Cuellar	Y	N	N	N	N	N	N
29 Green, G.	Y	N	N	N	N	N	N
30 Johnson, E.	Y	N	N	N	N	N	N
31 **Carter**	Y	Y	?	Y	Y	N	N
32 **Sessions**	Y	Y	Y	Y	Y	Y	Y
UTAH							
1 **Bishop**	Y	Y	Y	Y	Y	Y	Y
2 Matheson	Y	N	N	N	N	Y	N
3 **Chaffetz**	Y	Y	Y	Y	Y	Y	Y
VERMONT							
AL Welch	Y	N	N	N	N	N	N
VIRGINIA							
1 **Wittman**	Y	Y	Y	Y	Y	N	Y
2 Nye	Y	N	Y	Y	N	N	N
3 Scott	Y	?	?	?	?	?	?
4 **Forbes**	Y	Y	Y	Y	Y	N	N
5 Perriello	Y	N	N	N	N	N	N
6 **Goodlatte**	Y	Y	Y	Y	Y	Y	Y
7 **Cantor**	Y	Y	Y	Y	Y	N	Y
8 Moran	Y	N	N	N	N	N	N
9 Boucher	Y	N	N	N	N	N	N
10 **Wolf**	Y	Y	Y	Y	Y	N	N
11 Connolly	Y	N	N	N	N	N	N
WASHINGTON							
1 Inslee	Y	N	N	N	N	N	N
2 Larsen	Y	N	N	N	N	N	N
3 Baird	Y	N	N	N	N	N	N
4 **Hastings**	Y	Y	Y	Y	Y	N	N
5 **McMorris Rodgers**	Y	Y	Y	Y	Y	N	Y
6 Dicks	Y	N	N	N	N	N	N
7 McDermott	Y	N	N	N	N	N	N
8 **Reichert**	Y	Y	Y	Y	Y	N	N
9 Smith	Y	N	Y	N	N	N	N
WEST VIRGINIA							
1 Mollohan	Y	N	N	N	N	N	N
2 **Capito**	Y	Y	?	Y	Y	N	N
3 Rahall	Y	N	N	N	N	N	N
WISCONSIN							
1 **Ryan**	Y	Y	Y	Y	Y	Y	Y
2 Baldwin	Y	N	N	N	N	N	N
3 Kind	Y	N	N	N	N	Y	Y
4 Moore	Y	N	N	N	N	N	N
5 **Sensenbrenner**	N	Y	Y	Y	Y	Y	Y
6 **Petri**	Y	Y	Y	Y	Y	Y	Y
7 Obey	Y	N	N	N	N	N	N
8 Kagen	Y	N	N	N	N	N	N
WYOMING							
AL **Lummis**	N	Y	Y	Y	Y	Y	Y
DELEGATES							
Faleomavaega (A.S.)		?	?	?	?	?	?
Norton (D.C.)		–	–	N	N	N	N
Bordallo (Guam)		?	?	?	?	?	?
Sablan (N. Marianas)		N	N	N	N	N	N
Pierluisi (P.R.)		N	N	N	N	N	N
Christensen (V.I.)		N	N	N	N	N	N

IN THE HOUSE | By Vote Number

561. HR 3170. Fiscal 2010 Financial Services Appropriations/Proof of Concept Center. Flake, R-Ariz., amendment that would bar the use of funds appropriated in the bill for the Proof of Concept Center of Idaho TechConnect Inc. in Nampa, Idaho, and cut $285,000 intended for the project from the bill. Rejected in Committee of the Whole 94-336: R 86-89; D 8-247. July 16, 2009.

562. HR 3170. Fiscal 2010 Financial Services Appropriations/ Greenstone Group Project. Flake, R-Ariz., amendment that would bar the use of funds appropriated in the bill for the Greenstone Group project of the Northeast Entrepreneur Fund in Virginia, Minn., and cut $200,000 intended for the project from the bill. Rejected in Committee of the Whole 93-337: R 89-85; D 4-252. July 16, 2009.

563. HR 3170. Fiscal 2010 Financial Services Appropriations/Green Business Incubator Project. Flake, R-Ariz., amendment that would bar the use of funds appropriated in the bill for the Green Business Incubator project of Montgomery County, Md., and cut $150,000 intended for the project from the bill. Rejected in Committee of the Whole 114-318: R 111-64; D 3-254. July 16, 2009.

564. HR 3170. Fiscal 2010 Financial Services Appropriations/ Activity Based Total Accountability Project. Flake, R-Ariz., amendment that would bar the use of funds appropriated in the bill for the Activity Based Total Accountability project of the Florida Institute of Technology in Melbourne, Fla., and cut $100,000 intended for the project from the bill. Rejected in Committee of the Whole 102-326: R 95-79; D 7-247. July 16, 2009.

565. HR 3170. Fiscal 2010 Financial Services Appropriations/ Commercial Kitchen Business Incubator Project. Flake, R-Ariz., amendment that would bar the use of funds appropriated in the bill for the Commercial Kitchen Business Incubator project of the El Pajaro Community Development Corp. in Watsonville, Calif., and cut $90,000 intended for the project from the bill. Rejected in Committee of the Whole 120-311: R 112-63; D 8-248. July 16, 2009.

566. HR 3170. Fiscal 2010 Financial Services Appropriations/ Defense Procurement Assistance Program. Flake, R-Ariz., amendment that would bar the use of funds appropriated in the bill for the Defense Procurement Assistance Program of the Economic Growth Connection of Westmoreland in Greensburg, Pa., and cut $125,000 intended for the project from the bill. Rejected in Committee of the Whole 119-312: R 109-65; D 10-247. July 16, 2009.

567. HR 3170. Fiscal 2010 Financial Services Appropriations/ Myrtle Beach Conference Center. Flake, R-Ariz., amendment that would bar the use of funds appropriated in the bill for the Myrtle Beach International Trade and Conference Center in Myrtle Beach, S.C., and cut $100,000 intended for the project from the bill. Rejected in Committee of the Whole 99-332: R 88-85; D 11-247. July 16, 2009.

	561	562	563	564	565	566	567
ALABAMA							
1 Bonner	N	N	N	N	N	N	N
2 Bright	Y	N	Y	N	Y	Y	Y
3 Rogers	N	N	N	N	N	N	N
4 Aderholt	N	N	N	N	N	N	N
5 Griffith	N	N	N	N	N	N	N
6 Bachus	N	N	N	N	N	Y	N
7 Davis	N	N	N	N	N	N	N
ALASKA							
AL Young	N	N	Y	Y	Y	N	N
ARIZONA							
1 Kirkpatrick	N	N	N	N	N	N	N
2 Franks	Y	Y	Y	Y	Y	Y	Y
3 Shadegg	Y	Y	Y	Y	Y	Y	Y
4 Pastor	N	N	N	N	N	N	N
5 Mitchell	N	N	N	N	N	N	N
6 Flake	Y	Y	Y	Y	Y	Y	Y
7 Grijalva	N	N	N	N	N	N	N
8 Giffords	Y	N	N	N	N	N	Y
ARKANSAS							
1 Berry	N	N	N	N	N	N	N
2 Snyder	N	N	N	N	N	N	N
3 Boozman	Y	Y	Y	Y	Y	Y	Y
4 Ross	N	N	N	N	N	N	N
CALIFORNIA							
1 Thompson	N	N	N	N	N	N	N
2 Herger	Y	Y	Y	Y	Y	Y	Y
3 Lungren	Y	Y	Y	Y	Y	Y	Y
4 McClintock	Y	Y	Y	Y	Y	Y	Y
5 Matsui	N	N	N	N	N	N	N
6 Woolsey	N	N	N	N	N	N	N
7 Miller, George	N	N	N	N	N	N	N
8 Pelosi							
9 Lee	N	N	N	N	N	N	N
10 Vacant							
11 McNerney	N	N	N	N	N	N	N
12 Speier	N	N	N	N	N	Y	Y
13 Stark	N	N	N	N	N	N	N
14 Eshoo	N	N	N	?	N	N	N
15 Honda	N	N	N	N	N	N	N
16 Lofgren	N	N	N	N	N	N	N
17 Farr	N	N	N	N	N	N	N
18 Cardoza	N	N	N	N	N	N	N
19 Radanovich	N	N	N	N	Y	N	N
20 Costa	N	N	N	N	N	N	N
21 Nunes	Y	Y	Y	Y	Y	Y	N
22 McCarthy	N	Y	Y	Y	Y	Y	N
23 Capps	N	N	N	N	N	N	N
24 Gallegly	N	N	Y	N	Y	N	N
25 McKeon	N	N	N	N	N	N	?
26 Dreier	N	N	N	N	N	N	N
27 Sherman	N	N	N	N	N	N	N
28 Berman	N	N	N	N	N	N	N
29 Schiff	N	N	N	N	N	N	N
30 Waxman	N	N	N	N	N	N	N
31 Becerra	N	N	N	N	N	N	N
32 Chu	N	N	N	N	N	N	N
33 Watson	N	N	N	N	N	N	N
34 Roybal-Allard	N	N	N	N	N	N	N
35 Waters	N	N	N	N	N	N	N
36 Harman	N	N	N	N	N	N	N
37 Richardson	N	N	N	N	N	N	N
38 Napolitano	N	N	N	N	N	N	N
39 Sánchez, Linda	N	N	N	N	N	N	N
40 Royce	Y	Y	Y	Y	Y	Y	Y
41 Lewis	N	N	N	N	N	N	N
42 Miller, Gary	N	N	N	N	Y	N	N
43 Baca	N	N	N	N	N	N	N
44 Calvert	N	N	N	N	Y	N	N
45 Bono Mack	N	N	N	N	N	Y	N
46 Rohrabacher	Y	Y	Y	Y	Y	Y	Y
47 Sanchez, Loretta	N	N	N	N	N	N	N
48 Campbell	Y	Y	Y	Y	Y	Y	Y
49 Issa	Y	Y	Y	Y	Y	Y	Y
50 Bilbray	N	Y	N	N	N	N	N
51 Filner	N	N	N	N	N	N	N
52 Hunter	N	N	Y	N	Y	N	N
53 Davis	N	N	N	N	N	N	N
COLORADO							
1 DeGette	N	N	N	N	N	N	N
2 Polis	N	N	N	N	N	N	N
3 Salazar	N	N	N	N	N	N	N
4 Markey	N	N	N	N	N	N	N
5 Lamborn	Y	Y	Y	Y	Y	Y	Y
6 Coffman	Y	Y	Y	Y	Y	Y	Y
7 Perlmutter	Y	N	N	N	N	N	N
CONNECTICUT							
1 Larson	N	N	N	N	N	N	N
2 Courtney	N	N	N	N	N	N	N
3 DeLauro	N	N	N	N	N	N	N
4 Himes	N	N	N	N	N	N	N
5 Murphy	N	N	N	N	N	N	N
DELAWARE							
AL Castle	N	Y	Y	Y	Y	Y	N
FLORIDA							
1 Miller	Y	Y	Y	Y	Y	Y	N
2 Boyd	N	N	N	N	N	N	N
3 Brown	N	N	N	N	N	N	N
4 Crenshaw	N	N	N	N	N	N	N
5 Brown-Waite	Y	N	N	N	N	N	Y
6 Stearns	Y	Y	Y	N	Y	Y	Y
7 Mica	Y	N	N	N	N	N	N
8 Grayson	N	N	N	N	N	N	N
9 Bilirakis	N	N	Y	N	Y	N	N
10 Young	N	N	N	N	N	N	N
11 Castor	N	N	N	N	N	N	N
12 Putnam	N	N	N	N	N	N	N
13 Buchanan	N	N	N	N	N	Y	N
14 Mack	Y	Y	Y	Y	Y	Y	Y
15 Posey	N	N	N	N	N	N	N
16 Rooney	Y	Y	Y	N	Y	N	Y
17 Meek	N	N	N	N	N	N	N
18 Ros-Lehtinen	N	N	N	N	N	N	N
19 Wexler	N	N	N	N	N	N	N
20 Wasserman Schultz	N	N	N	N	N	N	N
21 Diaz-Balart, L.	N	N	N	N	N	N	N
22 Klein	N	N	N	N	N	N	N
23 Hastings	N	N	N	N	N	N	N
24 Kosmas	N	N	N	N	N	N	N
25 Diaz-Balart, M.	N	N	N	N	N	N	N
GEORGIA							
1 Kingston	N	Y	Y	N	N	N	N
2 Bishop	N	N	N	N	N	N	N
3 Westmoreland	Y	Y	Y	Y	Y	Y	Y
4 Johnson	N	N	N	N	N	N	N
5 Lewis	N	N	N	N	N	N	N
6 Price	Y	Y	Y	Y	Y	Y	Y
7 Linder	Y	Y	Y	Y	Y	Y	Y
8 Marshall	N	N	N	N	N	N	N
9 Deal	Y	Y	Y	N	Y	Y	Y
10 Broun	Y	Y	Y	Y	Y	Y	Y
11 Gingrey	N	Y	N	N	N	N	N
12 Barrow	N	N	N	N	N	N	N
13 Scott	N	N	N	N	N	N	N
HAWAII							
1 Abercrombie	N	N	N	N	N	N	N
2 Hirono	N	N	N	N	N	N	N
IDAHO							
1 Minnick	Y	Y	Y	Y	Y	Y	Y
2 Simpson	N	N	N	N	N	N	N
ILLINOIS							
1 Rush	N	N	N	N	N	N	N
2 Jackson	N	N	N	N	N	N	N
3 Lipinski	N	N	N	N	N	N	N
4 Gutierrez	N	N	N	N	N	N	N
5 Quigley	N	N	N	N	N	N	N
6 Roskam	N	N	Y	Y	Y	Y	Y
7 Davis	N	N	N	N	N	N	N
8 Bean	N	N	N	N	Y	Y	Y
9 Schakowsky	N	N	N	N	N	N	N
10 Kirk	N	Y	Y	Y	Y	Y	Y
11 Halvorson	N	N	N	N	N	Y	Y
12 Costello	N	N	N	N	N	N	N
13 Biggert	N	N	Y	N	N	N	N
14 Foster	N	N	N	N	N	N	N
15 Johnson	Y	Y	Y	Y	Y	Y	Y

	561	562	563	564	565	566	567
16 **Manzullo**	N	N	N	Y	Y	Y	Y
17 Hare	N	N	N	N	N	N	N
18 **Schock**	Y	N	N	N	N	Y	N
19 **Shimkus**	Y	Y	Y	Y	Y	Y	Y
INDIANA							
1 Visclosky	N	N	N	N	N	N	N
2 Donnelly	N	N	N	N	N	N	N
3 **Souder**	N	N	Y	Y	Y	Y	Y
4 **Buyer**	N	Y	Y	N	Y	Y	N
5 **Burton**	N	Y	Y	Y	Y	Y	N
6 **Pence**	?	?	?	?	?	?	?
7 Carson	N	N	N	N	N	N	N
8 Ellsworth	N	N	N	N	N	N	N
9 Hill	N	N	N	N	N	N	N
IOWA							
1 Braley	N	N	N	N	N	N	N
2 Loebsack	N	N	N	N	N	N	N
3 Boswell	N	N	N	N	N	N	N
4 **Latham**	N	N	N	N	N	N	N
5 **King**	Y	Y	Y	Y	Y	Y	Y
KANSAS							
1 **Moran**	Y	N	Y	Y	Y	Y	Y
2 **Jenkins**	Y	Y	Y	Y	Y	Y	Y
3 Moore	N	N	N	N	N	N	N
4 **Tiahrt**	N	N	N	N	N	N	N
KENTUCKY							
1 **Whitfield**	N	N	N	N	N	N	N
2 **Guthrie**	N	N	N	N	N	N	N
3 Yarmuth	N	N	N	N	N	N	N
4 **Davis**	N	N	N	N	N	Y	N
5 **Rogers**	N	N	N	N	N	N	N
6 Chandler	N	N	N	N	N	N	N
LOUISIANA							
1 **Scalise**	Y	N	Y	Y	Y	Y	Y
2 **Cao**	N	N	N	N	N	N	N
3 Melancon	N	N	N	N	N	N	N
4 **Fleming**	Y	Y	Y	P	Y	Y	Y
5 **Alexander**	N	N	N	N	N	N	N
6 **Cassidy**	Y	Y	Y	Y	Y	Y	Y
7 **Boustany**	Y	Y	Y	Y	Y	Y	Y
MAINE							
1 Pingree	N	N	N	N	N	N	N
2 Michaud	N	N	N	N	N	N	N
MARYLAND							
1 Kratovil	N	N	N	N	N	N	N
2 Ruppersberger	N	N	N	N	N	N	N
3 Sarbanes	N	N	N	N	N	N	N
4 Edwards	N	N	N	N	N	N	N
5 Hoyer	N	N	N	N	N	N	N
6 **Bartlett**	N	N	N	N	N	N	N
7 Cummings	N	N	N	N	N	N	N
8 Van Hollen	N	N	N	N	N	N	N
MASSACHUSETTS							
1 Olver	N	N	N	N	N	N	N
2 Neal	N	N	N	N	N	N	N
3 McGovern	N	N	N	N	N	N	N
4 Frank	N	N	N	N	N	N	N
5 Tsongas	N	N	N	N	N	N	N
6 Tierney	N	N	N	N	Y	N	N
7 Markey	N	N	N	N	?	N	N
8 Capuano	N	N	N	N	N	N	N
9 Lynch	N	N	N	N	N	N	N
10 Delahunt	N	N	N	N	N	N	N
MICHIGAN							
1 Stupak	N	N	N	N	N	N	N
2 **Hoekstra**	Y	Y	Y	Y	Y	Y	Y
3 **Ehlers**	Y	N	Y	Y	Y	Y	Y
4 **Camp**	N	N	Y	N	Y	N	N
5 Kildee	N	N	N	N	N	N	N
6 **Upton**	N	N	Y	N	Y	Y	Y
7 Schauer	Y	N	N	Y	Y	Y	Y
8 **Rogers**	Y	Y	Y	N	Y	Y	Y
9 Peters	N	N	N	N	N	N	N
10 **Miller**	N	N	N	N	N	N	N
11 **McCotter**	Y	Y	Y	Y	Y	Y	Y
12 Levin	N	N	N	N	N	N	N
13 Kilpatrick	N	N	N	N	N	N	N
14 Conyers	N	N	N	N	N	N	N
15 Dingell	N	N	N	N	N	N	N
MINNESOTA							
1 Walz	N	N	N	N	N	N	N
2 **Kline**	Y	Y	Y	Y	Y	Y	Y
3 **Paulsen**	Y	N	Y	N	Y	Y	Y
4 McCollum	N	N	N	?	N	N	N

	561	562	563	564	565	566	567
5 Ellison	?	N	N	N	N	N	N
6 **Bachmann**	Y	Y	Y	Y	Y	Y	Y
7 Peterson	N	N	N	N	N	N	N
8 Oberstar	N	N	N	N	N	N	N
MISSISSIPPI							
1 Childers	N	N	N	N	N	N	N
2 Thompson	N	N	N	N	N	N	N
3 **Harper**	N	N	N	N	N	N	N
4 Taylor	N	N	N	N	N	N	N
MISSOURI							
1 Clay	N	N	N	N	N	N	N
2 **Akin**	N	N	Y	N	N	N	Y
3 Carnahan	N	N	N	N	N	N	N
4 Skelton	N	N	N	N	N	N	N
5 Cleaver	N	N	N	N	N	N	N
6 **Graves**	Y	N	Y	Y	Y	Y	Y
7 **Blunt**	N	Y	Y	N	N	Y	N
8 **Emerson**	N	N	N	N	N	Y	N
9 **Luetkemeyer**	Y	Y	Y	Y	Y	Y	Y
MONTANA							
AL **Rehberg**	N	N	N	N	N	N	N
NEBRASKA							
1 **Fortenberry**	Y	Y	Y	Y	Y	Y	Y
2 **Terry**	Y	Y	Y	Y	Y	N	Y
3 **Smith**	Y	Y	Y	Y	Y	Y	Y
NEVADA							
1 Berkley	N	N	N	N	N	N	N
2 **Heller**	Y	Y	Y	Y	Y	Y	Y
3 Titus	N	N	N	N	N	N	N
NEW HAMPSHIRE							
1 Shea-Porter	N	N	N	N	N	N	N
2 Hodes	N	N	N	N	N	Y	N
NEW JERSEY							
1 Andrews	N	N	N	N	N	N	N
2 **LoBiondo**	N	N	N	N	N	N	N
3 Adler	N	N	N	N	N	N	N
4 **Smith**	N	N	N	N	N	N	N
5 **Garrett**	Y	Y	N	Y	Y	Y	Y
6 Pallone	N	N	N	N	N	N	N
7 **Lance**	N	N	Y	N	Y	Y	N
8 Pascrell	N	N	N	N	N	N	N
9 Rothman	N	N	N	N	N	N	N
10 Payne	N	N	N	N	N	N	N
11 **Frelinghuysen**	N	N	N	N	N	N	N
12 Holt	N	N	N	N	N	N	N
13 Sires	N	N	N	N	N	N	N
NEW MEXICO							
1 Heinrich	N	N	N	N	N	N	N
2 Teague	N	N	N	N	N	N	N
3 Lujan	N	N	N	N	N	N	N
NEW YORK							
1 Bishop	N	N	N	Y	N	N	N
2 Israel	N	N	N	N	N	N	N
3 **King**	N	N	N	N	N	N	N
4 McCarthy	N	N	N	N	N	N	N
5 Ackerman	N	N	N	N	N	N	N
6 Meeks	N	?	N	N	N	N	N
7 Crowley	N	N	N	N	N	N	N
8 Nadler	N	N	N	N	N	N	N
9 Weiner	N	N	N	N	N	N	N
10 Towns	N	N	N	N	N	N	N
11 Clarke	N	N	N	N	N	N	N
12 Velázquez	?	?	?	N	N	N	N
13 McMahon	N	N	N	N	N	N	N
14 Maloney	N	N	N	N	N	N	N
15 Rangel	N	N	N	N	N	N	N
16 Serrano	N	N	N	N	N	N	N
17 Engel	N	N	N	N	N	N	N
18 Lowey	N	N	N	N	N	N	N
19 Hall	N	N	N	N	N	N	N
20 Murphy	N	N	N	N	N	N	N
21 Tonko	N	N	N	N	N	N	N
22 Hinchey	N	N	N	N	N	N	N
23 **McHugh**	N	N	N	N	N	N	N
24 Arcuri	N	N	N	N	N	N	N
25 Maffei	N	N	N	N	N	N	N
26 **Lee**	N	N	N	Y	Y	Y	Y
27 Higgins	N	N	N	N	N	N	N
28 Slaughter	N	N	N	N	N	N	N
29 Massa	N	N	N	N	N	N	N
NORTH CAROLINA							
1 Butterfield	N	N	N	N	N	N	N
2 Etheridge	N	N	N	N	N	N	N
3 **Jones**	N	N	N	N	N	N	N
4 Price	N	N	N	N	N	N	N

	561	562	563	564	565	566	567
5 **Foxx**	Y	Y	Y	Y	Y	Y	Y
6 **Coble**	Y	Y	Y	Y	Y	Y	Y
7 McIntyre	N	N	N	N	N	N	N
8 Kissell	N	N	N	N	N	N	N
9 **Myrick**	Y	Y	Y	Y	Y	Y	Y
10 **McHenry**	Y	Y	Y	Y	Y	Y	Y
11 Shuler	N	N	N	N	N	N	N
12 Watt	N	N	N	N	N	N	N
13 Miller	N	N	N	N	N	N	N
NORTH DAKOTA							
AL Pomeroy	N	N	N	N	N	N	N
OHIO							
1 Driehaus	N	N	N	N	N	N	N
2 **Schmidt**	Y	Y	Y	Y	Y	Y	Y
3 **Turner**	N	N	N	N	N	N	N
4 **Jordan**	Y	Y	Y	Y	Y	Y	Y
5 **Latta**	Y	Y	Y	Y	Y	Y	Y
6 Wilson	N	N	N	N	N	N	N
7 **Austria**	Y	Y	N	Y	Y	Y	Y
8 **Boehner**	N	Y	Y	Y	Y	Y	Y
9 Kaptur	N	N	N	N	N	N	N
10 Kucinich	N	N	N	N	N	N	N
11 Fudge	N	N	N	N	N	N	N
12 **Tiberi**	Y	Y	Y	Y	Y	Y	Y
13 Sutton	N	N	N	N	N	N	N
14 **LaTourette**	N	?	N	N	N	N	N
15 Kilroy	N	N	N	N	N	N	N
16 Boccieri	N	N	N	N	N	N	N
17 Ryan	N	N	N	N	N	N	N
18 Space	N	N	N	N	N	N	N
OKLAHOMA							
1 **Sullivan**	Y	Y	Y	Y	Y	Y	Y
2 Boren	N	N	N	N	N	N	N
3 **Lucas**	?	?	?	?	?	?	?
4 **Cole**	N	N	N	N	N	N	N
5 **Fallin**	Y	Y	Y	Y	Y	Y	Y
OREGON							
1 Wu	N	N	N	N	N	N	N
2 **Walden**	N	N	Y	Y	Y	Y	Y
3 Blumenauer	N	N	N	N	N	N	N
4 DeFazio	N	N	N	N	N	N	N
5 Schrader	N	N	N	N	N	N	N
PENNSYLVANIA							
1 Brady	N	N	N	N	N	N	N
2 Fattah	N	N	N	N	N	N	N
3 Dahlkemper	N	N	N	N	N	N	N
4 Altmire	N	N	N	N	N	N	N
5 **Thompson**	N	N	N	N	N	N	N
6 **Gerlach**	N	N	Y	Y	N	N	N
7 Sestak	N	N	N	N	N	N	N
8 Murphy, P.	N	N	N	N	N	N	N
9 **Shuster**	N	N	N	N	N	N	N
10 Carney	N	N	N	N	N	N	N
11 Kanjorski	N	N	N	N	N	N	N
12 Murtha	N	N	N	N	N	N	N
13 Schwartz	N	N	N	N	N	N	N
14 Doyle	N	N	N	N	N	N	N
15 **Dent**	N	N	Y	Y	Y	N	N
16 **Pitts**	Y	Y	Y	Y	Y	Y	Y
17 Holden	N	N	N	N	N	N	N
18 **Murphy, T.**	N	N	N	N	N	N	N
19 **Platts**	N	N	Y	Y	Y	N	N
RHODE ISLAND							
1 Kennedy	N	N	N	–	N	N	N
2 Langevin	N	N	N	N	N	N	N
SOUTH CAROLINA							
1 **Brown**	N	N	N	N	N	N	N
2 **Wilson**	Y	Y	Y	Y	Y	Y	Y
3 **Barrett**	?	?	?	?	?	?	?
4 **Inglis**	Y	Y	Y	Y	Y	Y	Y
5 Spratt	N	N	N	N	N	N	N
6 Clyburn	N	N	N	N	N	N	N
SOUTH DAKOTA							
AL Herseth Sandlin	N	N	N	N	N	N	N
TENNESSEE							
1 **Roe**	Y	Y	Y	Y	Y	Y	Y
2 **Duncan**	Y	N	Y	Y	N	Y	N
3 **Wamp**	Y	Y	Y	Y	Y	Y	N
4 Davis	N	N	N	N	N	N	N
5 Cooper	Y	Y	Y	Y	Y	Y	Y
6 Gordon	N	N	N	?	N	N	N
7 **Blackburn**	Y	Y	Y	Y	Y	Y	Y
8 Tanner	N	N	N	N	N	N	N
9 Cohen	N	N	N	N	N	N	N

	561	562	563	564	565	566	567
TEXAS							
1 **Gohmert**	Y	Y	Y	Y	Y	Y	?
2 **Poe**	N	N	Y	N	Y	Y	Y
3 **Johnson, S.**	N	Y	Y	Y	Y	Y	N
4 **Hall**	N	N	N	N	Y	N	N
5 **Hensarling**	Y	Y	Y	Y	Y	Y	Y
6 **Barton**	N	N	Y	Y	Y	N	Y
7 **Culberson**	N	N	N	N	N	?	N
8 **Brady**	N	Y	Y	Y	Y	Y	Y
9 Green, A.	N	N	N	N	N	N	N
10 **McCaul**	Y	Y	Y	Y	Y	Y	Y
11 **Conaway**	Y	Y	Y	Y	Y	Y	Y
12 **Granger**	N	N	N	N	N	N	N
13 **Thornberry**	Y	Y	Y	Y	Y	Y	Y
14 **Paul**	Y	Y	Y	Y	Y	Y	Y
15 Hinojosa	N	N	N	N	N	N	N
16 Reyes	N	N	N	N	N	N	N
17 Edwards	N	N	N	N	N	N	N
18 Jackson Lee	N	N	N	N	N	N	N
19 **Neugebauer**	Y	Y	Y	Y	Y	Y	Y
20 Gonzalez	N	N	N	N	N	N	N
21 **Smith**	N	N	N	N	N	N	N
22 **Olson**	Y	Y	Y	N	Y	Y	Y
23 Rodriguez	N	N	N	N	N	N	N
24 **Marchant**	Y	Y	N	Y	Y	Y	Y
25 Doggett	N	N	N	N	N	N	N
26 **Burgess**	Y	Y	Y	Y	Y	Y	Y
27 Ortiz	N	N	N	N	N	N	N
28 Cuellar	N	N	N	N	N	N	N
29 Green, G.	N	N	N	N	N	N	N
30 Johnson, E.	N	N	N	N	N	N	N
31 **Carter**	N	N	Y	N	N	N	N
32 **Sessions**	Y	Y	Y	Y	Y	Y	Y
UTAH							
1 **Bishop**	Y	Y	Y	Y	Y	Y	N
2 Matheson	N	N	N	N	N	N	N
3 **Chaffetz**	Y	Y	Y	Y	Y	Y	Y
VERMONT							
AL Welch	N	N	N	N	N	N	N
VIRGINIA							
1 **Wittman**	Y	N	N	N	Y	Y	N
2 Nye	Y	N	N	Y	Y	N	Y
3 Scott	?	?	?	?	?	?	?
4 **Forbes**	Y	N	N	N	Y	Y	N
5 Perriello	N	N	N	N	N	N	N
6 **Goodlatte**	Y	Y	Y	Y	Y	Y	Y
7 **Cantor**	N	Y	Y	Y	Y	Y	Y
8 Moran	N	N	N	N	N	N	N
9 Boucher	?	N	N	N	N	N	N
10 **Wolf**	N	N	N	N	N	N	N
11 Connolly	N	N	N	N	N	N	N
WASHINGTON							
1 Inslee	N	N	N	N	N	N	N
2 Larsen	N	N	N	N	N	N	N
3 Baird	N	N	N	N	N	N	N
4 **Hastings**	N	N	N	N	N	N	N
5 **McMorris Rodgers**	N	Y	Y	Y	Y	Y	N
6 Dicks	N	N	N	N	N	N	N
7 McDermott	N	N	N	N	N	N	N
8 **Reichert**	N	N	N	N	N	N	N
9 Smith	N	N	N	N	N	N	N
WEST VIRGINIA							
1 Mollohan	N	N	N	N	N	N	N
2 **Capito**	N	N	N	N	N	N	N
3 Rahall	N	N	N	N	N	N	N
WISCONSIN							
1 **Ryan**	Y	Y	Y	Y	Y	Y	Y
2 Baldwin	N	N	N	N	N	N	N
3 Kind	Y	Y	Y	Y	Y	Y	Y
4 Moore	N	N	N	N	N	N	N
5 **Sensenbrenner**	Y	Y	Y	Y	Y	Y	Y
6 **Petri**	Y	Y	Y	Y	Y	Y	Y
7 Obey	N	N	N	N	N	N	N
8 Kagen	N	N	N	N	N	N	N
WYOMING							
AL **Lummis**	Y	Y	Y	Y	Y	Y	Y
DELEGATES							
Faleomavaega (A.S.)	?	?	?	?	?	?	?
Norton (D.C.)	N	N	N	N	N	?	N
Bordallo (Guam)	?	?	?	?	?	?	?
Sablan (N. Marianas)	N	N	N	N	N	N	N
Pierluisi (P.R.)	N	N	N	N	N	N	N
Christensen (V.I.)	N	N	N	N	?	N	N

IN THE HOUSE | By Vote Number

568. **HR 3170. Fiscal 2010 Financial Services Appropriations/Tech Belt Life Sciences Greenhouse Project.** Flake, R-Ariz., amendment that would bar the use of funds appropriated in the bill for the Tech Belt Life Sciences Greenhouse project of the Pittsburgh Life Sciences Greenhouse in Pittsburgh and cut $100,000 intended for the project from the bill. Rejected in Committee of the Whole 104-325: R 98-75; D 6-250. July 16, 2009.

569. **HR 3170. Fiscal 2010 Financial Services Appropriations/ California Infrastructure Projects.** Flake, R-Ariz., amendment that would bar the use of funds appropriated in the bill for an infrastructure expansion project to promote small business for the cities of Loma Linda and Grand Terrace, Calif., and cut $900,000 intended for the project from the bill. Rejected in Committee of the Whole 74-356: R 65-108; D 9-248. July 16, 2009.

570. **HR 3170. Fiscal 2010 Financial Services Appropriations/ Motion to Table.** Serrano, D-N.Y., motion to table (kill) the Tiahrt, R-Kan., appeal of the ruling of the chair with respect to the Serrano point of order that the Tiahrt motion to recommit the bill constituted legislating on an appropriations bill. The motion would recommit the bill to the Appropriations Committee with instructions that it be immediately reported back with language that would strike the word "federal" from a provision in the bill that would bar the use of federal funds for abortion services in the District of Columbia except when the life of the woman is endangered or in cases of rape or incest. Motion agreed to 225-195: R 0-169; D 225-26. July 16, 2009.

571. **HR 3170. Fiscal 2010 Financial Services Appropriations/ Passage.** Passage of the bill that would provide $46.2 billion in fiscal 2010 for the Treasury Department, the Office of Personnel Management and other agencies, and the District of Columbia. The bill includes $13.4 billion for the Treasury Department, of which $12.1 billion is for the IRS. It would appropriate $20.4 billion for the Office of Personnel Management and $6.9 billion for the operation of the federal court system. It would fund the Executive Office of the President and provide $768 million in federal payments for the District of Columbia government. Passed 219-208: R 4-170; D 215-38. A "yea" was a vote in support of the president's position. July 16, 2009.

572. **H Res 476. Black Music Month Anniversary/Adoption.** Watson, D-Calif., motion to suspend the rules and adopt the resolution that would state the House of Representatives celebrates the goals and ideals of the 30th anniversary of Black Music Month. Motion agreed to 418-0: R 170-0; D 248-0. A two-thirds majority of those present and voting (279 in this case) is required for adoption under suspension of the rules. July 16, 2009.

	568	569	570	571	572
ALABAMA					
1 Bonner	N	N	N	N	Y
2 Bright	Y	Y	N	N	Y
3 Rogers	N	N	N	N	Y
4 Aderholt	N	N	N	N	Y
5 Griffith	N	N	N	N	Y
6 Bachus	N	N	N	N	Y
7 Davis	N	N	N	N	Y
ALASKA					
AL Young	N	N	N	N	Y
ARIZONA					
1 Kirkpatrick	N	N	Y	N	Y
2 Franks	Y	Y	N	N	Y
3 Shadegg	Y	Y	N	N	Y
4 Pastor	N	N	Y	Y	Y
5 Mitchell	N	N	Y	N	Y
6 Flake	Y	Y	N	N	Y
7 Grijalva	N	N	Y	Y	Y
8 Giffords	Y	N	Y	Y	Y
ARKANSAS					
1 Berry	N	N	N	Y	Y
2 Snyder	N	N	Y	Y	Y
3 Boozman	Y	N	N	N	Y
4 Ross	N	N	N	N	Y
CALIFORNIA					
1 Thompson	N	N	Y	Y	Y
2 Herger	Y	Y	?	N	Y
3 Lungren	Y	N	N	N	Y
4 McClintock	Y	Y	N	N	Y
5 Matsui	N	N	Y	Y	Y
6 Woolsey	N	N	Y	Y	Y
7 Miller, George	N	N	Y	Y	Y
8 Pelosi					
9 Lee	N	N	Y	Y	Y
10 Vacant					
11 McNerney	N	N	Y	Y	Y
12 Speier	N	N	Y	Y	Y
13 Stark	N	N	Y	Y	Y
14 Eshoo	N	N	Y	Y	Y
15 Honda	N	N	Y	Y	Y
16 Lofgren	N	N	Y	Y	Y
17 Farr	N	N	Y	Y	Y
18 Cardoza	N	N	Y	Y	Y
19 Radanovich	N	N	N	N	?
20 Costa	N	N	Y	Y	Y
21 Nunes	Y	N	N	N	Y
22 McCarthy	Y	N	N	N	Y
23 Capps	N	N	Y	Y	Y
24 Gallegly	N	N	Y	N	Y
25 McKeon	N	N	N	N	Y
26 Dreier	N	N	N	N	Y
27 Sherman	N	N	?	Y	Y
28 Berman	N	N	Y	Y	Y
29 Schiff	N	N	Y	Y	Y
30 Waxman	N	N	Y	Y	Y
31 Becerra	N	N	Y	Y	Y
32 Chu	N	N	Y	Y	Y
33 Watson	N	N	Y	Y	Y
34 Roybal-Allard	N	N	Y	Y	Y
35 Waters	N	N	Y	Y	Y
36 Harman	N	N	Y	Y	?
37 Richardson	N	N	Y	Y	Y
38 Napolitano	N	N	Y	Y	Y
39 Sánchez, Linda	N	N	Y	Y	Y
40 Royce	Y	N	N	N	Y
41 Lewis	N	N	N	N	Y
42 Miller, Gary	N	N	N	N	?
43 Baca	N	N	Y	Y	Y
44 Calvert	N	N	N	N	Y
45 Bono Mack	N	N	N	N	Y
46 Rohrabacher	Y	Y	N	N	Y
47 Sanchez, Loretta	N	N	Y	Y	Y
48 Campbell	Y	Y	N	N	Y
49 Issa	Y	Y	N	N	Y
50 Bilbray	N	N	N	N	Y
51 Filner	N	N	Y	Y	Y
52 Hunter	Y	N	N	N	Y
53 Davis	N	N	Y	Y	Y

	568	569	570	571	572
COLORADO					
1 DeGette	N	N	Y	Y	Y
2 Polis	N	N	Y	Y	Y
3 Salazar	N	N	Y	Y	Y
4 Markey	N	N	Y	N	Y
5 Lamborn	Y	Y	N	N	Y
6 Coffman	Y	Y	N	N	Y
7 Perlmutter	N	N	Y	+	Y
CONNECTICUT					
1 Larson	N	N	Y	Y	Y
2 Courtney	N	N	Y	Y	Y
3 DeLauro	N	N	Y	Y	Y
4 Himes	N	N	Y	Y	Y
5 Murphy	N	N	Y	Y	Y
DELAWARE					
AL Castle	N	N	N	Y	Y
FLORIDA					
1 Miller	Y	Y	N	N	Y
2 Boyd	N	N	Y	Y	Y
3 Brown	N	N	Y	Y	Y
4 Crenshaw	N	N	N	N	Y
5 Brown-Waite	Y	N	N	N	Y
6 Stearns	Y	N	N	N	Y
7 Mica	Y	N	N	N	Y
8 Grayson	N	N	Y	Y	Y
9 Bilirakis	N	N	N	N	Y
10 Young	N	N	N	N	Y
11 Castor	N	N	Y	Y	Y
12 Putnam	N	N	N	N	Y
13 Buchanan	Y	N	N	P	Y
14 Mack	Y	N	N	N	Y
15 Posey	N	N	N	N	Y
16 Rooney	N	N	N	N	Y
17 Meek	N	N	Y	Y	Y
18 Ros-Lehtinen	N	N	N	N	Y
19 Wexler	N	N	N	N	Y
20 Wasserman Schultz	N	N	Y	Y	Y
21 Diaz-Balart, L.	N	N	N	N	Y
22 Klein	N	N	Y	Y	Y
23 Hastings	N	N	Y	Y	Y
24 Kosmas	N	N	Y	Y	Y
25 Diaz-Balart, M.	N	N	N	N	Y
GEORGIA					
1 Kingston	Y	N	N	N	Y
2 Bishop	N	N	Y	Y	Y
3 Westmoreland	Y	Y	N	N	Y
4 Johnson	N	N	Y	Y	Y
5 Lewis	N	N	Y	Y	Y
6 Price	Y	Y	N	N	Y
7 Linder	?	?	?	N	Y
8 Marshall	N	N	N	N	Y
9 Deal	Y	Y	N	N	Y
10 Broun	Y	Y	N	N	Y
11 Gingrey	N	Y	N	N	Y
12 Barrow	N	Y	Y	Y	Y
13 Scott	N	N	Y	Y	Y
HAWAII					
1 Abercrombie	N	N	Y	Y	Y
2 Hirono	N	N	Y	Y	Y
IDAHO					
1 Minnick	Y	Y	Y	Y	Y
2 Simpson	N	N	N	N	Y
ILLINOIS					
1 Rush	N	N	Y	Y	Y
2 Jackson	N	N	Y	Y	Y
3 Lipinski	N	N	N	N	Y
4 Gutierrez	N	N	Y	Y	Y
5 Quigley	N	N	Y	Y	Y
6 Roskam	Y	N	N	N	Y
7 Davis	N	N	Y	Y	Y
8 Bean	N	N	Y	Y	Y
9 Schakowsky	N	N	Y	Y	Y
10 Kirk	Y	N	N	N	Y
11 Halvorson	N	Y	Y	Y	Y
12 Costello	N	N	Y	Y	Y
13 Biggert	Y	N	N	N	Y
14 Foster	N	Y	Y	Y	Y
15 Johnson	Y	Y	N	N	Y

KEY   **Republicans**   Democrats

Y Voted for (yea)	X Paired against
# Paired for	– Announced against
+ Announced for	P Voted "present"
N Voted against (nay)	

C Voted "present" to avoid possible conflict of interest

? Did not vote or otherwise make a position known

	568	569	570	571	572
16 Manzullo	Y	N	N	N	Y
17 Hare	N	N	Y	Y	Y
18 Schock	Y	N	N	N	Y
19 Shimkus	Y	Y	N	N	Y
INDIANA					
1 Visclosky	N	N	Y	Y	Y
2 Donnelly	N	N	N	N	Y
3 Souder	N	N	N	N	Y
4 Buyer	N	N	N	N	Y
5 Burton	N	N	N	N	Y
6 Pence	?	?	?	?	?
7 Carson	N	N	Y	Y	Y
8 Ellsworth	N	N	N	N	Y
9 Hill	N	N	Y	N	Y
IOWA					
1 Braley	N	N	Y	Y	Y
2 Loebsack	N	N	Y	Y	Y
3 Boswell	N	N	Y	Y	Y
4 Latham	N	N	N	N	Y
5 King	?	Y	?	N	Y
KANSAS					
1 Moran	Y	Y	N	N	Y
2 Jenkins	Y	Y	N	N	Y
3 Moore	N	N	Y	N	Y
4 Tiahrt	N	N	N	N	Y
KENTUCKY					
1 Whitfield	N	N	N	N	Y
2 Guthrie	N	N	N	N	Y
3 Yarmuth	N	N	Y	Y	?
4 Davis	N	N	N	N	Y
5 Rogers	N	N	N	N	Y
6 Chandler	N	N	Y	Y	Y
LOUISIANA					
1 Scalise	Y	N	N	N	Y
2 Cao	N	N	N	N	Y
3 Melancon	N	N	N	N	Y
4 Fleming	Y	Y	N	N	Y
5 Alexander	N	N	N	N	Y
6 Cassidy	Y	Y	N	N	Y
7 Boustany	Y	Y	N	N	Y
MAINE					
1 Pingree	N	N	Y	Y	Y
2 Michaud	N	N	Y	Y	Y
MARYLAND					
1 Kratovil	N	N	Y	Y	Y
2 Ruppersberger	N	N	Y	Y	Y
3 Sarbanes	N	N	Y	Y	Y
4 Edwards	N	N	Y	Y	Y
5 Hoyer	N	N	Y	Y	Y
6 Bartlett	N	N	N	N	Y
7 Cummings	N	N	Y	Y	Y
8 Van Hollen	N	N	Y	Y	Y
MASSACHUSETTS					
1 Olver	N	N	Y	Y	Y
2 Neal	N	N	Y	Y	Y
3 McGovern	N	N	Y	Y	Y
4 Frank	N	N	Y	Y	Y
5 Tsongas	N	N	Y	Y	Y
6 Tierney	N	N	Y	Y	Y
7 Markey	N	N	?	Y	Y
8 Capuano	N	N	Y	Y	Y
9 Lynch	N	N	Y	Y	Y
10 Delahunt	N	N	Y	Y	?
MICHIGAN					
1 Stupak	N	N	N	N	Y
2 Hoekstra	Y	Y	N	N	Y
3 Ehlers	Y	Y	N	N	Y
4 Camp	N	N	N	N	Y
5 Kildee	N	N	Y	N	Y
6 Upton	N	N	N	N	Y
7 Schauer	Y	Y	Y	Y	Y
8 Rogers	Y	N	N	N	Y
9 Peters	N	N	Y	Y	Y
10 Miller	N	N	N	N	Y
11 McCotter	Y	Y	N	N	Y
12 Levin	N	N	Y	Y	Y
13 Kilpatrick	N	N	Y	Y	Y
14 Conyers	N	N	Y	Y	Y
15 Dingell	N	N	Y	N	Y
MINNESOTA					
1 Walz	N	N	Y	Y	Y
2 Kline	Y	Y	N	N	Y
3 Paulsen	N	N	N	N	Y
4 McCollum	N	N	Y	Y	Y

	568	569	570	571	572
5 Ellison	N	N	Y	Y	Y
6 Bachmann	Y	Y	N	N	Y
7 Peterson	N	N	N	N	Y
8 Oberstar	N	N	N	N	Y
MISSISSIPPI					
1 Childers	N	N	N	N	Y
2 Thompson	N	N	Y	Y	Y
3 Harper	N	N	N	N	Y
4 Taylor	N	N	N	N	Y
MISSOURI					
1 Clay	N	N	Y	Y	Y
2 Akin	Y	N	N	N	Y
3 Carnahan	N	N	Y	Y	Y
4 Skelton	N	N	N	N	Y
5 Cleaver	N	N	Y	Y	Y
6 Graves	Y	N	N	N	Y
7 Blunt	N	N	N	N	Y
8 Emerson	N	N	N	N	Y
9 Luetkemeyer	Y	Y	N	N	Y
MONTANA					
AL Rehberg	N	N	N	N	Y
NEBRASKA					
1 Fortenberry	Y	Y	N	N	Y
2 Terry	Y	N	N	N	Y
3 Smith	Y	Y	N	N	Y
NEVADA					
1 Berkley	N	N	Y	Y	Y
2 Heller	Y	Y	N	N	Y
3 Titus	N	N	Y	Y	Y
NEW HAMPSHIRE					
1 Shea-Porter	N	N	Y	Y	Y
2 Hodes	N	N	Y	Y	Y
NEW JERSEY					
1 Andrews	N	N	Y	Y	Y
2 LoBiondo	N	N	N	N	Y
3 Adler	N	N	Y	Y	Y
4 Smith	N	N	N	N	Y
5 Garrett	Y	Y	N	N	Y
6 Pallone	N	N	Y	Y	Y
7 Lance	N	N	N	N	Y
8 Pascrell	N	N	Y	Y	Y
9 Rothman	N	N	Y	Y	Y
10 Payne	N	N	Y	Y	Y
11 Frelinghuysen	N	N	N	N	Y
12 Holt	N	N	Y	Y	Y
13 Sires	N	N	Y	Y	Y
NEW MEXICO					
1 Heinrich	N	N	Y	Y	Y
2 Teague	N	N	Y	Y	Y
3 Lujan	N	N	Y	Y	Y
NEW YORK					
1 Bishop	N	N	Y	Y	Y
2 Israel	N	N	Y	Y	Y
3 King	N	N	N	N	Y
4 McCarthy	?	?	Y	Y	Y
5 Ackerman	N	N	Y	Y	Y
6 Meeks	N	N	Y	Y	Y
7 Crowley	N	N	Y	Y	Y
8 Nadler	N	N	Y	Y	Y
9 Weiner	N	N	Y	Y	Y
10 Towns	N	N	Y	Y	Y
11 Clarke	N	N	Y	Y	Y
12 Velázquez	N	N	Y	Y	Y
13 McMahon	N	N	Y	Y	Y
14 Maloney	N	N	Y	Y	Y
15 Rangel	N	N	Y	Y	Y
16 Serrano	N	N	Y	Y	?
17 Engel	N	N	Y	Y	Y
18 Lowey	N	N	Y	Y	Y
19 Hall	N	N	Y	Y	Y
20 Murphy	N	N	Y	Y	N
21 Tonko	N	N	Y	Y	Y
22 Hinchey	N	N	Y	Y	Y
23 McHugh	N	N	N	Y	?
24 Arcuri	N	N	Y	Y	Y
25 Maffei	N	N	Y	Y	Y
26 Lee	N	N	N	N	Y
27 Higgins	N	N	Y	Y	Y
28 Slaughter	N	N	Y	Y	Y
29 Massa	N	N	Y	Y	Y
NORTH CAROLINA					
1 Butterfield	N	N	Y	Y	Y
2 Etheridge	N	N	Y	Y	Y
3 Jones	N	N	N	N	Y
4 Price	N	N	Y	Y	Y

	568	569	570	571	572
5 Foxx	Y	Y	N	N	Y
6 Coble	Y	Y	N	N	Y
7 McIntyre	N	N	N	N	Y
8 Kissell	N	N	Y	Y	Y
9 Myrick	Y	Y	N	N	Y
10 McHenry	Y	Y	N	N	Y
11 Shuler	N	N	N	N	Y
12 Watt	N	N	Y	Y	Y
13 Miller	N	N	Y	Y	Y
NORTH DAKOTA					
AL Pomeroy	N	N	Y	Y	Y
OHIO					
1 Driehaus	N	N	N	N	Y
2 Schmidt	Y	Y	N	N	Y
3 Turner	N	N	N	N	Y
4 Jordan	Y	Y	N	N	Y
5 Latta	Y	Y	N	N	Y
6 Wilson	N	N	Y	N	Y
7 Austria	Y	Y	N	N	Y
8 Boehner	Y	Y	N	N	Y
9 Kaptur	N	N	Y	Y	Y
10 Kucinich	N	N	Y	Y	Y
11 Fudge	N	N	Y	Y	Y
12 Tiberi	Y	Y	N	N	Y
13 Sutton	N	N	Y	Y	Y
14 LaTourette	N	N	Y	Y	Y
15 Kilroy	N	N	Y	Y	Y
16 Boccieri	N	N	N	N	Y
17 Ryan	N	N	Y	Y	Y
18 Space	N	N	Y	Y	Y
OKLAHOMA					
1 Sullivan	Y	N	?	N	Y
2 Boren	N	N	N	N	Y
3 Lucas	?	?	?	?	?
4 Cole	N	N	N	N	Y
5 Fallin	Y	Y	N	N	Y
OREGON					
1 Wu	N	N	Y	Y	Y
2 Walden	Y	N	N	N	Y
3 Blumenauer	?	N	Y	Y	Y
4 DeFazio	N	N	Y	Y	Y
5 Schrader	N	N	Y	Y	Y
PENNSYLVANIA					
1 Brady	N	N	Y	Y	Y
2 Fattah	N	N	Y	Y	Y
3 Dahlkemper	N	N	N	N	Y
4 Altmire	N	N	N	N	Y
5 Thompson	N	N	N	N	Y
6 Gerlach	N	N	N	N	Y
7 Sestak	N	N	Y	Y	Y
8 Murphy, P.	N	N	Y	Y	Y
9 Shuster	N	N	?	N	Y
10 Carney	N	N	Y	Y	Y
11 Kanjorski	N	N	Y	Y	Y
12 Murtha	N	N	Y	Y	?
13 Schwartz	N	N	Y	Y	Y
14 Doyle	N	N	Y	Y	Y
15 Dent	N	N	N	N	Y
16 Pitts	Y	Y	N	N	Y
17 Holden	N	N	Y	Y	Y
18 Murphy, T.	N	N	N	N	Y
19 Platts	N	N	N	N	Y
RHODE ISLAND					
1 Kennedy	N	N	Y	Y	Y
2 Langevin	N	N	Y	Y	Y
SOUTH CAROLINA					
1 Brown	N	N	N	N	Y
2 Wilson	Y	Y	N	N	Y
3 Barrett	?	?	?	?	?
4 Inglis	Y	Y	N	N	Y
5 Spratt	N	N	Y	Y	Y
6 Clyburn	N	N	Y	Y	Y
SOUTH DAKOTA					
AL Herseth Sandlin	N	N	Y	Y	Y
TENNESSEE					
1 Roe	Y	N	N	N	Y
2 Duncan	Y	Y	N	N	Y
3 Wamp	N	N	N	N	Y
4 Davis	N	N	N	N	Y
5 Cooper	Y	Y	Y	Y	Y
6 Gordon	N	N	Y	Y	Y
7 Blackburn	Y	Y	N	N	Y
8 Tanner	N	N	Y	Y	Y
9 Cohen	N	N	Y	Y	Y

	568	569	570	571	572
TEXAS					
1 Gohmert	Y	?	N	N	?
2 Poe	Y	N	N	N	Y
3 Johnson, S.	Y	N	N	N	Y
4 Hall	Y	N	N	N	Y
5 Hensarling	Y	Y	?	N	Y
6 Barton	N	N	N	N	Y
7 Culberson	N	N	N	N	Y
8 Brady	Y	N	N	N	Y
9 Green, A.	N	N	Y	Y	Y
10 McCaul	Y	Y	N	N	Y
11 Conaway	Y	N	N	N	Y
12 Granger	N	N	N	N	Y
13 Thornberry	Y	Y	N	N	Y
14 Paul	Y	Y	N	N	Y
15 Hinojosa	N	N	Y	Y	Y
16 Reyes	N	N	Y	Y	Y
17 Edwards	N	N	Y	Y	Y
18 Jackson Lee	N	N	Y	Y	Y
19 Neugebauer	Y	Y	N	N	Y
20 Gonzalez	N	N	Y	Y	Y
21 Smith	N	N	N	N	Y
22 Olson	Y	N	N	N	Y
23 Rodriguez	N	N	Y	Y	Y
24 Marchant	Y	Y	N	N	Y
25 Doggett	N	N	Y	Y	Y
26 Burgess	Y	N	N	N	Y
27 Ortiz	N	N	Y	Y	Y
28 Cuellar	N	N	Y	Y	Y
29 Green, G.	N	N	Y	Y	Y
30 Johnson, E.	N	N	Y	Y	Y
31 Carter	N	N	N	N	Y
32 Sessions	Y	Y	N	N	Y
UTAH					
1 Bishop	N	N	N	N	Y
2 Matheson	N	N	Y	N	Y
3 Chaffetz	Y	Y	N	N	Y
VERMONT					
AL Welch	N	N	?	Y	Y
VIRGINIA					
1 Wittman	Y	N	N	N	Y
2 Nye	N	Y	Y	N	Y
3 Scott	?	?	?	?	?
4 Forbes	Y	N	N	N	Y
5 Perriello	N	N	Y	Y	Y
6 Goodlatte	Y	Y	N	N	Y
7 Cantor	Y	Y	N	N	Y
8 Moran	N	N	Y	Y	Y
9 Boucher	N	N	Y	Y	Y
10 Wolf	N	N	N	N	Y
11 Connolly	N	N	Y	Y	Y
WASHINGTON					
1 Inslee	N	N	Y	Y	Y
2 Larsen	N	N	Y	Y	Y
3 Baird	N	N	Y	Y	?
4 Hastings	Y	N	N	N	Y
5 McMorris Rodgers	Y	N	N	N	Y
6 Dicks	N	N	Y	Y	Y
7 McDermott	N	N	Y	Y	Y
8 Reichert	N	N	N	N	Y
9 Smith	N	N	Y	Y	Y
WEST VIRGINIA					
1 Mollohan	N	N	Y	N	Y
2 Capito	N	N	N	N	Y
3 Rahall	N	N	Y	N	Y
WISCONSIN					
1 Ryan	Y	Y	N	N	Y
2 Baldwin	N	N	Y	Y	Y
3 Kind	Y	Y	Y	Y	Y
4 Moore	N	N	Y	Y	Y
5 Sensenbrenner	Y	Y	N	N	Y
6 Petri	Y	Y	N	N	Y
7 Obey	N	N	Y	Y	Y
8 Kagen	N	N	Y	Y	Y
WYOMING					
AL Lummis	Y	Y	N	N	Y
DELEGATES					
Faleomavaega (A.S.)	?	?			
Norton (D.C.)	N	N			
Bordallo (Guam)	?	?			
Sablan (N. Marianas)	N	N			
Pierluisi (P.R.)	N	N			
Christensen (V.I.)	N	N			

IN THE HOUSE | By Vote Number

573. **Fairness Doctrine/Motion to Table.** McGovern, D-Mass., motion to table (kill) the Walden, R-Ore., appeal of the ruling of the chair that the Walden draft resolution does not constitute a point of privilege under Rule IX of the House. The draft resolution would require the rule (H Res 644) that provides for House floor consideration of the fiscal 2010 Financial Services appropriations bill (HR 3170) to allow for consideration of an amendment that would bar the use of funds in the bill to implement the Fairness Doctrine. Motion agreed to 238-174: R 0-170; D 238-4. July 17, 2009.

574. **HR 1018. Wild Free-Roaming Horses and Burros/Previous Question.** McGovern, D-Mass., motion to order the previous question (thus ending debate and possibility of amendment) on adoption of the rule (H Res 653) that would provide for House floor consideration of the bill that would require the Interior Department to identify new rangeland and establish sanctuaries for wild free-roaming horses and burros. Motion agreed to 232-188: R 2-170; D 230-18. July 17, 2009.

575. **HR 1018. Wild Free-Roaming Horses and Burros/Rule.** Adoption of the rule (H Res 653) to provide for House floor consideration of the bill that would require the Interior Department to identify new rangeland and establish sanctuaries for wild free-roaming horses and burros. Adopted 236-186: R 4-166; D 232-20. July 17, 2009.

576. **HR 1018. Wild Free-Roaming Horses and Burros/Republican Substitute.** Hastings, R-Wash., substitute amendment that would prohibit the sale or transfer of wild horses or burros or their remains for processing into commercial products. Rejected 74-348: R 60-111; D 14-237. July 17, 2009.

577. **HR 1018. Wild Free-Roaming Horses and Burros/Passage.** Passage of the bill that would require the Interior Department to identify new rangeland and establish sanctuaries for wild free-roaming horses and burros, implement sterilization techniques for fertility control, prohibit the killing of healthy animals, and implement aggressive marketing strategies for an existing adoption program. Passed 239-185: R 33-138; D 206-47. July 17, 2009.

578. **HR 3183. Fiscal 2010 Energy-Water Appropriations/Laboratory-Directed Research and Development.** Heinrich, D-N.M., amendment that would increase, from 6 percent to 7 percent, the share of funds the Energy Department could authorize for laboratory-directed research and development from funds provided for government-owned labs operated by contractors. Adopted in Committee of the Whole 424-0: R 171-0; D 253-0. July 17, 2009.

579. **HR 3183. Fiscal 2010 Energy-Water Appropriations/NRC Report to Congress.** Cao, R-La., amendment that would require the Nuclear Regulatory Commission, within 60 days of the bill's enactment, to provide a report to Congress identifying barriers to and recommendations for streamlining the issuance of combined construction and operating licenses for new nuclear reactors. Adopted in Committee of the Whole 423-1: R 170-0; D 253-1. July 17, 2009.

	573	574	575	576	577	578	579
ALABAMA							
1 Bonner	N	N	N	N	N	Y	Y
2 Bright	Y	Y	Y	N	N	Y	Y
3 Rogers	N	N	N	N	N	Y	Y
4 Aderholt	N	N	N	Y	N	Y	Y
5 Griffith	Y	N	N	N	N	Y	Y
6 Bachus	N	N	N	Y	N	Y	Y
7 Davis	Y	Y	Y	N	Y	Y	Y
ALASKA							
AL Young	?	N	N	N	N	Y	Y
ARIZONA							
1 Kirkpatrick	Y	Y	N	N	N	Y	Y
2 Franks	N	N	N	N	N	Y	Y
3 Shadegg	N	N	N	N	N	Y	Y
4 Pastor	Y	Y	Y	N	Y	Y	Y
5 Mitchell	Y	Y	Y	N	Y	Y	Y
6 Flake	N	N	N	N	N	Y	Y
7 Grijalva	Y	Y	Y	N	Y	Y	Y
8 Giffords	Y	Y	Y	N	N	Y	Y
ARKANSAS							
1 Berry	Y	Y	Y	N	Y	Y	Y
2 Snyder	Y	Y	Y	N	Y	Y	Y
3 Boozman	N	N	N	N	N	Y	Y
4 Ross	Y	N	N	Y	N	Y	Y
CALIFORNIA							
1 Thompson	Y	Y	Y	N	Y	Y	Y
2 Herger	N	N	N	N	N	Y	Y
3 Lungren	N	N	N	Y	N	Y	Y
4 McClintock	N	N	N	Y	N	Y	Y
5 Matsui	Y	Y	Y	N	Y	Y	Y
6 Woolsey	Y	Y	Y	N	Y	Y	Y
7 Miller, George	Y	Y	Y	N	Y	Y	Y
8 Pelosi							
9 Lee	Y	Y	Y	N	Y	Y	Y
10 Vacant							
11 McNerney	Y	Y	Y	N	Y	Y	Y
12 Speier	Y	Y	Y	N	Y	Y	Y
13 Stark	Y	Y	Y	N	Y	Y	Y
14 Eshoo	?	Y	Y	N	Y	Y	Y
15 Honda	Y	Y	Y	N	Y	Y	Y
16 Lofgren	Y	Y	Y	N	Y	Y	Y
17 Farr	Y	Y	Y	N	Y	Y	Y
18 Cardoza	Y	Y	Y	N	N	Y	Y
19 Radanovich	N	N	N	Y	N	Y	Y
20 Costa	Y	N	N	N	N	Y	Y
21 Nunes	N	N	N	N	N	Y	Y
22 McCarthy	?	N	N	N	N	Y	Y
23 Capps	Y	Y	Y	N	Y	Y	Y
24 Gallegly	N	N	N	N	Y	Y	Y
25 McKeon	N	N	N	N	N	Y	Y
26 Dreier	N	N	N	N	Y	Y	Y
27 Sherman	Y	Y	Y	N	Y	Y	Y
28 Berman	Y	Y	Y	N	Y	Y	Y
29 Schiff	Y	Y	Y	N	Y	Y	Y
30 Waxman	Y	Y	Y	N	Y	Y	Y
31 Becerra	Y	Y	Y	N	Y	Y	Y
32 Chu	Y	Y	Y	N	Y	Y	Y
33 Watson	Y	Y	Y	N	Y	Y	Y
34 Roybal-Allard	Y	Y	Y	N	Y	Y	Y
35 Waters	Y	Y	Y	N	Y	Y	Y
36 Harman	Y	Y	Y	N	Y	Y	?
37 Richardson	?	Y	Y	N	Y	Y	Y
38 Napolitano	Y	Y	Y	N	Y	Y	Y
39 Sánchez, Linda	Y	Y	Y	N	Y	Y	Y
40 Royce	N	N	N	N	Y	Y	Y
41 Lewis	N	N	N	Y	Y	Y	Y
42 Miller, Gary	?	?	?	?	?	?	?
43 Baca	Y	Y	Y	N	Y	Y	Y
44 Calvert	N	N	N	Y	Y	Y	Y
45 Bono Mack	N	N	N	Y	Y	Y	Y
46 Rohrabacher	N	N	N	N	N	Y	Y
47 Sanchez, Loretta	Y	Y	Y	Y	N	Y	Y
48 Campbell	N	N	N	N	Y	Y	Y
49 Issa	N	N	N	N	Y	Y	Y
50 Bilbray	N	N	N	Y	Y	Y	Y
51 Filner	Y	Y	Y	N	Y	Y	Y
52 Hunter	N	N	N	N	Y	Y	Y
53 Davis	Y	Y	Y	N	Y	Y	Y

	573	574	575	576	577	578	579
COLORADO							
1 DeGette	Y	Y	Y	N	Y	Y	Y
2 Polis	Y	Y	Y	N	Y	Y	Y
3 Salazar	Y	N	N	N	N	Y	Y
4 Markey	Y	N	N	N	N	Y	Y
5 Lamborn	N	N	N	Y	N	Y	Y
6 Coffman	N	N	N	Y	N	Y	Y
7 Perlmutter	Y	Y	Y	N	Y	Y	Y
CONNECTICUT							
1 Larson	Y	Y	Y	N	Y	Y	Y
2 Courtney	Y	Y	Y	N	Y	Y	Y
3 DeLauro	Y	Y	Y	N	Y	Y	Y
4 Himes	Y	Y	Y	N	Y	Y	Y
5 Murphy	Y	Y	Y	N	Y	Y	Y
DELAWARE							
AL Castle	N	N	N	N	Y	Y	Y
FLORIDA							
1 Miller	N	N	N	N	N	Y	Y
2 Boyd	Y	Y	Y	N	N	Y	Y
3 Brown	Y	Y	Y	N	Y	Y	Y
4 Crenshaw	N	N	N	N	Y	Y	Y
5 Brown-Waite	N	N	N	N	Y	Y	Y
6 Stearns	N	N	N	N	N	Y	Y
7 Mica	N	N	N	N	N	Y	Y
8 Grayson	Y	Y	Y	N	Y	Y	Y
9 Bilirakis	N	N	N	Y	N	Y	Y
10 Young	N	N	N	Y	N	Y	Y
11 Castor	Y	Y	Y	N	Y	Y	Y
12 Putnam	N	N	N	N	N	Y	Y
13 Buchanan	N	N	N	N	Y	Y	Y
14 Mack	N	N	N	N	N	Y	Y
15 Posey	N	N	N	Y	N	Y	Y
16 Rooney	N	N	N	Y	N	Y	Y
17 Meek	Y	Y	Y	N	Y	Y	Y
18 Ros-Lehtinen	N	N	Y	Y	Y	Y	Y
19 Wexler	Y	Y	Y	N	Y	Y	Y
20 Wasserman Schultz	?	Y	Y	N	Y	Y	Y
21 Diaz-Balart, L.	N	N	N	Y	N	Y	Y
22 Klein	Y	Y	Y	N	Y	Y	Y
23 Hastings	Y	Y	Y	N	Y	Y	Y
24 Kosmas	N	Y	Y	N	N	Y	Y
25 Diaz-Balart, M.	N	N	N	N	N	Y	Y
GEORGIA							
1 Kingston	N	N	N	N	N	Y	Y
2 Bishop	Y	Y	Y	N	Y	Y	Y
3 Westmoreland	–	–	–	–	–	+	+
4 Johnson	Y	Y	Y	N	Y	Y	Y
5 Lewis	Y	Y	Y	N	Y	Y	Y
6 Price	N	N	N	N	N	Y	Y
7 Linder	N	N	N	Y	N	Y	Y
8 Marshall	Y	Y	Y	N	Y	Y	Y
9 Deal	N	N	N	N	N	Y	Y
10 Broun	N	N	N	N	N	Y	Y
11 Gingrey	N	N	N	N	N	Y	Y
12 Barrow	Y	Y	Y	N	Y	Y	Y
13 Scott	Y	Y	Y	N	Y	Y	Y
HAWAII							
1 Abercrombie	Y	Y	Y	N	Y	Y	Y
2 Hirono	Y	Y	Y	N	Y	Y	Y
IDAHO							
1 Minnick	N	N	N	N	N	Y	Y
2 Simpson	N	N	N	N	N	Y	Y
ILLINOIS							
1 Rush	Y	Y	Y	N	Y	?	Y
2 Jackson	Y	Y	Y	N	Y	Y	Y
3 Lipinski	Y	Y	Y	N	Y	Y	Y
4 Gutierrez	?	Y	Y	N	Y	Y	Y
5 Quigley	Y	Y	Y	N	Y	Y	Y
6 Roskam	N	N	N	Y	N	Y	?
7 Davis	Y	Y	Y	N	Y	Y	Y
8 Bean	Y	Y	Y	N	Y	Y	Y
9 Schakowsky	?	Y	Y	N	Y	Y	Y
10 Kirk	N	N	N	Y	N	Y	Y
11 Halvorson	Y	Y	Y	N	Y	Y	Y
12 Costello	Y	Y	Y	N	Y	Y	Y
13 Biggert	N	N	N	Y	N	Y	Y
14 Foster	Y	Y	Y	N	Y	Y	Y
15 Johnson	N	N	N	N	Y	Y	Y

	573	574	575	576	577	578	579
16 **Manzullo**	N	N	N	Y	N	Y	Y
17 Hare	Y	Y	Y	N	Y	Y	Y
18 **Schock**	N	N	N	N	?	Y	Y
19 **Shimkus**	N	N	N	N	N	Y	Y
INDIANA							
1 Visclosky	Y	Y	Y	N	Y	P	Y
2 Donnelly	Y	N	N	N	Y	Y	Y
3 **Souder**	N	N	N	N	N	Y	Y
4 **Buyer**	N	N	N	N	N	Y	Y
5 **Burton**	N	N	N	N	Y	Y	Y
6 **Pence**	N	N	N	N	N	Y	Y
7 Carson	Y	Y	Y	Y	Y	Y	Y
8 Ellsworth	Y	N	N	N	N	Y	Y
9 Hill	Y	N	N	N	N	Y	Y
IOWA							
1 Braley	Y	+	Y	N	Y	Y	Y
2 Loebsack	Y	Y	Y	N	Y	Y	Y
3 Boswell	Y	Y	Y	N	N	Y	Y
4 **Latham**	N	N	N	N	N	Y	Y
5 **King**	N	N	N	N	N	Y	Y
KANSAS							
1 **Moran**	N	N	N	N	N	Y	Y
2 **Jenkins**	N	N	N	N	N	Y	Y
3 Moore	Y	N	Y	N	Y	Y	Y
4 **Tiahrt**	N	N	N	N	N	Y	Y
KENTUCKY							
1 **Whitfield**	N	Y	Y	N	Y	Y	Y
2 **Guthrie**	N	N	N	Y	N	Y	Y
3 Yarmuth	Y	Y	Y	N	Y	Y	Y
4 **Davis**	N	N	N	Y	N	Y	Y
5 **Rogers**	N	N	N	Y	N	Y	Y
6 Chandler	Y	Y	Y	N	Y	Y	Y
LOUISIANA							
1 **Scalise**	N	N	N	Y	N	Y	Y
2 **Cao**	N	N	N	Y	Y	Y	Y
3 Melancon	Y	Y	N	N	N	Y	Y
4 **Fleming**	N	N	N	Y	N	Y	Y
5 **Alexander**	N	N	N	N	N	Y	Y
6 **Cassidy**	N	N	N	N	N	?	Y
7 **Boustany**	N	N	N	Y	N	Y	Y
MAINE							
1 Pingree	Y	Y	Y	N	Y	Y	Y
2 Michaud	Y	Y	Y	N	Y	Y	Y
MARYLAND							
1 Kratovil	N	N	N	N	Y	Y	Y
2 Ruppersberger	Y	Y	Y	N	Y	Y	Y
3 Sarbanes	Y	Y	Y	N	Y	Y	Y
4 Edwards	Y	Y	Y	N	Y	Y	Y
5 Hoyer	Y	Y	Y	N	Y	Y	Y
6 **Bartlett**	N	N	N	Y	Y	Y	Y
7 Cummings	Y	Y	Y	N	Y	Y	Y
8 Van Hollen	Y	Y	Y	N	Y	Y	Y
MASSACHUSETTS							
1 Olver	Y	Y	Y	N	Y	Y	Y
2 Neal	Y	Y	Y	N	Y	Y	Y
3 McGovern	Y	Y	Y	N	Y	Y	Y
4 Frank	Y	Y	Y	N	Y	Y	Y
5 Tsongas	Y	Y	Y	N	Y	Y	Y
6 Tierney	Y	Y	Y	N	Y	Y	Y
7 Markey	Y	Y	Y	N	Y	Y	Y
8 Capuano	Y	Y	Y	N	Y	Y	Y
9 Lynch	Y	Y	Y	N	Y	Y	Y
10 Delahunt	Y	Y	Y	N	Y	Y	Y
MICHIGAN							
1 Stupak	Y	Y	Y	N	N	Y	Y
2 **Hoekstra**	N	N	N	N	N	Y	Y
3 **Ehlers**	N	N	N	N	N	Y	Y
4 **Camp**	N	N	N	N	N	Y	Y
5 Kildee	?	Y	Y	N	Y	Y	Y
6 **Upton**	N	N	N	N	Y	Y	Y
7 Schauer	Y	Y	Y	N	Y	Y	Y
8 **Rogers**	N	N	N	Y	N	Y	Y
9 Peters	Y	Y	Y	N	Y	Y	Y
10 **Miller**	N	N	N	N	Y	Y	Y
11 **McCotter**	N	N	N	N	Y	Y	Y
12 Levin	Y	Y	Y	N	Y	Y	Y
13 Kilpatrick	Y	Y	Y	N	Y	Y	Y
14 Conyers	Y	Y	Y	N	Y	Y	Y
15 Dingell	Y	Y	Y	N	Y	Y	Y
MINNESOTA							
1 Walz	Y	Y	Y	N	N	Y	Y
2 **Kline**	N	N	N	N	N	Y	Y
3 **Paulsen**	N	N	N	Y	N	Y	Y
4 McCollum	Y	Y	Y	N	Y	Y	Y

	573	574	575	576	577	578	579
5 Ellison	Y	+	Y	N	Y	Y	Y
6 **Bachmann**	N	N	N	N	N	Y	Y
7 Peterson	Y	Y	Y	N	N	?	?
8 Oberstar	Y	Y	Y	N	Y	Y	Y
MISSISSIPPI							
1 Childers	Y	N	N	N	N	Y	Y
2 Thompson	Y	Y	Y	N	Y	Y	Y
3 **Harper**	N	N	N	N	N	Y	Y
4 Taylor	?	?	?	?	?	?	?
MISSOURI							
1 Clay	Y	Y	Y	N	Y	Y	Y
2 **Akin**	N	N	N	N	N	Y	Y
3 Carnahan	Y	Y	Y	N	Y	Y	Y
4 Skelton	Y	Y	Y	N	N	Y	Y
5 Cleaver	Y	Y	Y	N	Y	Y	Y
6 **Graves**	–	–	–	–	–	+	+
7 **Blunt**	N	N	N	N	N	Y	Y
8 **Emerson**	N	N	N	N	N	Y	Y
9 **Luetkemeyer**	N	N	N	N	N	Y	Y
MONTANA							
AL **Rehberg**	N	N	N	N	N	Y	Y
NEBRASKA							
1 **Fortenberry**	N	N	N	N	N	Y	Y
2 **Terry**	N	N	N	N	N	Y	Y
3 **Smith**	N	N	N	N	N	Y	Y
NEVADA							
1 Berkley	Y	Y	Y	N	Y	Y	Y
2 **Heller**	N	N	N	Y	N	Y	Y
3 Titus	Y	Y	Y	N	Y	Y	Y
NEW HAMPSHIRE							
1 Shea-Porter	Y	Y	Y	?	Y	Y	Y
2 Hodes	Y	Y	Y	N	Y	Y	Y
NEW JERSEY							
1 Andrews	Y	Y	Y	N	Y	Y	Y
2 **LoBiondo**	N	N	N	N	Y	Y	Y
3 Adler	Y	Y	Y	N	Y	Y	Y
4 **Smith**	N	N	N	N	Y	Y	Y
5 **Garrett**	N	N	N	N	N	Y	Y
6 Pallone	Y	Y	Y	N	Y	Y	Y
7 **Lance**	N	N	N	N	Y	Y	Y
8 Pascrell	Y	Y	Y	N	Y	Y	Y
9 Rothman	Y	Y	Y	N	Y	Y	Y
10 Payne	Y	Y	Y	N	Y	Y	Y
11 **Frelinghuysen**	N	N	N	N	Y	Y	Y
12 Holt	Y	Y	Y	N	Y	Y	Y
13 Sires	Y	Y	Y	N	Y	Y	Y
NEW MEXICO							
1 Heinrich	Y	Y	Y	N	Y	Y	Y
2 Teague	Y	N	N	N	N	Y	Y
3 Lujan	Y	Y	Y	N	Y	Y	Y
NEW YORK							
1 Bishop	Y	Y	Y	N	Y	Y	Y
2 Israel	Y	Y	Y	N	Y	Y	Y
3 **King**	N	N	N	N	Y	Y	Y
4 McCarthy	?	Y	Y	N	Y	Y	Y
5 Ackerman	?	?	?	?	?	?	?
6 Meeks	Y	Y	Y	N	Y	Y	Y
7 Crowley	Y	Y	Y	N	Y	Y	Y
8 Nadler	Y	?	Y	N	Y	Y	N
9 Weiner	Y	Y	Y	N	Y	Y	Y
10 Towns	Y	Y	Y	N	Y	Y	Y
11 Clarke	Y	Y	Y	N	Y	Y	Y
12 Velázquez	Y	Y	Y	N	Y	Y	Y
13 McMahon	Y	Y	Y	N	Y	Y	Y
14 Maloney	Y	Y	Y	N	Y	Y	Y
15 Rangel	Y	?	Y	N	Y	Y	Y
16 Serrano	Y	Y	Y	N	Y	Y	Y
17 Engel	Y	Y	Y	N	Y	Y	Y
18 Lowey	Y	Y	Y	N	Y	Y	Y
19 Hall	Y	Y	Y	N	Y	Y	Y
20 Murphy	Y	Y	N	N	N	Y	Y
21 Tonko	Y	Y	Y	N	Y	Y	Y
22 Hinchey	Y	Y	Y	N	Y	Y	Y
23 **McHugh**	N	N	N	Y	N	Y	Y
24 Arcuri	Y	Y	Y	Y	N	Y	Y
25 Maffei	Y	Y	Y	N	Y	Y	Y
26 **Lee**	N	N	N	Y	N	Y	Y
27 Higgins	Y	Y	Y	N	Y	Y	Y
28 Slaughter	Y	Y	Y	?	Y	Y	Y
29 Massa	Y	Y	Y	N	Y	Y	Y
NORTH CAROLINA							
1 Butterfield	Y	Y	Y	N	Y	Y	Y
2 Etheridge	Y	Y	Y	N	Y	Y	Y
3 **Jones**	N	Y	Y	N	Y	Y	Y
4 Price	Y	Y	Y	N	Y	Y	Y

	573	574	575	576	577	578	579
5 **Foxx**	N	N	N	Y	N	Y	Y
6 **Coble**	N	N	Y	?	?	?	?
7 McIntyre	Y	Y	Y	Y	Y	Y	Y
8 Kissell	Y	Y	Y	N	Y	Y	Y
9 **Myrick**	N	N	N	Y	N	Y	Y
10 **McHenry**	N	N	N	N	N	Y	Y
11 Shuler	Y	N	N	Y	N	Y	Y
12 Watt	Y	Y	Y	N	Y	Y	Y
13 Miller	Y	Y	Y	N	Y	Y	Y
NORTH DAKOTA							
AL Pomeroy	Y	Y	Y	N	N	Y	Y
OHIO							
1 Driehaus	Y	Y	Y	N	N	Y	Y
2 **Schmidt**	N	N	N	Y	N	Y	Y
3 **Turner**	N	N	N	Y	Y	Y	Y
4 **Jordan**	N	N	N	N	N	Y	Y
5 **Latta**	N	N	N	N	N	Y	Y
6 Wilson	Y	Y	Y	N	Y	Y	Y
7 **Austria**	N	N	N	N	N	Y	Y
8 **Boehner**	N	N	N	Y	N	Y	Y
9 Kaptur	Y	Y	Y	N	Y	Y	Y
10 Kucinich	Y	Y	Y	N	Y	Y	Y
11 Fudge	Y	Y	Y	N	Y	Y	Y
12 **Tiberi**	N	N	N	Y	N	Y	Y
13 Sutton	?	Y	Y	N	Y	Y	Y
14 **LaTourette**	N	N	?	N	N	Y	Y
15 Kilroy	Y	Y	Y	N	Y	Y	Y
16 Boccieri	Y	Y	Y	N	N	Y	Y
17 Ryan	Y	Y	Y	N	Y	Y	Y
18 Space	Y	Y	N	N	N	Y	Y
OKLAHOMA							
1 **Sullivan**	N	N	N	N	N	Y	Y
2 Boren	Y	N	N	N	N	Y	Y
3 **Lucas**	?	?	?	?	?	?	?
4 **Cole**	N	N	N	N	N	Y	Y
5 **Fallin**	N	N	N	N	N	Y	Y
OREGON							
1 Wu	Y	Y	Y	N	Y	Y	Y
2 **Walden**	N	N	N	N	N	Y	Y
3 Blumenauer	Y	Y	Y	N	Y	Y	Y
4 DeFazio	Y	Y	Y	N	Y	Y	Y
5 Schrader	Y	Y	Y	N	Y	Y	Y
PENNSYLVANIA							
1 Brady	Y	Y	Y	N	Y	Y	Y
2 Fattah	Y	Y	Y	N	Y	Y	Y
3 Dahlkemper	Y	Y	Y	N	N	Y	Y
4 Altmire	Y	Y	Y	Y	Y	Y	Y
5 **Thompson**	N	N	N	Y	N	Y	Y
6 **Gerlach**	N	N	N	N	Y	Y	Y
7 Sestak	Y	Y	Y	N	Y	Y	Y
8 Murphy, P.	?	Y	Y	N	Y	Y	Y
9 **Shuster**	N	N	N	N	N	Y	Y
10 Carney	Y	Y	Y	Y	Y	Y	Y
11 Kanjorski	Y	Y	Y	N	Y	Y	Y
12 Murtha	Y	Y	Y	N	Y	Y	Y
13 Schwartz	Y	Y	Y	N	Y	Y	Y
14 Doyle	Y	Y	Y	N	Y	Y	Y
15 **Dent**	N	N	N	N	Y	Y	Y
16 **Pitts**	N	N	N	Y	N	Y	Y
17 Holden	Y	Y	Y	N	Y	Y	Y
18 **Murphy, T.**	N	N	N	Y	N	Y	Y
19 **Platts**	N	N	N	N	Y	Y	Y
RHODE ISLAND							
1 Kennedy	Y	Y	Y	N	Y	Y	Y
2 Langevin	Y	Y	Y	N	Y	Y	Y
SOUTH CAROLINA							
1 **Brown**	N	N	N	N	N	Y	Y
2 **Wilson**	N	N	N	Y	N	Y	Y
3 **Barrett**	?	?	?	?	?	?	?
4 **Inglis**	N	N	N	N	N	Y	Y
5 Spratt	Y	Y	Y	N	Y	Y	Y
6 Clyburn	Y	Y	Y	N	Y	Y	Y
SOUTH DAKOTA							
AL Herseth Sandlin	Y	Y	Y	Y	N	Y	Y
TENNESSEE							
1 **Roe**	N	N	N	N	N	Y	Y
2 **Duncan**	N	N	N	Y	N	Y	Y
3 **Wamp**	N	N	N	Y	N	Y	Y
4 Davis	Y	N	N	N	N	Y	Y
5 Cooper	Y	Y	Y	N	Y	Y	Y
6 Gordon	Y	Y	Y	N	Y	Y	Y
7 **Blackburn**	N	N	N	N	N	Y	Y
8 Tanner	Y	Y	Y	Y	N	Y	Y
9 Cohen	Y	Y	Y	N	Y	Y	Y

	573	574	575	576	577	578	579
TEXAS							
1 **Gohmert**	N	?	?	N	N	Y	?
2 **Poe**	N	N	N	N	N	Y	Y
3 **Johnson, S.**	N	N	N	Y	N	Y	Y
4 **Hall**	N	N	Y	Y	Y	Y	Y
5 **Hensarling**	N	N	N	N	N	Y	Y
6 **Barton**	N	N	N	Y	N	Y	Y
7 **Culberson**	N	N	N	N	N	Y	Y
8 **Brady**	N	N	?	N	N	Y	Y
9 Green, A.	Y	Y	Y	N	Y	Y	Y
10 **McCaul**	N	N	N	N	N	Y	Y
11 **Conaway**	N	N	N	N	N	Y	Y
12 **Granger**	N	N	N	N	N	Y	Y
13 **Thornberry**	N	N	N	N	N	Y	Y
14 **Paul**	N	N	N	N	N	Y	Y
15 Hinojosa	+	Y	Y	N	N	Y	Y
16 Reyes	?	Y	Y	N	Y	Y	Y
17 Edwards	Y	Y	Y	N	Y	Y	Y
18 Jackson Lee	Y	Y	Y	N	Y	Y	Y
19 **Neugebauer**	N	N	N	N	N	Y	Y
20 Gonzalez	Y	Y	?	N	Y	Y	Y
21 **Smith**	N	N	N	N	N	Y	Y
22 **Olson**	N	N	N	N	N	Y	Y
23 Rodriguez	N	Y	Y	N	N	Y	Y
24 **Marchant**	N	N	N	N	N	Y	Y
25 Doggett	Y	Y	Y	N	N	Y	Y
26 **Burgess**	N	N	N	Y	N	Y	Y
27 Ortiz	Y	Y	Y	N	Y	Y	Y
28 Cuellar	Y	Y	Y	N	N	Y	Y
29 Green, G.	Y	Y	Y	N	Y	Y	Y
30 Johnson, E.	Y	Y	Y	N	Y	Y	Y
31 **Carter**	N	N	N	N	N	Y	Y
32 **Sessions**	N	N	N	N	N	Y	Y
UTAH							
1 **Bishop**	N	N	N	?	N	Y	Y
2 Matheson	Y	N	N	N	N	Y	Y
3 **Chaffetz**	N	N	N	N	N	Y	Y
VERMONT							
AL Welch	Y	Y	Y	N	Y	Y	Y
VIRGINIA							
1 **Wittman**	N	N	N	N	N	Y	Y
2 Nye	Y	Y	Y	N	Y	Y	Y
3 Scott	Y	Y	Y	N	Y	Y	Y
4 **Forbes**	N	N	N	Y	N	Y	Y
5 Perriello	Y	N	Y	Y	N	Y	Y
6 **Goodlatte**	N	N	N	N	N	Y	Y
7 **Cantor**	?	N	N	N	N	Y	Y
8 Moran	Y	Y	Y	N	Y	Y	Y
9 Boucher	Y	Y	Y	Y	Y	Y	Y
10 **Wolf**	N	N	N	Y	N	Y	Y
11 Connolly	Y	Y	Y	N	Y	Y	Y
WASHINGTON							
1 Inslee	Y	Y	Y	N	Y	Y	Y
2 Larsen	Y	Y	Y	N	N	Y	Y
3 Baird	Y	Y	Y	N	Y	Y	Y
4 **Hastings**	N	N	N	Y	N	Y	Y
5 **McMorris Rodgers**	N	N	N	Y	N	Y	Y
6 Dicks	Y	Y	Y	N	Y	Y	Y
7 McDermott	Y	Y	Y	N	Y	Y	Y
8 **Reichert**	N	N	N	N	Y	Y	Y
9 Smith	Y	Y	Y	N	Y	Y	Y
WEST VIRGINIA							
1 Mollohan	Y	Y	Y	N	Y	Y	Y
2 **Capito**	N	N	N	Y	N	Y	Y
3 Rahall	Y	Y	Y	N	Y	Y	Y
WISCONSIN							
1 **Ryan**	N	N	N	N	N	Y	Y
2 Baldwin	Y	Y	Y	N	Y	Y	Y
3 Kind	Y	?	Y	N	N	Y	Y
4 Moore	Y	Y	Y	N	Y	Y	Y
5 **Sensenbrenner**	N	N	N	N	N	Y	Y
6 **Petri**	N	N	N	N	N	Y	Y
7 Obey	Y	Y	Y	N	Y	Y	Y
8 Kagen	Y	Y	Y	N	Y	Y	Y
WYOMING							
AL **Lummis**	N	N	N	N	N	Y	Y
DELEGATES							
Faleomavaega (A.S.)						?	?
Norton (D.C.)						Y	Y
Bordallo (Guam)						?	?
Sablan (N. Marianas)						Y	Y
Pierluisi (P.R.)						?	?
Christensen (V.I.)						Y	Y

IN THE HOUSE | By Vote Number

580. HR 3183. Fiscal 2010 Energy-Water Appropriations/ **Discretionary Spending Reduction.** Blackburn, R-Tenn., amendment that would reduce discretionary spending in the bill by 5 percent. Rejected in Committee of the Whole 167-259: R 147-25; D 20-234. A "nay" was a vote in support of the president's position. July 17, 2009.

581. HR 3183. Fiscal 2010 Energy-Water Appropriations/ **Housatonic River Net-Zero Energy Building.** Campbell, R-Calif., amendment that would bar the use of funds appropriated in the bill for the Housatonic River Net-Zero Energy Building project and cut $1 million intended for the project from the bill. Rejected in Committee of the Whole 121-303: R 118-54; D 3-249. July 17, 2009.

582. HR 3183. Fiscal 2010 Energy-Water Appropriations/ **Maret Center Project.** Flake, R-Ariz., amendment that would bar the use of funds appropriated in the bill for the Maret Center project and cut $1.5 million intended for the project from the bill. Rejected in Committee of the Whole 89-338: R 79-92; D 10-246. July 17, 2009.

583. HR 3183. Fiscal 2010 Energy-Water Appropriations/ **Consortium for Plant Biotechnology Research.** Flake, R-Ariz., amendment that would bar the use of funds appropriated in the bill for the Consortium for Plant Biotechnology Research and cut $3 million intended for the project from the bill. Rejected in Committee of the Whole 89-335: R 85-87; D 4-248. July 17, 2009.

584. HR 3183. Fiscal 2010 Energy-Water Appropriations/ **Ethanol From Agriculture Project.** Flake, R-Ariz., amendment that would bar the use of funds appropriated in the bill for the Ethanol From Agriculture project and cut $500,000 intended for the project from the bill. Rejected in Committee of the Whole 102-318: R 95-73; D 7-245. July 17, 2009.

585. HR 3183. Fiscal 2010 Energy-Water Appropriations/ **Fort Mason Center Pier 2 Project.** Flake, R-Ariz., amendment that would bar the use of funds appropriated in the bill for the Fort Mason Center Pier 2 project and cut $2 million intended for the project from the bill. Rejected in Committee of the Whole 125-301: R 120-51; D 5-250. July 17, 2009.

586. HR 3183. Fiscal 2010 Energy-Water Appropriations/ **Whitworth University Stem Equipment Project.** Flake, R-Ariz., amendment that would bar the use of funds appropriated in the bill for the Whitworth University Stem Equipment project and cut $300,000 intended for the project from the bill. Rejected in Committee of the Whole 81-341: R 74-98; D 7-243. July 17, 2009.

	580	581	582	583	584	585	586
ALABAMA							
1 Bonner	Y	N	N	N	N	N	N
2 Bright	Y	Y	Y	N	N	Y	Y
3 Rogers	Y	N	N	N	N	N	N
4 Aderholt	Y	N	N	N	N	N	N
5 Griffith	N	N	N	N	N	N	N
6 Bachus	Y	N	N	N	N	N	N
7 Davis	N	N	N	N	N	N	N
ALASKA							
AL Young	N	N	N	N	N	Y	N
ARIZONA							
1 Kirkpatrick	Y	N	N	N	N	N	N
2 Franks	Y	Y	Y	Y	Y	Y	Y
3 Shadegg	Y	Y	Y	Y	Y	Y	Y
4 Pastor	N	N	N	N	N	N	N
5 Mitchell	N	N	N	N	N	N	N
6 Flake	Y	Y	Y	Y	Y	Y	Y
7 Grijalva	N	N	N	N	N	N	N
8 Giffords	N	N	Y	N	Y	N	N
ARKANSAS							
1 Berry	N	N	N	N	N	N	N
2 Snyder	N	N	N	N	N	N	N
3 Boozman	Y	N	N	N	N	Y	N
4 Ross	N	N	N	N	N	N	N
CALIFORNIA							
1 Thompson	N	N	N	N	N	N	N
2 Herger	Y	Y	Y	Y	Y	Y	Y
3 Lungren	Y	Y	Y	N	Y	Y	Y
4 McClintock	Y	Y	Y	Y	Y	Y	Y
5 Matsui	N	N	N	N	N	N	N
6 Woolsey	N	N	N	N	N	N	N
7 Miller, George	N	N	N	N	N	N	N
8 Pelosi							
9 Lee	N	N	N	N	N	N	N
10 Vacant							
11 McNerney	N	N	N	N	N	N	N
12 Speier	N	N	N	N	Y	N	N
13 Stark	N	N	N	?	N	N	N
14 Eshoo	N	N	N	N	N	N	N
15 Honda	N	N	N	N	?	N	N
16 Lofgren	N	N	N	N	N	N	N
17 Farr	N	N	N	N	N	N	N
18 Cardoza	N	N	N	N	N	N	N
19 Radanovich	Y	Y	N	N	N	N	N
20 Costa	N	N	N	N	N	N	?
21 Nunes	Y	Y	Y	Y	Y	Y	Y
22 McCarthy	Y	Y	N	N	Y	Y	N
23 Capps	N	N	N	N	N	N	N
24 Gallegly	Y	Y	N	N	N	Y	N
25 McKeon	Y	Y	N	N	N	N	N
26 Dreier	Y	N	N	N	N	N	N
27 Sherman	N	N	N	N	N	N	N
28 Berman	N	N	N	N	N	N	N
29 Schiff	N	N	N	N	N	N	N
30 Waxman	N	N	N	N	N	N	N
31 Becerra	N	N	N	N	-	N	N
32 Chu	N	N	N	N	N	N	N
33 Watson	N	N	N	N	N	N	N
34 Roybal-Allard	N	N	N	?	N	N	?
35 Waters	N	?	N	N	N	N	N
36 Harman	N	N	N	?	N	N	N
37 Richardson	N	N	N	N	N	N	N
38 Napolitano	N	N	N	N	N	N	N
39 Sánchez, Linda	N	N	N	N	N	N	N
40 Royce	Y	Y	Y	Y	Y	Y	N
41 Lewis	Y	N	N	N	N	N	N
42 Miller, Gary	?	?	?	?	?	?	?
43 Baca	N	N	N	N	N	N	N
44 Calvert	Y	N	N	N	N	N	N
45 Bono Mack	Y	Y	Y	N	N	N	N
46 Rohrabacher	Y	Y	Y	Y	Y	N	N
47 Sanchez, Loretta	N	N	N	N	N	N	N
48 Campbell	Y	Y	Y	Y	Y	Y	Y
49 Issa	Y	Y	Y	Y	Y	Y	Y
50 Bilbray	Y	Y	Y	N	Y	N	N
51 Filner	N	N	N	N	N	N	N
52 Hunter	Y	Y	N	Y	Y	N	N
53 Davis	N	N	N	N	N	N	N
COLORADO							
1 DeGette	N	N	N	N	N	N	N
2 Polis	N	?	N	N	N	N	N
3 Salazar	N	N	N	N	N	N	N
4 Markey	Y	N	N	N	N	N	N
5 Lamborn	Y	Y	Y	Y	Y	Y	Y
6 Coffman	Y	Y	Y	Y	Y	Y	Y
7 Perlmutter	N	N	N	N	N	N	N
CONNECTICUT							
1 Larson	N	N	N	N	N	N	N
2 Courtney	N	N	N	N	N	N	N
3 DeLauro	N	N	N	N	N	N	N
4 Himes	N	N	N	N	N	N	N
5 Murphy	N	N	N	N	N	N	?
DELAWARE							
AL Castle	N	Y	N	N	N	N	N
FLORIDA							
1 Miller	Y	Y	Y	Y	Y	Y	Y
2 Boyd	N	N	N	N	N	N	N
3 Brown	N	N	N	N	N	N	N
4 Crenshaw	N	N	N	N	N	N	N
5 Brown-Waite	Y	Y	Y	N	Y	Y	Y
6 Stearns	Y	Y	Y	Y	Y	Y	Y
7 Mica	Y	N	N	N	N	N	N
8 Grayson	N	N	N	N	N	N	N
9 Bilirakis	Y	N	Y	Y	Y	N	Y
10 Young	Y	N	N	N	N	N	N
11 Castor	N	N	N	N	N	N	N
12 Putnam	Y	N	N	N	N	N	N
13 Buchanan	Y	N	N	+	Y	N	N
14 Mack	Y	Y	Y	Y	Y	Y	Y
15 Posey	Y	N	N	N	N	N	N
16 Rooney	Y	N	N	N	N	N	N
17 Meek	?	N	N	N	N	N	N
18 Ros-Lehtinen	Y	N	N	N	N	N	N
19 Wexler	N	N	N	N	N	N	N
20 Wasserman Schultz	N	N	N	N	N	N	N
21 Diaz-Balart, L.	N	N	N	N	N	N	N
22 Klein	N	N	N	N	N	N	N
23 Hastings	N	N	N	N	N	N	N
24 Kosmas	N	N	N	N	N	N	N
25 Diaz-Balart, M.	N	N	N	N	N	N	N
GEORGIA							
1 Kingston	Y	Y	N	Y	N	Y	Y
2 Bishop	N	N	N	N	N	N	N
3 Westmoreland	+	+	+	+	+	+	+
4 Johnson	N	N	N	N	N	N	N
5 Lewis	N	N	N	N	N	N	N
6 Price	Y	Y	Y	Y	Y	Y	Y
7 Linder	Y	Y	Y	Y	Y	Y	Y
8 Marshall	N	N	N	N	N	N	N
9 Deal	Y	Y	N	Y	Y	Y	Y
10 Broun	Y	Y	Y	Y	Y	Y	Y
11 Gingrey	Y	Y	Y	Y	Y	Y	Y
12 Barrow	N	N	N	N	N	N	N
13 Scott	N	N	N	N	N	N	N
HAWAII							
1 Abercrombie	N	N	N	N	N	N	N
2 Hirono	N	N	N	N	N	N	N
IDAHO							
1 Minnick	Y	Y	Y	Y	Y	Y	Y
2 Simpson	N	N	N	N	N	N	N
ILLINOIS							
1 Rush	N	N	N	N	N	N	N
2 Jackson	N	N	N	N	N	N	N
3 Lipinski	N	N	N	N	N	N	N
4 Gutierrez	N	N	N	N	N	N	N
5 Quigley	N	N	N	N	N	N	N
6 Roskam	Y	N	Y	N	Y	Y	N
7 Davis	N	N	N	N	N	N	N
8 Bean	Y	N	Y	Y	Y	Y	Y
9 Schakowsky	N	N	N	N	N	N	N
10 Kirk	Y	Y	Y	N	Y	N	N
11 Halvorson	N	N	N	N	N	N	N
12 Costello	N	N	N	N	N	N	N
13 Biggert	Y	N	N	N	N	N	N
14 Foster	N	N	N	N	N	N	N
15 Johnson	Y	Y	Y	N	Y	N	Y

KEY   **Republicans**   Democrats

Y Voted for (yea)	X Paired against	C Voted "present" to avoid possible conflict of interest
# Paired for	– Announced against	? Did not vote or otherwise make a position known
+ Announced for	P Voted "present"	
N Voted against (nay)		

	580	581	582	583	584	585	586
16 **Manzullo**	Y	Y	Y	Y	Y	Y	N
17 Hare	N	N	N	N	N	N	N
18 **Schock**	N	Y	N	N	?	N	N
19 **Shimkus**	Y	Y	Y	Y	Y	Y	Y
INDIANA							
1 Visclosky	N	N	N	N	N	N	N
2 Donnelly	N	N	N	N	N	N	N
3 **Souder**	Y	N	Y	Y	?	Y	Y
4 **Buyer**	Y	N	N	N	N	N	N
5 **Burton**	Y	Y	N	Y	Y	Y	Y
6 **Pence**	Y	Y	Y	Y	Y	Y	Y
7 Carson	N	N	N	N	N	N	N
8 Ellsworth	N	N	N	N	N	N	N
9 Hill	N	N	N	N	N	N	N
IOWA							
1 Braley	N	N	N	N	N	N	N
2 Loebsack	N	N	N	N	N	N	N
3 Boswell	N	N	N	N	N	N	N
4 **Latham**	N	N	N	N	N	N	N
5 **King**	Y	Y	Y	Y	N	Y	Y
KANSAS							
1 **Moran**	Y	Y	Y	Y	Y	Y	Y
2 **Jenkins**	Y	Y	Y	Y	Y	Y	Y
3 Moore	N	N	N	N	N	N	N
4 **Tiahrt**	Y	Y	N	N	N	N	N
KENTUCKY							
1 **Whitfield**	Y	N	N	N	N	N	N
2 **Guthrie**	Y	N	N	N	N	N	N
3 Yarmuth	N	N	N	N	N	N	N
4 **Davis**	Y	Y	N	N	Y	Y	N
5 **Rogers**	N	N	N	N	N	N	N
6 Chandler	N	N	N	N	N	N	N
LOUISIANA							
1 **Scalise**	N	Y	Y	Y	Y	Y	Y
2 **Cao**	N	N	N	N	N	N	N
3 Melancon	N	N	N	N	N	N	N
4 **Fleming**	Y	Y	N	Y	Y	Y	Y
5 **Alexander**	Y	N	N	N	N	N	N
6 **Cassidy**	N	Y	Y	Y	Y	Y	Y
7 **Boustany**	Y	Y	Y	Y	Y	Y	Y
MAINE							
1 Pingree	N	N	N	N	N	N	N
2 Michaud	N	N	N	N	N	N	N
MARYLAND							
1 Kratovil	Y	N	N	N	N	N	N
2 Ruppersberger	N	N	N	N	N	N	N
3 Sarbanes	N	N	N	N	N	N	N
4 Edwards	N	N	N	N	N	N	N
5 Hoyer	N	N	N	N	N	N	N
6 **Bartlett**	Y	Y	N	N	N	Y	N
7 Cummings	N	N	N	N	N	N	N
8 Van Hollen	N	N	N	N	N	N	?
MASSACHUSETTS							
1 Olver	N	N	N	N	N	?	N
2 Neal	N	N	N	N	N	N	N
3 McGovern	N	N	N	N	N	N	N
4 Frank	N	N	N	N	N	N	N
5 Tsongas	N	?	N	N	N	N	?
6 Tierney	N	?	N	N	N	N	N
7 Markey	N	N	N	N	N	N	N
8 Capuano	N	N	N	N	N	N	N
9 Lynch	N	N	N	N	N	N	N
10 Delahunt	N	N	N	N	N	N	N
MICHIGAN							
1 Stupak	N	N	N	N	N	N	N
2 **Hoekstra**	Y	Y	Y	Y	Y	Y	Y
3 **Ehlers**	N	Y	Y	N	Y	Y	N
4 **Camp**	Y	N	N	N	N	Y	N
5 Kildee	N	N	N	N	N	N	N
6 **Upton**	N	Y	N	N	Y	Y	Y
7 Schauer	N	N	Y	N	N	N	N
8 **Rogers**	Y	Y	Y	N	Y	Y	Y
9 Peters	Y	N	N	N	N	N	N
10 **Miller**	Y	N	N	N	N	N	N
11 **McCotter**	Y	Y	Y	N	Y	Y	Y
12 Levin	N	N	N	N	N	N	N
13 Kilpatrick	N	N	N	N	N	N	N
14 Conyers	N	N	N	N	N	N	N
15 Dingell	N	N	N	N	N	N	N
MINNESOTA							
1 Walz	N	N	N	N	N	N	N
2 **Kline**	Y	Y	Y	Y	Y	Y	Y
3 **Paulsen**	Y	Y	N	N	Y	Y	N
4 McCollum	N	N	N	N	N	N	N

	580	581	582	583	584	585	586
5 Ellison	N	N	N	N	N	N	N
6 **Bachmann**	Y	Y	N	Y	Y	Y	Y
7 Peterson	N	N	N	N	N	N	N
8 Oberstar	N	N	N	N	N	N	N
MISSISSIPPI							
1 Childers	Y	N	N	N	N	N	N
2 Thompson	N	N	N	N	N	N	N
3 **Harper**	Y	Y	N	N	N	Y	N
4 Taylor	?	?	?	?	?	?	?
MISSOURI							
1 Clay	N	N	N	N	N	N	N
2 **Akin**	Y	Y	N	Y	Y	Y	N
3 Carnahan	N	N	N	N	N	N	N
4 Skelton	N	N	N	N	N	N	N
5 Cleaver	N	N	N	N	N	N	N
6 **Graves**	+	+	?	+	?	+	+
7 **Blunt**	Y	N	N	N	N	Y	N
8 **Emerson**	N	N	N	N	N	N	N
9 **Luetkemeyer**	Y	Y	Y	Y	Y	Y	Y
MONTANA							
AL **Rehberg**	Y	N	N	N	N	N	N
NEBRASKA							
1 **Fortenberry**	N	Y	N	N	N	Y	Y
2 **Terry**	Y	Y	N	N	N	Y	N
3 **Smith**	Y	Y	N	Y	N	Y	N
NEVADA							
1 Berkley	N	N	N	?	N	N	N
2 **Heller**	Y	Y	Y	Y	Y	Y	Y
3 Titus	N	N	N	N	N	N	N
NEW HAMPSHIRE							
1 Shea-Porter	N	N	N	N	N	N	N
2 Hodes	N	N	N	N	N	N	N
NEW JERSEY							
1 Andrews	N	N	N	N	N	N	N
2 **LoBiondo**	N	N	N	N	N	N	N
3 Adler	Y	N	N	N	Y	N	N
4 **Smith**	N	N	N	N	N	N	N
5 **Garrett**	Y	Y	Y	Y	Y	Y	Y
6 Pallone	N	N	N	N	N	N	N
7 **Lance**	Y	Y	N	N	Y	Y	N
8 Pascrell	N	N	N	N	N	N	N
9 Rothman	N	N	N	N	N	N	N
10 Payne	N	N	N	N	N	N	N
11 **Frelinghuysen**	N	N	N	N	N	N	N
12 Holt	N	N	N	N	N	N	N
13 Sires	N	N	N	N	N	N	N
NEW MEXICO							
1 Heinrich	N	N	N	N	N	N	N
2 Teague	N	N	N	N	N	N	N
3 Lujan	N	N	N	N	N	N	N
NEW YORK							
1 Bishop	N	N	Y	N	N	N	Y
2 Israel	N	N	N	N	N	N	N
3 **King**	N	N	N	N	N	N	N
4 McCarthy	N	N	N	N	N	N	N
5 Ackerman	?	?	?	?	?	?	?
6 Meeks	N	N	N	N	N	N	N
7 Crowley	N	N	N	N	N	N	N
8 Nadler	N	N	N	N	N	N	N
9 Weiner	N	N	N	N	N	N	N
10 Towns	N	N	N	N	N	N	N
11 Clarke	N	N	N	N	N	N	N
12 Velázquez	N	N	N	N	N	N	N
13 McMahon	Y	N	Y	N	N	N	N
14 Maloney	N	N	N	N	?	N	N
15 Rangel	N	N	N	N	N	N	N
16 Serrano	N	N	N	N	N	N	N
17 Engel	N	N	N	N	N	N	N
18 Lowey	N	N	N	N	N	N	N
19 Hall	N	N	N	N	N	N	N
20 Murphy	N	N	N	N	N	N	N
21 Tonko	N	N	N	N	N	N	N
22 Hinchey	N	N	N	N	N	N	N
23 **McHugh**	N	N	N	N	N	N	N
24 Arcuri	Y	N	N	N	N	N	N
25 Maffei	N	N	N	N	N	N	N
26 **Lee**	Y	Y	N	N	N	Y	N
27 Higgins	N	N	N	N	N	N	N
28 Slaughter	?	N	N	N	N	N	N
29 Massa	N	N	N	N	N	N	N
NORTH CAROLINA							
1 Butterfield	N	N	N	N	N	N	N
2 Etheridge	N	N	N	N	N	N	N
3 **Jones**	Y	N	N	N	N	N	N
4 Price	N	N	N	N	N	N	N

	580	581	582	583	584	585	586
5 **Foxx**	Y	Y	Y	Y	Y	Y	Y
6 **Coble**	?	?	?	?	?	?	?
7 McIntyre	N	N	N	N	N	N	N
8 Kissell	N	N	N	N	N	N	N
9 **Myrick**	Y	Y	Y	Y	+	Y	Y
10 **McHenry**	Y	Y	Y	Y	Y	Y	Y
11 Shuler	N	N	N	N	N	N	N
12 Watt	N	N	N	N	N	N	N
13 Miller	N	N	N	N	N	N	N
NORTH DAKOTA							
AL Pomeroy	N	N	N	N	N	N	N
OHIO							
1 Driehaus	Y	N	N	N	N	N	N
2 **Schmidt**	Y	Y	Y	Y	Y	Y	Y
3 **Turner**	N	N	N	N	N	N	N
4 **Jordan**	Y	Y	Y	Y	Y	Y	Y
5 **Latta**	Y	Y	N	Y	Y	Y	Y
6 Wilson	N	N	N	N	N	N	N
7 **Austria**	Y	Y	Y	Y	N	Y	N
8 **Boehner**	Y	Y	Y	Y	Y	Y	Y
9 Kaptur	N	N	N	N	N	N	N
10 Kucinich	N	N	N	N	N	N	N
11 Fudge	N	N	N	N	N	N	N
12 **Tiberi**	Y	Y	Y	N	Y	Y	Y
13 Sutton	N	N	N	N	N	N	N
14 **LaTourette**	N	N	N	N	N	N	N
15 Kilroy	N	N	N	N	N	N	N
16 Boccieri	N	N	N	N	N	N	N
17 Ryan	N	N	N	N	N	N	N
18 Space	N	N	N	N	?	N	N
OKLAHOMA							
1 **Sullivan**	Y	Y	N	N	Y	Y	Y
2 Boren	Y	N	N	N	N	N	N
3 **Lucas**	?	?	?	?	?	?	?
4 **Cole**	Y	N	N	N	N	N	N
5 **Fallin**	Y	Y	Y	Y	Y	Y	Y
OREGON							
1 Wu	N	N	N	N	N	N	N
2 **Walden**	N	Y	N	N	Y	Y	N
3 Blumenauer	N	N	N	N	N	N	N
4 DeFazio	N	N	N	N	N	N	N
5 Schrader	N	N	N	N	N	N	?
PENNSYLVANIA							
1 Brady	N	N	N	N	N	N	N
2 Fattah	N	N	N	N	N	N	N
3 Dahlkemper	N	N	N	N	N	N	N
4 Altmire	Y	N	N	N	N	N	N
5 **Thompson**	Y	N	N	N	N	N	N
6 **Gerlach**	Y	Y	Y	Y	Y	Y	N
7 Sestak	N	N	N	N	N	N	N
8 Murphy, P.	Y	N	N	N	N	N	N
9 **Shuster**	Y	N	N	N	N	N	N
10 Carney	N	N	N	N	N	N	N
11 Kanjorski	N	N	N	N	N	N	N
12 Murtha	N	N	N	N	N	N	N
13 Schwartz	N	N	N	N	N	N	N
14 Doyle	N	N	N	N	N	N	N
15 **Dent**	Y	Y	N	Y	Y	Y	N
16 **Pitts**	Y	Y	Y	Y	Y	Y	Y
17 Holden	N	N	N	N	N	N	N
18 **Murphy, T.**	N	N	N	N	N	N	N
19 **Platts**	Y	Y	N	Y	Y	Y	N
RHODE ISLAND							
1 Kennedy	N	N	N	N	N	N	N
2 Langevin	N	N	N	N	N	N	N
SOUTH CAROLINA							
1 **Brown**	Y	N	N	N	N	N	N
2 **Wilson**	Y	Y	Y	Y	Y	Y	Y
3 **Barrett**	?	?	?	?	?	?	?
4 **Inglis**	Y	Y	Y	Y	Y	Y	Y
5 Spratt	N	N	N	N	N	N	N
6 Clyburn	N	N	N	N	N	N	N
SOUTH DAKOTA							
AL Herseth Sandlin	N	N	N	N	N	N	N
TENNESSEE							
1 **Roe**	Y	Y	Y	Y	Y	Y	Y
2 **Duncan**	Y	Y	Y	Y	Y	Y	Y
3 **Wamp**	Y	Y	N	Y	Y	Y	Y
4 Davis	N	N	N	N	N	N	N
5 Cooper	Y	Y	Y	Y	Y	Y	Y
6 Gordon	N	N	N	N	N	N	N
7 **Blackburn**	Y	Y	Y	Y	Y	Y	Y
8 Tanner	N	N	N	N	N	N	N
9 Cohen	N	N	N	N	N	N	N

	580	581	582	583	584	585	586
TEXAS							
1 **Gohmert**	Y	Y	?	Y	Y	Y	Y
2 **Poe**	Y	Y	Y	N	Y	Y	N
3 **Johnson, S.**	Y	Y	Y	Y	Y	Y	Y
4 **Hall**	Y	Y	N	N	N	N	N
5 **Hensarling**	Y	Y	Y	Y	Y	Y	Y
6 **Barton**	Y	Y	N	Y	Y	Y	N
7 **Culberson**	Y	N	N	N	N	Y	N
8 **Brady**	Y	Y	N	N	Y	?	N
9 Green, A.	N	N	N	N	N	N	N
10 **McCaul**	Y	Y	Y	Y	Y	Y	Y
11 **Conaway**	Y	Y	Y	Y	Y	Y	Y
12 **Granger**	Y	N	N	N	N	Y	N
13 **Thornberry**	Y	Y	Y	Y	Y	Y	Y
14 **Paul**	Y	Y	Y	Y	Y	Y	Y
15 Hinojosa	N	N	N	N	N	N	N
16 Reyes	N	N	N	N	N	N	N
17 Edwards	N	N	N	N	N	N	N
18 Jackson Lee	N	N	N	N	N	N	N
19 **Neugebauer**	Y	Y	Y	Y	Y	Y	Y
20 Gonzalez	N	N	N	N	N	N	N
21 **Smith**	Y	N	N	N	N	N	N
22 **Olson**	Y	Y	Y	Y	Y	Y	Y
23 Rodriguez	N	N	N	N	N	N	N
24 **Marchant**	Y	Y	Y	Y	Y	Y	Y
25 Doggett	N	N	N	N	N	N	N
26 **Burgess**	Y	Y	Y	Y	Y	Y	N
27 Ortiz	N	N	N	N	N	N	N
28 Cuellar	N	N	N	N	N	N	N
29 Green, G.	N	N	N	N	N	N	N
30 Johnson, E.	N	N	N	N	N	N	N
31 **Carter**	Y	N	N	N	N	Y	N
32 **Sessions**	Y	Y	Y	Y	Y	Y	Y
UTAH							
1 **Bishop**	Y	Y	Y	Y	Y	Y	N
2 Matheson	N	N	N	N	N	N	N
3 **Chaffetz**	Y	Y	Y	Y	Y	Y	Y
VERMONT							
AL Welch	N	N	N	N	N	N	N
VIRGINIA							
1 **Wittman**	Y	Y	N	Y	N	Y	N
2 Nye	N	N	Y	N	N	N	Y
3 Scott	N	N	N	N	N	N	N
4 **Forbes**	Y	Y	N	N	N	Y	N
5 Perriello	Y	N	N	N	N	N	N
6 **Goodlatte**	Y	Y	Y	Y	Y	Y	Y
7 **Cantor**	Y	Y	N	Y	Y	Y	N
8 Moran	N	N	N	N	N	N	N
9 Boucher	N	N	N	N	N	N	N
10 **Wolf**	Y	N	N	N	N	N	N
11 Connolly	N	N	N	N	N	N	N
WASHINGTON							
1 Inslee	N	N	N	N	N	N	N
2 Larsen	N	N	N	N	N	N	N
3 Baird	N	N	N	N	N	N	N
4 **Hastings**	Y	N	N	N	N	N	N
5 **McMorris Rodgers**	Y	Y	N	Y	Y	Y	N
6 Dicks	N	N	N	N	N	N	N
7 McDermott	N	N	N	N	N	N	N
8 **Reichert**	N	N	N	N	N	N	N
9 Smith	N	N	N	N	N	N	N
WEST VIRGINIA							
1 Mollohan	N	N	N	N	N	N	N
2 **Capito**	Y	N	N	N	N	N	N
3 Rahall	N	N	N	N	N	N	N
WISCONSIN							
1 **Ryan**	Y	Y	Y	Y	Y	Y	Y
2 Baldwin	N	N	N	N	N	N	N
3 Kind	N	N	Y	Y	N	Y	Y
4 Moore	N	N	N	N	N	N	N
5 **Sensenbrenner**	Y	Y	Y	Y	Y	Y	Y
6 **Petri**	Y	Y	Y	Y	Y	Y	Y
7 Obey	N	N	N	N	N	N	N
8 Kagen	N	N	N	N	N	N	N
WYOMING							
AL **Lummis**	Y	Y	Y	Y	Y	Y	Y
DELEGATES							
Faleomavaega (A.S.)	?	?	?	?	?	?	?
Norton (D.C.)	N	N	N	N	N	N	N
Bordallo (Guam)	?	?	?	?	?	?	?
Sablan (N. Marianas)	N	N	N	N	N	N	N
Pierluisi (P.R.)	?	?	?	?	?	?	?
Christensen (V.I.)	N	N	N	N	N	N	N

IN THE HOUSE | By Vote Number

587. HR 3183. Fiscal 2010 Energy-Water Appropriations/Urban Sustainability Initiative. Flake, R-Ariz., amendment that would bar the use of funds appropriated in the bill for the Boston Architectural College's Urban Sustainability Initiative and cut $1.6 million intended for the project from the bill. Rejected in Committee of the Whole 111-316: R 106-66; D 5-250. July 17, 2009.

588. HR 3183. Fiscal 2010 Energy-Water Appropriations/Energy Conservation and Efficiency Upgrade. Hensarling, R-Texas, amendment that would bar the use of funds appropriated in the bill for the Energy Conservation and Efficiency Upgrade of HVAC Controls project and cut $500,000 intended for the project from the bill. Rejected in Committee of the Whole 133-290: R 127-45; D 6-245. July 17, 2009.

589. HR 3183. Fiscal 2010 Energy-Water Appropriations/Pier 36 Removal. Hensarling, R-Texas, amendment that would bar the use of funds appropriated in the bill for the Pier 36 Removal project in California and cut $6.2 million intended for the project from the bill. Rejected in Committee of the Whole 128-299: R 125-46; D 3-253. July 17, 2009.

590. HR 3183. Fiscal 2010 Energy-Water Appropriations/Automated Remote Electric and Water Meters. Hensarling, R-Texas, amendment that would bar the use of funds appropriated in the bill for the Automated Remote Electric and Water Meters in South River project and cut $500,000 intended for the project from the bill. Rejected in Committee of the Whole 119-308: R 115-56; D 4-252. July 17, 2009.

591. HR 3183. Fiscal 2010 Energy-Water Appropriations/Recommit. Simpson, R-Idaho, motion to recommit the bill to the Appropriations Committee with instructions that it be immediately reported back with language that would eliminate $98 million for civilian nuclear waste disposal and $98 million for defense nuclear waste disposal. Motion rejected 30-388: R 7-164; D 23-224. July 17, 2009.

592. HR 3183. Fiscal 2010 Energy-Water Appropriations/Passage. Passage of the bill that would provide $33.3 billion in fiscal 2010 for energy and water development projects, including $26.9 billion for the Energy Department and $5.5 billion for the Army Corps of Engineers. It would appropriate $6.3 billion for nuclear weapons programs and $197 million for nuclear waste disposal, including the closure of the Yucca Mountain nuclear waste repository. The bill would provide $4.9 billion for Office of Science programs and $1 billion for the Interior Department's Bureau of Reclamation. Passed 320-97: R 79-90; D 241-7. A "yea" was a vote in support of the president's position. July 17, 2009.

593. Journal/Procedural Motion. Approval of the House Journal of July 17, 2009. Approved 233-159: R 25-135; D 208-24. July 20, 2009.

	587	588	589	590	591	592	593
ALABAMA							
1 Bonner	N	N	N	N	N	N	N
2 Bright	Y	Y	Y	Y	N	Y	?
3 Rogers	N	N	N	N	N	N	N
4 Aderholt	N	N	N	N	N	N	N
5 Griffith	N	N	N	N	N	Y	Y
6 Bachus	N	N	N	N	N	N	N
7 Davis	N	N	N	N	?	?	?
ALASKA							
AL Young	N	N	Y	N	N	Y	N
ARIZONA							
1 Kirkpatrick	N	N	N	N	N	Y	N
2 Franks	Y	Y	Y	Y	N	N	N
3 Shadegg	Y	Y	Y	Y	N	N	N
4 Pastor	N	N	N	N	N	N	Y
5 Mitchell	N	N	N	N	N	Y	Y
6 Flake	Y	Y	Y	Y	N	N	N
7 Grijalva	N	N	N	N	N	Y	?
8 Giffords	N	Y	N	Y	N	Y	Y
ARKANSAS							
1 Berry	N	N	N	N	N	Y	Y
2 Snyder	N	N	N	N	N	Y	Y
3 Boozman	Y	Y	Y	Y	N	Y	N
4 Ross	N	N	N	N	N	Y	Y
CALIFORNIA							
1 Thompson	N	N	N	N	N	Y	N
2 Herger	Y	Y	Y	Y	N	Y	N
3 Lungren	Y	Y	Y	Y	N	N	N
4 McClintock	Y	Y	Y	Y	N	N	Y
5 Matsui	N	N	N	N	N	Y	Y
6 Woolsey	N	N	N	N	Y	Y	Y
7 Miller, George	N	N	N	N	N	Y	Y
8 Pelosi							
9 Lee	N	N	N	N	N	Y	Y
10 Vacant							
11 McNerney	N	N	N	N	N	Y	Y
12 Speier	N	N	N	N	N	Y	Y
13 Stark	N	N	N	N	N	Y	?
14 Eshoo	N	N	N	N	N	Y	Y
15 Honda	N	N	N	N	Y	Y	Y
16 Lofgren	N	N	N	N	Y	Y	Y
17 Farr	N	N	N	N	Y	Y	Y
18 Cardoza	N	N	N	N	Y	Y	Y
19 Radanovich	N	Y	Y	N	N	N	Y
20 Costa	N	N	N	N	N	Y	?
21 Nunes	Y	Y	Y	Y	N	Y	N
22 McCarthy	Y	Y	Y	Y	N	Y	N
23 Capps	N	N	N	N	N	Y	Y
24 Gallegly	Y	Y	Y	N	N	Y	N
25 McKeon	Y	Y	Y	?	Y	Y	?
26 Dreier	N	N	N	N	N	Y	N
27 Sherman	N	N	N	N	N	Y	Y
28 Berman	N	N	N	N	Y	Y	Y
29 Schiff	N	N	N	N	N	Y	Y
30 Waxman	N	?	N	N	N	Y	Y
31 Becerra	N	N	N	N	N	Y	Y
32 Chu	N	N	N	N	N	Y	Y
33 Watson	N	N	N	N	N	Y	Y
34 Roybal-Allard	N	N	N	N	N	Y	Y
35 Waters	N	N	N	N	Y	Y	Y
36 Harman	N	N	N	N	N	Y	Y
37 Richardson	N	N	N	N	N	Y	Y
38 Napolitano	N	N	N	N	N	Y	Y
39 Sánchez, Linda	N	N	N	N	N	Y	Y
40 Royce	Y	Y	Y	N	Y	N	N
41 Lewis	N	Y	N	N	N	N	?
42 Miller, Gary	?	?	?	?	?	?	N
43 Baca	N	N	N	N	N	Y	Y
44 Calvert	N	Y	N	N	N	Y	N
45 Bono Mack	N	N	Y	N	N	N	N
46 Rohrabacher	Y	Y	Y	Y	N	N	?
47 Sanchez, Loretta	N	N	N	N	N	Y	?
48 Campbell	Y	Y	Y	N	N	Y	N
49 Issa	Y	Y	Y	N	N	Y	N
50 Bilbray	N	Y	Y	Y	N	Y	N
51 Filner	N	N	N	N	N	Y	Y
52 Hunter	Y	Y	Y	Y	N	Y	N
53 Davis	N	N	N	N	N	Y	Y

	587	588	589	590	591	592	593
COLORADO							
1 DeGette	N	N	N	N	N	Y	Y
2 Polis	N	N	N	N	N	Y	Y
3 Salazar	N	N	N	N	N	Y	Y
4 Markey	N	N	N	N	N	Y	Y
5 Lamborn	Y	Y	Y	Y	N	N	N
6 Coffman	Y	Y	Y	Y	N	Y	N
7 Perlmutter	N	N	N	N	N	Y	Y
CONNECTICUT							
1 Larson	N	N	N	N	N	Y	Y
2 Courtney	N	N	N	N	N	Y	Y
3 DeLauro	N	N	N	N	N	Y	Y
4 Himes	N	N	N	N	N	Y	Y
5 Murphy	N	N	N	N	N	Y	Y
DELAWARE							
AL Castle	N	Y	Y	Y	N	Y	Y
FLORIDA							
1 Miller	Y	Y	Y	Y	N	N	N
2 Boyd	N	N	N	N	N	Y	Y
3 Brown	N	N	N	Y	Y	Y	?
4 Crenshaw	N	N	N	N	Y	Y	?
5 Brown-Waite	Y	Y	Y	Y	N	Y	Y
6 Stearns	Y	Y	Y	Y	N	N	N
7 Mica	Y	N	Y	Y	N	N	N
8 Grayson	N	N	N	N	N	Y	Y
9 Bilirakis	Y	Y	Y	Y	N	N	N
10 Young	N	N	N	N	N	Y	N
11 Castor	N	N	N	N	N	?	Y
12 Putnam	N	Y	N	N	N	Y	N
13 Buchanan	N	Y	N	Y	N	Y	N
14 Mack	Y	Y	Y	Y	N	Y	N
15 Posey	N	N	Y	Y	N	Y	N
16 Rooney	Y	Y	Y	Y	N	Y	N
17 Meek	N	N	N	N	N	Y	N
18 Ros-Lehtinen	N	N	N	N	N	Y	N
19 Wexler	N	N	N	N	N	Y	N
20 Wasserman Schultz	N	N	N	N	N	Y	?
21 Diaz-Balart, L.	N	N	N	N	N	Y	N
22 Klein	N	N	N	N	N	Y	Y
23 Hastings	N	N	N	N	N	Y	Y
24 Kosmas	N	N	N	N	N	Y	Y
25 Diaz-Balart, M.	N	N	N	N	N	Y	N
GEORGIA							
1 Kingston	Y	Y	Y	Y	N	N	N
2 Bishop	N	N	N	N	N	Y	Y
3 Westmoreland	+	+	+	+	-	-	N
4 Johnson	N	N	N	N	N	Y	Y
5 Lewis	N	N	N	N	Y	Y	Y
6 Price	Y	Y	Y	Y	N	N	N
7 Linder	Y	Y	Y	Y	N	N	N
8 Marshall	N	N	N	N	N	Y	Y
9 Deal	Y	Y	Y	Y	N	N	N
10 Broun	Y	Y	Y	Y	N	N	N
11 Gingrey	Y	Y	Y	Y	N	N	N
12 Barrow	N	N	N	N	N	Y	Y
13 Scott	N	N	N	N	N	Y	Y
HAWAII							
1 Abercrombie	N	N	N	N	Y	Y	Y
2 Hirono	N	N	N	N	Y	Y	Y
IDAHO							
1 Minnick	Y	Y	Y	Y	N	Y	N
2 Simpson	N	N	N	N	N	Y	Y
ILLINOIS							
1 Rush	N	N	N	?	Y	Y	Y
2 Jackson	N	N	N	N	N	Y	Y
3 Lipinski	N	N	N	N	N	Y	Y
4 Gutierrez	N	?	N	N	N	Y	+
5 Quigley	N	N	N	N	N	Y	Y
6 Roskam	N	Y	Y	N	N	N	N
7 Davis	N	N	N	N	N	Y	?
8 Bean	Y	N	N	N	N	Y	Y
9 Schakowsky	N	N	N	N	Y	Y	Y
10 Kirk	Y	Y	Y	N	Y	N	?
11 Halvorson	N	N	N	N	N	Y	Y
12 Costello	N	N	N	?	?	Y	Y
13 Biggert	Y	Y	Y	N	N	Y	Y
14 Foster	N	Y	N	N	N	Y	Y
15 Johnson	Y	Y	Y	N	N	N	?

	587	588	589	590	591	592	593
16 **Manzullo**	Y	Y	Y	Y	N	N	–
17 Hare	N	N	N	N	N	Y	Y
18 **Schock**	Y	Y	N	Y	N	Y	N
19 **Shimkus**	Y	Y	Y	Y	N	N	N
INDIANA							
1 Visclosky	N	N	N	N	N	Y	Y
2 Donnelly	N	N	N	N	N	Y	Y
3 **Souder**	Y	Y	?	Y	Y	Y	N
4 **Buyer**	N	N	N	N	N	Y	N
5 **Burton**	Y	Y	Y	Y	N	N	N
6 **Pence**	Y	Y	Y	Y	N	N	N
7 Carson	N	N	N	N	N	Y	Y
8 Ellsworth	N	N	N	N	N	Y	N
9 Hill	N	N	N	N	N	Y	Y
IOWA							
1 Braley	?	N	N	N	N	Y	Y
2 Loebsack	N	N	N	N	N	Y	Y
3 Boswell	N	N	N	N	N	Y	+
4 **Latham**	N	N	N	N	N	Y	Y
5 **King**	Y	Y	Y	Y	N	N	N
KANSAS							
1 **Moran**	Y	Y	Y	Y	N	N	N
2 **Jenkins**	Y	Y	Y	Y	N	N	N
3 Moore	N	N	N	N	Y	N	Y
4 **Tiahrt**	N	N	Y	Y	N	N	N
KENTUCKY							
1 **Whitfield**	N	N	N	N	N	Y	N
2 **Guthrie**	N	N	N	N	N	Y	N
3 Yarmuth	N	N	N	N	N	Y	Y
4 **Davis**	N	Y	Y	N	N	N	N
5 **Rogers**	N	N	N	N	N	Y	N
6 Chandler	N	N	N	N	N	Y	N
LOUISIANA							
1 **Scalise**	Y	Y	Y	Y	N	Y	N
2 **Cao**	N	N	N	N	N	Y	N
3 Melancon	N	N	N	N	N	Y	N
4 **Fleming**	Y	Y	Y	Y	N	Y	N
5 **Alexander**	N	N	N	N	N	Y	N
6 **Cassidy**	Y	Y	Y	Y	N	Y	N
7 **Boustany**	Y	Y	Y	Y	N	Y	N
MAINE							
1 Pingree	N	N	N	N	N	Y	Y
2 Michaud	N	N	N	N	N	Y	Y
MARYLAND							
1 Kratovil	N	N	N	N	N	Y	N
2 Ruppersberger	N	?	N	N	N	Y	Y
3 Sarbanes	N	N	N	N	N	Y	Y
4 Edwards	N	N	N	N	Y	Y	Y
5 Hoyer	N	N	N	N	N	Y	Y
6 **Bartlett**	N	Y	Y	N	N	N	N
7 Cummings	N	N	N	N	N	Y	Y
8 Van Hollen	N	N	N	N	N	Y	Y
MASSACHUSETTS							
1 Olver	N	N	N	N	N	Y	Y
2 Neal	N	N	N	N	N	?	Y
3 McGovern	N	N	N	N	Y	Y	Y
4 Frank	N	N	N	N	N	Y	Y
5 Tsongas	N	N	N	N	N	Y	Y
6 Tierney	N	N	N	N	N	Y	Y
7 Markey	N	N	N	N	N	Y	Y
8 Capuano	N	N	N	N	N	Y	?
9 Lynch	N	N	N	N	N	Y	Y
10 Delahunt	N	N	N	N	N	Y	Y
MICHIGAN							
1 Stupak	N	N	N	N	N	Y	N
2 **Hoekstra**	Y	Y	Y	Y	N	N	N
3 **Ehlers**	Y	Y	Y	Y	N	Y	N
4 **Camp**	N	Y	Y	Y	N	Y	N
5 Kildee	N	N	N	N	N	Y	Y
6 **Upton**	Y	Y	Y	Y	N	Y	N
7 Schauer	N	Y	N	N	N	Y	Y
8 **Rogers**	Y	Y	Y	Y	N	N	N
9 Peters	N	N	N	N	N	Y	Y
10 **Miller**	N	N	N	N	N	Y	N
11 **McCotter**	Y	Y	Y	Y	Y	Y	N
12 Levin	N	N	N	N	N	Y	Y
13 Kilpatrick	N	N	N	N	N	Y	Y
14 Conyers	N	N	N	N	Y	N	+
15 Dingell	N	N	N	N	N	Y	Y
MINNESOTA							
1 Walz	N	N	N	N	N	Y	Y
2 **Kline**	Y	Y	Y	Y	N	N	N
3 **Paulsen**	Y	Y	Y	Y	N	N	Y
4 McCollum	N	N	N	N	N	Y	Y
5 Ellison	N	N	N	N	Y	Y	Y
6 **Bachmann**	Y	Y	Y	Y	N	N	Y
7 Peterson	N	N	N	N	N	Y	N
8 Oberstar	N	N	N	N	N	Y	Y
MISSISSIPPI							
1 Childers	N	N	N	N	N	Y	N
2 Thompson	N	N	N	N	N	Y	Y
3 **Harper**	Y	Y	Y	N	N	Y	Y
4 Taylor	?	?	?	?	?	?	Y
MISSOURI							
1 Clay	N	N	N	N	N	Y	Y
2 **Akin**	Y	Y	Y	Y	N	Y	N
3 Carnahan	N	N	N	N	N	Y	Y
4 Skelton	N	N	N	N	N	Y	Y
5 Cleaver	N	N	N	N	N	Y	Y
6 **Graves**	+	+	+	+	–	–	N
7 **Blunt**	Y	Y	Y	Y	N	N	N
8 **Emerson**	N	N	N	N	N	N	N
9 **Luetkemeyer**	Y	Y	Y	Y	N	Y	N
MONTANA							
AL **Rehberg**	N	N	N	N	N	Y	N
NEBRASKA							
1 **Fortenberry**	N	Y	Y	Y	N	Y	Y
2 **Terry**	N	Y	Y	Y	N	Y	N
3 **Smith**	Y	Y	Y	Y	N	Y	N
NEVADA							
1 Berkley	N	N	N	N	Y	Y	Y
2 **Heller**	Y	Y	Y	Y	Y	N	Y
3 Titus	N	N	N	N	Y	Y	Y
NEW HAMPSHIRE							
1 Shea-Porter	N	N	N	N	Y	Y	Y
2 Hodes	N	N	N	N	N	Y	Y
NEW JERSEY							
1 Andrews	N	N	N	N	N	Y	Y
2 **LoBiondo**	N	N	N	N	N	Y	N
3 Adler	N	N	N	N	N	Y	N
4 **Smith**	N	N	N	N	N	Y	Y
5 **Garrett**	Y	Y	Y	Y	N	N	N
6 Pallone	N	N	N	N	N	Y	Y
7 **Lance**	Y	Y	Y	N	N	Y	Y
8 Pascrell	N	N	N	N	N	Y	Y
9 Rothman	N	N	N	N	N	Y	Y
10 Payne	N	N	N	N	N	Y	Y
11 **Frelinghuysen**	N	N	N	N	N	Y	N
12 Holt	N	N	N	N	N	Y	Y
13 Sires	N	N	N	N	N	Y	?
NEW MEXICO							
1 Heinrich	N	N	N	N	N	Y	Y
2 Teague	N	N	N	N	N	Y	Y
3 Lujan	N	N	N	N	N	Y	Y
NEW YORK							
1 Bishop	N	N	N	N	N	Y	Y
2 Israel	N	N	N	N	N	Y	Y
3 **King**	N	N	N	N	N	Y	N
4 McCarthy	N	N	N	N	N	Y	+
5 Ackerman	?	?	?	?	?	?	Y
6 Meeks	N	N	N	N	N	Y	Y
7 Crowley	N	N	N	N	N	Y	Y
8 Nadler	N	N	N	N	N	Y	Y
9 Weiner	N	N	N	N	N	Y	Y
10 Towns	N	N	N	N	N	Y	?
11 Clarke	N	N	N	N	N	Y	Y
12 Velázquez	N	N	N	N	N	Y	Y
13 McMahon	N	?	N	N	N	Y	Y
14 Maloney	N	N	N	N	N	Y	?
15 Rangel	N	N	N	N	N	Y	Y
16 Serrano	N	N	N	N	N	Y	Y
17 Engel	N	N	N	N	N	Y	Y
18 Lowey	N	N	N	N	N	Y	Y
19 Hall	N	N	N	N	N	Y	Y
20 Murphy	N	N	N	N	N	Y	N
21 Tonko	N	N	N	N	N	Y	Y
22 Hinchey	N	N	N	N	N	Y	?
23 **McHugh**	N	N	N	N	N	Y	N
24 Arcuri	N	N	N	N	N	Y	N
25 Maffei	N	N	N	N	N	Y	Y
26 **Lee**	Y	Y	Y	N	N	Y	N
27 Higgins	N	N	N	N	N	Y	Y
28 Slaughter	N	N	N	N	N	Y	Y
29 Massa	N	N	N	N	N	Y	Y
NORTH CAROLINA							
1 Butterfield	N	N	N	N	N	Y	Y
2 Etheridge	N	N	N	N	N	Y	N
3 **Jones**	N	N	N	N	N	Y	Y
4 Price	N	N	N	N	N	Y	Y
5 **Foxx**	Y	Y	Y	Y	N	N	N
6 **Coble**	?	?	?	?	?	?	N
7 McIntyre	N	N	N	N	N	Y	Y
8 Kissell	N	N	N	N	N	Y	Y
9 **Myrick**	Y	Y	Y	Y	N	N	N
10 **McHenry**	Y	Y	Y	Y	N	N	N
11 Shuler	N	N	N	N	N	Y	N
12 Watt	N	N	N	N	N	Y	Y
13 Miller	N	N	N	N	N	Y	Y
NORTH DAKOTA							
AL Pomeroy	N	N	N	N	N	Y	Y
OHIO							
1 Driehaus	N	N	N	N	N	Y	Y
2 **Schmidt**	Y	Y	Y	Y	N	Y	N
3 **Turner**	N	N	N	N	N	Y	?
4 **Jordan**	Y	Y	Y	Y	N	N	N
5 **Latta**	Y	Y	Y	Y	N	N	N
6 Wilson	N	N	N	N	N	Y	Y
7 **Austria**	Y	Y	Y	Y	N	Y	N
8 **Boehner**	Y	Y	Y	Y	N	?	N
9 Kaptur	N	N	N	N	N	Y	Y
10 Kucinich	N	N	N	N	Y	N	Y
11 Fudge	N	N	N	N	N	Y	Y
12 **Tiberi**	Y	Y	Y	Y	N	Y	?
13 Sutton	N	N	N	N	N	Y	Y
14 **LaTourette**	N	N	N	N	N	Y	N
15 Kilroy	N	N	N	N	Y	Y	Y
16 Boccieri	N	N	N	N	N	Y	N
17 Ryan	N	N	N	N	N	Y	Y
18 Space	N	N	N	N	N	Y	Y
OKLAHOMA							
1 **Sullivan**	Y	Y	Y	Y	N	N	N
2 Boren	N	N	N	N	N	Y	Y
3 **Lucas**	?	?	?	?	?	?	?
4 **Cole**	N	N	N	N	N	N	N
5 **Fallin**	Y	Y	Y	Y	N	N	N
OREGON							
1 Wu	N	N	N	N	N	Y	N
2 **Walden**	Y	Y	Y	Y	N	Y	N
3 Blumenauer	N	N	N	N	Y	Y	Y
4 DeFazio	N	N	N	N	N	Y	Y
5 Schrader	N	?	N	N	N	Y	Y
PENNSYLVANIA							
1 Brady	N	N	N	N	N	Y	Y
2 Fattah	N	N	N	N	N	Y	Y
3 Dahlkemper	N	N	N	N	N	Y	Y
4 Altmire	N	N	N	N	N	Y	N
5 **Thompson**	N	N	N	N	N	Y	N
6 **Gerlach**	N	Y	Y	N	N	Y	Y
7 Sestak	N	N	N	N	N	Y	?
8 Murphy, P.	N	N	N	N	N	Y	Y
9 **Shuster**	N	N	N	N	N	Y	N
10 Carney	N	N	N	N	N	Y	N
11 Kanjorski	N	N	N	N	N	Y	Y
12 Murtha	N	N	N	N	N	Y	Y
13 Schwartz	N	N	N	N	N	Y	Y
14 Doyle	N	N	N	N	N	Y	Y
15 **Dent**	N	N	Y	N	N	Y	Y
16 **Pitts**	Y	Y	Y	Y	N	N	Y
17 Holden	N	N	N	N	N	Y	Y
18 **Murphy, T.**	N	N	N	N	N	Y	N
19 **Platts**	N	Y	Y	Y	N	N	N
RHODE ISLAND							
1 Kennedy	N	N	N	N	N	Y	Y
2 Langevin	N	N	N	N	N	Y	Y
SOUTH CAROLINA							
1 **Brown**	N	N	N	N	N	N	N
2 **Wilson**	Y	Y	Y	Y	N	N	N
3 **Barrett**	?	?	?	?	?	?	?
4 **Inglis**	Y	Y	N	Y	N	N	N
5 Spratt	N	N	N	N	N	Y	Y
6 Clyburn	N	N	N	N	N	Y	Y
SOUTH DAKOTA							
AL Herseth Sandlin	N	N	N	N	N	Y	Y
TENNESSEE							
1 **Roe**	Y	Y	Y	Y	N	Y	N
2 **Duncan**	Y	Y	Y	Y	N	N	N
3 **Wamp**	Y	Y	Y	Y	N	Y	N
4 Davis	N	N	N	N	N	Y	Y
5 Cooper	Y	Y	Y	Y	N	Y	Y
6 Gordon	N	N	N	N	?	Y	Y
7 **Blackburn**	Y	Y	Y	Y	N	N	N
8 Tanner	N	N	N	N	N	Y	Y
9 Cohen	N	N	N	N	N	Y	Y
TEXAS							
1 **Gohmert**	Y	Y	Y	Y	N	N	?
2 **Poe**	N	Y	Y	Y	N	N	N
3 **Johnson, S.**	Y	Y	Y	Y	N	N	N
4 **Hall**	Y	Y	Y	Y	N	Y	N
5 **Hensarling**	Y	Y	Y	Y	N	N	N
6 **Barton**	Y	Y	Y	Y	?	?	N
7 **Culberson**	N	Y	Y	N	N	N	N
8 **Brady**	Y	Y	Y	Y	N	N	?
9 Green, A.	N	N	N	N	N	Y	Y
10 **McCaul**	Y	Y	Y	Y	N	N	N
11 **Conaway**	Y	Y	Y	Y	N	N	?
12 **Granger**	N	Y	Y	N	N	Y	N
13 **Thornberry**	Y	Y	Y	Y	N	N	N
14 **Paul**	Y	Y	Y	Y	Y	?	Y
15 Hinojosa	N	N	N	N	N	Y	Y
16 Reyes	N	N	N	N	N	Y	Y
17 Edwards	N	N	N	N	N	Y	Y
18 Jackson Lee	N	N	N	N	Y	Y	Y
19 **Neugebauer**	Y	Y	Y	Y	N	N	N
20 Gonzalez	N	N	N	N	N	Y	Y
21 **Smith**	N	N	N	N	N	N	N
22 **Olson**	Y	Y	Y	Y	N	N	N
23 Rodriguez	N	N	N	N	N	Y	Y
24 **Marchant**	Y	Y	Y	Y	N	N	?
25 Doggett	N	N	N	N	Y	N	Y
26 **Burgess**	Y	Y	Y	Y	N	N	N
27 Ortiz	N	N	N	N	N	Y	Y
28 Cuellar	N	N	N	N	N	Y	Y
29 Green, G.	N	N	N	N	N	Y	Y
30 Johnson, E.	N	N	N	N	N	Y	Y
31 **Carter**	N	Y	Y	N	N	N	Y
32 **Sessions**	Y	Y	Y	Y	N	N	?
UTAH							
1 **Bishop**	Y	Y	Y	Y	Y	N	N
2 Matheson	N	N	N	N	N	N	Y
3 **Chaffetz**	Y	Y	Y	Y	Y	N	Y
VERMONT							
AL Welch	N	N	N	N	?	?	Y
VIRGINIA							
1 **Wittman**	N	Y	Y	Y	N	Y	–
2 Nye	N	N	N	N	N	N	N
3 Scott	N	N	N	N	N	Y	Y
4 **Forbes**	N	Y	Y	N	N	Y	?
5 Perriello	N	N	N	N	N	Y	Y
6 **Goodlatte**	Y	Y	Y	Y	N	N	Y
7 **Cantor**	Y	Y	Y	Y	N	N	N
8 Moran	N	N	N	N	?	Y	?
9 Boucher	N	N	N	N	N	Y	?
10 **Wolf**	N	N	N	N	N	N	N
11 Connolly	N	N	N	N	N	Y	N
WASHINGTON							
1 Inslee	N	N	N	N	N	Y	Y
2 Larsen	N	N	N	N	N	Y	?
3 Baird	N	N	N	N	Y	Y	Y
4 **Hastings**	N	Y	Y	Y	N	Y	N
5 **McMorris Rodgers**	Y	Y	Y	Y	N	Y	Y
6 Dicks	N	N	N	N	N	Y	Y
7 McDermott	N	N	N	N	N	Y	Y
8 **Reichert**	N	N	N	N	N	Y	N
9 Smith	N	N	N	N	N	Y	+
WEST VIRGINIA							
1 Mollohan	N	N	N	N	N	Y	Y
2 **Capito**	N	N	N	N	N	Y	Y
3 Rahall	N	N	N	N	N	Y	Y
WISCONSIN							
1 **Ryan**	Y	Y	Y	Y	N	N	N
2 Baldwin	N	N	N	N	N	Y	Y
3 Kind	Y	N	N	N	N	N	Y
4 Moore	N	N	N	N	N	Y	Y
5 **Sensenbrenner**	Y	Y	Y	Y	N	N	N
6 **Petri**	Y	Y	Y	Y	N	N	N
7 Obey	N	N	N	N	N	Y	Y
8 Kagen	N	N	N	N	N	Y	Y
WYOMING							
AL **Lummis**	Y	Y	Y	Y	N	N	N
DELEGATES							
Faleomavaega (A.S.)	?	?	?	?			
Norton (D.C.)	N	N	N	N			
Bordallo (Guam)	?	?	?	?			
Sablan (N. Marianas)	N	N	N	N			
Pierluisi (P.R.)	?	?	?	?			
Christensen (V.I.)	N	N	N	N			

IN THE HOUSE | By Vote Number

594. **H Res 607. 40th Anniversary of Moon Landing/Adoption.** Luján, D-N.M., motion to suspend the rules and adopt the resolution that would state the House of Representatives celebrates the 40th anniversary of the moon landing and honors the crew of Apollo 11 and all who contributed to the historic achievement. Motion agreed to 390-0: R 159-0; D 231-0. A two-thirds majority of those present and voting (260 in this case) is required for adoption under suspension of the rules. July 20, 2009.

595. **HR 2245. Astronaut Gold Medals/Passage.** Grayson, D-Fla., motion to suspend the rules and pass the bill that would authorize presentation of congressional gold medals to astronauts Neil A. Armstrong, Edwin E. "Buzz" Aldrin Jr., Michael Collins and John Herschel Glenn Jr., in recognition of their significant contributions to society. Motion agreed to 390-0: R 158-0; D 232-0. A two-thirds majority of those present and voting (260 in this case) is required for passage under suspension of the rules. July 20, 2009.

596. **H Con Res 164. Food and Nutrition Service Recognition/ Adoption.** Scott, D-Ga., motion to suspend the rules and adopt the concurrent resolution that would recognize the contributions of the Food and Nutrition Service of the Agriculture Department. Motion agreed to 422-0: R 176-0; D 246-0. A two-thirds majority of those present and voting (282 in this case) is required for adoption under suspension of the rules. July 21, 2009.

597. **HR 2729. National Environmental Research Parks/Passage.** Luján, D-N.M., motion to suspend the rules and pass the bill that would authorize $35 million per year in fiscal 2010-14 for the Energy Department to designate the seven existing National Environmental Research Parks as permanent research reserves to study the impact of human activities on the environment. Motion agreed to 330-96: R 80-95; D 250-1. A two-thirds majority of those present and voting (284 in this case) is required for passage under suspension of the rules. July 21, 2009.

598. **HR 1622. Natural Gas Vehicle Research/Passage.** Luján, D-N.M., motion to suspend the rules and pass the bill that would authorize $30 million per year in fiscal 2010-14 for the Energy Department to conduct a five-year program of research, development and demonstration related to natural gas vehicles. Motion agreed to 393-35: R 141-35; D 252-0. A two-thirds majority of those present and voting (286 in this case) is required for passage under suspension of the rules. July 21, 2009.

599. **H Res 507. National Dairy Month/Adoption.** Scott, D-Ga., motion to suspend the rules and adopt the resolution that would state the House of Representatives supports the goals of National Dairy Month. Motion agreed to 428-0: R 176-0; D 252-0. A two-thirds majority of those present and voting (286 in this case) is required for adoption under suspension of the rules. July 21, 2009.

600. **H Res 270. Hunters for the Hungry Programs/Adoption.** Scott, D-Ga., motion to suspend the rules and adopt the resolution that would recognize the cooperative efforts of hunters, sportsmen's associations, meat processors, meat inspectors and hunger relief organizations to establish Hunters for the Hungry programs across the nation to reduce hunger. Motion agreed to 418-1: R 170-0; D 248-1. A two-thirds majority of those present and voting (280 in this case) is required for adoption under suspension of the rules. July 21, 2009.

	594	595	596	597	598	599	600
ALABAMA							
1 Bonner	Y	Y	Y	Y	Y	Y	Y
2 Bright	?	?	Y	Y	Y	Y	Y
3 Rogers	Y	Y	Y	Y	Y	Y	Y
4 Aderholt	Y	Y	Y	Y	Y	Y	Y
5 Griffith	Y	Y	Y	Y	Y	Y	Y
6 Bachus	Y	Y	Y	N	Y	Y	Y
7 Davis	?	?	Y	Y	Y	Y	Y
ALASKA							
AL Young	Y	Y	Y	N	Y	Y	Y
ARIZONA							
1 Kirkpatrick	Y	Y	Y	Y	Y	Y	Y
2 Franks	Y	Y	Y	N	Y	Y	Y
3 Shadegg	Y	Y	Y	N	Y	Y	Y
4 Pastor	Y	Y	Y	Y	Y	Y	Y
5 Mitchell	Y	Y	Y	Y	Y	Y	Y
6 Flake	Y	Y	Y	N	Y	Y	Y
7 Grijalva	?	?	Y	Y	Y	Y	Y
8 Giffords	Y	Y	Y	Y	Y	Y	Y
ARKANSAS							
1 Berry	Y	Y	Y	Y	Y	Y	Y
2 Snyder	Y	Y	Y	Y	Y	Y	Y
3 Boozman	Y	Y	Y	N	Y	Y	Y
4 Ross	Y	Y	Y	Y	Y	Y	Y
CALIFORNIA							
1 Thompson	Y	Y	Y	Y	Y	Y	Y
2 Herger	Y	Y	Y	N	N	Y	Y
3 Lungren	Y	Y	Y	N	Y	Y	Y
4 McClintock	Y	Y	Y	N	N	Y	Y
5 Matsui	Y	Y	Y	Y	Y	Y	Y
6 Woolsey	Y	Y	Y	Y	Y	Y	Y
7 Miller, George	Y	Y	Y	Y	Y	Y	Y
8 Pelosi							
9 Lee	Y	Y	Y	Y	Y	Y	Y
10 Vacant							
11 McNerney	Y	Y	Y	Y	Y	Y	Y
12 Speier	Y	Y	Y	?	Y	Y	Y
13 Stark	?	?	Y	Y	Y	Y	Y
14 Eshoo	Y	Y	Y	Y	Y	Y	Y
15 Honda	Y	Y	Y	Y	Y	Y	Y
16 Lofgren	Y	Y	Y	Y	Y	Y	Y
17 Farr	Y	Y	Y	Y	Y	Y	Y
18 Cardoza	Y	Y	Y	Y	Y	Y	Y
19 Radanovich	Y	Y	Y	Y	Y	Y	Y
20 Costa	?	?	Y	Y	Y	Y	Y
21 Nunes	Y	Y	Y	Y	Y	Y	Y
22 McCarthy	Y	Y	Y	Y	Y	Y	Y
23 Capps	Y	Y	Y	Y	Y	Y	Y
24 Gallegly	Y	Y	Y	Y	Y	Y	Y
25 McKeon	?	?	Y	N	Y	Y	Y
26 Dreier	Y	Y	Y	N	Y	Y	Y
27 Sherman	Y	Y	Y	Y	Y	Y	Y
28 Berman	Y	Y	Y	Y	Y	Y	Y
29 Schiff	Y	Y	Y	Y	Y	Y	Y
30 Waxman	Y	Y	Y	Y	Y	Y	Y
31 Becerra	Y	Y	Y	Y	Y	Y	Y
32 Chu	Y	Y	Y	Y	Y	Y	Y
33 Watson	Y	Y	Y	Y	Y	Y	Y
34 Roybal-Allard	Y	Y	Y	Y	Y	Y	Y
35 Waters	Y	Y	Y	Y	Y	Y	Y
36 Harman	Y	Y	Y	Y	Y	Y	Y
37 Richardson	Y	Y	Y	Y	Y	Y	Y
38 Napolitano	Y	Y	Y	Y	Y	Y	Y
39 Sánchez, Linda	Y	Y	Y	Y	Y	Y	Y
40 Royce	Y	Y	Y	N	N	Y	Y
41 Lewis	?	?	Y	Y	Y	Y	Y
42 Miller, Gary	Y	Y	Y	Y	Y	Y	Y
43 Baca	Y	Y	Y	Y	Y	Y	Y
44 Calvert	Y	Y	Y	Y	Y	Y	Y
45 Bono Mack	Y	Y	Y	Y	Y	Y	Y
46 Rohrabacher	?	?	Y	N	N	Y	Y
47 Sanchez, Loretta	?	?	Y	Y	Y	Y	Y
48 Campbell	Y	Y	Y	N	N	Y	Y
49 Issa	Y	Y	Y	N	Y	Y	Y
50 Bilbray	Y	Y	Y	Y	Y	Y	Y
51 Filner	Y	Y	Y	Y	Y	Y	Y
52 Hunter	Y	Y	Y	N	Y	Y	Y
53 Davis	Y	Y	Y	Y	Y	Y	Y
COLORADO							
1 DeGette	Y	Y	Y	Y	Y	Y	Y
2 Polis	Y	Y	Y	Y	Y	Y	Y
3 Salazar	Y	Y	Y	Y	Y	Y	Y
4 Markey	Y	Y	Y	Y	Y	Y	Y
5 Lamborn	Y	Y	Y	N	N	Y	Y
6 Coffman	Y	Y	Y	N	Y	Y	Y
7 Perlmutter	Y	Y	Y	Y	Y	Y	Y
CONNECTICUT							
1 Larson	Y	Y	Y	Y	Y	Y	Y
2 Courtney	Y	Y	Y	Y	Y	Y	Y
3 DeLauro	Y	Y	Y	Y	Y	Y	Y
4 Himes	Y	Y	Y	Y	Y	Y	Y
5 Murphy	Y	Y	Y	?	Y	Y	Y
DELAWARE							
AL Castle	Y	Y	Y	N	Y	Y	Y
FLORIDA							
1 Miller	Y	Y	Y	Y	Y	Y	Y
2 Boyd	Y	Y	Y	Y	Y	Y	Y
3 Brown	?	?	Y	Y	Y	Y	Y
4 Crenshaw	?	?	Y	N	Y	Y	Y
5 Brown-Waite	Y	Y	Y	N	Y	Y	Y
6 Stearns	Y	Y	Y	N	Y	Y	Y
7 Mica	Y	Y	Y	N	Y	Y	Y
8 Grayson	Y	Y	Y	Y	Y	Y	Y
9 Bilirakis	Y	Y	Y	Y	Y	Y	Y
10 Young	Y	Y	Y	Y	Y	Y	Y
11 Castor	Y	Y	Y	Y	Y	Y	Y
12 Putnam	Y	Y	Y	Y	Y	Y	Y
13 Buchanan	Y	Y	Y	Y	Y	Y	Y
14 Mack	Y	Y	Y	N	Y	Y	Y
15 Posey	Y	Y	Y	Y	Y	Y	Y
16 Rooney	Y	Y	Y	N	Y	Y	Y
17 Meek	Y	Y	Y	Y	Y	Y	Y
18 Ros-Lehtinen	Y	Y	Y	Y	Y	Y	Y
19 Wexler	Y	Y	Y	Y	Y	Y	?
20 Wasserman Schultz	?	?	Y	Y	Y	Y	Y
21 Diaz-Balart, L.	Y	Y	Y	Y	Y	Y	Y
22 Klein	Y	Y	Y	Y	Y	Y	Y
23 Hastings	Y	Y	Y	Y	Y	Y	Y
24 Kosmas	Y	Y	Y	Y	Y	Y	Y
25 Diaz-Balart, M.	Y	Y	Y	Y	Y	Y	Y
GEORGIA							
1 Kingston	Y	Y	Y	N	N	Y	Y
2 Bishop	Y	Y	Y	Y	Y	Y	Y
3 Westmoreland	Y	Y	Y	N	N	Y	Y
4 Johnson	Y	Y	Y	Y	Y	Y	?
5 Lewis	Y	Y	Y	Y	Y	Y	Y
6 Price	Y	Y	Y	N	Y	Y	Y
7 Linder	Y	Y	Y	N	N	Y	?
8 Marshall	Y	Y	Y	Y	Y	Y	Y
9 Deal	Y	Y	Y	N	Y	Y	?
10 Broun	Y	Y	Y	N	N	Y	Y
11 Gingrey	Y	Y	Y	N	Y	Y	Y
12 Barrow	Y	Y	Y	Y	Y	Y	Y
13 Scott	Y	Y	Y	Y	Y	Y	Y
HAWAII							
1 Abercrombie	Y	Y	Y	Y	Y	Y	Y
2 Hirono	Y	Y	Y	Y	Y	Y	Y
IDAHO							
1 Minnick	Y	Y	Y	Y	Y	Y	Y
2 Simpson	Y	Y	Y	Y	Y	Y	?
ILLINOIS							
1 Rush	Y	Y	Y	Y	Y	Y	Y
2 Jackson	Y	Y	Y	Y	Y	Y	Y
3 Lipinski	Y	Y	Y	Y	Y	Y	Y
4 Gutierrez	+	+	Y	Y	Y	Y	Y
5 Quigley	Y	Y	Y	Y	Y	Y	Y
6 Roskam	Y	?	Y	N	Y	Y	Y
7 Davis	?	?	Y	Y	Y	Y	Y
8 Bean	Y	Y	Y	Y	Y	Y	Y
9 Schakowsky	Y	Y	Y	Y	Y	Y	Y
10 Kirk	?	?	+	+	+	+	+
11 Halvorson	Y	Y	Y	Y	Y	Y	Y
12 Costello	Y	Y	Y	Y	Y	Y	Y
13 Biggert	Y	Y	Y	Y	Y	Y	Y
14 Foster	Y	Y	Y	Y	Y	Y	Y
15 Johnson	?	?	Y	Y	Y	Y	Y

KEY **Republicans**   Democrats

Y Voted for (yea)	X Paired against	C Voted "present" to avoid possible conflict of interest
# Paired for	– Announced against	
+ Announced for	P Voted "present"	? Did not vote or otherwise make a position known
N Voted against (nay)		

	594	595	596	597	598	599	600
16 **Manzullo**	+	+	Y	N	N	Y	Y
17 Hare	Y	Y	Y	Y	Y	Y	Y
18 **Schock**	Y	Y	Y	N	Y	Y	Y
19 **Shimkus**	Y	Y	Y	N	Y	Y	Y
INDIANA							
1 Visclosky	Y	Y	Y	Y	Y	Y	Y
2 Donnelly	Y	Y	Y	Y	Y	Y	Y
3 **Souder**	Y	Y	Y	Y	Y	Y	Y
4 **Buyer**	Y	Y	Y	Y	Y	Y	Y
5 **Burton**	Y	Y	Y	N	Y	Y	?
6 **Pence**	Y	Y	Y	N	N	Y	Y
7 Carson	Y	Y	Y	Y	Y	Y	Y
8 Ellsworth	Y	Y	Y	Y	Y	Y	Y
9 Hill	Y	Y	?	Y	Y	Y	Y
IOWA							
1 Braley	Y	Y	Y	Y	Y	Y	Y
2 Loebsack	Y	Y	Y	Y	Y	Y	Y
3 Boswell	+	+	Y	Y	Y	Y	Y
4 **Latham**	Y	Y	Y	Y	Y	Y	Y
5 **King**	Y	Y	Y	N	N	Y	Y
KANSAS							
1 **Moran**	Y	Y	Y	N	Y	Y	Y
2 **Jenkins**	Y	Y	Y	N	Y	Y	Y
3 Moore	Y	Y	Y	Y	Y	Y	Y
4 **Tiahrt**	Y	Y	Y	Y	Y	Y	Y
KENTUCKY							
1 **Whitfield**	Y	Y	Y	N	N	Y	Y
2 **Guthrie**	Y	Y	Y	Y	Y	Y	Y
3 Yarmuth	Y	Y	Y	Y	Y	Y	Y
4 **Davis**	Y	Y	Y	Y	Y	Y	Y
5 **Rogers**	Y	Y	Y	Y	Y	Y	Y
6 Chandler	Y	Y	Y	Y	Y	Y	Y
LOUISIANA							
1 **Scalise**	Y	Y	Y	N	Y	Y	Y
2 **Cao**	Y	Y	Y	Y	Y	Y	Y
3 Melancon	Y	Y	Y	Y	Y	Y	Y
4 **Fleming**	Y	Y	Y	Y	Y	Y	Y
5 **Alexander**	Y	Y	Y	Y	Y	Y	Y
6 **Cassidy**	Y	Y	Y	Y	Y	Y	Y
7 **Boustany**	?	Y	Y	N	Y	Y	Y
MAINE							
1 Pingree	Y	Y	Y	Y	Y	Y	Y
2 Michaud	Y	Y	Y	Y	Y	Y	Y
MARYLAND							
1 Kratovil	Y	Y	Y	Y	Y	Y	Y
2 Ruppersberger	Y	Y	Y	Y	Y	Y	Y
3 Sarbanes	Y	Y	Y	Y	Y	Y	Y
4 Edwards	Y	Y	Y	Y	Y	Y	Y
5 Hoyer	Y	Y	Y	Y	Y	Y	Y
6 **Bartlett**	Y	Y	Y	Y	Y	Y	Y
7 Cummings	Y	Y	Y	Y	Y	Y	Y
8 Van Hollen	Y	Y	Y	Y	Y	Y	Y
MASSACHUSETTS							
1 Olver	Y	Y	Y	Y	Y	Y	Y
2 Neal	Y	Y	Y	Y	Y	Y	Y
3 McGovern	Y	Y	Y	Y	Y	Y	Y
4 Frank	Y	Y	Y	Y	Y	Y	Y
5 Tsongas	Y	Y	Y	Y	Y	Y	Y
6 Tierney	Y	Y	Y	N	Y	Y	Y
7 Markey	Y	Y	Y	Y	Y	Y	Y
8 Capuano	?	?	Y	Y	Y	Y	Y
9 Lynch	Y	Y	Y	Y	Y	Y	Y
10 Delahunt	Y	Y	Y	Y	Y	Y	Y
MICHIGAN							
1 Stupak	Y	Y	Y	Y	Y	Y	Y
2 **Hoekstra**	Y	Y	Y	N	Y	Y	Y
3 **Ehlers**	Y	Y	Y	Y	N	Y	Y
4 **Camp**	Y	Y	Y	Y	Y	Y	Y
5 Kildee	Y	Y	Y	Y	Y	Y	Y
6 **Upton**	Y	Y	Y	N	Y	Y	Y
7 Schauer	Y	Y	Y	Y	Y	Y	Y
8 **Rogers**	Y	Y	Y	Y	Y	Y	Y
9 Peters	Y	Y	Y	Y	Y	Y	Y
10 **Miller**	Y	Y	Y	Y	Y	Y	Y
11 **McCotter**	Y	Y	Y	Y	Y	Y	Y
12 Levin	Y	Y	Y	Y	Y	Y	Y
13 Kilpatrick	Y	Y	Y	Y	Y	Y	Y
14 Conyers	+	+	Y	Y	Y	Y	Y
15 Dingell	Y	Y	Y	Y	Y	Y	Y
MINNESOTA							
1 Walz	Y	Y	Y	Y	Y	Y	Y
2 **Kline**	Y	Y	Y	N	Y	Y	Y
3 **Paulsen**	Y	Y	Y	?	Y	Y	Y
4 McCollum	Y	Y	Y	Y	Y	Y	Y

	594	595	596	597	598	599	600
5 Ellison	Y	Y	Y	Y	Y	Y	Y
6 **Bachmann**	Y	Y	Y	Y	Y	Y	Y
7 Peterson	Y	Y	Y	Y	Y	Y	Y
8 Oberstar	Y	Y	Y	Y	Y	Y	Y
MISSISSIPPI							
1 Childers	Y	Y	Y	Y	Y	Y	Y
2 Thompson	Y	Y	Y	Y	Y	Y	Y
3 **Harper**	Y	Y	Y	N	N	Y	Y
4 Taylor	Y	Y	Y	Y	Y	Y	Y
MISSOURI							
1 Clay	Y	Y	Y	Y	Y	Y	Y
2 **Akin**	Y	Y	Y	N	N	Y	Y
3 Carnahan	Y	Y	Y	Y	Y	Y	Y
4 Skelton	Y	Y	Y	Y	Y	Y	Y
5 Cleaver	Y	Y	?	Y	Y	Y	Y
6 **Graves**	Y	Y	Y	N	Y	Y	Y
7 **Blunt**	Y	Y	Y	N	Y	Y	Y
8 **Emerson**	Y	Y	Y	Y	Y	Y	Y
9 **Luetkemeyer**	Y	Y	Y	Y	Y	Y	Y
MONTANA							
AL **Rehberg**	Y	Y	Y	Y	Y	Y	Y
NEBRASKA							
1 **Fortenberry**	Y	Y	Y	Y	Y	Y	Y
2 **Terry**	Y	Y	Y	Y	Y	Y	Y
3 **Smith**	Y	Y	Y	Y	Y	Y	Y
NEVADA							
1 Berkley	Y	Y	Y	Y	Y	Y	Y
2 **Heller**	Y	Y	Y	Y	Y	Y	Y
3 Titus	Y	Y	Y	Y	Y	Y	Y
NEW HAMPSHIRE							
1 Shea-Porter	Y	Y	Y	Y	Y	Y	Y
2 Hodes	Y	Y	Y	Y	Y	Y	Y
NEW JERSEY							
1 Andrews	Y	Y	Y	Y	Y	Y	Y
2 **LoBiondo**	Y	Y	Y	Y	Y	Y	Y
3 Adler	Y	Y	Y	Y	Y	Y	Y
4 **Smith**	Y	Y	Y	Y	Y	Y	?
5 **Garrett**	Y	Y	Y	N	N	Y	Y
6 Pallone	Y	Y	Y	Y	Y	Y	Y
7 **Lance**	Y	Y	Y	Y	Y	Y	Y
8 Pascrell	Y	Y	Y	Y	Y	Y	Y
9 Rothman	Y	Y	Y	Y	Y	Y	Y
10 Payne	Y	Y	Y	Y	Y	Y	Y
11 **Frelinghuysen**	Y	Y	Y	Y	Y	Y	Y
12 Holt	Y	Y	Y	Y	Y	Y	Y
13 Sires	?	?	Y	Y	Y	Y	Y
NEW MEXICO							
1 Heinrich	Y	Y	Y	Y	Y	Y	Y
2 Teague	Y	Y	Y	Y	Y	Y	Y
3 Lujan	Y	Y	Y	Y	Y	Y	Y
NEW YORK							
1 Bishop	Y	Y	Y	Y	Y	Y	Y
2 Israel	Y	Y	Y	Y	Y	Y	Y
3 **King**	Y	Y	Y	N	Y	Y	Y
4 McCarthy	+	+	+	+	+	+	+
5 Ackerman	Y	Y	Y	Y	Y	Y	Y
6 Meeks	Y	Y	Y	Y	Y	Y	Y
7 Crowley	Y	Y	Y	Y	+	+	Y
8 Nadler	Y	Y	Y	Y	Y	Y	Y
9 Weiner	Y	Y	Y	Y	Y	Y	Y
10 Towns	?	?	Y	Y	Y	Y	Y
11 Clarke	Y	Y	Y	Y	Y	Y	Y
12 Velázquez	Y	Y	Y	Y	Y	Y	Y
13 McMahon	Y	Y	?	Y	Y	Y	Y
14 Maloney	?	?	Y	Y	Y	Y	Y
15 Rangel	Y	Y	Y	Y	Y	Y	Y
16 Serrano	Y	Y	Y	Y	Y	Y	Y
17 Engel	Y	Y	Y	Y	Y	Y	Y
18 Lowey	Y	Y	Y	Y	Y	Y	Y
19 Hall	Y	Y	Y	Y	Y	Y	Y
20 Murphy	Y	Y	Y	Y	Y	Y	Y
21 Tonko	Y	Y	Y	Y	Y	Y	Y
22 Hinchey	?	?	Y	Y	Y	Y	Y
23 **McHugh**	Y	Y	?	Y	Y	Y	Y
24 Arcuri	Y	Y	Y	Y	Y	Y	Y
25 Maffei	Y	Y	Y	Y	Y	Y	Y
26 **Lee**	Y	Y	Y	Y	Y	Y	Y
27 Higgins	Y	Y	Y	Y	Y	Y	Y
28 Slaughter	Y	Y	Y	Y	Y	Y	Y
29 Massa	Y	Y	Y	Y	Y	Y	Y
NORTH CAROLINA							
1 Butterfield	Y	Y	Y	Y	Y	Y	Y
2 Etheridge	Y	Y	Y	Y	Y	Y	Y
3 **Jones**	Y	Y	Y	Y	Y	Y	Y
4 Price	Y	Y	Y	Y	Y	Y	Y

	594	595	596	597	598	599	600
5 **Foxx**	Y	Y	Y	N	Y	Y	Y
6 **Coble**	Y	Y	Y	N	N	Y	Y
7 McIntyre	Y	Y	Y	Y	Y	Y	Y
8 Kissell	Y	Y	Y	Y	Y	Y	Y
9 **Myrick**	Y	Y	Y	N	Y	Y	Y
10 **McHenry**	Y	Y	Y	N	Y	Y	Y
11 Shuler	Y	Y	Y	Y	Y	Y	Y
12 Watt	Y	Y	Y	Y	Y	Y	Y
13 Miller	Y	Y	Y	Y	Y	Y	Y
NORTH DAKOTA							
AL Pomeroy	Y	Y	Y	Y	Y	Y	Y
OHIO							
1 Driehaus	Y	Y	Y	Y	Y	Y	Y
2 **Schmidt**	Y	Y	Y	N	Y	Y	Y
3 **Turner**	+	+	Y	Y	Y	Y	Y
4 **Jordan**	Y	Y	Y	N	Y	Y	Y
5 **Latta**	Y	Y	Y	N	Y	Y	Y
6 Wilson	Y	Y	Y	Y	Y	Y	Y
7 **Austria**	Y	Y	Y	Y	Y	Y	Y
8 **Boehner**	Y	Y	Y	N	Y	Y	Y
9 Kaptur	Y	Y	Y	Y	Y	Y	Y
10 Kucinich	Y	Y	Y	Y	Y	Y	Y
11 Fudge	Y	Y	Y	Y	Y	Y	Y
12 **Tiberi**	?	?	Y	Y	Y	Y	Y
13 Sutton	Y	Y	Y	Y	Y	Y	?
14 **LaTourette**	Y	Y	Y	Y	Y	Y	Y
15 Kilroy	Y	Y	Y	Y	Y	Y	Y
16 Boccieri	Y	Y	Y	Y	Y	Y	Y
17 Ryan	Y	Y	Y	Y	Y	Y	Y
18 Space	Y	Y	Y	Y	Y	Y	Y
OKLAHOMA							
1 **Sullivan**	Y	Y	Y	?	Y	Y	Y
2 Boren	Y	Y	Y	Y	Y	Y	Y
3 **Lucas**	?	?	Y	Y	Y	Y	Y
4 **Cole**	Y	Y	Y	Y	Y	Y	Y
5 **Fallin**	Y	Y	Y	N	Y	Y	Y
OREGON							
1 Wu	Y	Y	Y	Y	Y	Y	Y
2 **Walden**	Y	Y	Y	N	N	Y	Y
3 Blumenauer	Y	Y	Y	Y	Y	Y	Y
4 DeFazio	Y	Y	Y	Y	Y	Y	Y
5 Schrader	Y	Y	Y	Y	Y	Y	Y
PENNSYLVANIA							
1 Brady	Y	Y	Y	Y	Y	Y	Y
2 Fattah	Y	Y	Y	Y	Y	Y	Y
3 Dahlkemper	Y	Y	Y	Y	Y	Y	Y
4 Altmire	Y	Y	Y	Y	Y	Y	Y
5 **Thompson**	Y	Y	Y	Y	Y	Y	Y
6 **Gerlach**	Y	Y	Y	Y	Y	Y	Y
7 Sestak	?	?	?	?	?	?	?
8 Murphy, P.	Y	Y	Y	Y	Y	Y	Y
9 **Shuster**	Y	Y	Y	N	Y	Y	Y
10 Carney	Y	Y	Y	Y	Y	Y	Y
11 Kanjorski	Y	Y	Y	Y	Y	Y	Y
12 Murtha	Y	Y	Y	Y	Y	Y	Y
13 Schwartz	Y	Y	Y	Y	Y	Y	Y
14 Doyle	?	Y	Y	Y	Y	Y	Y
15 **Dent**	Y	Y	Y	Y	Y	Y	Y
16 **Pitts**	Y	Y	Y	Y	Y	Y	Y
17 Holden	Y	Y	Y	Y	Y	Y	Y
18 **Murphy, T.**	Y	Y	Y	Y	Y	Y	Y
19 **Platts**	Y	Y	Y	N	Y	Y	Y
RHODE ISLAND							
1 Kennedy	Y	Y	Y	Y	Y	Y	Y
2 Langevin	Y	Y	Y	Y	Y	Y	Y
SOUTH CAROLINA							
1 **Brown**	Y	Y	Y	N	Y	Y	Y
2 **Wilson**	Y	?	Y	Y	Y	Y	Y
3 **Barrett**	?	?	Y	N	Y	Y	Y
4 **Inglis**	Y	Y	Y	Y	Y	Y	Y
5 Spratt	Y	Y	Y	Y	Y	Y	Y
6 Clyburn	Y	Y	Y	Y	Y	Y	Y
SOUTH DAKOTA							
AL Herseth Sandlin	Y	Y	Y	Y	Y	Y	Y
TENNESSEE							
1 **Roe**	Y	Y	Y	N	Y	Y	Y
2 **Duncan**	Y	Y	Y	N	N	Y	Y
3 **Wamp**	Y	Y	Y	Y	Y	Y	Y
4 Davis	Y	Y	?	Y	Y	Y	Y
5 Cooper	Y	Y	Y	Y	Y	Y	Y
6 Gordon	Y	Y	Y	Y	Y	Y	Y
7 **Blackburn**	Y	Y	Y	Y	?	?	Y
8 Tanner	Y	Y	Y	Y	Y	Y	Y
9 Cohen	Y	Y	Y	Y	Y	Y	Y

	594	595	596	597	598	599	600
TEXAS							
1 **Gohmert**	?	Y	Y	N	Y	Y	?
2 **Poe**	Y	Y	Y	N	Y	Y	Y
3 **Johnson, S.**	Y	Y	Y	N	Y	Y	Y
4 **Hall**	Y	Y	Y	N	Y	Y	Y
5 **Hensarling**	Y	Y	Y	N	N	Y	Y
6 **Barton**	Y	Y	Y	Y	Y	Y	Y
7 **Culberson**	Y	?	Y	N	N	Y	Y
8 **Brady**	+	+	Y	N	Y	Y	Y
9 Green, A.	Y	Y	Y	Y	Y	Y	Y
10 **McCaul**	Y	Y	Y	Y	Y	Y	Y
11 **Conaway**	?	?	Y	N	Y	Y	Y
12 **Granger**	Y	Y	Y	N	Y	Y	Y
13 **Thornberry**	Y	Y	Y	N	Y	Y	Y
14 **Paul**	Y	Y	Y	N	N	Y	Y
15 Hinojosa	Y	Y	Y	Y	Y	Y	Y
16 Reyes	Y	Y	?	Y	Y	Y	Y
17 Edwards	Y	Y	Y	Y	Y	Y	Y
18 Jackson Lee	Y	Y	Y	Y	Y	Y	Y
19 **Neugebauer**	Y	Y	Y	N	Y	Y	Y
20 Gonzalez	Y	Y	Y	Y	Y	Y	Y
21 **Smith**	Y	Y	Y	Y	Y	Y	Y
22 **Olson**	Y	Y	Y	N	Y	Y	Y
23 Rodriguez	Y	Y	Y	Y	Y	Y	Y
24 **Marchant**	?	?	Y	N	Y	Y	?
25 Doggett	Y	Y	Y	Y	Y	Y	Y
26 **Burgess**	Y	Y	Y	Y	Y	Y	Y
27 Ortiz	Y	Y	Y	Y	Y	Y	Y
28 Cuellar	Y	Y	Y	Y	Y	Y	Y
29 Green, G.	Y	Y	Y	Y	Y	Y	Y
30 Johnson, E.	Y	Y	Y	Y	Y	Y	Y
31 **Carter**	Y	Y	Y	N	Y	Y	Y
32 **Sessions**	?	?	Y	N	Y	Y	Y
UTAH							
1 **Bishop**	Y	Y	Y	N	N	Y	Y
2 Matheson	Y	Y	Y	Y	Y	Y	Y
3 **Chaffetz**	Y	Y	Y	N	N	Y	Y
VERMONT							
AL Welch	Y	Y	Y	Y	Y	Y	Y
VIRGINIA							
1 **Wittman**	+	+	Y	N	Y	Y	Y
2 Nye	Y	Y	Y	Y	Y	Y	Y
3 Scott	Y	Y	Y	Y	Y	Y	Y
4 **Forbes**	?	?	Y	N	Y	Y	Y
5 Perriello	Y	Y	Y	Y	Y	Y	Y
6 **Goodlatte**	Y	Y	Y	N	Y	Y	Y
7 **Cantor**	Y	Y	Y	N	Y	Y	Y
8 Moran	?	?	Y	Y	Y	Y	N
9 Boucher	?	?	Y	Y	Y	Y	Y
10 **Wolf**	Y	Y	Y	Y	Y	Y	Y
11 Connolly	Y	Y	Y	Y	Y	Y	Y
WASHINGTON							
1 Inslee	Y	Y	Y	Y	Y	Y	Y
2 Larsen	?	?	Y	Y	Y	Y	Y
3 Baird	Y	Y	Y	Y	Y	Y	Y
4 **Hastings**	Y	Y	Y	N	N	Y	Y
5 **McMorris Rodgers**	Y	Y	Y	Y	Y	Y	Y
6 Dicks	Y	Y	Y	Y	Y	Y	Y
7 McDermott	Y	Y	Y	Y	Y	Y	Y
8 **Reichert**	Y	Y	Y	Y	Y	Y	Y
9 Smith	+	+	Y	Y	Y	Y	Y
WEST VIRGINIA							
1 Mollohan	Y	Y	Y	Y	Y	Y	Y
2 **Capito**	Y	Y	Y	Y	Y	Y	Y
3 Rahall	Y	Y	Y	Y	Y	Y	Y
WISCONSIN							
1 **Ryan**	Y	Y	Y	N	N	Y	Y
2 Baldwin	Y	Y	Y	Y	Y	Y	Y
3 Kind	Y	Y	Y	Y	Y	Y	Y
4 Moore	Y	Y	?	Y	Y	Y	Y
5 **Sensenbrenner**	Y	Y	Y	N	N	Y	Y
6 **Petri**	Y	Y	Y	N	N	Y	Y
7 Obey	Y	Y	Y	Y	Y	Y	Y
8 Kagen	Y	Y	Y	Y	Y	Y	Y
WYOMING							
AL **Lummis**	Y	Y	Y	N	N	Y	Y
DELEGATES							
Faleomavaega (A.S.)							
Norton (D.C.)							
Bordallo (Guam)							
Sablan (N. Marianas)							
Pierluisi (P.R.)							
Christensen (V.I.)							

IN THE HOUSE | By Vote Number

601. **S Con Res 30. Bureau of Labor Statistics Anniversary/ Adoption.** Courtney, D-Conn., motion to suspend the rules and adopt the concurrent resolution that would commend the Bureau of Labor Statistics on its 125th anniversary. Motion agreed to 421-2: R 169-2; D 252-0. A two-thirds majority of those present and voting (282 in this case) is required for adoption under suspension of the rules. July 21, 2009.

602. **H Con Res 123. John Heisman Recognition/Adoption.** Courtney, D-Conn., motion to suspend the rules and adopt the concurrent resolution that would recognize the contributions that football player and coach John William Heisman made to the sport. Motion agreed to 423-0: R 174-0; D 249-0. A two-thirds majority of those present and voting (282 in this case) is required for adoption under suspension of the rules. July 21, 2009.

603. **HR 1933. Missing Child Center/Passage.** Johnson, D-Ga., motion to suspend the rules and pass the bill that would require the attorney general to make an annual grant to the A Child Is Missing Alert and Recovery Center to assist law enforcement agencies in the recovery of missing children, and authorize funding for the grants. Motion agreed to 417-5: R 169-5; D 248-0. A two-thirds majority of those present and voting (282 in this case) is required for passage under suspension of the rules. July 21, 2009.

604. **HR 2632. National Korean War Veterans Armistice Day/ Passage.** Johnson, D-Ga., motion to suspend the rules and pass the bill that would add July 27, National Korean War Veterans Armistice Day, to the days on which the American flag should be displayed. Motion agreed to 421-0: R 172-0; D 249-0. A two-thirds majority of those present and voting (281 in this case) is required for passage under suspension of the rules. July 21, 2009.

605. **H Res 667. Earmark Investigation/Motion to Table.** Andrews, D-N.J., motion to table (kill) the Flake, R-Ariz., privileged resolution that would instruct the Committee on Standards of Official Conduct to investigate the relationship between earmarks requested by members of Congress and the details of past campaign contributions. Motion agreed to 224-189: R 2-165; D 222-24. July 22, 2009.

606. **HR 2920. Statutory Pay-As-You-Go/Rule.** Adoption of the rule (H Res 665) to provide for House floor consideration of the bill that would establish a statutory requirement that new tax and mandatory spending legislation be budget-neutral, enforced annually by automatic, across-the-board spending cuts in non-exempt programs. Adopted 243-182: R 0-176; D 243-6. July 22, 2009.

607. **HR 1675. Housing for People With Disabilities/Passage.** Grayson, D-Fla., motion to suspend the rules and pass the bill that would make several changes to existing law addressing low-income housing programs for people with disabilities and authorize unspecified sums for fiscal 2010 through fiscal 2014. Motion agreed to 376-51: R 126-51; D 250-0. A two-thirds majority of those present and voting (285 in this case) is required for passage under suspension of the rules. July 22, 2009.

	601	602	603	604	605	606	607
ALABAMA							
1 Bonner	Y	Y	Y	Y	P	N	Y
2 Bright	Y	Y	Y	Y	N	Y	Y
3 Rogers	Y	Y	Y	Y	N	?	Y
4 Aderholt	Y	Y	Y	Y	N	N	Y
5 Griffith	Y	Y	Y	Y	Y	Y	Y
6 Bachus	Y	Y	Y	Y	N	N	Y
7 Davis	Y	Y	Y	Y	Y	Y	Y
ALASKA							
AL Young	N	Y	Y	Y	Y	N	Y
ARIZONA							
1 Kirkpatrick	Y	Y	Y	Y	N	Y	Y
2 Franks	Y	Y	Y	N	N	N	N
3 Shadegg	Y	Y	N	N	N	N	N
4 Pastor	Y	Y	Y	Y	Y	Y	Y
5 Mitchell	Y	Y	Y	Y	N	N	Y
6 Flake	Y	Y	N	Y	N	N	N
7 Grijalva	Y	Y	Y	Y	Y	Y	Y
8 Giffords	Y	Y	Y	Y	N	Y	Y
ARKANSAS							
1 Berry	Y	Y	Y	Y	Y	Y	Y
2 Snyder	Y	Y	Y	Y	Y	Y	Y
3 Boozman	Y	Y	Y	Y	N	N	Y
4 Ross	Y	Y	Y	Y	Y	Y	Y
CALIFORNIA							
1 Thompson	Y	Y	Y	Y	Y	Y	Y
2 Herger	Y	Y	Y	N	N	N	Y
3 Lungren	Y	Y	Y	N	N	N	Y
4 McClintock	Y	Y	Y	N	N	N	N
5 Matsui	Y	Y	Y	Y	Y	Y	Y
6 Woolsey	Y	Y	Y	Y	Y	Y	Y
7 Miller, George	Y	Y	Y	Y	Y	Y	Y
8 Pelosi							
9 Lee	Y	Y	Y	Y	Y	Y	Y
10 Vacant							
11 McNerney	Y	Y	Y	Y	N	Y	Y
12 Speier	Y	Y	?	Y	Y	Y	Y
13 Stark	Y	Y	Y	Y	Y	Y	Y
14 Eshoo	Y	Y	Y	Y	Y	Y	Y
15 Honda	Y	Y	Y	Y	Y	Y	Y
16 Lofgren	Y	Y	Y	Y	P	Y	Y
17 Farr	Y	Y	Y	Y	Y	Y	Y
18 Cardoza	Y	Y	Y	Y	Y	Y	Y
19 Radanovich	Y	Y	?	?	N	N	N
20 Costa	Y	Y	Y	Y	Y	Y	Y
21 Nunes	Y	Y	Y	Y	N	N	Y
22 McCarthy	Y	Y	Y	Y	N	N	Y
23 Capps	Y	Y	Y	Y	Y	Y	Y
24 Gallegly	Y	Y	Y	Y	N	N	Y
25 McKeon	Y	Y	Y	Y	N	N	Y
26 Dreier	Y	Y	Y	Y	N	N	Y
27 Sherman	Y	Y	Y	Y	Y	Y	Y
28 Berman	Y	Y	Y	Y	Y	Y	Y
29 Schiff	Y	Y	Y	Y	Y	Y	Y
30 Waxman	Y	Y	Y	Y	Y	Y	Y
31 Becerra	Y	Y	Y	Y	Y	?	Y
32 Chu	Y	Y	Y	Y	Y	Y	Y
33 Watson	Y	Y	Y	Y	Y	Y	Y
34 Roybal-Allard	Y	Y	Y	Y	Y	Y	Y
35 Waters	Y	Y	Y	Y	Y	Y	Y
36 Harman	Y	Y	Y	Y	Y	Y	Y
37 Richardson	Y	Y	Y	Y	Y	Y	Y
38 Napolitano	Y	Y	Y	Y	Y	Y	Y
39 Sánchez, Linda	Y	Y	Y	Y	Y	Y	Y
40 Royce	Y	Y	Y	N	N	N	N
41 Lewis	Y	Y	Y	?	N	N	Y
42 Miller, Gary	Y	Y	Y	N	N	N	Y
43 Baca	Y	Y	Y	Y	Y	Y	Y
44 Calvert	Y	Y	Y	Y	N	N	Y
45 Bono Mack	Y	Y	Y	Y	N	N	Y
46 Rohrabacher	Y	Y	N	N	N	N	N
47 Sanchez, Loretta	Y	Y	Y	Y	Y	Y	Y
48 Campbell	Y	Y	Y	Y	N	N	N
49 Issa	Y	Y	Y	Y	N	N	Y
50 Bilbray	Y	Y	Y	?	N	N	Y
51 Filner	Y	Y	Y	Y	Y	Y	Y
52 Hunter	Y	Y	Y	Y	N	N	Y
53 Davis	Y	Y	Y	Y	Y	Y	Y

	601	602	603	604	605	606	607
COLORADO							
1 DeGette	Y	Y	Y	Y	Y	Y	Y
2 Polis	Y	Y	Y	Y	Y	Y	Y
3 Salazar	Y	Y	Y	Y	Y	Y	Y
4 Markey	Y	Y	Y	Y	Y	Y	Y
5 Lamborn	Y	Y	Y	N	N	N	N
6 Coffman	Y	Y	Y	N	N	N	N
7 Perlmutter	Y	Y	Y	Y	Y	Y	Y
CONNECTICUT							
1 Larson	Y	Y	Y	Y	Y	Y	Y
2 Courtney	Y	Y	Y	Y	Y	Y	Y
3 DeLauro	Y	Y	Y	Y	Y	Y	Y
4 Himes	Y	Y	Y	Y	N	Y	Y
5 Murphy	Y	Y	Y	Y	Y	Y	Y
DELAWARE							
AL Castle	Y	Y	Y	Y	N	N	Y
FLORIDA							
1 Miller	Y	Y	Y	Y	N	N	Y
2 Boyd	Y	Y	Y	Y	Y	Y	Y
3 Brown	Y	Y	Y	Y	Y	Y	Y
4 Crenshaw	Y	Y	Y	Y	N	N	Y
5 Brown-Waite	Y	Y	Y	Y	N	N	Y
6 Stearns	Y	Y	Y	N	N	N	Y
7 Mica	Y	Y	Y	N	N	N	Y
8 Grayson	Y	Y	Y	Y	Y	Y	Y
9 Bilirakis	Y	Y	Y	Y	N	N	Y
10 Young	Y	Y	Y	?	?	?	Y
11 Castor	Y	Y	Y	P	Y	Y	Y
12 Putnam	Y	Y	Y	Y	Y	Y	Y
13 Buchanan	Y	Y	Y	Y	N	N	Y
14 Mack	Y	Y	Y	N	N	N	Y
15 Posey	Y	Y	Y	Y	N	N	Y
16 Rooney	Y	Y	Y	Y	N	N	Y
17 Meek	Y	Y	Y	?	?	Y	Y
18 Ros-Lehtinen	Y	Y	Y	Y	N	N	Y
19 Wexler	?	?	?	?	Y	Y	Y
20 Wasserman Schultz	Y	Y	Y	Y	Y	Y	Y
21 Diaz-Balart, L.	Y	Y	Y	P	N	N	Y
22 Klein	Y	Y	Y	Y	Y	Y	Y
23 Hastings	Y	Y	Y	Y	Y	Y	Y
24 Kosmas	Y	Y	Y	Y	Y	Y	Y
25 Diaz-Balart, M.	Y	Y	Y	Y	N	N	Y
GEORGIA							
1 Kingston	Y	Y	Y	N	N	N	N
2 Bishop	Y	Y	Y	Y	Y	Y	Y
3 Westmoreland	Y	Y	Y	N	N	N	N
4 Johnson	Y	Y	Y	Y	Y	Y	Y
5 Lewis	Y	Y	Y	Y	Y	Y	Y
6 Price	Y	Y	Y	N	N	N	N
7 Linder	Y	Y	Y	N	N	N	N
8 Marshall	Y	Y	Y	Y	Y	Y	Y
9 Deal	Y	Y	Y	Y	N	N	N
10 Broun	Y	N	Y	N	N	N	N
11 Gingrey	Y	Y	Y	N	N	N	N
12 Barrow	Y	Y	Y	Y	Y	Y	Y
13 Scott	Y	Y	Y	Y	Y	Y	Y
HAWAII							
1 Abercrombie	Y	Y	Y	Y	Y	Y	Y
2 Hirono	Y	Y	Y	Y	Y	Y	Y
IDAHO							
1 Minnick	Y	Y	Y	N	N	Y	Y
2 Simpson	?	?	?	?	N	N	Y
ILLINOIS							
1 Rush	Y	Y	Y	Y	Y	Y	Y
2 Jackson	Y	Y	Y	Y	Y	Y	Y
3 Lipinski	Y	Y	Y	Y	Y	Y	Y
4 Gutierrez	Y	Y	Y	Y	Y	Y	Y
5 Quigley	Y	Y	Y	Y	N	Y	Y
6 Roskam	Y	Y	Y	Y	N	N	Y
7 Davis	Y	Y	Y	Y	Y	Y	Y
8 Bean	Y	Y	Y	Y	Y	Y	Y
9 Schakowsky	Y	?	Y	Y	Y	Y	Y
10 Kirk	+	+	Y	Y	N	N	Y
11 Halvorson	Y	Y	Y	Y	Y	Y	Y
12 Costello	Y	Y	Y	Y	Y	Y	Y
13 Biggert	Y	Y	Y	Y	N	N	Y
14 Foster	Y	Y	Y	Y	N	Y	Y
15 Johnson	Y	Y	Y	Y	N	N	Y

KEY   **Republicans**   Democrats

Y Voted for (yea)	X Paired against	C Voted "present" to avoid possible conflict of interest
# Paired for	– Announced against	
+ Announced for	P Voted "present"	? Did not vote or otherwise make a position known
N Voted against (nay)		

	601	602	603	604	605	606	607
16 **Manzullo**	Y	Y	Y	Y	N	N	Y
17 Hare	Y	Y	Y	Y	Y	Y	Y
18 **Schock**	Y	Y	Y	Y	N	N	Y
19 **Shimkus**	Y	Y	Y	Y	N	N	Y
INDIANA							
1 Visclosky	Y	Y	Y	Y	N	Y	Y
2 Donnelly	Y	Y	Y	Y	N	Y	Y
3 **Souder**	Y	Y	Y	Y	N	N	Y
4 **Buyer**	Y	Y	Y	Y	N	N	Y
5 **Burton**	?	Y	Y	Y	N	N	Y
6 **Pence**	Y	Y	Y	Y	N	N	N
7 Carson	Y	Y	Y	Y	Y	Y	Y
8 Ellsworth	Y	Y	Y	Y	N	Y	Y
9 Hill	Y	Y	Y	Y	N	Y	Y
IOWA							
1 Braley	Y	Y	Y	Y	Y	Y	Y
2 Loebsack	Y	Y	Y	Y	N	Y	Y
3 Boswell	Y	Y	Y	Y	Y	Y	Y
4 **Latham**	Y	Y	Y	Y	N	N	Y
5 **King**	Y	Y	Y	Y	N	N	N
KANSAS							
1 **Moran**	Y	Y	Y	Y	N	N	Y
2 **Jenkins**	Y	Y	Y	Y	N	N	Y
3 Moore	Y	Y	Y	Y	Y	Y	Y
4 **Tiahrt**	Y	Y	Y	Y	N	N	Y
KENTUCKY							
1 **Whitfield**	Y	Y	Y	Y	N	N	Y
2 **Guthrie**	Y	Y	Y	Y	N	N	Y
3 Yarmuth	Y	Y	Y	Y	Y	Y	Y
4 **Davis**	Y	Y	Y	Y	N	N	Y
5 **Rogers**	Y	Y	Y	Y	N	N	Y
6 Chandler	Y	Y	Y	Y	P	?	Y
LOUISIANA							
1 **Scalise**	?	Y	Y	Y	N	N	N
2 **Cao**	Y	Y	Y	Y	N	N	Y
3 Melancon	Y	Y	Y	Y	Y	Y	Y
4 **Fleming**	Y	Y	Y	Y	N	N	Y
5 **Alexander**	Y	Y	Y	Y	N	N	Y
6 **Cassidy**	Y	Y	Y	Y	N	N	Y
7 **Boustany**	Y	Y	Y	Y	N	N	Y
MAINE							
1 Pingree	Y	Y	Y	Y	Y	Y	Y
2 Michaud	Y	Y	Y	Y	Y	N	Y
MARYLAND							
1 Kratovil	Y	Y	Y	Y	Y	Y	Y
2 Ruppersberger	Y	Y	Y	Y	Y	Y	Y
3 Sarbanes	Y	Y	Y	Y	Y	Y	Y
4 Edwards	Y	Y	Y	Y	Y	Y	Y
5 Hoyer	Y	Y	Y	Y	Y	Y	?
6 **Bartlett**	Y	Y	Y	Y	N	N	N
7 Cummings	Y	Y	Y	Y	Y	Y	Y
8 Van Hollen	Y	Y	Y	Y	Y	Y	Y
MASSACHUSETTS							
1 Olver	Y	Y	Y	Y	Y	Y	Y
2 Neal	Y	Y	Y	Y	Y	Y	Y
3 McGovern	Y	Y	Y	Y	Y	Y	Y
4 Frank	Y	Y	Y	Y	Y	Y	Y
5 Tsongas	Y	Y	Y	Y	Y	Y	Y
6 Tierney	Y	Y	Y	Y	Y	Y	Y
7 Markey	Y	Y	Y	Y	Y	Y	Y
8 Capuano	Y	Y	Y	Y	Y	Y	Y
9 Lynch	Y	Y	Y	Y	Y	Y	Y
10 Delahunt	Y	Y	Y	Y	Y	Y	Y
MICHIGAN							
1 Stupak	Y	Y	Y	Y	Y	Y	Y
2 **Hoekstra**	Y	Y	Y	Y	N	N	Y
3 **Ehlers**	Y	Y	Y	Y	N	N	Y
4 **Camp**	Y	Y	Y	Y	N	N	Y
5 Kildee	Y	Y	Y	Y	Y	Y	Y
6 **Upton**	Y	Y	Y	Y	N	N	Y
7 Schauer	Y	Y	Y	Y	Y	Y	Y
8 **Rogers**	Y	Y	Y	Y	N	N	Y
9 Peters	Y	Y	Y	Y	Y	Y	Y
10 **Miller**	Y	Y	Y	Y	N	N	Y
11 **McCotter**	Y	Y	Y	Y	N	N	Y
12 Levin	Y	Y	Y	Y	Y	Y	Y
13 Kilpatrick	Y	Y	Y	Y	Y	Y	Y
14 Conyers	Y	Y	Y	Y	Y	Y	Y
15 Dingell	Y	Y	Y	Y	Y	Y	Y
MINNESOTA							
1 Walz	Y	Y	Y	Y	N	Y	Y
2 **Kline**	Y	Y	Y	Y	N	N	Y
3 **Paulsen**	Y	Y	Y	Y	N	N	Y
4 McCollum	Y	Y	Y	Y	Y	Y	Y
5 Ellison	Y	Y	Y	?	Y	Y	Y
6 **Bachmann**	Y	Y	Y	Y	N	N	Y
7 Peterson	Y	Y	Y	Y	Y	Y	Y
8 Oberstar	Y	Y	Y	Y	Y	Y	Y
MISSISSIPPI							
1 Childers	Y	Y	Y	Y	N	Y	Y
2 Thompson	Y	Y	Y	Y	?	?	?
3 **Harper**	Y	Y	Y	Y	P	N	Y
4 Taylor	Y	Y	Y	Y	Y	N	Y
MISSOURI							
1 Clay	Y	Y	Y	Y	Y	N	Y
2 **Akin**	Y	Y	Y	Y	N	N	N
3 Carnahan	Y	Y	Y	Y	Y	Y	Y
4 Skelton	Y	Y	Y	Y	Y	Y	Y
5 Cleaver	Y	Y	Y	Y	Y	Y	Y
6 **Graves**	Y	Y	Y	Y	N	N	Y
7 **Blunt**	Y	Y	Y	Y	N	N	N
8 **Emerson**	Y	Y	Y	Y	N	N	Y
9 **Luetkemeyer**	Y	Y	Y	Y	N	N	Y
MONTANA							
AL **Rehberg**	Y	Y	Y	Y	N	N	Y
NEBRASKA							
1 **Fortenberry**	Y	Y	Y	Y	N	N	Y
2 **Terry**	Y	Y	Y	Y	N	N	Y
3 **Smith**	Y	Y	Y	Y	N	N	Y
NEVADA							
1 Berkley	Y	Y	Y	Y	Y	Y	Y
2 **Heller**	Y	Y	Y	Y	N	N	Y
3 Titus	Y	Y	Y	Y	Y	Y	Y
NEW HAMPSHIRE							
1 Shea-Porter	Y	Y	Y	Y	Y	Y	Y
2 Hodes	Y	Y	Y	Y	N	Y	Y
NEW JERSEY							
1 Andrews	Y	Y	Y	Y	Y	Y	Y
2 **LoBiondo**	Y	Y	Y	Y	N	N	Y
3 Adler	Y	Y	Y	Y	Y	Y	Y
4 **Smith**	?	Y	Y	Y	N	N	Y
5 **Garrett**	Y	Y	Y	Y	N	N	N
6 Pallone	Y	Y	Y	Y	Y	Y	Y
7 **Lance**	Y	Y	Y	Y	N	N	Y
8 Pascrell	Y	Y	Y	Y	Y	Y	Y
9 Rothman	Y	Y	Y	Y	Y	Y	Y
10 Payne	Y	Y	Y	Y	Y	Y	Y
11 **Frelinghuysen**	Y	Y	Y	Y	N	N	Y
12 Holt	Y	Y	Y	Y	Y	Y	Y
13 Sires	Y	Y	Y	?	Y	Y	Y
NEW MEXICO							
1 Heinrich	Y	Y	Y	Y	Y	Y	Y
2 Teague	Y	Y	Y	Y	N	Y	Y
3 Lujan	Y	Y	Y	Y	Y	Y	?
NEW YORK							
1 Bishop	Y	Y	Y	Y	Y	Y	Y
2 Israel	Y	Y	Y	Y	Y	Y	Y
3 **King**	Y	Y	Y	Y	N	N	Y
4 McCarthy	+	+	+	+	?	?	?
5 Ackerman	Y	Y	Y	Y	Y	Y	Y
6 Meeks	Y	Y	Y	Y	Y	Y	Y
7 Crowley	Y	Y	Y	Y	Y	Y	Y
8 Nadler	Y	Y	Y	Y	Y	Y	Y
9 Weiner	Y	Y	Y	Y	Y	Y	Y
10 Towns	Y	Y	Y	Y	Y	Y	Y
11 Clarke	Y	Y	Y	Y	Y	Y	Y
12 Velázquez	Y	Y	Y	Y	Y	Y	Y
13 McMahon	Y	Y	Y	Y	Y	Y	Y
14 Maloney	Y	Y	Y	Y	Y	Y	Y
15 Rangel	Y	Y	?	Y	Y	Y	Y
16 Serrano	Y	Y	Y	Y	Y	Y	Y
17 Engel	Y	Y	Y	Y	Y	Y	Y
18 Lowey	Y	Y	Y	Y	Y	Y	Y
19 Hall	Y	Y	Y	Y	Y	Y	Y
20 Murphy	Y	Y	Y	Y	N	Y	Y
21 Tonko	Y	Y	Y	Y	Y	Y	Y
22 Hinchey	Y	Y	Y	Y	Y	Y	Y
23 **McHugh**	Y	Y	Y	Y	N	N	Y
24 Arcuri	Y	Y	Y	Y	Y	Y	Y
25 Maffei	Y	Y	Y	Y	Y	Y	Y
26 **Lee**	Y	Y	Y	Y	N	N	Y
27 Higgins	Y	Y	Y	Y	Y	Y	Y
28 Slaughter	Y	Y	?	Y	Y	Y	Y
29 Massa	Y	Y	Y	Y	Y	Y	Y
NORTH CAROLINA							
1 Butterfield	Y	Y	Y	Y	P	Y	Y
2 Etheridge	Y	Y	Y	Y	Y	Y	Y
3 **Jones**	Y	Y	Y	Y	N	N	Y
4 Price	Y	Y	Y	Y	Y	Y	Y
5 **Foxx**	Y	Y	Y	Y	N	N	N
6 **Coble**	Y	Y	Y	Y	N	N	Y
7 McIntyre	Y	Y	Y	Y	Y	Y	Y
8 Kissell	Y	Y	Y	Y	Y	Y	Y
9 **Myrick**	Y	Y	Y	Y	P	N	N
10 **McHenry**	Y	Y	Y	Y	N	N	Y
11 Shuler	Y	Y	Y	Y	Y	N	Y
12 Watt	Y	Y	Y	Y	Y	Y	Y
13 Miller	Y	Y	Y	Y	Y	Y	Y
NORTH DAKOTA							
AL Pomeroy	Y	Y	Y	Y	Y	Y	Y
OHIO							
1 Driehaus	Y	Y	Y	Y	Y	Y	Y
2 **Schmidt**	Y	Y	Y	Y	N	N	Y
3 **Turner**	Y	Y	Y	Y	N	N	Y
4 **Jordan**	Y	Y	Y	Y	N	N	N
5 **Latta**	Y	Y	Y	Y	N	N	N
6 Wilson	Y	Y	Y	Y	Y	Y	Y
7 **Austria**	Y	Y	Y	Y	N	N	Y
8 **Boehner**	Y	Y	Y	Y	N	N	N
9 Kaptur	Y	Y	Y	Y	Y	Y	Y
10 Kucinich	Y	Y	Y	Y	Y	N	Y
11 Fudge	Y	Y	Y	Y	Y	Y	Y
12 **Tiberi**	Y	Y	Y	Y	N	N	Y
13 Sutton	Y	Y	Y	Y	Y	Y	Y
14 **LaTourette**	Y	Y	Y	Y	N	N	Y
15 Kilroy	Y	Y	Y	Y	Y	Y	Y
16 Boccieri	Y	Y	Y	Y	N	Y	Y
17 Ryan	Y	Y	Y	Y	Y	Y	Y
18 Space	Y	Y	Y	Y	Y	Y	Y
OKLAHOMA							
1 **Sullivan**	Y	Y	Y	Y	N	N	N
2 Boren	Y	Y	Y	Y	Y	Y	Y
3 **Lucas**	Y	Y	Y	Y	N	N	Y
4 **Cole**	Y	Y	Y	Y	N	N	Y
5 **Fallin**	Y	Y	Y	Y	N	N	Y
OREGON							
1 Wu	Y	Y	Y	Y	Y	Y	Y
2 **Walden**	Y	Y	Y	Y	P	N	Y
3 Blumenauer	Y	Y	Y	Y	Y	Y	Y
4 DeFazio	Y	Y	Y	Y	Y	Y	Y
5 Schrader	Y	Y	Y	Y	Y	Y	Y
PENNSYLVANIA							
1 Brady	Y	Y	Y	Y	Y	Y	Y
2 Fattah	Y	Y	Y	Y	Y	Y	Y
3 Dahlkemper	Y	Y	Y	Y	Y	Y	Y
4 Altmire	Y	Y	Y	Y	Y	Y	Y
5 **Thompson**	Y	Y	Y	Y	?	N	Y
6 **Gerlach**	Y	Y	Y	Y	N	N	Y
7 Sestak	?	?	?	?	Y	Y	Y
8 Murphy, P.	Y	Y	Y	Y	Y	Y	Y
9 **Shuster**	Y	Y	Y	Y	N	N	Y
10 Carney	Y	Y	Y	Y	Y	Y	Y
11 Kanjorski	Y	Y	Y	Y	Y	Y	Y
12 Murtha	Y	Y	Y	Y	Y	Y	Y
13 Schwartz	Y	Y	Y	Y	Y	Y	Y
14 Doyle	Y	Y	Y	Y	Y	Y	Y
15 **Dent**	Y	Y	Y	Y	P	N	Y
16 **Pitts**	Y	Y	Y	Y	N	N	Y
17 Holden	Y	Y	Y	Y	Y	Y	Y
18 **Murphy, T.**	Y	Y	Y	Y	Y	N	Y
19 **Platts**	Y	Y	Y	Y	N	N	Y
RHODE ISLAND							
1 Kennedy	Y	Y	Y	Y	?	?	?
2 Langevin	Y	Y	Y	Y	Y	Y	Y
SOUTH CAROLINA							
1 **Brown**	Y	Y	Y	Y	N	N	Y
2 **Wilson**	Y	Y	Y	Y	N	N	N
3 **Barrett**	Y	Y	Y	Y	N	N	N
4 **Inglis**	Y	Y	Y	Y	N	N	Y
5 Spratt	Y	Y	Y	Y	Y	Y	Y
6 Clyburn	Y	Y	Y	Y	Y	Y	Y
SOUTH DAKOTA							
AL Herseth Sandlin	Y	Y	Y	Y	N	Y	Y
TENNESSEE							
1 **Roe**	Y	Y	Y	Y	N	N	Y
2 **Duncan**	Y	Y	Y	Y	N	N	N
3 **Wamp**	Y	Y	Y	Y	N	N	Y
4 Davis	Y	Y	Y	Y	Y	Y	Y
5 Cooper	Y	+	+	+	Y	Y	Y
6 Gordon	Y	Y	Y	Y	Y	Y	Y
7 **Blackburn**	Y	Y	Y	Y	N	N	N
8 Tanner	Y	Y	Y	Y	Y	Y	Y
9 Cohen	Y	Y	Y	Y	Y	Y	Y
TEXAS							
1 **Gohmert**	?	?	?	Y	N	N	N
2 **Poe**	Y	Y	Y	Y	P	N	N
3 **Johnson, S.**	Y	Y	Y	Y	N	N	N
4 **Hall**	Y	Y	Y	Y	N	N	Y
5 **Hensarling**	Y	Y	Y	Y	N	N	N
6 **Barton**	Y	Y	Y	Y	N	N	N
7 **Culberson**	Y	Y	Y	Y	N	N	Y
8 **Brady**	Y	Y	Y	Y	N	N	N
9 Green, A.	Y	Y	Y	Y	Y	Y	Y
10 **McCaul**	Y	Y	Y	Y	N	N	Y
11 **Conaway**	Y	Y	Y	Y	P	N	N
12 **Granger**	Y	Y	Y	Y	N	N	Y
13 **Thornberry**	Y	Y	Y	Y	N	N	N
14 **Paul**	N	Y	N	?	N	N	N
15 Hinojosa	Y	Y	Y	Y	Y	Y	Y
16 Reyes	Y	Y	Y	Y	Y	Y	Y
17 Edwards	Y	Y	Y	Y	Y	Y	Y
18 Jackson Lee	Y	Y	Y	Y	Y	Y	Y
19 **Neugebauer**	Y	Y	Y	Y	N	N	N
20 Gonzalez	Y	Y	Y	Y	Y	Y	Y
21 **Smith**	Y	Y	Y	Y	N	N	Y
22 **Olson**	Y	Y	Y	Y	N	N	N
23 Rodriguez	Y	Y	Y	Y	Y	Y	Y
24 **Marchant**	Y	Y	Y	Y	N	N	Y
25 Doggett	Y	Y	Y	Y	Y	Y	Y
26 **Burgess**	Y	Y	Y	Y	N	N	N
27 Ortiz	Y	Y	Y	Y	Y	Y	Y
28 Cuellar	Y	Y	Y	Y	Y	Y	Y
29 Green, G.	Y	Y	Y	Y	Y	Y	Y
30 Johnson, E.	Y	Y	Y	Y	Y	Y	Y
31 **Carter**	Y	Y	Y	Y	N	N	N
32 **Sessions**	Y	Y	Y	Y	N	N	Y
UTAH							
1 **Bishop**	Y	Y	Y	Y	N	N	Y
2 Matheson	Y	Y	Y	Y	N	Y	Y
3 **Chaffetz**	Y	Y	Y	Y	N	N	N
VERMONT							
AL Welch	Y	Y	Y	Y	P	Y	Y
VIRGINIA							
1 **Wittman**	Y	Y	Y	Y	N	N	Y
2 Nye	Y	Y	Y	Y	Y	Y	Y
3 Scott	Y	Y	Y	Y	Y	Y	Y
4 **Forbes**	Y	Y	Y	Y	N	N	Y
5 Perriello	Y	Y	Y	Y	N	Y	Y
6 **Goodlatte**	Y	Y	Y	Y	N	N	Y
7 **Cantor**	Y	Y	Y	Y	N	N	Y
8 Moran	Y	Y	Y	Y	Y	Y	Y
9 Boucher	Y	Y	Y	Y	Y	Y	Y
10 **Wolf**	Y	Y	Y	Y	N	N	Y
11 Connolly	Y	Y	Y	Y	Y	Y	Y
WASHINGTON							
1 Inslee	Y	Y	Y	Y	Y	Y	Y
2 Larsen	Y	Y	Y	Y	Y	Y	Y
3 Baird	Y	Y	Y	Y	Y	Y	Y
4 **Hastings**	Y	Y	Y	Y	P	N	N
5 **McMorris Rodgers**	?	Y	Y	Y	N	N	Y
6 Dicks	Y	Y	Y	Y	Y	Y	Y
7 McDermott	Y	Y	Y	Y	Y	Y	Y
8 **Reichert**	Y	Y	Y	Y	N	N	Y
9 Smith	Y	Y	Y	Y	N	Y	Y
WEST VIRGINIA							
1 Mollohan	Y	Y	Y	Y	Y	Y	Y
2 **Capito**	Y	Y	Y	Y	N	N	Y
3 Rahall	Y	Y	Y	Y	Y	Y	Y
WISCONSIN							
1 **Ryan**	Y	+	+	+	N	N	Y
2 Baldwin	Y	Y	Y	Y	Y	Y	Y
3 Kind	Y	Y	Y	Y	Y	Y	Y
4 Moore	Y	Y	Y	Y	Y	Y	Y
5 **Sensenbrenner**	Y	Y	Y	Y	N	N	Y
6 **Petri**	Y	Y	Y	Y	N	N	Y
7 Obey	Y	?	Y	Y	Y	Y	Y
8 Kagen	Y	Y	Y	Y	Y	Y	Y
WYOMING							
AL **Lummis**	Y	Y	Y	Y	N	N	N
DELEGATES							
Faleomavaega (A.S.)							
Norton (D.C.)							
Bordallo (Guam)							
Sablan (N. Marianas)							
Pierluisi (P.R.)							
Christensen (V.I.)							

IN THE HOUSE | By Vote Number

608. **HR 2938. FERC Project Deadline Extension/Passage.** Costello, D-Ill., motion to suspend the rules and pass the bill that would authorize the Federal Energy Regulatory Commission (FERC) to extend the deadline by which initial construction is required on a hydroelectric power plant at the Melvin Price Locks and Dam on the Mississippi River at Alton, Ill., by as much as three consecutive two-year periods. Motion agreed to 418-0: R 170-0; D 248-0. A two-thirds majority of those present and voting (279 in this case) is required for passage under suspension of the rules. July 22, 2009.

609. **H Res 69. Diabetes Research and Awareness/Adoption.** Baca, D-Calif., motion to suspend the rules and adopt the resolution that would recognize the need to continue research related to diabetes and support the designation of a month as Latino Diabetes Awareness Month. Motion agreed to 420-0: R 172-0; D 248-0. A two-thirds majority of those present and voting (280 in this case) is required for adoption under suspension of the rules. July 22, 2009.

610. **HR 2920. Statutory Pay-As-You-Go/Republican Substitute.** Ryan, R-Wis., substitute amendment that would set discretionary spending caps in fiscal 2010-14, set total spending limits as a percentage of gross domestic product (GDP), and set deficit limits as a percentage of GDP in fiscal 2010 through fiscal 2019. Rejected 169-259: R 164-12; D 5-247. July 22, 2009.

611. **HR 2920. Statutory Pay-As-You-Go/Recommit.** Ryan, R-Wis., motion to recommit the bill to the Budget Committee with instructions that it be immediately reported back with language that would set discretionary spending caps in fiscal 2011-13, require the Congressional Budget Office to disclose the effect of legislation on the federal debt, and require CBO to score conference reports. Motion rejected 196-234: R 177-0; D 19-234. July 22, 2009.

612. **HR 2920. Statutory Pay-As-You-Go/Passage.** Passage of the bill that would establish a statutory requirement that new tax and mandatory spending legislation be budget-neutral, enforced by automatic, across-the-board spending cuts in non-exempt programs if the pay-as-you-go tally at the end of the year shows a deficit. Exempt programs would include legislation to extend middle-class tax cuts set to expire at the end of 2010, revise the estate tax, provide for an alternative minimum tax "patch" and prevent scheduled cuts in Medicare payments to physicians. Passed 265-166: R 24-153; D 241-13. A "yea" was a vote in support of the president's position. July 22, 2009.

613. **HR 3119. Lim Poon Lee Post Office/Passage.** Lynch, D-Mass., motion to suspend the rules and pass the bill that would designate a post office in San Francisco as the "Lim Poon Lee Post Office." Motion agreed to 426-0: R 177-0; D 249-0. A two-thirds majority of those present and voting (284 in this case) is required for passage under suspension of the rules. July 22, 2009.

614. **H Res 534. National Children and Families Day/Adoption.** Lynch, D-Mass., motion to suspend the rules and adopt the resolution that would support the goals of National Children and Families Day. Motion agreed to 429-0: R 177-0; D 252-0. A two-thirds majority of those present and voting (286 in this case) is required for adoption under suspension of the rules. July 22, 2009.

	608	609	610	611	612	613	614
ALABAMA							
1 **Bonner**	Y	Y	Y	Y	N	Y	Y
2 Bright	Y	Y	N	N	Y	Y	Y
3 **Rogers**	Y	Y	Y	Y	N	Y	Y
4 **Aderholt**	Y	Y	Y	Y	N	Y	Y
5 Griffith	Y	Y	N	Y	Y	Y	Y
6 **Bachus**	Y	Y	Y	Y	N	Y	Y
7 Davis	Y	Y	N	N	Y	Y	Y
ALASKA							
AL **Young**	Y	Y	Y	Y	N	Y	Y
ARIZONA							
1 Kirkpatrick	Y	Y	N	Y	Y	Y	Y
2 **Franks**	Y	Y	Y	Y	N	Y	Y
3 **Shadegg**	Y	Y	Y	Y	N	Y	Y
4 Pastor	Y	Y	N	N	Y	Y	Y
5 Mitchell	Y	Y	N	Y	Y	Y	Y
6 **Flake**	Y	Y	Y	Y	N	Y	Y
7 Grijalva	Y	?	N	N	Y	Y	Y
8 Giffords	Y	Y	N	N	Y	Y	Y
ARKANSAS							
1 Berry	Y	Y	N	Y	Y	Y	Y
2 Snyder	Y	Y	N	Y	Y	Y	Y
3 **Boozman**	Y	+	Y	Y	N	Y	Y
4 Ross	Y	Y	N	Y	Y	Y	Y
CALIFORNIA							
1 Thompson	Y	Y	N	N	Y	Y	Y
2 **Herger**	Y	Y	Y	Y	N	Y	Y
3 **Lungren**	Y	Y	Y	Y	N	Y	Y
4 **McClintock**	Y	Y	Y	Y	N	Y	Y
5 Matsui	Y	Y	N	N	Y	Y	Y
6 Woolsey	Y	Y	N	N	Y	Y	Y
7 Miller, George	Y	Y	N	N	Y	Y	Y
8 Pelosi					Y	Y	
9 Lee	Y	Y	N	N	N	Y	Y
10 Vacant							
11 McNerney	Y	Y	N	N	Y	Y	Y
12 Speier	Y	Y	N	N	Y	Y	Y
13 Stark	Y	Y	N	N	Y	Y	Y
14 Eshoo	Y	Y	N	N	Y	Y	Y
15 Honda	Y	Y	N	N	Y	Y	Y
16 Lofgren	Y	Y	N	N	Y	Y	Y
17 Farr	Y	Y	N	N	Y	Y	Y
18 Cardoza	Y	Y	N	N	Y	Y	Y
19 **Radanovich**	Y	Y	Y	Y	N	Y	Y
20 Costa	Y	Y	N	N	Y	Y	Y
21 **Nunes**	Y	Y	Y	Y	N	Y	Y
22 **McCarthy**	Y	Y	Y	Y	N	Y	Y
23 Capps	Y	Y	N	N	Y	Y	Y
24 **Gallegly**	Y	Y	Y	Y	N	Y	Y
25 **McKeon**	Y	Y	Y	Y	N	Y	Y
26 **Dreier**	Y	Y	Y	Y	N	Y	Y
27 Sherman	Y	Y	N	N	Y	Y	Y
28 Berman	Y	Y	N	N	Y	Y	Y
29 Schiff	Y	Y	N	N	Y	Y	Y
30 Waxman	Y	Y	N	N	Y	?	Y
31 Becerra	Y	Y	N	N	Y	Y	Y
32 Chu	Y	Y	N	N	Y	Y	Y
33 Watson	Y	Y	N	N	Y	Y	Y
34 Roybal-Allard	Y	Y	N	N	Y	Y	Y
35 Waters	Y	Y	N	N	Y	Y	Y
36 Harman	Y	Y	N	N	Y	Y	Y
37 Richardson	Y	Y	N	N	Y	Y	Y
38 Napolitano	Y	Y	N	N	Y	Y	Y
39 Sánchez, Linda	Y	Y	N	N	Y	Y	Y
40 **Royce**	Y	Y	Y	Y	N	Y	Y
41 **Lewis**	Y	Y	Y	Y	N	Y	Y
42 **Miller, Gary**	Y	Y	Y	Y	N	Y	Y
43 Baca	Y	Y	N	N	Y	Y	Y
44 **Calvert**	Y	Y	Y	Y	N	Y	Y
45 **Bono Mack**	Y	Y	Y	Y	N	Y	Y
46 **Rohrabacher**	Y	Y	Y	Y	N	Y	Y
47 Sanchez, Loretta	Y	Y	N	N	Y	Y	Y
48 **Campbell**	Y	Y	Y	Y	N	Y	Y
49 **Issa**	Y	Y	Y	Y	N	Y	Y
50 **Bilbray**	Y	Y	Y	Y	N	Y	Y
51 Filner	Y	Y	N	N	N	Y	Y
52 **Hunter**	Y	Y	Y	Y	N	Y	Y
53 Davis	Y	Y	N	N	Y	Y	Y

	608	609	610	611	612	613	614
COLORADO							
1 DeGette	Y	Y	N	N	Y	Y	Y
2 Polis	Y	Y	N	N	Y	Y	Y
3 Salazar	Y	Y	N	N	Y	Y	Y
4 Markey	Y	Y	N	N	Y	?	Y
5 **Lamborn**	Y	Y	Y	Y	N	Y	Y
6 **Coffman**	Y	Y	Y	Y	N	Y	Y
7 Perlmutter	Y	Y	N	N	Y	Y	Y
CONNECTICUT							
1 Larson	Y	Y	N	N	Y	Y	Y
2 Courtney	Y	Y	N	N	Y	Y	Y
3 DeLauro	Y	Y	N	N	Y	Y	Y
4 Himes	Y	Y	N	N	Y	Y	Y
5 Murphy	Y	Y	N	N	Y	Y	Y
DELAWARE							
AL **Castle**	Y	Y	Y	Y	Y	Y	Y
FLORIDA							
1 **Miller**	Y	Y	Y	Y	N	Y	Y
2 Boyd	Y	Y	N	N	Y	Y	Y
3 Brown	Y	Y	N	N	Y	Y	Y
4 **Crenshaw**	Y	Y	Y	Y	N	Y	Y
5 **Brown-Waite**	Y	Y	Y	Y	N	Y	Y
6 **Stearns**	Y	Y	Y	Y	N	Y	Y
7 **Mica**	Y	Y	Y	Y	N	Y	Y
8 Grayson	Y	Y	N	N	Y	Y	Y
9 **Bilirakis**	Y	Y	Y	Y	N	Y	Y
10 **Young**	?	?	Y	Y	Y	Y	Y
11 Castor	Y	Y	N	N	Y	Y	Y
12 **Putnam**	Y	Y	Y	Y	N	Y	Y
13 **Buchanan**	Y	Y	Y	Y	?	?	?
14 **Mack**	Y	Y	Y	Y	N	Y	Y
15 **Posey**	Y	Y	Y	Y	N	Y	Y
16 **Rooney**	Y	Y	Y	Y	N	Y	Y
17 Meek	Y	Y	N	N	Y	Y	Y
18 **Ros-Lehtinen**	Y	Y	Y	Y	N	Y	Y
19 Wexler	Y	Y	N	N	Y	Y	Y
20 Wasserman Schultz	Y	Y	N	N	Y	Y	Y
21 **Diaz-Balart, L.**	Y	Y	Y	Y	N	Y	Y
22 Klein	Y	Y	N	N	Y	Y	Y
23 Hastings	Y	Y	N	N	Y	Y	Y
24 Kosmas	Y	Y	N	Y	Y	Y	Y
25 **Diaz-Balart, M.**	Y	Y	Y	Y	N	Y	Y
GEORGIA							
1 **Kingston**	Y	Y	?	Y	N	Y	Y
2 Bishop	Y	Y	N	N	Y	Y	Y
3 **Westmoreland**	Y	Y	Y	Y	N	Y	Y
4 Johnson	Y	Y	N	N	Y	Y	Y
5 Lewis	Y	Y	N	N	Y	Y	Y
6 **Price**	Y	Y	Y	Y	N	Y	Y
7 **Linder**	Y	Y	Y	Y	N	Y	Y
8 Marshall	Y	Y	N	N	Y	Y	Y
9 **Deal**	Y	Y	Y	N	N	Y	Y
10 **Broun**	Y	Y	Y	Y	N	Y	Y
11 **Gingrey**	Y	Y	Y	Y	N	Y	Y
12 Barrow	Y	Y	N	N	Y	Y	Y
13 Scott	Y	Y	N	N	Y	Y	Y
HAWAII							
1 Abercrombie	Y	Y	N	N	Y	Y	Y
2 Hirono	Y	Y	N	N	Y	Y	Y
IDAHO							
1 **Minnick**	Y	Y	N	N	Y	Y	Y
2 **Simpson**	Y	Y	N	Y	Y	Y	Y
ILLINOIS							
1 Rush	Y	Y	N	N	Y	Y	Y
2 Jackson	Y	Y	N	N	Y	Y	Y
3 Lipinski	Y	Y	N	N	Y	Y	Y
4 Gutierrez	Y	Y	N	N	Y	Y	Y
5 Quigley	Y	Y	N	N	Y	Y	Y
6 **Roskam**	Y	Y	Y	Y	N	Y	Y
7 Davis	Y	Y	N	N	Y	Y	Y
8 Bean	Y	Y	N	N	Y	Y	Y
9 Schakowsky	Y	Y	N	N	Y	?	Y
10 **Kirk**	Y	Y	Y	Y	N	Y	Y
11 Halvorson	Y	Y	N	N	Y	Y	Y
12 Costello	Y	Y	N	N	Y	Y	Y
13 **Biggert**	Y	Y	Y	N	Y	Y	Y
14 Foster	Y	Y	N	Y	Y	Y	Y
15 Johnson	Y	Y	N	Y	Y	Y	Y

	608	609	610	611	612	613	614
16 **Manzullo**	Y	Y	Y	Y	N	Y	Y
17 Hare	Y	Y	N	N	Y	Y	Y
18 **Schock**	Y	Y	Y	Y	N	Y	Y
19 **Shimkus**	Y	Y	Y	Y	N	Y	Y
INDIANA							
1 Visclosky	Y	Y	N	N	Y	Y	Y
2 Donnelly	Y	Y	N	N	Y	Y	Y
3 **Souder**	Y	Y	Y	Y	N	Y	Y
4 **Buyer**	Y	Y	Y	Y	N	Y	Y
5 **Burton**	Y	Y	Y	Y	N	Y	Y
6 **Pence**	Y	Y	Y	Y	N	Y	Y
7 Carson	Y	Y	N	N	Y	Y	Y
8 Ellsworth	Y	Y	N	N	Y	Y	Y
9 Hill	Y	Y	N	N	Y	Y	Y
IOWA							
1 Braley	Y	Y	N	N	Y	Y	Y
2 Loebsack	Y	Y	N	N	Y	Y	Y
3 Boswell	Y	Y	N	N	Y	Y	Y
4 **Latham**	Y	Y	N	Y	Y	Y	Y
5 **King**	Y	Y	Y	Y	N	Y	Y
KANSAS							
1 **Moran**	Y	Y	Y	Y	Y	Y	Y
2 **Jenkins**	Y	Y	Y	Y	Y	Y	Y
3 Moore	Y	Y	N	N	Y	Y	Y
4 **Tiahrt**	Y	Y	Y	Y	N	Y	Y
KENTUCKY							
1 **Whitfield**	Y	Y	Y	Y	Y	Y	Y
2 **Guthrie**	Y	Y	Y	Y	N	Y	Y
3 Yarmuth	Y	Y	N	N	Y	Y	Y
4 **Davis**	Y	Y	Y	Y	N	Y	Y
5 **Rogers**	Y	Y	Y	Y	N	Y	Y
6 Chandler	Y	Y	N	N	Y	Y	Y
LOUISIANA							
1 **Scalise**	Y	Y	Y	Y	N	Y	Y
2 **Cao**	Y	Y	Y	Y	N	Y	Y
3 Melancon	?	Y	N	N	Y	Y	Y
4 **Fleming**	Y	Y	Y	Y	N	Y	Y
5 **Alexander**	Y	Y	N	Y	N	Y	Y
6 **Cassidy**	Y	Y	Y	Y	N	Y	Y
7 **Boustany**	Y	Y	Y	Y	N	Y	Y
MAINE							
1 Pingree	Y	Y	N	N	Y	Y	Y
2 Michaud	Y	Y	N	Y	Y	Y	Y
MARYLAND							
1 Kratovil	Y	Y	N	N	Y	Y	Y
2 Ruppersberger	Y	?	N	N	Y	Y	Y
3 Sarbanes	Y	Y	N	N	Y	Y	Y
4 Edwards	Y	?	N	N	Y	Y	Y
5 Hoyer	Y	Y	N	N	Y	Y	Y
6 **Bartlett**	Y	Y	Y	Y	N	Y	Y
7 Cummings	Y	Y	N	N	Y	Y	Y
8 Van Hollen	Y	Y	N	N	Y	Y	Y
MASSACHUSETTS							
1 Olver	Y	Y	N	N	Y	Y	Y
2 Neal	Y	Y	N	N	Y	Y	Y
3 McGovern	Y	Y	N	N	Y	Y	Y
4 Frank	Y	Y	N	N	Y	Y	Y
5 Tsongas	Y	Y	N	N	Y	Y	Y
6 Tierney	Y	Y	N	N	Y	Y	Y
7 Markey	Y	Y	N	N	Y	Y	Y
8 Capuano	Y	Y	N	N	Y	Y	Y
9 Lynch	Y	Y	N	N	Y	Y	Y
10 Delahunt	Y	Y	N	N	Y	Y	Y
MICHIGAN							
1 Stupak	Y	Y	N	N	N	Y	Y
2 **Hoekstra**	Y	Y	Y	Y	N	Y	Y
3 **Ehlers**	Y	Y	Y	Y	Y	Y	Y
4 **Camp**	Y	Y	Y	Y	N	Y	Y
5 Kildee	Y	Y	N	N	Y	Y	Y
6 **Upton**	Y	Y	Y	Y	Y	Y	Y
7 Schauer	Y	Y	N	N	Y	Y	Y
8 **Rogers**	Y	Y	Y	Y	N	Y	Y
9 Peters	Y	Y	N	Y	Y	Y	Y
10 **Miller**	Y	Y	Y	Y	Y	Y	Y
11 **McCotter**	?	?	Y	Y	Y	Y	Y
12 Levin	Y	Y	N	N	Y	Y	Y
13 Kilpatrick	Y	Y	N	N	N	Y	Y
14 Conyers	Y	Y	?	N	Y	Y	Y
15 Dingell	Y	Y	N	N	Y	Y	Y
MINNESOTA							
1 Walz	Y	Y	N	N	Y	Y	Y
2 **Kline**	Y	Y	Y	Y	N	Y	Y
3 **Paulsen**	Y	Y	Y	Y	N	Y	Y
4 McCollum	Y	Y	N	N	Y	Y	Y

	608	609	610	611	612	613	614
5 Ellison	Y	Y	N	N	Y	Y	Y
6 **Bachmann**	Y	Y	Y	Y	N	Y	Y
7 Peterson	Y	Y	N	N	Y	Y	Y
8 Oberstar	Y	Y	N	N	Y	Y	Y
MISSISSIPPI							
1 Childers	Y	Y	N	Y	Y	Y	Y
2 Thompson	?	?	?	?	?	?	?
3 **Harper**	Y	Y	Y	Y	N	Y	Y
4 Taylor	Y	Y	Y	Y	Y	Y	Y
MISSOURI							
1 Clay	Y	Y	Y	Y	N	Y	Y
2 **Akin**	Y	Y	Y	Y	N	Y	Y
3 Carnahan	Y	Y	N	N	Y	Y	Y
4 Skelton	Y	Y	N	N	Y	Y	Y
5 Cleaver	Y	Y	N	N	Y	?	Y
6 **Graves**	Y	Y	Y	Y	N	Y	Y
7 **Blunt**	Y	Y	Y	Y	N	Y	Y
8 **Emerson**	?	?	N	Y	Y	Y	Y
9 **Luetkemeyer**	Y	Y	Y	Y	N	Y	Y
MONTANA							
AL **Rehberg**	Y	Y	Y	Y	N	Y	Y
NEBRASKA							
1 **Fortenberry**	Y	Y	Y	Y	N	Y	Y
2 **Terry**	Y	Y	Y	Y	Y	Y	Y
3 **Smith**	Y	Y	Y	Y	N	Y	Y
NEVADA							
1 Berkley	Y	Y	N	N	Y	Y	Y
2 **Heller**	Y	Y	N	Y	N	Y	Y
3 Titus	Y	Y	N	N	Y	Y	Y
NEW HAMPSHIRE							
1 Shea-Porter	Y	Y	N	N	Y	Y	Y
2 Hodes	Y	Y	N	Y	Y	Y	Y
NEW JERSEY							
1 Andrews	Y	Y	N	N	Y	Y	Y
2 **LoBiondo**	Y	Y	Y	Y	N	Y	Y
3 Adler	Y	Y	Y	Y	Y	Y	Y
4 **Smith**	Y	Y	Y	Y	N	Y	Y
5 **Garrett**	Y	Y	Y	Y	N	Y	Y
6 Pallone	Y	Y	N	N	Y	Y	Y
7 **Lance**	Y	Y	Y	Y	N	Y	Y
8 Pascrell	Y	Y	N	N	Y	Y	Y
9 Rothman	Y	Y	N	N	Y	Y	Y
10 Payne	Y	Y	N	N	Y	Y	Y
11 **Frelinghuysen**	Y	Y	N	Y	N	Y	Y
12 Holt	Y	Y	N	N	Y	Y	Y
13 Sires	Y	Y	N	N	Y	Y	Y
NEW MEXICO							
1 Heinrich	Y	Y	N	N	Y	Y	Y
2 Teague	Y	Y	N	Y	Y	Y	Y
3 Lujan	Y	Y	N	N	Y	Y	Y
NEW YORK							
1 Bishop	Y	Y	N	N	Y	Y	Y
2 Israel	Y	Y	N	N	Y	Y	Y
3 **King**	Y	Y	Y	Y	N	Y	Y
4 McCarthy	?	?	?	?	?	?	?
5 Ackerman	?	Y	N	N	Y	Y	Y
6 Meeks	Y	Y	N	N	Y	Y	Y
7 Crowley	Y	Y	N	N	Y	Y	Y
8 Nadler	Y	Y	N	N	Y	Y	Y
9 Weiner	Y	Y	N	N	N	Y	Y
10 Towns	Y	Y	N	N	Y	Y	Y
11 Clarke	Y	Y	N	N	Y	Y	Y
12 Velázquez	Y	Y	N	N	Y	Y	Y
13 McMahon	Y	Y	Y	Y	Y	Y	Y
14 Maloney	Y	Y	N	N	Y	Y	Y
15 Rangel	Y	Y	N	N	Y	Y	Y
16 Serrano	Y	Y	N	N	Y	Y	Y
17 Engel	Y	Y	N	N	Y	Y	Y
18 Lowey	Y	Y	N	N	Y	Y	Y
19 Hall	Y	Y	N	N	Y	Y	Y
20 Murphy	Y	Y	N	Y	Y	Y	Y
21 Tonko	Y	Y	N	N	Y	Y	Y
22 Hinchey	Y	Y	N	N	N	Y	Y
23 **McHugh**	Y	Y	?	?	?	Y	Y
24 Arcuri	Y	Y	N	N	Y	Y	Y
25 Maffei	Y	Y	N	Y	Y	Y	Y
26 **Lee**	Y	Y	Y	Y	N	Y	Y
27 Higgins	Y	Y	N	N	Y	Y	Y
28 Slaughter	Y	Y	N	N	Y	Y	Y
29 Massa	Y	Y	N	N	Y	Y	Y
NORTH CAROLINA							
1 Butterfield	Y	Y	N	N	Y	Y	Y
2 Etheridge	Y	Y	N	N	Y	Y	Y
3 **Jones**	Y	Y	Y	Y	N	Y	Y
4 Price	Y	Y	N	N	Y	Y	Y

	608	609	610	611	612	613	614
5 **Foxx**	Y	Y	Y	Y	N	Y	Y
6 **Coble**	Y	Y	Y	Y	N	Y	Y
7 McIntyre	Y	Y	N	N	Y	Y	Y
8 Kissell	Y	Y	N	N	Y	Y	Y
9 **Myrick**	Y	Y	Y	Y	N	Y	Y
10 **McHenry**	Y	Y	Y	Y	N	Y	Y
11 Shuler	Y	Y	N	N	Y	Y	Y
12 Watt	Y	Y	N	N	Y	Y	Y
13 Miller	Y	Y	N	N	Y	Y	Y
NORTH DAKOTA							
AL Pomeroy	Y	Y	N	N	Y	Y	Y
OHIO							
1 Driehaus	Y	Y	N	N	Y	Y	Y
2 **Schmidt**	Y	Y	Y	Y	N	Y	Y
3 **Turner**	Y	Y	Y	Y	Y	Y	Y
4 **Jordan**	Y	Y	Y	Y	N	Y	Y
5 **Latta**	Y	Y	Y	Y	N	Y	Y
6 Wilson	Y	Y	N	N	Y	Y	Y
7 **Austria**	Y	Y	Y	Y	N	Y	Y
8 **Boehner**	Y	Y	Y	Y	N	Y	Y
9 Kaptur	Y	Y	N	N	Y	Y	?
10 Kucinich	Y	Y	N	N	N	Y	Y
11 Fudge	Y	Y	N	N	Y	Y	Y
12 **Tiberi**	Y	Y	Y	Y	Y	Y	Y
13 Sutton	Y	Y	N	N	Y	Y	Y
14 **LaTourette**	Y	Y	N	Y	Y	Y	Y
15 Kilroy	?	Y	N	N	Y	Y	Y
16 Boccieri	Y	Y	N	N	Y	Y	Y
17 Ryan	Y	Y	N	N	Y	Y	Y
18 Space	Y	Y	N	N	Y	Y	Y
OKLAHOMA							
1 **Sullivan**	?	Y	Y	Y	N	Y	Y
2 Boren	Y	Y	N	N	Y	Y	Y
3 **Lucas**	Y	Y	Y	Y	N	Y	Y
4 **Cole**	Y	Y	N	Y	N	Y	Y
5 **Fallin**	Y	Y	Y	Y	N	Y	Y
OREGON							
1 Wu	Y	Y	N	N	Y	Y	Y
2 **Walden**	Y	Y	Y	Y	N	Y	Y
3 Blumenauer	Y	Y	N	N	Y	Y	Y
4 DeFazio	Y	Y	N	N	Y	Y	Y
5 Schrader	?	Y	N	N	Y	Y	Y
PENNSYLVANIA							
1 Brady	Y	Y	N	N	Y	Y	Y
2 Fattah	Y	Y	N	N	Y	Y	Y
3 Dahlkemper	Y	Y	N	N	Y	Y	Y
4 Altmire	Y	Y	N	N	Y	Y	Y
5 **Thompson**	Y	Y	Y	Y	N	Y	Y
6 **Gerlach**	Y	Y	Y	Y	N	Y	Y
7 Sestak	Y	Y	N	N	Y	Y	Y
8 Murphy, P.	Y	Y	N	N	Y	Y	Y
9 **Shuster**	Y	Y	Y	Y	N	Y	Y
10 Carney	Y	Y	N	N	Y	Y	Y
11 Kanjorski	Y	Y	N	N	Y	Y	Y
12 Murtha	Y	Y	N	N	Y	Y	Y
13 Schwartz	Y	Y	N	N	Y	Y	Y
14 Doyle	Y	Y	N	N	Y	Y	Y
15 **Dent**	Y	Y	Y	Y	N	Y	Y
16 **Pitts**	Y	Y	Y	Y	N	Y	Y
17 Holden	Y	Y	N	N	Y	Y	Y
18 **Murphy, T.**	Y	Y	Y	Y	Y	Y	Y
19 **Platts**	Y	Y	Y	Y	N	Y	Y
RHODE ISLAND							
1 Kennedy	?	?	N	N	Y	Y	Y
2 Langevin	Y	Y	N	N	Y	Y	Y
SOUTH CAROLINA							
1 **Brown**	Y	Y	Y	Y	N	Y	Y
2 **Wilson**	Y	Y	Y	Y	N	Y	Y
3 **Barrett**	?	Y	Y	Y	N	Y	Y
4 **Inglis**	Y	Y	Y	Y	N	Y	Y
5 Spratt	Y	Y	N	N	Y	Y	Y
6 Clyburn	Y	Y	N	N	Y	Y	Y
SOUTH DAKOTA							
AL Herseth Sandlin	Y	Y	N	N	Y	Y	Y
TENNESSEE							
1 **Roe**	Y	Y	Y	Y	N	Y	Y
2 **Duncan**	Y	Y	Y	Y	N	Y	Y
3 **Wamp**	Y	Y	Y	Y	N	Y	Y
4 Davis	Y	Y	N	N	Y	Y	Y
5 Cooper	Y	Y	N	N	Y	Y	Y
6 Gordon	Y	Y	N	N	Y	?	Y
7 **Blackburn**	Y	Y	Y	Y	N	Y	Y
8 Tanner	Y	Y	N	N	Y	Y	Y
9 Cohen	Y	Y	N	N	Y	Y	Y

	608	609	610	611	612	613	614
TEXAS							
1 **Gohmert**	Y	Y	Y	Y	Y	Y	Y
2 **Poe**	Y	Y	Y	Y	N	Y	Y
3 **Johnson, S.**	Y	Y	Y	Y	N	Y	Y
4 **Hall**	Y	Y	Y	Y	Y	Y	Y
5 **Hensarling**	Y	Y	Y	Y	N	Y	Y
6 **Barton**	Y	Y	Y	Y	N	Y	Y
7 **Culberson**	Y	Y	Y	Y	N	Y	Y
8 **Brady**	?	Y	Y	Y	N	Y	Y
9 Green, A.	Y	Y	N	N	Y	Y	Y
10 **McCaul**	Y	Y	Y	Y	N	Y	Y
11 **Conaway**	Y	Y	Y	Y	N	Y	Y
12 **Granger**	Y	Y	N	Y	N	Y	Y
13 **Thornberry**	Y	Y	Y	Y	N	Y	Y
14 **Paul**	Y	?	Y	Y	N	Y	Y
15 Hinojosa	Y	Y	N	N	Y	Y	Y
16 Reyes	Y	Y	N	N	Y	Y	Y
17 Edwards	Y	Y	N	N	Y	Y	Y
18 Jackson Lee	Y	Y	N	N	Y	Y	Y
19 **Neugebauer**	Y	Y	Y	Y	N	Y	Y
20 Gonzalez	Y	Y	N	N	Y	Y	Y
21 **Smith**	Y	Y	Y	Y	N	Y	Y
22 **Olson**	Y	Y	Y	Y	N	Y	Y
23 Rodriguez	Y	Y	N	N	Y	Y	Y
24 **Marchant**	?	?	Y	Y	N	Y	Y
25 Doggett	Y	Y	N	N	Y	Y	Y
26 **Burgess**	Y	Y	Y	Y	N	Y	Y
27 Ortiz	Y	Y	N	N	Y	Y	Y
28 Cuellar	Y	Y	N	N	Y	Y	Y
29 Green, G.	Y	Y	N	N	Y	Y	Y
30 Johnson, E.	Y	Y	N	N	Y	Y	Y
31 **Carter**	Y	Y	N	Y	N	Y	Y
32 **Sessions**	Y	Y	Y	Y	N	Y	Y
UTAH							
1 **Bishop**	?	Y	Y	Y	N	Y	Y
2 Matheson	Y	Y	N	Y	Y	Y	Y
3 **Chaffetz**	Y	Y	Y	Y	N	Y	Y
VERMONT							
AL Welch	Y	Y	N	N	Y	Y	Y
VIRGINIA							
1 **Wittman**	Y	Y	Y	Y	N	Y	Y
2 Nye	Y	Y	N	Y	Y	Y	Y
3 Scott	Y	Y	N	N	Y	Y	Y
4 **Forbes**	Y	Y	Y	Y	N	Y	Y
5 Perriello	Y	Y	Y	Y	Y	Y	Y
6 **Goodlatte**	Y	Y	Y	Y	N	Y	Y
7 **Cantor**	Y	Y	Y	Y	N	Y	Y
8 Moran	Y	Y	N	N	Y	Y	Y
9 Boucher	Y	Y	N	N	Y	Y	Y
10 **Wolf**	Y	Y	Y	Y	Y	Y	Y
11 Connolly	Y	Y	N	N	Y	Y	Y
WASHINGTON							
1 Inslee	Y	Y	N	N	Y	Y	Y
2 Larsen	Y	Y	N	N	Y	Y	Y
3 Baird	Y	Y	N	N	Y	Y	Y
4 **Hastings**	Y	Y	Y	Y	N	Y	Y
5 **McMorris Rodgers**	Y	Y	Y	Y	N	Y	Y
6 Dicks	Y	Y	N	N	Y	Y	Y
7 McDermott	Y	Y	N	N	N	Y	Y
8 **Reichert**	Y	Y	Y	Y	N	Y	Y
9 Smith	Y	Y	N	N	Y	Y	Y
WEST VIRGINIA							
1 Mollohan	Y	?	N	N	Y	Y	Y
2 **Capito**	Y	Y	Y	Y	N	Y	Y
3 Rahall	Y	Y	N	N	Y	Y	Y
WISCONSIN							
1 **Ryan**	Y	Y	Y	Y	N	Y	Y
2 Baldwin	Y	Y	N	N	Y	Y	Y
3 Kind	Y	Y	N	N	Y	Y	Y
4 Moore	Y	Y	N	N	Y	Y	Y
5 **Sensenbrenner**	Y	Y	Y	Y	N	Y	Y
6 **Petri**	Y	Y	Y	Y	Y	Y	Y
7 Obey	Y	Y	N	N	Y	Y	Y
8 Kagen	Y	Y	N	N	Y	Y	Y
WYOMING							
AL **Lummis**	Y	Y	Y	Y	N	Y	Y
DELEGATES							
Faleomavaega (A.S.)							
Norton (D.C.)							
Bordallo (Guam)							
Sablan (N. Marianas)							
Pierluisi (P.R.)							
Christensen (V.I.)							

IN THE HOUSE | By Vote Number

615. HR 2972. Conrad DeRouen Post Office/Passage. Lynch, D-Mass., motion to suspend the rules and pass the bill that would designate a post office in Erath, La., as the "Conrad DeRouen Jr. Post Office." Motion agreed to 424-0: R 174-0; D 250-0. A two-thirds majority of those present and voting (283 in this case) is required for passage under suspension of the rules. July 22, 2009.

616. Discharge of Water Project Bill/Motion to Table. Jackson, D-Ill., motion to table (kill) the Nunes, R-Calif., appeal of the ruling of the chair that the draft resolution does not constitute a point of privilege under Rule IX of the House. The draft resolution would require the Natural Resources Committee to discharge a bill (HR 3105) for immediate consideration by the House. The bill would prevent the Bureau of Reclamation or any California state agency from restricting operations of the Central Valley Project, a water project in California, regarding any biologic opinion issued under the Endangered Species Act, if it would result in water delivery below the historic maximum. Motion agreed to 249-179: R 1-176; D 248-3. July 23, 2009.

617. HR 3288. Fiscal 2010 Transportation-HUD Appropriations/Rule. Adoption of the rule (H Res 669) to provide for House floor consideration of the bill that would appropriate $123.1 billion in fiscal 2010 for the departments of Transportation and Housing and Urban Development and related agencies. Adopted 235-183: R 0-170; D 235-13. July 23, 2009.

618. H Res 566. Los Angeles Lakers Tribute/Adoption. Lynch, D-Mass., motion to suspend the rules and adopt the resolution that would congratulate the Los Angeles Lakers for winning the 2008-09 NBA championship. Motion agreed to 413-8: R 168-5; D 245-3. A two-thirds majority of those present and voting (281 in this case) is required for adoption under suspension of the rules. July 23, 2009.

619. H Res 350. Harry Kalas Tribute/Adoption. Lynch, D-Mass., motion to suspend the rules and adopt the resolution that would honor the life and accomplishments of sports broadcaster Harry Kalas, who died April 13, 2009. Motion agreed to 426-0: R 175-0; D 251-0. A two-thirds majority of those present and voting (284 in this case) is required for adoption under suspension of the rules. July 23, 2009.

620. HR 3288. Fiscal 2010 Transportation-HUD Appropriations/Hope VI Program. Hensarling, R-Texas, amendment that would strike funding in the bill for the Hope VI housing program. Rejected in Committee of the Whole 152-276: R 144-30; D 8-246. A "nay" was a vote in support of the president's position. July 23, 2009.

621. HR 3288. Fiscal 2010 Transportation-HUD Appropriations/Capital Assistance for Rail. Latham, R-Iowa, amendment that would reduce funding for capital assistance for high-speed rail corridors and intercity passenger rail service by $3 billion and eliminate a provision that would allow the Transportation Department use $2 billion of the amount for a national infrastructure bank, if such a bank is authorized by Sept. 30, 2010. Rejected in Committee of the Whole 136-284: R 132-40; D 4-244. A "nay" was a vote in support of the president's position. July 23, 2009.

	615	616	617	618	619	620	621
ALABAMA							
1 **Bonner**	Y	N	N	Y	Y	N	Y
2 Bright	Y	Y	N	Y	Y	N	Y
3 **Rogers**	Y	N	N	Y	Y	N	N
4 **Aderholt**	Y	N	N	Y	Y	N	N
5 Griffith	Y	N	Y	Y	Y	N	N
6 **Bachus**	Y	N	N	Y	Y	Y	Y
7 Davis	Y	Y	Y	Y	Y	N	N
ALASKA							
AL **Young**	Y	N	N	Y	Y	Y	Y
ARIZONA							
1 Kirkpatrick	Y	Y	Y	Y	Y	N	Y
2 **Franks**	Y	N	N	Y	Y	Y	Y
3 **Shadegg**	Y	N	N	Y	Y	Y	Y
4 Pastor	Y	Y	Y	Y	Y	N	N
5 Mitchell	Y	Y	Y	Y	Y	N	N
6 **Flake**	Y	N	N	Y	Y	Y	Y
7 Grijalva	Y	Y	Y	Y	Y	N	N
8 Giffords	Y	Y	Y	Y	Y	N	N
ARKANSAS							
1 Berry	Y	Y	Y	Y	Y	N	N
2 Snyder	Y	Y	Y	Y	Y	N	N
3 **Boozman**	Y	N	N	Y	Y	Y	Y
4 Ross	Y	Y	Y	Y	Y	N	N
CALIFORNIA							
1 Thompson	Y	Y	Y	Y	Y	N	N
2 **Herger**	Y	N	N	Y	Y	Y	Y
3 **Lungren**	Y	N	N	Y	Y	Y	Y
4 **McClintock**	Y	N	N	Y	Y	Y	Y
5 Matsui	Y	Y	Y	Y	Y	N	N
6 Woolsey	Y	Y	Y	Y	Y	N	N
7 Miller, George	Y	Y	Y	Y	Y	N	N
8 Pelosi							
9 Lee	Y	Y	Y	Y	Y	N	N
10 Vacant							
11 McNerney	Y	Y	Y	Y	Y	N	N
12 Speier	Y	Y	?	Y	Y	N	N
13 Stark	Y	?	?	Y	Y	N	N
14 Eshoo	Y	Y	Y	Y	Y	N	N
15 Honda	?	Y	Y	Y	Y	N	N
16 Lofgren	Y	Y	Y	Y	Y	N	N
17 Farr	Y	Y	Y	Y	Y	N	N
18 Cardoza	Y	Y	Y	Y	Y	N	N
19 **Radanovich**	Y	N	N	Y	Y	Y	Y
20 Costa	Y	Y	Y	Y	Y	N	N
21 **Nunes**	Y	N	N	Y	Y	Y	Y
22 **McCarthy**	Y	N	N	Y	Y	Y	Y
23 Capps	Y	Y	Y	Y	Y	N	N
24 **Gallegly**	Y	N	N	Y	Y	Y	Y
25 **McKeon**	Y	N	N	Y	Y	Y	Y
26 **Dreier**	Y	N	N	Y	Y	Y	Y
27 Sherman	Y	Y	Y	Y	Y	N	N
28 Berman	Y	Y	Y	Y	Y	N	N
29 Schiff	Y	Y	Y	Y	Y	N	N
30 Waxman	Y	Y	Y	Y	Y	N	N
31 Becerra	Y	Y	Y	Y	Y	N	N
32 Chu	Y	Y	Y	Y	Y	N	N
33 Watson	Y	Y	Y	Y	Y	N	N
34 Roybal-Allard	Y	Y	Y	Y	Y	N	N
35 Waters	Y	Y	Y	Y	Y	N	N
36 Harman	Y	Y	Y	Y	Y	N	N
37 Richardson	Y	Y	Y	Y	Y	N	N
38 Napolitano	Y	Y	Y	Y	Y	N	N
39 Sánchez, Linda	Y	Y	Y	Y	Y	N	N
40 **Royce**	Y	N	N	Y	Y	Y	Y
41 **Lewis**	Y	N	N	Y	Y	Y	Y
42 **Miller, Gary**	Y	N	N	Y	Y	Y	Y
43 Baca	Y	Y	Y	Y	Y	N	N
44 **Calvert**	Y	N	N	Y	Y	Y	Y
45 **Bono Mack**	Y	N	N	Y	Y	Y	Y
46 **Rohrabacher**	Y	N	N	Y	Y	Y	Y
47 Sanchez, Loretta	Y	Y	Y	Y	Y	N	N
48 **Campbell**	Y	N	N	Y	Y	Y	Y
49 **Issa**	Y	N	N	Y	Y	Y	Y
50 **Bilbray**	Y	N	N	Y	Y	N	N
51 Filner	Y	Y	Y	Y	Y	N	N
52 **Hunter**	Y	N	N	Y	Y	Y	Y
53 Davis	Y	Y	Y	Y	Y	N	N

	615	616	617	618	619	620	621
COLORADO							
1 DeGette	Y	Y	Y	Y	Y	N	N
2 Polis	Y	Y	Y	Y	Y	N	N
3 Salazar	Y	Y	Y	Y	Y	N	N
4 Markey	Y	Y	Y	Y	Y	N	N
5 **Lamborn**	Y	N	N	Y	Y	Y	Y
6 **Coffman**	Y	N	N	Y	Y	Y	Y
7 Perlmutter	Y	Y	Y	N	Y	N	N
CONNECTICUT							
1 Larson	Y	Y	Y	Y	Y	N	N
2 Courtney	Y	Y	Y	P	Y	N	N
3 DeLauro	Y	Y	Y	Y	Y	N	N
4 Himes	Y	Y	Y	Y	Y	N	N
5 Murphy	Y	Y	Y	Y	Y	N	N
DELAWARE							
AL Castle	Y	N	N	Y	Y	N	N
FLORIDA							
1 **Miller**	Y	N	N	Y	Y	Y	Y
2 Boyd	Y	Y	Y	Y	Y	N	N
3 Brown	Y	Y	Y	Y	Y	N	N
4 **Crenshaw**	Y	N	N	Y	Y	N	N
5 **Brown-Waite**	Y	N	N	Y	Y	Y	Y
6 **Stearns**	Y	N	N	Y	Y	Y	Y
7 **Mica**	Y	N	N	Y	?	N	N
8 Grayson	Y	Y	Y	N	Y	N	N
9 **Bilirakis**	Y	N	N	Y	Y	Y	Y
10 **Young**	Y	N	N	Y	Y	Y	Y
11 Castor	Y	Y	Y	Y	Y	N	N
12 **Putnam**	Y	N	N	Y	Y	N	N
13 **Buchanan**	?	N	N	Y	Y	Y	Y
14 **Mack**	Y	N	N	Y	Y	Y	Y
15 **Posey**	Y	N	N	Y	Y	Y	Y
16 **Rooney**	Y	N	N	Y	Y	Y	Y
17 Meek	Y	Y	Y	Y	Y	N	N
18 **Ros-Lehtinen**	Y	N	N	Y	Y	N	N
19 Wexler	Y	Y	Y	Y	Y	N	N
20 Wasserman Schultz	Y	Y	Y	Y	Y	N	N
21 **Diaz-Balart, L.**	Y	N	N	Y	Y	N	N
22 Klein	Y	Y	Y	Y	Y	N	N
23 Hastings	Y	?	Y	Y	Y	N	N
24 Kosmas	Y	Y	Y	Y	Y	N	N
25 **Diaz-Balart, M.**	Y	N	N	Y	Y	N	N
GEORGIA							
1 **Kingston**	Y	N	N	Y	Y	Y	Y
2 Bishop	Y	Y	Y	Y	Y	N	N
3 **Westmoreland**	Y	N	N	Y	Y	Y	Y
4 Johnson	Y	Y	Y	Y	Y	N	N
5 Lewis	Y	Y	?	Y	Y	N	N
6 **Price**	Y	N	N	Y	Y	Y	Y
7 **Linder**	Y	N	N	Y	Y	Y	Y
8 Marshall	Y	Y	Y	Y	Y	N	N
9 **Deal**	Y	N	N	Y	Y	Y	Y
10 **Broun**	Y	N	N	Y	Y	Y	Y
11 **Gingrey**	Y	N	?	Y	Y	Y	Y
12 Barrow	Y	Y	Y	Y	Y	N	N
13 Scott	Y	Y	Y	Y	Y	N	N
HAWAII							
1 Abercrombie	Y	Y	Y	Y	Y	N	N
2 Hirono	Y	Y	Y	Y	Y	N	N
IDAHO							
1 Minnick	Y	N	N	Y	Y	N	N
2 **Simpson**	Y	N	N	Y	Y	Y	Y
ILLINOIS							
1 Rush	Y	Y	Y	Y	Y	N	N
2 Jackson	Y	Y	Y	Y	Y	N	N
3 Lipinski	Y	Y	Y	Y	Y	N	N
4 Gutierrez	Y	Y	Y	Y	Y	N	N
5 Quigley	Y	Y	Y	Y	Y	N	N
6 **Roskam**	Y	N	N	Y	Y	Y	Y
7 Davis	Y	Y	Y	Y	Y	N	?
8 Bean	Y	Y	Y	Y	?	N	N
9 Schakowsky	Y	Y	Y	Y	Y	N	N
10 **Kirk**	Y	N	N	Y	Y	Y	Y
11 Halvorson	Y	Y	Y	Y	Y	N	N
12 Costello	Y	Y	Y	Y	?	N	N
13 **Biggert**	Y	N	N	Y	Y	N	N
14 Foster	Y	Y	Y	Y	Y	N	N
15 **Johnson**	Y	N	N	Y	Y	Y	?

KEY   **Republicans**   Democrats

Y Voted for (yea)	**X** Paired against	**C** Voted "present" to avoid possible conflict of interest
# Paired for	**–** Announced against	
+ Announced for	**P** Voted "present"	**?** Did not vote or otherwise make a position known
N Voted against (nay)		

	615	616	617	618	619	620	621
16 **Manzullo**	Y	N	N	Y	Y	Y	N
17 Hare	Y	Y	Y	Y	Y	N	N
18 **Schock**	Y	N	N	Y	Y	Y	N
19 **Shimkus**	Y	N	N	Y	Y	Y	N
INDIANA							
1 Visclosky	Y	Y	Y	Y	Y	N	N
2 Donnelly	Y	Y	Y	P	Y	N	N
3 **Souder**	Y	N	N	Y	Y	Y	N
4 **Buyer**	Y	N	N	Y	Y	Y	Y
5 **Burton**	Y	N	N	Y	Y	Y	Y
6 **Pence**	Y	N	N	Y	?	Y	Y
7 Carson	Y	Y	Y	Y	Y	N	N
8 Ellsworth	Y	Y	N	Y	Y	N	N
9 Hill	Y	Y	N	Y	Y	N	N
IOWA							
1 Braley	Y	Y	Y	Y	Y	N	N
2 Loebsack	Y	Y	Y	Y	Y	N	N
3 Boswell	Y	Y	Y	Y	Y	N	N
4 **Latham**	Y	N	N	Y	Y	Y	Y
5 **King**	Y	N	N	Y	Y	Y	Y
KANSAS							
1 **Moran**	Y	N	N	Y	Y	Y	Y
2 **Jenkins**	Y	N	N	Y	Y	Y	Y
3 Moore	Y	Y	N	Y	Y	N	N
4 **Tiahrt**	Y	N	N	Y	Y	Y	Y
KENTUCKY							
1 **Whitfield**	Y	N	N	Y	Y	Y	Y
2 **Guthrie**	Y	N	N	Y	Y	Y	Y
3 Yarmuth	Y	Y	Y	Y	Y	N	N
4 **Davis**	Y	N	N	Y	Y	N	Y
5 **Rogers**	Y	N	N	Y	Y	Y	Y
6 Chandler	Y	Y	Y	Y	Y	N	N
LOUISIANA							
1 **Scalise**	Y	N	N	Y	Y	Y	Y
2 **Cao**	Y	N	N	Y	Y	N	N
3 Melancon	Y	Y	N	Y	Y	N	N
4 **Fleming**	Y	N	?	Y	Y	Y	Y
5 **Alexander**	Y	N	N	Y	Y	Y	Y
6 **Cassidy**	?	N	N	Y	Y	Y	Y
7 **Boustany**	Y	N	N	Y	Y	?	Y
MAINE							
1 Pingree	Y	Y	Y	Y	Y	N	N
2 Michaud	Y	Y	Y	Y	Y	N	N
MARYLAND							
1 Kratovil	Y	N	N	Y	Y	Y	N
2 Ruppersberger	Y	Y	Y	Y	Y	N	N
3 Sarbanes	Y	Y	Y	Y	Y	N	N
4 Edwards	Y	Y	Y	Y	Y	N	N
5 Hoyer	Y	Y	Y	Y	Y	N	N
6 **Bartlett**	Y	N	N	P	Y	Y	Y
7 Cummings	Y	Y	Y	Y	Y	N	N
8 Van Hollen	Y	Y	Y	Y	Y	N	N
MASSACHUSETTS							
1 Olver	Y	Y	?	Y	Y	N	N
2 Neal	Y	Y	Y	Y	Y	N	N
3 McGovern	Y	Y	Y	Y	Y	N	N
4 Frank	Y	Y	Y	Y	Y	N	N
5 Tsongas	?	Y	Y	Y	Y	N	N
6 Tierney	Y	Y	Y	Y	Y	N	N
7 Markey	Y	Y	Y	Y	Y	N	N
8 Capuano	Y	Y	Y	Y	Y	N	?
9 Lynch	Y	Y	Y	Y	Y	N	N
10 Delahunt	Y	Y	Y	Y	Y	N	N
MICHIGAN							
1 Stupak	Y	Y	Y	Y	Y	N	N
2 **Hoekstra**	Y	N	N	Y	Y	Y	Y
3 **Ehlers**	Y	N	N	Y	Y	Y	N
4 **Camp**	Y	N	N	Y	Y	Y	Y
5 Kildee	Y	Y	Y	Y	Y	N	N
6 **Upton**	Y	N	N	Y	Y	N	N
7 Schauer	Y	Y	?	Y	Y	N	N
8 **Rogers**	Y	N	N	Y	Y	Y	Y
9 Peters	Y	Y	Y	Y	Y	N	N
10 **Miller**	Y	N	N	Y	Y	N	N
11 **McCotter**	Y	N	N	Y	Y	Y	Y
12 Levin	Y	Y	Y	Y	Y	N	N
13 Kilpatrick	Y	Y	Y	Y	Y	N	N
14 Conyers	Y	Y	Y	Y	Y	N	N
15 Dingell	Y	Y	Y	Y	Y	N	N
MINNESOTA							
1 Walz	Y	Y	Y	Y	Y	N	N
2 **Kline**	Y	N	?	Y	Y	Y	Y
3 **Paulsen**	Y	N	N	Y	Y	Y	Y
4 McCollum	Y	Y	Y	Y	Y	N	N
5 Ellison	Y	Y	Y	Y	Y	N	N
6 **Bachmann**	Y	N	N	Y	Y	Y	Y
7 Peterson	Y	Y	?	Y	Y	N	N
8 Oberstar	Y	Y	Y	Y	Y	N	N
MISSISSIPPI							
1 Childers	Y	Y	Y	Y	Y	N	N
2 Thompson	?	Y	Y	Y	Y	N	N
3 **Harper**	Y	N	N	Y	Y	Y	Y
4 Taylor	Y	Y	Y	Y	Y	N	N
MISSOURI							
1 Clay	Y	Y	Y	Y	Y	N	N
2 **Akin**	Y	N	N	Y	Y	Y	Y
3 Carnahan	Y	Y	Y	?	Y	N	N
4 Skelton	Y	Y	Y	Y	Y	N	N
5 Cleaver	Y	Y	Y	Y	Y	N	?
6 **Graves**	Y	N	N	Y	Y	Y	N
7 **Blunt**	Y	N	?	Y	Y	Y	Y
8 **Emerson**	Y	N	N	Y	Y	Y	Y
9 **Luetkemeyer**	Y	N	N	Y	Y	Y	Y
MONTANA							
AL **Rehberg**	Y	N	N	Y	Y	Y	Y
NEBRASKA							
1 **Fortenberry**	Y	N	N	Y	Y	N	Y
2 **Terry**	Y	N	N	Y	Y	Y	?
3 **Smith**	Y	N	N	Y	Y	Y	Y
NEVADA							
1 Berkley	Y	Y	Y	Y	Y	N	N
2 **Heller**	Y	N	N	Y	Y	Y	Y
3 Titus	Y	Y	Y	Y	Y	N	N
NEW HAMPSHIRE							
1 Shea-Porter	Y	Y	Y	P	Y	N	?
2 Hodes	Y	Y	Y	P	Y	N	N
NEW JERSEY							
1 Andrews	Y	Y	Y	Y	Y	N	N
2 **LoBiondo**	Y	N	N	Y	Y	N	N
3 Adler	Y	Y	Y	Y	Y	N	N
4 **Smith**	Y	N	N	Y	Y	N	N
5 **Garrett**	Y	N	N	Y	Y	Y	Y
6 Pallone	Y	Y	Y	Y	Y	N	N
7 **Lance**	Y	N	N	Y	Y	Y	Y
8 Pascrell	Y	Y	Y	Y	Y	N	N
9 Rothman	Y	Y	Y	Y	Y	N	N
10 Payne	Y	Y	Y	Y	Y	N	N
11 **Frelinghuysen**	Y	N	N	Y	Y	Y	Y
12 Holt	Y	Y	Y	Y	Y	N	N
13 Sires	Y	Y	Y	Y	Y	N	N
NEW MEXICO							
1 Heinrich	Y	Y	Y	Y	Y	N	N
2 Teague	Y	Y	Y	Y	Y	Y	N
3 Lujan	Y	Y	Y	Y	Y	N	N
NEW YORK							
1 Bishop	Y	Y	Y	Y	Y	N	N
2 Israel	Y	Y	Y	Y	Y	N	?
3 **King**	Y	N	N	Y	Y	Y	N
4 McCarthy	?	?	?	?	?	?	?
5 Ackerman	Y	Y	Y	Y	Y	N	N
6 Meeks	Y	Y	Y	Y	Y	N	N
7 Crowley	Y	Y	Y	Y	Y	N	N
8 Nadler	Y	Y	Y	Y	Y	N	N
9 Weiner	Y	Y	Y	Y	Y	N	N
10 Towns	Y	Y	Y	Y	Y	N	N
11 Clarke	Y	Y	Y	Y	Y	N	N
12 Velázquez	Y	Y	Y	Y	Y	N	N
13 McMahon	Y	Y	Y	Y	Y	N	N
14 Maloney	Y	Y	Y	Y	Y	N	N
15 Rangel	Y	?	Y	Y	Y	N	N
16 Serrano	Y	Y	Y	Y	Y	N	N
17 Engel	Y	Y	Y	Y	Y	N	N
18 Lowey	Y	Y	Y	Y	Y	N	N
19 Hall	Y	Y	Y	Y	Y	N	?
20 Murphy	Y	Y	N	Y	Y	N	N
21 Tonko	Y	Y	Y	Y	Y	N	N
22 Hinchey	Y	Y	Y	Y	Y	N	N
23 **McHugh**	Y	N	N	Y	Y	Y	?
24 Arcuri	?	Y	Y	Y	Y	N	N
25 Maffei	Y	Y	Y	Y	Y	N	N
26 **Lee**	Y	N	N	Y	Y	Y	N
27 Higgins	Y	Y	Y	Y	Y	N	?
28 Slaughter	Y	Y	Y	Y	Y	?	N
29 Massa	Y	Y	Y	Y	Y	N	N
NORTH CAROLINA							
1 Butterfield	Y	Y	Y	Y	Y	N	N
2 Etheridge	Y	Y	Y	Y	Y	N	N
3 **Jones**	Y	N	N	Y	Y	N	Y
4 Price	Y	Y	Y	Y	Y	N	N
5 **Foxx**	Y	N	N	Y	Y	Y	Y
6 **Coble**	Y	N	N	Y	Y	Y	N
7 McIntyre	Y	Y	Y	Y	Y	N	N
8 Kissell	Y	Y	Y	Y	Y	N	N
9 **Myrick**	Y	N	N	Y	Y	N	N
10 **McHenry**	Y	N	N	Y	Y	Y	Y
11 Shuler	Y	Y	N	Y	Y	N	N
12 Watt	Y	Y	Y	Y	Y	N	N
13 Miller	Y	Y	Y	Y	Y	N	N
NORTH DAKOTA							
AL Pomeroy	Y	Y	Y	Y	Y	N	N
OHIO							
1 Driehaus	Y	Y	N	Y	Y	N	N
2 **Schmidt**	Y	N	N	Y	Y	Y	Y
3 **Turner**	Y	N	N	Y	Y	N	N
4 **Jordan**	Y	N	N	Y	Y	Y	Y
5 **Latta**	Y	N	N	Y	Y	Y	Y
6 Wilson	Y	Y	Y	Y	Y	N	N
7 **Austria**	Y	N	N	Y	Y	N	Y
8 **Boehner**	Y	N	N	Y	Y	Y	Y
9 Kaptur	Y	Y	Y	Y	Y	?	N
10 Kucinich	Y	Y	Y	Y	Y	N	N
11 Fudge	Y	Y	Y	Y	Y	N	N
12 **Tiberi**	Y	N	N	Y	Y	N	Y
13 Sutton	Y	Y	Y	Y	Y	N	N
14 **LaTourette**	Y	N	N	P	Y	N	N
15 Kilroy	Y	Y	Y	Y	Y	N	N
16 Boccieri	Y	Y	Y	Y	Y	N	N
17 Ryan	Y	Y	Y	Y	Y	?	N
18 Space	Y	Y	Y	Y	Y	N	N
OKLAHOMA							
1 **Sullivan**	Y	N	N	Y	Y	Y	N
2 Boren	Y	Y	Y	Y	Y	N	N
3 **Lucas**	Y	N	N	Y	Y	Y	Y
4 **Cole**	Y	N	N	Y	Y	Y	Y
5 **Fallin**	Y	N	N	Y	Y	Y	Y
OREGON							
1 Wu	Y	Y	Y	Y	Y	N	N
2 **Walden**	Y	N	N	Y	Y	N	N
3 Blumenauer	Y	Y	Y	Y	Y	N	N
4 DeFazio	Y	Y	Y	Y	Y	N	N
5 Schrader	Y	Y	Y	Y	?	N	N
PENNSYLVANIA							
1 Brady	Y	Y	Y	Y	Y	N	N
2 Fattah	Y	Y	Y	Y	Y	N	N
3 Dahlkemper	Y	Y	Y	Y	Y	N	N
4 Altmire	Y	Y	Y	Y	Y	N	N
5 **Thompson**	Y	N	N	Y	Y	Y	Y
6 **Gerlach**	Y	N	N	Y	Y	N	N
7 Sestak	Y	Y	Y	Y	Y	N	N
8 Murphy, P.	Y	Y	Y	Y	Y	N	N
9 **Shuster**	Y	N	N	Y	Y	Y	N
10 Carney	Y	Y	Y	N	Y	N	N
11 Kanjorski	Y	Y	Y	Y	Y	N	N
12 Murtha	Y	Y	Y	Y	Y	N	N
13 Schwartz	Y	Y	Y	Y	Y	N	N
14 Doyle	Y	Y	Y	Y	Y	N	N
15 **Dent**	Y	N	N	Y	Y	N	N
16 **Pitts**	Y	N	N	Y	Y	Y	Y
17 Holden	Y	Y	Y	Y	Y	N	N
18 **Murphy, T.**	Y	N	N	Y	Y	N	N
19 **Platts**	Y	N	N	Y	Y	?	N
RHODE ISLAND							
1 Kennedy	Y	Y	Y	Y	Y	N	?
2 Langevin	Y	Y	Y	Y	Y	N	N
SOUTH CAROLINA							
1 **Brown**	Y	N	N	Y	Y	Y	Y
2 **Wilson**	Y	N	N	Y	Y	Y	Y
3 **Barrett**	Y	N	N	Y	Y	?	?
4 **Inglis**	Y	N	N	Y	Y	Y	Y
5 Spratt	Y	Y	Y	Y	Y	N	?
6 Clyburn	Y	Y	Y	Y	Y	N	N
SOUTH DAKOTA							
AL Herseth Sandlin	Y	Y	Y	Y	Y	N	Y
TENNESSEE							
1 **Roe**	Y	N	N	N	Y	Y	Y
2 **Duncan**	Y	N	N	Y	Y	Y	Y
3 **Wamp**	Y	N	N	Y	Y	Y	Y
4 Davis	Y	Y	Y	Y	Y	N	N
5 Cooper	Y	Y	Y	Y	Y	Y	N
6 Gordon	Y	Y	Y	Y	Y	N	Y
7 **Blackburn**	Y	N	N	Y	Y	Y	N
8 Tanner	Y	Y	Y	Y	Y	N	N
9 Cohen	Y	Y	Y	Y	Y	N	N
TEXAS							
1 **Gohmert**	Y	N	N	Y	Y	Y	Y
2 **Poe**	Y	N	N	P	Y	N	N
3 **Johnson, S.**	Y	N	N	Y	Y	Y	Y
4 **Hall**	Y	N	N	Y	Y	N	Y
5 **Hensarling**	Y	N	N	Y	Y	Y	Y
6 **Barton**	Y	N	N	Y	Y	Y	Y
7 **Culberson**	Y	N	N	Y	Y	Y	Y
8 **Brady**	Y	N	N	Y	Y	Y	Y
9 Green, A.	Y	Y	Y	Y	Y	N	N
10 **McCaul**	Y	N	N	Y	Y	Y	Y
11 **Conaway**	Y	N	N	Y	Y	Y	Y
12 **Granger**	?	N	N	Y	Y	Y	Y
13 **Thornberry**	Y	N	N	Y	Y	Y	Y
14 **Paul**	Y	N	N	N	Y	Y	?
15 Hinojosa	Y	Y	Y	Y	Y	?	N
16 Reyes	Y	Y	Y	Y	Y	N	N
17 Edwards	Y	Y	Y	Y	Y	N	N
18 Jackson Lee	Y	Y	Y	Y	Y	N	N
19 **Neugebauer**	Y	N	N	Y	Y	Y	Y
20 Gonzalez	Y	Y	Y	Y	Y	N	N
21 **Smith**	Y	N	N	Y	Y	Y	Y
22 **Olson**	Y	N	N	Y	Y	Y	Y
23 Rodriguez	Y	Y	Y	Y	Y	N	N
24 **Marchant**	Y	N	N	Y	Y	Y	Y
25 Doggett	Y	Y	Y	Y	Y	N	N
26 **Burgess**	Y	N	N	Y	Y	Y	Y
27 Ortiz	Y	Y	Y	Y	Y	N	N
28 Cuellar	Y	Y	Y	Y	Y	N	N
29 Green, G.	Y	Y	Y	Y	Y	N	N
30 Johnson, E.	Y	Y	Y	Y	Y	N	N
31 **Carter**	?	N	N	Y	Y	Y	Y
32 **Sessions**	Y	N	N	Y	Y	Y	Y
UTAH							
1 **Bishop**	Y	?	?	?	?	?	?
2 Matheson	Y	Y	Y	Y	Y	N	?
3 **Chaffetz**	Y	N	N	Y	Y	Y	Y
VERMONT							
AL Welch	Y	Y	Y	Y	Y	N	N
VIRGINIA							
1 **Wittman**	Y	N	?	Y	Y	N	Y
2 Nye	Y	Y	N	Y	Y	N	N
3 Scott	Y	Y	Y	Y	Y	N	N
4 **Forbes**	Y	N	N	Y	Y	Y	Y
5 Perriello	Y	Y	N	Y	Y	?	N
6 **Goodlatte**	Y	N	N	Y	Y	Y	Y
7 **Cantor**	Y	N	?	Y	Y	Y	N
8 Moran	Y	Y	Y	Y	Y	N	N
9 Boucher	Y	Y	Y	Y	Y	N	N
10 **Wolf**	Y	N	N	Y	Y	N	Y
11 Connolly	Y	Y	Y	Y	Y	N	N
WASHINGTON							
1 Inslee	Y	Y	Y	Y	Y	N	N
2 Larsen	Y	Y	Y	?	Y	N	N
3 Baird	Y	Y	Y	Y	Y	N	N
4 **Hastings**	Y	N	N	Y	Y	Y	Y
5 **McMorris Rodgers**	Y	N	N	Y	Y	Y	Y
6 Dicks	Y	Y	Y	Y	Y	N	?
7 McDermott	Y	Y	Y	Y	Y	N	N
8 **Reichert**	Y	Y	N	Y	Y	Y	Y
9 Smith	Y	Y	Y	Y	Y	N	N
WEST VIRGINIA							
1 Mollohan	Y	Y	Y	Y	Y	N	N
2 **Capito**	Y	N	N	Y	Y	N	Y
3 Rahall	Y	Y	Y	Y	Y	N	N
WISCONSIN							
1 **Ryan**	Y	N	?	Y	Y	Y	Y
2 Baldwin	Y	Y	Y	Y	Y	N	N
3 Kind	Y	Y	Y	Y	Y	N	N
4 Moore	Y	Y	Y	Y	Y	?	?
5 **Sensenbrenner**	Y	N	N	N	Y	Y	Y
6 **Petri**	Y	N	N	P	Y	Y	Y
7 Obey	Y	Y	Y	Y	Y	N	N
8 Kagen	Y	Y	Y	Y	Y	N	N
WYOMING							
AL **Lummis**	Y	N	N	N	Y	Y	Y
DELEGATES							
Faleomavaega (A.S.)						N	N
Norton (D.C.)						N	N
Bordallo (Guam)						N	N
Sablan (N. Marianas)						N	N
Pierluisi (P.R.)						N	N
Christensen (V.I.)						N	N

IN THE HOUSE | By Vote Number

622. HR 3288. Fiscal 2010 Transportation-HUD Appropriations/ **Regional Airspace Redesign Project.** Frelinghuysen, R-N.J., amendment that would bar the use of funds by the Federal Aviation Administration to implement the New York/New Jersey/Philadelphia airspace redesign project. Rejected in Committee of the Whole 116-313: R 76-95; D 40-218. July 23, 2009.

623. HR 3288. Fiscal 2010 Transportation-HUD Appropriations/ **Discretionary Spending Cut.** Blackburn, R-Tenn., amendment that would reduce discretionary spending in the bill by 5 percent. Rejected in Committee of the Whole 181-252: R 161-14; D 20-238. A "nay" was a vote in support of the president's position. July 23, 2009.

624. HR 3288. Fiscal 2010 Transportation-HUD Appropriations/ **Spending Reduction.** Jordan, R-Ohio, amendment that would reduce spending in the bill by $20.1 billion. Rejected in Committee of the Whole 145-287: R 141-33; D 4-254. July 23, 2009.

625. HR 3288. Fiscal 2010 Transportation-HUD Appropriations/ **Spending Reduction.** Neugebauer, R-Texas, amendment that would reduce spending in the bill by $13.5 billion. Rejected in Committee of the Whole 166-267: R 152-23; D 14-244. July 23, 2009.

626. HR 3288. Fiscal 2010 Transportation-HUD Appropriations/ **Discretionary Spending Cut.** Stearns, R-Fla., amendment that would reduce discretionary spending in the bill by 25 percent. Rejected in Committee of the Whole 152-279: R 147-26; D 5-253. July 23, 2009.

627. HR 3288. Fiscal 2010 Transportation-HUD Appropriations/ **Grand Forks International Airport.** Flake, R-Ariz., amendment that would bar the use of funds appropriated in the bill for the terminal replacement project at Grand Forks International Airport in Grand Forks, N.D., and cut $500,000 intended for the project from the bill. Rejected in Committee of the Whole 108-327: R 102-73; D 6-254. July 23, 2009.

	622	623	624	625	626	627
ALABAMA						
1 Bonner	N	Y	Y	Y	Y	N
2 Bright	N	Y	N	Y	Y	Y
3 Rogers	N	Y	Y	Y	Y	N
4 Aderholt	N	Y	Y	Y	N	N
5 Griffith	N	N	N	N	N	N
6 Bachus	Y	Y	Y	Y	Y	N
7 Davis	N	N	N	N	N	N
ALASKA						
AL Young	N	N	N	N	N	N
ARIZONA						
1 Kirkpatrick	N	Y	Y	Y	Y	N
2 Franks	N	Y	Y	Y	Y	Y
3 Shadegg	N	Y	Y	Y	Y	Y
4 Pastor	N	N	N	N	N	N
5 Mitchell	N	Y	N	Y	N	N
6 Flake	N	Y	Y	Y	Y	Y
7 Grijalva	N	N	N	N	N	N
8 Giffords	N	N	N	N	N	N
ARKANSAS						
1 Berry	N	N	N	N	N	N
2 Snyder	N	N	N	N	N	N
3 Boozman	N	Y	Y	Y	Y	Y
4 Ross	N	N	N	N	?	N
CALIFORNIA						
1 Thompson	N	N	N	N	N	N
2 Herger	N	Y	Y	Y	Y	Y
3 Lungren	Y	Y	Y	Y	Y	Y
4 McClintock	N	Y	Y	Y	Y	Y
5 Matsui	N	N	N	N	N	N
6 Woolsey	N	N	N	?	N	N
7 Miller, George	N	N	N	N	N	N
8 Pelosi						
9 Lee	N	N	N	N	N	N
10 Vacant						
11 McNerney	N	Y	N	N	N	N
12 Speier	N	N	N	N	N	N
13 Stark	N	N	N	N	N	N
14 Eshoo	N	N	N	N	N	N
15 Honda	N	N	N	N	N	N
16 Lofgren	N	N	N	N	N	N
17 Farr	N	N	N	N	N	N
18 Cardoza	N	N	N	N	N	N
19 Radanovich	Y	Y	Y	Y	Y	N
20 Costa	N	N	N	N	N	N
21 Nunes	Y	Y	Y	Y	Y	Y
22 McCarthy	N	Y	Y	Y	Y	Y
23 Capps	N	N	N	N	N	N
24 Gallegly	Y	Y	Y	Y	Y	N
25 McKeon	Y	Y	Y	Y	Y	N
26 Dreier	Y	Y	Y	Y	Y	N
27 Sherman	N	N	N	N	N	N
28 Berman	N	N	N	N	N	N
29 Schiff	N	N	N	N	N	N
30 Waxman	N	N	N	N	N	N
31 Becerra	N	N	N	N	N	N
32 Chu	N	N	N	N	N	N
33 Watson	N	N	N	N	N	N
34 Roybal-Allard	N	N	N	N	N	N
35 Waters	N	N	N	N	N	N
36 Harman	N	N	N	N	N	N
37 Richardson	N	N	N	N	N	N
38 Napolitano	N	N	N	N	N	N
39 Sánchez, Linda	N	N	N	N	N	N
40 Royce	Y	Y	Y	Y	Y	Y
41 Lewis	Y	N	Y	N	Y	N
42 Miller, Gary	N	Y	Y	Y	Y	N
43 Baca	N	N	N	N	N	N
44 Calvert	Y	Y	Y	Y	Y	N
45 Bono Mack	Y	Y	Y	Y	Y	N
46 Rohrabacher	N	Y	Y	Y	Y	Y
47 Sanchez, Loretta	N	N	N	N	N	N
48 Campbell	Y	Y	Y	Y	Y	Y
49 Issa	Y	Y	Y	Y	Y	Y
50 Bilbray	N	N	N	N	N	Y
51 Filner	N	N	N	N	N	N
52 Hunter	N	Y	Y	Y	Y	Y
53 Davis	N	N	N	N	N	N
COLORADO						
1 DeGette	N	N	N	N	N	N
2 Polis	N	N	N	N	N	N
3 Salazar	N	N	N	N	N	N
4 Markey	N	N	N	N	N	N
5 Lamborn	Y	Y	Y	Y	Y	Y
6 Coffman	Y	Y	Y	Y	Y	Y
7 Perlmutter	N	N	N	N	N	N
CONNECTICUT						
1 Larson	N	N	N	N	N	N
2 Courtney	N	N	N	N	N	N
3 DeLauro	N	N	N	N	N	N
4 Himes	Y	N	N	N	N	N
5 Murphy	Y	N	N	N	N	N
DELAWARE						
AL Castle	N	Y	N	Y	Y	Y
FLORIDA						
1 Miller	Y	Y	Y	Y	Y	Y
2 Boyd	N	N	N	N	N	N
3 Brown	N	N	N	N	N	N
4 Crenshaw	N	Y	Y	Y	Y	N
5 Brown-Waite	Y	Y	Y	Y	Y	N
6 Stearns	Y	Y	Y	Y	Y	Y
7 Mica	N	Y	N	N	N	N
8 Grayson	N	N	N	N	N	N
9 Bilirakis	N	Y	N	Y	Y	N
10 Young	Y	Y	Y	N	Y	N
11 Castor	N	N	N	N	N	N
12 Putnam	N	Y	Y	Y	Y	N
13 Buchanan	Y	Y	N	N	N	Y
14 Mack	N	Y	Y	Y	Y	Y
15 Posey	Y	Y	Y	Y	Y	Y
16 Rooney	N	Y	Y	Y	Y	Y
17 Meek	N	N	N	N	N	N
18 Ros-Lehtinen	N	Y	Y	Y	Y	N
19 Wexler	Y	N	N	N	N	N
20 Wasserman Schultz	N	N	N	N	N	N
21 Diaz-Balart, L.	N	Y	Y	Y	Y	N
22 Klein	N	N	N	N	N	N
23 Hastings	N	N	N	N	N	N
24 Kosmas	N	N	N	N	N	N
25 Diaz-Balart, M.	N	Y	Y	Y	Y	N
GEORGIA						
1 Kingston	Y	Y	Y	Y	Y	Y
2 Bishop	N	N	N	N	N	N
3 Westmoreland	N	Y	Y	Y	Y	Y
4 Johnson	N	?	N	N	N	N
5 Lewis	N	N	N	N	N	N
6 Price	Y	Y	Y	Y	Y	Y
7 Linder	N	Y	Y	Y	Y	Y
8 Marshall	N	N	Y	N	N	N
9 Deal	N	Y	Y	Y	Y	N
10 Broun	N	Y	Y	Y	Y	Y
11 Gingrey	N	Y	Y	Y	Y	Y
12 Barrow	N	N	N	N	N	N
13 Scott	N	N	N	N	N	N
HAWAII						
1 Abercrombie	N	N	N	N	N	N
2 Hirono	N	N	N	N	N	N
IDAHO						
1 Minnick	N	N	Y	Y	Y	N
2 Simpson	Y	Y	N	N	N	N
ILLINOIS						
1 Rush	N	N	N	N	N	N
2 Jackson	N	N	N	N	N	N
3 Lipinski	N	N	N	N	N	N
4 Gutierrez	N	N	N	N	N	N
5 Quigley	N	N	N	N	N	N
6 Roskam	N	Y	Y	Y	Y	Y
7 Davis	N	N	N	N	N	N
8 Bean	N	Y	N	N	N	N
9 Schakowsky	N	N	N	N	N	N
10 Kirk	Y	Y	N	Y	Y	Y
11 Halvorson	N	N	N	N	N	N
12 Costello	N	N	N	N	N	N
13 Biggert	N	Y	Y	Y	Y	N
14 Foster	N	N	N	N	N	N
15 Johnson	Y	Y	Y	Y	Y	Y

KEY	**Republicans**	Democrats

Y Voted for (yea)	X Paired against	C Voted "present" to avoid possible conflict of interest
# Paired for	– Announced against	
+ Announced for	P Voted "present"	? Did not vote or otherwise make a position known
N Voted against (nay)		

	622	623	624	625	626	627
16 **Manzullo**	Y	Y	Y	Y	Y	Y
17 Hare	N	N	N	N	N	N
18 **Schock**	N	Y	N	N	N	Y
19 **Shimkus**	N	Y	Y	Y	Y	N
INDIANA						
1 Visclosky	Y	N	N	N	N	N
2 Donnelly	N	Y	N	Y	N	N
3 **Souder**	Y	Y	Y	Y	Y	N
4 **Buyer**	Y	Y	Y	Y	Y	N
5 **Burton**	N	Y	Y	Y	Y	Y
6 **Pence**	?	Y	Y	Y	Y	Y
7 Carson	N	N	N	N	N	N
8 Ellsworth	N	Y	N	N	N	N
9 Hill	N	N	N	N	N	N
IOWA						
1 Braley	N	N	N	N	N	N
2 Loebsack	N	N	N	N	N	N
3 Boswell	N	N	N	N	N	N
4 **Latham**	N	N	N	N	N	N
5 **King**	Y	Y	Y	Y	Y	Y
KANSAS						
1 **Moran**	N	Y	Y	Y	Y	Y
2 **Jenkins**	N	Y	N	N	Y	Y
3 Moore	N	N	N	N	N	N
4 **Tiahrt**	N	Y	Y	Y	Y	N
KENTUCKY						
1 **Whitfield**	Y	Y	N	N	Y	N
2 **Guthrie**	N	Y	Y	Y	Y	N
3 Yarmuth	N	N	N	N	N	N
4 **Davis**	N	Y	Y	Y	Y	N
5 **Rogers**	N	Y	N	N	N	N
6 Chandler	N	N	N	N	N	N
LOUISIANA						
1 **Scalise**	Y	Y	Y	Y	Y	Y
2 **Cao**	N	N	N	N	N	N
3 Melancon	N	N	N	N	N	N
4 **Fleming**	N	Y	Y	Y	Y	Y
5 **Alexander**	Y	Y	Y	Y	Y	N
6 **Cassidy**	Y	Y	Y	Y	Y	Y
7 **Boustany**	Y	Y	Y	Y	Y	Y
MAINE						
1 Pingree	N	N	N	N	N	N
2 Michaud	N	N	N	N	N	N
MARYLAND						
1 Kratovil	N	Y	Y	Y	Y	N
2 Ruppersberger	N	N	N	N	N	N
3 Sarbanes	N	N	N	N	N	N
4 Edwards	N	N	N	N	N	N
5 Hoyer	N	N	N	N	N	N
6 **Bartlett**	Y	Y	Y	Y	Y	Y
7 Cummings	N	N	N	N	N	N
8 Van Hollen	N	N	N	N	N	N
MASSACHUSETTS						
1 Olver	N	N	N	N	N	N
2 Neal	N	N	N	N	N	N
3 McGovern	N	N	N	N	N	N
4 Frank	N	N	N	N	N	N
5 Tsongas	Y	N	N	N	N	N
6 Tierney	Y	N	N	N	N	N
7 Markey	N	N	N	N	N	N
8 Capuano	N	N	N	N	N	N
9 Lynch	N	N	N	N	N	N
10 Delahunt	Y	N	N	N	N	N
MICHIGAN						
1 Stupak	N	N	N	N	N	N
2 **Hoekstra**	N	Y	Y	Y	Y	Y
3 **Ehlers**	N	N	N	Y	N	Y
4 **Camp**	N	Y	Y	Y	Y	Y
5 Kildee	N	N	N	N	N	N
6 **Upton**	N	Y	N	Y	Y	Y
7 Schauer	N	N	N	N	N	Y
8 **Rogers**	N	Y	Y	Y	Y	Y
9 Peters	N	Y	N	N	N	N
10 **Miller**	N	Y	Y	Y	Y	N
11 **McCotter**	Y	Y	Y	Y	Y	Y
12 Levin	N	N	N	N	N	N
13 Kilpatrick	N	N	N	N	N	N
14 Conyers	Y	N	N	?	N	N
15 Dingell	N	N	N	N	N	N
MINNESOTA						
1 Walz	N	N	N	N	N	N
2 **Kline**	N	Y	Y	Y	Y	Y
3 **Paulsen**	N	Y	Y	Y	Y	N
4 McCollum	N	N	N	N	N	N

	622	623	624	625	626	627
5 Ellison	N	N	N	N	N	N
6 **Bachmann**	N	Y	Y	Y	Y	Y
7 Peterson	N	N	N	N	N	N
8 Oberstar	N	N	N	N	N	N
MISSISSIPPI						
1 Childers	N	N	N	N	N	N
2 Thompson	N	N	N	N	N	N
3 **Harper**	Y	Y	Y	Y	Y	N
4 Taylor	N	Y	N	Y	N	N
MISSOURI						
1 Clay	N	N	N	N	N	N
2 **Akin**	Y	Y	Y	Y	Y	Y
3 Carnahan	N	N	N	N	N	N
4 Skelton	N	N	N	N	N	N
5 Cleaver	N	N	N	N	N	N
6 **Graves**	N	Y	Y	Y	Y	Y
7 **Blunt**	Y	Y	Y	Y	Y	Y
8 **Emerson**	N	Y	Y	Y	Y	N
9 **Luetkemeyer**	N	Y	Y	Y	Y	Y
MONTANA						
AL **Rehberg**	Y	Y	Y	Y	Y	Y
NEBRASKA						
1 **Fortenberry**	N	Y	N	Y	N	N
2 **Terry**	Y	Y	Y	Y	Y	Y
3 **Smith**	Y	Y	Y	Y	Y	Y
NEVADA						
1 Berkley	N	N	N	N	N	N
2 **Heller**	N	Y	Y	Y	Y	Y
3 Titus	N	N	N	N	N	N
NEW HAMPSHIRE						
1 Shea-Porter	N	N	N	N	N	N
2 Hodes	Y	N	N	N	N	N
NEW JERSEY						
1 Andrews	Y	N	N	N	N	N
2 **LoBiondo**	N	N	N	N	N	N
3 Adler	Y	Y	N	N	N	N
4 **Smith**	Y	N	N	N	N	N
5 **Garrett**	Y	Y	Y	Y	Y	Y
6 Pallone	Y	N	N	N	N	N
7 **Lance**	Y	Y	Y	Y	Y	Y
8 Pascrell	Y	N	N	N	N	N
9 Rothman	Y	N	N	N	N	N
10 Payne	Y	N	N	N	N	N
11 **Frelinghuysen**	Y	Y	N	N	N	N
12 Holt	Y	N	N	N	N	N
13 Sires	Y	N	N	N	N	N
NEW MEXICO						
1 Heinrich	N	Y	N	N	N	N
2 Teague	N	N	N	N	N	N
3 Lujan	N	N	N	N	N	N
NEW YORK						
1 Bishop	N	N	N	N	N	N
2 Israel	N	N	N	N	N	Y
3 **King**	N	Y	N	Y	N	N
4 McCarthy	?	?	?	?	?	?
5 Ackerman	N	N	N	N	N	N
6 Meeks	N	N	N	N	N	N
7 Crowley	N	N	N	N	N	N
8 Nadler	N	N	N	N	N	N
9 Weiner	N	N	N	N	N	N
10 Towns	N	N	N	N	N	N
11 Clarke	Y	N	N	N	N	N
12 Velázquez	N	N	N	N	N	N
13 McMahon	N	N	N	N	?	N
14 Maloney	N	N	N	N	N	N
15 Rangel	N	N	N	N	N	N
16 Serrano	N	N	N	N	N	N
17 Engel	Y	N	N	N	N	N
18 Lowey	N	N	N	N	N	N
19 Hall	N	N	N	N	N	N
20 Murphy	Y	Y	N	Y	N	N
21 Tonko	N	N	N	N	N	N
22 Hinchey	N	N	N	N	N	N
23 **McHugh**	Y	N	N	N	N	N
24 Arcuri	Y	Y	N	N	N	N
25 Maffei	N	N	N	N	N	N
26 **Lee**	N	Y	Y	Y	Y	N
27 Higgins	N	N	N	N	N	N
28 Slaughter	Y	N	N	N	N	N
29 Massa	Y	N	N	N	N	N
NORTH CAROLINA						
1 Butterfield	N	N	N	N	N	N
2 Etheridge	N	N	N	N	N	N
3 **Jones**	Y	Y	Y	Y	Y	N
4 Price	N	N	?	N	N	N

	622	623	624	625	626	627
5 **Foxx**	Y	Y	Y	Y	Y	Y
6 **Coble**	N	Y	Y	Y	Y	Y
7 McIntyre	N	N	N	N	N	N
8 Kissell	Y	N	N	N	N	N
9 **Myrick**	?	Y	Y	Y	Y	Y
10 **McHenry**	N	Y	Y	Y	Y	Y
11 Shuler	N	N	N	N	N	N
12 Watt	N	N	N	N	N	N
13 Miller	Y	N	N	N	N	N
NORTH DAKOTA						
AL Pomeroy	N	N	N	N	N	N
OHIO						
1 Driehaus	N	Y	N	Y	N	N
2 **Schmidt**	N	Y	Y	Y	Y	Y
3 **Turner**	Y	N	N	N	N	N
4 **Jordan**	N	Y	Y	Y	Y	Y
5 **Latta**	Y	Y	Y	Y	Y	Y
6 Wilson	N	N	N	N	N	N
7 **Austria**	N	Y	Y	Y	Y	N
8 **Boehner**	N	Y	Y	Y	Y	Y
9 Kaptur	N	N	N	N	N	N
10 Kucinich	Y	N	N	N	N	N
11 Fudge	N	N	N	N	N	N
12 **Tiberi**	N	Y	Y	Y	Y	Y
13 Sutton	N	N	N	N	N	N
14 **LaTourette**	N	N	N	N	N	N
15 Kilroy	N	N	N	N	N	N
16 Boccieri	Y	N	N	N	N	N
17 Ryan	N	N	N	N	N	N
18 Space	N	N	N	N	N	N
OKLAHOMA						
1 **Sullivan**	?	Y	Y	Y	Y	Y
2 Boren	Y	Y	N	Y	N	N
3 **Lucas**	Y	Y	Y	Y	Y	N
4 **Cole**	Y	Y	Y	Y	Y	N
5 **Fallin**	N	Y	Y	Y	Y	N
OREGON						
1 Wu	N	N	N	N	N	N
2 **Walden**	Y	Y	N	N	N	Y
3 Blumenauer	N	N	N	N	N	N
4 DeFazio	N	N	N	N	N	N
5 Schrader	N	N	N	N	N	N
PENNSYLVANIA						
1 Brady	Y	N	N	N	N	N
2 Fattah	Y	N	N	N	N	N
3 Dahlkemper	Y	N	N	N	N	N
4 Altmire	Y	Y	N	Y	N	N
5 **Thompson**	Y	Y	Y	Y	Y	N
6 **Gerlach**	Y	Y	N	N	Y	N
7 Sestak	Y	N	N	N	N	N
8 Murphy, P.	N	Y	N	N	N	N
9 **Shuster**	N	Y	Y	Y	Y	N
10 Carney	Y	N	N	N	N	N
11 Kanjorski	Y	N	N	N	N	N
12 Murtha	N	N	N	N	N	N
13 Schwartz	N	N	N	N	N	N
14 Doyle	N	N	N	N	N	N
15 **Dent**	N	Y	N	Y	Y	N
16 **Pitts**	Y	Y	Y	Y	Y	Y
17 Holden	N	N	N	N	N	N
18 **Murphy, T.**	N	N	N	N	N	N
19 **Platts**	Y	Y	N	N	N	N
RHODE ISLAND						
1 Kennedy	N	N	N	N	N	N
2 Langevin	N	N	N	N	N	N
SOUTH CAROLINA						
1 **Brown**	N	Y	Y	Y	Y	N
2 **Wilson**	Y	Y	Y	Y	Y	Y
3 **Barrett**	?	?	?	?	?	?
4 **Inglis**	N	Y	Y	Y	Y	Y
5 Spratt	?	?	?	N	N	N
6 Clyburn	N	N	N	N	N	N
SOUTH DAKOTA						
AL Herseth Sandlin	N	N	N	N	N	N
TENNESSEE						
1 **Roe**	Y	Y	Y	Y	Y	Y
2 **Duncan**	N	Y	Y	Y	Y	Y
3 **Wamp**	N	Y	Y	Y	Y	Y
4 Davis	N	N	N	N	N	N
5 Cooper	N	Y	N	N	N	Y
6 Gordon	N	N	N	N	N	N
7 **Blackburn**	Y	Y	Y	Y	Y	Y
8 Tanner	N	N	N	N	N	N
9 Cohen	N	N	N	N	N	N

	622	623	624	625	626	627
TEXAS						
1 **Gohmert**	Y	Y	Y	Y	Y	N
2 **Poe**	N	Y	Y	Y	Y	N
3 **Johnson, S.**	?	Y	Y	Y	Y	Y
4 **Hall**	N	Y	Y	Y	Y	N
5 **Hensarling**	Y	Y	Y	Y	Y	Y
6 **Barton**	N	Y	Y	Y	Y	N
7 **Culberson**	N	Y	?	Y	Y	N
8 **Brady**	N	Y	Y	Y	Y	Y
9 Green, A.	N	N	N	N	N	N
10 **McCaul**	N	Y	Y	Y	Y	Y
11 **Conaway**	Y	Y	Y	Y	Y	Y
12 **Granger**	N	Y	Y	Y	Y	N
13 **Thornberry**	N	Y	Y	Y	Y	Y
14 **Paul**	?	?	?	?	?	?
15 Hinojosa	N	N	N	N	N	N
16 Reyes	N	N	N	N	N	N
17 Edwards	Y	N	N	N	N	N
18 Jackson Lee	Y	N	N	N	N	N
19 **Neugebauer**	N	Y	Y	Y	Y	Y
20 Gonzalez	N	N	N	N	N	N
21 **Smith**	Y	Y	Y	Y	Y	N
22 **Olson**	N	Y	Y	Y	Y	Y
23 Rodriguez	N	N	N	N	N	N
24 **Marchant**	Y	Y	Y	Y	?	Y
25 Doggett	Y	N	N	N	N	N
26 **Burgess**	Y	Y	Y	Y	Y	Y
27 Ortiz	N	N	N	N	N	N
28 Cuellar	N	N	N	N	N	N
29 Green, G.	N	N	N	N	N	N
30 Johnson, E.	N	N	N	N	N	N
31 **Carter**	N	Y	Y	Y	Y	N
32 **Sessions**	N	Y	Y	Y	Y	Y
UTAH						
1 **Bishop**	?	?	?	?	?	?
2 Matheson	N	N	N	N	N	N
3 **Chaffetz**	N	Y	Y	Y	Y	Y
VERMONT						
AL Welch	N	N	N	N	N	N
VIRGINIA						
1 **Wittman**	Y	Y	Y	Y	Y	Y
2 Nye	N	Y	Y	Y	Y	N
3 Scott	N	N	N	N	N	N
4 **Forbes**	Y	Y	Y	Y	Y	Y
5 Perriello	N	N	N	N	N	N
6 **Goodlatte**	N	Y	Y	Y	Y	Y
7 **Cantor**	Y	Y	Y	Y	Y	Y
8 Moran	N	N	N	N	N	N
9 Boucher	N	N	N	N	N	N
10 **Wolf**	Y	N	N	N	N	N
11 Connolly	N	N	N	N	N	N
WASHINGTON						
1 Inslee	N	N	N	N	N	N
2 Larsen	N	N	N	N	N	N
3 Baird	N	N	N	N	N	N
4 **Hastings**	N	Y	Y	Y	Y	N
5 **McMorris Rodgers**	Y	Y	Y	Y	?	Y
6 Dicks	N	N	N	N	N	N
7 McDermott	N	N	N	N	N	N
8 **Reichert**	N	N	N	N	N	N
9 Smith	N	N	N	N	N	N
WEST VIRGINIA						
1 Mollohan	N	N	N	N	N	N
2 **Capito**	N	Y	Y	Y	Y	N
3 Rahall	N	N	N	N	N	N
WISCONSIN						
1 **Ryan**	Y	Y	Y	Y	Y	Y
2 Baldwin	N	N	N	N	N	N
3 Kind	N	N	N	N	N	Y
4 Moore	?	N	N	N	N	N
5 **Sensenbrenner**	Y	Y	Y	Y	Y	Y
6 **Petri**	N	Y	N	Y	Y	Y
7 Obey	N	N	N	N	N	N
8 Kagen	N	N	N	N	N	N
WYOMING						
AL **Lummis**	Y	Y	Y	Y	Y	Y
DELEGATES						
Faleomavaega (A.S.)	N	N	N	N	N	N
Norton (D.C.)	N	N	N	N	N	N
Bordallo (Guam)	N	N	N	N	N	N
Sablan (N. Marianas)	N	N	N	N	N	N
Pierluisi (P.R.)	N	N	N	N	N	N
Christensen (V.I.)	N	N	N	N	N	N

IN THE HOUSE | By Vote Number

628. HR 3288. Fiscal 2010 Transportation-HUD Appropriations/ **Murphy Theatre Community Center.** Flake, R-Ariz., amendment that would bar the use of funds appropriated in the bill for a building renovation project of the Murphy Theatre Community Center in Wilmington, Ohio, and cut $250,000 intended for the project from the bill. Rejected in Committee of the Whole 105-328: R 96-77; D 9-251. July 23, 2009.

629. HR 3288. Fiscal 2010 Transportation-HUD Appropriations/ **Triangle Building by Alianza Dominicana.** Flake, R-Ariz., amendment that would bar the use of funds appropriated in the bill for the construction of the Triangle Building by Alianza Dominicana in New York and cut $250,000 intended for the project from the bill. Rejected in Committee of the Whole 124-310: R 115-59; D 9-251. July 23, 2009.

630. HR 3288. Fiscal 2010 Transportation-HUD Appropriations/ **Local Economic Development Project.** Flake, R-Ariz., amendment that would bar the use of funds appropriated in the bill for the renovation of a vacant building for economic development by the city of Jal, N.M., and cut $400,000 intended for the project from the bill. Rejected in Committee of the Whole 125-310: R 118-57; D 7-253. July 23, 2009.

631. HR 3288. Fiscal 2010 Transportation-HUD Appropriations/ **Monroe County Farmer's Market.** Flake, R-Ariz., amendment that would bar the use of funds appropriated in the bill for the Monroe County Farmer's Market facility construction project of the Monroe County Fiscal Court and cut $250,000 intended for the project from the bill. Rejected in Committee of the Whole 98-331: R 89-84; D 9-247. July 23, 2009.

632. HR 3288. Fiscal 2010 Transportation-HUD Appropriations/ **Millennium Technology Park.** Flake, R-Ariz., amendment that would bar the use of funds appropriated in the bill for the Millennium Technology Park in New Castle, Pa., and cut $500,000 intended for the project from the bill. Rejected in Committee of the Whole 105-329: R 101-73; D 4-256. July 23, 2009.

	628	629	630	631	632
ALABAMA					
1 Bonner	N	N	N	N	N
2 Bright	Y	Y	Y	Y	Y
3 Rogers	N	N	N	N	N
4 Aderholt	N	N	N	N	N
5 Griffith	N	N	N	N	N
6 Bachus	N	N	N	N	N
7 Davis	N	N	N	N	N
ALASKA					
AL Young	N	N	N	N	N
ARIZONA					
1 Kirkpatrick	N	N	N	Y	N
2 Franks	Y	Y	Y	Y	?
3 Shadegg	Y	Y	Y	Y	Y
4 Pastor	N	N	N	N	N
5 Mitchell	N	N	N	N	N
6 Flake	Y	Y	Y	Y	Y
7 Grijalva	N	N	N	N	N
8 Giffords	N	N	N	N	N
ARKANSAS					
1 Berry	N	N	N	N	N
2 Snyder	N	N	N	N	N
3 Boozman	N	Y	Y	N	Y
4 Ross	N	N	N	N	N
CALIFORNIA					
1 Thompson	N	N	N	N	N
2 Herger	?	Y	Y	Y	Y
3 Lungren	Y	Y	Y	Y	Y
4 McClintock	Y	Y	Y	Y	Y
5 Matsui	N	N	N	N	N
6 Woolsey	N	N	N	N	N
7 Miller, George	N	N	N	N	N
8 Pelosi					
9 Lee	N	N	N	N	N
10 Vacant					
11 McNerney	N	N	N	N	N
12 Speier	N	N	N	N	N
13 Stark	N	N	N	N	N
14 Eshoo	N	N	N	N	N
15 Honda	N	N	N	N	N
16 Lofgren	N	N	N	N	N
17 Farr	N	N	N	N	N
18 Cardoza	N	N	N	N	N
19 Radanovich	N	N	N	N	N
20 Costa	N	N	N	N	N
21 Nunes	Y	Y	Y	Y	Y
22 McCarthy	Y	Y	Y	N	Y
23 Capps	N	N	N	N	N
24 Gallegly	N	N	N	N	N
25 McKeon	N	N	N	N	N
26 Dreier	N	N	N	N	N
27 Sherman	N	N	N	N	N
28 Berman	N	N	N	N	N
29 Schiff	N	N	N	N	N
30 Waxman	N	N	N	N	N
31 Becerra	N	N	N	N	N
32 Chu	N	N	N	N	N
33 Watson	N	N	N	N	N
34 Roybal-Allard	N	N	N	N	N
35 Waters	N	N	N	N	N
36 Harman	N	N	N	N	N
37 Richardson	N	N	N	N	N
38 Napolitano	N	N	N	N	N
39 Sánchez, Linda	N	N	N	N	N
40 Royce	Y	Y	Y	Y	Y
41 Lewis	Y	Y	N	N	N
42 Miller, Gary	N	N	N	N	N
43 Baca	N	N	N	N	N
44 Calvert	N	N	N	N	N
45 Bono Mack	Y	Y	Y	Y	Y
46 Rohrabacher	Y	Y	Y	Y	Y
47 Sanchez, Loretta	N	N	N	N	N
48 Campbell	Y	Y	Y	Y	Y
49 Issa	Y	Y	Y	Y	Y
50 Bilbray	Y	Y	Y	Y	Y
51 Filner	N	N	N	N	N
52 Hunter	Y	Y	Y	N	Y
53 Davis	N	N	N	N	N

	628	629	630	631	632
COLORADO					
1 DeGette	N	N	N	N	N
2 Polis	N	N	N	N	N
3 Salazar	N	N	N	N	N
4 Markey	N	N	N	N	N
5 Lamborn	Y	Y	Y	Y	Y
6 Coffman	Y	Y	Y	Y	Y
7 Perlmutter	N	N	N	N	N
CONNECTICUT					
1 Larson	N	N	N	N	N
2 Courtney	N	N	N	N	N
3 DeLauro	N	N	N	N	N
4 Himes	N	N	N	N	N
5 Murphy	N	N	N	N	N
DELAWARE					
AL Castle	Y	Y	Y	N	Y
FLORIDA					
1 Miller	Y	Y	Y	Y	Y
2 Boyd	N	N	N	N	N
3 Brown	N	N	N	N	N
4 Crenshaw	N	N	N	N	N
5 Brown-Waite	N	N	Y	N	N
6 Stearns	Y	Y	Y	Y	Y
7 Mica	N	Y	N	N	N
8 Grayson	N	N	N	N	N
9 Bilirakis	N	Y	Y	N	
10 Young	N	N	Y	N	N
11 Castor	N	N	N	N	N
12 Putnam	N	Y	N	N	N
13 Buchanan	N	N	N	N	N
14 Mack	Y	Y	Y	Y	Y
15 Posey	N	N	N	N	N
16 Rooney	Y	Y	Y	Y	N
17 Meek	N	N	N	N	N
18 Ros-Lehtinen	N	N	N	N	N
19 Wexler	N	N	N	N	N
20 Wasserman Schultz	N	N	N	N	N
21 Diaz-Balart, L.	N	N	N	N	N
22 Klein	N	N	N	N	N
23 Hastings	N	N	N	N	N
24 Kosmas	N	N	N	N	N
25 Diaz-Balart, M.	N	N	N	N	N
GEORGIA					
1 Kingston	Y	Y	Y	Y	N
2 Bishop	N	N	N	N	N
3 Westmoreland	Y	Y	Y	Y	Y
4 Johnson	N	N	N	?	N
5 Lewis	N	N	N	N	N
6 Price	Y	Y	Y	Y	Y
7 Linder	Y	Y	Y	Y	Y
8 Marshall	N	N	N	N	N
9 Deal	Y	Y	Y	Y	Y
10 Broun	Y	Y	Y	Y	Y
11 Gingrey	N	Y	Y	Y	Y
12 Barrow	N	N	N	N	N
13 Scott	N	N	N	N	N
HAWAII					
1 Abercrombie	N	N	N	N	N
2 Hirono	N	N	N	N	N
IDAHO					
1 Minnick	Y	Y	Y	Y	Y
2 Simpson	N	N	N	N	N
ILLINOIS					
1 Rush	N	N	N	N	N
2 Jackson	N	N	N	N	N
3 Lipinski	N	N	N	N	N
4 Gutierrez	N	N	N	N	N
5 Quigley	N	N	N	N	N
6 Roskam	Y	Y	Y	Y	Y
7 Davis	N	N	N	N	N
8 Bean	Y	Y	Y	Y	N
9 Schakowsky	N	N	N	N	N
10 Kirk	Y	Y	Y	N	Y
11 Halvorson	N	Y	Y	N	N
12 Costello	N	N	N	N	N
13 Biggert	N	Y	N	N	N
14 Foster	Y	Y	N	Y	N
15 Johnson	Y	Y	Y	N	Y

KEY	Republicans	Democrats		
Y Voted for (yea)		X Paired against		C Voted "present" to avoid possible conflict of interest
# Paired for		– Announced against		
+ Announced for		P Voted "present"		? Did not vote or otherwise make a position known
N Voted against (nay)				

	628	629	630	631	632
16 Manzullo	Y	Y	Y	Y	N
17 Hare	N	N	N	N	N
18 Schock	N	Y	Y	Y	N
19 Shimkus	Y	Y	Y	Y	Y
INDIANA					
1 Visclosky	N	N	N	N	N
2 Donnelly	N	N	N	N	N
3 Souder	Y	Y	Y	N	Y
4 Buyer	N	N	N	N	N
5 Burton	Y	Y	Y	Y	Y
6 Pence	Y	Y	Y	Y	Y
7 Carson	N	N	N	N	N
8 Ellsworth	N	N	N	N	N
9 Hill	N	N	N	N	N
IOWA					
1 Braley	N	N	N	N	N
2 Loebsack	N	N	N	N	N
3 Boswell	N	N	N	N	N
4 Latham	N	N	N	N	N
5 King	Y	Y	Y	?	Y
KANSAS					
1 Moran	Y	Y	Y	Y	Y
2 Jenkins	Y	Y	Y	Y	Y
3 Moore	N	N	N	N	N
4 Tiahrt	N	N	N	N	N
KENTUCKY					
1 Whitfield	N	N	N	N	N
2 Guthrie	N	Y	N	N	N
3 Yarmuth	N	N	N	N	N
4 Davis	N	N	Y	N	N
5 Rogers	N	N	N	N	N
6 Chandler	N	N	N	N	N
LOUISIANA					
1 Scalise	Y	Y	Y	Y	Y
2 Cao	N	N	N	N	N
3 Melancon	N	N	N	N	N
4 Fleming	Y	Y	Y	Y	Y
5 Alexander	N	N	N	N	N
6 Cassidy	Y	Y	Y	Y	Y
7 Boustany	Y	Y	Y	Y	Y
MAINE					
1 Pingree	N	N	N	N	N
2 Michaud	N	N	N	N	N
MARYLAND					
1 Kratovil	N	N	N	N	N
2 Ruppersberger	N	N	N	N	N
3 Sarbanes	N	N	N	N	N
4 Edwards	N	N	N	N	N
5 Hoyer	N	N	N	N	N
6 Bartlett	Y	Y	Y	N	Y
7 Cummings	N	N	N	N	N
8 Van Hollen	N	N	N	N	N
MASSACHUSETTS					
1 Olver	N	N	N	N	N
2 Neal	N	N	N	N	N
3 McGovern	N	N	N	N	N
4 Frank	N	N	N	N	N
5 Tsongas	N	N	N	N	N
6 Tierney	N	N	N	N	N
7 Markey	N	N	N	N	N
8 Capuano	N	N	N	N	N
9 Lynch	N	N	N	N	N
10 Delahunt	N	N	N	N	N
MICHIGAN					
1 Stupak	N	N	N	N	N
2 Hoekstra	Y	Y	Y	Y	Y
3 Ehlers	Y	Y	N	Y	N
4 Camp	N	N	N	N	N
5 Kildee	N	N	N	N	N
6 Upton	Y	Y	Y	N	Y
7 Schauer	Y	Y	Y	Y	Y
8 Rogers	Y	Y	Y	Y	Y
9 Peters	N	N	N	N	N
10 Miller	Y	Y	Y	Y	Y
11 McCotter	Y	Y	Y	Y	Y
12 Levin	N	N	N	N	N
13 Kilpatrick	N	N	N	N	N
14 Conyers	N	N	N	N	N
15 Dingell	N	N	N	N	N
MINNESOTA					
1 Walz	N	N	N	N	N
2 Kline	Y	Y	Y	Y	Y
3 Paulsen	Y	Y	Y	Y	N
4 McCollum	N	N	N	N	N

	628	629	630	631	632
5 Ellison	N	N	N	N	N
6 Bachmann	Y	Y	Y	Y	Y
7 Peterson	N	N	N	N	N
8 Oberstar	N	N	N	N	N
MISSISSIPPI					
1 Childers	N	N	N	N	N
2 Thompson	N	N	N	N	N
3 Harper	Y	N	Y	Y	N
4 Taylor	N	Y	N	N	N
MISSOURI					
1 Clay	N	N	N	N	N
2 Akin	Y	Y	Y	Y	Y
3 Carnahan	N	N	N	N	N
4 Skelton	N	N	N	N	N
5 Cleaver	N	N	N	N	N
6 Graves	Y	Y	Y	Y	Y
7 Blunt	N	Y	Y	Y	Y
8 Emerson	N	N	Y	N	N
9 Luetkemeyer	Y	Y	Y	Y	Y
MONTANA					
AL Rehberg	N	N	N	N	N
NEBRASKA					
1 Fortenberry	Y	Y	Y	Y	Y
2 Terry	Y	Y	Y	?	Y
3 Smith	Y	Y	Y	Y	Y
NEVADA					
1 Berkley	N	N	N	N	N
2 Heller	Y	Y	Y	Y	Y
3 Titus	N	N	N	N	N
NEW HAMPSHIRE					
1 Shea-Porter	N	N	N	N	N
2 Hodes	N	N	N	N	N
NEW JERSEY					
1 Andrews	N	N	N	N	N
2 LoBiondo	N	N	N	N	N
3 Adler	N	N	N	N	N
4 Smith	N	N	N	N	N
5 Garrett	Y	Y	Y	Y	Y
6 Pallone	N	N	N	N	N
7 Lance	Y	Y	Y	Y	Y
8 Pascrell	N	N	N	N	N
9 Rothman	N	N	N	N	N
10 Payne	N	N	N	N	N
11 Frelinghuysen	N	N	N	N	N
12 Holt	N	N	N	?	N
13 Sires	N	N	N	N	N
NEW YORK					
1 Bishop	N	N	N	N	N
2 Israel	N	N	N	N	N
3 King	N	N	N	N	N
4 McCarthy	?	?	?	?	?
5 Ackerman	N	N	N	N	N
6 Meeks	N	N	N	N	N
7 Crowley	N	N	N	N	N
8 Nadler	N	N	N	N	N
9 Weiner	N	N	N	N	N
10 Towns	N	N	N	N	N
11 Clarke	N	N	N	N	N
12 Velázquez	N	N	N	N	N
13 McMahon	Y	N	N	Y	N
14 Maloney	N	N	N	N	N
15 Rangel	N	N	N	N	N
16 Serrano	N	N	N	N	N
17 Engel	N	N	N	N	N
18 Lowey	N	N	N	N	N
19 Hall	N	N	N	N	N
20 Murphy	N	N	N	N	N
21 Tonko	N	N	N	N	N
22 Hinchey	N	N	N	N	N
23 McHugh	N	N	N	N	N
24 Arcuri	N	N	N	N	N
25 Maffei	N	N	N	N	N
26 Lee	Y	N	Y	N	N
27 Higgins	N	N	N	N	N
28 Slaughter	N	N	N	N	N
29 Massa	N	N	N	N	N
NORTH CAROLINA					
1 Butterfield	N	N	N	N	N
2 Etheridge	N	N	N	N	N
3 Jones	N	N	N	N	N
4 Price	N	N	N	N	N

	628	629	630	631	632
5 Foxx	Y	Y	Y	Y	Y
6 Coble	Y	Y	Y	N	Y
7 McIntyre	N	N	N	N	N
8 Kissell	N	N	N	N	N
9 Myrick	Y	Y	Y	Y	Y
10 McHenry	Y	Y	Y	Y	Y
11 Shuler	N	N	N	N	N
12 Watt	N	N	N	N	N
13 Miller	N	N	N	?	N
NORTH DAKOTA					
AL Pomeroy	N	N	N	N	N
OHIO					
1 Driehaus	N	N	N	N	N
2 Schmidt	N	Y	Y	Y	Y
3 Turner	N	N	N	N	N
4 Jordan	Y	Y	Y	Y	Y
5 Latta	N	Y	Y	Y	Y
6 Wilson	N	N	N	N	N
7 Austria	N	Y	Y	Y	Y
8 Boehner	N	Y	Y	Y	Y
9 Kaptur	N	N	N	N	N
10 Kucinich	N	N	N	N	N
11 Fudge	N	N	N	N	N
12 Tiberi	N	Y	Y	N	Y
13 Sutton	N	N	N	N	N
14 LaTourette	N	N	N	N	N
15 Kilroy	N	N	N	N	N
16 Boccieri	N	N	N	N	N
17 Ryan	N	N	N	N	N
18 Space	N	N	N	N	N
OKLAHOMA					
1 Sullivan	Y	Y	Y	Y	Y
2 Boren	N	N	N	N	N
3 Lucas	N	N	N	N	N
4 Cole	N	N	N	N	N
5 Fallin	Y	Y	Y	Y	Y
OREGON					
1 Wu	N	N	N	N	N
2 Walden	Y	Y	Y	N	Y
3 Blumenauer	N	N	N	N	N
4 DeFazio	N	N	N	N	N
5 Schrader	N	N	N	?	N
PENNSYLVANIA					
1 Brady	N	N	N	N	N
2 Fattah	N	N	N	N	N
3 Dahlkemper	N	N	N	N	N
4 Altmire	N	N	N	N	N
5 Thompson	N	N	N	N	N
6 Gerlach	?	N	N	N	N
7 Sestak	N	N	N	N	N
8 Murphy, P.	N	N	N	N	N
9 Shuster	N	N	N	N	N
10 Carney	N	N	N	N	N
11 Kanjorski	N	N	N	N	N
12 Murtha	N	N	N	N	N
13 Schwartz	N	N	N	N	N
14 Doyle	N	N	N	N	N
15 Dent	N	Y	N	N	N
16 Pitts	Y	Y	Y	Y	Y
17 Holden	N	N	N	N	N
18 Murphy, T.	N	N	N	N	N
19 Platts	N	Y	Y	N	N
RHODE ISLAND					
1 Kennedy	N	N	N	N	N
2 Langevin	N	N	N	N	N
SOUTH CAROLINA					
1 Brown	N	N	N	N	N
2 Wilson	Y	Y	Y	Y	Y
3 Barrett	?	?	?	?	?
4 Inglis	Y	Y	Y	Y	Y
5 Spratt	N	N	N	N	N
6 Clyburn	N	N	N	N	N
SOUTH DAKOTA					
AL Herseth Sandlin	N	N	N	N	N
TENNESSEE					
1 Roe	Y	Y	Y	Y	Y
2 Duncan	N	Y	Y	N	Y
3 Wamp	Y	Y	Y	Y	Y
4 Davis	N	N	N	N	N
5 Cooper	N	Y	Y	N	N
6 Gordon	N	N	N	N	N
7 Blackburn	Y	Y	Y	Y	Y
8 Tanner	N	N	N	N	N
9 Cohen	N	N	N	N	N

	628	629	630	631	632
TEXAS					
1 Gohmert	Y	Y	Y	Y	Y
2 Poe	Y	Y	Y	Y	Y
3 Johnson, S.	Y	Y	Y	Y	Y
4 Hall	Y	Y	Y	N	Y
5 Hensarling	Y	Y	Y	Y	Y
6 Barton	Y	N	Y	N	N
7 Culberson	N	N	N	N	N
8 Brady	N	Y	Y	N	Y
9 Green, A.	N	N	N	N	N
10 McCaul	Y	Y	Y	Y	Y
11 Conaway	Y	Y	Y	Y	Y
12 Granger	N	N	N	N	N
13 Thornberry	Y	Y	Y	Y	Y
14 Paul	?	?	?	?	?
15 Hinojosa	N	N	N	N	N
16 Reyes	N	N	N	N	N
17 Edwards	N	N	N	N	N
18 Jackson Lee	N	N	N	N	N
19 Neugebauer	Y	Y	Y	Y	Y
20 Gonzalez	N	N	N	N	N
21 Smith	N	N	N	N	N
22 Olson	Y	Y	Y	Y	Y
23 Rodriguez	N	N	N	N	N
24 Marchant	Y	Y	Y	Y	Y
25 Doggett	N	N	N	?	N
26 Burgess	Y	Y	Y	Y	Y
27 Ortiz	N	N	N	N	N
28 Cuellar	N	N	N	N	N
29 Green, G.	N	N	N	N	N
30 Johnson, E.	N	N	N	N	N
31 Carter	N	N	N	N	N
32 Sessions	Y	Y	Y	Y	Y
UTAH					
1 Bishop	?	?	?	?	?
2 Matheson	N	N	N	N	N
3 Chaffetz	Y	Y	Y	Y	N
VERMONT					
AL Welch	N	N	N	N	N
VIRGINIA					
1 Wittman	N	Y	Y	N	Y
2 Nye	Y	N	N	Y	N
3 Scott	N	N	N	N	N
4 Forbes	N	Y	Y	N	Y
5 Perriello	N	N	N	N	N
6 Goodlatte	Y	Y	Y	Y	Y
7 Cantor	N	Y	Y	Y	Y
8 Moran	N	N	N	N	N
9 Boucher	N	N	N	N	N
10 Wolf	N	N	N	N	N
11 Connolly	N	N	N	N	N
WASHINGTON					
1 Inslee	N	N	N	N	N
2 Larsen	N	N	N	N	N
3 Baird	N	N	N	N	N
4 Hastings	Y	Y	Y	Y	Y
5 McMorris Rodgers	N	Y	Y	N	Y
6 Dicks	N	N	N	N	N
7 McDermott	N	N	N	N	N
8 Reichert	N	N	N	N	N
9 Smith	N	N	N	N	N
WEST VIRGINIA					
1 Mollohan	N	N	N	N	N
2 Capito	N	N	N	N	N
3 Rahall	N	N	N	N	N
WISCONSIN					
1 Ryan	Y	Y	Y	Y	Y
2 Baldwin	N	N	N	N	N
3 Kind	Y	Y	Y	Y	Y
4 Moore	N	N	N	N	N
5 Sensenbrenner	Y	Y	Y	Y	Y
6 Petri	Y	Y	Y	Y	Y
7 Obey	N	N	N	N	N
8 Kagen	N	N	N	N	N
WYOMING					
AL Lummis	Y	+	Y	Y	Y
DELEGATES					
Faleomavaega (A.S.)	N	N	N	N	N
Norton (D.C.)	N	N	N	N	N
Bordallo (Guam)	N	N	N	N	N
Sablan (N. Marianas)	N	N	N	N	N
Pierluisi (P.R.)	N	N	N	N	N
Christensen (V.I.)	N	N	N	N	N

IN THE HOUSE | By Vote Number

633. HR 3288. Fiscal 2010 Transportation-HUD Appropriations/ **Rib Mountain.** Flake, R-Ariz., amendment that would bar the use of funds appropriated in the bill for the reconstruction of Rib Mountain in Wisconsin and cut $500,000 intended for the project from the bill. Rejected in Committee of the Whole 105-329: R 101-74; D 4-255. July 23, 2009.

634. HR 3288. Fiscal 2010 Transportation-HUD Appropriations/ **Doyle Drive Replacement Project.** Hensarling, R-Texas, amendment that would bar the use of funds appropriated in the bill for the Doyle Drive Replacement project in San Francisco and cut $2 million intended for the project from the bill. Rejected in Committee of the Whole 124-309: R 121-53; D 3-256. July 23, 2009.

635. HR 3288. Fiscal 2010 Transportation-HUD Appropriations/ **Philadelphia Museum of Art.** Hensarling, R-Texas, amendment that would bar the use of funds appropriated in the bill for the Philadelphia Museum of Art transportation improvement program and cut $750,000 intended for the project from the bill. Rejected in Committee of the Whole 109-326: R 105-70; D 4-256. July 23, 2009.

636. HR 3288. Fiscal 2010 Transportation-HUD Appropriations/ **Recommit.** Latham, R-Iowa, motion to recommit the bill to the Appropriations Committee with instructions that it be immediately reported back with language that would reduce appropriations back to the amount in the president's budget. Motion rejected 192-226: R 170-1; D 22-225. July 23, 2009.

637. HR 3288. Fiscal 2010 Transportation-HUD Appropriations/ **Passage.** Passage of the bill that would appropriate $123.1 billion in fiscal 2010, including $68.8 billion in discretionary spending, for the departments of Transportation and Housing and Urban Development and related agencies. It would provide a total of $75.8 billion for the Transportation Department, including $41.1 billion for the federal aid highway program, $16 billion for the Federal Aviation Administration, $10.5 billion for the Federal Transit Administration and $1.5 billion in grants to Amtrak. It would appropriate $47 billion for the Housing and Urban Development Department, including $18.2 billion for the Section 8 Tenant-Based Rental Assistance program. Passed 256-168: R 16-158; D 240-10. A "yea" was a vote in support of the president's position. July 23, 2009.

	633	634	635	636	637
ALABAMA					
1 **Bonner**	N	N	N	Y	N
2 Bright	Y	Y	Y	Y	Y
3 **Rogers**	N	N	N	Y	N
4 Aderholt	N	N	N	Y	N
5 Griffith	N	N	N	N	Y
6 **Bachus**	N	N	N	Y	N
7 Davis	N	N	N	N	Y
ALASKA					
AL **Young**	N	Y	N	Y	Y
ARIZONA					
1 Kirkpatrick	N	N	N	Y	Y
2 **Franks**	Y	Y	Y	Y	N
3 **Shadegg**	Y	Y	Y	Y	N
4 Pastor	N	N	N	N	Y
5 Mitchell	N	N	N	Y	Y
6 **Flake**	Y	Y	Y	Y	N
7 Grijalva	N	N	N	N	Y
8 Giffords	N	N	N	Y	Y
ARKANSAS					
1 Berry	N	N	N	?	Y
2 Snyder	N	N	N	N	Y
3 **Boozman**	Y	Y	Y	Y	N
4 Ross	N	N	N	N	Y
CALIFORNIA					
1 Thompson	N	N	N	N	Y
2 **Herger**	Y	Y	Y	Y	N
3 **Lungren**	Y	Y	Y	Y	N
4 **McClintock**	Y	Y	Y	Y	N
5 Matsui	N	N	N	N	Y
6 Woolsey	N	N	N	N	Y
7 Miller, George	N	N	N	N	Y
8 Pelosi					
9 Lee	N	N	N	N	Y
10 Vacant					
11 McNerney	N	N	N	Y	Y
12 Speier	N	N	N	N	Y
13 Stark	N	N	N	N	Y
14 Eshoo	N	N	N	N	Y
15 Honda	N	N	N	N	Y
16 Lofgren	N	N	N	N	Y
17 Farr	N	N	N	N	Y
18 Cardoza	N	N	N	N	Y
19 **Radanovich**	Y	Y	Y	Y	N
20 Costa	N	N	N	N	Y
21 **Nunes**	Y	Y	Y	Y	N
22 **McCarthy**	Y	Y	Y	Y	N
23 Capps	N	N	N	N	Y
24 **Gallegly**	N	N	N	Y	N
25 **McKeon**	N	Y	Y	Y	N
26 **Dreier**	N	N	N	Y	N
27 Sherman	N	N	N	N	Y
28 Berman	N	N	N	N	Y
29 Schiff	N	N	N	?	Y
30 Waxman	N	N	N	N	Y
31 Becerra	N	N	N	N	Y
32 Chu	N	N	N	N	Y
33 Watson	N	N	N	N	Y
34 Roybal-Allard	N	N	N	N	Y
35 Waters	N	N	N	N	Y
36 Harman	N	N	N	N	Y
37 Richardson	N	N	N	?	Y
38 Napolitano	N	N	N	N	Y
39 Sánchez, Linda	N	N	N	N	Y
40 **Royce**	Y	Y	Y	Y	N
41 **Lewis**	N	N	N	Y	N
42 **Miller, Gary**	N	N	N	Y	N
43 Baca	N	N	N	N	Y
44 **Calvert**	Y	Y	Y	Y	N
45 **Bono Mack**	Y	Y	Y	Y	N
46 **Rohrabacher**	Y	Y	Y	Y	Y
47 Sanchez, Loretta	N	N	N	N	Y
48 **Campbell**	Y	Y	Y	Y	N
49 **Issa**	Y	Y	Y	Y	N
50 **Bilbray**	Y	?	Y	Y	N
51 Filner	N	N	N	N	Y
52 **Hunter**	Y	Y	Y	Y	N
53 Davis	N	N	N	N	Y

	633	634	635	636	637
COLORADO					
1 DeGette	N	N	N	N	Y
2 Polis	N	N	N	N	Y
3 Salazar	N	N	N	N	Y
4 Markey	N	N	N	Y	Y
5 **Lamborn**	Y	Y	Y	Y	N
6 **Coffman**	Y	Y	Y	Y	N
7 Perlmutter	N	N	N	N	Y
CONNECTICUT					
1 Larson	N	N	N	N	Y
2 Courtney	N	N	N	N	Y
3 DeLauro	N	N	N	N	Y
4 Himes	N	N	N	N	Y
5 Murphy	N	N	N	N	?
DELAWARE					
AL **Castle**	N	Y	N	Y	N
FLORIDA					
1 **Miller**	Y	Y	Y	Y	N
2 Boyd	N	N	N	N	Y
3 Brown	N	N	N	N	Y
4 **Crenshaw**	N	N	N	Y	N
5 **Brown-Waite**	N	Y	N	Y	N
6 **Stearns**	Y	Y	Y	Y	N
7 **Mica**	N	Y	N	Y	N
8 Grayson	N	N	N	N	Y
9 **Bilirakis**	N	Y	Y	Y	N
10 **Young**	N	N	N	N	N
11 Castor	N	N	N	N	Y
12 **Putnam**	N	N	N	Y	N
13 **Buchanan**	N	Y	N	Y	N
14 **Mack**	Y	Y	Y	Y	N
15 **Posey**	N	N	Y	Y	N
16 **Rooney**	Y	Y	N	Y	N
17 Meek	N	N	N	N	Y
18 **Ros-Lehtinen**	N	N	N	N	Y
19 Wexler	N	N	N	N	Y
20 Wasserman Schultz	N	N	N	N	Y
21 **Diaz-Balart, L.**	N	N	N	Y	Y
22 Klein	N	N	N	N	Y
23 Hastings	N	N	N	N	Y
24 Kosmas	N	N	N	N	Y
25 **Diaz-Balart, M.**	N	N	N	Y	Y
GEORGIA					
1 **Kingston**	Y	Y	Y	Y	N
2 Bishop	N	N	N	N	Y
3 **Westmoreland**	Y	Y	Y	Y	N
4 Johnson	N	N	N	N	Y
5 Lewis	N	N	N	N	Y
6 **Price**	Y	Y	Y	Y	N
7 **Linder**	Y	Y	Y	Y	N
8 Marshall	N	N	N	Y	N
9 **Deal**	Y	Y	Y	Y	N
10 **Broun**	Y	Y	Y	Y	N
11 **Gingrey**	Y	Y	Y	Y	N
12 Barrow	N	N	N	N	Y
13 Scott	N	N	N	N	Y
HAWAII					
1 Abercrombie	N	N	N	N	?
2 Hirono	N	N	N	N	Y
IDAHO					
1 Minnick	Y	Y	Y	Y	N
2 **Simpson**	N	N	N	Y	N
ILLINOIS					
1 Rush	N	N	N	?	Y
2 Jackson	N	N	N	N	Y
3 Lipinski	N	N	N	N	Y
4 Gutierrez	N	N	N	N	Y
5 Quigley	N	N	N	N	Y
6 **Roskam**	Y	Y	Y	Y	N
7 Davis	N	N	N	N	Y
8 Bean	N	N	N	Y	Y
9 Schakowsky	N	N	N	N	Y
10 **Kirk**	Y	Y	Y	Y	N
11 Halvorson	N	N	N	N	Y
12 Costello	N	N	N	N	Y
13 **Biggert**	N	Y	N	Y	N
14 Foster	N	N	N	Y	Y
15 **Johnson**	Y	Y	Y	Y	N

KEY	Republicans	Democrats		
Y Voted for (yea)		X Paired against		C Voted "present" to avoid possible conflict of interest
# Paired for		– Announced against		
+ Announced for		P Voted "present"		? Did not vote or otherwise make a position known
N Voted against (nay)				

	633	634	635	636	637
16 Manzullo	N	N	Y	Y	N
17 Hare	N	N	N	N	Y
18 Schock	N	N	N	Y	N
19 Shimkus	Y	Y	Y	Y	N
INDIANA					
1 Visclosky	N	N	N	N	Y
2 Donnelly	N	N	N	Y	Y
3 Souder	Y	Y	N	Y	N
4 Buyer	N	N	N	Y	N
5 Burton	Y	Y	Y	Y	N
6 Pence	Y	Y	Y	Y	N
7 Carson	N	N	N	N	Y
8 Ellsworth	N	?	N	Y	Y
9 Hill	N	N	N	N	N
IOWA					
1 Braley	N	N	N	N	Y
2 Loebsack	N	N	N	N	Y
3 Boswell	N	N	N	N	Y
4 Latham	N	N	N	N	Y
5 King	Y	Y	Y	Y	N
KANSAS					
1 Moran	Y	Y	Y	Y	N
2 Jenkins	Y	Y	Y	Y	N
3 Moore	N	N	N	N	Y
4 Tiahrt	N	Y	Y	Y	N
KENTUCKY					
1 Whitfield	N	N	N	Y	N
2 Guthrie	N	N	N	Y	N
3 Yarmuth	N	N	N	N	Y
4 Davis	N	N	Y	Y	N
5 Rogers	N	N	N	Y	N
6 Chandler	N	N	N	N	Y
LOUISIANA					
1 Scalise	Y	Y	Y	Y	N
2 Cao	N	N	N	Y	N
3 Melancon	N	N	N	N	Y
4 Fleming	Y	Y	Y	Y	N
5 Alexander	N	N	N	Y	N
6 Cassidy	Y	Y	Y	Y	N
7 Boustany	Y	Y	Y	Y	N
MAINE					
1 Pingree	N	N	N	N	Y
2 Michaud	N	N	N	N	Y
MARYLAND					
1 Kratovil	N	N	N	Y	N
2 Ruppersberger	N	N	N	N	Y
3 Sarbanes	N	N	N	N	Y
4 Edwards	N	N	N	N	Y
5 Hoyer	N	N	N	N	Y
6 Bartlett	Y	Y	Y	Y	N
7 Cummings	N	N	N	N	Y
8 Van Hollen	N	N	N	N	Y
MASSACHUSETTS					
1 Olver	N	N	N	N	Y
2 Neal	N	N	N	N	Y
3 McGovern	N	N	N	N	Y
4 Frank	N	N	N	N	Y
5 Tsongas	N	N	N	N	Y
6 Tierney	N	N	N	N	Y
7 Markey	N	N	N	N	Y
8 Capuano	N	N	N	N	Y
9 Lynch	N	N	N	N	Y
10 Delahunt	N	N	N	N	Y
MICHIGAN					
1 Stupak	N	N	N	N	Y
2 Hoekstra	Y	Y	Y	Y	N
3 Ehlers	N	N	Y	Y	Y
4 Camp	N	N	N	Y	N
5 Kildee	N	N	N	N	Y
6 Upton	N	Y	N	Y	N
7 Schauer	N	N	N	N	Y
8 Rogers	Y	Y	Y	Y	N
9 Peters	N	N	N	Y	Y
10 Miller	N	N	N	Y	N
11 McCotter	Y	Y	Y	Y	N
12 Levin	N	N	N	N	Y
13 Kilpatrick	N	N	N	N	Y
14 Conyers	N	N	N	?	Y
15 Dingell	N	N	N	N	Y
MINNESOTA					
1 Walz	N	N	N	N	Y
2 Kline	Y	Y	Y	Y	N
3 Paulsen	Y	Y	Y	Y	N
4 McCollum	N	N	N	N	Y
5 Ellison	N	N	N	N	Y
6 Bachmann	Y	Y	Y	Y	N
7 Peterson	N	N	N	N	Y
8 Oberstar	N	N	N	N	Y
MISSISSIPPI					
1 Childers	N	N	N	N	Y
2 Thompson	N	N	N	N	Y
3 Harper	Y	Y	N	Y	N
4 Taylor	N	N	N	Y	N
MISSOURI					
1 Clay	N	N	N	N	Y
2 Akin	Y	Y	Y	Y	N
3 Carnahan	N	N	N	N	Y
4 Skelton	N	N	N	N	?
5 Cleaver	N	N	N	N	Y
6 Graves	Y	Y	Y	Y	N
7 Blunt	N	Y		?	?
8 Emerson	N	N	N	Y	
9 Luetkemeyer	Y	Y	Y	Y	N
MONTANA					
AL Rehberg	N	N	N	Y	N
NEBRASKA					
1 Fortenberry	N	Y	Y	Y	N
2 Terry	Y	Y	Y	Y	N
3 Smith	Y	Y	Y	Y	N
NEVADA					
1 Berkley	N	N	N	N	Y
2 Heller	Y	Y	Y	Y	N
3 Titus	N	N	N	N	Y
NEW HAMPSHIRE					
1 Shea-Porter	N	N	N	N	Y
2 Hodes	N	N	N	N	Y
NEW JERSEY					
1 Andrews	N	N	N	N	Y
2 LoBiondo	N	N	N	Y	Y
3 Adler	N	N	N	Y	Y
4 Smith	N	N	N	?	Y
5 Garrett	Y	Y	Y	Y	N
6 Pallone	N	N	N	N	Y
7 Lance	Y	Y	Y	Y	N
8 Pascrell	N	N	N	N	?
9 Rothman	N	N	N	N	Y
10 Payne	N	N	N	N	Y
11 Frelinghuysen	N	N	N	Y	N
12 Holt	N	N	N	N	Y
13 Sires	N	N	N	N	Y
NEW MEXICO					
1 Heinrich	N	N	N	N	Y
2 Teague	N	N	N	N	Y
3 Lujan	N	N	N	N	Y
NEW YORK					
1 Bishop	N	N	N	N	Y
2 Israel	N	N	N	N	Y
3 King	N	N	N	Y	N
4 McCarthy	?	?	?	?	?
5 Ackerman	N	N	N	N	Y
6 Meeks	N	N	N	N	Y
7 Crowley	N	N	N	N	Y
8 Nadler	N	N	N	N	Y
9 Weiner	N	N	N	N	Y
10 Towns	N	N	N	?	Y
11 Clarke	N	N	N	N	Y
12 Velázquez	N	N	N	N	Y
13 McMahon	N	N	N	N	Y
14 Maloney	N	N	N	N	Y
15 Rangel	N	N	N	N	Y
16 Serrano	N	N	N	N	Y
17 Engel	N	N	N	N	Y
18 Lowey	N	N	N	N	Y
19 Hall	N	N	N	N	Y
20 Murphy	N	N	N	Y	Y
21 Tonko	N	N	N	N	Y
22 Hinchey	N	N	N	N	Y
23 McHugh	N	N	N	Y	Y
24 Arcuri	N	N	N	N	Y
25 Maffei	N	N	N	N	Y
26 Lee	N	N	N	Y	N
27 Higgins	N	N	N	N	Y
28 Slaughter	N	N	N	N	Y
29 Massa	N	N	N	N	Y
NORTH CAROLINA					
1 Butterfield	N	N	N	N	Y
2 Etheridge	N	N	N	N	Y
3 Jones	N	Y	N	Y	N
4 Price	N	N	N	N	Y
5 Foxx	Y	Y	Y	Y	N
6 Coble	N	Y	Y	Y	Y
7 McIntyre	N	N	N	N	Y
8 Kissell	N	N	N	N	Y
9 Myrick	Y	Y	Y	Y	N
10 McHenry	Y	Y	Y	Y	N
11 Shuler	N	N	N	Y	Y
12 Watt	N	N	N	N	Y
13 Miller	N	N	N	N	Y
NORTH DAKOTA					
AL Pomeroy	N	N	N	N	Y
OHIO					
1 Driehaus	N	N	N	N	N
2 Schmidt	Y	Y	Y	Y	N
3 Turner	N	N	N	Y	Y
4 Jordan	Y	Y	Y	Y	N
5 Latta	Y	Y	Y	Y	N
6 Wilson	N	N	N	N	Y
7 Austria	Y	Y	N	Y	N
8 Boehner	Y	Y	Y	Y	N
9 Kaptur	N	N	N	?	Y
10 Kucinich	N	N	N	N	Y
11 Fudge	N	N	N	N	Y
12 Tiberi	Y	Y	Y	Y	N
13 Sutton	N	N	N	N	Y
14 LaTourette	N	Y	Y	Y	Y
15 Kilroy	N	N	N	N	Y
16 Boccieri	N	N	N	N	Y
17 Ryan	N	N	N	N	Y
18 Space	N	N	N	N	Y
OKLAHOMA					
1 Sullivan	Y	Y	Y	Y	N
2 Boren	N	N	N	Y	N
3 Lucas	N	N	N	Y	N
4 Cole	N	N	N	Y	N
5 Fallin	Y	Y	Y	Y	N
OREGON					
1 Wu	N	N	N	N	Y
2 Walden	Y	Y	Y	Y	N
3 Blumenauer	N	N	N	N	Y
4 DeFazio	N	N	N	N	Y
5 Schrader	N	N	N	N	Y
PENNSYLVANIA					
1 Brady	N	N	N	N	Y
2 Fattah	N	N	N	N	Y
3 Dahlkemper	N	N	N	Y	N
4 Altmire	N	N	N	N	Y
5 Thompson	N	N	N	Y	N
6 Gerlach	N	Y	N	Y	N
7 Sestak	N	N	N	N	Y
8 Murphy, P.	N	N	N	N	Y
9 Shuster	N	N	N	Y	N
10 Carney	N	N	N	N	Y
11 Kanjorski	N	N	N	N	Y
12 Murtha	N	N	N	N	Y
13 Schwartz	N	N	N	N	Y
14 Doyle	N	N	N	N	Y
15 Dent	N	Y	N	Y	N
16 Pitts	Y	Y	Y	Y	N
17 Holden	N	N	N	N	Y
18 Murphy, T.	N	N	N	Y	Y
19 Platts	N	Y	N	?	N
RHODE ISLAND					
1 Kennedy	N	N	N	N	Y
2 Langevin	N	N	N	N	Y
SOUTH CAROLINA					
1 Brown	N	N	N	Y	N
2 Wilson	Y	Y	Y	Y	N
3 Barrett	?	?	?	?	?
4 Inglis	Y	Y	Y	Y	N
5 Spratt	N	N	N	N	Y
6 Clyburn	N	N	N	N	Y
SOUTH DAKOTA					
AL Herseth Sandlin	N	N	N	N	Y
TENNESSEE					
1 Roe	Y	Y	Y	Y	N
2 Duncan	Y	Y	Y	?	N
3 Wamp	Y	Y	Y	Y	N
4 Davis	N	N	N	N	Y
5 Cooper	N	N	N	N	Y
6 Gordon	N	N	N	N	Y
7 Blackburn	Y	Y	Y	Y	N
8 Tanner	N	N	N	N	Y
9 Cohen	N	N	N	N	Y
TEXAS					
1 Gohmert	N	N	N	Y	N
2 Poe	Y	N	N	Y	N
3 Johnson, S.	Y	Y	Y	Y	N
4 Hall	N	N	Y	Y	N
5 Hensarling	Y	Y	Y	Y	N
6 Barton	N	Y	Y	Y	N
7 Culberson	N	N	N	Y	N
8 Brady	Y	Y	N	Y	N
9 Green, A.	N	N	N	N	Y
10 McCaul	Y	Y	Y	Y	N
11 Conaway	Y	Y	Y	Y	N
12 Granger	N	Y	N	Y	N
13 Thornberry	Y	Y	Y	Y	N
14 Paul	?	?	?	?	?
15 Hinojosa	N	N	N	N	Y
16 Reyes	N	N	N	N	Y
17 Edwards	N	N	N	N	Y
18 Jackson Lee	N	N	N	N	Y
19 Neugebauer	Y	Y	Y	Y	N
20 Gonzalez	N	N	N	N	Y
21 Smith	N	N	N	Y	N
22 Olson	Y	Y	Y	Y	N
23 Rodriguez	N	N	N	N	Y
24 Marchant	Y	Y	Y	Y	N
25 Doggett	N	N	N	N	Y
26 Burgess	Y	Y	Y	Y	N
27 Ortiz	N	N	N	N	Y
28 Cuellar	N	N	N	N	Y
29 Green, G.	N	N	N	N	Y
30 Johnson, E.	N	N	N	N	Y
31 Carter	N	Y	N	Y	N
32 Sessions	Y	Y	Y	Y	N
UTAH					
1 Bishop	?	?	?	?	?
2 Matheson	N	N	N	N	Y
3 Chaffetz	Y	Y	Y	Y	N
VERMONT					
AL Welch	N	N	N	N	Y
VIRGINIA					
1 Wittman	Y	Y	Y	Y	N
2 Nye	N	N	N	N	Y
3 Scott	N	N	N	N	Y
4 Forbes	N	Y	Y	Y	N
5 Perriello	N	N	N	N	Y
6 Goodlatte	Y	Y	Y	Y	N
7 Cantor	Y	Y	Y	Y	N
8 Moran	N	N	N	N	Y
9 Boucher	N	N	N	N	Y
10 Wolf	N	N	N	Y	Y
11 Connolly	N	N	N	N	Y
WASHINGTON					
1 Inslee	N	N	N	N	Y
2 Larsen	N	N	N	N	Y
3 Baird	N	N	N	N	Y
4 Hastings	N	Y	N	Y	N
5 McMorris Rodgers	Y	Y	Y	Y	N
6 Dicks	N	N	N	N	Y
7 McDermott	N	N	N	N	Y
8 Reichert	N	N	N	N	Y
9 Smith	N	N	N	N	Y
WEST VIRGINIA					
1 Mollohan	N	N	N	N	Y
2 Capito	N	N	N	Y	N
3 Rahall	N	N	N	N	Y
WISCONSIN					
1 Ryan	Y	Y	Y	Y	N
2 Baldwin	N	N	N	N	Y
3 Kind	Y	N	N	N	N
4 Moore	N	N	N	N	Y
5 Sensenbrenner	Y	Y	Y	Y	N
6 Petri	Y	Y	Y	Y	Y
7 Obey	N	N	N	N	Y
8 Kagen	N	N	N	N	Y
WYOMING					
AL **Lummis**	Y	Y	Y	Y	N
DELEGATES					
Faleomavaega (A.S.)	N	N			
Norton (D.C.)	N	N			
Bordallo (Guam)	N	N			
Sablan (N. Marianas)	?	N	N		
Pierluisi (P.R.)	N	N			
Christensen (V.I.)	N	N			

IN THE HOUSE | By Vote Number

638. Firearms in Federally Assisted Housing/Motion to Table. Hastings, D-Fla., motion to table (kill) the Price, R-Ga., appeal of the ruling of the chair that the Price draft resolution does not constitute a point of privilege under Rule IX of the House. The draft resolution would require the rule (H Res 669) for House floor consideration of the fiscal 2010 Transportation-HUD appropriations bill to allow an amendment that would bar the use of funds in the bill to restrict lawful possession or use of firearms in federally assisted housing. Motion agreed to 238-182: R 1-171; D 237-11. July 24, 2009.

639. HR 3293. Fiscal 2010 Labor-HHS-Education Appropriations/ Previous Question. Hastings, D-Fla., motion to order the previous question (thus ending debate and possibility of amendment) on adoption of the rule (H Res 673) that would provide for House floor consideration of the bill that would appropriate $730.5 billion in fiscal 2010 for the departments of Labor, Health and Human Services, and Education as well as related agencies. Motion agreed to 239-181: R 1-170; D 238-11. July 24, 2009.

640. HR 3293. Fiscal 2010 Labor-HHS-Education Appropriations/ Rule. Adoption of the rule (H Res 673) to provide for House floor consideration of the bill that would appropriate $730.5 billion in fiscal 2010 for the departments of Labor, Health and Human Services, and Education as well as related agencies. Adopted 232-187: R 0-172; D 232-15. July 24, 2009.

641. HR 3293. Fiscal 2010 Labor-HHS-Education Appropriations/ Manager's Amendment. Obey, D-Wis., amendment that would make increases and decreases to a number of programs funded in the bill. It would bar the use of funds in the bill to purchase lights bulbs that are not Energy Star qualified or do not have the Federal Energy Management Program designation. It also would bar the use of funds for first-class travel by federal employees. Adopted in Committee of the Whole 284-137: R 32-137; D 252-0. July 24, 2009.

642. HR 3293. Fiscal 2010 Labor-HHS-Education Appropriations/ Hypodermic Needles. Souder, R-Ind., amendment that would bar the use of funds in the bill to provide individuals with hypodermic needles or syringes. Rejected in Committee of the Whole 211-218: R 165-6; D 46-212. July 24, 2009.

643. HR 3293. Fiscal 2010 Labor-HHS-Education Appropriations/ Planned Parenthood. Pence, R-Ind., amendment that would bar funds from being available for Planned Parenthood for voluntary family planning. Rejected in Committee of the Whole 183-247: R 163-9; D 20-238. July 24, 2009.

644. HR 3293 Fiscal 2010 Labor-HHS-Education Appropriations/ Funding Reduction. Wittman, R-Va., amendment that would reduce funding in the bill by $803.3 million. Rejected in Committee of the Whole 199-229: R 167-4; D 32-225. July 24, 2009.

	638	639	640	641	642	643	644
ALABAMA							
1 Bonner	N	N	N	N	Y	Y	Y
2 Bright	N	Y	N	Y	Y	Y	Y
3 Rogers	N	N	N	N	Y	Y	Y
4 Aderholt	N	N	N	N	Y	Y	Y
5 Griffith	Y	Y	Y	Y	Y	Y	Y
6 Bachus	N	N	N	N	Y	Y	Y
7 Davis	Y	Y	Y	Y	N	N	N
ALASKA							
AL Young	N	N	N	N	Y	Y	Y
ARIZONA							
1 Kirkpatrick	Y	Y	Y	Y	N	N	Y
2 Franks	N	N	N	N	Y	Y	Y
3 Shadegg	N	N	N	N	Y	Y	Y
4 Pastor	Y	Y	Y	Y	N	N	N
5 Mitchell	Y	N	N	Y	Y	N	Y
6 Flake	N	N	N	N	Y	Y	Y
7 Grijalva	Y	Y	Y	Y	N	N	N
8 Giffords	Y	Y	Y	Y	N	N	Y
ARKANSAS							
1 Berry	Y	Y	Y	Y	N	N	N
2 Snyder	Y	Y	Y	Y	N	N	N
3 Boozman	N	N	N	N	Y	Y	Y
4 Ross	Y	Y	Y	Y	N	N	N
CALIFORNIA							
1 Thompson	Y	Y	Y	Y	N	N	N
2 Herger	N	N	N	N	Y	Y	Y
3 Lungren	N	N	N	N	Y	Y	Y
4 McClintock	N	N	N	N	Y	Y	Y
5 Matsui	Y	Y	Y	Y	N	N	N
6 Woolsey	Y	Y	Y	Y	N	N	N
7 Miller, George	Y	Y	Y	?	N	N	N
8 Pelosi							
9 Lee	Y	Y	Y	Y	N	N	N
10 Vacant							
11 McNerney	N	Y	Y	Y	N	N	N
12 Speier	Y	Y	Y	Y	N	N	N
13 Stark	Y	Y	?	Y	N	N	N
14 Eshoo	Y	Y	Y	Y	N	N	N
15 Honda	Y	Y	Y	Y	N	N	N
16 Lofgren	Y	?	Y	Y	N	N	N
17 Farr	Y	Y	Y	Y	N	N	N
18 Cardoza	Y	Y	Y	Y	N	N	N
19 Radanovich	N	N	N	N	Y	Y	Y
20 Costa	Y	Y	Y	Y	N	N	N
21 Nunes	N	N	N	N	Y	Y	Y
22 McCarthy	N	N	N	N	Y	Y	Y
23 Capps	Y	Y	Y	Y	N	N	N
24 Gallegly	N	N	N	N	Y	Y	Y
25 McKeon	N	N	N	N	Y	Y	Y
26 Dreier	N	N	N	N	Y	Y	Y
27 Sherman	Y	Y	Y	Y	N	N	N
28 Berman	Y	Y	Y	Y	N	N	N
29 Schiff	Y	Y	Y	Y	N	N	N
30 Waxman	Y	Y	Y	Y	N	N	N
31 Becerra	Y	Y	Y	Y	N	N	N
32 Chu	Y	Y	Y	Y	N	N	N
33 Watson	Y	Y	Y	Y	N	N	N
34 Roybal-Allard	Y	Y	Y	Y	N	N	N
35 Waters	Y	Y	Y	Y	N	N	N
36 Harman	Y	Y	Y	Y	N	N	N
37 Richardson	Y	Y	Y	Y	N	N	N
38 Napolitano	Y	Y	Y	Y	N	N	N
39 Sánchez, Linda	Y	Y	Y	Y	N	N	N
40 Royce	N	N	N	Y	Y	Y	Y
41 Lewis	N	N	N	N	Y	Y	Y
42 Miller, Gary	N	N	N	N	Y	Y	Y
43 Baca	Y	Y	Y	Y	N	N	N
44 Calvert	N	N	N	N	Y	Y	Y
45 Bono Mack	N	N	N	N	Y	Y	Y
46 Rohrabacher	N	N	N	N	Y	Y	Y
47 Sanchez, Loretta	Y	Y	Y	Y	N	N	N
48 Campbell	N	N	N	N	Y	Y	Y
49 Issa	N	N	N	N	Y	Y	Y
50 Bilbray	N	N	N	N	Y	Y	Y
51 Filner	Y	Y	Y	Y	N	N	N
52 Hunter	N	N	N	N	Y	Y	Y
53 Davis	Y	Y	Y	Y	N	N	N

	638	639	640	641	642	643	644
COLORADO							
1 DeGette	Y	Y	Y	Y	N	N	N
2 Polis	Y	Y	Y	Y	N	N	N
3 Salazar	Y	Y	Y	Y	N	N	N
4 Markey	Y	Y	Y	Y	N	N	N
5 Lamborn	N	N	N	N	Y	Y	Y
6 Coffman	N	N	N	N	Y	Y	Y
7 Perlmutter	Y	Y	Y	Y	N	N	N
CONNECTICUT							
1 Larson	Y	Y	Y	Y	N	N	N
2 Courtney	Y	Y	Y	Y	N	N	N
3 DeLauro	Y	Y	Y	Y	N	N	N
4 Himes	Y	Y	Y	Y	N	N	N
5 Murphy	Y	Y	Y	Y	N	N	N
DELAWARE							
AL Castle	N	N	N	Y	N	N	Y
FLORIDA							
1 Miller	N	N	N	N	Y	Y	Y
2 Boyd	Y	Y	Y	Y	Y	N	N
3 Brown	Y	Y	Y	Y	N	N	N
4 Crenshaw	N	N	N	N	Y	Y	Y
5 Brown-Waite	N	N	N	N	Y	Y	Y
6 Stearns	N	N	N	N	Y	Y	Y
7 Mica	N	N	N	N	Y	Y	Y
8 Grayson	Y	Y	Y	Y	N	N	N
9 Bilirakis	N	N	N	N	Y	Y	Y
10 Young	?	?	?	N	Y	Y	Y
11 Castor	Y	Y	Y	Y	N	N	N
12 Putnam	N	N	N	N	Y	Y	Y
13 Buchanan	N	N	N	N	Y	Y	Y
14 Mack	N	N	N	N	Y	Y	Y
15 Posey	N	N	N	N	Y	Y	Y
16 Rooney	N	N	N	N	Y	Y	Y
17 Meek	Y	Y	Y	Y	N	N	N
18 Ros-Lehtinen	N	N	N	N	Y	Y	Y
19 Wexler	Y	Y	Y	Y	N	N	?
20 Wasserman Schultz	Y	Y	Y	Y	N	N	N
21 Diaz-Balart, L.	N	N	N	N	Y	Y	Y
22 Klein	Y	Y	Y	Y	N	N	N
23 Hastings	Y	Y	Y	Y	N	N	N
24 Kosmas	N	Y	Y	Y	N	N	Y
25 Diaz-Balart, M.	N	N	N	N	Y	Y	Y
GEORGIA							
1 Kingston	N	N	?	Y	Y	Y	Y
2 Bishop	Y	Y	Y	Y	N	N	N
3 Westmoreland	N	N	N	N	Y	Y	Y
4 Johnson	?	?	Y	Y	N	N	N
5 Lewis	Y	Y	Y	Y	N	N	N
6 Price	N	N	N	N	Y	Y	Y
7 Linder	N	N	N	N	Y	Y	Y
8 Marshall	Y	Y	Y	Y	Y	Y	Y
9 Deal	N	N	N	N	Y	Y	Y
10 Broun	N	N	N	N	Y	Y	Y
11 Gingrey	N	N	N	N	Y	Y	Y
12 Barrow	Y	Y	Y	Y	Y	N	N
13 Scott	Y	Y	Y	Y	N	N	N
HAWAII							
1 Abercrombie	Y	Y	Y	Y	N	N	N
2 Hirono	Y	Y	Y	Y	N	N	N
IDAHO							
1 Minnick	N	N	N	Y	N	N	Y
2 Simpson	Y	N	N	N	Y	Y	Y
ILLINOIS							
1 Rush	Y	Y	Y	Y	N	N	N
2 Jackson	Y	Y	Y	Y	N	N	N
3 Lipinski	Y	Y	Y	Y	Y	Y	N
4 Gutierrez	Y	Y	Y	Y	N	N	N
5 Quigley	Y	Y	Y	Y	N	N	N
6 Roskam	N	N	N	N	Y	Y	Y
7 Davis	?	Y	Y	Y	N	N	N
8 Bean	Y	Y	Y	Y	N	N	Y
9 Schakowsky	Y	Y	Y	Y	N	N	N
10 Kirk	N	N	N	Y	Y	Y	Y
11 Halvorson	Y	Y	Y	Y	N	N	N
12 Costello	Y	Y	Y	Y	Y	Y	N
13 Biggert	N	N	N	Y	Y	N	Y
14 Foster	Y	Y	Y	Y	N	N	N
15 Johnson	N	N	N	N	Y	Y	Y

KEY   **Republicans**   Democrats

Y Voted for (yea)	X Paired against	C Voted "present" to avoid possible conflict of interest
# Paired for	– Announced against	
+ Announced for	P Voted "present"	? Did not vote or otherwise make a position known
N Voted against (nay)		

	638	639	640	641	642	643	644
16 **Manzullo**	N	N	N	N	?	Y	Y
17 Hare	Y	Y	Y	Y	N	N	N
18 **Schock**	N	N	N	Y	Y	Y	Y
19 **Shimkus**	N	N	N	N	Y	Y	Y
INDIANA							
1 Visclosky	Y	Y	Y	Y	N	N	N
2 Donnelly	Y	Y	Y	Y	Y	Y	Y
3 **Souder**	N	N	N	N	Y	Y	Y
4 **Buyer**	N	N	N	Y	Y	Y	Y
5 **Burton**	N	N	N	N	Y	Y	Y
6 **Pence**	N	N	N	N	Y	Y	+
7 Carson	Y	Y	Y	Y	N	N	N
8 Ellsworth	Y	N	N	Y	Y	Y	Y
9 Hill	N	N	N	Y	Y	N	Y
IOWA							
1 Braley	Y	Y	Y	Y	N	N	N
2 Loebsack	Y	Y	Y	Y	N	N	N
3 Boswell	Y	Y	Y	Y	Y	N	N
4 **Latham**	N	N	N	?	Y	Y	Y
5 **King**	N	N	N	N	Y	Y	Y
KANSAS							
1 **Moran**	N	N	N	N	Y	Y	Y
2 **Jenkins**	N	N	N	Y	Y	N	Y
3 Moore	Y	Y	Y	Y	N	N	N
4 **Tiahrt**	N	N	N	N	Y	Y	Y
KENTUCKY							
1 **Whitfield**	N	N	N	N	Y	Y	Y
2 **Guthrie**	N	N	N	N	Y	Y	Y
3 Yarmuth	Y	Y	Y	Y	N	N	N
4 **Davis**	N	N	N	N	Y	Y	Y
5 **Rogers**	N	N	N	N	Y	Y	Y
6 Chandler	Y	Y	Y	Y	Y	N	N
LOUISIANA							
1 **Scalise**	N	N	N	N	Y	Y	Y
2 **Cao**	N	N	N	Y	Y	Y	Y
3 Melancon	Y	N	N	Y	Y	Y	N
4 **Fleming**	N	N	N	N	Y	Y	Y
5 **Alexander**	N	N	N	N	Y	Y	Y
6 **Cassidy**	N	N	N	N	Y	Y	Y
7 **Boustany**	N	N	N	N	Y	Y	Y
MAINE							
1 Pingree	Y	Y	Y	Y	N	N	N
2 Michaud	Y	Y	Y	Y	N	N	N
MARYLAND							
1 Kratovil	N	N	N	Y	N	N	Y
2 Ruppersberger	Y	Y	Y	Y	N	N	N
3 Sarbanes	Y	Y	Y	Y	N	N	N
4 Edwards	Y	Y	Y	Y	N	N	N
5 Hoyer	Y	Y	Y	Y	N	N	N
6 **Bartlett**	N	N	N	N	Y	Y	Y
7 Cummings	Y	Y	Y	Y	N	N	N
8 Van Hollen	Y	Y	Y	Y	N	N	N
MASSACHUSETTS							
1 Olver	Y	Y	Y	Y	N	N	N
2 Neal	Y	Y	Y	Y	N	N	N
3 McGovern	?	Y	Y	Y	N	N	N
4 Frank	Y	Y	Y	Y	N	N	N
5 Tsongas	Y	Y	?	Y	N	N	N
6 Tierney	Y	Y	Y	Y	N	N	N
7 Markey	Y	Y	Y	Y	N	N	N
8 Capuano	Y	Y	Y	Y	N	N	N
9 Lynch	Y	Y	Y	Y	N	N	N
10 Delahunt	Y	Y	Y	Y	N	N	N
MICHIGAN							
1 Stupak	Y	Y	Y	Y	N	N	N
2 **Hoekstra**	N	Y	N	N	Y	Y	Y
3 **Ehlers**	N	N	N	Y	N	Y	Y
4 **Camp**	N	N	N	Y	Y	Y	Y
5 Kildee	Y	Y	Y	Y	N	N	N
6 **Upton**	N	N	N	Y	Y	N	Y
7 Schauer	Y	Y	Y	Y	N	N	N
8 **Rogers**	N	N	N	Y	Y	Y	Y
9 Peters	Y	Y	Y	Y	N	N	Y
10 **Miller**	N	N	N	Y	Y	Y	Y
11 **McCotter**	N	N	N	Y	Y	Y	Y
12 Levin	Y	Y	Y	Y	N	N	N
13 Kilpatrick	Y	Y	Y	Y	N	N	N
14 Conyers	Y	Y	Y	?	N	N	N
15 Dingell	Y	Y	Y	Y	N	N	N
MINNESOTA							
1 Walz	Y	Y	Y	Y	N	N	N
2 **Kline**	N	N	N	N	Y	Y	Y
3 **Paulsen**	N	N	N	Y	Y	Y	Y
4 McCollum	Y	Y	Y	Y	N	N	N
5 Ellison	Y	Y	Y	Y	N	N	N
6 **Bachmann**	N	N	N	N	Y	Y	Y
7 Peterson	Y	Y	Y	Y	Y	Y	N
8 Oberstar	Y	Y	Y	Y	N	N	N
MISSISSIPPI							
1 Childers	N	N	N	Y	Y	Y	Y
2 Thompson	Y	Y	Y	Y	N	N	N
3 **Harper**	N	N	N	N	Y	Y	Y
4 Taylor	N	Y	Y	Y	Y	Y	Y
MISSOURI							
1 Clay	Y	Y	Y	Y	N	N	N
2 **Akin**	N	N	N	N	Y	Y	Y
3 Carnahan	Y	Y	Y	Y	N	N	N
4 Skelton	Y	Y	Y	Y	Y	Y	N
5 Cleaver	Y	Y	Y	Y	N	N	N
6 **Graves**	N	N	N	N	Y	Y	Y
7 **Blunt**	N	N	N	N	Y	Y	Y
8 **Emerson**	N	N	N	?	N	Y	N
9 **Luetkemeyer**	N	N	N	N	Y	Y	Y
MONTANA							
AL **Rehberg**	N	N	N	N	Y	Y	Y
NEBRASKA							
1 **Fortenberry**	N	N	N	N	Y	Y	Y
2 **Terry**	N	N	N	Y	Y	Y	Y
3 **Smith**	N	N	N	N	Y	Y	Y
NEVADA							
1 Berkley	Y	Y	Y	Y	N	N	N
2 **Heller**	N	N	N	N	Y	Y	Y
3 Titus	Y	Y	Y	Y	N	N	Y
NEW HAMPSHIRE							
1 Shea-Porter	Y	Y	Y	Y	N	N	N
2 Hodes	Y	Y	Y	Y	N	N	N
NEW JERSEY							
1 Andrews	Y	Y	Y	Y	N	N	N
2 **LoBiondo**	N	N	N	Y	Y	Y	Y
3 Adler	Y	Y	Y	Y	N	N	Y
4 **Smith**	N	N	N	Y	Y	Y	Y
5 **Garrett**	N	N	N	Y	Y	Y	Y
6 Pallone	Y	Y	Y	Y	N	N	N
7 **Lance**	N	N	N	Y	Y	N	Y
8 Pascrell	Y	Y	Y	Y	N	N	N
9 Rothman	Y	Y	Y	Y	N	N	N
10 Payne	Y	Y	Y	Y	N	N	Y
11 **Frelinghuysen**	N	N	N	N	Y	N	Y
12 Holt	Y	Y	Y	Y	N	N	N
13 Sires	Y	Y	Y	?	N	N	N
NEW MEXICO							
1 Heinrich	Y	Y	Y	Y	N	N	Y
2 Teague	Y	Y	Y	Y	Y	N	Y
3 Lujan	Y	Y	Y	Y	N	N	N
NEW YORK							
1 Bishop	Y	N	N	Y	N	N	N
2 Israel	Y	Y	Y	Y	N	N	N
3 **King**	N	N	N	N	Y	Y	Y
4 McCarthy	+	+	+	+	–	–	–
5 Ackerman	Y	Y	Y	Y	N	N	N
6 Meeks	Y	Y	Y	Y	N	N	N
7 Crowley	Y	Y	Y	Y	N	N	N
8 Nadler	Y	Y	Y	Y	N	N	N
9 Weiner	Y	Y	Y	Y	N	N	N
10 Towns	Y	Y	Y	Y	N	N	N
11 Clarke	Y	Y	Y	?	N	N	N
12 Velázquez	Y	?	Y	Y	N	N	N
13 McMahon	Y	Y	Y	Y	Y	N	N
14 Maloney	Y	Y	Y	Y	N	N	N
15 Rangel	Y	Y	?	Y	N	?	?
16 Serrano	Y	Y	Y	Y	N	N	N
17 Engel	Y	Y	Y	Y	N	N	N
18 Lowey	Y	Y	Y	Y	N	N	N
19 Hall	Y	Y	Y	Y	Y	N	N
20 Murphy	?	?	?	Y	Y	N	Y
21 Tonko	Y	Y	Y	Y	N	N	N
22 Hinchey	Y	Y	Y	Y	N	N	N
23 **McHugh**	N	?	?	?	?	?	?
24 Arcuri	Y	Y	Y	Y	N	N	Y
25 Maffei	Y	Y	Y	Y	N	N	N
26 **Lee**	N	N	N	N	Y	Y	Y
27 Higgins	Y	Y	Y	Y	N	N	N
28 Slaughter	Y	Y	Y	Y	N	N	N
29 Massa	Y	Y	Y	Y	N	N	N
NORTH CAROLINA							
1 Butterfield	Y	Y	Y	Y	N	N	N
2 Etheridge	Y	Y	Y	Y	Y	N	N
3 **Jones**	N	N	N	N	Y	Y	Y
4 Price	Y	Y	Y	Y	N	N	N
5 **Foxx**	N	N	N	N	Y	Y	Y
6 **Coble**	N	N	N	N	Y	Y	Y
7 McIntyre	Y	Y	Y	Y	Y	Y	N
8 Kissell	Y	Y	Y	Y	N	N	N
9 **Myrick**	N	N	N	N	Y	Y	Y
10 **McHenry**	N	?	N	N	Y	Y	Y
11 Shuler	N	N	N	Y	Y	Y	N
12 Watt	Y	Y	Y	Y	N	N	N
13 Miller	Y	Y	Y	Y	N	N	N
NORTH DAKOTA							
AL Pomeroy	Y	Y	Y	Y	Y	N	N
OHIO							
1 Driehaus	Y	Y	N	Y	N	N	Y
2 **Schmidt**	N	N	N	N	Y	Y	Y
3 **Turner**	N	N	N	N	Y	Y	N
4 **Jordan**	N	N	N	N	Y	Y	Y
5 **Latta**	N	N	N	N	Y	Y	Y
6 Wilson	Y	Y	Y	Y	Y	Y	N
7 **Austria**	N	N	N	N	Y	Y	Y
8 **Boehner**	N	N	N	?	?	?	?
9 Kaptur	Y	Y	Y	Y	N	N	N
10 Kucinich	Y	Y	Y	Y	N	N	N
11 Fudge	Y	Y	Y	Y	N	N	N
12 **Tiberi**	N	N	N	N	Y	Y	Y
13 Sutton	?	Y	Y	Y	N	N	N
14 **LaTourette**	N	N	N	N	N	Y	Y
15 Kilroy	Y	Y	Y	Y	N	N	N
16 Boccieri	Y	Y	N	Y	N	N	N
17 Ryan	Y	Y	Y	Y	N	N	N
18 Space	Y	Y	Y	Y	N	N	N
OKLAHOMA							
1 **Sullivan**	N	N	N	N	Y	Y	Y
2 Boren	N	Y	Y	Y	Y	Y	N
3 **Lucas**	N	N	N	N	Y	Y	Y
4 **Cole**	N	N	N	Y	Y	Y	Y
5 **Fallin**	N	N	N	N	Y	Y	Y
OREGON							
1 Wu	Y	Y	Y	Y	N	N	N
2 **Walden**	N	N	N	N	Y	N	Y
3 Blumenauer	Y	Y	Y	Y	N	N	N
4 DeFazio	Y	Y	Y	Y	N	N	N
5 Schrader	Y	Y	Y	Y	N	N	N
PENNSYLVANIA							
1 Brady	Y	Y	Y	Y	N	N	N
2 Fattah	Y	Y	Y	Y	N	N	N
3 Dahlkemper	?	?	?	?	?	?	?
4 Altmire	Y	Y	Y	Y	N	N	Y
5 **Thompson**	N	N	N	N	Y	Y	Y
6 **Gerlach**	N	N	N	Y	Y	Y	Y
7 Sestak	Y	Y	Y	Y	N	N	N
8 Murphy, P.	Y	Y	Y	Y	N	N	Y
9 **Shuster**	N	N	N	N	Y	Y	Y
10 Carney	Y	Y	Y	Y	Y	N	N
11 Kanjorski	Y	Y	Y	Y	N	N	N
12 Murtha	Y	Y	Y	Y	N	N	N
13 Schwartz	Y	Y	Y	Y	N	N	N
14 Doyle	Y	Y	Y	Y	N	N	N
15 **Dent**	N	N	N	Y	Y	N	Y
16 **Pitts**	N	N	N	N	Y	Y	Y
17 Holden	Y	Y	Y	Y	Y	N	N
18 **Murphy, T.**	N	N	N	Y	Y	Y	N
19 **Platts**	N	N	N	Y	Y	Y	Y
RHODE ISLAND							
1 Kennedy	Y	Y	Y	Y	N	N	N
2 Langevin	Y	Y	Y	Y	N	N	N
SOUTH CAROLINA							
1 **Brown**	N	N	N	N	Y	Y	Y
2 **Wilson**	N	N	N	N	Y	Y	Y
3 **Barrett**	?	?	?	?	?	?	?
4 **Inglis**	N	N	N	Y	Y	Y	Y
5 Spratt	Y	Y	Y	Y	Y	N	N
6 Clyburn	Y	Y	?	Y	N	N	N
SOUTH DAKOTA							
AL Herseth Sandlin	Y	Y	N	Y	Y	N	N
TENNESSEE							
1 **Roe**	N	N	N	N	Y	Y	Y
2 **Duncan**	N	N	N	N	Y	Y	Y
3 **Wamp**	N	N	N	N	Y	Y	Y
4 Davis	Y	Y	Y	Y	Y	Y	N
5 Cooper	Y	Y	Y	Y	N	N	Y
6 Gordon	Y	Y	Y	Y	N	N	N
7 **Blackburn**	N	N	N	N	Y	Y	Y
8 Tanner	Y	Y	Y	?	N	N	N
9 Cohen	Y	Y	Y	Y	N	N	N
TEXAS							
1 **Gohmert**	N	N	N	N	Y	Y	Y
2 **Poe**	N	N	N	N	Y	Y	Y
3 **Johnson, S.**	N	N	N	N	Y	Y	Y
4 **Hall**	N	N	N	N	Y	Y	Y
5 **Hensarling**	N	N	N	N	Y	Y	Y
6 **Barton**	N	N	N	N	Y	Y	Y
7 **Culberson**	N	N	N	N	Y	Y	Y
8 **Brady**	N	N	N	N	Y	Y	Y
9 Green, A.	Y	Y	Y	Y	N	N	N
10 **McCaul**	N	N	N	N	Y	Y	Y
11 **Conaway**	N	N	N	N	Y	Y	Y
12 **Granger**	?	?	?	Y	Y	Y	Y
13 **Thornberry**	N	N	N	N	Y	Y	Y
14 **Paul**	?	?	?	?	?	?	?
15 Hinojosa	Y	Y	Y	Y	N	N	N
16 Reyes	Y	Y	Y	Y	N	N	N
17 Edwards	Y	Y	Y	Y	Y	N	N
18 Jackson Lee	Y	Y	Y	Y	N	N	N
19 **Neugebauer**	N	N	N	N	Y	Y	Y
20 Gonzalez	Y	Y	Y	Y	N	N	N
21 **Smith**	N	N	N	N	Y	Y	Y
22 **Olson**	N	N	N	N	Y	Y	Y
23 Rodriguez	Y	Y	Y	Y	Y	N	N
24 **Marchant**	N	N	N	N	Y	Y	Y
25 Doggett	Y	Y	Y	Y	N	N	N
26 **Burgess**	N	N	N	Y	Y	Y	Y
27 Ortiz	Y	Y	Y	Y	N	N	N
28 Cuellar	Y	Y	Y	Y	Y	N	N
29 Green, G.	Y	Y	Y	Y	Y	N	N
30 Johnson, E.	Y	Y	Y	Y	N	N	N
31 **Carter**	N	N	N	N	Y	Y	Y
32 **Sessions**	N	N	N	N	Y	Y	Y
UTAH							
1 **Bishop**	?	?	?	?	?	?	?
2 Matheson	Y	Y	Y	Y	N	N	Y
3 **Chaffetz**	N	N	N	N	Y	Y	Y
VERMONT							
AL Welch	Y	Y	Y	Y	N	N	N
VIRGINIA							
1 **Wittman**	N	N	N	N	Y	Y	Y
2 Nye	N	N	N	Y	Y	N	Y
3 Scott	Y	Y	Y	Y	N	N	N
4 **Forbes**	N	N	N	Y	Y	Y	Y
5 Perriello	Y	N	N	Y	N	N	Y
6 **Goodlatte**	N	N	N	N	Y	Y	Y
7 **Cantor**	N	N	N	N	Y	Y	Y
8 Moran	Y	Y	Y	Y	N	N	N
9 Boucher	Y	Y	Y	Y	Y	N	N
10 **Wolf**	N	N	N	N	Y	Y	Y
11 Connolly	Y	Y	Y	Y	N	N	N
WASHINGTON							
1 Inslee	Y	Y	Y	Y	N	N	N
2 Larsen	Y	Y	Y	Y	N	N	N
3 Baird	Y	Y	Y	Y	N	N	Y
4 **Hastings**	N	N	N	N	Y	Y	Y
5 **McMorris Rodgers**	N	N	N	N	Y	Y	Y
6 Dicks	Y	Y	Y	Y	N	N	N
7 McDermott	Y	Y	?	Y	N	N	N
8 **Reichert**	N	N	N	Y	Y	Y	N
9 Smith	Y	Y	Y	Y	N	N	Y
WEST VIRGINIA							
1 Mollohan	Y	Y	Y	Y	N	Y	N
2 **Capito**	N	N	N	?	?	?	?
3 Rahall	Y	Y	Y	Y	N	Y	N
WISCONSIN							
1 **Ryan**	N	N	N	Y	Y	Y	Y
2 Baldwin	Y	Y	Y	Y	N	N	N
3 Kind	Y	Y	Y	Y	N	N	N
4 Moore	Y	Y	Y	Y	N	N	N
5 **Sensenbrenner**	N	N	N	N	Y	Y	Y
6 **Petri**	N	N	N	Y	Y	Y	Y
7 Obey	Y	Y	Y	Y	N	N	N
8 Kagen	Y	Y	Y	Y	N	N	N
WYOMING							
AL **Lummis**	–	N	N	N	Y	Y	Y
DELEGATES							
Faleomavaega (A.S.)				Y	N	N	N
Norton (D.C.)				+	–	N	N
Bordallo (Guam)				Y	N	Y	N
Sablan (N. Marianas)				Y	N	N	N
Pierluisi (P.R.)				?	N	N	N
Christensen (V.I.)				Y	N	N	N

IN THE HOUSE | By Vote Number

**645. HR 3293. Fiscal 2010 Labor-HHS-Education Appropriations/
Recommit.** Tiahrt, R-Kan., motion to recommit the bill to the
Appropriations Committee with instructions that it be immediately
reported back with language that would increase funding for special
education by $1 billion and reduce several accounts, including those of
the National Institute of Allergy and Infectious Diseases, the
Education Department innovation and improvement programs,
and the Corporation for National and Community Service. Motion
rejected 171-248: R 168-0; D 3-248. A "nay" was a vote in support of the
president's position. July 24, 2009.

**646. HR 3293. Fiscal 2010 Labor-HHS-Education Appropriations/
Passage.** Passage of the bill that would appropriate $730.5 billion in
fiscal 2010, including $163.4 billion in discretionary funds, for the
departments of Labor, Health and Human Services, and Education and
related agencies. It would provide $67.8 billion for the Education
Department, including $17.8 billion for Pell Grants; $16 billion for the
Labor Department; and $603.5 billion for Health and Human
Services, including $31.3 billion for the National Institutes of Health.
Passed 264-153: R 20-148; D 244-5. A "yea" was a vote in support of
the president's position. July 24, 2009.

647. H Res 593. Hawaii's 50th Anniversary/Adoption. Clay, D-Mo.,
motion to suspend the rules and adopt the resolution that would
recognize the 50th anniversary of Hawaii becoming the 50th state.
Motion agreed to 378-0: R 158-0; D 220-0. A two-thirds majority of those
present and voting (252 in this case) is required for adoption under
suspension of the rules. July 27, 2009.

648. HR 1376. Waco Mammoth National Monument/Passage.
Bordallo, D-Guam, motion to suspend the rules and pass the bill that
would establish the Waco Mammoth National Monument in Texas in
the National Park System and authorize the Interior Department to
construct visitor facilities and acquire necessary land. Motion agreed
to 308-74: R 85-74; D 223-0. A two-thirds majority of those present and
voting (255 in this case) is required for passage under suspension of the
rules. July 27, 2009.

649. HR 1121. Blue Ridge Parkway Land Exchange/Passage.
Bordallo, D-Guam, motion to suspend the rules and pass the bill that
would authorize the Interior Department to exchange 20 acres of the
Blowing Rock Reservoir in the Blue Ridge Parkway for 192 acres owned
by the town of Blowing Rock, N.C., within three years. Motion agreed
to 377-0: R 157-0; D 220-0. A two-thirds majority of those present and
voting (252 in this case) is required for passage under suspension of the
rules. July 27, 2009.

650. HR 1293. Veterans' Home Health Services/Passage. Filner,
D-Calif., motion to suspend the rules and pass the bill that would
increase the maximum reimbursement amount for various expenses
related to improvements and necessary structural alterations to homes of
veterans with disabilities as part of home health services. Motion agreed
to 426-0: R 177-0; D 249-0. A two-thirds majority of those present and
voting (284 in this case) is required for passage under suspension of the
rules. July 28, 2009.

	645	646	647	648	649	650
ALABAMA						
1 Bonner	Y	N	Y	Y	Y	Y
2 Bright	N	Y	Y	Y	Y	Y
3 Rogers	Y	Y	Y	N	Y	Y
4 Aderholt	Y	N	Y	N	Y	Y
5 Griffith	N	Y	Y	Y	Y	Y
6 Bachus	Y	N	Y	Y	Y	Y
7 Davis	N	Y	?	?	?	Y
ALASKA						
AL Young	Y	Y	Y	Y	Y	Y
ARIZONA						
1 Kirkpatrick	N	Y	Y	Y	Y	Y
2 Franks	Y	N	Y	N	Y	Y
3 Shadegg	Y	N	Y	N	Y	Y
4 Pastor	N	Y	Y	Y	Y	Y
5 Mitchell	N	Y	Y	Y	Y	Y
6 Flake	Y	N	Y	N	Y	Y
7 Grijalva	N	Y	?	?	?	Y
8 Giffords	N	Y	Y	Y	Y	Y
ARKANSAS						
1 Berry	N	Y	Y	Y	Y	Y
2 Snyder	N	Y	Y	Y	Y	Y
3 Boozman	Y	N	Y	N	Y	Y
4 Ross	N	Y	Y	Y	Y	Y
CALIFORNIA						
1 Thompson	N	Y	Y	Y	Y	Y
2 Herger	Y	N	Y	N	Y	Y
3 Lungren	Y	N	Y	N	Y	Y
4 McClintock	Y	N	Y	N	Y	Y
5 Matsui	N	Y	Y	Y	Y	Y
6 Woolsey	N	Y	Y	Y	Y	Y
7 Miller, George	N	Y	Y	Y	Y	Y
8 Pelosi						
9 Lee	N	Y	Y	Y	Y	Y
10 Vacant						
11 McNerney	N	Y	Y	Y	Y	Y
12 Speier	N	Y	Y	Y	Y	Y
13 Stark	N	Y	Y	Y	Y	Y
14 Eshoo	N	Y	Y	Y	Y	Y
15 Honda	N	Y	Y	Y	Y	Y
16 Lofgren	N	Y	Y	Y	Y	Y
17 Farr	N	Y	Y	Y	Y	Y
18 Cardoza	N	Y	Y	Y	Y	Y
19 Radanovich	Y	N	?	?	?	Y
20 Costa	N	Y	Y	Y	Y	Y
21 Nunes	Y	N	Y	N	Y	Y
22 McCarthy	Y	N	Y	N	Y	Y
23 Capps	N	Y	Y	Y	Y	Y
24 Gallegly	Y	N	Y	N	Y	Y
25 McKeon	Y	N	Y	N	Y	Y
26 Dreier	Y	N	Y	N	Y	Y
27 Sherman	N	Y	Y	Y	Y	Y
28 Berman	N	Y	Y	Y	Y	Y
29 Schiff	N	Y	Y	Y	Y	Y
30 Waxman	N	Y	?	Y	Y	Y
31 Becerra	N	Y	Y	Y	Y	Y
32 Chu	N	Y	Y	Y	Y	Y
33 Watson	N	?	Y	Y	Y	Y
34 Roybal-Allard	N	Y	Y	Y	Y	Y
35 Waters	N	Y	?	?	?	Y
36 Harman	N	Y	Y	Y	Y	Y
37 Richardson	N	Y	Y	Y	Y	Y
38 Napolitano	N	Y	Y	Y	Y	Y
39 Sánchez, Linda	N	Y	Y	Y	Y	Y
40 Royce	Y	N	Y	N	Y	Y
41 Lewis	Y	N	Y	N	Y	Y
42 Miller, Gary	Y	N	Y	N	Y	Y
43 Baca	N	Y	Y	Y	Y	Y
44 Calvert	Y	N	Y	N	Y	Y
45 Bono Mack	Y	N	Y	Y	Y	Y
46 Rohrabacher	Y	N	?	?	?	Y
47 Sanchez, Loretta	N	Y	Y	Y	Y	Y
48 Campbell	Y	N	?	N	Y	Y
49 Issa	Y	N	Y	Y	Y	Y
50 Bilbray	Y	Y	Y	Y	Y	Y
51 Filner	N	Y	Y	Y	Y	Y
52 Hunter	Y	N	Y	N	Y	Y
53 Davis	N	Y	Y	Y	Y	Y

	645	646	647	648	649	650
COLORADO						
1 DeGette	N	Y	Y	Y	Y	Y
2 Polis	N	Y	Y	Y	Y	Y
3 Salazar	N	Y	Y	Y	Y	Y
4 Markey	N	Y	Y	Y	Y	Y
5 Lamborn	Y	N	Y	N	Y	Y
6 Coffman	Y	N	Y	N	Y	Y
7 Perlmutter	N	Y	Y	Y	Y	Y
CONNECTICUT						
1 Larson	N	Y	Y	Y	Y	Y
2 Courtney	N	Y	+	−	+	Y
3 DeLauro	N	Y	Y	Y	Y	Y
4 Himes	N	Y	Y	Y	Y	Y
5 Murphy	N	Y	?	Y	Y	Y
DELAWARE						
AL Castle	Y	Y	Y	Y	Y	Y
FLORIDA						
1 Miller	Y	N	Y	N	Y	Y
2 Boyd	N	Y	Y	Y	?	Y
3 Brown	N	Y	Y	Y	Y	Y
4 Crenshaw	Y	N	?	?	?	Y
5 Brown-Waite	Y	N	Y	N	Y	Y
6 Stearns	Y	N	Y	N	Y	Y
7 Mica	Y	N	Y	Y	Y	Y
8 Grayson	N	Y	Y	Y	Y	Y
9 Bilirakis	Y	N	Y	N	Y	Y
10 Young	Y	N	Y	Y	Y	Y
11 Castor	N	Y	Y	Y	Y	Y
12 Putnam	Y	N	Y	Y	Y	Y
13 Buchanan	Y	Y	Y	Y	Y	Y
14 Mack	Y	N	Y	N	Y	Y
15 Posey	Y	N	Y	N	Y	Y
16 Rooney	Y	N	Y	N	Y	Y
17 Meek	N	Y	Y	Y	Y	Y
18 Ros-Lehtinen	Y	Y	Y	Y	Y	Y
19 Wexler	?	?	Y	Y	Y	Y
20 Wasserman Schultz	N	Y	Y	Y	Y	Y
21 Diaz-Balart, L.	Y	N	Y	Y	Y	Y
22 Klein	N	Y	Y	Y	Y	Y
23 Hastings	N	Y	Y	Y	Y	Y
24 Kosmas	N	Y	Y	Y	Y	Y
25 Diaz-Balart, M.	Y	N	Y	Y	Y	Y
GEORGIA						
1 Kingston	Y	N	Y	N	Y	Y
2 Bishop	N	Y	Y	Y	Y	Y
3 Westmoreland	Y	N	Y	N	Y	Y
4 Johnson	N	Y	Y	Y	Y	Y
5 Lewis	N	Y	Y	Y	Y	Y
6 Price	Y	N	Y	N	Y	Y
7 Linder	Y	N	Y	N	Y	Y
8 Marshall	Y	Y	Y	Y	Y	Y
9 Deal	Y	N	?	?	?	Y
10 Broun	Y	N	Y	N	Y	Y
11 Gingrey	Y	?	Y	Y	Y	Y
12 Barrow	N	Y	Y	Y	Y	Y
13 Scott	N	Y	Y	Y	Y	Y
HAWAII						
1 Abercrombie	N	Y	Y	Y	Y	Y
2 Hirono	N	Y	Y	Y	Y	Y
IDAHO						
1 Minnick	N	Y	Y	Y	Y	Y
2 Simpson	Y	N	Y	N	Y	Y
ILLINOIS						
1 Rush	N	Y	?	?	?	Y
2 Jackson	N	Y	Y	Y	Y	Y
3 Lipinski	N	Y	Y	Y	Y	Y
4 Gutierrez	N	Y	?	?	?	Y
5 Quigley	N	Y	?	?	?	Y
6 Roskam	Y	N	Y	N	Y	Y
7 Davis	N	Y	?	?	?	Y
8 Bean	N	Y	Y	Y	Y	Y
9 Schakowsky	N	Y	Y	Y	Y	Y
10 Kirk	Y	N	Y	Y	Y	Y
11 Halvorson	N	Y	Y	Y	Y	Y
12 Costello	N	Y	?	?	?	?
13 Biggert	Y	N	Y	Y	Y	Y
14 Foster	N	Y	Y	Y	Y	Y
15 Johnson	Y	N	?	?	?	Y

KEY Republicans Democrats

Y	Voted for (yea)	X	Paired against	C	Voted "present" to avoid possible conflict of interest
#	Paired for	−	Announced against		
+	Announced for	P	Voted "present"	?	Did not vote or otherwise make a position known
N	Voted against (nay)				

	645	646	647	648	649	650
16 **Manzullo**	Y	N	Y	N	Y	Y
17 Hare	N	Y	Y	Y	Y	Y
18 **Schock**	Y	N	Y	N	Y	Y
19 **Shimkus**	Y	N	Y	Y	Y	Y
INDIANA						
1 Visclosky	N	Y	Y	Y	Y	Y
2 Donnelly	N	Y	Y	Y	Y	Y
3 **Souder**	Y	N	Y	Y	Y	?
4 **Buyer**	Y	N	Y	N	Y	Y
5 **Burton**	Y	N	Y	N	Y	Y
6 **Pence**	+	–	Y	N	Y	Y
7 Carson	N	Y	Y	Y	Y	Y
8 Ellsworth	N	Y	Y	Y	Y	Y
9 Hill	N	N	Y	Y	Y	Y
IOWA						
1 Braley	N	Y	+	+	+	Y
2 Loebsack	N	Y	Y	Y	Y	Y
3 Boswell	N	Y	Y	Y	Y	Y
4 **Latham**	Y	N	Y	Y	Y	Y
5 **King**	Y	N	Y	N	Y	Y
KANSAS						
1 **Moran**	Y	N	Y	N	Y	Y
2 **Jenkins**	Y	N	Y	Y	Y	Y
3 Moore	N	Y	Y	Y	Y	Y
4 **Tiahrt**	Y	N	Y	Y	Y	Y
KENTUCKY						
1 **Whitfield**	Y	N	Y	Y	Y	Y
2 **Guthrie**	Y	N	Y	Y	Y	Y
3 Yarmuth	N	Y	Y	Y	Y	Y
4 **Davis**	?	N	Y	N	Y	Y
5 **Rogers**	Y	N	Y	Y	Y	Y
6 Chandler	N	Y	Y	Y	Y	Y
LOUISIANA						
1 **Scalise**	Y	N	Y	N	Y	Y
2 **Cao**	Y	Y	Y	Y	Y	Y
3 Melancon	N	Y	Y	Y	Y	Y
4 **Fleming**	Y	N	Y	Y	Y	Y
5 **Alexander**	Y	Y	Y	N	Y	Y
6 **Cassidy**	Y	N	Y	Y	Y	Y
7 **Boustany**	Y	N	Y	N	Y	Y
MAINE						
1 Pingree	N	Y	Y	Y	Y	Y
2 Michaud	N	Y	Y	Y	Y	Y
MARYLAND						
1 Kratovil	N	N	Y	Y	Y	Y
2 Ruppersberger	N	Y	Y	Y	Y	Y
3 Sarbanes	N	Y	Y	Y	Y	Y
4 Edwards	N	Y	Y	Y	Y	Y
5 Hoyer	N	Y	Y	Y	Y	Y
6 **Bartlett**	Y	N	Y	N	Y	Y
7 Cummings	N	Y	Y	Y	Y	Y
8 Van Hollen	N	Y	Y	Y	Y	Y
MASSACHUSETTS						
1 Olver	N	Y	Y	Y	Y	Y
2 Neal	N	Y	Y	Y	Y	Y
3 McGovern	N	Y	Y	Y	Y	Y
4 Frank	N	Y	Y	Y	Y	Y
5 Tsongas	N	Y	?	?	?	Y
6 Tierney	N	Y	Y	Y	Y	Y
7 Markey	N	Y	Y	Y	Y	Y
8 Capuano	N	Y	Y	Y	Y	Y
9 Lynch	N	Y	?	?	?	Y
10 Delahunt	N	Y	Y	Y	Y	Y
MICHIGAN						
1 Stupak	N	Y	?	?	?	Y
2 **Hoekstra**	Y	N	?	?	?	Y
3 **Ehlers**	Y	Y	Y	Y	Y	Y
4 **Camp**	Y	N	?	?	?	Y
5 Kildee	N	Y	Y	Y	Y	Y
6 **Upton**	Y	Y	Y	Y	Y	Y
7 Schauer	N	Y	Y	Y	Y	Y
8 **Rogers**	Y	N	Y	Y	Y	Y
9 Peters	N	Y	Y	Y	Y	Y
10 **Miller**	Y	N	Y	Y	Y	Y
11 **McCotter**	Y	N	Y	Y	Y	Y
12 Levin	N	Y	Y	Y	Y	Y
13 Kilpatrick	N	Y	Y	Y	Y	Y
14 Conyers	N	Y	Y	Y	?	Y
15 Dingell	N	Y	Y	Y	Y	Y
MINNESOTA						
1 Walz	N	Y	Y	Y	Y	Y
2 **Kline**	Y	N	Y	Y	Y	Y
3 **Paulsen**	Y	N	Y	Y	Y	Y
4 McCollum	N	Y	Y	Y	Y	Y

	645	646	647	648	649	650
5 Ellison	–	Y	Y	Y	Y	Y
6 **Bachmann**	Y	N	Y	Y	Y	Y
7 Peterson	N	Y	Y	Y	Y	Y
8 Oberstar	N	Y	Y	Y	Y	Y
MISSISSIPPI						
1 Childers	N	Y	Y	Y	Y	Y
2 Thompson	N	Y	Y	Y	Y	Y
3 **Harper**	Y	N	Y	N	Y	Y
4 Taylor	Y	N	Y	Y	Y	Y
MISSOURI						
1 Clay	N	Y	Y	Y	Y	Y
2 **Akin**	Y	N	+	+	+	Y
3 Carnahan	N	Y	Y	Y	Y	Y
4 Skelton	N	Y	Y	Y	Y	Y
5 Cleaver	N	Y	Y	Y	Y	Y
6 **Graves**	Y	N	?	?	?	Y
7 **Blunt**	Y	N	Y	Y	Y	Y
8 **Emerson**	Y	N	Y	N	Y	Y
9 **Luetkemeyer**	Y	N	Y	N	Y	Y
MONTANA						
AL **Rehberg**	Y	N	Y	Y	Y	Y
NEBRASKA						
1 **Fortenberry**	Y	N	Y	Y	Y	Y
2 **Terry**	Y	N	Y	N	Y	Y
3 **Smith**	Y	N	Y	N	Y	Y
NEVADA						
1 Berkley	N	Y	Y	Y	Y	Y
2 **Heller**	Y	N	Y	N	Y	Y
3 Titus	N	Y	Y	Y	Y	Y
NEW HAMPSHIRE						
1 Shea-Porter	N	Y	Y	Y	Y	Y
2 Hodes	Y	Y	+	+	+	Y
NEW JERSEY						
1 Andrews	N	Y	Y	Y	Y	Y
2 **LoBiondo**	Y	Y	Y	Y	Y	Y
3 Adler	N	Y	Y	Y	Y	Y
4 **Smith**	Y	Y	Y	Y	Y	Y
5 **Garrett**	Y	N	Y	N	Y	Y
6 Pallone	N	Y	Y	Y	Y	Y
7 **Lance**	Y	N	Y	Y	Y	Y
8 Pascrell	N	Y	Y	Y	Y	Y
9 Rothman	N	Y	Y	Y	Y	Y
10 Payne	N	Y	Y	Y	Y	Y
11 **Frelinghuysen**	Y	N	Y	Y	Y	Y
12 Holt	N	Y	Y	Y	Y	Y
13 Sires	N	Y	?	?	?	Y
NEW MEXICO						
1 Heinrich	N	Y	Y	Y	Y	Y
2 Teague	N	Y	Y	Y	Y	Y
3 Lujan	N	Y	Y	Y	Y	Y
NEW YORK						
1 Bishop	N	Y	+	+	+	Y
2 Israel	N	Y	Y	Y	Y	Y
3 **King**	Y	Y	Y	Y	Y	Y
4 McCarthy	–	+	+	+	+	+
5 Ackerman	N	Y	Y	Y	?	Y
6 Meeks	N	Y	Y	Y	Y	Y
7 Crowley	N	Y	Y	Y	Y	Y
8 Nadler	N	Y	Y	Y	Y	Y
9 Weiner	N	Y	?	?	?	Y
10 Towns	N	Y	Y	Y	Y	Y
11 Clarke	N	Y	Y	Y	Y	Y
12 Velázquez	N	Y	Y	Y	Y	Y
13 McMahon	N	Y	Y	Y	Y	Y
14 Maloney	N	Y	?	?	?	Y
15 Rangel	N	Y	Y	Y	Y	Y
16 Serrano	N	Y	Y	Y	Y	Y
17 Engel	N	Y	?	?	?	Y
18 Lowey	N	Y	Y	Y	Y	Y
19 Hall	N	Y	Y	Y	Y	Y
20 Murphy	N	Y	Y	Y	Y	Y
21 Tonko	N	Y	Y	Y	Y	Y
22 Hinchey	N	Y	Y	Y	Y	Y
23 **McHugh**	?	?	Y	Y	Y	Y
24 Arcuri	N	Y	Y	Y	Y	Y
25 Maffei	N	Y	Y	Y	Y	Y
26 **Lee**	Y	N	Y	Y	Y	Y
27 Higgins	N	Y	?	?	?	Y
28 Slaughter	N	+	Y	Y	Y	+
29 Massa	N	Y	Y	Y	Y	Y
NORTH CAROLINA						
1 Butterfield	N	Y	Y	Y	Y	Y
2 Etheridge	N	Y	Y	Y	Y	Y
3 **Jones**	Y	?	Y	Y	Y	Y
4 Price	N	Y	Y	Y	Y	Y

	645	646	647	648	649	650
5 **Foxx**	Y	N	Y	N	Y	Y
6 **Coble**	Y	N	Y	N	Y	Y
7 McIntyre	N	Y	Y	Y	Y	Y
8 Kissell	N	Y	Y	Y	Y	Y
9 **Myrick**	Y	N	Y	Y	Y	Y
10 **McHenry**	Y	N	Y	N	Y	Y
11 Shuler	N	Y	Y	Y	Y	Y
12 Watt	N	Y	Y	Y	Y	Y
13 Miller	N	Y	?	?	?	Y
NORTH DAKOTA						
AL Pomeroy	N	Y	Y	Y	Y	Y
OHIO						
1 Driehaus	N	Y	Y	Y	Y	Y
2 **Schmidt**	Y	N	Y	N	Y	Y
3 **Turner**	Y	N	Y	Y	Y	Y
4 **Jordan**	Y	N	Y	N	Y	Y
5 **Latta**	Y	N	Y	N	Y	Y
6 Wilson	N	Y	Y	Y	Y	Y
7 **Austria**	Y	N	Y	Y	Y	Y
8 **Boehner**	?	?	Y	N	Y	Y
9 Kaptur	N	Y	Y	Y	Y	Y
10 Kucinich	N	Y	Y	Y	Y	Y
11 Fudge	N	Y	Y	Y	Y	Y
12 **Tiberi**	Y	N	?	?	?	Y
13 Sutton	N	Y	Y	Y	Y	Y
14 **LaTourette**	Y	N	Y	Y	Y	Y
15 Kilroy	N	Y	+	+	+	Y
16 Boccieri	N	Y	Y	Y	Y	Y
17 Ryan	N	Y	Y	Y	Y	?
18 Space	N	Y	Y	Y	Y	Y
OKLAHOMA						
1 **Sullivan**	Y	N	Y	N	Y	Y
2 Boren	N	Y	Y	Y	Y	Y
3 **Lucas**	Y	N	Y	Y	Y	Y
4 **Cole**	Y	N	Y	Y	Y	Y
5 **Fallin**	Y	N	Y	Y	Y	Y
OREGON						
1 Wu	N	Y	Y	Y	Y	Y
2 **Walden**	Y	N	Y	N	Y	Y
3 Blumenauer	N	Y	Y	Y	Y	Y
4 DeFazio	N	Y	Y	Y	Y	Y
5 Schrader	N	Y	Y	Y	Y	Y
PENNSYLVANIA						
1 Brady	N	Y	Y	Y	Y	Y
2 Fattah	N	Y	Y	Y	Y	Y
3 Dahlkemper	?	?	Y	Y	Y	Y
4 Altmire	N	Y	Y	Y	Y	Y
5 **Thompson**	Y	N	Y	N	Y	Y
6 **Gerlach**	Y	Y	Y	Y	Y	Y
7 Sestak	N	Y	?	?	?	Y
8 Murphy, P.	N	Y	Y	Y	Y	Y
9 **Shuster**	Y	N	Y	Y	?	Y
10 Carney	N	Y	Y	Y	Y	Y
11 Kanjorski	N	Y	Y	Y	Y	?
12 Murtha	N	Y	?	?	?	Y
13 Schwartz	N	Y	Y	Y	Y	Y
14 Doyle	N	Y	Y	Y	Y	Y
15 **Dent**	Y	Y	Y	Y	Y	Y
16 **Pitts**	Y	N	Y	Y	Y	Y
17 Holden	N	Y	Y	Y	Y	Y
18 **Murphy, T.**	Y	Y	Y	Y	Y	Y
19 **Platts**	Y	Y	?	?	?	Y
RHODE ISLAND						
1 Kennedy	N	Y	Y	Y	Y	Y
2 Langevin	N	Y	Y	Y	Y	Y
SOUTH CAROLINA						
1 **Brown**	Y	N	+	–	+	Y
2 **Wilson**	Y	N	Y	N	Y	Y
3 **Barrett**	?	?	?	?	?	Y
4 **Inglis**	Y	N	Y	N	Y	Y
5 Spratt	N	Y	Y	Y	Y	Y
6 Clyburn	N	Y	Y	Y	Y	?
SOUTH DAKOTA						
AL Herseth Sandlin	N	Y	Y	Y	Y	Y
TENNESSEE						
1 **Roe**	Y	N	Y	Y	Y	Y
2 **Duncan**	Y	N	Y	Y	Y	Y
3 **Wamp**	Y	N	?	?	?	Y
4 Davis	N	Y	Y	Y	Y	Y
5 Cooper	N	Y	Y	Y	Y	Y
6 Gordon	N	Y	Y	Y	Y	Y
7 **Blackburn**	Y	N	Y	Y	Y	Y
8 Tanner	N	Y	Y	Y	Y	Y
9 Cohen	N	Y	Y	Y	Y	Y

	645	646	647	648	649	650
TEXAS						
1 **Gohmert**	Y	N	Y	Y	Y	Y
2 **Poe**	Y	N	Y	Y	Y	Y
3 **Johnson, S.**	Y	N	Y	Y	Y	Y
4 **Hall**	Y	N	Y	Y	Y	Y
5 **Hensarling**	Y	N	Y	N	Y	Y
6 **Barton**	Y	N	Y	Y	Y	Y
7 **Culberson**	Y	N	Y	Y	Y	Y
8 **Brady**	Y	N	?	?	?	Y
9 Green, A.	N	Y	+	+	+	Y
10 **McCaul**	Y	N	Y	Y	Y	Y
11 **Conaway**	Y	N	Y	Y	Y	Y
12 **Granger**	Y	N	Y	Y	?	Y
13 **Thornberry**	Y	N	Y	Y	Y	Y
14 **Paul**	?	?	?	?	?	Y
15 Hinojosa	N	Y	Y	Y	Y	Y
16 Reyes	N	Y	Y	Y	Y	Y
17 Edwards	N	Y	Y	Y	Y	Y
18 Jackson Lee	N	+	Y	Y	Y	Y
19 **Neugebauer**	Y	N	Y	Y	Y	Y
20 Gonzalez	N	Y	Y	Y	Y	Y
21 **Smith**	Y	N	Y	Y	Y	Y
22 **Olson**	Y	N	?	?	?	Y
23 Rodriguez	N	Y	+	+	+	Y
24 **Marchant**	?	?	?	?	?	Y
25 Doggett	N	Y	Y	Y	Y	Y
26 **Burgess**	?	N	Y	Y	Y	Y
27 Ortiz	N	Y	?	?	?	Y
28 Cuellar	N	Y	?	?	?	Y
29 Green, G.	N	Y	Y	Y	Y	Y
30 Johnson, E.	N	Y	Y	Y	Y	Y
31 **Carter**	Y	N	?	?	?	Y
32 **Sessions**	Y	N	Y	N	Y	Y
UTAH						
1 **Bishop**	?	?	Y	N	Y	Y
2 Matheson	N	N	Y	Y	Y	Y
3 **Chaffetz**	Y	N	Y	N	Y	Y
VERMONT						
AL Welch	N	Y	Y	Y	Y	Y
VIRGINIA						
1 **Wittman**	Y	N	Y	N	Y	Y
2 Nye	N	N	Y	Y	Y	Y
3 Scott	N	Y	Y	Y	Y	Y
4 **Forbes**	Y	N	Y	N	Y	Y
5 Perriello	N	Y	Y	Y	Y	Y
6 **Goodlatte**	Y	N	Y	N	Y	Y
7 **Cantor**	Y	N	Y	N	Y	Y
8 Moran	N	Y	Y	Y	Y	Y
9 Boucher	N	Y	?	?	?	Y
10 **Wolf**	Y	Y	Y	Y	Y	Y
11 Connolly	N	Y	Y	Y	Y	Y
WASHINGTON						
1 Inslee	N	Y	Y	Y	Y	Y
2 Larsen	N	Y	?	?	?	Y
3 Baird	N	Y	Y	Y	Y	Y
4 **Hastings**	Y	N	Y	N	Y	Y
5 **McMorris Rodgers**	Y	N	Y	Y	Y	Y
6 Dicks	N	Y	Y	Y	Y	Y
7 McDermott	N	Y	Y	Y	Y	Y
8 **Reichert**	Y	Y	Y	Y	Y	Y
9 Smith	N	Y	+	+	+	Y
WEST VIRGINIA						
1 Mollohan	N	Y	Y	Y	Y	Y
2 **Capito**	?	?	Y	Y	Y	Y
3 Rahall	N	Y	Y	Y	Y	Y
WISCONSIN						
1 **Ryan**	Y	N	Y	N	Y	Y
2 Baldwin	N	Y	Y	Y	Y	Y
3 Kind	N	Y	Y	Y	Y	Y
4 Moore	N	Y	Y	Y	Y	Y
5 **Sensenbrenner**	Y	N	Y	N	Y	Y
6 **Petri**	Y	N	Y	N	Y	Y
7 Obey	N	Y	Y	Y	Y	Y
8 Kagen	N	Y	Y	Y	Y	Y
WYOMING						
AL **Lummis**	Y	N	Y	Y	Y	Y
DELEGATES						
Faleomavaega (A.S.)						
Norton (D.C.)						
Bordallo (Guam)						
Sablan (N. Marianas)						
Pierluisi (P.R.)						
Christensen (V.I.)						

IN THE HOUSE | By Vote Number

651. HR 556. **Southern Sea Otters/Passage.** Bordallo, D-Guam, motion to suspend the rules and pass the bill that would require the Interior Department to carry out a recovery and research program for southern sea otters along the California coast and authorize $5 million per year in fiscal 2010-15. Motion agreed to 316-107: R 70-105; D 246-2. A two-thirds majority of those present and voting (282 in this case) is required for passage under suspension of the rules. July 28, 2009.

652. HR 509. **Marine Turtle Conservation/Passage.** Bordallo, D-Guam, motion to suspend the rules and pass the bill that would reauthorize the Marine Turtle Conservation Act through fiscal 2014 and limit the amount spent in any fiscal year for projects related to the conservation of marine turtles in the United States to 20 percent of funds in the Interior Department's Marine Turtle Conservation Fund. Motion agreed to 354-72: R 107-70; D 247-2. A two-thirds majority of those present and voting (284 in this case) is required for passage under suspension of the rules. July 28, 2009.

653. H Res 616. **Louisiana State University Tribute/Adoption.** Grijalva, D-Ariz., motion to suspend the rules and adopt the resolution that would commend the Louisiana State University Tigers baseball team on winning the 2009 Division I College World Series. Motion agreed to 426-0: R 177-0; D 249-0. A two-thirds majority of those present and voting (284 in this case) is required for adoption under suspension of the rules. July 28, 2009.

654. HR 3326. **Fiscal 2010 Defense Appropriations/Previous Question.** Polis, D-Colo., motion to order the previous question (thus ending debate and possibility of amendment) on adoption of the rule (H Res 685) and a Polis amendment to the rule. The rule would provide for House floor consideration of the bill that would appropriate $636.6 billion for the Defense Department in fiscal 2010. The Polis amendment would specify that the amendments listed in the first section of the resolution would not be subject to a demand for division of the question in the House or Committee of the Whole. Motion agreed to 245-176: R 1-171; D 244-5. (Subsequently, the Polis amendment was adopted by voice vote.) July 29, 2009.

655. HR 3326. **Fiscal 2010 Defense Appropriations/Rule.** Adoption of the rule (H Res 685) to provide for House floor consideration of the bill that would appropriate $636.6 billion for the Defense Department in fiscal 2010. Adopted 241-185: R 0-174; D 241-11. July 29, 2009.

656. H Res 690. **Franking Commission Disapproval/Motion to Table.** Hoyer, D-Md., motion to table (kill) the Boehner, R-Ohio, privileged resolution that would state that the House views with disapproval the failure of the Democratic members of the Franking Commission to ensure the commission's Democratic staff carries out its responsibilities in a professional, fair and impartial manner. Motion agreed to 244-173: R 0-172; D 244-1. July 29, 2009.

657. HR 2749. **Food Safety Overhaul/Passage.** Dingell, D-Mich., motion to suspend the rules and pass the bill that would establish a risk-based inspection schedule for food facilities; impose criminal and civil penalties for violating food safety laws; authorize the Food and Drug Administration (FDA) to impose mandatory food quarantines; require food facilities to register with the FDA annually and pay a fee; and require facilities to implement written food safety plans. Motion rejected 280-150: R 50-127; D 230-23. A two-thirds majority of those present and voting (287 in this case) is required for passage under suspension of the rules. A "yea" was a vote in support of the president's position. July 29, 2009.

	651	652	653	654	655	656	657
ALABAMA							
1 Bonner	Y	Y	Y	?	?	?	N
2 Bright	?	N	Y	?	N	Y	Y
3 Rogers	N	Y	Y	?	N	N	N
4 Aderholt	Y	Y	Y	?	N	N	N
5 Griffith	Y	Y	Y	Y	Y	Y	N
6 Bachus	N	Y	Y	N	N	N	N
7 Davis	Y	Y	Y	?	Y	N	N
ALASKA							
AL Young	N	N	Y	N	N	N	N
ARIZONA							
1 Kirkpatrick	Y	Y	Y	Y	Y	Y	Y
2 Franks	N	N	Y	N	N	N	N
3 Shadegg	N	N	Y	N	N	N	N
4 Pastor	Y	Y	Y	Y	Y	Y	Y
5 Mitchell	Y	Y	Y	N	N	Y	Y
6 Flake	N	N	Y	N	N	N	N
7 Grijalva	Y	Y	Y	Y	Y	Y	Y
8 Giffords	Y	Y	Y	Y	Y	Y	Y
ARKANSAS							
1 Berry	Y	Y	Y	Y	Y	Y	Y
2 Snyder	Y	Y	Y	Y	N	Y	Y
3 Boozman	N	N	Y	N	N	N	N
4 Ross	Y	Y	Y	Y	Y	Y	Y
CALIFORNIA							
1 Thompson	Y	Y	Y	Y	Y	Y	Y
2 Herger	N	N	Y	N	N	N	N
3 Lungren	Y	Y	Y	N	N	N	N
4 McClintock	N	N	Y	N	N	N	N
5 Matsui	Y	Y	Y	Y	Y	Y	Y
6 Woolsey	Y	Y	Y	Y	Y	Y	Y
7 Miller, George	Y	Y	Y	Y	Y	Y	Y
8 Pelosi							
9 Lee	Y	Y	Y	Y	Y	Y	Y
10 Vacant							
11 McNerney	Y	Y	Y	Y	Y	Y	Y
12 Speier	Y	Y	Y	Y	Y	Y	Y
13 Stark	Y	Y	Y	Y	N	Y	Y
14 Eshoo	Y	Y	Y	Y	Y	Y	Y
15 Honda	Y	Y	Y	Y	Y	Y	Y
16 Lofgren	Y	Y	Y	Y	Y	P	Y
17 Farr	Y	Y	Y	Y	Y	Y	Y
18 Cardoza	Y	Y	Y	Y	Y	Y	Y
19 Radanovich	N	Y	Y	N	N	N	N
20 Costa	Y	Y	Y	Y	Y	Y	Y
21 Nunes	N	Y	Y	N	N	N	N
22 McCarthy	Y	Y	Y	N	N	N	N
23 Capps	Y	Y	Y	Y	Y	Y	Y
24 Gallegly	N	Y	Y	N	N	N	N
25 McKeon	Y	Y	Y	N	N	N	N
26 Dreier	N	Y	Y	N	N	N	N
27 Sherman	Y	Y	Y	Y	Y	P	Y
28 Berman	Y	Y	Y	Y	Y	Y	Y
29 Schiff	Y	Y	Y	Y	Y	Y	Y
30 Waxman	Y	Y	Y	Y	Y	Y	Y
31 Becerra	Y	Y	Y	Y	Y	Y	Y
32 Chu	Y	Y	Y	Y	Y	Y	Y
33 Watson	Y	Y	Y	Y	Y	?	Y
34 Roybal-Allard	Y	Y	Y	Y	Y	Y	Y
35 Waters	Y	Y	Y	Y	Y	Y	Y
36 Harman	Y	Y	Y	Y	Y	Y	Y
37 Richardson	Y	Y	Y	Y	Y	Y	Y
38 Napolitano	Y	Y	Y	Y	Y	Y	Y
39 Sánchez, Linda	Y	Y	Y	Y	Y	Y	Y
40 Royce	N	N	Y	N	N	N	N
41 Lewis	Y	Y	Y	N	N	N	N
42 Miller, Gary	N	Y	Y	N	N	N	N
43 Baca	Y	Y	Y	Y	Y	Y	Y
44 Calvert	Y	Y	Y	N	N	N	N
45 Bono Mack	Y	Y	Y	N	N	N	N
46 Rohrabacher	N	N	Y	N	N	N	N
47 Sanchez, Loretta	Y	Y	Y	Y	Y	Y	Y
48 Campbell	Y	Y	Y	N	N	N	N
49 Issa	N	N	Y	N	N	N	N
50 Bilbray	Y	Y	Y	N	N	N	N
51 Filner	Y	Y	Y	Y	Y	Y	Y
52 Hunter	N	N	Y	N	N	N	N
53 Davis	Y	Y	Y	Y	Y	P	Y
COLORADO							
1 DeGette	Y	Y	Y	Y	Y	Y	Y
2 Polis	Y	Y	Y	Y	Y	Y	Y
3 Salazar	Y	Y	Y	Y	Y	Y	N
4 Markey	N	Y	Y	Y	Y	Y	Y
5 Lamborn	N	N	Y	N	N	N	N
6 Coffman	N	N	Y	N	N	N	N
7 Perlmutter	Y	Y	Y	Y	Y	Y	Y
CONNECTICUT							
1 Larson	Y	Y	Y	Y	Y	Y	Y
2 Courtney	Y	Y	Y	Y	Y	Y	Y
3 DeLauro	Y	Y	Y	Y	Y	Y	Y
4 Himes	Y	Y	Y	Y	Y	Y	Y
5 Murphy	Y	Y	Y	Y	Y	Y	Y
DELAWARE							
AL Castle	Y	Y	Y	N	N	N	Y
FLORIDA							
1 Miller	N	N	Y	N	N	N	N
2 Boyd	Y	Y	Y	Y	Y	Y	Y
3 Brown	Y	Y	Y	Y	Y	Y	Y
4 Crenshaw	Y	Y	Y	N	N	N	N
5 Brown-Waite	N	Y	Y	N	N	N	N
6 Stearns	N	Y	Y	N	N	N	N
7 Mica	N	Y	Y	N	N	N	N
8 Grayson	Y	Y	Y	Y	Y	Y	Y
9 Bilirakis	Y	Y	Y	Y	N	N	Y
10 Young	Y	Y	Y	Y	N	N	Y
11 Castor	Y	Y	Y	Y	P	Y	Y
12 Putnam	Y	Y	Y	N	N	N	N
13 Buchanan	Y	Y	Y	N	N	N	N
14 Mack	N	N	Y	N	N	N	N
15 Posey	Y	Y	Y	N	N	N	N
16 Rooney	N	Y	Y	N	N	N	N
17 Meek	Y	Y	Y	Y	Y	Y	Y
18 Ros-Lehtinen	Y	Y	Y	Y	Y	Y	Y
19 Wexler	Y	Y	Y	Y	Y	Y	Y
20 Wasserman Schultz	Y	Y	Y	Y	Y	Y	Y
21 Diaz-Balart, L.	Y	Y	Y	N	N	N	Y
22 Klein	Y	Y	Y	Y	Y	Y	Y
23 Hastings	Y	Y	Y	Y	Y	Y	Y
24 Kosmas	Y	Y	Y	Y	Y	Y	Y
25 Diaz-Balart, M.	Y	Y	Y	N	N	N	Y
GEORGIA							
1 Kingston	N	Y	Y	N	N	N	N
2 Bishop	Y	Y	Y	Y	Y	Y	Y
3 Westmoreland	N	N	Y	N	N	N	N
4 Johnson	Y	Y	Y	Y	Y	Y	Y
5 Lewis	Y	Y	Y	Y	Y	Y	Y
6 Price	N	N	Y	N	N	N	N
7 Linder	N	N	Y	N	N	N	N
8 Marshall	Y	Y	Y	Y	Y	Y	Y
9 Deal	N	Y	Y	N	N	N	Y
10 Broun	N	N	Y	N	N	N	N
11 Gingrey	N	N	Y	N	N	N	Y
12 Barrow	Y	Y	Y	Y	Y	Y	Y
13 Scott	Y	Y	Y	Y	Y	Y	Y
HAWAII							
1 Abercrombie	Y	Y	Y	Y	Y	Y	Y
2 Hirono	Y	Y	Y	Y	Y	Y	Y
IDAHO							
1 Minnick	Y	Y	Y	N	N	Y	N
2 Simpson	Y	Y	Y	N	N	N	N
ILLINOIS							
1 Rush	Y	Y	Y	Y	Y	Y	Y
2 Jackson	Y	Y	Y	Y	Y	Y	Y
3 Lipinski	Y	Y	Y	Y	Y	Y	Y
4 Gutierrez	Y	Y	Y	Y	Y	Y	Y
5 Quigley	Y	Y	Y	Y	Y	Y	Y
6 Roskam	N	Y	Y	N	N	N	Y
7 Davis	Y	Y	Y	Y	Y	Y	Y
8 Bean	Y	Y	Y	Y	Y	Y	Y
9 Schakowsky	Y	Y	Y	Y	Y	Y	Y
10 Kirk	?	Y	Y	N	N	N	Y
11 Halvorson	Y	Y	Y	Y	Y	Y	Y
12 Costello	?	?	?	Y	Y	Y	Y
13 Biggert	Y	Y	Y	N	N	N	Y
14 Foster	Y	Y	Y	Y	Y	Y	Y
15 Johnson	Y	Y	Y	N	N	N	N

KEY	**Republicans**	Democrats	
Y Voted for (yea)		**X** Paired against	**C** Voted "present" to avoid possible conflict of interest
# Paired for		**–** Announced against	
+ Announced for		**P** Voted "present"	**?** Did not vote or otherwise make a position known
N Voted against (nay)			

	651	652	653	654	655	656	657
16 **Manzullo**	N	N	Y	N	N	N	N
17 Hare	Y	Y	Y	Y	Y	Y	Y
18 **Schock**	N	N	Y	N	N	N	N
19 **Shimkus**	N	N	Y	N	N	N	Y
INDIANA							
1 Visclosky	Y	Y	Y	Y	Y	Y	Y
2 Donnelly	Y	Y	Y	Y	Y	Y	Y
3 **Souder**	Y	Y	Y	N	N	N	N
4 **Buyer**	N	N	Y	N	N	N	Y
5 **Burton**	N	Y	Y	N	N	N	N
6 **Pence**	N	N	Y	N	?	N	N
7 Carson	Y	Y	Y	Y	Y	Y	Y
8 Ellsworth	Y	Y	Y	Y	Y	Y	Y
9 Hill	Y	Y	Y	N	N	Y	Y
IOWA							
1 Braley	Y	Y	Y	Y	Y	Y	Y
2 Loebsack	Y	Y	Y	Y	Y	Y	Y
3 Boswell	Y	Y	Y	Y	Y	Y	Y
4 **Latham**	Y	Y	Y	N	N	N	N
5 **King**	N	N	Y	N	N	N	N
KANSAS							
1 **Moran**	N	N	Y	N	N	N	N
2 **Jenkins**	N	N	Y	N	N	N	N
3 Moore	Y	Y	Y	Y	Y	Y	Y
4 **Tiahrt**	N	N	Y	N	N	N	N
KENTUCKY							
1 **Whitfield**	?	Y	Y	N	N	N	Y
2 **Guthrie**	Y	Y	Y	N	N	N	Y
3 Yarmuth	Y	Y	Y	Y	Y	Y	Y
4 **Davis**	N	Y	Y	N	N	N	N
5 **Rogers**	N	Y	Y	N	N	N	Y
6 Chandler	Y	Y	Y	Y	Y	P	Y
LOUISIANA							
1 **Scalise**	N	N	Y	N	N	N	Y
2 **Cao**	Y	Y	Y	N	N	N	Y
3 Melancon	Y	Y	Y	Y	Y	Y	Y
4 **Fleming**	N	Y	Y	N	N	N	N
5 **Alexander**	Y	Y	Y	N	N	N	N
6 **Cassidy**	N	Y	Y	N	N	N	N
7 **Boustany**	Y	Y	Y	N	N	N	N
MAINE							
1 Pingree	Y	Y	Y	Y	Y	Y	N
2 Michaud	Y	Y	Y	Y	Y	Y	Y
MARYLAND							
1 Kratovil	Y	Y	Y	N	N	Y	N
2 Ruppersberger	Y	Y	Y	Y	Y	Y	Y
3 Sarbanes	Y	Y	Y	Y	Y	Y	Y
4 Edwards	Y	Y	Y	Y	Y	P	Y
5 Hoyer	Y	Y	Y	Y	Y	Y	Y
6 **Bartlett**	N	Y	Y	N	N	N	N
7 Cummings	Y	Y	Y	Y	Y	Y	Y
8 Van Hollen	Y	Y	Y	Y	Y	Y	Y
MASSACHUSETTS							
1 Olver	Y	Y	Y	Y	Y	Y	Y
2 Neal	Y	Y	Y	Y	Y	Y	Y
3 McGovern	Y	Y	Y	Y	Y	Y	Y
4 Frank	Y	Y	Y	Y	Y	Y	Y
5 Tsongas	Y	Y	Y	Y	Y	Y	Y
6 Tierney	Y	Y	Y	Y	Y	Y	Y
7 Markey	Y	Y	Y	Y	Y	Y	Y
8 Capuano	Y	Y	Y	Y	Y	Y	Y
9 Lynch	Y	Y	Y	Y	Y	Y	Y
10 Delahunt	Y	Y	Y	Y	Y	Y	Y
MICHIGAN							
1 Stupak	Y	Y	Y	Y	Y	Y	Y
2 **Hoekstra**	N	N	Y	Y	N	N	N
3 **Ehlers**	Y	Y	Y	N	N	N	Y
4 **Camp**	Y	Y	Y	N	N	N	Y
5 Kildee	Y	Y	Y	Y	Y	Y	Y
6 **Upton**	Y	Y	Y	N	N	N	Y
7 Schauer	Y	Y	Y	Y	Y	Y	Y
8 **Rogers**	Y	Y	Y	N	N	N	Y
9 Peters	Y	Y	Y	Y	Y	Y	Y
10 **Miller**	Y	Y	Y	N	N	N	N
11 **McCotter**	Y	Y	Y	N	N	N	Y
12 Levin	Y	Y	Y	Y	Y	Y	Y
13 Kilpatrick	Y	Y	Y	Y	Y	Y	Y
14 Conyers	Y	Y	Y	Y	Y	Y	Y
15 Dingell	Y	Y	Y	Y	Y	Y	Y
MINNESOTA							
1 Walz	Y	Y	Y	?	?	Y	Y
2 **Kline**	Y	Y	Y	N	N	N	N
3 **Paulsen**	Y	Y	Y	N	N	N	Y
4 McCollum	Y	Y	Y	Y	Y	Y	Y

	651	652	653	654	655	656	657
5 Ellison	Y	Y	Y	Y	Y	Y	Y
6 **Bachmann**	N	N	Y	N	N	N	Y
7 Peterson	Y	Y	Y	Y	Y	Y	Y
8 Oberstar	Y	Y	Y	Y	Y	Y	Y
MISSISSIPPI							
1 Childers	Y	Y	Y	Y	Y	Y	N
2 Thompson	Y	Y	Y	Y	Y	Y	Y
3 **Harper**	N	N	Y	N	N	P	N
4 Taylor	Y	Y	Y	Y	Y	Y	N
MISSOURI							
1 Clay	Y	Y	Y	Y	Y	Y	Y
2 **Akin**	N	N	Y	N	N	N	N
3 Carnahan	Y	Y	Y	Y	Y	Y	Y
4 Skelton	Y	Y	Y	Y	Y	Y	Y
5 Cleaver	Y	Y	Y	Y	Y	Y	Y
6 **Graves**	N	N	Y	N	N	N	N
7 **Blunt**	N	N	Y	N	N	N	N
8 **Emerson**	Y	Y	Y	N	N	N	N
9 **Luetkemeyer**	N	N	Y	N	N	N	N
MONTANA							
AL **Rehberg**	Y	Y	Y	N	N	N	N
NEBRASKA							
1 **Fortenberry**	Y	Y	Y	N	N	N	Y
2 **Terry**	Y	Y	Y	N	N	N	Y
3 **Smith**	N	Y	Y	N	N	N	N
NEVADA							
1 Berkley	Y	Y	Y	Y	Y	Y	Y
2 **Heller**	Y	Y	Y	N	N	N	N
3 Titus	Y	Y	Y	Y	Y	Y	Y
NEW HAMPSHIRE							
1 Shea-Porter	Y	Y	Y	Y	Y	Y	Y
2 Hodes	Y	Y	Y	Y	Y	Y	Y
NEW JERSEY							
1 Andrews	Y	Y	Y	Y	Y	Y	Y
2 **LoBiondo**	Y	Y	Y	N	N	N	Y
3 Adler	Y	Y	Y	Y	Y	Y	Y
4 **Smith**	Y	Y	Y	N	N	N	Y
5 **Garrett**	N	N	Y	N	N	N	N
6 Pallone	Y	Y	Y	Y	Y	Y	Y
7 **Lance**	Y	Y	Y	–	N	N	Y
8 Pascrell	Y	Y	Y	Y	Y	Y	Y
9 Rothman	Y	Y	Y	Y	Y	Y	Y
10 Payne	Y	Y	Y	Y	Y	Y	Y
11 **Frelinghuysen**	Y	Y	Y	N	N	N	Y
12 Holt	Y	Y	Y	Y	Y	Y	Y
13 Sires	Y	Y	Y	Y	Y	Y	Y
NEW MEXICO							
1 Heinrich	Y	Y	Y	Y	Y	Y	N
2 Teague	N	N	Y	Y	Y	Y	N
3 Lujan	Y	Y	Y	Y	Y	Y	N
NEW YORK							
1 Bishop	Y	Y	Y	Y	Y	Y	Y
2 Israel	Y	Y	Y	Y	Y	Y	Y
3 **King**	Y	Y	Y	N	N	N	Y
4 McCarthy	+	+	+	?	?	?	?
5 Ackerman	Y	Y	Y	Y	Y	Y	Y
6 Meeks	Y	Y	Y	?	Y	Y	Y
7 Crowley	Y	Y	Y	Y	Y	Y	Y
8 Nadler	Y	Y	Y	Y	Y	Y	Y
9 Weiner	Y	Y	Y	Y	Y	Y	Y
10 Towns	Y	Y	Y	?	?	Y	Y
11 Clarke	Y	Y	Y	Y	Y	Y	Y
12 Velázquez	Y	Y	Y	Y	Y	Y	Y
13 McMahon	Y	Y	Y	Y	Y	Y	Y
14 Maloney	Y	Y	Y	Y	Y	Y	Y
15 Rangel	?	Y	Y	Y	Y	Y	Y
16 Serrano	Y	Y	Y	Y	Y	Y	Y
17 Engel	Y	Y	Y	Y	Y	Y	Y
18 Lowey	Y	Y	Y	Y	Y	Y	Y
19 Hall	Y	Y	Y	Y	Y	Y	Y
20 Murphy	Y	Y	Y	Y	N	Y	Y
21 Tonko	Y	Y	Y	Y	Y	Y	Y
22 Hinchey	Y	Y	Y	Y	Y	Y	N
23 **McHugh**	Y	Y	Y	N	N	N	?
24 Arcuri	Y	Y	Y	Y	Y	Y	N
25 Maffei	Y	Y	Y	Y	Y	Y	Y
26 **Lee**	Y	Y	Y	N	N	N	Y
27 Higgins	Y	Y	Y	Y	Y	Y	Y
28 Slaughter	+	+	+	Y	Y	Y	Y
29 Massa	Y	Y	Y	Y	Y	Y	N
NORTH CAROLINA							
1 Butterfield	Y	Y	Y	Y	Y	P	Y
2 Etheridge	Y	Y	Y	Y	Y	Y	Y
3 **Jones**	Y	Y	Y	N	N	N	N
4 Price	Y	Y	Y	Y	Y	Y	Y

	651	652	653	654	655	656	657
5 **Foxx**	N	N	Y	N	N	N	N
6 **Coble**	N	N	Y	N	N	N	N
7 McIntyre	Y	Y	Y	Y	Y	Y	Y
8 Kissell	Y	Y	Y	Y	Y	Y	Y
9 **Myrick**	N	Y	Y	N	N	N	N
10 **McHenry**	N	N	Y	N	N	N	N
11 Shuler	Y	Y	Y	N	N	Y	N
12 Watt	Y	Y	Y	Y	Y	Y	Y
13 Miller	Y	Y	Y	Y	Y	Y	Y
NORTH DAKOTA							
AL Pomeroy	Y	Y	Y	Y	Y	Y	Y
OHIO							
1 Driehaus	Y	Y	Y	Y	Y	Y	Y
2 **Schmidt**	?	?	Y	N	N	N	N
3 **Turner**	Y	Y	Y	N	N	N	Y
4 **Jordan**	N	N	Y	N	N	N	N
5 **Latta**	N	Y	Y	N	N	N	N
6 Wilson	Y	Y	Y	Y	Y	Y	Y
7 **Austria**	Y	Y	Y	N	N	N	N
8 **Boehner**	N	Y	Y	?	N	N	N
9 Kaptur	Y	Y	Y	Y	Y	Y	Y
10 Kucinich	Y	Y	Y	Y	N	N	Y
11 Fudge	Y	Y	Y	Y	Y	Y	Y
12 **Tiberi**	Y	Y	Y	N	N	N	Y
13 Sutton	Y	Y	Y	Y	Y	Y	Y
14 **LaTourette**	Y	Y	Y	N	N	N	Y
15 Kilroy	Y	Y	Y	Y	Y	Y	Y
16 Boccieri	Y	Y	Y	Y	Y	Y	Y
17 Ryan	Y	Y	Y	Y	Y	Y	Y
18 Space	Y	Y	Y	Y	Y	Y	Y
OKLAHOMA							
1 **Sullivan**	N	N	Y	N	N	N	N
2 Boren	Y	Y	Y	Y	Y	Y	Y
3 **Lucas**	Y	Y	Y	N	N	N	N
4 **Cole**	Y	Y	Y	N	N	N	N
5 **Fallin**	N	Y	Y	N	N	N	N
OREGON							
1 Wu	Y	Y	Y	Y	Y	Y	Y
2 **Walden**	N	Y	Y	N	N	N	Y
3 Blumenauer	Y	?	?	Y	N	Y	N
4 DeFazio	Y	Y	Y	Y	Y	Y	Y
5 Schrader	Y	Y	Y	Y	Y	Y	Y
PENNSYLVANIA							
1 Brady	Y	Y	Y	Y	Y	Y	Y
2 Fattah	Y	Y	Y	Y	Y	Y	Y
3 Dahlkemper	Y	Y	Y	Y	Y	Y	Y
4 Altmire	Y	Y	Y	Y	Y	Y	Y
5 **Thompson**	N	N	Y	N	N	N	N
6 **Gerlach**	Y	Y	Y	?	?	?	Y
7 Sestak	Y	Y	Y	Y	Y	Y	Y
8 Murphy, P.	Y	Y	Y	Y	Y	Y	Y
9 **Shuster**	N	Y	Y	N	N	N	N
10 Carney	Y	Y	Y	Y	Y	Y	Y
11 Kanjorski	?	?	?	Y	Y	Y	Y
12 Murtha	Y	Y	Y	Y	Y	Y	Y
13 Schwartz	Y	Y	Y	Y	Y	Y	Y
14 Doyle	Y	Y	Y	Y	Y	Y	Y
15 **Dent**	Y	Y	Y	N	N	P	Y
16 **Pitts**	Y	Y	Y	N	N	N	N
17 Holden	Y	Y	Y	Y	Y	Y	Y
18 **Murphy, T.**	Y	Y	Y	N	N	N	Y
19 **Platts**	Y	Y	Y	N	N	N	Y
RHODE ISLAND							
1 Kennedy	Y	Y	Y	Y	Y	Y	Y
2 Langevin	Y	Y	Y	Y	Y	Y	Y
SOUTH CAROLINA							
1 **Brown**	Y	Y	Y	N	N	N	N
2 **Wilson**	N	Y	Y	N	N	N	N
3 **Barrett**	N	Y	Y	N	?	?	N
4 **Inglis**	Y	Y	Y	N	N	N	N
5 Spratt	Y	Y	Y	Y	Y	Y	Y
6 Clyburn	?	?	?	Y	Y	Y	Y
SOUTH DAKOTA							
AL Herseth Sandlin	Y	Y	Y	Y	Y	Y	Y
TENNESSEE							
1 **Roe**	Y	Y	Y	N	N	N	N
2 **Duncan**	N	N	Y	N	N	N	N
3 **Wamp**	N	N	Y	N	N	N	N
4 Davis	Y	Y	Y	Y	Y	Y	?
5 Cooper	Y	Y	Y	Y	Y	Y	Y
6 Gordon	Y	Y	Y	Y	Y	Y	Y
7 **Blackburn**	N	N	Y	N	N	N	N
8 Tanner	Y	Y	Y	Y	Y	Y	Y
9 Cohen	Y	Y	Y	Y	Y	Y	Y

	651	652	653	654	655	656	657
TEXAS							
1 **Gohmert**	N	N	Y	N	N	N	N
2 **Poe**	N	N	Y	N	N	N	N
3 **Johnson, S.**	N	N	Y	N	N	N	N
4 **Hall**	N	N	Y	N	N	N	N
5 **Hensarling**	N	N	Y	N	N	N	N
6 **Barton**	N	Y	P	N	N	N	Y
7 **Culberson**	N	N	Y	N	N	N	N
8 **Brady**	N	N	Y	N	N	N	N
9 Green, A.	Y	Y	Y	Y	Y	Y	Y
10 **McCaul**	Y	Y	Y	N	N	N	N
11 **Conaway**	N	N	Y	N	N	P	N
12 **Granger**	N	N	Y	N	N	N	N
13 **Thornberry**	N	N	Y	N	N	N	N
14 **Paul**	N	N	Y	N	N	N	N
15 Hinojosa	Y	Y	Y	Y	Y	Y	Y
16 Reyes	Y	Y	Y	Y	Y	Y	Y
17 Edwards	Y	Y	Y	Y	Y	Y	Y
18 Jackson Lee	Y	Y	Y	Y	Y	Y	Y
19 **Neugebauer**	N	N	Y	N	N	N	N
20 Gonzalez	Y	Y	Y	Y	Y	Y	Y
21 **Smith**	Y	Y	Y	N	N	N	N
22 **Olson**	N	N	Y	N	N	N	N
23 Rodriguez	Y	Y	Y	Y	Y	Y	Y
24 **Marchant**	N	N	Y	N	N	N	Y
25 Doggett	Y	Y	Y	Y	Y	Y	Y
26 **Burgess**	N	N	Y	N	N	N	Y
27 Ortiz	Y	Y	Y	Y	Y	Y	Y
28 Cuellar	Y	Y	Y	Y	Y	Y	Y
29 Green, G.	Y	Y	Y	Y	Y	Y	Y
30 Johnson, E.	Y	Y	Y	Y	Y	Y	Y
31 **Carter**	N	Y	Y	N	N	N	N
32 **Sessions**	N	N	Y	N	N	N	N
UTAH							
1 **Bishop**	N	Y	Y	N	N	N	N
2 Matheson	Y	Y	Y	Y	Y	Y	Y
3 **Chaffetz**	N	N	Y	N	N	N	N
VERMONT							
AL Welch	Y	Y	Y	Y	Y	P	N
VIRGINIA							
1 **Wittman**	Y	Y	Y	N	N	N	N
2 Nye	Y	Y	Y	Y	Y	Y	Y
3 Scott	Y	Y	Y	Y	Y	Y	Y
4 **Forbes**	N	Y	Y	N	N	N	N
5 Perriello	Y	Y	Y	Y	Y	Y	N
6 **Goodlatte**	N	N	Y	N	N	N	N
7 **Cantor**	N	N	Y	N	N	N	N
8 Moran	Y	Y	Y	Y	Y	Y	Y
9 Boucher	Y	Y	Y	Y	Y	Y	Y
10 **Wolf**	Y	Y	Y	N	N	N	Y
11 Connolly	Y	Y	Y	Y	Y	Y	Y
WASHINGTON							
1 Inslee	Y	Y	Y	Y	Y	Y	Y
2 Larsen	Y	Y	Y	Y	Y	Y	Y
3 Baird	Y	Y	Y	Y	Y	Y	Y
4 **Hastings**	N	Y	Y	N	N	N	N
5 **McMorris Rodgers**	N	Y	Y	N	N	N	N
6 Dicks	Y	Y	Y	Y	Y	Y	Y
7 McDermott	Y	Y	Y	Y	Y	Y	Y
8 **Reichert**	Y	Y	Y	N	N	N	Y
9 Smith	Y	Y	Y	Y	Y	Y	Y
WEST VIRGINIA							
1 Mollohan	Y	Y	Y	Y	Y	Y	Y
2 **Capito**	Y	Y	Y	N	N	N	Y
3 Rahall	Y	Y	Y	Y	Y	Y	Y
WISCONSIN							
1 **Ryan**	N	N	Y	N	N	N	N
2 Baldwin	Y	Y	Y	Y	Y	Y	Y
3 Kind	Y	Y	Y	Y	Y	Y	N
4 Moore	Y	Y	Y	Y	Y	Y	Y
5 **Sensenbrenner**	N	N	Y	N	N	N	N
6 **Petri**	N	N	Y	N	N	N	N
7 Obey	Y	Y	Y	Y	Y	Y	Y
8 Kagen	Y	Y	Y	Y	Y	Y	N
WYOMING							
AL **Lummis**	N	N	Y	N	N	N	N
DELEGATES							
Faleomavaega (A.S.)							
Norton (D.C.)							
Bordallo (Guam)							
Sablan (N. Marianas)							
Pierluisi (P.R.)							
Christensen (V.I.)							

IN THE HOUSE | By Vote Number

658. **HR 1665. Coast Guard Acquisitions/Passage.** Cummings, D-Md., motion to suspend the rules and pass the bill that would restructure the Coast Guard's acquisitions system. The bill would bar the use of private-sector companies as lead systems integrators for acquisition contracts, require the use of full and open competition for acquisition contracts, and require the Coast Guard to create the position of chief acquisition officer and establish operational requirements for acquisitions before awarding the contracts. Motion agreed to 426-0: R 176-0; D 250-0. A two-thirds majority of those present and voting (284 in this case) is required for passage under suspension of the rules. July 29, 2009.

659. **HR 3357. Trust Funds Solvency/Passage.** Lewis, D-Ga., motion to suspend the rules and pass the bill that would transfer $7 billion from the Treasury to the Highway Trust Fund, increase the statutory level of the Unemployment Trust Fund by unspecified sums, increase the Federal Housing Administration mutual mortgage insurance program account to $400 billion and increase the Government National Mortgage Association Mortgage-Backed Securities Loan Guarantee Program account level to $400 billion. Motion agreed to 363-68: R 109-68; D 254-0. A two-thirds majority of those present and voting (288 in this case) is required for passage under suspension of the rules. July 29, 2009.

660. **H Res 496. Fall of Berlin Wall 20th Anniversary/Adoption.** Faleomavaega, D-A.S., motion to suspend the rules and adopt the resolution that would recognize the 20th anniversary of the fall of the Berlin Wall and acknowledge a triumph of democracy over communism. Motion agreed to 432-0: R 178-0; D 254-0. A two-thirds majority of those present and voting (288 in this case) is required for adoption under suspension of the rules. July 29, 2009.

661. **HR 3326. Fiscal 2010 Defense Appropriations/Manager's Amendment.** Murtha, D-Pa., amendment that would bar the use of funds in the bill for advance procurement of F-22 aircraft and shift $369 million that would be provided in the bill for advance procurement to other accounts, including the purchase of spare engines for F-22 and C-17 aircraft and the shutdown of the F-22 production line. The amendment would also revise funding for a number of other programs. Adopted in Committee of the Whole 269-165: R 26-152; D 243-13. A "yea" was a vote in support of the president's position. July 30, 2009.

662. **HR 3326. Fiscal 2010 Defense Appropriations/Drug Interdiction and Counter-Drug Activities.** Flake, R-Ariz., amendment that would reduce funding for drug interdiction and counter-drug activities of the Department of Defense by $160 million. Rejected in Committee of the Whole 48-373: R 42-129; D 6-244. July 30, 2009.

	658	659	660	661	662
ALABAMA					
1 Bonner	?	Y	Y	N	N
2 Bright	Y	Y	Y	N	N
3 Rogers	Y	Y	Y	N	N
4 Aderholt	Y	Y	Y	N	N
5 Griffith	Y	Y	Y	Y	N
6 Bachus	Y	N	Y	N	Y
7 Davis	Y	Y	Y	Y	N
ALASKA					
AL Young	Y	Y	Y	N	N
ARIZONA					
1 Kirkpatrick	Y	Y	Y	Y	N
2 Franks	Y	N	Y	N	N
3 Shadegg	Y	N	Y	N	?
4 Pastor	Y	Y	Y	Y	N
5 Mitchell	Y	Y	Y	Y	N
6 Flake	Y	N	Y	Y	Y
7 Grijalva	Y	Y	Y	Y	N
8 Giffords	Y	Y	Y	Y	N
ARKANSAS					
1 Berry	Y	Y	Y	Y	N
2 Snyder	Y	Y	Y	Y	N
3 Boozman	Y	Y	Y	N	N
4 Ross	Y	Y	Y	Y	N
CALIFORNIA					
1 Thompson	Y	Y	Y	Y	N
2 Herger	Y	N	Y	N	Y
3 Lungren	Y	Y	Y	N	N
4 McClintock	Y	N	Y	N	Y
5 Matsui	Y	Y	Y	Y	N
6 Woolsey	Y	Y	Y	N	N
7 Miller, George	Y	Y	Y	Y	N
8 Pelosi					
9 Lee	Y	Y	Y	N	N
10 Vacant					
11 McNerney	Y	Y	Y	Y	N
12 Speier	Y	Y	Y	Y	N
13 Stark	Y	Y	Y	N	Y
14 Eshoo	Y	Y	Y	Y	N
15 Honda	Y	Y	Y	Y	N
16 Lofgren	Y	Y	Y	Y	N
17 Farr	Y	Y	Y	Y	N
18 Cardoza	Y	Y	Y	Y	N
19 Radanovich	Y	N	Y	N	N
20 Costa	Y	Y	Y	Y	N
21 Nunes	Y	N	Y	N	N
22 McCarthy	Y	Y	Y	Y	N
23 Capps	Y	Y	Y	Y	N
24 Gallegly	Y	Y	Y	N	N
25 McKeon	Y	Y	Y	N	N
26 Dreier	Y	N	Y	N	N
27 Sherman	Y	Y	Y	Y	N
28 Berman	Y	Y	Y	Y	N
29 Schiff	Y	Y	Y	Y	N
30 Waxman	Y	Y	Y	Y	N
31 Becerra	Y	Y	Y	Y	N
32 Chu	Y	Y	Y	Y	N
33 Watson	Y	Y	Y	Y	N
34 Roybal-Allard	Y	Y	Y	Y	N
35 Waters	Y	Y	Y	Y	N
36 Harman	Y	Y	Y	Y	N
37 Richardson	Y	Y	Y	Y	N
38 Napolitano	Y	Y	Y	Y	N
39 Sánchez, Linda	Y	Y	Y	Y	N
40 Royce	Y	N	Y	N	Y
41 Lewis	Y	N	Y	N	N
42 Miller, Gary	Y	Y	Y	N	N
43 Baca	Y	Y	Y	Y	N
44 Calvert	Y	Y	Y	N	N
45 Bono Mack	Y	Y	Y	N	N
46 Rohrabacher	Y	N	Y	Y	Y
47 Sanchez, Loretta	Y	Y	Y	Y	N
48 Campbell	Y	N	Y	Y	Y
49 Issa	Y	N	Y	N	N
50 Bilbray	Y	Y	Y	N	N
51 Filner	Y	Y	Y	N	N
52 Hunter	Y	Y	Y	N	N
53 Davis	Y	Y	Y	Y	N

	658	659	660	661	662
COLORADO					
1 DeGette	Y	Y	Y	Y	N
2 Polis	Y	Y	Y	Y	N
3 Salazar	Y	Y	Y	Y	N
4 Markey	Y	Y	Y	Y	N
5 Lamborn	Y	N	Y	N	Y
6 Coffman	Y	N	Y	N	N
7 Perlmutter	Y	Y	Y	Y	N
CONNECTICUT					
1 Larson	Y	Y	Y	Y	N
2 Courtney	Y	Y	Y	Y	N
3 DeLauro	Y	Y	Y	Y	N
4 Himes	Y	Y	Y	Y	N
5 Murphy	Y	Y	Y	Y	N
DELAWARE					
AL Castle	Y	Y	Y	Y	Y
FLORIDA					
1 Miller	Y	Y	Y	N	Y
2 Boyd	Y	Y	Y	N	N
3 Brown	Y	Y	Y	Y	N
4 Crenshaw	Y	Y	Y	N	N
5 Brown-Waite	Y	Y	Y	N	N
6 Stearns	Y	N	Y	N	N
7 Mica	Y	Y	Y	N	N
8 Grayson	Y	Y	Y	Y	N
9 Bilirakis	Y	N	Y	N	N
10 Young	Y	Y	Y	N	N
11 Castor	Y	Y	Y	Y	N
12 Putnam	Y	Y	Y	N	N
13 Buchanan	Y	Y	Y	N	N
14 Mack	Y	N	Y	N	N
15 Posey	Y	Y	Y	N	N
16 Rooney	Y	Y	Y	N	N
17 Meek	Y	Y	Y	N	N
18 Ros-Lehtinen	Y	Y	Y	N	N
19 Wexler	Y	Y	Y	Y	N
20 Wasserman Schultz	Y	Y	Y	Y	N
21 Diaz-Balart, L.	Y	Y	Y	N	N
22 Klein	Y	Y	Y	Y	N
23 Hastings	Y	Y	Y	Y	N
24 Kosmas	Y	Y	Y	Y	N
25 Diaz-Balart, M.	Y	Y	Y	N	N
GEORGIA					
1 Kingston	Y	N	Y	N	?
2 Bishop	Y	Y	Y	Y	?
3 Westmoreland	Y	N	Y	N	Y
4 Johnson	Y	Y	Y	Y	N
5 Lewis	Y	Y	Y	N	N
6 Price	Y	N	Y	N	Y
7 Linder	Y	N	Y	N	Y
8 Marshall	Y	Y	Y	Y	N
9 Deal	Y	N	Y	N	Y
10 Broun	Y	N	Y	N	?
11 Gingrey	Y	N	Y	N	Y
12 Barrow	Y	Y	Y	Y	N
13 Scott	Y	Y	Y	Y	N
HAWAII					
1 Abercrombie	?	Y	Y	Y	N
2 Hirono	Y	Y	Y	Y	N
IDAHO					
1 Minnick	Y	Y	Y	N	Y
2 Simpson	Y	N	Y	N	N
ILLINOIS					
1 Rush	Y	Y	Y	Y	N
2 Jackson	Y	Y	Y	Y	N
3 Lipinski	Y	Y	Y	Y	?
4 Gutierrez	Y	Y	Y	Y	N
5 Quigley	Y	Y	Y	Y	N
6 Roskam	Y	Y	Y	N	N
7 Davis	Y	Y	Y	Y	N
8 Bean	Y	Y	Y	Y	N
9 Schakowsky	Y	Y	Y	Y	N
10 Kirk	Y	Y	Y	N	N
11 Halvorson	Y	Y	Y	Y	N
12 Costello	Y	Y	Y	Y	N
13 Biggert	Y	Y	Y	N	N
14 Foster	Y	Y	Y	Y	Y
15 Johnson	Y	Y	Y	Y	N

KEY   Republicans   Democrats

Y Voted for (yea)	**X** Paired against
# Paired for	**–** Announced against
+ Announced for	**P** Voted "present"
N Voted against (nay)	

C Voted "present" to avoid possible conflict of interest

? Did not vote or otherwise make a position known

	658	659	660	661	662
16 Manzullo	Y	Y	Y	N	N
17 Hare	Y	Y	Y	Y	N
18 Schock	Y	Y	Y	N	N
19 Shimkus	Y	N	Y	N	N
INDIANA					
1 Visclosky	Y	Y	Y	Y	N
2 Donnelly	Y	Y	Y	Y	N
3 Souder	Y	Y	Y	N	N
4 Buyer	Y	Y	Y	N	N
5 Burton	Y	Y	Y	N	Y
6 Pence	Y	Y	Y	N	?
7 Carson	Y	Y	Y	Y	N
8 Ellsworth	Y	Y	Y	Y	N
9 Hill	Y	Y	Y	Y	N
IOWA					
1 Braley	Y	Y	Y	Y	N
2 Loebsack	Y	Y	Y	Y	N
3 Boswell	Y	Y	Y	Y	N
4 Latham	Y	Y	Y	N	N
5 King	Y	Y	Y	N	N
KANSAS					
1 Moran	Y	Y	Y	N	Y
2 Jenkins	Y	Y	Y	N	Y
3 Moore	Y	Y	Y	Y	N
4 Tiahrt	Y	Y	Y	N	N
KENTUCKY					
1 Whitfield	Y	Y	Y	N	N
2 Guthrie	Y	Y	Y	N	N
3 Yarmuth	Y	Y	Y	Y	N
4 Davis	Y	Y	Y	N	N
5 Rogers	Y	Y	Y	N	N
6 Chandler	Y	Y	Y	Y	N
LOUISIANA					
1 Scalise	Y	N	Y	N	Y
2 Cao	Y	Y	Y	N	N
3 Melancon	Y	Y	Y	Y	N
4 Fleming	Y	Y	Y	N	N
5 Alexander	Y	Y	Y	N	N
6 Cassidy	Y	Y	Y	N	Y
7 Boustany	Y	Y	Y	N	Y
MAINE					
1 Pingree	Y	Y	Y	Y	N
2 Michaud	Y	Y	Y	Y	N
MARYLAND					
1 Kratovil	Y	Y	Y	Y	N
2 Ruppersberger	Y	Y	Y	Y	N
3 Sarbanes	Y	Y	Y	Y	N
4 Edwards	Y	Y	Y	Y	N
5 Hoyer	Y	Y	Y	Y	N
6 Bartlett	Y	N	Y	N	Y
7 Cummings	Y	Y	Y	Y	N
8 Van Hollen	Y	Y	Y	Y	N
MASSACHUSETTS					
1 Olver	Y	Y	Y	Y	?
2 Neal	Y	Y	Y	Y	N
3 McGovern	Y	Y	Y	Y	N
4 Frank	Y	Y	Y	Y	N
5 Tsongas	Y	Y	Y	Y	N
6 Tierney	Y	Y	Y	Y	N
7 Markey	Y	Y	Y	Y	N
8 Capuano	Y	Y	Y	Y	N
9 Lynch	Y	Y	Y	Y	N
10 Delahunt	Y	Y	Y	Y	N
MICHIGAN					
1 Stupak	Y	Y	Y	Y	N
2 Hoekstra	Y	Y	Y	N	N
3 Ehlers	Y	Y	Y	Y	N
4 Camp	Y	Y	Y	Y	N
5 Kildee	Y	Y	Y	Y	N
6 Upton	Y	Y	Y	Y	N
7 Schauer	Y	Y	Y	Y	N
8 Rogers	Y	Y	Y	N	N
9 Peters	Y	Y	Y	Y	N
10 Miller	Y	Y	Y	Y	N
11 McCotter	Y	Y	Y	Y	N
12 Levin	Y	Y	Y	Y	N
13 Kilpatrick	Y	Y	Y	Y	N
14 Conyers	Y	Y	Y	Y	N
15 Dingell	Y	Y	Y	Y	N
MINNESOTA					
1 Walz	Y	Y	Y	Y	N
2 Kline	Y	Y	Y	N	Y
3 Paulsen	Y	Y	Y	Y	N
4 McCollum	Y	Y	Y	Y	N

	658	659	660	661	662
5 Ellison	Y	Y	Y	Y	N
6 Bachmann	Y	Y	Y	N	Y
7 Peterson	Y	Y	Y	Y	N
8 Oberstar	Y	Y	Y	Y	N
MISSISSIPPI					
1 Childers	Y	Y	Y	Y	N
2 Thompson	Y	Y	Y	Y	N
3 Harper	Y	Y	Y	N	N
4 Taylor	Y	Y	Y	Y	N
MISSOURI					
1 Clay	Y	Y	Y	Y	N
2 Akin	Y	N	Y	N	N
3 Carnahan	Y	Y	Y	Y	N
4 Skelton	Y	Y	Y	Y	N
5 Cleaver	Y	Y	Y	Y	N
6 Graves	Y	Y	Y	N	N
7 Blunt	Y	Y	Y	N	N
8 Emerson	Y	Y	Y	N	N
9 Luetkemeyer	Y	Y	Y	N	N
MONTANA					
AL Rehberg	Y	Y	Y	N	N
NEBRASKA					
1 Fortenberry	Y	Y	Y	N	N
2 Terry	Y	Y	Y	N	N
3 Smith	Y	Y	Y	N	–
NEVADA					
1 Berkley	Y	Y	Y	Y	?
2 Heller	Y	Y	Y	Y	N
3 Titus	Y	Y	Y	Y	N
NEW HAMPSHIRE					
1 Shea-Porter	Y	Y	Y	Y	N
2 Hodes	Y	Y	Y	Y	N
NEW JERSEY					
1 Andrews	Y	Y	Y	Y	N
2 LoBiondo	Y	Y	Y	N	N
3 Adler	Y	Y	Y	N	N
4 Smith	Y	Y	Y	N	N
5 Garrett	Y	N	Y	Y	Y
6 Pallone	Y	Y	Y	Y	N
7 Lance	Y	N	Y	N	N
8 Pascrell	Y	Y	Y	Y	N
9 Rothman	Y	Y	Y	Y	N
10 Payne	Y	Y	Y	Y	N
11 Frelinghuysen	Y	Y	Y	N	N
12 Holt	Y	Y	Y	Y	N
13 Sires	Y	Y	Y	Y	N
NEW MEXICO					
1 Heinrich	Y	Y	Y	Y	N
2 Teague	Y	Y	Y	N	N
3 Lujan	Y	Y	Y	Y	N
NEW YORK					
1 Bishop	Y	Y	Y	Y	N
2 Israel	Y	Y	Y	Y	?
3 King	Y	Y	Y	N	N
4 McCarthy	?	?	?	?	?
5 Ackerman	Y	Y	Y	Y	N
6 Meeks	Y	Y	Y	Y	N
7 Crowley	Y	Y	Y	Y	N
8 Nadler	Y	Y	Y	Y	N
9 Weiner	Y	Y	Y	Y	N
10 Towns	Y	Y	Y	Y	N
11 Clarke	Y	Y	Y	Y	N
12 Velázquez	Y	Y	Y	N	N
13 McMahon	Y	Y	Y	Y	N
14 Maloney	Y	Y	Y	Y	N
15 Rangel	Y	Y	Y	Y	N
16 Serrano	Y	Y	Y	Y	N
17 Engel	Y	Y	Y	Y	N
18 Lowey	Y	Y	Y	Y	?
19 Hall	Y	Y	Y	+	–
20 Murphy	Y	Y	Y	Y	N
21 Tonko	Y	Y	Y	Y	N
22 Hinchey	Y	Y	Y	Y	?
23 McHugh	?	Y	Y	Y	N
24 Arcuri	Y	Y	Y	Y	N
25 Maffei	Y	Y	Y	Y	N
26 Lee	Y	Y	Y	N	N
27 Higgins	Y	Y	Y	Y	N
28 Slaughter	Y	Y	Y	Y	N
29 Massa	Y	Y	Y	Y	N
NORTH CAROLINA					
1 Butterfield	Y	Y	Y	Y	N
2 Etheridge	Y	Y	Y	Y	N
3 Jones	Y	Y	Y	Y	N
4 Price	Y	Y	Y	Y	N

	658	659	660	661	662
5 Foxx	Y	N	Y	N	Y
6 Coble	Y	Y	Y	N	Y
7 McIntyre	Y	Y	Y	Y	N
8 Kissell	Y	Y	Y	Y	N
9 Myrick	Y	N	Y	N	Y
10 McHenry	Y	Y	Y	N	Y
11 Shuler	Y	Y	Y	Y	N
12 Watt	Y	Y	Y	Y	N
13 Miller	Y	Y	Y	Y	N
NORTH DAKOTA					
AL Pomeroy	Y	Y	Y	Y	N
OHIO					
1 Driehaus	Y	Y	Y	Y	N
2 Schmidt	Y	Y	Y	N	Y
3 Turner	Y	Y	Y	Y	N
4 Jordan	Y	N	Y	N	N
5 Latta	Y	N	Y	N	N
6 Wilson	Y	Y	Y	Y	N
7 Austria	Y	Y	Y	N	N
8 Boehner	Y	N	Y	N	N
9 Kaptur	Y	Y	Y	Y	N
10 Kucinich	Y	Y	Y	N	N
11 Fudge	Y	Y	Y	Y	N
12 Tiberi	Y	Y	Y	N	N
13 Sutton	Y	Y	Y	Y	N
14 LaTourette	Y	Y	Y	N	N
15 Kilroy	Y	Y	Y	Y	N
16 Boccieri	Y	Y	Y	Y	N
17 Ryan	Y	Y	Y	Y	N
18 Space	Y	Y	Y	Y	N
OKLAHOMA					
1 Sullivan	Y	N	Y	N	N
2 Boren	Y	Y	Y	Y	N
3 Lucas	Y	Y	Y	N	N
4 Cole	Y	Y	Y	N	N
5 Fallin	Y	Y	Y	N	N
OREGON					
1 Wu	Y	Y	Y	Y	N
2 Walden	Y	Y	Y	N	N
3 Blumenauer	Y	Y	Y	Y	N
4 DeFazio	Y	Y	Y	Y	N
5 Schrader	?	Y	Y	Y	N
PENNSYLVANIA					
1 Brady	Y	Y	Y	Y	N
2 Fattah	Y	Y	Y	?	N
3 Dahlkemper	Y	Y	Y	Y	N
4 Altmire	Y	Y	Y	Y	N
5 Thompson	Y	Y	Y	N	N
6 Gerlach	Y	Y	Y	Y	N
7 Sestak	Y	Y	Y	Y	N
8 Murphy, P.	Y	Y	Y	Y	N
9 Shuster	Y	Y	Y	N	N
10 Carney	Y	Y	Y	Y	N
11 Kanjorski	Y	Y	Y	Y	N
12 Murtha	Y	N	Y	Y	N
13 Schwartz	Y	Y	Y	+	N
14 Doyle	Y	Y	Y	Y	N
15 Dent	Y	Y	Y	Y	N
16 Pitts	Y	N	Y	N	Y
17 Holden	Y	Y	Y	Y	N
18 Murphy, T.	Y	Y	Y	Y	–
19 Platts	Y	Y	Y	N	N
RHODE ISLAND					
1 Kennedy	Y	Y	Y	Y	N
2 Langevin	Y	Y	Y	Y	N
SOUTH CAROLINA					
1 Brown	Y	Y	Y	N	N
2 Wilson	Y	N	Y	N	Y
3 Barrett	Y	N	Y	N	Y
4 Inglis	Y	N	Y	N	Y
5 Spratt	Y	Y	Y	Y	N
6 Clyburn	Y	Y	Y	Y	N
SOUTH DAKOTA					
AL Herseth Sandlin	Y	Y	Y	Y	N
TENNESSEE					
1 Roe	Y	Y	Y	N	N
2 Duncan	Y	N	Y	Y	Y
3 Wamp	Y	Y	Y	N	N
4 Davis	?	?	Y	Y	N
5 Cooper	?	Y	Y	Y	N
6 Gordon	Y	Y	Y	Y	N
7 Blackburn	Y	N	Y	N	N
8 Tanner	Y	Y	Y	Y	N
9 Cohen	Y	Y	Y	Y	N

	658	659	660	661	662
TEXAS					
1 Gohmert	Y	N	Y	N	?
2 Poe	Y	Y	Y	N	N
3 Johnson, S.	Y	N	Y	N	N
4 Hall	Y	Y	Y	N	N
5 Hensarling	Y	N	Y	Y	Y
6 Barton	Y	N	Y	N	N
7 Culberson	Y	N	Y	N	N
8 Brady	Y	N	Y	N	N
9 Green, A.	Y	Y	Y	N	N
10 McCaul	Y	N	Y	N	N
11 Conaway	Y	N	Y	N	N
12 Granger	Y	N	Y	N	N
13 Thornberry	Y	N	Y	N	N
14 Paul	Y	N	Y	Y	Y
15 Hinojosa	Y	Y	Y	Y	N
16 Reyes	Y	Y	Y	Y	N
17 Edwards	Y	Y	Y	Y	N
18 Jackson Lee	Y	Y	Y	Y	N
19 Neugebauer	Y	N	Y	N	N
20 Gonzalez	Y	Y	Y	Y	N
21 Smith	Y	N	Y	N	N
22 Olson	Y	Y	Y	N	N
23 Rodriguez	Y	Y	Y	Y	N
24 Marchant	Y	N	Y	N	Y
25 Doggett	Y	Y	Y	Y	N
26 Burgess	Y	N	Y	N	N
27 Ortiz	Y	Y	Y	Y	N
28 Cuellar	Y	Y	Y	Y	N
29 Green, G.	Y	Y	Y	Y	N
30 Johnson, E.	Y	Y	Y	Y	N
31 Carter	Y	N	Y	N	N
32 Sessions	Y	N	Y	N	N
UTAH					
1 Bishop	Y	?	Y	N	N
2 Matheson	Y	Y	Y	Y	N
3 Chaffetz	Y	N	Y	N	N
VERMONT					
AL Welch	Y	Y	Y	Y	N
VIRGINIA					
1 Wittman	Y	Y	Y	N	N
2 Nye	Y	Y	Y	N	N
3 Scott	Y	Y	Y	Y	N
4 Forbes	Y	Y	Y	N	N
5 Perriello	Y	Y	Y	Y	N
6 Goodlatte	Y	N	Y	N	N
7 Cantor	Y	N	Y	N	Y
8 Moran	Y	Y	Y	Y	N
9 Boucher	Y	Y	Y	Y	N
10 Wolf	Y	Y	Y	N	N
11 Connolly	Y	Y	Y	Y	N
WASHINGTON					
1 Inslee	Y	Y	Y	Y	N
2 Larsen	Y	Y	Y	Y	N
3 Baird	Y	Y	Y	Y	N
4 Hastings	Y	Y	Y	N	N
5 McMorris Rodgers	Y	Y	Y	N	N
6 Dicks	Y	Y	Y	Y	N
7 McDermott	Y	Y	Y	Y	?
8 Reichert	Y	Y	Y	N	N
9 Smith	Y	Y	Y	Y	N
WEST VIRGINIA					
1 Mollohan	Y	Y	Y	Y	?
2 Capito	Y	Y	Y	N	N
3 Rahall	Y	Y	Y	Y	N
WISCONSIN					
1 Ryan	Y	Y	Y	Y	Y
2 Baldwin	Y	Y	Y	Y	N
3 Kind	Y	Y	Y	Y	N
4 Moore	Y	Y	Y	Y	N
5 Sensenbrenner	Y	N	Y	Y	Y
6 Petri	Y	Y	Y	Y	N
7 Obey	Y	Y	Y	Y	N
8 Kagen	Y	Y	Y	Y	N
WYOMING					
AL Lummis	Y	N	Y	N	Y
DELEGATES					
Faleomavaega (A.S.)				Y	N
Norton (D.C.)				+	N
Bordallo (Guam)				Y	N
Sablan (N. Marianas)				Y	N
Pierluisi (P.R.)				Y	N
Christensen (V.I.)				Y	N

IN THE HOUSE | By Vote Number

663. HR 3326. Fiscal 2010 Defense Appropriations/Kinetic Energy Interceptor. Tierney, D-Mass., amendment that would bar the use of funds in the Defense-wide research and development section of the bill for the Kinetic Energy Interceptor program. It would cut $80 million intended for the program from the bill total. Rejected in Committee of the Whole 124-307: R 14-163; D 110-144. July 30, 2009.

664. HR 3326. Fiscal 2010 Defense Appropriations/Enhanced Navy Shore Readiness Integration. Flake, R-Ariz., amendment that would bar the use of funds appropriated in the bill for the Enhanced Navy Shore Readiness Integration program. Rejected in Committee of the Whole 77-347: R 68-104; D 9-243. July 30, 2009.

665. HR 3326. Fiscal 2010 Defense Appropriations/Reduced Manning Situational Awareness. Flake, R-Ariz., amendment that would bar the use of funds appropriated in the bill for the Reduced Manning Situational Awareness program. Rejected in Committee of the Whole 69-351: R 57-116; D 12-235. July 30, 2009.

666. HR 3326. Fiscal 2010 Defense Appropriations/Gulf Range Mobile Instrumentation Capability. Flake, R-Ariz., amendment that would bar the use of funds appropriated in the bill for the Gulf Range Mobile Instrumentation Capability program. Rejected in Committee of the Whole 76-350: R 59-114; D 17-236. July 30, 2009.

667. HR 3326. Fiscal 2010 Defense Appropriations/Gunshot Localization System. Flake, R-Ariz., amendment that would bar the use of funds appropriated in the bill for an Ultra Low Profile EARS Gunshot Localization System. Rejected in Committee of the Whole 82-341: R 73-98; D 9-243. July 30, 2009.

668. HR 3326. Fiscal 2010 Defense Appropriations/Counter Air Defense Future Capabilities. Flake, R-Ariz., amendment that would bar the use of funds appropriated in the bill for AARGM Counter Air Defense Future Capabilities. Rejected in Committee of the Whole 78-348: R 71-101; D 7-247. July 30, 2009.

669. HR 3326. Fiscal 2010 Defense Appropriations/Ship Torpedo Defense Program. Flake, R-Ariz., amendment that would bar the use of funds appropriated in the bill for AN/SLQ-25D Integration, a next-generation system to counter undersea weapon threats. Rejected in Committee of the Whole 83-338: R 75-94; D 8-244. July 30, 2009.

	663	664	665	666	667	668	669
ALABAMA							
1 Bonner	N	P	P	P	P	P	P
2 Bright	Y	N	N	N	N	N	N
3 Rogers	N	N	N	N	N	N	N
4 Aderholt	N	N	N	N	N	N	?
5 Griffith	N	N	N	N	N	N	N
6 Bachus	N	N	N	N	N	N	N
7 Davis	N	N	N	N	N	N	N
ALASKA							
AL Young	N	N	N	N	N	N	N
ARIZONA							
1 Kirkpatrick	N	Y	Y	Y	Y	N	Y
2 Franks	N	N	N	N	N	N	N
3 Shadegg	N	Y	Y	Y	Y	Y	Y
4 Pastor	N	N	N	N	N	N	N
5 Mitchell	Y	N	N	N	N	N	N
6 Flake	N	Y	Y	Y	Y	Y	Y
7 Grijalva	Y	N	N	N	N	N	N
8 Giffords	Y	N	N	N	N	N	N
ARKANSAS							
1 Berry	N	N	?	N	N	N	N
2 Snyder	N	N	N	N	N	N	N
3 Boozman	N	N	N	N	N	Y	Y
4 Ross	N	N	N	N	N	N	N
CALIFORNIA							
1 Thompson	Y	N	N	N	N	N	N
2 Herger	N	Y	Y	Y	Y	Y	Y
3 Lungren	N	N	N	N	Y	N	Y
4 McClintock	N	Y	Y	Y	Y	Y	Y
5 Matsui	Y	N	N	N	N	N	N
6 Woolsey	?	N	N	N	N	N	N
7 Miller, George	Y	N	N	N	N	N	N
8 Pelosi							
9 Lee	Y	N	N	N	N	N	N
10 Vacant							
11 McNerney	N	N	N	N	N	N	N
12 Speier	Y	Y	Y	Y	Y	Y	Y
13 Stark	Y	Y	Y	?	Y	Y	Y
14 Eshoo	Y	N	N	N	N	N	N
15 Honda	Y	N	N	N	N	N	N
16 Lofgren	Y	P	P	P	P	P	P
17 Farr	Y	N	N	N	N	N	N
18 Cardoza	N	N	N	N	N	N	N
19 Radanovich	N	N	N	N	N	N	N
20 Costa	N	N	N	N	N	N	N
21 Nunes	N	Y	N	Y	Y	Y	Y
22 McCarthy	N	N	N	N	Y	N	N
23 Capps	Y	N	N	N	N	N	N
24 Gallegly	N	Y	N	N	N	N	N
25 McKeon	N	N	N	N	Y	N	N
26 Dreier	N	N	N	N	N	N	N
27 Sherman	Y	N	N	N	N	N	N
28 Berman	Y	N	N	N	N	N	N
29 Schiff	Y	N	N	N	N	N	N
30 Waxman	Y	N	N	N	N	N	N
31 Becerra	N	N	N	N	N	N	N
32 Chu	Y	N	N	N	N	N	N
33 Watson	N	N	N	N	N	N	N
34 Roybal-Allard	Y	N	N	N	N	N	N
35 Waters	N	N	N	N	N	N	N
36 Harman	N	N	N	N	N	N	N
37 Richardson	N	N	N	N	N	N	N
38 Napolitano	N	N	N	N	N	N	N
39 Sánchez, Linda	Y	N	N	N	N	N	N
40 Royce	N	Y	Y	Y	Y	Y	Y
41 Lewis	N	N	N	N	N	N	N
42 Miller, Gary	N	N	N	N	N	N	N
43 Baca	N	N	N	N	N	N	N
44 Calvert	N	N	N	N	N	N	N
45 Bono Mack	N	N	N	N	N	N	N
46 Rohrabacher	N	Y	Y	N	N	N	N
47 Sanchez, Loretta	Y	N	N	N	N	N	N
48 Campbell	N	Y	Y	Y	Y	Y	Y
49 Issa	N	Y	Y	Y	Y	Y	Y
50 Bilbray	N	N	N	N	N	N	N
51 Filner	Y	N	N	N	N	N	N
52 Hunter	N	N	N	N	N	N	N
53 Davis	Y	N	N	N	N	N	N

	663	664	665	666	667	668	669
COLORADO							
1 DeGette	N	N	N	N	N	N	N
2 Polis	Y	N	N	Y	N	N	N
3 Salazar	N	N	N	N	N	N	N
4 Markey	N	N	N	N	N	N	N
5 Lamborn	N	Y	Y	Y	Y	Y	Y
6 Coffman	N	Y	Y	Y	Y	Y	Y
7 Perlmutter	N	N	N	Y	N	N	N
CONNECTICUT							
1 Larson	N	N	N	N	N	N	N
2 Courtney	N	N	N	N	N	N	N
3 DeLauro	N	N	N	N	N	N	N
4 Himes	Y	N	N	N	N	N	N
5 Murphy	N	N	N	N	N	N	N
DELAWARE							
AL Castle	Y	Y	N	Y	Y	Y	Y
FLORIDA							
1 Miller	N	N	N	N	N	N	N
2 Boyd	N	N	N	N	N	N	N
3 Brown	N	N	N	N	N	N	N
4 Crenshaw	N	N	N	N	N	N	N
5 Brown-Waite	Y	N	N	N	N	N	N
6 Stearns	N	Y	N	Y	N	N	N
7 Mica	N	N	N	N	N	N	N
8 Grayson	N	N	N	N	N	N	N
9 Bilirakis	N	N	N	N	N	N	N
10 Young	N	N	N	N	N	N	N
11 Castor	Y	P	P	P	P	P	P
12 Putnam	N	N	N	N	N	N	N
13 Buchanan	N	?	N	N	N	N	N
14 Mack	N	N	N	N	N	N	N
15 Posey	N	N	N	N	N	N	N
16 Rooney	N	N	N	N	N	N	N
17 Meek	N	N	N	N	N	N	N
18 Ros-Lehtinen	N	N	N	N	N	N	N
19 Wexler	N	N	N	N	N	N	N
20 Wasserman Schultz	N	N	N	N	N	N	N
21 Diaz-Balart, L.	N	N	N	N	N	N	P
22 Klein	–	N	N	N	N	N	N
23 Hastings	N	N	N	N	N	N	N
24 Kosmas	N	N	N	N	N	N	N
25 Diaz-Balart, M.	N	N	N	N	N	N	N
GEORGIA							
1 Kingston	N	N	N	N	N	N	N
2 Bishop	N	N	N	N	N	N	N
3 Westmoreland	N	Y	Y	Y	Y	Y	Y
4 Johnson	Y	N	N	N	N	N	N
5 Lewis	Y	N	N	N	N	N	N
6 Price	N	Y	Y	Y	Y	Y	Y
7 Linder	N	Y	Y	Y	Y	Y	Y
8 Marshall	N	N	N	N	N	N	N
9 Deal	N	Y	Y	Y	Y	Y	Y
10 Broun	N	Y	Y	Y	Y	Y	Y
11 Gingrey	N	N	N	N	N	Y	Y
12 Barrow	N	N	N	N	N	N	N
13 Scott	N	N	N	N	N	N	N
HAWAII							
1 Abercrombie	N	N	N	N	N	N	N
2 Hirono	N	N	?	N	N	N	N
IDAHO							
1 Minnick	N	Y	Y	Y	Y	Y	Y
2 Simpson	N	N	N	N	N	N	N
ILLINOIS							
1 Rush	?	N	?	N	N	N	N
2 Jackson	N	N	N	N	N	N	N
3 Lipinski	N	N	N	N	N	N	N
4 Gutierrez	Y	N	N	N	N	N	N
5 Quigley	Y	N	N	N	N	N	N
6 Roskam	N	Y	Y	Y	Y	Y	Y
7 Davis	Y	N	N	N	N	N	N
8 Bean	N	N	N	N	N	N	N
9 Schakowsky	Y	N	N	N	N	N	N
10 Kirk	N	Y	N	N	Y	N	Y
11 Halvorson	Y	Y	Y	Y	Y	Y	Y
12 Costello	N	N	N	N	N	N	N
13 Biggert	Y	N	N	N	N	N	N
14 Foster	Y	Y	N	Y	Y	N	Y
15 Johnson	Y	Y	Y	Y	Y	Y	Y

KEY   **Republicans**   Democrats

Y Voted for (yea)	**X** Paired against	**C** Voted "present" to avoid possible conflict of interest
# Paired for	**–** Announced against	
+ Announced for	**P** Voted "present"	**?** Did not vote or otherwise make a position known
N Voted against (nay)		

	663	664	665	666	667	668	669
16 **Manzullo**	N	Y	N	Y	Y	Y	Y
17 Hare	Y	N	N	N	N	N	N
18 **Schock**	N	N	N	N	N	N	Y
19 **Shimkus**	N	Y	Y	N	Y	Y	Y
INDIANA							
1 Visclosky	Y	N	N	N	N	N	N
2 Donnelly	N	N	N	N	N	N	N
3 **Souder**	N	N	N	N	N	N	N
4 **Buyer**	N	N	N	N	N	N	N
5 **Burton**	N	Y	N	Y	Y	Y	Y
6 **Pence**	N	Y	Y	Y	Y	Y	Y
7 Carson	N	N	N	N	N	N	N
8 Ellsworth	Y	N	N	N	N	N	N
9 Hill	N	N	N	N	N	N	N
IOWA							
1 Braley	Y	N	N	N	N	N	N
2 Loebsack	Y	N	N	N	N	N	N
3 Boswell	Y	N	N	N	N	N	N
4 **Latham**	N	N	N	N	N	N	N
5 **King**	N	N	Y	Y	N	Y	Y
KANSAS							
1 **Moran**	N	Y	Y	Y	Y	Y	Y
2 **Jenkins**	Y	Y	Y	Y	Y	Y	Y
3 Moore	N	N	N	N	N	N	N
4 **Tiahrt**	N	N	N	N	N	N	N
KENTUCKY							
1 **Whitfield**	N	N	N	N	N	N	N
2 **Guthrie**	N	N	N	N	N	N	N
3 Yarmuth	Y	N	N	N	N	N	N
4 **Davis**	N	N	N	Y	N	N	N
5 **Rogers**	N	N	N	N	N	N	N
6 Chandler	N	P	P	P	P	P	P
LOUISIANA							
1 **Scalise**	N	Y	Y	Y	Y	Y	Y
2 **Cao**	N	N	N	N	N	N	N
3 Melancon	N	N	N	N	N	N	N
4 **Fleming**	N	N	N	N	N	N	N
5 **Alexander**	N	N	N	N	N	N	N
6 **Cassidy**	N	Y	Y	Y	Y	Y	Y
7 **Boustany**	N	Y	Y	Y	Y	Y	Y
MAINE							
1 Pingree	Y	N	N	N	N	N	N
2 Michaud	Y	N	N	N	N	N	N
MARYLAND							
1 Kratovil	N	N	N	N	N	N	N
2 Ruppersberger	N	N	N	N	N	N	N
3 Sarbanes	Y	N	N	N	N	N	N
4 Edwards	Y	N	N	N	N	N	N
5 Hoyer	Y	N	N	N	N	N	N
6 **Bartlett**	N	N	N	N	N	N	N
7 Cummings	N	N	N	N	N	N	N
8 Van Hollen	Y	N	N	N	N	N	N
MASSACHUSETTS							
1 Olver	Y	N	Y	N	N	N	N
2 Neal	Y	N	N	N	N	N	N
3 McGovern	Y	N	N	N	N	N	N
4 Frank	Y	N	N	N	N	N	N
5 Tsongas	Y	N	N	N	N	N	N
6 Tierney	Y	N	N	N	N	N	N
7 Markey	Y	N	N	N	N	N	N
8 Capuano	Y	N	N	N	N	N	N
9 Lynch	Y	N	N	N	N	N	N
10 Delahunt	Y	N	N	N	N	N	N
MICHIGAN							
1 Stupak	N	N	N	N	N	N	N
2 **Hoekstra**	Y	Y	Y	Y	Y	Y	Y
3 **Ehlers**	Y	Y	Y	N	Y	Y	Y
4 **Camp**	N	N	N	N	N	N	N
5 Kildee	N	N	N	N	N	N	N
6 **Upton**	N	N	N	N	Y	N	N
7 Schauer	Y	N	N	N	N	N	N
8 **Rogers**	N	N	N	N	N	N	N
9 Peters	Y	N	N	Y	N	N	N
10 **Miller**	N	N	N	N	N	N	N
11 **McCotter**	N	N	N	N	N	N	N
12 Levin	Y	N	N	N	N	N	N
13 Kilpatrick	N	N	N	N	N	N	N
14 Conyers	N	N	?	N	N	N	?
15 Dingell	N	N	N	N	N	N	N
MINNESOTA							
1 Walz	N	N	N	N	N	N	N
2 **Kline**	N	Y	Y	Y	Y	Y	Y
3 **Paulsen**	N	Y	N	Y	Y	N	N
4 McCollum	Y	N	N	N	N	N	N

	663	664	665	666	667	668	669
5 Ellison	N	N	?	N	N	N	N
6 **Bachmann**	N	Y	Y	Y	Y	Y	Y
7 Peterson	N	N	N	N	N	N	N
8 Oberstar	Y	N	N	N	N	N	N
MISSISSIPPI							
1 Childers	N	N	N	N	N	N	N
2 Thompson	N	N	N	N	N	N	N
3 **Harper**	N	P	P	P	P	P	P
4 Taylor	N	N	N	N	N	N	N
MISSOURI							
1 Clay	N	N	N	N	N	N	N
2 **Akin**	N	N	N	N	N	N	N
3 Carnahan	Y	N	N	N	N	N	N
4 Skelton	Y	N	N	N	N	N	N
5 Cleaver	N	N	N	N	N	N	N
6 **Graves**	N	Y	N	N	N	N	N
7 **Blunt**	N	N	N	N	Y	N	Y
8 **Emerson**	N	N	N	N	N	N	N
9 **Luetkemeyer**	N	N	N	N	N	N	N
MONTANA							
AL **Rehberg**	N	N	N	N	N	N	N
NEBRASKA							
1 **Fortenberry**	N	N	N	N	Y	Y	Y
2 **Terry**	N	N	Y	Y	Y	Y	Y
3 **Smith**	N	Y	Y	Y	Y	Y	Y
NEVADA							
1 Berkley	N	N	N	N	N	N	N
2 **Heller**	N	Y	Y	Y	Y	Y	Y
3 Titus	N	N	N	N	N	N	N
NEW HAMPSHIRE							
1 Shea-Porter	Y	N	N	N	N	N	N
2 Hodes	Y	N	N	N	N	N	N
NEW JERSEY							
1 Andrews	N	N	N	N	?	N	N
2 **LoBiondo**	N	N	N	N	N	N	N
3 Adler	N	N	N	N	N	N	N
4 **Smith**	N	N	N	N	N	N	N
5 **Garrett**	N	Y	Y	Y	Y	Y	Y
6 Pallone	N	N	N	N	N	N	N
7 **Lance**	N	N	N	N	N	N	N
8 Pascrell	N	N	N	N	N	N	N
9 Rothman	N	N	N	N	N	N	N
10 Payne	Y	N	N	N	N	N	?
11 **Frelinghuysen**	N	N	N	N	N	N	N
12 Holt	Y	N	N	N	N	N	N
13 Sires	N	N	N	N	N	N	N
NEW MEXICO							
1 Heinrich	Y	N	N	N	N	N	N
2 Teague	N	N	Y	N	N	N	N
3 Lujan	N	N	N	N	N	N	N
NEW YORK							
1 Bishop	Y	N	N	Y	N	N	N
2 Israel	Y	N	N	N	N	N	N
3 **King**	N	N	N	N	N	N	N
4 McCarthy	?	?	?	?	?	?	?
5 Ackerman	N	N	N	N	N	N	N
6 Meeks	N	N	N	N	N	N	N
7 Crowley	Y	N	N	N	N	N	N
8 Nadler	Y	N	N	N	N	N	N
9 Weiner	Y	N	N	N	N	N	N
10 Towns	N	N	N	N	N	N	N
11 Clarke	N	N	N	N	N	N	N
12 Velázquez	Y	N	N	N	N	N	N
13 McMahon	N	N	N	Y	N	N	N
14 Maloney	N	?	N	N	N	N	N
15 Rangel	N	N	N	N	N	N	N
16 Serrano	Y	N	N	N	N	N	N
17 Engel	N	N	N	N	N	N	N
18 Lowey	N	N	N	N	N	N	N
19 Hall	–	–	–	–	–	N	N
20 Murphy	Y	N	N	N	N	N	N
21 Tonko	Y	N	N	N	N	N	N
22 Hinchey	N	N	N	N	N	N	N
23 **McHugh**	N	N	N	N	N	N	N
24 Arcuri	Y	N	N	N	N	N	N
25 Maffei	Y	N	N	N	N	N	N
26 **Lee**	N	N	N	N	N	N	N
27 Higgins	N	N	N	N	N	N	N
28 Slaughter	Y	N	N	N	N	N	N
29 Massa	N	N	N	N	N	N	N
NORTH CAROLINA							
1 Butterfield	N	P	P	P	P	P	P
2 Etheridge	N	N	N	N	N	N	N
3 **Jones**	N	N	N	N	N	N	N
4 Price	Y	N	N	N	N	N	N

	663	664	665	666	667	668	669
5 **Foxx**	N	Y	Y	Y	Y	Y	Y
6 **Coble**	Y	Y	Y	Y	Y	Y	Y
7 McIntyre	N	N	N	N	N	N	N
8 Kissell	N	N	N	N	N	N	N
9 **Myrick**	N	Y	N	N	Y	Y	Y
10 **McHenry**	N	Y	Y	Y	Y	Y	Y
11 Shuler	N	N	N	N	N	N	N
12 Watt	Y	N	N	N	N	N	N
13 Miller	Y	N	N	N	N	N	N
NORTH DAKOTA							
AL Pomeroy	Y	N	N	N	N	N	N
OHIO							
1 Driehaus	N	N	N	Y	N	N	N
2 **Schmidt**	N	Y	Y	Y	Y	Y	Y
3 **Turner**	N	N	N	N	N	N	N
4 **Jordan**	N	Y	Y	Y	Y	Y	Y
5 **Latta**	N	N	N	N	N	N	N
6 Wilson	N	N	N	N	N	N	N
7 **Austria**	N	N	N	N	N	N	N
8 **Boehner**	N	Y	N	N	Y	Y	Y
9 Kaptur	Y	N	N	N	N	N	N
10 Kucinich	N	N	N	N	N	N	N
11 Fudge	N	N	N	N	N	N	N
12 **Tiberi**	N	N	N	N	N	N	N
13 Sutton	Y	N	N	N	N	N	?
14 **LaTourette**	N	N	N	N	N	N	N
15 Kilroy	Y	N	N	N	N	N	N
16 Boccieri	N	N	N	N	N	N	N
17 Ryan	N	N	N	N	N	N	N
18 Space	N	N	N	N	N	N	N
OKLAHOMA							
1 **Sullivan**	N	N	N	N	N	N	N
2 Boren	N	N	N	N	N	N	N
3 **Lucas**	N	N	N	N	N	N	N
4 **Cole**	?	N	N	N	N	N	?
5 **Fallin**	N	N	N	N	N	N	N
OREGON							
1 Wu	Y	N	N	N	N	N	N
2 **Walden**	Y	N	Y	Y	Y	Y	Y
3 Blumenauer	Y	Y	Y	N	Y	Y	N
4 DeFazio	Y	N	N	N	N	N	N
5 Schrader	N	N	N	N	N	N	N
PENNSYLVANIA							
1 Brady	N	N	N	N	N	N	N
2 Fattah	N	N	N	N	N	N	N
3 Dahlkemper	N	N	N	N	N	N	N
4 Altmire	N	N	N	N	N	N	N
5 **Thompson**	N	N	N	N	N	N	N
6 **Gerlach**	N	N	N	Y	Y	Y	N
7 Sestak	Y	N	N	N	N	N	N
8 Murphy, P.	Y	N	N	N	N	N	N
9 **Shuster**	N	N	N	N	N	N	N
10 Carney	N	N	N	N	N	N	N
11 Kanjorski	N	N	N	N	N	N	N
12 Murtha	N	N	N	N	N	N	N
13 Schwartz	N	N	N	N	N	N	N
14 Doyle	N	N	N	N	N	N	N
15 **Dent**	N	P	P	P	P	P	P
16 **Pitts**	N	Y	Y	Y	Y	Y	Y
17 Holden	N	N	N	N	N	N	N
18 **Murphy, T.**	N	N	N	N	N	N	N
19 **Platts**	N	N	N	Y	Y	Y	N
RHODE ISLAND							
1 Kennedy	N	N	N	N	N	N	N
2 Langevin	Y	N	N	N	N	N	N
SOUTH CAROLINA							
1 **Brown**	N	N	N	N	N	N	N
2 **Wilson**	N	N	N	N	N	N	N
3 **Barrett**	N	P	P	P	P	P	P
4 **Inglis**	N	Y	Y	Y	Y	Y	Y
5 Spratt	Y	N	N	N	N	N	N
6 Clyburn	N	N	N	N	N	N	N
SOUTH DAKOTA							
AL Herseth Sandlin	N	N	N	N	N	N	N
TENNESSEE							
1 **Roe**	N	Y	Y	Y	Y	Y	Y
2 **Duncan**	Y	Y	Y	N	Y	Y	Y
3 **Wamp**	N	Y	N	Y	Y	Y	Y
4 Davis	N	N	N	N	N	N	N
5 Cooper	N	Y	Y	Y	Y	Y	Y
6 Gordon	Y	N	N	N	N	N	N
7 **Blackburn**	N	Y	Y	N	Y	Y	Y
8 Tanner	N	N	N	N	N	N	N
9 Cohen	N	N	N	N	N	N	N

	663	664	665	666	667	668	669
TEXAS							
1 **Gohmert**	N	Y	Y	Y	Y	Y	?
2 **Poe**	N	N	N	N	N	N	Y
3 **Johnson, S.**	N	N	N	N	N	N	N
4 **Hall**	N	N	N	N	?	N	N
5 **Hensarling**	N	Y	Y	Y	Y	Y	Y
6 **Barton**	N	Y	N	N	Y	?	N
7 **Culberson**	N	N	N	N	N	N	N
8 **Brady**	N	N	N	N	N	Y	Y
9 Green, A.	N	N	N	N	N	N	N
10 **McCaul**	N	Y	Y	Y	Y	Y	Y
11 **Conaway**	N	P	P	P	P	P	P
12 **Granger**	N	N	N	N	N	N	N
13 **Thornberry**	N	N	N	N	N	N	N
14 **Paul**	Y	Y	N	N	N	N	N
15 Hinojosa	N	N	N	N	N	N	N
16 Reyes	N	N	N	N	N	N	N
17 Edwards	N	?	N	N	?	N	N
18 Jackson Lee	N	N	N	N	N	N	N
19 **Neugebauer**	N	N	N	N	N	N	N
20 Gonzalez	N	N	N	N	N	N	N
21 **Smith**	N	N	N	N	N	N	N
22 **Olson**	N	N	N	N	N	N	N
23 Rodriguez	?	N	?	N	N	?	N
24 **Marchant**	N	Y	Y	N	Y	Y	Y
25 Doggett	Y	N	Y	Y	N	N	N
26 **Burgess**	N	N	N	N	Y	Y	Y
27 Ortiz	N	N	N	N	N	N	N
28 Cuellar	N	N	N	N	N	N	N
29 Green, G.	?	N	N	N	N	N	N
30 Johnson, E.	N	N	?	N	N	N	N
31 **Carter**	N	N	N	N	N	N	N
32 **Sessions**	N	Y	Y	Y	Y	Y	Y
UTAH							
1 **Bishop**	N	N	N	N	N	N	N
2 Matheson	Y	N	N	N	N	N	N
3 **Chaffetz**	N	Y	Y	Y	Y	Y	Y
VERMONT							
AL Welch	Y	P	P	P	P	P	P
VIRGINIA							
1 **Wittman**	N	Y	Y	Y	P	Y	Y
2 Nye	N	N	N	Y	N	N	N
3 Scott	N	N	N	N	N	N	N
4 **Forbes**	N	Y	Y	N	N	Y	Y
5 Perriello	Y	N	N	N	N	N	N
6 **Goodlatte**	Y	Y	Y	N	Y	Y	Y
7 **Cantor**	N	Y	N	N	Y	Y	Y
8 Moran	Y	N	N	N	N	N	N
9 Boucher	N	N	N	N	N	N	N
10 **Wolf**	N	N	N	N	N	N	Y
11 Connolly	N	N	N	Y	N	N	N
WASHINGTON							
1 Inslee	Y	N	N	N	N	N	N
2 Larsen	Y	N	N	N	N	N	N
3 Baird	Y	N	N	N	N	N	N
4 **Hastings**	N	N	N	N	N	N	N
5 **McMorris Rodgers**	N	N	N	N	N	N	N
6 Dicks	N	N	N	N	N	N	N
7 McDermott	N	N	N	N	N	N	N
8 **Reichert**	N	N	N	N	N	N	N
9 Smith	N	N	N	N	N	N	N
WEST VIRGINIA							
1 Mollohan	N	N	N	N	N	N	N
2 **Capito**	N	N	N	N	N	N	N
3 Rahall	N	N	N	N	N	N	N
WISCONSIN							
1 **Ryan**	N	Y	Y	Y	Y	Y	Y
2 Baldwin	Y	N	N	N	N	N	N
3 Kind	Y	Y	Y	Y	Y	Y	Y
4 Moore	Y	N	N	N	N	N	N
5 **Sensenbrenner**	Y	Y	Y	Y	Y	Y	Y
6 **Petri**	Y	Y	Y	Y	Y	Y	Y
7 Obey	Y	N	N	N	N	N	N
8 Kagen	Y	N	N	Y	N	N	N
WYOMING							
AL **Lummis**	N	Y	Y	Y	Y	Y	Y
DELEGATES							
Faleomavaega (A.S.)	N	N	N	N	N	N	N
Norton (D.C.)	N	N	N	N	N	N	N
Bordallo (Guam)	Y	N	N	N	N	N	N
Sablan (N. Marianas)	N	N	N	N	N	N	N
Pierluisi (P.R.)	Y	N	N	N	N	N	N
Christensen (V.I.)	N	N	N	N	N	N	N

IN THE HOUSE | By Vote Number

670. HR 3326. Fiscal 2010 Defense Appropriations/Member Projects Reduction. Flake, R-Ariz., amendment that would bar the use of funds in the bill for 75 member-requested projects, including $8 million for the AN/SLQ-25D Integration, $6.3 million for the EP-3E Requirements Capability Migration Systems Integration Lab and $5 million for Submarine Navigation Decision Aids. Rejected in Committee of the Whole 118-304: R 99-70; D 19-234. July 30, 2009.

671. HR 3326. Fiscal 2010 Defense Appropriations/En Bloc Member Projects Reduction. Flake, R-Ariz., en bloc amendment that would bar the use of funds in the bill for 552 member-requested projects, including the Civil Air Patrol, Next Generation Wearable Video Capture System and a Kinetic Hydropower System Turbine. Rejected in Committee of the Whole 82-342: R 73-99; D 9-243. July 30, 2009.

672. HR 3326. Fiscal 2010 Defense Appropriations/Military Projects. Campbell, R-Calif., amendment that would bar the use of funds appropriated in the bill for Marine Corps operations and maintenance for the Modular General Purpose Tent System Type III or Rapid Deployable Shelter project and cut $3 million intended for the projects from the bill total. Rejected in Committee of the Whole 81-353: R 77-101; D 4-252. July 30, 2009.

673. HR 3326. Fiscal 2010 Defense Appropriations/Model for Green Laboratories and Clean Rooms. Campbell, R-Calif., amendment that would bar the use of funds appropriated in the bill for Army research and development for the Model for Green Laboratories and Clean Rooms project and cut $1.5 million intended for the project from the bill total. Rejected in Committee of the Whole 99-338: R 93-85; D 6-253. July 30, 2009.

674. HR 3326. Fiscal 2010 Defense Appropriations/Recommit. Frelinghuysen, R-N.J., motion to recommit the bill to the Appropriations Committee with instructions that it be reported back immediately after deleting a provision that would bar the use of funds in the bill for advance procurement of the F-22 aircraft; as well as inserting provisions to increase funding for Army military personnel by $100 million and Air Force aircraft procurement by $304.8 million, offset by a reduction of $404.8 million for Navy research, development, test and evaluation. Motion rejected 169-261: R 154-22; D 15-239. A "nay" was a vote in support of the president's position. July 30, 2009.

675. HR 3326. Fiscal 2010 Defense Appropriations/Passage. Passage of the bill that would appropriate $636.6 billion for the Defense Department in fiscal 2010. The total includes $154.1 billion for operations and maintenance; $104.8 billion for procurement; and $80.2 billion for research and development. It would provide $9.3 billion for ballistic missile defense, $29.9 billion for the Defense Health Program, and $122.4 billion for military personnel, including a 3.4 percent pay raise. It also includes $128.2 billion for overseas operations in Iraq and Afghanistan. Passed 400-30: R 170-7; D 230-23. July 30, 2009.

676. H Con Res 172. Adjournment/Adoption. Adoption of the concurrent resolution that would provide for adjournment of the House until 2 p.m. on Sept. 8, and the Senate until noon on Sept. 8. Adopted 231-191: R 11-165; D 220-26. July 30, 2009.

	670	671	672	673	674	675	676
ALABAMA							
1 Bonner	P	P	N	N	Y	Y	N
2 Bright	N	N	N	N	Y	Y	N
3 **Rogers**	N	N	N	N	Y	Y	N
4 **Aderholt**	N	N	N	Y	Y	Y	N
5 Griffith	N	N	N	N	N	N	Y
6 **Bachus**	N	N	N	N	Y	Y	N
7 Davis	N	N	N	N	Y	Y	Y
ALASKA							
AL **Young**	N	N	N	N	Y	Y	Y
ARIZONA							
1 Kirkpatrick	Y	N	N	N	Y	Y	Y
2 **Franks**	+	N	Y	Y	Y	Y	Y
3 **Shadegg**	Y	Y	Y	Y	Y	Y	N
4 Pastor	N	N	N	N	N	Y	Y
5 Mitchell	Y	N	N	N	N	Y	Y
6 **Flake**	Y	Y	Y	Y	N	N	N
7 Grijalva	N	N	N	N	N	Y	?
8 Giffords	Y	N	N	N	Y	Y	N
ARKANSAS							
1 Berry	N	N	N	N	N	N	Y
2 Snyder	N	N	N	N	N	Y	Y
3 **Boozman**	Y	N	Y	Y	Y	Y	N
4 Ross	N	N	N	N	N	Y	Y
CALIFORNIA							
1 Thompson	N	N	N	N	N	Y	Y
2 **Herger**	?	Y	Y	Y	Y	Y	N
3 **Lungren**	Y	Y	N	Y	Y	Y	N
4 **McClintock**	Y	Y	Y	Y	Y	Y	N
5 Matsui	N	N	N	N	N	Y	Y
6 Woolsey	N	N	N	N	N	Y	Y
7 Miller, George	N	N	N	N	N	N	Y
8 Pelosi							
9 Lee	N	N	N	N	N	N	Y
10 Vacant							
11 McNerney	N	N	N	N	N	Y	Y
12 Speier	Y	Y	Y	Y	N	N	Y
13 Stark	Y	Y	N	N	N	N	Y
14 Eshoo	N	N	N	N	N	Y	Y
15 Honda	N	N	N	N	N	Y	Y
16 Lofgren	P	P	N	N	N	N	?
17 Farr	N	N	N	N	N	Y	Y
18 Cardoza	N	N	N	N	N	Y	Y
19 **Radanovich**	N	N	N	N	Y	Y	N
20 Costa	N	N	N	N	N	Y	Y
21 **Nunes**	Y	Y	Y	Y	Y	Y	N
22 **McCarthy**	N	Y	Y	Y	Y	Y	N
23 Capps	N	N	N	N	N	Y	Y
24 **Gallegly**	Y	N	N	Y	Y	Y	N
25 **McKeon**	Y	N	N	Y	Y	Y	N
26 **Dreier**	N	N	N	N	Y	Y	N
27 Sherman	N	N	N	N	N	Y	Y
28 Berman	N	N	N	N	N	Y	Y
29 Schiff	N	N	N	N	N	Y	Y
30 Waxman	N	N	N	N	N	Y	Y
31 Becerra	N	N	N	N	N	Y	Y
32 Chu	N	N	N	N	N	Y	Y
33 Watson	N	N	N	N	N	Y	Y
34 Roybal-Allard	N	N	N	N	N	Y	Y
35 Waters	N	?	?	N	N	N	Y
36 Harman	N	N	N	N	N	Y	Y
37 Richardson	N	N	N	N	N	Y	Y
38 Napolitano	N	N	N	N	N	Y	Y
39 Sánchez, Linda	N	N	N	N	N	Y	Y
40 **Royce**	Y	Y	Y	Y	Y	N	N
41 **Lewis**	N	N	N	N	Y	Y	N
42 **Miller, Gary**	Y	N	N	Y	Y	Y	N
43 Baca	N	N	N	N	N	Y	Y
44 **Calvert**	N	N	N	Y	Y	Y	N
45 **Bono Mack**	Y	N	N	Y	Y	Y	N
46 **Rohrabacher**	Y	Y	Y	Y	N	Y	N
47 Sanchez, Loretta	N	N	N	N	N	Y	?
48 **Campbell**	Y	Y	Y	Y	N	N	N
49 **Issa**	Y	Y	Y	Y	Y	Y	N
50 **Bilbray**	N	N	N	N	Y	Y	N
51 Filner	N	N	N	N	N	N	Y
52 **Hunter**	N	N	N	Y	Y	Y	N
53 Davis	N	N	N	N	N	Y	Y

	670	671	672	673	674	675	676
COLORADO							
1 DeGette	N	N	N	N	N	Y	Y
2 Polis	N	N	N	N	N	Y	Y
3 Salazar	N	N	N	N	Y	Y	Y
4 Markey	Y	N	N	N	N	Y	Y
5 **Lamborn**	Y	Y	Y	Y	Y	Y	N
6 **Coffman**	Y	Y	Y	Y	Y	Y	N
7 Perlmutter	N	N	N	N	N	Y	Y
CONNECTICUT							
1 Larson	N	N	N	N	N	Y	Y
2 Courtney	N	N	N	N	N	Y	Y
3 DeLauro	N	N	N	N	N	Y	Y
4 Himes	Y	Y	N	N	N	Y	Y
5 Murphy	N	N	N	N	N	Y	Y
DELAWARE							
AL **Castle**	Y	N	N	Y	N	Y	N
FLORIDA							
1 **Miller**	N	N	N	Y	Y	Y	N
2 Boyd	N	N	N	N	Y	Y	Y
3 Brown	N	N	N	N	N	Y	Y
4 **Crenshaw**	N	N	N	N	Y	Y	N
5 **Brown-Waite**	Y	N	Y	N	Y	Y	N
6 **Stearns**	Y	Y	Y	Y	Y	Y	N
7 **Mica**	N	N	N	Y	Y	Y	N
8 Grayson	N	N	N	N	N	Y	Y
9 **Bilirakis**	Y	N	N	Y	Y	Y	N
10 **Young**	N	N	N	Y	Y	Y	?
11 Castor	P	P	N	N	N	Y	Y
12 **Putnam**	N	N	N	N	Y	Y	N
13 **Buchanan**	N	N	N	N	Y	Y	N
14 **Mack**	Y	N	N	Y	Y	Y	?
15 **Posey**	Y	N	N	Y	Y	Y	N
16 **Rooney**	Y	N	Y	Y	Y	Y	N
17 Meek	N	N	N	N	N	Y	Y
18 **Ros-Lehtinen**	N	N	N	N	Y	Y	N
19 Wexler	N	N	N	N	N	Y	Y
20 Wasserman Schultz	N	N	N	N	N	Y	Y
21 **Diaz-Balart, L.**	P	P	N	N	Y	Y	N
22 Klein	N	N	N	N	N	Y	Y
23 Hastings	N	N	N	N	N	Y	Y
24 Kosmas	N	N	N	N	Y	Y	N
25 **Diaz-Balart, M.**	N	N	N	N	Y	Y	N
GEORGIA							
1 **Kingston**	N	N	N	N	Y	Y	N
2 Bishop	N	N	N	N	N	Y	Y
3 **Westmoreland**	Y	Y	Y	Y	Y	Y	N
4 Johnson	N	N	N	N	N	Y	Y
5 Lewis	N	N	N	N	N	N	Y
6 **Price**	Y	Y	Y	Y	Y	Y	N
7 **Linder**	Y	Y	Y	Y	Y	Y	N
8 Marshall	N	N	N	N	Y	Y	Y
9 **Deal**	Y	Y	Y	Y	Y	Y	N
10 **Broun**	Y	Y	Y	Y	Y	Y	N
11 **Gingrey**	Y	N	N	Y	Y	Y	N
12 Barrow	N	N	N	N	Y	Y	Y
13 Scott	N	N	N	N	Y	Y	Y
HAWAII							
1 Abercrombie	N	N	N	N	N	Y	Y
2 Hirono	N	N	N	N	N	Y	Y
IDAHO							
1 Minnick	Y	Y	Y	Y	Y	Y	N
2 **Simpson**	N	N	N	Y	Y	Y	N
ILLINOIS							
1 Rush	N	N	N	?	N	Y	Y
2 Jackson	N	N	N	N	N	Y	Y
3 Lipinski	N	N	N	N	N	Y	Y
4 Gutierrez	N	N	N	N	N	Y	Y
5 Quigley	Y	N	N	N	N	Y	Y
6 **Roskam**	Y	Y	Y	Y	Y	Y	N
7 Davis	?	N	N	N	N	Y	Y
8 Bean	N	N	N	N	Y	Y	Y
9 Schakowsky	N	N	N	N	N	N	Y
10 **Kirk**	Y	Y	Y	Y	Y	Y	N
11 Halvorson	Y	Y	Y	Y	N	Y	N
12 Costello	N	N	N	N	N	Y	Y
13 **Biggert**	N	N	N	N	Y	Y	N
14 Foster	Y	N	N	N	N	Y	N
15 **Johnson**	Y	Y	Y	Y	N	Y	N

KEY   **Republicans**   Democrats

Y Voted for (yea)	X Paired against	C Voted "present" to avoid possible conflict of interest
# Paired for	– Announced against	
+ Announced for	P Voted "present"	? Did not vote or otherwise make a position known
N Voted against (nay)		

	670	671	672	673	674	675	676
16 **Manzullo**	Y	N	Y	Y	Y	Y	N
17 Hare	N	N	N	N	N	Y	Y
18 **Schock**	N	N	N	N	Y	Y	N
19 **Shimkus**	Y	Y	Y	Y	Y	Y	N
INDIANA							
1 Visclosky	N	N	N	N	N	Y	Y
2 Donnelly	N	N	N	N	N	Y	N
3 **Souder**	N	N	N	N	Y	Y	N
4 **Buyer**	Y	N	Y	N	Y	Y	N
5 **Burton**	Y	Y	Y	Y	Y	Y	N
6 **Pence**	Y	Y	Y	Y	Y	Y	N
7 Carson	N	N	N	N	N	Y	Y
8 Ellsworth	N	N	N	N	N	Y	N
9 Hill	N	N	N	N	N	Y	Y
IOWA							
1 Braley	N	N	N	N	N	Y	Y
2 Loebsack	N	N	N	N	N	Y	Y
3 Boswell	N	N	N	N	N	Y	Y
4 **Latham**	N	N	N	N	Y	Y	N
5 **King**	N	Y	Y	Y	Y	Y	N
KANSAS							
1 **Moran**	Y	Y	Y	Y	Y	Y	N
2 **Jenkins**	Y	Y	Y	Y	Y	Y	N
3 Moore	N	N	N	N	N	Y	Y
4 **Tiahrt**	N	N	N	N	Y	Y	N
KENTUCKY							
1 **Whitfield**	N	N	N	N	Y	Y	N
2 **Guthrie**	N	N	N	N	Y	Y	N
3 Yarmuth	N	N	N	N	N	Y	?
4 **Davis**	N	N	N	N	Y	Y	N
5 **Rogers**	N	N	N	N	Y	Y	N
6 Chandler	P	P	N	N	N	Y	Y
LOUISIANA							
1 **Scalise**	Y	Y	Y	Y	Y	Y	N
2 **Cao**	Y	N	N	N	Y	Y	Y
3 Melancon	N	N	N	N	N	Y	N
4 **Fleming**	N	Y	N	Y	Y	Y	N
5 **Alexander**	N	N	N	N	Y	Y	N
6 **Cassidy**	Y	Y	Y	Y	Y	Y	N
7 **Boustany**	Y	Y	Y	Y	Y	Y	N
MAINE							
1 Pingree	N	N	?	N	N	Y	Y
2 Michaud	N	N	N	N	N	Y	N
MARYLAND							
1 Kratovil	N	N	N	N	Y	Y	N
2 Ruppersberger	N	N	N	N	N	Y	Y
3 Sarbanes	N	N	N	N	N	Y	Y
4 Edwards	N	?	N	N	N	Y	Y
5 Hoyer	N	N	N	N	N	Y	Y
6 **Bartlett**	N	N	N	N	Y	Y	N
7 Cummings	N	N	N	N	N	Y	Y
8 Van Hollen	N	N	N	N	N	Y	?
MASSACHUSETTS							
1 Olver	N	N	N	N	N	Y	Y
2 Neal	N	N	N	N	N	Y	Y
3 McGovern	N	N	N	N	N	Y	Y
4 Frank	N	N	N	N	N	N	Y
5 Tsongas	N	N	N	N	N	Y	Y
6 Tierney	N	N	N	N	N	N	Y
7 Markey	N	N	N	N	N	Y	Y
8 Capuano	N	N	N	N	N	Y	Y
9 Lynch	N	N	N	N	N	Y	Y
10 Delahunt	N	N	N	N	N	Y	Y
MICHIGAN							
1 Stupak	N	N	N	N	N	Y	Y
2 **Hoekstra**	Y	Y	Y	Y	Y	Y	N
3 **Ehlers**	Y	Y	Y	Y	N	Y	Y
4 **Camp**	Y	N	N	N	N	Y	N
5 Kildee	N	N	N	N	N	Y	Y
6 **Upton**	Y	N	N	Y	N	Y	N
7 Schauer	N	N	N	N	N	Y	Y
8 **Rogers**	Y	N	Y	N	Y	Y	N
9 Peters	N	N	N	N	N	Y	N
10 **Miller**	Y	Y	N	N	N	Y	N
11 **McCotter**	Y	Y	N	N	Y	Y	N
12 Levin	N	N	N	N	N	Y	Y
13 Kilpatrick	N	N	N	N	N	Y	Y
14 Conyers	N	N	N	N	N	Y	Y
15 Dingell	N	N	N	N	N	Y	Y
MINNESOTA							
1 Walz	N	N	N	N	N	Y	Y
2 **Kline**	Y	Y	Y	Y	Y	Y	N
3 **Paulsen**	N	N	Y	Y	N	Y	N
4 McCollum	N	N	N	N	N	Y	Y

	670	671	672	673	674	675	676
5 Ellison	N	N	N	N	N	N	Y
6 **Bachmann**	Y	Y	Y	Y	Y	Y	N
7 Peterson	N	N	N	N	N	Y	Y
8 Oberstar	N	N	N	N	N	Y	Y
MISSISSIPPI							
1 Childers	N	N	N	N	N	Y	Y
2 Thompson	N	N	N	N	N	Y	Y
3 **Harper**	P	P	N	N	Y	Y	N
4 Taylor	N	N	N	N	N	Y	Y
MISSOURI							
1 Clay	N	N	N	N	N	Y	Y
2 **Akin**	N	N	N	N	Y	Y	N
3 Carnahan	N	N	N	N	N	Y	Y
4 Skelton	N	N	N	N	N	Y	Y
5 Cleaver	N	N	N	N	N	Y	Y
6 **Graves**	?	N	N	Y	Y	Y	N
7 **Blunt**	N	N	Y	Y	Y	Y	N
8 **Emerson**	N	Y	N	N	N	Y	N
9 **Luetkemeyer**	Y	Y	N	Y	Y	Y	N
MONTANA							
AL **Rehberg**	N	N	N	N	Y	Y	N
NEBRASKA							
1 **Fortenberry**	Y	Y	N	N	Y	Y	N
2 **Terry**	Y	N	N	Y	Y	Y	N
3 **Smith**	Y	Y	Y	Y	Y	Y	N
NEVADA							
1 Berkley	N	N	N	N	N	Y	Y
2 **Heller**	Y	Y	Y	Y	Y	Y	N
3 Titus	N	N	N	N	N	Y	Y
NEW HAMPSHIRE							
1 Shea-Porter	N	N	N	N	N	Y	Y
2 Hodes	Y	N	N	N	N	Y	Y
NEW JERSEY							
1 Andrews	N	N	N	N	N	Y	Y
2 **LoBiondo**	N	N	N	N	Y	Y	N
3 Adler	N	N	N	N	Y	Y	N
4 **Smith**	N	N	N	N	Y	Y	Y
5 **Garrett**	Y	Y	Y	Y	N	Y	N
6 Pallone	N	N	N	N	N	Y	Y
7 **Lance**	N	N	N	N	Y	Y	N
8 Pascrell	N	N	N	N	N	Y	Y
9 Rothman	N	N	N	N	N	Y	Y
10 Payne	N	N	N	N	N	N	?
11 **Frelinghuysen**	N	N	N	N	Y	Y	N
12 Holt	N	N	N	N	N	Y	Y
13 Sires	N	N	N	N	N	Y	Y
NEW MEXICO							
1 Heinrich	N	N	N	N	N	Y	Y
2 Teague	Y	N	N	N	Y	Y	Y
3 Lujan	N	N	N	N	N	Y	Y
NEW YORK							
1 Bishop	N	N	N	N	N	Y	N
2 Israel	N	N	N	N	N	Y	Y
3 **King**	N	N	N	N	Y	Y	N
4 McCarthy	?	?	?	?	?	?	?
5 Ackerman	N	N	N	N	N	Y	Y
6 Meeks	N	N	N	N	N	Y	Y
7 Crowley	N	N	N	N	N	Y	Y
8 Nadler	N	N	N	N	N	Y	Y
9 Weiner	N	N	N	N	N	Y	Y
10 Towns	N	N	N	N	N	N	Y
11 Clarke	N	N	N	N	N	Y	Y
12 Velázquez	N	N	N	N	N	Y	Y
13 McMahon	Y	N	N	N	N	Y	Y
14 Maloney	N	N	N	N	N	Y	Y
15 Rangel	N	N	N	N	N	Y	Y
16 Serrano	N	N	N	N	N	N	Y
17 Engel	N	N	N	N	N	Y	Y
18 Lowey	N	N	N	N	N	Y	Y
19 Hall	N	N	N	N	N	Y	Y
20 Murphy	N	N	N	N	N	Y	N
21 Tonko	N	?	N	N	N	Y	Y
22 Hinchey	N	N	N	N	N	Y	Y
23 **McHugh**	N	N	N	N	?	Y	N
24 Arcuri	N	N	N	N	N	Y	N
25 Maffei	N	N	N	N	N	Y	Y
26 **Lee**	N	N	N	N	Y	Y	N
27 Higgins	N	N	N	N	N	Y	Y
28 Slaughter	N	N	N	N	N	Y	Y
29 Massa	N	N	N	N	N	Y	N
NORTH CAROLINA							
1 Butterfield	P	P	N	N	N	Y	Y
2 Etheridge	N	N	N	N	N	Y	Y
3 **Jones**	Y	N	N	Y	N	Y	N
4 Price	N	N	N	N	N	Y	Y

	670	671	672	673	674	675	676
5 **Foxx**	Y	Y	Y	Y	Y	Y	N
6 **Coble**	N	N	Y	Y	N	Y	N
7 McIntyre	N	N	N	N	N	Y	Y
8 Kissell	N	N	N	N	N	Y	Y
9 **Myrick**	Y	Y	Y	Y	Y	Y	N
10 **McHenry**	Y	Y	Y	Y	Y	Y	N
11 Shuler	N	N	N	N	N	Y	N
12 Watt	N	N	N	N	N	N	Y
13 Miller	N	N	N	N	N	Y	Y
NORTH DAKOTA							
AL Pomeroy	N	N	N	N	N	Y	Y
OHIO							
1 Driehaus	N	N	N	N	N	Y	Y
2 **Schmidt**	Y	Y	Y	Y	Y	Y	N
3 **Turner**	N	N	N	N	Y	Y	N
4 **Jordan**	Y	N	Y	Y	Y	Y	N
5 **Latta**	Y	Y	N	N	Y	Y	N
6 Wilson	N	N	N	N	N	Y	Y
7 **Austria**	Y	N	N	Y	Y	Y	N
8 **Boehner**	Y	N	Y	Y	Y	Y	N
9 Kaptur	N	N	N	N	N	Y	Y
10 Kucinich	N	N	N	N	N	N	Y
11 Fudge	N	N	N	N	N	Y	Y
12 **Tiberi**	Y	Y	N	N	N	Y	N
13 Sutton	N	N	?	N	N	Y	Y
14 **LaTourette**	N	N	N	N	Y	Y	N
15 Kilroy	N	N	N	N	N	Y	Y
16 Boccieri	N	N	N	N	N	Y	Y
17 Ryan	N	N	N	N	N	Y	?
18 Space	N	N	N	N	N	Y	Y
OKLAHOMA							
1 **Sullivan**	N	N	N	N	Y	Y	N
2 Boren	N	N	N	N	N	Y	N
3 **Lucas**	N	N	N	N	Y	Y	N
4 **Cole**	N	N	N	N	Y	Y	N
5 **Fallin**	N	N	N	N	Y	Y	N
OREGON							
1 Wu	N	N	N	N	N	Y	Y
2 **Walden**	Y	Y	Y	Y	Y	Y	N
3 Blumenauer	N	N	N	N	N	N	Y
4 DeFazio	N	N	N	N	N	Y	Y
5 Schrader	N	N	N	N	N	Y	Y
PENNSYLVANIA							
1 Brady	N	N	N	N	N	Y	Y
2 Fattah	N	N	N	N	N	Y	Y
3 Dahlkemper	N	N	N	N	N	Y	Y
4 Altmire	N	N	N	N	N	Y	N
5 **Thompson**	N	N	N	N	Y	Y	N
6 **Gerlach**	Y	N	N	Y	N	Y	Y
7 Sestak	N	N	N	N	N	Y	N
8 Murphy, P.	N	N	N	N	N	Y	Y
9 **Shuster**	N	N	N	N	?	Y	N
10 Carney	N	N	N	N	N	Y	N
11 Kanjorski	N	N	N	N	N	Y	Y
12 Murtha	N	N	N	N	N	Y	Y
13 Schwartz	N	N	N	N	N	Y	+
14 Doyle	N	N	N	N	N	Y	Y
15 **Dent**	P	P	N	Y	N	Y	N
16 **Pitts**	Y	Y	Y	Y	Y	Y	N
17 Holden	N	N	N	N	N	Y	Y
18 **Murphy, T.**	N	N	N	N	N	?	N
19 **Platts**	Y	N	N	Y	Y	Y	N
RHODE ISLAND							
1 Kennedy	N	N	N	N	N	Y	Y
2 Langevin	N	N	N	N	N	Y	Y
SOUTH CAROLINA							
1 **Brown**	N	N	N	N	Y	Y	N
2 **Wilson**	N	N	N	N	Y	Y	N
3 **Barrett**	P	P	Y	Y	Y	Y	N
4 **Inglis**	Y	N	Y	Y	Y	Y	N
5 Spratt	N	N	N	N	N	?	Y
6 Clyburn	N	N	N	N	N	Y	Y
SOUTH DAKOTA							
AL Herseth Sandlin	N	N	N	N	N	Y	Y
TENNESSEE							
1 **Roe**	Y	Y	Y	Y	Y	Y	N
2 **Duncan**	Y	Y	Y	Y	Y	N	N
3 **Wamp**	Y	Y	Y	Y	Y	Y	N
4 Davis	N	N	N	N	N	Y	Y
5 Cooper	Y	Y	Y	Y	N	Y	Y
6 Gordon	N	N	N	N	N	Y	Y
7 **Blackburn**	Y	Y	Y	Y	Y	Y	N
8 Tanner	N	N	N	N	N	Y	Y
9 Cohen	N	N	N	N	N	Y	Y

	670	671	672	673	674	675	676
TEXAS							
1 **Gohmert**	Y	Y	Y	Y	Y	Y	Y
2 **Poe**	Y	N	N	Y	Y	Y	N
3 **Johnson, S.**	N	N	N	N	Y	Y	Y
4 **Hall**	Y	Y	N	Y	Y	Y	N
5 **Hensarling**	Y	Y	Y	Y	Y	Y	N
6 **Barton**	Y	N	N	N	Y	Y	N
7 **Culberson**	N	N	N	N	Y	Y	N
8 **Brady**	Y	N	N	Y	Y	Y	N
9 Green, A.	N	N	N	N	N	Y	Y
10 **McCaul**	Y	Y	Y	Y	Y	Y	N
11 **Conaway**	P	P	N	N	Y	Y	N
12 **Granger**	N	N	N	N	Y	Y	N
13 **Thornberry**	N	N	N	N	Y	Y	N
14 **Paul**	N	N	Y	Y	N	N	Y
15 Hinojosa	N	N	N	N	N	Y	Y
16 Reyes	N	N	N	N	N	Y	Y
17 Edwards	?	N	N	N	Y	Y	Y
18 Jackson Lee	N	N	N	N	N	Y	Y
19 **Neugebauer**	N	Y	N	N	Y	Y	N
20 Gonzalez	N	N	N	N	N	Y	Y
21 **Smith**	Y	N	N	N	Y	Y	N
22 **Olson**	N	N	N	N	Y	Y	Y
23 Rodriguez	N	N	N	N	N	Y	Y
24 **Marchant**	Y	Y	Y	N	Y	Y	N
25 Doggett	Y	Y	N	N	N	Y	Y
26 **Burgess**	Y	Y	Y	Y	Y	Y	N
27 Ortiz	N	N	N	N	N	Y	Y
28 Cuellar	N	N	N	N	N	Y	Y
29 Green, G.	N	N	N	N	N	Y	Y
30 Johnson, E.	N	N	N	N	N	Y	Y
31 **Carter**	N	N	N	N	Y	Y	N
32 **Sessions**	Y	Y	Y	Y	Y	Y	N
UTAH							
1 **Bishop**	Y	N	N	N	Y	Y	N
2 Matheson	N	N	N	N	N	Y	N
3 **Chaffetz**	Y	Y	Y	Y	Y	Y	N
VERMONT							
AL Welch	P	P	N	N	N	N	Y
VIRGINIA							
1 **Wittman**	Y	Y	Y	Y	Y	Y	N
2 Nye	N	N	N	N	N	N	Y
3 Scott	N	N	N	N	N	Y	Y
4 **Forbes**	Y	Y	Y	Y	Y	Y	N
5 Perriello	Y	N	N	N	Y	Y	N
6 **Goodlatte**	Y	Y	Y	Y	Y	Y	N
7 **Cantor**	Y	Y	Y	Y	Y	Y	N
8 Moran	N	N	N	N	N	Y	Y
9 Boucher	N	N	N	N	N	Y	Y
10 **Wolf**	N	N	N	N	Y	Y	N
11 Connolly	N	N	N	N	N	Y	Y
WASHINGTON							
1 Inslee	N	N	N	N	N	Y	Y
2 Larsen	N	N	N	N	N	Y	Y
3 Baird	N	N	N	N	N	Y	Y
4 **Hastings**	N	N	N	N	Y	Y	N
5 **McMorris Rodgers**	Y	Y	Y	Y	Y	Y	N
6 Dicks	N	N	N	N	N	Y	Y
7 McDermott	N	N	N	N	N	N	Y
8 **Reichert**	N	N	N	N	Y	Y	N
9 Smith	N	N	N	N	N	Y	Y
WEST VIRGINIA							
1 Mollohan	N	N	N	N	N	Y	Y
2 **Capito**	N	N	N	N	Y	Y	N
3 Rahall	N	N	N	N	N	Y	Y
WISCONSIN							
1 **Ryan**	Y	Y	Y	Y	N	Y	N
2 Baldwin	N	N	N	N	N	N	Y
3 Kind	Y	Y	N	Y	N	Y	Y
4 Moore	N	N	N	N	N	N	Y
5 **Sensenbrenner**	Y	Y	Y	Y	Y	N	N
6 **Petri**	Y	Y	Y	Y	N	Y	N
7 Obey	N	N	N	N	N	Y	Y
8 Kagen	N	N	N	N	N	Y	Y
WYOMING							
AL **Lummis**	Y	Y	Y	Y	Y	Y	Y
DELEGATES							
Faleomavaega (A.S.)	N	N	N	N			
Norton (D.C.)	N	N	N	N			
Bordallo (Guam)	N	N	N	N			
Sablan (N. Marianas)	N	N	?	N			
Pierluisi (P.R.)	N	N	N	N			
Christensen (V.I.)	N	N	N	N			

IN THE HOUSE | By Vote Number

677. **HR 2749. Food Safety Overhaul/Rule.** Adoption of the rule (H Res 691) to provide for House floor consideration of the bill that would make several changes to food safety laws, including establishing a risk-based inspection schedule for food facilities and imposing criminal and civil penalties for violations. Adopted 249-180: R 6-170; D 243-10. July 30, 2009.

678. **HR 2728. Library of Congress Law Library/Passage.** Lofgren, D-Calif., motion to suspend the rules and pass the bill that would authorize $3.5 million for the Library of Congress to administer the law library and require the Library of Congress to operate a William Orton Law Library Support Program. Motion agreed to 383-44: R 132-44; D 251-0. A two-thirds majority of those present and voting (285 in this case) is required for passage under suspension of the rules. July 30, 2009.

679. **HR 2749. Food Safety Overhaul/Recommit.** Lucas, R-Okla., motion to recommit the bill to the Energy and Commerce Committee with instructions that it be immediately reported back with language that would insert provisions related to defraying the cost of additional safety inspections of food as well as income loss related to an erroneous action by the government. Motion rejected 186-240: R 177-0; D 9-240. July 30, 2009.

680. **HR 2749. Food Safety Overhaul/Passage.** Passage of the bill that would revise food safety laws, including establishing a risk-based inspection schedule for food facilities and imposing criminal and civil penalties for violations. The bill would require facilities that serve U.S. customers to register with the Food and Drug Administration (FDA) and pay a registration fee. Farms, grocery stores and restaurants would be exempt. Frequency of inspections would range from every six months to every five years, depending on the level of risk at the facility. The bill would also authorize the FDA to impose mandatory food quarantines and require facilities to implement written food safety plans. Passed 283-142: R 54-122; D 229-20. A "yea" was a vote in support of the president's position. July 30, 2009.

681. **HR 1752. Salary Payment Date/Passage.** Davis, D-Calif., motion to suspend the rules and pass the bill that would authorize the House Administration Committee to provide for the payment of salaries for a given month on a date other than previously provided in order to conform to generally accepted accounting practices. Motion rejected 282-144: R 42-135; D 240-9. A two-thirds majority of those present and voting (284 in this case) is required for passage under suspension of the rules. July 30, 2009.

	677	678	679	680	681
ALABAMA					
1 **Bonner**	N	Y	Y	N	N
2 Bright	Y	Y	Y	N	Y
3 **Rogers**	N	Y	Y	N	N
4 **Aderholt**	N	Y	Y	N	N
5 Griffith	Y	Y	N	N	Y
6 **Bachus**	N	Y	Y	N	N
7 Davis	Y	Y	N	Y	Y
ALASKA					
AL **Young**	N	Y	Y	N	Y
ARIZONA					
1 Kirkpatrick	Y	Y	N	Y	Y
2 **Franks**	N	N	Y	N	N
3 **Shadegg**	N	N	Y	N	N
4 Pastor	Y	Y	N	Y	Y
5 Mitchell	N	Y	N	Y	Y
6 **Flake**	N	N	Y	N	N
7 Grijalva	Y	Y	N	Y	Y
8 Giffords	Y	Y	N	Y	Y
ARKANSAS					
1 Berry	Y	Y	N	Y	Y
2 Snyder	Y	Y	N	Y	Y
3 **Boozman**	N	Y	Y	N	N
4 Ross	Y	Y	N	Y	Y
CALIFORNIA					
1 Thompson	Y	Y	N	Y	Y
2 **Herger**	N	N	Y	N	N
3 **Lungren**	N	Y	Y	N	Y
4 **McClintock**	N	Y	Y	N	N
5 Matsui	Y	Y	N	Y	Y
6 Woolsey	Y	Y	N	N	Y
7 Miller, George	Y	Y	N	Y	Y
8 Pelosi					
9 Lee	Y	Y	N	Y	Y
10 Vacant					
11 McNerney	Y	Y	Y	Y	Y
12 Speier	Y	Y	N	Y	Y
13 Stark	Y	Y	N	Y	Y
14 Eshoo	Y	Y	N	Y	Y
15 Honda	Y	Y	N	Y	Y
16 Lofgren	Y	Y	N	Y	Y
17 Farr	Y	Y	N	Y	Y
18 Cardoza	Y	Y	N	Y	Y
19 **Radanovich**	N	Y	Y	N	Y
20 Costa	Y	Y	N	Y	Y
21 **Nunes**	N	Y	Y	N	Y
22 **McCarthy**	N	Y	Y	N	Y
23 Capps	Y	Y	N	Y	Y
24 **Gallegly**	N	Y	Y	N	N
25 **McKeon**	N	Y	Y	N	N
26 **Dreier**	N	N	Y	N	N
27 Sherman	Y	Y	N	Y	Y
28 Berman	Y	?	N	Y	?
29 Schiff	Y	Y	N	Y	Y
30 Waxman	Y	Y	N	Y	Y
31 Becerra	Y	Y	N	Y	Y
32 Chu	Y	Y	N	Y	Y
33 Watson	Y	Y	N	Y	Y
34 Roybal-Allard	Y	Y	N	Y	Y
35 Waters	Y	Y	N	Y	Y
36 Harman	Y	Y	N	Y	Y
37 Richardson	Y	Y	N	Y	Y
38 Napolitano	Y	Y	N	Y	Y
39 Sánchez, Linda	Y	Y	N	Y	Y
40 **Royce**	N	N	Y	N	N
41 **Lewis**	N	Y	Y	N	N
42 **Miller, Gary**	N	Y	Y	N	N
43 Baca	Y	Y	N	Y	Y
44 **Calvert**	N	Y	Y	N	N
45 **Bono Mack**	N	Y	Y	N	N
46 **Rohrabacher**	N	Y	Y	N	N
47 Sanchez, Loretta	?	?	?	?	?
48 **Campbell**	N	N	Y	N	N
49 **Issa**	N	Y	Y	N	N
50 **Bilbray**	N	Y	Y	N	Y
51 Filner	Y	Y	N	Y	Y
52 **Hunter**	N	Y	Y	N	N
53 Davis	Y	Y	N	Y	Y

	677	678	679	680	681
COLORADO					
1 DeGette	Y	Y	N	Y	Y
2 Polis	Y	Y	N	Y	Y
3 Salazar	N	Y	?	?	?
4 Markey	Y	Y	N	N	Y
5 **Lamborn**	N	N	Y	N	N
6 **Coffman**	N	N	Y	N	N
7 Perlmutter	Y	Y	N	Y	Y
CONNECTICUT					
1 Larson	Y	Y	N	Y	Y
2 Courtney	Y	Y	N	Y	Y
3 DeLauro	Y	Y	N	Y	Y
4 Himes	Y	Y	N	Y	Y
5 Murphy	Y	Y	N	Y	Y
DELAWARE					
AL **Castle**	Y	Y	Y	Y	Y
FLORIDA					
1 **Miller**	N	N	Y	N	N
2 Boyd	Y	Y	N	Y	Y
3 Brown	Y	Y	N	Y	Y
4 **Crenshaw**	N	Y	Y	N	N
5 **Brown-Waite**	N	Y	Y	N	N
6 **Stearns**	N	N	Y	N	N
7 **Mica**	N	Y	Y	N	N
8 Grayson	Y	Y	–	+	Y
9 **Bilirakis**	N	Y	Y	Y	Y
10 **Young**	?	?	Y	Y	Y
11 Castor	Y	Y	N	Y	Y
12 **Putnam**	N	Y	Y	Y	N
13 **Buchanan**	N	Y	Y	Y	Y
14 **Mack**	N	Y	Y	N	N
15 **Posey**	N	Y	Y	N	N
16 **Rooney**	N	N	Y	N	N
17 Meek	Y	Y	N	Y	Y
18 **Ros-Lehtinen**	N	Y	Y	N	N
19 Wexler	Y	Y	N	Y	Y
20 Wasserman Schultz	Y	Y	N	Y	Y
21 **Diaz-Balart, L.**	N	Y	Y	Y	N
22 Klein	Y	Y	N	Y	Y
23 Hastings	Y	Y	N	Y	Y
24 Kosmas	Y	Y	N	Y	Y
25 **Diaz-Balart, M.**	N	Y	Y	Y	N
GEORGIA					
1 **Kingston**	N	N	Y	N	N
2 Bishop	Y	Y	N	Y	Y
3 **Westmoreland**	N	N	Y	N	N
4 Johnson	Y	Y	N	Y	Y
5 Lewis	Y	Y	N	Y	Y
6 **Price**	–	–	Y	N	N
7 **Linder**	N	Y	?	?	?
8 Marshall	Y	Y	N	Y	Y
9 **Deal**	Y	N	Y	Y	Y
10 **Broun**	N	N	Y	N	Y
11 **Gingrey**	Y	N	Y	Y	N
12 Barrow	Y	Y	N	Y	Y
13 Scott	Y	Y	N	Y	Y
HAWAII					
1 Abercrombie	Y	Y	N	Y	Y
2 Hirono	Y	Y	N	Y	Y
IDAHO					
1 Minnick	N	Y	N	N	Y
2 **Simpson**	N	Y	Y	N	N
ILLINOIS					
1 Rush	Y	Y	N	Y	N
2 Jackson	Y	Y	N	Y	N
3 Lipinski	Y	Y	N	Y	Y
4 Gutierrez	Y	Y	N	Y	Y
5 Quigley	Y	Y	N	Y	Y
6 **Roskam**	N	N	Y	Y	N
7 Davis	Y	Y	N	Y	Y
8 Bean	Y	Y	N	Y	Y
9 Schakowsky	Y	Y	N	Y	Y
10 **Kirk**	N	Y	Y	Y	Y
11 Halvorson	Y	Y	N	Y	Y
12 Costello	Y	Y	N	Y	Y
13 **Biggert**	N	Y	Y	Y	N
14 Foster	Y	Y	N	Y	Y
15 **Johnson**	N	N	Y	N	N

KEY **Republicans** Democrats

Y Voted for (yea)	X Paired against	C Voted "present" to avoid possible conflict of interest
# Paired for	– Announced against	
+ Announced for	P Voted "present"	? Did not vote or otherwise make a position known
N Voted against (nay)		

Member	677	678	679	680	681
16 Manzullo	N	Y	Y	N	N
17 Hare	Y	Y	N	Y	Y
18 Schock	N	Y	Y	N	N
19 Shimkus	N	Y	Y	Y	N
INDIANA					
1 Visclosky	Y	Y	N	Y	Y
2 Donnelly	Y	Y	N	Y	Y
3 Souder	N	Y	Y	N	N
4 Buyer	Y	Y	Y	Y	N
5 Burton	N	Y	Y	N	N
6 Pence	N	Y	Y	N	N
7 Carson	Y	Y	N	Y	Y
8 Ellsworth	Y	Y	N	Y	Y
9 Hill	N	Y	N	Y	Y
IOWA					
1 Braley	Y	Y	N	Y	Y
2 Loebsack	Y	Y	N	Y	Y
3 Boswell	Y	Y	N	Y	Y
4 Latham	N	Y	Y	N	N
5 King	N	N	Y	N	Y
KANSAS					
1 Moran	N	Y	Y	N	N
2 Jenkins	N	Y	Y	N	Y
3 Moore	N	Y	N	Y	Y
4 Tiahrt	N	Y	Y	N	Y
KENTUCKY					
1 Whitfield	N	Y	Y	Y	N
2 Guthrie	N	Y	Y	Y	N
3 Yarmuth	Y	Y	N	Y	Y
4 Davis	N	Y	Y	N	N
5 Rogers	N	Y	Y	N	N
6 Chandler	Y	Y	N	Y	Y
LOUISIANA					
1 Scalise	N	N	Y	Y	N
2 Cao	N	Y	Y	Y	Y
3 Melancon	Y	Y	N	Y	Y
4 Fleming	N	Y	Y	N	N
5 Alexander	N	Y	Y	N	N
6 Cassidy	N	N	Y	N	N
7 Boustany	N	Y	Y	N	N
MAINE					
1 Pingree	Y	Y	N	N	Y
2 Michaud	Y	Y	N	Y	Y
MARYLAND					
1 Kratovil	N	Y	N	N	N
2 Ruppersberger	Y	Y	N	Y	Y
3 Sarbanes	Y	Y	N	Y	Y
4 Edwards	Y	Y	N	Y	Y
5 Hoyer	Y	Y	N	Y	Y
6 Bartlett	N	N	Y	N	N
7 Cummings	Y	Y	N	Y	Y
8 Van Hollen	Y	Y	N	Y	Y
MASSACHUSETTS					
1 Olver	Y	Y	N	Y	Y
2 Neal	Y	Y	N	Y	Y
3 McGovern	Y	Y	N	Y	Y
4 Frank	Y	Y	N	Y	Y
5 Tsongas	Y	Y	N	Y	Y
6 Tierney	Y	Y	N	Y	Y
7 Markey	Y	Y	N	Y	Y
8 Capuano	Y	Y	N	Y	Y
9 Lynch	Y	Y	N	Y	Y
10 Delahunt	Y	Y	N	Y	Y
MICHIGAN					
1 Stupak	Y	Y	N	Y	Y
2 Hoekstra	N	Y	Y	N	N
3 Ehlers	N	Y	Y	Y	N
4 Camp	N	Y	Y	Y	N
5 Kildee	Y	Y	N	Y	Y
6 Upton	Y	Y	Y	Y	N
7 Schauer	Y	Y	N	Y	Y
8 Rogers	N	Y	Y	Y	N
9 Peters	Y	Y	N	Y	Y
10 Miller	N	Y	Y	Y	N
11 McCotter	N	Y	Y	Y	N
12 Levin	Y	Y	N	Y	Y
13 Kilpatrick	Y	Y	N	Y	Y
14 Conyers	Y	Y	N	Y	Y
15 Dingell	Y	Y	N	Y	Y
MINNESOTA					
1 Walz	Y	Y	N	Y	Y
2 Kline	N	Y	Y	Y	N
3 Paulsen	N	Y	Y	Y	N
4 McCollum	Y	Y	N	Y	Y
5 Ellison	Y	Y	N	Y	Y
6 Bachmann	N	Y	Y	Y	N
7 Peterson	Y	Y	N	Y	Y
8 Oberstar	Y	Y	N	Y	Y
MISSISSIPPI					
1 Childers	Y	Y	N	N	Y
2 Thompson	Y	Y	N	Y	Y
3 Harper	N	Y	Y	N	N
4 Taylor	Y	Y	N	Y	Y
MISSOURI					
1 Clay	Y	Y	N	Y	Y
2 Akin	N	N	Y	–	N
3 Carnahan	Y	Y	N	Y	Y
4 Skelton	Y	Y	N	Y	Y
5 Cleaver	Y	Y	N	Y	Y
6 Graves	N	Y	Y	N	Y
7 Blunt	N	Y	Y	N	Y
8 Emerson	N	Y	Y	N	Y
9 Luetkemeyer	N	Y	Y	N	N
MONTANA					
AL Rehberg	N	Y	Y	N	N
NEBRASKA					
1 Fortenberry	N	Y	Y	Y	Y
2 Terry	N	Y	Y	Y	Y
3 Smith	N	Y	Y	N	N
NEVADA					
1 Berkley	Y	Y	N	Y	Y
2 Heller	N	Y	Y	N	N
3 Titus	Y	Y	N	Y	Y
NEW HAMPSHIRE					
1 Shea-Porter	Y	Y	N	Y	Y
2 Hodes	Y	Y	N	Y	Y
NEW JERSEY					
1 Andrews	Y	Y	N	Y	Y
2 LoBiondo	N	Y	Y	Y	Y
3 Adler	Y	Y	–	+	Y
4 Smith	N	Y	Y	Y	Y
5 Garrett	N	N	Y	N	N
6 Pallone	Y	Y	N	Y	Y
7 Lance	N	Y	Y	Y	Y
8 Pascrell	Y	Y	N	Y	Y
9 Rothman	Y	Y	N	Y	Y
10 Payne	Y	Y	N	Y	Y
11 Frelinghuysen	N	Y	Y	Y	Y
12 Holt	Y	Y	N	Y	Y
13 Sires	Y	Y	N	Y	Y
NEW MEXICO					
1 Heinrich	N	Y	N	N	Y
2 Teague	N	Y	N	N	Y
3 Lujan	Y	Y	N	N	Y
NEW YORK					
1 Bishop	Y	Y	N	Y	Y
2 Israel	Y	Y	N	Y	Y
3 King	N	Y	Y	Y	Y
4 McCarthy	?	?	?	?	?
5 Ackerman	Y	Y	N	Y	Y
6 Meeks	Y	Y	N	Y	Y
7 Crowley	Y	Y	N	Y	Y
8 Nadler	Y	Y	N	Y	Y
9 Weiner	Y	Y	N	Y	Y
10 Towns	Y	Y	N	Y	Y
11 Clarke	Y	Y	N	Y	Y
12 Velázquez	Y	Y	N	Y	Y
13 McMahon	Y	Y	N	Y	Y
14 Maloney	Y	Y	N	Y	Y
15 Rangel	Y	Y	N	Y	Y
16 Serrano	Y	Y	N	Y	Y
17 Engel	Y	Y	N	Y	Y
18 Lowey	Y	Y	N	Y	Y
19 Hall	Y	Y	N	Y	Y
20 Murphy	Y	Y	Y	Y	N
21 Tonko	Y	Y	N	Y	Y
22 Hinchey	Y	Y	N	N	Y
23 McHugh	N	Y	Y	Y	N
24 Arcuri	Y	Y	Y	N	N
25 Maffei	Y	Y	N	Y	Y
26 Lee	N	Y	Y	Y	Y
27 Higgins	Y	Y	N	Y	Y
28 Slaughter	Y	Y	N	Y	Y
29 Massa	Y	Y	N	N	Y
NORTH CAROLINA					
1 Butterfield	Y	Y	N	Y	Y
2 Etheridge	Y	Y	N	Y	Y
3 Jones	N	Y	Y	N	N
4 Price	Y	Y	N	Y	Y
5 Foxx	N	N	Y	N	N
6 Coble	N	N	Y	N	N
7 McIntyre	Y	Y	Y	Y	Y
8 Kissell	Y	Y	N	Y	N
9 Myrick	N	Y	Y	Y	N
10 McHenry	N	N	Y	N	N
11 Shuler	N	Y	N	N	Y
12 Watt	Y	Y	N	Y	Y
13 Miller	Y	Y	N	Y	Y
NORTH DAKOTA					
AL Pomeroy	Y	Y	N	Y	Y
OHIO					
1 Driehaus	Y	Y	N	Y	Y
2 Schmidt	N	Y	Y	N	N
3 Turner	N	Y	Y	Y	N
4 Jordan	N	N	Y	N	N
5 Latta	N	Y	Y	N	N
6 Wilson	Y	Y	N	Y	Y
7 Austria	N	Y	Y	Y	N
8 Boehner	N	Y	Y	N	N
9 Kaptur	Y	Y	N	Y	Y
10 Kucinich	Y	Y	N	Y	Y
11 Fudge	Y	Y	N	Y	Y
12 Tiberi	N	Y	Y	Y	N
13 Sutton	Y	Y	N	Y	Y
14 LaTourette	N	Y	Y	Y	N
15 Kilroy	Y	Y	N	Y	Y
16 Boccieri	Y	Y	N	Y	Y
17 Ryan	Y	Y	N	Y	Y
18 Space	Y	Y	N	Y	Y
OKLAHOMA					
1 Sullivan	N	Y	Y	N	N
2 Boren	Y	Y	Y	Y	Y
3 Lucas	N	Y	Y	N	Y
4 Cole	N	Y	Y	N	Y
5 Fallin	N	Y	Y	N	Y
OREGON					
1 Wu	Y	Y	N	Y	Y
2 Walden	N	Y	Y	Y	N
3 Blumenauer	Y	Y	N	Y	Y
4 DeFazio	Y	Y	N	Y	Y
5 Schrader	Y	Y	N	Y	Y
PENNSYLVANIA					
1 Brady	Y	Y	N	Y	Y
2 Fattah	Y	Y	N	Y	Y
3 Dahlkemper	Y	Y	N	Y	Y
4 Altmire	Y	Y	Y	Y	Y
5 Thompson	N	Y	Y	N	N
6 Gerlach	N	Y	Y	Y	Y
7 Sestak	Y	Y	N	Y	Y
8 Murphy, P.	Y	Y	N	Y	Y
9 Shuster	N	Y	Y	N	N
10 Carney	Y	Y	N	Y	Y
11 Kanjorski	Y	Y	N	Y	Y
12 Murtha	Y	Y	?	?	?
13 Schwartz	Y	Y	N	Y	Y
14 Doyle	Y	Y	N	Y	Y
15 Dent	N	Y	Y	Y	Y
16 Pitts	N	Y	Y	N	N
17 Holden	Y	Y	N	Y	Y
18 Murphy, T.	N	Y	Y	Y	Y
19 Platts	N	Y	Y	Y	Y
RHODE ISLAND					
1 Kennedy	Y	Y	N	Y	Y
2 Langevin	Y	Y	N	Y	Y
SOUTH CAROLINA					
1 Brown	N	Y	Y	N	Y
2 Wilson	N	N	Y	N	N
3 Barrett	N	Y	Y	N	N
4 Inglis	N	Y	Y	N	N
5 Spratt	Y	Y	N	Y	Y
6 Clyburn	Y	Y	N	Y	Y
SOUTH DAKOTA					
AL Herseth Sandlin	Y	Y	N	Y	Y
TENNESSEE					
1 Roe	N	Y	Y	N	N
2 Duncan	N	Y	Y	N	N
3 Wamp	N	Y	Y	N	Y
4 Davis	Y	Y	N	Y	Y
5 Cooper	Y	Y	N	Y	Y
6 Gordon	Y	Y	N	Y	Y
7 Blackburn	N	N	Y	N	N
8 Tanner	Y	Y	N	Y	Y
9 Cohen	Y	Y	N	Y	Y
TEXAS					
1 Gohmert	N	Y	Y	N	N
2 Poe	N	Y	Y	N	N
3 Johnson, S.	N	Y	Y	N	N
4 Hall	N	Y	Y	N	Y
5 Hensarling	N	N	Y	N	N
6 Barton	Y	Y	Y	Y	N
7 Culberson	N	Y	Y	N	Y
8 Brady	N	N	Y	N	Y
9 Green, A.	Y	Y	N	Y	Y
10 McCaul	N	Y	Y	N	Y
11 Conaway	N	Y	Y	N	N
12 Granger	N	Y	Y	N	N
13 Thornberry	N	Y	Y	N	N
14 Paul	N	N	Y	N	N
15 Hinojosa	Y	Y	N	Y	Y
16 Reyes	Y	Y	N	Y	Y
17 Edwards	Y	Y	Y	Y	Y
18 Jackson Lee	Y	Y	N	Y	Y
19 Neugebauer	N	N	Y	N	N
20 Gonzalez	Y	Y	N	Y	Y
21 Smith	N	Y	Y	N	N
22 Olson	N	N	Y	N	N
23 Rodriguez	Y	Y	N	Y	Y
24 Marchant	N	Y	Y	N	N
25 Doggett	Y	Y	N	Y	Y
26 Burgess	N	N	Y	N	N
27 Ortiz	Y	Y	N	Y	Y
28 Cuellar	Y	Y	N	Y	Y
29 Green, G.	Y	Y	N	Y	Y
30 Johnson, E.	Y	Y	N	Y	Y
31 Carter	N	N	Y	N	N
32 Sessions	N	N	Y	N	N
UTAH					
1 Bishop	N	Y	Y	N	N
2 Matheson	Y	Y	N	Y	Y
3 Chaffetz	N	Y	Y	N	N
VERMONT					
AL Welch	Y	Y	N	N	Y
VIRGINIA					
1 Wittman	N	Y	Y	N	Y
2 Nye	Y	Y	N	Y	Y
3 Scott	Y	Y	N	Y	Y
4 Forbes	N	Y	Y	N	Y
5 Perriello	N	Y	Y	N	Y
6 Goodlatte	N	Y	Y	N	N
7 Cantor	N	N	Y	N	N
8 Moran	Y	Y	N	Y	Y
9 Boucher	Y	Y	N	Y	Y
10 Wolf	N	Y	Y	Y	N
11 Connolly	Y	Y	N	Y	Y
WASHINGTON					
1 Inslee	Y	Y	N	Y	Y
2 Larsen	Y	Y	N	Y	Y
3 Baird	Y	Y	N	Y	?
4 Hastings	N	Y	Y	N	Y
5 McMorris Rodgers	N	Y	Y	N	Y
6 Dicks	Y	Y	N	Y	Y
7 McDermott	Y	Y	N	Y	Y
8 Reichert	N	Y	Y	N	Y
9 Smith	Y	Y	N	Y	Y
WEST VIRGINIA					
1 Mollohan	Y	Y	N	Y	Y
2 Capito	N	Y	Y	N	Y
3 Rahall	Y	Y	N	Y	Y
WISCONSIN					
1 Ryan	N	N	Y	N	N
2 Baldwin	Y	Y	N	Y	Y
3 Kind	Y	Y	N	Y	Y
4 Moore	Y	?	N	Y	Y
5 Sensenbrenner	N	N	Y	N	N
6 Petri	N	N	Y	N	N
7 Obey	Y	Y	N	Y	Y
8 Kagen	Y	Y	N	Y	Y
WYOMING					
AL Lummis	N	N	Y	N	N
DELEGATES					
Faleomavaega (A.S.)					
Norton (D.C.)					
Bordallo (Guam)					
Sablan (N. Marianas)					
Pierluisi (P.R.)					
Christensen (V.I.)					

IN THE HOUSE | By Vote Number

682. HR 3435. **Car Voucher Program Funding/Passage.** Obey, D-Wis., motion to suspend the rules and pass the bill that would provide $2 billion for the "Cash for Clunkers" vehicle trade-in program, which offers vouchers worth up to $4,500 toward the purchase of new vehicles to consumers who trade in their older, less-efficient models. The funds would be transferred from the Energy Department's innovative-technologies loan guarantee program. Motion agreed to 316-109: R 77-95; D 239-14. A two-thirds majority of those present and voting (284 in this case) is required for passage under suspension of the rules. A "yea" was a vote in support of the president's position. July 31, 2009.

683. HR 3269. **Executive Pay Overhaul/Time Limit.** Frank, D-Mass., amendment that would not allow for the recovery of incentive-based pay under compensation arrangements in effect on the date of the bill's enactment if the agreements are for a period of no more than two years. Adopted 242-178: R 1-169; D 241-9. July 31, 2009.

684. HR 3269. **Executive Pay Overhaul/Republican Substitute.** Garrett, R-N.J., substitute amendment that would require publicly traded companies to allow shareholders to take nonbinding votes every three years on executive compensation packages with allowances to opt out of such votes for five years. It also would allow state law to supersede federal law regarding independent compensation committees. It would omit language in the bill providing for regulations regarding incentive-based compensation agreements. Rejected 179-244: R 169-3; D 10-241. July 31, 2009.

685. HR 3269. **Executive Pay Overhaul/Recommit.** Sessions, R-Texas, motion to recommit the bill to the Financial Services Committee with instructions that it be immediately reported back with language that would not allow a shareholder's vote on executive compensation to be counted if the shareholder has spent more than a de minimis amount of money to influence the votes of others, unless the shareholder discloses details about the effort to influence the outcome. Motion rejected 178-244: R 172-0; D 6-244. July 31, 2009.

686. HR 3269. **Executive Pay Overhaul/Passage.** Passage of the bill that would require publicly traded companies to allow shareholders to take annual, nonbinding votes on executive compensation packages and on "golden parachute" compensation for outgoing executives in the event of a merger or acquisition. It would create new standards for corporate compensation committees and require federal financial agencies to issue regulations that restrict the use of employee compensation structures that pose a risk to financial institutions and the economy. As amended, it would not allow for the recovery of incentive-based pay under compensation arrangements in effect on the date of the bill's enactment if the agreements are for a period of no more than two years. Passed 237-185: R 2-169; D 235-16. July 31, 2009.

	682	683	684	685	686
ALABAMA					
1 Bonner	N	N	Y	Y	N
2 Bright	Y	N	Y	Y	N
3 Rogers	Y	N	Y	Y	N
4 Aderholt	Y	N	Y	Y	N
5 Griffith	Y	N	Y	Y	N
6 Bachus	Y	N	Y	Y	N
7 Davis	Y	Y	N	N	Y
ALASKA					
AL Young	N	N	Y	Y	N
ARIZONA					
1 Kirkpatrick	N	N	Y	N	N
2 Franks	N	N	Y	Y	N
3 Shadegg	N	N	Y	Y	N
4 Pastor	Y	Y	N	N	Y
5 Mitchell	N	N	N	N	N
6 Flake	N	N	Y	Y	N
7 Grijalva	Y	Y	N	N	?
8 Giffords	N	Y	N	N	Y
ARKANSAS					
1 Berry	Y	Y	N	N	N
2 Snyder	Y	Y	N	N	N
3 Boozman	N	N	Y	Y	N
4 Ross	Y	Y	N	N	N
CALIFORNIA					
1 Thompson	Y	Y	N	N	Y
2 Herger	N	N	Y	Y	N
3 Lungren	N	N	Y	Y	N
4 McClintock	N	N	Y	Y	N
5 Matsui	Y	Y	N	N	Y
6 Woolsey	Y	Y	N	?	Y
7 Miller, George	Y	Y	N	N	Y
8 Pelosi					
9 Lee	Y	Y	N	N	Y
10 Vacant					
11 McNerney	Y	Y	N	N	Y
12 Speier	Y	Y	N	N	Y
13 Stark	Y	Y	N	N	Y
14 Eshoo	Y	Y	N	N	Y
15 Honda	Y	Y	N	N	Y
16 Lofgren	Y	Y	N	N	Y
17 Farr	Y	Y	N	N	Y
18 Cardoza	Y	Y	N	N	Y
19 Radanovich	N	N	Y	Y	N
20 Costa	Y	Y	N	N	Y
21 Nunes	N	N	Y	Y	N
22 McCarthy	N	N	Y	Y	N
23 Capps	Y	Y	N	N	Y
24 Gallegly	N	N	Y	Y	N
25 McKeon	Y	N	Y	Y	N
26 Dreier	Y	N	Y	Y	N
27 Sherman	Y	Y	N	N	Y
28 Berman	Y	Y	N	N	Y
29 Schiff	Y	Y	N	N	Y
30 Waxman	Y	?	N	N	Y
31 Becerra	Y	Y	N	N	Y
32 Chu	Y	Y	N	N	Y
33 Watson	Y	Y	N	N	Y
34 Roybal-Allard	Y	Y	N	N	Y
35 Waters	Y	Y	N	N	Y
36 Harman	Y	Y	N	N	Y
37 Richardson	Y	Y	N	N	Y
38 Napolitano	Y	Y	N	N	Y
39 Sánchez, Linda	Y	Y	N	N	Y
40 Royce	N	N	Y	Y	N
41 Lewis	N	N	Y	Y	N
42 Miller, Gary	Y	N	Y	Y	N
43 Baca	Y	Y	N	N	Y
44 Calvert	N	N	Y	Y	N
45 Bono Mack	Y	N	Y	Y	N
46 Rohrabacher	N	N	Y	Y	N
47 Sanchez, Loretta	Y	Y	N	N	Y
48 Campbell	Y	N	Y	Y	N
49 Issa	Y	N	Y	Y	N
50 Bilbray	Y	N	?	Y	N
51 Filner	Y	Y	N	N	Y
52 Hunter	N	N	Y	Y	N
53 Davis	Y	Y	N	N	Y

	682	683	684	685	686
COLORADO					
1 DeGette	Y	Y	N	N	Y
2 Polis	N	Y	N	N	Y
3 Salazar	?	?	?	?	?
4 Markey	Y	N	Y	N	N
5 Lamborn	N	N	Y	Y	N
6 Coffman	N	N	Y	Y	N
7 Perlmutter	Y	Y	N	N	Y
CONNECTICUT					
1 Larson	Y	Y	N	N	Y
2 Courtney	Y	Y	N	N	Y
3 DeLauro	Y	Y	N	N	Y
4 Himes	Y	Y	N	N	Y
5 Murphy	Y	Y	N	N	Y
DELAWARE					
AL Castle	Y	N	Y	Y	N
FLORIDA					
1 Miller	N	N	Y	Y	N
2 Boyd	N	Y	N	N	N
3 Brown	Y	Y	N	N	Y
4 Crenshaw	N	N	Y	Y	N
5 Brown-Waite	Y	N	Y	Y	N
6 Stearns	Y	N	Y	Y	N
7 Mica	N	N	Y	Y	N
8 Grayson	Y	Y	N	N	Y
9 Bilirakis	N	N	Y	Y	N
10 Young	Y	N	Y	Y	N
11 Castor	Y	Y	N	N	Y
12 Putnam	Y	N	Y	Y	N
13 Buchanan	P	N	Y	Y	N
14 Mack	N	N	Y	Y	N
15 Posey	N	N	Y	Y	N
16 Rooney	N	N	Y	Y	N
17 Meek	Y	Y	N	N	Y
18 Ros-Lehtinen	Y	N	Y	Y	N
19 Wexler	Y	Y	N	N	Y
20 Wasserman Schultz	Y	Y	N	N	Y
21 Diaz-Balart, L.	Y	N	Y	Y	N
22 Klein	Y	Y	N	N	Y
23 Hastings	Y	Y	N	N	Y
24 Kosmas	Y	Y	N	N	Y
25 Diaz-Balart, M.	Y	N	Y	Y	N
GEORGIA					
1 Kingston	Y	N	Y	Y	N
2 Bishop	Y	Y	N	N	Y
3 Westmoreland	N	N	Y	Y	N
4 Johnson	Y	Y	N	N	Y
5 Lewis	Y	Y	N	N	Y
6 Price	N	N	Y	Y	N
7 Linder	?	?	?	?	?
8 Marshall	N	Y	N	N	Y
9 Deal	P	N	Y	Y	N
10 Broun	N	N	Y	Y	N
11 Gingrey	Y	N	Y	Y	N
12 Barrow	Y	Y	N	N	Y
13 Scott	Y	Y	N	N	Y
HAWAII					
1 Abercrombie	Y	Y	N	N	Y
2 Hirono	Y	Y	N	N	Y
IDAHO					
1 Minnick	Y	Y	Y	N	Y
2 Simpson	Y	N	Y	Y	N
ILLINOIS					
1 Rush	Y	Y	N	N	Y
2 Jackson	Y	Y	N	N	Y
3 Lipinski	Y	Y	N	N	Y
4 Gutierrez	Y	Y	?	N	Y
5 Quigley	Y	Y	N	N	Y
6 Roskam	N	N	Y	Y	N
7 Davis	Y	Y	N	N	Y
8 Bean	Y	Y	N	N	Y
9 Schakowsky	Y	Y	N	N	Y
10 Kirk	Y	N	Y	Y	N
11 Halvorson	Y	Y	N	N	Y
12 Costello	Y	Y	N	N	Y
13 Biggert	Y	N	Y	Y	N
14 Foster	Y	Y	N	N	Y
15 Johnson	N	N	Y	Y	N

KEY   **Republicans**   Democrats

Y Voted for (yea)	**X** Paired against	**C** Voted "present" to avoid possible conflict of interest
# Paired for	**–** Announced against	
+ Announced for	**P** Voted "present"	**?** Did not vote or otherwise make a position known
N Voted against (nay)		

	682	683	684	685	686
16 Manzullo	Y	N	Y	Y	N
17 Hare	Y	Y	N	N	Y
18 Schock	N	?	Y	Y	N
19 Shimkus	Y	N	Y	Y	N
INDIANA					
1 Visclosky	Y	Y	N	N	Y
2 Donnelly	Y	Y	N	N	Y
3 Souder	Y	N	Y	Y	N
4 Buyer	Y	N	Y	Y	N
5 Burton	Y	N	Y	Y	N
6 Pence	N	N	Y	Y	N
7 Carson	Y	Y	N	N	Y
8 Ellsworth	Y	Y	N	Y	Y
9 Hill	Y	Y	N	N	Y
IOWA					
1 Braley	Y	Y	N	N	Y
2 Loebsack	Y	Y	N	N	Y
3 Boswell	Y	Y	N	N	Y
4 Latham	Y	N	Y	Y	N
5 King	N	N	Y	Y	N
KANSAS					
1 Moran	N	N	Y	Y	N
2 Jenkins	N	N	Y	Y	N
3 Moore	Y	Y	N	N	Y
4 Tiahrt	Y	N	Y	Y	N
KENTUCKY					
1 Whitfield	N	Y	Y	Y	N
2 Guthrie	Y	N	Y	Y	N
3 Yarmuth	Y	Y	N	N	Y
4 Davis	Y	N	Y	Y	N
5 Rogers	N	N	Y	Y	N
6 Chandler	Y	Y	N	N	Y
LOUISIANA					
1 Scalise	N	N	Y	Y	N
2 Cao	Y	N	Y	Y	N
3 Melancon	Y	Y	N	N	Y
4 Fleming	N	N	Y	Y	N
5 Alexander	N	N	Y	Y	N
6 Cassidy	Y	N	Y	Y	N
7 Boustany	Y	N	Y	Y	N
MAINE					
1 Pingree	Y	Y	?	N	Y
2 Michaud	Y	Y	N	N	Y
MARYLAND					
1 Kratovil	Y	N	Y	Y	N
2 Ruppersberger	Y	Y	N	N	Y
3 Sarbanes	Y	Y	N	N	Y
4 Edwards	Y	Y	N	N	Y
5 Hoyer	Y	Y	N	N	Y
6 Bartlett	N	N	Y	Y	N
7 Cummings	Y	Y	N	N	Y
8 Van Hollen	Y	Y	N	N	Y
MASSACHUSETTS					
1 Olver	Y	?	N	N	Y
2 Neal	Y	Y	N	N	Y
3 McGovern	Y	Y	N	N	Y
4 Frank	Y	Y	N	N	Y
5 Tsongas	Y	Y	N	N	Y
6 Tierney	N	Y	N	N	Y
7 Markey	Y	Y	N	N	+
8 Capuano	Y	Y	N	N	Y
9 Lynch	Y	Y	N	N	Y
10 Delahunt	Y	Y	N	N	Y
MICHIGAN					
1 Stupak	Y	Y	N	N	Y
2 Hoekstra	Y	N	Y	Y	N
3 Ehlers	Y	N	Y	Y	N
4 Camp	Y	N	Y	Y	N
5 Kildee	Y	Y	N	N	Y
6 Upton	Y	N	Y	Y	N
7 Schauer	Y	Y	N	N	Y
8 Rogers	Y	N	Y	Y	N
9 Peters	Y	Y	N	N	Y
10 Miller	Y	N	Y	Y	N
11 McCotter	Y	N	Y	Y	N
12 Levin	Y	Y	N	N	Y
13 Kilpatrick	Y	Y	N	N	Y
14 Conyers	Y	Y	N	N	Y
15 Dingell	Y	Y	N	N	Y
MINNESOTA					
1 Walz	Y	Y	N	N	Y
2 Kline	Y	N	Y	Y	N
3 Paulsen	N	–	Y	Y	N
4 McCollum	Y	?	N	N	Y

	682	683	684	685	686
5 Ellison	Y	Y	N	N	Y
6 Bachmann	N	N	Y	Y	N
7 Peterson	N	Y	N	N	Y
8 Oberstar	Y	Y	N	N	Y
MISSISSIPPI					
1 Childers	Y	Y	N	N	Y
2 Thompson	Y	Y	N	N	Y
3 Harper	?	?	?	?	?
4 Taylor	Y	Y	N	N	Y
MISSOURI					
1 Clay	Y	Y	N	N	Y
2 Akin	N	N	Y	Y	N
3 Carnahan	Y	Y	N	N	Y
4 Skelton	Y	Y	N	?	Y
5 Cleaver	Y	Y	N	N	Y
6 Graves	N	N	Y	Y	N
7 Blunt	Y	N	Y	Y	N
8 Emerson	Y	N	Y	Y	N
9 Luetkemeyer	N	N	Y	Y	N
MONTANA					
AL Rehberg	Y	N	Y	Y	N
NEBRASKA					
1 Fortenberry	N	N	Y	Y	N
2 Terry	Y	N	Y	Y	N
3 Smith	N	N	Y	Y	N
NEVADA					
1 Berkley	Y	Y	N	N	Y
2 Heller	N	N	Y	Y	N
3 Titus	Y	Y	N	N	Y
NEW HAMPSHIRE					
1 Shea-Porter	Y	Y	N	N	Y
2 Hodes	Y	Y	N	N	Y
NEW JERSEY					
1 Andrews	Y	Y	N	N	Y
2 LoBiondo	Y	N	Y	Y	N
3 Adler	Y	Y	N	N	Y
4 Smith	Y	N	Y	N	Y
5 Garrett	N	N	Y	Y	N
6 Pallone	Y	Y	N	N	Y
7 Lance	Y	N	Y	Y	N
8 Pascrell	Y	Y	N	N	Y
9 Rothman	Y	Y	N	N	Y
10 Payne	Y	Y	N	N	Y
11 Frelinghuysen	N	N	Y	Y	N
12 Holt	Y	Y	N	N	Y
13 Sires	Y	Y	N	N	Y
NEW MEXICO					
1 Heinrich	Y	Y	N	N	Y
2 Teague	Y	N	Y	Y	N
3 Lujan	Y	Y	N	N	Y
NEW YORK					
1 Bishop	Y	Y	N	N	Y
2 Israel	Y	Y	N	N	Y
3 King	Y	N	Y	Y	N
4 McCarthy	+	+	–	–	+
5 Ackerman	Y	Y	N	N	Y
6 Meeks	Y	Y	N	N	Y
7 Crowley	Y	Y	N	N	Y
8 Nadler	Y	Y	N	N	Y
9 Weiner	Y	Y	N	N	Y
10 Towns	Y	Y	N	N	Y
11 Clarke	Y	Y	N	N	Y
12 Velázquez	Y	Y	N	N	Y
13 McMahon	Y	Y	Y	N	N
14 Maloney	Y	Y	N	?	Y
15 Rangel	Y	Y	N	N	Y
16 Serrano	Y	Y	N	N	Y
17 Engel	Y	Y	N	N	Y
18 Lowey	Y	Y	N	N	Y
19 Hall	Y	Y	N	N	Y
20 Murphy	N	Y	N	N	Y
21 Tonko	Y	Y	N	N	Y
22 Hinchey	Y	Y	N	N	Y
23 McHugh	Y	N	Y	?	?
24 Arcuri	Y	Y	N	N	Y
25 Maffei	Y	Y	N	N	Y
26 Lee	Y	N	Y	Y	+
27 Higgins	Y	Y	N	N	Y
28 Slaughter	Y	Y	N	N	Y
29 Massa	Y	Y	N	N	Y
NORTH CAROLINA					
1 Butterfield	Y	Y	N	N	Y
2 Etheridge	Y	Y	N	N	Y
3 Jones	Y	N	Y	Y	N
4 Price	Y	Y	N	N	Y

	682	683	684	685	686
5 Foxx	N	N	Y	Y	N
6 Coble	Y	N	Y	Y	N
7 McIntyre	Y	Y	N	N	Y
8 Kissell	Y	Y	N	N	Y
9 Myrick	N	N	Y	Y	N
10 McHenry	N	N	Y	Y	N
11 Shuler	Y	Y	N	N	Y
12 Watt	Y	Y	N	N	Y
13 Miller	Y	Y	N	N	Y
NORTH DAKOTA					
AL Pomeroy	Y	Y	N	N	Y
OHIO					
1 Driehaus	Y	Y	N	N	Y
2 Schmidt	N	N	Y	Y	N
3 Turner	Y	N	Y	Y	N
4 Jordan	N	N	Y	Y	N
5 Latta	N	N	Y	Y	N
6 Wilson	Y	Y	N	N	Y
7 Austria	Y	N	Y	Y	N
8 Boehner	N	N	Y	Y	N
9 Kaptur	Y	Y	N	N	Y
10 Kucinich	Y	Y	N	N	Y
11 Fudge	Y	Y	N	N	Y
12 Tiberi	Y	N	Y	Y	N
13 Sutton	Y	Y	N	N	Y
14 LaTourette	Y	N	Y	Y	N
15 Kilroy	Y	Y	N	N	Y
16 Boccieri	Y	Y	N	N	Y
17 Ryan	Y	Y	N	N	Y
18 Space	Y	Y	N	N	Y
OKLAHOMA					
1 Sullivan	N	N	Y	Y	N
2 Boren	Y	N	N	N	N
3 Lucas	N	N	Y	Y	N
4 Cole	N	N	Y	Y	N
5 Fallin	N	N	Y	Y	N
OREGON					
1 Wu	Y	Y	N	N	Y
2 Walden	Y	N	Y	Y	N
3 Blumenauer	N	Y	N	N	Y
4 DeFazio	Y	Y	N	N	Y
5 Schrader	N	Y	N	N	Y
PENNSYLVANIA					
1 Brady	Y	Y	N	N	Y
2 Fattah	Y	Y	N	N	Y
3 Dahlkemper	Y	Y	N	N	Y
4 Altmire	Y	N	N	N	Y
5 Thompson	N	Y	Y	Y	N
6 Gerlach	Y	N	Y	Y	N
7 Sestak	Y	Y	N	N	Y
8 Murphy, P.	Y	Y	N	N	Y
9 Shuster	Y	N	Y	Y	N
10 Carney	Y	Y	N	N	Y
11 Kanjorski	Y	Y	N	N	Y
12 Murtha	Y	Y	N	N	Y
13 Schwartz	Y	Y	N	N	Y
14 Doyle	Y	Y	N	N	Y
15 Dent	N	N	Y	Y	N
16 Pitts	Y	N	Y	Y	N
17 Holden	Y	Y	N	N	Y
18 Murphy, T.	Y	N	Y	Y	Y
19 Platts	Y	N	Y	Y	N
RHODE ISLAND					
1 Kennedy	Y	Y	N	N	Y
2 Langevin	Y	Y	N	N	Y
SOUTH CAROLINA					
1 Brown	N	N	Y	Y	N
2 Wilson	N	N	Y	Y	N
3 Barrett	N	N	Y	Y	N
4 Inglis	N	N	Y	Y	N
5 Spratt	Y	Y	N	N	Y
6 Clyburn	Y	Y	N	N	Y
SOUTH DAKOTA					
AL Herseth Sandlin	N	Y	N	N	Y
TENNESSEE					
1 Roe	Y	N	Y	Y	N
2 Duncan	Y	N	N	Y	Y
3 Wamp	Y	?	?	?	?
4 Davis	Y	Y	N	N	Y
5 Cooper	Y	Y	N	N	Y
6 Gordon	Y	Y	N	N	Y
7 Blackburn	N	N	Y	Y	N
8 Tanner	Y	Y	N	N	Y
9 Cohen	Y	Y	N	N	Y

	682	683	684	685	686
TEXAS					
1 Gohmert	?	?	?	?	?
2 Poe	Y	N	Y	Y	N
3 Johnson, S.	N	N	Y	Y	N
4 Hall	Y	N	Y	Y	N
5 Hensarling	N	N	Y	Y	N
6 Barton	Y	N	Y	Y	N
7 Culberson	N	N	Y	Y	N
8 Brady	N	N	Y	Y	N
9 Green, A.	Y	Y	N	N	Y
10 McCaul	?	?	?	?	?
11 Conaway	N	N	Y	Y	N
12 Granger	N	N	Y	Y	N
13 Thornberry	N	N	Y	Y	N
14 Paul	N	N	Y	Y	N
15 Hinojosa	Y	Y	N	N	Y
16 Reyes	Y	Y	N	N	Y
17 Edwards	Y	Y	N	N	Y
18 Jackson Lee	Y	Y	N	N	Y
19 Neugebauer	N	N	Y	Y	N
20 Gonzalez	Y	Y	N	N	Y
21 Smith	N	N	Y	Y	N
22 Olson	N	N	Y	Y	N
23 Rodriguez	Y	Y	N	N	Y
24 Marchant	Y	N	Y	Y	N
25 Doggett	Y	Y	N	N	Y
26 Burgess	Y	N	Y	Y	N
27 Ortiz	Y	Y	N	N	Y
28 Cuellar	Y	Y	N	N	Y
29 Green, G.	Y	Y	N	N	Y
30 Johnson, E.	Y	Y	N	N	Y
31 Carter	N	N	Y	Y	N
32 Sessions	N	N	Y	Y	N
UTAH					
1 Bishop	N	N	Y	Y	N
2 Matheson	Y	Y	N	N	Y
3 Chaffetz	N	N	Y	Y	N
VERMONT					
AL Welch	Y	Y	N	N	Y
VIRGINIA					
1 Wittman	N	N	Y	Y	N
2 Nye	Y	N	Y	Y	N
3 Scott	Y	Y	N	N	Y
4 Forbes	N	N	Y	Y	N
5 Perriello	Y	Y	N	N	Y
6 Goodlatte	N	N	Y	Y	N
7 Cantor	N	N	Y	Y	N
8 Moran	Y	Y	N	N	Y
9 Boucher	Y	Y	N	N	Y
10 Wolf	N	N	Y	Y	N
11 Connolly	Y	Y	N	N	Y
WASHINGTON					
1 Inslee	Y	Y	N	N	Y
2 Larsen	Y	Y	N	N	Y
3 Baird	N	Y	N	N	Y
4 Hastings	N	N	Y	Y	N
5 McMorris Rodgers	N	?	Y	Y	N
6 Dicks	Y	Y	N	N	Y
7 McDermott	Y	Y	N	N	Y
8 Reichert	Y	N	Y	Y	N
9 Smith	Y	Y	N	N	Y
WEST VIRGINIA					
1 Mollohan	Y	Y	N	N	Y
2 Capito	Y	N	Y	Y	N
3 Rahall	Y	Y	N	N	Y
WISCONSIN					
1 Ryan	N	N	Y	Y	N
2 Baldwin	Y	Y	N	N	Y
3 Kind	Y	Y	N	N	Y
4 Moore	Y	Y	N	N	Y
5 Sensenbrenner	N	N	Y	Y	N
6 Petri	Y	N	Y	Y	N
7 Obey	Y	Y	N	N	Y
8 Kagen	Y	Y	N	N	Y
WYOMING					
AL Lummis	N	N	Y	Y	N
DELEGATES					
Faleomavaega (A.S.)					
Norton (D.C.)					
Bordallo (Guam)					
Sablan (N. Marianas)					
Pierluisi (P.R.)					
Christensen (V.I.)					

HOUSE VOTES

IN THE HOUSE | By Vote Number

687. **HR 324. Santa Cruz Valley National Heritage Area/Passage.** Grijalva, D-Ariz., motion to suspend the rules and pass the bill that would establish the Santa Cruz Valley National Heritage Area in Santa Cruz and Pima counties in Arizona and authorize $1 million per fiscal year, with a maximum of $15 million. Motion rejected 249-145: R 16-145; D 233-0. A two-thirds majority of those present and voting (263 in this case) is required for passage under suspension of the rules. Sept. 8, 2009.

688. **HR 310. Boy Scouts Land Conveyance/Passage.** Grijalva, D-Ariz., motion to suspend the rules and pass the bill that would require the Agriculture Department to convey, for fair market value, about 140 acres in the Ouachita National Forest in Oklahoma to the Indian Nations Council Inc. of the Boy Scouts of America. Motion agreed to 388-0: R 162-0; D 226-0. A two-thirds majority of those present and voting (259 in this case) is required for passage under suspension of the rules. Sept. 8, 2009.

689. **HR 3123. Leadville Mine Drainage Tunnel/Passage.** Grijalva, D-Ariz., motion to suspend the rules and pass the bill that would require the Interior Department to maintain the structural integrity of the Leadville Mine Drainage Tunnel in Colorado to prevent tunnel failure and uncontrolled water release, and require the department to implement a specific remedy for the California Gulch superfund. Motion rejected 206-191: R 156-7; D 50-184. A two-thirds majority of those present and voting (265 in this case) is required for passage under suspension of the rules. Sept. 8, 2009.

690. **H Res 447. American Council of Engineering Companies Anniversary/Adoption.** Tonko, D-N.Y., motion to suspend the rules and adopt the resolution that would recognize the 100th anniversary of the American Council of Engineering Companies. Motion agreed to 420-0: R 175-0; D 245-0. A two-thirds majority of those present and voting (280 in this case) is required for adoption under suspension of the rules. Sept. 9, 2009.

691. **HR 2097. Star Spangled Banner Commemorative Coin/Passage.** Watt, D-N.C., motion to suspend the rules and pass the bill that would authorize the Treasury to mint coins commemorating the 200th anniversary of the writing of the "Star Spangled Banner." It would authorize surcharges on the coins to be paid to the Maryland War of 1812 Bicentennial Commission. Motion agreed to 419-1: R 173-1; D 246-0. A two-thirds majority of those present and voting (280 in this case) is required for passage under suspension of the rules. Sept. 9, 2009.

	687	688	689	690	691
ALABAMA					
1 Bonner	N	Y	Y	Y	Y
2 Bright	Y	Y	Y	Y	Y
3 Rogers	N	Y	Y	Y	Y
4 Aderholt	N	Y	Y	Y	Y
5 Griffith	Y	Y	Y	Y	Y
6 Bachus	N	Y	Y	Y	Y
7 Davis	?	?	?	Y	Y
ALASKA					
AL Young	?	?	?	?	?
ARIZONA					
1 Kirkpatrick	Y	Y	Y	Y	Y
2 Franks	N	Y	Y	Y	Y
3 Shadegg	N	Y	Y	Y	Y
4 Pastor	Y	Y	N	Y	Y
5 Mitchell	Y	Y	Y	Y	Y
6 Flake	N	Y	N	Y	Y
7 Grijalva	Y	Y	N	Y	Y
8 Giffords	Y	Y	N	Y	Y
ARKANSAS					
1 Berry	Y	Y	N	Y	Y
2 Snyder	Y	Y	Y	Y	Y
3 Boozman	N	Y	Y	Y	Y
4 Ross	Y	Y	Y	Y	Y
CALIFORNIA					
1 Thompson	Y	Y	N	Y	Y
2 Herger	N	Y	Y	Y	Y
3 Lungren	N	Y	Y	Y	Y
4 McClintock	N	Y	Y	Y	Y
5 Matsui	Y	Y	N	Y	Y
6 Woolsey	Y	P	N	Y	Y
7 Miller, George	Y	P	N	Y	Y
8 Pelosi					
9 Lee	Y	Y	N	Y	Y
10 Vacant					
11 McNerney	Y	Y	Y	Y	Y
12 Speier	Y	Y	N	Y	Y
13 Stark	Y	P	N	Y	Y
14 Eshoo	Y	Y	N	Y	Y
15 Honda	Y	Y	N	Y	Y
16 Lofgren	Y	Y	N	Y	Y
17 Farr	Y	Y	N	Y	Y
18 Cardoza	Y	Y	N	Y	Y
19 Radanovich	N	Y	Y	Y	Y
20 Costa	Y	Y	N	Y	Y
21 Nunes	N	Y	Y	Y	Y
22 McCarthy	N	Y	Y	Y	Y
23 Capps	Y	Y	N	Y	Y
24 Gallegly	?	?	?	Y	Y
25 McKeon	N	Y	Y	Y	Y
26 Dreier	?	?	?	Y	Y
27 Sherman	Y	Y	N	Y	Y
28 Berman	Y	Y	?	Y	Y
29 Schiff	Y	Y	N	Y	Y
30 Waxman	Y	P	N	Y	Y
31 Becerra	Y	Y	N	Y	Y
32 Chu	Y	Y	N	Y	Y
33 Watson	Y	Y	N	Y	Y
34 Roybal-Allard	Y	Y	N	Y	Y
35 Waters	Y	Y	N	Y	Y
36 Harman	Y	Y	N	Y	Y
37 Richardson	Y	Y	Y	Y	Y
38 Napolitano	Y	Y	N	Y	Y
39 Sánchez, Linda	Y	Y	N	Y	Y
40 Royce	N	Y	Y	Y	Y
41 Lewis	N	Y	Y	Y	Y
42 Miller, Gary	N	Y	Y	Y	Y
43 Baca	Y	Y	N	Y	Y
44 Calvert	N	Y	Y	Y	Y
45 Bono Mack	N	Y	Y	Y	Y
46 Rohrabacher	?	?	?	Y	Y
47 Sanchez, Loretta	?	?	?	Y	Y
48 Campbell	?	?	?	Y	Y
49 Issa	N	Y	Y	Y	Y
50 Bilbray	N	Y	Y	Y	Y
51 Filner	+	+	+	Y	Y
52 Hunter	N	Y	Y	Y	Y
53 Davis	Y	Y	N	Y	Y
COLORADO					
1 DeGette	Y	Y	N	Y	Y
2 Polis	?	?	?	Y	Y
3 Salazar	Y	Y	Y	Y	Y
4 Markey	Y	Y	N	Y	Y
5 Lamborn	N	Y	Y	Y	Y
6 Coffman	N	Y	Y	Y	Y
7 Perlmutter	Y	Y	Y	Y	Y
CONNECTICUT					
1 Larson	Y	Y	N	Y	Y
2 Courtney	Y	Y	N	Y	Y
3 DeLauro	Y	Y	N	Y	Y
4 Himes	Y	Y	N	Y	Y
5 Murphy	Y	Y	N	Y	Y
DELAWARE					
AL Castle	N	Y	Y	Y	Y
FLORIDA					
1 Miller	N	Y	Y	Y	Y
2 Boyd	+	+	+	+	+
3 Brown	?	?	?	Y	Y
4 Crenshaw	N	Y	Y	Y	Y
5 Brown-Waite	N	Y	Y	Y	Y
6 Stearns	N	Y	Y	Y	Y
7 Mica	N	Y	Y	Y	Y
8 Grayson	Y	Y	N	Y	Y
9 Bilirakis	N	Y	Y	Y	Y
10 Young	N	Y	Y	Y	Y
11 Castor	Y	Y	N	Y	Y
12 Putnam	N	Y	Y	Y	Y
13 Buchanan	N	Y	Y	Y	Y
14 Mack	N	Y	Y	Y	Y
15 Posey	N	Y	Y	Y	Y
16 Rooney	N	Y	Y	Y	Y
17 Meek	Y	Y	N	Y	Y
18 Ros-Lehtinen	Y	Y	Y	Y	Y
19 Wexler	Y	Y	N	Y	Y
20 Wasserman Schultz	Y	Y	N	Y	Y
21 Diaz-Balart, L.	Y	Y	Y	Y	Y
22 Klein	Y	Y	N	Y	Y
23 Hastings	Y	Y	N	Y	Y
24 Kosmas	Y	Y	N	Y	Y
25 Diaz-Balart, M.	Y	Y	Y	Y	Y
GEORGIA					
1 Kingston	N	Y	Y	Y	Y
2 Bishop	Y	Y	N	Y	Y
3 Westmoreland	N	Y	Y	Y	Y
4 Johnson	Y	Y	N	Y	Y
5 Lewis	Y	Y	N	Y	Y
6 Price	N	Y	Y	Y	Y
7 Linder	N	Y	Y	Y	Y
8 Marshall	Y	Y	Y	Y	Y
9 Deal	?	?	?	Y	Y
10 Broun	N	Y	N	Y	Y
11 Gingrey	N	Y	Y	Y	Y
12 Barrow	Y	Y	N	Y	Y
13 Scott	Y	Y	N	Y	Y
HAWAII					
1 Abercrombie	Y	Y	N	Y	Y
2 Hirono	Y	Y	N	Y	Y
IDAHO					
1 Minnick	Y	?	Y	Y	Y
2 Simpson	?	?	?	Y	Y
ILLINOIS					
1 Rush	?	?	?	Y	Y
2 Jackson	Y	Y	N	Y	Y
3 Lipinski	Y	Y	Y	Y	Y
4 Gutierrez	+	+	+	Y	Y
5 Quigley	Y	Y	Y	Y	Y
6 Roskam	N	Y	Y	Y	Y
7 Davis	Y	Y	N	?	?
8 Bean	Y	Y	Y	Y	Y
9 Schakowsky	Y	Y	N	Y	Y
10 Kirk	?	?	?	Y	Y
11 Halvorson	Y	Y	N	Y	Y
12 Costello	Y	Y	N	Y	Y
13 Biggert	N	Y	Y	Y	Y
14 Foster	Y	Y	Y	Y	Y
15 Johnson	N	Y	Y	Y	Y

KEY   **Republicans**   Democrats

Y Voted for (yea)	X Paired against
# Paired for	– Announced against
+ Announced for	P Voted "present"
N Voted against (nay)	C Voted "present" to avoid possible conflict of interest
	? Did not vote or otherwise make a position known

Member	687	688	689	690	691
16 Manzullo	N	Y	Y	Y	Y
17 Hare	Y	Y	N	Y	Y
18 Schock	N	Y	Y	Y	Y
19 Shimkus	?	?	?	Y	Y
INDIANA					
1 Visclosky	Y	Y	Y	Y	Y
2 Donnelly	Y	Y	Y	Y	Y
3 Souder	N	Y	Y	Y	Y
4 Buyer	N	Y	Y	Y	Y
5 Burton	N	Y	Y	Y	Y
6 Pence	N	Y	Y	Y	Y
7 Carson	Y	Y	N	Y	Y
8 Ellsworth	Y	Y	N	Y	Y
9 Hill	Y	Y	Y	Y	Y
IOWA					
1 Braley	Y	Y	N	Y	Y
2 Loebsack	Y	Y	N	Y	Y
3 Boswell	Y	Y	N	Y	Y
4 Latham	?	?	?	Y	Y
5 King	N	Y	Y	Y	Y
KANSAS					
1 Moran	N	Y	Y	Y	Y
2 Jenkins	N	Y	Y	Y	Y
3 Moore	Y	Y	N	Y	Y
4 Tiahrt	N	Y	Y	Y	Y
KENTUCKY					
1 Whitfield	Y	Y	Y	Y	Y
2 Guthrie	N	Y	Y	Y	Y
3 Yarmuth	Y	Y	N	Y	Y
4 Davis	N	Y	Y	Y	Y
5 Rogers	?	?	?	Y	Y
6 Chandler	Y	Y	N	Y	Y
LOUISIANA					
1 Scalise	N	Y	Y	Y	Y
2 Cao	Y	Y	Y	Y	Y
3 Melancon	Y	Y	Y	Y	Y
4 Fleming	N	Y	Y	Y	Y
5 Alexander	N	Y	Y	Y	Y
6 Cassidy	N	Y	Y	Y	Y
7 Boustany	N	Y	Y	Y	?
MAINE					
1 Pingree	Y	Y	N	Y	Y
2 Michaud	Y	Y	Y	Y	Y
MARYLAND					
1 Kratovil	Y	Y	Y	Y	Y
2 Ruppersberger	Y	Y	Y	Y	Y
3 Sarbanes	Y	Y	N	Y	Y
4 Edwards	Y	Y	N	Y	Y
5 Hoyer	Y	Y	N	Y	Y
6 Bartlett	N	Y	N	Y	Y
7 Cummings	Y	Y	N	Y	Y
8 Van Hollen	Y	Y	N	Y	Y
MASSACHUSETTS					
1 Olver	Y	Y	N	Y	Y
2 Neal	Y	Y	N	Y	Y
3 McGovern	Y	Y	N	Y	Y
4 Frank	Y	P	N	Y	Y
5 Tsongas	Y	Y	N	Y	Y
6 Tierney	Y	Y	N	Y	Y
7 Markey	?	?	?	Y	Y
8 Capuano	?	?	?	Y	Y
9 Lynch	Y	Y	N	?	?
10 Delahunt	?	?	?	?	?
MICHIGAN					
1 Stupak	Y	Y	N	Y	Y
2 Hoekstra	N	Y	Y	Y	Y
3 Ehlers	Y	Y	Y	Y	Y
4 Camp	N	Y	Y	Y	Y
5 Kildee	Y	Y	N	Y	Y
6 Upton	N	Y	Y	Y	Y
7 Schauer	Y	Y	N	Y	Y
8 Rogers	?	?	?	Y	Y
9 Peters	Y	Y	N	Y	Y
10 Miller	N	Y	Y	Y	Y
11 McCotter	N	Y	Y	Y	Y
12 Levin	Y	Y	N	Y	Y
13 Kilpatrick	?	Y	N	Y	Y
14 Conyers	Y	Y	N	Y	Y
15 Dingell	Y	Y	N	Y	Y
MINNESOTA					
1 Walz	Y	Y	N	Y	Y
2 Kline	N	Y	Y	Y	Y
3 Paulsen	N	Y	Y	Y	Y
4 McCollum	Y	Y	N	Y	Y

Member	687	688	689	690	691
5 Ellison	Y	Y	N	Y	Y
6 Bachmann	N	Y	Y	Y	Y
7 Peterson	Y	Y	N	Y	Y
8 Oberstar	Y	Y	Y	Y	Y
MISSISSIPPI					
1 Childers	Y	Y	Y	Y	Y
2 Thompson	Y	Y	N	Y	Y
3 Harper	N	Y	Y	Y	Y
4 Taylor	?	?	?	Y	Y
MISSOURI					
1 Clay	Y	Y	N	Y	Y
2 Akin	N	Y	Y	Y	Y
3 Carnahan	Y	Y	Y	Y	Y
4 Skelton	Y	Y	N	Y	Y
5 Cleaver	Y	Y	N	Y	Y
6 Graves	N	Y	Y	Y	Y
7 Blunt	N	Y	Y	Y	Y
8 Emerson	N	Y	Y	Y	Y
9 Luetkemeyer	N	Y	Y	Y	Y
MONTANA					
AL Rehberg	N	Y	Y	Y	Y
NEBRASKA					
1 Fortenberry	Y	Y	Y	Y	Y
2 Terry	N	Y	Y	Y	Y
3 Smith	N	Y	Y	Y	Y
NEVADA					
1 Berkley	?	?	?	Y	Y
2 Heller	N	Y	Y	Y	Y
3 Titus	Y	Y	Y	Y	Y
NEW HAMPSHIRE					
1 Shea-Porter	Y	Y	N	Y	Y
2 Hodes	Y	Y	N	Y	Y
NEW JERSEY					
1 Andrews	Y	Y	N	Y	Y
2 LoBiondo	Y	Y	Y	Y	Y
3 Adler	Y	Y	N	Y	Y
4 Smith	Y	Y	Y	?	?
5 Garrett	N	Y	Y	Y	Y
6 Pallone	Y	Y	N	Y	Y
7 Lance	Y	Y	Y	Y	Y
8 Pascrell	Y	Y	N	Y	Y
9 Rothman	Y	Y	N	Y	Y
10 Payne	Y	Y	N	Y	Y
11 Frelinghuysen	Y	Y	Y	Y	Y
12 Holt	Y	Y	N	Y	Y
13 Sires	Y	Y	N	Y	Y
NEW MEXICO					
1 Heinrich	Y	Y	N	Y	Y
2 Teague	Y	Y	Y	Y	Y
3 Lujan	Y	Y	N	Y	Y
NEW YORK					
1 Bishop	Y	Y	N	Y	Y
2 Israel	Y	Y	N	Y	Y
3 King	N	Y	Y	Y	Y
4 McCarthy	+	+	+	+	+
5 Ackerman	Y	Y	N	Y	Y
6 Meeks	Y	Y	N	Y	Y
7 Crowley	Y	Y	N	Y	Y
8 Nadler	Y	Y	N	Y	Y
9 Weiner	Y	Y	N	Y	Y
10 Towns	Y	Y	Y	Y	Y
11 Clarke	+	+	+	Y	Y
12 Velázquez	Y	Y	N	Y	Y
13 McMahon	Y	Y	N	Y	Y
14 Maloney	Y	Y	N	Y	Y
15 Rangel	Y	Y	N	Y	Y
16 Serrano	Y	Y	N	Y	Y
17 Engel	Y	Y	N	Y	Y
18 Lowey	Y	Y	N	Y	Y
19 Hall	Y	Y	Y	Y	Y
20 Murphy	Y	Y	Y	Y	Y
21 Tonko	Y	Y	N	Y	Y
22 Hinchey	Y	Y	N	Y	Y
23 McHugh	Y	Y	Y	Y	Y
24 Arcuri	Y	Y	N	Y	Y
25 Maffei	Y	Y	N	?	?
26 Lee	Y	Y	Y	Y	Y
27 Higgins	Y	Y	Y	Y	Y
28 Slaughter	Y	?	N	+	+
29 Massa	Y	Y	N	Y	Y
NORTH CAROLINA					
1 Butterfield	Y	Y	N	Y	Y
2 Etheridge	Y	Y	N	Y	Y
3 Jones	Y	Y	Y	Y	Y
4 Price	Y	Y	N	Y	Y

Member	687	688	689	690	691
5 Foxx	N	Y	Y	Y	Y
6 Coble	N	Y	N	Y	Y
7 McIntyre	Y	Y	Y	Y	Y
8 Kissell	Y	Y	N	Y	Y
9 Myrick	N	Y	Y	Y	Y
10 McHenry	N	Y	Y	Y	Y
11 Shuler	Y	Y	N	Y	Y
12 Watt	Y	Y	N	Y	Y
13 Miller	Y	Y	Y	Y	Y
NORTH DAKOTA					
AL Pomeroy	Y	Y	N	Y	Y
OHIO					
1 Driehaus	Y	Y	N	Y	Y
2 Schmidt	N	Y	Y	Y	Y
3 Turner	N	Y	Y	Y	Y
4 Jordan	N	Y	Y	Y	Y
5 Latta	N	Y	Y	Y	Y
6 Wilson	Y	Y	N	Y	Y
7 Austria	N	Y	Y	Y	Y
8 Boehner	N	Y	Y	Y	Y
9 Kaptur	Y	Y	N	Y	Y
10 Kucinich	Y	P	N	Y	Y
11 Fudge	Y	Y	N	Y	Y
12 Tiberi	N	Y	Y	Y	Y
13 Sutton	Y	Y	N	?	Y
14 LaTourette	?	?	Y	Y	Y
15 Kilroy	Y	Y	Y	Y	Y
16 Boccieri	Y	Y	Y	Y	Y
17 Ryan	?	Y	N	Y	Y
18 Space	Y	Y	Y	Y	Y
OKLAHOMA					
1 Sullivan	N	Y	Y	Y	Y
2 Boren	Y	Y	Y	Y	Y
3 Lucas	N	Y	Y	Y	Y
4 Cole	N	Y	Y	Y	Y
5 Fallin	N	Y	Y	Y	Y
OREGON					
1 Wu	Y	Y	N	Y	Y
2 Walden	N	Y	Y	Y	Y
3 Blumenauer	Y	Y	N	Y	Y
4 DeFazio	Y	Y	N	Y	Y
5 Schrader	Y	Y	N	Y	Y
PENNSYLVANIA					
1 Brady	Y	Y	N	Y	Y
2 Fattah	Y	Y	Y	Y	Y
3 Dahlkemper	Y	Y	Y	Y	Y
4 Altmire	Y	Y	Y	Y	Y
5 Thompson	N	Y	Y	Y	Y
6 Gerlach	−	+	+	Y	Y
7 Sestak	?	?	?	Y	Y
8 Murphy, P.	Y	Y	N	Y	Y
9 Shuster	N	Y	Y	Y	Y
10 Carney	?	?	?	Y	Y
11 Kanjorski	Y	Y	N	Y	Y
12 Murtha	?	?	?	Y	Y
13 Schwartz	Y	Y	N	Y	Y
14 Doyle	Y	Y	N	Y	Y
15 Dent	N	Y	Y	Y	Y
16 Pitts	N	Y	Y	Y	Y
17 Holden	Y	Y	N	Y	Y
18 Murphy, T.	Y	Y	Y	Y	Y
19 Platts	Y	Y	Y	Y	Y
RHODE ISLAND					
1 Kennedy	Y	Y	N	Y	Y
2 Langevin	Y	Y	N	Y	Y
SOUTH CAROLINA					
1 Brown	N	Y	Y	Y	Y
2 Wilson	N	Y	Y	Y	Y
3 Barrett	−	+	+	Y	Y
4 Inglis	N	Y	Y	Y	Y
5 Spratt	Y	Y	Y	Y	Y
6 Clyburn	Y	Y	N	Y	Y
SOUTH DAKOTA					
AL Herseth Sandlin	Y	Y	Y	Y	Y
TENNESSEE					
1 Roe	N	Y	Y	Y	Y
2 Duncan	N	Y	Y	Y	Y
3 Wamp	N	Y	Y	Y	Y
4 Davis	Y	Y	N	Y	Y
5 Cooper	Y	Y	N	Y	Y
6 Gordon	Y	Y	N	Y	Y
7 Blackburn	N	Y	Y	Y	Y
8 Tanner	?	?	?	?	?
9 Cohen	Y	Y	N	Y	Y

Member	687	688	689	690	691
TEXAS					
1 Gohmert	N	Y	Y	Y	Y
2 Poe	N	Y	Y	Y	Y
3 Johnson, S.	N	Y	Y	Y	Y
4 Hall	N	Y	Y	Y	Y
5 Hensarling	N	Y	Y	Y	Y
6 Barton	N	Y	Y	Y	Y
7 Culberson	N	Y	Y	Y	Y
8 Brady	?	?	?	Y	Y
9 Green, A.	Y	Y	N	Y	Y
10 McCaul	N	Y	Y	Y	Y
11 Conaway	N	Y	Y	Y	Y
12 Granger	N	Y	Y	Y	Y
13 Thornberry	N	Y	Y	Y	Y
14 Paul	N	Y	N	Y	N
15 Hinojosa	Y	Y	N	Y	Y
16 Reyes	Y	Y	N	Y	Y
17 Edwards	Y	Y	N	Y	Y
18 Jackson Lee	Y	Y	N	Y	Y
19 Neugebauer	N	Y	Y	Y	Y
20 Gonzalez	Y	Y	N	Y	Y
21 Smith	N	Y	Y	Y	Y
22 Olson	N	Y	Y	Y	Y
23 Rodriguez	?	?	?	Y	Y
24 Marchant	N	Y	Y	Y	Y
25 Doggett	Y	Y	N	Y	Y
26 Burgess	N	Y	Y	Y	Y
27 Ortiz	Y	Y	N	Y	Y
28 Cuellar	Y	Y	N	Y	Y
29 Green, G.	Y	Y	N	Y	Y
30 Johnson, E.	Y	Y	N	Y	Y
31 Carter	N	Y	Y	Y	Y
32 Sessions	N	Y	Y	Y	Y
UTAH					
1 Bishop	?	Y	Y	Y	Y
2 Matheson	Y	Y	N	Y	Y
3 Chaffetz	N	Y	Y	Y	Y
VERMONT					
AL Welch	Y	Y	N	Y	Y
VIRGINIA					
1 Wittman	N	Y	Y	Y	Y
2 Nye	Y	Y	Y	Y	Y
3 Scott	Y	Y	N	Y	Y
4 Forbes	N	Y	Y	Y	Y
5 Perriello	Y	Y	Y	Y	Y
6 Goodlatte	N	Y	Y	Y	Y
7 Cantor	N	Y	Y	Y	Y
8 Moran	Y	Y	N	Y	Y
9 Boucher	Y	Y	N	Y	Y
10 Wolf	N	Y	Y	Y	Y
11 Connolly	Y	Y	N	Y	Y
WASHINGTON					
1 Inslee	Y	Y	N	Y	Y
2 Larsen	Y	Y	N	Y	Y
3 Baird	Y	Y	N	Y	Y
4 Hastings	N	Y	Y	Y	Y
5 McMorris Rodgers	N	Y	Y	?	Y
6 Dicks	Y	Y	N	Y	Y
7 McDermott	Y	Y	N	Y	Y
8 Reichert	N	Y	Y	Y	Y
9 Smith	Y	Y	N	Y	Y
WEST VIRGINIA					
1 Mollohan	Y	Y	N	Y	Y
2 Capito	N	Y	Y	Y	Y
3 Rahall	Y	Y	N	Y	Y
WISCONSIN					
1 Ryan	N	Y	Y	Y	Y
2 Baldwin	Y	P	N	?	?
3 Kind	Y	Y	Y	Y	Y
4 Moore	Y	Y	N	Y	Y
5 Sensenbrenner	N	Y	Y	Y	Y
6 Petri	N	Y	N	Y	Y
7 Obey	Y	Y	N	Y	Y
8 Kagen	Y	Y	N	Y	Y
WYOMING					
AL Lummis	N	Y	Y	Y	Y
DELEGATES					
Faleomavaega (A.S.)					
Norton (D.C.)					
Bordallo (Guam)					
Sablan (N. Marianas)					
Pierluisi (P.R.)					
Christensen (V.I.)					

IN THE HOUSE | By Vote Number

692. **HR 2498. William Lipinski Federal Building/Passage.** Norton, D-D.C., motion to suspend the rules and pass the bill that would designate a federal building in Chicago as the "William O. Lipinski Federal Building." Motion agreed to 419-0: R 175-0; D 244-0. A two-thirds majority of those present and voting (280 in this case) is required for passage under suspension of the rules. Sept. 9, 2009.

693. **H Res 722. Sept. 11 Remembrance/Adoption.** Berman, D-Calif., motion to suspend the rules and adopt the resolution that would recognize Sept. 11 as a day of remembrance and service, extend sympathies to the victims of the 2001 terrorist attacks, honor the actions of first responders and armed forces, and express gratitude to the nations that continue to stand in solidarity against terrorism. Motion agreed to 416-0: R 172-0; D 244-0. A two-thirds majority of those present and voting (278 in this case) is required for adoption under suspension of the rules. Sept. 9, 2009.

694. **HR 965. Chesapeake Bay Gateways and Watertrails Network/Recommit.** Hastings, R-Wash., motion to recommit the bill to the Natural Resources Committee with instructions that it be reported back immediately with language that would prevent the bill's provisions from taking effect until the national deficit is less than $1 trillion. Motion rejected 194-229: R 175-0; D 19-229. Sept. 10, 2009.

695. **HR 965. Chesapeake Bay Gateways and Watertrails Network/Passage.** Passage of the bill that would permanently authorize the Chesapeake Bay Gateways and Watertrails Network and authorize such sums as necessary. Passed 311-107: R 65-107; D 246-0. Sept. 10, 2009.

	692	693	694	695
ALABAMA				
1 **Bonner**	Y	Y	Y	N
2 Bright	Y	Y	Y	Y
3 **Rogers**	Y	Y	Y	Y
4 **Aderholt**	Y	Y	Y	N
5 Griffith	Y	Y	Y	Y
6 **Bachus**	Y	Y	Y	N
7 Davis	Y	Y	N	Y
ALASKA				
AL **Young**	?	?	?	?
ARIZONA				
1 Kirkpatrick	Y	Y	N	Y
2 **Franks**	Y	Y	Y	N
3 **Shadegg**	Y	Y	Y	N
4 Pastor	Y	Y	N	Y
5 Mitchell	Y	Y	Y	Y
6 **Flake**	Y	Y	N	N
7 Grijalva	Y	Y	N	Y
8 Giffords	Y	Y	Y	Y
ARKANSAS				
1 Berry	Y	Y	N	Y
2 Snyder	Y	Y	N	Y
3 **Boozman**	Y	Y	Y	N
4 Ross	Y	Y	N	Y
CALIFORNIA				
1 Thompson	Y	Y	N	Y
2 **Herger**	Y	Y	Y	N
3 **Lungren**	Y	Y	Y	?
4 **McClintock**	Y	Y	Y	N
5 Matsui	Y	Y	N	Y
6 Woolsey	Y	Y	N	Y
7 Miller, George	Y	Y	N	Y
8 Pelosi		Y		
9 Lee	Y	Y	N	Y
10 Vacant				
11 McNerney	Y	Y	N	Y
12 Speier	Y	Y	N	Y
13 Stark	Y	Y	N	Y
14 Eshoo	Y	Y	N	Y
15 Honda	Y	Y	N	Y
16 Lofgren	Y	Y	N	Y
17 Farr	Y	Y	N	?
18 Cardoza	Y	Y	N	Y
19 **Radanovich**	Y	Y	Y	N
20 Costa	Y	Y	N	Y
21 **Nunes**	Y	Y	Y	N
22 **McCarthy**	Y	Y	Y	N
23 Capps	Y	Y	N	Y
24 **Gallegly**	Y	Y	Y	Y
25 **McKeon**	Y	Y	Y	N
26 **Dreier**	Y	Y	Y	N
27 Sherman	Y	Y	N	Y
28 Berman	Y	Y	N	Y
29 Schiff	Y	Y	N	Y
30 Waxman	Y	Y	N	Y
31 Becerra	Y	Y	N	Y
32 Chu	Y	Y	N	Y
33 Watson	Y	Y	N	Y
34 Roybal-Allard	Y	Y	N	Y
35 Waters	Y	Y	N	Y
36 Harman	Y	Y	N	Y
37 Richardson	Y	Y	N	Y
38 Napolitano	Y	Y	N	Y
39 Sánchez, Linda	Y	Y	N	Y
40 **Royce**	Y	Y	Y	N
41 **Lewis**	Y	Y	Y	N
42 **Miller, Gary**	Y	Y	Y	Y
43 Baca	Y	Y	N	Y
44 **Calvert**	Y	Y	Y	N
45 **Bono Mack**	Y	Y	Y	N
46 **Rohrabacher**	Y	Y	Y	Y
47 Sanchez, Loretta	Y	Y	N	Y
48 **Campbell**	Y	Y	Y	N
49 **Issa**	Y	Y	?	?
50 **Bilbray**	Y	Y	Y	Y
51 Filner	Y	Y	N	Y
52 **Hunter**	Y	Y	Y	N
53 Davis	Y	Y	N	Y

	692	693	694	695
COLORADO				
1 DeGette	Y	Y	N	Y
2 Polis	Y	Y	N	Y
3 Salazar	Y	Y	N	Y
4 Markey	Y	Y	N	Y
5 **Lamborn**	Y	Y	Y	N
6 **Coffman**	Y	Y	Y	N
7 Perlmutter	Y	Y	N	Y
CONNECTICUT				
1 Larson	Y	Y	N	Y
2 Courtney	Y	Y	N	Y
3 DeLauro	Y	Y	N	Y
4 Himes	Y	Y	N	Y
5 Murphy	Y	Y	N	Y
DELAWARE				
AL **Castle**	Y	Y	Y	Y
FLORIDA				
1 **Miller**	Y	Y	Y	N
2 Boyd	+	+	?	+
3 Brown	Y	Y	N	Y
4 **Crenshaw**	Y	Y	Y	N
5 **Brown-Waite**	Y	Y	Y	N
6 **Stearns**	Y	Y	Y	N
7 **Mica**	Y	Y	Y	N
8 Grayson	Y	Y	N	Y
9 **Bilirakis**	Y	Y	Y	Y
10 **Young**	Y	Y	Y	Y
11 Castor	Y	Y	N	Y
12 **Putnam**	Y	Y	Y	Y
13 **Buchanan**	Y	Y	Y	Y
14 **Mack**	Y	Y	Y	N
15 **Posey**	Y	Y	Y	N
16 **Rooney**	Y	Y	Y	Y
17 Meek	Y	Y	N	Y
18 **Ros-Lehtinen**	Y	?	Y	Y
19 Wexler	Y	Y	N	Y
20 Wasserman Schultz	Y	Y	N	Y
21 **Diaz-Balart, L.**	Y	Y	Y	Y
22 Klein	Y	Y	N	Y
23 Hastings	Y	Y	N	Y
24 Kosmas	Y	Y	N	Y
25 **Diaz-Balart, M.**	Y	Y	Y	Y
GEORGIA				
1 **Kingston**	Y	Y	Y	N
2 Bishop	Y	Y	N	Y
3 **Westmoreland**	Y	Y	Y	N
4 Johnson	Y	Y	N	Y
5 Lewis	Y	Y	N	Y
6 **Price**	Y	Y	Y	N
7 **Linder**	Y	Y	Y	N
8 Marshall	Y	Y	Y	Y
9 **Deal**	Y	Y	Y	N
10 **Broun**	Y	Y	Y	N
11 **Gingrey**	Y	Y	Y	N
12 Barrow	Y	Y	N	Y
13 Scott	Y	Y	N	Y
HAWAII				
1 Abercrombie	Y	Y	N	Y
2 Hirono	Y	Y	N	Y
IDAHO				
1 Minnick	Y	Y	N	Y
2 **Simpson**	Y	Y	Y	Y
ILLINOIS				
1 Rush	?	Y	N	?
2 Jackson	Y	Y	N	Y
3 Lipinski	Y	Y	N	Y
4 Gutierrez	Y	Y	N	Y
5 Quigley	Y	Y	N	Y
6 **Roskam**	Y	Y	?	?
7 Davis	?	?	?	?
8 Bean	Y	Y	N	Y
9 Schakowsky	Y	Y	N	Y
10 **Kirk**	Y	Y	Y	Y
11 Halvorson	Y	Y	N	Y
12 Costello	Y	Y	N	Y
13 **Biggert**	Y	Y	Y	Y
14 Foster	Y	Y	N	Y
15 **Johnson**	Y	Y	Y	Y

KEY	**Republicans**	Democrats		
Y Voted for (yea)		**X** Paired against		**C** Voted "present" to avoid possible conflict of interest
# Paired for		**–** Announced against		
+ Announced for		**P** Voted "present"		**?** Did not vote or otherwise make a position known
N Voted against (nay)				

	692	693	694	695
16 Manzullo	Y	Y	Y	N
17 Hare	Y	Y	N	Y
18 Schock	Y	Y	Y	Y
19 Shimkus	Y	Y	Y	N
INDIANA				
1 Visclosky	Y	Y	N	Y
2 Donnelly	Y	Y	N	Y
3 Souder	Y	Y	Y	N
4 Buyer	Y	Y	Y	N
5 Burton	Y	Y	Y	N
6 Pence	Y	Y	Y	N
7 Carson	Y	Y	N	Y
8 Ellsworth	Y	Y	N	Y
9 Hill	Y	Y	N	Y
IOWA				
1 Braley	Y	Y	N	Y
2 Loebsack	Y	Y	N	Y
3 Boswell	Y	Y	N	Y
4 Latham	Y	Y	Y	N
5 King	Y	Y	Y	N
KANSAS				
1 Moran	Y	Y	Y	N
2 Jenkins	Y	Y	Y	Y
3 Moore	Y	Y	N	Y
4 Tiahrt	Y	Y	Y	N
KENTUCKY				
1 Whitfield	Y	Y	Y	Y
2 Guthrie	Y	Y	Y	Y
3 Yarmuth	Y	Y	N	Y
4 Davis	Y	Y	Y	N
5 Rogers	Y	Y	Y	Y
6 Chandler	Y	Y	N	Y
LOUISIANA				
1 Scalise	Y	Y	Y	N
2 Cao	Y	Y	Y	Y
3 Melancon	Y	Y	Y	Y
4 Fleming	Y	Y	Y	N
5 Alexander	Y	Y	Y	Y
6 Cassidy	Y	Y	Y	N
7 Boustany	?	Y	Y	N
MAINE				
1 Pingree	Y	Y	N	Y
2 Michaud	Y	Y	N	Y
MARYLAND				
1 Kratovil	Y	Y	N	Y
2 Ruppersberger	Y	Y	N	Y
3 Sarbanes	Y	Y	N	Y
4 Edwards	Y	Y	N	Y
5 Hoyer	Y	Y	N	Y
6 Bartlett	Y	Y	Y	Y
7 Cummings	Y	Y	N	Y
8 Van Hollen	Y	Y	N	Y
MASSACHUSETTS				
1 Olver	Y	Y	N	Y
2 Neal	Y	Y	N	Y
3 McGovern	Y	Y	N	Y
4 Frank	?	Y	N	Y
5 Tsongas	Y	Y	N	Y
6 Tierney	Y	Y	N	Y
7 Markey	Y	Y	N	Y
8 Capuano	Y	Y	N	Y
9 Lynch	?	?	?	?
10 Delahunt	?	?	?	?
MICHIGAN				
1 Stupak	Y	Y	N	Y
2 Hoekstra	Y	Y	Y	N
3 Ehlers	Y	Y	Y	Y
4 Camp	Y	Y	Y	N
5 Kildee	Y	Y	N	Y
6 Upton	Y	Y	Y	Y
7 Schauer	Y	Y	N	Y
8 Rogers	Y	Y	Y	Y
9 Peters	Y	Y	N	Y
10 Miller	Y	Y	Y	Y
11 McCotter	Y	Y	Y	Y
12 Levin	Y	Y	N	Y
13 Kilpatrick	Y	Y	N	Y
14 Conyers	Y	Y	N	Y
15 Dingell	Y	Y	N	Y
MINNESOTA				
1 Walz	Y	Y	N	Y
2 Kline	Y	Y	Y	N
3 Paulsen	Y	Y	Y	Y
4 McCollum	Y	Y	N	Y

	692	693	694	695
5 Ellison	Y	Y	N	Y
6 Bachmann	Y	Y	Y	N
7 Peterson	Y	Y	N	Y
8 Oberstar	Y	Y	N	Y
MISSISSIPPI				
1 Childers	Y	Y	Y	Y
2 Thompson	Y	Y	N	Y
3 Harper	Y	Y	Y	N
4 Taylor	Y	Y	Y	Y
MISSOURI				
1 Clay	Y	Y	?	?
2 Akin	Y	Y	Y	N
3 Carnahan	Y	?	N	Y
4 Skelton	Y	Y	N	Y
5 Cleaver	Y	Y	N	Y
6 Graves	Y	Y	Y	N
7 Blunt	Y	Y	Y	Y
8 Emerson	Y	Y	Y	Y
9 Luetkemeyer	Y	Y	Y	N
MONTANA				
AL Rehberg	Y	Y	Y	Y
NEBRASKA				
1 Fortenberry	Y	Y	Y	Y
2 Terry	Y	Y	Y	?
3 Smith	Y	Y	Y	N
NEVADA				
1 Berkley	Y	Y	N	Y
2 Heller	Y	Y	Y	N
3 Titus	Y	Y	N	Y
NEW HAMPSHIRE				
1 Shea-Porter	Y	Y	N	Y
2 Hodes	Y	Y	N	Y
NEW JERSEY				
1 Andrews	Y	Y	N	Y
2 LoBiondo	Y	Y	Y	Y
3 Adler	Y	Y	Y	Y
4 Smith	?	?	Y	Y
5 Garrett	Y	Y	Y	N
6 Pallone	Y	Y	N	Y
7 Lance	Y	Y	Y	Y
8 Pascrell	Y	Y	N	Y
9 Rothman	Y	Y	N	Y
10 Payne	Y	Y	?	?
11 Frelinghuysen	Y	Y	Y	Y
12 Holt	Y	Y	N	Y
13 Sires	Y	Y	N	Y
NEW MEXICO				
1 Heinrich	Y	Y	N	Y
2 Teague	Y	Y	Y	Y
3 Lujan	Y	Y	N	Y
NEW YORK				
1 Bishop	Y	Y	N	Y
2 Israel	Y	Y	N	Y
3 King	Y	Y	Y	Y
4 McCarthy	+	+	−	+
5 Ackerman	Y	Y	N	Y
6 Meeks	Y	Y	N	Y
7 Crowley	Y	Y	N	Y
8 Nadler	Y	Y	N	Y
9 Weiner	Y	Y	N	Y
10 Towns	Y	Y	N	Y
11 Clarke	Y	Y	N	Y
12 Velázquez	Y	Y	N	Y
13 McMahon	Y	Y	N	Y
14 Maloney	Y	Y	N	Y
15 Rangel	Y	Y	N	Y
16 Serrano	Y	Y	N	Y
17 Engel	Y	Y	N	Y
18 Lowey	Y	Y	N	Y
19 Hall	Y	Y	N	Y
20 Murphy	Y	Y	N	Y
21 Tonko	Y	Y	N	Y
22 Hinchey	Y	Y	N	Y
23 McHugh	Y	+	Y	Y
24 Arcuri	Y	Y	Y	Y
25 Maffei	?	?	Y	Y
26 Lee	Y	Y	Y	N
27 Higgins	Y	Y	N	Y
28 Slaughter	+	+	N	Y
29 Massa	Y	Y	N	Y
NORTH CAROLINA				
1 Butterfield	Y	Y	N	Y
2 Etheridge	Y	Y	N	Y
3 Jones	Y	Y	Y	Y
4 Price	Y	Y	N	Y

	692	693	694	695
5 Foxx	Y	Y	Y	N
6 Coble	Y	?	Y	N
7 McIntyre	Y	Y	Y	Y
8 Kissell	Y	Y	N	Y
9 Myrick	Y	Y	Y	N
10 McHenry	Y	Y	Y	N
11 Shuler	Y	Y	Y	Y
12 Watt	Y	Y	N	Y
13 Miller	Y	Y	N	Y
NORTH DAKOTA				
AL Pomeroy	Y	Y	N	Y
OHIO				
1 Driehaus	Y	Y	Y	Y
2 Schmidt	Y	?	Y	Y
3 Turner	Y	Y	Y	Y
4 Jordan	Y	Y	N	N
5 Latta	Y	Y	Y	N
6 Wilson	Y	?	N	Y
7 Austria	Y	Y	Y	N
8 Boehner	Y	Y	Y	N
9 Kaptur	Y	Y	N	Y
10 Kucinich	Y	Y	N	Y
11 Fudge	Y	Y	N	Y
12 Tiberi	Y	Y	Y	N
13 Sutton	Y	Y	N	Y
14 LaTourette	Y	Y	Y	Y
15 Kilroy	Y	Y	N	Y
16 Boccieri	Y	Y	N	Y
17 Ryan	Y	Y	N	Y
18 Space	Y	Y	N	Y
OKLAHOMA				
1 Sullivan	Y	Y	Y	N
2 Boren	Y	Y	N	Y
3 Lucas	Y	Y	Y	N
4 Cole	Y	Y	Y	N
5 Fallin	Y	Y	Y	Y
OREGON				
1 Wu	Y	?	N	Y
2 Walden	Y	Y	Y	N
3 Blumenauer	Y	Y	N	Y
4 DeFazio	Y	Y	N	Y
5 Schrader	Y	Y	N	Y
PENNSYLVANIA				
1 Brady	Y	Y	N	Y
2 Fattah	Y	Y	N	Y
3 Dahlkemper	Y	Y	N	Y
4 Altmire	Y	Y	Y	Y
5 Thompson	Y	Y	Y	Y
6 Gerlach	Y	Y	Y	Y
7 Sestak	Y	Y	N	Y
8 Murphy, P.	Y	Y	N	Y
9 Shuster	Y	Y	Y	N
10 Carney	Y	Y	N	Y
11 Kanjorski	Y	Y	N	Y
12 Murtha	Y	Y	N	Y
13 Schwartz	Y	Y	N	Y
14 Doyle	Y	Y	N	Y
15 Dent	Y	Y	Y	Y
16 Pitts	Y	Y	Y	Y
17 Holden	Y	Y	N	Y
18 Murphy, T.	Y	Y	Y	Y
19 Platts	Y	Y	Y	Y
RHODE ISLAND				
1 Kennedy	Y	Y	N	Y
2 Langevin	Y	Y	N	Y
SOUTH CAROLINA				
1 Brown	Y	Y	Y	N
2 Wilson	Y	Y	Y	N
3 Barrett	Y	Y	Y	N
4 Inglis	Y	Y	Y	N
5 Spratt	Y	Y	N	Y
6 Clyburn	Y	Y	N	Y
SOUTH DAKOTA				
AL Herseth Sandlin	Y	Y	N	Y
TENNESSEE				
1 Roe	Y	Y	Y	?
2 Duncan	Y	Y	Y	N
3 Wamp	Y	Y	Y	N
4 Davis	Y	Y	N	Y
5 Cooper	Y	Y	N	Y
6 Gordon	Y	Y	N	Y
7 Blackburn	Y	Y	Y	N
8 Tanner	?	?	N	Y
9 Cohen	Y	Y	N	Y

	692	693	694	695
TEXAS				
1 Gohmert	Y	Y	Y	N
2 Poe	Y	Y	Y	N
3 Johnson, S.	Y	Y	Y	N
4 Hall	Y	Y	Y	N
5 Hensarling	Y	Y	Y	N
6 Barton	Y	Y	Y	N
7 Culberson	Y	Y	Y	N
8 Brady	Y	Y	Y	N
9 Green, A.	Y	Y	N	Y
10 McCaul	Y	Y	Y	Y
11 Conaway	Y	Y	Y	N
12 Granger	Y	Y	Y	N
13 Thornberry	Y	Y	Y	N
14 Paul	Y	Y	Y	N
15 Hinojosa	Y	Y	N	Y
16 Reyes	Y	Y	N	Y
17 Edwards	Y	Y	N	Y
18 Jackson Lee	Y	Y	N	Y
19 Neugebauer	Y	Y	N	Y
20 Gonzalez	Y	Y	N	Y
21 Smith	Y	Y	Y	Y
22 Olson	Y	Y	Y	N
23 Rodriguez	Y	Y	N	Y
24 Marchant	Y	Y	Y	N
25 Doggett	Y	Y	N	Y
26 Burgess	Y	Y	Y	N
27 Ortiz	Y	Y	N	Y
28 Cuellar	Y	Y	N	Y
29 Green, G.	Y	Y	N	Y
30 Johnson, E.	Y	Y	N	Y
31 Carter	Y	Y	Y	N
32 Sessions	Y	Y	Y	N
UTAH				
1 Bishop	Y	Y	Y	Y
2 Matheson	Y	Y	N	Y
3 Chaffetz	Y	Y	Y	N
VERMONT				
AL Welch	Y	Y	N	Y
VIRGINIA				
1 Wittman	Y	Y	Y	Y
2 Nye	Y	Y	Y	Y
3 Scott	Y	Y	N	Y
4 Forbes	Y	Y	Y	Y
5 Perriello	Y	Y	N	Y
6 Goodlatte	Y	Y	Y	Y
7 Cantor	Y	Y	Y	Y
8 Moran	Y	Y	N	Y
9 Boucher	Y	Y	N	Y
10 Wolf	Y	Y	Y	Y
11 Connolly	Y	Y	N	Y
WASHINGTON				
1 Inslee	Y	Y	N	Y
2 Larsen	Y	Y	N	Y
3 Baird	Y	Y	N	Y
4 Hastings	Y	Y	Y	N
5 McMorris Rodgers	Y	Y	Y	N
6 Dicks	Y	Y	N	Y
7 McDermott	Y	Y	N	Y
8 Reichert	Y	Y	Y	N
9 Smith	Y	Y	N	Y
WEST VIRGINIA				
1 Mollohan	Y	Y	N	Y
2 Capito	Y	Y	Y	Y
3 Rahall	Y	Y	N	Y
WISCONSIN				
1 Ryan	Y	Y	Y	N
2 Baldwin	?	?	N	Y
3 Kind	Y	Y	N	Y
4 Moore	Y	Y	N	Y
5 Sensenbrenner	Y	Y	Y	N
6 Petri	Y	Y	Y	Y
7 Obey	Y	Y	N	Y
8 Kagen	Y	Y	N	Y
WYOMING				
AL Lummis	Y	Y	Y	N
DELEGATES				
Faleomavaega (A.S.)				
Norton (D.C.)				
Bordallo (Guam)				
Sablan (N. Marianas)				
Pierluisi (P.R.)				
Christensen (V.I.)				

IN THE HOUSE | By Vote Number

696. **H Res 6. National Coach Appreciation Week/Adoption.** Sablan, D-N. Marianas, motion to suspend the rules and adopt the resolution that would recognize the contribution coaches make in the lives of children who participate in organized sports, and encourage the observation of National Coach Appreciation Week. Motion agreed to 388-0: R 156-0; D 232-0. A two-thirds majority of those present and voting (259 in this case) is required for adoption under suspension of the rules. Sept. 14, 2009.

697. **H Res 459. National Safety Month/Adoption.** Sablan, D-N. Marianas, motion to suspend the rules and adopt the resolution that would support the designation and encourage the observation of National Safety Month and recognize the National Safety Council for raising awareness about the need for safe practices in schools and workplaces. Motion agreed to 386-0: R 157-0; D 229-0. A two-thirds majority of those present and voting (258 in this case) is required for adoption under suspension of the rules. Sept. 14, 2009.

698. **H Con Res 59. Senior Caregiver Recognition/Adoption.** Sablan, D-N. Marianas, motion to suspend the rules and adopt the concurrent resolution that would recognize caregiving as a profession and encourage individuals to provide care to family, friends and neighbors. It would call on Congress to fund programs that address the needs of seniors and family caregivers and continue education on the options available to seniors who need care. Motion agreed to 387-0: R 156-0; D 231-0. A two-thirds majority of those present and voting (258 in this case) is required for adoption under suspension of the rules. Sept. 14, 2009.

699. **H Res 744. Disapproval of Rep. Wilson Conduct/Adoption.** Adoption of the privileged resolution that would express the House's disapproval of the behavior of Rep. Joe Wilson, R-S.C., in breaching decorum and degrading proceedings to the discredit of the House during the joint session of Congress on Sept. 9, 2009. Adopted 240-179: R 7-167; D 233-12. Sept. 15, 2009.

700. **H Res 317. Kansas City Animal Health Corridor/Adoption.** Holden, D-Pa., motion to suspend the rules and adopt the resolution that would recognize the region from Manhattan, Kan., to Columbia, Mo., as the Kansas City Animal Health Corridor, recognize the corridor as the national center of the animal health industry and support continued growth of the industry. Motion agreed to 312-108: R 111-63; D 201-45. A two-thirds majority of those present and voting (280 in this case) is required for adoption under suspension of the rules. Sept. 15, 2009.

701. **HR 22. Postal Service Retiree Health Benefits/Passage.** Towns, D-N.Y., motion to suspend the rules and pass the bill that would lower the amount the U.S. Postal Service is required to contribute to the Postal Service Retiree Health Benefits Fund in fiscal 2009 to $1.4 billion from $5.4 billion. Motion agreed to 388-32: R 142-32; D 246-0. A two-thirds majority of those present and voting (280 in this case) is required for passage under suspension of the rules. Sept. 15, 2009.

	696	697	698	699	700	701
ALABAMA						
1 Bonner	Y	Y	Y	N	Y	Y
2 Bright	Y	Y	Y	Y	Y	Y
3 Rogers	Y	Y	Y	N	N	Y
4 Aderholt	Y	Y	Y	N	N	Y
5 Griffith	Y	Y	Y	Y	Y	Y
6 Bachus	Y	Y	Y	N	N	Y
7 Davis	Y	Y	Y	Y	Y	Y
ALASKA						
AL Young	Y	Y	Y	N	Y	Y
ARIZONA						
1 Kirkpatrick	Y	Y	Y	Y	Y	Y
2 Franks	Y	Y	Y	N	N	N
3 Shadegg	Y	Y	Y	N	N	N
4 Pastor	Y	Y	Y	N	Y	Y
5 Mitchell	Y	Y	Y	Y	Y	Y
6 Flake	Y	Y	Y	N	N	N
7 Grijalva	?	?	?	Y	?	?
8 Giffords	Y	Y	Y	N	Y	Y
ARKANSAS						
1 Berry	Y	Y	Y	Y	Y	Y
2 Snyder	Y	Y	Y	Y	Y	Y
3 Boozman	Y	Y	Y	N	Y	Y
4 Ross	Y	Y	Y	Y	Y	Y
CALIFORNIA						
1 Thompson	Y	Y	Y	Y	Y	Y
2 Herger	Y	Y	Y	N	Y	Y
3 Lungren	Y	Y	Y	N	N	Y
4 McClintock	Y	Y	Y	N	Y	N
5 Matsui	Y	Y	Y	Y	Y	Y
6 Woolsey	+	+	+	Y	Y	Y
7 Miller, George	Y	Y	Y	Y	Y	Y
8 Pelosi				Y		
9 Lee	Y	Y	Y	Y	Y	Y
10 Vacant						
11 McNerney	Y	Y	Y	Y	Y	Y
12 Speier	Y	Y	Y	Y	Y	Y
13 Stark	Y	Y	Y	Y	Y	Y
14 Eshoo	Y	Y	Y	Y	Y	Y
15 Honda	Y	Y	Y	Y	N	Y
16 Lofgren	Y	Y	Y	Y	Y	Y
17 Farr	Y	Y	Y	Y	Y	Y
18 Cardoza	Y	Y	Y	Y	Y	Y
19 Radanovich	Y	Y	Y	N	N	Y
20 Costa	Y	Y	Y	Y	Y	Y
21 Nunes	Y	Y	Y	N	N	Y
22 McCarthy	Y	Y	Y	N	Y	Y
23 Capps	Y	Y	Y	Y	Y	Y
24 Gallegly	Y	Y	Y	N	Y	Y
25 McKeon	Y	Y	Y	N	Y	Y
26 Dreier	Y	Y	Y	N	Y	Y
27 Sherman	Y	Y	Y	Y	Y	Y
28 Berman	Y	Y	Y	Y	Y	Y
29 Schiff	Y	Y	Y	Y	Y	Y
30 Waxman	Y	Y	Y	Y	N	Y
31 Becerra	Y	Y	Y	Y	Y	Y
32 Chu	Y	Y	Y	Y	Y	Y
33 Watson	Y	Y	Y	Y	Y	Y
34 Roybal-Allard	Y	Y	Y	Y	Y	Y
35 Waters	?	?	?	?	?	?
36 Harman	Y	Y	Y	Y	Y	Y
37 Richardson	Y	Y	Y	Y	Y	Y
38 Napolitano	Y	Y	Y	Y	N	Y
39 Sánchez, Linda	Y	Y	Y	Y	Y	Y
40 Royce	Y	Y	Y	N	Y	N
41 Lewis	Y	Y	Y	N	Y	Y
42 Miller, Gary	Y	Y	Y	N	Y	Y
43 Baca	Y	Y	Y	Y	N	Y
44 Calvert	Y	Y	Y	N	Y	Y
45 Bono Mack	Y	Y	Y	N	Y	Y
46 Rohrabacher	?	?	?	Y	Y	Y
47 Sanchez, Loretta	Y	Y	Y	Y	Y	Y
48 Campbell	Y	Y	Y	N	Y	Y
49 Issa	?	?	?	N	N	Y
50 Bilbray	Y	Y	Y	N	N	Y
51 Filner	Y	Y	Y	Y	Y	Y
52 Hunter	Y	Y	Y	N	Y	Y
53 Davis	Y	Y	Y	Y	Y	Y

	696	697	698	699	700	701
COLORADO						
1 DeGette	?	?	?	Y	Y	Y
2 Polis	Y	Y	Y	Y	Y	Y
3 Salazar	Y	Y	Y	Y	Y	Y
4 Markey	Y	Y	Y	Y	Y	Y
5 Lamborn	Y	Y	Y	N	N	N
6 Coffman	Y	Y	Y	N	N	Y
7 Perlmutter	Y	Y	Y	Y	Y	Y
CONNECTICUT						
1 Larson	Y	Y	Y	Y	Y	+
2 Courtney	Y	Y	Y	N	Y	Y
3 DeLauro	Y	Y	Y	Y	Y	Y
4 Himes	Y	Y	Y	Y	Y	Y
5 Murphy	Y	Y	Y	Y	N	Y
DELAWARE						
AL Castle	Y	Y	Y	N	Y	Y
FLORIDA						
1 Miller	Y	Y	Y	N	Y	Y
2 Boyd	Y	Y	Y	Y	Y	Y
3 Brown	?	?	?	Y	Y	Y
4 Crenshaw	?	?	?	N	Y	Y
5 Brown-Waite	Y	Y	Y	N	N	Y
6 Stearns	Y	Y	Y	N	N	Y
7 Mica	Y	Y	Y	N	Y	Y
8 Grayson	Y	Y	Y	Y	Y	Y
9 Bilirakis	Y	Y	Y	N	Y	Y
10 Young	?	?	?	N	N	Y
11 Castor	Y	Y	Y	Y	Y	Y
12 Putnam	Y	Y	Y	N	Y	Y
13 Buchanan	Y	Y	Y	N	Y	Y
14 Mack	Y	Y	Y	N	N	N
15 Posey	Y	Y	Y	Y	Y	Y
16 Rooney	Y	Y	Y	N	Y	Y
17 Meek	Y	Y	Y	Y	Y	Y
18 Ros-Lehtinen	Y	Y	Y	N	Y	Y
19 Wexler	Y	Y	Y	Y	Y	Y
20 Wasserman Schultz	Y	Y	Y	Y	Y	Y
21 Diaz-Balart, L.	Y	Y	Y	Y	Y	Y
22 Klein	Y	Y	Y	Y	Y	Y
23 Hastings	Y	Y	Y	Y	Y	Y
24 Kosmas	Y	Y	Y	Y	Y	Y
25 Diaz-Balart, M.	Y	Y	Y	N	Y	Y
GEORGIA						
1 Kingston	Y	Y	Y	N	N	N
2 Bishop	Y	Y	Y	Y	N	Y
3 Westmoreland	Y	Y	Y	N	N	Y
4 Johnson	Y	Y	Y	Y	Y	Y
5 Lewis	Y	Y	Y	Y	Y	Y
6 Price	Y	Y	Y	N	N	N
7 Linder	Y	Y	Y	N	N	Y
8 Marshall	Y	Y	Y	Y	Y	Y
9 Deal	?	?	?	N	N	Y
10 Broun	Y	Y	Y	N	N	N
11 Gingrey	Y	Y	Y	N	N	Y
12 Barrow	Y	Y	Y	N	Y	Y
13 Scott	Y	Y	Y	N	Y	Y
HAWAII						
1 Abercrombie	Y	?	Y	Y	Y	Y
2 Hirono	Y	Y	Y	Y	Y	Y
IDAHO						
1 Minnick	Y	Y	Y	Y	Y	?
2 Simpson	Y	Y	Y	N	Y	Y
ILLINOIS						
1 Rush	?	?	?	Y	Y	Y
2 Jackson	Y	Y	Y	Y	Y	Y
3 Lipinski	?	?	?	Y	Y	Y
4 Gutierrez	Y	Y	Y	Y	Y	Y
5 Quigley	Y	Y	Y	Y	Y	Y
6 Roskam	Y	Y	Y	N	Y	N
7 Davis	?	?	?	Y	Y	Y
8 Bean	Y	Y	Y	Y	Y	Y
9 Schakowsky	Y	Y	Y	Y	Y	Y
10 Kirk	?	?	?	N	Y	Y
11 Halvorson	Y	Y	Y	Y	N	Y
12 Costello	Y	Y	Y	Y	Y	Y
13 Biggert	Y	Y	Y	N	Y	Y
14 Foster	Y	Y	Y	P	Y	Y
15 Johnson	Y	Y	Y	N	Y	Y

	696	697	698	699	700	701
16 **Manzullo**	Y	Y	Y	N	Y	Y
17 Hare	Y	Y	Y	Y	Y	Y
18 **Schock**	Y	Y	Y	N	Y	Y
19 **Shimkus**	?	?	?	N	Y	Y
INDIANA						
1 Visclosky	Y	Y	Y	Y	Y	Y
2 Donnelly	Y	Y	Y	Y	Y	Y
3 **Souder**	Y	Y	Y	N	Y	Y
4 **Buyer**	?	?	?	N	N	Y
5 **Burton**	Y	Y	Y	N	Y	Y
6 **Pence**	Y	Y	Y	N	Y	N
7 Carson	Y	Y	Y	Y	Y	Y
8 Ellsworth	Y	Y	Y	Y	Y	Y
9 Hill	Y	Y	Y	Y	Y	Y
IOWA						
1 Braley	Y	Y	Y	Y	Y	Y
2 Loebsack	Y	Y	Y	Y	Y	Y
3 Boswell	Y	Y	Y	Y	Y	Y
4 **Latham**	Y	Y	Y	N	N	Y
5 **King**	Y	Y	Y	N	N	Y
KANSAS						
1 **Moran**	?	?	?	N	Y	Y
2 **Jenkins**	Y	Y	Y	N	Y	Y
3 Moore	Y	Y	Y	Y	Y	Y
4 **Tiahrt**	Y	Y	Y	N	Y	Y
KENTUCKY						
1 **Whitfield**	Y	Y	Y	N	N	N
2 **Guthrie**	Y	Y	Y	N	Y	Y
3 Yarmuth	Y	Y	Y	Y	Y	Y
4 **Davis**	Y	Y	Y	N	Y	Y
5 **Rogers**	?	?	?	N	Y	Y
6 Chandler	Y	Y	Y	Y	Y	Y
LOUISIANA						
1 **Scalise**	Y	Y	Y	N	Y	N
2 **Cao**	Y	Y	Y	Y	Y	Y
3 Melancon	Y	Y	Y	Y	Y	Y
4 **Fleming**	Y	Y	Y	N	Y	Y
5 **Alexander**	?	?	?	N	Y	Y
6 **Cassidy**	Y	Y	Y	N	Y	Y
7 **Boustany**	Y	Y	Y	N	Y	Y
MAINE						
1 Pingree	Y	Y	Y	Y	Y	Y
2 Michaud	Y	Y	Y	Y	Y	Y
MARYLAND						
1 Kratovil	Y	Y	Y	Y	Y	Y
2 Ruppersberger	Y	Y	Y	Y	Y	Y
3 Sarbanes	Y	Y	Y	Y	Y	Y
4 Edwards	Y	Y	Y	Y	Y	Y
5 Hoyer	?	?	?	Y	Y	Y
6 **Bartlett**	Y	Y	Y	N	Y	N
7 Cummings	Y	Y	Y	Y	N	Y
8 Van Hollen	Y	Y	Y	Y	Y	Y
MASSACHUSETTS						
1 Olver	Y	Y	Y	Y	Y	Y
2 Neal	?	?	?	Y	Y	Y
3 McGovern	Y	Y	Y	Y	N	Y
4 Frank	Y	Y	Y	P	Y	Y
5 Tsongas	Y	Y	Y	Y	Y	Y
6 Tierney	Y	Y	Y	Y	Y	Y
7 Markey	?	?	?	Y	Y	Y
8 Capuano	?	?	?	Y	Y	Y
9 Lynch	?	?	?	?	?	?
10 Delahunt	Y	Y	Y	N	Y	Y
MICHIGAN						
1 Stupak	Y	Y	Y	Y	N	Y
2 **Hoekstra**	?	?	?	?	?	?
3 **Ehlers**	Y	Y	Y	N	N	Y
4 **Camp**	Y	Y	Y	N	N	Y
5 Kildee	Y	Y	Y	Y	Y	Y
6 **Upton**	Y	Y	Y	N	N	Y
7 Schauer	Y	Y	Y	Y	N	Y
8 **Rogers**	Y	Y	Y	N	N	Y
9 Peters	Y	Y	Y	Y	Y	Y
10 **Miller**	Y	Y	Y	N	N	Y
11 **McCotter**	Y	Y	Y	N	N	Y
12 Levin	Y	Y	Y	Y	Y	Y
13 Kilpatrick	Y	Y	Y	Y	Y	Y
14 Conyers	Y	Y	Y	Y	Y	Y
15 Dingell	Y	Y	Y	Y	N	Y
MINNESOTA						
1 Walz	Y	Y	Y	Y	Y	Y
2 **Kline**	Y	Y	Y	N	Y	Y
3 **Paulsen**	Y	Y	Y	N	Y	Y
4 McCollum	Y	Y	Y	Y	Y	Y

	696	697	698	699	700	701
5 Ellison	Y	Y	Y	Y	Y	Y
6 **Bachmann**	Y	Y	Y	N	Y	Y
7 Peterson	Y	Y	Y	Y	Y	Y
8 Oberstar	Y	Y	Y	Y	Y	Y
MISSISSIPPI						
1 Childers	Y	Y	Y	Y	Y	Y
2 Thompson	Y	Y	Y	Y	N	Y
3 **Harper**	?	?	?	N	N	Y
4 Taylor	Y	Y	Y	N	N	Y
MISSOURI						
1 Clay	Y	Y	Y	Y	Y	Y
2 **Akin**	Y	Y	Y	N	Y	N
3 Carnahan	Y	Y	Y	Y	Y	Y
4 Skelton	Y	Y	Y	P	Y	Y
5 Cleaver	Y	Y	Y	Y	Y	Y
6 **Graves**	Y	Y	Y	N	Y	Y
7 **Blunt**	?	?	?	N	Y	Y
8 **Emerson**	Y	Y	Y	Y	Y	Y
9 **Luetkemeyer**	Y	Y	Y	N	Y	Y
MONTANA						
AL **Rehberg**	Y	Y	Y	N	Y	Y
NEBRASKA						
1 **Fortenberry**	Y	Y	Y	N	N	Y
2 **Terry**	Y	Y	Y	N	Y	Y
3 **Smith**	Y	Y	Y	N	Y	Y
NEVADA						
1 Berkley	Y	Y	Y	Y	Y	Y
2 **Heller**	Y	Y	Y	N	Y	N
3 Titus	Y	Y	Y	Y	Y	Y
NEW HAMPSHIRE						
1 Shea-Porter	Y	Y	Y	P	Y	Y
2 Hodes	Y	Y	Y	N	Y	Y
NEW JERSEY						
1 Andrews	Y	Y	Y	Y	Y	Y
2 **LoBiondo**	Y	Y	Y	N	Y	Y
3 Adler	Y	Y	Y	Y	Y	Y
4 **Smith**	Y	Y	Y	N	Y	Y
5 **Garrett**	Y	Y	Y	N	Y	Y
6 Pallone	Y	Y	Y	Y	Y	Y
7 **Lance**	Y	Y	Y	N	Y	Y
8 Pascrell	Y	Y	Y	Y	Y	Y
9 Rothman	Y	Y	Y	Y	Y	Y
10 Payne	Y	Y	Y	Y	Y	Y
11 **Frelinghuysen**	?	?	?	N	Y	Y
12 Holt	Y	Y	Y	Y	Y	Y
13 Sires	Y	Y	Y	Y	N	Y
NEW MEXICO						
1 Heinrich	Y	Y	Y	Y	Y	Y
2 Teague	Y	Y	Y	N	N	Y
3 Lujan	Y	Y	Y	Y	Y	Y
NEW YORK						
1 Bishop	Y	Y	Y	Y	N	Y
2 Israel	?	?	?	Y	Y	Y
3 **King**	+	Y	Y	N	N	Y
4 McCarthy	Y	Y	Y	Y	Y	Y
5 Ackerman	?	?	?	?	?	?
6 Meeks	Y	Y	Y	Y	?	?
7 Crowley	Y	Y	Y	Y	N	Y
8 Nadler	Y	Y	Y	Y	Y	Y
9 Weiner	Y	Y	Y	Y	N	Y
10 Towns	?	?	?	Y	Y	Y
11 Clarke	Y	Y	Y	Y	Y	Y
12 Velázquez	Y	Y	Y	?	?	Y
13 McMahon	?	?	?	Y	N	Y
14 Maloney	Y	Y	Y	Y	Y	Y
15 Rangel	Y	Y	Y	Y	Y	Y
16 Serrano	Y	Y	Y	Y	Y	Y
17 Engel	Y	Y	Y	P	Y	Y
18 Lowey	Y	Y	Y	Y	Y	Y
19 Hall	Y	Y	Y	Y	Y	Y
20 Murphy	Y	Y	Y	Y	Y	Y
21 Tonko	Y	Y	Y	Y	Y	Y
22 Hinchey	Y	Y	Y	N	Y	Y
23 **McHugh**	?	?	?	?	?	?
24 Arcuri	Y	Y	Y	N	Y	Y
25 Maffei	Y	Y	Y	N	Y	Y
26 **Lee**	Y	Y	Y	N	N	Y
27 Higgins	Y	Y	Y	Y	Y	Y
28 Slaughter	Y	Y	Y	Y	Y	Y
29 Massa	Y	Y	Y	N	Y	Y
NORTH CAROLINA						
1 Butterfield	Y	Y	Y	Y	Y	Y
2 Etheridge	Y	Y	Y	Y	Y	Y
3 **Jones**	Y	Y	Y	Y	Y	Y
4 Price	Y	Y	Y	Y	Y	Y

	696	697	698	699	700	701
5 **Foxx**	Y	Y	Y	N	Y	Y
6 **Coble**	Y	Y	Y	N	N	Y
7 McIntyre	Y	Y	Y	Y	Y	Y
8 Kissell	Y	Y	Y	Y	Y	Y
9 **Myrick**	Y	Y	Y	N	Y	Y
10 **McHenry**	Y	Y	Y	N	Y	Y
11 Shuler	Y	Y	Y	Y	Y	Y
12 Watt	Y	Y	Y	Y	Y	Y
13 Miller	Y	Y	Y	Y	Y	Y
NORTH DAKOTA						
AL Pomeroy	Y	Y	Y	Y	Y	Y
OHIO						
1 Driehaus	Y	Y	Y	Y	Y	Y
2 **Schmidt**	Y	Y	Y	N	Y	Y
3 **Turner**	Y	Y	Y	N	Y	Y
4 **Jordan**	Y	Y	Y	N	Y	Y
5 **Latta**	Y	Y	Y	N	Y	Y
6 Wilson	Y	Y	Y	Y	Y	Y
7 **Austria**	Y	Y	Y	N	Y	Y
8 **Boehner**	Y	Y	Y	N	Y	N
9 Kaptur	Y	Y	Y	Y	Y	Y
10 Kucinich	Y	Y	Y	N	Y	Y
11 Fudge	Y	Y	Y	Y	N	Y
12 **Tiberi**	Y	Y	Y	N	Y	Y
13 Sutton	Y	Y	Y	Y	Y	Y
14 **LaTourette**	Y	Y	Y	N	Y	Y
15 Kilroy	Y	Y	Y	Y	Y	Y
16 Boccieri	Y	Y	Y	Y	Y	Y
17 Ryan	?	?	?	Y	Y	Y
18 Space	Y	Y	Y	Y	N	Y
OKLAHOMA						
1 **Sullivan**	Y	Y	Y	N	Y	N
2 Boren	Y	?	Y	Y	Y	Y
3 **Lucas**	Y	Y	Y	N	Y	Y
4 **Cole**	Y	Y	Y	N	Y	Y
5 **Fallin**	Y	Y	Y	N	Y	Y
OREGON						
1 Wu	Y	Y	Y	Y	Y	Y
2 **Walden**	Y	Y	Y	N	Y	Y
3 Blumenauer	?	?	?	Y	N	Y
4 DeFazio	Y	Y	Y	Y	Y	Y
5 Schrader	Y	Y	Y	Y	Y	Y
PENNSYLVANIA						
1 Brady	Y	Y	Y	Y	Y	Y
2 Fattah	Y	Y	Y	Y	Y	Y
3 Dahlkemper	Y	Y	Y	Y	Y	Y
4 Altmire	Y	Y	Y	Y	N	Y
5 **Thompson**	Y	Y	Y	N	Y	Y
6 **Gerlach**	+	+	+	N	Y	Y
7 Sestak	Y	Y	Y	?	?	?
8 Murphy, P.	Y	Y	Y	Y	N	Y
9 **Shuster**	Y	Y	Y	N	Y	Y
10 Carney	Y	Y	Y	Y	Y	Y
11 Kanjorski	Y	Y	Y	Y	Y	Y
12 Murtha	Y	Y	Y	Y	Y	Y
13 Schwartz	Y	Y	Y	Y	Y	Y
14 Doyle	Y	Y	?	Y	N	Y
15 **Dent**	Y	Y	Y	N	Y	Y
16 **Pitts**	Y	Y	Y	N	Y	Y
17 Holden	Y	Y	Y	Y	Y	Y
18 **Murphy, T.**	Y	Y	Y	N	Y	Y
19 **Platts**	Y	Y	Y	N	Y	Y
RHODE ISLAND						
1 Kennedy	Y	+	Y	Y	Y	Y
2 Langevin	Y	Y	Y	Y	Y	Y
SOUTH CAROLINA						
1 **Brown**	Y	Y	Y	N	Y	Y
2 **Wilson**	Y	Y	Y	N	Y	N
3 **Barrett**	?	?	?	?	?	?
4 **Inglis**	Y	Y	Y	Y	Y	Y
5 Spratt	Y	Y	Y	Y	Y	Y
6 Clyburn	Y	Y	Y	Y	Y	Y
SOUTH DAKOTA						
AL Herseth Sandlin	Y	Y	Y	Y	Y	Y
TENNESSEE						
1 **Roe**	Y	Y	Y	N	Y	Y
2 **Duncan**	Y	Y	Y	N	Y	N
3 **Wamp**	Y	Y	Y	N	Y	N
4 Davis	Y	Y	Y	Y	Y	Y
5 Cooper	Y	Y	Y	Y	Y	Y
6 Gordon	Y	Y	Y	Y	Y	Y
7 **Blackburn**	Y	Y	Y	N	Y	Y
8 Tanner	?	?	?	?	?	?
9 Cohen	Y	Y	Y	Y	Y	Y

	696	697	698	699	700	701
TEXAS						
1 **Gohmert**	Y	Y	Y	N	N	Y
2 **Poe**	Y	Y	Y	N	N	N
3 **Johnson, S.**	?	?	?	N	N	N
4 **Hall**	Y	Y	Y	N	N	Y
5 **Hensarling**	Y	Y	Y	N	N	N
6 **Barton**	Y	Y	Y	N	N	N
7 **Culberson**	Y	Y	Y	N	N	N
8 **Brady**	Y	Y	Y	N	N	N
9 Green, A.	Y	Y	Y	Y	Y	Y
10 **McCaul**	Y	Y	Y	N	N	Y
11 **Conaway**	Y	Y	Y	–	–	+
12 **Granger**	Y	Y	Y	N	N	Y
13 **Thornberry**	Y	Y	Y	N	N	Y
14 **Paul**	Y	Y	Y	N	N	N
15 Hinojosa	Y	Y	Y	Y	N	Y
16 Reyes	Y	Y	Y	Y	N	Y
17 Edwards	Y	Y	Y	Y	N	Y
18 Jackson Lee	Y	Y	Y	Y	Y	Y
19 **Neugebauer**	Y	Y	Y	N	N	N
20 Gonzalez	Y	Y	Y	Y	N	Y
21 **Smith**	Y	Y	Y	N	N	Y
22 **Olson**	Y	Y	Y	N	N	Y
23 Rodriguez	Y	Y	Y	Y	N	Y
24 **Marchant**	?	?	?	N	N	N
25 Doggett	Y	Y	Y	Y	N	Y
26 **Burgess**	?	?	?	N	N	Y
27 Ortiz	Y	Y	Y	Y	N	Y
28 Cuellar	Y	Y	Y	Y	N	Y
29 Green, G.	Y	Y	Y	Y	N	Y
30 Johnson, E.	Y	Y	Y	Y	N	Y
31 **Carter**	Y	Y	?	N	N	Y
32 **Sessions**	Y	Y	Y	N	N	Y
UTAH						
1 **Bishop**	Y	Y	Y	N	N	Y
2 Matheson	Y	Y	Y	Y	Y	Y
3 **Chaffetz**	Y	Y	Y	N	N	Y
VERMONT						
AL Welch	Y	Y	Y	Y	Y	Y
VIRGINIA						
1 **Wittman**	Y	Y	Y	N	Y	Y
2 Nye	Y	Y	Y	Y	Y	Y
3 Scott	Y	Y	Y	Y	Y	Y
4 **Forbes**	Y	Y	Y	N	Y	Y
5 Perriello	Y	Y	Y	Y	N	Y
6 **Goodlatte**	Y	Y	Y	N	Y	Y
7 **Cantor**	Y	Y	Y	N	Y	Y
8 Moran	Y	Y	Y	Y	Y	Y
9 Boucher	Y	Y	Y	Y	Y	Y
10 **Wolf**	Y	Y	Y	N	Y	Y
11 Connolly	Y	Y	Y	Y	Y	Y
WASHINGTON						
1 Inslee	Y	Y	Y	Y	Y	Y
2 Larsen	Y	Y	Y	Y	Y	Y
3 Baird	Y	Y	Y	Y	Y	Y
4 **Hastings**	Y	Y	Y	N	Y	Y
5 **McMorris Rodgers**	Y	Y	Y	N	Y	Y
6 Dicks	?	?	?	Y	Y	Y
7 McDermott	Y	Y	Y	N	Y	Y
8 **Reichert**	Y	Y	Y	N	Y	Y
9 Smith	+	+	+	Y	Y	Y
WEST VIRGINIA						
1 Mollohan	?	?	?	Y	Y	Y
2 **Capito**	Y	Y	Y	N	Y	Y
3 Rahall	Y	Y	Y	Y	N	Y
WISCONSIN						
1 **Ryan**	Y	Y	Y	N	N	N
2 Baldwin	Y	Y	Y	Y	Y	Y
3 Kind	Y	Y	Y	Y	Y	Y
4 Moore	Y	Y	Y	N	Y	Y
5 **Sensenbrenner**	Y	Y	Y	N	N	Y
6 **Petri**	Y	Y	Y	Y	N	Y
7 Obey	Y	Y	Y	Y	P	Y
8 Kagen	Y	Y	Y	Y	Y	Y
WYOMING						
AL **Lummis**	Y	Y	Y	N	N	Y
DELEGATES						
Faleomavaega (A.S.)						
Norton (D.C.)						
Bordallo (Guam)						
Sablan (N. Marianas)						
Pierluisi (P.R.)						
Christensen (V.I.)						

IN THE HOUSE | By Vote Number

702. HR 3137. Postal Service Donations for Plaques/Passage.
Towns, D-N.Y., motion to suspend the rules and pass the bill that would allow the U.S. Postal Service to accept monetary donations for plaques in connection with the commemorative designation of postal facilities and require the Postal Service, after receiving sufficient amounts, to provide a plaque within 120 days of a facility designation. Motion agreed to 414-0: R 170-0; D 244-0. A two-thirds majority of those present and voting (276 in this case) is required for passage under suspension of the rules. Sept. 15, 2009.

703. HR 3221. Student Loan Overhaul/Rule. Adoption of the rule (H Res 746) to provide for House floor consideration of the bill that would terminate the authority of the Federal Family Education Loan program to make or insure new loans after June 30, 2010, and direct the federal government to originate student loans. Adopted 241-179: R 0-173; D 241-6. Sept. 16, 2009.

704. H Res 260. Lowering Infant Mortality Rate/Adoption. Cohen, D-Tenn., motion to suspend the rules and adopt the resolution that would acknowledge the United States has a high infant mortality rate and support efforts to lower the rate and correct racial disparities in pre-natal care. Motion agreed to 415-0: R 171-0; D 244-0. A two-thirds majority of those present and voting (277 in this case) is required for adoption under suspension of the rules. Sept. 16, 2009.

705. HR 3246. Vehicle Research and Development Program/ Authorization Reduction. Hall, R-Texas, amendment that would reduce the bill's authorization to $2.2 billion from fiscal 2010 through 2013 and subsequently decrease the amounts provided for research projects on medium- and heavy-duty commercial vehicles to $800 million and user facilities to $100 million during that same period. Rejected in Committee of the Whole 179-253: R 161-13; D 18-240. Sept. 16, 2009.

706. HR 3246. Vehicle Research and Development Program/ Recreational Vehicles Research. Donnelly, D-Ind., amendment that would include recreational vehicles in a research and development program on advanced technologies for medium- and heavy-duty commercial and transit vehicles. Adopted in Committee of the Whole 369-62: R 118-57; D 251-5. Sept. 16, 2009.

707. HR 3246. Vehicle Research and Development Program/ Public-Private Partnerships. Massa, D-N.Y., amendment that would direct the Energy Department to support public-private partnerships dedicated to overcoming barriers in commercial application of "transformational" vehicle technologies that utilize specified facilities. Adopted in Committee of the Whole 416-14: R 158-14; D 258-0. Sept. 16, 2009.

	702	703	704	705	706	707
ALABAMA						
1 Bonner	Y	?	?	N	Y	Y
2 Bright	Y	Y	Y	Y	Y	Y
3 Rogers	Y	N	Y	N	Y	Y
4 Aderholt	Y	N	Y	Y	Y	Y
5 Griffith	Y	N	Y	N	Y	Y
6 Bachus	Y	N	Y	Y	Y	Y
7 Davis	Y	Y	Y	N	Y	Y
ALASKA						
AL Young	Y	N	Y	Y	Y	Y
ARIZONA						
1 Kirkpatrick	Y	Y	Y	Y	Y	Y
2 Franks	Y	N	Y	Y	Y	N
3 Shadegg	Y	N	Y	N	N	N
4 Pastor	Y	Y	Y	N	Y	Y
5 Mitchell	Y	Y	Y	Y	Y	Y
6 Flake	Y	N	Y	N	N	N
7 Grijalva	?	Y	Y	N	Y	Y
8 Giffords	Y	Y	Y	N	Y	Y
ARKANSAS						
1 Berry	Y	Y	Y	Y	Y	Y
2 Snyder	Y	Y	Y	N	Y	Y
3 Boozman	Y	N	Y	Y	Y	Y
4 Ross	Y	Y	Y	N	Y	Y
CALIFORNIA						
1 Thompson	Y	Y	Y	N	Y	Y
2 Herger	Y	N	Y	Y	Y	Y
3 Lungren	Y	N	Y	N	Y	Y
4 McClintock	Y	N	Y	Y	Y	N
5 Matsui	Y	Y	Y	N	Y	Y
6 Woolsey	Y	Y	Y	N	Y	Y
7 Miller, George	Y	Y	Y	N	Y	Y
8 Pelosi						
9 Lee	Y	Y	Y	N	Y	Y
10 Vacant						
11 McNerney	Y	Y	Y	Y	Y	Y
12 Speier	Y	Y	Y	N	Y	Y
13 Stark	Y	Y	Y	N	N	Y
14 Eshoo	Y	Y	Y	N	Y	Y
15 Honda	Y	Y	Y	N	Y	Y
16 Lofgren	Y	Y	?	N	Y	Y
17 Farr	Y	Y	Y	N	Y	Y
18 Cardoza	Y	Y	?	N	Y	Y
19 Radanovich	Y	N	Y	N	Y	Y
20 Costa	Y	Y	?	N	Y	Y
21 Nunes	Y	N	Y	N	N	Y
22 McCarthy	Y	N	Y	N	Y	Y
23 Capps	Y	Y	+	+	+	+
24 Gallegly	Y	N	Y	N	Y	Y
25 McKeon	Y	N	Y	Y	Y	Y
26 Dreier	Y	N	Y	Y	Y	Y
27 Sherman	Y	Y	Y	N	Y	Y
28 Berman	?	Y	Y	N	Y	Y
29 Schiff	Y	Y	Y	N	Y	Y
30 Waxman	Y	Y	Y	N	Y	Y
31 Becerra	Y	Y	Y	N	Y	Y
32 Chu	Y	Y	Y	N	Y	Y
33 Watson	Y	Y	Y	N	Y	Y
34 Roybal-Allard	Y	Y	Y	N	Y	Y
35 Waters	?	Y	Y	N	Y	Y
36 Harman	Y	Y	Y	N	Y	Y
37 Richardson	Y	Y	Y	N	Y	Y
38 Napolitano	Y	Y	Y	N	Y	Y
39 Sánchez, Linda	Y	?	?	N	Y	Y
40 Royce	Y	N	Y	Y	N	Y
41 Lewis	Y	N	Y	Y	Y	Y
42 Miller, Gary	Y	N	Y	Y	N	Y
43 Baca	Y	Y	Y	N	Y	Y
44 Calvert	Y	N	Y	Y	Y	Y
45 Bono Mack	Y	N	Y	Y	Y	Y
46 Rohrabacher	Y	N	Y	Y	N	Y
47 Sanchez, Loretta	Y	Y	Y	N	Y	Y
48 Campbell	Y	N	Y	Y	Y	Y
49 Issa	Y	N	Y	N	Y	Y
50 Bilbray	Y	N	Y	Y	Y	Y
51 Filner	Y	Y	Y	N	Y	Y
52 Hunter	Y	N	Y	Y	Y	Y
53 Davis	Y	Y	Y	N	Y	Y

	702	703	704	705	706	707
COLORADO						
1 DeGette	Y	?	Y	N	Y	Y
2 Polis	Y	Y	Y	N	Y	Y
3 Salazar	Y	Y	Y	N	Y	Y
4 Markey	Y	Y	Y	N	Y	Y
5 Lamborn	Y	N	Y	N	N	Y
6 Coffman	Y	N	Y	Y	Y	Y
7 Perlmutter	Y	Y	Y	N	Y	Y
CONNECTICUT						
1 Larson	Y	Y	Y	N	Y	Y
2 Courtney	Y	Y	Y	N	Y	Y
3 DeLauro	Y	Y	Y	N	Y	Y
4 Himes	Y	Y	Y	Y	Y	Y
5 Murphy	Y	Y	Y	N	Y	Y
DELAWARE						
AL Castle	Y	N	Y	N	N	Y
FLORIDA						
1 Miller	Y	N	Y	Y	Y	Y
2 Boyd	Y	N	Y	N	Y	Y
3 Brown	Y	Y	Y	N	Y	Y
4 Crenshaw	Y	N	Y	Y	Y	Y
5 Brown-Waite	Y	N	Y	Y	Y	Y
6 Stearns	Y	N	?	Y	Y	Y
7 Mica	Y	N	Y	Y	Y	Y
8 Grayson	Y	Y	Y	N	Y	Y
9 Bilirakis	Y	N	Y	Y	Y	Y
10 Young	Y	N	Y	Y	Y	Y
11 Castor	Y	Y	Y	N	Y	Y
12 Putnam	Y	N	Y	Y	Y	Y
13 Buchanan	Y	N	Y	Y	Y	Y
14 Mack	Y	N	Y	Y	Y	?
15 Posey	Y	N	Y	Y	Y	Y
16 Rooney	?	N	Y	N	N	N
17 Meek	Y	Y	Y	N	Y	Y
18 Ros-Lehtinen	Y	N	Y	Y	Y	Y
19 Wexler	Y	Y	Y	N	Y	Y
20 Wasserman Schultz	Y	Y	Y	N	Y	Y
21 Diaz-Balart, L.	Y	N	Y	Y	Y	Y
22 Klein	?	Y	Y	N	Y	Y
23 Hastings	Y	Y	Y	N	Y	Y
24 Kosmas	Y	Y	Y	N	Y	Y
25 Diaz-Balart, M.	Y	N	Y	Y	Y	Y
GEORGIA						
1 Kingston	Y	N	Y	Y	N	Y
2 Bishop	Y	?	?	N	Y	Y
3 Westmoreland	Y	N	Y	Y	Y	Y
4 Johnson	Y	Y	Y	N	Y	Y
5 Lewis	Y	Y	Y	N	Y	Y
6 Price	Y	N	?	Y	Y	Y
7 Linder	Y	N	Y	N	Y	Y
8 Marshall	Y	Y	Y	N	Y	Y
9 Deal	Y	N	Y	Y	Y	Y
10 Broun	Y	N	Y	N	N	N
11 Gingrey	Y	N	Y	N	Y	Y
12 Barrow	Y	Y	Y	N	Y	Y
13 Scott	Y	Y	Y	N	Y	Y
HAWAII						
1 Abercrombie	Y	Y	Y	N	Y	Y
2 Hirono	Y	Y	Y	N	Y	Y
IDAHO						
1 Minnick	Y	Y	Y	Y	Y	Y
2 Simpson	Y	N	Y	Y	Y	Y
ILLINOIS						
1 Rush	Y	Y	Y	N	Y	Y
2 Jackson	Y	Y	Y	N	Y	Y
3 Lipinski	Y	Y	Y	N	Y	Y
4 Gutierrez	Y	Y	Y	N	Y	Y
5 Quigley	Y	Y	Y	N	Y	Y
6 Roskam	Y	N	Y	Y	Y	Y
7 Davis	Y	Y	Y	N	?	Y
8 Bean	Y	Y	Y	N	Y	Y
9 Schakowsky	Y	Y	Y	N	Y	Y
10 Kirk	Y	N	Y	N	Y	Y
11 Halvorson	Y	Y	Y	N	Y	Y
12 Costello	Y	Y	Y	N	Y	Y
13 Biggert	Y	N	Y	N	Y	Y
14 Foster	Y	Y	Y	N	Y	Y
15 Johnson	Y	N	Y	Y	Y	Y

KEY   **Republicans**   Democrats

Y Voted for (yea)	X Paired against
# Paired for	− Announced against
+ Announced for	P Voted "present"
N Voted against (nay)	

C Voted "present" to avoid possible conflict of interest

? Did not vote or otherwise make a position known

	702	703	704	705	706	707
16 **Manzullo**	Y	N	Y	Y	Y	Y
17 Hare	Y	Y	Y	N	Y	Y
18 **Schock**	Y	N	Y	Y	Y	Y
19 **Shimkus**	Y	N	Y	Y	Y	Y
INDIANA						
1 Visclosky	Y	Y	Y	N	Y	Y
2 Donnelly	Y	Y	Y	N	Y	Y
3 **Souder**	Y	N	Y	Y	Y	Y
4 **Buyer**	Y	N	Y	Y	Y	Y
5 **Burton**	Y	N	Y	Y	Y	Y
6 **Pence**	Y	N	Y	Y	Y	Y
7 Carson	Y	Y	Y	N	Y	Y
8 Ellsworth	Y	Y	Y	N	Y	Y
9 Hill	Y	N	Y	N	Y	Y
IOWA						
1 Braley	Y	Y	Y	N	Y	Y
2 Loebsack	Y	Y	Y	N	Y	Y
3 Boswell	Y	Y	Y	N	Y	Y
4 **Latham**	Y	N	Y	Y	Y	Y
5 **King**	Y	N	Y	Y	Y	N
KANSAS						
1 **Moran**	Y	N	Y	Y	N	Y
2 **Jenkins**	Y	N	Y	Y	Y	Y
3 Moore	Y	N	Y	N	Y	Y
4 **Tiahrt**	Y	N	Y	Y	N	Y
KENTUCKY						
1 **Whitfield**	Y	N	Y	Y	Y	Y
2 **Guthrie**	Y	N	Y	Y	Y	Y
3 Yarmuth	Y	Y	Y	N	Y	Y
4 **Davis**	Y	N	Y	Y	Y	Y
5 **Rogers**	Y	N	Y	Y	Y	Y
6 Chandler	Y	Y	Y	N	Y	Y
LOUISIANA						
1 **Scalise**	Y	N	Y	Y	Y	Y
2 **Cao**	Y	N	Y	Y	Y	Y
3 Melancon	Y	Y	Y	N	Y	Y
4 **Fleming**	Y	N	Y	Y	N	Y
5 **Alexander**	Y	N	Y	Y	Y	Y
6 **Cassidy**	Y	N	Y	Y	Y	Y
7 **Boustany**	?	N	Y	Y	N	Y
MAINE						
1 Pingree	Y	Y	Y	N	Y	Y
2 Michaud	Y	Y	Y	N	Y	Y
MARYLAND						
1 Kratovil	Y	N	Y	Y	Y	Y
2 Ruppersberger	Y	Y	Y	N	Y	Y
3 Sarbanes	Y	Y	Y	N	Y	Y
4 Edwards	Y	Y	Y	N	Y	Y
5 Hoyer	Y	Y	Y	N	Y	Y
6 **Bartlett**	Y	N	Y	N	N	Y
7 Cummings	Y	Y	Y	N	Y	Y
8 Van Hollen	Y	Y	Y	N	Y	Y
MASSACHUSETTS						
1 Olver	Y	Y	Y	N	Y	Y
2 Neal	Y	Y	?	N	Y	Y
3 McGovern	Y	Y	Y	N	Y	Y
4 Frank	Y	Y	Y	N	Y	Y
5 Tsongas	Y	Y	Y	N	Y	Y
6 Tierney	Y	Y	Y	N	N	Y
7 Markey	Y	Y	Y	N	Y	Y
8 Capuano	Y	Y	Y	N	Y	Y
9 Lynch	?	Y	Y	N	Y	Y
10 Delahunt	Y	Y	Y	N	Y	Y
MICHIGAN						
1 Stupak	Y	Y	Y	N	Y	Y
2 **Hoekstra**	?	N	Y	N	Y	Y
3 **Ehlers**	Y	N	Y	N	Y	Y
4 **Camp**	Y	N	Y	N	Y	Y
5 Kildee	Y	Y	Y	N	Y	Y
6 **Upton**	Y	N	Y	N	Y	Y
7 Schauer	Y	Y	Y	N	Y	Y
8 **Rogers**	Y	N	Y	Y	Y	Y
9 Peters	Y	Y	Y	N	Y	Y
10 **Miller**	Y	N	Y	N	Y	Y
11 **McCotter**	Y	N	Y	N	Y	Y
12 Levin	Y	Y	Y	N	Y	Y
13 Kilpatrick	Y	Y	Y	N	Y	Y
14 Conyers	Y	?	?	N	Y	Y
15 Dingell	Y	Y	Y	N	Y	Y
MINNESOTA						
1 Walz	Y	Y	Y	N	Y	Y
2 **Kline**	Y	N	Y	Y	Y	Y
3 **Paulsen**	Y	N	Y	Y	Y	Y
4 McCollum	Y	Y	Y	N	Y	Y

	702	703	704	705	706	707
5 Ellison	Y	Y	Y	N	Y	Y
6 **Bachmann**	Y	N	Y	Y	Y	Y
7 Peterson	Y	Y	Y	N	Y	Y
8 Oberstar	Y	Y	Y	N	Y	Y
MISSISSIPPI						
1 Childers	Y	Y	Y	Y	Y	Y
2 Thompson	Y	Y	Y	N	Y	Y
3 **Harper**	Y	N	Y	Y	Y	Y
4 Taylor	Y	Y	Y	Y	Y	Y
MISSOURI						
1 Clay	Y	Y	Y	N	Y	Y
2 **Akin**	Y	N	Y	Y	Y	Y
3 Carnahan	Y	Y	Y	N	Y	Y
4 Skelton	Y	Y	Y	Y	Y	Y
5 Cleaver	Y	Y	Y	N	Y	Y
6 **Graves**	Y	N	Y	Y	N	Y
7 **Blunt**	Y	N	Y	Y	Y	Y
8 **Emerson**	Y	N	Y	Y	Y	Y
9 **Luetkemeyer**	Y	N	Y	Y	Y	Y
MONTANA						
AL **Rehberg**	Y	N	Y	Y	Y	Y
NEBRASKA						
1 **Fortenberry**	Y	N	Y	Y	N	Y
2 **Terry**	Y	N	Y	Y	Y	Y
3 **Smith**	Y	N	Y	Y	Y	Y
NEVADA						
1 Berkley	Y	Y	Y	N	Y	Y
2 **Heller**	Y	N	Y	Y	N	Y
3 Titus	Y	Y	Y	N	Y	Y
NEW HAMPSHIRE						
1 Shea-Porter	Y	Y	Y	N	Y	Y
2 Hodes	Y	Y	Y	N	Y	Y
NEW JERSEY						
1 Andrews	Y	Y	Y	N	Y	Y
2 **LoBiondo**	Y	N	Y	Y	Y	Y
3 Adler	Y	Y	Y	Y	Y	Y
4 **Smith**	Y	N	Y	Y	Y	Y
5 **Garrett**	Y	N	Y	Y	Y	Y
6 Pallone	Y	Y	Y	N	Y	Y
7 **Lance**	Y	N	Y	Y	Y	Y
8 Pascrell	Y	Y	Y	N	Y	Y
9 Rothman	Y	Y	Y	N	Y	Y
10 Payne	Y	Y	Y	N	Y	Y
11 **Frelinghuysen**	Y	N	Y	Y	Y	Y
12 Holt	Y	Y	Y	N	Y	Y
13 Sires	Y	Y	Y	N	Y	Y
NEW MEXICO						
1 Heinrich	Y	Y	Y	N	N	Y
2 Teague	Y	Y	Y	Y	Y	Y
3 Lujan	Y	Y	Y	N	Y	Y
NEW YORK						
1 Bishop	Y	Y	Y	N	Y	Y
2 Israel	Y	Y	Y	N	Y	Y
3 **King**	Y	N	Y	Y	Y	Y
4 McCarthy	Y	Y	Y	N	Y	Y
5 Ackerman	?	Y	Y	N	Y	Y
6 Meeks	?	Y	Y	N	Y	Y
7 Crowley	Y	Y	Y	N	Y	Y
8 Nadler	Y	Y	Y	N	Y	Y
9 Weiner	Y	Y	Y	N	Y	Y
10 Towns	Y	Y	Y	N	Y	Y
11 Clarke	?	Y	Y	N	?	Y
12 Velázquez	Y	Y	Y	N	Y	Y
13 McMahon	Y	Y	Y	Y	Y	Y
14 Maloney	Y	Y	Y	Y	Y	Y
15 Rangel	Y	Y	Y	N	Y	Y
16 Serrano	Y	Y	Y	N	Y	Y
17 Engel	Y	Y	Y	N	Y	Y
18 Lowey	Y	Y	Y	N	Y	Y
19 Hall	Y	Y	Y	N	Y	Y
20 Murphy	Y	Y	Y	Y	Y	Y
21 Tonko	Y	Y	Y	N	Y	Y
22 Hinchey	Y	Y	Y	N	Y	Y
23 **McHugh**	?	?	?	?	?	?
24 Arcuri	Y	Y	Y	N	Y	Y
25 Maffei	Y	Y	Y	N	Y	Y
26 **Lee**	Y	N	Y	Y	Y	Y
27 Higgins	Y	?	?	N	Y	Y
28 Slaughter	Y	Y	Y	N	Y	Y
29 Massa	Y	Y	Y	N	Y	Y
NORTH CAROLINA						
1 Butterfield	Y	Y	Y	N	Y	Y
2 Etheridge	Y	N	Y	N	Y	Y
3 **Jones**	Y	N	Y	Y	Y	Y
4 Price	Y	Y	Y	N	Y	Y

	702	703	704	705	706	707
5 **Foxx**	Y	N	Y	Y	N	Y
6 **Coble**	Y	N	Y	Y	N	Y
7 McIntyre	Y	Y	Y	N	Y	Y
8 Kissell	Y	Y	Y	N	Y	Y
9 **Myrick**	Y	N	Y	Y	Y	Y
10 **McHenry**	Y	N	Y	Y	Y	Y
11 Shuler	Y	Y	Y	N	Y	Y
12 Watt	Y	Y	Y	N	Y	Y
13 Miller	Y	Y	Y	N	Y	Y
NORTH DAKOTA						
AL Pomeroy	Y	Y	Y	N	N	Y
OHIO						
1 Driehaus	Y	Y	Y	N	Y	Y
2 **Schmidt**	Y	?	?	?	?	?
3 **Turner**	Y	N	Y	N	Y	Y
4 **Jordan**	Y	N	Y	Y	Y	Y
5 **Latta**	Y	N	Y	Y	Y	Y
6 Wilson	Y	?	Y	N	Y	Y
7 **Austria**	Y	N	Y	N	Y	Y
8 **Boehner**	Y	N	Y	Y	N	N
9 Kaptur	Y	Y	Y	N	Y	Y
10 Kucinich	Y	Y	Y	N	Y	Y
11 Fudge	Y	Y	Y	N	Y	Y
12 **Tiberi**	Y	N	Y	Y	Y	Y
13 Sutton	Y	Y	Y	N	Y	Y
14 **LaTourette**	Y	N	Y	Y	Y	Y
15 Kilroy	Y	Y	Y	N	Y	Y
16 Boccieri	Y	Y	Y	N	Y	Y
17 Ryan	Y	Y	Y	N	Y	Y
18 Space	Y	Y	Y	N	Y	Y
OKLAHOMA						
1 **Sullivan**	Y	N	Y	Y	N	Y
2 Boren	Y	Y	Y	N	Y	Y
3 **Lucas**	Y	N	Y	Y	Y	Y
4 **Cole**	Y	N	Y	Y	Y	Y
5 **Fallin**	Y	N	Y	Y	Y	Y
OREGON						
1 Wu	Y	Y	Y	N	Y	Y
2 **Walden**	Y	N	Y	Y	Y	Y
3 Blumenauer	?	Y	Y	N	Y	Y
4 DeFazio	Y	Y	Y	N	Y	Y
5 Schrader	Y	Y	Y	N	Y	Y
PENNSYLVANIA						
1 Brady	Y	Y	Y	N	Y	Y
2 Fattah	Y	Y	Y	N	Y	Y
3 Dahlkemper	Y	Y	Y	N	Y	Y
4 Altmire	Y	Y	Y	Y	Y	Y
5 **Thompson**	Y	N	Y	Y	Y	Y
6 **Gerlach**	Y	N	Y	Y	Y	Y
7 Sestak	?	?	?	?	?	?
8 Murphy, P.	Y	Y	Y	N	Y	Y
9 **Shuster**	?	N	Y	Y	Y	Y
10 Carney	Y	Y	Y	Y	Y	Y
11 Kanjorski	Y	Y	Y	N	Y	Y
12 Murtha	Y	Y	Y	N	Y	Y
13 Schwartz	Y	Y	Y	N	Y	Y
14 Doyle	Y	Y	Y	N	Y	Y
15 **Dent**	Y	N	Y	Y	N	Y
16 **Pitts**	Y	N	Y	Y	Y	Y
17 Holden	Y	Y	Y	N	Y	Y
18 **Murphy, T.**	Y	N	Y	N	N	Y
19 **Platts**	Y	N	Y	Y	Y	Y
RHODE ISLAND						
1 Kennedy	Y	Y	Y	N	Y	Y
2 Langevin	Y	Y	Y	N	Y	Y
SOUTH CAROLINA						
1 **Brown**	Y	N	Y	Y	Y	Y
2 **Wilson**	Y	N	Y	Y	Y	Y
3 **Barrett**	?	?	?	?	?	?
4 **Inglis**	Y	N	Y	Y	N	Y
5 Spratt	Y	Y	Y	N	Y	Y
6 Clyburn	Y	Y	Y	N	Y	Y
SOUTH DAKOTA						
AL Herseth Sandlin	Y	Y	Y	N	Y	Y
TENNESSEE						
1 **Roe**	Y	N	Y	Y	Y	Y
2 **Duncan**	Y	N	Y	Y	Y	Y
3 **Wamp**	?	N	Y	Y	Y	Y
4 Davis	Y	Y	Y	N	Y	Y
5 Cooper	Y	Y	Y	N	Y	Y
6 Gordon	Y	Y	Y	N	Y	Y
7 **Blackburn**	Y	N	Y	Y	Y	N
8 Tanner	?	?	?	?	?	?
9 Cohen	Y	Y	Y	N	Y	Y

	702	703	704	705	706	707
TEXAS						
1 **Gohmert**	Y	N	Y	?	N	Y
2 **Poe**	Y	N	Y	Y	N	N
3 **Johnson, S.**	Y	N	Y	Y	N	N
4 **Hall**	Y	N	Y	Y	N	Y
5 **Hensarling**	Y	N	Y	Y	N	Y
6 **Barton**	Y	N	Y	Y	N	Y
7 **Culberson**	Y	?	?	Y	Y	Y
8 **Brady**	Y	N	Y	Y	Y	Y
9 Green, A.	Y	Y	Y	N	Y	Y
10 **McCaul**	Y	N	Y	Y	N	Y
11 **Conaway**	+	N	Y	Y	N	Y
12 **Granger**	Y	N	Y	Y	N	Y
13 **Thornberry**	Y	N	Y	Y	N	Y
14 **Paul**	Y	N	Y	Y	N	N
15 Hinojosa	Y	Y	Y	N	Y	Y
16 Reyes	Y	Y	Y	N	Y	Y
17 Edwards	Y	Y	Y	N	Y	Y
18 Jackson Lee	Y	Y	Y	N	Y	Y
19 **Neugebauer**	Y	N	Y	Y	N	Y
20 Gonzalez	Y	Y	Y	N	Y	Y
21 **Smith**	Y	N	Y	Y	Y	Y
22 **Olson**	Y	N	Y	Y	Y	Y
23 Rodriguez	Y	Y	Y	N	Y	Y
24 **Marchant**	Y	N	Y	Y	N	Y
25 Doggett	Y	Y	Y	Y	N	Y
26 **Burgess**	Y	N	Y	Y	N	?
27 Ortiz	Y	Y	Y	N	Y	Y
28 Cuellar	Y	Y	Y	N	Y	Y
29 Green, G.	Y	Y	Y	N	Y	Y
30 Johnson, E.	Y	Y	Y	N	Y	Y
31 **Carter**	Y	N	Y	Y	N	Y
32 **Sessions**	Y	N	Y	Y	N	Y
UTAH						
1 **Bishop**	Y	N	Y	Y	N	Y
2 Matheson	Y	Y	Y	N	Y	Y
3 **Chaffetz**	Y	N	Y	Y	N	Y
VERMONT						
AL Welch	Y	Y	Y	N	Y	Y
VIRGINIA						
1 **Wittman**	Y	N	Y	Y	Y	Y
2 Nye	Y	Y	Y	N	Y	Y
3 Scott	Y	Y	Y	N	Y	Y
4 **Forbes**	Y	N	Y	Y	Y	Y
5 Perriello	Y	Y	Y	N	Y	Y
6 **Goodlatte**	Y	N	Y	Y	Y	Y
7 **Cantor**	Y	N	Y	Y	N	?
8 Moran	Y	Y	Y	N	Y	Y
9 Boucher	Y	Y	Y	N	Y	Y
10 **Wolf**	Y	N	Y	Y	Y	Y
11 Connolly	Y	Y	Y	N	Y	Y
WASHINGTON						
1 Inslee	Y	Y	Y	N	Y	Y
2 Larsen	Y	Y	Y	N	Y	Y
3 Baird	Y	Y	Y	N	Y	Y
4 **Hastings**	Y	N	Y	Y	N	Y
5 **McMorris Rodgers**	Y	N	Y	Y	Y	Y
6 Dicks	Y	Y	Y	N	Y	Y
7 McDermott	Y	Y	Y	N	Y	Y
8 **Reichert**	Y	N	Y	Y	Y	Y
9 Smith	Y	Y	Y	N	Y	Y
WEST VIRGINIA						
1 Mollohan	Y	Y	Y	N	Y	Y
2 **Capito**	Y	N	Y	Y	Y	Y
3 Rahall	Y	Y	Y	N	Y	Y
WISCONSIN						
1 **Ryan**	Y	N	Y	Y	N	N
2 Baldwin	Y	Y	Y	N	Y	Y
3 Kind	Y	Y	Y	N	Y	Y
4 Moore	Y	Y	Y	N	Y	Y
5 **Sensenbrenner**	Y	N	Y	Y	N	Y
6 **Petri**	Y	N	Y	Y	N	Y
7 Obey	Y	Y	Y	N	Y	Y
8 Kagen	Y	Y	Y	N	Y	Y
WYOMING						
AL **Lummis**	Y	N	Y	Y	N	N
DELEGATES						
Faleomavaega (A.S.)				N	Y	Y
Norton (D.C.)				N	Y	Y
Bordallo (Guam)				N	Y	Y
Sablan (N. Marianas)				N	Y	Y
Pierluisi (P.R.)				N	Y	Y
Christensen (V.I.)				N	Y	Y

IN THE HOUSE | By Vote Number

708. HR 3246. **Vehicle Research and Development Program/ Recommit.** Broun, R-Ga., motion to recommit the bill to the Science and Technology Committee with instructions that it be immediately reported back with language that would bar the legislation from taking effect until the federal deficit does not exceed $500 billion and no other funding is authorized for such Energy Department vehicle technologies research and development. Motion rejected 180-245: R 166-9; D 14-236. Sept. 16, 2009.

709. HR 3246. **Vehicle Research and Development Program/ Passage.** Passage of the bill that would require the Energy Department to conduct a research and development program on materials, technologies and processes to reduce petroleum use and emissions from passenger and commercial vehicles. It would authorize $2.9 billion from fiscal years 2010 to 2014 for the program, including $1.1 billion for research projects on medium- and heavy-duty commercial vehicles, $115 million for user facilities and $60 million for a non-road pilot program. Passed 312-114: R 62-113; D 250-1. Sept. 16, 2009.

710. HR 3221. **Student Loan Overhaul/School Construction Funding.** Hoekstra, R-Mich., amendment that would strike provisions in the bill that would authorize $6.6 billion for school construction programs in elementary and secondary public schools in 2010 and 2011, as well as community colleges in 2011. Rejected in Committee of the Whole 161-262: R 155-16; D 6-246. Sept. 17, 2009.

711. HR 3221. **Student Loan Overhaul/Duplicative Funding Ban.** McMorris Rodgers, R-Wash., amendment that would bar the use of school construction funds authorized in the bill to assist local educational agencies that receive funding for school modernization and repair under the 2009 economic stimulus law. Rejected in Committee of the Whole 167-251: R 164-6; D 3-245. Sept. 17, 2009.

712. HR 3221. **Student Loan Overhaul/American Graduation Initiative.** Foxx, R-N.C., amendment that would eliminate provisions in the bill related to the American Graduation Initiative, which includes grants for community college programs, and $7 billion in authorization for the initiative. Rejected in Committee of the Whole 126-301: R 126-45; D 0-256. A "nay" was a vote in support of the president's position. Sept. 17, 2009.

713. HR 3221. **Student Loan Overhaul/Financial Literacy Programs.** Himes, D-Conn., amendment that would make several modifications to the bill regarding financial literacy programs, including authorizing states to use certain grant funds for programs to provide financial literacy education and counseling to elementary, secondary and postsecondary students that include an examination of how financial planning may impact a student's ability to pursue postsecondary education. Adopted in Committee of the Whole 428-2: R 171-1; D 257-1. Sept. 17, 2009.

	708	709	710	711	712	713
ALABAMA						
1 Bonner	Y	Y	Y	Y	Y	Y
2 Bright	Y	Y	N	Y	N	Y
3 Rogers	Y	Y	Y	Y	Y	Y
4 Aderholt	Y	Y	Y	Y	Y	Y
5 Griffith	Y	Y	N	N	N	Y
6 Bachus	Y	Y	Y	Y	Y	Y
7 Davis	N	Y	N	N	N	Y
ALASKA						
AL Young	Y	Y	Y	Y	N	Y
ARIZONA						
1 Kirkpatrick	N	Y	N	N	N	Y
2 Franks	Y	N	Y	+	Y	Y
3 Shadegg	Y	N	Y	Y	Y	Y
4 Pastor	N	Y	N	N	N	Y
5 Mitchell	Y	Y	N	N	N	Y
6 Flake	Y	N	Y	Y	Y	Y
7 Grijalva	N	Y	N	N	N	Y
8 Giffords	N	Y	N	N	N	Y
ARKANSAS						
1 Berry	N	Y	N	N	N	Y
2 Snyder	N	Y	N	N	N	Y
3 Boozman	Y	N	Y	Y	N	Y
4 Ross	N	Y	N	N	N	Y
CALIFORNIA						
1 Thompson	N	Y	N	N	N	Y
2 Herger	Y	N	Y	Y	Y	Y
3 Lungren	Y	N	Y	Y	Y	Y
4 McClintock	Y	N	Y	Y	Y	Y
5 Matsui	N	Y	N	N	N	Y
6 Woolsey	N	Y	N	N	N	Y
7 Miller, George	N	Y	N	N	N	Y
8 Pelosi						
9 Lee	N	Y	N	N	N	Y
10 Vacant						
11 McNerney	N	Y	N	N	N	Y
12 Speier	N	Y	N	N	N	Y
13 Stark	N	Y	N	N	N	Y
14 Eshoo	N	Y	N	N	N	Y
15 Honda	N	Y	N	N	N	Y
16 Lofgren	N	Y	N	N	N	Y
17 Farr	N	Y	N	N	N	Y
18 Cardoza	N	Y	N	N	N	Y
19 Radanovich	Y	N	?	?	?	?
20 Costa	N	Y	?	?	?	?
21 Nunes	Y	N	+	+	+	+
22 McCarthy	Y	N	Y	Y	N	Y
23 Capps	–	+	N	N	N	Y
24 Gallegly	Y	N	Y	Y	Y	Y
25 McKeon	Y	N	Y	Y	Y	Y
26 Dreier	Y	N	Y	Y	N	Y
27 Sherman	N	Y	N	N	N	Y
28 Berman	N	Y	N	N	N	Y
29 Schiff	N	Y	N	N	N	Y
30 Waxman	N	Y	N	N	N	Y
31 Becerra	N	Y	N	N	N	Y
32 Chu	N	Y	N	N	N	Y
33 Watson	N	Y	N	N	N	Y
34 Roybal-Allard	N	Y	N	N	N	Y
35 Waters	N	Y	N	N	N	Y
36 Harman	N	Y	N	N	N	Y
37 Richardson	N	Y	N	N	N	Y
38 Napolitano	N	Y	N	N	N	Y
39 Sánchez, Linda	N	Y	N	N	N	Y
40 Royce	Y	N	Y	Y	Y	Y
41 Lewis	Y	N	Y	Y	Y	Y
42 Miller, Gary	Y	Y	Y	Y	Y	Y
43 Baca	N	Y	N	N	N	Y
44 Calvert	Y	Y	Y	Y	Y	Y
45 Bono Mack	Y	N	Y	Y	N	Y
46 Rohrabacher	Y	N	Y	Y	Y	Y
47 Sanchez, Loretta	N	Y	N	N	N	Y
48 Campbell	Y	N	Y	Y	Y	Y
49 Issa	Y	N	Y	Y	Y	Y
50 Bilbray	Y	Y	Y	Y	?	Y
51 Filner	N	Y	N	N	N	Y
52 Hunter	Y	N	Y	Y	Y	Y
53 Davis	N	Y	N	N	N	Y

	708	709	710	711	712	713
COLORADO						
1 DeGette	N	Y	N	N	N	Y
2 Polis	N	Y	N	N	N	Y
3 Salazar	N	Y	N	N	N	Y
4 Markey	N	Y	N	N	N	Y
5 Lamborn	Y	N	Y	Y	Y	Y
6 Coffman	Y	N	Y	Y	Y	Y
7 Perlmutter	N	Y	N	?	?	Y
CONNECTICUT						
1 Larson	N	Y	N	N	N	Y
2 Courtney	N	Y	N	N	N	Y
3 DeLauro	N	Y	N	N	N	Y
4 Himes	N	Y	N	Y	N	Y
5 Murphy	N	Y	N	N	N	Y
DELAWARE						
AL Castle	Y	Y	Y	Y	N	Y
FLORIDA						
1 Miller	Y	N	Y	Y	Y	Y
2 Boyd	N	Y	N	N	N	Y
3 Brown	N	Y	N	N	N	Y
4 Crenshaw	Y	N	Y	Y	Y	Y
5 Brown-Waite	Y	N	Y	Y	Y	Y
6 Stearns	Y	N	Y	Y	Y	Y
7 Mica	Y	N	Y	Y	Y	Y
8 Grayson	N	Y	N	N	N	Y
9 Bilirakis	Y	N	Y	Y	N	Y
10 Young	Y	N	Y	Y	Y	Y
11 Castor	N	Y	N	N	N	Y
12 Putnam	Y	Y	N	Y	N	Y
13 Buchanan	Y	N	Y	Y	N	Y
14 Mack	Y	N	Y	Y	Y	Y
15 Posey	Y	Y	N	Y	N	Y
16 Rooney	Y	N	Y	N	Y	Y
17 Meek	N	Y	N	N	N	Y
18 Ros-Lehtinen	Y	Y	N	N	N	Y
19 Wexler	N	Y	N	?	N	Y
20 Wasserman Schultz	N	Y	N	N	N	Y
21 Diaz-Balart, L.	Y	Y	N	N	Y	Y
22 Klein	N	Y	N	N	N	Y
23 Hastings	N	Y	N	N	N	Y
24 Kosmas	N	Y	N	N	N	Y
25 Diaz-Balart, M.	Y	Y	N	N	Y	Y
GEORGIA						
1 Kingston	Y	N	Y	Y	Y	Y
2 Bishop	N	Y	N	N	N	Y
3 Westmoreland	Y	N	Y	Y	Y	Y
4 Johnson	N	Y	?	N	N	Y
5 Lewis	N	Y	N	N	N	Y
6 Price	Y	N	Y	Y	Y	Y
7 Linder	Y	N	Y	Y	Y	Y
8 Marshall	N	Y	N	N	N	Y
9 Deal	Y	N	Y	Y	Y	Y
10 Broun	Y	Y	Y	Y	Y	Y
11 Gingrey	Y	N	Y	Y	Y	Y
12 Barrow	N	Y	N	N	N	Y
13 Scott	N	Y	N	N	N	Y
HAWAII						
1 Abercrombie	N	Y	?	?	?	?
2 Hirono	N	Y	N	N	N	Y
IDAHO						
1 Minnick	Y	Y	N	N	N	Y
2 Simpson	Y	N	N	N	Y	Y
ILLINOIS						
1 Rush	N	Y	N	N	N	Y
2 Jackson	N	Y	N	N	N	Y
3 Lipinski	N	Y	N	N	N	Y
4 Gutierrez	N	Y	N	N	N	Y
5 Quigley	N	Y	N	N	N	Y
6 Roskam	Y	N	Y	Y	N	Y
7 Davis	N	Y	N	N	N	Y
8 Bean	N	Y	Y	Y	N	Y
9 Schakowsky	N	Y	N	N	N	Y
10 Kirk	N	Y	N	N	N	Y
11 Halvorson	N	Y	N	N	N	Y
12 Costello	N	Y	N	N	N	Y
13 Biggert	N	Y	Y	Y	N	Y
14 Foster	N	Y	N	N	N	Y
15 Johnson	Y	Y	Y	Y	Y	Y

KEY	**Republicans**	Democrats		
Y	Voted for (yea)	X	Paired against	C Voted "present" to avoid possible conflict of interest
#	Paired for	–	Announced against	
+	Announced for	P	Voted "present"	? Did not vote or otherwise make a position known
N	Voted against (nay)			

	708	709	710	711	712	713
16 **Manzullo**	Y	N	Y	Y	Y	Y
17 Hare	N	Y	N	N	N	Y
18 **Schock**	Y	Y	Y	Y	Y	Y
19 **Shimkus**	Y	N	Y	Y	Y	Y
INDIANA						
1 Visclosky	N	Y	N	N	N	Y
2 Donnelly	N	Y	N	N	N	Y
3 **Souder**	N	Y	Y	Y	Y	Y
4 **Buyer**	Y	Y	Y	Y	Y	Y
5 **Burton**	Y	N	Y	Y	Y	Y
6 **Pence**	Y	N	Y	Y	Y	Y
7 Carson	N	Y	N	N	N	Y
8 Ellsworth	N	Y	N	N	N	Y
9 Hill	N	Y	N	N	N	Y
IOWA						
1 Braley	N	Y	N	?	N	Y
2 Loebsack	N	Y	N	N	N	Y
3 Boswell	N	Y	N	N	N	Y
4 **Latham**	Y	N	Y	Y	N	Y
5 **King**	Y	N	Y	Y	Y	Y
KANSAS						
1 **Moran**	Y	N	Y	Y	Y	Y
2 **Jenkins**	Y	Y	Y	Y	Y	Y
3 Moore	N	Y	?	N	N	Y
4 **Tiahrt**	Y	N	Y	Y	Y	Y
KENTUCKY						
1 **Whitfield**	Y	Y	Y	Y	N	Y
2 **Guthrie**	Y	N	Y	Y	N	Y
3 Yarmuth	N	Y	N	N	N	Y
4 **Davis**	Y	Y	Y	Y	N	Y
5 **Rogers**	Y	Y	Y	Y	N	Y
6 Chandler	N	?	N	N	N	Y
LOUISIANA						
1 **Scalise**	Y	N	Y	Y	Y	Y
2 **Cao**	Y	Y	N	Y	N	Y
3 Melancon	Y	Y	N	N	N	Y
4 **Fleming**	Y	N	Y	Y	Y	Y
5 **Alexander**	Y	N	Y	Y	Y	Y
6 **Cassidy**	Y	N	Y	Y	Y	Y
7 **Boustany**	Y	N	Y	Y	Y	Y
MAINE						
1 Pingree	N	Y	N	N	N	Y
2 Michaud	N	Y	N	N	N	Y
MARYLAND						
1 Kratovil	Y	Y	N	N	N	Y
2 Ruppersberger	N	Y	N	N	N	Y
3 Sarbanes	N	Y	N	N	N	Y
4 Edwards	N	Y	N	N	N	Y
5 Hoyer	N	Y	N	N	N	Y
6 **Bartlett**	Y	Y	Y	Y	Y	Y
7 Cummings	N	Y	N	N	N	Y
8 Van Hollen	N	Y	N	N	N	Y
MASSACHUSETTS						
1 Olver	N	Y	N	N	N	Y
2 Neal	N	Y	N	N	N	Y
3 McGovern	N	Y	N	N	N	Y
4 Frank	N	Y	N	N	N	Y
5 Tsongas	N	Y	N	N	N	Y
6 Tierney	N	Y	N	N	N	Y
7 Markey	N	Y	N	N	N	Y
8 Capuano	N	Y	N	N	N	Y
9 Lynch	N	Y	N	N	N	Y
10 Delahunt	N	Y	Y	N	N	Y
MICHIGAN						
1 Stupak	N	Y	N	N	N	Y
2 **Hoekstra**	Y	Y	Y	Y	N	Y
3 **Ehlers**	N	Y	Y	Y	N	Y
4 **Camp**	Y	Y	Y	Y	Y	Y
5 Kildee	N	Y	N	N	N	Y
6 **Upton**	N	Y	Y	Y	N	Y
7 Schauer	N	Y	N	N	N	Y
8 **Rogers**	Y	Y	Y	Y	N	Y
9 Peters	N	Y	Y	N	N	Y
10 **Miller**	N	Y	Y	Y	N	Y
11 **McCotter**	N	Y	Y	Y	N	Y
12 Levin	N	Y	N	N	N	Y
13 Kilpatrick	N	Y	N	N	N	Y
14 Conyers	N	Y	N	N	N	Y
15 Dingell	N	Y	?	?	?	Y
MINNESOTA						
1 Walz	N	Y	N	N	N	Y
2 **Kline**	Y	N	Y	Y	Y	Y
3 **Paulsen**	Y	Y	Y	Y	N	Y
4 McCollum	N	Y	N	N	N	Y
5 Ellison	?	Y	N	N	N	Y
6 **Bachmann**	Y	N	Y	Y	Y	Y
7 Peterson	N	Y	Y	N	N	Y
8 Oberstar	N	Y	N	N	N	Y
MISSISSIPPI						
1 Childers	Y	Y	N	N	N	Y
2 Thompson	N	Y	N	N	N	Y
3 **Harper**	Y	N	Y	Y	Y	Y
4 Taylor	Y	Y	N	N	N	Y
MISSOURI						
1 Clay	N	Y	N	N	N	Y
2 **Akin**	Y	N	Y	Y	Y	Y
3 Carnahan	N	Y	N	N	N	Y
4 Skelton	N	Y	N	N	N	Y
5 Cleaver	N	Y	N	N	N	Y
6 **Graves**	Y	N	Y	Y	Y	Y
7 **Blunt**	Y	N	Y	Y	N	Y
8 **Emerson**	Y	Y	Y	Y	Y	Y
9 **Luetkemeyer**	Y	N	Y	Y	Y	Y
MONTANA						
AL **Rehberg**	Y	N	Y	Y	Y	Y
NEBRASKA						
1 **Fortenberry**	Y	N	Y	Y	N	Y
2 **Terry**	Y	Y	Y	Y	N	Y
3 **Smith**	Y	Y	Y	Y	Y	Y
NEVADA						
1 Berkley	N	Y	N	N	N	Y
2 **Heller**	Y	N	Y	Y	N	Y
3 Titus	N	Y	N	N	N	Y
NEW HAMPSHIRE						
1 Shea-Porter	N	Y	N	N	N	Y
2 Hodes	N	Y	N	N	N	Y
NEW JERSEY						
1 Andrews	N	Y	N	N	N	Y
2 **LoBiondo**	Y	Y	N	Y	N	Y
3 Adler	Y	Y	N	N	N	Y
4 **Smith**	Y	Y	N	Y	N	Y
5 **Garrett**	Y	N	Y	Y	Y	Y
6 Pallone	N	Y	N	N	N	Y
7 **Lance**	Y	Y	Y	Y	Y	Y
8 Pascrell	N	Y	N	N	N	Y
9 Rothman	N	Y	N	N	N	Y
10 Payne	N	Y	N	N	N	Y
11 **Frelinghuysen**	Y	Y	Y	Y	Y	Y
12 Holt	N	Y	N	N	N	Y
13 Sires	N	Y	N	N	N	Y
NEW MEXICO						
1 Heinrich	N	Y	N	N	N	Y
2 Teague	Y	N	N	N	N	Y
3 Lujan	N	Y	N	N	N	Y
NEW YORK						
1 Bishop	N	Y	N	N	N	Y
2 Israel	N	Y	N	?	N	Y
3 **King**	Y	Y	N	Y	N	Y
4 McCarthy	N	Y	N	N	N	Y
5 Ackerman	N	Y	N	N	N	Y
6 Meeks	N	Y	N	N	N	Y
7 Crowley	N	Y	N	N	N	Y
8 Nadler	N	Y	N	N	N	Y
9 Weiner	N	Y	N	N	N	Y
10 Towns	N	Y	N	N	N	Y
11 Clarke	N	Y	N	N	N	Y
12 Velázquez	N	Y	N	N	N	Y
13 McMahon	Y	Y	N	N	N	Y
14 Maloney	N	Y	N	N	N	Y
15 Rangel	N	Y	N	?	N	Y
16 Serrano	N	Y	N	N	N	Y
17 Engel	N	Y	N	N	N	Y
18 Lowey	N	Y	N	N	N	Y
19 Hall	N	Y	N	N	N	Y
20 Murphy	N	Y	Y	N	N	Y
21 Tonko	N	Y	N	N	N	Y
22 Hinchey	N	Y	N	N	N	Y
23 **McHugh**	?	?	N	?	?	?
24 Arcuri	N	Y	N	N	N	Y
25 Maffei	N	Y	N	N	N	Y
26 **Lee**	Y	Y	Y	Y	N	Y
27 Higgins	N	Y	N	N	N	Y
28 Slaughter	N	Y	N	N	N	Y
29 Massa	N	Y	N	N	N	Y
NORTH CAROLINA						
1 Butterfield	N	Y	N	N	N	Y
2 Etheridge	N	Y	N	N	N	Y
3 **Jones**	Y	Y	Y	Y	Y	Y
4 Price	N	Y	N	N	N	Y
5 **Foxx**	Y	N	Y	Y	Y	Y
6 **Coble**	Y	Y	Y	Y	Y	Y
7 McIntyre	N	Y	N	N	N	Y
8 Kissell	N	Y	N	N	N	Y
9 **Myrick**	Y	N	Y	Y	Y	Y
10 **McHenry**	Y	N	Y	Y	Y	Y
11 Shuler	N	Y	N	N	N	Y
12 Watt	N	Y	N	?	N	Y
13 Miller	N	Y	N	N	N	Y
NORTH DAKOTA						
AL Pomeroy	N	Y	N	N	N	Y
OHIO						
1 Driehaus	N	Y	N	N	N	Y
2 **Schmidt**	?	N	Y	Y	Y	Y
3 **Turner**	Y	Y	Y	Y	N	Y
4 **Jordan**	Y	N	Y	Y	Y	Y
5 **Latta**	Y	N	Y	Y	Y	Y
6 Wilson	N	Y	N	N	N	Y
7 **Austria**	N	Y	Y	Y	Y	Y
8 **Boehner**	Y	N	Y	Y	Y	Y
9 Kaptur	N	Y	N	N	N	Y
10 Kucinich	N	Y	N	N	N	Y
11 Fudge	N	Y	N	N	N	Y
12 **Tiberi**	Y	Y	Y	Y	Y	?
13 Sutton	N	Y	?	N	N	Y
14 **LaTourette**	Y	Y	N	Y	N	Y
15 Kilroy	N	Y	N	N	N	Y
16 Boccieri	Y	Y	N	N	N	Y
17 Ryan	N	Y	N	?	N	Y
18 Space	N	Y	N	N	N	Y
OKLAHOMA						
1 **Sullivan**	Y	N	Y	Y	Y	Y
2 Boren	N	Y	N	N	N	Y
3 **Lucas**	Y	Y	Y	Y	Y	Y
4 **Cole**	Y	N	Y	Y	Y	Y
5 **Fallin**	Y	N	Y	Y	?	Y
OREGON						
1 Wu	N	Y	N	N	N	Y
2 **Walden**	Y	N	Y	Y	Y	Y
3 Blumenauer	N	Y	N	N	N	Y
4 DeFazio	N	Y	N	N	N	Y
5 Schrader	N	Y	N	N	N	Y
PENNSYLVANIA						
1 Brady	N	Y	N	N	N	Y
2 Fattah	N	Y	N	N	N	Y
3 Dahlkemper	N	Y	N	N	N	Y
4 Altmire	N	Y	N	N	N	Y
5 **Thompson**	Y	N	Y	Y	Y	Y
6 **Gerlach**	Y	Y	N	Y	N	Y
7 Sestak	?	?	N	N	N	Y
8 Murphy, P.	N	Y	N	N	N	Y
9 **Shuster**	Y	Y	Y	Y	Y	Y
10 Carney	N	Y	N	N	N	Y
11 Kanjorski	N	Y	N	N	N	Y
12 Murtha	N	Y	N	N	N	Y
13 Schwartz	N	Y	N	N	N	Y
14 Doyle	N	Y	N	N	N	Y
15 **Dent**	Y	Y	Y	Y	N	Y
16 **Pitts**	Y	Y	Y	Y	Y	Y
17 Holden	N	Y	N	N	N	Y
18 **Murphy, T.**	N	Y	Y	Y	N	Y
19 **Platts**	Y	Y	N	Y	N	Y
RHODE ISLAND						
1 Kennedy	N	Y	N	–	N	Y
2 Langevin	N	Y	N	N	N	Y
SOUTH CAROLINA						
1 **Brown**	Y	N	Y	Y	Y	Y
2 **Wilson**	Y	N	Y	Y	Y	Y
3 **Barrett**	?	?	?	?	?	?
4 **Inglis**	Y	Y	Y	Y	Y	Y
5 Spratt	N	Y	N	N	N	Y
6 Clyburn	?	Y	N	N	N	Y
SOUTH DAKOTA						
AL Herseth Sandlin	N	Y	N	N	N	Y
TENNESSEE						
1 **Roe**	Y	N	Y	Y	Y	Y
2 **Duncan**	Y	N	Y	Y	Y	Y
3 **Wamp**	Y	Y	Y	Y	Y	Y
4 Davis	N	Y	N	N	N	Y
5 Cooper	N	Y	N	N	N	Y
6 Gordon	N	Y	N	N	N	Y
7 **Blackburn**	Y	N	Y	Y	Y	Y
8 Tanner	?	?	?	?	?	?
9 Cohen	N	Y	N	N	N	Y
TEXAS						
1 **Gohmert**	Y	N	Y	Y	Y	Y
2 **Poe**	Y	N	Y	Y	Y	Y
3 **Johnson, S.**	Y	N	Y	Y	Y	N
4 **Hall**	Y	Y	Y	Y	N	Y
5 **Hensarling**	Y	N	Y	Y	Y	Y
6 **Barton**	Y	+	Y	Y	Y	Y
7 **Culberson**	Y	N	Y	+	Y	Y
8 **Brady**	Y	N	Y	Y	Y	Y
9 Green, A.	N	Y	N	N	N	Y
10 **McCaul**	Y	N	N	Y	Y	Y
11 **Conaway**	Y	N	Y	Y	Y	Y
12 **Granger**	Y	N	Y	Y	Y	Y
13 **Thornberry**	Y	N	Y	Y	Y	Y
14 **Paul**	Y	N	?	?	?	?
15 Hinojosa	N	Y	N	N	N	Y
16 Reyes	N	Y	N	N	N	Y
17 Edwards	N	Y	N	N	N	Y
18 Jackson Lee	N	Y	N	N	N	Y
19 **Neugebauer**	Y	N	Y	Y	Y	Y
20 Gonzalez	N	Y	N	N	N	Y
21 **Smith**	Y	N	Y	Y	Y	Y
22 **Olson**	Y	N	Y	Y	Y	Y
23 Rodriguez	N	Y	N	N	N	Y
24 **Marchant**	Y	N	?	Y	Y	Y
25 Doggett	N	Y	Y	Y	N	Y
26 **Burgess**	Y	N	Y	Y	N	Y
27 Ortiz	N	Y	N	N	N	Y
28 Cuellar	N	Y	N	N	N	Y
29 Green, G.	N	Y	N	N	N	Y
30 Johnson, E.	N	Y	N	N	N	Y
31 **Carter**	Y	N	Y	Y	Y	Y
32 **Sessions**	Y	N	Y	Y	Y	Y
UTAH						
1 **Bishop**	Y	N	?	Y	Y	Y
2 Matheson	N	Y	N	N	N	Y
3 **Chaffetz**	Y	N	Y	Y	Y	Y
VERMONT						
AL Welch	N	Y	N	N	N	Y
VIRGINIA						
1 **Wittman**	Y	N	Y	Y	N	Y
2 Nye	Y	Y	N	N	N	Y
3 Scott	N	Y	N	N	N	Y
4 **Forbes**	Y	N	Y	Y	N	Y
5 Perriello	Y	Y	N	N	N	Y
6 **Goodlatte**	Y	N	Y	Y	Y	Y
7 **Cantor**	Y	N	Y	?	Y	Y
8 Moran	N	Y	N	N	N	Y
9 Boucher	N	Y	N	N	N	Y
10 **Wolf**	Y	Y	Y	Y	N	Y
11 Connolly	N	Y	N	N	N	Y
WASHINGTON						
1 Inslee	N	Y	N	?	N	Y
2 Larsen	N	Y	N	N	N	Y
3 Baird	N	Y	N	N	N	Y
4 **Hastings**	Y	N	Y	Y	Y	Y
5 **McMorris Rodgers**	Y	N	Y	Y	Y	Y
6 Dicks	N	Y	N	N	N	Y
7 McDermott	N	Y	N	N	N	Y
8 **Reichert**	Y	Y	N	Y	N	Y
9 Smith	N	Y	N	N	N	N
WEST VIRGINIA						
1 Mollohan	N	Y	N	N	N	Y
2 **Capito**	Y	Y	Y	Y	Y	Y
3 Rahall	N	Y	?	N	N	Y
WISCONSIN						
1 **Ryan**	Y	N	Y	Y	Y	Y
2 Baldwin	N	Y	N	N	N	Y
3 Kind	N	Y	N	N	N	Y
4 Moore	N	Y	N	N	N	Y
5 **Sensenbrenner**	Y	N	Y	Y	Y	Y
6 **Petri**	Y	N	Y	Y	Y	Y
7 Obey	N	Y	N	N	N	Y
8 Kagen	N	Y	N	N	N	Y
WYOMING						
AL **Lummis**	Y	N	?	Y	Y	Y
DELEGATES						
Faleomavaega (A.S.)			?	N	N	Y
Norton (D.C.)			N	N	N	Y
Bordallo (Guam)			N	N	N	Y
Sablan (N. Marianas)			N	N	N	Y
Pierluisi (P.R.)			N	N	N	Y
Christensen (V.I.)			N	N	N	Y

IN THE HOUSE | By Vote Number

714. **HR 3221. Student Loan Overhaul/Armed Forces Credit Transfer.** Minnick, D-Idaho, amendment that would specify that academic credits earned while serving in the armed forces transferred between institutions of higher education would be part of a benchmark aimed at improving employment and education programs. The benchmark would be developed by an institution receiving one of the community college reform grants. Adopted in Committee of the Whole 428-0: R 171-0; D 257-0. Sept. 17, 2009.

715. **HR 3221. Student Loan Overhaul/Dislocated Workers.** Schauer, D-Mich., amendment that would direct the Education Department, in awarding grants to schools, states and nonprofits for programs to increase the number of individuals with postsecondary degrees or certificates, to give priority to applications that include activities to encourage dislocated workers to complete postsecondary education opportunities. Adopted in Committee of the Whole 425-5: R 168-5; D 257-0. Sept. 17, 2009.

716. **HR 3221. Student Loan Overhaul/Deficit Reduction.** Teague, D-N.M., amendment that would specify that all savings in federal expenditures not otherwise allocated in the bill be used for deficit reduction. Adopted in Committee of the Whole 425-0: R 171-0; D 254-0. Sept. 17, 2009.

717. **HR 3221. Student Loan Overhaul/Republican Substitute.** Guthrie, R-Ky., substitute amendment that would extend the temporary authority of the Education Department to purchase student loans to July 1, 2014, and require a study to be conducted to make recommendations for the development of a federal student loan program that incorporates a partnership between the federal government and the private sector. Rejected in Committee of the Whole 165-265: R 165-8; D 0-257. Sept. 17, 2009.

718. **HR 3221. Student Loan Overhaul/Recommit.** Issa, R-Calif., motion to recommit the bill to the Education and Labor Committee with instructions that it be immediately reported back with language that would bar federal agreements from being entered into with certain organizations, including the Association of Community Organizations for Reform Now (ACORN), prohibit federal funds from being provided to the organizations and bar federal employees or contractors from promoting the organizations. Motion agreed to 345-75: R 173-0; D 172-75. Sept. 17, 2009.

719. **HR 3221. Student Loan Overhaul/Passage.** Passage of the bill that would terminate the authority of the Federal Family Education Loan program to make or insure new loans after June 30, 2010, and direct the federal government to originate student loans. The legislation would provide for a competitive bidding process for entities to service the loans. The bill would make several modifications to education programs, including increasing funding for Pell grants, early-childhood education and community colleges. As amended, it would bar federal agreements from being entered into with certain organizations, including ACORN. Passed 253-171: R 6-167; D 247-4. A "yea" was a vote in support of the president's position. Sept. 17, 2009.

	714	715	716	717	718	719
ALABAMA						
1 **Bonner**	Y	Y	Y	Y	Y	N
2 Bright	Y	Y	Y	N	Y	Y
3 **Rogers**	Y	Y	Y	Y	Y	N
4 **Aderholt**	Y	Y	Y	Y	Y	N
5 Griffith	Y	Y	Y	N	Y	Y
6 **Bachus**	Y	Y	Y	Y	Y	N
7 Davis	Y	Y	Y	N	Y	Y
ALASKA						
AL **Young**	Y	Y	Y	Y	Y	N
ARIZONA						
1 Kirkpatrick	Y	Y	Y	N	Y	Y
2 **Franks**	Y	Y	Y	Y	Y	N
3 **Shadegg**	Y	Y	Y	Y	Y	N
4 Pastor	Y	Y	Y	N	Y	Y
5 Mitchell	Y	Y	Y	N	Y	Y
6 **Flake**	Y	N	Y	Y	Y	N
7 Grijalva	Y	Y	Y	N	N	Y
8 Giffords	Y	Y	Y	N	Y	Y
ARKANSAS						
1 Berry	Y	Y	Y	N	Y	Y
2 Snyder	Y	Y	Y	N	Y	Y
3 **Boozman**	Y	Y	Y	Y	Y	N
4 Ross	Y	Y	Y	N	Y	Y
CALIFORNIA						
1 Thompson	Y	Y	Y	N	Y	Y
2 **Herger**	Y	Y	Y	Y	Y	N
3 **Lungren**	Y	Y	Y	Y	Y	N
4 **McClintock**	Y	N	Y	Y	Y	N
5 Matsui	Y	Y	Y	N	Y	Y
6 Woolsey	Y	Y	Y	N	N	Y
7 Miller, George	Y	Y	Y	N	Y	Y
8 Pelosi						Y
9 Lee	Y	Y	Y	N	N	Y
10 Vacant						
11 McNerney	Y	Y	Y	N	Y	Y
12 Speier	Y	Y	Y	N	Y	Y
13 Stark	Y	Y	Y	N	N	Y
14 Eshoo	Y	Y	Y	N	Y	Y
15 Honda	Y	Y	Y	N	N	Y
16 Lofgren	Y	Y	Y	N	Y	Y
17 Farr	Y	Y	Y	N	Y	Y
18 Cardoza	Y	Y	Y	N	Y	Y
19 **Radanovich**	?	?	?	?	?	?
20 Costa	?	?	?	?	?	?
21 **Nunes**	+	+	+	+	+	–
22 **McCarthy**	Y	Y	Y	Y	Y	N
23 Capps	Y	Y	Y	N	Y	Y
24 **Gallegly**	Y	Y	Y	Y	Y	N
25 **McKeon**	Y	Y	Y	Y	Y	N
26 **Dreier**	Y	Y	Y	Y	Y	N
27 Sherman	Y	Y	Y	N	N	Y
28 Berman	Y	Y	?	N	Y	Y
29 Schiff	Y	Y	Y	N	Y	Y
30 Waxman	Y	Y	Y	N	N	Y
31 Becerra	Y	Y	Y	N	N	Y
32 Chu	Y	Y	Y	N	Y	Y
33 Watson	Y	Y	Y	N	N	Y
34 Roybal-Allard	Y	Y	Y	N	N	Y
35 Waters	Y	Y	Y	N	N	Y
36 Harman	Y	Y	Y	N	Y	Y
37 Richardson	Y	Y	Y	N	Y	Y
38 Napolitano	Y	Y	Y	N	Y	Y
39 Sánchez, Linda	Y	Y	Y	N	N	Y
40 **Royce**	Y	Y	Y	Y	Y	N
41 **Lewis**	Y	Y	Y	Y	Y	N
42 **Miller, Gary**	Y	Y	Y	Y	Y	N
43 Baca	Y	Y	Y	N	Y	Y
44 **Calvert**	Y	Y	Y	Y	Y	N
45 **Bono Mack**	Y	Y	Y	Y	Y	N
46 **Rohrabacher**	Y	Y	Y	Y	Y	N
47 Sanchez, Loretta	Y	Y	Y	N	Y	Y
48 **Campbell**	Y	Y	Y	Y	Y	N
49 **Issa**	Y	Y	Y	Y	Y	N
50 **Bilbray**	?	Y	Y	Y	Y	N
51 Filner	Y	Y	Y	N	N	Y
52 **Hunter**	Y	Y	Y	Y	Y	N
53 Davis	Y	Y	Y	N	Y	Y

	714	715	716	717	718	719
COLORADO						
1 DeGette	Y	Y	Y	N	N	Y
2 Polis	Y	Y	Y	N	N	Y
3 Salazar	Y	Y	Y	N	Y	Y
4 Markey	Y	Y	Y	N	Y	Y
5 **Lamborn**	Y	Y	Y	Y	Y	N
6 **Coffman**	Y	Y	Y	Y	Y	N
7 Perlmutter	Y	Y	Y	N	Y	Y
CONNECTICUT						
1 Larson	Y	Y	Y	N	Y	Y
2 Courtney	Y	Y	Y	N	Y	Y
3 DeLauro	Y	Y	Y	N	Y	Y
4 Himes	Y	Y	Y	N	Y	Y
5 Murphy	Y	Y	Y	N	Y	Y
DELAWARE						
AL **Castle**	Y	Y	Y	Y	Y	N
FLORIDA						
1 **Miller**	Y	Y	Y	Y	Y	N
2 Boyd	Y	Y	Y	N	Y	Y
3 Brown	Y	Y	Y	N	N	Y
4 **Crenshaw**	Y	Y	Y	Y	Y	N
5 **Brown-Waite**	Y	Y	Y	Y	Y	N
6 **Stearns**	Y	Y	Y	Y	Y	N
7 **Mica**	Y	Y	Y	Y	Y	N
8 Grayson	Y	Y	Y	N	N	Y
9 **Bilirakis**	Y	Y	Y	Y	Y	N
10 **Young**	Y	Y	Y	Y	Y	N
11 Castor	Y	Y	Y	N	N	Y
12 **Putnam**	Y	Y	Y	Y	Y	N
13 **Buchanan**	Y	Y	Y	Y	Y	N
14 **Mack**	Y	Y	Y	Y	Y	N
15 **Posey**	Y	Y	Y	Y	Y	N
16 **Rooney**	Y	Y	Y	Y	Y	N
17 Meek	Y	Y	Y	N	Y	Y
18 **Ros-Lehtinen**	Y	Y	Y	N	Y	Y
19 Wexler	Y	Y	Y	N	N	Y
20 Wasserman Schultz	Y	Y	Y	N	Y	Y
21 **Diaz-Balart, L.**	Y	Y	Y	Y	Y	N
22 Klein	Y	Y	Y	N	Y	Y
23 Hastings	Y	Y	Y	N	P	Y
24 Kosmas	Y	Y	Y	N	Y	Y
25 **Diaz-Balart, M.**	Y	Y	Y	Y	Y	N
GEORGIA						
1 **Kingston**	?	Y	Y	Y	Y	N
2 Bishop	Y	Y	?	N	Y	Y
3 **Westmoreland**	Y	Y	Y	Y	Y	N
4 Johnson	Y	Y	Y	N	Y	Y
5 Lewis	Y	Y	Y	N	N	Y
6 **Price**	Y	Y	Y	N	Y	N
7 **Linder**	Y	Y	Y	N	Y	N
8 Marshall	Y	Y	Y	Y	Y	Y
9 **Deal**	Y	Y	Y	Y	Y	N
10 **Broun**	Y	N	Y	Y	Y	N
11 **Gingrey**	Y	Y	Y	Y	Y	N
12 Barrow	Y	Y	Y	N	Y	Y
13 Scott	Y	Y	Y	N	N	Y
HAWAII						
1 Abercrombie	?	?	?	?	?	?
2 Hirono	Y	Y	Y	N	N	Y
IDAHO						
1 **Minnick**	Y	Y	Y	N	Y	Y
2 **Simpson**	Y	Y	Y	Y	Y	N
ILLINOIS						
1 Rush	Y	Y	Y	N	N	Y
2 Jackson	Y	Y	Y	N	N	Y
3 Lipinski	Y	Y	Y	N	Y	Y
4 Gutierrez	Y	Y	Y	N	Y	Y
5 Quigley	Y	Y	Y	N	Y	Y
6 **Roskam**	Y	Y	Y	Y	Y	N
7 Davis	Y	Y	Y	N	N	Y
8 Bean	Y	Y	Y	N	Y	Y
9 Schakowsky	Y	Y	Y	N	N	Y
10 **Kirk**	Y	Y	Y	N	Y	N
11 Halvorson	Y	Y	Y	N	Y	Y
12 Costello	Y	Y	Y	N	Y	Y
13 **Biggert**	Y	Y	Y	Y	Y	N
14 Foster	Y	Y	Y	N	Y	Y
15 **Johnson**	Y	Y	Y	Y	Y	Y

	714	715	716	717	718	719
16 **Manzullo**	Y	Y	Y	Y	Y	N
17 Hare	Y	Y	Y	N	Y	Y
18 **Schock**	Y	Y	Y	Y	Y	N
19 **Shimkus**	Y	Y	Y	Y	Y	N
INDIANA						
1 Visclosky	Y	Y	Y	N	Y	Y
2 Donnelly	Y	Y	Y	N	Y	Y
3 **Souder**	Y	Y	Y	Y	Y	N
4 **Buyer**	Y	Y	Y	Y	Y	N
5 **Burton**	Y	Y	Y	Y	Y	N
6 **Pence**	Y	Y	Y	Y	Y	N
7 Carson	Y	Y	Y	N	N	Y
8 Ellsworth	Y	Y	Y	N	Y	Y
9 Hill	Y	Y	Y	N	Y	Y
IOWA						
1 Braley	Y	Y	Y	N	Y	Y
2 Loebsack	Y	Y	Y	N	Y	Y
3 Boswell	Y	Y	Y	N	Y	Y
4 **Latham**	Y	Y	Y	Y	Y	N
5 **King**	Y	Y	Y	Y	Y	N
KANSAS						
1 **Moran**	Y	Y	Y	Y	Y	N
2 **Jenkins**	Y	Y	Y	Y	Y	N
3 Moore	Y	Y	Y	N	Y	Y
4 **Tiahrt**	Y	Y	Y	Y	Y	N
KENTUCKY						
1 **Whitfield**	Y	Y	Y	Y	Y	N
2 **Guthrie**	Y	Y	Y	Y	Y	N
3 Yarmuth	Y	Y	Y	N	Y	Y
4 **Davis**	Y	Y	Y	Y	Y	N
5 **Rogers**	Y	Y	Y	Y	Y	N
6 Chandler	Y	Y	Y	N	Y	Y
LOUISIANA						
1 **Scalise**	Y	Y	Y	Y	Y	N
2 **Cao**	Y	Y	Y	N	Y	Y
3 Melancon	Y	Y	Y	N	Y	Y
4 **Fleming**	Y	Y	Y	Y	Y	N
5 **Alexander**	Y	Y	Y	Y	Y	N
6 **Cassidy**	Y	Y	Y	Y	Y	N
7 **Boustany**	Y	Y	Y	Y	Y	N
MAINE						
1 Pingree	Y	Y	Y	N	Y	Y
2 Michaud	Y	Y	Y	N	Y	Y
MARYLAND						
1 Kratovil	Y	Y	Y	N	Y	Y
2 Ruppersberger	Y	Y	Y	N	Y	Y
3 Sarbanes	Y	Y	Y	N	Y	Y
4 Edwards	Y	Y	Y	N	N	Y
5 Hoyer	Y	Y	Y	N	Y	Y
6 **Bartlett**	Y	Y	Y	Y	Y	N
7 Cummings	Y	Y	Y	N	N	Y
8 Van Hollen	Y	Y	Y	N	Y	Y
MASSACHUSETTS						
1 Olver	Y	Y	Y	N	N	Y
2 Neal	Y	Y	Y	N	N	Y
3 McGovern	Y	Y	Y	N	N	Y
4 Frank	Y	Y	Y	N	?	?
5 Tsongas	Y	Y	Y	N	N	Y
6 Tierney	Y	Y	Y	N	Y	Y
7 Markey	Y	Y	Y	N	N	Y
8 Capuano	Y	Y	Y	N	N	Y
9 Lynch	Y	Y	Y	N	N	Y
10 Delahunt	Y	Y	Y	N	N	Y
MICHIGAN						
1 Stupak	Y	Y	Y	N	Y	Y
2 **Hoekstra**	Y	Y	Y	Y	Y	N
3 **Ehlers**	Y	Y	Y	Y	Y	N
4 **Camp**	Y	Y	Y	Y	Y	N
5 Kildee	Y	Y	Y	N	Y	Y
6 **Upton**	Y	Y	Y	Y	Y	N
7 Schauer	Y	Y	Y	N	Y	Y
8 **Rogers**	Y	Y	Y	Y	Y	N
9 Peters	Y	Y	Y	N	Y	Y
10 **Miller**	Y	Y	Y	Y	Y	N
11 **McCotter**	Y	Y	Y	Y	Y	N
12 Levin	Y	Y	Y	N	Y	Y
13 Kilpatrick	Y	Y	Y	N	N	Y
14 Conyers	Y	Y	Y	N	Y	+
15 Dingell	Y	Y	Y	N	Y	Y
MINNESOTA						
1 Walz	Y	Y	Y	N	Y	Y
2 **Kline**	Y	Y	Y	Y	Y	N
3 **Paulsen**	Y	Y	Y	Y	Y	N
4 McCollum	Y	Y	Y	N	N	Y

	714	715	716	717	718	719
5 Ellison	Y	Y	Y	N	N	Y
6 **Bachmann**	Y	Y	?	Y	Y	N
7 Peterson	Y	Y	Y	N	Y	Y
8 Oberstar	Y	Y	Y	N	Y	Y
MISSISSIPPI						
1 Childers	Y	Y	Y	N	Y	Y
2 Thompson	Y	Y	Y	N	N	Y
3 **Harper**	Y	Y	Y	Y	Y	N
4 Taylor	Y	Y	Y	N	Y	Y
MISSOURI						
1 Clay	Y	Y	Y	N	Y	Y
2 **Akin**	Y	Y	Y	Y	Y	N
3 Carnahan	?	?	Y	N	Y	Y
4 Skelton	Y	Y	Y	N	Y	Y
5 Cleaver	Y	Y	Y	N	N	Y
6 **Graves**	Y	Y	Y	Y	Y	N
7 **Blunt**	Y	Y	Y	Y	Y	N
8 **Emerson**	Y	Y	?	Y	Y	N
9 **Luetkemeyer**	Y	Y	Y	Y	Y	N
MONTANA						
AL **Rehberg**	Y	Y	Y	Y	Y	N
NEBRASKA						
1 **Fortenberry**	Y	Y	Y	Y	Y	N
2 **Terry**	Y	Y	Y	Y	Y	N
3 **Smith**	Y	Y	Y	Y	Y	N
NEVADA						
1 Berkley	Y	Y	Y	N	Y	Y
2 **Heller**	Y	Y	Y	Y	Y	N
3 Titus	Y	Y	Y	N	Y	Y
NEW HAMPSHIRE						
1 Shea-Porter	Y	Y	Y	N	Y	Y
2 Hodes	Y	Y	Y	N	Y	Y
NEW JERSEY						
1 Andrews	Y	Y	Y	N	Y	Y
2 **LoBiondo**	Y	Y	Y	Y	Y	N
3 Adler	Y	Y	Y	N	Y	Y
4 **Smith**	Y	Y	Y	Y	Y	N
5 **Garrett**	Y	Y	Y	Y	Y	N
6 Pallone	Y	Y	Y	N	N	Y
7 **Lance**	Y	Y	Y	Y	Y	N
8 Pascrell	Y	Y	Y	N	N	Y
9 Rothman	Y	Y	Y	N	N	Y
10 Payne	Y	Y	Y	N	N	Y
11 **Frelinghuysen**	Y	Y	Y	Y	Y	N
12 Holt	Y	Y	Y	N	N	Y
13 Sires	Y	Y	Y	N	N	Y
NEW MEXICO						
1 Heinrich	Y	Y	Y	N	Y	Y
2 Teague	Y	Y	Y	N	Y	Y
3 Lujan	Y	Y	Y	N	Y	Y
NEW YORK						
1 Bishop	Y	Y	Y	N	Y	Y
2 Israel	Y	Y	Y	N	Y	Y
3 **King**	Y	Y	Y	Y	Y	N
4 McCarthy	Y	Y	Y	N	Y	Y
5 Ackerman	Y	Y	Y	N	Y	Y
6 Meeks	Y	Y	Y	?	N	Y
7 Crowley	Y	Y	Y	N	N	Y
8 Nadler	Y	Y	Y	N	N	Y
9 Weiner	Y	Y	Y	N	N	Y
10 Towns	Y	Y	Y	N	N	Y
11 Clarke	Y	Y	Y	N	?	Y
12 Velázquez	Y	Y	?	N	N	Y
13 McMahon	Y	Y	Y	N	Y	N
14 Maloney	Y	Y	Y	N	N	Y
15 Rangel	Y	Y	Y	N	N	Y
16 Serrano	Y	Y	Y	N	N	Y
17 Engel	Y	Y	Y	N	N	Y
18 Lowey	Y	Y	Y	N	Y	Y
19 Hall	Y	Y	Y	N	Y	Y
20 Murphy	Y	Y	Y	N	Y	Y
21 Tonko	Y	Y	Y	N	Y	Y
22 Hinchey	Y	Y	Y	N	N	Y
23 **McHugh**	?	?	?	?	?	?
24 Arcuri	Y	Y	Y	N	Y	Y
25 Maffei	Y	Y	Y	N	Y	Y
26 **Lee**	Y	Y	Y	Y	Y	N
27 Higgins	Y	Y	Y	N	Y	Y
28 Slaughter	Y	Y	Y	N	N	Y
29 Massa	Y	Y	Y	N	Y	Y
NORTH CAROLINA						
1 Butterfield	Y	Y	Y	N	N	Y
2 Etheridge	Y	Y	Y	N	Y	Y
3 **Jones**	Y	Y	Y	Y	Y	N
4 Price	Y	Y	Y	N	N	Y

	714	715	716	717	718	719
5 **Foxx**	Y	Y	Y	N	Y	N
6 **Coble**	Y	Y	Y	Y	Y	N
7 McIntyre	Y	Y	Y	N	Y	Y
8 Kissell	Y	Y	Y	N	Y	Y
9 **Myrick**	Y	Y	Y	Y	Y	N
10 **McHenry**	Y	Y	Y	Y	Y	N
11 Shuler	Y	Y	Y	N	Y	Y
12 Watt	Y	Y	Y	N	P	Y
13 Miller	Y	Y	Y	N	Y	Y
NORTH DAKOTA						
AL Pomeroy	Y	Y	Y	N	Y	Y
OHIO						
1 Driehaus	Y	Y	Y	N	Y	Y
2 **Schmidt**	Y	Y	Y	Y	Y	N
3 **Turner**	Y	Y	Y	Y	Y	N
4 **Jordan**	Y	Y	Y	Y	Y	N
5 **Latta**	Y	Y	Y	Y	Y	N
6 Wilson	Y	Y	Y	N	Y	Y
7 **Austria**	Y	Y	Y	Y	Y	N
8 **Boehner**	Y	Y	Y	Y	Y	N
9 Kaptur	Y	Y	Y	N	Y	Y
10 Kucinich	Y	Y	Y	N	N	Y
11 Fudge	Y	Y	Y	N	N	Y
12 **Tiberi**	Y	Y	Y	Y	Y	N
13 Sutton	Y	Y	Y	N	Y	Y
14 **LaTourette**	Y	Y	Y	Y	Y	N
15 Kilroy	Y	Y	Y	N	Y	Y
16 Boccieri	Y	Y	Y	N	Y	Y
17 Ryan	Y	Y	Y	N	Y	Y
18 Space	Y	Y	Y	N	Y	Y
OKLAHOMA						
1 **Sullivan**	Y	Y	Y	Y	Y	N
2 Boren	Y	Y	Y	N	Y	Y
3 **Lucas**	Y	Y	Y	Y	Y	N
4 **Cole**	Y	Y	Y	Y	Y	N
5 **Fallin**	Y	Y	Y	Y	Y	N
OREGON						
1 Wu	Y	Y	Y	N	Y	Y
2 **Walden**	Y	Y	Y	Y	Y	N
3 Blumenauer	Y	Y	Y	N	Y	Y
4 DeFazio	Y	Y	Y	N	Y	Y
5 Schrader	Y	Y	Y	N	Y	Y
PENNSYLVANIA						
1 Brady	Y	Y	Y	N	N	Y
2 Fattah	Y	Y	Y	N	N	Y
3 Dahlkemper	Y	Y	Y	N	Y	Y
4 Altmire	Y	Y	Y	N	Y	Y
5 **Thompson**	Y	Y	Y	Y	Y	N
6 **Gerlach**	Y	Y	Y	Y	Y	N
7 Sestak	Y	Y	Y	N	Y	Y
8 Murphy, P.	Y	Y	Y	N	Y	Y
9 **Shuster**	Y	Y	Y	Y	Y	N
10 Carney	Y	Y	Y	N	Y	Y
11 Kanjorski	Y	Y	Y	N	Y	Y
12 Murtha	Y	Y	Y	N	Y	Y
13 Schwartz	Y	Y	Y	N	Y	Y
14 Doyle	Y	Y	Y	N	N	Y
15 **Dent**	Y	Y	Y	Y	Y	N
16 **Pitts**	Y	Y	Y	Y	Y	N
17 Holden	Y	Y	Y	N	Y	Y
18 **Murphy, T.**	Y	Y	Y	Y	Y	N
19 **Platts**	Y	Y	Y	N	Y	Y
RHODE ISLAND						
1 Kennedy	Y	Y	Y	N	Y	Y
2 Langevin	Y	Y	Y	N	Y	Y
SOUTH CAROLINA						
1 **Brown**	Y	Y	Y	Y	Y	N
2 **Wilson**	Y	Y	Y	Y	Y	N
3 **Barrett**	?	?	?	?	?	?
4 **Inglis**	Y	Y	Y	Y	Y	N
5 Spratt	Y	Y	Y	N	Y	Y
6 Clyburn	Y	Y	Y	N	N	Y
SOUTH DAKOTA						
AL Herseth Sandlin	Y	Y	Y	N	Y	N
TENNESSEE						
1 **Roe**	Y	Y	Y	Y	Y	N
2 **Duncan**	Y	Y	Y	Y	Y	N
3 **Wamp**	Y	Y	Y	Y	Y	N
4 Davis	Y	Y	Y	N	Y	Y
5 Cooper	Y	Y	Y	N	Y	Y
6 Gordon	Y	Y	Y	N	Y	Y
7 **Blackburn**	Y	Y	Y	Y	Y	N
8 Tanner	?	?	?	?	?	?
9 Cohen	Y	Y	Y	N	Y	Y

	714	715	716	717	718	719
TEXAS						
1 **Gohmert**	Y	Y	Y	Y	Y	N
2 **Poe**	Y	Y	Y	Y	Y	N
3 **Johnson, S.**	Y	N	Y	Y	Y	N
4 **Hall**	Y	Y	Y	Y	Y	N
5 **Hensarling**	Y	Y	Y	Y	Y	N
6 **Barton**	Y	Y	Y	Y	Y	N
7 **Culberson**	Y	Y	Y	Y	Y	N
8 **Brady**	Y	Y	Y	Y	Y	N
9 Green, A.	Y	Y	Y	N	N	Y
10 **McCaul**	Y	Y	Y	Y	Y	N
11 **Conaway**	Y	Y	Y	Y	Y	N
12 **Granger**	Y	Y	Y	Y	Y	N
13 **Thornberry**	Y	Y	Y	Y	Y	N
14 **Paul**	?	?	?	?	?	?
15 Hinojosa	Y	Y	Y	N	Y	Y
16 Reyes	Y	Y	Y	N	Y	Y
17 Edwards	Y	Y	Y	N	Y	Y
18 Jackson Lee	Y	Y	Y	N	N	Y
19 **Neugebauer**	Y	Y	Y	Y	Y	N
20 Gonzalez	Y	Y	Y	N	Y	Y
21 **Smith**	Y	Y	Y	Y	Y	N
22 **Olson**	Y	Y	Y	Y	Y	N
23 Rodriguez	Y	Y	Y	N	Y	Y
24 **Marchant**	Y	Y	Y	Y	Y	N
25 Doggett	Y	Y	Y	N	Y	Y
26 **Burgess**	Y	Y	Y	Y	Y	N
27 Ortiz	Y	Y	Y	N	Y	Y
28 Cuellar	Y	Y	Y	N	Y	Y
29 Green, G.	Y	Y	Y	N	Y	Y
30 Johnson, E.	Y	Y	Y	N	N	Y
31 **Carter**	Y	Y	Y	Y	Y	N
32 **Sessions**	Y	Y	Y	Y	Y	N
UTAH						
1 **Bishop**	Y	N	Y	Y	Y	N
2 Matheson	Y	Y	Y	N	Y	Y
3 **Chaffetz**	Y	Y	Y	Y	Y	N
VERMONT						
AL Welch	Y	Y	Y	N	Y	Y
VIRGINIA						
1 **Wittman**	Y	Y	Y	Y	Y	N
2 Nye	Y	Y	Y	N	Y	Y
3 Scott	Y	Y	?	N	N	Y
4 **Forbes**	Y	Y	Y	Y	Y	N
5 Perriello	Y	Y	Y	N	Y	Y
6 **Goodlatte**	Y	Y	Y	Y	Y	N
7 **Cantor**	Y	Y	Y	Y	Y	N
8 Moran	Y	Y	Y	N	N	Y
9 Boucher	Y	Y	Y	N	Y	Y
10 **Wolf**	Y	Y	Y	Y	Y	N
11 Connolly	Y	Y	Y	N	?	Y
WASHINGTON						
1 Inslee	Y	Y	Y	N	Y	Y
2 Larsen	Y	Y	Y	N	N	Y
3 Baird	Y	Y	Y	N	Y	Y
4 **Hastings**	Y	Y	Y	Y	Y	N
5 **McMorris Rodgers**	Y	Y	Y	Y	Y	N
6 Dicks	Y	Y	Y	N	Y	Y
7 McDermott	Y	Y	Y	N	N	Y
8 **Reichert**	Y	Y	Y	Y	Y	N
9 Smith	Y	Y	Y	N	Y	Y
WEST VIRGINIA						
1 Mollohan	Y	Y	Y	N	N	Y
2 **Capito**	Y	Y	Y	Y	Y	N
3 Rahall	Y	Y	Y	N	N	Y
WISCONSIN						
1 **Ryan**	Y	Y	Y	Y	Y	N
2 Baldwin	Y	Y	Y	N	N	Y
3 Kind	Y	Y	Y	N	Y	Y
4 Moore	Y	Y	Y	N	N	Y
5 **Sensenbrenner**	Y	Y	Y	Y	Y	N
6 **Petri**	Y	Y	Y	N	Y	Y
7 Obey	Y	Y	Y	N	Y	Y
8 Kagen	Y	Y	Y	N	Y	Y
WYOMING						
AL **Lummis**	Y	Y	Y	Y	Y	N
DELEGATES						
Faleomavaega (A.S.)	Y	Y	Y	N		
Norton (D.C.)	Y	Y	Y	N		
Bordallo (Guam)	Y	Y	Y	N		
Sablan (N. Marianas)	Y	Y	Y	N		
Pierluisi (P.R.)	Y	Y	Y	N		
Christensen (V.I.)	Y	Y	Y	N		

IN THE HOUSE | By Vote Number

720. H Res 441. Tribute to Catholic Nuns/Adoption. Lynch, D-Mass., motion to suspend the rules and adopt the resolution that would honor and commend Catholic nuns for their service and sacrifice throughout U.S. history. Motion agreed to 412-0: R 169-0; D 243-0. A two-thirds majority of those present and voting (275 in this case) is required for adoption under suspension of the rules. Sept. 22, 2009.

721. HR 2971. Martin Luther King Jr. Post Office/Passage. Lynch, D-Mass., motion to suspend the rules and pass the bill that would designate a post office in Portland, Ore., as the "Dr. Martin Luther King Jr. Post Office." Motion agreed to 411-0: R 170-0; D 241-0. A two-thirds majority of those present and voting (274 in this case) is required for passage under suspension of the rules. Sept. 22, 2009.

722. HR 3548. Unemployment Benefits Extension/Passage.
McDermott, D-Wash., motion to suspend the rules and pass the bill that would provide an additional 13 weeks of unemployment benefits for workers in states with a three-month average unemployment rate of at least 8.5 percent. Motion agreed to 331-83: R 104-66; D 227-17. A two-thirds majority of those present and voting (276 in this case) is required for passage under suspension of the rules. Sept. 22, 2009.

723. HR 324. Santa Cruz Valley National Heritage Area/Rule.
Adoption of the rule (H Res 760) to provide for House floor consideration of the bill that would establish the Santa Cruz Valley National Heritage Area in Santa Cruz and Pima counties in Arizona and authorize $1 million per fiscal year, with a maximum of $15 million. Adopted 244-177: R 1-172; D 243-5. Sept. 23, 2009.

724. H Res 765. Condolences for Georgia Flood Victims/Adoption.
Oberstar, D-Minn., motion to suspend the rules and adopt the resolution that would express condolences to the families of those killed during the storms and floods in Georgia between Sept. 18 and Sept. 21, 2009, and express gratitude to emergency personnel. Motion agreed to 421-0: R 173-0; D 248-0. A two-thirds majority of those present and voting (281 in this case) is required for adoption under suspension of the rules. Sept. 23, 2009.

725. HR 2215. John J. Shivnen Post Office/Passage. Lynch, D-Mass., motion to suspend the rules and pass the bill that would designate a post office in Garden City, Mich., as the "John J. Shivnen Post Office Building." Motion agreed to 423-0: R 172-0; D 251-0. A two-thirds majority of those present and voting (282 in this case) is required for passage under suspension of the rules. Sept. 23, 2009.

*Rep. John M. McHugh, R-N.Y., resigned Sept. 21 to become secretary of the Army. The last vote for which he was eligible was 719.

	720	721	722	723	724	725
ALABAMA						
1 **Bonner**	Y	Y	Y	N	Y	Y
2 Bright	Y	Y	Y	Y	Y	Y
3 **Rogers**	Y	Y	Y	N	Y	Y
4 **Aderholt**	Y	Y	Y	N	Y	Y
5 Griffith	Y	Y	Y	Y	Y	Y
6 **Bachus**	Y	Y	N	N	Y	Y
7 Davis	Y	Y	Y	Y	Y	Y
ALASKA						
AL **Young**	Y	Y	Y	N	Y	Y
ARIZONA						
1 Kirkpatrick	Y	Y	Y	Y	Y	Y
2 **Franks**	Y	Y	N	N	Y	Y
3 **Shadegg**	Y	Y	N	N	Y	Y
4 Pastor	Y	Y	Y	Y	Y	Y
5 Mitchell	Y	Y	Y	Y	Y	Y
6 **Flake**	Y	Y	N	N	Y	Y
7 Grijalva	?	?	?	Y	Y	Y
8 Giffords	Y	Y	Y	Y	Y	Y
ARKANSAS						
1 Berry	Y	Y	N	Y	Y	Y
2 Snyder	Y	Y	Y	Y	Y	Y
3 **Boozman**	Y	Y	N	N	Y	Y
4 Ross	Y	Y	N	Y	Y	Y
CALIFORNIA						
1 Thompson	Y	Y	Y	Y	Y	Y
2 **Herger**	Y	Y	Y	N	Y	Y
3 **Lungren**	Y	Y	N	N	Y	Y
4 **McClintock**	Y	Y	N	N	Y	Y
5 Matsui	?	Y	Y	Y	Y	Y
6 Woolsey	Y	Y	Y	Y	Y	Y
7 Miller, George	Y	Y	Y	Y	Y	Y
8 Pelosi						
9 Lee	Y	Y	Y	Y	Y	Y
10 Vacant						
11 McNerney	Y	Y	Y	Y	Y	Y
12 Speier	Y	Y	Y	Y	Y	Y
13 Stark	Y	Y	Y	Y	Y	Y
14 Eshoo	Y	Y	Y	Y	Y	Y
15 Honda	Y	Y	Y	Y	Y	Y
16 Lofgren	Y	Y	Y	Y	Y	Y
17 Farr	Y	Y	Y	Y	Y	Y
18 Cardoza	Y	Y	Y	Y	Y	Y
19 **Radanovich**	?	?	?	?	?	?
20 Costa	Y	Y	Y	Y	Y	Y
21 **Nunes**	Y	Y	N	N	Y	Y
22 **McCarthy**	Y	Y	Y	N	Y	Y
23 Capps	Y	Y	Y	Y	Y	Y
24 **Gallegly**	Y	Y	Y	N	Y	Y
25 **McKeon**	Y	Y	Y	N	Y	Y
26 **Dreier**	Y	Y	Y	N	Y	Y
27 Sherman	Y	Y	Y	Y	Y	Y
28 Berman	Y	Y	Y	Y	Y	Y
29 Schiff	Y	Y	Y	Y	Y	Y
30 Waxman	Y	Y	Y	Y	Y	Y
31 Becerra	Y	Y	Y	Y	Y	Y
32 Chu	Y	Y	Y	Y	Y	Y
33 Watson	Y	Y	Y	Y	Y	Y
34 Roybal-Allard	Y	Y	Y	Y	Y	Y
35 Waters	Y	Y	Y	Y	Y	Y
36 Harman	Y	Y	Y	Y	Y	Y
37 Richardson	Y	Y	Y	Y	Y	Y
38 Napolitano	Y	Y	Y	Y	Y	Y
39 Sánchez, Linda	Y	Y	Y	Y	Y	Y
40 **Royce**	Y	Y	Y	N	Y	Y
41 **Lewis**	Y	Y	Y	N	Y	Y
42 **Miller, Gary**	Y	Y	Y	N	Y	Y
43 Baca	Y	Y	Y	Y	Y	Y
44 **Calvert**	Y	Y	Y	N	Y	Y
45 **Bono Mack**	Y	Y	Y	N	Y	Y
46 **Rohrabacher**	?	?	?	N	Y	Y
47 Sanchez, Loretta	Y	Y	Y	Y	Y	Y
48 **Campbell**	Y	Y	Y	N	Y	Y
49 **Issa**	Y	Y	Y	N	Y	Y
50 **Bilbray**	Y	Y	Y	N	Y	Y
51 Filner	Y	Y	Y	Y	Y	Y
52 **Hunter**	Y	Y	N	N	Y	Y
53 Davis	Y	Y	Y	Y	Y	Y

	720	721	722	723	724	725
COLORADO						
1 DeGette	Y	Y	Y	Y	Y	Y
2 Polis	Y	Y	Y	Y	Y	Y
3 Salazar	Y	Y	Y	Y	Y	Y
4 Markey	Y	Y	N	Y	Y	Y
5 **Lamborn**	Y	Y	N	N	Y	Y
6 **Coffman**	Y	Y	N	N	Y	Y
7 Perlmutter	Y	Y	N	?	Y	Y
CONNECTICUT						
1 Larson	Y	Y	Y	Y	Y	Y
2 Courtney	Y	Y	N	Y	Y	Y
3 DeLauro	Y	Y	Y	Y	Y	Y
4 Himes	Y	Y	Y	Y	Y	Y
5 Murphy	Y	?	N	Y	?	Y
DELAWARE						
AL **Castle**	Y	Y	Y	N	Y	Y
FLORIDA						
1 **Miller**	Y	Y	N	N	Y	Y
2 Boyd	Y	Y	Y	Y	Y	Y
3 Brown	Y	Y	Y	Y	Y	Y
4 **Crenshaw**	Y	Y	Y	N	Y	Y
5 **Brown-Waite**	Y	Y	Y	N	Y	Y
6 **Stearns**	Y	Y	Y	N	Y	Y
7 **Mica**	Y	Y	Y	N	Y	Y
8 Grayson	Y	Y	Y	Y	Y	Y
9 **Bilirakis**	Y	Y	Y	N	Y	Y
10 **Young**	Y	Y	Y	N	Y	Y
11 Castor	Y	Y	Y	Y	Y	Y
12 **Putnam**	Y	Y	N	N	Y	Y
13 **Buchanan**	Y	Y	Y	N	Y	Y
14 **Mack**	Y	Y	N	N	Y	Y
15 **Posey**	Y	Y	Y	N	Y	Y
16 **Rooney**	Y	Y	Y	N	Y	Y
17 Meek	?	?	?	Y	Y	Y
18 **Ros-Lehtinen**	Y	Y	Y	N	Y	Y
19 Wexler	Y	Y	Y	Y	Y	Y
20 Wasserman Schultz	Y	Y	Y	Y	Y	Y
21 **Diaz-Balart, L.**	Y	Y	Y	N	Y	Y
22 Klein	Y	Y	Y	Y	Y	Y
23 Hastings	Y	Y	Y	Y	Y	Y
24 **Kosmas**	Y	Y	Y	Y	Y	Y
25 **Diaz-Balart, M.**	Y	Y	N	N	Y	Y
GEORGIA						
1 **Kingston**	Y	Y	N	N	Y	Y
2 Bishop	Y	Y	Y	Y	Y	Y
3 **Westmoreland**	Y	Y	N	N	Y	Y
4 Johnson	Y	Y	Y	Y	Y	Y
5 Lewis	Y	Y	Y	Y	Y	Y
6 **Price**	Y	Y	N	N	Y	Y
7 **Linder**	Y	Y	N	N	Y	Y
8 Marshall	Y	?	Y	Y	Y	Y
9 **Deal**	Y	Y	N	N	Y	Y
10 **Broun**	Y	Y	N	N	Y	Y
11 **Gingrey**	Y	Y	N	N	Y	Y
12 Barrow	Y	Y	Y	Y	Y	Y
13 Scott	Y	Y	Y	Y	Y	Y
HAWAII						
1 Abercrombie	?	?	?	?	?	?
2 Hirono	Y	Y	Y	Y	Y	Y
IDAHO						
1 Minnick	Y	Y	Y	Y	Y	Y
2 **Simpson**	Y	Y	Y	N	Y	Y
ILLINOIS						
1 Rush	?	?	?	Y	Y	Y
2 Jackson	?	?	?	Y	Y	Y
3 Lipinski	Y	Y	Y	Y	Y	Y
4 Gutierrez	+	+	+	Y	Y	Y
5 Quigley	Y	Y	Y	Y	Y	Y
6 **Roskam**	Y	Y	N	N	Y	Y
7 Davis	Y	Y	Y	Y	Y	Y
8 Bean	Y	Y	Y	Y	Y	Y
9 Schakowsky	Y	Y	Y	Y	Y	Y
10 **Kirk**	?	?	?	N	Y	Y
11 Halvorson	Y	Y	Y	Y	Y	Y
12 Costello	Y	Y	Y	Y	Y	Y
13 **Biggert**	Y	Y	Y	N	Y	Y
14 Foster	Y	Y	Y	N	Y	Y
15 **Johnson**	Y	Y	Y	N	Y	Y

KEY Republicans Democrats

Y Voted for (yea)	X Paired against
# Paired for	– Announced against
+ Announced for	P Voted "present"
N Voted against (nay)	
C Voted "present" to avoid possible conflict of interest	
? Did not vote or otherwise make a position known	

	720	721	722	723	724	725
16 **Manzullo**	Y	Y	Y	N	Y	Y
17 Hare	Y	Y	Y	Y	Y	Y
18 **Schock**	?	Y	Y	N	Y	Y
19 **Shimkus**	Y	Y	Y	N	Y	Y
INDIANA						
1 Visclosky	Y	Y	Y	Y	Y	Y
2 Donnelly	Y	Y	Y	Y	Y	Y
3 **Souder**	Y	Y	Y	N	Y	Y
4 **Buyer**	Y	Y	Y	N	Y	Y
5 **Burton**	Y	Y	Y	N	Y	Y
6 **Pence**	Y	Y	Y	N	Y	Y
7 Carson	Y	Y	Y	Y	Y	Y
8 Ellsworth	Y	Y	Y	Y	Y	Y
9 Hill	Y	Y	Y	N	Y	Y
IOWA						
1 Braley	Y	Y	N	Y	Y	Y
2 Loebsack	?	?	?	Y	Y	Y
3 Boswell	Y	Y	N	Y	Y	Y
4 **Latham**	Y	Y	Y	N	Y	Y
5 **King**	Y	Y	N	N	Y	Y
KANSAS						
1 **Moran**	Y	Y	N	N	Y	Y
2 **Jenkins**	Y	Y	N	N	Y	Y
3 Moore	Y	Y	Y	Y	Y	Y
4 **Tiahrt**	Y	Y	N	N	Y	Y
KENTUCKY						
1 **Whitfield**	Y	Y	Y	N	Y	Y
2 **Guthrie**	Y	Y	Y	N	Y	Y
3 Yarmuth	Y	Y	Y	Y	Y	Y
4 **Davis**	Y	Y	Y	N	Y	Y
5 **Rogers**	Y	Y	Y	N	Y	Y
6 Chandler	Y	Y	Y	Y	Y	Y
LOUISIANA						
1 **Scalise**	Y	Y	N	N	Y	Y
2 **Cao**	Y	Y	Y	N	Y	Y
3 Melancon	Y	Y	N	Y	Y	Y
4 **Fleming**	Y	Y	N	N	Y	Y
5 **Alexander**	Y	Y	Y	N	Y	Y
6 **Cassidy**	Y	Y	Y	N	Y	Y
7 **Boustany**	Y	Y	Y	N	Y	Y
MAINE						
1 Pingree	Y	Y	Y	Y	?	Y
2 Michaud	Y	Y	Y	Y	Y	Y
MARYLAND						
1 Kratovil	Y	Y	Y	Y	Y	Y
2 Ruppersberger	Y	Y	Y	Y	Y	Y
3 Sarbanes	Y	Y	Y	Y	Y	Y
4 Edwards	Y	Y	Y	Y	Y	Y
5 Hoyer	Y	Y	Y	Y	Y	Y
6 **Bartlett**	Y	Y	Y	N	Y	Y
7 Cummings	Y	Y	Y	Y	Y	Y
8 Van Hollen	Y	Y	Y	Y	Y	Y
MASSACHUSETTS						
1 Olver	Y	Y	Y	Y	Y	Y
2 Neal	Y	Y	Y	Y	Y	Y
3 McGovern	Y	Y	Y	Y	Y	Y
4 Frank	Y	Y	Y	Y	Y	Y
5 Tsongas	Y	Y	Y	Y	Y	Y
6 Tierney	Y	Y	Y	Y	Y	Y
7 Markey	Y	Y	Y	Y	Y	Y
8 Capuano	?	?	?	?	?	?
9 Lynch	Y	Y	Y	Y	Y	Y
10 Delahunt	?	?	?	?	?	?
MICHIGAN						
1 Stupak	Y	Y	Y	Y	Y	Y
2 **Hoekstra**	Y	Y	Y	N	Y	Y
3 **Ehlers**	Y	Y	Y	N	Y	Y
4 **Camp**	Y	Y	Y	N	Y	Y
5 Kildee	Y	Y	Y	Y	Y	Y
6 **Upton**	Y	Y	Y	N	Y	Y
7 Schauer	Y	Y	Y	Y	Y	Y
8 **Rogers**	Y	Y	Y	N	Y	Y
9 Peters	Y	Y	Y	Y	Y	Y
10 **Miller**	Y	Y	Y	N	Y	Y
11 **McCotter**	Y	Y	Y	N	Y	Y
12 Levin	Y	Y	Y	Y	Y	Y
13 Kilpatrick	Y	Y	Y	Y	Y	Y
14 Conyers	Y	Y	Y	Y	Y	Y
15 Dingell	Y	Y	Y	Y	Y	Y
MINNESOTA						
1 Walz	Y	Y	Y	Y	Y	Y
2 **Kline**	Y	Y	N	N	Y	Y
3 **Paulsen**	Y	Y	N	N	Y	Y
4 McCollum	Y	Y	Y	Y	Y	Y
5 Ellison	Y	Y	Y	Y	Y	Y
6 **Bachmann**	Y	Y	N	N	Y	Y
7 Peterson	Y	Y	Y	Y	Y	Y
8 Oberstar	Y	Y	Y	Y	Y	Y
MISSISSIPPI						
1 Childers	Y	Y	Y	N	Y	Y
2 Thompson	Y	Y	Y	Y	Y	Y
3 **Harper**	Y	Y	Y	N	Y	Y
4 Taylor	Y	Y	Y	Y	Y	Y
MISSOURI						
1 Clay	Y	Y	Y	Y	Y	Y
2 **Akin**	Y	Y	N	N	Y	Y
3 Carnahan	Y	Y	Y	Y	Y	Y
4 Skelton	Y	Y	Y	Y	Y	Y
5 Cleaver	Y	Y	Y	Y	Y	Y
6 **Graves**	Y	Y	Y	N	Y	Y
7 **Blunt**	Y	Y	Y	N	Y	Y
8 **Emerson**	Y	Y	Y	N	Y	Y
9 **Luetkemeyer**	Y	Y	Y	N	Y	Y
MONTANA						
AL **Rehberg**	Y	Y	Y	N	Y	Y
NEBRASKA						
1 **Fortenberry**	Y	Y	N	N	Y	Y
2 **Terry**	Y	Y	N	N	Y	Y
3 **Smith**	Y	Y	N	N	Y	Y
NEVADA						
1 Berkley	Y	Y	Y	Y	Y	Y
2 **Heller**	Y	Y	Y	N	Y	Y
3 Titus	Y	Y	Y	Y	Y	Y
NEW HAMPSHIRE						
1 Shea-Porter	Y	Y	Y	Y	Y	Y
2 Hodes	Y	Y	N	Y	Y	Y
NEW JERSEY						
1 Andrews	Y	Y	Y	Y	Y	Y
2 **LoBiondo**	Y	Y	Y	N	Y	Y
3 Adler	Y	Y	Y	Y	Y	Y
4 **Smith**	Y	Y	Y	?	?	?
5 **Garrett**	Y	Y	Y	N	Y	Y
6 Pallone	Y	Y	Y	Y	Y	Y
7 **Lance**	Y	Y	Y	N	Y	Y
8 Pascrell	Y	Y	Y	Y	Y	Y
9 Rothman	Y	Y	Y	Y	Y	Y
10 Payne	Y	Y	Y	Y	Y	Y
11 **Frelinghuysen**	Y	Y	Y	N	Y	Y
12 Holt	Y	Y	Y	Y	Y	Y
13 Sires	Y	Y	Y	Y	Y	Y
NEW MEXICO						
1 Heinrich	Y	Y	Y	Y	Y	Y
2 Teague	Y	Y	N	Y	Y	Y
3 Lujan	Y	Y	Y	Y	Y	Y
NEW YORK						
1 Bishop	Y	Y	Y	Y	Y	Y
2 Israel	Y	Y	Y	Y	Y	Y
3 **King**	Y	Y	Y	N	Y	Y
4 McCarthy	Y	Y	Y	Y	Y	Y
5 Ackerman	Y	Y	Y	Y	Y	Y
6 Meeks	Y	Y	Y	Y	Y	Y
7 Crowley	Y	Y	Y	Y	Y	Y
8 Nadler	Y	Y	Y	Y	Y	Y
9 Weiner	Y	Y	Y	Y	Y	Y
10 Towns	Y	Y	Y	Y	Y	Y
11 Clarke	Y	Y	Y	Y	Y	Y
12 Velázquez	Y	Y	Y	Y	Y	Y
13 McMahon	Y	Y	Y	Y	?	Y
14 Maloney	Y	Y	Y	Y	Y	Y
15 Rangel	Y	Y	Y	Y	Y	Y
16 Serrano	Y	Y	Y	Y	Y	Y
17 Engel	Y	Y	Y	Y	Y	Y
18 Lowey	Y	Y	Y	Y	Y	Y
19 Hall	Y	Y	Y	Y	Y	Y
20 Murphy	Y	Y	Y	Y	Y	Y
21 Tonko	Y	Y	Y	Y	Y	Y
22 Hinchey	Y	Y	Y	Y	Y	Y
23 Vacant*						
24 Arcuri	Y	Y	Y	Y	Y	Y
25 Maffei	Y	Y	Y	Y	Y	Y
26 **Lee**	Y	Y	Y	N	Y	Y
27 Higgins	Y	Y	Y	Y	Y	Y
28 Slaughter	Y	Y	Y	?	Y	Y
29 Massa	Y	Y	Y	Y	Y	Y
NORTH CAROLINA						
1 Butterfield	Y	Y	Y	Y	Y	Y
2 Etheridge	Y	Y	Y	Y	Y	Y
3 **Jones**	Y	Y	Y	N	Y	Y
4 Price	Y	Y	Y	Y	Y	Y
5 **Foxx**	Y	Y	N	N	Y	Y
6 **Coble**	Y	Y	Y	N	Y	Y
7 McIntyre	Y	Y	Y	Y	Y	Y
8 Kissell	Y	Y	Y	Y	Y	Y
9 **Myrick**	Y	Y	Y	N	Y	Y
10 **McHenry**	Y	Y	Y	N	Y	Y
11 Shuler	Y	Y	Y	N	Y	Y
12 Watt	Y	Y	Y	Y	Y	Y
13 Miller	Y	Y	Y	Y	Y	Y
NORTH DAKOTA						
AL Pomeroy	Y	Y	Y	Y	Y	Y
OHIO						
1 Driehaus	Y	Y	Y	Y	Y	Y
2 **Schmidt**	Y	Y	Y	N	Y	Y
3 **Turner**	Y	Y	Y	N	Y	Y
4 **Jordan**	Y	Y	N	N	Y	Y
5 **Latta**	Y	Y	N	N	Y	Y
6 Wilson	Y	Y	Y	Y	Y	Y
7 **Austria**	Y	Y	Y	N	Y	Y
8 **Boehner**	Y	Y	N	N	Y	Y
9 Kaptur	Y	Y	Y	Y	Y	Y
10 Kucinich	Y	Y	Y	Y	Y	Y
11 Fudge	Y	Y	Y	Y	Y	Y
12 **Tiberi**	Y	Y	Y	N	Y	Y
13 Sutton	Y	Y	Y	Y	Y	Y
14 **LaTourette**	Y	Y	Y	N	Y	Y
15 Kilroy	Y	Y	Y	Y	Y	Y
16 Boccieri	Y	Y	Y	Y	Y	Y
17 Ryan	Y	Y	Y	Y	Y	Y
18 Space	Y	Y	Y	Y	Y	Y
OKLAHOMA						
1 **Sullivan**	Y	Y	N	N	Y	Y
2 Boren	Y	Y	N	Y	Y	Y
3 **Lucas**	Y	Y	N	N	Y	Y
4 **Cole**	Y	Y	N	N	Y	Y
5 **Fallin**	Y	Y	N	N	Y	Y
OREGON						
1 Wu	?	?	?	Y	Y	Y
2 **Walden**	Y	Y	Y	N	Y	Y
3 Blumenauer	Y	Y	Y	Y	Y	Y
4 DeFazio	Y	Y	Y	Y	Y	Y
5 Schrader	Y	Y	Y	Y	Y	Y
PENNSYLVANIA						
1 Brady	Y	Y	Y	Y	Y	Y
2 Fattah	Y	Y	Y	?	Y	Y
3 Dahlkemper	Y	Y	Y	Y	Y	Y
4 Altmire	Y	Y	Y	N	Y	Y
5 **Thompson**	Y	Y	Y	N	Y	Y
6 **Gerlach**	?	?	?	N	Y	Y
7 Sestak	Y	Y	Y	Y	Y	Y
8 Murphy, P.	Y	Y	Y	Y	Y	Y
9 **Shuster**	Y	Y	Y	N	Y	Y
10 Carney	?	?	?	Y	Y	Y
11 Kanjorski	Y	Y	Y	Y	Y	Y
12 Murtha	Y	Y	Y	Y	Y	Y
13 Schwartz	Y	Y	Y	Y	Y	Y
14 Doyle	Y	Y	Y	?	?	?
15 **Dent**	Y	Y	Y	N	Y	Y
16 **Pitts**	Y	Y	N	N	Y	Y
17 Holden	Y	Y	Y	Y	Y	Y
18 **Murphy, T.**	Y	Y	Y	N	Y	Y
19 **Platts**	Y	Y	Y	N	Y	Y
RHODE ISLAND						
1 Kennedy	Y	Y	Y	Y	Y	Y
2 Langevin	Y	Y	Y	Y	Y	Y
SOUTH CAROLINA						
1 **Brown**	Y	Y	Y	N	Y	Y
2 **Wilson**	Y	Y	Y	N	Y	Y
3 **Barrett**	+	+	–	?	?	?
4 **Inglis**	Y	Y	Y	N	Y	Y
5 Spratt	Y	Y	Y	Y	Y	Y
6 Clyburn	Y	Y	Y	Y	Y	Y
SOUTH DAKOTA						
AL Herseth Sandlin	Y	?	Y	Y	Y	Y
TENNESSEE						
1 **Roe**	Y	Y	Y	N	Y	Y
2 **Duncan**	Y	Y	N	N	Y	Y
3 **Wamp**	Y	Y	Y	N	Y	Y
4 Davis	Y	Y	Y	Y	Y	Y
5 Cooper	Y	Y	Y	Y	Y	Y
6 Gordon	Y	Y	Y	Y	Y	Y
7 **Blackburn**	Y	Y	Y	N	Y	Y
8 Tanner	Y	Y	Y	Y	Y	Y
9 Cohen	Y	Y	Y	Y	Y	Y
TEXAS						
1 **Gohmert**	Y	Y	N	N	Y	Y
2 **Poe**	Y	Y	N	N	Y	Y
3 **Johnson, S.**	Y	Y	N	N	Y	Y
4 **Hall**	Y	Y	N	N	Y	Y
5 **Hensarling**	Y	Y	N	N	Y	Y
6 **Barton**	Y	Y	N	N	Y	Y
7 **Culberson**	Y	Y	N	N	Y	Y
8 **Brady**	Y	Y	N	N	Y	Y
9 Green, A.	Y	Y	Y	Y	Y	Y
10 **McCaul**	Y	Y	N	N	Y	Y
11 **Conaway**	Y	Y	N	N	Y	Y
12 **Granger**	Y	Y	N	N	Y	Y
13 **Thornberry**	Y	Y	N	N	Y	Y
14 **Paul**	Y	Y	N	N	Y	Y
15 Hinojosa	Y	Y	Y	Y	Y	Y
16 Reyes	Y	Y	Y	Y	Y	Y
17 Edwards	Y	Y	Y	Y	Y	Y
18 Jackson Lee	Y	Y	Y	Y	Y	Y
19 **Neugebauer**	Y	Y	N	N	Y	Y
20 Gonzalez	Y	Y	Y	Y	Y	Y
21 **Smith**	Y	Y	N	N	Y	Y
22 **Olson**	Y	Y	N	N	Y	Y
23 Rodriguez	Y	Y	Y	Y	Y	Y
24 **Marchant**	Y	Y	N	N	Y	Y
25 Doggett	Y	Y	Y	Y	Y	Y
26 **Burgess**	Y	Y	N	N	Y	Y
27 Ortiz	Y	Y	Y	Y	Y	Y
28 Cuellar	Y	Y	Y	Y	Y	Y
29 Green, G.	Y	Y	Y	Y	Y	Y
30 Johnson, E.	Y	Y	Y	Y	Y	Y
31 **Carter**	Y	Y	N	N	Y	Y
32 **Sessions**	Y	Y	N	N	Y	Y
UTAH						
1 **Bishop**	?	?	?	N	Y	Y
2 Matheson	Y	Y	N	Y	Y	Y
3 **Chaffetz**	Y	Y	N	N	Y	Y
VERMONT						
AL Welch	Y	Y	Y	Y	Y	Y
VIRGINIA						
1 **Wittman**	Y	Y	Y	N	Y	Y
2 Nye	Y	Y	N	Y	Y	Y
3 Scott	Y	Y	Y	Y	Y	Y
4 **Forbes**	Y	Y	Y	?	?	?
5 Perriello	Y	Y	N	Y	Y	Y
6 **Goodlatte**	Y	Y	N	N	Y	Y
7 **Cantor**	Y	Y	N	N	Y	?
8 Moran	Y	Y	N	Y	Y	Y
9 Boucher	Y	Y	Y	Y	Y	Y
10 **Wolf**	Y	Y	Y	N	Y	Y
11 Connolly	Y	Y	N	Y	Y	Y
WASHINGTON						
1 Inslee	Y	Y	Y	Y	Y	Y
2 Larsen	Y	Y	Y	Y	Y	Y
3 Baird	Y	Y	Y	Y	Y	Y
4 **Hastings**	?	?	?	N	Y	Y
5 **McMorris Rodgers**	Y	Y	Y	N	Y	Y
6 Dicks	Y	Y	Y	Y	Y	Y
7 McDermott	Y	Y	Y	Y	Y	Y
8 **Reichert**	Y	Y	Y	Y	Y	Y
9 Smith	Y	Y	Y	Y	Y	Y
WEST VIRGINIA						
1 Mollohan	Y	Y	Y	Y	Y	Y
2 **Capito**	Y	Y	Y	N	Y	Y
3 Rahall	Y	Y	Y	Y	Y	Y
WISCONSIN						
1 **Ryan**	Y	Y	Y	N	Y	Y
2 Baldwin	Y	Y	Y	Y	Y	Y
3 Kind	Y	Y	Y	Y	Y	Y
4 Moore	Y	Y	Y	Y	Y	Y
5 **Sensenbrenner**	Y	Y	Y	N	Y	Y
6 **Petri**	Y	Y	Y	N	Y	Y
7 Obey	Y	Y	Y	Y	Y	Y
8 Kagen	Y	Y	Y	Y	Y	Y
WYOMING						
AL **Lummis**	Y	Y	N	N	Y	Y
DELEGATES						
Faleomavaega (A.S.)						
Norton (D.C.)						
Bordallo (Guam)						
Sablan (N. Marianas)						
Pierluisi (P.R.)						
Christensen (V.I.)						

IN THE HOUSE | By Vote Number

726. **HR 3614. Small-Business Programs Extension/Passage.**
Velázquez, D-N.Y., motion to suspend the rules and pass the bill that would extend through Oct. 31, 2009, the authorization of programs under the Small Business Act and the Small Business Investment Act of 1958. Motion agreed to 417-2: R 168-2; D 249-0. A two-thirds majority of those present and voting (280 in this case) is required for passage under suspension of the rules. Sept. 23, 2009.

727. **HR 324. Santa Cruz Valley National Heritage Area/Recommit.**
Bishop, R-Utah, motion to recommit the bill to the Natural Resources Committee with instructions that it be reported back immediately with language specifying that private property could not be included in the National Heritage Area without written consent from the owner, and an owner with private property within the National Heritage Area boundary could have the property removed by written request. It would specify the legislation could not restrict the Homeland Security Department from achieving operational control within the National Heritage Area. Motion agreed to 259-167: R 174-0; D 85-167. Sept. 23, 2009.

728. **HR 324. Santa Cruz Valley National Heritage Area/Passage.**
Passage of the bill that would establish the Santa Cruz Valley National Heritage Area in Santa Cruz and Pima counties in Arizona and authorize $1 million per fiscal year, with a maximum of $15 million. It would specify private property could not be included in the National Heritage Area without written consent of the owner, and the bill could not restrict the Homeland Security Department from achieving operational control within the National Heritage Area. Passed 281-142: R 29-142; D 252-0. Sept. 23, 2009.

729. **H Res 696. Western Wyoming Community College Anniversary/Adoption.** Hirono, D-Hawaii, motion to suspend the rules and adopt the resolution that would congratulate Western Wyoming Community College on its 50th anniversary. Motion agreed to 418-0: R 171-0; D 247-0. A two-thirds majority of those present and voting (279 in this case) is required for adoption under suspension of the rules. Sept. 23, 2009.

730. **Procedural Motion/Motion to Adjourn.** Simpson, R-Idaho, motion to adjourn. Motion rejected 42-355: R 38-126; D 4-229. Sept. 23, 2009.

731. **HR 3617. Transportation Funding Extension/Passage.** Oberstar, D-Minn., motion to suspend the rules and pass the bill that would extend funding for federal highway, transit, motor carrier safety and highway safety programs from Oct. 1, 2009, through Dec. 31, 2009, or when a multi-year law reauthorizing the programs is enacted, whichever comes earlier. Motion agreed to 335-85: R 86-85; D 249-0. A two-thirds majority of those present and voting (280 in this case) is required for passage under suspension of the rules. Sept. 23, 2009.

	726	727	728	729	730	731
ALABAMA						
1 **Bonner**	Y	Y	N	Y	N	Y
2 **Bright**	Y	Y	Y	Y	N	Y
3 **Rogers**	Y	Y	N	Y	N	Y
4 **Aderholt**	Y	Y	N	Y	Y	N
5 Griffith	Y	Y	Y	Y	N	Y
6 **Bachus**	Y	Y	N	Y	?	Y
7 Davis	Y	Y	Y	Y	Y	Y
ALASKA						
AL **Young**	Y	Y	Y	Y	?	Y
ARIZONA						
1 Kirkpatrick	Y	Y	Y	Y	N	Y
2 **Franks**	Y	Y	N	Y	N	N
3 **Shadegg**	?	Y	N	Y	N	Y
4 Pastor	Y	N	Y	Y	Y	Y
5 Mitchell	Y	Y	Y	Y	N	Y
6 **Flake**	N	Y	N	Y	N	N
7 Grijalva	Y	N	Y	Y	N	Y
8 Giffords	Y	Y	Y	Y	?	Y
ARKANSAS						
1 Berry	Y	N	Y	Y	N	Y
2 Snyder	Y	N	Y	Y	N	Y
3 **Boozman**	Y	Y	N	Y	N	Y
4 Ross	Y	Y	Y	Y	N	Y
CALIFORNIA						
1 Thompson	Y	N	Y	Y	N	Y
2 **Herger**	Y	Y	N	N	N	N
3 **Lungren**	Y	Y	N	Y	N	Y
4 **McClintock**	Y	Y	N	N	N	N
5 Matsui	Y	N	Y	Y	N	Y
6 Woolsey	Y	N	Y	Y	N	Y
7 Miller, George	Y	N	Y	Y	N	Y
8 Pelosi						
9 Lee	Y	N	Y	Y	N	Y
10 Vacant						
11 McNerney	Y	Y	Y	Y	N	Y
12 Speier	Y	N	Y	?	?	?
13 Stark	Y	N	Y	?	?	?
14 Eshoo	Y	N	Y	Y	N	Y
15 Honda	Y	N	Y	Y	N	Y
16 Lofgren	Y	N	Y	Y	N	Y
17 Farr	Y	N	Y	Y	N	Y
18 Cardoza	Y	Y	Y	Y	N	Y
19 **Radanovich**	?	Y	N	Y	N	N
20 Costa	Y	Y	Y	Y	?	Y
21 **Nunes**	Y	Y	N	Y	N	Y
22 **McCarthy**	Y	Y	N	Y	Y	N
23 Capps	Y	N	Y	Y	N	Y
24 **Gallegly**	Y	Y	N	Y	N	Y
25 **McKeon**	Y	Y	N	Y	N	Y
26 **Dreier**	Y	Y	N	Y	N	N
27 Sherman	Y	N	Y	Y	N	Y
28 Berman	Y	N	Y	Y	N	Y
29 Schiff	Y	N	Y	Y	N	Y
30 Waxman	Y	N	Y	Y	N	Y
31 Becerra	?	N	Y	Y	N	Y
32 Chu	Y	N	Y	Y	N	Y
33 Watson	Y	N	Y	Y	N	Y
34 Roybal-Allard	Y	N	Y	Y	N	Y
35 Waters	Y	N	Y	?	?	Y
36 Harman	Y	Y	Y	Y	N	Y
37 Richardson	Y	Y	Y	Y	N	Y
38 Napolitano	Y	N	Y	Y	N	Y
39 Sánchez, Linda	Y	N	Y	Y	N	Y
40 **Royce**	Y	Y	N	Y	N	?
41 **Lewis**	Y	Y	N	Y	N	Y
42 **Miller, Gary**	Y	Y	N	Y	N	Y
43 Baca	Y	N	Y	Y	N	Y
44 **Calvert**	Y	Y	N	Y	N	Y
45 **Bono Mack**	Y	Y	N	Y	N	Y
46 **Rohrabacher**	Y	Y	N	Y	N	N
47 Sanchez, Loretta	Y	N	Y	Y	N	Y
48 **Campbell**	Y	Y	N	Y	Y	N
49 **Issa**	Y	Y	N	Y	N	N
50 **Bilbray**	Y	Y	N	Y	N	Y
51 Filner	Y	N	Y	Y	N	Y
52 **Hunter**	Y	Y	N	Y	N	Y
53 Davis	Y	N	Y	Y	N	Y

	726	727	728	729	730	731
COLORADO						
1 DeGette	Y	N	Y	Y	N	Y
2 Polis	Y	N	Y	Y	N	Y
3 Salazar	Y	N	Y	Y	N	Y
4 Markey	Y	Y	Y	Y	N	Y
5 **Lamborn**	Y	Y	N	Y	N	N
6 **Coffman**	Y	Y	N	Y	N	N
7 Perlmutter	Y	N	Y	Y	N	Y
CONNECTICUT						
1 Larson	Y	N	Y	Y	N	Y
2 Courtney	Y	N	Y	Y	N	Y
3 DeLauro	Y	N	Y	Y	N	Y
4 Himes	Y	Y	Y	Y	N	Y
5 Murphy	Y	N	Y	Y	N	Y
DELAWARE						
AL **Castle**	Y	Y	Y	Y	N	Y
FLORIDA						
1 **Miller**	Y	Y	N	Y	N	N
2 Boyd	Y	Y	Y	Y	N	Y
3 Brown	Y	N	Y	Y	N	Y
4 **Crenshaw**	Y	Y	N	Y	N	N
5 **Brown-Waite**	Y	Y	Y	Y	N	Y
6 **Stearns**	Y	Y	N	Y	N	Y
7 **Mica**	Y	Y	N	Y	N	Y
8 Grayson	Y	N	Y	Y	N	Y
9 **Bilirakis**	Y	Y	N	Y	N	Y
10 **Young**	Y	Y	N	Y	N	Y
11 Castor	Y	N	Y	Y	N	Y
12 **Putnam**	Y	N	N	Y	N	Y
13 **Buchanan**	Y	Y	Y	Y	N	N
14 **Mack**	Y	Y	N	Y	N	N
15 **Posey**	Y	Y	Y	Y	Y	N
16 **Rooney**	Y	Y	N	Y	N	N
17 Meek	Y	N	Y	Y	N	Y
18 **Ros-Lehtinen**	?	Y	Y	Y	N	Y
19 Wexler	Y	N	Y	Y	N	Y
20 Wasserman Schultz	Y	N	Y	Y	N	Y
21 **Diaz-Balart, L.**	Y	Y	Y	Y	N	Y
22 Klein	Y	Y	Y	Y	N	Y
23 Hastings	Y	N	Y	Y	N	Y
24 Kosmas	Y	Y	Y	Y	N	Y
25 **Diaz-Balart, M.**	Y	Y	?	Y	N	Y
GEORGIA						
1 **Kingston**	Y	Y	N	Y	N	N
2 Bishop	Y	Y	Y	Y	N	Y
3 **Westmoreland**	Y	Y	N	Y	N	N
4 Johnson	Y	N	Y	Y	N	Y
5 Lewis	Y	N	Y	Y	N	Y
6 **Price**	Y	Y	N	Y	N	N
7 **Linder**	Y	N	N	Y	N	N
8 Marshall	Y	Y	Y	?	?	?
9 **Deal**	Y	Y	N	Y	N	?
10 **Broun**	Y	N	N	Y	N	N
11 **Gingrey**	Y	Y	N	Y	N	N
12 Barrow	Y	Y	Y	Y	N	Y
13 Scott	Y	N	Y	Y	N	Y
HAWAII						
1 Abercrombie	?	N	Y	Y	–	Y
2 Hirono	Y	N	Y	Y	N	Y
IDAHO						
1 Minnick	Y	Y	Y	?	N	Y
2 **Simpson**	Y	Y	Y	Y	Y	Y
ILLINOIS						
1 Rush	Y	N	Y	Y	N	Y
2 Jackson	Y	N	Y	Y	N	Y
3 Lipinski	Y	Y	Y	Y	N	Y
4 Gutierrez	Y	N	Y	Y	N	Y
5 Quigley	Y	N	Y	Y	N	Y
6 **Roskam**	Y	Y	N	Y	?	N
7 Davis	Y	N	Y	Y	?	Y
8 Bean	Y	Y	Y	Y	?	Y
9 Schakowsky	Y	N	Y	Y	N	Y
10 **Kirk**	Y	Y	Y	Y	?	Y
11 Halvorson	Y	Y	Y	Y	N	Y
12 Costello	Y	Y	Y	Y	N	Y
13 **Biggert**	Y	Y	N	Y	N	Y
14 Foster	Y	Y	Y	Y	N	Y
15 Johnson	Y	Y	N	Y	Y	Y

	726	727	728	729	730	731
16 **Manzullo**	Y	Y	N	Y	N	Y
17 Hare	Y	N	Y	Y	N	Y
18 **Schock**	Y	Y	?	Y	N	Y
19 **Shimkus**	Y	Y	N	Y	N	Y
INDIANA						
1 Visclosky	Y	N	Y	Y	N	Y
2 Donnelly	Y	Y	Y	Y	N	Y
3 **Souder**	Y	Y	N	Y	Y	Y
4 **Buyer**	Y	Y	Y	Y	Y	N
5 **Burton**	Y	Y	N	Y	N	Y
6 **Pence**	Y	Y	N	Y	N	N
7 Carson	Y	N	Y	Y	N	Y
8 Ellsworth	Y	Y	Y	Y	N	Y
9 Hill	Y	Y	Y	Y	N	Y
IOWA						
1 Braley	Y	N	Y	Y	N	Y
2 Loebsack	Y	N	Y	Y	N	Y
3 Boswell	Y	Y	Y	Y	N	Y
4 **Latham**	Y	Y	N	Y	N	Y
5 **King**	Y	Y	N	Y	Y	N
KANSAS						
1 **Moran**	Y	Y	N	Y	?	Y
2 **Jenkins**	Y	Y	N	Y	N	Y
3 Moore	Y	N	Y	Y	N	Y
4 **Tiahrt**	Y	Y	N	Y	Y	N
KENTUCKY						
1 **Whitfield**	Y	Y	N	Y	N	Y
2 **Guthrie**	Y	Y	N	Y	N	Y
3 Yarmuth	Y	N	Y	Y	N	Y
4 **Davis**	Y	Y	N	Y	N	N
5 **Rogers**	Y	Y	N	Y	N	Y
6 Chandler	?	Y	Y	Y	N	Y
LOUISIANA						
1 **Scalise**	Y	Y	N	Y	N	N
2 **Cao**	Y	Y	N	Y	N	Y
3 Melancon	Y	Y	Y	Y	N	Y
4 **Fleming**	Y	Y	N	Y	N	Y
5 **Alexander**	Y	Y	N	Y	Y	Y
6 **Cassidy**	Y	Y	N	Y	N	Y
7 **Boustany**	Y	Y	N	Y	N	N
MAINE						
1 Pingree	Y	N	Y	Y	N	Y
2 Michaud	Y	N	Y	Y	N	Y
MARYLAND						
1 Kratovil	Y	Y	Y	Y	N	Y
2 Ruppersberger	Y	N	Y	Y	N	Y
3 Sarbanes	Y	N	Y	Y	N	Y
4 Edwards	Y	N	Y	Y	N	Y
5 Hoyer	Y	N	Y	Y	N	Y
6 **Bartlett**	Y	Y	N	?	Y	N
7 Cummings	Y	N	Y	Y	N	Y
8 Van Hollen	Y	N	Y	Y	N	Y
MASSACHUSETTS						
1 Olver	Y	N	Y	Y	N	Y
2 Neal	Y	N	Y	Y	N	Y
3 McGovern	Y	N	Y	Y	N	Y
4 Frank	Y	N	Y	Y	?	Y
5 Tsongas	Y	N	Y	Y	N	Y
6 Tierney	Y	N	Y	Y	N	Y
7 Markey	Y	N	Y	Y	N	Y
8 Capuano	?	?	?	?	?	?
9 Lynch	Y	Y	Y	Y	N	Y
10 Delahunt	?	?	?	?	?	?
MICHIGAN						
1 Stupak	Y	N	Y	Y	N	Y
2 **Hoekstra**	Y	Y	N	Y	N	N
3 **Ehlers**	Y	Y	Y	Y	N	Y
4 **Camp**	Y	Y	N	Y	N	Y
5 Kildee	Y	N	Y	Y	N	Y
6 **Upton**	Y	Y	Y	Y	N	Y
7 Schauer	Y	Y	Y	Y	N	Y
8 **Rogers**	Y	Y	N	Y	N	N
9 Peters	Y	Y	Y	Y	N	Y
10 **Miller**	Y	Y	N	Y	Y	Y
11 **McCotter**	Y	Y	N	Y	N	Y
12 Levin	Y	N	Y	Y	N	Y
13 Kilpatrick	Y	N	Y	Y	?	Y
14 Conyers	Y	N	Y	Y	N	Y
15 Dingell	Y	N	Y	Y	?	Y
MINNESOTA						
1 Walz	Y	Y	Y	Y	N	Y
2 **Kline**	Y	Y	N	Y	N	N
3 **Paulsen**	Y	Y	Y	Y	N	Y
4 McCollum	Y	N	Y	Y	N	Y

	726	727	728	729	730	731
5 Ellison	Y	N	Y	Y	N	Y
6 **Bachmann**	Y	Y	N	Y	N	N
7 Peterson	Y	Y	Y	Y	N	Y
8 Oberstar	Y	N	Y	Y	N	Y
MISSISSIPPI						
1 Childers	Y	Y	Y	Y	N	Y
2 Thompson	Y	N	Y	Y	N	Y
3 **Harper**	Y	Y	N	Y	N	N
4 Taylor	Y	Y	Y	Y	N	Y
MISSOURI						
1 Clay	Y	N	Y	Y	Y	Y
2 **Akin**	Y	Y	N	Y	Y	N
3 Carnahan	Y	N	Y	Y	N	Y
4 Skelton	Y	Y	Y	Y	N	Y
5 Cleaver	Y	N	Y	Y	N	Y
6 **Graves**	Y	Y	N	Y	N	Y
7 **Blunt**	Y	Y	N	Y	N	N
8 **Emerson**	Y	Y	N	Y	N	Y
9 **Luetkemeyer**	Y	Y	N	Y	N	Y
MONTANA						
AL **Rehberg**	Y	Y	N	Y	Y	Y
NEBRASKA						
1 **Fortenberry**	Y	Y	Y	Y	N	Y
2 **Terry**	Y	Y	N	Y	N	Y
3 **Smith**	Y	Y	N	Y	N	N
NEVADA						
1 Berkley	Y	Y	Y	Y	N	Y
2 **Heller**	Y	Y	N	Y	Y	N
3 Titus	Y	Y	Y	Y	N	Y
NEW HAMPSHIRE						
1 Shea-Porter	Y	N	Y	Y	N	Y
2 Hodes	Y	Y	Y	Y	N	Y
NEW JERSEY						
1 Andrews	Y	N	Y	Y	N	Y
2 **LoBiondo**	Y	Y	Y	Y	N	Y
3 Adler	Y	Y	Y	Y	Y	Y
4 **Smith**	?	?	?	?	?	?
5 **Garrett**	Y	Y	N	Y	Y	N
6 Pallone	Y	N	Y	Y	N	Y
7 **Lance**	Y	Y	Y	Y	N	Y
8 Pascrell	Y	N	Y	Y	N	Y
9 Rothman	Y	N	Y	Y	N	Y
10 Payne	Y	N	Y	Y	N	Y
11 **Frelinghuysen**	Y	Y	Y	Y	N	Y
12 Holt	Y	N	Y	Y	N	Y
13 Sires	Y	N	Y	Y	N	Y
NEW MEXICO						
1 Heinrich	Y	N	Y	Y	N	Y
2 Teague	Y	Y	Y	Y	N	Y
3 Lujan	Y	N	Y	Y	N	Y
NEW YORK						
1 Bishop	Y	Y	Y	Y	N	Y
2 Israel	Y	Y	Y	Y	N	Y
3 **King**	Y	Y	N	Y	N	Y
4 McCarthy	Y	Y	Y	Y	N	Y
5 Ackerman	Y	N	Y	Y	N	Y
6 Meeks	Y	N	Y	Y	?	Y
7 Crowley	Y	N	Y	Y	N	Y
8 Nadler	Y	N	Y	Y	N	Y
9 Weiner	Y	N	Y	Y	N	Y
10 Towns	Y	N	Y	Y	N	Y
11 Clarke	Y	N	Y	Y	N	Y
12 Velázquez	Y	N	Y	Y	N	Y
13 McMahon	Y	Y	Y	Y	N	Y
14 Maloney	Y	N	Y	Y	N	Y
15 Rangel	Y	N	Y	Y	N	Y
16 Serrano	Y	N	Y	Y	N	Y
17 Engel	Y	N	Y	Y	N	Y
18 Lowey	Y	N	Y	Y	?	Y
19 Hall	Y	N	Y	Y	N	Y
20 Murphy	Y	Y	Y	Y	N	Y
21 Tonko	Y	N	Y	Y	N	Y
22 Hinchey	Y	N	Y	Y	N	Y
23 Vacant						
24 Arcuri	Y	Y	Y	?	N	Y
25 Maffei	Y	Y	Y	Y	N	Y
26 **Lee**	Y	Y	N	Y	N	Y
27 Higgins	Y	N	Y	Y	N	Y
28 Slaughter	Y	N	Y	Y	?	Y
29 Massa	Y	Y	Y	Y	N	Y
NORTH CAROLINA						
1 Butterfield	Y	N	Y	Y	N	Y
2 Etheridge	Y	Y	Y	Y	?	Y
3 **Jones**	Y	Y	Y	Y	N	Y
4 Price	Y	N	Y	Y	N	Y

	726	727	728	729	730	731
5 **Foxx**	Y	Y	N	Y	Y	N
6 **Coble**	Y	Y	N	Y	N	N
7 McIntyre	Y	Y	Y	Y	N	Y
8 Kissell	Y	Y	Y	Y	N	Y
9 **Myrick**	Y	Y	N	Y	N	N
10 **McHenry**	Y	Y	N	Y	Y	N
11 Shuler	Y	Y	Y	Y	N	Y
12 Watt	Y	N	Y	Y	N	Y
13 Miller	Y	N	Y	Y	N	Y
NORTH DAKOTA						
AL Pomeroy	Y	N	Y	Y	N	Y
OHIO						
1 Driehaus	Y	Y	Y	Y	N	Y
2 **Schmidt**	Y	Y	N	Y	N	Y
3 **Turner**	Y	Y	Y	Y	N	Y
4 **Jordan**	Y	Y	N	Y	N	N
5 **Latta**	Y	Y	N	Y	N	N
6 Wilson	Y	N	Y	Y	N	Y
7 **Austria**	Y	Y	N	Y	N	Y
8 **Boehner**	Y	Y	N	?	?	N
9 Kaptur	Y	N	Y	Y	N	Y
10 Kucinich	Y	N	Y	Y	N	Y
11 Fudge	Y	N	Y	Y	N	Y
12 **Tiberi**	Y	Y	N	Y	N	N
13 Sutton	Y	N	Y	Y	N	Y
14 **LaTourette**	Y	Y	Y	Y	N	Y
15 Kilroy	Y	N	Y	Y	N	Y
16 Boccieri	Y	Y	Y	Y	N	Y
17 Ryan	Y	N	Y	Y	N	Y
18 Space	Y	Y	Y	Y	N	Y
OKLAHOMA						
1 **Sullivan**	Y	Y	N	Y	N	N
2 Boren	Y	Y	Y	Y	N	Y
3 **Lucas**	Y	Y	N	Y	N	N
4 **Cole**	Y	Y	N	Y	N	N
5 **Fallin**	Y	Y	N	Y	N	Y
OREGON						
1 Wu	Y	N	Y	Y	N	Y
2 **Walden**	Y	Y	N	Y	N	Y
3 Blumenauer	Y	N	Y	Y	N	Y
4 DeFazio	Y	N	Y	Y	N	Y
5 Schrader	Y	N	Y	Y	N	Y
PENNSYLVANIA						
1 Brady	Y	N	Y	Y	N	Y
2 Fattah	Y	N	Y	Y	N	Y
3 Dahlkemper	Y	Y	Y	Y	N	Y
4 Altmire	Y	Y	Y	Y	N	Y
5 **Thompson**	Y	Y	Y	Y	N	Y
6 **Gerlach**	Y	Y	Y	Y	N	Y
7 Sestak	Y	Y	Y	Y	N	Y
8 Murphy, P.	Y	Y	Y	Y	N	Y
9 **Shuster**	Y	Y	?	Y	N	Y
10 Carney	Y	Y	Y	Y	N	Y
11 Kanjorski	Y	Y	Y	Y	N	Y
12 Murtha	Y	N	Y	Y	N	Y
13 Schwartz	Y	Y	Y	Y	Y	Y
14 Doyle	?	?	?	?	?	?
15 **Dent**	Y	Y	Y	Y	N	Y
16 **Pitts**	Y	Y	N	Y	Y	N
17 Holden	Y	Y	Y	?	N	Y
18 **Murphy, T.**	Y	Y	Y	Y	N	Y
19 **Platts**	Y	Y	Y	Y	N	Y
RHODE ISLAND						
1 Kennedy	Y	N	Y	Y	?	Y
2 Langevin	Y	N	Y	Y	N	Y
SOUTH CAROLINA						
1 **Brown**	Y	Y	N	Y	N	Y
2 **Wilson**	Y	Y	N	Y	N	N
3 **Barrett**	?	?	?	?	?	?
4 **Inglis**	Y	Y	N	Y	Y	N
5 Spratt	Y	N	Y	Y	N	Y
6 Clyburn	Y	N	Y	Y	N	Y
SOUTH DAKOTA						
AL Herseth Sandlin	Y	Y	Y	Y	N	Y
TENNESSEE						
1 **Roe**	Y	Y	N	Y	N	N
2 **Duncan**	Y	Y	N	Y	N	N
3 **Wamp**	Y	Y	N	Y	N	Y
4 Davis	Y	Y	Y	Y	N	Y
5 Cooper	Y	N	Y	Y	N	Y
6 Gordon	Y	Y	Y	Y	N	Y
7 **Blackburn**	Y	Y	N	Y	Y	N
8 Tanner	Y	Y	Y	Y	N	Y
9 Cohen	Y	N	Y	Y	N	Y

	726	727	728	729	730	731
TEXAS						
1 **Gohmert**	Y	Y	N	Y	Y	Y
2 **Poe**	?	Y	N	Y	N	Y
3 **Johnson, S.**	Y	Y	N	Y	Y	N
4 **Hall**	Y	Y	N	Y	N	Y
5 **Hensarling**	Y	Y	N	Y	Y	N
6 **Barton**	Y	Y	N	Y	Y	Y
7 **Culberson**	Y	Y	N	Y	N	Y
8 **Brady**	Y	Y	N	Y	N	N
9 Green, A.	Y	N	Y	Y	N	Y
10 **McCaul**	Y	Y	N	Y	N	Y
11 **Conaway**	Y	Y	N	Y	N	N
12 **Granger**	Y	?	?	?	?	?
13 **Thornberry**	Y	Y	N	Y	Y	N
14 **Paul**	N	Y	N	Y	N	N
15 Hinojosa	Y	N	Y	Y	N	Y
16 Reyes	Y	N	Y	Y	N	Y
17 Edwards	Y	Y	Y	Y	?	Y
18 Jackson Lee	Y	N	Y	Y	N	Y
19 **Neugebauer**	Y	Y	N	Y	N	N
20 Gonzalez	Y	N	Y	Y	N	Y
21 **Smith**	Y	Y	N	Y	N	N
22 **Olson**	Y	Y	N	Y	Y	N
23 Rodriguez	Y	N	Y	Y	N	Y
24 **Marchant**	Y	Y	N	Y	?	Y
25 Doggett	Y	N	Y	?	N	Y
26 **Burgess**	Y	Y	N	Y	N	N
27 Ortiz	Y	N	Y	Y	–	Y
28 Cuellar	Y	Y	Y	Y	N	Y
29 Green, G.	Y	N	Y	Y	N	Y
30 Johnson, E.	Y	N	Y	Y	N	Y
31 **Carter**	Y	Y	N	Y	Y	N
32 **Sessions**	Y	Y	N	Y	?	N
UTAH						
1 **Bishop**	Y	Y	Y	Y	?	?
2 Matheson	Y	Y	Y	Y	N	Y
3 **Chaffetz**	Y	Y	N	Y	Y	N
VERMONT						
AL Welch	Y	N	Y	Y	N	Y
VIRGINIA						
1 **Wittman**	Y	Y	N	Y	N	Y
2 Nye	Y	Y	Y	Y	N	Y
3 Scott	Y	N	Y	Y	N	Y
4 **Forbes**	?	Y	N	Y	N	Y
5 Perriello	Y	Y	Y	Y	N	Y
6 **Goodlatte**	Y	Y	N	Y	N	N
7 **Cantor**	Y	Y	N	Y	N	N
8 Moran	Y	N	Y	Y	N	Y
9 Boucher	Y	Y	Y	Y	N	Y
10 **Wolf**	Y	Y	N	Y	N	N
11 Connolly	Y	N	Y	Y	N	Y
WASHINGTON						
1 Inslee	Y	N	Y	Y	N	Y
2 Larsen	Y	N	Y	Y	N	Y
3 Baird	Y	Y	Y	Y	N	Y
4 **Hastings**	Y	Y	N	Y	Y	N
5 **McMorris Rodgers**	Y	Y	N	Y	?	N
6 Dicks	Y	N	Y	Y	N	Y
7 McDermott	Y	N	Y	Y	N	Y
8 **Reichert**	Y	Y	Y	Y	N	Y
9 Smith	Y	N	Y	Y	N	Y
WEST VIRGINIA						
1 Mollohan	Y	N	Y	Y	N	Y
2 **Capito**	Y	Y	N	Y	N	Y
3 Rahall	Y	N	Y	Y	N	Y
WISCONSIN						
1 **Ryan**	Y	Y	N	Y	N	N
2 Baldwin	Y	N	Y	Y	N	Y
3 Kind	Y	Y	Y	Y	N	Y
4 Moore	Y	N	Y	Y	N	Y
5 **Sensenbrenner**	Y	Y	N	Y	Y	N
6 **Petri**	Y	Y	Y	Y	N	Y
7 Obey	Y	N	Y	Y	N	Y
8 Kagen	Y	Y	Y	Y	N	Y
WYOMING						
AL **Lummis**	Y	Y	N	?	N	N
DELEGATES						
Faleomavaega (A.S.)						
Norton (D.C.)						
Bordallo (Guam)						
Sablan (N. Marianas)						
Pierluisi (P.R.)						
Christensen (V.I.)						

IN THE HOUSE | By Vote Number

732. Procedural Motion/Motion to Adjourn. Kingston, R-Ga., motion to adjourn. Motion rejected 50-349: R 46-122; D 4-227. Sept. 23, 2009.

733. HR 2918. Fiscal 2010 Legislative Branch Appropriations/ Previous Question. Wasserman Schultz, D-Fla., motion to order the previous question (thus ending debate and possibility of amendment) on a motion that the House disagree to the Senate amendment and agree to a conference on the bill that would appropriate $3.7 billion in fiscal 2010 for legislative branch operations, excluding Senate operations. Motion agreed to 240-171: R 1-169; D 239-2. Sept. 23, 2009.

734. HR 2918. Fiscal 2010 Legislative Branch Appropriations/ Motion to Instruct. Aderholt, R-Ala., motion to instruct conferees to disagree to any proposition that would violate a rule that requires modifications to be germane; insist on provisions that do not allow the use of funds in the bill to restrict guided tours of the Capitol by members' offices; and approve the final conference agreement only if it has been available to the managers for at least 48 hours. Motion rejected 191-213: R 169-1; D 22-212. Sept. 23, 2009.

735. HR 3631. Medicare Premium Adjustment/Rule. Adoption of the rule (H Res 766) to provide for House floor consideration of a Medicare bill under suspension of the rules through the legislative day of Sept. 24, 2009. The bill would adjust 2010 Medicare premiums to equal 2009 premiums, paid for by a reduction of the same amount to Medicare Improvement Fund expenditures for fiscal 2014. Adopted 235-182: R 0-172; D 235-10. Sept. 24, 2009.

736. H Con Res 163. National Job Corps Day/Adoption. Lynch, D-Mass., motion to suspend the rules and adopt the concurrent resolution that would support the designation of National Job Corps Day and encourage states and local governments to observe the day with appropriate activities. Motion agreed to 413-4: R 167-4; D 246-0. A two-thirds majority of those present and voting (278 in this case) is required for adoption under suspension of the rules. Sept. 24, 2009.

737. HR 3631. Medicare Premium Adjustment/Passage. Pallone, D-N.J., motion to suspend the rules and pass the bill that would adjust 2010 Medicare premiums to equal 2009 premiums, paid for by a reduction of the same amount to Medicare Improvement Fund expenditures for fiscal 2014. Motion agreed to 406-18: R 161-13; D 245-5. A two-thirds majority of those present and voting (283 in this case) is required for passage under suspension of the rules. Sept. 24, 2009.

	732	733	734	735	736	737
ALABAMA						
1 Bonner	N	N	Y	N	Y	Y
2 Bright	N	Y	Y	N	Y	Y
3 Rogers	N	N	Y	N	Y	Y
4 Aderholt	Y	N	Y	N	Y	Y
5 Griffith	N	Y	N	Y	Y	Y
6 Bachus	N	N	Y	N	Y	Y
7 Davis	N	Y	N	Y	Y	Y
ALASKA						
AL Young	Y	N	Y	N	Y	Y
ARIZONA						
1 Kirkpatrick	N	Y	Y	Y	Y	Y
2 Franks	N	N	Y	N	Y	Y
3 Shadegg	Y	N	Y	N	Y	N
4 Pastor	N	Y	N	Y	Y	Y
5 Mitchell	N	N	Y	Y	Y	Y
6 Flake	Y	N	Y	N	N	N
7 Grijalva	?	Y	N	Y	Y	Y
8 Giffords	N	Y	Y	Y	Y	Y
ARKANSAS						
1 Berry	N	Y	N	Y	Y	Y
2 Snyder	N	Y	N	Y	Y	Y
3 Boozman	N	N	Y	N	Y	Y
4 Ross	N	Y	N	Y	Y	Y
CALIFORNIA						
1 Thompson	N	Y	N	Y	Y	Y
2 Herger	N	N	Y	N	Y	Y
3 Lungren	Y	N	Y	N	Y	Y
4 McClintock	N	N	Y	N	Y	N
5 Matsui	N	Y	N	Y	Y	Y
6 Woolsey	?	Y	N	Y	Y	Y
7 Miller, George	?	?	N	Y	Y	Y
8 Pelosi						
9 Lee	N	Y	N	Y	Y	Y
10 Vacant						
11 McNerney	N	?	N	Y	Y	Y
12 Speier	?	?	?	?	?	?
13 Stark	?	?	?	Y	Y	Y
14 Eshoo	N	Y	N	Y	Y	Y
15 Honda	N	?	N	Y	Y	Y
16 Lofgren	N	Y	N	Y	Y	Y
17 Farr	N	Y	N	Y	Y	Y
18 Cardoza	N	Y	N	Y	Y	Y
19 Radanovich	N	N	Y	N	Y	Y
20 Costa	N	Y	N	Y	Y	Y
21 Nunes	N	N	Y	N	Y	Y
22 McCarthy	N	N	Y	N	Y	Y
23 Capps	N	Y	N	Y	Y	Y
24 Gallegly	N	N	Y	N	Y	Y
25 McKeon	N	N	?	N	Y	Y
26 Dreier	N	N	Y	N	Y	Y
27 Sherman	N	Y	N	Y	Y	Y
28 Berman	N	Y	?	Y	Y	Y
29 Schiff	N	Y	N	Y	Y	Y
30 Waxman	N	?	?	Y	Y	Y
31 Becerra	N	Y	N	Y	Y	Y
32 Chu	N	Y	N	Y	Y	Y
33 Watson	N	Y	N	Y	Y	Y
34 Roybal-Allard	?	Y	N	Y	Y	Y
35 Waters	N	Y	N	Y	Y	Y
36 Harman	N	Y	N	Y	Y	Y
37 Richardson	N	?	?	Y	Y	Y
38 Napolitano	?	Y	N	Y	Y	Y
39 Sánchez, Linda	N	Y	N	Y	Y	Y
40 Royce	N	N	Y	N	Y	Y
41 Lewis	N	N	Y	N	Y	Y
42 Miller, Gary	N	N	Y	N	Y	Y
43 Baca	N	Y	N	Y	Y	Y
44 Calvert	N	N	Y	N	Y	Y
45 Bono Mack	N	N	Y	N	Y	Y
46 Rohrabacher	N	N	Y	N	Y	Y
47 Sanchez, Loretta	N	Y	N	Y	Y	Y
48 Campbell	Y	N	Y	N	Y	Y
49 Issa	N	N	Y	N	Y	Y
50 Bilbray	N	N	Y	N	Y	Y
51 Filner	N	Y	N	Y	Y	Y
52 Hunter	N	N	Y	N	Y	Y
53 Davis	N	Y	N	Y	Y	Y
COLORADO						
1 DeGette	N	Y	N	Y	Y	Y
2 Polis	N	Y	N	Y	Y	Y
3 Salazar	N	Y	N	Y	Y	Y
4 Markey	N	Y	N	Y	Y	Y
5 Lamborn	Y	N	Y	N	Y	N
6 Coffman	Y	N	Y	N	Y	Y
7 Perlmutter	N	Y	N	Y	Y	Y
CONNECTICUT						
1 Larson	?	Y	N	Y	+	Y
2 Courtney	N	Y	N	Y	Y	Y
3 DeLauro	N	Y	N	Y	Y	Y
4 Himes	Y	N	Y	N	Y	Y
5 Murphy	N	Y	N	Y	Y	Y
DELAWARE						
AL Castle	N	N	Y	N	Y	Y
FLORIDA						
1 Miller	N	N	Y	N	Y	Y
2 Boyd	?	?	?	Y	Y	Y
3 Brown	N	Y	N	Y	Y	Y
4 Crenshaw	N	N	Y	N	Y	Y
5 Brown-Waite	N	N	Y	N	Y	Y
6 Stearns	N	N	Y	N	Y	Y
7 Mica	N	N	Y	N	Y	Y
8 Grayson	N	Y	N	Y	Y	Y
9 Bilirakis	N	N	Y	N	Y	Y
10 Young	N	N	Y	N	Y	Y
11 Castor	N	Y	N	Y	Y	Y
12 Putnam	N	N	Y	N	Y	Y
13 Buchanan	N	N	Y	N	Y	Y
14 Mack	N	?	Y	N	Y	Y
15 Posey	N	N	Y	N	Y	Y
16 Rooney	N	N	Y	–	+	Y
17 Meek	?	N	Y	Y	Y	Y
18 Ros-Lehtinen	N	N	Y	N	Y	Y
19 Wexler	N	Y	N	Y	Y	Y
20 Wasserman Schultz	N	Y	N	Y	Y	Y
21 Diaz-Balart, L.	N	N	Y	N	Y	Y
22 Klein	N	Y	N	Y	Y	Y
23 Hastings	N	Y	N	Y	Y	Y
24 Kosmas	N	Y	N	Y	Y	Y
25 Diaz-Balart, M.	N	N	Y	N	Y	Y
GEORGIA						
1 Kingston	Y	N	Y	N	Y	Y
2 Bishop	N	Y	N	Y	Y	Y
3 Westmoreland	N	N	Y	N	Y	Y
4 Johnson	N	Y	N	?	Y	Y
5 Lewis	?	Y	N	?	?	Y
6 Price	Y	N	Y	N	Y	Y
7 Linder	Y	N	Y	N	Y	Y
8 Marshall	N	Y	Y	Y	Y	Y
9 Deal	N	N	Y	N	N	Y
10 Broun	Y	N	Y	N	N	N
11 Gingrey	Y	N	Y	N	Y	Y
12 Barrow	N	Y	N	Y	Y	Y
13 Scott	N	Y	N	Y	Y	Y
HAWAII						
1 Abercrombie	N	Y	N	Y	Y	Y
2 Hirono	N	Y	N	Y	Y	Y
IDAHO						
1 Minnick	N	N	N	Y	Y	Y
2 Simpson	N	N	Y	N	Y	Y
ILLINOIS						
1 Rush	?	Y	N	Y	Y	Y
2 Jackson	N	Y	N	Y	Y	Y
3 Lipinski	N	Y	N	Y	Y	Y
4 Gutierrez	N	Y	N	Y	Y	Y
5 Quigley	N	Y	N	Y	Y	Y
6 Roskam	?	N	Y	N	Y	Y
7 Davis	N	Y	N	Y	Y	Y
8 Bean	?	Y	?	Y	Y	N
9 Schakowsky	N	Y	N	Y	Y	Y
10 Kirk	N	N	Y	N	Y	Y
11 Halvorson	N	Y	N	Y	Y	Y
12 Costello	N	Y	N	Y	Y	Y
13 Biggert	N	N	Y	N	Y	Y
14 Foster	N	Y	N	Y	Y	Y
15 Johnson	N	N	N	N	Y	Y

KEY	**Republicans**	Democrats	
Y Voted for (yea)	X Paired against	C Voted "present" to avoid possible conflict of interest
# Paired for	– Announced against	
+ Announced for	P Voted "present"	? Did not vote or otherwise make a position known
N Voted against (nay)		

	732	733	734	735	736	737
16 **Manzullo**	N	N	Y	N	Y	Y
17 Hare	N	Y	N	Y	Y	Y
18 **Schock**	N	N	Y	N	Y	Y
19 **Shimkus**	?	N	Y	N	Y	Y
INDIANA						
1 Visclosky	N	Y	N	Y	Y	Y
2 Donnelly	N	Y	Y	Y	Y	Y
3 **Souder**	Y	N	Y	N	Y	Y
4 **Buyer**	Y	N	Y	N	Y	?
5 **Burton**	N	N	Y	N	Y	Y
6 **Pence**	N	N	Y	N	Y	N
7 Carson	N	Y	N	Y	Y	Y
8 Ellsworth	N	Y	Y	Y	Y	Y
9 Hill	N	Y	N	N	Y	N
IOWA						
1 Braley	N	Y	N	Y	Y	Y
2 Loebsack	N	Y	N	Y	Y	Y
3 Boswell	N	Y	N	Y	Y	Y
4 **Latham**	N	N	Y	N	Y	Y
5 **King**	Y	N	Y	N	Y	Y
KANSAS						
1 **Moran**	N	N	Y	N	Y	Y
2 **Jenkins**	N	N	Y	N	Y	Y
3 Moore	?	Y	N	N	Y	Y
4 **Tiahrt**	Y	N	Y	N	Y	Y
KENTUCKY						
1 **Whitfield**	N	N	Y	N	Y	Y
2 **Guthrie**	N	N	Y	N	Y	Y
3 Yarmuth	N	Y	N	Y	Y	Y
4 **Davis**	N	N	Y	N	Y	Y
5 **Rogers**	N	N	Y	N	Y	Y
6 Chandler	N	Y	N	N	Y	Y
LOUISIANA						
1 **Scalise**	N	N	Y	N	Y	Y
2 **Cao**	N	Y	Y	N	Y	Y
3 Melancon	N	Y	N	Y	Y	Y
4 **Fleming**	N	N	Y	N	Y	Y
5 **Alexander**	N	N	Y	N	Y	Y
6 **Cassidy**	N	N	Y	N	Y	Y
7 **Boustany**	N	N	Y	N	Y	Y
MAINE						
1 Pingree	N	Y	N	Y	Y	Y
2 Michaud	N	Y	N	Y	Y	Y
MARYLAND						
1 Kratovil	N	Y	Y	Y	Y	Y
2 Ruppersberger	N	Y	Y	Y	Y	Y
3 Sarbanes	?	Y	N	Y	Y	Y
4 Edwards	N	Y	N	Y	Y	Y
5 Hoyer	N	Y	N	Y	Y	N
6 **Bartlett**	Y	N	Y	N	Y	Y
7 Cummings	N	Y	N	Y	Y	Y
8 Van Hollen	N	Y	N	Y	Y	Y
MASSACHUSETTS						
1 Olver	N	Y	N	Y	Y	Y
2 Neal	N	Y	N	Y	Y	Y
3 McGovern	N	?	?	Y	Y	Y
4 Frank	N	Y	N	Y	Y	Y
5 Tsongas	N	Y	N	Y	Y	Y
6 Tierney	N	Y	N	Y	Y	Y
7 Markey	N	Y	N	Y	Y	Y
8 Capuano	?	?	?	Y	Y	Y
9 Lynch	N	Y	N	Y	Y	Y
10 Delahunt	?	?	?	?	?	?
MICHIGAN						
1 Stupak	N	Y	N	Y	Y	Y
2 **Hoekstra**	N	N	Y	N	Y	Y
3 **Ehlers**	N	N	Y	N	Y	Y
4 **Camp**	N	N	Y	N	Y	Y
5 Kildee	N	Y	N	Y	Y	Y
6 **Upton**	N	N	Y	N	Y	Y
7 Schauer	N	Y	N	Y	Y	Y
8 **Rogers**	N	N	Y	N	Y	Y
9 Peters	N	Y	N	Y	Y	Y
10 **Miller**	N	N	Y	N	Y	Y
11 **McCotter**	N	N	Y	N	Y	Y
12 Levin	N	Y	N	Y	Y	Y
13 Kilpatrick	N	Y	N	Y	Y	Y
14 Conyers	N	Y	N	+	+	Y
15 Dingell	N	Y	N	Y	Y	Y
MINNESOTA						
1 Walz	N	Y	N	Y	Y	Y
2 **Kline**	N	N	Y	N	Y	Y
3 **Paulsen**	N	N	Y	N	Y	Y
4 McCollum	N	Y	N	Y	Y	Y

	732	733	734	735	736	737
5 Ellison	N	Y	N	Y	Y	Y
6 **Bachmann**	N	N	Y	N	Y	Y
7 Peterson	N	Y	N	Y	Y	Y
8 Oberstar	N	Y	N	Y	Y	Y
MISSISSIPPI						
1 Childers	N	Y	Y	N	Y	Y
2 Thompson	?	Y	N	Y	Y	Y
3 **Harper**	Y	N	Y	N	Y	Y
4 Taylor	Y	Y	Y	N	Y	Y
MISSOURI						
1 Clay	Y	Y	Y	?	Y	Y
2 **Akin**	Y	N	Y	N	Y	N
3 Carnahan	N	Y	N	Y	Y	Y
4 Skelton	N	?	?	Y	Y	Y
5 Cleaver	N	Y	N	Y	Y	Y
6 **Graves**	N	N	Y	?	?	?
7 **Blunt**	N	N	?	N	Y	Y
8 **Emerson**	N	N	Y	N	Y	Y
9 **Luetkemeyer**	N	N	Y	N	Y	Y
MONTANA						
AL **Rehberg**	N	N	Y	N	Y	Y
NEBRASKA						
1 **Fortenberry**	N	N	Y	N	Y	Y
2 **Terry**	N	N	Y	N	Y	Y
3 **Smith**	N	N	Y	N	Y	Y
NEVADA						
1 Berkley	N	Y	N	Y	Y	Y
2 **Heller**	Y	N	Y	N	Y	Y
3 Titus	N	Y	N	Y	Y	Y
NEW HAMPSHIRE						
1 Shea-Porter	N	Y	N	Y	Y	Y
2 Hodes	N	Y	N	Y	Y	Y
NEW JERSEY						
1 Andrews	N	Y	N	Y	Y	Y
2 **LoBiondo**	N	N	Y	N	Y	Y
3 Adler	N	Y	N	Y	Y	Y
4 **Smith**	?	?	?	N	Y	Y
5 **Garrett**	Y	N	Y	N	Y	N
6 Pallone	N	Y	N	Y	Y	Y
7 **Lance**	N	N	Y	N	Y	Y
8 Pascrell	N	Y	N	Y	Y	Y
9 Rothman	N	Y	N	Y	Y	Y
10 Payne	N	Y	N	Y	Y	Y
11 **Frelinghuysen**	N	N	Y	N	Y	Y
12 Holt	N	Y	N	Y	Y	Y
13 Sires	N	Y	N	Y	Y	Y
NEW MEXICO						
1 Heinrich	N	Y	N	Y	Y	Y
2 Teague	N	Y	Y	Y	Y	Y
3 Lujan	N	Y	N	Y	Y	Y
NEW YORK						
1 Bishop	N	Y	N	Y	Y	Y
2 Israel	N	Y	N	?	?	?
3 **King**	N	N	Y	N	Y	Y
4 McCarthy	N	Y	N	Y	Y	Y
5 Ackerman	N	Y	N	Y	Y	Y
6 Meeks	N	Y	N	Y	Y	Y
7 Crowley	N	Y	N	Y	Y	Y
8 Nadler	N	Y	N	Y	Y	Y
9 Weiner	N	Y	N	Y	Y	Y
10 Towns	N	Y	N	?	?	Y
11 Clarke	N	Y	N	?	Y	Y
12 Velázquez	?	Y	N	Y	Y	Y
13 McMahon	N	Y	Y	Y	Y	Y
14 Maloney	N	Y	N	Y	Y	Y
15 Rangel	N	Y	N	Y	Y	Y
16 Serrano	N	Y	N	Y	Y	Y
17 Engel	N	Y	N	Y	Y	Y
18 Lowey	N	Y	N	Y	Y	Y
19 Hall	N	Y	N	Y	Y	Y
20 Murphy	?	Y	Y	N	Y	Y
21 Tonko	N	Y	N	Y	Y	Y
22 Hinchey	N	Y	N	Y	Y	Y
23 Vacant						
24 Arcuri	N	Y	N	Y	Y	Y
25 Maffei	N	Y	N	Y	Y	Y
26 **Lee**	N	N	Y	N	Y	Y
27 Higgins	N	Y	N	Y	Y	Y
28 Slaughter	N	Y	N	Y	Y	Y
29 Massa	N	Y	N	Y	Y	Y
NORTH CAROLINA						
1 Butterfield	N	Y	N	Y	Y	Y
2 Etheridge	N	Y	N	Y	Y	Y
3 **Jones**	N	N	Y	N	Y	Y
4 Price	N	Y	N	Y	Y	Y

	732	733	734	735	736	737
5 **Foxx**	N	N	Y	N	Y	Y
6 **Coble**	N	N	Y	N	Y	Y
7 McIntyre	N	Y	Y	Y	Y	Y
8 Kissell	N	Y	N	Y	Y	Y
9 **Myrick**	N	N	Y	N	Y	Y
10 **McHenry**	Y	N	Y	N	Y	Y
11 Shuler	N	Y	N	N	Y	Y
12 Watt	N	Y	N	Y	Y	Y
13 Miller	N	Y	N	Y	Y	Y
NORTH DAKOTA						
AL Pomeroy	N	Y	N	Y	Y	Y
OHIO						
1 Driehaus	N	Y	N	Y	Y	Y
2 **Schmidt**	N	N	Y	N	Y	Y
3 **Turner**	Y	N	Y	N	Y	Y
4 **Jordan**	Y	N	Y	N	Y	N
5 **Latta**	N	N	Y	N	Y	Y
6 Wilson	N	Y	?	Y	Y	Y
7 **Austria**	N	N	Y	N	Y	Y
8 **Boehner**	?	?	?	N	Y	Y
9 Kaptur	N	Y	N	Y	Y	Y
10 Kucinich	N	Y	N	Y	Y	Y
11 Fudge	N	Y	N	Y	Y	Y
12 **Tiberi**	N	N	Y	N	Y	Y
13 Sutton	N	Y	N	Y	Y	Y
14 **LaTourette**	Y	N	Y	N	Y	Y
15 Kilroy	N	Y	N	Y	Y	Y
16 Boccieri	N	Y	N	Y	Y	Y
17 Ryan	N	Y	N	Y	Y	Y
18 Space	N	Y	N	Y	Y	Y
OKLAHOMA						
1 **Sullivan**	Y	N	Y	N	Y	Y
2 Boren	N	Y	Y	Y	Y	Y
3 **Lucas**	N	N	Y	N	Y	Y
4 **Cole**	N	N	Y	N	Y	Y
5 **Fallin**	N	N	Y	?	?	Y
OREGON						
1 Wu	N	Y	N	Y	Y	Y
2 **Walden**	N	N	Y	N	Y	Y
3 Blumenauer	N	Y	N	Y	Y	Y
4 DeFazio	N	Y	N	Y	Y	Y
5 Schrader	N	Y	N	Y	?	Y
PENNSYLVANIA						
1 Brady	N	Y	N	Y	Y	Y
2 Fattah	N	Y	N	Y	Y	Y
3 Dahlkemper	N	Y	N	Y	Y	Y
4 Altmire	N	Y	Y	Y	Y	Y
5 **Thompson**	N	N	Y	N	Y	Y
6 **Gerlach**	N	N	Y	N	Y	Y
7 Sestak	?	?	?	Y	Y	Y
8 Murphy, P.	N	Y	N	Y	Y	Y
9 **Shuster**	N	N	Y	N	Y	Y
10 Carney	N	Y	N	Y	Y	Y
11 Kanjorski	N	Y	?	Y	Y	Y
12 Murtha	N	Y	?	Y	Y	Y
13 Schwartz	N	Y	N	Y	Y	Y
14 Doyle	?	?	?	?	?	?
15 **Dent**	N	N	Y	N	Y	Y
16 **Pitts**	Y	N	?	N	Y	Y
17 Holden	?	Y	N	Y	Y	Y
18 **Murphy, T.**	N	?	Y	N	Y	Y
19 **Platts**	N	N	Y	?	Y	Y
RHODE ISLAND						
1 Kennedy	N	Y	Y	Y	Y	Y
2 Langevin	N	Y	N	Y	Y	Y
SOUTH CAROLINA						
1 **Brown**	N	N	Y	N	Y	Y
2 **Wilson**	N	N	Y	N	Y	Y
3 **Barrett**	?	?	?	?	?	?
4 **Inglis**	Y	N	Y	N	Y	Y
5 Spratt	N	Y	N	Y	Y	Y
6 Clyburn	N	Y	N	Y	Y	Y
SOUTH DAKOTA						
AL Herseth Sandlin	N	Y	N	Y	Y	Y
TENNESSEE						
1 **Roe**	N	N	Y	N	Y	Y
2 **Duncan**	N	N	Y	N	Y	Y
3 **Wamp**	N	N	Y	N	Y	Y
4 Davis	N	Y	N	Y	Y	Y
5 Cooper	N	Y	N	Y	Y	Y
6 Gordon	N	Y	N	Y	Y	Y
7 **Blackburn**	?	N	Y	N	N	Y
8 Tanner	N	Y	N	Y	Y	Y
9 Cohen	N	Y	N	Y	Y	Y

	732	733	734	735	736	737
TEXAS						
1 **Gohmert**	Y	N	Y	N	?	Y
2 **Poe**	N	N	Y	N	Y	Y
3 **Johnson, S.**	Y	N	Y	N	Y	Y
4 **Hall**	N	N	Y	N	Y	Y
5 **Hensarling**	Y	N	Y	N	Y	N
6 **Barton**	Y	N	Y	N	Y	Y
7 **Culberson**	N	N	Y	N	Y	Y
8 **Brady**	N	N	Y	N	Y	Y
9 Green, A.	N	Y	N	Y	Y	Y
10 **McCaul**	?	N	Y	N	Y	Y
11 **Conaway**	N	N	Y	N	Y	Y
12 **Granger**	?	?	?	N	Y	Y
13 **Thornberry**	Y	N	Y	N	Y	Y
14 **Paul**	Y	N	Y	N	Y	Y
15 Hinojosa	N	Y	N	Y	Y	Y
16 Reyes	N	Y	N	Y	Y	Y
17 Edwards	N	Y	?	Y	Y	Y
18 Jackson Lee	Y	Y	N	Y	Y	Y
19 **Neugebauer**	N	N	Y	N	Y	Y
20 Gonzalez	N	Y	N	Y	Y	Y
21 **Smith**	N	N	Y	N	Y	Y
22 **Olson**	Y	N	Y	N	Y	Y
23 Rodriguez	N	Y	N	Y	Y	Y
24 **Marchant**	N	N	Y	N	Y	Y
25 Doggett	N	Y	N	Y	Y	Y
26 **Burgess**	N	N	Y	N	Y	Y
27 Ortiz	N	Y	N	Y	Y	Y
28 Cuellar	N	Y	N	Y	Y	Y
29 Green, G.	N	Y	N	Y	Y	Y
30 Johnson, E.	N	Y	?	Y	Y	Y
31 **Carter**	Y	N	Y	N	Y	Y
32 **Sessions**	Y	N	Y	N	Y	Y
UTAH						
1 **Bishop**	?	?	Y	N	?	Y
2 Matheson	N	Y	N	Y	Y	Y
3 **Chaffetz**	Y	N	Y	N	Y	N
VERMONT						
AL Welch	N	Y	N	Y	Y	Y
VIRGINIA						
1 **Wittman**	N	N	Y	N	Y	Y
2 Nye	N	Y	Y	Y	Y	Y
3 Scott	N	Y	N	Y	Y	Y
4 **Forbes**	N	N	Y	N	Y	Y
5 Perriello	N	Y	Y	Y	Y	Y
6 **Goodlatte**	N	N	Y	N	Y	Y
7 **Cantor**	N	N	Y	N	Y	Y
8 Moran	N	Y	?	Y	Y	?
9 Boucher	?	Y	N	Y	Y	Y
10 **Wolf**	Y	N	Y	N	Y	Y
11 Connolly	N	Y	N	Y	Y	Y
WASHINGTON						
1 Inslee	N	Y	N	Y	Y	Y
2 Larsen	N	Y	N	Y	Y	Y
3 Baird	N	Y	N	N	Y	N
4 **Hastings**	Y	N	Y	N	Y	Y
5 **McMorris Rodgers**	N	N	Y	N	Y	Y
6 Dicks	N	Y	?	Y	Y	Y
7 McDermott	N	Y	N	Y	Y	Y
8 **Reichert**	N	N	Y	N	Y	Y
9 Smith	N	Y	N	N	Y	N
WEST VIRGINIA						
1 Mollohan	N	Y	N	Y	Y	Y
2 **Capito**	N	N	Y	N	Y	Y
3 Rahall	N	Y	N	Y	Y	Y
WISCONSIN						
1 **Ryan**	N	N	Y	N	Y	N
2 Baldwin	N	Y	N	Y	Y	Y
3 Kind	N	Y	N	Y	Y	Y
4 Moore	N	Y	?	Y	Y	Y
5 **Sensenbrenner**	Y	N	Y	N	Y	Y
6 **Petri**	Y	N	Y	N	Y	Y
7 Obey	N	Y	N	Y	Y	Y
8 Kagen	N	Y	N	Y	Y	Y
WYOMING						
AL **Lummis**	Y	N	Y	N	Y	Y
DELEGATES						
Faleomavaega (A.S.)						
Norton (D.C.)						
Bordallo (Guam)						
Sablan (N. Marianas)						
Pierluisi (P.R.)						
Christensen (V.I.)						

IN THE HOUSE | By Vote Number

738. **HR 2918. Fiscal 2010 Legislative Branch Appropriations/Rule.** Adoption of the rule (H Res 772) to provide for House floor consideration of the conference report on the bill that would appropriate $4.7 billion in fiscal 2010 for legislative branch operations and provide continuing appropriations through Oct. 31, 2009, for all federal departments and agencies whose fiscal 2010 appropriations bills have not been enacted. Funding would mostly be set at fiscal 2009 levels. Adopted 209-189: R 1-164; D 208-25. Sept. 25, 2009.

739. **HR 2918. Fiscal 2010 Legislative Branch Appropriations/Conference Report.** Adoption of the conference report on the bill that would appropriate $4.7 billion in fiscal 2010 for legislative branch operations. It includes $1.3 billion for House operations, $926 million for Senate operations, $602 million for the Architect of the Capitol and $643 million for the Library of Congress. It would provide continuing appropriations through Oct. 31, 2009, for all federal departments and agencies whose fiscal 2010 appropriations bills have not been enacted. Funding would mostly be set at fiscal 2009 levels. Adopted (thus sent to the Senate) 217-190: R 5-162; D 212-28. Sept. 25, 2009.

740. **HR 905. Thunder Bay National Marine Sanctuary/Passage.** Bordallo, D-Guam, motion to suspend the rules and pass the bill that would extend the boundary of the Thunder Bay National Marine Sanctuary and Underwater Preserve to include the offshore waters of Presque Isle and Alcona counties in Michigan. Motion agreed to 286-107: R 58-105; D 228-2. A two-thirds majority of those present and voting (262 in this case) is required for passage under suspension of the rules. Sept. 29, 2009.

741. **H Res 16. National Life Insurance Awareness Month/Adoption.** Lynch, D-Mass., motion to suspend the rules and adopt the resolution that would support the goals and ideals of National Life Insurance Awareness Month. Motion agreed to 394-1: R 164-0; D 230-1. A two-thirds majority of those present and voting (264 in this case) is required for adoption under suspension of the rules. Sept. 29, 2009.

742. **HR 2997. Fiscal 2010 Agriculture Appropriations/Motion to Instruct.** Kingston, R-Ga., motion to instruct conferees to approve the final conference agreement only if it has been available to the managers for at least 72 hours. Motion agreed to 359-41: R 166-0; D 193-41. Sept. 29, 2009.

	738	739	740	741	742
ALABAMA					
1 **Bonner**	N	N	N	Y	Y
2 **Bright**	N	N	N	Y	Y
3 **Rogers**	N	Y	N	?	Y
4 **Aderholt**	N	N	Y	Y	Y
5 **Griffith**	N	N	Y	Y	Y
6 **Bachus**	N	N	Y	Y	Y
7 Davis	Y	Y	Y	Y	Y
ALASKA					
AL **Young**	?	N	N	Y	Y
ARIZONA					
1 Kirkpatrick	N	N	Y	Y	Y
2 **Franks**	N	N	N	Y	Y
3 **Shadegg**	N	N	N	Y	Y
4 Pastor	Y	Y	Y	Y	N
5 Mitchell	N	N	Y	Y	Y
6 **Flake**	N	N	N	Y	Y
7 Grijalva	Y	Y	Y	Y	N
8 Giffords	Y	N	Y	Y	Y
ARKANSAS					
1 Berry	Y	?	Y	Y	N
2 Snyder	Y	Y	Y	Y	Y
3 **Boozman**	N	N	N	Y	Y
4 Ross	Y	Y	Y	Y	Y
CALIFORNIA					
1 Thompson	Y	Y	Y	Y	Y
2 **Herger**	N	N	N	Y	Y
3 **Lungren**	N	N	N	Y	Y
4 **McClintock**	N	N	N	Y	Y
5 Matsui	Y	Y	Y	Y	N
6 Woolsey	Y	N	Y	Y	Y
7 Miller, George	Y	Y	?	?	?
8 Pelosi					
9 Lee	N	N	Y	Y	N
10 Vacant					
11 McNerney	Y	N	Y	Y	Y
12 Speier	?	?	Y	Y	N
13 Stark	Y	Y	Y	N	Y
14 Eshoo	Y	Y	Y	Y	Y
15 Honda	Y	Y	Y	Y	N
16 Lofgren	Y	Y	Y	Y	N
17 Farr	Y	Y	Y	Y	N
18 Cardoza	?	Y	Y	Y	Y
19 **Radanovich**	N	N	?	?	?
20 Costa	Y	Y	Y	Y	Y
21 **Nunes**	?	?	N	Y	Y
22 **McCarthy**	N	N	N	Y	Y
23 Capps	Y	Y	Y	Y	N
24 **Gallegly**	N	N	N	Y	Y
25 **McKeon**	N	N	N	Y	Y
26 **Dreier**	N	N	N	Y	Y
27 Sherman	Y	Y	Y	Y	Y
28 Berman	Y	Y	Y	Y	Y
29 Schiff	Y	Y	Y	Y	Y
30 Waxman	Y	Y	Y	Y	Y
31 Becerra	Y	N	Y	Y	N
32 Chu	Y	Y	Y	Y	Y
33 Watson	Y	Y	Y	Y	N
34 Roybal-Allard	Y	Y	Y	Y	N
35 Waters	?	Y	Y	Y	N
36 Harman	Y	Y	?	?	?
37 Richardson	Y	Y	+	Y	Y
38 Napolitano	Y	Y	Y	Y	N
39 Sánchez, Linda	Y	Y	Y	Y	N
40 **Royce**	N	N	?	Y	Y
41 **Lewis**	N	N	N	Y	Y
42 **Miller, Gary**	N	N	N	Y	Y
43 Baca	?	?	?	?	?
44 **Calvert**	N	N	N	Y	Y
45 **Bono Mack**	N	N	Y	Y	Y
46 **Rohrabacher**	N	N	?	?	?
47 Sanchez, Loretta	Y	Y	Y	Y	Y
48 **Campbell**	N	N	N	Y	Y
49 **Issa**	?	?	N	Y	Y
50 **Bilbray**	N	N	N	Y	Y
51 Filner	Y	Y	Y	Y	Y
52 **Hunter**	N	N	N	Y	Y
53 Davis	Y	Y	Y	Y	Y
COLORADO					
1 DeGette	Y	Y	Y	Y	Y
2 Polis	Y	Y	Y	Y	Y
3 Salazar	Y	Y	Y	Y	Y
4 Markey	Y	Y	Y	Y	N
5 **Lamborn**	N	N	N	Y	Y
6 **Coffman**	N	N	N	Y	Y
7 Perlmutter	Y	Y	Y	Y	Y
CONNECTICUT					
1 Larson	Y	Y	Y	Y	N
2 Courtney	Y	Y	Y	Y	Y
3 DeLauro	Y	Y	Y	Y	N
4 Himes	Y	Y	Y	Y	Y
5 Murphy	Y	Y	Y	Y	Y
DELAWARE					
AL **Castle**	N	N	N	Y	Y
FLORIDA					
1 **Miller**	N	N	N	Y	Y
2 Boyd	Y	Y	Y	Y	Y
3 Brown	Y	Y	Y	Y	Y
4 **Crenshaw**	N	N	N	Y	Y
5 **Brown-Waite**	N	N	Y	Y	Y
6 **Stearns**	N	N	N	Y	Y
7 **Mica**	?	?	Y	Y	Y
8 Grayson	Y	Y	+	Y	Y
9 **Bilirakis**	N	N	Y	Y	Y
10 **Young**	N	N	?	?	?
11 Castor	Y	Y	Y	Y	Y
12 **Putnam**	N	N	Y	Y	Y
13 **Buchanan**	N	N	Y	Y	Y
14 **Mack**	N	N	N	Y	Y
15 **Posey**	N	N	N	Y	Y
16 **Rooney**	N	N	Y	Y	Y
17 Meek	?	?	Y	Y	Y
18 **Ros-Lehtinen**	N	Y	Y	Y	Y
19 Wexler	Y	Y	?	?	?
20 Wasserman Schultz	Y	Y	?	?	?
21 **Diaz-Balart, L.**	N	Y	Y	Y	Y
22 Klein	Y	Y	Y	Y	Y
23 Hastings	Y	Y	Y	Y	Y
24 Kosmas	Y	Y	Y	Y	Y
25 **Diaz-Balart, M.**	N	Y	Y	Y	Y
GEORGIA					
1 **Kingston**	N	N	N	Y	Y
2 Bishop	Y	Y	Y	Y	Y
3 **Westmoreland**	N	N	N	Y	Y
4 Johnson	Y	Y	Y	Y	Y
5 Lewis	Y	Y	Y	Y	Y
6 **Price**	N	N	N	Y	Y
7 **Linder**	N	N	N	Y	Y
8 Marshall	Y	Y	Y	Y	Y
9 **Deal**	N	N	N	Y	Y
10 **Broun**	N	N	N	Y	Y
11 **Gingrey**	N	N	N	Y	Y
12 Barrow	Y	Y	Y	Y	Y
13 Scott	?	?	Y	Y	Y
HAWAII					
1 Abercrombie	?	Y	+	+	−
2 Hirono	Y	Y	Y	Y	N
IDAHO					
1 Minnick	N	N	Y	Y	Y
2 **Simpson**	N	N	N	Y	Y
ILLINOIS					
1 Rush	Y	Y	Y	Y	Y
2 Jackson	Y	Y	Y	Y	Y
3 Lipinski	Y	Y	Y	Y	Y
4 Gutierrez	Y	Y	Y	Y	Y
5 Quigley	Y	Y	Y	Y	Y
6 **Roskam**	N	N	N	Y	Y
7 Davis	Y	Y	+	+	+
8 Bean	N	Y	Y	Y	Y
9 Schakowsky	Y	N	Y	Y	N
10 **Kirk**	N	N	Y	Y	Y
11 Halvorson	Y	Y	Y	Y	Y
12 Costello	Y	Y	Y	Y	Y
13 **Biggert**	N	N	Y	Y	Y
14 Foster	Y	Y	Y	Y	Y
15 **Johnson**	N	N	Y	Y	Y

KEY	**Republicans**	Democrats

Y Voted for (yea)	X Paired against	C Voted "present" to avoid possible conflict of interest
# Paired for	− Announced against	
+ Announced for	P Voted "present"	? Did not vote or otherwise make a position known
N Voted against (nay)		

Name	738	739	740	741	742
16 Manzullo	N	N	N	Y	Y
17 Hare	Y	Y	Y	Y	Y
18 Schock	N	N	N	Y	Y
19 Shimkus	N	N	N	Y	Y
INDIANA					
1 Visclosky	Y	Y	Y	Y	N
2 Donnelly	Y	Y	Y	Y	Y
3 Souder	N	N	Y	Y	Y
4 Buyer	N	N	N	Y	Y
5 Burton	N	N	N	Y	Y
6 Pence	N	N	–	+	+
7 Carson	Y	Y	Y	Y	Y
8 Ellsworth	Y	Y	Y	Y	Y
9 Hill	?	?	Y	Y	Y
IOWA					
1 Braley	Y	Y	Y	Y	Y
2 Loebsack	?	?	Y	Y	Y
3 Boswell	Y	Y	Y	Y	Y
4 Latham	N	N	N	Y	Y
5 King	N	N	N	Y	Y
KANSAS					
1 Moran	N	N	N	Y	Y
2 Jenkins	N	N	N	Y	Y
3 Moore	Y	Y	Y	Y	Y
4 Tiahrt	N	N	N	Y	Y
KENTUCKY					
1 Whitfield	N	N	?	?	?
2 Guthrie	N	N	Y	Y	Y
3 Yarmuth	Y	Y	Y	?	Y
4 Davis	N	N	N	Y	Y
5 Rogers	N	N	Y	Y	Y
6 Chandler	Y	Y	Y	Y	Y
LOUISIANA					
1 Scalise	N	N	N	Y	Y
2 Cao	N	N	Y	Y	Y
3 Melancon	Y	Y	Y	Y	Y
4 Fleming	?	N	N	Y	Y
5 Alexander	N	N	N	Y	Y
6 Cassidy	N	N	N	Y	Y
7 Boustany	N	N	N	Y	Y
MAINE					
1 Pingree	Y	Y	Y	Y	Y
2 Michaud	Y	Y	Y	Y	Y
MARYLAND					
1 Kratovil	N	N	Y	Y	Y
2 Ruppersberger	Y	Y	Y	Y	Y
3 Sarbanes	Y	Y	?	?	Y
4 Edwards	N	N	Y	Y	Y
5 Hoyer	Y	Y	Y	Y	N
6 Bartlett	N	N	N	Y	Y
7 Cummings	Y	Y	Y	Y	Y
8 Van Hollen	Y	Y	Y	Y	Y
MASSACHUSETTS					
1 Olver	Y	Y	Y	Y	N
2 Neal	Y	Y	Y	Y	Y
3 McGovern	Y	Y	Y	Y	N
4 Frank	Y	Y	Y	Y	N
5 Tsongas	Y	Y	Y	Y	N
6 Tierney	Y	Y	Y	Y	?
7 Markey	Y	Y	Y	Y	Y
8 Capuano	+	+	?	?	+
9 Lynch	Y	Y	Y	Y	Y
10 Delahunt	?	?	Y	Y	N
MICHIGAN					
1 Stupak	Y	Y	Y	Y	Y
2 Hoekstra	N	N	Y	Y	Y
3 Ehlers	N	N	Y	Y	Y
4 Camp	N	N	Y	Y	Y
5 Kildee	Y	Y	Y	Y	Y
6 Upton	N	N	Y	Y	Y
7 Schauer	Y	Y	Y	Y	Y
8 Rogers	N	N	Y	Y	Y
9 Peters	Y	N	Y	Y	Y
10 Miller	N	N	Y	Y	Y
11 McCotter	N	N	Y	Y	Y
12 Levin	Y	Y	Y	Y	Y
13 Kilpatrick	Y	N	Y	Y	N
14 Conyers	?	Y	+	+	+
15 Dingell	Y	Y	Y	Y	Y
MINNESOTA					
1 Walz	Y	Y	Y	Y	Y
2 Kline	N	N	Y	Y	Y
3 Paulsen	N	N	Y	Y	Y
4 McCollum	Y	Y	?	?	Y
5 Ellison	Y	N	Y	Y	Y
6 Bachmann	N	N	N	Y	Y
7 Peterson	Y	Y	Y	Y	Y
8 Oberstar	Y	Y	Y	Y	Y
MISSISSIPPI					
1 Childers	Y	Y	Y	Y	Y
2 Thompson	Y	Y	Y	Y	Y
3 Harper	N	N	N	Y	Y
4 Taylor	N	N	Y	Y	?
MISSOURI					
1 Clay	?	Y	Y	Y	Y
2 Akin	N	N	N	Y	Y
3 Carnahan	Y	Y	Y	Y	Y
4 Skelton	Y	Y	Y	Y	N
5 Cleaver	Y	Y	Y	Y	Y
6 Graves	?	?	N	Y	Y
7 Blunt	?	?	N	Y	Y
8 Emerson	N	N	N	Y	Y
9 Luetkemeyer	N	N	N	Y	Y
MONTANA					
AL Rehberg	N	N	N	Y	Y
NEBRASKA					
1 Fortenberry	N	N	Y	Y	Y
2 Terry	N	N	N	Y	Y
3 Smith	N	N	N	Y	Y
NEVADA					
1 Berkley	Y	Y	Y	Y	Y
2 Heller	N	N	N	Y	Y
3 Titus	Y	Y	Y	Y	Y
NEW HAMPSHIRE					
1 Shea-Porter	Y	Y	Y	Y	Y
2 Hodes	Y	Y	Y	Y	Y
NEW JERSEY					
1 Andrews	Y	Y	Y	Y	Y
2 LoBiondo	N	N	Y	Y	Y
3 Adler	Y	Y	Y	Y	Y
4 Smith	N	N	Y	Y	Y
5 Garrett	N	N	N	Y	Y
6 Pallone	Y	Y	Y	Y	Y
7 Lance	N	N	Y	Y	Y
8 Pascrell	Y	Y	Y	Y	Y
9 Rothman	Y	Y	Y	Y	Y
10 Payne	Y	Y	Y	Y	N
11 Frelinghuysen	N	N	Y	Y	Y
12 Holt	N	Y	Y	Y	Y
13 Sires	Y	Y	?	?	?
NEW MEXICO					
1 Heinrich	Y	Y	Y	Y	Y
2 Teague	N	Y	?	?	?
3 Lujan	Y	Y	Y	Y	N
NEW YORK					
1 Bishop	Y	Y	Y	Y	Y
2 Israel	?	?	?	?	?
3 King	N	N	N	Y	Y
4 McCarthy	Y	Y	Y	Y	Y
5 Ackerman	?	?	Y	Y	Y
6 Meeks	Y	Y	Y	Y	Y
7 Crowley	Y	Y	Y	Y	Y
8 Nadler	N	N	Y	Y	Y
9 Weiner	Y	Y	Y	Y	Y
10 Towns	Y	N	Y	Y	Y
11 Clarke	N	?	Y	Y	N
12 Velázquez	Y	N	Y	Y	N
13 McMahon	Y	Y	Y	Y	Y
14 Maloney	Y	Y	?	?	?
15 Rangel	Y	Y	Y	Y	Y
16 Serrano	Y	Y	Y	Y	Y
17 Engel	?	Y	?	?	Y
18 Lowey	Y	Y	Y	Y	Y
19 Hall	Y	Y	Y	Y	Y
20 Murphy	N	Y	Y	Y	Y
21 Tonko	Y	Y	Y	Y	Y
22 Hinchey	Y	Y	Y	Y	Y
23 Vacant					
24 Arcuri	Y	Y	Y	Y	Y
25 Maffei	Y	Y	Y	Y	Y
26 Lee	N	N	Y	Y	Y
27 Higgins	?	?	Y	Y	?
28 Slaughter	Y	Y	?	?	Y
29 Massa	Y	N	Y	Y	N
NORTH CAROLINA					
1 Butterfield	Y	Y	?	?	?
2 Etheridge	Y	Y	Y	Y	Y
3 Jones	?	?	Y	Y	Y
4 Price	Y	Y	Y	Y	N
5 Foxx	N	N	N	Y	Y
6 Coble	N	N	N	Y	Y
7 McIntyre	Y	Y	Y	Y	Y
8 Kissell	Y	Y	Y	Y	Y
9 Myrick	N	N	N	Y	Y
10 McHenry	N	N	N	Y	Y
11 Shuler	N	Y	Y	Y	Y
12 Watt	Y	Y	Y	Y	Y
13 Miller	Y	Y	Y	Y	Y
NORTH DAKOTA					
AL Pomeroy	Y	Y	Y	Y	Y
OHIO					
1 Driehaus	N	N	Y	Y	Y
2 Schmidt	?	N	N	Y	Y
3 Turner	N	N	Y	Y	Y
4 Jordan	N	N	N	Y	Y
5 Latta	N	N	N	Y	Y
6 Wilson	Y	?	Y	Y	Y
7 Austria	N	N	Y	Y	Y
8 Boehner	N	N	–	Y	Y
9 Kaptur	Y	Y	Y	Y	Y
10 Kucinich	N	N	Y	Y	Y
11 Fudge	N	Y	Y	Y	N
12 Tiberi	N	N	?	Y	Y
13 Sutton	Y	Y	?	?	?
14 LaTourette	N	N	Y	Y	Y
15 Kilroy	Y	Y	Y	Y	Y
16 Boccieri	Y	Y	Y	Y	Y
17 Ryan	Y	Y	Y	Y	Y
18 Space	Y	Y	Y	Y	Y
OKLAHOMA					
1 Sullivan	?	?	N	Y	Y
2 Boren	Y	Y	Y	Y	Y
3 Lucas	N	N	N	Y	Y
4 Cole	N	N	N	Y	Y
5 Fallin	N	N	N	Y	Y
OREGON					
1 Wu	Y	Y	Y	Y	Y
2 Walden	N	N	N	Y	Y
3 Blumenauer	Y	Y	Y	Y	Y
4 DeFazio	Y	Y	Y	?	Y
5 Schrader	?	Y	Y	Y	Y
PENNSYLVANIA					
1 Brady	Y	Y	Y	Y	Y
2 Fattah	Y	Y	Y	Y	Y
3 Dahlkemper	Y	Y	Y	Y	Y
4 Altmire	Y	Y	N	Y	Y
5 Thompson	N	N	N	Y	Y
6 Gerlach	N	N	?	?	?
7 Sestak	Y	Y	?	?	?
8 Murphy, P.	Y	Y	Y	Y	Y
9 Shuster	N	N	Y	Y	Y
10 Carney	Y	Y	Y	Y	Y
11 Kanjorski	Y	Y	Y	Y	Y
12 Murtha	Y	Y	Y	Y	Y
13 Schwartz	Y	Y	Y	Y	Y
14 Doyle	?	?	Y	Y	Y
15 Dent	N	N	Y	Y	Y
16 Pitts	N	N	N	Y	Y
17 Holden	Y	Y	Y	Y	Y
18 Murphy, T.	N	N	Y	Y	Y
19 Platts	?	N	Y	Y	Y
RHODE ISLAND					
1 Kennedy	Y	Y	Y	Y	N
2 Langevin	?	Y	Y	Y	Y
SOUTH CAROLINA					
1 Brown	N	N	N	Y	Y
2 Wilson	N	?	N	Y	Y
3 Barrett	N	N	?	+	?
4 Inglis	N	N	N	Y	Y
5 Spratt	Y	Y	Y	Y	Y
6 Clyburn	Y	Y	Y	Y	N
SOUTH DAKOTA					
AL Herseth Sandlin	Y	Y	Y	Y	Y
TENNESSEE					
1 Roe	N	N	N	Y	Y
2 Duncan	N	N	Y	Y	Y
3 Wamp	N	N	?	?	?
4 Davis	Y	Y	Y	Y	Y
5 Cooper	Y	Y	Y	Y	Y
6 Gordon	Y	Y	Y	Y	Y
7 Blackburn	N	N	N	Y	Y
8 Tanner	Y	Y	Y	Y	Y
9 Cohen	Y	Y	Y	Y	Y
TEXAS					
1 Gohmert	N	N	?	?	?
2 Poe	N	?	N	Y	Y
3 Johnson, S.	N	N	N	Y	Y
4 Hall	N	N	N	Y	Y
5 Hensarling	N	N	N	Y	Y
6 Barton	N	N	N	Y	Y
7 Culberson	?	?	N	Y	Y
8 Brady	Y	N	N	Y	Y
9 Green, A.	Y	Y	Y	Y	Y
10 McCaul	N	Y	Y	Y	Y
11 Conaway	N	N	N	Y	Y
12 Granger	N	N	Y	Y	Y
13 Thornberry	N	N	N	Y	Y
14 Paul	N	N	?	?	?
15 Hinojosa	?	N	Y	Y	Y
16 Reyes	Y	Y	Y	Y	Y
17 Edwards	Y	Y	Y	Y	Y
18 Jackson Lee	N	N	?	+	?
19 Neugebauer	N	N	?	?	?
20 Gonzalez	Y	Y	Y	Y	Y
21 Smith	N	N	Y	Y	Y
22 Olson	N	N	Y	Y	Y
23 Rodriguez	Y	Y	Y	Y	Y
24 Marchant	N	N	Y	Y	Y
25 Doggett	Y	Y	Y	Y	Y
26 Burgess	N	N	N	Y	Y
27 Ortiz	Y	Y	+	Y	Y
28 Cuellar	Y	Y	Y	Y	Y
29 Green, G.	Y	Y	Y	Y	Y
30 Johnson, E.	?	?	Y	Y	N
31 Carter	N	N	N	Y	Y
32 Sessions	N	N	Y	Y	Y
UTAH					
1 Bishop	N	N	?	Y	Y
2 Matheson	Y	Y	Y	Y	Y
3 Chaffetz	N	N	N	Y	Y
VERMONT					
AL Welch	Y	Y	Y	Y	Y
VIRGINIA					
1 Wittman	N	N	N	Y	Y
2 Nye	N	N	Y	Y	Y
3 Scott	N	Y	Y	Y	Y
4 Forbes	N	N	N	Y	Y
5 Perriello	N	N	Y	Y	Y
6 Goodlatte	N	N	N	Y	Y
7 Cantor	N	N	N	?	Y
8 Moran	Y	Y	?	?	?
9 Boucher	Y	Y	Y	Y	Y
10 Wolf	N	N	N	Y	Y
11 Connolly	Y	Y	Y	Y	Y
WASHINGTON					
1 Inslee	Y	Y	Y	Y	Y
2 Larsen	Y	Y	Y	Y	Y
3 Baird	N	N	Y	Y	Y
4 Hastings	N	N	N	Y	Y
5 McMorris Rodgers	N	N	N	Y	Y
6 Dicks	Y	Y	Y	Y	Y
7 McDermott	Y	Y	Y	Y	N
8 Reichert	N	N	Y	Y	Y
9 Smith	Y	Y	+	Y	Y
WEST VIRGINIA					
1 Mollohan	Y	Y	Y	Y	Y
2 Capito	N	N	Y	Y	Y
3 Rahall	Y	Y	Y	Y	Y
WISCONSIN					
1 Ryan	N	N	Y	Y	Y
2 Baldwin	Y	Y	Y	Y	Y
3 Kind	Y	Y	Y	Y	Y
4 Moore	Y	Y	Y	Y	N
5 Sensenbrenner	N	N	Y	Y	Y
6 Petri	N	N	Y	Y	Y
7 Obey	Y	Y	Y	Y	N
8 Kagen	Y	Y	Y	Y	Y
WYOMING					
AL Lummis	N	N	N	Y	Y
DELEGATES					
Faleomavaega (A.S.)					
Norton (D.C.)					
Bordallo (Guam)					
Sablan (N. Marianas)					
Pierluisi (P.R.)					
Christensen (V.I.)					

IN THE HOUSE | By Vote Number

743. **HR 2442. Bay Area Water Recycling Program Expansion/ Passage.** Bordallo, D-Guam, motion to suspend the rules and pass the bill that would authorize $32.2 million in federal assistance for six water recycling programs in California that would be part of the Bay Area Regional Water Recycling Program. Motion rejected 240-170: R 2-169; D 238-1. A two-thirds majority of those present and voting (274 in this case) is required for passage under suspension of the rules. Sept. 30, 2009.

744. **HR 1771. NOAA Chesapeake Bay Office/Passage.** Bordallo, D-Guam, motion to suspend the rules and pass the bill that would authorize $78.9 million for the Chesapeake Bay Office of the National Oceanic and Atmospheric Administration for fiscal years 2011 through 2014. Motion agreed to 338-78: R 95-77; D 243-1. A two-thirds majority of those present and voting (278 in this case) is required for passage under suspension of the rules. Sept. 30, 2009.

745. **HR 1053. Chesapeake Bay Restoration Report/Passage.** Bordallo, D-Guam, motion to suspend the rules and pass the bill that would require the director of the Office of Management and Budget to submit a financial report to Congress listing all federal and state Chesapeake Bay watershed restoration activities. Motion agreed to 418-1: R 171-1; D 247-0. A two-thirds majority of those present and voting (280 in this case) is required for passage under suspension of the rules. Sept. 30, 2009.

746. **HR 2892. Fiscal 2010 Homeland Security Appropriations/ Motion to Instruct.** Rogers, R-Ky., motion to instruct conferees to recede to a Senate provision that would allow the Defense secretary to decide whether to make photos of Guantánamo Bay detainees public, insist on provisions to require that Guantánamo Bay detainees be on the no-fly list and be prohibited from entering the United States, and withhold approval of the final conference agreement unless it has been available to the managers for at least 72 hours. Motion agreed to 258-163: R 170-1; D 88-162. Oct. 1, 2009.

747. **H Res 517. University of Washington Women's Softball Team/ Adoption.** Chu, D-Calif., motion to suspend the rules and adopt the resolution that would congratulate the University of Washington women's softball team for winning the 2009 Women's College World Series. Motion agreed to 421-0: R 171-0; D 250-0. A two-thirds majority of those present and voting (281 in this case) is required for adoption under suspension of the rules. Oct. 1, 2009.

	743	744	745	746	747
ALABAMA					
1 Bonner	N	N	Y	Y	Y
2 Bright	N	N	Y	Y	Y
3 Rogers	N	Y	Y	Y	Y
4 Aderholt	N	Y	Y	Y	Y
5 Griffith	Y	Y	Y	Y	Y
6 Bachus	N	Y	Y	Y	Y
7 Davis	Y	Y	Y	Y	Y
ALASKA					
AL Young	N	Y	Y	Y	Y
ARIZONA					
1 Kirkpatrick	Y	Y	Y	Y	Y
2 Franks	N	N	Y	Y	Y
3 Shadegg	N	N	Y	?	?
4 Pastor	Y	Y	Y	N	Y
5 Mitchell	Y	Y	Y	Y	Y
6 Flake	N	N	Y	Y	Y
7 Grijalva	Y	Y	Y	N	Y
8 Giffords	Y	Y	Y	Y	Y
ARKANSAS					
1 Berry	Y	Y	Y	N	Y
2 Snyder	Y	Y	Y	N	Y
3 Boozman	N	Y	Y	N	Y
4 Ross	Y	Y	Y	Y	Y
CALIFORNIA					
1 Thompson	Y	Y	Y	N	Y
2 Herger	N	N	Y	Y	Y
3 Lungren	N	Y	Y	Y	Y
4 McClintock	N	N	Y	Y	Y
5 Matsui	Y	Y	Y	N	Y
6 Woolsey	Y	Y	Y	N	Y
7 Miller, George	+	Y	Y	N	Y
8 Pelosi					
9 Lee	Y	Y	Y	N	Y
10 Vacant					
11 McNerney	Y	Y	Y	Y	Y
12 Speier	Y	Y	Y	N	Y
13 Stark	Y	Y	Y	?	?
14 Eshoo	Y	Y	Y	N	Y
15 Honda	Y	Y	Y	N	Y
16 Lofgren	Y	Y	Y	N	Y
17 Farr	Y	Y	Y	N	Y
18 Cardoza	Y	Y	Y	Y	Y
19 Radanovich	N	N	Y	Y	Y
20 Costa	?	Y	Y	Y	Y
21 Nunes	N	Y	Y	Y	Y
22 McCarthy	N	N	Y	?	?
23 Capps	Y	Y	Y	N	Y
24 Gallegly	N	Y	Y	Y	Y
25 McKeon	N	Y	Y	Y	Y
26 Dreier	N	Y	Y	Y	Y
27 Sherman	Y	Y	Y	N	Y
28 Berman	Y	Y	Y	N	Y
29 Schiff	Y	Y	Y	N	Y
30 Waxman	?	Y	Y	N	Y
31 Becerra	?	Y	Y	N	Y
32 Chu	Y	Y	Y	N	Y
33 Watson	Y	Y	Y	N	Y
34 Roybal-Allard	Y	Y	Y	N	Y
35 Waters	Y	Y	Y	N	Y
36 Harman	Y	Y	Y	N	Y
37 Richardson	Y	Y	Y	N	Y
38 Napolitano	Y	Y	Y	N	Y
39 Sánchez, Linda	Y	Y	Y	N	Y
40 Royce	N	N	Y	Y	Y
41 Lewis	N	Y	Y	Y	Y
42 Miller, Gary	N	N	Y	Y	Y
43 Baca	Y	Y	Y	N	Y
44 Calvert	N	Y	Y	Y	Y
45 Bono Mack	N	Y	Y	Y	Y
46 Rohrabacher	N	Y	Y	Y	Y
47 Sanchez, Loretta	Y	Y	Y	Y	Y
48 Campbell	N	N	Y	Y	Y
49 Issa	N	N	Y	Y	Y
50 Bilbray	N	Y	Y	Y	Y
51 Filner	Y	Y	Y	N	Y
52 Hunter	N	N	Y	Y	Y
53 Davis	Y	Y	Y	N	Y

	743	744	745	746	747
COLORADO					
1 DeGette	Y	Y	Y	N	Y
2 Polis	Y	Y	Y	N	Y
3 Salazar	Y	Y	Y	N	Y
4 Markey	Y	Y	Y	Y	Y
5 Lamborn	N	N	Y	Y	Y
6 Coffman	N	N	Y	Y	Y
7 Perlmutter	Y	Y	Y	Y	Y
CONNECTICUT					
1 Larson	Y	Y	Y	N	Y
2 Courtney	Y	Y	Y	N	Y
3 DeLauro	Y	Y	Y	N	Y
4 Himes	Y	Y	Y	Y	Y
5 Murphy	Y	Y	Y	N	Y
DELAWARE					
AL Castle	N	Y	Y	Y	Y
FLORIDA					
1 Miller	N	N	Y	Y	Y
2 Boyd	Y	Y	Y	Y	Y
3 Brown	Y	Y	Y	N	Y
4 Crenshaw	N	Y	Y	Y	Y
5 Brown-Waite	N	N	Y	Y	Y
6 Stearns	N	N	Y	Y	Y
7 Mica	N	Y	Y	Y	Y
8 Grayson	Y	Y	Y	Y	Y
9 Bilirakis	N	N	Y	Y	Y
10 Young	?	?	?	Y	Y
11 Castor	Y	Y	Y	N	Y
12 Putnam	N	Y	Y	Y	Y
13 Buchanan	N	Y	Y	Y	Y
14 Mack	N	N	Y	Y	Y
15 Posey	N	Y	Y	Y	Y
16 Rooney	N	Y	Y	Y	Y
17 Meek	Y	Y	Y	N	Y
18 Ros-Lehtinen	N	Y	Y	Y	Y
19 Wexler	Y	Y	Y	N	Y
20 Wasserman Schultz	Y	Y	Y	N	Y
21 Diaz-Balart, L.	N	Y	Y	Y	Y
22 Klein	Y	Y	Y	N	Y
23 Hastings	Y	Y	Y	N	Y
24 Kosmas	Y	Y	Y	N	Y
25 Diaz-Balart, M.	N	Y	Y	Y	Y
GEORGIA					
1 Kingston	N	N	Y	Y	Y
2 Bishop	Y	Y	Y	Y	Y
3 Westmoreland	N	N	Y	Y	Y
4 Johnson	Y	Y	Y	N	Y
5 Lewis	Y	Y	Y	N	Y
6 Price	N	Y	Y	Y	Y
7 Linder	N	N	Y	Y	Y
8 Marshall	Y	Y	Y	Y	Y
9 Deal	N	N	Y	Y	Y
10 Broun	N	N	Y	Y	Y
11 Gingrey	N	Y	Y	Y	Y
12 Barrow	Y	Y	Y	Y	Y
13 Scott	Y	Y	Y	N	Y
HAWAII					
1 Abercrombie	+	+	+	N	Y
2 Hirono	Y	Y	Y	N	Y
IDAHO					
1 Minnick	Y	Y	Y	Y	Y
2 Simpson	N	Y	Y	Y	Y
ILLINOIS					
1 Rush	Y	Y	Y	Y	Y
2 Jackson	Y	Y	Y	N	Y
3 Lipinski	Y	Y	Y	Y	Y
4 Gutierrez	Y	Y	Y	N	Y
5 Quigley	Y	Y	Y	N	Y
6 Roskam	N	Y	Y	Y	Y
7 Davis	Y	Y	Y	N	Y
8 Bean	Y	Y	Y	Y	Y
9 Schakowsky	Y	Y	Y	N	Y
10 Kirk	N	Y	Y	Y	Y
11 Halvorson	Y	Y	Y	Y	Y
12 Costello	Y	Y	Y	Y	Y
13 Biggert	N	Y	Y	Y	Y
14 Foster	Y	Y	Y	Y	Y
15 Johnson	Y	Y	Y	Y	Y

KEY   **Republicans**   Democrats

Y Voted for (yea)	X Paired against	C Voted "present" to avoid possible conflict of interest
# Paired for	– Announced against	
+ Announced for	P Voted "present"	? Did not vote or otherwise make a position known
N Voted against (nay)		

	743	744	745	746	747
16 Manzullo	N	N	Y	Y	Y
17 Hare	Y	Y	Y	N	Y
18 Schock	N	Y	Y	N	Y
19 Shimkus	N	N	Y	Y	Y
INDIANA					
1 Visclosky	Y	Y	Y	N	Y
2 Donnelly	Y	Y	Y	Y	Y
3 Souder	N	N	Y	Y	Y
4 Buyer	N	N	?	Y	Y
5 Burton	N	N	Y	Y	Y
6 Pence	N	N	Y	Y	Y
7 Carson	Y	Y	Y	N	Y
8 Ellsworth	Y	Y	Y	Y	Y
9 Hill	Y	Y	Y	Y	Y
IOWA					
1 Braley	Y	Y	Y	N	Y
2 Loebsack	Y	Y	Y	N	Y
3 Boswell	Y	Y	Y	N	Y
4 Latham	N	Y	Y	Y	Y
5 King	N	N	Y	Y	Y
KANSAS					
1 Moran	N	N	Y	Y	Y
2 Jenkins	N	Y	Y	Y	Y
3 Moore	Y	?	Y	Y	Y
4 Tiahrt	N	N	Y	Y	Y
KENTUCKY					
1 Whitfield	?	?	?	?	?
2 Guthrie	N	Y	Y	Y	Y
3 Yarmuth	Y	Y	Y	Y	Y
4 Davis	N	N	Y	Y	Y
5 Rogers	N	Y	Y	Y	Y
6 Chandler	Y	Y	Y	Y	Y
LOUISIANA					
1 Scalise	N	N	Y	Y	Y
2 Cao	N	Y	Y	Y	Y
3 Melancon	Y	Y	Y	Y	Y
4 Fleming	N	N	Y	Y	Y
5 Alexander	N	N	Y	Y	Y
6 Cassidy	N	Y	Y	Y	Y
7 Boustany	N	N	Y	Y	Y
MAINE					
1 Pingree	Y	Y	Y	N	Y
2 Michaud	Y	Y	Y	Y	Y
MARYLAND					
1 Kratovil	Y	Y	Y	Y	Y
2 Ruppersberger	Y	Y	Y	N	Y
3 Sarbanes	Y	Y	Y	N	Y
4 Edwards	Y	Y	Y	N	Y
5 Hoyer	Y	Y	Y	N	Y
6 Bartlett	N	Y	Y	Y	Y
7 Cummings	Y	Y	Y	N	Y
8 Van Hollen	Y	Y	Y	N	Y
MASSACHUSETTS					
1 Olver	Y	Y	Y	N	Y
2 Neal	Y	Y	Y	N	Y
3 McGovern	Y	Y	Y	N	Y
4 Frank	Y	Y	Y	N	Y
5 Tsongas	Y	Y	Y	N	Y
6 Tierney	Y	Y	Y	N	Y
7 Markey	Y	Y	Y	N	Y
8 Capuano	?	?	?	?	?
9 Lynch	Y	Y	Y	Y	Y
10 Delahunt	Y	Y	Y	N	Y
MICHIGAN					
1 Stupak	Y	Y	Y	N	Y
2 Hoekstra	N	Y	Y	Y	Y
3 Ehlers	N	Y	Y	Y	Y
4 Camp	N	Y	Y	Y	Y
5 Kildee	Y	Y	Y	N	Y
6 Upton	N	Y	Y	Y	Y
7 Schauer	Y	Y	Y	N	Y
8 Rogers	N	Y	Y	Y	Y
9 Peters	Y	Y	Y	N	Y
10 Miller	N	Y	Y	Y	Y
11 McCotter	N	Y	Y	Y	Y
12 Levin	Y	Y	Y	N	Y
13 Kilpatrick	Y	Y	Y	N	Y
14 Conyers	+	?	?	N	Y
15 Dingell	Y	Y	Y	N	Y
MINNESOTA					
1 Walz	Y	Y	Y	N	Y
2 Kline	N	N	Y	Y	Y
3 Paulsen	N	Y	Y	Y	Y
4 McCollum	Y	Y	Y	N	Y

	743	744	745	746	747
5 Ellison	Y	Y	Y	N	Y
6 Bachmann	N	N	Y	Y	Y
7 Peterson	Y	Y	Y	Y	Y
8 Oberstar	Y	Y	Y	N	Y
MISSISSIPPI					
1 Childers	Y	Y	Y	Y	Y
2 Thompson	Y	Y	Y	N	Y
3 Harper	N	N	Y	Y	Y
4 Taylor	Y	Y	Y	Y	Y
MISSOURI					
1 Clay	Y	Y	Y	N	Y
2 Akin	N	?	Y	Y	Y
3 Carnahan	Y	Y	Y	Y	Y
4 Skelton	Y	Y	Y	Y	Y
5 Cleaver	Y	Y	Y	N	Y
6 Graves	N	N	Y	Y	Y
7 Blunt	N	Y	Y	Y	Y
8 Emerson	N	N	Y	Y	Y
9 Luetkemeyer	N	N	Y	Y	Y
MONTANA					
AL Rehberg	N	N	Y	Y	Y
NEBRASKA					
1 Fortenberry	N	Y	Y	Y	Y
2 Terry	N	N	Y	Y	Y
3 Smith	N	Y	Y	Y	Y
NEVADA					
1 Berkley	Y	Y	Y	N	Y
2 Heller	N	N	Y	Y	Y
3 Titus	Y	Y	Y	N	Y
NEW HAMPSHIRE					
1 Shea-Porter	Y	Y	Y	N	Y
2 Hodes	Y	Y	Y	N	Y
NEW JERSEY					
1 Andrews	Y	Y	Y	N	Y
2 LoBiondo	N	Y	Y	Y	Y
3 Adler	Y	Y	Y	?	?
4 Smith	N	Y	Y	Y	Y
5 Garrett	N	N	Y	Y	Y
6 Pallone	Y	Y	Y	N	Y
7 Lance	N	Y	Y	Y	Y
8 Pascrell	Y	Y	Y	N	Y
9 Rothman	Y	Y	Y	N	Y
10 Payne	Y	?	Y	N	Y
11 Frelinghuysen	N	Y	Y	Y	Y
12 Holt	Y	Y	Y	N	Y
13 Sires	Y	Y	Y	N	Y
NEW MEXICO					
1 Heinrich	Y	Y	Y	Y	Y
2 Teague	?	?	?	Y	Y
3 Lujan	Y	Y	Y	N	Y
NEW YORK					
1 Bishop	Y	Y	Y	Y	Y
2 Israel	Y	Y	Y	N	Y
3 King	N	Y	Y	Y	Y
4 McCarthy	Y	Y	Y	N	Y
5 Ackerman	Y	Y	Y	N	Y
6 Meeks	Y	Y	Y	N	Y
7 Crowley	Y	?	Y	N	Y
8 Nadler	Y	Y	Y	N	Y
9 Weiner	Y	Y	Y	N	Y
10 Towns	Y	Y	Y	N	Y
11 Clarke	Y	Y	Y	N	Y
12 Velázquez	Y	Y	Y	N	Y
13 McMahon	Y	Y	Y	Y	Y
14 Maloney	?	?	?	?	?
15 Rangel	?	Y	Y	N	Y
16 Serrano	Y	Y	Y	N	Y
17 Engel	Y	Y	Y	N	Y
18 Lowey	?	Y	Y	N	Y
19 Hall	Y	Y	Y	Y	Y
20 Murphy	Y	Y	Y	Y	Y
21 Tonko	Y	Y	Y	N	Y
22 Hinchey	Y	Y	Y	N	Y
23 Vacant					
24 Arcuri	Y	Y	Y	Y	Y
25 Maffei	Y	Y	Y	N	Y
26 Lee	N	Y	Y	N	Y
27 Higgins	Y	Y	Y	N	Y
28 Slaughter	+	Y	Y	N	Y
29 Massa	Y	Y	Y	N	Y
NORTH CAROLINA					
1 Butterfield	Y	Y	Y	N	Y
2 Etheridge	Y	Y	Y	N	Y
3 Jones	N	Y	Y	Y	Y
4 Price	Y	Y	Y	N	Y

	743	744	745	746	747
5 Foxx	N	N	Y	Y	Y
6 Coble	N	N	Y	Y	Y
7 McIntyre	Y	Y	Y	Y	Y
8 Kissell	Y	Y	Y	Y	Y
9 Myrick	–	N	Y	Y	Y
10 McHenry	N	Y	Y	Y	Y
11 Shuler	Y	Y	Y	Y	Y
12 Watt	Y	Y	Y	N	Y
13 Miller	Y	Y	Y	N	Y
NORTH DAKOTA					
AL Pomeroy	Y	Y	Y	Y	Y
OHIO					
1 Driehaus	Y	Y	Y	N	Y
2 Schmidt	N	N	Y	?	?
3 Turner	N	Y	Y	Y	Y
4 Jordan	N	N	Y	Y	Y
5 Latta	N	N	Y	Y	Y
6 Wilson	Y	Y	Y	Y	Y
7 Austria	N	Y	Y	Y	Y
8 Boehner	N	Y	Y	Y	Y
9 Kaptur	Y	Y	Y	Y	Y
10 Kucinich	Y	Y	Y	N	Y
11 Fudge	Y	Y	Y	N	Y
12 Tiberi	N	Y	Y	Y	Y
13 Sutton	?	?	?	N	Y
14 LaTourette	N	Y	Y	Y	Y
15 Kilroy	Y	Y	Y	N	Y
16 Boccieri	Y	Y	Y	Y	Y
17 Ryan	Y	Y	Y	N	Y
18 Space	Y	Y	Y	Y	Y
OKLAHOMA					
1 Sullivan	N	N	Y	Y	Y
2 Boren	Y	Y	Y	Y	Y
3 Lucas	N	Y	Y	Y	Y
4 Cole	N	Y	Y	Y	Y
5 Fallin	N	Y	Y	Y	Y
OREGON					
1 Wu	Y	Y	Y	N	Y
2 Walden	N	Y	Y	Y	Y
3 Blumenauer	Y	Y	Y	N	Y
4 DeFazio	Y	Y	Y	Y	Y
5 Schrader	Y	Y	Y	Y	Y
PENNSYLVANIA					
1 Brady	Y	Y	Y	N	Y
2 Fattah	Y	Y	Y	N	Y
3 Dahlkemper	Y	Y	Y	N	Y
4 Altmire	Y	Y	Y	Y	Y
5 Thompson	N	Y	Y	Y	Y
6 Gerlach	N	Y	Y	Y	Y
7 Sestak	Y	Y	Y	N	Y
8 Murphy, P.	Y	Y	Y	N	Y
9 Shuster	N	Y	Y	Y	Y
10 Carney	?	?	?	?	?
11 Kanjorski	Y	Y	Y	N	Y
12 Murtha	Y	Y	Y	N	Y
13 Schwartz	Y	Y	Y	N	Y
14 Doyle	Y	Y	?	N	Y
15 Dent	N	Y	Y	Y	Y
16 Pitts	N	Y	Y	Y	Y
17 Holden	Y	Y	Y	N	Y
18 Murphy, T.	N	Y	Y	Y	Y
19 Platts	N	Y	Y	Y	Y
RHODE ISLAND					
1 Kennedy	Y	Y	Y	N	Y
2 Langevin	Y	Y	Y	N	Y
SOUTH CAROLINA					
1 Brown	N	N	Y	Y	Y
2 Wilson	N	Y	Y	Y	Y
3 Barrett	?	?	?	?	?
4 Inglis	N	N	Y	Y	Y
5 Spratt	Y	Y	Y	N	Y
6 Clyburn	?	Y	Y	N	Y
SOUTH DAKOTA					
AL Herseth Sandlin	Y	Y	Y	Y	Y
TENNESSEE					
1 Roe	N	N	Y	Y	Y
2 Duncan	N	N	Y	Y	Y
3 Wamp	N	Y	Y	Y	Y
4 Davis	Y	Y	Y	N	Y
5 Cooper	Y	Y	Y	N	Y
6 Gordon	Y	Y	Y	N	Y
7 Blackburn	N	N	Y	Y	Y
8 Tanner	Y	Y	Y	N	Y
9 Cohen	Y	Y	Y	N	Y

	743	744	745	746	747
TEXAS					
1 Gohmert	N	N	Y	Y	Y
2 Poe	N	N	Y	Y	Y
3 Johnson, S.	N	N	Y	Y	Y
4 Hall	N	N	Y	Y	Y
5 Hensarling	N	N	Y	Y	Y
6 Barton	N	Y	Y	Y	Y
7 Culberson	N	N	Y	Y	Y
8 Brady	N	N	Y	Y	Y
9 Green, A.	Y	Y	Y	N	Y
10 McCaul	N	Y	Y	Y	Y
11 Conaway	N	N	Y	Y	Y
12 Granger	N	N	Y	Y	Y
13 Thornberry	N	N	Y	Y	Y
14 Paul	N	N	N	N	Y
15 Hinojosa	Y	Y	Y	N	Y
16 Reyes	Y	Y	Y	N	Y
17 Edwards	Y	Y	Y	N	Y
18 Jackson Lee	?	Y	Y	N	Y
19 Neugebauer	?	?	?	?	?
20 Gonzalez	Y	Y	Y	N	Y
21 Smith	N	Y	Y	Y	Y
22 Olson	N	Y	Y	Y	Y
23 Rodriguez	Y	Y	Y	N	Y
24 Marchant	N	N	Y	Y	Y
25 Doggett	Y	Y	Y	N	Y
26 Burgess	?	Y	Y	Y	Y
27 Ortiz	Y	Y	Y	N	Y
28 Cuellar	Y	Y	Y	N	Y
29 Green, G.	Y	Y	Y	N	Y
30 Johnson, E.	Y	Y	Y	N	Y
31 Carter	N	N	Y	Y	Y
32 Sessions	N	Y	Y	Y	Y
UTAH					
1 Bishop	N	Y	Y	Y	Y
2 Matheson	Y	Y	Y	Y	Y
3 Chaffetz	N	Y	Y	Y	Y
VERMONT					
AL Welch	Y	Y	Y	N	Y
VIRGINIA					
1 Wittman	Y	Y	Y	Y	Y
2 Nye	Y	Y	Y	Y	Y
3 Scott	Y	Y	Y	N	Y
4 Forbes	N	Y	Y	Y	Y
5 Perriello	Y	Y	Y	Y	Y
6 Goodlatte	N	Y	Y	Y	Y
7 Cantor	N	Y	Y	Y	Y
8 Moran	Y	Y	Y	N	Y
9 Boucher	Y	Y	Y	Y	Y
10 Wolf	N	Y	Y	Y	Y
11 Connolly	Y	Y	Y	N	Y
WASHINGTON					
1 Inslee	Y	Y	Y	N	Y
2 Larsen	Y	Y	Y	N	Y
3 Baird	Y	Y	Y	N	Y
4 Hastings	N	N	Y	Y	Y
5 McMorris Rodgers	N	Y	Y	Y	Y
6 Dicks	Y	?	Y	N	Y
7 McDermott	Y	Y	Y	N	Y
8 Reichert	N	N	Y	Y	Y
9 Smith	Y	Y	Y	N	Y
WEST VIRGINIA					
1 Mollohan	Y	Y	Y	Y	Y
2 Capito	N	Y	Y	Y	Y
3 Rahall	Y	Y	Y	N	Y
WISCONSIN					
1 Ryan	N	N	Y	Y	Y
2 Baldwin	Y	Y	Y	N	Y
3 Kind	Y	Y	Y	N	Y
4 Moore	Y	Y	Y	N	Y
5 Sensenbrenner	N	N	Y	Y	Y
6 Petri	N	Y	Y	Y	Y
7 Obey	Y	Y	Y	N	Y
8 Kagen	Y	Y	Y	N	Y
WYOMING					
AL Lummis	N	N	Y	Y	Y
DELEGATES					
Faleomavaega (A.S.)					
Norton (D.C.)					
Bordallo (Guam)					
Sablan (N. Marianas)					
Pierluisi (P.R.)					
Christensen (V.I.)					

IN THE HOUSE | By Vote Number

748. **H Res 487. Michigan State University State News Anniversary/Adoption.** Chu, D-Calif., motion to suspend the rules and adopt the resolution that would recognize the 100th anniversary of the State News at Michigan State University. Motion agreed to 413-0: R 168-0; D 245-0. A two-thirds majority of those present and voting (276 in this case) is required for adoption under suspension of the rules. Oct. 1, 2009.

749. **HR 3183. Fiscal 2010 Energy-Water Appropriations/Rule.** Adoption of the rule (H Res 788) that would provide for House floor consideration of the conference report on the bill that would appropriate $34 billion, including $33.5 billion in discretionary funds, for fiscal 2010 for energy and water development projects in the Energy Department, Army Corps of Engineers, Bureau of Reclamation and other agencies. Adopted 234-181: R 0-169; D 234-12. Oct. 1, 2009.

750. **H Res 692. Tay-Sachs Awareness Month/Adoption.** Pallone, D-N.J., motion to suspend the rules and adopt the resolution that would support the goals of Tay-Sachs Awareness Month and encourage research into Tay-Sachs disease. Motion agreed to 415-0: R 171-0; D 244-0. A two-thirds majority of those present and voting (277 in this case) is required for adoption under suspension of the rules. Oct. 1, 2009.

751. **H Con Res 151. Release of Liu Xiaobo/Adoption.** Berman, D-Calif., motion to suspend the rules and adopt the concurrent resolution that would express the sense of Congress that the Chinese government should release democracy activist Liu Xiaobo and begin making strides toward true representative democracy. Motion agreed to 410-1: R 167-1; D 243-0. A two-thirds majority of those present and voting (274 in this case) is required for adoption under suspension of the rules. Oct. 1, 2009.

752. **HR 3183. Fiscal 2010 Energy-Water Appropriations/Conference Report.** Adoption of the conference report on the bill that would appropriate $34 billion, including $33.5 billion in discretionary funds, in fiscal 2010 for energy and water development projects. It would provide $27.1 billion for the Energy Department, including $2.2 billion for renewable-energy programs and $6.4 billion to maintain and refurbish nuclear weapons. The total also includes $5.4 billion for the Army Corps of Engineers and $1.1 billion for the Interior Department's Bureau of Reclamation. Adopted (thus sent to the Senate) 308-114: R 70-102; D 238-12. A "yea" was a vote in support of the president's position. Oct. 1, 2009.

	748	749	750	751	752
ALABAMA					
1 Bonner	Y	N	Y	Y	Y
2 Bright	Y	N	Y	Y	Y
3 Rogers	Y	N	Y	Y	Y
4 Aderholt	Y	N	Y	Y	Y
5 Griffith	Y	N	Y	Y	Y
6 Bachus	Y	N	Y	Y	Y
7 Davis	Y	Y	Y	Y	Y
ALASKA					
AL Young	Y	N	Y	Y	N
ARIZONA					
1 Kirkpatrick	Y	Y	Y	Y	Y
2 Franks	Y	N	Y	Y	Y
3 Shadegg	?	N	Y	Y	N
4 Pastor	Y	Y	Y	Y	Y
5 Mitchell	Y	Y	Y	Y	Y
6 Flake	Y	N	Y	Y	Y
7 Grijalva	Y	Y	Y	Y	Y
8 Giffords	Y	Y	Y	Y	Y
ARKANSAS					
1 Berry	Y	Y	Y	Y	Y
2 Snyder	Y	Y	Y	Y	Y
3 Boozman	Y	N	Y	Y	N
4 Ross	Y	Y	Y	Y	Y
CALIFORNIA					
1 Thompson	Y	Y	Y	Y	Y
2 Herger	Y	N	Y	Y	Y
3 Lungren	Y	N	Y	Y	Y
4 McClintock	Y	N	Y	Y	N
5 Matsui	Y	Y	Y	Y	Y
6 Woolsey	Y	Y	Y	Y	Y
7 Miller, George	Y	Y	Y	Y	Y
8 Pelosi					
9 Lee	Y	Y	Y	Y	Y
10 Vacant					
11 McNerney	Y	Y	?	Y	Y
12 Speier	Y	Y	Y	Y	Y
13 Stark	?	Y	Y	Y	Y
14 Eshoo	Y	Y	Y	Y	Y
15 Honda	Y	Y	Y	Y	Y
16 Lofgren	Y	Y	Y	Y	Y
17 Farr	Y	Y	Y	Y	Y
18 Cardoza	Y	Y	Y	Y	Y
19 Radanovich	Y	N	Y	Y	N
20 Costa	Y	Y	Y	Y	Y
21 Nunes	Y	N	Y	Y	N
22 McCarthy	?	?	?	?	?
23 Capps	Y	Y	Y	Y	Y
24 Gallegly	Y	N	Y	Y	N
25 McKeon	Y	N	Y	Y	Y
26 Dreier	Y	N	Y	Y	Y
27 Sherman	Y	Y	Y	Y	Y
28 Berman	?	Y	Y	Y	Y
29 Schiff	Y	Y	Y	Y	Y
30 Waxman	Y	Y	Y	Y	Y
31 Becerra	Y	Y	Y	Y	Y
32 Chu	Y	Y	Y	Y	Y
33 Watson	Y	Y	Y	Y	Y
34 Roybal-Allard	Y	Y	Y	Y	Y
35 Waters	Y	Y	Y	Y	Y
36 Harman	Y	Y	Y	Y	Y
37 Richardson	Y	Y	Y	Y	Y
38 Napolitano	Y	Y	Y	Y	Y
39 Sánchez, Linda	Y	Y	Y	Y	Y
40 Royce	?	N	Y	Y	N
41 Lewis	Y	N	Y	Y	N
42 Miller, Gary	Y	N	Y	Y	N
43 Baca	Y	Y	Y	Y	Y
44 Calvert	Y	N	Y	Y	N
45 Bono Mack	Y	N	Y	Y	N
46 Rohrabacher	Y	N	Y	Y	Y
47 Sanchez, Loretta	Y	Y	Y	Y	Y
48 Campbell	Y	N	Y	Y	N
49 Issa	Y	N	Y	Y	N
50 Bilbray	Y	N	Y	Y	Y
51 Filner	Y	Y	Y	Y	Y
52 Hunter	Y	N	Y	Y	N
53 Davis	Y	Y	Y	Y	Y

	748	749	750	751	752
COLORADO					
1 DeGette	Y	Y	Y	Y	Y
2 Polis	Y	Y	Y	Y	Y
3 Salazar	Y	Y	Y	Y	Y
4 Markey	Y	Y	?	Y	Y
5 Lamborn	Y	?	?	?	N
6 Coffman	Y	N	Y	Y	N
7 Perlmutter	Y	Y	Y	Y	Y
CONNECTICUT					
1 Larson	Y	Y	Y	Y	Y
2 Courtney	Y	Y	Y	Y	Y
3 DeLauro	Y	Y	Y	Y	Y
4 Himes	Y	Y	Y	Y	Y
5 Murphy	Y	Y	Y	Y	Y
DELAWARE					
AL Castle	Y	N	Y	Y	Y
FLORIDA					
1 Miller	Y	N	Y	Y	N
2 Boyd	Y	Y	Y	Y	Y
3 Brown	Y	Y	Y	Y	Y
4 Crenshaw	Y	N	Y	Y	N
5 Brown-Waite	Y	N	Y	Y	N
6 Stearns	Y	N	Y	Y	Y
7 Mica	Y	N	Y	Y	N
8 Grayson	Y	Y	Y	Y	Y
9 Bilirakis	Y	N	Y	Y	N
10 Young	Y	N	Y	Y	Y
11 Castor	Y	Y	Y	Y	Y
12 Putnam	Y	N	Y	Y	N
13 Buchanan	Y	N	Y	Y	N
14 Mack	Y	N	Y	Y	N
15 Posey	Y	N	Y	Y	N
16 Rooney	Y	N	Y	Y	Y
17 Meek	Y	Y	Y	Y	Y
18 Ros-Lehtinen	Y	N	Y	Y	Y
19 Wexler	?	?	?	?	Y
20 Wasserman Schultz	Y	Y	Y	Y	Y
21 Diaz-Balart, L.	Y	N	Y	Y	Y
22 Klein	Y	Y	Y	Y	Y
23 Hastings	Y	Y	Y	Y	Y
24 Kosmas	Y	Y	Y	Y	Y
25 Diaz-Balart, M.	Y	N	Y	Y	Y
GEORGIA					
1 Kingston	Y	N	Y	Y	N
2 Bishop	Y	Y	Y	Y	N
3 Westmoreland	Y	N	Y	Y	N
4 Johnson	Y	Y	Y	Y	Y
5 Lewis	Y	Y	Y	Y	Y
6 Price	Y	N	Y	Y	N
7 Linder	Y	N	Y	Y	N
8 Marshall	Y	Y	Y	Y	N
9 Deal	Y	N	Y	?	N
10 Broun	Y	N	Y	Y	N
11 Gingrey	Y	?	Y	Y	N
12 Barrow	Y	Y	Y	Y	Y
13 Scott	Y	Y	Y	Y	Y
HAWAII					
1 Abercrombie	Y	Y	Y	Y	Y
2 Hirono	Y	Y	Y	Y	Y
IDAHO					
1 Minnick	Y	N	Y	Y	Y
2 Simpson	Y	N	Y	Y	Y
ILLINOIS					
1 Rush	?	Y	Y	Y	Y
2 Jackson	Y	Y	Y	Y	Y
3 Lipinski	Y	Y	Y	Y	Y
4 Gutierrez	Y	Y	Y	Y	Y
5 Quigley	Y	?	?	?	Y
6 Roskam	Y	N	Y	Y	N
7 Davis	Y	Y	Y	Y	Y
8 Bean	Y	Y	Y	Y	Y
9 Schakowsky	Y	Y	Y	Y	Y
10 Kirk	Y	N	Y	Y	Y
11 Halvorson	Y	Y	Y	Y	Y
12 Costello	Y	Y	Y	Y	Y
13 Biggert	Y	N	Y	Y	Y
14 Foster	Y	Y	Y	Y	Y
15 Johnson	Y	N	Y	Y	N

KEY	**Republicans**	Democrats		
Y Voted for (yea)		X Paired against		C Voted "present" to avoid possible conflict of interest
# Paired for		– Announced against		? Did not vote or otherwise make a position known
+ Announced for		P Voted "present"		
N Voted against (nay)				

Member	748	749	750	751	752
16 Manzullo	Y	N	Y	Y	N
17 Hare	Y	Y	Y	Y	Y
18 Schock	Y	N	Y	Y	N
19 Shimkus	Y	N	Y	Y	N
INDIANA					
1 Visclosky	Y	Y	Y	?	Y
2 Donnelly	Y	Y	Y	Y	Y
3 Souder	Y	?	Y	Y	Y
4 Buyer	Y	N	Y	Y	N
5 Burton	Y	N	Y	Y	N
6 Pence	Y	N	Y	Y	N
7 Carson	Y	Y	Y	Y	Y
8 Ellsworth	Y	N	Y	Y	Y
9 Hill	Y	Y	Y	Y	Y
IOWA					
1 Braley	Y	Y	Y	Y	Y
2 Loebsack	Y	Y	Y	Y	Y
3 Boswell	Y	Y	Y	Y	Y
4 Latham	Y	N	Y	Y	Y
5 King	Y	N	Y	Y	N
KANSAS					
1 Moran	Y	N	Y	Y	N
2 Jenkins	Y	N	Y	Y	N
3 Moore	Y	Y	Y	Y	Y
4 Tiahrt	Y	N	Y	Y	N
KENTUCKY					
1 Whitfield	?	?	?	?	?
2 Guthrie	Y	N	Y	Y	Y
3 Yarmuth	Y	Y	Y	Y	Y
4 Davis	Y	N	Y	Y	N
5 Rogers	Y	N	Y	Y	Y
6 Chandler	Y	Y	Y	Y	Y
LOUISIANA					
1 Scalise	Y	N	Y	Y	N
2 Cao	Y	N	Y	Y	Y
3 Melancon	Y	N	Y	Y	Y
4 Fleming	Y	N	Y	Y	N
5 Alexander	Y	N	Y	Y	Y
6 Cassidy	Y	N	Y	Y	Y
7 Boustany	Y	N	Y	Y	Y
MAINE					
1 Pingree	Y	Y	Y	Y	Y
2 Michaud	Y	Y	Y	Y	Y
MARYLAND					
1 Kratovil	Y	N	Y	Y	Y
2 Ruppersberger	Y	Y	Y	Y	Y
3 Sarbanes	Y	Y	Y	Y	Y
4 Edwards	Y	Y	Y	Y	Y
5 Hoyer	Y	Y	Y	Y	Y
6 Bartlett	Y	N	Y	Y	N
7 Cummings	Y	Y	Y	Y	Y
8 Van Hollen	Y	Y	Y	Y	Y
MASSACHUSETTS					
1 Olver	Y	Y	Y	Y	Y
2 Neal	Y	Y	Y	Y	Y
3 McGovern	Y	Y	Y	Y	Y
4 Frank	Y	Y	Y	Y	Y
5 Tsongas	Y	Y	Y	Y	Y
6 Tierney	Y	Y	Y	Y	Y
7 Markey	Y	Y	Y	Y	Y
8 Capuano	?	?	?	?	?
9 Lynch	Y	Y	Y	Y	Y
10 Delahunt	Y	Y	Y	Y	Y
MICHIGAN					
1 Stupak	Y	Y	Y	Y	Y
2 Hoekstra	Y	N	Y	Y	N
3 Ehlers	Y	N	Y	Y	Y
4 Camp	Y	N	Y	Y	Y
5 Kildee	Y	Y	Y	Y	Y
6 Upton	Y	N	Y	Y	Y
7 Schauer	Y	Y	Y	Y	Y
8 Rogers	Y	N	Y	Y	Y
9 Peters	Y	Y	Y	Y	Y
10 Miller	Y	N	Y	Y	Y
11 McCotter	Y	N	Y	Y	Y
12 Levin	Y	Y	Y	Y	Y
13 Kilpatrick	Y	Y	Y	Y	Y
14 Conyers	Y	Y	Y	?	Y
15 Dingell	Y	Y	Y	Y	Y
MINNESOTA					
1 Walz	Y	Y	Y	Y	Y
2 Kline	Y	N	Y	Y	N
3 Paulsen	Y	N	Y	Y	N
4 McCollum	Y	Y	Y	Y	Y

Member	748	749	750	751	752
5 Ellison	Y	Y	Y	?	Y
6 Bachmann	Y	N	Y	Y	N
7 Peterson	Y	Y	Y	Y	Y
8 Oberstar	Y	Y	Y	Y	Y
MISSISSIPPI					
1 Childers	Y	Y	Y	Y	Y
2 Thompson	Y	Y	Y	Y	Y
3 Harper	Y	N	Y	Y	Y
4 Taylor	Y	Y	Y	Y	Y
MISSOURI					
1 Clay	Y	Y	Y	Y	Y
2 Akin	Y	N	Y	Y	N
3 Carnahan	Y	Y	Y	Y	Y
4 Skelton	Y	Y	Y	Y	Y
5 Cleaver	Y	Y	Y	Y	Y
6 Graves	Y	N	Y	Y	N
7 Blunt	Y	N	Y	Y	N
8 Emerson	Y	N	Y	Y	N
9 Luetkemeyer	Y	N	Y	Y	Y
MONTANA					
AL Rehberg	Y	N	Y	Y	Y
NEBRASKA					
1 Fortenberry	Y	N	Y	Y	Y
2 Terry	Y	N	Y	Y	Y
3 Smith	Y	N	Y	Y	N
NEVADA					
1 Berkley	Y	Y	Y	Y	Y
2 Heller	?	N	Y	Y	N
3 Titus	Y	Y	Y	Y	Y
NEW HAMPSHIRE					
1 Shea-Porter	Y	Y	Y	Y	Y
2 Hodes	Y	Y	Y	Y	Y
NEW JERSEY					
1 Andrews	Y	Y	Y	Y	N
2 LoBiondo	Y	N	Y	Y	Y
3 Adler	?	?	?	?	?
4 Smith	Y	N	Y	Y	Y
5 Garrett	Y	N	Y	Y	N
6 Pallone	Y	Y	Y	Y	Y
7 Lance	Y	N	Y	Y	Y
8 Pascrell	Y	?	?	?	?
9 Rothman	Y	Y	Y	Y	Y
10 Payne	Y	Y	Y	Y	Y
11 Frelinghuysen	Y	N	Y	Y	Y
12 Holt	Y	Y	Y	Y	Y
13 Sires	Y	Y	Y	Y	Y
NEW MEXICO					
1 Heinrich	Y	Y	Y	Y	Y
2 Teague	Y	Y	Y	Y	Y
3 Lujan	Y	?	?	?	Y
NEW YORK					
1 Bishop	Y	Y	Y	Y	Y
2 Israel	Y	Y	Y	Y	Y
3 King	Y	N	Y	Y	Y
4 McCarthy	Y	Y	Y	Y	Y
5 Ackerman	Y	Y	Y	Y	Y
6 Meeks	Y	Y	Y	Y	Y
7 Crowley	Y	Y	Y	Y	Y
8 Nadler	Y	Y	Y	Y	Y
9 Weiner	Y	Y	Y	Y	Y
10 Towns	Y	Y	Y	Y	Y
11 Clarke	Y	Y	Y	Y	Y
12 Velázquez	Y	Y	Y	Y	Y
13 McMahon	Y	Y	Y	Y	Y
14 Maloney	?	?	?	?	?
15 Rangel	Y	Y	Y	Y	Y
16 Serrano	Y	Y	Y	Y	Y
17 Engel	Y	Y	Y	Y	Y
18 Lowey	Y	Y	Y	Y	Y
19 Hall	Y	Y	Y	Y	Y
20 Murphy	Y	N	Y	Y	Y
21 Tonko	Y	Y	Y	Y	Y
22 Hinchey	Y	Y	Y	Y	Y
23 Vacant					
24 Arcuri	Y	Y	Y	Y	Y
25 Maffei	Y	Y	Y	Y	Y
26 Lee	Y	N	Y	Y	Y
27 Higgins	Y	Y	Y	Y	Y
28 Slaughter	Y	Y	Y	Y	Y
29 Massa	?	Y	Y	Y	Y
NORTH CAROLINA					
1 Butterfield	Y	Y	Y	Y	Y
2 Etheridge	Y	Y	Y	Y	Y
3 Jones	Y	N	Y	Y	Y
4 Price	Y	Y	Y	Y	Y

Member	748	749	750	751	752
5 Foxx	Y	N	Y	Y	N
6 Coble	Y	N	Y	Y	N
7 McIntyre	Y	Y	Y	Y	Y
8 Kissell	Y	Y	Y	Y	Y
9 Myrick	Y	N	Y	Y	N
10 McHenry	Y	N	Y	Y	N
11 Shuler	Y	N	Y	Y	Y
12 Watt	Y	Y	Y	Y	Y
13 Miller	Y	Y	Y	?	Y
NORTH DAKOTA					
AL Pomeroy	Y	Y	Y	Y	Y
OHIO					
1 Driehaus	Y	Y	Y	Y	Y
2 Schmidt	?	?	?	?	?
3 Turner	Y	N	Y	Y	Y
4 Jordan	Y	N	Y	Y	N
5 Latta	Y	N	Y	Y	N
6 Wilson	?	Y	Y	Y	Y
7 Austria	Y	N	Y	Y	Y
8 Boehner	Y	N	Y	Y	N
9 Kaptur	Y	Y	Y	Y	Y
10 Kucinich	Y	N	Y	Y	N
11 Fudge	Y	Y	Y	Y	Y
12 Tiberi	Y	N	Y	?	Y
13 Sutton	Y	Y	Y	Y	Y
14 LaTourette	Y	Y	Y	Y	Y
15 Kilroy	Y	Y	Y	Y	Y
16 Boccieri	Y	Y	Y	Y	Y
17 Ryan	Y	Y	Y	Y	Y
18 Space	Y	Y	Y	Y	Y
OKLAHOMA					
1 Sullivan	Y	N	Y	Y	N
2 Boren	Y	Y	Y	Y	Y
3 Lucas	Y	N	Y	Y	N
4 Cole	Y	N	Y	Y	N
5 Fallin	Y	N	Y	Y	N
OREGON					
1 Wu	Y	Y	Y	Y	Y
2 Walden	Y	N	Y	Y	N
3 Blumenauer	Y	Y	Y	Y	Y
4 DeFazio	Y	Y	Y	Y	Y
5 Schrader	Y	Y	Y	Y	Y
PENNSYLVANIA					
1 Brady	Y	Y	Y	Y	Y
2 Fattah	Y	Y	Y	Y	Y
3 Dahlkemper	Y	Y	Y	Y	Y
4 Altmire	Y	Y	Y	Y	Y
5 Thompson	Y	N	Y	Y	Y
6 Gerlach	Y	N	Y	Y	Y
7 Sestak	Y	Y	Y	Y	Y
8 Murphy, P.	Y	Y	Y	Y	Y
9 Shuster	Y	N	Y	Y	Y
10 Carney	?	?	?	?	?
11 Kanjorski	Y	N	Y	Y	N
12 Murtha	Y	Y	Y	Y	Y
13 Schwartz	Y	Y	Y	Y	Y
14 Doyle	Y	Y	Y	Y	Y
15 Dent	Y	N	Y	Y	Y
16 Pitts	Y	N	Y	Y	N
17 Holden	Y	Y	Y	Y	Y
18 Murphy, T.	Y	N	Y	Y	Y
19 Platts	Y	N	Y	Y	N
RHODE ISLAND					
1 Kennedy	Y	Y	Y	Y	Y
2 Langevin	Y	Y	Y	Y	Y
SOUTH CAROLINA					
1 Brown	Y	N	Y	Y	N
2 Wilson	Y	N	Y	Y	N
3 Barrett	?	?	?	?	?
4 Inglis	Y	N	Y	Y	N
5 Spratt	Y	Y	Y	Y	Y
6 Clyburn	Y	Y	Y	Y	Y
SOUTH DAKOTA					
AL Herseth Sandlin	Y	Y	Y	Y	Y
TENNESSEE					
1 Roe	Y	N	Y	Y	N
2 Duncan	Y	N	Y	Y	N
3 Wamp	Y	N	Y	Y	Y
4 Davis	Y	Y	Y	Y	Y
5 Cooper	Y	Y	Y	Y	Y
6 Gordon	Y	Y	Y	?	Y
7 Blackburn	Y	N	Y	Y	N
8 Tanner	Y	Y	Y	Y	Y
9 Cohen	Y	Y	Y	Y	Y

Member	748	749	750	751	752
TEXAS					
1 Gohmert	Y	N	Y	?	N
2 Poe	Y	N	Y	Y	N
3 Johnson, S.	Y	N	Y	Y	N
4 Hall	Y	N	Y	Y	Y
5 Hensarling	Y	N	Y	Y	N
6 Barton	Y	N	Y	Y	N
7 Culberson	Y	N	Y	Y	N
8 Brady	Y	N	Y	Y	N
9 Green, A.	Y	Y	Y	Y	Y
10 McCaul	Y	N	Y	Y	N
11 Conaway	Y	N	Y	Y	N
12 Granger	Y	N	Y	Y	N
13 Thornberry	Y	N	Y	Y	N
14 Paul	Y	N	Y	N	N
15 Hinojosa	Y	Y	Y	Y	Y
16 Reyes	Y	Y	Y	Y	Y
17 Edwards	Y	Y	Y	Y	Y
18 Jackson Lee	Y	Y	Y	Y	Y
19 Neugebauer	?	?	?	?	?
20 Gonzalez	Y	Y	Y	Y	Y
21 Smith	Y	N	Y	Y	N
22 Olson	Y	N	Y	Y	N
23 Rodriguez	Y	Y	Y	Y	Y
24 Marchant	Y	N	Y	Y	N
25 Doggett	Y	Y	Y	Y	Y
26 Burgess	Y	N	Y	Y	N
27 Ortiz	Y	Y	Y	Y	Y
28 Cuellar	Y	Y	Y	Y	Y
29 Green, G.	Y	Y	Y	Y	Y
30 Johnson, E.	Y	Y	Y	Y	Y
31 Carter	?	N	Y	Y	N
32 Sessions	Y	N	Y	Y	N
UTAH					
1 Bishop	Y	N	Y	Y	N
2 Matheson	Y	Y	Y	Y	N
3 Chaffetz	Y	N	Y	Y	N
VERMONT					
AL Welch	Y	Y	Y	Y	Y
VIRGINIA					
1 Wittman	Y	N	Y	Y	Y
2 Nye	Y	N	Y	Y	Y
3 Scott	Y	Y	Y	Y	Y
4 Forbes	Y	N	Y	Y	Y
5 Perriello	Y	Y	Y	Y	Y
6 Goodlatte	Y	N	Y	Y	N
7 Cantor	Y	N	Y	Y	N
8 Moran	Y	Y	Y	Y	Y
9 Boucher	Y	Y	Y	Y	Y
10 Wolf	Y	N	Y	Y	Y
11 Connolly	Y	Y	Y	Y	Y
WASHINGTON					
1 Inslee	Y	?	Y	Y	Y
2 Larsen	Y	Y	Y	Y	Y
3 Baird	Y	N	Y	N	Y
4 Hastings	Y	N	Y	Y	N
5 McMorris Rodgers	Y	N	Y	Y	N
6 Dicks	Y	Y	Y	Y	Y
7 McDermott	Y	Y	Y	Y	Y
8 Reichert	Y	N	Y	Y	Y
9 Smith	Y	Y	Y	Y	Y
WEST VIRGINIA					
1 Mollohan	Y	Y	Y	Y	Y
2 Capito	Y	N	Y	Y	Y
3 Rahall	Y	Y	Y	Y	Y
WISCONSIN					
1 Ryan	Y	N	Y	Y	N
2 Baldwin	Y	Y	Y	Y	Y
3 Kind	Y	Y	Y	Y	Y
4 Moore	Y	Y	Y	Y	Y
5 Sensenbrenner	Y	N	Y	Y	N
6 Petri	Y	N	Y	Y	N
7 Obey	Y	Y	Y	Y	Y
8 Kagen	Y	Y	Y	Y	Y
WYOMING					
AL Lummis	Y	N	Y	Y	N

DELEGATES
Faleomavaega (A.S.)
Norton (D.C.)
Bordallo (Guam)
Sablan (N. Marianas)
Pierluisi (P.R.)
Christensen (V.I.)

IN THE HOUSE | By Vote Number

753. HR 2647. Fiscal 2010 Defense Authorization/Motion to Close **Conference.** Skelton, D-Mo., motion to close portions of the conference on the bill that would authorize $680.2 billion in discretionary funds for defense programs in fiscal 2010, including approximately $130 billion for the wars in Iraq and Afghanistan and other operations. Motion agreed to 405-7: R 164-2; D 241-5. Oct. 6, 2009.

754. HR 2647. Fiscal 2010 Defense Authorization/Motion to **Instruct.** Forbes, R-Va., motion to instruct conferees to disagree with Senate provisions that would extend federal hate crimes laws to cover offenses motivated by the victim's gender identity, sexual orientation or disability. Motion rejected 178-234: R 156-9; D 22-225. Oct. 6, 2009.

755. H Res 707. National Adult Education and Family Literacy **Week/Adoption.** Polis, D-Colo., motion to suspend the rules and adopt the resolution that would support the designation of National Adult Education and Family Literacy Week and request a presidential proclamation recognizing adult education and literacy programs. Motion agreed to 412-0: R 165-0; D 247-0. A two-thirds majority of those present and voting (275 in this case) is required for adoption under suspension of the rules. Oct. 6, 2009.

756. HR 2997. Fiscal 2010 Agriculture Appropriations/Previous **Question.** McGovern, D-Mass., motion to order the previous question (thus ending debate and possibility of amendment) on adoption of the rule (H Res 799) that would provide for House floor consideration of the conference report on the bill that would appropriate $121.2 billion in fiscal 2010 for the Department of Agriculture and related agencies, including the Food and Drug Administration. Motion agreed to 237-180: R 0-169; D 237-11. Oct. 7, 2009.

757. HR 2997. Fiscal 2010 Agriculture Appropriations/Rule.
Adoption of the rule (H Res 799) that would provide for House floor consideration of the conference report on the bill that would appropriate $121.2 billion in fiscal 2010 for the Department of Agriculture and related agencies, including the Food and Drug Administration. Adopted 241-178: R 0-170; D 241-8. Oct. 7, 2009.

	753	754	755	756	757
ALABAMA					
1 Bonner	Y	Y	Y	N	N
2 Bright	Y	Y	Y	N	N
3 Rogers	Y	Y	Y	N	N
4 Aderholt	Y	Y	Y	N	N
5 Griffith	Y	Y	Y	N	Y
6 Bachus	Y	Y	Y	N	N
7 Davis	Y	Y	Y	Y	Y
ALASKA					
AL Young	Y	Y	Y	N	N
ARIZONA					
1 Kirkpatrick	Y	N	Y	Y	Y
2 Franks	Y	Y	Y	N	N
3 Shadegg	Y	Y	Y	N	N
4 Pastor	Y	N	Y	Y	Y
5 Mitchell	Y	N	Y	N	N
6 Flake	Y	Y	Y	N	N
7 Grijalva	Y	N	Y	Y	Y
8 Giffords	Y	N	Y	Y	Y
ARKANSAS					
1 Berry	Y	Y	Y	Y	Y
2 Snyder	Y	N	Y	Y	Y
3 Boozman	Y	Y	Y	N	N
4 Ross	Y	Y	Y	Y	Y
CALIFORNIA					
1 Thompson	Y	N	Y	Y	Y
2 Herger	Y	Y	Y	N	N
3 Lungren	Y	Y	Y	N	N
4 McClintock	Y	Y	Y	N	N
5 Matsui	Y	N	Y	Y	Y
6 Woolsey	Y	N	Y	Y	Y
7 Miller, George	Y	N	Y	Y	Y
8 Pelosi					
9 Lee	Y	N	Y	Y	Y
10 Vacant					
11 McNerney	Y	N	Y	Y	Y
12 Speier	Y	N	Y	Y	Y
13 Stark	N	N	Y	Y	Y
14 Eshoo	Y	N	Y	Y	Y
15 Honda	Y	N	Y	Y	?
16 Lofgren	Y	N	Y	Y	Y
17 Farr	Y	N	Y	Y	Y
18 Cardoza	Y	N	Y	Y	Y
19 Radanovich	Y	Y	?	?	?
20 Costa	?	N	Y	Y	Y
21 Nunes	Y	Y	Y	N	N
22 McCarthy	Y	Y	Y	N	N
23 Capps	Y	N	Y	Y	Y
24 Gallegly	Y	Y	Y	N	N
25 McKeon	Y	Y	Y	N	N
26 Dreier	Y	Y	Y	N	N
27 Sherman	Y	N	Y	Y	Y
28 Berman	Y	N	Y	Y	Y
29 Schiff	Y	N	Y	Y	Y
30 Waxman	Y	N	Y	Y	Y
31 Becerra	Y	N	Y	Y	Y
32 Chu	Y	N	Y	Y	Y
33 Watson	Y	N	Y	Y	Y
34 Roybal-Allard	Y	N	Y	Y	Y
35 Waters	Y	N	Y	Y	Y
36 Harman	Y	N	Y	Y	Y
37 Richardson	Y	N	Y	Y	Y
38 Napolitano	Y	N	Y	Y	Y
39 Sánchez, Linda	Y	N	Y	Y	Y
40 Royce	Y	Y	Y	N	N
41 Lewis	Y	Y	Y	N	N
42 Miller, Gary	Y	Y	Y	N	N
43 Baca	Y	N	Y	Y	Y
44 Calvert	Y	Y	Y	N	N
45 Bono Mack	Y	Y	Y	N	N
46 Rohrabacher	?	?	?	N	N
47 Sanchez, Loretta	Y	N	Y	Y	Y
48 Campbell	Y	Y	Y	N	N
49 Issa	Y	Y	Y	N	N
50 Bilbray	Y	Y	Y	N	N
51 Filner	Y	N	Y	Y	Y
52 Hunter	Y	Y	Y	N	N
53 Davis	Y	N	Y	Y	Y
COLORADO					
1 DeGette	Y	N	Y	Y	Y
2 Polis	Y	N	Y	Y	Y
3 Salazar	Y	N	Y	Y	Y
4 Markey	Y	N	Y	Y	Y
5 Lamborn	Y	Y	Y	N	N
6 Coffman	Y	Y	Y	N	N
7 Perlmutter	Y	N	Y	Y	Y
CONNECTICUT					
1 Larson	Y	N	Y	+	+
2 Courtney	Y	N	Y	Y	Y
3 DeLauro	Y	N	Y	Y	Y
4 Himes	Y	N	Y	Y	Y
5 Murphy	Y	N	Y	Y	Y
DELAWARE					
AL Castle	Y	N	Y	N	N
FLORIDA					
1 Miller	Y	Y	Y	N	N
2 Boyd	Y	N	Y	Y	Y
3 Brown	?	?	?	?	?
4 Crenshaw	?	?	?	?	?
5 Brown-Waite	Y	Y	Y	N	N
6 Stearns	Y	Y	Y	N	N
7 Mica	Y	Y	Y	N	N
8 Grayson	Y	N	Y	Y	Y
9 Bilirakis	Y	Y	Y	N	N
10 Young	Y	Y	Y	N	N
11 Castor	Y	N	Y	Y	Y
12 Putnam	Y	Y	Y	N	N
13 Buchanan	Y	Y	Y	N	N
14 Mack	Y	Y	Y	N	N
15 Posey	Y	Y	Y	N	N
16 Rooney	Y	Y	Y	N	N
17 Meek	?	?	?	Y	Y
18 Ros-Lehtinen	?	–	Y	N	N
19 Wexler	Y	N	Y	Y	Y
20 Wasserman Schultz	Y	N	Y	Y	Y
21 Diaz-Balart, L.	?	?	?	N	N
22 Klein	Y	N	Y	Y	Y
23 Hastings	Y	N	Y	Y	Y
24 Kosmas	Y	N	Y	Y	Y
25 Diaz-Balart, M.	?	?	?	?	?
GEORGIA					
1 Kingston	Y	Y	Y	N	N
2 Bishop	Y	N	Y	Y	Y
3 Westmoreland	Y	Y	Y	?	N
4 Johnson	Y	N	Y	Y	Y
5 Lewis	Y	N	Y	Y	Y
6 Price	Y	Y	Y	N	N
7 Linder	Y	Y	Y	N	N
8 Marshall	Y	Y	Y	Y	Y
9 Deal	Y	Y	Y	N	N
10 Broun	Y	Y	Y	N	N
11 Gingrey	Y	Y	Y	N	N
12 Barrow	Y	N	Y	Y	Y
13 Scott	Y	N	Y	Y	Y
HAWAII					
1 Abercrombie	Y	N	Y	Y	Y
2 Hirono	Y	N	Y	Y	Y
IDAHO					
1 Minnick	Y	N	Y	N	N
2 Simpson	Y	Y	Y	N	N
ILLINOIS					
1 Rush	Y	N	Y	Y	Y
2 Jackson	Y	N	Y	Y	Y
3 Lipinski	Y	N	Y	Y	Y
4 Gutierrez	Y	N	Y	Y	Y
5 Quigley	Y	N	Y	Y	Y
6 Roskam	Y	Y	Y	N	N
7 Davis	Y	N	Y	Y	Y
8 Bean	Y	N	Y	Y	Y
9 Schakowsky	Y	N	Y	Y	Y
10 Kirk	Y	N	Y	N	N
11 Halvorson	Y	N	Y	Y	Y
12 Costello	Y	N	Y	Y	Y
13 Biggert	Y	N	Y	N	N
14 Foster	Y	N	Y	N	Y
15 Johnson	N	Y	Y	N	N

KEY	Republicans		Democrats		
Y Voted for (yea)		X Paired against		C Voted "present" to avoid possible conflict of interest	
# Paired for		– Announced against			
+ Announced for		P Voted "present"		? Did not vote or otherwise make a position known	
N Voted against (nay)					

	753	754	755	756	757
16 Manzullo	Y	Y	Y	N	N
17 Hare	Y	N	Y	Y	Y
18 Schock	Y	Y	Y	N	N
19 Shimkus	?	?	?	N	N
INDIANA					
1 Visclosky	?	?	?	Y	Y
2 Donnelly	Y	Y	Y	Y	Y
3 Souder	Y	Y	Y	N	N
4 Buyer	Y	Y	Y	N	N
5 Burton	Y	Y	Y	N	N
6 Pence	Y	Y	Y	N	N
7 Carson	Y	N	Y	Y	Y
8 Ellsworth	Y	Y	Y	Y	Y
9 Hill	Y	N	Y	Y	Y
IOWA					
1 Braley	Y	N	Y	+	Y
2 Loebsack	Y	N	Y	Y	Y
3 Boswell	Y	N	Y	Y	Y
4 Latham	Y	Y	Y	N	N
5 King	Y	+	Y	N	N
KANSAS					
1 Moran	Y	Y	Y	N	N
2 Jenkins	Y	Y	Y	N	N
3 Moore	Y	N	Y	Y	Y
4 Tiahrt	Y	Y	Y	N	N
KENTUCKY					
1 Whitfield	Y	Y	Y	N	N
2 Guthrie	Y	Y	Y	N	N
3 Yarmuth	Y	N	Y	Y	Y
4 Davis	Y	Y	Y	N	N
5 Rogers	Y	Y	Y	N	N
6 Chandler	Y	N	Y	Y	Y
LOUISIANA					
1 Scalise	Y	Y	Y	N	N
2 Cao	Y	N	Y	N	N
3 Melancon	Y	N	Y	Y	Y
4 Fleming	Y	Y	Y	N	N
5 Alexander	Y	Y	Y	N	N
6 Cassidy	Y	N	Y	N	N
7 Boustany	Y	Y	Y	N	N
MAINE					
1 Pingree	Y	N	Y	Y	Y
2 Michaud	Y	N	Y	Y	Y
MARYLAND					
1 Kratovil	Y	Y	Y	N	N
2 Ruppersberger	Y	N	Y	Y	Y
3 Sarbanes	Y	N	Y	Y	Y
4 Edwards	Y	N	Y	Y	Y
5 Hoyer	Y	N	Y	Y	Y
6 Bartlett	Y	Y	Y	N	N
7 Cummings	Y	N	Y	Y	Y
8 Van Hollen	Y	N	Y	Y	Y
MASSACHUSETTS					
1 Olver	Y	N	Y	Y	Y
2 Neal	Y	N	Y	Y	Y
3 McGovern	Y	N	Y	Y	Y
4 Frank	Y	N	Y	Y	Y
5 Tsongas	Y	N	Y	+	+
6 Tierney	Y	N	Y	Y	Y
7 Markey	Y	N	Y	Y	Y
8 Capuano	?	?	?	Y	Y
9 Lynch	Y	N	Y	Y	Y
10 Delahunt	Y	N	Y	Y	Y
MICHIGAN					
1 Stupak	Y	N	Y	Y	Y
2 Hoekstra	Y	Y	Y	N	N
3 Ehlers	Y	Y	Y	N	N
4 Camp	Y	Y	Y	N	N
5 Kildee	Y	N	Y	Y	Y
6 Upton	Y	Y	Y	N	N
7 Schauer	Y	N	Y	Y	Y
8 Rogers	Y	Y	Y	N	N
9 Peters	Y	N	Y	Y	Y
10 Miller	Y	Y	Y	N	N
11 McCotter	Y	Y	Y	N	N
12 Levin	Y	N	Y	Y	Y
13 Kilpatrick	Y	N	Y	Y	Y
14 Conyers	Y	N	Y	+	Y
15 Dingell	Y	N	Y	Y	Y
MINNESOTA					
1 Walz	Y	N	Y	Y	Y
2 Kline	Y	Y	Y	N	N
3 Paulsen	Y	Y	Y	N	N
4 McCollum	Y	N	Y	Y	Y

	753	754	755	756	757
5 Ellison	Y	N	Y	Y	Y
6 Bachmann	Y	Y	Y	?	?
7 Peterson	Y	Y	Y	Y	Y
8 Oberstar	Y	N	Y	Y	Y
MISSISSIPPI					
1 Childers	Y	Y	Y	Y	Y
2 Thompson	Y	N	Y	Y	Y
3 Harper	Y	Y	Y	N	N
4 Taylor	Y	Y	Y	N	N
MISSOURI					
1 Clay	Y	N	Y	Y	Y
2 Akin	Y	Y	Y	N	N
3 Carnahan	Y	N	Y	Y	Y
4 Skelton	Y	N	Y	Y	Y
5 Cleaver	Y	N	Y	Y	Y
6 Graves	Y	Y	Y	N	N
7 Blunt	Y	Y	Y	N	N
8 Emerson	Y	Y	Y	N	N
9 Luetkemeyer	Y	Y	Y	N	N
MONTANA					
AL Rehberg	Y	Y	Y	N	N
NEBRASKA					
1 Fortenberry	Y	Y	Y	N	N
2 Terry	Y	Y	Y	N	N
3 Smith	Y	Y	Y	N	N
NEVADA					
1 Berkley	Y	N	Y	Y	Y
2 Heller	Y	Y	Y	N	N
3 Titus	Y	N	Y	Y	Y
NEW HAMPSHIRE					
1 Shea-Porter	Y	N	Y	Y	Y
2 Hodes	Y	N	Y	Y	Y
NEW JERSEY					
1 Andrews	Y	N	Y	Y	Y
2 LoBiondo	Y	Y	Y	N	N
3 Adler	Y	N	Y	Y	Y
4 Smith	Y	Y	Y	N	N
5 Garrett	Y	Y	Y	N	N
6 Pallone	Y	N	Y	Y	Y
7 Lance	Y	Y	Y	N	N
8 Pascrell	Y	N	Y	Y	Y
9 Rothman	Y	N	Y	Y	Y
10 Payne	Y	N	Y	Y	Y
11 Frelinghuysen	Y	Y	Y	?	?
12 Holt	Y	N	Y	Y	Y
13 Sires	Y	N	Y	Y	Y
NEW MEXICO					
1 Heinrich	Y	N	Y	Y	Y
2 Teague	Y	Y	Y	Y	Y
3 Lujan	Y	N	Y	Y	Y
NEW YORK					
1 Bishop	Y	N	Y	Y	Y
2 Israel	Y	N	Y	Y	Y
3 King	Y	Y	Y	N	N
4 McCarthy	Y	N	Y	Y	Y
5 Ackerman	Y	N	Y	Y	Y
6 Meeks	Y	N	Y	Y	Y
7 Crowley	Y	N	Y	Y	Y
8 Nadler	Y	N	Y	Y	Y
9 Weiner	Y	N	Y	Y	Y
10 Towns	Y	N	Y	Y	Y
11 Clarke	Y	N	Y	Y	Y
12 Velázquez	Y	N	Y	Y	Y
13 McMahon	Y	N	Y	Y	Y
14 Maloney	?	?	?	?	?
15 Rangel	Y	N	Y	Y	Y
16 Serrano	Y	N	Y	Y	Y
17 Engel	Y	N	Y	?	Y
18 Lowey	Y	N	Y	Y	Y
19 Hall	Y	N	Y	Y	Y
20 Murphy	Y	Y	Y	Y	Y
21 Tonko	Y	N	Y	Y	Y
22 Hinchey	Y	N	Y	Y	Y
23 Vacant					
24 Arcuri	Y	N	Y	Y	Y
25 Maffei	Y	N	Y	Y	Y
26 Lee	Y	Y	Y	N	N
27 Higgins	Y	N	Y	Y	Y
28 Slaughter	Y	N	Y	Y	Y
29 Massa	Y	N	Y	Y	Y
NORTH CAROLINA					
1 Butterfield	Y	N	Y	Y	Y
2 Etheridge	Y	N	Y	Y	Y
3 Jones	Y	Y	Y	N	N
4 Price	Y	N	Y	Y	Y

	753	754	755	756	757
5 Foxx	Y	Y	Y	N	N
6 Coble	Y	Y	Y	N	N
7 McIntyre	Y	Y	Y	Y	Y
8 Kissell	Y	N	Y	Y	Y
9 Myrick	Y	Y	Y	N	N
10 McHenry	Y	Y	Y	N	N
11 Shuler	Y	Y	Y	Y	Y
12 Watt	Y	N	Y	Y	Y
13 Miller	Y	N	Y	Y	Y
NORTH DAKOTA					
AL Pomeroy	Y	N	Y	Y	Y
OHIO					
1 Driehaus	Y	N	Y	Y	Y
2 Schmidt	Y	Y	Y	N	N
3 Turner	Y	Y	Y	N	N
4 Jordan	Y	Y	Y	N	N
5 Latta	Y	Y	Y	N	N
6 Wilson	Y	N	Y	Y	Y
7 Austria	Y	Y	Y	N	N
8 Boehner	Y	Y	Y	N	N
9 Kaptur	Y	N	Y	Y	Y
10 Kucinich	N	N	Y	Y	Y
11 Fudge	Y	N	Y	Y	Y
12 Tiberi	Y	Y	Y	N	N
13 Sutton	Y	N	Y	Y	Y
14 LaTourette	Y	Y	Y	N	N
15 Kilroy	Y	N	Y	Y	Y
16 Boccieri	Y	N	Y	Y	Y
17 Ryan	Y	N	Y	Y	Y
18 Space	Y	N	Y	Y	Y
OKLAHOMA					
1 Sullivan	Y	Y	Y	N	N
2 Boren	Y	Y	Y	N	Y
3 Lucas	Y	Y	Y	N	N
4 Cole	Y	Y	Y	N	N
5 Fallin	Y	Y	Y	N	N
OREGON					
1 Wu	Y	N	Y	Y	Y
2 Walden	Y	N	Y	N	N
3 Blumenauer	N	N	Y	Y	Y
4 DeFazio	N	N	Y	Y	Y
5 Schrader	Y	N	Y	Y	Y
PENNSYLVANIA					
1 Brady	Y	N	Y	Y	Y
2 Fattah	Y	N	Y	Y	Y
3 Dahlkemper	Y	N	Y	Y	Y
4 Altmire	Y	N	Y	Y	Y
5 Thompson	Y	Y	Y	N	N
6 Gerlach	+	-	+	N	N
7 Sestak	Y	N	Y	Y	Y
8 Murphy, P.	Y	N	Y	Y	Y
9 Shuster	Y	Y	Y	N	N
10 Carney	?	?	?	?	?
11 Kanjorski	Y	N	Y	Y	Y
12 Murtha	Y	N	Y	Y	?
13 Schwartz	Y	N	Y	Y	Y
14 Doyle	Y	N	Y	Y	Y
15 Dent	Y	N	Y	Y	N
16 Pitts	Y	Y	Y	N	N
17 Holden	Y	N	Y	Y	Y
18 Murphy, T.	Y	Y	Y	N	N
19 Platts	Y	N	Y	N	N
RHODE ISLAND					
1 Kennedy	Y	N	Y	Y	Y
2 Langevin	Y	N	Y	Y	Y
SOUTH CAROLINA					
1 Brown	Y	Y	Y	N	N
2 Wilson	Y	Y	Y	N	N
3 Barrett	+	+	+	N	N
4 Inglis	Y	Y	Y	N	N
5 Spratt	Y	N	Y	Y	Y
6 Clyburn	Y	N	Y	Y	Y
SOUTH DAKOTA					
AL Herseth Sandlin	Y	N	Y	Y	Y
TENNESSEE					
1 Roe	Y	Y	Y	N	N
2 Duncan	Y	Y	Y	N	N
3 Wamp	Y	Y	Y	N	N
4 Davis	Y	N	Y	Y	Y
5 Cooper	Y	N	Y	Y	Y
6 Gordon	Y	N	Y	Y	Y
7 Blackburn	Y	Y	Y	N	N
8 Tanner	Y	Y	Y	Y	Y
9 Cohen	Y	N	Y	Y	Y

	753	754	755	756	757
TEXAS					
1 Gohmert	Y	Y	Y	N	N
2 Poe	Y	Y	Y	N	N
3 Johnson, S.	?	?	?	?	?
4 Hall	Y	Y	Y	N	N
5 Hensarling	Y	Y	Y	N	N
6 Barton	Y	Y	Y	N	N
7 Culberson	Y	Y	Y	N	N
8 Brady	Y	Y	Y	N	N
9 Green, A.	Y	N	Y	Y	Y
10 McCaul	Y	Y	Y	N	N
11 Conaway	Y	Y	Y	N	N
12 Granger	Y	Y	Y	N	N
13 Thornberry	Y	Y	Y	N	N
14 Paul	N	Y	Y	N	N
15 Hinojosa	?	?	?	Y	Y
16 Reyes	Y	N	Y	Y	Y
17 Edwards	Y	Y	Y	Y	Y
18 Jackson Lee	Y	N	Y	Y	Y
19 Neugebauer	?	?	?	?	?
20 Gonzalez	Y	N	Y	Y	Y
21 Smith	Y	Y	Y	N	N
22 Olson	?	?	?	N	N
23 Rodriguez	Y	N	Y	Y	Y
24 Marchant	Y	Y	Y	N	N
25 Doggett	Y	N	Y	Y	Y
26 Burgess	Y	Y	Y	N	N
27 Ortiz	Y	N	Y	Y	Y
28 Cuellar	Y	N	Y	Y	Y
29 Green, G.	Y	N	Y	Y	Y
30 Johnson, E.	Y	N	Y	Y	Y
31 Carter	Y	Y	Y	N	N
32 Sessions	Y	Y	Y	N	N
UTAH					
1 Bishop	Y	Y	Y	N	N
2 Matheson	Y	N	Y	Y	Y
3 Chaffetz	Y	Y	Y	N	N
VERMONT					
AL Welch	Y	N	Y	Y	Y
VIRGINIA					
1 Wittman	Y	Y	Y	N	N
2 Nye	Y	N	Y	N	N
3 Scott	Y	Y	Y	Y	Y
4 Forbes	Y	Y	Y	N	N
5 Perriello	Y	N	Y	Y	Y
6 Goodlatte	Y	Y	Y	N	N
7 Cantor	Y	Y	Y	N	N
8 Moran	?	?	?	Y	Y
9 Boucher	Y	N	Y	Y	Y
10 Wolf	Y	Y	Y	N	N
11 Connolly	Y	N	Y	Y	Y
WASHINGTON					
1 Inslee	Y	N	Y	Y	Y
2 Larsen	Y	N	Y	Y	Y
3 Baird	Y	N	Y	N	Y
4 Hastings	Y	Y	Y	N	N
5 McMorris Rodgers	Y	Y	Y	N	N
6 Dicks	Y	N	Y	Y	Y
7 McDermott	N	N	Y	Y	Y
8 Reichert	Y	Y	Y	N	N
9 Smith	Y	N	Y	N	Y
WEST VIRGINIA					
1 Mollohan	Y	N	Y	Y	Y
2 Capito	Y	Y	Y	N	N
3 Rahall	Y	N	Y	Y	Y
WISCONSIN					
1 Ryan	Y	Y	Y	N	N
2 Baldwin	Y	N	Y	Y	Y
3 Kind	Y	N	Y	Y	Y
4 Moore	Y	N	Y	Y	Y
5 Sensenbrenner	Y	Y	Y	N	N
6 Petri	Y	Y	Y	N	N
7 Obey	Y	N	Y	Y	Y
8 Kagen	Y	N	Y	Y	Y
WYOMING					
AL Lummis	Y	Y	Y	N	N
DELEGATES					
Faleomavaega (A.S.)					
Norton (D.C.)					
Bordallo (Guam)					
Sablan (N. Marianas)					
Pierluisi (P.R.)					
Christensen (V.I.)					

IN THE HOUSE | By Vote Number

758. **H Res 805. Rep. Rangel Removal From Chairmanship/Previous Question.** Crowley, D-N.Y., motion to order the previous question (thus ending debate and possibility of amendment) on the Crowley motion to refer the Carter, R-Texas, privileged resolution to the Standards of Official Conduct Committee. The Carter resolution would remove Rep. Charles B. Rangel, D-N.Y., as chairman of the Ways and Means Committee until the Standards of Official Conduct Committee completes its investigation into his finances. Motion agreed to 243-156: R 3-155; D 240-1. Oct. 7, 2009.

759. **H Res 805. Rep. Rangel Removal From Chairmanship/Motion to Refer.** Crowley, D-N.Y., motion to refer the Carter, R-Texas, privileged resolution to the Standards of Official Conduct Committee. The Carter resolution would remove Rep. Charles B. Rangel, D-N.Y., as chairman of the Ways and Means Committee until the Standards of Official Conduct Committee completes its investigation into his finances. Motion agreed to 246-153: R 6-151; D 240-2. Oct. 7, 2009.

760. **H Res 701. Dyke Marsh Wildlife Preserve/Adoption.** Bordallo, D-Guam, motion to suspend the rules and adopt the resolution that would mark the 50th anniversary of the designation of the Dyke Marsh Wildlife Preserve in Virginia as a protected wetland habitat. Motion agreed to 325-93: R 79-90; D 246-3. A two-thirds majority of those present and voting (279 in this case) is required for adoption under suspension of the rules. Oct. 7, 2009.

761. **HR 2997. Fiscal 2010 Agriculture Appropriations/Conference Report.** Adoption of the conference report on the bill that would appropriate $121.2 billion in fiscal 2010 for the Agriculture Department and related agencies, including $23.4 billion in discretionary funding. The bill would provide $20.9 billion in discretionary spending for the Agriculture Department and $2.4 billion for the Food and Drug Administration, excluding user fees. It includes $58.3 billion for the food stamp program and $17 billion for child nutrition. It also would drop a ban on Chinese poultry if the products meet U.S. safety standards. Adopted (thus sent to the Senate) 263-162: R 23-151; D 240-11. A "yea" was a vote in support of the president's position. Oct. 7, 2009.

762. **HR 1035. Office of Travel Promotion/Adoption.** Grijalva, D-Ariz., motion to suspend the rules and adopt the resolution (H Res 806) to concur in the Senate amendment to the bill with an amendment that would create a nonprofit corporation to attract foreign tourists to the United States, as well as an Office of Travel Promotion in the Commerce Department. The bill would direct the Morris K. Udall Foundation to award grants to the University of Arizona for the research and training of Native American and Alaska Native professionals in health care and public policy. Motion agreed to 358-66: R 108-66; D 250-0. A two-thirds majority of those present and voting (283 in this case) is required for adoption under suspension of the rules. Oct. 7, 2009.

	758	759	760	761	762
ALABAMA					
1 **Bonner**	P	P	N	N	Y
2 Bright	Y	Y	Y	Y	Y
3 **Rogers**	N	N	N	N	Y
4 **Aderholt**	N	N	N	N	Y
5 Griffith	Y	Y	Y	Y	Y
6 **Bachus**	N	N	N	N	N
7 Davis	Y	Y	Y	Y	Y
ALASKA					
AL **Young**	Y	Y	Y	Y	Y
ARIZONA					
1 Kirkpatrick	Y	Y	Y	Y	Y
2 **Franks**	N	N	N	N	N
3 **Shadegg**	N	N	N	N	N
4 Pastor	Y	Y	Y	Y	Y
5 Mitchell	Y	Y	Y	N	Y
6 **Flake**	N	N	N	N	N
7 Grijalva	Y	Y	Y	Y	Y
8 Giffords	Y	Y	Y	Y	Y
ARKANSAS					
1 Berry	Y	Y	Y	Y	Y
2 Snyder	Y	Y	Y	Y	Y
3 **Boozman**	N	N	N	N	Y
4 Ross	Y	Y	Y	Y	Y
CALIFORNIA					
1 Thompson	Y	Y	Y	Y	Y
2 **Herger**	N	N	N	N	N
3 **Lungren**	N	N	Y	N	N
4 **McClintock**	N	N	Y	N	N
5 Matsui	Y	Y	Y	Y	Y
6 Woolsey	Y	Y	Y	Y	Y
7 Miller, George	Y	Y	Y	Y	Y
8 Pelosi					
9 Lee	Y	Y	Y	Y	Y
10 Vacant					
11 McNerney	Y	Y	Y	Y	Y
12 Speier	?	Y	Y	Y	Y
13 Stark	Y	Y	Y	Y	Y
14 Eshoo	+	+	+	Y	Y
15 Honda	Y	Y	Y	Y	Y
16 Lofgren	?	?	+	Y	Y
17 Farr	Y	Y	Y	Y	Y
18 Cardoza	Y	Y	Y	Y	Y
19 **Radanovich**	?	?	?	?	?
20 Costa	Y	Y	Y	Y	Y
21 **Nunes**	N	N	N	N	N
22 **McCarthy**	N	N	N	N	Y
23 Capps	Y	Y	Y	Y	Y
24 **Gallegly**	N	N	Y	N	Y
25 **McKeon**	N	N	Y	N	Y
26 **Dreier**	N	N	N	N	Y
27 Sherman	Y	Y	Y	Y	Y
28 Berman	Y	Y	Y	Y	Y
29 Schiff	Y	Y	Y	Y	Y
30 Waxman	Y	Y	Y	Y	Y
31 Becerra	Y	Y	Y	Y	Y
32 Chu	Y	Y	Y	Y	Y
33 Watson	Y	Y	Y	Y	Y
34 Roybal-Allard	Y	Y	Y	Y	Y
35 Waters	Y	Y	Y	Y	Y
36 Harman	Y	Y	Y	Y	Y
37 Richardson	Y	Y	Y	Y	Y
38 Napolitano	Y	Y	Y	Y	Y
39 Sánchez, Linda	Y	Y	Y	Y	Y
40 **Royce**	N	N	?	N	Y
41 **Lewis**	N	N	Y	N	N
42 **Miller, Gary**	N	N	Y	N	N
43 Baca	Y	Y	Y	Y	Y
44 **Calvert**	N	N	Y	N	N
45 **Bono Mack**	N	N	Y	N	Y
46 **Rohrabacher**	Y	Y	N	N	N
47 Sanchez, Loretta	Y	Y	Y	Y	Y
48 **Campbell**	N	N	Y	N	Y
49 **Issa**	N	N	N	N	N
50 **Bilbray**	N	N	?	N	Y
51 Filner	Y	Y	Y	Y	Y
52 **Hunter**	N	N	N	N	Y
53 Davis	Y	Y	Y	Y	Y

	758	759	760	761	762
COLORADO					
1 DeGette	Y	Y	Y	Y	Y
2 Polis	Y	Y	Y	Y	Y
3 Salazar	Y	Y	Y	Y	Y
4 Markey	Y	Y	Y	Y	Y
5 **Lamborn**	N	N	N	N	N
6 **Coffman**	N	N	N	N	N
7 Perlmutter	Y	Y	Y	Y	Y
CONNECTICUT					
1 Larson	+	+	+	Y	Y
2 Courtney	Y	Y	Y	Y	Y
3 DeLauro	Y	Y	Y	Y	Y
4 Himes	Y	Y	Y	Y	Y
5 Murphy	Y	Y	Y	Y	Y
DELAWARE					
AL **Castle**	N	N	Y	N	Y
FLORIDA					
1 **Miller**	N	N	N	N	N
2 Boyd	Y	Y	Y	Y	Y
3 Brown	Y	Y	Y	Y	Y
4 **Crenshaw**	N	N	N	N	N
5 **Brown-Waite**	N	N	N	N	Y
6 **Stearns**	N	N	N	N	Y
7 **Mica**	N	N	Y	N	Y
8 Grayson	Y	Y	Y	Y	Y
9 **Bilirakis**	N	N	Y	N	Y
10 **Young**	N	N	Y	N	N
11 Castor	P	P	Y	Y	Y
12 **Putnam**	N	N	Y	N	Y
13 **Buchanan**	N	N	Y	N	Y
14 **Mack**	?	?	?	N	N
15 **Posey**	N	N	N	N	Y
16 **Rooney**	N	N	Y	Y	Y
17 Meek	Y	Y	Y	Y	Y
18 **Ros-Lehtinen**	N	N	Y	Y	Y
19 Wexler	Y	Y	Y	Y	Y
20 Wasserman Schultz	?	Y	Y	Y	Y
21 **Diaz-Balart, L.**	P	P	Y	Y	Y
22 Klein	Y	Y	Y	Y	Y
23 Hastings	Y	Y	Y	Y	Y
24 Kosmas	Y	Y	Y	Y	Y
25 **Diaz-Balart, M.**	?	?	?	Y	Y
GEORGIA					
1 **Kingston**	N	N	N	N	N
2 Bishop	Y	Y	Y	Y	Y
3 **Westmoreland**	N	N	N	N	N
4 Johnson	Y	Y	Y	Y	Y
5 Lewis	Y	Y	Y	Y	Y
6 **Price**	N	N	N	N	N
7 **Linder**	N	N	N	N	N
8 Marshall	Y	Y	Y	Y	Y
9 **Deal**	N	N	N	N	N
10 **Broun**	N	N	N	N	N
11 **Gingrey**	N	N	Y	N	N
12 Barrow	Y	Y	Y	Y	Y
13 Scott	Y	Y	Y	Y	Y
HAWAII					
1 Abercrombie	Y	Y	Y	Y	Y
2 Hirono	Y	Y	Y	Y	Y
IDAHO					
1 Minnick	Y	Y	Y	Y	Y
2 **Simpson**	N	P	Y	N	N
ILLINOIS					
1 Rush	Y	Y	Y	Y	Y
2 Jackson	Y	Y	Y	Y	Y
3 Lipinski	Y	Y	Y	Y	Y
4 Gutierrez	Y	Y	Y	Y	Y
5 Quigley	P	P	Y	Y	Y
6 **Roskam**	N	N	N	N	Y
7 Davis	Y	Y	Y	Y	Y
8 Bean	Y	Y	Y	Y	Y
9 Schakowsky	Y	Y	Y	Y	Y
10 **Kirk**	N	N	Y	N	Y
11 Halvorson	Y	Y	Y	Y	Y
12 Costello	Y	Y	Y	N	Y
13 **Biggert**	N	N	Y	N	Y
14 Foster	Y	Y	Y	Y	Y
15 **Johnson**	N	N	Y	N	Y

KEY	**Republicans**	Democrats		
Y Voted for (yea)		X Paired against		C Voted "present" to avoid possible conflict of interest
# Paired for		– Announced against		
+ Announced for		P Voted "present"		? Did not vote or otherwise make a position known
N Voted against (nay)				

	758	759	760	761	762
16 Manzullo	N	N	Y	N	N
17 Hare	Y	Y	Y	Y	Y
18 Schock	N	N	Y	Y	Y
19 Shimkus	N	N	N	N	N
INDIANA					
1 Visclosky	Y	Y	Y	Y	Y
2 Donnelly	Y	Y	Y	Y	Y
3 Souder	N	N	Y	Y	Y
4 Buyer	N	N	N	N	Y
5 Burton	P	P	N	N	N
6 Pence	N	N	N	N	N
7 Carson	Y	Y	Y	Y	Y
8 Ellsworth	Y	Y	Y	Y	Y
9 Hill	Y	Y	Y	N	Y
IOWA					
1 Braley	Y	Y	Y	Y	Y
2 Loebsack	Y	Y	Y	Y	Y
3 Boswell	Y	Y	Y	Y	Y
4 Latham	P	P	Y	N	Y
5 King	N	N	N	N	N
KANSAS					
1 Moran	N	N	N	N	Y
2 Jenkins	N	N	N	N	Y
3 Moore	Y	Y	Y	Y	Y
4 Tiahrt	N	N	N	N	N
KENTUCKY					
1 Whitfield	N	N	Y	N	Y
2 Guthrie	N	N	N	N	Y
3 Yarmuth	Y	Y	Y	Y	Y
4 Davis	N	N	N	N	Y
5 Rogers	N	N	Y	N	Y
6 Chandler	P	P	Y	Y	Y
LOUISIANA					
1 Scalise	N	N	N	N	N
2 Cao	N	N	Y	Y	Y
3 Melancon	Y	Y	Y	Y	Y
4 Fleming	N	N	N	N	Y
5 Alexander	N	N	Y	N	Y
6 Cassidy	N	N	N	N	Y
7 Boustany	N	N	Y	N	Y
MAINE					
1 Pingree	Y	Y	Y	Y	Y
2 Michaud	Y	Y	Y	Y	Y
MARYLAND					
1 Kratovil	Y	Y	Y	Y	Y
2 Ruppersberger	Y	Y	Y	?	Y
3 Sarbanes	Y	Y	Y	Y	Y
4 Edwards	Y	Y	Y	Y	Y
5 Hoyer	Y	Y	Y	Y	Y
6 Bartlett	P	N	Y	N	Y
7 Cummings	Y	Y	Y	Y	Y
8 Van Hollen	Y	Y	Y	Y	Y
MASSACHUSETTS					
1 Olver	Y	Y	Y	Y	Y
2 Neal	Y	Y	Y	Y	Y
3 McGovern	Y	?	Y	Y	Y
4 Frank	Y	Y	Y	Y	Y
5 Tsongas	+	+	+	+	+
6 Tierney	Y	Y	Y	Y	Y
7 Markey	Y	Y	Y	Y	Y
8 Capuano	Y	Y	Y	Y	Y
9 Lynch	Y	Y	Y	Y	Y
10 Delahunt	Y	Y	Y	Y	Y
MICHIGAN					
1 Stupak	Y	Y	Y	Y	Y
2 Hoekstra	N	N	N	N	N
3 Ehlers	N	N	Y	N	Y
4 Camp	N	N	N	N	Y
5 Kildee	Y	Y	Y	Y	Y
6 Upton	N	N	Y	N	Y
7 Schauer	Y	Y	Y	Y	Y
8 Rogers	N	N	Y	N	Y
9 Peters	P	P	Y	N	Y
10 Miller	N	N	Y	N	Y
11 McCotter	N	N	Y	N	Y
12 Levin	Y	Y	Y	Y	Y
13 Kilpatrick	Y	Y	Y	Y	Y
14 Conyers	Y	Y	Y	Y	Y
15 Dingell	Y	Y	Y	Y	Y
MINNESOTA					
1 Walz	Y	Y	Y	Y	Y
2 Kline	N	N	N	N	Y
3 Paulsen	N	N	Y	N	N
4 McCollum	Y	Y	Y	Y	Y

	758	759	760	761	762
5 Ellison	Y	Y	Y	Y	Y
6 Bachmann	N	N	N	N	N
7 Peterson	Y	Y	Y	Y	Y
8 Oberstar	Y	Y	Y	Y	Y
MISSISSIPPI					
1 Childers	Y	N	N	Y	Y
2 Thompson	Y	Y	Y	Y	Y
3 Harper	P	P	N	Y	Y
4 Taylor	N	N	Y	N	Y
MISSOURI					
1 Clay	Y	Y	Y	Y	Y
2 Akin	N	N	N	N	N
3 Carnahan	Y	Y	Y	Y	Y
4 Skelton	Y	Y	Y	Y	Y
5 Cleaver	Y	Y	Y	Y	Y
6 Graves	N	N	N	N	Y
7 Blunt	N	N	Y	N	Y
8 Emerson	N	N	Y	Y	Y
9 Luetkemeyer	N	N	Y	Y	Y
MONTANA					
AL Rehberg	N	N	Y	N	Y
NEBRASKA					
1 Fortenberry	N	N	Y	Y	Y
2 Terry	N	N	Y	N	Y
3 Smith	N	N	N	N	N
NEVADA					
1 Berkley	Y	Y	Y	Y	Y
2 Heller	N	N	N	N	Y
3 Titus	Y	Y	Y	Y	Y
NEW HAMPSHIRE					
1 Shea-Porter	Y	Y	Y	Y	Y
2 Hodes	Y	Y	Y	Y	Y
NEW JERSEY					
1 Andrews	Y	Y	Y	Y	Y
2 LoBiondo	N	N	Y	Y	Y
3 Adler	Y	Y	Y	N	Y
4 Smith	N	N	Y	N	Y
5 Garrett	N	N	N	N	N
6 Pallone	Y	Y	Y	Y	Y
7 Lance	N	N	Y	N	Y
8 Pascrell	Y	Y	Y	Y	Y
9 Rothman	Y	Y	Y	Y	Y
10 Payne	Y	Y	Y	Y	Y
11 Frelinghuysen	N	N	Y	N	Y
12 Holt	Y	Y	Y	Y	Y
13 Sires	Y	Y	Y	Y	Y
NEW MEXICO					
1 Heinrich	Y	Y	Y	Y	Y
2 Teague	Y	Y	Y	Y	Y
3 Lujan	Y	Y	Y	Y	Y
NEW YORK					
1 Bishop	Y	Y	Y	Y	Y
2 Israel	Y	Y	Y	Y	Y
3 King	Y	Y	Y	N	Y
4 McCarthy	Y	Y	Y	Y	Y
5 Ackerman	Y	Y	Y	Y	Y
6 Meeks	Y	Y	Y	Y	Y
7 Crowley	Y	Y	Y	Y	Y
8 Nadler	Y	Y	Y	Y	Y
9 Weiner	Y	Y	Y	Y	Y
10 Towns	Y	Y	Y	Y	Y
11 Clarke	Y	Y	Y	Y	Y
12 Velázquez	Y	Y	Y	Y	Y
13 McMahon	Y	Y	Y	Y	Y
14 Maloney	?	?	?	?	?
15 Rangel	Y	Y	Y	Y	Y
16 Serrano	Y	Y	Y	Y	Y
17 Engel	Y	Y	Y	Y	Y
18 Lowey	Y	Y	Y	Y	Y
19 Hall	Y	Y	Y	Y	Y
20 Murphy	Y	Y	Y	Y	Y
21 Tonko	Y	Y	Y	Y	Y
22 Hinchey	Y	Y	Y	Y	Y
23 Vacant					
24 Arcuri	Y	Y	Y	Y	Y
25 Maffei	Y	Y	Y	Y	Y
26 Lee	N	N	Y	Y	Y
27 Higgins	Y	Y	Y	Y	Y
28 Slaughter	Y	Y	Y	Y	Y
29 Massa	Y	Y	Y	Y	Y
NORTH CAROLINA					
1 Butterfield	P	P	Y	Y	Y
2 Etheridge	Y	Y	Y	Y	Y
3 Jones	N	Y	Y	N	Y
4 Price	Y	Y	Y	Y	Y

	758	759	760	761	762
5 Foxx	N	N	N	N	N
6 Coble	N	N	N	N	N
7 McIntyre	Y	Y	Y	Y	Y
8 Kissell	Y	Y	Y	Y	Y
9 Myrick	P	P	Y	N	Y
10 McHenry	N	N	N	N	N
11 Shuler	Y	Y	Y	Y	Y
12 Watt	Y	Y	Y	Y	Y
13 Miller	Y	Y	Y	Y	Y
NORTH DAKOTA					
AL Pomeroy	Y	Y	Y	Y	Y
OHIO					
1 Driehaus	Y	Y	Y	Y	Y
2 Schmidt	N	N	N	N	N
3 Turner	–	–	+	N	N
4 Jordan	N	N	N	N	N
5 Latta	N	N	N	N	N
6 Wilson	Y	Y	N	Y	Y
7 Austria	N	N	Y	N	Y
8 Boehner	N	N	N	N	Y
9 Kaptur	Y	Y	Y	Y	Y
10 Kucinich	Y	Y	Y	Y	Y
11 Fudge	Y	Y	Y	Y	Y
12 Tiberi	N	N	N	N	N
13 Sutton	Y	Y	Y	Y	Y
14 LaTourette	N	?	Y	N	Y
15 Kilroy	Y	Y	Y	Y	Y
16 Boccieri	Y	Y	Y	Y	Y
17 Ryan	Y	Y	Y	Y	Y
18 Space	Y	Y	Y	Y	?
OKLAHOMA					
1 Sullivan	N	N	N	N	N
2 Boren	Y	Y	N	Y	Y
3 Lucas	N	N	N	N	N
4 Cole	N	N	N	N	Y
5 Fallin	N	N	N	N	Y
OREGON					
1 Wu	Y	Y	Y	Y	Y
2 Walden	P	P	Y	N	Y
3 Blumenauer	Y	Y	Y	Y	Y
4 DeFazio	Y	Y	Y	Y	Y
5 Schrader	Y	Y	Y	Y	Y
PENNSYLVANIA					
1 Brady	Y	Y	Y	Y	Y
2 Fattah	Y	Y	Y	Y	Y
3 Dahlkemper	Y	Y	Y	Y	Y
4 Altmire	Y	Y	Y	N	Y
5 Thompson	N	N	N	N	N
6 Gerlach	N	N	N	N	Y
7 Sestak	Y	Y	Y	Y	Y
8 Murphy, P.	Y	Y	Y	Y	Y
9 Shuster	N	N	Y	N	Y
10 Carney	?	?	?	?	?
11 Kanjorski	Y	Y	Y	Y	Y
12 Murtha	Y	Y	Y	Y	Y
13 Schwartz	Y	Y	Y	Y	Y
14 Doyle	Y	Y	Y	Y	Y
15 Dent	P	P	Y	N	Y
16 Pitts	N	N	N	N	N
17 Holden	Y	Y	Y	Y	Y
18 Murphy, T.	N	N	Y	Y	Y
19 Platts	N	N	Y	N	Y
RHODE ISLAND					
1 Kennedy	Y	Y	Y	Y	Y
2 Langevin	Y	Y	Y	Y	Y
SOUTH CAROLINA					
1 Brown	N	N	N	N	Y
2 Wilson	N	N	N	N	Y
3 Barrett	N	N	N	N	N
4 Inglis	N	N	N	N	N
5 Spratt	Y	Y	Y	Y	Y
6 Clyburn	Y	Y	Y	Y	Y
SOUTH DAKOTA					
AL Herseth Sandlin	Y	Y	Y	Y	Y
TENNESSEE					
1 Roe	N	N	N	N	Y
2 Duncan	N	N	N	N	N
3 Wamp	N	N	N	N	Y
4 Davis	Y	Y	Y	Y	Y
5 Cooper	Y	Y	Y	Y	Y
6 Gordon	Y	Y	Y	Y	Y
7 Blackburn	N	N	N	N	N
8 Tanner	Y	Y	Y	Y	Y
9 Cohen	Y	Y	Y	Y	Y

	758	759	760	761	762
TEXAS					
1 Gohmert	N	N	N	N	N
2 Poe	P	P	N	N	N
3 Johnson, S.	?	?	?	?	?
4 Hall	N	N	N	N	N
5 Hensarling	N	N	N	N	N
6 Barton	N	N	N	Y	N
7 Culberson	N	N	N	N	N
8 Brady	N	N	N	N	N
9 Green, A.	Y	Y	Y	Y	Y
10 McCaul	P	P	Y	N	Y
11 Conaway	P	P	N	N	N
12 Granger	N	N	N	N	Y
13 Thornberry	N	N	N	N	N
14 Paul	N	Y	N	N	N
15 Hinojosa	Y	Y	Y	Y	Y
16 Reyes	Y	Y	Y	Y	Y
17 Edwards	Y	Y	Y	Y	Y
18 Jackson Lee	Y	Y	Y	Y	Y
19 Neugebauer	?	?	?	?	?
20 Gonzalez	Y	Y	Y	Y	Y
21 Smith	N	N	Y	N	Y
22 Olson	N	N	N	N	Y
23 Rodriguez	Y	Y	Y	Y	Y
24 Marchant	N	N	N	N	N
25 Doggett	Y	Y	Y	Y	Y
26 Burgess	N	N	Y	N	N
27 Ortiz	Y	Y	Y	Y	Y
28 Cuellar	Y	Y	Y	Y	Y
29 Green, G.	P	P	Y	Y	Y
30 Johnson, E.	Y	Y	Y	Y	?
31 Carter	N	N	N	N	Y
32 Sessions	N	N	N	N	Y
UTAH					
1 Bishop	N	N	N	N	Y
2 Matheson	Y	Y	Y	N	Y
3 Chaffetz	N	N	Y	N	Y
VERMONT					
AL Welch	P	P	Y	Y	Y
VIRGINIA					
1 Wittman	N	N	Y	N	Y
2 Nye	Y	Y	Y	N	Y
3 Scott	Y	Y	Y	Y	Y
4 Forbes	N	N	Y	N	Y
5 Perriello	Y	Y	Y	Y	Y
6 Goodlatte	N	N	Y	N	N
7 Cantor	N	N	Y	N	N
8 Moran	Y	Y	Y	Y	Y
9 Boucher	Y	Y	Y	Y	Y
10 Wolf	N	N	Y	N	Y
11 Connolly	Y	Y	Y	Y	Y
WASHINGTON					
1 Inslee	Y	Y	Y	Y	Y
2 Larsen	Y	Y	Y	Y	Y
3 Baird	Y	Y	Y	Y	Y
4 Hastings	P	P	N	N	Y
5 McMorris Rodgers	N	N	N	N	N
6 Dicks	Y	Y	Y	Y	Y
7 McDermott	Y	Y	Y	Y	Y
8 Reichert	N	N	Y	N	Y
9 Smith	Y	Y	Y	Y	Y
WEST VIRGINIA					
1 Mollohan	Y	Y	Y	Y	Y
2 Capito	N	N	N	N	Y
3 Rahall	Y	Y	Y	Y	Y
WISCONSIN					
1 Ryan	N	N	N	N	N
2 Baldwin	Y	Y	Y	Y	Y
3 Kind	Y	Y	Y	Y	Y
4 Moore	Y	Y	Y	Y	Y
5 Sensenbrenner	N	N	N	N	N
6 Petri	N	N	Y	N	Y
7 Obey	Y	Y	Y	Y	Y
8 Kagen	Y	Y	Y	Y	Y
WYOMING					
AL Lummis	N	N	N	N	Y
DELEGATES					
Faleomavaega (A.S.)					
Norton (D.C.)					
Bordallo (Guam)					
Sablan (N. Marianas)					
Pierluisi (P.R.)					
Christensen (V.I.)					

IN THE HOUSE | By Vote Number

763. **H Res 795. Flight 93 Memorial/Adoption.** Bordallo, D-Guam, motion to suspend the rules and adopt the resolution that would honor the Shanksville, Pa., community and the Flight 93 Ambassadors for their dedication to establishing a Flight 93 memorial and encourage the completion of a permanent memorial by Sept. 10, 2011. Motion agreed to 426-0: R 174-0; D 252-0. A two-thirds majority of those present and voting (284 in this case) is required for adoption under suspension of the rules. Oct. 7, 2009.

764. **HR 2647. Fiscal 2010 Defense Authorization/Previous Question.** Slaughter, D-N.Y., motion to order the previous question (thus ending debate and possibility of amendment) on adoption of the rule (H Res 808) and a Slaughter amendment. The rule would provide for House floor consideration of the conference report on the bill that would authorize $680.2 billion in discretionary spending for defense programs in fiscal 2010, including funds for operations in Iraq and Afghanistan. The amendment would provide for automatic House adoption of a concurrent resolution making technical corrections in the enrollment of the bill. Motion agreed to 237-187: R 0-175; D 237-12. (Subsequently, the Slaughter amendment was adopted by voice vote.) Oct. 8, 2009.

765. **HR 2647. Fiscal 2010 Defense Authorization/Rule.** Adoption of the rule (H Res 808) that would provide for House floor consideration of the conference report on the bill that would authorize $680.2 billion in discretionary spending for defense programs in fiscal 2010, including funds for operations in Iraq and Afghanistan. Adopted 234-188: R 1-174; D 233-14. A two-thirds majority of those present and voting (284 in this case) is required for adoption under suspension of the rules. Oct. 8, 2009.

766. **H Res 650. Recognizing Country Music/Adoption.** Polis, D-Colo., motion to suspend the rules and adopt the resolution that would declare country music to be a uniquely American art form and recognize country music for its contributions to American life and culture. Motion agreed to 421-0: R 175-0; D 246-0. A two-thirds majority of those present and voting (281 in this case) is required for adoption under suspension of the rules. Oct. 8, 2009.

767. **H J Res 26. Casimir Pulaski Honorary Citizenship/Passage.** Weiner, D-N.Y., motion to suspend the rules and pass the joint resolution that would posthumously grant honorary U.S. citizenship to Casimir Pulaski. Motion agreed to 422-0: R 174-0; D 248-0. A two-thirds majority of those present and voting (282 in this case) is required for passage under suspension of the rules. Oct. 8, 2009.

	763	764	765	766	767
ALABAMA					
1 **Bonner**	Y	N	N	Y	Y
2 Bright	Y	N	N	Y	Y
3 **Rogers**	Y	N	N	Y	Y
4 **Aderholt**	Y	N	N	Y	Y
5 Griffith	Y	N	N	Y	Y
6 **Bachus**	Y	N	N	Y	Y
7 Davis	Y	Y	Y	Y	Y
ALASKA					
AL **Young**	Y	N	N	Y	Y
ARIZONA					
1 Kirkpatrick	Y	Y	Y	Y	Y
2 **Franks**	Y	N	N	Y	Y
3 **Shadegg**	Y	N	N	Y	Y
4 Pastor	Y	Y	Y	Y	Y
5 Mitchell	Y	Y	Y	Y	Y
6 **Flake**	Y	N	N	Y	Y
7 Grijalva	Y	Y	Y	Y	Y
8 Giffords	Y	Y	Y	Y	Y
ARKANSAS					
1 Berry	Y	Y	Y	Y	Y
2 Snyder	Y	Y	Y	Y	Y
3 **Boozman**	Y	N	N	Y	Y
4 Ross	Y	Y	Y	Y	Y
CALIFORNIA					
1 Thompson	Y	Y	Y	Y	Y
2 **Herger**	Y	N	N	Y	Y
3 **Lungren**	Y	N	N	Y	Y
4 **McClintock**	Y	N	N	Y	Y
5 Matsui	Y	Y	Y	Y	Y
6 Woolsey	Y	Y	Y	Y	Y
7 Miller, George	Y	Y	Y	Y	Y
8 Pelosi					
9 Lee	Y	Y	Y	Y	Y
10 Vacant					
11 McNerney	Y	Y	Y	Y	Y
12 Speier	Y	Y	Y	Y	Y
13 Stark	Y	Y	Y	Y	Y
14 Eshoo	Y	Y	Y	Y	Y
15 Honda	Y	Y	Y	?	Y
16 Lofgren	Y	Y	Y	Y	Y
17 Farr	Y	Y	Y	Y	Y
18 Cardoza	Y	Y	Y	Y	Y
19 **Radanovich**	?	N	N	Y	Y
20 Costa	Y	Y	Y	Y	Y
21 **Nunes**	Y	N	N	Y	Y
22 **McCarthy**	Y	N	N	Y	Y
23 Capps	Y	Y	?	Y	Y
24 **Gallegly**	Y	N	N	Y	Y
25 **McKeon**	Y	N	N	Y	Y
26 **Dreier**	Y	N	N	Y	Y
27 Sherman	Y	Y	Y	Y	Y
28 Berman	Y	Y	Y	Y	Y
29 Schiff	Y	Y	Y	Y	Y
30 Waxman	Y	Y	Y	Y	Y
31 Becerra	Y	Y	Y	Y	Y
32 Chu	Y	Y	Y	Y	Y
33 Watson	Y	Y	Y	Y	Y
34 Roybal-Allard	Y	Y	Y	Y	Y
35 Waters	Y	Y	Y	Y	Y
36 Harman	Y	Y	Y	Y	Y
37 Richardson	Y	Y	Y	Y	Y
38 Napolitano	Y	Y	Y	Y	Y
39 Sánchez, Linda	Y	Y	Y	Y	Y
40 **Royce**	Y	N	N	Y	Y
41 **Lewis**	Y	N	N	Y	Y
42 **Miller, Gary**	Y	N	N	Y	Y
43 Baca	Y	Y	Y	Y	Y
44 **Calvert**	Y	N	N	Y	Y
45 **Bono Mack**	Y	N	N	Y	Y
46 **Rohrabacher**	Y	N	N	Y	Y
47 Sanchez, Loretta	Y	Y	Y	Y	Y
48 **Campbell**	Y	N	N	Y	Y
49 **Issa**	Y	N	N	Y	Y
50 **Bilbray**	Y	N	N	Y	Y
51 Filner	Y	Y	Y	Y	Y
52 **Hunter**	Y	N	N	Y	Y
53 Davis	Y	Y	Y	Y	Y

	763	764	765	766	767
COLORADO					
1 DeGette	Y	Y	Y	Y	Y
2 Polis	Y	Y	Y	Y	Y
3 Salazar	Y	Y	Y	Y	Y
4 Markey	Y	Y	Y	Y	Y
5 **Lamborn**	Y	N	N	Y	Y
6 **Coffman**	Y	N	N	Y	Y
7 Perlmutter	Y	Y	Y	Y	Y
CONNECTICUT					
1 Larson	Y	Y	Y	Y	Y
2 Courtney	Y	Y	Y	Y	Y
3 DeLauro	Y	Y	Y	Y	Y
4 Himes	Y	Y	Y	Y	Y
5 Murphy	Y	Y	Y	Y	Y
DELAWARE					
AL **Castle**	Y	N	N	Y	Y
FLORIDA					
1 **Miller**	Y	N	N	Y	Y
2 Boyd	Y	Y	Y	Y	Y
3 Brown	Y	Y	Y	Y	Y
4 **Crenshaw**	Y	N	N	Y	Y
5 **Brown-Waite**	Y	N	N	Y	Y
6 **Stearns**	Y	N	N	Y	Y
7 **Mica**	Y	N	N	Y	Y
8 Grayson	Y	Y	Y	Y	Y
9 **Bilirakis**	Y	N	N	Y	Y
10 **Young**	Y	N	N	Y	Y
11 Castor	Y	Y	Y	Y	Y
12 **Putnam**	Y	N	N	Y	Y
13 **Buchanan**	Y	N	N	Y	Y
14 **Mack**	Y	N	N	Y	Y
15 **Posey**	Y	N	N	Y	Y
16 **Rooney**	Y	N	N	Y	Y
17 Meek	Y	Y	Y	Y	Y
18 **Ros-Lehtinen**	Y	N	N	Y	Y
19 Wexler	Y	Y	Y	Y	Y
20 Wasserman Schultz	Y	Y	Y	Y	Y
21 **Diaz-Balart, L.**	Y	N	N	Y	Y
22 Klein	Y	Y	Y	?	Y
23 Hastings	Y	Y	Y	Y	Y
24 Kosmas	Y	Y	Y	Y	Y
25 **Diaz-Balart, M.**	Y	N	N	Y	Y
GEORGIA					
1 **Kingston**	Y	N	N	Y	Y
2 Bishop	Y	Y	Y	Y	Y
3 **Westmoreland**	Y	N	N	Y	Y
4 Johnson	Y	Y	?	Y	Y
5 Lewis	Y	Y	Y	Y	Y
6 **Price**	Y	N	N	Y	Y
7 **Linder**	Y	N	N	Y	Y
8 Marshall	Y	Y	Y	Y	Y
9 **Deal**	Y	N	N	Y	Y
10 **Broun**	Y	N	N	Y	Y
11 **Gingrey**	Y	N	N	Y	Y
12 Barrow	Y	Y	Y	Y	Y
13 Scott	Y	Y	Y	Y	Y
HAWAII					
1 Abercrombie	Y	Y	Y	Y	?
2 Hirono	Y	Y	Y	Y	Y
IDAHO					
1 Minnick	Y	Y	Y	Y	Y
2 **Simpson**	Y	N	N	Y	Y
ILLINOIS					
1 Rush	Y	Y	Y	Y	Y
2 Jackson	Y	Y	Y	Y	Y
3 Lipinski	Y	Y	Y	Y	Y
4 Gutierrez	Y	Y	Y	Y	Y
5 Quigley	Y	Y	Y	Y	Y
6 **Roskam**	Y	N	N	Y	Y
7 Davis	Y	Y	Y	Y	Y
8 Bean	Y	Y	Y	Y	Y
9 Schakowsky	Y	Y	Y	Y	Y
10 **Kirk**	Y	N	N	Y	Y
11 Halvorson	Y	Y	Y	Y	Y
12 Costello	Y	Y	Y	Y	Y
13 **Biggert**	Y	N	N	Y	Y
14 Foster	Y	N	Y	Y	Y
15 **Johnson**	Y	N	Y	Y	Y

KEY	**Republicans**		Democrats	
Y	Voted for (yea)		X	Paired against
#	Paired for		–	Announced against
+	Announced for		P	Voted "present"
N	Voted against (nay)			

C Voted "present" to avoid possible conflict of interest

? Did not vote or otherwise make a position known

	763	764	765	766	767
16 **Manzullo**	Y	N	N	Y	Y
17 Hare	Y	Y	Y	Y	Y
18 **Schock**	Y	N	N	Y	?
19 **Shimkus**	Y	N	N	Y	Y
INDIANA					
1 Visclosky	Y	Y	Y	Y	Y
2 Donnelly	Y	N	N	Y	Y
3 **Souder**	Y	N	N	Y	Y
4 **Buyer**	Y	N	N	Y	Y
5 **Burton**	Y	N	N	Y	Y
6 **Pence**	Y	N	N	Y	Y
7 Carson	Y	Y	Y	Y	Y
8 Ellsworth	Y	N	N	Y	Y
9 Hill	Y	Y	Y	Y	Y
IOWA					
1 Braley	Y	Y	Y	Y	Y
2 Loebsack	Y	Y	Y	Y	Y
3 Boswell	Y	Y	Y	Y	Y
4 **Latham**	Y	N	N	Y	Y
5 **King**	Y	N	N	Y	Y
KANSAS					
1 **Moran**	Y	N	N	Y	Y
2 **Jenkins**	Y	N	N	Y	Y
3 Moore	Y	Y	Y	Y	Y
4 **Tiahrt**	Y	N	N	Y	Y
KENTUCKY					
1 **Whitfield**	Y	N	N	Y	Y
2 **Guthrie**	Y	N	N	Y	Y
3 Yarmuth	Y	Y	Y	Y	Y
4 **Davis**	Y	N	N	Y	Y
5 **Rogers**	Y	N	N	Y	Y
6 Chandler	Y	Y	Y	Y	Y
LOUISIANA					
1 **Scalise**	Y	N	N	Y	Y
2 **Cao**	Y	N	N	Y	Y
3 Melancon	Y	Y	N	Y	Y
4 **Fleming**	Y	N	N	Y	Y
5 **Alexander**	Y	N	N	Y	Y
6 **Cassidy**	Y	N	N	Y	Y
7 **Boustany**	Y	N	N	Y	Y
MAINE					
1 Pingree	Y	Y	Y	Y	Y
2 Michaud	Y	Y	Y	Y	Y
MARYLAND					
1 Kratovil	Y	N	N	Y	Y
2 Ruppersberger	Y	Y	Y	Y	Y
3 Sarbanes	Y	Y	Y	Y	Y
4 Edwards	Y	Y	Y	Y	Y
5 Hoyer	Y	Y	Y	Y	Y
6 **Bartlett**	Y	N	N	Y	Y
7 Cummings	Y	Y	Y	Y	Y
8 Van Hollen	Y	Y	Y	Y	Y
MASSACHUSETTS					
1 Olver	Y	Y	Y	Y	Y
2 Neal	Y	Y	Y	Y	Y
3 McGovern	Y	Y	Y	Y	Y
4 Frank	Y	Y	Y	Y	Y
5 Tsongas	+	+	+	+	+
6 Tierney	Y	Y	Y	Y	Y
7 Markey	Y	Y	Y	Y	Y
8 Capuano	Y	Y	Y	Y	Y
9 Lynch	Y	Y	Y	Y	Y
10 Delahunt	Y	Y	Y	Y	Y
MICHIGAN					
1 Stupak	Y	Y	Y	Y	Y
2 **Hoekstra**	Y	N	N	Y	Y
3 **Ehlers**	Y	N	N	Y	Y
4 **Camp**	Y	N	N	Y	Y
5 Kildee	Y	Y	Y	Y	Y
6 **Upton**	Y	N	N	Y	Y
7 Schauer	Y	Y	Y	Y	Y
8 **Rogers**	Y	N	N	Y	Y
9 Peters	Y	Y	Y	Y	Y
10 **Miller**	Y	N	N	Y	Y
11 **McCotter**	Y	N	N	Y	Y
12 Levin	Y	Y	Y	Y	Y
13 Kilpatrick	Y	Y	Y	Y	Y
14 Conyers	Y	Y	Y	Y	Y
15 Dingell	Y	Y	Y	Y	Y
MINNESOTA					
1 Walz	Y	Y	Y	Y	Y
2 **Kline**	Y	N	N	Y	Y
3 **Paulsen**	Y	N	N	Y	Y
4 McCollum	Y	Y	Y	Y	Y

	763	764	765	766	767
5 Ellison	Y	Y	Y	Y	Y
6 **Bachmann**	Y	N	N	Y	Y
7 Peterson	Y	Y	Y	Y	Y
8 Oberstar	Y	?	?	?	Y
MISSISSIPPI					
1 Childers	Y	N	N	Y	Y
2 Thompson	Y	Y	Y	Y	Y
3 **Harper**	Y	N	N	Y	Y
4 Taylor	Y	N	N	Y	Y
MISSOURI					
1 Clay	Y	Y	Y	Y	Y
2 **Akin**	Y	N	N	Y	Y
3 Carnahan	Y	Y	Y	Y	Y
4 Skelton	Y	Y	Y	Y	Y
5 Cleaver	Y	Y	Y	Y	Y
6 **Graves**	Y	N	N	Y	Y
7 **Blunt**	Y	N	N	Y	Y
8 **Emerson**	Y	N	N	Y	Y
9 **Luetkemeyer**	Y	N	N	Y	Y
MONTANA					
AL **Rehberg**	Y	N	N	Y	Y
NEBRASKA					
1 **Fortenberry**	Y	N	N	Y	Y
2 **Terry**	Y	N	N	Y	Y
3 **Smith**	Y	N	N	Y	Y
NEVADA					
1 Berkley	Y	Y	Y	Y	Y
2 **Heller**	Y	N	N	Y	Y
3 Titus	Y	Y	Y	Y	Y
NEW HAMPSHIRE					
1 Shea-Porter	Y	Y	Y	Y	Y
2 Hodes	Y	Y	Y	Y	Y
NEW JERSEY					
1 Andrews	Y	Y	Y	Y	Y
2 **LoBiondo**	Y	N	N	Y	Y
3 Adler	Y	Y	Y	Y	Y
4 **Smith**	Y	N	N	Y	Y
5 **Garrett**	Y	N	N	Y	Y
6 Pallone	Y	Y	Y	Y	Y
7 **Lance**	Y	N	N	Y	Y
8 Pascrell	Y	Y	Y	Y	Y
9 Rothman	Y	Y	Y	Y	Y
10 Payne	Y	Y	Y	Y	Y
11 **Frelinghuysen**	Y	N	N	Y	Y
12 Holt	Y	Y	Y	Y	Y
13 Sires	Y	Y	Y	Y	Y
NEW MEXICO					
1 Heinrich	Y	Y	Y	Y	Y
2 Teague	Y	N	N	Y	Y
3 Lujan	Y	Y	Y	Y	Y
NEW YORK					
1 Bishop	Y	Y	Y	Y	Y
2 Israel	Y	Y	Y	Y	Y
3 **King**	Y	N	N	Y	Y
4 McCarthy	Y	Y	Y	Y	Y
5 Ackerman	Y	Y	Y	Y	Y
6 Meeks	Y	Y	Y	Y	Y
7 Crowley	Y	Y	Y	Y	Y
8 Nadler	Y	Y	Y	Y	Y
9 Weiner	Y	Y	Y	Y	Y
10 Towns	Y	Y	Y	Y	Y
11 Clarke	Y	Y	Y	Y	Y
12 Velázquez	Y	Y	Y	Y	Y
13 McMahon	Y	Y	Y	Y	Y
14 Maloney	?	?	?	?	?
15 Rangel	Y	Y	Y	Y	Y
16 Serrano	Y	Y	Y	Y	Y
17 Engel	Y	Y	Y	Y	Y
18 Lowey	Y	Y	Y	Y	Y
19 Hall	Y	Y	Y	Y	Y
20 Murphy	Y	Y	Y	Y	Y
21 Tonko	Y	Y	Y	Y	Y
22 Hinchey	Y	Y	Y	Y	Y
23 Vacant					
24 Arcuri	Y	Y	Y	Y	Y
25 Maffei	Y	Y	Y	Y	Y
26 **Lee**	Y	N	N	Y	Y
27 Higgins	Y	Y	Y	Y	Y
28 Slaughter	Y	Y	Y	Y	Y
29 Massa	Y	Y	Y	Y	Y
NORTH CAROLINA					
1 Butterfield	Y	Y	Y	Y	Y
2 Etheridge	Y	Y	Y	Y	Y
3 **Jones**	Y	N	N	Y	Y
4 Price	Y	Y	Y	Y	Y

	763	764	765	766	767
5 **Foxx**	Y	N	N	Y	Y
6 **Coble**	Y	N	N	Y	Y
7 McIntyre	Y	N	N	Y	Y
8 Kissell	Y	Y	Y	Y	Y
9 **Myrick**	Y	N	N	Y	Y
10 **McHenry**	Y	N	N	Y	Y
11 Shuler	Y	Y	N	Y	Y
12 Watt	Y	Y	Y	Y	Y
13 Miller	Y	Y	Y	Y	Y
NORTH DAKOTA					
AL Pomeroy	Y	Y	Y	Y	Y
OHIO					
1 Driehaus	Y	Y	Y	Y	Y
2 **Schmidt**	Y	N	N	Y	Y
3 **Turner**	Y	N	N	Y	Y
4 **Jordan**	Y	N	N	Y	Y
5 **Latta**	Y	N	N	Y	Y
6 Wilson	Y	Y	Y	Y	Y
7 **Austria**	Y	N	N	Y	Y
8 **Boehner**	Y	N	N	Y	Y
9 Kaptur	Y	?	?	?	?
10 Kucinich	Y	N	N	Y	Y
11 Fudge	Y	Y	Y	Y	Y
12 **Tiberi**	Y	N	N	Y	Y
13 Sutton	Y	?	Y	Y	Y
14 **LaTourette**	Y	N	N	Y	Y
15 Kilroy	Y	Y	Y	Y	Y
16 Boccieri	Y	Y	Y	Y	Y
17 Ryan	Y	Y	Y	Y	Y
18 Space	Y	Y	Y	Y	Y
OKLAHOMA					
1 **Sullivan**	Y	N	N	Y	Y
2 Boren	Y	N	N	Y	Y
3 **Lucas**	Y	N	N	Y	Y
4 **Cole**	Y	N	N	Y	Y
5 **Fallin**	Y	N	N	Y	Y
OREGON					
1 Wu	Y	Y	Y	Y	Y
2 **Walden**	Y	N	N	Y	Y
3 Blumenauer	Y	Y	Y	Y	Y
4 DeFazio	Y	Y	Y	Y	Y
5 Schrader	Y	Y	Y	Y	Y
PENNSYLVANIA					
1 Brady	Y	Y	Y	Y	Y
2 Fattah	Y	Y	Y	Y	Y
3 Dahlkemper	Y	Y	Y	Y	Y
4 Altmire	Y	Y	Y	Y	Y
5 **Thompson**	Y	N	N	Y	Y
6 **Gerlach**	Y	N	N	Y	Y
7 Sestak	Y	Y	Y	Y	Y
8 Murphy, P.	Y	Y	Y	Y	Y
9 **Shuster**	Y	N	N	Y	Y
10 Carney	?	?	?	?	?
11 Kanjorski	Y	Y	Y	Y	Y
12 Murtha	Y	Y	Y	Y	Y
13 Schwartz	Y	Y	Y	?	Y
14 Doyle	Y	Y	Y	Y	Y
15 **Dent**	Y	N	N	Y	Y
16 **Pitts**	Y	N	N	Y	Y
17 Holden	Y	Y	Y	Y	Y
18 **Murphy, T.**	Y	N	N	Y	Y
19 **Platts**	Y	N	N	Y	Y
RHODE ISLAND					
1 Kennedy	Y	Y	Y	Y	Y
2 Langevin	Y	Y	Y	Y	Y
SOUTH CAROLINA					
1 **Brown**	Y	N	N	Y	Y
2 **Wilson**	Y	N	N	Y	Y
3 **Barrett**	Y	N	N	Y	Y
4 **Inglis**	Y	N	N	Y	Y
5 Spratt	Y	Y	Y	Y	Y
6 Clyburn	Y	Y	Y	Y	Y
SOUTH DAKOTA					
AL Herseth Sandlin	Y	Y	Y	Y	Y
TENNESSEE					
1 **Roe**	Y	N	N	Y	Y
2 **Duncan**	Y	N	N	Y	Y
3 **Wamp**	Y	N	N	Y	Y
4 Davis	Y	Y	Y	Y	Y
5 Cooper	Y	Y	Y	Y	Y
6 Gordon	Y	Y	Y	Y	Y
7 **Blackburn**	Y	N	N	Y	Y
8 Tanner	Y	Y	Y	Y	Y
9 Cohen	Y	Y	Y	Y	Y

	763	764	765	766	767
TEXAS					
1 **Gohmert**	Y	N	N	Y	Y
2 **Poe**	Y	N	N	Y	Y
3 **Johnson, S.**	?	?	?	?	?
4 **Hall**	Y	N	N	Y	Y
5 **Hensarling**	Y	N	N	Y	Y
6 **Barton**	Y	N	N	Y	Y
7 **Culberson**	Y	N	N	Y	Y
8 **Brady**	Y	N	N	Y	Y
9 Green, A.	Y	Y	Y	Y	Y
10 **McCaul**	Y	N	N	Y	Y
11 **Conaway**	Y	N	N	Y	Y
12 **Granger**	Y	N	N	Y	Y
13 **Thornberry**	Y	N	N	Y	Y
14 **Paul**	Y	N	N	Y	Y
15 Hinojosa	Y	Y	Y	Y	?
16 Reyes	Y	Y	Y	Y	Y
17 Edwards	Y	Y	Y	Y	Y
18 Jackson Lee	Y	Y	Y	Y	Y
19 **Neugebauer**	?	?	?	?	?
20 Gonzalez	Y	Y	Y	Y	Y
21 **Smith**	Y	N	N	Y	Y
22 **Olson**	Y	N	N	Y	Y
23 Rodriguez	Y	Y	?	Y	Y
24 **Marchant**	Y	N	N	Y	Y
25 Doggett	Y	Y	Y	Y	Y
26 **Burgess**	Y	N	N	Y	Y
27 Ortiz	Y	Y	Y	Y	Y
28 Cuellar	Y	Y	Y	Y	Y
29 Green, G.	Y	Y	Y	Y	Y
30 Johnson, E.	Y	Y	Y	Y	Y
31 **Carter**	Y	N	N	Y	Y
32 **Sessions**	Y	N	N	Y	Y
UTAH					
1 **Bishop**	Y	N	N	Y	Y
2 Matheson	Y	Y	Y	Y	Y
3 **Chaffetz**	Y	N	N	Y	Y
VERMONT					
AL Welch	Y	Y	Y	Y	Y
VIRGINIA					
1 **Wittman**	Y	N	N	Y	Y
2 Nye	Y	Y	Y	Y	Y
3 Scott	Y	Y	Y	Y	Y
4 **Forbes**	Y	N	N	Y	Y
5 Perriello	Y	Y	Y	Y	Y
6 **Goodlatte**	Y	N	N	Y	Y
7 **Cantor**	Y	N	N	Y	Y
8 Moran	Y	Y	Y	?	?
9 Boucher	Y	Y	Y	Y	Y
10 **Wolf**	Y	N	N	Y	Y
11 Connolly	Y	Y	Y	Y	Y
WASHINGTON					
1 Inslee	Y	Y	Y	Y	Y
2 Larsen	Y	Y	Y	Y	Y
3 Baird	Y	Y	N	Y	Y
4 **Hastings**	Y	N	N	Y	Y
5 **McMorris Rodgers**	Y	N	N	Y	Y
6 Dicks	Y	Y	Y	Y	Y
7 McDermott	Y	Y	Y	Y	Y
8 **Reichert**	Y	N	N	Y	Y
9 Smith	Y	Y	Y	Y	Y
WEST VIRGINIA					
1 Mollohan	Y	Y	Y	Y	Y
2 **Capito**	Y	N	N	Y	Y
3 Rahall	Y	Y	Y	Y	Y
WISCONSIN					
1 **Ryan**	Y	N	N	Y	Y
2 Baldwin	Y	Y	Y	Y	Y
3 Kind	Y	Y	Y	Y	Y
4 Moore	Y	Y	Y	Y	Y
5 **Sensenbrenner**	Y	N	N	Y	Y
6 **Petri**	Y	N	N	Y	Y
7 Obey	Y	Y	Y	Y	Y
8 Kagen	Y	Y	Y	Y	Y
WYOMING					
AL **Lummis**	Y	N	N	Y	Y
DELEGATES					
Faleomavaega (A.S.)					
Norton (D.C.)					
Bordallo (Guam)					
Sablan (N. Marianas)					
Pierluisi (P.R.)					
Christensen (V.I.)					

IN THE HOUSE | By Vote Number

768. HR 3590. **Homebuyer Tax Credit Extension for Overseas Personnel/Passage.** Blumenauer, D-Ore., motion to suspend the rules and pass the bill that would extend a first-time-homebuyer tax credit through Nov. 30, 2010, for military, Foreign Service and intelligence agency personnel who are posted abroad for at least 90 days during 2009. The cost of the extension would be offset by an increase in penalties on partnerships or S-corporations that fail to file the correct tax form. Motion agreed to 416-0: R 173-0; D 243-0. A two-thirds majority of those present and voting (278 in this case) is required for passage under suspension of the rules. Oct. 8, 2009.

769. HR 2647. **Fiscal 2010 Defense Authorization/Motion to Recommit.** McKeon, R-Calif., motion to recommit the conference report on the bill to the conference committee with instructions that managers not accept provisions that would allow for the transfer or release of detainees held at Guantánamo Bay, Cuba, into the United States or its territories. It also would instruct managers to insist on a one-year expansion of eligibility that would allow all disabled military retirees to concurrently receive military retired pay and veterans' disability compensation. Motion rejected 208-216: R 174-0; D 34-216. Oct. 8, 2009.

770. HR 2647. **Fiscal 2010 Defense Authorization/Conference Report.** Adoption of the conference report on the bill that would authorize $680.2 billion in discretionary spending for defense programs in fiscal 2010, including approximately $130 billion for the wars in Iraq and Afghanistan and other operations. It would authorize $244.4 billion for operations and maintenance; $150.2 billion for military personnel; $24.6 billion for military construction, family housing and base closings; and $29.3 billion for the Defense Health Program. It would authorize a 3.4 percent pay raise for military personnel. It would prohibit detainees at Guantánamo Bay, Cuba, from being transferred to U.S. soil until the president submits a plan to Congress and consults with the governors of affected states. It would extend federal hate crimes laws to cover offenses motivated by a victim's gender identity, sexual orientation or disability. Adopted (thus sent to the Senate) 281-146: R 44-131; D 237-15. Oct. 8, 2009.

771. HR 1016. **Advance VA Health Care Budget/Adoption.** Filner, D-Calif., motion to suspend the rules and adopt the resolution (H Res 804) that would concur in the Senate amendment to the bill with an amendment that would require appropriations bills for the Department of Veterans Affairs to include advance appropriations for the following fiscal year for certain veterans' programs. The president would have to request the advance appropriations as part of his budget. Motion agreed to 419-1: R 171-1; D 248-0. A two-thirds majority of those present and voting (280 in this case) is required for adoption under suspension of the rules. A "yea" vote was a vote in support of the president's position. Oct. 8, 2009.

		768	769	770	771
ALABAMA					
1	**Bonner**	Y	Y	N	Y
2	Bright	Y	Y	N	Y
3	**Rogers**	Y	Y	N	Y
4	**Aderholt**	Y	Y	N	Y
5	Griffith	Y	Y	N	Y
6	**Bachus**	Y	Y	N	Y
7	Davis	Y	Y	Y	Y
ALASKA					
AL	**Young**	Y	Y	Y	Y
ARIZONA					
1	Kirkpatrick	Y	Y	Y	Y
2	**Franks**	Y	Y	N	Y
3	**Shadegg**	Y	Y	N	Y
4	Pastor	Y	N	Y	Y
5	Mitchell	Y	Y	Y	Y
6	**Flake**	Y	Y	N	Y
7	Grijalva	Y	N	Y	Y
8	Giffords	Y	N	Y	Y
ARKANSAS					
1	Berry	Y	N	Y	Y
2	Snyder	Y	N	Y	Y
3	**Boozman**	Y	Y	N	Y
4	Ross	Y	Y	Y	Y
CALIFORNIA					
1	Thompson	Y	N	Y	Y
2	**Herger**	Y	Y	N	?
3	**Lungren**	Y	Y	Y	Y
4	**McClintock**	Y	Y	N	Y
5	Matsui	Y	N	Y	Y
6	Woolsey	Y	N	Y	Y
7	Miller, George	Y	N	Y	?
8	Pelosi		N	Y	
9	Lee	Y	N	Y	Y
10	Vacant				
11	McNerney	Y	Y	Y	Y
12	Speier	?	N	Y	Y
13	Stark	Y	N	N	Y
14	Eshoo	Y	N	Y	Y
15	Honda	Y	N	Y	Y
16	Lofgren	Y	N	Y	Y
17	Farr	Y	N	Y	Y
18	Cardoza	Y	N	Y	Y
19	**Radanovich**	?	Y	N	Y
20	Costa	Y	N	Y	Y
21	**Nunes**	Y	Y	N	Y
22	**McCarthy**	Y	Y	N	Y
23	Capps	Y	N	Y	Y
24	**Gallegly**	Y	Y	Y	Y
25	**McKeon**	Y	Y	Y	Y
26	**Dreier**	Y	Y	N	Y
27	Sherman	Y	N	Y	Y
28	Berman	Y	N	Y	Y
29	Schiff	Y	N	Y	Y
30	Waxman	Y	N	Y	Y
31	Becerra	Y	N	Y	Y
32	Chu	Y	N	Y	Y
33	Watson	Y	N	Y	Y
34	Roybal-Allard	Y	N	Y	Y
35	Waters	Y	N	Y	Y
36	Harman	Y	N	Y	Y
37	Richardson	Y	N	Y	Y
38	Napolitano	Y	N	Y	Y
39	Sánchez, Linda	Y	N	Y	Y
40	**Royce**	Y	Y	N	Y
41	**Lewis**	Y	Y	N	Y
42	**Miller, Gary**	Y	Y	N	Y
43	Baca	Y	N	Y	Y
44	**Calvert**	Y	Y	Y	Y
45	**Bono Mack**	Y	Y	Y	Y
46	**Rohrabacher**	Y	Y	N	Y
47	Sanchez, Loretta	Y	N	Y	Y
48	**Campbell**	Y	?	?	?
49	**Issa**	Y	Y	N	Y
50	**Bilbray**	Y	Y	Y	Y
51	Filner	Y	N	N	Y
52	**Hunter**	Y	Y	Y	Y
53	Davis	Y	N	Y	Y
COLORADO					
1	DeGette	Y	N	Y	Y
2	Polis	Y	N	Y	Y
3	Salazar	Y	N	Y	Y
4	Markey	Y	Y	Y	Y
5	**Lamborn**	Y	Y	N	Y
6	**Coffman**	Y	Y	N	Y
7	Perlmutter	Y	N	Y	Y
CONNECTICUT					
1	Larson	Y	N	Y	Y
2	Courtney	Y	N	Y	Y
3	DeLauro	Y	N	Y	Y
4	Himes	Y	N	Y	Y
5	Murphy	Y	N	Y	Y
DELAWARE					
AL	**Castle**	Y	Y	Y	Y
FLORIDA					
1	**Miller**	Y	Y	N	Y
2	Boyd	Y	N	Y	Y
3	Brown	Y	N	Y	Y
4	**Crenshaw**	Y	Y	N	Y
5	**Brown-Waite**	Y	Y	Y	Y
6	**Stearns**	Y	Y	N	Y
7	**Mica**	Y	Y	N	Y
8	Grayson	Y	N	Y	Y
9	**Bilirakis**	Y	Y	N	Y
10	**Young**	Y	Y	Y	Y
11	Castor	Y	N	Y	Y
12	**Putnam**	Y	Y	N	Y
13	**Buchanan**	Y	Y	N	Y
14	**Mack**	Y	Y	N	Y
15	**Posey**	Y	Y	N	Y
16	**Rooney**	Y	Y	Y	Y
17	Meek	Y	N	Y	Y
18	**Ros-Lehtinen**	Y	Y	Y	Y
19	Wexler	Y	N	Y	Y
20	Wasserman Schultz	Y	N	Y	Y
21	**Diaz-Balart, L.**	Y	Y	Y	Y
22	Klein	Y	N	Y	Y
23	Hastings	Y	N	Y	Y
24	Kosmas	Y	Y	Y	Y
25	**Diaz-Balart, M.**	Y	Y	Y	Y
GEORGIA					
1	**Kingston**	Y	Y	N	Y
2	Bishop	Y	N	Y	Y
3	**Westmoreland**	Y	Y	N	Y
4	Johnson	Y	N	Y	Y
5	Lewis	Y	N	Y	Y
6	**Price**	Y	Y	N	Y
7	**Linder**	Y	Y	N	?
8	Marshall	?	Y	Y	Y
9	**Deal**	Y	Y	N	Y
10	**Broun**	Y	Y	N	Y
11	**Gingrey**	Y	Y	N	Y
12	Barrow	Y	Y	Y	Y
13	Scott	Y	N	Y	Y
HAWAII					
1	Abercrombie	Y	N	Y	Y
2	Hirono	Y	N	Y	Y
IDAHO					
1	Minnick	Y	Y	Y	Y
2	**Simpson**	Y	Y	N	Y
ILLINOIS					
1	Rush	Y	N	Y	Y
2	Jackson	Y	N	N	Y
3	Lipinski	Y	N	Y	Y
4	Gutierrez	Y	N	Y	Y
5	Quigley	Y	N	Y	Y
6	**Roskam**	Y	Y	N	Y
7	Davis	Y	N	Y	Y
8	Bean	Y	N	Y	Y
9	Schakowsky	Y	N	Y	?
10	**Kirk**	Y	Y	Y	Y
11	Halvorson	Y	N	Y	Y
12	Costello	Y	N	Y	Y
13	**Biggert**	Y	Y	Y	Y
14	Foster	Y	Y	Y	Y
15	**Johnson**	Y	Y	N	Y

KEY **Republicans** Democrats

Y Voted for (yea)	X Paired against	C Voted "present" to avoid possible conflict of interest
# Paired for	– Announced against	
+ Announced for	P Voted "present"	? Did not vote or otherwise make a position known
N Voted against (nay)		

	768	769	770	771
16 Manzullo	Y	Y	N	Y
17 Hare	Y	N	Y	Y
18 Schock	Y	Y	N	Y
19 Shimkus	Y	Y	N	Y
INDIANA				
1 Visclosky	Y	N	Y	Y
2 Donnelly	Y	Y	Y	Y
3 Souder	Y	Y	N	Y
4 Buyer	Y	Y	N	N
5 Burton	Y	Y	N	Y
6 Pence	Y	Y	N	Y
7 Carson	Y	N	Y	Y
8 Ellsworth	Y	N	Y	Y
9 Hill	Y	N	Y	Y
IOWA				
1 Braley	Y	N	Y	Y
2 Loebsack	Y	N	Y	Y
3 Boswell	Y	N	Y	Y
4 Latham	Y	Y	N	Y
5 King	Y	Y	N	Y
KANSAS				
1 Moran	Y	Y	N	Y
2 Jenkins	Y	Y	Y	Y
3 Moore	Y	N	Y	Y
4 Tiahrt	Y	Y	N	Y
KENTUCKY				
1 Whitfield	Y	Y	N	Y
2 Guthrie	Y	Y	N	Y
3 Yarmuth	Y	N	Y	Y
4 Davis	Y	Y	N	Y
5 Rogers	Y	Y	N	Y
6 Chandler	Y	N	Y	Y
LOUISIANA				
1 Scalise	Y	Y	N	Y
2 Cao	Y	Y	Y	Y
3 Melancon	Y	Y	Y	Y
4 Fleming	Y	Y	N	Y
5 Alexander	Y	Y	N	Y
6 Cassidy	Y	Y	Y	Y
7 Boustany	Y	Y	N	Y
MAINE				
1 Pingree	?	N	Y	Y
2 Michaud	Y	N	N	Y
MARYLAND				
1 Kratovil	Y	Y	Y	Y
2 Ruppersberger	Y	N	Y	Y
3 Sarbanes	Y	N	Y	Y
4 Edwards	Y	N	Y	Y
5 Hoyer	Y	N	Y	Y
6 Bartlett	Y	Y	N	Y
7 Cummings	Y	N	Y	?
8 Van Hollen	Y	N	Y	Y
MASSACHUSETTS				
1 Olver	Y	N	Y	Y
2 Neal	Y	N	Y	Y
3 McGovern	Y	N	Y	Y
4 Frank	Y	N	Y	Y
5 Tsongas	+	−	+	+
6 Tierney	Y	N	Y	Y
7 Markey	Y	N	Y	Y
8 Capuano	Y	N	Y	Y
9 Lynch	Y	N	Y	Y
10 Delahunt	Y	N	Y	Y
MICHIGAN				
1 Stupak	Y	N	Y	Y
2 Hoekstra	Y	Y	N	Y
3 Ehlers	Y	Y	N	Y
4 Camp	Y	Y	N	Y
5 Kildee	Y	N	Y	Y
6 Upton	Y	Y	Y	Y
7 Schauer	Y	N	Y	Y
8 Rogers	Y	Y	N	Y
9 Peters	Y	Y	Y	Y
10 Miller	Y	Y	Y	Y
11 McCotter	Y	Y	Y	Y
12 Levin	Y	N	Y	Y
13 Kilpatrick	Y	N	Y	Y
14 Conyers	?	N	N	Y
15 Dingell	Y	N	Y	Y
MINNESOTA				
1 Walz	Y	N	Y	Y
2 Kline	Y	Y	N	Y
3 Paulsen	Y	Y	Y	Y
4 McCollum	Y	N	Y	Y
5 Ellison	Y	N	Y	Y
6 Bachmann	Y	Y	N	Y
7 Peterson	Y	N	Y	Y
8 Oberstar	Y	N	Y	Y
MISSISSIPPI				
1 Childers	Y	Y	Y	Y
2 Thompson	Y	N	Y	Y
3 Harper	Y	Y	N	Y
4 Taylor	Y	Y	Y	Y
MISSOURI				
1 Clay	Y	N	Y	Y
2 Akin	Y	Y	N	Y
3 Carnahan	Y	N	Y	Y
4 Skelton	Y	N	Y	Y
5 Cleaver	Y	N	Y	Y
6 Graves	Y	Y	N	Y
7 Blunt	Y	Y	N	Y
8 Emerson	Y	Y	N	Y
9 Luetkemeyer	Y	Y	Y	Y
MONTANA				
AL Rehberg	Y	Y	Y	Y
NEBRASKA				
1 Fortenberry	Y	Y	N	Y
2 Terry	Y	Y	Y	Y
3 Smith	Y	Y	N	Y
NEVADA				
1 Berkley	Y	N	Y	Y
2 Heller	Y	Y	N	Y
3 Titus	Y	N	Y	Y
NEW HAMPSHIRE				
1 Shea-Porter	Y	N	Y	Y
2 Hodes	Y	Y	Y	Y
NEW JERSEY				
1 Andrews	Y	N	Y	Y
2 LoBiondo	Y	Y	Y	Y
3 Adler	Y	Y	Y	Y
4 Smith	Y	Y	N	Y
5 Garrett	Y	Y	N	Y
6 Pallone	Y	N	Y	Y
7 Lance	Y	Y	Y	Y
8 Pascrell	Y	N	Y	Y
9 Rothman	Y	N	Y	Y
10 Payne	Y	N	Y	Y
11 Frelinghuysen	Y	Y	Y	Y
12 Holt	Y	N	Y	Y
13 Sires	Y	N	Y	Y
NEW MEXICO				
1 Heinrich	Y	N	Y	Y
2 Teague	Y	Y	Y	Y
3 Lujan	Y	N	Y	Y
NEW YORK				
1 Bishop	Y	N	Y	Y
2 Israel	Y	N	Y	Y
3 King	Y	Y	Y	Y
4 McCarthy	?	N	Y	Y
5 Ackerman	Y	N	Y	Y
6 Meeks	Y	Y	Y	Y
7 Crowley	Y	N	Y	Y
8 Nadler	Y	N	Y	Y
9 Weiner	Y	N	Y	Y
10 Towns	Y	N	Y	Y
11 Clarke	Y	N	Y	Y
12 Velázquez	Y	N	Y	Y
13 McMahon	Y	Y	Y	Y
14 Maloney	?	?	?	?
15 Rangel	Y	N	Y	Y
16 Serrano	Y	N	Y	Y
17 Engel	Y	N	Y	Y
18 Lowey	Y	N	Y	Y
19 Hall	Y	Y	Y	Y
20 Murphy	Y	N	Y	Y
21 Tonko	Y	N	Y	Y
22 Hinchey	Y	N	Y	Y
23 Vacant				
24 Arcuri	Y	N	Y	Y
25 Maffei	Y	N	Y	Y
26 Lee	Y	Y	Y	Y
27 Higgins	Y	N	Y	Y
28 Slaughter	Y	−	+	+
29 Massa	Y	Y	Y	Y
NORTH CAROLINA				
1 Butterfield	Y	N	Y	Y
2 Etheridge	Y	N	Y	Y
3 Jones	Y	Y	N	Y
4 Price	Y	N	Y	Y
5 Foxx	Y	Y	N	Y
6 Coble	Y	Y	N	Y
7 McIntyre	Y	Y	N	Y
8 Kissell	Y	N	Y	Y
9 Myrick	Y	Y	N	Y
10 McHenry	Y	Y	N	Y
11 Shuler	Y	N	N	Y
12 Watt	Y	?	Y	Y
13 Miller	Y	N	Y	Y
NORTH DAKOTA				
AL Pomeroy	Y	N	Y	Y
OHIO				
1 Driehaus	Y	N	Y	Y
2 Schmidt	Y	Y	N	Y
3 Turner	Y	Y	Y	Y
4 Jordan	Y	Y	N	Y
5 Latta	Y	Y	N	Y
6 Wilson	Y	N	Y	Y
7 Austria	Y	Y	Y	Y
8 Boehner	Y	Y	N	Y
9 Kaptur	?	N	Y	Y
10 Kucinich	Y	P	N	Y
11 Fudge	Y	N	Y	Y
12 Tiberi	Y	Y	N	Y
13 Sutton	Y	N	Y	Y
14 LaTourette	Y	Y	N	Y
15 Kilroy	Y	N	Y	Y
16 Boccieri	Y	Y	Y	Y
17 Ryan	Y	N	Y	Y
18 Space	Y	Y	Y	Y
OKLAHOMA				
1 Sullivan	Y	Y	N	Y
2 Boren	Y	Y	N	Y
3 Lucas	Y	Y	N	Y
4 Cole	Y	Y	N	Y
5 Fallin	Y	Y	N	Y
OREGON				
1 Wu	Y	N	Y	Y
2 Walden	Y	Y	Y	Y
3 Blumenauer	Y	N	Y	Y
4 DeFazio	Y	N	Y	Y
5 Schrader	Y	N	Y	Y
PENNSYLVANIA				
1 Brady	Y	N	Y	Y
2 Fattah	Y	N	Y	Y
3 Dahlkemper	Y	Y	Y	Y
4 Altmire	Y	Y	Y	Y
5 Thompson	Y	Y	N	Y
6 Gerlach	Y	N	Y	Y
7 Sestak	Y	N	Y	Y
8 Murphy, P.	Y	N	Y	Y
9 Shuster	Y	Y	N	Y
10 Carney	?	?	?	?
11 Kanjorski	Y	N	Y	Y
12 Murtha	?	N	Y	Y
13 Schwartz	Y	N	Y	Y
14 Doyle	Y	N	Y	Y
15 Dent	Y	Y	Y	Y
16 Pitts	Y	Y	N	Y
17 Holden	Y	Y	Y	Y
18 Murphy, T.	Y	Y	N	Y
19 Platts	Y	Y	Y	Y
RHODE ISLAND				
1 Kennedy	Y	N	Y	Y
2 Langevin	Y	N	Y	Y
SOUTH CAROLINA				
1 Brown	Y	N	Y	Y
2 Wilson	Y	Y	N	Y
3 Barrett	Y	Y	N	Y
4 Inglis	Y	Y	N	Y
5 Spratt	Y	N	Y	Y
6 Clyburn	Y	N	Y	Y
SOUTH DAKOTA				
AL Herseth Sandlin	Y	N	Y	Y
TENNESSEE				
1 Roe	Y	Y	N	Y
2 Duncan	Y	Y	N	Y
3 Wamp	Y	Y	N	Y
4 Davis	Y	N	N	Y
5 Cooper	Y	N	Y	Y
6 Gordon	Y	N	Y	Y
7 Blackburn	Y	Y	N	Y
8 Tanner	Y	N	Y	Y
9 Cohen	Y	N	Y	Y
TEXAS				
1 Gohmert	Y	Y	N	Y
2 Poe	Y	Y	N	Y
3 Johnson, S.	?	?	?	?
4 Hall	Y	Y	N	Y
5 Hensarling	Y	Y	N	Y
6 Barton	Y	Y	N	Y
7 Culberson	Y	Y	N	Y
8 Brady	Y	Y	N	Y
9 Green, A.	Y	N	Y	Y
10 McCaul	Y	Y	N	Y
11 Conaway	Y	Y	N	Y
12 Granger	Y	Y	N	Y
13 Thornberry	Y	Y	N	Y
14 Paul	Y	P	N	Y
15 Hinojosa	Y	N	Y	Y
16 Reyes	Y	N	Y	Y
17 Edwards	Y	N	Y	Y
18 Jackson Lee	Y	N	Y	Y
19 Neugebauer	?	Y	N	Y
20 Gonzalez	Y	N	Y	Y
21 Smith	?	Y	N	Y
22 Olson	Y	Y	N	Y
23 Rodriguez	Y	N	Y	Y
24 Marchant	Y	Y	N	Y
25 Doggett	Y	N	Y	Y
26 Burgess	Y	Y	N	Y
27 Ortiz	Y	N	Y	Y
28 Cuellar	+	N	Y	Y
29 Green, G.	Y	N	Y	Y
30 Johnson, E.	Y	N	Y	Y
31 Carter	Y	Y	N	Y
32 Sessions	Y	Y	N	Y
UTAH				
1 Bishop	Y	Y	N	Y
2 Matheson	Y	N	Y	Y
3 Chaffetz	Y	Y	N	Y
VERMONT				
AL Welch	Y	N	N	Y
VIRGINIA				
1 Wittman	Y	Y	N	Y
2 Nye	Y	Y	Y	Y
3 Scott	Y	N	Y	Y
4 Forbes	Y	Y	N	Y
5 Perriello	Y	Y	Y	Y
6 Goodlatte	Y	Y	N	Y
7 Cantor	Y	Y	N	Y
8 Moran	?	N	Y	Y
9 Boucher	Y	N	Y	Y
10 Wolf	Y	Y	N	Y
11 Connolly	Y	N	Y	Y
WASHINGTON				
1 Inslee	Y	N	Y	Y
2 Larsen	Y	N	Y	Y
3 Baird	Y	N	N	Y
4 Hastings	Y	Y	N	?
5 McMorris Rodgers	Y	Y	N	Y
6 Dicks	Y	N	Y	Y
7 McDermott	Y	N	Y	Y
8 Reichert	Y	Y	Y	Y
9 Smith	Y	N	Y	Y
WEST VIRGINIA				
1 Mollohan	Y	N	Y	Y
2 Capito	Y	Y	Y	Y
3 Rahall	Y	N	Y	Y
WISCONSIN				
1 Ryan	Y	Y	N	Y
2 Baldwin	Y	N	Y	Y
3 Kind	Y	N	Y	Y
4 Moore	Y	N	Y	Y
5 Sensenbrenner	Y	Y	N	Y
6 Petri	Y	Y	N	Y
7 Obey	Y	N	Y	Y
8 Kagen	Y	N	Y	Y
WYOMING				
AL Lummis	Y	Y	N	Y
DELEGATES				
Faleomavaega (A.S.)				
Norton (D.C.)				
Bordallo (Guam)				
Sablan (N. Marianas)				
Pierluisi (P.R.)				
Christensen (V.I.)				

IN THE HOUSE | By Vote Number

772. **HR 3689. Vietnam Veterans Memorial Fund Extension/ Passage.** Sablan, D-N. Marianas, motion to suspend the rules and pass the bill that would extend the legislative authority of the Vietnam Veterans Memorial Fund Inc. to establish a Vietnam Veterans Memorial visitor center until Nov. 17, 2014. Motion agreed to 390-0: R 157-0; D 233-0. A two-thirds majority of those present and voting (260 in this case) is required for passage under suspension of the rules. Oct. 13, 2009.

773. **HR 3476. Delaware Water Gap Recreation/Passage.** Sablan, D-N. Marianas, motion to suspend the rules and pass the bill that would reauthorize the Delaware Water Gap National Recreation Area Citizen Advisory Committee through Oct. 30, 2038. Motion agreed to 384-1: R 154-1; D 230-0. A two-thirds majority of those present and voting (257 in this case) is required for passage under suspension of the rules. Oct. 13, 2009.

774. **H Res 659. Kappa Alpha Psi Fraternity Anniversary/ Adoption.** Sablan, D-N. Marianas, motion to suspend the rules and adopt the resolution that would recognize the 98th anniversary of Kappa Alpha Psi fraternity. Motion agreed to 392-0: R 158-0; D 234-0. A two-thirds majority of those present and voting (262 in this case) is required for adoption under suspension of the rules. Oct. 13, 2009.

775. **H Res 768. National Work and Family Month/Adoption.** Sablan, D-N. Marianas, motion to suspend the rules and adopt the resolution that would support the designation of October as National Work and Family Month. Motion agreed to 415-0: R 171-0; D 244-0. A two-thirds majority of those present and voting (277 in this case) is required for adoption under suspension of the rules. Oct. 14, 2009.

776. **HR 1327. Iranian Energy Sector Divestment/Passage.** Frank, D-Mass., motion to suspend the rules and pass the bill that would give state and local governments authority to divest their assets from and prohibit the investment of their assets in any company that invests $20 million or more in the Iranian energy sector, provides fuel infrastructure equipment to Iran, or extends $20 million or more in credit for investment in the Iranian energy sector. Motion agreed to 414-6: R 172-3; D 242-3. A two-thirds majority of those present and voting (280 in this case) is required for passage under suspension of the rules. Oct. 14, 2009.

777. **H Res 816. American Samoa Earthquake Victims/Adoption.** Faleomavaega, D-A.S., motion to suspend the rules and adopt the resolution that would express that the House mourns for the loss of life caused by the Sept. 29 earthquakes and tsunamis in American Samoa, Samoa and Tonga. Motion agreed to 422-0: R 175-0; D 247-0. A two-thirds majority of those present and voting (282 in this case) is required for adoption under suspension of the rules. Oct. 14, 2009.

	772	773	774	775	776	777
ALABAMA						
1 Bonner	?	?	?	Y	Y	Y
2 Bright	Y	Y	Y	Y	Y	Y
3 Rogers	Y	Y	Y	Y	Y	Y
4 Aderholt	Y	Y	Y	Y	Y	Y
5 Griffith	?	?	?	Y	Y	Y
6 Bachus	Y	Y	Y	Y	Y	Y
7 Davis	?	?	?	Y	Y	Y
ALASKA						
AL Young	Y	Y	Y	Y	Y	Y
ARIZONA						
1 Kirkpatrick	Y	Y	Y	Y	Y	Y
2 Franks	Y	Y	Y	Y	Y	Y
3 Shadegg	Y	Y	Y	Y	Y	Y
4 Pastor	Y	Y	Y	Y	Y	Y
5 Mitchell	Y	Y	Y	Y	Y	Y
6 Flake	Y	Y	Y	Y	N	Y
7 Grijalva	Y	?	Y	Y	Y	Y
8 Giffords	Y	Y	Y	Y	Y	Y
ARKANSAS						
1 Berry	Y	Y	Y	Y	Y	Y
2 Snyder	Y	Y	Y	Y	Y	Y
3 Boozman	Y	Y	Y	Y	Y	Y
4 Ross	Y	Y	Y	Y	Y	Y
CALIFORNIA						
1 Thompson	Y	Y	Y	Y	Y	Y
2 Herger	Y	Y	Y	Y	Y	Y
3 Lungren	Y	Y	Y	Y	Y	Y
4 McClintock	Y	Y	Y	Y	Y	Y
5 Matsui	Y	Y	Y	Y	Y	Y
6 Woolsey	Y	?	Y	Y	Y	Y
7 Miller, George	Y	Y	Y	Y	Y	Y
8 Pelosi						
9 Lee	Y	Y	Y	Y	Y	Y
10 Vacant						
11 McNerney	Y	Y	Y	Y	Y	Y
12 Speier	Y	Y	Y	Y	Y	Y
13 Stark	Y	Y	Y	Y	Y	Y
14 Eshoo	Y	Y	Y	Y	Y	Y
15 Honda	Y	Y	Y	Y	+	+
16 Lofgren	Y	Y	Y	Y	Y	Y
17 Farr	Y	Y	Y	Y	Y	Y
18 Cardoza	Y	Y	Y	Y	Y	Y
19 Radanovich	?	?	?	Y	Y	Y
20 Costa	Y	Y	Y	Y	Y	Y
21 Nunes	Y	Y	Y	Y	Y	Y
22 McCarthy	Y	Y	Y	Y	Y	Y
23 Capps	Y	Y	Y	Y	Y	Y
24 Gallegly	Y	Y	Y	Y	Y	Y
25 McKeon	Y	Y	Y	Y	Y	Y
26 Dreier	Y	Y	Y	Y	Y	Y
27 Sherman	Y	Y	Y	Y	Y	Y
28 Berman	Y	Y	Y	Y	Y	Y
29 Schiff	Y	Y	Y	Y	Y	Y
30 Waxman	Y	Y	Y	Y	Y	Y
31 Becerra	Y	+	Y	Y	Y	Y
32 Chu	Y	Y	Y	Y	Y	Y
33 Watson	Y	Y	Y	Y	Y	Y
34 Roybal-Allard	Y	Y	Y	Y	Y	Y
35 Waters	Y	Y	Y	Y	Y	Y
36 Harman	?	?	?	Y	Y	Y
37 Richardson	Y	Y	Y	Y	Y	Y
38 Napolitano	Y	Y	Y	Y	Y	Y
39 Sánchez, Linda	+	+	+	Y	Y	Y
40 Royce	Y	Y	Y	Y	Y	Y
41 Lewis	Y	Y	Y	Y	Y	Y
42 Miller, Gary	Y	Y	Y	Y	Y	Y
43 Baca	Y	Y	Y	Y	Y	Y
44 Calvert	Y	Y	Y	Y	Y	Y
45 Bono Mack	Y	Y	Y	Y	Y	Y
46 Rohrabacher	?	?	?	Y	Y	Y
47 Sanchez, Loretta	?	?	?	Y	Y	Y
48 Campbell	Y	Y	Y	Y	Y	Y
49 Issa	Y	Y	Y	Y	Y	Y
50 Bilbray	Y	Y	Y	Y	Y	Y
51 Filner	Y	Y	Y	Y	Y	Y
52 Hunter	Y	Y	Y	Y	Y	Y
53 Davis	Y	Y	Y	Y	Y	Y

	772	773	774	775	776	777
COLORADO						
1 DeGette	Y	Y	Y	Y	Y	Y
2 Polis	Y	Y	Y	Y	Y	Y
3 Salazar	Y	Y	Y	Y	Y	Y
4 Markey	Y	Y	Y	Y	Y	Y
5 Lamborn	Y	Y	Y	Y	Y	Y
6 Coffman	Y	Y	Y	Y	Y	Y
7 Perlmutter	Y	Y	Y	Y	Y	
CONNECTICUT						
1 Larson	Y	Y	Y	Y	Y	Y
2 Courtney	Y	Y	Y	Y	Y	Y
3 DeLauro	Y	Y	Y	Y	Y	Y
4 Himes	Y	Y	Y	Y	Y	Y
5 Murphy	Y	Y	Y	Y	Y	Y
DELAWARE						
AL Castle	Y	Y	Y	Y	Y	Y
FLORIDA						
1 Miller	+	+	+	Y	Y	Y
2 Boyd	Y	Y	Y	Y	Y	Y
3 Brown	Y	Y	Y	Y	Y	Y
4 Crenshaw	Y	Y	Y	Y	Y	Y
5 Brown-Waite	?	?	?	Y	Y	Y
6 Stearns	Y	Y	Y	Y	Y	Y
7 Mica	Y	Y	Y	Y	Y	Y
8 Grayson	Y	Y	Y	Y	Y	Y
9 Bilirakis	Y	Y	Y	?	Y	Y
10 Young	Y	Y	Y	Y	Y	Y
11 Castor	Y	Y	Y	Y	Y	Y
12 Putnam	+	+	+	Y	Y	Y
13 Buchanan	Y	Y	Y	Y	Y	Y
14 Mack	Y	?	Y	Y	Y	Y
15 Posey	Y	Y	Y	Y	Y	Y
16 Rooney	Y	Y	Y	Y	Y	Y
17 Meek	Y	Y	Y	Y	Y	Y
18 Ros-Lehtinen	Y	Y	Y	Y	Y	Y
19 Wexler	?	?	?	?	?	Y
20 Wasserman Schultz	Y	Y	Y	+	+	Y
21 Diaz-Balart, L.	?	?	?	Y	Y	Y
22 Klein	Y	Y	Y	Y	Y	Y
23 Hastings	Y	Y	Y	Y	Y	Y
24 Kosmas	Y	Y	Y	Y	Y	Y
25 Diaz-Balart, M.	Y	Y	Y	Y	Y	Y
GEORGIA						
1 Kingston	Y	Y	Y	Y	Y	Y
2 Bishop	Y	Y	Y	Y	Y	Y
3 Westmoreland	Y	Y	Y	Y	Y	Y
4 Johnson	Y	Y	Y	Y	Y	Y
5 Lewis	Y	Y	Y	Y	Y	Y
6 Price	Y	Y	Y	Y	Y	Y
7 Linder	Y	Y	Y	Y	Y	Y
8 Marshall	Y	Y	Y	Y	Y	Y
9 Deal	Y	Y	Y	Y	Y	Y
10 Broun	Y	Y	Y	Y	Y	Y
11 Gingrey	Y	?	Y	Y	Y	Y
12 Barrow	Y	Y	Y	Y	Y	Y
13 Scott	Y	Y	Y	Y	Y	Y
HAWAII						
1 Abercrombie	+	+	+	Y	Y	Y
2 Hirono	Y	Y	Y	?	?	Y
IDAHO						
1 Minnick	Y	Y	Y	Y	Y	Y
2 Simpson	Y	Y	Y	Y	Y	Y
ILLINOIS						
1 Rush	?	?	?	Y	Y	Y
2 Jackson	Y	Y	Y	Y	Y	Y
3 Lipinski	Y	Y	Y	Y	Y	Y
4 Gutierrez	Y	Y	Y	Y	Y	Y
5 Quigley	Y	Y	Y	Y	Y	Y
6 Roskam	?	?	?	Y	Y	Y
7 Davis	Y	Y	Y	Y	Y	Y
8 Bean	?	?	?	Y	Y	Y
9 Schakowsky	Y	Y	Y	Y	Y	Y
10 Kirk	Y	Y	Y	Y	Y	Y
11 Halvorson	Y	Y	Y	Y	Y	Y
12 Costello	?	?	?	Y	Y	Y
13 Biggert	Y	Y	Y	Y	Y	Y
14 Foster	Y	Y	Y	Y	Y	Y
15 Johnson	Y	Y	Y	Y	Y	Y

KEY   **Republicans**   Democrats

Y Voted for (yea)	X Paired against
# Paired for	– Announced against
+ Announced for	P Voted "present"
N Voted against (nay)	

C Voted "present" to avoid possible conflict of interest

? Did not vote or otherwise make a position known

	772	773	774	775	776	777
16 **Manzullo**	Y	Y	Y	Y	Y	Y
17 Hare	Y	Y	Y	Y	Y	Y
18 **Schock**	Y	Y	Y	?	Y	Y
19 **Shimkus**	?	?	?	Y	Y	Y
INDIANA						
1 Visclosky	Y	Y	Y	Y	Y	Y
2 Donnelly	Y	Y	Y	Y	Y	Y
3 **Souder**	Y	Y	Y	Y	Y	Y
4 **Buyer**	Y	Y	Y	Y	Y	Y
5 **Burton**	Y	Y	Y	Y	Y	Y
6 **Pence**	Y	Y	Y	Y	Y	Y
7 Carson	Y	Y	Y	Y	Y	Y
8 Ellsworth	Y	Y	Y	Y	Y	Y
9 Hill	Y	Y	Y	Y	Y	Y
IOWA						
1 Braley	Y	Y	Y	Y	Y	Y
2 Loebsack	Y	Y	Y	Y	Y	Y
3 Boswell	Y	Y	Y	Y	Y	Y
4 **Latham**	Y	Y	Y	Y	Y	Y
5 **King**	Y	Y	Y	Y	Y	Y
KANSAS						
1 **Moran**	?	?	?	Y	Y	Y
2 **Jenkins**	Y	Y	Y	Y	Y	Y
3 Moore	Y	Y	Y	Y	Y	Y
4 **Tiahrt**	Y	Y	Y	Y	Y	Y
KENTUCKY						
1 **Whitfield**	Y	Y	Y	Y	Y	Y
2 **Guthrie**	Y	Y	Y	Y	Y	Y
3 Yarmuth	Y	Y	Y	Y	Y	Y
4 **Davis**	Y	Y	Y	Y	Y	Y
5 **Rogers**	Y	Y	Y	Y	Y	Y
6 Chandler	Y	Y	Y	Y	Y	Y
LOUISIANA						
1 **Scalise**	Y	Y	Y	Y	Y	Y
2 **Cao**	Y	Y	Y	?	?	?
3 Melancon	Y	Y	Y	Y	Y	Y
4 **Fleming**	Y	Y	Y	Y	Y	Y
5 **Alexander**	Y	Y	Y	Y	Y	Y
6 **Cassidy**	Y	Y	Y	Y	Y	Y
7 **Boustany**	Y	Y	Y	Y	Y	Y
MAINE						
1 Pingree	Y	Y	Y	Y	Y	Y
2 Michaud	Y	Y	Y	Y	Y	Y
MARYLAND						
1 Kratovil	Y	Y	Y	Y	Y	Y
2 Ruppersberger	Y	Y	Y	Y	Y	Y
3 Sarbanes	Y	Y	Y	Y	Y	Y
4 Edwards	Y	Y	Y	Y	Y	Y
5 Hoyer	Y	Y	Y	Y	Y	Y
6 **Bartlett**	Y	Y	Y	Y	Y	Y
7 Cummings	Y	Y	Y	Y	Y	Y
8 Van Hollen	Y	Y	Y	Y	Y	Y
MASSACHUSETTS						
1 Olver	Y	Y	Y	Y	Y	Y
2 Neal	?	?	?	Y	Y	Y
3 McGovern	Y	Y	Y	Y	Y	Y
4 Frank	Y	Y	Y	Y	Y	Y
5 Tsongas	Y	Y	Y	Y	Y	Y
6 Tierney	Y	Y	Y	Y	Y	Y
7 Markey	Y	Y	Y	Y	Y	Y
8 Capuano	+	+	+	Y	Y	Y
9 Lynch	Y	Y	Y	Y	Y	Y
10 Delahunt	Y	Y	Y	Y	Y	Y
MICHIGAN						
1 Stupak	Y	Y	Y	Y	Y	Y
2 **Hoekstra**	?	?	?	Y	Y	Y
3 **Ehlers**	Y	Y	Y	Y	Y	Y
4 **Camp**	?	?	?	Y	Y	Y
5 Kildee	Y	Y	Y	Y	Y	Y
6 **Upton**	Y	Y	Y	Y	Y	Y
7 Schauer	Y	Y	Y	Y	Y	Y
8 **Rogers**	?	Y	Y	Y	Y	Y
9 Peters	Y	Y	Y	Y	Y	Y
10 **Miller**	Y	Y	Y	Y	Y	Y
11 **McCotter**	Y	Y	Y	Y	Y	Y
12 Levin	Y	Y	Y	Y	Y	Y
13 Kilpatrick	Y	Y	Y	Y	Y	Y
14 Conyers	+	+	Y	+	+	+
15 Dingell	Y	Y	Y	Y	Y	Y
MINNESOTA						
1 Walz	Y	Y	Y	Y	+	Y
2 **Kline**	Y	Y	Y	Y	Y	Y
3 **Paulsen**	Y	Y	Y	Y	Y	Y
4 McCollum	Y	Y	Y	Y	Y	Y

	772	773	774	775	776	777
5 Ellison	Y	Y	Y	Y	Y	Y
6 **Bachmann**	Y	Y	Y	Y	Y	Y
7 Peterson	Y	Y	Y	Y	Y	Y
8 Oberstar	Y	Y	Y	Y	Y	Y
MISSISSIPPI						
1 Childers	Y	Y	Y	Y	Y	Y
2 Thompson	Y	Y	Y	Y	Y	Y
3 **Harper**	Y	Y	Y	Y	Y	Y
4 Taylor	?	?	?	Y	Y	Y
MISSOURI						
1 Clay	Y	Y	Y	Y	Y	Y
2 **Akin**	Y	Y	Y	Y	Y	Y
3 Carnahan	Y	Y	Y	Y	Y	Y
4 Skelton	Y	Y	Y	Y	Y	Y
5 Cleaver	Y	Y	Y	Y	Y	Y
6 **Graves**	Y	Y	Y	Y	Y	Y
7 **Blunt**	?	?	?	Y	Y	Y
8 **Emerson**	Y	Y	Y	Y	Y	Y
9 **Luetkemeyer**	Y	Y	Y	Y	Y	Y
MONTANA						
AL **Rehberg**	Y	Y	Y	Y	Y	Y
NEBRASKA						
1 **Fortenberry**	Y	Y	Y	Y	Y	Y
2 **Terry**	Y	Y	Y	Y	Y	Y
3 **Smith**	Y	Y	Y	Y	Y	Y
NEVADA						
1 Berkley	Y	Y	Y	Y	Y	Y
2 **Heller**	Y	Y	Y	Y	Y	Y
3 Titus	Y	Y	Y	Y	Y	Y
NEW HAMPSHIRE						
1 Shea-Porter	Y	Y	Y	Y	Y	Y
2 Hodes	Y	Y	Y	Y	Y	Y
NEW JERSEY						
1 Andrews	Y	Y	Y	?	Y	Y
2 **LoBiondo**	Y	Y	Y	Y	Y	Y
3 Adler	Y	Y	Y	+	Y	Y
4 **Smith**	Y	Y	Y	Y	Y	Y
5 **Garrett**	Y	Y	Y	Y	Y	Y
6 Pallone	Y	Y	Y	Y	Y	Y
7 **Lance**	Y	Y	Y	Y	Y	Y
8 Pascrell	Y	Y	Y	Y	Y	Y
9 Rothman	Y	Y	Y	Y	Y	Y
10 Payne	Y	Y	Y	Y	Y	Y
11 **Frelinghuysen**	Y	Y	Y	Y	Y	Y
12 Holt	Y	Y	Y	+	Y	Y
13 Sires	?	?	?	Y	Y	Y
NEW MEXICO						
1 Heinrich	Y	Y	Y	Y	Y	Y
2 Teague	Y	Y	Y	Y	Y	Y
3 Lujan	Y	Y	Y	Y	Y	Y
NEW YORK						
1 Bishop	Y	Y	Y	Y	Y	Y
2 Israel	Y	Y	Y	Y	Y	Y
3 **King**	Y	Y	Y	Y	Y	Y
4 McCarthy	Y	Y	Y	Y	Y	Y
5 Ackerman	Y	Y	Y	Y	Y	Y
6 Meeks	Y	Y	Y	Y	Y	Y
7 Crowley	Y	Y	Y	Y	Y	Y
8 Nadler	Y	Y	Y	Y	Y	Y
9 Weiner	Y	Y	Y	Y	Y	Y
10 Towns	Y	Y	Y	Y	Y	Y
11 Clarke	?	Y	Y	Y	Y	Y
12 Velázquez	Y	Y	?	Y	Y	Y
13 McMahon	Y	Y	Y	Y	Y	Y
14 Maloney	?	?	?	Y	Y	Y
15 Rangel	Y	Y	Y	Y	Y	Y
16 Serrano	Y	Y	Y	?	Y	Y
17 Engel	?	?	?	Y	Y	Y
18 Lowey	Y	Y	Y	Y	Y	Y
19 Hall	Y	Y	Y	Y	Y	Y
20 Murphy	Y	Y	Y	Y	Y	Y
21 Tonko	Y	Y	Y	Y	Y	Y
22 Hinchey	Y	Y	Y	Y	N	Y
23 Vacant						
24 Arcuri	Y	Y	Y	Y	Y	Y
25 Maffei	Y	Y	Y	Y	Y	Y
26 **Lee**	Y	Y	Y	Y	Y	Y
27 Higgins	Y	Y	Y	Y	Y	Y
28 Slaughter	Y	Y	Y	Y	Y	Y
29 Massa	Y	Y	Y	Y	Y	Y
NORTH CAROLINA						
1 Butterfield	Y	?	Y	Y	Y	Y
2 Etheridge	Y	Y	Y	Y	Y	Y
3 **Jones**	Y	Y	Y	Y	N	Y
4 Price	Y	Y	Y	Y	Y	Y

	772	773	774	775	776	777
5 **Foxx**	Y	Y	Y	Y	Y	Y
6 **Coble**	Y	Y	Y	Y	Y	Y
7 McIntyre	Y	Y	Y	Y	Y	Y
8 Kissell	Y	Y	Y	Y	Y	Y
9 **Myrick**	Y	Y	Y	Y	Y	Y
10 **McHenry**	Y	Y	Y	Y	Y	Y
11 Shuler	Y	Y	Y	Y	Y	Y
12 Watt	Y	Y	Y	Y	Y	?
13 Miller	Y	Y	Y	Y	Y	Y
NORTH DAKOTA						
AL Pomeroy	?	?	?	Y	Y	Y
OHIO						
1 Driehaus	Y	Y	Y	Y	Y	Y
2 **Schmidt**	Y	Y	Y	Y	Y	Y
3 **Turner**	Y	Y	Y	Y	Y	Y
4 **Jordan**	Y	Y	Y	Y	Y	Y
5 **Latta**	Y	Y	Y	Y	Y	Y
6 Wilson	Y	Y	Y	Y	Y	Y
7 **Austria**	?	?	?	Y	Y	Y
8 **Boehner**	Y	Y	Y	Y	Y	Y
9 Kaptur	Y	Y	Y	Y	Y	Y
10 Kucinich	Y	Y	Y	Y	N	Y
11 Fudge	Y	Y	Y	Y	Y	Y
12 **Tiberi**	Y	Y	Y	Y	Y	Y
13 Sutton	Y	Y	Y	Y	Y	Y
14 **LaTourette**	Y	Y	Y	Y	Y	Y
15 Kilroy	Y	Y	Y	?	Y	Y
16 Boccieri	Y	Y	Y	Y	Y	Y
17 Ryan	Y	Y	Y	Y	Y	Y
18 Space	Y	Y	Y	Y	Y	Y
OKLAHOMA						
1 **Sullivan**	Y	Y	Y	Y	Y	Y
2 Boren	Y	Y	Y	Y	+	Y
3 **Lucas**	Y	Y	Y	Y	Y	Y
4 **Cole**	Y	Y	Y	+	Y	Y
5 **Fallin**	Y	Y	Y	Y	Y	Y
OREGON						
1 Wu	Y	Y	Y	Y	Y	Y
2 **Walden**	Y	Y	Y	Y	Y	Y
3 Blumenauer	Y	Y	Y	Y	Y	Y
4 DeFazio	Y	Y	Y	Y	Y	Y
5 Schrader	Y	?	Y	Y	Y	Y
PENNSYLVANIA						
1 Brady	Y	Y	Y	Y	Y	Y
2 Fattah	Y	Y	Y	Y	Y	Y
3 Dahlkemper	Y	Y	Y	Y	Y	Y
4 Altmire	Y	Y	Y	Y	Y	Y
5 **Thompson**	Y	Y	Y	Y	Y	Y
6 **Gerlach**	Y	Y	Y	Y	Y	Y
7 Sestak	Y	Y	Y	Y	Y	Y
8 Murphy, P.	Y	Y	Y	Y	Y	Y
9 **Shuster**	Y	Y	Y	+	+	+
10 Carney	?	?	?	?	?	?
11 Kanjorski	Y	Y	Y	Y	Y	Y
12 Murtha	Y	Y	Y	Y	Y	Y
13 Schwartz	Y	Y	Y	Y	Y	Y
14 Doyle	Y	Y	Y	Y	Y	Y
15 **Dent**	Y	Y	Y	Y	Y	Y
16 **Pitts**	Y	Y	Y	Y	Y	Y
17 Holden	Y	Y	Y	Y	Y	Y
18 **Murphy, T.**	Y	Y	Y	Y	Y	Y
19 **Platts**	?	?	?	Y	Y	Y
RHODE ISLAND						
1 Kennedy	Y	Y	Y	Y	Y	Y
2 Langevin	Y	Y	Y	Y	Y	Y
SOUTH CAROLINA						
1 **Brown**	Y	Y	Y	Y	Y	Y
2 **Wilson**	Y	Y	Y	Y	Y	Y
3 **Barrett**	?	?	?	Y	Y	Y
4 **Inglis**	Y	Y	Y	Y	Y	Y
5 Spratt	Y	Y	Y	Y	Y	Y
6 Clyburn	Y	Y	Y	Y	Y	Y
SOUTH DAKOTA						
AL Herseth Sandlin	Y	Y	Y	Y	+	Y
TENNESSEE						
1 **Roe**	Y	Y	Y	Y	Y	Y
2 **Duncan**	Y	Y	Y	Y	Y	Y
3 **Wamp**	?	?	?	Y	Y	Y
4 Davis	Y	Y	Y	Y	Y	Y
5 Cooper	Y	Y	Y	Y	Y	Y
6 Gordon	Y	Y	Y	Y	Y	Y
7 **Blackburn**	Y	Y	Y	Y	Y	Y
8 Tanner	Y	Y	Y	Y	Y	Y
9 Cohen	Y	Y	Y	Y	Y	Y

	772	773	774	775	776	777
TEXAS						
1 **Gohmert**	Y	Y	Y	Y	Y	Y
2 **Poe**	Y	Y	Y	Y	Y	Y
3 **Johnson, S.**	Y	Y	Y	Y	Y	Y
4 **Hall**	Y	Y	Y	Y	Y	Y
5 **Hensarling**	Y	Y	Y	Y	Y	Y
6 **Barton**	Y	Y	Y	Y	Y	Y
7 **Culberson**	Y	Y	Y	Y	Y	Y
8 **Brady**	Y	Y	Y	Y	Y	Y
9 Green, A.	Y	Y	Y	Y	Y	Y
10 **McCaul**	Y	Y	Y	Y	Y	Y
11 **Conaway**	Y	Y	Y	Y	Y	Y
12 **Granger**	?	?	?	Y	Y	Y
13 **Thornberry**	?	?	?	Y	Y	Y
14 **Paul**	Y	N	Y	Y	N	Y
15 Hinojosa	Y	Y	Y	Y	Y	Y
16 Reyes	Y	Y	Y	Y	Y	Y
17 Edwards	Y	Y	Y	Y	Y	Y
18 Jackson Lee	Y	Y	Y	Y	Y	Y
19 **Neugebauer**	Y	Y	Y	Y	Y	Y
20 Gonzalez	Y	Y	Y	Y	Y	Y
21 **Smith**	Y	Y	Y	Y	Y	Y
22 **Olson**	Y	?	Y	Y	Y	Y
23 Rodriguez	Y	Y	Y	Y	Y	Y
24 **Marchant**	Y	Y	Y	Y	Y	Y
25 Doggett	Y	Y	Y	Y	Y	Y
26 **Burgess**	Y	Y	Y	Y	Y	Y
27 Ortiz	Y	Y	Y	Y	Y	Y
28 Cuellar	?	?	Y	Y	Y	Y
29 Green, G.	Y	Y	?	Y	Y	Y
30 Johnson, E.	Y	Y	Y	Y	Y	Y
31 **Carter**	Y	Y	Y	Y	Y	Y
32 **Sessions**	Y	Y	Y	Y	Y	Y
UTAH						
1 **Bishop**	Y	Y	Y	?	Y	Y
2 Matheson	?	Y	Y	Y	Y	Y
3 **Chaffetz**	Y	Y	Y	Y	Y	Y
VERMONT						
AL Welch	Y	Y	Y	Y	Y	Y
VIRGINIA						
1 **Wittman**	Y	Y	Y	Y	Y	Y
2 Nye	Y	Y	Y	Y	Y	Y
3 Scott	Y	Y	Y	Y	Y	Y
4 **Forbes**	Y	Y	Y	Y	Y	Y
5 Perriello	Y	Y	Y	Y	Y	Y
6 **Goodlatte**	Y	Y	Y	Y	Y	Y
7 **Cantor**	Y	Y	Y	Y	Y	Y
8 Moran	Y	Y	Y	Y	Y	Y
9 Boucher	Y	Y	Y	Y	Y	Y
10 **Wolf**	Y	Y	Y	Y	Y	Y
11 Connolly	Y	Y	Y	Y	Y	Y
WASHINGTON						
1 Inslee	Y	Y	Y	Y	Y	Y
2 Larsen	Y	Y	Y	Y	Y	Y
3 Baird	Y	Y	Y	Y	Y	Y
4 **Hastings**	Y	Y	Y	Y	Y	Y
5 **McMorris Rodgers**	Y	Y	Y	Y	Y	Y
6 Dicks	Y	Y	Y	Y	Y	Y
7 McDermott	Y	Y	Y	Y	N	Y
8 **Reichert**	Y	Y	Y	Y	Y	Y
9 Smith	Y	Y	Y	Y	Y	Y
WEST VIRGINIA						
1 Mollohan	Y	Y	Y	?	?	?
2 **Capito**	Y	Y	Y	Y	Y	Y
3 Rahall	Y	Y	Y	Y	Y	Y
WISCONSIN						
1 **Ryan**	Y	Y	Y	Y	Y	Y
2 Baldwin	Y	Y	Y	Y	Y	Y
3 Kind	Y	Y	Y	Y	Y	Y
4 Moore	Y	Y	Y	Y	Y	Y
5 **Sensenbrenner**	Y	Y	Y	Y	Y	Y
6 **Petri**	Y	Y	Y	Y	Y	Y
7 Obey	Y	Y	Y	Y	Y	Y
8 Kagen	Y	Y	Y	Y	Y	Y
WYOMING						
AL **Lummis**	Y	Y	Y	Y	Y	Y
DELEGATES						
Faleomavaega (A.S.)						
Norton (D.C.)						
Bordallo (Guam)						
Sablan (N. Marianas)						
Pierluisi (P.R.)						
Christensen (V.I.)						

IN THE HOUSE | By Vote Number

778. **HR 3371. Increased Pilot Training/Passage.** Costello, D-Ill., motion to suspend the rules and pass the bill that would require commercial pilots to obtain licenses requiring 1,500 flight hours and receive training on recovery tactics for emergency situations and inclement weather. It would also require the Federal Aviation Administration to examine the impact of pilot fatigue and issue a new time and duty rule for pilots. Motion agreed to 409-11: R 163-11; D 246-0. A two-thirds majority of those present and voting (280 in this case) is required for passage under suspension of the rules. Oct. 14, 2009.

779. **H Res 786. Father Damien Canonization/Adoption.** Faleomavaega, D-A.S., motion to suspend the rules and adopt the resolution that would recognize the canonization of Father Damien de Veuster to sainthood. Motion agreed to 418-0: R 173-0; D 245-0. A two-thirds majority of those present and voting (279 in this case) is required for adoption under suspension of the rules. Oct. 14, 2009.

780. **HR 2892. Fiscal 2010 Homeland Security Appropriations/ Previous Question.** Hastings, D-Fla., motion to order the previous question (thus ending debate and possibility of amendment) on adoption of the rule (H Res 829) that would provide for House floor consideration of the conference report on the bill that would appropriate $44.1 billion, including $42.8 billion in discretionary funds, in fiscal 2010 for the Homeland Security Department. Motion agreed to 243-173: R 1-168; D 242-5. Oct. 15, 2009.

781. **HR 2892. Fiscal 2010 Homeland Security Appropriations/Rule.** Adoption of the rule (H Res 829) that would provide for House floor consideration of the conference report on the bill that would appropriate $44.1 billion, including $42.8 billion in discretionary funds, in fiscal 2010 for the Homeland Security Department. Adopted 239-174: R 0-170; D 239-4. Oct. 15, 2009.

782. **H Res 800. Philippines Storm Victims/Adoption.** Faleomavaega, D-A.S., motion to suspend the rules and adopt the resolution that would express that the House mourns the loss of life in the Philippines caused by Tropical Storm Ketsana and Typhoon Parma, and would urge the president to continue emergency aid to the Philippines. Motion agreed to 415-0: R 170-0; D 245-0. A two-thirds majority of those present and voting (277 in this case) is required for adoption under suspension of the rules. Oct. 15, 2009.

783. **HR 2892. Fiscal 2010 Homeland Security Appropriations/ Motion to Recommit.** Rogers, R-Ky., motion to recommit the conference report on the bill to the conference committee with instructions that managers not accept language that would allow detainees held at Guantánamo Bay, Cuba, to be brought into the United States for prosecution or incarceration. Motion rejected 193-224: R 168-1; D 25-223. A "nay" vote was a vote in support of the president's position. Oct. 15, 2009.

	778	779	780	781	782	783
ALABAMA						
1 **Bonner**	Y	Y	N	N	Y	Y
2 **Bright**	Y	Y	Y	N	?	Y
3 **Rogers**	Y	Y	?	N	Y	Y
4 **Aderholt**	Y	Y	N	N	Y	Y
5 Griffith	Y	Y	N	Y	Y	Y
6 **Bachus**	Y	Y	N	N	Y	Y
7 Davis	Y	Y	Y	Y	Y	Y
ALASKA						
AL **Young**	Y	Y	N	N	Y	Y
ARIZONA						
1 Kirkpatrick	Y	Y	Y	Y	Y	Y
2 **Franks**	Y	Y	N	N	Y	Y
3 **Shadegg**	Y	Y	N	N	Y	Y
4 Pastor	Y	Y	Y	Y	Y	N
5 Mitchell	Y	Y	Y	Y	Y	Y
6 **Flake**	N	Y	N	N	Y	Y
7 Grijalva	Y	Y	Y	Y	Y	N
8 Giffords	Y	Y	Y	Y	Y	N
ARKANSAS						
1 Berry	Y	Y	Y	Y	Y	N
2 Snyder	Y	Y	Y	Y	Y	N
3 **Boozman**	Y	Y	N	N	Y	Y
4 Ross	Y	Y	Y	Y	Y	N
CALIFORNIA						
1 Thompson	Y	Y	Y	Y	Y	N
2 **Herger**	Y	Y	N	N	Y	Y
3 **Lungren**	Y	Y	N	Y	Y	Y
4 **McClintock**	Y	Y	N	N	Y	Y
5 Matsui	Y	Y	Y	Y	Y	N
6 Woolsey	Y	Y	Y	Y	Y	N
7 Miller, George	Y	Y	Y	Y	Y	N
8 Pelosi						
9 Lee	Y	Y	Y	Y	Y	N
10 Vacant						
11 McNerney	Y	Y	Y	Y	Y	Y
12 Speier	Y	Y	Y	Y	Y	N
13 Stark	Y	Y	?	?	?	N
14 Eshoo	Y	Y	Y	Y	Y	N
15 Honda	+	+	?	Y	Y	N
16 Lofgren	Y	Y	Y	Y	Y	N
17 Farr	Y	Y	Y	Y	Y	N
18 Cardoza	Y	Y	Y	Y	Y	N
19 **Radanovich**	Y	Y	?	?	?	?
20 Costa	Y	Y	Y	Y	Y	N
21 **Nunes**	Y	Y	N	N	Y	Y
22 **McCarthy**	Y	Y	N	N	Y	Y
23 Capps	Y	?	Y	Y	Y	N
24 **Gallegly**	Y	Y	N	N	Y	Y
25 **McKeon**	Y	Y	N	N	Y	Y
26 **Dreier**	Y	Y	N	N	Y	Y
27 Sherman	Y	Y	Y	Y	Y	N
28 Berman	Y	Y	Y	Y	Y	N
29 Schiff	Y	Y	Y	Y	Y	N
30 Waxman	Y	Y	Y	Y	Y	N
31 Becerra	Y	Y	Y	Y	Y	N
32 Chu	Y	Y	Y	Y	Y	N
33 Watson	Y	Y	Y	Y	Y	N
34 Roybal-Allard	Y	Y	Y	Y	Y	N
35 Waters	Y	Y	Y	Y	Y	N
36 Harman	Y	Y	Y	Y	Y	N
37 Richardson	Y	Y	Y	Y	Y	N
38 Napolitano	Y	Y	Y	Y	Y	N
39 Sánchez, Linda	Y	Y	Y	Y	Y	N
40 **Royce**	Y	Y	N	N	Y	Y
41 **Lewis**	Y	Y	N	N	Y	Y
42 **Miller, Gary**	Y	Y	N	N	Y	Y
43 Baca	Y	Y	Y	Y	Y	N
44 **Calvert**	Y	Y	N	N	Y	Y
45 **Bono Mack**	Y	Y	N	N	Y	Y
46 **Rohrabacher**	Y	Y	N	N	Y	Y
47 Sanchez, Loretta	Y	Y	Y	Y	Y	N
48 **Campbell**	Y	Y	N	N	Y	Y
49 **Issa**	Y	Y	N	N	Y	Y
50 **Bilbray**	Y	Y	N	N	Y	Y
51 Filner	Y	Y	Y	Y	Y	Y
52 **Hunter**	Y	Y	N	N	Y	Y
53 Davis	Y	Y	Y	Y	Y	N

	778	779	780	781	782	783
COLORADO						
1 DeGette	Y	Y	Y	Y	Y	N
2 Polis	Y	Y	Y	Y	Y	N
3 Salazar	Y	Y	Y	Y	Y	N
4 Markey	Y	Y	Y	Y	Y	N
5 **Lamborn**	Y	Y	N	N	Y	Y
6 **Coffman**	Y	Y	N	N	Y	Y
7 Perlmutter	Y	Y	Y	Y	Y	N
CONNECTICUT						
1 Larson	Y	Y	Y	Y	Y	N
2 Courtney	Y	Y	Y	Y	Y	N
3 DeLauro	Y	Y	Y	Y	Y	N
4 Himes	Y	Y	Y	Y	Y	N
5 Murphy	Y	Y	Y	Y	Y	N
DELAWARE						
AL **Castle**	Y	Y	N	N	Y	Y
FLORIDA						
1 **Miller**	Y	Y	N	N	Y	Y
2 Boyd	Y	Y	?	?	+	?
3 Brown	Y	Y	Y	Y	Y	N
4 **Crenshaw**	Y	Y	N	N	Y	Y
5 **Brown-Waite**	Y	?	N	N	Y	Y
6 **Stearns**	Y	Y	N	N	Y	Y
7 **Mica**	Y	Y	N	N	Y	Y
8 Grayson	Y	Y	Y	Y	Y	N
9 **Bilirakis**	Y	Y	N	N	Y	Y
10 **Young**	Y	Y	N	N	Y	Y
11 Castor	Y	Y	Y	Y	Y	N
12 **Putnam**	Y	Y	N	N	Y	Y
13 **Buchanan**	Y	Y	N	N	Y	Y
14 **Mack**	Y	Y	N	N	Y	Y
15 **Posey**	Y	Y	N	N	Y	Y
16 **Rooney**	Y	Y	N	N	Y	Y
17 Meek	Y	Y	Y	Y	Y	N
18 **Ros-Lehtinen**	Y	Y	N	N	Y	Y
19 Wexler	?	?	Y	Y	Y	N
20 Wasserman Schultz	+	+	Y	Y	Y	N
21 **Diaz-Balart, L.**	Y	Y	N	N	Y	Y
22 Klein	Y	Y	Y	Y	Y	N
23 Hastings	Y	Y	Y	Y	Y	N
24 Kosmas	Y	Y	Y	Y	Y	N
25 **Diaz-Balart, M.**	Y	Y	N	N	Y	Y
GEORGIA						
1 **Kingston**	Y	Y	N	N	Y	Y
2 Bishop	Y	Y	Y	Y	Y	N
3 **Westmoreland**	N	Y	N	N	Y	Y
4 Johnson	Y	Y	Y	Y	Y	N
5 Lewis	Y	Y	Y	Y	Y	N
6 **Price**	N	Y	N	N	Y	Y
7 **Linder**	Y	Y	N	N	Y	Y
8 Marshall	Y	Y	Y	Y	Y	?
9 **Deal**	Y	Y	N	N	Y	Y
10 **Broun**	N	Y	N	N	Y	Y
11 **Gingrey**	Y	Y	N	N	Y	Y
12 Barrow	Y	Y	Y	Y	Y	Y
13 Scott	Y	Y	Y	Y	Y	N
HAWAII						
1 Abercrombie	Y	Y	Y	?	Y	N
2 Hirono	?	?	Y	+	Y	N
IDAHO						
1 Minnick	Y	Y	N	Y	Y	?
2 **Simpson**	Y	Y	N	N	Y	Y
ILLINOIS						
1 Rush	Y	Y	Y	Y	Y	N
2 Jackson	Y	Y	Y	Y	Y	N
3 Lipinski	Y	Y	Y	Y	Y	N
4 Gutierrez	Y	Y	Y	Y	Y	N
5 Quigley	Y	Y	Y	Y	Y	N
6 **Roskam**	Y	Y	N	N	Y	Y
7 Davis	Y	Y	Y	Y	Y	N
8 Bean	Y	Y	Y	Y	Y	N
9 Schakowsky	Y	Y	Y	Y	Y	N
10 **Kirk**	Y	Y	N	N	Y	Y
11 Halvorson	Y	Y	Y	Y	Y	N
12 Costello	Y	Y	Y	Y	Y	N
13 **Biggert**	Y	Y	N	N	Y	Y
14 Foster	Y	Y	Y	Y	Y	N
15 Johnson	Y	Y	N	N	Y	Y

KEY | **Republicans** | Democrats

Y	Voted for (yea)	X	Paired against	C	Voted "present" to avoid possible conflict of interest
#	Paired for	–	Announced against		
+	Announced for	P	Voted "present"	?	Did not vote or otherwise make a position known
N	Voted against (nay)				

	778	779	780	781	782	783
16 **Manzullo**	Y	Y	N	N	Y	Y
17 Hare	Y	Y	Y	Y	Y	N
18 **Schock**	Y	Y	?	N	Y	?
19 **Shimkus**	Y	Y	N	N	Y	Y
INDIANA						
1 Visclosky	Y	Y	Y	Y	Y	N
2 Donnelly	Y	Y	Y	Y	Y	Y
3 **Souder**	Y	Y	N	N	Y	Y
4 **Buyer**	Y	Y	N	N	Y	Y
5 **Burton**	Y	Y	N	N	Y	Y
6 **Pence**	Y	Y	N	N	Y	Y
7 Carson	Y	Y	Y	Y	Y	N
8 Ellsworth	Y	Y	Y	Y	Y	N
9 Hill	Y	Y	Y	Y	Y	N
IOWA						
1 Braley	Y	Y	Y	Y	Y	N
2 Loebsack	Y	Y	Y	Y	Y	N
3 Boswell	Y	?	Y	Y	Y	N
4 **Latham**	Y	Y	N	N	Y	Y
5 **King**	Y	Y	N	N	Y	Y
KANSAS						
1 **Moran**	Y	Y	N	N	Y	Y
2 **Jenkins**	Y	Y	N	N	Y	Y
3 Moore	Y	Y	Y	Y	Y	N
4 **Tiahrt**	Y	Y	N	N	Y	Y
KENTUCKY						
1 **Whitfield**	N	Y	N	N	Y	Y
2 **Guthrie**	Y	Y	N	N	Y	Y
3 Yarmuth	Y	Y	Y	Y	Y	N
4 **Davis**	Y	Y	N	N	Y	Y
5 **Rogers**	Y	Y	N	N	Y	Y
6 Chandler	Y	Y	Y	Y	Y	N
LOUISIANA						
1 **Scalise**	Y	Y	?	?	?	?
2 **Cao**	?	?	?	?	?	?
3 Melancon	Y	Y	?	?	?	?
4 **Fleming**	Y	Y	N	N	Y	Y
5 **Alexander**	Y	Y	N	N	Y	Y
6 **Cassidy**	Y	Y	N	N	Y	Y
7 **Boustany**	Y	Y	N	N	Y	Y
MAINE						
1 Pingree	Y	Y	Y	Y	Y	N
2 Michaud	Y	Y	Y	Y	Y	N
MARYLAND						
1 Kratovil	Y	Y	N	N	Y	Y
2 Ruppersberger	Y	Y	Y	Y	Y	N
3 Sarbanes	Y	Y	Y	Y	Y	N
4 Edwards	Y	Y	Y	Y	Y	N
5 Hoyer	Y	Y	Y	Y	Y	N
6 **Bartlett**	Y	Y	N	N	Y	Y
7 Cummings	Y	Y	Y	Y	Y	N
8 Van Hollen	Y	Y	Y	Y	Y	N
MASSACHUSETTS						
1 Olver	Y	Y	Y	Y	Y	N
2 Neal	Y	Y	Y	Y	Y	N
3 McGovern	Y	Y	Y	Y	Y	N
4 Frank	Y	Y	Y	Y	Y	N
5 Tsongas	Y	Y	Y	Y	Y	N
6 Tierney	Y	Y	Y	Y	Y	N
7 Markey	Y	Y	Y	Y	Y	N
8 Capuano	Y	Y	Y	Y	Y	N
9 Lynch	Y	Y	Y	Y	Y	N
10 Delahunt	Y	Y	Y	Y	Y	N
MICHIGAN						
1 Stupak	Y	Y	Y	Y	Y	N
2 **Hoekstra**	Y	Y	N	N	Y	Y
3 **Ehlers**	Y	Y	N	N	Y	Y
4 **Camp**	Y	Y	N	N	Y	Y
5 Kildee	Y	Y	Y	Y	Y	N
6 **Upton**	Y	Y	N	N	Y	Y
7 Schauer	Y	Y	Y	Y	Y	N
8 **Rogers**	Y	Y	N	N	Y	Y
9 Peters	Y	Y	Y	Y	Y	Y
10 **Miller**	Y	Y	N	N	Y	Y
11 **McCotter**	Y	Y	N	N	Y	Y
12 Levin	Y	Y	Y	Y	Y	N
13 Kilpatrick	Y	Y	Y	Y	Y	N
14 Conyers	+	+	Y	Y	Y	N
15 Dingell	Y	Y	Y	Y	Y	N
MINNESOTA						
1 Walz	Y	Y	Y	Y	Y	N
2 **Kline**	Y	Y	N	N	Y	Y
3 **Paulsen**	Y	Y	N	N	Y	Y
4 McCollum	Y	Y	?	?	?	?

	778	779	780	781	782	783
5 Ellison	Y	Y	Y	Y	Y	N
6 **Bachmann**	Y	Y	N	N	Y	Y
7 Peterson	Y	Y	Y	Y	Y	N
8 Oberstar	Y	Y	Y	Y	Y	N
MISSISSIPPI						
1 Childers	Y	Y	Y	Y	Y	Y
2 Thompson	Y	Y	Y	Y	Y	N
3 **Harper**	Y	Y	N	N	Y	Y
4 Taylor	Y	Y	Y	Y	Y	Y
MISSOURI						
1 Clay	Y	Y	Y	Y	Y	N
2 **Akin**	Y	Y	N	N	Y	Y
3 Carnahan	Y	Y	Y	Y	Y	N
4 Skelton	Y	Y	Y	Y	Y	N
5 Cleaver	Y	Y	Y	Y	Y	N
6 **Graves**	N	Y	N	N	Y	Y
7 **Blunt**	Y	Y	N	N	Y	?
8 **Emerson**	Y	Y	?	?	?	?
9 **Luetkemeyer**	Y	Y	N	N	Y	Y
MONTANA						
AL **Rehberg**	Y	Y	N	N	Y	Y
NEBRASKA						
1 **Fortenberry**	Y	Y	N	N	Y	Y
2 **Terry**	Y	Y	N	N	Y	Y
3 **Smith**	Y	Y	N	N	Y	Y
NEVADA						
1 Berkley	Y	Y	Y	Y	Y	N
2 **Heller**	Y	Y	N	N	Y	Y
3 Titus	Y	Y	Y	Y	Y	N
NEW HAMPSHIRE						
1 Shea-Porter	Y	Y	Y	Y	Y	Y
2 Hodes	Y	?	Y	Y	Y	Y
NEW JERSEY						
1 Andrews	Y	Y	Y	Y	Y	N
2 **LoBiondo**	Y	Y	N	N	Y	Y
3 Adler	Y	Y	Y	Y	Y	Y
4 **Smith**	Y	Y	N	N	Y	Y
5 **Garrett**	Y	Y	N	N	Y	Y
6 Pallone	Y	Y	Y	Y	Y	N
7 **Lance**	Y	Y	N	N	Y	Y
8 Pascrell	Y	Y	Y	Y	Y	N
9 Rothman	Y	Y	Y	Y	Y	N
10 Payne	Y	Y	Y	Y	Y	N
11 **Frelinghuysen**	Y	Y	N	N	Y	Y
12 Holt	Y	Y	Y	Y	Y	N
13 Sires	Y	Y	Y	Y	Y	N
NEW MEXICO						
1 Heinrich	Y	Y	Y	Y	Y	N
2 Teague	Y	Y	Y	Y	Y	Y
3 Lujan	Y	Y	Y	Y	Y	N
NEW YORK						
1 Bishop	Y	Y	Y	Y	Y	N
2 Israel	Y	Y	Y	Y	Y	N
3 **King**	Y	Y	N	N	Y	Y
4 McCarthy	Y	Y	Y	Y	Y	N
5 Ackerman	Y	Y	Y	Y	Y	N
6 Meeks	Y	Y	Y	Y	Y	N
7 Crowley	Y	Y	Y	Y	Y	N
8 Nadler	Y	Y	Y	Y	Y	N
9 Weiner	Y	Y	Y	?	Y	N
10 Towns	Y	Y	Y	?	Y	N
11 Clarke	Y	Y	Y	Y	Y	N
12 Velázquez	Y	Y	Y	Y	Y	N
13 McMahon	Y	Y	Y	Y	Y	Y
14 Maloney	Y	Y	Y	Y	Y	N
15 Rangel	Y	Y	Y	?	Y	N
16 Serrano	Y	Y	Y	Y	?	N
17 Engel	Y	Y	Y	Y	Y	N
18 Lowey	Y	Y	Y	Y	Y	N
19 Hall	Y	Y	Y	Y	Y	N
20 Murphy	Y	Y	Y	–	Y	N
21 Tonko	Y	Y	Y	Y	Y	N
22 Hinchey	Y	Y	Y	Y	Y	N
23 Vacant						
24 Arcuri	Y	Y	Y	Y	Y	N
25 Maffei	Y	Y	Y	Y	Y	N
26 **Lee**	Y	Y	N	N	Y	Y
27 Higgins	Y	Y	Y	Y	Y	N
28 Slaughter	Y	Y	Y	Y	Y	N
29 Massa	Y	Y	Y	Y	Y	N
NORTH CAROLINA						
1 Butterfield	Y	Y	Y	Y	Y	N
2 Etheridge	Y	Y	Y	Y	Y	N
3 **Jones**	Y	Y	N	N	Y	Y
4 Price	Y	Y	Y	Y	Y	N

	778	779	780	781	782	783
5 **Foxx**	Y	Y	N	N	Y	Y
6 **Coble**	Y	Y	N	N	Y	Y
7 McIntyre	Y	Y	Y	Y	Y	Y
8 Kissell	Y	Y	Y	Y	Y	N
9 **Myrick**	Y	Y	N	N	Y	Y
10 **McHenry**	Y	Y	N	N	Y	Y
11 Shuler	Y	Y	Y	Y	Y	N
12 Watt	Y	Y	Y	Y	Y	N
13 Miller	Y	Y	Y	Y	Y	N
NORTH DAKOTA						
AL Pomeroy	Y	Y	Y	Y	Y	N
OHIO						
1 Driehaus	Y	Y	Y	Y	Y	N
2 **Schmidt**	Y	Y	N	N	Y	Y
3 **Turner**	Y	Y	N	N	Y	Y
4 **Jordan**	Y	Y	N	N	Y	Y
5 **Latta**	Y	Y	N	N	Y	Y
6 Wilson	Y	Y	Y	Y	Y	N
7 **Austria**	Y	Y	N	N	Y	Y
8 **Boehner**	Y	Y	N	N	?	Y
9 Kaptur	Y	Y	Y	Y	Y	N
10 Kucinich	Y	Y	Y	Y	Y	N
11 Fudge	Y	Y	Y	Y	Y	N
12 **Tiberi**	Y	Y	N	N	Y	Y
13 Sutton	Y	Y	Y	Y	Y	N
14 **LaTourette**	Y	Y	N	N	Y	Y
15 Kilroy	Y	Y	Y	Y	Y	N
16 Boccieri	Y	Y	Y	Y	Y	N
17 Ryan	Y	Y	?	Y	Y	?
18 Space	Y	Y	Y	Y	Y	Y
OKLAHOMA						
1 **Sullivan**	Y	Y	N	N	Y	Y
2 Boren	Y	Y	Y	Y	Y	Y
3 **Lucas**	Y	Y	N	N	Y	Y
4 **Cole**	Y	Y	N	N	Y	Y
5 **Fallin**	Y	Y	N	N	Y	Y
OREGON						
1 Wu	Y	Y	Y	Y	Y	N
2 **Walden**	Y	Y	N	N	Y	Y
3 Blumenauer	Y	Y	Y	Y	Y	N
4 DeFazio	Y	Y	Y	Y	Y	N
5 Schrader	?	Y	Y	Y	Y	N
PENNSYLVANIA						
1 Brady	Y	Y	Y	Y	Y	N
2 Fattah	Y	Y	Y	Y	Y	N
3 Dahlkemper	Y	Y	Y	Y	Y	N
4 Altmire	Y	Y	Y	Y	Y	Y
5 **Thompson**	Y	Y	N	N	Y	Y
6 **Gerlach**	Y	Y	N	N	Y	Y
7 Sestak	Y	Y	Y	Y	Y	N
8 Murphy, P.	Y	Y	Y	Y	Y	N
9 **Shuster**	+	+	N	N	Y	Y
10 Carney	?	?	?	?	?	?
11 Kanjorski	Y	Y	Y	Y	Y	N
12 Murtha	Y	Y	Y	Y	Y	N
13 Schwartz	Y	Y	Y	Y	Y	N
14 Doyle	Y	Y	Y	Y	Y	N
15 **Dent**	Y	Y	N	N	Y	Y
16 **Pitts**	Y	Y	N	N	Y	Y
17 Holden	Y	Y	Y	Y	Y	Y
18 **Murphy, T.**	Y	Y	N	N	Y	Y
19 **Platts**	Y	Y	?	?	?	Y
RHODE ISLAND						
1 Kennedy	Y	Y	Y	Y	Y	N
2 Langevin	Y	Y	Y	Y	Y	N
SOUTH CAROLINA						
1 **Brown**	Y	Y	N	N	Y	Y
2 **Wilson**	Y	Y	N	N	Y	Y
3 **Barrett**	Y	Y	N	N	Y	Y
4 **Inglis**	N	Y	N	N	Y	Y
5 Spratt	Y	Y	Y	Y	Y	N
6 Clyburn	Y	Y	Y	Y	Y	N
SOUTH DAKOTA						
AL Herseth Sandlin	Y	Y	Y	Y	Y	Y
TENNESSEE						
1 **Roe**	Y	Y	N	N	Y	Y
2 **Duncan**	Y	Y	N	N	Y	Y
3 **Wamp**	Y	Y	N	N	Y	Y
4 Davis	Y	Y	Y	Y	Y	N
5 Cooper	Y	Y	Y	Y	Y	N
6 Gordon	Y	Y	Y	Y	?	N
7 **Blackburn**	N	Y	N	N	Y	Y
8 Tanner	Y	Y	Y	Y	Y	N
9 Cohen	Y	Y	Y	Y	Y	N

	778	779	780	781	782	783
TEXAS						
1 **Gohmert**	Y	Y	N	N	Y	Y
2 **Poe**	Y	Y	N	N	Y	Y
3 **Johnson, S.**	Y	Y	N	N	Y	Y
4 **Hall**	?	?	?	?	?	?
5 **Hensarling**	Y	Y	N	N	Y	Y
6 **Barton**	Y	Y	N	N	Y	Y
7 **Culberson**	Y	Y	N	N	Y	Y
8 **Brady**	Y	Y	N	N	Y	Y
9 Green, A.	Y	Y	Y	Y	Y	N
10 **McCaul**	Y	Y	N	N	Y	Y
11 **Conaway**	Y	Y	N	N	Y	Y
12 **Granger**	Y	Y	N	N	Y	Y
13 **Thornberry**	Y	Y	N	N	Y	Y
14 **Paul**	N	Y	N	N	Y	N
15 Hinojosa	Y	Y	Y	Y	Y	N
16 Reyes	Y	Y	Y	Y	Y	N
17 Edwards	Y	Y	Y	Y	Y	N
18 Jackson Lee	Y	Y	Y	Y	Y	N
19 **Neugebauer**	Y	Y	N	N	Y	Y
20 Gonzalez	Y	Y	Y	Y	Y	N
21 **Smith**	Y	Y	N	N	Y	Y
22 **Olson**	Y	Y	N	N	Y	Y
23 Rodriguez	Y	Y	Y	Y	Y	N
24 **Marchant**	Y	Y	N	N	Y	Y
25 Doggett	Y	Y	Y	Y	Y	N
26 **Burgess**	Y	Y	N	N	Y	Y
27 Ortiz	Y	Y	Y	Y	Y	N
28 Cuellar	Y	Y	Y	Y	Y	N
29 Green, G.	Y	Y	Y	Y	Y	N
30 Johnson, E.	?	Y	Y	Y	Y	N
31 **Carter**	Y	Y	N	N	Y	?
32 **Sessions**	Y	Y	N	N	Y	Y
UTAH						
1 **Bishop**	N	Y	N	N	Y	Y
2 Matheson	Y	Y	Y	Y	Y	N
3 **Chaffetz**	Y	Y	N	N	Y	Y
VERMONT						
AL Welch	Y	Y	Y	Y	Y	N
VIRGINIA						
1 **Wittman**	Y	Y	N	N	Y	Y
2 Nye	Y	Y	N	N	Y	N
3 Scott	Y	Y	Y	Y	Y	N
4 **Forbes**	Y	Y	N	N	Y	Y
5 Perriello	Y	Y	Y	Y	Y	N
6 **Goodlatte**	Y	Y	N	N	Y	Y
7 **Cantor**	Y	Y	N	N	Y	Y
8 Moran	Y	Y	Y	Y	Y	N
9 Boucher	Y	Y	Y	Y	Y	N
10 **Wolf**	Y	Y	N	N	Y	Y
11 Connolly	Y	Y	Y	Y	Y	N
WASHINGTON						
1 Inslee	Y	Y	Y	Y	Y	N
2 Larsen	Y	Y	Y	Y	Y	N
3 Baird	Y	Y	N	N	Y	N
4 **Hastings**	Y	Y	N	N	Y	Y
5 **McMorris Rodgers**	Y	Y	Y	–	Y	Y
6 Dicks	Y	Y	Y	Y	Y	N
7 McDermott	Y	Y	Y	Y	Y	N
8 **Reichert**	Y	Y	N	N	Y	Y
9 Smith	Y	Y	Y	Y	Y	N
WEST VIRGINIA						
1 Mollohan	?	?	?	?	?	?
2 **Capito**	Y	Y	N	N	Y	Y
3 Rahall	Y	Y	Y	Y	Y	N
WISCONSIN						
1 **Ryan**	Y	Y	N	N	Y	Y
2 Baldwin	Y	Y	Y	Y	Y	N
3 Kind	Y	Y	Y	Y	Y	N
4 Moore	Y	Y	Y	Y	Y	N
5 **Sensenbrenner**	N	Y	N	N	Y	Y
6 **Petri**	Y	Y	N	N	Y	Y
7 Obey	Y	Y	Y	Y	Y	N
8 Kagen	Y	Y	Y	Y	Y	N
WYOMING						
AL **Lummis**	Y	Y	N	N	Y	Y
DELEGATES						
Faleomavaega (A.S.)						
Norton (D.C.)						
Bordallo (Guam)						
Sablan (N. Marianas)						
Pierluisi (P.R.)						
Christensen (V.I.)						

IN THE HOUSE | By Vote Number

784. HR 2892. Fiscal 2010 Homeland Security Appropriations/ **Conference Report.** Adoption of the conference report on the bill that would provide $44.1 billion in fiscal 2010, including $42.8 billion in discretionary funds, for the Homeland Security Department and related activities. The total includes $10.1 billion for Customs and Border Protection; $7.7 billion for the Transportation Security Administration, including fees; $10.1 billion for the Coast Guard; $1.5 billion for the Secret Service; and $7.1 billion for the Federal Emergency Management Agency. It would prohibit the transfer of detainees held at Guantánamo Bay, Cuba, to the United States except for prosecution. It also would extend the authorization of the E-Verify program for three years. Adopted (thus sent to the Senate) 307-114: R 63-108; D 244-6. A "yea" was a vote in support of the president's position. Oct. 15, 2009.

785. HR 2423. George Kazen Courthouse/Passage. Hirono, D-Hawaii, motion to suspend the rules and pass the bill that would designate the federal building and U.S. courthouse in Laredo, Texas, as the "George P. Kazen Federal Building and United States Courthouse." Motion agreed to 421-0: R 171-0; D 250-0. A two-thirds majority of those present and voting (281 in this case) is required for passage under suspension of the rules. Oct. 15, 2009.

786. HR 2442. Bay Area Water Recycling Program Expansion/ **Previous Question.** Matsui, D-Calif., motion to order the previous question (thus ending debate and possibility of amendment) on adoption of the rule (H Res 830) that would provide for House floor consideration of the bill that would authorize $32.2 million in federal assistance for six water recycling programs in the San Francisco Bay area and add to amounts authorized under current law for two other projects. Motion agreed to 237-178: R 0-171; D 237-7. Oct. 15, 2009.

787. HR 2442. Bay Area Water Recycling Program Expansion/Rule. Adoption of the rule (H Res 830) that would provide for House floor consideration of the bill that would authorize $32.2 million in federal assistance for six water recycling programs in the San Francisco Bay Area and add to amounts authorized under current law for two other projects. Adopted 221-193: R 0-170; D 221-23. Oct. 15, 2009.

788. HR 2442. Bay Area Water Recycling Program Expansion/ **Motion to Table.** Miller, D-Calif., motion to table (kill) the Nunes, R-Calif., appeal of the ruling of the chair with respect to the Miller point of order that the Nunes motion to recommit the bill was not germane to the bill. The motion would recommit the bill to the Natural Resources Committee with instructions that it be immediately reported back with an amendment that would prohibit the Interior secretary from restricting, reducing or reallocating water stored in California Central Valley Project reservoirs to meet requirements under the Endangered Species Act, unless water can be purchased or leased. Motion agreed to 237-176: R 0-168; D 237-8. Oct. 15, 2009.

789. HR 2442. Bay Area Water Recycling Program Expansion/ **Passage.** Passage of the bill that would authorize $32.2 million in federal assistance for six water recycling programs in the San Francisco Bay Area. It also would add $5.9 million to amounts authorized under current law for two other projects and limit the federal share of the total project costs for the six projects to 25 percent. Passed 241-173: R 6-163; D 235-10. Oct. 15, 2009.

	784	785	786	787	788	789
ALABAMA						
1 Bonner	Y	Y	N	N	N	N
2 Bright	Y	Y	Y	N	Y	N
3 Rogers	Y	Y	N	N	N	N
4 Aderholt	Y	Y	N	N	N	N
5 Griffith	Y	Y	Y	N	N	Y
6 Bachus	N	Y	N	N	N	N
7 Davis	Y	Y	Y	Y	Y	Y
ALASKA						
AL Young	Y	Y	N	N	N	N
ARIZONA						
1 Kirkpatrick	Y	Y	Y	Y	Y	Y
2 Franks	N	Y	N	N	N	N
3 Shadegg	N	Y	N	N	N	N
4 Pastor	Y	Y	Y	Y	Y	Y
5 Mitchell	Y	Y	Y	Y	Y	Y
6 Flake	N	Y	N	N	N	N
7 Grijalva	Y	Y	Y	Y	Y	Y
8 Giffords	Y	Y	Y	Y	Y	Y
ARKANSAS						
1 Berry	Y	Y	Y	Y	Y	Y
2 Snyder	Y	Y	Y	Y	Y	Y
3 Boozman	N	Y	N	N	N	N
4 Ross	Y	Y	Y	N	Y	Y
CALIFORNIA						
1 Thompson	Y	Y	Y	Y	Y	Y
2 Herger	N	Y	N	?	N	N
3 Lungren	N	Y	N	N	N	N
4 McClintock	N	Y	N	N	N	N
5 Matsui	Y	Y	Y	Y	Y	Y
6 Woolsey	Y	Y	Y	Y	Y	Y
7 Miller, George	Y	Y	Y	Y	Y	Y
8 Pelosi						
9 Lee	Y	Y	Y	Y	Y	Y
10 Vacant						
11 McNerney	Y	Y	Y	Y	Y	Y
12 Speier	Y	Y	Y	Y	Y	Y
13 Stark	N	Y	Y	Y	Y	Y
14 Eshoo	Y	Y	Y	Y	Y	Y
15 Honda	Y	Y	Y	Y	Y	Y
16 Lofgren	Y	Y	Y	Y	?	?
17 Farr	Y	Y	Y	Y	Y	Y
18 Cardoza	Y	Y	Y	N	N	N
19 Radanovich	?	?	?	?	?	?
20 Costa	Y	Y	N	N	N	N
21 Nunes	N	Y	N	N	N	N
22 McCarthy	N	Y	N	N	N	N
23 Capps	Y	Y	Y	Y	Y	Y
24 Gallegly	Y	Y	N	N	N	N
25 McKeon	Y	Y	N	N	N	N
26 Dreier	N	Y	N	N	N	N
27 Sherman	Y	Y	Y	Y	Y	Y
28 Berman	Y	Y	Y	Y	Y	Y
29 Schiff	Y	Y	Y	Y	Y	Y
30 Waxman	Y	Y	Y	Y	Y	Y
31 Becerra	Y	Y	Y	Y	Y	Y
32 Chu	Y	Y	Y	Y	Y	Y
33 Watson	Y	Y	Y	Y	Y	Y
34 Roybal-Allard	Y	Y	Y	Y	Y	Y
35 Waters	Y	Y	?	?	Y	Y
36 Harman	Y	Y	Y	Y	Y	Y
37 Richardson	Y	Y	Y	Y	Y	Y
38 Napolitano	Y	Y	Y	Y	Y	Y
39 Sánchez, Linda	Y	Y	Y	Y	Y	
40 Royce	N	Y	N	N	N	N
41 Lewis	N	Y	N	N	N	N
42 Miller, Gary	Y	Y	N	N	N	N
43 Baca	Y	Y	Y	Y	Y	Y
44 Calvert	N	Y	N	N	N	N
45 Bono Mack	N	Y	N	N	N	N
46 Rohrabacher	Y	Y	N	N	N	N
47 Sanchez, Loretta	Y	Y	Y	Y	Y	Y
48 Campbell	N	Y	N	N	N	N
49 Issa	N	Y	N	N	N	N
50 Bilbray	Y	Y	N	N	N	N
51 Filner	Y	Y	Y	Y	Y	Y
52 Hunter	N	Y	N	N	N	N
53 Davis	Y	Y	Y	Y	Y	Y

	784	785	786	787	788	789
COLORADO						
1 DeGette	Y	Y	Y	Y	Y	Y
2 Polis	N	Y	Y	Y	Y	Y
3 Salazar	Y	Y	Y	Y	Y	Y
4 Markey	Y	Y	Y	Y	Y	Y
5 Lamborn	N	Y	N	N	N	N
6 Coffman	N	Y	N	N	N	N
7 Perlmutter	Y	Y	Y	Y	Y	Y
CONNECTICUT						
1 Larson	Y	Y	Y	Y	Y	Y
2 Courtney	Y	Y	Y	Y	Y	Y
3 DeLauro	Y	Y	Y	Y	Y	Y
4 Himes	Y	Y	Y	Y	Y	Y
5 Murphy	Y	Y	Y	Y	Y	Y
DELAWARE						
AL Castle	N	Y	N	N	N	N
FLORIDA						
1 Miller	N	?	N	N	N	N
2 Boyd	+	+	?	?	?	+
3 Brown	Y	Y	Y	Y	Y	Y
4 Crenshaw	N	Y	N	N	N	N
5 Brown-Waite	Y	Y	N	N	N	N
6 Stearns	N	Y	N	N	N	N
7 Mica	N	Y	N	N	N	N
8 Grayson	Y	Y	Y	Y	Y	Y
9 Bilirakis	Y	Y	N	N	N	N
10 Young	Y	Y	N	N	N	N
11 Castor	Y	Y	Y	Y	Y	Y
12 Putnam	N	Y	N	N	N	N
13 Buchanan	Y	Y	N	N	N	N
14 Mack	Y	Y	N	N	N	N
15 Posey	N	Y	N	N	N	N
16 Rooney	N	Y	N	N	N	N
17 Meek	Y	Y	Y	Y	Y	Y
18 Ros-Lehtinen	Y	Y	N	N	N	N
19 Wexler	Y	Y	Y	Y	Y	Y
20 Wasserman Schultz	Y	Y	?	?	Y	Y
21 Diaz-Balart, L.	Y	Y	N	N	N	N
22 Klein	Y	Y	Y	Y	Y	Y
23 Hastings	Y	Y	Y	Y	Y	Y
24 Kosmas	Y	Y	Y	Y	Y	Y
25 Diaz-Balart, M.	Y	Y	N	N	N	N
GEORGIA						
1 Kingston	N	Y	N	N	N	N
2 Bishop	Y	Y	Y	Y	Y	Y
3 Westmoreland	N	Y	N	N	N	N
4 Johnson	Y	Y	?	?	Y	Y
5 Lewis	Y	Y	Y	Y	Y	Y
6 Price	N	Y	N	N	N	N
7 Linder	N	Y	N	N	?	?
8 Marshall	Y	Y	Y	Y	Y	Y
9 Deal	N	Y	?	?	?	?
10 Broun	N	Y	N	N	N	N
11 Gingrey	N	Y	N	N	N	N
12 Barrow	Y	Y	Y	N	Y	Y
13 Scott	Y	Y	Y	Y	Y	Y
HAWAII						
1 Abercrombie	Y	Y	Y	Y	Y	Y
2 Hirono	Y	Y	Y	Y	Y	Y
IDAHO						
1 Minnick	Y	Y	N	N	N	N
2 Simpson	N	Y	N	N	N	N
ILLINOIS						
1 Rush	Y	Y	Y	Y	Y	Y
2 Jackson	Y	Y	Y	Y	Y	Y
3 Lipinski	Y	Y	Y	Y	Y	Y
4 Gutierrez	N	Y	Y	Y	Y	Y
5 Quigley	Y	Y	Y	Y	Y	Y
6 Roskam	N	Y	N	N	N	N
7 Davis	Y	Y	Y	Y	Y	Y
8 Bean	Y	Y	Y	Y	Y	Y
9 Schakowsky	Y	Y	Y	Y	Y	Y
10 Kirk	Y	Y	N	N	N	N
11 Halvorson	Y	Y	Y	Y	Y	Y
12 Costello	N	Y	Y	Y	Y	Y
13 Biggert	Y	Y	N	N	N	N
14 Foster	Y	Y	Y	Y	Y	Y
15 Johnson	N	Y	N	N	N	Y

KEY	**Republicans**	Democrats		
Y Voted for (yea)		X Paired against		C Voted "present" to avoid possible conflict of interest
# Paired for		– Announced against		
+ Announced for		P Voted "present"		? Did not vote or otherwise make a position known
N Voted against (nay)				

	784	785	786	787	788	789
16 **Manzullo**	Y	Y	N	N	N	N
17 Hare	Y	Y	Y	Y	Y	Y
18 **Schock**	Y	Y	N	N	N	N
19 **Shimkus**	Y	Y	N	N	N	N
INDIANA						
1 Visclosky	Y	Y	Y	Y	Y	Y
2 Donnelly	Y	Y	Y	Y	Y	Y
3 **Souder**	N	Y	N	N	N	N
4 **Buyer**	N	Y	N	N	N	N
5 **Burton**	N	Y	N	N	N	N
6 **Pence**	N	Y	N	N	N	N
7 Carson	Y	Y	Y	Y	Y	Y
8 Ellsworth	Y	Y	Y	N	Y	Y
9 Hill	Y	Y	N	N	Y	Y
IOWA						
1 Braley	Y	Y	Y	Y	Y	Y
2 Loebsack	Y	Y	Y	Y	Y	Y
3 Boswell	Y	Y	Y	N	?	?
4 **Latham**	Y	Y	N	N	N	N
5 **King**	N	Y	N	N	N	N
KANSAS						
1 **Moran**	N	Y	N	N	N	N
2 **Jenkins**	Y	Y	N	N	N	N
3 Moore	Y	Y	N	N	Y	Y
4 **Tiahrt**	N	Y	N	N	N	N
KENTUCKY						
1 **Whitfield**	Y	Y	N	N	N	N
2 **Guthrie**	N	Y	N	N	N	N
3 Yarmuth	Y	Y	Y	Y	Y	Y
4 **Davis**	N	Y	N	N	N	N
5 **Rogers**	Y	Y	N	N	N	N
6 Chandler	Y	Y	Y	Y	Y	Y
LOUISIANA						
1 **Scalise**	?	?	?	?	?	?
2 **Cao**	?	?	?	?	?	?
3 Melancon	?	?	?	?	?	?
4 **Fleming**	Y	Y	N	N	–	N
5 **Alexander**	Y	Y	N	N	N	N
6 **Cassidy**	Y	Y	N	N	N	N
7 **Boustany**	Y	Y	N	N	N	N
MAINE						
1 Pingree	Y	Y	Y	Y	Y	Y
2 Michaud	Y	Y	Y	Y	Y	Y
MARYLAND						
1 Kratovil	Y	Y	N	N	N	Y
2 Ruppersberger	Y	Y	Y	Y	Y	Y
3 Sarbanes	Y	Y	Y	Y	Y	Y
4 Edwards	Y	Y	Y	Y	Y	Y
5 Hoyer	Y	Y	Y	Y	Y	Y
6 **Bartlett**	N	Y	N	N	N	N
7 Cummings	Y	Y	Y	Y	Y	Y
8 Van Hollen	Y	Y	Y	Y	Y	Y
MASSACHUSETTS						
1 Olver	Y	Y	Y	?	Y	Y
2 Neal	Y	Y	Y	Y	Y	Y
3 McGovern	Y	Y	Y	Y	Y	Y
4 Frank	Y	Y	Y	Y	Y	Y
5 Tsongas	Y	Y	Y	Y	Y	Y
6 Tierney	Y	Y	Y	Y	Y	Y
7 Markey	Y	Y	Y	Y	Y	Y
8 Capuano	Y	Y	Y	Y	Y	Y
9 Lynch	Y	Y	Y	Y	Y	Y
10 Delahunt	N	Y	Y	Y	Y	Y
MICHIGAN						
1 Stupak	Y	Y	Y	Y	Y	Y
2 **Hoekstra**	N	Y	N	N	N	N
3 **Ehlers**	N	Y	N	N	N	Y
4 **Camp**	Y	Y	N	N	N	N
5 Kildee	Y	Y	Y	Y	Y	Y
6 **Upton**	Y	Y	N	N	N	N
7 Schauer	Y	Y	Y	Y	Y	Y
8 **Rogers**	Y	Y	N	N	N	N
9 Peters	Y	Y	Y	Y	Y	Y
10 **Miller**	Y	Y	N	N	N	N
11 **McCotter**	Y	Y	N	N	N	N
12 Levin	Y	Y	Y	Y	Y	Y
13 Kilpatrick	Y	Y	Y	Y	Y	Y
14 Conyers	Y	Y	Y	Y	–	+
15 Dingell	Y	Y	Y	Y	Y	Y
MINNESOTA						
1 Walz	Y	Y	Y	Y	Y	Y
2 **Kline**	N	Y	N	N	N	N
3 **Paulsen**	N	Y	N	N	N	N
4 McCollum	?	?	?	?	?	?

	784	785	786	787	788	789
5 Ellison	Y	Y	Y	Y	Y	Y
6 **Bachmann**	N	Y	N	N	N	N
7 Peterson	Y	Y	Y	N	Y	N
8 Oberstar	Y	Y	Y	Y	Y	Y
MISSISSIPPI						
1 Childers	Y	Y	N	N	N	N
2 Thompson	Y	Y	Y	Y	Y	Y
3 **Harper**	Y	Y	N	N	N	?
4 Taylor	Y	Y	Y	N	Y	Y
MISSOURI						
1 Clay	Y	Y	Y	Y	Y	Y
2 **Akin**	N	Y	N	N	N	N
3 Carnahan	Y	Y	Y	Y	Y	Y
4 Skelton	Y	Y	Y	Y	Y	N
5 Cleaver	Y	Y	?	?	Y	Y
6 **Graves**	N	Y	N	N	N	N
7 **Blunt**	?	Y	N	N	N	N
8 **Emerson**	?	?	?	?	?	?
9 **Luetkemeyer**	Y	Y	N	N	N	N
MONTANA						
AL **Rehberg**	N	Y	N	N	N	N
NEBRASKA						
1 **Fortenberry**	Y	Y	N	N	N	N
2 **Terry**	Y	Y	N	N	N	N
3 **Smith**	Y	Y	N	N	N	N
NEVADA						
1 Berkley	Y	Y	Y	Y	Y	Y
2 **Heller**	Y	Y	N	N	N	N
3 Titus	Y	Y	Y	Y	Y	Y
NEW HAMPSHIRE						
1 Shea-Porter	Y	Y	Y	Y	Y	Y
2 Hodes	Y	Y	Y	Y	Y	Y
NEW JERSEY						
1 Andrews	Y	Y	Y	Y	Y	Y
2 **LoBiondo**	Y	Y	N	N	N	N
3 Adler	Y	Y	Y	Y	Y	Y
4 **Smith**	Y	Y	N	N	N	Y
5 **Garrett**	Y	Y	N	N	N	N
6 Pallone	Y	Y	Y	Y	Y	Y
7 **Lance**	Y	Y	N	N	N	N
8 Pascrell	Y	Y	Y	Y	Y	Y
9 Rothman	Y	Y	Y	Y	Y	Y
10 Payne	Y	Y	Y	Y	Y	Y
11 **Frelinghuysen**	Y	Y	N	N	N	N
12 Holt	Y	Y	Y	Y	Y	Y
13 Sires	Y	Y	Y	Y	Y	Y
NEW MEXICO						
1 Heinrich	Y	Y	Y	Y	Y	Y
2 Teague	Y	Y	Y	Y	Y	Y
3 Lujan	Y	Y	Y	Y	Y	Y
NEW YORK						
1 Bishop	Y	Y	Y	Y	Y	Y
2 Israel	Y	Y	Y	Y	Y	Y
3 **King**	Y	Y	N	N	N	N
4 McCarthy	Y	Y	Y	Y	Y	Y
5 Ackerman	Y	Y	Y	Y	Y	Y
6 Meeks	Y	Y	Y	Y	Y	Y
7 Crowley	Y	Y	Y	Y	Y	Y
8 Nadler	Y	Y	Y	Y	Y	Y
9 Weiner	Y	Y	Y	Y	Y	Y
10 Towns	Y	Y	Y	Y	Y	Y
11 Clarke	Y	Y	Y	Y	Y	Y
12 Velázquez	N	Y	Y	Y	Y	Y
13 McMahon	Y	Y	Y	Y	Y	Y
14 Maloney	Y	Y	Y	Y	Y	Y
15 Rangel	Y	Y	Y	Y	Y	Y
16 Serrano	Y	Y	Y	Y	Y	Y
17 Engel	Y	Y	Y	Y	Y	Y
18 Lowey	Y	Y	Y	Y	Y	Y
19 Hall	Y	Y	Y	Y	Y	Y
20 Murphy	Y	Y	Y	N	Y	Y
21 Tonko	Y	Y	Y	Y	Y	Y
22 Hinchey	Y	Y	Y	Y	Y	Y
23 Vacant						
24 Arcuri	Y	Y	Y	Y	Y	N
25 Maffei	Y	Y	Y	Y	Y	Y
26 **Lee**	Y	Y	N	N	N	N
27 Higgins	Y	Y	Y	Y	Y	Y
28 Slaughter	Y	Y	Y	Y	Y	Y
29 Massa	Y	Y	Y	Y	Y	Y
NORTH CAROLINA						
1 Butterfield	Y	Y	Y	Y	Y	Y
2 Etheridge	Y	Y	Y	Y	Y	Y
3 **Jones**	N	Y	N	N	N	N
4 Price	Y	Y	Y	Y	Y	Y

	784	785	786	787	788	789
5 **Foxx**	N	Y	N	N	–	N
6 **Coble**	N	Y	N	N	N	N
7 McIntyre	Y	Y	Y	Y	Y	Y
8 Kissell	Y	Y	Y	Y	Y	Y
9 **Myrick**	N	Y	N	N	N	N
10 **McHenry**	N	Y	N	N	N	N
11 Shuler	Y	Y	Y	N	Y	Y
12 Watt	Y	Y	Y	Y	Y	Y
13 Miller	Y	Y	Y	Y	Y	Y
NORTH DAKOTA						
AL Pomeroy	Y	Y	Y	Y	Y	Y
OHIO						
1 Driehaus	Y	Y	Y	Y	Y	Y
2 **Schmidt**	N	Y	N	N	N	N
3 **Turner**	N	Y	N	N	N	N
4 **Jordan**	N	Y	N	N	N	N
5 **Latta**	N	Y	N	N	N	N
6 Wilson	Y	Y	Y	Y	Y	Y
7 **Austria**	Y	Y	N	N	N	N
8 **Boehner**	N	Y	N	N	N	N
9 Kaptur	Y	Y	Y	Y	Y	Y
10 Kucinich	Y	Y	Y	Y	Y	Y
11 Fudge	Y	Y	Y	Y	Y	Y
12 **Tiberi**	Y	Y	N	N	N	N
13 Sutton	Y	Y	Y	Y	Y	Y
14 **LaTourette**	Y	Y	N	N	N	N
15 Kilroy	Y	Y	Y	Y	Y	Y
16 Boccieri	Y	Y	Y	Y	Y	Y
17 Ryan	Y	Y	Y	Y	Y	Y
18 Space	Y	Y	Y	Y	Y	Y
OKLAHOMA						
1 **Sullivan**	N	Y	N	N	N	N
2 Boren	Y	Y	Y	N	N	N
3 **Lucas**	N	Y	N	N	N	N
4 **Cole**	N	Y	N	N	N	N
5 **Fallin**	N	Y	N	N	N	N
OREGON						
1 Wu	Y	Y	Y	Y	Y	Y
2 **Walden**	Y	Y	N	N	N	Y
3 Blumenauer	Y	Y	Y	Y	Y	Y
4 DeFazio	Y	Y	Y	Y	?	?
5 Schrader	Y	Y	Y	Y	Y	Y
PENNSYLVANIA						
1 Brady	Y	Y	Y	Y	Y	Y
2 Fattah	Y	Y	Y	Y	Y	Y
3 Dahlkemper	Y	Y	Y	Y	Y	Y
4 Altmire	Y	Y	Y	N	N	Y
5 **Thompson**	N	Y	N	N	N	N
6 **Gerlach**	Y	Y	N	N	N	N
7 Sestak	Y	Y	Y	Y	Y	Y
8 Murphy, P.	Y	Y	Y	Y	Y	Y
9 **Shuster**	N	Y	N	N	N	N
10 Carney	?	?	?	?	?	?
11 Kanjorski	Y	Y	Y	Y	Y	Y
12 Murtha	Y	Y	Y	Y	Y	Y
13 Schwartz	Y	Y	Y	Y	Y	Y
14 Doyle	Y	Y	Y	Y	Y	Y
15 **Dent**	Y	Y	N	N	N	N
16 **Pitts**	Y	Y	N	N	N	N
17 Holden	Y	Y	Y	Y	Y	Y
18 **Murphy, T.**	N	Y	N	N	N	N
19 **Platts**	Y	Y	N	N	N	N
RHODE ISLAND						
1 Kennedy	Y	Y	Y	Y	Y	Y
2 Langevin	Y	Y	Y	Y	Y	Y
SOUTH CAROLINA						
1 **Brown**	N	Y	N	N	N	N
2 **Wilson**	N	Y	N	N	N	N
3 **Barrett**	N	Y	N	N	N	N
4 **Inglis**	N	Y	N	N	N	N
5 Spratt	Y	Y	Y	Y	Y	Y
6 Clyburn	Y	Y	Y	Y	Y	Y
SOUTH DAKOTA						
AL Herseth Sandlin	Y	Y	Y	N	Y	Y
TENNESSEE						
1 **Roe**	N	Y	N	N	N	N
2 **Duncan**	N	Y	N	N	N	N
3 **Wamp**	N	Y	N	N	N	N
4 Davis	Y	Y	Y	N	Y	Y
5 Cooper	Y	Y	Y	Y	Y	Y
6 Gordon	Y	Y	Y	Y	Y	Y
7 **Blackburn**	N	Y	N	N	N	N
8 Tanner	Y	Y	Y	N	Y	N
9 Cohen	Y	Y	Y	Y	Y	Y

	784	785	786	787	788	789
TEXAS						
1 **Gohmert**	N	Y	N	N	N	N
2 **Poe**	N	Y	N	N	N	N
3 **Johnson, S.**	N	Y	N	N	N	N
4 **Hall**	?	?	?	?	?	?
5 **Hensarling**	N	Y	N	N	N	N
6 **Barton**	N	Y	N	N	N	N
7 **Culberson**	N	Y	N	N	N	N
8 **Brady**	N	Y	N	N	N	N
9 Green, A.	Y	Y	Y	Y	Y	Y
10 **McCaul**	Y	Y	N	N	N	N
11 **Conaway**	N	Y	N	N	N	N
12 **Granger**	N	Y	N	N	N	N
13 **Thornberry**	N	Y	N	N	N	N
14 **Paul**	N	Y	N	N	N	N
15 Hinojosa	Y	Y	Y	Y	Y	Y
16 Reyes	Y	Y	Y	Y	Y	Y
17 Edwards	Y	Y	Y	Y	Y	Y
18 Jackson Lee	Y	Y	Y	Y	Y	Y
19 **Neugebauer**	N	Y	N	N	N	N
20 Gonzalez	Y	Y	Y	Y	Y	Y
21 **Smith**	Y	Y	N	N	N	N
22 **Olson**	N	Y	N	N	N	N
23 Rodriguez	Y	Y	Y	Y	Y	Y
24 **Marchant**	N	Y	N	N	N	N
25 Doggett	Y	Y	Y	Y	Y	Y
26 **Burgess**	N	Y	N	N	N	N
27 Ortiz	Y	Y	Y	Y	Y	Y
28 Cuellar	Y	Y	Y	Y	Y	Y
29 Green, G.	Y	Y	Y	Y	Y	Y
30 Johnson, E.	Y	Y	Y	Y	Y	Y
31 **Carter**	N	Y	N	N	N	N
32 **Sessions**	N	Y	N	N	N	N
UTAH						
1 **Bishop**	N	Y	N	N	N	N
2 Matheson	Y	Y	Y	Y	Y	Y
3 **Chaffetz**	N	Y	N	N	N	Y
VERMONT						
AL Welch	Y	Y	Y	Y	Y	Y
VIRGINIA						
1 **Wittman**	Y	Y	N	N	N	Y
2 Nye	Y	Y	Y	Y	Y	Y
3 Scott	Y	Y	Y	Y	Y	Y
4 **Forbes**	Y	Y	N	N	N	N
5 Perriello	Y	Y	Y	Y	Y	Y
6 **Goodlatte**	N	Y	N	N	N	N
7 **Cantor**	N	Y	N	N	N	N
8 Moran	Y	Y	Y	Y	Y	Y
9 Boucher	Y	Y	Y	Y	Y	Y
10 **Wolf**	Y	Y	N	N	N	N
11 Connolly	Y	Y	Y	Y	Y	Y
WASHINGTON						
1 Inslee	Y	Y	Y	Y	Y	Y
2 Larsen	Y	Y	Y	Y	Y	Y
3 Baird	Y	Y	N	Y	Y	Y
4 **Hastings**	Y	Y	N	N	N	N
5 **McMorris Rodgers**	Y	Y	N	N	N	N
6 Dicks	Y	Y	Y	Y	Y	Y
7 McDermott	Y	Y	Y	Y	Y	Y
8 **Reichert**	Y	Y	N	N	N	N
9 Smith	Y	Y	?	?	?	?
WEST VIRGINIA						
1 Mollohan	?	?	?	?	?	?
2 **Capito**	Y	Y	N	N	N	N
3 Rahall	Y	Y	Y	Y	Y	Y
WISCONSIN						
1 **Ryan**	N	Y	N	N	N	N
2 Baldwin	Y	Y	Y	Y	Y	Y
3 Kind	Y	Y	?	Y	Y	Y
4 Moore	Y	Y	Y	Y	Y	Y
5 **Sensenbrenner**	N	Y	N	N	N	N
6 **Petri**	N	Y	N	N	N	N
7 Obey	Y	Y	Y	Y	Y	Y
8 Kagen	Y	Y	Y	Y	Y	Y
WYOMING						
AL **Lummis**	N	Y	N	N	N	N
DELEGATES						
Faleomavaega (A.S.)						
Norton (D.C.)						
Bordallo (Guam)						
Sablan (N. Marianas)						
Pierluisi (P.R.)						
Christensen (V.I.)						

IN THE HOUSE | By Vote Number

790. HR 3763. Small Business Identity Theft Exemptions/Passage.
Adler, D-N.J., motion to suspend the rules and pass the bill that would exempt health care, accounting and legal practices with 20 or fewer employees and other small businesses from the Federal Trade Commission's identity theft regulations. Motion agreed to 400-0: D 234-0; R 166-0. A two-thirds majority of those present and voting (267 in this case) is required for passage under suspension of the rules. Oct. 20, 2009.

791. HR 3319. Jeremiah Paul McCleery Post Office/Passage. Lynch, D-Mass., motion to suspend the rules and pass the bill that would designate a post office in Portola, Calif., as the "Army Spc. Jeremiah Paul McCleery Post Office." Motion agreed to 401-0: D 236-0; R 165-0. A two-thirds majority of those present and voting (268 in this case) is required for passage under suspension of the rules. Oct. 20, 2009.

792. H Res 558. National Computer Science Week/Adoption.
Gordon, D-Tenn., motion to suspend the rules and adopt the resolution that would express House support for National Computer Science Week and encourage computer science education. Motion agreed to 405-0: D 239-0; R 166-0. A two-thirds majority of those present and voting (270 in this case) is required for adoption under suspension of the rules. Oct. 20, 2009.

793. S 1793. Ryan White HIV/AIDS Reauthorization/Passage.
Pallone, D-N.J., motion to suspend the rules and pass the bill that would reauthorize the Ryan White HIV/AIDS federal assistance program through fiscal 2013. The bill would authorize $2.35 billion in fiscal 2010 and increase the funding level each year, reaching $2.7 billion in fiscal 2013. It would remove a sunset provision in current law. Motion agreed to (thus clearing the measure for the president) 408-9: D 246-0; R 162-9. A two-thirds majority of those present and voting (278 in this case) is required for passage under suspension of the rules. A "yea" was a vote in support of the president's position. Oct. 21, 2009.

794. H Res 811. National Principals Month/Adoption. Davis, D-Calif., motion to suspend the rules and adopt the resolution that would support the designation of October 2009 as National Principals Month. Motion agreed to 411-0: D 242-0; R 169-0. A two-thirds majority of those present and voting (274 in this case) is required for adoption under suspension of the rules. Oct. 21, 2009.

795. H Res 837. Tribute to Kentucky Wesleyan College/Adoption.
Davis, D-Calif., motion to suspend the rules and adopt the resolution that would recognize Kentucky Wesleyan College for more than 150 years of service. Motion agreed to 415-0: D 244-0; R 171-0. A two-thirds majority of those present and voting (277 in this case) is required for adoption under suspension of the rules. Oct. 21, 2009.

	790	791	792	793	794	795
ALABAMA						
1 Bonner	Y	Y	Y	Y	Y	Y
2 Bright	Y	Y	Y	Y	Y	Y
3 Rogers	Y	Y	Y	Y	?	Y
4 Aderholt	Y	Y	Y	Y	Y	Y
5 Griffith	Y	Y	Y	Y	Y	Y
6 Bachus	Y	Y	Y	Y	Y	Y
7 Davis	Y	Y	Y	Y	Y	Y
ALASKA						
AL Young	?	?	?	?	?	?
ARIZONA						
1 Kirkpatrick	Y	Y	Y	Y	Y	Y
2 Franks	Y	Y	Y	Y	Y	Y
3 Shadegg	?	?	?	?	?	?
4 Pastor	Y	Y	Y	Y	Y	Y
5 Mitchell	Y	Y	Y	Y	Y	Y
6 Flake	Y	Y	Y	N	Y	Y
7 Grijalva	?	Y	Y	Y	Y	Y
8 Giffords	Y	Y	Y	Y	Y	Y
ARKANSAS						
1 Berry	Y	Y	Y	Y	Y	Y
2 Snyder	Y	Y	Y	Y	Y	Y
3 Boozman	Y	Y	Y	Y	Y	Y
4 Ross	Y	Y	Y	Y	Y	Y
CALIFORNIA						
1 Thompson	Y	Y	Y	Y	Y	Y
2 Herger	Y	Y	Y	Y	Y	Y
3 Lungren	Y	Y	Y	Y	Y	Y
4 McClintock	Y	Y	Y	Y	Y	Y
5 Matsui	Y	Y	Y	Y	Y	Y
6 Woolsey	Y	Y	Y	Y	Y	Y
7 Miller, George	Y	Y	Y	Y	Y	Y
8 Pelosi						
9 Lee	Y	Y	Y	Y	Y	Y
10 Vacant						
11 McNerney	Y	Y	Y	Y	Y	Y
12 Speier	Y	Y	Y	Y	Y	Y
13 Stark	Y	Y	Y	Y	Y	Y
14 Eshoo	Y	Y	Y	Y	Y	Y
15 Honda	Y	Y	Y	Y	Y	Y
16 Lofgren	?	?	?	?	?	?
17 Farr	Y	Y	Y	Y	Y	
18 Cardoza	Y	Y	Y	Y	Y	Y
19 Radanovich	Y	Y	Y	Y	Y	Y
20 Costa	Y	Y	Y	Y	Y	Y
21 Nunes	Y	Y	Y	Y	Y	Y
22 McCarthy	Y	Y	Y	Y	Y	Y
23 Capps	Y	Y	Y	Y	Y	Y
24 Gallegly	Y	Y	Y	Y	Y	Y
25 McKeon	Y	Y	Y	Y	Y	Y
26 Dreier	Y	Y	Y	Y	Y	Y
27 Sherman	Y	Y	Y	Y	Y	Y
28 Berman	Y	Y	Y	Y	Y	Y
29 Schiff	Y	Y	Y	Y	Y	Y
30 Waxman	Y	Y	Y	Y	Y	Y
31 Becerra	Y	Y	Y	Y	+	Y
32 Chu	Y	Y	Y	Y	Y	Y
33 Watson	Y	Y	Y	Y	Y	Y
34 Roybal-Allard	Y	Y	Y	Y	Y	Y
35 Waters	Y	Y	Y	Y	Y	Y
36 Harman	Y	Y	Y	Y	Y	Y
37 Richardson	Y	Y	Y	?	?	?
38 Napolitano	Y	Y	Y	Y	Y	Y
39 Sánchez, Linda	Y	Y	Y	Y	Y	Y
40 Royce	Y	Y	Y	Y	Y	Y
41 Lewis	Y	Y	Y	Y	Y	Y
42 Miller, Gary	Y	Y	Y	Y	Y	+
43 Baca	Y	Y	Y	Y	Y	Y
44 Calvert	Y	Y	Y	Y	Y	Y
45 Bono Mack	Y	Y	Y	Y	Y	Y
46 Rohrabacher	?	?	?	Y	Y	Y
47 Sanchez, Loretta	Y	Y	Y	Y	Y	Y
48 Campbell	Y	Y	Y	Y	Y	Y
49 Issa	Y	Y	Y	Y	Y	Y
50 Bilbray	Y	Y	Y	Y	Y	Y
51 Filner	Y	Y	Y	Y	Y	Y
52 Hunter	Y	Y	Y	Y	Y	Y
53 Davis	Y	Y	Y	Y	Y	Y

	790	791	792	793	794	795
COLORADO						
1 DeGette	Y	Y	Y	Y	Y	Y
2 Polis	Y	Y	Y	Y	Y	Y
3 Salazar	Y	Y	Y	Y	Y	
4 Markey	Y	Y	Y	Y	Y	
5 Lamborn	Y	Y	Y	Y	Y	Y
6 Coffman	Y	Y	Y	Y	Y	Y
7 Perlmutter	Y	Y	Y	Y	Y	
CONNECTICUT						
1 Larson	Y	Y	Y	Y	Y	Y
2 Courtney	Y	Y	Y	Y	Y	Y
3 DeLauro	Y	Y	Y	Y	Y	Y
4 Himes	Y	Y	Y	Y	Y	Y
5 Murphy	Y	Y	Y	Y	Y	Y
DELAWARE						
AL Castle	Y	Y	Y	Y	Y	
FLORIDA						
1 Miller	Y	Y	Y	Y	Y	Y
2 Boyd	Y	Y	Y	Y	Y	Y
3 Brown	Y	Y	Y	Y	Y	Y
4 Crenshaw	?	?	?	?	?	Y
5 Brown-Waite	Y	Y	Y	Y	Y	Y
6 Stearns	Y	Y	Y	Y	Y	Y
7 Mica	Y	Y	Y	Y	Y	Y
8 Grayson	Y	Y	Y	Y	Y	Y
9 Bilirakis	Y	Y	Y	Y	Y	Y
10 Young	Y	Y	Y	Y	?	Y
11 Castor	Y	Y	Y	Y	Y	Y
12 Putnam	Y	Y	Y	Y	Y	Y
13 Buchanan	Y	Y	Y	Y	Y	Y
14 Mack	Y	Y	Y	Y	Y	Y
15 Posey	Y	Y	Y	Y	Y	Y
16 Rooney	Y	Y	Y	Y	Y	Y
17 Meek	Y	Y	Y	Y	Y	Y
18 Ros-Lehtinen	Y	Y	Y	Y	Y	Y
19 Wexler	?	?	?	Y	Y	Y
20 Wasserman Schultz	+	+	+	Y	Y	Y
21 Diaz-Balart, L.	Y	Y	Y	Y	Y	Y
22 Klein	Y	Y	Y	Y	Y	Y
23 Hastings	Y	Y	Y	Y	Y	Y
24 Kosmas	Y	Y	Y	Y	Y	Y
25 Diaz-Balart, M.	Y	?	Y	Y	Y	Y
GEORGIA						
1 Kingston	Y	Y	Y	Y	Y	Y
2 Bishop	Y	Y	Y	Y	Y	Y
3 Westmoreland	Y	Y	Y	Y	Y	Y
4 Johnson	Y	Y	Y	Y	Y	Y
5 Lewis	Y	Y	Y	Y	Y	Y
6 Price	+	+	+	+	+	+
7 Linder	Y	Y	Y	Y	Y	Y
8 Marshall	Y	Y	Y	Y	Y	Y
9 Deal	?	?	?	Y	Y	Y
10 Broun	Y	Y	Y	N	Y	Y
11 Gingrey	Y	Y	Y	Y	Y	Y
12 Barrow	Y	Y	Y	Y	Y	Y
13 Scott	Y	Y	Y	Y	Y	Y
HAWAII						
1 Abercrombie	?	Y	Y	Y	Y	Y
2 Hirono	Y	Y	Y	Y	Y	?
IDAHO						
1 Minnick	Y	Y	Y	Y	Y	Y
2 Simpson	Y	Y	Y	Y	Y	Y
ILLINOIS						
1 Rush	Y	Y	Y	Y	?	Y
2 Jackson	Y	Y	Y	Y	Y	Y
3 Lipinski	Y	Y	Y	Y	Y	Y
4 Gutierrez	+	+	+	Y	Y	Y
5 Quigley	Y	Y	Y	Y	Y	Y
6 Roskam	Y	Y	Y	Y	Y	Y
7 Davis	Y	Y	Y	Y	Y	Y
8 Bean	?	?	?	?	?	?
9 Schakowsky	Y	Y	Y	Y	Y	Y
10 Kirk	Y	Y	Y	?	Y	Y
11 Halvorson	Y	Y	Y	Y	Y	Y
12 Costello	Y	Y	Y	Y	Y	Y
13 Biggert	Y	Y	Y	Y	Y	Y
14 Foster	Y	Y	Y	Y	Y	Y
15 Johnson	Y	Y	Y	Y	Y	Y

KEY   **Republicans**   Democrats

Y Voted for (yea)	X Paired against	C Voted "present" to avoid possible conflict of interest
# Paired for	– Announced against	
+ Announced for	P Voted "present"	? Did not vote or otherwise make a position known
N Voted against (nay)		

	790	791	792	793	794	795
16 **Manzullo**	Y	Y	Y	Y	Y	Y
17 Hare	Y	Y	Y	Y	Y	Y
18 **Schock**	Y	?	Y	Y	Y	Y
19 **Shimkus**	Y	Y	Y	Y	Y	Y
INDIANA						
1 Visclosky	Y	Y	Y	Y	Y	Y
2 Donnelly	Y	Y	Y	Y	Y	Y
3 **Souder**	Y	Y	Y	Y	Y	Y
4 **Buyer**	Y	Y	Y	Y	Y	Y
5 **Burton**	Y	Y	Y	Y	Y	Y
6 **Pence**	Y	Y	Y	Y	Y	Y
7 Carson	Y	Y	Y	Y	Y	Y
8 Ellsworth	Y	Y	Y	Y	Y	Y
9 Hill	Y	Y	Y	Y	Y	Y
IOWA						
1 Braley	Y	Y	Y	Y	Y	Y
2 Loebsack	Y	Y	Y	Y	Y	Y
3 Boswell	Y	Y	Y	Y	Y	Y
4 **Latham**	Y	Y	Y	Y	Y	Y
5 **King**	Y	Y	Y	Y	Y	Y
KANSAS						
1 **Moran**	Y	Y	Y	Y	Y	Y
2 **Jenkins**	Y	Y	Y	Y	Y	Y
3 Moore	Y	Y	Y	Y	Y	Y
4 **Tiahrt**	Y	Y	Y	Y	Y	Y
KENTUCKY						
1 **Whitfield**	Y	Y	Y	Y	Y	Y
2 **Guthrie**	Y	Y	Y	Y	Y	Y
3 Yarmuth	Y	Y	Y	Y	Y	Y
4 **Davis**	Y	Y	Y	Y	Y	Y
5 **Rogers**	Y	Y	Y	Y	Y	Y
6 Chandler	Y	Y	Y	Y	Y	Y
LOUISIANA						
1 **Scalise**	Y	Y	Y	Y	Y	Y
2 **Cao**	Y	Y	Y	Y	Y	Y
3 Melancon	Y	Y	Y	Y	Y	Y
4 **Fleming**	Y	Y	Y	Y	Y	Y
5 **Alexander**	Y	Y	Y	Y	Y	Y
6 **Cassidy**	Y	Y	Y	Y	Y	Y
7 **Boustany**	Y	Y	Y	Y	Y	Y
MAINE						
1 Pingree	Y	Y	Y	Y	Y	Y
2 Michaud	Y	Y	Y	Y	Y	Y
MARYLAND						
1 Kratovil	Y	Y	Y	Y	Y	Y
2 Ruppersberger	Y	Y	Y	Y	Y	Y
3 Sarbanes	Y	Y	Y	Y	Y	Y
4 Edwards	Y	Y	Y	?	?	?
5 Hoyer	Y	Y	Y	?	?	?
6 **Bartlett**	Y	Y	Y	Y	Y	Y
7 Cummings	Y	Y	Y	Y	Y	Y
8 Van Hollen	Y	Y	Y	?	?	?
MASSACHUSETTS						
1 Olver	Y	Y	Y	Y	Y	Y
2 Neal	Y	Y	Y	Y	Y	Y
3 McGovern	Y	Y	Y	Y	Y	Y
4 Frank	Y	Y	Y	Y	Y	Y
5 Tsongas	Y	Y	Y	Y	Y	Y
6 Tierney	Y	Y	Y	Y	Y	Y
7 Markey	Y	Y	Y	Y	Y	Y
8 Capuano	?	?	?	Y	Y	Y
9 Lynch	Y	Y	Y	Y	Y	Y
10 Delahunt	Y	Y	Y	Y	Y	Y
MICHIGAN						
1 Stupak	Y	Y	Y	Y	Y	Y
2 **Hoekstra**	Y	Y	Y	Y	Y	Y
3 **Ehlers**	Y	Y	Y	Y	Y	Y
4 **Camp**	Y	Y	Y	Y	Y	Y
5 Kildee	Y	Y	Y	Y	Y	Y
6 **Upton**	Y	Y	Y	Y	Y	Y
7 Schauer	Y	Y	Y	Y	Y	Y
8 **Rogers**	Y	Y	Y	Y	Y	Y
9 Peters	Y	Y	Y	Y	Y	Y
10 **Miller**	Y	Y	Y	Y	Y	Y
11 **McCotter**	Y	Y	Y	Y	Y	Y
12 Levin	Y	Y	Y	Y	Y	Y
13 Kilpatrick	Y	Y	Y	Y	Y	Y
14 Conyers	Y	Y	Y	Y	Y	Y
15 Dingell	Y	Y	Y	Y	Y	Y
MINNESOTA						
1 Walz	Y	Y	Y	Y	Y	Y
2 **Kline**	Y	Y	Y	Y	Y	Y
3 **Paulsen**	Y	Y	Y	Y	Y	Y
4 McCollum	Y	Y	Y	Y	?	Y
5 Ellison	Y	?	Y	Y	Y	Y
6 **Bachmann**	Y	Y	Y	Y	Y	Y
7 Peterson	Y	Y	Y	Y	Y	Y
8 Oberstar	Y	Y	Y	Y	Y	Y
MISSISSIPPI						
1 Childers	Y	Y	Y	Y	Y	Y
2 Thompson	Y	Y	Y	Y	Y	Y
3 **Harper**	Y	Y	Y	Y	Y	Y
4 Taylor	Y	Y	Y	Y	Y	Y
MISSOURI						
1 Clay	Y	Y	Y	Y	Y	Y
2 **Akin**	Y	Y	Y	Y	Y	Y
3 Carnahan	Y	Y	Y	Y	Y	Y
4 Skelton	Y	Y	Y	Y	Y	Y
5 Cleaver	Y	Y	Y	Y	Y	Y
6 **Graves**	Y	Y	Y	Y	Y	Y
7 **Blunt**	Y	Y	Y	Y	Y	Y
8 **Emerson**	Y	Y	Y	Y	Y	Y
9 **Luetkemeyer**	Y	Y	Y	Y	Y	Y
MONTANA						
AL **Rehberg**	Y	Y	Y	Y	Y	Y
NEBRASKA						
1 **Fortenberry**	Y	Y	Y	Y	Y	Y
2 **Terry**	Y	Y	Y	Y	Y	Y
3 **Smith**	Y	Y	Y	Y	Y	Y
NEVADA						
1 Berkley	Y	Y	Y	Y	Y	Y
2 **Heller**	Y	Y	Y	Y	Y	Y
3 Titus	Y	Y	Y	Y	Y	Y
NEW HAMPSHIRE						
1 Shea-Porter	Y	Y	Y	Y	Y	Y
2 Hodes	Y	Y	Y	Y	Y	Y
NEW JERSEY						
1 Andrews	?	?	Y	Y	Y	Y
2 **LoBiondo**	Y	Y	Y	Y	Y	Y
3 Adler	Y	Y	Y	Y	Y	Y
4 **Smith**	Y	Y	Y	Y	Y	Y
5 **Garrett**	Y	Y	Y	Y	Y	Y
6 Pallone	Y	Y	Y	Y	Y	Y
7 **Lance**	Y	Y	Y	Y	Y	Y
8 Pascrell	Y	Y	Y	Y	Y	Y
9 Rothman	Y	Y	Y	?	?	?
10 Payne	Y	Y	Y	Y	Y	Y
11 **Frelinghuysen**	Y	Y	Y	Y	Y	Y
12 Holt	Y	Y	Y	Y	Y	Y
13 Sires	?	?	?	Y	Y	Y
NEW MEXICO						
1 Heinrich	Y	Y	Y	Y	Y	Y
2 Teague	Y	Y	Y	Y	Y	Y
3 Lujan	Y	Y	Y	Y	Y	Y
NEW YORK						
1 Bishop	Y	Y	Y	Y	Y	Y
2 Israel	?	?	?	Y	Y	?
3 **King**	Y	Y	Y	Y	Y	Y
4 McCarthy	Y	Y	Y	Y	Y	Y
5 Ackerman	Y	Y	Y	?	?	?
6 Meeks	Y	Y	Y	Y	Y	Y
7 Crowley	?	?	?	Y	Y	Y
8 Nadler	Y	Y	Y	Y	Y	Y
9 Weiner	?	?	?	Y	Y	Y
10 Towns	Y	Y	Y	Y	Y	Y
11 Clarke	Y	Y	Y	Y	Y	Y
12 Velázquez	Y	Y	?	Y	Y	Y
13 McMahon	Y	Y	Y	Y	Y	Y
14 Maloney	+	+	+	Y	Y	Y
15 Rangel	Y	Y	Y	Y	Y	Y
16 Serrano	Y	Y	Y	Y	Y	Y
17 Engel	Y	Y	Y	Y	Y	Y
18 Lowey	+	+	+	Y	Y	Y
19 Hall	Y	Y	Y	Y	Y	Y
20 Murphy	Y	Y	Y	Y	Y	Y
21 Tonko	Y	Y	Y	Y	Y	Y
22 Hinchey	Y	Y	Y	Y	Y	Y
23 Vacant						
24 Arcuri	Y	Y	Y	Y	Y	Y
25 Maffei	Y	Y	Y	Y	Y	Y
26 **Lee**	Y	Y	Y	Y	Y	Y
27 Higgins	Y	Y	Y	Y	Y	Y
28 Slaughter	Y	Y	Y	Y	Y	Y
29 Massa	Y	Y	Y	Y	Y	Y
NORTH CAROLINA						
1 Butterfield	Y	Y	Y	Y	Y	Y
2 Etheridge	?	+	+	+	+	+
3 **Jones**	Y	Y	Y	Y	Y	Y
4 Price	Y	Y	Y	Y	Y	Y
5 **Foxx**	Y	Y	Y	N	Y	Y
6 **Coble**	Y	Y	Y	Y	Y	Y
7 McIntyre	Y	Y	Y	Y	Y	Y
8 Kissell	Y	Y	Y	Y	Y	Y
9 **Myrick**	Y	Y	Y	Y	Y	Y
10 **McHenry**	Y	Y	Y	Y	Y	Y
11 Shuler	?	?	?	Y	Y	Y
12 Watt	Y	Y	Y	Y	Y	Y
13 Miller	Y	Y	Y	Y	Y	Y
NORTH DAKOTA						
AL Pomeroy	Y	Y	Y	Y	Y	Y
OHIO						
1 Driehaus	Y	Y	Y	Y	Y	Y
2 **Schmidt**	Y	Y	Y	Y	Y	Y
3 **Turner**	Y	Y	Y	Y	Y	Y
4 **Jordan**	Y	Y	Y	Y	Y	Y
5 **Latta**	Y	Y	Y	Y	Y	Y
6 Wilson	Y	?	Y	Y	Y	Y
7 **Austria**	Y	Y	Y	Y	Y	Y
8 **Boehner**	?	Y	Y	Y	Y	Y
9 Kaptur	Y	Y	Y	Y	Y	Y
10 Kucinich	Y	Y	Y	Y	Y	Y
11 Fudge	Y	Y	Y	Y	Y	Y
12 **Tiberi**	Y	Y	Y	Y	Y	Y
13 Sutton	Y	Y	Y	Y	Y	Y
14 **LaTourette**	Y	Y	Y	Y	Y	Y
15 Kilroy	Y	Y	Y	Y	Y	Y
16 Boccieri	Y	Y	Y	Y	Y	Y
17 Ryan	Y	Y	Y	Y	Y	Y
18 Space	Y	Y	Y	Y	Y	Y
OKLAHOMA						
1 **Sullivan**	Y	Y	Y	Y	Y	Y
2 Boren	Y	Y	Y	Y	?	Y
3 **Lucas**	Y	Y	Y	Y	Y	Y
4 **Cole**	Y	Y	Y	Y	Y	Y
5 **Fallin**	Y	Y	Y	Y	Y	Y
OREGON						
1 Wu	Y	Y	Y	Y	Y	Y
2 **Walden**	?	?	?	?	?	?
3 Blumenauer	Y	Y	Y	Y	Y	Y
4 DeFazio	Y	Y	Y	Y	Y	Y
5 Schrader	Y	Y	Y	Y	Y	Y
PENNSYLVANIA						
1 Brady	Y	Y	Y	Y	Y	Y
2 Fattah	Y	Y	Y	Y	Y	Y
3 Dahlkemper	Y	Y	Y	Y	Y	Y
4 Altmire	Y	Y	Y	Y	Y	Y
5 **Thompson**	Y	Y	Y	Y	Y	Y
6 **Gerlach**	+	+	+	Y	Y	Y
7 Sestak	Y	Y	Y	Y	Y	Y
8 Murphy, P.	Y	Y	Y	Y	Y	Y
9 **Shuster**	Y	Y	Y	Y	Y	Y
10 Carney	Y	Y	Y	Y	Y	Y
11 Kanjorski	Y	?	Y	Y	Y	Y
12 Murtha	?	?	?	Y	Y	Y
13 Schwartz	?	Y	Y	Y	Y	Y
14 Doyle	Y	Y	Y	Y	Y	Y
15 **Dent**	Y	Y	Y	Y	Y	Y
16 **Pitts**	Y	Y	Y	Y	Y	Y
17 Holden	Y	Y	Y	Y	Y	Y
18 **Murphy, T.**	Y	Y	Y	Y	Y	Y
19 **Platts**	Y	Y	Y	Y	Y	Y
RHODE ISLAND						
1 Kennedy	Y	Y	Y	Y	Y	Y
2 Langevin	+	Y	Y	Y	Y	Y
SOUTH CAROLINA						
1 **Brown**	Y	Y	Y	Y	Y	Y
2 **Wilson**	Y	Y	Y	Y	Y	Y
3 **Barrett**	+	+	+	Y	Y	Y
4 **Inglis**	Y	Y	Y	Y	Y	Y
5 Spratt	?	Y	Y	Y	Y	Y
6 Clyburn	Y	Y	Y	Y	Y	Y
SOUTH DAKOTA						
AL Herseth Sandlin	Y	Y	Y	Y	Y	Y
TENNESSEE						
1 **Roe**	Y	Y	Y	Y	Y	Y
2 **Duncan**	Y	Y	Y	N	Y	Y
3 **Wamp**	Y	Y	Y	Y	Y	Y
4 Davis	Y	Y	Y	Y	Y	Y
5 Cooper	Y	Y	Y	Y	Y	Y
6 Gordon	Y	Y	Y	Y	Y	Y
7 **Blackburn**	Y	Y	Y	Y	Y	Y
8 Tanner	Y	Y	Y	Y	Y	Y
9 Cohen	Y	Y	Y	Y	Y	Y
TEXAS						
1 **Gohmert**	Y	Y	Y	N	Y	Y
2 **Poe**	Y	Y	Y	N	Y	Y
3 **Johnson, S.**	Y	Y	Y	Y	Y	Y
4 **Hall**	Y	Y	Y	Y	Y	Y
5 **Hensarling**	Y	Y	Y	Y	Y	Y
6 **Barton**	Y	Y	Y	Y	Y	Y
7 **Culberson**	Y	Y	Y	Y	Y	Y
8 **Brady**	Y	Y	Y	N	Y	Y
9 Green, A.	Y	Y	Y	Y	Y	Y
10 **McCaul**	Y	Y	Y	Y	Y	Y
11 **Conaway**	Y	Y	Y	Y	Y	Y
12 **Granger**	Y	Y	Y	Y	Y	Y
13 **Thornberry**	Y	Y	Y	Y	Y	Y
14 **Paul**	Y	Y	Y	N	Y	Y
15 Hinojosa	Y	Y	Y	Y	Y	Y
16 Reyes	Y	Y	Y	Y	Y	Y
17 Edwards	Y	Y	Y	Y	Y	Y
18 Jackson Lee	Y	Y	Y	Y	Y	Y
19 **Neugebauer**	Y	Y	Y	Y	Y	Y
20 Gonzalez	Y	Y	Y	Y	Y	Y
21 **Smith**	Y	Y	Y	Y	Y	Y
22 **Olson**	Y	Y	Y	Y	Y	Y
23 Rodriguez	Y	Y	Y	Y	Y	Y
24 **Marchant**	Y	Y	Y	Y	Y	Y
25 Doggett	Y	Y	Y	Y	Y	Y
26 **Burgess**	Y	Y	Y	Y	Y	Y
27 Ortiz	Y	Y	Y	Y	Y	Y
28 Cuellar	Y	Y	Y	Y	Y	Y
29 Green, G.	Y	Y	Y	Y	Y	Y
30 Johnson, E.	Y	Y	Y	Y	Y	Y
31 **Carter**	+	+	+	+	+	+
32 **Sessions**	Y	Y	Y	Y	Y	Y
UTAH						
1 **Bishop**	Y	Y	Y	Y	Y	Y
2 Matheson	Y	Y	Y	Y	Y	Y
3 **Chaffetz**	Y	Y	Y	Y	Y	Y
VERMONT						
AL Welch	Y	Y	Y	Y	Y	Y
VIRGINIA						
1 **Wittman**	Y	Y	Y	Y	Y	Y
2 Nye	Y	Y	Y	Y	Y	Y
3 Scott	Y	Y	Y	Y	Y	Y
4 **Forbes**	Y	Y	Y	Y	Y	Y
5 Perriello	Y	Y	Y	Y	Y	Y
6 **Goodlatte**	Y	Y	Y	Y	Y	Y
7 **Cantor**	Y	Y	Y	Y	Y	Y
8 Moran	Y	Y	Y	Y	Y	Y
9 Boucher	Y	Y	Y	Y	Y	Y
10 **Wolf**	Y	Y	Y	Y	Y	Y
11 Connolly	Y	Y	Y	Y	Y	Y
WASHINGTON						
1 Inslee	Y	Y	Y	Y	Y	Y
2 Larsen	Y	Y	Y	Y	Y	Y
3 Baird	Y	Y	Y	Y	Y	Y
4 **Hastings**	Y	Y	Y	Y	Y	Y
5 **McMorris Rodgers**	Y	Y	Y	Y	Y	Y
6 Dicks	Y	Y	Y	Y	Y	Y
7 McDermott	Y	Y	Y	Y	Y	Y
8 **Reichert**	Y	Y	Y	Y	Y	Y
9 Smith	Y	Y	Y	Y	Y	Y
WEST VIRGINIA						
1 Mollohan	Y	Y	Y	Y	Y	Y
2 **Capito**	Y	Y	Y	Y	Y	Y
3 Rahall	Y	Y	Y	Y	Y	Y
WISCONSIN						
1 **Ryan**	Y	Y	Y	Y	Y	Y
2 Baldwin	Y	Y	Y	Y	Y	Y
3 Kind	Y	Y	Y	Y	Y	Y
4 Moore	Y	Y	Y	Y	Y	Y
5 **Sensenbrenner**	Y	Y	Y	Y	Y	Y
6 **Petri**	Y	Y	Y	Y	Y	Y
7 Obey	Y	Y	Y	Y	Y	Y
8 Kagen	Y	Y	Y	Y	Y	Y
WYOMING						
AL **Lummis**	Y	Y	Y	N	Y	Y
DELEGATES						
Faleomavaega (A.S.)						
Norton (D.C.)						
Bordallo (Guam)						
Sablan (N. Marianas)						
Pierluisi (P.R.)						
Christensen (V.I.)						

IN THE HOUSE | By Vote Number

796. **H Res 660. Laurinburg Normal Industrial Institute Tribute/ Adoption.** Davis, D-Calif., motion to suspend the rules and adopt the resolution that would recognize the distinguished history of the Laurinburg Normal Industrial Institute. Motion agreed to 418-0: D 246-0; R 172-0. A two-thirds majority of those present and voting (279 in this case) is required for adoption under suspension of the rules. Oct. 21, 2009.

797. **S Con Res 43. Use of Capitol Rotunda/Adoption.** Brady, D-Pa., motion to suspend the rules and adopt the concurrent resolution that would authorize the use of the Capitol Rotunda on Oct. 28 for the presentation of a Congressional Gold Medal to former Sen. Edward Brooke, R-Mass. Motion agreed to 417-0: D 245-0; R 172-0. A two-thirds majority of those present and voting (278 in this case) is required for adoption under suspension of the rules. Oct. 21, 2009.

798. **HR 3585. Solar Energy Technology Programs/Previous Question.** Polis, D-Colo., motion to order the previous question (thus ending debate and possibility of amendment) on adoption of the rule (H Res 846) to provide for House floor consideration of the bill that would establish a Solar Technology Roadmap Committee and authorize $2.25 billion for fiscal 2011 through 2015. Motion agreed to 239-176: D 239-8; R 0-168. Oct. 22, 2009.

799. **HR 3585. Solar Energy Technology Programs/Rule.** Adoption of the rule (H Res 846) that would provide for House floor consideration of the bill that would establish a Solar Technology Roadmap Committee and authorize $2.25 billion for fiscal 2011 through 2015. Adopted 241-178: D 240-8; R 1-170. Oct. 22, 2009.

800. **H Res 797. National Cyber Security Awareness Month/ Adoption.** Gordon, D-Tenn., motion to suspend the rules and adopt the resolution that would support the designation of "National Cyber Security Awareness Month." Motion agreed to 415-0: D 245-0; R 170-0. A two-thirds majority of those present and voting (277 in this case) is required for adoption under suspension of the rules. Oct. 22, 2009.

801. **HR 3585. Solar Energy Technology Programs/Reduce Authorization.** Broun, R-Ga., amendment that would reduce the authorization of the Solar Technology Roadmap Committee to three years, from five years. It also would reduce to $250 million the amount authorized in each of those three years. Rejected in Committee of the Whole 162-256: D 7-243; R 155-13. Oct. 22, 2009.

	796	797	798	799	800	801
ALABAMA						
1 **Bonner**	Y	Y	N	N	Y	Y
2 **Bright**	Y	Y	N	N	Y	Y
3 **Rogers**	Y	Y	N	N	Y	Y
4 **Aderholt**	Y	Y	N	N	Y	Y
5 Griffith	Y	Y	N	N	Y	N
6 **Bachus**	Y	Y	N	N	Y	Y
7 Davis	Y	Y	?	?	?	?
ALASKA						
AL **Young**	?	?	?	?	?	?
ARIZONA						
1 Kirkpatrick	Y	Y	Y	Y	Y	N
2 **Franks**	Y	Y	N	N	Y	Y
3 **Shadegg**	?	?	N	N	Y	Y
4 Pastor	Y	Y	Y	Y	Y	N
5 Mitchell	Y	Y	Y	Y	Y	N
6 **Flake**	Y	Y	N	N	Y	Y
7 Grijalva	Y	Y	Y	Y	Y	N
8 Giffords	Y	Y	Y	Y	Y	N
ARKANSAS						
1 Berry	Y	Y	Y	Y	Y	N
2 Snyder	Y	Y	Y	Y	Y	N
3 **Boozman**	Y	Y	N	N	Y	Y
4 Ross	Y	Y	Y	Y	Y	N
CALIFORNIA						
1 Thompson	Y	Y	Y	Y	Y	N
2 **Herger**	Y	Y	N	N	Y	Y
3 **Lungren**	Y	Y	N	N	Y	Y
4 **McClintock**	Y	Y	N	N	Y	Y
5 Matsui	Y	Y	Y	Y	Y	N
6 Woolsey	Y	Y	Y	Y	Y	N
7 Miller, George	Y	Y	Y	Y	Y	N
8 Pelosi						
9 Lee	Y	Y	Y	Y	Y	N
10 Vacant						
11 McNerney	Y	Y	Y	Y	Y	N
12 Speier	Y	Y	Y	Y	Y	N
13 Stark	Y	Y	Y	Y	Y	N
14 Eshoo	Y	Y	Y	Y	Y	N
15 Honda	Y	Y	Y	Y	Y	N
16 Lofgren	?	?	?	?	?	?
17 Farr	Y	Y	Y	Y	Y	N
18 Cardoza	Y	Y	Y	Y	Y	N
19 **Radanovich**	Y	Y	?	?	?	Y
20 Costa	Y	Y	Y	Y	Y	N
21 **Nunes**	Y	Y	N	N	Y	Y
22 **McCarthy**	Y	Y	N	N	Y	Y
23 Capps	Y	Y	Y	Y	Y	N
24 **Gallegly**	Y	Y	N	N	Y	Y
25 **McKeon**	Y	Y	N	N	?	Y
26 **Dreier**	Y	Y	N	N	Y	Y
27 Sherman	Y	Y	Y	Y	Y	N
28 Berman	Y	Y	Y	Y	Y	N
29 Schiff	Y	Y	Y	Y	Y	N
30 Waxman	Y	Y	Y	Y	Y	N
31 Becerra	Y	Y	Y	Y	Y	N
32 Chu	Y	Y	Y	Y	Y	N
33 Watson	Y	Y	Y	Y	?	N
34 Roybal-Allard	Y	Y	Y	Y	Y	N
35 Waters	Y	Y	Y	Y	Y	N
36 Harman	Y	Y	Y	Y	Y	N
37 Richardson	?	?	?	?	?	?
38 Napolitano	Y	Y	Y	Y	Y	N
39 Sánchez, Linda	Y	Y	Y	Y	Y	N
40 **Royce**	Y	Y	N	N	Y	Y
41 **Lewis**	Y	Y	N	N	Y	Y
42 **Miller, Gary**	Y	Y	N	N	Y	Y
43 Baca	Y	Y	Y	Y	Y	N
44 **Calvert**	Y	Y	N	N	Y	Y
45 **Bono Mack**	Y	Y	N	N	Y	Y
46 **Rohrabacher**	Y	Y	N	N	Y	Y
47 Sanchez, Loretta	Y	Y	Y	Y	Y	N
48 **Campbell**	Y	Y	N	N	Y	Y
49 **Issa**	Y	Y	N	N	Y	Y
50 **Bilbray**	Y	Y	N	N	Y	Y
51 Filner	Y	Y	Y	Y	Y	N
52 **Hunter**	Y	Y	N	N	Y	Y
53 Davis	Y	Y	Y	Y	Y	N
COLORADO						
1 DeGette	Y	Y	Y	Y	Y	N
2 Polis	Y	Y	Y	Y	Y	N
3 Salazar	Y	Y	Y	Y	Y	N
4 Markey	Y	Y	Y	Y	Y	N
5 **Lamborn**	Y	Y	N	N	Y	Y
6 **Coffman**	Y	Y	N	N	Y	+
7 Perlmutter	Y	Y	Y	Y	Y	N
CONNECTICUT						
1 Larson	Y	Y	Y	Y	Y	N
2 Courtney	Y	Y	Y	Y	Y	N
3 DeLauro	Y	Y	Y	Y	Y	N
4 Himes	Y	Y	Y	Y	Y	N
5 Murphy	Y	Y	Y	Y	Y	N
DELAWARE						
AL **Castle**	Y	Y	N	N	Y	N
FLORIDA						
1 **Miller**	Y	Y	N	N	Y	Y
2 Boyd	Y	Y	Y	Y	Y	N
3 Brown	Y	Y	Y	Y	Y	N
4 **Crenshaw**	Y	Y	N	N	Y	Y
5 **Brown-Waite**	Y	Y	N	N	Y	Y
6 **Stearns**	Y	Y	N	N	Y	Y
7 **Mica**	Y	Y	N	N	Y	Y
8 Grayson	Y	Y	Y	Y	Y	N
9 **Bilirakis**	Y	Y	N	N	Y	Y
10 **Young**	Y	Y	N	N	Y	Y
11 Castor	Y	Y	Y	Y	Y	N
12 **Putnam**	Y	Y	N	N	Y	Y
13 **Buchanan**	Y	Y	N	N	Y	Y
14 **Mack**	Y	Y	N	N	Y	Y
15 **Posey**	Y	Y	N	N	Y	Y
16 **Rooney**	Y	Y	N	N	Y	Y
17 Meek	Y	Y	Y	Y	Y	N
18 **Ros-Lehtinen**	Y	Y	N	N	Y	Y
19 Wexler	Y	Y	Y	Y	Y	N
20 Wasserman Schultz	Y	Y	Y	Y	Y	N
21 **Diaz-Balart, L.**	Y	Y	N	N	Y	Y
22 Klein	Y	Y	Y	Y	Y	N
23 Hastings	Y	Y	Y	Y	Y	N
24 Kosmas	Y	Y	Y	Y	Y	N
25 **Diaz-Balart, M.**	Y	Y	N	N	Y	Y
GEORGIA						
1 **Kingston**	Y	Y	N	N	Y	Y
2 Bishop	Y	Y	Y	Y	Y	N
3 **Westmoreland**	Y	Y	N	N	Y	Y
4 Johnson	Y	Y	Y	Y	Y	N
5 Lewis	Y	Y	Y	Y	Y	N
6 **Price**	+	+	N	N	Y	+
7 **Linder**	Y	Y	N	N	Y	Y
8 Marshall	Y	Y	Y	Y	Y	N
9 **Deal**	Y	Y	N	N	Y	Y
10 **Broun**	Y	Y	N	N	Y	Y
11 **Gingrey**	Y	Y	?	N	Y	Y
12 Barrow	Y	Y	Y	Y	Y	N
13 Scott	Y	Y	Y	Y	Y	N
HAWAII						
1 Abercrombie	Y	Y	?	?	?	?
2 Hirono	Y	Y	Y	Y	Y	N
IDAHO						
1 Minnick	Y	Y	N	N	Y	Y
2 **Simpson**	Y	Y	N	N	Y	Y
ILLINOIS						
1 Rush	Y	Y	Y	Y	Y	N
2 Jackson	Y	Y	Y	Y	Y	N
3 Lipinski	Y	Y	Y	Y	Y	N
4 Gutierrez	Y	Y	Y	Y	Y	N
5 Quigley	Y	Y	Y	Y	Y	N
6 **Roskam**	Y	Y	N	N	Y	Y
7 Davis	Y	Y	Y	Y	Y	N
8 Bean	?	?	?	?	?	?
9 Schakowsky	Y	Y	Y	Y	Y	N
10 **Kirk**	Y	Y	N	N	Y	N
11 Halvorson	Y	Y	Y	Y	Y	N
12 Costello	Y	Y	Y	Y	Y	N
13 **Biggert**	Y	Y	N	N	Y	Y
14 Foster	Y	Y	Y	Y	Y	N
15 **Johnson**	Y	Y	N	N	Y	Y

KEY **Republicans** Democrats

Y Voted for (yea)	X Paired against
# Paired for	– Announced against
+ Announced for	P Voted "present"
N Voted against (nay)	

C Voted "present" to avoid possible conflict of interest

? Did not vote or otherwise make a position known

	796	797	798	799	800	801
16 **Manzullo**	Y	Y	N	N	Y	Y
17 Hare	Y	Y	Y	Y	Y	N
18 **Schock**	Y	Y	N	N	Y	Y
19 **Shimkus**	Y	Y	N	N	Y	Y
INDIANA						
1 Visclosky	Y	Y	Y	Y	Y	N
2 Donnelly	Y	Y	Y	Y	Y	N
3 **Souder**	Y	Y	N	N	Y	Y
4 **Buyer**	Y	Y	N	N	Y	?
5 **Burton**	Y	Y	N	N	Y	Y
6 **Pence**	Y	Y	N	N	Y	Y
7 Carson	Y	Y	Y	Y	Y	N
8 Ellsworth	Y	Y	Y	Y	Y	N
9 Hill	Y	Y	N	N	Y	N
IOWA						
1 Braley	Y	Y	Y	Y	Y	N
2 Loebsack	Y	Y	Y	Y	Y	N
3 Boswell	Y	Y	Y	Y	Y	N
4 **Latham**	Y	Y	N	N	Y	Y
5 **King**	Y	Y	N	N	Y	Y
KANSAS						
1 **Moran**	Y	Y	N	N	Y	Y
2 **Jenkins**	Y	Y	N	N	Y	Y
3 Moore	Y	Y	Y	Y	Y	N
4 **Tiahrt**	Y	Y	N	N	Y	Y
KENTUCKY						
1 **Whitfield**	Y	Y	N	N	Y	Y
2 **Guthrie**	Y	Y	N	N	Y	Y
3 Yarmuth	Y	Y	Y	Y	Y	N
4 **Davis**	Y	Y	N	N	Y	Y
5 **Rogers**	Y	Y	N	N	Y	Y
6 Chandler	Y	Y	Y	Y	Y	N
LOUISIANA						
1 **Scalise**	Y	Y	N	N	Y	Y
2 **Cao**	Y	Y	N	N	Y	Y
3 Melancon	Y	Y	Y	Y	Y	N
4 **Fleming**	Y	Y	N	N	Y	Y
5 **Alexander**	Y	Y	N	N	Y	Y
6 **Cassidy**	Y	Y	N	N	Y	Y
7 **Boustany**	Y	Y	N	N	Y	Y
MAINE						
1 Pingree	Y	Y	Y	Y	?	N
2 Michaud	Y	Y	Y	Y	Y	N
MARYLAND						
1 Kratovil	Y	Y	N	N	Y	N
2 Ruppersberger	Y	Y	Y	Y	Y	N
3 Sarbanes	Y	Y	Y	Y	Y	N
4 Edwards	?	?	Y	Y	Y	N
5 Hoyer	?	?	Y	Y	Y	N
6 **Bartlett**	Y	Y	N	N	Y	N
7 Cummings	Y	Y	Y	Y	Y	N
8 Van Hollen	?	?	Y	Y	Y	N
MASSACHUSETTS						
1 Olver	Y	Y	Y	Y	Y	N
2 Neal	Y	Y	Y	Y	Y	N
3 McGovern	Y	Y	Y	Y	Y	N
4 Frank	Y	Y	Y	Y	Y	N
5 Tsongas	Y	Y	Y	Y	Y	N
6 Tierney	Y	Y	Y	Y	Y	N
7 Markey	Y	Y	Y	Y	Y	N
8 Capuano	Y	Y	Y	Y	Y	N
9 Lynch	Y	Y	Y	Y	Y	N
10 Delahunt	Y	Y	Y	Y	Y	N
MICHIGAN						
1 Stupak	Y	Y	Y	Y	Y	N
2 **Hoekstra**	Y	Y	N	N	Y	Y
3 **Ehlers**	Y	Y	N	N	Y	N
4 **Camp**	Y	Y	N	N	Y	N
5 Kildee	Y	Y	Y	Y	Y	N
6 **Upton**	Y	Y	N	N	Y	Y
7 Schauer	Y	Y	Y	Y	?	N
8 **Rogers**	Y	Y	N	N	Y	Y
9 Peters	Y	Y	Y	Y	Y	N
10 **Miller**	Y	Y	N	N	Y	Y
11 **McCotter**	Y	Y	N	N	Y	Y
12 Levin	Y	Y	Y	Y	Y	N
13 Kilpatrick	Y	Y	Y	Y	Y	N
14 Conyers	Y	Y	Y	Y	Y	N
15 Dingell	Y	Y	Y	Y	Y	N
MINNESOTA						
1 Walz	Y	Y	Y	Y	Y	N
2 **Kline**	Y	Y	N	N	Y	Y
3 **Paulsen**	Y	Y	N	N	Y	Y
4 McCollum	Y	Y	Y	Y	Y	N

	796	797	798	799	800	801
5 Ellison	Y	Y	Y	Y	Y	N
6 **Bachmann**	Y	Y	N	N	Y	Y
7 Peterson	Y	Y	Y	Y	Y	N
8 Oberstar	Y	Y	Y	Y	Y	N
MISSISSIPPI						
1 Childers	Y	Y	N	N	Y	N
2 Thompson	Y	Y	Y	Y	Y	N
3 **Harper**	Y	Y	N	N	Y	Y
4 Taylor	Y	Y	N	N	Y	N
MISSOURI						
1 Clay	Y	Y	Y	Y	Y	N
2 **Akin**	Y	Y	N	N	Y	Y
3 Carnahan	Y	?	Y	Y	Y	N
4 Skelton	Y	Y	Y	Y	Y	Y
5 Cleaver	Y	Y	Y	Y	Y	N
6 **Graves**	Y	Y	N	N	Y	Y
7 **Blunt**	Y	Y	N	N	Y	Y
8 **Emerson**	Y	Y	N	N	Y	Y
9 **Luetkemeyer**	Y	Y	N	N	Y	Y
MONTANA						
AL **Rehberg**	Y	Y	N	N	Y	Y
NEBRASKA						
1 **Fortenberry**	Y	Y	N	N	Y	Y
2 **Terry**	Y	Y	N	N	Y	Y
3 **Smith**	Y	Y	N	N	Y	Y
NEVADA						
1 Berkley	Y	Y	Y	Y	Y	N
2 **Heller**	Y	Y	N	N	Y	Y
3 Titus	Y	Y	Y	Y	Y	N
NEW HAMPSHIRE						
1 Shea-Porter	Y	Y	Y	Y	Y	N
2 Hodes	Y	Y	Y	Y	Y	N
NEW JERSEY						
1 Andrews	Y	Y	Y	Y	Y	N
2 **LoBiondo**	Y	Y	N	N	Y	Y
3 Adler	Y	Y	Y	Y	Y	N
4 **Smith**	Y	Y	N	N	Y	N
5 **Garrett**	Y	Y	N	N	Y	Y
6 Pallone	Y	Y	Y	Y	Y	N
7 **Lance**	Y	Y	N	N	Y	Y
8 Pascrell	Y	Y	Y	Y	Y	N
9 Rothman	?	?	Y	Y	Y	N
10 Payne	Y	Y	Y	Y	Y	?
11 **Frelinghuysen**	Y	Y	N	N	Y	Y
12 Holt	Y	Y	Y	Y	Y	N
13 Sires	Y	Y	Y	Y	Y	N
NEW MEXICO						
1 Heinrich	Y	Y	Y	Y	Y	N
2 Teague	Y	Y	Y	Y	Y	N
3 Lujan	Y	Y	Y	Y	Y	N
NEW YORK						
1 Bishop	Y	Y	Y	Y	Y	N
2 Israel	Y	Y	Y	Y	Y	N
3 **King**	Y	Y	N	N	Y	Y
4 McCarthy	Y	Y	Y	Y	Y	N
5 Ackerman	?	?	Y	Y	Y	N
6 Meeks	Y	Y	Y	Y	Y	N
7 Crowley	Y	Y	Y	Y	Y	N
8 Nadler	Y	Y	Y	Y	Y	N
9 Weiner	Y	Y	Y	Y	?	N
10 Towns	Y	Y	Y	Y	Y	N
11 Clarke	Y	Y	Y	Y	Y	N
12 Velázquez	Y	Y	Y	Y	Y	N
13 McMahon	Y	Y	Y	Y	Y	N
14 Maloney	Y	Y	Y	Y	Y	N
15 Rangel	Y	Y	Y	Y	Y	N
16 Serrano	Y	Y	Y	Y	Y	N
17 Engel	Y	Y	Y	Y	Y	?
18 Lowey	Y	Y	Y	Y	Y	N
19 Hall	Y	Y	Y	Y	Y	N
20 Murphy	Y	Y	Y	Y	Y	Y
21 Tonko	Y	Y	Y	Y	Y	N
22 Hinchey	Y	Y	Y	Y	Y	N
23 Vacant						
24 Arcuri	Y	Y	Y	Y	Y	N
25 Maffei	Y	Y	Y	Y	Y	N
26 **Lee**	Y	Y	N	N	Y	Y
27 Higgins	Y	Y	Y	Y	Y	N
28 Slaughter	Y	Y	Y	Y	Y	N
29 Massa	Y	Y	Y	Y	Y	N
NORTH CAROLINA						
1 Butterfield	Y	Y	Y	Y	Y	N
2 Etheridge	+	+	Y	Y	Y	N
3 **Jones**	Y	Y	N	Y	Y	Y
4 Price	Y	Y	Y	Y	Y	N

	796	797	798	799	800	801
5 **Foxx**	Y	Y	N	N	Y	Y
6 **Coble**	Y	Y	N	N	Y	Y
7 McIntyre	Y	Y	Y	Y	Y	N
8 Kissell	Y	Y	Y	Y	Y	N
9 **Myrick**	Y	Y	N	N	Y	Y
10 **McHenry**	Y	Y	N	N	Y	Y
11 Shuler	Y	Y	Y	Y	Y	N
12 Watt	Y	Y	Y	Y	Y	N
13 Miller	Y	Y	Y	Y	Y	N
NORTH DAKOTA						
AL Pomeroy	Y	Y	Y	Y	Y	N
OHIO						
1 Driehaus	Y	Y	Y	Y	Y	N
2 **Schmidt**	Y	Y	N	N	Y	Y
3 **Turner**	Y	Y	N	N	Y	Y
4 **Jordan**	Y	Y	N	N	Y	Y
5 **Latta**	Y	Y	N	N	Y	Y
6 Wilson	Y	Y	Y	Y	Y	N
7 **Austria**	Y	Y	N	N	Y	Y
8 **Boehner**	Y	Y	N	N	Y	Y
9 Kaptur	Y	Y	Y	Y	Y	N
10 Kucinich	Y	Y	Y	Y	Y	N
11 Fudge	Y	Y	Y	Y	Y	N
12 **Tiberi**	Y	Y	N	N	Y	Y
13 Sutton	Y	Y	Y	Y	Y	N
14 **LaTourette**	Y	Y	N	N	Y	Y
15 Kilroy	Y	Y	Y	Y	Y	N
16 Boccieri	Y	Y	Y	Y	Y	N
17 Ryan	Y	Y	Y	Y	Y	N
18 Space	Y	Y	Y	Y	Y	N
OKLAHOMA						
1 **Sullivan**	Y	Y	N	N	Y	Y
2 Boren	Y	Y	Y	Y	Y	N
3 **Lucas**	Y	Y	N	N	Y	Y
4 **Cole**	Y	Y	?	N	Y	Y
5 **Fallin**	Y	Y	N	N	Y	Y
OREGON						
1 Wu	Y	Y	Y	Y	Y	N
2 **Walden**	?	?	?	?	?	?
3 Blumenauer	Y	Y	Y	Y	Y	N
4 DeFazio	Y	Y	Y	Y	Y	N
5 Schrader	Y	Y	Y	Y	Y	N
PENNSYLVANIA						
1 Brady	Y	Y	Y	Y	Y	N
2 Fattah	Y	Y	Y	Y	Y	Y
3 Dahlkemper	Y	Y	Y	Y	Y	Y
4 Altmire	Y	Y	Y	Y	Y	Y
5 **Thompson**	Y	Y	N	N	Y	Y
6 **Gerlach**	Y	Y	N	N	Y	Y
7 Sestak	Y	Y	Y	Y	Y	N
8 Murphy, P.	Y	Y	Y	Y	Y	N
9 **Shuster**	Y	Y	N	N	Y	Y
10 Carney	Y	Y	+	+	Y	N
11 Kanjorski	Y	Y	Y	Y	Y	N
12 Murtha	Y	Y	Y	Y	Y	N
13 Schwartz	Y	Y	Y	Y	Y	N
14 Doyle	Y	Y	Y	Y	Y	?
15 **Dent**	Y	Y	N	N	Y	Y
16 **Pitts**	Y	Y	N	N	Y	Y
17 Holden	Y	Y	Y	Y	Y	N
18 **Murphy, T.**	Y	Y	N	N	Y	N
19 **Platts**	Y	Y	N	N	Y	N
RHODE ISLAND						
1 Kennedy	Y	Y	Y	Y	Y	N
2 Langevin	Y	Y	Y	Y	Y	N
SOUTH CAROLINA						
1 **Brown**	Y	Y	N	N	Y	Y
2 **Wilson**	Y	Y	N	N	Y	Y
3 **Barrett**	Y	Y	?	?	?	?
4 **Inglis**	Y	Y	N	N	Y	Y
5 Spratt	Y	Y	Y	Y	Y	N
6 Clyburn	Y	Y	Y	Y	Y	N
SOUTH DAKOTA						
AL Herseth Sandlin	Y	Y	Y	Y	Y	N
TENNESSEE						
1 **Roe**	Y	Y	N	N	Y	Y
2 **Duncan**	Y	Y	N	N	Y	Y
3 **Wamp**	Y	Y	?	?	?	?
4 Davis	Y	Y	Y	Y	Y	N
5 Cooper	Y	Y	Y	Y	Y	N
6 Gordon	Y	Y	Y	Y	Y	N
7 **Blackburn**	Y	Y	N	N	Y	Y
8 Tanner	Y	Y	Y	Y	Y	N
9 Cohen	Y	Y	Y	Y	Y	N

	796	797	798	799	800	801
TEXAS						
1 **Gohmert**	Y	Y	?	?	?	?
2 **Poe**	Y	Y	N	N	Y	Y
3 **Johnson, S.**	Y	Y	N	N	Y	Y
4 **Hall**	Y	Y	N	N	Y	Y
5 **Hensarling**	Y	Y	N	N	Y	Y
6 **Barton**	Y	Y	N	N	Y	Y
7 **Culberson**	Y	Y	N	N	Y	Y
8 **Brady**	Y	Y	N	N	Y	Y
9 Green, A.	Y	Y	Y	Y	Y	N
10 **McCaul**	Y	Y	N	N	Y	N
11 **Conaway**	Y	Y	N	N	Y	Y
12 **Granger**	Y	Y	N	N	Y	Y
13 **Thornberry**	Y	Y	N	N	Y	Y
14 **Paul**	Y	Y	N	N	Y	Y
15 Hinojosa	Y	Y	?	?	?	?
16 Reyes	Y	Y	Y	Y	Y	N
17 Edwards	Y	Y	Y	Y	Y	N
18 Jackson Lee	Y	Y	Y	Y	Y	N
19 **Neugebauer**	Y	Y	N	N	Y	Y
20 Gonzalez	Y	Y	Y	Y	Y	N
21 **Smith**	Y	Y	?	N	Y	Y
22 **Olson**	Y	Y	N	N	Y	Y
23 Rodriguez	Y	Y	Y	Y	Y	N
24 **Marchant**	Y	Y	N	N	Y	Y
25 Doggett	Y	Y	Y	Y	Y	N
26 **Burgess**	Y	Y	N	N	Y	N
27 Ortiz	Y	Y	Y	Y	Y	N
28 Cuellar	Y	Y	Y	Y	Y	N
29 Green, G.	Y	Y	Y	Y	Y	N
30 Johnson, E.	Y	Y	Y	Y	Y	N
31 **Carter**	+	+	N	N	Y	Y
32 **Sessions**	Y	Y	N	N	Y	N
UTAH						
1 **Bishop**	Y	Y	N	N	Y	Y
2 Matheson	Y	Y	Y	Y	Y	N
3 **Chaffetz**	Y	Y	N	N	Y	Y
VERMONT						
AL Welch	Y	Y	Y	Y	Y	N
VIRGINIA						
1 **Wittman**	Y	Y	N	N	Y	Y
2 Nye	Y	Y	Y	Y	Y	N
3 Scott	Y	Y	Y	Y	Y	N
4 **Forbes**	Y	Y	N	N	Y	?
5 Perriello	Y	Y	Y	Y	Y	N
6 **Goodlatte**	Y	Y	N	N	Y	Y
7 **Cantor**	Y	Y	N	N	Y	Y
8 Moran	Y	Y	Y	Y	Y	N
9 Boucher	Y	Y	Y	Y	Y	N
10 **Wolf**	Y	Y	N	N	Y	N
11 Connolly	Y	Y	Y	Y	Y	N
WASHINGTON						
1 Inslee	Y	Y	Y	Y	Y	N
2 Larsen	Y	Y	Y	Y	Y	N
3 Baird	Y	Y	N	Y	Y	N
4 **Hastings**	Y	Y	N	N	Y	Y
5 **McMorris Rodgers**	Y	Y	N	N	Y	Y
6 Dicks	Y	Y	Y	Y	Y	N
7 McDermott	Y	Y	Y	Y	Y	N
8 **Reichert**	Y	Y	N	N	Y	Y
9 Smith	Y	Y	Y	Y	Y	N
WEST VIRGINIA						
1 Mollohan	Y	Y	Y	Y	Y	N
2 **Capito**	Y	Y	N	N	Y	Y
3 Rahall	Y	Y	Y	Y	Y	N
WISCONSIN						
1 **Ryan**	Y	Y	N	N	Y	Y
2 Baldwin	Y	Y	Y	Y	Y	N
3 Kind	Y	Y	Y	Y	Y	N
4 Moore	Y	Y	Y	Y	Y	N
5 **Sensenbrenner**	Y	Y	N	N	Y	Y
6 **Petri**	Y	Y	N	N	Y	Y
7 Obey	Y	Y	?	Y	Y	N
8 Kagen	Y	Y	Y	Y	Y	N
WYOMING						
AL **Lummis**	Y	Y	N	N	Y	Y
DELEGATES						
Faleomavaega (A.S.)						?
Norton (D.C.)						N
Bordallo (Guam)						N
Sablan (N. Marianas)						N
Pierluisi (P.R.)						N
Christensen (V.I.)						N

IN THE HOUSE | By Vote Number

802. **HR 3585. Solar Energy Technology Programs/Business Recommendations.** Kaptur, D-Ohio, amendment that would require the Energy Department Solar Technology Roadmap Committee to issue recommendations for linking solar power research to the development of commercial products that can be manufactured and sold domestically. Adopted in Committee of the Whole 395-24: D 251-0; R 144-24. Oct. 22, 2009.

803. **HR 3585. Solar Energy Technology Programs/Solar Energy Storage.** Klein, D-Fla., amendment that would include research on solar energy storage technology as an eligible use of funding under the bill's solar technology research and development grant program. Adopted in Committee of the Whole 414-5: D 250-0; R 164-5. Oct. 22, 2009.

804. **HR 3585. Solar Energy Technology Programs/Water-Efficient Solar Technology.** Titus, D-Nev., amendment that would include the development of solar technology products that are water-efficient as an eligible use of funds under the bill's solar technology grant program and direct the Solar Technology Roadmap Committee to review those products. Adopted in Committee of the Whole 407-9: D 247-1; R 160-8. Oct. 22, 2009.

805. **HR 3585. Solar Energy Technology Programs/Public Comment.** Heinrich, D-N.M., amendment that would require the Energy Department's Solar Technology Roadmap Committee to release a draft of its report one month prior to publication to allow for public comment. Adopted in Committee of the Whole 420-0: D 251-0; R 169-0. Oct. 22, 2009.

806. **HR 3585. Solar Energy Technology Programs/Solar Thermal and Photovoltaic Technologies.** Himes, D-Conn., amendment that would clarify that solar thermal technologies and concentrating solar photovoltaic technologies would be included within the scope of the bill's research and development program. Adopted in Committee of the Whole 410-6: D 247-0; R 163-6. Oct. 22, 2009.

	802	803	804	805	806
ALABAMA					
1 **Bonner**	Y	Y	Y	Y	Y
2 Bright	Y	Y	Y	Y	Y
3 **Rogers**	Y	Y	Y	Y	Y
4 **Aderholt**	Y	Y	Y	Y	Y
5 Griffith	Y	Y	Y	Y	Y
6 **Bachus**	Y	Y	Y	Y	Y
7 Davis	?	?	?	?	?
ALASKA					
AL **Young**	?	?	?	?	?
ARIZONA					
1 Kirkpatrick	Y	Y	Y	Y	Y
2 **Franks**	N	N	N	Y	N
3 **Shadegg**	N	Y	Y	Y	Y
4 Pastor	Y	Y	Y	Y	Y
5 Mitchell	Y	Y	Y	Y	Y
6 **Flake**	N	N	N	Y	N
7 Grijalva	Y	Y	Y	Y	Y
8 Giffords	Y	Y	Y	Y	Y
ARKANSAS					
1 Berry	?	Y	Y	Y	Y
2 Snyder	Y	Y	Y	Y	Y
3 **Boozman**	Y	Y	Y	Y	Y
4 Ross	Y	Y	Y	Y	Y
CALIFORNIA					
1 Thompson	Y	Y	Y	Y	Y
2 **Herger**	Y	Y	Y	Y	Y
3 **Lungren**	Y	Y	Y	Y	Y
4 **McClintock**	N	N	N	Y	N
5 Matsui	Y	Y	Y	Y	Y
6 Woolsey	Y	Y	Y	?	Y
7 Miller, George	Y	Y	Y	Y	Y
8 Pelosi					
9 Lee	Y	Y	Y	Y	Y
10 Vacant					
11 McNerney	Y	Y	Y	Y	Y
12 Speier	Y	Y	Y	Y	Y
13 Stark	Y	Y	Y	Y	Y
14 Eshoo	Y	Y	Y	Y	Y
15 Honda	Y	Y	Y	Y	Y
16 Lofgren	?	?	?	?	?
17 Farr	Y	Y	Y	Y	Y
18 Cardoza	?	?	?	?	?
19 **Radanovich**	Y	Y	Y	Y	Y
20 Costa	Y	Y	Y	Y	Y
21 **Nunes**	Y	Y	Y	Y	Y
22 **McCarthy**	Y	Y	Y	Y	Y
23 Capps	Y	Y	Y	Y	Y
24 **Gallegly**	Y	Y	Y	Y	Y
25 **McKeon**	Y	Y	Y	Y	Y
26 **Dreier**	?	?	?	?	?
27 Sherman	Y	Y	Y	Y	Y
28 Berman	Y	Y	Y	Y	Y
29 Schiff	Y	Y	Y	Y	Y
30 Waxman	Y	Y	Y	Y	?
31 Becerra	Y	Y	?	Y	Y
32 Chu	Y	Y	Y	Y	Y
33 Watson	Y	Y	Y	Y	Y
34 Roybal-Allard	Y	Y	Y	Y	Y
35 Waters	Y	?	Y	Y	Y
36 Harman	Y	Y	Y	Y	Y
37 Richardson	?	?	?	?	?
38 Napolitano	Y	Y	Y	Y	Y
39 Sánchez, Linda	Y	Y	Y	Y	Y
40 **Royce**	Y	Y	Y	Y	Y
41 **Lewis**	N	Y	Y	Y	Y
42 **Miller, Gary**	Y	Y	Y	Y	Y
43 Baca	Y	Y	Y	Y	Y
44 **Calvert**	Y	Y	Y	Y	Y
45 **Bono Mack**	Y	Y	Y	Y	Y
46 **Rohrabacher**	Y	Y	Y	Y	Y
47 Sanchez, Loretta	Y	Y	Y	Y	Y
48 **Campbell**	Y	Y	Y	Y	Y
49 **Issa**	Y	Y	Y	Y	Y
50 **Bilbray**	Y	Y	Y	Y	Y
51 Filner	Y	Y	Y	Y	Y
52 **Hunter**	Y	Y	Y	Y	Y
53 Davis	Y	Y	Y	?	?

	802	803	804	805	806
COLORADO					
1 DeGette	Y	Y	Y	Y	Y
2 Polis	Y	Y	Y	Y	Y
3 Salazar	Y	Y	Y	Y	Y
4 Markey	Y	Y	Y	Y	Y
5 **Lamborn**	Y	Y	Y	Y	Y
6 **Coffman**	Y	Y	Y	Y	Y
7 Perlmutter	Y	Y	Y	Y	Y
CONNECTICUT					
1 Larson	Y	Y	Y	Y	Y
2 Courtney	Y	Y	Y	Y	Y
3 DeLauro	Y	Y	Y	Y	Y
4 Himes	Y	Y	Y	Y	Y
5 Murphy	Y	Y	Y	Y	?
DELAWARE					
AL **Castle**	Y	Y	Y	Y	Y
FLORIDA					
1 **Miller**	N	Y	Y	Y	Y
2 Boyd	Y	Y	Y	Y	Y
3 Brown	Y	Y	Y	Y	Y
4 **Crenshaw**	Y	Y	Y	Y	Y
5 **Brown-Waite**	Y	Y	Y	Y	Y
6 **Stearns**	Y	Y	Y	Y	Y
7 **Mica**	Y	Y	Y	Y	Y
8 Grayson	Y	Y	Y	Y	Y
9 **Bilirakis**	Y	Y	Y	Y	Y
10 **Young**	Y	Y	Y	Y	Y
11 Castor	Y	Y	Y	Y	Y
12 **Putnam**	Y	Y	Y	Y	Y
13 **Buchanan**	Y	Y	Y	Y	Y
14 **Mack**	Y	Y	Y	Y	Y
15 **Posey**	Y	Y	Y	Y	Y
16 **Rooney**	N	Y	Y	Y	Y
17 Meek	Y	Y	Y	Y	Y
18 **Ros-Lehtinen**	Y	Y	Y	Y	Y
19 Wexler	Y	Y	Y	Y	Y
20 Wasserman Schultz	Y	Y	Y	Y	Y
21 **Diaz-Balart, L.**	Y	Y	Y	Y	Y
22 Klein	Y	Y	Y	Y	Y
23 Hastings	Y	Y	Y	Y	Y
24 Kosmas	Y	Y	Y	Y	Y
25 **Diaz-Balart, M.**	Y	Y	Y	Y	Y
GEORGIA					
1 **Kingston**	Y	Y	Y	Y	Y
2 Bishop	Y	Y	Y	Y	Y
3 **Westmoreland**	N	N	N	Y	Y
4 Johnson	Y	Y	Y	Y	Y
5 Lewis	Y	Y	Y	Y	Y
6 **Price**	N	Y	Y	Y	Y
7 **Linder**	Y	Y	Y	Y	Y
8 Marshall	Y	Y	Y	Y	Y
9 **Deal**	Y	Y	Y	Y	Y
10 **Broun**	N	N	N	Y	N
11 **Gingrey**	Y	Y	Y	Y	Y
12 Barrow	Y	Y	Y	Y	Y
13 Scott	Y	Y	Y	Y	Y
HAWAII					
1 Abercrombie	?	?	?	?	?
2 Hirono	Y	Y	Y	Y	Y
IDAHO					
1 Minnick	Y	Y	Y	Y	Y
2 **Simpson**	Y	Y	Y	Y	Y
ILLINOIS					
1 Rush	Y	Y	Y	Y	Y
2 Jackson	Y	Y	Y	Y	Y
3 Lipinski	Y	Y	Y	Y	Y
4 Gutierrez	Y	Y	Y	Y	Y
5 Quigley	Y	Y	Y	Y	Y
6 **Roskam**	Y	Y	Y	Y	Y
7 Davis	Y	Y	Y	Y	Y
8 Bean	?	?	?	?	?
9 Schakowsky	Y	Y	Y	Y	Y
10 **Kirk**	Y	Y	Y	Y	Y
11 Halvorson	Y	Y	Y	Y	Y
12 Costello	Y	Y	Y	Y	Y
13 **Biggert**	Y	Y	Y	Y	Y
14 Foster	Y	Y	Y	Y	Y
15 **Johnson**	Y	Y	Y	Y	Y

KEY   **Republicans**   Democrats

Y Voted for (yea)	**X** Paired against	**C** Voted "present" to avoid possible conflict of interest
# Paired for	**–** Announced against	
+ Announced for	**P** Voted "present"	**?** Did not vote or otherwise make a position known
N Voted against (nay)		

	802	803	804	805	806
16 Manzullo	Y	Y	Y	Y	Y
17 Hare	Y	Y	Y	Y	Y
18 Schock	Y	Y	Y	Y	Y
19 Shimkus	Y	Y	Y	Y	Y
INDIANA					
1 Visclosky	Y	Y	Y	Y	Y
2 Donnelly	Y	Y	Y	Y	Y
3 Souder	Y	Y	Y	Y	Y
4 Buyer	?	?	?	?	?
5 Burton	Y	Y	Y	Y	Y
6 Pence	Y	Y	Y	Y	Y
7 Carson	Y	Y	Y	Y	Y
8 Ellsworth	Y	Y	Y	Y	Y
9 Hill	Y	Y	Y	Y	Y
IOWA					
1 Braley	Y	?	Y	Y	Y
2 Loebsack	Y	Y	Y	Y	Y
3 Boswell	Y	Y	Y	Y	Y
4 Latham	Y	Y	Y	Y	Y
5 King	Y	Y	Y	Y	Y
KANSAS					
1 Moran	Y	Y	Y	Y	Y
2 Jenkins	Y	Y	Y	Y	Y
3 Moore	Y	Y	Y	Y	Y
4 Tiahrt	Y	Y	Y	Y	Y
KENTUCKY					
1 Whitfield	Y	Y	Y	Y	Y
2 Guthrie	Y	Y	Y	Y	Y
3 Yarmuth	Y	Y	Y	Y	Y
4 Davis	Y	Y	Y	Y	Y
5 Rogers	Y	Y	Y	Y	Y
6 Chandler	Y	Y	Y	Y	Y
LOUISIANA					
1 Scalise	Y	Y	Y	Y	Y
2 Cao	Y	Y	Y	Y	Y
3 Melancon	Y	Y	Y	Y	Y
4 Fleming	Y	Y	Y	Y	Y
5 Alexander	Y	Y	Y	Y	Y
6 Cassidy	Y	Y	Y	Y	Y
7 Boustany	Y	Y	Y	Y	Y
MAINE					
1 Pingree	Y	Y	Y	Y	Y
2 Michaud	Y	Y	Y	Y	Y
MARYLAND					
1 Kratovil	Y	Y	Y	Y	Y
2 Ruppersberger	Y	Y	Y	Y	Y
3 Sarbanes	Y	Y	Y	Y	Y
4 Edwards	Y	Y	Y	Y	Y
5 Hoyer	Y	Y	Y	Y	Y
6 Bartlett	Y	Y	Y	Y	Y
7 Cummings	Y	Y	Y	Y	Y
8 Van Hollen	Y	Y	Y	Y	Y
MASSACHUSETTS					
1 Olver	Y	Y	Y	Y	Y
2 Neal	Y	Y	Y	Y	Y
3 McGovern	Y	Y	Y	Y	Y
4 Frank	Y	Y	Y	Y	Y
5 Tsongas	Y	Y	Y	Y	Y
6 Tierney	Y	Y	Y	Y	Y
7 Markey	Y	Y	Y	Y	Y
8 Capuano	Y	Y	Y	Y	Y
9 Lynch	Y	Y	Y	Y	Y
10 Delahunt	Y	Y	Y	Y	Y
MICHIGAN					
1 Stupak	Y	Y	Y	Y	Y
2 Hoekstra	Y	Y	Y	Y	Y
3 Ehlers	Y	Y	Y	Y	Y
4 Camp	Y	Y	Y	Y	Y
5 Kildee	Y	Y	Y	Y	Y
6 Upton	Y	Y	Y	Y	Y
7 Schauer	Y	Y	Y	Y	Y
8 Rogers	Y	Y	Y	Y	Y
9 Peters	Y	Y	Y	Y	Y
10 Miller	Y	Y	Y	Y	Y
11 McCotter	Y	Y	Y	Y	Y
12 Levin	Y	Y	Y	Y	Y
13 Kilpatrick	Y	Y	Y	Y	Y
14 Conyers	Y	Y	Y	Y	Y
15 Dingell	Y	Y	Y	Y	Y
MINNESOTA					
1 Walz	Y	Y	Y	Y	Y
2 Kline	Y	Y	Y	Y	Y
3 Paulsen	Y	Y	Y	Y	Y
4 McCollum	Y	Y	Y	Y	Y

	802	803	804	805	806
5 Ellison	Y	Y	?	Y	Y
6 Bachmann	Y	Y	Y	Y	Y
7 Peterson	Y	Y	Y	Y	Y
8 Oberstar	Y	Y	Y	Y	Y
MISSISSIPPI					
1 Childers	Y	Y	Y	Y	Y
2 Thompson	Y	Y	Y	Y	Y
3 Harper	Y	Y	Y	Y	Y
4 Taylor	Y	Y	Y	Y	Y
MISSOURI					
1 Clay	Y	Y	Y	Y	Y
2 Akin	Y	Y	Y	Y	Y
3 Carnahan	Y	Y	Y	Y	Y
4 Skelton	Y	Y	Y	Y	Y
5 Cleaver	Y	Y	Y	Y	Y
6 Graves	Y	Y	Y	Y	Y
7 Blunt	N	Y	Y	Y	Y
8 Emerson	Y	Y	Y	Y	Y
9 Luetkemeyer	Y	Y	Y	Y	Y
MONTANA					
AL Rehberg	Y	Y	Y	Y	Y
NEBRASKA					
1 Fortenberry	Y	Y	Y	Y	Y
2 Terry	Y	Y	Y	Y	Y
3 Smith	Y	Y	Y	Y	Y
NEVADA					
1 Berkley	Y	Y	Y	Y	Y
2 Heller	Y	Y	Y	Y	Y
3 Titus	Y	Y	Y	Y	Y
NEW HAMPSHIRE					
1 Shea-Porter	Y	Y	Y	Y	Y
2 Hodes	Y	Y	Y	Y	Y
NEW JERSEY					
1 Andrews	Y	Y	Y	Y	Y
2 LoBiondo	Y	Y	Y	Y	Y
3 Adler	Y	Y	Y	Y	Y
4 Smith	Y	Y	Y	Y	Y
5 Garrett	N	Y	Y	Y	Y
6 Pallone	Y	Y	Y	Y	Y
7 Lance	Y	Y	Y	Y	Y
8 Pascrell	Y	Y	Y	Y	Y
9 Rothman	Y	Y	Y	Y	?
10 Payne	Y	Y	Y	Y	Y
11 Frelinghuysen	Y	Y	Y	Y	Y
12 Holt	Y	Y	Y	Y	Y
13 Sires	Y	Y	Y	Y	Y
NEW MEXICO					
1 Heinrich	Y	Y	Y	Y	Y
2 Teague	Y	Y	Y	Y	Y
3 Lujan	Y	Y	Y	Y	Y
NEW YORK					
1 Bishop	Y	Y	Y	Y	Y
2 Israel	Y	Y	Y	Y	Y
3 King	Y	Y	Y	Y	Y
4 McCarthy	Y	Y	?	Y	Y
5 Ackerman	Y	Y	?	Y	Y
6 Meeks	Y	Y	Y	Y	Y
7 Crowley	Y	Y	Y	Y	Y
8 Nadler	Y	Y	Y	Y	Y
9 Weiner	Y	Y	Y	Y	Y
10 Towns	Y	?	Y	Y	Y
11 Clarke	Y	Y	Y	Y	Y
12 Velázquez	Y	Y	Y	Y	Y
13 McMahon	Y	Y	Y	Y	Y
14 Maloney	Y	Y	Y	Y	Y
15 Rangel	Y	Y	Y	Y	Y
16 Serrano	Y	Y	Y	Y	Y
17 Engel	Y	Y	Y	Y	Y
18 Lowey	Y	Y	Y	Y	Y
19 Hall	Y	Y	Y	Y	Y
20 Murphy	Y	Y	Y	Y	Y
21 Tonko	Y	Y	Y	Y	Y
22 Hinchey	Y	Y	Y	Y	Y
23 Vacant					
24 Arcuri	Y	Y	Y	Y	Y
25 Maffei	Y	Y	Y	Y	Y
26 Lee	Y	Y	Y	Y	Y
27 Higgins	Y	Y	Y	Y	Y
28 Slaughter	Y	Y	Y	Y	Y
29 Massa	Y	Y	Y	Y	Y
NORTH CAROLINA					
1 Butterfield	Y	Y	Y	Y	Y
2 Etheridge	Y	Y	Y	Y	Y
3 Jones	Y	Y	Y	Y	Y
4 Price	Y	Y	Y	Y	Y

	802	803	804	805	806
5 Foxx	Y	Y	Y	Y	Y
6 Coble	N	Y	Y	Y	Y
7 McIntyre	Y	Y	Y	Y	Y
8 Kissell	Y	Y	Y	Y	Y
9 Myrick	Y	Y	Y	Y	Y
10 McHenry	Y	Y	Y	Y	Y
11 Shuler	Y	Y	Y	Y	Y
12 Watt	Y	Y	Y	Y	Y
13 Miller	Y	Y	Y	Y	Y
NORTH DAKOTA					
AL Pomeroy	Y	Y	Y	Y	Y
OHIO					
1 Driehaus	Y	Y	Y	Y	Y
2 Schmidt	Y	Y	Y	Y	Y
3 Turner	Y	Y	Y	Y	Y
4 Jordan	Y	Y	Y	Y	Y
5 Latta	Y	Y	Y	Y	Y
6 Wilson	Y	Y	Y	Y	Y
7 Austria	Y	Y	Y	Y	Y
8 Boehner	Y	Y	Y	Y	Y
9 Kaptur	Y	Y	Y	Y	Y
10 Kucinich	Y	Y	Y	Y	Y
11 Fudge	Y	Y	Y	Y	Y
12 Tiberi	Y	Y	Y	Y	Y
13 Sutton	Y	Y	Y	Y	Y
14 LaTourette	Y	Y	Y	Y	Y
15 Kilroy	Y	Y	Y	Y	Y
16 Boccieri	Y	Y	Y	Y	Y
17 Ryan	Y	Y	Y	Y	Y
18 Space	Y	Y	Y	Y	Y
OKLAHOMA					
1 Sullivan	Y	Y	?	Y	Y
2 Boren	Y	Y	Y	Y	Y
3 Lucas	Y	Y	Y	Y	Y
4 Cole	Y	Y	Y	Y	Y
5 Fallin	Y	Y	Y	Y	Y
OREGON					
1 Wu	Y	Y	Y	Y	Y
2 Walden	?	?	?	?	?
3 Blumenauer	Y	Y	Y	Y	Y
4 DeFazio	Y	Y	Y	Y	Y
5 Schrader	Y	Y	Y	Y	Y
PENNSYLVANIA					
1 Brady	Y	Y	Y	Y	Y
2 Fattah	Y	Y	Y	Y	Y
3 Dahlkemper	Y	Y	Y	Y	Y
4 Altmire	Y	Y	N	Y	Y
5 Thompson	Y	Y	Y	Y	Y
6 Gerlach	Y	Y	Y	Y	Y
7 Sestak	Y	Y	Y	Y	Y
8 Murphy, P.	Y	Y	Y	Y	Y
9 Shuster	Y	Y	Y	Y	Y
10 Carney	Y	Y	Y	Y	Y
11 Kanjorski	Y	Y	Y	Y	Y
12 Murtha	Y	Y	Y	Y	Y
13 Schwartz	Y	Y	Y	Y	Y
14 Doyle	Y	Y	Y	Y	Y
15 Dent	Y	Y	Y	Y	Y
16 Pitts	Y	Y	Y	Y	Y
17 Holden	Y	Y	Y	Y	Y
18 Murphy, T.	Y	Y	Y	Y	Y
19 Platts	Y	Y	Y	Y	Y
RHODE ISLAND					
1 Kennedy	Y	Y	Y	Y	Y
2 Langevin	Y	Y	Y	Y	Y
SOUTH CAROLINA					
1 Brown	Y	Y	Y	Y	Y
2 Wilson	N	Y	Y	Y	Y
3 Barrett	?	?	?	?	?
4 Inglis	Y	Y	Y	Y	Y
5 Spratt	Y	Y	Y	Y	Y
6 Clyburn	Y	Y	Y	Y	Y
SOUTH DAKOTA					
AL Herseth Sandlin	Y	Y	Y	Y	Y
TENNESSEE					
1 Roe	Y	Y	Y	Y	Y
2 Duncan	Y	Y	Y	Y	Y
3 Wamp	?	?	?	?	?
4 Davis	Y	Y	Y	Y	Y
5 Cooper	Y	Y	Y	Y	Y
6 Gordon	Y	Y	Y	?	Y
7 Blackburn	Y	Y	Y	Y	Y
8 Tanner	Y	Y	Y	Y	Y
9 Cohen	Y	Y	Y	Y	Y

	802	803	804	805	806
TEXAS					
1 Gohmert	?	?	?	?	?
2 Poe	N	Y	Y	Y	Y
3 Johnson, S.	N	Y	Y	Y	Y
4 Hall	Y	Y	Y	Y	Y
5 Hensarling	N	Y	Y	Y	Y
6 Barton	N	Y	Y	Y	Y
7 Culberson	Y	Y	Y	Y	Y
8 Brady	Y	Y	Y	Y	Y
9 Green, A.	Y	Y	Y	Y	Y
10 McCaul	Y	Y	Y	Y	Y
11 Conaway	Y	Y	Y	Y	Y
12 Granger	Y	Y	Y	Y	Y
13 Thornberry	Y	Y	Y	Y	Y
14 Paul	N	N	N	Y	N
15 Hinojosa	?	?	?	?	?
16 Reyes	Y	Y	Y	Y	Y
17 Edwards	Y	Y	?	Y	Y
18 Jackson Lee	Y	Y	Y	Y	Y
19 Neugebauer	Y	Y	Y	Y	Y
20 Gonzalez	Y	Y	Y	Y	Y
21 Smith	Y	Y	Y	Y	Y
22 Olson	Y	Y	Y	Y	Y
23 Rodriguez	Y	Y	?	Y	Y
24 Marchant	Y	Y	Y	Y	Y
25 Doggett	Y	Y	Y	Y	Y
26 Burgess	N	Y	Y	Y	Y
27 Ortiz	Y	Y	Y	Y	Y
28 Cuellar	Y	Y	Y	Y	Y
29 Green, G.	Y	Y	Y	Y	Y
30 Johnson, E.	Y	Y	Y	Y	Y
31 Carter	Y	Y	Y	Y	Y
32 Sessions	Y	Y	Y	Y	Y
UTAH					
1 Bishop	N	Y	Y	Y	Y
2 Matheson	Y	Y	Y	Y	Y
3 Chaffetz	Y	Y	Y	Y	Y
VERMONT					
AL Welch	Y	Y	Y	Y	Y
VIRGINIA					
1 Wittman	Y	Y	Y	Y	Y
2 Nye	Y	Y	Y	Y	Y
3 Scott	Y	Y	Y	Y	Y
4 Forbes	?	?	?	?	?
5 Perriello	Y	Y	Y	Y	Y
6 Goodlatte	Y	Y	Y	Y	Y
7 Cantor	?	Y	Y	Y	Y
8 Moran	Y	Y	Y	Y	Y
9 Boucher	Y	Y	Y	Y	Y
10 Wolf	Y	Y	Y	Y	Y
11 Connolly	Y	Y	Y	Y	Y
WASHINGTON					
1 Inslee	Y	Y	Y	Y	?
2 Larsen	Y	Y	Y	Y	Y
3 Baird	Y	Y	Y	Y	Y
4 Hastings	Y	Y	Y	Y	Y
5 McMorris Rodgers	Y	Y	Y	Y	Y
6 Dicks	Y	Y	Y	Y	Y
7 McDermott	Y	Y	Y	Y	Y
8 Reichert	N	Y	Y	Y	Y
9 Smith	Y	Y	Y	Y	Y
WEST VIRGINIA					
1 Mollohan	Y	Y	Y	Y	Y
2 Capito	Y	Y	Y	Y	Y
3 Rahall	Y	Y	Y	Y	Y
WISCONSIN					
1 Ryan	Y	Y	Y	Y	Y
2 Baldwin	Y	Y	Y	Y	Y
3 Kind	Y	Y	Y	Y	Y
4 Moore	Y	Y	Y	Y	Y
5 Sensenbrenner	N	Y	N	Y	N
6 Petri	N	Y	N	Y	Y
7 Obey	Y	Y	Y	Y	Y
8 Kagen	Y	Y	Y	Y	Y
WYOMING					
AL Lummis	Y	Y	Y	Y	Y
DELEGATES					
Faleomavaega (A.S.)	?	?	?	?	?
Norton (D.C.)	Y	Y	Y	Y	Y
Bordallo (Guam)	Y	Y	Y	Y	Y
Sablan (N. Marianas)	Y	Y	Y	Y	Y
Pierluisi (P.R.)	?	Y	Y	Y	Y
Christensen (V.I.)	Y	Y	Y	Y	Y

IN THE HOUSE | By Vote Number

807. **HR 3585. Solar Energy Technology Programs/Passage.** Passage of the bill that would direct the Energy secretary to establish a program to research and develop solar technologies and create a Solar Technology Roadmap Committee to examine current and future needs in solar technology. It would authorize $2.25 billion for the program from fiscal 2011 through 2015. It would direct the Energy secretary to award up to $300 million in competitive grants for projects to develop solar technologies that can be widely manufactured. Passed 310-106: D 247-0; R 63-106. Oct. 22, 2009.

808. **H Res 175. Condemning Iranian Government/Adoption.** Watson, D-Calif., motion to suspend the rules and adopt the resolution that would condemn the government of Iran for its persecution of the Baha'i minority and its violations of the International Covenants on Human Rights. Motion agreed to 407-2: D 244-1; R 163-1. A two-thirds majority of those present and voting (272 in this case) is required for adoption under suspension of the rules. Oct. 22, 2009.

809. **HR 3619. Coast Guard Authorization/Previous Question.** Matsui, D-Calif., motion to order the previous question (thus ending debate and possibility of amendment) on adoption of the rule (H Res 853) that would provide for House floor consideration of the bill that would authorize funding for the Coast Guard at $10 billion for fiscal 2010 and increase the number of military personnel by 1,500 for a total of 47,000 members. Motion agreed to 236-171: D 236-6; R 0-165. Oct. 22, 2009.

810. **HR 3619. Coast Guard Authorization/Rule.** Adoption of the rule (H Res 853) that would provide for House floor consideration of the bill that would authorize funding for the Coast Guard at $10 billion for fiscal 2010 and increase the number of military personnel by 1,500 for a total of 47,000 members. Adopted 213-192: D 213-27; R 0-165. Oct. 22, 2009.

811. **H Res 836. Support Teen Read Week/Adoption.** Davis, D-Calif., motion to suspend the rules and adopt the resolution that would express support for Teen Read Week. Motion agreed to 405-0: D 242-0; R 163-0. A two-thirds majority of those present and voting (270 in this case) is required for adoption under suspension of the rules. Oct. 22, 2009.

	807	808	809	810	811
ALABAMA					
1 Bonner	N	Y	N	N	Y
2 Bright	Y	Y	N	N	Y
3 Rogers	Y	Y	N	N	Y
4 Aderholt	Y	Y	N	N	Y
5 Griffith	Y	Y	Y	Y	Y
6 Bachus	N	Y	N	N	Y
7 Davis	?	?	?	?	?
ALASKA					
AL Young	?	?	?	?	?
ARIZONA					
1 Kirkpatrick	Y	Y	Y	Y	Y
2 Franks	N	Y	N	N	Y
3 Shadegg	N	Y	N	N	Y
4 Pastor	Y	Y	Y	Y	Y
5 Mitchell	Y	Y	Y	Y	Y
6 Flake	N	Y	N	N	Y
7 Grijalva	Y	Y	Y	Y	Y
8 Giffords	Y	Y	Y	Y	Y
ARKANSAS					
1 Berry	Y	Y	Y	Y	Y
2 Snyder	Y	Y	Y	N	Y
3 Boozman	N	Y	N	N	Y
4 Ross	Y	Y	Y	N	Y
CALIFORNIA					
1 Thompson	Y	Y	Y	Y	Y
2 Herger	N	?	N	N	Y
3 Lungren	Y	Y	N	N	?
4 McClintock	N	Y	N	N	Y
5 Matsui	Y	Y	Y	Y	Y
6 Woolsey	Y	Y	Y	Y	Y
7 Miller, George	Y	Y	Y	Y	Y
8 Pelosi					
9 Lee	Y	Y	Y	Y	Y
10 Vacant					
11 McNerney	Y	Y	Y	Y	Y
12 Speier	Y	Y	Y	Y	Y
13 Stark	Y	Y	Y	Y	Y
14 Eshoo	Y	Y	Y	Y	Y
15 Honda	Y	Y	Y	Y	Y
16 Lofgren	?	?	?	?	?
17 Farr	Y	Y	Y	Y	Y
18 Cardoza	?	?	?	?	?
19 Radanovich	N	Y	?	?	?
20 Costa	Y	Y	Y	N	Y
21 Nunes	N	Y	N	N	Y
22 McCarthy	N	Y	N	N	Y
23 Capps	Y	Y	Y	Y	Y
24 Gallegly	N	Y	N	N	Y
25 McKeon	Y	Y	N	N	Y
26 Dreier	?	?	?	?	?
27 Sherman	Y	Y	Y	Y	Y
28 Berman	Y	Y	Y	Y	Y
29 Schiff	Y	Y	Y	Y	Y
30 Waxman	Y	Y	Y	Y	Y
31 Becerra	Y	Y	Y	Y	Y
32 Chu	Y	Y	Y	Y	Y
33 Watson	Y	Y	Y	Y	Y
34 Roybal-Allard	Y	Y	Y	Y	Y
35 Waters	Y	Y	Y	Y	Y
36 Harman	Y	Y	Y	Y	Y
37 Richardson	?	?	?	?	?
38 Napolitano	Y	Y	Y	Y	Y
39 Sánchez, Linda	Y	Y	Y	Y	Y
40 Royce	N	Y	N	N	Y
41 Lewis	Y	Y	N	N	Y
42 Miller, Gary	N	Y	N	N	Y
43 Baca	Y	Y	Y	Y	Y
44 Calvert	Y	Y	N	N	Y
45 Bono Mack	Y	Y	N	N	Y
46 Rohrabacher	Y	Y	N	N	Y
47 Sanchez, Loretta	Y	Y	Y	Y	Y
48 Campbell	N	Y	N	N	Y
49 Issa	N	Y	N	N	Y
50 Bilbray	Y	Y	N	N	Y
51 Filner	Y	Y	Y	Y	Y
52 Hunter	N	Y	N	N	Y
53 Davis	Y	Y	Y	Y	Y

	807	808	809	810	811
COLORADO					
1 DeGette	Y	Y	Y	Y	Y
2 Polis	Y	Y	Y	Y	Y
3 Salazar	Y	Y	Y	Y	Y
4 Markey	Y	Y	Y	Y	Y
5 Lamborn	N	Y	N	N	Y
6 Coffman	N	Y	N	N	Y
7 Perlmutter	Y	Y	Y	?	Y
CONNECTICUT					
1 Larson	Y	Y	Y	Y	Y
2 Courtney	Y	Y	Y	Y	Y
3 DeLauro	Y	Y	Y	Y	Y
4 Himes	Y	Y	Y	Y	Y
5 Murphy	Y	Y	Y	Y	Y
DELAWARE					
AL Castle	Y	Y	N	N	Y
FLORIDA					
1 Miller	N	Y	N	N	Y
2 Boyd	Y	Y	Y	Y	Y
3 Brown	Y	Y	Y	Y	Y
4 Crenshaw	Y	Y	N	N	Y
5 Brown-Waite	N	Y	N	N	Y
6 Stearns	N	Y	N	N	Y
7 Mica	N	Y	N	N	Y
8 Grayson	Y	Y	Y	Y	Y
9 Bilirakis	N	Y	N	N	Y
10 Young	Y	Y	N	N	Y
11 Castor	Y	Y	Y	Y	Y
12 Putnam	Y	Y	N	N	Y
13 Buchanan	Y	Y	N	N	Y
14 Mack	N	Y	N	N	Y
15 Posey	Y	Y	N	N	Y
16 Rooney	Y	Y	N	N	Y
17 Meek	Y	Y	Y	Y	Y
18 Ros-Lehtinen	Y	Y	N	N	Y
19 Wexler	Y	Y	Y	Y	Y
20 Wasserman Schultz	Y	Y	Y	Y	Y
21 Diaz-Balart, L.	Y	Y	N	N	Y
22 Klein	Y	Y	Y	Y	Y
23 Hastings	Y	Y	Y	Y	Y
24 Kosmas	Y	Y	Y	Y	Y
25 Diaz-Balart, M.	Y	Y	N	N	Y
GEORGIA					
1 Kingston	N	Y	N	N	Y
2 Bishop	Y	Y	Y	Y	Y
3 Westmoreland	N	Y	N	N	Y
4 Johnson	Y	Y	Y	Y	Y
5 Lewis	Y	Y	Y	Y	Y
6 Price	N	Y	N	N	Y
7 Linder	N	?	N	N	Y
8 Marshall	Y	?	Y	Y	Y
9 Deal	N	Y	N	N	Y
10 Broun	N	Y	N	N	Y
11 Gingrey	N	Y	N	N	Y
12 Barrow	Y	Y	Y	Y	Y
13 Scott	Y	Y	Y	Y	Y
HAWAII					
1 Abercrombie	?	?	?	?	?
2 Hirono	Y	Y	Y	Y	Y
IDAHO					
1 Minnick	Y	Y	N	N	Y
2 Simpson	Y	Y	N	N	Y
ILLINOIS					
1 Rush	Y	Y	Y	Y	Y
2 Jackson	Y	Y	Y	Y	Y
3 Lipinski	Y	Y	Y	Y	Y
4 Gutierrez	Y	Y	Y	N	?
5 Quigley	Y	Y	Y	Y	Y
6 Roskam	N	Y	N	N	Y
7 Davis	Y	Y	Y	Y	Y
8 Bean	?	?	?	?	?
9 Schakowsky	Y	Y	Y	Y	Y
10 Kirk	Y	Y	N	N	Y
11 Halvorson	Y	Y	Y	Y	Y
12 Costello	Y	Y	N	N	Y
13 Biggert	Y	Y	?	?	?
14 Foster	Y	Y	Y	Y	Y
15 Johnson	Y	Y	N	N	Y

KEY   **Republicans**   Democrats

Y Voted for (yea)	X Paired against	C Voted "present" to avoid possible conflict of interest
# Paired for	– Announced against	
+ Announced for	P Voted "present"	? Did not vote or otherwise make a position known
N Voted against (nay)		

	807	808	809	810	811
16 Manzullo	N	Y	N	N	Y
17 Hare	Y	Y	Y	Y	Y
18 Schock	Y	Y	N	N	Y
19 Shimkus	N	Y	N	N	Y
INDIANA					
1 Visclosky	Y	Y	Y	Y	Y
2 Donnelly	Y	Y	Y	Y	Y
3 Souder	N	Y	N	N	Y
4 Buyer	?	?	?	?	?
5 Burton	N	Y	N	N	Y
6 Pence	N	Y	N	N	Y
7 Carson	Y	Y	Y	Y	Y
8 Ellsworth	Y	Y	Y	N	Y
9 Hill	Y	Y	Y	N	Y
IOWA					
1 Braley	Y	Y	Y	Y	Y
2 Loebsack	Y	Y	Y	Y	Y
3 Boswell	Y	Y	Y	Y	Y
4 Latham	N	Y	N	N	Y
5 King	N	Y	N	N	Y
KANSAS					
1 Moran	N	Y	N	N	Y
2 Jenkins	N	Y	N	N	Y
3 Moore	Y	Y	Y	N	Y
4 Tiahrt	N	Y	N	N	Y
KENTUCKY					
1 Whitfield	Y	Y	N	N	Y
2 Guthrie	N	Y	N	N	Y
3 Yarmuth	Y	Y	Y	Y	Y
4 Davis	N	Y	N	N	Y
5 Rogers	N	Y	N	N	Y
6 Chandler	Y	Y	Y	N	Y
LOUISIANA					
1 Scalise	N	Y	N	N	Y
2 Cao	Y	Y	N	N	Y
3 Melancon	Y	Y	Y	Y	Y
4 Fleming	N	Y	N	N	Y
5 Alexander	N	Y	N	N	Y
6 Cassidy	Y	Y	N	N	Y
7 Boustany	N	Y	N	N	Y
MAINE					
1 Pingree	Y	Y	Y	Y	Y
2 Michaud	Y	Y	Y	N	Y
MARYLAND					
1 Kratovil	Y	Y	Y	Y	Y
2 Ruppersberger	Y	Y	Y	Y	Y
3 Sarbanes	Y	Y	Y	Y	Y
4 Edwards	Y	Y	Y	Y	Y
5 Hoyer	Y	Y	Y	Y	Y
6 Bartlett	Y	Y	N	N	Y
7 Cummings	Y	Y	Y	Y	Y
8 Van Hollen	Y	Y	Y	Y	Y
MASSACHUSETTS					
1 Olver	Y	Y	Y	Y	Y
2 Neal	Y	Y	Y	Y	Y
3 McGovern	Y	Y	Y	Y	Y
4 Frank	Y	Y	?	?	?
5 Tsongas	Y	?	Y	Y	Y
6 Tierney	Y	Y	Y	Y	Y
7 Markey	Y	Y	Y	Y	Y
8 Capuano	Y	Y	Y	N	Y
9 Lynch	Y	Y	Y	Y	Y
10 Delahunt	Y	Y	Y	Y	Y
MICHIGAN					
1 Stupak	Y	Y	Y	Y	Y
2 Hoekstra	N	Y	N	N	Y
3 Ehlers	Y	Y	N	N	Y
4 Camp	Y	Y	N	N	Y
5 Kildee	Y	Y	Y	N	Y
6 Upton	Y	Y	N	N	Y
7 Schauer	Y	Y	Y	Y	Y
8 Rogers	Y	Y	?	?	?
9 Peters	Y	Y	Y	Y	Y
10 Miller	Y	Y	N	N	Y
11 McCotter	Y	Y	N	N	Y
12 Levin	Y	Y	Y	Y	Y
13 Kilpatrick	Y	Y	Y	Y	Y
14 Conyers	Y	Y	Y	Y	Y
15 Dingell	Y	Y	Y	Y	Y
MINNESOTA					
1 Walz	Y	Y	Y	N	Y
2 Kline	N	Y	N	N	Y
3 Paulsen	Y	Y	N	N	Y
4 McCollum	Y	Y	Y	Y	Y

	807	808	809	810	811
5 Ellison	Y	Y	Y	Y	Y
6 Bachmann	N	?	N	N	Y
7 Peterson	Y	Y	Y	Y	Y
8 Oberstar	Y	Y	Y	Y	Y
MISSISSIPPI					
1 Childers	Y	Y	N	N	Y
2 Thompson	Y	Y	Y	Y	Y
3 Harper	N	Y	N	N	Y
4 Taylor	Y	Y	N	N	Y
MISSOURI					
1 Clay	Y	Y	Y	Y	Y
2 Akin	N	Y	N	N	Y
3 Carnahan	Y	Y	Y	Y	Y
4 Skelton	Y	Y	Y	Y	Y
5 Cleaver	Y	Y	Y	Y	Y
6 Graves	N	Y	N	N	Y
7 Blunt	Y	Y	N	N	Y
8 Emerson	N	Y	N	N	Y
9 Luetkemeyer	N	Y	N	N	Y
MONTANA					
AL Rehberg	N	Y	N	N	Y
NEBRASKA					
1 Fortenberry	Y	Y	N	N	Y
2 Terry	Y	Y	N	N	Y
3 Smith	N	Y	N	N	Y
NEVADA					
1 Berkley	Y	Y	Y	Y	Y
2 Heller	Y	Y	N	N	Y
3 Titus	Y	Y	Y	Y	Y
NEW HAMPSHIRE					
1 Shea-Porter	Y	Y	Y	Y	Y
2 Hodes	Y	Y	Y	Y	Y
NEW JERSEY					
1 Andrews	Y	Y	Y	Y	Y
2 LoBiondo	Y	Y	N	N	Y
3 Adler	Y	Y	Y	N	Y
4 Smith	Y	Y	N	N	Y
5 Garrett	N	Y	N	N	Y
6 Pallone	Y	Y	Y	Y	Y
7 Lance	Y	Y	N	N	Y
8 Pascrell	Y	Y	?	?	?
9 Rothman	Y	Y	Y	Y	Y
10 Payne	Y	Y	Y	Y	Y
11 Frelinghuysen	Y	Y	N	N	Y
12 Holt	Y	Y	Y	Y	Y
13 Sires	Y	Y	Y	Y	Y
NEW MEXICO					
1 Heinrich	Y	Y	Y	Y	Y
2 Teague	Y	Y	Y	Y	Y
3 Lujan	Y	Y	Y	Y	Y
NEW YORK					
1 Bishop	Y	Y	Y	Y	Y
2 Israel	Y	Y	Y	Y	Y
3 King	Y	Y	N	N	Y
4 McCarthy	Y	Y	Y	Y	Y
5 Ackerman	Y	Y	Y	Y	Y
6 Meeks	Y	Y	Y	Y	Y
7 Crowley	Y	Y	Y	Y	Y
8 Nadler	Y	Y	Y	Y	Y
9 Weiner	Y	Y	Y	Y	Y
10 Towns	Y	Y	Y	Y	Y
11 Clarke	Y	Y	Y	Y	Y
12 Velázquez	Y	Y	Y	?	Y
13 McMahon	Y	Y	Y	Y	Y
14 Maloney	Y	Y	Y	Y	Y
15 Rangel	Y	Y	Y	?	Y
16 Serrano	Y	Y	Y	Y	Y
17 Engel	Y	Y	Y	Y	Y
18 Lowey	Y	Y	?	?	?
19 Hall	Y	Y	Y	Y	Y
20 Murphy	Y	Y	Y	N	Y
21 Tonko	Y	Y	Y	Y	Y
22 Hinchey	Y	Y	Y	Y	Y
23 Vacant					
24 Arcuri	Y	Y	Y	Y	Y
25 Maffei	Y	Y	Y	Y	Y
26 Lee	Y	Y	N	N	Y
27 Higgins	Y	Y	Y	Y	Y
28 Slaughter	Y	Y	Y	Y	Y
29 Massa	Y	Y	N	N	Y
NORTH CAROLINA					
1 Butterfield	Y	Y	Y	Y	Y
2 Etheridge	Y	Y	Y	Y	Y
3 Jones	N	Y	N	N	Y
4 Price	Y	Y	Y	Y	Y

	807	808	809	810	811
5 Foxx	N	Y	N	N	Y
6 Coble	N	Y	N	N	?
7 McIntyre	Y	Y	Y	Y	Y
8 Kissell	Y	Y	Y	Y	Y
9 Myrick	N	Y	N	N	Y
10 McHenry	N	Y	N	N	Y
11 Shuler	Y	Y	Y	N	Y
12 Watt	Y	Y	Y	Y	Y
13 Miller	Y	Y	Y	Y	Y
NORTH DAKOTA					
AL Pomeroy	Y	Y	Y	Y	Y
OHIO					
1 Driehaus	Y	Y	Y	Y	Y
2 Schmidt	N	Y	N	N	Y
3 Turner	Y	Y	N	N	Y
4 Jordan	N	Y	N	N	Y
5 Latta	N	Y	N	N	Y
6 Wilson	Y	Y	Y	Y	Y
7 Austria	N	Y	N	N	Y
8 Boehner	N	?	N	N	Y
9 Kaptur	Y	Y	Y	Y	Y
10 Kucinich	Y	N	Y	N	Y
11 Fudge	Y	Y	Y	Y	Y
12 Tiberi	Y	Y	N	N	Y
13 Sutton	Y	Y	Y	Y	Y
14 LaTourette	Y	Y	N	N	Y
15 Kilroy	Y	Y	Y	Y	Y
16 Boccieri	Y	Y	Y	Y	Y
17 Ryan	Y	Y	Y	Y	Y
18 Space	Y	Y	Y	N	Y
OKLAHOMA					
1 Sullivan	N	Y	N	N	Y
2 Boren	Y	Y	Y	Y	Y
3 Lucas	N	Y	N	N	Y
4 Cole	N	Y	N	N	Y
5 Fallin	N	Y	N	N	Y
OREGON					
1 Wu	Y	Y	Y	Y	Y
2 Walden	?	?	?	?	?
3 Blumenauer	Y	Y	Y	Y	Y
4 DeFazio	Y	Y	Y	Y	Y
5 Schrader	Y	Y	Y	Y	Y
PENNSYLVANIA					
1 Brady	Y	Y	Y	Y	Y
2 Fattah	Y	Y	Y	Y	Y
3 Dahlkemper	Y	Y	Y	N	Y
4 Altmire	Y	Y	N	N	Y
5 Thompson	Y	Y	N	N	Y
6 Gerlach	Y	Y	N	N	Y
7 Sestak	Y	Y	Y	Y	Y
8 Murphy, P.	Y	Y	Y	Y	Y
9 Shuster	N	Y	N	N	Y
10 Carney	Y	Y	Y	N	Y
11 Kanjorski	Y	Y	Y	Y	Y
12 Murtha	Y	Y	?	?	?
13 Schwartz	Y	Y	Y	Y	Y
14 Doyle	Y	Y	Y	Y	Y
15 Dent	Y	Y	N	N	Y
16 Pitts	N	Y	N	N	Y
17 Holden	Y	Y	Y	Y	Y
18 Murphy, T.	Y	Y	Y	N	Y
19 Platts	Y	Y	N	N	Y
RHODE ISLAND					
1 Kennedy	Y	Y	Y	Y	Y
2 Langevin	Y	Y	Y	Y	Y
SOUTH CAROLINA					
1 Brown	N	Y	N	N	Y
2 Wilson	N	Y	N	N	Y
3 Barrett	?	?	?	?	?
4 Inglis	N	Y	N	N	Y
5 Spratt	Y	Y	Y	Y	Y
6 Clyburn	Y	Y	Y	Y	Y
SOUTH DAKOTA					
AL Herseth Sandlin	Y	Y	Y	Y	Y
TENNESSEE					
1 Roe	Y	Y	N	N	Y
2 Duncan	N	Y	N	N	Y
3 Wamp	?	?	?	?	?
4 Davis	Y	Y	Y	Y	Y
5 Cooper	Y	Y	Y	Y	Y
6 Gordon	Y	Y	Y	Y	Y
7 Blackburn	N	Y	N	N	Y
8 Tanner	Y	Y	Y	Y	Y
9 Cohen	Y	Y	Y	Y	Y

	807	808	809	810	811
TEXAS					
1 Gohmert	?	?	?	?	?
2 Poe	N	Y	N	N	Y
3 Johnson, S.	N	Y	N	N	Y
4 Hall	Y	Y	N	N	Y
5 Hensarling	N	Y	N	N	Y
6 Barton	Y	Y	N	N	Y
7 Culberson	N	Y	N	N	Y
8 Brady	N	Y	N	N	Y
9 Green, A.	Y	Y	Y	Y	Y
10 McCaul	Y	Y	?	?	?
11 Conaway	N	Y	N	N	Y
12 Granger	N	Y	N	N	Y
13 Thornberry	N	Y	N	N	Y
14 Paul	N	N	N	N	Y
15 Hinojosa	?	?	?	?	?
16 Reyes	Y	Y	Y	Y	Y
17 Edwards	Y	Y	Y	Y	Y
18 Jackson Lee	Y	Y	Y	Y	Y
19 Neugebauer	N	Y	N	N	Y
20 Gonzalez	Y	Y	Y	Y	Y
21 Smith	Y	Y	N	N	Y
22 Olson	N	Y	N	N	Y
23 Rodriguez	Y	Y	Y	Y	Y
24 Marchant	N	Y	N	N	Y
25 Doggett	Y	Y	Y	Y	Y
26 Burgess	N	Y	N	N	Y
27 Ortiz	Y	Y	Y	Y	Y
28 Cuellar	Y	Y	Y	Y	Y
29 Green, G.	Y	Y	Y	Y	Y
30 Johnson, E.	Y	Y	Y	Y	Y
31 Carter	N	Y	N	N	Y
32 Sessions	N	Y	N	N	Y
UTAH					
1 Bishop	N	Y	N	N	Y
2 Matheson	Y	Y	Y	Y	Y
3 Chaffetz	N	Y	N	N	Y
VERMONT					
AL Welch	Y	Y	Y	Y	Y
VIRGINIA					
1 Wittman	Y	Y	N	N	Y
2 Nye	Y	Y	Y	Y	Y
3 Scott	Y	Y	Y	Y	Y
4 Forbes	?	?	?	?	?
5 Perriello	Y	Y	Y	Y	Y
6 Goodlatte	N	Y	N	N	Y
7 Cantor	N	Y	N	N	Y
8 Moran	Y	Y	Y	Y	Y
9 Boucher	Y	Y	Y	Y	Y
10 Wolf	Y	Y	N	N	Y
11 Connolly	Y	Y	Y	Y	Y
WASHINGTON					
1 Inslee	?	?	?	?	?
2 Larsen	Y	Y	Y	Y	Y
3 Baird	Y	Y	N	N	Y
4 Hastings	N	Y	N	N	Y
5 McMorris Rodgers	N	?	N	N	Y
6 Dicks	Y	Y	Y	Y	Y
7 McDermott	Y	Y	Y	Y	Y
8 Reichert	Y	Y	N	N	Y
9 Smith	Y	Y	Y	Y	Y
WEST VIRGINIA					
1 Mollohan	Y	Y	Y	Y	Y
2 Capito	Y	Y	N	N	Y
3 Rahall	Y	Y	Y	Y	Y
WISCONSIN					
1 Ryan	N	Y	N	N	Y
2 Baldwin	Y	Y	Y	Y	Y
3 Kind	Y	Y	Y	Y	Y
4 Moore	Y	Y	Y	Y	Y
5 Sensenbrenner	N	Y	N	N	Y
6 Petri	N	Y	N	N	Y
7 Obey	Y	Y	?	Y	Y
8 Kagen	Y	Y	Y	Y	Y
WYOMING					
AL Lummis	N	Y	N	N	Y
DELEGATES					
Faleomavaega (A.S.)					
Norton (D.C.)					
Bordallo (Guam)					
Sablan (N. Marianas)					
Pierluisi (P.R.)					
Christensen (V.I.)					

IN THE HOUSE | By Vote Number

812. HR 3619. Coast Guard Authorization/Infrastructure Report.
Kratovil, D-Md., amendment that would require the Coast Guard commandant to submit a report reviewing Coast Guard infrastructure needs and confirming that the Homeland Security Department has the appropriate technological capabilities. Adopted in Committee of the Whole 398-0: D 237-0; R 161-0. Oct. 23, 2009.

813. HR 3619. Coast Guard Authorization/Passage.
Passage of the bill that would authorize $10 billion for the Coast Guard for fiscal 2010, including $6.8 billion for operations and maintenance and $1.6 billion for acquisitions. It also would expand Coast Guard and Justice Department authority to prosecute people caught smuggling illegal immigrants by sea. Passed 385-11: D 234-1; R 151-10. Oct. 23, 2009.

814. H Res 368. University of Iowa Wrestling Team/Adoption.
Pierluisi, D-P.R., motion to suspend the rules and adopt the resolution that would congratulate the University of Iowa wrestling team for winning the 2009 NCAA Division I National Wrestling Championships. Motion agreed to 367-1: D 216-1; R 151-0. A two-thirds majority of those present and voting (246 in this case) is required for adoption under suspension of the rules. Oct. 26, 2009.

815. H Res 562. Syracuse University Men's Lacrosse Team/Adoption.
Pierluisi, D-P.R., motion to suspend the rules and adopt the resolution that would congratulate the Syracuse University men's lacrosse team for winning the 2009 NCAA Division I men's lacrosse tournament. Motion agreed to 359-1: D 213-1; R 146-0. A two-thirds majority of those present and voting (240 in this case) is required for adoption under suspension of the rules. Oct. 26, 2009.

816. HR 2996. Fiscal 2010 Interior-Environment Appropriations/Motion to Instruct.
Simpson, R-Idaho, motion to instruct conferees to insist on a provision that would bar the use of funds in the bill to implement any rule requiring reporting of greenhouse gas emissions from manure management systems and withhold approval of the final conference agreement unless it has been available to the managers in an electronic, searchable, downloadable form for at least 72 hours. Motion agreed to 267-147: D 99-147; R 168-0. Oct. 27, 2009.

	812	813	814	815	816
ALABAMA					
1 Bonner	Y	Y	Y	Y	Y
2 Bright	Y	Y	Y	Y	Y
3 Rogers	Y	Y	Y	Y	Y
4 Aderholt	Y	Y	Y	Y	Y
5 Griffith	Y	Y	Y	Y	Y
6 Bachus	Y	Y	Y	Y	Y
7 Davis	?	?	?	?	Y
ALASKA					
AL Young	?	?	Y	Y	Y
ARIZONA					
1 Kirkpatrick	Y	Y	Y	Y	?
2 Franks	Y	N	Y	Y	Y
3 Shadegg	Y	N	?	?	Y
4 Pastor	Y	Y	Y	Y	N
5 Mitchell	Y	Y	Y	Y	Y
6 Flake	Y	N	Y	Y	Y
7 Grijalva	Y	Y	?	?	N
8 Giffords	Y	Y	Y	Y	Y
ARKANSAS					
1 Berry	Y	N	N	N	Y
2 Snyder	Y	Y	Y	Y	N
3 Boozman	Y	Y	Y	Y	Y
4 Ross	Y	Y	Y	Y	Y
CALIFORNIA					
1 Thompson	Y	Y	+	+	Y
2 Herger	Y	Y	Y	Y	Y
3 Lungren	Y	Y	Y	Y	Y
4 McClintock	Y	Y	Y	Y	Y
5 Matsui	Y	Y	?	?	N
6 Woolsey	Y	Y	Y	Y	N
7 Miller, George	Y	Y	Y	Y	N
8 Pelosi					
9 Lee	Y	Y	?	?	N
10 Vacant					
11 McNerney	Y	Y	Y	Y	Y
12 Speier	Y	Y	Y	Y	Y
13 Stark	Y	Y	?	?	N
14 Eshoo	Y	Y	Y	Y	N
15 Honda	?	Y	Y	Y	N
16 Lofgren	?	?	Y	Y	N
17 Farr	Y	Y	Y	Y	N
18 Cardoza	+	+	Y	Y	Y
19 Radanovich	Y	Y	Y	Y	?
20 Costa	Y	Y	?	?	Y
21 Nunes	Y	Y	Y	Y	Y
22 McCarthy	Y	Y	?	?	Y
23 Capps	Y	Y	Y	N	N
24 Gallegly	Y	Y	Y	Y	Y
25 McKeon	Y	Y	Y	?	Y
26 Dreier	?	?	?	?	Y
27 Sherman	Y	Y	Y	N	N
28 Berman	Y	Y	Y	N	N
29 Schiff	Y	Y	Y	Y	N
30 Waxman	Y	Y	Y	Y	N
31 Becerra	Y	Y	Y	Y	N
32 Chu	Y	Y	Y	Y	N
33 Watson	Y	Y	Y	Y	N
34 Roybal-Allard	Y	Y	Y	Y	N
35 Waters	Y	Y	Y	Y	N
36 Harman	Y	Y	Y	Y	N
37 Richardson	?	?	?	+	Y
38 Napolitano	Y	Y	Y	Y	N
39 Sánchez, Linda	Y	Y	Y	Y	N
40 Royce	Y	N	Y	Y	Y
41 Lewis	Y	Y	Y	Y	Y
42 Miller, Gary	Y	Y	?	?	Y
43 Baca	?	?	Y	Y	Y
44 Calvert	+	?	Y	Y	Y
45 Bono Mack	Y	Y	Y	Y	Y
46 Rohrabacher	Y	Y	?	?	Y
47 Sanchez, Loretta	Y	Y	Y	Y	?
48 Campbell	Y	Y	Y	Y	Y
49 Issa	Y	Y	Y	Y	Y
50 Bilbray	Y	Y	Y	Y	Y
51 Filner	Y	Y	Y	Y	N
52 Hunter	Y	Y	Y	Y	Y
53 Davis	Y	Y	Y	Y	N

	812	813	814	815	816
COLORADO					
1 DeGette	Y	Y	Y	Y	N
2 Polis	Y	Y	Y	Y	N
3 Salazar	Y	Y	Y	Y	Y
4 Markey	Y	Y	Y	Y	Y
5 Lamborn	Y	Y	Y	Y	Y
6 Coffman	Y	Y	Y	?	Y
7 Perlmutter	Y	Y	Y	Y	N
CONNECTICUT					
1 Larson	Y	Y	Y	Y	N
2 Courtney	Y	N	Y	Y	N
3 DeLauro	Y	Y	Y	Y	N
4 Himes	Y	Y	Y	Y	N
5 Murphy	Y	Y	Y	Y	N
DELAWARE					
AL Castle	Y	Y	Y	Y	Y
FLORIDA					
1 Miller	Y	Y	Y	Y	Y
2 Boyd	Y	?	?	?	Y
3 Brown	Y	Y	?	?	N
4 Crenshaw	Y	Y	?	?	Y
5 Brown-Waite	Y	Y	?	?	Y
6 Stearns	Y	Y	Y	Y	Y
7 Mica	Y	Y	Y	Y	Y
8 Grayson	Y	Y	?	?	Y
9 Bilirakis	Y	Y	Y	Y	Y
10 Young	Y	Y	?	?	Y
11 Castor	Y	Y	?	?	?
12 Putnam	Y	Y	+	+	Y
13 Buchanan	Y	Y	Y	Y	Y
14 Mack	Y	Y	Y	Y	Y
15 Posey	Y	Y	Y	Y	Y
16 Rooney	Y	Y	Y	Y	Y
17 Meek	Y	Y	?	?	Y
18 Ros-Lehtinen	Y	Y	Y	Y	Y
19 Wexler	?	?	?	?	N
20 Wasserman Schultz	Y	Y	?	?	N
21 Diaz-Balart, L.	Y	Y	?	?	Y
22 Klein	Y	Y	+	+	N
23 Hastings	Y	Y	Y	Y	N
24 Kosmas	Y	Y	Y	Y	Y
25 Diaz-Balart, M.	Y	Y	Y	Y	Y
GEORGIA					
1 Kingston	Y	Y	Y	Y	Y
2 Bishop	?	?	Y	Y	Y
3 Westmoreland	Y	Y	Y	Y	Y
4 Johnson	Y	Y	Y	Y	N
5 Lewis	Y	Y	Y	Y	N
6 Price	Y	Y	Y	Y	Y
7 Linder	Y	Y	Y	Y	Y
8 Marshall	Y	Y	Y	Y	Y
9 Deal	Y	Y	?	?	?
10 Broun	Y	N	Y	Y	Y
11 Gingrey	Y	Y	Y	Y	Y
12 Barrow	Y	Y	Y	Y	Y
13 Scott	Y	Y	Y	Y	Y
HAWAII					
1 Abercrombie	?	?	?	?	?
2 Hirono	Y	Y	Y	Y	N
IDAHO					
1 Minnick	Y	Y	Y	Y	Y
2 Simpson	Y	Y	Y	Y	Y
ILLINOIS					
1 Rush	?	?	Y	Y	Y
2 Jackson	Y	Y	Y	Y	N
3 Lipinski	Y	Y	?	?	N
4 Gutierrez	Y	Y	?	?	Y
5 Quigley	Y	Y	Y	Y	N
6 Roskam	Y	Y	?	?	Y
7 Davis	Y	Y	?	?	N
8 Bean	?	?	Y	Y	N
9 Schakowsky	Y	Y	Y	Y	N
10 Kirk	Y	Y	?	?	Y
11 Halvorson	Y	Y	Y	Y	Y
12 Costello	Y	Y	Y	Y	Y
13 Biggert	?	?	Y	Y	Y
14 Foster	Y	Y	Y	Y	Y
15 Johnson	Y	Y	?	?	Y

KEY   **Republicans**   Democrats

Y Voted for (yea)	X Paired against
# Paired for	− Announced against
+ Announced for	P Voted "present"
N Voted against (nay)	

C Voted "present" to avoid possible conflict of interest

? Did not vote or otherwise make a position known

	812	813	814	815	816
16 Manzullo	Y	Y	Y	Y	Y
17 Hare	Y	Y	Y	Y	Y
18 Schock	Y	Y	Y	Y	Y
19 Shimkus	Y	Y	Y	Y	Y
INDIANA					
1 Visclosky	Y	Y	Y	Y	N
2 Donnelly	Y	Y	Y	Y	Y
3 Souder	Y	Y	?	?	Y
4 Buyer	?	?	Y	Y	Y
5 Burton	Y	Y	Y	Y	Y
6 Pence	Y	Y	Y	Y	Y
7 Carson	Y	Y	Y	Y	N
8 Ellsworth	Y	Y	Y	Y	Y
9 Hill	Y	Y	Y	Y	Y
IOWA					
1 Braley	+	+	Y	Y	Y
2 Loebsack	Y	Y	Y	Y	Y
3 Boswell	Y	Y	Y	Y	Y
4 Latham	Y	Y	Y	Y	Y
5 King	Y	N	Y	Y	Y
KANSAS					
1 Moran	Y	Y	Y	Y	Y
2 Jenkins	Y	Y	Y	Y	Y
3 Moore	Y	Y	Y	Y	Y
4 Tiahrt	Y	N	Y	Y	Y
KENTUCKY					
1 Whitfield	Y	Y	Y	Y	Y
2 Guthrie	Y	Y	Y	Y	Y
3 Yarmuth	Y	Y	Y	Y	N
4 Davis	Y	Y	Y	Y	Y
5 Rogers	Y	Y	Y	Y	Y
6 Chandler	Y	Y	Y	Y	N
LOUISIANA					
1 Scalise	Y	Y	Y	Y	Y
2 Cao	Y	Y	?	?	?
3 Melancon	?	?	?	?	Y
4 Fleming	Y	Y	Y	Y	Y
5 Alexander	Y	Y	Y	Y	Y
6 Cassidy	Y	Y	Y	Y	Y
7 Boustany	Y	Y	Y	Y	Y
MAINE					
1 Pingree	Y	Y	Y	Y	N
2 Michaud	Y	Y	Y	Y	Y
MARYLAND					
1 Kratovil	Y	Y	Y	Y	Y
2 Ruppersberger	Y	Y	Y	Y	N
3 Sarbanes	Y	Y	Y	Y	N
4 Edwards	Y	Y	Y	Y	N
5 Hoyer	Y	Y	Y	Y	N
6 Bartlett	Y	Y	Y	Y	Y
7 Cummings	Y	Y	?	?	N
8 Van Hollen	Y	Y	?	?	N
MASSACHUSETTS					
1 Olver	Y	Y	Y	Y	N
2 Neal	Y	Y	?	?	N
3 McGovern	Y	Y	Y	Y	N
4 Frank	Y	Y	Y	Y	N
5 Tsongas	Y	Y	Y	Y	N
6 Tierney	Y	Y	Y	Y	N
7 Markey	Y	Y	Y	Y	N
8 Capuano	?	?	?	?	N
9 Lynch	Y	Y	Y	Y	N
10 Delahunt	Y	Y	?	?	N
MICHIGAN					
1 Stupak	Y	Y	Y	Y	Y
2 Hoekstra	Y	Y	?	?	?
3 Ehlers	Y	Y	Y	Y	Y
4 Camp	Y	Y	Y	Y	Y
5 Kildee	Y	Y	Y	Y	N
6 Upton	Y	Y	Y	Y	Y
7 Schauer	Y	Y	Y	Y	Y
8 Rogers	+	?	Y	Y	Y
9 Peters	Y	Y	Y	Y	N
10 Miller	Y	Y	Y	Y	Y
11 McCotter	Y	Y	Y	Y	Y
12 Levin	Y	Y	Y	Y	N
13 Kilpatrick	Y	Y	Y	Y	N
14 Conyers	Y	Y	Y	Y	N
15 Dingell	Y	Y	Y	Y	N
MINNESOTA					
1 Walz	Y	Y	Y	Y	Y
2 Kline	Y	Y	Y	Y	Y
3 Paulsen	Y	Y	Y	Y	Y
4 McCollum	Y	Y	?	?	N

	812	813	814	815	816
5 Ellison	Y	Y	Y	Y	N
6 Bachmann	Y	Y	Y	Y	Y
7 Peterson	Y	Y	Y	Y	Y
8 Oberstar	Y	Y	Y	Y	Y
MISSISSIPPI					
1 Childers	Y	Y	Y	Y	Y
2 Thompson	Y	Y	Y	Y	N
3 Harper	Y	Y	Y	Y	Y
4 Taylor	Y	Y	Y	Y	Y
MISSOURI					
1 Clay	Y	Y	Y	Y	N
2 Akin	Y	Y	Y	Y	N
3 Carnahan	Y	Y	Y	Y	Y
4 Skelton	Y	Y	Y	Y	Y
5 Cleaver	Y	Y	Y	Y	Y
6 Graves	Y	Y	Y	Y	Y
7 Blunt	Y	Y	Y	Y	Y
8 Emerson	Y	Y	Y	?	Y
9 Luetkemeyer	Y	Y	Y	Y	Y
MONTANA					
AL Rehberg	Y	Y	Y	Y	Y
NEBRASKA					
1 Fortenberry	Y	Y	Y	Y	Y
2 Terry	Y	Y	Y	Y	Y
3 Smith	Y	Y	Y	Y	Y
NEVADA					
1 Berkley	Y	Y	Y	Y	N
2 Heller	Y	Y	Y	Y	Y
3 Titus	Y	Y	Y	Y	Y
NEW HAMPSHIRE					
1 Shea-Porter	Y	Y	Y	Y	N
2 Hodes	Y	Y	Y	Y	N
NEW JERSEY					
1 Andrews	Y	Y	Y	Y	N
2 LoBiondo	Y	Y	Y	Y	Y
3 Adler	Y	Y	Y	Y	Y
4 Smith	Y	Y	Y	Y	Y
5 Garrett	Y	Y	Y	Y	Y
6 Pallone	Y	Y	Y	Y	N
7 Lance	Y	Y	Y	Y	Y
8 Pascrell	Y	Y	Y	Y	?
9 Rothman	Y	Y	Y	Y	N
10 Payne	Y	Y	?	?	?
11 Frelinghuysen	Y	Y	Y	Y	Y
12 Holt	Y	Y	Y	Y	N
13 Sires	Y	Y	Y	Y	N
NEW MEXICO					
1 Heinrich	Y	Y	Y	Y	N
2 Teague	Y	Y	?	?	Y
3 Lujan	Y	Y	Y	Y	Y
NEW YORK					
1 Bishop	Y	Y	Y	Y	Y
2 Israel	Y	Y	Y	Y	?
3 King	Y	Y	?	?	Y
4 McCarthy	Y	Y	Y	Y	N
5 Ackerman	Y	Y	Y	Y	N
6 Meeks	Y	Y	Y	Y	N
7 Crowley	Y	Y	Y	Y	N
8 Nadler	?	Y	Y	Y	N
9 Weiner	Y	Y	Y	Y	N
10 Towns	Y	Y	?	?	N
11 Clarke	Y	Y	Y	Y	N
12 Velázquez	Y	Y	Y	Y	N
13 McMahon	Y	Y	Y	Y	Y
14 Maloney	?	?	?	?	N
15 Rangel	Y	Y	Y	Y	N
16 Serrano	Y	Y	Y	Y	N
17 Engel	?	Y	Y	Y	N
18 Lowey	Y	Y	Y	Y	N
19 Hall	Y	Y	Y	Y	N
20 Murphy	Y	Y	Y	Y	Y
21 Tonko	Y	Y	Y	Y	N
22 Hinchey	Y	Y	?	?	N
23 Vacant					
24 Arcuri	Y	Y	Y	Y	Y
25 Maffei	?	?	Y	Y	N
26 Lee	Y	Y	Y	Y	Y
27 Higgins	?	?	Y	Y	N
28 Slaughter	Y	Y	Y	Y	N
29 Massa	Y	Y	Y	Y	N
NORTH CAROLINA					
1 Butterfield	Y	Y	Y	Y	N
2 Etheridge	Y	Y	Y	Y	Y
3 Jones	?	?	Y	Y	Y
4 Price	?	Y	Y	Y	N

	812	813	814	815	816
5 Foxx	Y	Y	Y	Y	Y
6 Coble	Y	Y	Y	Y	Y
7 McIntyre	Y	Y	Y	Y	Y
8 Kissell	Y	Y	Y	Y	Y
9 Myrick	Y	Y	Y	Y	Y
10 McHenry	Y	Y	Y	Y	Y
11 Shuler	Y	Y	Y	Y	Y
12 Watt	Y	Y	Y	Y	N
13 Miller	Y	Y	Y	Y	N
NORTH DAKOTA					
AL Pomeroy	Y	Y	Y	Y	Y
OHIO					
1 Driehaus	Y	Y	Y	Y	Y
2 Schmidt	Y	Y	Y	Y	Y
3 Turner	Y	Y	Y	Y	Y
4 Jordan	Y	Y	Y	Y	Y
5 Latta	Y	Y	Y	Y	Y
6 Wilson	Y	Y	Y	Y	Y
7 Austria	Y	Y	Y	Y	Y
8 Boehner	Y	Y	Y	Y	Y
9 Kaptur	Y	Y	Y	Y	Y
10 Kucinich	Y	Y	Y	Y	N
11 Fudge	Y	Y	Y	Y	N
12 Tiberi	Y	Y	Y	Y	Y
13 Sutton	Y	Y	Y	Y	Y
14 LaTourette	Y	Y	Y	Y	Y
15 Kilroy	Y	Y	Y	Y	N
16 Boccieri	Y	Y	Y	Y	Y
17 Ryan	Y	Y	Y	Y	Y
18 Space	Y	Y	?	?	Y
OKLAHOMA					
1 Sullivan	Y	Y	Y	Y	Y
2 Boren	Y	Y	Y	Y	Y
3 Lucas	Y	Y	Y	Y	Y
4 Cole	Y	Y	Y	?	Y
5 Fallin	Y	Y	Y	Y	Y
OREGON					
1 Wu	Y	Y	Y	?	N
2 Walden	?	?	Y	Y	Y
3 Blumenauer	Y	Y	Y	Y	N
4 DeFazio	Y	Y	Y	Y	N
5 Schrader	Y	Y	Y	Y	Y
PENNSYLVANIA					
1 Brady	Y	Y	Y	Y	N
2 Fattah	Y	Y	Y	Y	N
3 Dahlkemper	Y	Y	Y	Y	N
4 Altmire	Y	Y	Y	Y	Y
5 Thompson	Y	Y	Y	Y	Y
6 Gerlach	Y	Y	+	+	+
7 Sestak	Y	Y	Y	Y	N
8 Murphy, P.	Y	Y	Y	Y	N
9 Shuster	Y	Y	Y	Y	Y
10 Carney	Y	Y	Y	Y	Y
11 Kanjorski	Y	Y	Y	Y	N
12 Murtha	Y	Y	Y	Y	N
13 Schwartz	Y	Y	Y	Y	N
14 Doyle	Y	Y	Y	Y	N
15 Dent	Y	Y	Y	Y	Y
16 Pitts	Y	Y	Y	Y	Y
17 Holden	Y	Y	?	?	Y
18 Murphy, T.	Y	Y	Y	Y	Y
19 Platts	Y	Y	Y	Y	Y
RHODE ISLAND					
1 Kennedy	Y	Y	Y	Y	N
2 Langevin	Y	Y	Y	Y	Y
SOUTH CAROLINA					
1 Brown	Y	Y	Y	Y	Y
2 Wilson	Y	Y	Y	Y	Y
3 Barrett	+	+	?	?	?
4 Inglis	Y	Y	Y	Y	Y
5 Spratt	Y	Y	Y	Y	Y
6 Clyburn	Y	Y	Y	Y	N
SOUTH DAKOTA					
AL Herseth Sandlin	Y	Y	Y	Y	Y
TENNESSEE					
1 Roe	Y	Y	?	?	Y
2 Duncan	Y	Y	Y	Y	Y
3 Wamp	?	?	?	?	Y
4 Davis	?	?	Y	Y	Y
5 Cooper	Y	Y	Y	Y	Y
6 Gordon	Y	Y	Y	Y	Y
7 Blackburn	Y	Y	Y	Y	Y
8 Tanner	Y	Y	Y	Y	Y
9 Cohen	Y	Y	Y	Y	N

	812	813	814	815	816
TEXAS					
1 Gohmert	?	?	Y	Y	Y
2 Poe	Y	Y	Y	Y	Y
3 Johnson, S.	Y	Y	?	?	?
4 Hall	Y	Y	Y	Y	?
5 Hensarling	Y	Y	Y	Y	Y
6 Barton	Y	Y	Y	Y	Y
7 Culberson	?	?	?	?	Y
8 Brady	Y	Y	Y	Y	Y
9 Green, A.	Y	Y	Y	Y	N
10 McCaul	?	?	Y	Y	Y
11 Conaway	Y	Y	Y	Y	Y
12 Granger	Y	Y	Y	Y	?
13 Thornberry	?	?	Y	Y	Y
14 Paul	Y	N	?	?	Y
15 Hinojosa	?	?	Y	Y	N
16 Reyes	Y	Y	Y	Y	Y
17 Edwards	Y	Y	Y	Y	Y
18 Jackson Lee	Y	Y	Y	Y	Y
19 Neugebauer	Y	Y	Y	Y	Y
20 Gonzalez	Y	Y	Y	Y	Y
21 Smith	Y	Y	Y	Y	Y
22 Olson	Y	Y	Y	Y	Y
23 Rodriguez	Y	Y	Y	Y	Y
24 Marchant	Y	Y	Y	Y	Y
25 Doggett	Y	Y	Y	Y	N
26 Burgess	Y	Y	Y	Y	Y
27 Ortiz	Y	Y	+	+	Y
28 Cuellar	Y	Y	Y	Y	Y
29 Green, G.	Y	Y	Y	Y	Y
30 Johnson, E.	Y	Y	Y	Y	Y
31 Carter	Y	Y	+	+	Y
32 Sessions	Y	Y	Y	Y	Y
UTAH					
1 Bishop	?	?	Y	Y	Y
2 Matheson	Y	Y	Y	Y	N
3 Chaffetz	Y	Y	Y	Y	Y
VERMONT					
AL Welch	Y	Y	Y	Y	N
VIRGINIA					
1 Wittman	Y	Y	Y	Y	Y
2 Nye	Y	Y	Y	Y	Y
3 Scott	Y	Y	Y	Y	?
4 Forbes	?	?	Y	Y	Y
5 Perriello	Y	Y	Y	Y	Y
6 Goodlatte	Y	Y	Y	Y	Y
7 Cantor	Y	Y	Y	Y	Y
8 Moran	Y	Y	Y	Y	Y
9 Boucher	Y	Y	Y	Y	Y
10 Wolf	Y	Y	Y	Y	Y
11 Connolly	Y	Y	Y	Y	N
WASHINGTON					
1 Inslee	?	?	Y	Y	N
2 Larsen	Y	Y	?	?	Y
3 Baird	Y	Y	Y	Y	N
4 Hastings	Y	Y	Y	Y	Y
5 McMorris Rodgers	Y	Y	Y	Y	Y
6 Dicks	Y	Y	Y	Y	N
7 McDermott	Y	Y	Y	Y	N
8 Reichert	Y	Y	Y	Y	Y
9 Smith	Y	Y	?	?	?
WEST VIRGINIA					
1 Mollohan	Y	Y	Y	Y	Y
2 Capito	Y	Y	Y	Y	Y
3 Rahall	Y	Y	Y	Y	Y
WISCONSIN					
1 Ryan	Y	N	Y	Y	Y
2 Baldwin	Y	Y	Y	Y	N
3 Kind	Y	Y	Y	Y	Y
4 Moore	Y	Y	?	?	N
5 Sensenbrenner	Y	N	Y	Y	Y
6 Petri	Y	Y	Y	Y	Y
7 Obey	Y	Y	Y	Y	N
8 Kagen	Y	Y	Y	Y	Y
WYOMING					
AL Lummis	Y	Y	Y	Y	Y
DELEGATES					
Faleomavaega (A.S.)	?				
Norton (D.C.)	Y				
Bordallo (Guam)	Y				
Sablan (N. Marianas)	Y				
Pierluisi (P.R.)	Y				
Christensen (V.I.)	Y				

IN THE HOUSE | By Vote Number

817. **HR 2489. National Geospatial Imagery Mapping Program/ Passage.** Pierluisi, D-P.R., motion to suspend the rules and pass the bill that would direct the Interior secretary to establish a national program through the U.S. Geological Survey to provide state and local governments increased access to satellite imagery. It would authorize $10 million a year for the program through fiscal 2019. Motion agreed to 379-33: D 243-1; R 136-32. A two-thirds majority of those present and voting (275 in this case) is required for passage under suspension of the rules. Oct. 27, 2009.

818. **H Res 854. Weber State University Anniversary/Adoption.** Pierluisi, D-P.R., motion to suspend the rules and adopt the resolution that would recognize the 120th anniversary of Weber State University. Motion agreed to 412-0: D 245-0; R 167-0. A two-thirds majority of those present and voting (275 in this case) is required for adoption under suspension of the rules. Oct. 27, 2009.

819. **S 1694. Interoperable Communications Grant Extension/ Passage.** Boucher, D-Va., motion to suspend the rules and pass the bill that would extend funding for a grant program to assist public safety agencies in using interoperable communications to Sept. 30, 2012. Motion agreed to 420-0: D 249-0; R 171-0. A two-thirds majority of those present and voting (280 in this case) is required for passage under suspension of the rules. Oct. 28, 2009.

820. **H Res 838. Welcoming Ecumenical Patriarch Bartholomew/ Adoption.** Carnahan, D-Mo., motion to suspend the rules and adopt the resolution that would welcome the Ecumenical Patriarch Bartholomew to the United States. Motion agreed to 424-0: D 249-0; R 175-0. A two-thirds majority of those present and voting (283 in this case) is required for adoption under suspension of the rules. Oct. 28, 2009.

821. **H Res 784. Tribute to Confucius/Adoption.** Carnahan, D-Mo., motion to suspend the rules and adopt the resolution that would recognize the 2,560th anniversary of the birth of Confucius. Motion agreed to 361-47: D 234-12; R 127-35. A two-thirds majority of those present and voting (272 in this case) is required for adoption under suspension of the rules. Oct. 28, 2009.

	817	818	819	820	821
ALABAMA					
1 **Bonner**	Y	Y	Y	Y	Y
2 Bright	Y	Y	Y	Y	?
3 **Rogers**	Y	Y	Y	Y	Y
4 **Aderholt**	Y	Y	?	Y	Y
5 Griffith	Y	Y	Y	Y	Y
6 **Bachus**	Y	Y	?	Y	Y
7 Davis	Y	Y	Y	Y	Y
ALASKA					
AL **Young**	Y	Y	Y	Y	N
ARIZONA					
1 Kirkpatrick	?	?	Y	Y	Y
2 **Franks**	N	Y	Y	Y	Y
3 **Shadegg**	N	Y	Y	Y	N
4 Pastor	Y	Y	Y	Y	Y
5 Mitchell	Y	Y	Y	Y	Y
6 **Flake**	N	Y	Y	Y	N
7 Grijalva	?	?	Y	Y	Y
8 Giffords	Y	Y	Y	Y	Y
ARKANSAS					
1 Berry	Y	Y	Y	Y	N
2 Snyder	Y	Y	Y	Y	Y
3 **Boozman**	Y	Y	Y	Y	Y
4 Ross	Y	Y	Y	Y	Y
CALIFORNIA					
1 Thompson	Y	Y	Y	Y	Y
2 **Herger**	N	Y	Y	Y	Y
3 **Lungren**	Y	Y	Y	Y	Y
4 **McClintock**	N	Y	Y	Y	Y
5 Matsui	Y	Y	Y	Y	Y
6 Woolsey	Y	Y	Y	+	Y
7 Miller, George	Y	Y	Y	Y	Y
8 Pelosi					
9 Lee	Y	Y	Y	Y	Y
10 Vacant					
11 McNerney	Y	Y	Y	Y	Y
12 Speier	Y	Y	Y	Y	Y
13 Stark	Y	Y	Y	Y	Y
14 Eshoo	Y	Y	Y	Y	?
15 Honda	Y	Y	Y	Y	Y
16 Lofgren	Y	Y	Y	Y	Y
17 Farr	Y	Y	Y	Y	?
18 Cardoza	Y	Y	Y	Y	Y
19 **Radanovich**	?	?	Y	N	N
20 Costa	Y	Y	Y	Y	Y
21 **Nunes**	Y	Y	Y	Y	P
22 **McCarthy**	Y	Y	Y	Y	Y
23 Capps	Y	Y	Y	Y	Y
24 **Gallegly**	Y	Y	Y	Y	Y
25 **McKeon**	Y	Y	Y	Y	Y
26 **Dreier**	Y	Y	Y	Y	Y
27 Sherman	Y	Y	Y	Y	Y
28 Berman	Y	Y	Y	Y	Y
29 Schiff	Y	Y	Y	Y	Y
30 Waxman	?	Y	Y	Y	Y
31 Becerra	Y	Y	Y	Y	Y
32 Chu	Y	Y	Y	Y	Y
33 Watson	Y	Y	Y	Y	Y
34 Roybal-Allard	Y	Y	Y	Y	Y
35 Waters	Y	Y	Y	Y	Y
36 Harman	Y	Y	Y	Y	Y
37 Richardson	Y	Y	Y	Y	Y
38 Napolitano	Y	Y	Y	Y	Y
39 Sánchez, Linda	Y	Y	Y	Y	Y
40 **Royce**	N	Y	Y	Y	Y
41 **Lewis**	Y	Y	Y	Y	Y
42 **Miller, Gary**	Y	Y	Y	Y	Y
43 Baca	Y	Y	Y	Y	Y
44 **Calvert**	Y	Y	Y	Y	Y
45 **Bono Mack**	Y	Y	Y	Y	Y
46 **Rohrabacher**	Y	Y	Y	Y	Y
47 Sanchez, Loretta	?	?	Y	Y	Y
48 **Campbell**	N	Y	Y	Y	P
49 **Issa**	N	Y	Y	Y	Y
50 **Bilbray**	Y	Y	Y	Y	Y
51 Filner	Y	Y	Y	Y	Y
52 **Hunter**	Y	Y	Y	Y	Y
53 Davis	Y	Y	Y	Y	Y

	817	818	819	820	821
COLORADO					
1 DeGette	Y	Y	Y	Y	Y
2 Polis	Y	Y	Y	Y	Y
3 Salazar	Y	Y	Y	Y	Y
4 Markey	Y	Y	Y	Y	Y
5 **Lamborn**	N	Y	Y	Y	Y
6 **Coffman**	Y	Y	Y	Y	Y
7 Perlmutter	Y	Y	Y	Y	Y
CONNECTICUT					
1 Larson	Y	Y	Y	Y	Y
2 Courtney	Y	Y	Y	Y	Y
3 DeLauro	Y	Y	Y	Y	Y
4 Himes	Y	Y	Y	Y	Y
5 Murphy	Y	Y	Y	Y	Y
DELAWARE					
AL **Castle**	Y	Y	Y	Y	Y
FLORIDA					
1 **Miller**	Y	Y	Y	Y	N
2 Boyd	Y	Y	Y	Y	Y
3 Brown	Y	Y	Y	Y	Y
4 **Crenshaw**	Y	Y	Y	Y	Y
5 **Brown-Waite**	Y	Y	Y	Y	P
6 **Stearns**	N	Y	Y	Y	Y
7 **Mica**	Y	Y	Y	Y	N
8 Grayson	Y	Y	Y	Y	Y
9 **Bilirakis**	Y	Y	Y	Y	Y
10 **Young**	Y	Y	Y	Y	N
11 Castor	?	?	Y	Y	Y
12 **Putnam**	Y	Y	Y	Y	Y
13 **Buchanan**	Y	Y	Y	Y	Y
14 **Mack**	Y	Y	Y	Y	Y
15 **Posey**	Y	?	Y	Y	Y
16 **Rooney**	N	Y	Y	Y	Y
17 Meek	Y	Y	Y	Y	Y
18 **Ros-Lehtinen**	Y	Y	Y	Y	Y
19 Wexler	Y	Y	Y	Y	Y
20 Wasserman Schultz	Y	Y	Y	Y	Y
21 **Diaz-Balart, L.**	Y	Y	Y	Y	Y
22 Klein	Y	Y	Y	Y	Y
23 Hastings	Y	Y	?	?	?
24 Kosmas	Y	Y	Y	Y	Y
25 **Diaz-Balart, M.**	Y	Y	Y	Y	Y
GEORGIA					
1 **Kingston**	N	Y	Y	Y	Y
2 Bishop	Y	Y	Y	Y	Y
3 **Westmoreland**	Y	Y	Y	Y	N
4 Johnson	Y	Y	Y	Y	Y
5 Lewis	Y	Y	Y	Y	Y
6 **Price**	Y	Y	Y	Y	Y
7 **Linder**	Y	Y	Y	Y	Y
8 Marshall	Y	Y	Y	Y	P
9 **Deal**	?	?	Y	Y	Y
10 **Broun**	N	Y	?	Y	N
11 **Gingrey**	Y	Y	Y	Y	Y
12 Barrow	Y	Y	Y	Y	Y
13 Scott	Y	Y	?	Y	Y
HAWAII					
1 Abercrombie	?	?	Y	Y	Y
2 Hirono	Y	Y	Y	Y	Y
IDAHO					
1 Minnick	Y	Y	Y	Y	Y
2 **Simpson**	Y	Y	Y	Y	N
ILLINOIS					
1 Rush	Y	Y	Y	Y	Y
2 Jackson	Y	Y	Y	Y	Y
3 Lipinski	Y	Y	Y	Y	Y
4 Gutierrez	Y	Y	Y	Y	Y
5 Quigley	Y	Y	Y	Y	Y
6 **Roskam**	Y	Y	Y	Y	Y
7 Davis	Y	Y	Y	Y	Y
8 Bean	Y	Y	Y	Y	Y
9 Schakowsky	Y	Y	Y	Y	Y
10 **Kirk**	Y	Y	Y	Y	Y
11 Halvorson	Y	Y	Y	Y	Y
12 Costello	Y	Y	Y	Y	Y
13 **Biggert**	Y	Y	Y	Y	Y
14 Foster	Y	Y	Y	Y	Y
15 **Johnson**	Y	Y	Y	Y	N

KEY	**Republicans**	Democrats

Y Voted for (yea)	X Paired against	C Voted "present" to avoid possible conflict of interest
# Paired for	– Announced against	
+ Announced for	P Voted "present"	? Did not vote or otherwise make a position known
N Voted against (nay)		

	817	818	819	820	821
16 Manzullo	N	Y	Y	Y	Y
17 Hare	Y	Y	Y	Y	Y
18 Schock	Y	Y	Y	Y	Y
19 Shimkus	Y	Y	Y	Y	N
INDIANA					
1 Visclosky	Y	Y	Y	Y	Y
2 Donnelly	Y	Y	Y	Y	P
3 Souder	Y	Y	Y	Y	N
4 Buyer	Y	Y	Y	Y	P
5 Burton	N	Y	Y	Y	P
6 Pence	N	Y	Y	Y	Y
7 Carson	Y	Y	Y	Y	Y
8 Ellsworth	Y	Y	Y	Y	N
9 Hill	Y	Y	Y	Y	Y
IOWA					
1 Braley	Y	Y	Y	Y	Y
2 Loebsack	Y	Y	Y	Y	Y
3 Boswell	Y	Y	Y	Y	Y
4 Latham	Y	Y	Y	Y	Y
5 King	Y	Y	Y	Y	Y
KANSAS					
1 Moran	Y	Y	Y	Y	Y
2 Jenkins	Y	Y	Y	Y	Y
3 Moore	Y	Y	Y	Y	Y
4 Tiahrt	Y	Y	Y	Y	Y
KENTUCKY					
1 Whitfield	Y	Y	Y	Y	Y
2 Guthrie	Y	Y	Y	Y	Y
3 Yarmuth	Y	Y	Y	Y	Y
4 Davis	Y	Y	Y	Y	N
5 Rogers	Y	Y	Y	Y	Y
6 Chandler	Y	Y	Y	Y	Y
LOUISIANA					
1 Scalise	N	Y	Y	Y	Y
2 Cao	Y	Y	Y	Y	Y
3 Melancon	Y	Y	Y	Y	Y
4 Fleming	Y	Y	Y	Y	N
5 Alexander	Y	Y	Y	Y	Y
6 Cassidy	Y	Y	Y	Y	Y
7 Boustany	Y	Y	Y	Y	Y
MAINE					
1 Pingree	Y	Y	Y	Y	Y
2 Michaud	Y	Y	Y	Y	Y
MARYLAND					
1 Kratovil	Y	Y	Y	Y	Y
2 Ruppersberger	Y	Y	Y	Y	Y
3 Sarbanes	Y	Y	Y	Y	Y
4 Edwards	Y	Y	Y	Y	Y
5 Hoyer	Y	Y	?	?	?
6 Bartlett	Y	Y	Y	Y	Y
7 Cummings	Y	Y	Y	Y	Y
8 Van Hollen	Y	Y	Y	Y	Y
MASSACHUSETTS					
1 Olver	Y	Y	Y	Y	Y
2 Neal	Y	Y	Y	Y	Y
3 McGovern	Y	Y	Y	Y	Y
4 Frank	Y	Y	Y	Y	Y
5 Tsongas	Y	Y	?	?	?
6 Tierney	N	Y	Y	Y	Y
7 Markey	Y	Y	Y	Y	Y
8 Capuano	Y	Y	Y	Y	Y
9 Lynch	Y	Y	Y	Y	Y
10 Delahunt	Y	Y	Y	Y	Y
MICHIGAN					
1 Stupak	Y	Y	Y	Y	Y
2 Hoekstra	?	?	Y	Y	N
3 Ehlers	Y	Y	Y	Y	Y
4 Camp	Y	Y	Y	Y	N
5 Kildee	Y	Y	Y	Y	Y
6 Upton	Y	Y	Y	Y	Y
7 Schauer	Y	Y	Y	Y	Y
8 Rogers	Y	Y	Y	Y	Y
9 Peters	Y	Y	Y	Y	Y
10 Miller	Y	Y	Y	Y	Y
11 McCotter	Y	Y	Y	Y	Y
12 Levin	Y	Y	Y	Y	Y
13 Kilpatrick	Y	Y	Y	Y	Y
14 Conyers	Y	Y	Y	Y	Y
15 Dingell	Y	Y	Y	Y	Y
MINNESOTA					
1 Walz	Y	Y	Y	Y	Y
2 Kline	Y	Y	Y	Y	Y
3 Paulsen	N	Y	Y	Y	Y
4 McCollum	Y	Y	Y	Y	Y

	817	818	819	820	821
5 Ellison	Y	Y	Y	Y	Y
6 Bachmann	Y	Y	Y	Y	Y
7 Peterson	Y	Y	Y	Y	Y
8 Oberstar	Y	Y	Y	Y	Y
MISSISSIPPI					
1 Childers	Y	Y	Y	Y	Y
2 Thompson	Y	Y	Y	Y	Y
3 Harper	Y	Y	Y	Y	Y
4 Taylor	Y	Y	Y	Y	N
MISSOURI					
1 Clay	Y	Y	Y	Y	Y
2 Akin	N	Y	Y	Y	N
3 Carnahan	Y	Y	Y	Y	Y
4 Skelton	Y	Y	Y	Y	N
5 Cleaver	Y	Y	Y	Y	Y
6 Graves	Y	Y	Y	Y	N
7 Blunt	Y	Y	Y	Y	Y
8 Emerson	Y	Y	Y	Y	N
9 Luetkemeyer	Y	Y	Y	Y	
MONTANA					
AL Rehberg	Y	Y	Y	Y	Y
NEBRASKA					
1 Fortenberry	Y	Y	Y	Y	P
2 Terry	Y	Y	Y	Y	Y
3 Smith	Y	Y	Y	Y	Y
NEVADA					
1 Berkley	Y	Y	Y	Y	Y
2 Heller	Y	Y	Y	Y	Y
3 Titus	Y	Y	Y	Y	Y
NEW HAMPSHIRE					
1 Shea-Porter	Y	Y	Y	Y	Y
2 Hodes	Y	Y	Y	Y	Y
NEW JERSEY					
1 Andrews	Y	Y	Y	Y	Y
2 LoBiondo	Y	Y	Y	Y	Y
3 Adler	Y	Y	Y	Y	Y
4 Smith	Y	Y	Y	Y	Y
5 Garrett	N	Y	Y	Y	Y
6 Pallone	Y	Y	Y	Y	Y
7 Lance	Y	Y	Y	Y	Y
8 Pascrell	?	?	Y	Y	Y
9 Rothman	Y	Y	Y	Y	Y
10 Payne	?	?	Y	Y	Y
11 Frelinghuysen	Y	Y	Y	Y	Y
12 Holt	Y	Y	Y	Y	Y
13 Sires	Y	Y	Y	Y	Y
NEW MEXICO					
1 Heinrich	Y	Y	Y	Y	Y
2 Teague	Y	Y	Y	Y	Y
3 Lujan	Y	Y	Y	Y	Y
NEW YORK					
1 Bishop	Y	Y	Y	Y	Y
2 Israel	?	?	Y	Y	Y
3 King	Y	Y	Y	Y	Y
4 McCarthy	Y	Y	Y	Y	Y
5 Ackerman	Y	Y	Y	Y	Y
6 Meeks	Y	Y	Y	Y	Y
7 Crowley	Y	Y	Y	Y	Y
8 Nadler	Y	Y	Y	Y	Y
9 Weiner	Y	Y	Y	Y	Y
10 Towns	Y	Y	Y	Y	Y
11 Clarke	Y	Y	Y	Y	Y
12 Velázquez	Y	Y	Y	Y	Y
13 McMahon	Y	Y	?	Y	Y
14 Maloney	Y	Y	Y	Y	Y
15 Rangel	Y	Y	Y	Y	Y
16 Serrano	Y	Y	Y	Y	Y
17 Engel	Y	Y	Y	Y	Y
18 Lowey	Y	Y	Y	Y	Y
19 Hall	Y	Y	Y	Y	Y
20 Murphy	Y	Y	Y	Y	Y
21 Tonko	Y	Y	Y	Y	Y
22 Hinchey	Y	Y	Y	Y	Y
23 Vacant					
24 Arcuri	Y	Y	Y	Y	Y
25 Maffei	Y	Y	Y	Y	Y
26 Lee	Y	Y	Y	Y	Y
27 Higgins	Y	Y	Y	Y	Y
28 Slaughter	Y	Y	Y	Y	Y
29 Massa	Y	Y	Y	Y	N
NORTH CAROLINA					
1 Butterfield	Y	Y	Y	Y	Y
2 Etheridge	Y	Y	Y	Y	Y
3 Jones	Y	Y	Y	Y	Y
4 Price	Y	Y	Y	Y	Y

	817	818	819	820	821
5 Foxx	Y	Y	Y	Y	P
6 Coble	N	Y	Y	Y	Y
7 McIntyre	Y	Y	Y	Y	Y
8 Kissell	Y	Y	Y	Y	Y
9 Myrick	Y	Y	Y	Y	Y
10 McHenry	Y	Y	Y	Y	P
11 Shuler	Y	Y	Y	Y	Y
12 Watt	Y	Y	Y	Y	Y
13 Miller	Y	Y	Y	Y	Y
NORTH DAKOTA					
AL Pomeroy	Y	Y	Y	Y	Y
OHIO					
1 Driehaus	Y	Y	Y	Y	N
2 Schmidt	Y	Y	Y	Y	Y
3 Turner	Y	Y	Y	Y	Y
4 Jordan	N	Y	Y	Y	N
5 Latta	Y	Y	Y	Y	N
6 Wilson	Y	Y	Y	Y	Y
7 Austria	Y	Y	Y	Y	Y
8 Boehner	Y	?	Y	Y	?
9 Kaptur	Y	Y	Y	Y	Y
10 Kucinich	Y	Y	Y	Y	Y
11 Fudge	Y	Y	Y	Y	Y
12 Tiberi	Y	Y	Y	Y	N
13 Sutton	Y	Y	Y	Y	Y
14 LaTourette	Y	Y	Y	Y	N
15 Kilroy	Y	Y	Y	Y	Y
16 Boccieri	Y	Y	Y	Y	N
17 Ryan	Y	Y	Y	Y	Y
18 Space	Y	Y	Y	Y	N
OKLAHOMA					
1 Sullivan	Y	Y	Y	Y	Y
2 Boren	Y	Y	Y	Y	Y
3 Lucas	Y	Y	Y	Y	Y
4 Cole	Y	Y	Y	Y	Y
5 Fallin	Y	Y	Y	Y	P
OREGON					
1 Wu	Y	Y	Y	Y	Y
2 Walden	Y	Y	Y	Y	N
3 Blumenauer	Y	Y	Y	Y	Y
4 DeFazio	Y	Y	Y	Y	Y
5 Schrader	Y	Y	Y	Y	Y
PENNSYLVANIA					
1 Brady	Y	Y	Y	Y	Y
2 Fattah	Y	Y	Y	Y	Y
3 Dahlkemper	Y	Y	Y	Y	Y
4 Altmire	Y	Y	Y	Y	N
5 Thompson	Y	Y	Y	Y	Y
6 Gerlach	+	+	Y	Y	Y
7 Sestak	Y	Y	Y	Y	Y
8 Murphy, P.	Y	Y	Y	?	Y
9 Shuster	Y	Y	Y	Y	Y
10 Carney	Y	Y	Y	Y	Y
11 Kanjorski	Y	Y	Y	Y	Y
12 Murtha	Y	Y	Y	Y	P
13 Schwartz	Y	Y	Y	Y	Y
14 Doyle	Y	Y	Y	Y	Y
15 Dent	Y	Y	Y	Y	Y
16 Pitts	Y	Y	Y	Y	Y
17 Holden	Y	Y	Y	Y	Y
18 Murphy, T.	Y	Y	Y	Y	Y
19 Platts	Y	Y	Y	Y	N
RHODE ISLAND					
1 Kennedy	Y	Y	Y	Y	Y
2 Langevin	Y	Y	Y	Y	Y
SOUTH CAROLINA					
1 Brown	Y	Y	Y	Y	Y
2 Wilson	Y	Y	Y	Y	Y
3 Barrett	?	?	?	?	?
4 Inglis	Y	Y	Y	Y	Y
5 Spratt	Y	Y	Y	Y	Y
6 Clyburn	Y	Y	Y	Y	Y
SOUTH DAKOTA					
AL Herseth Sandlin	Y	Y	Y	Y	Y
TENNESSEE					
1 Roe	Y	Y	Y	Y	P
2 Duncan	N	Y	Y	Y	Y
3 Wamp	Y	Y	Y	Y	Y
4 Davis	Y	Y	Y	Y	N
5 Cooper	Y	Y	Y	Y	Y
6 Gordon	Y	Y	Y	Y	Y
7 Blackburn	Y	Y	Y	Y	Y
8 Tanner	Y	Y	Y	Y	Y
9 Cohen	Y	Y	Y	Y	Y

	817	818	819	820	821
TEXAS					
1 Gohmert	Y	Y	?	Y	?
2 Poe	N	Y	Y	Y	N
3 Johnson, S.	?	?	Y	Y	N
4 Hall	?	?	?	?	?
5 Hensarling	N	Y	Y	Y	Y
6 Barton	Y	Y	Y	Y	N
7 Culberson	N	Y	Y	Y	Y
8 Brady	Y	Y	Y	Y	Y
9 Green, A.	Y	Y	Y	Y	Y
10 McCaul	Y	Y	Y	Y	Y
11 Conaway	N	Y	Y	Y	N
12 Granger	?	?	Y	Y	Y
13 Thornberry	Y	Y	Y	Y	Y
14 Paul	N	Y	Y	Y	Y
15 Hinojosa	Y	Y	Y	Y	Y
16 Reyes	Y	Y	Y	Y	Y
17 Edwards	Y	Y	Y	Y	Y
18 Jackson Lee	Y	Y	Y	Y	Y
19 Neugebauer	N	Y	Y	Y	P
20 Gonzalez	Y	Y	Y	Y	Y
21 Smith	Y	Y	Y	Y	Y
22 Olson	?	Y	Y	Y	Y
23 Rodriguez	Y	Y	Y	Y	Y
24 Marchant	N	Y	Y	Y	N
25 Doggett	Y	Y	Y	Y	Y
26 Burgess	Y	Y	Y	Y	N
27 Ortiz	Y	Y	Y	Y	Y
28 Cuellar	Y	Y	Y	Y	Y
29 Green, G.	Y	Y	Y	Y	Y
30 Johnson, E.	Y	Y	Y	Y	Y
31 Carter	Y	Y	Y	Y	N
32 Sessions	Y	Y	Y	Y	Y
UTAH					
1 Bishop	Y	Y	Y	Y	Y
2 Matheson	Y	Y	Y	Y	N
3 Chaffetz	Y	Y	Y	Y	N
VERMONT					
AL Welch	Y	Y	Y	Y	Y
VIRGINIA					
1 Wittman	Y	Y	Y	Y	Y
2 Nye	Y	Y	Y	Y	Y
3 Scott	?	?	Y	Y	Y
4 Forbes	Y	Y	Y	Y	Y
5 Perriello	Y	Y	Y	Y	Y
6 Goodlatte	Y	Y	Y	Y	Y
7 Cantor	Y	Y	Y	Y	Y
8 Moran	Y	Y	Y	Y	Y
9 Boucher	Y	Y	Y	Y	Y
10 Wolf	Y	Y	Y	Y	Y
11 Connolly	Y	Y	Y	Y	Y
WASHINGTON					
1 Inslee	Y	Y	Y	Y	Y
2 Larsen	Y	Y	Y	Y	Y
3 Baird	Y	Y	?	?	Y
4 Hastings	Y	Y	Y	Y	Y
5 McMorris Rodgers	Y	Y	Y	Y	Y
6 Dicks	Y	Y	Y	Y	Y
7 McDermott	Y	Y	Y	Y	Y
8 Reichert	Y	Y	Y	Y	Y
9 Smith	?	?	Y	Y	Y
WEST VIRGINIA					
1 Mollohan	Y	Y	Y	Y	Y
2 Capito	Y	Y	Y	Y	Y
3 Rahall	Y	Y	Y	Y	Y
WISCONSIN					
1 Ryan	Y	Y	Y	Y	Y
2 Baldwin	Y	Y	Y	Y	Y
3 Kind	Y	Y	Y	Y	Y
4 Moore	Y	Y	Y	Y	Y
5 Sensenbrenner	N	Y	Y	Y	N
6 Petri	N	Y	Y	Y	Y
7 Obey	Y	Y	Y	Y	Y
8 Kagen	Y	Y	Y	Y	Y
WYOMING					
AL Lummis	Y	Y	Y	Y	Y
DELEGATES					
Faleomavaega (A.S.)					
Norton (D.C.)					
Bordallo (Guam)					
Sablan (N. Marianas)					
Pierluisi (P.R.)					
Christensen (V.I.)					

IN THE HOUSE | By Vote Number

822. H Res 824. **Northwestern University Women's Lacrosse Team/ Adoption.** Pierluisi, D-P.R., motion to suspend the rules and adopt the resolution that would congratulate the Northwestern University women's lacrosse team for winning the 2009 NCAA women's lacrosse championship. Motion agreed to 416-0: D 247-0; R 169-0. A two-thirds majority of those present and voting (278 in this case) is required for adoption under suspension of the rules. Oct. 28, 2009.

823. HR 2996. **Fiscal 2010 Interior-Environment Appropriations/ Previous Question.** Hastings, D-Fla., motion to order the previous question (thus ending debate and possibility of amendment) on adoption of the rule (H Res 876) that would provide for House floor consideration of the conference report on the bill that would appropriate $32.3 billion in fiscal 2010 for the Interior Department, the EPA and related agencies. It also would provide continuing appropriations through Dec. 18, 2009, for all federal departments and agencies whose fiscal 2010 appropriations bills have not been enacted. Motion agreed to 236-183: D 236-10; R 0-173. Oct. 29, 2009.

824. HR 2996. **Fiscal 2010 Interior-Environment Appropriations/ Rule.** Adoption of the rule (H Res 876) that would provide for House floor consideration of the conference report on the bill that would appropriate $32.3 billion in fiscal 2010 for the Interior Department, the EPA and related agencies. It also would provide continuing appropriations through Dec. 18, 2009, for all federal departments and agencies whose fiscal 2010 appropriations bills have not been enacted. Adopted 232-184: D 232-15; R 0-169. Oct. 29, 2009.

825. S Con Res 45. **U.S. Citizens' Release From Iran/Adoption.** Carnahan, D-Mo., motion to suspend the rules and adopt the concurrent resolution that would state that Congress encourages the government of Iran to allow U.S. citizens Joshua Fattal, Shane Bauer and Sarah Shourd to be reunited with their families in the United States. Motion agreed to 423-0: D 250-0; R 173-0. A two-thirds majority of those present and voting (282 in this case) is required for adoption under suspension of the rules. Oct. 29, 2009.

826. HR 2996. **Fiscal 2010 Interior-Environment Appropriations/ Conference Report.** Adoption of the conference report on the bill that would appropriate $32.3 billion in fiscal 2010 for the Interior Department, the EPA and related agencies. The bill would provide $11 billion for the Interior Department, $10.3 billion for the EPA, $5.3 billion for the Forest Service and $4.1 billion for the Indian Health Service. The funding includes $3.4 billion to fight and prevent wildfires. It would provide continuing appropriations through Dec. 18, 2009, for all federal departments and agencies whose fiscal 2010 appropriations bills have not been enacted. Funding would continue at fiscal 2009 levels, with some exceptions. Adopted (thus sent to the Senate) 247-178: D 237-15; R 10-163. A "yea" was a vote in support of the president's position. Oct. 29, 2009.

	822	823	824	825	826
ALABAMA					
1 Bonner	Y	N	N	Y	N
2 Bright	Y	N	N	Y	N
3 Rogers	Y	N	N	Y	N
4 Aderholt	Y	N	N	Y	N
5 Griffith	Y	N	N	Y	N
6 Bachus	Y	N	N	Y	N
7 Davis	Y	Y	Y	Y	Y
ALASKA					
AL Young	Y	N	N	Y	N
ARIZONA					
1 Kirkpatrick	Y	Y	Y	Y	Y
2 Franks	Y	N	N	Y	N
3 Shadegg	Y	N	N	Y	N
4 Pastor	Y	Y	?	Y	Y
5 Mitchell	Y	N	N	Y	N
6 Flake	Y	N	N	Y	N
7 Grijalva	Y	Y	Y	Y	Y
8 Giffords	Y	Y	Y	Y	Y
ARKANSAS					
1 Berry	Y	Y	Y	Y	Y
2 Snyder	Y	Y	Y	Y	Y
3 Boozman	Y	N	N	Y	N
4 Ross	Y	Y	Y	Y	Y
CALIFORNIA					
1 Thompson	Y	Y	Y	Y	Y
2 Herger	?	N	N	Y	N
3 Lungren	Y	N	N	Y	N
4 McClintock	Y	N	N	Y	N
5 Matsui	Y	Y	Y	Y	Y
6 Woolsey	Y	Y	Y	Y	Y
7 Miller, George	Y	Y	Y	Y	Y
8 Pelosi					
9 Lee	Y	Y	Y	Y	Y
10 Vacant					
11 McNerney	Y	Y	Y	Y	Y
12 Speier	?	Y	Y	Y	Y
13 Stark	Y	Y	Y	Y	Y
14 Eshoo	?	Y	Y	Y	Y
15 Honda	Y	Y	Y	Y	Y
16 Lofgren	Y	Y	Y	Y	Y
17 Farr	?	Y	Y	Y	Y
18 Cardoza	Y	Y	N	Y	Y
19 Radanovich	?	N	N	Y	N
20 Costa	Y	N	N	Y	Y
21 Nunes	Y	?	?	Y	?
22 McCarthy	Y	N	N	Y	N
23 Capps	Y	Y	Y	Y	Y
24 Gallegly	Y	N	N	Y	N
25 McKeon	Y	N	N	Y	N
26 Dreier	Y	N	N	Y	N
27 Sherman	Y	Y	Y	Y	Y
28 Berman	Y	Y	Y	Y	Y
29 Schiff	Y	Y	Y	Y	Y
30 Waxman	Y	Y	?	Y	Y
31 Becerra	Y	Y	Y	Y	Y
32 Chu	Y	Y	Y	Y	Y
33 Watson	Y	Y	Y	Y	Y
34 Roybal-Allard	Y	Y	Y	Y	Y
35 Waters	Y	Y	Y	Y	Y
36 Harman	Y	Y	Y	Y	Y
37 Richardson	Y	Y	Y	Y	Y
38 Napolitano	Y	Y	Y	Y	Y
39 Sánchez, Linda	Y	Y	Y	Y	Y
40 Royce	Y	N	N	Y	N
41 Lewis	Y	N	N	Y	N
42 Miller, Gary	Y	N	N	Y	N
43 Baca	Y	Y	Y	Y	Y
44 Calvert	Y	N	N	Y	N
45 Bono Mack	Y	N	N	Y	N
46 Rohrabacher	Y	N	N	Y	N
47 Sanchez, Loretta	Y	Y	Y	Y	Y
48 Campbell	Y	N	N	Y	N
49 Issa	Y	N	N	Y	N
50 Bilbray	Y	N	N	Y	N
51 Filner	Y	Y	Y	Y	Y
52 Hunter	Y	N	N	Y	N
53 Davis	Y	Y	Y	Y	Y
COLORADO					
1 DeGette	Y	Y	Y	Y	Y
2 Polis	Y	Y	Y	Y	Y
3 Salazar	Y	Y	Y	Y	Y
4 Markey	Y	Y	Y	Y	Y
5 Lamborn	Y	N	N	Y	N
6 Coffman	Y	N	N	Y	N
7 Perlmutter	Y	Y	Y	Y	Y
CONNECTICUT					
1 Larson	Y	Y	Y	Y	Y
2 Courtney	Y	Y	Y	Y	Y
3 DeLauro	Y	Y	Y	Y	Y
4 Himes	Y	Y	Y	Y	Y
5 Murphy	Y	Y	Y	Y	
DELAWARE					
AL Castle	Y	N	N	Y	N
FLORIDA					
1 Miller	Y	N	N	Y	N
2 Boyd	Y	Y	Y	Y	Y
3 Brown	Y	Y	Y	Y	Y
4 Crenshaw	Y	N	N	Y	N
5 Brown-Waite	Y	N	N	Y	N
6 Stearns	Y	N	N	Y	N
7 Mica	Y	N	N	Y	N
8 Grayson	Y	Y	Y	Y	Y
9 Bilirakis	Y	N	N	Y	N
10 Young	Y	N	N	Y	N
11 Castor	Y	Y	Y	Y	Y
12 Putnam	Y	N	N	Y	N
13 Buchanan	Y	N	N	Y	N
14 Mack	Y	N	N	Y	N
15 Posey	Y	N	N	Y	N
16 Rooney	Y	N	N	Y	N
17 Meek	Y	Y	Y	Y	Y
18 Ros-Lehtinen	Y	N	N	Y	N
19 Wexler	Y	Y	Y	Y	Y
20 Wasserman Schultz	Y	Y	Y	Y	Y
21 Diaz-Balart, L.	Y	N	N	Y	N
22 Klein	Y	Y	Y	Y	Y
23 Hastings	?	Y	Y	Y	Y
24 Kosmas	Y	Y	Y	Y	Y
25 Diaz-Balart, M.	Y	N	N	Y	N
GEORGIA					
1 Kingston	Y	N	N	Y	N
2 Bishop	Y	Y	Y	Y	Y
3 Westmoreland	Y	N	N	Y	N
4 Johnson	Y	Y	Y	Y	Y
5 Lewis	Y	Y	Y	Y	Y
6 Price	Y	N	N	Y	N
7 Linder	Y	N	N	Y	N
8 Marshall	Y	Y	Y	Y	Y
9 Deal	Y	N	?	Y	N
10 Broun	Y	N	N	Y	N
11 Gingrey	Y	N	N	Y	N
12 Barrow	Y	Y	Y	Y	Y
13 Scott	Y	Y	Y	Y	Y
HAWAII					
1 Abercrombie	Y	?	?	?	Y
2 Hirono	Y	Y	?	Y	Y
IDAHO					
1 Minnick	Y	N	N	Y	N
2 Simpson	Y	N	N	Y	N
ILLINOIS					
1 Rush	Y	Y	Y	?	Y
2 Jackson	Y	Y	Y	Y	Y
3 Lipinski	Y	Y	Y	Y	Y
4 Gutierrez	Y	Y	Y	Y	Y
5 Quigley	Y	Y	Y	Y	Y
6 Roskam	Y	N	N	Y	N
7 Davis	Y	Y	Y	Y	Y
8 Bean	Y	Y	Y	Y	Y
9 Schakowsky	Y	Y	Y	Y	Y
10 Kirk	Y	N	N	Y	N
11 Halvorson	Y	Y	Y	Y	Y
12 Costello	Y	Y	Y	Y	Y
13 Biggert	Y	N	N	Y	N
14 Foster	Y	Y	Y	Y	Y
15 Johnson	Y	N	N	Y	N

KEY   **Republicans**   Democrats

Y Voted for (yea)	X Paired against
# Paired for	– Announced against
+ Announced for	P Voted "present"
N Voted against (nay)	

C Voted "present" to avoid possible conflict of interest

? Did not vote or otherwise make a position known

	822	823	824	825	826
16 Manzullo	Y	N	N	Y	N
17 Hare	Y	Y	Y	Y	Y
18 Schock	Y	N	N	Y	N
19 Shimkus	Y	N	N	Y	N
INDIANA					
1 Visclosky	Y	Y	Y	Y	Y
2 Donnelly	Y	Y	Y	Y	N
3 Souder	Y	N	N	Y	N
4 Buyer	Y	?	?	?	?
5 Burton	Y	N	N	Y	N
6 Pence	Y	N	N	Y	N
7 Carson	Y	Y	Y	Y	Y
8 Ellsworth	Y	Y	Y	Y	Y
9 Hill	Y	Y	Y	Y	N
IOWA					
1 Braley	Y	Y	Y	Y	Y
2 Loebsack	Y	Y	Y	Y	Y
3 Boswell	Y	Y	Y	Y	Y
4 Latham	Y	N	N	Y	N
5 King	?	N	N	Y	N
KANSAS					
1 Moran	Y	N	N	Y	N
2 Jenkins	Y	N	N	Y	N
3 Moore	Y	Y	Y	Y	N
4 Tiahrt	Y	N	N	Y	N
KENTUCKY					
1 Whitfield	Y	N	N	Y	N
2 Guthrie	Y	N	N	Y	N
3 Yarmuth	Y	Y	Y	Y	Y
4 Davis	Y	N	N	Y	N
5 Rogers	Y	N	N	Y	N
6 Chandler	Y	Y	Y	Y	Y
LOUISIANA					
1 Scalise	Y	N	N	Y	N
2 Cao	Y	N	N	Y	Y
3 Melancon	Y	Y	N	Y	Y
4 Fleming	Y	N	N	Y	N
5 Alexander	Y	N	N	Y	N
6 Cassidy	Y	N	N	Y	N
7 Boustany	Y	N	N	Y	N
MAINE					
1 Pingree	Y	Y	Y	Y	Y
2 Michaud	Y	?	Y	Y	Y
MARYLAND					
1 Kratovil	Y	N	N	Y	N
2 Ruppersberger	Y	Y	Y	Y	Y
3 Sarbanes	Y	Y	Y	Y	Y
4 Edwards	Y	Y	Y	Y	Y
5 Hoyer	?	Y	Y	Y	Y
6 Bartlett	Y	N	N	Y	N
7 Cummings	Y	Y	Y	Y	Y
8 Van Hollen	Y	?	Y	Y	Y
MASSACHUSETTS					
1 Olver	Y	Y	Y	Y	Y
2 Neal	Y	Y	Y	Y	Y
3 McGovern	Y	Y	Y	Y	Y
4 Frank	Y	Y	Y	Y	Y
5 Tsongas	?	Y	Y	Y	Y
6 Tierney	Y	Y	Y	Y	Y
7 Markey	Y	Y	Y	Y	Y
8 Capuano	Y	Y	Y	Y	Y
9 Lynch	Y	Y	Y	Y	Y
10 Delahunt	Y	Y	Y	Y	Y
MICHIGAN					
1 Stupak	Y	Y	Y	Y	Y
2 Hoekstra	Y	N	N	Y	N
3 Ehlers	Y	N	N	Y	N
4 Camp	Y	N	N	Y	N
5 Kildee	Y	Y	Y	Y	Y
6 Upton	Y	N	N	Y	N
7 Schauer	Y	Y	Y	Y	Y
8 Rogers	?	N	N	Y	N
9 Peters	Y	Y	Y	Y	Y
10 Miller	Y	N	N	Y	N
11 McCotter	Y	?	N	Y	N
12 Levin	Y	Y	Y	Y	Y
13 Kilpatrick	Y	Y	Y	Y	Y
14 Conyers	Y	Y	Y	Y	Y
15 Dingell	Y	Y	Y	Y	Y
MINNESOTA					
1 Walz	Y	Y	Y	Y	Y
2 Kline	Y	N	N	Y	N
3 Paulsen	Y	N	N	Y	N
4 McCollum	Y	Y	Y	Y	Y

	822	823	824	825	826
5 Ellison	Y	Y	Y	Y	Y
6 Bachmann	Y	N	N	Y	N
7 Peterson	Y	Y	Y	Y	Y
8 Oberstar	Y	?	Y	Y	Y
MISSISSIPPI					
1 Childers	Y	N	N	Y	N
2 Thompson	Y	Y	Y	Y	Y
3 Harper	Y	N	N	Y	N
4 Taylor	Y	N	N	Y	N
MISSOURI					
1 Clay	Y	Y	Y	Y	Y
2 Akin	Y	N	N	Y	N
3 Carnahan	Y	Y	Y	Y	Y
4 Skelton	Y	Y	Y	Y	Y
5 Cleaver	Y	Y	Y	Y	Y
6 Graves	Y	N	N	Y	N
7 Blunt	Y	N	N	Y	N
8 Emerson	Y	N	?	Y	N
9 Luetkemeyer	Y	N	N	Y	N
MONTANA					
AL Rehberg	Y	N	N	Y	N
NEBRASKA					
1 Fortenberry	Y	N	N	Y	N
2 Terry	Y	N	N	Y	N
3 Smith	Y	N	N	Y	N
NEVADA					
1 Berkley	Y	Y	Y	Y	Y
2 Heller	Y	N	N	Y	N
3 Titus	Y	Y	Y	Y	Y
NEW HAMPSHIRE					
1 Shea-Porter	Y	Y	Y	Y	Y
2 Hodes	Y	Y	Y	Y	Y
NEW JERSEY					
1 Andrews	Y	Y	Y	Y	Y
2 LoBiondo	Y	N	N	Y	Y
3 Adler	Y	Y	Y	Y	Y
4 Smith	Y	N	N	Y	Y
5 Garrett	Y	N	N	Y	N
6 Pallone	Y	Y	Y	Y	Y
7 Lance	Y	N	N	Y	Y
8 Pascrell	Y	Y	Y	Y	Y
9 Rothman	Y	Y	Y	Y	Y
10 Payne	Y	Y	Y	Y	Y
11 Frelinghuysen	Y	N	N	Y	Y
12 Holt	Y	Y	Y	Y	Y
13 Sires	Y	Y	Y	Y	Y
NEW MEXICO					
1 Heinrich	Y	Y	Y	Y	Y
2 Teague	Y	Y	Y	Y	Y
3 Lujan	Y	Y	Y	Y	Y
NEW YORK					
1 Bishop	Y	Y	Y	Y	Y
2 Israel	Y	Y	Y	Y	Y
3 King	Y	N	N	Y	N
4 McCarthy	Y	Y	Y	Y	Y
5 Ackerman	Y	Y	Y	Y	Y
6 Meeks	Y	Y	Y	Y	Y
7 Crowley	Y	Y	Y	Y	Y
8 Nadler	Y	Y	Y	Y	?
9 Weiner	Y	Y	Y	Y	Y
10 Towns	Y	Y	Y	Y	?
11 Clarke	Y	Y	Y	Y	Y
12 Velázquez	Y	?	?	Y	Y
13 McMahon	Y	Y	Y	Y	Y
14 Maloney	Y	Y	Y	Y	Y
15 Rangel	Y	Y	Y	Y	Y
16 Serrano	Y	Y	Y	Y	Y
17 Engel	Y	?	Y	Y	Y
18 Lowey	Y	Y	Y	Y	Y
19 Hall	Y	Y	Y	Y	Y
20 Murphy	Y	N	Y	Y	Y
21 Tonko	Y	Y	Y	Y	Y
22 Hinchey	Y	Y	Y	Y	Y
23 Vacant					
24 Arcuri	Y	Y	Y	Y	Y
25 Maffei	Y	Y	Y	Y	Y
26 Lee	Y	N	N	Y	N
27 Higgins	Y	Y	Y	Y	Y
28 Slaughter	Y	Y	Y	Y	Y
29 Massa	Y	Y	Y	Y	Y
NORTH CAROLINA					
1 Butterfield	Y	Y	Y	Y	Y
2 Etheridge	Y	Y	Y	Y	Y
3 Jones	Y	N	N	Y	N
4 Price	Y	Y	Y	Y	Y

	822	823	824	825	826
5 Foxx	Y	N	N	Y	N
6 Coble	Y	N	N	Y	N
7 McIntyre	Y	Y	Y	Y	Y
8 Kissell	Y	Y	Y	Y	Y
9 Myrick	Y	N	N	Y	N
10 McHenry	Y	N	N	Y	N
11 Shuler	Y	Y	Y	Y	Y
12 Watt	Y	Y	Y	Y	Y
13 Miller	Y	Y	Y	Y	Y
NORTH DAKOTA					
AL Pomeroy	Y	?	Y	Y	Y
OHIO					
1 Driehaus	Y	Y	Y	Y	Y
2 Schmidt	Y	N	N	Y	N
3 Turner	Y	N	N	?	N
4 Jordan	Y	N	N	Y	N
5 Latta	Y	N	N	Y	N
6 Wilson	Y	Y	Y	Y	Y
7 Austria	Y	N	N	Y	N
8 Boehner	Y	N	N	Y	N
9 Kaptur	Y	Y	Y	Y	Y
10 Kucinich	Y	Y	Y	Y	N
11 Fudge	Y	Y	Y	Y	Y
12 Tiberi	Y	N	N	Y	N
13 Sutton	Y	Y	Y	Y	Y
14 LaTourette	Y	N	?	Y	Y
15 Kilroy	Y	Y	Y	Y	Y
16 Boccieri	Y	Y	Y	Y	Y
17 Ryan	Y	Y	Y	Y	Y
18 Space	Y	Y	Y	Y	Y
OKLAHOMA					
1 Sullivan	Y	N	?	Y	N
2 Boren	Y	Y	Y	Y	Y
3 Lucas	Y	N	N	Y	N
4 Cole	Y	N	N	Y	Y
5 Fallin	Y	N	N	Y	Y
OREGON					
1 Wu	?	Y	Y	Y	Y
2 Walden	Y	N	N	Y	N
3 Blumenauer	Y	Y	Y	Y	Y
4 DeFazio	Y	Y	Y	Y	Y
5 Schrader	Y	Y	Y	Y	Y
PENNSYLVANIA					
1 Brady	Y	Y	Y	Y	Y
2 Fattah	Y	?	?	?	Y
3 Dahlkemper	Y	Y	Y	Y	Y
4 Altmire	Y	Y	Y	Y	Y
5 Thompson	Y	N	N	Y	Y
6 Gerlach	Y	N	N	Y	Y
7 Sestak	Y	Y	Y	Y	Y
8 Murphy, P.	Y	?	?	?	?
9 Shuster	?	N	N	Y	N
10 Carney	Y	Y	Y	Y	Y
11 Kanjorski	Y	Y	Y	Y	Y
12 Murtha	Y	Y	Y	Y	Y
13 Schwartz	Y	Y	Y	Y	Y
14 Doyle	Y	Y	Y	Y	Y
15 Dent	Y	N	N	Y	Y
16 Pitts	Y	N	N	Y	N
17 Holden	Y	Y	Y	Y	Y
18 Murphy, T.	Y	N	N	Y	?
19 Platts	Y	N	N	Y	N
RHODE ISLAND					
1 Kennedy	Y	Y	Y	Y	Y
2 Langevin	Y	Y	Y	Y	Y
SOUTH CAROLINA					
1 Brown	Y	N	N	Y	N
2 Wilson	Y	N	N	Y	N
3 Barrett	?	?	?	?	?
4 Inglis	Y	N	N	Y	N
5 Spratt	Y	Y	Y	Y	Y
6 Clyburn	Y	Y	Y	Y	Y
SOUTH DAKOTA					
AL Herseth Sandlin	Y	Y	Y	Y	Y
TENNESSEE					
1 Roe	Y	N	N	Y	N
2 Duncan	Y	N	N	Y	N
3 Wamp	Y	N	N	Y	N
4 Davis	Y	Y	Y	Y	Y
5 Cooper	Y	Y	Y	Y	Y
6 Gordon	Y	Y	Y	Y	Y
7 Blackburn	Y	N	N	Y	N
8 Tanner	Y	Y	Y	Y	Y
9 Cohen	Y	Y	Y	Y	Y

	822	823	824	825	826
TEXAS					
1 Gohmert	?	N	N	Y	N
2 Poe	Y	N	N	Y	N
3 Johnson, S.	Y	N	N	Y	N
4 Hall	?	N	N	Y	N
5 Hensarling	Y	N	N	Y	N
6 Barton	Y	N	N	Y	N
7 Culberson	Y	N	N	Y	N
8 Brady	Y	N	N	Y	N
9 Green, A.	Y	Y	Y	Y	Y
10 McCaul	Y	N	N	Y	N
11 Conaway	Y	N	N	Y	N
12 Granger	Y	N	N	Y	N
13 Thornberry	Y	N	N	Y	N
14 Paul	Y	N	N	Y	N
15 Hinojosa	Y	Y	Y	Y	Y
16 Reyes	Y	Y	Y	Y	Y
17 Edwards	Y	Y	Y	Y	Y
18 Jackson Lee	Y	Y	Y	Y	Y
19 Neugebauer	Y	N	N	Y	N
20 Gonzalez	Y	Y	Y	Y	Y
21 Smith	Y	N	N	Y	N
22 Olson	Y	N	N	Y	N
23 Rodriguez	Y	Y	Y	Y	Y
24 Marchant	Y	N	N	Y	N
25 Doggett	Y	Y	Y	Y	Y
26 Burgess	Y	N	?	Y	N
27 Ortiz	Y	Y	Y	Y	Y
28 Cuellar	Y	Y	Y	Y	Y
29 Green, G.	Y	Y	Y	Y	Y
30 Johnson, E.	Y	Y	Y	Y	Y
31 Carter	Y	N	N	Y	N
32 Sessions	Y	N	N	Y	N
UTAH					
1 Bishop	Y	N	N	Y	N
2 Matheson	Y	Y	Y	Y	Y
3 Chaffetz	Y	N	N	Y	N
VERMONT					
AL Welch	Y	Y	Y	Y	Y
VIRGINIA					
1 Wittman	Y	N	N	Y	N
2 Nye	Y	N	N	Y	N
3 Scott	Y	Y	Y	?	Y
4 Forbes	Y	N	N	Y	N
5 Perriello	Y	N	N	Y	N
6 Goodlatte	Y	N	N	Y	N
7 Cantor	Y	N	N	Y	N
8 Moran	Y	Y	Y	Y	Y
9 Boucher	Y	Y	Y	Y	Y
10 Wolf	Y	N	N	Y	N
11 Connolly	Y	?	Y	Y	Y
WASHINGTON					
1 Inslee	Y	Y	Y	Y	Y
2 Larsen	Y	Y	Y	Y	Y
3 Baird	?	N	N	Y	N
4 Hastings	Y	N	N	Y	N
5 McMorris Rodgers	Y	N	N	Y	N
6 Dicks	Y	Y	Y	Y	Y
7 McDermott	Y	Y	Y	Y	Y
8 Reichert	Y	N	N	Y	N
9 Smith	Y	Y	Y	Y	Y
WEST VIRGINIA					
1 Mollohan	Y	Y	Y	Y	Y
2 Capito	Y	N	N	Y	N
3 Rahall	Y	Y	Y	Y	Y
WISCONSIN					
1 Ryan	Y	N	N	Y	N
2 Baldwin	Y	Y	Y	Y	Y
3 Kind	Y	Y	Y	Y	Y
4 Moore	Y	Y	Y	Y	Y
5 Sensenbrenner	Y	N	N	Y	N
6 Petri	Y	N	N	Y	N
7 Obey	Y	Y	Y	Y	Y
8 Kagen	Y	Y	Y	Y	Y
WYOMING					
AL Lummis	Y	N	N	Y	N
DELEGATES					
Faleomavaega (A.S.)					
Norton (D.C.)					
Bordallo (Guam)					
Sablan (N. Marianas)					
Pierluisi (P.R.)					
Christensen (V.I.)					

IN THE HOUSE | By Vote Number

827. **H Res 783. Hispanic Heritage Month/Adoption.** Lynch, D-Mass., motion to suspend the rules and adopt the resolution that would recognize Hispanic Heritage Month and encourage Americans to observe the month with appropriate activities. Motion agreed to 423-0: D 251-0; R 172-0. A two-thirds majority of those present and voting (282 in this case) is required for adoption under suspension of the rules. Oct. 29, 2009.

828. **HR 3854. Small Business Administration Loans Financing/ Earmark Ban.** Flake, R-Ariz., amendment that would prohibit congressionally directed spending of grants made under a program for new businesses. Adopted in Committee of the Whole 370-55: D 203-53; R 167-2. Oct. 29, 2009.

829. **HR 3854. Small Business Administration Loans Financing/ Recommit.** Cantor, R-Va., motion to recommit the bill to the Small Business Committee with instructions that it be immediately reported back with an amendment that would require the Small Business Administration to study whether agency loans fail to provide adequate capital for businesses to offset increases in income taxes, health care expenses, energy costs and other provisions of the bill. Motion agreed to 272-149: D 101-149; R 171-0. Oct. 29, 2009.

830. **HR 3854. Small Business Administration Loans Financing/ Passage.** Passage of the bill that would reauthorize and modify the Small Business Administration (SBA) loan programs. It would authorize $20 billion in fiscal 2010 and 2011 for SBA 7(a) loans, and $9 billion in fiscal 2010 and $10 billion in fiscal 2011 for loans to small businesses working to address community development goals. It would extend some stimulus programs to allow the SBA to increase loan limits and authorize additional loans to renewable-energy industries and businesses in low-income communities and rural areas. It would provide loan guarantees to health care professionals purchasing health information technology. Passed 389-32: D 250-0; R 139-32. Oct. 29, 2009.

831. **H Res 729. National Firefighters Memorial Day/Adoption.** Lynch, D-Mass., motion to suspend the rules and adopt the resolution that would support the designation of a National Firefighters Memorial Day to commemorate federal, state and local firefighters killed or disabled in the line of duty. Motion agreed to 390-0: D 231-0; R 159-0. A two-thirds majority of those present and voting (260 in this case) is required for adoption under suspension of the rules. Oct. 29, 2009.

	827	828	829	830	831
ALABAMA					
1 **Bonner**	Y	Y	Y	Y	Y
2 Bright	Y	Y	Y	Y	Y
3 **Rogers**	Y	Y	Y	Y	Y
4 **Aderholt**	Y	Y	Y	Y	Y
5 Griffith	Y	Y	Y	Y	Y
6 **Bachus**	Y	Y	Y	Y	Y
7 Davis	Y	Y	Y	Y	Y
ALASKA					
AL **Young**	Y	N	Y	Y	Y
ARIZONA					
1 Kirkpatrick	Y	Y	Y	Y	Y
2 **Franks**	Y	Y	Y	N	Y
3 **Shadegg**	Y	Y	Y	N	?
4 Pastor	Y	Y	N	Y	Y
5 Mitchell	Y	Y	Y	Y	Y
6 **Flake**	Y	Y	Y	N	?
7 Grijalva	Y	N	N	N	?
8 Giffords	Y	Y	Y	Y	Y
ARKANSAS					
1 Berry	Y	Y	N	Y	Y
2 Snyder	Y	Y	Y	Y	Y
3 **Boozman**	Y	Y	Y	Y	Y
4 Ross	Y	Y	Y	Y	Y
CALIFORNIA					
1 Thompson	Y	Y	N	Y	Y
2 **Herger**	Y	Y	Y	Y	Y
3 **Lungren**	Y	Y	Y	Y	Y
4 **McClintock**	Y	Y	Y	N	Y
5 Matsui	Y	N	N	Y	Y
6 Woolsey	Y	N	N	Y	?
7 Miller, George	Y	N	N	Y	Y
8 Pelosi					
9 Lee	Y	N	N	Y	?
10 Vacant					
11 McNerney	Y	Y	Y	Y	Y
12 Speier	Y	Y	N	Y	Y
13 Stark	Y	N	N	Y	Y
14 Eshoo	Y	Y	N	Y	Y
15 Honda	Y	Y	N	Y	?
16 Lofgren	Y	Y	N	Y	Y
17 Farr	Y	Y	N	Y	Y
18 Cardoza	Y	Y	Y	Y	Y
19 **Radanovich**	Y	Y	Y	Y	Y
20 Costa	Y	Y	Y	Y	Y
21 **Nunes**	?	?	?	?	?
22 **McCarthy**	Y	Y	Y	Y	Y
23 Capps	Y	Y	N	Y	Y
24 **Gallegly**	Y	Y	Y	Y	?
25 **McKeon**	Y	Y	Y	Y	Y
26 **Dreier**	Y	Y	Y	Y	Y
27 Sherman	Y	N	N	Y	Y
28 Berman	Y	?	?	?	?
29 Schiff	Y	Y	N	Y	Y
30 Waxman	Y	Y	N	Y	?
31 Becerra	Y	Y	N	Y	Y
32 Chu	Y	Y	N	Y	Y
33 Watson	Y	Y	N	Y	Y
34 Roybal-Allard	Y	Y	N	Y	?
35 Waters	Y	Y	N	Y	Y
36 Harman	Y	Y	N	Y	Y
37 Richardson	Y	Y	Y	Y	Y
38 Napolitano	Y	Y	N	Y	Y
39 Sánchez, Linda	Y	Y	N	Y	?
40 **Royce**	Y	Y	Y	N	Y
41 **Lewis**	Y	Y	Y	N	Y
42 **Miller, Gary**	Y	Y	Y	Y	Y
43 **Baca**	Y	Y	N	Y	Y
44 **Calvert**	Y	Y	Y	Y	Y
45 **Bono Mack**	Y	Y	Y	Y	Y
46 **Rohrabacher**	Y	Y	Y	Y	Y
47 Sanchez, Loretta	Y	N	N	Y	?
48 **Campbell**	Y	Y	Y	N	Y
49 **Issa**	Y	Y	Y	N	Y
50 **Bilbray**	Y	Y	Y	Y	Y
51 Filner	Y	N	N	Y	Y
52 **Hunter**	Y	Y	Y	Y	Y
53 Davis	Y	Y	N	Y	Y
COLORADO					
1 DeGette	Y	Y	Y	Y	Y
2 Polis	Y	Y	Y	Y	Y
3 Salazar	Y	Y	N	Y	Y
4 Markey	Y	Y	Y	Y	Y
5 **Lamborn**	Y	Y	Y	N	Y
6 **Coffman**	?	Y	Y	Y	Y
7 Perlmutter	Y	Y	Y	Y	Y
CONNECTICUT					
1 Larson	Y	N	N	Y	?
2 Courtney	Y	Y	N	Y	Y
3 DeLauro	Y	Y	N	Y	Y
4 Himes	Y	Y	Y	Y	Y
5 Murphy	Y	Y	Y	Y	Y
DELAWARE					
AL **Castle**	Y	Y	Y	Y	Y
FLORIDA					
1 **Miller**	Y	Y	N	N	Y
2 Boyd	Y	Y	Y	Y	Y
3 Brown	Y	N	N	Y	Y
4 **Crenshaw**	Y	Y	Y	Y	Y
5 **Brown-Waite**	Y	?	?	?	?
6 **Stearns**	Y	Y	Y	Y	Y
7 **Mica**	Y	Y	Y	Y	Y
8 Grayson	Y	N	N	Y	Y
9 **Bilirakis**	Y	Y	Y	Y	Y
10 **Young**	Y	Y	Y	Y	Y
11 Castor	Y	Y	N	Y	Y
12 **Putnam**	Y	Y	Y	Y	Y
13 **Buchanan**	Y	Y	Y	Y	Y
14 **Mack**	Y	Y	Y	Y	Y
15 **Posey**	Y	Y	Y	Y	Y
16 **Rooney**	Y	Y	Y	Y	Y
17 Meek	Y	N	N	Y	Y
18 **Ros-Lehtinen**	Y	Y	Y	Y	?
19 Wexler	Y	N	N	Y	Y
20 Wasserman Schultz	Y	N	N	Y	Y
21 **Diaz-Balart, L.**	Y	Y	Y	Y	?
22 Klein	Y	Y	Y	Y	Y
23 Hastings	Y	N	N	Y	Y
24 Kosmas	Y	Y	Y	Y	Y
25 **Diaz-Balart, M.**	Y	Y	Y	Y	?
GEORGIA					
1 **Kingston**	Y	Y	N	N	Y
2 Bishop	Y	Y	Y	Y	Y
3 **Westmoreland**	Y	Y	Y	Y	Y
4 Johnson	?	Y	N	Y	Y
5 Lewis	Y	N	N	Y	Y
6 **Price**	Y	Y	N	N	Y
7 **Linder**	Y	?	Y	Y	Y
8 Marshall	Y	Y	Y	Y	Y
9 **Deal**	Y	Y	Y	Y	Y
10 **Broun**	Y	Y	N	N	Y
11 **Gingrey**	Y	Y	Y	Y	Y
12 Barrow	Y	Y	Y	Y	Y
13 Scott	Y	Y	N	Y	?
HAWAII					
1 Abercrombie	Y	Y	N	Y	Y
2 Hirono	Y	Y	N	Y	Y
IDAHO					
1 **Minnick**	Y	Y	Y	Y	Y
2 **Simpson**	Y	Y	Y	Y	Y
ILLINOIS					
1 Rush	Y	Y	Y	Y	Y
2 Jackson	Y	Y	N	Y	Y
3 Lipinski	Y	Y	Y	Y	Y
4 Gutierrez	?	Y	N	Y	Y
5 Quigley	Y	Y	N	Y	?
6 **Roskam**	Y	Y	Y	Y	Y
7 Davis	Y	Y	N	Y	Y
8 Bean	Y	Y	N	Y	Y
9 Schakowsky	Y	N	N	Y	?
10 **Kirk**	Y	Y	Y	Y	Y
11 Halvorson	Y	Y	N	Y	Y
12 Costello	Y	N	N	Y	Y
13 **Biggert**	Y	Y	Y	Y	Y
14 Foster	Y	Y	Y	Y	Y
15 **Johnson**	Y	Y	Y	Y	Y

KEY	**Republicans**	Democrats		
Y Voted for (yea)		X Paired against		C Voted "present" to avoid possible conflict of interest
# Paired for		– Announced against		
+ Announced for		P Voted "present"		? Did not vote or otherwise make a position known
N Voted against (nay)				

	827	828	829	830	831
16 **Manzullo**	Y	Y	Y	Y	Y
17 Hare	Y	Y	N	Y	Y
18 **Schock**	Y	Y	Y	Y	Y
19 **Shimkus**	Y	Y	Y	Y	Y
INDIANA					
1 Visclosky	Y	Y	N	Y	Y
2 Donnelly	Y	Y	Y	Y	Y
3 **Souder**	Y	Y	Y	Y	Y
4 **Buyer**	?	?	?	?	?
5 **Burton**	Y	Y	Y	N	Y
6 **Pence**	Y	Y	Y	Y	Y
7 Carson	Y	Y	N	Y	Y
8 Ellsworth	Y	Y	Y	Y	Y
9 Hill	Y	Y	Y	Y	Y
IOWA					
1 Braley	Y	Y	N	Y	Y
2 Loebsack	Y	Y	N	Y	?
3 Boswell	Y	Y	Y	Y	Y
4 **Latham**	Y	Y	Y	Y	Y
5 **King**	Y	Y	Y	Y	Y
KANSAS					
1 **Moran**	Y	Y	Y	Y	Y
2 **Jenkins**	Y	Y	Y	Y	Y
3 Moore	Y	Y	Y	Y	Y
4 **Tiahrt**	Y	Y	Y	Y	Y
KENTUCKY					
1 **Whitfield**	Y	Y	Y	Y	Y
2 **Guthrie**	Y	Y	Y	Y	Y
3 Yarmuth	Y	Y	N	Y	Y
4 **Davis**	Y	Y	Y	Y	Y
5 **Rogers**	Y	Y	Y	Y	Y
6 Chandler	Y	Y	Y	Y	Y
LOUISIANA					
1 **Scalise**	Y	Y	Y	Y	Y
2 **Cao**	Y	Y	Y	Y	Y
3 Melancon	Y	Y	Y	Y	Y
4 **Fleming**	Y	Y	Y	Y	Y
5 **Alexander**	Y	Y	Y	Y	Y
6 **Cassidy**	Y	Y	Y	Y	Y
7 **Boustany**	Y	Y	Y	Y	Y
MAINE					
1 Pingree	Y	Y	Y	Y	Y
2 Michaud	Y	Y	Y	Y	Y
MARYLAND					
1 Kratovil	Y	Y	N	Y	Y
2 Ruppersberger	Y	Y	Y	Y	Y
3 Sarbanes	Y	Y	N	Y	Y
4 Edwards	Y	N	N	Y	Y
5 Hoyer	Y	Y	N	Y	Y
6 **Bartlett**	Y	Y	Y	Y	Y
7 Cummings	Y	Y	Y	Y	Y
8 Van Hollen	Y	Y	Y	Y	Y
MASSACHUSETTS					
1 Olver	Y	Y	N	Y	Y
2 Neal	Y	N	N	Y	Y
3 McGovern	Y	Y	N	Y	Y
4 Frank	Y	N	N	Y	Y
5 Tsongas	Y	Y	N	Y	Y
6 Tierney	Y	Y	N	Y	Y
7 Markey	Y	Y	N	Y	Y
8 Capuano	Y	?	?	?	?
9 Lynch	Y	Y	Y	Y	Y
10 Delahunt	Y	N	N	Y	Y
MICHIGAN					
1 Stupak	Y	Y	N	Y	Y
2 **Hoekstra**	Y	Y	Y	Y	?
3 **Ehlers**	Y	Y	Y	Y	Y
4 **Camp**	Y	Y	Y	Y	Y
5 Kildee	Y	N	N	Y	Y
6 **Upton**	Y	Y	Y	Y	Y
7 Schauer	Y	Y	N	Y	Y
8 **Rogers**	Y	Y	Y	Y	Y
9 Peters	Y	Y	Y	Y	Y
10 **Miller**	Y	Y	Y	Y	Y
11 **McCotter**	Y	Y	Y	Y	Y
12 Levin	Y	Y	N	Y	Y
13 Kilpatrick	Y	N	N	Y	Y
14 Conyers	Y	N	N	Y	Y
15 Dingell	Y	Y	N	Y	Y
MINNESOTA					
1 Walz	Y	Y	N	Y	Y
2 **Kline**	Y	Y	Y	Y	Y
3 **Paulsen**	Y	Y	Y	Y	Y
4 McCollum	Y	Y	N	Y	Y

	827	828	829	830	831
5 Ellison	Y	N	N	Y	Y
6 **Bachmann**	Y	Y	Y	Y	Y
7 Peterson	Y	Y	Y	Y	Y
8 Oberstar	Y	Y	N	Y	Y
MISSISSIPPI					
1 Childers	Y	Y	Y	Y	Y
2 Thompson	Y	N	N	Y	Y
3 **Harper**	Y	Y	Y	Y	Y
4 Taylor	Y	Y	Y	Y	Y
MISSOURI					
1 Clay	Y	Y	N	Y	Y
2 **Akin**	Y	Y	Y	N	Y
3 Carnahan	Y	Y	Y	Y	Y
4 Skelton	Y	Y	Y	Y	Y
5 Cleaver	Y	Y	Y	Y	Y
6 **Graves**	Y	Y	Y	Y	Y
7 **Blunt**	Y	Y	Y	Y	Y
8 **Emerson**	Y	Y	Y	Y	Y
9 **Luetkemeyer**	Y	Y	Y	Y	Y
MONTANA					
AL **Rehberg**	Y	Y	Y	Y	Y
NEBRASKA					
1 **Fortenberry**	Y	Y	Y	Y	Y
2 **Terry**	Y	Y	Y	Y	Y
3 **Smith**	Y	Y	Y	Y	Y
NEVADA					
1 Berkley	Y	N	Y	Y	Y
2 **Heller**	Y	Y	Y	Y	Y
3 Titus	Y	Y	Y	Y	Y
NEW HAMPSHIRE					
1 Shea-Porter	Y	N	Y	Y	Y
2 Hodes	Y	Y	N	Y	Y
NEW JERSEY					
1 Andrews	Y	Y	N	Y	Y
2 **LoBiondo**	Y	Y	Y	Y	Y
3 Adler	Y	Y	Y	Y	Y
4 **Smith**	Y	Y	Y	Y	Y
5 **Garrett**	Y	Y	Y	N	?
6 Pallone	Y	Y	N	Y	Y
7 **Lance**	Y	Y	Y	Y	Y
8 Pascrell	Y	N	N	Y	Y
9 Rothman	Y	Y	Y	Y	Y
10 Payne	Y	?	?	?	?
11 **Frelinghuysen**	Y	Y	Y	Y	Y
12 Holt	Y	Y	N	Y	Y
13 Sires	Y	N	Y	Y	Y
NEW MEXICO					
1 Heinrich	Y	Y	Y	Y	Y
2 Teague	Y	Y	Y	Y	Y
3 Lujan	Y	Y	Y	Y	Y
NEW YORK					
1 Bishop	Y	Y	N	Y	Y
2 Israel	Y	Y	Y	Y	Y
3 **King**	Y	Y	Y	Y	Y
4 McCarthy	Y	Y	N	Y	Y
5 Ackerman	Y	Y	Y	Y	Y
6 Meeks	Y	N	N	Y	Y
7 Crowley	Y	?	?	?	?
8 Nadler	Y	N	N	Y	?
9 Weiner	Y	Y	Y	Y	Y
10 Towns	Y	Y	N	Y	Y
11 Clarke	Y	Y	N	Y	?
12 Velázquez	Y	Y	Y	Y	Y
13 McMahon	Y	Y	Y	Y	Y
14 Maloney	Y	Y	Y	Y	Y
15 Rangel	Y	N	N	Y	?
16 Serrano	Y	N	N	Y	Y
17 Engel	Y	Y	N	Y	Y
18 Lowey	Y	Y	Y	Y	Y
19 Hall	Y	Y	N	Y	Y
20 Murphy	Y	Y	Y	Y	?
21 Tonko	Y	N	Y	Y	Y
22 Hinchey	Y	N	N	Y	Y
23 Vacant					
24 Arcuri	Y	Y	Y	Y	Y
25 Maffei	Y	Y	Y	Y	Y
26 **Lee**	Y	Y	Y	Y	Y
27 Higgins	Y	Y	Y	Y	Y
28 Slaughter	Y	Y	N	Y	Y
29 Massa	Y	Y	Y	Y	Y
NORTH CAROLINA					
1 Butterfield	Y	N	N	Y	Y
2 Etheridge	Y	Y	Y	Y	Y
3 **Jones**	Y	Y	Y	Y	Y
4 Price	Y	Y	N	Y	Y

	827	828	829	830	831
5 **Foxx**	Y	Y	Y	N	Y
6 **Coble**	Y	Y	Y	Y	Y
7 McIntyre	Y	Y	Y	Y	Y
8 Kissell	Y	Y	Y	Y	Y
9 **Myrick**	Y	Y	Y	Y	Y
10 **McHenry**	Y	Y	Y	N	Y
11 Shuler	Y	Y	Y	Y	Y
12 Watt	Y	Y	N	Y	Y
13 Miller	Y	Y	Y	Y	Y
NORTH DAKOTA					
AL Pomeroy	Y	Y	Y	Y	Y
OHIO					
1 Driehaus	Y	Y	N	Y	Y
2 **Schmidt**	Y	Y	Y	Y	Y
3 **Turner**	Y	Y	Y	Y	Y
4 **Jordan**	Y	Y	Y	N	Y
5 **Latta**	Y	Y	Y	Y	Y
6 Wilson	Y	Y	Y	Y	Y
7 **Austria**	Y	Y	Y	Y	Y
8 **Boehner**	Y	Y	Y	Y	Y
9 Kaptur	Y	Y	N	Y	Y
10 Kucinich	Y	N	N	Y	Y
11 Fudge	Y	N	N	Y	Y
12 **Tiberi**	Y	Y	Y	Y	Y
13 Sutton	Y	Y	N	Y	Y
14 **LaTourette**	Y	Y	Y	Y	Y
15 Kilroy	Y	Y	Y	Y	Y
16 Boccieri	Y	Y	N	Y	Y
17 Ryan	Y	Y	N	Y	Y
18 Space	Y	Y	Y	Y	Y
OKLAHOMA					
1 **Sullivan**	Y	Y	Y	Y	?
2 Boren	Y	Y	Y	Y	Y
3 **Lucas**	Y	Y	Y	Y	Y
4 **Cole**	Y	Y	Y	Y	Y
5 **Fallin**	Y	Y	Y	Y	Y
OREGON					
1 Wu	Y	Y	Y	Y	Y
2 **Walden**	Y	Y	Y	Y	Y
3 Blumenauer	Y	Y	N	Y	Y
4 DeFazio	Y	Y	N	Y	Y
5 Schrader	Y	Y	Y	Y	Y
PENNSYLVANIA					
1 Brady	Y	N	N	Y	Y
2 Fattah	Y	Y	N	Y	Y
3 Dahlkemper	Y	Y	Y	Y	Y
4 Altmire	Y	Y	Y	Y	Y
5 **Thompson**	Y	Y	Y	Y	Y
6 **Gerlach**	Y	Y	Y	Y	Y
7 Sestak	Y	Y	N	Y	Y
8 Murphy, P.	?	?	?	?	?
9 **Shuster**	Y	Y	Y	Y	Y
10 Carney	Y	Y	Y	Y	Y
11 Kanjorski	Y	Y	N	Y	Y
12 Murtha	Y	N	N	Y	Y
13 Schwartz	Y	Y	N	Y	Y
14 Doyle	Y	N	N	Y	Y
15 **Dent**	Y	Y	Y	Y	Y
16 **Pitts**	Y	Y	Y	Y	Y
17 Holden	Y	N	N	Y	Y
18 **Murphy, T.**	?	?	?	?	?
19 **Platts**	Y	Y	Y	Y	Y
RHODE ISLAND					
1 Kennedy	Y	Y	N	Y	Y
2 Langevin	Y	Y	N	Y	Y
SOUTH CAROLINA					
1 **Brown**	Y	Y	Y	Y	Y
2 **Wilson**	Y	Y	Y	Y	Y
3 **Barrett**	?	?	?	?	?
4 **Inglis**	Y	Y	Y	Y	Y
5 Spratt	?	Y	Y	Y	Y
6 Clyburn	Y	N	N	Y	Y
SOUTH DAKOTA					
AL Herseth Sandlin	Y	Y	Y	Y	Y
TENNESSEE					
1 **Roe**	Y	Y	Y	Y	Y
2 **Duncan**	Y	Y	Y	N	Y
3 **Wamp**	Y	Y	Y	Y	Y
4 Davis	Y	Y	Y	Y	Y
5 Cooper	Y	Y	Y	Y	Y
6 Gordon	Y	Y	Y	Y	Y
7 **Blackburn**	Y	Y	Y	Y	Y
8 Tanner	Y	Y	Y	Y	Y
9 Cohen	Y	Y	N	Y	Y

	827	828	829	830	831
TEXAS					
1 **Gohmert**	Y	Y	Y	Y	Y
2 **Poe**	Y	Y	Y	Y	Y
3 **Johnson, S.**	Y	Y	Y	Y	Y
4 **Hall**	Y	Y	Y	Y	Y
5 **Hensarling**	Y	Y	Y	N	Y
6 **Barton**	Y	Y	Y	Y	?
7 **Culberson**	Y	Y	Y	N	Y
8 **Brady**	Y	Y	Y	Y	Y
9 Green, A.	Y	Y	N	Y	Y
10 **McCaul**	Y	Y	Y	Y	Y
11 **Conaway**	Y	?	?	?	?
12 **Granger**	Y	Y	Y	N	Y
13 **Thornberry**	Y	Y	Y	N	Y
14 **Paul**	Y	N	Y	N	Y
15 Hinojosa	Y	Y	N	Y	Y
16 Reyes	Y	N	N	Y	Y
17 Edwards	Y	Y	N	Y	Y
18 Jackson Lee	Y	Y	N	Y	Y
19 **Neugebauer**	Y	Y	Y	N	Y
20 Gonzalez	Y	Y	N	Y	?
21 **Smith**	Y	Y	Y	Y	?
22 **Olson**	Y	Y	Y	Y	Y
23 Rodriguez	Y	Y	Y	Y	Y
24 **Marchant**	Y	Y	Y	Y	Y
25 Doggett	Y	Y	N	Y	Y
26 **Burgess**	Y	Y	Y	N	Y
27 Ortiz	Y	Y	N	Y	Y
28 Cuellar	Y	Y	Y	Y	Y
29 Green, G.	Y	Y	N	Y	Y
30 Johnson, E.	Y	Y	N	Y	Y
31 **Carter**	Y	Y	Y	N	Y
32 **Sessions**	Y	Y	Y	Y	Y
UTAH					
1 **Bishop**	Y	?	Y	N	Y
2 Matheson	Y	Y	Y	Y	Y
3 **Chaffetz**	Y	Y	Y	Y	Y
VERMONT					
AL Welch	Y	Y	N	Y	Y
VIRGINIA					
1 **Wittman**	Y	Y	Y	Y	Y
2 Nye	Y	Y	Y	Y	Y
3 Scott	Y	Y	Y	Y	Y
4 **Forbes**	Y	Y	Y	Y	Y
5 Perriello	Y	Y	Y	Y	Y
6 **Goodlatte**	Y	Y	Y	Y	Y
7 **Cantor**	Y	Y	Y	Y	Y
8 Moran	Y	N	Y	Y	Y
9 Boucher	Y	Y	Y	Y	Y
10 **Wolf**	Y	Y	Y	Y	Y
11 Connolly	Y	Y	N	Y	Y
WASHINGTON					
1 Inslee	Y	Y	N	Y	Y
2 Larsen	Y	Y	N	Y	Y
3 Baird	Y	Y	Y	Y	Y
4 **Hastings**	Y	Y	Y	Y	Y
5 **McMorris Rodgers**	Y	Y	Y	Y	Y
6 Dicks	Y	Y	N	Y	Y
7 McDermott	Y	N	N	Y	Y
8 **Reichert**	Y	Y	Y	Y	Y
9 Smith	Y	Y	N	Y	Y
WEST VIRGINIA					
1 Mollohan	Y	Y	N	Y	Y
2 **Capito**	Y	Y	Y	Y	Y
3 Rahall	Y	N	N	Y	Y
WISCONSIN					
1 **Ryan**	Y	Y	Y	N	Y
2 Baldwin	Y	N	N	Y	Y
3 Kind	Y	Y	Y	Y	Y
4 Moore	Y	N	N	Y	Y
5 **Sensenbrenner**	Y	Y	Y	N	Y
6 **Petri**	Y	Y	Y	Y	Y
7 Obey	Y	Y	N	Y	Y
8 Kagen	Y	Y	N	Y	Y
WYOMING					
AL **Lummis**	Y	Y	Y	N	Y
DELEGATES					
Faleomavaega (A.S.)		Y			
Norton (D.C.)		Y			
Bordallo (Guam)		Y			
Sablan (N. Marianas)		Y			
Pierluisi (P.R.)		Y			
Christensen (V.I.)		N			

IN THE HOUSE | By Vote Number

832. **HR 1168. Veterans Job Training/Passage.** Walz, D-Minn., motion to suspend the rules and pass the bill that would authorize the Labor Department to pay a monthly training allowance of about $1,400 for each month a veteran is enrolled in an employment-training program that teaches a skill in demand. Eligible veterans could receive up to six months of training assistance every 10 years and a stipend of up to $5,000 for moving expenses related to job training. Motion agreed to 356-0: D 206-0; R 150-0. A two-thirds majority of those present and voting (238 in this case) is required for passage under suspension of the rules. Nov. 2, 2009.

833. **H Res 291. Assistance Dogs for Veterans/Adoption.** Walz, D-Minn., motion to suspend the rules and adopt the resolution that would acknowledge the importance of assistance dogs in helping wounded veterans and the work of the Tower of Hope organization in training and providing the dogs. Motion agreed to 351-0: D 203-0; R 148-0. A two-thirds majority of those present and voting (234 in this case) is required for adoption under suspension of the rules. Nov. 2, 2009.

834. **S 509. Walla Walla Veterans Medical Center/Passage.** Walz, D-Minn., motion to suspend the rules and pass the bill that would authorize $71 million for the construction of a multiple-specialty outpatient facility, campus renovation and upgrades, and additional parking at the Veterans Affairs Department's Medical Center in Walla Walla, Wash. Motion agreed to 352-0: D 205-0; R 147-0. A two-thirds majority of those present and voting (235 in this case) is required for passage under suspension of the rules. Nov. 2, 2009.

835. **HR 3949. Veterans' Small Business Assistance/Passage.** Walz, D-Minn., motion to suspend the rules and pass the bill that would require that small businesses included in a Veterans Affairs Department database be verified as owned or operated by former military service members. It also would authorize $25 million per year in fiscal 2011-13 for grants to state and local veterans' programs for outreach activities. Motion agreed to 382-2: D 222-0; R 160-2. A two-thirds majority of those present and voting (256 in this case) is required for passage under suspension of the rules. Nov. 3, 2009.

836. **H Res 398. Tribute to Berlin Airlift Veterans/Adoption.** Walz, D-Minn., motion to suspend the rules and adopt the resolution that would recognize the 60th anniversary of the Berlin Airlift and the veterans who lost their lives participating in the mission. Motion agreed to 367-0: D 219-0; R 148-0. A two-thirds majority of those present and voting (245 in this case) is required for adoption under suspension of the rules. Nov. 3, 2009.

837. **H Res 866. National Veterans Awareness Week/Adoption.** Walz, D-Minn., motion to suspend the rules and adopt the resolution that would express House recognition of National Veterans Awareness Week, support the designation of National Veterans History Project Week and encourage citizens to interview veterans in their families or communities. Motion agreed to 389-0: D 226-0; R 163-0. A two-thirds majority of those voting and present (260 in this case) is required for adoption under suspension of the rules. Nov. 3, 2009.

	832	833	834	835	836	837
ALABAMA						
1 **Bonner**	?	?	?	Y	Y	Y
2 Bright	Y	Y	Y	Y	Y	Y
3 **Rogers**	Y	Y	Y	Y	Y	Y
4 **Aderholt**	Y	Y	Y	Y	Y	Y
5 Griffith	Y	Y	Y	Y	Y	Y
6 **Bachus**	Y	Y	Y	Y	Y	Y
7 Davis	?	?	?	?	?	?
ALASKA						
AL **Young**	Y	Y	Y	Y	Y	Y
ARIZONA						
1 Kirkpatrick	Y	Y	Y	Y	Y	Y
2 **Franks**	Y	Y	Y	Y	+	Y
3 **Shadegg**	Y	Y	Y	Y	Y	Y
4 Pastor	Y	Y	Y	Y	Y	Y
5 Mitchell	Y	Y	Y	Y	Y	Y
6 **Flake**	Y	Y	Y	N	Y	Y
7 Grijalva	?	?	?	Y	Y	Y
8 Giffords	Y	Y	Y	Y	Y	Y
ARKANSAS						
1 Berry	Y	Y	Y	Y	Y	Y
2 Snyder	Y	Y	Y	Y	Y	Y
3 **Boozman**	Y	Y	Y	Y	Y	Y
4 Ross	Y	Y	Y	Y	Y	Y
CALIFORNIA						
1 Thompson	+	+	+	Y	Y	Y
2 **Herger**	Y	Y	Y	Y	Y	Y
3 **Lungren**	Y	Y	Y	Y	Y	Y
4 **McClintock**	Y	Y	Y	Y	Y	Y
5 Matsui	Y	Y	Y	Y	Y	Y
6 Woolsey	Y	Y	Y	Y	Y	Y
7 Miller, George	Y	Y	Y	Y	Y	Y
8 Pelosi						
9 Lee	Y	Y	Y	Y	Y	Y
10 Vacant						
11 McNerney	Y	Y	Y	Y	Y	Y
12 Speier	Y	Y	Y	?	Y	Y
13 Stark	?	?	?	Y	Y	Y
14 Eshoo	Y	Y	Y	Y	Y	Y
15 Honda	Y	Y	Y	Y	Y	Y
16 Lofgren	Y	Y	Y	Y	Y	Y
17 Farr	Y	Y	Y	Y	?	Y
18 Cardoza	Y	Y	Y	Y	Y	Y
19 **Radanovich**	Y	Y	?	Y	Y	Y
20 Costa	Y	Y	Y	Y	Y	Y
21 **Nunes**	+	+	+	+	+	+
22 **McCarthy**	Y	Y	Y	Y	?	Y
23 Capps	Y	Y	Y	Y	Y	Y
24 **Gallegly**	Y	Y	Y	Y	Y	Y
25 **McKeon**	Y	Y	Y	Y	Y	Y
26 **Dreier**	Y	Y	Y	Y	+	Y
27 Sherman	Y	Y	Y	Y	Y	Y
28 Berman	Y	Y	Y	Y	Y	Y
29 Schiff	Y	Y	Y	Y	Y	Y
30 Waxman	Y	Y	Y	Y	Y	Y
31 Becerra	+	+	?	Y	Y	Y
32 Chu	Y	Y	Y	Y	Y	Y
33 Watson	Y	Y	Y	Y	Y	Y
34 Roybal-Allard	Y	Y	Y	Y	Y	Y
35 Waters	?	?	?	Y	Y	Y
36 Harman	Y	Y	Y	Y	Y	Y
37 Richardson	Y	Y	Y	Y	Y	Y
38 Napolitano	Y	Y	Y	Y	Y	Y
39 Sánchez, Linda	Y	Y	Y	+	+	+
40 **Royce**	Y	Y	Y	Y	Y	Y
41 **Lewis**	Y	Y	Y	Y	Y	Y
42 **Miller, Gary**	Y	Y	Y	Y	Y	Y
43 Baca	Y	Y	Y	Y	Y	Y
44 **Calvert**	Y	Y	Y	Y	Y	Y
45 **Bono Mack**	Y	Y	Y	Y	Y	Y
46 **Rohrabacher**	Y	Y	Y	Y	Y	Y
47 Sanchez, Loretta	Y	Y	Y	Y	Y	Y
48 **Campbell**	Y	Y	Y	Y	Y	Y
49 **Issa**	Y	Y	Y	Y	Y	Y
50 **Bilbray**	Y	Y	Y	Y	Y	Y
51 Filner	Y	Y	Y	Y	Y	Y
52 **Hunter**	Y	Y	Y	Y	Y	Y
53 Davis	Y	Y	Y	Y	Y	Y

	832	833	834	835	836	837
COLORADO						
1 DeGette	Y	Y	Y	Y	Y	Y
2 Polis	Y	Y	Y	Y	Y	Y
3 Salazar	?	?	?	Y	Y	Y
4 Markey	Y	Y	Y	Y	Y	Y
5 **Lamborn**	?	?	?	Y	Y	Y
6 **Coffman**	Y	Y	Y	Y	Y	Y
7 Perlmutter	Y	Y	Y	Y	Y	Y
CONNECTICUT						
1 Larson	Y	Y	Y	Y	Y	Y
2 Courtney	Y	Y	Y	Y	Y	Y
3 DeLauro	Y	Y	Y	Y	Y	Y
4 Himes	?	?	?	Y	Y	Y
5 Murphy	Y	Y	Y	Y	Y	Y
DELAWARE						
AL **Castle**	Y	Y	Y	Y	Y	Y
FLORIDA						
1 **Miller**	Y	Y	Y	Y	Y	Y
2 Boyd	Y	Y	Y	Y	Y	Y
3 Brown	?	?	?	?	?	?
4 **Crenshaw**	?	?	?	?	?	?
5 **Brown-Waite**	Y	Y	Y	Y	Y	Y
6 **Stearns**	Y	Y	Y	Y	Y	Y
7 **Mica**	Y	Y	Y	Y	Y	Y
8 Grayson	Y	Y	Y	Y	Y	Y
9 **Bilirakis**	Y	Y	Y	Y	Y	Y
10 **Young**	Y	Y	Y	?	?	Y
11 Castor	Y	Y	Y	Y	Y	Y
12 **Putnam**	Y	Y	Y	Y	Y	Y
13 **Buchanan**	Y	?	Y	Y	Y	Y
14 **Mack**	Y	Y	Y	Y	Y	Y
15 **Posey**	Y	Y	Y	Y	Y	Y
16 **Rooney**	Y	Y	Y	Y	Y	Y
17 Meek	Y	Y	Y	Y	Y	Y
18 **Ros-Lehtinen**	Y	Y	Y	Y	Y	Y
19 Wexler	?	?	?	Y	Y	Y
20 Wasserman Schultz	Y	Y	Y	Y	Y	Y
21 **Diaz-Balart, L.**	Y	Y	Y	Y	Y	Y
22 Klein	Y	Y	Y	Y	Y	Y
23 Hastings	Y	Y	?	Y	Y	Y
24 Kosmas	Y	Y	Y	Y	Y	Y
25 **Diaz-Balart, M.**	Y	Y	Y	Y	Y	Y
GEORGIA						
1 **Kingston**	Y	Y	Y	?	?	?
2 Bishop	Y	Y	Y	Y	Y	Y
3 **Westmoreland**	Y	Y	Y	Y	Y	Y
4 Johnson	Y	Y	Y	Y	Y	Y
5 Lewis	Y	Y	Y	Y	Y	Y
6 **Price**	Y	Y	Y	+	+	+
7 **Linder**	?	?	?	Y	Y	Y
8 Marshall	Y	Y	Y	Y	Y	Y
9 **Deal**	?	?	?	?	?	?
10 **Broun**	?	+	+	Y	Y	Y
11 **Gingrey**	?	?	?	Y	Y	Y
12 Barrow	Y	Y	Y	Y	Y	Y
13 Scott	Y	Y	Y	Y	Y	Y
HAWAII						
1 Abercrombie	+	+	+	+	+	+
2 Hirono	Y	Y	Y	Y	Y	Y
IDAHO						
1 **Minnick**	Y	Y	Y	Y	Y	Y
2 **Simpson**	Y	Y	Y	Y	Y	Y
ILLINOIS						
1 Rush	?	?	?	Y	Y	Y
2 Jackson	Y	Y	Y	Y	Y	Y
3 Lipinski	?	?	?	?	?	?
4 Gutierrez	+	+	+	+	+	+
5 Quigley	Y	Y	Y	Y	Y	Y
6 **Roskam**	Y	Y	Y	Y	Y	Y
7 Davis	+	+	+	Y	Y	Y
8 Bean	Y	Y	Y	Y	Y	Y
9 Schakowsky	Y	Y	Y	Y	Y	Y
10 **Kirk**	Y	Y	Y	Y	Y	Y
11 Halvorson	Y	Y	Y	Y	Y	Y
12 Costello	Y	Y	Y	Y	Y	Y
13 **Biggert**	Y	Y	Y	Y	Y	Y
14 Foster	Y	Y	Y	Y	Y	Y
15 **Johnson**	+	+	+	+	+	+

KEY   Republicans   Democrats

Y	Voted for (yea)	X	Paired against	C	Voted "present" to avoid possible conflict of interest
#	Paired for	–	Announced against		
+	Announced for	P	Voted "present"	?	Did not vote or otherwise make a position known
N	Voted against (nay)				

	832	833	834	835	836	837
16 **Manzullo**	Y	Y	Y	Y	Y	Y
17 Hare	Y	Y	Y	Y	Y	Y
18 **Schock**	?	?	?	Y	Y	Y
19 **Shimkus**	?	?	?	Y	Y	Y
INDIANA						
1 Visclosky	Y	Y	Y	Y	Y	Y
2 Donnelly	Y	Y	Y	Y	Y	Y
3 **Souder**	?	?	?	Y	Y	Y
4 **Buyer**	Y	Y	Y	Y	Y	Y
5 **Burton**	Y	Y	Y	Y	Y	Y
6 **Pence**	Y	Y	Y	Y	?	Y
7 Carson	Y	Y	Y	Y	Y	Y
8 Ellsworth	Y	?	Y	Y	Y	Y
9 Hill	Y	Y	Y	Y	Y	Y
IOWA						
1 Braley	Y	Y	Y	Y	Y	Y
2 Loebsack	Y	Y	Y	Y	Y	Y
3 Boswell	Y	Y	Y	Y	Y	Y
4 **Latham**	Y	Y	Y	Y	Y	Y
5 **King**	Y	Y	Y	Y	Y	Y
KANSAS						
1 **Moran**	Y	Y	Y	?	Y	Y
2 **Jenkins**	Y	Y	Y	Y	Y	Y
3 Moore	Y	Y	Y	Y	Y	Y
4 **Tiahrt**	?	?	?	Y	Y	Y
KENTUCKY						
1 **Whitfield**	Y	Y	Y	Y	Y	Y
2 **Guthrie**	Y	Y	Y	Y	Y	Y
3 Yarmuth	Y	Y	Y	Y	Y	Y
4 **Davis**	Y	Y	Y	Y	Y	Y
5 **Rogers**	Y	Y	Y	Y	Y	Y
6 Chandler	Y	Y	Y	Y	Y	Y
LOUISIANA						
1 **Scalise**	Y	Y	Y	Y	Y	Y
2 **Cao**	Y	Y	Y	Y	Y	Y
3 Melancon	Y	Y	Y	Y	Y	Y
4 **Fleming**	Y	Y	Y	Y	Y	Y
5 **Alexander**	Y	Y	Y	Y	Y	Y
6 **Cassidy**	Y	+	Y	Y	Y	Y
7 **Boustany**	Y	Y	Y	Y	Y	Y
MAINE						
1 Pingree	Y	Y	Y	Y	Y	Y
2 Michaud	Y	Y	Y	Y	Y	Y
MARYLAND						
1 Kratovil	Y	Y	Y	Y	Y	Y
2 Ruppersberger	Y	Y	Y	Y	Y	Y
3 Sarbanes	?	?	?	Y	Y	Y
4 Edwards	Y	Y	Y	Y	Y	Y
5 Hoyer	Y	Y	Y	Y	Y	Y
6 **Bartlett**	Y	Y	Y	Y	Y	Y
7 Cummings	Y	Y	Y	Y	Y	Y
8 Van Hollen	Y	Y	Y	Y	Y	Y
MASSACHUSETTS						
1 Olver	?	Y	Y	Y	Y	Y
2 Neal	?	?	?	Y	Y	Y
3 McGovern	Y	Y	Y	Y	Y	Y
4 Frank	Y	Y	Y	Y	?	Y
5 Tsongas	Y	Y	Y	Y	Y	Y
6 Tierney	Y	Y	Y	Y	Y	Y
7 Markey	Y	Y	Y	Y	Y	Y
8 Capuano	?	?	?	?	?	?
9 Lynch	Y	Y	Y	Y	Y	Y
10 Delahunt	Y	Y	Y	Y	Y	Y
MICHIGAN						
1 Stupak	?	?	?	?	?	?
2 **Hoekstra**	?	?	?	?	?	?
3 **Ehlers**	Y	Y	Y	Y	Y	Y
4 **Camp**	Y	Y	Y	Y	?	Y
5 Kildee	Y	Y	Y	Y	Y	Y
6 **Upton**	Y	Y	Y	Y	Y	Y
7 Schauer	Y	Y	Y	Y	?	Y
8 **Rogers**	Y	Y	Y	Y	Y	Y
9 Peters	Y	Y	Y	Y	Y	Y
10 **Miller**	Y	Y	Y	Y	Y	Y
11 **McCotter**	Y	Y	Y	Y	?	Y
12 Levin	Y	Y	Y	Y	Y	Y
13 Kilpatrick	Y	Y	Y	Y	Y	Y
14 Conyers	+	+	+	+	+	+
15 Dingell	Y	Y	Y	Y	Y	Y
MINNESOTA						
1 Walz	Y	Y	Y	Y	Y	Y
2 **Kline**	Y	Y	Y	Y	?	Y
3 **Paulsen**	Y	Y	Y	Y	Y	Y
4 McCollum	Y	Y	Y	Y	Y	Y
5 Ellison	Y	Y	Y	Y	Y	Y
6 **Bachmann**	Y	Y	Y	Y	Y	Y
7 Peterson	Y	Y	Y	Y	Y	Y
8 Oberstar	Y	Y	Y	Y	Y	Y
MISSISSIPPI						
1 Childers	Y	Y	Y	Y	Y	Y
2 Thompson	Y	Y	Y	Y	Y	Y
3 **Harper**	Y	Y	Y	Y	Y	Y
4 Taylor	?	?	?	Y	Y	Y
MISSOURI						
1 Clay	Y	Y	Y	?	Y	Y
2 **Akin**	Y	Y	Y	Y	Y	Y
3 Carnahan	Y	Y	Y	Y	Y	Y
4 Skelton	Y	Y	Y	Y	Y	Y
5 Cleaver	Y	Y	Y	Y	Y	Y
6 **Graves**	Y	Y	Y	Y	Y	Y
7 **Blunt**	Y	Y	Y	Y	?	Y
8 **Emerson**	Y	Y	Y	Y	Y	Y
9 **Luetkemeyer**	Y	Y	Y	Y	Y	Y
MONTANA						
AL **Rehberg**	Y	Y	Y	Y	Y	Y
NEBRASKA						
1 **Fortenberry**	Y	Y	Y	Y	Y	Y
2 **Terry**	Y	Y	Y	Y	Y	Y
3 **Smith**	Y	Y	Y	Y	Y	Y
NEVADA						
1 Berkley	Y	Y	Y	Y	Y	Y
2 **Heller**	Y	Y	Y	Y	Y	Y
3 Titus	Y	Y	Y	Y	Y	Y
NEW HAMPSHIRE						
1 Shea-Porter	Y	Y	Y	Y	Y	Y
2 Hodes	Y	Y	Y	Y	Y	Y
NEW JERSEY						
1 Andrews	Y	Y	Y	?	?	?
2 **LoBiondo**	Y	Y	Y	Y	Y	Y
3 Adler	Y	Y	Y	Y	Y	Y
4 **Smith**	Y	Y	Y	Y	Y	Y
5 **Garrett**	Y	Y	Y	Y	Y	Y
6 Pallone	?	?	?	?	?	?
7 **Lance**	Y	Y	Y	Y	Y	Y
8 Pascrell	+	+	+	+	+	+
9 Rothman	Y	Y	Y	Y	Y	Y
10 Payne	?	?	?	?	?	?
11 **Frelinghuysen**	Y	Y	Y	Y	Y	Y
12 Holt	Y	Y	Y	?	?	?
13 Sires	?	?	?	?	?	?
NEW MEXICO						
1 Heinrich	Y	Y	Y	Y	Y	Y
2 Teague	+	?	?	Y	Y	Y
3 Lujan	Y	Y	Y	Y	Y	Y
NEW YORK						
1 Bishop	Y	Y	Y	Y	Y	Y
2 Israel	Y	Y	Y	Y	?	Y
3 **King**	?	?	?	Y	Y	Y
4 McCarthy	Y	Y	Y	Y	Y	Y
5 Ackerman	?	?	?	?	?	?
6 Meeks	?	?	?	?	?	?
7 Crowley	Y	Y	Y	Y	Y	Y
8 Nadler	Y	Y	Y	Y	Y	Y
9 Weiner	?	?	?	Y	Y	Y
10 Towns	Y	Y	Y	?	?	?
11 Clarke	?	?	?	Y	Y	Y
12 Velázquez	?	?	?	?	?	?
13 McMahon	Y	Y	Y	Y	Y	Y
14 Maloney	?	?	?	?	?	?
15 Rangel	Y	?	Y	Y	Y	Y
16 Serrano	Y	Y	Y	Y	Y	Y
17 Engel	Y	Y	Y	Y	Y	Y
18 Lowey	Y	Y	Y	Y	Y	Y
19 Hall	?	?	?	?	?	?
20 Murphy	Y	Y	Y	Y	Y	Y
21 Tonko	Y	Y	Y	Y	Y	Y
22 Hinchey	?	?	?	?	?	?
23 Vacant						
24 Arcuri	Y	Y	Y	Y	Y	Y
25 Maffei	Y	Y	Y	Y	Y	Y
26 **Lee**	Y	Y	Y	Y	Y	Y
27 Higgins	Y	Y	Y	Y	Y	Y
28 Slaughter	Y	Y	Y	Y	Y	Y
29 Massa	Y	Y	Y	Y	Y	Y
NORTH CAROLINA						
1 Butterfield	Y	Y	Y	Y	Y	Y
2 Etheridge	Y	Y	Y	Y	Y	Y
3 **Jones**	Y	Y	Y	Y	Y	Y
4 Price	Y	Y	Y	Y	Y	Y
5 **Foxx**	Y	Y	Y	Y	Y	Y
6 **Coble**	Y	Y	Y	Y	Y	Y
7 McIntyre	Y	Y	Y	Y	Y	Y
8 Kissell	Y	Y	Y	Y	Y	Y
9 **Myrick**	Y	Y	Y	Y	Y	Y
10 **McHenry**	Y	Y	Y	Y	Y	Y
11 Shuler	Y	Y	Y	Y	Y	Y
12 Watt	Y	Y	Y	Y	Y	Y
13 Miller	Y	Y	Y	Y	Y	Y
NORTH DAKOTA						
AL Pomeroy	Y	Y	Y	Y	Y	Y
OHIO						
1 Driehaus	Y	Y	Y	Y	Y	Y
2 **Schmidt**	Y	Y	Y	Y	Y	Y
3 **Turner**	Y	Y	Y	Y	Y	Y
4 **Jordan**	Y	Y	Y	Y	Y	Y
5 **Latta**	Y	Y	Y	Y	Y	Y
6 Wilson	Y	Y	Y	Y	Y	Y
7 **Austria**	Y	Y	Y	Y	Y	?
8 **Boehner**	Y	Y	Y	Y	+	Y
9 Kaptur	Y	Y	Y	Y	Y	Y
10 Kucinich	Y	Y	Y	Y	Y	Y
11 Fudge	Y	Y	Y	Y	Y	Y
12 **Tiberi**	?	?	?	Y	Y	Y
13 Sutton	Y	Y	Y	Y	Y	Y
14 **LaTourette**	Y	Y	Y	Y	Y	Y
15 Kilroy	Y	Y	Y	Y	Y	Y
16 Boccieri	Y	Y	Y	Y	Y	Y
17 Ryan	?	?	?	?	?	?
18 Space	Y	Y	Y	Y	Y	Y
OKLAHOMA						
1 **Sullivan**	Y	Y	Y	Y	Y	Y
2 Boren	?	?	?	Y	Y	Y
3 **Lucas**	?	?	?	Y	Y	Y
4 **Cole**	Y	Y	Y	+	+	+
5 **Fallin**	Y	Y	Y	Y	Y	Y
OREGON						
1 Wu	Y	Y	Y	Y	Y	Y
2 **Walden**	Y	Y	Y	Y	Y	Y
3 Blumenauer	?	?	?	Y	Y	Y
4 DeFazio	?	?	?	Y	Y	Y
5 Schrader	Y	Y	Y	Y	Y	Y
PENNSYLVANIA						
1 Brady	?	?	?	?	?	?
2 Fattah	Y	Y	Y	+	Y	Y
3 Dahlkemper	Y	Y	Y	Y	Y	Y
4 Altmire	Y	Y	Y	Y	Y	Y
5 **Thompson**	Y	Y	Y	Y	Y	Y
6 **Gerlach**	?	?	?	?	?	?
7 Sestak	Y	Y	Y	Y	Y	Y
8 Murphy, P.	?	?	?	?	?	?
9 **Shuster**	+	+	+	Y	Y	Y
10 Carney	+	+	+	+	+	+
11 Kanjorski	Y	?	Y	Y	Y	Y
12 Murtha	Y	Y	Y	Y	?	Y
13 Schwartz	Y	Y	Y	Y	Y	Y
14 Doyle	?	?	?	Y	Y	Y
15 **Dent**	Y	Y	Y	Y	Y	Y
16 **Pitts**	Y	Y	Y	Y	Y	Y
17 Holden	?	?	?	Y	Y	Y
18 **Murphy, T.**	Y	Y	Y	Y	Y	Y
19 **Platts**	Y	Y	Y	Y	Y	Y
RHODE ISLAND						
1 Kennedy	Y	Y	Y	Y	Y	Y
2 Langevin	Y	Y	Y	Y	Y	Y
SOUTH CAROLINA						
1 **Brown**	Y	Y	Y	Y	Y	Y
2 **Wilson**	Y	Y	Y	Y	Y	Y
3 **Barrett**	?	?	?	?	?	?
4 **Inglis**	Y	Y	Y	Y	Y	Y
5 Spratt	?	?	?	?	?	?
6 Clyburn	Y	Y	Y	Y	Y	Y
SOUTH DAKOTA						
AL Herseth Sandlin	Y	Y	Y	Y	Y	Y
TENNESSEE						
1 **Roe**	Y	Y	Y	Y	Y	Y
2 **Duncan**	Y	Y	Y	Y	Y	Y
3 **Wamp**	?	?	?	?	?	?
4 Davis	?	?	?	?	?	?
5 Cooper	Y	Y	Y	Y	Y	Y
6 Gordon	?	?	?	?	?	?
7 **Blackburn**	Y	Y	Y	Y	Y	Y
8 Tanner	Y	Y	Y	Y	Y	Y
9 Cohen	Y	Y	Y	Y	Y	Y
TEXAS						
1 **Gohmert**	Y	Y	Y	Y	Y	Y
2 **Poe**	+	+	+	Y	Y	Y
3 **Johnson, S.**	Y	Y	Y	Y	Y	Y
4 **Hall**	Y	Y	Y	Y	Y	Y
5 **Hensarling**	Y	Y	Y	Y	Y	Y
6 **Barton**	Y	Y	Y	Y	?	Y
7 **Culberson**	Y	Y	Y	Y	Y	Y
8 **Brady**	?	?	?	Y	Y	Y
9 Green, A.	Y	Y	Y	Y	Y	Y
10 **McCaul**	?	?	?	?	?	?
11 **Conaway**	Y	Y	Y	Y	Y	Y
12 **Granger**	?	?	?	?	?	?
13 **Thornberry**	Y	Y	Y	Y	Y	Y
14 **Paul**	Y	Y	Y	N	Y	Y
15 Hinojosa	Y	Y	Y	Y	Y	Y
16 Reyes	Y	Y	Y	Y	Y	Y
17 Edwards	Y	Y	Y	Y	Y	Y
18 Jackson Lee	Y	Y	Y	Y	Y	Y
19 **Neugebauer**	Y	Y	Y	Y	Y	Y
20 Gonzalez	Y	Y	Y	Y	Y	Y
21 **Smith**	Y	Y	Y	Y	Y	Y
22 **Olson**	Y	Y	Y	Y	Y	Y
23 Rodriguez	Y	Y	Y	Y	Y	Y
24 **Marchant**	Y	Y	Y	Y	Y	Y
25 Doggett	Y	Y	Y	Y	Y	Y
26 **Burgess**	Y	Y	Y	Y	Y	Y
27 Ortiz	Y	Y	Y	Y	Y	Y
28 Cuellar	Y	Y	Y	Y	Y	Y
29 Green, G.	Y	Y	Y	Y	Y	Y
30 Johnson, E.	Y	Y	Y	Y	Y	Y
31 **Carter**	Y	Y	Y	Y	?	Y
32 **Sessions**	Y	Y	Y	Y	?	Y
UTAH						
1 **Bishop**	Y	Y	?	Y	Y	Y
2 Matheson	Y	Y	Y	Y	Y	Y
3 **Chaffetz**	Y	Y	Y	Y	Y	Y
VERMONT						
AL Welch	Y	Y	Y	Y	Y	Y
VIRGINIA						
1 **Wittman**	Y	Y	Y	Y	Y	Y
2 Nye	Y	Y	Y	Y	Y	Y
3 Scott	Y	Y	Y	Y	Y	Y
4 **Forbes**	Y	Y	Y	Y	Y	Y
5 Perriello	Y	Y	Y	Y	Y	Y
6 **Goodlatte**	Y	Y	Y	Y	+	Y
7 **Cantor**	Y	Y	Y	Y	?	Y
8 Moran	Y	?	?	Y	Y	Y
9 Boucher	Y	Y	Y	Y	Y	Y
10 **Wolf**	Y	Y	Y	Y	Y	Y
11 Connolly	Y	Y	Y	Y	Y	Y
WASHINGTON						
1 Inslee	Y	Y	Y	Y	Y	Y
2 Larsen	Y	Y	Y	Y	Y	Y
3 Baird	Y	Y	Y	Y	Y	Y
4 **Hastings**	+	+	+	Y	Y	Y
5 **McMorris Rodgers**	?	?	?	Y	?	Y
6 Dicks	Y	Y	Y	Y	Y	Y
7 McDermott	Y	Y	Y	Y	Y	Y
8 **Reichert**	Y	Y	Y	Y	Y	Y
9 Smith	+	+	+	Y	Y	Y
WEST VIRGINIA						
1 Mollohan	Y	Y	Y	Y	Y	Y
2 **Capito**	Y	Y	Y	Y	Y	Y
3 Rahall	Y	Y	Y	?	?	Y
WISCONSIN						
1 **Ryan**	Y	Y	Y	Y	Y	Y
2 Baldwin	Y	Y	Y	Y	Y	Y
3 Kind	?	?	?	Y	Y	Y
4 Moore	Y	Y	Y	Y	Y	Y
5 **Sensenbrenner**	Y	Y	Y	Y	Y	Y
6 **Petri**	Y	Y	Y	Y	Y	Y
7 Obey	Y	Y	Y	Y	?	Y
8 Kagen	Y	Y	Y	Y	Y	Y
WYOMING						
AL **Lummis**	Y	Y	Y	Y	Y	Y
DELEGATES						
Faleomavaega (A.S.)						
Norton (D.C.)						
Bordallo (Guam)						
Sablan (N. Marianas)						
Pierluisi (P.R.)						
Christensen (V.I.)						

IN THE HOUSE | By Vote Number

838. **H Res 867. U.N. Report on Gaza/Adoption.** Berman, D-Calif., motion to suspend the rules and adopt the resolution that would call on the president and the secretary of State to continue to oppose any endorsement of a report by the United Nations on the conflict in Gaza and reaffirm the support of the House for the state of Israel. Motion agreed to 344-36: D 179-33; R 165-3. A two-thirds majority of those present and voting (254 in this case) is required for adoption under suspension of the rules. Nov. 3, 2009.

839. **HR 3157. Max J. Beilke VA Outpatient Clinic/Passage.** Walz, D-Minn., motion to suspend the rules and pass the bill that would designate an outpatient clinic in Alexandria, Minn., as the "Max J. Beilke Department of Veterans Affairs Outpatient Clinic." Motion agreed to 398-0: D 229-0; R 169-0. A two-thirds majority of those present and voting (266 in this case) is required for passage under suspension of the rules. Nov. 3, 2009.

840. **H Res 736. Tribute to the Gettysburg Address/Adoption.** Lynch, D-Mass., motion to suspend the rules and adopt the resolution that would honor President Abraham Lincoln's Gettysburg Address and encourage citizens to read the address on Dedication Day. Motion agreed to 393-0: D 225-0; R 168-0. A two-thirds majority of those present and voting (262 in this case) is required for adoption under suspension of the rules. Nov. 3, 2009.

841. **HR 3639. Expedited Credit Card Company Rules/Previous Question.** Perlmutter, D-Colo., motion to order the previous question (thus ending debate and possibility of amendment) on adoption of the rule (H Res 884) that would provide for House floor consideration of the bill that would move up the effective date of certain credit card rules enacted earlier this year. Motion agreed to 228-176: D 228-6; R 0-170. Nov. 4, 2009.

842. **HR 3639. Expedited Credit Card Company Rules/Rule.** Adoption of the rule (H Res 884) that would provide for House floor consideration of the bill that would move up the effective date of certain credit card rules enacted earlier this year. Adopted 234-175: D 233-6; R 1-169. Nov. 4, 2009.

843. **H Res 858. Tribute to Inter-American Foundation/Adoption.** Engel, D-N.Y., motion to suspend the rules and adopt the resolution that would recognize the 40th anniversary of the Inter-American Foundation and acknowledge the effectiveness of the grass-roots model for U.S. foreign aid. Motion agreed to 405-1: D 240-0; R 165-1. A two-thirds majority of those present and voting (271 in this case) is required for adoption under suspension of the rules. Nov. 4, 2009.

	838	839	840	841	842	843
ALABAMA						
1 **Bonner**	Y	Y	Y	N	N	Y
2 Bright	Y	Y	Y	Y	?	Y
3 **Rogers**	Y	Y	Y	N	N	Y
4 **Aderholt**	Y	Y	Y	N	N	Y
5 **Griffith**	Y	Y	Y	Y	Y	Y
6 **Bachus**	Y	Y	Y	N	N	Y
7 Davis	?	?	?	Y	Y	Y
ALASKA						
AL **Young**	Y	Y	Y	N	N	Y
ARIZONA						
1 Kirkpatrick	Y	Y	Y	Y	Y	Y
2 **Franks**	Y	Y	Y	N	N	Y
3 **Shadegg**	Y	Y	Y	N	N	Y
4 Pastor	N	Y	Y	Y	Y	Y
5 Mitchell	Y	Y	Y	N	N	Y
6 **Flake**	Y	Y	Y	N	N	Y
7 Grijalva	N	?	?	Y	Y	?
8 Giffords	Y	Y	Y	Y	Y	Y
ARKANSAS						
1 Berry	Y	Y	?	Y	Y	Y
2 Snyder	N	Y	Y	Y	Y	Y
3 **Boozman**	Y	Y	Y	N	N	Y
4 Ross	Y	Y	Y	Y	Y	Y
CALIFORNIA						
1 Thompson	Y	Y	Y	Y	Y	Y
2 **Herger**	Y	Y	Y	N	N	Y
3 **Lungren**	Y	Y	Y	N	N	Y
4 **McClintock**	Y	Y	Y	N	N	Y
5 Matsui	Y	Y	Y	Y	Y	Y
6 Woolsey	N	Y	Y	Y	Y	Y
7 Miller, George	N	Y	Y	Y	Y	Y
8 Pelosi						
9 Lee	N	Y	Y	+	Y	Y
10 Vacant						
11 McNerney	Y	Y	Y	?	?	?
12 Speier	P	Y	Y	Y	Y	?
13 Stark	N	Y	Y	Y	Y	Y
14 Eshoo	P	Y	Y	Y	Y	Y
15 Honda	P	Y	Y	Y	Y	Y
16 Lofgren	P	Y	Y	Y	Y	Y
17 Farr	P	Y	Y	Y	Y	Y
18 Cardoza	Y	Y	Y	Y	Y	?
19 **Radanovich**	Y	Y	Y	N	N	Y
20 Costa	Y	Y	Y	Y	Y	Y
21 **Nunes**	+	+	+	–	–	?
22 **McCarthy**	N	Y	Y	Y	Y	Y
23 Capps	N	Y	Y	Y	Y	Y
24 **Gallegly**	Y	Y	Y	N	N	Y
25 **McKeon**	Y	Y	Y	N	N	Y
26 **Dreier**	Y	Y	Y	N	N	Y
27 Sherman	Y	Y	Y	Y	Y	Y
28 Berman	Y	Y	Y	Y	Y	Y
29 Schiff	Y	Y	Y	Y	Y	Y
30 Waxman	Y	Y	Y	Y	Y	Y
31 Becerra	P	Y	Y	Y	Y	Y
32 Chu	Y	Y	Y	+	Y	Y
33 Watson	Y	Y	Y	Y	Y	Y
34 Roybal-Allard	Y	Y	Y	?	Y	Y
35 Waters	N	Y	Y	Y	Y	Y
36 Harman	Y	Y	Y	Y	Y	Y
37 Richardson	Y	Y	Y	Y	Y	Y
38 Napolitano	Y	Y	Y	Y	Y	Y
39 Sánchez, Linda	+	+	+	+	+	+
40 **Royce**	Y	Y	Y	N	N	Y
41 **Lewis**	Y	Y	Y	?	N	Y
42 **Miller, Gary**	Y	Y	Y	N	N	Y
43 Baca	Y	Y	Y	Y	Y	Y
44 **Calvert**	Y	Y	Y	N	N	Y
45 **Bono Mack**	Y	Y	Y	N	N	Y
46 **Rohrabacher**	Y	Y	Y	N	N	Y
47 Sanchez, Loretta	Y	Y	Y	Y	Y	Y
48 **Campbell**	Y	Y	Y	N	N	P
49 **Issa**	Y	Y	Y	N	N	Y
50 **Bilbray**	Y	Y	Y	N	N	Y
51 Filner	N	Y	Y	Y	Y	Y
52 **Hunter**	Y	Y	Y	N	N	Y
53 Davis	Y	Y	Y	Y	Y	Y

	838	839	840	841	842	843
COLORADO						
1 DeGette	Y	Y	Y	Y	Y	Y
2 Polis	Y	Y	Y	Y	Y	Y
3 Salazar	Y	Y	?	Y	Y	Y
4 Markey	Y	Y	Y	Y	Y	Y
5 **Lamborn**	Y	Y	Y	N	N	?
6 **Coffman**	Y	Y	Y	N	N	Y
7 Perlmutter	Y	Y	Y	Y	Y	Y
CONNECTICUT						
1 Larson	Y	Y	Y	Y	Y	Y
2 Courtney	Y	Y	Y	Y	Y	Y
3 DeLauro	Y	Y	Y	?	Y	Y
4 Himes	Y	Y	Y	Y	Y	Y
5 Murphy	Y	Y	Y	Y	Y	Y
DELAWARE						
AL **Castle**	Y	Y	Y	N	N	Y
FLORIDA						
1 **Miller**	Y	Y	Y	N	N	Y
2 Boyd	Y	Y	Y	Y	Y	Y
3 Brown	Y	Y	Y	Y	Y	Y
4 **Crenshaw**	Y	Y	Y	N	N	Y
5 **Brown-Waite**	Y	Y	Y	N	N	Y
6 **Stearns**	Y	Y	Y	N	N	Y
7 **Mica**	Y	Y	Y	N	N	Y
8 Grayson	Y	Y	Y	Y	Y	Y
9 **Bilirakis**	Y	Y	Y	N	N	Y
10 **Young**	Y	Y	Y	N	N	Y
11 Castor	Y	Y	Y	Y	Y	Y
12 **Putnam**	Y	Y	Y	N	N	Y
13 **Buchanan**	Y	Y	Y	N	N	Y
14 **Mack**	Y	Y	Y	N	N	Y
15 **Posey**	Y	Y	Y	N	N	Y
16 **Rooney**	Y	Y	Y	N	N	Y
17 Meek	Y	Y	Y	Y	Y	Y
18 **Ros-Lehtinen**	Y	Y	Y	N	N	Y
19 Wexler	Y	Y	Y	Y	Y	Y
20 Wasserman Schultz	Y	Y	Y	Y	Y	Y
21 **Diaz-Balart, L.**	Y	Y	Y	N	N	Y
22 Klein	Y	Y	Y	Y	?	Y
23 Hastings	Y	Y	Y	Y	Y	Y
24 Kosmas	Y	Y	Y	Y	Y	Y
25 **Diaz-Balart, M.**	Y	Y	Y	N	N	Y
GEORGIA						
1 **Kingston**	Y	Y	Y	N	N	Y
2 Bishop	Y	Y	Y	Y	Y	Y
3 **Westmoreland**	Y	Y	Y	N	N	Y
4 Johnson	P	Y	Y	?	Y	Y
5 Lewis	Y	Y	Y	?	Y	Y
6 **Price**	+	+	+	N	N	Y
7 **Linder**	Y	Y	Y	N	N	Y
8 Marshall	Y	Y	Y	?	Y	Y
9 **Deal**	?	?	?	?	?	?
10 **Broun**	Y	Y	Y	N	N	Y
11 **Gingrey**	Y	Y	Y	N	N	Y
12 Barrow	Y	Y	Y	Y	Y	Y
13 Scott	Y	Y	Y	Y	Y	Y
HAWAII						
1 Abercrombie	+	+	+	+	Y	Y
2 Hirono	P	Y	Y	Y	+	Y
IDAHO						
1 Minnick	Y	Y	Y	N	Y	Y
2 **Simpson**	Y	Y	Y	N	N	Y
ILLINOIS						
1 Rush	Y	Y	Y	Y	Y	Y
2 Jackson	Y	Y	Y	Y	Y	Y
3 Lipinski	Y	Y	Y	Y	Y	Y
4 Gutierrez	+	+	+	Y	Y	Y
5 Quigley	Y	Y	Y	Y	Y	Y
6 **Roskam**	Y	Y	Y	N	N	Y
7 Davis	Y	Y	Y	Y	?	Y
8 Bean	Y	Y	Y	Y	Y	Y
9 Schakowsky	Y	Y	Y	Y	Y	Y
10 **Kirk**	Y	Y	Y	–	–	Y
11 Halvorson	Y	Y	Y	Y	Y	Y
12 Costello	Y	Y	Y	Y	Y	Y
13 **Biggert**	Y	Y	Y	N	N	Y
14 Foster	Y	Y	Y	Y	Y	Y
15 **Johnson**	Y	Y	Y	N	N	Y

KEY — **Republicans** — Democrats

Y Voted for (yea)	X Paired against	C Voted "present" to avoid possible conflict of interest
# Paired for	– Announced against	
+ Announced for	P Voted "present"	? Did not vote or otherwise make a position known
N Voted against (nay)		

	838	839	840	841	842	843
16 **Manzullo**	Y	Y	Y	N	N	Y
17 Hare	Y	Y	Y	Y	Y	Y
18 **Schock**	Y	Y	Y	N	N	Y
19 **Shimkus**	Y	Y	Y	N	N	Y
INDIANA						
1 Visclosky	Y	Y	Y	Y	Y	Y
2 Donnelly	Y	Y	Y	Y	Y	Y
3 **Souder**	?	?	?	N	N	Y
4 **Buyer**	Y	Y	Y	N	N	Y
5 **Burton**	Y	Y	Y	N	N	Y
6 **Pence**	Y	Y	Y	N	N	Y
7 Carson	N	Y	Y	Y	Y	Y
8 Ellsworth	Y	Y	Y	Y	Y	Y
9 Hill	Y	Y	Y	N	N	Y
IOWA						
1 Braley	Y	Y	Y	+	+	+
2 Loebsack	P	Y	Y	Y	Y	Y
3 Boswell	Y	Y	Y	Y	Y	Y
4 **Latham**	Y	Y	Y	N	N	Y
5 **King**	Y	Y	Y	N	N	Y
KANSAS						
1 **Moran**	Y	Y	Y	N	N	Y
2 **Jenkins**	Y	Y	Y	N	N	Y
3 Moore	Y	Y	Y	Y	N	Y
4 **Tiahrt**	Y	Y	Y	N	N	Y
KENTUCKY						
1 **Whitfield**	Y	Y	Y	N	N	Y
2 **Guthrie**	Y	Y	Y	N	N	Y
3 Yarmuth	Y	Y	Y	Y	Y	Y
4 **Davis**	N	Y	Y	N	N	Y
5 **Rogers**	Y	Y	Y	N	N	Y
6 Chandler	Y	Y	Y	Y	Y	Y
LOUISIANA						
1 **Scalise**	Y	Y	Y	N	N	Y
2 **Cao**	Y	Y	Y	N	N	Y
3 Melancon	Y	Y	Y	Y	Y	Y
4 **Fleming**	Y	Y	Y	N	N	Y
5 **Alexander**	Y	Y	Y	N	N	Y
6 **Cassidy**	Y	Y	Y	N	N	Y
7 **Boustany**	N	Y	Y	N	N	Y
MAINE						
1 Pingree	?	?	?	Y	Y	Y
2 Michaud	Y	Y	Y	Y	Y	Y
MARYLAND						
1 Kratovil	Y	Y	?	N	N	Y
2 Ruppersberger	Y	Y	Y	Y	Y	Y
3 Sarbanes	Y	Y	Y	Y	Y	Y
4 Edwards	N	Y	Y	Y	Y	Y
5 Hoyer	Y	Y	Y	Y	Y	Y
6 **Bartlett**	Y	Y	Y	N	N	Y
7 Cummings	Y	Y	Y	Y	Y	Y
8 Van Hollen	Y	Y	Y	Y	Y	Y
MASSACHUSETTS						
1 Olver	N	Y	Y	Y	Y	Y
2 Neal	Y	Y	Y	Y	Y	Y
3 McGovern	N	Y	Y	Y	Y	Y
4 Frank	Y	Y	?	Y	Y	Y
5 Tsongas	Y	Y	Y	Y	Y	Y
6 Tierney	P	Y	Y	Y	?	Y
7 Markey	Y	Y	Y	Y	?	Y
8 Capuano	?	?	?	Y	Y	Y
9 Lynch	N	Y	Y	Y	Y	Y
10 Delahunt	P	Y	Y	Y	Y	Y
MICHIGAN						
1 Stupak	?	?	?	?	?	?
2 **Hoekstra**	Y	Y	Y	N	N	Y
3 **Ehlers**	Y	Y	Y	N	N	Y
4 **Camp**	Y	Y	Y	N	N	Y
5 Kildee	Y	Y	Y	Y	Y	Y
6 **Upton**	Y	Y	Y	N	N	Y
7 Schauer	Y	Y	Y	Y	Y	Y
8 **Rogers**	Y	Y	Y	N	N	Y
9 Peters	Y	Y	Y	Y	Y	Y
10 **Miller**	Y	Y	Y	N	N	Y
11 **McCotter**	Y	Y	Y	N	Y	Y
12 Levin	Y	Y	Y	Y	Y	Y
13 Kilpatrick	N	Y	Y	Y	Y	Y
14 Conyers	–	+	+	Y	Y	Y
15 Dingell	N	Y	Y	Y	Y	Y
MINNESOTA						
1 Walz	Y	Y	Y	Y	Y	Y
2 **Kline**	Y	Y	Y	N	N	Y
3 **Paulsen**	Y	Y	Y	N	N	Y
4 McCollum	N	Y	Y	Y	Y	Y

	838	839	840	841	842	843
5 Ellison	N	Y	Y	Y	Y	Y
6 **Bachmann**	+	Y	Y	?	N	Y
7 Peterson	Y	Y	Y	Y	Y	Y
8 Oberstar	Y	Y	Y	Y	Y	Y
MISSISSIPPI						
1 Childers	Y	Y	Y	Y	Y	Y
2 Thompson	Y	Y	Y	Y	Y	Y
3 **Harper**	Y	Y	Y	N	N	Y
4 Taylor	Y	Y	Y	N	N	Y
MISSOURI						
1 Clay	N	Y	Y	Y	Y	Y
2 **Akin**	Y	Y	Y	N	N	Y
3 Carnahan	Y	Y	Y	Y	Y	Y
4 Skelton	Y	Y	Y	Y	Y	Y
5 Cleaver	Y	Y	Y	Y	Y	Y
6 **Graves**	Y	Y	Y	N	N	Y
7 **Blunt**	Y	Y	Y	N	N	Y
8 **Emerson**	Y	Y	Y	N	N	Y
9 **Luetkemeyer**	Y	Y	Y	N	N	Y
MONTANA						
AL **Rehberg**	Y	Y	Y	N	N	Y
NEBRASKA						
1 **Fortenberry**	Y	Y	Y	N	N	Y
2 **Terry**	Y	Y	Y	N	N	Y
3 **Smith**	Y	Y	Y	N	N	Y
NEVADA						
1 Berkley	Y	Y	Y	Y	Y	Y
2 **Heller**	Y	Y	Y	N	N	Y
3 Titus	Y	Y	Y	Y	Y	Y
NEW HAMPSHIRE						
1 Shea-Porter	Y	Y	Y	+	Y	Y
2 Hodes	Y	Y	Y	Y	Y	Y
NEW JERSEY						
1 Andrews	Y	?	Y	Y	Y	?
2 **LoBiondo**	Y	Y	Y	N	N	Y
3 Adler	Y	Y	Y	Y	Y	Y
4 **Smith**	Y	Y	Y	N	N	Y
5 **Garrett**	Y	Y	Y	N	N	Y
6 Pallone	?	?	?	Y	Y	Y
7 **Lance**	Y	Y	Y	N	N	Y
8 Pascrell	+	+	+	Y	Y	Y
9 Rothman	Y	?	?	?	?	?
10 Payne	?	?	?	Y	Y	Y
11 **Frelinghuysen**	Y	Y	Y	N	N	Y
12 Holt	?	?	?	Y	Y	Y
13 Sires	?	?	?	Y	Y	Y
NEW MEXICO						
1 Heinrich	P	Y	Y	Y	Y	Y
2 Teague	Y	Y	Y	Y	Y	Y
3 Lujan	P	Y	Y	Y	Y	Y
NEW YORK						
1 Bishop	Y	Y	Y	Y	Y	Y
2 Israel	Y	Y	Y	Y	Y	Y
3 **King**	Y	Y	Y	N	N	Y
4 McCarthy	Y	Y	Y	Y	Y	Y
5 Ackerman	?	?	?	Y	Y	Y
6 Meeks	?	?	?	Y	Y	Y
7 Crowley	Y	Y	Y	Y	Y	Y
8 Nadler	Y	Y	Y	Y	Y	Y
9 Weiner	Y	Y	Y	Y	Y	Y
10 Towns	?	?	?	Y	Y	Y
11 Clarke	N	Y	Y	Y	Y	Y
12 Velázquez	?	?	?	Y	Y	Y
13 McMahon	Y	Y	Y	+	+	Y
14 Maloney	Y	Y	Y	Y	Y	Y
15 Rangel	Y	Y	Y	Y	Y	Y
16 Serrano	Y	Y	Y	Y	Y	Y
17 Engel	Y	Y	Y	Y	Y	Y
18 Lowey	Y	Y	Y	Y	Y	Y
19 Hall	?	?	?	Y	Y	Y
20 Murphy	Y	Y	Y	Y	Y	Y
21 Tonko	Y	Y	Y	Y	Y	Y
22 Hinchey	N	Y	Y	Y	Y	Y
23 Vacant						
24 Arcuri	Y	Y	Y	Y	Y	Y
25 Maffei	Y	Y	Y	Y	Y	Y
26 **Lee**	Y	Y	Y	N	N	Y
27 Higgins	Y	Y	Y	Y	Y	Y
28 Slaughter	Y	Y	Y	+	?	+
29 Massa	Y	Y	Y	Y	Y	Y
NORTH CAROLINA						
1 Butterfield	Y	Y	Y	Y	Y	Y
2 Etheridge	Y	Y	Y	Y	Y	Y
3 **Jones**	P	Y	Y	N	N	Y
4 Price	N	Y	Y	Y	Y	Y

	838	839	840	841	842	843
5 **Foxx**	Y	Y	Y	N	N	Y
6 **Coble**	Y	Y	Y	N	N	Y
7 McIntyre	Y	Y	Y	Y	Y	Y
8 Kissell	Y	Y	Y	Y	Y	Y
9 **Myrick**	Y	Y	Y	N	?	Y
10 **McHenry**	Y	Y	Y	N	N	Y
11 Shuler	Y	Y	Y	Y	N	Y
12 Watt	N	Y	Y	Y	Y	?
13 Miller	Y	Y	Y	Y	Y	Y
NORTH DAKOTA						
AL Pomeroy	Y	Y	Y	Y	Y	Y
OHIO						
1 Driehaus	Y	Y	Y	Y	Y	Y
2 **Schmidt**	Y	Y	Y	N	N	Y
3 **Turner**	Y	Y	Y	N	N	Y
4 **Jordan**	Y	Y	Y	N	N	Y
5 **Latta**	Y	Y	Y	N	N	Y
6 Wilson	Y	Y	Y	Y	Y	Y
7 **Austria**	Y	Y	Y	N	N	Y
8 **Boehner**	Y	Y	Y	N	N	?
9 Kaptur	P	Y	Y	Y	Y	Y
10 Kucinich	N	Y	Y	Y	Y	Y
11 Fudge	Y	Y	Y	Y	Y	Y
12 **Tiberi**	Y	Y	Y	N	N	Y
13 Sutton	Y	Y	Y	Y	Y	Y
14 **LaTourette**	Y	Y	Y	N	N	Y
15 Kilroy	Y	Y	Y	Y	Y	Y
16 Boccieri	Y	Y	Y	Y	Y	Y
17 Ryan	Y	Y	Y	?	Y	Y
18 Space	Y	Y	Y	Y	Y	Y
OKLAHOMA						
1 **Sullivan**	Y	Y	Y	N	N	?
2 Boren	Y	Y	Y	Y	Y	Y
3 **Lucas**	Y	Y	Y	N	N	Y
4 **Cole**	Y	Y	Y	N	N	Y
5 **Fallin**	Y	Y	Y	N	N	Y
OREGON						
1 Wu	P	Y	Y	Y	Y	Y
2 **Walden**	Y	Y	Y	N	N	Y
3 Blumenauer	N	Y	?	Y	Y	Y
4 DeFazio	P	Y	Y	Y	Y	Y
5 Schrader	Y	Y	Y	Y	Y	Y
PENNSYLVANIA						
1 Brady	?	?	?	Y	Y	Y
2 Fattah	Y	Y	Y	Y	Y	Y
3 Dahlkemper	P	Y	Y	Y	Y	Y
4 Altmire	Y	Y	Y	Y	Y	Y
5 **Thompson**	Y	Y	Y	N	N	Y
6 **Gerlach**	Y	Y	Y	?	?	?
7 Sestak	Y	Y	Y	Y	Y	Y
8 Murphy, P.	?	?	?	?	?	?
9 **Shuster**	Y	Y	Y	N	N	Y
10 Carney	Y	Y	Y	Y	Y	Y
11 Kanjorski	Y	Y	Y	Y	Y	Y
12 Murtha	Y	?	?	Y	Y	Y
13 Schwartz	Y	Y	Y	Y	Y	Y
14 Doyle	Y	Y	Y	Y	Y	Y
15 **Dent**	Y	Y	Y	N	N	Y
16 **Pitts**	Y	Y	Y	N	N	Y
17 Holden	Y	Y	Y	Y	Y	Y
18 **Murphy, T.**	Y	Y	Y	N	N	Y
19 **Platts**	Y	Y	Y	N	N	Y
RHODE ISLAND						
1 Kennedy	Y	Y	Y	Y	Y	Y
2 Langevin	Y	Y	Y	Y	Y	Y
SOUTH CAROLINA						
1 **Brown**	Y	Y	Y	N	N	Y
2 **Wilson**	Y	Y	Y	N	N	Y
3 **Barrett**	?	?	?	?	?	?
4 **Inglis**	Y	Y	Y	N	N	Y
5 Spratt	Y	Y	Y	Y	Y	Y
6 Clyburn	Y	Y	Y	Y	Y	Y
SOUTH DAKOTA						
AL Herseth Sandlin	Y	Y	Y	Y	Y	Y
TENNESSEE						
1 **Roe**	Y	Y	Y	N	N	Y
2 **Duncan**	P	Y	Y	N	N	Y
3 **Wamp**	?	?	?	N	N	Y
4 Davis	?	?	?	?	?	?
5 Cooper	P	Y	Y	Y	Y	Y
6 Gordon	?	?	?	Y	Y	Y
7 **Blackburn**	Y	Y	Y	N	N	Y
8 Tanner	Y	Y	Y	Y	Y	Y
9 Cohen	Y	Y	Y	Y	Y	Y

	838	839	840	841	842	843
TEXAS						
1 **Gohmert**	Y	Y	Y	N	N	P
2 **Poe**	Y	Y	Y	N	N	Y
3 **Johnson, S.**	Y	Y	Y	N	N	Y
4 **Hall**	Y	Y	Y	N	N	Y
5 **Hensarling**	Y	Y	Y	N	N	Y
6 **Barton**	Y	Y	Y	N	N	Y
7 **Culberson**	Y	Y	Y	N	?	Y
8 **Brady**	Y	Y	Y	N	N	Y
9 Green, A.	Y	Y	Y	Y	Y	Y
10 **McCaul**	Y	Y	Y	N	N	?
11 **Conaway**	Y	Y	Y	N	N	Y
12 **Granger**	Y	Y	Y	N	N	Y
13 **Thornberry**	Y	Y	Y	N	N	Y
14 **Paul**	N	Y	?	N	N	N
15 Hinojosa	Y	Y	Y	Y	Y	Y
16 Reyes	Y	Y	Y	Y	Y	Y
17 Edwards	Y	Y	Y	Y	Y	Y
18 Jackson Lee	Y	Y	Y	Y	Y	Y
19 **Neugebauer**	Y	Y	Y	N	N	Y
20 Gonzalez	Y	Y	Y	Y	Y	Y
21 **Smith**	Y	Y	Y	N	N	Y
22 **Olson**	Y	Y	Y	N	N	Y
23 Rodriguez	Y	Y	Y	Y	Y	Y
24 **Marchant**	Y	Y	Y	N	N	Y
25 Doggett	N	Y	Y	Y	Y	Y
26 **Burgess**	Y	Y	Y	N	N	Y
27 Ortiz	Y	Y	Y	Y	Y	Y
28 Cuellar	Y	Y	Y	Y	Y	Y
29 Green, G.	Y	Y	Y	Y	Y	Y
30 Johnson, E.	N	Y	Y	Y	Y	Y
31 **Carter**	Y	Y	Y	N	N	Y
32 **Sessions**	Y	Y	Y	N	N	Y
UTAH						
1 **Bishop**	Y	Y	Y	N	N	Y
2 Matheson	Y	Y	Y	Y	Y	Y
3 **Chaffetz**	Y	Y	Y	N	N	Y
VERMONT						
AL Welch	P	Y	Y	Y	Y	Y
VIRGINIA						
1 **Wittman**	Y	?	?	N	N	Y
2 Nye	Y	Y	Y	Y	Y	Y
3 Scott	Y	Y	Y	Y	Y	Y
4 **Forbes**	Y	Y	Y	N	N	Y
5 Perriello	Y	Y	Y	Y	Y	Y
6 **Goodlatte**	Y	Y	Y	N	N	Y
7 **Cantor**	Y	?	?	N	N	Y
8 Moran	N	Y	Y	?	Y	Y
9 Boucher	?	Y	Y	Y	?	?
10 **Wolf**	Y	Y	Y	N	N	Y
11 Connolly	Y	Y	Y	Y	Y	Y
WASHINGTON						
1 Inslee	Y	Y	Y	Y	Y	?
2 Larsen	Y	Y	Y	Y	Y	Y
3 Baird	N	Y	Y	N	Y	Y
4 **Hastings**	Y	Y	Y	N	N	Y
5 **McMorris Rodgers**	Y	Y	Y	N	N	Y
6 Dicks	Y	Y	Y	Y	Y	Y
7 McDermott	N	Y	Y	Y	Y	Y
8 **Reichert**	Y	Y	Y	N	N	?
9 Smith	Y	Y	Y	Y	Y	Y
WEST VIRGINIA						
1 Mollohan	Y	Y	Y	Y	Y	Y
2 **Capito**	Y	Y	Y	N	N	Y
3 Rahall	N	Y	Y	Y	Y	Y
WISCONSIN						
1 **Ryan**	Y	Y	Y	N	N	Y
2 Baldwin	N	Y	Y	Y	Y	Y
3 Kind	Y	Y	Y	Y	Y	Y
4 Moore	Y	Y	Y	Y	Y	Y
5 **Sensenbrenner**	Y	Y	Y	N	N	Y
6 **Petri**	Y	Y	Y	N	N	Y
7 Obey	P	Y	Y	?	Y	Y
8 Kagen	Y	Y	Y	Y	Y	Y
WYOMING						
AL **Lummis**	Y	Y	Y	N	N	Y
DELEGATES						
Faleomavaega (A.S.)						
Norton (D.C.)						
Bordallo (Guam)						
Sablan (N. Marianas)						
Pierluisi (P.R.)						
Christensen (V.I.)						

IN THE HOUSE | By Vote Number

844. H Res 839. **Madagascar Resource Extraction/Adoption.**
Berman, D-Calif., motion to suspend the rules and adopt the resolution that would condemn the March 2009 coup d'etat in Madagascar and support the people of Madagascar in undertaking a democratic, consensual process to restore constitutional governance. It would also condemn the illegal extraction of natural resources in Madagascar. Motion agreed to 409-5: D 243-0; R 166-5. A two-thirds majority of those present and voting (276 in this case) is required for adoption under suspension of the rules. Nov. 4, 2009.

845. HR 3639. **Expedited Credit Card Company Rules/Fee Reduction Implementation.** Hensarling, R-Texas, amendment that would clarify that interest rate or fee reductions would not be subject to a 45-day waiting period. Adopted in Committee of the Whole 427-0: D 254-0; R 173-0. Nov. 4, 2009.

846. HR 3639. **Expedited Credit Card Company Rules/Credit Card Company Exemption.** McCarthy, D-N.Y., amendment that would exempt credit card companies from accelerated provisions requiring them to apply customer payments in excess of minimum amounts to the highest rate balance if they have not increased interest rates or fees. Adopted in Committee of the Whole 427-0: D 254-0; R 173-0. Nov. 4, 2009.

847. HR 3639. **Expedited Credit Card Company Rules/Enactment Date.** Maffei, D-N.Y., amendment that would set the effective date for credit card company regulations enacted earlier this year to the date of the underlying bill's enactment. Adopted in Committee of the Whole 251-174: D 243-10; R 8-164. Nov. 4, 2009.

848. HR 3639. **Expedited Credit Card Company Rules/Credit Score Impact.** Sutton, D-Ohio, amendment that would prohibit creditors or consumer reporting agencies from lowering a consumer's credit score because the consumer closed a credit account within 45 days of receiving a notice of a fee increase. Adopted in Committee of the Whole 353-71: D 248-2; R 105-69. Nov. 4, 2009.

849. HR 3639. **Expedited Credit Card Company Rules/Rate Increase Moratorium.** Sutton, D-Ohio, amendment that would prohibit increases in annual percentage rates, fees or finance charges, as well as changes to the terms for repayment of outstanding balances, for nine months after the bill's enactment. Adopted in Committee of the Whole 249-173: D 228-20; R 21-153. Nov. 4, 2009.

	844	845	846	847	848	849
ALABAMA						
1 **Bonner**	Y	Y	Y	N	Y	N
2 Bright	Y	Y	Y	N	Y	N
3 **Rogers**	Y	Y	Y	N	Y	Y
4 **Aderholt**	Y	Y	Y	N	Y	Y
5 Griffith	Y	Y	Y	Y	Y	?
6 **Bachus**	Y	Y	Y	N	N	N
7 Davis	Y	Y	Y	Y	Y	Y
ALASKA						
AL **Young**	Y	Y	Y	N	Y	Y
ARIZONA						
1 Kirkpatrick	Y	Y	Y	N	Y	N
2 **Franks**	N	Y	Y	N	N	N
3 **Shadegg**	Y	Y	Y	N	Y	N
4 Pastor	Y	Y	Y	Y	Y	Y
5 Mitchell	Y	Y	Y	Y	Y	Y
6 **Flake**	Y	Y	Y	N	N	N
7 Grijalva	Y	Y	Y	Y	Y	Y
8 Giffords	Y	Y	Y	N	Y	Y
ARKANSAS						
1 Berry	Y	Y	Y	Y	Y	Y
2 Snyder	Y	Y	Y	Y	Y	Y
3 **Boozman**	Y	Y	Y	N	Y	N
4 Ross	Y	Y	Y	Y	Y	Y
CALIFORNIA						
1 Thompson	Y	Y	Y	Y	Y	Y
2 **Herger**	Y	Y	Y	N	Y	N
3 **Lungren**	Y	Y	Y	N	Y	N
4 **McClintock**	N	Y	Y	N	N	N
5 Matsui	Y	Y	Y	Y	Y	Y
6 Woolsey	Y	Y	Y	Y	Y	Y
7 Miller, George	Y	Y	Y	Y	Y	Y
8 Pelosi						
9 Lee	Y	Y	Y	Y	Y	Y
10 Vacant						
11 McNerney	?	Y	Y	Y	Y	Y
12 Speier	Y	Y	Y	Y	Y	Y
13 Stark	Y	Y	Y	Y	Y	Y
14 Eshoo	Y	Y	Y	Y	Y	Y
15 Honda	Y	Y	Y	Y	Y	Y
16 Lofgren	Y	Y	Y	Y	Y	Y
17 Farr	Y	Y	Y	Y	Y	Y
18 Cardoza	Y	Y	Y	Y	Y	N
19 **Radanovich**	Y	Y	Y	N	N	N
20 Costa	Y	Y	Y	Y	Y	Y
21 **Nunes**	+	+	+	−	−	−
22 **McCarthy**	Y	Y	Y	N	Y	N
23 Capps	Y	Y	Y	Y	Y	Y
24 **Gallegly**	Y	Y	Y	N	N	N
25 **McKeon**	Y	Y	Y	N	N	N
26 **Dreier**	Y	Y	Y	N	N	N
27 Sherman	Y	Y	Y	Y	Y	Y
28 Berman	Y	Y	Y	Y	Y	Y
29 Schiff	Y	Y	Y	Y	Y	Y
30 Waxman	Y	Y	Y	Y	Y	Y
31 Becerra	Y	Y	Y	Y	?	Y
32 Chu	Y	Y	Y	Y	Y	Y
33 Watson	Y	Y	Y	Y	Y	Y
34 Roybal-Allard	Y	Y	Y	Y	Y	Y
35 Waters	Y	Y	Y	Y	Y	?
36 Harman	Y	Y	Y	Y	Y	Y
37 Richardson	Y	Y	Y	Y	Y	Y
38 Napolitano	Y	Y	Y	Y	Y	Y
39 Sánchez, Linda	+	+	+	+	+	+
40 **Royce**	Y	Y	Y	N	N	N
41 **Lewis**	Y	Y	Y	N	N	N
42 **Miller, Gary**	Y	Y	Y	N	N	N
43 Baca	Y	Y	Y	Y	Y	?
44 **Calvert**	Y	Y	Y	N	N	N
45 **Bono Mack**	Y	Y	Y	N	Y	Y
46 **Rohrabacher**	Y	Y	Y	N	N	N
47 Sanchez, Loretta	Y	Y	Y	Y	Y	Y
48 **Campbell**	N	Y	Y	N	Y	N
49 **Issa**	Y	Y	Y	N	N	N
50 **Bilbray**	Y	Y	Y	N	Y	N
51 Filner	Y	Y	Y	Y	Y	Y
52 **Hunter**	Y	Y	Y	N	Y	N
53 Davis	Y	Y	Y	Y	Y	Y

	844	845	846	847	848	849
COLORADO						
1 DeGette	Y	Y	Y	Y	Y	Y
2 Polis	Y	Y	Y	Y	Y	Y
3 Salazar	Y	Y	Y	Y	Y	Y
4 Markey	Y	Y	Y	Y	Y	N
5 **Lamborn**	Y	Y	Y	N	N	N
6 **Coffman**	Y	+	+	−	Y	N
7 Perlmutter	Y	Y	Y	Y	Y	Y
CONNECTICUT						
1 Larson	Y	Y	Y	Y	Y	Y
2 Courtney	Y	Y	Y	Y	Y	Y
3 DeLauro	Y	Y	Y	Y	Y	Y
4 Himes	Y	Y	Y	N	N	N
5 Murphy	Y	Y	Y	Y	Y	Y
DELAWARE						
AL **Castle**	Y	Y	Y	N	N	N
FLORIDA						
1 **Miller**	Y	Y	Y	N	N	N
2 Boyd	Y	Y	Y	Y	Y	Y
3 Brown	Y	Y	Y	Y	Y	Y
4 **Crenshaw**	Y	Y	Y	N	N	N
5 **Brown-Waite**	Y	Y	Y	N	Y	N
6 **Stearns**	Y	Y	Y	N	Y	N
7 **Mica**	Y	Y	Y	N	N	N
8 Grayson	Y	Y	Y	Y	Y	Y
9 **Bilirakis**	Y	Y	Y	N	Y	N
10 **Young**	Y	Y	Y	N	Y	N
11 Castor	Y	Y	Y	Y	Y	Y
12 **Putnam**	Y	Y	Y	N	Y	N
13 **Buchanan**	Y	Y	Y	N	Y	Y
14 **Mack**	Y	Y	Y	N	N	N
15 **Posey**	Y	Y	Y	N	Y	N
16 **Rooney**	Y	Y	Y	N	Y	N
17 Meek	Y	Y	Y	Y	Y	Y
18 **Ros-Lehtinen**	Y	Y	Y	N	Y	Y
19 Wexler	Y	Y	Y	?	Y	Y
20 Wasserman Schultz	Y	Y	Y	?	Y	Y
21 **Diaz-Balart, L.**	Y	Y	Y	N	Y	N
22 Klein	Y	Y	Y	Y	Y	Y
23 Hastings	Y	Y	Y	Y	?	Y
24 Kosmas	Y	Y	Y	Y	Y	N
25 **Diaz-Balart, M.**	Y	Y	Y	N	Y	N
GEORGIA						
1 **Kingston**	Y	Y	Y	N	Y	N
2 Bishop	Y	Y	Y	Y	Y	Y
3 **Westmoreland**	Y	Y	Y	N	N	N
4 Johnson	Y	Y	Y	Y	Y	Y
5 Lewis	Y	Y	Y	Y	Y	Y
6 **Price**	Y	Y	Y	N	N	N
7 **Linder**	Y	Y	Y	N	N	N
8 Marshall	Y	Y	Y	Y	Y	Y
9 **Deal**	?	?	?	?	?	?
10 **Broun**	Y	Y	Y	N	N	N
11 **Gingrey**	Y	Y	Y	N	N	N
12 Barrow	Y	Y	Y	Y	Y	Y
13 Scott	Y	Y	Y	Y	Y	Y
HAWAII						
1 Abercrombie	Y	Y	Y	Y	Y	Y
2 Hirono	Y	Y	Y	Y	Y	Y
IDAHO						
1 Minnick	Y	Y	Y	Y	Y	Y
2 **Simpson**	Y	Y	Y	Y	Y	N
ILLINOIS						
1 Rush	Y	Y	Y	Y	Y	Y
2 Jackson	Y	Y	Y	Y	Y	Y
3 Lipinski	Y	Y	Y	Y	Y	Y
4 Gutierrez	Y	Y	Y	Y	Y	?
5 Quigley	Y	Y	Y	Y	Y	Y
6 **Roskam**	Y	Y	Y	N	Y	N
7 Davis	Y	Y	Y	Y	Y	Y
8 Bean	Y	Y	Y	Y	Y	N
9 Schakowsky	Y	Y	Y	Y	Y	Y
10 **Kirk**	Y	Y	Y	N	Y	N
11 Halvorson	Y	Y	Y	Y	Y	Y
12 Costello	Y	Y	Y	Y	Y	Y
13 **Biggert**	Y	Y	Y	N	Y	N
14 Foster	Y	Y	Y	Y	Y	Y
15 **Johnson**	Y	Y	Y	N	Y	N

	844	845	846	847	848	849
16 **Manzullo**	Y	Y	Y	N	Y	N
17 Hare	Y	Y	Y	Y	Y	Y
18 **Schock**	Y	Y	Y	N	N	N
19 **Shimkus**	Y	Y	Y	N	Y	N
INDIANA						
1 Visclosky	Y	Y	Y	Y	Y	Y
2 Donnelly	Y	Y	Y	Y	Y	Y
3 **Souder**	Y	Y	Y	N	Y	N
4 **Buyer**	Y	Y	Y	N	Y	Y
5 **Burton**	Y	Y	Y	N	N	N
6 **Pence**	Y	Y	Y	N	N	N
7 Carson	Y	Y	Y	Y	Y	Y
8 Ellsworth	Y	Y	Y	Y	Y	Y
9 Hill	Y	Y	Y	Y	Y	Y
IOWA						
1 Braley	+	+	+	+	+	+
2 Loebsack	Y	Y	Y	Y	Y	Y
3 Boswell	Y	Y	Y	Y	Y	Y
4 **Latham**	Y	Y	Y	Y	Y	Y
5 **King**	Y	Y	Y	N	N	N
KANSAS						
1 **Moran**	Y	Y	Y	N	Y	Y
2 **Jenkins**	Y	Y	Y	N	Y	N
3 Moore	Y	Y	Y	Y	Y	Y
4 **Tiahrt**	Y	Y	Y	N	Y	N
KENTUCKY						
1 **Whitfield**	Y	Y	Y	N	Y	N
2 **Guthrie**	Y	Y	Y	N	Y	N
3 Yarmuth	Y	Y	Y	Y	?	Y
4 **Davis**	Y	Y	Y	N	N	N
5 **Rogers**	Y	Y	Y	N	Y	N
6 Chandler	Y	Y	Y	Y	Y	Y
LOUISIANA						
1 **Scalise**	Y	Y	Y	N	N	N
2 **Cao**	Y	Y	Y	N	Y	Y
3 Melancon	Y	Y	Y	Y	Y	Y
4 **Fleming**	Y	Y	Y	N	Y	N
5 **Alexander**	Y	Y	Y	N	Y	N
6 **Cassidy**	?	Y	Y	N	Y	N
7 **Boustany**	Y	Y	Y	N	Y	N
MAINE						
1 Pingree	Y	Y	Y	Y	Y	Y
2 Michaud	Y	Y	Y	Y	Y	Y
MARYLAND						
1 Kratovil	Y	Y	Y	Y	Y	N
2 Ruppersberger	Y	Y	Y	Y	Y	Y
3 Sarbanes	Y	Y	Y	Y	Y	Y
4 Edwards	Y	Y	Y	Y	Y	Y
5 Hoyer	Y	Y	Y	Y	Y	Y
6 **Bartlett**	Y	Y	Y	N	Y	N
7 Cummings	Y	Y	Y	Y	Y	Y
8 Van Hollen	Y	Y	Y	Y	Y	Y
MASSACHUSETTS						
1 Olver	Y	Y	Y	Y	Y	Y
2 Neal	Y	Y	Y	Y	Y	Y
3 McGovern	Y	Y	Y	Y	Y	Y
4 Frank	Y	Y	Y	Y	Y	Y
5 Tsongas	Y	Y	Y	Y	Y	Y
6 Tierney	Y	Y	Y	Y	Y	Y
7 Markey	Y	Y	Y	Y	Y	Y
8 Capuano	Y	Y	Y	Y	Y	Y
9 Lynch	Y	Y	Y	Y	Y	Y
10 Delahunt	Y	Y	Y	Y	Y	Y
MICHIGAN						
1 Stupak	?	?	?	?	?	?
2 **Hoekstra**	Y	Y	Y	N	Y	N
3 **Ehlers**	Y	Y	Y	N	Y	N
4 **Camp**	Y	Y	Y	N	Y	N
5 Kildee	Y	Y	Y	Y	Y	Y
6 **Upton**	Y	Y	Y	N	Y	N
7 Schauer	Y	Y	Y	Y	Y	Y
8 **Rogers**	Y	Y	Y	N	Y	N
9 Peters	Y	Y	Y	Y	Y	Y
10 **Miller**	Y	Y	Y	N	Y	N
11 **McCotter**	Y	Y	Y	N	Y	N
12 Levin	Y	Y	Y	Y	Y	Y
13 Kilpatrick	Y	Y	Y	Y	Y	Y
14 Conyers	Y	Y	Y	Y	Y	Y
15 Dingell	Y	Y	Y	Y	Y	Y
MINNESOTA						
1 Walz	Y	Y	Y	Y	Y	Y
2 **Kline**	Y	Y	Y	N	Y	N
3 **Paulsen**	Y	Y	Y	N	Y	N
4 McCollum	Y	Y	Y	Y	Y	Y

	844	845	846	847	848	849
5 Ellison	Y	Y	Y	Y	Y	Y
6 **Bachmann**	Y	Y	Y	N	N	N
7 Peterson	Y	Y	Y	Y	Y	Y
8 Oberstar	Y	Y	Y	Y	Y	Y
MISSISSIPPI						
1 Childers	Y	Y	Y	Y	Y	N
2 Thompson	Y	Y	Y	Y	Y	Y
3 **Harper**	Y	Y	Y	N	Y	N
4 Taylor	Y	Y	Y	N	Y	N
MISSOURI						
1 Clay	Y	Y	Y	Y	Y	Y
2 **Akin**	Y	Y	Y	?	N	N
3 Carnahan	Y	Y	Y	Y	Y	Y
4 Skelton	Y	Y	Y	N	Y	Y
5 Cleaver	Y	Y	Y	Y	Y	Y
6 **Graves**	Y	Y	Y	N	Y	N
7 **Blunt**	Y	Y	Y	Y	Y	N
8 **Emerson**	Y	Y	Y	Y	Y	N
9 **Luetkemeyer**	Y	Y	Y	N	N	N
MONTANA						
AL **Rehberg**	Y	Y	Y	N	Y	N
NEBRASKA						
1 **Fortenberry**	Y	Y	Y	N	Y	N
2 **Terry**	Y	Y	Y	N	Y	N
3 **Smith**	Y	Y	Y	N	Y	N
NEVADA						
1 Berkley	Y	Y	Y	Y	Y	Y
2 **Heller**	Y	Y	Y	N	Y	N
3 Titus	Y	Y	Y	Y	Y	Y
NEW HAMPSHIRE						
1 Shea-Porter	Y	Y	Y	Y	Y	Y
2 Hodes	Y	Y	Y	Y	Y	Y
NEW JERSEY						
1 Andrews	Y	Y	Y	Y	Y	Y
2 **LoBiondo**	Y	Y	Y	N	Y	Y
3 Adler	Y	Y	Y	Y	Y	Y
4 **Smith**	Y	Y	Y	N	Y	Y
5 **Garrett**	Y	Y	Y	N	N	N
6 Pallone	Y	Y	Y	Y	Y	Y
7 **Lance**	Y	Y	Y	N	Y	N
8 Pascrell	Y	Y	Y	Y	Y	Y
9 Rothman	?	Y	Y	?	Y	Y
10 Payne	Y	Y	Y	Y	Y	Y
11 **Frelinghuysen**	Y	Y	Y	N	Y	N
12 Holt	Y	Y	Y	Y	Y	Y
13 Sires	Y	Y	Y	Y	Y	Y
NEW MEXICO						
1 Heinrich	Y	Y	Y	Y	Y	Y
2 Teague	Y	Y	Y	Y	Y	Y
3 Lujan	Y	Y	Y	Y	Y	Y
NEW YORK						
1 Bishop	Y	Y	Y	Y	Y	Y
2 Israel	Y	Y	Y	Y	Y	Y
3 **King**	Y	Y	Y	N	N	N
4 McCarthy	?	Y	Y	N	Y	N
5 Ackerman	Y	Y	Y	Y	Y	Y
6 Meeks	Y	Y	Y	Y	?	Y
7 Crowley	Y	Y	Y	Y	Y	Y
8 Nadler	Y	Y	Y	Y	Y	Y
9 Weiner	Y	Y	Y	Y	Y	Y
10 Towns	Y	Y	Y	Y	Y	Y
11 Clarke	Y	Y	Y	Y	Y	Y
12 Velázquez	Y	Y	Y	Y	Y	Y
13 McMahon	Y	Y	Y	Y	N	N
14 Maloney	Y	Y	Y	Y	Y	Y
15 Rangel	Y	Y	Y	Y	Y	Y
16 Serrano	Y	Y	Y	Y	Y	Y
17 Engel	Y	Y	Y	Y	Y	Y
18 Lowey	Y	Y	Y	Y	Y	Y
19 Hall	Y	Y	Y	Y	Y	Y
20 Murphy	Y	Y	Y	Y	Y	N
21 Tonko	Y	Y	Y	Y	Y	Y
22 Hinchey	Y	Y	Y	Y	Y	Y
23 Vacant						
24 Arcuri	Y	Y	Y	Y	Y	Y
25 Maffei	Y	Y	Y	Y	Y	Y
26 **Lee**	Y	Y	Y	N	N	N
27 Higgins	Y	Y	Y	Y	Y	Y
28 Slaughter	Y	Y	?	Y	Y	Y
29 Massa	Y	Y	Y	Y	Y	Y
NORTH CAROLINA						
1 Butterfield	?	Y	Y	Y	Y	Y
2 Etheridge	Y	Y	Y	Y	Y	Y
3 **Jones**	Y	Y	Y	Y	Y	Y
4 Price	Y	Y	Y	Y	Y	Y

	844	845	846	847	848	849
5 **Foxx**	Y	Y	Y	N	N	N
6 **Coble**	Y	Y	Y	N	Y	N
7 McIntyre	Y	Y	Y	Y	Y	Y
8 Kissell	Y	Y	Y	Y	Y	Y
9 **Myrick**	Y	Y	Y	N	Y	N
10 **McHenry**	Y	Y	Y	N	Y	N
11 Shuler	Y	Y	Y	Y	Y	N
12 Watt	Y	Y	Y	Y	Y	Y
13 Miller	Y	Y	Y	Y	Y	Y
NORTH DAKOTA						
AL Pomeroy	Y	Y	Y	Y	Y	Y
OHIO						
1 Driehaus	Y	Y	Y	Y	Y	Y
2 **Schmidt**	Y	Y	Y	N	N	N
3 **Turner**	Y	Y	Y	N	Y	N
4 **Jordan**	Y	Y	Y	N	N	N
5 **Latta**	Y	Y	Y	N	N	N
6 Wilson	Y	Y	Y	Y	Y	Y
7 **Austria**	Y	Y	Y	N	N	N
8 **Boehner**	?	Y	Y	N	N	N
9 Kaptur	Y	Y	Y	Y	Y	Y
10 Kucinich	Y	Y	Y	Y	Y	Y
11 Fudge	Y	Y	Y	Y	Y	Y
12 **Tiberi**	Y	Y	Y	N	Y	N
13 Sutton	Y	Y	Y	Y	Y	Y
14 **LaTourette**	Y	Y	Y	Y	Y	N
15 Kilroy	Y	Y	Y	Y	Y	Y
16 Boccieri	Y	Y	Y	Y	Y	Y
17 Ryan	Y	Y	Y	Y	Y	Y
18 Space	Y	Y	Y	Y	Y	Y
OKLAHOMA						
1 **Sullivan**	Y	Y	Y	N	N	N
2 Boren	Y	Y	Y	Y	Y	N
3 **Lucas**	Y	Y	Y	N	N	N
4 **Cole**	Y	Y	Y	N	N	N
5 **Fallin**	Y	Y	Y	N	Y	N
OREGON						
1 Wu	Y	Y	Y	Y	Y	Y
2 **Walden**	Y	Y	Y	N	Y	N
3 Blumenauer	Y	Y	Y	Y	Y	Y
4 DeFazio	Y	Y	Y	Y	Y	Y
5 Schrader	?	Y	Y	Y	Y	Y
PENNSYLVANIA						
1 Brady	Y	Y	Y	Y	Y	Y
2 Fattah	Y	Y	Y	Y	Y	Y
3 Dahlkemper	Y	Y	Y	Y	Y	N
4 Altmire	Y	Y	Y	Y	Y	N
5 **Thompson**	Y	Y	Y	N	N	N
6 **Gerlach**	?	?	?	?	?	?
7 Sestak	Y	Y	Y	Y	Y	Y
8 Murphy, P.	?	?	?	?	?	?
9 **Shuster**	Y	Y	Y	N	Y	N
10 Carney	Y	Y	Y	Y	Y	Y
11 Kanjorski	?	Y	Y	Y	Y	Y
12 Murtha	Y	Y	Y	Y	Y	Y
13 Schwartz	Y	Y	Y	Y	Y	Y
14 Doyle	Y	Y	Y	Y	Y	Y
15 **Dent**	Y	Y	Y	N	Y	Y
16 **Pitts**	Y	Y	Y	N	Y	N
17 Holden	Y	Y	Y	Y	Y	Y
18 **Murphy, T.**	Y	Y	Y	N	Y	Y
19 **Platts**	Y	Y	Y	Y	Y	Y
RHODE ISLAND						
1 Kennedy	Y	Y	Y	Y	Y	Y
2 Langevin	Y	Y	Y	Y	Y	Y
SOUTH CAROLINA						
1 **Brown**	Y	Y	Y	N	Y	N
2 **Wilson**	Y	Y	Y	N	Y	N
3 **Barrett**	?	Y	Y	N	N	N
4 **Inglis**	Y	Y	Y	N	N	N
5 Spratt	Y	Y	Y	Y	Y	Y
6 Clyburn	Y	Y	Y	Y	Y	Y
SOUTH DAKOTA						
AL Herseth Sandlin	Y	Y	Y	N	Y	N
TENNESSEE						
1 **Roe**	Y	Y	Y	N	Y	N
2 **Duncan**	Y	Y	Y	N	Y	N
3 **Wamp**	Y	Y	Y	N	Y	N
4 Davis	?	?	?	?	?	?
5 Cooper	Y	Y	Y	Y	Y	Y
6 Gordon	Y	Y	Y	Y	Y	Y
7 **Blackburn**	Y	Y	Y	N	Y	N
8 Tanner	Y	Y	Y	Y	Y	N
9 Cohen	Y	Y	Y	Y	Y	Y

	844	845	846	847	848	849
TEXAS						
1 **Gohmert**	Y	Y	Y	N	Y	N
2 **Poe**	Y	Y	Y	N	N	N
3 **Johnson, S.**	Y	Y	Y	N	N	N
4 **Hall**	Y	Y	Y	N	N	N
5 **Hensarling**	Y	Y	Y	N	N	N
6 **Barton**	Y	Y	Y	N	Y	Y
7 **Culberson**	Y	Y	Y	N	Y	N
8 **Brady**	Y	Y	Y	N	N	N
9 Green, A.	Y	Y	Y	Y	Y	Y
10 **McCaul**	Y	Y	Y	N	N	N
11 **Conaway**	Y	Y	Y	N	N	N
12 **Granger**	Y	Y	Y	N	N	N
13 **Thornberry**	Y	Y	Y	N	N	N
14 **Paul**	N	Y	Y	N	N	N
15 Hinojosa	Y	Y	Y	Y	Y	Y
16 Reyes	Y	Y	Y	Y	Y	Y
17 Edwards	Y	Y	Y	Y	Y	Y
18 Jackson Lee	Y	Y	Y	Y	Y	Y
19 **Neugebauer**	Y	Y	Y	N	N	N
20 Gonzalez	Y	Y	Y	Y	Y	?
21 **Smith**	Y	Y	Y	N	N	N
22 **Olson**	Y	Y	Y	N	N	N
23 Rodriguez	Y	Y	Y	Y	Y	Y
24 **Marchant**	Y	Y	Y	N	N	N
25 Doggett	Y	Y	Y	Y	Y	Y
26 **Burgess**	Y	Y	Y	N	N	N
27 Ortiz	Y	Y	Y	Y	Y	Y
28 Cuellar	Y	Y	Y	Y	Y	Y
29 Green, G.	Y	Y	Y	Y	Y	Y
30 Johnson, E.	Y	Y	Y	Y	Y	Y
31 **Carter**	Y	Y	Y	N	N	N
32 **Sessions**	Y	Y	Y	N	N	N
UTAH						
1 **Bishop**	N	Y	Y	N	Y	N
2 Matheson	Y	Y	Y	Y	Y	N
3 **Chaffetz**	Y	Y	Y	N	Y	N
VERMONT						
AL Welch	Y	Y	Y	Y	Y	Y
VIRGINIA						
1 **Wittman**	Y	Y	Y	N	Y	N
2 Nye	Y	Y	Y	Y	Y	Y
3 Scott	Y	Y	Y	Y	Y	Y
4 **Forbes**	Y	Y	Y	N	Y	Y
5 Perriello	Y	Y	Y	Y	Y	Y
6 **Goodlatte**	Y	Y	Y	N	Y	N
7 **Cantor**	Y	Y	Y	N	N	N
8 Moran	Y	Y	Y	Y	Y	Y
9 Boucher	Y	Y	Y	N	Y	?
10 **Wolf**	Y	Y	Y	N	Y	N
11 Connolly	Y	Y	Y	Y	Y	Y
WASHINGTON						
1 Inslee	Y	Y	Y	Y	Y	Y
2 Larsen	Y	Y	Y	Y	Y	Y
3 Baird	Y	Y	Y	Y	Y	Y
4 **Hastings**	Y	Y	Y	N	N	N
5 **McMorris Rodgers**	Y	Y	Y	N	N	N
6 Dicks	Y	Y	Y	Y	Y	Y
7 McDermott	Y	Y	Y	Y	Y	Y
8 **Reichert**	Y	Y	Y	Y	Y	N
9 Smith	Y	Y	Y	Y	Y	Y
WEST VIRGINIA						
1 Mollohan	Y	Y	Y	Y	Y	Y
2 **Capito**	Y	Y	Y	N	Y	Y
3 Rahall	Y	Y	Y	Y	Y	Y
WISCONSIN						
1 **Ryan**	Y	Y	Y	N	N	N
2 Baldwin	Y	Y	Y	Y	Y	Y
3 Kind	Y	Y	Y	Y	Y	?
4 Moore	?	Y	Y	Y	Y	Y
5 **Sensenbrenner**	Y	Y	Y	N	Y	N
6 **Petri**	Y	Y	Y	N	Y	N
7 Obey	Y	Y	Y	Y	Y	Y
8 Kagen	Y	Y	Y	Y	Y	Y
WYOMING						
AL **Lummis**	Y	Y	Y	N	Y	Y
DELEGATES						
Faleomavaega (A.S.)		Y	Y	Y	Y	Y
Norton (D.C.)		?	?	?	?	?
Bordallo (Guam)		Y	Y	Y	Y	Y
Sablan (N. Marianas)		Y	Y	Y	Y	Y
Pierluisi (P.R.)		?	Y	Y	Y	Y
Christensen (V.I.)		Y	Y	Y	Y	Y

IN THE HOUSE | By Vote Number

850. HR 3639. Expedited Credit Card Company Rules/Recommit.
Castle, R-Del., motion to recommit the bill to the House Financial Services Committee with instructions that it be immediately reported back with an amendment that would require the Federal Reserve Board to submit a report to Congress stating whether implementation of regulations by Dec. 1, 2009, is feasible. It would make the bill ineffective if the Federal Reserve determines that implementation is not feasible by that date. Motion rejected 171-253: D 3-247; R 168-6. Nov. 4, 2009.

851. HR 3639. Expedited Credit Card Company Rules/Passage.
Passage of the bill that would move up the effective date of certain credit card rules enacted earlier this year. As amended, it would make those rules take effect on the date of this bill's enactment. The regulations that would take effect at that time include restrictions on when companies may increase annual percentage interest rates retroactively on an existing balance, and restrictions on computing interest charges on balances from more than one billing cycle. Passed 331-92: D 248-1; R 83-91. Nov. 4, 2009.

852. H Res 863. Pneumonia Prevention and Treatment/Adoption.
Engel, D-N.Y., motion to suspend the rules and adopt the resolution that would acknowledge the House's commitment to international child survival and development programs related to the prevention and treatment of pneumonia. Motion agreed to 421-1: D 250-0; R 171-1. A two-thirds majority of those present and voting (282 in this case) is required for adoption under suspension of the rules. Nov. 4, 2009.

853. H Res 641. Tribute to Radio Free Europe/Adoption.
Berman, D-Calif., motion to suspend the rules and adopt the resolution that would recognize the 60th anniversary of Radio Free Europe/Radio Liberty and honor the organization's contribution to freedom. Motion agreed to 422-1: D 250-0; R 172-1. A two-thirds majority of those present and voting (282 in this case) is required for adoption under suspension of the rules. Nov. 4, 2009.

854. H Res 711. Sri Lankan Release of Tamil Refugees/Adoption.
Berman, D-Calif., motion to suspend the rules and adopt the resolution that would urge the Sri Lankan government to guarantee the safety and release of Tamil refugees and internally displaced persons. Motion agreed to 421-1: D 249-0; R 172-1. A two-thirds majority of those present and voting (282 in this case) is required for adoption under suspension of the rules. Nov. 4, 2009.

	850	851	852	853	854
ALABAMA					
1 **Bonner**	Y	N	Y	Y	Y
2 Bright	N	Y	Y	Y	Y
3 **Rogers**	Y	Y	Y	Y	Y
4 **Aderholt**	Y	Y	Y	Y	Y
5 Griffith	N	Y	Y	Y	Y
6 **Bachus**	Y	N	Y	Y	Y
7 Davis	N	Y	Y	Y	Y
ALASKA					
AL **Young**	Y	Y	Y	Y	Y
ARIZONA					
1 Kirkpatrick	N	Y	Y	Y	Y
2 **Franks**	Y	N	Y	Y	Y
3 **Shadegg**	Y	N	Y	Y	Y
4 Pastor	N	Y	Y	Y	Y
5 Mitchell	N	Y	Y	Y	Y
6 **Flake**	Y	N	Y	Y	Y
7 Grijalva	N	Y	Y	?	?
8 Giffords	N	Y	Y	Y	Y
ARKANSAS					
1 Berry	N	Y	Y	Y	Y
2 Snyder	N	Y	Y	Y	Y
3 **Boozman**	Y	Y	Y	Y	Y
4 Ross	N	Y	Y	Y	Y
CALIFORNIA					
1 Thompson	N	Y	Y	Y	Y
2 **Herger**	Y	N	Y	Y	Y
3 **Lungren**	Y	Y	Y	Y	Y
4 **McClintock**	Y	N	Y	Y	Y
5 Matsui	N	Y	Y	Y	Y
6 Woolsey	N	Y	Y	Y	Y
7 Miller, George	N	Y	Y	Y	Y
8 Pelosi					
9 Lee	N	Y	Y	Y	Y
10 Vacant					
11 McNerney	N	Y	Y	Y	Y
12 Speier	N	Y	Y	Y	Y
13 Stark	N	Y	Y	Y	Y
14 Eshoo	N	Y	Y	Y	Y
15 Honda	N	Y	Y	Y	Y
16 Lofgren	N	Y	Y	Y	Y
17 Farr	N	Y	Y	Y	Y
18 Cardoza	N	Y	Y	Y	Y
19 **Radanovich**	Y	N	Y	Y	Y
20 Costa	N	Y	Y	Y	Y
21 **Nunes**	+	–	+	+	+
22 **McCarthy**	Y	N	Y	Y	Y
23 Capps	N	Y	Y	Y	Y
24 **Gallegly**	Y	Y	Y	Y	Y
25 **McKeon**	Y	N	Y	Y	Y
26 **Dreier**	Y	Y	Y	Y	Y
27 Sherman	N	Y	Y	Y	Y
28 Berman	N	Y	Y	Y	Y
29 Schiff	N	Y	Y	Y	Y
30 Waxman	N	Y	Y	Y	Y
31 Becerra	N	Y	Y	Y	Y
32 Chu	N	Y	Y	Y	Y
33 Watson	N	Y	Y	Y	Y
34 Roybal-Allard	N	Y	Y	Y	Y
35 Waters	N	Y	Y	Y	Y
36 Harman	N	Y	Y	Y	Y
37 Richardson	N	Y	Y	Y	Y
38 Napolitano	N	Y	Y	Y	Y
39 Sánchez, Linda	–	+	+	+	+
40 **Royce**	Y	N	Y	Y	Y
41 **Lewis**	Y	N	Y	Y	Y
42 **Miller, Gary**	Y	N	Y	Y	Y
43 Baca	N	Y	Y	Y	Y
44 **Calvert**	Y	Y	Y	Y	Y
45 **Bono Mack**	Y	Y	Y	Y	Y
46 **Rohrabacher**	Y	N	Y	Y	Y
47 Sanchez, Loretta	N	Y	Y	Y	Y
48 **Campbell**	Y	N	Y	Y	Y
49 **Issa**	Y	Y	Y	Y	Y
50 **Bilbray**	Y	Y	Y	Y	Y
51 Filner	N	Y	Y	Y	Y
52 **Hunter**	Y	Y	Y	Y	Y
53 Davis	N	Y	Y	Y	Y

	850	851	852	853	854
COLORADO					
1 DeGette	N	Y	Y	Y	Y
2 Polis	N	Y	Y	Y	Y
3 Salazar	N	Y	Y	Y	Y
4 Markey	N	Y	Y	Y	Y
5 **Lamborn**	Y	N	Y	Y	Y
6 **Coffman**	Y	N	Y	Y	Y
7 Perlmutter	N	Y	Y	Y	Y
CONNECTICUT					
1 Larson	N	Y	Y	Y	?
2 Courtney	N	Y	Y	Y	Y
3 DeLauro	N	Y	Y	Y	Y
4 Himes	N	Y	Y	Y	Y
5 Murphy	N	Y	Y	Y	Y
DELAWARE					
AL **Castle**	Y	N	Y	Y	Y
FLORIDA					
1 **Miller**	Y	N	Y	Y	Y
2 Boyd	N	Y	Y	Y	Y
3 Brown	N	Y	Y	Y	Y
4 **Crenshaw**	Y	Y	Y	Y	Y
5 **Brown-Waite**	Y	Y	Y	Y	Y
6 **Stearns**	Y	N	Y	Y	Y
7 **Mica**	Y	N	Y	Y	Y
8 Grayson	N	Y	Y	Y	Y
9 **Bilirakis**	Y	Y	Y	Y	Y
10 **Young**	Y	Y	Y	Y	Y
11 Castor	N	Y	Y	Y	Y
12 **Putnam**	Y	Y	Y	Y	Y
13 **Buchanan**	Y	Y	Y	Y	Y
14 **Mack**	Y	Y	Y	Y	Y
15 **Posey**	Y	Y	Y	Y	Y
16 **Rooney**	Y	Y	Y	Y	Y
17 Meek	N	Y	Y	Y	Y
18 **Ros-Lehtinen**	Y	Y	Y	Y	Y
19 Wexler	N	Y	Y	Y	Y
20 Wasserman Schultz	N	Y	Y	Y	Y
21 **Diaz-Balart, L.**	Y	Y	Y	Y	Y
22 Klein	N	Y	Y	Y	Y
23 Hastings	N	Y	Y	Y	Y
24 Kosmas	N	Y	Y	Y	Y
25 **Diaz-Balart, M.**	Y	Y	Y	Y	Y
GEORGIA					
1 **Kingston**	Y	Y	Y	Y	Y
2 Bishop	N	Y	Y	Y	Y
3 **Westmoreland**	Y	N	Y	Y	Y
4 Johnson	N	Y	Y	Y	Y
5 Lewis	N	Y	Y	Y	Y
6 **Price**	Y	N	Y	Y	Y
7 **Linder**	Y	N	Y	Y	Y
8 Marshall	N	Y	Y	Y	Y
9 **Deal**	?	?	?	?	?
10 **Broun**	Y	N	Y	Y	Y
11 **Gingrey**	Y	N	Y	Y	Y
12 Barrow	N	Y	Y	Y	Y
13 Scott	N	Y	Y	Y	Y
HAWAII					
1 Abercrombie	N	Y	Y	Y	Y
2 Hirono	N	Y	Y	Y	Y
IDAHO					
1 Minnick	N	Y	Y	Y	Y
2 **Simpson**	N	Y	Y	Y	Y
ILLINOIS					
1 Rush	N	Y	Y	Y	Y
2 Jackson	N	Y	Y	Y	Y
3 Lipinski	N	Y	Y	Y	Y
4 Gutierrez	N	Y	Y	Y	Y
5 Quigley	N	Y	Y	Y	Y
6 **Roskam**	Y	N	Y	Y	Y
7 Davis	N	Y	Y	Y	Y
8 Bean	N	Y	Y	Y	Y
9 Schakowsky	N	Y	Y	Y	Y
10 **Kirk**	Y	Y	Y	Y	Y
11 Halvorson	N	Y	Y	Y	Y
12 Costello	N	Y	Y	Y	Y
13 **Biggert**	Y	Y	Y	Y	Y
14 Foster	N	Y	Y	Y	Y
15 **Johnson**	Y	Y	Y	Y	Y

KEY   **Republicans**   Democrats

Y Voted for (yea)	X Paired against	C Voted "present" to avoid possible conflict of interest
# Paired for	– Announced against	
+ Announced for	P Voted "present"	? Did not vote or otherwise make a position known
N Voted against (nay)		

	850	851	852	853	854
16 **Manzullo**	Y	N	Y	Y	Y
17 Hare	N	Y	Y	Y	Y
18 **Schock**	Y	Y	Y	Y	Y
19 **Shimkus**	Y	Y	Y	Y	Y
INDIANA					
1 Visclosky	N	Y	Y	Y	Y
2 Donnelly	N	Y	Y	Y	Y
3 **Souder**	Y	Y	Y	Y	Y
4 **Buyer**	Y	Y	Y	Y	Y
5 **Burton**	Y	N	Y	Y	Y
6 **Pence**	Y	N	Y	Y	Y
7 Carson	N	Y	Y	Y	Y
8 Ellsworth	N	Y	Y	Y	Y
9 Hill	N	Y	Y	Y	Y
IOWA					
1 Braley	–	+	+	+	+
2 Loebsack	N	Y	Y	Y	Y
3 Boswell	N	Y	Y	Y	Y
4 **Latham**	N	Y	Y	Y	Y
5 **King**	Y	N	Y	Y	Y
KANSAS					
1 **Moran**	Y	Y	Y	Y	Y
2 **Jenkins**	Y	N	Y	Y	Y
3 Moore	N	Y	Y	Y	Y
4 **Tiahrt**	Y	N	Y	Y	Y
KENTUCKY					
1 **Whitfield**	Y	Y	Y	Y	Y
2 **Guthrie**	Y	N	Y	Y	Y
3 Yarmuth	N	Y	Y	Y	Y
4 **Davis**	Y	N	Y	Y	Y
5 **Rogers**	Y	Y	Y	Y	Y
6 Chandler	N	+	Y	Y	Y
LOUISIANA					
1 **Scalise**	Y	N	Y	Y	Y
2 **Cao**	Y	Y	Y	Y	Y
3 Melancon	Y	Y	Y	Y	Y
4 **Fleming**	Y	N	Y	Y	Y
5 **Alexander**	Y	N	Y	Y	Y
6 **Cassidy**	Y	Y	Y	Y	Y
7 **Boustany**	Y	N	Y	Y	Y
MAINE					
1 Pingree	N	Y	Y	Y	Y
2 Michaud	N	Y	Y	Y	Y
MARYLAND					
1 Kratovil	N	Y	Y	Y	Y
2 Ruppersberger	N	Y	Y	Y	Y
3 Sarbanes	N	Y	Y	Y	Y
4 Edwards	N	Y	Y	Y	Y
5 Hoyer	N	Y	Y	Y	Y
6 **Bartlett**	Y	Y	Y	Y	Y
7 Cummings	N	Y	Y	Y	Y
8 Van Hollen	N	Y	Y	Y	Y
MASSACHUSETTS					
1 Olver	N	Y	Y	Y	Y
2 Neal	N	Y	Y	Y	Y
3 McGovern	N	Y	Y	Y	Y
4 Frank	N	Y	Y	Y	Y
5 Tsongas	N	Y	Y	Y	Y
6 Tierney	N	Y	Y	Y	Y
7 Markey	N	Y	Y	Y	Y
8 Capuano	N	Y	?	Y	Y
9 Lynch	N	Y	Y	Y	Y
10 Delahunt	N	Y	Y	Y	Y
MICHIGAN					
1 Stupak	?	?	?	?	?
2 **Hoekstra**	Y	Y	Y	Y	Y
3 **Ehlers**	Y	Y	Y	Y	Y
4 **Camp**	Y	Y	Y	Y	Y
5 Kildee	N	Y	Y	Y	Y
6 **Upton**	Y	Y	Y	Y	Y
7 Schauer	N	Y	Y	Y	Y
8 **Rogers**	Y	Y	Y	Y	Y
9 Peters	N	Y	Y	Y	Y
10 **Miller**	Y	Y	Y	Y	Y
11 **McCotter**	Y	Y	Y	Y	Y
12 Levin	N	Y	Y	Y	Y
13 Kilpatrick	N	Y	Y	Y	Y
14 Conyers	N	Y	Y	Y	Y
15 Dingell	N	Y	Y	Y	Y
MINNESOTA					
1 Walz	N	Y	Y	Y	Y
2 **Kline**	Y	N	Y	Y	Y
3 **Paulsen**	Y	Y	Y	Y	Y
4 McCollum	N	?	Y	Y	Y

	850	851	852	853	854
5 Ellison	N	Y	Y	Y	Y
6 **Bachmann**	Y	N	Y	Y	Y
7 Peterson	N	Y	Y	Y	Y
8 Oberstar	N	Y	Y	Y	Y
MISSISSIPPI					
1 Childers	N	Y	Y	Y	Y
2 Thompson	N	Y	Y	Y	Y
3 **Harper**	Y	N	Y	Y	Y
4 Taylor	N	Y	Y	Y	Y
MISSOURI					
1 Clay	N	Y	Y	Y	Y
2 **Akin**	Y	N	Y	Y	Y
3 Carnahan	N	Y	Y	Y	Y
4 Skelton	N	Y	Y	Y	Y
5 Cleaver	N	Y	Y	Y	Y
6 **Graves**	Y	Y	Y	Y	Y
7 **Blunt**	Y	Y	Y	Y	Y
8 **Emerson**	N	Y	Y	Y	Y
9 **Luetkemeyer**	Y	N	Y	Y	Y
MONTANA					
AL **Rehberg**	Y	Y	Y	Y	Y
NEBRASKA					
1 **Fortenberry**	Y	Y	Y	Y	Y
2 **Terry**	Y	N	Y	Y	Y
3 **Smith**	Y	N	Y	Y	Y
NEVADA					
1 Berkley	N	Y	Y	Y	Y
2 **Heller**	Y	N	Y	Y	Y
3 Titus	N	Y	Y	Y	Y
NEW HAMPSHIRE					
1 Shea-Porter	N	Y	Y	Y	Y
2 Hodes	N	Y	Y	Y	Y
NEW JERSEY					
1 Andrews	N	Y	Y	Y	Y
2 **LoBiondo**	Y	Y	Y	Y	Y
3 Adler	N	Y	Y	Y	Y
4 **Smith**	Y	Y	Y	Y	Y
5 **Garrett**	Y	N	Y	Y	Y
6 Pallone	N	Y	Y	Y	Y
7 **Lance**	Y	Y	Y	Y	Y
8 Pascrell	N	Y	Y	Y	Y
9 Rothman	N	Y	Y	Y	Y
10 Payne	N	Y	Y	Y	Y
11 **Frelinghuysen**	Y	Y	Y	Y	Y
12 Holt	N	Y	Y	Y	Y
13 Sires	N	Y	Y	Y	Y
NEW MEXICO					
1 Heinrich	N	Y	Y	Y	Y
2 Teague	N	Y	Y	Y	Y
3 Lujan	N	Y	Y	Y	Y
NEW YORK					
1 Bishop	N	Y	Y	Y	Y
2 Israel	N	Y	Y	Y	Y
3 **King**	Y	Y	Y	Y	Y
4 McCarthy	N	Y	Y	Y	Y
5 Ackerman	N	Y	Y	Y	Y
6 Meeks	N	Y	Y	Y	Y
7 Crowley	N	Y	Y	Y	Y
8 Nadler	N	Y	Y	Y	Y
9 Weiner	N	Y	Y	Y	Y
10 Towns	N	Y	Y	Y	Y
11 Clarke	N	Y	Y	Y	Y
12 Velázquez	N	Y	Y	Y	Y
13 McMahon	Y	Y	Y	Y	Y
14 Maloney	N	Y	Y	Y	Y
15 Rangel	N	Y	Y	Y	Y
16 Serrano	N	Y	Y	Y	Y
17 Engel	N	Y	Y	Y	Y
18 Lowey	N	Y	Y	Y	Y
19 Hall	N	Y	Y	Y	Y
20 Murphy	N	Y	Y	Y	Y
21 Tonko	N	Y	Y	Y	Y
22 Hinchey	N	Y	Y	Y	Y
23 Vacant					
24 Arcuri	N	Y	Y	Y	Y
25 Maffei	N	Y	Y	Y	Y
26 **Lee**	Y	Y	Y	Y	Y
27 Higgins	N	Y	Y	Y	Y
28 Slaughter	N	Y	Y	Y	Y
29 Massa	N	Y	Y	Y	Y
NORTH CAROLINA					
1 Butterfield	N	Y	Y	Y	Y
2 Etheridge	N	Y	Y	Y	Y
3 **Jones**	N	Y	Y	Y	Y
4 Price	N	Y	Y	Y	Y

	850	851	852	853	854
5 **Foxx**	Y	N	Y	Y	Y
6 **Coble**	Y	N	Y	Y	Y
7 McIntyre	N	Y	Y	Y	Y
8 Kissell	N	Y	Y	Y	Y
9 **Myrick**	Y	N	Y	Y	Y
10 **McHenry**	Y	N	Y	Y	Y
11 Shuler	N	Y	Y	Y	Y
12 Watt	N	Y	Y	Y	Y
13 Miller	N	Y	Y	Y	Y
NORTH DAKOTA					
AL Pomeroy	N	Y	Y	Y	Y
OHIO					
1 Driehaus	N	Y	Y	Y	Y
2 **Schmidt**	Y	N	Y	Y	Y
3 **Turner**	Y	Y	Y	Y	Y
4 **Jordan**	Y	N	?	?	?
5 **Latta**	Y	N	Y	Y	Y
6 Wilson	N	Y	Y	Y	Y
7 **Austria**	Y	N	Y	Y	Y
8 **Boehner**	Y	N	Y	Y	Y
9 Kaptur	N	Y	Y	Y	Y
10 Kucinich	N	Y	Y	Y	Y
11 Fudge	N	Y	Y	Y	Y
12 **Tiberi**	Y	Y	Y	Y	Y
13 Sutton	N	Y	Y	Y	Y
14 **LaTourette**	N	Y	Y	Y	Y
15 Kilroy	N	Y	Y	Y	Y
16 Boccieri	N	Y	Y	Y	Y
17 Ryan	N	Y	Y	Y	Y
18 Space	N	Y	Y	Y	Y
OKLAHOMA					
1 **Sullivan**	Y	N	Y	Y	Y
2 Boren	N	Y	Y	Y	Y
3 **Lucas**	Y	N	Y	Y	Y
4 **Cole**	Y	N	Y	Y	Y
5 **Fallin**	Y	N	Y	Y	Y
OREGON					
1 Wu	N	Y	Y	Y	Y
2 **Walden**	Y	Y	Y	Y	Y
3 Blumenauer	N	Y	Y	Y	Y
4 DeFazio	N	Y	Y	Y	Y
5 Schrader	N	Y	Y	Y	Y
PENNSYLVANIA					
1 Brady	N	Y	Y	Y	Y
2 Fattah	N	Y	Y	Y	Y
3 Dahlkemper	N	Y	Y	Y	Y
4 Altmire	N	Y	Y	Y	Y
5 **Thompson**	Y	N	Y	Y	Y
6 **Gerlach**	?	?	Y	Y	Y
7 Sestak	N	Y	Y	Y	Y
8 Murphy, P.	?	?	?	?	?
9 **Shuster**	Y	Y	+	+	+
10 Carney	N	Y	Y	Y	Y
11 Kanjorski	N	Y	Y	Y	Y
12 Murtha	N	Y	Y	Y	Y
13 Schwartz	N	Y	Y	Y	Y
14 Doyle	N	Y	Y	Y	Y
15 **Dent**	Y	Y	Y	Y	Y
16 **Pitts**	Y	N	Y	Y	Y
17 Holden	N	Y	Y	Y	Y
18 **Murphy, T.**	Y	Y	Y	Y	Y
19 **Platts**	Y	Y	Y	Y	Y
RHODE ISLAND					
1 Kennedy	N	Y	Y	Y	Y
2 Langevin	N	Y	Y	Y	Y
SOUTH CAROLINA					
1 **Brown**	Y	Y	Y	Y	Y
2 **Wilson**	Y	Y	Y	Y	Y
3 **Barrett**	Y	N	Y	Y	Y
4 **Inglis**	Y	N	Y	Y	Y
5 Spratt	N	Y	Y	Y	Y
6 Clyburn	N	Y	Y	Y	Y
SOUTH DAKOTA					
AL Herseth Sandlin	Y	N	Y	Y	Y
TENNESSEE					
1 **Roe**	Y	Y	Y	Y	Y
2 **Duncan**	Y	Y	Y	Y	Y
3 **Wamp**	Y	Y	Y	Y	Y
4 Davis	?	Y	Y	Y	Y
5 Cooper	N	Y	Y	Y	Y
6 Gordon	N	Y	Y	Y	Y
7 **Blackburn**	Y	N	Y	Y	Y
8 Tanner	N	Y	Y	Y	Y
9 Cohen	N	Y	Y	Y	Y

	850	851	852	853	854
TEXAS					
1 **Gohmert**	Y	N	Y	Y	Y
2 **Poe**	Y	N	Y	Y	Y
3 **Johnson, S.**	Y	N	Y	Y	Y
4 **Hall**	Y	N	Y	Y	Y
5 **Hensarling**	Y	N	Y	Y	Y
6 **Barton**	Y	Y	Y	Y	Y
7 **Culberson**	Y	N	Y	Y	Y
8 **Brady**	Y	N	Y	Y	Y
9 Green, A.	N	Y	Y	Y	Y
10 **McCaul**	Y	Y	Y	Y	Y
11 **Conaway**	Y	N	Y	Y	Y
12 **Granger**	Y	N	Y	Y	Y
13 **Thornberry**	Y	N	Y	Y	Y
14 **Paul**	N	N	N	N	N
15 Hinojosa	N	Y	Y	Y	Y
16 Reyes	N	Y	Y	Y	Y
17 Edwards	N	Y	Y	Y	Y
18 Jackson Lee	N	Y	Y	Y	Y
19 **Neugebauer**	Y	N	Y	Y	Y
20 Gonzalez	N	Y	Y	Y	Y
21 **Smith**	Y	Y	Y	Y	Y
22 **Olson**	Y	N	Y	Y	Y
23 Rodriguez	N	Y	Y	Y	Y
24 **Marchant**	Y	N	Y	Y	Y
25 Doggett	N	Y	Y	Y	Y
26 **Burgess**	Y	Y	Y	Y	Y
27 Ortiz	N	Y	Y	Y	Y
28 Cuellar	N	Y	Y	Y	Y
29 Green, G.	N	Y	Y	Y	Y
30 Johnson, E.	N	Y	Y	Y	Y
31 **Carter**	Y	N	Y	Y	Y
32 **Sessions**	Y	N	Y	Y	Y
UTAH					
1 **Bishop**	Y	N	?	Y	Y
2 Matheson	N	Y	Y	Y	Y
3 **Chaffetz**	Y	N	Y	Y	Y
VERMONT					
AL Welch	N	Y	Y	Y	Y
VIRGINIA					
1 **Wittman**	Y	Y	Y	Y	Y
2 Nye	N	Y	Y	Y	Y
3 Scott	N	Y	Y	Y	Y
4 **Forbes**	Y	Y	Y	Y	Y
5 Perriello	N	Y	Y	Y	Y
6 **Goodlatte**	Y	N	Y	Y	Y
7 **Cantor**	Y	N	Y	Y	Y
8 Moran	N	Y	Y	Y	Y
9 Boucher	N	Y	Y	Y	Y
10 **Wolf**	Y	Y	Y	Y	Y
11 Connolly	N	Y	Y	Y	Y
WASHINGTON					
1 Inslee	N	Y	Y	Y	Y
2 Larsen	N	Y	Y	Y	Y
3 Baird	N	Y	Y	Y	Y
4 **Hastings**	Y	N	Y	Y	Y
5 **McMorris Rodgers**	Y	N	Y	Y	Y
6 Dicks	N	Y	Y	Y	Y
7 McDermott	N	Y	Y	Y	Y
8 **Reichert**	Y	Y	Y	Y	Y
9 Smith	N	Y	Y	Y	Y
WEST VIRGINIA					
1 Mollohan	N	Y	Y	Y	Y
2 **Capito**	Y	Y	Y	Y	Y
3 Rahall	N	Y	Y	Y	Y
WISCONSIN					
1 **Ryan**	Y	N	Y	Y	Y
2 Baldwin	N	Y	Y	Y	Y
3 Kind	N	Y	Y	Y	Y
4 Moore	N	Y	Y	Y	Y
5 **Sensenbrenner**	Y	N	Y	Y	Y
6 **Petri**	Y	Y	Y	Y	Y
7 Obey	N	Y	Y	Y	Y
8 Kagen	N	Y	Y	Y	Y
WYOMING					
AL **Lummis**	Y	N	Y	Y	Y
DELEGATES					
Faleomavaega (A.S.)					
Norton (D.C.)					
Bordallo (Guam)					
Sablan (N. Marianas)					
Pierluisi (P.R.)					
Christensen (V.I.)					

IN THE HOUSE | By Vote Number

855. H Res 856. Tribute to the *USS New York*/Adoption. Taylor, D-Miss., motion to suspend the rules and adopt the resolution that would recognize the commissioning of the *USS New York* LPD 21. Motion agreed to 420-0: D 249-0; R 171-0. A two-thirds majority of those present and voting (280 in this case) is required for adoption under suspension of the rules. Nov. 4, 2009.

856. HR 2868. Chemical Plant Security/Previous Question. Hastings, D-Fla., motion to order the previous question (thus ending debate and possibility of amendment) on adoption of the rule (H Res 885) that would provide for House floor consideration of the bill that would authorize a total of $900 million in fiscal 2011 through 2013 for the Department of Homeland Security to conduct assessments and set security standards for chemical plants. Motion agreed to 241-180: D 241-7; R 0-173. Nov. 5, 2009.

857. HR 2868. Chemical Plant Security/Rule. Adoption of the rule (H Res 885) that would provide for House floor consideration of the bill that would authorize a total of $900 million in fiscal 2011 through 2013 for the Department of Homeland Security to conduct assessments and set security standards for chemical plants. Adopted 233-182: D 233-11; R 0-171. Nov. 5, 2009.

858. H Res 868. Tribute to Female Members of the Armed Forces/Adoption. Davis, D-Calif., motion to suspend the rules and adopt the resolution that would recognize the service and achievements of current and former female members of the armed forces. Motion agreed to 366-0: D 245-0; R 121-0. A two-thirds majority of those present and voting (244 in this case) is required for adoption under suspension of the rules. Nov. 5, 2009.

859. HR 3548. Unemployment Benefits Extension/Passage. Rangel, D-N.Y., motion to suspend the rules and concur in the Senate amendment to the bill that would extend unemployment benefits by 14 weeks for individuals who have used their regular 26 weeks of state compensation and provide an additional six weeks to jobless individuals in states with unemployment rates of 8.5 percent or higher. It would extend an $8,000 tax credit for first-time homebuyers and create a $6,500 homebuyer tax credit for certain homeowners who have lived in their current homes for at least five consecutive years. Motion agreed to (thus clearing the bill for the president) 403-12: D 247-0; R 156-12. A two-thirds majority of those present and voting (277 in this case) is required for passage under suspension of the rules. Nov. 5, 2009.

	855	856	857	858	859
ALABAMA					
1 Bonner	Y	N	N	Y	Y
2 Bright	Y	Y	Y	Y	Y
3 Rogers	Y	N	N	Y	Y
4 Aderholt	Y	?	?	?	?
5 Griffith	Y	Y	N	Y	Y
6 Bachus	Y	N	N	Y	Y
7 Davis	Y	Y	Y	Y	Y
ALASKA					
AL Young	Y	N	N	Y	Y
ARIZONA					
1 Kirkpatrick	Y	Y	Y	Y	Y
2 Franks	Y	N	N	Y	N
3 Shadegg	Y	N	N	?	N
4 Pastor	Y	Y	Y	Y	Y
5 Mitchell	Y	Y	Y	Y	Y
6 Flake	Y	N	N	Y	N
7 Grijalva	?	Y	Y	Y	Y
8 Giffords	Y	Y	Y	Y	Y
ARKANSAS					
1 Berry	Y	Y	Y	Y	Y
2 Snyder	Y	Y	Y	Y	Y
3 Boozman	Y	N	N	Y	Y
4 Ross	Y	Y	Y	Y	Y
CALIFORNIA					
1 Thompson	Y	Y	Y	Y	Y
2 Herger	Y	N	N	Y	Y
3 Lungren	Y	N	N	Y	Y
4 McClintock	Y	N	N	Y	N
5 Matsui	Y	Y	Y	Y	Y
6 Woolsey	Y	Y	Y	Y	Y
7 Miller, George	Y	Y	Y	Y	Y
8 Pelosi					
9 Lee	Y	Y	Y	Y	Y
10 Garamendi*				Y	Y
11 McNerney	Y	Y	Y	Y	Y
12 Speier	Y	?	Y	Y	Y
13 Stark	Y	Y	Y	?	Y
14 Eshoo	Y	Y	Y	Y	Y
15 Honda	Y	Y	Y	Y	?
16 Lofgren	Y	Y	Y	?	Y
17 Farr	Y	Y	Y	Y	Y
18 Cardoza	Y	Y	Y	Y	Y
19 Radanovich	Y	N	N	Y	N
20 Costa	Y	Y	Y	Y	Y
21 Nunes	+	?	?	?	?
22 McCarthy	Y	N	N	Y	Y
23 Capps	Y	Y	Y	Y	Y
24 Gallegly	Y	N	N	?	Y
25 McKeon	Y	N	N	Y	Y
26 Dreier	Y	N	N	Y	Y
27 Sherman	Y	Y	Y	Y	Y
28 Berman	Y	Y	Y	Y	Y
29 Schiff	Y	Y	Y	Y	Y
30 Waxman	Y	Y	Y	Y	Y
31 Becerra	Y	Y	Y	Y	Y
32 Chu	Y	Y	Y	Y	Y
33 Watson	Y	Y	Y	Y	Y
34 Roybal-Allard	Y	Y	Y	Y	Y
35 Waters	Y	Y	Y	?	Y
36 Harman	Y	Y	Y	Y	Y
37 Richardson	Y	Y	Y	Y	Y
38 Napolitano	Y	Y	Y	Y	Y
39 Sánchez, Linda	?	?	?	?	?
40 Royce	Y	N	N	?	Y
41 Lewis	Y	N	N	Y	Y
42 Miller, Gary	Y	N	N	Y	Y
43 Baca	Y	Y	Y	Y	Y
44 Calvert	Y	N	N	Y	Y
45 Bono Mack	Y	N	N	Y	Y
46 Rohrabacher	Y	N	N	Y	Y
47 Sanchez, Loretta	Y	Y	Y	Y	Y
48 Campbell	Y	N	N	Y	Y
49 Issa	Y	N	N	Y	Y
50 Bilbray	Y	N	N	?	Y
51 Filner	Y	Y	Y	Y	Y
52 Hunter	Y	N	N	Y	Y
53 Davis	Y	Y	Y	Y	Y
COLORADO					
1 DeGette	Y	Y	Y	Y	Y
2 Polis	Y	Y	Y	Y	Y
3 Salazar	Y	Y	Y	Y	Y
4 Markey	Y	Y	Y	Y	Y
5 Lamborn	Y	N	N	Y	Y
6 Coffman	Y	N	N	+	Y
7 Perlmutter	Y	Y	Y	Y	Y
CONNECTICUT					
1 Larson	Y	Y	Y	Y	Y
2 Courtney	Y	Y	Y	Y	Y
3 DeLauro	Y	Y	Y	Y	Y
4 Himes	Y	Y	Y	Y	Y
5 Murphy	Y	Y	Y	Y	Y
DELAWARE					
AL Castle	Y	N	N	Y	Y
FLORIDA					
1 Miller	Y	N	N	?	Y
2 Boyd	Y	Y	Y	Y	Y
3 Brown	Y	Y	Y	Y	Y
4 Crenshaw	Y	N	N	Y	Y
5 Brown-Waite	Y	N	N	?	Y
6 Stearns	Y	N	N	+	Y
7 Mica	Y	N	N	+	Y
8 Grayson	Y	Y	Y	Y	Y
9 Bilirakis	Y	N	N	Y	Y
10 Young	Y	N	N	Y	Y
11 Castor	Y	Y	Y	Y	Y
12 Putnam	Y	N	N	Y	Y
13 Buchanan	Y	N	N	Y	Y
14 Mack	Y	N	N	Y	Y
15 Posey	Y	N	N	?	Y
16 Rooney	Y	N	N	Y	Y
17 Meek	Y	Y	Y	Y	Y
18 Ros-Lehtinen	Y	N	N	Y	Y
19 Wexler	Y	Y	?	Y	Y
20 Wasserman Schultz	Y	Y	Y	Y	Y
21 Diaz-Balart, L.	Y	N	N	Y	Y
22 Klein	Y	Y	Y	Y	Y
23 Hastings	Y	Y	Y	Y	Y
24 Kosmas	Y	Y	Y	Y	Y
25 Diaz-Balart, M.	Y	N	N	?	Y
GEORGIA					
1 Kingston	Y	N	N	Y	Y
2 Bishop	Y	Y	Y	Y	Y
3 Westmoreland	Y	N	N	Y	Y
4 Johnson	Y	Y	Y	Y	Y
5 Lewis	Y	Y	Y	Y	Y
6 Price	Y	N	N	?	N
7 Linder	Y	N	N	?	N
8 Marshall	Y	Y	Y	Y	Y
9 Deal	?	N	N	Y	Y
10 Broun	Y	N	N	?	N
11 Gingrey	Y	N	N	+	Y
12 Barrow	Y	Y	Y	Y	Y
13 Scott	Y	Y	Y	Y	Y
HAWAII					
1 Abercrombie	Y	Y	Y	Y	Y
2 Hirono	Y	Y	Y	Y	Y
IDAHO					
1 Minnick	Y	N	N	Y	Y
2 Simpson	Y	N	N	Y	Y
ILLINOIS					
1 Rush	Y	Y	Y	Y	Y
2 Jackson	Y	Y	Y	Y	Y
3 Lipinski	Y	Y	Y	Y	Y
4 Gutierrez	Y	Y	Y	Y	Y
5 Quigley	Y	Y	Y	Y	Y
6 Roskam	Y	N	N	Y	Y
7 Davis	Y	Y	Y	Y	Y
8 Bean	Y	Y	Y	Y	Y
9 Schakowsky	Y	Y	Y	Y	Y
10 Kirk	Y	N	N	Y	Y
11 Halvorson	Y	Y	Y	Y	Y
12 Costello	Y	Y	Y	Y	Y
13 Biggert	Y	N	N	+	Y
14 Foster	Y	Y	Y	Y	Y
15 Johnson	Y	N	N	Y	Y

KEY	**Republicans**	Democrats

Y Voted for (yea)	X Paired against	C Voted "present" to avoid possible conflict of interest
# Paired for	– Announced against	
+ Announced for	P Voted "present"	? Did not vote or otherwise make a position known
N Voted against (nay)		

*Rep. John Garamendi, D-Calif., was sworn in Nov. 5 to fill the seat vacated by fellow Democrat Ellen O. Tauscher, who resigned June 26 to become an undersecretary of State. The first vote for which Garamendi was eligible was 858.

	855	856	857	858	859
16 Manzullo	Y	N	N	Y	Y
17 Hare	Y	Y	Y	Y	Y
18 Schock	Y	N	N	Y	Y
19 Shimkus	Y	N	N	Y	Y
INDIANA					
1 Visclosky	Y	Y	Y	Y	Y
2 Donnelly	Y	Y	Y	Y	Y
3 Souder	Y	N	N	Y	Y
4 Buyer	Y	N	N	+	Y
5 Burton	Y	N	N	Y	Y
6 Pence	Y	N	N	?	Y
7 Carson	Y	Y	Y	Y	Y
8 Ellsworth	Y	Y	?	Y	Y
9 Hill	Y	N	N	?	Y
IOWA					
1 Braley	?	+	+	+	+
2 Loebsack	Y	Y	Y	Y	Y
3 Boswell	Y	Y	Y	Y	Y
4 Latham	Y	N	N	Y	Y
5 King	Y	N	N	?	Y
KANSAS					
1 Moran	Y	N	N	Y	Y
2 Jenkins	Y	N	N	Y	Y
3 Moore	Y	Y	Y	Y	Y
4 Tiahrt	Y	N	N	?	Y
KENTUCKY					
1 Whitfield	Y	N	N	Y	Y
2 Guthrie	Y	N	N	Y	Y
3 Yarmuth	Y	Y	Y	Y	Y
4 Davis	Y	N	N	+	+
5 Rogers	Y	N	N	?	Y
6 Chandler	Y	Y	Y	Y	Y
LOUISIANA					
1 Scalise	Y	N	N	Y	N
2 Cao	Y	N	N	Y	Y
3 Melancon	Y	Y	Y	Y	Y
4 Fleming	Y	N	N	?	Y
5 Alexander	Y	N	N	Y	Y
6 Cassidy	Y	N	N	Y	Y
7 Boustany	Y	N	N	?	Y
MAINE					
1 Pingree	Y	Y	Y	Y	Y
2 Michaud	Y	Y	Y	Y	Y
MARYLAND					
1 Kratovil	Y	N	N	Y	Y
2 Ruppersberger	Y	Y	Y	Y	Y
3 Sarbanes	Y	Y	Y	Y	Y
4 Edwards	Y	Y	Y	Y	Y
5 Hoyer	Y	Y	Y	Y	Y
6 Bartlett	Y	N	N	Y	Y
7 Cummings	Y	Y	Y	Y	Y
8 Van Hollen	Y	Y	Y	Y	Y
MASSACHUSETTS					
1 Olver	Y	Y	Y	?	Y
2 Neal	Y	Y	Y	Y	Y
3 McGovern	Y	Y	Y	Y	Y
4 Frank	Y	Y	Y	Y	Y
5 Tsongas	Y	Y	Y	Y	Y
6 Tierney	Y	Y	Y	Y	Y
7 Markey	Y	Y	Y	Y	Y
8 Capuano	Y	?	?	?	?
9 Lynch	Y	Y	Y	Y	Y
10 Delahunt	Y	Y	?	Y	Y
MICHIGAN					
1 Stupak	?	?	?	?	?
2 Hoekstra	Y	N	N	Y	Y
3 Ehlers	Y	N	N	Y	Y
4 Camp	Y	N	N	Y	Y
5 Kildee	Y	Y	Y	Y	Y
6 Upton	Y	N	N	Y	Y
7 Schauer	Y	Y	Y	Y	Y
8 Rogers	Y	?	?	?	+
9 Peters	Y	Y	Y	Y	Y
10 Miller	Y	N	N	?	Y
11 McCotter	Y	Y	Y	Y	Y
12 Levin	Y	Y	Y	Y	Y
13 Kilpatrick	Y	Y	Y	Y	Y
14 Conyers	Y	Y	Y	Y	Y
15 Dingell	Y	Y	Y	Y	Y
MINNESOTA					
1 Walz	Y	Y	Y	Y	Y
2 Kline	Y	N	N	Y	Y
3 Paulsen	Y	N	N	Y	Y
4 McCollum	Y	Y	Y	Y	Y

	855	856	857	858	859
5 Ellison	Y	Y	Y	Y	Y
6 Bachmann	Y	N	N	?	Y
7 Peterson	Y	Y	Y	Y	Y
8 Oberstar	Y	Y	Y	Y	Y
MISSISSIPPI					
1 Childers	Y	N	N	Y	Y
2 Thompson	Y	Y	Y	Y	Y
3 Harper	Y	N	N	Y	+
4 Taylor	Y	N	N	Y	Y
MISSOURI					
1 Clay	Y	Y	Y	Y	Y
2 Akin	Y	N	N	?	Y
3 Carnahan	Y	Y	Y	Y	Y
4 Skelton	Y	Y	Y	Y	Y
5 Cleaver	Y	Y	Y	Y	Y
6 Graves	Y	N	N	Y	Y
7 Blunt	Y	N	N	?	Y
8 Emerson	Y	N	N	Y	Y
9 Luetkemeyer	Y	N	N	Y	Y
MONTANA					
AL Rehberg	Y	N	N	Y	Y
NEBRASKA					
1 Fortenberry	Y	N	N	Y	Y
2 Terry	Y	N	N	Y	Y
3 Smith	Y	N	N	Y	Y
NEVADA					
1 Berkley	Y	Y	Y	Y	Y
2 Heller	Y	N	N	Y	Y
3 Titus	Y	Y	Y	Y	Y
NEW HAMPSHIRE					
1 Shea-Porter	Y	Y	Y	Y	Y
2 Hodes	Y	Y	Y	Y	Y
NEW JERSEY					
1 Andrews	Y	Y	?	Y	Y
2 LoBiondo	Y	N	N	Y	Y
3 Adler	Y	Y	Y	Y	Y
4 Smith	Y	N	N	Y	Y
5 Garrett	Y	N	?	?	N
6 Pallone	Y	Y	Y	Y	Y
7 Lance	Y	N	N	Y	Y
8 Pascrell	Y	Y	Y	Y	Y
9 Rothman	Y	Y	Y	Y	Y
10 Payne	Y	Y	Y	Y	Y
11 Frelinghuysen	Y	N	N	Y	Y
12 Holt	Y	Y	Y	Y	Y
13 Sires	Y	Y	Y	Y	Y
NEW MEXICO					
1 Heinrich	Y	Y	Y	Y	Y
2 Teague	Y	Y	Y	Y	Y
3 Lujan	Y	Y	Y	Y	Y
NEW YORK					
1 Bishop	Y	Y	Y	Y	Y
2 Israel	Y	Y	Y	Y	Y
3 King	Y	N	N	Y	Y
4 McCarthy	Y	Y	Y	Y	Y
5 Ackerman	Y	Y	Y	Y	Y
6 Meeks	Y	Y	Y	Y	Y
7 Crowley	Y	Y	Y	Y	Y
8 Nadler	Y	Y	Y	Y	Y
9 Weiner	Y	Y	Y	Y	Y
10 Towns	Y	Y	?	Y	Y
11 Clarke	Y	Y	Y	Y	Y
12 Velázquez	Y	Y	Y	Y	Y
13 McMahon	Y	Y	Y	Y	Y
14 Maloney	Y	Y	Y	Y	Y
15 Rangel	Y	Y	Y	Y	Y
16 Serrano	Y	Y	Y	Y	Y
17 Engel	Y	Y	Y	Y	Y
18 Lowey	Y	Y	Y	Y	Y
19 Hall	Y	Y	Y	Y	Y
20 Murphy	Y	Y	N	Y	Y
21 Tonko	Y	Y	Y	Y	Y
22 Hinchey	Y	Y	Y	Y	Y
23 Vacant					
24 Arcuri	Y	Y	Y	Y	Y
25 Maffei	Y	Y	Y	Y	Y
26 Lee	Y	N	N	?	Y
27 Higgins	Y	Y	Y	Y	Y
28 Slaughter	Y	Y	Y	Y	Y
29 Massa	Y	Y	Y	Y	Y
NORTH CAROLINA					
1 Butterfield	Y	Y	Y	Y	Y
2 Etheridge	Y	Y	Y	Y	Y
3 Jones	Y	N	N	Y	Y
4 Price	Y	Y	Y	Y	Y

	855	856	857	858	859
5 Foxx	Y	N	N	+	Y
6 Coble	Y	N	N	Y	Y
7 McIntyre	Y	Y	Y	Y	Y
8 Kissell	Y	Y	Y	Y	Y
9 Myrick	Y	N	N	+	Y
10 McHenry	Y	N	N	Y	Y
11 Shuler	Y	Y	N	Y	Y
12 Watt	Y	Y	Y	Y	Y
13 Miller	?	Y	Y	Y	Y
NORTH DAKOTA					
AL Pomeroy	Y	Y	Y	?	Y
OHIO					
1 Driehaus	Y	Y	Y	Y	Y
2 Schmidt	Y	N	N	?	Y
3 Turner	Y	N	N	Y	Y
4 Jordan	?	N	N	Y	Y
5 Latta	Y	N	N	Y	Y
6 Wilson	Y	Y	Y	Y	Y
7 Austria	Y	N	N	Y	Y
8 Boehner	Y	N	N	?	Y
9 Kaptur	Y	Y	Y	Y	Y
10 Kucinich	Y	Y	Y	Y	Y
11 Fudge	Y	Y	Y	Y	Y
12 Tiberi	Y	N	N	Y	Y
13 Sutton	Y	Y	Y	Y	Y
14 LaTourette	Y	N	N	Y	Y
15 Kilroy	Y	Y	Y	Y	Y
16 Boccieri	Y	Y	N	?	Y
17 Ryan	Y	Y	Y	Y	Y
18 Space	Y	Y	Y	Y	Y
OKLAHOMA					
1 Sullivan	Y	N	N	?	Y
2 Boren	Y	Y	Y	Y	Y
3 Lucas	Y	N	N	Y	Y
4 Cole	Y	N	N	Y	+
5 Fallin	Y	N	N	Y	Y
OREGON					
1 Wu	Y	Y	Y	Y	Y
2 Walden	Y	N	N	Y	Y
3 Blumenauer	Y	Y	Y	Y	Y
4 DeFazio	Y	Y	Y	Y	Y
5 Schrader	Y	Y	Y	Y	Y
PENNSYLVANIA					
1 Brady	Y	?	?	?	?
2 Fattah	Y	Y	Y	Y	Y
3 Dahlkemper	Y	Y	Y	Y	Y
4 Altmire	Y	N	N	N	Y
5 Thompson	Y	N	N	+	Y
6 Gerlach	Y	N	N	Y	Y
7 Sestak	Y	Y	Y	Y	Y
8 Murphy, P.	?	?	?	?	?
9 Shuster	+	N	N	?	Y
10 Carney	Y	Y	Y	Y	Y
11 Kanjorski	Y	Y	Y	Y	Y
12 Murtha	Y	Y	Y	Y	Y
13 Schwartz	Y	Y	Y	Y	Y
14 Doyle	Y	Y	Y	Y	Y
15 Dent	Y	N	N	Y	Y
16 Pitts	Y	N	N	Y	Y
17 Holden	Y	Y	Y	Y	Y
18 Murphy, T.	Y	N	N	Y	Y
19 Platts	Y	N	N	Y	Y
RHODE ISLAND					
1 Kennedy	Y	Y	Y	Y	Y
2 Langevin	Y	Y	Y	Y	Y
SOUTH CAROLINA					
1 Brown	Y	N	N	?	Y
2 Wilson	Y	N	N	+	Y
3 Barrett		N	N	?	Y
4 Inglis	Y	N	N	Y	Y
5 Spratt	Y	Y	Y	Y	Y
6 Clyburn	Y	Y	Y	Y	Y
SOUTH DAKOTA					
AL Herseth Sandlin	Y	Y	Y	Y	+
TENNESSEE					
1 Roe	Y	N	N	Y	Y
2 Duncan	Y	N	N	Y	Y
3 Wamp	Y	N	N	?	Y
4 Davis	Y	Y	Y	Y	Y
5 Cooper	Y	Y	Y	Y	Y
6 Gordon	Y	Y	Y	Y	Y
7 Blackburn	Y	N	N	Y	Y
8 Tanner	Y	Y	Y	Y	Y
9 Cohen	Y	Y	Y	Y	Y

	855	856	857	858	859
TEXAS					
1 Gohmert	Y	?	?	?	Y
2 Poe	Y	N	?	?	+
3 Johnson, S.	Y	N	N	Y	Y
4 Hall	Y	N	N	Y	Y
5 Hensarling	Y	N	N	Y	Y
6 Barton	Y	N	N	Y	Y
7 Culberson	Y	N	N	Y	?
8 Brady	Y	N	N	Y	Y
9 Green, A.	Y	Y	Y	Y	Y
10 McCaul	Y	N	N	Y	Y
11 Conaway	Y	N	N	Y	Y
12 Granger	Y	N	N	?	Y
13 Thornberry	Y	N	N	Y	Y
14 Paul	?	N	N	Y	N
15 Hinojosa	Y	Y	Y	Y	Y
16 Reyes	Y	Y	Y	Y	Y
17 Edwards	Y	Y	Y	Y	Y
18 Jackson Lee	Y	Y	Y	Y	Y
19 Neugebauer	Y	N	N	?	Y
20 Gonzalez	Y	Y	Y	Y	Y
21 Smith	Y	N	N	Y	Y
22 Olson	Y	N	N	?	Y
23 Rodriguez	Y	Y	Y	Y	Y
24 Marchant	Y	N	N	Y	Y
25 Doggett	Y	Y	Y	Y	Y
26 Burgess	Y	N	N	?	N
27 Ortiz	Y	Y	Y	Y	Y
28 Cuellar	Y	Y	Y	Y	Y
29 Green, G.	Y	Y	Y	Y	Y
30 Johnson, E.	Y	Y	Y	Y	Y
31 Carter	Y	N	N	?	Y
32 Sessions	Y	N	N	Y	?
UTAH					
1 Bishop	Y	N	N	Y	Y
2 Matheson	Y	Y	Y	Y	Y
3 Chaffetz	Y	N	N	?	Y
VERMONT					
AL Welch	Y	Y	Y	Y	Y
VIRGINIA					
1 Wittman	Y	N	N	Y	Y
2 Nye	Y	Y	Y	Y	Y
3 Scott	Y	Y	Y	Y	Y
4 Forbes	Y	N	N	Y	Y
5 Perriello	Y	Y	Y	Y	Y
6 Goodlatte	Y	N	N	Y	Y
7 Cantor	?	N	N	Y	Y
8 Moran	Y	Y	Y	Y	Y
9 Boucher	Y	Y	Y	Y	Y
10 Wolf	Y	N	N	Y	Y
11 Connolly	Y	Y	Y	Y	Y
WASHINGTON					
1 Inslee	Y	Y	Y	Y	Y
2 Larsen	Y	Y	Y	Y	Y
3 Baird	Y	N	N	Y	Y
4 Hastings	Y	N	N	?	Y
5 McMorris Rodgers	Y	N	N	?	Y
6 Dicks	Y	Y	Y	Y	Y
7 McDermott	Y	Y	Y	Y	Y
8 Reichert	Y	N	N	Y	Y
9 Smith	Y	Y	Y	Y	Y
WEST VIRGINIA					
1 Mollohan	Y	Y	Y	Y	Y
2 Capito	Y	N	N	Y	Y
3 Rahall	Y	Y	Y	Y	Y
WISCONSIN					
1 Ryan	Y	N	N	Y	Y
2 Baldwin	Y	Y	Y	Y	Y
3 Kind	Y	Y	Y	Y	Y
4 Moore	Y	Y	Y	Y	Y
5 Sensenbrenner	Y	N	N	Y	Y
6 Petri	Y	N	N	Y	Y
7 Obey	Y	Y	Y	Y	+
8 Kagen	Y	Y	Y	Y	Y
WYOMING					
AL Lummis	Y	N	N	?	Y
DELEGATES					
Faleomavaega (A.S.)					
Norton (D.C.)					
Bordallo (Guam)					
Sablan (N. Marianas)					
Pierluisi (P.R.)					
Christensen (V.I.)					

IN THE HOUSE | By Vote Number

860. **H Con Res 139. Tribute to First Air Force Academy Class/Adoption.** Davis, D-Calif., motion to suspend the rules and adopt the concurrent resolution that would recognize the first graduating class of the Air Force Academy on the 50th anniversary of their graduation. Motion agreed to 411-0: D 244-0; R 167-0. A two-thirds majority of those present and voting (274 in this case) is required for adoption under the suspension of the rules. Nov. 5, 2009.

861. **H Res 880. Tribute to Career and Technical Colleges/Adoption.** Bishop, D-N.Y., motion to suspend the rules and adopt the resolution that would recognize the efforts of career and technical colleges to educate and train workers for positions in high-demand industries. Motion agreed to 409-0: D 242-0; R 167-0. A two-thirds majority of those present and voting (273 in this case) is required for adoption under suspension of the rules. Nov. 5, 2009.

862. **HR 1849. World War I Centennial Commission/Passage.** Davis, D-Ill., motion to suspend the rules and pass the bill that would authorize $500,000 from fiscal 2010 through 2019 to establish a Commission on the Commemoration of the Centennial of World War I and designate the Liberty Memorial in Kansas City, Mo., as the National World War I Memorial. Motion agreed to 418-1: D 249-0; R 169-1. A two-thirds majority of those present and voting (280 in this case) is required for passage under suspension of the rules. Nov. 5, 2009.

863. **HR 3276. Medical Isotope Development/Passage.** Markey, D-Mass., motion to suspend the rules and pass the bill that would authorize $163 million from fiscal 2010 through 2014 to establish a program under the Department of Energy to evaluate and support projects for domestic production of molybdenum-99 without the use of highly enriched uranium. Motion agreed to 400-17: D 248-0; R 152-17. A two-thirds majority of those present and voting (278 in this case) is required for passage under suspension of the rules. Nov. 5, 2009.

864. **H Res 878. National Family Literacy Day/Adoption.** Bishop, D-N.Y., motion to suspend the rules and adopt the resolution that would support the goals and ideals of National Family Literacy Day and recognize the benefits of parental involvement in a child's education. Motion agreed to 409-0: D 242-0; R 167-0. A two-thirds majority of those present and voting (273 in this case) is required for adoption under suspension of the rules. Nov. 5, 2009.

	860	861	862	863	864
ALABAMA					
1 **Bonner**	Y	Y	Y	Y	Y
2 Bright	Y	Y	Y	Y	Y
3 **Rogers**	Y	Y	Y	Y	Y
4 **Aderholt**	?	?	?	?	?
5 Griffith	Y	Y	Y	Y	Y
6 **Bachus**	Y	Y	Y	?	?
7 Davis	Y	Y	Y	Y	Y
ALASKA					
AL **Young**	Y	Y	Y	Y	Y
ARIZONA					
1 Kirkpatrick	Y	Y	Y	Y	Y
2 **Franks**	Y	Y	Y	Y	Y
3 **Shadegg**	Y	Y	Y	N	Y
4 Pastor	Y	Y	Y	Y	Y
5 Mitchell	Y	Y	Y	Y	Y
6 **Flake**	Y	Y	Y	N	Y
7 Grijalva	Y	Y	Y	Y	Y
8 Giffords	Y	Y	Y	Y	Y
ARKANSAS					
1 Berry	Y	Y	Y	Y	Y
2 Snyder	Y	Y	Y	Y	Y
3 **Boozman**	Y	Y	Y	Y	Y
4 Ross	Y	Y	Y	Y	Y
CALIFORNIA					
1 Thompson	Y	Y	Y	Y	Y
2 **Herger**	Y	Y	Y	Y	Y
3 **Lungren**	Y	Y	Y	Y	Y
4 **McClintock**	Y	Y	Y	Y	Y
5 Matsui	Y	Y	Y	Y	Y
6 Woolsey	Y	Y	Y	Y	?
7 Miller, George	Y	Y	Y	Y	Y
8 Pelosi					
9 Lee	Y	Y	Y	Y	Y
10 Garamendi	Y	Y	Y	Y	Y
11 McNerney	Y	Y	Y	Y	Y
12 Speier	Y	Y	Y	Y	Y
13 Stark	Y	Y	?	?	?
14 Eshoo	Y	Y	Y	Y	Y
15 Honda	Y	Y	Y	Y	Y
16 Lofgren	Y	Y	Y	Y	Y
17 Farr	Y	Y	Y	Y	Y
18 Cardoza	Y	Y	Y	Y	Y
19 **Radanovich**	Y	Y	Y	Y	Y
20 Costa	Y	Y	Y	Y	Y
21 **Nunes**	?	?	?	?	?
22 **McCarthy**	Y	Y	Y	Y	Y
23 Capps	Y	Y	Y	Y	Y
24 **Gallegly**	Y	Y	Y	Y	Y
25 **McKeon**	Y	Y	Y	Y	Y
26 **Dreier**	Y	Y	Y	Y	Y
27 Sherman	Y	Y	Y	Y	Y
28 Berman	Y	Y	Y	Y	Y
29 Schiff	Y	Y	Y	Y	Y
30 Waxman	Y	Y	Y	Y	Y
31 Becerra	Y	Y	Y	Y	Y
32 Chu	Y	Y	Y	Y	Y
33 Watson	Y	Y	Y	Y	Y
34 Roybal-Allard	Y	Y	Y	Y	Y
35 Waters	Y	Y	Y	Y	Y
36 Harman	Y	Y	Y	Y	Y
37 Richardson	Y	Y	Y	Y	Y
38 Napolitano	Y	Y	Y	Y	Y
39 Sánchez, Linda	?	?	?	?	?
40 **Royce**	Y	Y	Y	N	Y
41 **Lewis**	Y	Y	Y	Y	Y
42 **Miller, Gary**	Y	Y	Y	Y	Y
43 Baca	Y	Y	Y	Y	Y
44 **Calvert**	Y	Y	Y	Y	Y
45 **Bono Mack**	Y	Y	Y	Y	Y
46 **Rohrabacher**	Y	Y	Y	Y	Y
47 Sanchez, Loretta	Y	Y	Y	Y	Y
48 **Campbell**	Y	Y	Y	N	Y
49 **Issa**	Y	Y	Y	Y	Y
50 **Bilbray**	Y	Y	Y	Y	Y
51 Filner	Y	Y	Y	Y	Y
52 **Hunter**	Y	Y	Y	Y	Y
53 Davis	Y	Y	Y	Y	Y

	860	861	862	863	864
COLORADO					
1 DeGette	Y	Y	Y	Y	?
2 Polis	Y	Y	Y	Y	Y
3 Salazar	Y	Y	Y	Y	Y
4 Markey	Y	Y	Y	Y	Y
5 **Lamborn**	Y	Y	Y	N	Y
6 **Coffman**	Y	Y	Y	Y	Y
7 Perlmutter	Y	Y	Y	Y	Y
CONNECTICUT					
1 Larson	Y	Y	Y	Y	Y
2 Courtney	Y	Y	Y	Y	Y
3 DeLauro	Y	Y	Y	Y	?
4 Himes	Y	Y	Y	Y	Y
5 Murphy	Y	Y	Y	Y	Y
DELAWARE					
AL **Castle**	Y	Y	Y	Y	Y
FLORIDA					
1 **Miller**	Y	Y	Y	Y	Y
2 Boyd	Y	Y	Y	Y	Y
3 Brown	Y	Y	Y	Y	Y
4 **Crenshaw**	Y	Y	Y	Y	Y
5 **Brown-Waite**	Y	Y	Y	Y	Y
6 **Stearns**	Y	Y	Y	Y	Y
7 **Mica**	Y	Y	Y	Y	Y
8 Grayson	Y	Y	Y	Y	Y
9 **Bilirakis**	Y	Y	Y	Y	Y
10 **Young**	Y	Y	Y	Y	Y
11 Castor	Y	Y	Y	Y	Y
12 **Putnam**	Y	Y	Y	Y	Y
13 **Buchanan**	Y	Y	Y	Y	Y
14 **Mack**	Y	Y	Y	Y	Y
15 **Posey**	Y	Y	Y	Y	Y
16 **Rooney**	Y	Y	Y	N	Y
17 Meek	Y	Y	Y	Y	Y
18 **Ros-Lehtinen**	Y	Y	Y	Y	Y
19 Wexler	Y	Y	Y	Y	Y
20 Wasserman Schultz	Y	Y	Y	Y	Y
21 **Diaz-Balart, L.**	Y	Y	Y	Y	Y
22 Klein	Y	Y	Y	Y	Y
23 Hastings	Y	Y	Y	Y	Y
24 Kosmas	Y	Y	Y	Y	Y
25 **Diaz-Balart, M.**	Y	Y	Y	Y	Y
GEORGIA					
1 **Kingston**	Y	Y	Y	N	Y
2 Bishop	Y	Y	Y	Y	Y
3 **Westmoreland**	Y	Y	Y	N	Y
4 Johnson	Y	Y	Y	Y	Y
5 Lewis	Y	Y	Y	Y	Y
6 **Price**	Y	Y	Y	Y	Y
7 **Linder**	Y	Y	Y	Y	Y
8 Marshall	Y	Y	Y	Y	Y
9 **Deal**	?	?	?	?	?
10 **Broun**	Y	Y	Y	N	Y
11 **Gingrey**	Y	Y	Y	Y	Y
12 Barrow	Y	Y	Y	Y	Y
13 Scott	Y	Y	Y	Y	Y
HAWAII					
1 Abercrombie	Y	Y	Y	Y	Y
2 Hirono	Y	Y	Y	Y	Y
IDAHO					
1 Minnick	Y	Y	Y	Y	Y
2 **Simpson**	Y	Y	Y	Y	Y
ILLINOIS					
1 Rush	Y	Y	Y	Y	Y
2 Jackson	Y	Y	Y	Y	Y
3 Lipinski	Y	Y	Y	Y	Y
4 Gutierrez	Y	?	Y	Y	Y
5 Quigley	Y	Y	Y	Y	Y
6 **Roskam**	Y	Y	Y	Y	Y
7 Davis	?	Y	Y	Y	Y
8 Bean	Y	Y	Y	Y	Y
9 Schakowsky	Y	Y	Y	Y	Y
10 **Kirk**	Y	Y	Y	Y	Y
11 Halvorson	Y	Y	Y	Y	Y
12 Costello	Y	Y	Y	Y	Y
13 **Biggert**	Y	Y	Y	Y	Y
14 Foster	Y	Y	Y	Y	Y
15 Johnson	Y	Y	Y	Y	Y

KEY **Republicans** Democrats

Y Voted for (yea)	X Paired against
# Paired for	– Announced against
+ Announced for	P Voted "present"
N Voted against (nay)	

C Voted "present" to avoid possible conflict of interest

? Did not vote or otherwise make a position known

	860	861	862	863	864
16 Manzullo	Y	Y	Y	Y	Y
17 Hare	Y	Y	Y	Y	Y
18 Schock	Y	Y	Y	Y	Y
19 Shimkus	Y	Y	Y	Y	Y
INDIANA					
1 Visclosky	Y	Y	Y	Y	Y
2 Donnelly	Y	Y	Y	Y	Y
3 Souder	Y	Y	Y	Y	Y
4 Buyer	Y	Y	Y	Y	Y
5 Burton	Y	Y	Y	Y	Y
6 Pence	?	?	Y	N	Y
7 Carson	Y	Y	Y	Y	Y
8 Ellsworth	Y	Y	Y	Y	Y
9 Hill	Y	?	Y	Y	Y
IOWA					
1 Braley	+	+	Y	Y	Y
2 Loebsack	Y	Y	Y	Y	Y
3 Boswell	Y	Y	Y	Y	Y
4 Latham	Y	Y	Y	Y	Y
5 King	Y	Y	Y	Y	Y
KANSAS					
1 Moran	Y	Y	Y	Y	Y
2 Jenkins	Y	Y	Y	Y	Y
3 Moore	Y	Y	Y	Y	Y
4 Tiahrt	Y	Y	Y	Y	Y
KENTUCKY					
1 Whitfield	Y	Y	Y	Y	Y
2 Guthrie	Y	Y	Y	Y	Y
3 Yarmuth	Y	Y	Y	Y	Y
4 Davis	+	+	Y	Y	Y
5 Rogers	Y	Y	Y	Y	Y
6 Chandler	Y	Y	Y	Y	?
LOUISIANA					
1 Scalise	Y	Y	Y	Y	Y
2 Cao	Y	Y	Y	Y	Y
3 Melancon	Y	Y	Y	Y	Y
4 Fleming	Y	Y	Y	Y	Y
5 Alexander	Y	Y	Y	Y	Y
6 Cassidy	Y	Y	Y	Y	Y
7 Boustany	Y	Y	Y	Y	Y
MAINE					
1 Pingree	Y	Y	Y	Y	Y
2 Michaud	Y	Y	Y	Y	Y
MARYLAND					
1 Kratovil	Y	Y	Y	Y	Y
2 Ruppersberger	Y	Y	Y	Y	Y
3 Sarbanes	Y	Y	Y	Y	Y
4 Edwards	Y	Y	Y	Y	Y
5 Hoyer	Y	Y	Y	Y	?
6 Bartlett	Y	Y	Y	Y	Y
7 Cummings	?	Y	Y	Y	Y
8 Van Hollen	Y	Y	Y	Y	Y
MASSACHUSETTS					
1 Olver	Y	Y	Y	Y	Y
2 Neal	Y	Y	Y	Y	Y
3 McGovern	Y	Y	Y	Y	Y
4 Frank	Y	Y	Y	Y	Y
5 Tsongas	Y	Y	Y	Y	Y
6 Tierney	Y	Y	Y	Y	Y
7 Markey	Y	Y	Y	Y	Y
8 Capuano	?	?	?	?	?
9 Lynch	Y	Y	Y	Y	Y
10 Delahunt	Y	Y	Y	Y	Y
MICHIGAN					
1 Stupak	?	?	?	?	?
2 Hoekstra	Y	Y	Y	Y	Y
3 Ehlers	Y	Y	Y	Y	Y
4 Camp	Y	Y	Y	Y	Y
5 Kildee	Y	Y	Y	Y	Y
6 Upton	Y	Y	Y	Y	Y
7 Schauer	Y	Y	Y	Y	Y
8 Rogers	?	?	?	?	?
9 Peters	Y	Y	Y	Y	Y
10 Miller	Y	Y	Y	Y	Y
11 McCotter	Y	Y	Y	Y	Y
12 Levin	Y	Y	Y	Y	Y
13 Kilpatrick	Y	Y	Y	Y	Y
14 Conyers	Y	Y	Y	Y	?
15 Dingell	Y	Y	Y	Y	Y
MINNESOTA					
1 Walz	Y	Y	Y	Y	Y
2 Kline	Y	Y	Y	Y	Y
3 Paulsen	Y	Y	Y	Y	Y
4 McCollum	Y	Y	Y	Y	Y

	860	861	862	863	864
5 Ellison	Y	Y	Y	?	Y
6 Bachmann	Y	Y	Y	Y	Y
7 Peterson	Y	Y	Y	Y	Y
8 Oberstar	Y	Y	Y	Y	Y
MISSISSIPPI					
1 Childers	Y	Y	Y	Y	Y
2 Thompson	Y	Y	Y	Y	Y
3 Harper	Y	Y	Y	Y	Y
4 Taylor	Y	Y	Y	Y	Y
MISSOURI					
1 Clay	Y	Y	Y	Y	Y
2 Akin	Y	Y	Y	Y	Y
3 Carnahan	Y	Y	Y	Y	Y
4 Skelton	Y	Y	Y	Y	Y
5 Cleaver	Y	Y	Y	Y	Y
6 Graves	Y	Y	Y	Y	Y
7 Blunt	Y	Y	Y	Y	Y
8 Emerson	Y	Y	Y	Y	Y
9 Luetkemeyer	Y	Y	Y	Y	Y
MONTANA					
AL Rehberg	Y	Y	Y	Y	Y
NEBRASKA					
1 Fortenberry	Y	Y	Y	Y	Y
2 Terry	Y	Y	Y	Y	Y
3 Smith	Y	Y	Y	Y	Y
NEVADA					
1 Berkley	Y	Y	Y	Y	Y
2 Heller	Y	Y	Y	Y	Y
3 Titus	Y	Y	Y	Y	Y
NEW HAMPSHIRE					
1 Shea-Porter	Y	Y	Y	Y	Y
2 Hodes	Y	Y	Y	Y	?
NEW JERSEY					
1 Andrews	Y	Y	Y	Y	Y
2 LoBiondo	Y	Y	Y	Y	Y
3 Adler	Y	Y	Y	Y	Y
4 Smith	Y	Y	Y	Y	Y
5 Garrett	Y	Y	Y	Y	Y
6 Pallone	Y	Y	Y	Y	Y
7 Lance	Y	Y	Y	Y	Y
8 Pascrell	Y	Y	Y	Y	Y
9 Rothman	Y	Y	Y	Y	Y
10 Payne	Y	Y	Y	Y	Y
11 Frelinghuysen	Y	Y	Y	Y	Y
12 Holt	Y	Y	Y	Y	Y
13 Sires	Y	Y	Y	Y	Y
NEW MEXICO					
1 Heinrich	Y	Y	Y	Y	Y
2 Teague	Y	Y	Y	Y	Y
3 Lujan	Y	Y	Y	Y	Y
NEW YORK					
1 Bishop	Y	Y	Y	Y	Y
2 Israel	Y	Y	Y	Y	Y
3 King	Y	Y	Y	Y	Y
4 McCarthy	Y	Y	Y	Y	Y
5 Ackerman	Y	Y	Y	Y	Y
6 Meeks	Y	Y	Y	Y	Y
7 Crowley	Y	Y	Y	Y	Y
8 Nadler	Y	Y	?	?	?
9 Weiner	Y	Y	Y	Y	Y
10 Towns	Y	Y	Y	Y	Y
11 Clarke	Y	Y	Y	Y	Y
12 Velázquez	Y	Y	Y	Y	Y
13 McMahon	Y	Y	Y	Y	Y
14 Maloney	Y	Y	Y	Y	Y
15 Rangel	Y	Y	Y	Y	Y
16 Serrano	Y	Y	Y	Y	Y
17 Engel	Y	Y	Y	Y	Y
18 Lowey	Y	Y	Y	Y	Y
19 Hall	Y	Y	Y	Y	Y
20 Murphy	Y	Y	Y	Y	Y
21 Tonko	Y	Y	Y	Y	Y
22 Hinchey	Y	Y	Y	Y	Y
23 Vacant					
24 Arcuri	Y	Y	Y	Y	Y
25 Maffei	Y	Y	Y	Y	Y
26 Lee	Y	?	Y	Y	Y
27 Higgins	Y	Y	Y	Y	Y
28 Slaughter	Y	Y	Y	Y	Y
29 Massa	Y	Y	Y	Y	Y
NORTH CAROLINA					
1 Butterfield	Y	Y	Y	Y	Y
2 Etheridge	Y	Y	Y	Y	Y
3 Jones	Y	Y	Y	Y	Y
4 Price	Y	Y	Y	Y	Y

	860	861	862	863	864
5 Foxx	Y	Y	Y	Y	Y
6 Coble	Y	Y	Y	Y	Y
7 McIntyre	Y	Y	Y	Y	Y
8 Kissell	Y	Y	Y	Y	Y
9 Myrick	Y	Y	Y	Y	Y
10 McHenry	Y	Y	Y	Y	Y
11 Shuler	Y	Y	Y	Y	Y
12 Watt	Y	Y	Y	Y	Y
13 Miller	Y	Y	Y	Y	Y
NORTH DAKOTA					
AL Pomeroy	Y	Y	Y	Y	Y
OHIO					
1 Driehaus	Y	Y	Y	Y	Y
2 Schmidt	Y	Y	Y	Y	Y
3 Turner	Y	Y	Y	Y	Y
4 Jordan	Y	Y	Y	N	Y
5 Latta	Y	Y	Y	Y	Y
6 Wilson	Y	Y	Y	Y	Y
7 Austria	Y	Y	Y	Y	Y
8 Boehner	?	?	Y	Y	Y
9 Kaptur	Y	Y	Y	Y	Y
10 Kucinich	Y	Y	Y	Y	Y
11 Fudge	Y	Y	Y	Y	Y
12 Tiberi	Y	Y	Y	Y	Y
13 Sutton	Y	Y	Y	Y	Y
14 LaTourette	Y	Y	Y	Y	Y
15 Kilroy	Y	Y	Y	Y	Y
16 Boccieri	Y	Y	Y	Y	Y
17 Ryan	Y	Y	Y	Y	Y
18 Space	Y	Y	Y	Y	Y
OKLAHOMA					
1 Sullivan	Y	Y	Y	Y	Y
2 Boren	Y	Y	Y	Y	Y
3 Lucas	Y	Y	Y	Y	Y
4 Cole	+	+	Y	Y	Y
5 Fallin	Y	Y	Y	Y	Y
OREGON					
1 Wu	Y	Y	Y	Y	Y
2 Walden	Y	Y	Y	Y	Y
3 Blumenauer	Y	Y	Y	Y	Y
4 DeFazio	Y	Y	Y	Y	Y
5 Schrader	Y	Y	Y	Y	Y
PENNSYLVANIA					
1 Brady	?	?	?	?	?
2 Fattah	Y	Y	Y	Y	Y
3 Dahlkemper	Y	Y	Y	Y	Y
4 Altmire	Y	Y	Y	Y	Y
5 Thompson	Y	Y	Y	Y	Y
6 Gerlach	Y	Y	Y	Y	Y
7 Sestak	Y	Y	Y	Y	Y
8 Murphy, P.	?	?	?	?	?
9 Shuster	Y	Y	Y	Y	Y
10 Carney	Y	Y	Y	Y	Y
11 Kanjorski	Y	Y	Y	Y	Y
12 Murtha	Y	Y	Y	Y	Y
13 Schwartz	Y	Y	Y	Y	Y
14 Doyle	Y	Y	Y	Y	Y
15 Dent	Y	Y	Y	Y	Y
16 Pitts	Y	Y	Y	Y	Y
17 Holden	Y	Y	Y	Y	Y
18 Murphy, T.	Y	Y	Y	Y	Y
19 Platts	Y	Y	Y	Y	Y
RHODE ISLAND					
1 Kennedy	?	?	Y	Y	Y
2 Langevin	?	?	Y	Y	Y
SOUTH CAROLINA					
1 Brown	Y	Y	Y	Y	Y
2 Wilson	Y	Y	Y	Y	Y
3 Barrett	Y	Y	Y	Y	Y
4 Inglis	Y	Y	Y	Y	Y
5 Spratt	Y	Y	Y	Y	Y
6 Clyburn	Y	Y	Y	Y	Y
SOUTH DAKOTA					
AL Herseth Sandlin	+	+	Y	Y	Y
TENNESSEE					
1 Roe	Y	Y	Y	Y	Y
2 Duncan	Y	Y	Y	Y	Y
3 Wamp	Y	Y	Y	Y	Y
4 Davis	Y	Y	Y	Y	Y
5 Cooper	Y	Y	Y	Y	Y
6 Gordon	?	Y	Y	Y	Y
7 Blackburn	Y	Y	Y	Y	Y
8 Tanner	Y	Y	Y	Y	Y
9 Cohen	Y	Y	Y	Y	Y

	860	861	862	863	864
TEXAS					
1 Gohmert	Y	Y	?	?	?
2 Poe	Y	Y	Y	N	Y
3 Johnson, S.	?	?	?	?	?
4 Hall	Y	Y	Y	Y	Y
5 Hensarling	Y	Y	Y	N	Y
6 Barton	Y	Y	Y	Y	Y
7 Culberson	Y	Y	Y	Y	Y
8 Brady	Y	Y	Y	Y	?
9 Green, A.	Y	Y	Y	Y	Y
10 McCaul	Y	Y	Y	Y	Y
11 Conaway	Y	Y	Y	N	Y
12 Granger	Y	Y	Y	Y	Y
13 Thornberry	Y	Y	Y	Y	Y
14 Paul	Y	Y	N	N	Y
15 Hinojosa	Y	Y	Y	Y	Y
16 Reyes	Y	Y	Y	Y	Y
17 Edwards	Y	Y	Y	Y	Y
18 Jackson Lee	Y	Y	Y	Y	Y
19 Neugebauer	Y	Y	Y	Y	Y
20 Gonzalez	Y	Y	Y	Y	Y
21 Smith	Y	Y	Y	Y	Y
22 Olson	Y	Y	Y	Y	Y
23 Rodriguez	Y	Y	Y	Y	Y
24 Marchant	Y	Y	Y	Y	Y
25 Doggett	Y	Y	Y	Y	Y
26 Burgess	Y	Y	Y	Y	Y
27 Ortiz	Y	Y	Y	Y	Y
28 Cuellar	Y	Y	Y	Y	Y
29 Green, G.	Y	Y	Y	Y	Y
30 Johnson, E.	Y	Y	Y	Y	Y
31 Carter	Y	Y	Y	Y	?
32 Sessions	Y	Y	Y	Y	Y
UTAH					
1 Bishop	Y	Y	Y	Y	Y
2 Matheson	Y	Y	Y	Y	Y
3 Chaffetz	Y	Y	Y	N	Y
VERMONT					
AL Welch	Y	Y	Y	Y	Y
VIRGINIA					
1 Wittman	Y	Y	Y	Y	Y
2 Nye	Y	Y	Y	Y	Y
3 Scott	Y	Y	Y	Y	Y
4 Forbes	Y	Y	?	?	Y
5 Perriello	Y	Y	Y	Y	Y
6 Goodlatte	Y	Y	Y	Y	Y
7 Cantor	?	?	Y	Y	Y
8 Moran	Y	Y	Y	Y	Y
9 Boucher	Y	Y	Y	Y	Y
10 Wolf	Y	Y	Y	Y	Y
11 Connolly	Y	?	Y	Y	Y
WASHINGTON					
1 Inslee	Y	Y	Y	Y	Y
2 Larsen	Y	Y	Y	Y	Y
3 Baird	Y	?	Y	Y	Y
4 Hastings	Y	Y	Y	Y	Y
5 McMorris Rodgers	Y	Y	Y	Y	Y
6 Dicks	?	?	Y	Y	Y
7 McDermott	Y	Y	Y	Y	Y
8 Reichert	Y	Y	Y	Y	Y
9 Smith	Y	Y	Y	Y	Y
WEST VIRGINIA					
1 Mollohan	Y	Y	Y	Y	Y
2 Capito	Y	Y	Y	Y	Y
3 Rahall	Y	Y	Y	Y	Y
WISCONSIN					
1 Ryan	Y	Y	Y	Y	Y
2 Baldwin	Y	Y	Y	Y	Y
3 Kind	Y	Y	Y	Y	Y
4 Moore	Y	Y	Y	Y	Y
5 Sensenbrenner	Y	Y	Y	N	Y
6 Petri	Y	Y	Y	Y	Y
7 Obey	Y	?	Y	Y	Y
8 Kagen	Y	Y	Y	Y	Y
WYOMING					
AL Lummis	Y	Y	Y	Y	Y
DELEGATES					
Faleomavaega (A.S.)					
Norton (D.C.)					
Bordallo (Guam)					
Sablan (N. Marianas)					
Pierluisi (P.R.)					
Christensen (V.I.)					

IN THE HOUSE | By Vote Number

865. **H Con Res 210. Adjournment/Adoption.** Adoption of the concurrent resolution that would provide for adjournment of the House until 2 p.m. Monday, Nov. 16, 2009, and the Senate until 12 p.m. Monday, Nov. 16, 2009. Adopted 235-179: D 231-14; R 4-165. Nov. 6, 2009.

866. **H Res 893. Tribute to New York Yankees/Adoption.** Towns, D-N.Y., motion to suspend the rules and adopt the resolution that would congratulate the New York Yankees for winning the 2009 Major League Baseball World Series. Motion agreed to 386-17: D 228-10; R 158-7. A two-thirds majority of those present and voting (269 in this case) is required for adoption under suspension of the rules. Nov. 6, 2009.

867. **HR 3788. Joseph A. Tomci Post Office Building/Passage.** Davis, D-Ill., motion to suspend the rules and pass the bill that would designate a post office in Stow, Ohio, as the "Cpl. Joseph A. Tomci Post Office." Motion agreed to 415-1: D 247-1; R 168-0. A two-thirds majority of those present and voting (278 in this case) is required for passage under suspension of the rules. Nov. 6, 2009.

868. **S 1211. Jack F. Kemp Post Office Building/Passage.** Davis, D-Ill., motion to suspend the rules and pass the bill to designate a post office in Orchard Park, N.Y., as the "Jack F. Kemp Post Office," after the former Republican congressman from New York, who died in May 2009. Motion agreed to 408-0: D 242-0; R 166-0. A two-thirds majority of those present and voting (272 in this case) is required for passage under suspension of the rules. Nov. 6, 2009.

869. **HR 2868. Chemical Plant Security/Substitute.** Thompson, D-Miss., substitute amendment that would make technical corrections and allow the secretary of Homeland Security to release information on chemical plants that is not detrimental to the safety of the facility or if it has been obtained through a third-party source. Adopted in Committee of the Whole 253-168: D 253-0; R 0-168. Nov. 6, 2009.

870. **HR 2868. Chemical Plant Security/Federal Regulation Pre-emption.** Barton, R-Texas, amendment that would prohibit state or local laws from pre-empting Homeland Security Department and EPA regulations. Rejected in Committee of the Whole 165-262: D 18-240; R 147-22. Nov. 6, 2009.

871. **HR 2868. Chemical Plant Security/Existing Program Reauthorization.** Dent, R-Pa., amendment that would strike provisions on chemical facilities and reauthorize the existing chemical plant safety program administered by the Department of Homeland Security until Oct. 1, 2012. Rejected in Committee of the Whole 186-241: D 17-241; R 169-0. Nov. 6, 2009.

	865	866	867	868	869	870	871
ALABAMA							
1 Bonner	N	Y	Y	Y	N	Y	Y
2 Bright	Y	Y	Y	Y	Y	Y	Y
3 Rogers	N	Y	Y	Y	N	Y	Y
4 Aderholt	?	?	?	?	?	?	?
5 Griffith	Y	Y	Y	Y	Y	Y	Y
6 Bachus	N	Y	Y	Y	N	Y	Y
7 Davis	Y	Y	Y	Y	Y	N	N
ALASKA							
AL Young	N	Y	Y	Y	N	Y	Y
ARIZONA							
1 Kirkpatrick	Y	Y	Y	Y	Y	N	N
2 Franks	N	Y	Y	Y	N	Y	Y
3 Shadegg	N	Y	Y	Y	N	Y	Y
4 Pastor	Y	Y	Y	Y	Y	N	N
5 Mitchell	N	Y	Y	Y	Y	N	N
6 Flake	N	Y	Y	Y	N	N	Y
7 Grijalva	Y	Y	Y	Y	Y	N	N
8 Giffords	Y	Y	Y	Y	Y	N	N
ARKANSAS							
1 Berry	Y	N	N	Y	Y	N	N
2 Snyder	Y	Y	Y	Y	Y	N	N
3 Boozman	N	Y	Y	Y	N	Y	Y
4 Ross	Y	Y	Y	Y	Y	N	N
CALIFORNIA							
1 Thompson	Y	Y	Y	Y	Y	N	N
2 Herger	N	Y	Y	Y	N	Y	Y
3 Lungren	N	N	Y	Y	N	Y	Y
4 McClintock	N	Y	Y	Y	N	Y	Y
5 Matsui	Y	Y	Y	Y	Y	N	N
6 Woolsey	Y	Y	Y	+	Y	N	N
7 Miller, George	Y	Y	Y	Y	Y	N	N
8 Pelosi							
9 Lee	Y	Y	Y	Y	Y	N	N
10 Garamendi	Y	Y	Y	Y	Y	N	N
11 McNerney	Y	Y	Y	Y	Y	N	N
12 Speier	Y	Y	Y	Y	?	N	N
13 Stark	Y	Y	Y	Y	Y	N	N
14 Eshoo	Y	Y	Y	Y	Y	N	N
15 Honda	Y	Y	Y	Y	Y	N	N
16 Lofgren	Y	Y	Y	?	Y	N	N
17 Farr	Y	Y	Y	Y	Y	N	?
18 Cardoza	Y	Y	Y	Y	Y	N	N
19 Radanovich	N	N	Y	Y	N	Y	Y
20 Costa	Y	Y	Y	Y	?	N	N
21 Nunes	?	?	?	?	?	?	?
22 McCarthy	N	Y	Y	Y	N	Y	Y
23 Capps	Y	Y	Y	Y	Y	N	N
24 Gallegly	N	Y	Y	Y	N	Y	Y
25 McKeon	N	Y	?	Y	N	Y	Y
26 Dreier	N	Y	Y	Y	N	Y	Y
27 Sherman	Y	Y	Y	Y	Y	N	N
28 Berman	Y	Y	Y	Y	Y	N	N
29 Schiff	Y	Y	Y	Y	Y	N	N
30 Waxman	Y	Y	Y	Y	Y	N	N
31 Becerra	Y	Y	Y	Y	Y	N	N
32 Chu	Y	Y	Y	Y	Y	N	N
33 Watson	Y	Y	Y	Y	Y	N	N
34 Roybal-Allard	Y	Y	Y	Y	Y	N	N
35 Waters	Y	Y	Y	Y	Y	N	N
36 Harman	Y	Y	Y	Y	Y	N	N
37 Richardson	Y	Y	Y	Y	Y	N	N
38 Napolitano	Y	Y	Y	Y	Y	N	N
39 Sánchez, Linda	+	?	+	+	+	–	–
40 Royce	N	Y	Y	Y	N	Y	Y
41 Lewis	N	Y	Y	Y	N	Y	Y
42 Miller, Gary	N	Y	Y	Y	N	Y	Y
43 Baca	Y	Y	Y	Y	Y	N	N
44 Calvert	N	Y	Y	Y	N	Y	Y
45 Bono Mack	N	Y	Y	Y	N	Y	Y
46 Rohrabacher	N	N	Y	Y	N	Y	Y
47 Sanchez, Loretta	Y	Y	Y	?	Y	N	N
48 Campbell	N	N	Y	Y	N	Y	Y
49 Issa	N	Y	Y	Y	N	Y	Y
50 Bilbray	N	Y	Y	Y	N	Y	Y
51 Filner	N	Y	Y	Y	Y	N	N
52 Hunter	N	N	Y	Y	N	Y	Y
53 Davis	Y	Y	Y	Y	Y	N	N

	865	866	867	868	869	870	871
COLORADO							
1 DeGette	Y	Y	Y	Y	Y	N	N
2 Polis	Y	Y	Y	Y	Y	N	N
3 Salazar	Y	Y	Y	Y	N	N	Y
4 Markey	N	Y	Y	Y	Y	N	N
5 Lamborn	N	Y	Y	Y	N	Y	Y
6 Coffman	N	Y	Y	?	N	Y	Y
7 Perlmutter	Y	Y	Y	Y	Y	N	N
CONNECTICUT							
1 Larson	Y	Y	Y	Y	Y	N	N
2 Courtney	Y	Y	Y	Y	Y	N	N
3 DeLauro	Y	Y	Y	Y	Y	N	N
4 Himes	N	Y	Y	Y	Y	N	N
5 Murphy	Y	N	Y	Y	Y	N	N
DELAWARE							
AL Castle	N	Y	Y	Y	N	N	Y
FLORIDA							
1 Miller	N	Y	Y	Y	N	Y	Y
2 Boyd	Y	Y	Y	Y	Y	N	N
3 Brown	Y	Y	Y	Y	Y	N	N
4 Crenshaw	N	Y	Y	Y	N	Y	Y
5 Brown-Waite	N	Y	Y	Y	N	Y	Y
6 Stearns	N	Y	Y	Y	N	Y	Y
7 Mica	N	Y	Y	Y	N	Y	Y
8 Grayson	Y	Y	Y	Y	Y	N	N
9 Bilirakis	N	Y	Y	Y	N	Y	Y
10 Young	N	Y	Y	Y	N	Y	Y
11 Castor	Y	Y	Y	Y	Y	N	N
12 Putnam	N	Y	Y	Y	N	Y	Y
13 Buchanan	N	Y	Y	Y	N	Y	Y
14 Mack	N	Y	Y	Y	N	Y	Y
15 Posey	N	?	Y	Y	N	Y	Y
16 Rooney	N	N	Y	Y	N	Y	Y
17 Meek	Y	Y	Y	Y	Y	N	N
18 Ros-Lehtinen	N	Y	Y	Y	N	Y	Y
19 Wexler	Y	Y	Y	Y	Y	N	N
20 Wasserman Schultz	?	Y	Y	Y	Y	N	N
21 Diaz-Balart, L.	N	Y	Y	Y	N	Y	Y
22 Klein	Y	Y	Y	Y	Y	N	N
23 Hastings	Y	Y	Y	Y	Y	N	N
24 Kosmas	N	Y	Y	Y	Y	N	N
25 Diaz-Balart, M.	N	Y	Y	Y	N	Y	Y
GEORGIA							
1 Kingston	N	Y	Y	Y	N	Y	Y
2 Bishop	Y	Y	Y	Y	?	N	N
3 Westmoreland	N	Y	Y	?	N	Y	Y
4 Johnson	?	Y	Y	Y	Y	N	N
5 Lewis	Y	Y	Y	Y	Y	N	N
6 Price	N	Y	Y	Y	N	Y	Y
7 Linder	N	Y	Y	Y	N	Y	Y
8 Marshall	Y	P	Y	Y	Y	Y	Y
9 Deal	N	Y	Y	Y	N	Y	Y
10 Broun	?	?	?	?	N	N	Y
11 Gingrey	N	Y	Y	Y	N	Y	Y
12 Barrow	Y	Y	Y	Y	Y	N	Y
13 Scott	Y	Y	Y	Y	N	N	N
HAWAII							
1 Abercrombie	Y	Y	Y	Y	Y	N	N
2 Hirono	Y	Y	Y	Y	Y	N	N
IDAHO							
1 Minnick	N	Y	Y	Y	Y	Y	Y
2 Simpson	N	Y	Y	Y	N	Y	Y
ILLINOIS							
1 Rush	Y	Y	Y	Y	Y	N	N
2 Jackson	Y	Y	Y	Y	Y	N	N
3 Lipinski	Y	Y	Y	Y	Y	N	N
4 Gutierrez	Y	Y	Y	Y	Y	N	N
5 Quigley	Y	Y	Y	Y	Y	N	N
6 Roskam	N	Y	Y	Y	N	Y	Y
7 Davis	Y	Y	Y	Y	Y	N	N
8 Bean	Y	Y	Y	Y	Y	N	N
9 Schakowsky	Y	Y	Y	Y	Y	N	N
10 Kirk	N	Y	Y	Y	N	Y	Y
11 Halvorson	Y	Y	Y	Y	Y	N	N
12 Costello	Y	Y	Y	Y	Y	N	N
13 Biggert	N	Y	Y	Y	N	Y	Y
14 Foster	Y	Y	Y	Y	Y	N	N
15 Johnson	N	Y	Y	Y	N	Y	Y

*Rep. Bill Owens, D-N.Y., was sworn in Nov. 6 to fill the seat vacated by Republican John M. McHugh, who resigned Sept. 21 to become secretary of the Army. The first vote for which Owens was eligible was 867.

	865	866	867	868	869	870	871
16 **Manzullo**	N	Y	Y	Y	N	N	Y
17 Hare	Y	Y	Y	Y	Y	N	N
18 **Schock**	N	Y	Y	?	N	Y	?
19 **Shimkus**	N	Y	Y	Y	N	Y	Y
INDIANA							
1 Visclosky	Y	Y	Y	Y	Y	N	N
2 Donnelly	N	Y	Y	Y	Y	N	Y
3 **Souder**	N	P	Y	Y	N	Y	Y
4 **Buyer**	N	Y	Y	Y	N	Y	Y
5 **Burton**	N	Y	Y	Y	N	Y	Y
6 **Pence**	N	Y	Y	Y	N	Y	Y
7 Carson	Y	Y	Y	Y	Y	N	N
8 Ellsworth	Y	Y	Y	Y	Y	Y	Y
9 Hill	Y	Y	Y	Y	Y	N	N
IOWA							
1 Braley	Y	N	Y	Y	Y	N	N
2 Loebsack	Y	Y	Y	Y	Y	N	N
3 Boswell	Y	Y	Y	Y	Y	Y	N
4 **Latham**	N	Y	Y	Y	N	Y	Y
5 **King**	N	Y	Y	Y	N	Y	Y
KANSAS							
1 **Moran**	N	Y	Y	Y	N	Y	Y
2 **Jenkins**	N	Y	Y	Y	N	Y	Y
3 Moore	Y	Y	Y	Y	Y	N	N
4 **Tiahrt**	N	Y	Y	Y	N	Y	Y
KENTUCKY							
1 **Whitfield**	N	Y	Y	Y	N	Y	Y
2 **Guthrie**	N	Y	Y	Y	N	Y	Y
3 Yarmuth	Y	Y	Y	Y	Y	N	N
4 **Davis**	N	?	Y	Y	N	Y	Y
5 **Rogers**	N	Y	Y	Y	N	Y	Y
6 Chandler	?	?	?	?	?	?	?
LOUISIANA							
1 **Scalise**	N	Y	Y	Y	N	Y	Y
2 **Cao**	Y	Y	Y	Y	N	Y	Y
3 Melancon	Y	Y	Y	Y	Y	N	N
4 **Fleming**	N	Y	Y	Y	N	Y	Y
5 **Alexander**	N	Y	Y	Y	N	Y	Y
6 **Cassidy**	?	?	?	?	?	?	Y
7 **Boustany**	N	Y	Y	Y	N	Y	Y
MAINE							
1 Pingree	Y	Y	Y	Y	Y	N	N
2 Michaud	Y	Y	Y	Y	Y	N	N
MARYLAND							
1 Kratovil	N	Y	Y	Y	Y	N	N
2 Ruppersberger	Y	Y	Y	Y	Y	N	N
3 Sarbanes	Y	Y	Y	Y	Y	N	N
4 Edwards	Y	Y	Y	Y	Y	N	N
5 Hoyer	Y	Y	Y	Y	Y	N	N
6 **Bartlett**	N	Y	Y	Y	N	Y	Y
7 Cummings	Y	Y	Y	Y	Y	N	N
8 Van Hollen	Y	Y	Y	Y	Y	N	N
MASSACHUSETTS							
1 Olver	Y	P	Y	Y	Y	N	N
2 Neal	Y	Y	Y	Y	Y	N	N
3 McGovern	?	?	?	?	Y	N	N
4 Frank	Y	Y	Y	?	Y	N	N
5 Tsongas	Y	P	Y	Y	Y	N	N
6 Tierney	Y	Y	Y	Y	Y	N	N
7 Markey	Y	Y	Y	Y	Y	N	N
8 Capuano	Y	Y	Y	Y	Y	N	N
9 Lynch	Y	Y	Y	Y	Y	N	N
10 Delahunt	Y	N	Y	Y	Y	N	N
MICHIGAN							
1 Stupak	?	?	?	Y	Y	N	N
2 **Hoekstra**	N	Y	Y	Y	N	Y	Y
3 **Ehlers**	?	?	?	?	?	?	?
4 **Camp**	N	Y	Y	Y	N	Y	Y
5 Kildee	Y	Y	Y	Y	Y	N	N
6 **Upton**	N	Y	Y	Y	N	Y	Y
7 Schauer	Y	Y	Y	Y	Y	N	N
8 **Rogers**	?	?	?	?	?	?	?
9 Peters	Y	Y	Y	Y	Y	N	N
10 **Miller**	N	Y	Y	Y	N	Y	Y
11 **McCotter**	N	Y	Y	Y	N	Y	Y
12 Levin	Y	Y	Y	Y	Y	N	N
13 Kilpatrick	Y	Y	Y	Y	Y	N	N
14 Conyers	+	+	Y	Y	Y	N	N
15 Dingell	Y	Y	Y	Y	Y	N	N
MINNESOTA							
1 Walz	Y	Y	Y	Y	Y	N	N
2 **Kline**	N	Y	Y	Y	N	Y	Y
3 **Paulsen**	N	Y	Y	Y	N	Y	Y
4 McCollum	Y	Y	Y	Y	Y	N	N
5 Ellison	Y	Y	Y	?	Y	N	N
6 **Bachmann**	N	Y	Y	Y	N	Y	Y
7 Peterson	Y	Y	Y	Y	Y	N	N
8 Oberstar	Y	P	Y	Y	Y	N	N
MISSISSIPPI							
1 Childers	Y	Y	Y	Y	Y	N	N
2 Thompson	Y	Y	Y	Y	Y	N	N
3 **Harper**	N	Y	Y	Y	N	Y	Y
4 Taylor	N	Y	Y	Y	Y	N	Y
MISSOURI							
1 Clay	?	?	?	Y	Y	N	N
2 **Akin**	N	Y	Y	Y	N	Y	Y
3 Carnahan	Y	Y	Y	Y	Y	N	N
4 Skelton	Y	Y	Y	Y	Y	N	Y
5 Cleaver	Y	Y	Y	Y	Y	N	N
6 **Graves**	N	Y	Y	Y	N	Y	Y
7 **Blunt**	N	Y	Y	Y	N	Y	Y
8 **Emerson**	N	Y	Y	Y	?	Y	Y
9 **Luetkemeyer**	N	Y	Y	Y	N	Y	Y
MONTANA							
AL **Rehberg**	N	Y	Y	Y	N	Y	Y
NEBRASKA							
1 **Fortenberry**	N	Y	Y	Y	N	Y	Y
2 **Terry**	N	Y	Y	Y	N	Y	Y
3 **Smith**	N	Y	Y	Y	N	Y	Y
NEVADA							
1 Berkley	Y	Y	Y	Y	Y	N	N
2 **Heller**	Y	Y	Y	Y	N	Y	Y
3 Titus	Y	Y	Y	Y	Y	N	N
NEW HAMPSHIRE							
1 Shea-Porter	Y	Y	Y	Y	Y	Y	N
2 Hodes	Y	P	Y	Y	Y	N	N
NEW JERSEY							
1 Andrews	Y	Y	Y	Y	Y	Y	N
2 **LoBiondo**	N	Y	Y	Y	N	N	Y
3 Adler	N	N	Y	Y	Y	N	N
4 **Smith**	N	Y	Y	Y	N	N	Y
5 **Garrett**	N	Y	Y	Y	N	Y	Y
6 Pallone	Y	Y	Y	Y	Y	N	N
7 **Lance**	N	Y	Y	Y	N	N	Y
8 Pascrell	Y	Y	Y	Y	Y	N	N
9 Rothman	Y	Y	Y	Y	Y	N	N
10 Payne	Y	Y	Y	Y	Y	N	N
11 **Frelinghuysen**	N	Y	Y	Y	N	N	Y
12 Holt	Y	Y	Y	Y	Y	N	N
13 Sires	Y	Y	Y	Y	Y	N	N
NEW MEXICO							
1 Heinrich	Y	Y	Y	Y	Y	N	N
2 Teague	Y	Y	Y	Y	Y	Y	Y
3 Lujan	Y	Y	Y	Y	Y	N	N
NEW YORK							
1 Bishop	Y	Y	Y	Y	Y	N	N
2 Israel	Y	Y	Y	Y	Y	N	N
3 **King**	N	Y	Y	Y	N	Y	Y
4 McCarthy	Y	Y	Y	Y	Y	N	N
5 Ackerman	Y	Y	Y	Y	Y	N	N
6 Meeks	Y	Y	Y	Y	?	N	N
7 Crowley	Y	Y	Y	?	Y	N	N
8 Nadler	Y	Y	Y	Y	Y	N	N
9 Weiner	Y	Y	Y	Y	Y	N	N
10 Towns	Y	Y	Y	Y	Y	N	N
11 Clarke	Y	Y	Y	Y	Y	N	N
12 Velázquez	Y	Y	Y	Y	Y	N	N
13 McMahon	Y	Y	Y	Y	Y	N	N
14 Maloney	Y	Y	Y	Y	Y	N	N
15 Rangel	Y	Y	Y	?	Y	N	N
16 Serrano	Y	Y	Y	Y	Y	N	N
17 Engel	Y	Y	Y	Y	Y	N	N
18 Lowey	Y	Y	Y	Y	Y	N	N
19 Hall	Y	Y	Y	Y	Y	N	N
20 Murphy	N	Y	Y	Y	Y	N	N
21 Tonko	Y	Y	Y	Y	Y	N	N
22 Hinchey	Y	Y	Y	Y	Y	N	N
23 Owens*			Y	Y	Y	N	N
24 Arcuri	Y	Y	Y	Y	Y	N	N
25 Maffei	N	Y	Y	Y	Y	N	N
26 **Lee**	N	Y	Y	Y	N	Y	Y
27 Higgins	Y	Y	Y	Y	Y	N	N
28 Slaughter	Y	Y	Y	?	Y	N	N
29 Massa	N	Y	Y	Y	Y	N	N
NORTH CAROLINA							
1 Butterfield	Y	Y	Y	Y	Y	N	N
2 Etheridge	Y	Y	Y	Y	Y	N	N
3 **Jones**	N	Y	Y	Y	N	N	Y
4 Price	Y	Y	Y	Y	Y	N	N
5 **Foxx**	N	Y	Y	Y	N	Y	Y
6 **Coble**	N	Y	Y	Y	N	Y	Y
7 McIntyre	Y	Y	Y	Y	Y	N	N
8 Kissell	Y	Y	Y	Y	Y	N	N
9 **Myrick**	N	Y	Y	Y	N	Y	Y
10 **McHenry**	N	Y	Y	Y	N	Y	Y
11 Shuler	Y	Y	Y	Y	Y	N	N
12 Watt	Y	Y	Y	Y	Y	N	N
13 Miller	Y	Y	Y	Y	Y	N	N
NORTH DAKOTA							
AL Pomeroy	Y	Y	Y	Y	Y	N	N
OHIO							
1 Driehaus	Y	P	Y	Y	Y	N	N
2 **Schmidt**	N	Y	Y	Y	N	Y	Y
3 **Turner**	N	Y	Y	Y	N	Y	Y
4 **Jordan**	N	Y	Y	Y	N	Y	Y
5 **Latta**	N	Y	Y	Y	N	Y	Y
6 Wilson	Y	Y	Y	Y	Y	N	N
7 **Austria**	N	Y	Y	Y	N	Y	Y
8 **Boehner**	N	Y	Y	Y	?	?	Y
9 Kaptur	Y	N	Y	Y	Y	N	N
10 Kucinich	Y	Y	Y	Y	Y	N	N
11 Fudge	Y	Y	Y	Y	Y	N	N
12 **Tiberi**	N	Y	Y	Y	N	Y	Y
13 Sutton	Y	Y	Y	Y	Y	N	N
14 **LaTourette**	N	Y	Y	Y	N	Y	Y
15 Kilroy	Y	Y	Y	Y	Y	N	N
16 Boccieri	Y	Y	Y	Y	Y	N	N
17 Ryan	Y	Y	Y	Y	Y	N	N
18 Space	Y	Y	Y	Y	Y	N	Y
OKLAHOMA							
1 **Sullivan**	N	Y	Y	Y	N	Y	Y
2 Boren	Y	Y	Y	Y	Y	Y	Y
3 **Lucas**	N	Y	Y	Y	N	Y	Y
4 **Cole**	N	Y	Y	Y	N	Y	Y
5 **Fallin**	N	Y	Y	Y	N	Y	Y
OREGON							
1 Wu	Y	Y	Y	Y	Y	N	N
2 **Walden**	N	Y	Y	Y	N	Y	Y
3 Blumenauer	Y	Y	Y	Y	Y	N	N
4 DeFazio	Y	P	Y	Y	Y	N	N
5 Schrader	Y	Y	Y	Y	Y	N	N
PENNSYLVANIA							
1 Brady	Y	Y	Y	Y	Y	N	N
2 Fattah	Y	Y	Y	Y	Y	N	N
3 Dahlkemper	Y	Y	Y	Y	Y	N	N
4 Altmire	Y	N	Y	Y	Y	Y	N
5 **Thompson**	N	Y	Y	Y	N	Y	Y
6 **Gerlach**	N	Y	Y	Y	N	N	Y
7 Sestak	N	Y	Y	Y	Y	N	N
8 Murphy, P.	?	?	?	?	?	?	?
9 **Shuster**	N	Y	Y	Y	N	Y	Y
10 Carney	Y	Y	Y	Y	Y	N	N
11 Kanjorski	Y	Y	Y	Y	Y	N	N
12 Murtha	Y	Y	Y	Y	Y	N	N
13 Schwartz	Y	N	Y	Y	Y	N	N
14 Doyle	Y	Y	Y	Y	Y	N	N
15 **Dent**	N	Y	Y	Y	N	Y	Y
16 **Pitts**	N	Y	Y	Y	N	Y	Y
17 Holden	Y	Y	Y	Y	Y	N	N
18 **Murphy, T.**	N	Y	Y	Y	N	Y	Y
19 **Platts**	N	Y	Y	Y	N	N	Y
RHODE ISLAND							
1 Kennedy	Y	Y	Y	Y	Y	N	N
2 Langevin	Y	P	Y	Y	Y	N	N
SOUTH CAROLINA							
1 **Brown**	N	Y	Y	Y	N	Y	Y
2 **Wilson**	N	Y	Y	Y	N	Y	Y
3 **Barrett**	N	Y	Y	Y	N	Y	Y
4 **Inglis**	N	Y	Y	Y	N	Y	Y
5 Spratt	Y	Y	Y	Y	Y	N	Y
6 Clyburn	Y	Y	Y	Y	Y	N	N
SOUTH DAKOTA							
AL Herseth Sandlin	Y	Y	Y	Y	Y	N	N
TENNESSEE							
1 **Roe**	N	Y	Y	Y	N	Y	Y
2 **Duncan**	N	Y	Y	Y	N	Y	Y
3 **Wamp**	N	Y	Y	Y	N	N	Y
4 Davis	Y	Y	Y	Y	Y	N	N
5 Cooper	Y	Y	Y	Y	Y	Y	N
6 Gordon	Y	Y	?	?	Y	Y	N
7 **Blackburn**	N	Y	Y	Y	N	Y	Y
8 Tanner	Y	Y	Y	Y	Y	N	N
9 Cohen	Y	Y	Y	Y	Y	Y	N
TEXAS							
1 **Gohmert**	N	?	Y	Y	N	Y	Y
2 **Poe**	N	Y	Y	Y	N	Y	Y
3 **Johnson, S.**	N	Y	Y	Y	N	Y	Y
4 **Hall**	N	Y	Y	Y	N	Y	Y
5 **Hensarling**	N	Y	Y	Y	N	Y	Y
6 **Barton**	N	Y	Y	Y	N	Y	Y
7 **Culberson**	N	Y	Y	Y	N	N	Y
8 **Brady**	N	Y	Y	Y	N	Y	Y
9 Green, A.	Y	Y	Y	Y	Y	N	N
10 **McCaul**	N	Y	Y	Y	N	Y	Y
11 **Conaway**	?	?	?	?	?	?	?
12 **Granger**	N	Y	Y	Y	N	Y	Y
13 **Thornberry**	N	Y	Y	Y	N	N	Y
14 **Paul**	N	Y	Y	Y	N	N	Y
15 Hinojosa	Y	Y	Y	Y	Y	N	N
16 Reyes	Y	Y	Y	Y	Y	N	N
17 Edwards	Y	Y	Y	Y	Y	N	N
18 Jackson Lee	Y	Y	Y	Y	Y	N	N
19 **Neugebauer**	N	Y	Y	Y	N	N	Y
20 Gonzalez	Y	Y	Y	Y	Y	N	N
21 **Smith**	N	Y	Y	Y	N	Y	Y
22 **Olson**	Y	Y	Y	Y	N	Y	Y
23 Rodriguez	Y	Y	Y	Y	Y	N	N
24 **Marchant**	N	Y	Y	Y	N	Y	?
25 Doggett	Y	Y	Y	Y	Y	N	N
26 **Burgess**	N	Y	Y	Y	N	Y	Y
27 Ortiz	Y	Y	Y	Y	Y	N	N
28 Cuellar	Y	Y	Y	Y	Y	N	N
29 Green, G.	Y	Y	Y	Y	Y	N	Y
30 Johnson, E.	Y	Y	Y	Y	?	N	N
31 **Carter**	–	+	+	+	+	+	+
32 **Sessions**	N	Y	Y	Y	N	Y	Y
UTAH							
1 **Bishop**	N	Y	Y	Y	N	Y	Y
2 Matheson	Y	Y	Y	Y	Y	Y	N
3 **Chaffetz**	Y	Y	Y	Y	N	Y	Y
VERMONT							
AL Welch	Y	P	Y	Y	Y	N	N
VIRGINIA							
1 **Wittman**	N	Y	Y	Y	N	Y	Y
2 Nye	Y	Y	Y	Y	Y	N	N
3 Scott	Y	Y	Y	Y	Y	N	N
4 **Forbes**	N	Y	Y	Y	N	Y	Y
5 Perriello	?	Y	Y	Y	Y	N	N
6 **Goodlatte**	N	Y	Y	Y	N	Y	Y
7 **Cantor**	N	Y	Y	Y	N	Y	Y
8 Moran	Y	Y	Y	Y	Y	N	N
9 Boucher	Y	Y	Y	Y	Y	Y	N
10 **Wolf**	N	Y	Y	Y	N	Y	Y
11 Connolly	Y	Y	Y	Y	Y	N	N
WASHINGTON							
1 Inslee	Y	Y	Y	Y	Y	N	N
2 Larsen	Y	Y	Y	?	Y	N	N
3 Baird	N	Y	Y	Y	Y	N	Y
4 **Hastings**	N	Y	Y	Y	N	Y	Y
5 **McMorris Rodgers**	N	Y	Y	Y	N	Y	Y
6 Dicks	Y	Y	?	?	Y	N	N
7 McDermott	Y	Y	Y	Y	Y	?	N
8 **Reichert**	N	Y	Y	Y	N	Y	Y
9 Smith	Y	Y	Y	Y	Y	N	N
WEST VIRGINIA							
1 Mollohan	Y	Y	Y	Y	Y	N	N
2 **Capito**	N	Y	Y	Y	N	N	Y
3 Rahall	Y	N	Y	Y	Y	N	N
WISCONSIN							
1 **Ryan**	N	Y	Y	Y	N	Y	Y
2 Baldwin	Y	Y	Y	Y	Y	N	N
3 Kind	Y	Y	Y	Y	Y	N	N
4 Moore	?	?	Y	Y	Y	N	N
5 **Sensenbrenner**	N	N	Y	Y	N	Y	Y
6 **Petri**	N	Y	Y	Y	N	Y	Y
7 Obey	Y	Y	Y	Y	Y	N	N
8 Kagen	Y	P	?	Y	Y	N	N
WYOMING							
AL **Lummis**	N	Y	Y	Y	N	Y	Y
DELEGATES							
Faleomavaega (A.S.)					Y	N	N
Norton (D.C.)					?	?	?
Bordallo (Guam)					Y	N	N
Sablan (N. Marianas)					Y	N	N
Pierluisi (P.R.)					Y	N	N
Christensen (V.I.)					?	N	N

IN THE HOUSE | By Vote Number

872. HR 2868. Chemical Plant Security/Study of Potential Terrorist Attacks.
Dent, R-Pa., amendment that would strike provisions in the bill that would require chemical facility operators to investigate and implement methods to prevent the adverse impact of a terrorist attack. Rejected in Committee of the Whole 193-236: D 22-236; R 171-0. Nov. 6, 2009.

873. HR 2868. Chemical Plant Security/Civil Lawsuits.
McCaul, R-Texas, amendment that would strike provisions in the bill that would permit citizens to file a lawsuit against anyone in violation of the safety regulations in the underlying bill. Rejected in Committee of the Whole 196-232: D 28-231; R 168-1. Nov. 6, 2009.

874. HR 2868. Chemical Plant Security/Recommit.
Dent, R-Pa., motion to recommit the bill to the House Homeland Security Committee with instructions that it be immediately reported back with an amendment that would permit chemical facilities to not implement inherently safer technologies if it would reduce the operations of the facility when national unemployment is above 4 percent. Motion rejected 189-236: D 19-235; R 170-1. Nov. 6, 2009.

875. HR 2868. Chemical Plant Security/Passage.
Passage of the bill that would authorize $900 million in fiscal 2011 through 2013 for the Department of Homeland Security to conduct assessments and codify security standards for chemical plants. It would direct the agency to identify chemical plants according to a risk-based tier system, require plant operators to submit site security plans, and establish training standards and background checks for employees. It would also authorize the EPA to regulate the security of community water systems serving more than 3,300 people and other public water systems that present a security risk. It would authorize $315 million in fiscal 2011 for grants to states and nonprofits to help develop security plans for covered public water systems. Passed 230-193: D 230-21; R 0-172. Nov. 6, 2009.

876. HR 3737. Small Business Administration Microloan Program/Passage.
Velázquez, D-N.Y., motion to suspend the rules and pass the bill that would authorize such sums as necessary for the Small Business Administration's microloan program to provide $80 million in technical assistance grants and $110 million in direct loans in fiscal 2010 and 2011. It would expand program eligibility for intermediary lenders and specify that no loan can be made if the total amount outstanding and committed to one lender exceeds $1 million in the first year of the lender's participation in the program and $7 million in years thereafter. Motion agreed to 405-23: D 252-0; R 153-23. A two-thirds majority of those present and voting (286 in this case) is required for passage under suspension of the rules. Nov. 7, 2009.

877. HR 1838. Women's Business Center Grants/Passage.
Velázquez, D-N.Y., motion to suspend the rules and pass the bill that would authorize up to $20 million in fiscal 2010 and $22 million in fiscal 2011 for matching grants for women's business centers, with 40 percent for new centers. New centers would receive up to $150,000 annually for five years. Existing centers would be eligible to apply for grants of $100,000 annually. Motion agreed to 428-4: D 256-0; R 172-4. A two-thirds majority of those present and voting (288 in this case) is required for passage under suspension of the rules. Nov. 7, 2009.

	872	873	874	875	876	877
ALABAMA						
1 Bonner	Y	Y	Y	N	Y	Y
2 Bright	Y	Y	Y	N	Y	Y
3 Rogers	Y	Y	Y	N	Y	Y
4 Aderholt	?	?	?	?	Y	Y
5 Griffith	Y	Y	Y	N	Y	Y
6 Bachus	Y	Y	Y	N	Y	Y
7 Davis	N	N	N	Y	Y	Y
ALASKA						
AL Young	Y	Y	Y	N	?	?
ARIZONA						
1 Kirkpatrick	N	N	Y	Y	Y	Y
2 Franks	Y	Y	Y	N	N	Y
3 Shadegg	Y	Y	Y	N	N	Y
4 Pastor	N	N	Y	Y	Y	Y
5 Mitchell	N	N	Y	Y	Y	Y
6 Flake	Y	Y	Y	N	N	N
7 Grijalva	N	N	N	Y	Y	Y
8 Giffords	N	N	N	Y	Y	Y
ARKANSAS						
1 Berry	Y	Y	N	N	Y	Y
2 Snyder	N	N	N	Y	Y	Y
3 Boozman	Y	Y	Y	N	Y	Y
4 Ross	N	N	N	N	Y	Y
CALIFORNIA						
1 Thompson	N	N	N	Y	Y	Y
2 Herger	Y	Y	Y	N	Y	Y
3 Lungren	Y	Y	Y	N	Y	Y
4 McClintock	Y	Y	Y	N	N	N
5 Matsui	N	N	N	Y	Y	Y
6 Woolsey	N	N	N	Y	Y	Y
7 Miller, George	N	N	N	Y	Y	Y
8 Pelosi						
9 Lee	N	N	N	Y	Y	Y
10 Garamendi	N	N	N	Y	Y	Y
11 McNerney	N	N	Y	Y	Y	Y
12 Speier	N	N	N	Y	Y	Y
13 Stark	N	N	N	Y	Y	Y
14 Eshoo	N	N	N	Y	Y	Y
15 Honda	N	N	N	Y	Y	Y
16 Lofgren	N	N	N	Y	Y	Y
17 Farr	N	N	N	Y	Y	Y
18 Cardoza	N	N	N	N	Y	Y
19 Radanovich	Y	Y	Y	N	Y	Y
20 Costa	N	Y	Y	Y	Y	Y
21 Nunes	?	?	N	N	Y	Y
22 McCarthy	Y	Y	Y	N	Y	Y
23 Capps	N	N	N	Y	Y	Y
24 Gallegly	Y	Y	Y	N	Y	Y
25 McKeon	Y	Y	Y	N	Y	Y
26 Dreier	Y	Y	Y	N	Y	Y
27 Sherman	N	N	N	Y	Y	Y
28 Berman	N	N	N	Y	Y	Y
29 Schiff	N	N	N	Y	Y	Y
30 Waxman	N	N	N	Y	Y	Y
31 Becerra	N	N	N	Y	Y	Y
32 Chu	N	N	N	Y	Y	Y
33 Watson	N	N	N	Y	Y	Y
34 Roybal-Allard	N	N	N	Y	Y	Y
35 Waters	N	N	N	?	Y	Y
36 Harman	N	N	N	Y	Y	Y
37 Richardson	N	N	N	Y	Y	Y
38 Napolitano	N	N	N	Y	Y	Y
39 Sánchez, Linda	−	−	−	+	Y	Y
40 Royce	Y	Y	Y	N	Y	Y
41 Lewis	Y	Y	Y	N	Y	Y
42 Miller, Gary	Y	Y	Y	N	Y	Y
43 Baca	N	N	N	Y	Y	Y
44 Calvert	Y	Y	Y	N	Y	Y
45 Bono Mack	Y	Y	Y	N	Y	Y
46 Rohrabacher	Y	Y	Y	N	N	Y
47 Sanchez, Loretta	N	N	N	Y	Y	Y
48 Campbell	Y	Y	Y	N	N	Y
49 Issa	Y	Y	?	N	Y	Y
50 Bilbray	Y	Y	Y	N	Y	Y
51 Filner	N	N	N	Y	Y	Y
52 Hunter	Y	Y	Y	N	Y	Y
53 Davis	N	N	N	Y	Y	Y

	872	873	874	875	876	877
COLORADO						
1 DeGette	N	N	N	Y	Y	Y
2 Polis	N	N	N	Y	Y	Y
3 Salazar	N	Y	N	Y	Y	Y
4 Markey	N	N	N	N	Y	Y
5 Lamborn	Y	Y	Y	N	N	Y
6 Coffman	Y	Y	Y	N	Y	Y
7 Perlmutter	N	N	N	Y	Y	Y
CONNECTICUT						
1 Larson	N	N	N	Y	Y	Y
2 Courtney	N	N	N	Y	Y	Y
3 DeLauro	N	N	N	Y	Y	Y
4 Himes	N	N	N	Y	Y	Y
5 Murphy	N	N	N	Y	Y	Y
DELAWARE						
AL Castle	Y	Y	Y	N	Y	Y
FLORIDA						
1 Miller	Y	Y	Y	N	Y	Y
2 Boyd	N	N	N	Y	Y	Y
3 Brown	N	N	N	Y	Y	Y
4 Crenshaw	Y	Y	Y	N	Y	Y
5 Brown-Waite	Y	Y	Y	N	Y	Y
6 Stearns	Y	Y	Y	N	Y	Y
7 Mica	Y	Y	Y	N	Y	Y
8 Grayson	N	N	N	Y	Y	Y
9 Bilirakis	Y	Y	Y	N	Y	Y
10 Young	Y	Y	Y	N	Y	Y
11 Castor	N	N	N	Y	Y	Y
12 Putnam	Y	Y	Y	N	Y	Y
13 Buchanan	Y	Y	Y	N	Y	Y
14 Mack	Y	Y	Y	N	Y	Y
15 Posey	Y	Y	Y	N	Y	Y
16 Rooney	Y	Y	Y	N	Y	Y
17 Meek	N	N	N	Y	Y	Y
18 Ros-Lehtinen	Y	Y	Y	N	Y	Y
19 Wexler	N	N	N	Y	Y	Y
20 Wasserman Schultz	N	N	N	Y	Y	Y
21 Diaz-Balart, L.	Y	Y	Y	N	Y	Y
22 Klein	N	N	N	Y	Y	Y
23 Hastings	N	N	N	Y	Y	Y
24 Kosmas	N	N	N	Y	Y	Y
25 Diaz-Balart, M.	Y	Y	Y	N	Y	Y
GEORGIA						
1 Kingston	Y	Y	Y	N	Y	Y
2 Bishop	N	N	N	Y	Y	Y
3 Westmoreland	Y	Y	Y	N	Y	Y
4 Johnson	N	N	N	Y	Y	Y
5 Lewis	N	N	N	Y	Y	Y
6 Price	Y	Y	Y	N	N	Y
7 Linder	Y	Y	Y	N	Y	Y
8 Marshall	Y	Y	Y	N	Y	Y
9 Deal	Y	Y	Y	N	Y	Y
10 Broun	Y	Y	Y	N	N	N
11 Gingrey	Y	Y	Y	N	Y	Y
12 Barrow	N	N	N	Y	Y	Y
13 Scott	N	N	N	Y	Y	Y
HAWAII						
1 Abercrombie	N	N	N	Y	Y	Y
2 Hirono	N	N	N	Y	Y	Y
IDAHO						
1 Minnick	Y	Y	Y	N	Y	Y
2 Simpson	Y	Y	Y	N	Y	Y
ILLINOIS						
1 Rush	N	N	N	Y	Y	Y
2 Jackson	N	N	N	Y	Y	Y
3 Lipinski	N	N	N	Y	Y	Y
4 Gutierrez	N	N	N	Y	Y	Y
5 Quigley	N	N	N	Y	Y	Y
6 Roskam	Y	Y	Y	N	Y	Y
7 Davis	N	N	N	Y	Y	Y
8 Bean	N	Y	N	Y	Y	Y
9 Schakowsky	N	N	N	Y	Y	Y
10 Kirk	Y	Y	Y	N	Y	Y
11 Halvorson	Y	N	N	Y	Y	Y
12 Costello	Y	N	N	Y	Y	Y
13 Biggert	Y	Y	Y	N	Y	Y
14 Foster	N	N	N	Y	Y	Y
15 Johnson	Y	N	Y	N	Y	Y

	872	873	874	875	876	877
16 **Manzullo**	Y	Y	Y	N	Y	Y
17 Hare	N	N	Y	N	Y	Y
18 **Schock**	Y	Y	Y	N	Y	Y
19 **Shimkus**	Y	Y	Y	N	Y	Y
INDIANA						
1 Visclosky	N	N	N	Y	Y	Y
2 Donnelly	Y	Y	Y	Y	Y	Y
3 **Souder**	Y	Y	Y	N	Y	Y
4 **Buyer**	Y	Y	Y	N	Y	Y
5 **Burton**	Y	Y	Y	N	Y	Y
6 **Pence**	Y	Y	Y	N	Y	Y
7 Carson	N	N	N	Y	Y	Y
8 Ellsworth	Y	Y	N	Y	Y	Y
9 Hill	N	N	N	Y	Y	Y
IOWA						
1 Braley	N	N	N	Y	Y	Y
2 Loebsack	N	N	N	Y	Y	Y
3 Boswell	Y	Y	N	Y	Y	Y
4 **Latham**	Y	Y	Y	N	Y	Y
5 **King**	Y	?	Y	N	Y	Y
KANSAS						
1 **Moran**	Y	Y	Y	N	Y	Y
2 **Jenkins**	Y	Y	Y	N	Y	Y
3 Moore	N	N	N	Y	Y	Y
4 **Tiahrt**	Y	Y	Y	N	Y	Y
KENTUCKY						
1 **Whitfield**	Y	Y	Y	N	Y	Y
2 **Guthrie**	Y	Y	Y	N	Y	Y
3 Yarmuth	N	N	N	Y	Y	Y
4 **Davis**	Y	Y	Y	N	Y	Y
5 **Rogers**	Y	Y	Y	N	Y	Y
6 Chandler	?	?	?	?	Y	Y
LOUISIANA						
1 **Scalise**	Y	Y	Y	N	Y	Y
2 **Cao**	Y	Y	Y	N	Y	Y
3 Melancon	N	N	N	Y	Y	Y
4 **Fleming**	Y	Y	Y	N	Y	Y
5 **Alexander**	Y	Y	Y	N	Y	Y
6 **Cassidy**	Y	Y	Y	N	Y	Y
7 **Boustany**	Y	Y	Y	N	Y	Y
MAINE						
1 Pingree	N	N	N	Y	Y	Y
2 Michaud	N	N	N	Y	Y	Y
MARYLAND						
1 Kratovil	N	Y	N	Y	Y	Y
2 Ruppersberger	N	N	N	Y	Y	Y
3 Sarbanes	N	N	N	Y	Y	Y
4 Edwards	N	N	N	Y	Y	Y
5 Hoyer	N	N	N	Y	Y	Y
6 **Bartlett**	Y	Y	Y	N	Y	Y
7 Cummings	N	N	N	Y	?	Y
8 Van Hollen	N	N	N	Y	Y	Y
MASSACHUSETTS						
1 Olver	N	N	N	Y	Y	Y
2 Neal	N	N	N	Y	Y	Y
3 McGovern	N	N	N	Y	Y	Y
4 Frank	N	N	N	Y	Y	Y
5 Tsongas	N	N	N	Y	Y	Y
6 Tierney	N	N	N	Y	Y	Y
7 Markey	N	N	N	Y	Y	Y
8 Capuano	N	N	N	Y	Y	Y
9 Lynch	N	N	N	Y	Y	Y
10 Delahunt	N	N	N	Y	Y	Y
MICHIGAN						
1 Stupak	N	N	N	Y	Y	Y
2 **Hoekstra**	Y	Y	Y	N	Y	Y
3 **Ehlers**	?	?	?	?	Y	Y
4 **Camp**	Y	Y	Y	N	Y	Y
5 Kildee	N	N	N	Y	Y	Y
6 **Upton**	Y	Y	Y	N	Y	Y
7 Schauer	N	N	N	Y	Y	Y
8 **Rogers**	?	?	?	?	Y	Y
9 Peters	N	N	N	Y	Y	Y
10 **Miller**	Y	Y	Y	N	Y	Y
11 **McCotter**	Y	Y	Y	N	Y	Y
12 Levin	N	N	N	Y	Y	Y
13 Kilpatrick	N	N	N	Y	Y	Y
14 Conyers	N	N	N	Y	?	Y
15 Dingell	N	N	N	Y	Y	Y
MINNESOTA						
1 Walz	N	N	N	Y	Y	Y
2 **Kline**	Y	Y	Y	N	Y	Y
3 **Paulsen**	Y	Y	Y	N	Y	Y
4 McCollum	N	N	N	Y	Y	Y

	872	873	874	875	876	877
5 Ellison	N	N	N	Y	Y	Y
6 **Bachmann**	Y	Y	Y	N	N	Y
7 Peterson	N	N	N	Y	Y	Y
8 Oberstar	N	N	N	Y	Y	Y
MISSISSIPPI						
1 Childers	N	N	Y	Y	Y	Y
2 Thompson	N	N	N	Y	Y	Y
3 **Harper**	Y	Y	Y	N	Y	Y
4 Taylor	Y	Y	Y	N	Y	Y
MISSOURI						
1 Clay	N	N	N	Y	Y	Y
2 **Akin**	Y	Y	Y	N	Y	Y
3 Carnahan	N	N	N	Y	Y	Y
4 Skelton	Y	N	N	N	Y	Y
5 Cleaver	?	N	N	?	Y	Y
6 **Graves**	Y	Y	Y	N	Y	Y
7 **Blunt**	Y	Y	Y	N	Y	Y
8 **Emerson**	Y	Y	Y	N	Y	Y
9 **Luetkemeyer**	Y	Y	Y	N	Y	Y
MONTANA						
AL **Rehberg**	Y	Y	Y	N	Y	Y
NEBRASKA						
1 **Fortenberry**	Y	Y	Y	N	Y	Y
2 **Terry**	Y	Y	Y	N	Y	Y
3 **Smith**	Y	Y	Y	N	Y	Y
NEVADA						
1 Berkley	N	N	N	Y	Y	Y
2 **Heller**	Y	Y	Y	N	Y	Y
3 Titus	N	N	N	Y	Y	Y
NEW HAMPSHIRE						
1 Shea-Porter	N	N	N	Y	Y	Y
2 Hodes	N	N	N	Y	Y	Y
NEW JERSEY						
1 Andrews	N	N	N	Y	Y	Y
2 **LoBiondo**	Y	Y	Y	N	Y	Y
3 Adler	N	Y	N	Y	Y	Y
4 **Smith**	Y	Y	Y	N	Y	Y
5 **Garrett**	Y	Y	Y	N	Y	Y
6 Pallone	N	N	N	Y	Y	Y
7 **Lance**	Y	Y	Y	N	Y	Y
8 Pascrell	N	N	N	Y	Y	Y
9 Rothman	N	N	N	Y	Y	Y
10 Payne	N	N	N	Y	Y	Y
11 **Frelinghuysen**	Y	Y	Y	N	Y	Y
12 Holt	N	N	N	Y	Y	Y
13 Sires	N	N	N	Y	Y	Y
NEW MEXICO						
1 Heinrich	N	N	N	Y	Y	Y
2 Teague	Y	Y	Y	N	Y	Y
3 Lujan	N	N	N	Y	Y	Y
NEW YORK						
1 Bishop	N	N	N	Y	Y	Y
2 Israel	N	N	N	Y	Y	Y
3 **King**	Y	Y	Y	N	Y	Y
4 McCarthy	N	N	N	Y	Y	Y
5 Ackerman	N	N	N	Y	Y	Y
6 Meeks	N	N	N	Y	Y	Y
7 Crowley	N	N	N	Y	Y	Y
8 Nadler	N	N	N	Y	Y	Y
9 Weiner	N	N	N	Y	Y	Y
10 Towns	N	N	N	Y	Y	Y
11 Clarke	N	N	N	Y	Y	Y
12 Velázquez	N	N	N	Y	Y	Y
13 McMahon	N	Y	N	Y	Y	Y
14 Maloney	N	N	N	Y	Y	Y
15 Rangel	N	N	N	Y	Y	Y
16 Serrano	N	N	N	Y	Y	Y
17 Engel	N	N	N	Y	?	Y
18 Lowey	N	N	N	Y	Y	Y
19 Hall	N	N	N	Y	Y	Y
20 Murphy	N	Y	N	Y	Y	Y
21 Tonko	N	N	N	Y	Y	Y
22 Hinchey	N	N	N	Y	?	?
23 Owens	N	N	N	Y	Y	Y
24 Arcuri	Y	Y	N	Y	Y	Y
25 Maffei	N	N	N	Y	Y	Y
26 **Lee**	Y	Y	Y	N	Y	Y
27 Higgins	N	N	N	Y	Y	Y
28 Slaughter	N	N	N	Y	Y	Y
29 Massa	N	N	Y	Y	Y	Y
NORTH CAROLINA						
1 Butterfield	N	N	N	Y	Y	Y
2 Etheridge	N	N	N	Y	Y	Y
3 **Jones**	Y	Y	Y	N	Y	Y
4 Price	N	N	N	Y	Y	Y

	872	873	874	875	876	877
5 **Foxx**	Y	Y	Y	N	N	Y
6 **Coble**	Y	Y	Y	N	Y	Y
7 McIntyre	N	N	N	Y	Y	Y
8 Kissell	N	N	N	Y	Y	Y
9 **Myrick**	Y	Y	Y	N	N	Y
10 **McHenry**	Y	Y	Y	N	N	Y
11 Shuler	N	N	N	Y	Y	Y
12 Watt	N	Y	N	Y	Y	Y
13 Miller	N	N	N	Y	Y	Y
NORTH DAKOTA						
AL Pomeroy	Y	Y	N	Y	Y	Y
OHIO						
1 Driehaus	N	N	N	Y	Y	Y
2 **Schmidt**	Y	Y	Y	N	Y	Y
3 **Turner**	Y	Y	Y	N	Y	Y
4 **Jordan**	Y	Y	Y	N	N	Y
5 **Latta**	Y	Y	Y	N	Y	Y
6 Wilson	N	N	N	Y	Y	Y
7 **Austria**	Y	Y	Y	N	Y	Y
8 **Boehner**	Y	Y	Y	N	Y	Y
9 Kaptur	N	N	N	Y	Y	Y
10 Kucinich	N	N	N	Y	Y	Y
11 Fudge	N	N	N	Y	Y	Y
12 **Tiberi**	Y	Y	Y	N	Y	Y
13 Sutton	N	N	N	Y	Y	Y
14 **LaTourette**	Y	Y	Y	N	Y	Y
15 Kilroy	N	N	N	Y	Y	Y
16 Boccieri	N	N	N	N	Y	Y
17 Ryan	N	N	N	Y	Y	Y
18 Space	Y	N	Y	N	Y	Y
OKLAHOMA						
1 **Sullivan**	Y	Y	Y	N	Y	Y
2 Boren	Y	Y	Y	N	Y	Y
3 **Lucas**	Y	Y	Y	N	Y	Y
4 **Cole**	Y	Y	Y	N	Y	Y
5 **Fallin**	Y	Y	Y	N	Y	Y
OREGON						
1 Wu	N	N	N	Y	Y	Y
2 **Walden**	Y	Y	Y	N	Y	Y
3 Blumenauer	N	N	N	Y	Y	Y
4 DeFazio	N	N	N	Y	Y	Y
5 Schrader	N	N	N	Y	Y	Y
PENNSYLVANIA						
1 Brady	N	N	N	Y	Y	Y
2 Fattah	N	N	N	Y	Y	Y
3 Dahlkemper	N	Y	N	Y	Y	Y
4 Altmire	N	Y	N	Y	Y	Y
5 **Thompson**	Y	Y	Y	N	Y	Y
6 **Gerlach**	Y	Y	Y	N	Y	Y
7 Sestak	N	N	N	Y	Y	Y
8 Murphy, P.	?	?	?	?	Y	Y
9 **Shuster**	Y	Y	Y	N	Y	Y
10 Carney	N	N	N	Y	Y	Y
11 Kanjorski	N	N	N	Y	Y	Y
12 Murtha	N	N	N	Y	Y	Y
13 Schwartz	N	N	N	Y	Y	Y
14 Doyle	N	N	N	Y	Y	Y
15 **Dent**	Y	Y	Y	N	Y	Y
16 **Pitts**	Y	Y	Y	N	Y	Y
17 Holden	Y	N	N	Y	Y	Y
18 **Murphy, T.**	Y	Y	Y	N	Y	Y
19 **Platts**	Y	Y	Y	N	Y	Y
RHODE ISLAND						
1 Kennedy	N	N	N	Y	Y	Y
2 Langevin	N	N	N	Y	?	Y
SOUTH CAROLINA						
1 **Brown**	Y	Y	Y	N	Y	Y
2 **Wilson**	Y	Y	Y	N	Y	Y
3 **Barrett**	Y	Y	Y	N	Y	Y
4 **Inglis**	Y	Y	Y	N	Y	Y
5 Spratt	N	Y	N	Y	Y	Y
6 Clyburn	N	N	N	Y	Y	Y
SOUTH DAKOTA						
AL Herseth Sandlin	Y	N	Y	N	Y	Y
TENNESSEE						
1 **Roe**	Y	Y	Y	N	Y	Y
2 **Duncan**	Y	Y	Y	N	N	Y
3 **Wamp**	Y	Y	Y	N	Y	Y
4 Davis	N	N	N	Y	Y	Y
5 Cooper	N	Y	N	Y	Y	Y
6 Gordon	N	Y	N	Y	Y	Y
7 **Blackburn**	Y	Y	Y	N	Y	Y
8 Tanner	Y	N	N	Y	Y	Y
9 Cohen	N	N	N	Y	Y	Y

	872	873	874	875	876	877
TEXAS						
1 **Gohmert**	Y	?	Y	N	Y	Y
2 **Poe**	Y	Y	Y	N	Y	Y
3 **Johnson, S.**	Y	Y	Y	N	Y	Y
4 **Hall**	Y	Y	Y	N	Y	Y
5 **Hensarling**	Y	Y	Y	N	N	Y
6 **Barton**	Y	Y	Y	N	Y	Y
7 **Culberson**	Y	Y	Y	N	N	Y
8 **Brady**	Y	Y	Y	N	Y	Y
9 Green, A.	N	N	N	Y	Y	Y
10 **McCaul**	Y	Y	Y	N	Y	Y
11 **Conaway**	?	?	?	?	N	Y
12 **Granger**	Y	Y	Y	N	Y	Y
13 **Thornberry**	Y	Y	Y	N	Y	Y
14 **Paul**	Y	Y	Y	N	N	N
15 Hinojosa	N	N	N	Y	Y	Y
16 Reyes	N	N	N	Y	Y	Y
17 Edwards	N	N	N	Y	Y	Y
18 Jackson Lee	N	N	N	Y	Y	Y
19 **Neugebauer**	Y	Y	Y	N	N	Y
20 Gonzalez	N	N	N	Y	Y	Y
21 **Smith**	Y	Y	Y	N	Y	Y
22 **Olson**	Y	Y	Y	N	Y	Y
23 Rodriguez	N	N	N	Y	Y	Y
24 **Marchant**	Y	Y	Y	N	Y	Y
25 Doggett	N	N	N	Y	Y	Y
26 **Burgess**	Y	Y	Y	N	N	Y
27 Ortiz	N	N	N	Y	Y	Y
28 Cuellar	N	N	N	Y	Y	Y
29 Green, G.	N	N	N	Y	Y	Y
30 Johnson, E.	N	N	N	Y	Y	Y
31 **Carter**	–	+	+	–	Y	Y
32 **Sessions**	Y	Y	Y	N	Y	Y
UTAH						
1 **Bishop**	Y	Y	Y	N	Y	Y
2 Matheson	N	N	N	Y	Y	Y
3 **Chaffetz**	Y	Y	Y	N	N	Y
VERMONT						
AL Welch	N	N	N	Y	Y	Y
VIRGINIA						
1 **Wittman**	Y	Y	Y	N	Y	Y
2 Nye	N	N	N	Y	Y	Y
3 Scott	N	N	N	Y	Y	Y
4 **Forbes**	Y	Y	Y	N	Y	Y
5 Perriello	N	N	Y	N	Y	Y
6 **Goodlatte**	Y	Y	Y	N	Y	Y
7 **Cantor**	Y	Y	Y	N	Y	Y
8 Moran	N	N	N	Y	Y	Y
9 Boucher	N	N	N	Y	Y	Y
10 **Wolf**	Y	Y	Y	N	Y	Y
11 Connolly	N	N	N	Y	Y	Y
WASHINGTON						
1 Inslee	N	N	N	Y	Y	Y
2 Larsen	N	N	N	Y	Y	Y
3 Baird	Y	Y	Y	N	Y	Y
4 **Hastings**	Y	Y	Y	N	Y	Y
5 **McMorris Rodgers**	Y	Y	Y	N	Y	Y
6 Dicks	N	N	N	Y	Y	Y
7 McDermott	N	N	N	?	Y	Y
8 **Reichert**	Y	Y	Y	N	Y	Y
9 Smith	N	N	N	Y	Y	Y
WEST VIRGINIA						
1 Mollohan	N	N	N	Y	Y	Y
2 **Capito**	Y	Y	Y	N	Y	Y
3 Rahall	N	N	N	Y	Y	Y
WISCONSIN						
1 **Ryan**	Y	Y	Y	N	Y	Y
2 Baldwin	N	N	N	Y	Y	Y
3 Kind	N	N	N	Y	Y	Y
4 Moore	N	N	N	Y	Y	Y
5 **Sensenbrenner**	Y	Y	Y	N	Y	Y
6 **Petri**	Y	Y	Y	N	Y	Y
7 Obey	N	N	N	Y	Y	Y
8 Kagen	N	N	N	Y	Y	Y
WYOMING						
AL **Lummis**	Y	Y	Y	N	Y	Y
DELEGATES						
Faleomavaega (A.S.)	N	N				
Norton (D.C.)	?	?				
Bordallo (Guam)	N	N				
Sablan (N. Marianas)	N	N				
Pierluisi (P.R.)	N	N				
Christensen (V.I.)	N	N				

IN THE HOUSE | By Vote Number

878. HR 1845. Small-Business Development Center Grants/ Passage. Velázquez, D-N.Y., motion to suspend the rules and pass the bill that would authorize $150 million in fiscal 2010 and $160 million in fiscal 2011 for the Small Business Administration's development center program and require that new grants go to higher education institutions that are fully accredited. It would prohibit the administration from interfering in grant recipients' hiring practices and limit states other than California and Texas to one center each. Motion agreed to 412-20: D 256-0; R 156-20. A two-thirds majority of those present and voting (288 in this case) is required for passage under suspension of the rules. Nov. 7, 2009.

879. H Res 700. National School Psychology Week/Adoption. Loebsack, D-Iowa, motion to suspend the rules and adopt the resolution that would support the designation of National School Psychology Week and would honor and recognize the contributions of school psychologists to the success of students. Motion agreed to 431-1: D 257-0; R 174-1. A two-thirds majority of those present and voting (288 in this case) is required for adoption under suspension of the rules. Nov. 7, 2009.

880. H Res 877. Support of Huang Qi and Tan Zuoren/Adoption. Berman, D-Calif., motion to suspend the rules and adopt the resolution that would express support for Huang Qi and Tan Zuoren for engaging in peaceful expression as they seek answers and justice for the parents of the children killed in the Sichuan earthquake in May 2008. It also would call on China to provide them the right of freedom of speech and the right to make suggestions to officials free from suppression and retaliation. Motion agreed to 426-1: D 253-0; R 173-1. A two-thirds majority of those present and voting (285 in this case) is required for adoption under suspension of the rules. Nov. 7, 2009.

881. HR 3962, HR 3961. Health Care Overhaul, Medicare Physician Payment/Previous Question. Slaughter, D-N.Y., motion to order the previous question (thus ending debate and possibility of amendment) on adoption of the rule (H Res 903) that would provide for House floor consideration of the bill (HR 3962) that would overhaul the health care system and the bill (HR 3961) that would update the Medicare payment rates for physician services. Motion agreed to 247-187: D 247-10; R 0-177. Nov. 7, 2009.

882. HR 3962, HR 3961. Health Care Overhaul, Medicare Physician Payment/Rule. Adoption of the rule (H Res 903) that would provide for House floor consideration of the bill (HR 3962) that would overhaul the health care system and the bill (HR 3961) that would update the Medicare payment rates for physician services. Adopted 242-192: D 242-15; R 0-177. Nov. 7, 2009.

883. H Res 892. Anniversary of End of Cold War/Adoption. Berman, D-Calif., motion to suspend the rules and adopt the resolution that would recognize the events of 1989 that helped lead to the end of the Cold War and congratulate the countries of central and Eastern Europe for the progress they have made in the past 20 years. Motion agreed to 431-1: D 256-0; R 175-1. A two-thirds majority of those present and voting (288 in this case) is required for adoption under suspension of the rules. Nov. 7, 2009.

	878	879	880	881	882	883
ALABAMA						
1 Bonner	Y	Y	Y	N	N	Y
2 Bright	Y	Y	Y	N	N	Y
3 Rogers	Y	Y	Y	N	N	Y
4 Aderholt	Y	Y	Y	N	N	Y
5 Griffith	Y	Y	Y	N	N	Y
6 Bachus	Y	Y	Y	N	N	Y
7 Davis	Y	Y	Y	N	N	Y
ALASKA						
AL Young	?	?	?	N	N	Y
ARIZONA						
1 Kirkpatrick	Y	Y	Y	Y	Y	Y
2 Franks	N	Y	Y	N	N	Y
3 Shadegg	N	Y	Y	N	N	Y
4 Pastor	Y	Y	Y	Y	Y	Y
5 Mitchell	Y	Y	Y	Y	Y	Y
6 Flake	N	Y	Y	N	N	Y
7 Grijalva	Y	Y	Y	Y	Y	Y
8 Giffords	Y	Y	Y	Y	Y	Y
ARKANSAS						
1 Berry	Y	Y	Y	Y	Y	Y
2 Snyder	Y	Y	Y	Y	Y	Y
3 Boozman	Y	Y	Y	N	N	Y
4 Ross	Y	Y	Y	Y	Y	Y
CALIFORNIA						
1 Thompson	Y	Y	Y	Y	Y	Y
2 Herger	Y	Y	Y	N	N	Y
3 Lungren	Y	Y	Y	N	N	Y
4 McClintock	N	Y	Y	N	N	Y
5 Matsui	Y	Y	Y	Y	Y	Y
6 Woolsey	Y	Y	Y	Y	Y	Y
7 Miller, George	Y	Y	Y	Y	Y	Y
8 Pelosi						
9 Lee	Y	Y	Y	Y	Y	Y
10 Garamendi	Y	Y	Y	Y	Y	Y
11 McNerney	Y	Y	Y	Y	Y	Y
12 Speier	Y	Y	Y	Y	Y	Y
13 Stark	?	Y	Y	Y	Y	Y
14 Eshoo	Y	Y	Y	Y	Y	Y
15 Honda	Y	Y	Y	Y	Y	Y
16 Lofgren	Y	Y	Y	Y	Y	Y
17 Farr	Y	Y	Y	Y	Y	Y
18 Cardoza	Y	Y	Y	Y	Y	Y
19 Radanovich	Y	Y	Y	N	N	Y
20 Costa	Y	Y	Y	Y	Y	Y
21 Nunes	Y	Y	Y	N	N	Y
22 McCarthy	Y	Y	Y	N	N	Y
23 Capps	Y	Y	Y	Y	Y	Y
24 Gallegly	Y	Y	Y	N	N	Y
25 McKeon	Y	Y	Y	N	N	Y
26 Dreier	Y	Y	Y	N	N	Y
27 Sherman	Y	Y	Y	Y	Y	Y
28 Berman	Y	Y	Y	Y	Y	Y
29 Schiff	Y	Y	Y	Y	Y	Y
30 Waxman	Y	Y	Y	Y	Y	Y
31 Becerra	Y	Y	Y	Y	Y	Y
32 Chu	Y	Y	Y	Y	Y	Y
33 Watson	Y	Y	Y	Y	Y	Y
34 Roybal-Allard	Y	Y	Y	Y	Y	Y
35 Waters	Y	Y	Y	Y	Y	Y
36 Harman	Y	Y	Y	Y	Y	Y
37 Richardson	Y	Y	Y	Y	Y	Y
38 Napolitano	Y	Y	Y	Y	Y	Y
39 Sánchez, Linda	Y	Y	Y	Y	Y	Y
40 Royce	N	Y	Y	N	N	Y
41 Lewis	Y	Y	Y	N	N	Y
42 Miller, Gary	Y	Y	Y	N	N	Y
43 Baca	Y	Y	Y	Y	Y	Y
44 Calvert	Y	Y	Y	N	N	Y
45 Bono Mack	Y	?	Y	N	N	Y
46 Rohrabacher	N	Y	Y	N	N	Y
47 Sanchez, Loretta	Y	Y	Y	N	N	Y
48 Campbell	N	Y	N	N	N	Y
49 Issa	Y	Y	Y	N	N	Y
50 Bilbray	Y	Y	Y	N	N	Y
51 Filner	Y	Y	Y	Y	Y	Y
52 Hunter	Y	Y	Y	N	N	Y
53 Davis	Y	Y	Y	Y	Y	Y

	878	879	880	881	882	883
COLORADO						
1 DeGette	Y	Y	Y	Y	Y	Y
2 Polis	Y	Y	Y	Y	Y	Y
3 Salazar	Y	Y	Y	Y	Y	Y
4 Markey	Y	Y	Y	Y	Y	Y
5 Lamborn	N	Y	Y	N	N	Y
6 Coffman	Y	Y	Y	N	N	Y
7 Perlmutter	Y	Y	Y	Y	Y	Y
CONNECTICUT						
1 Larson	Y	Y	Y	Y	Y	Y
2 Courtney	Y	Y	Y	Y	Y	Y
3 DeLauro	Y	Y	Y	Y	Y	Y
4 Himes	Y	Y	Y	Y	Y	Y
5 Murphy	Y	Y	Y	Y	Y	Y
DELAWARE						
AL Castle	Y	Y	Y	N	N	Y
FLORIDA						
1 Miller	Y	Y	Y	N	N	Y
2 Boyd	Y	Y	Y	Y	Y	Y
3 Brown	Y	Y	Y	Y	Y	Y
4 Crenshaw	Y	Y	Y	N	N	Y
5 Brown-Waite	Y	Y	Y	N	N	Y
6 Stearns	Y	Y	Y	N	N	Y
7 Mica	Y	Y	Y	N	N	Y
8 Grayson	Y	Y	Y	Y	Y	Y
9 Bilirakis	Y	Y	Y	N	N	Y
10 Young	Y	Y	Y	N	N	Y
11 Castor	Y	Y	Y	Y	Y	Y
12 Putnam	Y	Y	Y	N	N	Y
13 Buchanan	Y	Y	Y	N	N	Y
14 Mack	Y	Y	Y	N	N	Y
15 Posey	Y	Y	Y	N	N	Y
16 Rooney	Y	Y	Y	N	N	Y
17 Meek	Y	Y	Y	Y	Y	Y
18 Ros-Lehtinen	Y	Y	Y	N	N	Y
19 Wexler	Y	Y	Y	Y	Y	Y
20 Wasserman Schultz	Y	Y	Y	Y	Y	Y
21 Diaz-Balart, L.	Y	Y	Y	N	N	Y
22 Klein	Y	Y	Y	Y	Y	Y
23 Hastings	Y	Y	Y	Y	Y	Y
24 Kosmas	Y	Y	Y	Y	Y	Y
25 Diaz-Balart, M.	Y	Y	Y	N	N	Y
GEORGIA						
1 Kingston	Y	Y	Y	N	N	Y
2 Bishop	Y	Y	Y	Y	Y	Y
3 Westmoreland	Y	Y	Y	N	N	Y
4 Johnson	Y	Y	Y	Y	Y	Y
5 Lewis	Y	Y	Y	Y	Y	Y
6 Price	Y	Y	Y	N	N	Y
7 Linder	Y	Y	Y	N	N	Y
8 Marshall	Y	Y	Y	Y	Y	Y
9 Deal	Y	Y	Y	N	N	Y
10 Broun	N	Y	Y	N	N	Y
11 Gingrey	Y	Y	Y	N	N	?
12 Barrow	Y	Y	Y	Y	Y	Y
13 Scott	Y	Y	Y	Y	Y	Y
HAWAII						
1 Abercrombie	Y	Y	Y	Y	Y	Y
2 Hirono	Y	Y	Y	Y	Y	Y
IDAHO						
1 Minnick	Y	Y	Y	N	N	Y
2 Simpson	Y	Y	Y	N	N	Y
ILLINOIS						
1 Rush	Y	Y	?	Y	Y	Y
2 Jackson	Y	Y	Y	Y	Y	Y
3 Lipinski	Y	Y	Y	Y	Y	Y
4 Gutierrez	Y	Y	Y	Y	Y	Y
5 Quigley	Y	Y	Y	Y	Y	Y
6 Roskam	Y	Y	Y	N	N	Y
7 Davis	Y	Y	Y	Y	Y	Y
8 Bean	Y	Y	Y	Y	Y	Y
9 Schakowsky	Y	Y	Y	Y	Y	Y
10 Kirk	Y	Y	Y	N	N	Y
11 Halvorson	Y	Y	Y	Y	Y	Y
12 Costello	Y	Y	Y	Y	Y	Y
13 Biggert	Y	Y	Y	N	N	Y
14 Foster	Y	Y	Y	Y	Y	Y
15 Johnson	Y	Y	Y	N	N	Y

KEY **Republicans** Democrats

Y	Voted for (yea)	X	Paired against
#	Paired for	–	Announced against
+	Announced for	P	Voted "present"
N	Voted against (nay)		

C Voted "present" to avoid possible conflict of interest
? Did not vote or otherwise make a position known

	878	879	880	881	882	883
16 **Manzullo**	Y	Y	Y	N	N	Y
17 Hare	Y	Y	Y	Y	Y	Y
18 **Schock**	Y	Y	Y	N	N	Y
19 **Shimkus**	Y	Y	Y	N	N	Y
INDIANA						
1 Visclosky	Y	Y	Y	Y	Y	Y
2 Donnelly	Y	Y	Y	Y	Y	Y
3 **Souder**	Y	Y	Y	N	N	Y
4 **Buyer**	Y	Y	Y	N	N	Y
5 **Burton**	Y	Y	Y	N	N	Y
6 **Pence**	Y	Y	Y	N	N	Y
7 Carson	Y	Y	Y	Y	Y	Y
8 Ellsworth	Y	Y	Y	Y	Y	Y
9 Hill	Y	Y	Y	Y	Y	Y
IOWA						
1 Braley	Y	Y	?	Y	Y	Y
2 Loebsack	Y	Y	Y	Y	Y	Y
3 Boswell	Y	Y	Y	Y	Y	Y
4 **Latham**	Y	Y	Y	N	N	Y
5 **King**	Y	Y	Y	N	N	Y
KANSAS						
1 **Moran**	Y	Y	Y	N	N	Y
2 **Jenkins**	Y	Y	Y	N	N	Y
3 Moore	Y	Y	?	Y	Y	Y
4 **Tiahrt**	Y	Y	Y	N	N	Y
KENTUCKY						
1 **Whitfield**	Y	Y	Y	N	N	Y
2 **Guthrie**	Y	Y	Y	N	N	Y
3 Yarmuth	Y	Y	Y	Y	Y	Y
4 **Davis**	Y	Y	Y	N	N	Y
5 **Rogers**	Y	Y	Y	N	N	Y
6 Chandler	Y	Y	Y	Y	Y	Y
LOUISIANA						
1 **Scalise**	Y	Y	Y	N	N	Y
2 **Cao**	Y	Y	Y	N	N	Y
3 Melancon	Y	Y	Y	N	N	Y
4 **Fleming**	Y	Y	Y	N	N	Y
5 **Alexander**	Y	Y	Y	N	N	Y
6 **Cassidy**	Y	Y	Y	N	N	Y
7 **Boustany**	Y	Y	Y	N	N	Y
MAINE						
1 Pingree	Y	Y	Y	Y	Y	Y
2 Michaud	Y	Y	Y	Y	Y	Y
MARYLAND						
1 Kratovil	Y	Y	Y	Y	N	Y
2 Ruppersberger	Y	Y	Y	Y	Y	Y
3 Sarbanes	Y	Y	Y	Y	Y	Y
4 Edwards	Y	Y	Y	Y	Y	Y
5 Hoyer	Y	Y	Y	Y	Y	Y
6 **Bartlett**	Y	Y	Y	N	N	Y
7 Cummings	Y	Y	Y	Y	Y	Y
8 Van Hollen	Y	Y	Y	Y	Y	Y
MASSACHUSETTS						
1 Olver	Y	Y	Y	Y	Y	Y
2 Neal	Y	Y	Y	Y	Y	Y
3 McGovern	Y	Y	Y	Y	Y	Y
4 Frank	Y	Y	Y	Y	Y	Y
5 Tsongas	Y	Y	Y	Y	Y	Y
6 Tierney	Y	Y	Y	Y	Y	Y
7 Markey	Y	Y	Y	Y	Y	Y
8 Capuano	Y	Y	Y	Y	Y	Y
9 Lynch	Y	Y	Y	Y	Y	Y
10 Delahunt	Y	Y	Y	Y	Y	Y
MICHIGAN						
1 Stupak	Y	Y	Y	Y	Y	Y
2 **Hoekstra**	Y	Y	Y	N	N	Y
3 **Ehlers**	Y	Y	Y	N	N	Y
4 **Camp**	Y	Y	Y	N	N	Y
5 Kildee	Y	Y	Y	Y	Y	Y
6 **Upton**	Y	Y	Y	N	N	Y
7 Schauer	Y	Y	Y	Y	Y	Y
8 **Rogers**	Y	Y	Y	N	N	Y
9 Peters	Y	Y	Y	Y	Y	Y
10 **Miller**	Y	Y	Y	N	N	Y
11 **McCotter**	Y	Y	Y	N	N	Y
12 Levin	Y	Y	Y	Y	Y	Y
13 Kilpatrick	Y	Y	Y	Y	Y	Y
14 Conyers	Y	Y	Y	Y	Y	Y
15 Dingell	Y	Y	Y	Y	Y	Y
MINNESOTA						
1 Walz	Y	Y	Y	Y	Y	Y
2 **Kline**	Y	Y	Y	N	N	Y
3 **Paulsen**	Y	Y	Y	N	N	Y
4 McCollum	Y	Y	Y	Y	Y	Y

	878	879	880	881	882	883
5 Ellison	Y	Y	Y	Y	Y	Y
6 **Bachmann**	N	Y	Y	N	N	Y
7 Peterson	Y	Y	Y	Y	Y	Y
8 Oberstar	Y	Y	Y	Y	Y	Y
MISSISSIPPI						
1 Childers	Y	Y	Y	N	N	Y
2 Thompson	Y	Y	Y	Y	Y	Y
3 **Harper**	Y	Y	Y	N	N	Y
4 Taylor	Y	Y	Y	N	N	Y
MISSOURI						
1 Clay	Y	Y	Y	Y	Y	Y
2 **Akin**	N	Y	Y	N	N	Y
3 Carnahan	Y	Y	Y	Y	Y	Y
4 Skelton	Y	Y	Y	Y	N	Y
5 Cleaver	Y	Y	Y	Y	Y	Y
6 **Graves**	Y	Y	Y	N	N	Y
7 **Blunt**	Y	Y	Y	N	N	Y
8 **Emerson**	Y	Y	Y	N	N	Y
9 **Luetkemeyer**	Y	Y	Y	N	N	Y
MONTANA						
AL **Rehberg**	Y	Y	Y	N	N	Y
NEBRASKA						
1 **Fortenberry**	Y	Y	Y	N	N	Y
2 **Terry**	Y	Y	Y	N	N	Y
3 **Smith**	Y	Y	Y	N	N	Y
NEVADA						
1 Berkley	Y	Y	Y	Y	Y	Y
2 **Heller**	Y	Y	Y	N	N	Y
3 Titus	Y	Y	Y	Y	Y	Y
NEW HAMPSHIRE						
1 Shea-Porter	Y	Y	Y	Y	Y	Y
2 Hodes	Y	Y	Y	Y	Y	Y
NEW JERSEY						
1 Andrews	Y	Y	Y	Y	Y	Y
2 **LoBiondo**	Y	Y	Y	N	N	Y
3 Adler	Y	Y	Y	Y	Y	Y
4 **Smith**	Y	Y	Y	N	N	Y
5 **Garrett**	N	Y	Y	N	N	Y
6 Pallone	Y	Y	Y	Y	Y	Y
7 **Lance**	Y	Y	Y	N	N	Y
8 Pascrell	Y	Y	Y	Y	Y	Y
9 Rothman	Y	Y	Y	Y	Y	Y
10 Payne	Y	Y	Y	Y	Y	Y
11 **Frelinghuysen**	Y	Y	Y	N	N	Y
12 Holt	Y	Y	Y	Y	Y	Y
13 Sires	Y	Y	Y	Y	Y	Y
NEW MEXICO						
1 Heinrich	Y	Y	Y	Y	Y	Y
2 Teague	Y	Y	Y	Y	Y	Y
3 Lujan	Y	Y	Y	Y	Y	Y
NEW YORK						
1 Bishop	Y	Y	Y	Y	Y	Y
2 Israel	Y	Y	Y	Y	Y	Y
3 **King**	Y	Y	Y	N	N	Y
4 McCarthy	Y	Y	Y	Y	Y	Y
5 Ackerman	Y	Y	Y	Y	Y	Y
6 Meeks	Y	Y	Y	Y	Y	Y
7 Crowley	Y	Y	Y	Y	Y	Y
8 Nadler	Y	Y	Y	Y	Y	Y
9 Weiner	Y	Y	Y	Y	Y	Y
10 Towns	Y	Y	Y	Y	Y	Y
11 Clarke	Y	Y	Y	Y	Y	Y
12 Velázquez	Y	Y	Y	Y	Y	Y
13 McMahon	Y	Y	Y	Y	Y	Y
14 Maloney	Y	Y	Y	Y	Y	Y
15 Rangel	Y	Y	Y	Y	Y	Y
16 Serrano	Y	Y	Y	Y	Y	Y
17 Engel	Y	Y	Y	Y	Y	Y
18 Lowey	Y	Y	Y	Y	Y	Y
19 Hall	Y	Y	Y	Y	Y	Y
20 Murphy	Y	Y	Y	Y	Y	Y
21 Tonko	Y	Y	Y	Y	Y	Y
22 Hinchey	Y	Y	Y	Y	Y	Y
23 Owens	Y	Y	Y	Y	Y	Y
24 Arcuri	Y	Y	Y	Y	Y	Y
25 Maffei	Y	Y	Y	Y	Y	Y
26 **Lee**	Y	Y	Y	N	N	Y
27 Higgins	Y	Y	Y	Y	Y	Y
28 Slaughter	Y	Y	Y	Y	Y	Y
29 Massa	Y	Y	Y	Y	Y	Y
NORTH CAROLINA						
1 Butterfield	Y	Y	Y	Y	Y	Y
2 Etheridge	Y	Y	Y	Y	Y	Y
3 **Jones**	Y	Y	Y	N	N	Y
4 Price	Y	Y	Y	Y	Y	Y

	878	879	880	881	882	883
5 **Foxx**	N	Y	Y	N	N	Y
6 **Coble**	Y	Y	Y	N	N	Y
7 McIntyre	Y	Y	Y	Y	Y	Y
8 Kissell	Y	Y	Y	Y	Y	Y
9 **Myrick**	Y	Y	Y	N	N	Y
10 **McHenry**	Y	Y	Y	N	N	Y
11 Shuler	Y	Y	Y	Y	N	Y
12 Watt	Y	Y	Y	Y	Y	Y
13 Miller	Y	Y	Y	Y	Y	Y
NORTH DAKOTA						
AL Pomeroy	Y	Y	Y	Y	Y	Y
OHIO						
1 Driehaus	Y	Y	Y	Y	Y	Y
2 **Schmidt**	Y	Y	Y	N	N	Y
3 **Turner**	Y	Y	Y	N	N	Y
4 **Jordan**	Y	Y	Y	N	N	Y
5 **Latta**	Y	Y	Y	N	N	Y
6 Wilson	Y	Y	Y	Y	Y	Y
7 **Austria**	Y	Y	Y	N	N	Y
8 **Boehner**	Y	Y	Y	N	N	Y
9 Kaptur	Y	Y	Y	Y	Y	Y
10 Kucinich	Y	Y	Y	Y	Y	Y
11 Fudge	Y	Y	Y	Y	Y	Y
12 **Tiberi**	Y	Y	Y	N	N	Y
13 Sutton	Y	Y	Y	Y	Y	Y
14 **LaTourette**	Y	Y	Y	N	N	Y
15 Kilroy	Y	Y	Y	Y	Y	Y
16 Boccieri	Y	Y	Y	Y	Y	Y
17 Ryan	Y	Y	Y	Y	Y	Y
18 Space	Y	Y	Y	Y	Y	Y
OKLAHOMA						
1 **Sullivan**	Y	Y	Y	N	N	Y
2 Boren	Y	Y	Y	N	N	Y
3 **Lucas**	Y	Y	Y	N	N	Y
4 **Cole**	Y	Y	Y	N	N	Y
5 **Fallin**	Y	Y	Y	N	N	Y
OREGON						
1 Wu	Y	Y	Y	Y	Y	Y
2 **Walden**	Y	Y	Y	N	N	Y
3 Blumenauer	Y	Y	Y	Y	Y	Y
4 DeFazio	Y	Y	Y	Y	Y	Y
5 Schrader	Y	Y	Y	Y	Y	Y
PENNSYLVANIA						
1 Brady	Y	Y	Y	Y	Y	Y
2 Fattah	Y	Y	Y	Y	Y	Y
3 Dahlkemper	Y	Y	Y	Y	Y	Y
4 Altmire	Y	Y	Y	Y	N	Y
5 **Thompson**	Y	Y	Y	N	N	Y
6 **Gerlach**	Y	Y	Y	N	N	Y
7 Sestak	Y	Y	Y	Y	Y	Y
8 Murphy, P.	Y	Y	Y	Y	Y	Y
9 **Shuster**	Y	Y	Y	N	N	Y
10 Carney	Y	Y	Y	Y	Y	Y
11 Kanjorski	Y	Y	Y	Y	Y	Y
12 Murtha	Y	Y	Y	Y	Y	Y
13 Schwartz	Y	Y	Y	Y	Y	Y
14 Doyle	Y	Y	Y	Y	Y	Y
15 **Dent**	Y	Y	Y	N	N	Y
16 **Pitts**	Y	Y	Y	N	N	Y
17 Holden	Y	Y	Y	Y	Y	Y
18 **Murphy, T.**	Y	Y	Y	N	N	Y
19 **Platts**	Y	Y	Y	N	N	Y
RHODE ISLAND						
1 Kennedy	Y	Y	Y	Y	Y	Y
2 Langevin	Y	Y	Y	Y	Y	Y
SOUTH CAROLINA						
1 **Brown**	Y	Y	Y	N	N	Y
2 **Wilson**	Y	Y	Y	N	N	Y
3 **Barrett**	Y	Y	Y	N	N	Y
4 **Inglis**	Y	Y	Y	N	N	Y
5 Spratt	Y	Y	Y	Y	Y	Y
6 Clyburn	Y	Y	Y	Y	Y	Y
SOUTH DAKOTA						
AL Herseth Sandlin	Y	Y	Y	Y	Y	Y
TENNESSEE						
1 **Roe**	Y	Y	Y	N	N	Y
2 **Duncan**	N	Y	Y	N	N	Y
3 **Wamp**	Y	Y	Y	N	N	Y
4 Davis	Y	Y	Y	Y	Y	Y
5 Cooper	Y	Y	Y	Y	Y	Y
6 Gordon	Y	Y	Y	Y	Y	Y
7 **Blackburn**	Y	Y	?	N	N	Y
8 Tanner	Y	Y	Y	Y	Y	Y
9 Cohen	Y	Y	Y	Y	Y	Y

	878	879	880	881	882	883
TEXAS						
1 **Gohmert**	Y	Y	Y	N	N	Y
2 **Poe**	Y	Y	Y	N	N	Y
3 **Johnson, S.**	Y	Y	Y	N	N	Y
4 **Hall**	Y	Y	Y	N	N	Y
5 **Hensarling**	N	Y	Y	N	N	Y
6 **Barton**	Y	Y	Y	N	N	Y
7 **Culberson**	N	Y	Y	N	N	Y
8 **Brady**	Y	Y	Y	N	N	Y
9 Green, A.	Y	Y	Y	Y	Y	Y
10 **McCaul**	Y	Y	Y	N	N	Y
11 **Conaway**	N	Y	Y	N	N	Y
12 **Granger**	Y	Y	Y	N	N	Y
13 **Thornberry**	Y	Y	Y	N	N	Y
14 **Paul**	N	N	N	N	N	N
15 Hinojosa	Y	Y	Y	Y	Y	Y
16 Reyes	Y	Y	Y	Y	Y	Y
17 Edwards	Y	Y	Y	Y	Y	Y
18 Jackson Lee	Y	Y	Y	Y	Y	Y
19 **Neugebauer**	N	Y	Y	N	N	Y
20 Gonzalez	Y	Y	Y	Y	Y	Y
21 **Smith**	Y	Y	Y	N	N	Y
22 **Olson**	Y	Y	Y	N	N	Y
23 Rodriguez	Y	Y	Y	Y	Y	Y
24 **Marchant**	Y	Y	?	N	N	Y
25 Doggett	Y	Y	Y	Y	Y	Y
26 **Burgess**	Y	Y	Y	N	N	Y
27 Ortiz	Y	Y	Y	Y	Y	Y
28 Cuellar	Y	Y	Y	Y	Y	Y
29 Green, G.	Y	Y	?	Y	Y	Y
30 Johnson, E.	Y	Y	Y	Y	Y	Y
31 **Carter**	Y	Y	Y	N	N	Y
32 **Sessions**	Y	Y	Y	N	N	Y
UTAH						
1 **Bishop**	Y	Y	Y	N	N	Y
2 Matheson	Y	Y	Y	Y	Y	Y
3 **Chaffetz**	Y	Y	Y	N	N	Y
VERMONT						
AL Welch	Y	Y	Y	Y	Y	Y
VIRGINIA						
1 **Wittman**	Y	Y	Y	N	N	Y
2 Nye	Y	Y	Y	Y	Y	Y
3 Scott	Y	Y	Y	Y	Y	Y
4 **Forbes**	Y	Y	Y	N	N	Y
5 Perriello	Y	Y	Y	Y	Y	Y
6 **Goodlatte**	Y	Y	Y	N	N	Y
7 **Cantor**	Y	Y	Y	N	N	Y
8 Moran	Y	Y	Y	Y	Y	?
9 Boucher	Y	Y	Y	Y	Y	Y
10 **Wolf**	Y	Y	Y	N	N	Y
11 Connolly	Y	Y	Y	Y	Y	Y
WASHINGTON						
1 Inslee	Y	Y	Y	Y	Y	Y
2 Larsen	Y	Y	Y	Y	Y	Y
3 Baird	Y	Y	Y	Y	N	Y
4 **Hastings**	Y	Y	Y	N	N	Y
5 **McMorris Rodgers**	Y	Y	Y	N	N	Y
6 Dicks	Y	Y	Y	Y	Y	Y
7 McDermott	Y	Y	Y	Y	Y	Y
8 **Reichert**	Y	Y	Y	N	N	Y
9 Smith	Y	Y	Y	Y	Y	Y
WEST VIRGINIA						
1 Mollohan	Y	Y	Y	Y	Y	Y
2 **Capito**	Y	Y	Y	N	N	Y
3 Rahall	Y	Y	Y	Y	Y	Y
WISCONSIN						
1 **Ryan**	Y	Y	Y	N	N	Y
2 Baldwin	Y	Y	Y	Y	Y	Y
3 Kind	Y	Y	Y	Y	Y	Y
4 Moore	Y	Y	Y	Y	Y	Y
5 **Sensenbrenner**	Y	Y	Y	N	N	Y
6 **Petri**	Y	Y	Y	N	N	Y
7 Obey	Y	Y	Y	Y	Y	Y
8 Kagen	Y	Y	Y	Y	Y	Y
WYOMING						
AL **Lummis**	N	Y	Y	N	N	Y
DELEGATES						
Faleomavaega (A.S.)						
Norton (D.C.)						
Bordallo (Guam)						
Sablan (N. Marianas)						
Pierluisi (P.R.)						
Christensen (V.I.)						

IN THE HOUSE | By Vote Number

884. **HR 3962. Health Care Overhaul/Abortion Funding Ban.** Stupak, D-Mich., amendment that would bar the use of federal funds authorized in the bill to pay for abortion or to cover any part of the costs of any health plan that includes abortion coverage, unless the pregnancy is the result of rape or incest or would endanger the woman's life. Individuals with subsidized policies who also want abortion coverage would have to purchase it separately, using their own money. The amendment would prohibit individuals from using affordability credits to purchase a plan that provides for elective abortions. Adopted 240-194: D 64-194; R 176-0. Nov. 7, 2009.

885. **HR 3962. Health Care Overhaul/Republican Substitute.** Boehner, R-Ohio, substitute amendment that would require each state to establish a reinsurance health care program or high-risk pool by 2010, allow small businesses to pool together through association health plans, and allow consumers to purchase licensed health insurance in any state, not just their state of residence. It would prohibit any federal funding from being used to pay for abortions, unless the pregnancy is the result of rape or incest or the woman's life is in danger; provide incentives for states that reduce health care costs and the average number of uninsured non-elderly residents; establish a statute of limitations on starting a health care lawsuit; and cap the awards that plaintiffs and their attorneys could receive in medical malpractice cases. Rejected 176-258: D 0-257; R 176-1. A "nay" vote was a vote in support of the president's position. Nov. 7, 2009.

886. **HR 3962. Health Care Overhaul/Recommit.** Cantor, R-Va., motion to recommit the bill to the House Energy and Commerce Committee with instructions that it be immediately reported back with an amendment that would create a fund that aims to preserve access to the Medicare Advantage program and establish new regulations for medical malpractice lawsuits. Motion rejected 187-247: D 13-244; R 174-3. Nov. 7, 2009.

887. **HR 3962. Health Care Overhaul/Passage.** Passage of the bill that would overhaul the nation's health insurance system and require most individuals to buy health insurance by 2013. It would create an agency tasked with establishing a federal health insurance exchange, including a government-run "public option," to allow individuals without coverage to purchase insurance. Those who do not obtain coverage would be subject to an excise tax, with hardship waivers. Employers would be required to offer health insurance or contribute to a fund for coverage; non-compliance could bring penalties of up to 8 percent of their payrolls. It would provide tax credits to certain small businesses for providing coverage and provide subsidies to individuals making up to four times the federal poverty level, excluding illegal immigrants. The bill would bar the use of federal funds to provide abortions, except in cases of rape or incest or if the woman's life is in danger. Insurance companies could not deny or reduce coverage based on pre-existing medical conditions. Passed 220-215: D 219-39; R 1-176. A "yea" vote was a vote in support of the president's position. Nov. 7, 2009.

888. **H Res 895. Tribute to Fort Hood Victims/Adoption.** Skelton, D-Mo., motion to suspend the rules and adopt the resolution that would honor the lives of the U.S. Army soldiers and citizens who died or were wounded in the attack at Fort Hood, Texas, on Nov. 5, 2009. Motion agreed to 428-0: D 253-0; R 175-0. A two-thirds majority of those present and voting (286 in this case) is required for adoption under suspension of the rules. Nov. 7, 2009.

	884	885	886	887	888
ALABAMA					
1 **Bonner**	Y	Y	Y	N	Y
2 **Bright**	Y	N	Y	N	Y
3 **Rogers**	Y	Y	Y	N	Y
4 **Aderholt**	Y	Y	Y	N	Y
5 **Griffith**	Y	N	Y	N	Y
6 **Bachus**	Y	Y	Y	N	Y
7 Davis	Y	N	N	N	Y
ALASKA					
AL **Young**	Y	Y	Y	N	Y
ARIZONA					
1 Kirkpatrick	N	N	N	Y	Y
2 **Franks**	Y	Y	Y	N	Y
3 **Shadegg**	P	Y	Y	N	Y
4 Pastor	N	N	N	Y	Y
5 Mitchell	N	N	N	Y	Y
6 **Flake**	Y	Y	N	N	Y
7 Grijalva	N	N	N	Y	Y
8 Giffords	N	N	N	Y	Y
ARKANSAS					
1 Berry	Y	N	N	Y	Y
2 Snyder	Y	N	N	Y	Y
3 **Boozman**	Y	Y	Y	N	Y
4 Ross	Y	N	N	N	Y
CALIFORNIA					
1 Thompson	N	N	N	Y	Y
2 **Herger**	Y	Y	Y	N	Y
3 **Lungren**	Y	Y	Y	N	Y
4 **McClintock**	Y	Y	Y	N	Y
5 Matsui	N	N	N	Y	Y
6 Woolsey	N	N	N	Y	Y
7 Miller, George	N	N	N	Y	Y
8 Pelosi	N			Y	Y
9 Lee	N	N	N	Y	Y
10 Garamendi	N	N	N	Y	Y
11 McNerney	N	N	N	Y	Y
12 Speier	N	N	N	Y	Y
13 Stark	N	N	N	Y	Y
14 Eshoo	N	N	N	Y	Y
15 Honda	N	N	N	Y	Y
16 Lofgren	N	N	N	Y	Y
17 Farr	N	N	N	Y	Y
18 Cardoza	Y	N	Y	Y	Y
19 **Radanovich**	Y	Y	Y	N	Y
20 Costa	Y	N	Y	Y	Y
21 **Nunes**	Y	Y	Y	N	Y
22 **McCarthy**	Y	Y	Y	N	Y
23 Capps	N	N	N	Y	Y
24 **Gallegly**	Y	Y	Y	N	Y
25 **McKeon**	Y	Y	Y	N	Y
26 **Dreier**	Y	Y	Y	N	Y
27 Sherman	N	N	N	Y	Y
28 Berman	N	N	N	Y	Y
29 Schiff	N	N	N	Y	Y
30 Waxman	N	N	N	Y	Y
31 Becerra	N	N	N	Y	Y
32 Chu	N	N	N	Y	Y
33 Watson	N	N	N	Y	Y
34 Roybal-Allard	N	N	N	Y	Y
35 Waters	N	N	N	Y	Y
36 Harman	N	N	N	Y	Y
37 Richardson	N	N	N	Y	Y
38 Napolitano	N	N	N	Y	Y
39 Sánchez, Linda	N	N	N	Y	Y
40 **Royce**	Y	Y	Y	N	Y
41 **Lewis**	Y	Y	Y	N	Y
42 **Miller, Gary**	Y	Y	Y	N	Y
43 Baca	Y	N	Y	N	Y
44 **Calvert**	Y	Y	Y	N	Y
45 **Bono Mack**	Y	Y	Y	N	Y
46 **Rohrabacher**	Y	Y	Y	N	Y
47 Sanchez, Loretta	N	N	N	Y	Y
48 **Campbell**	Y	Y	Y	N	Y
49 **Issa**	Y	Y	Y	N	Y
50 **Bilbray**	Y	Y	Y	N	Y
51 Filner	N	N	N	Y	Y
52 **Hunter**	Y	Y	Y	N	Y
53 Davis	N	N	N	Y	Y
COLORADO					
1 DeGette	N	N	N	Y	Y
2 Polis	N	N	N	Y	Y
3 Salazar	Y	N	N	Y	Y
4 Markey	N	N	N	Y	Y
5 **Lamborn**	Y	Y	Y	N	Y
6 **Coffman**	Y	Y	Y	N	Y
7 Perlmutter	N	N	N	Y	Y
CONNECTICUT					
1 Larson	N	N	N	Y	Y
2 Courtney	N	N	N	Y	Y
3 DeLauro	N	N	N	Y	Y
4 Himes	N	N	N	Y	Y
5 Murphy	N	N	N	Y	Y
DELAWARE					
AL **Castle**	Y	Y	Y	N	Y
FLORIDA					
1 **Miller**	Y	Y	Y	N	Y
2 Boyd	N	N	N	N	Y
3 Brown	N	N	N	Y	Y
4 **Crenshaw**	Y	Y	Y	N	Y
5 **Brown-Waite**	Y	Y	Y	N	Y
6 **Stearns**	Y	Y	Y	N	Y
7 **Mica**	Y	Y	Y	N	Y
8 Grayson	N	N	N	Y	Y
9 **Bilirakis**	Y	Y	Y	N	Y
10 **Young**	Y	Y	Y	N	Y
11 Castor	N	N	N	Y	Y
12 **Putnam**	Y	Y	Y	N	Y
13 **Buchanan**	Y	Y	Y	N	Y
14 **Mack**	Y	Y	Y	N	Y
15 **Posey**	Y	Y	Y	N	Y
16 **Rooney**	Y	Y	Y	N	Y
17 Meek	N	N	N	Y	Y
18 **Ros-Lehtinen**	Y	Y	Y	N	Y
19 Wexler	N	N	N	Y	Y
20 Wasserman Schultz	N	N	N	Y	Y
21 **Diaz-Balart, L.**	Y	Y	Y	N	Y
22 Klein	N	N	N	Y	Y
23 Hastings	N	N	N	Y	?
24 Kosmas	N	N	N	N	Y
25 **Diaz-Balart, M.**	Y	Y	Y	N	Y
GEORGIA					
1 **Kingston**	Y	Y	Y	N	Y
2 Bishop	Y	N	N	Y	Y
3 **Westmoreland**	Y	Y	Y	N	Y
4 Johnson	N	N	N	Y	Y
5 Lewis	N	N	N	Y	Y
6 **Price**	Y	Y	Y	N	Y
7 **Linder**	Y	Y	Y	N	?
8 Marshall	Y	N	N	N	?
9 **Deal**	Y	Y	Y	N	Y
10 **Broun**	Y	Y	Y	N	Y
11 **Gingrey**	Y	Y	Y	N	Y
12 Barrow	Y	N	N	N	Y
13 Scott	N	N	N	Y	Y
HAWAII					
1 Abercrombie	N	N	N	Y	Y
2 Hirono	N	N	N	Y	Y
IDAHO					
1 Minnick	N	N	Y	N	Y
2 **Simpson**	Y	Y	Y	N	Y
ILLINOIS					
1 Rush	N	N	N	Y	Y
2 Jackson	N	N	N	Y	Y
3 Lipinski	Y	N	N	Y	Y
4 Gutierrez	N	N	N	Y	Y
5 Quigley	N	N	N	Y	Y
6 **Roskam**	Y	Y	Y	N	Y
7 Davis	N	N	N	Y	Y
8 Bean	N	N	N	Y	Y
9 Schakowsky	N	N	N	Y	Y
10 **Kirk**	Y	Y	Y	N	Y
11 Halvorson	N	N	N	Y	Y
12 Costello	N	N	N	Y	Y
13 **Biggert**	Y	Y	Y	N	Y
14 Foster	N	N	N	Y	Y
15 **Johnson**	Y	N	N	N	Y

	884	885	886	887	888
16 Manzullo	Y	Y	Y	N	Y
17 Hare	N	N	N	Y	Y
18 Schock	Y	Y	Y	N	Y
19 Shimkus	Y	Y	Y	N	Y
INDIANA					
1 Visclosky	N	N	N	Y	Y
2 Donnelly	Y	N	N	Y	Y
3 Souder	Y	Y	Y	N	Y
4 Buyer	Y	Y	Y	N	Y
5 Burton	Y	Y	Y	N	Y
6 Pence	Y	Y	Y	N	Y
7 Carson	N	N	N	Y	Y
8 Ellsworth	Y	N	Y	N	Y
9 Hill	Y	N	N	Y	Y
IOWA					
1 Braley	N	N	N	Y	Y
2 Loebsack	N	N	N	Y	Y
3 Boswell	N	N	N	Y	Y
4 Latham	Y	Y	Y	N	Y
5 King	Y	Y	Y	N	Y
KANSAS					
1 Moran	Y	Y	Y	N	Y
2 Jenkins	Y	Y	Y	N	Y
3 Moore	N	N	N	Y	Y
4 Tiahrt	Y	Y	Y	N	Y
KENTUCKY					
1 Whitfield	Y	Y	Y	N	Y
2 Guthrie	Y	Y	Y	N	Y
3 Yarmuth	N	N	N	Y	Y
4 Davis	Y	Y	Y	N	Y
5 Rogers	Y	Y	Y	N	Y
6 Chandler	Y	N	N	N	Y
LOUISIANA					
1 Scalise	Y	Y	Y	N	Y
2 Cao	Y	Y	Y	Y	Y
3 Melancon	Y	N	N	N	Y
4 Fleming	Y	Y	Y	N	Y
5 Alexander	Y	Y	Y	N	Y
6 Cassidy	Y	Y	Y	N	Y
7 Boustany	Y	Y	Y	N	Y
MAINE					
1 Pingree	N	N	N	Y	Y
2 Michaud	Y	N	N	Y	Y
MARYLAND					
1 Kratovil	N	N	N	N	Y
2 Ruppersberger	N	N	N	Y	Y
3 Sarbanes	N	N	N	Y	Y
4 Edwards	N	N	N	Y	Y
5 Hoyer	N	N	N	Y	Y
6 Bartlett	Y	Y	Y	N	Y
7 Cummings	N	N	N	Y	Y
8 Van Hollen	N	N	N	Y	Y
MASSACHUSETTS					
1 Olver	N	N	N	Y	Y
2 Neal	Y	N	N	Y	Y
3 McGovern	N	N	N	Y	Y
4 Frank	N	N	N	Y	Y
5 Tsongas	N	N	N	Y	Y
6 Tierney	N	N	N	Y	Y
7 Markey	N	N	N	Y	Y
8 Capuano	N	N	N	Y	Y
9 Lynch	Y	N	N	Y	Y
10 Delahunt	N	N	N	Y	Y
MICHIGAN					
1 Stupak	Y	N	N	Y	Y
2 Hoekstra	Y	Y	Y	N	Y
3 Ehlers	Y	Y	Y	N	Y
4 Camp	Y	Y	Y	N	Y
5 Kildee	Y	N	N	Y	Y
6 Upton	Y	Y	Y	N	Y
7 Schauer	N	N	N	Y	Y
8 Rogers	Y	Y	Y	N	Y
9 Peters	N	N	N	Y	Y
10 Miller	Y	Y	Y	N	Y
11 McCotter	Y	Y	Y	N	Y
12 Levin	N	N	N	Y	Y
13 Kilpatrick	N	N	N	Y	Y
14 Conyers	N	N	N	Y	Y
15 Dingell	N	N	N	Y	Y
MINNESOTA					
1 Walz	N	N	N	Y	Y
2 Kline	Y	Y	Y	N	Y
3 Paulsen	Y	Y	Y	N	Y
4 McCollum	N	N	N	Y	Y

	884	885	886	887	888
5 Ellison	N	N	N	Y	Y
6 Bachmann	Y	Y	Y	N	Y
7 Peterson	Y	N	N	N	Y
8 Oberstar	Y	N	N	Y	Y
MISSISSIPPI					
1 Childers	Y	N	Y	N	Y
2 Thompson	N	N	N	Y	Y
3 Harper	Y	Y	Y	N	Y
4 Taylor	Y	N	N	N	Y
MISSOURI					
1 Clay	N	N	N	Y	Y
2 Akin	Y	Y	Y	N	Y
3 Carnahan	N	N	N	Y	Y
4 Skelton	Y	N	N	Y	Y
5 Cleaver	N	N	N	Y	Y
6 Graves	Y	Y	Y	N	Y
7 Blunt	Y	Y	Y	N	Y
8 Emerson	Y	Y	Y	N	Y
9 Luetkemeyer	Y	Y	Y	N	Y
MONTANA					
AL Rehberg	Y	Y	Y	N	Y
NEBRASKA					
1 Fortenberry	Y	Y	Y	N	Y
2 Terry	Y	Y	Y	N	Y
3 Smith	Y	Y	Y	N	Y
NEVADA					
1 Berkley	N	N	N	Y	Y
2 Heller	Y	Y	Y	N	Y
3 Titus	N	N	N	Y	Y
NEW HAMPSHIRE					
1 Shea-Porter	N	N	N	Y	Y
2 Hodes	N	N	N	Y	Y
NEW JERSEY					
1 Andrews	N	N	N	Y	Y
2 LoBiondo	Y	Y	Y	N	Y
3 Adler	N	N	N	N	Y
4 Smith	Y	Y	Y	N	Y
5 Garrett	Y	Y	Y	N	Y
6 Pallone	N	N	N	Y	Y
7 Lance	Y	Y	Y	N	Y
8 Pascrell	N	N	N	Y	Y
9 Rothman	N	N	N	Y	Y
10 Payne	N	N	N	Y	Y
11 Frelinghuysen	Y	Y	Y	N	Y
12 Holt	N	N	N	Y	Y
13 Sires	N	N	N	Y	Y
NEW MEXICO					
1 Heinrich	N	N	N	Y	Y
2 Teague	Y	N	N	N	Y
3 Lujan	N	N	N	Y	Y
NEW YORK					
1 Bishop	N	N	N	Y	Y
2 Israel	N	N	N	Y	Y
3 King	Y	Y	Y	N	Y
4 McCarthy	N	N	N	Y	Y
5 Ackerman	N	N	N	Y	?
6 Meeks	N	N	N	Y	Y
7 Crowley	N	N	N	Y	Y
8 Nadler	N	N	N	Y	Y
9 Weiner	N	N	N	Y	Y
10 Towns	N	N	N	Y	Y
11 Clarke	N	N	N	Y	Y
12 Velázquez	N	N	N	Y	?
13 McMahon	N	N	N	N	Y
14 Maloney	N	N	N	Y	Y
15 Rangel	N	N	N	Y	Y
16 Serrano	N	N	N	Y	Y
17 Engel	N	N	N	Y	Y
18 Lowey	N	N	N	Y	Y
19 Hall	N	N	N	Y	Y
20 Murphy	N	N	Y	N	Y
21 Tonko	N	N	N	Y	Y
22 Hinchey	N	N	N	Y	Y
23 Owens	N	N	N	Y	Y
24 Arcuri	N	N	N	Y	Y
25 Maffei	N	N	N	Y	Y
26 Lee	Y	Y	Y	N	Y
27 Higgins	N	N	N	Y	Y
28 Slaughter	N	N	N	Y	Y
29 Massa	N	N	N	N	Y
NORTH CAROLINA					
1 Butterfield	N	N	N	Y	Y
2 Etheridge	Y	N	N	Y	Y
3 Jones	Y	Y	Y	N	Y
4 Price	N	N	N	Y	Y

	884	885	886	887	888
5 Foxx	Y	Y	Y	N	Y
6 Coble	Y	Y	Y	N	Y
7 McIntyre	Y	N	N	N	Y
8 Kissell	N	N	N	N	Y
9 Myrick	Y	Y	Y	N	Y
10 McHenry	Y	Y	Y	N	Y
11 Shuler	Y	N	N	N	Y
12 Watt	N	N	N	Y	Y
13 Miller	N	N	N	Y	Y
NORTH DAKOTA					
AL Pomeroy	Y	N	Y	Y	Y
OHIO					
1 Driehaus	Y	N	N	Y	Y
2 Schmidt	Y	Y	Y	N	Y
3 Turner	Y	Y	Y	N	Y
4 Jordan	Y	Y	Y	N	Y
5 Latta	Y	Y	Y	N	Y
6 Wilson	Y	N	N	Y	Y
7 Austria	Y	Y	Y	N	Y
8 Boehner	Y	Y	Y	N	Y
9 Kaptur	Y	N	N	Y	Y
10 Kucinich	N	N	N	Y	Y
11 Fudge	N	N	N	Y	Y
12 Tiberi	Y	Y	Y	N	Y
13 Sutton	N	N	N	Y	Y
14 LaTourette	Y	Y	Y	N	?
15 Kilroy	N	N	N	Y	Y
16 Boccieri	Y	N	N	Y	Y
17 Ryan	Y	N	N	Y	Y
18 Space	Y	N	N	Y	Y
OKLAHOMA					
1 Sullivan	Y	Y	Y	N	Y
2 Boren	Y	N	Y	N	Y
3 Lucas	Y	Y	Y	N	Y
4 Cole	Y	Y	Y	N	Y
5 Fallin	Y	Y	Y	N	Y
OREGON					
1 Wu	N	N	N	Y	Y
2 Walden	Y	Y	Y	N	Y
3 Blumenauer	N	N	N	Y	Y
4 DeFazio	N	N	N	Y	Y
5 Schrader	N	N	N	Y	Y
PENNSYLVANIA					
1 Brady	N	N	N	Y	Y
2 Fattah	N	N	N	Y	Y
3 Dahlkemper	Y	N	N	Y	Y
4 Altmire	Y	N	N	N	Y
5 Thompson	Y	Y	Y	N	Y
6 Gerlach	Y	Y	Y	N	Y
7 Sestak	N	N	N	Y	Y
8 Murphy, P.	N	N	N	Y	Y
9 Shuster	Y	Y	Y	N	Y
10 Carney	Y	N	N	Y	Y
11 Kanjorski	Y	N	N	Y	Y
12 Murtha	Y	N	N	Y	Y
13 Schwartz	N	N	N	Y	Y
14 Doyle	N	N	N	Y	Y
15 Dent	Y	Y	Y	N	Y
16 Pitts	Y	Y	Y	N	Y
17 Holden	Y	N	N	Y	Y
18 Murphy, T.	Y	Y	Y	N	Y
19 Platts	Y	Y	Y	N	Y
RHODE ISLAND					
1 Kennedy	N	N	N	Y	Y
2 Langevin	Y	N	N	Y	Y
SOUTH CAROLINA					
1 Brown	Y	Y	Y	N	Y
2 Wilson	Y	Y	Y	N	Y
3 Barrett	Y	Y	Y	N	Y
4 Inglis	Y	Y	Y	N	Y
5 Spratt	Y	N	N	Y	Y
6 Clyburn	N	N	N	Y	Y
SOUTH DAKOTA					
AL Herseth Sandlin	N	N	N	N	Y
TENNESSEE					
1 Roe	Y	Y	Y	N	Y
2 Duncan	Y	Y	Y	N	Y
3 Wamp	Y	Y	Y	N	Y
4 Davis	Y	N	N	Y	Y
5 Cooper	Y	N	N	Y	Y
6 Gordon	Y	N	N	Y	Y
7 Blackburn	Y	Y	Y	N	Y
8 Tanner	Y	N	N	Y	Y
9 Cohen	N	N	N	Y	Y

	884	885	886	887	888
TEXAS					
1 Gohmert	Y	Y	Y	N	Y
2 Poe	Y	Y	Y	N	Y
3 Johnson, S.	Y	Y	Y	N	Y
4 Hall	Y	Y	Y	N	Y
5 Hensarling	Y	Y	Y	N	Y
6 Barton	Y	Y	Y	N	Y
7 Culberson	Y	Y	Y	N	Y
8 Brady	Y	Y	Y	N	Y
9 Green, A.	N	N	N	Y	Y
10 McCaul	Y	Y	Y	N	Y
11 Conaway	Y	Y	Y	N	Y
12 Granger	Y	Y	Y	N	Y
13 Thornberry	Y	Y	Y	N	Y
14 Paul	Y	Y	N	N	Y
15 Hinojosa	N	N	N	Y	Y
16 Reyes	Y	N	N	Y	Y
17 Edwards	N	N	N	Y	Y
18 Jackson Lee	N	N	N	Y	Y
19 Neugebauer	Y	Y	Y	N	Y
20 Gonzalez	N	N	N	Y	Y
21 Smith	Y	Y	Y	N	Y
22 Olson	Y	Y	Y	N	Y
23 Rodriguez	Y	N	N	Y	Y
24 Marchant	Y	Y	Y	N	Y
25 Doggett	N	N	N	Y	Y
26 Burgess	Y	Y	Y	N	Y
27 Ortiz	Y	N	N	Y	Y
28 Cuellar	Y	N	Y	Y	Y
29 Green, G.	N	N	N	Y	Y
30 Johnson, E.	N	N	N	Y	Y
31 Carter	Y	Y	Y	N	Y
32 Sessions	Y	Y	Y	N	Y
UTAH					
1 Bishop	Y	Y	Y	N	Y
2 Matheson	Y	N	N	N	Y
3 Chaffetz	Y	Y	Y	N	Y
VERMONT					
AL Welch	N	N	N	Y	Y
VIRGINIA					
1 Wittman	Y	Y	Y	N	Y
2 Nye	N	N	N	N	Y
3 Scott	N	N	N	Y	Y
4 Forbes	Y	Y	Y	N	Y
5 Perriello	Y	N	N	N	Y
6 Goodlatte	Y	Y	Y	N	Y
7 Cantor	Y	Y	Y	N	Y
8 Moran	N	N	N	Y	Y
9 Boucher	N	N	N	N	Y
10 Wolf	Y	Y	Y	N	Y
11 Connolly	N	N	N	Y	Y
WASHINGTON					
1 Inslee	N	N	N	Y	Y
2 Larsen	N	N	N	Y	Y
3 Baird	N	N	N	Y	Y
4 Hastings	Y	Y	Y	N	Y
5 McMorris Rodgers	Y	Y	Y	N	Y
6 Dicks	N	N	N	Y	?
7 McDermott	N	N	N	Y	Y
8 Reichert	Y	Y	Y	N	Y
9 Smith	N	N	N	Y	Y
WEST VIRGINIA					
1 Mollohan	Y	N	N	Y	Y
2 Capito	Y	Y	Y	N	Y
3 Rahall	Y	N	N	Y	Y
WISCONSIN					
1 Ryan	Y	Y	Y	N	Y
2 Baldwin	N	N	N	Y	Y
3 Kind	N	N	N	Y	Y
4 Moore	N	N	N	Y	Y
5 Sensenbrenner	Y	Y	Y	N	Y
6 Petri	Y	Y	Y	N	Y
7 Obey	N	N	N	Y	Y
8 Kagen	N	N	N	Y	Y
WYOMING					
AL Lummis	Y	Y	Y	N	Y
DELEGATES					
Faleomavaega (A.S.)					
Norton (D.C.)					
Bordallo (Guam)					
Sablan (N. Marianas)					
Pierluisi (P.R.)					
Christensen (V.I.)					

IN THE HOUSE | By Vote Number

889. S 1314. Martin Luther King Jr. Post Office/Passage.
Blumenauer, D-Ore., motion to suspend the rules and pass the bill that would designate a post office in Portland, Ore., as the "Dr. Martin Luther King Jr. Post Office." Motion agreed to 373-0: D 218-0; R 155-0. A two-thirds majority of those present and voting (249 in this case) is required for passage under suspension of the rules. Nov. 16, 2009.

890. HR 3539. Patricia McGinty-Juhl Post Office/Passage.
Lynch, D-Mass., motion to suspend the rules and pass the bill that would designate a post office in Harrison, N.J., as the "Patricia D. McGinty-Juhl Post Office Building." Motion agreed to 367-0: D 215-0; R 152-0. A two-thirds majority of those present and voting (245 in this case) is required for passage under suspension of the rules. Nov. 16, 2009.

891. HR 3767. W. Hazen Hillyard Post Office/Passage.
Lynch, D-Mass., motion to suspend the rules and pass the bill that would designate a post office in Smithfield, Utah, as the "W. Hazen Hillyard Post Office Building." Motion agreed to 368-0: D 217-0; R 151-0. A two-thirds majority of those present and voting (246 in this case) is required for passage under suspension of the rules. Nov. 16, 2009.

892. HR 3360. Cruise Vessel Safety Regulations/Passage.
Cummings, D-Md., motion to suspend the rules and pass the bill that would require cruise ships with at least 250 passengers to report onboard crimes to federal officials and meet specific design and construction standards to increase ship safety. It would impose a civil penalty of up to $50,000 and a criminal penalty of up to one year in prison or $250,000 for non-compliance. Motion agreed to 416-4: D 249-0; R 167-4. A two-thirds majority of those present and voting (280 in this case) is required for passage under suspension of the rules. Nov. 17, 2009.

893. H Res 841. Drive Safer Sunday/Adoption.
Bishop, D-N.Y., motion to suspend the rules and adopt the resolution that would support the designation of Drive Safer Sunday on Nov. 29, 2009. Motion agreed to 413-1: D 245-0; R 168-1. A two-thirds majority of those present and voting (276 in this case) is required for adoption under suspension of the rules. Nov. 17, 2009.

894. Journal/Procedural Motion.
Approval of the House Journal of Monday, Nov. 16, 2009. Approved 243-177: D 218-32; R 25-145. Nov. 17, 2009.

	889	890	891	892	893	894
ALABAMA						
1 **Bonner**	?	?	?	Y	Y	N
2 Bright	Y	Y	Y	Y	Y	N
3 **Rogers**	Y	Y	Y	Y	Y	N
4 **Aderholt**	Y	Y	Y	Y	Y	N
5 Griffith	Y	Y	Y	Y	Y	N
6 **Bachus**	Y	Y	Y	Y	Y	N
7 Davis	?	?	?	?	?	?
ALASKA						
AL **Young**	Y	Y	Y	Y	Y	N
ARIZONA						
1 Kirkpatrick	?	?	?	Y	Y	N
2 **Franks**	Y	Y	Y	Y	Y	N
3 **Shadegg**	Y	Y	Y	Y	Y	N
4 Pastor	Y	Y	Y	Y	Y	Y
5 Mitchell	?	?	?	Y	Y	N
6 **Flake**	Y	Y	N	Y	N	N
7 Grijalva	?	?	?	Y	Y	Y
8 Giffords	?	?	?	Y	Y	N
ARKANSAS						
1 Berry	Y	Y	Y	Y	Y	Y
2 Snyder	Y	Y	Y	Y	Y	Y
3 **Boozman**	Y	Y	Y	Y	Y	Y
4 Ross	Y	Y	Y	Y	Y	Y
CALIFORNIA						
1 Thompson	Y	Y	Y	Y	Y	N
2 **Herger**	Y	Y	Y	Y	Y	N
3 **Lungren**	Y	Y	Y	Y	Y	Y
4 **McClintock**	Y	Y	Y	Y	Y	Y
5 Matsui	Y	Y	Y	Y	Y	Y
6 Woolsey	Y	Y	Y	Y	Y	Y
7 Miller, George	Y	Y	Y	Y	Y	Y
8 Pelosi						
9 Lee	Y	Y	Y	Y	Y	Y
10 Garamendi	Y	Y	Y	Y	Y	Y
11 McNerney	Y	Y	Y	Y	Y	Y
12 Speier	Y	?	Y	Y	Y	Y
13 Stark	?	?	Y	Y	Y	Y
14 Eshoo	Y	Y	Y	Y	Y	Y
15 Honda	Y	Y	Y	Y	Y	Y
16 Lofgren	Y	Y	Y	Y	Y	Y
17 Farr	Y	Y	Y	Y	Y	Y
18 Cardoza	Y	Y	Y	Y	?	N
19 **Radanovich**	Y	Y	Y	Y	Y	Y
20 Costa	Y	?	Y	Y	Y	N
21 **Nunes**	Y	Y	Y	Y	Y	Y
22 **McCarthy**	Y	Y	Y	Y	Y	N
23 Capps	Y	Y	Y	Y	Y	Y
24 **Gallegly**	Y	Y	Y	Y	Y	Y
25 **McKeon**	?	?	?	Y	Y	N
26 **Dreier**	Y	Y	Y	Y	Y	Y
27 Sherman	Y	Y	Y	Y	Y	Y
28 Berman	?	?	?	Y	?	Y
29 Schiff	Y	Y	Y	Y	Y	Y
30 Waxman	?	?	?	Y	Y	Y
31 Becerra	Y	Y	Y	Y	Y	Y
32 Chu	Y	Y	Y	Y	Y	Y
33 Watson	Y	Y	Y	Y	Y	Y
34 Roybal-Allard	Y	Y	Y	Y	Y	Y
35 Waters	Y	Y	Y	Y	Y	Y
36 Harman	?	?	?	Y	Y	Y
37 Richardson	Y	Y	Y	Y	Y	Y
38 Napolitano	Y	Y	Y	Y	Y	Y
39 Sánchez, Linda	Y	Y	Y	Y	Y	Y
40 **Royce**	Y	Y	Y	Y	Y	N
41 **Lewis**	Y	Y	Y	Y	?	N
42 **Miller, Gary**	Y	Y	Y	Y	Y	N
43 Baca	Y	Y	Y	Y	Y	Y
44 **Calvert**	Y	Y	Y	Y	Y	N
45 **Bono Mack**	Y	Y	Y	Y	Y	N
46 **Rohrabacher**	?	?	?	?	?	?
47 Sanchez, Loretta	Y	Y	Y	Y	Y	Y
48 **Campbell**	Y	Y	Y	Y	Y	N
49 **Issa**	Y	Y	Y	Y	Y	N
50 **Bilbray**	Y	Y	Y	Y	Y	N
51 Filner	Y	Y	Y	Y	Y	Y
52 **Hunter**	Y	Y	Y	Y	Y	N
53 Davis	+	+	+	Y	Y	Y

	889	890	891	892	893	894
COLORADO						
1 DeGette	?	?	?	Y	Y	Y
2 Polis	Y	Y	Y	Y	Y	Y
3 Salazar	Y	Y	Y	Y	Y	Y
4 Markey	?	?	?	Y	Y	N
5 **Lamborn**	Y	Y	Y	Y	Y	N
6 **Coffman**	Y	Y	Y	Y	Y	N
7 Perlmutter	Y	Y	Y	Y	Y	Y
CONNECTICUT						
1 Larson	Y	Y	Y	Y	?	Y
2 Courtney	Y	Y	Y	Y	Y	Y
3 DeLauro	Y	Y	Y	Y	Y	Y
4 Himes	Y	Y	Y	Y	Y	N
5 Murphy	Y	Y	Y	Y	Y	Y
DELAWARE						
AL **Castle**	Y	Y	Y	Y	Y	Y
FLORIDA						
1 **Miller**	Y	Y	Y	Y	Y	N
2 Boyd	Y	Y	Y	Y	Y	Y
3 Brown	Y	Y	Y	Y	Y	Y
4 **Crenshaw**	?	?	?	Y	Y	N
5 **Brown-Waite**	Y	Y	Y	Y	Y	N
6 **Stearns**	Y	Y	Y	Y	Y	N
7 **Mica**	Y	Y	Y	Y	Y	N
8 Grayson	Y	Y	Y	Y	Y	Y
9 **Bilirakis**	Y	Y	Y	Y	Y	N
10 **Young**	Y	Y	Y	?	?	?
11 Castor	Y	Y	Y	Y	Y	Y
12 **Putnam**	Y	Y	Y	Y	Y	N
13 **Buchanan**	Y	Y	Y	Y	Y	N
14 **Mack**	Y	Y	Y	Y	Y	N
15 **Posey**	Y	Y	Y	Y	Y	N
16 **Rooney**	Y	?	Y	Y	Y	Y
17 Meek	Y	Y	Y	Y	Y	Y
18 **Ros-Lehtinen**	Y	Y	Y	Y	Y	N
19 Wexler	?	?	?	Y	Y	Y
20 Wasserman Schultz	Y	Y	Y	Y	Y	Y
21 **Diaz-Balart, L.**	Y	Y	Y	Y	Y	N
22 Klein	Y	Y	Y	Y	Y	Y
23 Hastings	Y	Y	Y	Y	Y	Y
24 Kosmas	Y	Y	Y	Y	Y	Y
25 **Diaz-Balart, M.**	Y	Y	Y	Y	Y	N
GEORGIA						
1 **Kingston**	Y	Y	Y	Y	Y	N
2 Bishop	Y	Y	Y	Y	Y	Y
3 **Westmoreland**	Y	Y	Y	Y	Y	Y
4 Johnson	Y	Y	Y	Y	Y	Y
5 Lewis	Y	Y	Y	?	Y	Y
6 **Price**	Y	Y	Y	Y	Y	N
7 **Linder**	Y	Y	Y	Y	Y	N
8 Marshall	Y	Y	Y	Y	Y	Y
9 **Deal**	?	?	?	?	?	?
10 **Broun**	Y	Y	Y	N	Y	N
11 **Gingrey**	?	?	?	Y	Y	N
12 Barrow	Y	Y	Y	Y	Y	Y
13 Scott	Y	Y	Y	Y	Y	Y
HAWAII						
1 Abercrombie	Y	Y	Y	Y	Y	Y
2 Hirono	Y	Y	Y	Y	Y	Y
IDAHO						
1 **Minnick**	Y	Y	Y	Y	Y	N
2 **Simpson**	Y	Y	Y	Y	Y	N
ILLINOIS						
1 Rush	?	?	?	Y	Y	Y
2 Jackson	Y	Y	Y	Y	Y	Y
3 Lipinski	Y	Y	Y	Y	Y	N
4 Gutierrez	?	?	?	Y	Y	Y
5 Quigley	Y	Y	Y	Y	Y	Y
6 **Roskam**	?	?	?	Y	Y	N
7 Davis	Y	Y	Y	?	?	?
8 Bean	Y	Y	Y	Y	Y	Y
9 Schakowsky	Y	Y	Y	Y	Y	Y
10 **Kirk**	Y	Y	Y	Y	Y	Y
11 Halvorson	Y	Y	Y	Y	Y	Y
12 Costello	?	?	?	Y	Y	Y
13 **Biggert**	Y	Y	Y	Y	Y	N
14 Foster	Y	Y	Y	Y	Y	N
15 **Johnson**	Y	Y	Y	Y	Y	Y

KEY **Republicans** Democrats

Y Voted for (yea)	X Paired against	C Voted "present" to avoid possible conflict of interest
# Paired for	– Announced against	
+ Announced for	P Voted "present"	? Did not vote or otherwise make a position known
N Voted against (nay)		

	889	890	891	892	893	894
16 **Manzullo**	Y	Y	Y	Y	Y	N
17 Hare	Y	Y	Y	Y	Y	Y
18 **Schock**	?	?	?	Y	Y	Y
19 **Shimkus**	Y	Y	Y	Y	Y	N
INDIANA						
1 Visclosky	Y	Y	Y	Y	Y	Y
2 Donnelly	Y	Y	Y	Y	Y	N
3 **Souder**	Y	?	Y	Y	Y	N
4 **Buyer**	Y	Y	Y	Y	Y	N
5 **Burton**	Y	Y	Y	Y	Y	N
6 **Pence**	Y	Y	Y	Y	Y	N
7 Carson	Y	Y	Y	Y	Y	Y
8 Ellsworth	Y	Y	Y	Y	Y	N
9 Hill	Y	Y	Y	Y	Y	Y
IOWA						
1 Braley	?	?	?	Y	Y	Y
2 Loebsack	Y	Y	Y	Y	Y	Y
3 Boswell	Y	Y	Y	Y	Y	Y
4 **Latham**	Y	Y	Y	Y	Y	Y
5 **King**	Y	Y	Y	Y	Y	N
KANSAS						
1 **Moran**	Y	Y	Y	Y	Y	N
2 **Jenkins**	Y	Y	Y	Y	Y	N
3 Moore	Y	Y	Y	Y	Y	Y
4 **Tiahrt**	?	?	?	?	?	?
KENTUCKY						
1 **Whitfield**	Y	Y	Y	Y	Y	N
2 **Guthrie**	Y	Y	Y	Y	Y	N
3 Yarmuth	Y	Y	Y	Y	Y	Y
4 **Davis**	Y	Y	Y	Y	Y	N
5 **Rogers**	Y	Y	Y	Y	Y	N
6 Chandler	Y	Y	Y	Y	Y	Y
LOUISIANA						
1 **Scalise**	Y	Y	Y	Y	Y	N
2 **Cao**	Y	Y	Y	Y	Y	N
3 Melancon	Y	Y	Y	Y	Y	N
4 **Fleming**	Y	Y	Y	Y	Y	N
5 **Alexander**	?	?	?	Y	Y	N
6 **Cassidy**	Y	Y	Y	Y	Y	N
7 **Boustany**	Y	Y	Y	Y	Y	N
MAINE						
1 Pingree	?	?	?	?	?	?
2 Michaud	Y	Y	Y	Y	Y	Y
MARYLAND						
1 Kratovil	Y	Y	Y	Y	Y	N
2 Ruppersberger	Y	Y	Y	Y	Y	Y
3 Sarbanes	Y	Y	Y	Y	Y	Y
4 Edwards	Y	Y	Y	Y	Y	Y
5 Hoyer	Y	Y	Y	Y	Y	Y
6 **Bartlett**	Y	Y	Y	Y	Y	N
7 Cummings	Y	Y	Y	Y	Y	Y
8 Van Hollen	Y	Y	Y	Y	Y	Y
MASSACHUSETTS						
1 Olver	Y	Y	Y	Y	?	Y
2 Neal	?	?	?	Y	Y	Y
3 McGovern	?	?	?	Y	Y	Y
4 Frank	Y	Y	Y	Y	Y	Y
5 Tsongas	Y	Y	Y	Y	Y	Y
6 Tierney	Y	Y	Y	Y	Y	Y
7 Markey	Y	Y	Y	Y	Y	Y
8 Capuano	?	?	?	?	?	?
9 Lynch	?	?	?	Y	Y	Y
10 Delahunt	?	?	?	?	?	?
MICHIGAN						
1 Stupak	Y	Y	Y	Y	Y	N
2 **Hoekstra**	?	?	?	Y	Y	N
3 **Ehlers**	Y	Y	Y	Y	Y	N
4 **Camp**	Y	Y	Y	Y	Y	N
5 Kildee	Y	Y	Y	Y	Y	Y
6 **Upton**	Y	Y	Y	Y	Y	N
7 Schauer	Y	Y	Y	Y	Y	Y
8 **Rogers**	Y	Y	Y	Y	Y	N
9 Peters	Y	Y	Y	Y	Y	Y
10 **Miller**	Y	Y	Y	Y	Y	N
11 **McCotter**	Y	Y	Y	Y	Y	N
12 Levin	Y	Y	Y	Y	Y	Y
13 Kilpatrick	?	?	?	Y	Y	Y
14 Conyers	Y	Y	Y	Y	Y	Y
15 Dingell	Y	Y	Y	Y	Y	Y
MINNESOTA						
1 Walz	Y	Y	Y	Y	Y	Y
2 **Kline**	Y	Y	Y	Y	Y	N
3 **Paulsen**	Y	Y	Y	Y	Y	Y
4 McCollum	Y	Y	Y	Y	Y	Y

	889	890	891	892	893	894
5 Ellison	Y	Y	Y	Y	Y	Y
6 **Bachmann**	Y	Y	Y	Y	Y	N
7 Peterson	Y	Y	Y	Y	Y	N
8 Oberstar	Y	Y	Y	Y	Y	Y
MISSISSIPPI						
1 Childers	Y	Y	Y	Y	Y	N
2 Thompson	Y	Y	Y	Y	Y	Y
3 **Harper**	Y	Y	Y	Y	Y	Y
4 Taylor	Y	Y	Y	Y	Y	N
MISSOURI						
1 Clay	Y	Y	Y	Y	Y	Y
2 **Akin**	Y	Y	Y	Y	Y	N
3 Carnahan	Y	Y	Y	Y	Y	Y
4 Skelton	?	?	?	Y	Y	Y
5 Cleaver	Y	Y	Y	Y	Y	Y
6 **Graves**	?	?	?	Y	Y	N
7 **Blunt**	Y	Y	Y	Y	Y	N
8 **Emerson**	Y	Y	Y	Y	Y	N
9 **Luetkemeyer**	Y	Y	Y	Y	Y	N
MONTANA						
AL **Rehberg**	Y	Y	Y	Y	Y	N
NEBRASKA						
1 **Fortenberry**	Y	Y	Y	Y	Y	N
2 **Terry**	Y	Y	Y	Y	Y	N
3 **Smith**	Y	Y	Y	Y	Y	N
NEVADA						
1 Berkley	Y	Y	Y	Y	Y	Y
2 **Heller**	Y	Y	Y	Y	Y	Y
3 Titus	Y	Y	Y	Y	Y	N
NEW HAMPSHIRE						
1 Shea-Porter	Y	Y	Y	Y	Y	Y
2 Hodes	Y	Y	Y	Y	Y	Y
NEW JERSEY						
1 Andrews	Y	Y	Y	Y	Y	Y
2 **LoBiondo**	Y	Y	Y	Y	Y	N
3 Adler	Y	Y	Y	Y	Y	Y
4 **Smith**	Y	Y	Y	Y	Y	N
5 **Garrett**	Y	Y	Y	Y	Y	N
6 Pallone	Y	Y	Y	Y	Y	Y
7 **Lance**	Y	Y	Y	Y	Y	Y
8 Pascrell	Y	Y	Y	Y	Y	Y
9 Rothman	Y	Y	Y	Y	Y	Y
10 Payne	Y	Y	Y	Y	Y	Y
11 **Frelinghuysen**	Y	Y	Y	Y	Y	N
12 Holt	Y	Y	Y	Y	Y	Y
13 Sires	Y	Y	Y	Y	Y	Y
NEW MEXICO						
1 Heinrich	?	?	?	Y	Y	Y
2 Teague	?	?	?	Y	Y	Y
3 Lujan	?	?	?	Y	Y	Y
NEW YORK						
1 Bishop	Y	Y	Y	Y	Y	Y
2 Israel	?	?	?	Y	Y	Y
3 **King**	Y	Y	Y	Y	Y	N
4 McCarthy	Y	Y	Y	Y	Y	Y
5 Ackerman	Y	Y	Y	Y	Y	Y
6 Meeks	?	?	?	Y	Y	Y
7 Crowley	Y	Y	Y	Y	Y	Y
8 Nadler	Y	Y	Y	Y	Y	Y
9 Weiner	Y	Y	Y	Y	Y	Y
10 Towns	Y	Y	Y	Y	Y	Y
11 Clarke	Y	Y	Y	Y	Y	Y
12 Velázquez	Y	Y	Y	Y	Y	Y
13 McMahon	Y	Y	Y	Y	Y	Y
14 Maloney	Y	Y	Y	Y	Y	Y
15 Rangel	Y	Y	Y	Y	Y	Y
16 Serrano	Y	Y	Y	Y	Y	Y
17 Engel	Y	Y	Y	Y	Y	Y
18 Lowey	?	?	?	Y	Y	Y
19 Hall	Y	?	Y	Y	Y	Y
20 Murphy	Y	Y	Y	Y	Y	N
21 Tonko	Y	Y	Y	Y	Y	Y
22 Hinchey	Y	Y	Y	Y	Y	Y
23 Owens	Y	Y	Y	Y	Y	Y
24 Arcuri	Y	Y	Y	Y	Y	N
25 Maffei	?	?	?	Y	Y	Y
26 **Lee**	Y	Y	Y	Y	Y	N
27 Higgins	Y	Y	Y	Y	Y	Y
28 Slaughter	Y	Y	Y	Y	Y	Y
29 Massa	Y	Y	Y	Y	Y	Y
NORTH CAROLINA						
1 Butterfield	Y	Y	Y	Y	Y	Y
2 Etheridge	Y	Y	Y	Y	Y	Y
3 **Jones**	Y	Y	Y	Y	Y	Y
4 Price	Y	Y	Y	Y	Y	Y

	889	890	891	892	893	894
5 **Foxx**	Y	Y	Y	Y	Y	N
6 **Coble**	Y	Y	Y	Y	Y	N
7 McIntyre	Y	Y	Y	Y	Y	Y
8 Kissell	?	?	?	Y	Y	Y
9 **Myrick**	Y	Y	Y	Y	Y	N
10 **McHenry**	Y	Y	Y	Y	Y	Y
11 Shuler	Y	Y	Y	Y	Y	N
12 Watt	Y	Y	Y	Y	Y	Y
13 Miller	Y	Y	Y	Y	Y	Y
NORTH DAKOTA						
AL Pomeroy	Y	Y	Y	Y	Y	Y
OHIO						
1 Driehaus	Y	Y	Y	Y	Y	Y
2 **Schmidt**	Y	Y	Y	Y	Y	N
3 **Turner**	Y	Y	Y	Y	Y	N
4 **Jordan**	Y	Y	Y	Y	Y	N
5 **Latta**	Y	Y	Y	Y	Y	N
6 Wilson	Y	Y	Y	Y	Y	Y
7 **Austria**	Y	Y	Y	Y	Y	N
8 **Boehner**	Y	Y	?	Y	Y	N
9 Kaptur	Y	Y	Y	Y	Y	Y
10 Kucinich	Y	Y	Y	Y	Y	Y
11 Fudge	Y	Y	Y	Y	Y	Y
12 **Tiberi**	Y	Y	Y	Y	?	Y
13 Sutton	Y	Y	Y	Y	Y	Y
14 **LaTourette**	?	?	?	Y	Y	N
15 Kilroy	+	+	+	Y	Y	Y
16 Boccieri	Y	Y	Y	Y	Y	Y
17 Ryan	Y	Y	Y	Y	Y	Y
18 Space	Y	Y	Y	Y	Y	Y
OKLAHOMA						
1 **Sullivan**	Y	Y	Y	Y	Y	N
2 Boren	Y	Y	Y	Y	Y	N
3 **Lucas**	Y	Y	Y	Y	Y	N
4 **Cole**	Y	Y	+	Y	Y	N
5 **Fallin**	Y	Y	Y	Y	Y	N
OREGON						
1 Wu	Y	Y	Y	Y	Y	Y
2 **Walden**	Y	Y	?	Y	Y	N
3 Blumenauer	Y	Y	Y	Y	Y	Y
4 DeFazio	Y	Y	Y	Y	Y	Y
5 Schrader	Y	Y	Y	Y	Y	Y
PENNSYLVANIA						
1 Brady	Y	Y	Y	Y	Y	Y
2 Fattah	Y	Y	Y	Y	Y	Y
3 Dahlkemper	Y	Y	Y	Y	Y	Y
4 Altmire	Y	Y	Y	Y	Y	N
5 **Thompson**	Y	Y	Y	Y	Y	N
6 **Gerlach**	+	+	+	Y	Y	Y
7 Sestak	Y	Y	Y	Y	Y	Y
8 Murphy, P.	?	?	?	Y	Y	Y
9 **Shuster**	Y	Y	Y	Y	Y	N
10 Carney	Y	Y	Y	Y	Y	N
11 Kanjorski	Y	Y	Y	Y	Y	Y
12 Murtha	Y	Y	Y	Y	Y	Y
13 Schwartz	Y	Y	Y	Y	Y	Y
14 Doyle	Y	Y	Y	Y	Y	Y
15 **Dent**	Y	Y	Y	Y	Y	Y
16 **Pitts**	Y	Y	Y	Y	Y	Y
17 Holden	Y	Y	Y	Y	Y	Y
18 **Murphy, T.**	?	?	?	Y	Y	N
19 **Platts**	?	?	?	Y	Y	N
RHODE ISLAND						
1 Kennedy	Y	Y	Y	Y	Y	Y
2 Langevin	Y	Y	Y	Y	Y	Y
SOUTH CAROLINA						
1 **Brown**	?	?	?	?	?	?
2 **Wilson**	Y	Y	Y	Y	Y	N
3 **Barrett**	+	+	+	?	?	?
4 **Inglis**	Y	Y	Y	Y	Y	N
5 Spratt	Y	Y	Y	Y	Y	Y
6 Clyburn	Y	Y	Y	Y	Y	Y
SOUTH DAKOTA						
AL Herseth Sandlin	Y	Y	Y	Y	Y	Y
TENNESSEE						
1 **Roe**	Y	Y	Y	Y	Y	N
2 **Duncan**	Y	Y	Y	Y	Y	N
3 **Wamp**	?	?	?	Y	Y	N
4 Davis	Y	Y	Y	Y	Y	Y
5 Cooper	Y	Y	Y	Y	Y	Y
6 Gordon	Y	Y	Y	Y	Y	N
7 **Blackburn**	Y	Y	Y	Y	Y	N
8 Tanner	?	?	?	?	?	?
9 Cohen	Y	Y	Y	Y	Y	Y

	889	890	891	892	893	894
TEXAS						
1 **Gohmert**	Y	Y	?	Y	Y	P
2 **Poe**	Y	Y	Y	Y	Y	N
3 **Johnson, S.**	Y	Y	Y	Y	Y	N
4 **Hall**	Y	Y	Y	Y	Y	N
5 **Hensarling**	Y	Y	Y	Y	Y	N
6 **Barton**	Y	Y	Y	Y	Y	N
7 **Culberson**	Y	Y	Y	Y	Y	N
8 **Brady**	?	?	?	Y	Y	N
9 Green, A.	Y	Y	Y	Y	Y	Y
10 **McCaul**	Y	?	Y	Y	Y	N
11 **Conaway**	Y	Y	Y	Y	Y	N
12 **Granger**	Y	Y	Y	Y	Y	N
13 **Thornberry**	Y	Y	Y	Y	Y	N
14 **Paul**	Y	Y	Y	N	N	Y
15 Hinojosa	Y	Y	Y	Y	Y	Y
16 Reyes	Y	Y	Y	Y	Y	Y
17 Edwards	Y	Y	Y	Y	Y	Y
18 Jackson Lee	+	+	+	+	?	+
19 **Neugebauer**	Y	Y	Y	Y	Y	N
20 Gonzalez	Y	Y	Y	Y	Y	Y
21 **Smith**	Y	Y	Y	Y	Y	N
22 **Olson**	Y	Y	Y	Y	Y	N
23 Rodriguez	Y	Y	Y	Y	Y	Y
24 **Marchant**	Y	Y	Y	Y	Y	N
25 Doggett	Y	Y	Y	Y	Y	Y
26 **Burgess**	Y	Y	Y	Y	Y	N
27 Ortiz	Y	Y	Y	Y	Y	Y
28 Cuellar	Y	Y	Y	Y	Y	N
29 Green, G.	Y	Y	Y	Y	Y	Y
30 Johnson, E.	Y	Y	Y	Y	Y	Y
31 **Carter**	Y	Y	Y	Y	Y	N
32 **Sessions**	Y	Y	Y	Y	Y	N
UTAH						
1 **Bishop**	Y	Y	Y	Y	Y	N
2 Matheson	Y	Y	Y	Y	Y	Y
3 **Chaffetz**	Y	Y	Y	Y	Y	Y
VERMONT						
AL Welch	Y	Y	Y	Y	Y	Y
VIRGINIA						
1 **Wittman**	Y	Y	Y	Y	Y	N
2 Nye	Y	Y	Y	Y	Y	N
3 Scott	Y	Y	Y	Y	Y	Y
4 **Forbes**	Y	Y	Y	Y	Y	N
5 Perriello	Y	Y	Y	Y	Y	Y
6 **Goodlatte**	Y	Y	Y	Y	Y	Y
7 **Cantor**	?	?	?	Y	Y	N
8 Moran	?	?	?	Y	Y	Y
9 Boucher	Y	Y	Y	Y	Y	Y
10 **Wolf**	Y	Y	Y	Y	Y	N
11 Connolly	Y	Y	Y	Y	Y	N
WASHINGTON						
1 Inslee	Y	Y	Y	Y	Y	Y
2 Larsen	Y	Y	Y	Y	Y	Y
3 Baird	Y	Y	Y	Y	Y	Y
4 **Hastings**	?	?	?	Y	Y	N
5 **McMorris Rodgers**	Y	Y	Y	Y	Y	N
6 Dicks	Y	Y	Y	Y	Y	Y
7 McDermott	Y	Y	Y	Y	Y	Y
8 **Reichert**	Y	Y	Y	Y	Y	N
9 Smith	+	+	+	Y	Y	Y
WEST VIRGINIA						
1 Mollohan	Y	Y	Y	Y	Y	Y
2 **Capito**	Y	Y	Y	Y	Y	Y
3 Rahall	Y	Y	Y	Y	Y	Y
WISCONSIN						
1 **Ryan**	Y	Y	Y	Y	Y	N
2 Baldwin	Y	Y	Y	Y	Y	Y
3 Kind	Y	Y	Y	Y	Y	Y
4 Moore	Y	Y	?	Y	Y	Y
5 **Sensenbrenner**	Y	Y	Y	Y	Y	N
6 **Petri**	Y	Y	Y	Y	Y	N
7 Obey	Y	Y	Y	Y	?	Y
8 Kagen	Y	Y	Y	Y	Y	Y
WYOMING						
AL **Lummis**	Y	Y	Y	N	Y	N
DELEGATES						
Faleomavaega (A.S.)						
Norton (D.C.)						
Bordallo (Guam)						
Sablan (N. Marianas)						
Pierluisi (P.R.)						
Christensen (V.I.)						

IN THE HOUSE | By Vote Number

895. **H Res 891. Tribute to California Crash Victims/Adoption.** Cummings, D-Md., motion to suspend the rules and adopt the resolution that would express gratitude for the service of Coast Guard and Marine Corps pilots and crew members lost off the coast of California on Oct. 29, 2009, and extend condolences to the victims' families, friends and loved ones. Motion agreed to 419-0: D 247-0; R 172-0. A two-thirds majority of those present and voting (280 in this case) is required for adoption under suspension of the rules. Nov. 17, 2009.

896. **H Con Res 214. Adjournment/Adoption.** Adoption of the concurrent resolution that would provide for adjournment of the House until 2 p.m. Tuesday, Dec. 1, 2009, and the Senate until noon Monday, Nov. 30, 2009. Adopted 243-166: D 226-16; R 17-150. Nov. 18, 2009.

897. **HR 3791. Firefighter Organization Grants/Previous Question.** Pingree, D-Maine, motion to order the previous question (thus ending debate and possibility of amendment) on adoption of the rule (H Res 909) that would provide for House floor consideration of the bill that would authorize $2.2 billion per year in fiscal 2010 through 2014 for Federal Emergency Management Agency grant programs for firefighting organizations. Motion agreed to 242-174: D 242-5; R 0-169. Nov. 18, 2009.

898. **HR 3791. Firefighter Organization Grants/Rule.** Adoption of the rule (H Res 909) that would provide for House floor consideration of the bill that would authorize $2.2 billion per year from fiscal 2010 through 2014 for Federal Emergency Management Agency grant programs for firefighting organizations. Adopted 245-173: D 245-2; R 0-171. Nov. 18, 2009.

899. **HR 3791. Firefighter Organization Grants/Best Practices and Safety.** Perlmutter, D-Colo., amendment that would require the Homeland Security secretary to conduct a survey of fire departments to determine compliance with best practices for personnel and safety, and establish a task force to increase firefighter safety. Adopted in Committee of the Whole 358-75: D 259-0; R 99-75. Nov. 18, 2009.

900. **HR 3791. Firefighter Organization Grants/Earmarks Ban.** Flake, R-Ariz., amendment that would prohibit congressionally directed spending of funds appropriated to carry out the bill's provisions. Adopted in Committee of the Whole 371-63: D 199-61; R 172-2. Nov. 18, 2009.

	895	896	897	898	899	900
ALABAMA						
1 Bonner	Y	N	N	N	N	Y
2 Bright	Y	?	N	Y	Y	Y
3 Rogers	Y	N	N	N	N	Y
4 Aderholt	Y	N	N	N	N	Y
5 Griffith	Y	Y	Y	Y	Y	Y
6 Bachus	Y	N	N	N	N	Y
7 Davis	?	Y	Y	Y	Y	Y
ALASKA						
AL Young	Y	Y	N	N	Y	Y
ARIZONA						
1 Kirkpatrick	Y	Y	Y	Y	Y	Y
2 Franks	Y	N	N	N	N	Y
3 Shadegg	Y	N	N	N	N	Y
4 Pastor	Y	Y	Y	Y	Y	N
5 Mitchell	Y	N	Y	Y	Y	Y
6 Flake	Y	N	N	N	N	Y
7 Grijalva	Y	Y	Y	Y	Y	Y
8 Giffords	Y	N	Y	Y	Y	Y
ARKANSAS						
1 Berry	Y	Y	Y	Y	Y	Y
2 Snyder	Y	Y	Y	Y	Y	Y
3 Boozman	Y	N	N	N	N	Y
4 Ross	Y	Y	Y	Y	Y	Y
CALIFORNIA						
1 Thompson	Y	Y	Y	Y	Y	N
2 Herger	Y	N	N	N	N	Y
3 Lungren	Y	N	N	N	N	Y
4 McClintock	Y	N	N	N	N	Y
5 Matsui	Y	Y	Y	Y	Y	Y
6 Woolsey	Y	Y	Y	Y	Y	N
7 Miller, George	Y	Y	Y	Y	Y	Y
8 Pelosi						
9 Lee	Y	Y	Y	Y	Y	N
10 Garamendi	Y	?	Y	Y	Y	N
11 McNerney	Y	Y	Y	Y	Y	Y
12 Speier	Y	Y	Y	Y	Y	Y
13 Stark	Y	Y	Y	Y	Y	Y
14 Eshoo	Y	Y	Y	Y	Y	Y
15 Honda	Y	?	Y	Y	Y	Y
16 Lofgren	Y	Y	Y	Y	Y	Y
17 Farr	Y	Y	Y	Y	Y	Y
18 Cardoza	Y	Y	Y	Y	Y	Y
19 Radanovich	Y	N	N	N	N	Y
20 Costa	Y	?	?	Y	Y	Y
21 Nunes	Y	N	N	N	N	Y
22 McCarthy	Y	N	N	N	N	Y
23 Capps	Y	Y	Y	Y	Y	Y
24 Gallegly	Y	N	N	N	N	Y
25 McKeon	Y	N	N	N	N	Y
26 Dreier	Y	N	N	N	N	Y
27 Sherman	Y	Y	Y	Y	Y	N
28 Berman	Y	Y	Y	Y	Y	N
29 Schiff	Y	Y	Y	Y	Y	Y
30 Waxman	Y	Y	Y	Y	Y	Y
31 Becerra	Y	Y	Y	Y	Y	Y
32 Chu	Y	Y	Y	Y	Y	Y
33 Watson	Y	Y	Y	Y	Y	Y
34 Roybal-Allard	Y	Y	Y	Y	Y	Y
35 Waters	Y	Y	Y	Y	Y	Y
36 Harman	Y	Y	Y	Y	Y	Y
37 Richardson	Y	Y	Y	Y	Y	Y
38 Napolitano	?	Y	Y	Y	Y	N
39 Sánchez, Linda	Y	Y	Y	Y	Y	Y
40 Royce	Y	N	N	N	N	Y
41 Lewis	Y	N	N	N	N	N
42 Miller, Gary	Y	N	N	N	Y	Y
43 Baca	Y	Y	Y	Y	Y	Y
44 Calvert	Y	N	N	N	Y	Y
45 Bono Mack	Y	N	N	N	Y	Y
46 Rohrabacher	?	N	N	N	N	Y
47 Sanchez, Loretta	Y	Y	Y	Y	Y	Y
48 Campbell	Y	N	N	N	N	Y
49 Issa	Y	N	N	N	N	Y
50 Bilbray	Y	N	N	Y	N	Y
51 Filner	Y	Y	Y	Y	Y	N
52 Hunter	Y	N	N	N	Y	Y
53 Davis	Y	Y	Y	Y	Y	Y
COLORADO						
1 DeGette	Y	Y	Y	Y	Y	Y
2 Polis	Y	Y	Y	Y	Y	Y
3 Salazar	Y	?	Y	Y	Y	Y
4 Markey	Y	Y	Y	Y	Y	Y
5 Lamborn	Y	N	N	N	N	Y
6 Coffman	Y	N	N	N	N	Y
7 Perlmutter	Y	Y	Y	Y	Y	Y
CONNECTICUT						
1 Larson	Y	Y	Y	Y	Y	Y
2 Courtney	Y	Y	Y	Y	Y	Y
3 DeLauro	Y	Y	Y	Y	Y	N
4 Himes	Y	N	Y	Y	Y	Y
5 Murphy	Y	Y	Y	Y	Y	Y
DELAWARE						
AL Castle	Y	N	N	N	Y	Y
FLORIDA						
1 Miller	Y	N	N	N	N	Y
2 Boyd	Y	Y	Y	Y	Y	Y
3 Brown	Y	Y	Y	Y	Y	N
4 Crenshaw	Y	N	N	N	Y	Y
5 Brown-Waite	Y	N	N	N	Y	Y
6 Stearns	Y	N	N	N	N	Y
7 Mica	Y	N	N	N	N	Y
8 Grayson	Y	Y	Y	Y	Y	Y
9 Bilirakis	Y	?	N	N	Y	Y
10 Young	Y	Y	N	N	Y	Y
11 Castor	Y	Y	Y	Y	Y	Y
12 Putnam	Y	N	N	N	N	Y
13 Buchanan	Y	N	N	N	N	Y
14 Mack	Y	N	N	N	N	Y
15 Posey	Y	N	N	N	N	Y
16 Rooney	Y	N	N	N	N	Y
17 Meek	Y	Y	Y	Y	Y	Y
18 Ros-Lehtinen	Y	N	N	N	Y	Y
19 Wexler	Y	?	?	?	Y	Y
20 Wasserman Schultz	Y	Y	Y	Y	Y	N
21 Diaz-Balart, L.	Y	N	N	N	N	Y
22 Klein	Y	Y	Y	Y	Y	Y
23 Hastings	Y	Y	Y	Y	Y	N
24 Kosmas	Y	N	Y	Y	Y	Y
25 Diaz-Balart, M.	Y	N	N	N	N	Y
GEORGIA						
1 Kingston	Y	N	N	N	N	Y
2 Bishop	Y	Y	Y	Y	Y	Y
3 Westmoreland	Y	N	N	N	N	Y
4 Johnson	Y	Y	Y	Y	Y	Y
5 Lewis	Y	Y	Y	Y	Y	Y
6 Price	Y	N	N	N	N	Y
7 Linder	Y	N	N	N	N	Y
8 Marshall	Y	Y	Y	Y	Y	Y
9 Deal	?	?	?	?	N	Y
10 Broun	Y	N	N	N	N	Y
11 Gingrey	Y	N	N	N	N	Y
12 Barrow	Y	Y	Y	Y	Y	Y
13 Scott	Y	Y	Y	Y	Y	Y
HAWAII						
1 Abercrombie	Y	Y	Y	Y	Y	N
2 Hirono	Y	Y	Y	Y	Y	Y
IDAHO						
1 Minnick	Y	N	N	Y	Y	Y
2 Simpson	Y	N	N	N	N	Y
ILLINOIS						
1 Rush	Y	Y	Y	Y	Y	Y
2 Jackson	Y	Y	Y	Y	Y	N
3 Lipinski	Y	Y	Y	Y	Y	N
4 Gutierrez	Y	?	Y	Y	Y	Y
5 Quigley	Y	Y	Y	Y	Y	Y
6 Roskam	Y	N	N	N	Y	Y
7 Davis	?	Y	Y	Y	Y	Y
8 Bean	Y	Y	Y	Y	Y	Y
9 Schakowsky	Y	Y	Y	Y	Y	Y
10 Kirk	Y	N	N	N	Y	Y
11 Halvorson	Y	Y	Y	Y	Y	Y
12 Costello	Y	Y	Y	Y	Y	N
13 Biggert	Y	N	N	N	Y	Y
14 Foster	Y	Y	Y	Y	Y	Y
15 Johnson	Y	N	N	N	N	Y

KEY   **Republicans**   Democrats

Y Voted for (yea)	X Paired against	C Voted "present" to avoid possible conflict of interest
# Paired for	– Announced against	? Did not vote or otherwise make a position known
+ Announced for	P Voted "present"	
N Voted against (nay)		

	895	896	897	898	899	900
16 **Manzullo**	Y	N	N	N	N	Y
17 Hare	Y	Y	Y	Y	Y	N
18 **Schock**	Y	N	N	N	N	Y
19 **Shimkus**	Y	N	N	N	N	Y
INDIANA						
1 Visclosky	Y	Y	Y	Y	Y	Y
2 Donnelly	Y	N	Y	Y	Y	Y
3 **Souder**	Y	N	N	N	N	Y
4 **Buyer**	Y	N	N	N	N	Y
5 **Burton**	Y	N	N	N	Y	Y
6 **Pence**	Y	N	N	N	N	Y
7 Carson	Y	Y	Y	Y	Y	N
8 Ellsworth	Y	N	Y	Y	Y	Y
9 Hill	Y	Y	Y	Y	Y	Y
IOWA						
1 Braley	Y	Y	Y	Y	Y	Y
2 Loebsack	Y	Y	Y	Y	Y	Y
3 Boswell	Y	Y	Y	Y	Y	Y
4 **Latham**	Y	N	N	N	Y	Y
5 **King**	Y	N	N	N	N	Y
KANSAS						
1 **Moran**	Y	N	N	N	Y	Y
2 **Jenkins**	Y	N	N	N	Y	Y
3 Moore	Y	Y	Y	Y	Y	Y
4 **Tiahrt**	?	N	N	N	Y	Y
KENTUCKY						
1 **Whitfield**	Y	N	N	N	Y	Y
2 **Guthrie**	Y	N	N	N	Y	Y
3 Yarmuth	Y	+	+	?	Y	Y
4 **Davis**	Y	N	N	N	Y	Y
5 **Rogers**	Y	N	N	N	Y	Y
6 Chandler	Y	Y	Y	Y	Y	Y
LOUISIANA						
1 **Scalise**	Y	N	N	N	N	Y
2 **Cao**	Y	N	?	N	Y	Y
3 Melancon	Y	Y	Y	Y	Y	Y
4 **Fleming**	Y	N	N	N	Y	Y
5 **Alexander**	Y	N	N	N	Y	Y
6 **Cassidy**	Y	N	N	N	Y	Y
7 **Boustany**	Y	N	N	N	N	Y
MAINE						
1 Pingree	Y	Y	Y	Y	Y	Y
2 Michaud	Y	Y	Y	Y	Y	Y
MARYLAND						
1 Kratovil	Y	N	Y	Y	Y	Y
2 Ruppersberger	Y	Y	Y	Y	Y	N
3 Sarbanes	Y	Y	Y	Y	Y	Y
4 Edwards	Y	Y	Y	Y	Y	Y
5 Hoyer	Y	Y	Y	Y	Y	Y
6 **Bartlett**	Y	Y	N	N	N	Y
7 Cummings	Y	Y	Y	Y	Y	N
8 Van Hollen	Y	Y	Y	Y	Y	Y
MASSACHUSETTS						
1 Olver	Y	Y	Y	Y	Y	N
2 Neal	Y	Y	Y	Y	Y	N
3 McGovern	Y	Y	Y	Y	Y	Y
4 Frank	Y	Y	Y	Y	Y	Y
5 Tsongas	Y	Y	Y	Y	Y	Y
6 Tierney	Y	Y	Y	Y	Y	Y
7 Markey	Y	Y	Y	Y	Y	Y
8 Capuano	?	?	?	?	Y	Y
9 Lynch	Y	Y	Y	Y	Y	Y
10 Delahunt	?	Y	Y	Y	Y	N
MICHIGAN						
1 Stupak	Y	Y	Y	Y	Y	Y
2 **Hoekstra**	Y	N	N	N	N	Y
3 **Ehlers**	Y	Y	N	N	Y	Y
4 **Camp**	Y	N	N	N	Y	Y
5 Kildee	Y	Y	Y	Y	Y	N
6 **Upton**	Y	N	N	N	Y	Y
7 Schauer	Y	N	Y	Y	Y	Y
8 **Rogers**	Y	N	N	N	Y	Y
9 Peters	Y	Y	Y	Y	Y	Y
10 **Miller**	Y	N	N	N	Y	Y
11 **McCotter**	Y	N	N	N	Y	Y
12 Levin	Y	Y	Y	Y	Y	Y
13 Kilpatrick	Y	Y	Y	Y	Y	N
14 Conyers	Y	Y	Y	Y	Y	Y
15 Dingell	Y	?	?	?	Y	Y
MINNESOTA						
1 Walz	Y	Y	Y	Y	Y	Y
2 **Kline**	Y	N	N	N	Y	Y
3 **Paulsen**	Y	N	N	N	Y	Y
4 McCollum	Y	Y	Y	Y	Y	Y
5 Ellison	Y	Y	Y	Y	Y	Y
6 **Bachmann**	Y	N	N	N	Y	Y
7 Peterson	Y	Y	Y	Y	Y	Y
8 Oberstar	Y	Y	Y	Y	Y	N
MISSISSIPPI						
1 Childers	Y	Y	Y	Y	Y	Y
2 Thompson	Y	Y	Y	Y	Y	N
3 **Harper**	Y	N	N	N	Y	Y
4 Taylor	Y	Y	N	N	Y	Y
MISSOURI						
1 Clay	Y	Y	Y	Y	Y	Y
2 **Akin**	Y	N	N	N	N	Y
3 Carnahan	Y	Y	Y	Y	Y	Y
4 Skelton	Y	Y	Y	Y	Y	Y
5 Cleaver	Y	Y	Y	Y	Y	Y
6 **Graves**	Y	N	N	N	Y	Y
7 **Blunt**	Y	?	N	N	Y	Y
8 **Emerson**	Y	N	N	N	Y	Y
9 **Luetkemeyer**	Y	N	N	N	Y	Y
MONTANA						
AL **Rehberg**	Y	N	N	N	Y	Y
NEBRASKA						
1 **Fortenberry**	Y	N	N	N	Y	Y
2 **Terry**	Y	N	N	N	Y	Y
3 **Smith**	Y	N	N	N	Y	Y
NEVADA						
1 Berkley	Y	Y	Y	Y	Y	Y
2 **Heller**	Y	Y	N	N	Y	Y
3 Titus	Y	Y	Y	Y	Y	Y
NEW HAMPSHIRE						
1 Shea-Porter	Y	Y	Y	Y	Y	Y
2 Hodes	Y	Y	Y	Y	Y	Y
NEW JERSEY						
1 Andrews	Y	Y	Y	Y	Y	Y
2 **LoBiondo**	Y	N	N	N	N	Y
3 Adler	Y	N	Y	Y	Y	Y
4 **Smith**	Y	N	N	N	Y	Y
5 **Garrett**	Y	Y	N	N	N	Y
6 Pallone	Y	Y	Y	Y	Y	Y
7 **Lance**	Y	N	N	N	Y	Y
8 Pascrell	Y	Y	Y	Y	Y	Y
9 Rothman	Y	+	+	+	+	–
10 Payne	Y	Y	Y	Y	Y	N
11 **Frelinghuysen**	Y	N	N	N	Y	Y
12 Holt	Y	Y	Y	Y	Y	Y
13 Sires	Y	Y	Y	Y	Y	N
NEW MEXICO						
1 Heinrich	Y	Y	Y	Y	Y	Y
2 Teague	Y	Y	Y	Y	Y	Y
3 Lujan	Y	Y	Y	Y	Y	Y
NEW YORK						
1 Bishop	Y	Y	Y	Y	Y	Y
2 Israel	?	Y	Y	Y	Y	Y
3 **King**	Y	N	N	N	Y	Y
4 McCarthy	Y	Y	Y	Y	Y	Y
5 Ackerman	Y	Y	Y	Y	Y	Y
6 Meeks	Y	Y	Y	Y	Y	Y
7 Crowley	Y	+	+	+	Y	Y
8 Nadler	Y	Y	Y	Y	Y	N
9 Weiner	Y	Y	Y	Y	Y	Y
10 Towns	Y	Y	Y	Y	Y	N
11 Clarke	Y	Y	Y	Y	Y	Y
12 Velázquez	Y	Y	Y	Y	Y	Y
13 McMahon	Y	Y	Y	Y	Y	Y
14 Maloney	Y	?	Y	Y	Y	Y
15 Rangel	Y	Y	?	Y	Y	Y
16 Serrano	Y	Y	Y	?	Y	Y
17 Engel	Y	Y	Y	Y	Y	Y
18 Lowey	Y	Y	Y	Y	Y	Y
19 Hall	Y	Y	Y	Y	Y	N
20 Murphy	Y	N	Y	Y	Y	Y
21 Tonko	Y	Y	Y	Y	Y	Y
22 Hinchey	Y	Y	Y	Y	Y	N
23 Owens	Y	Y	Y	Y	Y	Y
24 Arcuri	Y	N	Y	Y	Y	Y
25 Maffei	Y	Y	Y	Y	Y	Y
26 **Lee**	Y	N	N	N	Y	Y
27 Higgins	Y	Y	Y	Y	Y	Y
28 Slaughter	Y	Y	Y	Y	Y	Y
29 Massa	Y	Y	Y	Y	Y	Y
NORTH CAROLINA						
1 Butterfield	Y	Y	Y	Y	Y	Y
2 Etheridge	Y	Y	Y	Y	Y	Y
3 **Jones**	Y	Y	N	N	Y	Y
4 Price	Y	Y	Y	Y	Y	N
5 **Foxx**	Y	N	N	N	N	Y
6 **Coble**	Y	N	N	N	Y	Y
7 McIntyre	Y	Y	Y	Y	Y	Y
8 Kissell	Y	Y	Y	Y	Y	Y
9 **Myrick**	Y	N	N	N	N	Y
10 **McHenry**	Y	N	N	N	Y	Y
11 Shuler	Y	N	Y	N	Y	Y
12 Watt	Y	Y	Y	Y	Y	N
13 Miller	Y	Y	Y	Y	Y	Y
NORTH DAKOTA						
AL Pomeroy	Y	Y	Y	Y	Y	Y
OHIO						
1 Driehaus	Y	Y	Y	Y	Y	Y
2 **Schmidt**	Y	N	N	N	Y	Y
3 **Turner**	Y	N	N	N	Y	Y
4 **Jordan**	Y	N	N	N	Y	Y
5 **Latta**	Y	N	N	N	Y	Y
6 Wilson	Y	Y	Y	Y	Y	Y
7 **Austria**	Y	N	N	N	Y	Y
8 **Boehner**	Y	N	N	N	N	Y
9 Kaptur	Y	Y	Y	Y	Y	N
10 Kucinich	Y	Y	N	Y	Y	N
11 Fudge	Y	Y	Y	Y	Y	N
12 **Tiberi**	Y	N	N	N	Y	Y
13 Sutton	Y	Y	Y	Y	Y	Y
14 **LaTourette**	Y	N	N	N	Y	Y
15 Kilroy	Y	Y	Y	Y	Y	Y
16 Boccieri	Y	Y	Y	Y	Y	Y
17 Ryan	Y	Y	Y	Y	Y	N
18 Space	Y	Y	Y	Y	Y	Y
OKLAHOMA						
1 **Sullivan**	Y	?	?	N	N	Y
2 Boren	Y	N	Y	Y	Y	Y
3 **Lucas**	Y	N	N	N	Y	Y
4 **Cole**	Y	N	N	N	Y	Y
5 **Fallin**	Y	N	N	N	Y	Y
OREGON						
1 Wu	Y	Y	Y	Y	Y	Y
2 **Walden**	Y	Y	N	N	N	Y
3 Blumenauer	Y	Y	Y	Y	Y	Y
4 DeFazio	Y	Y	Y	Y	Y	Y
5 Schrader	Y	Y	Y	Y	Y	Y
PENNSYLVANIA						
1 Brady	Y	Y	Y	Y	Y	N
2 Fattah	Y	Y	Y	Y	Y	N
3 Dahlkemper	Y	Y	Y	Y	Y	Y
4 Altmire	Y	N	Y	Y	Y	Y
5 **Thompson**	Y	N	N	N	Y	Y
6 **Gerlach**	Y	–	–	+	+	+
7 Sestak	Y	Y	Y	Y	Y	Y
8 Murphy, P.	Y	Y	Y	Y	Y	Y
9 **Shuster**	Y	N	N	N	Y	Y
10 Carney	Y	N	Y	Y	Y	Y
11 Kanjorski	Y	Y	Y	Y	Y	Y
12 Murtha	Y	Y	Y	Y	Y	N
13 Schwartz	Y	Y	Y	Y	Y	Y
14 Doyle	Y	Y	Y	Y	Y	N
15 **Dent**	Y	Y	N	N	Y	Y
16 **Pitts**	Y	?	?	N	Y	Y
17 Holden	Y	Y	Y	Y	Y	Y
18 **Murphy, T.**	Y	–	–	–	Y	Y
19 **Platts**	Y	Y	N	N	Y	Y
RHODE ISLAND						
1 Kennedy	Y	Y	Y	Y	Y	Y
2 Langevin	Y	Y	Y	Y	Y	Y
SOUTH CAROLINA						
1 **Brown**	?	?	?	?	?	?
2 **Wilson**	Y	N	N	N	N	Y
3 **Barrett**	?	?	?	?	?	?
4 **Inglis**	Y	N	N	N	N	Y
5 Spratt	Y	Y	Y	Y	Y	Y
6 Clyburn	Y	Y	Y	Y	Y	N
SOUTH DAKOTA						
AL Herseth Sandlin	Y	Y	Y	Y	Y	Y
TENNESSEE						
1 **Roe**	Y	N	N	N	Y	Y
2 **Duncan**	Y	N	N	N	N	Y
3 **Wamp**	Y	N	N	N	Y	Y
4 Davis	Y	Y	Y	Y	Y	Y
5 Cooper	Y	?	?	Y	Y	Y
6 Gordon	?	Y	Y	?	Y	Y
7 **Blackburn**	Y	N	N	N	Y	Y
8 Tanner	?	?	?	?	?	?
9 Cohen	Y	Y	Y	Y	Y	N
TEXAS						
1 **Gohmert**	Y	Y	N	N	N	Y
2 **Poe**	Y	N	N	N	N	Y
3 **Johnson, S.**	Y	N	N	N	N	Y
4 **Hall**	Y	N	N	N	Y	Y
5 **Hensarling**	Y	N	N	N	N	Y
6 **Barton**	Y	N	N	N	N	Y
7 **Culberson**	Y	N	N	N	Y	Y
8 **Brady**	Y	N	N	N	N	Y
9 Green, A.	Y	Y	Y	Y	Y	Y
10 **McCaul**	Y	N	N	N	Y	Y
11 **Conaway**	Y	N	N	N	N	Y
12 **Granger**	Y	N	N	?	Y	Y
13 **Thornberry**	Y	N	N	N	N	Y
14 **Paul**	Y	Y	N	N	N	N
15 Hinojosa	Y	Y	Y	Y	Y	Y
16 Reyes	Y	Y	Y	Y	Y	Y
17 Edwards	Y	Y	Y	Y	Y	Y
18 Jackson Lee	+	Y	Y	Y	Y	N
19 **Neugebauer**	Y	N	N	N	N	Y
20 Gonzalez	Y	Y	Y	Y	Y	Y
21 **Smith**	Y	N	N	N	Y	Y
22 **Olson**	Y	Y	N	N	Y	Y
23 Rodriguez	Y	Y	Y	Y	Y	Y
24 **Marchant**	Y	N	N	N	Y	Y
25 Doggett	Y	Y	Y	Y	Y	Y
26 **Burgess**	Y	N	N	N	N	Y
27 Ortiz	Y	Y	Y	Y	Y	Y
28 Cuellar	Y	Y	Y	Y	Y	Y
29 Green, G.	?	Y	Y	Y	Y	Y
30 Johnson, E.	Y	Y	Y	Y	Y	N
31 **Carter**	Y	N	N	N	N	Y
32 **Sessions**	Y	N	N	N	N	Y
UTAH						
1 **Bishop**	Y	N	N	N	N	Y
2 Matheson	Y	Y	Y	Y	Y	Y
3 **Chaffetz**	Y	Y	N	N	N	Y
VERMONT						
AL Welch	Y	Y	Y	Y	Y	Y
VIRGINIA						
1 **Wittman**	Y	N	N	N	N	Y
2 Nye	Y	Y	Y	Y	Y	Y
3 Scott	Y	Y	Y	Y	Y	Y
4 **Forbes**	Y	N	N	N	N	Y
5 Perriello	Y	Y	Y	Y	Y	Y
6 **Goodlatte**	Y	N	N	N	N	Y
7 **Cantor**	Y	?	N	N	N	Y
8 Moran	Y	Y	Y	Y	Y	N
9 Boucher	Y	Y	Y	Y	Y	Y
10 **Wolf**	Y	N	N	N	Y	Y
11 Connolly	Y	Y	Y	Y	Y	Y
WASHINGTON						
1 Inslee	Y	Y	Y	Y	Y	Y
2 Larsen	Y	Y	Y	Y	Y	Y
3 Baird	Y	Y	N	Y	Y	Y
4 **Hastings**	Y	N	N	N	Y	Y
5 **McMorris Rodgers**	Y	N	N	N	N	Y
6 Dicks	Y	Y	Y	Y	Y	Y
7 McDermott	Y	Y	Y	Y	Y	N
8 **Reichert**	Y	N	N	N	Y	Y
9 Smith	Y	Y	Y	Y	Y	Y
WEST VIRGINIA						
1 Mollohan	Y	Y	Y	Y	Y	Y
2 **Capito**	Y	N	N	N	Y	Y
3 Rahall	Y	Y	Y	Y	Y	N
WISCONSIN						
1 **Ryan**	Y	N	N	N	N	Y
2 Baldwin	Y	Y	Y	Y	Y	Y
3 Kind	Y	Y	Y	Y	Y	Y
4 Moore	Y	Y	Y	Y	?	N
5 **Sensenbrenner**	Y	N	N	N	N	Y
6 **Petri**	Y	N	N	N	N	Y
7 Obey	Y	Y	Y	Y	Y	N
8 Kagen	Y	Y	Y	Y	Y	Y
WYOMING						
AL **Lummis**	Y	Y	N	N	N	Y
DELEGATES						
Faleomavaega (A.S.)					?	?
Norton (D.C.)					Y	Y
Bordallo (Guam)					Y	N
Sablan (N. Marianas)					Y	Y
Pierluisi (P.R.)					Y	Y
Christensen (V.I.)					Y	Y

IN THE HOUSE | By Vote Number

901. HR 3791. Firefighter Organization Grants/Passage.
Passage of the bill that would authorize $2.2 billion per year from fiscal 2010 through 2014 for Federal Emergency Management Agency grant programs for firefighting organizations. It would authorize $1 billion per year for the Assistance to Firefighters Grants program to purchase equipment and $1.2 billion per year for the Staffing for Adequate Fire and Emergency Response program to hire and retain personnel. As amended, it would require the Homeland Security secretary to conduct a survey of firefighter organizations to determine compliance with best practices and establish a safety task force. Passed 395-31: D 252-0; R 143-31. Nov. 18, 2009.

902. HR 2781. Molalla River Designation/Previous Question.
Cardoza, D-Calif., motion to order the previous question (thus ending debate and possibility of amendment) on adoption of the rule (H Res 908) that would provide for House floor consideration of the bill that would designate segments of the Molalla River in Oregon as part of the National Wild and Scenic Rivers System. Motion agreed to 241-176: D 241-5; R 0-171. Nov. 19, 2009.

903. HR 2781. Molalla River Designation/Rule.
Adoption of the rule (H Res 908) that would provide for House floor consideration of the bill that would designate segments of the Molalla River in Oregon as part of the National Wild and Scenic Rivers System. Adopted 244-176: D 243-5; R 1-171. Nov. 19, 2009.

904. S 1599. Reserve Officers Association/Passage.
Chu, D-Calif., motion to suspend the rules and pass the bill that would update and expand positions included in the federal charter of the Reserve Officers Association. Motion agreed to 425-0: D 252-0; R 173-0. A two-thirds majority of those present and voting (284 in this case) is required for passage under suspension of the rules. Nov. 19, 2009.

905. HR 2781. Molalla River Designation/Passage.
Passage of the bill that would designate segments of the Molalla River in Oregon as a recreational river in the National Wild and Scenic Rivers System. Passed 292-133: D 252-0; R 40-133. Nov. 19, 2009.

	901	902	903	904	905
ALABAMA					
1 **Bonner**	Y	N	N	Y	N
2 Bright	Y	Y	Y	Y	Y
3 **Rogers**	Y	N	N	Y	N
4 **Aderholt**	Y	N	N	Y	N
5 Griffith	Y	Y	Y	Y	Y
6 **Bachus**	Y	N	N	Y	N
7 Davis	Y	Y	Y	Y	Y
ALASKA					
AL **Young**	Y	N	N	Y	N
ARIZONA					
1 Kirkpatrick	Y	Y	Y	Y	Y
2 **Franks**	N	N	N	Y	N
3 **Shadegg**	N	N	N	Y	N
4 Pastor	Y	Y	Y	Y	Y
5 Mitchell	Y	Y	Y	Y	Y
6 **Flake**	N	N	N	Y	N
7 Grijalva	Y	Y	Y	Y	Y
8 Giffords	Y	Y	Y	Y	Y
ARKANSAS					
1 Berry	Y	Y	Y	Y	Y
2 Snyder	Y	Y	Y	Y	Y
3 **Boozman**	Y	N	N	Y	N
4 Ross	Y	Y	Y	Y	Y
CALIFORNIA					
1 Thompson	Y	Y	Y	Y	Y
2 **Herger**	N	N	N	Y	N
3 **Lungren**	Y	N	N	Y	N
4 **McClintock**	N	N	N	Y	N
5 Matsui	Y	Y	Y	Y	Y
6 Woolsey	Y	Y	Y	Y	Y
7 Miller, George	Y	+	+	+	+
8 Pelosi					
9 Lee	Y	Y	Y	Y	Y
10 Garamendi	Y	Y	Y	Y	Y
11 McNerney	Y	Y	Y	Y	Y
12 Speier	Y	Y	Y	Y	Y
13 Stark	Y	Y	Y	Y	Y
14 Eshoo	Y	Y	Y	Y	Y
15 Honda	Y	Y	Y	Y	Y
16 Lofgren	Y	Y	Y	Y	Y
17 Farr	Y	Y	Y	Y	Y
18 Cardoza	Y	Y	Y	Y	Y
19 **Radanovich**	Y	N	N	Y	N
20 Costa	Y	Y	Y	Y	Y
21 **Nunes**	Y	N	N	Y	N
22 **McCarthy**	Y	N	N	Y	N
23 Capps	Y	Y	Y	Y	Y
24 **Gallegly**	Y	N	N	Y	N
25 **McKeon**	Y	N	N	Y	N
26 **Dreier**	Y	N	N	Y	N
27 Sherman	Y	Y	Y	Y	Y
28 Berman	Y	Y	Y	Y	Y
29 Schiff	Y	Y	Y	Y	Y
30 Waxman	Y	Y	Y	Y	Y
31 Becerra	Y	Y	Y	Y	Y
32 Chu	Y	Y	Y	Y	Y
33 Watson	Y	Y	Y	Y	Y
34 Roybal-Allard	Y	Y	Y	Y	Y
35 Waters	Y	Y	Y	Y	Y
36 Harman	Y	Y	Y	Y	Y
37 Richardson	Y	Y	Y	Y	Y
38 Napolitano	Y	Y	Y	Y	Y
39 Sánchez, Linda	Y	Y	Y	Y	Y
40 **Royce**	N	N	N	Y	N
41 **Lewis**	Y	N	N	Y	N
42 **Miller, Gary**	Y	N	N	Y	N
43 Baca	Y	Y	Y	Y	Y
44 **Calvert**	Y	N	N	Y	N
45 **Bono Mack**	Y	N	N	Y	N
46 **Rohrabacher**	Y	N	N	Y	N
47 Sanchez, Loretta	Y	Y	Y	Y	Y
48 **Campbell**	N	N	N	Y	N
49 **Issa**	N	N	N	Y	N
50 **Bilbray**	Y	N	N	Y	N
51 Filner	Y	Y	Y	Y	Y
52 **Hunter**	Y	N	N	Y	N
53 Davis	Y	Y	Y	Y	Y

	901	902	903	904	905
COLORADO					
1 DeGette	Y	Y	Y	Y	Y
2 Polis	Y	Y	Y	Y	Y
3 Salazar	Y	Y	Y	Y	Y
4 Markey	Y	Y	Y	Y	Y
5 **Lamborn**	N	N	N	Y	N
6 **Coffman**	N	N	N	Y	N
7 Perlmutter	Y	Y	Y	Y	Y
CONNECTICUT					
1 Larson	Y	Y	Y	Y	Y
2 Courtney	Y	Y	Y	Y	Y
3 DeLauro	Y	Y	Y	Y	Y
4 Himes	Y	Y	Y	Y	Y
5 Murphy	Y	Y	Y	Y	Y
DELAWARE					
AL **Castle**	Y	N	Y	Y	Y
FLORIDA					
1 **Miller**	Y	N	N	Y	N
2 Boyd	Y	Y	Y	Y	Y
3 Brown	Y	Y	Y	Y	Y
4 **Crenshaw**	Y	N	N	Y	N
5 **Brown-Waite**	Y	N	N	Y	Y
6 **Stearns**	Y	N	N	Y	N
7 **Mica**	N	N	N	Y	N
8 Grayson	Y	Y	Y	Y	Y
9 **Bilirakis**	Y	N	N	Y	N
10 **Young**	Y	N	N	Y	N
11 Castor	Y	Y	Y	Y	Y
12 **Putnam**	Y	N	N	Y	N
13 **Buchanan**	Y	N	N	Y	Y
14 **Mack**	N	N	N	Y	N
15 **Posey**	Y	N	N	Y	N
16 **Rooney**	Y	N	N	Y	N
17 Meek	Y	Y	Y	Y	Y
18 **Ros-Lehtinen**	Y	N	N	Y	N
19 Wexler	Y	Y	Y	Y	Y
20 Wasserman Schultz	Y	Y	Y	Y	Y
21 **Diaz-Balart, L.**	Y	N	N	Y	N
22 Klein	Y	Y	Y	Y	Y
23 Hastings	Y	Y	Y	Y	Y
24 Kosmas	Y	Y	Y	Y	Y
25 **Diaz-Balart, M.**	Y	N	N	Y	N
GEORGIA					
1 **Kingston**	N	N	N	Y	N
2 Bishop	Y	Y	Y	Y	Y
3 **Westmoreland**	Y	N	N	Y	N
4 Johnson	Y	Y	Y	Y	Y
5 Lewis	Y	?	?	Y	Y
6 **Price**	Y	N	N	Y	N
7 **Linder**	N	N	N	Y	N
8 Marshall	Y	Y	Y	Y	Y
9 **Deal**	Y	N	N	Y	N
10 **Broun**	N	N	N	Y	N
11 **Gingrey**	Y	N	N	Y	N
12 Barrow	Y	Y	Y	Y	Y
13 Scott	Y	Y	Y	Y	Y
HAWAII					
1 Abercrombie	Y	?	?	?	Y
2 Hirono	Y	Y	Y	Y	Y
IDAHO					
1 Minnick	Y	N	N	Y	Y
2 **Simpson**	Y	N	N	Y	Y
ILLINOIS					
1 Rush	Y	Y	Y	Y	Y
2 Jackson	Y	Y	Y	Y	Y
3 Lipinski	Y	Y	Y	Y	Y
4 Gutierrez	Y	Y	?	Y	Y
5 Quigley	Y	Y	Y	Y	Y
6 **Roskam**	Y	N	N	Y	Y
7 Davis	Y	Y	Y	Y	Y
8 Bean	Y	Y	Y	Y	Y
9 Schakowsky	Y	Y	Y	Y	Y
10 **Kirk**	Y	N	N	Y	Y
11 Halvorson	Y	Y	Y	Y	Y
12 Costello	Y	Y	Y	Y	Y
13 **Biggert**	Y	N	N	Y	Y
14 Foster	Y	Y	Y	Y	Y
15 **Johnson**	Y	N	N	Y	Y

KEY   **Republicans**   Democrats

Y Voted for (yea)	X Paired against	C Voted "present" to avoid possible conflict of interest
# Paired for	– Announced against	
+ Announced for	P Voted "present"	? Did not vote or otherwise make a position known
N Voted against (nay)		

	901	902	903	904	905
16 Manzullo	Y	N	N	Y	N
17 Hare	Y	Y	Y	Y	Y
18 Schock	Y	N	N	Y	N
19 Shimkus	Y	N	N	Y	N
INDIANA					
1 Visclosky	Y	Y	Y	Y	Y
2 Donnelly	Y	N	N	Y	Y
3 Souder	Y	N	N	Y	N
4 Buyer	Y	N	N	Y	N
5 Burton	Y	N	N	Y	N
6 Pence	Y	N	N	Y	N
7 Carson	Y	Y	Y	Y	Y
8 Ellsworth	Y	Y	Y	Y	Y
9 Hill	?	Y	Y	Y	Y
IOWA					
1 Braley	Y	Y	Y	Y	Y
2 Loebsack	Y	Y	Y	Y	Y
3 Boswell	Y	Y	Y	Y	Y
4 Latham	Y	N	N	Y	N
5 King	N	N	N	Y	N
KANSAS					
1 Moran	Y	N	N	Y	N
2 Jenkins	Y	N	N	Y	N
3 Moore	Y	Y	Y	Y	Y
4 Tiahrt	Y	N	N	Y	N
KENTUCKY					
1 Whitfield	Y	N	N	Y	Y
2 Guthrie	Y	N	N	Y	N
3 Yarmuth	Y	Y	Y	Y	Y
4 Davis	Y	N	N	Y	N
5 Rogers	Y	N	N	Y	Y
6 Chandler	Y	Y	Y	Y	Y
LOUISIANA					
1 Scalise	Y	N	N	Y	N
2 Cao	Y	N	N	Y	N
3 Melancon	Y	Y	Y	Y	?
4 Fleming	Y	N	N	Y	N
5 Alexander	Y	N	N	Y	N
6 Cassidy	Y	N	N	Y	N
7 Boustany	Y	?	?	Y	N
MAINE					
1 Pingree	Y	Y	Y	Y	Y
2 Michaud	Y	Y	Y	Y	Y
MARYLAND					
1 Kratovil	Y	Y	Y	Y	Y
2 Ruppersberger	Y	Y	Y	Y	Y
3 Sarbanes	Y	Y	Y	Y	Y
4 Edwards	Y	Y	Y	Y	Y
5 Hoyer	Y	Y	Y	Y	Y
6 Bartlett	Y	N	N	Y	Y
7 Cummings	Y	Y	Y	Y	Y
8 Van Hollen	Y	Y	Y	Y	Y
MASSACHUSETTS					
1 Olver	Y	Y	Y	Y	Y
2 Neal	?	Y	Y	Y	Y
3 McGovern	Y	Y	Y	Y	Y
4 Frank	Y	Y	Y	Y	Y
5 Tsongas	Y	Y	Y	Y	Y
6 Tierney	Y	Y	Y	Y	Y
7 Markey	Y	Y	Y	Y	Y
8 Capuano	Y	?	?	?	?
9 Lynch	Y	Y	Y	Y	Y
10 Delahunt	Y	Y	Y	Y	Y
MICHIGAN					
1 Stupak	?	Y	Y	Y	Y
2 Hoekstra	Y	N	N	Y	N
3 Ehlers	Y	N	N	Y	Y
4 Camp	Y	N	?	Y	Y
5 Kildee	Y	Y	Y	Y	Y
6 Upton	Y	N	N	Y	Y
7 Schauer	Y	Y	Y	Y	Y
8 Rogers	Y	N	N	Y	N
9 Peters	Y	Y	Y	Y	Y
10 Miller	Y	N	N	Y	Y
11 McCotter	Y	N	N	Y	Y
12 Levin	Y	Y	Y	Y	Y
13 Kilpatrick	Y	Y	Y	Y	Y
14 Conyers	Y	Y	Y	Y	Y
15 Dingell	Y	Y	Y	Y	Y
MINNESOTA					
1 Walz	Y	Y	Y	Y	Y
2 Kline	Y	N	N	Y	N
3 Paulsen	Y	N	N	Y	Y
4 McCollum	Y	Y	Y	Y	Y

	901	902	903	904	905
5 Ellison	Y	Y	Y	Y	Y
6 Bachmann	Y	N	N	Y	N
7 Peterson	Y	Y	Y	Y	Y
8 Oberstar	Y	Y	Y	Y	Y
MISSISSIPPI					
1 Childers	Y	N	N	Y	Y
2 Thompson	Y	Y	Y	Y	Y
3 Harper	Y	N	N	Y	N
4 Taylor	Y	N	N	Y	Y
MISSOURI					
1 Clay	Y	Y	Y	Y	Y
2 Akin	N	N	N	Y	N
3 Carnahan	Y	Y	Y	Y	Y
4 Skelton	Y	?	Y	Y	Y
5 Cleaver	Y	Y	Y	Y	Y
6 Graves	Y	N	N	Y	N
7 Blunt	Y	N	N	Y	N
8 Emerson	Y	N	N	Y	N
9 Luetkemeyer	Y	N	N	Y	N
MONTANA					
AL Rehberg	Y	N	N	Y	N
NEBRASKA					
1 Fortenberry	Y	N	N	Y	Y
2 Terry	Y	N	N	Y	N
3 Smith	Y	N	N	Y	N
NEVADA					
1 Berkley	Y	Y	Y	Y	Y
2 Heller	Y	N	N	Y	N
3 Titus	Y	Y	Y	Y	Y
NEW HAMPSHIRE					
1 Shea-Porter	Y	Y	Y	Y	Y
2 Hodes	Y	Y	Y	Y	Y
NEW JERSEY					
1 Andrews	Y	Y	Y	Y	Y
2 LoBiondo	Y	N	N	Y	Y
3 Adler	Y	Y	Y	Y	Y
4 Smith	Y	N	N	Y	Y
5 Garrett	Y	N	N	Y	N
6 Pallone	Y	Y	Y	Y	Y
7 Lance	Y	N	N	Y	Y
8 Pascrell	Y	Y	Y	Y	Y
9 Rothman	+	Y	Y	Y	+
10 Payne	Y	Y	Y	Y	Y
11 Frelinghuysen	Y	N	N	Y	Y
12 Holt	Y	Y	Y	Y	Y
13 Sires	Y	Y	Y	Y	Y
NEW MEXICO					
1 Heinrich	Y	Y	Y	Y	Y
2 Teague	Y	Y	Y	Y	Y
3 Lujan	Y	Y	Y	Y	Y
NEW YORK					
1 Bishop	Y	Y	Y	Y	Y
2 Israel	Y	Y	Y	Y	Y
3 King	Y	N	N	Y	N
4 McCarthy	Y	Y	Y	Y	Y
5 Ackerman	Y	Y	Y	Y	Y
6 Meeks	Y	Y	Y	Y	Y
7 Crowley	Y	Y	Y	Y	Y
8 Nadler	Y	?	Y	Y	Y
9 Weiner	Y	Y	Y	Y	Y
10 Towns	Y	Y	Y	Y	Y
11 Clarke	Y	?	Y	Y	Y
12 Velázquez	Y	Y	Y	Y	Y
13 McMahon	Y	Y	Y	Y	Y
14 Maloney	Y	Y	Y	Y	Y
15 Rangel	Y	Y	Y	Y	Y
16 Serrano	Y	Y	Y	Y	Y
17 Engel	Y	?	Y	Y	Y
18 Lowey	Y	Y	Y	Y	Y
19 Hall	Y	Y	Y	Y	Y
20 Murphy	Y	Y	Y	Y	Y
21 Tonko	Y	Y	Y	Y	Y
22 Hinchey	Y	Y	Y	Y	Y
23 Owens	Y	Y	Y	Y	Y
24 Arcuri	Y	Y	Y	Y	Y
25 Maffei	Y	Y	Y	Y	Y
26 Lee	Y	N	N	Y	N
27 Higgins	Y	Y	Y	Y	Y
28 Slaughter	Y	Y	Y	Y	Y
29 Massa	Y	Y	Y	Y	Y
NORTH CAROLINA					
1 Butterfield	Y	Y	Y	Y	Y
2 Etheridge	Y	Y	Y	Y	Y
3 Jones	Y	N	N	Y	Y
4 Price	Y	Y	Y	Y	Y

	901	902	903	904	905
5 Foxx	Y	N	N	Y	N
6 Coble	Y	N	N	Y	N
7 McIntyre	Y	Y	Y	Y	Y
8 Kissell	Y	Y	Y	Y	Y
9 Myrick	Y	N	N	Y	N
10 McHenry	Y	N	N	Y	N
11 Shuler	Y	Y	N	Y	N
12 Watt	Y	Y	?	Y	Y
13 Miller	Y	Y	Y	Y	Y
NORTH DAKOTA					
AL Pomeroy	Y	Y	Y	Y	Y
OHIO					
1 Driehaus	Y	Y	Y	Y	Y
2 Schmidt	Y	N	N	Y	N
3 Turner	Y	N	N	Y	N
4 Jordan	N	N	N	Y	N
5 Latta	Y	N	N	Y	N
6 Wilson	Y	Y	Y	?	Y
7 Austria	Y	N	N	Y	N
8 Boehner	Y	N	N	Y	N
9 Kaptur	Y	Y	Y	Y	Y
10 Kucinich	Y	Y	Y	Y	Y
11 Fudge	Y	Y	Y	Y	Y
12 Tiberi	Y	N	N	Y	N
13 Sutton	Y	Y	Y	Y	Y
14 LaTourette	Y	N	N	Y	N
15 Kilroy	Y	Y	Y	Y	Y
16 Boccieri	Y	Y	Y	Y	Y
17 Ryan	Y	Y	Y	Y	Y
18 Space	Y	Y	Y	Y	Y
OKLAHOMA					
1 Sullivan	Y	N	N	Y	N
2 Boren	Y	Y	Y	Y	Y
3 Lucas	Y	N	N	Y	N
4 Cole	Y	N	N	Y	N
5 Fallin	Y	N	N	Y	N
OREGON					
1 Wu	Y	?	Y	Y	Y
2 Walden	Y	N	N	Y	Y
3 Blumenauer	Y	Y	Y	Y	Y
4 DeFazio	Y	Y	Y	Y	Y
5 Schrader	Y	Y	Y	Y	Y
PENNSYLVANIA					
1 Brady	Y	Y	Y	Y	Y
2 Fattah	Y	Y	Y	Y	Y
3 Dahlkemper	Y	Y	Y	Y	Y
4 Altmire	Y	Y	Y	Y	Y
5 Thompson	Y	N	N	Y	N
6 Gerlach	+	N	N	Y	Y
7 Sestak	Y	Y	Y	Y	Y
8 Murphy, P.	Y	Y	Y	Y	Y
9 Shuster	Y	N	N	Y	N
10 Carney	Y	Y	Y	Y	Y
11 Kanjorski	Y	Y	Y	Y	Y
12 Murtha	Y	Y	Y	Y	Y
13 Schwartz	Y	Y	Y	Y	Y
14 Doyle	Y	Y	Y	Y	Y
15 Dent	Y	N	N	Y	Y
16 Pitts	Y	N	N	Y	N
17 Holden	Y	Y	Y	Y	Y
18 Murphy, T.	Y	N	N	Y	?
19 Platts	Y	N	N	Y	Y
RHODE ISLAND					
1 Kennedy	Y	Y	?	Y	Y
2 Langevin	Y	Y	Y	Y	Y
SOUTH CAROLINA					
1 Brown	?	?	?	?	?
2 Wilson	Y	N	N	Y	N
3 Barrett	?	N	N	Y	N
4 Inglis	N	N	N	Y	N
5 Spratt	Y	Y	Y	Y	Y
6 Clyburn	Y	Y	Y	Y	Y
SOUTH DAKOTA					
AL Herseth Sandlin	Y	Y	Y	Y	Y
TENNESSEE					
1 Roe	Y	N	N	Y	N
2 Duncan	Y	N	N	Y	N
3 Wamp	Y	N	N	Y	N
4 Davis	Y	Y	Y	Y	Y
5 Cooper	Y	Y	Y	Y	Y
6 Gordon	Y	Y	Y	Y	Y
7 Blackburn	Y	N	N	Y	N
8 Tanner	?	Y	Y	Y	Y
9 Cohen	Y	Y	Y	Y	Y

	901	902	903	904	905
TEXAS					
1 Gohmert	Y	?	N	Y	N
2 Poe	Y	N	N	Y	N
3 Johnson, S.	N	N	N	Y	N
4 Hall	Y	N	N	Y	N
5 Hensarling	N	N	N	Y	N
6 Barton	Y	N	N	Y	N
7 Culberson	N	N	N	Y	N
8 Brady	Y	N	N	Y	N
9 Green, A.	Y	Y	Y	Y	Y
10 McCaul	Y	?	?	?	?
11 Conaway	N	N	N	Y	N
12 Granger	Y	N	N	Y	N
13 Thornberry	Y	N	N	Y	N
14 Paul	N	N	N	Y	N
15 Hinojosa	Y	Y	Y	Y	Y
16 Reyes	Y	Y	Y	Y	Y
17 Edwards	Y	Y	Y	Y	Y
18 Jackson Lee	Y	Y	Y	Y	Y
19 Neugebauer	N	N	N	Y	N
20 Gonzalez	Y	Y	Y	Y	Y
21 Smith	Y	N	N	?	N
22 Olson	Y	N	N	Y	N
23 Rodriguez	Y	Y	Y	Y	Y
24 Marchant	Y	N	N	Y	N
25 Doggett	Y	Y	Y	Y	Y
26 Burgess	Y	?	N	Y	N
27 Ortiz	Y	Y	Y	Y	Y
28 Cuellar	Y	Y	Y	Y	Y
29 Green, G.	Y	Y	Y	Y	Y
30 Johnson, E.	Y	Y	Y	Y	Y
31 Carter	N	?	?	?	?
32 Sessions	Y	N	N	Y	N
UTAH					
1 Bishop	N	N	N	Y	N
2 Matheson	Y	Y	Y	Y	Y
3 Chaffetz	N	N	N	Y	N
VERMONT					
AL Welch	Y	Y	Y	Y	Y
VIRGINIA					
1 Wittman	Y	N	N	Y	N
2 Nye	Y	Y	Y	Y	Y
3 Scott	Y	Y	Y	Y	Y
4 Forbes	Y	N	N	Y	N
5 Perriello	Y	Y	Y	Y	Y
6 Goodlatte	Y	N	N	Y	N
7 Cantor	Y	N	N	Y	N
8 Moran	Y	?	?	?	Y
9 Boucher	Y	Y	Y	Y	Y
10 Wolf	Y	N	N	Y	Y
11 Connolly	Y	Y	Y	Y	Y
WASHINGTON					
1 Inslee	Y	Y	Y	Y	Y
2 Larsen	Y	Y	Y	Y	Y
3 Baird	Y	N	N	Y	Y
4 Hastings	Y	N	N	Y	N
5 McMorris Rodgers	Y	N	N	Y	N
6 Dicks	Y	Y	Y	Y	Y
7 McDermott	Y	?	?	Y	Y
8 Reichert	Y	N	N	Y	Y
9 Smith	Y	Y	Y	Y	Y
WEST VIRGINIA					
1 Mollohan	Y	Y	Y	Y	Y
2 Capito	Y	N	N	Y	N
3 Rahall	Y	Y	Y	Y	Y
WISCONSIN					
1 Ryan	Y	N	N	Y	N
2 Baldwin	Y	Y	Y	Y	Y
3 Kind	Y	Y	Y	Y	Y
4 Moore	Y	Y	Y	Y	?
5 Sensenbrenner	N	N	N	Y	N
6 Petri	Y	N	N	Y	N
7 Obey	Y	Y	Y	Y	Y
8 Kagen	Y	Y	Y	Y	Y
WYOMING					
AL Lummis	N	N	N	Y	N
DELEGATES					
Faleomavaega (A.S.)					
Norton (D.C.)					
Bordallo (Guam)					
Sablan (N. Marianas)					
Pierluisi (P.R.)					
Christensen (V.I.)					

IN THE HOUSE | By Vote Number

906. H Con Res 212. Velvet Revolution Anniversary/Adoption.
Ackerman, D-N.Y., motion to suspend the rules and adopt the resolution that would recognize the 20th anniversary of the collapse of the communist regimes in Central and Eastern Europe and commemorate the 20th anniversary of the Velvet Revolution in Czechoslovakia. Motion agreed to 426-0: D 252-0; R 174-0. A two-thirds majority (284 in this case) is required for adoption under suspension of the rules. Nov. 19, 2009.

907. HR 3961. Medicare Physician Reimbursement/Motion to Table.
Waxman, D-Calif., motion to table (kill) the Gingrey, R-Ga., appeal of the ruling of the chair with respect to the Waxman point of order that the Gingrey motion to recommit the bill was not germane to the bill. The motion would recommit the bill to the Energy and Commerce Committee with instructions that it be immediately reported back with an amendment that would increase Medicare physician reimbursement rates by 2 percent from 2010 through 2013, modify medical malpractice regulations and establish a Food and Drug Administration approval pathway for generic biologic drugs. Motion agreed to 251-177: D 251-3; R 0-174. Nov. 19, 2009.

908. HR 3961. Medicare Physician Reimbursement/Recommit.
Cantor, R-Va., motion to recommit the bill to the House Energy and Commerce Committee with instructions that it be immediately reported back with an amendment that would require the Health and Human Services Department to pay for up to $22.3 billion of costs resulting from adjustments to the Medicare physician reimbursement rate. Motion rejected 177-252: D 11-244; R 166-8. Nov. 19, 2009.

909. HR 3961. Medicare Physician Reimbursement/Passage.
Passage of the bill that would create a new Medicare payment formula for physician services. It would block a 21 percent cut scheduled to take effect in January 2010 and would increase the payment rate based on the Medicare economic index. It also would establish a new payment formula in 2011 based on spending in different service categories and allow physician expenditures on primary and preventive treatment to increase by one additional percentage point. Passed 243-183: D 242-11; R 1-172. (Pursuant to the rule, language was incorporated upon the bill's passage to add statutory pay-as-you-go rules that would require most new spending and tax cuts to be offset.) A "yea" vote was a vote in support of the president's position. Nov. 19, 2009.

910. HR 1834. Native American Small Businesses/Passage.
Velázquez, D-N.Y., motion to suspend the rules and pass the bill that would authorize funding in fiscal 2010 and 2011 to establish a Tribal Business Information Center in the Small Business Administration (SBA) to provide Native Americans with entrepreneurial development assistance, develop Small Business Development Center grants for Native Americans and establish an SBA Office of Native American Affairs. Motion agreed to 343-55: D 235-0; R 108-55. A two-thirds majority of those present and voting (266 in this case) is required for passage under suspension of the rules. Nov. 19, 2009.

	906	907	908	909	910
ALABAMA					
1 **Bonner**	Y	N	Y	N	Y
2 Bright	Y	Y	N	Y	Y
3 **Rogers**	Y	N	Y	N	Y
4 **Aderholt**	Y	N	Y	N	Y
5 Griffith	Y	Y	N	Y	Y
6 **Bachus**	Y	N	Y	N	Y
7 Davis	Y	Y	N	Y	Y
ALASKA					
AL **Young**	Y	N	Y	N	Y
ARIZONA					
1 Kirkpatrick	Y	Y	N	Y	Y
2 **Franks**	Y	N	Y	N	?
3 **Shadegg**	Y	N	Y	N	N
4 Pastor	Y	Y	N	Y	Y
5 Mitchell	Y	Y	N	Y	Y
6 **Flake**	Y	N	Y	N	?
7 Grijalva	Y	Y	N	Y	Y
8 Giffords	Y	Y	N	Y	Y
ARKANSAS					
1 Berry	Y	Y	N	Y	?
2 Snyder	Y	Y	N	Y	?
3 **Boozman**	Y	N	Y	N	Y
4 Ross	Y	Y	N	Y	?
CALIFORNIA					
1 Thompson	Y	Y	N	Y	Y
2 **Herger**	Y	N	Y	N	N
3 **Lungren**	Y	N	Y	N	Y
4 **McClintock**	Y	N	Y	N	N
5 Matsui	Y	Y	N	Y	Y
6 Woolsey	Y	Y	N	Y	Y
7 Miller, George	+	+	−	+	+
8 Pelosi					
9 Lee	Y	Y	N	Y	Y
10 Garamendi	Y	Y	N	Y	Y
11 McNerney	Y	Y	N	Y	Y
12 Speier	Y	Y	N	Y	Y
13 Stark	Y	Y	N	Y	Y
14 Eshoo	Y	Y	N	Y	Y
15 Honda	Y	Y	N	Y	Y
16 Lofgren	Y	Y	N	Y	Y
17 Farr	Y	Y	N	Y	Y
18 Cardoza	Y	Y	N	Y	Y
19 **Radanovich**	Y	N	Y	N	Y
20 Costa	Y	Y	N	Y	Y
21 **Nunes**	Y	N	Y	N	?
22 **McCarthy**	Y	N	Y	N	Y
23 Capps	Y	Y	N	Y	Y
24 **Gallegly**	Y	N	Y	N	?
25 **McKeon**	Y	N	Y	N	Y
26 **Dreier**	Y	N	Y	N	Y
27 Sherman	Y	Y	N	Y	Y
28 Berman	Y	Y	N	Y	Y
29 Schiff	Y	Y	N	Y	Y
30 Waxman	Y	Y	N	Y	Y
31 Becerra	Y	Y	N	Y	Y
32 Chu	Y	Y	N	Y	Y
33 Watson	Y	Y	N	Y	Y
34 Roybal-Allard	Y	Y	N	Y	Y
35 Waters	Y	Y	N	Y	Y
36 Harman	Y	Y	N	Y	Y
37 Richardson	Y	Y	N	Y	Y
38 Napolitano	Y	Y	N	Y	Y
39 Sánchez, Linda	Y	Y	N	Y	Y
40 **Royce**	Y	N	Y	N	N
41 **Lewis**	Y	N	Y	N	Y
42 **Miller, Gary**	Y	N	Y	N	?
43 Baca	Y	Y	N	Y	Y
44 **Calvert**	Y	N	Y	N	Y
45 **Bono Mack**	Y	N	Y	N	Y
46 **Rohrabacher**	Y	N	Y	N	N
47 Sanchez, Loretta	Y	Y	Y	Y	Y
48 **Campbell**	Y	N	Y	N	N
49 **Issa**	Y	N	N	N	Y
50 **Bilbray**	Y	N	Y	N	Y
51 Filner	Y	Y	N	Y	Y
52 **Hunter**	Y	N	Y	N	Y
53 Davis	Y	Y	N	Y	Y

	906	907	908	909	910
COLORADO					
1 DeGette	Y	Y	N	Y	Y
2 Polis	Y	Y	N	Y	Y
3 Salazar	Y	Y	N	Y	Y
4 Markey	Y	Y	N	Y	Y
5 **Lamborn**	Y	N	Y	N	N
6 **Coffman**	Y	N	Y	N	Y
7 Perlmutter	Y	Y	N	Y	Y
CONNECTICUT					
1 Larson	Y	Y	N	Y	Y
2 Courtney	Y	Y	N	Y	Y
3 DeLauro	Y	Y	N	Y	Y
4 Himes	Y	Y	N	Y	Y
5 Murphy	Y	Y	N	Y	Y
DELAWARE					
AL **Castle**	Y	N	Y	N	Y
FLORIDA					
1 **Miller**	Y	N	Y	N	N
2 Boyd	Y	Y	N	Y	?
3 Brown	Y	Y	N	Y	Y
4 **Crenshaw**	Y	N	Y	N	Y
5 **Brown-Waite**	Y	N	Y	N	N
6 **Stearns**	Y	N	Y	N	N
7 **Mica**	Y	N	Y	N	N
8 Grayson	Y	Y	N	Y	Y
9 **Bilirakis**	Y	N	Y	N	Y
10 **Young**	Y	N	Y	N	?
11 Castor	Y	Y	N	Y	Y
12 **Putnam**	Y	N	Y	N	N
13 **Buchanan**	Y	N	Y	N	Y
14 **Mack**	Y	N	Y	N	Y
15 **Posey**	Y	N	Y	N	N
16 **Rooney**	Y	N	Y	N	Y
17 Meek	Y	Y	N	Y	Y
18 **Ros-Lehtinen**	Y	N	Y	N	?
19 Wexler	Y	?	N	Y	Y
20 Wasserman Schultz	Y	Y	N	Y	Y
21 **Diaz-Balart, L.**	Y	N	Y	N	Y
22 Klein	Y	Y	N	Y	Y
23 Hastings	Y	Y	N	Y	Y
24 Kosmas	Y	Y	N	Y	Y
25 **Diaz-Balart, M.**	Y	N	Y	N	Y
GEORGIA					
1 **Kingston**	Y	N	Y	N	N
2 Bishop	Y	Y	N	Y	Y
3 **Westmoreland**	Y	N	Y	N	N
4 Johnson	Y	Y	N	Y	Y
5 Lewis	Y	Y	N	Y	Y
6 **Price**	Y	N	Y	N	N
7 **Linder**	Y	N	Y	N	N
8 Marshall	Y	Y	Y	Y	Y
9 **Deal**	Y	N	Y	N	Y
10 **Broun**	Y	N	N	N	N
11 **Gingrey**	Y	N	N	N	N
12 Barrow	Y	Y	N	Y	Y
13 Scott	Y	Y	N	Y	Y
HAWAII					
1 Abercrombie	Y	Y	N	Y	Y
2 Hirono	Y	Y	N	Y	Y
IDAHO					
1 Minnick	Y	N	Y	Y	Y
2 **Simpson**	Y	N	Y	N	Y
ILLINOIS					
1 Rush	Y	Y	N	Y	Y
2 Jackson	Y	Y	N	Y	Y
3 Lipinski	Y	Y	N	Y	Y
4 Gutierrez	Y	Y	N	Y	?
5 Quigley	Y	Y	N	Y	Y
6 **Roskam**	Y	N	Y	N	Y
7 Davis	Y	Y	N	Y	Y
8 Bean	Y	Y	N	Y	Y
9 Schakowsky	Y	Y	N	Y	Y
10 **Kirk**	Y	N	Y	N	Y
11 Halvorson	Y	Y	N	Y	Y
12 Costello	Y	Y	N	Y	Y
13 **Biggert**	Y	N	Y	N	Y
14 Foster	Y	Y	N	Y	Y
15 **Johnson**	Y	N	Y	N	Y

KEY	Republicans	Democrats		
Y Voted for (yea)		X Paired against		C Voted "present" to avoid possible conflict of interest
# Paired for		− Announced against		
+ Announced for		P Voted "present"		? Did not vote or otherwise make a position known
N Voted against (nay)				

	906	907	908	909	910
16 Manzullo	Y	N	Y	N	N
17 Hare	Y	Y	N	Y	Y
18 Schock	Y	N	Y	N	Y
19 Shimkus	Y	N	Y	N	N
INDIANA					
1 Visclosky	Y	Y	N	Y	Y
2 Donnelly	Y	Y	N	Y	Y
3 Souder	Y	N	Y	N	N
4 Buyer	Y	N	Y	N	Y
5 Burton	Y	N	Y	N	N
6 Pence	Y	N	Y	N	N
7 Carson	Y	Y	N	Y	?
8 Ellsworth	Y	Y	N	Y	Y
9 Hill	Y	Y	N	Y	Y
IOWA					
1 Braley	Y	Y	N	Y	Y
2 Loebsack	Y	Y	N	Y	Y
3 Boswell	Y	Y	N	Y	Y
4 Latham	Y	N	Y	N	Y
5 King	Y	N	Y	N	N
KANSAS					
1 Moran	Y	N	Y	N	N
2 Jenkins	Y	N	Y	N	Y
3 Moore	Y	Y	N	Y	Y
4 Tiahrt	Y	N	Y	N	N
KENTUCKY					
1 Whitfield	Y	N	Y	N	N
2 Guthrie	Y	N	Y	N	Y
3 Yarmuth	Y	Y	N	Y	Y
4 Davis	Y	N	Y	N	Y
5 Rogers	Y	N	Y	N	Y
6 Chandler	Y	Y	N	Y	Y
LOUISIANA					
1 Scalise	Y	N	Y	N	N
2 Cao	Y	N	Y	N	Y
3 Melancon	?	?	?	?	?
4 Fleming	Y	N	Y	N	Y
5 Alexander	Y	N	Y	N	Y
6 Cassidy	Y	N	Y	N	Y
7 Boustany	Y	N	Y	N	Y
MAINE					
1 Pingree	Y	Y	N	Y	Y
2 Michaud	Y	Y	N	Y	Y
MARYLAND					
1 Kratovil	Y	Y	N	Y	Y
2 Ruppersberger	Y	Y	N	Y	Y
3 Sarbanes	Y	Y	N	Y	Y
4 Edwards	Y	Y	N	Y	Y
5 Hoyer	Y	Y	N	Y	Y
6 Bartlett	Y	N	Y	N	N
7 Cummings	Y	Y	N	Y	Y
8 Van Hollen	Y	Y	N	Y	Y
MASSACHUSETTS					
1 Olver	Y	Y	N	Y	Y
2 Neal	Y	Y	N	Y	Y
3 McGovern	Y	Y	N	Y	Y
4 Frank	Y	Y	N	Y	Y
5 Tsongas	Y	Y	N	Y	Y
6 Tierney	Y	Y	N	Y	Y
7 Markey	Y	Y	N	Y	Y
8 Capuano	Y	Y	N	Y	Y
9 Lynch	Y	Y	N	Y	Y
10 Delahunt	Y	Y	N	Y	?
MICHIGAN					
1 Stupak	Y	Y	Y	Y	Y
2 Hoekstra	Y	N	Y	N	Y
3 Ehlers	Y	N	Y	N	Y
4 Camp	Y	N	Y	N	Y
5 Kildee	Y	Y	N	Y	Y
6 Upton	Y	N	Y	N	Y
7 Schauer	Y	Y	N	Y	Y
8 Rogers	Y	N	Y	N	Y
9 Peters	Y	Y	N	Y	Y
10 Miller	Y	N	Y	N	Y
11 McCotter	Y	N	Y	N	Y
12 Levin	Y	Y	N	Y	Y
13 Kilpatrick	Y	Y	N	Y	Y
14 Conyers	Y	Y	N	Y	Y
15 Dingell	Y	Y	N	Y	Y
MINNESOTA					
1 Walz	Y	Y	N	Y	Y
2 Kline	Y	N	Y	N	Y
3 Paulsen	Y	N	Y	N	Y
4 McCollum	Y	Y	N	Y	Y

	906	907	908	909	910
5 Ellison	Y	Y	N	Y	?
6 Bachmann	Y	N	Y	N	N
7 Peterson	Y	Y	Y	N	Y
8 Oberstar	Y	Y	N	Y	Y
MISSISSIPPI					
1 Childers	Y	Y	Y	Y	Y
2 Thompson	Y	Y	N	Y	Y
3 Harper	Y	N	Y	N	N
4 Taylor	Y	Y	Y	N	Y
MISSOURI					
1 Clay	Y	Y	N	Y	Y
2 Akin	Y	N	Y	N	N
3 Carnahan	Y	Y	N	Y	Y
4 Skelton	Y	Y	N	Y	Y
5 Cleaver	Y	Y	N	Y	Y
6 Graves	Y	N	Y	N	Y
7 Blunt	Y	N	N	N	Y
8 Emerson	Y	N	Y	N	Y
9 Luetkemeyer	Y	N	Y	N	Y
MONTANA					
AL Rehberg	Y	N	Y	N	Y
NEBRASKA					
1 Fortenberry	Y	N	Y	N	Y
2 Terry	Y	N	Y	N	Y
3 Smith	Y	N	Y	N	Y
NEVADA					
1 Berkley	Y	N	Y	Y	Y
2 Heller	Y	N	Y	N	Y
3 Titus	Y	Y	N	Y	Y
NEW HAMPSHIRE					
1 Shea-Porter	Y	Y	N	Y	Y
2 Hodes	Y	Y	N	Y	Y
NEW JERSEY					
1 Andrews	Y	Y	N	Y	Y
2 LoBiondo	Y	N	Y	N	Y
3 Adler	Y	Y	Y	N	Y
4 Smith	Y	N	Y	N	Y
5 Garrett	Y	N	Y	N	N
6 Pallone	Y	Y	N	Y	Y
7 Lance	Y	N	Y	N	Y
8 Pascrell	Y	Y	N	Y	?
9 Rothman	+	Y	N	Y	Y
10 Payne	Y	Y	N	Y	?
11 Frelinghuysen	Y	N	Y	N	Y
12 Holt	Y	Y	N	Y	Y
13 Sires	Y	Y	N	Y	Y
NEW MEXICO					
1 Heinrich	Y	Y	N	Y	Y
2 Teague	Y	Y	N	Y	Y
3 Lujan	Y	Y	N	Y	Y
NEW YORK					
1 Bishop	Y	Y	N	Y	Y
2 Israel	Y	Y	N	Y	Y
3 King	Y	N	Y	N	Y
4 McCarthy	Y	Y	N	Y	Y
5 Ackerman	Y	Y	N	Y	Y
6 Meeks	Y	Y	N	Y	?
7 Crowley	Y	Y	N	Y	Y
8 Nadler	Y	Y	N	Y	?
9 Weiner	Y	Y	N	Y	Y
10 Towns	Y	Y	N	?	Y
11 Clarke	Y	Y	N	Y	Y
12 Velázquez	Y	Y	N	Y	Y
13 McMahon	Y	Y	Y	N	Y
14 Maloney	Y	Y	N	Y	Y
15 Rangel	Y	Y	N	Y	?
16 Serrano	Y	Y	N	Y	Y
17 Engel	Y	Y	N	Y	Y
18 Lowey	Y	Y	N	Y	Y
19 Hall	Y	Y	N	Y	Y
20 Murphy	Y	Y	N	Y	Y
21 Tonko	Y	Y	N	Y	Y
22 Hinchey	Y	Y	N	Y	?
23 Owens	Y	Y	N	Y	Y
24 Arcuri	Y	Y	N	Y	Y
25 Maffei	Y	Y	N	Y	Y
26 Lee	Y	N	Y	N	Y
27 Higgins	Y	Y	N	Y	Y
28 Slaughter	Y	Y	N	Y	Y
29 Massa	Y	Y	N	Y	Y
NORTH CAROLINA					
1 Butterfield	Y	Y	N	Y	Y
2 Etheridge	Y	Y	N	Y	Y
3 Jones	Y	N	Y	N	Y
4 Price	Y	Y	N	Y	Y

	906	907	908	909	910
5 Foxx	Y	N	Y	N	N
6 Coble	Y	N	Y	N	N
7 McIntyre	Y	Y	N	Y	Y
8 Kissell	Y	Y	N	Y	Y
9 Myrick	Y	N	Y	N	Y
10 McHenry	Y	N	Y	N	N
11 Shuler	Y	Y	N	Y	Y
12 Watt	Y	Y	N	Y	Y
13 Miller	Y	Y	N	Y	Y
NORTH DAKOTA					
AL Pomeroy	Y	Y	N	Y	Y
OHIO					
1 Driehaus	Y	Y	N	Y	Y
2 Schmidt	Y	N	Y	N	Y
3 Turner	Y	N	Y	N	Y
4 Jordan	Y	N	Y	N	N
5 Latta	Y	N	Y	N	N
6 Wilson	Y	Y	N	Y	Y
7 Austria	Y	N	Y	N	Y
8 Boehner	Y	N	Y	N	N
9 Kaptur	Y	Y	N	Y	Y
10 Kucinich	Y	Y	N	Y	Y
11 Fudge	Y	Y	N	Y	Y
12 Tiberi	Y	N	Y	N	Y
13 Sutton	Y	Y	N	Y	Y
14 LaTourette	Y	N	Y	N	Y
15 Kilroy	Y	Y	N	Y	Y
16 Boccieri	Y	Y	N	Y	Y
17 Ryan	Y	Y	N	Y	Y
18 Space	Y	Y	N	Y	Y
OKLAHOMA					
1 Sullivan	Y	N	Y	N	Y
2 Boren	Y	Y	N	Y	Y
3 Lucas	Y	N	Y	N	Y
4 Cole	Y	N	N	N	Y
5 Fallin	Y	N	Y	N	?
OREGON					
1 Wu	Y	Y	N	Y	Y
2 Walden	Y	N	Y	N	Y
3 Blumenauer	Y	Y	N	Y	Y
4 DeFazio	Y	Y	N	Y	Y
5 Schrader	Y	Y	N	Y	Y
PENNSYLVANIA					
1 Brady	Y	Y	N	Y	Y
2 Fattah	Y	Y	N	Y	Y
3 Dahlkemper	Y	Y	N	Y	Y
4 Altmire	Y	Y	Y	Y	Y
5 Thompson	Y	N	Y	N	Y
6 Gerlach	Y	N	Y	N	Y
7 Sestak	Y	Y	N	Y	Y
8 Murphy, P.	Y	Y	N	Y	Y
9 Shuster	Y	N	Y	N	Y
10 Carney	Y	N	Y	N	Y
11 Kanjorski	Y	Y	N	Y	Y
12 Murtha	?	Y	N	Y	Y
13 Schwartz	Y	Y	N	Y	Y
14 Doyle	Y	Y	N	Y	?
15 Dent	Y	N	Y	N	Y
16 Pitts	Y	N	Y	N	N
17 Holden	Y	Y	N	Y	Y
18 Murphy, T.	Y	N	Y	N	Y
19 Platts	Y	N	N	N	Y
RHODE ISLAND					
1 Kennedy	Y	Y	N	+	Y
2 Langevin	Y	Y	N	Y	Y
SOUTH CAROLINA					
1 Brown	?	?	?	?	?
2 Wilson	Y	N	Y	N	Y
3 Barrett	Y	N	Y	N	Y
4 Inglis	Y	N	N	N	N
5 Spratt	Y	Y	N	Y	Y
6 Clyburn	Y	Y	N	Y	Y
SOUTH DAKOTA					
AL Herseth Sandlin	Y	Y	N	Y	Y
TENNESSEE					
1 Roe	Y	N	Y	N	Y
2 Duncan	Y	N	Y	N	N
3 Wamp	Y	N	Y	N	?
4 Davis	Y	Y	N	Y	Y
5 Cooper	Y	Y	N	Y	Y
6 Gordon	Y	Y	N	Y	Y
7 Blackburn	Y	N	Y	N	?
8 Tanner	Y	Y	N	Y	Y
9 Cohen	Y	Y	N	Y	Y

	906	907	908	909	910
TEXAS					
1 Gohmert	Y	N	Y	N	N
2 Poe	Y	N	Y	N	N
3 Johnson, S.	Y	N	Y	N	Y
4 Hall	Y	N	Y	N	Y
5 Hensarling	Y	N	Y	N	N
6 Barton	Y	N	Y	N	N
7 Culberson	Y	N	Y	N	N
8 Brady	Y	N	N	–	Y
9 Green, A.	Y	Y	N	Y	Y
10 McCaul	?	?	?	?	?
11 Conaway	Y	N	Y	N	N
12 Granger	Y	N	Y	N	Y
13 Thornberry	Y	N	Y	N	N
14 Paul	Y	N	Y	N	N
15 Hinojosa	Y	Y	N	Y	Y
16 Reyes	Y	Y	N	Y	Y
17 Edwards	Y	Y	N	Y	Y
18 Jackson Lee	Y	Y	N	Y	?
19 Neugebauer	Y	N	Y	N	N
20 Gonzalez	Y	Y	N	Y	Y
21 Smith	Y	N	Y	N	N
22 Olson	Y	N	Y	N	Y
23 Rodriguez	Y	Y	N	Y	Y
24 Marchant	Y	N	Y	N	N
25 Doggett	Y	Y	N	Y	Y
26 Burgess	Y	N	Y	N	Y
27 Ortiz	Y	Y	N	Y	Y
28 Cuellar	Y	Y	N	Y	Y
29 Green, G.	Y	Y	N	Y	Y
30 Johnson, E.	Y	Y	N	Y	?
31 Carter	?	?	?	?	?
32 Sessions	Y	N	Y	N	Y
UTAH					
1 Bishop	Y	N	Y	N	Y
2 Matheson	Y	Y	N	Y	Y
3 Chaffetz	Y	N	Y	N	Y
VERMONT					
AL Welch	Y	Y	N	Y	?
VIRGINIA					
1 Wittman	Y	N	Y	N	Y
2 Nye	Y	Y	N	Y	Y
3 Scott	Y	Y	N	Y	Y
4 Forbes	Y	N	Y	N	Y
5 Perriello	Y	Y	N	Y	?
6 Goodlatte	Y	N	Y	N	N
7 Cantor	Y	N	Y	N	Y
8 Moran	Y	Y	N	Y	Y
9 Boucher	Y	Y	N	Y	Y
10 Wolf	Y	N	Y	N	N
11 Connolly	Y	Y	N	Y	Y
WASHINGTON					
1 Inslee	Y	Y	N	Y	Y
2 Larsen	Y	Y	N	Y	Y
3 Baird	Y	Y	N	N	Y
4 Hastings	Y	N	Y	N	Y
5 McMorris Rodgers	Y	N	Y	N	Y
6 Dicks	Y	Y	N	Y	Y
7 McDermott	Y	Y	N	Y	Y
8 Reichert	Y	N	Y	N	Y
9 Smith	Y	Y	N	N	Y
WEST VIRGINIA					
1 Mollohan	Y	Y	N	Y	Y
2 Capito	Y	N	Y	N	Y
3 Rahall	Y	Y	N	Y	Y
WISCONSIN					
1 Ryan	Y	N	Y	N	Y
2 Baldwin	Y	Y	N	Y	Y
3 Kind	Y	Y	N	Y	Y
4 Moore	?	Y	N	Y	Y
5 Sensenbrenner	Y	N	Y	N	Y
6 Petri	Y	N	Y	N	Y
7 Obey	Y	Y	N	Y	Y
8 Kagen	Y	Y	N	Y	Y
WYOMING					
AL Lummis	Y	N	Y	N	N
DELEGATES					
Faleomavaega (A.S.)					
Norton (D.C.)					
Bordallo (Guam)					
Sablan (N. Marianas)					
Pierluisi (P.R.)					
Christensen (V.I.)					

IN THE HOUSE | By Vote Number

911. **HR 3029. Gas Turbine Research Program/Passage.** Tonko, D-N.Y., motion to suspend the rules and pass the bill that would require the Energy Department to establish a research and development program to increase the efficiency of gas turbines used in combined and simple cycle power generation systems. Motion agreed to 266-118: D 224-1; R 42-117. A two-thirds majority of those present and voting (256 in this case) is required for passage under suspension of the rules. Dec. 1, 2009.

912. **H Res 727. Ovarian Cancer Awareness/Adoption.** Lynch, D-Mass., motion to suspend the rules and adopt the resolution that would express support for greater awareness of ovarian cancer. Motion agreed to 385-0: D 226-0; R 159-0. A two-thirds majority of those present and voting (257 in this case) is required for adoption under suspension of the rules. Dec. 1, 2009.

913. **HR 3667. Clyde L. Hillhouse Post Office/Passage.** Lynch, D-Mass., motion to suspend the rules and pass the bill that would designate a post office in White Springs, Fla., as the "Clyde L. Hillhouse Post Office Building." Motion agreed to 386-0: D 225-0; R 161-0. A two-thirds majority of those present and voting (258 in this case) is required for passage under suspension of the rules. Dec. 1, 2009.

914. **H Res 494. Tribute to 30th Infantry Division Soldiers/ Adoption.** Kissell, D-N.C., motion to suspend the rules and adopt the resolution that would recognize the service of the 30th Infantry Division soldiers during World War II. Motion agreed to 415-0: D 247-0; R 168-0. A two-thirds majority of those present and voting (277 in this case) is required for adoption under suspension of the rules. Dec. 2, 2009.

915. **H Con Res 129. Tribute to Submarine Force/Adoption.** Kissell, D-N.C., motion to suspend the rules and adopt the concurrent resolution that would congratulate the U.S. submarine force for completing 1,000 *Ohio*-class ballistic missile submarine patrols. Motion agreed to 412-0: D 247-0; R 165-0. A two-thirds majority of those present and voting (275 in this case) is required for adoption under suspension of the rules. Dec. 2, 2009.

916. **H Res 861. National Military Family Month/Adoption.** Kissell, D-N.C., motion to suspend the rules and adopt the resolution that would recognize the goals and ideals of National Military Family Month and honor the sacrifices and dedication of military families, as well as their contributions to the United States. Motion agreed to 417-0: D 249-0; R 168-0. A two-thirds majority of those present and voting (278 in this case) is required for adoption under suspension of the rules. Dec. 2, 2009.

917. **H Res 897. Teaching About Veterans/Adoption.** Bishop, D-N.Y., motion to suspend the rules and adopt the resolution that would recognize the importance of teaching elementary and secondary school students about the sacrifices made by veterans. Motion agreed to 419-0: D 250-0; R 169-0. A two-thirds majority of those present and voting (280 in this case) is required for adoption under suspension of the rules. Dec. 2, 2009.

	911	912	913	914	915	916	917
ALABAMA							
1 Bonner	N	Y	Y	Y	Y	Y	Y
2 Bright	N	Y	Y	Y	Y	Y	Y
3 Rogers	Y	Y	Y	Y	Y	Y	Y
4 Aderholt	?	?	?	?	?	?	?
5 Griffith	?	?	?	Y	Y	Y	Y
6 Bachus	N	Y	Y	Y	Y	Y	Y
7 Davis	Y	Y	Y	?	?	?	?
ALASKA							
AL Young	?	?	?	?	?	?	?
ARIZONA							
1 Kirkpatrick	Y	Y	Y	Y	Y	Y	Y
2 Franks	N	Y	Y	Y	Y	Y	Y
3 Shadegg	N	Y	Y	Y	Y	Y	Y
4 Pastor	Y	Y	Y	Y	Y	Y	Y
5 Mitchell	Y	Y	Y	Y	Y	Y	Y
6 Flake	?	?	?	Y	Y	Y	Y
7 Grijalva	?	?	?	Y	Y	Y	Y
8 Giffords	Y	Y	Y	Y	Y	Y	Y
ARKANSAS							
1 Berry	?	Y	Y	Y	Y	Y	Y
2 Snyder	Y	Y	Y	Y	Y	Y	Y
3 Boozman	N	Y	Y	Y	Y	Y	Y
4 Ross	Y	Y	Y	Y	Y	Y	Y
CALIFORNIA							
1 Thompson	Y	Y	Y	Y	Y	Y	Y
2 Herger	N	Y	Y	Y	Y	Y	Y
3 Lungren	?	?	?	Y	Y	Y	Y
4 McClintock	N	Y	Y	Y	Y	Y	Y
5 Matsui	Y	Y	Y	Y	Y	Y	Y
6 Woolsey	Y	Y	Y	Y	Y	Y	Y
7 Miller, George	Y	Y	Y	Y	Y	Y	Y
8 Pelosi							
9 Lee	Y	Y	Y	Y	Y	Y	Y
10 Garamendi	Y	Y	Y	Y	Y	Y	Y
11 McNerney	Y	Y	Y	Y	Y	Y	Y
12 Speier	Y	Y	Y	Y	Y	Y	Y
13 Stark	?	?	?	Y	Y	Y	Y
14 Eshoo	Y	Y	Y	Y	Y	Y	Y
15 Honda	Y	Y	?	Y	Y	Y	Y
16 Lofgren	Y	Y	Y	Y	Y	Y	Y
17 Farr	?	?	?	Y	Y	Y	Y
18 Cardoza	Y	Y	Y	Y	Y	Y	Y
19 Radanovich	?	Y	Y	?	?	?	?
20 Costa	Y	Y	Y	Y	Y	Y	Y
21 Nunes	N	Y	Y	Y	Y	Y	Y
22 McCarthy	N	Y	Y	Y	Y	Y	Y
23 Capps	Y	Y	Y	Y	Y	Y	Y
24 Gallegly	N	Y	Y	Y	Y	Y	Y
25 McKeon	N	Y	Y	Y	Y	Y	Y
26 Dreier	N	Y	Y	Y	Y	Y	Y
27 Sherman	Y	Y	Y	Y	Y	Y	Y
28 Berman	Y	?	Y	Y	Y	Y	Y
29 Schiff	Y	Y	Y	Y	Y	Y	Y
30 Waxman	Y	Y	Y	Y	Y	Y	Y
31 Becerra	Y	Y	Y	Y	Y	Y	Y
32 Chu	Y	Y	Y	Y	Y	Y	Y
33 Watson	Y	Y	Y	Y	Y	Y	Y
34 Roybal-Allard	Y	Y	Y	Y	Y	Y	Y
35 Waters	Y	Y	Y	Y	Y	Y	Y
36 Harman	?	?	?	Y	Y	Y	Y
37 Richardson	Y	Y	Y	Y	Y	Y	Y
38 Napolitano	Y	Y	Y	Y	Y	Y	Y
39 Sánchez, Linda	Y	Y	Y	Y	Y	Y	Y
40 Royce	N	Y	Y	Y	Y	Y	Y
41 Lewis	N	Y	Y	Y	Y	Y	Y
42 Miller, Gary	Y	Y	Y	Y	Y	Y	Y
43 Baca	Y	Y	Y	Y	Y	Y	Y
44 Calvert	Y	Y	Y	Y	Y	Y	Y
45 Bono Mack	N	Y	Y	Y	Y	Y	Y
46 Rohrabacher	Y	Y	Y	Y	Y	Y	Y
47 Sanchez, Loretta	?	?	?	Y	Y	Y	Y
48 Campbell	N	Y	Y	Y	Y	Y	Y
49 Issa	N	Y	Y	Y	Y	Y	Y
50 Bilbray	Y	Y	Y	+	Y	Y	Y
51 Filner	Y	Y	Y	Y	Y	Y	Y
52 Hunter	N	Y	Y	Y	Y	Y	Y
53 Davis	Y	Y	Y	Y	Y	Y	Y

	911	912	913	914	915	916	917
COLORADO							
1 DeGette	Y	Y	Y	Y	Y	Y	Y
2 Polis	Y	Y	Y	Y	Y	Y	Y
3 Salazar	Y	Y	Y	Y	Y	Y	Y
4 Markey	Y	Y	Y	Y	Y	Y	Y
5 Lamborn	N	Y	Y	Y	Y	Y	Y
6 Coffman	N	Y	Y	Y	Y	Y	Y
7 Perlmutter	Y	Y	Y	Y	Y	Y	Y
CONNECTICUT							
1 Larson	Y	Y	?	Y	Y	Y	Y
2 Courtney	Y	Y	Y	Y	Y	Y	Y
3 DeLauro	Y	Y	Y	Y	Y	Y	Y
4 Himes	Y	Y	Y	Y	Y	Y	Y
5 Murphy	?	?	?	Y	Y	Y	Y
DELAWARE							
AL Castle	Y	Y	Y	Y	Y	Y	Y
FLORIDA							
1 Miller	N	Y	Y	Y	Y	Y	Y
2 Boyd	Y	Y	Y	Y	Y	Y	Y
3 Brown	Y	Y	Y	Y	Y	Y	Y
4 Crenshaw	N	Y	Y	Y	Y	Y	Y
5 Brown-Waite	Y	Y	Y	Y	Y	Y	Y
6 Stearns	N	Y	Y	Y	Y	Y	Y
7 Mica	N	Y	Y	Y	Y	Y	Y
8 Grayson	Y	Y	Y	Y	Y	Y	Y
9 Bilirakis	N	Y	Y	Y	Y	Y	Y
10 Young	Y	Y	Y	Y	Y	Y	Y
11 Castor	Y	Y	Y	Y	Y	Y	Y
12 Putnam	Y	Y	Y	+	Y	Y	Y
13 Buchanan	Y	Y	Y	Y	Y	Y	Y
14 Mack	N	Y	Y	Y	Y	Y	Y
15 Posey	Y	Y	Y	Y	Y	Y	Y
16 Rooney	N	Y	Y	Y	Y	Y	Y
17 Meek	?	?	?	Y	Y	Y	Y
18 Ros-Lehtinen	Y	Y	Y	Y	Y	Y	Y
19 Wexler	?	?	?	?	?	?	?
20 Wasserman Schultz	Y	Y	Y	Y	Y	Y	Y
21 Diaz-Balart, L.	Y	Y	Y	Y	Y	Y	Y
22 Klein	Y	Y	Y	Y	Y	Y	Y
23 Hastings	Y	Y	Y	Y	Y	Y	Y
24 Kosmas	Y	Y	Y	Y	Y	Y	Y
25 Diaz-Balart, M.	Y	Y	Y	Y	Y	Y	Y
GEORGIA							
1 Kingston	?	?	?	Y	Y	Y	Y
2 Bishop	Y	Y	Y	Y	Y	Y	Y
3 Westmoreland	N	?	Y	Y	Y	Y	Y
4 Johnson	Y	Y	Y	Y	Y	Y	Y
5 Lewis	Y	Y	Y	Y	Y	Y	Y
6 Price	N	Y	Y	Y	Y	Y	Y
7 Linder	N	Y	Y	Y	Y	Y	Y
8 Marshall	?	?	?	Y	Y	Y	Y
9 Deal	?	?	?	?	?	?	?
10 Broun	N	Y	Y	Y	Y	Y	Y
11 Gingrey	N	Y	Y	Y	Y	Y	Y
12 Barrow	?	?	?	?	?	?	?
13 Scott	Y	Y	Y	Y	Y	Y	Y
HAWAII							
1 Abercrombie	+	+	+	Y	Y	Y	Y
2 Hirono	Y	Y	Y	Y	Y	Y	Y
IDAHO							
1 Minnick	?	?	?	Y	Y	Y	Y
2 Simpson	N	Y	Y	Y	Y	Y	Y
ILLINOIS							
1 Rush	?	?	?	Y	Y	Y	Y
2 Jackson	Y	Y	Y	Y	Y	Y	Y
3 Lipinski	Y	Y	Y	Y	Y	Y	Y
4 Gutierrez	Y	Y	Y	Y	Y	Y	Y
5 Quigley	Y	Y	?	Y	Y	Y	Y
6 Roskam	N	Y	Y	Y	Y	Y	Y
7 Davis	?	?	?	Y	Y	Y	Y
8 Bean	Y	Y	Y	Y	Y	Y	Y
9 Schakowsky	Y	Y	Y	Y	Y	Y	Y
10 Kirk	?	?	?	Y	Y	Y	Y
11 Halvorson	Y	Y	Y	Y	Y	Y	Y
12 Costello	Y	Y	Y	Y	Y	Y	Y
13 Biggert	Y	Y	Y	Y	Y	Y	Y
14 Foster	Y	Y	Y	Y	Y	Y	Y
15 Johnson	Y	Y	Y	Y	Y	Y	Y

	911	912	913	914	915	916	917
16 **Manzullo**	N	Y	Y	Y	Y	Y	Y
17 Hare	Y	Y	Y	Y	Y	Y	Y
18 **Schock**	Y	Y	Y	?	Y	Y	Y
19 **Shimkus**	?	?	?	Y	Y	Y	Y
INDIANA							
1 Visclosky	Y	Y	Y	Y	Y	Y	Y
2 Donnelly	Y	Y	Y	Y	Y	Y	Y
3 **Souder**	N	Y	Y	Y	Y	Y	Y
4 **Buyer**	N	Y	Y	Y	Y	Y	Y
5 **Burton**	N	Y	Y	Y	Y	Y	Y
6 **Pence**	N	Y	Y	Y	Y	Y	Y
7 Carson	Y	Y	Y	Y	Y	Y	Y
8 Ellsworth	Y	Y	Y	Y	Y	Y	Y
9 Hill	Y	Y	Y	Y	Y	Y	Y
IOWA							
1 Braley	+	+	+	Y	Y	Y	Y
2 Loebsack	Y	Y	Y	Y	Y	Y	Y
3 Boswell	Y	Y	Y	Y	Y	Y	Y
4 **Latham**	N	Y	Y	Y	Y	Y	Y
5 **King**	N	Y	Y	Y	?	Y	Y
KANSAS							
1 **Moran**	?	?	?	Y	Y	Y	Y
2 **Jenkins**	N	Y	Y	Y	Y	Y	Y
3 Moore	Y	Y	Y	Y	Y	Y	Y
4 **Tiahrt**	N	Y	Y	Y	Y	Y	Y
KENTUCKY							
1 **Whitfield**	N	Y	Y	Y	Y	Y	Y
2 **Guthrie**	N	Y	Y	Y	Y	Y	Y
3 Yarmuth	Y	Y	Y	Y	Y	Y	Y
4 **Davis**	–	+	+	Y	Y	Y	Y
5 **Rogers**	N	Y	Y	Y	Y	Y	Y
6 Chandler	Y	Y	Y	Y	Y	Y	Y
LOUISIANA							
1 **Scalise**	N	Y	Y	Y	Y	Y	Y
2 **Cao**	?	Y	Y	?	?	Y	Y
3 Melancon	Y	Y	Y	?	?	?	?
4 **Fleming**	N	Y	Y	Y	Y	Y	Y
5 **Alexander**	N	Y	Y	Y	Y	Y	Y
6 **Cassidy**	N	Y	Y	Y	Y	Y	Y
7 **Boustany**	N	Y	Y	Y	Y	Y	Y
MAINE							
1 Pingree	Y	Y	Y	Y	Y	Y	Y
2 Michaud	Y	Y	Y	Y	Y	Y	Y
MARYLAND							
1 Kratovil	Y	Y	Y	Y	Y	Y	Y
2 Ruppersberger	Y	Y	Y	Y	Y	Y	Y
3 Sarbanes	Y	Y	Y	Y	Y	Y	Y
4 Edwards	Y	Y	Y	Y	Y	Y	Y
5 Hoyer	Y	Y	Y	Y	Y	Y	Y
6 **Bartlett**	Y	Y	Y	Y	Y	Y	Y
7 Cummings	Y	Y	Y	Y	Y	Y	Y
8 Van Hollen	Y	Y	Y	Y	Y	Y	Y
MASSACHUSETTS							
1 Olver	Y	Y	Y	Y	Y	Y	Y
2 Neal	Y	Y	Y	Y	Y	Y	Y
3 McGovern	Y	Y	Y	Y	Y	Y	Y
4 Frank	Y	Y	Y	Y	Y	Y	Y
5 Tsongas	Y	Y	Y	Y	Y	Y	Y
6 Tierney	Y	Y	Y	Y	Y	Y	Y
7 Markey	Y	Y	Y	Y	Y	Y	Y
8 Capuano	?	?	?	?	?	?	?
9 Lynch	Y	Y	Y	Y	Y	Y	Y
10 Delahunt	Y	Y	Y	Y	Y	Y	Y
MICHIGAN							
1 Stupak	Y	Y	Y	Y	Y	Y	Y
2 **Hoekstra**	N	Y	Y	Y	Y	Y	Y
3 **Ehlers**	Y	Y	Y	Y	Y	Y	Y
4 **Camp**	N	Y	Y	Y	Y	Y	Y
5 Kildee	Y	Y	Y	Y	Y	Y	Y
6 **Upton**	N	Y	Y	Y	Y	Y	Y
7 Schauer	Y	Y	Y	Y	Y	Y	Y
8 **Rogers**	Y	Y	Y	Y	Y	Y	Y
9 Peters	Y	Y	Y	Y	Y	Y	Y
10 **Miller**	N	Y	Y	Y	Y	Y	Y
11 **McCotter**	Y	Y	Y	Y	Y	Y	Y
12 Levin	Y	Y	Y	Y	Y	Y	Y
13 Kilpatrick	Y	Y	Y	Y	Y	Y	Y
14 Conyers	+	+	+	Y	Y	Y	Y
15 Dingell	?	?	?	Y	Y	Y	Y
MINNESOTA							
1 Walz	Y	Y	Y	Y	Y	Y	Y
2 **Kline**	N	Y	Y	Y	Y	Y	Y
3 **Paulsen**	N	Y	Y	Y	Y	Y	Y
4 McCollum	?	?	?	Y	Y	Y	Y
5 Ellison	Y	Y	Y	Y	Y	Y	Y
6 **Bachmann**	N	Y	Y	Y	Y	Y	Y
7 Peterson	Y	Y	Y	Y	Y	Y	Y
8 Oberstar	?	Y	Y	Y	Y	Y	Y
MISSISSIPPI							
1 Childers	Y	Y	Y	Y	Y	Y	Y
2 Thompson	Y	Y	Y	Y	Y	Y	Y
3 **Harper**	N	Y	Y	Y	Y	Y	Y
4 Taylor	Y	Y	Y	Y	Y	Y	Y
MISSOURI							
1 Clay	Y	Y	Y	Y	Y	Y	Y
2 **Akin**	N	Y	Y	Y	Y	Y	Y
3 Carnahan	Y	Y	Y	Y	Y	Y	Y
4 Skelton	Y	Y	Y	Y	Y	Y	Y
5 Cleaver	Y	Y	Y	Y	Y	Y	Y
6 **Graves**	?	?	?	Y	Y	Y	Y
7 **Blunt**	?	?	?	Y	Y	Y	Y
8 **Emerson**	N	Y	Y	Y	Y	Y	Y
9 **Luetkemeyer**	N	Y	Y	Y	Y	Y	Y
MONTANA							
AL **Rehberg**	–	+	+	Y	Y	Y	Y
NEBRASKA							
1 **Fortenberry**	Y	Y	Y	Y	Y	Y	Y
2 **Terry**	N	Y	Y	Y	Y	Y	Y
3 **Smith**	Y	Y	Y	Y	Y	Y	Y
NEVADA							
1 Berkley	Y	Y	Y	Y	Y	Y	Y
2 **Heller**	Y	Y	Y	Y	Y	Y	Y
3 Titus	Y	Y	Y	Y	Y	Y	Y
NEW HAMPSHIRE							
1 Shea-Porter	Y	Y	Y	Y	Y	Y	Y
2 Hodes	Y	Y	Y	Y	Y	Y	Y
NEW JERSEY							
1 Andrews	Y	Y	Y	Y	Y	Y	Y
2 **LoBiondo**	Y	Y	Y	Y	Y	Y	Y
3 Adler	Y	Y	Y	Y	Y	Y	Y
4 **Smith**	Y	Y	Y	Y	Y	Y	Y
5 **Garrett**	N	Y	Y	Y	Y	Y	Y
6 Pallone	Y	Y	Y	Y	Y	Y	Y
7 **Lance**	Y	Y	Y	Y	Y	Y	Y
8 Pascrell	Y	Y	Y	Y	Y	Y	Y
9 Rothman	Y	Y	Y	Y	Y	Y	Y
10 Payne	?	?	?	Y	Y	Y	Y
11 **Frelinghuysen**	Y	Y	Y	Y	Y	Y	Y
12 Holt	Y	Y	Y	Y	Y	Y	Y
13 Sires	Y	Y	Y	Y	Y	Y	Y
NEW MEXICO							
1 Heinrich	Y	Y	Y	Y	Y	Y	Y
2 Teague	Y	Y	Y	Y	Y	Y	Y
3 Lujan	Y	Y	Y	Y	Y	Y	Y
NEW YORK							
1 Bishop	Y	Y	Y	Y	Y	Y	Y
2 Israel	Y	Y	Y	Y	Y	Y	Y
3 **King**	Y	Y	Y	Y	Y	Y	Y
4 McCarthy	Y	Y	Y	Y	Y	Y	Y
5 Ackerman	Y	Y	Y	Y	Y	Y	Y
6 Meeks	Y	Y	Y	Y	Y	Y	Y
7 Crowley	Y	Y	Y	Y	Y	Y	Y
8 Nadler	Y	Y	Y	Y	Y	Y	Y
9 Weiner	Y	Y	Y	Y	Y	Y	Y
10 Towns	Y	Y	Y	Y	Y	Y	Y
11 Clarke	Y	Y	Y	Y	Y	Y	Y
12 Velázquez	Y	Y	Y	Y	Y	Y	Y
13 McMahon	Y	Y	Y	Y	Y	Y	Y
14 Maloney	Y	Y	Y	Y	Y	Y	Y
15 Rangel	Y	?	Y	Y	Y	Y	Y
16 Serrano	Y	Y	Y	Y	Y	Y	Y
17 Engel	Y	Y	Y	Y	Y	Y	Y
18 Lowey	Y	Y	Y	Y	Y	Y	Y
19 Hall	?	?	?	Y	Y	Y	Y
20 Murphy	Y	Y	Y	?	Y	Y	Y
21 Tonko	Y	Y	Y	Y	Y	Y	Y
22 Hinchey	Y	Y	Y	?	Y	Y	Y
23 Owens	Y	Y	Y	Y	Y	Y	Y
24 Arcuri	Y	Y	Y	Y	Y	Y	Y
25 Maffei	Y	Y	Y	Y	Y	Y	Y
26 **Lee**	Y	Y	Y	Y	Y	Y	Y
27 Higgins	Y	Y	Y	Y	Y	Y	Y
28 Slaughter	Y	Y	Y	Y	Y	Y	Y
29 Massa	Y	Y	Y	Y	Y	Y	Y
NORTH CAROLINA							
1 Butterfield	Y	Y	Y	Y	Y	Y	Y
2 Etheridge	Y	Y	Y	Y	Y	Y	Y
3 **Jones**	Y	Y	Y	Y	Y	Y	Y
4 Price	Y	Y	Y	Y	Y	Y	Y
5 **Foxx**	N	Y	Y	Y	Y	Y	Y
6 **Coble**	N	Y	Y	Y	Y	Y	Y
7 McIntyre	Y	Y	Y	Y	Y	Y	Y
8 Kissell	Y	Y	Y	Y	Y	Y	Y
9 **Myrick**	N	Y	Y	Y	Y	?	Y
10 **McHenry**	N	Y	Y	Y	Y	Y	Y
11 Shuler	Y	Y	Y	Y	Y	Y	Y
12 Watt	Y	Y	Y	Y	Y	Y	Y
13 Miller	Y	Y	Y	Y	Y	Y	Y
NORTH DAKOTA							
AL Pomeroy	Y	Y	Y	Y	Y	Y	Y
OHIO							
1 Driehaus	Y	Y	Y	Y	Y	Y	Y
2 **Schmidt**	N	Y	Y	Y	Y	Y	Y
3 **Turner**	N	Y	Y	Y	Y	Y	Y
4 **Jordan**	N	Y	Y	Y	Y	Y	Y
5 **Latta**	N	Y	Y	Y	Y	Y	Y
6 Wilson	Y	Y	Y	Y	Y	Y	Y
7 **Austria**	N	Y	Y	Y	Y	Y	Y
8 **Boehner**	N	Y	Y	Y	Y	Y	Y
9 Kaptur	Y	Y	Y	Y	Y	Y	Y
10 Kucinich	Y	Y	Y	Y	Y	Y	Y
11 Fudge	Y	Y	Y	Y	Y	Y	Y
12 **Tiberi**	N	Y	Y	Y	Y	Y	Y
13 Sutton	Y	Y	Y	Y	Y	Y	Y
14 **LaTourette**	Y	Y	Y	Y	Y	Y	Y
15 Kilroy	Y	Y	Y	Y	Y	Y	Y
16 Boccieri	Y	Y	Y	Y	Y	Y	Y
17 Ryan	Y	Y	Y	Y	?	Y	Y
18 Space	Y	Y	Y	Y	Y	Y	Y
OKLAHOMA							
1 **Sullivan**	N	Y	Y	Y	Y	Y	Y
2 Boren	Y	Y	Y	Y	Y	Y	Y
3 **Lucas**	N	Y	Y	Y	Y	Y	Y
4 **Cole**	N	Y	Y	Y	Y	Y	Y
5 **Fallin**	N	Y	Y	Y	Y	Y	Y
OREGON							
1 Wu	Y	Y	Y	Y	Y	Y	Y
2 **Walden**	N	Y	Y	Y	Y	Y	Y
3 Blumenauer	Y	Y	Y	Y	Y	Y	Y
4 DeFazio	Y	Y	Y	Y	Y	Y	Y
5 Schrader	Y	Y	Y	?	?	?	Y
PENNSYLVANIA							
1 Brady	Y	Y	Y	Y	Y	Y	Y
2 Fattah	Y	Y	Y	Y	Y	Y	Y
3 Dahlkemper	Y	Y	Y	Y	Y	Y	Y
4 Altmire	Y	Y	Y	Y	Y	Y	Y
5 **Thompson**	N	Y	Y	Y	Y	Y	Y
6 **Gerlach**	+	+	+	Y	Y	Y	Y
7 Sestak	Y	Y	Y	Y	Y	Y	Y
8 Murphy, P.	Y	Y	Y	Y	Y	Y	Y
9 **Shuster**	N	Y	Y	Y	Y	Y	Y
10 Carney	+	+	+	Y	Y	Y	Y
11 Kanjorski	Y	Y	Y	Y	Y	Y	Y
12 Murtha	?	?	?	Y	Y	Y	Y
13 Schwartz	Y	Y	Y	Y	Y	Y	Y
14 Doyle	Y	Y	Y	Y	Y	Y	Y
15 **Dent**	Y	Y	Y	Y	Y	Y	Y
16 **Pitts**	N	Y	Y	Y	Y	Y	Y
17 Holden	Y	Y	Y	Y	Y	Y	Y
18 **Murphy, T.**	Y	Y	Y	+	+	+	+
19 **Platts**	N	Y	Y	Y	Y	Y	Y
RHODE ISLAND							
1 Kennedy	Y	Y	Y	Y	Y	Y	Y
2 Langevin	Y	Y	Y	Y	Y	Y	Y
SOUTH CAROLINA							
1 **Brown**	N	Y	Y	Y	Y	Y	Y
2 **Wilson**	N	Y	Y	Y	Y	Y	Y
3 **Barrett**	?	?	?	?	?	?	?
4 **Inglis**	Y	Y	Y	Y	Y	Y	Y
5 Spratt	Y	Y	Y	Y	Y	Y	Y
6 Clyburn	Y	Y	Y	Y	Y	Y	Y
SOUTH DAKOTA							
AL Herseth Sandlin	Y	Y	Y	Y	Y	Y	Y
TENNESSEE							
1 **Roe**	N	Y	Y	Y	Y	Y	Y
2 **Duncan**	N	Y	Y	Y	Y	Y	Y
3 **Wamp**	?	?	?	Y	Y	Y	Y
4 Davis	Y	Y	Y	Y	Y	Y	Y
5 Cooper	Y	Y	Y	Y	Y	Y	Y
6 Gordon	Y	Y	Y	Y	Y	Y	Y
7 **Blackburn**	Y	Y	Y	Y	?	Y	Y
8 Tanner	?	?	?	Y	Y	Y	Y
9 Cohen	Y	Y	Y	Y	Y	Y	Y
TEXAS							
1 **Gohmert**	N	Y	Y	Y	Y	Y	Y
2 **Poe**	N	Y	Y	Y	Y	Y	Y
3 **Johnson, S.**	N	Y	Y	Y	Y	Y	Y
4 **Hall**	Y	Y	Y	Y	Y	Y	Y
5 **Hensarling**	N	Y	Y	Y	Y	Y	Y
6 **Barton**	N	Y	Y	Y	Y	Y	Y
7 **Culberson**	N	Y	Y	Y	Y	Y	Y
8 **Brady**	N	Y	Y	Y	Y	Y	Y
9 Green, A.	Y	Y	Y	Y	Y	Y	Y
10 **McCaul**	N	Y	Y	Y	Y	Y	Y
11 **Conaway**	N	Y	Y	Y	Y	Y	Y
12 **Granger**	Y	?	Y	Y	Y	Y	Y
13 **Thornberry**	Y	Y	Y	Y	Y	Y	Y
14 **Paul**	N	Y	Y	Y	Y	Y	Y
15 Hinojosa	Y	Y	Y	Y	Y	Y	Y
16 Reyes	Y	Y	Y	Y	Y	Y	Y
17 Edwards	Y	Y	Y	Y	Y	Y	Y
18 Jackson Lee	Y	Y	Y	Y	Y	Y	Y
19 **Neugebauer**	N	Y	Y	Y	Y	Y	Y
20 Gonzalez	?	?	?	?	?	?	?
21 **Smith**	Y	Y	Y	Y	Y	Y	Y
22 **Olson**	N	Y	Y	Y	Y	Y	Y
23 Rodriguez	Y	Y	Y	Y	Y	Y	Y
24 **Marchant**	N	Y	Y	Y	Y	Y	Y
25 Doggett	Y	Y	Y	Y	Y	Y	Y
26 **Burgess**	N	Y	Y	Y	Y	Y	Y
27 Ortiz	Y	Y	Y	Y	Y	Y	Y
28 Cuellar	Y	Y	Y	Y	Y	Y	Y
29 Green, G.	Y	Y	Y	Y	Y	Y	Y
30 Johnson, E.	Y	Y	Y	Y	Y	Y	Y
31 **Carter**	N	Y	Y	Y	Y	Y	Y
32 **Sessions**	N	Y	Y	Y	Y	Y	Y
UTAH							
1 **Bishop**	N	Y	Y	?	?	?	?
2 Matheson	Y	Y	Y	Y	Y	Y	Y
3 **Chaffetz**	N	Y	Y	Y	Y	Y	Y
VERMONT							
AL Welch	Y	Y	Y	Y	Y	Y	Y
VIRGINIA							
1 **Wittman**	N	Y	Y	Y	Y	Y	Y
2 Nye	Y	Y	Y	Y	Y	Y	Y
3 Scott	Y	Y	Y	Y	Y	Y	Y
4 **Forbes**	Y	Y	Y	Y	Y	Y	Y
5 Perriello	Y	Y	Y	Y	Y	Y	Y
6 **Goodlatte**	N	Y	Y	Y	Y	Y	Y
7 **Cantor**	N	Y	Y	Y	Y	?	?
8 Moran	?	?	?	?	?	?	?
9 Boucher	Y	Y	Y	Y	Y	Y	Y
10 **Wolf**	N	Y	Y	Y	Y	Y	Y
11 Connolly	Y	Y	Y	Y	Y	Y	Y
WASHINGTON							
1 Inslee	Y	Y	Y	Y	Y	Y	Y
2 Larsen	?	?	?	Y	Y	Y	Y
3 Baird	Y	Y	Y	Y	Y	Y	Y
4 **Hastings**	N	Y	Y	Y	Y	Y	Y
5 **McMorris Rodgers**	N	Y	Y	Y	Y	Y	Y
6 Dicks	?	Y	Y	Y	Y	Y	Y
7 McDermott	Y	Y	Y	Y	Y	Y	Y
8 **Reichert**	Y	Y	Y	Y	Y	Y	Y
9 Smith	Y	Y	Y	Y	Y	Y	Y
WEST VIRGINIA							
1 Mollohan	?	?	?	Y	Y	Y	Y
2 **Capito**	Y	Y	Y	Y	Y	Y	Y
3 Rahall	Y	Y	Y	Y	Y	Y	Y
WISCONSIN							
1 **Ryan**	N	Y	Y	Y	Y	Y	Y
2 Baldwin	Y	Y	Y	Y	Y	Y	Y
3 Kind	Y	Y	Y	Y	Y	Y	Y
4 Moore	Y	Y	Y	Y	Y	Y	Y
5 **Sensenbrenner**	N	Y	Y	Y	Y	Y	Y
6 **Petri**	Y	Y	Y	Y	Y	Y	Y
7 Obey	Y	Y	Y	Y	Y	Y	Y
8 Kagen	Y	Y	Y	Y	Y	Y	Y
WYOMING							
AL **Lummis**	N	Y	Y	Y	Y	Y	Y
DELEGATES							
Faleomavaega (A.S.)							
Norton (D.C.)							
Bordallo (Guam)							
Sablan (N. Marianas)							
Pierluisi (P.R.)							
Christensen (V.I.)							

IN THE HOUSE | By Vote Number

918. **HR 3634. George Kell Post Office/Passage.** Lynch, D-Mass., motion to suspend the rules and pass the bill that would designate a post office in Swifton, Ark., as the "George Kell Post Office." Motion agreed to 415-0: D 247-0; R 168-0. A two-thirds majority of those present and voting (277 in this case) is required for passage under suspension of the rules. Dec. 2, 2009.

919. **HR 515. Low-Level Radioactive Waste Import Ban/Passage.** Gordon, D-Tenn., motion to suspend the rules and pass the bill that would bar the Nuclear Regulatory Commission from issuing permits to import low-level radioactive waste into the United States. The president could provide a waiver under certain circumstances. Motion agreed to 309-112: D 247-1; R 62-111. A two-thirds majority of those present and voting (281 in this case) is required for passage under suspension of the rules. Dec. 2, 2009.

920. **H Con Res 197. Contaminated Drywall Assistance/Adoption.** Waters, D-Calif., motion to suspend the rules and adopt the concurrent resolution that would encourage banks and mortgage servicers to assist families affected by contaminated drywall and allow temporary forbearance without penalty on home mortgage payments. Motion agreed to 419-1: D 247-0; R 172-1. A two-thirds majority of those present and voting (280 in this case) is required for adoption under suspension of the rules. Dec. 2, 2009.

921. **HR 1242. TARP Funds Database/Passage.** Maloney, D-N.Y., motion to suspend the rules and pass the bill that would require the Treasury secretary to establish and maintain an electronic database tracking the status of funds distributed under the Troubled Asset Relief Program. Motion agreed to 421-0: D 248-0; R 173-0. A two-thirds majority of those present and voting (281 in this case) is required for passage under suspension of the rules. Dec. 2, 2009.

922. **HR 3980. FEMA Grant Regulations/Passage.** Cuellar, D-Texas, motion to suspend the rules and pass the bill that would require the Federal Emergency Management Agency (FEMA) administrator to submit a report to Congress that identifies redundant rules and regulations for FEMA grant recipients and includes a plan to improve methods of measuring performance. Motion agreed to 414-0: D 243-0; R 171-0. A two-thirds majority of those present and voting (276 in this case) is required for passage under suspension of the rules. Dec. 2, 2009.

923. **HR 4154. Estate Tax Extension/Previous Question.** Polis, D-Colo., motion to order the previous question (thus ending debate and possibility of amendment) on adoption of the rule (H Res 941) that would provide for House floor consideration of the bill that would permanently extend current estate and gift tax levels. Motion agreed to 228-187: D 228-16; R 0-171. Dec. 3, 2009.

924. **HR 4154. Estate Tax Extension/Rule.** Adoption of the rule (H Res 941) that would provide for House floor consideration of the bill that would permanently extend current estate and gift tax levels. Adopted 223-192: D 223-21; R 0-171. Dec. 3, 2009.

	918	919	920	921	922	923	924
ALABAMA							
1 Bonner	Y	N	Y	Y	Y	N	N
2 Bright	Y	Y	Y	Y	?	Y	Y
3 Rogers	Y	Y	Y	Y	Y	N	N
4 Aderholt	?	?	?	?	?	N	N
5 Griffith	Y	Y	Y	Y	Y	N	N
6 Bachus	Y	N	Y	Y	Y	N	N
7 Davis	?	Y	Y	Y	Y	Y	Y
ALASKA							
AL Young	?	?	?	?	?	?	?
ARIZONA							
1 Kirkpatrick	Y	Y	Y	Y	Y	Y	Y
2 Franks	Y	N	Y	Y	Y	N	N
3 Shadegg	Y	N	Y	Y	Y	N	N
4 Pastor	Y	Y	Y	Y	Y	Y	Y
5 Mitchell	Y	Y	Y	Y	Y	Y	Y
6 Flake	Y	N	Y	Y	Y	N	N
7 Grijalva	Y	Y	Y	Y	?	Y	Y
8 Giffords	Y	Y	Y	Y	+	Y	Y
ARKANSAS							
1 Berry	Y	Y	Y	Y	Y	Y	Y
2 Snyder	Y	Y	Y	Y	Y	Y	Y
3 Boozman	Y	Y	Y	Y	Y	N	N
4 Ross	Y	Y	Y	Y	Y	N	N
CALIFORNIA							
1 Thompson	Y	Y	Y	Y	Y	Y	Y
2 Herger	Y	N	Y	Y	Y	N	N
3 Lungren	Y	N	Y	Y	Y	N	N
4 McClintock	Y	N	N	Y	Y	N	N
5 Matsui	Y	Y	Y	Y	Y	Y	Y
6 Woolsey	Y	Y	Y	Y	Y	Y	Y
7 Miller, George	Y	Y	Y	Y	Y	Y	Y
8 Pelosi							
9 Lee	Y	Y	Y	Y	Y	Y	Y
10 Garamendi	?	Y	Y	Y	Y	Y	Y
11 McNerney	Y	Y	Y	Y	Y	Y	Y
12 Speier	?	Y	Y	Y	Y	Y	Y
13 Stark	Y	Y	Y	Y	Y	Y	Y
14 Eshoo	Y	Y	Y	Y	Y	Y	Y
15 Honda	Y	Y	Y	Y	Y	Y	Y
16 Lofgren	Y	Y	Y	Y	Y	Y	Y
17 Farr	Y	Y	Y	Y	Y	Y	Y
18 Cardoza	Y	Y	Y	Y	Y	Y	Y
19 Radanovich	?	N	Y	Y	Y	N	N
20 Costa	Y	Y	Y	Y	Y	Y	Y
21 Nunes	Y	N	Y	Y	Y	N	N
22 McCarthy	Y	Y	Y	Y	Y	N	N
23 Capps	Y	Y	Y	Y	Y	Y	Y
24 Gallegly	Y	Y	Y	Y	Y	N	N
25 McKeon	Y	Y	Y	Y	Y	N	N
26 Dreier	Y	N	Y	Y	Y	N	N
27 Sherman	Y	Y	Y	Y	Y	Y	Y
28 Berman	Y	Y	Y	Y	Y	Y	Y
29 Schiff	Y	Y	Y	Y	Y	Y	Y
30 Waxman	Y	Y	Y	Y	Y	Y	Y
31 Becerra	Y	Y	Y	Y	Y	Y	Y
32 Chu	Y	Y	Y	Y	Y	Y	Y
33 Watson	Y	Y	Y	Y	Y	Y	Y
34 Roybal-Allard	Y	Y	Y	Y	Y	Y	Y
35 Waters	Y	Y	Y	Y	?	Y	Y
36 Harman	Y	Y	Y	Y	Y	Y	Y
37 Richardson	Y	Y	Y	Y	Y	Y	Y
38 Napolitano	Y	Y	Y	Y	Y	Y	Y
39 Sánchez, Linda	Y	Y	Y	Y	Y	Y	Y
40 Royce	Y	N	Y	Y	Y	N	N
41 Lewis	Y	N	Y	Y	Y	N	N
42 Miller, Gary	Y	N	Y	Y	Y	N	N
43 Baca	Y	Y	Y	Y	Y	Y	Y
44 Calvert	Y	N	Y	Y	Y	N	N
45 Bono Mack	Y	N	Y	Y	Y	N	N
46 Rohrabacher	Y	N	Y	Y	Y	N	N
47 Sanchez, Loretta	Y	Y	Y	Y	Y	Y	Y
48 Campbell	Y	N	Y	Y	Y	N	N
49 Issa	Y	N	Y	Y	Y	N	N
50 Bilbray	Y	Y	Y	Y	Y	N	N
51 Filner	Y	Y	Y	Y	Y	Y	Y
52 Hunter	Y	Y	Y	Y	Y	N	N
53 Davis	Y	Y	Y	Y	Y	Y	Y

	918	919	920	921	922	923	924
COLORADO							
1 DeGette	Y	Y	Y	Y	Y	Y	Y
2 Polis	Y	Y	Y	Y	Y	Y	Y
3 Salazar	Y	Y	Y	Y	Y	Y	Y
4 Markey	Y	Y	Y	Y	Y	Y	Y
5 Lamborn	Y	N	Y	Y	Y	N	N
6 Coffman	Y	N	Y	Y	Y	N	N
7 Perlmutter	Y	Y	Y	Y	Y	?	Y
CONNECTICUT							
1 Larson	Y	Y	Y	Y	Y	Y	Y
2 Courtney	Y	Y	Y	Y	Y	Y	Y
3 DeLauro	Y	Y	Y	Y	Y	Y	Y
4 Himes	Y	Y	Y	Y	Y	N	N
5 Murphy	Y	Y	Y	Y	Y	Y	Y
DELAWARE							
AL Castle	Y	Y	Y	Y	Y	N	N
FLORIDA							
1 Miller	Y	N	Y	Y	Y	N	N
2 Boyd	Y	Y	Y	Y	Y	Y	Y
3 Brown	Y	Y	Y	Y	?	Y	Y
4 Crenshaw	Y	N	Y	Y	Y	N	N
5 Brown-Waite	Y	N	Y	Y	Y	N	N
6 Stearns	Y	N	Y	Y	Y	N	N
7 Mica	Y	N	Y	Y	Y	N	N
8 Grayson	Y	Y	Y	Y	Y	Y	Y
9 Bilirakis	Y	N	Y	Y	Y	N	N
10 Young	Y	Y	Y	Y	Y	N	N
11 Castor	Y	Y	Y	Y	Y	Y	Y
12 Putnam	Y	Y	Y	Y	Y	N	N
13 Buchanan	Y	Y	Y	Y	Y	N	N
14 Mack	Y	N	Y	Y	Y	N	N
15 Posey	Y	Y	Y	Y	Y	N	N
16 Rooney	Y	Y	Y	Y	Y	N	N
17 Meek	Y	Y	Y	Y	Y	Y	Y
18 Ros-Lehtinen	?	Y	Y	Y	Y	N	N
19 Wexler	Y	Y	Y	Y	Y	Y	Y
20 Wasserman Schultz	Y	Y	Y	Y	Y	Y	Y
21 Diaz-Balart, L.	Y	Y	Y	Y	Y	N	N
22 Klein	Y	Y	Y	Y	Y	Y	Y
23 Hastings	Y	Y	Y	Y	Y	Y	Y
24 Kosmas	Y	Y	Y	Y	Y	Y	Y
25 Diaz-Balart, M.	Y	Y	Y	Y	Y	N	N
GEORGIA							
1 Kingston	Y	N	Y	Y	Y	N	N
2 Bishop	Y	Y	Y	Y	Y	Y	Y
3 Westmoreland	Y	N	Y	Y	Y	N	N
4 Johnson	Y	Y	Y	Y	Y	Y	Y
5 Lewis	Y	Y	Y	Y	Y	Y	Y
6 Price	Y	N	Y	Y	Y	N	N
7 Linder	Y	N	Y	Y	Y	N	N
8 Marshall	Y	Y	Y	Y	Y	Y	Y
9 Deal	?	Y	Y	Y	Y	N	N
10 Broun	Y	N	Y	Y	Y	N	N
11 Gingrey	Y	N	Y	Y	Y	?	N
12 Barrow	?	?	?	?	?	?	?
13 Scott	Y	Y	Y	Y	Y	Y	Y
HAWAII							
1 Abercrombie	Y	Y	Y	Y	Y	Y	Y
2 Hirono	Y	Y	Y	Y	?	?	?
IDAHO							
1 Minnick	Y	Y	Y	Y	Y	N	N
2 Simpson	Y	N	Y	Y	Y	N	N
ILLINOIS							
1 Rush	Y	Y	Y	Y	Y	Y	Y
2 Jackson	Y	Y	Y	Y	Y	Y	Y
3 Lipinski	Y	Y	Y	Y	Y	Y	Y
4 Gutierrez	Y	Y	Y	Y	Y	Y	Y
5 Quigley	Y	Y	Y	Y	Y	Y	Y
6 Roskam	Y	N	Y	Y	Y	N	N
7 Davis	Y	Y	Y	Y	Y	Y	Y
8 Bean	Y	Y	Y	Y	Y	Y	Y
9 Schakowsky	Y	Y	Y	Y	Y	Y	Y
10 Kirk	Y	Y	Y	Y	Y	N	N
11 Halvorson	Y	Y	Y	Y	Y	Y	Y
12 Costello	Y	Y	Y	Y	Y	Y	Y
13 Biggert	Y	N	Y	Y	Y	N	N
14 Foster	Y	Y	Y	Y	Y	Y	Y
15 Johnson	Y	Y	Y	Y	Y	N	N

KEY

Republicans	Democrats	
Y Voted for (yea)	**X** Paired against	**C** Voted "present" to avoid possible conflict of interest
# Paired for	**−** Announced against	**?** Did not vote or otherwise make a position known
+ Announced for	**P** Voted "present"	
N Voted against (nay)		

	918	919	920	921	922	923	924
16 **Manzullo**	Y	Y	Y	Y	Y	N	N
17 Hare	Y	Y	Y	Y	Y	Y	Y
18 **Schock**	Y	N	Y	Y	Y	N	N
19 **Shimkus**	Y	N	Y	Y	Y	N	N
INDIANA							
1 Visclosky	Y	Y	Y	Y	Y	Y	Y
2 Donnelly	Y	Y	Y	Y	Y	N	N
3 **Souder**	Y	N	Y	Y	Y	N	N
4 **Buyer**	Y	Y	Y	Y	Y	N	N
5 **Burton**	Y	N	Y	Y	Y	N	N
6 **Pence**	Y	N	Y	Y	?	N	N
7 Carson	Y	Y	Y	Y	Y	Y	Y
8 Ellsworth	Y	Y	Y	Y	Y	Y	N
9 Hill	Y	Y	Y	Y	Y	N	N
IOWA							
1 Braley	Y	Y	Y	Y	Y	Y	?
2 Loebsack	Y	Y	Y	Y	Y	Y	Y
3 Boswell	Y	Y	Y	Y	Y	Y	Y
4 **Latham**	Y	N	Y	Y	Y	N	N
5 **King**	Y	N	Y	Y	Y	N	N
KANSAS							
1 **Moran**	Y	N	Y	Y	Y	N	N
2 **Jenkins**	Y	N	Y	Y	Y	N	N
3 Moore	Y	Y	Y	Y	Y	Y	Y
4 **Tiahrt**	Y	N	Y	Y	Y	N	N
KENTUCKY							
1 **Whitfield**	Y	N	Y	Y	Y	N	N
2 **Guthrie**	Y	Y	Y	Y	Y	N	N
3 Yarmuth	Y	Y	Y	Y	Y	Y	Y
4 **Davis**	Y	N	Y	Y	Y	N	N
5 **Rogers**	Y	N	Y	Y	Y	N	N
6 Chandler	Y	Y	Y	Y	Y	Y	Y
LOUISIANA							
1 **Scalise**	Y	N	Y	Y	Y	N	N
2 **Cao**	Y	Y	Y	Y	Y	N	N
3 Melancon	?	?	?	?	?	?	?
4 **Fleming**	Y	N	Y	Y	Y	N	N
5 **Alexander**	Y	N	Y	Y	Y	N	N
6 **Cassidy**	Y	N	Y	Y	Y	N	N
7 **Boustany**	Y	N	Y	Y	Y	N	N
MAINE							
1 Pingree	Y	Y	Y	Y	Y	Y	Y
2 Michaud	Y	Y	Y	Y	Y	Y	Y
MARYLAND							
1 Kratovil	Y	Y	Y	Y	Y	N	N
2 Ruppersberger	Y	Y	Y	Y	Y	Y	Y
3 Sarbanes	Y	Y	Y	Y	Y	Y	Y
4 Edwards	Y	Y	Y	Y	Y	Y	Y
5 Hoyer	Y	Y	Y	Y	Y	Y	Y
6 **Bartlett**	Y	N	Y	Y	Y	N	N
7 Cummings	Y	Y	Y	Y	Y	Y	Y
8 Van Hollen	Y	Y	Y	Y	Y	Y	Y
MASSACHUSETTS							
1 Olver	Y	Y	Y	Y	Y	Y	Y
2 Neal	Y	Y	Y	Y	Y	Y	Y
3 McGovern	Y	Y	Y	Y	Y	?	?
4 Frank	Y	Y	Y	Y	Y	Y	Y
5 Tsongas	Y	Y	Y	Y	Y	Y	Y
6 Tierney	Y	Y	?	Y	Y	Y	Y
7 Markey	Y	Y	Y	Y	Y	Y	Y
8 Capuano	?	?	?	?	?	?	?
9 Lynch	Y	Y	Y	Y	Y	Y	Y
10 Delahunt	Y	Y	Y	Y	Y	Y	Y
MICHIGAN							
1 Stupak	Y	Y	Y	Y	Y	Y	Y
2 **Hoekstra**	Y	N	Y	Y	Y	N	N
3 **Ehlers**	Y	N	Y	Y	Y	N	N
4 **Camp**	Y	Y	Y	Y	Y	N	N
5 Kildee	Y	Y	Y	Y	Y	Y	Y
6 **Upton**	Y	N	Y	Y	Y	N	N
7 Schauer	Y	Y	Y	Y	Y	Y	Y
8 **Rogers**	Y	Y	Y	Y	Y	N	N
9 Peters	Y	Y	Y	Y	Y	Y	Y
10 **Miller**	Y	N	Y	Y	Y	N	N
11 **McCotter**	Y	Y	Y	Y	Y	N	N
12 Levin	Y	Y	Y	Y	Y	Y	Y
13 Kilpatrick	Y	Y	Y	Y	Y	Y	Y
14 Conyers	Y	Y	Y	Y	Y	Y	Y
15 Dingell	Y	Y	Y	Y	Y	Y	Y
MINNESOTA							
1 Walz	Y	Y	Y	Y	Y	Y	Y
2 **Kline**	Y	N	Y	Y	Y	N	N
3 **Paulsen**	Y	Y	Y	Y	Y	N	N
4 McCollum	Y	Y	Y	Y	Y	Y	Y
5 Ellison	Y	Y	Y	Y	Y	Y	Y
6 **Bachmann**	Y	N	Y	Y	Y	N	N
7 Peterson	Y	Y	Y	Y	Y	Y	Y
8 Oberstar	Y	Y	Y	Y	Y	Y	Y
MISSISSIPPI							
1 Childers	Y	Y	Y	Y	Y	N	N
2 Thompson	Y	Y	Y	Y	Y	Y	Y
3 **Harper**	Y	N	Y	Y	Y	N	N
4 Taylor	Y	N	Y	Y	Y	N	N
MISSOURI							
1 Clay	Y	Y	Y	Y	Y	Y	Y
2 **Akin**	Y	N	Y	Y	Y	N	N
3 Carnahan	Y	Y	Y	Y	Y	Y	Y
4 Skelton	Y	Y	Y	Y	Y	Y	N
5 Cleaver	Y	Y	Y	Y	Y	Y	Y
6 **Graves**	Y	N	Y	Y	Y	N	N
7 **Blunt**	Y	N	Y	Y	Y	N	N
8 **Emerson**	Y	N	Y	Y	Y	N	N
9 **Luetkemeyer**	Y	Y	Y	Y	Y	N	N
MONTANA							
AL **Rehberg**	Y	N	Y	Y	Y	N	N
NEBRASKA							
1 **Fortenberry**	Y	Y	Y	Y	Y	N	N
2 **Terry**	Y	Y	Y	Y	Y	N	N
3 **Smith**	Y	Y	Y	Y	Y	N	N
NEVADA							
1 Berkley	Y	Y	Y	Y	Y	Y	Y
2 **Heller**	Y	Y	Y	Y	Y	N	N
3 Titus	Y	Y	Y	Y	Y	Y	Y
NEW HAMPSHIRE							
1 Shea-Porter	Y	?	?	?	?	Y	Y
2 Hodes	Y	?	?	?	?	Y	Y
NEW JERSEY							
1 Andrews	Y	Y	Y	Y	Y	Y	Y
2 **LoBiondo**	Y	Y	Y	Y	Y	N	N
3 Adler	Y	Y	Y	Y	Y	Y	Y
4 **Smith**	Y	Y	Y	Y	Y	N	N
5 **Garrett**	Y	Y	Y	Y	Y	N	N
6 Pallone	Y	Y	Y	Y	Y	Y	Y
7 **Lance**	Y	Y	Y	Y	Y	N	N
8 Pascrell	Y	Y	Y	Y	Y	Y	Y
9 Rothman	Y	Y	Y	Y	Y	Y	Y
10 Payne	Y	Y	Y	Y	Y	Y	Y
11 **Frelinghuysen**	Y	N	Y	Y	Y	N	N
12 Holt	Y	Y	Y	Y	Y	Y	Y
13 Sires	Y	Y	Y	Y	Y	Y	Y
NEW MEXICO							
1 Heinrich	Y	Y	Y	Y	Y	Y	Y
2 Teague	Y	Y	Y	Y	Y	N	N
3 Lujan	Y	Y	Y	Y	Y	Y	Y
NEW YORK							
1 Bishop	Y	Y	Y	Y	Y	N	N
2 Israel	Y	Y	Y	Y	Y	Y	Y
3 **King**	Y	Y	Y	Y	Y	N	N
4 McCarthy	Y	Y	Y	Y	Y	Y	Y
5 Ackerman	Y	Y	Y	Y	Y	Y	Y
6 Meeks	Y	Y	Y	Y	Y	Y	Y
7 Crowley	Y	Y	Y	Y	Y	Y	Y
8 Nadler	Y	Y	Y	Y	Y	Y	Y
9 Weiner	Y	Y	Y	Y	Y	Y	Y
10 Towns	Y	Y	Y	Y	Y	Y	Y
11 Clarke	Y	Y	Y	Y	Y	Y	Y
12 Velázquez	Y	Y	Y	Y	Y	Y	Y
13 McMahon	Y	Y	Y	Y	Y	Y	Y
14 Maloney	Y	Y	Y	Y	Y	Y	Y
15 Rangel	Y	Y	Y	Y	Y	Y	Y
16 Serrano	Y	Y	Y	Y	Y	Y	Y
17 Engel	Y	Y	Y	Y	Y	Y	Y
18 Lowey	Y	Y	Y	Y	Y	Y	Y
19 Hall	Y	Y	Y	Y	Y	Y	Y
20 Murphy	Y	Y	Y	Y	Y	Y	Y
21 Tonko	Y	Y	Y	Y	Y	Y	Y
22 Hinchey	Y	Y	Y	Y	Y	Y	Y
23 Owens	Y	Y	Y	Y	Y	Y	Y
24 Arcuri	Y	Y	Y	Y	Y	?	Y
25 Maffei	Y	Y	Y	Y	Y	Y	Y
26 **Lee**	Y	Y	Y	Y	Y	N	N
27 Higgins	Y	?	?	?	?	Y	Y
28 Slaughter	Y	Y	Y	Y	Y	Y	Y
29 Massa	Y	Y	Y	Y	Y	Y	Y
NORTH CAROLINA							
1 Butterfield	Y	Y	Y	Y	Y	Y	Y
2 Etheridge	Y	Y	Y	Y	Y	Y	Y
3 **Jones**	Y	Y	Y	Y	Y	N	N
4 Price	Y	Y	Y	Y	Y	Y	Y
5 **Foxx**	Y	N	Y	Y	Y	N	N
6 **Coble**	Y	N	Y	Y	Y	N	N
7 McIntyre	Y	Y	Y	Y	Y	Y	Y
8 Kissell	Y	Y	Y	Y	Y	Y	Y
9 **Myrick**	Y	N	Y	Y	Y	N	N
10 **McHenry**	Y	N	Y	Y	Y	N	N
11 Shuler	Y	Y	Y	Y	Y	Y	N
12 Watt	Y	Y	Y	Y	Y	Y	Y
13 Miller	Y	Y	Y	Y	Y	Y	Y
NORTH DAKOTA							
AL Pomeroy	Y	Y	Y	Y	Y	Y	Y
OHIO							
1 Driehaus	Y	Y	Y	Y	Y	Y	Y
2 **Schmidt**	Y	N	Y	Y	Y	N	N
3 **Turner**	Y	Y	Y	Y	Y	N	N
4 **Jordan**	Y	N	Y	Y	Y	N	N
5 **Latta**	Y	N	Y	Y	Y	N	N
6 Wilson	Y	Y	Y	Y	Y	Y	Y
7 **Austria**	Y	N	Y	Y	Y	N	N
8 **Boehner**	Y	N	Y	Y	Y	N	?
9 Kaptur	Y	Y	Y	Y	Y	N	N
10 Kucinich	Y	Y	Y	Y	Y	Y	Y
11 Fudge	Y	Y	Y	Y	Y	Y	Y
12 **Tiberi**	Y	Y	Y	Y	Y	N	N
13 Sutton	Y	Y	Y	Y	Y	?	?
14 **LaTourette**	Y	Y	Y	Y	Y	N	N
15 Kilroy	Y	Y	Y	Y	Y	Y	Y
16 Boccieri	Y	Y	Y	Y	Y	Y	Y
17 Ryan	Y	Y	Y	Y	Y	?	Y
18 Space	Y	Y	Y	Y	Y	Y	Y
OKLAHOMA							
1 **Sullivan**	Y	N	Y	Y	Y	N	N
2 Boren	Y	Y	Y	Y	Y	Y	Y
3 **Lucas**	Y	N	Y	Y	Y	?	?
4 **Cole**	Y	N	Y	Y	Y	N	N
5 **Fallin**	Y	N	Y	Y	Y	N	N
OREGON							
1 Wu	Y	Y	Y	Y	Y	Y	Y
2 **Walden**	Y	Y	Y	Y	Y	N	N
3 Blumenauer	Y	Y	Y	Y	Y	Y	Y
4 DeFazio	Y	Y	Y	Y	Y	Y	?
5 Schrader	Y	Y	Y	Y	Y	Y	Y
PENNSYLVANIA							
1 Brady	Y	Y	Y	Y	Y	Y	Y
2 Fattah	Y	Y	Y	Y	Y	Y	Y
3 Dahlkemper	Y	Y	Y	Y	Y	Y	Y
4 Altmire	Y	Y	Y	Y	Y	Y	Y
5 **Thompson**	Y	Y	Y	Y	Y	N	N
6 **Gerlach**	Y	Y	Y	Y	Y	–	–
7 Sestak	Y	Y	Y	Y	Y	Y	Y
8 Murphy, P.	Y	Y	Y	Y	Y	Y	Y
9 **Shuster**	Y	Y	Y	Y	Y	N	N
10 Carney	Y	Y	Y	Y	Y	Y	Y
11 Kanjorski	Y	Y	Y	Y	Y	Y	Y
12 Murtha	Y	Y	Y	Y	Y	Y	Y
13 Schwartz	Y	Y	Y	Y	Y	Y	Y
14 Doyle	Y	Y	Y	Y	Y	Y	Y
15 **Dent**	Y	Y	Y	Y	Y	N	N
16 **Pitts**	Y	N	Y	Y	Y	N	N
17 Holden	Y	Y	Y	Y	Y	Y	Y
18 **Murphy, T.**	+	N	Y	Y	Y	N	N
19 **Platts**	Y	Y	Y	Y	Y	N	N
RHODE ISLAND							
1 Kennedy	Y	Y	Y	Y	Y	Y	Y
2 Langevin	Y	Y	Y	Y	Y	Y	Y
SOUTH CAROLINA							
1 **Brown**	Y	Y	Y	Y	Y	N	N
2 **Wilson**	Y	N	Y	Y	Y	N	N
3 **Barrett**	?	?	?	?	?	N	N
4 **Inglis**	Y	N	Y	Y	Y	N	N
5 Spratt	Y	Y	Y	Y	Y	Y	Y
6 Clyburn	Y	Y	Y	Y	Y	Y	Y
SOUTH DAKOTA							
AL Herseth Sandlin	Y	Y	Y	Y	Y	Y	Y
TENNESSEE							
1 **Roe**	Y	N	Y	Y	Y	N	N
2 **Duncan**	Y	Y	Y	Y	Y	N	N
3 **Wamp**	Y	Y	Y	Y	Y	N	N
4 Davis	Y	Y	Y	Y	Y	Y	Y
5 Cooper	Y	Y	Y	Y	Y	Y	Y
6 Gordon	Y	Y	Y	Y	Y	?	?
7 **Blackburn**	Y	N	Y	Y	Y	N	N
8 Tanner	Y	Y	Y	Y	Y	Y	Y
9 Cohen	Y	Y	Y	Y	Y	Y	Y
TEXAS							
1 **Gohmert**	Y	N	Y	Y	Y	N	N
2 **Poe**	Y	N	Y	Y	Y	N	N
3 **Johnson, S.**	Y	N	Y	Y	Y	N	N
4 **Hall**	Y	N	Y	Y	Y	N	N
5 **Hensarling**	Y	N	Y	Y	Y	N	N
6 **Barton**	Y	N	Y	Y	Y	N	N
7 **Culberson**	Y	N	Y	Y	Y	N	N
8 **Brady**	Y	N	Y	Y	?	N	N
9 Green, A.	Y	Y	Y	Y	Y	Y	Y
10 **McCaul**	Y	N	Y	Y	Y	N	N
11 **Conaway**	Y	N	Y	Y	Y	N	N
12 **Granger**	Y	N	Y	Y	Y	N	N
13 **Thornberry**	Y	N	Y	Y	Y	N	N
14 **Paul**	Y	N	Y	Y	Y	N	N
15 Hinojosa	Y	Y	Y	Y	Y	Y	Y
16 Reyes	Y	Y	Y	Y	Y	Y	Y
17 Edwards	Y	Y	Y	Y	Y	Y	Y
18 Jackson Lee	Y	Y	Y	Y	Y	Y	Y
19 **Neugebauer**	Y	Y	Y	Y	Y	N	N
20 Gonzalez	?	?	?	?	?	?	?
21 **Smith**	Y	N	Y	Y	Y	N	N
22 **Olson**	Y	N	Y	Y	Y	N	N
23 Rodriguez	Y	Y	Y	Y	Y	Y	Y
24 **Marchant**	Y	N	Y	Y	Y	N	N
25 Doggett	Y	Y	Y	Y	Y	Y	Y
26 **Burgess**	Y	N	Y	Y	Y	?	?
27 Ortiz	Y	Y	Y	Y	Y	Y	Y
28 Cuellar	Y	Y	Y	Y	Y	Y	Y
29 Green, G.	Y	Y	Y	Y	Y	Y	Y
30 Johnson, E.	Y	Y	Y	Y	Y	Y	Y
31 **Carter**	Y	N	Y	Y	Y	N	N
32 **Sessions**	Y	N	Y	Y	Y	N	N
UTAH							
1 **Bishop**	?	?	?	?	?	?	?
2 Matheson	Y	Y	Y	Y	Y	Y	Y
3 **Chaffetz**	Y	Y	Y	Y	Y	N	N
VERMONT							
AL Welch	Y	Y	Y	Y	Y	Y	?
VIRGINIA							
1 **Wittman**	Y	Y	Y	Y	Y	N	N
2 Nye	Y	Y	Y	Y	Y	N	N
3 Scott	Y	Y	Y	Y	Y	Y	Y
4 **Forbes**	Y	Y	Y	Y	Y	N	N
5 Perriello	Y	Y	Y	Y	Y	N	N
6 **Goodlatte**	Y	Y	Y	Y	Y	N	N
7 **Cantor**	?	Y	Y	Y	Y	N	N
8 Moran	?	?	?	?	?	?	?
9 Boucher	Y	Y	Y	Y	Y	Y	Y
10 **Wolf**	Y	Y	Y	Y	Y	N	N
11 Connolly	Y	Y	Y	Y	Y	Y	Y
WASHINGTON							
1 Inslee	Y	Y	Y	Y	Y	Y	Y
2 Larsen	Y	?	?	?	?	Y	Y
3 Baird	Y	Y	Y	Y	Y	N	N
4 **Hastings**	Y	N	Y	Y	Y	N	N
5 **McMorris Rodgers**	?	N	Y	Y	Y	N	N
6 Dicks	Y	Y	Y	Y	Y	Y	Y
7 McDermott	Y	Y	Y	Y	Y	Y	Y
8 **Reichert**	Y	Y	Y	Y	Y	N	N
9 Smith	Y	Y	Y	Y	Y	Y	Y
WEST VIRGINIA							
1 Mollohan	Y	Y	Y	Y	Y	Y	Y
2 **Capito**	Y	Y	Y	Y	Y	N	N
3 Rahall	Y	Y	Y	Y	Y	Y	Y
WISCONSIN							
1 **Ryan**	Y	N	Y	Y	Y	N	N
2 Baldwin	Y	Y	Y	Y	Y	Y	Y
3 Kind	Y	Y	Y	Y	Y	Y	Y
4 Moore	Y	Y	Y	Y	Y	Y	Y
5 **Sensenbrenner**	Y	N	Y	Y	Y	N	N
6 **Petri**	Y	Y	Y	Y	Y	N	N
7 Obey	Y	Y	Y	Y	Y	Y	Y
8 Kagen	Y	Y	Y	Y	Y	Y	?
WYOMING							
AL **Lummis**	Y	Y	Y	Y	Y	N	N
DELEGATES							
Faleomavaega (A.S.)							
Norton (D.C.)							
Bordallo (Guam)							
Sablan (N. Marianas)							
Pierluisi (P.R.)							
Christensen (V.I.)							

IN THE HOUSE | By Vote Number

925. Procedural Motion/Journal. Approval of the House Journal of Wednesday, Dec. 2, 2009. Approved 250-169: D 224-24; R 26-145. Dec. 3, 2009.

926. H Res 28. Surface Transportation Safety/Adoption. Jackson Lee, D-Texas, motion to suspend the rules and adopt the resolution that would express the sense of the House that the Transportation Security Administration should continue to increase security on rail, mass transit and other surface transportation systems. Motion agreed to 417-3: D 249-0; R 168-3. A two-thirds majority of those present and voting (280 in this case) is required for adoption under suspension of the rules. Dec. 3, 2009.

927. HR 4154. Estate Tax Extension/Motion to Table. Pomeroy, D-N.D., motion to table (kill) the Heller, R-Nev., appeal of the ruling of the chair with respect to the Pomeroy point of order that the Heller motion to recommit the bill violates the House pay-as-you-go budget rule because it would increase the deficit. The motion would recommit the bill to the Ways and Means Committee with instructions that it be immediately reported back with an amendment that would repeal the estate tax. Motion agreed to 234-186: D 234-15; R 0-171. Dec. 3, 2009.

928. HR 4154. Estate Tax Extension/Recommit. Heller, R-Nev., motion to recommit the bill to the House Ways and Means Committee with instructions that it be immediately reported back with an amendment that would repeal the estate tax through Dec. 31, 2011. Motion rejected 187-233: D 18-233; R 169-0. Dec. 3, 2009.

929. HR 4154. Estate Tax Extension/Passage. Passage of the bill that would make permanent the current estate and gift tax levels, which set a 45 percent top tax rate and a $3.5 million per-person exemption amount from the tax. Passed 225-200: D 225-26; R 0-174. (Pursuant to the rule, language was incorporated upon the bill's passage to add statutory pay-as-you-go rules that would require most new mandatory spending and tax cuts to be offset.) Dec. 3, 2009.

930. HR 3570. Satellite Television Regulations/Passage. Conyers, D-Mich., motion to suspend the rules and pass the bill that would extend and modify regulations governing satellite television carriers' distribution of local broadcast stations to markets without local affiliates. It also would require satellite television providers to continue carrying multicast affiliates. Motion agreed to 394-11: D 238-0; R 156-11. A two-thirds majority of those present and voting (270 in this case) is required for passage under suspension of the rules. Dec. 3, 2009.

	925	926	927	928	929	930
ALABAMA						
1 Bonner	N	Y	N	Y	N	Y
2 Bright	N	Y	N	Y	N	Y
3 Rogers	N	Y	N	Y	N	Y
4 Aderholt	N	Y	N	Y	N	Y
5 Griffith	Y	Y	N	Y	N	Y
6 Bachus	N	Y	N	Y	N	Y
7 Davis	Y	Y	Y	N	Y	Y
ALASKA						
AL Young	?	?	?	?	?	?
ARIZONA						
1 Kirkpatrick	N	Y	N	Y	N	Y
2 Franks	N	Y	N	Y	N	Y
3 Shadegg	N	Y	N	Y	N	Y
4 Pastor	Y	Y	Y	N	Y	Y
5 Mitchell	N	Y	N	Y	N	Y
6 Flake	N	N	N	Y	N	N
7 Grijalva	Y	Y	Y	N	Y	Y
8 Giffords	N	Y	N	Y	Y	?
ARKANSAS						
1 Berry	Y	Y	Y	N	Y	Y
2 Snyder	Y	Y	Y	N	Y	Y
3 Boozman	N	Y	N	Y	N	Y
4 Ross	Y	Y	Y	N	Y	Y
CALIFORNIA						
1 Thompson	N	Y	Y	N	Y	Y
2 Herger	N	Y	N	Y	N	Y
3 Lungren	N	Y	N	Y	N	Y
4 McClintock	Y	Y	N	Y	N	N
5 Matsui	Y	Y	Y	N	Y	Y
6 Woolsey	Y	Y	Y	N	Y	Y
7 Miller, George	Y	Y	Y	N	Y	Y
8 Pelosi						
9 Lee	Y	Y	Y	N	Y	Y
10 Garamendi	Y	Y	Y	N	Y	Y
11 McNerney	Y	Y	Y	N	Y	Y
12 Speier	Y	Y	Y	N	Y	Y
13 Stark	Y	Y	Y	N	N	Y
14 Eshoo	Y	Y	Y	N	Y	Y
15 Honda	Y	Y	Y	N	Y	Y
16 Lofgren	Y	Y	Y	N	Y	Y
17 Farr	Y	Y	Y	N	Y	Y
18 Cardoza	Y	Y	Y	N	Y	Y
19 Radanovich	N	Y	N	Y	N	Y
20 Costa	N	Y	N	Y	N	Y
21 Nunes	N	Y	N	Y	N	Y
22 McCarthy	Y	Y	Y	N	Y	Y
23 Capps	Y	Y	Y	N	Y	Y
24 Gallegly	N	Y	N	Y	N	Y
25 McKeon	N	Y	N	Y	N	Y
26 Dreier	N	Y	N	Y	N	Y
27 Sherman	Y	Y	Y	N	Y	?
28 Berman	Y	Y	Y	N	Y	Y
29 Schiff	Y	Y	Y	N	Y	Y
30 Waxman	Y	Y	Y	N	Y	Y
31 Becerra	Y	Y	Y	N	N	Y
32 Chu	Y	Y	Y	N	Y	Y
33 Watson	Y	Y	Y	N	Y	Y
34 Roybal-Allard	Y	Y	Y	N	Y	Y
35 Waters	Y	Y	Y	N	Y	Y
36 Harman	Y	Y	Y	N	Y	Y
37 Richardson	Y	Y	Y	N	Y	Y
38 Napolitano	Y	Y	Y	N	Y	Y
39 Sánchez, Linda	Y	Y	Y	N	N	Y
40 Royce	N	Y	N	+	N	Y
41 Lewis	N	Y	N	Y	N	Y
42 Miller, Gary	N	Y	N	Y	N	Y
43 Baca	Y	Y	Y	N	Y	Y
44 Calvert	N	Y	N	Y	N	Y
45 Bono Mack	N	Y	?	Y	N	Y
46 Rohrabacher	N	Y	N	Y	N	Y
47 Sanchez, Loretta	Y	Y	Y	N	Y	Y
48 Campbell	N	Y	N	Y	N	?
49 Issa	N	Y	N	Y	N	Y
50 Bilbray	Y	Y	Y	N	Y	N
51 Filner	Y	Y	Y	N	Y	Y
52 Hunter	N	Y	N	Y	N	Y
53 Davis	Y	Y	Y	N	Y	Y

	925	926	927	928	929	930
COLORADO						
1 DeGette	Y	Y	Y	N	Y	Y
2 Polis	Y	Y	Y	N	Y	Y
3 Salazar	Y	Y	Y	N	Y	?
4 Markey	N	Y	Y	N	Y	Y
5 Lamborn	N	Y	N	Y	N	Y
6 Coffman	N	Y	N	Y	N	Y
7 Perlmutter	Y	Y	Y	N	Y	?
CONNECTICUT						
1 Larson	Y	Y	Y	N	Y	Y
2 Courtney	Y	Y	Y	N	Y	Y
3 DeLauro	Y	Y	Y	N	Y	Y
4 Himes	Y	Y	Y	N	N	Y
5 Murphy	Y	Y	Y	N	N	Y
DELAWARE						
AL Castle	Y	Y	N	Y	N	Y
FLORIDA						
1 Miller	N	Y	N	Y	N	Y
2 Boyd	Y	Y	Y	N	Y	Y
3 Brown	Y	Y	Y	N	Y	Y
4 Crenshaw	N	Y	N	Y	N	Y
5 Brown-Waite	N	Y	N	Y	N	?
6 Stearns	N	Y	N	Y	N	Y
7 Mica	N	Y	N	Y	N	Y
8 Grayson	Y	Y	Y	N	Y	Y
9 Bilirakis	N	Y	N	Y	N	Y
10 Young	N	Y	N	Y	N	Y
11 Castor	Y	Y	Y	N	Y	Y
12 Putnam	Y	Y	N	Y	N	?
13 Buchanan	N	Y	N	Y	N	Y
14 Mack	Y	Y	N	Y	N	Y
15 Posey	Y	Y	N	Y	N	Y
16 Rooney	N	?	N	Y	N	Y
17 Meek	Y	Y	Y	N	Y	Y
18 Ros-Lehtinen	N	Y	N	Y	N	Y
19 Wexler	Y	Y	Y	N	Y	Y
20 Wasserman Schultz	Y	Y	Y	N	Y	Y
21 Diaz-Balart, L.	N	Y	N	Y	N	Y
22 Klein	Y	Y	Y	N	Y	Y
23 Hastings	Y	Y	Y	N	Y	Y
24 Kosmas	Y	Y	Y	N	Y	Y
25 Diaz-Balart, M.	N	Y	N	Y	N	Y
GEORGIA						
1 Kingston	N	Y	N	Y	N	Y
2 Bishop	Y	Y	Y	N	Y	?
3 Westmoreland	N	Y	N	Y	N	Y
4 Johnson	Y	Y	Y	N	Y	Y
5 Lewis	Y	Y	Y	N	Y	Y
6 Price	N	?	N	Y	N	Y
7 Linder	N	Y	?	N	Y	Y
8 Marshall	N	Y	Y	N	Y	Y
9 Deal	N	Y	N	Y	N	Y
10 Broun	N	Y	N	Y	N	Y
11 Gingrey	N	Y	N	Y	N	Y
12 Barrow	?	?	?	?	?	?
13 Scott	Y	Y	Y	N	Y	Y
HAWAII						
1 Abercrombie	Y	Y	Y	N	Y	Y
2 Hirono	Y	Y	Y	N	Y	Y
IDAHO						
1 Minnick	N	Y	N	Y	Y	Y
2 Simpson	N	Y	N	Y	N	Y
ILLINOIS						
1 Rush	Y	Y	Y	N	Y	Y
2 Jackson	Y	Y	Y	N	Y	Y
3 Lipinski	Y	Y	Y	N	Y	Y
4 Gutierrez	Y	Y	Y	N	Y	Y
5 Quigley	Y	Y	Y	N	Y	Y
6 Roskam	N	Y	N	+	N	Y
7 Davis	Y	Y	Y	N	Y	Y
8 Bean	Y	Y	Y	N	N	?
9 Schakowsky	Y	Y	Y	N	Y	Y
10 Kirk	Y	Y	N	Y	N	Y
11 Halvorson	N	Y	Y	N	Y	Y
12 Costello	Y	Y	Y	N	Y	Y
13 Biggert	Y	Y	N	Y	N	Y
14 Foster	Y	Y	Y	N	Y	Y
15 Johnson	Y	Y	N	Y	N	Y

KEY   Republicans   Democrats

Y Voted for (yea)	X Paired against	C Voted "present" to avoid possible conflict of interest
# Paired for	– Announced against	
+ Announced for	P Voted "present"	? Did not vote or otherwise make a position known
N Voted against (nay)		

	925	926	927	928	929	930
16 **Manzullo**	N	Y	N	Y	N	Y
17 Hare	Y	Y	Y	N	Y	Y
18 **Schock**	N	Y	?	Y	N	Y
19 **Shimkus**	N	Y	N	Y	N	Y
INDIANA						
1 Visclosky	Y	Y	Y	N	Y	Y
2 Donnelly	N	Y	Y	N	Y	Y
3 **Souder**	N	Y	N	Y	N	Y
4 **Buyer**	N	Y	N	Y	N	Y
5 **Burton**	N	Y	N	Y	N	Y
6 **Pence**	N	Y	N	Y	N	Y
7 Carson	Y	Y	Y	N	Y	Y
8 Ellsworth	Y	Y	N	Y	Y	Y
9 Hill	Y	Y	Y	N	Y	Y
IOWA						
1 Braley	Y	Y	Y	N	Y	?
2 Loebsack	Y	Y	Y	N	Y	Y
3 Boswell	Y	Y	Y	N	Y	Y
4 **Latham**	Y	Y	N	Y	N	Y
5 **King**	N	Y	N	Y	N	Y
KANSAS						
1 **Moran**	N	Y	N	Y	N	Y
2 **Jenkins**	N	Y	N	Y	N	Y
3 Moore	Y	Y	Y	N	Y	Y
4 **Tiahrt**	N	Y	N	Y	N	Y
KENTUCKY						
1 **Whitfield**	Y	Y	N	Y	N	Y
2 **Guthrie**	N	Y	N	Y	N	Y
3 Yarmuth	Y	Y	Y	N	Y	Y
4 **Davis**	N	Y	N	Y	N	Y
5 **Rogers**	N	Y	N	Y	N	?
6 Chandler	Y	Y	Y	N	Y	Y
LOUISIANA						
1 **Scalise**	N	Y	N	Y	N	Y
2 **Cao**	N	Y	N	Y	N	Y
3 Melancon	?	?	?	?	?	?
4 **Fleming**	N	Y	N	Y	N	Y
5 **Alexander**	N	Y	N	Y	N	Y
6 **Cassidy**	N	Y	N	Y	N	N
7 **Boustany**	N	Y	N	Y	N	Y
MAINE						
1 Pingree	Y	Y	Y	N	Y	Y
2 Michaud	Y	Y	Y	N	Y	Y
MARYLAND						
1 Kratovil	Y	Y	N	N	N	Y
2 Ruppersberger	Y	Y	Y	N	N	Y
3 Sarbanes	Y	Y	Y	N	Y	Y
4 Edwards	Y	Y	Y	N	Y	Y
5 Hoyer	Y	Y	Y	N	Y	Y
6 **Bartlett**	N	Y	N	Y	N	Y
7 Cummings	Y	Y	Y	N	Y	Y
8 Van Hollen	Y	Y	Y	N	Y	Y
MASSACHUSETTS						
1 Olver	Y	Y	Y	N	Y	Y
2 Neal	Y	Y	Y	N	Y	Y
3 McGovern	?	?	?	?	?	?
4 Frank	Y	Y	Y	N	Y	Y
5 Tsongas	Y	Y	Y	N	Y	Y
6 Tierney	Y	Y	Y	N	Y	Y
7 Markey	Y	Y	Y	N	Y	Y
8 Capuano	?	?	?	?	+	?
9 Lynch	Y	Y	Y	N	Y	Y
10 Delahunt	Y	Y	Y	N	Y	Y
MICHIGAN						
1 Stupak	N	Y	Y	N	Y	Y
2 **Hoekstra**	N	Y	N	Y	N	Y
3 **Ehlers**	N	Y	N	Y	N	Y
4 **Camp**	N	Y	N	Y	N	Y
5 Kildee	Y	Y	Y	N	Y	Y
6 **Upton**	N	Y	N	Y	N	Y
7 Schauer	Y	Y	Y	Y	N	Y
8 **Rogers**	N	Y	N	Y	N	Y
9 Peters	Y	Y	Y	N	Y	Y
10 **Miller**	N	Y	N	Y	N	Y
11 **McCotter**	Y	Y	N	Y	N	Y
12 Levin	Y	Y	Y	N	Y	Y
13 Kilpatrick	Y	Y	Y	N	N	Y
14 Conyers	Y	Y	Y	N	Y	Y
15 Dingell	Y	Y	Y	N	Y	Y
MINNESOTA						
1 Walz	Y	Y	Y	N	N	Y
2 **Kline**	N	Y	N	Y	N	Y
3 **Paulsen**	Y	Y	N	Y	N	Y
4 McCollum	Y	Y	Y	N	Y	Y

	925	926	927	928	929	930
5 Ellison	Y	Y	Y	N	Y	Y
6 **Bachmann**	N	Y	N	Y	N	Y
7 Peterson	Y	Y	Y	N	Y	Y
8 Oberstar	Y	Y	Y	N	Y	Y
MISSISSIPPI						
1 Childers	Y	Y	Y	N	Y	Y
2 Thompson	Y	Y	Y	N	Y	Y
3 **Harper**	N	Y	N	Y	N	Y
4 Taylor	Y	Y	N	N	Y	Y
MISSOURI						
1 Clay	Y	Y	Y	N	Y	Y
2 **Akin**	N	Y	N	Y	N	Y
3 Carnahan	Y	?	Y	N	Y	Y
4 Skelton	Y	Y	Y	Y	Y	Y
5 Cleaver	Y	Y	Y	N	Y	Y
6 **Graves**	N	Y	N	Y	N	Y
7 **Blunt**	N	Y	N	Y	N	Y
8 **Emerson**	N	Y	N	Y	N	Y
9 **Luetkemeyer**	Y	Y	N	Y	N	Y
MONTANA						
AL **Rehberg**	N	Y	N	Y	N	Y
NEBRASKA						
1 **Fortenberry**	N	Y	N	Y	N	Y
2 **Terry**	N	Y	N	Y	N	Y
3 **Smith**	N	Y	N	Y	N	N
NEVADA						
1 Berkley	Y	Y	Y	N	Y	Y
2 **Heller**	Y	Y	N	Y	N	Y
3 Titus	N	Y	Y	N	Y	Y
NEW HAMPSHIRE						
1 Shea-Porter	Y	Y	Y	N	Y	Y
2 Hodes	Y	Y	Y	N	Y	Y
NEW JERSEY						
1 Andrews	Y	Y	Y	N	Y	?
2 **LoBiondo**	N	Y	N	Y	N	Y
3 Adler	N	Y	Y	Y	Y	Y
4 **Smith**	N	Y	N	Y	N	Y
5 **Garrett**	N	Y	N	Y	N	N
6 Pallone	Y	Y	Y	N	Y	Y
7 **Lance**	Y	Y	N	Y	N	Y
8 Pascrell	Y	Y	Y	N	Y	Y
9 Rothman	Y	Y	Y	N	Y	Y
10 Payne	Y	Y	Y	N	Y	Y
11 **Frelinghuysen**	N	Y	N	Y	N	Y
12 Holt	Y	Y	Y	N	Y	Y
13 Sires	Y	Y	Y	N	Y	Y
NEW MEXICO						
1 Heinrich	Y	Y	Y	N	Y	Y
2 Teague	N	Y	Y	Y	Y	Y
3 Lujan	Y	Y	Y	N	Y	Y
NEW YORK						
1 Bishop	Y	Y	Y	N	Y	Y
2 Israel	Y	Y	Y	N	Y	Y
3 **King**	N	Y	N	Y	N	Y
4 McCarthy	Y	Y	Y	N	Y	Y
5 Ackerman	Y	Y	Y	N	Y	?
6 Meeks	Y	Y	Y	N	Y	Y
7 Crowley	Y	Y	Y	N	Y	Y
8 Nadler	Y	Y	Y	N	Y	Y
9 Weiner	Y	Y	Y	N	Y	Y
10 Towns	Y	Y	Y	N	Y	Y
11 Clarke	Y	Y	Y	N	Y	Y
12 Velázquez	Y	Y	Y	N	Y	Y
13 McMahon	Y	Y	Y	N	Y	Y
14 Maloney	Y	Y	Y	N	Y	Y
15 Rangel	Y	Y	Y	N	Y	Y
16 Serrano	Y	Y	Y	N	Y	Y
17 Engel	Y	Y	Y	N	Y	Y
18 Lowey	Y	Y	Y	N	Y	Y
19 Hall	Y	Y	Y	N	Y	Y
20 Murphy	Y	Y	Y	N	Y	Y
21 Tonko	Y	Y	Y	N	Y	Y
22 Hinchey	Y	Y	Y	N	Y	Y
23 Owens	Y	Y	Y	N	N	Y
24 Arcuri	N	Y	Y	N	Y	Y
25 Maffei	Y	Y	Y	N	Y	Y
26 **Lee**	N	Y	N	Y	N	Y
27 Higgins	Y	Y	Y	N	Y	Y
28 Slaughter	Y	Y	Y	N	N	+
29 Massa	Y	Y	Y	N	Y	Y
NORTH CAROLINA						
1 Butterfield	Y	Y	Y	N	Y	Y
2 Etheridge	Y	Y	Y	N	Y	Y
3 **Jones**	N	Y	N	Y	N	Y
4 Price	Y	Y	Y	N	Y	Y

	925	926	927	928	929	930
5 **Foxx**	N	Y	N	Y	N	N
6 **Coble**	N	Y	N	Y	N	Y
7 McIntyre	Y	Y	N	Y	Y	Y
8 Kissell	Y	Y	N	Y	Y	Y
9 **Myrick**	N	Y	N	Y	N	Y
10 **McHenry**	N	Y	N	Y	N	Y
11 Shuler	N	Y	Y	N	Y	Y
12 Watt	?	Y	Y	N	Y	Y
13 Miller	Y	Y	Y	N	Y	Y
NORTH DAKOTA						
AL Pomeroy	Y	Y	Y	N	Y	Y
OHIO						
1 Driehaus	Y	Y	Y	N	Y	Y
2 **Schmidt**	N	Y	N	Y	N	Y
3 **Turner**	N	Y	N	Y	N	Y
4 **Jordan**	N	Y	N	Y	N	Y
5 **Latta**	N	Y	N	Y	N	N
6 Wilson	Y	Y	Y	N	Y	Y
7 **Austria**	N	Y	N	Y	N	Y
8 **Boehner**	N	Y	N	+	N	Y
9 Kaptur	Y	Y	Y	N	N	Y
10 Kucinich	Y	Y	Y	N	Y	Y
11 Fudge	Y	Y	Y	N	Y	Y
12 **Tiberi**	Y	Y	N	Y	N	Y
13 Sutton	Y	Y	Y	N	Y	Y
14 **LaTourette**	N	Y	N	Y	N	Y
15 Kilroy	N	Y	Y	N	Y	Y
16 Boccieri	N	Y	Y	N	Y	Y
17 Ryan	Y	Y	Y	N	Y	Y
18 Space	Y	Y	N	Y	N	Y
OKLAHOMA						
1 **Sullivan**	N	Y	N	Y	N	Y
2 Boren	Y	Y	Y	Y	Y	Y
3 **Lucas**	?	?	?	?	?	?
4 **Cole**	N	Y	N	Y	N	Y
5 **Fallin**	N	Y	N	Y	N	?
OREGON						
1 Wu	Y	Y	Y	N	Y	Y
2 **Walden**	N	Y	N	Y	N	Y
3 Blumenauer	Y	Y	Y	N	Y	Y
4 DeFazio	Y	Y	Y	N	Y	Y
5 Schrader	Y	Y	Y	N	Y	Y
PENNSYLVANIA						
1 Brady	Y	Y	Y	N	Y	Y
2 Fattah	Y	Y	Y	N	Y	Y
3 Dahlkemper	N	Y	Y	N	Y	Y
4 Altmire	N	Y	Y	N	Y	Y
5 **Thompson**	N	Y	N	Y	N	Y
6 **Gerlach**	N	Y	N	Y	N	Y
7 Sestak	Y	Y	N	N	Y	Y
8 Murphy, P.	Y	Y	Y	N	Y	Y
9 **Shuster**	N	Y	N	Y	N	Y
10 Carney	Y	Y	Y	N	Y	?
11 Kanjorski	Y	Y	Y	N	Y	Y
12 Murtha	Y	Y	Y	N	Y	Y
13 Schwartz	Y	Y	Y	N	Y	Y
14 Doyle	Y	Y	Y	N	Y	Y
15 **Dent**	Y	Y	N	Y	N	Y
16 **Pitts**	N	Y	N	Y	N	Y
17 Holden	Y	Y	Y	N	Y	Y
18 **Murphy, T.**	N	Y	N	Y	N	Y
19 **Platts**	N	Y	N	Y	N	Y
RHODE ISLAND						
1 Kennedy	Y	Y	Y	N	Y	Y
2 Langevin	Y	Y	Y	N	Y	Y
SOUTH CAROLINA						
1 **Brown**	N	Y	N	Y	N	Y
2 **Wilson**	N	Y	N	Y	N	Y
3 **Barrett**	N	Y	N	Y	N	Y
4 **Inglis**	N	Y	N	Y	N	Y
5 Spratt	Y	Y	Y	N	Y	Y
6 Clyburn	Y	Y	Y	N	Y	Y
SOUTH DAKOTA						
AL Herseth Sandlin	Y	Y	Y	N	Y	Y
TENNESSEE						
1 **Roe**	N	Y	N	Y	N	Y
2 **Duncan**	N	Y	N	Y	N	N
3 **Wamp**	N	Y	N	Y	N	Y
4 Davis	Y	Y	Y	N	Y	Y
5 Cooper	Y	Y	Y	N	Y	Y
6 Gordon	?	?	Y	N	Y	Y
7 **Blackburn**	Y	Y	N	Y	N	Y
8 Tanner	Y	Y	Y	N	Y	Y
9 Cohen	Y	Y	Y	N	Y	Y

	925	926	927	928	929	930
TEXAS						
1 **Gohmert**	P	Y	N	Y	N	Y
2 **Poe**	N	Y	N	Y	N	Y
3 **Johnson, S.**	N	Y	N	Y	N	Y
4 **Hall**	N	Y	N	Y	N	Y
5 **Hensarling**	N	Y	N	Y	N	Y
6 **Barton**	N	Y	N	Y	N	Y
7 **Culberson**	N	Y	N	Y	N	N
8 **Brady**	N	Y	N	Y	N	Y
9 Green, A.	Y	Y	Y	N	Y	Y
10 **McCaul**	N	Y	N	Y	N	Y
11 **Conaway**	N	Y	N	Y	N	Y
12 **Granger**	N	Y	N	Y	N	Y
13 **Thornberry**	N	Y	N	Y	N	Y
14 **Paul**	Y	N	N	?	N	N
15 Hinojosa	Y	Y	Y	N	Y	Y
16 Reyes	Y	Y	Y	N	Y	Y
17 Edwards	Y	Y	?	N	Y	Y
18 Jackson Lee	Y	Y	Y	N	Y	Y
19 **Neugebauer**	N	Y	N	Y	N	Y
20 Gonzalez	?	?	?	?	?	?
21 **Smith**	N	Y	N	Y	N	Y
22 **Olson**	N	Y	N	Y	N	Y
23 Rodriguez	Y	Y	Y	N	Y	Y
24 **Marchant**	N	Y	N	Y	N	?
25 Doggett	Y	Y	Y	N	N	Y
26 **Burgess**	?	?	N	Y	N	Y
27 Ortiz	Y	Y	Y	N	Y	Y
28 Cuellar	Y	Y	Y	N	Y	Y
29 Green, G.	?	Y	Y	N	Y	Y
30 Johnson, E.	Y	Y	Y	N	Y	?
31 **Carter**	N	Y	N	Y	N	Y
32 **Sessions**	N	Y	N	Y	N	Y
UTAH						
1 **Bishop**	?	?	?	?	?	?
2 Matheson	Y	Y	Y	N	Y	Y
3 **Chaffetz**	Y	Y	N	Y	N	Y
VERMONT						
AL Welch	Y	Y	Y	N	Y	Y
VIRGINIA						
1 **Wittman**	Y	Y	N	Y	N	Y
2 Nye	N	Y	Y	N	Y	Y
3 Scott	Y	Y	Y	N	N	Y
4 **Forbes**	N	Y	N	Y	N	Y
5 Perriello	N	Y	Y	N	Y	Y
6 **Goodlatte**	Y	Y	N	Y	N	Y
7 **Cantor**	?	Y	N	Y	N	Y
8 Moran	?	?	?	?	?	?
9 Boucher	Y	Y	Y	N	Y	Y
10 **Wolf**	N	Y	N	Y	N	Y
11 Connolly	N	Y	Y	N	Y	Y
WASHINGTON						
1 Inslee	Y	Y	Y	N	Y	Y
2 Larsen	Y	Y	Y	N	Y	Y
3 Baird	Y	Y	?	N	N	Y
4 **Hastings**	N	Y	N	Y	N	Y
5 **McMorris Rodgers**	N	Y	N	Y	N	Y
6 Dicks	Y	Y	Y	N	Y	Y
7 McDermott	Y	Y	Y	N	N	Y
8 **Reichert**	N	Y	N	Y	N	Y
9 Smith	Y	Y	Y	N	Y	Y
WEST VIRGINIA						
1 Mollohan	Y	Y	Y	N	Y	Y
2 **Capito**	Y	Y	N	Y	N	Y
3 Rahall	Y	Y	Y	N	Y	Y
WISCONSIN						
1 **Ryan**	N	Y	N	Y	N	Y
2 Baldwin	Y	Y	Y	N	Y	Y
3 Kind	Y	Y	Y	N	Y	Y
4 Moore	Y	Y	Y	N	Y	Y
5 **Sensenbrenner**	N	Y	N	Y	N	Y
6 **Petri**	Y	Y	N	Y	N	Y
7 Obey	Y	Y	Y	N	Y	Y
8 Kagen	Y	Y	N	N	Y	Y
WYOMING						
AL **Lummis**	N	N	N	Y	N	N
DELEGATES						
Faleomavaega (A.S.)						
Norton (D.C.)						
Bordallo (Guam)						
Sablan (N. Marianas)						
Pierluisi (P.R.)						
Christensen (V.I.)						

IN THE HOUSE | By Vote Number

931. **HR 3288. Fiscal 2010 Transportation-HUD Appropriations/ Motion to Instruct.** Latham, R-Iowa, motion to instruct conferees to disagree with any congressionally directed spending items added to the Transportation-HUD bill in conference and to withhold approval of the final conference agreement unless it has been available to the managers in searchable electronic form for at least 72 hours. Motion agreed to 212-193: D 47-193; R 165-0. Dec. 8, 2009.

932. **H Con Res 199. Tribute to Company E/Adoption.** Bordallo, D-Guam, motion to suspend the rules and adopt the concurrent resolution that would recognize the historic and continued contributions of Company E of the 100th Battalion of the 442nd Infantry of the U.S. Army to the citizens of the Northern Mariana Islands and the United States. Motion agreed to 400-0: D 236-0; R 164-0. A two-thirds majority of those present and voting (267 in this case) is required for adoption under suspension of the rules. Dec. 8, 2009.

933. **H Con Res 206. Tribute to Fort Gordon Personnel/Adoption.** Bordallo, D-Guam, motion to suspend the rules and adopt the concurrent resolution that would recognize the soldiers, their families and the civilian personnel at Fort Gordon in Georgia for their service and dedication to the United States. Motion agreed to 404-0: D 239-0; R 165-0. A two-thirds majority of those present and voting (270 in this case) is required for adoption under suspension of the rules. Dec. 8, 2009.

934. **H Res 940. Tribute to National Guard/Adoption.** Bordallo, D-Guam, motion to suspend the rules and adopt the resolution that would recognize the members of the National Guard for their service in response to the attacks on Sept. 11, 2001, and for their continuing role in homeland security and military operations. It also would state the support of Congress for providing the National Guard with the necessary resources to ensure readiness. Motion agreed to 401-0: D 236-0; R 165-0. A two-thirds majority of those present and voting (268 in this case) is required for adoption under suspension of the rules. Dec. 8, 2009.

935. **H Res 845. U.S. Air Force Energy Savings/Adoption.** Bordallo, D-Guam, motion to suspend the rules and adopt the resolution that would recognize the energy savings achieved by the U.S. Air Force and the leadership of the 7th Bomb Wing at Dyess Air Force Base. Motion agreed to 409-0: D 241-0; R 168-0. A two-thirds majority of those present and voting (273 in this case) is required for adoption under suspension of the rules. Dec. 8, 2009.

936. **HR 2278. Report on Middle Eastern Media Outlets/Passage.** Costa, D-Calif., motion to suspend the rules and pass the bill that would require the president to submit a report to Congress on Middle Eastern media outlets and satellite companies that incite anti-American violence through their programming. Motion agreed to 395-3: D 226-2; R 169-1. A two-thirds majority of those present and voting (266 in this case) is required for passage under suspension of the rules. Dec. 8, 2009.

	931	932	933	934	935	936
ALABAMA						
1 Bonner	Y	Y	Y	Y	Y	Y
2 Bright	Y	Y	Y	Y	Y	Y
3 **Rogers**	Y	Y	Y	Y	Y	Y
4 **Aderholt**	Y	Y	Y	Y	Y	Y
5 Griffith	Y	Y	Y	Y	Y	Y
6 **Bachus**	Y	Y	Y	Y	Y	Y
7 Davis	?	?	?	?	?	?
ALASKA						
AL **Young**	Y	Y	Y	Y	Y	Y
ARIZONA						
1 Kirkpatrick	?	?	?	Y	Y	Y
2 **Franks**	Y	Y	Y	Y	Y	Y
3 **Shadegg**	Y	Y	Y	Y	Y	Y
4 Pastor	N	Y	Y	Y	Y	Y
5 Mitchell	Y	Y	Y	Y	Y	Y
6 **Flake**	Y	Y	Y	Y	Y	Y
7 Grijalva	N	Y	Y	Y	?	Y
8 Giffords	Y	Y	Y	Y	Y	Y
ARKANSAS						
1 Berry	N	Y	Y	Y	Y	Y
2 Snyder	N	Y	Y	Y	Y	Y
3 **Boozman**	Y	Y	Y	Y	Y	Y
4 Ross	N	Y	Y	Y	Y	Y
CALIFORNIA						
1 Thompson	N	Y	Y	Y	Y	Y
2 **Herger**	Y	Y	Y	Y	Y	Y
3 **Lungren**	Y	Y	Y	Y	Y	Y
4 **McClintock**	Y	Y	Y	Y	Y	Y
5 Matsui	N	Y	Y	Y	Y	Y
6 Woolsey	N	Y	Y	Y	Y	P
7 Miller, George	N	Y	Y	Y	Y	Y
8 Pelosi						
9 Lee	N	Y	Y	Y	Y	P
10 Garamendi	N	Y	Y	Y	Y	Y
11 McNerney	Y	Y	Y	Y	Y	Y
12 Speier	N	Y	Y	Y	Y	Y
13 Stark	N	Y	Y	Y	Y	P
14 Eshoo	N	Y	Y	Y	Y	Y
15 Honda	N	Y	Y	Y	Y	N
16 Lofgren	N	Y	Y	Y	Y	Y
17 Farr	N	Y	Y	Y	Y	Y
18 Cardoza	N	Y	Y	Y	Y	Y
19 **Radanovich**	Y	Y	Y	Y	?	?
20 Costa	Y	Y	Y	Y	Y	Y
21 **Nunes**	Y	Y	Y	Y	Y	Y
22 **McCarthy**	Y	Y	Y	Y	Y	Y
23 Capps	N	Y	Y	Y	Y	Y
24 **Gallegly**	Y	Y	Y	Y	Y	Y
25 **McKeon**	Y	Y	Y	Y	Y	Y
26 **Dreier**	Y	Y	Y	Y	Y	Y
27 Sherman	N	Y	Y	Y	Y	Y
28 Berman	?	?	?	?	?	?
29 Schiff	N	Y	Y	Y	Y	Y
30 Waxman	N	Y	Y	Y	Y	Y
31 Becerra	N	Y	Y	Y	Y	Y
32 Chu	N	Y	Y	?	Y	Y
33 Watson	N	Y	Y	Y	Y	Y
34 Roybal-Allard	N	Y	Y	Y	Y	Y
35 Waters	N	Y	Y	?	Y	P
36 Harman	N	Y	Y	Y	Y	Y
37 Richardson	Y	Y	Y	Y	Y	Y
38 Napolitano	N	Y	Y	Y	Y	Y
39 Sánchez, Linda	N	Y	Y	Y	Y	Y
40 **Royce**	Y	Y	Y	Y	Y	Y
41 **Lewis**	Y	Y	Y	Y	Y	Y
42 **Miller, Gary**	?	?	?	?	?	?
43 Baca	N	Y	Y	Y	Y	Y
44 **Calvert**	Y	Y	Y	Y	Y	Y
45 **Bono Mack**	Y	Y	Y	Y	?	?
46 **Rohrabacher**	Y	Y	Y	Y	Y	Y
47 Sanchez, Loretta	N	Y	Y	Y	Y	Y
48 **Campbell**	?	?	?	?	Y	Y
49 **Issa**	Y	Y	Y	Y	Y	Y
50 **Bilbray**	Y	Y	Y	Y	Y	Y
51 Filner	N	Y	Y	Y	Y	Y
52 **Hunter**	Y	Y	Y	Y	Y	Y
53 Davis	N	Y	Y	Y	Y	Y

	931	932	933	934	935	936
COLORADO						
1 DeGette	N	Y	Y	Y	Y	Y
2 Polis	N	Y	Y	Y	Y	Y
3 Salazar	N	Y	Y	Y	Y	Y
4 Markey	N	Y	Y	Y	Y	Y
5 **Lamborn**	Y	Y	Y	Y	Y	Y
6 **Coffman**	Y	Y	Y	Y	Y	Y
7 Perlmutter	N	Y	Y	Y	Y	Y
CONNECTICUT						
1 Larson	N	?	Y	Y	Y	Y
2 Courtney	N	Y	Y	Y	Y	Y
3 DeLauro	N	Y	Y	?	Y	Y
4 Himes	Y	Y	Y	Y	Y	Y
5 Murphy	Y	Y	Y	Y	Y	Y
DELAWARE						
AL **Castle**	Y	Y	Y	Y	Y	Y
FLORIDA						
1 **Miller**	Y	Y	Y	Y	Y	Y
2 Boyd	N	Y	Y	Y	Y	Y
3 Brown	N	Y	Y	Y	Y	Y
4 **Crenshaw**	Y	Y	Y	Y	Y	Y
5 **Brown-Waite**	Y	Y	Y	Y	Y	Y
6 **Stearns**	Y	Y	Y	Y	Y	Y
7 **Mica**	Y	Y	Y	Y	Y	Y
8 Grayson	N	Y	Y	Y	Y	Y
9 **Bilirakis**	Y	Y	Y	Y	Y	Y
10 **Young**	Y	Y	Y	Y	Y	Y
11 Castor	N	Y	Y	Y	Y	Y
12 **Putnam**	Y	Y	Y	Y	Y	Y
13 **Buchanan**	Y	Y	Y	Y	Y	Y
14 **Mack**	Y	Y	Y	Y	Y	Y
15 **Posey**	Y	Y	Y	Y	Y	Y
16 **Rooney**	Y	?	Y	Y	Y	Y
17 Meek	N	Y	Y	Y	Y	Y
18 **Ros-Lehtinen**	Y	Y	Y	Y	Y	Y
19 Wexler	?	?	?	?	Y	Y
20 Wasserman Schultz	N	Y	Y	Y	Y	Y
21 **Diaz-Balart, L.**	Y	Y	Y	Y	Y	Y
22 Klein	Y	Y	Y	Y	Y	Y
23 Hastings	N	Y	Y	Y	Y	Y
24 Kosmas	Y	Y	Y	Y	Y	?
25 **Diaz-Balart, M.**	Y	Y	Y	Y	Y	Y
GEORGIA						
1 **Kingston**	Y	Y	Y	Y	Y	Y
2 Bishop	N	Y	Y	Y	Y	Y
3 **Westmoreland**	Y	Y	Y	Y	Y	Y
4 Johnson	N	?	?	?	Y	Y
5 Lewis	N	Y	Y	Y	Y	Y
6 **Price**	Y	Y	Y	Y	Y	Y
7 **Linder**	Y	Y	Y	Y	Y	Y
8 Marshall	Y	Y	Y	Y	Y	Y
9 **Deal**	Y	Y	Y	Y	Y	Y
10 **Broun**	?	?	?	?	+	+
11 **Gingrey**	Y	Y	Y	Y	Y	Y
12 Barrow	Y	Y	Y	Y	Y	Y
13 Scott	N	Y	Y	Y	Y	Y
HAWAII						
1 Abercrombie	?	?	?	?	?	?
2 Hirono	N	Y	Y	Y	Y	Y
IDAHO						
1 **Minnick**	Y	Y	Y	Y	Y	Y
2 **Simpson**	Y	Y	Y	Y	?	Y
ILLINOIS						
1 Rush	Y	Y	Y	Y	Y	Y
2 Jackson	N	Y	Y	Y	Y	Y
3 Lipinski	?	?	?	?	Y	Y
4 Gutierrez	N	Y	Y	Y	Y	?
5 Quigley	N	Y	Y	Y	Y	Y
6 **Roskam**	Y	Y	Y	Y	Y	Y
7 Davis	N	Y	Y	Y	Y	Y
8 Bean	Y	Y	Y	Y	Y	Y
9 Schakowsky	N	Y	Y	Y	Y	Y
10 **Kirk**	Y	Y	Y	Y	Y	Y
11 Halvorson	N	Y	Y	Y	Y	Y
12 Costello	N	Y	Y	Y	Y	Y
13 **Biggert**	Y	Y	Y	Y	Y	Y
14 Foster	Y	Y	Y	Y	Y	Y
15 **Johnson**	+	?	+	+	Y	Y

KEY	**Republicans**	Democrats		
Y Voted for (yea)		X Paired against		C Voted "present" to avoid possible conflict of interest
# Paired for		– Announced against		
+ Announced for		P Voted "present"		? Did not vote or otherwise make a position known
N Voted against (nay)				

	931	932	933	934	935	936
16 **Manzullo**	Y	Y	Y	Y	Y	Y
17 Hare	N	Y	Y	Y	Y	Y
18 **Schock**	Y	Y	Y	Y	Y	Y
19 **Shimkus**	Y	Y	Y	Y	Y	Y
INDIANA						
1 Visclosky	N	Y	Y	Y	Y	Y
2 Donnelly	Y	Y	Y	Y	Y	Y
3 **Souder**	Y	Y	Y	Y	Y	Y
4 **Buyer**	Y	Y	Y	Y	Y	Y
5 **Burton**	Y	Y	Y	Y	Y	Y
6 **Pence**	Y	Y	Y	?	?	?
7 Carson	N	Y	Y	Y	Y	Y
8 Ellsworth	Y	Y	Y	Y	Y	Y
9 Hill	N	Y	Y	Y	Y	Y
IOWA						
1 Braley	Y	Y	Y	Y	Y	Y
2 Loebsack	N	Y	Y	Y	Y	Y
3 Boswell	N	Y	Y	Y	Y	Y
4 **Latham**	Y	Y	Y	Y	Y	Y
5 **King**	Y	Y	Y	Y	Y	Y
KANSAS						
1 **Moran**	Y	Y	Y	Y	Y	Y
2 **Jenkins**	Y	Y	Y	Y	Y	Y
3 Moore	N	Y	Y	Y	Y	Y
4 **Tiahrt**	Y	Y	Y	Y	Y	Y
KENTUCKY						
1 **Whitfield**	Y	Y	Y	Y	Y	Y
2 **Guthrie**	Y	Y	Y	Y	Y	Y
3 Yarmuth	N	Y	Y	Y	Y	Y
4 **Davis**	Y	Y	Y	Y	Y	Y
5 **Rogers**	Y	Y	Y	Y	Y	Y
6 Chandler	N	Y	Y	Y	Y	Y
LOUISIANA						
1 **Scalise**	Y	Y	Y	Y	Y	Y
2 **Cao**	Y	Y	Y	Y	Y	Y
3 Melancon	N	Y	Y	Y	?	?
4 **Fleming**	Y	Y	Y	Y	Y	Y
5 **Alexander**	Y	Y	Y	Y	Y	Y
6 **Cassidy**	Y	Y	Y	Y	Y	Y
7 **Boustany**	Y	Y	Y	Y	Y	Y
MAINE						
1 Pingree	N	Y	Y	Y	Y	Y
2 Michaud	Y	Y	Y	Y	Y	Y
MARYLAND						
1 Kratovil	Y	Y	Y	Y	Y	Y
2 Ruppersberger	N	Y	Y	Y	Y	Y
3 Sarbanes	N	Y	Y	Y	Y	Y
4 Edwards	N	Y	Y	Y	Y	P
5 Hoyer	N	Y	Y	Y	Y	Y
6 **Bartlett**	Y	Y	Y	Y	Y	Y
7 Cummings	N	Y	Y	Y	Y	Y
8 Van Hollen	N	Y	Y	Y	Y	Y
MASSACHUSETTS						
1 Olver	N	Y	Y	Y	Y	Y
2 Neal	?	?	?	?	Y	Y
3 McGovern	N	Y	Y	Y	Y	Y
4 Frank	N	Y	Y	Y	Y	Y
5 Tsongas	N	Y	Y	Y	?	?
6 Tierney	N	Y	Y	Y	Y	Y
7 Markey	N	Y	Y	Y	Y	Y
8 Capuano	?	?	?	?	?	?
9 Lynch	N	Y	Y	Y	Y	Y
10 Delahunt	?	?	?	?	Y	Y
MICHIGAN						
1 Stupak	N	Y	Y	Y	Y	Y
2 **Hoekstra**	?	?	?	?	?	?
3 **Ehlers**	Y	Y	Y	Y	Y	Y
4 **Camp**	Y	Y	Y	Y	Y	Y
5 Kildee	N	Y	Y	Y	Y	Y
6 **Upton**	Y	Y	Y	Y	Y	Y
7 Schauer	N	Y	Y	Y	Y	Y
8 **Rogers**	Y	Y	Y	Y	Y	Y
9 Peters	N	Y	Y	Y	Y	Y
10 **Miller**	Y	Y	Y	Y	Y	Y
11 **McCotter**	Y	Y	Y	Y	Y	Y
12 Levin	N	Y	Y	Y	Y	Y
13 Kilpatrick	N	Y	Y	Y	Y	Y
14 Conyers	N	Y	Y	Y	Y	Y
15 Dingell	N	Y	Y	Y	Y	Y
MINNESOTA						
1 Walz	N	Y	Y	Y	Y	Y
2 **Kline**	Y	Y	Y	Y	Y	Y
3 **Paulsen**	Y	Y	Y	Y	Y	Y
4 McCollum	N	Y	Y	Y	Y	Y

	931	932	933	934	935	936
5 Ellison	N	Y	Y	Y	Y	Y
6 **Bachmann**	Y	Y	Y	Y	Y	Y
7 Peterson	N	Y	Y	Y	Y	Y
8 Oberstar	N	Y	Y	Y	Y	Y
MISSISSIPPI						
1 Childers	Y	Y	Y	Y	Y	Y
2 Thompson	N	Y	Y	Y	Y	Y
3 **Harper**	Y	Y	Y	Y	Y	Y
4 Taylor	Y	Y	Y	Y	Y	Y
MISSOURI						
1 Clay	N	Y	Y	Y	Y	Y
2 **Akin**	Y	Y	Y	Y	Y	Y
3 Carnahan	N	Y	Y	Y	Y	Y
4 Skelton	Y	Y	Y	Y	Y	Y
5 Cleaver	N	Y	Y	Y	Y	Y
6 **Graves**	Y	Y	Y	Y	Y	Y
7 **Blunt**	Y	Y	Y	Y	Y	Y
8 **Emerson**	Y	Y	Y	Y	Y	Y
9 **Luetkemeyer**	Y	Y	Y	Y	Y	Y
MONTANA						
AL **Rehberg**	Y	Y	Y	Y	Y	Y
NEBRASKA						
1 **Fortenberry**	Y	Y	Y	Y	Y	Y
2 **Terry**	Y	Y	Y	Y	Y	Y
3 **Smith**	Y	Y	Y	Y	Y	Y
NEVADA						
1 Berkley	N	Y	Y	Y	Y	Y
2 **Heller**	Y	Y	Y	Y	Y	Y
3 Titus	N	Y	Y	Y	Y	Y
NEW HAMPSHIRE						
1 Shea-Porter	N	Y	Y	Y	Y	Y
2 Hodes	Y	Y	Y	Y	Y	Y
NEW JERSEY						
1 Andrews	N	Y	Y	Y	Y	Y
2 **LoBiondo**	Y	Y	Y	Y	Y	Y
3 Adler	Y	Y	Y	Y	Y	Y
4 **Smith**	Y	Y	Y	Y	Y	Y
5 **Garrett**	Y	?	?	Y	Y	Y
6 Pallone	N	Y	Y	Y	Y	Y
7 **Lance**	Y	Y	Y	Y	Y	Y
8 Pascrell	N	Y	Y	Y	Y	Y
9 Rothman	N	Y	Y	Y	Y	Y
10 Payne	N	Y	Y	Y	?	?
11 **Frelinghuysen**	Y	Y	Y	Y	Y	Y
12 Holt	N	Y	Y	Y	Y	Y
13 Sires	N	Y	Y	Y	Y	Y
NEW MEXICO						
1 Heinrich	N	Y	Y	?	Y	Y
2 Teague	Y	Y	Y	Y	Y	Y
3 Lujan	N	Y	Y	Y	Y	Y
NEW YORK						
1 Bishop	N	Y	Y	Y	Y	Y
2 Israel	N	Y	Y	Y	Y	Y
3 **King**	Y	Y	Y	Y	Y	Y
4 McCarthy	N	Y	Y	Y	Y	Y
5 Ackerman	N	Y	Y	Y	Y	Y
6 Meeks	N	Y	Y	Y	Y	Y
7 Crowley	N	Y	Y	Y	Y	Y
8 Nadler	N	Y	Y	Y	Y	Y
9 Weiner	N	Y	Y	Y	Y	Y
10 Towns	?	?	?	?	Y	Y
11 Clarke	N	Y	Y	Y	Y	Y
12 Velázquez	N	Y	Y	Y	Y	Y
13 McMahon	N	Y	Y	Y	Y	Y
14 Maloney	N	Y	Y	Y	Y	Y
15 Rangel	N	Y	Y	Y	Y	Y
16 Serrano	N	?	Y	Y	Y	Y
17 Engel	N	Y	Y	Y	Y	Y
18 Lowey	N	Y	Y	Y	Y	Y
19 Hall	Y	Y	Y	Y	Y	Y
20 Murphy	Y	Y	Y	Y	Y	Y
21 Tonko	N	Y	Y	Y	Y	Y
22 Hinchey	N	Y	Y	Y	Y	Y
23 Owens	Y	Y	Y	Y	Y	?
24 Arcuri	?	?	?	?	?	?
25 Maffei	N	Y	Y	Y	Y	Y
26 **Lee**	Y	Y	Y	Y	Y	Y
27 Higgins	N	Y	Y	Y	Y	Y
28 Slaughter	N	Y	Y	Y	Y	Y
29 Massa	N	Y	Y	Y	Y	Y
NORTH CAROLINA						
1 Butterfield	N	Y	Y	Y	Y	Y
2 Etheridge	N	Y	Y	Y	Y	Y
3 **Jones**	Y	Y	Y	Y	Y	Y
4 Price	N	Y	Y	Y	Y	Y

	931	932	933	934	935	936
5 **Foxx**	Y	Y	Y	Y	Y	Y
6 **Coble**	Y	Y	Y	Y	Y	Y
7 McIntyre	Y	Y	Y	Y	Y	Y
8 Kissell	N	Y	Y	Y	Y	Y
9 **Myrick**	Y	Y	Y	Y	Y	Y
10 **McHenry**	Y	Y	Y	Y	Y	Y
11 Shuler	N	Y	Y	Y	Y	Y
12 Watt	N	Y	Y	Y	Y	P
13 Miller	N	Y	Y	Y	Y	Y
NORTH DAKOTA						
AL Pomeroy	Y	Y	Y	Y	Y	Y
OHIO						
1 Driehaus	N	Y	Y	Y	Y	Y
2 **Schmidt**	Y	Y	Y	Y	Y	Y
3 **Turner**	Y	Y	Y	Y	Y	Y
4 **Jordan**	Y	Y	Y	Y	Y	Y
5 **Latta**	Y	Y	Y	Y	Y	Y
6 Wilson	N	Y	Y	Y	Y	Y
7 **Austria**	Y	Y	Y	Y	Y	Y
8 **Boehner**	Y	Y	Y	Y	Y	Y
9 Kaptur	N	Y	Y	Y	Y	Y
10 Kucinich	N	?	Y	Y	Y	P
11 Fudge	N	Y	Y	Y	Y	Y
12 **Tiberi**	Y	Y	Y	Y	Y	Y
13 Sutton	N	Y	Y	Y	Y	Y
14 **LaTourette**	Y	Y	Y	Y	Y	Y
15 Kilroy	N	Y	Y	Y	Y	Y
16 Boccieri	Y	Y	Y	Y	Y	Y
17 Ryan	N	Y	Y	Y	Y	Y
18 Space	Y	Y	Y	Y	Y	Y
OKLAHOMA						
1 **Sullivan**	Y	Y	Y	Y	Y	Y
2 Boren	Y	Y	Y	Y	Y	Y
3 **Lucas**	Y	Y	Y	Y	Y	Y
4 **Cole**	Y	Y	Y	Y	Y	Y
5 **Fallin**	?	?	?	?	Y	Y
OREGON						
1 Wu	N	Y	Y	Y	Y	Y
2 **Walden**	Y	Y	Y	Y	Y	Y
3 Blumenauer	N	Y	Y	Y	Y	Y
4 DeFazio	N	Y	Y	Y	Y	Y
5 Schrader	Y	Y	Y	Y	Y	?
PENNSYLVANIA						
1 Brady	N	Y	Y	Y	Y	Y
2 Fattah	N	Y	Y	Y	Y	Y
3 Dahlkemper	Y	Y	Y	Y	Y	Y
4 Altmire	Y	Y	Y	Y	Y	Y
5 **Thompson**	Y	Y	Y	Y	Y	Y
6 **Gerlach**	Y	Y	Y	Y	Y	Y
7 Sestak	Y	Y	Y	Y	Y	Y
8 Murphy, P.	N	Y	Y	Y	Y	Y
9 **Shuster**	Y	Y	Y	Y	Y	Y
10 Carney	Y	Y	Y	Y	?	?
11 Kanjorski	N	Y	Y	Y	Y	Y
12 Murtha	?	?	?	?	?	?
13 Schwartz	N	Y	Y	Y	Y	Y
14 Doyle	N	Y	Y	Y	Y	Y
15 **Dent**	Y	Y	Y	Y	Y	Y
16 **Pitts**	Y	Y	Y	Y	Y	Y
17 Holden	N	Y	Y	Y	Y	Y
18 **Murphy, T.**	Y	Y	Y	Y	Y	Y
19 **Platts**	Y	Y	Y	Y	Y	Y
RHODE ISLAND						
1 Kennedy	N	Y	Y	Y	Y	Y
2 Langevin	N	Y	Y	Y	Y	Y
SOUTH CAROLINA						
1 **Brown**	Y	Y	Y	Y	Y	Y
2 **Wilson**	Y	Y	Y	Y	Y	Y
3 **Barrett**	?	?	?	?	?	?
4 **Inglis**	Y	Y	Y	Y	Y	Y
5 Spratt	N	Y	Y	Y	Y	Y
6 Clyburn	N	Y	Y	Y	Y	Y
SOUTH DAKOTA						
AL Herseth Sandlin	N	Y	Y	Y	Y	Y
TENNESSEE						
1 **Roe**	Y	Y	Y	Y	Y	Y
2 **Duncan**	Y	Y	Y	Y	Y	Y
3 **Wamp**	Y	Y	Y	Y	Y	Y
4 Davis	N	Y	Y	Y	Y	Y
5 Cooper	Y	Y	Y	Y	Y	Y
6 Gordon	N	Y	Y	Y	Y	Y
7 **Blackburn**	Y	Y	Y	Y	Y	Y
8 Tanner	N	Y	Y	Y	Y	Y
9 Cohen	N	Y	Y	Y	Y	Y

	931	932	933	934	935	936
TEXAS						
1 **Gohmert**	Y	Y	Y	Y	Y	Y
2 **Poe**	Y	Y	Y	Y	?	Y
3 **Johnson, S.**	?	+	?	?	Y	Y
4 **Hall**	?	?	?	?	Y	Y
5 **Hensarling**	Y	Y	Y	Y	Y	Y
6 **Barton**	Y	Y	Y	Y	Y	Y
7 **Culberson**	Y	Y	Y	Y	Y	Y
8 **Brady**	Y	Y	Y	Y	Y	Y
9 Green, A.	N	Y	Y	Y	Y	Y
10 **McCaul**	Y	Y	Y	Y	Y	Y
11 **Conaway**	Y	Y	Y	Y	Y	Y
12 **Granger**	Y	Y	Y	Y	Y	Y
13 **Thornberry**	Y	Y	Y	Y	Y	Y
14 **Paul**	?	?	?	?	Y	N
15 Hinojosa	N	Y	Y	Y	Y	Y
16 Reyes	N	Y	Y	Y	Y	Y
17 Edwards	N	Y	Y	Y	Y	Y
18 Jackson Lee	N	Y	Y	Y	Y	Y
19 **Neugebauer**	Y	Y	Y	Y	Y	Y
20 Gonzalez	N	Y	Y	Y	Y	Y
21 **Smith**	Y	Y	Y	Y	Y	Y
22 **Olson**	Y	Y	Y	Y	Y	Y
23 Rodriguez	N	Y	Y	Y	Y	Y
24 **Marchant**	Y	Y	Y	Y	Y	Y
25 Doggett	Y	Y	Y	Y	Y	Y
26 **Burgess**	Y	Y	Y	Y	Y	Y
27 Ortiz	N	Y	Y	Y	Y	Y
28 Cuellar	Y	Y	Y	Y	Y	Y
29 Green, G.	N	Y	Y	Y	Y	Y
30 Johnson, E.	N	Y	Y	Y	Y	N
31 **Carter**	Y	Y	Y	Y	Y	Y
32 **Sessions**	Y	Y	Y	Y	Y	Y
UTAH						
1 **Bishop**	Y	Y	Y	Y	Y	Y
2 Matheson	N	Y	Y	Y	Y	Y
3 **Chaffetz**	Y	Y	Y	Y	Y	Y
VERMONT						
AL Welch	N	Y	Y	Y	Y	Y
VIRGINIA						
1 **Wittman**	Y	Y	Y	Y	Y	Y
2 Nye	Y	Y	Y	Y	Y	Y
3 Scott	N	Y	Y	Y	Y	Y
4 **Forbes**	Y	Y	Y	Y	Y	Y
5 Perriello	Y	Y	Y	Y	Y	Y
6 **Goodlatte**	Y	Y	Y	Y	Y	Y
7 **Cantor**	Y	Y	Y	Y	Y	Y
8 Moran	?	?	?	?	?	?
9 Boucher	?	?	?	?	?	?
10 **Wolf**	Y	Y	Y	Y	Y	Y
11 Connolly	N	Y	Y	Y	Y	Y
WASHINGTON						
1 Inslee	N	Y	Y	Y	Y	Y
2 Larsen	N	Y	Y	Y	Y	Y
3 Baird	Y	Y	Y	Y	Y	Y
4 **Hastings**	Y	Y	Y	Y	Y	Y
5 **McMorris Rodgers**	Y	Y	Y	Y	Y	Y
6 Dicks	N	Y	Y	Y	Y	Y
7 McDermott	N	Y	Y	Y	Y	P
8 **Reichert**	?	?	?	?	?	?
9 Smith	+	+	+	+	+	+
WEST VIRGINIA						
1 Mollohan	N	Y	Y	Y	Y	Y
2 **Capito**	Y	Y	Y	Y	Y	Y
3 Rahall	N	Y	Y	Y	Y	Y
WISCONSIN						
1 **Ryan**	Y	Y	Y	Y	Y	Y
2 Baldwin	N	Y	Y	Y	Y	Y
3 Kind	?	?	?	?	?	?
4 Moore	N	Y	Y	Y	Y	P
5 **Sensenbrenner**	Y	Y	Y	Y	Y	Y
6 **Petri**	?	Y	Y	Y	Y	Y
7 Obey	N	Y	Y	Y	Y	Y
8 Kagen	?	?	?	?	?	?
WYOMING						
AL **Lummis**	Y	Y	Y	Y	Y	Y
DELEGATES						
Faleomavaega (A.S.)						
Norton (D.C.)						
Bordallo (Guam)						
Sablan (N. Marianas)						
Pierluisi (P.R.)						
Christensen (V.I.)						

IN THE HOUSE | By Vote Number

937. **H Res 915. Condemnation of Hungarian State Radio Licenses/ Adoption.** Engel, D-N.Y., motion to suspend the rules and adopt the resolution that would condemn the recent action by the Hungarian National Radio and Television Board to award national community radio licenses, and encourage the republic to respect the rule of law, treat foreign investors fairly and maintain a free press. Motion agreed to 333-74: D 182-55; R 151-19. A two-thirds majority of those present and voting (272 in this case) is required for adoption under suspension of the rules. Dec. 8, 2009.

938. **H Res 907. 100th Anniversary of the Bronx Grand Concourse/ Adoption.** Larsen, D-Wash., motion to suspend the rules and adopt the resolution that would recognize the 100th anniversary of the Grand Concourse, a four-mile thoroughfare in the Bronx, New York City. Motion agreed to 405-0: D 238-0; R 167-0. A two-thirds majority of those present and voting (270 in this case) is required for adoption under suspension of the rules. Dec. 8, 2009.

939. **HR 4213. Tax Extensions/Previous Question.** Arcuri, D-N.Y., motion to order the previous question (thus ending debate and possibility of amendment) on adoption of the rule (H Res 955) to provide for House floor consideration of the bill that would extend dozens of expiring tax provisions, including tax incentives for research and development and investment in restaurants and retail businesses. Motion agreed to 239-182: D 239-8; R 0-174. Dec. 9, 2009.

940. **HR 4213. Tax Extensions/Rule.** Adoption of the rule (H Res 955) to provide for House floor consideration of the bill that would extend dozens of expiring tax provisions, including tax incentives for research and development and investment in restaurants and retail businesses. Adopted 237-182: D 237-9; R 0-173. Dec. 9, 2009.

941. **HR 3951. Roy Rondeno Sr. Post Office/Passage.** Lynch, D-Mass., motion to suspend the rules and pass the bill that would designate a post office in New Orleans as the "Roy Rondeno Sr. Post Office Building." Motion agreed to 417-1: D 245-1; R 172-0. A two-thirds majority of those present and voting (279 in this case) is required for passage under suspension of the rules. Dec. 9, 2009.

942. **HR 4213. Tax Extensions/Motion to Table.** Neal, D-Mass., motion to table (kill) the Camp, R-Mich., appeal of the ruling of the chair with respect to the Neal point of order that the Camp motion to recommit the bill violates the House pay-as-you-go budget rule because it would increase the deficit. The Camp motion would recommit the bill to the Ways and Means Committee with instructions that it be immediately reported back with amendments that would eliminate modifications to the tax rate on investment management services, add language to increase the exemption amount for the alternative minimum tax and extend provisions allowing businesses to deduct equipment purchases through 2010. Motion agreed to 251-172: D 250-1; R 1-171. Dec. 9, 2009.

	937	938	939	940	941	942
ALABAMA						
1 **Bonner**	Y	Y	N	N	Y	N
2 Bright	Y	Y	N	Y	Y	Y
3 **Rogers**	Y	Y	N	N	Y	N
4 **Aderholt**	Y	Y	N	N	Y	N
5 Griffith	Y	Y	Y	Y	Y	Y
6 **Bachus**	Y	Y	N	N	Y	N
7 Davis	?	?	Y	Y	Y	Y
ALASKA						
AL **Young**	N	Y	N	N	Y	N
ARIZONA						
1 Kirkpatrick	Y	Y	Y	Y	Y	Y
2 **Franks**	Y	Y	N	N	Y	N
3 **Shadegg**	Y	Y	N	N	Y	N
4 Pastor	N	Y	Y	Y	Y	Y
5 Mitchell	Y	Y	N	N	Y	Y
6 **Flake**	Y	Y	N	N	Y	N
7 Grijalva	?	?	Y	Y	Y	Y
8 Giffords	Y	Y	Y	Y	Y	Y
ARKANSAS						
1 Berry	Y	Y	Y	Y	Y	Y
2 Snyder	N	Y	Y	Y	Y	Y
3 **Boozman**	Y	Y	N	N	Y	N
4 Ross	Y	Y	Y	Y	Y	Y
CALIFORNIA						
1 Thompson	Y	Y	Y	Y	Y	Y
2 **Herger**	Y	Y	N	N	Y	N
3 **Lungren**	Y	Y	N	N	Y	N
4 **McClintock**	Y	Y	N	N	Y	N
5 Matsui	Y	Y	Y	Y	Y	Y
6 Woolsey	N	Y	Y	Y	Y	Y
7 Miller, George	Y	Y	Y	Y	Y	Y
8 Pelosi						
9 Lee	N	Y	Y	Y	Y	Y
10 Garamendi	Y	Y	Y	Y	Y	Y
11 McNerney	Y	Y	Y	Y	Y	Y
12 Speier	P	Y	Y	Y	Y	Y
13 Stark	N	Y	Y	Y	Y	Y
14 Eshoo	Y	Y	Y	Y	Y	Y
15 Honda	Y	Y	Y	Y	Y	Y
16 Lofgren	N	Y	Y	Y	Y	Y
17 Farr	Y	Y	Y	Y	Y	Y
18 Cardoza	Y	Y	Y	Y	Y	Y
19 **Radanovich**	?	?	?	?	?	?
20 Costa	Y	Y	Y	Y	Y	Y
21 **Nunes**	N	Y	N	N	Y	N
22 **McCarthy**	Y	Y	N	N	Y	N
23 Capps	Y	Y	Y	Y	Y	Y
24 **Gallegly**	Y	Y	N	N	Y	N
25 **McKeon**	Y	Y	N	N	Y	N
26 **Dreier**	Y	Y	N	N	Y	N
27 Sherman	Y	Y	Y	Y	Y	Y
28 Berman	?	?	Y	Y	Y	Y
29 Schiff	Y	Y	Y	Y	Y	Y
30 Waxman	Y	Y	Y	Y	Y	Y
31 Becerra	N	Y	Y	Y	Y	Y
32 Chu	Y	Y	Y	Y	Y	Y
33 Watson	Y	Y	Y	Y	Y	Y
34 Roybal-Allard	Y	?	Y	Y	Y	Y
35 Waters	N	?	Y	Y	Y	Y
36 Harman	Y	Y	Y	Y	Y	Y
37 Richardson	Y	Y	Y	Y	Y	Y
38 Napolitano	N	Y	Y	Y	Y	Y
39 Sánchez, Linda	Y	Y	Y	Y	Y	Y
40 **Royce**	Y	Y	N	N	Y	N
41 **Lewis**	Y	Y	N	N	Y	N
42 **Miller, Gary**	Y	Y	N	N	Y	N
43 Baca	Y	Y	Y	Y	Y	Y
44 **Calvert**	Y	Y	N	N	Y	N
45 **Bono Mack**	?	?	N	N	Y	N
46 **Rohrabacher**	Y	Y	N	N	Y	N
47 Sanchez, Loretta	Y	?	?	?	?	?
48 **Campbell**	Y	Y	N	N	Y	N
49 **Issa**	Y	Y	N	N	Y	N
50 **Bilbray**	Y	Y	N	N	Y	N
51 Filner	Y	Y	Y	Y	Y	Y
52 **Hunter**	Y	Y	N	N	Y	N
53 Davis	Y	Y	Y	Y	Y	Y

	937	938	939	940	941	942
COLORADO						
1 DeGette	Y	Y	Y	Y	Y	Y
2 Polis	Y	Y	Y	Y	Y	Y
3 Salazar	Y	Y	Y	Y	Y	Y
4 Markey	Y	Y	Y	Y	Y	Y
5 **Lamborn**	Y	Y	N	N	Y	N
6 **Coffman**	Y	Y	N	N	?	N
7 Perlmutter	Y	Y	Y	Y	Y	Y
CONNECTICUT						
1 Larson	Y	Y	+	+	+	Y
2 Courtney	Y	Y	Y	Y	Y	Y
3 DeLauro	Y	Y	Y	Y	Y	Y
4 Himes	Y	Y	Y	Y	Y	Y
5 Murphy	Y	Y	Y	Y	Y	Y
DELAWARE						
AL **Castle**	Y	Y	N	N	Y	N
FLORIDA						
1 **Miller**	?	Y	N	N	Y	N
2 Boyd	Y	Y	Y	Y	?	Y
3 Brown	Y	Y	Y	Y	Y	Y
4 **Crenshaw**	Y	Y	N	N	Y	N
5 **Brown-Waite**	Y	Y	N	N	Y	N
6 **Stearns**	Y	Y	N	N	Y	N
7 **Mica**	Y	Y	N	N	Y	N
8 Grayson	Y	Y	Y	Y	Y	Y
9 **Bilirakis**	Y	Y	N	N	Y	N
10 **Young**	Y	Y	N	N	Y	N
11 Castor	Y	Y	Y	Y	Y	Y
12 **Putnam**	Y	Y	N	N	Y	N
13 **Buchanan**	Y	Y	N	N	Y	N
14 **Mack**	Y	Y	N	N	Y	N
15 **Posey**	Y	Y	N	N	Y	N
16 **Rooney**	Y	Y	N	N	Y	N
17 Meek	Y	Y	Y	Y	Y	Y
18 **Ros-Lehtinen**	Y	Y	N	N	Y	N
19 Wexler	?	Y	Y	Y	Y	Y
20 Wasserman Schultz	Y	Y	Y	Y	Y	Y
21 **Diaz-Balart, L.**	N	Y	N	N	Y	N
22 Klein	Y	Y	Y	Y	Y	Y
23 Hastings	Y	Y	Y	Y	Y	Y
24 Kosmas	Y	Y	Y	Y	Y	Y
25 **Diaz-Balart, M.**	N	Y	N	N	Y	N
GEORGIA						
1 **Kingston**	Y	Y	N	N	Y	N
2 Bishop	Y	Y	Y	Y	Y	Y
3 **Westmoreland**	Y	Y	N	N	Y	N
4 Johnson	Y	Y	Y	Y	Y	Y
5 Lewis	Y	Y	?	?	?	?
6 **Price**	Y	Y	N	N	Y	N
7 **Linder**	Y	Y	N	?	Y	N
8 Marshall	Y	Y	Y	Y	Y	Y
9 **Deal**	Y	Y	N	N	Y	N
10 **Broun**	+	+	N	N	Y	N
11 **Gingrey**	Y	Y	N	N	Y	N
12 **Barrow**	Y	Y	Y	Y	Y	Y
13 Scott	Y	Y	Y	Y	Y	Y
HAWAII						
1 Abercrombie	?	?	Y	Y	Y	Y
2 Hirono	N	Y	Y	Y	Y	Y
IDAHO						
1 Minnick	Y	Y	Y	Y	Y	Y
2 **Simpson**	Y	Y	N	N	Y	N
ILLINOIS						
1 Rush	Y	Y	Y	?	Y	Y
2 Jackson	Y	Y	Y	Y	Y	Y
3 Lipinski	Y	Y	Y	Y	Y	Y
4 Gutierrez	Y	Y	Y	Y	Y	Y
5 Quigley	Y	Y	Y	Y	Y	Y
6 **Roskam**	Y	Y	N	N	Y	N
7 Davis	Y	Y	Y	Y	Y	Y
8 Bean	Y	Y	Y	Y	Y	Y
9 Schakowsky	Y	Y	Y	Y	Y	Y
10 **Kirk**	Y	Y	N	N	Y	N
11 Halvorson	Y	Y	Y	Y	Y	Y
12 Costello	N	Y	Y	Y	Y	Y
13 **Biggert**	Y	Y	N	N	Y	N
14 Foster	Y	Y	Y	Y	Y	Y
15 **Johnson**	Y	Y	N	N	Y	N

KEY   **Republicans**   Democrats

Y Voted for (yea)	**X** Paired against	**C** Voted "present" to avoid possible conflict of interest
# Paired for	**–** Announced against	
+ Announced for	**P** Voted "present"	**?** Did not vote or otherwise make a position known
N Voted against (nay)		

	937	938	939	940	941	942
16 **Manzullo**	Y	Y	N	N	Y	N
17 Hare	Y	Y	Y	Y	Y	Y
18 **Schock**	Y	Y	N	N	Y	N
19 **Shimkus**	Y	Y	N	N	Y	N
INDIANA						
1 Visclosky	Y	Y	Y	Y	Y	Y
2 Donnelly	Y	Y	N	N	Y	Y
3 **Souder**	Y	Y	N	N	Y	N
4 **Buyer**	Y	Y	N	N	Y	N
5 **Burton**	Y	Y	N	N	Y	N
6 **Pence**	Y	Y	N	N	Y	N
7 Carson	Y	Y	Y	Y	Y	Y
8 Ellsworth	Y	Y	Y	Y	Y	Y
9 Hill	Y	Y	N	N	Y	Y
IOWA						
1 Braley	Y	Y	Y	Y	Y	Y
2 Loebsack	N	Y	Y	Y	Y	Y
3 Boswell	Y	Y	Y	Y	Y	Y
4 **Latham**	Y	Y	N	N	Y	N
5 **King**	Y	Y	N	N	Y	N
KANSAS						
1 **Moran**	Y	Y	N	N	Y	N
2 **Jenkins**	Y	Y	N	N	Y	N
3 Moore	Y	Y	Y	Y	Y	Y
4 **Tiahrt**	Y	Y	N	N	Y	N
KENTUCKY						
1 **Whitfield**	N	Y	N	N	Y	N
2 **Guthrie**	Y	Y	N	N	Y	N
3 Yarmuth	Y	Y	Y	Y	Y	Y
4 **Davis**	Y	Y	N	N	Y	N
5 **Rogers**	Y	Y	N	N	Y	N
6 Chandler	Y	Y	Y	Y	?	Y
LOUISIANA						
1 **Scalise**	Y	Y	N	N	Y	N
2 **Cao**	Y	Y	N	N	Y	Y
3 Melancon	?	?	Y	?	Y	Y
4 **Fleming**	Y	Y	N	N	Y	N
5 **Alexander**	Y	Y	N	N	Y	N
6 **Cassidy**	Y	Y	N	N	Y	N
7 **Boustany**	Y	Y	N	N	Y	N
MAINE						
1 Pingree	N	Y	Y	Y	Y	Y
2 Michaud	N	Y	Y	Y	Y	Y
MARYLAND						
1 Kratovil	Y	Y	N	N	Y	Y
2 Ruppersberger	Y	Y	Y	Y	Y	Y
3 Sarbanes	Y	Y	Y	Y	Y	Y
4 Edwards	N	Y	Y	Y	Y	Y
5 Hoyer	Y	?	Y	Y	Y	Y
6 **Bartlett**	Y	Y	N	N	Y	N
7 Cummings	Y	Y	Y	Y	Y	Y
8 Van Hollen	Y	Y	Y	Y	Y	Y
MASSACHUSETTS						
1 Olver	N	Y	Y	Y	Y	Y
2 Neal	Y	Y	Y	Y	Y	Y
3 McGovern	N	Y	Y	Y	Y	Y
4 Frank	Y	Y	Y	Y	Y	Y
5 Tsongas	?	?	Y	Y	Y	Y
6 Tierney	N	Y	Y	Y	Y	Y
7 Markey	N	Y	Y	Y	Y	Y
8 Capuano	?	?	?	?	?	Y
9 Lynch	N	Y	Y	Y	Y	Y
10 Delahunt	Y	Y	Y	Y	Y	Y
MICHIGAN						
1 Stupak	Y	Y	Y	Y	Y	Y
2 **Hoekstra**	?	?	N	N	Y	N
3 **Ehlers**	Y	Y	N	N	Y	N
4 **Camp**	Y	Y	N	N	Y	N
5 Kildee	N	Y	Y	Y	Y	Y
6 **Upton**	Y	Y	N	N	Y	N
7 Schauer	Y	Y	Y	Y	Y	Y
8 **Rogers**	Y	Y	N	N	Y	N
9 Peters	Y	Y	Y	Y	Y	Y
10 **Miller**	N	Y	N	N	Y	N
11 **McCotter**	N	Y	N	N	Y	N
12 Levin	Y	Y	Y	Y	Y	Y
13 Kilpatrick	N	Y	Y	Y	Y	Y
14 Conyers	N	Y	Y	Y	Y	Y
15 Dingell	N	Y	?	?	?	Y
MINNESOTA						
1 Walz	N	Y	Y	Y	Y	Y
2 **Kline**	Y	Y	N	N	Y	N
3 **Paulsen**	Y	Y	N	N	Y	N
4 McCollum	Y	Y	Y	Y	Y	Y

	937	938	939	940	941	942
5 Ellison	Y	Y	Y	Y	Y	Y
6 **Bachmann**	Y	Y	N	N	Y	N
7 Peterson	Y	Y	Y	Y	Y	Y
8 Oberstar	Y	Y	Y	Y	Y	Y
MISSISSIPPI						
1 Childers	Y	Y	Y	Y	Y	Y
2 Thompson	Y	Y	Y	Y	Y	Y
3 **Harper**	Y	Y	N	N	Y	N
4 Taylor	N	Y	Y	N	Y	Y
MISSOURI						
1 Clay	Y	Y	Y	Y	Y	Y
2 **Akin**	Y	Y	N	N	Y	N
3 Carnahan	Y	Y	Y	Y	Y	Y
4 Skelton	Y	Y	Y	Y	Y	Y
5 Cleaver	Y	Y	Y	Y	Y	Y
6 **Graves**	Y	Y	N	N	Y	N
7 **Blunt**	Y	Y	N	N	Y	N
8 **Emerson**	Y	Y	N	N	Y	N
9 **Luetkemeyer**	Y	Y	N	N	Y	N
MONTANA						
AL **Rehberg**	Y	Y	N	N	Y	N
NEBRASKA						
1 **Fortenberry**	Y	Y	N	N	Y	N
2 **Terry**	Y	Y	N	N	Y	N
3 **Smith**	Y	Y	N	N	Y	N
NEVADA						
1 Berkley	Y	Y	Y	Y	Y	Y
2 **Heller**	Y	Y	N	N	Y	N
3 Titus	Y	Y	Y	Y	Y	Y
NEW HAMPSHIRE						
1 Shea-Porter	Y	Y	Y	Y	Y	Y
2 Hodes	Y	Y	Y	Y	Y	Y
NEW JERSEY						
1 Andrews	Y	Y	Y	Y	Y	Y
2 **LoBiondo**	Y	Y	N	N	Y	N
3 Adler	Y	Y	Y	Y	Y	Y
4 **Smith**	Y	Y	N	N	Y	N
5 **Garrett**	Y	?	N	N	Y	N
6 Pallone	Y	Y	Y	Y	Y	Y
7 **Lance**	Y	Y	N	N	Y	N
8 Pascrell	Y	Y	Y	Y	Y	Y
9 Rothman	Y	Y	Y	Y	Y	Y
10 Payne	?	?	Y	Y	Y	Y
11 **Frelinghuysen**	Y	Y	N	N	Y	N
12 Holt	Y	Y	Y	Y	Y	Y
13 Sires	Y	Y	Y	Y	Y	Y
NEW MEXICO						
1 Heinrich	Y	Y	N	N	Y	Y
2 Teague	Y	Y	Y	Y	Y	Y
3 Lujan	Y	Y	Y	Y	Y	Y
NEW YORK						
1 Bishop	Y	Y	Y	Y	Y	Y
2 Israel	Y	Y	Y	Y	Y	Y
3 **King**	Y	Y	N	N	Y	N
4 McCarthy	P	Y	Y	Y	Y	Y
5 Ackerman	Y	Y	Y	Y	Y	Y
6 Meeks	Y	Y	Y	Y	Y	Y
7 Crowley	Y	Y	Y	Y	Y	Y
8 Nadler	Y	Y	Y	Y	Y	Y
9 Weiner	Y	Y	Y	Y	Y	Y
10 Towns	Y	Y	Y	Y	Y	Y
11 Clarke	N	Y	Y	Y	Y	Y
12 Velázquez	N	Y	Y	Y	Y	Y
13 McMahon	N	Y	Y	Y	Y	Y
14 Maloney	Y	Y	Y	Y	Y	Y
15 Rangel	Y	Y	Y	Y	Y	Y
16 Serrano	N	Y	Y	Y	Y	Y
17 Engel	Y	Y	Y	Y	Y	Y
18 Lowey	Y	Y	Y	Y	Y	Y
19 Hall	Y	Y	Y	Y	Y	Y
20 Murphy	Y	Y	Y	Y	Y	Y
21 Tonko	Y	Y	Y	Y	Y	Y
22 Hinchey	N	Y	Y	Y	Y	Y
23 Owens	Y	Y	Y	Y	Y	Y
24 Arcuri	?	?	Y	Y	Y	Y
25 Maffei	Y	Y	Y	Y	Y	Y
26 **Lee**	Y	Y	N	N	Y	N
27 Higgins	Y	Y	Y	Y	Y	Y
28 Slaughter	Y	Y	Y	Y	Y	Y
29 Massa	N	Y	Y	Y	Y	Y
NORTH CAROLINA						
1 Butterfield	Y	Y	Y	Y	Y	Y
2 Etheridge	Y	Y	Y	Y	Y	Y
3 **Jones**	N	Y	N	N	Y	N
4 Price	Y	Y	Y	Y	Y	Y

	937	938	939	940	941	942
5 **Foxx**	Y	Y	N	N	Y	N
6 **Coble**	Y	Y	N	N	Y	N
7 McIntyre	Y	Y	Y	Y	Y	Y
8 Kissell	Y	Y	Y	Y	Y	Y
9 **Myrick**	Y	Y	N	N	Y	N
10 **McHenry**	Y	Y	N	N	Y	N
11 Shuler	Y	Y	N	N	Y	Y
12 Watt	Y	Y	Y	Y	Y	Y
13 Miller	Y	Y	Y	Y	Y	Y
NORTH DAKOTA						
AL Pomeroy	Y	Y	Y	Y	Y	Y
OHIO						
1 Driehaus	N	Y	Y	Y	Y	Y
2 **Schmidt**	N	Y	N	N	Y	N
3 **Turner**	N	Y	N	N	Y	N
4 **Jordan**	Y	Y	N	N	Y	N
5 **Latta**	Y	Y	N	N	Y	N
6 Wilson	Y	Y	Y	Y	Y	Y
7 **Austria**	Y	Y	N	N	Y	N
8 **Boehner**	Y	?	N	N	Y	N
9 Kaptur	N	Y	Y	Y	Y	Y
10 Kucinich	N	Y	?	Y	Y	Y
11 Fudge	N	Y	?	?	?	?
12 **Tiberi**	N	Y	N	N	Y	N
13 Sutton	Y	Y	Y	Y	Y	Y
14 **LaTourette**	N	Y	N	N	Y	?
15 Kilroy	N	Y	Y	Y	Y	Y
16 Boccieri	N	Y	Y	Y	Y	Y
17 Ryan	N	Y	Y	Y	Y	Y
18 Space	Y	Y	Y	Y	Y	Y
OKLAHOMA						
1 **Sullivan**	Y	Y	N	N	Y	N
2 Boren	Y	Y	Y	Y	Y	Y
3 **Lucas**	Y	Y	N	N	Y	N
4 **Cole**	N	Y	N	N	Y	N
5 **Fallin**	Y	Y	N	N	Y	N
OREGON						
1 Wu	Y	Y	Y	Y	Y	Y
2 **Walden**	Y	Y	N	N	Y	N
3 Blumenauer	N	Y	Y	Y	Y	Y
4 DeFazio	N	Y	Y	Y	Y	Y
5 Schrader	Y	Y	Y	Y	N	Y
PENNSYLVANIA						
1 Brady	Y	Y	Y	Y	Y	Y
2 Fattah	Y	Y	Y	Y	Y	Y
3 Dahlkemper	N	Y	Y	Y	Y	Y
4 Altmire	Y	Y	Y	N	Y	Y
5 **Thompson**	Y	Y	N	N	Y	N
6 **Gerlach**	Y	Y	N	N	Y	N
7 Sestak	Y	Y	Y	Y	Y	Y
8 Murphy, P.	Y	Y	Y	Y	Y	Y
9 **Shuster**	N	Y	N	N	Y	N
10 Carney	?	?	Y	Y	Y	Y
11 Kanjorski	Y	Y	Y	Y	Y	Y
12 Murtha	?	?	Y	Y	Y	?
13 Schwartz	Y	Y	Y	Y	Y	Y
14 Doyle	Y	Y	Y	Y	Y	Y
15 **Dent**	Y	Y	N	N	Y	N
16 **Pitts**	Y	Y	N	N	Y	N
17 Holden	Y	Y	Y	Y	Y	Y
18 **Murphy, T.**	Y	Y	N	N	Y	N
19 **Platts**	Y	Y	N	N	Y	N
RHODE ISLAND						
1 Kennedy	Y	Y	Y	Y	Y	Y
2 Langevin	Y	Y	Y	Y	Y	Y
SOUTH CAROLINA						
1 **Brown**	Y	Y	N	N	Y	N
2 **Wilson**	Y	Y	N	N	Y	N
3 **Barrett**	?	?	?	?	?	?
4 **Inglis**	Y	Y	N	N	Y	N
5 Spratt	Y	Y	Y	Y	Y	Y
6 Clyburn	Y	Y	Y	Y	Y	Y
SOUTH DAKOTA						
AL Herseth Sandlin	Y	Y	Y	Y	Y	Y
TENNESSEE						
1 **Roe**	Y	Y	N	N	Y	N
2 **Duncan**	N	Y	N	N	Y	N
3 **Wamp**	Y	Y	N	N	Y	N
4 Davis	Y	Y	Y	Y	Y	Y
5 Cooper	Y	Y	Y	Y	Y	Y
6 Gordon	Y	Y	Y	Y	Y	Y
7 **Blackburn**	Y	Y	N	N	Y	N
8 Tanner	P	Y	Y	Y	Y	Y
9 Cohen	N	Y	Y	Y	Y	Y

	937	938	939	940	941	942
TEXAS						
1 **Gohmert**	Y	Y	N	N	Y	N
2 **Poe**	Y	Y	N	N	Y	N
3 **Johnson, S.**	Y	Y	N	N	Y	N
4 **Hall**	Y	Y	N	N	Y	N
5 **Hensarling**	Y	Y	N	N	Y	N
6 **Barton**	Y	Y	N	N	Y	N
7 **Culberson**	Y	?	N	N	Y	N
8 **Brady**	Y	Y	N	N	Y	N
9 Green, A.	Y	Y	Y	Y	Y	Y
10 **McCaul**	Y	Y	N	N	Y	N
11 **Conaway**	Y	Y	N	N	Y	N
12 **Granger**	Y	Y	?	?	?	?
13 **Thornberry**	Y	Y	N	N	Y	N
14 **Paul**	N	Y	N	?	Y	N
15 Hinojosa	Y	Y	Y	Y	Y	Y
16 Reyes	N	Y	Y	Y	Y	Y
17 Edwards	Y	Y	Y	Y	Y	Y
18 Jackson Lee	Y	Y	Y	Y	Y	Y
19 **Neugebauer**	Y	?	N	N	Y	N
20 Gonzalez	Y	Y	Y	Y	Y	Y
21 **Smith**	Y	Y	N	N	Y	N
22 **Olson**	Y	Y	N	N	Y	N
23 Rodriguez	Y	Y	Y	Y	Y	Y
24 **Marchant**	Y	Y	N	N	Y	N
25 Doggett	N	Y	Y	Y	Y	Y
26 **Burgess**	Y	Y	N	N	Y	N
27 Ortiz	Y	Y	Y	Y	Y	Y
28 Cuellar	Y	Y	Y	Y	Y	Y
29 Green, G.	Y	Y	Y	Y	Y	Y
30 Johnson, E.	N	Y	Y	Y	Y	Y
31 **Carter**	Y	Y	N	N	Y	–
32 **Sessions**	Y	Y	N	N	Y	N
UTAH						
1 **Bishop**	N	Y	N	N	Y	N
2 Matheson	Y	Y	Y	Y	Y	Y
3 **Chaffetz**	N	Y	N	N	Y	N
VERMONT						
AL Welch	N	Y	Y	Y	Y	Y
VIRGINIA						
1 **Wittman**	Y	Y	N	N	Y	N
2 Nye	Y	Y	Y	Y	Y	N
3 Scott	Y	Y	?	?	?	Y
4 **Forbes**	Y	Y	N	N	Y	N
5 Perriello	N	Y	N	Y	Y	Y
6 **Goodlatte**	Y	Y	N	N	Y	N
7 **Cantor**	Y	Y	N	N	Y	N
8 Moran	?	?	?	?	?	?
9 Boucher	?	?	Y	Y	Y	Y
10 **Wolf**	Y	Y	N	N	Y	N
11 Connolly	Y	Y	Y	Y	Y	Y
WASHINGTON						
1 Inslee	Y	Y	Y	Y	Y	Y
2 Larsen	Y	Y	Y	Y	Y	Y
3 Baird	Y	Y	Y	Y	Y	Y
4 **Hastings**	Y	Y	N	N	Y	N
5 **McMorris Rodgers**	Y	Y	N	N	Y	N
6 Dicks	Y	Y	Y	Y	Y	Y
7 McDermott	N	Y	Y	Y	Y	Y
8 **Reichert**	?	?	N	N	Y	N
9 Smith	+	+	Y	Y	Y	Y
WEST VIRGINIA						
1 Mollohan	N	Y	Y	Y	Y	Y
2 **Capito**	Y	Y	N	N	Y	N
3 Rahall	N	Y	Y	Y	Y	Y
WISCONSIN						
1 **Ryan**	Y	Y	N	N	Y	N
2 Baldwin	N	Y	?	?	?	?
3 Kind	?	?	Y	Y	Y	Y
4 Moore	N	Y	Y	Y	Y	Y
5 **Sensenbrenner**	Y	Y	N	N	Y	N
6 **Petri**	N	Y	N	N	Y	N
7 Obey	Y	Y	Y	Y	Y	Y
8 Kagen	?	?	Y	Y	Y	Y
WYOMING						
AL **Lummis**	Y	Y	N	N	Y	N
DELEGATES						
Faleomavaega (A.S.)						
Norton (D.C.)						
Bordallo (Guam)						
Sablan (N. Marianas)						
Pierluisi (P.R.)						
Christensen (V.I.)						

IN THE HOUSE | By Vote Number

943. **HR 4213. Tax Extensions/Passage.** Passage of the bill that would extend expiring tax provisions through 2010, including the tax credit for research and development, incentives to invest in restaurants and retail businesses, rules for active financing income, state and local sales tax deductions, deductions for teachers' expenses, and deductions for tuition expenses, as well as a 2008 deduction for state and local property taxes. It would be offset by modifications to the tax rate on investment management services and reporting requirements for foreign financial institutions. Passed 241-181: D 239-10; R 2-171. A "yea" was a vote in support of the president's position. Dec. 9, 2009.

944. **HR 3603. Ocmulgee National Monument/Passage.** Bordallo, D-Guam, motion to suspend the rules and pass the bill that would redesignate the Ocmulgee National Monument in Macon, Ga., as the "Ocmulgee Mounds National Monument." Motion agreed to 419-0: D 248-0; R 171-0. A two-thirds majority of those present and voting (280 in this case) is required for passage under suspension of the rules. Dec. 9, 2009.

945. **HR 4173. Financial Industry Regulation Overhaul/Rule.** Adoption of the rule (H Res 956) to provide for House floor consideration of the bill that would overhaul financial industry regulation. Adopted 235-177: D 235-7; R 0-170. Dec. 9, 2009.

946. **HR 86. California Seacoast Preservation/Passage.** Bordallo, D-Guam, motion to suspend the rules and pass the bill that would designate the rocks and small islands on the seacoast of Orange County, Calif., as part of the California Coastal National Monument. It also would repeal the reservation of a lighthouse on the Orange County coast. Motion agreed to 397-4: D 228-2; R 169-2. A two-thirds majority of those present and voting (268 in this case) is required for passage under suspension of the rules. Dec. 9, 2009.

947. **HR 3288. Fiscal 2010 Omnibus Appropriations/Previous Question.** McGovern, D-Mass., motion to order the previous question (thus ending debate and possibility of amendment) on adoption of the rule (H Res 961) to provide for House floor consideration of the conference report on the bill that would provide fiscal 2010 appropriations for federal departments and agencies covered by six unfinished fiscal 2010 spending bills. Motion agreed to 227-187: D 227-17; R 0-170. Dec. 10, 2009.

948. **HR 3288. Fiscal 2010 Omnibus Appropriations/Rule.** Adoption of the rule (H Res 961) to provide for House floor consideration of the conference report on the bill that would provide fiscal 2010 appropriations for federal departments and agencies covered by six unfinished fiscal 2010 spending bills. Adopted 221-200: D 221-29; R 0-171. Dec. 10, 2009.

	943	944	945	946	947	948
ALABAMA						
1 **Bonner**	N	Y	N	Y	N	N
2 Bright	Y	Y	N	Y	N	N
3 **Rogers**	N	Y	N	Y	N	N
4 **Aderholt**	N	Y	N	Y	N	N
5 Griffith	Y	Y	N	Y	N	N
6 **Bachus**	N	Y	N	?	N	N
7 Davis	Y	Y	Y	Y	Y	Y
ALASKA						
AL **Young**	N	Y	N	N	N	N
ARIZONA						
1 Kirkpatrick	Y	Y	N	Y	Y	N
2 **Franks**	N	Y	N	Y	N	N
3 **Shadegg**	N	Y	N	Y	N	N
4 Pastor	Y	Y	?	?	Y	Y
5 Mitchell	N	Y	N	Y	N	N
6 **Flake**	N	Y	N	Y	N	N
7 Grijalva	Y	Y	Y	?	Y	Y
8 Giffords	Y	Y	Y	Y	N	N
ARKANSAS						
1 Berry	Y	Y	?	?	Y	Y
2 Snyder	Y	Y	Y	Y	Y	Y
3 **Boozman**	N	Y	N	Y	N	N
4 Ross	Y	Y	Y	Y	Y	N
CALIFORNIA						
1 Thompson	Y	Y	Y	Y	Y	Y
2 **Herger**	N	Y	N	Y	N	N
3 **Lungren**	N	Y	N	Y	N	N
4 **McClintock**	N	Y	N	Y	N	N
5 Matsui	Y	Y	Y	Y	Y	Y
6 Woolsey	Y	Y	+	?	Y	Y
7 Miller, George	Y	Y	?	?	Y	Y
8 Pelosi						
9 Lee	Y	Y	Y	Y	Y	Y
10 Garamendi	Y	Y	Y	Y	Y	Y
11 McNerney	Y	Y	Y	?	Y	Y
12 Speier	Y	Y	Y	Y	Y	Y
13 Stark	Y	Y	?	?	Y	Y
14 Eshoo	Y	Y	Y	Y	Y	Y
15 Honda	Y	Y	Y	Y	Y	Y
16 Lofgren	Y	Y	Y	Y	Y	Y
17 Farr	Y	Y	Y	Y	Y	Y
18 Cardoza	Y	Y	Y	Y	Y	Y
19 **Radanovich**	?	?	?	?	?	?
20 Costa	Y	Y	Y	Y	?	Y
21 **Nunes**	N	Y	N	Y	N	N
22 **McCarthy**	N	Y	N	Y	N	N
23 Capps	Y	Y	Y	Y	Y	Y
24 **Gallegly**	N	Y	N	Y	N	N
25 **McKeon**	N	?	N	Y	?	N
26 **Dreier**	N	Y	N	Y	N	N
27 Sherman	Y	Y	Y	Y	Y	Y
28 Berman	Y	Y	Y	Y	Y	Y
29 Schiff	Y	Y	Y	Y	Y	Y
30 Waxman	Y	Y	Y	Y	Y	Y
31 Becerra	Y	Y	Y	Y	Y	Y
32 Chu	Y	Y	Y	Y	Y	Y
33 Watson	Y	Y	Y	Y	Y	Y
34 Roybal-Allard	Y	Y	Y	Y	Y	Y
35 Waters	Y	Y	Y	Y	?	Y
36 Harman	Y	Y	Y	?	Y	Y
37 Richardson	Y	Y	Y	Y	Y	Y
38 Napolitano	Y	Y	Y	Y	N	Y
39 Sánchez, Linda	Y	Y	Y	Y	Y	Y
40 **Royce**	N	Y	N	Y	N	N
41 **Lewis**	N	Y	N	Y	N	N
42 **Miller, Gary**	N	Y	N	Y	N	N
43 Baca	Y	Y	Y	Y	Y	Y
44 **Calvert**	N	Y	N	Y	N	N
45 **Bono Mack**	N	Y	N	Y	N	N
46 **Rohrabacher**	N	Y	N	Y	N	N
47 Sanchez, Loretta	?	?	?	?	Y	Y
48 **Campbell**	N	Y	N	Y	N	N
49 **Issa**	N	Y	N	Y	N	N
50 **Bilbray**	N	Y	N	Y	N	N
51 Filner	Y	Y	Y	Y	Y	Y
52 **Hunter**	N	Y	?	Y	N	N
53 Davis	Y	Y	Y	Y	Y	Y

	943	944	945	946	947	948
COLORADO						
1 DeGette	Y	Y	?	?	Y	Y
2 Polis	N	Y	Y	Y	Y	Y
3 Salazar	Y	Y	Y	Y	Y	Y
4 Markey	Y	Y	Y	Y	Y	Y
5 **Lamborn**	N	Y	N	Y	N	N
6 **Coffman**	N	Y	N	Y	N	N
7 Perlmutter	Y	Y	Y	Y	Y	Y
CONNECTICUT						
1 Larson	Y	Y	Y	Y	Y	Y
2 Courtney	Y	?	Y	Y	Y	Y
3 DeLauro	Y	Y	Y	Y	Y	Y
4 Himes	N	Y	Y	Y	Y	Y
5 Murphy	Y	Y	Y	Y	Y	Y
DELAWARE						
AL **Castle**	N	Y	N	Y	N	N
FLORIDA						
1 **Miller**	N	Y	N	Y	N	N
2 Boyd	Y	Y	Y	Y	Y	Y
3 Brown	Y	Y	Y	N	Y	N
4 **Crenshaw**	N	Y	N	Y	N	N
5 **Brown-Waite**	N	Y	N	Y	N	N
6 **Stearns**	N	Y	N	Y	N	N
7 **Mica**	N	Y	N	Y	–	–
8 Grayson	Y	Y	Y	Y	Y	Y
9 **Bilirakis**	N	Y	N	?	N	N
10 **Young**	N	Y	N	Y	N	N
11 Castor	Y	Y	Y	Y	Y	Y
12 **Putnam**	N	Y	N	Y	N	N
13 **Buchanan**	N	Y	N	Y	N	N
14 **Mack**	N	Y	N	Y	N	N
15 **Posey**	N	Y	N	Y	N	N
16 **Rooney**	N	Y	N	Y	N	N
17 Meek	Y	Y	Y	Y	Y	Y
18 **Ros-Lehtinen**	N	Y	N	Y	N	N
19 Wexler	N	Y	?	?	Y	Y
20 Wasserman Schultz	Y	Y	Y	Y	?	Y
21 **Diaz-Balart, L.**	N	Y	N	Y	N	N
22 Klein	N	Y	Y	Y	Y	Y
23 Hastings	Y	Y	Y	Y	Y	Y
24 Kosmas	Y	Y	Y	Y	Y	Y
25 **Diaz-Balart, M.**	N	Y	N	Y	N	N
GEORGIA						
1 **Kingston**	N	Y	N	Y	N	N
2 Bishop	Y	Y	Y	Y	Y	Y
3 **Westmoreland**	N	Y	N	Y	N	N
4 Johnson	Y	Y	Y	Y	Y	Y
5 Lewis	?	?	?	?	Y	Y
6 **Price**	N	Y	N	Y	N	N
7 **Linder**	N	Y	N	Y	N	N
8 Marshall	Y	Y	Y	Y	Y	Y
9 **Deal**	N	Y	N	Y	N	N
10 **Broun**	N	Y	N	Y	N	N
11 **Gingrey**	N	Y	N	Y	N	N
12 Barrow	Y	Y	Y	Y	Y	Y
13 Scott	Y	Y	Y	Y	Y	Y
HAWAII						
1 Abercrombie	Y	Y	Y	Y	Y	Y
2 Hirono	Y	Y	Y	Y	Y	Y
IDAHO						
1 Minnick	Y	Y	Y	Y	Y	N
2 **Simpson**	N	Y	N	Y	N	N
ILLINOIS						
1 Rush	Y	Y	Y	Y	Y	Y
2 Jackson	Y	Y	Y	Y	Y	Y
3 Lipinski	Y	Y	Y	Y	Y	N
4 Gutierrez	Y	Y	Y	Y	Y	Y
5 Quigley	Y	Y	Y	Y	Y	Y
6 **Roskam**	N	Y	N	Y	N	N
7 Davis	Y	Y	Y	Y	Y	Y
8 Bean	Y	Y	Y	Y	Y	Y
9 Schakowsky	Y	Y	Y	Y	Y	Y
10 **Kirk**	N	Y	N	Y	N	N
11 Halvorson	Y	Y	Y	?	Y	Y
12 Costello	Y	Y	Y	Y	Y	Y
13 **Biggert**	N	Y	N	Y	N	N
14 Foster	Y	Y	Y	Y	Y	Y
15 **Johnson**	N	Y	N	Y	N	N

KEY	**Republicans**	Democrats	
Y	Voted for (yea)	X Paired against	C Voted "present" to avoid possible conflict of interest
#	Paired for	– Announced against	
+	Announced for	P Voted "present"	? Did not vote or otherwise make a position known
N	Voted against (nay)		

	943	944	945	946	947	948
16 **Manzullo**	N	Y	N	Y	N	N
17 Hare	Y	Y	Y	Y	Y	Y
18 **Schock**	N	Y	N	Y	N	N
19 **Shimkus**	N	Y	N	Y	N	N
INDIANA						
1 Visclosky	Y	Y	Y	Y	Y	Y
2 Donnelly	Y	Y	Y	Y	N	N
3 **Souder**	N	Y	N	Y	N	N
4 **Buyer**	N	Y	?	?	?	?
5 **Burton**	N	Y	N	Y	N	N
6 **Pence**	N	Y	N	Y	N	N
7 Carson	Y	Y	Y	Y	Y	Y
8 Ellsworth	Y	Y	Y	Y	N	N
9 Hill	Y	Y	Y	Y	N	N
IOWA						
1 Braley	Y	Y	Y	Y	?	Y
2 Loebsack	Y	Y	Y	Y	Y	Y
3 Boswell	Y	Y	Y	Y	Y	Y
4 **Latham**	N	Y	N	Y	N	N
5 **King**	N	Y	N	Y	N	N
KANSAS						
1 **Moran**	N	Y	N	Y	N	N
2 **Jenkins**	N	Y	N	Y	N	N
3 Moore	Y	Y	Y	Y	Y	Y
4 **Tiahrt**	N	Y	N	Y	N	N
KENTUCKY						
1 **Whitfield**	N	Y	N	Y	N	N
2 **Guthrie**	N	Y	N	Y	N	N
3 Yarmuth	Y	Y	Y	Y	Y	Y
4 **Davis**	N	Y	N	Y	N	N
5 **Rogers**	N	Y	N	Y	N	N
6 Chandler	Y	Y	Y	Y	Y	Y
LOUISIANA						
1 **Scalise**	N	Y	N	Y	N	N
2 **Cao**	Y	Y	N	Y	N	N
3 Melancon	Y	Y	Y	?	Y	Y
4 **Fleming**	N	Y	N	Y	N	N
5 **Alexander**	N	Y	N	Y	N	N
6 **Cassidy**	N	Y	N	Y	N	N
7 **Boustany**	N	Y	N	Y	N	N
MAINE						
1 Pingree	Y	Y	Y	Y	Y	Y
2 Michaud	Y	Y	Y	Y	Y	Y
MARYLAND						
1 Kratovil	Y	Y	Y	Y	N	N
2 Ruppersberger	Y	Y	Y	Y	Y	Y
3 Sarbanes	Y	Y	Y	Y	Y	Y
4 Edwards	Y	Y	Y	Y	Y	Y
5 Hoyer	Y	Y	Y	Y	Y	Y
6 **Bartlett**	N	Y	N	Y	?	?
7 Cummings	Y	Y	Y	Y	Y	Y
8 Van Hollen	Y	Y	Y	Y	Y	Y
MASSACHUSETTS						
1 Olver	Y	Y	Y	Y	Y	Y
2 Neal	Y	Y	Y	Y	Y	Y
3 McGovern	Y	Y	Y	Y	Y	Y
4 Frank	Y	Y	Y	Y	Y	Y
5 Tsongas	Y	Y	Y	Y	Y	Y
6 Tierney	Y	Y	Y	Y	Y	Y
7 Markey	Y	Y	Y	Y	Y	Y
8 Capuano	Y	Y	Y	Y	Y	Y
9 Lynch	Y	Y	Y	Y	Y	Y
10 Delahunt	Y	Y	Y	?	Y	Y
MICHIGAN						
1 Stupak	Y	Y	Y	Y	N	N
2 **Hoekstra**	N	Y	N	Y	N	N
3 **Ehlers**	N	Y	N	Y	N	N
4 **Camp**	N	Y	N	Y	N	N
5 Kildee	Y	Y	Y	Y	Y	Y
6 **Upton**	N	Y	N	Y	N	N
7 Schauer	Y	Y	Y	Y	Y	Y
8 **Rogers**	N	Y	N	Y	N	N
9 Peters	Y	Y	Y	Y	Y	Y
10 **Miller**	N	Y	N	Y	N	N
11 **McCotter**	N	Y	N	Y	N	N
12 Levin	Y	Y	Y	Y	Y	Y
13 Kilpatrick	Y	Y	Y	Y	Y	Y
14 Conyers	Y	Y	Y	Y	Y	Y
15 Dingell	Y	Y	Y	Y	Y	Y
MINNESOTA						
1 Walz	Y	Y	Y	Y	Y	Y
2 **Kline**	N	Y	N	Y	N	N
3 **Paulsen**	N	Y	N	Y	N	N
4 McCollum	Y	Y	Y	Y	Y	Y

	943	944	945	946	947	948
5 Ellison	Y	Y	Y	Y	Y	Y
6 **Bachmann**	N	Y	N	Y	N	N
7 Peterson	Y	Y	Y	Y	Y	Y
8 Oberstar	Y	Y	Y	Y	Y	Y
MISSISSIPPI						
1 Childers	Y	Y	Y	Y	N	N
2 Thompson	Y	Y	Y	Y	N	N
3 **Harper**	N	Y	N	Y	N	N
4 Taylor	N	Y	N	Y	N	N
MISSOURI						
1 Clay	Y	Y	Y	Y	Y	Y
2 **Akin**	N	Y	N	Y	N	N
3 Carnahan	Y	Y	Y	Y	Y	Y
4 Skelton	Y	Y	Y	N	Y	N
5 Cleaver	Y	Y	Y	Y	Y	Y
6 **Graves**	N	Y	N	Y	N	N
7 **Blunt**	N	Y	N	Y	N	N
8 **Emerson**	N	Y	N	N	N	N
9 **Luetkemeyer**	N	Y	N	Y	N	N
MONTANA						
AL **Rehberg**	N	Y	N	Y	N	N
NEBRASKA						
1 **Fortenberry**	N	Y	N	Y	N	N
2 **Terry**	N	Y	N	Y	N	N
3 **Smith**	N	Y	N	Y	N	N
NEVADA						
1 Berkley	Y	Y	Y	Y	Y	Y
2 **Heller**	N	Y	N	Y	N	N
3 Titus	Y	Y	Y	Y	Y	Y
NEW HAMPSHIRE						
1 Shea-Porter	Y	Y	Y	Y	Y	Y
2 Hodes	Y	Y	Y	Y	Y	Y
NEW JERSEY						
1 Andrews	Y	Y	Y	Y	Y	Y
2 **LoBiondo**	N	Y	N	Y	N	N
3 Adler	Y	Y	Y	Y	Y	Y
4 **Smith**	N	Y	N	Y	N	N
5 **Garrett**	N	Y	N	Y	N	N
6 Pallone	Y	Y	Y	Y	Y	Y
7 **Lance**	N	Y	N	Y	N	N
8 Pascrell	Y	Y	Y	Y	Y	Y
9 Rothman	Y	Y	Y	Y	Y	Y
10 Payne	Y	Y	?	?	Y	Y
11 **Frelinghuysen**	N	Y	N	Y	N	N
12 Holt	Y	Y	Y	Y	Y	Y
13 Sires	Y	Y	Y	Y	?	Y
NEW MEXICO						
1 Heinrich	Y	Y	Y	Y	?	Y
2 Teague	Y	Y	Y	Y	Y	Y
3 Lujan	Y	Y	Y	Y	Y	Y
NEW YORK						
1 Bishop	Y	Y	Y	Y	Y	Y
2 Israel	Y	Y	Y	Y	Y	Y
3 **King**	N	Y	N	Y	N	N
4 McCarthy	Y	Y	Y	Y	Y	Y
5 Ackerman	Y	Y	Y	Y	Y	Y
6 Meeks	Y	Y	Y	Y	?	Y
7 Crowley	Y	Y	Y	Y	Y	Y
8 Nadler	Y	Y	Y	Y	Y	Y
9 Weiner	Y	Y	Y	Y	Y	Y
10 Towns	Y	Y	Y	Y	Y	Y
11 Clarke	Y	Y	Y	Y	Y	Y
12 Velázquez	Y	Y	Y	Y	Y	Y
13 McMahon	Y	Y	Y	Y	Y	Y
14 Maloney	Y	Y	Y	Y	Y	Y
15 Rangel	Y	Y	Y	Y	Y	Y
16 Serrano	Y	Y	Y	Y	Y	Y
17 Engel	Y	Y	Y	Y	?	Y
18 Lowey	Y	Y	Y	Y	Y	Y
19 Hall	Y	Y	Y	Y	Y	Y
20 Murphy	Y	Y	Y	Y	Y	N
21 Tonko	Y	Y	Y	Y	Y	Y
22 Hinchey	?	Y	Y	Y	Y	Y
23 Owens	Y	Y	Y	Y	Y	Y
24 Arcuri	Y	?	Y	Y	Y	Y
25 Maffei	N	Y	Y	Y	Y	Y
26 **Lee**	N	Y	?	Y	N	N
27 Higgins	Y	Y	Y	Y	Y	?
28 Slaughter	Y	Y	Y	Y	Y	Y
29 Massa	Y	Y	Y	Y	Y	Y
NORTH CAROLINA						
1 Butterfield	Y	Y	Y	Y	Y	Y
2 Etheridge	Y	Y	Y	Y	Y	Y
3 **Jones**	Y	Y	N	Y	N	N
4 Price	Y	Y	Y	Y	Y	Y

	943	944	945	946	947	948
5 **Foxx**	N	Y	N	Y	N	N
6 **Coble**	N	Y	N	Y	N	N
7 McIntyre	Y	Y	Y	Y	N	N
8 Kissell	Y	Y	Y	Y	Y	Y
9 **Myrick**	N	Y	N	Y	N	N
10 **McHenry**	N	Y	?	Y	N	N
11 Shuler	Y	Y	N	?	Y	N
12 Watt	Y	Y	Y	Y	Y	?
13 Miller	Y	Y	Y	Y	Y	Y
NORTH DAKOTA						
AL Pomeroy	Y	Y	Y	Y	Y	Y
OHIO						
1 Driehaus	Y	Y	Y	Y	N	N
2 **Schmidt**	N	Y	N	Y	N	N
3 **Turner**	N	Y	N	Y	N	N
4 **Jordan**	N	Y	N	Y	N	N
5 **Latta**	N	Y	N	Y	N	N
6 Wilson	Y	Y	Y	Y	Y	Y
7 **Austria**	N	Y	N	Y	N	N
8 **Boehner**	N	Y	N	Y	N	N
9 Kaptur	?	Y	N	Y	Y	Y
10 Kucinich	Y	Y	Y	Y	Y	N
11 Fudge	?	?	?	?	Y	Y
12 **Tiberi**	N	Y	N	Y	N	N
13 Sutton	Y	Y	Y	Y	Y	+
14 **LaTourette**	N	?	N	Y	N	N
15 Kilroy	Y	Y	Y	Y	Y	Y
16 Boccieri	Y	Y	Y	Y	Y	Y
17 Ryan	Y	Y	Y	Y	Y	Y
18 Space	Y	Y	Y	Y	Y	Y
OKLAHOMA						
1 **Sullivan**	N	Y	N	Y	N	N
2 Boren	Y	Y	Y	Y	N	N
3 **Lucas**	N	Y	N	Y	N	N
4 **Cole**	N	Y	N	Y	N	N
5 **Fallin**	N	Y	N	Y	N	N
OREGON						
1 Wu	Y	Y	Y	Y	Y	Y
2 **Walden**	N	Y	N	Y	N	N
3 Blumenauer	Y	Y	Y	Y	Y	Y
4 DeFazio	Y	Y	Y	Y	Y	Y
5 Schrader	N	Y	Y	Y	Y	Y
PENNSYLVANIA						
1 Brady	Y	Y	Y	Y	Y	Y
2 Fattah	Y	Y	Y	Y	Y	Y
3 Dahlkemper	Y	Y	Y	Y	Y	N
4 Altmire	Y	Y	Y	Y	Y	Y
5 **Thompson**	N	Y	N	Y	N	N
6 **Gerlach**	N	Y	N	Y	N	N
7 Sestak	Y	Y	Y	Y	Y	Y
8 Murphy, P.	Y	Y	Y	Y	Y	Y
9 **Shuster**	N	Y	N	Y	N	N
10 Carney	Y	Y	Y	Y	Y	N
11 Kanjorski	Y	Y	Y	Y	Y	Y
12 Murtha	?	?	?	?	?	?
13 Schwartz	Y	Y	Y	Y	Y	Y
14 Doyle	Y	?	Y	Y	Y	Y
15 **Dent**	N	Y	N	Y	N	N
16 **Pitts**	N	Y	N	Y	N	N
17 Holden	Y	Y	Y	?	Y	Y
18 **Murphy, T.**	N	Y	N	Y	N	N
19 **Platts**	N	Y	N	Y	N	N
RHODE ISLAND						
1 Kennedy	Y	Y	Y	N	Y	Y
2 Langevin	Y	Y	Y	Y	Y	Y
SOUTH CAROLINA						
1 **Brown**	N	Y	N	Y	N	N
2 **Wilson**	N	Y	N	Y	N	N
3 **Barrett**	?	?	?	?	?	?
4 **Inglis**	N	Y	N	Y	N	N
5 Spratt	Y	Y	Y	Y	Y	Y
6 Clyburn	Y	Y	Y	Y	Y	Y
SOUTH DAKOTA						
AL Herseth Sandlin	Y	Y	Y	Y	Y	Y
TENNESSEE						
1 **Roe**	N	Y	N	Y	N	N
2 **Duncan**	N	Y	N	Y	N	N
3 **Wamp**	N	Y	N	Y	N	N
4 Davis	Y	Y	?	?	Y	?
5 Cooper	Y	Y	Y	Y	Y	Y
6 Gordon	Y	Y	Y	Y	Y	Y
7 **Blackburn**	N	Y	N	Y	N	N
8 Tanner	Y	Y	Y	Y	?	Y
9 Cohen	Y	Y	Y	Y	Y	Y

	943	944	945	946	947	948
TEXAS						
1 **Gohmert**	N	Y	N	Y	N	N
2 **Poe**	N	Y	N	Y	N	N
3 **Johnson, S.**	N	Y	N	Y	N	N
4 **Hall**	N	Y	N	Y	N	N
5 **Hensarling**	N	Y	N	Y	N	N
6 **Barton**	N	Y	N	Y	N	N
7 **Culberson**	N	Y	N	Y	N	N
8 **Brady**	N	Y	N	Y	N	N
9 Green, A.	Y	Y	Y	Y	Y	Y
10 **McCaul**	N	Y	N	Y	N	N
11 **Conaway**	N	Y	N	Y	N	N
12 **Granger**	?	?	?	?	N	N
13 **Thornberry**	N	Y	N	Y	N	N
14 **Paul**	N	Y	N	Y	N	N
15 Hinojosa	Y	Y	Y	Y	Y	Y
16 Reyes	Y	Y	Y	Y	Y	Y
17 Edwards	Y	Y	Y	Y	Y	Y
18 Jackson Lee	Y	Y	Y	Y	?	Y
19 **Neugebauer**	N	Y	N	Y	N	N
20 Gonzalez	Y	Y	Y	Y	Y	Y
21 **Smith**	N	Y	N	Y	N	N
22 **Olson**	N	Y	N	Y	N	N
23 Rodriguez	Y	Y	Y	Y	Y	Y
24 **Marchant**	N	Y	N	Y	N	N
25 Doggett	Y	Y	Y	?	Y	Y
26 **Burgess**	N	Y	N	Y	N	N
27 Ortiz	Y	Y	Y	Y	Y	Y
28 Cuellar	Y	Y	Y	Y	Y	Y
29 Green, G.	Y	Y	Y	Y	Y	Y
30 Johnson, E.	Y	Y	Y	Y	Y	Y
31 **Carter**	–	+	N	Y	N	N
32 **Sessions**	N	Y	N	Y	N	N
UTAH						
1 **Bishop**	N	Y	N	Y	N	N
2 Matheson	Y	Y	Y	Y	Y	Y
3 **Chaffetz**	N	Y	N	Y	N	N
VERMONT						
AL Welch	Y	Y	Y	Y	Y	Y
VIRGINIA						
1 **Wittman**	N	Y	N	Y	N	?
2 Nye	Y	Y	Y	Y	Y	Y
3 Scott	Y	Y	Y	Y	Y	Y
4 **Forbes**	N	Y	N	Y	N	N
5 Perriello	Y	Y	Y	Y	Y	Y
6 **Goodlatte**	N	Y	N	Y	N	N
7 **Cantor**	N	Y	N	Y	?	N
8 Moran	?	?	?	?	?	?
9 Boucher	Y	Y	Y	Y	Y	Y
10 **Wolf**	N	Y	N	Y	N	N
11 Connolly	Y	Y	Y	Y	Y	Y
WASHINGTON						
1 Inslee	Y	Y	Y	Y	Y	Y
2 Larsen	Y	Y	Y	Y	Y	Y
3 Baird	Y	Y	Y	?	N	N
4 **Hastings**	N	Y	N	Y	N	N
5 **McMorris Rodgers**	N	Y	N	Y	N	N
6 Dicks	Y	Y	Y	Y	Y	Y
7 McDermott	Y	Y	Y	Y	Y	Y
8 **Reichert**	N	Y	N	Y	N	N
9 Smith	N	Y	Y	Y	Y	Y
WEST VIRGINIA						
1 Mollohan	Y	Y	Y	Y	Y	Y
2 **Capito**	N	Y	N	Y	N	N
3 Rahall	Y	Y	Y	Y	Y	Y
WISCONSIN						
1 **Ryan**	N	Y	N	Y	N	N
2 Baldwin	?	?	?	?	?	?
3 Kind	Y	Y	Y	Y	Y	Y
4 Moore	Y	Y	Y	Y	Y	Y
5 **Sensenbrenner**	N	Y	N	Y	N	N
6 **Petri**	N	Y	N	Y	N	N
7 Obey	Y	Y	Y	?	Y	Y
8 Kagen	Y	Y	Y	?	Y	Y
WYOMING						
AL **Lummis**	N	Y	N	Y	N	N
DELEGATES						
Faleomavaega (A.S.)						
Norton (D.C.)						
Bordallo (Guam)						
Sablan (N. Marianas)						
Pierluisi (P.R.)						
Christensen (V.I.)						

IN THE HOUSE | By Vote Number

949. **HR 3288. Fiscal 2010 Omnibus Appropriations/Conference Report.** Adoption of the conference report on the bill that would provide $446.8 billion in discretionary spending in fiscal 2010 for federal departments and agencies covered by six unfinished fiscal 2010 spending bills. The measure incorporates the following bills: Commerce-Justice-Science; Financial Services; Labor-HHS-Education; Military Construction-VA; State-Foreign Operations; and Transportation-HUD. It also would prohibit the release or transfer of detainees held in Guantánamo Bay, Cuba, into the United States for any reason other than prosecution. Adopted (thus sent to the Senate) 221-202: D 221-28; R 0-174. A "yea" was a vote in support of the president's position. Dec. 10, 2009.

950. **HR 4017. Ann Marie Blute Post Office/Passage.** Lynch, D-Mass., motion to suspend the rules and pass the bill that would designate a post office in Shrewsbury, Mass., as the "Ann Marie Blute Post Office." Motion agreed to 419-0: D 247-0; R 172-0. A two-thirds majority of those present and voting is (280 in this case) required for passage under suspension of the rules. Dec. 10, 2009.

951. **HR 4173. Financial Industry Regulation Overhaul/Same-Day Consideration.** Adoption of the rule (H Res 962) that would waive the two-thirds majority vote requirement for same-day consideration of resolutions reported from the Rules Committee on the legislative day of Dec. 10, 2009, that provide for further consideration of the bill that would overhaul financial industry regulations. Adopted 239-183: D 239-12; R 0-171. Dec. 10, 2009.

952. **HR 4173. Financial Industry Regulation Overhaul/Rule.** Adoption of the rule (H Res 964) that would provide for further House floor consideration of the bill that would overhaul financial industry regulations. Adopted 238-186: D 238-14; R 0-172. Dec. 10, 2009.

953. **HR 4173. Financial Industry Regulation Overhaul/Manager's Amendment.** Frank, D-Mass., amendment that would expand federal pre-emption by permitting the Office of the Comptroller of the Currency to overrule state consumer financial laws if they impair national bank business and authorize $4 billion of Troubled Asset Relief Program funds for housing relief. It also would stipulate that Consumer Financial Protection Agency regulations would not supersede state or federal consumer protection standards. It would clarify that the Financial Services Oversight Council would be the chief regulatory body for systemic-risk regulation, and increase the ability of the Federal Reserve to prevent mergers, acquisitions and consolidations of non-bank financial holding companies. Adopted in Committee of the Whole 240-182: D 239-10; R 1-172. Dec. 10, 2009.

	949	950	951	952	953
ALABAMA					
1 **Bonner**	N	Y	N	N	N
2 Bright	N	Y	Y	Y	N
3 **Rogers**	N	Y	N	N	N
4 **Aderholt**	N	Y	N	N	N
5 Griffith	Y	Y	N	N	N
6 **Bachus**	N	Y	N	N	N
7 Davis	Y	Y	Y	Y	Y
ALASKA					
AL **Young**	N	Y	N	N	N
ARIZONA					
1 Kirkpatrick	Y	Y	N	N	Y
2 **Franks**	N	Y	N	N	N
3 **Shadegg**	N	Y	N	N	N
4 Pastor	Y	Y	Y	Y	Y
5 Mitchell	N	Y	N	N	Y
6 **Flake**	N	Y	N	N	N
7 Grijalva	Y	Y	Y	Y	Y
8 Giffords	Y	Y	Y	Y	Y
ARKANSAS					
1 Berry	Y	Y	Y	Y	N
2 Snyder	Y	Y	Y	Y	Y
3 **Boozman**	N	Y	N	N	N
4 Ross	Y	Y	Y	Y	Y
CALIFORNIA					
1 Thompson	Y	Y	Y	Y	Y
2 **Herger**	N	Y	N	N	N
3 **Lungren**	N	Y	N	N	N
4 **McClintock**	N	Y	N	N	N
5 Matsui	Y	Y	Y	Y	Y
6 Woolsey	Y	Y	Y	Y	Y
7 Miller, George	Y	Y	Y	Y	Y
8 Pelosi					
9 Lee	Y	Y	Y	Y	Y
10 Garamendi	Y	Y	Y	Y	Y
11 McNerney	Y	Y	Y	Y	Y
12 Speier	?	Y	Y	Y	Y
13 Stark	Y	?	Y	Y	Y
14 Eshoo	Y	Y	Y	Y	Y
15 Honda	Y	Y	Y	Y	Y
16 Lofgren	Y	Y	Y	?	?
17 Farr	Y	Y	Y	Y	Y
18 Cardoza	Y	Y	Y	?	Y
19 **Radanovich**	N	Y	?	?	?
20 Costa	Y	Y	Y	Y	Y
21 **Nunes**	N	Y	N	N	N
22 **McCarthy**	N	Y	N	N	N
23 Capps	Y	Y	Y	Y	Y
24 **Gallegly**	N	Y	N	N	N
25 **McKeon**	N	Y	N	N	N
26 **Dreier**	N	Y	N	N	N
27 Sherman	Y	Y	Y	Y	Y
28 Berman	Y	Y	Y	Y	Y
29 Schiff	Y	Y	Y	Y	Y
30 Waxman	Y	Y	Y	Y	Y
31 Becerra	Y	?	Y	Y	Y
32 Chu	Y	Y	Y	Y	Y
33 Watson	Y	Y	Y	Y	Y
34 Roybal-Allard	Y	Y	Y	Y	Y
35 Waters	Y	Y	Y	Y	Y
36 Harman	Y	Y	Y	N	Y
37 Richardson	Y	Y	Y	Y	?
38 Napolitano	Y	Y	Y	Y	Y
39 Sánchez, Linda	Y	Y	Y	Y	Y
40 **Royce**	N	Y	N	N	N
41 **Lewis**	N	Y	N	N	N
42 **Miller, Gary**	N	Y	N	N	N
43 Baca	Y	Y	Y	Y	Y
44 **Calvert**	N	Y	N	N	N
45 **Bono Mack**	N	Y	N	N	N
46 **Rohrabacher**	N	Y	N	N	N
47 Sanchez, Loretta	Y	Y	Y	Y	Y
48 **Campbell**	N	Y	N	N	N
49 **Issa**	N	Y	N	N	N
50 **Bilbray**	N	Y	N	N	N
51 Filner	Y	Y	Y	Y	Y
52 **Hunter**	N	Y	N	N	N
53 Davis	Y	Y	Y	Y	Y

	949	950	951	952	953
COLORADO					
1 DeGette	Y	Y	Y	Y	Y
2 Polis	?	Y	Y	Y	Y
3 Salazar	Y	Y	Y	Y	Y
4 Markey	Y	Y	Y	Y	Y
5 **Lamborn**	N	Y	N	N	N
6 **Coffman**	N	Y	N	N	N
7 Perlmutter	Y	Y	Y	Y	Y
CONNECTICUT					
1 Larson	Y	Y	Y	Y	Y
2 Courtney	Y	Y	Y	Y	Y
3 DeLauro	Y	Y	Y	Y	Y
4 Himes	Y	Y	Y	Y	Y
5 Murphy	Y	Y	Y	Y	Y
DELAWARE					
AL **Castle**	N	Y	N	N	N
FLORIDA					
1 **Miller**	N	Y	N	N	N
2 Boyd	Y	Y	Y	Y	Y
3 Brown	P	Y	Y	Y	Y
4 **Crenshaw**	N	Y	N	N	N
5 **Brown-Waite**	N	Y	N	N	N
6 **Stearns**	N	Y	N	N	N
7 **Mica**	–	+	–	?	N
8 Grayson	Y	Y	Y	Y	Y
9 **Bilirakis**	N	Y	N	N	N
10 **Young**	N	Y	N	N	N
11 Castor	Y	Y	Y	Y	Y
12 **Putnam**	N	Y	N	N	N
13 **Buchanan**	N	Y	N	N	N
14 **Mack**	N	Y	N	N	N
15 **Posey**	N	Y	N	N	N
16 **Rooney**	N	Y	N	N	N
17 Meek	Y	Y	Y	Y	N
18 **Ros-Lehtinen**	N	Y	N	N	N
19 Wexler	Y	Y	Y	Y	Y
20 Wasserman Schultz	Y	Y	Y	Y	Y
21 **Diaz-Balart, L.**	N	Y	N	N	N
22 Klein	Y	Y	Y	Y	Y
23 Hastings	Y	Y	?	Y	Y
24 Kosmas	Y	Y	Y	Y	Y
25 **Diaz-Balart, M.**	N	Y	N	N	N
GEORGIA					
1 **Kingston**	N	Y	N	N	N
2 Bishop	Y	Y	Y	Y	Y
3 **Westmoreland**	N	Y	N	N	N
4 Johnson	Y	Y	Y	Y	?
5 Lewis	Y	Y	Y	Y	Y
6 **Price**	N	Y	N	N	N
7 **Linder**	N	?	N	N	N
8 Marshall	N	Y	Y	Y	Y
9 **Deal**	N	Y	?	?	?
10 **Broun**	N	Y	N	N	N
11 **Gingrey**	N	Y	N	N	N
12 Barrow	Y	Y	Y	Y	Y
13 Scott	Y	Y	Y	Y	+
HAWAII					
1 Abercrombie	Y	Y	Y	Y	Y
2 Hirono	Y	Y	Y	Y	Y
IDAHO					
1 Minnick	N	Y	Y	Y	Y
2 **Simpson**	N	Y	N	N	N
ILLINOIS					
1 Rush	Y	Y	Y	Y	Y
2 Jackson	Y	Y	Y	Y	Y
3 Lipinski	N	Y	Y	Y	Y
4 Gutierrez	Y	Y	Y	Y	Y
5 Quigley	Y	Y	Y	Y	Y
6 **Roskam**	N	Y	N	N	N
7 Davis	Y	Y	Y	Y	Y
8 Bean	Y	Y	Y	Y	Y
9 Schakowsky	Y	Y	Y	Y	Y
10 **Kirk**	N	Y	N	N	N
11 Halvorson	Y	Y	Y	Y	Y
12 Costello	N	Y	Y	Y	Y
13 **Biggert**	N	Y	N	N	N
14 Foster	Y	Y	N	Y	Y
15 **Johnson**	N	Y	N	N	N

	949	950	951	952	953
16 Manzullo	N	Y	N	N	N
17 Hare	Y	Y	Y	Y	Y
18 Schock	N	Y	N	N	N
19 Shimkus	N	Y	N	N	N
INDIANA					
1 Visclosky	Y	Y	Y	Y	Y
2 Donnelly	N	Y	Y	N	Y
3 Souder	N	Y	N	N	N
4 Buyer	?	?	?	?	N
5 Burton	N	Y	N	N	N
6 Pence	N	Y	N	N	N
7 Carson	Y	Y	Y	Y	Y
8 Ellsworth	N	Y	N	Y	Y
9 Hill	Y	Y	Y	N	Y
IOWA					
1 Braley	Y	Y	Y	Y	Y
2 Loebsack	Y	Y	Y	Y	Y
3 Boswell	Y	Y	Y	Y	Y
4 Latham	N	Y	N	N	N
5 King	N	Y	N	N	N
KANSAS					
1 Moran	N	Y	N	N	N
2 Jenkins	N	Y	N	N	N
3 Moore	Y	Y	Y	Y	Y
4 Tiahrt	N	Y	N	N	N
KENTUCKY					
1 Whitfield	N	Y	N	N	N
2 Guthrie	N	Y	N	N	N
3 Yarmuth	Y	Y	Y	Y	Y
4 Davis	N	?	N	N	N
5 Rogers	N	Y	N	N	N
6 Chandler	Y	Y	Y	Y	Y
LOUISIANA					
1 Scalise	N	Y	N	N	N
2 Cao	N	Y	N	N	N
3 Melancon	N	Y	Y	Y	Y
4 Fleming	N	Y	N	N	N
5 Alexander	N	Y	N	N	N
6 Cassidy	N	Y	N	N	N
7 Boustany	N	Y	N	N	N
MAINE					
1 Pingree	Y	Y	Y	Y	Y
2 Michaud	Y	Y	Y	Y	Y
MARYLAND					
1 Kratovil	N	Y	N	Y	Y
2 Ruppersberger	Y	Y	Y	Y	Y
3 Sarbanes	Y	Y	Y	Y	Y
4 Edwards	Y	Y	Y	Y	Y
5 Hoyer	Y	Y	?	Y	?
6 Bartlett	N	Y	N	N	N
7 Cummings	Y	Y	Y	Y	Y
8 Van Hollen	Y	?	Y	Y	Y
MASSACHUSETTS					
1 Olver	Y	Y	Y	Y	Y
2 Neal	Y	Y	Y	Y	Y
3 McGovern	Y	Y	Y	Y	Y
4 Frank	?	Y	Y	Y	Y
5 Tsongas	Y	Y	Y	Y	Y
6 Tierney	Y	Y	Y	Y	Y
7 Markey	Y	Y	Y	Y	Y
8 Capuano	Y	Y	Y	Y	Y
9 Lynch	Y	Y	Y	Y	Y
10 Delahunt	Y	Y	Y	Y	Y
MICHIGAN					
1 Stupak	N	Y	Y	Y	Y
2 Hoekstra	N	Y	N	N	N
3 Ehlers	N	Y	N	N	N
4 Camp	N	Y	N	N	N
5 Kildee	Y	Y	Y	Y	Y
6 Upton	N	Y	N	N	N
7 Schauer	Y	Y	Y	Y	?
8 Rogers	N	Y	N	N	N
9 Peters	Y	Y	Y	Y	Y
10 Miller	N	Y	N	N	N
11 McCotter	N	Y	N	N	N
12 Levin	Y	Y	Y	Y	Y
13 Kilpatrick	Y	Y	Y	Y	Y
14 Conyers	Y	Y	Y	Y	Y
15 Dingell	Y	Y	Y	Y	Y
MINNESOTA					
1 Walz	Y	Y	Y	Y	Y
2 Kline	N	Y	N	N	N
3 Paulsen	N	Y	N	N	N
4 McCollum	Y	Y	Y	Y	Y

	949	950	951	952	953
5 Ellison	Y	Y	Y	Y	Y
6 Bachmann	N	Y	N	N	N
7 Peterson	N	Y	Y	Y	Y
8 Oberstar	Y	Y	Y	Y	Y
MISSISSIPPI					
1 Childers	N	Y	Y	Y	Y
2 Thompson	Y	Y	Y	Y	Y
3 Harper	N	Y	N	N	N
4 Taylor	N	Y	N	N	Y
MISSOURI					
1 Clay	Y	Y	Y	Y	Y
2 Akin	N	Y	N	N	N
3 Carnahan	Y	Y	Y	Y	Y
4 Skelton	Y	Y	Y	Y	Y
5 Cleaver	Y	Y	Y	Y	Y
6 Graves	N	Y	N	N	N
7 Blunt	N	Y	N	N	N
8 Emerson	N	Y	N	N	N
9 Luetkemeyer	N	Y	N	N	N
MONTANA					
AL Rehberg	N	Y	N	N	N
NEBRASKA					
1 Fortenberry	N	Y	N	N	N
2 Terry	N	Y	N	N	N
3 Smith	N	Y	N	N	N
NEVADA					
1 Berkley	Y	Y	Y	Y	Y
2 Heller	N	Y	N	N	N
3 Titus	Y	Y	Y	Y	Y
NEW HAMPSHIRE					
1 Shea-Porter	Y	Y	?	Y	Y
2 Hodes	Y	Y	Y	Y	Y
NEW JERSEY					
1 Andrews	Y	Y	Y	Y	Y
2 LoBiondo	N	Y	N	N	N
3 Adler	N	Y	Y	Y	Y
4 Smith	N	Y	N	N	N
5 Garrett	N	Y	N	N	N
6 Pallone	Y	Y	Y	Y	Y
7 Lance	N	Y	N	N	N
8 Pascrell	Y	Y	Y	Y	Y
9 Rothman	Y	Y	Y	Y	Y
10 Payne	Y	Y	Y	Y	Y
11 Frelinghuysen	N	Y	N	N	N
12 Holt	Y	Y	Y	Y	Y
13 Sires	Y	Y	Y	Y	Y
NEW MEXICO					
1 Heinrich	Y	Y	Y	Y	Y
2 Teague	Y	N	Y	Y	Y
3 Lujan	Y	Y	Y	Y	Y
NEW YORK					
1 Bishop	Y	Y	Y	Y	Y
2 Israel	Y	Y	Y	Y	Y
3 King	N	Y	N	N	N
4 McCarthy	Y	Y	Y	Y	Y
5 Ackerman	Y	Y	Y	Y	Y
6 Meeks	Y	?	Y	Y	Y
7 Crowley	Y	Y	Y	Y	Y
8 Nadler	Y	Y	Y	Y	Y
9 Weiner	Y	Y	Y	Y	Y
10 Towns	Y	Y	Y	Y	Y
11 Clarke	Y	Y	Y	Y	+
12 Velázquez	Y	Y	Y	Y	Y
13 McMahon	Y	Y	Y	Y	Y
14 Maloney	Y	Y	Y	Y	Y
15 Rangel	Y	Y	Y	Y	Y
16 Serrano	Y	Y	Y	Y	Y
17 Engel	Y	Y	Y	Y	Y
18 Lowey	Y	Y	Y	Y	Y
19 Hall	Y	Y	Y	Y	Y
20 Murphy	Y	Y	Y	Y	Y
21 Tonko	Y	Y	Y	Y	Y
22 Hinchey	Y	Y	Y	Y	Y
23 Owens	N	Y	Y	Y	Y
24 Arcuri	Y	Y	Y	Y	Y
25 Maffei	Y	Y	Y	Y	Y
26 Lee	N	Y	N	N	N
27 Higgins	Y	Y	Y	Y	Y
28 Slaughter	Y	Y	Y	Y	?
29 Massa	Y	Y	Y	Y	N
NORTH CAROLINA					
1 Butterfield	Y	Y	Y	Y	Y
2 Etheridge	Y	Y	Y	Y	Y
3 Jones	N	Y	N	N	N
4 Price	Y	Y	Y	Y	Y

	949	950	951	952	953
5 Foxx	N	Y	N	N	N
6 Coble	N	Y	N	N	N
7 McIntyre	Y	Y	Y	Y	Y
8 Kissell	Y	Y	Y	Y	Y
9 Myrick	N	Y	N	N	N
10 McHenry	N	Y	?	N	?
11 Shuler	Y	Y	N	N	Y
12 Watt	Y	Y	Y	Y	Y
13 Miller	Y	Y	Y	Y	Y
NORTH DAKOTA					
AL Pomeroy	Y	Y	Y	Y	Y
OHIO					
1 Driehaus	N	Y	Y	Y	Y
2 Schmidt	N	Y	N	N	N
3 Turner	N	Y	N	N	N
4 Jordan	N	Y	N	N	N
5 Latta	N	Y	N	N	N
6 Wilson	Y	Y	Y	Y	Y
7 Austria	N	Y	N	N	N
8 Boehner	N	Y	N	N	N
9 Kaptur	Y	Y	Y	N	Y
10 Kucinich	N	Y	Y	Y	Y
11 Fudge	Y	Y	Y	Y	Y
12 Tiberi	N	Y	N	N	N
13 Sutton	Y	Y	Y	Y	Y
14 LaTourette	N	Y	N	N	N
15 Kilroy	Y	Y	Y	Y	Y
16 Boccieri	N	Y	N	N	Y
17 Ryan	Y	Y	Y	Y	Y
18 Space	Y	Y	Y	Y	Y
OKLAHOMA					
1 Sullivan	N	Y	N	N	N
2 Boren	N	Y	N	N	N
3 Lucas	N	Y	N	N	N
4 Cole	N	Y	N	N	N
5 Fallin	N	Y	N	N	N
OREGON					
1 Wu	Y	Y	Y	Y	Y
2 Walden	N	Y	N	N	N
3 Blumenauer	Y	Y	Y	Y	Y
4 DeFazio	Y	Y	Y	Y	?
5 Schrader	Y	?	Y	Y	Y
PENNSYLVANIA					
1 Brady	Y	Y	Y	Y	Y
2 Fattah	Y	Y	Y	Y	Y
3 Dahlkemper	N	Y	Y	Y	Y
4 Altmire	Y	Y	Y	Y	Y
5 Thompson	N	Y	N	N	N
6 Gerlach	N	Y	N	N	N
7 Sestak	Y	Y	Y	Y	Y
8 Murphy, P.	Y	Y	Y	Y	Y
9 Shuster	N	Y	N	N	N
10 Carney	N	Y	N	N	Y
11 Kanjorski	Y	Y	Y	Y	Y
12 Murtha	?	?	?	?	?
13 Schwartz	Y	Y	Y	Y	Y
14 Doyle	Y	Y	Y	Y	Y
15 Dent	N	Y	N	N	N
16 Pitts	N	Y	N	N	N
17 Holden	Y	Y	Y	Y	?
18 Murphy, T.	N	Y	N	N	N
19 Platts	N	Y	N	N	N
RHODE ISLAND					
1 Kennedy	Y	Y	Y	Y	Y
2 Langevin	Y	Y	Y	Y	Y
SOUTH CAROLINA					
1 Brown	N	Y	N	N	N
2 Wilson	N	Y	N	N	N
3 Barrett	?	?	?	?	?
4 Inglis	N	Y	N	N	N
5 Spratt	Y	Y	Y	Y	Y
6 Clyburn	Y	Y	Y	Y	Y
SOUTH DAKOTA					
AL Herseth Sandlin	Y	Y	Y	Y	Y
TENNESSEE					
1 Roe	N	Y	N	N	N
2 Duncan	N	Y	N	N	N
3 Wamp	N	Y	N	N	N
4 Davis	Y	Y	Y	Y	Y
5 Cooper	-	Y	Y	Y	Y
6 Gordon	N	Y	Y	Y	Y
7 Blackburn	N	Y	N	N	N
8 Tanner	N	Y	Y	Y	Y
9 Cohen	Y	Y	Y	Y	Y

	949	950	951	952	953
TEXAS					
1 Gohmert	N	Y	N	N	N
2 Poe	N	Y	N	N	N
3 Johnson, S.	N	Y	N	N	N
4 Hall	N	Y	N	N	N
5 Hensarling	N	Y	N	N	N
6 Barton	N	Y	N	N	N
7 Culberson	N	Y	N	N	N
8 Brady	N	Y	N	N	N
9 Green, A.	Y	Y	Y	Y	Y
10 McCaul	N	Y	N	N	N
11 Conaway	N	Y	N	N	N
12 Granger	N	Y	N	N	N
13 Thornberry	N	Y	N	N	N
14 Paul	N	Y	N	N	N
15 Hinojosa	Y	Y	Y	Y	Y
16 Reyes	Y	Y	Y	Y	Y
17 Edwards	Y	?	Y	Y	Y
18 Jackson Lee	Y	Y	Y	Y	Y
19 Neugebauer	N	Y	N	N	N
20 Gonzalez	Y	Y	Y	Y	Y
21 Smith	N	Y	N	N	N
22 Olson	N	Y	N	N	N
23 Rodriguez	Y	Y	Y	Y	Y
24 Marchant	N	Y	N	N	N
25 Doggett	Y	Y	Y	Y	Y
26 Burgess	N	Y	N	N	N
27 Ortiz	Y	Y	Y	Y	Y
28 Cuellar	Y	Y	Y	N	Y
29 Green, G.	Y	Y	Y	Y	Y
30 Johnson, E.	Y	Y	Y	Y	Y
31 Carter	N	Y	N	N	N
32 Sessions	N	Y	N	N	N
UTAH					
1 Bishop	N	Y	N	N	Y
2 Matheson	N	Y	Y	N	Y
3 Chaffetz	N	Y	N	N	N
VERMONT					
AL Welch	Y	Y	Y	Y	Y
VIRGINIA					
1 Wittman	N	Y	N	N	N
2 Nye	Y	Y	Y	Y	Y
3 Scott	Y	Y	Y	Y	Y
4 Forbes	N	Y	N	N	N
5 Perriello	Y	Y	N	N	Y
6 Goodlatte	N	Y	N	N	N
7 Cantor	N	Y	N	N	N
8 Moran	?	?	?	?	?
9 Boucher	Y	Y	Y	Y	Y
10 Wolf	N	Y	N	N	N
11 Connolly	Y	Y	Y	Y	Y
WASHINGTON					
1 Inslee	Y	Y	Y	Y	Y
2 Larsen	Y	Y	Y	Y	Y
3 Baird	N	Y	Y	Y	Y
4 Hastings	N	Y	N	N	N
5 McMorris Rodgers	N	Y	N	N	N
6 Dicks	Y	Y	Y	Y	Y
7 McDermott	Y	Y	Y	Y	Y
8 Reichert	N	Y	N	N	N
9 Smith	Y	Y	Y	Y	Y
WEST VIRGINIA					
1 Mollohan	Y	Y	Y	Y	Y
2 Capito	N	Y	N	N	N
3 Rahall	Y	Y	Y	Y	Y
WISCONSIN					
1 Ryan	N	Y	N	N	N
2 Baldwin	?	?	?	?	?
3 Kind	N	Y	Y	Y	Y
4 Moore	Y	Y	Y	Y	Y
5 Sensenbrenner	N	Y	N	N	N
6 Petri	N	Y	N	N	N
7 Obey	Y	?	Y	Y	Y
8 Kagen	Y	Y	Y	Y	Y
WYOMING					
AL Lummis	N	Y	N	N	N
DELEGATES					
Faleomavaega (A.S.)					Y
Norton (D.C.)					Y
Bordallo (Guam)					?
Sablan (N. Marianas)					Y
Pierluisi (P.R.)					Y
Christensen (V.I.)					Y

H-323

IN THE HOUSE | By Vote Number

954. HR 4173. Financial Industry Regulation Overhaul/Credit-Rating Agency Lawsuits. Sessions, R-Texas, amendment that would strike provisions in the bill that would allow private lawsuits to be brought against credit-rating agencies. Rejected in Committee of the Whole 172-257: D 4-252; R 168-5. Dec. 10, 2009.

955. HR 4173. Financial Industry Regulation Overhaul/Conflicts of Interest. Lynch, D-Mass., amendment that would establish governance rules for clearinghouses and swap-exchange facilities to prevent conflicts of interest. Adopted in Committee of the Whole 228-202: D 210-46; R 18-156. Dec. 10, 2009.

956. HR 4173. Financial Industry Regulation Overhaul/Major Swap Participant Definition. Murphy, D-N.Y., amendment that would define "major swap participant" as a firm having a significant impact on the financial system. Adopted in Committee of the Whole 304-124: D 131-124; R 173-0. Dec. 10, 2009.

957. HR 4173. Financial Industry Regulation Overhaul/End User Swap Margins. Frank, D-Mass., amendment that would authorize prudential regulators, the Commodity Futures Trading Commission, and the Securities and Exchange Commission to set margins or collateral requirements in swap and security-based swap transactions involving end users. Rejected in Committee of the Whole 150-280: D 149-107; R 1-173. Dec. 10, 2009.

958. HR 4173. Financial Industry Regulation Overhaul/Registered Swap Facilities. Stupak, D-Mich., amendment that would require all non-cleared swaps to be executed on a registered swap execution facility. Rejected in Committee of the Whole 98-330: D 95-160; R 3-170. Dec. 10, 2009.

959. HR 4173. Financial Industry Regulation Overhaul/Swap Regulation and Invalidation. Stupak, D-Mich., amendment that would authorize the Commodity Futures Trading Commission and the Securities and Exchange Commission to ban abusive swaps, amend any proposed commercial risk definition to disregard balance sheet risk and invalidate illegal swaps entered into after enactment of the bill. Rejected in Committee of the Whole 150-279: D 145-110; R 5-169. Dec. 10, 2009.

	954	955	956	957	958	959
ALABAMA						
1 Bonner	Y	N	Y	N	N	N
2 Bright	N	N	Y	N	N	N
3 Rogers	Y	N	Y	N	N	N
4 Aderholt	Y	N	Y	N	N	N
5 Griffith	N	N	Y	N	N	N
6 Bachus	Y	N	Y	N	N	N
7 Davis	N	Y	Y	N	N	N
ALASKA						
AL Young	Y	N	Y	N	N	N
ARIZONA						
1 Kirkpatrick	N	N	Y	N	N	N
2 Franks	Y	N	Y	N	N	N
3 Shadegg	Y	N	Y	N	N	N
4 Pastor	N	Y	N	Y	Y	Y
5 Mitchell	N	N	Y	N	N	N
6 Flake	Y	N	Y	N	N	N
7 Grijalva	N	Y	N	Y	Y	?
8 Giffords	N	Y	Y	N	N	N
ARKANSAS						
1 Berry	N	Y	Y	N	N	N
2 Snyder	N	N	Y	N	N	N
3 Boozman	Y	N	Y	N	N	N
4 Ross	N	Y	Y	N	N	N
CALIFORNIA						
1 Thompson	N	Y	Y	Y	N	Y
2 Herger	Y	N	Y	N	N	N
3 Lungren	Y	N	Y	N	N	N
4 McClintock	Y	N	Y	N	N	N
5 Matsui	N	Y	Y	Y	N	Y
6 Woolsey	N	Y	N	Y	Y	Y
7 Miller, George	N	Y	N	Y	Y	Y
8 Pelosi						
9 Lee	N	Y	N	Y	Y	Y
10 Garamendi	N	Y	N	Y	Y	Y
11 McNerney	N	Y	Y	N	N	N
12 Speier	N	Y	Y	Y	Y	N
13 Stark	N	Y	N	Y	Y	Y
14 Eshoo	N	Y	N	Y	Y	Y
15 Honda	N	Y	N	Y	Y	Y
16 Lofgren	?	?	?	?	?	?
17 Farr	N	Y	N	Y	Y	Y
18 Cardoza	N	N	Y	N	N	N
19 Radanovich	?	?	?	?	?	?
20 Costa	N	N	Y	N	N	N
21 Nunes	Y	N	Y	N	N	N
22 McCarthy	Y	N	Y	N	N	N
23 Capps	N	Y	N	Y	Y	Y
24 Gallegly	Y	N	Y	N	N	N
25 McKeon	Y	N	Y	N	N	N
26 Dreier	Y	N	Y	N	N	N
27 Sherman	N	Y	N	Y	Y	Y
28 Berman	N	Y	N	Y	Y	Y
29 Schiff	N	Y	N	Y	Y	Y
30 Waxman	N	Y	N	Y	Y	Y
31 Becerra	N	Y	N	Y	Y	Y
32 Chu	N	Y	N	Y	Y	Y
33 Watson	N	Y	N	Y	Y	Y
34 Roybal-Allard	N	Y	N	Y	Y	Y
35 Waters	N	Y	N	Y	N	Y
36 Harman	N	Y	Y	N	N	N
37 Richardson	?	?	?	?	?	?
38 Napolitano	N	Y	N	Y	N	Y
39 Sánchez, Linda	N	Y	N	Y	Y	Y
40 Royce	Y	N	Y	N	N	N
41 Lewis	Y	N	Y	N	N	N
42 Miller, Gary	Y	N	Y	N	N	N
43 Baca	N	Y	Y	N	N	N
44 Calvert	Y	N	Y	N	N	N
45 Bono Mack	Y	N	Y	N	N	N
46 Rohrabacher	N	N	Y	N	N	N
47 Sanchez, Loretta	N	Y	N	Y	Y	Y
48 Campbell	Y	N	Y	N	N	N
49 Issa	Y	N	Y	N	N	N
50 Bilbray	Y	Y	Y	N	N	N
51 Filner	N	Y	N	Y	Y	Y
52 Hunter	Y	N	Y	N	N	N
53 Davis	N	Y	Y	N	N	N
COLORADO						
1 DeGette	N	Y	N	Y	Y	Y
2 Polis	N	N	Y	N	N	N
3 Salazar	N	Y	Y	N	N	N
4 Markey	N	Y	Y	N	N	N
5 Lamborn	Y	N	Y	N	N	N
6 Coffman	Y	N	Y	N	N	N
7 Perlmutter	N	N	Y	N	N	N
CONNECTICUT						
1 Larson	N	Y	N	Y	Y	Y
2 Courtney	N	Y	N	Y	Y	Y
3 DeLauro	N	Y	N	Y	Y	Y
4 Himes	N	N	Y	N	N	N
5 Murphy	N	Y	Y	N	Y	Y
DELAWARE						
AL Castle	Y	Y	Y	N	N	N
FLORIDA						
1 Miller	Y	N	Y	N	N	N
2 Boyd	N	N	Y	N	N	N
3 Brown	N	Y	Y	N	N	N
4 Crenshaw	Y	N	Y	N	N	N
5 Brown-Waite	Y	N	Y	N	N	N
6 Stearns	Y	Y	Y	N	N	N
7 Mica	Y	N	Y	N	N	N
8 Grayson	N	Y	N	Y	Y	Y
9 Bilirakis	Y	Y	Y	N	N	N
10 Young	Y	N	Y	N	N	N
11 Castor	N	Y	N	Y	Y	Y
12 Putnam	Y	N	Y	N	N	N
13 Buchanan	Y	N	Y	N	N	N
14 Mack	Y	N	Y	N	N	N
15 Posey	Y	N	Y	N	N	N
16 Rooney	Y	N	Y	N	N	N
17 Meek	N	N	Y	N	N	N
18 Ros-Lehtinen	Y	N	Y	N	N	N
19 Wexler	N	Y	N	Y	N	Y
20 Wasserman Schultz	N	Y	Y	Y	N	N
21 Diaz-Balart, L.	N	N	Y	N	N	N
22 Klein	N	N	Y	N	N	Y
23 Hastings	N	Y	N	Y	N	Y
24 Kosmas	N	N	Y	N	N	N
25 Diaz-Balart, M.	N	N	Y	N	?	N
GEORGIA						
1 Kingston	Y	N	Y	N	N	N
2 Bishop	N	Y	Y	N	N	N
3 Westmoreland	Y	N	Y	N	N	N
4 Johnson	N	Y	N	Y	N	Y
5 Lewis	N	Y	Y	Y	N	Y
6 Price	Y	N	Y	N	N	N
7 Linder	Y	N	Y	N	N	N
8 Marshall	N	Y	Y	N	N	N
9 Deal	?	?	?	?	?	?
10 Broun	Y	N	Y	N	N	N
11 Gingrey	Y	N	Y	N	N	N
12 Barrow	N	Y	Y	N	N	N
13 Scott	N	Y	Y	N	N	N
HAWAII						
1 Abercrombie	N	Y	N	Y	Y	Y
2 Hirono	N	Y	N	Y	Y	Y
IDAHO						
1 Minnick	N	Y	Y	N	N	N
2 Simpson	Y	N	Y	N	N	N
ILLINOIS						
1 Rush	N	Y	Y	Y	N	N
2 Jackson	N	Y	N	Y	N	Y
3 Lipinski	N	Y	Y	N	N	N
4 Gutierrez	N	N	N	N	?	Y
5 Quigley	N	Y	N	Y	N	N
6 Roskam	Y	N	Y	N	N	N
7 Davis	N	Y	Y	Y	N	Y
8 Bean	N	N	Y	N	N	N
9 Schakowsky	N	Y	N	Y	Y	Y
10 Kirk	Y	N	Y	N	N	N
11 Halvorson	N	Y	Y	N	N	N
12 Costello	N	Y	?	Y	N	N
13 Biggert	Y	N	Y	N	N	N
14 Foster	N	N	Y	N	N	N
15 Johnson	N	Y	N	Y	N	N

	954	955	956	957	958	959
16 **Manzullo**	Y	N	Y	N	N	N
17 Hare	N	Y	N	Y	Y	Y
18 **Schock**	Y	N	Y	N	N	N
19 **Shimkus**	Y	N	Y	N	N	N
INDIANA						
1 Visclosky	N	Y	N	Y	Y	Y
2 Donnelly	N	Y	Y	N	Y	Y
3 **Souder**	Y	N	Y	N	N	N
4 **Buyer**	Y	N	Y	N	N	N
5 **Burton**	Y	N	Y	N	N	N
6 **Pence**	Y	N	Y	N	N	N
7 Carson	N	Y	N	Y	N	Y
8 Ellsworth	N	Y	N	N	N	N
9 Hill	N	N	Y	N	N	N
IOWA						
1 Braley	N	Y	N	Y	Y	Y
2 Loebsack	N	Y	N	N	Y	Y
3 Boswell	N	Y	Y	N	N	N
4 **Latham**	Y	N	Y	N	N	N
5 **King**	Y	N	Y	N	N	N
KANSAS						
1 **Moran**	Y	N	Y	N	N	N
2 **Jenkins**	Y	N	Y	N	N	N
3 Moore	N	N	Y	Y	N	N
4 **Tiahrt**	Y	N	Y	N	N	N
KENTUCKY						
1 **Whitfield**	Y	N	Y	N	N	N
2 **Guthrie**	Y	N	Y	N	N	N
3 Yarmuth	N	Y	Y	Y	Y	Y
4 **Davis**	Y	N	Y	Y	N	N
5 **Rogers**	Y	N	Y	N	N	N
6 Chandler	N	Y	Y	N	Y	Y
LOUISIANA						
1 **Scalise**	Y	N	Y	N	N	N
2 **Cao**	Y	N	Y	N	N	N
3 Melancon	N	Y	Y	N	N	N
4 **Fleming**	Y	N	Y	N	N	N
5 **Alexander**	Y	N	Y	N	N	N
6 **Cassidy**	Y	N	Y	N	N	Y
7 **Boustany**	Y	N	Y	N	N	N
MAINE						
1 Pingree	N	Y	N	Y	Y	Y
2 Michaud	N	Y	Y	Y	Y	Y
MARYLAND						
1 Kratovil	N	N	Y	N	N	N
2 Ruppersberger	N	Y	Y	N	N	N
3 Sarbanes	N	Y	N	Y	Y	Y
4 Edwards	N	Y	N	Y	Y	Y
5 Hoyer	N	Y	Y	N	N	N
6 **Bartlett**	Y	N	Y	N	N	N
7 Cummings	N	Y	Y	Y	Y	N
8 Van Hollen	N	Y	N	Y	Y	Y
MASSACHUSETTS						
1 Olver	N	Y	N	Y	Y	Y
2 Neal	N	Y	N	Y	N	Y
3 McGovern	N	Y	N	Y	Y	Y
4 Frank	N	Y	N	Y	N	Y
5 Tsongas	N	Y	N	Y	Y	Y
6 Tierney	N	Y	N	Y	Y	Y
7 Markey	N	Y	N	Y	Y	Y
8 Capuano	N	Y	N	Y	N	Y
9 Lynch	N	Y	N	Y	Y	Y
10 Delahunt	N	Y	N	Y	N	Y
MICHIGAN						
1 Stupak	N	Y	N	Y	Y	Y
2 **Hoekstra**	Y	N	Y	N	N	N
3 **Ehlers**	Y	N	Y	N	N	N
4 **Camp**	Y	N	Y	N	N	N
5 Kildee	N	Y	N	Y	Y	Y
6 **Upton**	Y	Y	Y	N	N	N
7 Schauer	N	Y	Y	N	N	N
8 **Rogers**	Y	N	Y	N	N	N
9 Peters	N	N	Y	N	N	N
10 **Miller**	Y	N	Y	N	N	N
11 **McCotter**	Y	Y	Y	N	N	N
12 Levin	N	Y	Y	Y	N	Y
13 Kilpatrick	N	Y	N	Y	N	Y
14 Conyers	N	Y	N	Y	Y	N
15 Dingell	N	Y	N	Y	Y	Y
MINNESOTA						
1 Walz	N	Y	Y	N	N	N
2 **Kline**	Y	N	Y	N	N	N
3 **Paulsen**	Y	N	Y	N	N	N
4 McCollum	N	Y	N	Y	N	Y

	954	955	956	957	958	959
5 Ellison	N	Y	Y	Y	Y	Y
6 **Bachmann**	Y	N	Y	N	N	N
7 Peterson	N	Y	N	N	N	N
8 Oberstar	N	Y	N	Y	N	N
MISSISSIPPI						
1 Childers	N	Y	Y	N	N	N
2 Thompson	N	Y	Y	Y	N	N
3 **Harper**	Y	Y	Y	N	N	N
4 Taylor	N	Y	Y	N	N	N
MISSOURI						
1 Clay	N	Y	N	Y	N	Y
2 **Akin**	Y	N	Y	N	N	N
3 Carnahan	N	Y	Y	Y	N	N
4 Skelton	N	Y	Y	N	N	N
5 Cleaver	N	Y	N	Y	N	Y
6 **Graves**	Y	N	Y	N	N	N
7 **Blunt**	Y	N	Y	N	N	N
8 **Emerson**	Y	Y	Y	N	N	N
9 **Luetkemeyer**	Y	N	Y	N	N	N
MONTANA						
AL **Rehberg**	Y	N	Y	N	N	N
NEBRASKA						
1 **Fortenberry**	Y	Y	Y	N	N	N
2 **Terry**	Y	N	Y	N	N	N
3 **Smith**	Y	N	Y	N	N	N
NEVADA						
1 Berkley	N	Y	Y	Y	N	Y
2 **Heller**	Y	N	Y	N	N	N
3 Titus	N	N	N	Y	Y	Y
NEW HAMPSHIRE						
1 Shea-Porter	N	Y	Y	Y	Y	Y
2 Hodes	N	Y	Y	N	N	Y
NEW JERSEY						
1 Andrews	N	Y	N	Y	Y	Y
2 **LoBiondo**	Y	N	Y	N	N	N
3 Adler	N	N	Y	N	N	N
4 **Smith**	Y	N	Y	N	N	N
5 **Garrett**	Y	N	Y	N	N	N
6 Pallone	N	Y	N	Y	Y	Y
7 **Lance**	Y	N	Y	N	N	N
8 Pascrell	N	Y	N	Y	Y	Y
9 Rothman	N	Y	N	Y	Y	Y
10 Payne	N	Y	N	Y	Y	Y
11 **Frelinghuysen**	Y	N	Y	N	N	N
12 Holt	N	Y	N	Y	N	Y
13 Sires	N	Y	N	Y	Y	Y
NEW MEXICO						
1 Heinrich	N	Y	Y	N	Y	N
2 Teague	Y	N	Y	N	N	N
3 Lujan	N	Y	Y	Y	Y	Y
NEW YORK						
1 Bishop	N	Y	N	Y	N	Y
2 Israel	N	Y	N	Y	Y	Y
3 **King**	Y	N	Y	N	N	N
4 McCarthy	N	N	Y	N	N	N
5 Ackerman	N	Y	N	Y	N	Y
6 Meeks	N	Y	Y	N	N	N
7 Crowley	N	N	Y	N	N	N
8 Nadler	N	Y	N	Y	Y	Y
9 Weiner	N	N	N	N	N	Y
10 Towns	N	Y	Y	N	N	N
11 Clarke	N	Y	N	Y	Y	Y
12 Velázquez	N	Y	N	Y	N	Y
13 McMahon	Y	N	Y	N	N	N
14 Maloney	N	N	Y	Y	N	N
15 Rangel	N	Y	Y	Y	N	Y
16 Serrano	N	Y	N	Y	Y	Y
17 Engel	N	Y	Y	Y	N	Y
18 Lowey	N	Y	N	Y	Y	Y
19 Hall	N	Y	Y	Y	N	Y
20 Murphy	N	N	Y	N	N	N
21 Tonko	N	Y	N	Y	N	Y
22 Hinchey	N	Y	N	Y	Y	Y
23 Owens	N	Y	Y	N	N	N
24 Arcuri	N	Y	Y	N	N	N
25 Maffei	N	N	Y	N	N	N
26 **Lee**	Y	N	Y	N	N	N
27 Higgins	N	Y	Y	N	N	N
28 Slaughter	?	?	?	?	?	?
29 Massa	N	Y	Y	N	N	N
NORTH CAROLINA						
1 Butterfield	N	Y	Y	Y	N	Y
2 Etheridge	N	N	Y	N	N	N
3 **Jones**	Y	Y	Y	N	N	N
4 Price	N	Y	N	Y	N	Y

	954	955	956	957	958	959
5 **Foxx**	Y	N	Y	N	N	N
6 **Coble**	Y	N	Y	N	N	N
7 McIntyre	N	Y	Y	N	N	N
8 Kissell	N	Y	Y	N	N	N
9 **Myrick**	Y	N	Y	N	N	N
10 **McHenry**	Y	N	Y	N	N	N
11 Shuler	N	Y	Y	N	N	N
12 Watt	N	Y	N	Y	N	Y
13 Miller	N	Y	N	Y	N	Y
NORTH DAKOTA						
AL Pomeroy	N	Y	Y	N	N	N
OHIO						
1 Driehaus	N	Y	Y	Y	N	Y
2 **Schmidt**	Y	N	Y	N	N	N
3 **Turner**	Y	N	Y	N	N	N
4 **Jordan**	Y	N	Y	N	N	N
5 **Latta**	Y	N	Y	N	N	N
6 Wilson	N	Y	Y	Y	N	N
7 **Austria**	Y	N	Y	N	N	N
8 **Boehner**	Y	N	Y	N	N	N
9 Kaptur	N	Y	N	Y	Y	Y
10 Kucinich	N	Y	N	Y	Y	Y
11 Fudge	N	Y	N	Y	N	Y
12 **Tiberi**	Y	N	Y	N	N	N
13 Sutton	N	Y	N	Y	Y	Y
14 **LaTourette**	Y	N	Y	N	N	N
15 Kilroy	N	Y	N	Y	N	Y
16 Boccieri	N	Y	Y	N	N	N
17 Ryan	N	Y	N	Y	Y	Y
18 Space	N	Y	Y	N	N	N
OKLAHOMA						
1 **Sullivan**	Y	N	?	N	N	N
2 Boren	N	Y	Y	N	N	N
3 **Lucas**	Y	N	Y	N	N	N
4 **Cole**	Y	N	Y	N	N	N
5 **Fallin**	Y	N	Y	N	N	N
OREGON						
1 Wu	N	Y	N	Y	Y	Y
2 **Walden**	Y	N	Y	N	N	N
3 Blumenauer	N	Y	Y	Y	Y	Y
4 DeFazio	N	Y	Y	Y	Y	Y
5 Schrader	Y	N	Y	Y	N	N
PENNSYLVANIA						
1 Brady	N	Y	N	Y	N	Y
2 Fattah	N	Y	N	Y	N	Y
3 Dahlkemper	N	Y	N	N	N	N
4 Altmire	N	N	Y	N	N	N
5 **Thompson**	Y	N	Y	N	N	N
6 **Gerlach**	Y	Y	Y	N	N	N
7 Sestak	N	Y	N	Y	N	Y
8 Murphy, P.	N	Y	Y	N	Y	Y
9 **Shuster**	Y	N	Y	N	N	N
10 Carney	N	Y	Y	N	N	Y
11 Kanjorski	N	Y	N	Y	N	Y
12 Murtha	?	?	?	?	?	?
13 Schwartz	N	Y	Y	N	N	N
14 Doyle	N	Y	N	Y	Y	Y
15 **Dent**	Y	Y	Y	N	N	N
16 **Pitts**	Y	N	Y	N	N	N
17 Holden	N	Y	Y	N	N	N
18 **Murphy, T.**	Y	N	Y	N	N	N
19 **Platts**	Y	Y	Y	N	N	N
RHODE ISLAND						
1 Kennedy	N	Y	N	Y	Y	Y
2 Langevin	N	Y	N	Y	Y	Y
SOUTH CAROLINA						
1 **Brown**	Y	N	Y	N	N	N
2 **Wilson**	Y	N	Y	N	N	N
3 **Barrett**	?	?	?	?	?	?
4 **Inglis**	Y	Y	Y	N	N	N
5 Spratt	N	Y	Y	Y	N	N
6 Clyburn	N	Y	N	Y	Y	Y
SOUTH DAKOTA						
AL Herseth Sandlin	N	Y	Y	N	N	N
TENNESSEE						
1 **Roe**	Y	N	Y	N	N	N
2 **Duncan**	Y	Y	Y	N	N	N
3 **Wamp**	Y	N	Y	N	N	N
4 Davis	N	N	Y	N	N	N
5 Cooper	N	N	Y	N	N	N
6 Gordon	N	N	Y	N	N	N
7 **Blackburn**	Y	N	Y	N	N	N
8 Tanner	N	N	Y	N	N	N
9 Cohen	N	Y	N	Y	Y	Y

	954	955	956	957	958	959
TEXAS						
1 **Gohmert**	N	Y	Y	N	N	Y
2 **Poe**	Y	N	Y	N	N	N
3 **Johnson, S.**	Y	N	Y	N	N	N
4 **Hall**	Y	N	Y	N	N	Y
5 **Hensarling**	Y	N	Y	N	N	N
6 **Barton**	Y	Y	Y	N	Y	N
7 **Culberson**	Y	N	Y	N	N	N
8 **Brady**	Y	N	Y	N	N	N
9 Green, A.	N	Y	N	Y	N	Y
10 **McCaul**	?	N	Y	N	N	N
11 **Conaway**	Y	N	Y	N	N	N
12 **Granger**	Y	N	Y	N	N	N
13 **Thornberry**	Y	N	Y	N	N	N
14 **Paul**	Y	N	Y	N	N	N
15 Hinojosa	N	Y	N	Y	N	Y
16 Reyes	N	Y	N	Y	N	Y
17 Edwards	N	Y	Y	N	N	N
18 Jackson Lee	N	Y	N	N	N	N
19 **Neugebauer**	Y	N	Y	N	N	N
20 Gonzalez	N	Y	Y	N	N	N
21 **Smith**	Y	N	Y	N	N	N
22 **Olson**	Y	N	Y	N	N	N
23 Rodriguez	N	N	Y	N	N	N
24 **Marchant**	Y	N	Y	N	N	N
25 Doggett	N	Y	N	Y	Y	Y
26 **Burgess**	Y	N	Y	N	N	N
27 Ortiz	N	Y	Y	N	N	N
28 Cuellar	N	Y	Y	N	N	N
29 Green, G.	N	Y	Y	N	N	Y
30 Johnson, E.	N	Y	N	N	N	N
31 **Carter**	Y	N	Y	N	N	N
32 **Sessions**	Y	N	Y	N	N	N
UTAH						
1 **Bishop**	Y	N	Y	N	N	N
2 Matheson	N	N	Y	N	N	N
3 **Chaffetz**	Y	N	Y	N	N	N
VERMONT						
AL Welch	N	Y	N	Y	Y	Y
VIRGINIA						
1 **Wittman**	Y	N	Y	N	N	N
2 Nye	Y	N	Y	N	N	N
3 Scott	N	Y	N	Y	N	Y
4 **Forbes**	Y	N	Y	N	N	N
5 Perriello	N	Y	N	Y	Y	Y
6 **Goodlatte**	Y	N	Y	N	N	N
7 **Cantor**	Y	N	Y	N	N	N
8 Moran	?	?	?	?	?	?
9 Boucher	N	Y	Y	N	N	N
10 **Wolf**	Y	N	Y	N	N	N
11 Connolly	N	N	Y	N	N	N
WASHINGTON						
1 Inslee	N	Y	Y	N	N	Y
2 Larsen	N	N	Y	N	N	N
3 Baird	N	Y	Y	N	N	N
4 **Hastings**	Y	N	Y	N	N	N
5 **McMorris Rodgers**	Y	N	Y	N	N	N
6 Dicks	N	Y	Y	N	N	Y
7 McDermott	N	Y	N	Y	Y	Y
8 **Reichert**	Y	N	Y	N	N	N
9 Smith	N	N	Y	N	N	N
WEST VIRGINIA						
1 Mollohan	N	Y	Y	N	N	N
2 **Capito**	Y	Y	Y	N	N	N
3 Rahall	N	Y	Y	N	N	Y
WISCONSIN						
1 **Ryan**	Y	N	Y	N	N	N
2 Baldwin	?	?	?	?	?	?
3 Kind	N	N	Y	N	N	N
4 Moore	N	Y	N	Y	N	Y
5 **Sensenbrenner**	Y	N	Y	N	N	Y
6 **Petri**	Y	N	Y	N	N	N
7 Obey	N	Y	N	Y	Y	Y
8 Kagen	N	Y	Y	N	N	N
WYOMING						
AL **Lummis**	Y	N	Y	N	N	N
DELEGATES						
Faleomavaega (A.S.)	N	Y	N	Y	Y	Y
Norton (D.C.)	N	Y	N	Y	N	Y
Bordallo (Guam)	?	?	?	?	?	?
Sablan (N. Marianas)	N	Y	N	Y	N	Y
Pierluisi (P.R.)	N	Y	N	Y	Y	Y
Christensen (V.I.)	N	Y	Y	Y	Y	Y

IN THE HOUSE | By Vote Number

960. HR 4173. Financial Industry Regulation Overhaul/External Audit Requirements.
Kanjorski, D-Pa., amendment that would strike provisions in the bill exempting public companies with less than $75 million in market capitalization from the external audit of internal controls required under the Sarbanes-Oxley Act. Rejected in Committee of the Whole 153-271: D 152-101; R 1-170. Dec. 11, 2009.

961. HR 4173. Financial Industry Regulation Overhaul/Credit Rating Agency Exemptions.
McCarthy, R-Calif., amendment that would strike a section of the bill repealing a rule that exempts credit rating agencies registered with the Securities and Exchange Commission from liability as "experts" under the Securities Act. Rejected in Committee of the Whole 166-259: D 4-249; R 162-10. Dec. 11, 2009.

962. HR 4173. Financial Industry Regulation Overhaul/Unrecovered TARP Funds.
Peters, D-Mich., amendment that would authorize the Federal Deposit Insurance Corporation to shift some of the money out of a new Systemic Dissolution Fund to be created in the bill for non-bank financial institutions and use the funds instead to make up shortfalls in repayments to the Troubled Asset Relief Program. Adopted in Committee of the Whole 228-198: D 228-25; R 0-173. Dec. 11, 2009.

963. HR 4173. Financial Industry Regulation Overhaul/Mortgage Loans Modification.
Marshall, D-Ga., amendment that would allow bankruptcy courts to modify the terms of mortgages on primary residences by extending repayment periods, reducing excessive interest rates and fees and adjusting the principal balance to the home's fair market value. It also would authorize the Department of Veterans Affairs, Federal Housing Administration and Rural Housing Service to facilitate mortgage modifications. Rejected in Committee of the Whole 188-241: D 184-71; R 4-170. Dec. 11, 2009.

964. HR 4173. Financial Industry Regulation Overhaul/Reverse Mortgage Transactions.
Schakowsky, D-Ill., amendment that would authorize the director of the Consumer Financial Protection Agency to regulate reverse mortgage transactions within one year of the bill's enactment. Adopted in Committee of the Whole 277-149: D 251-0; R 26-149. Dec. 11, 2009.

965. HR 4173. Financial Industry Regulation Overhaul/Consumer Financial Protection Council.
Minnick, D-Idaho, amendment that would replace the Consumer Financial Protection Agency to be created under the bill with a council of regulators authorized to issue rules on the safety and soundness of financial institutions and products. The council would include the secretaries of Treasury and Housing and Urban Development, the chairman of the Federal Reserve, and the chairmen of the Commodity Futures Trading Commission and the Securities and Exchange Commission. Rejected in Committee of the Whole 208-223: D 33-223; R 175-0. A "nay" was a vote in support of the president's position. Dec. 11, 2009.

966. HR 4173. Financial Industry Regulation Overhaul/Republican Substitute.
Bachus, R-Ala., substitute amendment that would establish a new chapter of the bankruptcy code to resolve certain non-bank financial institutions, create a consumer protection council tasked with developing new consumer protections, regulate over-the-counter financial derivatives markets, address executive compensation, overhaul Fannie Mae and Freddie Mac and create a Federal Insurance Office. It also would require the Treasury Department to approve Federal Reserve emergency lending. Rejected in Committee of the Whole 175-251: D 3-248; R 172-3. Dec. 11, 2009.

	960	961	962	963	964	965	966
ALABAMA							
1 Bonner	N	Y	N	N	N	Y	Y
2 Bright	N	N	Y	N	Y	Y	Y
3 Rogers	N	Y	N	N	N	Y	Y
4 Aderholt	?	Y	N	N	N	Y	Y
5 Griffith	N	N	N	N	Y	Y	Y
6 Bachus	N	Y	N	N	N	Y	Y
7 Davis	N	N	Y	Y	Y	N	N
ALASKA							
AL Young	?	?	?	?	?	?	?
ARIZONA							
1 Kirkpatrick	N	N	Y	Y	Y	Y	N
2 Franks	N	Y	N	N	N	Y	Y
3 Shadegg	N	Y	N	N	N	Y	Y
4 Pastor	Y	N	Y	Y	Y	N	N
5 Mitchell	N	N	Y	N	Y	Y	N
6 Flake	N	Y	N	N	N	Y	Y
7 Grijalva	Y	N	Y	Y	Y	N	N
8 Giffords	Y	N	Y	Y	Y	N	N
ARKANSAS							
1 Berry	N	N	Y	Y	Y	N	N
2 Snyder	N	N	Y	Y	Y	N	N
3 Boozman	N	Y	N	N	N	Y	Y
4 Ross	N	N	N	N	Y	Y	N
CALIFORNIA							
1 Thompson	Y	N	Y	Y	Y	N	N
2 Herger	N	Y	N	N	N	Y	Y
3 Lungren	N	Y	N	N	N	Y	Y
4 McClintock	N	Y	N	N	N	Y	Y
5 Matsui	Y	N	Y	Y	Y	N	N
6 Woolsey	Y	N	Y	Y	Y	N	N
7 Miller, George	Y	N	Y	Y	Y	N	N
8 Pelosi					N		
9 Lee	Y	N	Y	Y	Y	N	N
10 Garamendi	Y	N	Y	Y	Y	N	N
11 McNerney	N	N	Y	Y	Y	N	N
12 Speier	Y	Y	Y	Y	Y	N	N
13 Stark	Y	N	Y	Y	Y	N	N
14 Eshoo	Y	N	Y	Y	Y	N	N
15 Honda	N	N	Y	Y	Y	N	N
16 Lofgren	+	-	+	+	+	-	-
17 Farr	Y	N	Y	Y	Y	N	N
18 Cardoza	N	N	N	Y	Y	N	N
19 Radanovich	?	?	?	N	N	Y	Y
20 Costa	N	N	N	Y	Y	N	N
21 Nunes	N	Y	N	N	N	Y	Y
22 McCarthy	N	Y	N	N	N	Y	Y
23 Capps	Y	N	Y	Y	Y	N	N
24 Gallegly	N	Y	N	N	N	Y	Y
25 McKeon	N	Y	N	N	N	Y	Y
26 Dreier	N	Y	N	N	N	Y	Y
27 Sherman	Y	Y	Y	Y	Y	N	N
28 Berman	Y	N	Y	Y	Y	N	N
29 Schiff	Y	N	Y	Y	Y	N	N
30 Waxman	Y	N	Y	Y	Y	N	N
31 Becerra	Y	N	Y	Y	Y	N	N
32 Chu	Y	N	Y	Y	Y	N	N
33 Watson	Y	N	Y	Y	Y	N	N
34 Roybal-Allard	Y	N	Y	Y	Y	N	N
35 Waters	Y	N	Y	Y	?	N	N
36 Harman	Y	N	N	Y	Y	N	N
37 Richardson	N	N	Y	Y	Y	N	N
38 Napolitano	Y	N	Y	Y	Y	N	N
39 Sánchez, Linda	Y	N	Y	Y	Y	N	N
40 Royce	N	Y	N	N	N	Y	Y
41 Lewis	N	Y	N	N	N	Y	Y
42 Miller, Gary	N	Y	N	N	N	Y	Y
43 Baca	N	N	Y	Y	Y	N	N
44 Calvert	N	Y	N	N	N	Y	N
45 Bono Mack	N	Y	N	N	N	Y	Y
46 Rohrabacher	N	Y	N	N	N	Y	Y
47 Sanchez, Loretta	N	N	Y	Y	Y	N	N
48 Campbell	N	Y	N	N	N	Y	Y
49 Issa	N	Y	N	N	N	Y	Y
50 Bilbray	N	Y	N	N	Y	Y	Y
51 Filner	?	N	Y	Y	Y	N	N
52 Hunter	N	Y	N	N	N	Y	Y
53 Davis	Y	N	Y	Y	Y	N	N
COLORADO							
1 DeGette	Y	N	Y	Y	Y	N	N
2 Polis	N	N	N	N	Y	N	N
3 Salazar	N	N	Y	Y	Y	N	N
4 Markey	N	N	Y	N	Y	Y	N
5 Lamborn	N	Y	N	N	N	Y	Y
6 Coffman	N	Y	N	N	N	Y	Y
7 Perlmutter	Y	N	Y	Y	Y	N	N
CONNECTICUT							
1 Larson	Y	N	Y	Y	Y	N	N
2 Courtney	Y	N	Y	Y	Y	N	N
3 DeLauro	Y	N	Y	Y	Y	N	N
4 Himes	Y	N	Y	Y	Y	N	N
5 Murphy	Y	N	Y	Y	Y	N	?
DELAWARE							
AL Castle	N	Y	N	N	Y	Y	Y
FLORIDA							
1 Miller	N	Y	N	N	N	Y	Y
2 Boyd	N	N	Y	N	Y	Y	N
3 Brown	Y	N	Y	Y	Y	N	N
4 Crenshaw	N	Y	N	N	N	Y	Y
5 Brown-Waite	N	N	N	N	Y	Y	Y
6 Stearns	N	N	N	N	N	Y	Y
7 Mica	N	Y	N	N	N	Y	Y
8 Grayson	Y	N	Y	Y	Y	N	N
9 Bilirakis	N	Y	N	N	N	Y	Y
10 Young	N	N	N	N	N	Y	Y
11 Castor	Y	N	Y	Y	Y	N	N
12 Putnam	N	Y	N	N	N	Y	Y
13 Buchanan	N	Y	N	N	N	Y	Y
14 Mack	N	Y	N	N	N	Y	Y
15 Posey	N	Y	N	N	N	Y	Y
16 Rooney	N	Y	N	N	N	Y	Y
17 Meek	Y	N	Y	Y	Y	N	N
18 Ros-Lehtinen	N	Y	N	Y	Y	Y	N
19 Wexler	?	?	?	Y	Y	N	N
20 Wasserman Schultz	Y	N	Y	Y	Y	N	N
21 Diaz-Balart, L.	N	N	N	?	Y	Y	N
22 Klein	Y	N	Y	Y	Y	N	N
23 Hastings	Y	N	Y	Y	Y	N	N
24 Kosmas	N	N	Y	N	Y	Y	N
25 Diaz-Balart, M.	N	N	N	N	Y	Y	Y
GEORGIA							
1 Kingston	N	Y	N	N	N	Y	Y
2 Bishop	N	N	Y	N	Y	Y	N
3 Westmoreland	N	Y	N	N	N	Y	Y
4 Johnson	Y	N	Y	Y	Y	N	N
5 Lewis	Y	N	Y	Y	Y	N	N
6 Price	N	Y	N	N	N	Y	Y
7 Linder	N	Y	N	N	N	Y	Y
8 Marshall	N	N	Y	Y	Y	N	N
9 Deal	N	Y	N	N	N	Y	Y
10 Broun	N	Y	N	N	N	Y	Y
11 Gingrey	N	Y	N	N	N	Y	Y
12 Barrow	N	N	N	Y	Y	Y	N
13 Scott	Y	N	Y	N	Y	N	N
HAWAII							
1 Abercrombie	Y	N	Y	Y	Y	N	N
2 Hirono	Y	N	Y	Y	Y	N	N
IDAHO							
1 Minnick	N	N	Y	N	Y	Y	N
2 Simpson	N	Y	N	N	N	Y	Y
ILLINOIS							
1 Rush	N	N	Y	Y	Y	N	N
2 Jackson	Y	N	Y	Y	Y	N	N
3 Lipinski	Y	N	Y	Y	Y	N	N
4 Gutierrez	Y	N	Y	Y	Y	N	N
5 Quigley	N	N	Y	Y	Y	N	N
6 Roskam	N	Y	N	N	N	Y	Y
7 Davis	Y	N	Y	Y	Y	N	N
8 Bean	N	N	Y	Y	Y	N	N
9 Schakowsky	Y	N	Y	Y	Y	N	N
10 Kirk	N	?	N	N	Y	Y	Y
11 Halvorson	N	N	Y	Y	Y	N	N
12 Costello	N	N	Y	Y	Y	N	N
13 Biggert	N	Y	N	N	Y	Y	N
14 Foster	N	N	Y	Y	Y	N	N
15 Johnson	N	N	N	N	N	Y	Y

KEY Republicans Democrats

Y Voted for (yea)	X Paired against	C Voted "present" to avoid possible conflict of interest
# Paired for	- Announced against	
+ Announced for	P Voted "present"	? Did not vote or otherwise make a position known
N Voted against (nay)		

	960	961	962	963	964	965	966
16 **Manzullo**	N	Y	N	N	N	Y	Y
17 Hare	Y	N	Y	Y	Y	N	N
18 **Schock**	N	Y	N	N	N	Y	Y
19 **Shimkus**	N	Y	N	N	N	Y	Y
INDIANA							
1 Visclosky	N	N	N	Y	Y	N	N
2 Donnelly	N	N	Y	N	Y	N	N
3 **Souder**	N	N	N	N	N	Y	Y
4 **Buyer**	N	Y	N	N	N	Y	Y
5 **Burton**	N	Y	N	N	N	Y	Y
6 **Pence**	N	Y	N	N	N	Y	Y
7 Carson	Y	N	Y	Y	Y	N	N
8 Ellsworth	N	N	Y	N	Y	N	N
9 Hill	N	N	Y	N	Y	Y	N
IOWA							
1 Braley	Y	N	Y	Y	Y	N	N
2 Loebsack	Y	N	Y	Y	Y	N	N
3 Boswell	Y	N	Y	N	Y	N	N
4 **Latham**	N	Y	N	N	Y	Y	Y
5 **King**	N	Y	N	N	N	Y	Y
KANSAS							
1 **Moran**	N	Y	N	N	N	Y	Y
2 **Jenkins**	N	Y	N	N	N	Y	Y
3 Moore	Y	N	Y	Y	Y	N	N
4 **Tiahrt**	N	Y	N	N	N	Y	Y
KENTUCKY							
1 **Whitfield**	N	Y	N	N	N	Y	Y
2 **Guthrie**	N	Y	N	N	N	Y	Y
3 Yarmuth	Y	N	Y	Y	Y	N	N
4 **Davis**	N	Y	N	N	N	Y	Y
5 **Rogers**	N	Y	N	N	N	Y	Y
6 Chandler	N	N	Y	N	Y	Y	N
LOUISIANA							
1 **Scalise**	N	Y	N	N	N	Y	Y
2 **Cao**	N	Y	N	N	Y	Y	Y
3 Melancon	N	N	Y	N	Y	Y	N
4 **Fleming**	N	Y	N	N	N	Y	Y
5 **Alexander**	N	Y	N	N	N	Y	Y
6 **Cassidy**	N	Y	N	N	N	Y	Y
7 **Boustany**	N	Y	N	N	N	Y	Y
MAINE							
1 Pingree	Y	N	Y	Y	Y	N	N
2 Michaud	Y	N	Y	Y	Y	N	N
MARYLAND							
1 Kratovil	Y	N	N	N	Y	Y	N
2 Ruppersberger	N	N	Y	Y	Y	N	N
3 Sarbanes	Y	N	Y	Y	Y	N	N
4 Edwards	Y	N	Y	Y	Y	N	N
5 Hoyer	Y	N	Y	Y	Y	N	N
6 **Bartlett**	N	Y	N	N	N	Y	Y
7 Cummings	Y	N	Y	Y	Y	N	N
8 Van Hollen	Y	N	Y	Y	Y	N	N
MASSACHUSETTS							
1 Olver	Y	N	Y	Y	Y	N	N
2 Neal	N	N	Y	Y	Y	N	N
3 McGovern	Y	N	Y	Y	Y	N	N
4 Frank	Y	N	Y	Y	Y	N	N
5 Tsongas	Y	N	Y	Y	Y	N	N
6 Tierney	Y	N	Y	Y	Y	N	N
7 Markey	Y	N	Y	Y	Y	N	N
8 Capuano	Y	N	Y	Y	Y	N	N
9 Lynch	Y	N	Y	Y	Y	N	N
10 Delahunt	Y	N	Y	Y	Y	N	N
MICHIGAN							
1 Stupak	N	N	Y	N	Y	N	N
2 **Hoekstra**	N	Y	N	N	N	Y	Y
3 **Ehlers**	N	Y	N	N	N	Y	Y
4 **Camp**	N	Y	N	N	N	Y	Y
5 Kildee	Y	N	Y	Y	Y	N	N
6 **Upton**	N	Y	N	N	Y	Y	Y
7 Schauer	N	N	Y	Y	Y	N	N
8 **Rogers**	N	Y	N	N	Y	Y	Y
9 Peters	N	N	Y	Y	Y	N	N
10 **Miller**	N	Y	N	N	N	Y	Y
11 **McCotter**	N	Y	N	N	N	Y	Y
12 Levin	Y	N	Y	Y	Y	N	N
13 Kilpatrick	Y	N	Y	Y	?	N	N
14 Conyers	Y	N	Y	Y	Y	N	N
15 Dingell	Y	N	Y	Y	Y	N	N
MINNESOTA							
1 Walz	N	N	Y	N	Y	N	N
2 **Kline**	N	Y	N	N	N	Y	Y
3 **Paulsen**	N	Y	N	N	Y	Y	Y
4 McCollum	N	N	Y	Y	Y	N	N
5 Ellison	Y	N	Y	Y	Y	N	N
6 **Bachmann**	?	Y	N	N	N	Y	Y
7 Peterson	N	N	N	N	Y	N	N
8 Oberstar	Y	N	Y	Y	Y	N	?
MISSISSIPPI							
1 Childers	N	N	Y	N	Y	Y	N
2 Thompson	Y	N	Y	Y	Y	N	N
3 **Harper**	N	Y	N	N	N	Y	Y
4 Taylor	Y	N	N	Y	Y	Y	N
MISSOURI							
1 Clay	Y	N	Y	Y	Y	N	N
2 **Akin**	N	Y	N	N	N	Y	Y
3 Carnahan	N	N	Y	Y	Y	N	N
4 Skelton	N	N	Y	N	Y	Y	N
5 Cleaver	Y	N	Y	Y	Y	N	N
6 **Graves**	N	Y	N	N	N	Y	Y
7 **Blunt**	N	Y	N	N	N	Y	Y
8 **Emerson**	N	Y	N	N	Y	Y	Y
9 **Luetkemeyer**	N	Y	N	N	N	Y	Y
MONTANA							
AL **Rehberg**	N	Y	N	N	N	Y	Y
NEBRASKA							
1 **Fortenberry**	N	N	N	N	Y	Y	Y
2 **Terry**	N	Y	N	N	N	Y	Y
3 **Smith**	N	Y	N	N	N	Y	Y
NEVADA							
1 Berkley	Y	N	Y	Y	Y	N	N
2 **Heller**	N	Y	N	N	N	Y	Y
3 Titus	N	N	Y	Y	Y	N	N
NEW HAMPSHIRE							
1 Shea-Porter	Y	N	Y	Y	Y	N	N
2 Hodes	Y	N	Y	Y	Y	N	N
NEW JERSEY							
1 Andrews	Y	N	Y	Y	Y	N	N
2 **LoBiondo**	N	Y	N	N	Y	Y	Y
3 Adler	N	N	Y	Y	Y	N	N
4 **Smith**	N	Y	N	N	Y	Y	Y
5 **Garrett**	N	Y	N	N	N	Y	Y
6 Pallone	Y	N	Y	Y	Y	N	N
7 **Lance**	N	Y	N	N	Y	Y	Y
8 Pascrell	Y	N	Y	Y	Y	N	N
9 Rothman	Y	N	Y	Y	Y	N	N
10 Payne	Y	N	Y	Y	Y	N	N
11 **Frelinghuysen**	N	Y	N	N	N	Y	Y
12 Holt	Y	N	Y	Y	Y	N	N
13 Sires	Y	N	Y	Y	Y	N	N
NEW MEXICO							
1 Heinrich	N	N	Y	Y	Y	N	N
2 Teague	N	N	Y	N	Y	Y	N
3 Lujan	N	N	Y	Y	Y	N	N
NEW YORK							
1 Bishop	Y	N	Y	Y	Y	N	N
2 Israel	Y	N	Y	Y	Y	N	N
3 **King**	N	Y	N	N	N	Y	Y
4 McCarthy	N	N	Y	Y	Y	N	N
5 Ackerman	Y	N	Y	Y	Y	N	Y
6 Meeks	N	N	Y	Y	Y	N	N
7 Crowley	Y	N	Y	Y	Y	N	N
8 Nadler	Y	N	Y	Y	Y	N	N
9 Weiner	Y	N	Y	Y	Y	N	N
10 Towns	Y	N	Y	Y	Y	N	N
11 Clarke	Y	N	Y	Y	Y	N	N
12 Velázquez	N	N	Y	Y	Y	N	N
13 McMahon	N	Y	N	N	Y	N	N
14 Maloney	Y	N	Y	Y	Y	N	N
15 Rangel	Y	N	Y	Y	?	N	N
16 Serrano	Y	N	Y	Y	Y	N	N
17 Engel	Y	N	Y	Y	Y	N	N
18 Lowey	Y	N	Y	Y	Y	N	N
19 Hall	N	N	Y	Y	Y	N	N
20 Murphy	N	N	N	N	Y	N	N
21 Tonko	Y	N	Y	Y	Y	N	N
22 Hinchey	Y	N	Y	Y	Y	N	N
23 Owens	N	N	Y	N	Y	N	N
24 Arcuri	N	N	N	N	Y	N	N
25 Maffei	N	N	N	Y	Y	N	N
26 **Lee**	N	Y	N	N	N	Y	Y
27 Higgins	Y	?	Y	Y	Y	N	N
28 Slaughter	?	?	?	?	?	?	?
29 Massa	Y	N	Y	N	Y	Y	N
NORTH CAROLINA							
1 Butterfield	Y	N	Y	Y	Y	N	N
2 Etheridge	N	N	N	Y	Y	N	N
3 **Jones**	N	N	N	Y	N	Y	Y
4 Price	Y	N	Y	Y	Y	N	N
5 **Foxx**	N	Y	N	N	N	Y	Y
6 **Coble**	N	Y	N	N	N	Y	Y
7 McIntyre	N	N	Y	N	Y	Y	?
8 Kissell	N	N	Y	N	Y	N	N
9 **Myrick**	N	Y	N	N	N	Y	Y
10 **McHenry**	N	Y	N	N	N	Y	Y
11 Shuler	N	Y	Y	N	Y	Y	N
12 Watt	Y	N	Y	Y	Y	N	N
13 Miller	Y	N	Y	Y	Y	N	N
NORTH DAKOTA							
AL Pomeroy	N	N	Y	N	Y	N	N
OHIO							
1 Driehaus	N	N	Y	N	Y	N	N
2 **Schmidt**	N	Y	N	N	N	Y	Y
3 **Turner**	N	Y	N	Y	N	Y	Y
4 **Jordan**	N	Y	N	N	N	Y	Y
5 **Latta**	N	Y	N	N	N	Y	Y
6 Wilson	Y	N	Y	N	Y	N	N
7 **Austria**	N	Y	N	N	N	Y	Y
8 **Boehner**	N	Y	N	N	N	Y	Y
9 Kaptur	Y	N	Y	Y	Y	N	N
10 Kucinich	Y	N	Y	Y	Y	N	N
11 Fudge	Y	N	Y	Y	Y	N	N
12 **Tiberi**	N	Y	N	N	N	Y	Y
13 Sutton	Y	N	Y	Y	Y	N	N
14 **LaTourette**	N	Y	N	N	N	Y	Y
15 Kilroy	Y	N	Y	Y	Y	N	N
16 Boccieri	N	N	Y	N	Y	N	N
17 Ryan	N	N	Y	Y	Y	N	N
18 Space	N	N	Y	N	Y	Y	N
OKLAHOMA							
1 **Sullivan**	N	Y	N	N	N	Y	Y
2 Boren	N	N	N	N	Y	Y	N
3 **Lucas**	N	Y	N	N	N	Y	Y
4 **Cole**	N	Y	N	N	N	Y	Y
5 **Fallin**	N	Y	N	N	N	Y	Y
OREGON							
1 Wu	Y	N	Y	Y	Y	N	N
2 **Walden**	N	Y	N	N	N	Y	Y
3 Blumenauer	Y	N	Y	Y	Y	N	N
4 DeFazio	Y	N	Y	Y	Y	N	N
5 Schrader	N	N	Y	N	Y	N	N
PENNSYLVANIA							
1 Brady	Y	N	Y	Y	Y	N	N
2 Fattah	Y	N	Y	Y	Y	N	N
3 Dahlkemper	Y	N	Y	N	Y	N	N
4 Altmire	N	N	Y	N	Y	N	N
5 **Thompson**	N	Y	N	N	N	Y	Y
6 **Gerlach**	N	Y	N	N	N	Y	Y
7 Sestak	Y	N	Y	Y	Y	N	N
8 Murphy, P.	Y	N	Y	Y	Y	N	N
9 **Shuster**	N	Y	N	N	N	Y	Y
10 Carney	N	N	Y	N	Y	N	N
11 Kanjorski	N	N	Y	Y	Y	N	N
12 Murtha	?	?	?	?	?	?	?
13 Schwartz	N	N	Y	Y	Y	N	N
14 Doyle	Y	N	Y	Y	Y	N	N
15 **Dent**	N	Y	N	N	N	Y	Y
16 **Pitts**	N	Y	N	N	N	Y	Y
17 Holden	N	N	Y	N	Y	N	N
18 **Murphy, T.**	N	Y	N	N	N	Y	Y
19 **Platts**	N	Y	N	N	Y	Y	Y
RHODE ISLAND							
1 Kennedy	Y	N	Y	Y	Y	N	N
2 Langevin	Y	N	Y	Y	Y	N	N
SOUTH CAROLINA							
1 **Brown**	N	Y	N	N	N	Y	Y
2 **Wilson**	N	Y	N	N	N	Y	Y
3 **Barrett**	–	+	–	N	N	Y	Y
4 **Inglis**	N	Y	N	N	N	Y	Y
5 Spratt	N	N	N	N	Y	N	N
6 Clyburn	Y	N	Y	Y	?	N	N
SOUTH DAKOTA							
AL Herseth Sandlin	N	N	Y	N	Y	Y	N
TENNESSEE							
1 **Roe**	N	Y	N	N	N	Y	Y
2 **Duncan**	N	Y	N	N	N	Y	Y
3 **Wamp**	N	Y	N	N	Y	Y	Y
4 Davis	N	N	N	N	Y	Y	N
5 Cooper	N	N	N	Y	Y	N	N
6 Gordon	N	N	N	N	Y	N	N
7 **Blackburn**	N	Y	N	N	N	Y	Y
8 Tanner	N	N	Y	N	Y	N	N
9 Cohen	Y	Y	Y	Y	Y	N	N
TEXAS							
1 **Gohmert**	N	N	N	N	N	Y	Y
2 **Poe**	N	Y	N	N	N	Y	Y
3 **Johnson, S.**	N	Y	N	N	N	Y	Y
4 **Hall**	N	Y	N	N	N	Y	Y
5 **Hensarling**	N	Y	N	N	N	Y	Y
6 **Barton**	N	Y	N	N	N	Y	Y
7 **Culberson**	N	Y	N	N	N	Y	Y
8 **Brady**	N	Y	N	N	N	Y	Y
9 Green, A.	Y	N	?	Y	Y	N	N
10 **McCaul**	N	Y	N	N	N	Y	Y
11 **Conaway**	Y	Y	N	N	N	Y	Y
12 **Granger**	N	Y	N	N	N	Y	Y
13 **Thornberry**	N	Y	N	N	N	Y	Y
14 **Paul**	N	Y	N	Y	N	Y	Y
15 Hinojosa	N	N	Y	Y	Y	N	N
16 Reyes	Y	N	Y	N	Y	N	N
17 Edwards	N	N	Y	N	Y	N	N
18 Jackson Lee	Y	N	Y	Y	Y	N	N
19 **Neugebauer**	N	Y	N	N	N	Y	Y
20 Gonzalez	Y	N	Y	Y	Y	N	N
21 **Smith**	N	Y	N	N	N	Y	Y
22 **Olson**	N	Y	N	N	N	Y	Y
23 Rodriguez	Y	N	Y	N	Y	Y	N
24 **Marchant**	N	Y	N	N	N	Y	Y
25 Doggett	Y	N	Y	Y	Y	N	N
26 **Burgess**	N	Y	N	N	N	Y	Y
27 Ortiz	N	N	Y	N	Y	Y	N
28 Cuellar	N	N	Y	N	Y	Y	N
29 Green, G.	Y	N	Y	Y	Y	N	N
30 Johnson, E.	Y	N	Y	Y	Y	N	N
31 **Carter**	N	Y	N	N	N	Y	Y
32 **Sessions**	?	?	?	?	?	?	?
UTAH							
1 **Bishop**	N	Y	N	N	N	Y	Y
2 Matheson	N	N	Y	N	Y	Y	N
3 **Chaffetz**	N	Y	N	N	N	Y	Y
VERMONT							
AL Welch	Y	N	Y	Y	Y	N	N
VIRGINIA							
1 **Wittman**	N	Y	N	N	N	Y	Y
2 Nye	N	N	N	N	Y	N	N
3 Scott	N	N	Y	Y	Y	N	N
4 **Forbes**	N	Y	N	N	N	Y	Y
5 Perriello	N	N	Y	N	Y	N	N
6 **Goodlatte**	N	Y	N	N	N	Y	Y
7 **Cantor**	N	Y	N	N	N	Y	Y
8 Moran	?	?	?	?	?	?	?
9 Boucher	N	N	Y	N	Y	Y	N
10 **Wolf**	N	Y	N	N	N	Y	Y
11 Connolly	N	N	Y	N	Y	N	N
WASHINGTON							
1 Inslee	N	N	Y	Y	Y	N	N
2 Larsen	N	N	Y	N	Y	N	N
3 Baird	N	N	Y	Y	Y	N	N
4 **Hastings**	N	Y	N	N	N	Y	Y
5 **McMorris Rodgers**	N	Y	N	N	N	Y	Y
6 Dicks	N	N	Y	Y	Y	N	N
7 McDermott	Y	N	Y	Y	Y	N	N
8 **Reichert**	N	Y	N	N	N	Y	Y
9 Smith	N	N	N	N	Y	N	N
WEST VIRGINIA							
1 Mollohan	N	N	Y	N	Y	N	N
2 **Capito**	N	Y	N	N	Y	Y	Y
3 Rahall	Y	N	Y	N	Y	N	N
WISCONSIN							
1 **Ryan**	N	Y	N	N	N	Y	Y
2 Baldwin	?	?	?	?	?	?	?
3 Kind	N	N	N	N	Y	N	N
4 Moore	Y	N	N	Y	Y	N	N
5 **Sensenbrenner**	N	Y	N	N	N	Y	Y
6 **Petri**	N	Y	N	N	Y	Y	Y
7 Obey	Y	N	Y	Y	Y	N	N
8 Kagen	N	N	Y	Y	Y	N	N
WYOMING							
AL **Lummis**	N	Y	N	N	N	Y	Y
DELEGATES							
Faleomavaega (A.S.)	?	?	?	Y	Y	N	N
Norton (D.C.)	Y	N	Y	+	+	–	–
Bordallo (Guam)	?	?	?	?	?	?	?
Sablan (N. Marianas)	N	N	Y	Y	Y	N	N
Pierluisi (P.R.)	?	?	?	?	?	?	?
Christensen (V.I.)	Y	N	Y	Y	Y	N	N

IN THE HOUSE | By Vote Number

967. **HR 4173. Financial Industry Regulation Overhaul/Recommit.**
Dent, R-Pa., motion to recommit the bill to the House Financial Services Committee with instructions that it be reported back immediately with an amendment that would repeal the Troubled Asset Relief Program and lower the national debt limit. Motion rejected 190-232: D 19-232; R 171-0. Dec. 11, 2009.

968. **HR 4173. Financial Industry Regulation Overhaul/Passage.**
Passage of the bill that would overhaul federal regulation of the financial services industry. It would establish a process for dissolving failing financial institutions that pose risks to the entire financial system and create a Consumer Financial Protection Agency. It would regulate the financial derivatives market, require registration of all credit rating firms, strengthen investor protections and require a registry of private capital investment advisers. As amended, the bill would set national mortgage standards, allow the Office of the Comptroller of the Currency to over-rule state consumer finance laws if they impair national bank business and authorize the use of $4 billion of Troubled Asset Relief Program funds for housing relief. Passed 223-202: D 223-27; R 0-175. A "yea" was a vote in support of the president's position. Dec. 11, 2009.

969. **H Res 779. Runaway Youth Prevention/Adoption.** Lynch, D-Mass., motion to suspend the rules and adopt the resolution that would recognize the importance of youth runaway prevention. Motion agreed to 341-0: D 202-0; R 139-0. A two-thirds majority of those present and voting (228 in this case) is required for adoption under suspension of the rules. Dec. 14, 2009.

970. **H Res 942. Real Salt Lake Soccer Cup Win/Adoption.** Lynch, D-Mass., motion to suspend the rules and adopt the resolution that would commend the Real Salt Lake soccer club for winning the 2009 Major League Soccer cup, the first in the franchise's history. Motion agreed to 347-0: D 208-0; R 139-0. A two-thirds majority of those present and voting (232 in this case) is required for adoption under suspension of the rules. Dec. 14, 2009.

971. **H Res 894. 50th Anniversary of 'Kind of Blue'/Adoption.** Conyers, D-Mich., motion to suspend the rules and adopt the resolution that would recognize the 50th anniversary of the recording of the album "Kind of Blue" and the national importance of jazz. Motion agreed to 409-0: D 244-0; R 165-0. A two-thirds majority of those present and voting (273 in this case) is required for adoption under suspension of the rules. Dec. 15, 2009.

972. **HR 1517. Permanent U.S. Customs and Border Protection Appointments/Passage.** Cuellar, D-Texas, motion to suspend the rules and pass the bill that would authorize the commissioner of U.S. Customs and Border Protection to convert employees serving a limited overseas appointment to a permanent position if they have successfully completed two years of service. Motion agreed to 414-1: D 248-0; R 166-1. A two-thirds majority of those present and voting (277 in this case) is required for passage under suspension of the rules. Dec. 15, 2009.

973. **HR 3978. Terrorism Preparedness Gifts/Passage.** Cuellar, D-Texas, motion to suspend the rules and pass the bill that would authorize the secretary of Homeland Security to accept gifts of property or services related to terrorism preparedness and response. It also would require the secretary to submit an annual report to Congress on gifts received by the agency. Motion agreed to 413-1: D 249-0; R 164-1. A two-thirds majority of those present and voting (276 in this case) is required for passage under suspension of the rules. Dec. 15, 2009.

	967	968	969	970	971	972	973
ALABAMA							
1 Bonner	Y	N	?	?	?	?	?
2 Bright	Y	N	Y	Y	Y	Y	Y
3 Rogers	Y	N	Y	Y	Y	Y	Y
4 Aderholt	Y	N	Y	Y	Y	Y	Y
5 Griffith	Y	N	Y	Y	Y	Y	Y
6 Bachus	Y	N	Y	Y	Y	Y	Y
7 Davis	N	Y	?	?	Y	Y	Y
ALASKA							
AL Young	?	?	?	?	Y	Y	Y
ARIZONA							
1 Kirkpatrick	Y	N	?	?	Y	Y	Y
2 Franks	Y	N	Y	Y	Y	Y	Y
3 Shadegg	Y	N	Y	Y	Y	Y	Y
4 Pastor	N	Y	Y	Y	Y	Y	Y
5 Mitchell	Y	N	Y	Y	Y	Y	Y
6 Flake	Y	N	Y	Y	Y	Y	Y
7 Grijalva	N	Y	?	?	Y	Y	Y
8 Giffords	Y	Y	Y	Y	Y	Y	Y
ARKANSAS							
1 Berry	N	N	Y	Y	Y	Y	Y
2 Snyder	N	Y	Y	Y	Y	Y	Y
3 Boozman	Y	N	Y	Y	Y	Y	Y
4 Ross	N	N	Y	Y	Y	Y	Y
CALIFORNIA							
1 Thompson	N	Y	+	+	Y	Y	Y
2 Herger	Y	N	Y	Y	?	Y	Y
3 Lungren	Y	N	Y	Y	Y	Y	Y
4 McClintock	Y	N	Y	Y	Y	Y	Y
5 Matsui	N	Y	Y	Y	Y	Y	Y
6 Woolsey	N	Y	Y	Y	Y	Y	Y
7 Miller, George	N	Y	?	Y	Y	Y	Y
8 Pelosi							
9 Lee	N	Y	Y	Y	Y	Y	Y
10 Garamendi	N	Y	Y	Y	Y	Y	Y
11 McNerney	N	Y	Y	Y	Y	Y	Y
12 Speier	N	Y	Y	Y	Y	Y	Y
13 Stark	N	Y	?	Y	Y	Y	Y
14 Eshoo	N	Y	+	+	Y	Y	Y
15 Honda	N	Y	Y	Y	Y	Y	Y
16 Lofgren	–	+	Y	Y	Y	Y	Y
17 Farr	N	Y	Y	Y	Y	Y	Y
18 Cardoza	N	Y	Y	Y	Y	Y	Y
19 Radanovich	Y	N	?	?	?	?	?
20 Costa	N	Y	?	Y	Y	Y	Y
21 Nunes	Y	N	Y	Y	Y	Y	Y
22 McCarthy	Y	N	Y	Y	Y	Y	Y
23 Capps	N	Y	Y	Y	Y	Y	Y
24 Gallegly	Y	N	Y	Y	Y	Y	Y
25 McKeon	Y	N	Y	Y	Y	Y	Y
26 Dreier	Y	N	Y	Y	Y	Y	Y
27 Sherman	N	Y	Y	Y	Y	Y	Y
28 Berman	N	Y	?	Y	Y	Y	Y
29 Schiff	N	Y	Y	Y	Y	Y	Y
30 Waxman	N	Y	Y	Y	Y	Y	Y
31 Becerra	N	Y	Y	Y	Y	Y	Y
32 Chu	N	Y	?	Y	Y	Y	Y
33 Watson	N	Y	Y	Y	Y	Y	Y
34 Roybal-Allard	N	Y	Y	Y	Y	Y	Y
35 Waters	N	Y	Y	Y	Y	Y	Y
36 Harman	N	Y	Y	Y	Y	Y	Y
37 Richardson	N	Y	?	Y	Y	Y	Y
38 Napolitano	N	Y	Y	Y	Y	Y	Y
39 Sánchez, Linda	N	Y	Y	Y	Y	Y	Y
40 Royce	Y	N	Y	Y	Y	Y	Y
41 Lewis	Y	N	Y	Y	Y	Y	Y
42 Miller, Gary	Y	N	Y	Y	Y	Y	Y
43 Baca	N	Y	Y	Y	Y	Y	Y
44 Calvert	Y	N	Y	Y	Y	Y	Y
45 Bono Mack	Y	N	?	?	Y	Y	Y
46 Rohrabacher	Y	N	?	?	Y	Y	Y
47 Sanchez, Loretta	N	Y	?	?	?	?	?
48 Campbell	Y	N	Y	Y	Y	Y	Y
49 Issa	Y	N	Y	Y	Y	Y	Y
50 Bilbray	Y	N	Y	Y	Y	Y	Y
51 Filner	N	Y	Y	Y	Y	Y	Y
52 Hunter	Y	N	Y	Y	Y	Y	Y
53 Davis	N	Y	Y	Y	Y	Y	Y
COLORADO							
1 DeGette	N	Y	Y	Y	Y	Y	Y
2 Polis	N	Y	Y	Y	Y	Y	Y
3 Salazar	N	Y	Y	Y	?	?	?
4 Markey	N	Y	Y	Y	Y	Y	Y
5 Lamborn	Y	N	Y	Y	Y	Y	Y
6 Coffman	Y	N	Y	Y	Y	Y	Y
7 Perlmutter	N	Y	Y	Y	Y	Y	Y
CONNECTICUT							
1 Larson	N	Y	?	Y	Y	Y	Y
2 Courtney	N	Y	Y	Y	Y	Y	Y
3 DeLauro	N	Y	?	Y	Y	Y	Y
4 Himes	N	Y	Y	Y	Y	Y	Y
5 Murphy	N	Y	Y	Y	Y	Y	Y
DELAWARE							
AL Castle	Y	N	Y	Y	Y	Y	Y
FLORIDA							
1 Miller	Y	N	Y	Y	Y	Y	Y
2 Boyd	N	Y	Y	Y	Y	Y	Y
3 Brown	N	Y	Y	Y	Y	Y	Y
4 Crenshaw	Y	N	Y	Y	Y	Y	Y
5 Brown-Waite	Y	N	Y	Y	Y	Y	Y
6 Stearns	Y	N	Y	Y	Y	Y	Y
7 Mica	?	N	+	+	Y	Y	Y
8 Grayson	N	Y	?	Y	Y	Y	Y
9 Bilirakis	Y	N	Y	Y	Y	Y	Y
10 Young	Y	N	?	?	?	?	?
11 Castor	N	Y	Y	Y	Y	Y	Y
12 Putnam	Y	N	Y	Y	Y	Y	Y
13 Buchanan	Y	N	Y	Y	Y	Y	Y
14 Mack	Y	N	?	?	Y	Y	Y
15 Posey	Y	N	Y	Y	Y	Y	Y
16 Rooney	Y	N	Y	Y	Y	Y	Y
17 Meek	N	Y	Y	Y	Y	Y	Y
18 Ros-Lehtinen	Y	N	Y	Y	Y	Y	Y
19 Wexler	N	Y	?	?	Y	Y	Y
20 Wasserman Schultz	N	Y	?	Y	Y	Y	Y
21 Diaz-Balart, L.	Y	N	Y	Y	Y	Y	Y
22 Klein	N	Y	+	+	Y	Y	Y
23 Hastings	N	Y	Y	?	Y	Y	Y
24 Kosmas	Y	Y	Y	Y	Y	Y	Y
25 Diaz-Balart, M.	Y	N	Y	Y	Y	Y	Y
GEORGIA							
1 Kingston	Y	N	Y	Y	Y	Y	Y
2 Bishop	Y	Y	Y	Y	Y	Y	Y
3 Westmoreland	Y	N	Y	Y	Y	Y	Y
4 Johnson	N	Y	Y	Y	Y	Y	Y
5 Lewis	N	Y	?	Y	Y	Y	Y
6 Price	Y	N	Y	Y	Y	Y	Y
7 Linder	Y	N	Y	Y	Y	Y	Y
8 Marshall	N	Y	Y	Y	Y	Y	Y
9 Deal	Y	N	?	?	?	?	?
10 Broun	Y	N	Y	Y	Y	Y	Y
11 Gingrey	Y	N	Y	Y	Y	Y	Y
12 Barrow	N	Y	Y	Y	Y	Y	Y
13 Scott	N	Y	Y	Y	Y	Y	Y
HAWAII							
1 Abercrombie	N	Y	?	?	?	?	?
2 Hirono	N	Y	Y	Y	Y	Y	Y
IDAHO							
1 Minnick	Y	Y	Y	Y	Y	Y	Y
2 Simpson	Y	N	?	?	Y	Y	Y
ILLINOIS							
1 Rush	N	Y	?	?	Y	Y	Y
2 Jackson	N	Y	Y	Y	Y	Y	Y
3 Lipinski	N	Y	Y	Y	Y	Y	Y
4 Gutierrez	N	Y	?	?	Y	Y	Y
5 Quigley	N	Y	Y	Y	Y	Y	Y
6 Roskam	Y	N	Y	Y	?	Y	Y
7 Davis	N	Y	?	?	Y	Y	Y
8 Bean	N	Y	Y	Y	Y	Y	Y
9 Schakowsky	N	Y	Y	Y	Y	Y	Y
10 Kirk	Y	N	Y	Y	Y	Y	Y
11 Halvorson	Y	N	Y	Y	Y	Y	Y
12 Costello	N	Y	Y	Y	Y	Y	Y
13 Biggert	Y	N	Y	Y	Y	Y	Y
14 Foster	N	Y	Y	Y	Y	Y	Y
15 Johnson	Y	N	+	+	+	+	+

	967	968	969	970	971	972	973
16 **Manzullo**	Y	N	Y	Y	Y	Y	Y
17 Hare	N	Y	Y	Y	Y	Y	Y
18 **Schock**	Y	N	Y	Y	Y	Y	Y
19 **Shimkus**	Y	N	Y	Y	Y	Y	Y
INDIANA							
1 Visclosky	N	N	Y	Y	Y	Y	Y
2 Donnelly	N	Y	Y	Y	Y	Y	Y
3 **Souder**	?	N	?	?	Y	Y	Y
4 **Buyer**	Y	N	Y	Y	Y	Y	Y
5 **Burton**	Y	N	Y	Y	Y	Y	Y
6 **Pence**	Y	N	Y	Y	Y	Y	Y
7 Carson	N	Y	Y	Y	Y	Y	Y
8 Ellsworth	N	Y	Y	Y	Y	Y	Y
9 Hill	N	N	Y	Y	Y	Y	Y
IOWA							
1 Braley	N	Y	+	+	Y	Y	Y
2 Loebsack	N	Y	?	?	Y	Y	Y
3 Boswell	N	Y	Y	Y	Y	Y	Y
4 **Latham**	Y	N	Y	Y	Y	Y	Y
5 **King**	Y	N	Y	Y	Y	Y	Y
KANSAS							
1 **Moran**	Y	N	?	?	Y	Y	Y
2 **Jenkins**	Y	N	Y	Y	Y	Y	Y
3 Moore	N	Y	Y	Y	Y	Y	Y
4 **Tiahrt**	Y	N	Y	Y	Y	Y	Y
KENTUCKY							
1 **Whitfield**	Y	N	Y	Y	Y	Y	Y
2 **Guthrie**	Y	N	+	+	Y	Y	Y
3 Yarmuth	N	Y	Y	Y	Y	Y	Y
4 **Davis**	Y	N	Y	Y	Y	Y	Y
5 **Rogers**	Y	N	Y	Y	Y	Y	Y
6 Chandler	Y	N	Y	Y	Y	Y	Y
LOUISIANA							
1 **Scalise**	Y	N	Y	Y	Y	Y	Y
2 **Cao**	?	N	Y	Y	Y	Y	Y
3 Melancon	N	Y	Y	Y	Y	Y	Y
4 **Fleming**	Y	N	Y	Y	Y	Y	Y
5 **Alexander**	Y	N	?	?	Y	Y	Y
6 **Cassidy**	Y	N	Y	Y	Y	Y	?
7 **Boustany**	Y	N	?	?	Y	Y	Y
MAINE							
1 Pingree	N	Y	Y	Y	Y	Y	Y
2 Michaud	N	Y	?	?	Y	Y	Y
MARYLAND							
1 Kratovil	Y	Y	Y	Y	Y	Y	Y
2 Ruppersberger	N	Y	Y	Y	Y	Y	Y
3 Sarbanes	N	Y	Y	Y	Y	Y	Y
4 Edwards	N	Y	Y	Y	Y	Y	Y
5 Hoyer	N	Y	Y	Y	Y	Y	Y
6 **Bartlett**	Y	N	Y	Y	Y	Y	Y
7 Cummings	N	Y	Y	Y	Y	Y	Y
8 Van Hollen	N	Y	Y	Y	Y	Y	Y
MASSACHUSETTS							
1 Olver	N	Y	Y	Y	Y	Y	Y
2 Neal	N	Y	?	?	Y	Y	Y
3 McGovern	N	Y	Y	Y	Y	Y	Y
4 Frank	N	Y	?	?	Y	Y	Y
5 Tsongas	N	Y	Y	Y	Y	Y	Y
6 Tierney	N	Y	Y	Y	Y	Y	Y
7 Markey	N	Y	Y	Y	Y	Y	Y
8 Capuano	N	Y	Y	Y	Y	Y	Y
9 Lynch	N	?	Y	Y	Y	Y	Y
10 Delahunt	N	Y	Y	Y	Y	Y	Y
MICHIGAN							
1 Stupak	N	N	Y	Y	Y	Y	Y
2 **Hoekstra**	Y	N	?	?	Y	Y	Y
3 **Ehlers**	Y	N	Y	Y	Y	Y	Y
4 **Camp**	Y	N	Y	Y	Y	Y	Y
5 Kildee	N	Y	Y	Y	Y	Y	Y
6 **Upton**	Y	N	Y	Y	Y	Y	Y
7 Schauer	N	Y	Y	Y	Y	Y	Y
8 **Rogers**	Y	N	Y	Y	Y	Y	Y
9 Peters	N	Y	Y	Y	Y	Y	Y
10 **Miller**	Y	N	Y	Y	Y	Y	Y
11 **McCotter**	Y	N	Y	Y	Y	Y	Y
12 Levin	N	Y	Y	Y	Y	Y	Y
13 Kilpatrick	N	Y	Y	Y	Y	Y	Y
14 Conyers	N	Y	Y	Y	Y	Y	Y
15 Dingell	N	Y	Y	Y	Y	Y	Y
MINNESOTA							
1 Walz	N	Y	Y	Y	Y	Y	Y
2 **Kline**	Y	N	Y	Y	Y	Y	Y
3 **Paulsen**	Y	N	?	?	Y	Y	Y
4 McCollum	N	Y	Y	Y	Y	Y	Y

	967	968	969	970	971	972	973
5 Ellison	N	Y	Y	Y	Y	Y	Y
6 **Bachmann**	Y	N	Y	Y	Y	Y	Y
7 Peterson	N	Y	Y	Y	Y	Y	Y
8 Oberstar	?	?	Y	Y	Y	Y	Y
MISSISSIPPI							
1 Childers	Y	Y	?	?	Y	Y	Y
2 Thompson	N	Y	Y	Y	Y	Y	Y
3 **Harper**	Y	N	Y	Y	Y	Y	Y
4 Taylor	Y	N	?	?	Y	Y	Y
MISSOURI							
1 Clay	N	Y	?	?	?	?	?
2 **Akin**	Y	N	Y	Y	Y	Y	Y
3 Carnahan	N	Y	Y	Y	Y	Y	Y
4 Skelton	N	N	?	?	Y	Y	Y
5 Cleaver	N	Y	Y	Y	Y	Y	Y
6 **Graves**	Y	N	?	?	Y	Y	Y
7 **Blunt**	Y	N	?	?	Y	Y	Y
8 **Emerson**	Y	N	Y	Y	Y	Y	Y
9 **Luetkemeyer**	Y	N	Y	Y	Y	Y	Y
MONTANA							
AL **Rehberg**	Y	N	Y	Y	Y	Y	Y
NEBRASKA							
1 **Fortenberry**	Y	N	Y	Y	Y	Y	Y
2 **Terry**	Y	N	Y	Y	Y	Y	Y
3 **Smith**	Y	N	Y	Y	Y	Y	Y
NEVADA							
1 Berkley	N	Y	Y	Y	Y	Y	Y
2 **Heller**	Y	N	Y	Y	+	+	?
3 Titus	N	Y	Y	Y	Y	Y	Y
NEW HAMPSHIRE							
1 Shea-Porter	N	Y	Y	Y	Y	Y	Y
2 Hodes	N	Y	?	?	?	?	?
NEW JERSEY							
1 Andrews	N	Y	Y	Y	Y	Y	Y
2 **LoBiondo**	Y	N	Y	Y	Y	Y	Y
3 Adler	N	Y	Y	Y	Y	Y	Y
4 **Smith**	Y	N	?	+	Y	Y	Y
5 **Garrett**	Y	N	Y	Y	Y	Y	Y
6 Pallone	N	Y	Y	Y	Y	Y	Y
7 **Lance**	Y	N	Y	Y	Y	Y	Y
8 Pascrell	N	Y	+	+	?	Y	Y
9 Rothman	N	Y	Y	Y	Y	Y	Y
10 Payne	N	Y	Y	Y	Y	Y	Y
11 **Frelinghuysen**	Y	N	Y	Y	Y	Y	Y
12 Holt	N	Y	Y	Y	Y	Y	Y
13 Sires	N	Y	Y	Y	Y	Y	Y
NEW MEXICO							
1 Heinrich	N	Y	Y	Y	Y	Y	Y
2 Teague	Y	N	Y	Y	Y	Y	Y
3 Lujan	N	Y	Y	Y	Y	Y	Y
NEW YORK							
1 Bishop	N	Y	Y	Y	Y	Y	Y
2 Israel	N	Y	Y	Y	Y	Y	Y
3 **King**	Y	N	Y	Y	Y	Y	Y
4 McCarthy	N	Y	+	+	Y	Y	Y
5 Ackerman	N	Y	Y	Y	Y	Y	Y
6 Meeks	N	Y	?	?	Y	Y	Y
7 Crowley	N	Y	?	?	Y	Y	Y
8 Nadler	N	Y	Y	Y	Y	Y	Y
9 Weiner	?	Y	?	?	Y	Y	Y
10 Towns	N	Y	Y	Y	Y	Y	Y
11 Clarke	N	Y	Y	Y	Y	Y	Y
12 Velázquez	N	Y	Y	Y	Y	Y	Y
13 McMahon	N	Y	Y	Y	Y	Y	Y
14 Maloney	N	Y	+	+	Y	Y	Y
15 Rangel	N	?	Y	Y	Y	?	Y
16 Serrano	N	Y	Y	Y	Y	Y	Y
17 Engel	N	Y	Y	Y	Y	Y	Y
18 Lowey	N	Y	Y	Y	Y	Y	Y
19 Hall	N	Y	Y	Y	Y	Y	Y
20 Murphy	N	Y	Y	Y	Y	Y	Y
21 Tonko	N	Y	Y	Y	Y	Y	Y
22 Hinchey	N	Y	?	?	?	?	Y
23 Owens	N	Y	Y	Y	Y	Y	Y
24 Arcuri	N	Y	Y	Y	Y	Y	Y
25 Maffei	N	Y	?	?	?	Y	Y
26 **Lee**	Y	N	Y	Y	Y	Y	Y
27 Higgins	N	Y	?	?	Y	Y	Y
28 Slaughter	?	?	Y	Y	Y	Y	Y
29 Massa	Y	N	Y	Y	Y	Y	Y
NORTH CAROLINA							
1 Butterfield	N	Y	Y	Y	Y	Y	Y
2 Etheridge	N	Y	Y	Y	Y	Y	Y
3 **Jones**	Y	N	Y	Y	Y	Y	Y
4 Price	N	Y	Y	Y	Y	Y	Y

	967	968	969	970	971	972	973
5 **Foxx**	Y	N	Y	Y	Y	Y	Y
6 **Coble**	Y	N	?	?	Y	Y	Y
7 McIntyre	Y	N	Y	Y	Y	Y	Y
8 Kissell	N	Y	Y	Y	Y	Y	Y
9 **Myrick**	?	N	+	+	Y	Y	Y
10 **McHenry**	Y	N	Y	Y	Y	Y	Y
11 Shuler	N	Y	?	?	?	?	?
12 Watt	N	Y	Y	Y	Y	Y	Y
13 Miller	N	Y	Y	Y	Y	Y	?
NORTH DAKOTA							
AL Pomeroy	N	Y	Y	Y	Y	Y	Y
OHIO							
1 Driehaus	N	Y	Y	Y	Y	Y	Y
2 **Schmidt**	Y	N	Y	Y	Y	Y	Y
3 **Turner**	Y	N	Y	Y	Y	Y	Y
4 **Jordan**	Y	N	+	+	Y	Y	Y
5 **Latta**	Y	N	Y	Y	Y	Y	Y
6 Wilson	N	Y	Y	Y	Y	Y	Y
7 **Austria**	Y	N	?	?	Y	Y	Y
8 **Boehner**	Y	N	Y	Y	Y	Y	Y
9 Kaptur	N	N	Y	Y	Y	Y	Y
10 Kucinich	N	N	Y	Y	Y	Y	Y
11 Fudge	N	Y	Y	Y	Y	Y	Y
12 **Tiberi**	Y	N	?	?	Y	Y	Y
13 Sutton	N	Y	Y	Y	Y	Y	Y
14 **LaTourette**	Y	N	Y	Y	?	?	?
15 Kilroy	N	Y	Y	Y	+	Y	Y
16 Boccieri	N	Y	Y	Y	Y	Y	Y
17 Ryan	N	Y	Y	Y	Y	Y	Y
18 Space	N	N	Y	Y	Y	Y	Y
OKLAHOMA							
1 **Sullivan**	Y	N	Y	Y	Y	Y	Y
2 Boren	Y	N	Y	Y	Y	Y	Y
3 **Lucas**	Y	N	Y	Y	Y	Y	Y
4 **Cole**	Y	N	Y	Y	Y	Y	Y
5 **Fallin**	Y	N	Y	Y	Y	Y	Y
OREGON							
1 Wu	N	Y	Y	Y	Y	Y	Y
2 **Walden**	Y	N	Y	Y	Y	Y	Y
3 Blumenauer	N	Y	Y	Y	Y	Y	Y
4 DeFazio	N	Y	Y	Y	Y	Y	Y
5 Schrader	N	N	Y	Y	Y	Y	Y
PENNSYLVANIA							
1 Brady	N	Y	Y	Y	Y	Y	Y
2 Fattah	N	Y	Y	Y	Y	Y	Y
3 Dahlkemper	N	Y	Y	Y	Y	Y	Y
4 Altmire	N	Y	Y	Y	Y	Y	Y
5 **Thompson**	Y	N	Y	Y	Y	Y	Y
6 **Gerlach**	Y	N	+	+	Y	Y	Y
7 Sestak	N	Y	?	?	Y	Y	Y
8 Murphy, P.	N	Y	?	?	Y	Y	Y
9 **Shuster**	Y	N	Y	Y	Y	Y	?
10 Carney	N	Y	?	?	Y	Y	Y
11 Kanjorski	N	Y	Y	Y	Y	Y	Y
12 Murtha	N	Y	?	?	?	?	?
13 Schwartz	N	Y	Y	Y	Y	Y	Y
14 Doyle	N	Y	Y	Y	Y	Y	Y
15 **Dent**	Y	N	Y	Y	Y	Y	Y
16 **Pitts**	Y	N	Y	Y	Y	Y	Y
17 Holden	N	Y	Y	Y	Y	Y	Y
18 **Murphy, T.**	Y	N	Y	Y	Y	Y	Y
19 **Platts**	Y	N	Y	Y	Y	Y	Y
RHODE ISLAND							
1 Kennedy	N	Y	Y	Y	Y	Y	Y
2 Langevin	N	Y	+	+	Y	Y	Y
SOUTH CAROLINA							
1 **Brown**	Y	N	Y	Y	Y	Y	Y
2 **Wilson**	Y	N	+	+	Y	Y	Y
3 **Barrett**	Y	N	+	+	+	+	?
4 **Inglis**	Y	N	Y	Y	Y	Y	Y
5 Spratt	N	Y	Y	Y	Y	Y	Y
6 Clyburn	N	Y	?	?	Y	Y	Y
SOUTH DAKOTA							
AL Herseth Sandlin	N	Y	Y	Y	Y	Y	Y
TENNESSEE							
1 **Roe**	Y	N	Y	Y	Y	Y	Y
2 **Duncan**	Y	N	Y	Y	Y	Y	Y
3 **Wamp**	Y	N	?	?	Y	Y	Y
4 Davis	N	N	Y	Y	Y	Y	Y
5 Cooper	N	Y	Y	Y	Y	Y	Y
6 Gordon	N	Y	Y	Y	Y	Y	Y
7 **Blackburn**	Y	N	Y	Y	Y	Y	Y
8 Tanner	N	Y	Y	Y	Y	Y	Y
9 Cohen	N	Y	Y	Y	Y	Y	Y

	967	968	969	970	971	972	973
TEXAS							
1 **Gohmert**	Y	N	?	?	Y	Y	Y
2 **Poe**	Y	N	Y	Y	Y	Y	Y
3 **Johnson, S.**	Y	N	Y	Y	?	?	?
4 **Hall**	Y	N	Y	Y	Y	Y	Y
5 **Hensarling**	Y	N	Y	Y	Y	Y	Y
6 **Barton**	Y	N	?	?	Y	Y	Y
7 **Culberson**	Y	N	Y	Y	Y	Y	Y
8 **Brady**	Y	N	Y	Y	Y	Y	Y
9 Green, A.	N	Y	Y	Y	Y	Y	Y
10 **McCaul**	Y	N	Y	Y	Y	Y	Y
11 **Conaway**	Y	N	Y	Y	Y	Y	Y
12 **Granger**	Y	N	Y	Y	Y	Y	Y
13 **Thornberry**	Y	N	Y	Y	Y	Y	Y
14 **Paul**	Y	N	?	?	Y	N	N
15 Hinojosa	N	Y	?	?	Y	Y	Y
16 Reyes	N	Y	Y	Y	Y	Y	Y
17 Edwards	N	N	?	?	Y	Y	Y
18 Jackson Lee	N	Y	Y	Y	Y	Y	Y
19 **Neugebauer**	Y	N	+	+	Y	Y	Y
20 Gonzalez	N	Y	Y	Y	Y	Y	Y
21 **Smith**	Y	N	Y	Y	Y	Y	Y
22 **Olson**	Y	N	Y	Y	Y	Y	Y
23 Rodriguez	Y	Y	Y	Y	Y	Y	Y
24 **Marchant**	Y	N	?	?	Y	Y	Y
25 Doggett	N	Y	Y	Y	Y	Y	Y
26 **Burgess**	Y	N	Y	Y	Y	Y	Y
27 Ortiz	N	N	Y	Y	Y	Y	Y
28 Cuellar	N	N	Y	Y	Y	Y	Y
29 Green, G.	N	N	Y	Y	Y	Y	Y
30 Johnson, E.	N	Y	Y	Y	Y	Y	Y
31 **Carter**	Y	N	Y	Y	Y	Y	Y
32 **Sessions**	?	?	Y	Y	Y	Y	Y
UTAH							
1 **Bishop**	Y	N	?	?	?	?	?
2 Matheson	N	Y	Y	Y	Y	Y	Y
3 **Chaffetz**	Y	N	Y	Y	Y	Y	Y
VERMONT							
AL Welch	N	Y	?	?	Y	Y	Y
VIRGINIA							
1 **Wittman**	Y	N	Y	Y	Y	Y	Y
2 Nye	Y	Y	Y	Y	Y	Y	Y
3 Scott	N	Y	Y	Y	Y	Y	Y
4 **Forbes**	Y	N	Y	Y	Y	Y	Y
5 Perriello	N	N	Y	Y	Y	Y	Y
6 **Goodlatte**	Y	N	?	?	Y	Y	Y
7 **Cantor**	Y	N	Y	Y	Y	Y	Y
8 Moran	?	?	?	?	?	Y	Y
9 Boucher	N	N	?	?	Y	Y	Y
10 **Wolf**	Y	N	?	?	Y	Y	Y
11 Connolly	N	Y	Y	Y	Y	Y	Y
WASHINGTON							
1 Inslee	N	Y	Y	Y	Y	Y	Y
2 Larsen	N	Y	Y	Y	Y	Y	Y
3 Baird	N	Y	Y	Y	Y	Y	Y
4 **Hastings**	Y	N	Y	Y	Y	Y	Y
5 **McMorris Rodgers**	Y	N	Y	Y	Y	Y	Y
6 Dicks	N	Y	Y	Y	Y	Y	Y
7 McDermott	N	Y	Y	Y	Y	Y	Y
8 **Reichert**	Y	N	Y	Y	Y	Y	Y
9 Smith	N	Y	+	?	Y	Y	Y
WEST VIRGINIA							
1 Mollohan	N	Y	Y	Y	Y	Y	Y
2 **Capito**	Y	N	Y	Y	Y	Y	Y
3 Rahall	N	Y	Y	Y	Y	Y	Y
WISCONSIN							
1 **Ryan**	Y	N	Y	Y	Y	Y	Y
2 Baldwin	?	?	Y	Y	Y	Y	Y
3 Kind	N	Y	Y	Y	Y	Y	Y
4 Moore	N	Y	Y	Y	Y	Y	Y
5 **Sensenbrenner**	Y	N	Y	Y	Y	Y	Y
6 **Petri**	Y	N	Y	Y	Y	Y	Y
7 Obey	N	Y	Y	Y	Y	Y	Y
8 Kagen	N	Y	Y	Y	Y	Y	Y
WYOMING							
AL **Lummis**	Y	N	Y	Y	Y	Y	Y
DELEGATES							
Faleomavaega (A.S.)							
Norton (D.C.)							
Bordallo (Guam)							
Sablan (N. Marianas)							
Pierluisi (P.R.)							
Christensen (V.I.)							

IN THE HOUSE | By Vote Number

974. **H Res 971. Mammography Insurance Coverage/Adoption.**
Capps, D-Calif., motion to suspend the rules and adopt the resolution that would express the sense of the House that the U.S. Preventive Services Task Force guidelines should not be used by insurers to prohibit or deny coverage for mammography services. Motion agreed to 426-0: D 253-0; R 173-0. A two-thirds majority of those present and voting (284 in this case) is required for adoption under suspension of the rules. Dec. 15, 2009.

975. **HR 2194. Iran Sanctions/Passage.** Berman, D-Calif., motion to suspend the rules and pass the bill that would impose sanctions against companies that supply Iran with, or support its domestic production of, gasoline and other refined-petroleum products. Motion agreed to 412-12: D 241-9; R 171-3. A two-thirds majority of those present and voting (283 in this case) is required for passage under suspension of the rules. Dec. 15, 2009.

976. **H Res 150. Tribute to A. Philip Randolph/Adoption.** Conyers, D-Mich., motion to suspend the rules and adopt the resolution that would recognize civil rights leader A. Philip Randolph for his leadership and work to end discrimination and secure equal employment opportunities for all Americans. Motion agreed to 395-23: D 253-0; R 142-23. A two-thirds majority of those present and voting (279 in this case) is required for adoption under suspension of the rules. Dec. 15, 2009.

977. **S 1472. Justice Department Human Rights Division/Passage.** Conyers, D-Mich., motion to suspend the rules and pass the bill that would require the attorney general to create a Justice Department division to focus on enforcing human rights laws. Motion agreed to 416-3: D 249-0; R 167-3. A two-thirds majority of those present and voting (280 in this case) is required for passage under suspension of the rules. Dec. 15, 2009.

978. **H Con Res 223. Adjournment/Adoption.** Adoption of the concurrent resolution that would provide for the sine die adjournment of the first session of the 111th Congress and would provide for the adjournment of the House until noon on Jan. 12, 2010, and the Senate until noon on Jan. 19, 2010, in the second session. Adopted 222-195: D 216-29; R 6-166. Dec. 16, 2009.

979. **H Res 973. Same-Day Consideration/Previous Question.** Pingree, D-Maine, motion to order the previous question (thus ending debate and possibility of amendment) on adoption of the rule (H Res 973) that would waive the two-thirds majority vote requirement for same-day consideration of resolutions reported from the Rules Committee on the legislative day of Dec. 16. Motion agreed to 226-192: D 226-20; R 0-172. Dec. 16, 2009.

980. **H Res 973. Same-Day Consideration/Rule.** Adoption of the rule (H Res 973) that would waive the two-thirds majority vote requirement for same-day consideration of resolutions reported from the Rules Committee on the legislative day of Dec. 16. Adopted 218-202: D 218-29; R 0-173. Dec. 16, 2009.

	974	975	976	977	978	979	980
ALABAMA							
1 Bonner	Y	Y	Y	Y	N	N	N
2 Bright	Y	Y	Y	Y	Y	N	Y
3 Rogers	Y	Y	Y	Y	N	N	N
4 Aderholt	Y	Y	N	Y	N	N	N
5 Griffith	Y	Y	Y	Y	N	N	N
6 Bachus	Y	Y	Y	Y	N	N	N
7 Davis	Y	Y	Y	Y	Y	Y	Y
ALASKA							
AL Young	Y	Y	Y	N	?	N	N
ARIZONA							
1 Kirkpatrick	Y	Y	Y	Y	N	N	N
2 Franks	Y	N	Y	N	N	N	N
3 Shadegg	Y	N	Y	N	N	N	N
4 Pastor	Y	Y	Y	Y	Y	Y	Y
5 Mitchell	Y	Y	Y	N	N	N	N
6 Flake	N	Y	N	Y	N	N	N
7 Grijalva	Y	Y	Y	Y	Y	Y	Y
8 Giffords	Y	Y	Y	N	N	N	N
ARKANSAS							
1 Berry	Y	Y	Y	Y	Y	Y	Y
2 Snyder	Y	Y	Y	Y	Y	Y	Y
3 Boozman	Y	Y	Y	N	N	N	N
4 Ross	Y	Y	Y	Y	Y	Y	Y
CALIFORNIA							
1 Thompson	Y	Y	Y	Y	Y	?	Y
2 Herger	Y	Y	Y	N	N	N	N
3 Lungren	Y	Y	Y	N	N	N	N
4 McClintock	Y	Y	Y	N	N	N	N
5 Matsui	Y	Y	Y	Y	Y	Y	Y
6 Woolsey	Y	Y	Y	Y	Y	Y	Y
7 Miller, George	Y	Y	Y	Y	Y	Y	Y
8 Pelosi							
9 Lee	Y	P	Y	Y	Y	Y	Y
10 Garamendi	Y	Y	Y	Y	Y	Y	Y
11 McNerney	Y	Y	Y	Y	Y	Y	Y
12 Speier	Y	Y	Y	Y	?	?	?
13 Stark	Y	N	Y	Y	Y	Y	Y
14 Eshoo	Y	Y	Y	Y	Y	Y	Y
15 Honda	Y	Y	Y	Y	Y	Y	Y
16 Lofgren	Y	Y	Y	Y	Y	Y	Y
17 Farr	Y	Y	Y	Y	Y	Y	Y
18 Cardoza	Y	Y	Y	Y	?	?	Y
19 Radanovich	?	?	?	?	–	?	+
20 Costa	Y	Y	Y	Y	Y	Y	Y
21 Nunes	Y	Y	Y	Y	N	N	N
22 McCarthy	Y	Y	N	Y	N	N	N
23 Capps	Y	Y	Y	Y	Y	Y	Y
24 Gallegly	Y	Y	Y	Y	N	N	N
25 McKeon	Y	Y	Y	N	N	N	N
26 Dreier	Y	Y	Y	N	N	N	N
27 Sherman	Y	Y	Y	Y	Y	Y	Y
28 Berman	Y	Y	Y	Y	Y	Y	Y
29 Schiff	Y	Y	Y	Y	Y	Y	Y
30 Waxman	Y	Y	Y	Y	Y	Y	Y
31 Becerra	Y	Y	Y	Y	Y	Y	Y
32 Chu	Y	Y	Y	Y	Y	Y	Y
33 Watson	Y	Y	Y	Y	Y	Y	Y
34 Roybal-Allard	Y	Y	Y	Y	Y	Y	Y
35 Waters	Y	P	Y	Y	Y	Y	Y
36 Harman	Y	Y	Y	Y	Y	Y	Y
37 Richardson	Y	Y	Y	Y	Y	Y	Y
38 Napolitano	Y	Y	Y	Y	Y	Y	Y
39 Sánchez, Linda	Y	Y	Y	Y	Y	Y	Y
40 Royce	Y	Y	Y	N	N	N	N
41 Lewis	Y	Y	Y	Y	N	N	N
42 Miller, Gary	Y	Y	Y	Y	N	N	N
43 Baca	Y	Y	Y	Y	Y	Y	Y
44 Calvert	Y	Y	Y	Y	N	N	N
45 Bono Mack	Y	Y	Y	Y	N	N	N
46 Rohrabacher	Y	Y	Y	Y	N	N	N
47 Sanchez, Loretta	?	?	?	?	Y	Y	Y
48 Campbell	Y	Y	N	Y	N	N	N
49 Issa	Y	Y	Y	Y	N	N	N
50 Bilbray	Y	Y	Y	Y	N	N	N
51 Filner	Y	Y	Y	Y	+	+	+
52 Hunter	Y	Y	Y	Y	N	N	N
53 Davis	Y	Y	Y	?	Y	Y	Y

	974	975	976	977	978	979	980
COLORADO							
1 DeGette	Y	Y	Y	Y	Y	Y	Y
2 Polis	?	Y	Y	Y	Y	Y	Y
3 Salazar	Y	Y	Y	Y	Y	Y	Y
4 Markey	Y	Y	Y	Y	N	Y	Y
5 Lamborn	Y	Y	N	N	N	N	N
6 Coffman	Y	Y	N	N	N	N	N
7 Perlmutter	Y	Y	Y	Y	Y	Y	Y
CONNECTICUT							
1 Larson	Y	Y	Y	Y	Y	Y	Y
2 Courtney	Y	Y	Y	Y	Y	Y	Y
3 DeLauro	Y	Y	Y	Y	Y	Y	Y
4 Himes	Y	Y	Y	Y	N	Y	Y
5 Murphy	Y	Y	Y	Y	Y	Y	Y
DELAWARE							
AL Castle	Y	Y	Y	Y	N	N	N
FLORIDA							
1 Miller	Y	Y	N	Y	N	N	N
2 Boyd	Y	Y	Y	Y	Y	Y	Y
3 Brown	Y	Y	Y	Y	Y	Y	Y
4 Crenshaw	Y	Y	Y	Y	N	N	N
5 Brown-Waite	Y	Y	Y	Y	N	N	N
6 Stearns	Y	Y	Y	Y	N	N	N
7 Mica	Y	Y	Y	N	N	N	N
8 Grayson	Y	Y	Y	Y	Y	Y	Y
9 Bilirakis	Y	Y	Y	N	N	N	N
10 Young	Y	Y	Y	Y	N	N	N
11 Castor	Y	Y	Y	Y	Y	Y	Y
12 Putnam	Y	Y	Y	N	N	N	N
13 Buchanan	Y	Y	Y	Y	N	N	N
14 Mack	Y	Y	Y	N	N	N	N
15 Posey	Y	Y	Y	N	N	N	N
16 Rooney	Y	Y	N	Y	N	N	N
17 Meek	Y	Y	Y	Y	Y	Y	Y
18 Ros-Lehtinen	Y	Y	Y	N	N	N	N
19 Wexler	Y	Y	Y	?	?	?	?
20 Wasserman Schultz	Y	Y	Y	Y	Y	Y	Y
21 Diaz-Balart, L.	Y	Y	?	?	N	N	N
22 Klein	Y	Y	Y	Y	Y	Y	Y
23 Hastings	Y	Y	Y	Y	Y	Y	Y
24 Kosmas	Y	Y	Y	N	N	Y	N
25 Diaz-Balart, M.	Y	Y	?	?	N	N	N
GEORGIA							
1 Kingston	Y	Y	N	Y	N	N	N
2 Bishop	Y	Y	Y	Y	Y	Y	Y
3 Westmoreland	Y	Y	N	N	N	N	N
4 Johnson	Y	Y	Y	Y	Y	Y	Y
5 Lewis	Y	Y	Y	Y	Y	Y	Y
6 Price	Y	Y	?	Y	N	N	N
7 Linder	Y	Y	Y	Y	N	N	N
8 Marshall	Y	Y	Y	Y	Y	N	N
9 Deal	?	?	?	?	N	N	N
10 Broun	Y	N	N	N	N	N	N
11 Gingrey	Y	Y	N	N	N	N	N
12 Barrow	Y	Y	Y	Y	Y	N	N
13 Scott	Y	Y	Y	Y	Y	Y	Y
HAWAII							
1 Abercrombie	Y	Y	Y	?	Y	Y	Y
2 Hirono	Y	Y	Y	Y	Y	Y	Y
IDAHO							
1 Minnick	Y	Y	Y	Y	N	N	N
2 Simpson	Y	Y	Y	Y	?	?	?
ILLINOIS							
1 Rush	Y	Y	Y	Y	Y	Y	Y
2 Jackson	Y	Y	Y	Y	Y	Y	Y
3 Lipinski	Y	Y	Y	Y	Y	Y	Y
4 Gutierrez	Y	Y	Y	Y	Y	Y	Y
5 Quigley	Y	Y	Y	Y	Y	Y	Y
6 Roskam	Y	Y	Y	Y	N	N	N
7 Davis	Y	Y	Y	Y	Y	Y	Y
8 Bean	Y	Y	Y	Y	Y	Y	Y
9 Schakowsky	Y	Y	Y	Y	Y	Y	Y
10 Kirk	Y	Y	Y	Y	N	N	N
11 Halvorson	Y	Y	Y	Y	Y	Y	N
12 Costello	Y	Y	Y	Y	Y	Y	Y
13 Biggert	Y	Y	Y	Y	N	N	N
14 Foster	Y	Y	Y	Y	Y	N	N
15 Johnson	Y	Y	Y	Y	Y	N	N

	974	975	976	977	978	979	980
16 **Manzullo**	Y	Y	Y	Y	N	N	N
17 Hare	Y	Y	Y	Y	Y	Y	Y
18 **Schock**	Y	Y	Y	Y	N	N	N
19 **Shimkus**	Y	Y	Y	Y	N	N	N
INDIANA							
1 Visclosky	Y	Y	Y	Y	Y	Y	Y
2 Donnelly	Y	Y	Y	Y	N	Y	N
3 **Souder**	Y	Y	Y	Y	N	N	N
4 **Buyer**	Y	Y	Y	Y	N	N	N
5 **Burton**	Y	Y	N	Y	N	N	N
6 **Pence**	Y	Y	Y	Y	N	N	N
7 Carson	Y	Y	Y	Y	Y	Y	Y
8 Ellsworth	Y	Y	Y	Y	N	N	N
9 Hill	Y	Y	Y	Y	Y	N	N
IOWA							
1 Braley	Y	Y	Y	Y	Y	Y	Y
2 Loebsack	Y	Y	Y	Y	Y	Y	Y
3 Boswell	Y	Y	Y	Y	Y	Y	Y
4 **Latham**	Y	Y	Y	Y	N	N	N
5 **King**	Y	Y	?	?	N	N	N
KANSAS							
1 **Moran**	Y	Y	Y	Y	N	N	N
2 **Jenkins**	Y	Y	Y	Y	N	N	N
3 Moore	Y	Y	Y	Y	Y	Y	?
4 **Tiahrt**	Y	Y	+	Y	N	N	N
KENTUCKY							
1 **Whitfield**	Y	Y	Y	Y	N	N	N
2 **Guthrie**	Y	Y	Y	Y	N	N	N
3 Yarmuth	Y	Y	Y	Y	Y	Y	Y
4 **Davis**	Y	Y	Y	Y	N	N	N
5 **Rogers**	Y	Y	Y	Y	N	N	N
6 Chandler	Y	Y	Y	Y	Y	Y	Y
LOUISIANA							
1 **Scalise**	Y	Y	N	Y	N	N	N
2 **Cao**	Y	Y	Y	Y	N	N	N
3 Melancon	Y	Y	Y	Y	Y	Y	N
4 **Fleming**	Y	Y	N	Y	N	N	N
5 **Alexander**	Y	Y	Y	Y	N	N	N
6 **Cassidy**	Y	Y	Y	Y	N	N	N
7 **Boustany**	Y	Y	Y	Y	N	N	N
MAINE							
1 Pingree	Y	Y	Y	Y	Y	Y	Y
2 Michaud	Y	Y	Y	Y	Y	Y	Y
MARYLAND							
1 Kratovil	Y	Y	Y	Y	N	N	N
2 Ruppersberger	Y	Y	Y	Y	Y	Y	Y
3 Sarbanes	Y	Y	Y	Y	Y	Y	Y
4 Edwards	Y	Y	Y	Y	Y	Y	Y
5 Hoyer	Y	Y	Y	Y	Y	Y	Y
6 **Bartlett**	Y	Y	Y	Y	N	N	N
7 Cummings	Y	Y	Y	Y	Y	Y	Y
8 Van Hollen	Y	Y	Y	Y	Y	Y	Y
MASSACHUSETTS							
1 Olver	Y	Y	Y	Y	Y	Y	Y
2 Neal	Y	Y	Y	Y	Y	Y	Y
3 McGovern	Y	Y	Y	Y	Y	Y	Y
4 Frank	Y	Y	Y	?	Y	Y	Y
5 Tsongas	Y	Y	Y	Y	Y	Y	Y
6 Tierney	Y	Y	Y	Y	Y	Y	Y
7 Markey	Y	Y	Y	Y	?	Y	Y
8 Capuano	Y	Y	Y	Y	Y	Y	Y
9 Lynch	Y	N	Y	Y	Y	Y	Y
10 Delahunt	Y	Y	Y	Y	Y	Y	Y
MICHIGAN							
1 Stupak	Y	Y	Y	Y	Y	Y	Y
2 **Hoekstra**	Y	Y	Y	Y	N	N	N
3 **Ehlers**	Y	Y	Y	Y	Y	N	N
4 **Camp**	Y	Y	Y	Y	N	N	N
5 Kildee	Y	Y	Y	Y	Y	Y	Y
6 **Upton**	Y	Y	Y	Y	N	N	N
7 Schauer	Y	Y	Y	Y	Y	Y	Y
8 **Rogers**	Y	Y	Y	Y	N	N	N
9 Peters	Y	Y	Y	Y	N	N	N
10 **Miller**	Y	Y	Y	Y	N	N	N
11 **McCotter**	Y	Y	Y	Y	N	N	N
12 Levin	Y	Y	Y	Y	Y	Y	Y
13 Kilpatrick	Y	P	Y	Y	Y	Y	Y
14 Conyers	Y	N	Y	Y	Y	Y	Y
15 Dingell	Y	Y	Y	Y	Y	Y	Y
MINNESOTA							
1 Walz	Y	Y	Y	Y	Y	Y	Y
2 **Kline**	Y	Y	Y	Y	N	N	N
3 **Paulsen**	Y	Y	Y	Y	N	N	N
4 McCollum	Y	Y	Y	Y	Y	Y	Y

	974	975	976	977	978	979	980
5 Ellison	Y	Y	Y	Y	Y	Y	Y
6 **Bachmann**	Y	Y	Y	Y	N	N	N
7 Peterson	Y	Y	Y	Y	Y	Y	Y
8 Oberstar	Y	Y	Y	Y	Y	Y	Y
MISSISSIPPI							
1 Childers	Y	Y	Y	Y	N	N	N
2 Thompson	Y	Y	Y	Y	Y	Y	Y
3 **Harper**	Y	Y	Y	Y	N	N	N
4 Taylor	Y	Y	Y	Y	Y	N	N
MISSOURI							
1 Clay	?	?	?	?	?	?	?
2 **Akin**	Y	Y	N	Y	N	N	N
3 Carnahan	Y	Y	Y	Y	Y	Y	Y
4 Skelton	Y	Y	Y	Y	Y	Y	Y
5 Cleaver	Y	Y	Y	Y	Y	Y	Y
6 **Graves**	Y	Y	Y	Y	N	N	N
7 **Blunt**	Y	Y	Y	Y	N	N	N
8 **Emerson**	Y	Y	Y	Y	N	N	N
9 **Luetkemeyer**	Y	Y	Y	Y	N	N	N
MONTANA							
AL **Rehberg**	Y	Y	Y	Y	N	N	N
NEBRASKA							
1 **Fortenberry**	Y	Y	Y	Y	N	N	N
2 **Terry**	Y	Y	Y	Y	N	N	N
3 **Smith**	Y	Y	Y	Y	N	N	N
NEVADA							
1 Berkley	Y	Y	Y	Y	Y	Y	Y
2 **Heller**	Y	Y	Y	Y	N	N	N
3 Titus	Y	Y	Y	?	Y	Y	Y
NEW HAMPSHIRE							
1 Shea-Porter	Y	Y	Y	Y	Y	Y	Y
2 Hodes	Y	Y	Y	Y	Y	Y	Y
NEW JERSEY							
1 Andrews	Y	Y	Y	Y	Y	Y	Y
2 **LoBiondo**	Y	Y	Y	Y	N	N	N
3 Adler	Y	Y	Y	Y	N	Y	N
4 **Smith**	Y	Y	Y	Y	N	N	N
5 **Garrett**	Y	Y	N	Y	N	N	N
6 Pallone	Y	Y	Y	Y	Y	Y	Y
7 **Lance**	Y	Y	Y	Y	N	N	N
8 Pascrell	Y	Y	Y	Y	Y	Y	Y
9 Rothman	Y	Y	Y	Y	Y	Y	Y
10 Payne	Y	Y	Y	Y	Y	Y	Y
11 **Frelinghuysen**	Y	Y	Y	Y	N	N	N
12 Holt	Y	Y	Y	Y	Y	Y	Y
13 Sires	Y	Y	Y	Y	Y	Y	Y
NEW MEXICO							
1 Heinrich	Y	Y	Y	Y	Y	Y	Y
2 Teague	Y	Y	Y	Y	Y	N	N
3 Lujan	Y	Y	Y	Y	Y	Y	Y
NEW YORK							
1 Bishop	Y	Y	Y	Y	N	N	N
2 Israel	Y	Y	Y	Y	Y	Y	Y
3 **King**	Y	Y	Y	Y	N	N	N
4 McCarthy	Y	Y	Y	Y	Y	Y	Y
5 Ackerman	Y	Y	Y	Y	Y	Y	Y
6 Meeks	Y	Y	Y	Y	Y	Y	Y
7 Crowley	Y	Y	Y	Y	Y	Y	Y
8 Nadler	Y	Y	Y	Y	Y	Y	Y
9 Weiner	Y	Y	Y	Y	Y	Y	Y
10 Towns	Y	Y	Y	Y	Y	Y	Y
11 Clarke	Y	Y	Y	Y	Y	Y	Y
12 Velázquez	Y	Y	Y	Y	Y	Y	Y
13 McMahon	Y	Y	Y	Y	N	Y	N
14 Maloney	Y	Y	Y	Y	Y	Y	Y
15 Rangel	Y	Y	Y	Y	Y	Y	Y
16 Serrano	Y	Y	Y	Y	Y	Y	Y
17 Engel	Y	Y	Y	Y	?	Y	Y
18 Lowey	Y	Y	Y	Y	Y	Y	Y
19 Hall	Y	Y	Y	Y	?	?	?
20 Murphy	Y	Y	Y	Y	N	Y	N
21 Tonko	Y	Y	Y	Y	Y	Y	Y
22 Hinchey	Y	N	Y	Y	Y	Y	Y
23 Owens	Y	Y	Y	Y	Y	Y	Y
24 Arcuri	Y	Y	Y	Y	N	Y	Y
25 Maffei	Y	Y	Y	Y	N	Y	Y
26 **Lee**	Y	Y	Y	Y	N	N	N
27 Higgins	Y	Y	Y	Y	Y	Y	Y
28 Slaughter	Y	Y	Y	Y	Y	Y	Y
29 Massa	Y	Y	Y	Y	N	Y	Y
NORTH CAROLINA							
1 Butterfield	Y	Y	Y	Y	Y	Y	Y
2 Etheridge	Y	Y	Y	Y	Y	Y	Y
3 **Jones**	Y	Y	Y	Y	N	N	N
4 Price	Y	Y	Y	Y	Y	Y	Y

	974	975	976	977	978	979	980
5 **Foxx**	Y	Y	Y	Y	N	N	N
6 **Coble**	Y	Y	Y	Y	N	N	N
7 McIntyre	Y	Y	Y	Y	Y	Y	Y
8 Kissell	Y	Y	Y	Y	Y	Y	Y
9 **Myrick**	Y	Y	Y	Y	N	N	N
10 **McHenry**	Y	Y	Y	Y	N	N	N
11 Shuler	Y	Y	Y	Y	Y	Y	Y
12 Watt	Y	Y	Y	Y	Y	Y	Y
13 Miller	Y	Y	Y	Y	Y	Y	Y
NORTH DAKOTA							
AL Pomeroy	Y	Y	Y	Y	Y	Y	Y
OHIO							
1 Driehaus	Y	Y	Y	Y	N	N	N
2 **Schmidt**	Y	Y	Y	Y	N	N	N
3 **Turner**	Y	Y	Y	Y	N	N	N
4 **Jordan**	Y	Y	N	Y	N	N	N
5 **Latta**	Y	Y	Y	Y	N	N	N
6 Wilson	Y	Y	Y	Y	Y	Y	Y
7 **Austria**	Y	Y	Y	Y	N	N	N
8 **Boehner**	Y	Y	Y	Y	N	N	N
9 Kaptur	Y	Y	Y	Y	?	?	Y
10 Kucinich	Y	N	Y	Y	Y	Y	N
11 Fudge	Y	Y	Y	Y	Y	Y	Y
12 **Tiberi**	Y	Y	Y	Y	N	N	N
13 Sutton	Y	Y	Y	Y	Y	Y	Y
14 **LaTourette**	Y	Y	Y	Y	N	N	N
15 Kilroy	Y	Y	Y	Y	N	Y	Y
16 Boccieri	Y	Y	Y	Y	N	Y	Y
17 Ryan	Y	Y	Y	Y	Y	Y	Y
18 Space	Y	Y	Y	Y	N	Y	N
OKLAHOMA							
1 **Sullivan**	Y	Y	Y	Y	N	N	N
2 Boren	Y	Y	Y	Y	Y	Y	Y
3 **Lucas**	Y	Y	Y	Y	N	N	N
4 **Cole**	Y	Y	Y	Y	N	N	N
5 **Fallin**	Y	Y	Y	Y	N	N	N
OREGON							
1 Wu	Y	Y	Y	Y	Y	Y	Y
2 **Walden**	Y	Y	Y	Y	N	N	N
3 Blumenauer	Y	N	Y	Y	Y	Y	Y
4 DeFazio	Y	Y	Y	Y	Y	Y	Y
5 Schrader	Y	Y	Y	Y	Y	Y	Y
PENNSYLVANIA							
1 Brady	Y	Y	Y	Y	Y	Y	Y
2 Fattah	Y	Y	Y	Y	Y	Y	Y
3 Dahlkemper	Y	Y	Y	Y	N	Y	Y
4 Altmire	Y	Y	Y	Y	N	N	N
5 **Thompson**	Y	Y	Y	Y	N	N	N
6 **Gerlach**	Y	Y	Y	Y	N	N	N
7 Sestak	Y	Y	Y	Y	N	Y	Y
8 Murphy, P.	Y	Y	Y	Y	Y	Y	Y
9 **Shuster**	Y	Y	Y	Y	N	N	N
10 Carney	Y	Y	Y	Y	N	N	N
11 Kanjorski	Y	Y	Y	Y	Y	Y	Y
12 Murtha	?	?	?	?	?	?	?
13 Schwartz	Y	Y	Y	Y	Y	Y	Y
14 Doyle	Y	Y	Y	Y	Y	Y	Y
15 **Dent**	Y	Y	Y	Y	N	N	N
16 **Pitts**	Y	Y	?	Y	N	N	N
17 Holden	Y	Y	Y	Y	Y	Y	Y
18 **Murphy, T.**	Y	Y	Y	Y	N	N	N
19 **Platts**	Y	Y	Y	Y	N	N	N
RHODE ISLAND							
1 Kennedy	Y	Y	Y	Y	Y	Y	Y
2 Langevin	Y	Y	Y	Y	Y	Y	Y
SOUTH CAROLINA							
1 **Brown**	Y	Y	Y	Y	N	N	N
2 **Wilson**	Y	Y	Y	Y	N	N	N
3 **Barrett**	+	+	+	+	–	–	–
4 **Inglis**	Y	Y	Y	Y	N	N	N
5 Spratt	Y	Y	?	?	Y	Y	Y
6 Clyburn	Y	Y	Y	Y	Y	Y	Y
SOUTH DAKOTA							
AL Herseth Sandlin	Y	Y	Y	Y	Y	Y	Y
TENNESSEE							
1 **Roe**	Y	Y	Y	Y	N	N	N
2 **Duncan**	Y	N	Y	Y	N	N	N
3 **Wamp**	Y	Y	Y	Y	N	N	N
4 Davis	Y	Y	Y	Y	Y	Y	Y
5 Cooper	Y	Y	Y	Y	Y	Y	Y
6 Gordon	Y	Y	Y	Y	Y	Y	Y
7 **Blackburn**	Y	Y	Y	Y	N	N	N
8 Tanner	Y	Y	Y	Y	Y	Y	Y
9 Cohen	Y	Y	Y	Y	Y	Y	Y

	974	975	976	977	978	979	980
TEXAS							
1 **Gohmert**	Y	Y	?	Y	Y	N	N
2 **Poe**	Y	Y	N	Y	N	N	N
3 **Johnson, S.**	Y	Y	Y	Y	N	N	N
4 **Hall**	Y	Y	Y	Y	N	N	N
5 **Hensarling**	Y	Y	N	Y	N	N	N
6 **Barton**	Y	Y	Y	Y	N	N	N
7 **Culberson**	Y	Y	Y	Y	N	N	N
8 **Brady**	Y	Y	Y	Y	N	N	N
9 Green, A.	Y	Y	Y	Y	Y	Y	Y
10 **McCaul**	Y	Y	Y	Y	N	N	N
11 **Conaway**	Y	Y	N	Y	N	N	N
12 **Granger**	Y	Y	Y	Y	N	N	N
13 **Thornberry**	Y	Y	Y	Y	N	N	N
14 **Paul**	Y	N	Y	N	?	?	?
15 Hinojosa	Y	Y	Y	Y	Y	Y	Y
16 Reyes	Y	Y	Y	Y	Y	Y	Y
17 Edwards	Y	Y	Y	Y	Y	Y	Y
18 Jackson Lee	Y	Y	Y	Y	Y	Y	Y
19 **Neugebauer**	Y	Y	N	Y	N	N	N
20 Gonzalez	Y	Y	Y	Y	Y	Y	Y
21 **Smith**	Y	Y	Y	Y	N	N	N
22 **Olson**	Y	Y	Y	Y	Y	N	N
23 Rodriguez	Y	Y	Y	Y	Y	Y	Y
24 **Marchant**	Y	Y	Y	Y	N	N	N
25 Doggett	Y	Y	Y	Y	Y	Y	Y
26 **Burgess**	Y	Y	?	Y	N	N	N
27 Ortiz	Y	Y	Y	Y	Y	Y	Y
28 Cuellar	Y	Y	Y	Y	Y	Y	Y
29 Green, G.	Y	Y	Y	Y	Y	Y	Y
30 Johnson, E.	Y	P	Y	Y	?	?	?
31 **Carter**	Y	Y	Y	Y	N	N	N
32 **Sessions**	Y	Y	Y	Y	N	?	N
UTAH							
1 **Bishop**	?	Y	Y	Y	N	N	N
2 Matheson	Y	Y	Y	Y	Y	Y	Y
3 **Chaffetz**	Y	Y	Y	Y	Y	N	N
VERMONT							
AL Welch	Y	Y	Y	Y	Y	Y	Y
VIRGINIA							
1 **Wittman**	Y	Y	Y	Y	N	N	N
2 Nye	Y	Y	Y	Y	N	N	N
3 Scott	Y	Y	Y	Y	Y	Y	Y
4 **Forbes**	Y	Y	?	Y	N	N	N
5 Perriello	Y	Y	Y	Y	N	N	N
6 **Goodlatte**	Y	Y	Y	Y	N	N	N
7 **Cantor**	Y	Y	Y	Y	N	N	N
8 Moran	Y	Y	Y	Y	?	?	?
9 Boucher	Y	Y	Y	Y	Y	Y	Y
10 **Wolf**	Y	Y	Y	Y	N	N	N
11 Connolly	Y	Y	Y	Y	Y	Y	Y
WASHINGTON							
1 Inslee	Y	Y	Y	Y	Y	Y	Y
2 Larsen	Y	Y	Y	Y	Y	Y	Y
3 Baird	Y	Y	Y	Y	Y	N	N
4 **Hastings**	Y	Y	Y	Y	N	N	N
5 **McMorris Rodgers**	Y	Y	Y	Y	N	N	N
6 Dicks	Y	Y	Y	Y	Y	Y	Y
7 McDermott	Y	N	Y	Y	Y	Y	Y
8 **Reichert**	Y	Y	Y	Y	N	N	N
9 Smith	Y	Y	Y	Y	Y	Y	Y
WEST VIRGINIA							
1 Mollohan	Y	Y	Y	Y	Y	Y	Y
2 **Capito**	Y	Y	Y	?	N	N	N
3 Rahall	Y	Y	Y	Y	Y	Y	Y
WISCONSIN							
1 **Ryan**	Y	Y	Y	Y	N	N	N
2 Baldwin	Y	N	Y	Y	Y	Y	Y
3 Kind	Y	Y	Y	Y	Y	Y	Y
4 Moore	Y	N	Y	Y	Y	Y	Y
5 **Sensenbrenner**	Y	Y	Y	Y	N	N	N
6 **Petri**	Y	Y	Y	Y	N	N	N
7 Obey	Y	Y	Y	Y	Y	Y	Y
8 Kagen	Y	Y	Y	Y	Y	Y	Y
WYOMING							
AL **Lummis**	Y	Y	Y	Y	N	N	N
DELEGATES							
Faleomavaega (A.S.)							
Norton (D.C.)							
Bordallo (Guam)							
Sablan (N. Marianas)							
Pierluisi (P.R.)							
Christensen (V.I.)							

IN THE HOUSE | By Vote Number

981. H Con Res 160. Tribute to American Kennel Club/Adoption.
Lynch, D-Mass., motion to suspend the rules and adopt the concurrent resolution that would honor the American Kennel Club for its service to dog owners and the public. Motion agreed to 419-0: D 246-0; R 173-0. A two-thirds majority of those present and voting (280 in this case) is required for adoption under suspension of the rules. Dec. 16, 2009.

982. HR 3326, H J Res 64, HR 4314, HR 2847. Year-End Funding Bills and Debt Limit/Previous Question. Pingree, D-Maine, motion to order the previous question (thus ending debate and possibility of amendment) on adoption of the rule (H Res 976) to provide for House floor consideration of measures that would provide fiscal 2010 appropriations for the Defense Department, continue appropriations through Dec. 23 for federal departments whose fiscal 2010 appropriations bills have not been enacted, increase the debt limit by $290 billion, and fund infrastructure projects. Motion agreed to 235-193: D 235-18; R 0-175. Dec. 16, 2009.

983. HR 3326, H J Res 64, HR 4314, HR 2847. Year-End Funding Bills and Debt Limit/Rule. Adoption of the rule (H Res 976) to provide for House floor consideration of the measures that would provide fiscal 2010 appropriations for the Defense Department, continue appropriations through Dec. 23 for federal departments whose fiscal 2010 appropriations bills have not been enacted, increase the debt limit by $290 billion, and fund infrastructure projects. Adopted 228-201: D 228-26; R 0-175. Dec. 16, 2009.

984. H Res 905. 70th Anniversary of Justice Brandeis' Retirement/Adoption. Cohen, D-Tenn., motion to suspend the rules and adopt the resolution that would recognize the 70th anniversary of Justice Louis D. Brandeis' retirement from the Supreme Court and the contribution he made to American jurisprudence. Motion agreed to 423-1: D 251-0; R 172-1. A two-thirds majority of those present and voting (283 in this case) is required for adoption under suspension of the rules. Dec. 16, 2009.

985. HR 3326. Fiscal 2010 Defense Appropriations/Motion to Concur. Murtha, D-Pa., motion to concur in the Senate amendment with a House amendment to the bill that would appropriate $636.4 billion in discretionary funding for the Defense Department in fiscal 2010, including $128.2 billion for war operations. The House amendment would raise military pay by 3.4 percent. It would extend unemployment benefits and COBRA health care premium subsidies through Feb. 28, 2010. It would extend expiring provisions of the anti-terrorism law known as the Patriot Act, certain transportation and flood insurance programs, and some Small Business Administration loan programs through Feb. 28, 2010. It also would provide $400 million for the food stamp program and funding to prevent a scheduled cut in Medicare payments to physicians until Feb. 28, 2010. Motion agreed to 395-34: D 231-23; R 164-11. Dec. 16, 2009.

986. HR 1110. Caller ID Protections/Passage. Conyers, D-Mich., motion to suspend the rules and pass the bill that would make it a federal crime to manipulate caller identification information to commit identity theft or other forms of fraud. Motion agreed to 418-1: D 249-0; R 169-1. A two-thirds majority of those present and voting (280 in this case) is required for passage under suspension of the rules. Dec. 16, 2009.

	981	982	983	984	985	986
ALABAMA						
1 Bonner	Y	N	N	Y	Y	?
2 Bright	Y	N	N	Y	Y	Y
3 Rogers	Y	N	N	Y	Y	Y
4 Aderholt	Y	N	N	Y	Y	Y
5 Griffith	Y	N	N	Y	Y	Y
6 Bachus	Y	N	N	Y	Y	Y
7 Davis	Y	Y	Y	Y	Y	Y
ALASKA						
AL Young	Y	N	N	N	Y	Y
ARIZONA						
1 Kirkpatrick	Y	N	N	Y	Y	Y
2 Franks	Y	N	N	Y	Y	Y
3 Shadegg	Y	N	N	Y	Y	Y
4 Pastor	Y	Y	Y	?	Y	?
5 Mitchell	Y	N	N	Y	Y	Y
6 Flake	Y	N	N	Y	N	Y
7 Grijalva	Y	Y	Y	Y	Y	Y
8 Giffords	Y	N	N	Y	Y	Y
ARKANSAS						
1 Berry	Y	Y	Y	Y	Y	Y
2 Snyder	Y	Y	Y	Y	Y	Y
3 Boozman	Y	N	N	Y	Y	Y
4 Ross	Y	Y	Y	Y	Y	Y
CALIFORNIA						
1 Thompson	Y	Y	Y	Y	Y	Y
2 Herger	Y	N	N	Y	Y	Y
3 Lungren	Y	N	N	Y	Y	Y
4 McClintock	Y	N	N	Y	Y	Y
5 Matsui	Y	Y	Y	Y	Y	Y
6 Woolsey	Y	Y	Y	Y	N	Y
7 Miller, George	Y	Y	Y	Y	Y	Y
8 Pelosi						
9 Lee	Y	Y	Y	Y	N	Y
10 Garamendi	Y	Y	Y	Y	Y	Y
11 McNerney	Y	Y	Y	Y	Y	Y
12 Speier	?	?	?	?	?	?
13 Stark	Y	Y	N	Y	N	Y
14 Eshoo	Y	Y	Y	Y	+	Y
15 Honda	Y	Y	Y	Y	Y	?
16 Lofgren	Y	Y	Y	Y	N	Y
17 Farr	Y	Y	Y	Y	Y	Y
18 Cardoza	?	?	?	?	Y	Y
19 Radanovich	+	–	–	+	+	+
20 Costa	Y	Y	Y	Y	Y	Y
21 Nunes	Y	N	N	Y	Y	Y
22 McCarthy	Y	N	N	Y	Y	Y
23 Capps	Y	Y	Y	Y	Y	Y
24 Gallegly	Y	N	N	Y	Y	Y
25 McKeon	Y	N	N	Y	Y	Y
26 Dreier	Y	N	N	Y	Y	Y
27 Sherman	Y	Y	Y	Y	Y	Y
28 Berman	Y	Y	Y	Y	Y	Y
29 Schiff	Y	Y	Y	Y	Y	Y
30 Waxman	Y	Y	Y	Y	Y	Y
31 Becerra	Y	Y	Y	Y	Y	Y
32 Chu	Y	Y	Y	Y	Y	Y
33 Watson	Y	Y	Y	Y	Y	Y
34 Roybal-Allard	Y	Y	Y	Y	Y	Y
35 Waters	Y	Y	Y	Y	Y	Y
36 Harman	Y	Y	Y	Y	Y	Y
37 Richardson	Y	Y	Y	Y	Y	Y
38 Napolitano	Y	Y	Y	Y	Y	Y
39 Sánchez, Linda	Y	Y	Y	Y	Y	Y
40 Royce	Y	N	N	Y	Y	Y
41 Lewis	Y	N	N	Y	Y	Y
42 Miller, Gary	Y	N	N	Y	Y	Y
43 Baca	Y	Y	Y	Y	Y	Y
44 Calvert	Y	N	N	Y	Y	Y
45 Bono Mack	Y	N	N	Y	Y	Y
46 Rohrabacher	Y	N	N	?	Y	Y
47 Sanchez, Loretta	Y	Y	Y	Y	Y	Y
48 Campbell	Y	N	N	Y	N	Y
49 Issa	Y	N	N	Y	Y	Y
50 Bilbray	Y	N	N	Y	Y	Y
51 Filner	+	Y	Y	Y	N	Y
52 Hunter	Y	N	N	Y	Y	Y
53 Davis	Y	Y	Y	Y	Y	Y

	981	982	983	984	985	986
COLORADO						
1 DeGette	Y	Y	Y	Y	Y	Y
2 Polis	Y	Y	Y	Y	N	Y
3 Salazar	Y	Y	Y	Y	Y	Y
4 Markey	Y	Y	Y	Y	Y	Y
5 Lamborn	Y	N	N	Y	Y	Y
6 Coffman	Y	N	N	Y	Y	Y
7 Perlmutter	Y	Y	Y	Y	Y	Y
CONNECTICUT						
1 Larson	Y	+	+	+	Y	Y
2 Courtney	Y	Y	Y	Y	Y	Y
3 DeLauro	Y	Y	Y	Y	Y	Y
4 Himes	Y	N	N	Y	Y	?
5 Murphy	Y	Y	Y	Y	Y	Y
DELAWARE						
AL Castle	Y	N	N	Y	Y	Y
FLORIDA						
1 Miller	Y	N	N	Y	Y	Y
2 Boyd	Y	Y	N	Y	Y	Y
3 Brown	Y	Y	Y	Y	Y	Y
4 Crenshaw	Y	N	N	Y	Y	Y
5 Brown-Waite	Y	N	N	Y	Y	Y
6 Stearns	Y	N	N	Y	Y	Y
7 Mica	Y	N	N	Y	Y	Y
8 Grayson	Y	Y	Y	Y	N	Y
9 Bilirakis	Y	N	N	Y	Y	Y
10 Young	Y	N	N	Y	Y	?
11 Castor	Y	Y	Y	Y	Y	Y
12 Putnam	Y	N	N	Y	Y	Y
13 Buchanan	Y	N	N	Y	Y	Y
14 Mack	Y	N	N	Y	Y	Y
15 Posey	Y	N	N	Y	Y	Y
16 Rooney	Y	N	N	Y	Y	Y
17 Meek	Y	Y	Y	Y	Y	Y
18 Ros-Lehtinen	Y	N	N	Y	Y	Y
19 Wexler	Y	Y	Y	Y	Y	Y
20 Wasserman Schultz	Y	Y	Y	Y	Y	Y
21 Diaz-Balart, L.	Y	N	N	Y	Y	Y
22 Klein	Y	Y	Y	Y	Y	Y
23 Hastings	Y	Y	Y	Y	Y	Y
24 Kosmas	Y	N	N	Y	Y	Y
25 Diaz-Balart, M.	Y	N	N	Y	Y	Y
GEORGIA						
1 Kingston	Y	N	N	Y	Y	Y
2 Bishop	Y	Y	Y	Y	Y	Y
3 Westmoreland	Y	?	N	Y	Y	Y
4 Johnson	Y	Y	Y	Y	Y	Y
5 Lewis	Y	Y	Y	Y	N	Y
6 Price	Y	N	N	Y	Y	Y
7 Linder	Y	N	N	Y	Y	?
8 Marshall	Y	Y	Y	Y	Y	Y
9 Deal	Y	N	N	Y	Y	Y
10 Broun	Y	N	N	Y	Y	Y
11 Gingrey	Y	N	N	Y	Y	?
12 Barrow	Y	Y	Y	Y	Y	Y
13 Scott	Y	Y	Y	Y	Y	Y
HAWAII						
1 Abercrombie	Y	Y	Y	Y	Y	Y
2 Hirono	Y	Y	Y	Y	+	+
IDAHO						
1 Minnick	Y	N	N	Y	Y	Y
2 Simpson	?	N	N	Y	Y	Y
ILLINOIS						
1 Rush	Y	Y	Y	Y	Y	Y
2 Jackson	Y	Y	Y	Y	Y	Y
3 Lipinski	Y	Y	Y	Y	Y	Y
4 Gutierrez	Y	Y	Y	Y	Y	Y
5 Quigley	Y	Y	Y	Y	N	Y
6 Roskam	Y	N	N	Y	Y	Y
7 Davis	Y	Y	Y	Y	Y	Y
8 Bean	Y	Y	Y	Y	Y	Y
9 Schakowsky	Y	Y	Y	Y	Y	Y
10 Kirk	Y	N	N	?	Y	Y
11 Halvorson	Y	Y	Y	Y	Y	Y
12 Costello	Y	Y	Y	Y	N	Y
13 Biggert	Y	N	N	Y	Y	Y
14 Foster	Y	Y	Y	Y	Y	Y
15 Johnson	Y	N	N	Y	Y	Y

	981	982	983	984	985	986
16 **Manzullo**	Y	N	N	Y	Y	Y
17 Hare	Y	Y	Y	Y	Y	Y
18 **Schock**	Y	N	N	Y	Y	Y
19 **Shimkus**	Y	N	N	Y	N	Y
INDIANA						
1 Visclosky	Y	Y	Y	Y	Y	Y
2 Donnelly	Y	Y	N	Y	Y	Y
3 **Souder**	Y	N	N	Y	?	Y
4 **Buyer**	Y	N	N	Y	Y	Y
5 **Burton**	Y	N	N	Y	Y	Y
6 **Pence**	Y	N	N	Y	Y	Y
7 Carson	Y	Y	Y	Y	Y	Y
8 Ellsworth	Y	N	N	Y	Y	Y
9 Hill	Y	N	N	Y	Y	Y
IOWA						
1 Braley	Y	Y	Y	Y	Y	Y
2 Loebsack	Y	Y	Y	Y	Y	Y
3 Boswell	Y	Y	Y	Y	Y	Y
4 **Latham**	Y	N	N	Y	Y	Y
5 **King**	Y	N	N	Y	Y	Y
KANSAS						
1 **Moran**	Y	N	N	Y	Y	Y
2 **Jenkins**	Y	N	N	Y	Y	Y
3 Moore	Y	Y	Y	Y	Y	Y
4 **Tiahrt**	Y	N	N	Y	Y	Y
KENTUCKY						
1 **Whitfield**	Y	N	N	Y	Y	Y
2 **Guthrie**	Y	N	N	Y	Y	Y
3 Yarmuth	Y	Y	Y	Y	Y	Y
4 **Davis**	Y	N	N	Y	Y	Y
5 **Rogers**	Y	N	N	Y	Y	Y
6 Chandler	Y	Y	Y	Y	Y	Y
LOUISIANA						
1 **Scalise**	Y	N	N	Y	Y	Y
2 **Cao**	Y	N	N	Y	Y	Y
3 Melancon	Y	N	N	Y	Y	Y
4 **Fleming**	Y	N	N	Y	Y	Y
5 **Alexander**	Y	N	N	Y	Y	Y
6 **Cassidy**	Y	N	N	Y	Y	Y
7 **Boustany**	Y	N	N	Y	Y	Y
MAINE						
1 Pingree	Y	Y	Y	Y	Y	Y
2 Michaud	Y	Y	Y	Y	Y	Y
MARYLAND						
1 Kratovil	Y	N	N	Y	Y	Y
2 Ruppersberger	Y	Y	Y	Y	Y	Y
3 Sarbanes	Y	Y	Y	Y	Y	Y
4 Edwards	Y	Y	Y	Y	Y	Y
5 Hoyer	Y	Y	Y	Y	Y	Y
6 **Bartlett**	Y	N	N	Y	Y	Y
7 Cummings	Y	Y	Y	Y	Y	Y
8 Van Hollen	Y	Y	Y	Y	Y	Y
MASSACHUSETTS						
1 Olver	Y	Y	Y	Y	Y	Y
2 Neal	Y	Y	Y	Y	Y	Y
3 McGovern	Y	Y	Y	Y	Y	Y
4 Frank	Y	Y	Y	Y	Y	Y
5 Tsongas	Y	Y	Y	Y	Y	Y
6 Tierney	Y	Y	Y	Y	Y	Y
7 Markey	Y	Y	Y	Y	Y	Y
8 Capuano	Y	Y	Y	Y	Y	Y
9 Lynch	?	Y	Y	Y	Y	Y
10 Delahunt	Y	Y	Y	Y	Y	Y
MICHIGAN						
1 Stupak	Y	Y	Y	Y	Y	Y
2 **Hoekstra**	Y	N	N	Y	Y	Y
3 **Ehlers**	Y	N	N	Y	N	Y
4 **Camp**	Y	N	N	Y	Y	Y
5 Kildee	Y	Y	Y	Y	Y	Y
6 **Upton**	Y	N	N	Y	Y	Y
7 Schauer	Y	Y	Y	Y	Y	Y
8 **Rogers**	Y	N	N	Y	Y	Y
9 Peters	Y	Y	N	Y	Y	Y
10 **Miller**	Y	N	N	Y	Y	Y
11 **McCotter**	Y	N	N	Y	Y	Y
12 Levin	Y	Y	Y	Y	Y	Y
13 Kilpatrick	Y	Y	Y	Y	Y	Y
14 Conyers	Y	Y	Y	?	Y	?
15 Dingell	Y	Y	Y	Y	Y	Y
MINNESOTA						
1 Walz	Y	Y	Y	Y	Y	Y
2 **Kline**	Y	N	N	Y	Y	Y
3 **Paulsen**	Y	N	N	Y	Y	Y
4 McCollum	Y	Y	Y	Y	Y	Y

	981	982	983	984	985	986
5 Ellison	Y	Y	Y	Y	N	Y
6 **Bachmann**	Y	N	N	Y	Y	Y
7 Peterson	Y	Y	Y	Y	Y	Y
8 Oberstar	Y	Y	Y	Y	Y	Y
MISSISSIPPI						
1 Childers	Y	Y	Y	Y	Y	Y
2 Thompson	Y	Y	Y	Y	Y	Y
3 **Harper**	Y	N	N	Y	Y	Y
4 Taylor	Y	Y	Y	Y	Y	Y
MISSOURI						
1 Clay	?	Y	Y	Y	Y	Y
2 **Akin**	Y	N	N	Y	Y	Y
3 Carnahan	Y	Y	Y	Y	Y	Y
4 Skelton	Y	Y	Y	Y	Y	Y
5 Cleaver	Y	Y	Y	Y	Y	Y
6 **Graves**	Y	N	N	Y	Y	Y
7 **Blunt**	Y	N	N	Y	Y	Y
8 **Emerson**	Y	N	N	Y	Y	Y
9 **Luetkemeyer**	Y	N	N	Y	Y	Y
MONTANA						
AL **Rehberg**	Y	N	N	Y	Y	Y
NEBRASKA						
1 **Fortenberry**	Y	N	N	Y	Y	Y
2 **Terry**	Y	N	N	Y	Y	Y
3 **Smith**	Y	N	N	Y	Y	Y
NEVADA						
1 Berkley	Y	Y	Y	Y	Y	Y
2 **Heller**	Y	N	N	Y	Y	?
3 Titus	Y	Y	Y	Y	Y	Y
NEW HAMPSHIRE						
1 Shea-Porter	Y	Y	Y	Y	Y	Y
2 Hodes	Y	Y	Y	Y	Y	Y
NEW JERSEY						
1 Andrews	Y	Y	Y	Y	Y	Y
2 **LoBiondo**	Y	N	N	Y	Y	Y
3 Adler	Y	Y	Y	Y	Y	Y
4 **Smith**	Y	N	N	Y	Y	Y
5 **Garrett**	Y	N	N	Y	Y	Y
6 Pallone	Y	Y	Y	Y	Y	Y
7 **Lance**	Y	N	N	Y	Y	Y
8 Pascrell	Y	Y	Y	Y	Y	Y
9 Rothman	Y	Y	Y	Y	Y	Y
10 Payne	Y	Y	Y	Y	N	Y
11 **Frelinghuysen**	Y	N	N	Y	Y	Y
12 Holt	Y	Y	Y	Y	Y	Y
13 Sires	Y	Y	Y	Y	Y	Y
NEW MEXICO						
1 Heinrich	Y	Y	Y	Y	Y	Y
2 Teague	Y	Y	Y	Y	Y	Y
3 Lujan	Y	Y	Y	Y	Y	Y
NEW YORK						
1 Bishop	Y	Y	Y	Y	Y	Y
2 Israel	Y	Y	Y	Y	Y	Y
3 **King**	Y	N	N	Y	Y	Y
4 McCarthy	Y	Y	Y	Y	Y	Y
5 Ackerman	Y	Y	Y	Y	Y	Y
6 Meeks	Y	Y	Y	Y	Y	Y
7 Crowley	Y	Y	Y	Y	Y	Y
8 Nadler	Y	Y	Y	Y	N	Y
9 Weiner	Y	Y	Y	Y	Y	Y
10 Towns	Y	Y	Y	Y	N	Y
11 Clarke	Y	Y	Y	Y	N	Y
12 Velázquez	Y	Y	Y	Y	N	Y
13 McMahon	?	N	N	?	Y	Y
14 Maloney	Y	Y	Y	Y	Y	Y
15 Rangel	Y	Y	Y	Y	Y	Y
16 Serrano	Y	Y	Y	Y	N	Y
17 Engel	Y	Y	Y	Y	Y	Y
18 Lowey	Y	Y	Y	Y	Y	Y
19 Hall	?	Y	Y	Y	Y	Y
20 Murphy	Y	Y	N	Y	Y	Y
21 Tonko	Y	Y	Y	Y	Y	Y
22 Hinchey	Y	Y	Y	Y	Y	Y
23 Owens	Y	Y	Y	Y	Y	Y
24 Arcuri	Y	Y	Y	Y	Y	Y
25 Maffei	Y	Y	Y	Y	Y	Y
26 **Lee**	Y	N	N	Y	Y	Y
27 Higgins	Y	Y	Y	Y	Y	Y
28 Slaughter	+	Y	Y	Y	Y	Y
29 Massa	Y	Y	Y	Y	Y	Y
NORTH CAROLINA						
1 Butterfield	Y	Y	Y	Y	Y	Y
2 Etheridge	Y	Y	Y	Y	Y	Y
3 **Jones**	Y	N	N	Y	Y	Y
4 Price	Y	Y	Y	Y	Y	Y

	981	982	983	984	985	986
5 **Foxx**	Y	N	N	Y	Y	Y
6 **Coble**	Y	N	N	Y	Y	Y
7 McIntyre	Y	Y	Y	Y	Y	Y
8 Kissell	Y	Y	Y	Y	Y	Y
9 **Myrick**	Y	N	N	Y	Y	Y
10 **McHenry**	Y	N	N	Y	Y	Y
11 Shuler	Y	Y	Y	Y	Y	Y
12 Watt	Y	Y	Y	Y	Y	Y
13 Miller	Y	Y	Y	Y	Y	Y
NORTH DAKOTA						
AL Pomeroy	Y	Y	Y	Y	Y	Y
OHIO						
1 Driehaus	Y	N	N	Y	Y	Y
2 **Schmidt**	Y	N	N	Y	Y	Y
3 **Turner**	Y	N	N	Y	Y	Y
4 **Jordan**	Y	N	N	Y	Y	Y
5 **Latta**	Y	N	N	Y	Y	Y
6 Wilson	Y	Y	Y	Y	Y	Y
7 **Austria**	Y	N	N	Y	Y	Y
8 **Boehner**	Y	N	N	?	Y	Y
9 Kaptur	Y	Y	Y	Y	Y	?
10 Kucinich	Y	Y	N	Y	N	Y
11 Fudge	Y	Y	Y	Y	Y	Y
12 **Tiberi**	Y	N	N	Y	Y	Y
13 Sutton	Y	Y	Y	Y	Y	Y
14 **LaTourette**	Y	N	N	Y	Y	Y
15 Kilroy	Y	Y	Y	Y	Y	Y
16 Boccieri	Y	Y	Y	Y	Y	Y
17 Ryan	Y	Y	Y	Y	Y	Y
18 Space	Y	N	N	Y	Y	Y
OKLAHOMA						
1 **Sullivan**	Y	N	?	Y	Y	Y
2 Boren	Y	Y	Y	Y	Y	Y
3 **Lucas**	Y	N	N	Y	Y	Y
4 **Cole**	Y	N	N	Y	Y	Y
5 **Fallin**	Y	N	N	Y	Y	Y
OREGON						
1 Wu	Y	Y	N	Y	N	Y
2 **Walden**	Y	N	N	Y	Y	Y
3 Blumenauer	Y	Y	Y	Y	Y	Y
4 DeFazio	Y	Y	Y	Y	Y	Y
5 Schrader	Y	Y	Y	Y	Y	Y
PENNSYLVANIA						
1 Brady	Y	Y	Y	Y	Y	Y
2 Fattah	Y	Y	Y	Y	Y	Y
3 Dahlkemper	Y	N	N	Y	Y	Y
4 Altmire	Y	Y	Y	Y	Y	Y
5 **Thompson**	Y	N	N	Y	Y	Y
6 **Gerlach**	Y	N	N	Y	Y	Y
7 Sestak	Y	Y	Y	Y	Y	Y
8 Murphy, P.	Y	?	Y	Y	Y	Y
9 **Shuster**	Y	N	N	Y	Y	Y
10 Carney	Y	Y	Y	Y	Y	Y
11 Kanjorski	Y	Y	Y	Y	Y	Y
12 Murtha	?	Y	Y	Y	Y	Y
13 Schwartz	Y	Y	Y	Y	Y	Y
14 Doyle	Y	Y	Y	Y	Y	Y
15 **Dent**	Y	N	N	Y	Y	Y
16 **Pitts**	Y	N	N	Y	Y	Y
17 Holden	Y	Y	Y	Y	Y	Y
18 **Murphy, T.**	Y	N	N	Y	Y	Y
19 **Platts**	Y	N	N	Y	Y	Y
RHODE ISLAND						
1 Kennedy	Y	Y	Y	Y	Y	Y
2 Langevin	Y	Y	Y	Y	Y	Y
SOUTH CAROLINA						
1 **Brown**	Y	N	N	Y	Y	Y
2 **Wilson**	Y	N	N	Y	Y	Y
3 **Barrett**	+	N	N	Y	Y	Y
4 **Inglis**	Y	N	N	Y	Y	Y
5 Spratt	Y	Y	Y	Y	Y	Y
6 Clyburn	Y	Y	Y	Y	Y	Y
SOUTH DAKOTA						
AL Herseth Sandlin	Y	Y	Y	Y	Y	Y
TENNESSEE						
1 **Roe**	Y	N	N	Y	Y	Y
2 **Duncan**	Y	N	N	Y	N	Y
3 **Wamp**	Y	N	N	Y	Y	Y
4 Davis	Y	Y	Y	Y	Y	Y
5 Cooper	Y	Y	Y	Y	Y	Y
6 Gordon	Y	Y	Y	Y	Y	Y
7 **Blackburn**	Y	N	N	Y	Y	Y
8 Tanner	Y	Y	N	Y	Y	Y
9 Cohen	Y	Y	Y	Y	Y	Y

	981	982	983	984	985	986
TEXAS						
1 **Gohmert**	Y	N	N	Y	N	Y
2 **Poe**	Y	N	N	Y	Y	Y
3 **Johnson, S.**	Y	N	N	Y	Y	Y
4 **Hall**	Y	N	N	Y	Y	Y
5 **Hensarling**	Y	N	N	Y	Y	Y
6 **Barton**	Y	N	N	Y	Y	Y
7 **Culberson**	Y	N	N	Y	Y	Y
8 **Brady**	Y	N	N	Y	Y	Y
9 Green, A.	Y	Y	Y	Y	Y	Y
10 **McCaul**	Y	N	N	Y	Y	Y
11 **Conaway**	Y	N	N	Y	Y	Y
12 **Granger**	Y	N	N	Y	Y	Y
13 **Thornberry**	Y	N	N	Y	Y	Y
14 **Paul**	?	N	N	Y	N	N
15 Hinojosa	Y	Y	Y	Y	Y	Y
16 Reyes	Y	Y	Y	Y	Y	Y
17 Edwards	Y	Y	Y	Y	Y	Y
18 Jackson Lee	Y	Y	Y	Y	Y	Y
19 **Neugebauer**	Y	N	N	Y	Y	Y
20 Gonzalez	Y	Y	Y	Y	Y	Y
21 **Smith**	Y	N	N	Y	Y	Y
22 **Olson**	Y	N	N	Y	Y	Y
23 Rodriguez	Y	Y	Y	Y	Y	Y
24 **Marchant**	Y	N	N	Y	Y	Y
25 Doggett	Y	Y	Y	Y	Y	Y
26 **Burgess**	Y	N	N	Y	Y	Y
27 Ortiz	Y	Y	Y	Y	Y	Y
28 Cuellar	Y	Y	Y	Y	Y	Y
29 Green, G.	Y	Y	Y	Y	Y	Y
30 Johnson, E.	?	Y	Y	Y	Y	Y
31 **Carter**	Y	N	N	Y	Y	Y
32 **Sessions**	Y	N	N	Y	Y	Y
UTAH						
1 **Bishop**	Y	N	N	Y	N	Y
2 Matheson	Y	Y	Y	Y	Y	Y
3 **Chaffetz**	Y	N	N	Y	N	Y
VERMONT						
AL Welch	Y	Y	Y	Y	N	Y
VIRGINIA						
1 **Wittman**	Y	N	N	Y	Y	Y
2 Nye	Y	Y	Y	Y	Y	Y
3 Scott	Y	Y	Y	Y	Y	Y
4 **Forbes**	Y	N	N	Y	Y	Y
5 Perriello	Y	N	Y	Y	Y	Y
6 **Goodlatte**	Y	N	N	Y	Y	Y
7 **Cantor**	Y	N	N	Y	Y	Y
8 Moran	?	Y	Y	Y	Y	Y
9 Boucher	Y	Y	Y	Y	Y	Y
10 **Wolf**	Y	N	N	Y	Y	?
11 Connolly	Y	Y	Y	Y	Y	Y
WASHINGTON						
1 Inslee	Y	Y	Y	Y	Y	Y
2 Larsen	Y	Y	Y	Y	Y	Y
3 Baird	Y	N	N	Y	Y	Y
4 **Hastings**	Y	N	N	Y	Y	Y
5 **McMorris Rodgers**	Y	N	N	Y	Y	Y
6 Dicks	Y	Y	Y	Y	Y	?
7 McDermott	Y	Y	Y	Y	N	Y
8 **Reichert**	Y	N	N	Y	Y	Y
9 Smith	Y	Y	Y	Y	Y	Y
WEST VIRGINIA						
1 Mollohan	Y	Y	Y	Y	Y	Y
2 **Capito**	Y	N	N	Y	Y	Y
3 Rahall	Y	Y	Y	Y	Y	Y
WISCONSIN						
1 **Ryan**	Y	N	N	Y	Y	Y
2 Baldwin	Y	Y	Y	Y	N	Y
3 Kind	Y	Y	Y	Y	Y	Y
4 Moore	Y	Y	Y	Y	Y	Y
5 **Sensenbrenner**	Y	N	N	Y	Y	Y
6 **Petri**	Y	N	N	Y	Y	Y
7 Obey	Y	Y	Y	Y	Y	Y
8 Kagen	Y	Y	Y	Y	N	Y
WYOMING						
AL **Lummis**	Y	N	N	Y	N	Y
DELEGATES						
Faleomavaega (A.S.)						
Norton (D.C.)						
Bordallo (Guam)						
Sablan (N. Marianas)						
Pierluisi (P.R.)						
Christensen (V.I.)						

IN THE HOUSE | By Vote Number

987. Procedural Matter/Quorum Call.* A quorum was present with 415 members responding (20 members did not respond). Dec. 16, 2009.

988. HR 4314. Debt Limit Increase/Passage. Passage of the bill that would increase the federal debt limit to $12.4 trillion. Passed 218-214: D 218-39; R 0-175. Dec. 16, 2009.

989. HR 3714. Global Press Freedom/Passage. Berman, D-Calif., motion to suspend the rules and pass the bill that would require the State Department to include information on the freedom of the press in country reports. Motion agreed to 403-12: D 246-0; R 157-12. A two-thirds majority of those present and voting (277 in this case) is required for passage under suspension of the rules. Dec. 16, 2009.

990. Procedural Matter/Quorum Call.* A quorum was present with 429 members responding (six members did not respond). Dec. 16, 2009.

991. HR 2847. Jobs Funding and Year-End Extensions/Motion to Concur. Obey, D-Wis., motion to concur in the Senate amendment to the bill with a House amendment that would appropriate $154.4 billion for infrastructure projects, jobs programs, and aid to state and local governments. It would redirect $75 billion of the money from the Troubled Asset Relief Program, with $48.3 billion for infrastructure projects and $26.7 billion for aid to help state and local governments preserve public jobs. It also would extend unemployment benefits, COBRA health care premium subsidies and provisions requiring the federal government to assume an increased share of Medicaid funding through June 30, 2010. It would extend federal highway, transit and safety programs through the end of fiscal 2010 and would expand eligibility for the child tax credit. Motion agreed to 217-212: D 217-38; R 0-174. Dec. 16, 2009.

	988	989	991
ALABAMA			
1 **Bonner**	N	Y	N
2 Bright	N	Y	N
3 **Rogers**	N	Y	N
4 **Aderholt**	N	Y	N
5 Griffith	N	Y	N
6 **Bachus**	N	Y	N
7 Davis	Y	Y	Y
ALASKA			
AL **Young**	N	Y	N
ARIZONA			
1 Kirkpatrick	N	Y	N
2 **Franks**	N	Y	N
3 **Shadegg**	N	Y	N
4 Pastor	Y	Y	Y
5 Mitchell	N	Y	N
6 **Flake**	N	Y	N
7 Grijalva	Y	Y	Y
8 Giffords	N	Y	Y
ARKANSAS			
1 Berry	Y	Y	Y
2 Snyder	Y	Y	Y
3 **Boozman**	N	Y	N
4 Ross	Y	Y	Y
CALIFORNIA			
1 Thompson	Y	Y	Y
2 **Herger**	N	Y	N
3 **Lungren**	N	Y	N
4 **McClintock**	N	N	N
5 Matsui	Y	Y	Y
6 Woolsey	Y	Y	Y
7 Miller, George	Y	Y	Y
8 Pelosi	Y		Y
9 Lee	Y	Y	Y
10 Garamendi	Y	Y	Y
11 McNerney	N	Y	Y
12 Speier	?	?	?
13 Stark	Y	Y	Y
14 Eshoo	Y	Y	Y
15 Honda	Y	Y	Y
16 Lofgren	Y	Y	Y
17 Farr	Y	Y	Y
18 Cardoza	Y	Y	Y
19 **Radanovich**	–	+	–
20 Costa	Y	Y	Y
21 **Nunes**	N	Y	N
22 **McCarthy**	N	Y	N
23 Capps	Y	Y	Y
24 **Gallegly**	N	Y	N
25 **McKeon**	N	Y	N
26 **Dreier**	N	Y	N
27 Sherman	Y	Y	Y
28 Berman	Y	Y	Y
29 Schiff	Y	Y	Y
30 Waxman	Y	?	Y
31 Becerra	Y	Y	Y
32 Chu	Y	Y	Y
33 Watson	Y	Y	Y
34 Roybal-Allard	Y	Y	Y
35 Waters	Y	Y	Y
36 Harman	Y	Y	Y
37 Richardson	Y	Y	Y
38 Napolitano	Y	Y	Y
39 Sánchez, Linda	Y	Y	Y
40 **Royce**	N	Y	N
41 **Lewis**	N	Y	N
42 **Miller, Gary**	N	Y	N
43 Baca	Y	Y	Y
44 **Calvert**	N	Y	N
45 **Bono Mack**	N	Y	N
46 **Rohrabacher**	N	Y	N
47 Sanchez, Loretta	Y	Y	Y
48 **Campbell**	N	Y	N
49 **Issa**	N	Y	N
50 **Bilbray**	N	Y	N
51 Filner	Y	Y	Y
52 **Hunter**	N	Y	N
53 Davis	Y	Y	Y

	988	989	991
COLORADO			
1 DeGette	Y	Y	Y
2 Polis	Y	Y	Y
3 Salazar	Y	Y	Y
4 Markey	N	Y	N
5 **Lamborn**	N	Y	N
6 **Coffman**	N	Y	N
7 Perlmutter	Y	Y	Y
CONNECTICUT			
1 Larson	Y	Y	Y
2 Courtney	Y	Y	Y
3 DeLauro	Y	Y	Y
4 Himes	Y	Y	N
5 Murphy	Y	Y	Y
DELAWARE			
AL **Castle**	N	Y	N
FLORIDA			
1 **Miller**	N	Y	N
2 Boyd	Y	Y	N
3 Brown	Y	Y	Y
4 **Crenshaw**	N	Y	N
5 **Brown-Waite**	N	N	N
6 **Stearns**	N	Y	N
7 **Mica**	N	Y	N
8 Grayson	N	Y	N
9 **Bilirakis**	N	Y	N
10 **Young**	?	?	?
11 Castor	Y	Y	Y
12 **Putnam**	N	Y	N
13 **Buchanan**	N	Y	N
14 **Mack**	N	Y	N
15 **Posey**	N	Y	N
16 **Rooney**	N	Y	N
17 Meek	N	Y	N
18 **Ros-Lehtinen**	N	Y	N
19 Wexler	Y	Y	Y
20 Wasserman Schultz	N	?	Y
21 **Diaz-Balart, L.**	N	Y	N
22 Klein	Y	Y	Y
23 Hastings	Y	Y	Y
24 Kosmas	Y	Y	N
25 **Diaz-Balart, M.**	N	Y	N
GEORGIA			
1 **Kingston**	N	Y	N
2 Bishop	Y	Y	Y
3 **Westmoreland**	N	Y	N
4 Johnson	Y	Y	Y
5 Lewis	Y	Y	Y
6 **Price**	N	Y	N
7 **Linder**	N	Y	?
8 Marshall	Y	Y	Y
9 **Deal**	N	N	N
10 **Broun**	N	N	N
11 **Gingrey**	N	Y	N
12 Barrow	Y	Y	Y
13 Scott	Y	Y	Y
HAWAII			
1 Abercrombie	Y	Y	Y
2 Hirono	Y	Y	Y
IDAHO			
1 Minnick	N	Y	N
2 **Simpson**	N	Y	N
ILLINOIS			
1 Rush	Y	Y	Y
2 Jackson	Y	Y	Y
3 Lipinski	Y	Y	Y
4 Gutierrez	Y	Y	Y
5 Quigley	Y	Y	N
6 **Roskam**	N	Y	N
7 Davis	Y	Y	Y
8 Bean	Y	Y	N
9 Schakowsky	Y	Y	Y
10 **Kirk**	N	Y	N
11 Halvorson	N	Y	Y
12 Costello	Y	Y	Y
13 **Biggert**	N	Y	N
14 Foster	N	Y	N
15 **Johnson**	N	Y	N

KEY   **Republicans**   Democrats

Y	Voted for (yea)	X	Paired against
#	Paired for	–	Announced against
+	Announced for	P	Voted "present"
N	Voted against (nay)	C	Voted "present" to avoid possible conflict of interest
		?	Did not vote or otherwise make a position known

* CQ does not include quorum calls in its vote charts.

	988	989	991
16 Manzullo	N	Y	N
17 Hare	Y	Y	Y
18 Schock	N	Y	N
19 Shimkus	N	Y	N
INDIANA			
1 Visclosky	N	Y	Y
2 Donnelly	N	Y	N
3 Souder	N	Y	N
4 Buyer	N	?	N
5 Burton	N	Y	N
6 Pence	N	Y	N
7 Carson	Y	Y	Y
8 Ellsworth	N	Y	N
9 Hill	Y	Y	N
IOWA			
1 Braley	Y	Y	Y
2 Loebsack	Y	Y	Y
3 Boswell	Y	Y	Y
4 Latham	N	Y	N
5 King	N	?	N
KANSAS			
1 Moran	N	Y	N
2 Jenkins	N	Y	N
3 Moore	Y	Y	Y
4 Tiahrt	N	Y	N
KENTUCKY			
1 Whitfield	N	?	N
2 Guthrie	N	Y	N
3 Yarmuth	Y	Y	Y
4 Davis	N	Y	N
5 Rogers	N	Y	N
6 Chandler	Y	Y	Y
LOUISIANA			
1 Scalise	N	Y	N
2 Cao	N	Y	N
3 Melancon	N	Y	N
4 Fleming	N	Y	N
5 Alexander	N	Y	N
6 Cassidy	N	Y	N
7 Boustany	N	Y	N
MAINE			
1 Pingree	Y	Y	Y
2 Michaud	Y	Y	Y
MARYLAND			
1 Kratovil	N	Y	N
2 Ruppersberger	Y	Y	Y
3 Sarbanes	Y	Y	Y
4 Edwards	Y	Y	Y
5 Hoyer	Y	Y	Y
6 Bartlett	N	Y	N
7 Cummings	Y	Y	Y
8 Van Hollen	Y	Y	Y
MASSACHUSETTS			
1 Olver	Y	Y	Y
2 Neal	Y	Y	Y
3 McGovern	Y	Y	Y
4 Frank	Y	Y	Y
5 Tsongas	Y	Y	Y
6 Tierney	Y	Y	Y
7 Markey	Y	Y	Y
8 Capuano	Y	Y	Y
9 Lynch	Y	Y	Y
10 Delahunt	Y	Y	Y
MICHIGAN			
1 Stupak	Y	Y	Y
2 Hoekstra	N	Y	N
3 Ehlers	N	Y	N
4 Camp	N	Y	N
5 Kildee	Y	Y	Y
6 Upton	N	Y	N
7 Schauer	Y	Y	Y
8 Rogers	N	Y	N
9 Peters	N	Y	N
10 Miller	N	Y	N
11 McCotter	N	Y	N
12 Levin	Y	Y	Y
13 Kilpatrick	Y	?	Y
14 Conyers	Y	Y	Y
15 Dingell	Y	Y	Y
MINNESOTA			
1 Walz	Y	Y	Y
2 Kline	N	Y	N
3 Paulsen	N	Y	N
4 McCollum	Y	Y	Y

	988	989	991
5 Ellison	Y	Y	Y
6 Bachmann	N	Y	N
7 Peterson	Y	?	N
8 Oberstar	Y	Y	Y
MISSISSIPPI			
1 Childers	N	Y	N
2 Thompson	Y	Y	Y
3 Harper	N	Y	N
4 Taylor	N	Y	N
MISSOURI			
1 Clay	Y	Y	Y
2 Akin	N	Y	N
3 Carnahan	Y	Y	Y
4 Skelton	Y	Y	Y
5 Cleaver	Y	Y	Y
6 Graves	N	Y	N
7 Blunt	N	Y	N
8 Emerson	N	Y	N
9 Luetkemeyer	N	Y	N
MONTANA			
AL Rehberg	N	Y	N
NEBRASKA			
1 Fortenberry	N	Y	N
2 Terry	N	Y	N
3 Smith	N	Y	N
NEVADA			
1 Berkley	Y	Y	Y
2 Heller	N	Y	N
3 Titus	N	?	Y
NEW HAMPSHIRE			
1 Shea-Porter	Y	Y	Y
2 Hodes	N	Y	N
NEW JERSEY			
1 Andrews	Y	Y	Y
2 LoBiondo	N	Y	N
3 Adler	N	Y	N
4 Smith	N	Y	N
5 Garrett	N	N	N
6 Pallone	Y	Y	Y
7 Lance	N	Y	N
8 Pascrell	Y	Y	Y
9 Rothman	Y	Y	Y
10 Payne	Y	Y	Y
11 Frelinghuysen	N	Y	N
12 Holt	Y	Y	Y
13 Sires	Y	Y	Y
NEW MEXICO			
1 Heinrich	Y	Y	Y
2 Teague	N	Y	N
3 Lujan	Y	Y	Y
NEW YORK			
1 Bishop	Y	Y	Y
2 Israel	Y	Y	Y
3 King	N	Y	N
4 McCarthy	Y	Y	Y
5 Ackerman	Y	Y	Y
6 Meeks	Y	Y	Y
7 Crowley	Y	Y	Y
8 Nadler	Y	Y	Y
9 Weiner	Y	Y	Y
10 Towns	Y	Y	Y
11 Clarke	Y	Y	Y
12 Velázquez	Y	Y	Y
13 McMahon	Y	Y	Y
14 Maloney	Y	Y	Y
15 Rangel	Y	Y	Y
16 Serrano	Y	Y	Y
17 Engel	Y	Y	Y
18 Lowey	Y	?	Y
19 Hall	Y	Y	Y
20 Murphy	N	?	Y
21 Tonko	Y	Y	Y
22 Hinchey	Y	Y	Y
23 Owens	N	Y	Y
24 Arcuri	Y	Y	N
25 Maffei	N	?	Y
26 Lee	N	Y	N
27 Higgins	Y	Y	Y
28 Slaughter	Y	Y	Y
29 Massa	N	Y	Y
NORTH CAROLINA			
1 Butterfield	Y	Y	Y
2 Etheridge	Y	Y	Y
3 Jones	N	Y	N
4 Price	Y	Y	Y

	988	989	991
5 Foxx	N	N	N
6 Coble	N	Y	N
7 McIntyre	N	Y	Y
8 Kissell	N	Y	Y
9 Myrick	N	Y	N
10 McHenry	N	Y	N
11 Shuler	Y	Y	Y
12 Watt	Y	Y	Y
13 Miller	Y	Y	Y
NORTH DAKOTA			
AL Pomeroy	Y	Y	N
OHIO			
1 Driehaus	N	Y	N
2 Schmidt	N	Y	N
3 Turner	N	Y	N
4 Jordan	N	?	N
5 Latta	N	Y	N
6 Wilson	Y	?	Y
7 Austria	N	Y	N
8 Boehner	N	?	N
9 Kaptur	Y	Y	Y
10 Kucinich	N	Y	Y
11 Fudge	Y	Y	Y
12 Tiberi	N	Y	N
13 Sutton	Y	Y	Y
14 LaTourette	N	Y	N
15 Kilroy	Y	Y	Y
16 Boccieri	N	Y	Y
17 Ryan	Y	Y	Y
18 Space	N	Y	N
OKLAHOMA			
1 Sullivan	N	Y	N
2 Boren	Y	Y	N
3 Lucas	N	Y	N
4 Cole	N	Y	N
5 Fallin	N	Y	N
OREGON			
1 Wu	Y	Y	Y
2 Walden	N	Y	N
3 Blumenauer	Y	Y	Y
4 DeFazio	Y	Y	Y
5 Schrader	Y	Y	N
PENNSYLVANIA			
1 Brady	Y	Y	Y
2 Fattah	Y	Y	Y
3 Dahlkemper	Y	Y	Y
4 Altmire	Y	Y	Y
5 Thompson	N	Y	N
6 Gerlach	N	Y	N
7 Sestak	Y	Y	Y
8 Murphy, P.	Y	Y	Y
9 Shuster	N	Y	N
10 Carney	N	Y	Y
11 Kanjorski	Y	Y	Y
12 Murtha	Y	?	?
13 Schwartz	Y	Y	Y
14 Doyle	Y	Y	Y
15 Dent	N	Y	N
16 Pitts	N	Y	N
17 Holden	Y	Y	Y
18 Murphy, T.	N	Y	N
19 Platts	N	Y	N
RHODE ISLAND			
1 Kennedy	Y	Y	Y
2 Langevin	Y	Y	Y
SOUTH CAROLINA			
1 Brown	N	Y	N
2 Wilson	N	Y	N
3 Barrett	N	Y	N
4 Inglis	N	Y	N
5 Spratt	Y	Y	Y
6 Clyburn	Y	Y	Y
SOUTH DAKOTA			
AL Herseth Sandlin	Y	Y	N
TENNESSEE			
1 Roe	N	Y	N
2 Duncan	N	N	N
3 Wamp	N	Y	N
4 Davis	Y	Y	Y
5 Cooper	Y	Y	Y
6 Gordon	Y	Y	Y
7 Blackburn	N	Y	N
8 Tanner	Y	Y	Y
9 Cohen	Y	Y	Y

	988	989	991
TEXAS			
1 Gohmert	N	N	N
2 Poe	N	Y	N
3 Johnson, S.	N	Y	N
4 Hall	N	Y	N
5 Hensarling	N	Y	N
6 Barton	N	N	N
7 Culberson	N	Y	N
8 Brady	N	Y	N
9 Green, A.	Y	Y	Y
10 McCaul	N	Y	N
11 Conaway	N	N	N
12 Granger	N	Y	N
13 Thornberry	N	Y	N
14 Paul	N	N	N
15 Hinojosa	Y	Y	Y
16 Reyes	Y	Y	Y
17 Edwards	Y	Y	Y
18 Jackson Lee	Y	Y	Y
19 Neugebauer	N	Y	N
20 Gonzalez	Y	Y	Y
21 Smith	N	Y	N
22 Olson	N	Y	N
23 Rodriguez	Y	Y	Y
24 Marchant	N	N	N
25 Doggett	Y	Y	Y
26 Burgess	N	Y	N
27 Ortiz	Y	Y	Y
28 Cuellar	Y	Y	Y
29 Green, G.	Y	Y	Y
30 Johnson, E.	Y	Y	?
31 Carter	N	Y	N
32 Sessions	N	Y	N
UTAH			
1 Bishop	N	?	N
2 Matheson	Y	Y	N
3 Chaffetz	N	Y	N
VERMONT			
AL Welch	Y	Y	Y
VIRGINIA			
1 Wittman	N	Y	N
2 Nye	N	Y	N
3 Scott	Y	Y	Y
4 Forbes	N	Y	N
5 Perriello	N	Y	Y
6 Goodlatte	N	Y	N
7 Cantor	N	Y	N
8 Moran	Y	Y	Y
9 Boucher	Y	Y	Y
10 Wolf	N	Y	N
11 Connolly	Y	Y	Y
WASHINGTON			
1 Inslee	Y	Y	Y
2 Larsen	Y	Y	Y
3 Baird	Y	Y	Y
4 Hastings	N	Y	N
5 McMorris Rodgers	N	Y	N
6 Dicks	Y	Y	Y
7 McDermott	Y	Y	Y
8 Reichert	N	Y	N
9 Smith	Y	Y	N
WEST VIRGINIA			
1 Mollohan	Y	Y	Y
2 Capito	N	Y	N
3 Rahall	Y	Y	Y
WISCONSIN			
1 Ryan	N	Y	N
2 Baldwin	Y	Y	Y
3 Kind	Y	Y	N
4 Moore	Y	Y	Y
5 Sensenbrenner	N	Y	N
6 Petri	N	Y	N
7 Obey	Y	Y	Y
8 Kagen	Y	Y	Y
WYOMING			
AL Lummis	N	N	N
DELEGATES			
Faleomavaega (A.S.)			
Norton (D.C.)			
Bordallo (Guam)			
Sablan (N. Marianas)			
Pierluisi (P.R.)			
Christensen (V.I.)			

House Roll Call Index by Subject

SENATE
ROLL CALL
VOTES

Senate Roll Call Index
By Bill Number

SENATE VOTES

S 22, S-4
S 160, S-16, S-17
S 181, S-4, S-5, S-6
S 386, S-33, S-35
S 454, S-37, S-39
S 896, S-35, S-36, S-37
S 1023, S-42, S-43, S-55
S 1256, S-40, S-41
S 1390, S-47, S-48, S-49
S 1776, S-65
S 1963, S-70
S 2346, S-40

S Con Res 13, S-26, S-27, S-28, S-29, S-30, S-31, S-33, S-34, S-35

S J Res 5, S-4

HOUSE VOTES

HR 1, S-10, S-11, S-12, S-13, S-14, S-15, S-16
HR 146, S-22, S-23
HR 627, S-38, S-39
HR 1105, S-18, S-19, S-20, S-21
HR 1388, S-24, S-25
HR 2346, S-39, S-42
HR 2647, S-65
HR 2847, S-64, S-67, S-68
HR 2892, S-43, S-44, S-45, S-46, S-65
HR 2918, S-43, S-44, S-61
HR 2996, S-58, S-59, S-60, S-66
HR 2997, S-52, S-53, S-64
HR 3082, S-69
HR 3183, S-50, S-64
HR 3288, S-56, S-57, S-58, S-75
HR 3326, S-61, S-62, S-63, S-76
HR 3357, S-51
HR 3435, S-53, S-54
HR 3548, S-66, S-67
HR 3590, S-70, S-71, S-72, S-73, S-74, S-75, S-76, S-77, S-78
HR 4314, S-78

IN THE SENATE | By Vote Number

1. **S 22. Public Lands Designation/Cloture.** Motion to invoke cloture (thus limiting debate) on the motion to proceed to the bill that would designate new wilderness areas, wild and scenic rivers, and historic rivers and codify a National Landscape Conservation System. Motion agreed to 66-12: R 12-12; D 52-0; I 2-0. Three-fifths of the total Senate (59) is required to invoke cloture. Jan. 11, 2009.

2. **S 22. Public Lands Designation/Cloture.** Motion to invoke cloture (thus limiting debate) on the bill that would designate new wilderness areas, wild and scenic rivers, and historic rivers and codify a National Landscape Conservation System. Motion agreed to 68-24: R 17-23; D 49-1; I 2-0. Three-fifths of the total Senate (59) is required to invoke cloture. Jan. 14, 2009.

3. **S 22. Public Lands Designation/Passage.** Passage of the bill that would designate more than 2 million new acres of protected wilderness areas nationwide, in addition to wild and scenic rivers, historic sites and expansions of national parks. It would authorize new water projects and allow three water settlements in Western states. The bill also would codify a National Landscape Conservation System to improve management of protected federal land. Passed 73-21: R 19-21; D 52-0; I 2-0. Jan. 15, 2009.

4. **S 181. Wage Discrimination/Cloture.** Motion to invoke cloture (thus limiting debate) on the motion to proceed to the bill that would amend the 1964 Civil Rights Act to allow employees to file charges of pay discrimination within 180 days of the last paycheck affected by the alleged discriminatory decision. Motion agreed to 72-23: R 17-23; D 53-0; I 2-0. Three-fifths of the total Senate (59) is required to invoke cloture. Jan. 15, 2009.

5. **S J Res 5. Troubled Asset Relief Program Disapproval/Passage.** Passage of the joint resolution that would prevent the release of the second half of the $700 billion provided under the 2008 financial industry bailout law. Rejected 42-52: R 33-6; D 8-45; I 1-1. Jan. 15, 2009.

	1	2	3	4	5
ALABAMA					
Shelby	N	N	N	N	Y
Sessions	N	N	N	N	Y
ALASKA					
Murkowski	Y	Y	Y	Y	Y
Begich	Y	Y	Y	Y	N
ARIZONA					
McCain	N	N	N	Y	Y
Kyl	?	N	N	N	N
ARKANSAS					
Lincoln	Y	Y	Y	Y	Y
Pryor	Y	Y	Y	Y	N
CALIFORNIA					
Feinstein	Y	Y	Y	Y	N
Boxer	Y	Y	Y	Y	N
COLORADO					
Salazar	Y	Y	Y	Y	N
Udall	Y	Y	Y	Y	N
CONNECTICUT					
Dodd	Y	Y	Y	Y	N
Lieberman	Y	Y	Y	Y	N
DELAWARE					
Biden	?	?	?	Y	N
Carper	Y	Y	Y	Y	N
FLORIDA					
Nelson	Y	Y	Y	Y	N
Martinez	?	Y	Y	Y	Y
GEORGIA					
Chambliss	?	N	N	N	Y
Isakson	N	N	N	N	Y
HAWAII					
Inouye	Y	Y	Y	Y	N
Akaka	Y	Y	Y	Y	N
IDAHO					
Crapo	Y	Y	Y	N	Y
Risch	Y	Y	Y	N	Y
ILLINOIS					
Durbin	Y	Y	Y	Y	N
Burris*					N
INDIANA					
Lugar	Y	Y	Y	N	N
Bayh	Y	Y	Y	Y	Y
IOWA					
Grassley	N	N	N	Y	Y
Harkin	Y	Y	Y	Y	N
KANSAS					
Brownback	N	N	N	Y	Y
Roberts	?	Y	N	N	Y
KENTUCKY					
McConnell	?	N	N	Y	Y
Bunning	–	–	–	–	+
LOUISIANA					
Landrieu	Y	Y	Y	Y	N
Vitter	?	N	N	N	Y
MAINE					
Snowe	Y	Y	Y	Y	N
Collins	Y	Y	Y	Y	Y
MARYLAND					
Mikulski	Y	Y	Y	Y	N
Cardin	Y	Y	Y	Y	N
MASSACHUSETTS					
Kennedy	?	?	?	?	X
Kerry	Y	Y	Y	Y	N
MICHIGAN					
Levin	Y	Y	Y	Y	N
Stabenow	Y	?	Y	Y	N
MINNESOTA					
Klobuchar	Y	Y	Y	Y	N
Vacant					
MISSISSIPPI					
Cochran	Y	Y	Y	N	Y
Wicker	Y	Y	Y	Y	Y
MISSOURI					
Bond	?	Y	Y	Y	Y
McCaskill	Y	Y	Y	Y	N

	1	2	3	4	5
MONTANA					
Baucus	Y	Y	Y	Y	N
Tester	Y	Y	Y	Y	#
NEBRASKA					
Nelson	Y	Y	Y	Y	Y
Johanns	N	N	N	N	Y
NEVADA					
Reid	Y	Y	Y	Y	N
Ensign	?	N	N	N	Y
NEW HAMPSHIRE					
Gregg	?	Y	Y	Y	N
Shaheen	Y	Y	Y	Y	Y
NEW JERSEY					
Lautenberg	Y	Y	Y	Y	N
Menendez	Y	Y	Y	Y	N
NEW MEXICO					
Bingaman	Y	Y	Y	Y	N
Udall	Y	Y	Y	Y	N
NEW YORK					
Schumer	Y	Y	Y	Y	N
Clinton	Y	Y	Y	Y	N
NORTH CAROLINA					
Burr	?	N	N	Y	Y
Hagan	Y	Y	Y	Y	N
NORTH DAKOTA					
Conrad	Y	?	Y	Y	N
Dorgan	Y	Y	Y	Y	Y
OHIO					
Voinovich	?	Y	Y	Y	N
Brown	?	?	?	?	X
OKLAHOMA					
Inhofe	N	N	N	N	Y
Coburn	N	N	N	N	Y
OREGON					
Wyden	Y	Y	Y	Y	Y
Merkley	Y	Y	Y	Y	N
PENNSYLVANIA					
Specter	?	N	N	Y	N
Casey	Y	Y	Y	Y	N
RHODE ISLAND					
Reed	Y	Y	Y	Y	N
Whitehouse	Y	Y	Y	Y	N
SOUTH CAROLINA					
Graham	–	Y	N	N	Y
DeMint	N	N	N	N	Y
SOUTH DAKOTA					
Johnson	Y	Y	Y	Y	N
Thune	N	N	N	N	Y
TENNESSEE					
Alexander	–	N	Y	Y	N
Corker	N	N	Y	Y	Y
TEXAS					
Hutchison	?	N	N	Y	Y
Cornyn	–	N	N	N	Y
UTAH					
Hatch	Y	Y	Y	N	#
Bennett	Y	Y	Y	Y	Y
VERMONT					
Leahy	Y	Y	Y	Y	N
Sanders	Y	Y	Y	Y	Y
VIRGINIA					
Webb	Y	Y	Y	Y	N
Warner	Y	Y	Y	Y	N
WASHINGTON					
Murray	Y	Y	Y	Y	N
Cantwell	Y	Y	Y	Y	Y
WEST VIRGINIA					
Byrd	Y	Y	Y	Y	N
Rockefeller	Y	Y	Y	Y	N
WISCONSIN					
Kohl	Y	Y	Y	Y	N
Feingold	Y	N	Y	Y	Y
WYOMING					
Enzi	Y	N	N	N	Y
Barrasso	Y	Y	Y	N	Y

KEY	**Republicans**	Democrats	*Independents*
Y Voted for (yea)	X Paired against	C Voted "present" to avoid possible conflict of interest
# Paired for	– Announced against	
+ Announced for	P Voted "present"	? Did not vote or otherwise make a position known
N Voted against (nay)		

*Sen. Roland W. Burris, D-Ill., was sworn in Jan. 15, 2009. The first vote for which he was eligible was vote 5.

IN THE SENATE | By Vote Number

6. Clinton Nomination/Confirmation. Confirmation of President Obama's nomination of Hillary Rodham Clinton of New York to be secretary of State. Confirmed 94-2: R 39-2; D 53-0; I 2-0. A "yea" was a vote in support of the president's position. Jan. 21, 2009.

7. S 181. Wage Discrimination/Substitute. Hutchison, R-Texas, substitute amendment that would amend the 1964 Civil Rights Act to allow employees to file charges of pay discrimination within 180 days of the point at which the worker should have or "be expected to have" enough information to suspect discrimination. Rejected 40-55: R 40-1; D 0-53; I 0-2. Jan. 22, 2009.

8. S 181. Wage Discrimination/Employer Defense. Mikulski, D-Md., motion to table (kill) the Specter, R-Pa., amendment that would allow employers to use the defense that an employee was aware of wage discrepancies and went along with them willingly. Motion agreed to 53-43: R 1-40; D 50-3; I 2-0. Jan. 22, 2009.

9. S 181. Wage Discrimination/Case Limitation. Mikulski, D-Md., motion to table (kill) the Specter, R-Pa., amendment that would limit the bill's application to wage discrimination cases only. Motion agreed to 55-39: R 2-39; D 51-0; I 2-0. Jan. 22, 2009.

10. S 181. Wage Discrimination/Statute of Limitations. Mikulski, D-Md., motion to table (kill) the Enzi, R-Wyo., amendment that would strike language in the bill amending the Civil Rights Act of 1964 and the Age Discrimination in Employment Act of 1967, affirming that the statute of limitations applies to the date that hiring and pay decisions are initially made. Motion agreed to 55-41: R 1-40; D 52-1; I 2-0. Jan. 22, 2009.

	6	7	8	9	10
ALABAMA					
Shelby	Y	Y	N	N	N
Sessions	Y	Y	N	N	N
ALASKA					
Murkowski	Y	Y	N	N	N
Begich	Y	N	Y	Y	Y
ARIZONA					
McCain	Y	Y	N	N	N
Kyl	Y	Y	N	N	N
ARKANSAS					
Lincoln	Y	N	Y	Y	Y
Pryor	Y	N	Y	Y	Y
CALIFORNIA					
Feinstein	Y	N	Y	?	Y
Boxer	Y	N	Y	Y	Y
COLORADO					
Udall	Y	N	Y	Y	Y
Vacant¹					
CONNECTICUT					
Dodd	Y	N	Y	Y	Y
Lieberman	Y	N	Y	Y	Y
DELAWARE					
Carper	Y	N	Y	Y	Y
Kaufman²	Y	N	Y	Y	Y
FLORIDA					
Nelson	Y	N	Y	Y	Y
Martinez	Y	Y	N	N	N
GEORGIA					
Chambliss	Y	Y	N	N	N
Isakson	Y	Y	N	N	N
HAWAII					
Inouye	Y	N	Y	?	Y
Akaka	Y	N	Y	Y	Y
IDAHO					
Crapo	Y	Y	N	N	N
Risch	Y	Y	N	N	N
ILLINOIS					
Durbin	Y	N	Y	Y	Y
Burris	Y	N	Y	Y	Y
INDIANA					
Lugar	Y	Y	N	N	N
Bayh	Y	N	Y	Y	Y
IOWA					
Grassley	Y	Y	N	N	N
Harkin	Y	?	Y	Y	Y
KANSAS					
Brownback	Y	Y	N	N	N
Roberts	Y	Y	N	N	N
KENTUCKY					
McConnell	Y	Y	N	N	N
Bunning	Y	Y	N	N	N
LOUISIANA					
Landrieu	Y	N	N	Y	Y
Vitter	N	Y	N	N	N
MAINE					
Snowe	Y	N	Y	Y	Y
Collins	Y	Y	N	Y	N
MARYLAND					
Mikulski	Y	N	Y	Y	Y
Cardin	Y	N	Y	Y	Y
MASSACHUSETTS					
Kennedy	?	?	?	?	?
Kerry	Y	N	Y	Y	Y
MICHIGAN					
Levin	Y	N	Y	Y	Y
Stabenow	Y	N	Y	Y	Y
MINNESOTA					
Klobuchar	Y	N	Y	Y	Y
Vacant					
MISSISSIPPI					
Cochran	Y	Y	N	N	N
Wicker	Y	Y	N	N	N
MISSOURI					
Bond	Y	Y	N	N	N
McCaskill	Y	N	Y	Y	Y
MONTANA					
Baucus	Y	N	Y	Y	Y
Tester	Y	N	Y	Y	Y
NEBRASKA					
Nelson	Y	N	N	Y	Y
Johanns	Y	Y	N	Y	Y
NEVADA					
Reid	Y	N	Y	Y	Y
Ensign	Y	Y	N	N	N
NEW HAMPSHIRE					
Gregg	Y	Y	N	N	N
Shaheen	Y	N	Y	Y	Y
NEW JERSEY					
Lautenberg	Y	N	Y	Y	Y
Menendez	Y	N	Y	Y	Y
NEW MEXICO					
Bingaman	Y	N	Y	Y	Y
Udall	Y	N	Y	Y	Y
NEW YORK					
Schumer	Y	N	Y	Y	Y
Clinton³	?				
NORTH CAROLINA					
Burr	Y	Y	N	N	N
Hagan	Y	N	Y	Y	Y
NORTH DAKOTA					
Conrad	Y	N	Y	Y	Y
Dorgan	Y	N	Y	Y	Y
OHIO					
Voinovich	Y	Y	N	N	N
Brown	Y	N	Y	Y	Y
OKLAHOMA					
Inhofe	Y	Y	N	N	N
Coburn	Y	Y	N	N	N
OREGON					
Wyden	Y	N	Y	Y	Y
Merkley	Y	N	Y	Y	Y
PENNSYLVANIA					
Specter	Y	Y	N	N	N
Casey	Y	N	Y	Y	Y
RHODE ISLAND					
Reed	Y	N	Y	Y	Y
Whitehouse	Y	N	Y	Y	Y
SOUTH CAROLINA					
Graham	Y	Y	N	N	N
DeMint	N	Y	N	N	N
SOUTH DAKOTA					
Johnson	Y	N	Y	Y	Y
Thune	Y	Y	N	N	N
TENNESSEE					
Alexander	Y	Y	N	N	N
Corker	Y	Y	N	N	N
TEXAS					
Hutchison	Y	Y	N	N	N
Cornyn	Y	Y	N	N	N
UTAH					
Hatch	Y	Y	N	N	N
Bennett	Y	Y	N	N	N
VERMONT					
Leahy	Y	N	Y	Y	Y
Sanders	Y	N	Y	Y	Y
VIRGINIA					
Webb	Y	N	Y	N	Y
Warner	Y	N	Y	Y	Y
WASHINGTON					
Murray	Y	N	Y	Y	Y
Cantwell	Y	N	Y	Y	Y
WEST VIRGINIA					
Byrd	Y	N	Y	Y	Y
Rockefeller	Y	N	Y	Y	Y
WISCONSIN					
Kohl	Y	N	Y	Y	Y
Feingold	Y	N	Y	Y	Y
WYOMING					
Enzi	Y	Y	N	N	N
Barrasso	Y	Y	N	N	N

¹Sen. Ken Salazar, D-Colo., resigned Jan. 20 to become secretary of the Interior. The last vote for which he was eligible was vote 5.

²Sen. Ted Kaufman, D-Del., was sworn in Jan. 16 to fill the seat vacated by fellow Democrat Joseph R. Biden Jr., who resigned Jan. 15 to become vice president. The first vote for which Kaufman was eligible was vote 6; the last vote for which Biden was eligible was vote 5.

³Sen. Hillary Rodham Clinton, D-N.Y., resigned Jan. 21 to become secretary of State. The last vote for which she was eligible was vote 6.

KEY	**Republicans**	Democrats	*Independents*
Y Voted for (yea)		**X** Paired against	**C** Voted "present" to avoid possible conflict of interest
# Paired for		**–** Announced against	
+ Announced for		**P** Voted "present"	**?** Did not vote or otherwise make a position known
N Voted against (nay)			

IN THE SENATE | By Vote Number

11. **S 181. Wage Discrimination/Union Discrimination.** Mikulski, D-Md., motion to table (kill) the DeMint, R-S.C., amendment that would repeal provisions to authorize the firing of workers for refusing to pay union dues or fees. It also would ban discrimination of workers who do not wish to a join a union. Motion agreed to 66-31: R 10-31; D 54-0; I 2-0. Jan. 22, 2009.

12. **S 181. Wage Discrimination/Time Limitations.** Mikulski, D-Md., motion to table (kill) the Isakson, R-Ga., amendment that would limit the bill's provisions to wage discrimination claims that result from employer decisions made on or after the date of the bill's enactment. Motion agreed to 59-38: R 3-38; D 54-0; I 2-0. Jan. 22, 2009.

13. **S 181. Wage Discrimination/Construction Project Agreements.** Mikulski, D-Md., motion to table (kill) the Vitter, R-La., amendment that would prohibit federal agencies that award funds for construction projects from discriminating against a party because it did or did not sign or adhere to an agreement with a labor organization. Motion agreed to 59-38: R 3-38; D 54-0; I 2-0. Jan. 22, 2009.

14. **S 181. Wage Discrimination/Passage.** Passage of the bill that would amend the 1964 Civil Rights Act to clarify time limits for workers to file employment discrimination lawsuits. The bill would allow workers who allege discrimination based on race, gender, national origin, religion, age or disability to file charges of pay discrimination within 180 days of the last received paycheck affected by the alleged discriminatory decision. The bill would renew the statute of limitations with each act of discrimination. Passed 61-36: R 5-36; D 54-0; I 2-0. (By unanimous consent, the Senate agreed to raise the majority requirement for passage of the bill to 59 votes.) Jan. 22, 2009.

	11	12	13	14			11	12	13	14
ALABAMA						**MONTANA**				
Shelby	N	N	N	N		Baucus	Y	Y	Y	Y
Sessions	N	N	N	N		Tester	Y	Y	Y	Y
ALASKA						**NEBRASKA**				
Murkowski	Y	N	Y	Y		Nelson	Y	Y	Y	Y
Begich	Y	Y	Y	Y		**Johanns**	Y	N	N	N
ARIZONA						**NEVADA**				
McCain	N	N	N	N		Reid	Y	Y	Y	Y
Kyl	N	N	N	N		**Ensign**	N	N	N	N
ARKANSAS						**NEW HAMPSHIRE**				
Lincoln	Y	Y	Y	Y		**Gregg**	Y	N	N	N
Pryor	Y	Y	Y	Y		Shaheen	Y	Y	Y	Y
CALIFORNIA						**NEW JERSEY**				
Feinstein	Y	Y	Y	Y		Lautenberg	Y	Y	Y	Y
Boxer	Y	Y	Y	Y		Menendez	Y	Y	Y	Y
COLORADO						**NEW MEXICO**				
Udall	Y	Y	Y	Y		Bingaman	Y	Y	Y	Y
Bennet*	Y	Y	Y	Y		Udall	Y	Y	Y	Y
CONNECTICUT						**NEW YORK**				
Dodd	Y	Y	Y	Y		Schumer	Y	Y	Y	Y
Lieberman	Y	Y	Y	Y		Vacant				
DELAWARE						**NORTH CAROLINA**				
Carper	Y	Y	Y	Y		**Burr**	N	N	N	N
Kaufman	Y	Y	Y	Y		Hagan	Y	Y	Y	Y
FLORIDA						**NORTH DAKOTA**				
Nelson	Y	Y	Y	Y		Conrad	Y	Y	Y	Y
Martinez	Y	N	N	N		Dorgan	Y	Y	Y	Y
GEORGIA						**OHIO**				
Chambliss	N	N	N	N		**Voinovich**	Y	N	Y	N
Isakson	N	N	N	N		Brown	Y	Y	Y	Y
HAWAII						**OKLAHOMA**				
Inouye	Y	Y	Y	Y		**Inhofe**	N	N	N	N
Akaka	Y	Y	Y	Y		**Coburn**	N	N	N	N
IDAHO						**OREGON**				
Crapo	N	N	N	N		Wyden	Y	Y	Y	Y
Risch	N	N	N	N		Merkley	Y	Y	Y	Y
ILLINOIS						**PENNSYLVANIA**				
Durbin	Y	Y	Y	Y		**Specter**	Y	Y	Y	Y
Burris	Y	Y	Y	Y		Casey	Y	Y	Y	Y
INDIANA						**RHODE ISLAND**				
Lugar	N	N	N	N		Reed	Y	Y	Y	Y
Bayh	Y	Y	Y	Y		Whitehouse	Y	Y	Y	Y
IOWA						**SOUTH CAROLINA**				
Grassley	N	N	N	N		**Graham**	N	N	N	N
Harkin	Y	Y	Y	Y		**DeMint**	N	N	N	N
KANSAS						**SOUTH DAKOTA**				
Brownback	N	N	N	N		Johnson	Y	Y	Y	Y
Roberts	N	N	N	N		**Thune**	N	N	N	N
KENTUCKY						**TENNESSEE**				
McConnell	N	N	N	N		**Alexander**	Y	N	N	N
Bunning	N	N	N	N		**Corker**	N	N	N	N
LOUISIANA						**TEXAS**				
Landrieu	Y	Y	Y	Y		**Hutchison**	N	N	N	Y
Vitter	N	N	N	N		**Cornyn**	N	N	N	N
MAINE						**UTAH**				
Snowe	Y	Y	Y	N		**Hatch**	N	N	N	N
Collins	Y	Y	N	Y		**Bennett**	N	N	N	N
MARYLAND						**VERMONT**				
Mikulski	Y	Y	Y	Y		Leahy	Y	Y	Y	Y
Cardin	Y	Y	Y	Y		*Sanders*	Y	Y	Y	Y
MASSACHUSETTS						**VIRGINIA**				
Kennedy	?	?	?	?		Webb	Y	Y	Y	Y
Kerry	Y	Y	Y	Y		Warner	Y	Y	Y	Y
MICHIGAN						**WASHINGTON**				
Levin	Y	Y	Y	Y		Murray	Y	Y	Y	Y
Stabenow	Y	Y	Y	Y		Cantwell	Y	Y	Y	Y
MINNESOTA						**WEST VIRGINIA**				
Klobuchar	Y	Y	Y	Y		Byrd	Y	Y	Y	Y
Vacant						Rockefeller	Y	Y	Y	Y
MISSISSIPPI						**WISCONSIN**				
Cochran	N	N	N	N		Kohl	Y	Y	Y	Y
Wicker	N	N	N	N		Feingold	Y	Y	Y	Y
MISSOURI						**WYOMING**				
Bond	Y	N	N	N		**Enzi**	N	N	N	N
McCaskill	Y	Y	Y	Y		**Barrasso**	N	N	N	N

KEY	**Republicans**	Democrats	*Independents*
Y Voted for (yea)		X Paired against	C Voted "present" to avoid possible conflict of interest
# Paired for		– Announced against	
+ Announced for		P Voted "present"	? Did not vote or otherwise make a position known
N Voted against (nay)			

*Sen. Michael Bennet, D-Colo., was sworn in Jan. 22 to fill the seat vacated by fellow Democrat Ken Salazar, who resigned Jan. 20 to become secretary of Interior. The first vote for which Bennet was eligible was vote 11.

IN THE SENATE | By Vote Number

15. **Geithner Nomination/Confirmation.** Confirmation of President Obama's nomination of Timothy F. Geithner of New York to be secretary of the Treasury. Confirmed 60-34: R 10-30; D 49-3; I 1-1. A "yea" was a vote in support of the president's position. Jan. 26, 2009.

16. **HR 2. Children's Health Insurance/Cost-Sharing Requirement.** Pryor, D-Ark., motion to table (kill) the DeMint, R-S.C., amendment to the Reid, D-Nev., substitute amendment. The DeMint amendment would require states to impose cost sharing for children enrolled in the Children's Health Insurance Program or Medicaid whose family income exceeds 200 percent of the federal poverty level. The total cost sharing would not exceed 5 percent of the family's income for that year. The substitute would expand the State Children's Health Insurance Program by $32.8 billion over 4½ years. Motion agreed to 60-37: R 4-36; D 54-1; I 2-0. Jan. 27, 2009.

17. **Tarullo Nomination/Confirmation.** Confirmation of President Obama's nomination of Daniel K. Tarullo of Massachusetts to be a member of the board of governors of the Federal Reserve System. Confirmed 96-1: R 39-1; D 55-0; I 2-0. A "yea" was a vote in support of the president's position. Jan. 27, 2009.

18. **HR 2. Children's Health Insurance/Substitute.** McConnell, R-Ky., substitute amendment that would expand the State Children's Health Insurance Program by $19.3 billion over 4½ years. It would phase out coverage for adults other than pregnant women. It would provide funds to target low-income children and increase the amount states are allowed to provide in premium assistance for the purchase of private insurance. Rejected 32-65: R 32-8; D 0-55; I 0-2. Jan. 28, 2009.

19. **HR 2. Children's Health Insurance/"Mexico City Policy."** Martinez, R-Fla., amendment that would reinstate the so-called Mexico City policy, which bars U.S. aid to international family planning organizations that perform or promote abortions, even if they use their own funds to do so. Rejected 37-60: R 36-4; D 1-54; I 0-2. A "nay" was a vote in support of the president's position. Jan. 28, 2009.

20. **HR 2. Children's Health Insurance/Shortfall States.** Baucus, D-Mont., motion to table (kill) the Cornyn, R-Texas, amendment that would bar states that allow coverage of children whose family incomes are above 200 percent of the federal poverty level from being considered shortfall states. Unspent funds not distributed to those states would be committed to covering low-income children, including through enrollment and outreach programs. Motion agreed to 64-33: R 8-32; D 54-1; I 2-0. Jan. 28, 2009.

	15	16	17	18	19	20
ALABAMA						
Shelby	Y	N	Y	Y	Y	N
Sessions	N	N	Y	Y	Y	N
ALASKA						
Murkowski	N	N	Y	N	N	Y
Begich	Y	Y	Y	N	N	Y
ARIZONA						
McCain	N	N	Y	Y	Y	N
Kyl	N	N	Y	Y	Y	N
ARKANSAS						
Lincoln	Y	Y	Y	N	N	Y
Pryor	Y	Y	Y	N	N	Y
CALIFORNIA						
Feinstein	Y	Y	Y	N	N	Y
Boxer	Y	Y	Y	N	N	Y
COLORADO						
Udall	Y	Y	Y	N	N	Y
Bennet	Y	Y	Y	N	N	Y
CONNECTICUT						
Dodd	Y	Y	Y	N	N	Y
Lieberman	Y	Y	Y	N	N	Y
DELAWARE						
Carper	Y	Y	Y	N	N	Y
Kaufman	Y	Y	Y	N	N	Y
FLORIDA						
Nelson	Y	Y	Y	N	N	Y
Martinez	N	N	Y	Y	Y	N
GEORGIA						
Chambliss	N	?	?	?	?	?
Isakson	N	N	Y	Y	Y	Y
HAWAII						
Inouye	Y	Y	Y	N	N	Y
Akaka	Y	Y	Y	N	N	Y
IDAHO						
Crapo	Y	N	Y	Y	Y	N
Risch	N	N	Y	Y	Y	N
ILLINOIS						
Durbin	Y	Y	Y	N	N	Y
Burris	Y	Y	Y	N	N	Y
INDIANA						
Lugar	N	N	Y	N	Y	N
Bayh	Y	Y	Y	N	N	Y
IOWA						
Grassley	N	N	Y	N	Y	N
Harkin	N	Y	Y	N	N	Y
KANSAS						
Brownback	N	N	Y	N	Y	N
Roberts	N	N	Y	Y	Y	N
KENTUCKY						
McConnell	N	N	Y	Y	Y	N
Bunning	N	N	N	Y	Y	N
LOUISIANA						
Landrieu	Y	Y	Y	N	N	Y
Vitter	N	N	Y	Y	Y	Y
MAINE						
Snowe	Y	N	Y	N	N	Y
Collins	N	Y	Y	N	N	Y
MARYLAND						
Mikulski	Y	Y	Y	N	N	Y
Cardin	Y	Y	Y	N	N	Y
MASSACHUSETTS						
Kennedy	?	?	?	?	?	?
Kerry	Y	Y	Y	N	N	Y
MICHIGAN						
Levin	Y	Y	Y	N	N	Y
Stabenow	Y	Y	Y	N	N	Y
MINNESOTA						
Klobuchar	Y	Y	Y	N	N	Y
Vacant						
MISSISSIPPI						
Cochran	N	N	Y	Y	Y	N
Wicker	N	N	Y	Y	Y	N
MISSOURI						
Bond	?	Y	Y	N	Y	Y
McCaskill	Y	N	Y	N	N	Y
MONTANA						
Baucus	Y	Y	Y	N	N	Y
Tester	Y	Y	Y	N	N	Y
NEBRASKA						
Nelson	Y	Y	Y	N	N	Y
Johanns	N	N	Y	Y	Y	N
NEVADA						
Reid	Y	Y	Y	N	N	Y
Ensign	Y	N	Y	Y	Y	N
NEW HAMPSHIRE						
Gregg	Y	N	Y	Y	Y	N
Shaheen	Y	Y	Y	N	N	Y
NEW JERSEY						
Lautenberg	Y	Y	Y	N	N	Y
Menendez	Y	Y	Y	N	N	Y
NEW MEXICO						
Bingaman	Y	Y	Y	N	N	Y
Udall	Y	Y	Y	N	N	Y
NEW YORK						
Schumer	Y	Y	Y	N	N	Y
Gillibrand*		Y	Y	N	N	Y
NORTH CAROLINA						
Burr	N	N	Y	Y	Y	N
Hagan	Y	Y	Y	N	N	Y
NORTH DAKOTA						
Conrad	Y	Y	Y	N	N	Y
Dorgan	Y	Y	Y	N	N	Y
OHIO						
Voinovich	Y	N	Y	Y	Y	Y
Brown	?	Y	Y	N	N	Y
OKLAHOMA						
Inhofe	N	N	Y	Y	Y	N
Coburn	N	N	Y	Y	Y	N
OREGON						
Wyden	?	Y	Y	N	N	Y
Merkley	Y	Y	Y	N	N	Y
PENNSYLVANIA						
Specter	N	Y	Y	N	N	Y
Casey	Y	Y	Y	N	N	Y
RHODE ISLAND						
Reed	Y	Y	Y	N	N	Y
Whitehouse	Y	Y	Y	N	N	Y
SOUTH CAROLINA						
Graham	N	Y	Y	Y	Y	N
DeMint	N	N	Y	Y	Y	N
SOUTH DAKOTA						
Johnson	Y	Y	Y	N	N	Y
Thune	N	N	Y	Y	Y	N
TENNESSEE						
Alexander	N	N	Y	Y	Y	N
Corker	Y	N	Y	Y	Y	N
TEXAS						
Hutchison	N	Y	Y	Y	Y	N
Cornyn	Y	N	Y	Y	Y	N
UTAH						
Hatch	Y	N	Y	N	N	Y
Bennett	N	N	Y	Y	Y	N
VERMONT						
Leahy	Y	Y	Y	N	N	Y
Sanders	N	Y	Y	N	N	Y
VIRGINIA						
Webb	Y	Y	Y	N	N	Y
Warner	Y	Y	Y	N	N	Y
WASHINGTON						
Murray	Y	Y	Y	N	N	Y
Cantwell	Y	Y	Y	N	N	Y
WEST VIRGINIA						
Byrd	N	Y	Y	N	N	Y
Rockefeller	Y	Y	Y	N	N	Y
WISCONSIN						
Kohl	Y	Y	Y	N	N	Y
Feingold	N	Y	Y	N	N	Y
WYOMING						
Enzi	N	N	Y	Y	Y	N
Barrasso	N	N	Y	Y	Y	N

KEY   **Republicans**   Democrats   *Independents*

Y Voted for (yea)	X Paired against	C Voted "present" to avoid possible conflict of interest
# Paired for	– Announced against	
+ Announced for	P Voted "present"	? Did not vote or otherwise make a position known
N Voted against (nay)		

IN THE SENATE | By Vote Number

21. **HR 2. Children's Health Insurance/Eligibility Cap.** Roberts, R-Kan., amendment that would prohibit states from covering children under the State Children's Health Insurance Program (SCHIP) if their gross family incomes are above $65,000 or the median state income, whichever is lower. It would also prohibit states from covering children under Medicaid if their family income is at a level above the income eligibility for SCHIP. Rejected 36-60: R 35-5; D 1-53; I 0-2. Jan. 28, 2009.

22. **HR 2. Children's Health Insurance/Crowd-Out.** Kyl, R-Ariz., amendment that would require each state to submit a plan detailing how it would implement best practices to limit the crowding out of the lowest-income children by those from families with higher incomes. It would require the Health and Human Services secretary to ensure that states that cover higher-income populations under the State Children's Health Insurance Program also cover a target rate of low-income children, or the state would not receive federal funding for the higher-income population coverage. Rejected 42-56: R 41-0; D 1-54; I 0-2. Jan. 28, 2009.

23. **HR 2. Children's Health Insurance/HHS Recommendations.** Murkowski, R-Alaska, amendment that would require the Health and Human Services secretary to develop recommendations on best practices for states to address crowd-out within 12 months. As of Oct. 1, 2010, and every year thereafter, each state would be required to show it is covering 80 percent of children whose family incomes are below 200 percent of the federal poverty level, or it would not receive funds to cover children whose family incomes are below 300 percent of the federal poverty level. Rejected 47-51: R 41-0; D 6-49; I 0-2. Jan. 28, 2009.

24. **HR 2. Children's Health Insurance/Premium Assistance Subsidies.** Coburn, R-Okla., amendment that would require states that want to expand program coverage beyond the eligibility requirements in the bill to use premium-assistance subsidies to cover the expanded population, if the subsidy is cost-effective. It would redefine "cost-effective" to help states determine if subsidies were eligible. Health plans purchased in the private market would have to have similar benefits to those under the State Children's Health Insurance Program. It would institute a six-month waiting period between the time a child has private insurance and when the child enrolls in a premium assistance subsidy. Rejected 36-62: R 36-5; D 0-55; I 0-2. Jan. 29, 2009.

25. **HR 2. Children's Health Insurance/Matching Rate.** Baucus, D-Mont., motion to table (kill) the Bunning, R-Ky., amendment that would bar states from receiving the State Children's Health Insurance Program Enhanced-Federal Medical Assistance Percentage matching rate for covering families whose incomes are above 300 percent of the federal poverty level. Instead, states would receive the lower Medicaid matching rate. Exceptions would be made for states that enact state laws to cover families above 300 percent of the federal poverty level. Motion agreed to 54-44: R 0-41; D 52-3; I 2-0. Jan. 29, 2009.

26. **HR 2. Children's Health Insurance/Low-Income Children Definition.** Hatch, R-Utah, amendment that would allow states to define the phrase "low-income children" to include "an unborn child" for purposes of eligibility under the State Children's Health Insurance Program. Rejected 39-59: R 37-4; D 2-53; I 0-2. Jan. 29, 2009.

	21	22	23	24	25	26		21	22	23	24	25	26
ALABAMA							**MONTANA**						
Shelby	Y	Y	Y	Y	N	Y	Baucus	N	N	N	N	Y	N
Sessions	Y	Y	Y	Y	N	Y	Tester	N	N	N	N	Y	N
ALASKA							**NEBRASKA**						
Murkowski	N	Y	Y	N	N	N	Nelson	Y	Y	Y	N	N	Y
Begich	N	N	Y	N	N	N	Johanns	Y	Y	Y	Y	N	Y
ARIZONA							**NEVADA**						
McCain	Y	Y	Y	Y	N	Y	Reid	N	N	N	N	Y	N
Kyl	Y	Y	Y	Y	N	Y	Ensign	Y	Y	Y	Y	N	Y
ARKANSAS							**NEW HAMPSHIRE**						
Lincoln	N	N	N	N	Y	N	Gregg	Y	Y	Y	Y	N	Y
Pryor	N	N	N	N	Y	N	Shaheen	N	N	N	N	Y	N
CALIFORNIA							**NEW JERSEY**						
Feinstein	N	N	N	N	Y	N	Lautenberg	N	N	N	N	Y	N
Boxer	N	N	N	N	Y	N	Menendez	N	N	N	N	Y	N
COLORADO							**NEW MEXICO**						
Udall	N	N	N	N	Y	N	Bingaman	N	N	Y	N	Y	N
Bennet	N	N	N	N	Y	N	Udall	N	N	N	N	Y	N
CONNECTICUT							**NEW YORK**						
Dodd	N	N	N	N	Y	N	Schumer	N	N	N	N	Y	N
Lieberman	N	N	N	N	Y	N	Gillibrand	N	N	N	N	Y	N
DELAWARE							**NORTH CAROLINA**						
Carper	N	Y	Y	N	N	N	Burr	Y	Y	Y	Y	N	Y
Kaufman	N	N	N	N	Y	N	Hagan	N	N	N	N	Y	N
FLORIDA							**NORTH DAKOTA**						
Nelson	N	N	N	N	Y	N	Conrad	N	N	N	N	Y	N
Martinez	Y	Y	Y	Y	N	Y	Dorgan	N	N	N	N	Y	N
GEORGIA							**OHIO**						
Chambliss	?	Y	Y	Y	N	Y	**Voinovich**	Y	Y	Y	Y	N	Y
Isakson	Y	Y	Y	Y	N	Y	Brown	N	N	N	N	Y	N
HAWAII							**OKLAHOMA**						
Inouye	N	N	N	N	Y	N	**Inhofe**	Y	Y	Y	Y	N	Y
Akaka	N	N	N	N	Y	N	**Coburn**	Y	Y	Y	Y	N	Y
IDAHO							**OREGON**						
Crapo	Y	Y	Y	Y	N	Y	Wyden	N	N	N	N	Y	N
Risch	Y	Y	Y	Y	N	Y	Merkley	N	N	N	N	Y	N
ILLINOIS							**PENNSYLVANIA**						
Durbin	N	N	N	N	Y	N	**Specter**	N	Y	Y	N	N	N
Burris	N	N	N	N	Y	N	Casey	N	N	N	N	Y	Y
INDIANA							**RHODE ISLAND**						
Lugar	Y	Y	Y	Y	N	Y	Reed	N	N	N	N	Y	N
Bayh	N	N	N	N	Y	N	Whitehouse	N	N	N	N	Y	N
IOWA							**SOUTH CAROLINA**						
Grassley	Y	Y	Y	Y	N	Y	**Graham**	Y	Y	Y	Y	N	Y
Harkin	N	N	N	N	Y	N	**DeMint**	Y	Y	Y	Y	N	Y
KANSAS							**SOUTH DAKOTA**						
Brownback	Y	Y	Y	Y	N	Y	Johnson	N	N	N	N	Y	N
Roberts	Y	Y	Y	Y	N	Y	**Thune**	Y	Y	Y	Y	N	Y
KENTUCKY							**TENNESSEE**						
McConnell	Y	Y	Y	Y	N	Y	**Alexander**	Y	Y	Y	Y	N	Y
Bunning	Y	Y	Y	Y	N	Y	**Corker**	Y	Y	Y	Y	N	Y
LOUISIANA							**TEXAS**						
Landrieu	?	N	N	N	Y	N	**Hutchison**	Y	Y	Y	Y	N	Y
Vitter	Y	Y	Y	Y	N	Y	**Cornyn**	Y	Y	Y	Y	N	Y
MAINE							**UTAH**						
Snowe	N	Y	N	Y	N	N	**Hatch**	Y	Y	Y	Y	N	Y
Collins	N	Y	Y	N	N	N	**Bennett**	Y	Y	Y	Y	N	Y
MARYLAND							**VERMONT**						
Mikulski	N	N	N	N	Y	N	Leahy	N	N	N	N	Y	N
Cardin	N	N	N	N	Y	N	*Sanders*	N	N	N	N	Y	N
MASSACHUSETTS							**VIRGINIA**						
Kennedy	?	?	?	?	?	?	Webb	N	N	N	N	Y	N
Kerry	N	N	N	N	Y	N	Warner	N	N	N	N	Y	N
MICHIGAN							**WASHINGTON**						
Levin	N	N	N	N	Y	N	Murray	N	N	N	N	Y	N
Stabenow	N	N	N	N	Y	N	Cantwell	N	N	N	N	Y	N
MINNESOTA							**WEST VIRGINIA**						
Klobuchar	N	Y	Y	N	Y	N	Byrd	N	N	N	N	Y	N
Vacant							Rockefeller	N	N	N	N	Y	N
MISSISSIPPI							**WISCONSIN**						
Cochran	Y	Y	Y	Y	N	Y	Kohl	N	N	N	N	N	N
Wicker	Y	Y	Y	Y	N	Y	Feingold	N	N	N	N	Y	N
MISSOURI							**WYOMING**						
Bond	N	Y	Y	Y	N	Y	**Enzi**	Y	Y	Y	Y	N	Y
McCaskill	N	N	Y	N	Y	N	**Barrasso**	Y	Y	Y	Y	N	Y

KEY	**Republicans**	Democrats	*Independents*		
Y	Voted for (yea)	X	Paired against	C	Voted "present" to avoid possible conflict of interest
#	Paired for	−	Announced against		
+	Announced for	P	Voted "present"	?	Did not vote or otherwise make a position known
N	Voted against (nay)				

IN THE SENATE | By Vote Number

27. **HR 2. Children's Health Insurance/Tax Deduction.** DeMint, R-S.C., amendment that would provide a tax deduction of up to $1,500 per year per child for qualified health care costs. No deduction would be allowed if the child is eligible for a federal health assistance program. Families that earn enough to qualify for the alternative minimum tax would not be eligible for the deduction. Rejected 40-58: R 35-6; D 5-50; I 0-2. Jan. 29, 2009.

28. **HR 2. Children's Health Insurance/Private Health Plans.** Coburn, R-Okla., amendment that would require the Health and Human Services secretary to create a new program in two years to provide private health insurance for children who are eligible for the State Children's Health Insurance Program (SCHIP) and Medicaid and whose family incomes are under 300 percent of the federal poverty level. It would fund SCHIP at current levels through 2010. The private plans would be competitively bid and would pay benefits equivalent to current SCHIP benefits. Any additional funding would require offsets. Rejected 36-62: R 36-5; D 0-55; I 0-2. Jan. 29, 2009.

29. **HR 2. Children's Health Insurance/Express Lane Applications.** Bingaman, D-N.M., amendment that would allow families to consent to expedited, or Express Lane, applications for coverage in writing, over the phone, orally, through electronic signatures or by any other means qualified by the Health and Human Services secretary. States could rely on gross income or adjusted gross income in determining eligibility for the State Children's Health Insurance Program. Adopted 55-43: R 3-38; D 50-5; I 2-0. Jan. 29, 2009.

30. **HR 2. Children's Health Insurance/Enrollment Campaign.** Hutchison, R-Texas, amendment that would allow the five states with the highest number of uninsured children to retain through 2012 their allotments provided before 2009. It would make it easier for states with more than the national average of uninsured children to receive bonus grants. Rejected 17-81: R 8-33; D 9-46; I 0-2. Jan. 29, 2009.

31. **HR 2. Children's Health Insurance/Passage.** Passage of the bill that would reauthorize the State Children's Health Insurance Program for 4½ years and increase funding by $32.8 billion. To offset the cost of the expansion, it would increase the federal tax on cigarettes to 62 cents per pack and raise taxes on other tobacco products. It would remove a five-year waiting period for new legal immigrants, including pregnant women, and loosen citizenship and eligibility documentation requirements. The bill would limit program eligibility to families earning three times the federal poverty level or less and would require states to phase out coverage of childless adults. Passed 66-32: R 9-32; D 55-0; I 2-0. Jan. 29, 2009.

	27	28	29	30	31		27	28	29	30	31
ALABAMA						**MONTANA**					
Shelby	Y	Y	N	N	N	Baucus	N	N	Y	Y	Y
Sessions	Y	Y	N	N	N	Tester	N	N	Y	N	Y
ALASKA						**NEBRASKA**					
Murkowski	Y	N	N	N	Y	Nelson	Y	N	Y	N	Y
Begich	N	N	Y	N	Y	Johanns	Y	Y	N	N	N
ARIZONA						**NEVADA**					
McCain	N	Y	N	N	N	Reid	N	N	Y	Y	Y
Kyl	Y	Y	N	N	N	Ensign	Y	Y	N	Y	N
ARKANSAS						**NEW HAMPSHIRE**					
Lincoln	N	N	Y	N	Y	Gregg	Y	Y	N	N	Y
Pryor	N	N	Y	N	Y	Shaheen	N	N	Y	N	Y
CALIFORNIA						**NEW JERSEY**					
Feinstein	N	N	N	N	Y	Lautenberg	N	N	Y	N	Y
Boxer	N	N	N	N	Y	Menendez	N	N	Y	N	Y
COLORADO						**NEW MEXICO**					
Udall	N	N	Y	Y	Y	Bingaman	N	N	Y	Y	Y
Bennet	N	N	Y	Y	Y	Udall	N	N	Y	Y	Y
CONNECTICUT						**NEW YORK**					
Dodd	N	N	Y	N	Y	Schumer	N	N	Y	N	Y
Lieberman	N	N	Y	N	Y	Gillibrand	N	N	Y	N	Y
DELAWARE						**NORTH CAROLINA**					
Carper	N	N	Y	N	Y	Burr	Y	Y	N	N	N
Kaufman	N	N	Y	N	Y	Hagan	N	N	Y	N	Y
FLORIDA						**NORTH DAKOTA**					
Nelson	N	N	Y	Y	Y	Conrad	N	N	Y	N	Y
Martinez	N	Y	N	Y	Y	Dorgan	N	N	Y	N	Y
GEORGIA						**OHIO**					
Chambliss	Y	Y	N	N	N	**Voinovich**	N	N	N	N	N
Isakson	Y	Y	N	N	N	Brown	N	N	Y	N	Y
HAWAII						**OKLAHOMA**					
Inouye	N	N	Y	Y	Y	**Inhofe**	Y	Y	N	Y	N
Akaka	N	N	Y	N	Y	**Coburn**	Y	Y	N	N	N
IDAHO						**OREGON**					
Crapo	Y	Y	N	N	N	Wyden	N	N	Y	N	Y
Risch	Y	Y	N	N	N	Merkley	N	N	Y	N	Y
ILLINOIS						**PENNSYLVANIA**					
Durbin	N	N	Y	N	Y	Specter	N	N	Y	N	Y
Burris	N	N	Y	N	Y	Casey	N	N	Y	N	Y
INDIANA						**RHODE ISLAND**					
Lugar	Y	Y	N	N	N	Reed	N	N	Y	N	Y
Bayh	Y	N	Y	Y	Y	Whitehouse	N	N	Y	N	Y
IOWA						**SOUTH CAROLINA**					
Grassley	Y	Y	N	N	N	**Graham**	Y	Y	N	N	N
Harkin	N	N	Y	N	Y	**DeMint**	Y	Y	N	N	N
KANSAS						**SOUTH DAKOTA**					
Brownback	Y	Y	N	N	N	Johnson	N	N	Y	N	Y
Roberts	Y	Y	N	N	N	**Thune**	Y	Y	N	N	N
KENTUCKY						**TENNESSEE**					
McConnell	Y	Y	N	N	N	**Alexander**	Y	Y	N	N	Y
Bunning	Y	Y	N	N	N	**Corker**	Y	Y	N	N	Y
LOUISIANA						**TEXAS**					
Landrieu	N	N	Y	N	Y	**Hutchison**	Y	Y	N	Y	N
Vitter	Y	Y	N	N	N	**Cornyn**	Y	Y	N	Y	N
MAINE						**UTAH**					
Snowe	N	N	Y	N	Y	**Hatch**	Y	Y	N	N	N
Collins	N	N	N	N	Y	**Bennett**	Y	Y	N	N	N
MARYLAND						**VERMONT**					
Mikulski	N	N	Y	N	Y	Leahy	N	N	Y	N	Y
Cardin	N	N	Y	N	Y	*Sanders*	N	N	Y	N	Y
MASSACHUSETTS						**VIRGINIA**					
Kennedy	?	?	?	?	?	Webb	Y	N	N	N	Y
Kerry	N	N	Y	N	Y	Warner	N	N	N	N	Y
MICHIGAN						**WASHINGTON**					
Levin	N	N	Y	N	Y	Murray	N	N	Y	N	Y
Stabenow	N	N	Y	N	Y	Cantwell	Y	N	Y	N	Y
MINNESOTA						**WEST VIRGINIA**					
Klobuchar	N	N	Y	N	Y	Byrd	N	N	Y	N	Y
Vacant						Rockefeller	N	N	Y	N	Y
MISSISSIPPI						**WISCONSIN**					
Cochran	Y	Y	N	N	N	Kohl	N	N	Y	N	Y
Wicker	Y	Y	N	N	N	Feingold	N	N	Y	N	Y
MISSOURI						**WYOMING**					
Bond	Y	Y	N	Y	N	**Enzi**	Y	Y	N	Y	N
McCaskill	Y	N	Y	N	Y	**Barrasso**	Y	Y	N	Y	N

KEY	**Republicans**	Democrats	*Independents*		
Y	Voted for (yea)	X	Paired against	C	Voted "present" to avoid possible conflict of interest
#	Paired for	–	Announced against		
+	Announced for	P	Voted "present"	?	Did not vote or otherwise make a position known
N	Voted against (nay)				

IN THE SENATE | By Vote Number

32. **Holder Nomination/Confirmation.** Confirmation of President Obama's nomination of Eric H. Holder Jr. of the District of Columbia to be attorney general. Confirmed 75-21: R 19-21; D 54-0; I 2-0. A "yea" was a vote in support of the president's position. Feb. 2, 2009.

33. **HR 1. Economic Stimulus/Infrastructure Funding.** Murray, D-Wash., motion to waive the Budget Act with respect to the Inhofe, R-Okla., point of order against the Murray amendment to the Reid, D-Nev., substitute. The Murray amendment would provide an additional $25 billion for infrastructure projects, with transportation funding increasing from $45.5 billion to more than $63.5 billion and Environmental Protection Agency sewer and water grants increasing $7 billion. The substitute would provide $884.5 billion for tax cuts and additional spending to stimulate the economy, including a provision to exempt additional taxpayers from the alternative minimum tax in 2009. Among other things, it also would provide $27 billion to extend and expand federal unemployment insurance through Dec. 31, 2009, and $87 billion to reimburse state Medicaid programs. Motion rejected 58-39: R 2-38; D 54-1; I 2-0. A three-fifths majority (60) of the total Senate is required to waive the Budget Act. (Subsequently, the chair upheld the point of order, and the amendment fell.) Feb. 3, 2009.

34. **HR 1. Economic Stimulus/Movie Production Tax Break.** Coburn, R-Okla., amendment to the Reid, D-Nev., substitute. The Coburn amendment would remove a tax provision that would make movie productions eligible for an additional 50 percent depreciation deduction in the first year. Adopted 52-45: R 38-2; D 13-42; I 1-1. Feb. 3, 2009.

35. **HR 1. Economic Stimulus/Car Tax Deduction.** Mikulski, D-Md., motion to waive the Budget Act with respect to the Grassley, R-Iowa, point of order against the Mikulski amendment to the Reid, D-Nev., substitute. The Mikulski amendment would create a temporary tax deduction for interest payments on car loans and for state excise and sales taxes paid on new cars. It would apply to purchases made from Nov. 12, 2008, to Jan. 1, 2010, and be available to individuals with adjusted gross incomes up to $125,000, or married couples making $250,000. Motion agreed to 71-26: R 31-9; D 38-17; I 2-0. A three-fifths majority (60) of the total Senate is required to waive the Budget Act. (Subsequently, the amendment was adopted by voice vote.) Feb. 3, 2009.

36. **HR 1. Economic Stimulus/Repatriated Earnings.** Boxer, D-Calif., motion to waive the Budget Act with respect to the Baucus, D-Mont., point of order against the Boxer amendment to the Reid, D-Nev., substitute. The Boxer amendment would reduce the tax rate that corporations pay when they repatriate earnings from overseas to 5.25 percent for 2009 or 2010. Motion rejected 42-55: R 33-7; D 8-47; I 1-1. A three-fifths majority (60) of the total Senate is required to waive the Budget Act. (Subsequently, the chair upheld the point of order, and the amendment fell.) Feb. 3, 2009.

	32	33	34	35	36		32	33	34	35	36
ALABAMA						**MONTANA**					
Shelby	N	N	Y	Y	Y	Baucus	Y	Y	N	N	N
Sessions	Y	N	Y	N	N	Tester	Y	Y	N	Y	N
ALASKA						**NEBRASKA**					
Murkowski	Y	N	Y	Y	N	Nelson	Y	Y	N	Y	Y
Begich	+	Y	N	Y	N	Johanns	N	N	Y	Y	Y
ARIZONA						**NEVADA**					
McCain	Y	N	Y	Y	Y	Reid	Y	Y	N	Y	Y
Kyl	Y	N	Y	N	Y	Ensign	N	N	Y	Y	Y
ARKANSAS						**NEW HAMPSHIRE**					
Lincoln	Y	Y	N	Y	N	Gregg	Y	?	?	?	?
Pryor	Y	Y	Y	Y	Y	Shaheen	Y	Y	N	Y	N
CALIFORNIA						**NEW JERSEY**					
Feinstein	Y	Y	N	Y	Y	Lautenberg	Y	Y	N	Y	N
Boxer	Y	Y	N	Y	N	Menendez	Y	Y	N	Y	N
COLORADO						**NEW MEXICO**					
Udall	Y	Y	Y	N	N	Bingaman	Y	Y	N	N	N
Bennet	Y	Y	Y	N	N	Udall	Y	Y	N	N	N
CONNECTICUT						**NEW YORK**					
Dodd	Y	Y	N	Y	N	Schumer	Y	Y	N	Y	N
Lieberman	Y	Y	Y	Y	Y	Gillibrand	Y	Y	N	Y	N
DELAWARE						**NORTH CAROLINA**					
Carper	Y	Y	Y	N	N	Burr	N	N	Y	Y	N
Kaufman	Y	Y	N	Y	N	Hagan	Y	Y	Y	Y	N
FLORIDA						**NORTH DAKOTA**					
Nelson	Y	Y	N	Y	N	Conrad	Y	Y	N	N	N
Martinez	?	N	Y	Y	Y	Dorgan	Y	Y	Y	Y	N
GEORGIA						**OHIO**					
Chambliss	Y	N	Y	Y	Y	**Voinovich**	Y	N	N	N	Y
Isakson	Y	N	Y	Y	Y	Brown	Y	Y	N	Y	N
HAWAII						**OKLAHOMA**					
Inouye	Y	Y	N	Y	N	**Inhofe**	N	N	Y	Y	Y
Akaka	Y	Y	N	N	Y	**Coburn**	N	N	Y	Y	Y
IDAHO						**OREGON**					
Crapo	N	N	Y	Y	Y	Wyden	Y	Y	N	N	N
Risch	N	N	Y	Y	Y	Merkley	Y	Y	N	N	N
ILLINOIS						**PENNSYLVANIA**					
Durbin	Y	Y	N	Y	N	**Specter**	Y	Y	Y	Y	Y
Burris	Y	Y	N	Y	N	Casey	Y	Y	Y	N	N
INDIANA						**RHODE ISLAND**					
Lugar	Y	N	Y	Y	Y	Reed	Y	Y	N	Y	N
Bayh	Y	Y	Y	Y	Y	Whitehouse	Y	Y	N	Y	N
IOWA						**SOUTH CAROLINA**					
Grassley	Y	N	Y	N	N	**Graham**	Y	N	Y	Y	Y
Harkin	Y	Y	N	N	N	**DeMint**	N	N	Y	N	Y
KANSAS						**SOUTH DAKOTA**					
Brownback	N	N	Y	Y	Y	Johnson	Y	Y	Y	N	N
Roberts	N	N	Y	Y	Y	**Thune**	N	N	Y	Y	Y
KENTUCKY						**TENNESSEE**					
McConnell	N	N	Y	N	Y	**Alexander**	Y	N	Y	Y	Y
Bunning	N	N	Y	N	Y	**Corker**	Y	N	Y	Y	Y
LOUISIANA						**TEXAS**					
Landrieu	Y	N	N	Y	N	**Hutchison**	N	N	Y	Y	Y
Vitter	N	N	N	Y	Y	**Cornyn**	N	N	Y	Y	Y
MAINE						**UTAH**					
Snowe	Y	N	Y	Y	N	**Hatch**	Y	N	Y	Y	Y
Collins	Y	N	Y	Y	N	**Bennett**	Y	N	Y	Y	Y
MARYLAND						**VERMONT**					
Mikulski	Y	Y	N	Y	N	Leahy	Y	Y	N	Y	N
Cardin	Y	Y	N	Y	N	*Sanders*	Y	Y	N	Y	N
MASSACHUSETTS						**VIRGINIA**					
Kennedy	?	?	?	?	?	Webb	Y	Y	Y	Y	N
Kerry	Y	Y	N	N	N	Warner	Y	Y	N	Y	Y
MICHIGAN						**WASHINGTON**					
Levin	Y	Y	N	Y	N	Murray	Y	Y	N	Y	N
Stabenow	Y	Y	N	Y	N	Cantwell	Y	Y	N	N	N
MINNESOTA						**WEST VIRGINIA**					
Klobuchar	Y	Y	N	Y	N	Byrd	Y	Y	Y	Y	N
Vacant						Rockefeller	Y	Y	N	N	N
MISSISSIPPI						**WISCONSIN**					
Cochran	N	N	Y	Y	Y	Kohl	Y	Y	N	Y	N
Wicker	N	N	Y	Y	Y	Feingold	Y	Y	Y	Y	N
MISSOURI						**WYOMING**					
Bond	Y	Y	Y	Y	Y	**Enzi**	N	N	Y	N	N
McCaskill	Y	Y	Y	Y	N	**Barrasso**	N	N	Y	N	N

KEY	**Republicans**	Democrats	*Independents*		
Y	Voted for (yea)	X	Paired against	C	Voted "present" to avoid possible conflict of interest
#	Paired for	–	Announced against		
+	Announced for	P	Voted "present"	?	Did not vote or otherwise make a position known
N	Voted against (nay)				

IN THE SENATE | By Vote Number

37. **HR 1. Economic Stimulus/Reduced Spending.** Vitter, R-La., amendment to the Reid, D-Nev., substitute. The Vitter amendment would strike approximately $35 billion from the bill by reducing authorized amounts or eliminating some items. It would bar the use of funds for gambling institutions, aquariums, zoos, golf courses, swimming pools or a Mob Museum. It also would bar the application of the Davis-Bacon Act, which requires government contractors to pay employees the prevailing wage, for any construction projects under the bill. Rejected 32-65: R 32-8; D 0-55; I 0-2. Feb. 4, 2009.

38. **HR 1. Economic Stimulus/Tax Rate Reductions.** DeMint, R-S.C., motion to waive the Budget Act with respect to the Baucus, D-Mont., point of order against the DeMint substitute amendment to the Reid, D-Nev., substitute. The DeMint substitute would make permanent a number of tax reductions scheduled to expire in 2011, including the 15 percent rate on dividends and capital gains, so-called marriage penalty relief, and the $1,000-per-child tax credit. It would repeal the alternative minimum tax, reduce the top business tax rate from 35 percent to 25 percent, and repeal the estate tax for estates worth less than $5 million. Motion rejected 36-61: R 36-4; D 0-55; I 0-2. A three-fifths majority (60) of the total Senate is required to waive the Budget Act. (Subsequently, the chair upheld the point of order, and the amendment fell.) Feb. 4, 2009.

39. **HR 1. Economic Stimulus/Funding Deadline.** Thune, R-S.D., amendment to the Reid, D-Nev., substitute. The Thune amendment would ban funding in the bill for any program not authorized before Feb. 1, 2009. Rejected 35-62: R 35-5; D 0-55; I 0-2. Feb. 4, 2009.

40. **HR 1. Economic Stimulus/Deficit Reduction.** McCain, R-Ariz., motion to waive the Budget Act with respect to the Conrad, D-N.D., point of order against the McCain amendment to the Reid, D-Nev., substitute. The McCain amendment would require spending cuts after two consecutive quarters of economic growth greater than 2 percent of the inflation-adjusted gross domestic product. Once the trigger is met, all unobligated appropriations in the bill would be rescinded. Also, the president's next budget after the two quarters of growth would have to balance within five years and restore a discretionary spending cap for five years as the budget baseline. Motion rejected 44-53: R 40-0; D 3-52; I 1-1. A three-fifths majority (60) of the total Senate is required to waive the Budget Act. (Subsequently, the chair upheld the point of order, and the amendment fell.) Feb. 4, 2009.

41. **HR 1. Economic Stimulus/Defense Department Procurement.** Inhofe, R-Okla., motion to waive the Budget Act with respect to the Baucus, D-Mont., point of order against the Inhofe amendment to the Reid, D-Nev., substitute. The Inhofe amendment would provide $5.2 billion for Department of Defense procurement, offset by various cuts in the bill, including $2 billion for "green" energy for office buildings, $1 billion for the Census Bureau, $650 million for digital television coupons and $850 million for Amtrak. Motion rejected 38-59: R 37-3; D 0-55; I 1-1. A three-fifths majority vote (60) of the total Senate is required to waive the Budget Act. (Subsequently, the chair upheld the point of order, and the amendment fell.) Feb. 4, 2009.

	37	38	39	40	41			37	38	39	40	41
ALABAMA							**MONTANA**					
Shelby	N	Y	Y	Y	Y		Baucus	N	N	N	N	N
Sessions	Y	Y	Y	Y	Y		Tester	N	N	N	N	N
ALASKA							**NEBRASKA**					
Murkowski	N	Y	Y	Y	Y		Nelson	N	N	N	Y	N
Begich	N	N	N	N	N		**Johanns**	Y	Y	Y	Y	Y
ARIZONA							**NEVADA**					
McCain	Y	Y	Y	Y	Y		Reid	N	N	N	N	N
Kyl	Y	Y	Y	Y	Y		**Ensign**	Y	Y	Y	Y	Y
ARKANSAS							**NEW HAMPSHIRE**					
Lincoln	N	N	N	N	N		**Gregg**	?	?	?	?	?
Pryor	N	N	N	N	N		Shaheen	N	N	N	N	N
CALIFORNIA							**NEW JERSEY**					
Feinstein	N	N	N	N	N		Lautenberg	N	N	N	N	N
Boxer	N	N	N	N	N		Menendez	N	N	N	N	N
COLORADO							**NEW MEXICO**					
Udall	N	N	N	N	N		Bingaman	N	N	N	N	N
Bennet	N	N	N	N	N		Udall	N	N	N	N	N
CONNECTICUT							**NEW YORK**					
Dodd	N	N	N	N	N		Schumer	N	N	N	N	N
Lieberman	N	N	N	Y	Y		Gillibrand	N	N	N	N	N
DELAWARE							**NORTH CAROLINA**					
Carper	N	N	N	N	N		**Burr**	Y	Y	Y	Y	Y
Kaufman	N	N	N	N	N		Hagan	N	N	N	N	N
FLORIDA							**NORTH DAKOTA**					
Nelson	N	N	N	N	N		Conrad	N	N	N	N	N
Martinez	Y	Y	N	Y	Y		Dorgan	N	N	N	N	N
GEORGIA							**OHIO**					
Chambliss	Y	Y	Y	Y	Y		Voinovich	N	N	Y	N	N
Isakson	Y	Y	Y	Y	Y		Brown	N	N	N	N	N
HAWAII							**OKLAHOMA**					
Inouye	N	N	N	N	N		**Inhofe**	Y	Y	Y	Y	Y
Akaka	N	N	N	N	N		**Coburn**	Y	Y	Y	Y	Y
IDAHO							**OREGON**					
Crapo	Y	Y	Y	Y	Y		Wyden	N	N	N	N	N
Risch	Y	Y	Y	Y	Y		Merkley	N	N	N	N	N
ILLINOIS							**PENNSYLVANIA**					
Durbin	N	N	N	N	N		**Specter**	N	N	N	Y	N
Burris	N	N	N	N	N		Casey	N	N	N	N	N
INDIANA							**RHODE ISLAND**					
Lugar	N	Y	N	Y	Y		Reed	N	N	N	N	N
Bayh	N	N	N	Y	N		Whitehouse	N	N	N	N	N
IOWA							**SOUTH CAROLINA**					
Grassley	Y	Y	Y	Y	Y		**Graham**	Y	Y	Y	Y	Y
Harkin	N	N	N	N	N		**DeMint**	Y	Y	Y	Y	Y
KANSAS							**SOUTH DAKOTA**					
Brownback	Y	Y	Y	Y	Y		Johnson	N	N	N	N	N
Roberts	Y	Y	Y	Y	Y		**Thune**	Y	Y	Y	Y	Y
KENTUCKY							**TENNESSEE**					
McConnell	Y	Y	Y	Y	Y		**Alexander**	Y	Y	Y	Y	N
Bunning	Y	Y	Y	Y	Y		**Corker**	Y	Y	Y	Y	N
LOUISIANA							**TEXAS**					
Landrieu	N	N	N	N	N		**Hutchison**	N	Y	Y	Y	N
Vitter	Y	Y	Y	Y	Y		**Cornyn**	Y	Y	Y	Y	Y
MAINE							**UTAH**					
Snowe	N	N	N	N	Y		**Hatch**	Y	Y	Y	Y	Y
Collins	N	N	N	Y	Y		**Bennett**	Y	Y	Y	Y	Y
MARYLAND							**VERMONT**					
Mikulski	N	N	N	N	N		Leahy	N	N	N	N	N
Cardin	N	N	N	N	N		*Sanders*	N	N	N	N	N
MASSACHUSETTS							**VIRGINIA**					
Kennedy	?	?	?	?	?		Webb	N	N	N	N	N
Kerry	N	N	N	N	N		Warner	N	N	N	N	N
MICHIGAN							**WASHINGTON**					
Levin	N	N	N	N	N		Murray	N	N	N	N	N
Stabenow	N	N	N	N	N		Cantwell	N	N	N	N	N
MINNESOTA							**WEST VIRGINIA**					
Klobuchar	N	N	N	N	N		Byrd	N	N	N	N	N
Vacant							Rockefeller	N	N	N	N	N
MISSISSIPPI							**WISCONSIN**					
Cochran	Y	Y	Y	Y	Y		Kohl	N	N	N	N	N
Wicker	Y	Y	Y	Y	Y		Feingold	N	N	N	N	N
MISSOURI							**WYOMING**					
Bond	Y	Y	Y	Y	Y		**Enzi**	Y	Y	Y	Y	Y
McCaskill	N	N	N	Y	N		**Barrasso**	Y	Y	Y	Y	Y

KEY	**Republicans**	Democrats	*Independents*	
Y Voted for (yea)	X Paired against	C Voted "present" to avoid possible conflict of interest
# Paired for	– Announced against	
+ Announced for	P Voted "present"	? Did not vote or otherwise make a position known
N Voted against (nay)		

IN THE SENATE | By Vote Number

42. **HR 1. Economic Stimulus/Tax Rate Reduction.** Cornyn, R-Texas, motion to waive the Budget Act with respect to the Baucus, D-Mont., point of order against the Cornyn amendment to the Reid, D-Nev., substitute. The Cornyn amendment would strike the Making Work Pay tax credit and replace it with a reduction in the lowest marginal tax rate from 10 percent to 5 percent for 2009 and 2010. Motion rejected 37-60: R 37-3; D 0-55; I 0-2. A three-fifths majority (60) of the total Senate is required to waive the Budget Act. (Subsequently, the chair upheld the point of order, and the amendment fell.) Feb. 4, 2009.

43. **HR 1. Economic Stimulus/Social Security Benefits.** Bunning, R-Ky., motion to waive the Budget Act with respect to the Baucus, D-Mont., point of order against the Bunning amendment to the Reid, D-Nev., substitute. The Bunning amendment would repeal the 1993 tax increase in Social Security benefits for one year, effective Dec. 31, 2008. It would be offset by various cuts in the bill, except those designated for the Department of Veterans Affairs. Motion rejected 39-57: R 37-2; D 2-53; I 0-2. A three-fifths majority (60) of the total Senate is required to waive the Budget Act. (Subsequently, the chair upheld the point of order, and the amendment fell.) Feb. 4, 2009.

44. **HR 1. Economic Stimulus/"Buy American" Provision.** McCain, R-Ariz., amendment to the Reid, D-Nev., substitute. The McCain amendment would strike the "Buy American" provision in the bill, which would require that only U.S.-made manufactured goods and materials be used in projects funded by the bill. Rejected 31-65: R 30-9; D 0-55; I 1-1. Feb. 4, 2009.

45. **HR 1. Economic Stimulus/Republican Substitute.** McCain, R-Ariz., motion to waive the Budget Act with respect to the Baucus, D-Mont., point of order against the McCain substitute amendment to the Reid, D-Nev., substitute. The McCain substitute would provide $421 billion in tax cuts and additional spending, including $275 billion in income tax reductions and corporate tax breaks, $32 billion in spending and tax breaks aimed at preventing foreclosures and stimulating the housing market, and $45 billion in transportation infrastructure investments. It would extend eligibility for unemployment insurance benefits until Dec. 31, 2009. Motion rejected 40-57: R 40-0; D 0-55; I 0-2. A three-fifths majority (60) of the total Senate is required to waive the Budget Act. (Subsequently, the chair upheld the point of order, and the amendment fell.) A "nay" was a vote in support of the president's position. Feb. 5, 2009.

46. **HR 1. Economic Stimulus/Earmark Point of Order.** Feingold, D-Wis., amendment to the Reid, D-Nev., substitute. The Feingold amendment would create a 60-vote point of order in spending bills against unauthorized earmarks and require disclosure of lobbying by recipients of federal funds. Rejected 32-65: R 26-14; D 5-50; I 1-1. Feb. 5, 2009.

	42	43	44	45	46
ALABAMA					
Shelby	Y	Y	Y	Y	N
Sessions	Y	Y	Y	Y	Y
ALASKA					
Murkowski	Y	Y	Y	Y	N
Begich	N	N	N	N	N
ARIZONA					
McCain	Y	Y	Y	Y	Y
Kyl	Y	Y	Y	Y	Y
ARKANSAS					
Lincoln	N	N	N	N	N
Pryor	N	N	N	N	N
CALIFORNIA					
Feinstein	N	N	N	N	N
Boxer	N	N	N	N	N
COLORADO					
Udall	N	N	N	N	N
Bennet	N	N	N	N	N
CONNECTICUT					
Dodd	N	N	N	N	N
Lieberman	N	N	Y	N	Y
DELAWARE					
Carper	N	N	N	N	N
Kaufman	N	N	N	N	Y
FLORIDA					
Nelson	N	N	N	N	N
Martinez	Y	Y	Y	Y	Y
GEORGIA					
Chambliss	Y	Y	Y	Y	Y
Isakson	Y	Y	Y	Y	Y
HAWAII					
Inouye	N	N	N	N	N
Akaka	N	N	N	N	N
IDAHO					
Crapo	Y	Y	Y	Y	Y
Risch	Y	Y	Y	Y	Y
ILLINOIS					
Durbin	N	N	N	N	N
Burris	N	N	N	N	N
INDIANA					
Lugar	Y	Y	Y	Y	N
Bayh	N	Y	N	N	Y
IOWA					
Grassley	Y	Y	N	Y	Y
Harkin	N	N	N	N	N
KANSAS					
Brownback	Y	Y	N	Y	N
Roberts	Y	Y	Y	Y	N
KENTUCKY					
McConnell	Y	Y	Y	Y	N
Bunning	Y	Y	Y	Y	N
LOUISIANA					
Landrieu	N	N	N	N	N
Vitter	Y	Y	N	Y	Y
MAINE					
Snowe	N	N	N	Y	Y
Collins	N	N	N	Y	N
MARYLAND					
Mikulski	N	N	N	N	N
Cardin	N	N	N	N	N
MASSACHUSETTS					
Kennedy	?	?	?	?	?
Kerry	N	N	N	N	N
MICHIGAN					
Levin	N	N	N	N	N
Stabenow	N	N	N	N	N
MINNESOTA					
Klobuchar	N	N	N	N	N
Vacant					
MISSISSIPPI					
Cochran	Y	Y	Y	Y	N
Wicker	Y	Y	Y	Y	N
MISSOURI					
Bond	Y	Y	Y	Y	N
McCaskill	N	N	N	N	Y

	42	43	44	45	46
MONTANA					
Baucus	N	N	N	N	N
Tester	N	N	N	N	N
NEBRASKA					
Nelson	N	Y	N	N	N
Johanns	Y	Y	Y	Y	Y
NEVADA					
Reid	N	N	N	N	N
Ensign	Y	Y	Y	Y	Y
NEW HAMPSHIRE					
Gregg	?	?	?	?	?
Shaheen	N	N	N	N	N
NEW JERSEY					
Lautenberg	N	N	N	N	N
Menendez	N	N	N	N	N
NEW MEXICO					
Bingaman	N	N	N	N	N
Udall	N	N	N	N	N
NEW YORK					
Schumer	N	N	N	N	N
Gillibrand	N	N	N	N	N
NORTH CAROLINA					
Burr	Y	Y	N	Y	Y
Hagan	N	N	N	N	N
NORTH DAKOTA					
Conrad	N	N	N	N	N
Dorgan	N	N	N	N	N
OHIO					
Voinovich	N	?	?	Y	Y
Brown	N	N	N	N	N
OKLAHOMA					
Inhofe	Y	Y	Y	Y	Y
Coburn	Y	Y	Y	Y	Y
OREGON					
Wyden	N	N	N	N	N
Merkley	N	N	N	N	N
PENNSYLVANIA					
Specter	Y	Y	N	Y	N
Casey	N	N	N	N	N
RHODE ISLAND					
Reed	N	N	N	N	N
Whitehouse	N	N	N	N	N
SOUTH CAROLINA					
Graham	Y	Y	N	Y	Y
DeMint	Y	Y	Y	Y	Y
SOUTH DAKOTA					
Johnson	N	N	N	N	N
Thune	Y	Y	Y	Y	Y
TENNESSEE					
Alexander	Y	Y	Y	Y	N
Corker	Y	Y	Y	Y	Y
TEXAS					
Hutchison	Y	Y	N	Y	Y
Cornyn	Y	Y	Y	Y	Y
UTAH					
Hatch	Y	Y	Y	Y	Y
Bennett	Y	Y	Y	Y	N
VERMONT					
Leahy	N	N	N	N	N
Sanders	N	N	N	N	N
VIRGINIA					
Webb	N	N	N	N	N
Warner	N	N	N	N	N
WASHINGTON					
Murray	N	N	N	N	N
Cantwell	N	N	N	N	Y
WEST VIRGINIA					
Byrd	N	N	N	N	N
Rockefeller	N	N	N	N	N
WISCONSIN					
Kohl	N	N	N	N	N
Feingold	N	N	N	N	Y
WYOMING					
Enzi	Y	Y	Y	Y	Y
Barrasso	Y	Y	Y	Y	Y

KEY   Republicans   Democrats   *Independents*

Y	Voted for (yea)	X	Paired against
#	Paired for	–	Announced against
+	Announced for	P	Voted "present"
N	Voted against (nay)		
		C	Voted "present" to avoid possible conflict of interest
		?	Did not vote or otherwise make a position known

IN THE SENATE | By Vote Number

47. **HR 1. Economic Stimulus/Religious Instruction.** DeMint, R-S.C., amendment to the Reid, D-Nev., substitute. The DeMint amendment would eliminate funding prohibitions for the renovation or repair of higher education facilities used for sectarian instruction, religious worship, or a school or department of divinity. Rejected 43-54: R 38-2; D 4-51; I 1-1. Feb. 5, 2009.

48. **HR 1. Economic Stimulus/Housing and Tax Substitute.** Ensign, R-Nev., motion to waive the Budget Act with respect to the Baucus, D-Mont., point of order against the Ensign substitute amendment to the Reid, D-Nev., substitute. The Ensign substitute would strike the underlying stimulus provisions and replace them with provisions that focus on housing and taxes. It would require the Treasury to establish a homeowner security program. Refinanced mortgages that met conforming loan limits would be guaranteed a 30-year rate of 4 percent to 4.5 percent. It would reduce the marginal income tax rate for two years from 15 percent to 10 percent and from 10 percent to 5 percent. It would extend bonus depreciation for 2009, provide a tax credit to businesses that hire veterans and provide a one-time tax credit for homebuyers of $15,000 or 10 percent of the purchase price of a principal residence, whichever is lower. Motion rejected 35-62: R 35-5; D 0-55; I 0-2. A three-fifths majority (60) of the total Senate is required to waive the Budget Act. (Subsequently, the chair upheld the point of order, and the amendment fell.) A "nay" was a vote in support of the president's position. Feb. 5, 2009.

49. **HR 1. Economic Stimulus/Tax Provisions Substitute.** Thune, R-S.D., motion to waive the Budget Act with respect to the Baucus, D-Mont., point of order against the Thune substitute amendment to the Reid, D-Nev., substitute. The Thune substitute would replace the underlying stimulus with tax provisions. It would reduce the 10 percent and 15 percent tax rates to 5 percent and 10 percent in 2009, extend alternative minimum tax relief in 2009 and 2010, and extend and expand the homebuyer credit. Motion rejected 37-60: R 37-3; D 0-55; I 0-2. A three-fifths majority (60) of the total Senate is required to waive the Budget Act. (Subsequently, the chair upheld the point of order, and the amendment fell.) Feb. 5, 2009.

50. **HR 1. Economic Stimulus/Competitive Procedures.** Baucus, D-Mont., motion to table (kill) the Coburn, R-Okla., amendment to the Reid, D-Nev., substitute. The Coburn amendment would require the use of competitive procedures in awarding grants, contracts and cooperative agreements funded in the bill. Motion rejected 1-96: R 1-39; D 0-55; I 0-2. Feb. 5, 2009.

	47	48	49	50			47	48	49	50
ALABAMA						**MONTANA**				
Shelby	Y	Y	Y	N		Baucus	N	N	N	N
Sessions	Y	Y	Y	N		Tester	N	N	N	N
ALASKA						**NEBRASKA**				
Murkowski	Y	Y	Y	N		Nelson	Y	N	N	N
Begich	N	N	N	N		**Johanns**	Y	Y	Y	N
ARIZONA						**NEVADA**				
McCain	Y	Y	Y	N		Reid	N	N	N	N
Kyl	Y	Y	Y	N		**Ensign**	Y	Y	Y	N
ARKANSAS						**NEW HAMPSHIRE**				
Lincoln	N	N	N	N		**Gregg**	?	?	?	?
Pryor	N	N	N	N		Shaheen	N	N	N	N
CALIFORNIA						**NEW JERSEY**				
Feinstein	N	N	N	N		Lautenberg	N	N	N	N
Boxer	N	N	N	N		Menendez	N	N	N	N
COLORADO						**NEW MEXICO**				
Udall	N	N	N	N		Bingaman	N	N	N	N
Bennet	N	N	N	N		Udall	N	N	N	N
CONNECTICUT						**NEW YORK**				
Dodd	N	N	N	N		Schumer	N	N	N	N
Lieberman	Y	N	N	N		Gillibrand	N	N	N	N
DELAWARE						**NORTH CAROLINA**				
Carper	N	N	N	N		**Burr**	Y	Y	Y	N
Kaufman	N	N	N	N		Hagan	N	N	N	N
FLORIDA						**NORTH DAKOTA**				
Nelson	N	N	N	N		Conrad	Y	N	N	N
Martinez	Y	Y	Y	N		Dorgan	Y	N	N	N
GEORGIA						**OHIO**				
Chambliss	Y	Y	Y	N		**Voinovich**	Y	N	N	Y
Isakson	Y	Y	Y	N		Brown	N	N	N	N
HAWAII						**OKLAHOMA**				
Inouye	N	N	N	N		**Inhofe**	Y	Y	Y	N
Akaka	N	N	N	N		**Coburn**	Y	Y	Y	N
IDAHO						**OREGON**				
Crapo	Y	Y	Y	N		Wyden	N	N	N	N
Risch	Y	Y	Y	N		Merkley	N	N	N	N
ILLINOIS						**PENNSYLVANIA**				
Durbin	N	N	N	N		**Specter**	Y	Y	Y	N
Burris	N	N	N	N		Casey	N	N	N	N
INDIANA						**RHODE ISLAND**				
Lugar	Y	Y	Y	N		Reed	N	N	N	N
Bayh	Y	N	N	N		Whitehouse	N	N	N	N
IOWA						**SOUTH CAROLINA**				
Grassley	Y	Y	Y	N		**Graham**	Y	Y	Y	N
Harkin	N	N	N	N		**DeMint**	Y	N	Y	N
KANSAS						**SOUTH DAKOTA**				
Brownback	Y	Y	Y	N		Johnson	N	N	N	N
Roberts	Y	Y	Y	N		**Thune**	Y	Y	Y	N
KENTUCKY						**TENNESSEE**				
McConnell	Y	Y	Y	N		**Alexander**	Y	Y	Y	N
Bunning	Y	N	Y	N		**Corker**	Y	Y	Y	N
LOUISIANA						**TEXAS**				
Landrieu	N	N	N	N		**Hutchison**	Y	Y	Y	N
Vitter	Y	Y	Y	N		**Cornyn**	Y	Y	Y	N
MAINE						**UTAH**				
Snowe	N	N	N	N		**Hatch**	Y	Y	Y	N
Collins	N	N	N	N		**Bennett**	Y	Y	Y	N
MARYLAND						**VERMONT**				
Mikulski	N	N	N	N		Leahy	N	N	N	N
Cardin	N	N	N	N		*Sanders*	N	N	N	N
MASSACHUSETTS						**VIRGINIA**				
Kennedy	?	?	?	?		Webb	N	N	N	N
Kerry	N	N	N	N		Warner	N	N	N	N
MICHIGAN						**WASHINGTON**				
Levin	N	N	N	N		Murray	N	N	N	N
Stabenow	N	N	N	N		Cantwell	N	N	N	N
MINNESOTA						**WEST VIRGINIA**				
Klobuchar	N	N	N	N		Byrd	N	N	N	N
Vacant						Rockefeller	N	N	N	N
MISSISSIPPI						**WISCONSIN**				
Cochran	Y	Y	Y	N		Kohl	N	N	N	N
Wicker	Y	Y	Y	N		Feingold	N	N	N	N
MISSOURI						**WYOMING**				
Bond	Y	Y	Y	N		**Enzi**	Y	Y	Y	N
McCaskill	N	N	N	N		**Barrasso**	Y	Y	Y	N

KEY	**Republicans**	Democrats	*Independents*		
Y	Voted for (yea)	X	Paired against	C	Voted "present" to avoid possible conflict of interest
#	Paired for	–	Announced against		
+	Announced for	P	Voted "present"	?	Did not vote or otherwise make a position known
N	Voted against (nay)				

IN THE SENATE | By Vote Number

51. **HR 1. Economic Stimulus/Spending Allocation.** Coburn, R-Okla., amendment to the Reid, D-Nev., substitute. The Coburn amendment would bar the use of funds in the bill for purposes such as zoos, community parks, museums and highway beautification projects. As introduced, the substitute would provide $884.5 billion in tax cuts and additional spending to stimulate the economy, including a provision to exempt additional taxpayers from the alternative minimum tax in 2009. It would also provide $27 billion to extend and expand federal unemployment insurance through Dec. 31, 2009; $87 billion to reimburse state Medicaid programs; and $27.1 billion for highway programs. Adopted 73-24: R 40-0; D 33-22; I 0-2. Feb. 6, 2009.

52. **HR 1. Economic Stimulus/Competitive Procedures.** Coburn, R-Okla., amendment to the Reid, D-Nev., substitute. The Coburn amendment would require the use of competitive procedures in awarding grants, contracts and cooperative agreements funded in the bill. Adopted 97-0: R 40-0; D 55-0; I 2-0. Feb. 6, 2009.

53. **HR 1. Economic Stimulus/Foreclosure Mitigation.** Graham, R-S.C., amendment to the Reid, D-Nev., substitute. The Graham amendment would create a Federal Deposit Insurance Corporation (FDIC) loan modification program to provide incentives to lenders. The FDIC could take other steps if it certified to Congress that those efforts would have an equal or greater impact or be more cost-effective than the new program. It would shift $22.7 billion to the program. Rejected 39-57: R 36-3; D 3-52; I 0-2. Feb. 6, 2009.

54. **HR 1. Economic Stimulus/State Medicaid Formula.** Grassley, R-Iowa, amendment to the Reid, D-Nev., substitute. The Grassley amendment would replace the underlying Medicaid Federal Medical Assistance Percentages formula in the measure with a flat increase of 9.5 percent for every state for nine consecutive quarters. Rejected 47-49: R 36-3; D 11-44; I 0-2. Feb. 6, 2009.

55. **HR 1. Economic Stimulus/Electric Vehicle Technology.** Cantwell, D-Wash., motion to waive the Budget Act with respect to the Sessions, R-Ala., point of order against the Cantwell amendment to the Reid, D-Nev., substitute. The Cantwell amendment would allow 100 percent expensing of equipment placed in service before Jan. 1, 2012, that is used for manufacturing electric plug-in vehicles. It would increase tax credits for the cost of converting existing cars to plug-ins. It also would shorten the depreciation schedule for "smart meter" equipment to five years. Motion agreed to 80-16: R 23-16; D 55-0; I 2-0. A three-fifths majority vote (60) of the total Senate is required to waive the Budget Act. (Subsequently, the amendment was adopted by voice vote.) Feb. 6, 2009.

56. **HR 1. Economic Stimulus/ACORN Funding Ban.** Vitter, R-La., amendment to the Reid, D-Nev., substitute. The Vitter amendment would bar funds in the bill from being provided, either directly or indirectly, to the Association of Community Organizations for Reform Now (ACORN). Rejected 45-51: R 39-0; D 6-49; I 0-2. Feb. 6, 2009.

57. **HR 1. Economic Stimulus/Capital Loss Deduction.** Bunning, R-Ky., amendment to the Reid, D-Nev., substitute. The Bunning amendment would allow individuals to deduct up to $15,000 in capital losses for 2009, up from the current $3,000 limit. It is also intended to remove a provision that would allow corporations to apply general business tax credits against tax payments for the previous five years. Current law allows a one-year carryback. Rejected 41-55: R 38-1; D 3-52; I 0-2. Feb. 6, 2009.

	51	52	53	54	55	56	57		51	52	53	54	55	56	57
ALABAMA								**MONTANA**							
Shelby	Y	Y	Y	Y	N	Y	Y	Baucus	Y	Y	N	N	Y	Y	N
Sessions	Y	Y	Y	Y	N	Y	Y	Tester	Y	Y	N	N	Y	Y	N
ALASKA								**NEBRASKA**							
Murkowski	Y	Y	Y	Y	Y	Y	Y	Nelson	Y	Y	N	Y	Y	Y	N
Begich	Y	Y	N	N	Y	N	N	**Johanns**	Y	Y	Y	Y	N	Y	Y
ARIZONA								**NEVADA**							
McCain	Y	Y	Y	Y	Y	Y	Y	Reid	N	Y	N	N	Y	N	N
Kyl	Y	Y	Y	Y	N	Y	Y	**Ensign**	Y	Y	Y	N	Y	Y	Y
ARKANSAS								**NEW HAMPSHIRE**							
Lincoln	Y	Y	N	Y	Y	N	N	**Gregg**	?	?	?	?	?	?	?
Pryor	Y	Y	N	Y	Y	N	N	Shaheen	N	Y	N	Y	Y	N	N
CALIFORNIA								**NEW JERSEY**							
Feinstein	Y	Y	N	N	Y	N	N	Lautenberg	N	Y	N	N	Y	N	N
Boxer	N	Y	N	N	Y	N	N	Menendez	N	Y	N	N	Y	N	N
COLORADO								**NEW MEXICO**							
Udall	Y	Y	N	N	Y	N	Y	Bingaman	Y	Y	N	Y	Y	N	N
Bennet	Y	Y	N	N	Y	N	N	Udall	Y	Y	N	Y	Y	N	N
CONNECTICUT								**NEW YORK**							
Dodd	N	Y	N	N	Y	N	N	Schumer	N	Y	N	N	Y	N	N
Lieberman	N	Y	N	N	Y	N	N	Gillibrand	N	Y	N	N	Y	N	N
DELAWARE								**NORTH CAROLINA**							
Carper	Y	Y	N	N	Y	N	N	**Burr**	Y	Y	Y	Y	Y	Y	Y
Kaufman	N	Y	N	N	Y	N	N	Hagan	N	Y	N	N	Y	Y	N
FLORIDA								**NORTH DAKOTA**							
Nelson	Y	Y	N	N	Y	N	N	Conrad	Y	Y	Y	Y	Y	N	N
Martinez	Y	Y	Y	N	Y	Y	Y	Dorgan	Y	Y	Y	Y	N	N	N
GEORGIA								**OHIO**							
Chambliss	Y	Y	Y	Y	Y	Y	Y	**Voinovich**	Y	Y	Y	Y	Y	Y	Y
Isakson	Y	Y	Y	Y	Y	Y	Y	Brown	Y	Y	N	N	Y	N	N
HAWAII								**OKLAHOMA**							
Inouye	N	Y	N	N	Y	N	N	**Inhofe**	Y	Y	Y	Y	N	Y	Y
Akaka	N	Y	N	N	Y	N	N	**Coburn**	Y	Y	Y	Y	N	Y	Y
IDAHO								**OREGON**							
Crapo	Y	Y	Y	Y	Y	Y	Y	Wyden	Y	Y	N	N	Y	N	N
Risch	Y	Y	Y	Y	Y	Y	Y	Merkley	Y	Y	N	N	Y	N	N
ILLINOIS								**PENNSYLVANIA**							
Durbin	N	Y	N	N	Y	N	N	**Specter**	Y	Y	N	Y	Y	Y	Y
Burris	N	Y	N	N	Y	N	N	Casey	Y	Y	N	N	Y	N	N
INDIANA								**RHODE ISLAND**							
Lugar	Y	Y	Y	Y	Y	Y	Y	Reed	N	Y	N	N	Y	N	N
Bayh	Y	Y	N	N	Y	Y	N	Whitehouse	N	Y	N	N	Y	N	N
IOWA								**SOUTH CAROLINA**							
Grassley	Y	Y	Y	Y	N	Y	Y	**Graham**	Y	Y	Y	Y	Y	Y	Y
Harkin	N	Y	N	Y	N	N	N	**DeMint**	Y	Y	Y	Y	N	Y	Y
KANSAS								**SOUTH DAKOTA**							
Brownback	Y	Y	Y	Y	Y	Y	Y	Johnson	Y	Y	N	N	Y	N	N
Roberts	Y	Y	Y	Y	Y	Y	Y	**Thune**	Y	Y	Y	Y	Y	Y	Y
KENTUCKY								**TENNESSEE**							
McConnell	Y	Y	Y	Y	N	Y	Y	**Alexander**	Y	Y	Y	Y	Y	Y	Y
Bunning	Y	Y	N	Y	N	Y	Y	**Corker**	Y	Y	Y	Y	Y	Y	Y
LOUISIANA								**TEXAS**							
Landrieu	N	Y	N	N	Y	N	Y	**Hutchison**	Y	Y	?	?	?	?	?
Vitter	Y	Y	Y	N	Y	Y	Y	**Cornyn**	Y	Y	Y	Y	N	Y	Y
MAINE								**UTAH**							
Snowe	Y	Y	N	Y	Y	Y	N	**Hatch**	Y	Y	Y	Y	Y	Y	Y
Collins	Y	Y	N	Y	Y	Y	Y	**Bennett**	Y	Y	Y	Y	Y	Y	Y
MARYLAND								**VERMONT**							
Mikulski	Y	Y	N	N	Y	N	N	Leahy	N	Y	N	N	Y	N	N
Cardin	Y	Y	N	N	Y	N	N	*Sanders*	N	Y	N	N	Y	N	N
MASSACHUSETTS								**VIRGINIA**							
Kennedy	?	?	?	?	?	?	?	Webb	N	Y	N	N	Y	N	Y
Kerry	N	Y	N	N	Y	N	N	Warner	Y	Y	N	N	Y	N	N
MICHIGAN								**WASHINGTON**							
Levin	N	Y	N	N	Y	N	N	Murray	Y	Y	N	N	Y	N	N
Stabenow	Y	Y	N	N	Y	N	N	Cantwell	Y	Y	N	N	Y	N	N
MINNESOTA								**WEST VIRGINIA**							
Klobuchar	Y	Y	N	N	Y	N	N	Byrd	Y	Y	N	N	Y	Y	N
Vacant								Rockefeller	N	Y	N	N	Y	N	N
MISSISSIPPI								**WISCONSIN**							
Cochran	Y	Y	Y	Y	N	Y	Y	Kohl	Y	Y	N	N	Y	N	N
Wicker	Y	Y	Y	Y	N	Y	Y	Feingold	Y	Y	Y	N	Y	N	N
MISSOURI								**WYOMING**							
Bond	Y	Y	Y	Y	Y	Y	Y	**Enzi**	Y	Y	Y	Y	N	Y	Y
McCaskill	Y	Y	N	N	Y	N	N	**Barrasso**	Y	Y	Y	Y	N	Y	Y

KEY   **Republicans**   Democrats   *Independents*

Y Voted for (yea)	**X** Paired against	**C** Voted "present" to avoid possible conflict of interest
# Paired for	**–** Announced against	
+ Announced for	**P** Voted "present"	**?** Did not vote or otherwise make a position known
N Voted against (nay)		

IN THE SENATE | By Vote Number

58. **HR 1. Economic Stimulus/Tax Rebate.** Thune, R-S.D., motion to waive the Budget Act with respect to the Baucus, D-Mont., point of order against the Thune substitute amendment to the Reid, D-Nev., substitute. The Thune substitute would replace the bill text with an across-the-board tax rebate available for the 2009 tax year. Individuals who filed tax returns in 2007 with an adjusted gross income below $250,000 would be eligible. The rebate would provide $5,143 for single filers and $10,286 for joint filers. Motion rejected 35-61: R 35-4; D 0-55; I 0-2. A three-fifths majority vote (60) of the total Senate is required to waive the Budget Act. (Subsequently, the chair upheld the point of order, and the amendment fell; subsequent to that, Reid withdrew his substitute.) Feb. 7, 2009 (in the session that began and the Congressional Record dated Feb. 6).

59. **HR 1. Economic Stimulus/Cloture.** Motion to invoke cloture (thus limiting debate) on the Reid, D-Nev. (for Nelson, D-Neb., and Collins, R-Maine), substitute amendment that would provide approximately $838 billion in tax cuts and additional spending to stimulate the economy, including a provision to exempt additional taxpayers from paying the alternative minimum tax in 2009. It would provide funds for a state fiscal stabilization fund and a one-time payment to seniors, disabled veterans and those who receive disability payments. The amendment would expand bonus depreciation for 2009, increase weekly unemployment benefits and provide an additional 20 weeks of unemployment benefits (an additional 33 weeks in states with high unemployment rates). It would suspend federal income tax on the first $2,400 of unemployment benefits for 2009. It would also expand the current homeownership tax credit by up to $15,000 and allow the credit for purchases of a primary residence. It would temporarily increase federal Medicaid matching payments for states by an estimated $87 billion. Motion agreed to 61-36: R 3-36; D 56-0; I 2-0. Three-fifths of the total Senate (60) is required to invoke cloture. Feb. 9, 2009.

60. **HR 1. Economic Stimulus/Substitute.** Motion to waive the Budget Act with respect to the Sessions, R-Ala., point of order against the Reid, D-Nev. (for Nelson, D-Neb., and Collins, R-Maine), substitute amendment. Motion agreed to 61-37: R 3-37; D 56-0; I 2-0. A three-fifths majority vote (60) of the total Senate is required to waive the Budget Act. (Subsequently, the amendment was adopted by unanimous consent.) Feb. 10, 2009.

61. **HR 1. Economic Stimulus/Passage.** Passage of the bill that would provide approximately $838 billion in tax cuts and additional spending to stimulate the economy, including a provision to exempt additional taxpayers from paying the alternative minimum tax in 2009. It would provide funds for a state fiscal stabilization fund and a one-time payment to seniors, disabled veterans and those who receive disability payments. The bill would expand bonus depreciation for 2009, increase weekly unemployment benefits and provide an additional 20 weeks of unemployment benefits (an additional 33 weeks in states with high unemployment rates). It would suspend federal income tax on the first $2,400 of unemployment benefits for 2009. It would also expand the current homeownership tax credit by up to $15,000 and allow the credit for purchases of a primary residence. It would temporarily increase federal Medicaid matching payments for states by an estimated $87 billion. Passed 61-37: R 3-37; D 56-0; I 2-0. A "yea" was a vote in support of the president's position. Feb. 10, 2009.

62. **Lynn Nomination/Confirmation.** Confirmation of President Obama's nomination of William Lynn of Virginia to be deputy secretary of Defense. Confirmed 93-4: R 37-3; D 54-1; I 2-0. A "yea" was a vote in support of the president's position. Feb. 11, 2009.

	58	59	60	61	62
ALABAMA					
Shelby	Y	N	N	N	Y
Sessions	Y	N	N	N	Y
ALASKA					
Murkowski	Y	N	N	N	Y
Begich	N	Y	Y	Y	Y
ARIZONA					
McCain	Y	N	N	N	Y
Kyl	Y	N	N	N	Y
ARKANSAS					
Lincoln	N	Y	Y	Y	Y
Pryor	N	Y	Y	Y	Y
CALIFORNIA					
Feinstein	N	Y	Y	Y	Y
Boxer	N	Y	Y	Y	Y
COLORADO					
Udall	N	Y	Y	Y	Y
Bennet	N	Y	Y	Y	Y
CONNECTICUT					
Dodd	N	Y	Y	Y	Y
Lieberman	N	Y	Y	Y	Y
DELAWARE					
Carper	N	Y	Y	Y	Y
Kaufman	N	Y	Y	Y	Y
FLORIDA					
Nelson	N	Y	Y	Y	Y
Martinez	Y	N	N	N	Y
GEORGIA					
Chambliss	Y	N	N	N	Y
Isakson	Y	N	N	N	Y
HAWAII					
Inouye	N	Y	Y	Y	Y
Akaka	N	Y	Y	Y	Y
IDAHO					
Crapo	Y	N	N	N	Y
Risch	Y	N	N	N	Y
ILLINOIS					
Durbin	N	Y	Y	Y	Y
Burris	N	Y	Y	Y	Y
INDIANA					
Lugar	Y	N	N	N	Y
Bayh	N	Y	Y	Y	Y
IOWA					
Grassley	Y	N	N	N	N
Harkin	N	Y	Y	Y	Y
KANSAS					
Brownback	Y	N	N	N	Y
Roberts	Y	N	N	N	Y
KENTUCKY					
McConnell	Y	N	N	N	Y
Bunning	Y	N	N	N	Y
LOUISIANA					
Landrieu	N	Y	Y	Y	Y
Vitter	Y	N	N	N	Y
MAINE					
Snowe	N	Y	Y	Y	Y
Collins	N	Y	Y	Y	Y
MARYLAND					
Mikulski	N	Y	Y	Y	Y
Cardin	N	Y	Y	Y	Y
MASSACHUSETTS					
Kennedy	?	Y	Y	Y	?
Kerry	N	Y	Y	Y	Y
MICHIGAN					
Levin	N	Y	Y	Y	Y
Stabenow	N	Y	Y	Y	Y
MINNESOTA					
Klobuchar	N	Y	Y	Y	Y
Vacant					
MISSISSIPPI					
Cochran	Y	N	N	N	Y
Wicker	Y	N	N	N	Y
MISSOURI					
Bond	Y	N	N	N	Y
McCaskill	N	Y	Y	Y	N
MONTANA					
Baucus	N	Y	Y	Y	Y
Tester	N	Y	Y	Y	Y
NEBRASKA					
Nelson	N	Y	Y	Y	Y
Johanns	Y	N	N	N	Y
NEVADA					
Reid	N	Y	Y	Y	Y
Ensign	N	N	N	N	Y
NEW HAMPSHIRE					
Gregg	?	?	?	?	?
Shaheen	N	Y	Y	Y	Y
NEW JERSEY					
Lautenberg	N	Y	Y	Y	Y
Menendez	N	Y	Y	Y	Y
NEW MEXICO					
Bingaman	N	Y	Y	Y	Y
Udall	N	Y	Y	Y	Y
NEW YORK					
Schumer	N	Y	Y	Y	Y
Gillibrand	N	Y	Y	Y	Y
NORTH CAROLINA					
Burr	Y	N	N	N	Y
Hagan	N	Y	Y	Y	Y
NORTH DAKOTA					
Conrad	N	Y	Y	Y	Y
Dorgan	N	Y	Y	Y	Y
OHIO					
Voinovich	N	N	N	N	Y
Brown	N	Y	Y	Y	Y
OKLAHOMA					
Inhofe	Y	N	N	N	Y
Coburn	Y	N	N	N	N
OREGON					
Wyden	N	Y	Y	Y	Y
Merkley	N	Y	Y	Y	Y
PENNSYLVANIA					
Specter	Y	Y	Y	Y	Y
Casey	N	Y	Y	Y	Y
RHODE ISLAND					
Reed	N	Y	Y	Y	Y
Whitehouse	N	Y	Y	Y	Y
SOUTH CAROLINA					
Graham	Y	N	N	N	Y
DeMint	Y	N	N	N	Y
SOUTH DAKOTA					
Johnson	N	Y	Y	Y	Y
Thune	Y	N	N	N	Y
TENNESSEE					
Alexander	Y	N	N	N	Y
Corker	Y	N	N	N	Y
TEXAS					
Hutchison	?	N	N	N	Y
Cornyn	Y	-	N	N	N
UTAH					
Hatch	Y	N	N	N	Y
Bennett	Y	N	N	N	Y
VERMONT					
Leahy	N	Y	Y	Y	Y
Sanders	N	Y	Y	Y	Y
VIRGINIA					
Webb	N	Y	Y	Y	Y
Warner	N	Y	Y	Y	Y
WASHINGTON					
Murray	N	Y	Y	Y	Y
Cantwell	N	Y	Y	Y	Y
WEST VIRGINIA					
Byrd	N	Y	Y	Y	Y
Rockefeller	N	Y	Y	Y	Y
WISCONSIN					
Kohl	N	Y	Y	Y	Y
Feingold	N	Y	Y	Y	Y
WYOMING					
Enzi	Y	N	N	N	Y
Barrasso	Y	N	N	N	Y

KEY   **Republicans**   Democrats   *Independents*

Y Voted for (yea)	X Paired against	C Voted "present" to avoid possible conflict of interest
# Paired for	- Announced against	
+ Announced for	P Voted "present"	? Did not vote or otherwise make a position known
N Voted against (nay)		

IN THE SENATE | By Vote Number

63. **HR 1. Economic Stimulus/Conference Report.** Motion to waive the Budget Act with respect to the McCain, R-Ariz., point of order against the emergency designation of the conference report on the bill that would provide an estimated $787.2 billion in tax cuts and spending increases to stimulate the economy, prevent the alternative minimum tax from applying to millions of additional taxpayers in 2009 and increase the ceiling on federal borrowing. Motion agreed to 60-38: R 3-38; D 55-0; I 2-0. A three-fifths majority (60) of the total Senate is required to waive the Budget Act. (Senators cast a single vote that applied to votes 63 and 64.) Feb. 13, 2009.

64. **HR 1. Economic Stimulus/Conference Report.** Adoption of the conference report on the bill that would provide an estimated $787.2 billion in tax cuts and spending increases to stimulate the economy. It would prevent the alternative minimum tax from applying to millions of additional taxpayers in 2009 and increase the ceiling on federal borrowing by $789 billion to $12.104 trillion. The tax provisions, estimated to cost $211.8 billion through 2019, include extending current accelerated depreciation allowances for businesses, suspending taxes on the first $2,400 of unemployment benefits for 2009 and expanding a number of individual tax credits. Mandatory spending increases, expected to cost $267 billion through 2019, include an extension of unemployment and welfare benefits, Medicaid payments to states and grants for health information technology. Discretionary spending, estimated at $308.3 billion through 2019, includes grants for state and local schools and funds for public housing, transportation and nutrition assistance. Adopted (thus cleared for the president) 60-38: R 3-38; D 55-0; I 2-0. (By unanimous consent, the Senate agreed to raise the majority requirement for adoption of the conference report to 60 votes. Senators cast a single vote that applied to votes 63 and 64.) A "yea" was a vote in support of the president's position. Feb. 13, 2009.

65. **S 160. District of Columbia Voting Rights/Cloture.** Motion to invoke cloture (thus limiting debate) on the Reid, D-Nev., motion to proceed to the bill that would increase the membership of the House of Representatives to 437 by granting a seat to the District of Columbia and an additional seat to Utah for the 112th Congress. Motion agreed to 62-34: R 8-32; D 52-2; I 2-0. Three-fifths of the total Senate (60) is required to invoke cloture. Feb. 24, 2009.

66. **Solis Nomination/Confirmation.** Confirmation of President Obama's nomination of Hilda L. Solis of California to be secretary of Labor. Confirmed 80-17: R 24-17; D 54-0; I 2-0. A "yea" was a vote in support of the president's position. Feb. 24, 2009.

67. **S 160. District of Columbia Voting Rights/Constitutional Violation.** McCain, R-Ariz., point of order that the bill is out of order because it violates Article I, Section 2, of the Constitution, which states that the House "shall be composed of members chosen every second year by the people of the several states." Point of order rejected 36-62: R 35-6; D 1-54; I 0-2. Feb. 25, 2009.

68. **S 160. District of Columbia Voting Rights/Substitute.** Coburn, R-Okla., substitute amendment that would strike the text of the underlying bill and insert provisions that would exempt residents of the District of Columbia from paying the individual federal income tax. Rejected 7-91: R 7-34; D 0-55; I 0-2. Feb. 25, 2009.

	63	64	65	66	67	68
ALABAMA						
Shelby	N	N	N	N	Y	N
Sessions	N	N	N	N	Y	N
ALASKA						
Murkowski	N	N	Y	Y	Y	N
Begich	Y	Y	Y	Y	N	N
ARIZONA						
McCain	N	N	N	Y	Y	N
Kyl	N	N	N	N	Y	Y
ARKANSAS						
Lincoln	Y	Y	Y	Y	N	N
Pryor	Y	Y	Y	Y	N	N
CALIFORNIA						
Feinstein	Y	Y	Y	Y	N	N
Boxer	Y	Y	Y	Y	N	N
COLORADO						
Udall	Y	Y	Y	Y	N	N
Bennet	Y	Y	Y	Y	N	N
CONNECTICUT						
Dodd	Y	Y	Y	Y	N	N
Lieberman	Y	Y	Y	Y	N	N
DELAWARE						
Carper	Y	Y	Y	Y	N	N
Kaufman	Y	Y	Y	Y	N	N
FLORIDA						
Nelson	Y	Y	Y	Y	N	N
Martinez	N	N	N	Y	Y	N
GEORGIA						
Chambliss	N	N	N	Y	Y	N
Isakson	N	N	N	Y	Y	N
HAWAII						
Inouye	Y	Y	Y	Y	N	N
Akaka	Y	Y	Y	Y	N	N
IDAHO						
Crapo	N	N	N	N	Y	N
Risch	N	N	N	N	Y	N
ILLINOIS						
Durbin	Y	Y	Y	Y	N	N
Burris	Y	Y	Y	Y	N	N
INDIANA						
Lugar	N	N	N	Y	Y	N
Bayh	Y	Y	Y	Y	N	N
IOWA						
Grassley	N	N	N	Y	Y	N
Harkin	Y	Y	+	+	N	N
KANSAS						
Brownback	N	N	N	Y	Y	N
Roberts	N	N	N	N	Y	N
KENTUCKY						
McConnell	N	N	N	Y	Y	N
Bunning	N	N	N	N	Y	Y
LOUISIANA						
Landrieu	Y	Y	Y	Y	N	N
Vitter	N	N	N	N	Y	N
MAINE						
Snowe	Y	Y	Y	Y	N	N
Collins	Y	Y	Y	Y	N	N
MARYLAND						
Mikulski	Y	Y	Y	Y	N	N
Cardin	Y	Y	Y	Y	N	N
MASSACHUSETTS						
Kennedy	?	?	?	?	?	?
Kerry	Y	Y	Y	Y	N	N
MICHIGAN						
Levin	Y	Y	Y	Y	N	N
Stabenow	Y	Y	Y	Y	N	N
MINNESOTA						
Klobuchar	Y	Y	Y	Y	N	N
Vacant						
MISSISSIPPI						
Cochran	N	N	Y	Y	Y	N
Wicker	N	N	N	N	Y	Y
MISSOURI						
Bond	N	N	N	N	Y	N
McCaskill	Y	Y	Y	Y	N	N

	63	64	65	66	67	68
MONTANA						
Baucus	Y	Y	N	Y	N	N
Tester	Y	Y	Y	Y	N	N
NEBRASKA						
Nelson	Y	Y	Y	Y	N	N
Johanns	N	N	N	Y	Y	N
NEVADA						
Reid	Y	Y	Y	Y	N	N
Ensign	N	N	N	N	Y	N
NEW HAMPSHIRE						
Gregg	N	N	N	Y	Y	N
Shaheen	Y	Y	Y	Y	N	N
NEW JERSEY						
Lautenberg	Y	Y	Y	Y	N	N
Menendez	Y	Y	Y	Y	N	N
NEW MEXICO						
Bingaman	Y	Y	Y	Y	N	N
Udall	Y	Y	Y	Y	N	N
NEW YORK						
Schumer	Y	Y	Y	Y	N	N
Gillibrand	Y	Y	Y	Y	N	N
NORTH CAROLINA						
Burr	N	N	N	N	Y	Y
Hagan	Y	Y	Y	Y	N	N
NORTH DAKOTA						
Conrad	Y	Y	Y	Y	N	N
Dorgan	Y	Y	Y	Y	N	N
OHIO						
Voinovich	N	N	Y	Y	N	N
Brown	Y	Y	Y	Y	N	N
OKLAHOMA						
Inhofe	N	N	N	N	Y	N
Coburn	N	N	N	N	Y	Y
OREGON						
Wyden	Y	Y	Y	Y	N	N
Merkley	Y	Y	Y	Y	N	N
PENNSYLVANIA						
Specter	Y	Y	Y	Y	N	N
Casey	Y	Y	Y	Y	N	N
RHODE ISLAND						
Reed	Y	Y	Y	Y	N	N
Whitehouse	Y	Y	Y	Y	N	N
SOUTH CAROLINA						
Graham	N	N	N	Y	Y	Y
DeMint	N	N	-	N	Y	Y
SOUTH DAKOTA						
Johnson	Y	Y	Y	Y	N	N
Thune	N	N	N	N	Y	N
TENNESSEE						
Alexander	N	N	N	Y	Y	N
Corker	N	N	N	Y	Y	N
TEXAS						
Hutchison	N	N	N	Y	Y	N
Cornyn	N	N	N	N	Y	N
UTAH						
Hatch	N	N	N	Y	Y	N
Bennett	N	N	N	Y	Y	N
VERMONT						
Leahy	Y	Y	Y	Y	N	N
Sanders	Y	Y	Y	Y	N	N
VIRGINIA						
Webb	Y	Y	Y	Y	N	N
Warner	Y	Y	Y	Y	N	N
WASHINGTON						
Murray	Y	Y	Y	Y	N	N
Cantwell	Y	Y	Y	Y	N	N
WEST VIRGINIA						
Byrd	Y	Y	Y	Y	N	N
Rockefeller	Y	Y	Y	Y	N	N
WISCONSIN						
Kohl	Y	Y	Y	Y	N	N
Feingold	Y	Y	Y	Y	N	N
WYOMING						
Enzi	N	N	N	Y	Y	N
Barrasso	N	N	N	Y	Y	N

KEY   **Republicans**   Democrats   *Independents*

Y Voted for (yea)	X Paired against	C Voted "present" to avoid possible conflict of interest
# Paired for	– Announced against	
+ Announced for	P Voted "present"	? Did not vote or otherwise make a position known
N Voted against (nay)		

IN THE SENATE | By Vote Number

69. **S 160. District of Columbia Voting Rights/Retrocession.** Kyl, R-Ariz., amendment that would cede most land in the District of Columbia to the state of Maryland, except for land including the White House, the Capitol building, the Supreme Court building and federal office buildings, if Maryland enacted legislation to accept it. The District of Columbia would no longer have a delegate in the House. Until the first reapportionment after the bill's enactment, the delegate would serve as a representative from the state of Maryland. This temporary addition of a House member would not change the permanent size of the House. The amendment would repeal the 23rd Amendment to the Constitution, which gives the District of Columbia three electoral votes. Rejected 30-67: R 29-11; D 1-54; I 0-2. Feb. 26, 2009.

70. **S 160. District of Columbia Voting Rights/Fairness Doctrine.** Durbin, D-Ill., amendment that would require the Federal Communications Commission (FCC) to encourage diversity in media ownership and ensure broadcast station licenses are used in the public interest. It would state that the FCC's obligation is not limited by language proposed in the DeMint, R-S.C., amendment, except for provisions prohibiting the FCC from requiring broadcasters to present opposing viewpoints on issues of public interest. The DeMint amendment would bar the FCC from reinstating a rule known as the "fairness doctrine," which required broadcasters to air discussions of controversial issues and present opposing viewpoints. Adopted 57-41: R 0-41; D 55-0; I 2-0. Feb. 26, 2009.

71. **S 160. District of Columbia Voting Rights/Fairness Doctrine.** DeMint, R-S.C., amendment that would bar the Federal Communications Commission from reinstating a rule known as the "fairness doctrine," which required broadcasters to air discussions of controversial issues and present opposing viewpoints. The amendment also would bar requirements for programming quotas or guidelines on issues of public importance. Adopted 87-11: R 41-0; D 45-10; I 1-1. Feb. 26, 2009.

72. **S 160. District of Columbia Voting Rights/District Gun Laws.** Ensign, R-Nev., amendment that would ban the District of Columbia from prohibiting an individual from possessing firearms and repeal District laws barring possession of semiautomatic firearms. It would repeal the District's mandates for firearm registration and the requirement that firearms be disassembled or secured with a trigger lock in the home. District residents would be allowed to purchase firearms in Maryland and Virginia. Adopted 62-36: R 40-1; D 22-33; I 0-2. Feb. 26, 2009.

73. **S 160. District of Columbia Voting Rights/Passage.** Passage of the bill that would add two seats in the House of Representatives, expanding the total to 437 members. It would add a seat for the District of Columbia and provide an extra seat for Utah in the 112th Congress. The District of Columbia's seat would be permanent; beginning with the 113th Congress, the second seat would be apportioned based on 2010 census figures. The bill would increase the size of the Electoral College to accommodate the change. As amended, it also would repeal a number of District of Columbia gun restrictions. Passed 61-37: R 6-35; D 53-2; I 2-0. By unanimous consent, the Senate agreed to raise the majority requirement for passage of the bill to 60 votes. Feb. 26, 2009.

	69	70	71	72	73			69	70	71	72	73
ALABAMA							**MONTANA**					
Shelby	Y	N	Y	Y	N		Baucus	N	Y	Y	Y	N
Sessions	N	N	Y	Y	N		Tester	N	Y	Y	Y	Y
ALASKA							**NEBRASKA**					
Murkowski	N	N	Y	Y	N		Nelson	N	Y	Y	Y	Y
Begich	N	Y	Y	Y	Y		**Johanns**	N	N	Y	Y	N
ARIZONA							**NEVADA**					
McCain	Y	N	Y	Y	N		Reid	N	Y	Y	Y	Y
Kyl	Y	N	Y	Y	N		**Ensign**	N	N	Y	Y	N
ARKANSAS							**NEW HAMPSHIRE**					
Lincoln	N	Y	Y	Y	Y		**Gregg**	N	N	Y	Y	N
Pryor	N	Y	Y	Y	Y		Shaheen	N	Y	Y	N	Y
CALIFORNIA							**NEW JERSEY**					
Feinstein	N	Y	N	N	Y		Lautenberg	N	Y	Y	N	Y
Boxer	N	Y	Y	N	Y		Menendez	N	Y	Y	N	Y
COLORADO							**NEW MEXICO**					
Udall	N	Y	Y	Y	Y		Bingaman	N	Y	N	N	Y
Bennet	N	Y	Y	Y	Y		Udall	N	Y	Y	Y	Y
CONNECTICUT							**NEW YORK**					
Dodd	N	Y	Y	N	Y		Schumer	N	Y	Y	N	Y
Lieberman	N	Y	Y	N	Y		Gillibrand	N	Y	Y	N	Y
DELAWARE							**NORTH CAROLINA**					
Carper	N	Y	Y	N	Y		**Burr**	Y	N	Y	Y	N
Kaufman	N	Y	Y	N	Y		Hagan	N	Y	Y	Y	Y
FLORIDA							**NORTH DAKOTA**					
Nelson	N	Y	Y	N	Y		Conrad	N	Y	Y	Y	Y
Martinez	Y	N	Y	Y	N		Dorgan	N	Y	N	Y	Y
GEORGIA							**OHIO**					
Chambliss	Y	N	Y	Y	N		**Voinovich**	N	N	Y	Y	Y
Isakson	Y	N	Y	Y	N		Brown	N	Y	Y	N	Y
HAWAII							**OKLAHOMA**					
Inouye	N	Y	Y	N	Y		**Inhofe**	Y	N	Y	Y	N
Akaka	N	Y	Y	Y	Y		**Coburn**	Y	N	Y	Y	N
IDAHO							**OREGON**					
Crapo	Y	N	Y	Y	N		Wyden	N	Y	Y	N	Y
Risch	Y	N	Y	Y	N		Merkley	N	Y	Y	N	Y
ILLINOIS							**PENNSYLVANIA**					
Durbin	N	Y	Y	N	Y		Specter	N	N	Y	Y	Y
Burris	N	Y	Y	N	Y		Casey	N	Y	Y	Y	Y
INDIANA							**RHODE ISLAND**					
Lugar	N	N	Y	N	Y		Reed	N	Y	N	N	Y
Bayh	N	Y	Y	Y	Y		Whitehouse	N	Y	N	N	Y
IOWA							**SOUTH CAROLINA**					
Grassley	Y	N	Y	Y	N		**Graham**	Y	N	Y	Y	N
Harkin	N	Y	N	N	Y		**DeMint**	Y	N	Y	Y	N
KANSAS							**SOUTH DAKOTA**					
Brownback	N	N	Y	Y	N		Johnson	Y	Y	N	Y	Y
Roberts	Y	N	Y	Y	N		**Thune**	Y	N	Y	Y	N
KENTUCKY							**TENNESSEE**					
McConnell	Y	N	Y	Y	N		**Alexander**	Y	N	Y	Y	N
Bunning	Y	N	Y	Y	N		**Corker**	+	N	Y	Y	N
LOUISIANA							**TEXAS**					
Landrieu	N	Y	Y	Y	Y		**Hutchison**	Y	N	Y	Y	N
Vitter	Y	N	Y	Y	N		**Cornyn**	Y	N	Y	Y	N
MAINE							**UTAH**					
Snowe	N	N	Y	Y	Y		**Hatch**	Y	N	Y	Y	Y
Collins	N	N	Y	Y	Y		**Bennett**	Y	N	Y	Y	N
MARYLAND							**VERMONT**					
Mikulski	N	Y	Y	N	Y		Leahy	N	Y	Y	N	Y
Cardin	N	Y	Y	N	Y		*Sanders*	N	Y	N	N	Y
MASSACHUSETTS							**VIRGINIA**					
Kennedy	?	?	?	?	?		Webb	N	Y	Y	Y	Y
Kerry	N	Y	N	N	Y		Warner	N	Y	Y	Y	Y
MICHIGAN							**WASHINGTON**					
Levin	N	Y	Y	N	Y		Murray	N	Y	Y	N	Y
Stabenow	N	Y	Y	N	Y		Cantwell	N	Y	Y	N	Y
MINNESOTA							**WEST VIRGINIA**					
Klobuchar	N	Y	Y	N	Y		Byrd	N	Y	Y	Y	N
Vacant							Rockefeller	N	Y	N	N	Y
MISSISSIPPI							**WISCONSIN**					
Cochran	Y	N	Y	Y	N		Kohl	N	Y	Y	N	Y
Wicker	Y	N	Y	Y	N		Feingold	N	Y	Y	Y	Y
MISSOURI							**WYOMING**					
Bond	Y	N	Y	Y	N		**Enzi**	Y	N	Y	Y	N
McCaskill	N	Y	Y	Y	Y		**Barrasso**	Y	N	Y	Y	N

KEY	**Republicans**	Democrats	*Independents*		
Y	Voted for (yea)	X	Paired against	C	Voted "present" to avoid possible conflict of interest
#	Paired for	–	Announced against		
+	Announced for	P	Voted "present"	?	Did not vote or otherwise make a position known
N	Voted against (nay)				

IN THE SENATE | By Vote Number

74. HR 1105. Fiscal 2009 Omnibus Appropriations/Substitute.
McCain, R-Ariz., substitute amendment that would strike the text of the bill and insert provisions that would continue funding for most domestic agencies and programs at fiscal 2008 levels through Sept. 30, 2009. Rejected 32-63: R 30-9; D 2-52; I 0-2. March 3, 2009.

75. HR 1105. Fiscal 2009 Omnibus Appropriations/Commit.
Ensign, R-Nev., motion to commit the bill to the Appropriations Committee with instructions that it be reported back with discretionary funding levels reduced by $19 billion for fiscal 2009 and $3.2 billion for fiscal 2010. Motion rejected 33-61: R 33-6; D 0-53; I 0-2. March 3, 2009.

76. HR 1105. Fiscal 2009 Omnibus Appropriations/Commit.
Hutchison, R-Texas, motion to commit the bill to the Appropriations Committee with instructions that it be reported back with cuts that would bring total non-security funding to the fiscal 2008 funding level, adjusted for inflation. The reduction would come from cuts to items that are non-essential or are duplicative of funding in the 2009 economic stimulus law. Motion rejected 40-55: R 35-4; D 5-49; I 0-2. March 3, 2009.

77. HR 1105 Fiscal 2009 Omnibus Appropriations/Competitive Procedures. Coburn, R-Okla., amendment that would require the use of competitive procedures in awarding grants, contracts and cooperative agreements funded in the bill. Rejected 38-57: R 31-8; D 7-47; I 0-2. March 4, 2009.

78. HR 1105. Fiscal 2009 Omnibus Appropriations/Civil Rights Crimes. Coburn, R-Okla., amendment that would shift $10 million appropriated in the bill for grants to state or local law enforcement for expenses related to prosecuting unsolved civil rights crimes. The amendment would shift the funding from a Justice Department program that coordinates existing anti-crime and human services programs in high-crime neighborhoods. Rejected 37-58: R 36-3; D 1-53; I 0-2. March 4, 2009.

79. HR 1105. Fiscal 2009 Omnibus Appropriations/Individual Member Projects. Coburn, R-Okla., amendment that would bar the use of funds in the bill for 11 specific member projects, including spending on the Old Tiger Stadium Conservancy in Michigan, the Polynesian Voyaging Society in Hawaii, odor and manure management research in Iowa, and the California National Historic Trail Interpretive Center in Nevada. Rejected 34-61: R 29-10; D 5-49; I 0-2. March 4, 2009.

80. HR 1105. Fiscal 2009 Omnibus Appropriations/Individual Member Projects. Coburn, R-Okla., amendment that would bar the use of funds in the bill for 13 specific member projects, including spending for an anti-idling lithium ion battery program in California, an adaptive liquid crystal windows project in Ohio, and renovation and equipment at Carnegie Mellon University in Pittsburgh and Nazareth Hospital in Philadelphia. Rejected 43-52: R 37-2; D 6-48; I 0-2. March 4, 2009.

	74	75	76	77	78	79	80			74	75	76	77	78	79	80
ALABAMA									**MONTANA**							
Shelby	N	N	N	Y	Y	N	Y		Baucus	N	N	N	N	N	N	N
Sessions	+	?	?	?	?	?	?		Tester	N	N	N	N	N	N	N
ALASKA									**NEBRASKA**							
Murkowski	N	Y	Y	N	N	N	Y		Nelson	N	N	Y	N	N	N	N
Begich	N	N	N	N	N	N	N		**Johanns**	?	?	?	?	?	?	?
ARIZONA									**NEVADA**							
McCain	Y	Y	Y	Y	Y	Y	Y		Reid	N	N	N	N	N	N	N
Kyl	Y	Y	Y	Y	Y	Y	Y		**Ensign**	Y	Y	Y	Y	Y	Y	Y
ARKANSAS									**NEW HAMPSHIRE**							
Lincoln	N	N	N	N	N	N	Y		**Gregg**	Y	Y	Y	Y	N	Y	Y
Pryor	N	N	N	N	N	N	N		Shaheen	N	N	N	N	N	N	N
CALIFORNIA									**NEW JERSEY**							
Feinstein	N	N	N	N	N	N	N		Lautenberg	N	N	N	N	N	N	N
Boxer	N	N	N	N	N	N	N		Menendez	N	N	N	N	N	N	N
COLORADO									**NEW MEXICO**							
Udall	N	N	N	N	N	Y	N		Bingaman	N	N	N	N	N	N	N
Bennet	N	N	N	N	N	Y	N		Udall	N	N	N	N	N	N	N
CONNECTICUT									**NEW YORK**							
Dodd	N	N	N	N	N	N	N		Schumer	N	N	N	N	N	N	N
Lieberman	N	N	N	N	N	N	N		Gillibrand	N	N	N	N	N	N	N
DELAWARE									**NORTH CAROLINA**							
Carper	N	N	N	N	N	N	N		**Burr**	Y	Y	Y	Y	Y	Y	Y
Kaufman	N	N	N	N	N	N	N		Hagan	N	N	N	Y	N	N	N
FLORIDA									**NORTH DAKOTA**							
Nelson	N	N	N	N	N	Y	Y		Conrad	?	?	?	?	?	?	?
Martinez	Y	Y	Y	Y	Y	Y	Y		Dorgan	N	N	N	N	N	N	N
GEORGIA									**OHIO**							
Chambliss	Y	Y	Y	Y	Y	Y	Y		**Voinovich**	Y	Y	Y	Y	Y	N	N
Isakson	Y	Y	Y	Y	Y	Y	Y		Brown	N	N	N	N	N	N	N
HAWAII									**OKLAHOMA**							
Inouye	N	N	N	N	N	N	N		**Inhofe**	Y	Y	Y	Y	Y	Y	Y
Akaka	N	N	N	N	N	N	N		**Coburn**	Y	Y	Y	Y	Y	Y	Y
IDAHO									**OREGON**							
Crapo	Y	Y	Y	Y	Y	Y	Y		Wyden	N	N	N	N	N	N	N
Risch	Y	Y	Y	Y	Y	Y	Y		Merkley	N	N	N	N	N	N	N
ILLINOIS									**PENNSYLVANIA**							
Durbin	N	N	N	N	N	N	N		**Specter**	N	N	N	N	N	N	N
Burris	N	N	N	N	N	N	N		Casey	N	N	N	N	N	N	N
INDIANA									**RHODE ISLAND**							
Lugar	Y	Y	Y	N	Y	Y	Y		Reed	N	N	N	N	N	N	N
Bayh	Y	?	Y	N	Y	Y	Y		Whitehouse	N	N	N	N	N	N	N
IOWA									**SOUTH CAROLINA**							
Grassley	Y	Y	Y	Y	Y	Y	Y		**Graham**	Y	Y	Y	Y	Y	Y	Y
Harkin	N	N	N	N	N	N	N		**DeMint**	Y	Y	Y	Y	Y	Y	Y
KANSAS									**SOUTH DAKOTA**							
Brownback	Y	Y	Y	Y	Y	Y	Y		Johnson	N	N	N	N	N	N	N
Roberts	Y	Y	Y	Y	Y	Y	Y		**Thune**	Y	Y	Y	Y	Y	Y	Y
KENTUCKY									**TENNESSEE**							
McConnell	Y	Y	Y	Y	Y	Y	Y		**Alexander**	N	Y	Y	Y	Y	N	Y
Bunning	Y	Y	Y	Y	Y	Y	Y		**Corker**	Y	Y	Y	Y	Y	Y	Y
LOUISIANA									**TEXAS**							
Landrieu	N	N	N	N	N	N	N		**Hutchison**	Y	Y	Y	N	Y	Y	Y
Vitter	Y	Y	Y	Y	Y	Y	Y		**Cornyn**	Y	Y	Y	Y	Y	Y	Y
MAINE									**UTAH**							
Snowe	N	N	N	N	N	N	N		**Hatch**	Y	Y	Y	Y	Y	Y	Y
Collins	N	N	Y	N	Y	N	Y		**Bennett**	N	Y	Y	Y	Y	N	Y
MARYLAND									**VERMONT**							
Mikulski	N	N	N	N	N	N	N		Leahy	N	N	N	N	N	N	N
Cardin	N	N	N	N	N	N	N		*Sanders*	N	N	N	N	N	N	N
MASSACHUSETTS									**VIRGINIA**							
Kennedy	?	?	?	?	?	?	?		Webb	N	N	N	Y	N	N	N
Kerry	N	N	N	N	N	N	N		Warner	N	N	N	Y	N	N	N
MICHIGAN									**WASHINGTON**							
Levin	N	N	N	N	N	N	N		Murray	N	N	N	N	N	N	N
Stabenow	N	N	N	N	N	N	N		Cantwell	N	N	N	N	N	N	N
MINNESOTA									**WEST VIRGINIA**							
Klobuchar	N	N	Y	Y	N	N	Y		Byrd	N	N	N	N	N	N	N
Vacant									Rockefeller	N	N	N	N	N	N	N
MISSISSIPPI									**WISCONSIN**							
Cochran	N	N	Y	N	Y	N	Y		Kohl	N	N	N	N	N	N	N
Wicker	Y	Y	Y	N	Y	Y	Y		Feingold	N	N	N	Y	N	Y	Y
MISSOURI									**WYOMING**							
Bond	N	N	N	N	N	N	Y		**Enzi**	Y	Y	Y	Y	Y	Y	Y
McCaskill	Y	N	Y	Y	N	N	N		**Barrasso**	Y	Y	Y	Y	Y	Y	Y

KEY	**Republicans**	Democrats	*Independents*		
Y	Voted for (yea)	X	Paired against	C	Voted "present" to avoid possible conflict of interest
#	Paired for	–	Announced against		
+	Announced for	P	Voted "present"	?	Did not vote or otherwise make a position known
N	Voted against (nay)				

IN THE SENATE | By Vote Number

81. **HR 1105. Fiscal 2009 Omnibus Appropriations/Abortion and Sterilization.** Wicker, R-Miss., amendment that would eliminate language in the bill that would allow the U.N. Population Fund to use funds from the bill for specific purposes, including providing contraceptives and reducing child marriage, even if those funds would otherwise be withheld from UNFPA under U.S. laws barring funds for groups that support or participate in coercive abortion programs. Rejected 39-55: R 36-3; D 3-50; I 0-2. March 5, 2009.

82. **HR 1105. Fiscal 2009 Omnibus Appropriations/Polar Bear Regulations.** Murkowski, R-Alaska, amendment that would preserve a public comment period for proposed changes to regulations under the Endangered Species Act, specifically sections on protecting polar bears and on regulating carbon dioxide. The amendment would also preserve judicial review of new regulations for those sections. Rejected 42-52: R 39-0; D 3-50; I 0-2. March 5, 2009.

83. **HR 1105. Fiscal 2009 Omnibus Appropriations/U.N. Payment.** Inhofe, R-Okla., amendment that would bar the use of funds in the bill for any U.S. dues contribution or voluntary payment to the United Nations if the organization implements or imposes any tax on U.S. persons. Rejected 43-51: R 39-0; D 4-49; I 0-2. March 5, 2009.

84. **HR 1105. Fiscal 2009 Omnibus Appropriations/American Indian Health Fund.** Thune, R-S.D., motion to waive the Budget Act with respect to the Feinstein, D-Calif., point of order against the Thune amendment that would shift $400 million appropriated in the bill to an emergency fund to promote health and safety among American Indians. The funds would be provided through a 0.1 percent decrease in spending for other programs in the bill. Motion rejected 26-68: R 25-14; D 1-52; I 0-2. A three-fifths majority vote (60) of the total Senate is required to waive the Budget Act. (Subsequently, the chair upheld the point of order, and the amendment fell.) March 5, 2009.

85. **HR 1105. Fiscal 2009 Omnibus Appropriations/Iran Business.** Kyl, R-Ariz., amendment that would bar the use of funds in the bill for a federal contract with any company that does business in Iran's energy sector. The president could waive the ban if he determined it to be necessary for the national security interests of the United States and submitted a report to Congress. Rejected 41-53: R 36-3; D 4-49; I 1-1. March 5, 2009.

	81	82	83	84	85
ALABAMA					
Shelby	Y	Y	Y	Y	Y
Sessions	?	?	?	?	?
ALASKA					
Murkowski	Y	Y	Y	Y	N
Begich	N	Y	N	N	N
ARIZONA					
McCain	Y	Y	Y	Y	Y
Kyl	Y	Y	Y	Y	Y
ARKANSAS					
Lincoln	N	Y	N	N	N
Pryor	N	N	N	N	N
CALIFORNIA					
Feinstein	N	N	N	N	N
Boxer	N	N	N	N	N
COLORADO					
Udall	N	N	N	N	N
Bennet	N	N	N	N	N
CONNECTICUT					
Dodd	N	N	N	N	N
Lieberman	N	N	N	N	Y
DELAWARE					
Carper	N	N	N	N	N
Kaufman	N	N	N	N	N
FLORIDA					
Nelson	N	N	N	N	Y
Martinez	Y	Y	Y	N	Y
GEORGIA					
Chambliss	Y	Y	Y	Y	Y
Isakson	Y	Y	Y	Y	Y
HAWAII					
Inouye	N	N	N	N	N
Akaka	N	N	N	N	N
IDAHO					
Crapo	Y	Y	Y	Y	Y
Risch	Y	Y	Y	Y	Y
ILLINOIS					
Durbin	N	N	N	N	N
Burris	N	N	N	N	N
INDIANA					
Lugar	Y	Y	Y	N	N
Bayh	Y	N	Y	N	Y
IOWA					
Grassley	Y	Y	Y	Y	Y
Harkin	N	N	N	N	N
KANSAS					
Brownback	Y	Y	Y	Y	Y
Roberts	Y	Y	Y	Y	Y
KENTUCKY					
McConnell	Y	Y	Y	Y	Y
Bunning	Y	Y	Y	N	Y
LOUISIANA					
Landrieu	?	?	?	?	?
Vitter	Y	Y	Y	N	Y
MAINE					
Snowe	N	Y	Y	N	Y
Collins	N	Y	Y	N	Y
MARYLAND					
Mikulski	N	N	N	N	N
Cardin	N	N	N	N	N
MASSACHUSETTS					
Kennedy	?	?	?	?	?
Kerry	N	N	N	N	N
MICHIGAN					
Levin	N	N	N	N	N
Stabenow	N	N	N	N	N
MINNESOTA					
Klobuchar	N	N	N	N	N
Vacant					
MISSISSIPPI					
Cochran	Y	Y	Y	N	Y
Wicker	Y	Y	Y	Y	Y
MISSOURI					
Bond	Y	Y	Y	Y	Y
McCaskill	N	N	N	N	N
MONTANA					
Baucus	N	N	N	N	N
Tester	N	N	N	N	N
NEBRASKA					
Nelson	Y	Y	Y	N	Y
Johanns	?	?	?	?	?
NEVADA					
Reid	N	N	N	N	N
Ensign	Y	Y	Y	Y	Y
NEW HAMPSHIRE					
Gregg	Y	Y	Y	N	Y
Shaheen	N	N	N	N	N
NEW JERSEY					
Lautenberg	N	N	N	N	N
Menendez	N	N	N	N	N
NEW MEXICO					
Bingaman	N	N	N	N	N
Udall	N	N	N	N	N
NEW YORK					
Schumer	N	N	N	N	N
Gillibrand	N	N	N	N	N
NORTH CAROLINA					
Burr	Y	Y	Y	Y	Y
Hagan	N	N	N	N	N
NORTH DAKOTA					
Conrad	?	?	?	?	?
Dorgan	N	N	Y	N	N
OHIO					
Voinovich	Y	Y	Y	N	Y
Brown	N	N	N	N	N
OKLAHOMA					
Inhofe	Y	Y	Y	Y	Y
Coburn	Y	Y	Y	Y	Y
OREGON					
Wyden	N	N	N	N	N
Merkley	N	N	N	N	N
PENNSYLVANIA					
Specter	N	Y	Y	N	Y
Casey	Y	N	N	N	N
RHODE ISLAND					
Reed	N	N	N	N	N
Whitehouse	N	N	N	N	N
SOUTH CAROLINA					
Graham	Y	Y	Y	Y	Y
DeMint	Y	Y	Y	N	Y
SOUTH DAKOTA					
Johnson	N	N	N	N	N
Thune	Y	Y	Y	Y	Y
TENNESSEE					
Alexander	Y	Y	Y	N	Y
Corker	Y	Y	Y	N	N
TEXAS					
Hutchison	Y	Y	Y	N	Y
Cornyn	Y	Y	Y	Y	Y
UTAH					
Hatch	Y	Y	Y	Y	Y
Bennett	Y	Y	Y	Y	Y
VERMONT					
Leahy	N	N	N	N	N
Sanders	N	N	N	N	N
VIRGINIA					
Webb	N	N	N	N	N
Warner	N	N	N	N	N
WASHINGTON					
Murray	N	N	N	N	N
Cantwell	N	N	N	N	N
WEST VIRGINIA					
Byrd	N	N	N	N	N
Rockefeller	N	N	N	N	N
WISCONSIN					
Kohl	N	N	N	N	N
Feingold	N	N	Y	N	Y
WYOMING					
Enzi	Y	Y	Y	Y	Y
Barrasso	Y	Y	Y	Y	Y

KEY	Republicans	Democrats	*Independents*	
Y	Voted for (yea)	X	Paired against	C Voted "present" to avoid possible conflict of interest
#	Paired for	–	Announced against	
+	Announced for	P	Voted "present"	? Did not vote or otherwise make a position known
N	Voted against (nay)			

IN THE SENATE | By Vote Number

86. HR 1105. Fiscal 2009 Omnibus Appropriations/Individual **Member Projects.** McCain, R-Ariz., amendment that would bar the use of funds in the bill for any project not listed in the bill text, even if it is in the accompanying managers' statement. Rejected 32-63: R 28-10; D 4-51; I 0-2. March 9, 2009.

87. HR 1105. Fiscal 2009 Omnibus Appropriations/Gaza **Countersmuggling Efforts.** Kyl, R-Ariz., amendment that would require the secretary of State to issue a report on whether additional funds provided to the government of Egypt could be used to expand countersmuggling efforts in Gaza. Rejected 34-61: R 31-7; D 3-52; I 0-2. March 9, 2009.

88. HR 1105. Fiscal 2009 Omnibus Appropriations/Gaza **Reconstruction Efforts.** Kyl, R-Ariz., amendment that would require the secretary of State to certify, before funds are made available for reconstruction efforts in Gaza, that those funds would not be diverted to Hamas or entities controlled by Hamas. Rejected 39-56: R 33-5; D 5-50; I 1-1. March 9, 2009.

89. HR 1105. Fiscal 2009 Omnibus Appropriations/HIV/AIDS **Funding.** Enzi, R-Wyo., amendment that would bar the use of funds in the bill to change the formula for how HIV/AIDS funding would be distributed. Rejected 42-53: R 38-0; D 4-51; I 0-2. March 9, 2009.

90. HR 1105. Fiscal 2009 Omnibus Appropriations/State **Attorneys General.** Cornyn, R-Texas, amendment that would prohibit state attorneys general who hire outside legal experts and witnesses in civil actions from paying them through a contingency fee agreement in which they would receive a share of any award or settlement. Rejected 32-64: R 32-8; D 0-54; I 0-2. March 10, 2009.

91. HR 1105. Fiscal 2009 Omnibus Appropriations/Federal **Contractor Obligations.** Cornyn, R-Texas, amendment that would bar the use of funds in the bill to implement a January 2009 executive order in a manner that conflicts with a February 2001 executive order. The 2009 executive order allows the secretary of Labor to prescribe the content of notices required to be posted by federal contractors. The 2001 order prescribed the exact language, explaining workers' rights to decide not to join unions or pay union dues. Rejected 38-59: R 38-2; D 0-55; I 0-2. March 10, 2009.

92. HR 1105. Fiscal 2009 Omnibus Appropriations/Fairness **Doctrine.** Thune, R-S.D., amendment that would bar the use of funds in the bill for the Federal Communications Commission to reinstate a rule known as the "fairness doctrine," which required broadcasters to air discussions of controversial views and present opposing viewpoints. Rejected 47-50: R 40-0; D 7-48; I 0-2. March 10, 2009.

	86	87	88	89	90	91	92
ALABAMA							
Shelby	N	Y	Y	Y	N	Y	Y
Sessions	Y	Y	Y	Y	Y	Y	Y
ALASKA							
Murkowski	N	Y	Y	Y	Y	Y	Y
Begich	N	N	N	N	N	N	Y
ARIZONA							
McCain	Y	Y	Y	Y	Y	Y	Y
Kyl	Y	Y	Y	Y	Y	Y	Y
ARKANSAS							
Lincoln	N	N	N	N	N	N	N
Pryor	N	N	N	N	N	N	N
CALIFORNIA							
Feinstein	N	N	N	N	N	N	N
Boxer	N	N	N	N	N	N	N
COLORADO							
Udall	N	N	N	N	N	N	Y
Bennet	N	N	N	N	N	N	N
CONNECTICUT							
Dodd	N	N	N	N	N	N	N
Lieberman	N	N	Y	N	N	N	N
DELAWARE							
Carper	N	N	N	Y	N	N	N
Kaufman	N	N	N	N	N	N	N
FLORIDA							
Nelson	N	N	Y	Y	N	N	N
Martinez	Y	Y	Y	Y	N	Y	Y
GEORGIA							
Chambliss	Y	Y	Y	Y	Y	Y	Y
Isakson	Y	Y	Y	Y	Y	Y	Y
HAWAII							
Inouye	N	N	N	N	N	N	N
Akaka	N	N	N	N	N	N	N
IDAHO							
Crapo	Y	Y	Y	Y	N	Y	Y
Risch	Y	Y	Y	Y	N	Y	Y
ILLINOIS							
Durbin	N	N	N	N	N	N	N
Burris	N	N	N	N	N	N	N
INDIANA							
Lugar	Y	N	N	Y	Y	Y	Y
Bayh	Y	Y	N	N	N	Y	Y
IOWA							
Grassley	Y	Y	Y	Y	Y	Y	Y
Harkin	N	N	N	N	N	N	N
KANSAS							
Brownback	Y	Y	Y	Y	Y	Y	Y
Roberts	N	Y	Y	Y	Y	Y	Y
KENTUCKY							
McConnell	Y	Y	Y	Y	Y	Y	Y
Bunning	Y	Y	Y	Y	Y	Y	Y
LOUISIANA							
Landrieu	N	N	N	N	N	N	N
Vitter	Y	Y	Y	Y	Y	Y	Y
MAINE							
Snowe	N	Y	Y	Y	Y	Y	Y
Collins	N	Y	Y	Y	Y	Y	Y
MARYLAND							
Mikulski	N	N	N	N	N	N	N
Cardin	N	N	N	N	N	N	N
MASSACHUSETTS							
Kennedy	?	?	?	?	?	?	?
Kerry	N	N	N	N	N	N	N
MICHIGAN							
Levin	N	N	N	N	N	N	N
Stabenow	N	N	N	N	N	N	N
MINNESOTA							
Klobuchar	N	N	Y	N	N	N	Y
Vacant							
MISSISSIPPI							
Cochran	N	N	N	Y	Y	Y	Y
Wicker	N	N	Y	Y	Y	Y	Y
MISSOURI							
Bond	N	N	Y	Y	Y	Y	Y
McCaskill	Y	N	N	Y	N	N	N
MONTANA							
Baucus	N	N	N	N	N	N	N
Tester	N	N	N	N	N	N	N
NEBRASKA							
Nelson	N	Y	Y	Y	N	N	Y
Johanns	?	?	?	?	?	?	?
NEVADA							
Reid	N	N	N	N	N	N	N
Ensign	Y	Y	Y	Y	Y	Y	Y
NEW HAMPSHIRE							
Gregg	Y	N	N	Y	Y	Y	Y
Shaheen	N	N	N	N	N	N	N
NEW JERSEY							
Lautenberg	N	N	N	N	N	N	N
Menendez	N	N	N	N	N	N	N
NEW MEXICO							
Bingaman	N	N	N	N	N	N	N
Udall	N	N	N	N	N	N	N
NEW YORK							
Schumer	N	N	N	N	N	N	N
Gillibrand	N	N	N	?	N	N	N
NORTH CAROLINA							
Burr	Y	Y	Y	Y	Y	Y	Y
Hagan	N	N	N	N	N	N	N
NORTH DAKOTA							
Conrad	N	N	N	N	N	N	N
Dorgan	N	N	N	N	N	N	N
OHIO							
Voinovich	Y	N	N	Y	Y	N	Y
Brown	N	N	N	N	N	N	N
OKLAHOMA							
Inhofe	Y	Y	Y	Y	Y	Y	Y
Coburn	Y	Y	Y	Y	Y	Y	Y
OREGON							
Wyden	N	N	N	N	N	N	N
Merkley	N	N	N	N	N	N	N
PENNSYLVANIA							
Specter	N	Y	Y	Y	N	N	Y
Casey	N	N	Y	N	N	N	N
RHODE ISLAND							
Reed	N	N	N	N	N	N	N
Whitehouse	N	N	N	N	N	N	N
SOUTH CAROLINA							
Graham	Y	Y	Y	Y	N	Y	Y
DeMint	Y	Y	Y	Y	Y	Y	Y
SOUTH DAKOTA							
Johnson	N	N	N	N	N	N	N
Thune	Y	Y	Y	Y	Y	Y	Y
TENNESSEE							
Alexander	N	Y	Y	Y	Y	Y	Y
Corker	Y	N	N	Y	Y	Y	Y
TEXAS							
Hutchison	?	?	?	?	Y	Y	Y
Cornyn	Y	Y	Y	Y	Y	Y	Y
UTAH							
Hatch	Y	Y	Y	Y	N	Y	Y
Bennett	?	?	?	?	N	Y	Y
VERMONT							
Leahy	N	N	N	N	N	N	N
Sanders	N	N	N	N	N	N	N
VIRGINIA							
Webb	N	N	N	N	N	Y	Y
Warner	N	N	N	N	N	N	N
WASHINGTON							
Murray	N	N	N	N	N	N	N
Cantwell	Y	N	N	N	N	N	N
WEST VIRGINIA							
Byrd	N	N	N	N	N	N	N
Rockefeller	N	N	N	N	N	N	N
WISCONSIN							
Kohl	N	N	N	N	N	N	N
Feingold	Y	Y	Y	N	N	N	N
WYOMING							
Enzi	Y	Y	Y	Y	Y	Y	Y
Barrasso	Y	Y	Y	Y	Y	Y	Y

KEY   **Republicans**   Democrats   *Independents*

Y Voted for (yea)	X Paired against	C Voted "present" to avoid possible conflict of interest
# Paired for	– Announced against	
+ Announced for	P Voted "present"	? Did not vote or otherwise make a position known
N Voted against (nay)		

IN THE SENATE | By Vote Number

93. **HR 1105. Fiscal 2009 Omnibus Appropriations/E-Verify.** Leahy, D-Vt., motion to table (kill) the Sessions, R-Ala., amendment that would extend through 2014 a voluntary, Internet-based program known as E-Verify to determine if employees are legally entitled to work in the United States. Motion agreed to 50-47: R 0-40; D 48-7; I 2-0. March 10, 2009.

94. **HR 1105. Fiscal 2009 Omnibus Appropriations/D.C. School Voucher Program.** Ensign, R-Nev., amendment that would strike a provision to eliminate funds for the District of Columbia school voucher program after the 2009-10 school year, unless the program is reauthorized by Congress and approved by the District government. Rejected 39-58: R 36-4; D 2-53; I 1-1. March 10, 2009.

95. **HR 1105. Fiscal 2009 Omnibus Appropriations/Automatic COLA.** Reid, D-Nev., motion to table (kill) the Vitter, R-La., amendment that would repeal the provision of current law that provides for automatic cost-of-living adjustments for members of Congress. Motion agreed to 52-45: R 5-35; D 45-10; I 2-0. March 10, 2009.

96. **HR 1105. Fiscal 2009 Omnibus Appropriations/Cloture.** Motion to invoke cloture (thus limiting debate) on the bill that would provide $410 billion in discretionary spending in fiscal 2009 for federal departments and agencies covered by nine unfinished fiscal 2009 spending bills. Those bills are: Agriculture, Commerce-Justice-Science, Energy-Water, Financial Services, Interior-Environment, Labor-HHS-Education, Legislative Branch, State-Foreign Operations and Transportation-HUD. It would also provide $100 million for the U.S. Secret Service and block the automatic cost-of-living adjustment for members of Congress in 2010. Motion agreed to 62-35: R 8-32; D 52-3; I 2-0. Three-fifths of the total Senate (60) is required to invoke cloture. (Subsequently, the Senate passed the bill by voice vote, thus clearing the measure for the president.) March 10, 2009.

97. **Ogden Nomination/Confirmation.** Confirmation of President Obama's nomination of David W. Ogden of Virginia to be deputy attorney general. Confirmed 65-28: R 11-27; D 52-1; I 2-0. A "yea" was a vote in support of the president's position. March 12, 2009.

98. **Perrelli Nomination/Confirmation.** Confirmation of President Obama's nomination of Thomas J. Perrelli of Virginia to be associate attorney general. Confirmed 72-20: R 17-20; D 53-0; I 2-0. A "yea" was a vote in support of the president's position. March 12, 2009.

	93	94	95	96	97	98			93	94	95	96	97	98
ALABAMA								**MONTANA**						
Shelby	N	Y	N	Y	N	N		Baucus	N	N	Y	Y	Y	Y
Sessions	N	Y	N	N	N	Y		Tester	N	N	N	Y	Y	Y
ALASKA								**NEBRASKA**						
Murkowski	N	N	N	Y	N	Y		Nelson	N	N	N	Y	Y	Y
Begich	Y	N	Y	Y	Y	Y		**Johanns**	?	?	?	?	?	?
ARIZONA								**NEVADA**						
McCain	N	Y	N	N	Y	Y		Reid	Y	N	Y	Y	Y	Y
Kyl	N	Y	N	N	Y	Y		**Ensign**	N	Y	N	N	N	N
ARKANSAS								**NEW HAMPSHIRE**						
Lincoln	Y	N	N	Y	Y	Y		**Gregg**	N	Y	Y	N	Y	Y
Pryor	Y	N	Y	Y	Y	Y		Shaheen	Y	N	Y	Y	Y	Y
CALIFORNIA								**NEW JERSEY**						
Feinstein	Y	N	Y	Y	Y	Y		Lautenberg	Y	N	Y	Y	Y	Y
Boxer	Y	N	Y	Y	Y	Y		Menendez	Y	N	Y	Y	Y	Y
COLORADO								**NEW MEXICO**						
Udall	Y	N	Y	Y	Y	Y		Bingaman	Y	N	Y	Y	Y	Y
Bennet	Y	N	Y	Y	Y	Y		Udall	Y	N	Y	Y	Y	Y
CONNECTICUT								**NEW YORK**						
Dodd	Y	N	N	Y	Y	Y		Schumer	Y	N	Y	Y	Y	Y
Lieberman	Y	Y	Y	Y	Y	Y		Gillibrand	Y	N	Y	Y	Y	Y
DELAWARE								**NORTH CAROLINA**						
Carper	Y	N	Y	Y	Y	Y		**Burr**	N	Y	N	N	N	N
Kaufman	Y	N	Y	Y	Y	Y		Hagan	Y	N	Y	Y	?	?
FLORIDA								**NORTH DAKOTA**						
Nelson	Y	N	Y	Y	Y	Y		Conrad	Y	N	Y	Y	Y	Y
Martinez	N	Y	Y	N	N	?		Dorgan	Y	N	Y	Y	Y	Y
GEORGIA								**OHIO**						
Chambliss	N	Y	N	N	N	N		**Voinovich**	N	Y	N	Y	Y	Y
Isakson	N	Y	N	N	?	?		Brown	Y	N	Y	Y	Y	Y
HAWAII								**OKLAHOMA**						
Inouye	Y	N	Y	Y	Y	Y		**Inhofe**	N	Y	N	N	N	N
Akaka	Y	N	Y	Y	Y	Y		**Coburn**	N	Y	N	N	N	N
IDAHO								**OREGON**						
Crapo	N	N	N	N	N	N		Wyden	Y	N	N	Y	Y	Y
Risch	N	Y	N	N	N	N		Merkley	Y	N	Y	Y	Y	Y
ILLINOIS								**PENNSYLVANIA**						
Durbin	Y	N	Y	Y	Y	Y		**Specter**	N	N	N	Y	Y	Y
Burris	Y	N	Y	Y	Y	Y		Casey	Y	N	Y	Y	N	Y
INDIANA								**RHODE ISLAND**						
Lugar	N	Y	Y	N	Y	Y		Reed	Y	N	Y	Y	Y	Y
Bayh	N	N	N	N	Y	Y		Whitehouse	Y	N	Y	Y	Y	Y
IOWA								**SOUTH CAROLINA**						
Grassley	N	Y	N	N	N	N		**Graham**	N	Y	N	N	Y	Y
Harkin	Y	N	Y	Y	Y	Y		**DeMint**	N	Y	N	N	N	N
KANSAS								**SOUTH DAKOTA**						
Brownback	N	Y	N	N	N	N		Johnson	Y	N	Y	Y	Y	Y
Roberts	N	Y	N	N	N	N		**Thune**	N	Y	N	N	N	N
KENTUCKY								**TENNESSEE**						
McConnell	N	Y	N	N	N	Y		**Alexander**	N	Y	N	Y	Y	Y
Bunning	N	Y	N	N	N	N		**Corker**	N	Y	N	N	N	Y
LOUISIANA								**TEXAS**						
Landrieu	Y	N	Y	Y	Y	Y		**Hutchison**	N	Y	N	N	N	N
Vitter	N	Y	N	N	N	N		**Cornyn**	N	Y	N	N	-	+
MAINE								**UTAH**						
Snowe	N	N	N	Y	Y	Y		**Hatch**	N	Y	N	N	N	Y
Collins	N	Y	N	N	Y	Y		**Bennett**	N	Y	N	N	N	Y
MARYLAND								**VERMONT**						
Mikulski	Y	N	Y	Y	Y	Y		Leahy	Y	N	Y	Y	Y	Y
Cardin	Y	N	Y	Y	Y	Y		*Sanders*	Y	N	Y	Y	Y	Y
MASSACHUSETTS								**VIRGINIA**						
Kennedy	?	?	?	?	?	?		Webb	N	N	N	Y	Y	Y
Kerry	Y	N	Y	Y	Y	Y		Warner	Y	Y	Y	Y	Y	Y
MICHIGAN								**WASHINGTON**						
Levin	Y	N	Y	Y	Y	Y		Murray	Y	N	Y	Y	Y	Y
Stabenow	Y	N	Y	Y	Y	Y		Cantwell	Y	N	Y	Y	Y	Y
MINNESOTA								**WEST VIRGINIA**						
Klobuchar	N	N	N	Y	Y	Y		Byrd	Y	Y	Y	Y	?	?
Vacant								Rockefeller	Y	N	Y	Y	Y	Y
MISSISSIPPI								**WISCONSIN**						
Cochran	N	Y	Y	Y	N	N		Kohl	Y	N	Y	Y	Y	Y
Wicker	N	Y	Y	Y	N	N		Feingold	Y	N	N	N	Y	Y
MISSOURI								**WYOMING**						
Bond	N	Y	N	Y	Y	Y		**Enzi**	N	Y	N	N	N	N
McCaskill	N	N	N	N	Y	Y		**Barrasso**	N	Y	N	N	N	N

KEY	**Republicans**	Democrats	*Independents*		
Y	Voted for (yea)	X	Paired against	C	Voted "present" to avoid possible conflict of interest
#	Paired for	-	Announced against		
+	Announced for	P	Voted "present"	?	Did not vote or otherwise make a position known
N	Voted against (nay)				

IN THE SENATE | By Vote Number

99. **HR 146. Public Lands Bill/Cloture.** Motion to invoke cloture (thus limiting debate) on the motion to proceed to the bill that would authorize $10 million annually from fiscal 2010 to 2014 for matching grants to states and localities to acquire and protect significant battlefields and sites related to the Revolutionary War and the War of 1812. The bill was intended as a vehicle for an omnibus lands bill. Motion agreed to 73-21: R 16-21; D 55-0; I 2-0. Three-fifths of the total Senate (60) is required to invoke cloture. March 16, 2009.

100. **Kirk Nomination/Confirmation.** Confirmation of President Obama's nomination of Ron Kirk of Texas to be U.S. trade representative. Confirmed 92-5: R 38-3; D 53-1; I 1-1. A "yea" was a vote in support of the president's position. March 18, 2009.

101. **HR 146. Public Lands Bill/New Construction Ban.** Bingaman, D-N.M., motion to table (kill) the Coburn, R-Okla., amendment to the Bingaman, D-N.M., substitute. The Coburn amendment would ban any new construction in national parks until the Interior secretary determines that all existing sites, structures and trails are fully operational and accessible to the public. The substitute would strike the text of the underlying bill and insert provisions that would designate more than 2 million acres of new protected wilderness areas nationwide, in addition to wild and scenic rivers, historic sites and expansions of national parks. Motion agreed to 79-19: R 22-19; D 55-0; I 2-0. March 18, 2009.

102. **HR 146. Public Lands Bill/Renewable Energy.** Bingaman, D-N.M., motion to table (kill) the Coburn, R-Okla., amendment to the Bingaman substitute. The Coburn amendment would specify that nothing in the bill would restrict the development of renewable energy on public land. Motion agreed to 65-33: R 9-32; D 54-1; I 2-0. March 18, 2009.

103. **HR 146. Public Lands Bill/Eminent Domain.** Bingaman, D-N.M., motion to table (kill) the Coburn, R-Okla., amendment to the Bingaman substitute. The Coburn amendment would bar the use of eminent domain to acquire land or interest in land under the bill. Motion agreed to 63-35: R 10-31; D 51-4; I 2-0. March 18, 2009.

	99	100	101	102	103
ALABAMA					
Shelby	N	Y	N	N	N
Sessions	N	Y	Y	N	N
ALASKA					
Murkowski	Y	Y	Y	Y	Y
Begich	Y	Y	Y	Y	N
ARIZONA					
McCain	N	Y	N	N	N
Kyl	Y	Y	Y	N	N
ARKANSAS					
Lincoln	Y	Y	Y	Y	Y
Pryor	Y	Y	Y	Y	Y
CALIFORNIA					
Feinstein	Y	Y	Y	Y	Y
Boxer	Y	Y	Y	Y	Y
COLORADO					
Udall	Y	Y	Y	Y	Y
Bennet	Y	Y	Y	Y	Y
CONNECTICUT					
Dodd	Y	Y	Y	Y	Y
Lieberman	Y	Y	Y	Y	Y
DELAWARE					
Carper	Y	Y	Y	Y	Y
Kaufman	Y	Y	Y	Y	Y
FLORIDA					
Nelson	Y	Y	Y	Y	Y
Martinez	?	Y	Y	Y	Y
GEORGIA					
Chambliss	?	Y	N	N	N
Isakson	N	N	N	N	N
HAWAII					
Inouye	Y	Y	Y	Y	Y
Akaka	Y	Y	Y	Y	Y
IDAHO					
Crapo	Y	Y	Y	Y	Y
Risch	Y	Y	Y	N	N
ILLINOIS					
Durbin	Y	+	Y	Y	Y
Burris	Y	Y	Y	Y	Y
INDIANA					
Lugar	Y	Y	Y	N	N
Bayh	Y	Y	Y	Y	Y
IOWA					
Grassley	N	Y	N	N	N
Harkin	Y	Y	Y	Y	Y
KANSAS					
Brownback	N	Y	Y	N	N
Roberts	N	Y	Y	N	N
KENTUCKY					
McConnell	N	Y	N	N	N
Bunning	N	N	N	N	N
LOUISIANA					
Landrieu	Y	Y	Y	Y	Y
Vitter	?	Y	N	N	N
MAINE					
Snowe	Y	Y	Y	Y	Y
Collins	Y	Y	Y	Y	Y
MARYLAND					
Mikulski	Y	Y	Y	Y	Y
Cardin	Y	Y	Y	Y	Y
MASSACHUSETTS					
Kennedy	?	?	?	?	?
Kerry	Y	Y	Y	Y	Y
MICHIGAN					
Levin	Y	Y	Y	Y	Y
Stabenow	Y	Y	Y	Y	Y
MINNESOTA					
Klobuchar	Y	Y	Y	Y	Y
Vacant					
MISSISSIPPI					
Cochran	Y	Y	Y	N	Y
Wicker	Y	Y	N	N	N
MISSOURI					
Bond	Y	N	Y	N	N
McCaskill	Y	Y	Y	Y	Y

	99	100	101	102	103
MONTANA					
Baucus	Y	Y	Y	Y	Y
Tester	Y	Y	Y	Y	Y
NEBRASKA					
Nelson	Y	Y	Y	N	N
Johanns	?	Y	Y	N	N
NEVADA					
Reid	Y	Y	Y	Y	Y
Ensign	N	Y	N	N	N
NEW HAMPSHIRE					
Gregg	N	Y	Y	N	Y
Shaheen	Y	Y	Y	Y	Y
NEW JERSEY					
Lautenberg	Y	Y	Y	Y	Y
Menendez	Y	Y	Y	Y	Y
NEW MEXICO					
Bingaman	Y	Y	Y	Y	Y
Udall	Y	Y	Y	Y	Y
NEW YORK					
Schumer	Y	Y	Y	Y	Y
Gillibrand	Y	Y	Y	Y	Y
NORTH CAROLINA					
Burr	N	Y	N	N	N
Hagan	Y	Y	Y	Y	Y
NORTH DAKOTA					
Conrad	Y	Y	Y	Y	Y
Dorgan	Y	Y	Y	Y	Y
OHIO					
Voinovich	Y	Y	Y	Y	Y
Brown	Y	Y	Y	Y	Y
OKLAHOMA					
Inhofe	N	Y	N	N	N
Coburn	N	Y	N	N	N
OREGON					
Wyden	Y	Y	Y	Y	Y
Merkley	Y	Y	Y	Y	Y
PENNSYLVANIA					
Specter	Y	Y	Y	N	Y
Casey	Y	Y	Y	Y	Y
RHODE ISLAND					
Reed	Y	Y	Y	Y	Y
Whitehouse	Y	Y	Y	Y	Y
SOUTH CAROLINA					
Graham	N	Y	N	N	N
DeMint	N	Y	N	N	N
SOUTH DAKOTA					
Johnson	Y	Y	Y	Y	Y
Thune	N	Y	N	N	N
TENNESSEE					
Alexander	N	Y	Y	Y	Y
Corker	N	Y	N	Y	N
TEXAS					
Hutchison	N	Y	Y	N	N
Cornyn	N	Y	N	N	N
UTAH					
Hatch	Y	Y	N	N	N
Bennett	Y	Y	Y	N	N
VERMONT					
Leahy	Y	Y	Y	Y	Y
Sanders	Y	N	Y	Y	Y
VIRGINIA					
Webb	Y	Y	Y	N	N
Warner	Y	Y	Y	Y	Y
WASHINGTON					
Murray	Y	Y	Y	Y	Y
Cantwell	Y	Y	Y	Y	Y
WEST VIRGINIA					
Byrd	Y	N	Y	N	N
Rockefeller	Y	Y	Y	Y	Y
WISCONSIN					
Kohl	Y	Y	Y	Y	Y
Feingold	Y	Y	Y	Y	Y
WYOMING					
Enzi	Y	Y	N	N	N
Barrasso	Y	Y	N	N	N

KEY   **Republicans**   Democrats   *Independents*

Y Voted for (yea)	X Paired against	C Voted "present" to avoid possible conflict of interest
# Paired for	– Announced against	
+ Announced for	P Voted "present"	? Did not vote or otherwise make a position known
N Voted against (nay)		

IN THE SENATE | By Vote Number

104. **HR 146. Public Lands Bill/Annual Lands Report.** Bingaman, D-N.M., motion to table (kill) the Coburn, R-Okla., amendment to the Bingaman substitute. The Coburn amendment would require an annual, publicly available report on how much land each federal department owns and the total cost of maintaining and operating that land. Motion agreed to 58-39: R 3-38; D 53-1; I 2-0. March 19, 2009.

105. **HR 146. Public Lands Bill/Individual Member Projects.** Bingaman, D-N.M., motion to table (kill) the Coburn, R-Okla., amendment to the Bingaman substitute. The Coburn amendment would bar the use of funds in the bill for specific member projects, including a celebration of the 450th anniversary of St. Augustine, Fla.; the National Tropical Botanical Garden; and a project in California to restore salmon populations in the San Joaquin River. Motion agreed to 70-27: R 16-25; D 52-2; I 2-0. (Subsequently, the Bingaman substitute amendment was adopted by unanimous consent.) March 19, 2009.

106. **HR 146. Public Lands Bill/Passage.** Passage of the bill that would designate more than 2 million new acres of protected wilderness areas nationwide, in addition to wild and scenic rivers, historic sites and expansions of national parks. It would authorize new water projects and allow water settlements in Western states. It also would codify a system to improve management of protected federal land. It would specify that the provisions would not restrict access for hunting, fishing or trapping activities otherwise allowed by law and would not affect state authority to regulate these activities. Passed 77-20: R 21-20; D 54-0; I 2-0. (By unanimous consent, the Senate agreed to raise the majority requirement for passage of the bill to 60 votes.) March 19, 2009.

107. **Kagan Nomination/Confirmation.** Confirmation of President Obama's nomination of Elena Kagan of Massachusetts to be U.S. solicitor general. Confirmed 61-31: R 7-31; D 52-0; I 2-0. A "yea" was a vote in support of the president's position. March 19, 2009.

	104	105	106	107
ALABAMA				
Shelby	N	Y	Y	N
Sessions	N	N	N	N
ALASKA				
Murkowski	Y	Y	Y	N
Begich	Y	Y	Y	Y
ARIZONA				
McCain	N	N	N	N
Kyl	N	N	N	Y
ARKANSAS				
Lincoln	Y	Y	Y	Y
Pryor	Y	Y	Y	Y
CALIFORNIA				
Feinstein	Y	Y	Y	Y
Boxer	Y	Y	Y	?
COLORADO				
Udall	Y	Y	Y	Y
Bennet	Y	Y	Y	Y
CONNECTICUT				
Dodd	Y	Y	Y	Y
Lieberman	Y	Y	Y	Y
DELAWARE				
Carper	Y	Y	Y	Y
Kaufman	Y	Y	Y	Y
FLORIDA				
Nelson	Y	Y	Y	Y
Martinez	Y	Y	N	Y
GEORGIA				
Chambliss	N	N	N	N
Isakson	N	N	N	N
HAWAII				
Inouye	Y	Y	Y	Y
Akaka	Y	Y	Y	Y
IDAHO				
Crapo	N	Y	Y	N
Risch	N	Y	Y	N
ILLINOIS				
Durbin	Y	Y	Y	Y
Burris	Y	Y	Y	Y
INDIANA				
Lugar	N	N	Y	Y
Bayh	Y	N	Y	Y
IOWA				
Grassley	N	N	N	N
Harkin	Y	Y	Y	Y
KANSAS				
Brownback	N	N	N	N
Roberts	N	N	Y	N
KENTUCKY				
McConnell	N	N	N	N
Bunning	N	N	N	N
LOUISIANA				
Landrieu	Y	Y	Y	Y
Vitter	N	N	N	N
MAINE				
Snowe	N	Y	Y	Y
Collins	N	Y	Y	Y
MARYLAND				
Mikulski	Y	Y	Y	Y
Cardin	Y	Y	Y	Y
MASSACHUSETTS				
Kennedy	?	?	?	?
Kerry	Y	Y	Y	Y
MICHIGAN				
Levin	Y	Y	Y	Y
Stabenow	Y	Y	Y	Y
MINNESOTA				
Klobuchar	?	?	?	?
Vacant				
MISSISSIPPI				
Cochran	N	Y	Y	?
Wicker	N	Y	Y	N
MISSOURI				
Bond	N	Y	Y	N
McCaskill	N	Y	Y	Y

	104	105	106	107
MONTANA				
Baucus	Y	Y	Y	Y
Tester	Y	Y	Y	Y
NEBRASKA				
Nelson	Y	Y	Y	Y
Johanns	N	N	N	N
NEVADA				
Reid	Y	Y	Y	Y
Ensign	N	N	N	?
NEW HAMPSHIRE				
Gregg	N	Y	Y	Y
Shaheen	Y	Y	Y	Y
NEW JERSEY				
Lautenberg	Y	Y	Y	Y
Menendez	Y	Y	Y	Y
NEW MEXICO				
Bingaman	Y	Y	Y	Y
Udall	Y	Y	Y	Y
NEW YORK				
Schumer	Y	Y	Y	Y
Gillibrand	Y	Y	Y	Y
NORTH CAROLINA				
Burr	N	N	N	N
Hagan	Y	Y	Y	Y
NORTH DAKOTA				
Conrad	Y	Y	Y	Y
Dorgan	Y	Y	Y	Y
OHIO				
Voinovich	N	Y	Y	N
Brown	Y	Y	Y	Y
OKLAHOMA				
Inhofe	N	N	N	N
Coburn	N	N	N	Y
OREGON				
Wyden	Y	Y	Y	Y
Merkley	Y	Y	Y	Y
PENNSYLVANIA				
Specter	N	Y	Y	N
Casey	Y	Y	Y	Y
RHODE ISLAND				
Reed	Y	Y	Y	Y
Whitehouse	Y	Y	Y	Y
SOUTH CAROLINA				
Graham	N	N	N	?
DeMint	N	N	N	N
SOUTH DAKOTA				
Johnson	Y	Y	Y	Y
Thune	N	N	N	N
TENNESSEE				
Alexander	Y	Y	Y	N
Corker	N	N	Y	N
TEXAS				
Hutchison	N	N	N	N
Cornyn	N	N	N	N
UTAH				
Hatch	N	Y	Y	Y
Bennett	N	Y	Y	N
VERMONT				
Leahy	Y	Y	Y	Y
Sanders	Y	Y	Y	Y
VIRGINIA				
Webb	Y	Y	Y	Y
Warner	Y	Y	Y	Y
WASHINGTON				
Murray	Y	Y	Y	?
Cantwell	Y	Y	Y	Y
WEST VIRGINIA				
Byrd	Y	Y	Y	Y
Rockefeller	Y	Y	Y	Y
WISCONSIN				
Kohl	Y	Y	Y	Y
Feingold	Y	N	Y	Y
WYOMING				
Enzi	N	N	Y	N
Barrasso	N	N	Y	N

KEY	**Republicans**	Democrats	*Independents*	
Y	Voted for (yea)	X	Paired against	C Voted "present" to avoid possible conflict of interest
#	Paired for	–	Announced against	
+	Announced for	P	Voted "present"	? Did not vote or otherwise make a position known
N	Voted against (nay)			

IN THE SENATE | By Vote Number

108. HR 1388. National Service Programs/Cloture. Motion to invoke cloture (thus limiting debate) on the Reid, D-Nev., motion to proceed to the bill that would reauthorize Corporation for National Community Service programs through fiscal 2014 and increase the education reward for full-time service volunteers. Motion agreed to 74-14: R 23-14; D 49-0; I 2-0. Three-fifths of the total Senate (60) is required to invoke cloture. March 23, 2009.

109. Kris Nomination/Confirmation. Confirmation of President Obama's nomination of David S. Kris of Maryland to be assistant attorney general. Confirmed 97-0: R 40-0; D 55-0; I 2-0. A "yea" was a vote in support of the president's position. March 25, 2009.

110. HR 1388. National Service Programs/FDIC Borrowing Authority. Crapo, R-Idaho, motion to waive the Budget Act with respect to the Mikulski, D-Md., point of order against the Crapo amendment to the Mikulski substitute. The Crapo amendment would increase the borrowing authority of the Federal Deposit Insurance Corporation from $30 billion to $100 billion and allow a temporary increase up to $500 billion if the FDIC board of directors, the Federal Reserve, and the Treasury secretary determine it is necessary. The substitute would reauthorize and expand Corporation for National and Community Service programs through fiscal 2014 and increase the education reward for full-time service volunteers. Motion rejected 48-49: R 40-0; D 8-47; I 0-2. A three-fifths majority vote (60) of the total Senate is required to waive the Budget Act. (Subsequently, the chair upheld the point of order, and the amendment fell.) March 25, 2009.

111. HR 1388. National Service Programs/Nonprofit Training Program. Mikulski, D-Md., motion to table (kill) the Ensign, R-Nev., amendment to the Baucus, D-Mont., amendment to the Mikulski substitute. The Ensign amendment would clarify that certain crisis pregnancy centers and organizations that serve battered women or victims of rape or incest would be eligible for a nonprofit capacity-building program. The Baucus amendment would authorize $5 million per year in additional funds over five years for a capacity-building program to provide training opportunities for small and midsize charities. Motion agreed to 56-41: R 2-38; D 52-3; I 2-0. (Subsequently, the Baucus amendment was adopted by unanimous consent.) March 25, 2009.

	108	109	110	111
ALABAMA				
Shelby	N	Y	Y	N
Sessions	N	Y	Y	N
ALASKA				
Murkowski	Y	Y	Y	N
Begich	?	Y	N	Y
ARIZONA				
McCain	Y	Y	Y	N
Kyl	N	Y	Y	N
ARKANSAS				
Lincoln	Y	Y	Y	Y
Pryor	?	Y	N	Y
CALIFORNIA				
Feinstein	Y	Y	N	Y
Boxer	+	Y	N	Y
COLORADO				
Udall	Y	Y	N	Y
Bennet	Y	Y	N	Y
CONNECTICUT				
Dodd	Y	Y	N	Y
Lieberman	Y	Y	N	Y
DELAWARE				
Carper	Y	Y	N	Y
Kaufman	Y	Y	N	Y
FLORIDA				
Nelson	?	Y	N	Y
Martinez	?	Y	Y	N
GEORGIA				
Chambliss	Y	Y	Y	N
Isakson	Y	Y	Y	N
HAWAII				
Inouye	?	Y	N	Y
Akaka	Y	Y	N	Y
IDAHO				
Crapo	N	Y	Y	N
Risch	N	Y	Y	N
ILLINOIS				
Durbin	Y	Y	N	Y
Burris	Y	Y	N	Y
INDIANA				
Lugar	Y	Y	Y	N
Bayh	Y	Y	N	Y
IOWA				
Grassley	Y	Y	Y	N
Harkin	+	Y	N	Y
KANSAS				
Brownback	N	Y	Y	N
Roberts	N	Y	Y	N
KENTUCKY				
McConnell	N	Y	Y	N
Bunning	N	Y	Y	N
LOUISIANA				
Landrieu	?	Y	N	Y
Vitter	?	Y	Y	N
MAINE				
Snowe	Y	Y	Y	Y
Collins	Y	Y	Y	Y
MARYLAND				
Mikulski	Y	Y	N	Y
Cardin	Y	Y	N	Y
MASSACHUSETTS				
Kennedy	Y	?	?	?
Kerry	Y	Y	N	Y
MICHIGAN				
Levin	Y	Y	N	Y
Stabenow	Y	Y	N	Y
MINNESOTA				
Klobuchar	Y	Y	N	Y
Vacant				
MISSISSIPPI				
Cochran	Y	Y	Y	N
Wicker	Y	Y	Y	N
MISSOURI				
Bond	Y	Y	Y	N
McCaskill	Y	Y	Y	Y

	108	109	110	111
MONTANA				
Baucus	Y	Y	Y	Y
Tester	Y	Y	Y	Y
NEBRASKA				
Nelson	Y	Y	Y	N
Johanns	Y	Y	Y	N
NEVADA				
Reid	Y	Y	N	Y
Ensign	N	Y	Y	N
NEW HAMPSHIRE				
Gregg	Y	Y	Y	N
Shaheen	Y	Y	N	Y
NEW JERSEY				
Lautenberg	Y	Y	N	Y
Menendez	Y	Y	N	Y
NEW MEXICO				
Bingaman	Y	Y	N	Y
Udall	Y	Y	N	Y
NEW YORK				
Schumer	Y	Y	N	Y
Gillibrand	Y	Y	N	Y
NORTH CAROLINA				
Burr	Y	Y	Y	N
Hagan	Y	Y	N	Y
NORTH DAKOTA				
Conrad	Y	Y	N	N
Dorgan	Y	Y	Y	Y
OHIO				
Voinovich	Y	Y	Y	N
Brown	Y	Y	N	Y
OKLAHOMA				
Inhofe	N	Y	Y	N
Coburn	N	Y	Y	N
OREGON				
Wyden	Y	Y	N	Y
Merkley	Y	Y	N	Y
PENNSYLVANIA				
Specter	Y	Y	N	Y
Casey	Y	Y	N	N
RHODE ISLAND				
Reed	Y	Y	N	Y
Whitehouse	Y	Y	N	Y
SOUTH CAROLINA				
Graham	Y	Y	Y	N
DeMint	N	Y	Y	N
SOUTH DAKOTA				
Johnson	Y	Y	N	Y
Thune	N	Y	Y	N
TENNESSEE				
Alexander	Y	Y	Y	N
Corker	Y	Y	Y	N
TEXAS				
Hutchison	Y	Y	Y	N
Cornyn	–	Y	Y	N
UTAH				
Hatch	Y	Y	Y	N
Bennett	Y	Y	Y	N
VERMONT				
Leahy	Y	Y	N	Y
Sanders	Y	Y	N	Y
VIRGINIA				
Webb	Y	Y	N	Y
Warner	Y	Y	N	Y
WASHINGTON				
Murray	Y	Y	N	Y
Cantwell	Y	Y	Y	Y
WEST VIRGINIA				
Byrd	Y	Y	N	Y
Rockefeller	Y	Y	N	Y
WISCONSIN				
Kohl	Y	Y	N	Y
Feingold	Y	Y	Y	Y
WYOMING				
Enzi	?	?	?	?
Barrasso	Y	Y	Y	N

KEY	**Republicans**	Democrats	*Independents*

Y Voted for (yea)	X Paired against
# Paired for	– Announced against
+ Announced for	P Voted "present"
N Voted against (nay)	

C Voted "present" to avoid possible conflict of interest

? Did not vote or otherwise make a position known

IN THE SENATE | By Vote Number

112. HR 1388. National Service Programs/Federal Income Tax Deduction.
Baucus, D-Mont., amendment to the Mikulski, D-Md., substitute. The Baucus amendment would express the sense of the Senate that Congress should preserve the federal income tax deduction for charitable giving. Adopted 56-41: R 0-41; D 54-0; I 2-0. March 26, 2009.

113. HR 1388. National Service Programs/Federal Income Tax Deduction.
Thune, R-S.D., amendment to the Mikulski, D-Md., substitute. The Thune amendment would express the sense of the Senate that Congress should preserve the full federal income tax deduction for charitable giving. Rejected 48-49: R 41-0; D 6-48; I 1-1. March 26, 2009.

114. HR 1388. National Service Programs/ACORN Funding Ban.
Mikulski, D-Md., motion to table (kill) the Vitter, R-La., amendment to the Mikulski substitute. The Vitter amendment would prohibit the Association of Community Organizations for Reform Now (ACORN), or any organizations affiliated with ACORN, from receiving assistance under the bill. Motion agreed to 53-43: R 0-43; D 51-2; I 2-0. March 26, 2009.

115. HR 1388. National Service Programs/Passage.
Passage of the bill that would reauthorize Corporation for National and Community Service programs through fiscal 2014, increase the education reward for full-time service volunteers from $4,725 to $5,350 and make the reward equal to the maximum annual Pell grant thereafter. Volunteers older than 55 could transfer the education reward to a child or grandchild. It would authorize funding from fiscal 2010 to 2014 for AmeriCorps, Volunteers in the Service to America program, Learn and Serve America, the Retired and Senior Volunteer Program, the Foster Grandparent Program, and the Senior Companion Program. States would be required to match corporation service funds for state commissions on national service. It also would bar participants in national service programs from engaging in certain activities, such as lobbying or providing abortion services or referrals. It would designate $5 million a year from fiscal 2010 to 2014 to provide grants to nonprofit organizations that provide development assistance to small and midsize charities. Passed 79-19: R 22-19; D 55-0; I 2-0. (By unanimous consent, the Senate agreed to raise the majority requirement for passage of the bill to 60 votes.) A "yea" was a vote in support of the president's position. March 26, 2009.

	112	113	114	115
ALABAMA				
Shelby	N	Y	N	N
Sessions	N	Y	N	N
ALASKA				
Murkowski	N	Y	N	Y
Begich	Y	N	Y	Y
ARIZONA				
McCain	N	Y	N	Y
Kyl	N	Y	N	N
ARKANSAS				
Lincoln	Y	Y	Y	Y
Pryor	Y	N	Y	Y
CALIFORNIA				
Feinstein	Y	N	Y	Y
Boxer	Y	Y	Y	Y
COLORADO				
Udall	Y	N	Y	Y
Bennet	Y	N	Y	Y
CONNECTICUT				
Dodd	Y	N	Y	Y
Lieberman	Y	Y	Y	Y
DELAWARE				
Carper	Y	N	Y	Y
Kaufman	Y	N	Y	Y
FLORIDA				
Nelson	Y	N	Y	Y
Martinez	N	Y	N	Y
GEORGIA				
Chambliss	N	Y	N	Y
Isakson	N	Y	N	Y
HAWAII				
Inouye	Y	N	Y	Y
Akaka	Y	N	Y	Y
IDAHO				
Crapo	N	Y	N	N
Risch	N	Y	N	N
ILLINOIS				
Durbin	Y	N	Y	Y
Burris	Y	N	+	Y
INDIANA				
Lugar	N	Y	N	Y
Bayh	Y	Y	Y	Y
IOWA				
Grassley	N	Y	N	Y
Harkin	Y	N	Y	Y
KANSAS				
Brownback	N	Y	N	N
Roberts	N	Y	N	N
KENTUCKY				
McConnell	N	Y	N	N
Bunning	N	Y	N	N
LOUISIANA				
Landrieu	Y	N	Y	Y
Vitter	N	Y	N	Y
MAINE				
Snowe	N	Y	N	Y
Collins	N	Y	N	Y
MARYLAND				
Mikulski	Y	N	Y	Y
Cardin	Y	N	Y	Y
MASSACHUSETTS				
Kennedy	?	?	?	Y
Kerry	Y	N	Y	Y
MICHIGAN				
Levin	Y	N	Y	Y
Stabenow	Y	N	Y	Y
MINNESOTA				
Klobuchar	Y	N	Y	Y
Vacant				
MISSISSIPPI				
Cochran	N	Y	N	Y
Wicker	N	Y	N	Y
MISSOURI				
Bond	N	Y	N	Y
McCaskill	Y	N	Y	Y

	112	113	114	115
MONTANA				
Baucus	Y	N	Y	Y
Tester	Y	N	Y	Y
NEBRASKA				
Nelson	Y	Y	N	Y
Johanns	N	Y	N	Y
NEVADA				
Reid	Y	N	Y	Y
Ensign	N	Y	N	N
NEW HAMPSHIRE				
Gregg	N	Y	N	Y
Shaheen	Y	N	Y	Y
NEW JERSEY				
Lautenberg	Y	N	Y	Y
Menendez	Y	N	Y	Y
NEW MEXICO				
Bingaman	Y	N	Y	Y
Udall	Y	N	Y	Y
NEW YORK				
Schumer	Y	N	Y	Y
Gillibrand	Y	N	Y	Y
NORTH CAROLINA				
Burr	N	Y	N	Y
Hagan	Y	Y	Y	Y
NORTH DAKOTA				
Conrad	Y	N	Y	Y
Dorgan	?	?	?	?
OHIO				
Voinovich	N	Y	N	Y
Brown	Y	N	Y	Y
OKLAHOMA				
Inhofe	N	Y	N	N
Coburn	N	Y	N	N
OREGON				
Wyden	Y	N	Y	Y
Merkley	Y	N	Y	Y
PENNSYLVANIA				
Specter	N	Y	N	Y
Casey	Y	N	Y	Y
RHODE ISLAND				
Reed	Y	N	Y	Y
Whitehouse	Y	N	Y	Y
SOUTH CAROLINA				
Graham	N	Y	N	N
DeMint	N	Y	N	N
SOUTH DAKOTA				
Johnson	Y	N	Y	Y
Thune	N	Y	N	N
TENNESSEE				
Alexander	N	Y	N	Y
Corker	N	Y	N	N
TEXAS				
Hutchison	N	Y	N	Y
Cornyn	N	Y	N	N
UTAH				
Hatch	N	Y	N	Y
Bennett	N	Y	N	Y
VERMONT				
Leahy	Y	N	Y	Y
Sanders	Y	N	Y	Y
VIRGINIA				
Webb	Y	Y	Y	Y
Warner	Y	N	Y	Y
WASHINGTON				
Murray	Y	N	Y	Y
Cantwell	Y	N	Y	Y
WEST VIRGINIA				
Byrd	Y	N	N	Y
Rockefeller	Y	N	Y	Y
WISCONSIN				
Kohl	Y	N	Y	Y
Feingold	Y	N	Y	Y
WYOMING				
Enzi	N	Y	N	Y
Barrasso	N	Y	N	N

KEY	**Republicans**	Democrats	*Independents*
Y Voted for (yea)		X Paired against	C Voted "present" to avoid possible conflict of interest
# Paired for		− Announced against	
+ Announced for		P Voted "present"	? Did not vote or otherwise make a position known
N Voted against (nay)			

IN THE SENATE | By Vote Number

116. **S Con Res 13. Fiscal 2010 Budget Resolution/Energy Prices.**
Boxer, D-Calif., amendment to a provision that would allow a deficit-neutral increase in the resolution's discretionary spending cap for any future climate change legislation. The amendment would require that such legislation does not increase the overall price burden to consumers through revenues and policies. Adopted 54-43: R 0-41; D 52-2; I 2-0. March 31, 2009.

117. **S Con Res 13. Fiscal 2010 Budget Resolution/Energy Prices.**
Thune, R-S.D., amendment to a provision that would allow a deficit-neutral increase in the resolution's discretionary spending cap for future climate change legislation. The amendment would require that such legislation does not increase electricity or gasoline prices. Adopted 89-8: R 40-1; D 47-7; I 2-0. March 31, 2009.

118. **S Con Res 13. Fiscal 2010 Budget Resolution/Public Debt Increase.** Gregg, R-N.H., amendment that would create a 60-vote point of order against any budget resolution that shows an increase in the public debt over the fiscal years covered by the resolution by an amount equal to or greater than the debt accumulated from 1789 to January 20, 2009. Rejected 43-54: R 41-0; D 2-52; I 0-2. March 31, 2009.

119. **S Con Res 13. Fiscal 2010 Budget Resolution/Public Debt.**
Alexander, R-Tenn., amendment that would create a 60-vote point of order against the consideration of any budget resolution that projects a public debt level in fiscal 2009 through the next 10 fiscal years that is greater than 90 percent of the gross domestic product. Rejected 43-55: R 41-0; D 2-53; I 0-2. April 1, 2009.

120. **S Con Res 13. Fiscal 2010 Budget Resolution/Non-defense Discretionary Spending.** Sessions, R-Ala., amendment that would adjust the resolution to allow non-defense discretionary spending to be set at fiscal 2009 levels for fiscal 2010 and 2011, and allow it to increase by 1 percent annually in fiscal 2012 through 2014. Rejected 40-58: R 39-2; D 1-54; I 0-2. A "nay" was a vote in support of the president's position. April 1, 2009.

121. **S Con Res 13. Fiscal 2010 Budget Resolution/Tax Increase.**
Ensign, R-Nev., amendment that would create a 60-vote point of order against any legislation that assumes an increase in taxes on individuals with annual incomes of $200,000 or less ($250,000 for joint filers). Adopted 98-0: R 41-0; D 55-0; I 2-0. April 1, 2009.

122. **S Con Res 13. Fiscal 2010 Budget Resolution/Income Tax Rates.** Cornyn, R-Texas, amendment that would create a 60-vote point of order against any legislation that assumes an increase in income tax rates. Adopted 82-16: R 40-1; D 41-14; I 1-1. April 1, 2009.

	116	117	118	119	120	121	122
ALABAMA							
Shelby	N	Y	Y	Y	Y	Y	Y
Sessions	N	Y	Y	Y	Y	Y	Y
ALASKA							
Murkowski	N	Y	Y	Y	Y	Y	Y
Begich	Y	Y	N	N	N	Y	Y
ARIZONA							
McCain	N	Y	Y	Y	Y	Y	Y
Kyl	N	Y	Y	Y	Y	Y	Y
ARKANSAS							
Lincoln	Y	Y	N	N	N	Y	Y
Pryor	Y	Y	N	N	N	Y	Y
CALIFORNIA							
Feinstein	Y	N	N	N	N	Y	Y
Boxer	Y	Y	N	N	N	Y	Y
COLORADO							
Udall	Y	Y	N	N	N	Y	Y
Bennet	Y	Y	N	N	N	Y	Y
CONNECTICUT							
Dodd	Y	Y	N	N	N	Y	Y
Lieberman	Y	Y	N	N	N	Y	Y
DELAWARE							
Carper	Y	Y	N	N	N	Y	Y
Kaufman	Y	Y	N	N	N	Y	Y
FLORIDA							
Nelson	Y	Y	N	N	N	Y	Y
Martinez	N	Y	Y	Y	N	Y	Y
GEORGIA							
Chambliss	N	Y	Y	Y	Y	Y	Y
Isakson	N	Y	Y	Y	Y	Y	Y
HAWAII							
Inouye	Y	Y	N	N	N	Y	Y
Akaka	Y	Y	N	N	N	Y	Y
IDAHO							
Crapo	N	Y	Y	Y	Y	Y	Y
Risch	N	Y	Y	Y	Y	Y	Y
ILLINOIS							
Durbin	Y	N	N	N	N	Y	N
Burris	Y	Y	N	N	N	Y	Y
INDIANA							
Lugar	N	Y	Y	Y	Y	Y	Y
Bayh	Y	Y	N	N	Y	Y	Y
IOWA							
Grassley	N	Y	Y	Y	Y	Y	Y
Harkin	Y	Y	N	N	N	Y	N
KANSAS							
Brownback	N	Y	Y	Y	Y	Y	Y
Roberts	N	Y	Y	Y	Y	Y	Y
KENTUCKY							
McConnell	N	Y	Y	Y	Y	Y	Y
Bunning	N	Y	Y	Y	Y	Y	Y
LOUISIANA							
Landrieu	Y	Y	N	N	N	Y	Y
Vitter	N	Y	Y	Y	Y	Y	Y
MAINE							
Snowe	N	Y	Y	Y	Y	Y	Y
Collins	N	Y	Y	Y	N	Y	Y
MARYLAND							
Mikulski	Y	Y	N	N	N	Y	Y
Cardin	Y	N	N	N	N	Y	N
MASSACHUSETTS							
Kennedy	?	?	?	?	?	?	?
Kerry	Y	Y	N	N	N	Y	N
MICHIGAN							
Levin	Y	Y	N	N	N	Y	Y
Stabenow	Y	Y	N	N	N	Y	Y
MINNESOTA							
Klobuchar	Y	Y	N	Y	N	Y	Y
Vacant							
MISSISSIPPI							
Cochran	N	Y	Y	Y	Y	Y	Y
Wicker	N	Y	Y	Y	Y	Y	Y
MISSOURI							
Bond	N	Y	Y	Y	Y	Y	Y
McCaskill	Y	Y	N	N	N	Y	Y

	116	117	118	119	120	121	122
MONTANA							
Baucus	Y	Y	N	N	N	Y	Y
Tester	Y	Y	N	N	N	Y	Y
NEBRASKA							
Nelson	Y	Y	Y	Y	N	Y	Y
Johanns	N	Y	Y	Y	Y	Y	Y
NEVADA							
Reid	Y	Y	N	N	N	Y	Y
Ensign	N	Y	Y	Y	Y	Y	Y
NEW HAMPSHIRE							
Gregg	N	Y	Y	Y	Y	Y	Y
Shaheen	Y	Y	N	N	N	Y	Y
NEW JERSEY							
Lautenberg	Y	Y	N	N	N	Y	Y
Menendez	Y	N	N	N	N	Y	Y
NEW MEXICO							
Bingaman	N	N	N	N	N	Y	N
Udall	Y	N	N	N	N	Y	Y
NEW YORK							
Schumer	Y	Y	N	N	N	Y	Y
Gillibrand	?	?	?	N	N	Y	Y
NORTH CAROLINA							
Burr	N	Y	Y	Y	Y	Y	Y
Hagan	Y	Y	N	N	N	Y	Y
NORTH DAKOTA							
Conrad	Y	Y	N	N	N	Y	Y
Dorgan	Y	Y	N	N	N	Y	Y
OHIO							
Voinovich	N	Y	Y	Y	Y	Y	N
Brown	Y	Y	N	N	N	Y	N
OKLAHOMA							
Inhofe	N	Y	Y	Y	Y	Y	Y
Coburn	N	Y	Y	Y	Y	Y	Y
OREGON							
Wyden	Y	Y	N	N	N	Y	N
Merkley	Y	Y	N	N	N	Y	N
PENNSYLVANIA							
Specter	N	Y	Y	Y	Y	Y	N
Casey	Y	Y	N	N	N	Y	N
RHODE ISLAND							
Reed	Y	Y	N	N	N	Y	N
Whitehouse	Y	N	N	N	N	Y	N
SOUTH CAROLINA							
Graham	N	Y	Y	Y	Y	Y	Y
DeMint	N	Y	Y	Y	Y	Y	Y
SOUTH DAKOTA							
Johnson	Y	Y	N	N	N	Y	Y
Thune	N	Y	Y	Y	Y	Y	Y
TENNESSEE							
Alexander	N	Y	Y	Y	Y	Y	Y
Corker	N	N	Y	Y	Y	Y	Y
TEXAS							
Hutchison	N	Y	Y	Y	Y	Y	Y
Cornyn	N	Y	Y	Y	Y	Y	Y
UTAH							
Hatch	N	Y	Y	Y	Y	Y	Y
Bennett	N	Y	Y	Y	Y	Y	Y
VERMONT							
Leahy	Y	Y	N	N	N	Y	Y
Sanders	Y	Y	N	N	N	Y	Y
VIRGINIA							
Webb	Y	Y	N	N	N	Y	Y
Warner	Y	Y	N	N	N	Y	Y
WASHINGTON							
Murray	Y	Y	N	N	N	Y	Y
Cantwell	Y	Y	N	N	N	Y	Y
WEST VIRGINIA							
Byrd	N	Y	N	N	N	Y	N
Rockefeller	Y	Y	N	N	N	Y	N
WISCONSIN							
Kohl	Y	Y	N	N	N	Y	Y
Feingold	Y	Y	N	N	N	Y	N
WYOMING							
Enzi	N	Y	Y	Y	Y	Y	Y
Barrasso	N	Y	Y	Y	Y	Y	Y

IN THE SENATE | By Vote Number

123. **S Con Res 13. Fiscal 2010 Budget Resolution/Bipartisan Fiscal Commission.** Gregg, R-N.H., amendment that would allow a deficit-neutral increase in the discretionary spending cap in order to fund the creation of a bipartisan task force to examine long-term fiscal imbalances facing the nation. The commission would report legislative recommendations to address the imbalances with a majority approval of each party. Rejected 44-54: R 40-1; D 3-52; I 1-1. April 1, 2009.

124. **S Con Res 13. Fiscal 2010 Budget Resolution/Discretionary Funding Cap.** Crapo, R-Idaho, amendment that would expand a provision creating a 60-vote point of order against any legislation that exceeds the fiscal 2009 and 2010 discretionary funding caps in the resolution. The amendment would extend the point of order to caps for fiscal 2011 and 2012. Rejected 43-55: R 41-0; D 2-53; I 0-2. April 1, 2009.

125. **S Con Res 13. Fiscal 2010 Budget Resolution/Climate Change Legislation.** Whitehouse, D-R.I., motion to waive the Budget Act with respect to the Gregg, R-N.H., point of order against the Whitehouse amendment that would prohibit the use of reconciliation in the Senate for climate change or clean-energy legislation. The prohibition could be waived if the Senate finds that climate change is a threat to the U.S. economy, public health or national security. Motion rejected 42-56: R 0-41; D 40-15; I 2-0. A three-fifths majority vote (60) of the total Senate is required to waive the Budget Act. (Subsequently, the chair upheld the point of order, and the amendment fell.) April 1, 2009.

126. **S Con Res 13. Fiscal 2010 Budget Resolution/Prohibit Reconciliation.** Johanns, R-Neb., amendment that would prohibit the use of reconciliation in the Senate for climate change or clean-energy legislation involving a cap-and-trade system. Adopted 67-31: R 41-0; D 26-29; I 0-2. April 1, 2009.

127. **S Con Res 13. Fiscal 2010 Budget Resolution/Comparative Effectiveness.** Kyl, R-Ariz., amendment that would prohibit the use of information obtained from research comparing the effectiveness of different treatments for specific medical conditions to deny coverage of products or services under federal health care programs such as Medicare. Rejected 44-54: R 41-0; D 2-53; I 1-1. April 1, 2009.

128. **S Con Res 13. Fiscal 2010 Budget Resolution/Means Test.** Ensign, R-Nev., amendment that would adjust the resolution with the intention of allowing for a requirement that higher-income Medicare prescription drugs beneficiaries pay a larger share of their Medicare Part D premiums. Rejected 39-58: R 37-3; D 2-53; I 0-2. April 2, 2009.

129. **S Con Res 13. Fiscal 2010 Budget Resolution/Substitute.** McCain, R-Ariz., substitute amendment that would allow up to $17.5 trillion in discretionary spending for fiscal 2010 to 2015. It would call for an increase of $190 billion for defense and $25 billion for veterans' programs. It would assume an extension of the 2001 and 2003 tax cuts. It would allow a deficit-neutral increase in the discretionary spending cap to allow for the creation of a commission to retool Medicare, Medicaid and Social Security to find savings. It would also allow deficit-neutral discretionary increases for a health care overhaul, benefits for disabled military retirees and their families, and an overhaul of the tax code. Rejected 38-60: R 38-3; D 0-55; I 0-2. A "nay" was a vote in support of the president's position. April 2, 2009.

	123	124	125	126	127	128	129
ALABAMA							
Shelby	Y	Y	N	Y	Y	Y	Y
Sessions	Y	Y	N	Y	Y	Y	Y
ALASKA							
Murkowski	Y	Y	N	Y	Y	?	Y
Begich	N	N	N	Y	N	N	N
ARIZONA							
McCain	Y	Y	N	Y	Y	Y	Y
Kyl	Y	Y	N	Y	Y	Y	Y
ARKANSAS							
Lincoln	N	N	N	Y	N	N	N
Pryor	N	N	Y	Y	N	N	N
CALIFORNIA							
Feinstein	N	N	Y	N	N	Y	N
Boxer	N	N	Y	N	N	N	N
COLORADO							
Udall	N	N	Y	N	N	N	N
Bennet	N	N	Y	Y	N	N	N
CONNECTICUT							
Dodd	N	N	Y	N	N	N	N
Lieberman	Y	N	Y	N	Y	N	N
DELAWARE							
Carper	N	N	Y	N	N	N	N
Kaufman	N	N	Y	N	N	N	N
FLORIDA							
Nelson	N	N	Y	N	N	N	N
Martinez	Y	Y	N	Y	Y	N	Y
GEORGIA							
Chambliss	Y	Y	N	Y	Y	Y	Y
Isakson	Y	Y	N	Y	Y	Y	Y
HAWAII							
Inouye	N	N	Y	N	N	N	N
Akaka	N	N	Y	N	N	N	N
IDAHO							
Crapo	Y	Y	N	Y	Y	Y	Y
Risch	Y	Y	N	Y	Y	Y	Y
ILLINOIS							
Durbin	N	N	Y	N	N	N	N
Burris	N	N	Y	N	N	N	N
INDIANA							
Lugar	Y	Y	N	Y	Y	Y	Y
Bayh	N	Y	Y	Y	N	N	N
IOWA							
Grassley	Y	Y	N	Y	Y	Y	Y
Harkin	N	N	Y	N	N	N	N
KANSAS							
Brownback	Y	Y	N	Y	Y	Y	Y
Roberts	Y	Y	N	Y	Y	Y	Y
KENTUCKY							
McConnell	Y	Y	N	Y	Y	Y	Y
Bunning	Y	Y	N	Y	Y	Y	Y
LOUISIANA							
Landrieu	N	N	Y	Y	N	N	N
Vitter	Y	Y	N	Y	Y	Y	Y
MAINE							
Snowe	N	Y	N	Y	N	N	N
Collins	Y	Y	N	Y	Y	Y	Y
MARYLAND							
Mikulski	N	N	Y	N	N	N	N
Cardin	N	N	Y	N	N	N	N
MASSACHUSETTS							
Kennedy	?	?	?	?	?	?	?
Kerry	N	N	Y	N	N	N	N
MICHIGAN							
Levin	N	N	N	Y	N	N	N
Stabenow	N	N	N	Y	N	N	N
MINNESOTA							
Klobuchar	N	N	Y	Y	N	N	N
Vacant							
MISSISSIPPI							
Cochran	Y	Y	N	Y	Y	Y	Y
Wicker	Y	Y	N	Y	Y	N	Y
MISSOURI							
Bond	Y	Y	N	Y	Y	Y	Y
McCaskill	N	N	N	Y	N	N	N
MONTANA							
Baucus	N	N	Y	Y	N	N	N
Tester	N	N	Y	Y	N	N	N
NEBRASKA							
Nelson	Y	Y	N	Y	Y	N	N
Johanns	Y	Y	N	Y	Y	Y	Y
NEVADA							
Reid	N	N	Y	N	N	N	N
Ensign	Y	Y	N	Y	Y	Y	Y
NEW HAMPSHIRE							
Gregg	Y	Y	N	Y	Y	Y	Y
Shaheen	N	N	Y	N	N	N	N
NEW JERSEY							
Lautenberg	N	N	Y	N	N	N	N
Menendez	N	N	Y	N	N	N	N
NEW MEXICO							
Bingaman	N	N	Y	N	N	N	N
Udall	N	N	Y	N	N	N	N
NEW YORK							
Schumer	N	N	Y	N	N	N	N
Gillibrand	N	N	Y	N	N	N	N
NORTH CAROLINA							
Burr	Y	Y	N	Y	Y	Y	Y
Hagan	N	N	N	Y	N	N	N
NORTH DAKOTA							
Conrad	N	N	Y	Y	N	N	N
Dorgan	N	N	N	Y	N	N	N
OHIO							
Voinovich	Y	Y	N	Y	Y	Y	Y
Brown	N	N	Y	N	N	N	N
OKLAHOMA							
Inhofe	Y	Y	N	Y	Y	Y	Y
Coburn	Y	Y	N	Y	Y	Y	Y
OREGON							
Wyden	N	N	Y	N	N	N	N
Merkley	N	N	Y	N	N	N	N
PENNSYLVANIA							
Specter	Y	Y	N	Y	Y	Y	Y
Casey	N	N	Y	Y	N	N	N
RHODE ISLAND							
Reed	N	N	Y	N	N	N	N
Whitehouse	N	N	Y	N	N	N	N
SOUTH CAROLINA							
Graham	Y	Y	N	Y	Y	Y	Y
DeMint	Y	Y	N	Y	Y	Y	Y
SOUTH DAKOTA							
Johnson	N	N	Y	N	N	N	N
Thune	Y	Y	N	Y	Y	Y	Y
TENNESSEE							
Alexander	Y	Y	N	Y	Y	Y	Y
Corker	Y	Y	N	Y	Y	Y	N
TEXAS							
Hutchison	Y	Y	N	Y	Y	Y	Y
Cornyn	Y	Y	N	Y	Y	Y	Y
UTAH							
Hatch	Y	Y	N	Y	Y	Y	Y
Bennett	Y	Y	N	Y	Y	Y	Y
VERMONT							
Leahy	N	N	Y	N	N	N	N
Sanders	N	N	Y	N	N	N	N
VIRGINIA							
Webb	Y	N	Y	Y	N	N	N
Warner	Y	N	Y	Y	N	N	N
WASHINGTON							
Murray	N	N	Y	N	N	N	N
Cantwell	N	N	Y	N	N	N	N
WEST VIRGINIA							
Byrd	N	N	N	Y	N	N	N
Rockefeller	N	N	N	Y	N	N	N
WISCONSIN							
Kohl	N	N	Y	Y	N	N	N
Feingold	N	N	Y	Y	N	N	N
WYOMING							
Enzi	Y	Y	N	Y	Y	Y	Y
Barrasso	Y	Y	N	Y	Y	Y	Y

KEY   **Republicans**   Democrats   *Independents*

Y Voted for (yea)	X Paired against
# Paired for	− Announced against
+ Announced for	P Voted "present"
N Voted against (nay)	C Voted "present" to avoid possible conflict of interest
	? Did not vote or otherwise make a position known

IN THE SENATE | By Vote Number

130. **S Con Res 13. Fiscal 2010 Budget Resolution/Federal Reserve Banks.** Dodd, D-Conn., amendment to a provision that would allow a deficit-neutral increase in the resolution's discretionary spending cap for legislation to increase transparency at the Federal Reserve. The amendment would add a detailed list of disclosure requirements that would have to be in such legislation. Adopted 96-2: R 39-2; D 55-0; I 2-0. April 2, 2009.

131. **S Con Res 13. Fiscal 2010 Budget Resolution/Federal Reserve Banks.** Sanders, I-Vt., amendment to a provision that would allow a deficit-neutral increase in the resolution's discretionary spending cap for legislation to increase transparency at the Federal Reserve. The amendment would require additional disclosure from Federal Reserve banks, including the identification of institutions provided assistance under federal lending programs since March 24, 2005, the amount of assistance given, and how the funds are being used. Adopted 59-39: R 21-20; D 37-18; I 1-1. April 2, 2009.

132. **S Con Res 13. Fiscal 2010 Budget Resolution/Recommit.** Johanns, R-Neb., motion to recommit the resolution to the Senate Budget Committee with instructions that it limit the increase in aggregate non-defense, non-veteran spending above fiscal 2009 levels to the Congressional Budget Office's projected rate of inflation. Motion rejected 43-55: R 41-0; D 2-53; I 0-2. April 2, 2009.

133. **S Con Res 13. Fiscal 2010 Budget Resolution/Mortgage Relief.** Reed, D-R.I., amendment that would allow a deficit-neutral increase in the resolution's discretionary spending cap to pay for the impact of any legislation that affirms that the remaining funds in the Troubled Asset Relief Program would be used to help save homes and small businesses; help the municipal bond market; expand credit; and provide resources to the Government Accountability Office, the special inspector general for the program, and the congressional oversight panel. Adopted 56-42: R 1-40; D 53-2; I 2-0. April 2, 2009.

134. **S Con Res 13. Fiscal 2010 Budget Resolution/Mortgage Relief Funds.** Vitter, R-La., amendment that would adjust the resolution to allow for the recovery of funds approved as part of the 2008 mortgage-backed securities buyout, except for $100 billion in the Treasury Department's public-private "legacy asset" purchasing program. Rejected 28-70: R 26-15; D 2-53; I 0-2. April 2, 2009.

135. **S Con Res 13. Fiscal 2010 Budget Resolution/Energy Taxes.** Graham, R-S.C., amendment that would create a 60-vote point of order against any legislation that includes an energy tax increase that would be widely applicable to individual taxpayers with annual incomes of $200,000 or less ($250,000 or less for joint filers). Adopted 65-33: R 41-0; D 24-31; I 0-2. April 2, 2009.

136. **S Con Res 13. Fiscal 2010 Budget Resolution/Energy Revenue Sharing.** Landrieu, D-La., amendment that would allow a deficit-neutral increase in the resolution's discretionary spending cap to pay for the impact of any legislation that would require that 50 percent of revenue from outer continental shelf leases be distributed among coastal energy-producing states and/or allocated for the conduct of alternative-energy research and the support of parks and wildlife. Rejected 36-61: R 29-11; D 7-48; I 0-2. April 2, 2009.

	130	131	132	133	134	135	136
ALABAMA							
Shelby	Y	N	Y	N	Y	Y	Y
Sessions	Y	Y	Y	N	Y	Y	?
ALASKA							
Murkowski	Y	N	Y	N	Y	Y	Y
Begich	Y	Y	N	Y	N	Y	Y
ARIZONA							
McCain	Y	Y	Y	N	Y	Y	Y
Kyl	Y	N	Y	N	N	Y	Y
ARKANSAS							
Lincoln	Y	Y	N	Y	N	Y	N
Pryor	Y	Y	N	Y	N	Y	N
CALIFORNIA							
Feinstein	Y	Y	N	Y	N	N	N
Boxer	Y	Y	N	Y	N	N	N
COLORADO							
Udall	Y	N	N	Y	N	N	N
Bennet	Y	N	N	Y	N	N	N
CONNECTICUT							
Dodd	Y	N	N	Y	N	N	N
Lieberman	Y	N	N	Y	N	N	N
DELAWARE							
Carper	Y	N	N	Y	N	N	Y
Kaufman	Y	N	N	Y	N	N	N
FLORIDA							
Nelson	Y	Y	N	Y	N	Y	N
Martinez	Y	N	Y	N	N	Y	N
GEORGIA							
Chambliss	Y	N	Y	N	N	Y	Y
Isakson	Y	N	Y	N	N	Y	Y
HAWAII							
Inouye	Y	Y	N	N	N	N	N
Akaka	Y	Y	N	Y	N	N	N
IDAHO							
Crapo	Y	Y	Y	N	Y	Y	Y
Risch	Y	Y	Y	N	Y	Y	Y
ILLINOIS							
Durbin	Y	Y	N	Y	N	N	N
Burris	Y	Y	N	Y	N	N	N
INDIANA							
Lugar	Y	N	N	N	N	Y	N
Bayh	Y	N	Y	N	N	Y	N
IOWA							
Grassley	Y	Y	Y	N	N	Y	Y
Harkin	Y	Y	N	Y	N	N	N
KANSAS							
Brownback	Y	Y	Y	N	Y	Y	Y
Roberts	Y	Y	Y	N	Y	Y	Y
KENTUCKY							
McConnell	Y	N	Y	N	N	Y	Y
Bunning	Y	Y	Y	N	Y	Y	Y
LOUISIANA							
Landrieu	Y	Y	N	Y	N	Y	Y
Vitter	Y	Y	Y	N	Y	Y	Y
MAINE							
Snowe	Y	Y	Y	N	N	Y	N
Collins	Y	Y	Y	N	Y	Y	N
MARYLAND							
Mikulski	Y	Y	N	N	N	N	N
Cardin	Y	Y	N	Y	N	N	N
MASSACHUSETTS							
Kennedy	?	?	?	?	?	?	?
Kerry	Y	Y	N	Y	N	N	N
MICHIGAN							
Levin	Y	Y	N	Y	N	N	N
Stabenow	Y	Y	N	Y	N	N	N
MINNESOTA							
Klobuchar	Y	Y	N	Y	N	Y	N
Vacant							
MISSISSIPPI							
Cochran	Y	N	Y	N	N	Y	Y
Wicker	Y	N	Y	N	Y	Y	Y
MISSOURI							
Bond	Y	N	Y	N	Y	Y	Y
McCaskill	Y	Y	N	Y	N	Y	N
MONTANA							
Baucus	Y	N	N	Y	N	Y	N
Tester	Y	Y	N	Y	N	Y	N
NEBRASKA							
Nelson	Y	N	Y	N	Y	Y	Y
Johanns	Y	N	Y	N	Y	Y	Y
NEVADA							
Reid	Y	Y	N	Y	N	N	N
Ensign	Y	Y	Y	N	Y	Y	Y
NEW HAMPSHIRE							
Gregg	N	N	Y	N	N	Y	N
Shaheen	Y	N	N	Y	N	N	N
NEW JERSEY							
Lautenberg	Y	N	N	Y	N	N	N
Menendez	Y	N	N	Y	N	N	N
NEW MEXICO							
Bingaman	Y	N	N	Y	N	N	N
Udall	Y	Y	N	Y	N	N	N
NEW YORK							
Schumer	Y	N	N	Y	N	N	N
Gillibrand	Y	N	N	Y	N	N	N
NORTH CAROLINA							
Burr	Y	Y	Y	N	Y	Y	Y
Hagan	Y	Y	N	Y	N	Y	N
NORTH DAKOTA							
Conrad	Y	Y	N	Y	N	Y	N
Dorgan	Y	Y	N	Y	N	Y	N
OHIO							
Voinovich	Y	N	Y	N	Y	Y	N
Brown	Y	Y	N	N	N	N	N
OKLAHOMA							
Inhofe	Y	Y	Y	N	Y	Y	Y
Coburn	Y	Y	Y	N	Y	Y	Y
OREGON							
Wyden	Y	Y	N	Y	N	Y	N
Merkley	Y	Y	N	Y	N	N	N
PENNSYLVANIA							
Specter	Y	Y	Y	N	Y	Y	N
Casey	Y	Y	N	Y	N	Y	N
RHODE ISLAND							
Reed	Y	N	N	Y	N	N	N
Whitehouse	Y	Y	N	Y	N	N	N
SOUTH CAROLINA							
Graham	Y	Y	Y	N	Y	Y	Y
DeMint	Y	Y	Y	N	Y	Y	Y
SOUTH DAKOTA							
Johnson	Y	N	N	Y	N	Y	N
Thune	Y	Y	Y	N	Y	Y	Y
TENNESSEE							
Alexander	N	N	Y	N	N	Y	N
Corker	Y	N	Y	N	N	Y	Y
TEXAS							
Hutchison	Y	Y	Y	N	Y	Y	Y
Cornyn	Y	Y	Y	N	Y	Y	Y
UTAH							
Hatch	Y	N	Y	N	N	Y	N
Bennett	Y	N	Y	N	Y	Y	Y
VERMONT							
Leahy	Y	Y	N	Y	N	N	N
Sanders	Y	Y	N	Y	N	N	N
VIRGINIA							
Webb	Y	Y	N	Y	N	Y	N
Warner	Y	N	N	Y	N	N	Y
WASHINGTON							
Murray	Y	Y	N	Y	N	Y	N
Cantwell	Y	Y	N	Y	N	Y	N
WEST VIRGINIA							
Byrd	Y	Y	N	Y	N	Y	N
Rockefeller	Y	Y	N	Y	N	N	N
WISCONSIN							
Kohl	Y	N	N	Y	N	Y	N
Feingold	Y	Y	N	N	N	Y	N
WYOMING							
Enzi	Y	N	Y	N	Y	Y	Y
Barrasso	Y	N	Y	N	Y	Y	Y

KEY   Republicans   Democrats   *Independents*

Y Voted for (yea)
X Paired against
C Voted "present" to avoid possible conflict of interest
\# Paired for
– Announced against
\+ Announced for
P Voted "present"
? Did not vote or otherwise make a position known
N Voted against (nay)

IN THE SENATE | By Vote Number

137. **S Con Res 13. Fiscal 2010 Budget Resolution/After-School Programs.** Boxer, D-Calif., amendment that would allow a deficit-neutral increase in the discretionary spending cap in order to increase funding for before-school, after-school and summer programs. Adopted 89-9: R 32-9; D 55-0; I 2-0. April 2, 2009.

138. **S Con Res 13. Fiscal 2010 Budget Resolution/Charitable Donation Deduction.** Thune, R-S.D., amendment that would create a 60-vote point of order against any legislation that would increase revenues above a certain level. The amendment is aimed at legislation that would not allow taxpayers to deduct the full value of their charitable donations. Adopted 94-3: R 40-0; D 53-2; I 1-1. April 2, 2009.

139. **S Con Res 13. Fiscal 2010 Budget Resolution/Alternative Minimum Tax.** Grassley, R-Iowa, amendment that would adjust the resolution to allow for legislation that would prevent the alternative minimum tax from applying to millions of additional taxpayers through fiscal 2014. Rejected 40-58: R 39-2; D 1-54; I 0-2. April 2, 2009.

140. **S Con Res 13. Fiscal 2010 Budget Resolution/National Usury Law.** Sanders, I-Vt., amendment that would allow a deficit-neutral increase in the discretionary spending cap to establish a national usury law. Rejected 31-67: R 0-41; D 30-25; I 1-1. April 2, 2009.

141. **S Con Res 13. Fiscal 2010 Budget Resolution/Climate Change Legislation.** Stabenow, D-Mich., amendment that would allow for climate change legislation that would create new jobs in "clean" technology, diversify the domestic clean-energy supply, provide incentives for cost savings through energy efficiencies, and provide voluntary opportunities for agriculture and forestry communities to contribute to reducing greenhouse gas levels. Adopted 73-25: R 17-24; D 54-1; I 2-0. April 2, 2009.

142. **S Con Res 13. Fiscal 2010 Budget Resolution/Job Losses.** Bond, R-Mo., amendment that would create a 60-vote point of order against any legislation that causes significant job losses in manufacturing-dependent or coal-dependent regions of the United States. Adopted 54-44: R 41-0; D 13-42; I 0-2. April 2, 2009.

143. **S Con Res 13. Fiscal 2010 Budget Resolution/Stimulus Funds.** Bennett, R-Utah, amendment that would allow for a reduction in out-year spending caps to compensate for the amount of stimulus funds from the 2009 economic recovery package that will be spent after the economy is projected to recover. Rejected 42-56: R 41-0; D 1-54; I 0-2. April 2, 2009.

	137	138	139	140	141	142	143
ALABAMA							
Shelby	Y	Y	Y	N	N	Y	Y
Sessions	N	Y	Y	N	N	Y	Y
ALASKA							
Murkowski	Y	Y	Y	N	N	Y	Y
Begich	Y	Y	N	Y	Y	N	N
ARIZONA							
McCain	N	Y	Y	N	N	Y	Y
Kyl	N	Y	Y	N	N	Y	Y
ARKANSAS							
Lincoln	Y	Y	N	N	Y	Y	N
Pryor	Y	Y	N	N	Y	Y	N
CALIFORNIA							
Feinstein	Y	Y	N	Y	Y	N	N
Boxer	Y	Y	N	Y	Y	N	N
COLORADO							
Udall	Y	Y	N	N	Y	N	N
Bennet	Y	Y	N	N	Y	N	N
CONNECTICUT							
Dodd	Y	Y	N	Y	Y	N	N
Lieberman	Y	Y	N	N	Y	N	N
DELAWARE							
Carper	Y	Y	N	N	Y	N	N
Kaufman	Y	Y	N	Y	Y	N	N
FLORIDA							
Nelson	Y	Y	N	N	Y	N	N
Martinez	Y	Y	Y	N	Y	Y	Y
GEORGIA							
Chambliss	Y	Y	Y	N	N	Y	Y
Isakson	Y	Y	Y	N	N	Y	Y
HAWAII							
Inouye	Y	Y	N	N	Y	N	N
Akaka	Y	Y	N	N	Y	N	N
IDAHO							
Crapo	Y	Y	Y	N	Y	Y	Y
Risch	Y	Y	Y	N	Y	Y	Y
ILLINOIS							
Durbin	Y	Y	N	Y	Y	N	N
Burris	Y	Y	N	Y	Y	N	N
INDIANA							
Lugar	Y	Y	Y	N	Y	Y	N
Bayh	Y	Y	N	N	Y	Y	N
IOWA							
Grassley	Y	Y	Y	N	Y	Y	Y
Harkin	Y	Y	N	Y	Y	N	N
KANSAS							
Brownback	Y	Y	Y	N	Y	Y	Y
Roberts	Y	Y	Y	N	Y	Y	Y
KENTUCKY							
McConnell	Y	Y	Y	N	N	Y	Y
Bunning	N	Y	N	N	N	Y	Y
LOUISIANA							
Landrieu	Y	Y	N	N	N	Y	N
Vitter	Y	Y	Y	N	N	Y	Y
MAINE							
Snowe	Y	Y	Y	N	Y	Y	Y
Collins	Y	Y	Y	N	Y	Y	Y
MARYLAND							
Mikulski	Y	Y	N	Y	Y	N	N
Cardin	Y	Y	N	Y	Y	N	N
MASSACHUSETTS							
Kennedy	?	?	?	?	?	?	?
Kerry	Y	Y	N	Y	Y	N	N
MICHIGAN							
Levin	Y	Y	N	Y	Y	N	N
Stabenow	Y	Y	N	N	Y	N	N
MINNESOTA							
Klobuchar	Y	Y	N	N	Y	N	N
Vacant							
MISSISSIPPI							
Cochran	Y	Y	Y	N	N	Y	Y
Wicker	Y	Y	Y	N	N	Y	Y
MISSOURI							
Bond	Y	Y	Y	N	Y	Y	Y
McCaskill	Y	N	N	Y	Y	N	N

	137	138	139	140	141	142	143
MONTANA							
Baucus	Y	Y	N	N	Y	Y	N
Tester	Y	Y	N	N	Y	Y	N
NEBRASKA							
Nelson	Y	Y	Y	N	Y	Y	Y
Johanns	Y	Y	Y	N	Y	Y	Y
NEVADA							
Reid	Y	Y	N	Y	Y	N	N
Ensign	Y	Y	Y	N	N	Y	Y
NEW HAMPSHIRE							
Gregg	N	Y	N	N	N	Y	Y
Shaheen	Y	Y	N	Y	Y	N	N
NEW JERSEY							
Lautenberg	Y	Y	N	Y	Y	N	N
Menendez	Y	Y	N	Y	Y	N	N
NEW MEXICO							
Bingaman	Y	Y	N	N	Y	N	N
Udall	Y	Y	N	N	Y	N	N
NEW YORK							
Schumer	Y	Y	N	Y	Y	N	N
Gillibrand	Y	Y	N	Y	Y	N	N
NORTH CAROLINA							
Burr	Y	Y	N	N	Y	Y	Y
Hagan	Y	Y	N	N	Y	Y	N
NORTH DAKOTA							
Conrad	Y	Y	N	N	Y	N	N
Dorgan	Y	Y	N	N	Y	Y	N
OHIO							
Voinovich	N	Y	N	N	Y	Y	Y
Brown	Y	Y	N	N	Y	N	N
OKLAHOMA							
Inhofe	N	Y	Y	N	N	Y	Y
Coburn	N	Y	Y	N	N	Y	Y
OREGON							
Wyden	Y	Y	N	N	Y	N	N
Merkley	Y	Y	N	Y	Y	N	N
PENNSYLVANIA							
Specter	Y	+	N	N	N	Y	Y
Casey	Y	Y	N	Y	Y	N	N
RHODE ISLAND							
Reed	Y	Y	N	Y	Y	N	N
Whitehouse	Y	N	N	Y	Y	N	N
SOUTH CAROLINA							
Graham	Y	Y	Y	N	Y	Y	Y
DeMint	N	Y	Y	N	N	Y	Y
SOUTH DAKOTA							
Johnson	Y	Y	N	N	Y	N	N
Thune	Y	Y	Y	N	Y	Y	Y
TENNESSEE							
Alexander	Y	Y	Y	N	N	Y	Y
Corker	Y	Y	Y	N	N	Y	Y
TEXAS							
Hutchison	Y	Y	Y	N	N	Y	Y
Cornyn	Y	Y	Y	N	N	Y	Y
UTAH							
Hatch	Y	Y	Y	N	N	Y	Y
Bennett	Y	Y	Y	N	N	Y	Y
VERMONT							
Leahy	Y	Y	N	Y	Y	N	N
Sanders	Y	N	N	Y	Y	N	N
VIRGINIA							
Webb	Y	Y	N	N	Y	N	N
Warner	Y	Y	N	N	Y	N	N
WASHINGTON							
Murray	Y	Y	N	N	Y	N	N
Cantwell	Y	Y	N	N	Y	N	N
WEST VIRGINIA							
Byrd	Y	Y	N	Y	Y	N	N
Rockefeller	Y	Y	N	Y	Y	Y	N
WISCONSIN							
Kohl	Y	Y	N	Y	Y	N	N
Feingold	Y	Y	N	Y	Y	Y	N
WYOMING							
Enzi	Y	Y	Y	N	N	Y	Y
Barrasso	Y	Y	Y	N	N	Y	Y

KEY   **Republicans**   Democrats   *Independents*

Y Voted for (yea)	X Paired against	C Voted "present" to avoid possible conflict of interest
# Paired for	– Announced against	
+ Announced for	P Voted "present"	? Did not vote or otherwise make a position known
N Voted against (nay)		

IN THE SENATE | By Vote Number

144. S Con Res 13. Fiscal 2010 Budget Resolution/Legislative Transparency.
Cornyn, R-Texas, motion to waive the Budget Act with respect to the Conrad, D-N.D., point of order against the Cornyn amendment for not being germane. The Cornyn amendment would create a 60-vote point of order against final passage of any legislation that has not been made available for public review on a congressional Web site for five days. It would apply to the legislation's text and the Congressional Budget Office score. Motion rejected 46-52: R 41-0; D 5-50; I 0-2. A three-fifths majority (60) of the total Senate is required to waive the Budget Act. (Subsequently, the chair upheld the point of order, and the amendment fell.) April 2, 2009.

145. S Con Res 13. Fiscal 2010 Budget Resolution/Transport of Firearms on Amtrak.
Gregg, R-N.H., motion to waive the Budget Act with respect to the Lautenberg, D-N.J., point of order against the Wicker, R-Miss., amendment for not being germane. The Wicker amendment would stipulate that a provision that would allow a deficit-neutral increase in the discretionary spending cap for transportation could not apply to financial assistance for Amtrak unless passengers are allowed to transport firearms in their checked baggage. Motion agreed to 63-35: R 40-1; D 22-33; I 1-1. A three-fifths majority (60) of the total Senate is required to waive the Budget Act. (Subsequently, the amendment was adopted by voice vote.) April 2, 2009.

146. S Con Res 13. Fiscal 2010 Budget Resolution/Estate Tax.
Lincoln, D-Ark., amendment that would allow a deficit-neutral increase in the discretionary spending cap to pay for the impact of any legislation that would establish an estate tax exemption level of $5 million, indexed for inflation, a maximum estate tax rate of 35 percent, a reunification of the estate and gift credits, and portability of exemption between spouses. Adopted 51-48: R 41-0; D 10-46; I 0-2. April 2, 2009.

147. S Con Res 13. Fiscal 2010 Budget Resolution/Estate Tax.
Durbin, D-Ill., amendment that would create a 60-vote point of order against any legislation that would provide estate tax relief beyond what is already assumed in the budget resolution, unless an equal amount of tax relief is provided to individuals earning less than $100,000 per year and such relief is in addition to the amounts assumed in the budget resolution. Adopted 56-43: R 0-41; D 54-2; I 2-0. April 2, 2009.

148. S Con Res 13. Fiscal 2010 Budget Resolution/Auto Bailouts.
DeMint, R-S.C., amendment that would adjust the resolution for the purpose of blocking the use of funds approved as part of the 2008 mortgage-backed securities buyout to provide further bailouts to auto manufacturers. Rejected 31-66: R 30-11; D 1-53; I 0-2. April 2, 2009.

149. S Con Res 13. Fiscal 2010 Budget Resolution/Earmark Policy.
DeMint, R-S.C., motion to waive the Budget Act with respect to the Conrad, D-N.D., point of order against the DeMint amendment for not being germane. The DeMint amendment would create a 60-vote point of order against any legislation that includes earmarks for private or for-profit entities that are not competitively bid, have not been subject to public hearings or have not been posted on a member's Web site for at least 72 hours. Motion rejected 28-69: R 24-17; D 3-51; I 1-1. A three-fifths majority (60) of the total Senate is required to waive the Budget Act. (Subsequently, the chair upheld the point of order, and the amendment fell.) April 2, 2009.

	144	145	146	147	148	149
ALABAMA						
Shelby	Y	Y	Y	N	Y	N
Sessions	Y	Y	Y	N	Y	Y
ALASKA						
Murkowski	Y	Y	Y	N	Y	N
Begich	N	Y	N	Y	N	N
ARIZONA						
McCain	Y	Y	Y	N	Y	Y
Kyl	Y	Y	Y	N	Y	Y
ARKANSAS						
Lincoln	N	Y	Y	Y	N	N
Pryor	N	N	Y	Y	N	N
CALIFORNIA						
Feinstein	N	N	N	Y	N	N
Boxer	N	N	N	Y	N	N
COLORADO						
Udall	N	Y	N	Y	N	N
Bennet	N	Y	N	Y	N	N
CONNECTICUT						
Dodd	N	N	N	Y	N	N
Lieberman	N	N	N	Y	N	Y
DELAWARE						
Carper	N	N	N	Y	N	N
Kaufman	N	N	N	Y	N	N
FLORIDA						
Nelson	N	N	Y	N	N	N
Martinez	Y	Y	Y	N	N	Y
GEORGIA						
Chambliss	Y	Y	Y	N	Y	Y
Isakson	Y	Y	Y	N	Y	Y
HAWAII						
Inouye	N	N	N	Y	N	N
Akaka	N	N	N	Y	N	N
IDAHO						
Crapo	Y	Y	Y	N	Y	Y
Risch	Y	Y	Y	N	Y	Y
ILLINOIS						
Durbin	N	N	N	Y	N	N
Burris	N	N	N	Y	N	N
INDIANA						
Lugar	Y	Y	Y	Y	N	N
Bayh	Y	Y	Y	Y	N	N
IOWA						
Grassley	Y	Y	Y	N	Y	Y
Harkin	N	N	N	Y	N	N
KANSAS						
Brownback	Y	Y	Y	N	N	N
Roberts	Y	Y	Y	N	Y	N
KENTUCKY						
McConnell	Y	Y	Y	N	Y	N
Bunning	Y	Y	Y	N	Y	Y
LOUISIANA						
Landrieu	Y	Y	Y	N	N	N
Vitter	Y	Y	Y	N	Y	Y
MAINE						
Snowe	Y	Y	Y	N	N	Y
Collins	Y	N	Y	N	Y	N
MARYLAND						
Mikulski	N	N	N	Y	N	N
Cardin	N	N	N	Y	N	N
MASSACHUSETTS						
Kennedy	?	?	N	Y	?	?
Kerry	N	N	N	Y	N	N
MICHIGAN						
Levin	N	N	N	Y	N	N
Stabenow	N	N	N	Y	N	N
MINNESOTA						
Klobuchar	Y	Y	N	Y	N	N
Vacant						
MISSISSIPPI						
Cochran	Y	Y	Y	N	Y	N
Wicker	Y	Y	Y	N	Y	N
MISSOURI						
Bond	Y	Y	Y	N	N	N
McCaskill	N	N	N	Y	N	N
MONTANA						
Baucus	N	Y	Y	Y	N	N
Tester	N	Y	Y	Y	N	N
NEBRASKA						
Nelson	Y	Y	Y	Y	Y	N
Johanns	Y	Y	Y	N	Y	Y
NEVADA						
Reid	N	Y	N	Y	N	N
Ensign	Y	Y	Y	N	Y	Y
NEW HAMPSHIRE						
Gregg	Y	Y	Y	N	Y	N
Shaheen	N	Y	N	Y	N	N
NEW JERSEY						
Lautenberg	N	N	N	Y	N	N
Menendez	N	N	N	Y	N	N
NEW MEXICO						
Bingaman	N	Y	N	Y	N	N
Udall	N	Y	N	Y	N	N
NEW YORK						
Schumer	N	N	N	Y	N	N
Gillibrand	N	N	N	Y	N	N
NORTH CAROLINA						
Burr	Y	Y	Y	N	Y	Y
Hagan	N	Y	N	Y	N	N
NORTH DAKOTA						
Conrad	N	N	N	Y	N	N
Dorgan	N	Y	N	Y	N	N
OHIO						
Voinovich	Y	Y	Y	N	N	N
Brown	N	N	N	Y	N	N
OKLAHOMA						
Inhofe	Y	Y	Y	N	Y	Y
Coburn	Y	Y	Y	N	Y	Y
OREGON						
Wyden	N	N	N	Y	N	N
Merkley	N	N	N	Y	N	N
PENNSYLVANIA						
Specter	Y	Y	Y	N	N	N
Casey	N	Y	N	Y	N	N
RHODE ISLAND						
Reed	N	N	N	Y	N	N
Whitehouse	N	N	N	Y	N	N
SOUTH CAROLINA						
Graham	Y	Y	Y	N	Y	Y
DeMint	Y	Y	Y	N	Y	Y
SOUTH DAKOTA						
Johnson	N	Y	N	Y	N	N
Thune	Y	Y	Y	N	Y	N
TENNESSEE						
Alexander	Y	Y	Y	N	N	N
Corker	Y	Y	Y	N	N	Y
TEXAS						
Hutchison	Y	Y	Y	N	N	N
Cornyn	Y	Y	Y	N	Y	Y
UTAH						
Hatch	Y	Y	Y	N	N	N
Bennett	Y	Y	Y	N	N	N
VERMONT						
Leahy	N	Y	N	Y	N	N
Sanders	N	Y	N	Y	N	N
VIRGINIA						
Webb	N	Y	N	Y	N	N
Warner	N	N	N	Y	N	N
WASHINGTON						
Murray	N	N	N	Y	N	N
Cantwell	N	Y	N	Y	N	N
WEST VIRGINIA						
Byrd	N	N	N	Y	?	?
Rockefeller	N	N	N	Y	N	N
WISCONSIN						
Kohl	N	Y	N	Y	N	N
Feingold	N	Y	N	Y	N	Y
WYOMING						
Enzi	Y	Y	Y	N	Y	Y
Barrasso	Y	Y	Y	N	Y	Y

KEY   **Republicans**   Democrats   *Independents*

Y Voted for (yea)	X Paired against	C Voted "present" to avoid possible conflict of interest
# Paired for	– Announced against	
+ Announced for	P Voted "present"	? Did not vote or otherwise make a position known
N Voted against (nay)		

IN THE SENATE | By Vote Number

150. S Con Res 13. Fiscal 2010 Budget Resolution/Border Fence.
Motion to waive the Budget Act with respect to the Conrad, D-N.D., point of order against the Sessions, R-Ala., amendment. The Sessions amendment would create a 60-vote point of order against any appropriations legislation that fails to fully fund construction of Southwest border fencing. Motion rejected 36-61: R 34-7; D 2-52; I 0-2. A three-fifths majority (60) of the total Senate is required to waive the Budget Act. (Subsequently, the chair upheld the point of order, and the amendment fell.) April 2, 2009.

151. S Con Res 13. Fiscal 2010 Budget Resolution/Consumer
Product Safety. DeMint, R-S.C., amendment that would allow a deficit-neutral increase in the discretionary spending cap to pay for the impact of any legislation that funds certain consumer product safety programs. Rejected 39-58: R 35-6; D 4-50; I 0-2. April 2, 2009.

152. S Con Res 13. Fiscal 2010 Budget Resolution/Health
Providers. Coburn, R-Okla., amendment that would amend a provision allowing a deficit-neutral increase in the resolution's discretionary spending cap for a health care overhaul. The amendment would allow for a prohibition on discrimination or coercion against health providers who object to performing or participating in specific medical procedures or to prescribing certain pharmaceutical drugs on the grounds that such actions violate their moral or religious convictions. Rejected 41-56: R 38-3; D 3-51; I 0-2. April 2, 2009.

153. S Con Res 13. Fiscal 2010 Budget Resolution/Drug Testing.
Vitter, R-La., amendment that would allow the chairman of the Budget Committee to revise allocations in the resolution for legislation that would require states to operate a drug-testing program as part of their Temporary Assistance for Needy Families program, provide for treatment of those who test positive for illegal drug use and withhold program assistance for two years to individuals who test positive for illegal drug use after receiving treatment. Rejected 18-79: R 18-23; D 0-54; I 0-2. April 2, 2009.

154. S Con Res 13. Fiscal 2010 Budget Resolution/Adoption.
Adoption of the concurrent resolution that would set broad spending and revenue targets over the next five years. The resolution would allow up to $1.08 trillion in discretionary spending for fiscal 2010 and increase discretionary spending by $490 billion over five years. It would assume a three-year adjustment to prevent additional taxpayers from paying the alternative minimum tax. It would create numerous exceptions to the discretionary spending limit, including one to allow for health care changes and one for a cap-and-trade program for carbon emissions. It also would assume a deficit of $1.7 trillion in fiscal 2009 and $1.2 trillion in fiscal 2010. Adopted 55-43: R 0-41; D 53-2; I 2-0. April 2, 2009.

	150	151	152	153	154		150	151	152	153	154
ALABAMA						**MONTANA**					
Shelby	Y	Y	Y	N	N	Baucus	N	N	N	N	Y
Sessions	Y	Y	Y	N	N	Tester	N	N	N	N	Y
ALASKA						**NEBRASKA**					
Murkowski	N	Y	Y	N	N	Nelson	Y	Y	Y	N	N
Begich	N	Y	N	N	Y	Johanns	Y	N	Y	N	N
ARIZONA						**NEVADA**					
McCain	Y	N	Y	N	N	Reid	N	N	N	N	Y
Kyl	Y	Y	Y	Y	N	Ensign	Y	Y	Y	Y	N
ARKANSAS						**NEW HAMPSHIRE**					
Lincoln	N	N	N	N	Y	Gregg	Y	N	Y	N	N
Pryor	N	N	Y	N	Y	Shaheen	N	N	N	N	Y
CALIFORNIA						**NEW JERSEY**					
Feinstein	N	N	N	N	Y	Lautenberg	N	N	N	N	Y
Boxer	N	N	N	N	Y	Menendez	N	N	N	N	Y
COLORADO						**NEW MEXICO**					
Udall	N	N	N	N	Y	Bingaman	N	N	N	N	Y
Bennet	N	N	N	N	Y	Udall	N	N	N	N	Y
CONNECTICUT						**NEW YORK**					
Dodd	N	N	N	N	Y	Schumer	N	N	N	N	Y
Lieberman	N	N	N	N	Y	Gillibrand	N	N	N	N	Y
DELAWARE						**NORTH CAROLINA**					
Carper	N	N	N	N	Y	Burr	Y	Y	Y	Y	N
Kaufman	N	N	N	N	Y	Hagan	N	Y	N	N	Y
FLORIDA						**NORTH DAKOTA**					
Nelson	N	N	N	N	Y	Conrad	N	N	N	N	Y
Martinez	N	N	Y	N	N	Dorgan	N	N	N	N	Y
GEORGIA						**OHIO**					
Chambliss	Y	Y	Y	Y	N	Voinovich	N	Y	Y	N	N
Isakson	Y	Y	Y	Y	N	Brown	N	N	N	N	Y
HAWAII						**OKLAHOMA**					
Inouye	N	N	N	N	Y	**Inhofe**	Y	Y	Y	Y	N
Akaka	N	N	N	N	Y	**Coburn**	Y	Y	Y	Y	N
IDAHO						**OREGON**					
Crapo	Y	Y	Y	Y	N	Wyden	N	N	N	N	Y
Risch	Y	Y	Y	Y	N	Merkley	N	N	N	N	Y
ILLINOIS						**PENNSYLVANIA**					
Durbin	N	N	N	N	Y	Specter	N	Y	N	N	N
Burris	N	N	N	N	Y	Casey	N	N	Y	N	Y
INDIANA						**RHODE ISLAND**					
Lugar	N	Y	Y	N	N	Reed	N	N	N	N	Y
Bayh	Y	N	N	N	N	Whitehouse	N	N	N	N	Y
IOWA						**SOUTH CAROLINA**					
Grassley	Y	Y	Y	Y	N	Graham	Y	Y	Y	N	N
Harkin	N	N	N	N	Y	**DeMint**	Y	Y	Y	Y	N
KANSAS						**SOUTH DAKOTA**					
Brownback	Y	Y	Y	Y	N	Johnson	N	N	N	N	Y
Roberts	Y	Y	Y	N	N	**Thune**	Y	Y	Y	N	N
KENTUCKY						**TENNESSEE**					
McConnell	Y	Y	Y	Y	N	**Alexander**	Y	Y	Y	N	N
Bunning	Y	Y	Y	Y	N	**Corker**	Y	Y	Y	N	N
LOUISIANA						**TEXAS**					
Landrieu	N	N	N	N	Y	**Hutchison**	Y	Y	Y	N	N
Vitter	Y	Y	Y	Y	N	**Cornyn**	Y	N	Y	Y	N
MAINE						**UTAH**					
Snowe	N	Y	N	N	N	**Hatch**	Y	Y	Y	N	N
Collins	N	N	N	N	N	**Bennett**	Y	Y	Y	N	N
MARYLAND						**VERMONT**					
Mikulski	N	N	N	N	Y	Leahy	N	N	N	N	Y
Cardin	N	N	N	N	Y	*Sanders*	N	N	N	N	Y
MASSACHUSETTS						**VIRGINIA**					
Kennedy	?	?	?	?	Y	Webb	N	N	N	N	Y
Kerry	N	N	N	N	Y	Warner	N	N	N	N	Y
MICHIGAN						**WASHINGTON**					
Levin	N	N	N	N	Y	Murray	N	N	N	N	Y
Stabenow	N	N	N	N	Y	Cantwell	N	N	N	N	Y
MINNESOTA						**WEST VIRGINIA**					
Klobuchar	N	Y	N	N	Y	Byrd	?	?	?	?	?
Vacant						Rockefeller	N	N	N	N	Y
MISSISSIPPI						**WISCONSIN**					
Cochran	Y	Y	Y	N	N	Kohl	N	N	N	N	Y
Wicker	Y	Y	Y	N	N	Feingold	N	N	N	N	Y
MISSOURI						**WYOMING**					
Bond	Y	Y	Y	N	N	**Enzi**	Y	Y	Y	Y	N
McCaskill	N	N	N	N	Y	**Barrasso**	Y	Y	Y	Y	N

KEY	**Republicans**	Democrats	*Independents*		
Y	Voted for (yea)	X	Paired against	C	Voted "present" to avoid possible conflict of interest
#	Paired for	–	Announced against		
+	Announced for	P	Voted "present"	?	Did not vote or otherwise make a position known
N	Voted against (nay)				

IN THE SENATE | By Vote Number

155. West Nomination/Confirmation. Confirmation of President Obama's nomination of Tony West of California to be assistant attorney general. Confirmed 82-4: R 31-4; D 50-0; I 1-0. A "yea" was a vote in support of the president's position. April 20, 2009.

156. Breuer Nomination/Confirmation. Confirmation of President Obama's nomination of Lanny A. Breuer of the District of Columbia to be assistant attorney general. Confirmed 88-0: R 36-0; D 51-0; I 1-0. A "yea" was a vote in support of the president's position. April 20, 2009.

157. Varney Nomination/Confirmation. Confirmation of President Obama's nomination of Christine Anne Varney of the District of Columbia to be assistant attorney general. Confirmed 87-1: R 35-1; D 51-0; I 1-0. A "yea" was a vote in support of the president's position. April 20, 2009.

158. Hill Nomination/Cloture. Motion to invoke cloture (thus limiting debate) on the nomination of Christopher Hill of Rhode Island to be ambassador to Iraq. Motion agreed to 73-17: R 20-17; D 52-0; I 1-0. Three-fifths of the total Senate (60) is required to invoke cloture. April 20, 2009.

159. Hill Nomination/Confirmation. Confirmation of President Obama's nomination of Christopher Hill of Rhode Island to be ambassador to Iraq. Confirmed 73-23: R 17-23; D 54-0; I 2-0. A "yea" was a vote in support of the president's position. April 21, 2009.

	155	156	157	158	159		155	156	157	158	159
ALABAMA						**MONTANA**					
Shelby	N	Y	Y	N	N	Baucus	Y	Y	Y	Y	Y
Sessions	Y	Y	Y	N	N	Tester	Y	Y	Y	Y	Y
ALASKA						**NEBRASKA**					
Murkowski	Y	Y	Y	Y	Y	Nelson	Y	Y	Y	Y	Y
Begich	+	+	+	+	Y	**Johanns**	Y	Y	Y	Y	Y
ARIZONA						**NEVADA**					
McCain	?	?	?	?	N	Reid	Y	Y	Y	Y	Y
Kyl	?	?	?	?	N	**Ensign**	Y	Y	Y	N	N
ARKANSAS						**NEW HAMPSHIRE**					
Lincoln	Y	Y	Y	Y	Y	**Gregg**	Y	Y	Y	Y	Y
Pryor	Y	Y	Y	Y	Y	Shaheen	Y	Y	Y	Y	Y
CALIFORNIA						**NEW JERSEY**					
Feinstein	Y	Y	Y	Y	Y	Lautenberg	Y	Y	Y	Y	Y
Boxer	Y	Y	Y	Y	Y	Menendez	Y	Y	Y	Y	Y
COLORADO						**NEW MEXICO**					
Udall	Y	Y	Y	Y	Y	Bingaman	Y	Y	Y	Y	Y
Bennet	Y	Y	Y	Y	Y	Udall	Y	Y	Y	Y	Y
CONNECTICUT						**NEW YORK**					
Dodd	+	+	+	Y	Y	Schumer	Y	Y	Y	Y	Y
Lieberman	?	?	?	?	Y	Gillibrand	Y	Y	Y	Y	Y
DELAWARE						**NORTH CAROLINA**					
Carper	Y	Y	Y	Y	Y	**Burr**	Y	Y	Y	N	N
Kaufman	Y	Y	Y	Y	Y	Hagan	Y	Y	Y	Y	Y
FLORIDA						**NORTH DAKOTA**					
Nelson	Y	Y	Y	Y	Y	Conrad	Y	Y	Y	Y	Y
Martinez	Y	Y	Y	Y	Y	Dorgan	Y	Y	Y	Y	Y
GEORGIA						**OHIO**					
Chambliss	N	Y	Y	Y	Y	**Voinovich**	Y	Y	Y	Y	Y
Isakson	N	Y	Y	Y	Y	Brown	Y	Y	Y	Y	Y
HAWAII						**OKLAHOMA**					
Inouye	Y	Y	Y	Y	Y	**Inhofe**	Y	Y	Y	N	N
Akaka	Y	Y	Y	Y	Y	**Coburn**	Y	Y	Y	N	N
IDAHO						**OREGON**					
Crapo	Y	Y	Y	N	N	Wyden	?	?	?	?	Y
Risch	Y	Y	Y	N	N	Merkley	Y	Y	Y	Y	Y
ILLINOIS						**PENNSYLVANIA**					
Durbin	+	Y	Y	Y	Y	**Specter**	Y	Y	Y	Y	Y
Burris	Y	Y	Y	Y	Y	Casey	Y	Y	Y	Y	Y
INDIANA						**RHODE ISLAND**					
Lugar	Y	Y	Y	Y	Y	Reed	Y	Y	Y	Y	Y
Bayh	Y	Y	Y	Y	Y	Whitehouse	Y	Y	Y	Y	Y
IOWA						**SOUTH CAROLINA**					
Grassley	Y	Y	Y	N	N	**Graham**	Y	Y	Y	Y	N
Harkin	Y	Y	Y	Y	Y	**DeMint**	Y	Y	Y	N	N
KANSAS						**SOUTH DAKOTA**					
Brownback	Y	Y	Y	N	N	Johnson	Y	Y	Y	Y	Y
Roberts	?	?	?	?	?	**Thune**	Y	Y	Y	Y	N
KENTUCKY						**TENNESSEE**					
McConnell	Y	Y	Y	N	N	**Alexander**	Y	Y	Y	Y	Y
Bunning	N	Y	N	N	N	**Corker**	Y	Y	Y	Y	Y
LOUISIANA						**TEXAS**					
Landrieu	Y	Y	Y	Y	Y	**Hutchison**	Y	Y	Y	Y	Y
Vitter	Y	Y	Y	N	N	**Cornyn**	Y	Y	Y	N	N
MAINE						**UTAH**					
Snowe	Y	Y	Y	Y	Y	**Hatch**	Y	Y	Y	Y	N
Collins	Y	Y	Y	Y	Y	**Bennett**	?	?	?	?	N
MARYLAND						**VERMONT**					
Mikulski	Y	Y	Y	Y	Y	Leahy	Y	Y	Y	Y	Y
Cardin	Y	Y	Y	Y	Y	*Sanders*	Y	Y	Y	Y	Y
MASSACHUSETTS						**VIRGINIA**					
Kennedy	?	?	?	?	?	Webb	Y	Y	Y	Y	Y
Kerry	Y	Y	Y	Y	Y	Warner	Y	Y	Y	Y	Y
MICHIGAN						**WASHINGTON**					
Levin	Y	Y	Y	Y	Y	Murray	Y	Y	Y	Y	Y
Stabenow	Y	Y	Y	Y	Y	Cantwell	Y	Y	Y	Y	Y
MINNESOTA						**WEST VIRGINIA**					
Klobuchar	Y	Y	Y	Y	Y	Byrd	Y	Y	Y	Y	Y
Vacant						Rockefeller	?	?	?	?	?
MISSISSIPPI						**WISCONSIN**					
Cochran	?	?	?	Y	Y	Kohl	Y	Y	Y	Y	Y
Wicker	?	Y	Y	N	N	Feingold	Y	Y	Y	Y	Y
MISSOURI						**WYOMING**					
Bond	Y	Y	Y	N	N	**Enzi**	Y	Y	Y	Y	Y
McCaskill	Y	Y	Y	Y	Y	**Barrasso**	Y	Y	Y	Y	Y

KEY	**Republicans**	Democrats	*Independents*	
Y Voted for (yea)		**X** Paired against	**C** Voted "present" to avoid possible conflict of interest
# Paired for		**–** Announced against	
+ Announced for		**P** Voted "present"	**?** Did not vote or otherwise make a position known
N Voted against (nay)			

IN THE SENATE | By Vote Number

160. **S 386. Financial Fraud/Obligation Definition.** Kyl, R-Ariz., amendment that would clarify the term "obligation" in the bill by removing contingent duties from the definition and by making other technical changes. Adopted 94-1: R 40-0; D 53-0; I 1-1. April 22, 2009.

161. **S 386. Financial Fraud/Economy Commission.** Isakson, R-Ga., amendment that would establish a new 10-member bipartisan commission to investigate factors that may have led to the current economic situation. It would authorize $5 million for the commission, which would be required to issue its findings and recommendations by Dec. 15, 2010. Adopted 92-4: R 36-4; D 54-0; I 2-0. April 22, 2009.

162. **S 386. Financial Fraud/Whistleblower Reward Cap.** Kyl, R-Ariz., amendment that would cap the amount whistleblowers can collect at $50 million per case or 300 percent of the expenses, fees and costs incurred by private citizens as a result of fraud committed by government contractors, whichever is greater. Rejected 31-61: R 30-9; D 1-51; I 0-1. April 23, 2009.

163. **S Con Res 13. Fiscal 2010 Budget Resolution/Motion to Instruct.** Stabenow, D-Mich., motion to instruct conferees to insist that the conference report include a reserve fund for future legislation that would create new jobs in "clean technology," diversify the domestic clean-energy supply, provide incentives for cost savings through energy efficiencies, and provide voluntary opportunities for agriculture and forestry communities to contribute to reducing greenhouse gas levels. Motion agreed to 57-37: R 3-36; D 52-1; I 2-0. April 23, 2009.

164. **S Con Res 13. Fiscal 2010 Budget Resolution/Motion to Instruct.** Johanns, R-Neb., motion to instruct conferees to insist that, if a deficit-neutral reserve fund for clean energy and environmental preservation remains in the resolution, it includes language that prohibits the use of reconciliation for any climate change legislation. Motion agreed to 66-28: R 39-0; D 27-26; I 0-2. April 23, 2009.

	160	161	162	163	164
ALABAMA					
Shelby	Y	Y	Y	N	Y
Sessions	Y	Y	Y	N	Y
ALASKA					
Murkowski	Y	Y	Y	N	Y
Begich	Y	Y	N	Y	Y
ARIZONA					
McCain	Y	N	Y	N	Y
Kyl	Y	N	Y	N	Y
ARKANSAS					
Lincoln	Y	Y	N	Y	Y
Pryor	Y	Y	N	Y	Y
CALIFORNIA					
Feinstein	Y	Y	N	Y	N
Boxer	Y	Y	N	Y	N
COLORADO					
Udall	Y	Y	N	N	Y
Bennet	Y	Y	N	Y	Y
CONNECTICUT					
Dodd	Y	Y	N	Y	N
Lieberman	Y	Y	?	Y	N
DELAWARE					
Carper	Y	Y	N	Y	Y
Kaufman	Y	Y	N	Y	N
FLORIDA					
Nelson	Y	Y	N	Y	N
Martinez	Y	Y	N	N	Y
GEORGIA					
Chambliss	Y	Y	Y	N	Y
Isakson	Y	Y	Y	N	Y
HAWAII					
Inouye	Y	Y	N	Y	N
Akaka	Y	Y	N	Y	N
IDAHO					
Crapo	Y	Y	N	N	Y
Risch	Y	Y	N	N	Y
ILLINOIS					
Durbin	Y	Y	–	Y	N
Burris	Y	Y	N	Y	Y
INDIANA					
Lugar	Y	Y	Y	Y	Y
Bayh	Y	Y	N	Y	Y
IOWA					
Grassley	Y	N	N	N	Y
Harkin	Y	Y	N	Y	N
KANSAS					
Brownback	Y	Y	Y	N	Y
Roberts	?	?	?	?	?
KENTUCKY					
McConnell	Y	Y	Y	N	Y
Bunning	Y	N	Y	N	Y
LOUISIANA					
Landrieu	Y	Y	N	N	Y
Vitter	Y	Y	Y	N	Y
MAINE					
Snowe	Y	Y	N	Y	Y
Collins	Y	Y	N	Y	Y
MARYLAND					
Mikulski	Y	Y	N	Y	N
Cardin	Y	Y	N	Y	N
MASSACHUSETTS					
Kennedy	?	?	?	?	?
Kerry	?	Y	N	Y	N
MICHIGAN					
Levin	Y	Y	N	Y	Y
Stabenow	Y	Y	N	Y	Y
MINNESOTA					
Klobuchar	Y	Y	N	Y	Y
Vacant					
MISSISSIPPI					
Cochran	Y	Y	Y	N	Y
Wicker	Y	Y	Y	N	Y
MISSOURI					
Bond	Y	Y	Y	N	Y
McCaskill	Y	Y	N	Y	Y

	160	161	162	163	164
MONTANA					
Baucus	Y	Y	N	Y	Y
Tester	Y	Y	N	Y	Y
NEBRASKA					
Nelson	Y	Y	N	Y	Y
Johanns	Y	Y	N	N	Y
NEVADA					
Reid	Y	Y	N	Y	N
Ensign	Y	Y	Y	N	Y
NEW HAMPSHIRE					
Gregg	Y	Y	Y	N	Y
Shaheen	Y	Y	N	Y	N
NEW JERSEY					
Lautenberg	Y	Y	?	Y	N
Menendez	Y	Y	N	Y	N
NEW MEXICO					
Bingaman	Y	Y	Y	Y	Y
Udall	Y	Y	N	Y	N
NEW YORK					
Schumer	Y	Y	N	Y	N
Gillibrand	Y	Y	N	Y	N
NORTH CAROLINA					
Burr	Y	Y	Y	N	Y
Hagan	Y	Y	N	Y	Y
NORTH DAKOTA					
Conrad	Y	Y	N	Y	Y
Dorgan	Y	Y	N	Y	Y
OHIO					
Voinovich	Y	Y	N	?	?
Brown	Y	Y	N	Y	N
OKLAHOMA					
Inhofe	Y	Y	Y	N	Y
Coburn	Y	Y	Y	N	Y
OREGON					
Wyden	Y	Y	N	Y	N
Merkley	Y	Y	N	Y	N
PENNSYLVANIA					
Specter	Y	Y	Y	N	Y
Casey	Y	Y	N	Y	Y
RHODE ISLAND					
Reed	Y	Y	N	Y	N
Whitehouse	Y	Y	N	?	?
SOUTH CAROLINA					
Graham	Y	Y	N	N	Y
DeMint	Y	Y	Y	N	Y
SOUTH DAKOTA					
Johnson	Y	Y	N	Y	N
Thune	Y	Y	Y	N	Y
TENNESSEE					
Alexander	Y	Y	+	N	Y
Corker	Y	Y	Y	N	Y
TEXAS					
Hutchison	Y	Y	N	Y	Y
Cornyn	Y	Y	Y	N	Y
UTAH					
Hatch	Y	Y	Y	N	Y
Bennett	Y	Y	Y	N	Y
VERMONT					
Leahy	Y	Y	N	Y	N
Sanders	N	Y	N	Y	N
VIRGINIA					
Webb	Y	Y	N	Y	Y
Warner	Y	Y	N	Y	Y
WASHINGTON					
Murray	Y	Y	N	Y	Y
Cantwell	Y	Y	N	Y	Y
WEST VIRGINIA					
Byrd	Y	Y	N	Y	Y
Rockefeller	?	?	?	?	?
WISCONSIN					
Kohl	Y	Y	N	Y	Y
Feingold	Y	Y	N	Y	Y
WYOMING					
Enzi	Y	Y	Y	N	Y
Barrasso	Y	Y	Y	N	Y

KEY	**Republicans**	Democrats	*Independents*	
Y Voted for (yea)		X Paired against		C Voted "present" to avoid possible conflict of interest
# Paired for		– Announced against		
+ Announced for		P Voted "present"		? Did not vote or otherwise make a position known
N Voted against (nay)				

IN THE SENATE | By Vote Number

165. S Con Res 13. Fiscal 2010 Budget Resolution/Motion to Instruct.
Gregg, R-N.H., motion to instruct conferees to insist that the conference report limit the increase in the public debt for the period of 2009 through 2019 to an amount no greater than the amount of public debt accumulated from 1789 to Jan. 20, 2009. Motion rejected 40-54: R 39-0; D 1-52; I 0-2. April 23, 2009.

166. S Con Res 13. Fiscal 2010 Budget Resolution/Motion to Instruct.
Sessions, R-Ala., motion to instruct conferees to insist on provisions that would adjust the budget resolution to allow non-defense discretionary spending to be set at fiscal 2009 levels for fiscal 2010-11 and allow it to increase by 1 percent annually for fiscal 2012-14. Motion rejected 38-56: R 37-2; D 1-52; I 0-2. April 23, 2009.

167. S Con Res 13. Fiscal 2010 Budget Resolution/Motion to Instruct.
Cornyn, R-Texas, motion to instruct conferees to insist that the conference report include a 60-vote point of order against any legislation that assumes an increase in income tax rates on small businesses. Motion agreed to 84-9: R 38-1; D 44-8; I 2-0. April 23, 2009.

168. S Con Res 13. Fiscal 2010 Budget Resolution/Motion to Instruct.
DeMint, R-S.C., motion to instruct conferees to insist that the conference report include a 60-vote point of order against legislation that would interfere with taxpayers' ability to keep their health care plans or choose their doctors, or that would decrease the number of individuals enrolled in private health insurance while increasing the number enrolled in government-run insurance plans. Motion agreed to 79-14: R 39-0; D 39-13; I 1-1. April 23, 2009.

169. S Con Res 13. Fiscal 2010 Budget Resolution/Motion to Instruct.
Vitter, R-La., motion to instruct conferees to insist that if a reserve fund related to energy and environment remains in the resolution, it include a requirement that future legislation not increase the cost of domestic energy production, not increase energy costs for domestic industries or families, and not enhance foreign competitiveness against U.S. businesses. Motion agreed to 63-30: R 39-0; D 24-29; I 0-1. April 23, 2009.

	165	166	167	168	169
ALABAMA					
Shelby	Y	Y	Y	Y	Y
Sessions	Y	Y	Y	Y	Y
ALASKA					
Murkowski	Y	?	?	?	?
Begich	N	N	Y	Y	Y
ARIZONA					
McCain	Y	Y	Y	Y	Y
Kyl	Y	Y	Y	Y	Y
ARKANSAS					
Lincoln	N	N	Y	Y	Y
Pryor	N	N	Y	Y	Y
CALIFORNIA					
Feinstein	N	N	Y	Y	N
Boxer	N	N	Y	Y	N
COLORADO					
Udall	N	N	Y	Y	Y
Bennet	N	N	Y	Y	Y
CONNECTICUT					
Dodd	N	N	Y	Y	N
Lieberman	N	N	Y	Y	N
DELAWARE					
Carper	N	N	Y	Y	Y
Kaufman	N	N	Y	Y	N
FLORIDA					
Nelson	N	N	Y	Y	Y
Martinez	Y	Y	Y	Y	Y
GEORGIA					
Chambliss	Y	Y	Y	Y	Y
Isakson	Y	Y	Y	Y	Y
HAWAII					
Inouye	N	N	Y	Y	N
Akaka	N	N	Y	Y	N
IDAHO					
Crapo	Y	Y	Y	Y	Y
Risch	Y	Y	Y	Y	Y
ILLINOIS					
Durbin	N	N	N	N	N
Burris	N	N	Y	N	N
INDIANA					
Lugar	Y	Y	Y	Y	Y
Bayh	N	Y	Y	Y	Y
IOWA					
Grassley	Y	Y	Y	Y	Y
Harkin	N	N	N	N	N
KANSAS					
Brownback	Y	Y	Y	Y	Y
Roberts	?	?	?	?	?
KENTUCKY					
McConnell	Y	Y	Y	Y	Y
Bunning	Y	Y	Y	Y	Y
LOUISIANA					
Landrieu	N	N	?	?	Y
Vitter	Y	Y	Y	Y	Y
MAINE					
Snowe	Y	Y	Y	Y	Y
Collins	Y	N	Y	Y	Y
MARYLAND					
Mikulski	N	N	Y	N	N
Cardin	N	N	Y	N	N
MASSACHUSETTS					
Kennedy	?	?	?	?	?
Kerry	N	N	N	N	N
MICHIGAN					
Levin	N	N	Y	N	N
Stabenow	N	N	Y	N	Y
MINNESOTA					
Klobuchar	N	N	Y	Y	Y
Vacant					
MISSISSIPPI					
Cochran	Y	Y	Y	Y	Y
Wicker	Y	Y	Y	Y	Y
MISSOURI					
Bond	Y	Y	Y	Y	Y
McCaskill	N	N	Y	N	Y
MONTANA					
Baucus	N	N	Y	Y	Y
Tester	N	N	Y	Y	N
NEBRASKA					
Nelson	Y	N	Y	Y	Y
Johanns	Y	Y	Y	Y	Y
NEVADA					
Reid	N	N	Y	Y	Y
Ensign	Y	Y	Y	Y	Y
NEW HAMPSHIRE					
Gregg	Y	Y	Y	Y	Y
Shaheen	N	N	Y	Y	N
NEW JERSEY					
Lautenberg	N	N	Y	Y	N
Menendez	N	N	Y	Y	N
NEW MEXICO					
Bingaman	N	N	N	N	N
Udall	N	N	Y	N	N
NEW YORK					
Schumer	N	N	Y	Y	N
Gillibrand	N	N	Y	Y	N
NORTH CAROLINA					
Burr	Y	Y	Y	Y	Y
Hagan	N	N	Y	Y	Y
NORTH DAKOTA					
Conrad	N	N	Y	Y	Y
Dorgan	N	N	Y	Y	Y
OHIO					
Voinovich	?	N	N	Y	Y
Brown	N	N	N	N	N
OKLAHOMA					
Inhofe	Y	Y	Y	Y	Y
Coburn	Y	Y	Y	Y	Y
OREGON					
Wyden	N	N	Y	Y	N
Merkley	N	N	Y	N	N
PENNSYLVANIA					
Specter	Y	Y	Y	Y	Y
Casey	N	N	Y	Y	N
RHODE ISLAND					
Reed	N	N	Y	Y	N
Whitehouse	?	?	?	?	?
SOUTH CAROLINA					
Graham	Y	Y	Y	Y	Y
DeMint	Y	Y	Y	Y	Y
SOUTH DAKOTA					
Johnson	N	N	Y	Y	Y
Thune	Y	Y	Y	Y	Y
TENNESSEE					
Alexander	Y	Y	Y	Y	Y
Corker	Y	Y	Y	Y	Y
TEXAS					
Hutchison	Y	Y	Y	Y	Y
Cornyn	Y	Y	Y	Y	Y
UTAH					
Hatch	Y	Y	Y	Y	Y
Bennett	Y	Y	Y	Y	Y
VERMONT					
Leahy	N	N	Y	Y	N
Sanders	N	N	Y	N	?
VIRGINIA					
Webb	N	N	Y	Y	Y
Warner	N	N	N	N	N
WASHINGTON					
Murray	N	N	Y	Y	N
Cantwell	N	N	Y	Y	N
WEST VIRGINIA					
Byrd	N	N	N	Y	Y
Rockefeller	?	?	?	?	?
WISCONSIN					
Kohl	N	N	Y	Y	N
Feingold	N	N	N	Y	Y
WYOMING					
Enzi	Y	Y	Y	Y	Y
Barrasso	Y	Y	Y	Y	Y

KEY   **Republicans**   Democrats   *Independents*

Y Voted for (yea)	X Paired against	C Voted "present" to avoid possible conflict of interest
# Paired for	– Announced against	
+ Announced for	P Voted "present"	? Did not vote or otherwise make a position known
N Voted against (nay)		

IN THE SENATE | By Vote Number

170. **S 386. Financial Fraud/Cloture.** Motion to invoke cloture (thus limiting debate) on the Leahy, D-Vt., substitute that would expand federal fraud laws to cover funds paid under the economic stimulus package and the 2008 Troubled Assets Relief Program, as well as mortgage lenders not directly regulated or insured by the federal government. Motion agreed to 84-4: R 28-4; D 54-0; I 2-0. Three-fifths of the total Senate (60) is required to invoke cloture. (Subsequently, the substitute was adopted by voice vote.) April 27, 2009.

171. **S 386. Financial Fraud/Passage.** Passage of the bill that would expand federal fraud laws to cover funds paid under the economic stimulus package and the 2008 Troubled Assets Relief Program, as well as to mortgage lenders not directly regulated or insured by the federal government. It would authorize an additional $165 million per year for the Justice Department in fiscal 2010 and 2011, the hiring of more federal prosecutors and FBI agents, and additional funds in fiscal 2010 and 2011 for the Secret Service, the U.S. Postal Inspection Service and the Department of Housing and Urban Development. Passed 92-4: R 36-4; D 54-0; I 2-0. A "yea" was a vote in support of the president's position. April 28, 2009.

172. **Sebelius Nomination/Confirmation.** Confirmation of President Obama's nomination of Kathleen Sebelius of Kansas to be secretary of Health and Human Services. Confirmed 65-31: R 9-31; D 54-0; I 2-0. (By unanimous consent, the Senate agreed to raise the majority requirement for confirmation to 60 votes.) A "yea" was a vote in support of the president's position. April 28, 2009.

173. **S Con Res 13. Fiscal 2010 Budget Resolution/Conference Report.** Adoption of the conference report on the concurrent resolution that would allow up to $1.086 trillion in non-emergency discretionary spending for fiscal 2010, plus $130 billion in fiscal 2010 for operations in Iraq and Afghanistan. It would assume $764 billion in tax cuts over five years, including an extension of the 2001 and 2003 tax cuts for households earning less than $250,000 annually, a three-year adjustment to prevent additional taxpayers from paying the alternative minimum tax and a permanent extension of the 2009 estate tax levels. It includes reconciliation instructions to House and Senate committees to report a total of $2 billion in savings, presumably from health care and student loan programs, by Oct. 15. It would create a deficit-neutral reserve fund for health care and climate change legislation. Adopted, thus cleared, 53-43: R 0-40; D 51-3; I 2-0. April 29, 2009.

174. **S 896. Housing Loans Modification/'Cramdown' Provision.** Durbin, D-Ill., amendment that would allow bankruptcy judges to write down the principal and interest rates of certain mortgages on primary homes if the homeowner and creditor have not been able to reach agreement on a reasonable modification of the loan. The amendment would apply only to borrowers who are at least 60 days delinquent on payments for loans originated before Jan. 1, 2009, and would set the maximum value of loans that qualify at $729,000. Rejected 45-51: R 0-39; D 43-12; I 2-0. (By unanimous consent, the Senate agreed to raise the majority requirement for adoption of the amendment to 60 votes.) April 30, 2009.

175. **Strickland Nomination/Confirmation.** Confirmation of President Obama's nomination of Thomas L. Strickland of Colorado to be assistant secretary of the Interior for fish and wildlife. Confirmed 89-2: R 32-2; D 55-0; I 2-0. (By unanimous consent, the Senate agreed to raise the majority requirement for confirmation to 60 votes.) A "yea" was a vote in support of the president's position. April 30, 2009.

	170	171	172	173	174	175
ALABAMA						
Shelby	Y	Y	N	N	N	Y
Sessions	Y	?	?	–	?	?
ALASKA						
Murkowski	Y	Y	N	N	N	Y
Begich	Y	Y	Y	Y	Y	Y
ARIZONA						
McCain	Y	Y	N	N	N	Y
Kyl	N	N	N	N	N	Y
ARKANSAS						
Lincoln	Y	Y	Y	N	Y	N
Pryor	Y	Y	Y	Y	N	Y
CALIFORNIA						
Feinstein	Y	Y	Y	Y	Y	Y
Boxer	Y	Y	Y	Y	Y	Y
COLORADO						
Udall	Y	Y	Y	Y	Y	Y
Bennet	Y	Y	Y	N	Y	Y
CONNECTICUT						
Dodd	Y	Y	Y	Y	Y	Y
Lieberman	Y	Y	Y	Y	Y	Y
DELAWARE						
Carper	Y	Y	Y	Y	N	Y
Kaufman	Y	Y	Y	Y	Y	Y
FLORIDA						
Nelson	Y	Y	Y	Y	Y	Y
Martinez	?	Y	N	N	N	Y
GEORGIA						
Chambliss	Y	Y	N	N	N	Y
Isakson	Y	Y	N	N	N	Y
HAWAII						
Inouye	Y	Y	Y	Y	Y	Y
Akaka	Y	Y	Y	Y	Y	Y
IDAHO						
Crapo	Y	Y	N	N	N	Y
Risch	Y	Y	N	N	N	Y
ILLINOIS						
Durbin	Y	Y	Y	Y	Y	Y
Burris	Y	Y	Y	Y	Y	Y
INDIANA						
Lugar	Y	Y	Y	N	N	Y
Bayh	Y	Y	Y	N	Y	Y
IOWA						
Grassley	Y	Y	N	N	N	Y
Harkin	Y	Y	Y	Y	Y	Y
KANSAS						
Brownback	?	Y	Y	N	N	Y
Roberts	?	Y	Y	N	N	Y
KENTUCKY						
McConnell	Y	Y	N	N	N	Y
Bunning	+	Y	N	N	N	N
LOUISIANA						
Landrieu	?	Y	Y	Y	N	Y
Vitter	?	Y	N	N	N	Y
MAINE						
Snowe	Y	Y	Y	N	N	Y
Collins	Y	Y	Y	N	N	Y
MARYLAND						
Mikulski	Y	Y	Y	Y	Y	Y
Cardin	Y	Y	Y	Y	Y	Y
MASSACHUSETTS						
Kennedy	Y	?	+	?	?	?
Kerry	Y	Y	Y	Y	Y	Y
MICHIGAN						
Levin	Y	Y	Y	Y	Y	Y
Stabenow	Y	Y	Y	Y	Y	Y
MINNESOTA						
Klobuchar	Y	Y	Y	Y	Y	Y
Vacant						
MISSISSIPPI						
Cochran	Y	Y	N	N	N	Y
Wicker	Y	Y	N	N	N	N
MISSOURI						
Bond	Y	Y	Y	N	N	Y
McCaskill	Y	Y	Y	Y	Y	Y

	170	171	172	173	174	175
MONTANA						
Baucus	Y	Y	Y	Y	N	Y
Tester	Y	Y	Y	Y	N	Y
NEBRASKA						
Nelson	Y	Y	Y	N	N	Y
Johanns	Y	Y	N	N	N	Y
NEVADA						
Reid	Y	Y	Y	Y	Y	Y
Ensign	?	Y	N	N	N	?
NEW HAMPSHIRE						
Gregg	Y	Y	Y	N	N	Y
Shaheen	Y	Y	Y	Y	Y	Y
NEW JERSEY						
Lautenberg	Y	Y	Y	Y	Y	Y
Menendez	Y	Y	Y	Y	Y	Y
NEW MEXICO						
Bingaman	Y	Y	Y	Y	Y	Y
Udall	Y	Y	Y	Y	Y	Y
NEW YORK						
Schumer	Y	Y	Y	Y	Y	Y
Gillibrand	Y	Y	Y	Y	Y	Y
NORTH CAROLINA						
Burr	?	Y	N	N	N	Y
Hagan	Y	Y	Y	Y	Y	Y
NORTH DAKOTA						
Conrad	Y	Y	Y	Y	N	Y
Dorgan	Y	Y	Y	Y	N	Y
OHIO						
Voinovich	?	Y	Y	N	N	Y
Brown	Y	Y	Y	Y	Y	Y
OKLAHOMA						
Inhofe	N	N	N	N	N	Y
Coburn	N	N	N	N	N	?
OREGON						
Wyden	Y	Y	Y	Y	Y	Y
Merkley	Y	Y	Y	Y	Y	Y
PENNSYLVANIA						
Specter*	Y	Y	Y	Y	Y	Y
Casey	Y	Y	Y	Y	Y	Y
RHODE ISLAND						
Reed	Y	Y	Y	Y	Y	Y
Whitehouse	Y	Y	Y	Y	Y	Y
SOUTH CAROLINA						
Graham	Y	Y	N	N	N	?
DeMint	N	N	N	N	N	Y
SOUTH DAKOTA						
Johnson	Y	Y	Y	Y	N	Y
Thune	Y	Y	N	N	N	Y
TENNESSEE						
Alexander	Y	Y	N	N	N	Y
Corker	Y	Y	N	N	N	Y
TEXAS						
Hutchison	Y	Y	N	N	N	Y
Cornyn	+	Y	N	N	N	Y
UTAH						
Hatch	Y	Y	N	N	N	Y
Bennett	Y	Y	N	N	N	?
VERMONT						
Leahy	Y	Y	Y	Y	Y	Y
Sanders	Y	Y	Y	Y	Y	Y
VIRGINIA						
Webb	Y	Y	Y	Y	Y	Y
Warner	Y	Y	Y	Y	Y	Y
WASHINGTON						
Murray	Y	Y	Y	Y	Y	Y
Cantwell	Y	Y	Y	Y	Y	Y
WEST VIRGINIA						
Byrd	Y	Y	Y	N	N	Y
Rockefeller	?	+	+	?	?	?
WISCONSIN						
Kohl	Y	Y	Y	Y	Y	Y
Feingold	Y	Y	Y	Y	Y	Y
WYOMING						
Enzi	Y	Y	N	N	N	Y
Barrasso	Y	Y	N	N	N	Y

KEY	**Republicans**	Democrats	*Independents*		
Y	Voted for (yea)		X	Paired against	C Voted "present" to avoid possible conflict of interest
#	Paired for		–	Announced against	
+	Announced for		P	Voted "present"	? Did not vote or otherwise make a position known
N	Voted against (nay)				

*Pennsylvania Sen. Arlen Specter switched party affiliation from Republican to Democrat, effective April 30, 2009. The first vote he cast as a Democrat was vote 174.

IN THE SENATE | By Vote Number

176. S 896. Housing Loans Modification/Mortgage Relief Funds.
Vitter, R-La., amendment to the Dodd, D-Conn., substitute amendment. The Vitter amendment would allow for the repayment of funds approved as part of the 2008 Troubled Asset Relief Program, if the recipient meets capitalization requirements to continue operating. The recipient would not be required to repurchase warrants from the government as a condition of the repayment. The substitute would increase the Federal Deposit Insurance Corporation's borrowing authority to $100 billion, with the option of further increasing it to $500 billion. It would also extend an increase in FDIC deposit insurance to Dec. 31, 2013. Rejected 39-53: R 33-4; D 6-47; I 0-2. May 4, 2009.

177. S 896. Housing Loans Modification/FHA Solvency.
Vitter, R-La., amendment to the Dodd, D-Conn., substitute amendment. The Vitter amendment would establish that the primary responsibility of Federal Housing Administration (FHA) is to maintain its solvency. It would require the FHA commissioner to temporarily suspend any program determined to threaten FHA solvency, and recommend legislation to address such issues. Rejected 36-56: R 36-1; D 0-53; I 0-2. May 4, 2009.

178. S 896. Housing Loans Modification/Safe Harbor.
Corker, R-Tenn., amendment to the Dodd, D-Conn., substitute amendment. The Corker amendment would require lenders participating in mortgage modification programs to consider all other mitigation efforts, including foreclosure and refinancing, before qualifying for protection from investor lawsuits. Rejected 31-63: R 31-8; D 0-53; I 0-2. May 5, 2009.

179. S 896. Housing Loans Modification/TARP Funds.
Thune, R-S.D., amendment to the Dodd, D-Conn., substitute. The Thune amendment would prohibit the Treasury Department from redeploying funds returned by financial institutions under the Troubled Asset Relief Program. Rejected 47-48: R 39-1; D 8-45; I 0-2. May 5, 2009.

180. S 896. Housing Loans Modification/Conflict-of-Interest Rules.
Ensign, R-Nev., amendment to the Boxer, D-Calif., amendment to the Dodd, D-Conn., substitute. The Ensign amendment would make minor and technical changes to the Boxer amendment. The Boxer amendment would outline conflict-of-interest rules for managers of the Treasury Department's public-private "legacy asset" purchasing program. It would direct $15 million from the Troubled Asset Relief Program for the program's special inspector general to audit the Treasury's purchasing program, among others. Adopted 96-0: R 40-0; D 54-0; I 2-0. (Subsequently, the Boxer amendment, as amended, was adopted by unanimous consent.) May 5, 2009.

181. S 896. Housing Loans Modification/TARP Funds and Common Stock.
DeMint, R-S.C., amendment to the Dodd, D-Conn., substitute. The DeMint amendment would prevent the Treasury Department from using funds from the Troubled Asset Relief Program to acquire common stock in financial institutions receiving Treasury Department assistance or to convert preferred stock or future capital purchases into common stock. Rejected 36-59: R 36-4; D 0-53; I 0-2. May 5, 2009.

	176	177	178	179	180	181
ALABAMA						
Shelby	Y	Y	Y	Y	Y	Y
Sessions	Y	Y	Y	Y	Y	Y
ALASKA						
Murkowski	Y	Y	Y	Y	Y	Y
Begich	N	N	N	N	Y	N
ARIZONA						
McCain	?	?	?	Y	Y	Y
Kyl	Y	Y	Y	Y	Y	Y
ARKANSAS						
Lincoln	Y	N	N	Y	Y	N
Pryor	N	N	N	Y	Y	N
CALIFORNIA						
Feinstein	N	N	N	Y	Y	N
Boxer	N	N	N	N	Y	N
COLORADO						
Udall	N	N	N	Y	Y	N
Bennet	N	N	N	Y	Y	N
CONNECTICUT						
Dodd	N	N	N	Y	Y	N
Lieberman	N	N	N	Y	Y	N
DELAWARE						
Carper	N	N	N	Y	Y	N
Kaufman	N	N	N	N	Y	N
FLORIDA						
Nelson	N	N	N	N	Y	N
Martinez	?	?	N	Y	Y	N
GEORGIA						
Chambliss	Y	Y	N	Y	Y	Y
Isakson	Y	Y	N	Y	Y	Y
HAWAII						
Inouye	N	N	N	N	Y	N
Akaka	N	N	N	N	Y	N
IDAHO						
Crapo	Y	Y	Y	Y	Y	Y
Risch	Y	Y	Y	Y	Y	Y
ILLINOIS						
Durbin	N	N	N	N	Y	N
Burris	N	N	N	N	Y	N
INDIANA						
Lugar	N	Y	N	N	Y	Y
Bayh	Y	N	N	N	Y	?
IOWA						
Grassley	Y	Y	Y	Y	Y	Y
Harkin	N	N	N	N	Y	N
KANSAS						
Brownback	Y	Y	Y	Y	Y	Y
Roberts	Y	Y	Y	Y	Y	Y
KENTUCKY						
McConnell	Y	Y	Y	Y	Y	Y
Bunning	Y	Y	Y	Y	Y	Y
LOUISIANA						
Landrieu	N	N	N	N	Y	N
Vitter	Y	Y	Y	Y	Y	Y
MAINE						
Snowe	Y	Y	N	Y	Y	N
Collins	Y	Y	N	Y	Y	N
MARYLAND						
Mikulski	N	N	N	Y	Y	N
Cardin	N	N	N	Y	Y	N
MASSACHUSETTS						
Kennedy	?	?	?	?	?	?
Kerry	N	N	N	N	Y	N
MICHIGAN						
Levin	N	N	N	Y	Y	N
Stabenow	N	N	N	Y	Y	N
MINNESOTA						
Klobuchar	N	N	N	Y	Y	N
Vacant						
MISSISSIPPI						
Cochran	Y	Y	Y	Y	Y	Y
Wicker	Y	Y	Y	Y	Y	Y
MISSOURI						
Bond	Y	Y	Y	Y	Y	Y
McCaskill	N	N	N	N	Y	N
MONTANA						
Baucus	N	N	N	?	Y	N
Tester	N	N	N	Y	Y	N
NEBRASKA						
Nelson	Y	N	N	Y	Y	N
Johanns	Y	Y	Y	Y	Y	Y
NEVADA						
Reid	N	N	N	N	Y	N
Ensign	Y	Y	N	Y	Y	Y
NEW HAMPSHIRE						
Gregg	N	Y	Y	Y	Y	Y
Shaheen	?	?	?	N	Y	N
NEW JERSEY						
Lautenberg	N	N	N	Y	Y	N
Menendez	N	N	N	N	Y	N
NEW MEXICO						
Bingaman	N	N	N	Y	Y	N
Udall	N	N	N	Y	Y	N
NEW YORK						
Schumer	N	N	N	Y	Y	N
Gillibrand	N	N	N	N	Y	N
NORTH CAROLINA						
Burr	Y	Y	Y	N	Y	Y
Hagan	N	N	N	N	Y	N
NORTH DAKOTA						
Conrad	N	N	N	Y	Y	N
Dorgan	Y	N	N	Y	Y	N
OHIO						
Voinovich	Y	N	N	Y	Y	Y
Brown	N	N	N	N	Y	N
OKLAHOMA						
Inhofe	Y	Y	Y	Y	Y	Y
Coburn	?	?	Y	Y	Y	Y
OREGON						
Wyden	N	N	N	Y	Y	N
Merkley	N	N	N	N	Y	N
PENNSYLVANIA						
Specter	N	N	N	Y	Y	N
Casey	N	N	N	N	Y	N
RHODE ISLAND						
Reed	N	N	N	Y	Y	N
Whitehouse	N	N	N	N	Y	N
SOUTH CAROLINA						
Graham	Y	Y	Y	Y	Y	Y
DeMint	Y	Y	Y	Y	Y	Y
SOUTH DAKOTA						
Johnson	?	?	?	?	?	?
Thune	Y	Y	Y	Y	Y	Y
TENNESSEE						
Alexander	N	Y	Y	Y	Y	Y
Corker	N	Y	Y	Y	N	Y
TEXAS						
Hutchison	Y	Y	Y	Y	Y	Y
Cornyn	Y	Y	Y	Y	Y	Y
UTAH						
Hatch	Y	Y	Y	Y	Y	Y
Bennett	Y	Y	Y	Y	Y	N
VERMONT						
Leahy	N	N	N	N	Y	N
Sanders	N	N	N	N	Y	N
VIRGINIA						
Webb	Y	N	N	N	Y	N
Warner	N	N	N	N	Y	N
WASHINGTON						
Murray	N	N	N	Y	Y	N
Cantwell	N	N	N	Y	Y	N
WEST VIRGINIA						
Byrd	N	N	N	N	Y	N
Rockefeller	?	?	?	?	?	?
WISCONSIN						
Kohl	Y	N	N	Y	Y	N
Feingold	N	N	N	Y	Y	N
WYOMING						
Enzi	Y	Y	Y	Y	Y	Y
Barrasso	Y	Y	Y	Y	Y	Y

KEY   **Republicans**   Democrats   *Independents*

Y Voted for (yea)	X Paired against	C Voted "present" to avoid possible conflict of interest
# Paired for	– Announced against	
+ Announced for	P Voted "present"	? Did not vote or otherwise make a position known
N Voted against (nay)		

IN THE SENATE | By Vote Number

182. **S 896. Housing Loans Modification/Foreclosed Property Notification.** Kerry, D-Mass., amendment to the Dodd, D-Conn., substitute. The Kerry amendment would require that new successors could not claim interest in a property in the case of foreclosure on a federally related mortgage loan unless the tenants had received at least 90 days' notice to vacate the property. The amendment would not affect state and local laws; its provisions would expire Dec. 31, 2012. Adopted 57-39: R 1-39; D 54-0; I 2-0. May 6, 2009.

183. **S 896. Housing Loans Modification/Sale of Unused Federal Properties.** Coburn, R-Okla., motion to waive the Budget Act with respect to the Dodd, D-Conn., point of order against the Coburn amendment to the Reed, D-R.I., amendment to the Dodd substitute for not being germane. The Coburn amendment would establish a pilot program in the Office of Management and Budget to sell federal properties that are not being used. The Reed amendment would expand a program to provide federal funds for homeless shelters, education and other assistance for the homeless. It would authorize $2.2 billion for the program in fiscal 2010. Motion rejected 50-46: R 39-1; D 11-43; I 0-2. A three-fifths majority (60) of the total Senate is required to waive the Budget Act. (Subsequently, the chair upheld the point of order, and the Coburn amendment fell. Then the Reed amendment was adopted by voice vote.) May 6, 2009.

184. **S 896. Housing Loans Modification/Comptroller General Audits.** Grassley, R-Iowa, amendment to the Dodd, D-Conn., substitute. The Grassley amendment would give the comptroller general access upon request to information, data, records, books and accounts for audits of any entity receiving funding from or established by the Federal Reserve. The comptroller general would be able to conduct audits and on-site investigations when appropriate. Adopted 95-1: R 39-1; D 54-0; I 2-0. (Subsequently, the Dodd substitute amendment was adopted by unanimous consent.) May 6, 2009.

185. **S 896. Housing Loans Modification/Passage.** Passage of the bill that would ease the application and eligibility requirements for the Hope for Homeowners Program. It would increase, to $250,000, Federal Deposit Insurance Corporation and National Credit Union Administration deposit insurance coverage on individual bank accounts until Dec. 31, 2013. It would increase the FDIC's borrowing authority to $100 billion from $30 billion and provide temporary authority for further increases to $500 billion if deemed necessary. The bill includes a safe-harbor provision to protect lenders from legal liability if certain criteria are met during the loan modification process. Passed 91-5: R 35-5; D 54-0; I 2-0. A "yea" was a vote in support of the president's position. May 6, 2009.

186. **S 454. Defense Department Procurement/Passage.** Passage of the bill that would overhaul major elements of the Defense Department's weapons acquisition process. The Pentagon would have to require competition and issue regulations regarding conflicts of interest for the military's major acquisitions programs. It would direct the department to issue reports on rebuilding its system engineering capabilities and consider possible trade-offs among cost, schedule and performance for alternatives on major defense acquisitions. Passed 93-0: R 39-0; D 52-0; I 2-0. A "yea" was a vote in support of the president's position. May 7, 2009.

187. **Kerlikowske Nomination/Confirmation.** Confirmation of President Obama's nomination of R. Gil Kerlikowske of Washington to be director of National Drug Control Policy. Confirmed 91-1: R 37-1; D 52-0; I 2-0. A "yea" was a vote in support of the president's position. May 7, 2009.

	182	183	184	185	186	187			182	183	184	185	186	187
ALABAMA								**MONTANA**						
Shelby	N	Y	Y	Y	Y	Y		Baucus	Y	N	Y	Y	Y	Y
Sessions	N	Y	Y	Y	Y	Y		Tester	Y	N	Y	Y	Y	Y
ALASKA								**NEBRASKA**						
Murkowski	N	Y	Y	Y	Y	Y		Nelson	Y	Y	Y	Y	Y	Y
Begich	Y	N	Y	Y	Y	Y		**Johanns**	N	Y	Y	Y	Y	Y
ARIZONA								**NEVADA**						
McCain	N	Y	Y	Y	Y	Y		Reid	Y	N	Y	Y	Y	Y
Kyl	N	Y	Y	Y	Y	Y		**Ensign**	N	Y	Y	Y	Y	Y
ARKANSAS								**NEW HAMPSHIRE**						
Lincoln	Y	Y	Y	Y	Y	Y		**Gregg**	N	Y	Y	N	Y	Y
Pryor	Y	Y	Y	Y	Y	Y		Shaheen	Y	N	Y	Y	Y	Y
CALIFORNIA								**NEW JERSEY**						
Feinstein	Y	N	Y	Y	Y	Y		Lautenberg	Y	N	Y	Y	?	?
Boxer	Y	N	Y	Y	Y	Y		Menendez	Y	N	Y	Y	+	+
COLORADO								**NEW MEXICO**						
Udall	Y	N	Y	Y	Y	Y		Bingaman	Y	N	Y	Y	Y	Y
Bennet	Y	N	Y	Y	Y	Y		Udall	Y	N	Y	Y	Y	Y
CONNECTICUT								**NEW YORK**						
Dodd	Y	N	Y	Y	Y	Y		Schumer	Y	N	Y	Y	Y	Y
Lieberman	Y	N	Y	Y	Y	Y		Gillibrand	Y	N	Y	Y	Y	Y
DELAWARE								**NORTH CAROLINA**						
Carper	Y	Y	Y	Y	Y	Y		**Burr**	N	Y	Y	Y	Y	Y
Kaufman	Y	N	Y	Y	Y	Y		Hagan	Y	N	Y	Y	Y	Y
FLORIDA								**NORTH DAKOTA**						
Nelson	Y	N	Y	Y	Y	Y		Conrad	Y	Y	Y	Y	Y	Y
Martinez	N	Y	Y	Y	Y	Y		Dorgan	Y	Y	Y	Y	Y	Y
GEORGIA								**OHIO**						
Chambliss	N	Y	Y	Y	Y	Y		**Voinovich**	N	Y	Y	Y	Y	Y
Isakson	N	Y	Y	Y	Y	Y		Brown	Y	N	Y	Y	Y	Y
HAWAII								**OKLAHOMA**						
Inouye	Y	N	Y	Y	Y	Y		**Inhofe**	N	Y	Y	N	Y	Y
Akaka	Y	N	Y	Y	Y	Y		**Coburn**	N	Y	Y	N	Y	N
IDAHO								**OREGON**						
Crapo	N	Y	Y	Y	Y	Y		Wyden	Y	N	Y	Y	Y	Y
Risch	N	Y	Y	Y	Y	Y		Merkley	Y	N	Y	Y	Y	Y
ILLINOIS								**PENNSYLVANIA**						
Durbin	Y	N	Y	Y	Y	Y		Specter	Y	N	Y	Y	Y	Y
Burris	Y	N	Y	Y	Y	Y		Casey	Y	N	Y	Y	Y	Y
INDIANA								**RHODE ISLAND**						
Lugar	N	Y	Y	Y	Y	Y		Reed	Y	N	Y	Y	Y	Y
Bayh	Y	Y	Y	Y	Y	Y		Whitehouse	Y	N	Y	Y	Y	Y
IOWA								**SOUTH CAROLINA**						
Grassley	N	Y	Y	Y	Y	Y		**Graham**	N	Y	Y	Y	Y	Y
Harkin	Y	N	Y	Y	Y	Y		**DeMint**	N	Y	Y	N	Y	Y
KANSAS								**SOUTH DAKOTA**						
Brownback	N	Y	Y	Y	Y	Y		Johnson	?	?	?	?	?	?
Roberts	N	Y	Y	Y	Y	Y		**Thune**	N	Y	Y	Y	Y	Y
KENTUCKY								**TENNESSEE**						
McConnell	N	Y	Y	Y	Y	Y		**Alexander**	N	Y	N	Y	Y	Y
Bunning	N	Y	N	Y	Y	Y		**Corker**	N	Y	Y	Y	Y	Y
LOUISIANA								**TEXAS**						
Landrieu	Y	N	Y	Y	Y	Y		**Hutchison**	N	Y	Y	Y	Y	Y
Vitter	N	Y	Y	Y	Y	?		**Cornyn**	N	Y	Y	Y	Y	Y
MAINE								**UTAH**						
Snowe	Y	Y	Y	Y	Y	Y		**Hatch**	N	Y	Y	Y	Y	Y
Collins	N	Y	Y	Y	Y	Y		**Bennett**	N	Y	Y	Y	Y	Y
MARYLAND								**VERMONT**						
Mikulski	Y	N	Y	Y	Y	Y		Leahy	Y	N	Y	Y	Y	Y
Cardin	Y	N	Y	Y	Y	Y		*Sanders*	Y	N	Y	Y	Y	Y
MASSACHUSETTS								**VIRGINIA**						
Kennedy	?	?	?	?	?	?		Webb	Y	Y	Y	Y	Y	Y
Kerry	Y	N	Y	Y	Y	Y		Warner	Y	Y	Y	Y	Y	Y
MICHIGAN								**WASHINGTON**						
Levin	Y	N	Y	Y	Y	Y		Murray	Y	N	Y	Y	Y	Y
Stabenow	Y	N	Y	Y	Y	Y		Cantwell	Y	N	Y	Y	Y	Y
MINNESOTA								**WEST VIRGINIA**						
Klobuchar	Y	Y	Y	Y	Y	Y		Byrd	Y	N	Y	Y	Y	Y
Vacant								Rockefeller	?	?	?	+	+	?
MISSISSIPPI								**WISCONSIN**						
Cochran	N	Y	Y	Y	Y	Y		Kohl	Y	N	Y	Y	Y	Y
Wicker	N	Y	Y	Y	Y	Y		Feingold	Y	N	Y	Y	Y	Y
MISSOURI								**WYOMING**						
Bond	N	N	Y	Y	?	?		**Enzi**	N	Y	Y	Y	Y	Y
McCaskill	Y	Y	Y	Y	Y	Y		**Barrasso**	N	Y	Y	Y	Y	Y

KEY   **Republicans**   Democrats   *Independents*

Y Voted for (yea)	X Paired against	C Voted "present" to avoid possible conflict of interest
# Paired for	– Announced against	
+ Announced for	P Voted "present"	? Did not vote or otherwise make a position known
N Voted against (nay)		

IN THE SENATE | By Vote Number

188. **HR 627. Credit Card Company Regulations/Firearms in National Parks.** Coburn, R-Okla., amendment to the Dodd, D-Conn., substitute. The Coburn amendment would bar the Interior Department from prohibiting an individual from possessing a firearm in a national park or wildlife refuge. The substitute would impose restrictions on credit card company lending practices, including prohibiting companies from raising rates on cardholders during an account's first year. It would require companies to give at least 45 days' notice before increasing an annual percentage rate or changing an open-ended contract and would restrict companies from computing interest charges on balances from more than one billing cycle. Adopted 67-29: R 39-1; D 27-27; I 1-1. (By unanimous consent, the Senate agreed to raise the majority requirement for adoption of the amendment to 60 votes.) May 12, 2009.

189. **Hayes Nomination/Cloture.** Motion to invoke cloture (thus limiting debate) on the nomination of David J. Hayes of Virginia to be deputy secretary of the Interior Department. Motion rejected 57-39: R 2-38; D 53-1; I 2-0. Three-fifths of the total Senate (60) is required to invoke cloture. May 13, 2009.

190. **HR 627. Credit Card Company Regulations/Identity Check Requirements.** Vitter, R-La., amendment to the Dodd, D-Conn., substitute. The Vitter amendment would require the Federal Reserve to set rules to require credit card issuers to verify the identity of individuals. Acceptable identification for opening an account would be a Social Security card, driver's license, passport or photo ID card issued by the Homeland Security Department. Rejected 28-65: R 28-11; D 0-52; I 0-2. May 13, 2009.

191. **HR 627. Credit Card Company Regulations/National Credit Usury Rate.** Sanders, I-Vt., motion to waive the Budget Act with respect to the Shelby, R-Ala., point of order against the Sanders amendment to the Dodd, D-Conn., substitute. The Sanders amendment would limit the annual percentage rate applicable to a credit extension to 15 percent. Exceptions would be allowed if money market interest rates rose over a six-month period or if interest rate levels threatened the soundness of lenders. Motion rejected 33-60: R 1-38; D 31-21; I 1-1. A three-fifths majority vote (60) of the total Senate is required to waive the Budget Act. (Subsequently, the chair upheld the point of order, and the amendment fell.) May 13, 2009.

192. **HR 627. Credit Card Company Regulations/National Debt Disclosure.** Gregg, R-N.H., motion to waive the Budget Act with respect to the Sanders, I-Vt., point of order against the Gregg amendment to the Dodd, D-Conn., substitute. The Gregg amendment would require all appropriations bills to include the current federal debt level, the debt level per citizen and the effects of the bill on the national debt level. The requirement could be waived by a three-fifths majority of the Senate. Tax instruction forms would have to include information on individual taxpayer shares of the federal public debt. Motion rejected 59-35: R 40-0; D 19-33; I 0-2. A three-fifths majority vote (60) of the total Senate is required to waive the Budget Act. (Subsequently, the chair upheld the point of order, and the amendment fell.) May 13, 2009.

	188	189	190	191	192
ALABAMA					
Shelby	Y	N	Y	N	Y
Sessions	Y	N	Y	N	Y
ALASKA					
Murkowski	Y	N	N	N	Y
Begich	Y	Y	N	Y	N
ARIZONA					
McCain	Y	N	Y	N	Y
Kyl	Y	Y	Y	N	Y
ARKANSAS					
Lincoln	Y	Y	N	N	Y
Pryor	Y	Y	N	N	Y
CALIFORNIA					
Feinstein	N	Y	N	Y	Y
Boxer	N	Y	N	Y	Y
COLORADO					
Udall	Y	Y	N	Y	Y
Bennet	Y	Y	N	Y	Y
CONNECTICUT					
Dodd	N	Y	N	Y	N
Lieberman	N	Y	N	N	N
DELAWARE					
Carper	N	Y	N	N	N
Kaufman	N	Y	N	N	N
FLORIDA					
Nelson	Y	Y	N	N	Y
Martinez	Y	N	N	N	Y
GEORGIA					
Chambliss	Y	N	Y	N	Y
Isakson	Y	N	Y	N	Y
HAWAII					
Inouye	N	Y	N	Y	N
Akaka	N	Y	N	N	N
IDAHO					
Crapo	Y	N	Y	N	Y
Risch	Y	N	Y	N	Y
ILLINOIS					
Durbin	N	Y	N	Y	N
Burris	N	Y	N	Y	N
INDIANA					
Lugar	Y	N	N	N	Y
Bayh	Y	Y	N	N	Y
IOWA					
Grassley	Y	N	Y	Y	Y
Harkin	N	Y	N	Y	N
KANSAS					
Brownback	Y	N	Y	N	Y
Roberts	Y	N	Y	N	Y
KENTUCKY					
McConnell	Y	N	Y	N	Y
Bunning	Y	N	Y	N	Y
LOUISIANA					
Landrieu	Y	Y	N	N	N
Vitter	Y	N	Y	N	Y
MAINE					
Snowe	Y	Y	N	N	Y
Collins	Y	N	N	N	Y
MARYLAND					
Mikulski	?	?	?	?	?
Cardin	N	Y	N	Y	Y
MASSACHUSETTS					
Kennedy	?	?	?	?	?
Kerry	N	+	N	Y	N
MICHIGAN					
Levin	N	Y	N	N	N
Stabenow	N	Y	N	N	N
MINNESOTA					
Klobuchar	Y	Y	N	Y	Y
Vacant					
MISSISSIPPI					
Cochran	Y	N	Y	N	Y
Wicker	Y	N	Y	N	Y
MISSOURI					
Bond	Y	N	Y	N	Y
McCaskill	N	Y	N	Y	N

	188	189	190	191	192
MONTANA					
Baucus	Y	Y	N	N	N
Tester	Y	Y	N	N	N
NEBRASKA					
Nelson	Y	Y	N	N	Y
Johanns	Y	N	Y	N	Y
NEVADA					
Reid	Y	N	N	Y	N
Ensign	Y	N	N	N	Y
NEW HAMPSHIRE					
Gregg	Y	N	N	N	Y
Shaheen	Y	Y	N	N	N
NEW JERSEY					
Lautenberg	N	Y	N	Y	N
Menendez	N	Y	N	Y	N
NEW MEXICO					
Bingaman	N	Y	N	N	N
Udall	N	Y	N	N	N
NEW YORK					
Schumer	N	Y	N	N	N
Gillibrand	N	Y	N	Y	Y
NORTH CAROLINA					
Burr	Y	N	Y	N	Y
Hagan	Y	Y	N	N	Y
NORTH DAKOTA					
Conrad	Y	Y	N	Y	Y
Dorgan	Y	Y	N	Y	Y
OHIO					
Voinovich	Y	N	Y	?	Y
Brown	N	Y	N	Y	N
OKLAHOMA					
Inhofe	Y	N	Y	N	Y
Coburn	Y	N	Y	N	Y
OREGON					
Wyden	Y	Y	N	Y	Y
Merkley	Y	Y	N	Y	N
PENNSYLVANIA					
Specter	Y	Y	N	N	Y
Casey	Y	Y	N	N	Y
RHODE ISLAND					
Reed	N	Y	N	Y	N
Whitehouse	N	Y	?	?	?
SOUTH CAROLINA					
Graham	Y	N	Y	N	Y
DeMint	Y	N	Y	N	Y
SOUTH DAKOTA					
Johnson	N	Y	N	N	N
Thune	Y	N	Y	N	Y
TENNESSEE					
Alexander	N	N	N	N	Y
Corker	Y	N	N	N	Y
TEXAS					
Hutchison	Y	N	?	N	Y
Cornyn	Y	N	Y	N	Y
UTAH					
Hatch	Y	N	N	N	Y
Bennett	Y	N	N	N	Y
VERMONT					
Leahy	Y	Y	?	?	?
Sanders	Y	Y	N	Y	N
VIRGINIA					
Webb	Y	Y	N	Y	N
Warner	Y	Y	N	N	N
WASHINGTON					
Murray	N	Y	N	N	N
Cantwell	N	Y	N	N	N
WEST VIRGINIA					
Byrd	Y	Y	N	N	N
Rockefeller	?	Y	?	?	?
WISCONSIN					
Kohl	Y	Y	N	Y	Y
Feingold	Y	Y	N	Y	Y
WYOMING					
Enzi	Y	N	Y	N	Y
Barrasso	Y	N	Y	N	Y

KEY   **Republicans**   Democrats   *Independents*

Y Voted for (yea)	X Paired against
# Paired for	– Announced against
+ Announced for	P Voted "present"
N Voted against (nay)	

C Voted "present" to avoid possible conflict of interest

? Did not vote or otherwise make a position known

IN THE SENATE | By Vote Number

193. HR 627. **Credit Card Company Regulations/Cloture.** Motion to invoke cloture (thus limiting debate) on the Dodd, D-Conn., substitute amendment that would impose restrictions on credit card company lending practices, including prohibiting companies from raising rates on cardholders during an account's first year. It would require companies to give at least 45 days' notice before increasing an annual percentage rate or changing an open-ended contract and would restrict companies from computing interest charges on balances based on more than one billing cycle. Motion agreed to 92-2: R 37-2; D 53-0; I 2-0. Three-fifths of the total Senate (60) is required to invoke cloture. (Subsequently, the Dodd substitute was adopted by unanimous consent.) May 19, 2009.

194. HR 627. **Credit Card Company Regulations/Passage.** Passage of the bill that would impose restrictions on credit card company lending practices. The bill would restrict when companies could increase the annual percentage interest rate retroactively on existing balances, require companies to give at least 45 days' notice before increasing an annual percentage rate or changing an open-ended contract, and restrict companies from computing interest charges based on balances from more than one billing cycle. The term "fixed rate" could only be used for a rate that will not change over a set period. Credit cards could not be issued to consumers under age 21 without a cosigner's acceptance of financial liability or a demonstrated ability to repay the credit extension. The bill's provisions would take effect nine months after enactment. Passed 90-5: R 35-4; D 53-1; I 2-0. A "yea" was a vote in support of the president's position. May 19, 2009.

195. **Gensler Nomination/Confirmation.** Confirmation of President Obama's nomination of Gary Gensler of Maryland to be commissioner of the Commodity Futures Trading Commission. Confirmed 88-6: R 38-0; D 49-5; I 1-1. A "yea" was a vote in support of the president's position. May 19, 2009.

196. HR 2346. **Fiscal 2009 Supplemental/Guantánamo Bay Prison Closing.** Inouye, D-Hawaii, amendment that would bar the use of funds in the bill or any prior act to transfer or release any detainee at the detention facility in Guantánamo Bay, Cuba, to the United States. It would remove $50 million in the bill for closing the prison and relocating the prisoners and military personnel at the facility, as well as $30 million for Justice Department responsibilities related to Guantánamo operations. Adopted 90-6: R 40-0; D 48-6; I 2-0. A "nay" was a vote in support of the president's position. May 20, 2009.

197. S 454. **Weapons Acquisition Overhaul/Conference Report.** Adoption of the conference report on the bill that would overhaul major elements of the Defense Department's weapons acquisition process. The Pentagon would have to require competition and revise regulations regarding conflicts of interest for major acquisitions programs. It would establish the position of director of cost assessment and program evaluation. It would also require the Defense secretary to designate a director to oversee developmental testing and evaluation, and a director to oversee systems engineering. It would require the Pentagon to ensure that cost, performance and schedule objectives are balanced. Adopted 95-0: R 39-0; D 54-0; I 2-0. A "yea" was a vote in support of the president's position. May 20, 2009.

	193	194	195	196	197
ALABAMA					
Shelby	Y	Y	Y	Y	Y
Sessions	Y	Y	Y	Y	Y
ALASKA					
Murkowski	Y	Y	Y	Y	Y
Begich	Y	Y	Y	Y	Y
ARIZONA					
McCain	Y	Y	Y	Y	Y
Kyl	N	N	Y	Y	Y
ARKANSAS					
Lincoln	Y	Y	Y	Y	Y
Pryor	Y	Y	Y	Y	Y
CALIFORNIA					
Feinstein	Y	Y	Y	Y	Y
Boxer	Y	Y	Y	Y	Y
COLORADO					
Udall	Y	Y	Y	Y	Y
Bennet	Y	Y	Y	Y	Y
CONNECTICUT					
Dodd	Y	Y	Y	Y	Y
Lieberman	Y	Y	Y	Y	Y
DELAWARE					
Carper	Y	Y	Y	Y	Y
Kaufman	Y	Y	Y	Y	Y
FLORIDA					
Nelson	Y	Y	Y	Y	Y
Martinez	Y	Y	Y	Y	Y
GEORGIA					
Chambliss	Y	Y	Y	Y	Y
Isakson	Y	Y	Y	Y	Y
HAWAII					
Inouye	Y	Y	Y	Y	Y
Akaka	Y	Y	Y	Y	Y
IDAHO					
Crapo	Y	Y	Y	Y	Y
Risch	Y	Y	Y	Y	Y
ILLINOIS					
Durbin	Y	Y	Y	N	Y
Burris	Y	Y	Y	Y	Y
INDIANA					
Lugar	Y	Y	Y	Y	Y
Bayh	Y	Y	Y	Y	Y
IOWA					
Grassley	Y	Y	Y	Y	Y
Harkin	Y	Y	Y	N	Y
KANSAS					
Brownback	Y	Y	Y	Y	Y
Roberts	Y	Y	Y	Y	Y
KENTUCKY					
McConnell	Y	Y	Y	Y	Y
Bunning	Y	Y	Y	Y	Y
LOUISIANA					
Landrieu	Y	Y	Y	Y	Y
Vitter	Y	Y	Y	Y	Y
MAINE					
Snowe	Y	Y	Y	Y	Y
Collins	Y	Y	Y	Y	Y
MARYLAND					
Mikulski	Y	Y	Y	Y	Y
Cardin	Y	Y	Y	Y	Y
MASSACHUSETTS					
Kennedy	?	?	?	?	?
Kerry	Y	Y	Y	Y	Y
MICHIGAN					
Levin	Y	Y	Y	N	Y
Stabenow	Y	Y	Y	Y	Y
MINNESOTA					
Klobuchar	Y	Y	Y	Y	Y
Vacant					
MISSISSIPPI					
Cochran	Y	Y	Y	Y	Y
Wicker	Y	Y	Y	Y	Y
MISSOURI					
Bond	Y	Y	Y	Y	Y
McCaskill	Y	Y	Y	Y	Y
MONTANA					
Baucus	Y	Y	Y	Y	Y
Tester	Y	Y	Y	Y	Y
NEBRASKA					
Nelson	Y	Y	Y	Y	Y
Johanns	Y	Y	Y	Y	Y
NEVADA					
Reid	Y	Y	Y	Y	Y
Ensign	?	+	?	Y	Y
NEW HAMPSHIRE					
Gregg	Y	Y	Y	Y	Y
Shaheen	Y	Y	N	Y	Y
NEW JERSEY					
Lautenberg	Y	Y	Y	Y	Y
Menendez	Y	Y	Y	Y	Y
NEW MEXICO					
Bingaman	Y	Y	Y	Y	Y
Udall	Y	Y	Y	Y	Y
NEW YORK					
Schumer	Y	Y	Y	Y	Y
Gillibrand	Y	Y	Y	Y	Y
NORTH CAROLINA					
Burr	Y	Y	Y	Y	Y
Hagan	Y	Y	Y	Y	Y
NORTH DAKOTA					
Conrad	Y	Y	Y	Y	Y
Dorgan	Y	Y	N	Y	Y
OHIO					
Voinovich	Y	Y	?	Y	Y
Brown	?	+	?	Y	Y
OKLAHOMA					
Inhofe	Y	Y	Y	Y	Y
Coburn	Y	Y	Y	Y	Y
OREGON					
Wyden	Y	Y	Y	Y	Y
Merkley	Y	Y	N	Y	Y
PENNSYLVANIA					
Specter	Y	Y	Y	Y	Y
Casey	Y	Y	Y	Y	Y
RHODE ISLAND					
Reed	Y	Y	Y	N	Y
Whitehouse	Y	Y	Y	N	Y
SOUTH CAROLINA					
Graham	Y	Y	Y	Y	Y
DeMint	Y	Y	Y	Y	Y
SOUTH DAKOTA					
Johnson	Y	N	Y	Y	Y
Thune	N	N	Y	Y	Y
TENNESSEE					
Alexander	Y	N	Y	Y	Y
Corker	Y	Y	Y	Y	Y
TEXAS					
Hutchison	Y	Y	Y	Y	Y
Cornyn	Y	Y	Y	Y	Y
UTAH					
Hatch	Y	Y	Y	Y	Y
Bennett	Y	N	Y	Y	?
VERMONT					
Leahy	Y	Y	Y	N	Y
Sanders	Y	Y	N	Y	Y
VIRGINIA					
Webb	Y	Y	Y	Y	Y
Warner	Y	Y	Y	Y	Y
WASHINGTON					
Murray	Y	Y	N	Y	Y
Cantwell	Y	Y	N	Y	Y
WEST VIRGINIA					
Byrd	?	?	?	?	?
Rockefeller	?	+	?	?	+
WISCONSIN					
Kohl	Y	Y	Y	Y	Y
Feingold	Y	Y	Y	Y	Y
WYOMING					
Enzi	Y	Y	Y	Y	Y
Barrasso	Y	Y	Y	Y	Y

KEY **Republicans**   Democrats   *Independents*

Y Voted for (yea)	X Paired against	C Voted "present" to avoid possible conflict of interest
# Paired for	– Announced against	
+ Announced for	P Voted "present"	? Did not vote or otherwise make a position known
N Voted against (nay)		

IN THE SENATE | By Vote Number

198. **HR 2346. Fiscal 2009 Supplemental/Guantánamo Detainee Report.** McConnell, R-Ky., amendment that would require the president to submit a report to Congress every 90 days on the prisoner population at the detention facility at Guantánamo Bay, Cuba. The report would include each detainee's name and country of origin, a summary of the evidence and information used to justify his detention, measures taken to transfer the detainee and an individual threat assessment. It would ban the transfer of any detainee to another country until the president submits the first report within 60 days of the bill's enactment or certifies to Congress that such action would pose no threat to members of the U.S. military. Adopted 92-3: R 39-0; D 51-3; I 2-0. May 20, 2009.

199. **HR 2346. Fiscal 2009 Supplemental/Guantánamo Detainee Relocation.** Brownback, R-Kan., amendment that would express the sense of the Senate that the Defense secretary should consult with state and local government officials before making any decision about where detainees at the detention facility at Guantánamo Bay, Cuba, may be transferred if the prison is closed due to a presidential executive order. Adopted 94-0: R 38-0; D 54-0; I 2-0. May 20, 2009.

200. **HR 2346. Fiscal 2009 Supplemental/Cloture.** Motion to invoke cloture (thus limiting debate) on the bill that would appropriate $91.3 billion in emergency supplemental funds for fiscal 2009, including funding for the wars in Iraq and Afghanistan and pandemic flu preparations. Motion agreed to 94-1: R 39-0; D 53-1; I 2-0. Three-fifths of the total Senate (60) is required to invoke cloture. May 21, 2009.

201. **HR 2346. Fiscal 2009 Supplemental/International Monetary Fund.** DeMint, R-S.C., amendment that would strike provisions for increased funding for new U.S. commitments to the International Monetary Fund. Rejected 30-64: R 27-12; D 2-51; I 1-1. A "nay" was a vote in support of the president's position. May 21, 2009.

202. **HR 2346. Fiscal 2009 Supplemental/Passage.** Passage of the bill that would appropriate $91.3 billion in emergency supplemental funds for fiscal 2009, including funding for the wars in Iraq and Afghanistan and pandemic flu preparations. It would provide $73 billion for the Department of Defense, $6.9 billion for the State Department and foreign operations and $1.5 billion to address potential pandemic flu. It would provide $5 billion in budget authority for about $108 billion in funding for new commitments to the International Monetary Fund. It would also bar the use of funds to release detainees at the detention facility at Guantánamo Bay, Cuba, into the United States. It would ban the disclosure of certain photographs related to the treatment of individuals detained by the U.S. military after Sept. 11, 2001, under the Freedom of Information Act. Passed 86-3: R 38-1; D 47-1; I 1-1. A "yea" was a vote in support of the president's position. May 21, 2009.

203. **HR 1256. Tobacco Regulation/Cloture.** Reid, D-Nev., motion to invoke cloture (thus limiting debate) on the motion to proceed to the bill that would give the Food and Drug Administration the authority to regulate tobacco products. Motion agreed to 84-11: R 29-10; D 53-1; I 2-0. Three-fifths of the total Senate (60) is required to invoke cloture. June 2, 2009.

	198	199	200	201	202	203		198	199	200	201	202	203
ALABAMA							**MONTANA**						
Shelby	Y	Y	Y	Y	Y	Y	Baucus	Y	Y	Y	N	Y	Y
Sessions	Y	Y	Y	Y	Y	Y	Tester	Y	Y	Y	N	Y	Y
ALASKA							**NEBRASKA**						
Murkowski	Y	Y	Y	N	Y	Y	Nelson	Y	Y	Y	N	Y	Y
Begich	Y	Y	Y	N	?	?	**Johanns**	Y	Y	Y	Y	Y	Y
ARIZONA							**NEVADA**						
McCain	Y	Y	Y	Y	Y	Y	Reid	Y	Y	Y	N	Y	Y
Kyl	Y	Y	Y	Y	Y	Y	**Ensign**	Y	Y	Y	Y	Y	Y
ARKANSAS							**NEW HAMPSHIRE**						
Lincoln	Y	Y	Y	N	Y	Y	**Gregg**	Y	Y	Y	N	Y	Y
Pryor	Y	Y	Y	N	Y	Y	Shaheen	Y	Y	Y	N	?	Y
CALIFORNIA							**NEW JERSEY**						
Feinstein	Y	Y	Y	N	Y	Y	Lautenberg	Y	Y	Y	N	Y	Y
Boxer	Y	Y	Y	N	Y	Y	Menendez	Y	Y	Y	N	Y	Y
COLORADO							**NEW MEXICO**						
Udall	Y	Y	Y	N	?	Y	Bingaman	Y	Y	Y	N	Y	Y
Bennet	Y	Y	Y	N	Y	Y	Udall	Y	Y	Y	N	Y	Y
CONNECTICUT							**NEW YORK**						
Dodd	Y	Y	Y	N	Y	Y	Schumer	Y	Y	Y	N	Y	Y
Lieberman	Y	Y	Y	N	Y	Y	Gillibrand	Y	Y	Y	N	Y	Y
DELAWARE							**NORTH CAROLINA**						
Carper	Y	Y	Y	N	?	Y	**Burr**	Y	Y	Y	N	Y	N
Kaufman	Y	Y	Y	N	Y	Y	Hagan	Y	Y	Y	N	?	N
FLORIDA							**NORTH DAKOTA**						
Nelson	Y	Y	Y	N	Y	Y	Conrad	Y	Y	Y	N	Y	Y
Martinez	Y	Y	Y	N	Y	?	Dorgan	Y	Y	Y	N	Y	Y
GEORGIA							**OHIO**						
Chambliss	Y	Y	Y	Y	Y	Y	**Voinovich**	Y	Y	Y	N	Y	Y
Isakson	Y	Y	Y	Y	Y	Y	Brown	Y	Y	Y	N	Y	Y
HAWAII							**OKLAHOMA**						
Inouye	Y	Y	Y	N	Y	Y	**Inhofe**	Y	Y	Y	Y	Y	N
Akaka	Y	Y	Y	N	Y	Y	**Coburn**	Y	?	Y	Y	N	N
IDAHO							**OREGON**						
Crapo	Y	Y	Y	Y	Y	Y	Wyden	Y	Y	Y	N	Y	Y
Risch	Y	Y	Y	Y	Y	Y	Merkley	Y	Y	Y	N	Y	Y
ILLINOIS							**PENNSYLVANIA**						
Durbin	N	Y	Y	N	Y	Y	Specter	Y	Y	Y	N	Y	Y
Burris	N	Y	Y	N	Y	Y	Casey	Y	Y	Y	N	Y	Y
INDIANA							**RHODE ISLAND**						
Lugar	Y	Y	Y	N	Y	Y	Reed	Y	Y	Y	N	Y	Y
Bayh	Y	Y	Y	Y	Y	Y	Whitehouse	Y	Y	Y	N	Y	Y
IOWA							**SOUTH CAROLINA**						
Grassley	Y	Y	Y	Y	Y	Y	**Graham**	Y	Y	Y	Y	Y	Y
Harkin	Y	Y	Y	N	Y	Y	**DeMint**	Y	Y	Y	Y	Y	N
KANSAS							**SOUTH DAKOTA**						
Brownback	Y	Y	Y	Y	Y	N	Johnson	Y	Y	Y	N	Y	Y
Roberts	Y	Y	Y	Y	Y	N	**Thune**	Y	Y	Y	Y	Y	Y
KENTUCKY							**TENNESSEE**						
McConnell	Y	Y	Y	Y	Y	N	**Alexander**	Y	Y	Y	N	Y	Y
Bunning	Y	Y	Y	Y	Y	N	**Corker**	Y	Y	Y	N	Y	Y
LOUISIANA							**TEXAS**						
Landrieu	Y	Y	Y	N	Y	Y	**Hutchison**	Y	Y	Y	Y	Y	Y
Vitter	Y	Y	Y	Y	Y	Y	**Cornyn**	Y	Y	Y	Y	Y	Y
MAINE							**UTAH**						
Snowe	Y	Y	Y	N	Y	Y	**Hatch**	+	+	+	+	+	N
Collins	Y	Y	Y	N	Y	Y	**Bennett**	Y	Y	Y	Y	Y	Y
MARYLAND							**VERMONT**						
Mikulski	Y	Y	Y	N	Y	Y	Leahy	N	Y	Y	N	Y	Y
Cardin	Y	Y	Y	N	Y	Y	*Sanders*	Y	Y	Y	Y	N	Y
MASSACHUSETTS							**VIRGINIA**						
Kennedy	?	?	?	?	?	?	Webb	Y	Y	Y	N	Y	Y
Kerry	Y	Y	Y	N	Y	Y	Warner	Y	Y	Y	N	Y	Y
MICHIGAN							**WASHINGTON**						
Levin	Y	Y	Y	N	Y	Y	Murray	Y	Y	Y	?	?	Y
Stabenow	Y	Y	Y	N	Y	Y	Cantwell	Y	Y	Y	N	Y	Y
MINNESOTA							**WEST VIRGINIA**						
Klobuchar	Y	Y	Y	N	Y	Y	Byrd	?	?	?	?	?	?
Vacant							Rockefeller	?	?	?	?	+	Y
MISSISSIPPI							**WISCONSIN**						
Cochran	Y	Y	Y	N	Y	Y	Kohl	Y	Y	Y	N	Y	Y
Wicker	Y	Y	Y	N	Y	Y	Feingold	Y	Y	N	N	Y	Y
MISSOURI							**WYOMING**						
Bond	Y	Y	Y	N	Y	N	**Enzi**	Y	Y	Y	Y	Y	Y
McCaskill	Y	Y	Y	N	Y	Y	**Barrasso**	Y	Y	Y	Y	Y	Y

KEY	**Republicans**	Democrats	*Independents*	
Y	Voted for (yea)	X	Paired against	C Voted "present" to avoid possible conflict of interest
#	Paired for	–	Announced against	
+	Announced for	P	Voted "present"	? Did not vote or otherwise make a position known
N	Voted against (nay)			

IN THE SENATE | By Vote Number

204.
HR 1256. Tobacco Regulation/Cloture. Motion to invoke cloture (thus limiting debate) on the Dodd, D-Conn., substitute amendment that would allow the Food and Drug Administration (FDA) to regulate the manufacture, sale and promotion of tobacco products. It also would levy user fees on tobacco products to help pay for the cost of the regulation. Motion agreed to 61-30: R 7-29; D 52-1; I 2-0. Three-fifths of the total Senate (60) is required to invoke cloture. June 8, 2009.

205.
HR 1256. Tobacco Regulation/Republican Substitute. Burr, R-N.C., substitute amendment to the Dodd, D-Conn., substitute. The Burr substitute would establish a Tobacco Harm Reduction Center within the Department of Health and Human Services to regulate tobacco products, funded by industry-paid user fees. It would provide funding for smoking cessation and prevention programs and encourage current smokers to use less harmful, smokeless tobacco products. It would also place restrictions on print advertising for tobacco manufacturers. Rejected 36-60: R 35-5; D 1-53; I 0-2. June 9, 2009.

206.
HR 1256. Tobacco Regulation/Cloture. Motion to invoke cloture (thus limiting debate) on the bill that would allow the FDA to regulate the manufacture, sale and promotion of tobacco products. It also would levy user fees on tobacco products to help pay for the cost of the regulation. Motion agreed to 67-30: R 11-29; D 54-1; I 2-0. Three-fifths of the total Senate (60) is required to invoke cloture. June 10, 2009.

207.
HR 1256. Tobacco Regulation/Passage. Passage of the bill that would allow the Food and Drug Administration to regulate the manufacture, sale and promotion of tobacco products. It would require new, larger labels warning consumers of the health risks associated with tobacco products and clarify that the FDA does not endorse the safety of such products. It would establish standards for tobacco products marketed as lower in health risks. The FDA could regulate the amount of nicotine but not ban any class of tobacco products or eliminate nicotine levels completely. The bill would restrict the additives that can be included in cigarettes and ban flavors, except for menthol. It would require tobacco manufacturers and importers to pay quarterly user fees to help cover the cost of the regulation. Passed 79-17: R 23-16; D 54-1; I 2-0. (Prior to passage, the Dodd amendment was adopted by voice vote.) A "yea" was a vote in support of the president's position. June 11, 2009.

	204	205	206	207		204	205	206	207
ALABAMA					**MONTANA**				
Shelby	N	Y	N	Y	Baucus	Y	N	Y	Y
Sessions	N	Y	N	Y	Tester	Y	N	Y	Y
ALASKA					**NEBRASKA**				
Murkowski	Y	Y	Y	Y	Nelson	Y	N	Y	Y
Begich	Y	N	Y	Y	Johanns	N	Y	Y	Y
ARIZONA					**NEVADA**				
McCain	N	Y	N	Y	Reid	Y	N	Y	Y
Kyl	N	Y	N	N	Ensign	N	Y	N	N
ARKANSAS					**NEW HAMPSHIRE**				
Lincoln	Y	N	Y	Y	Gregg	?	Y	Y	Y
Pryor	Y	N	Y	Y	Shaheen	Y	N	Y	Y
CALIFORNIA					**NEW JERSEY**				
Feinstein	Y	N	Y	Y	Lautenberg	Y	N	Y	Y
Boxer	Y	N	Y	Y	Menendez	Y	N	Y	Y
COLORADO					**NEW MEXICO**				
Udall	Y	N	Y	Y	Bingaman	Y	N	Y	Y
Bennet	Y	N	Y	Y	Udall	Y	N	Y	Y
CONNECTICUT					**NEW YORK**				
Dodd	Y	N	Y	Y	Schumer	Y	N	Y	Y
Lieberman	Y	N	Y	Y	Gillibrand	?	N	Y	Y
DELAWARE					**NORTH CAROLINA**				
Carper	Y	N	Y	Y	Burr	N	Y	N	N
Kaufman	Y	N	Y	Y	Hagan	N	Y	N	N
FLORIDA					**NORTH DAKOTA**				
Nelson	Y	N	Y	Y	Conrad	Y	N	Y	Y
Martinez	N	Y	N	Y	Dorgan	Y	N	Y	Y
GEORGIA					**OHIO**				
Chambliss	N	Y	N	N	**Voinovich**	N	Y	N	Y
Isakson	N	Y	N	N	Brown	Y	N	Y	Y
HAWAII					**OKLAHOMA**				
Inouye	Y	N	Y	Y	**Inhofe**	N	Y	N	N
Akaka	Y	N	Y	Y	**Coburn**	N	Y	N	N
IDAHO					**OREGON**				
Crapo	?	Y	N	Y	Wyden	Y	N	Y	Y
Risch	N	Y	N	Y	Merkley	Y	N	Y	Y
ILLINOIS					**PENNSYLVANIA**				
Durbin	Y	N	Y	Y	Specter	Y	N	Y	Y
Burris	Y	N	Y	Y	Casey	Y	N	Y	Y
INDIANA					**RHODE ISLAND**				
Lugar	Y	N	Y	Y	Reed	Y	N	Y	Y
Bayh	Y	N	Y	Y	Whitehouse	Y	N	Y	Y
IOWA					**SOUTH CAROLINA**				
Grassley	Y	N	Y	Y	**Graham**	N	Y	N	N
Harkin	Y	N	Y	Y	**DeMint**	N	Y	N	N
KANSAS					**SOUTH DAKOTA**				
Brownback	N	Y	N	N	Johnson	Y	N	Y	Y
Roberts	?	Y	N	N	**Thune**	N	Y	Y	Y
KENTUCKY					**TENNESSEE**				
McConnell	N	Y	N	N	**Alexander**	N	Y	N	N
Bunning	N	Y	N	N	**Corker**	N	Y	Y	Y
LOUISIANA					**TEXAS**				
Landrieu	Y	N	Y	Y	**Hutchison**	?	Y	Y	Y
Vitter	N	Y	N	Y	**Cornyn**	Y	N	Y	Y
MAINE					**UTAH**				
Snowe	Y	N	Y	Y	**Hatch**	N	Y	N	N
Collins	Y	N	Y	Y	**Bennett**	N	Y	N	N
MARYLAND					**VERMONT**				
Mikulski	Y	N	Y	Y	Leahy	Y	N	Y	Y
Cardin	Y	N	Y	Y	*Sanders*	Y	N	Y	Y
MASSACHUSETTS					**VIRGINIA**				
Kennedy	?	?	?	?	Webb	Y	N	Y	Y
Kerry	Y	N	Y	Y	Warner	Y	N	Y	Y
MICHIGAN					**WASHINGTON**				
Levin	Y	N	Y	Y	Murray	Y	N	Y	Y
Stabenow	?	N	Y	Y	Cantwell	Y	N	Y	Y
MINNESOTA					**WEST VIRGINIA**				
Klobuchar	Y	N	Y	Y	Byrd	?	?	?	?
Vacant					Rockefeller	Y	N	Y	Y
MISSISSIPPI					**WISCONSIN**				
Cochran	Y	Y	N	Y	Kohl	Y	N	Y	Y
Wicker	N	Y	N	Y	Feingold	Y	N	Y	Y
MISSOURI					**WYOMING**				
Bond	N	Y	N	–	**Enzi**	N	Y	N	Y
McCaskill	Y	?	Y	Y	**Barrasso**	N	Y	N	Y

KEY   **Republicans**   Democrats   *Independents*

Y Voted for (yea)	X Paired against	C Voted "present" to avoid possible conflict of interest
# Paired for	– Announced against	? Did not vote or otherwise make a position known
+ Announced for	P Voted "present"	
N Voted against (nay)		

IN THE SENATE | By Vote Number

208. **S 1023. Foreign Tourism Promotion/Cloture.** Motion to invoke cloture (thus limiting debate) on the motion to proceed to the bill that would create an Office of Travel Promotion in the Commerce Department and a nonprofit corporation to attract foreign tourists to the United States. Motion agreed to 90-3: R 35-3; D 53-0; I 2-0. Three-fifths of the total Senate (60) is required to invoke cloture. June 16, 2009.

209. **HR 2346. Fiscal 2009 Supplemental/Conference Report Point of Order.** Inouye, D-Hawaii, motion to waive Senate rules with respect to all points of order against the conference report on the bill that would appropriate $105.9 billion in emergency supplemental funds for fiscal 2009, including funding for the wars in Iraq and Afghanistan and pandemic flu preparations. Motion agreed to 60-36: R 4-35; D 54-1; I 2-0. A three-fifths majority vote (60) of the total Senate is required to waive Senate Rule XLIV. Under the rule, a senator may raise a point of order against provisions of a conference report that constitute new direct spending. A "yea" was a vote in support of the president's position. June 18, 2009.

210. **HR 2346. Fiscal 2009 Supplemental/Conference Report.** Adoption of the conference report on the bill that would appropriate $105.9 billion in emergency supplemental funds for fiscal 2009, including funding for the wars in Iraq and Afghanistan and pandemic flu preparations. It would provide $79.9 billion for defense funding, $10.4 billion for foreign aid and stabilization programs, and $7.7 billion to address potential pandemic flu. It would provide $534.4 million for $500 per month in additional pay to military personnel in extended enlistments, $5 billion related to International Monetary Fund activities and $1 billion for a program to encourage consumers to trade in their cars for new, more fuel-efficient vehicles. It also would bar the use of funds in the bill to release detainees at the facility at Guantánamo Bay, Cuba, into the United States. Adopted (thus cleared for the president) 91-5: R 36-3; D 54-1; I 1-1. A "yea" was a vote in support of the president's position. June 18, 2009.

	208	209	210			208	209	210
ALABAMA					**MONTANA**			
Shelby	Y	N	Y		Baucus	Y	Y	Y
Sessions	Y	N	Y		Tester	Y	Y	Y
ALASKA					**NEBRASKA**			
Murkowski	Y	N	Y		Nelson	Y	N	Y
Begich	Y	Y	Y		**Johanns**	Y	N	Y
ARIZONA					**NEVADA**			
McCain	Y	N	Y		Reid	Y	Y	Y
Kyl	Y	N	Y		**Ensign**	?	?	?
ARKANSAS					**NEW HAMPSHIRE**			
Lincoln	Y	Y	Y		**Gregg**	?	N	Y
Pryor	Y	Y	Y		Shaheen	Y	Y	Y
CALIFORNIA					**NEW JERSEY**			
Feinstein	Y	Y	Y		Lautenberg	Y	Y	Y
Boxer	Y	Y	Y		Menendez	Y	Y	Y
COLORADO					**NEW MEXICO**			
Udall	Y	Y	Y		Bingaman	Y	Y	Y
Bennet	Y	Y	Y		Udall	Y	Y	Y
CONNECTICUT					**NEW YORK**			
Dodd	Y	Y	Y		Schumer	Y	Y	Y
Lieberman	Y	Y	Y		Gillibrand	Y	Y	Y
DELAWARE					**NORTH CAROLINA**			
Carper	Y	Y	Y		**Burr**	Y	N	Y
Kaufman	Y	Y	Y		Hagan	Y	Y	Y
FLORIDA					**NORTH DAKOTA**			
Nelson	Y	Y	Y		Conrad	Y	Y	Y
Martinez	Y	N	Y		Dorgan	Y	Y	Y
GEORGIA					**OHIO**			
Chambliss	Y	N	Y		**Voinovich**	Y	Y	Y
Isakson	Y	N	Y		Brown	Y	Y	Y
HAWAII					**OKLAHOMA**			
Inouye	Y	Y	Y		**Inhofe**	Y	N	Y
Akaka	Y	Y	Y		**Coburn**	N	N	N
IDAHO					**OREGON**			
Crapo	Y	N	Y		Wyden	Y	Y	Y
Risch	Y	N	Y		Merkley	Y	Y	Y
ILLINOIS					**PENNSYLVANIA**			
Durbin	+	Y	Y		Specter	Y	Y	Y
Burris	Y	Y	Y		Casey	Y	Y	Y
INDIANA					**RHODE ISLAND**			
Lugar	Y	N	Y		Reed	Y	Y	Y
Bayh	Y	Y	Y		Whitehouse	Y	Y	Y
IOWA					**SOUTH CAROLINA**			
Grassley	Y	N	Y		**Graham**	Y	N	Y
Harkin	Y	Y	Y		**DeMint**	N	N	N
KANSAS					**SOUTH DAKOTA**			
Brownback	Y	N	Y		Johnson	Y	Y	Y
Roberts	Y	N	Y		**Thune**	Y	N	Y
KENTUCKY					**TENNESSEE**			
McConnell	Y	N	Y		**Alexander**	Y	N	Y
Bunning	N	N	Y		**Corker**	Y	N	Y
LOUISIANA					**TEXAS**			
Landrieu	Y	Y	Y		**Hutchison**	Y	N	Y
Vitter	Y	N	Y		**Cornyn**	Y	N	Y
MAINE					**UTAH**			
Snowe	Y	N	Y		**Hatch**	Y	N	Y
Collins	Y	Y	Y		**Bennett**	Y	N	Y
MARYLAND					**VERMONT**			
Mikulski	Y	Y	Y		Leahy	Y	Y	Y
Cardin	Y	Y	Y		*Sanders*	Y	Y	N
MASSACHUSETTS					**VIRGINIA**			
Kennedy	?	?	?		Webb	Y	Y	Y
Kerry	Y	Y	Y		Warner	Y	Y	Y
MICHIGAN					**WASHINGTON**			
Levin	Y	Y	Y		Murray	Y	Y	Y
Stabenow	Y	Y	Y		Cantwell	Y	Y	Y
MINNESOTA					**WEST VIRGINIA**			
Klobuchar	Y	Y	Y		Byrd	?	?	?
Vacant					Rockefeller	?	Y	Y
MISSISSIPPI					**WISCONSIN**			
Cochran	Y	Y	Y		Kohl	Y	Y	Y
Wicker	Y	N	Y		Feingold	Y	N	N
MISSOURI					**WYOMING**			
Bond	Y	Y	Y		**Enzi**	Y	N	N
McCaskill	Y	Y	Y		**Barrasso**	Y	N	Y

KEY	Republicans	Democrats	*Independents*	
Y Voted for (yea)		X Paired against		C Voted "present" to avoid possible conflict of interest
# Paired for		– Announced against		
+ Announced for		P Voted "present"		? Did not vote or otherwise make a position known
N Voted against (nay)				

IN THE SENATE | By Vote Number

211. **S 1023. Foreign Tourism Promotion/Cloture.** Motion to invoke cloture (thus limiting debate) on the Dorgan, D-N.D., amendment that would make perfecting changes to the bill. Motion rejected 53-34: R 2-33; D 49-1; I 2-0. Three-fifths of the total Senate (60) is required to invoke cloture. June 22, 2009.

212. **Koh Nomination/Cloture.** Motion to invoke cloture (thus limiting debate) on the nomination of Harold Hongju Koh of Connecticut to be State Department legal adviser. Motion agreed to 65-31: R 8-31; D 55-0; I 2-0. Three-fifths of the total Senate (60) is required to invoke cloture. June 24, 2009.

213. **Koh Nomination/Confirmation.** Confirmation of President Obama's nomination of Harold Hongju Koh of Connecticut to be State Department legal adviser. Confirmed 62-35: R 5-35; D 55-0; I 2-0. A "yea" was a vote in support of the president's position. June 25, 2009.

214. **HR 2918. Fiscal 2010 Legislative Branch Appropriations/ Commit.** Nelson, D-Neb., motion to table (kill) the Vitter, R-La., motion to commit the bill to the Appropriations Committee with instructions that it be reported back with aggregate funding levels equal to the fiscal 2009 levels, except for funds related to the security of the Capitol complex. Motion agreed to 65-31: R 12-27; D 51-4; I 2-0. June 25, 2009.

	211	212	213	214
ALABAMA				
Shelby	N	N	N	Y
Sessions	N	N	N	N
ALASKA				
Murkowski	?	N	N	Y
Begich	?	Y	Y	Y
ARIZONA				
McCain	N	N	N	N
Kyl	N	N	N	N
ARKANSAS				
Lincoln	Y	Y	Y	Y
Pryor	Y	Y	Y	Y
CALIFORNIA				
Feinstein	Y	Y	Y	Y
Boxer	Y	Y	Y	Y
COLORADO				
Udall	?	Y	Y	Y
Bennet	Y	Y	Y	N
CONNECTICUT				
Dodd	Y	Y	Y	Y
Lieberman	Y	Y	Y	Y
DELAWARE				
Carper	Y	Y	Y	Y
Kaufman	Y	Y	Y	Y
FLORIDA				
Nelson	Y	Y	Y	Y
Martinez	Y	Y	Y	N
GEORGIA				
Chambliss	N	N	N	N
Isakson	N	N	N	N
HAWAII				
Inouye	Y	Y	Y	Y
Akaka	Y	Y	Y	Y
IDAHO				
Crapo	N	N	N	N
Risch	N	N	N	N
ILLINOIS				
Durbin	Y	Y	Y	Y
Burris	Y	Y	Y	Y
INDIANA				
Lugar	N	Y	Y	Y
Bayh	Y	Y	Y	Y
IOWA				
Grassley	N	N	N	N
Harkin	Y	Y	Y	Y
KANSAS				
Brownback	N	N	N	N
Roberts	?	N	N	Y
KENTUCKY				
McConnell	N	N	N	N
Bunning	N	N	N	N
LOUISIANA				
Landrieu	Y	Y	Y	Y
Vitter	?	N	N	N
MAINE				
Snowe	N	Y	Y	Y
Collins	N	Y	Y	Y
MARYLAND				
Mikulski	Y	Y	Y	Y
Cardin	Y	Y	Y	Y
MASSACHUSETTS				
Kennedy	?	?	?	?
Kerry	Y	Y	Y	Y
MICHIGAN				
Levin	Y	Y	Y	Y
Stabenow	Y	Y	Y	Y
MINNESOTA				
Klobuchar	Y	Y	Y	N
Vacant				
MISSISSIPPI				
Cochran	N	?	N	Y
Wicker	N	N	N	Y
MISSOURI				
Bond	N	N	N	Y
McCaskill	Y	Y	Y	N

	211	212	213	214
MONTANA				
Baucus	Y	Y	Y	Y
Tester	?	Y	Y	Y
NEBRASKA				
Nelson	Y	Y	Y	Y
Johanns	N	N	N	N
NEVADA				
Reid	N	Y	Y	Y
Ensign	Y	N	N	N
NEW HAMPSHIRE				
Gregg	N	Y	N	N
Shaheen	Y	Y	Y	Y
NEW JERSEY				
Lautenberg	Y	Y	Y	Y
Menendez	Y	Y	Y	Y
NEW MEXICO				
Bingaman	Y	Y	Y	Y
Udall	Y	Y	Y	Y
NEW YORK				
Schumer	Y	Y	Y	Y
Gillibrand	Y	Y	Y	Y
NORTH CAROLINA				
Burr	N	N	N	N
Hagan	Y	Y	Y	Y
NORTH DAKOTA				
Conrad	Y	Y	Y	Y
Dorgan	Y	Y	Y	Y
OHIO				
Voinovich	?	Y	Y	Y
Brown	Y	Y	Y	Y
OKLAHOMA				
Inhofe	N	N	N	?
Coburn	N	N	N	N
OREGON				
Wyden	?	Y	Y	Y
Merkley	Y	Y	Y	Y
PENNSYLVANIA				
Specter	?	Y	Y	Y
Casey	Y	Y	Y	Y
RHODE ISLAND				
Reed	Y	Y	Y	Y
Whitehouse	Y	Y	Y	Y
SOUTH CAROLINA				
Graham	N	N	N	N
DeMint	N	N	N	N
SOUTH DAKOTA				
Johnson	Y	Y	Y	Y
Thune	N	N	N	N
TENNESSEE				
Alexander	N	Y	N	Y
Corker	N	N	N	N
TEXAS				
Hutchison	?	N	N	N
Cornyn	N	N	N	N
UTAH				
Hatch	N	Y	N	N
Bennett	N	N	N	Y
VERMONT				
Leahy	Y	Y	Y	Y
Sanders	Y	Y	Y	Y
VIRGINIA				
Webb	Y	Y	Y	Y
Warner	Y	Y	Y	Y
WASHINGTON				
Murray	Y	Y	Y	Y
Cantwell	Y	Y	Y	Y
WEST VIRGINIA				
Byrd	?	?	?	?
Rockefeller	Y	Y	Y	Y
WISCONSIN				
Kohl	Y	Y	Y	Y
Feingold	Y	Y	Y	N
WYOMING				
Enzi	N	N	N	N
Barrasso	N	N	N	N

KEY	**Republicans**	Democrats	*Independents*
Y Voted for (yea)	X Paired against		C Voted "present" to avoid possible conflict of interest
# Paired for	– Announced against		
+ Announced for	P Voted "present"		? Did not vote or otherwise make a position known
N Voted against (nay)			

IN THE SENATE | By Vote Number

215. HR 2918. Fiscal 2010 Legislative Branch Appropriations/ **Durham Museum Photo Archive.** McCain, R-Ariz., amendment to the Nelson, D-Neb., substitute amendment. The McCain amendment would bar the use of funds appropriated in the bill for the Durham Museum in Omaha, Neb., to preserve the museum's photo archive collection of materials about Nebraska and the American West. The substitute would appropriate $4.7 billion in fiscal 2010 for legislative branch operations. Rejected 31-61: R 27-10; D 4-49; I 0-2. July 6, 2009.

216. HR 2918. Fiscal 2010 Legislative Branch Appropriations/ **Constitutional Point of Order.** Question of whether the Senate is in order to consider the Nelson, D-Neb., substitute amendment. Coburn, R-Okla., raised a point of order that the substitute violates Article I, Section 8 of the Constitution in conjunction with the 10th Amendment to the Constitution because it would provide $200,000 for the Durham Museum in Omaha, Neb., to preserve the museum's photo archive collection of materials about Nebraska and the American West. Amendment ruled in order 70-23: R 15-23; D 53-0; I 2-0. July 6, 2009.

217. HR 2918. Fiscal 2010 Legislative Branch Appropriations/ **Passage.** Passage of the bill that would appropriate $4.7 billion in fiscal 2010 for legislative branch operations, including $934 billion for operations of the Senate, $639 million for the Library of Congress, $554 million for the Government Accountability Office and $332 million for the Capitol Police. It would also include funding for House operations. Passed 67-25: R 17-21; D 48-4; I 2-0. (Prior to passage, the Nelson substitute amendment was adopted by voice vote.) July 6, 2009.

218. HR 2892. Fiscal 2010 Homeland Security Appropriations/ **Bus Security Grant.** McCain, R-Ariz., amendment to the Reid substitute amendment. The McCain amendment would eliminate $6 million for the Over-the-Road Bus Security Assistance grant program under the Federal Emergency Management Agency. The substitute would provide $44.3 billion in fiscal 2010 for the Homeland Security Department and related activities, including $43 billion in discretionary spending. Rejected 47-51: R 35-5; D 12-44; I 0-2. July 7, 2009.

219. HR 2892. Fiscal 2010 Homeland Security Appropriations/ **E-Verify for Government Contractors.** Schumer, D-N.Y., motion to table (kill) the Sessions, R-Ala., amendment to the Reid, D-Nev., substitute amendment. The Sessions amendment would make the Homeland Security Department's E-Verify program permanent and compel federal agencies to require government contractors to check employee citizenship status in the E-Verify system. Motion rejected 44-53: R 0-40; D 43-12; I 1-1. July 8, 2009.

220. HR 2892. Fiscal 2010 Homeland Security Appropriations/ **Border Fence Construction.** DeMint, R-S.C., amendment to the Reid, D-Nev., substitute amendment. The DeMint amendment would require the fence built along the U.S.-Mexican border to prevent pedestrian traffic and reach completion by Dec. 31, 2010. Adopted 54-44: R 33-7; D 21-35; I 0-2. July 8, 2009.

	215	216	217	218	219	220
ALABAMA						
Shelby	N	Y	Y	N	N	Y
Sessions	Y	N	N	Y	N	Y
ALASKA						
Murkowski	N	Y	Y	Y	N	N
Begich	N	Y	Y	N	Y	N
ARIZONA						
McCain	Y	N	Y	N	Y	N
Kyl	Y	N	N	Y	N	Y
ARKANSAS						
Lincoln	N	Y	Y	Y	N	Y
Pryor	N	Y	Y	N	N	Y
CALIFORNIA						
Feinstein	N	Y	Y	N	Y	Y
Boxer	N	Y	Y	N	Y	Y
COLORADO						
Udall	N	Y	N	Y	Y	N
Bennet	N	Y	N	Y	Y	N
CONNECTICUT						
Dodd	N	Y	Y	N	Y	N
Lieberman	N	Y	Y	N	N	N
DELAWARE						
Carper	N	Y	Y	N	Y	N
Kaufman	N	Y	Y	N	Y	N
FLORIDA						
Nelson	N	Y	Y	Y	Y	Y
Martinez	Y	N	N	Y	N	N
GEORGIA						
Chambliss	Y	N	N	Y	N	Y
Isakson	+	-	-	Y	N	Y
HAWAII						
Inouye	N	Y	Y	N	Y	N
Akaka	N	Y	Y	N	Y	N
IDAHO						
Crapo	Y	N	N	Y	N	Y
Risch	Y	N	N	Y	N	Y
ILLINOIS						
Durbin	N	Y	Y	N	Y	N
Burris	N	Y	Y	N	Y	N
INDIANA						
Lugar	Y	N	Y	Y	N	N
Bayh	Y	Y	Y	Y	Y	Y
IOWA						
Grassley	Y	Y	N	Y	N	Y
Harkin	N	Y	Y	N	?	N
KANSAS						
Brownback	?	?	?	Y	N	Y
Roberts	Y	N	N	Y	N	Y
KENTUCKY						
McConnell	Y	Y	Y	Y	N	Y
Bunning	Y	N	N	Y	N	Y
LOUISIANA						
Landrieu	N	Y	?	N	N	Y
Vitter	Y	N	N	Y	N	Y
MAINE						
Snowe	N	Y	Y	Y	N	Y
Collins	N	Y	Y	Y	N	N
MARYLAND						
Mikulski	N	Y	Y	N	Y	N
Cardin	N	Y	Y	N	Y	N
MASSACHUSETTS						
Kennedy	?	?	?	?	?	?
Kerry	N	Y	Y	N	Y	N
MICHIGAN						
Levin	N	Y	Y	N	Y	N
Stabenow	N	Y	Y	N	Y	Y
MINNESOTA						
Klobuchar	N	Y	Y	N	Y	N
Franken*				N	Y	N
MISSISSIPPI						
Cochran	N	Y	Y	N	N	N
Wicker	?	Y	Y	Y	N	Y
MISSOURI						
Bond	N	Y	Y	Y	N	Y
McCaskill	Y	Y	N	Y	N	Y
MONTANA						
Baucus	N	Y	Y	N	N	Y
Tester	N	Y	Y	N	N	Y
NEBRASKA						
Nelson	N	Y	Y	N	N	Y
Johanns	Y	N	Y	Y	N	Y
NEVADA						
Reid	N	Y	Y	N	Y	N
Ensign	Y	N	N	Y	N	N
NEW HAMPSHIRE						
Gregg	N	Y	Y	N	N	Y
Shaheen	N	Y	Y	Y	N	N
NEW JERSEY						
Lautenberg	N	Y	Y	N	Y	N
Menendez	N	Y	Y	N	Y	N
NEW MEXICO						
Bingaman	N	Y	Y	N	Y	N
Udall	?	?	?	Y	Y	N
NEW YORK						
Schumer	N	Y	Y	N	Y	N
Gillibrand	N	Y	Y	N	Y	N
NORTH CAROLINA						
Burr	Y	N	N	Y	N	Y
Hagan	Y	Y	Y	N	Y	N
NORTH DAKOTA						
Conrad	N	Y	N	Y	N	Y
Dorgan	N	Y	Y	N	N	Y
OHIO						
Voinovich	N	Y	Y	N	N	N
Brown	N	Y	Y	N	Y	N
OKLAHOMA						
Inhofe	Y	N	N	Y	N	Y
Coburn	Y	N	N	Y	N	Y
OREGON						
Wyden	N	Y	Y	N	Y	Y
Merkley	N	Y	Y	N	Y	Y
PENNSYLVANIA						
Specter	N	Y	Y	N	Y	Y
Casey	N	Y	Y	N	Y	N
RHODE ISLAND						
Reed	N	Y	Y	N	Y	N
Whitehouse	N	Y	Y	N	Y	N
SOUTH CAROLINA						
Graham	Y	N	N	Y	N	Y
DeMint	Y	N	N	Y	N	Y
SOUTH DAKOTA						
Johnson	N	Y	Y	N	Y	N
Thune	Y	N	N	Y	N	Y
TENNESSEE						
Alexander	Y	N	N	N	N	Y
Corker	Y	Y	Y	Y	N	Y
TEXAS						
Hutchison	Y	Y	Y	Y	N	Y
Cornyn	Y	N	N	Y	N	Y
UTAH						
Hatch	N	Y	Y	Y	N	Y
Bennett	N	Y	Y	Y	N	Y
VERMONT						
Leahy	N	Y	Y	N	Y	N
Sanders	N	Y	Y	N	Y	N
VIRGINIA						
Webb	N	Y	Y	Y	Y	Y
Warner	N	Y	Y	Y	Y	N
WASHINGTON						
Murray	?	?	?	N	Y	N
Cantwell	N	Y	Y	N	Y	N
WEST VIRGINIA						
Byrd	?	?	?	?	?	?
Rockefeller	N	Y	Y	N	N	Y
WISCONSIN						
Kohl	N	Y	Y	N	Y	N
Feingold	Y	Y	Y	Y	Y	N
WYOMING						
Enzi	Y	N	N	Y	N	Y
Barrasso	Y	N	N	Y	N	Y

KEY   Republicans   Democrats   *Independents*

Y Voted for (yea)	X Paired against	C Voted "present" to avoid possible conflict of interest
# Paired for	– Announced against	
+ Announced for	P Voted "present"	? Did not vote or otherwise make a position known
N Voted against (nay)		

*Sen. Al Franken, D-Minn., was sworn in July 7, 2009, after he was certified the winner of that state's contested election. The first vote for which he was eligible was vote 218.

IN THE SENATE | By Vote Number

221. HR 2892. Fiscal 2010 Homeland Security Appropriations/ **FEMA Grants.** Feingold, D-Wis., amendment to the Reid, D-Nev., substitute amendment. The Feingold amendment would require the administrator of the Federal Emergency Management Agency (FEMA) to award grants from FEMA's National Predisaster Mitigation Fund by competitive bid and without regard to congressionally directed spending. Rejected 38-60: R 25-15; D 12-44; I 1-1. July 8, 2009.

222. HR 2892. Fiscal 2010 Homeland Security Appropriations/ **Loran-C Funding.** McCain, R-Ariz., amendment to the Reid, D-Nev., substitute amendment. The McCain amendment would strike provisions providing for the termination of Loran-C, a land-based radio navigation system. Rejected 37-61: R 31-9; D 6-50; I 0-2. A "nay" was a vote in support of the president's position. July 8, 2009.

223. HR 2892. Fiscal 2010 Homeland Security Appropriations/ **Whitefish Emergency Operations Center.** Kyl, R-Ariz., amendment to the Reid, D-Nev., substitute amendment. The Kyl amendment would strike a provision directing $900,000 to the Whitefish Emergency Operations Center in Whitefish, Mont. Rejected 36-59: R 34-6; D 2-51; I 0-2. July 9, 2009.

224. HR 2892. Fiscal 2010 Homeland Security Appropriations/ **Advanced Training Center.** McCain, R-Ariz., amendment to the Reid, D-Nev., substitute amendment. The McCain amendment would strike a provision directing $39.7 million to the Advanced Training Center in Harpers Ferry, W.Va. Rejected 35-61: R 32-7; D 3-52; I 0-2. July 9, 2009.

	221	222	223	224			221	222	223	224
ALABAMA						**MONTANA**				
Shelby	N	N	N	N		Baucus	N	N	N	N
Sessions	N	Y	Y	Y		Tester	N	N	N	N
ALASKA						**NEBRASKA**				
Murkowski	N	N	Y	N		Nelson	N	N	N	N
Begich	N	N	N	N		**Johanns**	Y	Y	Y	Y
ARIZONA						**NEVADA**				
McCain	Y	Y	Y	Y		Reid	N	N	N	N
Kyl	Y	Y	Y	Y		**Ensign**	Y	Y	Y	Y
ARKANSAS						**NEW HAMPSHIRE**				
Lincoln	N	N	N	N		**Gregg**	Y	Y	Y	N
Pryor	N	N	N	N		Shaheen	N	N	N	N
CALIFORNIA						**NEW JERSEY**				
Feinstein	Y	N	N	N		Lautenberg	N	N	N	N
Boxer	N	N	N	N		Menendez	N	N	N	N
COLORADO						**NEW MEXICO**				
Udall	N	Y	N	N		Bingaman	Y	N	N	N
Bennet	N	Y	N	N		Udall	Y	N	N	N
CONNECTICUT						**NEW YORK**				
Dodd	N	N	?	?		Schumer	N	N	N	N
Lieberman	Y	N	N	N		Gillibrand	N	N	N	N
DELAWARE						**NORTH CAROLINA**				
Carper	Y	N	N	N		**Burr**	Y	Y	Y	Y
Kaufman	Y	N	N	N		Hagan	N	N	N	N
FLORIDA						**NORTH DAKOTA**				
Nelson	N	N	N	N		Conrad	Y	Y	N	N
Martinez	Y	Y	Y	Y		Dorgan	N	N	N	N
GEORGIA						**OHIO**				
Chambliss	Y	Y	Y	Y		**Voinovich**	N	N	N	N
Isakson	Y	Y	Y	Y		Brown	N	N	N	N
HAWAII						**OKLAHOMA**				
Inouye	N	N	N	N		**Inhofe**	Y	Y	Y	Y
Akaka	N	N	N	N		**Coburn**	Y	Y	Y	Y
IDAHO						**OREGON**				
Crapo	Y	Y	Y	Y		Wyden	N	N	N	N
Risch	Y	Y	Y	Y		Merkley	N	N	N	N
ILLINOIS						**PENNSYLVANIA**				
Durbin	N	N	N	N		Specter	N	N	N	N
Burris	N	N	N	N		Casey	N	N	N	N
INDIANA						**RHODE ISLAND**				
Lugar	Y	Y	Y	Y		Reed	N	N	N	N
Bayh	Y	Y	N	Y		Whitehouse	N	N	N	N
IOWA						**SOUTH CAROLINA**				
Grassley	N	Y	Y	Y		**Graham**	Y	Y	Y	Y
Harkin	N	N	N	N		**DeMint**	Y	Y	Y	Y
KANSAS						**SOUTH DAKOTA**				
Brownback	N	N	Y	Y		Johnson	N	N	N	N
Roberts	N	Y	Y	Y		**Thune**	Y	Y	Y	Y
KENTUCKY						**TENNESSEE**				
McConnell	N	Y	Y	Y		**Alexander**	N	N	N	N
Bunning	Y	Y	Y	Y		**Corker**	Y	Y	Y	Y
LOUISIANA						**TEXAS**				
Landrieu	N	N	N	N		**Hutchison**	N	Y	Y	N
Vitter	Y	Y	Y	Y		**Cornyn**	Y	Y	Y	Y
MAINE						**UTAH**				
Snowe	Y	N	N	Y		**Hatch**	N	Y	Y	Y
Collins	N	N	Y	N		**Bennett**	N	N	Y	Y
MARYLAND						**VERMONT**				
Mikulski	N	N	N	N		Leahy	N	N	N	N
Cardin	N	N	N	N		*Sanders*	N	N	N	N
MASSACHUSETTS						**VIRGINIA**				
Kennedy	?	?	?	?		Webb	Y	N	N	N
Kerry	N	N	N	N		Warner	N	N	N	N
MICHIGAN						**WASHINGTON**				
Levin	N	N	N	N		Murray	N	N	N	N
Stabenow	N	N	N	N		Cantwell	N	N	?	N
MINNESOTA						**WEST VIRGINIA**				
Klobuchar	Y	N	N	N		Byrd	?	?	?	?
Franken	Y	N	N	N		Rockefeller	N	N	?	N
MISSISSIPPI						**WISCONSIN**				
Cochran	N	Y	N	N		Kohl	N	N	N	N
Wicker	Y	Y	Y	Y		Feingold	Y	Y	Y	Y
MISSOURI						**WYOMING**				
Bond	N	N	N	?		**Enzi**	Y	Y	Y	Y
McCaskill	Y	Y	Y	Y		**Barrasso**	Y	Y	Y	Y

KEY	**Republicans**	Democrats	*Independents*	
Y	Voted for (yea)	X	Paired against	C	Voted "present" to avoid possible conflict of interest
#	Paired for	–	Announced against	
+	Announced for	P	Voted "present"	?	Did not vote or otherwise make a position known
N	Voted against (nay)			

IN THE SENATE | By Vote Number

225. **HR 2892. Fiscal 2010 Homeland Security Appropriations/ Prescription Drug Importation.** Vitter, R-La., amendment to the Dodd, D-Conn., amendment to the Reid, D-Nev., substitute. The Vitter amendment would bar U.S. Customs and Border Protection from using funds appropriated in the bill to prevent individuals from importing prescription drugs from Canada. The Dodd amendment would increase firefighter assistance grants under the Federal Emergency Management Agency by $10 million, offset by a reduction of $4.5 million from the Transportation Security Administration's aviation security program and $5.5 million from FEMA's trucking security program. Adopted 55-36: R 10-27; D 43-9; I 2-0. (Subsequently, the Dodd amendment, as amended, was adopted by voice vote.) July 9, 2009.

226. **HR 2892. Fiscal 2010 Homeland Security Appropriations/ Competitive Bidding Exemptions.** Murray, D-Wash., amendment to the Reid, D-Nev., substitute. The Murray amendment would require appropriated funds used for contracts or grants to be awarded using a competitive bidding process, with the exception of awards to small businesses or businesses owned by women or minorities. Adopted 67-24: R 13-24; D 52-0; I 2-0. July 9, 2009.

227. **HR 2892. Fiscal 2010 Homeland Security Appropriations/ Competitive Bidding.** Coburn, R-Okla., amendment to the Reid, D-Nev., substitute. The Coburn amendment would require appropriated funds used for contracts or grants to be awarded using a competitive bidding process. Rejected 31-60: R 27-10; D 4-48; I 0-2. July 9, 2009.

228. **HR 2892. Fiscal 2010 Homeland Security Appropriations/ Firefighter Assistance Grants.** Sanders, I-Vt., amendment to the Reid, D-Nev., substitute. The Sanders amendment would increase FEMA firefighter assistance grants by $100 million, offset by a reduction of the same amount from the Homeland Security Department's Science and Technology Directorate research, development, acquisition and operations account. Rejected 32-58: R 3-34; D 28-23; I 1-1. (Subsequently, the Reid substitute amendment was adopted by unanimous consent.) July 9, 2009.

229. **HR 2892. Fiscal 2010 Homeland Security Appropriations/ Passage.** Passage of the bill that would provide $44.3 billion in fiscal 2010 for the Homeland Security Department and related activities, including $42.9 billion in discretionary spending. The total would include $16 billion for Customs and Border Protection; $5.7 billion for Immigration and Customs Enforcement; $7.7 billion for the Transportation Security Administration, including fees; $10.2 billion for the Coast Guard; $1.5 billion for the Secret Service; and $7.1 billion for FEMA. Passed 84-6: R 32-5; D 50-1; I 2-0. A "yea" was a vote in support of the president's position. July 9, 2009.

	225	226	227	228	229
ALABAMA					
Shelby	Y	N	Y	N	Y
Sessions	Y	N	Y	N	Y
ALASKA					
Murkowski	N	Y	N	N	Y
Begich	Y	Y	N	N	Y
ARIZONA					
McCain	Y	N	Y	N	N
Kyl	N	N	Y	N	Y
ARKANSAS					
Lincoln	Y	Y	N	Y	Y
Pryor	Y	Y	N	N	Y
CALIFORNIA					
Feinstein	Y	Y	N	Y	Y
Boxer	Y	Y	Y	Y	Y
COLORADO					
Udall	N	Y	N	Y	Y
Bennet	Y	Y	N	Y	Y
CONNECTICUT					
Dodd	?	?	?	?	?
Lieberman	Y	Y	N	N	Y
DELAWARE					
Carper	N	Y	Y	Y	Y
Kaufman	Y	Y	N	Y	Y
FLORIDA					
Nelson	Y	Y	N	N	Y
Martinez	?	?	?	?	?
GEORGIA					
Chambliss	N	N	Y	N	Y
Isakson	N	N	Y	N	Y
HAWAII					
Inouye	Y	Y	N	N	Y
Akaka	Y	Y	N	N	Y
IDAHO					
Crapo	N	N	Y	N	Y
Risch	N	N	Y	N	Y
ILLINOIS					
Durbin	Y	Y	N	Y	Y
Burris	?	?	?	?	?
INDIANA					
Lugar	N	N	Y	N	Y
Bayh	N	Y	N	N	N
IOWA					
Grassley	Y	Y	Y	N	Y
Harkin	Y	Y	N	Y	Y
KANSAS					
Brownback	N	Y	Y	N	Y
Roberts	N	Y	N	N	Y
KENTUCKY					
McConnell	N	Y	Y	N	Y
Bunning	N	N	Y	N	Y
LOUISIANA					
Landrieu	Y	Y	N	N	Y
Vitter	Y	N	Y	N	Y
MAINE					
Snowe	Y	Y	N	Y	Y
Collins	Y	Y	N	N	Y
MARYLAND					
Mikulski	N	Y	N	Y	Y
Cardin	Y	Y	N	Y	Y
MASSACHUSETTS					
Kennedy	?	?	?	?	?
Kerry	N	Y	N	N	Y
MICHIGAN					
Levin	Y	Y	N	N	Y
Stabenow	Y	Y	N	N	Y
MINNESOTA					
Klobuchar	Y	Y	N	Y	Y
Franken	Y	Y	N	Y	Y
MISSISSIPPI					
Cochran	N	Y	N	N	Y
Wicker	N	Y	Y	N	Y
MISSOURI					
Bond	?	?	?	?	?
McCaskill	Y	Y	Y	N	Y
MONTANA					
Baucus	Y	Y	N	Y	Y
Tester	Y	Y	N	Y	Y
NEBRASKA					
Nelson	Y	Y	N	N	Y
Johanns	N	N	Y	Y	Y
NEVADA					
Reid	Y	Y	N	N	Y
Ensign	N	N	Y	N	N
NEW HAMPSHIRE					
Gregg	N	N	Y	N	Y
Shaheen	Y	Y	N	Y	Y
NEW JERSEY					
Lautenberg	N	Y	N	N	Y
Menendez	N	Y	N	N	Y
NEW MEXICO					
Bingaman	Y	Y	N	N	Y
Udall	Y	Y	N	N	Y
NEW YORK					
Schumer	Y	Y	N	Y	Y
Gillibrand	Y	Y	N	Y	Y
NORTH CAROLINA					
Burr	N	N	Y	N	N
Hagan	N	Y	N	N	Y
NORTH DAKOTA					
Conrad	Y	Y	N	Y	Y
Dorgan	Y	Y	N	Y	Y
OHIO					
Voinovich	N	Y	N	N	Y
Brown	Y	Y	N	Y	Y
OKLAHOMA					
Inhofe	?	?	?	?	?
Coburn	N	N	Y	N	N
OREGON					
Wyden	Y	Y	N	Y	Y
Merkley	Y	Y	N	Y	Y
PENNSYLVANIA					
Specter	Y	Y	N	Y	Y
Casey	Y	Y	N	Y	Y
RHODE ISLAND					
Reed	?	?	?	?	+
Whitehouse	Y	Y	N	Y	Y
SOUTH CAROLINA					
Graham	N	N	Y	N	Y
DeMint	Y	N	Y	N	N
SOUTH DAKOTA					
Johnson	Y	Y	N	Y	Y
Thune	Y	N	Y	Y	Y
TENNESSEE					
Alexander	N	Y	N	N	Y
Corker	Y	N	Y	N	Y
TEXAS					
Hutchison	N	Y	N	N	Y
Cornyn	N	N	Y	N	Y
UTAH					
Hatch	N	Y	N	N	Y
Bennett	N	N	N	N	Y
VERMONT					
Leahy	Y	Y	N	+	+
Sanders	Y	Y	N	Y	Y
VIRGINIA					
Webb	Y	Y	Y	N	Y
Warner	Y	Y	N	Y	Y
WASHINGTON					
Murray	N	Y	N	N	Y
Cantwell	Y	Y	N	N	Y
WEST VIRGINIA					
Byrd	?	?	?	?	?
Rockefeller	?	?	?	?	+
WISCONSIN					
Kohl	Y	Y	N	Y	Y
Feingold	Y	Y	Y	Y	Y
WYOMING					
Enzi	N	N	Y	N	Y
Barrasso	N	N	Y	N	Y

KEY   **Republicans**   Democrats   *Independents*

Y Voted for (yea)	X Paired against
# Paired for	– Announced against
+ Announced for	P Voted "present"
N Voted against (nay)	

C Voted "present" to avoid possible conflict of interest

? Did not vote or otherwise make a position known

IN THE SENATE | By Vote Number

230. **Groves Nomination/Cloture.** Motion to invoke cloture (thus limiting debate) on the nomination of Robert M. Groves of Michigan to be Census Bureau director. Motion agreed to 76-15: R 20-15; D 54-0; I 2-0. Three-fifths of the total Senate (60) is required to invoke cloture. (Subsequently, the nomination was confirmed by voice vote.) July 13, 2009.

231. S 1390. Fiscal 2010 Defense Authorization/Hate Crimes

Study. Hatch, R-Utah, amendment to the Leahy, D-Vt., amendment. The Hatch amendment would prevent the provisions of the Leahy amendment from taking effect. It would require a study and report comparing the investigation, prosecution and sentencing in states that have differing laws on hate crimes and allow the attorney general to provide grants and assistance to particular states if the study showed such assistance was needed. The Leahy amendment would expand federal hate crimes law to cover crimes based on sexual orientation, gender identity or disability. Violent crimes that involve a weapon and are motivated by those factors would be punishable by a fine and up to 10 years in prison. Crimes involving kidnapping, rape or murder would be punishable by life in prison. The amendment would authorize funds for grants to state and local law enforcement agencies to investigate and prosecute hate crimes and for additional Justice Department law enforcement personnel to prevent and respond to federal hate crimes. Rejected 29-62: R 29-4; D 0-56; I 0-2. July 16, 2009.

232. S 1390. Fiscal 2010 Defense Authorization/First Amendment

Protection. Brownback, R-Kan., amendment to the Leahy, D-Vt., amendment. The Brownback amendment would prohibit the provisions of the underlying amendment from being applied in a manner that violates the rights provided by the First Amendment to the Constitution or that burdens any exercise of those rights that is not intended to plan or incite violence against another individual. Adopted 78-13: R 33-0; D 43-13; I 2-0. July 16, 2009.

233. S 1390. Fiscal 2010 Defense Authorization/Cloture. Motion

to invoke cloture (thus limiting debate) on the Leahy, D-Vt., amendment. Motion agreed to 63-28: R 5-28; D 56-0; I 2-0. Three-fifths of the total Senate (60) is required to invoke cloture. (Subsequently, the Leahy amendment was adopted by voice vote.) July 16, 2009.

	230	231	232	233		230	231	232	233
ALABAMA					**MONTANA**				
Shelby	N	Y	Y	N	Baucus	Y	N	Y	Y
Sessions	N	Y	Y	N	Tester	Y	N	Y	Y
ALASKA					**NEBRASKA**				
Murkowski	Y	Y	Y	Y	Nelson	Y	N	Y	Y
Begich	Y	N	Y	Y	Johanns	Y	Y	Y	N
ARIZONA					**NEVADA**				
McCain	Y	Y	Y	N	Reid	Y	N	N	Y
Kyl	Y	Y	Y	N	Ensign	N	Y	Y	N
ARKANSAS					**NEW HAMPSHIRE**				
Lincoln	Y	N	Y	Y	Gregg	Y	?	?	?
Pryor	Y	N	Y	Y	Shaheen	Y	N	Y	Y
CALIFORNIA					**NEW JERSEY**				
Feinstein	Y	N	Y	Y	Lautenberg	Y	N	N	Y
Boxer	Y	N	Y	Y	Menendez	Y	N	Y	Y
COLORADO					**NEW MEXICO**				
Udall	Y	N	Y	Y	Bingaman	Y	N	Y	Y
Bennet	Y	N	Y	Y	Udall	Y	N	Y	Y
CONNECTICUT					**NEW YORK**				
Dodd	Y	N	Y	Y	Schumer	Y	N	N	Y
Lieberman	Y	N	Y	Y	Gillibrand	Y	N	N	Y
DELAWARE					**NORTH CAROLINA**				
Carper	Y	N	Y	Y	Burr	Y	Y	Y	N
Kaufman	Y	N	Y	Y	Hagan	Y	N	Y	Y
FLORIDA					**NORTH DAKOTA**				
Nelson	Y	N	Y	Y	Conrad	Y	N	Y	Y
Martinez	Y	?	?	?	Dorgan	Y	N	Y	Y
GEORGIA					**OHIO**				
Chambliss	N	Y	Y	N	Voinovich	?	N	Y	Y
Isakson	N	Y	Y	N	Brown	Y	N	N	Y
HAWAII					**OKLAHOMA**				
Inouye	Y	N	Y	Y	Inhofe	Y	Y	Y	N
Akaka	Y	N	N	Y	Coburn	Y	Y	Y	N
IDAHO					**OREGON**				
Crapo	N	Y	Y	N	Wyden	Y	N	Y	Y
Risch	N	Y	Y	N	Merkley	Y	N	Y	Y
ILLINOIS					**PENNSYLVANIA**				
Durbin	Y	N	Y	Y	Specter	Y	N	Y	Y
Burris	Y	N	N	Y	Casey	Y	N	Y	Y
INDIANA					**RHODE ISLAND**				
Lugar	?	N	Y	Y	Reed	Y	N	N	Y
Bayh	Y	N	Y	Y	Whitehouse	Y	N	N	Y
IOWA					**SOUTH CAROLINA**				
Grassley	Y	Y	Y	N	Graham	Y	?	?	?
Harkin	Y	N	N	Y	DeMint	?	Y	Y	N
KANSAS					**SOUTH DAKOTA**				
Brownback	N	Y	Y	N	Johnson	Y	N	Y	Y
Roberts	N	Y	Y	N	Thune	Y	Y	Y	N
KENTUCKY					**TENNESSEE**				
McConnell	Y	Y	Y	N	Alexander	Y	?	?	?
Bunning	N	?	?	?	Corker	Y	?	?	?
LOUISIANA					**TEXAS**				
Landrieu	Y	N	Y	Y	Hutchison	?	Y	Y	N
Vitter	N	Y	Y	N	Cornyn	N	Y	Y	N
MAINE					**UTAH**				
Snowe	Y	N	Y	Y	Hatch	Y	Y	Y	N
Collins	Y	N	Y	Y	Bennett	?	Y	Y	N
MARYLAND					**VERMONT**				
Mikulski	Y	N	N	Y	Leahy	Y	N	N	Y
Cardin	Y	N	N	Y	*Sanders*	Y	N	Y	Y
MASSACHUSETTS					**VIRGINIA**				
Kennedy	?	?	?	?	Webb	Y	N	Y	Y
Kerry	Y	N	Y	Y	Warner	Y	N	Y	Y
MICHIGAN					**WASHINGTON**				
Levin	Y	N	Y	Y	Murray	Y	N	Y	Y
Stabenow	?	N	Y	Y	Cantwell	Y	N	Y	Y
MINNESOTA					**WEST VIRGINIA**				
Klobuchar	Y	N	Y	Y	Byrd	?	?	?	?
Franken	Y	N	Y	Y	Rockefeller	?	N	Y	Y
MISSISSIPPI					**WISCONSIN**				
Cochran	Y	Y	Y	N	Kohl	Y	N	Y	Y
Wicker	N	Y	Y	N	Feingold	Y	N	Y	Y
MISSOURI					**WYOMING**				
Bond	Y	?	?	?	Enzi	N	Y	Y	N
McCaskill	Y	N	Y	Y	Barrasso	N	Y	Y	N

KEY	**Republicans**	Democrats	*Independents*		
Y	Voted for (yea)	X	Paired against	C	Voted "present" to avoid possible conflict of interest
#	Paired for	–	Announced against		
+	Announced for	P	Voted "present"	?	Did not vote or otherwise make a position known
N	Voted against (nay)				

IN THE SENATE | By Vote Number

234. **S 1390. Fiscal 2010 Defense Authorization/Crimes Against Military Members.** Sessions, R-Ala., amendment that would make it a federal crime to knowingly assault, batter or destroy property of a member of the U.S. armed forces or an immediate family member because of the servicemember's military service or status. Acts of assault would be punishable by up to a $10,000 fine and two years in prison; assault or battery resulting in bodily injury, by a $2,500 minimum fine and up to 10 years in prison. Destruction of property would be punishable by up to $100,000 and five years in prison. Individuals subject to the Uniform Code of Military Justice would be excluded. Adopted 92-0: R 36-0; D 54-0; I 2-0. July 20, 2009.

235. **S 1390. Fiscal 2010 Defense Authorization/F-22 Aircraft.** Levin, D-Mich., amendment that would strike $1.75 billion for the procurement of F-22A aircraft. It would increase the authorization for operations and maintenance by $350 million for the Army, $100 million for the Navy, $250 million for the Air Force and $150 million defensewide. It would increase the authorization for military personnel by $400 million and general Defense Department activities by $500 million. Adopted 58-40: R 15-25; D 42-14; I 1-1. A "yea" was a vote in support of the president's position. July 21, 2009.

236. **S 1390. Fiscal 2010 Defense Authorization/Army Active-Duty End Strength.** Lieberman, I-Conn., amendment that would authorize the Defense Department to increase the active-duty end strength for the Army by 30,000 above the 2010 baseline for fiscal 2010-12. For fiscal 2010, the department would get the funding from reserve funds or through an emergency supplemental. For fiscal 2011 and 2012, it would be required to include the necessary funding in its budget. The provisions could not be construed to limit the president's authority to waive statutory end strength in a time of war or national emergency. Adopted 93-1: R 39-0; D 52-1; I 2-0. July 21, 2009.

237. **S 1390. Fiscal 2010 Defense Authorization/Concealed Firearms Across State Lines.** Thune, R-S.D., amendment that would allow individuals with a valid permit or who are legally entitled in their home states to carry concealed firearms to do so in any state that issues permits for concealed firearms or does not prohibit residents from carrying them. Individuals carrying concealed firearms outside their states of residence would be required to carry a valid photo ID and would not be prohibited under federal law from possessing firearms. They would be subject to that state's laws on carrying concealed firearms. Rejected 58-39: R 38-2; D 20-35; I 0-2. (By unanimous consent, the Senate agreed to raise the majority requirement for adoption of the amendment to 60 votes.) July 22, 2009.

238. **S 1390. Fiscal 2010 Defense Authorization/North Korea Review.** Kerry, D-Mass., amendment that would require the president to submit a report to Congress, within 30 days of the bill's enactment, examining North Korea's conduct since June 26, 2008, to determine whether the country meets criteria for being listed as a state sponsor of terrorism. It would express a sense of the Senate that North Korea is a threat to international peace and security, and that, if the United States determines North Korea has assisted terrorists, the State Department should immediately list it as a state sponsor of terrorism. Adopted 66-31: R 9-31; D 55-0; I 2-0. July 22, 2009.

	234	235	236	237	238		234	235	236	237	238
ALABAMA						**MONTANA**					
Shelby	Y	Y	Y	Y	N	Baucus	Y	N	Y	Y	Y
Sessions	Y	N	Y	Y	N	Tester	Y	N	Y	Y	Y
ALASKA						**NEBRASKA**					
Murkowski	?	N	Y	Y	Y	Nelson	Y	Y	Y	Y	Y
Begich	Y	N	Y	Y	Y	Johanns	Y	N	Y	Y	N
ARIZONA						**NEVADA**					
McCain	Y	Y	Y	Y	N	Reid	Y	Y	Y	Y	Y
Kyl	Y	Y	Y	Y	N	Ensign	Y	Y	Y	Y	N
ARKANSAS						**NEW HAMPSHIRE**					
Lincoln	Y	Y	Y	Y	Y	Gregg	Y	Y	Y	Y	Y
Pryor	Y	Y	Y	Y	Y	Shaheen	Y	N	Y	N	Y
CALIFORNIA						**NEW JERSEY**					
Feinstein	Y	N	Y	N	Y	Lautenberg	Y	Y	Y	N	Y
Boxer	Y	N	Y	N	Y	Menendez	Y	Y	Y	N	Y
COLORADO						**NEW MEXICO**					
Udall	Y	Y	Y	Y	Y	Bingaman	Y	N	Y	N	Y
Bennet	Y	Y	Y	Y	Y	Udall	Y	N	Y	Y	Y
CONNECTICUT						**NEW YORK**					
Dodd	Y	N	Y	N	Y	Schumer	Y	Y	Y	N	Y
Lieberman	Y	N	Y	N	Y	Gillibrand	Y	Y	Y	N	Y
DELAWARE						**NORTH CAROLINA**					
Carper	Y	Y	Y	N	Y	Burr	Y	N	Y	Y	N
Kaufman	Y	Y	Y	N	Y	Hagan	Y	Y	Y	Y	Y
FLORIDA						**NORTH DAKOTA**					
Nelson	Y	Y	Y	N	Y	Conrad	Y	Y	Y	Y	Y
Martinez	?	N	Y	Y	N	Dorgan	Y	Y	Y	Y	Y
GEORGIA						**OHIO**					
Chambliss	Y	N	Y	Y	N	**Voinovich**	Y	Y	Y	N	Y
Isakson	Y	N	Y	Y	N	Brown	Y	Y	Y	N	Y
HAWAII						**OKLAHOMA**					
Inouye	Y	N	Y	N	Y	**Inhofe**	Y	N	Y	Y	N
Akaka	Y	N	Y	N	Y	**Coburn**	Y	Y	Y	Y	N
IDAHO						**OREGON**					
Crapo	Y	N	?	Y	N	Wyden	Y	Y	Y	N	Y
Risch	Y	N	Y	Y	N	Merkley	Y	Y	Y	N	Y
ILLINOIS						**PENNSYLVANIA**					
Durbin	Y	Y	Y	N	Y	Specter	Y	Y	?	N	Y
Burris	Y	Y	Y	N	Y	Casey	Y	Y	Y	Y	Y
INDIANA						**RHODE ISLAND**					
Lugar	Y	Y	Y	N	Y	Reed	Y	Y	Y	N	Y
Bayh	Y	Y	Y	Y	Y	Whitehouse	Y	Y	Y	N	Y
IOWA						**SOUTH CAROLINA**					
Grassley	Y	N	Y	Y	Y	**Graham**	Y	Y	Y	Y	N
Harkin	Y	Y	Y	N	Y	**DeMint**	Y	Y	Y	Y	N
KANSAS						**SOUTH DAKOTA**					
Brownback	Y	N	Y	Y	N	Johnson	Y	Y	Y	Y	Y
Roberts	Y	N	Y	Y	N	**Thune**	Y	N	Y	Y	N
KENTUCKY						**TENNESSEE**					
McConnell	Y	N	Y	Y	N	**Alexander**	Y	Y	Y	Y	Y
Bunning	Y	N	Y	Y	N	**Corker**	Y	Y	Y	Y	Y
LOUISIANA						**TEXAS**					
Landrieu	?	Y	Y	Y	Y	**Hutchison**	Y	N	Y	Y	N
Vitter	Y	N	Y	Y	N	**Cornyn**	Y	N	Y	Y	N
MAINE						**UTAH**					
Snowe	Y	N	Y	Y	Y	**Hatch**	Y	N	Y	Y	N
Collins	Y	N	Y	Y	Y	**Bennett**	?	N	Y	Y	N
MARYLAND						**VERMONT**					
Mikulski	?	?	?	?	?	Leahy	Y	Y	Y	N	Y
Cardin	Y	Y	Y	N	Y	*Sanders*	Y	Y	Y	N	Y
MASSACHUSETTS						**VIRGINIA**					
Kennedy	?	?	?	?	?	Webb	Y	Y	?	Y	Y
Kerry	Y	Y	Y	N	Y	Warner	Y	Y	Y	Y	Y
MICHIGAN						**WASHINGTON**					
Levin	Y	Y	Y	N	Y	Murray	Y	N	Y	N	Y
Stabenow	Y	Y	Y	N	Y	Cantwell	Y	N	Y	N	Y
MINNESOTA						**WEST VIRGINIA**					
Klobuchar	Y	Y	Y	N	Y	Byrd	?	N	?	?	?
Franken	Y	Y	Y	N	Y	Rockefeller	Y	Y	Y	N	Y
MISSISSIPPI						**WISCONSIN**					
Cochran	Y	N	Y	Y	N	Kohl	Y	Y	Y	N	Y
Wicker	Y	N	Y	Y	N	Feingold	Y	Y	N	Y	Y
MISSOURI						**WYOMING**					
Bond	?	Y	Y	Y	N	**Enzi**	Y	Y	Y	Y	N
McCaskill	Y	Y	Y	Y	N	**Barrasso**	Y	Y	Y	Y	N

KEY	**Republicans**	Democrats	*Independents*	
Y Voted for (yea)		X Paired against		C Voted "present" to avoid possible conflict of interest
# Paired for		− Announced against		
+ Announced for		P Voted "present"		? Did not vote or otherwise make a position known
N Voted against (nay)				

IN THE SENATE | By Vote Number

239. S 1390. Fiscal 2010 Defense Authorization/North Korea Terrorism Sponsor Designation.
Brownback, R-Kan., amendment that would express a sense of the Senate that the State Department should designate North Korea as a state sponsor of terrorism. Rejected 43-54: R 38-2; D 4-51; I 1-1. July 22, 2009.

240. S 1390. Fiscal 2010 Defense Authorization/Joint Strike Fighter Program.
Bayh, D-Ind., amendment that would withhold 10 percent of the funds authorized in the bill for the F-35 Joint Strike Fighter program until the Defense Department certifies to Congress that sufficient funds have been obligated in fiscal 2010 for an alternate engine program. It would also make changes in authorized funding for other weapons programs. Rejected 38-59: R 14-26; D 23-32; I 1-1. A "nay" was a vote in support of the president's position. July 23, 2009.

241. S 1390. Fiscal 2010 Defense Authorization/Rayon Fiber Procurement.
Isakson, R-Ga., amendment that would repeal the Jan. 28, 2013, sunset of the Defense Department's authority to procure fire-resistant rayon fiber from foreign countries for uniforms. Rejected 40-54: R 32-7; D 8-45; I 0-2. July 23, 2009.

242. S 1390. Fiscal 2010 Defense Authorization/Passage.
Passage of the bill that would authorize $679.8 billion for defense programs in fiscal 2010, including $129.3 billion for the wars in Iraq and Afghanistan. Excluding the war funding, the authorization includes $155.6 billion for operations and maintenance; $107.2 billion for procurement; $135.6 billion for military personnel; $22.8 billion for military construction, family housing and base closure; $79.9 billion for research, development, testing and evaluation; and $27.9 billion for the Defense Health Program. The bill would authorize a 3.4 percent pay increase for military personnel and would expand federal hate crime law to cover crimes based on sexual orientation, gender identity or disability. Passed 87-7: R 34-5; D 52-1; I 1-1. A "yea" was a vote in support of the president's position. July 23, 2009.

	239	240	241	242			239	240	241	242
ALABAMA						**MONTANA**				
Shelby	Y	N	Y	Y		Baucus	N	Y	N	Y
Sessions	Y	N	Y	Y		Tester	N	N	N	Y
ALASKA						**NEBRASKA**				
Murkowski	Y	Y	Y	Y		Nelson	Y	N	N	Y
Begich	N	Y	N	Y		Johanns	Y	Y	Y	Y
ARIZONA						**NEVADA**				
McCain	Y	N	Y	Y		Reid	N	N	Y	Y
Kyl	Y	N	Y	Y		Ensign	Y	N	Y	Y
ARKANSAS						**NEW HAMPSHIRE**				
Lincoln	Y	N	N	Y		Gregg	Y	N	Y	Y
Pryor	N	N	N	Y		Shaheen	N	N	N	Y
CALIFORNIA						**NEW JERSEY**				
Feinstein	N	N	N	?		Lautenberg	N	Y	N	Y
Boxer	N	N	N	Y		Menendez	N	N	N	Y
COLORADO						**NEW MEXICO**				
Udall	N	N	N	Y		Bingaman	N	N	N	Y
Bennet	N	N	N	Y		Udall	N	N	N	Y
CONNECTICUT						**NEW YORK**				
Dodd	N	N	Y	Y		Schumer	N	N	Y	Y
Lieberman	Y	N	N	Y		Gillibrand	N	Y	N	Y
DELAWARE						**NORTH CAROLINA**				
Carper	N	Y	N	Y		**Burr**	Y	Y	N	Y
Kaufman	N	N	N	Y		Hagan	N	Y	N	Y
FLORIDA						**NORTH DAKOTA**				
Nelson	Y	N	N	Y		Conrad	N	Y	N	Y
Martinez	Y	N	N	Y		Dorgan	N	Y	N	Y
GEORGIA						**OHIO**				
Chambliss	Y	N	Y	Y		**Voinovich**	Y	Y	Y	Y
Isakson	Y	N	Y	Y		Brown	N	Y	N	Y
HAWAII						**OKLAHOMA**				
Inouye	N	Y	N	Y		**Inhofe**	Y	N	Y	Y
Akaka	N	N	N	Y		**Coburn**	Y	N	Y	N
IDAHO						**OREGON**				
Crapo	Y	N	Y	Y		Wyden	N	N	N	Y
Risch	Y	N	Y	Y		Merkley	N	N	N	Y
ILLINOIS						**PENNSYLVANIA**				
Durbin	N	N	N	Y		Specter	N	N	N	Y
Burris	N	Y	N	Y		Casey	N	N	N	Y
INDIANA						**RHODE ISLAND**				
Lugar	N	Y	Y	Y		Reed	N	N	Y	Y
Bayh	Y	Y	Y	Y		Whitehouse	N	N	Y	Y
IOWA						**SOUTH CAROLINA**				
Grassley	Y	N	N	Y		**Graham**	Y	Y	N	Y
Harkin	N	N	N	Y		**DeMint**	Y	N	N	N
KANSAS						**SOUTH DAKOTA**				
Brownback	Y	N	Y	Y		Johnson	N	N	N	Y
Roberts	Y	N	Y	Y		**Thune**	Y	Y	Y	Y
KENTUCKY						**TENNESSEE**				
McConnell	Y	Y	Y	Y		**Alexander**	Y	N	Y	Y
Bunning	Y	Y	N	Y		**Corker**	N	Y	Y	Y
LOUISIANA						**TEXAS**				
Landrieu	N	Y	?	Y		**Hutchison**	Y	Y	Y	Y
Vitter	Y	Y	N	N		**Cornyn**	Y	Y	Y	Y
MAINE						**UTAH**				
Snowe	Y	N	Y	Y		**Hatch**	Y	N	Y	Y
Collins	Y	N	Y	Y		**Bennett**	Y	N	?	?
MARYLAND						**VERMONT**				
Mikulski	?	?	?	?		Leahy	N	Y	N	Y
Cardin	N	N	N	Y		*Sanders*	N	Y	N	N
MASSACHUSETTS						**VIRGINIA**				
Kennedy	?	?	?	?		Webb	N	Y	N	Y
Kerry	N	Y	N	Y		Warner	N	Y	?	Y
MICHIGAN						**WASHINGTON**				
Levin	N	Y	N	Y		Murray	N	Y	N	Y
Stabenow	N	Y	N	Y		Cantwell	N	Y	N	Y
MINNESOTA						**WEST VIRGINIA**				
Klobuchar	N	N	N	Y		Byrd	?	?	?	?
Franken	N	N	Y	Y		Rockefeller	N	N	N	?
MISSISSIPPI						**WISCONSIN**				
Cochran	Y	Y	Y	Y		Kohl	N	N	N	Y
Wicker	Y	N	N	Y		Feingold	N	Y	N	N
MISSOURI						**WYOMING**				
Bond	Y	N	Y	Y		**Enzi**	Y	N	Y	N
McCaskill	N	Y	Y	Y		**Barrasso**	Y	N	Y	N

KEY   **Republicans**   Democrats   *Independents*

Y Voted for (yea)	X Paired against	C Voted "present" to avoid possible conflict of interest
# Paired for	– Announced against	
+ Announced for	P Voted "present"	? Did not vote or otherwise make a position known
N Voted against (nay)		

IN THE SENATE | By Vote Number

243. HR 3183. Fiscal 2010 Energy-Water Appropriations/ **Unauthorized Funding Ban.** McCain, R-Ariz., amendment to the Dorgan, D-N.D., substitute amendment. The McCain amendment would bar the use of funds in the bill for unauthorized projects. The substitute would provide $34.3 billion in fiscal 2010 for energy and water development projects, including $5.4 billion for the Army Corps of Engineers and $27.4 billion for the Energy Department, of which $10 billion would be for the National Nuclear Security Administration. Rejected 25-72: R 22-18; D 3-52; I 0-2. July 28, 2009.

244. HR 3183. Fiscal 2010 Energy-Water Appropriations/TARP **Funding.** Alexander, R-Tenn., motion to waive the Congressional Budget Act with respect to the Dorgan, D-N.D., point of order against the Alexander amendment to the Dorgan substitute amendment. The Alexander amendment would prohibit the Treasury Department from providing further funds under the Troubled Asset Relief Program to automobile manufacturers and would state that Treasury has a fiduciary duty to each eligible taxpayer to maximize the return of funds provided under the program. Motion rejected 38-59: R 37-3; D 1-54; I 0-2. A three-fifths majority vote (60) of the total Senate is required to waive the Congressional Budget Act. (Subsequently, the chair upheld the point of order, and the amendment fell.) July 29, 2009.

245. HR 3183. Fiscal 2010 Energy-Water Appropriations/Energy **Department Administration.** Coburn, R-Okla., amendment to the Dorgan, D-N.D., substitute amendment. The Coburn amendment would reduce agency administration funding for the Energy Department by $14 million. Rejected 35-62: R 30-10; D 5-50; I 0-2. July 29, 2009.

246. HR 3183. Fiscal 2010 Energy-Water Appropriations/ **Federal Contracts.** Dorgan, D-N.D., amendment to the Dorgan substitute amendment. The Dorgan amendment would bar the use of funds for the Energy Department to enter into an unauthorized federal contract unless the contract is in accordance with the Federal Property and Administrative Services Act of 1949 and the Federal Acquisition Regulation. Adopted 79-18: R 23-17; D 54-1; I 2-0. July 29, 2009.

247. HR 3183. Fiscal 2010 Energy-Water Appropriations/ **Competitive Procedures.** Coburn, R-Okla., amendment to the Dorgan, D-N.D., substitute. The Coburn amendment would bar the use of funds in the bill for any grants or for payments in connection with a contract unless the grant or contract is awarded using competitive procedures as defined by federal law. Rejected 26-71: R 23-17; D 3-52; I 0-2. July 29, 2009.

248. HR 3183. Fiscal 2010 Energy-Water Appropriations/Passage. Passage of the bill that would provide $34.3 billion in fiscal 2010 for energy and water development projects, including $5.4 billion for the Army Corps of Engineers and $27.4 billion for the Energy Department, of which $10 billion would be for the National Nuclear Security Administration. The funding also includes $1.1 billion for the Interior Department's Bureau of Reclamation. Passed 85-9: R 31-8; D 53-1; I 1-0. (Before passage, the Dorgan, D-N.D., substitute was adopted by voice vote.) A "yea" was a vote in support of the president's position. July 29, 2009.

	243	244	245	246	247	248
ALABAMA						
Shelby	N	Y	N	Y	N	Y
Sessions	N	Y	Y	N	Y	Y
ALASKA						
Murkowski	N	Y	N	Y	N	Y
Begich	N	N	N	Y	N	Y
ARIZONA						
McCain	Y	Y	Y	N	Y	N
Kyl	Y	Y	Y	N	Y	N
ARKANSAS						
Lincoln	N	N	N	Y	N	Y
Pryor	N	N	N	Y	N	Y
CALIFORNIA						
Feinstein	N	N	N	Y	N	Y
Boxer	N	N	N	Y	N	Y
COLORADO						
Udall	N	N	N	Y	N	Y
Bennet	N	N	N	Y	N	Y
CONNECTICUT						
Dodd	N	N	N	Y	N	Y
Lieberman	N	N	N	Y	N	+
DELAWARE						
Carper	N	N	N	Y	Y	Y
Kaufman	N	N	N	Y	N	Y
FLORIDA						
Nelson	N	N	N	Y	N	Y
Martinez	Y	Y	Y	Y	Y	?
GEORGIA						
Chambliss	Y	Y	Y	N	Y	N
Isakson	Y	Y	Y	N	Y	N
HAWAII						
Inouye	N	N	N	Y	N	Y
Akaka	N	N	N	Y	N	Y
IDAHO						
Crapo	Y	Y	Y	Y	Y	Y
Risch	Y	Y	Y	Y	Y	Y
ILLINOIS						
Durbin	N	N	N	Y	N	Y
Burris	N	N	N	Y	N	Y
INDIANA						
Lugar	Y	N	Y	Y	N	Y
Bayh	Y	N	Y	Y	N	Y
IOWA						
Grassley	Y	Y	Y	N	Y	Y
Harkin	N	N	N	Y	N	Y
KANSAS						
Brownback	N	Y	N	Y	N	Y
Roberts	N	Y	N	Y	N	Y
KENTUCKY						
McConnell	N	Y	Y	Y	N	Y
Bunning	Y	Y	Y	N	Y	Y
LOUISIANA						
Landrieu	N	N	N	Y	N	Y
Vitter	Y	Y	Y	N	Y	Y
MAINE						
Snowe	N	Y	N	Y	N	Y
Collins	N	Y	N	Y	N	Y
MARYLAND						
Mikulski	?	?	?	?	?	?
Cardin	N	N	N	Y	N	Y
MASSACHUSETTS						
Kennedy	?	?	?	?	?	?
Kerry	N	N	N	Y	N	Y
MICHIGAN						
Levin	N	N	N	Y	N	Y
Stabenow	N	N	N	Y	N	Y
MINNESOTA						
Klobuchar	N	Y	N	Y	N	Y
Franken	N	N	N	Y	N	Y
MISSISSIPPI						
Cochran	N	Y	N	Y	N	Y
Wicker	N	Y	Y	Y	N	Y
MISSOURI						
Bond	N	Y	N	Y	N	Y
McCaskill	Y	N	Y	N	Y	N

	243	244	245	246	247	248
MONTANA						
Baucus	N	N	N	Y	N	Y
Tester	N	N	N	Y	N	Y
NEBRASKA						
Nelson	N	N	Y	Y	N	Y
Johanns	Y	Y	Y	N	Y	Y
NEVADA						
Reid	N	N	N	Y	N	Y
Ensign	N	Y	Y	N	Y	N
NEW HAMPSHIRE						
Gregg	N	Y	Y	Y	N	Y
Shaheen	N	N	N	Y	N	Y
NEW JERSEY						
Lautenberg	N	N	N	Y	N	Y
Menendez	N	N	N	Y	N	+
NEW MEXICO						
Bingaman	N	N	N	Y	N	Y
Udall	N	N	N	Y	N	Y
NEW YORK						
Schumer	N	N	N	Y	N	Y
Gillibrand	N	N	N	Y	N	Y
NORTH CAROLINA						
Burr	Y	Y	Y	N	Y	Y
Hagan	N	N	N	Y	N	Y
NORTH DAKOTA						
Conrad	N	N	N	Y	N	Y
Dorgan	N	N	N	Y	N	Y
OHIO						
Voinovich	N	N	N	Y	N	Y
Brown	N	N	N	Y	N	Y
OKLAHOMA						
Inhofe	Y	Y	Y	N	Y	N
Coburn	Y	Y	Y	N	Y	N
OREGON						
Wyden	N	N	N	Y	N	Y
Merkley	N	N	N	Y	N	Y
PENNSYLVANIA						
Specter	N	N	N	Y	N	Y
Casey	N	N	N	Y	N	Y
RHODE ISLAND						
Reed	N	N	N	Y	N	Y
Whitehouse	N	N	N	Y	N	Y
SOUTH CAROLINA						
Graham	Y	Y	Y	N	Y	Y
DeMint	Y	Y	Y	N	Y	N
SOUTH DAKOTA						
Johnson	N	N	N	Y	N	Y
Thune	Y	Y	Y	Y	Y	Y
TENNESSEE						
Alexander	N	Y	N	Y	N	Y
Corker	Y	N	Y	Y	Y	Y
TEXAS						
Hutchison	N	Y	Y	Y	N	Y
Cornyn	Y	Y	Y	N	Y	Y
UTAH						
Hatch	N+	Y	N	Y	N	Y
Bennett	N	Y	N	Y	N	Y
VERMONT						
Leahy	N	N	N	Y	N	Y
Sanders	N	N	N	Y	N	Y
VIRGINIA						
Webb	N	N	N	Y	N	Y
Warner	N	N	N	Y	N	Y
WASHINGTON						
Murray	N	N	N	Y	N	Y
Cantwell	N	N	N	Y	N	Y
WEST VIRGINIA						
Byrd	?	?	?	?	?	?
Rockefeller	N	N	N	Y	N	Y
WISCONSIN						
Kohl	N	N	N	Y	N	Y
Feingold	Y	N	Y	Y	Y	Y
WYOMING						
Enzi	Y	Y	Y	N	Y	Y
Barrasso	Y	Y	Y	N	Y	Y

KEY **Republicans** Democrats *Independents*

Y	Voted for (yea)	X	Paired against	C	Voted "present" to avoid possible conflict of interest
#	Paired for	–	Announced against		
+	Announced for	P	Voted "present"	?	Did not vote or otherwise make a position known
N	Voted against (nay)				

IN THE SENATE | By Vote Number

249. HR 3357. Trust Funds Solvency/Highway Trust Fund Offset.
Vitter, R-La., amendment that would strike language in the bill that would provide $7 billion from the Treasury for the Highway Trust Fund, and take money instead from unobligated funds made available under the 2009 economic stimulus law. Rejected 42-55: R 40-0; D 2-53; I 0-2. July 30, 2009.

250. HR 3357. Trust Funds Solvency/Unemployment Trust Fund Offset.
Ensign, R-Nev., amendment that would rescind $7.5 billion from unobligated funds made available under the 2009 economic stimulus law, excluding funding for veterans' programs, to offset funding in the bill for the Unemployment Trust Fund. It would require the Office of Management and Budget to report to Congress on the amounts rescinded as they apply to each congressional committee. Rejected 41-56: R 39-1; D 2-53; I 0-2. July 30, 2009.

251. HR 3357. Trust Funds Solvency/Repeal of Highway Trust Fund Rescission.
Bond, R-Mo., motion to waive the Congressional Budget Act with respect to the Durbin, D-Ill., point of order against the Bond amendment. The Bond amendment would repeal provisions of current law rescinding $8.6 billion from the Highway Trust Fund on Sept. 30. Motion rejected 34-63: R 22-18; D 11-44; I 1-1. A three-fifths majority vote (60) of the total Senate is required to waive the Congressional Budget Act. (Subsequently, the chair upheld the point of order, and the amendment fell.) July 30, 2009.

252. HR 3357. Trust Funds Solvency/Total Funding Offset.
Sessions, R-Ala., amendment that would rescind unobligated funds made available under the 2009 economic stimulus law to fund the bill's provisions. Rejected 40-57: R 38-2; D 2-53; I 0-2. July 30, 2009.

253. HR 3357. Trust Funds Solvency/Motion to Waive.
Boxer, D-Calif., motion to waive the Budget Act with respect to the Vitter, R-La., point of order against the bill that would transfer $7 billion from the Treasury to the Highway Trust Fund and increase funding authorizations for several other programs. Motion agreed to 71-26: R 15-25; D 54-1; I 2-0. A three-fifths majority vote (60) of the total Senate is required to waive the Budget Act. July 30, 2009.

254. HR 3357. Trust Funds Solvency/Passage.
Passage of the bill that would transfer $7 billion from the Treasury to the Highway Trust Fund, increase the statutory level of the Unemployment Trust Fund by unspecified sums, increase the Federal Housing Administration Mutual Mortgage Insurance program account to $400 billion and increase the Government National Mortgage Association Mortgage-Backed Securities Loan Guarantee Program account level to $400 billion. Passed (thus cleared for the president) 79-17: R 22-17; D 55-0; I 2-0. July 30, 2009.

	249	250	251	252	253	254
ALABAMA						
Shelby	Y	Y	Y	Y	Y	Y
Sessions	Y	Y	N	Y	N	N
ALASKA						
Murkowski	Y	Y	Y	Y	Y	Y
Begich	N	N	Y	N	Y	Y
ARIZONA						
McCain	Y	Y	N	Y	N	N
Kyl	Y	Y	N	Y	N	N
ARKANSAS						
Lincoln	Y	Y	N	N	N	Y
Pryor	N	N	N	N	Y	Y
CALIFORNIA						
Feinstein	N	N	N	N	Y	Y
Boxer	N	N	N	N	Y	Y
COLORADO						
Udall	N	N	Y	N	Y	Y
Bennet	N	N	Y	N	Y	Y
CONNECTICUT						
Dodd	N	N	N	N	Y	Y
Lieberman	N	N	N	N	Y	Y
DELAWARE						
Carper	N	N	N	N	Y	Y
Kaufman	N	N	N	N	Y	Y
FLORIDA						
Nelson	N	N	Y	N	Y	Y
Martinez	Y	Y	Y	Y	Y	Y
GEORGIA						
Chambliss	Y	Y	Y	Y	N	Y
Isakson	Y	Y	Y	Y	N	Y
HAWAII						
Inouye	N	N	N	N	Y	Y
Akaka	N	N	N	N	Y	Y
IDAHO						
Crapo	Y	Y	Y	Y	Y	Y
Risch	Y	Y	Y	Y	Y	Y
ILLINOIS						
Durbin	N	N	N	N	Y	Y
Burris	N	N	N	N	Y	Y
INDIANA						
Lugar	Y	Y	N	Y	Y	Y
Bayh	N	N	N	Y	Y	Y
IOWA						
Grassley	Y	Y	N	Y	N	Y
Harkin	N	N	Y	N	Y	Y
KANSAS						
Brownback	Y	Y	N	Y	N	Y
Roberts	Y	Y	Y	Y	Y	Y
KENTUCKY						
McConnell	Y	Y	N	Y	N	N
Bunning	Y	Y	N	Y	N	N
LOUISIANA						
Landrieu	N	N	N	N	Y	Y
Vitter	Y	Y	N	Y	N	Y
MAINE						
Snowe	Y	Y	N	Y	Y	Y
Collins	Y	N	Y	N	Y	Y
MARYLAND						
Mikulski	?	?	?	?	?	?
Cardin	N	N	N	N	Y	Y
MASSACHUSETTS						
Kennedy	?	?	?	?	?	?
Kerry	N	N	N	N	Y	Y
MICHIGAN						
Levin	N	N	N	N	Y	Y
Stabenow	N	N	N	N	Y	Y
MINNESOTA						
Klobuchar	N	N	N	N	Y	Y
Franken	N	N	N	N	Y	Y
MISSISSIPPI						
Cochran	Y	Y	Y	Y	Y	Y
Wicker	Y	Y	Y	Y	Y	Y
MISSOURI						
Bond	Y	Y	Y	Y	Y	Y
McCaskill	N	N	Y	N	Y	Y

	249	250	251	252	253	254
MONTANA						
Baucus	N	N	N	N	Y	Y
Tester	N	N	N	N	Y	Y
NEBRASKA						
Nelson	Y	Y	Y	Y	Y	Y
Johanns	Y	Y	N	Y	N	N
NEVADA						
Reid	N	N	N	N	Y	Y
Ensign	Y	Y	N	Y	N	N
NEW HAMPSHIRE						
Gregg	Y	Y	Y	Y	N	N
Shaheen	N	N	Y	N	Y	Y
NEW JERSEY						
Lautenberg	N	N	N	N	Y	Y
Menendez	N	N	N	N	Y	Y
NEW MEXICO						
Bingaman	N	N	N	N	Y	Y
Udall	N	N	N	N	Y	Y
NEW YORK						
Schumer	N	N	N	N	Y	Y
Gillibrand	N	N	N	N	Y	Y
NORTH CAROLINA						
Burr	Y	Y	N	Y	N	N
Hagan	N	N	N	N	Y	Y
NORTH DAKOTA						
Conrad	N	N	N	N	Y	Y
Dorgan	N	N	N	N	Y	Y
OHIO						
Voinovich	Y	Y	Y	Y	Y	Y
Brown	N	N	N	N	Y	Y
OKLAHOMA						
Inhofe	Y	Y	Y	Y	Y	?
Coburn	Y	Y	N	Y	N	N
OREGON						
Wyden	N	N	Y	N	Y	Y
Merkley	N	N	N	N	Y	Y
PENNSYLVANIA						
Specter	N	N	N	N	Y	Y
Casey	N	N	N	N	Y	Y
RHODE ISLAND						
Reed	N	N	N	N	Y	Y
Whitehouse	N	N	N	N	Y	Y
SOUTH CAROLINA						
Graham	Y	Y	N	Y	N	Y
DeMint	Y	Y	N	Y	N	N
SOUTH DAKOTA						
Johnson	N	N	N	N	Y	Y
Thune	Y	Y	Y	Y	N	N
TENNESSEE						
Alexander	Y	Y	Y	Y	Y	Y
Corker	Y	Y	N	Y	N	N
TEXAS						
Hutchison	Y	Y	Y	Y	N	Y
Cornyn	Y	Y	Y	Y	N	Y
UTAH						
Hatch	Y	Y	Y	Y	N	Y
Bennett	Y	Y	Y	Y	N	N
VERMONT						
Leahy	N	N	N	N	Y	Y
Sanders	N	N	Y	N	Y	Y
VIRGINIA						
Webb	N	N	N	N	Y	Y
Warner	N	N	N	N	Y	Y
WASHINGTON						
Murray	N	N	N	N	Y	Y
Cantwell	N	N	N	N	Y	Y
WEST VIRGINIA						
Byrd	?	?	?	?	?	?
Rockefeller	N	N	N	N	Y	Y
WISCONSIN						
Kohl	N	N	N	N	Y	Y
Feingold	N	N	N	N	Y	Y
WYOMING						
Enzi	Y	Y	Y	Y	N	N
Barrasso	Y	Y	Y	Y	N	N

KEY	**Republicans**	Democrats	*Independents*
Y	Voted for (yea)	X Paired against	C Voted "present" to avoid possible conflict of interest
#	Paired for	– Announced against	
+	Announced for	P Voted "present"	? Did not vote or otherwise make a position known
N	Voted against (nay)		

IN THE SENATE | By Vote Number

255. HR 2997. Fiscal 2010 Agriculture Appropriations/Cloture. Motion to invoke cloture (thus limiting debate) on the Kohl, D-Wis., substitute amendment that would provide $124.5 billion in fiscal 2010 for the Agriculture Department and related agencies, including $23.1 billion in discretionary spending. Motion agreed to 83-11: R 28-11; D 54-0; I 1-0. Three-fifths of the total Senate (60) is required to invoke cloture. Aug. 3, 2009.

256. HR 2997. Fiscal 2010 Agriculture Appropriations/High Energy Cost Grants. McCain, R-Ariz., amendment to the Kohl, D-Wis., substitute amendment. The McCain amendment would strike provisions that would appropriate $17.5 million for the High Energy Cost Grant Program. Rejected 41-55: R 27-13; D 14-41; I 0-1. Aug. 3, 2009.

257. HR 2997. Fiscal 2010 Agriculture Appropriations/Watershed and Flood Prevention. McCain, R-Ariz., amendment to the Kohl, D-Wis., substitute amendment. The McCain amendment would strike provisions that would appropriate $24.4 million for the Small Watershed Program. Rejected 27-70: R 20-20; D 7-48; I 0-2. Aug. 4, 2009.

258. HR 2997. Fiscal 2010 Agriculture Appropriations/Educational Television Station Grants. Coburn, R-Okla., amendment to the Kohl, D-Wis., substitute amendment. The Coburn amendment would strike provisions that would appropriate $5 million for grants for non-commercial educational television broadcast stations that serve rural areas and are qualified for Corporation for Public Broadcasting grants. Rejected 37-60: R 31-9; D 5-50; I 1-1. Aug. 4, 2009.

259. HR 2997. Fiscal 2010 Agriculture Appropriations/Commit. Coburn, R-Okla., motion to commit the bill to the Appropriations Committee with instructions that it be reported back with an aggregate discretionary funding level that is 2 percent above the fiscal 2009 level. Motion rejected 32-65: R 30-10; D 2-53; I 0-2. A "nay" was a vote in support of the president's position. Aug. 4, 2009.

260. HR 2997. Fiscal 2010 Agriculture Appropriations/Farm Service Agency Funding Increase. Sanders, I-Vt., motion to waive the Budget Act with respect to the Brownback, R-Kan., point of order against the Sanders amendment to the Kohl, D-Wis., substitute amendment. The Sanders amendment would increase the amount provided for the Farm Service Agency's salaries and expenses by $350 million. Motion agreed to 60-37: R 4-36; D 54-1; I 2-0. A three-fifths majority (60) of the total Senate is required to waive the Budget Act. (Subsequently, the Sanders amendment was adopted by voice vote.) Aug. 4, 2009.

	255	256	257	258	259	260
ALABAMA						
Shelby	Y	N	N	N	N	N
Sessions	Y	Y	Y	Y	Y	N
ALASKA						
Murkowski	Y	N	N	N	N	N
Begich	Y	N	N	N	N	Y
ARIZONA						
McCain	N	Y	Y	Y	Y	N
Kyl	N	Y	Y	Y	Y	N
ARKANSAS						
Lincoln	Y	N	N	N	N	Y
Pryor	Y	N	N	N	N	Y
CALIFORNIA						
Feinstein	Y	N	N	N	N	Y
Boxer	Y	N	N	N	N	Y
COLORADO						
Udall	Y	Y	N	Y	N	Y
Bennet	Y	N	N	N	N	Y
CONNECTICUT						
Dodd	Y	N	N	N	N	Y
Lieberman	+	+	N	Y	N	Y
DELAWARE						
Carper	Y	N	Y	Y	N	N
Kaufman	Y	Y	Y	N	N	Y
FLORIDA						
Nelson	Y	N	N	N	N	Y
Martinez	Y	Y	Y	Y	Y	N
GEORGIA						
Chambliss	Y	Y	N	Y	Y	N
Isakson	Y	Y	N	Y	Y	N
HAWAII						
Inouye	Y	N	N	N	N	Y
Akaka	Y	N	N	N	N	Y
IDAHO						
Crapo	Y	N	Y	Y	Y	N
Risch	Y	N	Y	Y	Y	N
ILLINOIS						
Durbin	Y	N	N	N	N	Y
Burris	Y	N	N	N	N	Y
INDIANA						
Lugar	Y	Y	N	Y	Y	N
Bayh	Y	Y	Y	Y	Y	Y
IOWA						
Grassley	Y	Y	Y	Y	Y	Y
Harkin	Y	N	N	N	N	Y
KANSAS						
Brownback	Y	N	N	N	N	N
Roberts	Y	N	N	N	N	N
KENTUCKY						
McConnell	Y	Y	Y	Y	Y	N
Bunning	N	Y	Y	Y	Y	N
LOUISIANA						
Landrieu	Y	N	N	N	N	Y
Vitter	N	Y	N	Y	Y	N
MAINE						
Snowe	Y	N	N	N	Y	Y
Collins	Y	N	N	N	N	Y
MARYLAND						
Mikulski	?	?	?	?	?	?
Cardin	Y	Y	N	N	N	Y
MASSACHUSETTS						
Kennedy	?	?	?	?	?	?
Kerry	Y	N	N	N	N	Y
MICHIGAN						
Levin	Y	N	N	N	N	Y
Stabenow	Y	N	N	N	N	Y
MINNESOTA						
Klobuchar	Y	Y	N	N	N	Y
Franken	Y	N	N	N	N	Y
MISSISSIPPI						
Cochran	?	N	N	N	N	N
Wicker	Y	N	N	Y	Y	N
MISSOURI						
Bond	Y	N	N	N	N	Y
McCaskill	Y	Y	Y	Y	Y	Y
MONTANA						
Baucus	Y	N	N	N	N	Y
Tester	Y	N	N	N	N	Y
NEBRASKA						
Nelson	Y	Y	N	N	N	Y
Johanns	N	Y	Y	Y	Y	N
NEVADA						
Reid	Y	N	N	N	N	Y
Ensign	N	Y	N	Y	Y	N
NEW HAMPSHIRE						
Gregg	N	Y	Y	Y	Y	N
Shaheen	Y	Y	N	N	N	Y
NEW JERSEY						
Lautenberg	Y	N	N	N	N	Y
Menendez	?	Y	Y	N	N	Y
NEW MEXICO						
Bingaman	Y	N	N	N	N	Y
Udall	Y	N	N	N	N	Y
NEW YORK						
Schumer	Y	N	N	N	N	Y
Gillibrand	Y	N	N	N	N	Y
NORTH CAROLINA						
Burr	Y	Y	Y	Y	Y	N
Hagan	Y	N	N	N	N	Y
NORTH DAKOTA						
Conrad	Y	Y	N	N	N	Y
Dorgan	Y	Y	N	N	N	Y
OHIO						
Voinovich	Y	Y	N	N	N	N
Brown	Y	N	N	N	N	Y
OKLAHOMA						
Inhofe	Y	Y	N	Y	Y	N
Coburn	Y	Y	Y	Y	Y	N
OREGON						
Wyden	Y	N	N	N	N	Y
Merkley	Y	Y	N	N	N	Y
PENNSYLVANIA						
Specter	Y	N	N	N	N	Y
Casey	Y	N	N	N	N	Y
RHODE ISLAND						
Reed	Y	N	N	N	N	Y
Whitehouse	Y	Y	N	N	N	Y
SOUTH CAROLINA						
Graham	Y	Y	Y	Y	Y	N
DeMint	N	Y	Y	Y	Y	N
SOUTH DAKOTA						
Johnson	Y	N	N	N	N	Y
Thune	Y	Y	Y	Y	Y	N
TENNESSEE						
Alexander	Y	Y	N	Y	N	N
Corker	N	Y	Y	Y	Y	N
TEXAS						
Hutchison	Y	Y	N	Y	Y	N
Cornyn	Y	Y	Y	Y	Y	N
UTAH						
Hatch	Y	N	N	Y	N	Y
Bennett	Y	N	N	N	N	N
VERMONT						
Leahy	Y	N	N	N	N	Y
Sanders	Y	N	N	N	N	Y
VIRGINIA						
Webb	Y	N	Y	N	N	Y
Warner	Y	N	N	N	N	Y
WASHINGTON						
Murray	Y	N	N	N	N	Y
Cantwell	Y	N	N	N	N	Y
WEST VIRGINIA						
Byrd	?	?	?	?	?	?
Rockefeller	Y	N	N	N	N	Y
WISCONSIN						
Kohl	Y	N	N	N	N	Y
Feingold	Y	Y	Y	Y	N	Y
WYOMING						
Enzi	N	Y	Y	Y	Y	N
Barrasso	N	Y	Y	Y	Y	N

KEY   **Republicans**   Democrats   *Independents*

Y Voted for (yea)

Paired for

+ Announced for

N Voted against (nay)

X Paired against

– Announced against

P Voted "present"

C Voted "present" to avoid possible conflict of interest

? Did not vote or otherwise make a position known

IN THE SENATE | By Vote Number

261. HR 2997. Fiscal 2010 Agriculture Appropriations/Passage.
Passage of the bill that would provide $124.2 billion in fiscal 2010 for the Agriculture Department and related agencies, including $23.4 billion in discretionary spending. It would appropriate $61.4 billion for the food stamp program, $16.8 billion for the child nutrition program, $7.6 billion for the Women, Infants and Children program, and $2.4 billion for the Food and Drug Administration. Passed 80-17: R 24-16; D 54-1; I 2-0. (Before passage, the Kohl, D-Wis., substitute amendment, as amended, was adopted by voice vote.) A "yea" was a vote in support of the president's position. Aug. 4, 2009.

262. Sotomayor Nomination/Confirmation.
Confirmation of President Obama's nomination of Sonia Sotomayor of New York to be an associate justice of the U.S. Supreme Court. Confirmed 68-31: R 9-31; D 57-0; I 2-0. A "yea" was a vote in support of the president's position. Aug. 6, 2009.

263. HR 3435. Car Voucher Program Funding/Qualification Restrictions.
Harkin, D-Iowa, motion to table (kill) the Harkin amendment that would restrict those eligible to receive vouchers under the program to individuals who filed federal income taxes for 2008 and who make less than $50,000 annually, or $75,000 annually for joint filers. Motion agreed to 65-32: R 8-32; D 55-0; I 2-0. Aug. 6, 2009.

264. HR 3435. Car Voucher Program Funding/Program Termination.
Kyl, R-Ariz., substitute amendment that would terminate the "cash for clunkers" program on Aug. 8, 2009. It would not provide new funding for the program beyond the $1 billion already appropriated, except for funds needed to meet obligations through the termination date. The Transportation Department would have to maintain a database of information on vehicle identification numbers of vehicles traded in and those purchased under the program, the amount of money the federal government has obligated and the amount remaining. Rejected 40-57: R 36-4; D 4-51; I 0-2. Aug. 6, 2009.

265. HR 3435. Car Voucher Program Funding/Budget Revisions.
Gregg, R-N.H., motion to waive the Budget Act with respect to the Murray, D-Wash., point of order against the Gregg amendment that would revise allocations in the fiscal 2010 budget resolution by decreasing the fiscal 2010 discretionary spending cap by $2 billion. Motion rejected 46-51: R 39-1; D 7-48; I 0-2. A three-fifths majority vote (60) of the total Senate is required to waive the Budget Act. (Subsequently, the chair upheld the point of order, and the amendment fell.) Aug. 6, 2009.

	261	262	263	264	265
ALABAMA					
Shelby	Y	N	N	Y	Y
Sessions	N	N	N	Y	Y
ALASKA					
Murkowski	Y	N	N	Y	Y
Begich	Y	Y	Y	N	N
ARIZONA					
McCain	N	N	N	Y	Y
Kyl	N	N	N	Y	Y
ARKANSAS					
Lincoln	Y	Y	Y	N	Y
Pryor	Y	Y	Y	N	N
CALIFORNIA					
Feinstein	Y	Y	Y	N	N
Boxer	Y	Y	Y	N	N
COLORADO					
Udall	Y	Y	Y	N	N
Bennet	Y	Y	Y	N	Y
CONNECTICUT					
Dodd	Y	Y	Y	N	N
Lieberman	Y	Y	Y	N	N
DELAWARE					
Carper	Y	Y	Y	N	N
Kaufman	Y	Y	Y	N	N
FLORIDA					
Nelson	Y	Y	Y	N	N
Martinez	Y	Y	N	Y	Y
GEORGIA					
Chambliss	N	N	N	Y	Y
Isakson	N	N	N	Y	Y
HAWAII					
Inouye	Y	Y	Y	N	N
Akaka	Y	Y	Y	N	N
IDAHO					
Crapo	Y	N	Y	Y	Y
Risch	Y	N	Y	Y	Y
ILLINOIS					
Durbin	Y	Y	Y	N	N
Burris	Y	Y	Y	N	N
INDIANA					
Lugar	Y	Y	N	Y	Y
Bayh	N	Y	Y	Y	Y
IOWA					
Grassley	Y	N	N	Y	Y
Harkin	Y	Y	Y	N	N
KANSAS					
Brownback	Y	N	N	Y	Y
Roberts	Y	N	N	Y	Y
KENTUCKY					
McConnell	Y	N	N	Y	Y
Bunning	N	N	N	Y	Y
LOUISIANA					
Landrieu	Y	Y	Y	N	N
Vitter	Y	N	N	Y	Y
MAINE					
Snowe	Y	Y	Y	Y	Y
Collins	Y	Y	Y	N	Y
MARYLAND					
Mikulski	?	Y	?	?	?
Cardin	Y	Y	Y	N	N
MASSACHUSETTS					
Kennedy	?	?	?	?	?
Kerry	Y	Y	Y	N	N
MICHIGAN					
Levin	Y	Y	Y	N	N
Stabenow	Y	Y	Y	N	N
MINNESOTA					
Klobuchar	Y	Y	Y	N	N
Franken	Y	Y	Y	N	N
MISSISSIPPI					
Cochran	Y	N	N	Y	Y
Wicker	Y	N	Y	Y	Y
MISSOURI					
Bond	Y	Y	N	N	Y
McCaskill	Y	Y	Y	Y	Y
MONTANA					
Baucus	Y	Y	Y	N	N
Tester	Y	Y	Y	N	N
NEBRASKA					
Nelson	Y	Y	Y	Y	Y
Johanns	Y	N	N	Y	Y
NEVADA					
Reid	Y	Y	Y	N	N
Ensign	N	N	N	Y	Y
NEW HAMPSHIRE					
Gregg	N	Y	N	Y	Y
Shaheen	Y	Y	Y	N	N
NEW JERSEY					
Lautenberg	Y	Y	Y	N	N
Menendez	Y	Y	Y	N	N
NEW MEXICO					
Bingaman	Y	Y	Y	N	N
Udall	Y	Y	Y	N	N
NEW YORK					
Schumer	Y	Y	Y	N	N
Gillibrand	Y	Y	Y	N	N
NORTH CAROLINA					
Burr	N	N	N	Y	Y
Hagan	Y	Y	Y	N	N
NORTH DAKOTA					
Conrad	Y	Y	Y	N	Y
Dorgan	Y	Y	Y	N	N
OHIO					
Voinovich	Y	Y	Y	N	N
Brown	Y	Y	Y	N	N
OKLAHOMA					
Inhofe	N	N	N	Y	Y
Coburn	N	N	N	Y	Y
OREGON					
Wyden	Y	Y	Y	N	N
Merkley	Y	Y	Y	N	N
PENNSYLVANIA					
Specter	Y	Y	Y	N	N
Casey	Y	Y	Y	N	N
RHODE ISLAND					
Reed	Y	Y	Y	N	N
Whitehouse	Y	Y	Y	N	N
SOUTH CAROLINA					
Graham	N	Y	N	Y	Y
DeMint	N	N	N	Y	Y
SOUTH DAKOTA					
Johnson	Y	Y	Y	N	N
Thune	Y	N	N	Y	Y
TENNESSEE					
Alexander	Y	Y	N	Y	Y
Corker	N	N	N	Y	Y
TEXAS					
Hutchison	Y	N	Y	Y	Y
Cornyn	Y	N	N	Y	Y
UTAH					
Hatch	Y	N	N	Y	Y
Bennett	Y	N	N	Y	Y
VERMONT					
Leahy	Y	Y	Y	N	N
Sanders	Y	Y	Y	N	N
VIRGINIA					
Webb	Y	Y	Y	N	N
Warner	Y	Y	Y	Y	Y
WASHINGTON					
Murray	Y	Y	Y	N	N
Cantwell	Y	Y	Y	N	N
WEST VIRGINIA					
Byrd	?	Y	?	?	?
Rockefeller	Y	Y	Y	N	N
WISCONSIN					
Kohl	Y	Y	Y	N	N
Feingold	Y	Y	Y	N	N
WYOMING					
Enzi	N	N	N	Y	Y
Barrasso	N	N	N	Y	Y

KEY   Republicans   Democrats   *Independents*

Y Voted for (yea)	X Paired against
# Paired for	– Announced against
+ Announced for	P Voted "present"
N Voted against (nay)	

C Voted "present" to avoid possible conflict of interest

? Did not vote or otherwise make a position known

IN THE SENATE | By Vote Number

266. HR 3435. Car Voucher Program Funding/Vehicle Donation.
Coburn, R-Okla., motion to waive the Budget Act with respect to the Murray, D-Wash., point of order against the Coburn amendment that would allow dealers to donate vehicles traded in under the program to families that cannot afford a vehicle, or to tax-exempt organizations that certify they will use the vehicles to assist those in need, including selling the vehicles to raise money for the organization. Motion rejected 41-56: R 37-3; D 4-51; I 0-2. A three-fifths majority vote (60) of the total Senate is required to waive the Budget Act. (Subsequently, the chair upheld the point of order, and the amendment fell.) Aug. 6, 2009.

267. HR 3435. Car Voucher Program Funding/Troubled Asset Relief Program.
Vitter, R-La., amendment that would not allow for further extensions of the Troubled Asset Relief Program beyond Dec. 31, 2009. Rejected 41-56: R 38-2; D 3-52; I 0-2. Aug. 6, 2009.

268. HR 3435. Car Voucher Program Funding/Homebuyer Credit.
Isakson, R-Ga., motion to waive the Budget Act with respect to the Levin, D-Mich., point of order against the Isakson amendment that would repeal the current $8,000 first-time homebuyer tax credit and create a new credit of up to $15,000 for the purchase of a principal residence ($7,500 each for married individuals filing separately). Only homes purchased within one year of the bill's enactment would be eligible, and recipients would be allowed only one credit. Motion rejected 47-50: R 39-1; D 8-47; I 0-2. A three-fifths majority vote (60) of the total Senate is required to waive the Budget Act. (Subsequently, the chair upheld the point of order, and the amendment fell.) Aug. 6, 2009.

269. HR 3435. Car Voucher Program Funding/Emergency Designation.
Murray, D-Wash., motion to waive the Budget Act with respect to the Kyl, R-Ariz., point of order against the emergency designation of the bill that would provide $2 billion for the "cash for clunkers" vehicle trade-in program. Motion agreed to 60-37: R 5-35; D 53-2; I 2-0. A three-fifths majority vote (60) of the total Senate is required to waive the Budget Act. Aug. 6, 2009.

270. HR 3435. Car Voucher Program Funding/Passage.
Passage of the bill that would provide $2 billion for the "cash for clunkers" vehicle trade-in program, which offers vouchers worth up to $4,500 toward the purchase of new vehicles to consumers who trade in their older, less efficient models. The funds would be transferred from the Energy Department's innovative technologies loan guarantee program. Passed (thus cleared for the president) 60-37: R 7-33; D 51-4; I 2-0. A "yea" was a vote in support of the president's position. Aug. 6, 2009.

	266	267	268	269	270
ALABAMA					
Shelby	Y	Y	Y	N	N
Sessions	Y	Y	Y	N	N
ALASKA					
Murkowski	Y	Y	Y	N	N
Begich	N	N	N	Y	Y
ARIZONA					
McCain	Y	Y	Y	N	N
Kyl	Y	Y	Y	N	N
ARKANSAS					
Lincoln	N	Y	Y	Y	Y
Pryor	N	N	N	Y	Y
CALIFORNIA					
Feinstein	N	N	N	Y	Y
Boxer	N	N	N	Y	Y
COLORADO					
Udall	N	N	N	Y	Y
Bennet	N	N	N	Y	Y
CONNECTICUT					
Dodd	N	N	N	Y	Y
Lieberman	N	N	N	Y	Y
DELAWARE					
Carper	Y	N	N	Y	Y
Kaufman	N	N	N	Y	Y
FLORIDA					
Nelson	N	N	N	Y	Y
Martinez	Y	Y	Y	N	N
GEORGIA					
Chambliss	Y	Y	Y	N	N
Isakson	Y	Y	Y	N	N
HAWAII					
Inouye	N	N	N	Y	Y
Akaka	N	N	N	Y	Y
IDAHO					
Crapo	Y	Y	Y	N	N
Risch	Y	Y	Y	N	N
ILLINOIS					
Durbin	N	N	N	Y	Y
Burris	N	N	N	Y	Y
INDIANA					
Lugar	Y	Y	Y	N	N
Bayh	N	Y	Y	Y	Y
IOWA					
Grassley	Y	Y	Y	N	N
Harkin	N	N	N	Y	Y
KANSAS					
Brownback	Y	Y	Y	Y	Y
Roberts	Y	Y	Y	N	N
KENTUCKY					
McConnell	Y	Y	Y	N	N
Bunning	Y	Y	Y	N	N
LOUISIANA					
Landrieu	N	N	N	Y	Y
Vitter	Y	Y	Y	N	N
MAINE					
Snowe	N	Y	Y	Y	Y
Collins	N	Y	Y	Y	Y
MARYLAND					
Mikulski	?	?	?	?	?
Cardin	N	N	N	Y	Y
MASSACHUSETTS					
Kennedy	?	?	?	?	?
Kerry	N	N	N	Y	Y
MICHIGAN					
Levin	N	N	N	Y	Y
Stabenow	N	N	N	Y	Y
MINNESOTA					
Klobuchar	N	N	Y	Y	Y
Franken	N	N	N	Y	Y
MISSISSIPPI					
Cochran	Y	Y	Y	N	N
Wicker	Y	Y	Y	N	N
MISSOURI					
Bond	Y	Y	Y	Y	Y
McCaskill	N	N	N	N	N

	266	267	268	269	270
MONTANA					
Baucus	N	N	N	Y	Y
Tester	N	N	N	Y	Y
NEBRASKA					
Nelson	Y	Y	Y	N	N
Johanns	Y	Y	Y	N	N
NEVADA					
Reid	N	N	N	Y	Y
Ensign	Y	Y	Y	N	N
NEW HAMPSHIRE					
Gregg	Y	N	Y	N	N
Shaheen	N	N	N	Y	Y
NEW JERSEY					
Lautenberg	N	N	N	Y	Y
Menendez	N	N	Y	Y	Y
NEW MEXICO					
Bingaman	N	N	N	Y	Y
Udall	N	N	N	Y	Y
NEW YORK					
Schumer	N	N	N	Y	Y
Gillibrand	N	N	N	Y	Y
NORTH CAROLINA					
Burr	Y	Y	Y	N	N
Hagan	N	N	N	Y	Y
NORTH DAKOTA					
Conrad	N	N	N	Y	Y
Dorgan	Y	N	N	Y	Y
OHIO					
Voinovich	N	N	Y	Y	Y
Brown	N	N	N	Y	Y
OKLAHOMA					
Inhofe	Y	Y	Y	N	N
Coburn	Y	Y	Y	N	N
OREGON					
Wyden	N	N	N	Y	Y
Merkley	N	N	N	Y	Y
PENNSYLVANIA					
Specter	N	N	Y	Y	Y
Casey	N	N	N	Y	Y
RHODE ISLAND					
Reed	N	N	N	Y	Y
Whitehouse	N	N	N	Y	Y
SOUTH CAROLINA					
Graham	Y	Y	Y	N	N
DeMint	Y	Y	N	N	N
SOUTH DAKOTA					
Johnson	N	N	N	Y	Y
Thune	Y	Y	Y	N	N
TENNESSEE					
Alexander	Y	Y	Y	N	Y
Corker	Y	Y	Y	N	Y
TEXAS					
Hutchison	Y	Y	Y	N	N
Cornyn	Y	Y	Y	N	N
UTAH					
Hatch	Y	Y	Y	N	N
Bennett	Y	Y	Y	N	N
VERMONT					
Leahy	N	N	Y	Y	N
Sanders	N	N	N	Y	Y
VIRGINIA					
Webb	Y	N	N	Y	N
Warner	N	N	N	Y	N
WASHINGTON					
Murray	N	N	N	Y	Y
Cantwell	N	N	N	Y	Y
WEST VIRGINIA					
Byrd	?	?	?	?	?
Rockefeller	N	N	N	Y	Y
WISCONSIN					
Kohl	N	N	N	Y	Y
Feingold	N	N	N	Y	Y
WYOMING					
Enzi	Y	Y	Y	N	N
Barrasso	Y	Y	Y	N	N

KEY   **Republicans**   Democrats   *Independents*

Y Voted for (yea)	X Paired against	C Voted "present" to avoid possible conflict of interest
# Paired for	– Announced against	
+ Announced for	P Voted "present"	? Did not vote or otherwise make a position known
N Voted against (nay)		

IN THE SENATE | By Vote Number

271. **S 1023. Foreign Tourism Promotion/Cloture.** Motion to invoke cloture (thus limiting debate) on the Dorgan, D-N.D., amendment that would make perfecting changes to the bill. Motion agreed to 80-19: R 21 19; D 57-0; I 2-0. Three-fifths of the total Senate (60) is required to invoke cloture. Sept. 8, 2009.

272. **S 1023. Foreign Tourism Promotion/Passage.** Passage of the bill that would create a nonprofit corporation to attract foreign tourists to the United States and an Office of Travel Promotion in the Commerce Department. It would require the Homeland Security Department to assess a $10 fee on users of a visa-waiver program. Money from the fee would be used to provide the nonprofit corporation up to $10 million for fiscal 2010 and to provide matching funds for up to $100 million annually in corporate contributions in fiscal 2011 through 2014. Passed 79-19: R 21-19; D 56-0; I 2-0. Sept. 9, 2009.

273. **Sunstein Nomination/Cloture.** Motion to invoke cloture (thus limiting debate) on the nomination of Cass R. Sunstein of Massachusetts to be administrator of the Office of Management and Budget's Office of Information and Regulatory Affairs. Motion agreed to 63-35: R 7-32; D 54-3; I 2-0. Three-fifths of the total Senate (59) is required to invoke cloture. Sept. 9, 2009.

274. **Sunstein Nomination/Confirmation.** Confirmation of President Obama's nomination of Cass R. Sunstein of Massachusetts to be administrator of the Office of Management and Budget's Office of Information and Regulatory Affairs. Confirmed 57-40: R 6-34; D 50-5; I 1-1. A "yea" was a vote in support of the president's position. Sept. 10, 2009.

State / Senator	271	272	273	274
ALABAMA				
Shelby	Y	Y	N	N
Sessions	N	N	N	N
ALASKA				
Murkowski	Y	Y	N	N
Begich	Y	Y	Y	N
ARIZONA				
McCain	N	N	N	N
Kyl	N	N	N	N
ARKANSAS				
Lincoln	Y	Y	N	N
Pryor	Y	Y	N	N
CALIFORNIA				
Feinstein	Y	Y	Y	Y
Boxer	Y	Y	Y	?
COLORADO				
Udall	Y	Y	Y	Y
Bennet	Y	Y	Y	Y
CONNECTICUT				
Dodd	Y	Y	Y	Y
Lieberman	Y	Y	Y	Y
DELAWARE				
Carper	Y	Y	Y	Y
Kaufman	Y	Y	Y	Y
FLORIDA				
Nelson	Y	Y	Y	Y
Martinez[1]	Y	Y		
LeMieux[1]				N
GEORGIA				
Chambliss	Y	N	N	N
Isakson	Y	Y	N	N
HAWAII				
Inouye	Y	Y	Y	Y
Akaka	Y	Y	Y	Y
IDAHO				
Crapo	N	N	N	N
Risch	N	N	N	N
ILLINOIS				
Durbin	Y	Y	Y	Y
Burris	Y	Y	Y	Y
INDIANA				
Lugar	Y	Y	Y	Y
Bayh	Y	Y	Y	Y
IOWA				
Grassley	N	N	N	N
Harkin	Y	Y	Y	Y
KANSAS				
Brownback	N	N	N	N
Roberts	N	N	N	N
KENTUCKY				
McConnell	N	N	N	N
Bunning	N	N	N	N
LOUISIANA				
Landrieu	Y	?	Y	Y
Vitter	Y	N	N	N
MAINE				
Snowe	Y	Y	Y	Y
Collins	Y	Y	Y	Y
MARYLAND				
Mikulski	Y	Y	Y	Y
Cardin	Y	Y	Y	Y
MASSACHUSETTS				
Kerry	Y	Y	Y	Y
Vacant[2]				
MICHIGAN				
Levin	Y	Y	Y	Y
Stabenow	Y	Y	Y	Y
MINNESOTA				
Klobuchar	Y	Y	Y	Y
Franken	Y	Y	Y	Y
MISSISSIPPI				
Cochran	Y	N	N	N
Wicker	Y	N	N	N
MISSOURI				
Bond	Y	N	N	N
McCaskill	Y	Y	Y	Y
MONTANA				
Baucus	Y	Y	Y	Y
Tester	Y	Y	Y	Y
NEBRASKA				
Nelson	Y	Y	Y	N
Johanns	Y	Y	N	N
NEVADA				
Reid	Y	Y	Y	Y
Ensign	Y	Y	N	N
NEW HAMPSHIRE				
Gregg	N	N	Y	N
Shaheen	Y	Y	Y	Y
NEW JERSEY				
Lautenberg	Y	Y	Y	Y
Menendez	Y	Y	Y	Y
NEW MEXICO				
Bingaman	Y	Y	Y	Y
Udall	Y	Y	Y	Y
NEW YORK				
Schumer	Y	Y	Y	Y
Gillibrand	Y	Y	Y	Y
NORTH CAROLINA				
Burr	N	N	N	N
Hagan	Y	Y	Y	Y
NORTH DAKOTA				
Conrad	Y	Y	Y	Y
Dorgan	Y	Y	Y	Y
OHIO				
Voinovich	Y	Y	Y	Y
Brown	Y	Y	Y	Y
OKLAHOMA				
Inhofe	N	N	N	N
Coburn	N	N	N	N
OREGON				
Wyden	Y	Y	Y	Y
Merkley	Y	Y	Y	Y
PENNSYLVANIA				
Specter	Y	Y	Y	Y
Casey	Y	Y	Y	Y
RHODE ISLAND				
Reed	Y	Y	Y	Y
Whitehouse	Y	Y	Y	Y
SOUTH CAROLINA				
Graham	Y	Y	N	N
DeMint	N	N	N	N
SOUTH DAKOTA				
Johnson	Y	Y	Y	Y
Thune	Y	Y	N	N
TENNESSEE				
Alexander	Y	Y	N	N
Corker	Y	Y	N	N
TEXAS				
Hutchison	N	N	N	N
Cornyn	N	N	N	N
UTAH				
Hatch	Y	Y	Y	Y
Bennett	Y	Y	Y	Y
VERMONT				
Leahy	Y	Y	Y	Y
Sanders	Y	Y	Y	N
VIRGINIA				
Webb	Y	Y	N	N
Warner	Y	Y	Y	Y
WASHINGTON				
Murray	Y	Y	Y	Y
Cantwell	Y	Y	Y	Y
WEST VIRGINIA				
Byrd	Y	Y	Y	?
Rockefeller	Y	Y	Y	Y
WISCONSIN				
Kohl	Y	Y	Y	Y
Feingold	Y	Y	Y	Y
WYOMING				
Enzi	N	Y	N	N
Barrasso	N	Y	N	N

KEY	**Republicans**	Democrats	*Independents*
Y Voted for (yea)	X Paired against		C Voted "present" to avoid possible conflict of interest
# Paired for	– Announced against		
+ Announced for	P Voted "present"		? Did not vote or otherwise make a position known
N Voted against (nay)			

[1] Sen. George LeMieux, R-Fla., was sworn in Sept. 10 to fill the seat vacated by the Sept. 9 resignation of fellow Republican Mel Martinez. The last vote for which Martinez was eligible was vote 272; the first vote for which LeMieux was eligible was vote 274.

[2] Sen. Edward M. Kennedy, D-Mass., died Aug. 25. The last vote for which he was eligible was vote 270.

IN THE SENATE | By Vote Number

275. HR 3288. Fiscal 2010 Transportation-HUD Appropriations/ **ACORN Funding Ban.** Johanns, R-Neb., amendment that would bar the use of funds in the bill for the Association of Community Organizations for Reform Now (ACORN) or its subsidiaries. Adopted 83-7: R 33-0; D 49-6; I 1-1. Sept. 14, 2009.

276. HR 3288. Fiscal 2010 Transportation-HUD Appropriations/ **Redirect Funding to NextGen Technology.** Murray, D-Wash., motion to table (kill) the McCain, R-Ariz., amendment that would make funds provided for congressionally directed spending items in the bill available for the Transportation Department to use for NextGen technology, a satellite GPS system for air traffic control. Motion agreed to 68-26: R 16-23; D 50-3; I 2-0. Sept. 15, 2009.

277. HR 3288. Fiscal 2010 Transportation-HUD Appropriations/ **Apportionment Requirement Ban.** Coburn, R-Okla., amendment that would bar the use of funds in the bill to require a state to use 10 percent of the surface transportation program funds apportioned to it for transportation enhancement activities such as footpaths, bike trails and barriers to keep animals off highways. Rejected 39-59: R 33-7; D 5-51; I 1-1. Sept. 16, 2009.

278. HR 3288. Fiscal 2010 Transportation-HUD Appropriations/ **Museum Funding Ban.** Coburn, R-Okla., amendment that would bar the use of funds in the bill for museums. Rejected 41-57: R 34-6; D 7-49; I 0-2. Sept. 16, 2009.

279. HR 3288. Fiscal 2010 Transportation-HUD Appropriations/ **Firearms Transport on Amtrak.** Wicker, R-Miss., amendment that would bar the use of funds in the bill for Amtrak from being available after March 31, 2010, unless Amtrak passengers are allowed to transport firearms and ammunition in their checked baggage. Adopted 68-30: R 40-0; D 27-29; I 1-1. Sept. 16, 2009.

	275	276	277	278	279			275	276	277	278	279
ALABAMA							**MONTANA**					
Shelby	Y	Y	N	N	Y		Baucus	Y	Y	N	N	Y
Sessions	Y	Y	Y	Y	Y		Tester	Y	Y	N	N	Y
ALASKA							**NEBRASKA**					
Murkowski	Y	Y	N	Y	Y		Nelson	Y	Y	N	N	Y
Begich	Y	Y	N	N	Y		Johanns	Y	N	Y	Y	Y
ARIZONA							**NEVADA**					
McCain	?	N	Y	Y	Y		Reid	Y	Y	N	N	Y
Kyl	Y	N	Y	Y	Y		Ensign	Y	N	Y	Y	Y
ARKANSAS							**NEW HAMPSHIRE**					
Lincoln	Y	Y	N	N	Y		Gregg	?	Y	Y	Y	Y
Pryor	Y	Y	N	N	N		Shaheen	Y	Y	N	N	Y
CALIFORNIA							**NEW JERSEY**					
Feinstein	Y	Y	N	N	N		Lautenberg	Y	Y	N	N	N
Boxer	Y	Y	N	N	N		Menendez	Y	Y	N	N	N
COLORADO							**NEW MEXICO**					
Udall	Y	Y	N	Y	Y		Bingaman	Y	Y	N	N	N
Bennet	Y	Y	N	Y	Y		Udall	Y	Y	N	N	N
CONNECTICUT							**NEW YORK**					
Dodd	Y	Y	N	N	N		Schumer	Y	Y	N	N	N
Lieberman	Y	Y	Y	N	N		Gillibrand	N	Y	N	N	N
DELAWARE							**NORTH CAROLINA**					
Carper	Y	Y	N	N	N		Burr	?	N	Y	Y	Y
Kaufman	Y	Y	N	N	N		Hagan	Y	Y	N	N	Y
FLORIDA							**NORTH DAKOTA**					
Nelson	Y	Y	N	N	Y		Conrad	Y	Y	N	Y	Y
LeMieux	Y	N	Y	Y	Y		Dorgan	Y	Y	N	N	Y
GEORGIA							**OHIO**					
Chambliss	Y	N	Y	Y	Y		Voinovich	Y	Y	N	Y	Y
Isakson	Y	N	Y	Y	Y		Brown	Y	?	N	N	N
HAWAII							**OKLAHOMA**					
Inouye	Y	Y	N	N	N		Inhofe	Y	Y	Y	Y	Y
Akaka	Y	Y	N	N	N		Coburn	?	N	Y	Y	Y
IDAHO							**OREGON**					
Crapo	Y	N	Y	Y	Y		Wyden	Y	Y	N	N	N
Risch	Y	N	Y	Y	Y		Merkley	Y	Y	N	N	Y
ILLINOIS							**PENNSYLVANIA**					
Durbin	N	Y	N	N	N		Specter	Y	?	N	N	N
Burris	N	Y	N	N	N		Casey	N	Y	N	N	Y
INDIANA							**RHODE ISLAND**					
Lugar	Y	Y	Y	Y	Y		Reed	Y	Y	N	N	N
Bayh	Y	N	Y	Y	Y		Whitehouse	N	Y	N	N	N
IOWA							**SOUTH CAROLINA**					
Grassley	Y	N	Y	Y	Y		Graham	+	N	Y	Y	Y
Harkin	Y	Y	N	N	N		DeMint	Y	N	Y	Y	Y
KANSAS							**SOUTH DAKOTA**					
Brownback	Y	Y	Y	Y	Y		Johnson	Y	Y	N	N	Y
Roberts	Y	Y	Y	Y	Y		Thune	Y	N	Y	Y	Y
KENTUCKY							**TENNESSEE**					
McConnell	Y	Y	Y	Y	Y		Alexander	Y	Y	Y	N	Y
Bunning	Y	N	Y	Y	Y		Corker	Y	N	Y	Y	Y
LOUISIANA							**TEXAS**					
Landrieu	Y	Y	N	N	Y		Hutchison	?	?	Y	Y	Y
Vitter	?	N	Y	Y	Y		Cornyn	Y	N	Y	Y	Y
MAINE							**UTAH**					
Snowe	Y	N	N	Y	Y		Hatch	Y	N	Y	Y	Y
Collins	Y	Y	N	Y	Y		Bennett	Y	Y	N	Y	Y
MARYLAND							**VERMONT**					
Mikulski	+	Y	N	N	N		Leahy	N	Y	N	N	Y
Cardin	Y	Y	N	N	N		*Sanders*	N	Y	N	N	Y
MASSACHUSETTS							**VIRGINIA**					
Kerry	Y	Y	N	N	N		Webb	Y	Y	N	N	Y
Vacant							Warner	Y	Y	N	N	Y
MICHIGAN							**WASHINGTON**					
Levin	Y	Y	N	N	N		Murray	Y	Y	N	N	N
Stabenow	Y	Y	N	N	N		Cantwell	Y	?	N	N	N
MINNESOTA							**WEST VIRGINIA**					
Klobuchar	Y	Y	Y	Y	Y		Byrd	?	?	?	?	?
Franken	Y	Y	N	N	N		Rockefeller	Y	Y	N	N	N
MISSISSIPPI							**WISCONSIN**					
Cochran	Y	Y	N	N	Y		Kohl	Y	Y	N	Y	Y
Wicker	Y	Y	Y	N	Y		Feingold	Y	N	Y	Y	Y
MISSOURI							**WYOMING**					
Bond	Y	Y	N	N	Y		Enzi	Y	N	Y	Y	Y
McCaskill	Y	N	Y	Y	Y		Barrasso	Y	N	Y	Y	Y

KEY   **Republicans**   Democrats   *Independents*

Y Voted for (yea)	X Paired against	C Voted "present" to avoid possible conflict of interest
# Paired for	– Announced against	
+ Announced for	P Voted "present"	? Did not vote or otherwise make a position known
N Voted against (nay)		

IN THE SENATE | By Vote Number

280. HR 3288. Fiscal 2010 Transportation-HUD Appropriations/ **Public Housing Community Service.** Vitter, R-La., amendment that would bar the use of funds in the bill to restrict implementation or enforcement of the requirement that certain adult residents of public housing projects contribute eight hours of community service each month. Adopted 73-25: R 40-0; D 32-24; I 1-1. Sept. 16, 2009.

281. HR 3288. Fiscal 2010 Transportation-HUD Appropriations/ **Stimulus Law Signs.** Gregg, R-N.H., amendment that would bar the use of funds made available under the 2009 economic stimulus law for physical signage to indicate that a project is being funded by that law. Rejected 45-52: R 40-0; D 5-50; I 0-2. Sept. 16, 2009.

282. HR 3288. Fiscal 2010 Transportation-HUD Appropriations/ **Recommit.** Ensign, R-Nev., motion to recommit the bill to the Senate Appropriations Committee with instructions that it be reported back with changes that would reduce funding in the bill by $12.7 billion. Motion rejected 33-64: R 31-9; D 2-53; I 0-2. A "nay" was a vote in support of the president's position. Sept. 16, 2009.

283. HR 3288. Fiscal 2010 Transportation-HUD Appropriations/ **New Orleans Housing Restrictions.** Vitter, R-La., amendment that would bar funds in the bill from being provided to households that include an individual who lives in federally subsidized housing in New Orleans and is in a street gang, or has been convicted of manufacturing or distributing a controlled substance or possessing a controlled substance with the intent to manufacture or distribute. Rejected 34-62: R 34-6; D 0-54; I 0-2. Sept. 17, 2009.

284. HR 3288. Fiscal 2010 Transportation-HUD Appropriations/ **John Murtha Johnstown-Cambria County Airport.** DeMint, R-S.C., amendment that would prohibit the Transportation Department from using funds in the bill for, or in connection with operations of, the John Murtha Johnstown-Cambria County Airport in Pennsylvania. Funding for air traffic control operations related to the airport would be permitted. Rejected 43-53: R 38-2; D 5-49; I 0-2. Sept. 17, 2009.

	280	281	282	283	284
ALABAMA					
Shelby	Y	Y	N	Y	Y
Sessions	Y	Y	Y	Y	Y
ALASKA					
Murkowski	Y	Y	N	N	Y
Begich	Y	N	N	N	N
ARIZONA					
McCain	Y	Y	Y	Y	Y
Kyl	Y	Y	Y	Y	Y
ARKANSAS					
Lincoln	Y	N	N	N	N
Pryor	N	N	N	N	N
CALIFORNIA					
Feinstein	Y	N	N	N	N
Boxer	Y	N	N	N	N
COLORADO					
Udall	Y	N	N	N	N
Bennet	Y	N	N	N	N
CONNECTICUT					
Dodd	Y	N	N	N	N
Lieberman	Y	N	N	N	N
DELAWARE					
Carper	N	N	N	N	N
Kaufman	Y	N	N	N	N
FLORIDA					
Nelson	Y	N	N	N	N
LeMieux	Y	Y	Y	Y	Y
GEORGIA					
Chambliss	Y	Y	Y	Y	Y
Isakson	Y	Y	Y	Y	Y
HAWAII					
Inouye	N	N	N	N	N
Akaka	N	N	N	N	N
IDAHO					
Crapo	Y	Y	Y	Y	Y
Risch	Y	Y	Y	Y	Y
ILLINOIS					
Durbin	Y	N	N	N	N
Burris	N	N	N	N	N
INDIANA					
Lugar	Y	Y	Y	Y	Y
Bayh	Y	N	Y	N	Y
IOWA					
Grassley	Y	Y	Y	Y	Y
Harkin	N	N	N	N	N
KANSAS					
Brownback	Y	Y	N	Y	Y
Roberts	Y	Y	Y	N	Y
KENTUCKY					
McConnell	Y	Y	Y	Y	Y
Bunning	Y	Y	Y	Y	Y
LOUISIANA					
Landrieu	N	N	N	?	?
Vitter	Y	Y	Y	Y	Y
MAINE					
Snowe	Y	Y	Y	Y	Y
Collins	Y	Y	N	N	Y
MARYLAND					
Mikulski	N	N	N	N	N
Cardin	N	N	N	N	N
MASSACHUSETTS					
Kerry	N	N	N	N	N
Vacant					
MICHIGAN					
Levin	N	N	N	N	N
Stabenow	N	N	N	N	N
MINNESOTA					
Klobuchar	Y	Y	N	N	N
Franken	N	N	N	N	N
MISSISSIPPI					
Cochran	Y	Y	N	Y	Y
Wicker	Y	Y	Y	Y	Y
MISSOURI					
Bond	Y	Y	N	N	Y
McCaskill	Y	N	Y	N	Y
MONTANA					
Baucus	Y	N	N	N	N
Tester	Y	N	N	N	N
NEBRASKA					
Nelson	Y	N	N	N	N
Johanns	Y	Y	Y	Y	Y
NEVADA					
Reid	N	N	N	N	N
Ensign	Y	Y	Y	Y	Y
NEW HAMPSHIRE					
Gregg	Y	Y	Y	Y	Y
Shaheen	N	Y	N	N	N
NEW JERSEY					
Lautenberg	N	N	N	N	N
Menendez	N	N	N	N	N
NEW MEXICO					
Bingaman	Y	N	N	N	N
Udall	Y	N	N	N	N
NEW YORK					
Schumer	Y	Y	N	N	N
Gillibrand	Y	Y	N	N	N
NORTH CAROLINA					
Burr	Y	Y	Y	Y	Y
Hagan	Y	N	N	N	N
NORTH DAKOTA					
Conrad	Y	N	N	N	N
Dorgan	Y	N	N	N	N
OHIO					
Voinovich	Y	Y	N	N	Y
Brown	N	N	N	N	N
OKLAHOMA					
Inhofe	Y	Y	Y	Y	Y
Coburn	Y	Y	Y	Y	Y
OREGON					
Wyden	Y	N	N	N	N
Merkley	Y	N	N	N	Y
PENNSYLVANIA					
Specter	Y	N	N	?	?
Casey	N	N	N	N	N
RHODE ISLAND					
Reed	N	N	N	N	N
Whitehouse	N	N	N	N	N
SOUTH CAROLINA					
Graham	Y	Y	Y	Y	Y
DeMint	Y	Y	Y	Y	Y
SOUTH DAKOTA					
Johnson	N	N	N	N	N
Thune	Y	Y	Y	Y	Y
TENNESSEE					
Alexander	Y	Y	N	Y	Y
Corker	Y	Y	N	N	Y
TEXAS					
Hutchison	Y	Y	Y	Y	Y
Cornyn	Y	Y	Y	Y	Y
UTAH					
Hatch	Y	Y	N	Y	Y
Bennett	Y	Y	N	Y	Y
VERMONT					
Leahy	Y	N	N	N	N
Sanders	N	N	N	N	N
VIRGINIA					
Webb	Y	N	N	N	N
Warner	Y	N	N	N	N
WASHINGTON					
Murray	N	N	N	N	N
Cantwell	N	N	N	N	N
WEST VIRGINIA					
Byrd	?	?	?	?	?
Rockefeller	Y	?	?	N	N
WISCONSIN					
Kohl	Y	N	N	N	Y
Feingold	Y	N	N	N	Y
WYOMING					
Enzi	Y	Y	Y	Y	Y
Barrasso	Y	Y	Y	Y	Y

KEY	**Republicans**	Democrats	*Independents*		
Y	Voted for (yea)	X	Paired against	C	Voted "present" to avoid possible conflict of interest
#	Paired for	–	Announced against		
+	Announced for	P	Voted "present"	?	Did not vote or otherwise make a position known
N	Voted against (nay)				

IN THE SENATE | By Vote Number

285. HR 3288. Fiscal 2010 Transportation-HUD Appropriations/ **Brownfields Economic Development Initiative.** McCain, R-Ariz., amendment that would bar the use of funds in the bill for the Housing and Urban Development Department's Brownfields Economic Development Initiative program. Rejected 37-60: R 34-6; D 3-52; I 0-2. Sept. 17, 2009.

286. HR 3288. Fiscal 2010 Transportation-HUD Appropriations/ **Recommit.** Kyl, R-Ariz., motion to recommit the bill to the Appropriations Committee with instructions that it be reported back immediately with language that would rescind any unobligated funds from the 2009 economic stimulus law that are duplicated in the measure and are not in a highway account. Motion rejected 34-64: R 34-6; D 0-56; I 0-2. Sept. 17, 2009.

287. HR 3288. Fiscal 2010 Transportation-HUD Appropriations/ **Passage.** Passage of the bill that would appropriate $122 billion in fiscal 2010, including $67.7 billion in discretionary spending, for the departments of Transportation and Housing and Urban Development and related agencies. It would provide $75.8 billion for the Transportation Department, including $15.6 billion for the Federal Aviation Administration, $42.7 billion for the Federal Highway Administration and $11.1 billion for the Federal Transit Administration. It would provide $45.8 billion for the Housing and Urban Development Department, including $18.1 billion for tenant-based rental assistance for public and Indian housing, $9.3 billion for housing programs, and $8.6 billion for community planning and development. Funding in the bill for Amtrak would be frozen after March 31, 2010, unless Amtrak passengers are allowed to transport firearms in their checked baggage. Passed 73-25: R 17-23; D 54-2; I 2-0. A "yea" was a vote in support of the president's position. Sept. 17, 2009.

288. Lynch Nomination/Confirmation. Confirmation of President Obama's nomination of Gerard E. Lynch of New York to be a judge on the Court of Appeals for the 2nd Circuit. Confirmed 94-3: R 36-3; D 56-0; I 2-0. A "yea" was a vote in support of the president's position. Sept. 17, 2009.

289. HR 2996. Fiscal 2010 Interior-Environment Appropriations/ **ACORN Funding Ban.** Johanns, R-Neb., amendment that would bar funds in the bill from being provided to the Association of Community Organizations for Reform Now (ACORN) or its subsidiaries. Adopted 85-11: R 39-0; D 45-10; I 1-1. Sept. 17, 2009.

	285	286	287	288	289
ALABAMA					
Shelby	Y	N	Y	Y	Y
Sessions	Y	Y	N	Y	Y
ALASKA					
Murkowski	N	Y	Y	Y	Y
Begich	N	N	Y	Y	Y
ARIZONA					
McCain	Y	Y	N	Y	Y
Kyl	Y	Y	N	Y	Y
ARKANSAS					
Lincoln	N	N	Y	Y	Y
Pryor	N	N	Y	Y	Y
CALIFORNIA					
Feinstein	N	N	Y	Y	N
Boxer	N	N	Y	Y	Y
COLORADO					
Udall	N	N	Y	Y	Y
Bennet	N	N	Y	Y	Y
CONNECTICUT					
Dodd	N	N	Y	Y	Y
Lieberman	N	N	Y	Y	Y
DELAWARE					
Carper	N	N	Y	Y	Y
Kaufman	N	N	Y	Y	Y
FLORIDA					
Nelson	N	N	Y	Y	Y
LeMieux	Y	Y	N	Y	Y
GEORGIA					
Chambliss	Y	Y	N	Y	Y
Isakson	Y	Y	N	Y	Y
HAWAII					
Inouye	N	N	Y	Y	Y
Akaka	N	N	Y	Y	N
IDAHO					
Crapo	Y	Y	N	Y	Y
Risch	Y	Y	N	Y	Y
ILLINOIS					
Durbin	N	N	Y	Y	N
Burris	N	N	Y	Y	N
INDIANA					
Lugar	N	Y	Y	Y	Y
Bayh	Y	N	N	Y	Y
IOWA					
Grassley	Y	Y	N	Y	Y
Harkin	N	N	Y	Y	N
KANSAS					
Brownback	Y	Y	Y	Y	Y
Roberts	Y	Y	Y	Y	Y
KENTUCKY					
McConnell	Y	Y	N	Y	Y
Bunning	Y	Y	N	N	Y
LOUISIANA					
Landrieu	?	?	?	?	?
Vitter	Y	Y	N	Y	Y
MAINE					
Snowe	Y	N	Y	Y	Y
Collins	N	N	Y	Y	Y
MARYLAND					
Mikulski	N	N	Y	Y	Y
Cardin	N	N	Y	Y	Y
MASSACHUSETTS					
Kerry	N	N	Y	Y	Y
Vacant					
MICHIGAN					
Levin	N	N	Y	Y	Y
Stabenow	N	N	Y	Y	Y
MINNESOTA					
Klobuchar	N	N	Y	Y	Y
Franken	N	N	Y	Y	Y
MISSISSIPPI					
Cochran	Y	N	Y	Y	Y
Wicker	Y	Y	Y	Y	Y
MISSOURI					
Bond	N	N	Y	Y	Y
McCaskill	Y	N	N	Y	Y

	285	286	287	288	289
MONTANA					
Baucus	N	N	Y	Y	Y
Tester	N	N	Y	Y	Y
NEBRASKA					
Nelson	N	N	Y	Y	Y
Johanns	Y	Y	Y	Y	Y
NEVADA					
Reid	N	N	Y	Y	Y
Ensign	Y	Y	N	Y	Y
NEW HAMPSHIRE					
Gregg	Y	Y	Y	Y	Y
Shaheen	N	N	Y	Y	Y
NEW JERSEY					
Lautenberg	N	N	Y	Y	Y
Menendez	N	N	Y	Y	Y
NEW MEXICO					
Bingaman	N	N	Y	Y	N
Udall	N	N	Y	Y	Y
NEW YORK					
Schumer	N	N	Y	Y	Y
Gillibrand	N	N	Y	Y	N
NORTH CAROLINA					
Burr	Y	Y	N	Y	Y
Hagan	N	N	Y	Y	Y
NORTH DAKOTA					
Conrad	N	N	Y	Y	Y
Dorgan	N	N	Y	Y	Y
OHIO					
Voinovich	N	N	Y	Y	Y
Brown	N	N	Y	Y	Y
OKLAHOMA					
Inhofe	Y	Y	N	N	Y
Coburn	Y	Y	N	N	Y
OREGON					
Wyden	N	N	Y	Y	Y
Merkley	N	N	Y	Y	Y
PENNSYLVANIA					
Specter	N	N	Y	Y	Y
Casey	N	N	Y	Y	N
RHODE ISLAND					
Reed	N	N	Y	Y	Y
Whitehouse	N	N	Y	Y	N
SOUTH CAROLINA					
Graham	Y	Y	N	Y	Y
DeMint	Y	Y	N	Y	Y
SOUTH DAKOTA					
Johnson	N	N	Y	Y	Y
Thune	Y	Y	N	Y	Y
TENNESSEE					
Alexander	N	Y	Y	Y	Y
Corker	Y	Y	N	Y	Y
TEXAS					
Hutchison	Y	Y	N	Y	Y
Cornyn	Y	Y	N	Y	Y
UTAH					
Hatch	Y	Y	Y	Y	Y
Bennett	Y	Y	Y	Y	Y
VERMONT					
Leahy	N	N	Y	Y	N
Sanders	N	N	Y	Y	N
VIRGINIA					
Webb	N	N	Y	Y	Y
Warner	N	N	Y	Y	Y
WASHINGTON					
Murray	N	N	Y	Y	?
Cantwell	N	N	Y	Y	Y
WEST VIRGINIA					
Byrd	?	N	Y	Y	Y
Rockefeller	N	N	Y	Y	Y
WISCONSIN					
Kohl	N	N	Y	Y	Y
Feingold	Y	N	Y	Y	Y
WYOMING					
Enzi	Y	Y	N	?	?
Barrasso	Y	Y	N	Y	Y

KEY   **Republicans**   Democrats   *Independents*

Y Voted for (yea)	X Paired against	C Voted "present" to avoid possible conflict of interest
# Paired for	− Announced against	
+ Announced for	P Voted "present"	? Did not vote or otherwise make a position known
N Voted against (nay)		

IN THE SENATE | By Vote Number

290. HR 2996. Fiscal 2010 Interior-Environment Appropriations/ **Civil Rights History Project.** Feinstein, D-Calif., amendment that would allow $250,000 of the funding provided in the bill for the Smithsonian Institution's salaries and expenses to be made available to carry out activities under the Civil Rights History Project Act of 2009. Adopted 95-0: R 39-0; D 54-0; I 2-0. Sept. 22, 2009.

291. HR 2996. Fiscal 2010 Interior-Environment Appropriations/ **Des Moines Art Center.** McCain, R-Ariz., amendment that would bar the use of funds in the bill for the Des Moines Art Center in Iowa. Rejected 27-70: R 26-14; D 1-54; I 0-2. Sept. 22, 2009.

292. HR 2996. Fiscal 2010 Interior-Environment Appropriations/ **Motion to Table.** Feinstein, D-Calif., motion to table (kill) the DeMint, R-S.C., motion to recommit the bill to the Senate Appropriations Committee with instructions that it be reported back immediately with language that would bar the use of funds in the bill for the Interior Department to restrict, reduce or reallocate any water based on biological opinions published by the U.S. Fish and Wildlife Service and the National Marine Fisheries Service. The opinions state that operations of the Federal Central Valley Project and the California State Water Project jeopardize the existence of certain fish and wildlife. Motion agreed to 61-36: R 4-36; D 55-0; I 2-0. Sept. 22, 2009.

293. HR 2996. Fiscal 2010 Interior-Environment Appropriations/ **Motion to Table.** Feinstein, D-Calif., motion to table (kill) the Vitter, R-La., motion to recommit the bill to the Senate Appropriations Committee with instructions that it be reported back immediately with an amendment that would bar the use of funds in the bill to delay the Outer Continental Shelf Oil and Gas Leasing Program. Motion agreed to 56-42: R 0-40; D 54-2; I 2-0. Sept. 23, 2009.

294. HR 2996. Fiscal 2010 Interior-Environment Appropriations/ **Motion to Table.** Feinstein, D-Calif., motion to table (kill) the McCaskill, D-Mo., amendment that would require the Interior Department to distribute the funds in the bill appropriated for the Save America's Treasures program in the form of competitive grants to be awarded to collections or historic property that are threatened or endangered, have a clear public benefit and are feasible. Motion agreed to 72-26: R 18-22; D 52-4; I 2-0. Sept. 23, 2009.

	290	291	292	293	294		290	291	292	293	294
ALABAMA						**MONTANA**					
Shelby	Y	N	N	N	Y	Baucus	Y	N	Y	Y	Y
Sessions	Y	Y	N	N	N	Tester	Y	N	Y	Y	Y
ALASKA						**NEBRASKA**					
Murkowski	Y	N	N	N	Y	Nelson	Y	N	Y	N	Y
Begich	Y	N	Y	N	Y	Johanns	Y	Y	N	N	N
ARIZONA						**NEVADA**					
McCain	Y	Y	N	N	N	Reid	Y	N	Y	Y	Y
Kyl	Y	Y	N	N	N	Ensign	Y	Y	N	N	N
ARKANSAS						**NEW HAMPSHIRE**					
Lincoln	?	?	?	Y	Y	Gregg	Y	Y	N	N	Y
Pryor	Y	N	Y	Y	Y	Shaheen	Y	N	Y	Y	Y
CALIFORNIA						**NEW JERSEY**					
Feinstein	Y	N	Y	Y	Y	Lautenberg	Y	N	Y	Y	Y
Boxer	Y	N	Y	Y	Y	Menendez	Y	N	Y	Y	Y
COLORADO						**NEW MEXICO**					
Udall	Y	N	Y	Y	Y	Bingaman	Y	N	Y	Y	Y
Bennet	Y	N	Y	Y	Y	Udall	Y	N	Y	Y	Y
CONNECTICUT						**NEW YORK**					
Dodd	Y	N	Y	Y	Y	Schumer	Y	N	Y	Y	Y
Lieberman	Y	N	Y	Y	Y	Gillibrand	Y	N	Y	Y	Y
DELAWARE						**NORTH CAROLINA**					
Carper	Y	N	Y	Y	Y	Burr	Y	Y	N	N	N
Kaufman	Y	N	Y	Y	N	Hagan	Y	N	Y	Y	Y
FLORIDA						**NORTH DAKOTA**					
Nelson	Y	N	Y	N	Y	Conrad	Y	N	Y	Y	Y
LeMieux	Y	Y	N	N	Y	Dorgan	Y	N	Y	Y	Y
GEORGIA						**OHIO**					
Chambliss	Y	Y	N	N	N	Voinovich	Y	N	Y	N	Y
Isakson	Y	Y	N	N	N	Brown	Y	N	Y	Y	Y
HAWAII						**OKLAHOMA**					
Inouye	Y	N	Y	Y	Y	Inhofe	Y	Y	N	N	N
Akaka	Y	N	Y	Y	Y	Coburn	?	Y	N	N	N
IDAHO						**OREGON**					
Crapo	Y	Y	N	N	N	Wyden	Y	N	Y	Y	Y
Risch	Y	Y	N	N	N	Merkley	Y	N	Y	Y	Y
ILLINOIS						**PENNSYLVANIA**					
Durbin	Y	N	Y	Y	Y	Specter	Y	N	Y	Y	Y
Burris	Y	N	Y	Y	Y	Casey	Y	N	Y	Y	Y
INDIANA						**RHODE ISLAND**					
Lugar	Y	Y	N	N	Y	Reed	Y	N	Y	Y	Y
Bayh	Y	N	Y	N	N	Whitehouse	Y	N	Y	Y	Y
IOWA						**SOUTH CAROLINA**					
Grassley	Y	N	N	N	N	Graham	Y	Y	N	N	Y
Harkin	Y	N	Y	Y	Y	DeMint	Y	Y	N	N	N
KANSAS						**SOUTH DAKOTA**					
Brownback	Y	N	N	N	Y	Johnson	Y	N	Y	Y	Y
Roberts	Y	N	N	N	Y	Thune	Y	Y	N	N	N
KENTUCKY						**TENNESSEE**					
McConnell	Y	Y	N	N	Y	Alexander	Y	N	Y	N	Y
Bunning	Y	Y	N	N	N	Corker	Y	Y	N	N	N
LOUISIANA						**TEXAS**					
Landrieu	Y	N	Y	Y	Y	Hutchison	Y	Y	N	N	Y
Vitter	Y	Y	N	N	N	Cornyn	Y	Y	N	N	N
MAINE						**UTAH**					
Snowe	Y	N	Y	N	Y	Hatch	Y	N	N	N	Y
Collins	Y	N	Y	N	Y	Bennett	Y	N	N	N	Y
MARYLAND						**VERMONT**					
Mikulski	Y	N	Y	Y	Y	Leahy	Y	N	Y	Y	Y
Cardin	Y	N	Y	Y	Y	Sanders	Y	N	Y	Y	Y
MASSACHUSETTS						**VIRGINIA**					
Kerry	Y	N	Y	Y	Y	Webb	Y	N	Y	Y	Y
Vacant						Warner	Y	N	Y	Y	Y
MICHIGAN						**WASHINGTON**					
Levin	Y	N	Y	Y	Y	Murray	Y	N	Y	Y	Y
Stabenow	Y	N	Y	Y	Y	Cantwell	Y	N	Y	Y	Y
MINNESOTA						**WEST VIRGINIA**					
Klobuchar	Y	N	Y	Y	Y	Byrd	?	?	?	?	?
Franken	Y	N	Y	Y	Y	Rockefeller	Y	N	Y	Y	Y
MISSISSIPPI						**WISCONSIN**					
Cochran	Y	N	N	N	Y	Kohl	?	N	Y	Y	Y
Wicker	Y	N	N	N	Y	Feingold	Y	Y	Y	Y	N
MISSOURI						**WYOMING**					
Bond	Y	N	N	N	Y	Enzi	Y	Y	N	N	N
McCaskill	Y	N	Y	N	N	Barrasso	Y	Y	N	N	N

KEY	**Republicans**	Democrats	*Independents*	
Y	Voted for (yea)	X Paired against	C Voted "present" to avoid possible conflict of interest
#	Paired for	- Announced against	
+	Announced for	P Voted "present"	? Did not vote or otherwise make a position known
N	Voted against (nay)		

IN THE SENATE | By Vote Number

295. HR 2996. Fiscal 2010 Interior-Environment Appropriations/ **Climate Change Assistant.** Feinstein, D-Calif., motion to table (kill) the Vitter, R-La., amendment that would bar funds in the bill from being provided to departments or agencies led by appointees confirmed by the Senate who implement policies of the assistant to the president for energy and climate change, known as the White House Climate Change "czar." Motion agreed to 57-41: R 1-39; D 54-2; I 2-0. A "yea" was a vote in support of the president's position. Sept. 24, 2009.

296. HR 2996. Fiscal 2010 Interior-Environment Appropriations/ **Recommit.** Feinstein, D-Calif., motion to table (kill) the Ensign, R-Nev., motion to recommit the bill to the Senate Appropriations Committee with instructions that it be reported back with changes that would reduce discretionary funding in the bill by $4.3 billion. Motion agreed to 64-34: R 8-32; D 54-2; I 2-0. Sept. 24, 2009.

297. HR 2996. Fiscal 2010 Interior-Environment Appropriations/ **Federal Land Acquisition Fund Requirement.** Feinstein, D-Calif., motion to table (kill) the Coburn, R-Okla., amendment that would require that funds in the bill taken from the Land and Water Conservation Fund for federal land acquisition be used for maintenance, repair or rehabilitation projects for constructed assets. Motion agreed to 79-19: R 22-18; D 55-1; I 2-0. Sept. 24, 2009.

298. HR 2996. Fiscal 2010 Interior-Environment Appropriations/ **Passage.** Passage of the bill that would provide $32.1 billion in fiscal 2010 discretionary spending for the Interior Department, the EPA and related agencies. The total includes $10.2 billion for the EPA and $11.1 billion for the Interior Department, including $1.1 billion for the Bureau of Land Management, $1.6 billion for the U.S. Fish and Wildlife Service, and $2.7 billion for the National Park Service. It also includes $5.3 billion for the U.S. Forest Service and $4 billion for the Indian Health Service. Passed 77-21: R 20-20; D 55-1; I 2-0. A "yea" was a vote in support of the president's position. Sept. 24, 2009.

299. **Viken Nomination/Confirmation.** Confirmation of President Obama's nomination of Jeffrey L. Viken of South Dakota to be a judge for the U.S. District Court for the District of South Dakota. Confirmed 99-0: R 40-0; D 57-0; I 2-0. A "yea" was a vote in support of the president's position. Sept. 29, 2009.

	295	296	297	298	299
ALABAMA					
Shelby	N	Y	Y	Y	Y
Sessions	N	N	Y	N	Y
ALASKA					
Murkowski	N	Y	Y	Y	Y
Begich	Y	Y	Y	Y	Y
ARIZONA					
McCain	N	N	Y	N	Y
Kyl	N	N	N	N	Y
ARKANSAS					
Lincoln	Y	Y	Y	Y	Y
Pryor	Y	Y	Y	Y	Y
CALIFORNIA					
Feinstein	Y	Y	Y	Y	Y
Boxer	Y	Y	Y	Y	Y
COLORADO					
Udall	Y	Y	Y	Y	Y
Bennet	Y	Y	Y	Y	Y
CONNECTICUT					
Dodd	Y	Y	Y	Y	Y
Lieberman	Y	Y	Y	Y	Y
DELAWARE					
Carper	Y	Y	Y	Y	Y
Kaufman	Y	Y	Y	Y	Y
FLORIDA					
Nelson	Y	Y	Y	Y	Y
LeMieux	N	N	Y	N	Y
GEORGIA					
Chambliss	N	N	N	N	Y
Isakson	N	N	Y	Y	Y
HAWAII					
Inouye	Y	Y	Y	Y	Y
Akaka	Y	Y	Y	Y	Y
IDAHO					
Crapo	N	N	N	Y	Y
Risch	N	N	N	Y	Y
ILLINOIS					
Durbin	Y	Y	Y	Y	Y
Burris	Y	Y	Y	Y	Y
INDIANA					
Lugar	N	N	N	Y	Y
Bayh	Y	N	Y	N	Y
IOWA					
Grassley	N	N	N	N	Y
Harkin	Y	Y	Y	Y	Y
KANSAS					
Brownback	N	N	Y	Y	Y
Roberts	N	N	Y	Y	Y
KENTUCKY					
McConnell	N	N	Y	N	Y
Bunning	N	N	N	N	Y
LOUISIANA					
Landrieu	Y	Y	Y	Y	Y
Vitter	N	N	Y	N	Y
MAINE					
Snowe	Y	N	Y	Y	Y
Collins	N	Y	Y	Y	Y
MARYLAND					
Mikulski	Y	Y	Y	Y	Y
Cardin	Y	Y	Y	Y	Y
MASSACHUSETTS					
Kerry	Y	Y	Y	Y	Y
Kirk*					Y
MICHIGAN					
Levin	Y	Y	Y	Y	Y
Stabenow	Y	Y	Y	Y	Y
MINNESOTA					
Klobuchar	Y	Y	Y	Y	Y
Franken	Y	Y	Y	Y	Y
MISSISSIPPI					
Cochran	N	Y	Y	Y	Y
Wicker	N	N	N	Y	Y
MISSOURI					
Bond	N	Y	Y	Y	Y
McCaskill	N	N	Y	Y	Y

	295	296	297	298	299
MONTANA					
Baucus	Y	Y	Y	Y	Y
Tester	Y	Y	Y	Y	Y
NEBRASKA					
Nelson	N	Y	Y	Y	Y
Johanns	N	N	N	Y	Y
NEVADA					
Reid	Y	Y	Y	Y	Y
Ensign	N	N	N	N	Y
NEW HAMPSHIRE					
Gregg	N	N	Y	Y	Y
Shaheen	Y	Y	Y	Y	Y
NEW JERSEY					
Lautenberg	Y	Y	Y	Y	Y
Menendez	Y	Y	Y	Y	Y
NEW MEXICO					
Bingaman	Y	Y	Y	Y	Y
Udall	Y	Y	Y	Y	Y
NEW YORK					
Schumer	Y	Y	Y	Y	Y
Gillibrand	Y	Y	Y	Y	Y
NORTH CAROLINA					
Burr	N	N	N	Y	Y
Hagan	Y	Y	Y	Y	Y
NORTH DAKOTA					
Conrad	Y	Y	N	Y	Y
Dorgan	Y	Y	Y	Y	Y
OHIO					
Voinovich	N	Y	Y	Y	Y
Brown	Y	Y	Y	Y	Y
OKLAHOMA					
Inhofe	N	N	N	N	Y
Coburn	N	N	N	N	Y
OREGON					
Wyden	Y	Y	Y	Y	Y
Merkley	Y	Y	Y	Y	Y
PENNSYLVANIA					
Specter	Y	Y	Y	Y	Y
Casey	Y	Y	Y	Y	Y
RHODE ISLAND					
Reed	Y	Y	Y	Y	Y
Whitehouse	Y	Y	Y	Y	Y
SOUTH CAROLINA					
Graham	N	N	N	Y	Y
DeMint	N	N	N	N	Y
SOUTH DAKOTA					
Johnson	Y	Y	Y	Y	Y
Thune	N	N	N	N	Y
TENNESSEE					
Alexander	N	Y	Y	Y	Y
Corker	N	N	Y	N	Y
TEXAS					
Hutchison	N	N	Y	Y	Y
Cornyn	N	N	N	N	Y
UTAH					
Hatch	N	N	N	Y	Y
Bennett	N	Y	Y	Y	Y
VERMONT					
Leahy	Y	Y	Y	Y	Y
Sanders	Y	Y	Y	Y	Y
VIRGINIA					
Webb	Y	Y	Y	Y	Y
Warner	Y	Y	Y	Y	Y
WASHINGTON					
Murray	Y	Y	Y	Y	Y
Cantwell	Y	Y	Y	Y	Y
WEST VIRGINIA					
Byrd	?	?	?	?	?
Rockefeller	Y	Y	Y	Y	Y
WISCONSIN					
Kohl	Y	Y	Y	Y	Y
Feingold	Y	Y	Y	Y	Y
WYOMING					
Enzi	N	N	N	N	Y
Barrasso	N	N	N	N	Y

KEY	Republicans	Democrats	*Independents*	
Y	Voted for (yea)	X	Paired against	
#	Paired for	–	Announced against	
+	Announced for	P	Voted "present"	
N	Voted against (nay)			
C	Voted "present" to avoid possible conflict of interest			
?	Did not vote or otherwise make a position known			

*Sen. Paul G. Kirk Jr., D-Mass., was sworn in Sept. 25 to fill temporarily the seat vacated by the Aug. 25 death of fellow Democrat Edward M. Kennedy. The first vote for which Kirk was eligible was vote 299.

IN THE SENATE | By Vote Number

300. HR 2918. **Fiscal 2010 Legislative Branch Appropriations/ Conference Report Points of Order.** Nelson, D-Neb., motion to waive Senate Rule 28 with respect to points of order against the conference report on the bill that would appropriate $4.7 billion in fiscal 2010 for legislative branch operations and provide continuing appropriations through Oct. 31, 2009, for all federal departments and agencies whose fiscal 2010 appropriations bills have not been enacted. Motion agreed to 61-39: R 2-38; D 57-1; I 2-0. A three-fifths majority vote (60) of the total Senate is required to waive Senate Rule 28. (Under the rule, a senator may raise a point of order against provisions of a conference report that were not in the bill passed by either chamber.) Sept. 30, 2009.

301. HR 2918. **Fiscal 2010 Legislative Branch Appropriations/ Conference Report Points of Order.** Nelson, D-Neb., motion to waive the Budget Act with respect to points of order against the conference report on the bill that would appropriate $4.7 billion in fiscal 2010 for legislative branch operations and provide continuing appropriations through Oct. 31, 2009, for all federal departments and agencies whose fiscal 2010 appropriations bills have not been enacted. Motion agreed to 61-39: R 2-38; D 57-1; I 2-0. A three-fifths majority vote (60) of the total Senate is required to waive the Budget Act. Sept. 30, 2009.

302. HR 2918. **Fiscal 2010 Legislative Branch Appropriations/ Conference Report.** Adoption of the conference report on the bill that would appropriate $4.7 billion in fiscal 2010 for legislative branch operations. It includes $1.3 billion for operations of the House, $926 million for Senate operations, $602 million for the Architect of the Capitol and $643 million for the Library of Congress. It would provide continuing appropriations through Oct. 31, 2009, for all federal departments and agencies whose fiscal 2010 appropriations bills have not been enacted. Funding would mostly be set at fiscal 2009 levels. Adopted (thus cleared for the president) 62-38: R 5-35; D 55-3; I 2-0. Sept. 30, 2009.

303. HR 3326. **Fiscal 2010 Defense Appropriations/Air Force Aircraft Funding Shift.** McCain, R-Ariz., motion to waive the Budget Act with respect to the Inouye, D-Hawaii, point of order against the McCain amendment that would shift $2.5 billion provided in the bill for Air Force aircraft procurement to Army overseas contingency operations, and general operations and maintenance. Motion rejected 34-64: R 16-24; D 17-39; I 1-1. A three-fifths majority vote (60) of the total Senate is required to waive the Budget Act. (Subsequently, the chair upheld the point of order, and the amendment fell.) Sept. 30, 2009.

304. HR 3326. **Fiscal 2010 Defense Appropriations/Congressional Testimony.** Levin, D-Mich., amendment that would call for congressional testimony of senior civilian and military officials in hearings on Afghanistan and Pakistan resources and strategies. The hearings would take place after the president has announced a decision on those matters. The officials testifying would include the secretaries of Defense and State, the chairman of the Joint Chiefs of Staff, the commander of U.S. Central Command, the commander of U.S. forces for Afghanistan, and the U.S. ambassadors to Afghanistan and Pakistan. Adopted 60-39: R 1-39; D 57-0; I 2-0. Oct. 1, 2009.

305. HR 3326. **Fiscal 2010 Defense Appropriations/Congressional Testimony.** McCain, R-Ariz., amendment that would require congressional testimony, no later than Nov. 15, 2009, from senior officials including the U.S. ambassador to Afghanistan and the commanders of U.S. Central Command and U.S. forces in Afghanistan, on their recommendations regarding additional forces and resources required to achieve U.S. policy objectives in Afghanistan and Pakistan. Rejected 40-59: R 40-0; D 0-57; I 0-2. A "nay" was a vote in support of the president's position. Oct. 1, 2009.

	300	301	302	303	304	305
ALABAMA						
Shelby	N	N	N	N	N	Y
Sessions	N	N	N	Y	N	Y
ALASKA						
Murkowski	N	N	Y	N	N	Y
Begich	Y	Y	Y	N	Y	N
ARIZONA						
McCain	N	N	N	Y	N	Y
Kyl	N	N	N	Y	N	Y
ARKANSAS						
Lincoln	Y	Y	Y	N	Y	N
Pryor	Y	Y	Y	N	Y	N
CALIFORNIA						
Feinstein	Y	Y	Y	N	Y	N
Boxer	Y	Y	Y	N	Y	N
COLORADO						
Udall	Y	Y	Y	Y	Y	N
Bennet	Y	Y	N	Y	Y	N
CONNECTICUT						
Dodd	Y	Y	Y	N	?	N
Lieberman	Y	Y	Y	N	Y	N
DELAWARE						
Carper	Y	Y	Y	Y	Y	N
Kaufman	Y	Y	Y	Y	Y	N
FLORIDA						
Nelson	Y	Y	Y	Y	Y	N
LeMieux	N	N	N	Y	N	Y
GEORGIA						
Chambliss	N	N	N	N	N	Y
Isakson	N	N	N	N	N	Y
HAWAII						
Inouye	Y	Y	Y	N	Y	N
Akaka	Y	Y	Y	N	Y	N
IDAHO						
Crapo	N	N	N	N	N	Y
Risch	N	N	N	N	N	Y
ILLINOIS						
Durbin	Y	Y	Y	N	Y	N
Burris	Y	Y	Y	N	Y	N
INDIANA						
Lugar	N	N	N	Y	N	Y
Bayh	Y	Y	Y	N	Y	?
IOWA						
Grassley	N	N	N	N	N	Y
Harkin	Y	Y	Y	N	Y	N
KANSAS						
Brownback	N	N	N	N	N	Y
Roberts	N	N	N	N	N	Y
KENTUCKY						
McConnell	N	N	N	Y	N	Y
Bunning	N	N	N	N	N	Y
LOUISIANA						
Landrieu	Y	Y	Y	?	Y	N
Vitter	N	N	N	Y	N	Y
MAINE						
Snowe	N	N	Y	N	N	Y
Collins	N	Y	Y	N	N	Y
MARYLAND						
Mikulski	Y	Y	Y	N	Y	N
Cardin	Y	Y	Y	Y	Y	N
MASSACHUSETTS						
Kerry	Y	Y	Y	N	Y	N
Kirk	Y	Y	Y	N	Y	N
MICHIGAN						
Levin	Y	Y	Y	Y	Y	N
Stabenow	Y	Y	Y	N	Y	N
MINNESOTA						
Klobuchar	Y	Y	Y	Y	Y	N
Franken	Y	Y	Y	Y	Y	N
MISSISSIPPI						
Cochran	Y	Y	Y	N	N	Y
Wicker	N	N	N	N	N	Y
MISSOURI						
Bond	N	N	N	N	N	Y
McCaskill	Y	Y	N	N	Y	N

	300	301	302	303	304	305
MONTANA						
Baucus	Y	Y	Y	N	Y	N
Tester	Y	Y	Y	N	Y	N
NEBRASKA						
Nelson	Y	Y	Y	N	Y	N
Johanns	N	N	N	N	N	Y
NEVADA						
Reid	Y	Y	Y	N	Y	N
Ensign	N	N	N	Y	N	Y
NEW HAMPSHIRE						
Gregg	N	N	N	Y	N	Y
Shaheen	Y	Y	Y	N	Y	N
NEW JERSEY						
Lautenberg	Y	Y	Y	N	Y	N
Menendez	Y	Y	Y	N	Y	N
NEW MEXICO						
Bingaman	Y	Y	Y	N	Y	N
Udall	Y	Y	Y	N	Y	N
NEW YORK						
Schumer	Y	Y	Y	N	Y	N
Gillibrand	Y	Y	Y	N	Y	N
NORTH CAROLINA						
Burr	N	N	N	N	N	Y
Hagan	Y	Y	Y	N	Y	N
NORTH DAKOTA						
Conrad	Y	Y	Y	Y	Y	N
Dorgan	Y	Y	Y	Y	Y	N
OHIO						
Voinovich	Y	N	N	Y	N	Y
Brown	Y	Y	Y	N	Y	N
OKLAHOMA						
Inhofe	N	N	N	N	N	Y
Coburn	N	N	N	N	N	Y
OREGON						
Wyden	Y	Y	Y	N	Y	N
Merkley	Y	Y	Y	Y	Y	N
PENNSYLVANIA						
Specter	Y	Y	Y	N	Y	N
Casey	Y	Y	Y	N	Y	N
RHODE ISLAND						
Reed	Y	Y	Y	N	Y	N
Whitehouse	Y	Y	Y	N	Y	N
SOUTH CAROLINA						
Graham	N	N	N	N	N	Y
DeMint	N	N	N	N	N	Y
SOUTH DAKOTA						
Johnson	Y	Y	Y	N	Y	N
Thune	N	N	N	Y	N	Y
TENNESSEE						
Alexander	N	N	N	Y	N	Y
Corker	N	N	N	Y	N	Y
TEXAS						
Hutchison	N	N	N	N	N	Y
Cornyn	N	N	N	N	N	Y
UTAH						
Hatch	N	N	N	N	N	Y
Bennett	N	N	N	N	N	Y
VERMONT						
Leahy	Y	Y	Y	N	Y	N
Sanders	Y	Y	Y	Y	Y	N
VIRGINIA						
Webb	Y	Y	Y	Y	Y	N
Warner	Y	Y	Y	Y	Y	N
WASHINGTON						
Murray	Y	Y	Y	N	Y	N
Cantwell	Y	Y	Y	N	Y	N
WEST VIRGINIA						
Byrd	Y	Y	Y	?	Y	N
Rockefeller	Y	Y	Y	N	Y	N
WISCONSIN						
Kohl	Y	Y	Y	N	Y	N
Feingold	N	N	N	Y	Y	N
WYOMING						
Enzi	N	N	N	Y	N	Y
Barrasso	N	N	N	Y	N	Y

KEY	**Republicans**	Democrats	*Independents*
Y Voted for (yea)	**X** Paired against		**C** Voted "present" to avoid possible conflict of interest
# Paired for	**–** Announced against		**?** Did not vote or otherwise make a position known
+ Announced for	**P** Voted "present"		
N Voted against (nay)			

IN THE SENATE | By Vote Number

306. **Perez Nomination/Confirmation.** Confirmation of President Obama's nomination of Thomas E. Perez of Maryland to be assistant attorney general for the Justice Department's Civil Rights Division. Confirmed 72-22: R 17-22; D 55-0; I 0-0. A "yea" was a vote in support of the president's position. Oct. 6, 2009.

307. **HR 3326. Fiscal 2010 Defense Appropriations/Center on Climate Change and National Security.** Barrasso, R-Wyo., amendment that would bar use of funds in the bill for the CIA's Center on Climate Change and National Security. Rejected 38-60: R 38-2; D 0-56; I 0-2. Oct. 6, 2009.

308. **HR 3326. Fiscal 2010 Defense Appropriations/Sexual Assault Arbitration Settlements.** Franken, D-Minn., amendment that would bar the use of funds in the bill for any federal contract with a contractor or subcontractor who requires employees or independent contractors to sign statements requiring mandatory arbitration related to civil rights or sexual harassment as a condition of their employment. Adopted 68-30: R 10-30; D 56-0; I 2-0. Oct. 6, 2009.

309. **HR 3326. Fiscal 2010 Defense Appropriations/Aircraft Retirement Report.** Bond, R-Mo., amendment that would require the Air Force to submit a report to congressional defense committees before retiring any tactical aircraft as announced in the Combat Air Forces structuring plan in May 2009. The report would describe plans for personnel and bases affected by aircraft retirement, and plans for filling force structure and capability gaps. It would explain criteria for selecting bases and aircraft to retire, estimate the funds saved and outline how those funds would be spent. Adopted 91-7: R 33-7; D 56-0; I 2-0. Oct. 6, 2009.

310. **HR 3326. Fiscal 2010 Defense Appropriations/Reserve and National Guard Modernization.** Coburn, R-Okla., amendment that would require the chiefs of the Reserve and National Guard to provide Congress and the Defense secretary with a modernization priority assessment for their respective components of the Reserve and National Guard within 30 days of enactment if they want to get $1.5 billion that would be available for obligation in the bill. Rejected 28-70: R 26-14; D 2-54; I 0-2. Oct. 6, 2009.

	306	307	308	309	310
ALABAMA					
Shelby	N	Y	N	Y	Y
Sessions	N	Y	N	N	Y
ALASKA					
Murkowski	Y	Y	Y	Y	Y
Begich	Y	N	Y	Y	N
ARIZONA					
McCain	N	Y	N	N	Y
Kyl	Y	Y	N	N	Y
ARKANSAS					
Lincoln	Y	N	Y	Y	N
Pryor	Y	N	Y	Y	N
CALIFORNIA					
Feinstein	Y	N	Y	Y	N
Boxer	Y	N	Y	Y	N
COLORADO					
Udall	+	N	Y	Y	N
Bennet	Y	N	Y	Y	N
CONNECTICUT					
Dodd	Y	N	Y	Y	N
Lieberman	?	N	Y	Y	N
DELAWARE					
Carper	Y	N	Y	Y	Y
Kaufman	Y	N	Y	Y	N
FLORIDA					
Nelson	Y	N	Y	Y	N
LeMieux	Y	Y	Y	Y	Y
GEORGIA					
Chambliss	N	Y	N	Y	Y
Isakson	N	Y	N	Y	Y
HAWAII					
Inouye	Y	N	Y	Y	N
Akaka	Y	N	Y	Y	N
IDAHO					
Crapo	N	Y	N	Y	N
Risch	N	Y	N	Y	N
ILLINOIS					
Durbin	Y	N	Y	Y	N
Burris	Y	N	Y	Y	N
INDIANA					
Lugar	Y	Y	Y	Y	N
Bayh	Y	N	Y	Y	N
IOWA					
Grassley	Y	Y	Y	Y	N
Harkin	Y	N	Y	Y	N
KANSAS					
Brownback	N	Y	N	Y	N
Roberts	N	Y	N	Y	N
KENTUCKY					
McConnell	N	Y	N	Y	Y
Bunning	N	Y	N	Y	Y
LOUISIANA					
Landrieu	Y	N	Y	Y	N
Vitter	N	Y	N	Y	Y
MAINE					
Snowe	Y	N	Y	Y	N
Collins	Y	N	Y	Y	Y
MARYLAND					
Mikulski	Y	N	Y	Y	N
Cardin	Y	N	Y	Y	N
MASSACHUSETTS					
Kerry	Y	N	Y	Y	N
Kirk	Y	N	Y	Y	N
MICHIGAN					
Levin	Y	N	Y	Y	N
Stabenow	Y	N	Y	Y	N
MINNESOTA					
Klobuchar	Y	N	Y	Y	N
Franken	Y	N	Y	Y	N
MISSISSIPPI					
Cochran	N	Y	N	Y	N
Wicker	N	Y	N	Y	Y
MISSOURI					
Bond	Y	N	Y	Y	N
McCaskill	Y	N	Y	Y	N

	306	307	308	309	310
MONTANA					
Baucus	Y	N	Y	Y	N
Tester	Y	N	Y	Y	N
NEBRASKA					
Nelson	Y	N	Y	Y	N
Johanns	Y	Y	N	N	Y
NEVADA					
Reid	Y	N	Y	Y	N
Ensign	N	Y	N	Y	Y
NEW HAMPSHIRE					
Gregg	Y	Y	N	N	Y
Shaheen	Y	N	Y	Y	N
NEW JERSEY					
Lautenberg	Y	N	Y	Y	N
Menendez	Y	N	Y	Y	N
NEW MEXICO					
Bingaman	Y	N	Y	Y	N
Udall	Y	N	Y	Y	N
NEW YORK					
Schumer	Y	N	Y	Y	N
Gillibrand	Y	N	Y	Y	N
NORTH CAROLINA					
Burr	?	Y	N	Y	Y
Hagan	Y	N	Y	Y	N
NORTH DAKOTA					
Conrad	Y	N	Y	Y	N
Dorgan	Y	N	Y	Y	N
OHIO					
Voinovich	Y	Y	Y	Y	N
Brown	Y	N	Y	Y	N
OKLAHOMA					
Inhofe	N	Y	N	Y	Y
Coburn	N	Y	N	N	Y
OREGON					
Wyden	Y	N	Y	Y	N
Merkley	Y	N	Y	Y	N
PENNSYLVANIA					
Specter	?	?	?	?	?
Casey	Y	N	Y	Y	N
RHODE ISLAND					
Reed	Y	N	Y	Y	N
Whitehouse	Y	N	Y	Y	N
SOUTH CAROLINA					
Graham	Y	Y	N	N	Y
DeMint	N	Y	N	Y	Y
SOUTH DAKOTA					
Johnson	Y	N	Y	Y	N
Thune	N	Y	N	Y	Y
TENNESSEE					
Alexander	Y	Y	N	Y	N
Corker	Y	Y	N	Y	Y
TEXAS					
Hutchison	Y	Y	Y	Y	N
Cornyn	Y	Y	N	Y	N
UTAH					
Hatch	Y	Y	Y	Y	N
Bennett	N	Y	Y	Y	N
VERMONT					
Leahy	Y	N	Y	Y	N
Sanders	?	N	Y	Y	N
VIRGINIA					
Webb	Y	N	Y	Y	N
Warner	Y	N	Y	Y	N
WASHINGTON					
Murray	Y	N	Y	Y	N
Cantwell	Y	N	Y	Y	N
WEST VIRGINIA					
Byrd	?	?	?	?	?
Rockefeller	Y	N	Y	Y	N
WISCONSIN					
Kohl	Y	N	Y	Y	N
Feingold	Y	N	Y	Y	N
WYOMING					
Enzi	N	Y	N	Y	Y
Barrasso	N	Y	N	Y	Y

KEY	**Republicans**	Democrats	*Independents*

Y Voted for (yea)	X Paired against	C Voted "present" to avoid possible conflict of interest
# Paired for	– Announced against	
+ Announced for	P Voted "present"	? Did not vote or otherwise make a position known
N Voted against (nay)		

IN THE SENATE | By Vote Number

311.
HR 3326. Fiscal 2010 Defense Appropriations/Operations and Maintenance Funds Earmark Ban. Coburn, R-Okla., amendment that would bar the use of funds in the bill for congressionally directed spending items paid from amounts appropriated for operations and maintenance of the Defense Department or branches of the U.S. armed forces. Rejected 25-73: R 22-18; D 3-53; I 0-2. Oct. 6, 2009.

312.
HR 3326. Fiscal 2010 Defense Appropriations/Air Force Aircraft Procurement Reduction. McCain, R-Ariz., amendment that would reduce the amount provided for Air Force aircraft procurement by $2.5 billion. Rejected 30-68: R 14-26; D 15-41; I 1-1. Oct. 6, 2009.

313.
HR 3326. Fiscal 2010 Defense Appropriations/Congressionally Directed Spending Regulations. Inouye, D-Hawaii, amendment that would subject congressionally directed spending items in the bill for for-profit entities to acquisition regulations for full and open competition. The regulations would not apply to contracts awarded by means required by federal statute, pursuant to the Small Business Act or that are less than the threshold defined by current federal law. Adopted 77-21: R 21-19; D 54-2; I 2-0. Oct. 6, 2009.

314.
HR 3326. Fiscal 2010 Defense Appropriations/Hypersonic Wind Tunnel Program. McCain, R-Ariz., amendment that would reduce the amount provided in the bill for Army research, development, testing and evaluation by $9.5 million, with the reduction to be taken from the MARIAH Hypersonic Wind Tunnel Development Program. Rejected 43-55: R 40-0; D 3-53; I 0-2. Oct. 6, 2009.

315.
HR 3326. Fiscal 2010 Defense Appropriations/Passage.
Passage of the bill that would provide $636.3 billion in discretionary appropriations for the Defense Department in fiscal 2010, including $128.2 billion for operations in Afghanistan and Iraq. The total includes $154.1 billion for operations and maintenance, $108 billion for procurement, and $78.4 billion for research and development. It would provide $28.3 billion for the Defense Health Program and $124.8 billion for military personnel. It would fund an active-duty end strength of 1.4 million and a reserve component end strength of 844,500. Passed 93-7: R 34-6; D 57-1; I 2-0. A "yea" was a vote in support of the president's position. Oct. 6, 2009.

	311	312	313	314	315
ALABAMA					
Shelby	N	N	Y	Y	Y
Sessions	Y	Y	N	Y	Y
ALASKA					
Murkowski	N	N	Y	Y	Y
Begich	N	N	Y	N	Y
ARIZONA					
McCain	Y	Y	N	Y	N
Kyl	Y	Y	N	Y	Y
ARKANSAS					
Lincoln	N	N	Y	N	Y
Pryor	N	N	Y	N	Y
CALIFORNIA					
Feinstein	N	N	Y	N	Y
Boxer	N	N	Y	N	Y
COLORADO					
Udall	N	Y	Y	N	Y
Bennet	N	Y	Y	N	Y
CONNECTICUT					
Dodd	N	N	Y	N	Y
Lieberman	N	N	Y	N	Y
DELAWARE					
Carper	N	Y	Y	N	Y
Kaufman	N	Y	Y	N	Y
FLORIDA					
Nelson	N	N	Y	N	Y
LeMieux	Y	Y	N	Y	Y
GEORGIA					
Chambliss	Y	N	Y	Y	Y
Isakson	Y	N	Y	Y	Y
HAWAII					
Inouye	N	N	Y	N	Y
Akaka	N	N	Y	N	Y
IDAHO					
Crapo	Y	N	N	Y	Y
Risch	Y	N	N	Y	Y
ILLINOIS					
Durbin	N	N	Y	N	Y
Burris	N	N	Y	N	Y
INDIANA					
Lugar	Y	Y	Y	Y	Y
Bayh	Y	N	Y	Y	Y
IOWA					
Grassley	Y	N	N	Y	N
Harkin	N	N	Y	N	Y
KANSAS					
Brownback	N	N	Y	Y	Y
Roberts	N	N	Y	Y	Y
KENTUCKY					
McConnell	N	Y	Y	Y	Y
Bunning	Y	N	N	Y	Y
LOUISIANA					
Landrieu	N	N	Y	N	Y
Vitter	Y	N	N	Y	Y
MAINE					
Snowe	N	N	Y	Y	Y
Collins	N	N	Y	Y	Y
MARYLAND					
Mikulski	N	N	Y	N	Y
Cardin	N	Y	Y	N	Y
MASSACHUSETTS					
Kerry	N	N	Y	N	Y
Kirk	N	N	Y	N	Y
MICHIGAN					
Levin	N	Y	Y	N	Y
Stabenow	N	N	Y	N	Y
MINNESOTA					
Klobuchar	N	Y	Y	N	Y
Franken	N	Y	Y	N	Y
MISSISSIPPI					
Cochran	N	N	Y	Y	Y
Wicker	N	N	Y	Y	Y
MISSOURI					
Bond	N	N	Y	Y	Y
McCaskill	Y	N	N	Y	Y
MONTANA					
Baucus	N	N	Y	N	Y
Tester	N	N	Y	N	Y
NEBRASKA					
Nelson	N	N	Y	N	Y
Johanns	Y	N	N	Y	Y
NEVADA					
Reid	N	N	Y	N	Y
Ensign	Y	N	N	Y	Y
NEW HAMPSHIRE					
Gregg	N	Y	Y	Y	Y
Shaheen	N	N	Y	N	Y
NEW JERSEY					
Lautenberg	N	N	Y	N	Y
Menendez	N	N	Y	N	Y
NEW MEXICO					
Bingaman	N	N	Y	N	Y
Udall	N	N	Y	N	Y
NEW YORK					
Schumer	N	N	Y	N	Y
Gillibrand	N	N	Y	N	Y
NORTH CAROLINA					
Burr	Y	N	N	Y	Y
Hagan	N	N	Y	N	Y
NORTH DAKOTA					
Conrad	N	Y	Y	N	Y
Dorgan	N	Y	Y	N	Y
OHIO					
Voinovich	N	Y	Y	Y	Y
Brown	N	N	Y	N	Y
OKLAHOMA					
Inhofe	Y	N	Y	Y	Y
Coburn	Y	Y	N	Y	N
OREGON					
Wyden	N	N	Y	N	Y
Merkley	N	Y	Y	N	Y
PENNSYLVANIA					
Specter	?	?	?	?	Y
Casey	N	N	Y	N	Y
RHODE ISLAND					
Reed	N	N	Y	N	Y
Whitehouse	N	N	Y	N	Y
SOUTH CAROLINA					
Graham	N	N	Y	N	Y
DeMint	Y	N	N	Y	N
SOUTH DAKOTA					
Johnson	N	N	Y	N	Y
Thune	Y	Y	N	Y	Y
TENNESSEE					
Alexander	N	Y	Y	Y	Y
Corker	N	Y	N	Y	Y
TEXAS					
Hutchison	N	N	Y	Y	Y
Cornyn	Y	N	Y	Y	Y
UTAH					
Hatch	N	N	Y	Y	Y
Bennett	N	N	Y	Y	Y
VERMONT					
Leahy	N	N	Y	N	Y
Sanders	N	Y	Y	N	Y
VIRGINIA					
Webb	N	Y	Y	N	Y
Warner	N	Y	Y	N	Y
WASHINGTON					
Murray	N	N	Y	N	Y
Cantwell	N	N	Y	N	Y
WEST VIRGINIA					
Byrd	?	?	?	?	Y
Rockefeller	N	N	Y	N	Y
WISCONSIN					
Kohl	N	Y	Y	N	Y
Feingold	Y	Y	N	Y	N
WYOMING					
Enzi	Y	Y	N	Y	N
Barrasso	Y	Y	N	Y	N

KEY Republicans Democrats *Independents*

Y Voted for (yea)	X Paired against
# Paired for	– Announced against
+ Announced for	P Voted "present"
N Voted against (nay)	

C Voted "present" to avoid possible conflict of interest

? Did not vote or otherwise make a position known

IN THE SENATE | By Vote Number

316. HR 2847. Fiscal 2010 Commerce-Justice-Science Appropriations/Local Immigration Enforcement. Menendez, D-N.J., motion to table (kill) the Vitter, R-La., amendment that would bar the use of Community Oriented Policing Services funds in the bill for jurisdictions that prohibit local law enforcement from cooperating with federal immigration officials. Motion agreed to 61-38: R 3-37; D 56-1; I 2-0. Oct. 7, 2009.

317. HR 2847. Fiscal 2010 Commerce-Justice-Science Appropriations/Telecommunications Grants. McCain, R-Ariz., amendment that would strike the $20 million the bill would provide for Commerce Department grants for the planning and construction of public telecommunications facilities. Rejected 33-64: R 32-7; D 1-55; I 0-2. Oct. 8, 2009.

318. HR 2997. Fiscal 2010 Agriculture Appropriations/Conference Report. Adoption of the conference report on the bill that would appropriate $121.2 billion in fiscal 2010 for the Agriculture Department and related agencies, including $23.4 billion in discretionary funding. The bill would provide $20.9 billion in discretionary spending for the Agriculture Department and $2.4 billion for the Food and Drug Administration, excluding user fees. It includes $58.3 billion for the food stamp program and $17 billion for child nutrition. It also would drop a ban on Chinese poultry if the products meet U.S. safety standards. Adopted (thus cleared for the president) 76-22: R 19-21; D 55-1; I 2-0. A "yea" was a vote in support of the president's position. Oct. 8, 2009.

319. HR 2847. Fiscal 2010 Commerce-Justice-Science Appropriations/Recommit. Ensign, R-Nev., motion to recommit the bill to the Senate Appropriations Committee with instructions that it be reported back with changes that would reduce funding in the bill by $3.4 billion, excluding amounts provided for the Census Bureau. Motion rejected 33-65: R 31-9; D 2-54; I 0-2. A "nay" was a vote in support of the president's position. Oct. 8, 2009.

320. HR 2847. Fiscal 2010 Commerce-Justice-Science Appropriations/Cloture. Motion to invoke cloture (thus limiting debate) on the Mikulski, D-Md., substitute amendment that would provide $65.1 billion in fiscal 2010 for the departments of Commerce and Justice and for other agencies, such as NASA and the National Science Foundation, including $64.9 billion in discretionary funding. Motion rejected 56-38: R 0-37; D 54-1; I 2-0. Three-fifths of the total Senate (60) is required to invoke cloture. Oct. 13, 2009.

321. HR 3183. Fiscal 2010 Energy-Water Appropriations/Cloture. Motion to invoke cloture (thus limiting debate) on the conference report on the bill that would appropriate $34 billion in fiscal 2010, including $33.5 billion in discretionary funds, for energy and water development projects. Motion agreed to 79-17: R 22-17; D 55-0; I 2-0. Three-fifths of the total Senate (60) is required to invoke cloture. Oct. 14, 2009.

322. HR 3183. Fiscal 2010 Energy-Water Appropriations/Conference Report. Adoption of the conference report on the bill that would appropriate $34 billion in fiscal 2010, including $33.5 billion in discretionary funds, for energy and water development projects. It includes $27.1 billion for the Energy Department, $5.4 billion for the Army Corps of Engineers and $1.1 billion for the Interior Department's Bureau of Reclamation. The measure would provide $197 million for the nuclear waste repository at Yucca Mountain and establish a commission to recommend alternatives to the facility. Adopted (thus cleared for the president) 80-17: R 24-15; D 54-2; I 2-0. A "yea" was a vote in support of the president's position. Oct. 15, 2009.

	316	317	318	319	320	321	322
ALABAMA							
Shelby	N	N	Y	N	N	Y	Y
Sessions	N	Y	N	Y	N	N	N
ALASKA							
Murkowski	Y	N	Y	N	N	Y	Y
Begich	Y	N	Y	N	?	?	Y
ARIZONA							
McCain	N	Y	N	Y	N	N	N
Kyl	N	Y	N	Y	N	N	Y
ARKANSAS							
Lincoln	Y	N	Y	N	Y	Y	Y
Pryor	Y	N	Y	N	Y	Y	Y
CALIFORNIA							
Feinstein	Y	N	Y	N	Y	Y	Y
Boxer	Y	N	Y	N	Y	Y	Y
COLORADO							
Udall	Y	N	Y	N	Y	Y	Y
Bennet	Y	N	Y	N	Y	Y	Y
CONNECTICUT							
Dodd	Y	N	Y	N	Y	Y	Y
Lieberman	Y	N	Y	N	Y	Y	Y
DELAWARE							
Carper	Y	N	Y	N	Y	Y	Y
Kaufman	Y	N	Y	N	Y	Y	Y
FLORIDA							
Nelson	Y	N	Y	N	Y	Y	Y
LeMieux	N	Y	N	N	N	Y	Y
GEORGIA							
Chambliss	N	Y	N	Y	N	N	N
Isakson	N	Y	N	Y	N	N	N
HAWAII							
Inouye	Y	N	Y	N	?	Y	Y
Akaka	Y	N	Y	N	Y	Y	Y
IDAHO							
Crapo	N	Y	Y	Y	N	Y	Y
Risch	N	Y	Y	Y	N	Y	Y
ILLINOIS							
Durbin	Y	N	Y	N	Y	Y	Y
Burris	Y	N	Y	N	Y	Y	Y
INDIANA							
Lugar	N	Y	Y	Y	Y	Y	Y
Bayh	Y	Y	N	Y	Y	Y	N
IOWA							
Grassley	N	Y	N	Y	N	N	N
Harkin	Y	N	Y	N	Y	Y	Y
KANSAS							
Brownback	N	Y	Y	Y	N	Y	Y
Roberts	N	Y	Y	Y	N	Y	Y
KENTUCKY							
McConnell	N	Y	N	Y	N	Y	Y
Bunning	N	Y	N	Y	N	N	N
LOUISIANA							
Landrieu	N	N	Y	N	Y	Y	?
Vitter	N	N	Y	Y	N	Y	Y
MAINE							
Snowe	Y	N	Y	N	N	Y	Y
Collins	N	N	Y	N	N	Y	Y
MARYLAND							
Mikulski	Y	N	Y	N	Y	Y	Y
Cardin	Y	N	Y	N	Y	Y	Y
MASSACHUSETTS							
Kerry	Y	–	+	–	Y	+	+
Kirk	Y	N	Y	N	Y	Y	Y
MICHIGAN							
Levin	Y	N	Y	N	Y	Y	Y
Stabenow	Y	N	Y	N	Y	Y	Y
MINNESOTA							
Klobuchar	Y	N	Y	N	Y	Y	Y
Franken	Y	N	Y	N	Y	Y	Y
MISSISSIPPI							
Cochran	N	Y	Y	N	N	Y	?
Wicker	N	Y	Y	Y	?	N	Y
MISSOURI							
Bond	N	N	Y	N	N	Y	Y
McCaskill	Y	N	Y	Y	Y	Y	N

	316	317	318	319	320	321	322
MONTANA							
Baucus	Y	N	Y	N	Y	Y	Y
Tester	Y	N	Y	N	Y	Y	Y
NEBRASKA							
Nelson	Y	N	Y	N	Y	Y	Y
Johanns	N	Y	Y	Y	N	N	N
NEVADA							
Reid	Y	N	Y	N	Y	Y	Y
Ensign	N	Y	N	Y	N	N	N
NEW HAMPSHIRE							
Gregg	Y	N	Y	N	Y	Y	Y
Shaheen	Y	N	Y	N	Y	Y	Y
NEW JERSEY							
Lautenberg	Y	N	Y	N	Y	Y	Y
Menendez	Y	N	Y	N	Y	Y	Y
NEW MEXICO							
Bingaman	Y	N	Y	N	Y	Y	Y
Udall	Y	N	Y	N	Y	Y	Y
NEW YORK							
Schumer	Y	N	Y	N	Y	Y	Y
Gillibrand	Y	N	Y	N	Y	Y	Y
NORTH CAROLINA							
Burr	N	N	Y	N	?	N	N
Hagan	Y	N	Y	N	Y	Y	Y
NORTH DAKOTA							
Conrad	Y	N	Y	N	Y	Y	Y
Dorgan	Y	N	Y	N	Y	Y	Y
OHIO							
Voinovich	Y	?	Y	Y	N	Y	Y
Brown	Y	N	Y	N	Y	Y	Y
OKLAHOMA							
Inhofe	N	Y	N	Y	N	N	N
Coburn	N	Y	N	Y	N	N	N
OREGON							
Wyden	Y	N	Y	N	Y	Y	Y
Merkley	Y	N	Y	N	Y	Y	Y
PENNSYLVANIA							
Specter	Y	N	Y	N	Y	Y	Y
Casey	Y	N	Y	N	Y	Y	Y
RHODE ISLAND							
Reed	Y	N	Y	N	Y	Y	Y
Whitehouse	Y	N	Y	N	Y	Y	Y
SOUTH CAROLINA							
Graham	N	Y	N	Y	N	N	N
DeMint	N	Y	N	Y	N	N	N
SOUTH DAKOTA							
Johnson	Y	N	Y	N	Y	Y	Y
Thune	N	Y	N	Y	N	Y	Y
TENNESSEE							
Alexander	N	Y	N	Y	N	N	Y
Corker	N	Y	N	Y	N	N	N
TEXAS							
Hutchison	N	Y	Y	Y	?	?	N
Cornyn	N	Y	N	Y	N	N	N
UTAH							
Hatch	N	Y	Y	N	N	N	Y
Bennett	N	Y	Y	N	N	Y	Y
VERMONT							
Leahy	Y	N	Y	N	Y	Y	Y
Sanders	Y	N	Y	N	Y	Y	Y
VIRGINIA							
Webb	Y	N	Y	N	Y	Y	Y
Warner	Y	N	Y	N	Y	Y	Y
WASHINGTON							
Murray	Y	N	Y	N	Y	Y	Y
Cantwell	Y	N	Y	N	Y	Y	Y
WEST VIRGINIA							
Byrd	?	?	?	?	?	Y	Y
Rockefeller	Y	N	Y	N	Y	Y	Y
WISCONSIN							
Kohl	Y	N	Y	N	Y	Y	Y
Feingold	Y	N	Y	N	Y	Y	Y
WYOMING							
Enzi	N	Y	N	Y	N	Y	Y
Barrasso	N	Y	N	Y	N	Y	Y

KEY **Republicans** Democrats *Independents*

Y Voted for (yea)	X Paired against	C Voted "present" to avoid possible conflict of interest
# Paired for	– Announced against	
+ Announced for	P Voted "present"	? Did not vote or otherwise make a position known
N Voted against (nay)		

IN THE SENATE | By Vote Number

323. HR 2892. Fiscal 2010 Homeland Security Appropriations/
Conference Report. Adoption of the conference report on the bill that would provide $44.1 billion in fiscal 2010, including $42.8 billion in discretionary funds, for the Homeland Security Department and related activities. The total includes $10.1 billion for Customs and Border Protection; $7.7 billion for the Transportation Security Administration, not including offsetting fees; $10.1 billion for the Coast Guard; $1.5 billion for the Secret Service; and $7.1 billion for the Federal Emergency Management Agency. It would prohibit the transfer of detainees held at Guantánamo Bay, Cuba, to the United States except for prosecution. It also would extend the authorization of the E-Verify program for three years. Adopted (thus cleared for the president) 79-19: D 55-1; R 22-18; I 2-0. A "yea" was a vote in support of the president's position. Oct. 20, 2009.

324. Lange Nomination/Confirmation. Confirmation of President Obama's nomination of Roberto A. Lange of South Dakota to be a judge for the U.S. District Court of the District of South Dakota. Confirmed 100-0: D 58-0; R 40-0; I 2-0. A "yea" was a vote in support of the president's position. Oct. 21, 2009.

325. S 1776. Medicare Reimbursement Formula/Cloture. Motion to invoke cloture (thus limiting debate) on the Reid, D-Nev., motion to proceed to the bill that would sunset the formula that modifies Medicare reimbursements for physicians each year and replace it with a formula that keeps the reimbursement rate constant. Motion rejected 47-53: D 46-12; R 0-40; I 1-1. Three-fifths of the total Senate (60) is required to invoke cloture. Oct. 21, 2009.

326. HR 2647. Fiscal 2010 Defense Authorization/Cloture. Motion to invoke cloture (thus limiting debate) on the conference report on the bill that would authorize $680.2 billion in discretionary funding for defense programs in fiscal 2010, including approximately $130 billion for the wars in Iraq and Afghanistan and other operations. Motion agreed to 64-35: D 57-1; R 5-34; I 2-0. Three-fifths of the total Senate (60) is required to invoke cloture. Oct. 22, 2009.

327. HR 2647. Fiscal 2010 Defense Authorization/Conference
Report. Adoption of the conference report on the bill that would authorize $680.2 billion in discretionary spending for defense programs in fiscal 2010, including approximately $130 billion for the wars in Iraq and Afghanistan and other operations. It would authorize $244.4 billion for operations and maintenance; $150.2 billion for military personnel; $24.6 billion for military construction, family housing and base closings; and $29.3 billion for the Defense Health Program. It would authorize a 3.4 percent pay raise for military personnel. It would prohibit detainees at Guantánamo Bay, Cuba, from being transferred to U.S. soil until the president submits a plan to Congress and consults with the governors of affected states. It also would extend federal hate crime laws to cover offenses motivated by a victim's gender identity, sexual orientation or disability. Adopted (thus cleared for the president) 68-29: D 56-1; R 10-28; I 2-0. Oct. 22, 2009.

	323	324	325	326	327
ALABAMA					
Shelby	Y	Y	N	N	N
Sessions	N	Y	N	N	N
ALASKA					
Murkowski	Y	Y	N	Y	?
Begich	Y	Y	Y	Y	Y
ARIZONA					
McCain	N	Y	N	N	Y
Kyl	N	Y	N	N	N
ARKANSAS					
Lincoln	Y	Y	Y	Y	Y
Pryor	Y	Y	Y	Y	Y
CALIFORNIA					
Feinstein	Y	Y	Y	Y	Y
Boxer	Y	Y	Y	Y	Y
COLORADO					
Udall	Y	Y	Y	Y	Y
Bennet	Y	Y	Y	Y	Y
CONNECTICUT					
Dodd	Y	Y	Y	Y	Y
Lieberman	Y	Y	N	Y	Y
DELAWARE					
Carper	Y	Y	Y	Y	Y
Kaufman	Y	Y	Y	Y	Y
FLORIDA					
Nelson	Y	Y	N	Y	Y
LeMieux	Y	Y	N	N	N
GEORGIA					
Chambliss	N	Y	N	N	N
Isakson	N	Y	N	N	N
HAWAII					
Inouye	Y	Y	Y	Y	Y
Akaka	Y	Y	Y	Y	Y
IDAHO					
Crapo	N	Y	N	N	N
Risch	N	Y	N	N	N
ILLINOIS					
Durbin	Y	Y	Y	Y	Y
Burris	Y	Y	Y	Y	Y
INDIANA					
Lugar	Y	Y	N	Y	Y
Bayh	N	Y	N	Y	Y
IOWA					
Grassley	Y	Y	N	N	N
Harkin	Y	Y	Y	Y	Y
KANSAS					
Brownback	Y	Y	N	N	N
Roberts	Y	Y	N	N	N
KENTUCKY					
McConnell	Y	Y	N	N	N
Bunning	N	Y	N	N	N
LOUISIANA					
Landrieu	Y	Y	Y	Y	Y
Vitter	Y	Y	N	N	N
MAINE					
Snowe	Y	Y	N	Y	Y
Collins	Y	Y	N	Y	Y
MARYLAND					
Mikulski	Y	Y	Y	Y	Y
Cardin	Y	Y	Y	Y	Y
MASSACHUSETTS					
Kerry	+	Y	Y	Y	Y
Kirk	Y	Y	Y	Y	Y
MICHIGAN					
Levin	Y	Y	Y	Y	Y
Stabenow	Y	Y	Y	Y	Y
MINNESOTA					
Klobuchar	Y	Y	Y	Y	Y
Franken	Y	Y	Y	Y	Y
MISSISSIPPI					
Cochran	Y	Y	N	N	N
Wicker	N	Y	N	N	N
MISSOURI					
Bond	Y	Y	N	N	Y
McCaskill	Y	Y	N	N	Y
MONTANA					
Baucus	Y	Y	Y	Y	Y
Tester	Y	Y	N	Y	Y
NEBRASKA					
Nelson	Y	Y	Y	Y	Y
Johanns	Y	Y	N	N	N
NEVADA					
Reid	Y	Y	Y	Y	Y
Ensign	N	Y	N	N	Y
NEW HAMPSHIRE					
Gregg	Y	Y	N	N	Y
Shaheen	Y	Y	Y	Y	Y
NEW JERSEY					
Lautenberg	Y	Y	Y	Y	Y
Menendez	Y	Y	Y	Y	Y
NEW MEXICO					
Bingaman	Y	Y	Y	Y	Y
Udall	Y	Y	Y	Y	Y
NEW YORK					
Schumer	Y	Y	Y	Y	Y
Gillibrand	Y	Y	Y	Y	Y
NORTH CAROLINA					
Burr	N	Y	N	N	N
Hagan	?	Y	Y	Y	Y
NORTH DAKOTA					
Conrad	Y	Y	N	Y	Y
Dorgan	Y	Y	N	Y	Y
OHIO					
Voinovich	Y	Y	N	Y	Y
Brown	Y	Y	Y	Y	Y
OKLAHOMA					
Inhofe	N	Y	N	N	N
Coburn	N	Y	N	N	N
OREGON					
Wyden	Y	Y	N	Y	Y
Merkley	Y	Y	Y	Y	Y
PENNSYLVANIA					
Specter	Y	Y	Y	Y	Y
Casey	Y	Y	Y	Y	Y
RHODE ISLAND					
Reed	Y	Y	Y	Y	Y
Whitehouse	Y	Y	Y	Y	Y
SOUTH CAROLINA					
Graham	Y	Y	N	N	N
DeMint	N	Y	N	N	N
SOUTH DAKOTA					
Johnson	Y	Y	Y	Y	Y
Thune	Y	Y	N	N	N
TENNESSEE					
Alexander	Y	Y	N	N	N
Corker	N	Y	N	N	N
TEXAS					
Hutchison	N	Y	N	N	N
Cornyn	Y	Y	N	N	Y
UTAH					
Hatch	Y	Y	N	?	–
Bennett	Y	Y	N	N	N
VERMONT					
Leahy	Y	Y	Y	Y	Y
Sanders	Y	Y	Y	Y	Y
VIRGINIA					
Webb	Y	Y	N	Y	Y
Warner	Y	Y	N	Y	Y
WASHINGTON					
Murray	Y	Y	Y	Y	Y
Cantwell	Y	Y	Y	Y	Y
WEST VIRGINIA					
Byrd	Y	Y	N	Y	?
Rockefeller	Y	Y	Y	Y	Y
WISCONSIN					
Kohl	Y	Y	N	Y	Y
Feingold	Y	Y	N	N	N
WYOMING					
Enzi	N	Y	N	N	N
Barrasso	N	Y	N	N	N

KEY	**Republicans**	Democrats	*Independents*	
Y Voted for (yea)		X Paired against		C Voted "present" to avoid possible conflict of interest
# Paired for		– Announced against		
+ Announced for		P Voted "present"		? Did not vote or otherwise make a position known
N Voted against (nay)				

IN THE SENATE | By Vote Number

328. **Berger Nomination/Confirmation.** Confirmation of President Obama's nomination of Irene Berger of West Virginia to be a judge for the U.S. District Court for the Southern District of West Virginia. Confirmed 97-0: D 56-0; R 39-0; I 2-0. A "yea" was a vote in support of the president's position. Oct. 27, 2009.

329. **HR 3548. Unemployment Benefits Extension/Cloture.** Motion to invoke cloture (thus limiting debate) on the Reid, D-Nev., motion to proceed to the bill that would provide additional unemployment benefits for U.S. workers and extend through 2010 a tax rate of 6.2 percent on certain wages. Motion agreed to 87-13: D 58-0; R 27-13; I 2-0. Three-fifths of the total Senate (60) is required to invoke cloture. Oct. 27, 2009.

330. **HR 2996. Fiscal 2010 Interior-Environment Appropriations/ Conference Report Point of Order.** Feinstein, D-Calif., motion to waive Senate Rule 28 with respect to the McCain, R-Ariz., point of order against the conference report on the bill that would appropriate $32.3 billion in fiscal 2010 for the Interior Department, the EPA and related agencies. It also would provide continuing appropriations through Dec. 18, 2009, for all federal departments and agencies whose fiscal 2010 appropriations bills have not been enacted. Motion agreed to 60-40: D 58-0; R 0-40; I 2-0. Three-fifths of the total Senate (60) is required to waive Senate Rule 28. (Under the rule, a senator may raise a point of order against provisions of a conference report that were not in the bill passed by either chamber.) Oct. 29, 2009.

331. **HR 2996. Fiscal 2010 Interior-Environment Appropriations/ Conference Report.** Adoption of the conference report on the bill that would appropriate $32.3 billion in fiscal 2010 for the Interior Department, the EPA and related agencies. The bill would provide $11 billion for the Interior Department, $10.3 billion for the EPA, $5.3 billion for the Forest Service and $4.1 billion for the Indian Health Service. The funding includes $3.4 billion to fight and prevent wildfires. It would provide continuing appropriations through Dec. 18, 2009, for all federal departments and agencies whose fiscal 2010 appropriations bills have not been enacted. Funding would continue at fiscal 2009 levels, with some exceptions. Adopted (thus cleared for the president) 72-28: D 55-3; R 15-25; I 2-0. A "yea" was a vote in support of the president's position. Oct. 29, 2009.

	328	329	330	331
ALABAMA				
Shelby	Y	Y	N	Y
Sessions	Y	N	N	N
ALASKA				
Murkowski	Y	Y	N	Y
Begich	Y	Y	Y	Y
ARIZONA				
McCain	Y	Y	N	N
Kyl	Y	Y	N	N
ARKANSAS				
Lincoln	Y	Y	Y	Y
Pryor	Y	Y	Y	Y
CALIFORNIA				
Feinstein	Y	Y	Y	Y
Boxer	Y	Y	Y	Y
COLORADO				
Udall	Y	Y	Y	Y
Bennet	Y	Y	Y	Y
CONNECTICUT				
Dodd	Y	Y	Y	Y
Lieberman	Y	Y	Y	Y
DELAWARE				
Carper	Y	Y	Y	Y
Kaufman	Y	Y	Y	Y
FLORIDA				
Nelson	Y	Y	Y	Y
LeMieux	Y	Y	N	N
GEORGIA				
Chambliss	Y	Y	N	N
Isakson	Y	Y	N	Y
HAWAII				
Inouye	Y	Y	Y	Y
Akaka	Y	Y	Y	Y
IDAHO				
Crapo	Y	Y	N	Y
Risch	Y	Y	N	Y
ILLINOIS				
Durbin	Y	Y	Y	Y
Burris	Y	Y	Y	Y
INDIANA				
Lugar	Y	Y	N	N
Bayh	Y	Y	Y	N
IOWA				
Grassley	Y	N	N	N
Harkin	Y	Y	Y	Y
KANSAS				
Brownback	Y	Y	N	Y
Roberts	Y	Y	N	Y
KENTUCKY				
McConnell	Y	Y	N	N
Bunning	Y	N	N	N
LOUISIANA				
Landrieu	Y	Y	Y	Y
Vitter	Y	N	N	N
MAINE				
Snowe	Y	Y	N	N
Collins	Y	Y	N	Y
MARYLAND				
Mikulski	Y	Y	Y	Y
Cardin	Y	Y	Y	Y
MASSACHUSETTS				
Kerry	Y	Y	Y	Y
Kirk	Y	Y	Y	Y
MICHIGAN				
Levin	Y	Y	Y	Y
Stabenow	Y	Y	Y	Y
MINNESOTA				
Klobuchar	Y	Y	Y	Y
Franken	Y	Y	Y	Y
MISSISSIPPI				
Cochran	Y	Y	N	Y
Wicker	Y	Y	N	N
MISSOURI				
Bond	Y	N	N	Y
McCaskill	Y	Y	Y	N

	328	329	330	331
MONTANA				
Baucus	Y	Y	Y	Y
Tester	Y	Y	Y	Y
NEBRASKA				
Nelson	Y	Y	Y	Y
Johanns	Y	N	N	N
NEVADA				
Reid	Y	Y	Y	Y
Ensign	Y	Y	N	N
NEW HAMPSHIRE				
Gregg	Y	Y	N	Y
Shaheen	Y	Y	Y	Y
NEW JERSEY				
Lautenberg	Y	Y	Y	Y
Menendez	?	Y	Y	Y
NEW MEXICO				
Bingaman	Y	Y	Y	Y
Udall	Y	Y	Y	Y
NEW YORK				
Schumer	Y	Y	Y	Y
Gillibrand	Y	Y	Y	Y
NORTH CAROLINA				
Burr	Y	Y	N	N
Hagan	Y	Y	Y	Y
NORTH DAKOTA				
Conrad	Y	Y	Y	Y
Dorgan	Y	Y	Y	Y
OHIO				
Voinovich	Y	Y	N	Y
Brown	Y	Y	Y	Y
OKLAHOMA				
Inhofe	Y	N	N	N
Coburn	Y	N	N	N
OREGON				
Wyden	Y	Y	Y	Y
Merkley	Y	Y	Y	Y
PENNSYLVANIA				
Specter	Y	Y	Y	Y
Casey	Y	Y	Y	Y
RHODE ISLAND				
Reed	Y	Y	Y	Y
Whitehouse	Y	Y	Y	Y
SOUTH CAROLINA				
Graham	Y	N	N	N
DeMint	?	N	N	N
SOUTH DAKOTA				
Johnson	Y	Y	Y	Y
Thune	Y	Y	N	N
TENNESSEE				
Alexander	Y	Y	N	Y
Corker	Y	Y	N	N
TEXAS				
Hutchison	Y	Y	N	N
Cornyn	Y	N	N	N
UTAH				
Hatch	Y	N	N	N
Bennett	Y	Y	N	Y
VERMONT				
Leahy	?	Y	Y	Y
Sanders	Y	Y	Y	Y
VIRGINIA				
Webb	Y	Y	Y	Y
Warner	Y	Y	Y	Y
WASHINGTON				
Murray	Y	Y	Y	Y
Cantwell	Y	Y	Y	Y
WEST VIRGINIA				
Byrd	Y	Y	Y	Y
Rockefeller	Y	Y	Y	Y
WISCONSIN				
Kohl	Y	Y	Y	Y
Feingold	Y	Y	Y	N
WYOMING				
Enzi	Y	N	N	N
Barrasso	Y	N	N	N

KEY **Republicans** Democrats *Independents*

Y	Voted for (yea)	X	Paired against	C	Voted "present" to avoid possible conflict of interest
#	Paired for	–	Announced against	
+	Announced for	P	Voted "present"	?	Did not vote or otherwise make a position known
N	Voted against (nay)			

IN THE SENATE | By Vote Number

332. HR 3548. Unemployment Benefits Extension/Cloture.
Motion to invoke cloture (thus limiting debate) on the Baucus, D-Mont., substitute amendment that would extend unemployment benefits by 14 weeks for individuals who have used their regular 26 weeks of state compensation and provide an additional six weeks to jobless individuals in high-unemployment states. It would create a $6,500 homebuyer tax credit for certain homeowners and extend an $8,000 tax credit for first-time homebuyers. Motion agreed to 85-2: D 55-0; R 28-2; I 2-0. Three-fifths of the total Senate (60) is required to invoke cloture. (Subsequently, the Baucus substitute amendment was adopted by voice vote.) Nov. 2, 2009.

333. HR 3548. Unemployment Benefits Extension/Cloture.
Motion to invoke cloture (thus limiting debate) on the bill that would extend unemployment benefits by 14 weeks for individuals who have used their regular 26 weeks of state compensation and provide an additional six weeks to jobless individuals in high-unemployment states. It would create a $6,500 homebuyer tax credit for certain homeowners and extend an $8,000 tax credit for first-time homebuyers. Motion agreed to 97-1: D 56-0; R 39-1; I 2-0. Three-fifths of the total Senate (60) is required to invoke cloture. Nov. 4, 2009.

334. HR 3548. Unemployment Benefits Extension/Passage.
Passage of the bill that would extend unemployment benefits by 14 weeks for individuals who have used their regular 26 weeks of state compensation and provide an additional six weeks to jobless individuals in states with unemployment rates of 8.5 percent or above. The bill would extend an $8,000 tax credit for first-time homebuyers and create a $6,500 home-buyer tax credit for certain homeowners who have lived in their current homes for at least five consecutive years. The bill would allow businesses to use net operating losses from 2008 and 2009 to offset profits from five previous years. Passed 98-0: D 56-0; R 40-0; I 2-0. Nov. 4, 2009.

335. HR 2847. Fiscal 2010 Commerce-Justice-Science Appropriations/Cloture.
Motion to invoke cloture (thus limiting debate) on the Mikulski, D-Md., substitute amendment that would provide $64.9 billion in discretionary funding in fiscal 2010 for the departments of Commerce and Justice and other agencies such as NASA and the National Science Foundation, including $64.9 billion in discretionary funding. Motion agreed to 60-39: D 58-0; R 0-39; I 2-0. Three-fifths of the total Senate (60) is required to invoke cloture. Nov. 5, 2009.

336. HR 2847. Fiscal 2010 Commerce-Justice-Science Appropriations/Political Science Program Funding Ban.
Coburn, R-Okla., amendment that would bar the use of funds in the bill for the National Science Foundation's Political Science Program. Rejected 36-62: D 5-51; R 31-9; I 0-2. Nov. 5, 2009.

	332	333	334	335	336			332	333	334	335	336
ALABAMA							**MONTANA**					
Shelby	Y	Y	Y	N	Y		Baucus	Y	Y	Y	Y	Y
Sessions	?	Y	Y	N	Y		Tester	Y	Y	Y	Y	N
ALASKA							**NEBRASKA**					
Murkowski	?	Y	Y	N	Y		Nelson	Y	Y	Y	Y	Y
Begich	Y	Y	Y	Y	N		Johanns	Y	Y	Y	N	N
ARIZONA							**NEVADA**					
McCain	Y	Y	Y	?	Y		Reid	Y	Y	Y	Y	N
Kyl	Y	Y	Y	N	Y		Ensign	Y	Y	Y	N	Y
ARKANSAS							**NEW HAMPSHIRE**					
Lincoln	Y	Y	Y	Y	N		Gregg	?	Y	Y	N	N
Pryor	Y	Y	Y	Y	N		Shaheen	Y	Y	Y	Y	N
CALIFORNIA							**NEW JERSEY**					
Feinstein	Y	Y	Y	Y	N		Lautenberg	Y	Y	Y	Y	N
Boxer	Y	Y	Y	Y	N		Menendez	?	Y	Y	Y	N
COLORADO							**NEW MEXICO**					
Udall	Y	Y	Y	Y	N		Bingaman	Y	Y	Y	Y	N
Bennet	Y	Y	Y	Y	N		Udall	Y	Y	Y	Y	N
CONNECTICUT							**NEW YORK**					
Dodd	Y	Y	Y	Y	N		Schumer	Y	Y	Y	Y	N
Lieberman	Y	Y	Y	Y	N		Gillibrand	Y	Y	Y	Y	N
DELAWARE							**NORTH CAROLINA**					
Carper	Y	Y	Y	Y	N		Burr	Y	Y	Y	N	N
Kaufman	Y	Y	Y	Y	N		Hagan	Y	Y	Y	Y	N
FLORIDA							**NORTH DAKOTA**					
Nelson	Y	Y	Y	Y	N		Conrad	Y	Y	Y	Y	N
LeMieux	Y	Y	Y	N	Y		Dorgan	Y	Y	Y	Y	N
GEORGIA							**OHIO**					
Chambliss	Y	Y	Y	N	Y		**Voinovich**	Y	Y	Y	N	Y
Isakson	?	Y	Y	N	Y		Brown	Y	Y	Y	Y	N
HAWAII							**OKLAHOMA**					
Inouye	Y	Y	Y	Y	N		**Inhofe**	Y	Y	Y	N	Y
Akaka	Y	Y	Y	Y	N		**Coburn**	?	Y	Y	N	Y
IDAHO							**OREGON**					
Crapo	Y	Y	Y	N	Y		Wyden	Y	Y	Y	Y	N
Risch	Y	Y	Y	N	Y		Merkley	Y	Y	Y	Y	N
ILLINOIS							**PENNSYLVANIA**					
Durbin	Y	Y	Y	Y	N		Specter	Y	Y	Y	Y	N
Burris	Y	Y	Y	Y	N		Casey	Y	Y	Y	Y	N
INDIANA							**RHODE ISLAND**					
Lugar	Y	Y	Y	N	Y		Reed	Y	Y	Y	Y	N
Bayh	Y	Y	Y	Y	Y		Whitehouse	Y	Y	Y	Y	N
IOWA							**SOUTH CAROLINA**					
Grassley	Y	Y	Y	N	Y		**Graham**	Y	Y	Y	N	Y
Harkin	Y	Y	Y	Y	N		**DeMint**	N	N	Y	N	Y
KANSAS							**SOUTH DAKOTA**					
Brownback	Y	Y	Y	N	Y		Johnson	Y	Y	Y	Y	N
Roberts	Y	Y	Y	N	Y		**Thune**	Y	Y	Y	N	Y
KENTUCKY							**TENNESSEE**					
McConnell	Y	Y	Y	N	Y		**Alexander**	Y	Y	Y	N	N
Bunning	+	Y	Y	N	Y		**Corker**	?	Y	Y	N	Y
LOUISIANA							**TEXAS**					
Landrieu	Y	Y	Y	Y	?		**Hutchison**	?	Y	Y	N	N
Vitter	Y	Y	Y	N	Y		**Cornyn**	+	Y	Y	N	N
MAINE							**UTAH**					
Snowe	Y	Y	Y	N	N		**Hatch**	Y	Y	Y	N	Y
Collins	Y	Y	Y	N	N		**Bennett**	?	Y	Y	N	Y
MARYLAND							**VERMONT**					
Mikulski	Y	Y	Y	Y	N		Leahy	?	Y	Y	Y	N
Cardin	Y	Y	Y	Y	N		*Sanders*	Y	Y	Y	Y	N
MASSACHUSETTS							**VIRGINIA**					
Kerry	Y	Y	Y	Y	N		Webb	Y	Y	Y	Y	Y
Kirk	Y	Y	Y	Y	N		Warner	Y	Y	Y	Y	N
MICHIGAN							**WASHINGTON**					
Levin	Y	Y	Y	Y	N		Murray	Y	Y	Y	Y	N
Stabenow	Y	Y	Y	Y	N		Cantwell	Y	Y	Y	Y	N
MINNESOTA							**WEST VIRGINIA**					
Klobuchar	Y	Y	Y	Y	N		Byrd	Y	?	?	Y	?
Franken	Y	Y	Y	Y	N		Rockefeller	Y	Y	Y	Y	N
MISSISSIPPI							**WISCONSIN**					
Cochran	Y	Y	Y	N	N		Kohl	Y	Y	Y	Y	N
Wicker	Y	Y	Y	N	Y		Feingold	Y	Y	Y	Y	N
MISSOURI							**WYOMING**					
Bond	N	Y	Y	N	N		**Enzi**	Y	Y	Y	N	Y
McCaskill	?	?	?	Y	N		**Barrasso**	Y	Y	Y	N	Y

KEY	**Republicans**	Democrats	*Independents*		
Y Voted for (yea)		**X** Paired against		**C** Voted "present" to avoid possible conflict of interest	
# Paired for		**–** Announced against			
+ Announced for		**P** Voted "present"		**?** Did not vote or otherwise make a position known	
N Voted against (nay)					

IN THE SENATE | By Vote Number

337. **HR 2847. Fiscal 2010 Commerce-Justice-Science Appropriations/Office of Inspector General.** Coburn, R-Okla., motion to waive the Budget Act with respect to the Mikulski, D-Md., point of order against the Coburn amendment that would increase the amount appropriated to the Office of Inspector General of the Commerce Department by $4.5 million, offset by a decrease of $5 million for the modernization and renovation of the Herbert C. Hoover Commerce Department building in Washington, D.C. Motion rejected 42-57: D 5-52; R 37-3; I 0-2. A three-fifths majority vote (60) of the total Senate is required to waive the Budget Act. (Subsequently, the chair upheld the point of order, and the amendment fell.) Nov. 5, 2009.

338. **HR 2847. Fiscal 2010 Commerce-Justice-Science Appropriations/Sept. 11 Terrorist Attacks Prosecution.** Reed, D-R.I., motion to table (kill) the Graham, R-S.C., amendment that would bar the use of Justice Department funds under the bill to prosecute in a regular federal court anyone linked to the Sept. 11 terrorist attacks. Motion agreed to 54-45: D 53-4; R 0-40; I 1-1. Nov. 5, 2009.

339. **HR 2847. Fiscal 2010 Commerce-Justice-Science Appropriations/State Criminal Assistance Program.** Ensign, R-Nev., motion to waive the Budget Act with respect to the Mikulski, D-Md., point of order against the Ensign amendment that would increase the amount provided for the State Criminal Assistance Program by $172 million. It would strike $124.7 million provided for the National Institute of Standards and Technology's Hollings Manufacturing Extension Partnership and $69.9 million for the institute's Technology Innovation Program. Motion rejected 32-67: D 8-49; R 24-16; I 0-2. A three-fifths majority vote (60) of the total Senate is required to waive the Budget Act. (Subsequently, the chair upheld the point of order, and the amendment fell.) Nov. 5, 2009.

340. **HR 2847. Fiscal 2010 Commerce-Justice-Science Appropriations/Passage.** Passage of the bill that would appropriate $64.9 billion in discretionary funding in fiscal 2010 for the departments of Commerce and Justice and other agencies such as NASA and the National Science Foundation. It would provide $14.1 billion for the Commerce Department and $27.4 billion for the Justice Department. It would fund NASA at $18.7 billion, the National Science Foundation at $6.9 billion and the National Oceanic and Atmospheric Administration at $4.8 billion. Passed 71-28: D 55-2; R 14-26; I 2-0. A "yea" was a vote in support of the president's position. Nov. 5, 2009.

341. **Moreno Nomination/Confirmation.** Confirmation of President Obama's nomination of Ignacia S. Moreno of New York to be an assistant attorney general. Confirmed 93-0: D 55-0; R 36-0; I 2-0. A "yea" was a vote in support of the president's position. Nov. 5, 2009.

342. **Davis Nomination/Confirmation.** Confirmation of President Obama's nomination of Andre M. Davis of Maryland to be a judge for the 4th U.S. Circuit Court of Appeals. Confirmed 72-16: D 54-0; R 16-16; I 2-0. A "yea" was a vote in support of the president's position. Nov. 9, 2009.

343. **Honeywell Nomination/Confirmation.** Confirmation of President Obama's nomination of Charlene Edwards Honeywell of Florida to be a judge for the U.S. District Court for the Middle District of Florida. Confirmed 88-0: D 54-0; R 32-0; I 2-0. A "yea" was a vote in support of the president's position. Nov. 9, 2009.

	337	338	339	340	341	342	343
ALABAMA							
Shelby	Y	N	N	Y	Y	N	Y
Sessions	Y	N	N	N	Y	N	Y
ALASKA							
Murkowski	N	N	Y	Y	Y	Y	Y
Begich	N	Y	N	Y	Y	Y	Y
ARIZONA							
McCain	Y	N	Y	N	Y	Y	Y
Kyl	Y	N	Y	N	Y	Y	Y
ARKANSAS							
Lincoln	Y	N	Y	Y	Y	Y	Y
Pryor	N	N	N	Y	Y	Y	Y
CALIFORNIA							
Feinstein	N	Y	Y	Y	Y	Y	Y
Boxer	N	Y	Y	Y	Y	Y	Y
COLORADO							
Udall	N	Y	N	Y	Y	Y	Y
Bennet	N	Y	N	Y	Y	Y	Y
CONNECTICUT							
Dodd	N	Y	N	Y	Y	Y	Y
Lieberman	N	N	N	Y	Y	Y	Y
DELAWARE							
Carper	N	Y	N	Y	?	Y	Y
Kaufman	N	Y	N	Y	Y	Y	Y
FLORIDA							
Nelson	N	Y	N	Y	?	?	?
LeMieux	Y	N	Y	Y	Y	Y	Y
GEORGIA							
Chambliss	Y	N	Y	N	?	?	?
Isakson	Y	N	Y	N	+	−	?
HAWAII							
Inouye	N	Y	N	Y	Y	Y	Y
Akaka	N	Y	N	Y	Y	Y	Y
IDAHO							
Crapo	Y	N	Y	N	Y	N	Y
Risch	Y	N	Y	N	?	?	?
ILLINOIS							
Durbin	N	Y	N	Y	Y	Y	Y
Burris	N	Y	N	Y	Y	Y	Y
INDIANA							
Lugar	Y	N	N	Y	Y	Y	Y
Bayh	Y	Y	N	N	Y	Y	Y
IOWA							
Grassley	Y	N	Y	N	Y	N	Y
Harkin	N	Y	N	Y	Y	Y	Y
KANSAS							
Brownback	Y	N	Y	N	Y	N	Y
Roberts	Y	N	Y	N	Y	N	Y
KENTUCKY							
McConnell	Y	N	Y	N	Y	Y	Y
Bunning	Y	N	N	N	Y	N	Y
LOUISIANA							
Landrieu	N	Y	N	Y	?	Y	Y
Vitter	Y	N	N	Y	Y	N	Y
MAINE							
Snowe	Y	N	N	Y	Y	Y	Y
Collins	Y	N	Y	Y	Y	Y	Y
MARYLAND							
Mikulski	N	Y	N	Y	Y	Y	Y
Cardin	N	Y	N	Y	Y	Y	Y
MASSACHUSETTS							
Kerry	N	Y	N	Y	Y	+	+
Kirk	N	Y	N	Y	Y	Y	Y
MICHIGAN							
Levin	N	Y	N	Y	Y	Y	Y
Stabenow	N	Y	N	Y	Y	Y	Y
MINNESOTA							
Klobuchar	N	Y	N	Y	Y	Y	Y
Franken	N	Y	N	Y	Y	Y	Y
MISSISSIPPI							
Cochran	Y	N	N	Y	Y	Y	Y
Wicker	Y	N	Y	N	Y	Y	Y
MISSOURI							
Bond	N	N	N	Y	Y	?	?
McCaskill	Y	Y	N	Y	Y	Y	Y

	337	338	339	340	341	342	343
MONTANA							
Baucus	Y	Y	Y	Y	Y	Y	Y
Tester	N	Y	Y	Y	Y	Y	Y
NEBRASKA							
Nelson	N	Y	Y	Y	Y	Y	Y
Johanns	Y	N	Y	N	Y	N	Y
NEVADA							
Reid	N	Y	N	Y	Y	Y	Y
Ensign	Y	N	Y	N	Y	N	Y
NEW HAMPSHIRE							
Gregg	Y	N	N	Y	Y	?	?
Shaheen	N	Y	N	Y	Y	Y	Y
NEW JERSEY							
Lautenberg	N	Y	N	Y	Y	Y	Y
Menendez	N	Y	N	Y	Y	Y	Y
NEW MEXICO							
Bingaman	N	Y	N	Y	Y	Y	Y
Udall	N	Y	N	Y	Y	Y	Y
NEW YORK							
Schumer	N	Y	N	Y	Y	Y	Y
Gillibrand	N	Y	N	Y	Y	Y	Y
NORTH CAROLINA							
Burr	Y	N	N	Y	N	?	?
Hagan	N	Y	Y	Y	Y	Y	Y
NORTH DAKOTA							
Conrad	N	Y	N	Y	Y	Y	Y
Dorgan	N	Y	N	Y	?	?	Y
OHIO							
Voinovich	N	N	N	Y	?	Y	Y
Brown	N	Y	N	Y	Y	Y	Y
OKLAHOMA							
Inhofe	Y	N	N	N	Y	N	Y
Coburn	Y	N	Y	N	Y	N	Y
OREGON							
Wyden	N	Y	N	Y	Y	Y	Y
Merkley	N	Y	N	Y	Y	Y	Y
PENNSYLVANIA							
Specter	N	Y	N	Y	Y	Y	Y
Casey	N	Y	N	Y	Y	Y	Y
RHODE ISLAND							
Reed	N	Y	N	Y	Y	Y	Y
Whitehouse	N	Y	N	Y	Y	Y	Y
SOUTH CAROLINA							
Graham	Y	N	Y	N	Y	Y	Y
DeMint	Y	N	Y	N	+	N	Y
SOUTH DAKOTA							
Johnson	N	Y	N	Y	Y	Y	Y
Thune	Y	N	Y	N	Y	N	Y
TENNESSEE							
Alexander	Y	N	N	Y	Y	Y	Y
Corker	Y	N	N	Y	Y	Y	Y
TEXAS							
Hutchison	Y	N	Y	Y	Y	?	?
Cornyn	Y	N	Y	N	Y	+	+
UTAH							
Hatch	Y	N	N	Y	Y	Y	Y
Bennett	Y	N	N	Y	Y	Y	Y
VERMONT							
Leahy	N	Y	N	Y	Y	Y	Y
Sanders	N	Y	N	Y	Y	Y	Y
VIRGINIA							
Webb	N	N	N	Y	Y	Y	Y
Warner	N	Y	N	Y	Y	Y	Y
WASHINGTON							
Murray	N	Y	N	Y	Y	Y	Y
Cantwell	N	N	N	Y	Y	Y	Y
WEST VIRGINIA							
Byrd	?	?	?	?	?	?	?
Rockefeller	N	Y	N	Y	Y	Y	Y
WISCONSIN							
Kohl	N	Y	N	Y	Y	Y	Y
Feingold	Y	Y	N	Y	Y	Y	Y
WYOMING							
Enzi	Y	N	Y	N	Y	N	Y
Barrasso	Y	N	Y	N	Y	N	Y

KEY   **Republicans**   Democrats   *Independents*

Y Voted for (yea)	X Paired against	C Voted "present" to avoid possible conflict of interest
# Paired for	− Announced against	
+ Announced for	P Voted "present"	? Did not vote or otherwise make a position known
N Voted against (nay)		

IN THE SENATE | By Vote Number

344. HR 3082. Fiscal 2010 Military Construction-VA **Appropriations/Report Posting Requirement.** Coburn, R-Okla., amendment to the Johnson, D-S.D., substitute amendment. The Coburn amendment would require a federal agency submitting a report to a congressional appropriations committee to post the report on its Web site unless it contains proprietary information or doing so would compromise national security. The substitute would provide $133.9 billion in fiscal 2010 for the Veterans Affairs Department, military construction and military housing, including $76.7 billion in discretionary funding. Adopted 93-0: D 55-0; R 37-0; I 1-0. Nov. 16, 2009.

345. HR 3082. Fiscal 2010 Military Construction-VA **Appropriations/Commit.** Coburn, R-Okla., motion to commit the bill to the Appropriations Committee with instructions that it be reported back with an increase in funding for care and payments to caregivers of disabled veterans, offset by a reduction in funding for earmarks not requested by the president and other programs. Motion rejected 24-69: D 2-53; R 22-15; I 0-1. Nov. 16, 2009.

346. HR 3082. Fiscal 2010 Military Construction-VA **Appropriations/Homeless Veterans Housing.** Johnson, D-S.D., amendment to the Johnson substitute amendment. The Johnson amendment would increase the amount provided for the Veterans Affairs Department by $50 million for the purpose of renovating the department's buildings to convert them into housing with support services for homeless veterans. It would be offset by a reduction of the same amount to the Homeowners Assistance Fund. Adopted 98-1: D 57-0; R 39-1; I 2-0. Nov. 17, 2009.

347. HR 3082. Fiscal 2010 Military Construction-VA **Appropriations/Detention Facilities.** Johnson, D-S.D., motion to table (kill) the Inhofe, R-Okla., amendment to the Johnson substitute amendment. The Inhofe amendment would bar the use of funds in the bill to construct or modify facilities in the United States or its territories to hold individuals who were detained as of Oct. 1, 2009, at the Guantánamo Bay, Cuba, detention facility. Motion agreed to 57-43: D 56-2; R 0-40; I 1-1. A "yea" was a vote in support of the president's position. Nov. 17, 2009.

348. HR 3082. Fiscal 2010 Military Construction-VA **Appropriations/Passage.** Passage of the bill that would provide $133.9 billion in fiscal 2010 for the Veterans Affairs Department, military construction and military housing, including $76.7 billion in discretionary funding. It would provide $109 billion for the VA, including $44.7 billion for veterans' health programs. The total includes $11.3 billion for military construction, $2.3 billion for military family housing and $7.9 billion for the latest round of base realignment and closure. The bill would also provide $48.2 billion in advance fiscal 2011 appropriations for three veterans' medical care accounts. Passed 100-0: D 58-0; R 40-0; I 2-0. A "yea" was a vote in support of the president's position. Nov. 17, 2009.

	344	345	346	347	348
ALABAMA					
Shelby	Y	N	Y	N	Y
Sessions	Y	Y	Y	N	Y
ALASKA					
Murkowski	Y	N	Y	N	Y
Begich	Y	N	Y	Y	Y
ARIZONA					
McCain	Y	Y	Y	N	Y
Kyl	Y	Y	Y	N	Y
ARKANSAS					
Lincoln	Y	N	Y	N	Y
Pryor	Y	N	Y	N	Y
CALIFORNIA					
Feinstein	Y	N	Y	Y	Y
Boxer	Y	N	Y	Y	Y
COLORADO					
Udall	Y	N	Y	Y	Y
Bennet	Y	N	Y	Y	Y
CONNECTICUT					
Dodd	Y	N	Y	Y	Y
Lieberman	+	–	Y	N	Y
DELAWARE					
Carper	Y	N	Y	Y	Y
Kaufman	+	+	Y	Y	Y
FLORIDA					
Nelson	Y	N	Y	Y	Y
LeMieux	Y	Y	Y	N	Y
GEORGIA					
Chambliss	Y	Y	Y	N	Y
Isakson	+	+	Y	N	Y
HAWAII					
Inouye	Y	N	Y	Y	Y
Akaka	Y	N	Y	Y	Y
IDAHO					
Crapo	Y	Y	Y	N	Y
Risch	Y	Y	Y	N	Y
ILLINOIS					
Durbin	Y	N	Y	Y	Y
Burris	Y	N	Y	Y	Y
INDIANA					
Lugar	Y	N	Y	N	Y
Bayh	Y	Y	Y	Y	Y
IOWA					
Grassley	Y	Y	Y	N	Y
Harkin	Y	N	Y	Y	Y
KANSAS					
Brownback	Y	Y	Y	N	Y
Roberts	Y	Y	Y	N	Y
KENTUCKY					
McConnell	Y	Y	Y	N	Y
Bunning	Y	Y	Y	N	Y
LOUISIANA					
Landrieu	Y	N	Y	Y	Y
Vitter	?	?	Y	N	Y
MAINE					
Snowe	Y	N	Y	N	Y
Collins	Y	N	Y	N	Y
MARYLAND					
Mikulski	Y	N	Y	Y	Y
Cardin	Y	N	Y	Y	Y
MASSACHUSETTS					
Kerry	Y	N	Y	Y	Y
Kirk	Y	N	Y	Y	Y
MICHIGAN					
Levin	Y	N	Y	Y	Y
Stabenow	Y	N	Y	Y	Y
MINNESOTA					
Klobuchar	Y	N	Y	Y	Y
Franken	Y	N	Y	Y	Y
MISSISSIPPI					
Cochran	Y	N	Y	N	Y
Wicker	Y	N	Y	N	Y
MISSOURI					
Bond	Y	N	Y	N	Y
McCaskill	Y	Y	Y	Y	Y
MONTANA					
Baucus	Y	N	Y	Y	Y
Tester	Y	N	Y	Y	Y
NEBRASKA					
Nelson	Y	N	Y	Y	Y
Johanns	Y	Y	Y	N	Y
NEVADA					
Reid	Y	N	Y	Y	Y
Ensign	Y	Y	Y	N	Y
NEW HAMPSHIRE					
Gregg	Y	N	Y	N	Y
Shaheen	Y	N	Y	Y	Y
NEW JERSEY					
Lautenberg	Y	N	Y	Y	Y
Menendez	Y	N	Y	Y	Y
NEW MEXICO					
Bingaman	Y	N	Y	Y	Y
Udall	Y	N	Y	Y	Y
NEW YORK					
Schumer	Y	N	Y	Y	Y
Gillibrand	Y	N	Y	Y	Y
NORTH CAROLINA					
Burr	Y	Y	Y	N	Y
Hagan	Y	N	Y	Y	Y
NORTH DAKOTA					
Conrad	Y	N	Y	Y	Y
Dorgan	Y	N	Y	Y	Y
OHIO					
Voinovich	Y	N	Y	N	Y
Brown	Y	N	Y	Y	Y
OKLAHOMA					
Inhofe	Y	N	Y	N	Y
Coburn	Y	Y	N	N	Y
OREGON					
Wyden	Y	N	Y	Y	Y
Merkley	Y	N	Y	Y	Y
PENNSYLVANIA					
Specter	Y	N	Y	Y	Y
Casey	Y	N	Y	Y	Y
RHODE ISLAND					
Reed	Y	N	Y	Y	Y
Whitehouse	?	?	Y	Y	Y
SOUTH CAROLINA					
Graham	?	?	Y	N	Y
DeMint	Y	Y	Y	N	Y
SOUTH DAKOTA					
Johnson	Y	N	Y	Y	Y
Thune	Y	Y	Y	N	Y
TENNESSEE					
Alexander	Y	N	Y	N	Y
Corker	Y	N	Y	N	Y
TEXAS					
Hutchison	Y	Y	Y	N	Y
Cornyn	Y	Y	Y	N	Y
UTAH					
Hatch	Y	N	Y	N	Y
Bennett	Y	N	Y	N	Y
VERMONT					
Leahy	Y	N	Y	Y	Y
Sanders	Y	N	Y	Y	Y
VIRGINIA					
Webb	Y	N	Y	Y	Y
Warner	Y	N	Y	Y	Y
WASHINGTON					
Murray	Y	N	Y	Y	Y
Cantwell	Y	N	Y	Y	Y
WEST VIRGINIA					
Byrd	?	?	?	Y	Y
Rockefeller	Y	N	Y	Y	Y
WISCONSIN					
Kohl	Y	N	Y	Y	Y
Feingold	Y	N	Y	Y	Y
WYOMING					
Enzi	Y	Y	Y	N	Y
Barrasso	Y	Y	Y	N	Y

KEY	**Republicans**	Democrats	*Independents*	
Y	Voted for (yea)		X	Paired against	C	Voted "present" to avoid possible conflict of interest
#	Paired for		–	Announced against	
+	Announced for		P	Voted "present"	?	Did not vote or otherwise make a position known
N	Voted against (nay)				

IN THE SENATE | By Vote Number

349. **Hamilton Nomination/Cloture.** Motion to invoke cloture (thus limiting debate) on the nomination of David F. Hamilton of Indiana to be a judge for the 7th U.S. Circuit Court of Appeals. Motion agreed to 70-29: D 58-0; R 10-29; I 2-0. Three-fifths of the total Senate (60) is required to invoke cloture. Nov. 17, 2009.

350. **Hamilton Nomination/Confirmation.** Confirmation of President Obama's nomination of David F. Hamilton of Indiana to be a judge for the 7th U.S. Circuit Court of Appeals. Confirmed 59-39: D 56-0; R 1-39; I 2-0. A "yea" was a vote in support of the president's position. Nov. 19, 2009.

351. **S 1963. Veterans' Family Caregiver Assistance/Funding Offset.** Coburn, R-Okla., amendment that would require the State Department to offset the costs of the bill from funding for contributions to international organizations and peacekeeping activities. It would also expand the eligibility for family caregiver assistance beyond veterans who have been injured after Sept. 10, 2001, to all veterans who require hospitalization, nursing home care or other residential care. Rejected 32-66: D 1-55; R 31-9; I 0-2. Nov. 19, 2009.

352. **S 1963. Veterans' Family Caregiver Assistance/Passage.** Passage of the bill that would authorize funding for the Veterans Affairs Department to provide training, counseling, health care and a stipend to family caregivers of veterans who have been seriously injured or had an injury aggravated in the line of duty after Sept. 10, 2001. The bill would require the Office of Rural Health to develop a five-year plan defining goals for recruitment and retention of health care personnel in rural areas and care improvement. It would authorize $3 million annually from fiscal 2010 to 2014 for grants to veteran service organizations to assist veterans in rural areas in traveling to medical facilities. Passed 98-0: D 56-0; R 40-0; I 2-0. Nov. 19, 2009.

353. **HR 3590. Health Care Overhaul 'Shell' Bill/Cloture.** Motion to invoke cloture (thus limiting debate) on the motion to proceed to the bill that is intended to serve as the vehicle for legislation that would overhaul the health care system. The bill as currently written would extend a tax credit for first-time homebuyers for military and other federal employees posted abroad. Motion agreed to 60-39: D 58-0; R 0-39; I 2-0. Three-fifths of the total Senate (60) is required to invoke cloture. (Subsequently, the motion to proceed was agreed to by unanimous consent.) Nov. 21, 2009.

	349	350	351	352	353
ALABAMA					
Shelby	N	N	Y	Y	N
Sessions	N	N	Y	Y	N
ALASKA					
Murkowski	Y	N	Y	Y	N
Begich	Y	Y	N	Y	Y
ARIZONA					
McCain	N	N	Y	Y	N
Kyl	N	N	Y	Y	N
ARKANSAS					
Lincoln	Y	Y	N	Y	Y
Pryor	Y	Y	N	Y	Y
CALIFORNIA					
Feinstein	Y	Y	N	Y	Y
Boxer	Y	Y	N	Y	Y
COLORADO					
Udall	Y	Y	N	Y	Y
Bennet	Y	Y	N	Y	Y
CONNECTICUT					
Dodd	Y	Y	N	Y	Y
Lieberman	Y	Y	N	Y	Y
DELAWARE					
Carper	Y	Y	N	Y	Y
Kaufman	Y	Y	N	Y	Y
FLORIDA					
Nelson	Y	Y	N	Y	Y
LeMieux	N	N	Y	Y	N
GEORGIA					
Chambliss	Y	N	Y	Y	N
Isakson	N	N	Y	Y	N
HAWAII					
Inouye	Y	Y	N	Y	Y
Akaka	Y	Y	N	Y	Y
IDAHO					
Crapo	N	N	Y	Y	N
Risch	N	N	Y	Y	N
ILLINOIS					
Durbin	Y	Y	N	Y	Y
Burris	Y	Y	N	Y	Y
INDIANA					
Lugar	Y	Y	N	Y	N
Bayh	Y	Y	Y	Y	Y
IOWA					
Grassley	N	N	N	Y	N
Harkin	Y	Y	N	Y	Y
KANSAS					
Brownback	N	N	Y	Y	N
Roberts	N	N	Y	Y	N
KENTUCKY					
McConnell	N	N	Y	Y	N
Bunning	N	N	Y	Y	N
LOUISIANA					
Landrieu	Y	Y	N	Y	Y
Vitter	N	N	Y	Y	N
MAINE					
Snowe	Y	N	N	Y	N
Collins	Y	N	N	Y	N
MARYLAND					
Mikulski	Y	Y	N	Y	Y
Cardin	Y	Y	N	Y	Y
MASSACHUSETTS					
Kerry	Y	Y	N	Y	Y
Kirk	Y	Y	N	Y	Y
MICHIGAN					
Levin	Y	Y	N	Y	Y
Stabenow	Y	Y	N	Y	Y
MINNESOTA					
Klobuchar	Y	Y	N	Y	Y
Franken	Y	Y	N	Y	Y
MISSISSIPPI					
Cochran	N	N	N	Y	N
Wicker	N	N	Y	Y	N
MISSOURI					
Bond	N	N	N	Y	N
McCaskill	Y	Y	Y	Y	Y
MONTANA					
Baucus	Y	?	?	?	Y
Tester	Y	Y	N	Y	Y
NEBRASKA					
Nelson	Y	Y	N	Y	Y
Johanns	N	N	Y	Y	N
NEVADA					
Reid	Y	Y	N	Y	Y
Ensign	N	N	Y	Y	N
NEW HAMPSHIRE					
Gregg	Y	N	Y	Y	N
Shaheen	Y	Y	N	Y	Y
NEW JERSEY					
Lautenberg	Y	Y	N	Y	Y
Menendez	Y	Y	N	Y	Y
NEW MEXICO					
Bingaman	Y	Y	N	Y	Y
Udall	Y	Y	N	Y	Y
NEW YORK					
Schumer	Y	Y	N	Y	Y
Gillibrand	Y	Y	N	Y	Y
NORTH CAROLINA					
Burr	N	N	Y	Y	N
Hagan	Y	Y	N	Y	Y
NORTH DAKOTA					
Conrad	Y	Y	N	Y	Y
Dorgan	Y	Y	N	Y	Y
OHIO					
Voinovich	N	N	N	Y	?
Brown	Y	Y	N	Y	Y
OKLAHOMA					
Inhofe	N	N	Y	Y	N
Coburn	N	N	Y	Y	N
OREGON					
Wyden	Y	Y	N	Y	Y
Merkley	Y	Y	N	Y	Y
PENNSYLVANIA					
Specter	Y	Y	N	Y	Y
Casey	Y	Y	N	Y	Y
RHODE ISLAND					
Reed	Y	Y	N	Y	Y
Whitehouse	Y	Y	N	Y	Y
SOUTH CAROLINA					
Graham	N	N	Y	Y	N
DeMint	N	N	Y	Y	N
SOUTH DAKOTA					
Johnson	Y	Y	N	Y	Y
Thune	Y	N	Y	Y	N
TENNESSEE					
Alexander	Y	N	Y	Y	N
Corker	N	N	N	Y	N
TEXAS					
Hutchison	?	N	Y	Y	N
Cornyn	Y	N	Y	Y	N
UTAH					
Hatch	Y	N	Y	Y	N
Bennett	N	N	Y	Y	N
VERMONT					
Leahy	Y	Y	N	Y	Y
Sanders	Y	Y	N	Y	Y
VIRGINIA					
Webb	Y	Y	N	Y	Y
Warner	Y	Y	N	Y	Y
WASHINGTON					
Murray	Y	Y	N	Y	Y
Cantwell	Y	Y	N	Y	Y
WEST VIRGINIA					
Byrd	Y	?	?	?	Y
Rockefeller	Y	Y	N	Y	Y
WISCONSIN					
Kohl	Y	Y	N	Y	Y
Feingold	Y	Y	N	Y	Y
WYOMING					
Enzi	N	N	Y	Y	N
Barrasso	N	N	Y	Y	N

KEY   **Republicans**   Democrats   *Independents*

Y Voted for (yea)	X Paired against
# Paired for	– Announced against
+ Announced for	P Voted "present"
N Voted against (nay)	

C   Voted "present" to avoid possible conflict of interest

?   Did not vote or otherwise make a position known

IN THE SENATE | By Vote Number

354. **Nguyen Nomination/Confirmation.** Confirmation of President Obama's nomination of Jacqueline H. Nguyen of California to be a judge for the U.S. District Court of the Central District of California. Confirmed 97-0: D 56-0; R 39-0; I 2-0. A "yea" was a vote in support of the president's position. Dec. 1, 2009.

355. **HR 3590. Health Care Overhaul/Women's Preventive Care Screening.** Mikulski, D-Md., amendment to the Reid, D-Nev., substitute amendment. The Mikulski amendment would require group health care plans and health insurance issuers to provide coverage, without any cost-sharing requirements for additional preventive care and screening for women. It would bar the U.S. Preventive Service Task Force's most recent recommendations on breast cancer screening, mammography and prevention from being used to determine coverage. The substitute would create health insurance marketplaces, establish a public health insurance option from which states could opt out, require most individuals to obtain insurance and set requirements for coverage by insurance companies. Adopted 61-39: D 56-2; R 3-37; I 2-0. (By unanimous consent, the Senate agreed to raise the majority requirement for adoption of the Mikulski amendment to 60 votes.) Dec. 3, 2009.

356. **HR 3590. Health Care Overhaul/Use of Task Force Recommendation.** Murkowski, R-Alaska, amendment to the Reid, D-Nev., substitute amendment. The Murkowski amendment would prohibit the secretary of Health and Human Services from using any recommendation made by the U.S. Preventive Services Task Force to deny individuals coverage of an item or service. It would strike language requiring health insurance issuers to provide coverage, without cost-sharing requirements, on items and services that receive a certain rating from the task force. It would specify that the bill would not authorize government agencies to define abortion services as preventive. Rejected 41-59: D 1-57; R 40-0; I 0-2. (By unanimous consent, the Senate agreed to raise the majority requirement for adoption of the Murkowski amendment to 60 votes.) Dec. 3, 2009.

357. **HR 3590. Health Care Overhaul/Medicare Benefits.** Bennet, D-Colo., amendment to the Reid, D-Nev., substitute amendment. The Bennet amendment would clarify that the bill's provisions would not result in a reduction in guaranteed Medicare benefits. It would require that savings from Medicare cuts be used to extend the solvency of the Medicare trust funds, reduce premiums and reduce other cost-sharing for beneficiaries, expand benefits, and protect access to Medicare providers. Adopted 100-0: D 58-0; R 40-0; I 2-0. (By unanimous consent, the Senate agreed to raise the majority requirement for adoption of the Bennet amendment to 60 votes.) Dec. 3, 2009.

358. **HR 3590. Health Care Overhaul/Commit.** McCain, R-Ariz., motion to commit the bill to the Finance Committee with instructions that it be reported back after striking provisions that would cut $440.5 billion from Medicare programs, including $118.1 billion from Medicare Advantage and $150 billion from providers. It would express the sense of the Senate that any savings to health trust funds resulting from the bill be used to strengthen Medicare. Motion rejected 42-58: D 2-56; R 40-0; I 0-2. (By unanimous consent, the Senate agreed to raise the majority requirement for agreeing to the McCain motion to 60 votes.) A "nay" was a vote in support of the president's position. Dec. 3, 2009.

	354	355	356	357	358			354	355	356	357	358
ALABAMA							**MONTANA**					
Shelby	Y	N	Y	Y	Y		Baucus	Y	Y	N	Y	N
Sessions	?	N	Y	Y	Y		Tester	Y	Y	N	Y	N
ALASKA							**NEBRASKA**					
Murkowski	Y	N	Y	Y	Y		Nelson	Y	N	Y	Y	Y
Begich	?	Y	N	Y	N		Johanns	Y	N	Y	Y	Y
ARIZONA							**NEVADA**					
McCain	Y	N	Y	Y	Y		Reid	Y	Y	N	Y	N
Kyl	Y	N	Y	Y	Y		Ensign	Y	N	Y	Y	Y
ARKANSAS							**NEW HAMPSHIRE**					
Lincoln	Y	Y	N	Y	Y		Gregg	Y	N	Y	Y	Y
Pryor	Y	Y	N	Y	N		Shaheen	Y	Y	N	Y	N
CALIFORNIA							**NEW JERSEY**					
Feinstein	Y	Y	N	Y	N		Lautenberg	Y	Y	N	Y	N
Boxer	Y	Y	N	Y	N		Menendez	Y	Y	N	Y	N
COLORADO							**NEW MEXICO**					
Udall	Y	Y	N	Y	N		Bingaman	Y	Y	N	Y	N
Bennet	Y	Y	N	Y	N		Udall	Y	Y	N	Y	N
CONNECTICUT							**NEW YORK**					
Dodd	Y	Y	N	Y	N		Schumer	Y	Y	N	Y	N
Lieberman	Y	Y	N	Y	N		Gillibrand	Y	Y	N	Y	N
DELAWARE							**NORTH CAROLINA**					
Carper	Y	Y	N	Y	N		Burr	Y	N	Y	Y	Y
Kaufman	Y	Y	N	Y	N		Hagan	Y	Y	N	Y	N
FLORIDA							**NORTH DAKOTA**					
Nelson	Y	Y	N	Y	N		Conrad	Y	Y	N	Y	N
LeMieux	Y	N	Y	Y	Y		Dorgan	Y	Y	N	Y	N
GEORGIA							**OHIO**					
Chambliss	Y	N	Y	Y	Y		Voinovich	Y	N	Y	Y	Y
Isakson	Y	N	Y	Y	Y		Brown	Y	Y	N	Y	N
HAWAII							**OKLAHOMA**					
Inouye	Y	Y	N	Y	N		Inhofe	Y	N	Y	Y	Y
Akaka	Y	Y	N	Y	N		Coburn	Y	N	Y	Y	Y
IDAHO							**OREGON**					
Crapo	Y	N	Y	Y	Y		Wyden	Y	Y	N	Y	N
Risch	Y	N	Y	Y	Y		Merkley	Y	Y	N	Y	N
ILLINOIS							**PENNSYLVANIA**					
Durbin	Y	Y	N	Y	N		Specter	Y	Y	N	Y	N
Burris	Y	Y	N	Y	N		Casey	Y	Y	N	Y	N
INDIANA							**RHODE ISLAND**					
Lugar	Y	N	Y	Y	Y		Reed	Y	Y	N	Y	N
Bayh	Y	Y	N	Y	N		Whitehouse	Y	Y	N	Y	N
IOWA							**SOUTH CAROLINA**					
Grassley	Y	N	Y	Y	Y		Graham	Y	N	Y	Y	Y
Harkin	Y	Y	N	Y	N		DeMint	Y	N	Y	Y	Y
KANSAS							**SOUTH DAKOTA**					
Brownback	Y	N	Y	Y	Y		Johnson	Y	Y	N	Y	N
Roberts	Y	N	Y	Y	Y		Thune	Y	N	Y	Y	Y
KENTUCKY							**TENNESSEE**					
McConnell	Y	N	Y	Y	Y		Alexander	Y	N	Y	Y	Y
Bunning	Y	N	Y	Y	Y		Corker	Y	N	Y	Y	Y
LOUISIANA							**TEXAS**					
Landrieu	Y	Y	N	Y	N		Hutchison	Y	N	Y	Y	Y
Vitter	Y	Y	Y	Y	Y		Cornyn	Y	N	Y	Y	Y
MAINE							**UTAH**					
Snowe	Y	Y	Y	Y	Y		Hatch	Y	N	Y	Y	Y
Collins	Y	Y	Y	Y	Y		Bennett	Y	N	Y	Y	Y
MARYLAND							**VERMONT**					
Mikulski	Y	Y	N	Y	N		Leahy	Y	Y	N	Y	N
Cardin	Y	Y	N	Y	N		*Sanders*	Y	Y	N	Y	N
MASSACHUSETTS							**VIRGINIA**					
Kerry	Y	Y	N	Y	N		Webb	Y	Y	N	Y	Y
Kirk	Y	Y	N	Y	N		Warner	Y	Y	N	Y	N
MICHIGAN							**WASHINGTON**					
Levin	Y	Y	N	Y	N		Murray	Y	Y	N	Y	N
Stabenow	Y	Y	N	Y	N		Cantwell	Y	Y	N	Y	N
MINNESOTA							**WEST VIRGINIA**					
Klobuchar	Y	Y	N	Y	N		Byrd	?	Y	N	Y	N
Franken	Y	Y	N	Y	N		Rockefeller	Y	Y	N	Y	N
MISSISSIPPI							**WISCONSIN**					
Cochran	Y	N	Y	Y	Y		Kohl	Y	Y	N	Y	N
Wicker	Y	N	Y	Y	Y		Feingold	Y	N	N	Y	N
MISSOURI							**WYOMING**					
Bond	Y	N	Y	Y	Y		Enzi	Y	N	Y	Y	Y
McCaskill	Y	Y	N	Y	N		Barrasso	Y	N	Y	Y	Y

KEY	**Republicans**	Democrats	*Independents*		
Y	Voted for (yea)		X	Paired against	C Voted "present" to avoid possible conflict of interest
#	Paired for		–	Announced against	
+	Announced for		P	Voted "present"	? Did not vote or otherwise make a position known
N	Voted against (nay)				

IN THE SENATE | By Vote Number

359. HR 3590. **Health Care Overhaul/Social Security and CLASS Program.** Whitehouse, D-R.I, amendment to the Reid, D-Nev., substitute amendment. The Whitehouse amendment would express the sense of the Senate that the additional surplus in the Social Security Trust Fund should be reserved for Social Security and that the net savings generated by the Community Living Assistance Services and Supports (CLASS) program, which would be created under the substitute, should be reserved for that program. The substitute would create marketplaces for purchasing health insurance, create a public health insurance option from which states could opt out, require most individuals to obtain insurance, and impose requirements on insurance companies regarding the coverage that they offer. Adopted 98-0: D 57-0; R 39-0; I 2-0. (By unanimous consent, the Senate agreed to raise the majority requirement for adoption of the Whitehouse amendment to 60 votes.) Dec. 4, 2009.

360. HR 3590. **Health Care Overhaul/CLASS Program.** Thune, R-S.D., amendment to the Reid, D-Nev., substitute amendment. The Thune amendment would strike the section of the substitute that would establish the Community Living Assistance Services and Supports (CLASS) program, a new voluntary insurance program to help individuals with functional limitations purchase community living assistance services. Rejected 51-47: D 11-46; R 39-0; I 1-1. (By unanimous consent, the Senate agreed to raise the majority requirement for adoption of the Thune amendment to 60 votes.) Dec. 4, 2009.

361. HR 3590. **Health Care Overhaul/Medicare Advantage.** Stabenow, D-Mich., amendment to the Reid, D-Nev., substitute amendment. The Stabenow amendment would stipulate that nothing in the bill would result in the reduction or elimination of any benefits guaranteed by law to participants in Medicare Advantage plans. Adopted 97-1: D 57-0; R 38-1; I 2-0. (By unanimous consent, the Senate agreed to raise the majority requirement for adoption of the Stabenow amendment to 60 votes.) Dec. 4, 2009.

362. HR 3590. **Health Care Overhaul/Commit.** Hatch, R-Utah, motion to commit the bill to the Finance Committee with instructions that it be reported back with changes that would eliminate cuts in payments to Medicare Advantage plans totaling $120 billion. Motion rejected 41-57: D 2-55; R 39-0; I 0-2. (By unanimous consent, the Senate agreed to raise the majority requirement for agreeing to the Hatch motion to 60 votes.) Dec. 4, 2009.

363. HR 3590. **Health Care Overhaul/Home Health Benefits.** Kerry, D-Mass., amendment to the Reid, D-Nev., substitute amendment. The Kerry amendment would stipulate that nothing in the bill would result in the reduction of guaranteed home health benefits. Adopted 96-0: D 57-0; R 37-0; I 2-0. (By unanimous consent, the Senate agreed to raise the majority requirement for adoption of the Kerry amendment to 60 votes.) Dec. 5, 2009.

	359	360	361	362	363
ALABAMA					
Shelby	Y	Y	Y	Y	Y
Sessions	Y	Y	Y	Y	Y
ALASKA					
Murkowski	Y	Y	Y	Y	Y
Begich	Y	N	Y	N	Y
ARIZONA					
McCain	Y	Y	Y	Y	Y
Kyl	Y	Y	Y	Y	Y
ARKANSAS					
Lincoln	Y	Y	Y	N	Y
Pryor	Y	N	Y	N	Y
CALIFORNIA					
Feinstein	Y	N	Y	N	Y
Boxer	Y	N	Y	N	Y
COLORADO					
Udall	Y	Y	Y	N	Y
Bennet	Y	N	Y	N	Y
CONNECTICUT					
Dodd	Y	N	Y	N	Y
Lieberman	Y	Y	Y	N	Y
DELAWARE					
Carper	Y	Y	Y	N	Y
Kaufman	Y	N	Y	N	Y
FLORIDA					
Nelson	Y	N	Y	N	Y
LeMieux	Y	Y	Y	Y	Y
GEORGIA					
Chambliss	Y	Y	Y	Y	Y
Isakson	Y	Y	Y	Y	Y
HAWAII					
Inouye	Y	N	Y	N	Y
Akaka	Y	N	Y	N	Y
IDAHO					
Crapo	Y	Y	Y	Y	Y
Risch	Y	Y	Y	Y	Y
ILLINOIS					
Durbin	Y	N	Y	N	Y
Burris	Y	N	Y	N	Y
INDIANA					
Lugar	Y	Y	Y	Y	Y
Bayh	Y	Y	Y	N	Y
IOWA					
Grassley	Y	Y	Y	Y	Y
Harkin	Y	N	Y	N	Y
KANSAS					
Brownback	Y	Y	Y	Y	Y
Roberts	Y	Y	Y	Y	Y
KENTUCKY					
McConnell	Y	Y	Y	Y	Y
Bunning	+	+	+	+	+
LOUISIANA					
Landrieu	Y	Y	Y	N	Y
Vitter	Y	Y	Y	Y	Y
MAINE					
Snowe	Y	Y	Y	Y	Y
Collins	Y	Y	Y	Y	Y
MARYLAND					
Mikulski	Y	N	Y	N	Y
Cardin	Y	N	Y	N	Y
MASSACHUSETTS					
Kerry	Y	N	Y	N	Y
Kirk	Y	N	Y	N	Y
MICHIGAN					
Levin	Y	N	Y	N	Y
Stabenow	Y	N	Y	N	Y
MINNESOTA					
Klobuchar	Y	N	Y	N	Y
Franken	Y	N	Y	N	Y
MISSISSIPPI					
Cochran	Y	Y	Y	Y	Y
Wicker	Y	Y	Y	Y	Y
MISSOURI					
Bond	Y	Y	Y	Y	Y
McCaskill	Y	Y	Y	N	Y

	359	360	361	362	363
MONTANA					
Baucus	Y	Y	Y	N	Y
Tester	Y	N	Y	N	Y
NEBRASKA					
Nelson	Y	Y	Y	Y	Y
Johanns	Y	Y	Y	Y	Y
NEVADA					
Reid	Y	N	Y	N	Y
Ensign	Y	Y	Y	Y	Y
NEW HAMPSHIRE					
Gregg	Y	Y	Y	Y	Y
Shaheen	Y	N	Y	N	Y
NEW JERSEY					
Lautenberg	Y	N	Y	N	Y
Menendez	Y	N	Y	N	Y
NEW MEXICO					
Bingaman	Y	N	Y	N	Y
Udall	Y	N	Y	N	Y
NEW YORK					
Schumer	Y	N	Y	N	Y
Gillibrand	Y	N	Y	N	Y
NORTH CAROLINA					
Burr	Y	Y	Y	Y	Y
Hagan	Y	N	Y	N	Y
NORTH DAKOTA					
Conrad	Y	Y	Y	N	Y
Dorgan	Y	N	Y	N	Y
OHIO					
Voinovich	Y	Y	Y	Y	Y
Brown	Y	N	Y	N	Y
OKLAHOMA					
Inhofe	Y	Y	Y	Y	?
Coburn	Y	Y	N	Y	Y
OREGON					
Wyden	Y	N	Y	N	Y
Merkley	Y	N	Y	N	Y
PENNSYLVANIA					
Specter	Y	N	Y	N	Y
Casey	Y	N	Y	N	Y
RHODE ISLAND					
Reed	Y	N	Y	N	Y
Whitehouse	Y	N	Y	N	Y
SOUTH CAROLINA					
Graham	Y	Y	Y	Y	?
DeMint	Y	Y	Y	Y	Y
SOUTH DAKOTA					
Johnson	Y	N	Y	N	Y
Thune	Y	Y	Y	Y	Y
TENNESSEE					
Alexander	Y	Y	Y	Y	Y
Corker	Y	Y	Y	Y	Y
TEXAS					
Hutchison	Y	Y	Y	Y	Y
Cornyn	Y	Y	Y	Y	Y
UTAH					
Hatch	Y	Y	Y	Y	Y
Bennett	Y	Y	Y	Y	Y
VERMONT					
Leahy	Y	N	Y	N	Y
Sanders	Y	N	Y	N	Y
VIRGINIA					
Webb	Y	Y	Y	Y	Y
Warner	Y	Y	Y	N	Y
WASHINGTON					
Murray	Y	N	Y	N	Y
Cantwell	Y	N	Y	N	Y
WEST VIRGINIA					
Byrd	?	?	?	?	?
Rockefeller	Y	N	Y	N	Y
WISCONSIN					
Kohl	Y	N	Y	N	Y
Feingold	Y	N	Y	N	Y
WYOMING					
Enzi	Y	Y	Y	Y	Y
Barrasso	Y	Y	Y	Y	Y

KEY   **Republicans**   Democrats   *Independents*

Y Voted for (yea)	X Paired against	C Voted "present" to avoid possible conflict of interest
# Paired for	– Announced against	
+ Announced for	P Voted "present"	? Did not vote or otherwise make a position known
N Voted against (nay)		

IN THE SENATE | By Vote Number

364. **HR 3590. Health Care Overhaul/Commit.** Johanns, R-Neb., motion to commit the bill to the Finance Committee with instructions that it be reported back with changes that would eliminate $42.1 billion in cuts to payments to home health agencies, which provide health care support and services in qualified patients' homes. Motion rejected 41-53: D 4-52; R 37-0; I 0-1. (By unanimous consent, the Senate agreed to raise the majority requirement for agreeing to the Johanns motion to 60 votes.) Dec. 5, 2009.

365. **HR 3590. Health Care Overhaul/Insurance Executive Salary Tax Deductions.** Lincoln, D-Ark., amendment to the Reid, D-Nev., substitute amendment. The Lincoln amendment would limit the annual tax deductions that health insurance companies can take for executive salaries to $400,000 or the compensation level of the U.S. president. It would require any savings to go to the Medicare Trust Fund. Rejected 56-42: D 54-3; R 1-38; I 1-1. (By unanimous consent, the Senate agreed to raise the majority requirement for adoption of the Lincoln amendment to 60 votes.) Dec. 6, 2009.

366. **HR 3590. Health Care Overhaul/Medical Malpractice Attorney Fees.** Ensign, R-Nev., amendment to the Reid, D-Nev., substitute amendment. The Ensign amendment would limit plaintiff attorney fees in medical malpractice suits to no more than 33.3 percent of the first $150,000 of the settlement recovered, plus 25 percent of any amount recovered in excess of that, unless otherwise determined by state law. It also would allow for new calculations of the limits if the settlement includes periodic or future damages payments. Rejected 32-66: D 4-53; R 27-12; I 1-1. (By unanimous consent, the Senate agreed to raise the majority requirement for adoption of the Ensign amendment to 60 votes.) Dec. 6, 2009.

367. **HR 3590. Health Care Overhaul/Enrollee Satisfaction Survey.** Pryor, D-Ark., amendment to the Reid, D-Nev., substitute amendment. The Pryor amendment would require the Health and Human Services Department to create a system to survey enrollee satisfaction with health care plans under the insurance exchanges created by the substitute and post information online to allow individuals to compare satisfaction levels. Plans with more than 500 enrollees in the previous year would be rated. Adopted 98-0: D 56-0; R 40-0; I 2-0. (By unanimous consent, the Senate agreed to raise the majority requirement for adoption of the Pryor amendment to 60 votes.) Dec. 7, 2009.

	364	365	366	367
ALABAMA				
Shelby	Y	N	N	Y
Sessions	Y	N	Y	Y
ALASKA				
Murkowski	Y	N	Y	Y
Begich	N	Y	N	Y
ARIZONA				
McCain	Y	N	Y	Y
Kyl	Y	N	Y	Y
ARKANSAS				
Lincoln	Y	Y	Y	Y
Pryor	N	Y	N	Y
CALIFORNIA				
Feinstein	N	Y	N	Y
Boxer	N	Y	N	Y
COLORADO				
Udall	N	Y	N	Y
Bennet	N	Y	N	Y
CONNECTICUT				
Dodd	N	Y	N	Y
Lieberman	N	N	Y	Y
DELAWARE				
Carper	N	N	N	Y
Kaufman	N	Y	N	Y
FLORIDA				
Nelson	N	Y	N	Y
LeMieux	Y	N	N	Y
GEORGIA				
Chambliss	Y	N	N	Y
Isakson	Y	N	Y	Y
HAWAII				
Inouye	N	Y	N	Y
Akaka	N	Y	N	Y
IDAHO				
Crapo	Y	N	N	Y
Risch	Y	N	N	Y
ILLINOIS				
Durbin	N	Y	N	Y
Burris	N	Y	N	Y
INDIANA				
Lugar	Y	N	Y	Y
Bayh	Y	Y	N	Y
IOWA				
Grassley	Y	N	Y	Y
Harkin	N	Y	N	Y
KANSAS				
Brownback	Y	N	Y	Y
Roberts	Y	N	Y	Y
KENTUCKY				
McConnell	Y	N	Y	Y
Bunning	+	–	+	Y
LOUISIANA				
Landrieu	N	Y	N	Y
Vitter	Y	N	Y	Y
MAINE				
Snowe	Y	Y	Y	Y
Collins	Y	N	N	Y
MARYLAND				
Mikulski	N	Y	N	Y
Cardin	N	Y	N	Y
MASSACHUSETTS				
Kerry	N	Y	N	Y
Kirk	N	Y	N	Y
MICHIGAN				
Levin	N	Y	N	Y
Stabenow	N	Y	N	Y
MINNESOTA				
Klobuchar	N	Y	N	Y
Franken	N	Y	N	Y
MISSISSIPPI				
Cochran	Y	N	N	Y
Wicker	Y	N	N	Y
MISSOURI				
Bond	Y	N	Y	Y
McCaskill	N	Y	N	Y

	364	365	366	367
MONTANA				
Baucus	N	Y	N	Y
Tester	N	Y	N	Y
NEBRASKA				
Nelson	Y	Y	N	Y
Johanns	Y	N	N	Y
NEVADA				
Reid	N	Y	N	Y
Ensign	Y	N	Y	Y
NEW HAMPSHIRE				
Gregg	Y	N	Y	Y
Shaheen	N	Y	N	Y
NEW JERSEY				
Lautenberg	N	Y	N	Y
Menendez	N	Y	N	Y
NEW MEXICO				
Bingaman	N	N	N	Y
Udall	N	Y	N	Y
NEW YORK				
Schumer	N	Y	N	Y
Gillibrand	N	Y	N	Y
NORTH CAROLINA				
Burr	Y	N	Y	Y
Hagan	N	Y	Y	Y
NORTH DAKOTA				
Conrad	N	N	N	Y
Dorgan	N	Y	N	Y
OHIO				
Voinovich	Y	N	Y	Y
Brown	N	Y	*N	Y
OKLAHOMA				
Inhofe	?	N	Y	Y
Coburn	Y	N	Y	Y
OREGON				
Wyden	N	Y	N	Y
Merkley	N	Y	N	Y
PENNSYLVANIA				
Specter	N	Y	N	?
Casey	N	Y	N	Y
RHODE ISLAND				
Reed	N	Y	N	Y
Whitehouse	N	Y	N	Y
SOUTH CAROLINA				
Graham	?	N	N	Y
DeMint	Y	N	Y	Y
SOUTH DAKOTA				
Johnson	N	Y	N	Y
Thune	Y	N	Y	Y
TENNESSEE				
Alexander	Y	N	Y	Y
Corker	Y	N	Y	Y
TEXAS				
Hutchison	Y	N	Y	Y
Cornyn	Y	N	Y	Y
UTAH				
Hatch	Y	N	N	Y
Bennett	Y	N	N	Y
VERMONT				
Leahy	?	Y	N	Y
Sanders	?	Y	N	Y
VIRGINIA				
Webb	Y	Y	N	Y
Warner	N	Y	Y	Y
WASHINGTON				
Murray	N	Y	N	Y
Cantwell	N	Y	N	Y
WEST VIRGINIA				
Byrd	?	?	?	?
Rockefeller	N	Y	N	Y
WISCONSIN				
Kohl	N	Y	Y	Y
Feingold	N	Y	N	Y
WYOMING				
Enzi	Y	N	Y	Y
Barrasso	Y	N	Y	Y

KEY   **Republicans**   Democrats   *Independents*

Y Voted for (yea)	X Paired against	C Voted "present" to avoid possible conflict of interest
# Paired for	– Announced against	
+ Announced for	P Voted "present"	? Did not vote or otherwise make a position known
N Voted against (nay)		

IN THE SENATE | By Vote Number

368. HR 3590. **Health Care Overhaul/Offset Certification.** Gregg, R-N.H., amendment to the Reid, D-Nev., substitute amendment. The Gregg amendment would prohibit revenue-reducing or spending provisions from being implemented until the Office of Management and Budget and the Centers for Medicare and Medicaid Services certify that the provisions are offset by projected savings for 10 years after the measure is fully implemented. Rejected 43-56: D 3-54; R 40-0; I 0-2. (By unanimous consent, the Senate agreed to raise the majority requirement for adoption of the Gregg amendment to 60 votes.) Dec. 7, 2009.

369. HR 3590. **Health Care Overhaul/Abortion Funding Ban.** Boxer, D-Calif., motion to table the Nelson, D-Neb., amendment to the Reid, D-Nev., substitute amendment. The Nelson amendment would bar the use of funds authorized in the bill to pay for an abortion or to cover any part of the costs of a health care plan that includes abortion coverage, except under certain circumstances. Individuals with subsidized policies who also want abortion coverage would have to purchase it separately, using their own money. Insurance issuers would be allowed to offer separate supplemental coverage for abortions as long as it is not funded under the bill. Health benefit plans participating in the exchanges created by the bill could not discriminate against providers or facilities for not covering or providing abortion services. Motion agreed to 54-45: D 50-7; R 2-38; I 2-0. Dec. 8, 2009.

370. HR 3590. **Health Care Overhaul/Commit.** McCain, R-Ariz., motion to commit the bill to the Finance Committee with instructions that it be reported back with changes that would allow all Medicare Advantage enrollees to retain their existing benefits. Rejected 42-57: D 2-55; R 40-0; I 0-2. (By unanimous consent, the Senate agreed to raise the majority requirement for agreeing to the McCain motion to 60 votes.) Dec. 8, 2009.

371. HR 3288. **Fiscal 2010 Omnibus Appropriations/Motion to Proceed.** Reid, D-Nev., motion to proceed to the conference report on the bill that would provide fiscal 2010 appropriations for federal departments and agencies covered by six unfinished fiscal 2010 spending bills. Motion agreed to 56-43: D 54-3; R 0-40; I 2-0. Dec. 10, 2009.

	368	369	370	371
ALABAMA				
Shelby	Y	N	Y	N
Sessions	Y	N	Y	N
ALASKA				
Murkowski	Y	N	N	N
Begich	N	Y	N	Y
ARIZONA				
McCain	Y	N	Y	N
Kyl	Y	N	Y	N
ARKANSAS				
Lincoln	N	Y	N	Y
Pryor	N	N	N	Y
CALIFORNIA				
Feinstein	N	Y	N	Y
Boxer	N	Y	N	Y
COLORADO				
Udall	N	Y	N	Y
Bennet	N	Y	N	Y
CONNECTICUT				
Dodd	N	Y	N	Y
Lieberman	N	Y	N	Y
DELAWARE				
Carper	N	Y	N	Y
Kaufman	N	N	N	Y
FLORIDA				
Nelson	N	Y	N	Y
LeMieux	Y	N	Y	N
GEORGIA				
Chambliss	Y	N	Y	N
Isakson	Y	N	Y	N
HAWAII				
Inouye	N	Y	N	Y
Akaka	N	Y	N	Y
IDAHO				
Crapo	Y	N	Y	N
Risch	Y	N	Y	N
ILLINOIS				
Durbin	N	Y	N	Y
Burris	N	Y	N	Y
INDIANA				
Lugar	Y	N	Y	N
Bayh	Y	N	N	N
IOWA				
Grassley	Y	N	Y	N
Harkin	N	Y	N	Y
KANSAS				
Brownback	Y	N	Y	N
Roberts	Y	N	Y	N
KENTUCKY				
McConnell	Y	N	Y	N
Bunning	Y	N	Y	N
LOUISIANA				
Landrieu	N	Y	N	Y
Vitter	Y	N	Y	N
MAINE				
Snowe	Y	Y	Y	N
Collins	Y	Y	Y	N
MARYLAND				
Mikulski	N	Y	N	Y
Cardin	N	Y	N	Y
MASSACHUSETTS				
Kerry	N	Y	N	Y
Kirk	N	Y	N	Y
MICHIGAN				
Levin	N	Y	N	Y
Stabenow	N	Y	N	Y
MINNESOTA				
Klobuchar	N	Y	N	Y
Franken	N	Y	N	Y
MISSISSIPPI				
Cochran	Y	N	Y	N
Wicker	Y	N	Y	N
MISSOURI				
Bond	Y	N	Y	N
McCaskill	N	Y	N	Y

	368	369	370	371
MONTANA				
Baucus	N	Y	N	Y
Tester	N	Y	N	Y
NEBRASKA				
Nelson	Y	N	Y	Y
Johanns	Y	N	Y	N
NEVADA				
Reid	N	Y	N	Y
Ensign	Y	N	Y	N
NEW HAMPSHIRE				
Gregg	Y	N	Y	N
Shaheen	N	Y	N	Y
NEW JERSEY				
Lautenberg	N	Y	N	Y
Menendez	N	Y	N	N
NEW MEXICO				
Bingaman	N	Y	N	Y
Udall	N	Y	N	Y
NEW YORK				
Schumer	N	Y	N	Y
Gillibrand	N	Y	N	Y
NORTH CAROLINA				
Burr	Y	N	Y	N
Hagan	N	Y	N	Y
NORTH DAKOTA				
Conrad	N	N	N	Y
Dorgan	N	N	N	Y
OHIO				
Voinovich	Y	N	Y	N
Brown	N	Y	N	Y
OKLAHOMA				
Inhofe	Y	N	Y	N
Coburn	Y	N	Y	N
OREGON				
Wyden	N	Y	N	Y
Merkley	N	Y	N	Y
PENNSYLVANIA				
Specter	N	Y	N	Y
Casey	N	N	N	Y
RHODE ISLAND				
Reed	N	Y	N	Y
Whitehouse	N	Y	N	Y
SOUTH CAROLINA				
Graham	Y	N	Y	N
DeMint	Y	N	Y	N
SOUTH DAKOTA				
Johnson	N	Y	N	Y
Thune	Y	N	Y	N
TENNESSEE				
Alexander	Y	N	Y	N
Corker	Y	N	Y	N
TEXAS				
Hutchison	Y	N	Y	N
Cornyn	Y	N	Y	N
UTAH				
Hatch	Y	N	Y	N
Bennett	Y	N	Y	N
VERMONT				
Leahy	N	Y	N	Y
Sanders	N	Y	N	Y
VIRGINIA				
Webb	Y	Y	Y	Y
Warner	N	Y	N	Y
WASHINGTON				
Murray	N	Y	N	Y
Cantwell	N	Y	N	Y
WEST VIRGINIA				
Byrd	?	?	?	?
Rockefeller	N	Y	N	Y
WISCONSIN				
Kohl	N	Y	N	Y
Feingold	N	Y	N	N
WYOMING				
Enzi	Y	N	Y	N
Barrasso	Y	N	Y	N

KEY	**Republicans**	Democrats	*Independents*		
Y	Voted for (yea)	X	Paired against	C	Voted "present" to avoid possible conflict of interest
#	Paired for	–	Announced against		
+	Announced for	P	Voted "present"	?	Did not vote or otherwise make a position known
N	Voted against (nay)				

IN THE SENATE | By Vote Number

372. **HR 3288. Fiscal 2010 Omnibus Appropriations/Conference Report Point of Order.** Inouye, D-Hawaii, motion to waive Senate Rule 28 with respect to the McCain, R-Ariz., point of order against the conference report on the bill that would provide $446.8 billion in discretionary spending for federal departments and agencies covered by six unfinished fiscal 2010 spending bills. Motion agreed to 60-36: D 55-3; R 3-33; I 2-0. Three-fifths of the total Senate (60) is required to waive Senate Rule 28. (Under the rule, a senator may raise a point of order against provisions of a conference report that were not in the bill as passed by either chamber.) Dec. 11, 2009.

373. **HR 3288. Fiscal 2010 Omnibus Appropriations/Cloture.** Motion to invoke cloture (thus limiting debate) on the conference report on the bill that would provide $446.8 billion in discretionary spending for federal departments and agencies covered by six unfinished fiscal 2010 spending bills. Motion agreed to 60-34: D 55-3; R 3-31; I 2-0. Three-fifths of the total Senate (60) is required to invoke cloture. Dec. 12, 2009.

374. **HR 3288. Fiscal 2010 Omnibus Appropriations/Conference Report.** Adoption of the conference report on the bill that would provide $446.8 billion in discretionary spending for federal departments and agencies covered by six unfinished fiscal 2010 spending bills. Adopted (thus cleared for the president) 57-35: D 52-3; R 3-32; I 2-0. A "yea" was a vote in support of the president's position. Dec. 13, 2009.

375. **HR 3590. Health Care Overhaul/Tax Increases.** Baucus, D-Mont., amendment to the Reid, D-Nev., substitute amendment. The Baucus amendment would express a sense of the Senate that the chamber should reject procedural maneuvers that would raise taxes on middle class families. The substitute would create marketplaces for purchasing health insurance, create a public health insurance option from which states could opt out, require most individuals to obtain insurance and impose requirements on insurance companies regarding the coverage that they offer. Adopted 97-1: D 56-1; R 39-0; I 2-0. (By unanimous consent, the Senate agreed to raise the majority requirement for adoption of the Baucus amendment to 60 votes.) Dec. 15, 2009.

376. **HR 3590. Health Care Overhaul/Commit.** Crapo, R-Idaho, motion to commit the bill to the Finance Committee with instructions that it be reported back with changes that would provide that no provision of the measure could result in a federal tax increase for individuals with adjusted gross incomes of less than $200,000 and married individuals with adjusted gross incomes of less than $250,000. Motion rejected 45-54: D 5-52; R 40-0; I 0-2. (By unanimous consent, the Senate agreed to raise the majority requirement for agreeing to the Crapo motion to 60 votes.) Dec. 15, 2009.

377. **HR 3590. Health Care Overhaul/Prescription Drug Importation.** Dorgan, D-N.D., amendment to the Reid, D-Nev., substitute amendment. The Dorgan amendment would allow registered importers and exporters to import prescription drugs into the United States and allow individuals to purchase them from registered exporters for personal use. It would establish new registration and inspection requirements and require the Department of Health and Human Services to designate countries from which drugs can be imported. Rejected 51-48: D 27-30; R 23-17; I 1-1. (By unanimous consent, the Senate agreed to raise the majority requirement for adoption of the Dorgan amendment to 60 votes.) A "nay" was a vote in support of the president's position. Dec. 15, 2009.

	372	373	374	375	376	377
ALABAMA						
Shelby	N	Y	Y	Y	Y	Y
Sessions	N	N	N	Y	Y	Y
ALASKA						
Murkowski	N	N	N	Y	Y	Y
Begich	Y	Y	Y	Y	N	Y
ARIZONA						
McCain	N	N	N	Y	Y	Y
Kyl	N	N	N	Y	Y	N
ARKANSAS						
Lincoln	Y	Y	Y	Y	Y	Y
Pryor	Y	Y	Y	Y	N	Y
CALIFORNIA						
Feinstein	Y	Y	Y	Y	N	Y
Boxer	Y	Y	Y	Y	N	Y
COLORADO						
Udall	Y	Y	Y	Y	N	N
Bennet	Y	Y	Y	Y	N	Y
CONNECTICUT						
Dodd	Y	Y	Y	Y	N	N
Lieberman	Y	Y	Y	Y	N	N
DELAWARE						
Carper	Y	Y	Y	Y	N	N
Kaufman	Y	Y	Y	Y	N	N
FLORIDA						
Nelson	Y	Y	Y	Y	N	Y
LeMieux	N	N	N	Y	Y	Y
GEORGIA						
Chambliss	N	N	N	Y	Y	N
Isakson	N	N	N	Y	N	N
HAWAII						
Inouye	Y	Y	Y	Y	N	N
Akaka	Y	Y	Y	Y	N	N
IDAHO						
Crapo	N	N	N	Y	Y	Y
Risch	N	N	N	Y	Y	Y
ILLINOIS						
Durbin	Y	Y	Y	Y	N	N
Burris	Y	Y	Y	Y	N	N
INDIANA						
Lugar	N	?	N	?	Y	N
Bayh	N	N	N	Y	Y	N
IOWA						
Grassley	N	N	N	Y	Y	Y
Harkin	Y	Y	Y	Y	N	Y
KANSAS						
Brownback	N	N	N	Y	N	N
Roberts	N	N	N	Y	Y	N
KENTUCKY						
McConnell	N	N	N	Y	Y	Y
Bunning	-	-	-	Y	Y	N
LOUISIANA						
Landrieu	Y	Y	Y	Y	N	N
Vitter	N	N	N	Y	Y	Y
MAINE						
Snowe	N	N	N	Y	Y	Y
Collins	Y	Y	Y	Y	Y	Y
MARYLAND						
Mikulski	Y	Y	Y	Y	N	N
Cardin	Y	Y	Y	Y	N	N
MASSACHUSETTS						
Kerry	Y	Y	Y	Y	N	N
Kirk	Y	Y	Y	Y	N	N
MICHIGAN						
Levin	Y	Y	Y	Y	N	N
Stabenow	Y	Y	Y	Y	N	Y
MINNESOTA						
Klobuchar	Y	Y	Y	Y	Y	Y
Franken	Y	Y	Y	Y	N	Y
MISSISSIPPI						
Cochran	Y	Y	Y	Y	Y	N
Wicker	N	N	N	Y	Y	Y
MISSOURI						
Bond	Y	?	?	Y	Y	Y
McCaskill	N	N	N	Y	N	Y
MONTANA						
Baucus	Y	Y	Y	Y	N	N
Tester	Y	Y	Y	Y	N	N
NEBRASKA						
Nelson	Y	Y	Y	N	Y	Y
Johanns	N	N	N	Y	Y	Y
NEVADA						
Reid	Y	Y	Y	Y	N	Y
Ensign	N	N	N	Y	Y	N
NEW HAMPSHIRE						
Gregg	N	N	N	Y	Y	N
Shaheen	Y	Y	Y	Y	N	N
NEW JERSEY						
Lautenberg	Y	Y	Y	Y	N	N
Menendez	Y	Y	Y	Y	N	N
NEW MEXICO						
Bingaman	Y	Y	Y	Y	N	Y
Udall	Y	Y	Y	Y	N	Y
NEW YORK						
Schumer	Y	Y	Y	Y	N	N
Gillibrand	Y	Y	Y	Y	N	N
NORTH CAROLINA						
Burr	?	N	N	Y	Y	N
Hagan	Y	Y	Y	Y	N	N
NORTH DAKOTA						
Conrad	Y	Y	Y	Y	N	Y
Dorgan	Y	Y	?	Y	N	Y
OHIO						
Voinovich	N	N	?	Y	Y	N
Brown	Y	Y	Y	Y	N	Y
OKLAHOMA						
Inhofe	N	N	?	Y	Y	N
Coburn	?	?	?	Y	Y	Y
OREGON						
Wyden	Y	Y	Y	Y	N	Y
Merkley	Y	Y	?	Y	N	Y
PENNSYLVANIA						
Specter	Y	Y	Y	Y	N	N
Casey	Y	Y	Y	Y	N	N
RHODE ISLAND						
Reed	Y	Y	Y	Y	N	N
Whitehouse	Y	Y	Y	Y	N	N
SOUTH CAROLINA						
Graham	N	?	N	Y	Y	Y
DeMint	N	?	N	Y	Y	Y
SOUTH DAKOTA						
Johnson	Y	Y	Y	Y	N	Y
Thune	N	N	N	Y	Y	Y
TENNESSEE						
Alexander	N	N	N	Y	Y	Y
Corker	N	N	N	Y	Y	Y
TEXAS						
Hutchison	?	N	N	Y	Y	Y
Cornyn	N	N	N	Y	Y	Y
UTAH						
Hatch	N	N	N	Y	Y	N
Bennett	N	N	N	Y	Y	N
VERMONT						
Leahy	Y	Y	Y	Y	N	Y
Sanders	Y	Y	Y	Y	N	Y
VIRGINIA						
Webb	Y	Y	Y	Y	N	Y
Warner	Y	Y	Y	Y	N	N
WASHINGTON						
Murray	Y	Y	?	Y	N	N
Cantwell	Y	Y	Y	Y	N	N
WEST VIRGINIA						
Byrd	Y	Y	Y	?	?	?
Rockefeller	Y	Y	Y	Y	N	N
WISCONSIN						
Kohl	Y	Y	Y	Y	N	Y
Feingold	N	N	N	Y	Y	N
WYOMING						
Enzi	N	N	N	Y	Y	N
Barrasso	N	N	N	Y	Y	N

KEY   **Republicans**   Democrats   *Independents*

Y Voted for (yea)	X Paired against	C Voted "present" to avoid possible conflict of interest
# Paired for	- Announced against	
+ Announced for	P Voted "present"	? Did not vote or otherwise make a position known
N Voted against (nay)		

IN THE SENATE | By Vote Number

378. **HR 3590. Health Care Overhaul/Prescription Drug Importation Safety Certification.** Lautenberg, D-N.J., amendment to the Reid, D-Nev., substitute amendment. The Lautenberg amendment would allow registered importers and exporters to import prescription drugs into the United States and allow individuals to purchase them from registered exporters for personal use. It would not take effect until the Department of Health and Human Services certified to Congress that implementation would not pose additional risk to the public's health and safety and would reduce cost for Americans. It also would establish new registration and inspection requirements and require the department to designate countries from which drugs can be imported. Rejected 56-43: D 32-25; R 23-17; I 1-1. (By unanimous consent, the Senate agreed to raise the majority requirement for adoption of the Lautenberg amendment to 60 votes.) Dec. 15, 2009.

379. **HR 3590. Health Care Overhaul/Motion to Table.** Sanders, I-Vt., motion to table (kill) the Hutchison, R-Texas, motion to commit the bill to the Finance Committee with instructions that it be reported back with changes that would align the effective dates of all taxes, fees and tax increases included in the substitute with the effective dates of the major insurance provisions in the measure, while maintaining the deficit neutrality of the legislation over the 10-year budget time frame. Motion agreed to 56-41: D 54-2; R 0-39; I 2-0. Dec. 16, 2009.

380. **Procedural Motion/Recess.** Reid, D-Nev., motion to recess until 12:01 a.m. on Friday, Dec. 18, 2009. Motion agreed to 59-38: D 57-0; R 0-38; I 2-0. Dec. 17, 2009.

381. **HR 3326. Fiscal 2010 Defense Appropriations/Cloture.** Motion to invoke cloture (thus limiting debate) on the motion to concur in the House amendment to the Senate amendment to the bill. The House amendment would appropriate $636.4 billion in discretionary funds for the Defense Department in fiscal 2010, raise military pay by 3.4 percent and extend several expiring programs through Feb. 28, 2010. Motion agreed to 63-33: D 58-0; R 3-33; I 2-0. Three-fifths of the total Senate (60) is required to invoke cloture. Dec. 18, 2009.

382. **HR 3326. Fiscal 2010 Defense Appropriations/Motion to Table.** Reid, D-Nev., motion to table (kill) the Reid motion to concur in the House amendment to the Senate amendment to the bill with an amendment that would change the effective date of the bill. Motion agreed to 63-35: D 58-0; R 4-35; I 1-0. Dec. 19, 2009.

383. **HR 3326. Fiscal 2010 Defense Appropriations/Motion to Waive.** Reid, D-Nev., motion to waive the Budget Act with respect to the Coburn, R-Okla., point of order against the Reid motion to concur in the House amendment to the Senate amendment to the bill. Motion agreed to 63-35: D 58-0; R 4-35; I 1-0. A three-fifths majority vote (60) of the total Senate is required to waive the Budget Act. Dec. 19, 2009.

384. **HR 3326. Fiscal 2010 Defense Appropriations/Motion to Concur.** Reid, D-Nev., motion to concur in the House amendment to the Senate amendment to the bill that would appropriate $636.4 billion in discretionary funds for the Defense Department in fiscal 2010, including $128.2 billion for war operations. It also would raise military pay by 3.4 percent. It would extend unemployment benefits and COBRA health care premium subsidies; expiring provisions of the anti-terrorism law known as the Patriot Act, and certain transportation and flood insurance programs through Feb. 28, 2010. It also would provide $400 million for the food stamp program and prevent a scheduled cut in Medicare payments to physicians until Feb. 28, 2010. Motion agreed to (thus clearing the bill for the president) 88-10: D 57-1; R 30-9; I 1-0. Dec. 19, 2009.

	378	379	380	381	382	383	384
ALABAMA							
Shelby	Y	N	N	N	N	N	Y
Sessions	N	N	N	N	N	N	N
ALASKA							
Murkowski	Y	N	N	N	N	N	Y
Begich	N	Y	Y	Y	Y	Y	Y
ARIZONA							
McCain	N	N	N	N	N	N	N
Kyl	N	N	N	N	N	N	Y
ARKANSAS							
Lincoln	Y	Y	Y	Y	Y	Y	Y
Pryor	N	Y	Y	Y	Y	Y	Y
CALIFORNIA							
Feinstein	N	Y	Y	Y	Y	Y	Y
Boxer	Y	Y	Y	Y	Y	Y	Y
COLORADO							
Udall	Y	Y	Y	Y	Y	Y	Y
Bennet	N	Y	Y	Y	Y	Y	Y
CONNECTICUT							
Dodd	Y	Y	Y	Y	Y	Y	Y
Lieberman	Y	Y	Y	Y	?	?	+
DELAWARE							
Carper	Y	Y	Y	Y	Y	Y	Y
Kaufman	Y	Y	Y	Y	Y	Y	Y
FLORIDA							
Nelson	N	Y	Y	Y	Y	Y	Y
LeMieux	Y	N	N	N	N	N	Y
GEORGIA							
Chambliss	Y	N	?	?	N	N	Y
Isakson	Y	N	N	N	N	N	Y
HAWAII							
Inouye	N	Y	Y	Y	Y	Y	Y
Akaka	Y	Y	Y	Y	Y	Y	Y
IDAHO							
Crapo	Y	N	N	N	N	N	Y
Risch	Y	N	N	N	N	N	Y
ILLINOIS							
Durbin	Y	Y	Y	Y	Y	Y	Y
Burris	Y	Y	Y	Y	Y	Y	Y
INDIANA							
Lugar	Y	N	N	N	N	N	Y
Bayh	Y	N	Y	Y	Y	Y	Y
IOWA							
Grassley	N	N	N	N	N	N	Y
Harkin	N	Y	Y	Y	Y	Y	Y
KANSAS							
Brownback	Y	N	N	N	N	N	Y
Roberts	Y	N	N	N	N	N	Y
KENTUCKY							
McConnell	N	N	N	N	N	N	Y
Bunning	Y	N	N	–	N	N	Y
LOUISIANA							
Landrieu	Y	Y	Y	Y	Y	Y	Y
Vitter	N	N	N	N	N	N	Y
MAINE							
Snowe	N	N	N	Y	Y	Y	Y
Collins	N	N	N	Y	Y	Y	Y
MARYLAND							
Mikulski	Y	Y	Y	Y	Y	Y	Y
Cardin	Y	Y	Y	Y	Y	Y	Y
MASSACHUSETTS							
Kerry	Y	+	Y	Y	Y	Y	Y
Kirk	Y	Y	Y	Y	Y	Y	Y
MICHIGAN							
Levin	N	Y	Y	Y	Y	Y	Y
Stabenow	N	Y	Y	Y	Y	Y	Y
MINNESOTA							
Klobuchar	N	Y	Y	Y	Y	Y	Y
Franken	N	Y	Y	Y	Y	Y	Y
MISSISSIPPI							
Cochran	Y	N	N	N	Y	Y	Y
Wicker	N	N	N	N	N	N	Y
MISSOURI							
Bond	Y	N	N	?	Y	Y	Y
McCaskill	N	Y	Y	Y	Y	Y	Y

	378	379	380	381	382	383	384
MONTANA							
Baucus	Y	Y	Y	Y	Y	Y	Y
Tester	Y	Y	Y	Y	Y	Y	Y
NEBRASKA							
Nelson	Y	N	Y	Y	Y	Y	Y
Johanns	N	N	N	N	N	N	N
NEVADA							
Reid	Y	Y	Y	Y	Y	Y	Y
Ensign	Y	N	N	N	N	N	Y
NEW HAMPSHIRE							
Gregg	N	N	N	N	?	?	?
Shaheen	N	Y	Y	Y	Y	Y	Y
NEW JERSEY							
Lautenberg	Y	Y	Y	Y	Y	Y	Y
Menendez	Y	Y	Y	Y	Y	Y	Y
NEW MEXICO							
Bingaman	N	Y	Y	Y	Y	Y	Y
Udall	N	Y	Y	Y	Y	Y	Y
NEW YORK							
Schumer	Y	Y	Y	Y	Y	Y	Y
Gillibrand	Y	Y	Y	Y	Y	Y	Y
NORTH CAROLINA							
Burr	Y	N	N	N	N	N	N
Hagan	Y	Y	Y	Y	Y	Y	Y
NORTH DAKOTA							
Conrad	N	Y	Y	Y	Y	Y	Y
Dorgan	N	Y	Y	Y	Y	Y	Y
OHIO							
Voinovich	Y	N	N	N	N	N	Y
Brown	N	Y	Y	Y	Y	Y	Y
OKLAHOMA							
Inhofe	Y	?	N	N	N	N	Y
Coburn	N	N	N	N	N	N	N
OREGON							
Wyden	N	Y	Y	Y	Y	Y	Y
Merkley	N	Y	Y	Y	Y	Y	Y
PENNSYLVANIA							
Specter	Y	Y	Y	Y	Y	Y	Y
Casey	Y	Y	Y	Y	Y	Y	Y
RHODE ISLAND							
Reed	Y	Y	Y	Y	Y	Y	Y
Whitehouse	N	Y	Y	Y	Y	Y	Y
SOUTH CAROLINA							
Graham	N	N	N	N	N	N	Y
DeMint	N	N	N	N	N	N	N
SOUTH DAKOTA							
Johnson	Y	Y	Y	Y	Y	Y	Y
Thune	N	N	N	N	N	N	N
TENNESSEE							
Alexander	Y	N	N	N	N	N	Y
Corker	N	N	N	N	N	N	Y
TEXAS							
Hutchison	Y	N	Y	N	N	N	Y
Cornyn	Y	N	N	–	N	N	Y
UTAH							
Hatch	N	N	N	N	N	N	Y
Bennett	Y	N	N	N	N	N	Y
VERMONT							
Leahy	N	Y	Y	Y	Y	Y	Y
Sanders	N	Y	Y	Y	Y	Y	Y
VIRGINIA							
Webb	N	Y	Y	Y	Y	Y	Y
Warner	Y	Y	Y	Y	Y	Y	Y
WASHINGTON							
Murray	Y	Y	Y	Y	Y	Y	Y
Cantwell	Y	Y	Y	Y	Y	Y	Y
WEST VIRGINIA							
Byrd	?	?	?	Y	Y	Y	Y
Rockefeller	Y	Y	Y	Y	Y	Y	Y
WISCONSIN							
Kohl	N	Y	Y	Y	Y	Y	Y
Feingold	N	Y	Y	Y	Y	Y	N
WYOMING							
Enzi	Y	N	?	N	N	N	N
Barrasso	Y	N	N	N	N	N	N

KEY   **Republicans**   Democrats   *Independents*

Y Voted for (yea)	X Paired against
# Paired for	– Announced against
+ Announced for	P Voted "present"
N Voted against (nay)	

C   Voted "present" to avoid possible conflict of interest

?   Did not vote or otherwise make a position known

IN THE SENATE | By Vote Number

385. **HR 3590. Health Care Overhaul/Cloture.** Motion to invoke cloture (thus limiting debate) on the Reid, D-Nev., manager's amendment to the Reid substitute amendment. Motion agreed to 60-40: D 58-0; R 0-40; I 2-0. Three-fifths of the total Senate (60) is required to invoke cloture. A "yea" was a vote in support of the president's position. Dec. 21, 2009.

386. **HR 3590. Health Care Overhaul/Enactment Date.** Reid, D-Nev., motion to table (kill) the Reid amendment to the Reid substitute amendment. The Reid amendment would change the effective date of the measure. Motion agreed to 60-39: D 58-0; R 0-39; I 2-0. Dec. 22, 2009.

387. **HR 3590. Health Care Overhaul/Manager's Amendment.** Reid, D-Nev., manager's amendment to the Reid substitute amendment. The manager's amendment would create a system of national private insurance plans supervised by the Office of Personnel Management. The amendment would strike provisions in the substitute that would create a public health insurance option. It would increase the percentage of revenue that insurers covering employees of large businesses must spend on medical claims and further expand Medicaid coverage. It would require every exchange to offer at least one plan that does not cover abortion and would lay out a financial structure for insurance plans to cover abortion if they do not use federal subsidies to pay for the procedure. Adopted 60-39: D 58-0; R 0-39; I 2-0. Dec. 22, 2009.

388. **HR 3590. Health Care Overhaul/Cloture.** Motion to invoke cloture (thus limiting debate) on the Reid, D-Nev., substitute amendment. Motion agreed to 60-39: D 58-0; R 0-39; I 2-0. Three-fifths of the total Senate (60) is required to invoke cloture. Dec. 22, 2009.

389. **HR 3590. Health Care Overhaul/Constitutional Point of Order.** Ensign, R-Nev., point of order that the Reid, D-Nev., substitute amendment violates the enumerated powers of Congress under Article I, Section 8 of the Constitution and the Fifth Amendment because it would require most individuals to obtain health insurance. Point of order rejected 39-60: D 0-58; R 39-0; I 0-2. Dec. 23, 2009.

390. **HR 3590. Health Care Overhaul/Unfunded Intergovernmental Mandate.** Baucus, D-Mont., motion to waive the Budget Act with respect to the Corker, R-Tenn., point of order against the Reid, D-Nev., substitute amendment. Corker raised a point of order that the Reid substitute violates the Budget Act because it contains an unfunded intergovernmental mandate in excess of the annual statutory limit of $69 million within the next five years. Motion agreed to 55-44: D 53-5; R 0-39; I 2-0. (A simple majority vote is required to waive a budget point of order for unfunded mandates.) Dec. 23, 2009.

391. **HR 3590. Health Care Overhaul/Earmark Disclosure.** Baucus, D-Mont., motion to table (kill) the Cornyn, R-Texas, appeal of the ruling of the chair rejecting the Cornyn point of order against the Reid, D-Nev., substitute amendment. Cornyn raised a point of order that the Reid substitute violates Senate rules requiring that a senator who proposes an amendment containing any congressionally directed spending items ensure as soon as practicable that the list of such items be printed in the Congressional Record. Motion agreed to 57-42: D 55-3; R 0-39; I 2-0. Dec. 23, 2009.

	385	386	387	388	389	390	391			385	386	387	388	389	390	391
ALABAMA									**MONTANA**							
Shelby	N	N	N	N	Y	N	N		Baucus	Y	Y	Y	Y	N	Y	Y
Sessions	N	N	N	N	Y	N	N		Tester	Y	Y	Y	Y	N	Y	Y
ALASKA									**NEBRASKA**							
Murkowski	N	N	N	N	Y	N	N		Nelson	Y	Y	Y	Y	N	N	Y
Begich	Y	Y	Y	Y	N	Y	Y		**Johanns**	N	N	N	N	Y	N	N
ARIZONA									**NEVADA**							
McCain	N	N	N	N	Y	N	N		Reid	Y	Y	Y	Y	N	Y	Y
Kyl	N	N	N	N	Y	N	N		**Ensign**	N	N	N	N	Y	N	N
ARKANSAS									**NEW HAMPSHIRE**							
Lincoln	Y	Y	Y	Y	N	Y	Y		**Gregg**	N	N	N	N	Y	N	N
Pryor	Y	Y	Y	Y	N	Y	Y		Shaheen	Y	Y	Y	Y	N	N	Y
CALIFORNIA									**NEW JERSEY**							
Feinstein	Y	Y	Y	Y	N	Y	Y		Lautenberg	Y	Y	Y	Y	N	Y	Y
Boxer	Y	Y	Y	Y	N	Y	Y		Menendez	Y	Y	Y	Y	N	Y	Y
COLORADO									**NEW MEXICO**							
Udall	Y	Y	Y	Y	N	Y	Y		Bingaman	Y	Y	Y	Y	N	Y	Y
Bennet	Y	Y	Y	Y	N	Y	N		Udall	Y	Y	Y	Y	N	Y	Y
CONNECTICUT									**NEW YORK**							
Dodd	Y	Y	Y	Y	N	Y	Y		Schumer	Y	Y	Y	Y	N	Y	Y
Lieberman	Y	Y	Y	Y	N	Y	Y		Gillibrand	Y	Y	Y	Y	N	Y	Y
DELAWARE									**NORTH CAROLINA**							
Carper	Y	Y	Y	Y	N	Y	Y		**Burr**	N	N	N	N	Y	N	N
Kaufman	Y	Y	Y	Y	N	Y	Y		Hagan	Y	Y	Y	Y	N	Y	Y
FLORIDA									**NORTH DAKOTA**							
Nelson	Y	Y	Y	Y	N	Y	Y		Conrad	Y	Y	Y	Y	N	Y	Y
LeMieux	N	N	N	N	Y	N	N		Dorgan	Y	Y	Y	Y	N	Y	Y
GEORGIA									**OHIO**							
Chambliss	N	N	N	N	Y	N	N		**Voinovich**	N	N	N	N	Y	N	N
Isakson	N	N	N	N	Y	N	N		Brown	Y	Y	Y	Y	N	Y	Y
HAWAII									**OKLAHOMA**							
Inouye	Y	Y	Y	Y	N	Y	Y		**Inhofe**	N	?	?	?	Y	N	N
Akaka	Y	Y	Y	Y	N	Y	Y		**Coburn**	N	N	N	N	Y	N	N
IDAHO									**OREGON**							
Crapo	N	N	N	N	Y	N	N		Wyden	Y	Y	Y	Y	N	Y	Y
Risch	N	N	N	N	Y	N	N		Merkley	Y	Y	Y	Y	N	Y	Y
ILLINOIS									**PENNSYLVANIA**							
Durbin	Y	Y	Y	Y	N	Y	Y		Specter	Y	Y	Y	Y	N	Y	Y
Burris	Y	Y	Y	Y	N	Y	Y		Casey	Y	Y	Y	Y	N	Y	Y
INDIANA									**RHODE ISLAND**							
Lugar	N	N	N	N	Y	N	N		Reed	Y	Y	Y	Y	N	Y	Y
Bayh	Y	Y	Y	Y	N	N	N		Whitehouse	Y	Y	Y	Y	N	Y	Y
IOWA									**SOUTH CAROLINA**							
Grassley	N	N	N	N	Y	N	N		**Graham**	N	N	N	N	Y	N	N
Harkin	Y	Y	Y	Y	N	Y	Y		**DeMint**	N	N	N	N	Y	N	N
KANSAS									**SOUTH DAKOTA**							
Brownback	N	N	N	N	Y	N	N		Johnson	Y	Y	Y	Y	N	Y	Y
Roberts	N	N	N	N	Y	N	N		**Thune**	N	N	N	N	Y	N	N
KENTUCKY									**TENNESSEE**							
McConnell	N	N	N	N	Y	N	N		**Alexander**	N	N	N	N	Y	N	N
Bunning	N	N	N	N	+	–	–		**Corker**	N	N	N	N	Y	N	N
LOUISIANA									**TEXAS**							
Landrieu	Y	Y	Y	Y	N	Y	Y		**Hutchison**	N	N	N	N	Y	N	N
Vitter	N	N	N	N	Y	N	N		**Cornyn**	N	N	N	N	Y	N	N
MAINE									**UTAH**							
Snowe	N	N	N	N	Y	N	N		**Hatch**	N	N	N	N	Y	N	N
Collins	N	N	N	N	Y	N	N		**Bennett**	N	N	N	N	Y	N	N
MARYLAND									**VERMONT**							
Mikulski	Y	Y	Y	Y	N	Y	Y		Leahy	Y	Y	Y	Y	N	Y	Y
Cardin	Y	Y	Y	Y	N	Y	Y		*Sanders*	Y	Y	Y	Y	N	Y	Y
MASSACHUSETTS									**VIRGINIA**							
Kerry	Y	Y	Y	Y	N	Y	Y		Webb	Y	Y	Y	Y	N	N	Y
Kirk	Y	Y	Y	Y	N	Y	Y		Warner	Y	Y	Y	Y	N	N	Y
MICHIGAN									**WASHINGTON**							
Levin	Y	Y	Y	Y	N	Y	Y		Murray	Y	Y	Y	Y	N	Y	Y
Stabenow	Y	Y	Y	Y	N	Y	Y		Cantwell	Y	Y	Y	Y	N	Y	Y
MINNESOTA									**WEST VIRGINIA**							
Klobuchar	Y	Y	Y	Y	N	Y	Y		Byrd	Y	Y	Y	Y	N	Y	Y
Franken	Y	Y	Y	Y	N	Y	Y		Rockefeller	Y	Y	Y	Y	N	Y	Y
MISSISSIPPI									**WISCONSIN**							
Cochran	N	N	N	N	Y	N	N		Kohl	Y	Y	Y	Y	N	Y	Y
Wicker	N	N	N	N	Y	N	N		Feingold	Y	Y	Y	Y	N	Y	Y
MISSOURI									**WYOMING**							
Bond	N	N	N	N	Y	N	N		**Enzi**	N	N	N	N	Y	N	N
McCaskill	Y	Y	Y	Y	N	Y	N		**Barrasso**	N	N	N	N	Y	N	N

KEY	**Republicans**		Democrats		*Independents*	
Y	Voted for (yea)		X	Paired against		C	Voted "present" to avoid possible conflict of interest
#	Paired for		–	Announced against		
+	Announced for		P	Voted "present"		?	Did not vote or otherwise make a position known
N	Voted against (nay)					

IN THE SENATE | By Vote Number

392. **HR 3590. Health Care Overhaul/Constitutional Point of Order.** Hutchison, R-Texas, point of order that the Reid, D-Nev., substitute amendment violates the 10th Amendment to the Constitution because it would pre-empt states' regulatory authority over health insurance. Point of order rejected 39-60: D 0-58; R 39-0; I 0-2. Dec. 23, 2009.

393. **HR 3590. Health Care Overhaul/Vote-Trading Ban.** Baucus, D-Mont., motion to table (kill) the DeMint, R-S.C., motion to suspend Senate Rule 22 to permit the consideration of DeMint amendment. The DeMint amendment would make it out of order in the Senate to consider a congressionally directed spending item, a limited tax benefit, or a limited tariff benefit if a senator has conditioned the inclusion of language to provide funding for a congressionally directed spending item, a limited tax benefit or a limited tariff benefit in any amendment, bill, joint resolution or conference report on a bill, or on any vote cast by any senator. The amendment would apply to future legislation. Motion agreed to 53-46: D 51-7; R 0-39; I 2-0. Dec. 23, 2009.

394. **HR 3590. Health Care Overhaul/Substitute.** Reid, D-Nev., substitute amendment that would create marketplaces for purchasing health insurance, create a system of national private insurance plans supervised by the Office of Personnel Management, require most individuals to obtain insurance and impose requirements on insurance companies regarding the coverage that they offer. It also would expand eligibility for Medicaid, shrink by $500 in 2010 the coverage gap under the Medicare Part D prescription drug program, and create an advisory board to reduce the per capita growth rate in Medicare spending. Adopted 60-39: D 58-0; R 0-39; I 2-0. Dec. 23, 2009.

395. **HR 3590. Health Care Overhaul/Cloture.** Motion to invoke cloture (thus limiting debate) on the bill. Motion agreed to 60-39: D 58-0; R 0-39; I 2-0. Three-fifths of the total Senate (60) is required to invoke cloture. Dec. 23, 2009.

396. **HR 3590. Health Care Overhaul/Passage.** Passage of the bill, as amended, that would overhaul the nation's health insurance system and require most individuals to buy health insurance by 2014. It would create a system of national private insurance plans supervised by the Office of Personnel Management and create state-run marketplaces for purchasing health insurance. Those who do not obtain coverage would be subject to an excise tax, with some exceptions. Employers with 50 or more workers would have to provide coverage or pay a fine if any employee gets a subsided plan on the exchange. The bill would provide tax credits to certain small businesses for providing coverage and provide subsidies to individuals making up to four times the federal poverty level, excluding illegal immigrants. It would bar use of federal funds to pay for abortions in the new programs created under the bill, except in cases of rape, incest or if the woman's life is in danger. It would bar insurance companies from denying coverage based on pre-existing medical conditions beginning in 2014, and also bar them from dropping coverage of people who become ill. It would expand eligibility for Medicaid, shrink the coverage gap under the Medicare Part D prescription drug program and create an advisory board to reduce the per capita growth rate in Medicare spending. Passed 60-39: D 58-0; R 0-39; I 2-0. A "yea" was a vote in support of the president's position. Dec. 24, 2009.

397. **HR 4314. Debt Limit Increase/Passage.** Passage of the bill that would increase the federal debt limit by $290 billion to $12.4 trillion. Passed (thus cleared for the president) 60-39: D 57-1; R 1-38; I 2-0. (By unanimous consent, the Senate agreed to raise the majority requirement for passage of the bill to 60 votes.) Dec. 24, 2009.

	392	393	394	395	396	397
ALABAMA						
Shelby	Y	N	N	N	N	N
Sessions	Y	N	N	N	N	N
ALASKA						
Murkowski	Y	N	N	N	N	N
Begich	N	Y	Y	Y	Y	Y
ARIZONA						
McCain	Y	N	N	N	N	N
Kyl	Y	N	N	N	N	N
ARKANSAS						
Lincoln	N	Y	Y	Y	Y	Y
Pryor	N	Y	Y	Y	Y	Y
CALIFORNIA						
Feinstein	N	Y	Y	Y	Y	Y
Boxer	N	Y	Y	Y	Y	Y
COLORADO						
Udall	N	Y	Y	Y	Y	Y
Bennet	N	Y	Y	Y	Y	Y
CONNECTICUT						
Dodd	N	Y	Y	Y	Y	Y
Lieberman	N	Y	Y	Y	Y	Y
DELAWARE						
Carper	N	Y	Y	Y	Y	Y
Kaufman	N	Y	Y	Y	Y	Y
FLORIDA						
Nelson	N	Y	Y	Y	Y	Y
LeMieux	Y	N	N	N	N	N
GEORGIA						
Chambliss	Y	N	N	N	N	N
Isakson	Y	N	N	N	N	N
HAWAII						
Inouye	N	Y	Y	Y	Y	Y
Akaka	N	Y	Y	Y	Y	Y
IDAHO						
Crapo	Y	N	N	N	N	N
Risch	Y	N	N	N	N	N
ILLINOIS						
Durbin	N	Y	Y	Y	Y	Y
Burris	N	Y	Y	Y	Y	Y
INDIANA						
Lugar	Y	N	N	N	N	N
Bayh	N	N	Y	Y	Y	Y
IOWA						
Grassley	Y	N	N	N	N	N
Harkin	N	Y	Y	Y	Y	Y
KANSAS						
Brownback	Y	N	N	N	N	N
Roberts	Y	N	N	N	N	N
KENTUCKY						
McConnell	Y	N	N	N	N	N
Bunning	+	-	-	-	-	-
LOUISIANA						
Landrieu	N	Y	Y	Y	Y	Y
Vitter	Y	N	N	N	N	N
MAINE						
Snowe	Y	N	N	N	N	N
Collins	Y	N	N	N	N	N
MARYLAND						
Mikulski	N	Y	Y	Y	Y	Y
Cardin	N	Y	Y	Y	Y	Y
MASSACHUSETTS						
Kerry	N	Y	Y	Y	Y	Y
Kirk	N	Y	Y	Y	Y	Y
MICHIGAN						
Levin	N	Y	Y	Y	Y	Y
Stabenow	N	Y	Y	Y	Y	Y
MINNESOTA						
Klobuchar	N	Y	Y	Y	Y	Y
Franken	N	Y	Y	Y	Y	Y
MISSISSIPPI						
Cochran	Y	N	N	N	N	N
Wicker	Y	N	N	N	N	N
MISSOURI						
Bond	Y	N	N	N	N	N
McCaskill	N	N	Y	Y	Y	Y

	392	393	394	395	396	397
MONTANA						
Baucus	N	Y	Y	Y	Y	Y
Tester	N	Y	Y	Y	Y	Y
NEBRASKA						
Nelson	N	N	Y	Y	Y	Y
Johanns	Y	N	N	N	N	N
NEVADA						
Reid	N	Y	Y	Y	Y	Y
Ensign	Y	N	N	N	N	N
NEW HAMPSHIRE						
Gregg	Y	N	N	N	N	N
Shaheen	N	Y	Y	Y	Y	Y
NEW JERSEY						
Lautenberg	N	Y	Y	Y	Y	Y
Menendez	N	Y	Y	Y	Y	Y
NEW MEXICO						
Bingaman	N	Y	Y	Y	Y	Y
Udall	N	Y	Y	Y	Y	Y
NEW YORK						
Schumer	N	Y	Y	Y	Y	Y
Gillibrand	N	Y	Y	Y	Y	Y
NORTH CAROLINA						
Burr	Y	N	N	N	N	N
Hagan	N	Y	Y	Y	Y	Y
NORTH DAKOTA						
Conrad	N	Y	Y	Y	Y	Y
Dorgan	N	Y	Y	Y	Y	Y
OHIO						
Voinovich	Y	N	N	N	N	Y
Brown	N	Y	Y	Y	Y	Y
OKLAHOMA						
Inhofe	Y	N	N	N	N	N
Coburn	Y	N	N	N	N	N
OREGON						
Wyden	N	Y	Y	Y	Y	Y
Merkley	N	N	Y	Y	Y	Y
PENNSYLVANIA						
Specter	N	Y	Y	Y	Y	Y
Casey	N	Y	Y	Y	Y	Y
RHODE ISLAND						
Reed	N	Y	Y	Y	Y	Y
Whitehouse	N	Y	Y	Y	Y	Y
SOUTH CAROLINA						
Graham	Y	N	N	N	N	N
DeMint	Y	N	N	N	N	N
SOUTH DAKOTA						
Johnson	N	Y	Y	Y	Y	Y
Thune	Y	N	N	N	N	N
TENNESSEE						
Alexander	Y	N	N	N	N	N
Corker	Y	N	N	N	N	N
TEXAS						
Hutchison	Y	N	N	N	N	N
Cornyn	Y	N	N	N	N	N
UTAH						
Hatch	Y	N	N	N	N	N
Bennett	Y	N	N	N	N	N
VERMONT						
Leahy	N	Y	Y	Y	Y	Y
Sanders	N	Y	Y	Y	Y	Y
VIRGINIA						
Webb	N	N	Y	Y	Y	Y
Warner	N	N	Y	Y	Y	Y
WASHINGTON						
Murray	N	Y	Y	Y	Y	Y
Cantwell	N	Y	Y	Y	Y	Y
WEST VIRGINIA						
Byrd	N	Y	Y	Y	Y	Y
Rockefeller	N	Y	Y	Y	Y	Y
WISCONSIN						
Kohl	N	Y	Y	Y	Y	Y
Feingold	N	N	Y	Y	Y	Y
WYOMING						
Enzi	Y	N	N	N	N	N
Barrasso	Y	N	N	N	N	N

KEY **Republicans** Democrats *Independents*

Y Voted for (yea)	**X** Paired against
# Paired for	**-** Announced against
+ Announced for	**P** Voted "present"
N Voted against (nay)	

C Voted "present" to avoid possible conflict of interest

? Did not vote or otherwise make a position known

Senate Roll Call Index by Subject